Harold D. Templeins
1931

A GUIDE TO HISTORICAL LITERATURE

Edited by ❧ ❧ ❧ William Henry Allison
Sidney Bradshaw Fay ❧ Augustus Hunt Shearer
and Henry Robinson Shipman ❧ ❧ ❧ ❧

NEW YORK: THE MACMILLAN COMPANY
1931

Printed in the United States of America by
J. J. LITTLE AND IVES COMPANY, NEW YORK

PREFACE

At its meeting in Cleveland in December, 1919, the American Historical Association appointed a special committee, with Professor George M. Dutcher of Wesleyan University as chairman, to coöperate with the American Library Association in the preparation of a manual of historical literature, on the same general plan as that of Professor C. K. Adams, published in 1882. The present *Guide* is the result of this action of eleven years ago. It was apparent almost from the beginning that not a new edition of Adams, but a new work such as was made necessary by the passage of time, was desirable.

Its limitations should be made plain, for they are many. To supply an exhaustive, or even a reasonably complete, bibliography in any field was out of the question in so compendious a work. Our purpose has been to furnish a carefully chosen list of available books in each of the several fields to the English reading audience, primarily to libraries, teachers, and graduate students.

The scheme of classification has presented difficulties, as must always be the case in a compilation of the kind. For a general outline of it, see Index I.

The plan of the volume is largely the work of Professor Dutcher, who served as chairman of the committee in charge of its preparation from 1920 to December, 1928, when he was succeeded by Henry R. Shipman and Sidney B. Fay. To Professor Dutcher are due our most sincere thanks for his years of friendly coöperation and unselfish service. We wish to acknowledge our indebtedness for many helpful suggestions to Professors Alice M. Baldwin, A. B. Benson, G. L. Burr, S. B. Harding and C. H. Hull, to Mr. R. L. Morrow, Mr. G. W. Robinson and Miss Anna M. Monrad; and for aid in the preparation of the manuscript to Mrs. Alexander Cowie, Miss Margaret Crawford, Miss Ruth M. Lind, Mr. L. G. Wells and Professor L. J. Meyer. We wish to express especially also our appreciation of the generous assistance given us by the section editors, more than three hundred reviewers, and by the Macmillan Company.

WILLIAM H. ALLISON
SIDNEY B. FAY
AUGUSTUS H. SHEARER
HENRY R. SHIPMAN

December, 1930.

PREFACE

CONTENTS

LIST OF CONTRIBUTORS OF REVIEWS

The following List of Contributors, arranged alphabetically according to the last names, includes persons who have edited various chapters or written book reviews. The chapters in which reviews of the respective reviewers and editors appear are indicated in the parentheses following the names. Contributors whose names are marked with an asterisk (*) are deceased.

EA   EDITH ABBOTT, Professor of Social Economy, and Dean, Graduate School of Social Service and Administration, University of Chicago (§ X)

WCA   WILBUR CORTEZ ABBOTT, Francis Lee Higginson Professor of History, Harvard University (§ K)

EDA   *EPHRAIM D. ADAMS, Professor of History, Stanford University (§ X)

RGA   RANDOLPH G. ADAMS, Custodian William L. Clements Library and Professor of History, University of Michigan (§ X)

RGAN   ROBERT G. ALBION, Associate Professor of History, Princeton University (§ IK)

HBA   HARTLEY BURR ALEXANDER, Professor of Philosophy, University of Nebraska (§ D)

GWA   GARDNER WELD ALLEN, Member of Naval History Society (§ L)

TGA   THOMAS GEORGE ALLEN, Secretary of Oriental Museum and Institute, Assistant Professor of Egyptology, University of Chicago, (§ C)

JMSA   JOHN MAUDRIDGE SNOWDEN ALLISON, Professor of History, Yale University (§ M)

WHA   WILLIAM H. ALLISON, Professor Emeritus of Ecclesiastical History, Colgate-Rochester Divinity School, Rochester, New York, and Consultant in Church and General History, Library of Congress (§ BFIUX)

CWA   *CLARENCE W. ALVORD, Professor of History, University of Minnesota (§ KX)

HVA   HERMAN V. AMES, Professor of American Constitutional History and Dean of the Graduate School, University of Pennsylvania (§ X)

DRA   DICE ROBINS ANDERSON, President, Randolph-Macon Woman's College (§ X)

FMA   FRANK MALOY ANDERSON, Professor of History, Dartmouth College (§ JT)

JBA   JOHN BENJAMIN ANDERSON, Professor of Christian Theology and Ethics, Colgate-Rochester Divinity School (§ F)

AIA   ARTHUR I. ANDREWS, Cambridge, Massachusetts (§ UW)

CMA   CHARLES M. ANDREWS, Farnam Professor of American History, Yale University (§ X)

GFA   GEORGE FREDERICK ANDREWS, Fellow of the Royal Geographical Society (§ W)

ACA   ANDREW C. ARMSTRONG, Professor Emeritus of Philosophy, Wesleyan University, Middletown, Connecticut (§ B)

KA   KAN-ICHI ASAKAWA, Associate Professor of History and Curator of the Japanese and Chinese Collections, Yale University (§ U)

JCA   JOSEPH CULLEN AYER, JR., Professor of Ecclesiastical History, Divinity School of the Protestant Episcopal Church, Philadelphia (§ F)

EBB   EARLE BROWNELL BABCOCK, Professor of Romance Languages and Literatures, New York University (§ O)

ESBr   E. S. BAGGER, Magyar Editor and Publicist (§ T)

ESB   EDWIN SWIFT BALCH, Philadelphia, Pennsylvania; Fellow of the Royal Geographical Society (§ K)

JFB   JAMES F. BALDWIN, Professor of History, Vassar College (§ L)

SEB   STANLEY E. BALDWIN, Professor of Rhetoric, Colgate University (§ U)

ECB   EUGENE CAMPBELL BARKER, Professor of American History, University of Texas (§ Y)

HEBs   HARRY ELMER BARNES, Formerly Professor of Historical Sociology, Smith College (§ BM)

FB   FREDERICK BARRY, Professor of the History of Science, Columbia University (§ D)

AHB   ARTHUR H. BASYE, Professor of History, Dartmouth College (§ HKL)

JCB JENS CHRISTIAN BAY, Medical Reference Librarian, John Crerar Library, Chicago, Illinois (§ R)

CLB CARL L. BECKER, Professor of History, Cornell University (§ BKX)

HCB HERBERT CLIFFORD BELL, Professor of History, Wesleyan University (§ IL)

ABB ADOLPHE BURNET BENSON, Associate Professor of German and Scandinavian, Yale University (§ R)

EJB ELBERT J. BENTON, Professor of History and Dean of the Graduate School, Western Reserve University (§ X)

BWB BLISS WASHINGTON BILLINGS, Professor of Occidental History, Chosen Christian College, Seoul, Korea (§ U)

RPB ROBERT P. BLAKE, Professor of History, Harvard University (§ S)

GHB GEORGE H. BLAKESLEE, Professor of History and International Relations, Clark University (§ V)

JB JOSHUA BLOCH, Curator of the Jewish Collection, New York Public Library (§ B)

ELB ERNEST LUDLOW BOGART, Professor of Economics, University of Illinois (§ X)

CSB CHAUNCY SMALL BOUCHER, Professor of American History and Dean of the College of Arts, Literature and Science, University of Chicago (§ X)

HEB HENRY E. BOURNE, Managing Editor, *American Historical Review* and Consultant in European History, Library of Congress (§ BIM)

PHB PERCY HOLMES BOYNTON, Professor of English, University of Chicago (§ X)

RWB RICHARD W. BOYNTON, Professor of Philosophy, University of Buffalo (§ B)

WB WITT BOWDEN, Professor of History, Atlantic Institute, Hampton Roads, Va. (§ I)

EEB EDGAR EWING BRANDON, Professor of Romance Languages, Miami University (§ Y)

JHB JAMES HENRY BREASTED, Director of the Oriental Institute, Professor of Egyptology and Oriental History, University of Chicago (§ C)

JBB JOHN BARTLETT BREBNER, Assistant Professor of History, Columbia University (§ Z)

JPB JULIAN PLEASANT BRETZ, Professor of American History, Cornell University (§ X)

APB ALBERT PERRY BRIGHAM, Professor Emeritus of Geology, Colgate University (§ U)

RCB ROBERT CLARKSON BROOKS, Professor of Political Science, Swarthmore College (§ BP)

LFB LOUISE FARGO BROWN, Professor of History, Vassar College (§ JK)

WAB WILLIAM ADAMS BROWN, Roosevelt Professor of Ecclesiastical History, Union Theological Seminary (§ F)

SJB SOLON J. BUCK, Professor of History, University of Minnesota, and Superintendent, Minnesota Historical Society (§ X)

RLB RAYMOND LESLIE BUELL, Foreign Policy Association, New York (§ U)

LJB LAWRENCE JOHNSTON BURPEE, President, Canadian Historical Association (§ Z)

TWB THOMAS WAINWRIGHT BUSSOM, Professor of Romance Languages, Wesleyan University (§ N)

HCBR *HOWARD CROSBY BUTLER, Professor of Architecture, Princeton University (§ G)

EHB EUGENE HUGH BYRNE, Professor of History, University of Wisconsin (§ HO)

WSC WILLIAM S. CARPENTER, Professor of Politics, Princeton University (§ B)

SJC SHIRLEY JACKSON CASE, Professor of Early Church History and New Testament Interpretation, University of Chicago (§ F)

WGC WILLIAM GEORGE CHANTER, Professor of Ethics and Religion, Wesleyan University (§ C)

EPCE EUGENE PARKER CHASE, Professor of Government, Lafayette College (§ KL)

GHC GEORGE HENRY CHASE, Professor of Archæology and Curator of Classical Antiquities, Harvard University (§ D)

EPC EDWARD POTTS CHEYNEY, Professor of History, University of Pennsylvania (§ IKL)

OPC OLIVER PERRY CHITWOOD, Professor of History, West Virginia University (§ J)

FAC FRANCIS A. CHRISTIE, Professor Emeritus of Church History, Meadeville Theological Seminary (§ FL)

AVC ALFRED VANCE CHURCHILL, Professor of Art, Smith College (§ B)

VSC   Victor Selden Clark, Consultant in Economics, Library of Congress (§ G)

ACCo Arthur Charles Cole, Professor of American History, Western Reserve University (§ X)

TC   Theodore Collier, Professor of History, Brown University (§ BI)

AHUC Arthur Humphrey Urquhart Colquhoun, Deputy-Minister of Education, Ontario (§ Z)

ACC   *Archibald Cary Coolidge, Professor of History, Harvard University (§ T)

ESC   Edward S. Corwin, McCormick Professor of Jurisprudence, Princeton University (§ B)

IJC   Isaac J. Cox, Professor of History, Northwestern University (§ KY)

AOC   Avery Odelle Craven, Professor of American History, University of Chicago (§ X)

CCC   Clarence Cory Crawford, Professor of History, University of Kansas (§ L)

MWC   Morris William Croll, Professor of English, Princeton University (§ B)

ALC   Arthur L. Cross, Professor of History, University of Michigan (§ L)

ENC   Eugene N. Curtis, Professor of History, Goucher College (§ M)

CWD   Charles Wendell David, Professor of History, Bryn Mawr College (§ HI)

WMD   William Morris Davis, Professor Emeritus of Geology, Harvard University (§ M)

WSD   *William Stearns Davis, formerly Professor of History, University of Minnesota (§ EM)

CD   Clive Day, Professor of Economic History, Yale University (§ KV)

ND   Niels Debel, Professor of Political Science, Goucher College (§ R)

TD   Tyler Dennett, Historical Adviser, State Department, Washington, D. C. (§ U)

ALPD *Alfred L. P. Dennis, Professor of History and International Relations, Clark University (§ V)

HBD   Henry Bronson Dewing, President, Athens College (Greece) (§ H)

RBD   ROLAND B. DIXON, Professor of Anthropology, Harvard University (§ B)

WLD   WALTER LOUIS DORN, Professor of History, Ohio State University (§ M)

AGD   ARTHUR GEORGE DOUGHTY, Keeper of Public Records, Public Archives of Canada, Ottawa (§ Z)

EWD   EARLE W. DOW, Professor of European History, University of Michigan (§ FHMP)

CAD   CHARLES AVERY DRAVO, Lt. Colonel, U. S. Army, and Professor of Military Science and Tactics, University of Pennsylvania (§ I)

SPD   STEPHEN P. DUGGAN, Director, Institute of International Education (§ T)

FD   FREDERIC DUNCALF, Professor of European History, University of Texas (§ H)

TSD   THOMAS SHEARER DUNCAN, Professor of Greek and Latin, Washington University (§ D)

GMD   GEORGE MATHEW DUTCHER, Hedding Professor of History, Wesleyan University (§ ABCDEFHJKLMNOPQRSTUVWXYZ)

GHE   GEORGE HAROLD EDGELL, Professor of Fine Arts and Dean of the Faculty of Architecture, Harvard University (§ H)

EEY   ELOISE ELLERY, Professor of History, Vassar College (§ IM)

EE   EPHRAIM EMERTON, Professor Emeritus of Ecclesiastical History, Harvard University (§ F)

APE   AUSTIN P. EVANS, Professor of History, Columbia University (§ F)

FEF   FRANK EDGAR FARLEY, Olin Professor of English Literature, Wesleyan University (§ BX)

SBF   SIDNEY BRADSHAW FAY, Professor of History, Harvard University and Radcliffe College (§ ABFGHIJMNPSTW)

WSF   WILLIAM SCOTT FERGUSON, McLean Professor of Ancient and Modern History, Harvard University (§ CD)

RHF   ROBERT HERNDON FIFE, Professor of Germanic Languages and Literatures, Columbia University (§ BP)

CRF   CARL RUSSELL FISH, Professor of History, University of Wisconsin (§ X)

COF CLYDE OLIN FISHER, Professor of Economics, Wesleyan University (§ BX)

GMF GALEN MERRIAM FISHER, Secretary of Institute of Social and Religious Research (§ U)

DJF DANIEL JOHNSON FLEMING, Professor of Missions, Union Theological Seminary (§ F)

ACF ALEXANDER C. FLICK, State Historian and Director of Archives, Albany, New York (§ BF)

FMF FRED MORROW FLING, Professor of European History, University of Nebraska (§ JM)

GTF GEORGE TOBIAS FLOM, Professor of Scandinavian Languages, University of Illinois (§ R)

GSF GUY STANTON FORD, Professor of History and Dean of the Graduate School, University of Minnesota (§ IP)

HDF *HERBERT D. FOSTER, Professor of History, Dartmouth College (§ FIM)

HNF HAROLD NORTH FOWLER, Professor Emeritus of Greek, College for Women, Western Reserve University, and Consultant in Classics, Library of Congress (§ M)

TF TENNEY FRANK, Professor of Latin, Johns Hopkins University (§ CE)

CEF CHARLES EDMUND FRYER, Professor of History, McGill University (§ LZ)

WFG WILLIAM FREEMAN GALPIN, Associate Professor of Political Science and History, Syracuse University (§ L)

HG HECTOR GARNEAU, Librarian, Civic Library, Montreal (§ Z)

JWG JAMES WILFORD GARNER, Professor of Political Science, University of Illinois (§ I)

HNG HARRY NELSON GAY, Rome, Italy (§ KW)

RHG ROBERT H. GEORGE, Associate Professor of History, Brown University (§ IKM)

HAG HERBERT ADAMS GIBBONS, Formerly Professor of History and Political Economy, Robert College, Constantinople (§ K)

WAG WILLIAM ALVA GIFFORD, Professor of Ecclesiastical History, Wesleyan Theological College, Montreal (§ L)

JEG JAMES EDWARD GILLESPIE, Associate Professor of History, Pennsylvania State College (§ L)

LHG LAWRENCE HENRY GIPSON, Professor of History and Government, Lehigh University (§ K)

KG   KNUT GJERSET, Professor of History, Luther College, Decorah, Iowa (§ R)

AAG   A. A. GOLDENWEISER, Lecturer on Anthropology and Sociology, New School of Social Research, New York City (§ AB)

RG   RICHARD JAMES HORATIO GOTTHEIL, Professor of Semitic Languages, Columbia University; Head of the Oriental Department, New York Public Library (§ G)

WLG   WILLIAM LAWSON GRAN, Principal, Upper Canada College, Toronto (§ KZ)

HLG   HOWARD L. GRAY, Professor of History, Bryn Mawr College (§ LO)

WDG   WILLIAM D. GRAY, Professor of History, Smith College (§ E)

AWG   ADOLPHUS WILLIAM GREELY, Major General retired, United States Army, Chief Signal Officer, United States of America, 1887-1906 (§ K)

KRG   KENT ROBERTS GREENFIELD, Professor of Modern European History, Johns Hopkins University (§ J)

HEG   HERBERT ERNEST GREGORY, Silliman Professor of Geology, Yale University; Director of the Bernice P. Bishop Museum, Honolulu (§ V)

ALG   ALBERT LÉON GUÉRARD, Professor of General Literature, Leland Stanford University (§ M)

PG   PETER GUILDAY, Professor of Church History, Catholic University of America (§ BF)

CWH   CHARLES WILSON HACKETT, Professor of Latin-American History, University of Texas (§ Y)

WPH   WALTER P. HALL, Professor of History, Princeton University (§ L)

MSH   MAX SYLVIUS HANDMAN, Professor of Sociology, University of Texas (§ T)

SBH   *SAMUEL BANNISTER HARDING, Professor of History, University of Minnesota (§ B)

CHHG   CLARENCE H. HARING, Professor of Latin-American History and Economics, Harvard University (§ KNY)

SNH   SAMUEL N. HARPER, Professor of Russian Language and Institutions, University of Chicago (§ S)

GAH   GUSTAVUS ADOLPHUS HARRER, Professor of Latin, University of North Carolina (§ E)

CHH	CHARLES HOMER HASKINS, Henry Charles Lea Professor of Medieval History, Harvard University (§ H)
TRH	THOMAS ROBSON HAY, Pittsburgh, Pennsylvania (§ J)
JRH	JOSEPH RALSTON HAYDEN, Professor of Political Science, University of Michigan (§ L)
PJH	PATRICK J. HEALY, Professor of Church History and Dean of the Faculty of Theology, Catholic University of America (§ F)
WAH	WILLIAM ARTHUR HEIDEL, Research Professor of Greek Language and Literature, Wesleyan University (§ ABDE)
HH	HALLDOR HERMANNSSON, Professor of Scandinavian Languages and Curator of Fiske Icelandic Collection, Cornell University (§ R)
JWH	JOSEPH WILLIAM HEWITT, Professor of Classics, Wesleyan University (§ DE)
JCH	JOHN C. HILDT, Professor of History, Smith College (§ O)
FHH	FRANK H. HODDER, Professor of American History, University of Kansas (§ K)
EWH	EDWARD WASHBURN HOPKINS, Professor Emeritus of Sanskrit and Comparative Philology, Yale University (§ U)
SKH	STANLEY K. HORNBECK, State Department, Washington, D. C. (§ U)
HLH	HALFORD L. HOSKINS, Professor of History, Tufts College (§ I)
ACH	ARTHUR CHARLES HOWLAND, Professor of Medieval History, University of Pennsylvania (§ F)
EMH	EDWARD MASLIN HULME, Professor of Medieval History, Leland Stanford University (§ I)
AWH	ARTHUR W. HUMMEL, Chief of the Chinese Literature Division, Library of Congress (§ U)
EFH	EDWARD FRANK HUMPHREY, Professor of History, Trinity College, Hartford, Connecticut (§ BK)
IH	ISAAC HUSICK, Professor of Philosophy, University of Pennsylvania (§ I)
DDI	DALLAS D. IRVINE, Instructor in History, University of Pennsylvania (§ I)
AVWJ	ABRAHAM VALENTINE WILLIAMS JACKSON, Professor of Indo-Iranian Languages, Columbia University (§ C)

FJFJ   FREDERICK JOHN FOAKES JACKSON, Professor of Christian Institutions, Union Theological Seminary (§ FO)

JFJ   J. FRANKLIN JAMESON, Chief of Division of Manuscripts, Library of Congress, Washington, D. C. (§ QX)

MWJ   MARCUS W. JERNEGAN, Professor of American History, University of Chicago (§ X)

JRJ   JAMES RICHARD JEWETT, Professor of Arabic, Harvard University (§ G)

ACJ   ALLAN CHESTER JOHNSON, Professor of Classics, Princeton University (§ B)

NTJ   NELSON T. JOHNSON, Department of State, Washington, D. C. (§ U)

CKJ   CECIL KNIGHT JONES, Library of Congress, Washington, D. C. (§ Y)

GJ   *GUERNSEY JONES, Professor of English History, University of Nebraska (§ IL)

PVBJ   PAUL VAN BRUNT JONES, Associate Professor of History, University of Illinois (§ L)

TFJ   THEODORE F. JONES, Professor of History, New York University (§ O)

EJ   EINAR JORANSON, Associate Professor of History, University of Chicago (§ R)

AGK   ALBERT GALLOWAY KELLER, Professor of Science of Society, Yale University (§ K)

RHK   RALPH HAYWARD KENISTON, Professor of the Spanish Language, University of Chicago (§ Y)

WPMK   WILLIAM PAUL MCCLURE KENNEDY, Professor of History, University of Toronto (§ Z)

RJK   ROBERT J. KERNER, Professor of History, University of California (§ ST)

CWK   CLINTON WALKER KEYES, Professor of Greek and Latin, Columbia University (§ E)

FK   FISKE KIMBALL, Director of the Pennsylvania Museum, Philadelphia, Pennsylvania (§ O)

FJK   FRANK JOSEPH KLINGBERG, Professor of History, University of California at Los Angeles (§ K)

PK   PAUL KNAPLUND, Professor of History, University of Wisconsin (§ R)

DCK   DANIEL C. KNOWLTON, Associate Professor of Education, New York University (§ B)

HLK   HARRY LYMAN KOOPMAN, Librarian and John Hay Professor of Bibliography, Brown University (§ ABL)

SAK   *SERGIEI A. KORFF, Professor of the History of Eastern Europe, Columbia University (§ S)

ACK   AUGUST CHARLES KREY, Professor of History, University of Minnesota (§ H)

LL   LANE LANCASTER, Associate Professor of History and Government, Wesleyan University (§ JX)

WLLr   WILLIAM L. LANGER, Assistant Professor of History, Harvard University (§ J)

HHL   HUGH HORNBY LANGTON, Formerly Librarian, University of Toronto (§ Z)

WTL   WILLIAM THOMAS LAPRADE, Professor of English and European History, Duke University, Durham, North Carolina (§ ABL)

LML   LAURENCE M. LARSON, Professor of History, University of Illinois (§ LR)

KSL   KENNETH S. LATOURETTE, Professor of Missions, Yale University (§ U)

HBL   HENRY BARRETT LEARNED, Washington, D. C. (§ X)

DBL   DANIEL BELL LEARY, Professor of Psychology, University of Buffalo (§ B)

KCL   KARL CLAYTON LEEBRICK, Professor of International Affairs and Dean of College of Liberal Arts, Syracuse University (§ V)

LZL   LEON ZELENKA LERANDO, Assistant Professor of Spanish, Lafayette College (§ ST)

WEL   WILLIAM E. LINGELBACH, Professor of European History, University of Pennsylvania (§ I)

JBL   JOSEPH BYRNE LOCKEY, Professor of History, University of California at Los Angeles (§ Y)

FWL   FREDERICK WILLIAM LOETSCHER, Professor of Church History, Princeton Theological Seminary (§ F)

CLL   CARL LUDWIG LOKKE, Assistant Professor of History, Smith College (§ M)

RHL   ROBERT H. LORD, S. J., Formerly Professor of History, Harvard University (§ ST)

SML   SUSAN M. LOUGH, Professor of History, Westhampton College, University of Richmond (§ L)

DDL   DANIEL DAVID LUCKENBILL, Professor of Semitic Languages and Literatures, University of Chicago (§ C)

AHL   ALBERT HOWE LYBYER, Professor of History, University of Illinois (§ BTU)

DAMC   DAVID ALOYSIUS MCCABE, Professor of Economics, Princeton University (§ B)

DBM   DUNCAN BLACK MACDONALD, Professor of Semitic Languages, Hartford Theological Seminary (§ GW)

DMcF   DONALD MCFAYDEN, Professor of History, Washington University (§ ABCD)

DM   DAVID MAGIE, Formerly Professor of Classics, Princeton University (§ E)

ACMcG   ARTHUR C. MCGIFFERT, Professor Emeritus of Church History and formerly President, Union Theological Seminary (§ F)

CEMcG   CONSTANTINE EDWARD MCGUIRE, Research Associate, Institute of Economics, Washington, D. C. (§ N)

CHM   CHARLES HOWARD MCILWAIN, Eaton Professor of the Science of Government, Harvard University (§ BHL)

WWM   WALTER WALLACE MCLAREN, Professor of Economics, Williams College (§ U)

ACMcL   ANDREW C. MCLAUGHLIN, Professor of History, University of Chicago (§ X)

JBMcM   JAMES ADELBERT MCMILLEN, Librarian, State University and Agricultural College, Baton Rouge, La. (§ D)

JTMcN   JOHN THOMAS MCNEILL, Professor of Church History, Knox College, Toronto (§ F)

RVDM   RALPH VAN DEMAN MAGOFFIN, Professor of Classics, New York University (§ E)

PAM   PERCY ALVIN MARTIN, Professor of European History, Stanford University (§ Y)

SM   SHAILER MATHEWS, Dean of the Divinity School, University of Chicago (§ F)

JGUM   JULES GOTE ULTIMUS MAURITZSON, Professor of Swedish Language and Literature, and Dean, Augustana College, Rock Island, Illinois (§ S)

FEM   FRANK E. MELVIN, Professor of European History, University of Kansas (§ I)

CEM   CHARLES E. MERRIAM, Professor of Political Science, University of Chicago (§ PX)

RBM   ROGER B. MERRIMAN, Gurney Professor of History, Harvard University (§ KLM)

LRM   LEWIS REX MILLER, Formerly Tutor in History, Harvard University (§ U)

HAM   HARRY A. MILLIS, Professor of Economics, University of Chicago (§ X)

SKM   SIDNEY K. MITCHELL, Professor of History, Yale University (§ L)

CHMo   CONRAD HENRY MOEHLMANN, Colgate Professor of the History of Christianity, Colgate-Rochester Theological Seminary (§ F)

JWM   JOHN WILDMAN MONCRIEF, Associate Professor Emeritus of Church History, University of Chicago (§ F)

JAM   JAMES ALLAN MONTGOMERY, Professor of Hebrew, University of Pennsylvania; Editor, *Journal of American Oriental Society* (§ C)

GFM   GEORGE FOOT MOORE, Professor Emeritus of the History of Religion, Harvard University (§ F)

CRM   CHARLES RUFUS MOREY, Professor of Art and Archæology, Princeton University (§ H)

WTM   WILLIAM T. MORGAN, Professor of History, Indiana University (§ L)

JLM   JOHN LYLE MORISON, Professor of Colonial History, Queen's University, Kingston (§ Z)

WAM   WILLIAM ALFRED MORRIS, Professor of English History, University of California (§ L)

DCM   DANA C. MUNRO, Dodge Professor of Medieval History, Princeton University (§ GH)

WBM   WILLIAM B. MUNRO, Jonathan Trumbull Professor of American History and Government, Harvard University (§ Z)

RAN   RICHARD A. NEWHALL, Professor of European History, Williams College (§ BHJM)

RHN   ROBERT HASTINGS NICHOLS, Professor of Church History, Auburn Theological Seminary (§ F)

WN   WALLACE NOTESTEIN, Sterling Professor of English History, Yale University (§ L)

JFO'H   JOHN FRANCIS O'HARA, Chaplain and former Dean of School of Commerce, University of Notre Dame (§ Y)

CHO   CHARLES HENRY OLDFATHER, Professor of Greek and
         Ancient History, Wabash College (§ E)

WAO   WILLIAM ABBOTT OLDFATHER, Professor of Classics, Uni-
         versity of Illinois (§ E)

ATO   ALBERT TEN EYCK OLMSTEAD, Professor of Oriental His-
         tory, Oriental Institute, University of Chicago (§ C)

JEO   JULIUS EMIL OLSEN, Professor of Scandinavian Languages
         and Literatures, University of Wisconsin (§ R)

JSO   JULIA S. ORVIS, Professor of History, Wellesley College
         (§ S)

LBP   LAURENCE B. PACKARD, Professor of History, Amherst Col-
         lege (§ AJM)

SRP   SIDNEY R. PACKARD, Professor of History, Smith College
         (§ M)

LJP   *LOUIS J. PAETOW, Professor of Medieval History, Uni-
         versity of California (§ H)

EWP   EDWIN W. PAHLOW, Professor of Principles and Practice
         of Historical Methods, Ohio State University (§ Q)

JHP   JOSEPH HEDERSHOT PARK, Professor of History, New York
         University (§ O)

JP   JULIAN PARK, Professor of History, University of Buffalo
         (§ I)

COP   CHARLES OSCAR PAULLIN, Research Staff, Division of His-
         torical Research, Carnegie Institution, Washington, D. C.
         (§ L)

FLP   FREDERICK LOGAN PAXSON, Professor of American History,
         University of Wisconsin (§ X)

TCP   THEODORE CALVIN PEASE, Professor of History, University
         of Illinois (§ LX)

CP   CLARENCE PERKINS, Professor of European History, Uni-
         versity of North Dakota (§ J)

DP   DEXTER PERKINS, Professor of History, University of
         Rochester (§ B)

UBP   ULRICH B. PHILLIPS, Professor of American History, Yale
         University (§ X)

AEP   *ARISTIDES EVANGELUS PHOUTRIDES, Assistant Professor of
         Greek, Yale University (§ T)

ECP   EDMUND COLIN PIESSE, Formerly Director of the Pacific
         Branch in the Commonwealth of Australia, Prime Minister's
         Department (§ V)

FWP   FRANK WESLEY PITMAN, Professor of History, Pomona College (§ BKV)

WP   WILLIAM POPPER, Professor of Semitic Languages, University of California (§ G)

GMP   GEORGE M. PRIEST, Professor of Germanic Languages and Literature, Princeton University (§ P)

HIP   HERBERT INGRAM PRIESTLY, Professor of Mexican History, University of California; Librarian of Bancroft Library (§ Y)

RP   RUTH PUTNAM, Washington, D. C. (§ Q)

JSR   JESSE S. REEVES, Professor of Political Science, University of Michigan (§ LX)

FHR   FRANCES H. RELF, Professor of History, Wells College (§ L)

GWRı   GEORGE WARREN RICHARDS, President and Professor of Church History, Theological Seminary of the Reformed Church in the United States, Lancaster, Pennsylvania (§ F)

TWR   THAD W. RIKER, Professor of Modern European History, University of Texas (§ L)

JFR   JAMES FRED RIPPY, Professor of History, Duke University (§ XY)

JAR   JAMES A. ROBERTSON, Research Professor of American History, John B. Stetson University, Deland, Florida; Managing Editor, *Hispanic American Historical Review* (§ VY)

WSR   WILLIAM S. ROBERTSON, Professor of History, University of Illinois (§ Y)

FNR   FRED N. ROBINSON, Professor of English, Harvard University (§ A)

GTR   GEROID TANQUARY ROBINSON, Lecturer in History, Columbia University (§ S)

WWR   WILLIAM WALKER ROCKWELL, Professor of Church History and Librarian, Union Theological Seminary (§ F)

RWR   *ROBERT WILLIAM ROGERS, Professor Emeritus of Hebrew and Old Testament Exegesis, Drew Theological Seminary; and Professor Emeritus of Ancient Literature, Princeton University (§ BC)

WTR   WINIFRED T. ROOT, Professor of History, Iowa State University (§LXU)

HKR HENRY KALLOCH ROWE, Professor of Social Science and History, Newton Theological Institution, Newton Centre, Massachusetts (§ F)

LSR LEO S. ROWE, Director-General of Pan-American Union, Washington, D. C. (§ Y)

COS CARL ORTWIN SAUER, Professor of Geography, University of California (§ L)

DSS DAVID SCHLEY SCHAFF, Professor Emeritus of Ecclesiastical History and History of Doctrine, Western Theological Seminary, Pittsburgh, Pennsylvania (§ F)

FS FERDINAND SCHEVILL, Professor of Modern History, University of Chicago (§ IT)

AS ALBERT SCHINZ, Professor of French Literature, University of Pennsylvania (§ M)

NS NATHANIEL SCHMIDT, Professor of Semitic Languages and Literatures, Cornell University (§ G)

BES BERNADOTTE E. SCHMITT, Professor of Modern History, University of Chicago; Editor, *Journal of Modern History*, (§ JLT)

RLS ROBERT LIVINGSTON SCHUYLER, Professor of History, Columbia University (§ K)

EFS ERNEST FINDLAY SCOTT, Professor of Biblical Theology, Union Theological Seminary (§ F)

GCS GEORGE C. SELLERY, Professor of History, University of Wisconsin (§ B)

CS CHARLES SEYMOUR, Provost and Professor of History, Yale University (§ ST)

AHS AUGUSTUS HUNT SHEARER, Librarian, Grosvenor Library, Buffalo (§ ABKJLMT and "Library Collections" in all §§)

WRS WILLIAM R. SHEPHERD, Professor of History, Columbia University (§ Y)

HRS HENRY R. SHIPMAN, Associate Professor of History, Princeton University (§ ABFGIJKLMPSTUXY)

WHS WILBUR H. SIEBERT, Research Professor of European History, Ohio State University (§ U)

ST. GLS ST. GEORGE LEAKIN SIOUSSAT, Professor of American History, University of Pennsylvania (§ IX)

PWS PRESTON WILLIAM SLOSSON, Professor of History, University of Michigan (§ JL)

EBS   EARL BALDWIN SMITH, Professor of Art and Archæology, Princeton University (§ EBM)

JMPS   JOHN MERLIN POWIS SMITH, Professor of Semitic Languages and Literatures, University of Chicago; Editor, *American Journal of Semitic Languages and Literature* (§ C)

PS   PRESERVED SMITH, Professor of History, Cornell University (§ FMP)

EGS   EDWARD GLEASON SPAULDING, Professor of Philosophy, Princeton University (§ BI)

OLS   OLIVER LYMAN SPAULDING, JR., Colonel, United States Army (§ IL)

MS   MARTIN SPRENGLING, Professor of Semitic Languages and Literatures, University of Chicago (§ G)

OWS   ORLANDO WORTH STEPHENSON, Assistant Professor of History, University of Michigan (§ L)

WES   WAYNE EDSON STEVENS, Professor of History, Dartmouth College (§ J)

WKS   WILLIAM K. STEWART, Professor of Comparative Literature, Dartmouth College (§ J)

FLS   FRANCIS L. STRICKLAND, Professor of History and Psychology of Religion, Boston University (§ B)

JES   JAMES E. SWAIN, Professor of European History, Muhlenberg College (§ I)

JWS   JOSEPH WARD SWAIN, Assistant Professor of History, University of Illinois (§ AB)

AHSw   ALFRED HENRY SWEET, Professor of European History, Washington and Jefferson University (§ L)

BST   BENJAMIN S. TERRY, Professor Emeritus of English History, University of Chicago (§ L)

ST   SHIPLEY THOMAS, Author, New York City (§ J)

FLT   FREDERICK LINCOLN THOMPSON, Professor of History, Amherst College (§ B)

JWT   JAMES WESTFALL THOMPSON, Professor of Medieval History, University of Chicago (§ AFHMP)

LT   LYNN THORNDIKE, Professor of History, Columbia University (§ H)

GRT   GEORGE REEVES THROOP, Professor of Greek, Washington University (§ D)

CCT   CHARLES CUTLER TORREY, Professor of Semitic Languages, Yale University (§ G)

MET   MARY E. TOWNSEND, Assistant Professor of History, Teachers College, Columbia University (§ K)

NMT   *NORMAN M. TRENHOLME, Professor of History, University of Missouri (§ BI)

HET   HARRIET E. TUELL, Head of Department of History, High School, Somerville, Massachusetts (§ K)

MWT   *MASON W. TYLER, Assistant Professor of History, University of Minnesota (§ LTW)

RMT   ROLLA MILTON TRYON, Professor of the Teaching of History, University of Chicago (§ X)

LFU   LAURA FOSTER ULLRICK, Head of History Department, New Trier Township High School, Kenilworth, Illinois (§ Y)

FHU   FRANK H. UNDERHILL, Professor of History, University of Toronto (§ Z)

APU   ABBOTT PAYSON USHER, Associate Professor of Economics, Harvard University (§ M)

HBVH   HENRY BARTLETT VAN HOESEN, Associate Librarian, and Associate Professor of Bibliography, Brown University (§ AB)

CHVT   *CLAUDE H. VAN TYNE, Professor of History, University of Michigan (§ X)

HMV   HARRY M. VARRELL, Professor of History, Simmons College (§ B)

HMVE   HAROLD M. VINACKE, Professor of Political Science, University of Cincinnati (§ U)

JMV   JOHN MARTIN VINCENT, Professor Emeritus of History, Johns Hopkins University (§ A)

HHW   *HENRY HOMMERSLEY WALKER, Professor of Ecclesiastical History, Chicago Theological Seminary (§ F)

WWA   *WILLISTON WALKER, Professor of Ecclesiastical History, Yale University (§ F)

WSW   WILLIAM STEWART WALLACE, Librarian, University of Toronto (§ Z)

HBW   HENRY BRADFORD WASHBURN, Dean of Episcopal Theological School, Cambridge, Massachusetts (§ F)

WRW   WILLIAM RANDALL WATERMAN, Assistant Professor of History, Dartmouth College (§ J)

APW   A. P. WATTS, Assistant Professor of European History, University of Pennsylvania (§ I)

TW   THOMAS WEARING, Dean of Colgate-Rochester Divinity School (§ F)

HW   HUTTON WEBSTER, Formerly Professor of Social Anthropology, University of Nebraska (§ BI)

RDW   ROY DICKINSON WELCH, Professor of Music, Smith College (§ B)

ARW   ABDEL ROSS WENTZ, Professor of Church History, Lutheran Theological Seminary, Gettysburg, Pennsylvania (§ F)

TJW   THOMAS J. WERTENBAKER, Edwards Professor of American History, Princeton University (§ J)

ABWt   ALLEN BROWN WEST, Professor of Classics, University of Cincinnati (§ E)

WLW   WILLIAM LINN WESTERMANN, Professor of History, Columbia University (§ E)

ABW   ALBERT BEEBE WHITE, Professor of History, University of Minnesota (§ L)

LDW   LEONARD DUPEE WHITE, Professor of Political Science, University of Chicago (§ X)

LAW   LESLIE A. WHITE, Assistant Professor of Anthropology, University of Michigan (§ A)

PLW   *PAUL LAMBERT WHITE, Instructor in History, Yale University (§ KM)

DSW   DERWENT STAINTHORPE WHITTLESEY, Associate Professor of Geography, University of Chicago (§ X)

JHW   JOHN HENRY WIGMORE, Dean of the Faculty of Law, Northwestern University (§ G)

WJW   WILLIAM JOHN WILKINSON, Professor of History, Colby College (§ X)

JFW   JAMES F. WILLARD, Professor of History, University of Colorado (§ H)

FWW   *FREDERICK WELLS WILLIAMS, Assistant Professor Emeritus of Modern Oriental History, Yale University (§ U)

MWW   MARY WILHELMINA WILLIAMS, Professor of History, Goucher College (§ Y)

GGW   GEORGE GRAFTON WILSON, Professor of International Law, Harvard University (§ B)

JGW   JOHN GARRETT WINTER, Director of the Museum of Classical Archæology, and Professor of the Latin Language and Literature, University of Michigan (§ E)

WW   WILLIAM WOOD, Lieutenant-Colonel, Reserve of Officers, Canadian Militia (§ Z)

HEW   HOMER EDWARDS WOODBRIDGE, Professor of English, Wesleyan University (§ L)

WHW   WILLIAM HOYT WORRELL, Associate Professor of Semitics, University of Michigan (§ G)

JEW   JESSE ERWIN WRENCH, Professor of History, University of Missouri (§ GU)

CHCW   CHARLES HENRY CONRAD WRIGHT, Professor of French Language and Literature, Harvard University (§ KM)

CWW   CHESTER WHITNEY WRIGHT, Professor of Political Economy, University of Chicago (§ X)

HMW   HENRY MERRITT WRISTON, President, Lawrence College, Wisconsin (§ BX)

GMW   GEORGE M. WRONG, Professor Emeritus of History, University of Toronto (§ Z)

JTY   JAMES T. YOUNG, Professor of Public Administration, University of Pennsylvania (§ I)

A GUIDE TO HISTORICAL LITERATURE

GUIDE TO
HISTORICAL LITERATURE

SECTION A

HISTORY AND AUXILIARY SCIENCES

Editor

JOHN MARTIN VINCENT

Professor of European History, Emeritus, Johns Hopkins University

CONTENTS

INTRODUCTION

Ever since Thucydides, historians have casually indicated in their writings their views as to the nature and significance of history and the ·rules which should govern its study and writing. From the Renaissance onwards, notably by Bodin (cf. A221) these attempts at definition and the establishment of principles and methods have been repeated.

Yet historical study made no great advance until the nineteenth century when the rise of nationalism and the remarkable growth of the natural sciences added a new incentive to historical research. With this growth of the natural sciences came the development of an elaborate and well-established method of investigation and exposition which constrained the historian to assert the independence of his position and to insist that history had a method of its own, no less important than scientific method, for the extension and testing of human knowledge. The

1

attention of historians was, consequently, directed to the definition of their own field of study, to discussion of the aims and methods to be pursued, and to consideration of the instruments to be utilized. The thorough and systematic elaboration of the conclusions was first achieved by Bernheim (cf. A281b) in 1889. Since then he and numerous others have amplified his exposition and modified it in detail, but have not substantially altered the fundamental principles

The interpretation of history, however, has remained the subject of ceaseless debate ever since Karl Marx wrenched its discussion away from the philosophers and expounded a distinctly pragmatic conception of human experience in social relations.

The growth of democracy and the enormous extension of popular education have given history a place of peculiar prominence in the curriculum all the way from the elementary school to the university. The professionalization of the study and writing, as well as of the teaching, of history, has consequently progressed with enormous rapidity, especially within the past generation.

In view of these various developments, the student of history is required to concern himself constantly with questions of definition, interpretation, purpose, method, and instruments, and must consider each of these with due attention to the relations of history to other fields of study, and to the utilization of the results attained by the experts in those other fields, for the improvement and enrichment of history itself.

This section, therefore, is devoted to works dealing with the definition and interpretation of history, with the formulation of its methods and the utilization of its instruments, with its relations to other branches of learning, especially to those closely allied subjects customarily called the auxiliary sciences, and with historiography. So far as it has been reasonably practicable, the selection of titles has been confined to works in English, though, in most cases, titles in other languages might be readily multiplied.

BIBLIOGRAPHY

This subsection includes bibliographies of bibliography, bibliographies of historical bibliography, and general bibliographies of special subjects allied to history. In the subsection on bibliography in § B will be found general bibliographies, technically so-called; general catalogues; bibliographies of periodicals; periodical publications useful for current bibliography, especially of history and allied subjects; and general bibliographies of history.

A1a Kroeger, Alice B. *Guide to the study and use of reference books.* 1902. 3rd rev. ed. by I. G. Mudge, Chicago, 1917. [American Library Association.]

b Mudge, Isadore G. *New guide to reference books.* 1923, rev. ed. 1929. [American Library Association.]

b. Practically an enlarged and revised edition of *a.* Both contain classified bibliographical lists of reference books prepared primarily for use of reference librarians. Contain not merely general reference works, but also those in various special fields including history, biography, geography, social sciences, government documents, and bibliography. Though special attention is given to English and American publications, the more important works in the leading European languages are also included. GMD

A2a Josephson, Aksel G. S. *Bibliographies of bibliographies, chronologically arranged with occasional notes and an index.* 1901. 2nd rev. ed., Chicago, 1913. [Bibliographical Society of Chicago.]

b Stein, Henri. *Manuel de bibliographie générale: bibliotheca bibliographica nova.* Paris, 1897. [Manuels de bibliographie historique.]

c Schneider, Georg. *Handbuch der Bibliographie.* 1923. 2nd ed. Leipzig, 1924.

d Van Hoesen, Henry Bartlett (with collaboration of Walter, Frank Keller). *Bibliography, practical, enumerative, historical. An introductory manual.* N. Y. 1928. [Bibliography.]

a. Brief but useful; deals with bibliographical theory; provides a practical bibliography of bibliographies, catalogues, periodicals, etc. *b.* General bibliography of bibliographies of sciences, arts, literature, history, and biography; includes lists of catalogues published by important libraries; carefully done, but out of date.   HRS

c. Most extensive and important selective bibliography of bibliographies. Consists of two parts: theoretical and enumerative. The historical student will find particularly useful the sections devoted to national bibliographies and the bibliographies of society publications, periodicals, public documents, and biographies. Does not cover subject bibliographies. Review, L. Halphen, *Rev. Hist.* 147:102, Sept. 1924.   HBVH

d. Designed primarily as a text-book. Excellent manual, notable particularly for its valuable discussion of the principal subject bibliographies in all departments of knowledge.   HRS

A3a Langlois, Charles V. *Manuel de bibliographie historique.* 2 v. Paris, 1901-04. [1, Instruments bibliographiques, 1896, 2nd rev. ed., 1901; 2, Histoire et organisation des études historiques, 1904.]

b Coulter, Edith M. *Guide to historical bibliographies, a critical and systematic bibliography for advanced students.* Berkeley, 1927.

a. Epoch-making and fundamental work in historical studies; not merely a list of titles of works instrumental in bibliographical research, but rich in comment on the books cited and in valuable suggestions and discussions of bibliographical method. V. 1. Primarily a systematic annotated bibliography of bibliographies and other aids to historical study. V. 2. After a rapid survey of historiography from the Renaissance to the close of the eighteenth century, the development and organization of historical studies in the principal European countries in the nineteenth century are set forth with abundant bibliographical references and critical comments. Most consideration is given to publications of sources; some attention is given to writers on method in history and to the auxiliary sciences. Countries outside Europe receive little or no space. Review, C. H. Haskins, *A.H.R.* 2:320, Jan. 1897; 6:831, July 1901; 9:768, July 1904.   JMV, GMD

b. Brief but helpful introduction to the subject.   HRS

A4a Sonnenschein, William Swan. *Best books: a reader's guide to the choice of the best available books (about 100,000) in every department of science, art, and literature, with the dates of the first and last editions, and the price, size, and publisher's name (both English and American) of each book; a contribution towards systematic bibliography, with complete authors and subjects indexes.* 1887. 3rd rev. ed., 2 v., London and N. Y., 1910. V. 3, 1923; v. 4, 1926.

b Robertson, John M. *Courses of study.* 1904. 2nd rev. ed., London, 1908. [Rationalist Press Association.]

a. Fairly successful attempt at the difficult undertaking of listing the best available books in English; arrangement is by subject; annotations are few and brief; includes very useful, well-selected bibliographies of history and related subjects. *b.* With the aim of "encouraging and assisting private students to acquire knowledge in all the main branches of liberal culture," by listing important works on most subjects, but excluding literature and with an emphasis on history and allied topics, the compiler attempts to guide the general reader in "courses of study." There are brief comments on many of the books and indications as to the order in which they should be read.   HRS

A5 Wyer, James I. *Bibliography of the study and teaching of history.* Washington, D. C., 1900. [American Historical Association, *Annual report, 1899,* 1:561-612.]

Chiefly devoted to the educational side of the matter, but contains also a well-selected list of works on research; brief comments.   JMV

A6a Wright, John K. *Aids to geographical research: bibliographies and periodicals.* N. Y. 1923. [American Geographical Society, Research series.]

b Regel, Fritz. *Geographieunterricht.* Dresden, 1910.

a. Contains classified lists of bibliographies of geography, of maps, and of other works containing geographical information; a list of periodicals; and other material to guide the student of geography, who will find it an indispensable aid to his research. For current publications, cf. (A957a) *Bibliographie géographique annuelle.*   GMD
b. Useful manual, containing select lists which do not duplicate those in *a.*
                                                                                    HRS

A7 Ripley, William Z. *Selected bibliography of the anthropology and ethnology of Europe.* Boston, 1899.

Prepared as a supplement to the author's (A56c) *Races of Europe;* useful, but seriously needs revision to include later publications.   GMD

A8a Huch, Friedrich August. *Versuch einer Litteratur der Diplomatik.* 2 v., Erlangen, 1792.

b Oesterley, Hermann. *Wegweiser durch die Literatur der Urkundensammlungen.* 2 v. Berlin, 1885-86.

c Mariette, Nicodéme. *Bibliographie générale de la sigillographie, in Bibliographie moderne.* 22: 130, 1924-25 (A943).

a and *b.* Bibliographical helps in the study of diplomatic. *c.* Excellent bibliography of sigillography, not as yet completed. There is no up-to-date bibliography of the rest of the field of diplomatic.   HRS

A9 Moore, Margaret F. *Two select bibliographies of medieval historical study.* London, 1912. [Studies in Economics and Political Science. No. 2.]

Contains a classified list of works relating to English paleography and diplomatic.   JMV

A10a Gilkey, M. A. *American and English genealogies in the Library.* [Library of Congress.] Washington. 2nd ed. 1919.

b Gundlach, O. *Bibliotheca familiarum nobilium: repertorium gedruckter Familien-Geschichten und Familien-Nachrichten.* 1883. 3rd ed., 2 v. Neustrelitz. 1897.

a. Valuable list, running to nearly 7,000 titles, including a few periodical articles. *b.* Published genealogies of families of all nations. Valuable. HRS

A11a Gomme, Sir George L., ed. *Index of archaeological papers, 1665–1890.* London, 1907.

b *Annual index of archaeological papers, 1891–1910.* 20 v. in 15. London, 1892-1914.

c *Year's work in archaeology,* 1921 ff. London, 1922 ff.

Standard works; devoted primarily to English publications; published under the auspices of the Congress of Archaeological Societies and of the Society of Antiquaries. GMD

A12 *List of works in the New York Public Library relating to numismatics.* N. Y. 1914; also as Bulletin, 17-18, 1913-14. [New York Public Library.]

Most extensive recent bibliography of numismatics. HRS

A13a The Fabian Society, ed. *What to read on social and economic subjects.* 1891. 6th rev. ed., London, 1921. [Fabian tracts.]

b Grandin, A. *Bibliographie générale des sciences juridiques, politiques, économiques, et sociales de 1800 à 1925–1926.* 3 v. Paris, 1926.

c Greer, Sarah. *Bibliography of public administration.* N. Y. 1926. [National Institute of Public Administration.]

a. Well-selected lists, mainly of English works. *b.* Devoted primarily to French works; an annual supplement is contemplated. *c.* Titles arranged under eleven topics; prepared especially for students of American conditions. GMD

Library collections.—The Library of Congress, the greater public libraries, and each of the larger university libraries contain considerable collections on the various topics covered in this section; some of these are preëminent in special fields. For works on archeology Harvard is especially conspicuous, as well as for the excellence of its collections on history and allied subjects in general. In anthropology extensive collections are to be found in the libraries of the American Museum of Natural History, New York, and of the Field Columbian Museum, Chicago; in the Library of Congress and the libraries of the Smithsonian Institution and the National Museum, Washington; and the libraries of Harvard, Yale, Columbia, and of the Universities of Pennsylvania, Chicago, Washington (Seattle), and California. For geography there are the large accumulations of the American Geographical Society, New York; of the National Geographic Society, Washington; and of Clark University, Worcester; for genealogy and heraldry, those of the New England Historical and Genealogical Society, Boston; the New York Genealogical and Biographical Society, New York; and the genealogical section of the New York Public Library. The libraries of state historical societies are usually rich in the biographical and genealogical records of their respective regions. Numismatics is specially represented by the library and museum of the American Numismatic Society, New York. For works on the teaching of history the library of Columbia University is particularly strong.

AHS

GEOGRAPHY AND ATLASES

The earth is the stage on which human beings enact history. Consequently, a knowledge of geography, the scientific study of that stage, is indispensable to the historian. Buckle enumerated "those physical agents . . . by which the human race is most profoundly influenced" as "climate, food, soil, and the general aspect of nature." The first three, he added, have "originated the most important consequences in regard to the general organization of society." Appreciation of this relation of geography to history has been reflected in the writings of each generation from the sixteenth century onward. Since the publications of Buckle (B209) and Marx (A222a) in the middle of the nineteenth century, few historians have ventured to ignore the significance of man's environment for his history, the particular aspect of geography with which this subsection is first concerned.

As man is affected by his environment, so history is determined by geography. Works which deal with man's choice of places for his residence and areas for his exploitation and control and with the shifting boundaries by which he has defined them in different periods are classified as historical geography. Man has also invented a highly conventionalized type of picture to exhibit his views of the earth and of man's relation thereto, which are called maps, or when bound together in collections, atlases. Historical geography, therefore, and the atlases which illustrate it, constitute the second class of works noticed in this subsection.

There are scholarly volumes on ancient, medieval, and modern geography, and on special regions or countries: these appear in appropriate sections of the *Guide*. General geographic works of descriptive or informational character are listed in § B.

A41a Keltie, John Scott, and **Howarth, O. J. R.** *History of geography.* N. Y. and London, 1913. [History of the sciences.]

   b Vivien de Saint-Martin, Louis. *Histoire de la géographie et des découvertes géographiques depuis les temps les plus reculés jusqu'à nos jours.* 1 v. and atlas, Paris, 1873-74.

   c Günther, Siegmund. *Geschichte der Erdkunde.* Wien, 1904. [Die Erdkunde, ed. by Max Klar.]

   d Stevenson, Edward L. *Terrestrial and celestial globes: their history and construction.* 2 v. New Haven, 1921.

   a. Convenient brief survey. *b.* Old standard work. *c.* Comprehensive, systematic, and scholarly. *d.* Important specialized study by an expert. Review, V. H. Paltsits, *A.H.R.* 27:543, Apr. 1922.   GMD

A42a George, Hereford B. *Relations of geography and history.* 1901. 5th rev. and enl. ed. by O. J. R. Howarth and C. B. Fawcett, Oxford, 1924.

   b Engeln, Oscar D. von. *Inheriting the earth, or the geographical factor in national development.* N. Y. and London, 1922. (Bibliographical footnotes.)

   c Ratzel, Friedrich. *Anthropogeographie.* 2 v. 1882-91. 4th ed. of v. 1, Stuttgart, 1921; 2nd ed. of v. 2, Stuttgart, 1912. (Bibliothek geographischer Handbücher.)

   d —— *Politische Geographie.* 1897. 3rd rev. ed. by Eugen Oberhummer, Berlin, 1923.

e Semple, Ellen C. *Influences of geographic environment, on the basis of Ratzel's system of anthropo-geography.* N. Y. and London, 1911.

f Febvre, Lucien, and **Battaillon, Lionel.** *A geographical introduction to history.* London and N. Y. 1925. [History of civilization v. 10. (B153a.)] (Bibliography.) Tr. by E. G. Mountford and J. H. Paxton of *La terre et l'évolution humaine,* Paris 1922. [L'évolution de l'humanité. v. 4, (B153b.)]

g Vidal de La Blache, P. and **Gallois, L.,** eds. *Geographie universelle.* Cf. (A43d.) [1, M. Demangeon, *Les Isles Britanniques;* 2, A. Demangeon, *Belgique, Pays bas, Luxembourg;* 15, P. Denis, *Amérique du Sud.* 2 v.] Paris, 1927ff. (Photographic illustrations and bibliographies.)

a. Excellent brief treatment by a student of history; shows the effect of geographical conditions upon the political destiny of states. Position of towns, nature of frontiers, presence of Alpine passes, conditions in the Danube basin, and similar questions are discussed in the light of events of the past. Review, *Bull. of the Amer. Geog. Soc.* 35:103, 1903; of 5th ed., J. E. Morris, *History* 11:304, Jan. 1927. *b.* Introductory survey by a professor of geography; strongly emphasizes the importance of environment and of man's response thereto; pays special attention to the exploitation of the tropics and the question of so-called backward races. Review, *Spectator* 129:877, Dec. 9, 1922. *c.* Ratzel was one of the pioneers in the observation of people, especially his own, in their environment. Since his day advance has been made in this field, but the nature of the study was definitely indicated in his work, which has served as the basis for the various recent studies of the subject. *d.* Supplements *c*; an inquiry into the relations between geography and national policy with the thesis that the state adjusts itself during the course of its development to the geographic conditions in which it finds itself, exploiting its natural advantages to build up political power and to overcome the handicaps of its environment. Has also served as a basis for many articles and treatises, some friendly and some hostile to Ratzel's ideas. Review, E. C. Semple, *Geographical Rev.* 14:666, Oct. 1924. *e.* Suggestive study, because it makes available in English in summary form Ratzel's work and because of the writer's own researches and numerous illuminating, though not always conclusive, interpretations. Review, O. G. Libby, *A.H.R.* 17:355, Jan. 1912. Also cf. the author's (X41a) *American history and its geographic conditions.*

JMV, HRS

f. Highly controversial work by a follower of Vidal de la Blache (cf. A43d). In opposition to Ratzel and the neo-Ratzelians like Miss Semple, Febvre believes that geographers should study the relations between actual human societies and their environment because the environment offers various possibilities to man from which men select according to their ideas and character. The environment does not, he thinks, compel men to any particular occupation or way of living. *g.* Universal geography (to be 15 v. in 22), four volumes of which have appeared, emphasizing the connection between geography and history. Excellent. Review of *f,* M. Jefferson, *A.H.R.* 28:291, Jan. 1923; M. Jefferson, *Geographical Rev.* 13:147, Jan. 1923. *g.* v. 1. Ch. Bémont, *Rev. Hist.* 156:337, Nov. 1927; *Geographical Rev.* 17:507, July 1927. v. 2, L. Eisenmann, *Rev. Hist.* 156:385, Nov. 1927. HRS

A43a Brunhes, Jean. *Étude de géographie humaine: l'irrigation, ses conditions géographiques, ses modes, et son organisation dans la péninsule ibérique et dans l'Afrique du Nord.* Paris, 1902. (Extensive bibliography.)

b ——— *Human geography: an attempt at a positive classification, principles, and examples.* Ed. by I. Bowman and R. E. Dodge. Chicago, 1920; London, 1922. Tr. by T. C. LeCompte from *La géographie humaine, essai de classification positive, principes, et exemples,* 1910; 2nd rev. ed., Paris, 1912. (Bibliographical footnotes.)

c Brunhes, Jean, and **Vallaux, Camille.** *La géographie de l'histoire, géographie de la paix et de la guerre sur terre et sur mer.* Paris, 1921.

d Vidal de La Blache, Paul. *Principles of human geography.* N. Y. and London, 1926. Cf. (A42g.) Tr. by M. T. Bingham from *Principes de géographie humaine,* ed. by E. de Martonne, Paris, 1922.

a. Exhaustive study of a problem of human geography specialized both as to subject and region. *b.* Systematic analysis of the problems of human geography by the foremost French authority. The English translation has been edited by leading American scholars. Review, *Geographical Journal* 37:559, May 1911; 60:80, July 1922. *c.* Excellent survey of the relations between geography and history with special emphasis on such questions as food supply, migrations and settlements of peoples, geographical factors in the formation of states, and character of frontiers; supplemented by an extended study of geographic factors in war with specific reference to the World War and the treaties by which it was concluded. Review, H. Hauser, *Rev. Hist.* 141:99, Sept. 1922. *d.* Systematic presentation, by another eminent French authority, of the correlation between historical events and physical environment, with special reference to the historical evolution of civilization. Edited from the author's manuscripts after his death. Review, *Geographical Rev.* 13:144, Jan. 1923.

Also cf. (B153*a,* v. 3) Perrier, *Earth before history.* Review, *A.H.R.* 28:347, Jan. 1923; (B153*a,* v. 10) Febvre, *Geographical introduction to history.* Review, M. Jefferson, *A.H.R.* 28:291, Jan. 1923; and (M42) for special studies by Brunhes and Vidal de La Blache relating to France.   GMD

A44a Huntington, Ellsworth, and others. *Climatic factor as illustrated in arid America.* Washington, 1914. [Carnegie Institution of Washington.] (Bibliography.)

b Huntington, Ellsworth. *Civilization and climate.* 1915. 3rd rev. ed., New Haven, 1924; London, 1925. (Bibliography.)

c ——— *Character of races as influenced by physical environment, national selection, and historical development.* N. Y. and London, 1924. (Bibliography.)

d ——— *The human habitat.* N. Y. and London, 1927.

e Huntington, Ellsworth, and **Cushing, Sumner W.** *Principles of human geography.* 1920. 3rd rev. ed., N. Y., 1924; London, 1925.

a. Study of the arid regions of Arizona, New Mexico, and Mexico with respect to topography and vegetation; adduces strong evidence that the prehistoric civilization must have declined under slow climatic changes. Review, F. E. Lloyd, *Science,* n.s. 41:864, June 11, 1915. *b.* Carries the investigation beyond the familiar generalities about the zones of civilizations. Special studies are made of industrial groups to show the difference in activity at different seasons and under variation of temperature. The results not only give direction to the study of the past, but are also of great economic interest for the present. Fundamentally revised and thoroughly rewritten in third edition. Review, R. H. Whitbeck, *A.H.R.* 21:781, July 1916; C. E. A. Winslow, *Geographical Rev.* 3:252, March 1917.   JMV *c.* Written as supplement and corrective to earlier editions of *b*; studies of conditions in China, Iceland, and elsewhere lead to recognition of natural selection as well as physical environment as factors in historical development. Review, C. Becker, *A.H.R.* 30:570, Apr. 1925. *d.* Study of man's distribution on the earth's surface. Review, (London) *Times Lit. Suppl.* 27:120, Feb. 23, 1928. *e.* Clear and interesting text-book; emphasizes the response of man to geographic surroundings, particularly the effects of climate on man's activities. Review, H. H. Barrows, *Geographical Rev.* 12:157, Jan. 1922. HRS

A45a Fairgrieve, James. *Geography and world power.* 1917. 2nd rev. ed., London and N. Y., 1921.

b Cornish, Vaughan. *Great capitals: an historical geography.* London and N. Y., 1923.

a. Compact in form but broad in treatment; written "to show how the history of the world has been controlled by those conditions and phenomena which we class together as geography." The author goes back into early history, using Egypt to show the effect of the desert; Greece and Carthage to illustrate the influence of the enclosed sea; Holland, France, and Great Britain to reveal the determination of their development by the ocean. Useful summary if read with the understanding that the broad general statements are subject to modifications. *b.* Another lucid survey of the relations between geography and history; approaches the problem from a different angle, the location of great cities. Review, *E.H.R.* 39:159, Jan. 1924. JMV

A46a Maguire, Thomas M. *Outlines of military geography.* Cambridge, Eng., 1899; N. Y., 1900. [Cambridge geographical series.]

b May, Edward S. *Introduction to military geography.* London, 1909.

c MacDonnell, A. C. *Outlines of military geography.* London, 1911.

d Gregory, Herbert E., ed. *Military geology and topography: a presentation of certain phases of geology, geography and topography for military purposes.* [Publications of National Research Council.] New Haven and Oxford, 1918.

e Whitbeck, Ray H. *Industrial geography: production, manufacture, commerce.* N. Y., 1924.

f Whitbeck, Ray H., and **Finch, Vernor C.** *Economic geography.* N. Y. and London, 1924.

g Chisholm, George G. *Handbook of commercial geography.* 1889. 9th rev. ed., London and N. Y., 1922.

h Newbigin, Marion I. *Commercial geography.* N. Y. and London, 1924. [Home university library.]

i Jones, W. D. and **Whittlesey, D. S.** *An introduction to economic geography.* 2 v. Chicago, 1924-1926.

j Partsch, Joseph. *Geographie des Welthandels.* Breslau, 1927.

Not infrequently the historian finds it necessary to consider distinctly technical cases of the relations between geographical factors and historical events. Perhaps in no case do these relations require such careful attention as in the study of military operations. Though these considerations will appear most clearly in detailed studies of special campaigns, by writers fully conversant with their significance, such as (I536*b*) Oman, *History of the peninsular war, a, b,* and *c* will introduce the reader to the principal problems. *a.* Though by a civilian, empha-

sizes strategical considerations more than geographical factors. Review, Sir T. H.
Holdich, *Geographical Journal*, 15:239, March 1900. *b.* By a British general;
gives more attention to geographical matters; provides plenty of illustrative incidents. Review, *Geographical Journal*, 35:717, June 1910. *c.* By a British colonel
of engineers; comprehensive; includes discussion of recent operations and military
problems of the time. Review, *Geographical Journal*, 38:616, Dec. 1911. Also cf.
(J41a) Johnson, *Topography and strategy in the war*. *d.* Joint product of
eighteen geologists and geographers. Text-book prepared for use of Students
Army Training Corps. Emphasizes "facts and principles of geological and
geographical science which have proved to be applicable to military problems."
Excellent. Review, D. W. Johnson, *Geographical Review*, 9:61, Jan. 1920. *e.*
Treatise on economic geography; emphasizes problems of production. *f.* More
general text-book; gives major attention to the United States and Canada.
g. Latest thorough revision of a work which has been standard for a generation;
presents a wealth of information. *h.* Competent discussion of principles and
causes. *i.* Excellent practical text-book including an analysis of principles and a
survey of the main facts of world economic geography. Review of *e, f, g, h,*
and *i,* I. Bowman, *Geographical Review*, 15:285, Apr. 1925. *j.* Posthumous work
of merit by a follower of Ratzel. Treats of, first, the varying conditions, density
of population, races, language, religion and political organization under which
man lives and which give rise to exchanges and, second, the distribution of the
world's goods which give rise to world trade. An important contribution to the
literature of geography. Review, E. Van Cleef, *Geographical Review*, 18:171,
Jan. 1928.   GMD, HRS

A47a Dominian, Leon. *Frontiers of language and nationality in Europe.* N. Y.
and London, 1917. [American Geographical Society of New York.] (Bibliography.)

b Newbigin, Marion I. *Geographical aspects of Balkan problems in their
relation to the great European war.* London and N. Y., 1915. (Bibliographies.)

c ——— *Frequented ways, a general survey of the land forms, climates, and
vegetation of western Europe, considered in their relation to the life of
man, including a detailed study of some typical regions.* London and Boston, 1922.

d ——— *Mediterranean lands: an introductory study in human and historical geography.* London and N. Y., 1924. (Bibliographies.)

a. Endeavors "to show that language exerts a strong formative influence upon
nationality . . . but underlying the currents of national feeling, or of speech, is
found the persistent action of the land." Studies the more important concrete
problems in Europe, especially in the Balkans of which he has first-hand knowledge. Illuminating maps. Good, readable treatment. Review, C. D. Buck,
A.H.R. 23:171, Oct. 1917. *b.* Important contribution to the complicated study
of the Balkans, for it deals with both topography and racial conditions. Review,
Athenaeum, 2:445, Dec. 11, 1915; D. W. Johnson, *Geographical Rev.* 1:391, May
1916. *c.* Presents the principal geographical features of western Europe as
viewed from the main routes of travel. Review, *Spectator* 129:213, Aug. 12,
1922; A. P. Brigham, *Geographical Rev.* 13:483, July 1923. *d.* Written as a
college text-book to illustrate the relations of geography and history in the
development of western civilization. Review, (London) *Times Lit. Supplement.*

23:751, Nov. 20, 1924; W. E. Lunt, *Geographical Review*, 16:166, Jan. 1926. *b, c,* and *d.* Together, these three complementary works cover the European regions which have been most important historically.　　　　　GMD

A48 Freeman, Edward A. *Historical geography of Europe.* 1881. 3rd rev. ed. by J. B. Bury, 1 v. and atlas, London and N. Y., 1903.

Concerns itself chiefly with the history of the political boundaries of Europe. Atlas contains sixty-five maps. Both in text and in maps the pioneer English work on historical geography; still very useful. Review, E. W. Dow, *A.H.R.* 9:603, Apr. 1904.　　　　　JMV

A49a Poole, Reginald Lane, ed. *Historical atlas of modern Europe from the decline of the Roman empire, comprising also maps of parts of Asia and of the New World connected with European history.* 30 pts. in 1 v. Oxford and N. Y., 1896-1902.

b Schrader, Franz, ed. *Atlas de géographie historique.* 1896. Rev. ed., Paris, 1907.

c Vidal de La Blache, Paul M. J. *Histoire et géographie; atlas générale.* 1891-95. new and enl. ed., Paris, 1913.

d Droysen, Gustav. *Allgemeiner historischer Hand-atlas in Sechsundneunzig Karten mit erläuterndem Text.* Ed. by R. Andree. Leipzig, 1886.

e Spruner von Merz, Karl. *Historisch-geographischer Hand-Atlas.* 3 v., 1846-51. 3rd rev. ed., of v. 1-2 by H. T. Menke, Gotha, 1865-80; 2nd rev. ed. of v. 3, Gotha, 1855; new rev. ed. by M. Sieglin of v. 1, pt. 1-6, Gotha, 1893-1909. [1, *Atlas antiquus;* 2, *Historisch-geographischer Hand-Atlas zur Geschichté der Staaten Europas vom Anfang des Mittelalters bis auf die neueste Zeit;* 3, *Historisch-geographischer Hand-Atlas zur Geschichte Asiens, Afrikas, Amerikas, und Australiens.*]

All in folio size with numerous double-page maps and explanatory text. The consequent wealth of detail is much greater than in the simpler quarto works (cf. A50) intended for students. These five atlases embodying the results of the highest scholarship in admirably executed maps are among the foremost works of their sort. *a.* The technical execution owes much to the best German examples but a decided improvement lies in the arrangement of the maps of each country in a consecutive group. The text intermingled with the maps is written by authors having special knowledge of the country or the period. Review, pt. 1-7, G. LeStrange, *E.H.R.* 12:604, July 1897; pt. 8-30, *ibid.* 18:138, Jan. 1903. A good octavo atlas for modern times forms v. 14 of (I121) *Cambridge modern history. b.* A score of leading French scholars collaborated in the production of the 55 double-page maps and nearly 300 insets and smaller sketch-maps and plans. About one-third of the material deals with ancient history. The maps for medieval and modern times include some for Asia, Africa, and America as well as Europe. The limitation of detail and simplicity of treatment render the maps perhaps less scholarly than those in *c, d,* and *e,* but much clearer and more illuminating. *c.* Scholarly production with 420 maps, only about half of which are historical; excellent index of 46,000 names, 3500 additional names in the latest edition. Review, G. Monod, *Rev. Hist.* 46:386, July 1891; 57:140, Jan. 1895. *d.* Covers ancient and modern history, the combined work of a learned historian and an eminent geographer. *e.* Long the standard work; thoroughly comprehensive in scope. Though still in print, now out-of-date and largely, but not entirely, replaced by *a, b,* and *c.*　　　　　JMV, HRS

A50a **Shepherd, William R.** *Historical atlas.* 1911. 7th rev. ed., N. Y. and London, 1929. [American historical series.]

b **Dow, Earle W.** *Atlas of European history.* London and N. Y., 1907.

c **Putzger, Friedrich W.** *Historical school atlas of ancient, mediaeval, and modern history.* American ed. by E. G. Lemcke, N. Y., 1903. Tr. from *Historischer Schul-Atlas zur alten, mittleren, und neuen Geschichte.* 1877, 47th rev. ed. by A. Baldamus, E. Schwabe, and J. Koch, Bielefeld, 1926.

d **Muir, Ramsay,** and **Philip, George.** *Putnam's new school atlas of universal history.* N. Y., 1929.

e **Muir, Ramsay.** *New school atlas of modern history.* 1911. 2nd ed., entitled *Hammond's new historical atlas for students,* N. Y., 1914. 6th rev. and enl. ed. by R. Muir, G. Philip, and R. M. McElroy, as *Putnam's historical atlas, mediaeval and modern,* N. Y. and London, 1927. (London ed. as *Philip's historical atlas.*)

f **Meyer, Hermann J.** *Historischer Handatlas mit 62 Hauptkarten, vielen Nebenkarten, einem Geschichtsabriss in tabellarischer Form und 10 Registerblättern.* Leipzig and Wien, 1911.

a. Within the compass of a moderate-sized volume, this work offers historical data from the fifteenth century B.C. down to the present time. The 164 maps with their insets cover as many periods and episodes as could well be expected and include much matter of economic and social character. Where the scale of the map is sufficiently large, the higher elevations are indicated by hatching which gives a subdued effect of mountainous country without interfering with the political coloration. Naturally the greater part of the atlas is devoted to the eastern hemisphere, but the history of North America is illustrated by more than twenty maps. Review, S. B. Fay, *A.H.R.* 17:676, Apr. 1912. *b.* Begins with the ancient eastern empires and justifies its title by confining its maps, with few exceptions, to the eastern hemisphere. The periods are well chosen and the maps abundant to illustrate the progress of European history. The data given are exclusively political. Physical features are rarely indicated. Review, W. R. Manning, *A.H.R.* 13:668, Apr. 1908. *c.* Long in use as a text-book, and for scale and plan served as a model for *a* and *b,* but contains much material not reproduced in either. *d.* Covers ancient, medieval and modern history in 56 plates containing 145 maps with an introduction illustrated by maps and plans in black and white; a good small atlas, carefully made. *e.* Beginning with the barbarian invasions about 395 A.D., some ninety-six plates containing 229 colored maps and diagrams are devoted to the history of Europe and its expansion, including the United States. Physical features are indicated in many cases and sometimes by shaded hatching, by contour lines, and by graded tints in the same map. There are also special maps illustrating physical, economic, anthropological, linguistic, and cultural factors. The color scheme is vivid but agreeable to the eye. Review, (London) *Times Lit. Suppl.* 26:462, July 7, 1927. *f.* Perhaps the most satisfactory historical atlas of relatively small size. Similar in scope to *a*; one-third of the maps relate to ancient history. On the back of each map is printed a convenient chronological table, adequate to illustrate the situation portrayed in the particular map. Many of the maps are admirably executed though there is a tendency to overload them with detail.

All five works contain indexes of place names. *a* and *b.* Contain no explanatory text; *c* and *d,* a slight amount; *e,* has a useful introduction of about eighty pages; *f*, contains the fullest supply of explanatory data. All are quarto sizes except 2nd ed. of *e*, which is octavo.

JMV, HRS

ANTHROPOLOGY

No less significant to the historian than geography is anthropology, which studies, in the broadest fashion, man as the thinking animal who acts upon the earthly stage. More precisely, anthropology is the science which deals with the differentiation between man and other animals and with the wide range of factors relating to the physical and intellectual nature and development of the human race. In practice the emphasis has been placed on the study of primitive peoples. The term, as here, is customarily used to include as well the more special fields of ethnography and ethnology. Ethnography is descriptive and classifies mankind into races and records their diverse characteristics. Ethnology is analytical and examines the scientific bases for the classification and embodies in scientific principles the deductions from study of the characters and practices of the several races.

These sciences are, on the whole, modern developments and their progress has been so rapid in recent years as to render antiquated, in whole or in considerable part, earlier works in the field. Works devoted to the ethnography of the several countries appear in the proper sections of this *Guide,* and general works on prehistoric peoples are listed in § B. This subsection is limited to a few important general works on anthropology and on the basic problems of racial classification.

A51a Tylor, Sir Edward B. *Anthropology, an introduction to the study of man and civilization.* 1881. Reprint, London and N. Y., 1904. [International scientific series.] (Brief bibliography.)

    b Marett, Robert R. *Anthropology.* London and N. Y., 1912. [Home university library.] (Brief bibliography.)

    c Kroeber, Alfred L. *Anthropology.* N. Y., 1923; London, 1924.

    d Schwalbe, Gustav; Fischer, Eugen; and others. *Anthropologie.* Leipzig, 1923. [Die Kultur der Gegenwart.]

    e Haddon, Alfred C., and **Quiggin, A. Hingston.** *History of anthropology.* London, 1910; N. Y., 1911. [History of the sciences.]

a. Although out of date, contains enough concrete material skilfully analyzed to make it perhaps the best brief introduction to the science of cultural anthropology. Review, *Nation* (N. Y.) 33:181, Sept. 1, 1881. *b.* Primer; very different in scope and treatment; little specific description; no attempt at systematization or thoroughness; but presents the point of view of modern anthropology with great clarity and suggestiveness. As a companion volume to *a,* it is invaluable. Review, *Athenaeum* 1:229, Feb. 24, 1912. *c.* More recent work; fully up to date; also more comprehensive and thorough; deals with the history of early civilizations. Review, *Hist. Outlook* 15:320, Oct. 1924.   AAG

d. Systematic treatise by leading scholars; includes ethnography, ethnology, and prehistory, as well as the various topics belonging more strictly to anthropology. *e.* Useful, systematic survey. Review, *Nature* 86:308, May 4, 1911.

GMD

A52a Tylor, Sir Edward B. *Primitive culture: researches into the development of mythology, philosophy, religion, art, language, and custom.* 1871. 4th rev. ed., 2 v., London, 1903.

b —— *Researches into the early history of mankind and the development of civilization.* 1865. 2nd ed. London, 1870. 1st American ed., Boston, 1878.

c Goldenweiser, Alexander A. *Early civilization: an introduction to anthropology.* N. Y,. 1922; London, 1923. (Bibliography.) (B310a.)

d Lowie, Robert H. *Primitive society.* N. Y., 1920; London, 1921. (Bibliography.)

e —— *Primitive religion.* N. Y., 1924; London, 1925.

f Mason, Otis T. *Woman's share in primitive culture.* N. Y. and London, 1894. [Anthropological series.]

g —— *Origins of invention: a study of industry among primitive peoples.* N. Y. and London, 1895. [Contemporary science series.]

a. For long an anthropological classic; still remains the best general presentation of primitive religion. Equally useful as a rather moderate illustration of the evolutionary viewpoint and of the comparative treatment of data characteristic of Tylor's day. Review, *Nature* 4:117, June 15, 1871; 4:138, June 22, 1871. *b.* Studies antecedent to *a.* Though an old book, still useful. *c.* May be used as an introduction to several phases of modern anthropology. Descriptive sketches of several primitive civilizations are presented; a comparative section deals with primitive economic conditions, art, religion, and social organization; the theories of primitive mentality advanced by Spencer, Frazer, Durkheim, and others are discussed. Review, H. E. Barnes, *A.H.R.* 28:293, Jan. 1923. *d* and *e.* Lowie discusses the facts and problems of primitive social and economic organization on the basis of abundant material, and with critical insight fairly typical of the younger American school of anthropologists trained and inspired by Professor Franz Boas. Review of *d*, E. Sapir, *Dial* 69:528, Nov. 1920; of *e*, A. Goldenweiser, *Nation* (N. Y.) 119:733, Dec. 31, 1924. *f* and *g.* While old and not free from misstatements, these are the only general works on the subjects, and, as such, deserve perusal. Review of *f*, *Nature* 51:244, Jan. 10, 1895; of *g*, *ibid.* 51:557, Apr. 11, 1895.   AAG

A53a Boas, Franz. *Mind of primitive man.* N. Y., 1911. [Lowell Institute lectures.] (Bibliography.)

b Lowie, Robert H. *Culture and ethnology.* N. Y., 1917. (Bibliography.)

c Wissler, Clark. *Man and culture.* N. Y. and London, 1923. [Crowell's social science series.]

d Schmidt, Max. *Primitive races of mankind.* London, 1927. Tr. by A. K. Dallas from *Völkerkunde,* Berlin, 1924.

e Buschan, Georg, and others. *Illustrierte Völkerkunde.* 2 v. in 3. Stuttgart, 1922-26.

a. Has no peer as a fairly elementary theoretical discussion of such problems as the relation of culture to physical environment, racial traits, and the characteristics of the primitive mind. *b.* The first four chapters ought to prove illuminating to those interested in the relations of culture to race, environment, and psychology. Review, A. A. Goldenweiser, *A.H.R.* 23:836, July 1918. *c.* Able study of the factors and processes of human culture; comprehensive and systematic; based upon the most recent researches. Review, *Hist. Outlook* 15:320, Oct. 1924.   AAG

d. Comprehensive text-book of ethnology and ethnography by a professor at the University of Berlin. Review, (London) *Times Lit. Suppl.* 26:690, Oct. 6, 1927. *e.* An ethnological introduction is followed by careful descriptions of the several races and their cultures by competent scholars; richly illustrated.

Also cf. (Y53a) Wissler, *American Indian,* and works listed in (X54).

GMD

A54a Lévy-Bruhl, Lucien. *Primitive Mentality.* N. Y. 1923. Tr. by L. A. Clare from *La mentalité primitive.* Paris, 1922. [Travaux de l'année sociologique.]

b Radin, Paul. *Primitive man as a philosopher.* N. Y. and London, 1928.

a. Notable book on the psychological traits of man at the dawn of history. Should be compared with the opposing views expressed in *b.* Review, R. E. Park, *Am. Journ. of Sociol.* 29:503, Jan. 1924.   HEBS

b. Study of the mentality of primitive man, particularly the emotional and intellectual life of certain North American Indians, the Maori, certain African peoples and the Papuans, on the basis of statements, myths, and songs as given by the natives themselves. A suggestive book. Review, (London) *Times Lit. Suppl.* 26:988, Dec. 29, 1927.   HRS

A55a Ratzel, Friedrich. *History of mankind.* 3 v. London and N. Y., 1896-98. Tr. by A. J. Butler from *Völkerkunde,* 1886-88, 2nd rev. ed., 2 v., Leipzig, 1894-95.

b Wundt, Wilhelm M. *Elements of folk-psychology, outlines of a psychological history of the development of mankind.* London and N. Y., 1916. Tr. by E. L. Schaub from *Elemente der Völkerpsychologie, Grundlinien einer psychologischen Entwicklungsgeschichte der Menschheit,* Leipzig, 1912.

c Durkheim, David Émile. *Elementary forms of the religious life, a study in religious sociology.* London and N. Y., 1915. Tr. by J. W. Swain from *Les formes élementaires de la vie religieuse, le système totémique en Australie,* Paris, 1912.

a. Epoch-making at the time of its appearance; brought to a focus most of the anthropological knowledge of the day and completely superseded earlier works; still makes good reading; the numerous illustrations are most helpful. Review, *Nature* 60:269, July 20, 1899. *b* and *c.* Of very different order. While neither author was an anthropologist, both had delved deeply into primitive customs and lore. For the student with a philosophical background their books are veritable mines of information and suggestion. Review of *b, Athenaeum* 609, Dec. 1916; of *c, Nation* (N. Y.) 103:39, July 13, 1916.   AAG

A56a Dixon, Roland B. *Racial history of man.* N. Y. and London, 1923. (Extensive bibliography.)

b Deniker, Joseph. *Races of man, an outline of anthropology and ethnography.* London and N. Y., 1900. [Contemporary science series.] Tr. from *Les races et les peuples de la terre, éléments d'anthropologie et d'ethnographie,* Paris, 1900.

c Ripley, William Z. *Races of Europe, a sociological study, accompanied by a supplementary bibliography of the anthropology and ethnology of Europe.* 1899. Reprint, N. Y. and London, 1910. [Lowell Institute lectures.]

d Sergi, Giuseppe. *Mediterranean race, a study of the origin of European peoples.* 1901. Latest ed., London and N. Y., 1913. [Contemporary science series.] Tr. from *Origine e diffusione della stirpe Mediterranea,* Roma, 1895.

e Haddon, Alfred C. *Wanderings of peoples.* Cambridge, Eng., 1911. [Cambridge manuals of science and literature.] (Bibliographies.)

f Simar, Théophile. *Race myth, a study of the notion of race.* N. Y., 1925. Tr. by A. A. Goldenweiser, from *Étude critique sur la formation de la doctrine des races au XVIIIᵉ siècle et son expansion au XIXᵉ. siècle.* Bruxelles, 1922.

g Hankins, Frank H. *Racial basis of civilization: a critique of the Nordic doctrine.* N. Y. and London, 1926.

h Günther, Hans F. K. *Racial elements of European history.* N. Y., 1927. Tr. by G. C. Wheeler from *Rassenkunde Europas,* 2nd rev. ed., München, 1926.

a. Most recent discussion of the classification of human races; systematic treatise based upon physical anthropology. Though by an eminent scholar, its conclusions have been severely criticized. Review, A. Hrdlička, *A.H.R.* 28:723, July 1923; F. Starr, *Amer. Pol. Sci. Rev.* 17:675, Nov. 1923. *b.* This somewhat confused work was long the only general study of the subject available in English. Review, A. C. Haddon, *Nature* 61:462, March 15, 1900. *c.* More discriminating, although here also the author falls into numerous errors of judgment and perspective. Review, A. C. Haddon, *Nature* 62:27, May 10, 1900. *d.* Greatly superior to *b* and *c.* While it covers but a small section of the ground of physical anthropology, the author's familiarity with modern statistical procedure greatly enhances its value for the more advanced student. The English edition is a new work rather than a translation. Review, A. C. Haddon, *Nature* 64:370, Aug. 15, 1901. *e.* Illuminating little volume, but to be used with caution. Review, *Nature* 88:209, Dec. 14, 1911. *f.* Traces critically the growth of exaggerated ideas of race and of the superiority of a particular group.   AAG

g. Work of sound scholarship; discriminating in discussion; conservative in conclusions; undermines the glorification of race; exhibits the principal historical groups in Europe as political rather than anthropological. Review, T. P. Peardon, *Pol. Sci. Quar.* 42:629, Dec. 1927. *h.* Discusses, from the standpoint of the somatologist, the European racial types; emphasizes the claims of the Nordics to psychic preëminence; laments the rapid "denordization" of the world. Review, (London) *Times Lit. Suppl.* 26:866, Nov. 24, 1927.

Also cf. (B153*a,* v. 15) Pittard, *Race and history.* Review, A. Hrdlička, *A.H.R.* 30:109, Oct. 1924.   HRS

A57 Boas, Franz. *Anthropology and modern life.*

A discussion of current problems—such as race and immigration, eugenics, social change, education, etc., in the light of modern anthropology. Critical, analytical, and close to important issues of today. An excellent volume for the intelligent lay reader.   LAW

A58 Thomas, William Isaac. *Source book for social origins.* Boston, 1909.

An excellent collection of studies of all major phases of primitive life, together with exhaustive bibliographies.   LAW

VALUE AND AIMS OF HISTORY

Every age, guided by its circumstances and problems, discovers its peculiar fascination in the drama of history. Consequently, each generation selects from the past those personages, episodes, and motives which interest it, and depicts them with fresh colors. Thus, each generation recreates history in its own image. Explanation of the nature and usefulness of history has had, therefore, a history of its own. Conceptions have tended to broaden and thinking about what history is has become clearer. This process of the definition of history has been affected to no small degree by advances in other fields of investigation, notably, in more recent times, by progress in scientific thought and method. Since, then, later views are more fully perfected, works here cited are chosen from those of recent date. An interesting comparison with these views may be obtained from (G66) Ibn Khaldūn, *Les prolégomènes,* a discussion by an Arab historian of the fourteenth century.

A201 Stubbs, William. *Seventeen lectures on the study of mediaeval and modern history and kindred subjects, delivered at Oxford . . . in the years 1867-- 1884.* 1886. 3rd ed., Oxford and N. Y., 1900.

Statutory lectures by a profound scholar and exact investigator (cf. L535), as Regius professor of modern history at Oxford. The first five are expositions of the modern conditions of historical study and of the methods of research; adapted to the layman rather than to the professional historian. The other lectures (cf. L125b) relate to special topics in English and European history. Review, *Spectator* 59:1282, Sept. 25, 1886.   JMV

A202 Lecky, William E. H. *Political value of history.* London, 1892. Reprinted in *Historical and political essays,* 1908, new ed., London and N. Y., 1910.

An address to the workingmen of Birmingham, by the author of (L352a) *History of England in the eighteenth century;* (B645a) *History of European morals;* and (B645 b) *History of rationalism.* Gives a popular exposition of the value of history, with warnings of what it does not teach; shows how human will and moral forces work as well as natural causes. The volume of collected essays also includes one entitled "Thoughts on history" and some excellent biographical studies. Review, C. Becker, *A.H.R.* 16:856, July 1911.   JMV

A203 Harrison, Frederic. *Meaning of history, and other historical pieces.* London and N. Y., 1894.

The veteran essayist and lecturer assembled under one cover a variety of papers on historical topics including four on the uses and importance of its study. His wide range of allusion and his criticism of outworn methods afford stimulating reading. Review, *Spectator* 74:108, Jan. 26, 1895.   JMV

A204 Lamprecht, Karl G. *What is history? Five lectures on the modern science of history.* N. Y. and London, 1905. Tr. by E. A. Andrews from *Moderne Geschichtswissenschaft,* 1904, 2nd ed., Berlin, 1909.

The author of the voluminous (P121) *Deutsche Geschichte* here presents his historical creed. He regards history as a series of phenomena which can be classified, or, at least, explained in phases of social psychology and, in this volume, he enlarges upon the argument. According to the author, each period of history is characterized by some dominant quality of its inner life, which qualities spring, for the most part, from political and economic evolution. The somewhat heavy style should not obscure the fact that much has been contributed to the understanding of the past through the results of modern psychological research. Review, A. C. Tilton, *A.H.R.* 11:119, Oct. 1905.   JMV

A207 Robinson, James H. *New history, essays illustrating the modern historical outlook.* 1912. New ed., N. Y. and London, 1913.

Essays in historical criticism collected under a common title. With entertaining sarcasm the author of (B651a) *Mind in the making* points out numerous fallacious beliefs which have become embalmed in history because of lack of critical examination, and various misconceptions on the part of older writers on the relative importance of events. The modern historian should accept assistance from all the sciences, both in the clarification of his materials and in the adjustment of his ideas. Review, E. W. Dow, *A.H.R.* 17:809, July 1912.   JMV

A208 Woodbridge, Frederick J. E. *Purpose of history.* N. Y. and London, 1916. [University of North Carolina, McNair lectures.]

These three brilliant lectures are the reflection of a metaphysician. A distinction is drawn between the facts of history and the historian's interpretation of them; the former are fixed, the latter is developing and itself has a history; this interpretation alone shows purpose, it alone makes the past important for us today. Review, H. J. Laski, *Dial* 62:59, Jan. 25, 1917.   JWS

A209a Teggart, Frederick J. *Prolegomena to history: the relation of history to literature, philosophy, and science.* Berkeley, 1916. [University of California publications in history, 4:155-292.] (Bibliography.)

   b —— *Processes of history.* New Haven and London, 1918.

   c —— *Theory of history.* New Haven, 1925.

a. Study of the preliminary conceptions needed in the approach to historical study and research. Amplified by abundant quotations from writers upon science, philosophy, and literary art, as well as from historians. Review, F. M. Fling, *A.H.R.* 22:617, Apr. 1917. *b.* In an attempt to answer the questions whether the problems in historical research have been correctly stated, and whether the fundamental processes have been properly described, the author reviews the definitions of history, the geographical factor, and the human factor in the development of civilization. Shows the influence on historical research of modern tendencies in the natural sciences. Review, C. Becker, *A.H.R.* 24:266, Jan. 1919.   JMV
c. Attacks the general problem in a somewhat different way. First, the author finds that the limitations of the traditional historiography have existed because writers have confined themselves to narratives and have been interested largely in the deeds and motives of persons. The attempts which have been made at a synthesis in history he believes inadequate. Secondly, he suggests a better utilization of the results of the study of evolution. Thirdly, he urges that an inquiry be instituted as to the reasons "for the differences in institutions, arts, and forms of knowledge among different peoples." This could be made fruitful by examining the cultures of the present day, by investigating the activities of mankind as they have been slowly modified in the past, and by inquiring why these activities have changed radically at particular moments. Such an inquiry, he hopes, "will afford a basis for scientific investigation in the field of the humanities," and will

result in a new and more satisfactory synthesis. A thoughtful book. Review, H. E. Barnes, *Nation* (N. Y.) 123:223, Sept. 8, 1926. HRS

A210 Cheyney, Edward Potts. *Law in history and other essays.* N. Y. 1927.

Six essays on the science of history written during a period of twenty years by a leading authority. Most striking perhaps is that which gives the volume its title, the presidential address delivered at the meeting of the American Historical Association in 1923 and a later essay on "History among the Sciences." Review, E. E. Aubrey, *A.H.R.* 33:618, Apr. 1928. HRS

A211 Scott, Ernest. *History and historical problems.* Melbourne, 1925.

Series of lectures to history teachers on such topics as the purpose of history, principles of historical inquiry, and the relation of history to geography, physical science, education and patriotism. Scholarly, well written and stimulating. Review, H. P. Gallinger, *A.H.R.* 32:149, Oct. 1926; A. Gardner, *E.H.R.* 41:623, Oct. 1926. HRS

A212 Sée, Henri. *Science et philosophie de l'histoire.* Paris, 1928.

Suggestive, pleasantly written, but somewhat slender essay by a distinguished economic historian, in which he raises and answers such questions as how far can history be considered a science and is a philosophy of a scientific history possible. Among writers on the general subject whose ideas he expounds and criticizes Sée admires particularly Cournot in his *Considérations sur la marche des idées et des événements.* The second part of the volume includes miscellaneous critical essays. Review, *Rev. des Quest. Hist.* 109:442, Oct. 1928; A. P. Usher, *A.H.R.* 34:787, July 1929. HRS

THE INTERPRETATION OF HISTORY

In recent years there has appeared a group of books which at the same time contribute to the discussion of the purpose of history and to the formation of a philosophy of history. The authors of these volumes address themselves to the single problem of the interpretation of the facts of history. The following titles further illustrate the different solutions, more or less novel, which have been advanced.

In other portions of this section will be found the works of those who approach the question from the point of view of (A41 ff.) geography, (A51 ff.) race, and (A301 ff.) language.

A221 Bodin, Jean. *Methodus ad facilem historiarum cognitionem.* Paris, 1566.

A brilliant achievement for its time, the height of the religious wars. Bodin in writing upon the philosophy of history approaches the subject in a scientific spirit and points out the influence of geographic situation, climate and soil on the character and fortunes of nations. The value of writers, as based upon opportunities for knowledge or patriotic and religious bias, is estimated. HRS

A222a Marx, Karl. *Contribution to the critique of political economy.* 1904. Rev. ed., Chicago, 1911. Tr. by N. I. Stone from *Zur Kritik der politischen Oekonomie.* 1859; rev. ed. by K. Kautsky, Stuttgart, 1897.

b Bober, Mandell Morton. *Karl Marx's interpretation of history.* Cambridge, 1927. [Harvard economic studies, no. 31.] (Bibliography.)

   c **William, Maurice.** *Social interpretation of history, a refutation of the Marxian economic interpretation of history.* 1920. 2nd rev. ed., Long Island City, 1921.

   a. Contains the definite exposition of Marx's economic interpretation of history which had been foreshadowed in his earlier works and which was further elaborated in (I581*a*) *Das Kapital.* In the field of historical studies this work has wielded an influence sometimes compared to that in the biological sciences exercised by Darwin's great work published in the same year.   GMD

   b. Able summary of the social philosophy of Marx and Engels, with a running fire of criticism; followed by five chapters of appraisal. Well written and very useful to students of the economic interpretation of history or of Marxism. Review, M. M. Knight, *Pol. Sci. Quart.* 43:299, June 1928.   HRS

   c. Not a critique of this specific work but of the complete presentation of Marx's views; written by "a disciple of Marxian socialism" in the light of the Soviet experiment in Russia; primarily a socialist tract.   GMD

A223a Rogers, James E. Thorold. *The economic interpretation of history.* N. Y. 1888.

   b **Seligman, Edwin R. A.** *Economic interpretation of history.* 1902. Rev. ed. N. Y. 1917.

   c **Sée, Henri.** *Matérialisme historique et interprétation économique de l'histoire.* Paris, 1927. [Études economiques et sociales, v. 26.]

   a. The scholarly investigator and voluminous writer on medieval agriculture and prices in England here gives his estimate of the part played by economic questions in history. It is, however, not an abstract discussion of theory, but a treatment of his view of economic topics amply fortified by citations from all parts of English history and expressed with much vigor of opinion.

   b. The first half of this book, by a professor of economics, deals with the history of the theory of economic effect from the eighteenth century onward. This is followed by the author's views of historical study. He does not adhere to a strictly materialistic conception of human development, but, while recognizing spiritual and mental elements, points out the great importance of economic factors in social history.   JMV

   c. Study of origin, nature and influence of Marx's ideas. Review, E. G. Ledos, *Rev. des Quest. Hist.* 108:160, Jan. 1928.   GMD

A224 Renard, Georges. *La méthode scientifique de l'histoire littéraire.* Paris, 1900.

To the student of civilization in general it is important to determine the mutual relations between literature and the other factors in the history of a people. The analyses in this book will assist in estimating the weight to be given to politics, the family, religion, the arts, and other elements in the life of the nation.   JMV

A225 Trevelyan, George Macaulay. *Clio, a muse and other essays, literary and pedestrian.* London, 1913.

As the "scientific" historian revolted against the "literary" historian, so this essay represents the revolt against the so-called "scientific" historian. Trevelyan concludes that the true value of history is educational, by causing men to reflect on the past, and that causal laws cannot be deduced as in the natural sciences. He emphasizes the view that the historian should cultivate the art of narration and must possess imagination. A most interesting forecast of the revaluation of the German schools and methods of historiography which was one of the characteristic accompaniments of the War of 1914. Review, *Spectator* 111:918, Nov. 29, 1913.   HRS

A227a Berr, Henri. *La synthèse en histoire, essai critique et théorique.* Paris, 1911.

b ——— *L'histoire traditionelle et la synthèse historique.* Paris, 1921.

These books by the director of the *Revue de synthèse historique* survey the fundamental problems of historical method. The aim of *a* is to distinguish between the synthesis of mere learning and the higher "scientific synthesis," to determine the problems which face the latter and to show how it is different from the philosophy of history. The greater part of it is devoted to an analysis of three causes which the author believes explain the past of mankind; accidental, e.g. geographical influence; necessary in the sociological sense; and logical, e.g. the implications of social consciousness. The book is an important contribution in a highly controversial field. Review, J. H. Robinson, *A.H.R.* 17:643, Apr. 1912. In *b* the author wishes to complement *a*, in which he has presented in abstract his theories of a true synthesis, by discussing the ideas of those who have criticized it adversely and also the tendencies in historiography which favor it. To that end the work and ideas of eminent historians, Tamizey de Larroque, Halphen, Xénopol, and at greater length of Lacombe, are analyzed. Helpful as an explanation of *a*.   HRS

A229a Mathews, Shailer. *Spiritual interpretation of history.* Cambridge, Mass., 1916. [Noble lectures.]

b McLaughlin, Robert. *Spiritual element in history.* N. Y. and Cincinnati, 1926.

a. A fair and moderate statement of the importance of spiritual factors in history, neither belittling the significance of material influences nor attempting to establish relative values. A suggestive indication of those phases of progress in which spiritual forces have coöperated with other historical influences in promoting the substitution of moral for physical force, in increasing the worth of the individual and in transforming mere legal rights into a broader social justice. Review, *A.H.R.* 23:124, Oct. 1917.   LBP

b. Essay on the final meaning of history. It is justifiable, Mr. McLaughlin believes, to infer the existence of certain laws of history as a result of comparing and describing historical events. The laws discovered are sequence, unity and progress. We must infer also a vast mind energy which expresses itself in various forms of energy that take shape in historical events. Involved in this process human life has a goal-perfected personality, already exhibited in Christ. Thoughtful, but full of questionable generalizations. Review, F. A. Christie, *A.H.R.* 32:825, July 1927.   HRS

A230 Adams, Henry. *The tendency of history.* N. Y. [Reprint of an essay in *Degradation of democratic dogma.* N. Y. 1919.]

Brilliant essay on "progress," with the thesis that mankind has not shown in its history any general or certain tendency to progress or to unity; that the assumption of an evolution toward a more perfect society is an illusion dispelled by the findings of modern scientists. Review (cf. *Degradation of democratic*

Dogma), C. Becker, *A.H.R.* 25:480, Apr. 1920; W. A. Dunning, *Pol. Sci. Quart.* 36:127, Mar. 1921.

HRS

HISTORIOGRAPHY

As Buckle once remarked, "There will always be a connection between the way in which men contemplate the past and the way in which they contemplate the present." Each century has its own historical standpoint; thus the doctrine of evolution affected profoundly the conception of history in the second half of the nineteenth century. The following typical works will serve to introduce the student to the extensive literature of historiography.

A241a Shotwell, James T. History. *Encyclopaedia Britannica.* 11th ed. v. 13, 527-533. Cambridge, Eng., 1910.

b Barnes, Harry E. History, its rise and development; a survey of the progress of historical writing from its origins to the present day. *Encyclopedia Americana,* 14:205-264, N. Y. 1919. (Bibliographies.)

c Mortet, Charles, and **Mortet, Victor.** La science de l'histoire. *Grande encyclopédie,* 20:121-150. Paris, 1893.

Both *b* and *c* appear in separate reprints. *b.* A comprehensive contribution, occupying sixty pages, with extended development of topics. A convenient starting point for the student of historiography. *a* and *c.* Illuminating articles.

JMV

A242 Shotwell, James T. *Introduction to the history of history.* N. Y. 1922. [Records of civilization, sources and studies.] Also as (B61.1).

A "history of antique historiography," which perhaps should more properly be called an account of the sources for the study of ancient history. Brief but clear analyses of existing materials with studies of some of the ancient and medieval writers. Good guide to the whole subject. Review, W. S. Ferguson, *A.H.R.* 28:286, Jan. 1923.

HRS

A243 Croce, Benedetto. *History: its theory and practice.* N. Y., 1921. Tr. by D. Ainslie from *Filosofia dello spirito:* v. 4, *Teoria e storia della storiografia,* Bari, 1917.

Really philosophy of history, but also historiography in the sense that in the attempt to define what history is the author reviews the whole development of man's attitude toward the subject. In spite of considerable obscurity of language the practical worker will find stimulating queries as to the object of research. Pt. 1. An attempt to formulate the theory of historiography. Pt. 2. An essay on the development of historiography since the Greco-Roman times. The theory formulated in pt. 1 is that history and philosophy are identical, philosophy being essentially methodological rather than metaphysical and history being reality as it exists in contemporary thought, being thus entire and true in all times for that time. Pt. 2. Deals with the gradual emergence of the theory formulated in pt. 1. Review, F. T. Teggart, *A.H.R.* 28:288, Jan. 1923; Preserved Smith, *Nation* (N. Y.) 114:750, June 21, 1922; I. Babbitt, *Yale Rev.* 14:377, Jan. 1925.

WTL

A244 Ritter, Moritz. *Die Entwicklung der Geschichtswissenschaft in den führenden Werken betrachtet.* München, 1919.

One of the foremost German historians of the last generation, in a series of lectures, illustrates the progress of history writing by studies of the typical historians of various periods from Thucydides to Ranke. An able and illuminating work. Review, A. W. Ward, *E.H.R.* 39:420, July 1924. GMD

A245 Guilday, Peter, ed. *Church historians.* N. Y. 1926.

An excellent volume of biographical and critical essays on noteworthy historians read at a meeting of the American Catholic Historical Association in December, 1925. The titles range from Eusebius to Ludwig Pastor. In each case the essayist has attempted to give the point of view of his author and his conception of his task. "The sketches of Moehler by L. F. Miller and of Hergenröther by H. C. Fischer are two of special interest." Review by J. C. Ayer, *A.H.R.* 32:296, Jan. 1927. HRS

A246a Flint, Robert. *Philosophy of history in Europe,* v. 1, *Philosophy of history in France and Germany.* London, 1874.

   b —— *History of the philosophy of history,* v. 1, *Historical philosophy in France and French Belgium and Switzerland.* N. Y., 1894.

In *b* the author, who was a professor of divinity at Edinburgh, began a revision of *a*. No other volumes of either ever appeared. *b*. In reality a history of historiography in France, Belgium, and Switzerland from the Middle Ages to modern times, pointing out in particular how the advances in political science have broadened the scope of research and enlarged the content of the word history. Review, Lord Acton, (B243a) *History of freedom and other essays,* ch. 17. JMV

A247 Fueter, Eduard. *Geschichte der neueren Historiographie.* Berlin, 1911. [Handbuch der mittelalterlichen und neueren Geschichte. Abt. I. Allgemeines.] Tr. into French by E. Jeanmaire as *Histoire de l'historiographie moderne,* Paris, 1914.

An encyclopedic treatise on the history of history writing from the Renaissance to about 1870. Biographical sketches of the conspicuous historians of Europe and America are followed by critical estimates of their work and their position in the development of scientific research and in the changing conception of human history. Because of the brevity of these estimates one may not always agree with the unmodified conclusions of the author, but to the advanced student of history the work is indispensable. The French translation is in some respects better than the original, of which it is really a second edition. Review, J. T. Shotwell, *A.H.R.* 17:812, July 1912. JMV

A248 Black, John B. *The art of history: a study of four great historians of the eighteenth century.* N. Y. 1926.

Thoughtful essays on the literary and historical method of Voltaire, Hume, Robertson and Gibbon. Review, C. Becker, *A.H.R.* 32:295, Jan. 1927; A. Gardner, *E.H.R.* 41:460, July 1926. HRS

A249a Gooch, George P. *History and historians in the nineteenth century.* London and N. Y., 1913.

   b *Geschichtswissenschaft der Gegenwart in Selbstdarstellungen.* 2 v. [Die Wissenschaft der Gegenwart in Selbstdarstellungen.]

a. "The object of this work is to summarize and assess the manifold achievements of historical research and production during the last hundred years, to portray the masters of the craft, to trace the development of scientific method, to measure the political, religious, and racial influences that have contributed to the making of celebrated books, and to analyze their effect on the life and thought of the time." These promises are amply fulfilled in a manner both scholarly and interesting and, notwithstanding certain omissions, the book affords the best introduction to the modern school of historians. Review, J. T. Shotwell, *A.H.R.* 19:151, Oct. 1913.   JMV

For German historians in general cf. (P3).

b. Autobiographies of living historians, for the most part Germans, few from other countries, none from France or Belgium. Review, G. Allemang, *Rev. des Quest. Hist.* 105:420, Oct. 1926.   GMD

A250 *Histoire et historiens depuis cinquante ans.* 2 v. Paris, 1927. [Bibliothèque de la Revue Historique.]

Survey of historical progress in methods, organization and results made during the last fifty years; prepared under the auspices of the *Revue Historique,* chapters in most cases by notable scholar of the country concerned. A very illuminating and valuable publication. Review, J. F. Jameson, *A.H.R.* 34:92, Oct. 1928.
                                                                          HRS

A251 Rein, Adolf. *Das Problem der europäischen Expansion in der Geschichtsschreibung.* Hamburg, 1929. [V. I, Übersee-Geschichte.]

Brief but suggestive essay on the influence of over-sea discoveries, conquests and colonies on European historiography from the sixteenth century to the present day.   HRS

THE TEACHING OF HISTORY

An entirely new outlook upon history and its significance was revealed when it became a subject of academic instruction. The introduction of history into the curricula of schools and colleges had rarely occurred prior to the nineteenth century, and only toward the close of that century had its adoption become general. Today history is taught in every grade from the elementary school to the university practically throughout the world. This sudden development has produced a flood of writings upon the teaching of history to which the works cited below afford a reasonable introduction.

A261a Johnson, Henry. *Teaching of history in elementary and secondary schools.* N. Y., 1915. [Teachers' professional library.] (Bibliography.)

b Bourne, Henry E. *Teaching of history and civics in the elementary and secondary school.* 1902. Rev. ed., N. Y., 1910. [American teachers' series.] (Bibliography.)

a. Chapters forming a brief history of history teaching in Europe and America are followed by discussions of aims and methods of instruction, based largely on the author's experience. The clear exposition is assisted by a carefully selected bibliography arranged under topics. This part of the work is so well done that readers may be referred to it without enlarging this list. Review, A. E. McKinley, *A.H.R.* 21:333, Jan. 1916. *b.* Also a review of present methods with suggestions, with an additional section devoted to plans for courses of study in all the fields of history likely to be used in schools. Review, M. Farrand, *A.H.R.* 8:516, Apr. 1903.   JMV

A262a Klapper, Paul. *Teaching of history.* N. Y., 1926.

b Dawson, Edgar. *Teaching of the social studies.* N. Y., 1927. [Teachers' professional library.]

a. Intended for teachers in American elementary and junior high schools, by a teacher of English. "Seeks to evolve a system of teaching the social environment that will contribute significantly towards the development of civic-mindedness in young people"; to provide apparatus for Americanization through history teaching. Practical and suggestive. Review, B. Brebner, *Hist. Out.* 19:236, May 1928. *b.* Essays by specialists on geography, biology, psychology, economics, political science, ethics, history, and sociology, presenting these fields from the point of view of the demands of the junior and senior high school; with the object of showing what correlation in instruction is possible and advisable. Review, D. C. Knowlton, *A.H.R.* 33:678, Apr. 1928. HRS

A264 Pierce, Bessie Louise. *Public opinion and the teaching of history in the United States.* N. Y. 1926.

Scathing analysis of the racial, regional and class attempts to control the teaching of history in the public schools of the United States, particularly since the World War. A depressing study in loyalties. Review, C. J. H. Hayes, *A.H.R.* 33:360, Jan. 1928. HRS

A265 Scherer, Emil Clemens. *Geschichte und Kirchengeschichte an den Deutschen Universitäten.* Freiburg im Br., 1927.

Account of the teaching of history in German universities from the age of Humanism to the end of the eighteenth century with special treatment of Catholic universities. Scholarly and most instructive as to the evolution of what has been considered history, its differentiation into subjects treated separately and the introduction of critical methods. Review, F. A. Christie, *A.H.R.* 33:390, Jan. 1928. HRS

METHODS OF HISTORICAL RESEARCH

As distinguished from essays which treat of different aspects of research and interpretation, the works next under consideration are classifications of the whole subject, giving in greater or less detail an organic system of historical investigation and expounding the mutual dependence between the sciences which aid in the determination of facts. Although the study of documents, chronology, language, and other auxiliaries had been progressing for centuries, and the new spirit of scientific research had entered with the early nineteenth century, it was near the close of that period before the matter was systematized in text-books of method.

A281a Droysen, Johann G. *Outline of the principles of history.* Boston, 1893. Tr. by E. B. Andrews from *Grundriss der Historik,* 1858. 3rd ed., Leipzig, 1882. New German ed. E. Rothacker, ed. Halle, 1925.

b Bernheim, Ernst. *Lehrbuch der historischen Methode und der Geschichtsphilosophie.* 1889. 6th ed., Leipzig, 1908.

c Dow, Earle W. *Principles of a note-system for historical studies.* N. Y. and London, 1924.

a. This eminent German professor (cf. P288) lectured for many years on methods of historical research and prepared for his students a syllabus of the principles of criticism and interpretation. These doctrines, condensed into about a hundred paragraphs, are rational and precise, but without the expanded lectures they are difficult to understand and sometimes obscure. Droysen deserves great credit for this pioneer work. An appendix on "The elevation of history to the rank of a science" is an important review of (B209) Buckle, *History of civilization in England*. Review of new German ed. *Hist. Zeit.* 133:126, 1925. *b.* Foremost both in time and in completeness; valuable not for the invention of new terms or new methods, but for the organization of criticism, evidence, interpretation, and conclusion into a logical system, fortified by illustrative examples. Every work of the kind since has been indebted to Bernheim. The later editions give more space to the subject of philosophy of history, and they have additional value because of their references to the newer literature.			JMV

c. Attempt to solve the difficulties connected with note-making and note-using. Helpful little book, with excellent illustrative examples. Review, M. W. Jernegan, *A.H.R.* 30:381, Jan. 1925.			HRS

A282 Freeman, Edward A. *Methods of historical study: eight lectures read in the University of Oxford in . . . 1884, with the inaugural lecture on The Office of the Historical Professor.* London, 1886.

The author of (L241a) *History of the Norman Conquest* and of a wide variety of (B242) *Historical essays* succeeded, late in life, to the chair held by Stubbs at Oxford. The historian of long experience addresses the beginner, in plain and forceful language, about the character of historical materials and the nature of historical evidence. Review, A. W. Ward, *E.H.R.* 2:358, Apr. 1887.			JMV

A283a Jusserand, Jean Jules; Abbott, Wilbur Cortez; Colby, Charles W.; Bassett, John Spencer. *The writing of history.* N. Y. 1926.

b Thayer, William Roscoe. *Art of biography.* N. Y. 1920.

a. Four stimulating essays by leading historians on the work of the historian, a report of a committee of the American Historical Association to investigate the writing of history in the United States. Included also are letters on the same subject by Dr. J. F. Jameson and Dr. Ellery Sedgwick. Review, A. Johnson, *A.H.R.* 32:293, Jan. 1927; (London) *Times Lit. Suppl.* 25:749, Oct. 28, 1926. *b.* Traces briefly the art of biography from the dawn of history to the time of writing with apt descriptions of notable biographies and the conclusion that today a personality is approached as "a problem to be solved rather than as a life to be exhibited." Review, A. Henderson, *A.H.R.* 28:574, Apr. 1923.			HRS

A284a Mabillon, Jean. *De re diplomatica libri VI in quibus quidquid ad veterum instrumentorum antiquitatem, materiam, scripturam et stilium; quidquid ad sigilla, monogrammata, subscriptiones ac notas chronologicas; quidquid inde ad antiquariam, historicam, foresemque disciplinam pertinet explicatur et illustratur.* 1681, 3rd ed. 2 v. (Supplement (*b*) reprinted as v. 2.) Napoli, 1789.

b —— *Librorum de re diplomatica supplementum.* Luteciae Parisiorum, 1704.

c Ranke, Leopold von. *Zur Kritik neuerer Geschichtschreiber.* Berlin and Leipzig, 1824.

a. First treatise on methodology and still a classic work on the critical method of determining the authenticity of documents; in fact Mabillon created the science of diplomatic. *b.* A supplement to *a.* Other writers soon followed this first attempt to formulate rules of historical method; notably Lenglet du Fresnoy, in *Méthode pour étudier l'histoire* in 1713, Henri Griffet in *Traité des différentes sortes des preuves qui servent à etablir la vérité de l'histoire* in 1769, and the German theologian and philosopher Johann Martin Chladenius who in *Allgemeine Geschichtswissenschaft* (1752) first attacked from the angle of psychology the problem of how an historian can arrive at certainty. It was left for Ranke in *c,* a critical dissertation on the historians of the period 1494-1514, published as an appendix to his *Geschichte der romanischen und germanischen Völker von 1494 bis 1514,* to show how untrustworthy was much of traditional modern history, and to do with Niebuhr (cf. E251*a Römische Geschichte*) for internal and interpretative criticism what Mabillon's book on diplomatic had done for the critical study of texts; cf. (A289*b*) Johnson, chap. 5; and (P252). HRS

A285 Feder, S. J. Alfred. *Lehrbuch der geschichtlichen Methode.* 1919, 3rd rev. ed., Regensburg, 1924.

Clear and well-written treatise by a professor in a Catholic theological seminary. Noteworthy for its interesting defense of the possibility and provableness of miracles. In this and in matters concerning ecclesiastical history and tradition the author stands decidedly on Catholic ground. Review, F. S. Betten, S.J., *Cath. Hist. Rev.,* new series, 2:98, Apr. 1922. HRS

A286a Wolf, Gustav. *Einführung in das Studium der neueren Geschichte.* Berlin, 1910.

b Bauer, Wilhelm. *Einführung in das Studium der Geschichte.* Tübingen, 1921.

a. An elaborate work on the sources of modern history, to be regarded as a complement to (A281*b*) Bernheim, *Lehrbuch.* The materials are duly classified for description and interpretation, and of the almost overwhelming abundance of modern documents no species appears to have been omitted. It is at the same time a bibliographical handbook of the most important things in modern German history and an indispensable guide for the advanced student of the period in general. The theory and method of history are discussed by a master in the field of ancient history in (C571*c*) E. Meyer, *Kleine Schriften.* JMV

b. Useful volume containing practical advice for graduate students, a satisfactory section on problems, philosophical and technical, which have been discussed by many historians during the last generation, and a treatment of instruments of work—with a list of titles arranged in order of the steps in historical research, but not always clearly classified. Review, L. Halphen, *Rev. Hist.* 141:100, Sept. 1922. HRS

A287 Langlois, Charles V. and **Seignobos, Charles.** *Introduction to the study of history.* 1898. Reprint, N. Y., 1912. Tr. by G. B. Berry from *Introduction aux études historiques,* Paris, 1898.

The authors disavow any intention to provide a system, or a complete text-book, but undertake rather an essay on the method of historical research. At the same time the treatment is systematically pursued within established rubrics, taking up in logical order the external and internal criticism of materials and the con-

structive processes of historical narrative. Furthermore, it is readable and interesting to others than professional students. Reviews, C. H. Haskins, *A.H.R.*
3:517, Apr. 1898; E. C. Burnett, *A.H.R.* 4:383, Jan. 1899.   JMV

A288a Seignobos, Charles. *La méthode historique appliquée aux sciences
sociales.* Paris, 1901.

b Strong, Thomas B., ed. *Lectures on the method of science.* Oxford,
1906.

a. Treats of the methods to be used by the student of social and economic
history, with particular reference to the materials to be met in this field. The
object of such study requires that great care be taken in the making of conclusions; for the clarification of ideas as well as for the cautions given, this book
is helpful. Review, C. H. Haskins, *A.H.R.* 7:390, Jan. 1902.   JMV
b. Includes a paper by the editor on "Scientific method as applied to history"
in which the nature of historical proof is discussed and interesting comparisons
with natural science presented.   GMD

A289a George, Hereford B. *Historical evidence.* Oxford, 1909.

b Johnson, Allen. *The historian and historical evidence.* N. Y. 1926.

c Crump, Charles George. *History and historical research.* London, 1928.

a. This admirable little book is a study of judgments and conclusions. The
analytical table of contents is in itself an illuminating arrangement of the
materials of history; the discussions are brief introductions to the evidence
afforded by writers, documents, relics, and physical facts. The illustrative examples are cited with such aptness that the exposition is not only instructive but
readable.   JMV
b. Introductory essay, showing the results of clear thinking on the subject of
historical evidence and the nature of historical proof. The chapter on assessment
of evidence is brief, but particularly intelligent. Review, G. C. Sellery, *A.H.R.*
32:148, Oct. 1, 1926. *c.* Probably no "other book will prove so attractive and
so helpful to the beginner as the brief manual of Mr. Crump." Review by P.
Smith, *Jour. of Mod. Hist.* 1:141, March 1929.   HRS

A290 Vincent, John M. *Historical research: an outline of theory and practice.*
1911. Reprint, N. Y. 1929. (Bibliography.)

Primarily intended for the beginner in serious historical study, it presents a
rapid view of the classification of historical materials, the methods by which
they are tested, and the inferences to be drawn from each kind of evidence. The
auxiliary sciences are in so many instances employed only in medieval history
that the illustrative examples from that period are very much in evidence, but
there is also continuous treatment of modern sources, with the expectation that
drill in reasoning will be mutually helpful in either field. The work is practical
rather than philosophical. Review, E. B. Krehbiel, *A.H.R.* 17:810, July 1912.
        HRS

A291 Fling, Fred M. *Writing of history.* New Haven, 1920.

Compact little treatise on the nature of historical materials and the evidence
which they afford. Considerable space is devoted to the criticism of sources
preparatory to the process of construction. The illustrative examples are taken

almost exclusively from the French Revolution, a field in which the author has been a deep explorer, thus rendering the book a valuable aid, not only to the study of method, but to modern history as well. Review, H. E. Bourne, *A.H.R.* 26:305, Jan. 1921.   JMV

A292a Poole, Reginald Lane. *Chronicles and annals.* Oxford, 1926.

b Lanzoni, Mgr. *Genesi svolgimento e tramonto delle leggende storiche critiche.* Roma, 1927.

a. Admirable little book tracing chronicles and annals from the earliest type of medieval chronicle on the Continent to the narrative history of the twelfth century. Review, C. W. Previté-Orton, *E.H.R.* 41:462, July 1926.   HRS
b. Analytical and critical study of legends, their origins, their end and their relations to history. Review, Cizam, *Rev. des Quest. Hist.* 108:144, Jan. 1928.
                                                                                  GMD

A293a Salmon, Lucy M. *The newspaper and the historian.* Oxford and N. Y., 1923.

b —— *The newspaper and authority.* Oxford and N. Y., 1923.

a. A discussion of the newspaper as historical material, with numerous examples to illustrate its usefulness to the historian. One of the first efforts to deal systematically with the special problems of research and method which confront the student in dealing with the more recent periods of history. Review, F. M. Fling, *Pol. Sci. Quar.* 39:709, Dec. 1924. *b.* An account of censorship and government control of the newspaper press, with liberal attention to the period since the beginning of the World War. Together these companion volumes by an experienced teacher of history, with their wealth of illustrative material, constitute a valuable contribution to historical method. Review, *Historical Outlook,* 15:417, Dec. 1924.   GMD

A294 Meister, Aloys, ed. *Grundriss der Geschichtswissenschaft zur Einführung in das Studium der deutschen Geschichte des Mittelalters und der Neuzeit.* 2 v., issued in pts. Leipzig, 1906-27. [V. 1, B. Bretholz, *Lateinische Paläographie;* R. Thommen, *Urkundenlehre, Grundbegriffe, Königs- und Kaiserurkunden;* L. Schmitz-Kallenberg, *Urkundenlehre Papsturkunden;* H. Steinacker, *Urkundenlehre, Privaturkunden mit Ausschluss von Königs- und Papsturkunden;* R. Heuberger, *Allgemeine Urkundenlehre für Deutschland und Italien;* H. Grotefend, *Chronologie des deutschen Mittelalters und der Neuzeit;* T. Ilgen, *Sphragistik;* E. Gritzner, *Heraldik;* F. Friedensburg, *Numismatik;* O. Forst-Battaglia, *Genealogie;* R. Kötzschke, *Quellen und Grundbegriffe der historischen Geographie Deutschlands und seiner Nachbarländer;* A. Meister, *Grundzüge der historischen Methode;* O. Braun, *Geschichtsphilosophie;* M. Jansen, *Quellen und Historiographie der deutschen Geschichte bis 1500.* V. 2, R. Kötzschke, *Deutsche Wirtschaftsgeschichte bis zum 17. Jahrhundert;* H. Sieveking, *Grundzüge der neueren Wirtschaftsgeschichte vom 17. Jahrhundert bis zur Gegenwart;* A. Meister, *Deutsche Verfassungsgeschichte von den Anfängen bis ins 15. Jahrhundert;* F. Hartung, *Deutsche Verfassungsgeschichte vom 15. Jahrhundert bis zur Gegenwart;* C. Freiherr von Schwerin, *Deutsche Rechtsgeschichte;* A. Werminghoff, *Verfassungsgeschichte der deutschen Kirche im Mittelalter;* E. Sehling, *Geschichte der protestantischen Kirchenverfassung.* Ergänzungsband: 1. H. Steinacker, *Die antiken Grundlagen der frühmittelalterlichen Privatkunde.*]

The series is designed, when completed, to cover every important aspect of historical methodology, criticism, and interpretation. Each part is written by an expert and is a comprehensive synthetic presentation of the subject fully abreast of the latest historical scholarship. There are two series, the parts of the first series dealing with the technique of historical method, those of the second with interpretation and presentation of the most important phases of German history, both medieval and modern. The nature and content of each part is accurately described in its title. That these monographs supply a real want is shown by the fact that nearly half of them have passed into a second edition, and some into a third. The treatises combine clearness of presentation with careful detailed work. They are models of luminous compression, and are good, sound manuals for advanced students of history. JWT

A295 **Johnson, Charles; Whitney, J. P.;** and **Temperley, Harold W. V.,** ed. *Helps for students of history.* V. 1-51, London and N. Y., 1918-24. [1, R. C. Fowler, *Episcopal registers of England and Wales;* 2, F. J. C. Hearnshaw, *Municipal records;* 3, R. L. Poole, *Medieval reckonings of time;* 4, C. Johnson, *Public record office;* 5, *id., Care of documents;* 6, C. G. Crump, *Logic of history;* 7, R. H. Murray, *Short guide to the principal classes of documents preserved in the Public Record Office, Dublin;* 8, A. A. Tilley, *French wars of religion;* 9-11, A. W. Ward, *Period of congresses,* 3 v.; 12, *id., Securities of peace;* 13, A. A. Tilley, *French renaissance;* 14, W. Cunningham, *Hints on the study of English economic history;* 15, A. H. Thompson, *Parish history and records;* 16, A. P. Newton, *Introduction to the study of colonial history;* 17, M. R. James, *Wanderings and homes of manuscripts;* 18, C. Jenkins, *Ecclesiastical records;* 19, C. R. Fish, *Introduction to the history of American diplomacy;* 20, A. Souter, *Hints on translation from Latin into English;* 21, *id., Hints on the study of Latin;* 22, R. A. Roberts, *Reports of the Historical Manuscripts Commission;* 23, A. G. Little, *Guide to Franciscan studies;* 24, J. W. Adamson, *Guide to the history of education;* 25, W. F. Reddaway, *Introduction to the study of Russian history;* 26, W. Cunningham, *Monuments of English municipal life;* 27, C. Bémont, *La Guyenne pendant la domination anglaise, 1152-1453;* 28, R. L. Marshall, *Historical criticism of documents;* 29, G. P. Gooch, *French revolution;* 30, H. S. Kingsford, *Seals;* 31, J. P. Gilson, *Students' guide to the manuscripts of the British Museum;* 32, R. H. Murray, *Short guide to some manuscripts in the library of Trinity College, Dublin;* 33, *id., Ireland, 1494-1603;* 34, *id., Ireland, 1603-1714;* 35, *id., Ireland, 1714-1829;* 36, G. F. Hill, *Coins and medals;* 37, W. Miller, *Latin Orient;* 38, *id., Turkish restoration in Greece, 1718-1797;* 39, J. H. Pollen, *Sources for the history of Roman Catholics in England, Ireland, and Scotland;* 40, J. E. W. Wallis, *English regnal years and titles;* 41, R. Cohen, *Knights of Malta, 1523-1798;* 42, C. G. Botha, *Records for the early history of South Africa;* 43, *Western manuscripts of the Bodleian Library;* 44, H. J. Fleure, *Geographical factors;* 45, C. S. S. Higham, *Colonial entry-books;* 46, H. G. Aldis, *University library, Cambridge;* 47, G. Davies, *Student's guide to the manuscripts relating to English history in the seventeenth century in the Bodleian Library;* 48, W. H. R. Rivers, *History and ethnology;* 49, A. G. Ogilvie, *Some aspects of boundary settlement at Peace Conference;* 50, C. Johnson, *Mechanical processes of the historian;* 51, E. R. Adair, *Sources for the history of the council in the 16th and 17th centuries.*]

A series of brief primers admirably fulfilling the promise of the title, on the nature of historical materials, on national and local records, chronology, sources for various periods, and other topics, written by experts in each field. JMV

PHILOLOGY

Philology, the science of the structure and development of language, is of primary importance to the historian as an auxiliary science. Philological study ought logically to precede historical research in every instance where the docu-ments to be employed are not in a form in which they can be readily understood. For example, the language used in itself often affords evidence which requires special rules for its interpretation. It may supply the clue to the date of a document or betray the source of a body of literature. Thus it is the linguistic analysis of the New Testament which has led to the assumption of earlier Aramaic versions of certain books and consequently, to certain theories about their date and origin. Or again for many years the chronicle of Croyland Abbey covering the period 625-1089 was considered genuine. Philological research in the nineteenth century showed that Latin terms frequently employed in the docu-ment came into use one or two centuries later than the dates of the documents which appear in the chronicle. Feudal terms, too, unknown in Britain before the Conquest, were used in charters alleged to be of an early Saxon period. On the basis of this and other evidence the whole chronicle was declared a forgery.

In a more direct way knowledge of a language may be useful—in avoiding the pitfalls of the man who, thinking that he knows the language, mistranslates official documents. Instances have occurred of such mistranslation by government officials with unfortunate consequences.

Language also may be a factor of significance in the development of a people or an indication of the relations of different peoples.

The extraordinary abundance of philological literature forbids the citation of more than a few titles. The works named will serve as a general introduction to linguistic science and give some description of its problems and methods.

A301a Jespersen, Otto. *Language: its nature, development, and origin.* N. Y. 1922.

b Paul, Hermann. *Principles of the history of language.* N. Y. 1889. Tr. by H. A. Strong and others from *Prinzipien der Sprachgeschichte,* 1880. 5th ed. Halle, 1920.

c Bloomfield, Leonard. *An introduction to the study of language.* N. Y. 1914.

d Sapir, Edward. *Language: an introduction to the study of speech.* N. Y. 1921.

e Whitney, William Dwight. *Language and the study of language.* 1867; 5th ed. N. Y. 1892.

f ———— *The life and growth of language.* N. Y. 1875. [International scientific series, v. 16.]

g Gabelentz, Georg von der. *Die Sprachwissenschaft, ihre Aufgaben, Methoden, und bisherigen Ergebnisse.* 1891. 2nd enl. ed., Leipzig, 1901.

h Sweet, Henry. *The history of language.* London, 1900.

i Wyld, Henry Cecil. *The historical study of the mother tongue: an intro-duction to philological method.* N. Y., 1906. (Bibliography.)

a. Perhaps affords the English-speaking reader the best general introduction to the subject. It gives a brief but excellent survey of the history of linguistic theory, and then discusses, in terms as untechnical as possible, and with abundant illustration, the nature of language and the processes of its growth and change. The treatises, *b, c,* and *d,* are more systematic, suited to accompany formal courses of study and in fact commonly used as text-books. All are competent statements of present knowledge and opinion. The works, *e, f, g,* and *h,* illustrate very well the development of the science during the past fifty years. *g.* Gives a very help-

ful exposition of philological method, particularly as applied to the English
language.   FNR

A302a Sweet, Henry. *Primer of phonetics.* Oxford, 1892.

    b Jespersen, Otto. *Lehrbuch der Phonetik.* 1904. 2nd ed. Leipzig and
Berlin, 1913. Tr. by H. Davidson from *Fonetik: en systematik frem-
stelling af laeren om sproglyd.* København, 1897-1899.

    c Sievers, Edward. *Grundzüge der Phonetik: zur Einführung in das Stu-
dium der Lautlehre der Indogermanischen Sprachen.* 1881. 5th ed.
Leipzig, 1901. [Bibliothek indogermanischer Grammatiken. v. 1.]

Reference may be made to these volumes for a convenient introduction to
phonetics, the physiological basis which underlies the study of sound and change.
                                                                          FNR

A303a Brugmann, Karl. *Elements of the comparative grammar of the Indo-
Germanic languages.* 5 v., N. Y. 1888-1895. Tr. by R. S. Conway and
W. H. D. Rouse from *Grundriss der indogermanischen Sprachen,* 5 v. in 6,
1886-1900. 2nd ed. Brugmann, Karl, and Delbrück, Berthold. 2 v. in 5,
Strassburg, 1897-1913.

    b Meillet, Antoine. *Linguistique historique et linguistique générale.* Paris,
1921.

Treatises on comparative grammar and comparative syntax.   HRS

A304a Brockelmann, Carl. *Kurzgefasste vergleichende Grammatik der semitischen Sprachen.* Berlin, 1908. [Porta linguarum orientalium Sammlung
von Lehrbüchern für das Studium der orientalischen Sprachen.]

    b —— *Grundriss der vergleichenden Grammatik der semitischen Sprachen.*
Berlin, 1908.

    c —— *Semitische Sprachwissenschaft.* 1906. 2nd ed., Berlin, 1916.
[Sammlung Göschen.]

Works on Semitic languages in general.   HRS

A305a Finck, Franz Nikolaus. *Die Sprachstämme des Erdkreises.* Leipzig,
1909. [Aus Natur und Geisteswelt.]

    b —— *Die Haupttypen des Sprachbaus.* Leipzig, 1910. [Aus Natur und
Geisteswelt.]

    c Meillet, Antoine, and **Cohen, Marcel,** eds. *Les langues du monde.* Paris,
1924.

The description and classification of the languages of mankind is briefly discussed in (A301h). *a, b,* and *c.* More complete and recent treatises on the subject.   FNR

A306a Usener, Hermann. *Philologie und Geschichtswissenschaft.* Bonn, 1882.

    b Wundt, Wilhelm. *Völkerpsychologie: eine Untersuchung der Entwickel-
ungsgesetze von Sprache, Mythus, und Sitte,* 10 v. in 13. Leizpig, 1900-
1926.

    c Vendryes, Joseph. *Language, a linguistic introduction to history.* Lon-
don, 1925 (also as B153*a*, no. 5). Tr. by P. Rudin from *Le langage:
introduction linguistique à l'histoire.* Paris, 1921 (also as B153*b*, no. 3).

Treat of the relations of philology and history. *b* and *c.* Especially valuable as
setting forth problems of current interest. Wundt, who writes as a psychologist,
deals largely with questions about the origin and development of language, and

his theories have been the subject of animated discussion among experts in linguistics. Vendryes, who is primarily a philologist, is more concerned with the ascertained facts of the history of language. But he shows fully, and very suggestively, their bearing on race psychology and social history. *a.* Briefer study. FNR

DIPLOMATIC AND SIGILLOGRAPHY

Diplomatic has been defined as the science of ancient writings, literary and public documents, letters, decrees and charters which has for its object to decipher such old writings and to ascertain their authenticity, dates, signatures, etc. Obviously this science is essential for the student of many fields of history, modern as well as medieval or ancient, for the scholar should realize that modern official papers need technical examination as well as do those of an earlier period. He should know also the nature and practices of the offices in which public documents were customarily prepared and are preserved.

Seals, too, have their importance, because for many years a guarantee of authenticity of legal and official documents has been an emblem known as a seal, and forgeries may often be detected by examination of this feature of the paper, which testifies to a legal transaction.

In the absence of a general work to introduce the student to the use of archives reference should be made to special works such as (H1a) Paetow, and those listed under (L5), (M11), (P6), and (X4).

A321 Rosenmund, Richard. *Die Fortschritte der Diplomatik seit Mabillon vornehmlich in Deutschland—Österreich.* München und Leipzig. 1897. [V. 4 *Historische Bibliothek.*]

Good introduction to the great works in diplomatic down to 1879.

For the beginning of diplomatic reference should be made to (A284a) Mabillon, *De Re Diplomatica,* a very famous and influential work, containing "not only a careful exposition of the way in which charters were prepared, but by a minute description of the material and the ink used, and of the handwriting characteristic of different chanceries"—with many illustrative specimens of handwriting. By it and by its supplement (A284b) Mabillon became the father of a new auxiliary science. HRS

A322 Jenkinson, Hilary. *Manual of archive administration, including the problems of war archives and archive making.* Oxford, 1922. [Economic and social history of the world war, British series.]

Excellent brief manual of value both to the archivist and to the historian. Part 5 is devoted to "war archives" of the World War. Review, V. H. Paltsits, *A.H.R.* 28:524, Apr. 1923. HRS

A323 Fournier, Paul E. L. *Conseils pratiques pour le classement et l'inventaire des archives et l'édition des documents historiques écrits.* Paris, 1924.

Brief but serviceable manual on classification of archives and editing of documents. HRS

A324a Rye, Walter. *Records and record searching: a guide to the genealogist and topographer.* London, 1888.

b Phillimore, William P. W. *How to write the history of a family: a guide for the genealogist.* 1887. 2nd ed., London and Boston. 1888.

c —— *Parish historian: a short initial guide for writing, printing and illustrating the history of a parish.* London, 1905.

d **Scott, Henry T.,** and **Davey, Samuel.** *Guide to the collector of historical documents, literary manuscripts and autograph letters,* etc. London, 1891.

e **Coke, Mrs. Emma E. (Thoyta).** *How to study and decipher old documents.* 1893. 3rd ed., London, 1909.

Popular writings on old English records have not been wanting, particularly such as offer assistance to amateur students of genealogy and local history. Among these, the above deserve mention here because written by persons of long experience in the examination of such documents. Although written for the special purposes named, these books have a value for the general student because of the suggestive explanations of sources which might otherwise escape attention. *e.* "A key to the family deed chest."   JMV

A325a Hall, Hubert. *Studies in English official historical documents.* Cambridge, England, 1908.

b —— ed. *Formula book of English official historical documents.* 2 v. Cambridge, England, 1908-09. 1, *Diplomatic documents;* 2, *Ministerial and judicial records.*

c **Loewe, Victor.** *Das deutsche Archivwesen.* Breslau, 1921.

A systematic treatment of English diplomatics has been slow in development. Only in recent years has the matter reached publication in the scientific form that it deserves. English public records are beyond comparison the most complete and continuous, but the classifications of forms and procedures by modern writers remained far behind those of Germany and France. A long step forward was made by *a.* Description of the archive system is followed by explanation of the legal and historical importance of the various kinds of documents. The work is indispensable to the student of original records as well as to the understanding of the printed reproductions. Reviews, C. H. Haskins, *A.H.R.* 14:558, Apr. 1909; 15:643, Apr. 1910.   JMV

c. Description of German archives.   HRS

A326a Bresslau, Harry. *Handbuch der Urkundenlehre für Deutschland und Italien.* 1889. 2nd ed., 2 v., Leipzig, 1912-15.

b **Giry, Arthur.** *Manuel de diplomatique.* Paris. New ed., 2 v., Paris, 1925.

c **Redlich, Oswald.** *Allgemeine Einleitung zur Urkundenlehre.* München, 1907. [(B170) Below and Meinecke, Handbuch der mittelalterlichen und neueren Geschichte, pt. 4.]

d **Erben, Wilhelm.** *Die Kaiser- und Königsurkunden des Mittelalters in Deutschland, Frankreich, und Italien.* München, 1910. (B170.)

e **Redlich, Oswald.** *Die Privaturkunden des Mittelalters.* München, 1911. (B170.)

In the midst of a multitude of works of smaller compass and monographs on particular topics, these manuals stand out as monuments in this field of learning. They cover all the auxiliary sciences which are concerned in the criticism of documents, such as paleography, chronology, heraldry, and seals, and demonstrate how much of a science the identification and interpretation of these sources has become. Between them the documents of France, the German Empire, and the

Papacy, that is to say the principal medieval systems of the continent, are comprehensively treated so far as form and content are concerned.

Several of the volumes in (A294) Meister, *Grundriss der Geschichtswissenschaft* furnish brief expositions of diplomatic in various aspects, especially Steinacker (A294, Ergänzungsband), which covers an earlier period in diplomatic than do the books listed under (A325).   JMV, HRS

A327 *Bulletin of the Institute of Historical Research.* 1 ff. London, 1925 ff.

Scattered through the volumes of this bulletin will be found many articles of value to the archivist and researcher; e.g., the report on editing historical documents made by a committee of Anglo-American historians. *Bull. of Instit. of Hist. Research,* 1:6, 1923.   HRS

A331a Ewald, Wilhelm. *Siegelkunde.* München, 1914. [(B170) Below and
    Meinecke, Handbuch der mittelalterlichen und neueren Geschichte, pt. 4.]
  b Grand, Ernest D. *Sigillographie.* (B23b) *Grande encyclopédie,* 30:1-9,
    Paris, 1900. (Extensive bibliography.)

Originally the legal value of a document and later its authenticity and historical importance depended much upon the seals attached thereto, consequently the serious works on historical method all contain chapters or parts treating of sigillography. In modern times these matters have lost their contemporary importance, but for some six centuries of European history the study cannot be omitted. Review of *a,* C. H. Haskins, *A.H.R.* 20:426, Jan. 1915. Also cf. (A326a) Bresslau, (A326b) Giry, (A341b) Prou, (A294) Meister.   JMV

A332a Birch, Walter de Gray. *Seals.* London, 1907. [Connoisseur's library.]
  b Maxwell-Lyte, Sir H. C. *Historical notes on the use of the great seal
    of England.* London, 1926.

a. Elaborately illustrated and interesting treatise on seals, from the earliest times to the date of publication, confining its attention principally to British seals. Useful glossary of conventional terms. *b.* Well-documented and learned work on the antiquities and technique of the English chancery by a deputy keeper of the public records. Reviews, T. F. Tout, *E.H.R.* 42:630, Oct. 1927; C. Bémont, *Rev. Hist.* 156:399, Nov. 1927.   HRS

PALEOGRAPHY

Paleography, the sum of the various kinds of knowledge required for the deciphering of ancient and medieval manuscripts, necessarily is considered as an auxiliary science to history or, rather, to the historical study of antiquity and the middle ages. Originally a part of diplomatic, it was developed in the eighteenth century as a distinct field, while more recently the discovery in Egypt of ancient documents and manuscripts on papyrus has brought into existence a specialized study, known as papyrology.

In addition to the brief list which follows, sections D and E should be consulted for works on ancient paleography, E for those on papyrology.

A341a Lehmann, Paul Joachim. *Zur Paläographie und Handschriftenkunde.*
    München, 1909. [V. 1 of Traube, Ludwig, *Vorlesungen und Abhandlungen,*
    München, 1909.]

   b **Prou, Maurice.** *Manuel de paléographie latine et française du sixième au dix-septième siècle.* 1889. 3rd ed., Paris, 1910. (Bibliography.)

   c **Johnson, Charles,** and **Jenkinson, Hilary.** *English court hand, A.D. 1066 to 1500, illustrated chiefly from the public records.* 1 v. and atlas of plates. Oxford, 1915. (Bibliography.)

   d **Jenkinson, Hilary.** *Palaeography and the practical study of court hand.* Cambridge, Eng., 1915.

   e **Wright, Andrew.** *Court hand restored; or, the student's assistant in reading old deeds, charters, records, etc.* 1776. 10th rev. ed. by C. T. Marvin, London, 1912.

   f **Martin, Charles Trice.** *The record interpreter.* 1892. 2nd ed., London, 1910.

a. In addition to chapters on the foundations of paleography and on Latin handwriting, contains a clear and interesting sketch of the history of paleography, one of the few treatments of the subject.   HRS

In addition to the chapters on manuscripts in the general works on diplomatics, such as those of (A326) Bresslau, Giry, and others, there are elaborate treatises on paleography alone which leave practically nothing uncovered in that science. The scholarship of France, Germany, and Austria has brought to light and systematized great quantities of documents, of which large numbers have been reproduced in facsimile for the use of students. As references to these collections are to be found in the various text-books only the above outstanding works need be mentioned here. *b.* The 3rd ed. has been entirely revised and is accompanied by a portfolio of plates illustrating the various periods of medieval writing. It is the authoritative work of an eminent archivist and professor in the École des Chartes at Paris. *c.* A brief introduction leads to methods of abbreviation and then to the history of individual letters. This part is illustrated by woodcuts showing the letters in large dimensions, so as to emphasize the characteristics of the different periods. The plates in the atlas are admirable for clearness. *d.* An essay which should be read in connection with *c,* and which sets limits to the value of paleography alone in determining the origin of a document and argues that it is inadequate except in the earlier periods when materials are rare. Conclusions from handwriting and from diplomatic usage must both be backed up by careful study of administrative history. *e.* An old book but still a convenience. The original introduction was written in 1773, but the series of progressive plates has been so useful that the work has been repeatedly reprinted and enlarged. The glossary of unusual Latin words and names of places is not the least of its conveniences. Review of *c,* C. H. Haskins, *A.H.R.* 21:342, Jan. 1916; of *d,* C. H. Haskins, *A.H.R.* 21:139, Oct. 1915; *E.H.R.* 31:756, Oct. 1915.
                                                                              JMV

f. Collection of abbreviations, Latin words and names used in English historical manuscripts and records.   HRS

A342a Thompson, Sir Edward Maunde. *Introduction to Greek and Latin palaeography.* Oxford, 1912. (Bibliography.)

   b **Steffens, Franz.** *Lateinische Paläographie mit gegenüberstehender Transcription nebst Erläuterungen und einer systematischen Darstellung der Entwickelung der lateinischen Schrift.* Freiburg (Switz.), 1903.

a. Now somewhat out of date; an enlarged edition of the author's "handbook" on the subject, originally written for the International Science series and therefore presented in a manner both scholarly and easily understood by the beginner. Includes English charter writing as far as the seventeenth century; furnished with abundant facsimiles.

    b. Excellent treatise.
JMV
HRS

A343 Berger, Philippe. *Histoire de l'écriture dans l'antiquité.* 1891. 2nd ed., Paris, 1892. [Musée pédagogique et Bibliothèque centrale et de l'enseignement primaire. Mémoires et documents. No. 98.]

Good account. Cf. also chapter by E. A. Lowe on handwriting in (H104*e*) *Legacy of the Middle Ages* for most recent short treatment of Latin writing; (B611*a*) Mason, *History of the art of writing* and (B611*b*) Williams, *History of the art of writing* for general books on writing.
HRS

A344a Lindsay, Wallace Martin. *Notae Latinae.* Cambridge (Eng.), 1915.

  b Schiaparelli, Luigi. *Avviamento alla studio delle abbreviature latinae nel mediaevo.* Firenze, 1926.

Treatises on abbreviations, *b* particularly good.
HRS

A345a Bond, Edward A., and Thompson, Sir Edward M. *Facsimiles of manuscripts and inscriptions.* Series I, 3 v., 260 plates. London, 1873-83; Series II, 2 v., 105 plates, London, 1884-94; indices, 1901. [Palaeographical Society.]

  b Thompson, Sir Edward Maunde; Warner, Sir George F.; Kenyon, Sir Frederic G.; Gilson, Julius P.; and Herbert, J. A. *Facsimiles of manuscripts and inscriptions.* Series I, 2 v., 250 plates, London, 1903-12; indices, 1914; Series II, pt. 1-11, 180 plates to 1926, London, 1913-26. [New Palaeographical Society.]

  c Wright, William. *Facsimiles of manuscripts and inscriptions.* (Oriental series.) 100 plates, London, 1875-1883. [Palaeographical Society.]

  d Arndt, Wilhelm. *Schrifttafeln zur Erlernung der lateinischen Palaeographie.* Original title, *Schrifttafeln zum Gebrauch bei Vorlesungen und zum Selbstunterricht.* 1874. 4th ed. of pt. 1 by M. Tangl, Berlin, 1904; 3rd ed. of pt. 2 by M. Tangl, Berlin, 1898; pt. 3, ed. by M. Tangl, Berlin, 1903.

  e Prou, Maurice. *Manuel de paléographie: recueil de fac-similés d'écritures du XIIe au XVIIe siècle, manuscrits latins et français.* 1892. *Nouveau recueil* 1896. *Supplément, du Ve au XVIIe siècle,* 1904. 4th rev. ed., Paris, 1924.

  f *Recueil de fac-similés.* 185 plates. Paris, 1880 (pref. 1887). [Société de l'École des Chartes.]

  g *Album paléographique: ou recueil de documents importants rélatifs à l'histoire et à la littérature nationales, reproduits en héliogravure d'après les originaux avec des notices explicatives.* 50 facsimiles. Paris, 1887. [Société de l'École des Chartes.] (Bibliographies.)

Portfolios of folio-size plates with excellent facsimiles of selected typical manuscripts and with letter-press containing transliterations and critical data. Useful for illustrative purposes and for training students. *a, b,* and *c.* Practically a single monumental enterprise now including 550 plates from manuscripts and inscriptions. *d.* Contains 70 plates. *e.* Three portfolios of 12 plates each; 3rd ed. includes an album of 24 plates.

f and *g.* Portfolios of plates, explanatory text with each facsimile, *g* with introduction by A. Giry. From 1835 the École des Chartes has been publishing two other series similar in character, including twelve hundred plates to 1923; this publication, however, is available only at the School. HRS

A346 Chroust, Anton. *Monumenta Palaeographica: Denkmäler der Schreibkunst des Mittelalters.* Series I, 3 v. Series II, 3 v. München, 1902-14.

Excellent reproductions by modern processes from various fields of literature and diplomatic. The tables of contents are particularly useful in that they provide not only a list of plates, but also a chronological list, a topographical list indicating the different schools and chanceries, and an index of examples showing the different forms of script. JMV

CHRONOLOGY

An understanding of the science of computing dates is of the highest importance to the student of history, for annalists, historians and biographers make continual use of time expressions which require explanation and the analogies of modern times are misleading. The date, too, is an indispensable factor in a document. Names and contents may serve to indicate the general period in which the instrument was issued, but something more exact is required to give the general connections.

A361a Grotefend, Hermann. *Zeitrechnung des deutschen Mittelalters und der Neuzeit.* 2 v. Hannover, 1891-98.

b —— *Taschenbuch der Zeitrechnung des deutschen Mittelalters und der Neuzeit.* 1898. 3rd ed., Hannover, 1910.

Books which bear the title chronology cover a wide variety of matters, ranging from astronomical calculations to handy books of dates. Those which are of particular interest to the student of documents usually combine a historical view of the development of time reckoning systems with practical tables of dates. Scientific attainment in this field has been very marked in Germany and the work of the greatest value to the investigator is *a*. Cf. also by the same author an introduction to the subject in (A294), Meister, *Grundriss der Geschichtswissenschaft,* v. 1. JMV

A362a Ginzel, Friedrich K. *Handbuch der mathematischen und technischen Chronologie: das Zeitrechnungswesen der Völker.* 3 v. Leipzig, 1906-14. (Bibliographies.)

b Schram, Robert. *Kalendariographische und chronologische Tafeln.* Leipzig, 1908.

a. An exhaustive study of the calendars of all peoples. V. 1. Deals with the astronomical and other fundamental questions and with the calendars of ancient Egypt and Babylonia, of India and China, and of the Mohammedans. V. 2. Treats those of the Jews, Greeks, and Romans. V. 3. Contains the study of medieval and modern calendars and chronology. Each volume is thoroughly documented and supplemented with numerous useful tables. It is inevitable that an attempt of a single individual to cover such a vast range of material cannot be free from errors. None the less, the student will find no single work of equal usefulness. For the calendars and systems of chronology of the ancient East, of classical antiquity, and of early Christian times, the articles in (F22) Hastings, *Encyclopaedia of religion and ethics,* are the best summaries of recent scholarship.

b. Collection of tables for various eras; convenient for synchronizing dates given in different systems of time-reckoning. Practically a supplement to *a.* WAH

A363 Dantine, Maur-François; Clémencet, Charles; and Durand, Ursin. *L'art de vérifier les dates.* 1750. 2nd rev. ed. [by F. Clément], 1770; 3rd rev. ed. [by F. Clément], 4 v., 1784-92; 4th rev. ed. by N. V. de Saint-Allais, J. B. P. J. de Courcelles, Marquis de Fortia d'Urban, and D. B. Warden, 44 v. (including 3 index v.; two more projected v. did not appear), Paris, 1818-44.

Of the 4th ed., besides the octavo cited above, there are also folio and quarto impressions. The best work was done by Clément whose manuscript notes were used by the compilers of the 4th ed. in continuing the work. Clément and his predecessors were Benedictine scholars whose industrious researches in chronology are recorded in this immense compilation which consists largely of tables of events and established dates and furnishes lists of rulers for practically every royal dynasty and for numerous princely and noble families. The 3rd ed. includes the essential portion of the work and for most purposes is as useful as the 4th, which has additional volumes on the pre-Christian period and on the period from 1770 to 1827. The work of the continuators is more diffuse and less satisfactory. For the historical student who ventures off the beaten paths this vast storehouse of facts is a convenient guide and time-saver, though later researches have corrected it in many points. Described by (A361) Grotefend as unreliable. GMD

A364 Mas Latrie, Comte Jaçques M. J. Louis de. *Trésor de chronologie, d'histoire, et de géographie pour l'étude et l'emploi des documents du moyen âge.* Paris, 1889.

Similar to (A363) in plan; a folio volume of materials presented in condensed form for use in connection with the study of medieval documents. Also described by (A361) Grotefend as unreliable. JMV

A365a Bond, John J. *Handy book of rules and tables for verifying dates with the Christian era.* 1866. 4th ed., London, 1889.

b Philip, Alexander. *The calendar: its history, structure, and improvement.* Cambridge, Eng., 1921.

c MacDonald, James C. *Chronologies and calendars.* London, 1897.

a. Written by an official of the English Public Record Office, this work has been before the public for half a century. Its numerous reprintings have been justified by its convenience. The eras of all the nations, ancient and modern, are explained and rules given for determining religious festivals and other movable dates. Especially useful are the extensive tables giving the exact regnal years and leading dates of English sovereigns. *b.* Clear, concise account of the various systems of time-reckoning. JMV
c. Clear but brief description of the principal chronologies, calendars, and chronological principles which have been used by man. Very useful. HRS

A366a Ploetz, Carl. *Epitome of ancient, medieval, and modern history.* 1884. Recent rev. ed., continued to date by Harry E. Barnes, Boston, 1925. Tr. by W. H. Tillinghast from (7th rev. ed. by O. Meltzer, Berlin, 1880) *Auszug aus der alten, mittleren, und neueren Geschichte,* 1863. 17th rev. ed. by M. Hoffman, Leipzig, 1910.

b **Haydn, Joseph T.** *Dictionary of dates and universal information relating to all ages and nations.* 1841. 25th rev. ed. by B. Vincent, N. Y., 1911.

c **Lewis, Charlton T.,** ed. *Harper's book of facts.* N. Y., 1895.

d **Little, Charles E.** *Cyclopedia of classified dates.* N. Y. and London, 1900.

e **Hart, Rabie J.** *Chronos, a handbook of comparative chronology.* London, 1912. (Bibliography.)

f **Hassall, Arthur.** *Handbook of European history, 476–1871, chronologically arranged.* London and N. Y., 1898.

g **Putnam, George P.** *Putnam's handbook of universal history, a series of chronological tables presenting, in parallel columns, a record of the more noteworthy events in the history of the world from the earliest times down to the present day.* 1870. Rev. 10th ed. by G. H. Putnam, N. Y. and London, 1928.

Innumerable books of dates have been compiled, ranging from connected chronicles to dictionaries of events in alphabetical order. Most of these are useful in their way and among the larger ones there is not much choice, except that the more modern works are likely to be correct, since they have had, or should have had, the benefit of later historical discoveries and criticism. Furthermore, it should always be held in mind that these are not final authorities or incontrovertible proof of the statements made, and that, in spite of the best intentions, or the most meticulous care, errors will creep in. Dates in ancient history are particularly subject to caution owing to progress in archeological discovery. *a.* One of the old standbys in this field, presenting dated outlines of the countries of western Europe and America, each treated separately. *b.* An alphabetical arrangement of events and subjects, which under various editors and revisions, has, for three-quarters of a century, proved its usefulness. The 25th ed. records events to Oct. 1910. *c.* "A classified history of the world embracing science, literature and art." Arrangement also alphabetical, with great emphasis on American history. *d.* Countries appear in alphabetical order. Short periods are given topically, e.g., army, navy, church, society, etc., with an elaborate index. *e.* Important events in the countries of the civilized world are arranged by centuries from the beginning of history to 1700 A.D. Among other uses it is a convenient guide for travellers and students of art. Review, J. M. Vincent, *A.H.R.* 18:382, Jan. 1913. *f* and *g.* Chronological lists of events arranged in parallel columns by countries and subjects. Extremely convenient for reference in regard to the synchronism of events. *g.* Covers a longer period than *f* and is more accurate. Review of *a* (1925 ed.) *A.H.R.* 31:557, Apr. 1926.   JMV

A367 Stokvis, A. M. H. J. *Manuel d'histoire, de généalogie et de chronologie de tous les états du globe depuis les temps les plus reculés jusqu'à nos jours.* 3 v. Leide, 1888-1889.

A useful compilation containing tables of sovereigns and governors of all states which have played any part in the world's history. Brief introductions on the states or provinces listed are added in many cases, also the Roman calendar with the feasts and saints' days, and a table to determine the days of the week for all dates.   HRS

A368 Muralt, Eduard von. *Essai de chronologie byzantine, 1057-1453.* 2 v., Bâle, 1871.

Scholarly treatise on Byzantine chronology.
For other special calendars, cf. (B622f) Heidel, *Day of Yahweh,* for calendar of Israel; (D31, VI, 12) Gow, *Calendar,* for the Greek; (D35) Kubitschek, *Zeitrechnung,* for the Roman; S. B. Burnaby, *Jewish and Mohammedan Calendars,* London, 1901, for the Moslem; Babinger, *Geschichtsschreiber der Osmanen,* supplement, by J. Mayr, for the Turkish calendar; G. Vilain, *Le Calendrier républicain,* (M931a) *La Révolution française,* v. 7, 1884-85, for the French revolutionary calendar.   HRS

GENEALOGY AND HERALDRY

Genealogy is the study of pedigrees. Heraldry is the body of doctrine which prescribes the rules by which coats of arms are composed; in its widest scope it has to do with honorary distinctions of all kinds. Both can be classed as sciences auxiliary to history.

A381 Heydenreich, Eduard K. H., and others. *Handbuch der praktischen Genealogie.* 2 v. Leipzig, 1913. (Bibliographies.)

In coöperation with various other scholars the author has not only treated the theory of family history, but has systematically considered every class of materials from which information on that subject is likely to be obtained. It is a Bernheim devoted to a special branch of history, but the discussion of the values and weaknesses of the various kinds of documents is equally valuable to the general student. Cf. (A324b) Phillimore, *How to write the history of a family.*   JMV

A382a Grote, Hermann. *Stammtafeln, mit Anhang: Calendarium medii aevi.* Leipzig, 1877.

   b Lorenz, Ottokar. *Genealogische Hand- und Schul-Atlas.* 1892. 3rd rev. ed. by E. Devrient, Berlin.

   c Grünewaldt, M. von. *Historische Stammtafeln: ein Beitrag zum Geschichtsstudium in Schule und Haus.* Frankfurt, 1889.

   d George, Hereford B. *Genealogical tables illustrative of modern history.* 1874. 5th rev. ed., by J. R. H. Weaver, Oxford, 1916.

These, together with v. 13 of (I121) *Cambridge modern history,* are convenient manuals containing tables of the more important ruling houses and of other prominent families. *a.* The best of the group, but now antiquated. Review, *Hist. Zeit.* 39:486, 1878. *b.* Review, *ibid.* 102:655, 1909. *d.* Review, *A.H.R.* 22:435, Jan. 1917.
Elaborate studies of the genealogy of the leading ruling houses exist, but more useful to the historical student are the massive compilations on the noble families of England, France, Germany, and other countries, which also contain a wealth of heraldic data. For a list of the more important of these works see article "Genealogy" in *Encyclopaedia Britannica,* 11th ed.   JMV

A401a Hauptmann, Felix. *Wappenkunde,* München, 1914. [(B170) Below and Meinecke, Handbuch der mittelalterlichen und neueren Geschichte, pt. 4.]

   b Woodward, John, and **Burnett, George.** *Treatise on heraldry, British and foreign.* 2 v., Edinburgh, 1892.

   c Boutell, Charles. *English heraldry.* 1867. 10th rev. ed. by A. C. Fox-Davies, London, 1908.

d Hope, Sir William H. St. John. *Grammar of English heraldry.* Cambridge, Eng., and N. Y., 1913. [Cambridge manuals of science and literature.]

e ——— *Heraldry for craftsmen and designers.* N. Y., 1913.

f Pedrich, Gale. *Manual of heraldry.* London, 1911.

In each of the important countries of Europe heraldry has given rise to an extensive literature. Part of this treats of the theory of the subject and part consists of compilations of coats of arms and descriptions for reference. Each country has its own lists of arms, just as it has its own related genealogies. The artistic taste of one country differs from another, and thus the explanatory literature accumulates, but the underlying theory is the same for all. Consequently the theoretical chapters in an English work will give a satisfactory introduction to all the rest.

a. Good but brief. *b.* The explanation of forms and heraldic terms is accompanied by abundant illustrations in color taken from the actual coats of arms of historic families. *c.* An older work, but has manifested its usefulness in repeated editions. *d.* A convenient little handbook in which the forms and terminology are explained in a simple manner. *e.* Equally simple in form, intended as a guide for artists so that the employment of heraldry may be exact as well as ornamental. Numerous color plates and text illustrations. JMV

f. History of heraldry; deals at some length with the most famous devices like that of the Lion, the Bull, etc. Chapters on the influence of heraldry upon art, architecture, archeology, genealogy, poetry and literature. HRS

ARCHEOLOGY AND EPIGRAPHY

Archeology, which has been defined as the science of the treatment of the material remains of the human past, and epigraphy, which devotes itself to inscriptions, are also helpful to the student of history. They are of use in exploring many fields and should not be thought of as confined only to the period and content included under the headings—Ancient, Orient, Greece, and Rome.

A421a Petrie, William Flinders. *Methods and aims in archaeology.* London and N. Y., 1904.

b Deonna, W. *L'archéologie; son domaine son but.* Paris, 1922. [Bibliothèque de philosophie scientifique.]

c Hogarth, David George, ed. *Authority and archaeology: sacred and profane. Essays on the relation of monuments to Biblical and classical literature.* London and N. Y., 1899.

a. Very practical handbook, giving directions for the excavation, recording, and preservation of relics—with a chapter on the nature of archeological evidence of the first importance, coming as it does from one of the foremost Egyptologists. A chapter by Petrie on the nature of "Archeological evidence" is to be found also in (A288b) *Lectures on the method of science.* JMV

b. Systematic and philosophical treatment in which the author, in addition to interesting theories as to the nature and aims of archeology, pleads for a definition of the subject wider and more scientific than has been given it in the past, for a synthesis grouping all pertinent facts without restriction of time or space to make archeology truly a history and science of art. Review, G. Guérin, *Rev. Hist.* 146:25, July 1924. *c.* Masterly, although somewhat antiquated, essays on

Hebrew, classical and early Christian monuments by authorities in each field; with a penetrating introductory chapter on the nature of archeology by the editor.

HRS

For special works on the archeology of the Near East in ancient times, of Greece and of Rome, §§ C, D, and E should be consulted.

NUMISMATICS

The study of coins and medals contributes largely to a knowledge of history. Coins are abundant and often continuous, thereby supplying a gap left vacant by the fragmentary remains of other forms of art. The emblems on coins, too, are often extremely informing. Finally, accumulated instances of widely scattered money bear important testimony concerning movements of civilization: e.g., important trade routes of antiquity or middle ages can often be traced by hoards dug up along the routes.

A441a Hill, George Francis. *Coins and medals.* London, 1920. [Helps for students of history, no. 36 (A295).] (Bibliography.)

b Poole, Stanley Lane, ed. *Coins and medals: their place in history and art.* 1885. 3rd ed. London, 1894.

c MacDonald, George. *Coin types, their origin and development.* Glasgow, 1905.

a. Excellent, but brief, introduction to the subject. *b.* Very illuminating work, provides a wealth of genealogical, biographical and other data; contains a short account of English coins by C. F. Keary. *c.* Lectures addressed to popular audiences.

JMV, HRS

A442a Luschin von Ebengreuth, Arnold. *Allgemeine Münzkunde und Geldgeschichte des Mittelalters und der neueren Zeit.* München, 1904, 2nd ed. 1926. (Bibliography.) [Below and Meinecke (B170).]

b Friedensburg, Ferdinand. *Münzkunde und Geldgeschichte der Einzelstaaten des Mittelalters und der neueren Zeit.* München, 1926.

c —— *Die Münze in der Kulturgeschichte.* 1909. 2nd ed. Berlin, 1926.

a. Scholarly and solid treatise on the coinage of medieval and modern times, discussing the coins themselves, the history of money and its significance for the history of those who used it, and the economic laws governing the issue of these currencies. Illustrated. *b.* Briefer and less satisfactory. *c.* Excellent treatment of numismatics from the cultural side. Review of *a* and *b*, S. P. Noe, *A.H.R.* 32:89, Oct. 1926; of *c*, Th. Reinach, *Rev. Critique*, 62:125, Apr. 1927. HRS

Books on Greek and Roman coinage will be found in sections D and E, particularly D685 and E691-695.

PERIODICALS

Bibliography and Library Resources. (A941) *Library journal*, N. Y., 1877 ff.; (A942) *Library association record*, London, 1899 ff.; (A942.1) Bibliographical society of America, *Papers*, N. Y., 1906 ff.; (A942.2) Bibliographical society, London, *Publications*, London, 1897 ff.; Transactions, London. 1893-1919; continued 1892 ff. in (A942.3) *Library*, London, 1899 ff.; (A943) *Bibliographe moderne*, Paris, 1897 ff.; (A944) *Revue des bibliothèques*, Paris, 1891 ff.; (A945) *Archiv für Bibliographie* (Buch und Bibliothekswesen) Linz, 1926 ff.; (A946) *Zentralblatt für Bibliothekswesen*, Leipzig, 1884 ff.; also Beihefte (including annual *Bibliographie des Bibliotheks und Buchwesens*, 1888 ff.).

Geography. (A951) *Geographical review* (formerly entitled *Bulletin*), quarterly, N. Y., 1851 ff. [American Geographical Society] ; (A952) *National geographic magazine*, monthly, Washington, 1888 ff. [National Geographic Society] ; (A953) *Journal of geography* (successor to *Journal of school geography* and *Bulletin of the American Bureau of Geography*), monthly, Lancaster, Pa., and Madison, Wis., 1897 ff.; (A954) *Geographical journal*, monthly, London, 1893 ff. [Royal Geographical Society] ; (A955) *Scottish geographical magazine*, monthly, Edinburgh, 1885 ff. [Royal Scottish Geographical Society] ; (A956) *La géographie*, monthly, Paris, 1900 ff. [Société de Géographie] ; (A957.1) *Annales de géographie*, bi-monthly, Paris, 1891 ff., which includes (A957.2) *Bibliographie géographique annuelle*, Paris, 1891 ff.; (A958) *Revue de géographie*, Paris, 1877 ff. (published annually since 1906) ; (A959) *Beiträge zur Geophysik, Zeitschrift für Physikalische Erdkunde*, Leipzig, 1887 ff.; (A960) *Deutsche Rundschau für Geographie und Statistik*, Wien, 1878 ff.; (A961) *Geographischer Anzeiger, Blätter für den geographischen Unterricht*, Gotha, 1899 ff.; (A962) *Geographischer Jahresbericht aus Österreich, in Verbindung mit dem Bericht des Vereins der Geographen an der Universität Wien*, annual, Wien, 1894 ff.; (A963) *Geographische Zeitschrift*, monthly, Leipzig, 1895 ff.; (A964) *Mitteilungen der Geographischen Gesellschaft in München*, München, 1904 ff. (*Jahresberichte*, 1869-1903) ; (A965) *Petermanns Mitteilungen aus Justus Perthes' geographischer Anstalt*, Gotha, 1855 ff.; (A966) *Mitteilungen der Geographischen Gesellschaft*, Wien, 1856 ff.; (A967) *Zeitschrift für Geopolitik*, monthly, Berlin, 1924 ff.; (A968) *Bolletino della Società Geografica Italiana*, Roma, 1868 ff.

Anthropology. (A971) *American anthropologist*, quarterly, Washington, 1888 ff. [American Anthropological Association] ; (A972) *Man*, monthly, London, 1901 ff. [Anthropological Institute of Great Britain and Ireland] ; (A973) *Folklore*, quarterly, London, 1890 ff. [Folklore Society] ; (A974) *L'Anthropologie* (formerly entitled *Matériaux pour l'histoire primitive et naturelle de l'homme*), bi-monthly, Paris, 1865-1885, 1890 ff.; (A975) *Bulletin et mémoires de la société d'anthropologie* (formerly entitled *Bulletin de la société d'anthropologie de Paris*), 1860 ff.; (A976) *Archiv für Anthropologie*, quarterly, Brunswick, 1866 ff. [Deutsche Gesellschaft für Anthropologie] ; (A977) *Zeitschrift für Ethnologie*, Berlin, 1869 ff. [Berliner Gesellschaft für Anthropologie] ; (A978) *Mannus*, Würzburg, 1909 ff. [Deutsche Gesellschaft für Vorgeschichte] ; (A979) *Anthropos*, Wien, 1909 ff.; (A980) *Anthropologischer Anzeiger*, quarterly, Stuttgart, 1924 ff.; (A981) *Prähistorische Zeitschrift*, Berlin, 1909 ff. [Deutsche Gesellschaft für Anthropologie] ; (A982) *Urgeschichtlicher Anzeiger*, Wien, 1924 ff.; (A983) *Vorgeschichtliches Jahrbuch*, annual, Berlin, 1926 ff. [Gesellschaft für vorgeschichtliche Forschung].

Teaching of History. (A991) *Historical outlook*, Philadelphia, 1909 ff., monthly (as *History teachers' magazine*, 1909-1918) (B941f4) ; (A992) *History*, London, 1912 ff., quarterly (B941f5) [The History Association].

Philology. (A1001) *Modern language notes*, monthly, Baltimore, 1886 ff.; (A1002) *Modern language review*, quarterly, Cambridge, England, 1905 ff.; (A1003) *Literaturblatt für germanische und romanische Philologie*, Heilbronn, 1880 ff.; (A1004) *Indo-germanisches Jahrbuch*, annual, Strassburg, 1914 ff. [Indo-germanische Gesellschaft]. Other periodicals dealing with special fields of literature will be found listed in the periodical sub-sections of many sections, particularly of §§ C, D, E, and H.

Diplomatic and Sigillography. (A1011) *Archiv für Urkundenforschung*, Leipzig, 1907 ff.; (A1012) *Archivalische Zeitschrift*, Stuttgart, 1876 ff. [Bayerisches Reichsarchiv].

Paleography. Periodicals under this heading will be found listed in the periodical subsections of §§ D and E.

Genealogy and Heraldry. (A1021) *New England historical and genealogical register,* quarterly, Boston, 1847 ff. [New England Historic Genealogical Society] ; (A1022) *New York genealogical and biographical record,* quarterly, N. Y., 1870 ff. [New York Genealogical and Biographical Society; (1023) *The genealogist,* London, 1877 ff.; (A1024) *Familiengeschichtliche Bibliographie,* Leipzig, 1925 ff. [Zentralstelle für deutsche Personen und Familiengeschichte] ; (A1025) *Vierteljahrsschrift für Wappen-, Siegel- und Familienkunde,* quarterly, Berlin, 1874-1922 (1874-1889 as *Vierteljahrsschrift für Heraldik, Spragistik, und Genealogie*) [Herold, Verein für Wappen-, Siegel- und Familienkunde] ; (A1026) *Zeitschrift für historische Waffenkunde,* Leipzig, 1897 ff.

Archeology and Epigraphy. Periodicals under this heading will be found listed in the periodical subsections of §§ C, D and E.

Numismatics. (A1041) *American journal of numismatics,* quarterly, N. Y., 1882 ff. [American Numismatic Society] ; (A1042) *The numismatist,* monthly, Lewisburg, Ohio, 18 ff. [American Numismatic Association] ; (A1043) *Numismatic chronicle,* quarterly, London, 1836 ff. [Royal Numismatic Society of England] ; (A1044) *The British numismatic journal and proceedings of the British numismatic society,* London, 1904 ff.; (A1045) *Revue numismatique,* Paris, 1836 ff. [Société Française de Numismatique] ; (A1046) *Bulletin international de numismatique,* Paris, 1902-1904; (A1047) *Revue Belge de numismatique et de sigillographie,* Bruxelles, quarterly, 1842 ff.; (A1048) *Revue Suisse de numismatique,* Genève, 1891 ff.; (A1049) *Rivista Italiana di numismatica,* Milano, 1888 ff.; (A1050) *Zeitschrift für Numismatik,* Berlin, 1874 ff.; (A1051) *Numismatische Zeitschrift,* Wien, 1870 ff.; (A1052) *Journal international d'archéologie numismatique; Ephemēris diethnēs nomismatikēs archaiologikēs,* 4 nos. yearly, Athenai, 1898-1920 [Numismatic Society of Greece].   DMCF, HRS

SECTION B

GENERAL HISTORY

Editor

HENRY ROBINSON SHIPMAN

Associate Professor of History, Princeton University

CONTENTS

INTRODUCTION

A section on General History omits by necessity all literature which deals specifically with the history of a nation or with any of the periods or topics to which a section of this *Guide* is devoted. Books dealing with such subjects should be looked for elsewhere, for example, works which cover general European history from or after the period of the Renaissance will be found in section I. The allocation of books to sections may seem arbitrary, but the reader will readily discover the work in which he is interested by consulting the index.

BIBLIOGRAPHY

The bibliographies listed in this section include the most important works dealing with American, English, French, and German publications which the student will find it necessary to use. Corresponding works for publications in other languages will be found listed in the sections dealing with the nations concerned,

46

since their value to the student is primarily for the special fields of these chapters; as general works they are of minor importance.

B1a Peddie, Robert A. *National bibliographies, a descriptive catalogue of the works which register the books published in each country.* London, 1912.

b *Selected national bibliographies.* 1900. 3rd rev. ed., Albany, N. Y., 1915. [New York State Library, Library school bulletin, no. 38.]

Lists of national bibliographies, that is, of works listing all publications in a country regardless of subject. The more important of these works in English, French, and German, are cited in this section (B2, 3, 4, 5); and for other countries in the sections concerned. GMD

B2a Evans, Charles, ed. *American bibliography: a chronological dictionary of all books, pamphlets, and periodical publications printed in the United States of America from the genesis of printing in 1639 down to and including the year 1820.* V. 1–10 (to 1795–6), Chicago, 1903–29.

b Sabin, Joseph, ed. *Dictionary of books relating to America from its discovery to the present time.* V. 1–20 (through Smith). N. Y., 1868–1928.

c Roorbach, Orville A., ed. *Bibliotheca americana: catalogue of American publications including reprints and original works from 1820 to 1860 inclusive, together with a list of periodicals published in the United States.* 4 v. N. Y., 1852–60.

d Kelly, James, ed. *American catalogue of books, original and reprints, published in the United States from Jan. 1861 to Jan. 1871.* 2 v., N. Y., 1868–71.

e *American catalogue: books in print,* July 1, 1876. 2 v. in 5. N. Y., 1878–81. Books recorded including reprints and importations, 1876 to 1910. 7 v., N. Y., 1885–1911.

f *The United States catalogue; books in print 1899 ff.* Minneapolis and N. Y., 1900 ff. [*Books in print 1899,* 1900; 2nd ed., *Books in print 1902,* 1903; *Supplement for 1902–1905,* 1906; 3rd ed., *Books in print 1912,* 1912; *Supplement for 1912–1917,* 1918; *Supplement for Jan. 1918–June 1921,* 1921; *Supplement for July 1921–June 1924,* 1924.]

g *The United States catalogue: annual cumulative book index.* N. Y., 1898 ff.; *monthly cumulated book index.* N. Y., 1898 ff.

h Stevens, Henry, ed. *Bibliotheca historica, or a catalogue of 5000 vols. of books and manuscripts relating chiefly to the history and literature of North and South America.* Boston, 1870.

i Church, Elihu Dwight. *Catalogue of books relating to the discovery and early history of North and South America, forming a part of his library.* (Comp. and annotated by G. W. Cole), 5 v. N. Y., 1907.

j *Publishers' trade list annual.* N. Y. 1873 ff.

a. List of books printed in the United States prior to 1820. *a* and *b* are two invaluable bibliographical enterprises, both incomplete, *a* arranged chronologically, *b* arranged alphabetically. As a later work *a* is in general superior to *b,* it has also indices giving authors, publishers and subjects, but at present each contains some material not in the other. *c, d, e,* and *f.* Current lists of publications issued in the United States, usually including reprints and in some cases importations; *e* has the alphabetical arrangement with authors and titles grouped together, and subjects alphabetized separately to 1900; since then authors, titles, subjects and series have been grouped in one alphabet; *f,* author, title, and subject in one alphabet. For weekly lists of new publications, cf. (B18a) *Publishers' Weekly.*

GMD

h. Catalogue of valuable books prepared for a sale of books held in Boston in 1870; a valuable introduction and learned notes accompany the volume. cf. Y236. *i.* Monumental work; includes 1385 entries of books arranged by date of publication from the earliest period to 1884; alphabetical and title index; contains many facsimile reproductions of title pages, colophons, etc. Review, W. N. C. Carlton, *Bibliog. Society of Am. Papers,* 7:41, 1912–1913. *j.* American publishers' catalogues bound together in an annual volume; no index.   HRS

B3a *London catalogue of books published in London from 1800 to 1822.* London, 1822.

  b *Books published in Great Britain from 1814 to 1846.* London, 1855.

  c *Books published in Great Britain from 1831 to 1855.* London, 1855.

  d *British catalogue of books published Oct. 1837 to 1852.* London, 1853. *Index to British catalogue, 1837–1857.* London, 1858.

  e *English catalogue of books published from 1801 to 1836.* Ed. by R. Peddie and Q. Waddington. London, 1914.

  f *English catalogue of books published from 1835 to 1920.* London, 1864 ff.

  g *English catalogue of books* [annual]. London, 1837 ff. Index, 4 v., 1858–93.

  h *Whitaker's cumulative book list.* London, 1925 ff.

  i *Reference catalogue of current literature, containing the full titles of books now in print and on sale.* London, 3 v. [11 v. in 25 to date], 1874 ff.

a, b, c, d, e. Taken together these works furnish lists of English publications from 1800 to 1852, but the others, which are seriously incomplete, are now quite replaced by *e.* Other issues and supplements of the London catalogue other than *a, b,* and *c* contain practically nothing in addition to the materials in these three. *f.* Current lists of publications in the United Kingdom since 1835; a series appearing at intervals of several years (now quinquennial). Inferior to (B2f) *United States catalogue* in completeness of the lists and in fullness of data on individual titles. Weekly lists of new publications are contained in (B18b) *Publisher's circular. g.* Annual series whose contents are cumulated from time to time in *f.* The most recent volumes are supplements to the latest volume of *f.* Weekly lists of new publications will be found in (B18b). *h.* A new annual volume, arranged by classes, with an alphabetical index of authors and titles intermingled. *i.* British publishers' catalogues bound together (at present in 2 v.) ; publication appears at intervals from one to five years, with very useful index by authors and titles (v. 1).   HRS

B4a Brunet, Jacques C., ed. *Manuel du libraire et de l'amateur de livres.* 1810. 5th ed., 6 v., Paris, 1860–65. *Supplement,* ed. by P. Deschamps and G. Brunet, 2 v., Paris, 1878–80.

  b Quérard, Joseph M., ed. *La France littéraire ou dictionnaire bibliographique des savants, historiens, et gens de lettres de la France ainsi que des littérateurs étrangers qui ont écrit en Français plus particulièrement pendant des XVIIIe et XIXe siècles.* 12 v. Paris, 1827–64.

  c Quérard, Joseph M., and others, eds. *La littérature française contemporaine.* 6 v. Paris, 1842–57.

  d Lorenz, Otto, ed. *Catalogue général de la librairie française depuis 1840.* 11 v. Paris, 1867–92. Continuation ed. by D. Jordell, v. 12 ff., Paris, 1892 ff.

  e *Catalogue mensuel de la librairie française.* Paris, 1876 ff.

a. One of the foremost bibliographical works; specially valuable for publications prior to the nineteenth century. *b* and *c.* Record publications of the eighteenth century and the first half of the nineteenth, with useful additional notes. *d.* List of current publications since 1840 issued in France or in the French language. In addition to a list of authors, there is also an extensive subject index. *e.* Annual volumes of current publications later cummulated in *d*, to which the latest volumes form a supplement. Weekly list of French publications will be found in (B18c) *Bibliographie de la France.* GMD

B5a Heinsius, Wilhelm, and others, ed. *Allgemeines Bücher-Lexicon oder vollständiges alphabetisches Verzeichniss der von 1700 erschienenen Bücher, welche im Deutschland und in den durch Sprache und Literatur damit verwandten Ländern gedruckt worden sind.* 19 v. Leipzig, 1812–1894.

b Kayser, Christian G. and others, ed. *Vollständiges Bücher-Lexicon; ein Verzeichniss der seit dem Jahre 1750 im deutschen Buchhandel erschienenen Bücher und Landkarten.* 36 v. Leipzig, 1834–1912.

c Kirchhoff, Albrecht, and others, ed. *Hinrichs' Fünfjähriger Katalog der im deutschen Buchhandel erschienenen Bücher, Zeitschriften, Landkarten, usw.* 13 v. Leipzig, 1856–1913.

d *Deutsches Bücherverzeichnis, eine Zusammenstellung der im deutschen Buchhandel erschienenen Bücher, Zeitschriften, und Landkarten; nebst Stich- und Schlagwortregister bearbeitet von der Bibliographischen Abteilung des Börsenvereins der Deutschen Buchhändler.* 11 v. Leipzig, 1916–27.

e *Hinrichs' Halbjahrs-Katalog der im deutschen Buchhandel erschienenen Bücher, Zeitschriften, Landkarten, usw. . . . herausgegeben und verlegt von der J. C. Hinrichs' schen Buchhandlung.* 235 v. Leipzig, 1798–1916.

f *Halbjahrsverzeichnis der im deutschen Buchhandel erschienenen Bücher Zeitschriften, und Landkarten, bearbeitet von der Bibliographischen Abteilung des Börsenvereins der deutschen Buchhändler.* V. 236 ff. Leipzig, 1916 ff.

a, b, c. These three trade catalogues, including respectively publications from 1700 to 1892 inclusive, from 1750 to 1910 inclusive, and from 1851 to 1912 inclusive, have been replaced and material continued by *d,* which at present includes publications from 1911 to 1920. Each volume of *c* includes a period of five, later three, years. *e,* continued by *f,* furnishes a semi-annual service of similar character. Hinrichs also issued weekly (1842 ff.), monthly (1866 ff.), and quarterly lists (1846 ff.) ; and also quinquennial catalogues (1851 ff). GMD

B6a *United States, Library of Congress.* Catalogue in form of separate author cards. Washington, 1898 ff.

b *Peabody Institute. Catalogue of the library of the Peabody Institute of the city of Baltimore.* 5 v. Baltimore, 1883–92. *Second catalogue, including additions made since 1882.* 8 v. Baltimore, 1896–1905.

c *Brown University. John Carter Brown Library. Bibliotheca americana: catalogue of the John Carter Brown library.* 2 v. in 4. Providence, 1919–22. To be 5 v.

a. The Library of Congress now contains over 3,000,000 volumes and is the second largest library in the world. It is especially strong in history. A catalogue, therefore, of these collections approaches the nature of a universal bibliography. This catalogue was started on cards in 1898 and these cards have been sold for the use of other libraries since 1901. Depository sets of Library of Congress cards are to be found in 47 libraries in the United States and 7 abroad. Besides these, proof sets are to be found in many libraries. In addition to its own books the Library of Congress in certain cases prints cards for books in other libraries. The bibliographical information on the Library of Congress cards is very carefully prepared and its accuracy and completeness may usually be assumed. One may feel reasonably sure of finding cards for American copyrighted publications since copies of these must be deposited in the Library of Congress. The student who has access to one of these depositories of the Library of Congress cards will find that they furnish one of the most important bibliographical aids, particularly to American publications. *b.* Probably the most useful printed catalogue in book form issued by an American library. *c.* Admirable bibliographical enterprise listing, with valuable bibliographical notes, the contents of a library which confines itself to books published in America prior to 1800 or relating thereto.   GMD

B8a *British Museum catalogue of printed books.* Ed. by R. Garnett and A. W. ˙K. Miller. 78 v. London, 1881–1900. *Supplement, containing all books acquired by the Museum from 1882 to 1899 which were not incorporated in the general catalogue.* 12 v. London, 1900. *Subject index of the modern works added to the library of the British Museum in the years 1881–1900,* ed. by G. K. Fortescue. 3 v. London, 1902–03; *Subject index for 1901–05,* London, 1906; *for 1906–10,* London, 1911; *for 1911–15,* London, 1918; *for 1916–20,* London, 1922. Later accessions in pamphlets published irregularly.

   b *Catalogue of the London Library.* 1842. Latest ed. edited by C. T. H. Wright and C. J. Purnell, 2 v. London, 1913–14. *Supplement, 1913–20, 1920–28,* London, 1929. *Subject index to the London Library,* v. 1, ed. by C. T. H. Wright, v. 2 by C. T. H. Wright and C. J. Purnell, London, 1909–23.

   a. The most important printed catalogue in book form of a library and consequently one of the most valuable bibliographical aids, especially for British and continental European publications. The subject index is sometimes a convenient guide to modern works. *b.* More convenient than *a* for ready reference, because of its compact character. The London Library is by no means so large as the British Museum but it does contain a very extensive collection, especially of publications since 1800.   GMD

B9 *Catalogue général des livres imprimés de la Bibliothèque Nationale.* V. 1–97 (to Liek), Paris, 1897 ff.

   At present the most complete printed catalogue in book form of a library, next to (B8*a*) *British Museum catalogue.* Naturally the first work to be consulted for French publications but its usefulness is by no means limited thereto.   GMD

B10a Richardson, Ernest Cushing. *A union list of collections on European history in American libraries.* Princeton, 1912. Supplement, the original list with revisions and additions of books added to the libraries in 1912–1915, Princeton, 1915. Alphabetical subject index, ed. by A. H. Shearer, Princeton, 1915.

   b Herre, Paul; Hofmeister, Adolf; and **Stübe, Rudolf.** *Quellenkunde zur Weltgeschichte.* Leipzig, 1910.

   c Baker, Ernest Albert. *Guide to historical fiction.* London, 1914.

   d Nield, Jonathan. *Guide to the best historical novels and tales.* 1902. 5th rev. ed., London, 1929.

   a. Compiled for the Committee on Bibliography of the American Historical Association. Lists approximately 2,000 sets of collected works, especially of source materials, by various authors and editors on European history in possession of ninety-four important American libraries. Very useful in guiding students to location of sets and serviceable as a purchase list. *b.* Well-selected historical bibliography to about 1910. *c.* Based on writer's smaller book, *History in Fiction,* 1907. Lists and brief descriptions of historical novels in English. Arranged by countries and periods within the history of a country. *d.* Another guide with chronological arrangement. Excellent indexes. HRS

B11a Peet, Hubert W., ed. *Sell's world's press.* V. 1–36. London, 1884–1921.

b Godet, Marcel. *Index bibliographicus: repertoire internationale des sources de bibliographie courante (périodiques et institutions).* Genève, 1925. [Publications de Société des Nations, Commission de Co-operation intellectuelle.]

a. Calls itself "the handbook of the fourth estate." Lists British and a few foreign newspapers and periodicals, and contains current information about journalists and journalism in the British Empire. HLK
b. List of periodicals which keep abreast of new developments in art, science, and other fields of knowledge by means of articles, reviews, and bibliography. These periodicals represent a large number of countries; listed according to decimal classification; data given are often incomplete. Valuable because it contains the essential titles of periodicals in its field, but to the historical student more valuable for periodicals in kindred fields than for historical periodicals.

HBVH

B12a Adams, Charles Kendall. *Manual of historical literature, comprising brief descriptions of the most important histories in English, French, and German, together with practical suggestions as to methods and courses of historical study.* 1882. 3rd rev. ed., N. Y., 1889.

b Andrews, Charles M.; Gambrill, J. Montgomery; Tall, Lida L. *Bibliography of history for schools and libraries.* N. Y., 1910.

a. Pioneer work of great usefulness; selected bibliography of historical literature arranged by topics and countries, with illuminating critical comments; mainly restricted to European countries and the United States. The student will still find it valuable, as a complement to the present *Guide,* for works issued prior to this publication; the final edition contains a large number of titles not in the smaller editions. *b.* Small list, carefully selected with reference to courses in history in secondary schools in the United States. Systematically arranged with brief critical comments. GMD, HRS

B13 Oettinger, Édouard M., ed. *Bibliographie biographique, ou dictionnaire de 26,000 ouvrages tant anciens que modernes relatifs à l'histoire de la vie publique et privée des hommes célèbres de tous les temps et de toutes les nations.* 1850. 2nd ed., 2 v., Bruxelles, 1854.

Valuable list of authorities for the biography of eminent persons. GMD

B14a New York Public Library. *Bulletin.* N. Y., 1897 ff.

b Library of Congress. *List of books on special subjects.* Washington, 1898 ff. (For complete list of latest catalogues cf. *Publications issued by the library since 1897,* under the headings of "Catalogs and lists," and "Bibliographies.")

These publications contain selected lists of books and sometimes of periodical articles on special topics. Many of them dealt with subjects of current interest at the time of publication. *a.* Periodical publication, containing, in addition to selected lists and lists of accessions, other bibliographical information. *b.* Lists on special subjects published from time to time.   GMD

B15a Historical Association. *Annual bulletin of historical literature.* London, 1911 ff.

   b *Jahresberichte der Geschichtswissenschaft, im Auftrage der Historischen Gesellschaft zu Berlin herausgegeben.* 56 v. (1878–1913). Berlin, 1880–1916.

   a. Selected critical list of historical publications chiefly English, issued during the preceding year. *b.* Extraordinarily comprehensive and accurate classified list of historical publications, appearing in the year concerned; includes both books and periodical articles in the leading European languages; invaluable bibliographical aid for every student of history. Its discontinuance with the volume for 1913 is a genuine misfortune, although it has been succeeded by (P1*d*) *Jahresberichte der deutschen Geschichte,* covering German history only.   GMD

B16a *Union list of serials in the libraries of the United States and Canada.* Gregory, Winifred, ed. N. Y., 1927.

   b Poole, **William F.,** and **Fletcher, William I.,** eds. *Poole's index to periodical literature,* 1802–1906. 1 v. and 5 supplements. Boston, 1881–1908.

   c *Readers' guide to periodical literature,* 1899–1921. 5 v. N. Y., 1905–22.

   d *Supplement,* 1907–19. 2 v. N. Y., 1916–20.

   e *International index to periodicals,* 1920–21 ff. V. 1–2 forming v. 8–10 of the whole series, N. Y., 1921 ff.

   f Faxon, Frederick Winthrop, ed. *Magazine subject-index,* Vol. 1, Boston, 1908.

   g —— *Annual magazine subject-index,* 1908 ff. v. 2 ff., Boston, 1909.

   a. Indispensable reference book; lists serials published to January, 1920, but excludes all American newspapers, foreign newspapers published since 1820, and government serials. Gives locations in American libraries.   HRS

   b. Indexes 470 British and American periodicals, representing 12,241 volumes and 590,000 articles; contains only subject entries; the principal clue to the contents of nineteenth century magazine literature in the English language. *c.* Cumulative; continued in monthly and annual issues. Full dictionary index, under author, subject and, when necessary, title. Does for twentieth century magazines what *b* did for those of the nineteenth century, and with greater fullness and exactness. V. 2–3. Also indexes 597 composite books. *d.* Indexes a select list of periodicals not in *c.* Includes certain composite books, foreign periodicals, and society transactions. *e.* Continuation of *c* and *d.* Indexes over 200 periodicals, chiefly in the humanities and sciences, including at least 75 foreign magazines. *f.* Indexes 79 American and British periodicals, 44 from their first issues to the end of 1907, 35 for 1907 only. *g.* Continuation of *f.* From 1909 on has pt. 2, "Dramatic index." It includes transactions of local historical societies, continuing the work of (X1*c*) Griffin. Out of 166 periodicals for 1920, 25 are British and 9 Canadian.   HLK

B17 *Gesamtverzeichnis der ausländischen Zeitschriften* (G.A.Z.) 1914–24. (To be in 10 v.) V. 1–2 (to Digest). Leipzig, 1927 ff.

   Union list of foreign periodicals in German libraries; covers only years 1914–24. Review, E. G. Ledos, *Rev. des Quest. Hist.* 107:295, Oct. 1927.   GMD

B18a *Publishers' weekly.* N. Y. 1872 ff.

  b *Publishers' circular and booksellers' record.* London, 1837 ff. (Semi-monthly before 1890, weekly since that date.)

  c *Bibliographie de la France; journal général de l'imprimerie et de la librairie.* Paris, 1811 ff. (Weekly.)

  d *Das deutsche Buch; Monatsschrift für die Neuerscheinungen deutscher Verlager.* Leipzig, 1921 ff.

  e *Jahresberichte des Literarisches Zentralblattes über die wichtigsten wissen-schaftlichen Neuerscheinungen des gesamten deutschen Sprachgebietes.* 1924 ff. Ed. by Hans Ruppert. Leipzig, 1925 ff.

Periodical lists of new publications. No one of them is absolutely complete for its country, but *a, b* and *d* are approximately so. *a.* Publications in the United States; *b,* in England; *c,* in France; *d,* in Germany.   GMD
  e. Annual record of German publications in philology.   DMCF

B19a *Book review digest.* Minneapolis, 1905 ff. (Monthly and annual.)

  b *Nation* (N. Y.). N. Y., 1865 ff. (Weekly.)

  c *Athenaeum.* 162 v., London, 1828–1921. (Weekly to 1915, monthly to 1919, weekly to Feb. 1921, when merged with *d.*)

  d *Nation* (London). London, 1890 ff. (Weekly.)

  e *Saturday review of politics, literature, science, and art.* London, 1856 ff.

  f *Spectator.* London, 1828 ff. (Weekly.)

  g *New Statesman.* London, 1913 ff. (Weekly.)

  h *Journal des savants.* Paris, 1817 ff. (Monthly.)

  i *Revue critique d'histoire et de littérature.* Paris, 1866 ff. (Semi-monthly.)

  j *Göttingische gelehrte Anzeigen.* Berlin, 1739 ff.

  k *Literarisches Zentralblatt für Deutschland.* Leipzig, 1850 ff. (Weekly.)

  l *Deutsche Literaturzeitung.* Berlin, 1880 ff. (Weekly.)

  m *Times* (London) *Literary Supplement.* London, 1902 ff. (Weekly.)

Leading critical literary reviews which are of special value for their reviews of historical publications; nearly all contain selected lists of new publications; review articles are usually by competent scholars. *a.* Cumulative publication of press comments on new publications; useful but not scholarly. *h.* Especially valu-able for ancient, medieval, and oriental topics. *j.* Usually limited to a few ex-tended highly scholarly reviews. All the remaining titles are of weekly literary reviews of substantially similar type.   GMD

ENCYCLOPEDIAS AND WORKS OF REFERENCE

Encyclopedias are in the main of two types, the dictionary and the monographic. The former lists a greater number and variety of vocabulary words and corre-spondingly subdivides the material into relatively short articles, while the latter restricts the vocabulary and confines the material as much as possible under comprehensive titles.

The first edition of B22b was an aggregation of a few monographs, and, not-withstanding its increase in size and scope, has never departed from its original form, with the result that one must consult the index frequently to find a sub-ject. Many cross references, too, are necessary and are given. The dictionary type requires no index and does away with as many cross references as possible. While (B22b) is still the archetype of the monographic encyclopedia, (B21a and b), (B23b and c), and (B24b and d) are dictionary-like in arrangement.   HRS

B21a *Encyclopedia americana.* Rines, George E., and others, eds. 1903–04. 2nd ed., 30 v., 1918–20. Latest ed., N. Y., 1929. (Bibliographies.)

   b *New international encyclopedia.* Colby, Frank M., and Williams, Talcott, eds. 24 v. N. Y., 1902–04. 2nd rev. ed. 1922; *Supplement* v., 1924. [Reprint, 1927, in 25 single or 13 double v.]

   c *Century cyclopedia of names.* Smith, Benjamin E., ed. 1894. Rev. ed., N. Y., 1911. [V. 11 of *Century dictionary.*]

   a. Strongest in science and technology; many biographies of contemporaries, history of each century from first to twentieth; 412 pages on World War ("War, European"); chief articles signed; many illustrations; pronunciation indicated. *b.* Excellent, well-rounded encyclopedia; very strong in biography; authors of principal articles indicated; v. 24 is supplementary. *c.* Extensive and valuable pronouncing and etymological dictionary of names in geography, biography, mythology, history, ethnology, art, architecture, fiction, etc., with brief explanatory notes. Contains in appendixes chronological table of the chief events of history, lists of rulers, genealogical charts, chronological outlines of European and American literature.   HLK, HRS

B22a *Chambers' encyclopaedia, a dictionary of universal knowledge.* 2 v., London, 1728. Latest ed., 10 v., London and Philadelphia, 1923–27.

   b *Encyclopaedia britannica.* 1768–71. 9th ed., 25 v., 1875–89; supplement to 9th ed., 4 v., 1889–90; 10th ed., 11 v., supplementing 9th ed., 1902–03; 11th ed., 28 v. and index, 1910–11; 12th ed., 3 v., supplementing 11th ed., 1922; 13th ed., 3 v., supplementing 11th and 12th ed.; and new and enl. index vol., 1926; 14th ed., 23 v. and v. containing index and maps. (Excellent bibliographies.)

   a. Convenient and inexpensive; many brief articles; long a popular work; latest edition only fairly satisfactory. *b.* Perhaps the foremost encyclopedia; notable for its long and authoritative articles; the chief historical articles are in most cases excellent. The 9th ed. is still valuable, for many articles not included in later editions in the form in which they appeared in the 9th were of great value. The 10th edition is still useful for its treatment of events in the score of years immediately preceding its publication. The 11th edition contains more short articles than previous issues. The supplementary volumes called the 12th edition deal with events and topics from 1910 to 1921 and have good articles on the World War. The 14th ed. is excellent. Many illustrations and maps throughout the work. Index volumes to 11th and 14th eds. are indispensable.   HLK, HRS

B23a *Encyclopédie; ou, dictionnaire raisonné des sciences, des arts, et des métiers.* Diderot, Denis, and D'Alembert, Jean L. 17 v., Paris and Neufchastel, 1751–65; *Supplement,* 4 v., Paris and Amsterdam, 1776–77. *Recueil de planches,* 11 v. Paris, 1762–72; *Supplement,* 1 v., Paris, 1777.

   b *La grande encyclopédie.* Berthelot, André; Derenbourg, Hartwig; Dreyfus, F. Camille, and others, eds. 31 v. Paris, 1885–1901. (Bibliographies.)

   c *Grand dictionnaire universel du XIXe siècle.* LaRousse, Pierre, ed. 15 v. and 2 v. *Supplement,* Paris, 1866–90. (Bibliographies.)

d *Nouveau Larousse illustré; dictionnaire universel encyclopédique.* Augé, Claude, ed. 7 v. Paris, 1898–1904. 1 v. supplement, Paris, 1906–07.

e —— *Larousse universel en deux volumes; nouveau dictionnaire encyclopédique.* 2 v. Paris, 1922–23. [Earlier ed. with title *Le Larousse pour tous,* 2 v., 1910.]

f —— *Petit Larousse illustré; nouveau dictionnaire encyclopédique.* Paris, 1906. Frequently reprinted.

a. This famous work, to which the leading French scholars of the eighteenth century contributed, was the most elaborate effort of the sort which had yet been made, and has furnished a model for many later encyclopedias. The student of the eighteenth century will find the work of great value. *b.* Most important French encyclopedia; long signed articles; many minor entries. Especially strong on medieval and renaissance topics and on European history, biography, and literature. *c.* No longer up to date for modern subjects, but still a mine of information on European literature, history, and biography. Particularly useful for its many articles on individual works of literature. Has a great number of brief entries and includes also those appropriate to a dictionary. *d.* Convenient work with many brief articles; neither an abridgment of *c* nor a supplement, but an independent work. *e* and *f.* Convenient handbooks with a very large number of titles but very brief articles. Naturally *e* is more useful than *f,* which is very highly condensed. HLK

B24a *Allgemeine Encyclopädie der Wissenschaften und Künste in alphabetischer Folge von genannten Schriftstellern.* Ersch, Johann S. and Gruber, Johann C., eds. 1st series, 99 v. Leipzig, 1818–32. 2nd series, 43 v., Leipzig, 1827–89. 3rd series, 25 v., Leipzig, 1830–50.

b *Konversations-Lexikon.* 1810–11. Brockhaus, Friedrich A., and others, eds. 14th rev. ed., 16 v. and 1 v. supplement. 1898. Rev. ed., 17 v., Leipzig, 1920.

c *Brockhaus' kleines Konversations-lexikon.* 4 v. 1854–56 (later Brockhaus' Handbuch des Wissens). 6th rev. ed., 4 v., Leipzig, 1925.

d *Meyers grosses Konversations-Lexikon.* 1842–53. 6th rev. ed., 20 v. and 4 v. supplement, Leipzig, 1902–12; Kriegsnachtrag, 3 v., Leipzig, 1916–20.

a. In general comparable to (B23*c*) as an extraordinary mine of information on all manner of topics for the period prior to its publication. Contains much material not to be found in any later work, though most later works are greatly indebted to it. *b.* Long the standard German encyclopedia; numerous brief articles. *c.* Condensation of *b.* *d.* Usually has longer and better major articles than *b* and also more nearly up to date. The best German encyclopedia for current use. GMD

B25 *Political handbook of the world: parliaments, parties, and press.* Malcolm W. Davis and Walter H. Mallory, eds. [Council on Foreign Relations.] Cambridge, Mass., 1928 ff.

Gives essential information on the composition of governments of the world, the character and aims of political parties, and the affiliation and tendencies of leading newspapers. Very useful. HRS

B26 *Encyclopedia of the social sciences.* Seligman, Edwin R. A., and others, eds. To be in about 10 v.   V. 1, ff., N. Y., 1929 ff.

To provide for scholars a synopsis of progress in various fields of social science and to "furnish a repository of facts and principles for the use of the legislator, the editor, the business man, the publicist and others interested."   HRS

YEARBOOKS

Yearbooks are an important source of historical and statistical information. Hans Goldschmidt, in *Jahrbücher als Quelle Weltwirtschaftlicher Forschung* in *Weltwirtschaftliches Archiv* (15:481–520, 1919–20, Jena), lists the regional yearbooks of the world and gives a critical estimate of the value of each.

B27a *American annual cyclopaedia and register of important events of the year 1861* [to 1902]. Beginning with v. for 1875, title changed to *Appleton's annual cyclopaedia.* 42 v. N. Y., 1862–1903. Index for years 1876–1887, N. Y., 1888.

  b *American year book: a record of events and progress.* Ed. by S. N. D. North and E. G. Wickware, 1910–19; by A. B. Hart, 1925 ff., N. Y., 1911–20, 1926 ff.

  c *International year book: a compendium of the world's progress in every department of human knowledge for the year 1898* [to 1902]. Ed. by F. M. Colby and others. 5 v. N. Y., 1899–1903. Revised with title *New international year book* [1907 ff.]. N. Y., 1908 ff.

  d *Americana annual: an encyclopedia of current events* [1923 ff.]. Ed. by A. H. McDannald and others. N. Y., 1923 ff.

Encyclopedic yearbooks published in the United States. Similar works limited in scope mainly to a single country or region will be found in the appropriate sections. *a* and *b*. Supplements to American cyclopaedia; *c*, to (B21*b*) *New international encyclopaedia; d*, to (B21*a*) *Encyclopedia Americana. a, c*, and *d*, used encyclopedic arrangement. *b*. Materials arranged under about thirty leading topics. The volumes of *a, b*, and *c* present events occurring in the year indicated by the titles; *d*, the events of the year preceding the title date. *a*. Special attention to political and other events, with biographical sketches of eminent persons deceased within the year. *b*. Valuable accounts of international affairs, of political events in the leading countries, and of progress in the more important fields of human endeavor. *c*. Similar to *a*, though the number of articles is larger; even greater emphasis is placed upon special articles with reference to the leading countries and other important topics. The events of the year 1903–1906 are summarized in the volume for 1907. *d*. Contains more, but briefer articles than *c*. Attempts to furnish a compressed presentation of data rather than expository accounts.   GMD

B28a *Annual register; or a view of the history, politicks and literature of the year 1758* [to date]. Present title, *Annual register; a review of public events at home and abroad,* ed. by M. Epstein. London, 1761 ff.

  b *Statesman's year-book; statistical and historical annual of the states of the world for the year 1864* [to date]. Rev. after official returns. At present, ed. by J. S. Keltie and M. Epstein. London, 1864 ff.

  c *Europa: an annual survey of economic and social conditions; a directory of the League of Nations and of international societies, a European Who's who in politics, trade, science, art and literature.* London, 1926 ff.

d *Hazell's annual for 1886* [to 1923] ; *a cyclopaedic record of men and topics of the day.* [Rev. to Nov. or Dec. of the previous year.] Ed. by E. D. Price, W. Palmer, H. Hall, T. A. Ingram. 38 v., London, 1886–1923.

e *Year-book of social progress; being a summary of recent legislation, official reports, and voluntary effort, with regard to the welfare of the people.* London, 1912 ff.

Principal British year-books. *a.* Originated and for some years edited and largely written by Edmund Burke. Each volume contains sections on English history, foreign and colonial history, chronicle of events, retrospect of literature, science and art, obituary, index. English affairs receive the larger share of attention. Gives some documents and many abstracts of political speeches, covers events of year indicated by the title. *b.* The most important general political year-book. Treats first of the British Empire, next the United States, and then the other countries of the world in alphabetical order. Not a record of events, but a systematic presentation of statistics and other data on existing conditions. Issued about the middle of the year which it is dated. Reliable, impartial, authoritative. *c.* Also issued about the middle of the year of publication. Contains a great deal of somewhat miscellaneous information—valuable for its directory of the League of Nations. *d.* Concise annual encyclopedia of biographical, political, and economic information, general in scope but predominantly British. Its record of current events for the year preceding its date makes it an invaluable companion to *b.* *e.* Useful for the special field indicated by its title. HLK, HRS

B29a Lesur, Charles L., and others, ed. *Annuaire historique universel; ou, Histoire politique pour 1818–61, comprenant en outre un aperçu de la littérature française, une chronique judiciaire, un tableau de la littérature étrangère, avec un appendice contenant les actes publics, traités . . . et un article variétés renfermant une petite chronique des événements, les plus remarquables et une notice nécrologique.* 44 v., Paris, 1821–66.

b Lebon, André, ed. *L'année politique,* 1874–1905 ff. Paris. 1875–1906.

c Viallate, Achille, and **Caudel, Maurice**, ed. *La vie politique dans les deux mondes.* 1906 ff. Paris, 1908 ff. [Bibliothèque d'histoire contemporaine.]

d *Annuaire général.* 1919 ff. (from 1919–1926 as *Annuaire général de la France et de l'étranger*). Paris, 1919 ff.

e *Annuaire de la législation du travail.* 1897 ff. Bruxelles, 1898 ff. [Belgian office of labor.]

f *Larousse Mensuel.* V. 1 ff. and index, Paris, 1907 ff.

a. Corresponds to (B28*a*) *Annual register* for England, continued by *b* and *c*. *d.* Corresponds to (B28*b*) *Statesman's Year-book.* *e.* Annual digest of social legislation in all countries. *f.* A supplement issued in monthly parts to (B23*d*) *Nouveau Larousse illustré.* *a* and *b* cover events indicated by the title, while *c* and *d* record events of the year preceding the date of publication. GMD

B30a Schulthess, H., and others, ed. *Europäischer Geschichtskalender.* 1880–1917, 1919 ff. Nordlingen and München, 1861–1920, 1923 ff.

b Jellinek, George; Laband, Paul; and **Piloty, Robert**, ed. *Jahrbuch des öffentlichen Rechts der Gegenwart.* Tübingen, 1907 ff.

c Schiemann, Theodor. *Deutschland und die grosse Politik.* Berlin, 1902 ff.

d Egelhaaf, Gottlob, and **Haug, Hermann**, eds. *Historisch-politische Jahresübersicht für 1913.* Stuttgart, 1914 ff. A continuation of *Politische Jahresübersicht für 1908* (1912). Stuttgart, 1909–1913.

a. Annual record of events. *b.* An invaluable compilation of information and discussion on current questions of international law. *a* and *b* cover events indicated by the title; *b* and *d* record events of the year preceding the date of publication. *c.* A re-issue in book form of the weekly summary of political events appearing in *Neue preussische Zeitung* (*Kreuzzeitung*). *d.* Another annual record of events.   GMD, HRS

B31a *Gothäischer genealogischer Hofkalender nebst diplomatischstatistischem Jahrbuch [Almanach de Gotha; annuaire généalogique, diplomatique, et statistique],* 1763 ff. Gotha, 1764 ff.

  b *Gothäisches Jahrbuch für Diplomatie, Verwaltung und Wirtschaft.* Gotha, 1926 ff.

  c *World almanac for 1868* [to date]. N. Y., 1868 ff. Titles vary.

  d *Chicago daily news almanack and year-book.* Ed. by J. Langland. Chicago, 1885 ff.

  e Whitaker, Joseph. *Almanack for the year of our Lord 1869* [to date], *containing an account of the astronomical and other phenomena, a vast amount of information respecting the government, finances, population, commerce, and general statistics of the British Empire throughout the world, with some notice of other countries.* London, 1869 ff.

  f *Almanach Hachette: petite encyclopédie de la vie pratique pour 1894* [to 1918]. V. 1–25, Paris, 1893–1917.

Valuable assemblages of official and governmental data. *a.* Issued simultaneously in French and German. Primarily a record of genealogical data of ruling families, with lists of officials of all countries. Since 1849, when the final clause was added to the title, increasing attention has been given to the presentation of statistical data for each country. *b.* Continues from 1926 the lists of officials which formed the second part of *a,* the *Diplomatisches Jahrbuch. c.* Perhaps the most important "information desk" reference book in existence. Chiefly statistical. Kept well up to date. The back volumes remain useful for the study of their period. Each volume has a full index. Up to 1915 each had also an index to the chief articles in the preceding volumes. In the issues for 1915–18 this information was incorporated in the annual index. *d.* Political, statistical, and other information on worldwide range of subjects. More than 200 of its 1000 pages are devoted to Illinois and Chicago. *e.* Devoted chiefly to political and economic affairs; especially valuable for British matters. *f.* Most useful French almanac, though its peculiar selection of material does not render it as useful as the others for political and official information. *a, c, d, e.* Each is published at the end of the year preceding its date; e.g. *World Almanac 1929* was published late in 1928, while in case of *f* events recorded occur in year of date on title page.

                                                          HLK, HRS

B32a *Minerva: Jahrbuch der gelehrten Welt,* 1891 ff. Title of v. 1 *Minerva: Jahrbuch der Universitäten der Welt,* ed. by R. Kupula and K. Trübner. At present 2 v. with 3rd v. (Register) ed. by G. Lüdtke and F. Richter. Leipzig, 1892 ff. *Supplement, Minerva: Handbuch der gelehrten Welt,* ed. by G. Lüdtke and J. Beugel. V. 1, Strassburg, 1911 (only issued in this year).

  b *Index generalis: annuaire général des universités, grandes écoles, académies, archives, bibliothèques, instituts scientifiques, jardins botaniques et zoologiques, musées, observatoires, sociétés savantes* [1919 to date]. Title of v. 1, *Index generalis, annuaire général des universités,* ed. by R. de Montessus de Ballore. Paris, 1920 ff.

c *Year book of the universities of the Empire.* [1914 to date.] London, 1914 ff.

d *Year book of the scientific and learned societies of Great Britain and Ireland: a record of the work done in science, literature and art during the session by numerous societies and governmental institutions.* [Title varies.] London, 1894 ff.

a and *b*. Yearbooks furnishing, in succinct form, information about universities and scientific institutions with lists of their officers and professors together with indexes of personal names. *a*. Publication suspended during the World War. Volumes issued immediately after the war were seriously incomplete. Arranged alphabetically by names of cities in which institutions are located. Contents entirely in German. The supplement contains brief histories of the various universities and other institutions. *b*. Arranged by countries. In countries using the more familiar languages, the data are presented in the vernacular, thus those relating to the United States and the British Empire are in English. In other cases, French is used. Now somewhat superior to *a*, especially for data on scientific and other learned societies. *c*. Gives information about universities of the British Empire. *d*. Record of the work done in science, literature, and art during the year concerned by numerous British societies and government institutions. Includes bibliographical and historical societies. V. 1, for 1884, contained historical information regarding the societies which has not been reprinted in later issues.   HLK

B33 Harbottle, Thomas Bonfield. *Dictionary of historical allusions.* 1903. 2nd ed., N. Y., 1904.

Useful compilation.   HRS

GEOGRAPHY AND ATLASES

Works on historical geography and the relations of geography and history will be found in the preceding section (A41–50). In the present sub-section are listed only geographical works of a descriptive or merely informational character.

B41 Thomas, Joseph, and **Baldwin, Thomas,** eds. *Lippincott's new gazetteer.* 1855. Rev. ed., by Angelo Heilprin and Louis Heilprin, Philadelphia, 1922.

Pronouncing geographical dictionary of the world. The edition of 1922 is the revision of 1906 with a conspectus giving the American census figures for 1910 and 1920. Very complete and satisfactory for the period before the recent great political changes.   HLK

B42a Reclus, Jean J. Élisée. *Earth and its inhabitants: the universal geography.* 19 v. London, 1878–94. V. 1–4, ed. by E. C. Ravenstein; v. 5, 6, by E. G. Ravenstein and A. H. Keane; v. 7–19, by A. H. Keane. Tr. from *Nouvelle géographie universelle,* 19 v., Paris, 1875–94. [1, *Southern Europe;* 2, *France, Switzerland;* 3, *Austria-Hungary, Germany, Belgium, Netherlands;* 4, *British Isles;* 5, *Northeastern Atlantic, Islands of Northern Atlantic, Scandinavia, European Islands of the Arctic Ocean, Russia in Europe;* 6, *Asiatic Russia;* 7, *Eastern Asia;* 8, *India and Indo-China;* 9, *Southwestern Asia;* 10, *Northeastern Africa;* 11, *Northwestern Africa;* 12, *West Africa;* 13, *Southern and Eastern Africa;* 14, *Australasia;* 15, *North America;* 16, *United States;* 17, *Mexico, Central America, West Indies;* 18, *South America, the Andes Regions;* 19, *Amazonia and La Plata.*] (Bibliographies.)

b Herbertson, Fanny D. *Clarendon geography.* 2 v. in 6 pt. Oxford, 1912–13. 1, *Principles;* 2, *British Isles;* 3, *Europe;* 4, *Asia;* 5, *Africa and Australasia;* 6, *America.* There are rev. ed. of the parts. (Bibliographies.)

c Bowman, Isaiah. *The new world: problems in political geography.* 1921. New rev. ed., N. Y. 1928. (Very good bibliography.)

d Moncrieff, Ascot Robert Hope. *New world of today, with economic data supplied by L. W. Lyde and I. J. Curnow and a series of maps to date by John Bartholomew & Son, Ltd.* 8 v. London, 1920–22.

a. Still the best available descriptive geography of a comprehensive sort on a large scale, though seriously out of date. *b.* Later and briefer work. *c.* Best brief presentation of geographical data with reference to conditions since the World War. Review, R. H. Lord, *A.H.R.* 27:568, Apr. 1922. *d.* Similar to *c,* but more extensive; popular; many illustrations; good maps.   GMD, HRS

B43a *Baedeker's guide books.* Leipzig, 1839 ff. Many ed. of each v. [The following appear in both English and German, most of them in French also. 1, *Great Britain,* 8th ed. 1927; 2, *London,* 18th ed. 1923; 3, *Northern France,* 5th ed. 1909; 4, *Southern France,* 13th ed. 1929; 5, *Paris,* 19th ed. 1924; 6, *Belgium and Holland,* 15th ed. 1910; 7, *Northern Germany,* 17th ed. 1925; 8, *Southern Germany,* 13th ed. 1929; 9, *Rhine,* 18th ed. 1926; 10, *Berlin,* 6th ed. 1923; 11, *Switzerland,* 27th ed. 1928; 12, *Tyrol and the Dolomites,* 13th ed. 1927; 13, *Austria,* 11th ed. 1911; 14, *Mediterranean,* 1911; 15, *Italy,* 3rd ed., 1928; 16, *Northern Italy,* 14th ed. 1913; 17, *Central Italy,* 15th ed. 1909; 18, *Southern Italy,* 16th ed. 1912; 19, *Spain and Portugal,* 4th ed. 1913; 20, *Greece,* 4th ed. 1909; 21, *Egypt and the Sudan,* 7th ed. 1914; 22, *Palestine,* 5th ed. 1912; 23, *Norway, Sweden, and Denmark,* 10th ed. 1912; 24, *Russia,* 1914; 25, *Dominion of Canada,* 4th ed. 1922; 26, *United States,* 4th ed. 1909; 27, *Manual of the Russian Language,* 1914. The following are in German only: 28, *Konstantinopel, Balkanstaaten, Kleinasien,* 2nd ed. 1914; 29, *Indien,* 1914.]

b *Murray's hand books.* London, 1836 ff. Many ed. of each v. [1, *India, Burma and Ceylon;* 2, *Egypt and the Sudan;* 3, *North Germany; Northern Europe;* 4, *Rome and Compagna;* 5, *Switzerland and the adjacent regions of the Alps;* 6, *Algeria and Tunis;* 7, *Asia Minor, Transcaucasia, Persia,* etc.; 8, *Central Italy;* 9, *Constantinople, Brusa, and the Troad;* 10, *Denmark, with Schleswig-Holstein and Iceland;* 11, *France;* 12, *Greece;* 13, *Holland and Belgium;* 14, *Ireland;* 15, *Japan;* 16, *New Zealand;* 17, *Northern Italy;* 18, *Norway;* 19, *Portugal;* 20, *Russia, Poland, Finland;* 21, *Scotland;* 22, *Southern Italy and Sicily;* 23, *South Germany;* 24, *Spain;* 25, *Sweden;* 26, *Syria and Palestine;* 27, *Corsica and Sardinia;* 28, *Turkey;* 29, *The Continent;* 30, *Riviera;* 31, *Paris;* 32, *Mediterranean;* 33, *Rome.*]

c Muirhead, Findlay, ed. *Guide books,* London, 1922 ff. [1, *England,* 2nd ed. 1924; 2, *Wales,* 2nd ed. 1926; 3, *Scotland,* 1927; 4, *London,* 3rd ed. 1927; 5, *Short guide to London,* 1927; 6, *Paris,* 2nd ed. 1927; 7, *North Western France,* 1926; 8, *Brittany,* 1925; 9, *Normandy,* 1925; 10, *North Eastern France,* 1922; 11, *French Alps,* 2nd ed. 1926; 12, *Southern France,* 1926; 13, *Belgium,* 2nd ed. 1924; 14, *Switzerland,* 1923; 15, *Northern Italy,* 1924; 16, *Southern Italy,* 1925.] [Blue guides.]

Travelers' guide books are extremely convenient sources of information on a wide range of historical and geographical topics. They frequently contain useful general articles in addition to the customary information on routes and places. Old editions provide data on conditions at particular past dates. *a.* Titles and contents differ somewhat in successive editions, and in the editions in the three different languages. Materials skilfully condensed and admirably arranged;

excellent maps and plans. On the whole the best series of guides available prior to the World War; recent editions fully maintain earlier standards. *b.* As a rule, materials are less compactly presented and the treatment is more elaborately descriptive. *c.* Recent works prepared primarily for the English tourists of the Post-war period; consequently the number of volumes is still very limited. Numerous other series of guides have been attempted in various countries in the last generation, but, with an occasional exception, the volumes do not measure up to those in the series here mentioned. There are, however, frequently special books for single cities or localities which are highly valuable. It is, however, impossible, except in a very few cases, to refer to them in this work. GMD

B44a Behm, Ernst, and **Wagner, Hermann von,** eds. *Geographisches Jahrbuch.* Gotha, 1866 ff. (V. 43, 1929.)

b Haach, Hermann, ed. *Geographen-Kalender.* V. 1–12, Gotha, 1903–14.

a. Best systematic record of the progress of geography in all departments. *b.* In addition to lists of geographers and geographical societies, it contains bibliographies of current publications and records of exploring and scientific expeditions and of other events relevant to geography and geographical science. FWP

B45a *Times survey atlas of the world: a comprehensive series of new and authentic maps reduced from the national surveys of the world and the special surveys of travellers and explorers, with general index of over two hundred thousand names.* John G. Bartholomew, ed. 112 plates, London, 1922.

b *Daily Telegraph victory atlas of the world; a series of 150 plates containing over 450 maps and diagrams compiled from the latest and most authentic sources.* Alexander Gross, ed. 150 plates. London, 1922.

c *Harmsworth's atlas of the world and pictorial gazetteer, with an atlas of the great war, containing 485 colored maps and plans, 3540 photographic views, and index to 120,000 names.* 1907. Rev. ed. by J. A. Hammerton. 179 plates. London, 1922.

d Saint-Martin, Vivien de, and **Schrader, Franz.** *Atlas universel de géographie; dressé sous la direction de F. Schrader d'après les sources originales et les documents les plus recents, comprenant 80 cartes gravées sur cuivre et tirées en lithographie, avec un index alphabétique des noms contenus dans l'atlas.* 1881–1911. 80 plates. Paris, 1923.

e Stieler, Adolf. *Hand-Atlas.* 1896. 10th rev. ed. (also in English), by H. Haack. 108 plates. Gotha, 1920–25.

f Andree, Richard. *Allgemeiner Hand-Atlas, in 228 Haupt- und 198 Nebenkarten, mit Vollständigem alphabetischem Namenverzeichnis in besonderem Bande.* 1881. 8th rev. ed. by E. Ambrosius, 132 plates, Leipzig, 1922.

g Westermann, George. *Weltatlas: 130 Haupt- und 117 Nebenkarten auf 106 Kartenblättern mit erläuterndem Text und einem alphabetischen Namenverzeichnis.* 1921. 3rd rev. ed. by A. Liebers and others. 106 plates. Braunschweig, 1922.

h Baratta, Mario, and **Visintin, Luigi.** *Grande atlante geografico; 102 tavole de geografia fisica, politica, ed economica, con 250 carte e cartine ed indice dei nomi.* 86 plates. Novara, 1922.

i *Meyers geographischer Handatlas.* 2nd ed., 1900. 92 main maps and 99 inset maps. 7th rev. ed. Leipzig, 1928.

Most important general atlases published since the World War, showing the new boundaries. Each contains an index of place names. All are folio size except *g, h,* and *i,* the largest scale maps being in *b.* All give chief attention to political geography and the location of places except *g* and *h,* which emphasize physical and economic features. The maps in *a,* however, also exhibit admirably the physical relief. *a, d, e,* and *f* are generally recognized as the best available reference atlases; each of these and *h* are based upon the latest information available from explorations, governmental publications, and other sources. *e.* Generally regarded as the handiest of the four just mentioned, being less bulky than the others, but it suffers from having its maps overloaded with detail. In this respect *f* is superior, and for various regions affords the best available maps. *a.* Especially excellent for the regions in the British Empire. It is also the best of the works in English though *b* has the advantage of being cheaper. *e.* Distinctly popular work; new edition differs considerably from the first, which contained many useful maps not reproduced. *g.* Contains a section of historical maps which has passed through several editions as a separate work. Review of all eight, W. L. G. Joerg, *Geographical Review,* 13 : 583, Oct. 1923.   GMD

i. Indicates physical relief excellently, is clear and detailed, and especially good for central Europe.   SBF

B46a *Century atlas of the world.* Ed. by B. E. Smith, 1897. 16th rev. ed., N. Y., 1914.

b *Rand McNally commercial atlas of America and foreign countries.* 2 pts. Pt. I, 1869. 58th ed., Chicago, 1927; Pt. 2, 1919. 2nd ed., Chicago, 1921.

c *Hammond's modern atlas of the world.* (C. S. Hammond & Co.) N. Y., 1924.

d *Hammond's business atlas of economic geography; a new series of maps showing relief of land, rainfall, mineral products, etc.* (C. S. Hammond & Co.) N. Y., 1919.

e *Putnam's handy map book.* (G. P. Putnam's Sons.) N. Y., 1925.

f *Oxford economic atlas, with introduction by L. W. Lyde.* (John Bartholomew.) 6th rev. ed., London, 1925.

g *Putnam's economic atlas: a systematic survey of the world's trade, economic resources, and communications, issued under the auspices of the Association of British Chambers of Commerce,* ed. by George Philip and T. Swinburne Sheldrake. London and N. Y., 1925. [Also published under the title: Chambers of Commerce atlas.]

h Schrader, Franz; Prudent, F.; and **Anthoine, E.** *Atlas de géographie moderne.* 1890. Rev. ed., Paris, 1908.

i Spamer, Otto, ed. *Grosser Handatlas.* 1897. 2nd rev. ed. by A. Hettner. Leipzig, 1900.

j *Neuer Handatlas über alle Teile der Erde.* 1893–95. 4th rev. ed. by E. Debes, Leipzig, 1911–13.

k Friederichsen, Maximilian H., ed. *Methodischer Atlas zur Länderkunde von Europa.* Leipzig, 1914 ff. [1, *Ost-Europa und die Ost-seeländer;* 2, *Die Nordseeländer und Frankreich;* 3, *Die iberische und italienische Halbinseln.*]

l Goode, John Paul, ed. *Goode's school atlas, physical, political, and economic, for American schools and colleges.* N. Y., 1923.

m Bartholomew, John G., ed. *Oxford advanced atlas.* 2nd ed. rev., London, 1924.

n Philip, George, ed. *Philip's senior school atlas.* London, 1921.

o Visintin, Luigi, ed. *Atlante geographico Metodico.* Novara, 1921.

a, b, c, d, e. Recent American atlases. *a* contains the best maps but is now out of date. *b* and *c* have large scale folio maps showing post-war boundaries and they locate and index a vast number of places. *e.* Small volume; 300 pages of maps and indexes; maps very legible. *d, f, g.* Good economic atlases. *g.* Folio; perhaps the best economic atlas yet published. *h, i, j.* Though published before the war, each of these large general atlases contains various maps which are still valuable. *k.* Extensive new work in course of publication; gives special attention to the factors of physical and economic geography; limited to Europe. *l, m, n, o.* Excellent recent school geographies with numerous small maps emphasizing not so much the political features, as the various other elements of interest which enter into the modern scientific geography. HRS, GMD

COLLECTIONS OF SOURCES

Very few general collections of sources are listed below. In the appropriate sections source collections and source books will be found under the title numbers assigned to this heading.

B61 **Shotwell, James T.,** and **Evans, Arthur P.,** eds. *Records of civilization; sources and studies.* V. 1–10, N. Y., 1915–29. (Bibliographies.) [1, J. T. Shotwell, *Introduction to the history of history,* 1922; 2, G. W. Botsford and E. H. Sihler, ed., *Hellenic civilization,* 1915; 3, (H203b) E. Brehaut, tr., *History of the Franks by Gregory, Bishop of Tours,* 1916; 4, L. R. Loomis, tr., *Book of the Popes (Liber pontificalis),* 1916; 5, J. A. Bewer, *Literature of the Old Testament in its historical development,* 1922; 6, J. T. Shotwell and Louise R. Loomis, *See of Peter,* 1927; 7, J. A. Montgomery, *History of Yaballaha III,* 1927; 8, J. B. Williams, *Guide to the printed materials for English social and economic history, 1750–1850,* 2 vs., 1927; 9, C. C. Mierow, tr., *Two cities by Otto, Bishop of Freising,* 1929; 10, P. K. Hitti, tr., *An Arab gentleman and warrior in the period of the Crusades. Memoirs of Usamah ibn-Murshid (Kitab al-i tibar).* 1929.]

Excellent volumes forming part of a series to make accessible in English important sources and critical discussion of them. 1, cf. (A242). 2, General source book for Greek social history. Review by P. Shorey, *A.H.R.* 21: 586, Apr. 1916. 3 and 4, Each deals with but a single source. 3, Cf. (H203b). 4, E. Emerton, *A.H.R.* 22: 697, Apr. 1917. 5, H. Neumann, *Freeman,* 6: 403, Jan. 3, 1923. 6, Documentary study tracing the doctrinal basis for the primacy of Rome and the rise of the Roman pontiff to preëminence in the universal church. Review, F. A. Christie, *A.H.R.* 33:848, July 1928. 7, Annotated translation from the Syriac of part of the history by Yaballaha III, Nestorian patriarch, and by his vicar, Mongol ambassador to the Frankish courts at the end of the thirteenth century. Review, J. K. Wright, *A.H.R.* 33: 430, Jan. 1928. 8, Scholarly and helpful selection, evolution and classification of (part 1) bibliographies and works of general reference covering the field of English social and economic history, 1750–1850, and (part 2) of titles centering around two main themes: economic theory, conditions and problems; and social relations broadly defined. Review, W. Bowden, *A.H.R.* 32:359, Jan. 1927; *E.H.R.* 43: 151, Jan. 1928. 9, Chronicle of universal history to 1146 A.D.; first translation in full in any modern language. Review, A. A. Beaumont, *A.H.R.* 34: 566, April 1929. 10, Review, D. B. Macdonald, *A.H.R.* 35: 154, Oct. 1929. HRS

B62 Schmitt, Bernadotte E., ed. *Landmarks in History.* N. Y. 1927 ff. [1. G. G. Andrews, *Constitution in the early French Revolution,* 1927; 2, A. Hyma, *Luther's theological development from Erfurt to Augsburg,* 1928; 3, F. L. Benns, *Irish question,* 1928; 4, W. Bowden, *Industrial Revolution, 1775–1825;* 5, F. C. Palm, *Establishment of French absolutism, 1574–1610;* 6, F. Schevill, *First century of Italian humanism;* 7, G. G. Andrews, *Parliamentary reform in England, 1830–1832.*]

Series of source books to cover field of modern European history from the Renaissance to the World War. Extracts from the chief sources for the study of each problem bound separately. Useful and well done.   HRS

B63 Webster, Hutton, ed. *Historical selections.* Boston, 1929.

Nearly six hundred brief selections in English or English translation for all ages and lands, chiefly illustrations of cultural development.   GMD

SHORTER GENERAL HISTORIES

In the sub-sections which follow it will be possible to follow roughly the course of historiography during the last few decades. Since George Park Fisher wrote his *Outlines* (101a) in 1881, the scope of history has gradually widened until it has come to include many aspects, if not every aspect, of the life of humanity. It is a truism to say that a writer of history reflects the interests of the age in which he writes. Interests have changed enormously since Fisher's day and Freeman's remark that history is merely past politics is noteworthy chiefly as recording the prevalent view of a generation now past.

Naturally the growth of nations and the rise and fall of parties hold their place in our narratives; but the influence of physical phenomena upon human society, economic conditions of life, the ever-changing relations of social classes, the new forms of religions and philosophic thought, characteristic tendencies in literature and art, the progress of science, the development of legal doctrine and practice, these and their complex interactions one upon another all command the attention of the historian of today and make his task increasingly difficult. In both shorter and longer works the widening scope of history is evident and in the later sub-sections of this section will be found volumes devoted especially to a number of the special interests just mentioned.

Most recent histories covering a large field have been the coöperative product of associations of scholars. There are doubtless necessary deficiencies in works carried out by this method: a series of monographs can hardly have coördination or unity, even under the most inspiring editorial control. Yet in the conditions imposed by modern specialization it is hard to see how else longer and comprehensive works can be produced. Few adequately trained historians are now willing to undertake alone a history of the world, or even of a long epoch.

B101a Fisher, George P. *Outlines of universal history, designed as a text-book and for private reading.* 1885. Rev. ed., N. Y. 1904.

b Wells, Herbert G. *Outline of history, being a plain history of life and mankind.* 2 v., 1920. 3rd ed., 1 v., 1921. 4th ed., 2 v., London and N. Y., 1926.

c —— *Short history of the world.* London and N. Y., 1924. (Bibliographies.)

d Van Loon, Hendrik W. *Story of mankind.* 1921. (Bibliography.)

e **Parsons, Geoffrey.** *Stream of history.* N. Y. and London, 1928.

f **Hillyer, Virgil M.** *Child's history of the world.* N. Y. and London, 1926.

g **Webster, Hutton.** *World history.* Rev. ed., Boston, 1925. (Bibliography.)

These surveys include the Far East and the American continents, besides tracing the development of civilization from its early homes in the Nile and Tigris-Euphrates valleys and its spread to Europe and the west. *a.* By a trained historian. Although it contains chapters on the history of literature, art, and science, the author emphasizes the outstanding political developments of the period covered, carrying the narrative in the final revision only to 1901. *b.* Work of a novelist and social reformer, written "plainly for the general reader." Essentially an attempt to interpret the past rather than a narrative of events. The group of scholars who have checked the facts used by the author, are not at all responsible for the interpretation which he has given. The author is interested in deducing general laws from his data and in demonstrating the wisdom of certain social and political theories. Review, C. Becker, *A.H.R.* 26: 641, July 1921. *c.* More generalized history, planned and written afresh; not a condensation of *b;* corrects many errors of facts made in *b.* Review, C. Becker, *A.H.R.* 28: 573, Apr. 1923. *d.* Like *b,* begins with prehistoric times but the treatment is much briefer and more elementary. As such it appeals to a wider circle of readers, to some children as well as to their elders. The author paints a series of word pictures of human progress which he reënforces by means of characteristic sketches and diagrams from his own hand. Both Wells and Van Loon stress the development of mankind and nationalities rather than the fortunes of political units. Both close their narratives with the Paris conference of 1919. Review, R. A. Maurer, *A.H.R.* 29: 156, Oct. 1923. DCK.

e. "The writer," so Mr. Parsons says in his preface, "has aimed to tell the whole story of man and his earth and to tell it so swiftly and simply that its essential parts will stand forth in their due relationships unobscured by detail." This aim has been well carried out in the six hundred odd pages of text and the description is accurate. With no hesitation on the part of the author in saying in regard to controversial questions that he does not know (always to be admired), that he believes no one knows, the reader is swept through the long story from the earliest days of the earth to the close of the Great War most enthusiastically. Well written and very clear. One of the best world histories in one volume. Review, *A.H.R.* 34: 149, Oct. 1928. *f.* Charming book for the very young with appropriate illustrations. Review, F. Morehouse, *Hist. Outlook,* 16: 126, Mar. 1925. *g.* Narrative account from prehistoric times to the Washington Conference in 1922, with half the space devoted to the period since 1789. A history of the race rather than of nations, with strong interest in social progress; but does not seek to propound an interpretation or favorite theories. Safe and readable. Abundant maps. Review, E. F. Jacob, *History* n. s. 8: 246, Jan. 1924. HRS

B102a **Adams, George Burton.** *European history: an outline of its development.* N. Y., 1899. (Brief bibliography.)

b **Grant, Arthur J.** *History of Europe.* 1913. Rev. ed., N. Y., 1918. (Bibliographies.)

    c Robinson, James Harvey. *Introduction to the history of western Europe.*
Boston and London, 1902. Rev. ed., 2 v., N. Y. and London, 1924–26.
New brief ed., 1925.

    d Robinson, James H.; Breasted, James H.; and Smith, Edward P.
*General history of Europe from the origins of civilization to the present
time.* N. Y., 1921. Also, 2 v. ed., N. Y., 1921. (Excellent selected
bibliography.)

    e Breasted, James H.; Robinson, James H.; and Beard, Charles A.
Outlines of European history. 2 v., N. Y., 1912–14. Rev. ed. of v. 2, 1927.
(Bibliography.)

    f Breasted, James Henry. *Ancient times.* N. Y., 1916. (For the most
part reprinted as *Conquest of civilization,* N. Y., 1926.)

    g Robinson, James Harvey. *Medieval and modern times.* N. Y., 1926.
(New and rev. ed.) (For the most part reprinted as *Ordeal of civilization.* N. Y., 1926.)

    a and *b.* Treatment restricted to an account of European progress, noting the
spread of European culture to other continents. Comparatively little space is
devoted in either of these volumes to developments since 1871. Both accounts
end with the opening of the present century. *b.* Written primarily for English
readers; omits all references to the separate history of the British Isles, in the
interest of proportion and a better perspective. Illustrated with several well-
executed maps and diagrams. *d.* Designed primarily as a text-book; a more
detailed narrative covering the same period, but omitting references to Asiatic
development except as it profoundly modifies the current of European and
western progress. *e.* A still more detailed account of which v. 1 is ancient and
medieval history, v. 2, our own times. *c.* A pioneer book of its type in the text-
book world in its omissions of many facts and emphasis upon important events
and upon the cultural side. The revised two-volume edition covers recent years
and includes many short extracts from the sources. An admirable text. Review
of *c,* P. van Dyke, *A.H.R.* 9: 132, Oct. 1903. *f.* Expansion of the first part of *e,*
vol. 1. *g.* Abridgment of the latter part of *e* and of *g.* Review of *f* (*Conquest
of civilization*), R. W. Rogers, *A.H.R.* 32: 830, July, 1927; of *g* (*Ordeal of
civilization*), T. Collier, *A.H.R.* 32: 842, July, 1927.   HRS, DCK

B103a Botsford, George W., and **Botsford, Jay B.** *Brief history of the
world, with especial reference to social and economic conditions.* 1917.
Rev. ed., N. Y. 1920. (Brief bibliography.)

    a. Authors concern themselves with the history of civilization, reducing to a
minimum the details of political history. Covers the World War, and is unique
in the condensation which the authors have attained and in the relatively large
amount of concrete data on social and economic conditions from ancient times
to the present day.   DCK

B104a Duruy, Victor. *General history of the world.* N. Y., 1898. Tr. by E. A.
Grosvenor from *Abrégé de l'histoire universelle,* Paris, 1873.

    b Marvin, Francis S. *Living past: a sketch of western progress.* London,
1913.

    c Happold, F. Christopher. *Adventure of man: a brief history of the
world.* London, 1926.

    d Weber, Nicholas A. *General history of the Christian era.* Washington,
1919.

a. Old, but in its new form still very useful compendium of world history; a good reference book. *b.* Very original survey of the social and intellectual history of mankind from the ice age to the twentieth century; a masterpiece in its compass; well written and thoughtful. Review, J. T. Shotwell, *A.H.R.* 19:580, 1914. *c.* Clever little book for the young reader. Progress of man is recorded in thirty-five "adventures." Well illustrated. Review, (London) *Times Lit. Suppl.* 25:657, Sept. 30, 1926.   HRS

d. Excellent text, the "encyclopedic tendency" dominant in so many short histories is successfully avoided, and the large important issues are treated in a thorough manner. Very clear; style remarkably good.   PG

B105 Petit, Maxime, ed. *Histoire générale des peuples.* 3 v., Paris, 1925–26.

Coöperative and somewhat popular account with many illustrations, photographic reproductions of documents, and maps. Very well done. Review, E. G. Ledos, *Rev. des Quest. Hist.* of v. 1, 102:462, April 1925; 103:151, July 1925; ibid., 103:443, Oct. 1925; 104:426, April 1926; of v. 2, ibid., 106:174, Jan. 1927.   HRS

B106 Newhall, Richard A.; Packard, Sidney R.; and **Packard, Lawrence B.,** eds. *Berkshire studies in European history.* N. Y. 1927 ff. [1, R. A. Newhall, *Crusades;* 2, S. R. Packard, *Europe and the Church under Innocent III;* 3, L. B. Packard, *Commercial revolution;* 4, F. C. Dietz, *Industrial revolution;* 5, J. K. Wright, *Geographical basis of European history;* 6, G. Brunn, *Enlightened despots;* 7, S. Baldwin, *Organization of medieval Christianity;* 8, L. B. Packard, *Age of Louis XIV;* 9, A. H. Buffinton, *Second hundred years' war, 1689–1815;* 10, D. E. Owen, *Imperialism and nationalism in the Far East;* 11, H. L. Hoskins, *European imperialism in Africa;* 12, R. G. Trotter, *British Empire-Commonwealth.*]

Pocket-size booklets, each intended to furnish the student with a week's "collateral reading" in special fields where an "assignment" of the right length is not readily available. Useful for the purpose.   HRS

B107 Robinson, George W. *Outlines of historical study.* N. Y., 1927.

"An introduction to historical study and an outline" comprising twelve chapters of illustrative selections from various authors, chronological outlines and searching questions covering history from ancient Greece to a recent date. Three supplementary chapters include a chronological table of inventions and discoveries, short accounts of great historians and their works, and historical maxims and reflections. A unique and helpful guide.   HRS

LONGER GENERAL HISTORIES

B121 *New Larned history for ready reference, reading, and research.* 1894–95. Rev. ed. by D. E. Smith, C. Seymour, A. H. Shearer, D. C. Knowlton. 12 v. Springfield, Mass., 1922–24. (Bibliographies.)

All subjects and phases of history, i.e., countries, peoples, events, movements, institutions, are arranged alphabetically, with succinct quotations given in succession, generally chronological, from accounts by established historians, with many cross references, eliminating repetition, making a complete treatment. Includes subjects of social and economic value not formerly classed with history, while many subjects are completely new. The World War is treated by a very complete series of quotations and references. Many documents, maps, illustrations, genealogies, chronologies.   AHS

B132 **Hassall, Arthur,** ed. *Periods of European history, 476–1899.* 8 v. London, 1893–1901. [1, C. W. C. Oman, *Dark Ages, 476–918;* 2, T. F. Tout, *Empire and the papacy, 918–1273;* 3, R. Lodge, *Close of the middle ages, 1273–1494;* 4, A. H. Johnson, *Europe in the sixteenth century, 1494–1598;* 5, H. O. Wakeman, *Ascendancy of France, 1598–1715;* 6, A. Hassall, *Balance of power, 1715–1789;* 7, H. M. Stephens, *Revolutionary Europe, 1789–1815;* 8, W. A. Phillips, *Modern Europe, 1815–1899.*]

After the lapse of a generation, these books are still probably the most useful handbooks of European political history in English. The treatment is confined to continental affairs, considering England only in its international relations. V. 1–4. Suffer somewhat from their age but there is nothing yet to replace them. V. 7–8. In great part superseded by more recent works of similar character and scope, but there is, as yet, practically nothing in English which treats the seventeenth and eighteenth centuries in such fashion as v. 5 and 6. Review of v. 2, *A.H.R.* 4:142, Oct. 1898; v. 3, J. H. Robinson, *A.H.R.* 7:396, Jan. 1902; v. 6, H. M. Stephens, *A.H.R.* 3:349, Jan. 1898; v. 8, C. M. Andrews, *A.H.R.* 7:984, July 1902.   RAN

B133a **Cox, George W.,** and **Sankey, Charles,** eds. *Epochs of ancient history.* 10 v., London, 1876–81. [1, G. W. Cox, *Greeks and the Persians;* 2, id., *Athenian empire;* 3, C. Sankey, *Spartan and Theban supremacies;* 4, A. M. Curteis, *Rise of the Macedonian empire;* 5, W. Ihne, *Rome to its destruction by the Gauls;* 6, R. B. Smith, *Rome and Carthage, the Punic Wars;* 7, A. H. Beesley, *Gracchi, Marius, and Sulla;* 8, C. Merivale, *Roman triumvirates;* 9, W. W. Capes, *Early Roman empire;* 10, id., *Roman empire of the second century.*] 11 v., N. Y. [V. 1, S. G. W. Benjamin, *Troy, its legend, history, and literature;* other v. same.]

b **Morris, Edward E.,** and others, eds. *Epochs of modern history.* 19 v., London, 1874–88. [1, R. W. Church, *Beginning of the middle ages;* 2, A. H. Johnson, *Normans in Europe;* 3, G. W. Cox, *Crusades;* 4, W. Stubbs, *Early Plantagenets;* 5, W. Warburton, *Edward the Third;* 6, J. Gairdner, *Houses of Lancaster and York;* 7, G. E. Moberly, *Early Tudors;* 8, F. Seebohm, *Era of the Protestant revolution;* 9, M. Creighton, *Age of Elizabeth;* 10, S. R. Gardiner, *First two Stuarts and the Puritan revolution;* 11, id., *Thirty years' war;* 12, O. Airy, *English restoration and Louis XIV;* 13, E. Hale, *Fall of the Stuarts and Western Europe;* 14, E. E. Morris, *Age of Anne;* 15, id., *Early Hanoverians;* 16, F. W. Longman, *Frederick the Great and the seven years' war;* 17, J. M. Ludlow, *War of American Independence;* 18, Mrs. S. R. Gardiner, *French revolution;* 19, J. McCarthy, *Epoch of reform.*] 18 v., N. Y. [Same omitting v. 17, and substituting for v. 18, W. O. Morris, *French revolution and first empire.*]

Commonplace works of popularization now very much out of date. They provide a somewhat detailed narrative of events. *a.* Should not be used with any confidence, and more recent works, if available, are to be preferred. The volume on Carthage is one of the few works in English which treats that subject. *b.* Has a marked English emphasis which may easily be misleading. Volumes by Stubbs, Seebohm, Creighton, and Gardiner are entitled to the consideration due to distinguished authorship, but they are, generally speaking, not the best treatment of their respective subjects now easily accessible in most libraries.   RAN

B134 **Williams, Henry Smith,** ed. *Historians' history of the world; a comprehensive narrative of the rise and development of nations as recorded by over two thousand of the great writers of all ages.* 25 v., London and N. Y., 1904–05. (Bibliographies.) [1, *Prolegomena, Egypt, Mesopotamia;*

2, *Israel, India, Persia, Phoenicia, minor nations of western Asia;* 3, *Greece to the Peloponnesian war;* 4, *Greece to the Roman conquest;* 5, *Roman republic;* 6, *Early Roman empire;* 7, *Later Roman empire;* 8, *Parthians, Sassanids, and Arabs, the crusades and the papacy;* 9, *Italy;* 10, *Spain and Portugal;* 11, *France, 843–1715;* 12, *France, 1715–1815;* 13, *France, 1815–1904, Netherlands;* 14, *The Netherlands (concluded), the Germanic empires;* 15, *Germanic empires (concluded);* 16, *Scandinavia, Switzerland to 1715;* 17, *Switzerland (concluded), Russia and Poland;* 18, *England to 1485;* 19, *England, 1485–1642;* 20, *England, 1642–1791;* 21, *Scotland, Ireland, England since 1792;* 22, *British colonies, United States (early colonial period);* 23, *United States (concluded), Spanish America;* 24, *Poland, The Balkans, Turkey, minor eastern states, China, Japan;* 25, *Index.*]

Attempt to produce a world history by joining together selections from labors of many writers of greatly varying degrees of worth, of different times, and of widely divergent conceptions of history and historical evidence. This has been quite skilfully accomplished and an interesting continuous narrative has been, in large measure, secured. It should be added that in very many cases literary and dramatic rather than historical value seems to have determined the choice of the fragments.

FLT

B135 **Lodge, Henry C.,** ed. *History of nations.* 25 v., Philadelphia, 1906–08. (Bibliographies.) [1, A. H. Sayce, *Ancient empires of the east;* 2, C. W. C. Oman, *Greece;* 3, T. Mommsen, *Rome;* 4, J. H. Cabot, ed., *Italy;* 5, Sir W. W. Hunter, *India;* 6, Sir R. K. Douglas, *China;* 7, Japan Department of Education, *Japan;* 8, G. M. Adam, *Spain and Portugal;* 9, E. Bonne-chose, *France;* 10, F. A. A. Mignet, *French revolution;* 11, S. R. Gardiner, *England;* 12, P. W. Joyce, *Ireland;* 13, T. Grattan, *Holland and Belgium,* — C. Dandliker, *Switzerland;* 14, Sir E. S. Creasy, *Turkey;* 15, W. R. Morfill, *Russia and Poland;* 16, E. C. Otte, *Norway, Sweden, and Denmark,* — G. F. Surface, *Polar research;* 17, L. P. M. Leger, *Austria-Hungary;* 18, B. Taylor, *Germany;* 19, J. S. Keltie, *Africa;* 20, E. J. Payne, *Colonies of the world;* 21, A. J. Deberle, *South America;* 22, B. Mayer, *Mexico, Central America, and West Indies;* 23–24, J. W. Garner, *United States;* 25, J. E. Burdick, *General index.*]

This series consists of standard or well-known works, often condensed, sometimes continued, and all edited by American scholars. The editing, as well as the original works, varies greatly in merit, but on the whole, the result is a series of reliable and creditable but somewhat antiquated narratives. GMD

B136 *Story of the nations.* 76 v., N. Y., 1882–1917. [1, A. Gilman, *Rome;* 2, J. K. Hosmer, *Jews;* 3, S. Baring-Gould, *Germany;* 4, A. J. Church, *Carthage;* 5, J. P. Mahaffy, *Alexander's Empire;* 6, S. Lane-Poole, *Moors in Spain;* 7, G. Rawlinson, *Ancient Egypt;* 8, A. Vambéry, *Hungary;* 9, A. Gilman, *Saracens;* 10, E. Lawless, *Ireland;* 11, Z. A. Ragozin, *Chaldea;* 12, H. Bradley, *Goths;* 13, Z. A. Ragozin, *Assyria;* 14, S. Lane-Poole, *Turkey;* 15, J. E. Thorold Rogers, *Holland;* 16, G. Masson, *Mediaeval France;* 17, S. G. W. Benjamin, *Persia;* 18, G. Rawlinson, *Phoenicia;* 19, Z. A. Ragozin, *Media;* 20, H. Zimmern, *Hansa Towns;* 21, A. J. Church, *Early Britain;* 22, S. Lane-Poole, *Barbary corsairs;* 23, W. R. Morfill, *Russia;* 24, W. D. Morrison, *Jews under the Romans;* 25, J. Mackintosh, *Scotland;* 26, Mrs. L. Hug and R. Stead, *Switzerland;* 27, S. Hale, *Mexico;* 28, H. M. Stephens, *Portugal;* 29, S. O. Jewett, *Normans;* 30, C. W. C. Oman, *Byzantine Empire;* 31, E. A. Freeman, *Sicily; Phoenician, Greek, and Roman;* 32, B. Duffy, *Tuscan republics;* 33, W. R. Morfill, *Poland;* 34, G. Rawlinson, *Parthia;* 35, G. Tregarthen, *Australian commonwealth;* 36, H. E. Watts, *Christian recovery of Spain;* 37, D. Murray, *Japan;* 38, G. M. Theal, *South Africa;* 39, A. Wiel, *Venice;* 40, T. A. Archer, and

C. L. Kingsford, *Crusades;* 41, Z. A. Ragozin, *Vedic India;* 42, J. Rodway, *West Indies and the Spanish Main;* 43, C. E. Maurice, *Bohemia;* 44, W. Miller, *Balkans;* 45, J. G. Bourinot, *Canada;* 46, R. W. Frazer, *British India;* 47, A. LeBon, *Modern France;* 48, L. Sergeant, *Franks;* 49, S. Whitman, *Austria;* 50, J. McCarthy, *Modern England before the reform bill;* 51, R. K. Douglas, *China;* 52, J. McCarthy, *Modern England from the reform bill to the present time;* 53, M. A. S. Hume, *Modern Spain;* 54, P. Orsi, *Modern Italy;* 55, H. H. Boyesen, *Norway;* 56, O. M. Edwards, *Wales;* 57, W. Miller, *Mediaeval Rome;* 58, W. Barry, *Papal monarchy;* 59, S. Lane-Poole, *Mediaeval India under Mohammedan rule;* 60, T. W. Rhys-Davids, *Buddhist India;* 61, E. Jenks, *Parliamentary England;* 62, M. Bateson, *Mediaeval England;* 63, L. C. Jane, *Coming of Parliament: England from 1350 to 1660;* 64, E. S. Shuckburgh, *Greece from the earliest times to A.D. 14;* 65, H. S. Jones, *Roman Empire;* 66, J. Stefansson, *Denmark and Sweden with Iceland and Finland;* 67, A. T. Story, *Building of the British empire,* 2 v.; 68, J. A. Harrison, *Greece;* 69, T. C. Dawson, *South American republic,* 2 v.; 70, E. E. Hale, *Spain;* 71, H. A. Smith, *Thirteen colonies,* 2 v.; 72, A. K. Fiske, *West Indies;* 73, E. E. Sparks, *United States of America,* 2 v.] Later reprints of most v.; rev. ed. of several v.

Distinctly popular. Volumes have all been confided to competent, in some cases to expert, writers and the result is a very attractive work covering the history of the world in a manner most useful for the general reader.   FLT

B137a **Buchan, John,** ed. *Nations of today, a new history of the world.* V. 1–12, N. Y., 1923 ff. [1, *British America;* 2, *Baltic and Caucasian republics;* 3, *France;* 4, *Jugo-Slavia;* 5, *Japan;* 6, *Italy;* 7, *Belgium and Luxembourg;* 8, *Bulgaria and Romania;* 9, *Great Britain,* 2 v.; 10, *India;* 11, *Ireland.*]

   b **Fisher, Herbert A. L.,** ed. *Modern world.* 15 v., N. Y. and London, 1924 ff. [1, G. P. Gooch, *Germany;* 2, Stephen Gwynn, *Ireland;* 3, N. Makeev and V. O'Hara, *Russia;* 4, G. G. Hardy, *Norway;* 5, Sir Valentine Chirol, *India;* 6, W. R. Inge, *England;* 7, S. Huddleston, *France;* 8, Arnold Toynbee, *Turkey;* 9, Geo. Young, *Egypt;* 10, W. Miller, *Greece;* 11, J. H. Finley, *America;* 13, A. Edwards, *Chile;* 14, V. W. H. W. Koo, *China;* 15, A. Lunn, *Switzerland;* 16, L. Villari, *Italy.*]

   a. Attempt to furnish a history of each of the important existing nations. Each volume is a collaborated work by experts in the field. In addition to a lively survey of the historical development of each nation, its present political organization and economic condition are described. Review, S. B. Fay, *Yale Review,* 14: 406, Jan. 1925.   GMD

   b. Another series with emphasis on modern happenings. Review of v. 1, G. S. Ford, *A.H.R.* 31 : 525, Apr. 1926; v. 2, (London) *Times Lit. Suppl.* 23 : 602, Oct. 2, 1924; v. 3, F. A. Golder, *A.H.R.* 31 : 788, July 1926; v. 4, P. Knaplund, *A.H.R.* 31 : 827, July 1926; v. 5, (London) *Times Lit. Suppl.* 25 : 89, Feb. 11, 1926; v. 6, 25 : 603, Sept. 16, 1926; v. 7, 25 : 954, Dec. 30, 1926; v. 8, 25 : 455, July 8, 1926; v. 9, 26 : 527, Aug. 4, 1927; v. 10, 27 : 303, Apr. 26, 1928; A. H. Lybyer, *A.H.R.* 34 : 125, Oct. 1928.   HRS

B138a **Murray, Gilbert; Fisher, Herbert A. L.; Brewster, William;** and **Thomson, John A.,** eds. *Home university library.* About 130 v. London and N. Y., 1911 ff. (Bibliographies.)

   b **Rhys, Ernest,** ed. *Everyman's library.* About 850 v. London and N. Y., 1906 ff.

   c *Temple cyclopaedic primers.* 48 v., London and N. Y., 1900–24.

These collections of small books at low prices include many volumes on history and related subjects. As a rule, though brief, the volumes are written by competent scholars and furnish commendable outlines of the subjects concerned. *a.* Collection of new books by competent authorities on topics in literature, art, history, geography, social science, philosophy, religion, and natural science. The volumes have a uniform length of 60,000 words and include indexes and other aids. *b.* Collection of reprints of standard works in literature, history, economics, philosophy, and occasionally other topics, including translations of numerous works in languages other than English. *c.* Shorter series similar to *a.* About one-half of the volumes pertain to history and related subjects. GMD

B152 Lavisse, Ernest, and **Rambaud, Alfred.** *Histoire générale du 4ᵉ siècle à nos jours.* 12 v., 1893–1901. (Critical bibliographies.) 3rd rev. ed., Paris, 1925. [1, *395–1095;* 2, *1095–1270;* 3, *1270–1492;* 4, *1492–1559;* 5, *1559–1648;* 6, *1648–1715;* 7, *1715–1788;* 8, *1789–1799;* 9, *1800–1815;* 10, *1815–1847;* 11, *1848–1870;* 12, *1870–1900.*]

Standard history of civilization since classic times; a work of collaboration, to which the various chapters have been contributed by specialists and scholars of established reputation in their respective fields, among others, Lavisse, Rambaud, Luchaire, Lacroix, Langlois, Seignobos, Bémont, Denis, Pirenne, Leger, Debidour, Martin, Aulard, Houssaye (for full list of contributors cf. appendix, v. 12). Not narrowly political in scope, but surveys the whole course of medieval and modern civilization, and pays due attention to economic, social, and cultural factors. The chapters naturally vary in merit, but the whole work is characterized by sound scholarship and strict scientific objectivity. Review, v. 1, *Rev. Hist.* 52: 336, July, 1893; of v. 7–9, H. M. Stephens, *A.H.R.* 3: 349, Jan. 1898; 3: 715, July 1898; 4: 351, Jan. 1899. TC

B153a Berr, Henri; Ogden, C. K.; Renard, G.; and **Barbes, H. E.,** ed., *History of civilization.* To be about 200 v. London and N. Y., 1924 ff. [1, W. H. R. Rivers, *Social organization;* 2, E. H. Parker, *Thousand years of the Tartars;* 3, Edmond Perrier, *Earth before history;* 4 (B301*d*), Jacques de Morgan, *Prehistoric man;* 5 (A306*c*), Joseph Vendryes, *Language;* 6, Pierre de Labriolle, *History and literature of Christianity;* 7, C. E. Fox, *Threshold of the Pacific;* 8, M. Dorothy George, *London life in the eighteenth century;* 9, Adolf Reichwein, *China and Europe;* 10, Lucien Febvre, *Geographical introduction to history;* 11 (B311*b*), V. Gordon Childe, *Dawn of European civilization;* 12, Gustave Glotz, *Aegean civilization;* 13 (C602*d*), L. Delaporte, *Mesopotamia: the Babylonian and Assyrian civilizations;* 14, L. H. Dudley Buxton, *Peoples of Asia;* 15, E. Pittard, *Race and history; an ethnological introduction to history;* 16, A. P. Newton and others, *Travel and travellers of the middle ages;* 17 (B575, v. 1), G. Glotz, *Ancient Greece at work;* 18 (B575, v. 7), G. Renard and G. Weulersse, *Life and work in modern Europe;* 19, D. A. Mackenzie, *Migration of symbols and their relations to beliefs and customs;* 20, V. G. Childe, *Aryans; Indo-European origins;* 21, A. Moret and G. Davy, *From tribe to empire: social organization among primitives and in the ancient East;* 22, A. Moret, *Nile and Egyptian civilization;* 23, A. Jardé, *Formation of the Greek people;* 24, A. de Ridder and W. Deonna, *Art in Greece;* 25, L. Homo, *Primitive Italy;* 26, A. Grenier, *Roman spirit in religion, thought and art;* 27, J. Declareuil, *Rome, the law giver;* 28, P. Louis, *Ancient Rome at work;* 29, V. Chapot, *Roman world;* 30, C. Huart, *Ancient Persia and the Iranian civilization;* 31, E. J. Thomas, *Life of Buddha;* 32, P. Boissonnade, *Life and work in medieval Europe;* 33, A. R. Burns, *Money and monetary policy in early times;* 34, A. R.

Burns, *Geography and witchcraft;* 35, C. G. Cumston, *Introduction to the history of medicine from the time of the Pharaohs to the end of the eighteenth century;* 36, M. Summers, *History of witchcraft and demonology;* 37, R. Karsten, *Civilization of the South American Indians, with special reference to magic and religion;* 38, P. Jouguet, *Macedonian imperialism;* 39, E. Prestage, *Chivalry;* 40, C. Gray, *History of music;* 41, W. C. MacLeod, *American Indian frontier;* 42, L. Robin, *Greek thought.*]

b Berr, Henri, ed. *L'évolution de l'humanité: synthèse collective.* To be 100 v. Paris, 1920 ff. [1, E. Perrier, *La terre avant l'histoire;* 2 (B301d), J. J. M. de Morgan, *L'humanité préhistorique;* 3 (A306c), J. Vendryes, *Le langage;* 4, L. Febvre and L. Battaillon, *La terre et l'évolution humaine;* 5, E. Pittard, *Les races et l'histoire;* 6, A. Moret and G. Davy, *Des clans aux empires;* 7, A. Moret, *Le Nile et la civilisation égyptienne;* 8 (C602d), L. Delaporte, *La Mesopotamie; les civilisations Babylonienne et Assyrienne;* 9, G. Glotz, *La civilisation égéenne;* 10, A. Jardé, *La formation du peuple grec;* 12, A. H. Ridder and W. Deonna, *L'art en Grèce;* 13, L. Robin, *La pensée grecque;* 15, P. Jouguet, *L'imperialisme macédonien;* 16 (E106c), L. P. Homo, *L'Italie primitive;* 17, A. Grenier, *Le génie romain dans la religion la pensée et l'art;* 18, L. Homo, *Les institutions politiques Romaines, de la cité à l'état;* 19, J. Declareuil, *Rome et l'organisation du droit;* 20, J. Toutain, *L'économie antique;* 22, V. Chapot, *L'empire romain;* 24, C. I. Huart, *La perse antique.*]

a. Includes translations from *b,* from B575, and the following original volumes 1, 2, 6, 7, 8, 9, 11, 14, 16, 19, 20, 31, 33, 34, 35, 36, 37, 39, 40, 41, cf. *A.H.R.* 28:784, July 1923. The aim of the series is to summarize in one synthesis the most recent findings of all students of civilization. Each volume is complete in itself, but the volumes supplement one another when considered in relation to a particular subject or period. A series of high character, in many of the volumes interesting suggestions abound and the pages of "conclusions" with which the volumes end summarize well the chief results of each study. Review of v. 1, 3, 4, 7, (London) *Times Lit. Suppl.* 203, p. 77, Feb. 5, 1925; v. 6, J. C. Ayer, *A.H.R.* 30:789, July 1925; v. 8, W. P. Hall, *A.H.R.* 31:127, Oct. 1925; v. 9, K. S. Latourette, *A.H.R.* 31:129, Oct. 1925; v. 11, M. Rostovtzeff, *A.H.R.* 31:499, Apr 1926; v. 14, *A.H.R.* 31:498; v. 16, (London) *Times Lit. Suppl.* 25:441, July 1, 1926; v. 19, 25:313, Apr. 29, 1926; v. 20, 25:686, Oct. 14, 1926; v. 21, 25:541, Aug. 19, 1926; v. 34 and 36, G. L. Burr, *A.H.R.* 34:324, Jan. 1929.

b. Cf. *Rev. Hist.* 136:121. More satisfactory than *a,* because M. Berr's plan for a complete synthesis is maintained throughout. As in the case of those volumes of *a* which form part of *b,* a preface by Berr precedes each volume. When fully published *b* will be a very satisfactory survey of the world's history in its broadest aspects. Review of v. 1, *A.H.R.* 28:347, Jan. 1923; v. 2, 27:539, Apr. 1922; v. 3, F. Edgerton, 27:772, July 1921; v. 4, M. Jefferson, 28:291, Jan. 1923; v. 5, A. Hrdlicka, 30:109, Oct. 1924; v. 6, D. D. Luckenbill, 29:158, Oct. 1923; v. 7, T. G. Allen, 32:300, Jan. 1927; v. 9, F. M. Robinson, 29:588, Apr. 1924; v. 10, D. M. Robinson, 29:112, Oct. 1923; v. 12, W. W. Hyde, 30:124, Oct. 1924; v. 13, H. N. Gardiner, 29:743, July 1924; v. 15, W. S. Ferguson, 33:95, Oct. 1927; v. 17, C. H. Moore, 31:159, Oct. 1925; v. 18, D. McFayden, 33:98, Oct. 1927; v. 20, M. Besnier, *Rev. des Quest. Hist.* 108:456, Apr. 1928; v. 22, R. V. D. Magoffin, *A.H.R.* 33:97, Oct. 1927; v. 24, R. W. Rogers, 31:301, Jan. 1926.   HRS

B161 Heeren, Arnold H. L.; Ukert, Friedrich A.; Giesebrecht, Wilhelm von; Lamprecht, Karl; and Oncken, Hermann, ed. *Allgemeine Staatengeschichte.* About 60 separate works. Hamburg and Gotha, 1829 ff. [I. *Geschichte der europäischen Staaten:* 1, J. Pfister, *Geschichte der Teutschen,* 5 v. with Register, 1829–36; 2, H. Leo, *Geschichte der italienischen Staaten,* 5 v. with Register, 1830–37; 3, C. W. Böttiger and T. Flathe, *Geschichte des Kurstaates und Königreiches Sachsen,* 3 v. with Register, 1830–73; 4, E. Geijer, F. Carlson, and L. Stavenow, *Geschichte Schwedens,* 7 v., 1832–1908; 5, N. G. von Kampen, *Geschichte der Niederlande,* 2 v. with Register, 1831–33; 6, J. M. Lappenberg, R. Pauli, and M. Brosch, *Geschichte von England,* 10 v. with Register, 1834–98; 7, (N201) F. W. Lembke, H. Schäfer, and F. Schirrmacher, *Geschichte von Spanien,* 7 v., 1831–1902; 8, J. Graf von Mailath, *Geschichte des oesterreichischen Kaiserstaates,* 5 v. with Register, 1834–50; 9, G. A. H. Stenzel, *Geschichte des preussichen Staates,* 5 v. with Register, 1830–54; 10, P. Strahl and E. Herrmann, *Geschichte des russischen Staates,* 7 v., 1832–66; 11, E. A. Schmidt, *Geschichte von Frankreich,* 4 v., 1835–48; 12, (N1122) H. Schäfer, *Geschichte von Portugal,* 5 v. with Register, 1836–54; 13, (R201) F. C. Dahlmann and D. Schäfer, *Geschichte von Dänemark,* 4 v., 1840–93; 14, J. W. Zinkeisen, *Geschichte des osmanischen Reiches in Europa,* 7 v., 1840–63; 15, W. Wachsmuth, *Geschichte Frankreichs im Revolutionszeitalter,* 4 v., 1840–44; 16, (S1201a) R. Roepell and J. Caro, *Geschichte Polens,* 5 v., 1840–88; 17, F. Bülau, *Geschichte Deutschlands,* 1806–30, 1 v., 1842; 18, G. F. Hertzberg, *Geschichte Griechenlands seit dem Absterben des antiken Lebens bis zur Gegenwart,* 4 v. with Register, 1876–79; 19, A. von Reumont, *Geschichte Toskanas seit dem Ende des florentinischen Freistaates,* 2 v., 1876–77; 20, K. Hillebrand, *Geschichte Frankreichs,* 2 v., and Supplement, 1877–81; 21, S. Riezler, *Geschichte Baierns,* 8 v., 1878–1914; 22, K. T. Wenzelburger, *Geschichte der Niederlande,* 2 v., 1879–86; 23, M. Brosch, *Geschichte des Kirchenstaates,* 2 v. with Register, 1880–82; 24, F. Reimann, *Neuere Geschichte des preussischen Staates vom Hubertusburger Frieden bis zum Wiener Kongress,* 2 v., 1882–88; 25, P. Stälin, *Geschichte Württembergs,* 1 v. in 2, 1882–87; 26, F. Dahn, *Deutsche Geschichte,* 1 v. in 2, with Register, 1883–88; 27, A. Dove, *Das Zeitalter Friedrichs des grossen und Josephs II,* v. 1, 1883; 28, (P422c) A. Huber, *Geschichte Österreichs,* 6 v., 1885–1921; 29, (P466) J. Dierauer, *Geschichte der schweizerischen Eidgenossenschaft,* 5 v., 1887–1917; 30, A. Bachmann, *Geschichte Böhmens,* v. 1, 1899; 31, A. Brückner, *Geschichte Russlands bis zur Ende des achtzehnten Jahrhunderts,* 2 v., 1896–1913; 32, (M421) K. Hillebrand, *Geschichte Frankreichs während des Julikönigtums,* 1830–48, 1 v. with Register, 1898; 33, H. Pirenne, *Geschichte Belgiens,* v. 1–4, 1899–1913; 34, P. J. Blok, *Geschichte der Niederlande,* 6 v., 1902–18; 35, M. G. Schybergson, *Geschichte Finnlands,* 1 v., 1896; 36, A. Kleinschmidt, *Geschichte des Königreiches Westfalen,* 1 v., 1893–; 37, (O202b) L. Hartmann, *Geschichte Italiens im Mittelalter,* 4 v., 1902–13; 38, (N256) K. Häbler, *Geschichte Spaniens unter den Habsburgern,* 1 v., 1907; 39, N. Jorga, *Geschichte des osmanischen Reiches,* 5 v., 1908–13; 40, C. Jirecek, *Geschichte Serbiens,* 2 v., 1911–18; 41, B. Bretholz, *Neuere Geschichte Böhmens,* 1 v., 1920; 42, (O461c) H. Kretzschmayr, *Geschichte von Venedig,* 2 v., 1905–1920; 43, E. Zivier, *Neuere Geschichte Polens,* 1 v., 1915. II. *Geschichte der ausseuropäischen Staaten:* O. Nachod, *Geschichte von Japan,* 1906. [1. *Die Urzeit* (bis 645 n. chr.).] III. *Deutsche Landesgeschichten:* 1, Kaindl, *Geschichte der Deutschen in den Karpathenländern.* 3 v., 1907–11; 2, K. Lohmeyer, *Geschichte von Ost- und Westpreussen,* 1 v., 1908; 3, H. Widmann, *Geschichte Salzburgs,* 3 v., 1907–14; 4, A. Wohlwill, *Neuere Geschichte der freien und Hansestadt Hamburg insbesondere von 1789–1815,* 1 v., 1914; 5, H. Pirchegger, *Geschichte der Steiermark,* 1 v., 1920; 6, (P408) O. Vitense, *Geschichte von Mecklenburg,* 1 v., 1920; 7, M. Wehrmann, *Geschichte von Pommern,* 1 v., 1919; 8, E. Baasch, *Geschichte Hamburgs, 1814–1918,* 2 v., 1924–25; 9, M. Vancsa, *Geschichte Nieder- und Ober-oesterreichs,* 2 v., 1905–27.]

In 1822 Friedrich Perthes conceived the plan of publishing a collection of comprehensive histories of the several European countries, each country to be assigned to a German historian of repute, under the general title, *Geschichte der europäischen Staaten.* The first editors were Heeren and Ukert. Giesebrecht became editor in 1874, Lamprecht in 1896, Oncken in 1917. In 1902 Lamprecht enlarged the scope of the series, giving it the general title, *Allgemeine Staaten-geschichte,* and dividing it into the three *Abteilungen* as indicated above. With three exceptions, all of the works published up to that date belonged to the first *Abteilung.* In the case of some countries, however, a second work has been written for the series. The series is naturally of very unequal merit, and though each of the works was a scholarly product at the time of publication, many volumes have become sadly antiquated. Among the more notable works recently published in the series are Hartmann's *Italien im Mittelalter,* Blok's *Niederlande,* and Pirenne's *Belgien.* For projected volumes, cf. *A.H.R.* 26: 156, Oct. 1920.   CLB

B162 Oncken, Wilhelm, ed. *Allgemeine Geschichte in Einzeldarstellungen.* 46 v., Berlin, 1879–93. Section I, *Geschichte des Altertums:* 1, E. Meyer, *Geschichte des alten Aegyptens;* 2, F. Hommel, *Geschichte Babyloniens und Assyriens;* 3, S. Lefmann, *Geschichte des alten Indiens;* 4, pt. 1, F. Justi, *Geschichte des alten Persiens:* pt. 2, R. Pietschmann, *Geschichte der Phönizier;* 5, G. F. Hertzberg, *Geschichte von Hellas und Rom,* 2 v.; 6, B. Stade, *Geschichte des Volkes Israel,* 2 v.; section II, *Geschichte des Mittelalters:* 1, G. F. Hertzberg, *Geschichte des Römischen Kaiserreiches;* 2, F. Dahn, *Urgeschichte der germanischen und romanischen Völker,* 4 v.; 3, E. Winkelmann, *Geschichte der Angelsachsen bis zum Tode König Aelfreds;* 4, A. Müller, *Der Islam im Morgen- und Abendland,* 2 v.; 5, B. Kugler, *Geschichte der Kreuzzüge;* 6, H. Prutz, *Staatengeschichte des Abendlandes im Mittelalter von Karl des Grossen bis auf Maximilian,* 2 v.; 7, G. F. Hertzberg, *Geschichte der byzantiner und des osmanischen Reiches bis gegen Ende des sechszehnten Jahrhunderts;* 8, L. Geiger, *Renaissance und Humanismus in Italien und Deutschland;* 9, S. Ruge, *Geschichte des Zeitalters der Entdeckungen;* 10, (S122) T. Schiemann, *Polen und Livland bis ins 17. Jahrhundert,* 2 v.; section III, *Geschichte der neueren Zeit:* 1, F. Bezold, *Geschichte der deutschen Reformation;* 2, M. Philippson, *Westeuropa im Zeitalter von Philipp II, Elizabeth, und Heinrich IV;* 3, pt. 1, G. Droysen, *Geschichte der Gegen-Reformation;* pt. 2, G. Winter, *Geschichte des dreissigjährigen Krieges;* 4, A. Stern, *Geschichte der Revolution in England;* 5, M. Philippson, *Das Zeitalter Ludwigs des Vierzehnten;* 6, A. Brückner, *Peter der Grosse;* 7, (P282) B, Erdmanns-dörffer, *Deutsche Geschichte 1648–1740,* 2 v.; 8, W. Oncken, *Das Zeitalter Friedrichs des Grossen,* 2 v.; 9, A. Wolf, *Oesterreich unter Maria Theresia, Josef II, und Leopold II;* 10, (S254a) A. Brückner, *Katharina die Zweite:* section IV, *Geschichte der neuesten Zeit;* 1, W. Oncken, *Das Zeitalter der Revolution, des Kaiserreiches, und der Befreiungskriege,* 2 v.; 2, T. Flathe, *Das Zeitalter der Restauration und Revolution;* 3, C. Bulle, *Geschichte des Zweiten Kaiserreiches und des Königreiches Italien;* 4, F. Bamberg, *Geschichte der orientalischen Angelegenheit im Zeitraume des Pariser und des Berliner Friedens;* 6, (P331g) W. Oncken, *Das Zeitalter des Kaisers Wilhelm,* 2 v.; O. Henne am Rhyn, *Namen und Sach-Register.*

Co-operative universal history initiated by the publishing house of Grote in Berlin. The authors were all reputable scholars, but as the series was designed for the general public, the external apparatus of erudition was omitted; the volumes were provided with illustrations. Erdmannsdörffer's *Deutsche Geschichte* may be noted as one of the best of the series.   CLB

B163a Ranke, Leopold von, and others. *Weltgeschichte.* 9 v., 1881–88. New ed., 8 v., München, 1922. 1, *Die aelteste historische Völkergruppe und die Griechen;* 2, *Die römische Republik und ihre Weltherrschaft;* 3, *Das altrömische Kaiserthum;* 4, *Das Kaiserthum in Constantinopel und der Ursprung romanischgermanischer Königreiche;* 5, *Die arabische Weltherrschaft und das Reich Karls des Grossen;* 6, *Zersetzung des karolingischen, Begründung des deutschen Reiches;* 7, *Höhe und Niedergang des deutschen Kaiserthums: Die Hierarchie unter Gregor VII;* 8, *Kreuzzüge und papstliche Weltherrschaft (XII. und XIII. Jahrhundert);* 9, *Zeiten des Uebergangs zur modernen Welt (XIV. und XV. Jahrhundert); Ueber die Epochen der neueren Geschichte.*

b Masur, Gerhard. *Rankes Begriff der Weltgeschichte.* München, 1926.

After passing his eightieth birthday, Ranke undertook the writing of a universal history. As was to be feared, it remained a torso. He saw v. 1–6 through the press, and nearly completed the manuscript of v. 7 before his death in 1886. He began with the history of the Hebrews, Egyptians, and Greeks and carried the story through the Middle Ages as far as the time of Henry IV and Gregory VII. The last two volumes, comprising the later Middle Ages to the fifteenth century, were put together by his students from notes of Ranke's lectures of twenty years earlier. These two volumes, as well as the first two, which have been rendered somewhat antiquated by modern researches in Ancient and Oriental History, are less valuable than the central part of the work on the mingling of the Latin and Teutonic races and on the early Middle Ages. Though the octogenarian master did not always reach the high critical level of his earlier years, his Universal History is still of value for its readableness, breadth of view, suggestive parallels, and thoughtful reflections on the wider aspects of the political development of mankind. One goes to it, not for facts, but for ideas and for the mature philosophy of history of one of Germany's greatest historians. For appreciations of Ranke, cf. (A249a) Gooch, *History and historians of the nineteenth century* and (B247) E. G. Bourne, *Essays in historical criticism,* ch. 10–11. Review, *Hist. Zeit.* 51:31, 1883; 52:491, 1894; 55:187, 1886; 56:5, 1886; 58:336, 1887; 65:288, 1890.

SBF

b. After an illuminating introduction on the difficulties inherent in the conception of "Weltgeschichte" and a sketch of the development of Weltgeschichte from the beginning of Christian thought to the time of Ranke, Masur analyses clearly Ranke's own ideas in regard to world-history. Review, F. J. Teggart, *A.H.R.* 32:151, Oct. 1926.

HRS

B164a Weber, Georg. *Outlines of universal history, from the creation of the world to the present time.* Boston, 1853. Tr. by M. Behr from *Lehr und Handbuch der Weltgeschichte,* 2 v., 1847; 22nd rev. ed. by A. Baldamus, 4 v., Leipzig, 1912–14; 23rd rev. ed., of v. 3, Leipzig, 1922–24.

b —— *Allgemeine Weltgeschichte.* 1857–81. 19 v. 3rd rev. ed., Leipzig, 1920. [1, *Geschichte des Morgenlandes;* 2, *Geschichte des hellenischen Volkes;* 3, *Römische Geschichte bis zum Ende der Republic und Geschichte der Alexandronischhellenischen Welt;* 4, *Geschichte des römischen Kaiserreichs, der Völkerwanderung, und der neuen Staatenbildungen;* 5–8, *Geschichte des Mittelalters;* 9, *Geschichte der Völker und Staaten im Uebergang vom Mittelalter zur Neuzeit;* 10, *Das Zeitalter der Reformation;* 11, *Geschichte der Gegenreformation und der Religionskriege;* 12, *Die Zeit der unumschränkten Fürstenmacht im 17. und 18. Jahrhundert;* 13, *Das Zeitalter der Reformen und Revolutionen;* 14–15, *Geschichte des 19. Jahrhunderts;* 16–19, *Register.*]

a. Small general history long widely used. *b.* The first edition resembled *a* in following closely the point of view of orthodox Protestantism, beginning with a paraphrase of the book of Genesis. The second edition departed considerably in the direction of liberalism, omitting, for example, the Biblical account before the time of Abraham. Contains a narrative of selected events in the world's history, presented in chronological order with clearness, consistency, and animation; the history of art, literature, industry, and philosophy are presented as well as political history; one of the best of the German universal histories.

AHL

B165 Wright, John H., ed. *History of all nations from the earliest times.* 24 v., Philadelphia, 1902. V. 1–19 condensed tr. with additions by J. Hunter, J. H. Myers and others, from *Allgemeine Weltgeschichte,* by T. Flathe and others. Berlin, 1885–92. 1, F. Justi, *Egypt and western Asia in antiquity;* 2, id. *Central and eastern Asia in antiquity;* 3, G. F. Hertzberg, *Ancient Greece;* 4, id. *Republican Rome;* 5, id. *Imperial Rome;* 6, J. A. G. von Pflugk-Harttung, *Great migrations;* 7, *Early middle ages;* 8, H. Prutz, *Age of Charlemagne;* 9, id. *Age of feudalism and theocracy;* 10, id. *Age of the renaissance;* 11, M. Philippson, *Age of the reformation;* 12, id. *Religious wars;* 13, id. *Age of Louis XIV;* 14, id. *Age of the European balance of power;* 15, id. *Age of Frederick the Great;* 16, T. Flathe, *French Revolution and the rise of Napoleon;* 17, id. *Napoleonic empire;* 18, id. *Restoration and revolution;* 19, id. *Reconstruction of Europe;* 20, C. M. Andrews, *Contemporary Europe, Asia, and Africa;* 21, J. Fiske, *Colonization of the New World;* 22, id. *Independence of the New World;* 23, id. *Modern development of the New World;* v. 24, *General index.*

Co-operative work; the parts are uneven in their value and interest; contains many illustrations of considerable value to the student. The writers are generally specialists in their respective fields, but prone to exaggerate the importance of their topics.

FLT

B166 Helmolt, Hans F., ed. *History of the world, a survey of man's record.* 8 v., N. Y., 1902–07. Tr. from *Weltgeschichte,* 1899–1907; 2nd rev. ed. by A. Tille, 9 v., Leipzig, 1913–22. [1, *Prehistory; America and the Pacific Ocean;* 2, *Eastern Asia and Oceania; the Indian Ocean;* 3, *West Asia and Africa;* 4, *Mediterranean countries;* 5, *Southeastern and eastern Europe;* 6, *Central and northern Europe;* 7, *Western Europe;* 8, *Western Europe: the Atlantic Ocean.*] (Brief bibliography.)

The first German edition which the English translation followed with some adaptations, was prepared by 30 collaborators. As a universal history, the plan of this work is unique—so to arrange the material as to give proper recognition to the influence of physical environment in shaping human progress, to write a history of the world from the standpoint of ethnography and geography. The authors have failed to harmonize the conclusions of these sciences in one connected narrative with the natural sequence of historical development. The proportions of the work are unfortunate, yet the chapters on the historical importance of oceans are full of interest, as are some of the essays on economic development, containing, as they do, many suggestive generalizations. Rev. of v. 1, 4, 7, E. G. Bourne, *A.H.R.* 9: 116, Oct. 1903; v. 2, K. Asakawa, *A.H.R.* 10: 134, Oct. 1904; v. 3, C. H. Toy, *A.H.R.* 9: 398, Jan. 1904; v. 5, A. C. Coolidge, *A.H.R.* 14: 97, Oct. 1908; v. 6, 8, S. B. Fay, *A.H.R.* 13: 353, 835, Jan., July 1908.

HRS

B167 **Lindner, Theodor.** *Weltgeschichte seit der Völkerwanderung.* 9 v., Stuttgart, 1901–16. 1, *Der Ursprung der byzantinischen, islamischen, abendländisch-christlichen, chinesischen, und indischen Kultur;* 2, *Niedergang der islamischen und der byzantinischen Kultur: Bildung der europäischen Staaten;* 3, *Vom dreizehnten Jahrhundert bis zum Ende der Konzile: Die abendländisch-christliche Kultur: Anfänge einer neuen Zeit;* 4, *Der Stillstand des Orients und das Aufsteigen Europas: Die deutsche Reformation;* 5, *Die Kämpfe um die Reformation: Der Übergang in die heutige Zeit;* 6, *Das neue europäische Staatensystem: Absolutismus und Merkantilismus: Die geistige Befreiung und die Aufklärung: Asien und Afrika;* 7, *Amerika-Europa bis zum Beginn der französischen Revolution: Die Revolution und die Republik: Napoleon;* 8, *Das europäische Geistesleben im Anfang des neunzehnten Jahrhunderts: Europa bis zum Julirevolution 1830. Europa von der Julirevolution bis zur Februarrevolution: Revolution und Reaktion: Der Übergang zu unserer Zeit 1848–1859;* 9, *Die Zeit Bismarcks: Die aussereuropäischen Staaten: Die letzten Jahrzehnte des alten Europa: Der Ursprung des Weltkrieges bis zu den Kriegserklärungen.* (Bibliography.)

The introduction, enlarged and published separately (Stuttgart, 1904), deals with the philosophy of history. A well-rounded account; the order is chronological, with emphasis throughout on developments and history of civilizations, especially in Western Europe. Review of v. 1, 2, 3, E. W. Dow, *A.H.R.* 8:161, Oct. 1902; 9:606, Apr. 1904; v. 4, A. C. Tilton, 15:136, Oct. 1909; 16:612, Apr. 1911; v. 9, M. W. Tyler, 25:103, Oct. 1919. AHL

B168a **Pflugk-Harttung, Julius A. G.**, and others, ed. *Weltgeschichte; die Entwicklung der Menschheit in Staat und Gesellschaft, in Kultur und Geistesleben,* 7 v., Berlin, 1908–1925. [1, *Altertum;* 2, *Mittelalter;* 3, *Orient;* 4, *Neuzeit, 1500–1650;* 5, *Neuzeit, 1650–1815;* 6, *Neuzeit seit 1815;* 7, *Neueste zeit. 1890–1925.*]

b **Hartmann, Ludo M.**, ed. *Weltgeschichte in gemeinverständlicher Darstellung,* v. 1–10, Gotha, 1919–25. To be 20 v. [1, E. Ranslik, E. Kohn, E. G. Klauber, *Einleitung und Geschichte des alten Orients;* 2, E. Ciccotti, *Griechische Geschichte;* 3, L. M. Hartmann, J. Kromayer, *Römische Geschichte;* 4, S. Hellmann, *Das Mittelalter bis zum Ausgange der Kreuzzüge;* 5, K. Kaser, *Das späte Mittelalter;* 6, Pt. 1, K. Kaser, *Das Zeitalter der Reformation und Gegenreformation;* 7, Pt. 1, G. Bourgin, *Die französische Revolution;* 8, L. M. Hartmann, *Das neunzehnte Jahrhundert.*

c **Delbrück, Hans.** *Weltgeschichte: Vorlesungen gehalten an der Universität Berlin.* 1896–1920. V. 1–5. [1, *Das Altertum;* 2, *Das Mittelalter;* 3, *Neuzeit bis zum Tode Friedrichs des Grossen;* 4, *Neuzeit, die Revolutions-periode;* 5, *Neuzeit von 1852 bis 1888.*] Berlin, 1923 ff.

d **Cartellieri, Alexander.** *Weltgeschichte als Machtgeschichte.* München, 1927. [V. 1, *382–911, die Zeit der Reichsgründungen.*] (Bibliography.)

a. Excellent; well illustrated with pictures and facsimiles. Sections are written by specialists who can speak with authority. V. 7 covers the period 1890–1925; carefully done. HRS

b. Creditable German post-war undertaking. Emphasis on social, economic, and domestic concerns rather than on military and diplomatic affairs and personalities. The scope is unfortunate as it is too large for a short history or manual, and yet it does not afford space for adequate treatment, especially of the modern period, so that it fails to rank with (I121) *Cambridge modern history,* or (B152) Lavisse and Rambaud, *Histoire générale.* Consequently the authors have not been encouraged to write from other than secondary sources. Review of v. 4–5,

A.H.R. 26: 495, Apr. 1921; 26: 761, July 1921; v. 6, P. Smith, 28: 578, Oct. 1923;
v. 7, C. Christol, 28: 581, Oct. 1923. GMD
 c. Well-written narrative by a distinguished German scholar; product of years
of study and thought; emphasizes political events and constitutional developments,
in v. 2, particularly those in Germany and Italy. Review of v. 2, *Pol. Sci. Quart.*
41: 649, Dec. 1926. *d.* Undertakes to portray universal history from the standpoint of Might; considers the struggle for power from an eternally unchanging
characteristic of human experience. Well written and skilfully unified account,
but neglects important phases of human development. Horizon largely confined
to the Mediterranean basin. Review, C. C. Mierow, *A.H.R.* 33: 174, Oct. 1927;
id. Speculum, 2: 468, Oct. 1927; L. Halphen, *Rev. Hist.* 155: 170, May 1927.
HRS

 B169a Glotz, Gustave, ed. *Histoire générale,* Paris, 1925. [I, *Histoire ancienne,*
  pt. 1, A. Moret, *Histoire de l'Orient;* pt. 2, G. Glotz and R. Cohen, *Histoire de la Grèce:* 1, **Des origines aux guerres mèdiques;* 2, **La Grèce
  au Ve siècle;* 3, *La Grèce du IVe siècle à la conquête romaine;* pt. 3,
  Histoire romaine:* 1, **E. Pais, Des origines à l'achèvement de la conquête,*
  (*146 avant J. C.*) ; 2, G. Bloch and J. Carponino, *La République romaine
  de 146 av. J. C. à la mort de César;* 3, L. Homo, *Le Haut Empire;* 4, M.
  Besnier, *Le Bas Empire jusqu'en 395;* II, *Histoire du moyen âge:* 1, **F.
  Lot (and others), *Les destinées de l'empire en Occident de 395 à 888;*
  2, (1) M. Fliche, *Le Sacerdoce et l'Empire de 888 à 1122,* (2) F. Lot,
  L'Europe occidentale de 888 à 1122; 3, C. Diehl, *Le Monde oriental de
  395 à 1261;* 4, (1) M. Jordan, *L'Allemagne et l'Italie de 1122 à 1273,* (2)
  N. C. Petit-Dutaillis, *L'Europe occidentale de 1122 à 1270;* 5, E. Perrin,
  La décadence de la papauté, L'Allemagne et l'Italie de 1273 à 1402; 6, A.
  Coville, *L'Europe occidentale de 1270 à 1380;* 7, J. Calmette, *L'Europe
  occidentale de 1381 à 1492;* 8, C. Diehl, *L'Europe septentrionale, l'Europe
  orientale et l'Asie, du milieu du XIIIe siècle à la fin du XVe;* 9, H. Pirenne
  (and others), *La civilisation occidentale du XIIe siècle à la fin du XVe.*]
 b Halphen, Louis, and **Sagnac, Philippe,** ed. *Peuples et civilisations:
  histoire général.* Paris, 1926 ff. [1, G. Fougères and others, *Les
  premières civilisations;* 3, A. Piganiol, *La conquête romaine;* 5, L. Halphen,
  Les barbares, des grandes invasions aux conquêtes turques du XIe siècle.]
 c Cavaignac, Eugéne, ed. *Histoire du monde.* Paris, 1924 ff. [1, E.
  Cavaignac, *Prolégomènes;* 4, H. Maspero, *La Chine antique;* 8, L. Bouvat,
  L'Empire mongole, 2e phase; 12, P. Vaucher, *Le monde anglo-saxon au
  XIXe siècle.*]

 a, b, c. Uncompleted co-operative French world histories all excellent as far
as published. *b,* to be twenty volumes in all, allots seven to ancient times and
the Middle Ages, while *a* devotes twenty-eight to the same period. *c* reserves
six volumes to India, Central Asia, and China. Review of *b,* v. 1, R. W. Rogers,
A.H.R. 32: 299, Jan. 1927; v. 3, T. Frank, 33: 372, Jan. 1928; v. 5, F. Duncalf,
32: 573, Apr. 1927. Review of I, pt. 2, M. Besnier, *Rev. des Quest. Hist.* 105: 231,
July 1926. Review of *c,* v. 1, A. Vincent, *Rev. des Quest. Hist.* 104: 232, Jan. 1926;
v. 4 and 8, L. Halphen, *Rev. Hist.* 157: 138, Jan. 1928. HRS

 B170 Below, Georg von, and **Meinecke, Friedrich,** eds. *Handbuch der mittel-
  alterlichen und neueren Geschichte.* V. 1–23, München, 1903–29. [I,
  Allgemeines: 1, (A247) E. Fueter, *Geschichte der neueren Historiographie;*
  2, (P3d) Georg von Below, *Die deutsche Geschichtschreibung von den
  Befreiungskriegen bis zu unsern Tagen;* II, *Politische Geschichte:* 1,
  (H105) J. Loserth, *Geschichte des späteren Mittelalters;* 2, E. Fueter,
  Geschichte des europäischen Staatensystems, 1492–1559; 3, M. Immich,
 * Indicates volumes already published.

Geschichte des europäischen Staatensystems, 1660–1789; 4, A. Wahl, *Geschichte des europäischen Staatensystems,* 1789–1815; 5, L. Schmidt, *Allgemeine Geschichte der germanischen Völker bis zur Mitte des sechsten Jahrhunderts;* 6, W. Plattzhoff, *Geschichte des europäischen Staatensystems,* 1559–1660; III, *Verfassung, Recht, Wirtschaft:* 1, (H572) A. Schaube, *Handelsgeschichte der romanischen Völker des Mittelmeergebiets bis zum Ende der Kreuzzüge;* 2, R. Holtzmann, *Französische Verfassungsgeschichte von der Mitte des neunten Jahrhunderts bis zur Revolution;* 3, J. Hatschek, *Englische Verfassungsgeschichte bis zum Regierungsantritt der Königin Viktoria;* 4, R. His, *Geschichte des deutschen Strafrechts bis zur Carolina;* 5, J. Kulischer, *Allgemeine Wirtschaftsgeschichte des Mittelalters und der Neuzeit,* 2 v.; IV, *Hilfswissenschaften und Altertümer:* 1, (A326c) W. Erben, L. Schmitz-Kallenberg, and O. Redlich, *Urkundenlehre;* 2, (A331) W. Ewald, *Siegelkunde;* 3, F. Hauptmann, *Wappenkunde;* 4, (P41b) K. Kretschmer, *Historische Geographie von Mitteleuropa;* 5, A. Schultz, *Das häusliche Leben der europäischen Kulturvölker von Mittelalter bis zur zweiten Hälfte des achtzehnten Jahrhunderts;* 6, (A442) A. Luschin von Ebengreuth, *Allgemeine Münzkunde und Geldgeschichte des Mittelalters und der neueren Zeit.*]

A series which aims to cover the history of medieval and modern times methodologically and constitutionally. Very useful volumes written by specialists.

HRS

B171a *Aus Natur und Geisteswelt.* V. 1–1008 in 1929. Leipzig, 1898. The volumes are classified under the following subjects: 1, Religion, Philosophie, und Psychologie; 2, Pädagogik und Bildungswesen; 3, Sprache, Literatur, bildende Kunst, und Musik; 4, Geschichte, Kulturgeschichte, und Geographie; 5, Mathematik, Naturwissenschaften, und Medizin; 6, Recht, Wirtschaft, und Technik. (Brief bibliographies.)

b *Sammlung Göschen.* V. 1–1005 in 1929, Leipzig, 1889 ff. The volumes are classified under the following subjects: Philosophie, Sprachwissenschaft, Literaturgeschichte, Geschichte, Geographie, Mathematik; Naturwissenschaft, Physik, Chemie, Technologie, Ingenieurwissenschaften, Rechts- und Staatswissenschaften, Volkswirtschaft, Theologie und Religionswissenschaften, Pädagogik, Kunst, Musik, Land- und Forstwirtschaft, Handelswissenschaft, Militärwissenschaft, Verschiedenes. (Bibliographies.)

c *Reclams Universal Bibliothek.* V. 1–7040 in 1929. Leipzig, 1867 ff.

d *Wissenschaft und Bildung.* V. 1–252 in 1929, Leipzig, 1907 ff. The volumes are classified under the following subjects: Religion; Philosophie, Pädagogik; Sprache, Literatur; Kunst; Geschichte; Bürgerkunde, Volkswirtschaftslehre; Zoologie, Botanik; Anthropologie; Hygiene; Geologie, Astronomie, Meteorologie; Physik, Technik.

Collections of small books at low prices, on a wide range of topics, which include many volumes on history and related subjects. As a rule, though brief, the volumes are written by competent scholars and furnish commendable outlines of the subjects concerned. *a.* All are original monographs. Among the more than 100 volumes on historical topics are several monographs on special topics which are among the most convenient presentations of the subjects concerned. The volumes average somewhat less than 50,000 words. A few of the volumes contain maps. *b.* Original monographs averaging about 40,000 words; illustrated. Thus far, less than 50 volumes deal with historical subjects. *c.* Reprints and translations of the chief literary works in all the more important languages, including particularly translations of the Greek and Roman classics into German. The series also contains numerous biographical works. *d.* The contents of the series extend over a somewhat wider range than *a.* The number of historical volumes is less than thirty and these belong largely within the field of *Kulturgeschichte*. Contain maps and excellent illustrations. Original monographs averaging about 30,000 words.   GMD

B172 Hammerton, John A. *Universal history of the world.* V. 1–4, London, 1928 ff. [1, *Earliest times to Egyptian empire;* 2, *Hittites to the Peloponnesian war;* 3, *Roman history to Hadrian;* 4, *Antonines to the Middle Ages.*]

Series aimed at the general reader, with chapters by "150 of our foremost living authorities," contributors who are largely the same as those who contributed to the Cambridge histories. Well illustrated, readable; neglects neither chronicle nor interpretation. Review of v. 1, (London) *Times Lit. Suppl.* 27 : 424, June 7, 1928; v. 4, 27 : 1004, Dec. 20, 1928.   HRS

B173. Montel, Paul, ed. *Collection Armand Colin,* Paris, 1921 ff.

Small volumes by French authorities, similar in character to those in (B138*a*) Home University Library series.   HRS

PHILOSOPHY OF HISTORY

B201 Bossuet, Jacques B. *Discours sur l'histoire universelle.* 1681. Recent ed., Paris, 1909.

This is perhaps the last great literary expression of the "Christian epic." The first part gives a summary of events from Adam to Charlemagne, the second discusses Judaism and Christianity, while the last describes the four great empires,—Scythian, Assyrian, Persian and Greek. The author's purpose is to show that religion offers man his only hope. Cf. (A247) Fueter.   JWS

B202 Vico, Giovanni B. *Principi di una scienza nuova interno alla commune natura delle nazioni.* 1725. 3rd ed., 2 v., Napoli, 1794. French abridged tr. by J. Michelet, *Principes de la philosophie de l'histoire.* Paris, 1827.

Progress from early barbarism, Vico thought, is in cycles of three ages, characterized respectively by gods, heroes, and men; the driving force is in three ideas, Providence, the family, and the future life. In this highly original work, Vico anticipated many of the conclusions of (E251*a*) Niebuhr and Wolf concerning antiquity.   JWS

B203a Montesquieu, Charles de Secondat, Baron de. *Considerations on the causes of the grandeur and decadence of the Romans.* N. Y., 1882. Tr. by J. Baker from *Considérations sur les causes de la grandeur des Romains et de leur décadence.* 1734; in v. 2 of *Oeuvres complètes de Montesquieu* ed. by E. Laboulaye, 7 v. Paris, 1875–9. (Many other ed.)

b ―――― *The spirit of the laws.* London, 1750. Rev. ed. 2 v., London, 1902. (Bohn's standard lib.) Tr. by T. Nugent from *L'esprit des lois,* Genève, 1748; v. 3–6 of *Oeuvres complètes de Montesquieu* ed. by E. Laboulaye, 7 v. Paris, 1875–9. (Many other ed.)

a. Account of the rise and fall of Roman power. Though often inaccurate in detail, and sometimes uncritical in spirit, it is still stimulating and valuable. The most remarkable and trenchant part of the book is chapter 6, which analyzes Roman methods and the causes of Roman success.

b. This famous treatise examines three types of government, despotism, monarchy, and republic, the weaknesses of each, and the relation of each to education, legislation, war and conquest, and other matters. Discusses the influence of climate, geography, national psychology, population, commerce, and religion on the spirit of the laws. Chapters on liberty, with their discussion of the separation of powers and checks and balances in government, are especially noteworthy, in interest and influence alike. Cf. (A247) Fueter.   DP

B204 Condorcet, Jean A. N. de Caritat, Marquis de. *Outlines of an historical view of the progress of the human mind.* London, 1795. Tr. from *Esquisse d'un tableau historique des progrès de l'esprit humain.* 1795. First part only. More complete form in *Oeuvres complètes,* 1801–04, 2nd rev. ed., 12 v., Paris, 1847–49.

This little book is the classic statement of the historical views of the "philosophes" and idealists of the French Revolution, of their hatred of priests and monarchs and their faith in human perfectibility. The author presents philosophical reflections upon the advance of humanity from the earliest barbarism to 1789, and closes with a glowing picture of future progress. The 1795 edition includes only a portion of the author's uncompleted manuscript.   JWS

B205 Herder, Johann G. *Outlines of philosophy of the history of man.* 1800. 2nd ed., 2 v., London, 1803. Tr. by T. Churchill from *Ideen zur Philosophie der Geschichte der Menscheit,* 4 v., Leipzig, 1784–91.

The history of mankind presented as an organic whole. Beginning with description of the earth among the planets and man among the animals, traces the history of mankind to the Middle Ages in accordance with the scientific knowledge of the time. Eloquent presentation of progressive development of mankind toward ideals of humanity and complete happiness. Discussion mixed with poetic ideas and fanciful speculations, but interesting for early evolutionary conceptions and highly idealistic presentation of contemporary views of perfectibility of man. Cf. (A247) Fueter.   RHF

B207 Hegel, Georg W. F. *Philosophy of history.* 1857. Latest ed., London, 1902. [Bohn's library.] Tr. by J. Sibree from *Die Philosophie der Geschichte,* Berlin, 1837. (V. 9 of *Werke.*)

Lectures at Berlin university 1822 to 1831. History is conceived as man's progress in the conception of freedom. Traces evolution of idea of freedom from Orient to Occident and in the several historical epochs, with its realization among Germanic peoples. Basing on postulates of theory of the "intellectual absolute," seeks to unite the idea of freedom with the principle of authority, culminating in the state. Dialectical in method. Grandiose conception of history as march of the absolute spirit through the ages. Cf. (A247) Fueter.   RHF

B208 Comte, Auguste. *The positive philosophy.* 2 v. London and N. Y., 1854. Tr. by H. Martineau from *Cours de philosophie positive,* 1830–42. Recent ed., 3 v., London, 1896. [Bohn's philosophical library.]

This is one of the seminal books of the 19th century. Believing that "all we know is phenomena," the author in his famous "law of the three stages," teaches that in every department of thought the human mind passes through first the theological, then the metaphysical stage, to arrive finally at the positive, or rigorously and objectively scientific. His discussion of principles is of lasting importance, while his illustrations have mostly become antiquated. He is credited with having founded the science of sociology, and his treatment of "Social physics," which fills the second volume, is still significant. Comte's work was reduced by the most brilliant Englishwoman of her time from the six huge volumes of the original to the moderate compass of 1000 pages, and gives the best available formulation of the so-called positive philosophy, or positivism.

RWB

B209 Buckle, Henry T. *A history of civilization in England.* *2* v., 1857–61. Rev. ed. from 2nd London ed., introduction by A. Brisbane, 4 v., N. Y., 1913.

This classic and once very popular and widely read work attempts to prove that all political, social, and intellectual development is due to physical agencies such as climate, soil, food, and aspects of nature. Buckle was an empiricist who lacked a sound evolutionary basis for his views. Cf. (A247) Fueter.   NMT

B210 Bagehot, Walter. *Physics and politics.* 1873. Rev. ed., N. Y., 1902. [International scientific series.]

Early attempt to formulate by analogy with the natural sciences the laws of what the author calls "verifiable progress." He concludes that in prehistoric times human beings were in the process of establishing by struggles with each other groups held together by ties of custom that ultimately became almost rigid. Progress has come in historical times from the practice of government by discussion, the beginning of which practice he does not undertake to place.   WTL

B211 Spengler, Oswald. *The decline of the west.* 2 v. N. Y., 1926–28. Tr. by C. F. Atkinson from *Der Untergang des Abendlandes; Umrisse einer Morphologie der Weltgeschichte.* München, 1920–22. [1, *Gestalt und Wirklichkeit;* 2, *Welthistorische Perspektiven.*]

The most popular political-historical philosopher of post-war Germany in this strange book is attempting to establish a parallelism between the various epochs of civilization. Rejecting the traditional interpretation, which sees world history "is a sort of tapeworm adding on to itself one epoch after another," he would make of history a series of cycles which complete themselves. Within the culture of any cycle the arts and sciences, including political development and religion, rise, culminate and decline together and this process must repeat itself in every epoch. In vol. 2 Spengler's principal preoccupation is in drawing an analogy between our own civilization and past civilizations of a similar type. Such civilizations are rationalistic in religion and politics, romantic in art and literature, and doomed to stagnation. The book is pessimistic in tone, and dogmatic in statement, but most vigorous in style,—an antidote to optimism. Review of v. 1, (London) *Times Lit. Suppl.* 25 : 942, Dec. 23, 1926, and E. E. Sperry, *A.H.R.* 32 : 826, July 1927; v. 2, *A.H.R.* 34 : 556, Apr 1929.   HRS, RHF

HISTORICAL ESSAYS

B241 Macaulay, Thomas B., Baron. *Critical and miscellaneous essays.* 5 v. 1841–44. Recent ed., 2 v., Oxford, 1914. [Oxford standard authors.]

Some fifty essays, most of them originally published in the *Edinburgh Review* and dealing mostly with British subjects. Brilliant in style, full of dramatic interest, and abounding in knowledge, they are dogmatic in tone and uneven in value. The greatest historical worth is in those essays which deal with seventeenth and eighteenth century England.   HMV

B242 Freeman, Edward A. *Historical essays.* 4 v. London, 1871–92.

These volumes contain most of Freeman's ephemeral writings taken from various English reviews. Very few of them possess historical value but a number show keen insight into contemporary English politics, especially in regard to the Near East, and indicate the wide range of the author's studies and reading. In general the essays fall under the three heads of English history, continental European history and architecture, and contemporary problems of politics and government. Review of v. 4, G. W. Prothero, *E.H.R.* 8 : 384, Apr. 1893. NMT

B243a Acton, John E. E. D., Baron. *History of freedom and other essays.* Ed. by J. N. Figgis and R. V. Laurence. London, 1907.

b ———— *Historical essays and studies.* Ed. by J. N. Figgis and R. V. Laurence. London, 1907.

Thirty-seven essays on various subjects, reprinted from English reviews, written from the view-point of a Catholic and a critical individualist. The most important theme is the author's strong defense of religious toleration and political freedom. He regards the Middle Ages with much sympathy, has a strong antipathy to the ecclesiastical state of the Reformation, and distrust of the equalitarian aspects of the French Revolution and modern democracy. Review of *a* and *b*, P. V. M. Benecke, *E.H.R.* 23 : 538, July 1908. HMV

B244 Morley, John, Viscount. *Critical miscellanies.* 1871–77. Rev. ed., 4 v., London and N. Y., 1886–1908.

These volumes consist of a collection of essays on various phases of the history of thought and culture. The subjects treated vary all the way from Greek social thought to a critical estimate of contemporary democracy. Especially important are the essays on the leading French thinkers of the eighteenth century. V. 4 contains two notable papers on the chief Renaissance historians, Machiavelli and Guicciardini. HEB

B245a Bryce, James, Viscount. *Studies in history and jurisprudence.* 2 v., London and N. Y., 1901.

b ———— *World history.* Oxford, 1920. [British academy annual]; [Raleigh lecture, 1919.]

a. Two readable volumes of learned and suggestive essays, comparing the history and law of Rome and England, and dealing with "Nature of the State," "Law of nature," "Relations of law and religion," etc. Review, W. G. P. Smith, *E.H.R.* 77 : 540, July 1902. *b.* A brilliant essay on the process and the forces whereby races and states have been drawn together into one common life, the progress achieved, and the hopes we may cherish for the future. GCS

B246 Maitland, Frederick W. *Collected papers.* 3 v., Cambridge, Eng., 1911.

Delightful papers, most of them on legal subjects, by the "greatest historian of the law of England." Review, R. L. Poole, *E.H.R.* 26 : 832, Oct. 1911. For work of Maitland as whole cf. P. Vinogradoff, *E.H.R.* 22 : 280, Apr. 1907; (A249a) Gooch, *History and Historians of the Nineteenth Century,* p. 393. HRS

B247 Bourne, Edward G. *Essays in historical criticism.* London and N. Y., 1901. [Yale bicentennial publications.]

Well described by the title; acute analytical discussions of vexed historical questions; with a few critical estimates of eminent historians. Review, J. F. Jameson, *A.H.R.* 7:745, July 1902.   HRS

B248 Aulard, François V. A. *Études et leçons sur la révolution française.* Ser. 1–9, 9 v. Paris, 1893–1924. [Bibliothèque de l'histoire contemporaine.]

Short essays, embodying the results of the long and fruitful researches of one of the greatest authorities on the Revolution.   HRS

B249 Meinecke, Friedrich. *Weltburgertum und Nationalstaat: Studien zur Genesis des deutschen Nationalstaates.* 1908. 7th ed., München, 1928.

Brilliant essays by one of Germany's foremost living historians and political philosophers on the genesis and development of problems "vital to the life of states and nations," using the history of Germany to illustrate his interpretation. Review, G. S. Ford, *A.H.R.* 34:826, July 1929.   HRS

PREHISTORIC TIMES

B301a Avebury, John Lubbock, Baron. *Prehistoric times, as illustrated by ancient remains and the manners and customs of modern savages.* 1865. 7th rev. ed., London and N. Y., 1913.

b Sollas, William J. *Ancient hunters and their modern representatives.* 1911. 3rd rev. ed., London, 1924.

c Osborn, Henry F. *Men of the old stone age, their environment, life, and art.* 1915. 3rd ed., N. Y., 1918. (Bibliography.)

d Morgan, Jacques de. *Prehistoric man.* London and N. Y., 1924. Tr. from (B153b) *L'humanité préhistorique,* Paris, 1921.

e Tyler, John M. *New stone age in northern Europe.* N. Y., 1921. (Bibliography.)

a. Justly famous work, by a pioneer in the field. Now antiquated. *b.* Account of palaeolithic man; suggestive comparisons of such a man with the Australian aborigines, Bushmen, and Eskimos of today. Especially strong on the geological side. Richly illustrated; now one of the best books in the field. *c.* Fullest and most satisfactory treatment of palaeolithic man and his culture; scientific in temper, interestingly written, lavishly illustrated; contains useful maps. *d.* General account, by a competent authority, of the material culture, fine arts, religion, and intellectual accomplishments of prehistoric man. Cf. (B153b), v. 2, J. de Morgan, *L'humanité préhistorique.*   HW

e. Popular and readable work; one of the few solid books in English on the neolithic period; contains useful recent bibliography (pp. 293–307) of prehistoric archaeology; sufficient for most purposes. Review, *A.H.R.* 27:94, Oct. 1921.

HRS

B302 MacCurdy, George G. *Human origins: a manual of prehistory.* 2 v. N. Y. and London, 1924.

V. 1. Treats the Old Stone Age; v. 2, the New Stone Age and Ages of Bronze and Iron. The outcome of many years of study and field work by a thoroughly competent scholar. Recommended as a comprehensive, reliable survey of European prehistory. Fully illustrated. Review, A. L. Kroeber, *A.H.R.* 30: 568, Apr. 1925. HW

B303a Macalister, Robert A. S. *Text-book of European archaeology.* V. 1, *Palaeolithic period.* Cambridge, Eng., London, 1921.

b Müller, Sophus O. *Urgeschichte Europas: Grundzüge einer prähistorischer Archäologie.* Strassburg, 1905. Tr. by O. L. Jiriczek from the Danish original. Also French tr.

a. Attractively written and profusely illustrated. Perhaps the best introduction to the entire field. *b.* Complete survey in two hundred pages, with useful references and illustrations. The Stone Age receives very brief treatment, most of the space being devoted to the Bronze and Iron Ages. HW

B304a Wilder, Harris H. *Man's prehistoric past.* 1923. 2nd rev. ed., N. Y., 1924.

b Elliot, George F. Scott. *Prehistoric man and his story.* 1915. 3rd ed., London, 1920. [Story library.]

c Cleland, Herdman F. *Our prehistoric ancestors.* N. Y., 1928.

Popular works, covering both European and American archeology; well adapted to the needs of the general reader. Review of *a, A.H.R.* 29: 365, Jan. 1924.

HW, HRS

B305a Geikie, James. *Antiquity of man in Europe.* Edinburgh, 1914. [Munro lectures, 1913.]

b Burkitt, Miles C. *Prehistory: a study of early cultures in Europe and the Mediterranean basin.* Cambridge, Eng., 1921. (Bibliography.)

c —— *Our forerunners.* N. Y. and London, 1923. [Home university library.]

d —— *Our early ancestors.* Cambridge, Eng., 1926.

e Vulliarmy, Colwyn E. *Our prehistoric forerunners.* London, 1925.

a. By an eminent geologist long interested in prehistoric problems. *b.* Very scholarly; intended for advanced students. HW
c. Compact version of *b.* *d.* Popular introduction to the study of the Mesolithic, Neolithic and Copper Ages. Review, (London) *Times Lit. Suppl.* 26: 27, Jan. 13, 1927. *e.* Excellent, recent manual. Review, G. Guerin, *Rev. Hist.* 151: 110, Jan. 1926. HRS

B306a Keith, Sir Arthur. *Antiquity of man.* 1915. 2nd rev. ed., 2 v. London, 1924.

b Goury, Georges. *Origine et évolution de l'homme.* Paris, 1927. [Précis d'archéologie préhistorique.]

a. Most complete and authoritative treatment of the subject, at least from an anatomical standpoint, in any language. HW
b. Scholarly and careful account of prehistory from the earliest times through the mesolithic period, based on latest researches in the field. Review, G. G. MacCurdy, *A.H.R.* 33: 902, July 1928. HRS

B307a Boule, Marcellin. *Fossil men: elements of human palaeontology.* Edinburgh. 1923. Tr. by Jessie E. Ritchie and James Ritchie from 2nd rev. ed. of *Les hommes fossiles: élements de paléontologie humaine.* Paris, 1923.

b Obermaier, Hugo. *Fossil man in Spain.* New Haven, 1924. Tr. from *El hombre fósil,* Madrid, 1916. [Hispanic Society of America.]

a. Work of a French authority, distinguished for his researches and discoveries in the field. Combines successfully the anatomical, geological, and palaeontological evidence for the antiquity of man, not only in Europe, but also in the other continents. Review, of French ed., G. Guérin, *Rev. Hist.* 144: 245, Nov. 1923.

b. Broader in scope than its title indicates; a general account largely at first-hand, of the antiquity of man in western Europe, with special reference to the Iberian Peninsula.   HW

B308 Dechellette, Joseph. *Manuel d'archéologie préhistorique, celtique, et gallo-romaine.* 2 v. in 6. Paris, 1908–14.

Complete, scholarly account of ancient Gaul, from the earliest appearance of man in that region to the fall of the Roman Empire. Fully annotated and indexed; many excellent illustrations. V. 1. Deals with palaeolithic and neo-lithic culture. V. 2–6. Deal with the culture of the Bronze and Iron Ages.

                                                                HW

B309a Carnoy, Albert J. *Les Indo-Européens: préhistoire des langues, des moeurs, et des croyances de l'Europe.* Bruxelles, 1921.

b Feist, Sigmund. *Kultur, Ausbreitung, und Herkunft der Indogermanen.* Berlin, 1913.

c Hirt, Hermann. *Die Indogermanen, ihre Verbreitung, ihre Urheimat, und ihre Kultur.* 2 v. Strassburg, 1905–07.

d Schrader, Otto. *Reallexikon der indogermanischen Altertumskunde.* Strassburg, 1901.

**e —— ** *Prehistoric antiquities of the Aryan peoples.* London, 1890. Tr. by F. B. Jevons from 2nd rev. ed. of *Sprachvergleichung und Urgeschichte,* 1883. 3rd rev. ed., 2 v., Jena, 1906–07.

f Bender, Harold H. *Home of the Indo-Europeans.* Princeton, 1922.

g Childe, Vere Gordon. *Aryans: a study of Indo-European origins.* N. Y. and London, 1925. (B153a)

a. Very clear, well written, and more compact than *b* and *c.* Provides an admirable introduction to the subject. Review, F. Edgerton, *A.H.R.* 27: 540, Apr. 1922. *b.* Learned, critical survey of the early linguistic history, ethnography, and civilization of the Indo-European peoples. On the whole, preferable to *c, d,* and *e* in the same field, and characterized by greater circumspectness. *c.* Magisterial work, which has a place beside *d* and *e.* *f.* Brief but scholarly summary.

                                                                HW

g. Good recent account, by a British archaeologist. Review, (London) *Times Lit. Suppl.* 25: 686, Oct. 14, 1926.   HRS

B310a Goldenweiser, Alexander A. *Early civilization: an introduction to anthropology.* N. Y., 1922. (A52c)

b Klaatsch, Hermann. *Evolution and progress of mankind.* London, 1923. Tr. by Joseph McCabe from *Entwickelung des Menschengeschlechts.* Wien, 1911–13, ed., and enlarged by Adolf Heilbron.

a. Part 2 of this excellent book, in which the industrial life, art, religion, and social organization of primitive men are admirably described and critically analyzed, is of great value to the historian and student of cultural and social evolution. Review, H. E. Barnes, *A.H.R.* 28: 293, Jan. 1923. HRS

b. Intended, primarily, for the general public, but also of value to the specialist.
HW

B311a Myres, John L. *Dawn of history.* N. Y., 1911. [Home university library.] (Brief bibliography.)

b Childe, Vere G. *Dawn of European civilization.* N. Y. and London, 1925. (B153*a*)

a. Admirable little book by a good scholar, on the transition from prehistoric to historic times in the Near East and in Europe. HW

b. Attempts, on the basis of much archeological evidence, to bring into some sort of relation with one another the facts concerning the neolithic and subsequent primitive cultures of Europe and Western Asia. Good illustrations and maps; well-balanced account. Review, M. Rostovtzeff, *A.H.R.* 31 : 499, Apr. 1926.
HRS

B312a Ebert, Max, ed. *Reallexikon der Vorgeschichte.* V. 1–12 (to Südliches Afrika). Berlin, 1924 ff.

b Ebert, Max. *Vorgeschichtliches Jahrbuch.* Berlin, 1926 ff. [Gesellschaft für Vorgeschichtliche Forschung.]

a. Well-illustrated, scholarly reference book. Especially valuable for the most recent data on many topics in prehistory. *b.* Annual containing a bibliography of publications in the field of prehistory for the preceding year. Annuals covering the years 1924, 1925, and 1926 have been published. Indispensable. HRS

Library Collections.—Valuable collections dealing with prehistoric times may be found in the libraries of Harvard University, Columbia University, Yale University, and the Peabody Museum of Cambridge, Mass., Boston Public Library, New York Public Library, the Library of Congress, and the Field Museum of Natural History, Chicago. AHS

HISTORY OF THE JEWS

The books included in this sub-section are limited mainly to those which deal with the post-biblical history of the Jews. In section *C* will be found works covering earlier Jewish history, in section *F* those which deal with the period of the early Christian church, and in many other sections, in particular in the national sections, volumes are listed dealing with Jewish activities in a country or referring to Jews as they have played a rôle in the history of a period.

The current literature on Jewish history may be found in (C996) *Jewish Quarterly Review,* and in (C997) *Revue des études juives,* although other special periodicals and many of the general historical reviews listed in (B941) ff. discuss new works of interest appropriate to this sub-section.

For all topics connected with the Jews, (F28) *Jewish Encyclopedia* is almost indispensable.

B331 New York Public Library Reference Department. *List of works relating to the history and condition of the Jews in various countries.* N. Y. 1914.

A very serviceable bibliography. HRS

B335a Hosmer, James K. *Story of the Jews, ancient mediaeval, and modern.* N. Y. and London, 1887. (Story of the nations series.)

b Goodman, Paul. *History of the Jews.* N. Y., 1919.

c Deutsch, Gotthard. *History of the Jews.* N. Y., 1921.

d Magnus, Lady Katie. *Outlines of Jewish history from B.C. 586 to C.E. 1885.* London, 1924.

e Browne, Lewis. *Stranger than Fiction: a short history of the Jews from the earliest times to the present day.* N. Y., 1925. (English ed., as *Story of the Jews,* London, 1926.)

Short, one-volume histories. *a.* Really a series of popular essays. *b.* Sympathetic, scholarly and readable; perhaps the best short account in English. *c.* Confines itself to a brief statement of facts. *d.* Good outline. *e.* Popular, but critical; covers in good proportion the period from the early days of the Old Testament narrative to the Zionist movement.   JB

B336a Kottek, Heimann. *Geschichte der Juden.* Frankfurt-am-Main, 1915.

b Elbogen, Ismar. *Geschichte der Juden seit dem Untergang des jüdischen Staates.* Leipzig, 1920.

c Hauser, Otto. *Geschichte des Judentums.* Weimar, 1921.

a. Clear outline. *b.* Most noteworthy; a very valuable and accurate book, very scholarly, but also popular; a most comprehensive presentation of Hebrew history in one volume. *c.* Very interesting as a history written from an anti-Jewish standpoint by a German professor.   JB

B337a Myers, Jack M. *Story of the Jewish people, being a history of the Jewish people since Bible times.* 3 v. London, 1909–25.

b Brann, Marcus. *Geschichte der Juden und ihrer Literatur vom Auszug aus Aegypten bis zum Abschluss des Talmud.* 1893–96. 3rd rev. and enl. ed., 3 v. in 1, Breslau, 1910.

c Margolis, Max L., and **Marx, Alexander.** *History of the Jewish people.* Philadelphia, 1927.

Somewhat longer than books listed under B335 and 336. *a.* Text-book of post-Biblical history for school and home; well written. *b.* Covers different period (circa B.C. 1500–A.D. 300); devotes more attention to culture.   JB
c. General history, woven around the successive centres of Jewish culture. Scholarly and well compressed, but with perhaps too much emphasis on Palestine. Review, (London) *Times Lit. Suppl.* 26: 764, Oct. 27, 1927.   HRS

B338a Graetz, Heinrich H. *History of the Jews.* 5 v., London, 1891–92. American ed. with index v., 6 v., Philadelphia, 1891–98. Ed. and abridged tr. by B. Löwy, from *Geschichte der Juden,* 11 v., Leipzig, 1853–75. Another American ed., *Popular history of the Jews,* ed. by A. Harkavy and M. Raisin, tr. by A. B. Rhim, 6 v., N. Y., 1919.

b Szold, Henrietta, comp. *Tables of Jewish history; a chronological summary of the history of the Jews.* Philadelphia, 1898.

a. Still the only general history of the Jews worthy in any way of common use. Interesting; written with fire, passion, and enthusiasm for Judaism, by a Jew. It has the defects of its qualities, and is justly open in places to the charge of prejudice against some individuals among the Jews, and to anti-Christian feeling not always under perfect restraint. The earlier volumes scarcely represent the modern scientific attitude to biblical criticism, not because of any unwillingness in its author, but because much water has run under the bridge since his death in 1891. The index by Henrietta Szold, issued as a supplementary volume by the Jewish Publication Society of Philadelphia with the American edition, is most useful. *b*. Reprinted from v. 6 of *a*. RWR

B339a Dubnow, S. Markovich. *Weltgeschichte des jüdischen Volkes von seinen Uranfängen bis zur Gegenwart.* 10 v., rev. and tr. from Russian original, Berlin 1925–1929. Bibliographies. (Also Yiddish tr. of Russian original.)

b —— *Outline of Jewish history.* 3 v. N. Y., 1925. Tr. from Russian.

a. Masterly work, admirable in every way. Now complete in the new German edition it is the most complete and authoritative history of the Jews in a western language.

b. Somewhat dull summary intended as a text-book for elementary schools; far inferior to *a*. No reference to Hebrews in the United States. JB

B349 Wolf, Lucien. *Notes on the diplomatic history of the Jewish question, with texts of treaty stipulations and other official documents.* London, 1919.

Used in connection with the Peace Conference of 1919. Valuable study, with full transcripts of documents covering the various phases of the Jewish question in diplomatic history from 1744 to 1917. Review, M. J. Kohler, *Jewish Quart. Rev.* new series, 11 : 120, 1920–21. HRS

B351 Wininger, Sal. *Grosse jüdische National-Biographie.* To be 5 v. V. 1–4, Cernăufi, 1925 ff.

Will contain upwards of eight thousand biographical notices of celebrated Jews and Jewesses of all times and countries. HRS

B355 Strassburger, B. *Geschichte der Erziehung und des Unterrichts für den Israeliten, von der vortalmudischen Zeit bis auf die Gegenwart.* Breslau, 1885.

Only available history of Jewish education; account adequate at the time of writing. JB

B360a Karpeles, Gustav. *Die Geschichte der jüdischen Literatur.* 1886. 3rd ed., 2 v., 1920–21. Also tr. into French, Russian, and Hebrew.

b Abrahams, Israel. *Chapters on Jewish literature.* Philadelphia, 1899.

c Steinschneider, Moritz. *Die Geschichtsliteratur der Juden in Druckwerken und Handschriften zusammengestellt.* V. 1, *Bibliographie der hebräischen Schriften.* Frankfurt-am-Main, 1905.

a. Only readable book on the subject; well-written, comprehensive survey.
b. Sparkling essays covering the period from A.D. 20 to 1786, the death of Moses Mendelssohn. *c*. Only v. 1 of this magisterial undertaking has appeared. JB

DIPLOMATIC, MILITARY, AND NAVAL HISTORY

B501 Hill, David J. *History of diplomacy in the international development of Europe.* V. 1–3, N. Y. and London, 1905–14. (Bibliography.)

V. 1. Covers the period from B.C. 30 to A.D. 1313; deals with the struggle for universal empire. V. 2. Emphasizes the establishment of territorial sovereignty; continues the history to 1648. V. 3. Entitled "The development of absolutism, 1648–1789"; shows the play of diplomatic motives and the development of modern diplomatic policies; contains maps and tables. Review, v. 1–2, G. L. Burr, *A.H.R.* 11 : 358, Jan. 1906; 12 : 617, Apr. 1907'; v. 3, S. B. Fay, *A.H.R.* 20 : 401, Jan. 1915.   GGW

B502a Myers, Denys P. *Manual of collections of treaties and of collections relating to treaties.* Cambridge, Mass., 1922. [Harvard bibliographies.]

    b Potter, Pitman B. *Freedom of the seas in history, law and politics.* N. Y., 1924.

    a. Excellent bibliography of "Collections of Treaties" and a section of 150 pages relating to international administration, listing publications emanating from a large number of bureaus, unions, commissions, etc., created by international agreement. The thousands of titles in the bibliography are annotated in a manner useful to both librarian and student. Very convenient compilation. Review, F. G. Davenport, *A.H.R.* 28 : 296, Jan. 1923.   b. Valuable discussion of this subject in ancient, medieval, and modern times.   HRS

B511a Delbrück, Hans. *Geschichte der Kriegskunst in Rahmen der politischen Geschichte.* V. 1–4, Berlin, 1900–27. 3rd ed., v. 1–2, 1920–21. 2nd ed., v. 3, 1907.

    b Spaulding, Oliver L., Jr.; Nickerson, Hoffman; and Wright, John W. *Warfare: a study of military methods from the earliest times.* N. Y., 1925. (Bibliography.)

    a. Through the interpretation of the significance of warfare on land Professor Delbrück endeavors to interpret the historical development of continental Europe from the days of the Persian wars to the early nineteenth century.   GGW
    b. Not a complete history of warfare, but an introductory survey to death of Frederick the Great; clear and scholarly account; many maps and plans. Review, *A.H.R.* Boak, *A.H.R.* 31 : 102, Oct. 1925.   HRS

B515 Pollard, Hugh B. C. *History of fire arms.* London, 1926.

    Admirable book of great interest for the historian as well as for the collector; many illustrations. Ends with the outbreak of the World War. Review, (London) *Times Lit. Suppl.* 25 : 313, Apr. 29, 1926.   HRS

B521 Stevens, William O., and Westcott, Allan F. *History of sea power.* N. Y., 1920. (Good bibliography.)

    Brief account of sea power from the earliest times to 1920; fully illustrated with charts and diagrams; well indexed. Nearly one-third of the volume is devoted to the period since 1898, which has put to a test many of the earlier theories. Review, R. W. Neeser, *Yale Rev.* 9 : 215, Oct. 1921.   GGW

B528 Meigs, John Forsyth. *Story of the seaman; being an account of the ways and appliances of seafarers and of ships from the earliest times until now.* 2 v. N. Y., 1925.

    Complete story of the art and science of the seaman; interesting; well illustrated.   HRS

B529a Anderson, Romola, and **Anderson, Roger C.** *The sailing ship: six thousand years of history.* London, 1926.

b Holland, Rupert S. *Historic ships.* Philadelphia, 1926.

a. Concise summary of the latest knowledge of the sailing ship from the dawn of history to the voyages of the clipper in the nineteenth century. Written for the general reader. Technical terms are avoided. Distinct contribution to the history of civilization. Review, (London) *Times Lit. Suppl.* 25:834, Nov. 25, 1926. *b.* Description of ships from the viking age to the present day, with illustrations in color from paintings made for the 1926 year-book of the United States Naval Academy. HRS

CONSTITUTIONAL AND LEGAL HISTORY—POLITICAL THEORY

B551a Vinogradoff, Sir Paul G. *Outlines of historical jurisprudence.* V. 1–2, Oxford, 1920–23. [1, *Introduction; tribal law;* 2, (D551d) *Jurisprudence of the Greek city.*]

b —— *Common sense in law.* N. Y., 1914. [Home university library.]

a. The author proposes in this work to trace the development of the recurring themes of jurisprudence, such as marriage, property, succession, in six different —and roughly speaking, successive—types of society, the totemistic, the tribal, the ancient city state, the medieval regime of feudal and canon law, and modern individual society which tends to give place to socialism. V. 1. Divided into two parts, an introduction which deals first with the relation of law to logic, psychology, social science, and political theory, and second, with the methods and schools of jurisprudence. This is followed by the most comprehensive and satisfactory treatment of primitive or tribal law in an English book. V. 2. Deals in detail with the jurisprudence of the Greek city state, particularly with that of Athens and Sparta; it is less concerned with the Greek conception of law in the abstract. Review, v. 1, R. Pound, *Harvard Law Rev.* 35:774, Apr. 1921; v. 2, E. Barker, *E.H.R.* 39:424, July 1924. *b.* Contains no historical matter, but treats of legal rights and duties and the sources of the rules which the courts enforce as law; an admirable little sketch. CHM, ESC

B552 Marquardsen, Heinrich, ed. *Handbuch des öffentlichen Rechts der Gegenwart in Monographien.* 4 v. in about 40 pts. Reprints of many parts. 1883–92. Rev. ed. of v. 2–3 in 20 pts., 1894–1919, with Einleitungsband by G. Jellinek, P. Laband, and R. Piloty, in about 17 pts., Freiburg and Tübingen, 1893–1917.

Voluminous collection of monographs on public law in European states and on kindred subjects. Most of the authors are German jurists, although a few titles are by other Continental scholars. Noteworthy volumes are those of C. Gareis, *Allgemeines Staatsrecht,* a solid and learned study of universal public law; P. Hinschius, *Staat and Kirche,* a brief account, largely historical, of the relations of church and state, by probably the greatest of modern canonists; and two books by H. Rehm, *Geschichte der Staatsrechtswissenschaft* and *Allgemeine Staatslehre.* The first of Rehm's volumes is one of the best general histories of political ideas from the Greeks to modern times. Emphasis is on Greek writers. The second volume is a systematic account of the various branches of the science of politics, an analytical study—in contrast with the historical method of the first book. CHM

B561a **Pollock, Sir Frederick.** *Introduction to the history of the science of politics.* 1890. Rev. ed., N. Y., 1911.

b **Janet, Paul A. R.** *Histoire de la science politique dans ses rapports avec la morale.* 1858. 4th rev. ed., 2 v., Paris, 1913.

c **Gettell, Raymond.** *History of political thought.* N. Y., 1924.

d **Murray, Robert.** *History of political science from Plato to the present.* Cambridge, England, 1926.

e **Engelmann, Geza.** *Political philosophy from Plato to Jeremy Bentham.* N. Y. and London, 1927. Tr. by K. F. Geiser from *Meisterwerke der Staatsphilosophie.* 1923.

f **Mohl, Robert von.** *Encyclopädie der Staatswissenschaften.* 1859. 2nd ed., Tübingen, 1872.

a, b, c, d are histories of political thought,—there are many other good ones; histories of political thought during special periods or fields of history will be found in appropriate sections of Dunning (H561) and (I553*a, b*). Of the books listed above *a*, a slender volume, is more than a mere summary of the ideas of writers; its outstanding quality is the integration of political thought with practical politics and with philosophical writing in general, an excellent outline, while *b* is perhaps the best compact comprehensive account of the history of political thought to the close of the eighteenth century. Penetrating analysis, particularly of French authors, with some tendency to underestimate the importance of English writers. *c.* A more comprehensive account than that of *a*, but briefer than *b*, necessarily rather summary in treatment. Review, A. N. Holcombe, *Amer. Pol. Sci. Rev.* 18:801, Nov. 1924.   HRS, HMW

d. The author, attempting to cover so great a field of political thought, is obliged to omit many writers. Three-fourths of the volume deals with the period since the Reformation, and devotes much attention to American thinkers. The chapters on "The Utilitarians and Democracy" and "The Prophet in Politics," which is an exposition of the philosophy of Mazzini, are the most distinctive contributions. Review, (London) *Times Lit. Suppl.* 25:71, Feb. 4, 1926; G. P. Gooch, *Contemp. Rev.* 129:389, Mar. 1926.   WSC

e. Digest of leading ideas in Plato's *Republic,* Aristotle's *Politics,* Aquinas's *Government of princes,* Hobbes's *De cive,* Spinoza's *Tractatus politicus,* Locke's *Civil government,* Montesquieu's *Spirit of laws,* Rousseau's *Social contract, The Federalist,* and Bentham's *Introduction to a project for a· constitutional code.* Well done. Excellent introduction by Professor O. Jaszi describes the setting of each treatise. Review, F. W. Coker, *A.H.R.* 33:622, Apr. 1928.   HRS

f. Standard German treatise on political science. An encyclopedia, not in the sense of an alphabetically arranged series of articles, but in the sense of a comprehensive treatment. Now seriously out of date. Also cf. (P531) Conrad, *Handwörterbuch der Staatswissenschaften,* and (B565) Jellinek.   CMM

B562 **Holtzendorff, Franz J. W. P. von,** ed. *Encyklopädie der Rechtswissenschaft in systematischer Bearbeitung.* 1880–1890. 6th rev. ed., 2 v., Leipzig, 1904.

Indispensable. Encyclopedia in the form of small treatises on various subjects connected with political science, in most cases by the most eminent German authorities on those subjects. Noteworthy is a section on canon law by Stutz, perhaps the leading authority since the death of Hinschius. The older editions are in a sense not superseded by the latest edition, because valuable articles are not always repeated, e.g., the fifth edition contains articles which do not appear in the sixth.

CHM

B564 Pound, Roscoe. *Interpretations of legal history.* N. Y., 1923. [Cambridge studies in English legal history.]

Critical discussion of various schools of jurisprudence, historical, analytical, and sociological. Review, S. E. Baldwin, *A.H.R.* 29: 322, Jan. 1924. CHM

B565 Jellinek, Georg. *Allgemeine Staatslehre.* 1900. 4th rev. ed., Berlin, 1922.

Standard text-book in Germany on the theory of the state. Excellent systematic account of the state in its origin, functions, and ends, with some treatment of the theories on all these subjects. CHM

B566a Vierkandt, Alfred, and others. *Allgemeine Verfassungs- und Verwaltungsgeschichte.* Leipzig, 1911. [(B606) Die Kultur der Gegenwart, v. 2, pt. 2, 1.]

b Kohler, Joseph, and **Wenger, Leopold.** *Allgemeine Rechtsgeschichte.* Leipzig, 1914. [(B606) Die Kultur der Gegenwart, v. 2, pt. 7, 1.]

a. First volume of a general history of political and constitutional developments; deals with the forms of society in Oriental states, with the origin of European political society in the Greek and Roman states, and with the constitutional history of Germany to 1806; a brief summary of knowledge at the time of publication. Well done and useful. Review, E. H. McNeal, *A.H.R.* 18: 346, Jan. 1913. *b.* Brief summary of oriental law and law under Greeks and Romans.

HRS

ECONOMIC AND SOCIAL HISTORY

B571a Cunningham, William. *Essay on western civilization in its economic aspects.* 2 v., Cambridge, Eng., 1898–1900. [Cambridge historical series.]

b Gras, Norman S. B. *Introduction to economic history.* N. Y., 1922. [Harper's historical series.] (Useful bibliography.)

c Weber, Max. *General economic history.* N. Y. and London, 1927. (Adelphi economic series.) Tr. by F. H. Knight from *Wirtschaftsgeschichte: Abriss der universalen Sozial- und Wirtschaftsgeschichte, aus der nachgelassenen Vorlesungen bearbeitet von M. Palyi.* München, 1923.

d Knight, Melvin M., ed. *Economic history of Europe.* 2 v. and 1 v., N. Y. 1926–28. [1, M. M. Knight, *To the end of the middle ages;* 2, M. M. Knight, H. E. Barnes, and F. Flugel, *In modern times.*]

a. Historical survey of economic development along broad lines of influence. No attempt is made by the author to be interpretative or to supply any large amount of data but the work is suggestive and valuable for its ideas as to historical influences. Review, B. Perrin, *A.H.R.* 4: 135, Oct. 1898; E. P. Cheyney, *ibid.* 6: 774, July 1901; W. W. Fowler, *E.H.R.* 13: 744, Oct. 1898; 16: 753, Oct. 1901. *b.* Well worked-out and scholarly interpretation of economic history and development along the five main lines of collectional, cultural nomadic, settled village, town, and metropolitan economy. Useful charts. Important and suggestive work for both historians and economists. Review, V. S. Clark, *A.H.R.* 28: 345, Jan. 1923.

NMT

c. "Systematic exposition of important phases of the sociological interpretation of economic history." Reviews the economic organizations of the ancient world and the Middle Ages with references to Indian and Chinese civilization as an aid to attacking the main problem of the book, how the economic system of capitalism came to develop when and as it did. Chapters on development of lordship, extension of manorial system, and the evolution of the capitalistic spirit are noteworthy. Important and very suggestive contribution to economic history. Review, A. P. Usher, *A.E.R.* 18: 104, Mar. 1928; (London) *Times Lit. Suppl.,* 27: 2, Jan. 5, 1928. d. Systematic narrative of the economic development of Europe through post-war developments, with emphasis on business organization. Able conspectus, but not always clear as a result of over-condensation. Review of v. 1, H. L. Gray, *A.H.R.* 32: 568, Apr. 1927; v. 2, *A.H.R.* 33: 858, July 1928.

HRS

B572 **Brodnitz, Georg,** ed. *Handbuch der Wirtschaftsgeschichte.* V. 1–2, Jena, 1918–24. [1, G. Brodnitz, *Englische Wirtschaftsgeschichte;* 2, Kötzschke, Rudolph, *Wirtschaftsgeschichte des Mittelalters.*]

V. 1. First of a series of handbooks on the economic history of various countries; carries the economic history of England down to the end of the Middle Ages. Comparatively little space is given to developments before the Norman Conquest. The story is organized around the substitution of voluntary relations in land holding and agricultural labor for feudal ties, the rise of mercantile and industrial capital, and the growth of foreign trade in the hands of Englishmen. These are frequently contrasted with developments on the Continent, particularly in Germany. Legal and political influences are strongly emphasized. References to authorities are abundant. Review, *E.H.R.* 37: 154, Jan. 1922. DAMC

V. 2. General economic history of the Middle Ages, covering the period from about 400 to 1500, but emphasizing the period 800 to 1100. Agriculture occupies much attention but the crusades, money economy, and economic ideas are not neglected. Although Europe in general from England to Byzantium is dealt with, Germany occupies the centre of the stage. A volume packed with information about medieval economic history. Review, Sir Paul Vinogradoff, *E.H.R.* 40: 264, Apr. 1925; N. S. B. Gras, *A.H.R.* 30: 343, Jan. 1925. HRS

B573a **Gras, Norman S. B.** *History of agriculture in Europe and America.* N. Y., 1925. (Bibliography.)

b **Meitzen, August.** *Siedelung und Agrarwesen der West- und Ostgermanen, der Kelten, Römer, Finnen, und Slaven.* 3 v. and atlas. Berlin, 1895.

a. Good survey of agriculture from the earliest stages. Emphasizes the social, political, and institutional rather than the technical sides of agriculture. Review, T. N. Carver, *A.H.R.* 31: 299, Jan. 1926. b. Massive treatise on the settlement and agricultural methods of the primitive Germans, Celts, Romans, and other peoples. Meitzen's most important contribution to the controversy over the free mark community was the introduction of a typical form of Germanic settlement. A Germanic people, he was led to believe after long study of the rural economy of western Europe, will normally settle in a nucleated village, a Celtic people in isolated homesteads. Although battles are still fought over this agrarian problem, Meitzen should be given credit for putting the Germanistic doctrine on a new and more secure footing. HRS

B575 **Renard, Georges,** ed. *Histoire universelle du travail.* 8 v., Paris, 1912–27. [1, G. Glotz, *Le travail dans la Grèce ancienne;* 2, P. Louis, *Le travail dans le monde romain;* 3, P. M. Boissonnade, *Le travail dans l'Europe chrétienne au moyen âge;* 4, H. L. Capitan and H. Lorin, *Le travail en Amérique avant et après Colomb;* 5, B. Nogaro and W. Ouahid, *L'évolution du commerce;* 6, G. Renard and A. Dulas, *L'évolution industrielle et agricole depuis cent cinquante ans;* 7, G. Renard and G. Weulersse, *Le travail dans l'Europe moderne;* 8, G. Renard, *Le travail dans le préhistoire.* (V. 1 also as B153a, v. 17; v. 2 as B153a, v. 28; v. 3 as B153a, v. 32; v. 7, as B153a, v. 18.)]

One of the few comprehensive histories of labor. Of the volumes, each of which is written by an authority, Glotz is particularly noteworthy, for it is not only a history of labor in ancient Greece, but a most meritorious economic history of Greece of the period, very clear and well organized. Review, v. 1, W. L. Westermann, *A.H.R.* 26:492, Apr. 1921; v. 2, *Rev. Hist.* 112:108, Jan. 1913; v. 4, H. Hauser, *Rev. Hist.* 118:336, March 1915; v. 5, *Rev. Hist.* 116:349, July 1914; v. 6, C. Seignobos, *Rev. Hist.* 113:391, July 1913; v. 7, A. Hewes, *A.H.R.* 28:158, Oct. 1922.   HRS

B576a **Day, Clive.** *History of commerce.* 1907. Rev. ed., N. Y., 1922. [Longman's commercial text-books.] (Bibliographies.)

b **Segre, Arturo.** *Storia del commercio.* 1915. 2nd rev. ed., 2 v., Turin, 1923–24. [1, *Dalle origini alla rivoluzione francese,* 2, 1789–1922.] [Biblioteca dell'insegnamento commerciale e professionale.] (Excellent bibliographies.)

a. Divided into five parts: ancient, medieval, modern, recent, and United States. Necessarily, the space devoted to each part is very brief, but is proportioned in such way as to give greater importance to the later divisions. Best comprehensive book on the subject in English; written with thorough grasp; a mine of information as well as a piece of good literature. Supplementary material in the 1922 edition brings the account to the date of publication. Review, J. P. Goode, *Jour. of Pol. Econ.* 16:309, May 1908.   COF
b. Good manual summarizing the history of commerce of the world; emphasizes Italian commerce. Review, C. Day, *A.H.R.* 30:112, Oct. 1924.   HRS

B581a **Beer, Max.** *General history of socialism and social struggles.* 5 v., London, 1922–25. [1, *Social struggle in antiquity;* 2, *Social struggles in the middle ages;* 3, *Social struggles and socialist forerunners;* 4, *Social struggles and thought, 1750–1860;* 5, *Social struggles and modern socialism.*] Tr. by H. J. Stenning from *Allgemeine Geschichte des Socialismus und der sozialen Kämpfe.* 5 v., Berlin, 1919–22.

b **Laidler, Harry W.** *History of socialistic thought.* N. Y., 1927.

a. History of radical movements and doctrines from the ancient Oriental period to the present time; written from the standpoint of a moderate Marxian. While a partisan interpretation, it is full of interesting and important material for the student of economic and social history and social theory. The emphasis is distinctly on the history of reform doctrines and programs rather than upon the actual struggles of social classes in the past.   HEBS
b. Able and exhaustive survey of socialism as a school of thought, a system of social philosophy, from early times to the communism of the Russian Bolsheviks in 1927. Well written and fair. Review, P. F. Brissenden, *Pol. Sci. Quart.* 43:464, Sept. 1928.   HRS

B582 Carr-Saunders, Alexander M. *Population problem: a study in human evolution.* Oxford, 1922.

Comprehensive and well-documented study of population growth and modes of population limitation from primitive times to our own; attempts to estimate and indicate the relation between population conditions and the progress of human culture at large. Unquestionably the most important work for the historian which has thus far been written on the population problem. Review, F. H. Hankins, *Journal of Social Forces,* V. 2, 2 : 287, Jan. 1924.   HEBS

B583 Sumner, William G. *Folkways: a study of the sociological importance of usages, manners, customs, mores, and morals.* Boston, 1907.

Elaborate collection of descriptive material to illustrate the sociological or comparative theory of morality, as expressed in the theses that "the mores can make anything right and prevent condemnation of anything." Aside from the first four chapters, it contains little in the way of abstract theory, but is confined to a frank, objective, and candid description of the nature and genesis of many of the more important customs and institutions. An invaluable aid to the legal, institutional, cultural, and sociological historian. Review, G. E. Vincent, *Amer. Jour. of Sociology* 13 : 414, Nov. 1907; H. E. Barnes, 25 : 3, July 1919.   HEBS

B584a Kidd, Benjamin. *Social evolution.* 1894. Rev. ed. N. Y., 1921.

    b —— *Principles of western. civilization.* N. Y., 1902.

    c —— *Science of power.* N. Y., 1918.

Works of an English social philosopher who lays particular stress upon the "irrational and altruistic" influence of religion in social evolution and cultural progress. Progress consists in a triumph of super-rational altruism over rational individualism. *c.* Repudiates some of the philosophy of *a* and *b.* Review of *a,* H. E. Barnes, *Amer. Jour. of Sociology,* 27 : 581, Mar. 1922; A. A. Tenney, *Pol. Sci. Quart.* 34 : 335, June 1919.   HEBS

B586 Müller-Lyer, Franz. *History of social development.* N. Y., 1921. Tr. by E. Lake and H. A. Lake from *Die Entwicklungsstufen der Menschheit,* 6 v., München, 1910–20.

Series of interesting essays on the nature and development of institutions in general, the history of food products and material culture, the growth of the structure and organization of labor, the evolution of social and economic specialization and coöperation, and the stages of cultural evolution. Not a coherent or organically unified book, but probably the best brief work on cultural history in its sociological and ethnographic aspects. Review of original German ed., *Sociological Rev.* 3 : 164, April 1910.   HEBS

B587a Wallas, Graham. *Great society.* N. Y., 1914.

    b —— *Our social heritage.* New Haven, 1921.

a. Socio-psychological analysis of the problems created by the reaction of the Industrial Revolution upon modern society, with constructive proposals for their solution. Review, H. E. Barnes, *Amer. Jour. of Sociology,* 28 : 189, Sept. 1922. *b.* The author contrasts the significance of nature and nurture in modern society, concludes that we must depend almost entirely upon improvements in the latter, and sets forth a program for the reconstruction of social institutions, especially the development of adequate forms of national and international coöperation. Review, H. E. Barnes, *Amer. Jour. of Sociology*, 28 : 194, Sept. 1922.   HEBS

B588 Ogburn, William F. *Social change with respect to culture and original nature.* N. Y., 1922.

Analyzes the problems of institutional and cultural change from the standpoint of history, psychology, and sociology. Considers the various types of culture in their relation to each other and with respect to their relative rates of change and alteration. The factors of social stability and social change are analyzed in a penetrating manner, indicating the bearing of these problems upon the most effective functioning of the human personality. A most significant sociological contribution to the subject of historical causation. Review, W. A. Orton, *Amer. Econ. Rev.* 13 : 468, Sept. 1923.   HEBS

CULTURAL HISTORY, GENERAL

B601 Voltaire, François Marie Arouet de. *Essay on universal history.* 4 v. Dublin, 1759. Tr. by T. Nugent from *Essai aur l'histoire générale et sur les moeurs et l'esprit des nations, depuis Charlemagne jusqu'à nos jours.* 7 v. Paris, 1756. Many later ed.

A most important and influential book, one of the foundations of modern historiography. In contrast with the narrow and unscientific conception of universal history of the preceding century typified by (B201) Bossuet, *Discourse on universal history.* Voltaire made a serious attempt to write a history of the world, not only free from theological bias, but also relating economic and cultural with political history. Europe as a whole was his subject, not separate states or movements. Weak on the Middle Ages, although full of interesting suggestions such as the debt of medieval culture to the Arabs, which it is said Voltaire was the first to point out, it is far more reliable as Voltaire approaches his own day. Attacks on the Church, typically Voltairean, mar the whole as an historical work, but its influence on historical writing was enormous. To us of the present day it is perhaps best described as a curiosity. For estimate of Voltaire, cf. (A247) Fueter, French ed., p. 434.   HRS

B602 Guizot, François P. G. *General history of civilization in modern Europe.* N. Y., 1846. [V. 1 of *History of civilization from the fall of the Roman empire to the French revolution.*] Tr. by W. Hazlitt from *Histoire générale de la civilisation en Europe,* 1828. [V. 1 of *Cours d'histoire moderne professé à la faculté des lettres.*] 19th ed., Paris, 1882. There are other English translations.

In these fourteen lectures, intended as an introduction to the study of the history of France, Guizot reviews the institutional history of Europe from the break-up of the Roman Empire to the eighteenth century. Civilization, as he uses the terms, means substantially those ideas and institutions that he supported while a minister under Louis Philippe; the lectures naturally deal with the growth of these institutions and notions. France is the chief subject of his study, because he felt that France had been the "center, the focus of European civilization." Cf. (M601) Guizot, *History of civilization in France.*   WTL

B604 Henne-Am-Rhyn, Otto. *Allgemeine Kulturgeschichte von der Urzeit bis auf die Gegenwart.* 6 v. Leipzig, 1877–78. V. 7, 1897. [1, *Die Urzeit und die morgenländischen Völker;* 2, *Die Hellenen und Römer;* 3, *Kulturgeschichte des Mittelalters;* 4, *Das Zeitalter der Reformation;* 5, *Das Zeitalter der Aufklärung;* 6, *Die neueste Zeit;* 7, *Die jüngste Zeit.*]

One of the older general histories of civilization, which blazed the way for more recent studies. Well written, scholarly, and scientific in its point of view.

ACF

B605a Richet, Charles. *Allgemeine Kulturgeschichte: Versuch einer Geschichte der Menschheit von den aeltesten Tagen bis zur Gegenwart.* 2 v. München, 1920.

b Thorndike, Lynn. *Short history of civilization.* N. Y., 1926.

a. Attempts to determine from a study of the past what it contributes to human progress. The essential service of the past to the present, Richet holds, has been the development of scientific knowledge, the increase of understanding and intelligence. For this reason he devotes his entire second volume to the period since 1789. An optimistic book. Review, C. Becker, *A.H.R.* 27:90, Oct. 1921. *b.* Briefer narrative with a different proportion: about half the book deals with the period before 800 A.D. A popular condensation. Review, E. M. Hulme, *A.H.R.* 32:555, Apr. 1927.

HRS

B606 Hinneberg, Paul, ed. *Die Kultur der Gegenwart, ihre Entwicklung und ihre Ziele.* V. 1–37, Berlin, 1905–21. [I. *Die geisteswissenschaftlichen Kulturgebiete,* 1st half, *Religion und Philosophie, Literatur, Musik, und Kunst:* 1, pt. 1, W. Lexis and others, *Die allgemeinen Grundlagen der Kultur der Gegenwart;* 3, pt. 1, E. Lehmann and others, *Die Religion des Orients und die altgermanische Religion;* 4, pt. 1, J. Wellhausen, K. Müller, and others, *Geschichte der christlichen Religion;* pt. 2, E. Troeltsch, J. Pohle, and others, *Systematische christliche Religion;* 5, W. Wundt, M. Oldenberg, and others, *Allgemeine Geschichte der Philosophie;* 6, W. Dilthey, A. Riehl, W. Wundt, R. Eucken, and others, *Systematische Philosophie;* 7, E. Schmidt, C. Bezold, and others, *Die orientalischen Literaturen;* 8, K. Krumbacher, F. Leo, W. Norden, and others, *Die griechische und lateinische Literatur und Sprache;* 9, A. Bezzenberger, A. Brückner, and others, *Die osteuropäischen Literaturen und die slawischen Sprachen;* 11, pt. 1, H. Zimmer, K. Meyer, and others, *Die romanischen Literaturen und Sprachen mit Einschluss des Keltischen.* II. *Die geisteswissenschaftlichen Kulturgebiete,* 2nd half, *Staat und Gesellschaft, Recht und Wirtschaft:* 2, pt. 1, A. Vierkandt, L. Wenger, and others, *Allgemeine Verfassungs- und Verwaltungsgeschichte;* 4, 1 v., Wilamowitz-Moellendorff and B. Niese, *Staat und Gesellschaft der Griechen und Römer;* 5, pt. 1, F. von Bezold, E. Gothein, and R. Koser, *Staat und Gesellschaft der neueren Zeit;* 7, pt. 1, J. Kohler and others, *Allgemeine Rechtsgeschichte mit Geschichte der Rechtswissenschaft;* 8, R. Stammler, R. Sohm, and others, *Systematische Rechtswissenschaft;* 10, pt. 1, W. Lexis, *Allgemeine Volkswirtschaftslehre;* III. *Die mathematischen, naturwissenschaftlichen und medizinischen Kulturgebiete:* 1, F. Klein, ed., *Die mathematischen Wissenschaften;* 3, E. Lecher, ed., *Anorganische Naturwissenschaften;* pt. 1, E. Warburg, ed., *Physik;* pt. 2, E. von Meyer, ed., *Chemie;* pt. 3, J. Hartmann, ed., *Astronomie;* 4, R. von Wettstein, ed., *Organische Naturwissenschaften;* pt. 1, C. Chun and W. L. Johannsen, ed., *Allgemeine Biologie;* pt. 2, E. Strassburger and R. von Hertwig, ed., *Zellen- und Gewebelehre, Morphologie und Entwicklungsgeschichte,* 2 v.; pt. 3, G. Haberlandt, ed., *Physiologie und Ökologie;* pt. 4, R. von Hertwig and R. von Wettstein, ed., *Abstammungslehre, Systematik, Paläontologie, Biogeographie;* 7, C. Stumpf, ed., *Natur-*

philosophie und Psychologie; pt. 1, C. Stumpf, ed., *Naturphilosophie:* IV. *Die technischen Kulturgebiete;* 12, M. Schwarte, ed., *Technik des Kriegs-wesens.* (Brief bibliographies.)

A coöperative work of German scholars to explain the cultural and political basis for contemporary civilization. On the whole, little use has been made of original sources. The contributions vary in value and are encyclopaedic in character. Review of II, 5, pt. 1, G. S. Ford, *A.H.R.* 14: 575, Apr. 1909; and *E.H.R.* 24: 831, Oct. 1909; of II, 2, pt. 1, *E.H.R.* 29: 179, Jan. 1914.

ACF

B607 Iorga, Nicolae. *Essai de synthèse de l'histoire de l'humanité.* 4 v. Paris, 1925–28. [1, *Histoire ancienne;* 2, *Histoire du moyen âge;* 3, *Epoque moderne;* 4, *Epoque contemporaine.*]

The well-known Rumanian historian has undertaken a survey of human progress within limited scope. V. 1. Gives unusually full attention to the period prior to the classical age of Greece and closes with the triumph of Christianity in the Roman empire. V. 2. Has been criticized as based too exclusively on chronicles. Review of v. 2, B. A. Pocquet du Haut-Jusse, *Rev. des Quest. Hist.* 108: 221, Jan. 1928.

GMD

B610 Randall, John H. *Making of the modern mind, a survey of the intellectual background of the present age.* N. Y., 1926.

Brilliant interpretation of history well described by its subtitle a "synthetic record of social change." The closing two-fifths of the book analyzes the modern mind, that "complex of beliefs, ideals and aspirations found in present-day society," in which old inherited beliefs and the findings of modern science struggle for mastery. The earlier portion considers the birth in the Middle Ages and growth of this complex, with the thesis that the economic interest of the increasingly dominant middle class has been an important cause of this historical product and largely explains it. Very well written; a distinct contribution to a highly controversial subject. Review, F. A. Christie, *A.H.R.* 32: 79, Oct. 1926.

HRS

B611a Mason, William A. *History of the art of writing.* N. Y., 1920.

b Williams, Henry S. *History of the art of writing.* 4 v., N. Y., 1902. [Same work also published as *Manuscripts—comprehending the history of the art of writing.*]

c Carter, Thomas F. *Invention of printing and its spread westward.* N. Y., 1925.

a. Discusses with many illustrations the principal forms of writing known to have been used by mankind. Follows the geographical order of (B166) Helmolt, *Weltgeschichte,* 1st ed., and covers from the earliest times to the invention of printing with movable types. Such unsolved problems as the possible connection of the Chinese and Babylonian systems of writing, the origin of the Phoenician alphabet, and the identity of the inventor of printing are discussed without an attempt at final solution. Review, R. W. Rogers, *A.H.R.* 26: 491, Apr. 1921. *b.* Excellent selection of illustrative plates which are described briefly in accompanying text.

AHL

c. Gives an account of the inventions in China which preceded block printing, of the early history of Chinese block printing and movable type, and of the course of printing westward. A distinct contribution is the discussion of the close connection between inventions in China and important developments in western Europe. Review, G. P. Winship, *A.H.R.* 32: 86, Oct. 1926.

HRS

CULTURAL HISTORY—RELIGIONS

B621a Toy, Crawford H. *Introduction to the history of religions.* Boston, 1913. [Handbook on the history of religions.]

  b Moore, George F. *History of religions.* 2 v. N. Y., 1913–19. [International theological library.]

  c Jevons, Frank B. *Introduction to the history of religion.* 1896. 7th rev. ed., London, 1910. [Handbook of theology.]

  d King, Irving. *Development of religion, a study in anthropology and social psychology.* N. Y., 1910. (Bibliography.)

  e Frazer, James G. *Golden bough.* 2 v. London and N. Y., 1890. Several later ed. Abridged 1 v. ed., N. Y., 1922.

a. Encyclopedic work, descriptive in purpose, rich in facts cited from original sources, and admirable in arrangement. *b.* V. 1. Comprises the religions of China, Japan, Egypt, Babylonia and Assyria, India, Persia, Greece, and Rome. V. 2. Includes Mohammedanism, Judaism, and Christianity. Probably the best treatment in one work of the more highly organized religions of the world. Review of v. 2, F. A. Christie, *A.H.R.* 25: 702, July 1920. *c.* The author, as in *e,* is an anthropologist, but he maintains the independent origin of religion separate from magic. Like Frazer he often takes no account of the genetic aspects of the development of human experience. Valuable nevertheless as a descriptive work. *d.* Sets forth the sociological theory of the origin of religion, following essentially the French School of Durkheim. With all its failure to take account of the individual factors in the early stages of religion's development, the treatment is adequate from the point of view of social psychology. *e.* Elaborately written to defend the theory that in early culture religion grew out of man's recognition of the failure of preceding magic. Too much reasoning power attributed to primitive people. Valuable as a source book of significant facts in spite of its psychological shortcomings.   FLS

B622a Dussaud, René. *Introduction à l'histoire des religions.* Paris, 1914.

  b Reinach, Salomon. *Orpheus, a general history of religions.* N. Y., 1909. (Bibliography.) Tr. by F. Simmons from *Orpheus, histoire générale des religions,* Paris, 1909.

  c —— *Cults, myths, and religions.* London, 1912. Abridged tr. by E. Frost from v. 1–3 of *Cultes, mythes, et religions,* 5 v., 1905–23; 3rd rev. ed., Paris, 1922–25.

  d Chantepie de la Saussaye, Pierre D. *Manual of the science of religion.* London, 1891. Tr. by B. S. Colyer-Fergusson from *Lehrbuch der Religionsgeschichte,* 1887–89; 3rd ed., 2 v., Tübingen, 1905. French tr. by P. Bettelheim and others from 2nd German ed., *Manuel d'histoire des religions,* Paris, 1904. (Excellent bibliographies.)

  e Hopkins, E. Washburn. *Origin and evolution of religion.* New Haven, 1923.

  f Heidel, William A. *Day of Yahweh: a study of sacred days and ritual forms in the ancient Near East.* N. Y. and London, 1929. [American Historical Association.]

a. Maintains the thesis that religion is essentially composed of beliefs and rites whose purpose is to amplify and perpetuate the principle of existence in man, individually or in corporate groups, and in nature. Treats briefly primitive cults and beliefs from this point of view. Interesting and valuable interpretations. *b.* Survey of the leading religions of the world, but chiefly devoted to the history of the Christian church and its manifold schisms. Its conciseness and mass of detail are compensated for by keen observation and scholarly criticism. *c.* Collections of essays dealing largely with primitive Greek and Roman cults. V. 1, most important for the student of religions as it contains valuable studies of primitive beliefs and practices. The remainder of the work consists of isolated studies, which, however, are valuable for the originality of their interpretation. *d.* Study of the phenomena and history of all important religions except Judaism and Christianity. In the third edition each subject has been treated by specialists. Full and authoritative.

ACJ

f. Illuminating study of the history of sacred days and ritual forms of the ancient Hebrews with elaborate citations of Egyptian, Babylonian, old Persian, Greek, Arabic, and other parallels. Includes important contributions to the history of the calendar.

GMD

CULTURAL HISTORY, EDUCATION, THOUGHT, PHILOSOPHY, SCIENCE

B641a Monroe, Paul. *Textbook in the history of education.* 1905. Reprint, N. Y., 1911.

b —— ed. *Cyclopedia of education.* 5 v. N. Y., 1911–13.

c Cubberley, Ellwood P. *History of education.* N. Y., 1920. [Riverside textbooks in education.]

d Graves, Frank P. *Student's history of education.* N. Y., 1915.

e Schmid, Karl A. *Geschichte der Erziehung.* 5 v. Stuttgart, 1884–1902. (Bibliography.)

Monroe differs from Cubberley in that he is primarily concerned with the social background, the general philosophy and the material culture of each period both as a cause and a reflection of educational theory. His treatment of practice is in terms of his more general philosophical survey. *c.* Cubberley, on the other hand, is interested more in the practice, the administration, and the machinery of education. The two volumes, *a* and *c,* each supplemented by the author's collections of source material, make good parallel reading. *b.* Monroe's cyclopedia gives further details on most of the topics of his history. *d.* More popular treatment from a point of view intermediate between that of Monroe and Cubberley.

DBL

e. Encyclopedic history, particularly complete on medieval education and on the developments during the Renaissance and Reformation.

EGS

B642a Thilly, Frank. *History of philosophy.* 1914. Rev. ed. N. Y., 1920.

b Rogers, Arthur K. *Student's history of philosophy.* 1901. Rev. ed., N. Y., 1907. (Bibliographies.)

c Weber, Emile A. *History of philosophy.* 1896. New ed., N. Y., 1912. Tr. by F. Thilly from *Histoire de la philosophie européenne,* 1872; 7th ed., Paris, 1905. (Bibliography.)

d Windelband, Wilhelm. *History of philosophy, with especial reference to the formation and development of its problems and conceptions.* N. Y., 1893, 2nd enl. ed., 1901. Tr. by J. A. H. Tufts from *Die Geschichte der* *neueren 'Philosophie in ihrem Zusammenhange mit der allgemeinen Cultur und den besonderen Wissenschaften dargestellt.* 2 v., 1878–80. 5th ed., v. 1–2, 1st ed., v. 3, Leipzig, 1911.

e **Ueberweg, Friedrich.** *History of philosophy from Thales to the present time.* 1872–74. 5th ed. 2 v., N. Y., 1910. [Theological and philosophical library.] Tr. by G. S. Morris from 4th ed. of *Grundriss der Geschichte der Philosophie von Thales bis auf die Gegenwart,* 3 v., 1862–66; 10th rev. ed., of v. 2 by M. Baumgarten, Berlin, 1915; 11th rev. ed. of v. 1, 3, 4, by K. Praechter and others, Berlin, 1914–20.

f **Ziegler, Theobald.** *Die geistigen und socialen Strömungen des neunzehnten Jahrhunderts.* Berlin, 1899.

g **Marvin, Walter T.** *History of European philosophy, an introductory book.* N. Y., 1917. (Bibliography.)

a. Comprehensive account of the entire history of philosophy, in moderate compass, by a competent scholar and experienced teacher of the subject. Until recently English-speaking students and readers have been dependent on histories of philosophy translated from foreign languages. This work has the advantage of being written by an American acquainted with the difficulties and needs of his readers and is one of the best of this class. It contains some discussion of the connections of philosophy and culture. *b.* Another good survey of similar scope. *c.* Good translation of one of the best compendious histories of the entire course of philosophy. The author, himself bi-lingual, was formerly professor at the University of Strasburg, and thus located at the meeting point of Gallic and Teutonic cultures. The account of medieval philosophy is especially valuable for a discussion of moderate compass. *d.* Altogether the best survey of the relations of philosophy to other types of thought and to general culture in the modern age. V. 1. Gives a complete account to the close of the eighteenth century. V. 2. Describes the German movement to about 1840. V. 3. Unfinished, was to bring the work down to date. For this last period special treatises, e.g., *f,* must be consulted. *e.* Standard account of the whole range of development of philosophic thought, frequently revised to keep abreast of scholarly research.   ACA

g. Begins with the pre-philosophic and pre-scientific period and shows the inheritance and gradual transformation of the ideas of this period in the philosophy and science of later periods. Presents philosophical movements with general history as a background.   EGS

B643a **Erdmann, Johann E.** *History of philosophy.* 3 v. London, 1890–91. 4th ed., 1897. Tr. by W. S. Hough from 3rd ed. of *Grundriss der Geschichte der Philosophie,* 3 v., Berlin, 1878; 1st ed., 1865; 4th ed., 1896.

b **Janet, Paul,** and **Scailles, Gabriel.** *History of the problems of philosophy.* 2 v. London, 1902. Tr. by A. Monahan, under editorship of H. Jones, from *Histoire de la philosophie: les problèmes et les écoles,* 1887; 2nd ed., Paris, 1894.

a. Excellent general history, giving the biographies of the leading philosophers, ancient, medieval and modern, and a critical presentation of their works. *b.* V. 1, Problems of psychology. V. 2, Ethics, metaphysics and theodicy. The history of each of these four specific problems is treated separately. A somewhat brief, yet an excellent presentation and a very useful supplement to those works which do not segregate problems.   EGS

B644 Draper, John W. *History of the intellectual development of Europe.* 1863. Rev. ed., 2 v., N. Y., 1904.

This "philosophical examination of the intellectual and political history of nations" was written in pre-psychology days, and touches but lightly upon things intellectual. Rather it is general history reviewed in the light of the "control of natural law in the shaping of human affairs" and the "law" is Buckle's "influence of nature." Review, *North Amer. Rev.* 97 : 291, July 1863.   EFH

B645a Lecky, William E. H. *History of European morals from Augustus to Charlemagne.* 1869. Rev. ed., 2 v., London and N. Y., 1905.

b —— *History of the rise and influence of the spirit of rationalism in Europe.* 1865. Rev. ed., 2 v., London and N. Y., 1914.

Erudite works, by a disciple of Buckle, designed to present the history of the imposition of "certain theological opinions" upon the world (morals) and a "history of their decay" (rationalism). In *a* the appropriateness of virtues to their age is considered. The fundamental thesis in *b* is that the pressure of the general intellectual influences of the time determines the predispositions which ultimately regulate the details of belief. Cf. (A249*a*) G. P. Gooch, *History and historians,* p. 365.   GCS

B646 Taylor, Henry O. *Freedom of the mind in history.* N. Y., 1923.

Reviews the progress of man in the course of history toward freedom in reference to political institutions, religion, philosophy, and science (ancient and medieval), religious reform (Luther and Calvin), metaphysical and epistemological thinking (Descartes, Locke, Kant, Berkeley), scientific investigation and interpretation (Greek and modern), art and literature; closing with a consideration of the prospect for the future. The book thus deals in good part with matters touched on in previous books by its author but viewed from a different angle, and is eminently readable and suggestive. Review, D. J. Hill, *A.H.R.* 29 : 525, Apr. 1924.   WAH

B647 Robertson, John M. *Short history of free thought, ancient and modern.* 2 v., N. Y., 1906.

Comprehensive history of the development of rationalism, written from the standpoint of a courageous, if somewhat exuberant and belligerent, advocate of free-thought. Contains much curious and recondite information, some of which is either unverifiable or interpreted in an unusual manner. The chief defect, however, is the relatively little space devoted to the period since 1700. More satisfactory as an introduction to (B645*b*) Lecky, than as a history of rationalism complete in itself.   HEBS

B648a Bury, John B. *Idea of progress; an inquiry into its origin and growth.* London and N. Y., 1920.

b —— *History of freedom of thought.* London and N. Y., 1913. [Home university library.]

a. Discussion of the "idea of progress" as conceived by the French philosophers and scientifically supported by the doctrine of evolution. Review, P. V. M. Benecke, *E.H.R.* 35 : 581, Oct. 1920. *b.* "Freedom of thought" is defined almost exclusively in terms of emancipation from religious intolerance, which, arising in the Middle Ages, has been destroyed by the rationalists of the 17th and 18th centuries, and by the development of science in the 19th. Review, *Athenaeum* 2: 108, Aug. 2, 1913.   HMV

B649a White, Andrew D. *History of the warfare of science with theology in christendom.* 1896. New ed., 2 v., N. Y., 1910.

 b ――― *Seven great statesmen in the warfare of humanity with unreason.* N. Y., 1910.

  a. Searching and very readable work on the efforts of dogmatic theologians (Catholic and Protestant) to hamper scientific investigation and teaching on evolution, the sciences, higher criticism, etc.; written to liberate science and to strengthen religion. Cf. *Autobiography* 2: 495. *b.* Less unified work dealing admirably with Grotius and Thomasius, allusively rather than concretely with Sarpi and, from another standpoint, with Turgot, Stein, Cavour, and Bismarck— the last uncritically. Review, G. S. Ford, *A.H.R.* 16: 602, Apr. 1911.   GCS

B650a Osborn, Henry F. *From the Greeks to Darwin.* N. Y., 1894. [Columbia Univ. biological series.]

 b Van Loon, Hendrik W. *Tolerance.* N. Y., 1925.

  a. Standard history, in English, of the development of the evolutionary hypothesis. Written from the standpoint of the zoologist, stressing the growth of the theories concerning organic evolution rather than analyzing the development of the philosophy of evolution and indicating its significance for the history of ideas and culture.   HEBS
  b. Brilliant survey of the struggle for tolerance from ancient times in Greece to the present. Review, Frances Bartlett, *Boston Transcript,* Dec. 5, 1925; T. A. Miller, *Sat. Rev. of Lit.* 2: 293, Nov. 14, 1925.   GMD

B651a Robinson, James H. *Mind in the making: the relation of intelligence to social reform.* N. Y., 1921.

 b Stawell, Florence M., and **Marvin, Francis S.** *Making of the western mind.* N. Y., 1923.

 c Barnes, Harry E. *New history and the social studies.* N. Y., 1925.

  a. "Study of how man has come to be as he is and to believe as he does." This pragmatic review exhibits the socio-psychological remains which the epochs of history have deposited upon the contemporary mind. By exposing the various vestiges of fossilized social traditions,—likes, dislikes, dreams, inhibitions, taboos, mysteries, moralities,—the author would break the shackles of historical prejudices and emancipate a creative intelligence. Stimulating and remarkable book; perhaps an *apologia pro vita sua.* Review, W. A. Brown, *Yale Rev.* 11: 856, July 1922.
                                                                                           EFH, HRS
  b. Compilation to give the general reader some idea of the history and development of European civilization; covers in tabloid form the contributions of each period in literature, art, science, philosophy, and politics. A sound little book. Review, (London) *Times Lit. Suppl.* 22: 155, Mar. 8, 1923.   HRS
  c. Notable effort to define and integrate the work of students of history, psychology, anthropology, sociology, economics, political science, and ethics. The author surveys, with wide-sweeping bibliographical references, recent progress in each of these fields and attempts a synthetic program for their further coöperation. His contention is that "Sociology has become one of the most severely

inductive of the social sciences. . . . It would be far better if historians as a group were consciously to recognize that they cannot adequately or accurately assemble or interpret the facts of history without the aid of sociology." In spite of his over-confident optimism as to the "scientific" character and the value of the results hitherto achieved by the various "social sciences," his volume is a stimulating challenge to historians to become more conversant with these newer aids to historical interpretation. Review, F. J. Teggart, *A.H.R.* 31 : 297, Jan. 1926; A. P. Usher, *Amer. Econ. Rev.* 15 : 736, Dec. 1925; A. W. Small, *Amer. Journ. of Sociology,* 31 : 89, July 1925; T. V. Smith, *Amer. Pol. Sci. Rev.* 19 : 826, Nov. 1925.   SBF

B653a Thomson, J. Arthur, ed. *Outline of science.* 4 v. N. Y., 1922. (Bibliography.)

b Libby, Walter. *Introduction to the history of science.* N. Y., 1917.

c Sedgwick, William T., and **Tyler, Harry W.** *Short history of science.* 1917. Last ed., N. Y., 1925. (Good bibliography.)

d Thomson, J. Arthur. *Science of life.* London, 1899. [Victorian era series.]

e Rice, William N. *Christian faith in an age of science.* 1903. New ed., N. Y., 1904.

f Whewell, William. *History of the inductive sciences, from the earliest time to the present.* 3 v. 1837. 3rd rev. ed., 2 v., N. Y., 1865.

g Williams, Henry S., and **Williams, Edward H.,** ed. *History of science.* 10 v. N. Y., 1909–10. Published also under title *Everyday science,* 10 v., N. Y., 1909–10.

h Williams, Henry S. *Story of nineteenth century science.* N. Y., 1900.

i Korschelt, Eugene, and others. *Handwörterbuch der Naturwissenschaften.* 10 v., Jena, 1912–15.

j Dana, Edward S., and others, ed. *Century of science in America,* with special reference to the *American Journal of Science,* 1818–1918. New Haven, 1918.

k Whetham, William C. D., and **Whetham, Catherine D.** *Science and the human mind: a critical and historical account of the development of natural knowledge.* London and N. Y., 1912. (Bibliography.)

l Woodruff, Lorande L., ed. *Development of the sciences.* New Haven, 1923.

a. Covers the entire field of contemporary science except pure mathematics. Little attention is paid to the history or interpretation of science. Well illustrated, popular account by various scholars.   EGS
b. Brief survey written on broad general lines; emphasizes practical achievements rather than the advance of scientific theory. Review, L. Thorndike, *A.H.R.* 23 : 125, Oct. 1917. *c.* Another text-book somewhat longer, more thorough on period before nineteenth century; emphasizes somewhat the mathematical and physical sciences. Review, L. Thorndike, *A.H.R.* 23 :609, Apr. 1918. *d.* Convenient for the developments of biological science in the nineteenth century. *e.* Contains excellent clear brief account of the revolutionary discoveries in the several sciences in the eighteenth and nineteenth centuries, together with some comment on their relations with Christian thought. Cf. (B649a) A. D. White, *Warfare of Science with Theology.* *f.* Classic work, still valuable for the earlier

period. Unfortunately no work of similar breadth and thoroughness of scholarship and of such philosophical grasp is available for the remarkable progress made in the period since its original publication. *g.* Extended compilation with sections on the several sciences, with special reference to their development in the nineteenth century. Intended for the general reader. *h.* Abridged presentation of the same materials. *i.* Encyclopedic work including biographical sketches of eminent scientists. Review, *Nature,* 113: 419, Mar. 22, 1924. *j.* Collection of monographs by leading American scholars on the developments in their respective fields of science in the century preceding 1918.   GMD

k. Excellent though brief account, stressing the important points in the development of science, philosophy, religion, and theology. *l.* Excellent popular essays aiming to cover the history of mathematics, physics, chemistry, astronomy, geology, and biology.   EGS

B654 Sarton, George. *Introduction to the history of science.* V. 1, *From Homer to Omar Khayyam,* Washington, 1927. [Carnegie Institution of Washington.]

Aims to give the main facts "concerning men of science together with a list of important editions and translations of the works of each individual and a critical bibliography of the treatment of that individual and his works by modern scholars," treating the subject in the main by fifty-year periods. Very useful reference book. Review, L. Thorndike, *A.H.R.* 33: 363, Jan. 1928.   HRS

B655a Ball, Walter R. *Short account of the history of mathematics.* 1888. 5th ed., N. Y., 1912. (Bibliography.)

b Cajori, Florian. *History of physics in its elementary branches, including the evolution of physical laboratories.* N. Y., 1899.

c Moore, Forris J. *History of chemistry.* N. Y., 1918. [International chemical series.]

d Zittel, Karl A. von. *History of geology and paleontology to the end of the nineteenth century.* London, 1901. [Contemporary science series.] Tr. by M. M. Ogilvie-Gordon from *Geschichte der Geologie und Paläontologie bis Ende des neunzehnten Jahrhunderts.* Leipzig, 1899. [Geschichte der Wissenschaften in Deutschland, unsere Zeit.]

e Berry, Arthur. *Short history of astronomy.* London, 1898. [University extension manuals.]

f Nordenskiöld, Erik. *History of biology.* London, 1929. (Bibliography.) Tr. by L. B. Eyre from *Biologius historia.* 3 v. Stockholm, 1920–24.

g Pillsbury, Walter B. *History of psychology.* N. Y., 1929. (Bibliography.)

h Mach, Ernst. *Science of mechanics: a critical and historical exposition of its principles.* Chicago, 1893. 4th rev. ed., Chicago, 1919. Tr. by T. J. McCormack from 2nd ed. of *Die Mechanik in ihrer Entwickelung, historisch-kritisch dargestellt.* 1883. 7th rev. ed., Leipzig, 1912. Jourdain, P. E. B. Supplement to 3rd Eng. ed. containing Mach's additions to 7th German ed. Chicago, 1915.

a, b, c, d, e, f, g. Good histories of their respective fields of science; introductions rather than exhaustive studies. *h.* Best history of mechanics, both critical and constructive; a classic of its kind. Regards scientific concepts and theories as practical intellectual instruments. Mach was one of the earliest pragmatists.
EGS, HRS

B656a **Libby, Walter.** *History of medicine in its salient features.* N. Y., 1922.

b **Garrison, Fielding H.** *Introduction to the history of medicine.* 1913. 3rd rev. ed., Philadelphia, 1921. (Bibliography.)

c **Baas, Johann H.** *Outlines of the history of medicine and the medical profession.* N. Y., 1889. Tr. by H. E. Henderson from *Grundriss der Geschichte der Medicin,* Stuttgart, 1876.

d **Haeser, Heinrich.** *Lehrbuch der Geschichte der Medicin und der epidemischen Krankheiten.* 1845. 3rd rev. ed., 3 v., Jena, 1875–92. (Bibliographies.)

e **Pagel, Julius L.** *Einführung in die Geschichte der Medizin.* 1898. 2nd rev. ed., by Karl Sudhell, Berlin, 1915.

f **Puschmann, Theodor; Pagel, Julius L.; and Neuburger, Max,** ed. *Handbuch der. Geschichte der Medizin.* 3 v. Jena, 1903–05. (Bibliography.)

g **Neuburger, Max.** *History of medicine:* V. 1, v. 2, pt. 1, London, 1910–1925. Tr. by Ernest Playfair from *Geschichte der Medizin,* 2 v. Stuttgart, 1906–11. (Bibliography.)

h **Osler, Sir William.** *Evolution of modern medicine.* Ed. by F. Garrison and others. New Haven, 1921. [Silliman memorial lectures.]

i **Buck, Albert H.** *Growth of medicine from the earliest times to about 1800.* New Haven, 1917.

j **Cumston, Charles G.** *History of medicine.* N. Y. and London, 1926. [(B153a) History of civilization.]

a. Recent brief survey of the principal topics in the progress of medical science. *b.* Usually regarded as the standard work in English. Traces the development of medical science from ancient Egypt through the Greek, Roman, Byzantine, Arabic, and Medieval times with increasing fulness of treatment for later periods. Nearly half the work is on the period since 1800. The narrative is closely packed with data especially of a biographical sort. Extensive chronological appendix. A book for consultation rather than reading. *c.* Standard one-volume German work. The English version contains revisions and additions by both the author and the translator, with especial reference to America. More comprehensive and thorough than *b* for earlier periods, but not so full on nineteenth century. For most purposes replaced by *b.* *d.* Monumental work on the subject. V. 1 devoted to antiquity and the middle ages; v. 2 to modern times. V. 3 is a history of epidemics. *e.* Readable series of lectures constructed on the biographical method, by one eminent authority and fully revised by another. *f.* Coöperative work by various specialists. Though the monographs are somewhat unequal in value, the work is valuable for reference purposes. *g.* Well-written narrative on broader lines, less overloaded with data and biographical details than *b* and *c.* By an eminent authority and translated under the supervision of Sir William Celer. V. 1 of translation includes part of v. 2 of original. *h.* Series of six lectures delivered in 1913 on Greek, Medieval, Renaissance, and Modern periods, with a general introduction and with a conclusion on the rise of preventive medicine. Excellent general survey of most important aspects of the subject.   GMD

i. Fascinating book, beautifully illustrated. Chapters on oriental medicine, the Arab renaissance, and the advance of surgery during medieval times are particularly interesting. Review, F. H. Garrison, *Yale Rev.* 7: 205, Oct. 1917. *j.* Summary for the general reader of the principal theories, books, and discoveries in the history of medicine from early times to the end of the eighteenth century. Review, (London) *Times Lit. Suppl.* 26:4, Jan. 6, 1927.   HRS

CULTURAL HISTORY, LITERATURE, ART, MUSIC

B661 **Magnus, Laurie.** *Dictionary of European literature designed as a companion to English studies.* London and N. Y., 1926.

Remarkably successful pioneer work covering the whole period since the submergence of classical antiquity and all the foreign literatures (including medieval and Renaissance Latin) which have any importance for the study of English. The titles include not only authors and important works, but also literary movements, types, and periods. (Metrical and rhetorical titles are properly excluded.) The articles, though necessarily short, are interesting, partly because the compiler has introduced well-chosen criticism and commentary as well as information.

                                                                              MWC

B662a **Loliée, Frederic.** *Short history of comparative literature from its earliest times to the present day.* N. Y., 1906. Tr. by M. D. Power from *Histoire des littératures comparées des origines au XXᵉ siècle,* 1903; 2nd ed., Paris, 1907.

   b **Wendell, Barrett.** *Traditions of European literature from Homer to Dante.* N. Y., 1920. (Bibliography.)

   c **Drinkwater, John,** ed. *Outline of literature.* 3 v. N. Y., 1923–24.

   d **Saintsbury, George B.,** ed. *Periods of European literature.* 12 v. N. Y., 1897–1907.

   e **Stern, Adolf.** *Geschichte der neueren Litteraturen.* 7 v. Leipzig, 1882.

   f **Zimmer, Heinrich** (and others). *Die romanischen Literaturen und Sprachen, mit Einschluss des Keltischen.* Berlin, 1909. [(B606) Hinneberg, *Die Kultur der Gegenwart.* v. 11, pt. 1.] (Excellent bibliographies.)

   a. The author attempts the impossible task of presenting a history of the literature of the whole world in 375 pages. He succeeds in making a striking and surprisingly readable summary, with interesting, if not very important generalizations. There are not a few inaccuracies, especially in the field of English and American literature, and a great many typographical errors. *b.* A survey of two thousand years of European literature, divided into five books dealing respectively with the traditions of Greece, Rome, Christianity, Christendom, and the Middle Ages. Based upon a course of lectures given repeatedly at Harvard University and intended to afford the present day American some acquaintance with the more important authors and developments of thought and literary expression and with their place in the intellectual heritage of today. Written in clear, simple, readable style by a master-hand.   FEF

   c. Hastily-written and perfunctory work which does not fulfill the promise of the title, and deserves mention only because of the rarity of "universal" histories of literature. Some of the chapters are written by the editor, some by contributors. *d.* Most notable attempt in English to write the history of European literature from the fall of Rome to the present time. This great purpose is largely defeated, however, by the failure of the editor to mature a significant or philosophical plan, and by the mechanical and encyclopedic method of some of the contributors. Two of the volumes display a breadth of view adequate to the idea of the series, and are valuable works of criticism:—*Dark Ages,* by W. P. Ker, and *First part of the seventeenth century,* by H. J. C. Grierson. There is no bibliographical material except in rare foot-notes. *e.* This elaborate survey begins with the beginning of the fourteenth century (Dante) and ends at about 1875, and includes not only the major fields, but also such minor literatures as the Portuguese, Roumanian, and many others. In the last volume there is a chapter on North American literature. The author has attempted to give unity to the discussion by treating all the phenomena of each period with reference to a leading idea. For instance, the last two volumes are called *Liberalism and Democracy* (middle of the nineteenth century) and *Realism and Pessimism* (third quarter of the century). *f.* Written by the best-equipped German specialists in their fields. The section devoted to the Celtic literatures and languages is particularly valuable for its comprehensiveness and for the comparative success of the various writers in relating the different branches of the Celtic civilization. MWC

B663a Saintsbury, George E. B. *History of criticism and literary taste in Europe from the earliest texts to the present day.* 1900–04. 2nd ed., 3 v., N. Y., 1902–06.

b Gayley, Charles M., and Scott, Fred N. *Introduction to the methods and materials of literary criticism.* Boston, 1899.

c Gayley, Charles M., and Kurtz, Benjamin P. *Methods and materials of literary criticism.* Boston, 1920.

a. Comprehensive, not very detailed survey; less searching than the scholar could wish in spite of the author's enormous reading; useful so far as its facts are concerned as a general work of reference; impaired in its judgments by the author's personal prejudices. V. 1. Deals with the classical and medieval period. V. 2. Begins with the Renaissance and ends with the close of the eighteenth century. V. 3. Treats of the romantic movement and the modern period. *b* and *c.* Two parts of a serial work, of which the final (third) volume has not appeared. *b.* Deals with the history of aesthetics and poetics from Aristotle to the present time. *c.* Presents the materials for the study of epic and lyric. The method is chiefly that of a bibliography, with extended comment indicating the character and content of the works cited. Useful work of reference. MWC

B664a *Grimm library.* 14 v. in 19. London, 1894–1909.

b *Popular studies in mythology, romance, and folk-lore.* 16 v. London, 1899–1908.

a. Series of volumes by various authors dealing with important themes in romantic literature and tracing them to their origins in primitive mythology and folk-lore. Although Arthurian and other Celtic topics predominate, the range is wide, embracing, for instance, classical, Hindu, and primitive American myths. The following titles will indicate the character of the themes:—*Cuchullin Saga,* by Eleanor Hull, 1898; *Legend of Perseus,* by E. S. Hartland, 3 v., 1894; *Legend of Sir Perceval,* by Jessie L. Weston, 2 v., 1906. *b.* Similar in content to the preceding, but containing briefer and less ambitious studies. Typical titles are: *Celtic Influence upon Medieval Romance,* by Alfred Nutt; *King Arthur and his Knights,* by Jessie L. Weston. MWC

B671a Sandys, John E. *History of classical scholarship.* 3 v. N. Y., 1903–08.

b Norden, Edouard. *Die Antike Kunstprosa vom VI Jahrhundert vor Christ bis in die Zeit der Renaissance.* 1 v. in 2. Leipzig, 1898, later editions, 1905, 1915–18.

a. Admirable history of classical scholarship since the sixth century B.C., with a great wealth of biographical detail. The characterization of the various great periods of civilization, though brief, is always illuminating. Pioneer work of great value in the history of humanism. WEL

b. Standard work of great erudition. The only attempt to give a complete account of the theory and practice of prose-style from its beginnings in Greece through the Renaissance. Of course the work is primarily devoted to the ancient art of style, and the prose-theories of the middle ages and the Renaissance are treated only as they are related to the prose of classical antiquity. The period of the church-fathers, however, is fully and excellently treated. MWC

B681 Gardner, Helen. *Art through the ages.* London and N. Y., 1927.

Discusses the development of the arts of all nations including India, China, and Japan, with a final chapter on contemporary art. Well-proportioned, conveniently organized, scholarly in background, and liberal in point of view. An admirable survey. Review, (London) *Times Lit. Suppl.* 26:901, Dec. 1, 1927. EBB, HRS

B682a Thieme, Ulrich, and Becker, Felix. *Allgemeines Lexikon der bildenden Künstler von der Antike bis zur Gegenwart.* V. 1–23. Leipzig, 1907 ff.

b Reinach, Salomon. *Apollo; an illustrated manual of the history of art throughout the ages.* 1905. Last rev. ed., N. Y., 1922. Tr. by F. Simmons from *Apollo, histoire des arts plastiques,* 1904; 4th ed., Paris, 1907. (Bibliography.)

c Van Dyke, John C., ed. *College histories of art.* 3 v. N. Y., 1894–96. Many later ed. [V. 1, J. C. Van Dyke, *Textbook of the history of painting,* 1894; new ed., N. Y., 1915 (Bibliography); v. 2, A. D. F. Hamlin, *Textbook of the history of architecture,* 1896; rev. ed., N. Y., 1922; v. 3, A. Marquand and A. L. Frothingham, Jr., *Textbook of the history of sculpture,* 1896; rev. ed., N. Y., 1911.]

d Lübke, Wilhelm. *Outlines of the history of art.* 1878. Rev. ed., largely rewritten by R. Sturgis, 2 v., N. Y., 1904. Tr. by C. Cook, from 7th ed. of *Grundriss der Kunstgeschichte,* 1860; 7th ed., 2 v. Stuttgart, 1876.

e Michel, André, ed. *Histoire de l'art depuis les premiers temps chrétiens jusqu'à nos jours.* V. 1–8 in 16. Paris, 1905–28. (Bibliographies.)

f Faure, Élie. *History of Art.* V. 1–4. N. Y., 1921–22. Tr. by W. Pach from *Histoire de l'art.* Paris, 1909–21.

g Springer, Anton H. *Handbuch der Kunstgeschichte.* 1 v. Later enlarged to 5 v. 11th ed. of v. 1, Stuttgart, 1920; 11th ed. of v. 2, Stuttgart, 1921; 10th ed. of v. 3, Stuttgart, 1918; 9th ed. of v. 4, Leipzig, 1914; 9th ed. of v. 5, Stuttgart, 1924.

h Marcel, Henry, ed. *Manuels d'histoire de l'art.* V. 1–6. Paris, 1908–23. [1, Louis Hourticq, *La peinture;* 2–3, François Benoit, *L'architecture;* 4, Gaston Migeon, *Les arts du tissu;* 5, Louis Gillet, *La peinture, XVIIe et XVIIIe siècles;* 6, Charles Picard, *La sculpture antique des origines à Phidias.*]

i **Marriott, Charles,** ed. *Universal arts series.* V. 1-4. N. Y., 1920-23.
[1, A. Fenn, *Design and tradition;* 2, C. Marriott, *Modern movements in painting;* 3, E. J. Sullivan, *Art of illustration;* 4, C. L. Hind, *Landscape painting from Giotto to the present day.*]

a. As yet incomplete (to Mander), but thoroughly done. Most fundamental source for biographical and other facts connected with art. *b.* Sound descriptive review of art in all its branches from the origins to the close of the nineteenth century. Readable but very brief on any one period and style; not analytical, but suggestive in its introductions and conclusions at the beginning and end of each chapter. *c.* Long well-known, but now out of date. *d.* Fully illustrated; covers all countries and periods; standard work, but now somewhat out of date and not always reliable. *e.* Coöperative work; best general history of art, although completed only to the end of the eighteenth century; clear and full. Omitting ancient art, and the arts of the Orient, it begins with the early Christian period. Uneven in excellence, as is every work of collaboration, yet in general every field and period are treated by a recognized expert. The minor arts receive adequate consideration. *f.* Stimulating, suggestive, interpretive, and synthetic treatment of all arts and all periods. M. Faure discusses as a philosopher and psychologist the relations of literature and music to the graphic and plastic arts and even attempts to forecast in the final volume art's future. *g.* By contrast, a good solid prosaic book. *h.* Each volume is intended to be a scholarly résumé, in some detail, of the separate arts in different periods with the idea of being both popular and instructive. Some volumes are very brilliant, all are good. Gillet is perhaps the best, very clear and logical; a good analysis of the elements of architecture which go to make up style. *i.* Incomplete series dealing with painting, sculpture, and the minor arts; distinctly popular, but written by good men.   EBS, HRS

B683 Pijoan y Soteras, Jose. *History of Art.* 3 v. N. Y. and London, 1927-28. (Bibliographies.) Tr. by R. L. Roys, *Historia del arte; el arte al traves de la historia,* 3 v., Barcelona, 1914-16.

Exceptionally valuable for the very large and well-chosen list of illustrations covering the whole history of art. The text is somewhat uneven in value, especially when dealing with controversial questions. Review of v. 1, 2, (London) *Times Lit. Suppl.* 26: 638, Sept. 22, 1927.   EBB

B684a Fergusson, James. *History of architecture in all countries, from the earliest times to the present day.* 1862-67. (Originally published as *Handbook of Architecture,* 1855.) 3rd rev. ed., by R. P. Spiers and R. Kerr, 5 v., London, 1893-1902.

   b **Fletcher, Banister,** and **Fletcher, Banister F.** *History of architecture on the comparative method.* 1896. 7th rev. ed., London, 1924. (Bibliography.)

   c **Kimball,˙Sidney,** and **Edgell, George H.** *History of architecture.* London and N. Y., 1918. [Harper's fine art series.]

   d **Choisy, Auguste.** *Histoire de l'architecture.* Paris, 1899.

   e **Simpson, Frederick M.** *History of architectural development.* 3 v. N. Y., 1909.

   f *Catalogue of books relating to architecture, construction and decoration in the Public Library of the city of Boston.* Boston, 1894. 2nd rev. ed., Boston, 1914.

g Dehio, George C., and **Bezold, Gustav von.** *Die kirchliche Baukunst des Abendlandes, historisch und systematisch dargestellt.* 2 v. and atlas. Stuttgart, 1887–1901.

a. A remarkable book for its time. Its generalizations are still recognized as true, but in details slightly out of date. *b.* Perhaps the best concise résumé of the history of architecture, giving both the facts and the comparative details, but above all valuable for its illustrations and plans. Excellent ready reference book. *c.* Still more concise, but a very satisfactory outline. *d.* Very scientific and structurally speculative. *e.* Complete narrative of continuous development, well arranged in topics, with excellent illustrations. *f.* Reliable and most useful. *g.* Pictures only; accurate; a very important aid to study. EBS, HRS

B685a Chase, George H., and **Post, Chandler R.** *History of sculpture.* N. Y., 1924. (Good bibliography.)

 b Post, Chandler R. *History of European and American sculpture from the early Christian period to the present day.* Cambridge, 1921. (Bibliography.)

 c Muther, Richard. *History of modern painting.* Rev. ed., continued by the author to the end of the nineteenth century. 4 v. N. Y., 1907. Tr. from *Geschichte der Malerei,* 5 v., Leipzig, 1899–1900.

a. Very successful summary, with sound generalizations. *b.* Scholarly and accurate in a smaller field. *c.* Comprehensive and reliable. EBS, HRS

B686a Knackfuss, Hermann, ed. *Künstler-Monographien.* Bielefeld, 1895 ff.

 b —— *Klassiker der Kunst in Gesamtausgaben.* Stuttgart, 1905 ff.

a. This series of inexpensive, richly illustrated, monographs includes volumes on many leading artists. They are written by scholars for a popular audience. Knackfuss himself has written the volumes on Dürer, Holbein the Younger, and Menzel. Many of them have been issued in English translation. SBF
b. Each volume consists of three parts: introduction, plates, and notes. The chief value of the series is in the plates, which in many cases show approximately all of the known works of the artist; but the introductions are carefully written by good scholars and are useful. Most of the 29 volumes that have appeared have been on artists from Giotto to Rembrandt; three on modern German artists. MWC

B691a Pratt, Waldo S. *History of music.* 1907. 4th ed., N. Y., 1911.

 b Hadow, William N., ed. *Oxford history of music.* 6 v. Oxford and N. Y., 1901–05.

 c Combarieu, Jules. *Histoire de la musique des origines au début du XXᵉ siècle.* 3 v. Paris, 1913–19.

 d Grove, Sir George. *Dictionary of music and musicians.* 4 v. London, 1879. Latest ed., by H. C. Colles, 5 v., London, 1927–28. American supplement, v. 6 of complete work, ed. by W. S. Pratt and C. N. Boyd, 1920. New ed., N. Y., 1928.

 e Riemann, Hugo. *Handbuch der Musikgeschichte.* 1904–13. Rev. ed., 2 v. in 3, Leipzig, 1922.

 f Parry, Sir Charles H. H. *Evolution of the art of music.* 1896. 4th ed., London, 1905. [International scientific series.]

a. Compendious reference book for students. Encyclopedic, it touches practically every phase of the subject from primitive music to the developments of the late nineteenth century. Large number of biographical notes. *b.* Fully illustrated and documented account from origins of polyphony through the late nineteenth century. V. 1 and 2, most scholarly and detailed treatment in English of the polyphonic schools. Entire work authoritative. *c.* Most important general history in French since Fetis. French contributions to the art fully treated. Social and intellectual backgrounds touched on. The least controversial volume is the first, which contains the author's theory of the origin of music and an excellent study of the music of antiquity. *d.* In spite of disproportion and omissions, the standard reference work in English. *e.* Scholarly, if ponderous, account, thoroughly illustrated with musical quotations, treating the subject from antiquity to the end of the eighteenth century.   RDW

f. Brief survey of the development of musical form from its elements in folksong to program music and other forms of modernism. The title is exact; not a history of music.   MWC

BIOGRAPHICAL DICTIONARIES

B701a Michaud, Joseph, and **Michaud, Louis G.** *Biographie universelle, ancienne et moderne.* 52 v. 1811–28; supplement v. 53–85, 1852–62. Rev. ed., 45 v. Paris, 1853–66. (Bibliographies.)

b Hoefer, Jean C. F., ed. *Nouvelle biographie générale.* 46 v., Paris, 1851–66. (Bibliographies.)

c Vapereau, Louis Gustav. *Dictionnaire universel des contemporains.* 1858. 6th rev. ed., Paris, 1892.

d Thomas, Joseph, ed. *Lippincott's universal pronouncing dictionary of biography and mythology.* 1870–74. 4th rev. ed., 2 v., Philadelphia, 1915.

e Oettinger, Edouard M., and **Schram-MacDonald, Hugo,** ed. *Moniteur des dates.* V. 1–6, Dresden, 1866–68; v. 7–8, 1st supplement, Leipzig, 1873–80; v. 9, 2nd supplement, Leipzig, 1882.

f Haydn, Joseph. *Book of dignities.* 1851. 3rd ed., by H. Ockerby, London, 1894.

g Patrick, David, and **Groome, Francis H.** *Chamber's biographical dictionary: the great of all times and nations.* Philadelphia and London, 1898; latest ed. 1920.

h Hyamson, Albert M. *Dictionary of universal biography of all ages and of all peoples.* N. Y. and London, 1916.

i Garollo, Gottardo. *Dizzionario biografico universale.* 2 v., Milano, 1907. (O22a)

a. Excellent general biographical dictionary with articles varying in length in accordance with the importance of the subjects; greatly improved in the 2nd ed., which was issued to offset the appearance of *b,* whose similarity of character gave rise to important litigation. The student will frequently find it desirable to consult both if possible, as they often supplement one another and as the better article on a particular personage may sometimes be in one, sometimes in the other. Both works are excellent specimens of the historical scholarship of their period. *c.* Convenient supplement to *a* and *b,* with brief articles on celebrities living at the date of publication of the successive editions, each of which contains materials not in the others. *d.* Admirable general biographical dictionary with a vast number of brief notices, especially valuable for authoritative pronunciation of names. *e.* Despite the French title the contents are in German. Many thousands of brief notices averaging four to six lines each. Surpasses all other works in the number of names contained. Various useful appendices of chronological character. *f.* Contains chronological lists of rulers and of important civil and ecclesiastical officials; particularly complete on the British side.   GMD

g and *h.* Good small biographical dictionaries. *g.* Marks pronunciation of difficult foreign names and has an index of selected pseudonyms and nicknames. *h.* Gives only brief information of the "title a line" type. *i.* Useful because it includes a larger proportion of Italian names than other biographical dictionaries.   HRS

B702a *Who's Who: an annual biographical dictionary.* London, 1849 ff. (L23*a*)

 b *Who's Who in America.* Chicago, 1899 ff. (X28)

 c *Who's who and why: a biographical dictionary of men and women of Canada and Newfoundland.* Toronto, 1921 ff. (Z801)

 d *Wer ists? Unsere Zeitgenossen. Zeitgenossen Lexikon enthaltend. Biographien nebst Bibliographie.* Leipzig, 1905 ff. (No issues 1915–21.) (P22*c*)

 e *Qui êtes-vous? Annuaire des contemporains.* Paris, 1908–1924. (No issue 1911–23, 1909–10 in 1 v.) (M25)

 f *Chi è?* 1908. Rev. ed., Roma, 1928. (O22*b*)

Annual or biennial dictionaries containing brief outlines of careers of eminent living people, especially titled persons, officials, and authors, usually compiled from data furnished by the individual concerned. Scores of such publications now exist, the more important of which are here cited. *a.* The standard work of its kind. Principally British, but containing the names of a few foreigners. With annual obituary list. *b.* Biographical dictionary, revised and reissued biennially, of the notable men and women of the United States. Contains pronunciation of difficult names, birth and residence statistics, and geographical index. *c.* Annual illustrated biographical record of men and women of the time, not only of Canada, but of all the British possessions in the western hemisphere. Not alphabetical, but supplied with an index. Has one or two portraits on each page. *d, e,* and *f.* German, French and Italian works similar to *a.*   HLK

COLLECTED BIOGRAPHIES

B711a Abbott, Evelyn, ed. *Heroes of the nations.* 52 v. London and N. Y., 1890–1919. [1, E. Abbott, *Pericles;* 2, E. Armstrong, *Lorenzo de' Medici;* 3, R. N. Bain, *Charles XII;* 4, C. R. Beasley, *Prince Henry the Navigator;* 5, H. R. F. Bourne, *Sir Philip Sidney;* 6, A. G. Bradley, *Owen Glyndower;* 7, N. Brooks, *Abraham Lincoln;* 8, W. C. Church, *Ulysses S. Grant;* 9, W. B. Clark, *The Cid Campeador;* 10, Edmund Curtis, *Roger of Sicily;* 11, H. C. W. Davis, *Charlemagne;* 12, R. Dunlop, *Daniel O'Connell;* 13, C. Firth, *Oliver Cromwell;* 14, J. B. Firth, *Constantine the Great;* 15, J. B. Firth, *Augustus Caesar;* 16, C. R. L. Fletcher, *Gustavus Adalphus;* 17, W. W. Fowler, *Julius Caesar;* 18, A. Gardner, *Julian, Philosopher and Emperor;* 19, W. D. Green, *Wm. Pitt, Earl of Chatham;* 20, J. A. Harrison, *George Washington;* 21, A. Hassall, *Louis XIV;* 22, J. W. Headlam, *Bismarck;* 23, E. F. Henderson, *Blucher;* 24, T. Hodgkin, *Theodoric the Goth;* 25, W. Irving, *Columbus;* 26, E. Jenks, *Edward Plantagenet;* 27, C. L. Kingsford, *Henry V;* 28, S. Lane Poole, *Saladin;* 29, L. M. Larson, *Canute the Great;* 30, E. A. Lees, *Alfred the Great;* 31, F. A. MacNutt, *Fernando Cortez;* 32, D. S. Margoliouth, *Mohammed;* 33, H. Maxwell, *Robert the Bruce;* 34, W. O'C. Morris, *Hannibal;* 35,

W. O'C. Morris, *Napoleon;* 36, W. O'C. Morris, *Wellington;* 37, Mrs.
M. O. W. Oliphant, *Jeanne d'Arc;* 38, P. Orsi, *Cavour;* 39, J. B. Perkins,
Richelieu; 40, F. Perry, *Saint Louis;* 41, A. W. Pickard-Cambridge,
Demosthenes; 42, I. L. Plunkett, *Isabel of Castille;* 43, R. Putnam, *Charles
the Bold;* 44, R. Putnam, *William the Silent;* 45, W. F. Reddaway,
Frederick the Great; 46, W. C. Russell, *Horatio Nelson;* 47, L. Sergeant,
John Wyclif; 48, J. L. Strachan-Davidson, *Cicero;* 49, F. M. Stenton,
William the Conqueror; 50, B. I. Wheeler, *Alexander the Great;* 51, H. A.
White, *Robert E. Lee;* 52, P. F. Willert, *Henry of Navarre.*]

  b *Foreign statesmen.* 11 v. London, 1896–1906. [1, J. F. Bright, *Joseph
II;* 2, J. F. Bright, *Maria Theresa;* 3, K. D. Ewart, *Cosmo de Medici;*
4, F. Harrison, *William the Silent;* 5, A. Hassall, *Mazarin;* 6, T. Hodgkin,
Charles the Great; 7, M. A. S. Hume, *Philip II of Spain;* 8, W. H.
Hutton, *Philip Augustus;* 9, R. Lodge, *Richelieu;* 10, E. Martinengo-
Cesaresco, *Cavour;* 11, P. F. Willert, *Mirabeau.*]

    Biographical series. Many volumes of merit, but varying greatly in quality.
Review of *a,* v. 2, J. H. Robinson, *A.H.R.* 2:134, Oct. 1895; v. 6, E. P. Cheyney,
A.H.R. 7:545, Apr. 1902; v. 8, H. V. Boynton, *A.H.R.* 3:569, Apr. 1898; v. 12,
V. Coffin, *A.H.R.* 6:567, Apr. 1899; v. 13, G. Jones, *A.H.R.* 7:130, Oct. 1901;
v. 14, C. H. Haskins, *A.H.R.* 11:432, Jan. 1906; v. 15, G. W. Botsford, *A.H.R.*
9:130, Oct. 1903; v. 18, A. C. McGiffert, *A.H.R.* 1:318, Jan. 1896; v. 19, A. G.
Porritt, *A.H.R.* 7:559, Apr. 1902; v. 20, *A.H.R.* 12:897, July 1907; v. 21, J. B.
Perkins, *A.H.R.* 1:335, Jan. 1896; v. 26, G. E. Howard, *A.H.R.* 8:117, Oct.
1902; v. 27, E. P. Cheyney, *A.H.R.* 8:121, Oct. 1902; v. 28, J. R. Jewett, *A.H.R.*
7:107, July 1899; v. 29, W. E. Lunt, *A.H.R.* 18:789, July 1913; v. 31, G. P.
Winship, *A.H.R.* 15:670, Apr. 1910; v. 32, J. R. Jewett, *A.H.R.* 11:880, July
1906; v. 36, R. M. Johnston, *A.H.R.* 10:692, Apr. 1905; v. 38, *A.H.R.* 20:204,
Oct. 1914; v. 39, H. E. Bourne, *A.H.R.* 6:561, Apr. 1899; v. 40, J. W. Thompson,
A.H.R. 7:120, Oct. 1901; v. 42, *A.H.R.* 25:88, Oct. 1919; v. 43, J. W. Thompson,
A.H.R. 14:343, Jan. 1909; v. 45, E. F. Henderson, *A.H.R.* 10:652, Apr. 1905;
v. 50, *A.H.R.* 6:113, Oct. 1900. Review of *b,* v. 3, F. Schwill, *A.H.R.* 5:332,
Jan. 1900; v. 5, S. B. Fay, *A.H.R.* 9:609, Apr. 1904; v. 6, *A.H.R.* 4:192, Oct.
1898; v. 8, H. M. Stephens, *A.H.R.* 2:370, Jan. 1898; v. 9, W. Walker, *A.H.R.*
3:384, Jan. 1897; v. 10, W. R. Thayer, *A.H.R.* 4:725, July 1899; v. 11, F. M.
Fling, *A.H.R.* 5:130, Oct. 1899.   HRS

ACADEMIES

B921 In many countries, especially on the European continent, there exist academies of sciences which publish abstracts or in some cases the complete
papers presented at their meetings. For many of these academies, the
papers interesting to the historian will be found either in an historical
section or in a philological-historical section of the publications. The sub-
sections on Academy and Society Publications of §§ M.P.S., etc., should
be consulted for these series.   HRS

PERIODICALS

    Periodicals must always be of great value to the historian, containing as they
do so much material not afterwards printed in book form. Naturally those
reviews which have to do specifically with history are of the greatest value,
partly because of the critical notices of new books which appear in them, by

means of which the student is able to follow the growing literature of his subject.
The list of periodicals which follows is merely representative, not by any means
exhaustive.

B941a American Periodicals. (General)

1, *American review of reviews*, N. Y., 1890 ff. (monthly) ; 2, *Living age*,
Boston, 1844 ff. (weekly), (as *Littell's living age*, 1844–1896), (monthly) ;
3, *Century*, N. Y., v. 1–117, 1870–1929 (as *Scribner's Monthly*, 1870–1881) ;
4, *Harper's Monthly magazine*, N. Y., 1850 ff. (monthly) ; 5, *Scribner's
magazine*, N. Y., 1887 ff. (monthly) ; 6, *Atlantic monthly*, Boston, 1857 ff.
(monthly) ; 7, *North American Review*, Boston, 1815–1877, N. Y., 1878 ff.
(now quarterly) ; 8, *Forum*, N. Y., 1886 ff. (monthly) ; 9, *Yale Review*,
New Haven, 1892 ff. (quarterly).

b British Periodicals. (General)

1, *Fortnightly review*, London, 1865 ff. (fortnightly) ; 2, *Contemporary
review*, London, 1866 ff. (monthly) ; 3, *Nineteenth century and after*,
London, 1877 ff. (monthly) ; 4, *Westminster review*, 181 v., London, 1824–
1871 (monthly) ; 5, *Edinburgh review*, Edinburgh and London, 1802 ff.
(quarterly) ; 6, *Quarterly review*, London, 1809 ff. (quarterly) ; 7, *National
review*, London, 1883 ff. (monthly) ; 8, *Dublin review*, London, 1836 ff.
(monthly).

c French Periodicals. (General)

1, *Revue des Deux Mondes*, Paris, 1829 ff. (fortnightly) ; 2, *Le corre-
spondant*, Paris, 1843 ff. (monthly) ; 3, *Revue de Paris*, Paris, 1894 ff.
(fortnightly) ; 4, *Revue politique et litteraire; revue bleue*, Paris, 1863 ff.
(monthly) ; 5, *Mercure de France*, Paris, 1890 ff. (monthly) ; 6, *Revue
hebdomadaire du Journal des débats*, Paris, 1909 ff. (weekly) ; 7, *Journal
des savants*, n. series, Paris, 1903 ff.

d Italian Periodicals. (General)

1, *Nuova antologia di lettere, scienze, ed arti*, Firenze and Roma, 1866 ff.
(monthly) ; 2, *Rivista d'Italia*, Roma, 1898 ff. (monthly).

e German and Austrian Periodicals. (General)

1, *Deutsche Rundschau*, Berlin, 1874 ff. (monthly) (P946) ; 2, *Oesterreichische Rundschau*, Wien, 1904 ff. (weekly) ; 3, *Westermann's Monatshefte*, Braunschweig, 1856 ff. (monthly) ; 4, *Velhagen und Klasings
Monatschrift*, Leipzig, 1886 ff. (monthly) ; 5, *Preussische Jahrbücher*,
Berlin, 1838 ff. (monthly). (P947)

f General Historical Reviews.

1, *American historical review*, N. Y., 1896 ff. (quarterly) ; 2, *English
historical review*, London, 1886 ff. (quarterly) ; the two leading historical
reviews in English; of the two the English Historical Review is less
general and more national in its interest than is the American review ;
3, *Cambridge history journal*, London, 1923 ff. (annual) ; 4, *Historical
outlook*, Philadelphia, 1909 ff. (monthly) (as *History teachers' magazine*,
1909–18) ; 5, *History*, London, 1912 ff. (monthly) ; two journals devoted
primarily to the interests of teachers of history; 6, *Economic history
review*, London, 1927 ff. (annual) ; 7, *Journal of economics and business
history*, Cambridge, 1928 ff. (quarterly) ; 8, *Social Science Abstracts*,
N. Y., 1929 ff. (monthly), containing systematic abstracts of new information in the field of the social sciences ; 9, *Revue historique*, Paris,
1876 ff. (bi-monthly) ; 10, *Revue des questions historiques*, Paris, 1866 ff.
(quarterly) ; 11, *Revue d'histoire diplomatique*, Paris, 1877 ff. (quarterly) ;
12, *Revue de synthèse historique*, Paris, 1900 ff. (bi-monthly) ; 13, *Revue
des études historiques*, Paris, 1851 ff. (quarterly). Of the French journals the *Revue Historique* is well known for its excellent critical reviews
and bibliographical notes, while the *Revue de Synthèse Historique* aims to
deal with the synthesis of history—its relations to religions, sciences,
literature and the arts, to historical psychology as well as to economic

and political history in the endeavor to make use of all of these subjects and achieve a unified whole; 14, *Historische Zeitschrift*, München, 1859 ff.; deals mainly with German history and contains excellent critical reviews; 15, *Historische Vierteljahrsschrift*, Leipzig, 1898 ff. (as *Deutsche Zeitschrift für Geschichteswissenschaft*, 14 v., Freiburg, 1889–1898 (quarterly); valuable for its supplements containing classified bibliographical lists of current works; 16, *Historisches Jahrbuch*, Bonn, 1880 ff. (quarterly); 17, *Archiv für Kulturgeschichte*, Berlin, 1903 ff. (quarterly) and *Isis*, Bruxelles, 1913 ff. (quarterly); reviews devoted to cultural history; 18, *Revue de l'histoire des religions*, 86 v., Paris, 1880–1922 (quarterly); and 19, *Revue d'histoire ecclesiastique*, Louvain, 1900 ff. for the subject of church history (quarterly).

g International Relations.

1, *Foreign affairs*, N. Y., 1922 ff. (quarterly); 2, *American journal of international law*, N. Y., 1907 ff. (quarterly); 3, *Zeitschrift für Völkerrecht*, Breslau, 1906 ff. (bi-monthly); 4, *Current history*, N. Y., 1914 ff. (monthly).

h Current Politics and Political Science.

1, *Political science quarterly*, N. Y., 1886 ff. (quarterly); 2, *New Statesman*, London, 1913 ff. (weekly); 3, *American political science review*, Baltimore, 1907 ff. (quarterly); 4, *Revue politique et parlementaire*, Paris, 1894 ff. (monthly).

i Illustrated Periodicals.

1, *Illustrated London news*, London, 1843 ff. (weekly); 2, *L'Illustration*, Paris, 1843 ff. (weekly): 3, *Illustrierte Zeitung*, Leipzig, 1843 ff. (weekly); 4, *Harper's weekly*, 62 v., N. Y., 1857–1916 (weekly). HRS

SECTION C

NEAR EAST IN ANCIENT TIMES

Editor

ALBERT TEN EYCK OLMSTEAD

Professor of Oriental History in the Oriental Institute of the
University of Chicago

CONTENTS

INTRODUCTION

No field of history has such fascinating interest as this one which deals with the most ancient written records of human activities and of organized states. Few triumphs of modern scholarship have been more romantic than the decipherment of the hieroglyphics of ancient Egypt and of the cuneiform writings of the early peoples of the Mesopotamian regions. The secrets of the daily life—even the very bodies—of these peoples who lived centuries before the rise of Greece and Rome have been revealed by the excavations conducted by skilled archeologists. Not only have the meager records transmitted by Hebrew and Greek writers concerning the ancient nations of the Nile and Euphrates valleys been substantiated and amplified but records of kings and regnal years have been recovered for centuries hitherto accounted prehistoric or legendary.

So rapidly, indeed, are new discoveries enlarging and defining knowledge of the ancient Near East that historical works concerning them become superannuated as speedily as do those on contemporary times. Many works but recently accounted the highest products of scholarship find no place in the accompanying lists because they have been entirely superseded by works embodying later results. It is necessary, moreover, to incorporate in the notices concerning many of the books listed the word "superannuated" though they are the latest substantial works on the subject, for historical writers have been unable to keep pace with the excavators and research workers. Even the scholarly periodicals cannot keep the eager student up to date on this most ancient field of history; he must turn to the daily newspaper to secure the latest data on the second or fourth pre-Christian millennium. Consequently the selection of titles for this section has been a peculiarly difficult problem. The safest solution, namely, omission in case of doubt, has usually been followed. In some cases, however, works have been included because they are widely known or frequently found on the shelves of public libraries; the critical reviews will put the reader on his guard in using such books.

Though it may seem that the political records of these most ancient states have little more than a curious interest, there is no question of the vital importance for the history of religion attributable to the wealth of materials which are reshaping the conceptions of religious developments among the Israelites and the Greeks. No less significance for the history of law, of art, and of language and literature attaches to the discovery of the code of Hammurabi, to the works of skilled craftsmanship recently unearthed at Ur and at Egyptian Thebes, to the unriddling of the Hittite language, and to many another amazing revelation of the venerable antecedents of modern culture. Much of this material is only available in technical journals and reports, but so far as possible an effort has been made to give the reader and student references to works which will provide suitable introductions to these most interesting subjects. For obvious reasons, disproportionate space has been given to books on topics related to Old Testament history, but even so, it has been quite impossible to cite other than the most obvious and indispensable works from this voluminous literature.

Finally, it should be observed that this section includes, in addition to the works lying wholly in its field, those books which deal with the entire field of ancient history and consequently devote their earlier pages to some consideration of the history of the ancient Near East, though their main content relates to the history of Greece and Rome.

BIBLIOGRAPHY

C1a Weidner, Ernst F. *Die Assyriologie, 1914-1922, wissenschaftliche Forschungsergebnisse in bibliographischer Form.* Leipzig, 1922.

b *Bibliographie zum Jahrbuch des Deutschen Archäologischen Instituts, 1920-1922.* Berlin, 1924.

The best general collection of bibliographical data for this field will be found in (G3) *Orientalische Bibliographie* and its predecessors. This work may be supplemented by (C955) *Die orientalistische Literaturzeitung* and other journals listed later in this section. *a.* Systematic lists of books, pamphlets, and periodical articles published in western European languages in the nine years indicated. The word Assyriology is interpreted broadly enough to include not merely the Assyrians, but also their neighbors and the various cultural aspects of their life as well as their history. *b.* Similar list covering the various phases

of archeology in the Orient and in the Mediterranean countries for the three
years indicated in the title. For Palestine, cf. the work of (G2a) Roericht and
(G2b) Thomsen.   GMD

Library collections.—Valuable collections are found in the university libraries
of Chicago, Columbia, Cornell (Eisenlohr collection), Harvard, Illinois, Michigan
(papyri), Johns Hopkins, Pennsylvania (Jastrow and Caspari collections), Princeton (Paton and Brünnow collections), and Yale (American Oriental Society
library, 6,000 v.), Egyptology is especially represented at Chicago and Cornell;
Assyriology at Chicago, Illinois, Pennsylvania, and Yale; Hebrew and Iranian
at Columbia. There is an Oriental Room, with good collections in all fields, at
the New York Public Library. The General Theological Seminary, New York
City, has the Schrader collection of Assyriology. The Cleveland Public Library
possesses the White collection of Orientalia. Important collections of Biblical
literature exist in the libraries of General Theological Seminary, New York City;
Princeton Theological Seminary, Princeton, N. J.; Union Theological Seminary,
New York City; and Western Theological Seminary, Evanston, Ill. Collections
of Hebraica are found in the libraries of Dropsie College, Philadelphia; Hebrew
Union College, Cincinnati; and Jewish Theological Seminary, New York City.
                                                                              AHS

ENCYCLOPEDIAS AND WORKS OF REFERENCE

C21 **Cheyne, Thomas K.,** and **Black, John Sutherland,** ed. *Encyclopaedia
biblica, a critical dictionary of the literary, political, and religious history,
the archaeology, geography, and natural history of the Bible.* 4 v. N. Y.
and London, 1899–1903.

Represents the extreme higher criticism; peculiar personal views are often
advanced; but the work is packed with learned information. Reference should
also be made to (F21a) Hastings, *Dictionary of the Bible,* (F22) Hastings,
Encyclopædia of religion and ethics, (F25) *Catholic encyclopedia,* and (F28)
Jewish encyclopedia.   JMPS

GEOGRAPHY

C41 **Hogarth, David G.** *Nearer east.* 1902. New ed., N. Y., 1915. [Apple-
ton's world series, regions of the world.]

The first part deals with the physical conditions exhibited in the region; the
second, with man, his distribution, grouping, and life conditions. Review, I. Bowman, *Bulletin of the Amer. Geog. Soc.* 38:86, Feb., 1906.   ATO

C42a **Smith, Sir George A.,** and **Bartholomew, John G.** *Atlas of the historical
geography of the Holy Land.* London, 1915.

b **Smith, Sir George A.** *Historical geography of the Holy Land, especially
in relation to the history of Israel and of the early church, 1894.* 14th ed.,
N. Y., 1908. (Bibliography.)

c ——— *Jerusalem, the topography, economics, and history from the earliest
times to A. D. 70.* 2 v. London and N. Y., 1907-08.

a. Contains an introduction with the names and authorities, and reviews the
problems; the detail maps have colored contours, others illustrate different periods
or racial or economic factors. Some of the maps rank among the best for ancient
oriental history. Review, J. A. Montgomery, *Jewish Quar. Rev.* 8:505, Apr.,

1918. *b.* One of the most brilliant examples of anthropo-geography. *c.* Applies the method in more detail to Jerusalem, with special attention to archeology. Review, J. A. Montgomery, *Jewish Quar. Rev.* 1:123, July 1910.   JMPS

C43a Anderson, John G. C. *Asia Minor.* London, 1903. [Murray's handy classical maps.]

  b Ramsay, Sir William M. *Historical geography of Asia Minor.* London, 1890. [Royal Geographical Society, Supplementary papers, v. 4.]

  a. Contains a map of Asia Minor indicating ancient sites and lines of communication and having colored contours. *b.* Standard manual of historical geography for the region. Cf. also (D35, 3) Hommel.   ATO

SOURCE BOOKS AND COLLECTIONS OF SOURCES

C61a Wachsmuth, Curt. *Einleitung in das Studium der alten Geschichte.* Leipzig, 1895.

  b Schaefer, Arnold. *Abriss der Quellenkunde der griechischen und römischen Geschichte.* 1867. 4th rev. ed. by H. Nissen, 2 v., Leipzig, 1889.

  c Strehl, Willy, and **Soltau, Wilhelm.** *Grundriss der alten Geschichte und Quellenkunde.* 1901. 2nd rev. ed., 2 v., Breslau, 1913.

  a. Useful description of the main sources for the history of the ancient Near East, Greece, and Rome in a single volume, though badly in need of revision. *b.* Still useful, particularly for the literary sources. *c.* Scholarly survey of ancient history, oriental, Greek, and Roman, with a discussion of the sources and of the main German works.   DMCF

C62a Botsford, George W., and **Botsford, Lillie S.** *Source-book of ancient history.* N. Y., 1912. (Bibliographies.)

  b Davis, William S. *Readings in ancient history, illustrative extracts from the sources.* 2 v. Boston, 1912–13. [1, *Greece and the East*; 2, *Rome and the West*.]

  c Webster, Hutton. *Readings in ancient history.* Boston, 1913.

  Brief collections of extracts from ancient sources illustrative of history prior to A. D. 800, with emphasis on the Greek and Roman periods. *a.* Review, V. Adams, *History Teacher's Magazine* 4:27, Jan. 1913. *b.* Superior to *a.* and *c.* in its selections for the history of the ancient Near East. Review, V. Adams, *History Teacher's Magazine* 5:194, June 1914. For better selections, though prepared for a special purpose, cf. (C305*a*) Barton, *Archaeology and the Bible,* and (C305*b*) Rogers, *Cuneiform parallels to the Old Testament.*   ATO

C71a Birch, Samuel, ed. *Records of the past, being English translations of the Assyrian and Egyptian monuments.* 12 v. London, 1874–81.

  b Sayce, Archibald H., ed. *Records of the past, being English translations of the ancient monuments of Egypt and western Asia, new series.* 6 v. London, 1889–93.

  Originally represented the best scholarship; now entirely antiquated; the materials are now all available in later, authoritative books. Cf. (C81) Breasted, *Ancients records of Egypt,* and (C91 *b, c, d*) and (C305 *a, b*).   ATO

C81 Breasted, James H. *Ancient records of Egypt, historical documents from the earliest times to the Persian conquest, collected, edited, and translated.*

with commentary. 5 v. Chicago, 1906–07. [W. R. Harper, Ancient records, 2nd series.] (Bibliography.)

Standard translation of all Egyptian records of a more narrowly historical character. Review, C. Johnston, *A.H.R.* 12:858, July 1907.   TGA

C82 Budge, Sir E. A. T. Wallis, ed. and tr. *Book of the dead, the chapters of the coming forth by day: the Egyptian text according to the Theban recension in hieroglyphic, ed. from papyri with translation and vocabulary.* 3 v. London, 1897. Rev. ed. of tr., 3 v. in 1, London and N. Y., 1923.

Best edition at present available, but all translations of this very obscure work should be used with caution.   TGA

C83 Winckler, Hugo. *Tell el Amarna letters.* N. Y., 1896. Tr. by J. M. P. Metcalf from *Die Thontafeln von Tell-el-Amarna,* Berlin, 1896. [(C91c) E. Schrader, Keilinschriftliche Bibliothek.]

English translation of a large number of these important letters which threw much light upon the history not only of Egypt under the eighteenth dynasty but of the nations of southwestern Asia. The best edition of these letters is, however, by Knudtzon in (C91d) *Vorderasiatische Bibliothek.*   ATO

C84a Egypt Exploration Fund. *Memoirs.* London, 1885 ff.

   b ———— *Archaeological survey of Egypt.* London, 1893 ff.

   c Egypt Exploration Fund, Graeco-Roman Branch. *Memoirs.* London, 1898 ff.

   d British School of Archaeology in Egypt and Egyptian Research Account. *Publications.* London, 1896 ff.

Publications of inscriptions, papyri, and other results of archeological research, conducted under British auspices in Egypt. *c.* This remarkable collection of papyri throws a flood of light on the Ptolemaic and Roman periods. *d.* Embodies the researches of Professor Flinders Petrie and his co-workers. Similar publications have been issued under the auspices of Egyptian, French, and German organizations and of special expeditions which have conducted excavations in Egypt.   GMD

C91a Olmstead, Albert T. *Assyrian historiography, a source study.* Columbia, Mo., 1916. [University of Missouri studies, social science series.] (Extensive bibliography.)

   b Harper, Robert F., ed. *Assyrian and Babylonian literature, selected translations.* N. Y., 1901. [World's great books, Aldine edition.]

   c Schrader, Eberhard, ed. *Keilinschriftliche Bibliothek; Sammlung von assyrischen und babylonischen Texten in Umschrift und Uebersetzung,* 7 v. in 6. Berlin, 1889–1915.

   d ———— *Vorderasiatische Bibliothek.* 7 v. Leipzig, 1907–16.

   e Luckenbill, D. D., ed. *Ancient records of Assyria and Babylonia.* 2 v. Chicago, 1927.

a. Full discussion of source problems in Assyrian history. Review, R. W. Rogers, *A.H.R.* 20:692, Apr. 1917. *b.* The only fairly complete collection of Assyrian and Babylonian sources available in English, though badly antiquated. *c.* Fuller collection in German, also antiquated. *d.* Up to date, but only a few volumes have been published. For adequate translations of the inscriptions which bear on the Bible cf. (C305a) Barton, *Archaeology and the Bible*, and (C305b) Rogers, *Cuneiform parallels to the Old Testament. e.* Best translation of the Assyrian royal annals. Review, I. W. Raymond, *Hist. Outlook*, 18:229, May 1927.   ATO

C96a King, Leonard W., and **Thompson, Reginald C.,** ed. *Sculptures and Inscription of Darius the Great on the rock of Behistun in Persia; a new collation of the Persian, Susian, and Babylonian texts, with English translations.* London, 1907.

b Weissbach, Franz H. *Die Keilinschriften der Achämeniden.* Leipzig, 1911. [(C91d) Vorderasiatische Bibliothek.]

a. Edition of chief source for the earlier Persian history. *b.* Complete collection of all cuneiform sources for the Achaemenid period.   AVWJ

SHORTER GENERAL HISTORIES

C101a Breasted, James H. *Ancient times, a history of the early world.* Boston, 1916. (Brief bibliography.) New ed.: *Conquest of Civilization*, N. Y. and London, 1926.

b Westermann, William L. *Story of the ancient nations, a textbook for high schools.* N. Y., 1912. [Twentieth century textbooks.] (Brief bibliography.)

c Botsford, George W. *History of the ancient world.* N. Y., 1911. (Brief bibliography.)

d Goodspeed, George S. *History of the ancient world.* 1904. Rev. ed. by W. S. Ferguson and S. P. R. Chadwick, N. Y., 1912. (Brief bibliography.)

e Morey, William C. *Outlines of ancient history, for the use of high schools and academies.* 1906. Rev. ed. under the title *Ancient peoples*, N. Y., 1915. (Brief bibliography.)

f Myers, Philip V. N. *Ancient history.* 1882. Rev. ed., Boston, 1916. (Brief bibliography.)

g Webster, Hutton. *Ancient history.* Boston, 1913. (Brief bibliographies.)

h West, Willis M. *Ancient world from the earliest times to 800 A. D.* 1902. Rev. ed., Boston, 1913. (Brief bibliography.)

i Rostovtsev, Mikhail I. *History of the ancient world.* Tr. from the Russian by J. D. Duff. Oxford, 1927.

Though all these works were written as text-books for high school use, they are also the most convenient introductions to the field of ancient history to A. D. 800 as a whole available for the general reader. All these works, especially *a.*, are excellently illustrated; all have been frequently reprinted with more or less revision. *a, b, c,* and *d.* Works of specialists in the field of ancient history and consequently authoritative accounts. *a.* Because of its scholarship and its attractive style affords the best available account in brief compass of the ancient Near East. *b.* and *c.* Excel in their accounts of ancient Greece. *b.* Especially commendable for its treatment of the economic factors. *i.* Excellent brief review of ancient history. Adequate attention is given to the Near East. Especially notable for the economic interpretation and for the elaborate and beautiful illustrations, many of them new. Review, A. T. Olmstead, *A.H.R.* 32:831, July, 1927.   ATO, DMCF

C102a Myres, John L. *Dawn of history.* London and N. Y., 1911. [Home university library.]

b Hogarth, David G. *Ancient East.* London and N. Y., 1915. [Home university library.]

c Hall, Harry R. H. *Ancient history of the Near East from the earliest times to the battle of Salamis.* London and N. Y., 1913.

a. and *b.* Together afford very brief surveys by experts. *c.* Valuable for its correlation of the oriental civilizations with those of the Aegean. Review, J. H. Breasted, *A.H.R.* 19:582, Apr. 1914. ATO

LONGER GENERAL HISTORIES

C121 Cambridge *ancient history.* Ed. by J. B. Bury, S. A. Cook, and F. E. Adcock. V. 1–7, Cambridge, Eng., and N. Y., 1921–26. [1, *Egypt and Babylonia to 1580 B. C.; 2, Egyptian and Hittite empires to 1000 B. C.; 3, Assyrian empire; 4, Persian empire and the West.*] (Extensive bibliographies and 2 v. of plates.)

Similar to the *Cambridge* (I121) *Modern and* (H121) *Medieval* histories, each chapter written by an expert. Planned to cover the period prior to A. D. 325. As compared with the modern and medieval series, much more attention is devoted to non-political history. Discussions of origins are especially good, in particular the introductory chapters on prehistory. The most up-to-date history of the peoples considered. Each volume contains a goodly number of especially prepared maps and plans. Review, v. 1, D. D. Luckenbill, *Amer. Jour. of Semitic Languages,* 41:66, Oct. 1924; R. W. Rogers, *A.H.R.* 29:316, Jan. 1924; v. 2, R. W. Rogers, *ibid.* 30:578, Apr. 1925. V. 3. Includes the history of Assyria from B. C. 1100 to its fall, of the later Babylonian empire, of Egypt to the Persian invasion, of the kingdoms of Israel and Judah, of the peoples and states of Asia Minor to the Persian conquest, and of the Greek peoples in the era of colonization. Review, R. W. Rogers, *A.H.R.* 31:755, July 1926. V. 4. Completes the history to B. C. 478 by dealing with early classical Greece, Persia, Carthage, the Etruscans, and various cultural topics. ATO

C122a Rawlinson, George. *Five great monarchies of the ancient eastern world, or the history, geography, and antiquities of Chaldaea, Assyria, Babylon, Media, and Persia, collected and illustrated from ancient and modern sources.* 1862–67. 2nd rev. ed., 3 v., London, 1871. Several reprints.

b ——— *Sixth great oriental monarchy, or the geography, history, and antiquities of Parthia, collected and illustrated from ancient and modern sources.* London and N. Y., 1873. Later reprints.

c ——— *Seventh great oriental monarchy, or the geography, history, and antiquities of the Sassanian or new Persian empire, collected and illustrated from ancient and modern sources.* 2 v. London, 1876. Later reprints.

d ——— *History of ancient Egypt.* 2 v., London, 1881. Reprint, N. Y., 1882.

Formerly standard works; now badly antiquated; still chiefly useful as the only works containing references to all the passages in the Greek and Roman authors relating to the various periods of Persian and Parthian history and culture. Well illustrated. ATO

C123a Maspero, Sir Gaston C. C. *Dawn of civilization, Egypt and Chaldea.* 1884, 5th ed., reprint, N. Y., 1922. Ed. by A. H. Sayce and tr. by M. L. McClure from *Histoire ancienne des peuples de l'orient classique,* v. 1, *Les origines, Egypte et Chaldée,* Paris, 1894. (Extensive bibliography.)

b —— *Struggle of the nations, Egypt, Syria, and Assyria.* 1897, 2nd ed., London, 1910. Ed. by A. H. Sayce and tr. by M. L. McClure from *Histoire ancienne des peuples de l'orient classique,* v. 2, *Les premières melées des peuples,* Paris, 1896. (Extensive bibliography.)

c —— *Passing of the empires, 850 B. C. to 330 B. C.* N. Y., 1900. Ed. by A. H. Sayce and tr. by M. L. McClure from *Histoire ancienne des peuples de l'orient classique,* v. 3, *Les empires,* Paris, 1899. (Extensive bibliography.)

d —— *Histoire ancienne des peuples de l'Orient.* 1875, 6th rev. ed., 1904; 7th ed., reprint, Paris, 1905.

a., b., and *c.* Most elaborate presentation of the ancient history of the Near East, but not entirely up to date even when published. *a.* Even the latest reprint entirely inadequate. *d.* Excellent summary of the larger work; especially good on Egypt. Review, C. H. Toy, *A.H.R.* 9:770, July 1904. ATO

C124 Meyer, Eduard. *Geschichte des Altertums.* V. 1, 3, 4, 5 in 5 v. Stuttgart, 1884–1902. [1, pt. 1, *Einleitung, Elemente der Anthropologie,* 4th ed., 1921; pt. 2, *Die ältesten geschichtlichen Völker und Kulturen bis zum sechzehnten Jahrhundert,* 4th ed., 1921; 3, *Das Perserreich und die Griechen, bis zu den Friedensschlüssen von 448 und 446 vor Christus,* 2nd ed., 1912; 4, *Das Perserreich und die Griechen, Athen vom Frieden von 446 bis zur Capitulation Athens im Jahre 404 vor Christus,* 2nd ed., 1912; 5, *Das Perserreich und die Griechen, der Ausgang der griechischen Geschichte,* 3rd ed., 1921.] (Detailed bibliography, largely German.) Supplements: *Die ältere Chronologie Babyloniens, Assyriens und Aegyptens,* 1925; *Die Zeit der aegyptischen Grossmachts,* 2nd ed., 1928.

Standard work in German, though still incomplete. The most noteworthy contributions are the introduction on anthropology and the section on the most ancient times rather than the more exhaustive treatment of the Greco-Persian period. ATO

C125 Cavaignac, Eugène. *Histoire de l'antiquité.* 4 v. Paris, 1913–20.

Ends at about B. C. 110. The latest and most complete attempt by a trained scholar to furnish an extended survey for substantially the whole field of pre-Christian history. Especially important for the incorporation of the results of recent studies by French and Belgian scholars, in the economic history of the period. Unfortunately defaced by many inaccuracies. Review, H. J. Cunningham, *E.H.R.* 29:540, July 1914; H. S. Jones, *E.H.R.* 35:435, July 1920.

DMCF

C126 Bilabel, Friedrich, and **Grohmann, A.** *Geschichte Vorderasiens und Aegyptens vom 16. Jahrhundert v. Chr. bis auf die Neuzeit.* V. 1. Heidelberg, 1927.

V. 1, by Bilabel, is a general sketch from the 16th to the 11th century B.C., with detailed investigation of various problems, giving many new views. ATO

C127a **Morgan, Jacques de.** *Préhistorie orientale.* 3 v. Paris, 1925–1927.

b **Blanckenhorn, M.** *Steinzeit Palästina, Syriens und Nordafricas.* Berlin, 1921.

a. Full synthesis of existing information on the origins and developments of civilization; admirable, illuminating, and indispensable for beginnings of history. Review, A. Vincent, *Rev. des Quest. Hist.* 104:148, Jan. 1926; 107:420, Oct. 1927. *b.* Brief but excellent survey of the present situation of prehistoric studies in the Near East. ATO

EGYPT

C201 **Maspero, Sir Gaston C. C.** *Egyptian archaeology.* London, 1887. Tr. by A. B. Edwards from *L'archéologie égyptienne,* Paris, 1887. 6th ed., *Manual of Egyptian archaeology and guide to the study of antiques in Egypt,* N. Y., 1914, tr. by A. S. Johns from 4th ed., Paris, 1911.

Best introduction to the subject; a necessary foundation for the study of Egyptian history. Numerous illustrations. JHB

C202a **Breasted, James H.** *History of Egypt from the earliest times to the Persian conquest.* 1905. 2nd ed., 1909. Reprint, N. Y., 1924.

b ——— *History of the ancient Egyptians.* 1908. Reprint, N. Y., 1911. [Historical series for Bible students.] (Bibliography.)

a. Standard history of Egypt, attractively written and beautifully illustrated. Review, W. Max Müller, *A.H.R.* 11:866, July 1906. *b.* Abridged form of *a.* The contributions of Professor Breasted and others to (C121) *Cambridge ancient history* should be consulted for the results of later researches. TGA

C203 **Petrie, Sir William M. Flinders,** ed. *History of Egypt.* 6 v. London, 1898–1905. Various reprints of the several volumes, with slight revisions. [1, W. M. F. Petrie, *From the earliest times to the sixteenth dynasty; 2, id., During the seventeenth and eighteenth dynasties; 3, id., From the nineteenth to the thirtieth dynasties; 4,* J. P. Mahaffy, *Under the Ptolemaic dynasty; 5,* J. G. Milne, *Under Roman rule; 6,* S. Lane Poole, *In the middle ages.*] (Bibliographies.)

V. 1–3. Comprehensive account; useful for the student; too technical for the general reader. Review, T. E. Peet, *Journal of Egyptian Archaeology,* 9:123, 1923. Cf., for reviews of v. 4 (D352d); v. 5, (E391); v. 6, (G271). TGA

C204a **Champollion, Jean François.** *Lettre à M. Dacier, secretaire perpétuel de l'académie des inscriptions, relative à l'alphabet des hiéroglyphes phonétiques employés par les anciens Egyptiens pour inscrire sur les monuments les titres, les noms, et les surnoms des souverains grecs et romains.* Paris, 1822.

b ——— *Précis du système hiéroglyphique des anciens Egyptiens, ou, recherches sur les élémens premiers de cette écriture sacrée, sur leurs diverses combinaisons, et sur les rapports de ce système avec les autres méthodes graphiques égyptiennes,* 2 v. 1824. 2nd rev. ed., including *a,* Paris, 1827–28.

c **Moret, A.** *Le Nil et la civilisation égyptienne.* Paris, 1927. [L'évolution de l'humanité.] [Eng. tran. in (B153a) History of civilization.]

a. First publication of the decipherment of the Egyptian hieroglyphics. *b.* First systematic study of the hieroglyphics. JHB *c.* One of the best of the series; not a narrative, but a synthesis of social, religious, and intellectual development. Review, R. Weill, *Rev. Critique* 61:390, Oct. 15, 1927.

ATO

BABYLONIA AND ASSYRIA

C251 Handcock, Percy S. P. *Mesopotamian archaeology, an introduction to the archaeology of Babylonia and Assyria.* London and N. Y., 1912.

This handbook of archeology for the region is the best available introduction to the study of the history and culture of Babylonia and Assyria. Review, I. M. Price, *Amer. Jour. of Semitic Languages,* 29:63, Oct. 1912.

DDL

C252a Goodspeed, George S. *History of the Babylonians and Assyrians.* N. Y., 1902. [Historical series for Bible students.] (Bibliography.)

   b Johns, Claude H. W. *Ancient Assyria.* Cambridge, Eng., and N. Y., 1912. [Cambridge manuals of science and literature.]

   c ——— *Ancient Babylonia.* Cambridge, Eng., and N. Y., 1913. [Cambridge manuals of science and literature.]

   d Winckler, Hugo.—*History of Babylonia and Assyria.* N. Y., 1907. Tr. and ed. by J. A. Craig from *Das alte Westasien.* [(B166) Helmolt, History of the world.]

   e Woolley, C. Leonard. *Sumerians.* London, 1929.

a. Good single volume survey, which needs revision at many points in light of later discoveries and researches. *b.* and *c.* Convenient chronological summaries of information from inscriptions. *d.* Brilliant but erratic; antiquated. *e.* Brief but excellent sketch of Babylonian history to the end of the First Dynasty of Babylon. Emphasizes the results of the latest excavations. Review, A. T. Olmstead, *A.H.R.* 34:864, July 1929.

ATO

C253a Rogers, Robert W. *History of Babylonia and Assyria.* 1900. 6th rev. ed., 2 v., N. Y., 1915. (Excellent bibliography.)

   b King, Leonard W. *History of Sumer and Akkad, an account of the early races of Babylonia from prehistoric times to the foundation of the Babylonian monarchy.* London and N. Y., 1910. [History of Babylonia and Assyria, v. 1.]

   c ——— *History of Babylon from the foundation of the monarchy to the Persian conquest.* London and N. Y., 1915. [History of Babylonia and Assyria, v. 2.]

a. Largely taken up with a fascinating and accurate account of the discovery and decipherment of the cuneiform inscriptions. V. 2. Presents the narrative history with the omission of unessential details. Review, A. T. Olmstead, *History Teacher's Magazine,* 7:31, Jan. 1916. *b.* and *c.* Full histories from the sources, but without bibliography. Review, A. T. Olmstead, *Amer. Jour. of Theol.,* 20:277, Apr. 1916.

ATO

C254a Olmstead, Albert T. *History of Assyria.* N. Y. and London, 1923.

   b Smith, Sidney. *Early history of Assyria.* London, 1927.

a. Standard history of Assyria; the narrative is enlivened by full use of numerous letters and other material of human interest; excellent illustrations. Review, R. W. Rogers, *A.H.R.* 29:529, Apr. 1924; T. J. Meek, *Amer. Jour. of Semitic Languages,* 41:140, Jan. 1925.

DDL

b. Detailed investigation in the light of the latest discoveries.   ATO

Also cf. (C121) *Cambridge ancient history;* and Delaporte, *Mesopotamia, the civilizations of Babylonia and Assyria,* N. Y., 1925 [(B153a) History of civilization]; tr. by V. G. Childe from *La Mésopotamie, les civilisations babylonienne et assyrienne* [(B153b) L'évolution de l'humanité].

C255a Gadd, Cyril J. *Fall of Nineveh, the newly discovered Babylonian chronicle, no. 21,901, in the British Museum, ed. with transliteration, translation, notes, etc.* Oxford and N. Y., 1923.

b Lewy, Julius. *Forschungen zur alten Geschichte Vorderasiens.* Leipzig, 1925. [*Mitteilungen der Vorderasiatisch-Aegyptischen Gesellschaft,* 1924, pt. 2.]

Both contain transliterations and translations of the chronicle, which throws important light not only on the overthrow of Assyria and the accompanying rise of the new Babylonian empire and of Media, but also upon the Jewish and Egyptian history of the period. Both works expound the significance of the new data which are among the most notable recent additions to knowledge of ancient Oriental history.   GMD

PALESTINE: OLD TESTAMENT HISTORY

C301 Kent, Charles F. *Student's Old Testament, logically and chronologically arranged and translated.* V. 1–5, N. Y., 1904–14. (Brief bibliographies.)

New translation on the basis of an emended text, with indication of the various literary sources. Does not contain Proverbs and the didactic poems announced to appear in v. 6. Review, A. S. Carrier, *Amer. Jour. of Theol.* 10:137, Jan. 1906.   JMPS

C302a *International critical commentary.* Ed. by Samuel R. Driver and others. Edinburgh and N. Y., 1895 ff.

b *Cambridge Bible for schools and colleges.* Ed. by John J. Stewart Perowne, Alexander F. Kirkpatrick and Alexander Nairne. 59 v. Cambridge, Eng., and N. Y., 1880–1912.

c *(New) Century Bible.* Ed. by Walter F. Adeney. 34 v. London and N. Y., 1901–13.

d *Expositor's Bible.* Ed. by William Robertson Nicoll. 50 v. London and N. Y., 1887–96. Later cheaper reprints.

e *Westminster commentaries.* Ed. by Walter Lock. London, 1899 ff.

Leading commentaries in English on the Bible, embodying the results of modern scholarship. In each series reprints and revised editions of individual volumes have often appeared. Most of the volumes in these several works are edited by British scholars, but some are by Americans, notably in *a.* In each of the series members of various denominations are represented among the editors of the several volumes, though Anglicans predominate in *a., b.,* and *e.,* and nonconformists in *c* and *d. a.* Thoroughly scholarly work addressed to scholars; full attention is paid to textual criticism and to other critical problems which are treated in the light of the most recent researches. It may, however, be easily used by general readers, as the sections which demand a knowledge of Hebrew are distinguished by being printed in smaller type. *b.* Complete for the Old and New Testaments, but with only a few volumes of the Apocrypha. For some books the text of the authorized version is used, for others, the revised version, and in a few cases both versions are given in separate editions. The text is presented with introduction and notes, primarily intended to elucidate the English texts. Small handy volumes intended for student use. *c.* Complete; similar in form and method to *b.* Usually follows the text of the revised version. Aims to "present in lucid form the results of the best modern scholarship." *d.* Complete. Avoids mere annotation and critical apparatus; distinctly expository and homiletic. "It aims at bringing out the general teaching of each book and of each of the divisions into which the book naturally falls." *e.* Thus far only fifteen volumes have appeared, representing much less than one half the necessary number. Based on the English text and addressed to the general reader, thus contrasting with *a.* The object "is primarily exegetical, to interpret the author's meaning to the present generation." It tries "to combine a hearty acceptance of critical principles with loyalty to the Catholic faith." WGC

C303a Gray, George B. *Critical introduction to the Old Testament.* London, 1912. N. Y., 1913.

  b Driver, Samuel R. *Introduction to the literature of the Old Testament.* 1891. 11th ed., N. Y., 1913. [International and theological library.] (Bibliographies.)

  c Orr, James. *Problem of the Old Testament, considered with reference to recent criticism.* N. Y., 1906. [Bross library.]

a. Brief sketch of biblical literature from the modern point of view. *b.* Represents a more cautious critical attitude; in spite of slight revision in the numerous editions, it is no longer abreast of present day opinion. *c.* Ablest criticism of the modern critical theory. Review, K. Fullerton, *Amer. Jour. of Theol.* 10:705, Oct. 1906. JMPS

C304a Smith, Henry P. *Old Testament history.* N. Y., 1903. [International theological library.]

  b Kent, Charles F. *History of the Hebrew people.* 2 v. N. Y., 1896–97. [Historical series for Bible students.]

  c —— *History of the Jewish people during the Babylonian, Persian, and Greek periods.* N. Y., 1899. [Historical series for Bible students.]

  d Peritz, Ismar J. *Old Testament history.* N. Y., 1915. (Bibliography.)

  e Wade, George Woosung. *Old Testament history.* 1901. 8th rev.. ed., N. Y., 1916. (Bibliography.)

a. An interpretation of the Old Testament rather than a history of the Hebrews or of Palestine. The approach is critical, but little attention is paid to extra-biblical sources. Review, J. A. Kelso, *Amer. Jour. of Theol.* 8:382, Apr. 1904. *b.* Briefer outline which permits the reader to work out the critical problems for himself; closes with the Babylonian conquest. Review, G. F. Moore, *A.H.R.* 2:708, July 1897. *c.* Similar work continuing the narrative to B. C. 165. Review, G. F. Moore, *A.H.R.* 5:547, Apr. 1900. *d.* Text-book, with moderately critical view. Review, A. R. Gordon, *Harvard Theological Rev.* 9:241, Apr. 1916. *e.* Similar to *d.* Extends to the post-exilic period. Review, J. D. Davis, *Amer. Jour. of Theol.* 6:775, Oct. 1902. For full discussions of the Hebrews in their relation to the other peoples of the ancient Near East, cf. (C202a) Breasted, *History of Egypt;* (C123c) Maspero, *Passing of the empires;*

(C253a) Rogers, *History of Babylonia and Assyria;* (C254) Olmstead, *History of Assyria.* JMPS

C305a Barton, George A. *Archaeology and the Bible.* 1916. 3rd ed., Philadelphia, 1921. [Green fund.]

  b Rogers, Robert W. *Cuneiform parallels to the Old Testament.* N. Y., 1912. (Selected bibliography.)

  c Jastrow, Morris, Jr. *Hebrew and Babylonian tradition..* N. Y., 1914. [Haskell lectures.]

  d Grant, Elihu. *Orient in Bible times.* Philadelphia and London, 1920. (Bibliographies.)

  e McCurdy, James F. *History, prophecy, and the monuments, or Israel and the nations.* 1894–1901. New ed., 3 v. in 1, N. Y., 1911.

  f Handcock, Percy S. P. *Archaeology of the Holy Land.* London and N. Y., 1916.

a. Prepared for the American Sunday School Union. After brief sketches of Near Eastern history and of the excavations, a translation is given of all the inscriptions bearing directly on the Bible. Where there is dispute as to the influences exerted, conservative and liberal opinions are given without comment. Numerous small cuts from an atlas of Biblical illustration. Review, M. Kellner, *Harvard Theological Rev.* 11:208, Apr. 1918. *b.* Presents the cuneiform material in *a.* in much fuller form and adds more background material, with elaborate illustrations. Review, D. G. Lyon, *Harvard Theological Rev.* 7:133, Jan. 1914. *c.* Compares Babylonian and Hebrew thought and seeks to minimize the influence of the former on the latter. Review, J. Hoschander, *Jewish Quart. Rev.* 5:615, Apr. 1915. *d.* Describes the ancient Near East as background for the Bible. *e.* Excellent study, now somewhat out of date. *f.* Well illustrated sketch; based on recent excavations; confined to Palestine proper.

ATO

PEOPLES OF SYRIA

C351a Paton, Lewis B. *Early history of Syria and Palestine.* N. Y., 1901. [Semitic series.] (Bibliography.)

  b Rawlinson, George. *History of Phoenicia.* London and N. Y., 1889.

  c Pietschmann, Richard. *Geschichte der Phönizier.* Berlin, 1889 [(B162) Oncken, Allgemeine Geschichte.]

  d Clay, Albert T. *Empire of the Amorites.* New Haven, 1919. [Yale oriental series.]

  e Kraeling, Emil G. H. *Aram and Israel or the Aramaeans in Syria and Mesopotamia.* N. Y., 1918. [Columbia University oriental studies, v. 13.]

  f MacAlister, Robert A. Stewart. *Philistines, their history and civilization.* London, 1913. [Schweich lectures.]

  g Montgomery, James A. *Samaritans, the earliest Jewish sect, their history, theology, and literature.* Philadelphia, 1907. [Bohlen lectures.] (Bibliography.)

  h Contenau, G. *Civilization Phénicienne.* Paris, 1926.

  i Hogarth, David G. *Kings of the Hittites.* London, 1926.

a. Scholarly survey of Syrian history, including relations with neighboring peoples, down to the Persian conquest. *b.* Latest detailed account in English, now sadly antiquated. *c.* Valuably supplements *b.* at many points. *d.* Deals with the Amorites as founders of both an empire and a culture; many of the conclusions are contested. Review, A. T. Olmstead, *Amer. Jour. of Theol.* 23:525, Oct. 1919. *e.* While chiefly interested in the relations of the Arameans with the Hebrews, it gives a good picture of the various Aramean states of Syria and Mesopotamia. Review, D. D. Luckenbill, *Amer. Jour. of Theol.* 23:127, Jan. 1919. *f.* Collects the available materials on the Philistines, with especial reference to their Aegean connections and their archeology. Review, A. T. Olmstead, *History Teacher's Magazine,* 6:25, Jan. 1915. *g.* Minutely describes everything known about the Samaritans, in both ancient and modern times. *h.* Latest and best history; includes history, religion, art, and literature. Review, A. Vincent, *Rev. des Quest. Hist.* 107:428, Oct. 1927. *i.* Brief account, not of the Hittite empire, but of the later rulers of North Syria who are more or less correctly called "Hittite". Review, A. T. Olmstead, *Art and Archæology,* 23:191, Apr. 1927.

For the minor peoples good accounts are often found in the general histories already mentioned, cf. (C121) *Cambridge ancient history,* (C123) Maspero, (C124) Meyer, and the several works listed under (C304). ATO

ASIA MINOR

C401a Garstang, John. *Land of the Hittites, an account of recent explorations and discoveries in Asia Minor, with descriptions of the Hittite monuments.* London, 1910. (Bibliography.)

b Meyer, Eduard. *Reich und Kultur der Chetiter.* Berlin, 1914. [Kunst und Altertum, alte Kulturen im Lichte neuer Forschung.]

c Olmstead, Albert T.; Charles, Benson B.; and Wrench, Jesse E. *Travels and studies in the Nearer East.* Ithaca, N. Y., 1911. [Hittite inscriptions, v. 1, pt. 2.]

d Alexander, Leigh. *Kings of Lydia and a rearrangement of some fragments from Nicolaus of Damascus.* Princeton, 1914.

a. Devoted especially to the geography and to a detailed examination of the monuments. *b.* Brilliant historical sketch. *c.* Latest publication of texts in the pictographic writing. Review, D. D. Luckenbill, *Classical Philology,* 7:257, Apr. 1912. *d.* Only recent volume in English on Lydia. No book as yet gives a general view of the results of the recent discoveries at the Hittite capital by the Deutsche Orient-Gesellschaft or of those at Sardis in Lydia by the Princeton expedition. For the most recent general account in English of the Hittites, cf. (C121) *Cambridge ancient history.* ATO

C402 Buckler, William H., and Calder, William M., ed. *Anatolian studies presented to Sir William Mitchell Ramsay.* London and N. Y., 1923. [University of Manchester publications.]

Collection of thirty-two studies by as many scholars, more than half of whom represent nationalities other than British. They cover a wide range of topics and chronology relating to the history of Asia Minor, and present the results of the most recent scholarship. Review, W. W. Hyde, *A.H.R.* 30:117, Oct. 1924; A. J. Toynbee, *E. H. R.* 39:451, July 1924. ATO

PERSIA

C451 Geiger, Wilhelm, and **Kuhn, Ernst,** ed. *Grundriss der iranischen Philologie.* 2 v. Strassburg, 1895–1904.

Series of essays by leading Iranian scholars which furnishes the fundamentals for Iranian study.   AVWJ

C452a Justi, Ferdinand. *Geschichte des alten Persiens.* Berlin, 1878–79. [(B162) Oncken, Allgemeine Geschichte.]

 b Prásek, Justin V. *Geschichte der Meder und Perser.* Gotha, 1906–10. [Handbücher der Altengeschichte.] (Extensive bibliography.)

a. Scholarly compendium, now somewhat out of date. *b.* Discusses in detail the earlier history of the Medes and Persians. Review, A. V. W. Jackson, *A.H.R.* 13: 119, Oct. 1907. The best description of the Achæmenid empire is found in (C123c) Maspero, *Passing of the empires.* The older account in (C122) Rawlinson, *Ancient monarchies,* is supplemented by his later works on the Parthian and Sassanid kingdoms which still remain useful. The most recent account of all these periods, though not directly from the sources, is contained in (U302c) Sykes, *History of Persia.* The ancient history and archeology of Persia are presented in relation to geography in (U302d) Jackson, *Persia past and present.*
                                                                              AVWJ

C453 Rogers, Robert W. *History of Persia.* N. Y., 1929. Full up-to-date narrative history of the Achæmenid empire.   ATO

LEGAL HISTORY

C551a Johns, Claude H. W. *Babylonian and Assyrian laws, contracts, and letters.* N. Y., 1904. [Library of ancient inscriptions, v. 6.] (Bibliography.)

 b Harper, Robert F. *Code of Hammurabi, king of Babylon, about 2250 B. C., autographed text, transliteration, translation.* . . . 1904. 2nd ed., 2 v., Chicago, 1904.

 c Kohler, Josef and **Ungnad, Arthur.** *Hammurabis Gesetz.* 5 v. Leipzig, 1904–11.

 d King, Leonard W., ed. *Letters and inscriptions of Hammurabi, king of Babylon, about B. C. 2200, to which are added a series of letters of other kings of the first dynasty of Babylon; the original Babylonian texts,* . . . *with English translations.* . . . 3 v. London, 1898–1900. [Luzac's Semitic text and translation series.]

a. Good collection of translations of non-historical sources. Contains good translation of the code of Hammurabi which will also be found in (C305a) Barton, *Archaeology and the Bible,* with a comparison, paragraph by paragraph, with the biblical codes; and in (C305b) Rogers, *Cuneiform parallels to the Old Testament.* *b.* Standard edition of the code. *c.* Technical legal discussion of the code; utilizes all the business documents. *d.* Original publication of the letters; given better in (C91d) *Vorderasiatische Bibliothek.*   ATO

ECONOMIC AND SOCIAL HISTORY

C571a Wallon, Henri. *Histoire de l'esclavage dans l'antiquité.* 1847–48. Rev. ed., Paris, 1879.

b Ward, Cyrenus Osborne. *Ancient lowly, a history of the ancient working people from the earliest known period to the adoption of Christianity by Constantine.* 1889–1900. New ed., 2 v., Chicago, 1906. (Bibliography.)

c Meyer, Eduard. *Kleine Schriften.* 1910. 2nd ed., Halle, 1925. [*Zur Theorie und Methodik der Geschichte; Die wirtschaftliche Entwicklung des Altertums; Die Sklaverei im Altertum; The development of individuality in ancient history; Der Gang der alten Geschichte, Hellas und Rom; Alexander der Grosse und die Absolute Monarchie; Die Mosesagen und die Lewiten; Der Ursprung des Tribunats und die Gemeinde der vier Tribus; Untersuchungen zur Geschichte der Gracchen; Kaiser Augustus.*] V. 2, Halle, 1925.

Contributions to the economic and social history of the ancient world in general, though mainly relating to the Greek and Roman periods. The widespread existence of slavery and its importance in the economic, social, and political life of antiquity are properly emphasized. *a.* Still the best general account of the subject but needs to be supplemented and corrected by later studies, such as that in *c.* *b.* Written with a socialistic bias. Review of *c.*, V. Ehrenberg, *Hist. Zeit.* 133:265, 1925.

DMCF

CULTURAL HISTORY: GENERAL

C601a Erman, Adolf. *Life in ancient Egypt.* London and N. Y., 1894. Tr. by H. M. Tirard from *Aegypten und Aegyptisches Leben im Altertum,* 1885–87. Rev. ed. by Herman Ranke, Tübingen, 1922–23.

b Steindorff, Georg. *Die Blütezeit des Pharaonenreichs.* 1900. 2nd ed., Leipzig and Bielefeld, 1926. [Monographien zur Weltgeschichte.]

c Maspero, Sir Gaston C. C. *Popular stories of ancient Egypt.* N. Y. and London, 1915. Tr. by Mrs. C. H. W. Johns from *Les contes populaires de l'Égypte ancienne,* 1882, 4th ed., Paris, 1911.

a. Only full description of everyday life in Egypt; now antiquated, but there is a new edition of the German original. Fully illustrated. Review, T. G. Allen, *Amer. Jour. of Semitic Languages,* 40:142, Jan. 1924. *b.* Brilliant brief statement of Egyptian culture. *c.* Gives the most important sources which are absent from (C81) Breasted, *Ancient records of Egypt;* chiefly valuable for cultural history.

JHB.

C602a Jastrow, Morris, Jr. *Civilization of Babylonia and Assyria, its remains, language, history, religion, commerce, law, art, and literature.* Philadelphia and London, 1915. [Westbrook lectures.]

b Sayce, Archibald H. *Babylonians and Assyrians, life and customs.* N. Y., 1899. [Semitic series.]

c Meissner, Bruno. *Babylonien und Assyrien.* 2 v. Heidelberg, 1920–25. [Kulturgeschichtliche Bibliothek, v. 1–2.] (Good bibliography, largely German.)

d Delaporte, Louis. *Mesopotamia, the Babylonian and Assyrian civilizations.* N. Y., 1928. [(B153*a*) History of civilization.] Tr. from *La Mesopotamie, les civilisations babylonienne et assyrienne.* Paris, 1923. [(B153*b*) L'évolution de l'humanité.]

a. General view of the civilization of the Tigris-Euphrates valleys. Review, D. D. Luckenbill, *Amer. Jour. of Semitic Languages,* 33:252, Apr. 1917. *b.* Brief, good view of cultural developments, now largely supplanted by *a.* *c.* Deals with the cultural life in its broadest aspect. *d.* Latest work on the subject. Review, R. W. Rogers, *A.H.R.* 28:726, July 1923. DDL

C603 MacAlister, Robert A. S. *History of civilization in Palestine.* Cambridge, Eng. and N. Y., 1912. [Cambridge manuals of science and literature.] (Bibliography.)

Archeological view of the culture of Palestine, both Hebrew and non-Hebrew. Review, G. A. Barton, *Amer. Jour. of Semitic Languages,* 29:225, Apr. 1913.
ATO

C604 De Burgh, William G. *Legacy of the ancient world.* London and N. Y., 1924. (Bibliography.)

Belongs to the type of books (cf. D603 and E601) which have recently attempted to demonstrate the contributions of Greece and Rome to modern civilization, but is the only one to include in its scope the more ancient nations of the Near East. Emphasizes religious factors, notably the religion of Israel. Review, L. Van Hook, *A.H.R.* 30:120, Oct. 1924. GMD

C605 Hammerton, John A., ed. *Wonders of the past: the romance of antiquity and its splendours.* 4 v. N. Y. and London, 1923–24.

The main archeological discoveries of modern times in the Old World and America described in a series of popular articles, mostly by eminent specialists. Sumptuously illustrated. DMCF

CULTURAL HISTORY: RELIGION

C621a Breasted, James H. *Development of religion and thought in ancient Egypt.* N. Y., 1912. [Morse lectures.]

  b Steindorff, Georg. *Religion of the ancient Egyptians.* N. Y. and London, 1905. [American lectures on the history of religions.]

  c Erman, Adolf. *Handbook of Egyptian religion.* London and N. Y., 1907. Tr. by A. S. Griffith from *Die ägyptische Religion,* Berlin, 1905. [Handbücher der Königlichen Museen zu Berlin.]

a. and *b.* Brief topical presentations of the chief features of the religion of ancient Egypt in lecture form. *a.* Later and much superior to *b.* in its exposition of the historical evolution of Egyptian religion. Review of *a.,* N. Schmidt, *A.H.R.* 19:133, Oct. 1913. *c.* Fully illustrated manual. TGA

C622a Jastrow, Morris, Jr. *Aspects of religious belief and practice in Babylonia and Assyria.* N. Y. and London, 1911. [American lectures on the history of religions.]

  b —— *Die Religion Babyloniens und Assyriens.* 2 v. Giessen, 1902–12.

a. Somewhat popular presentation in English of the main results of *b.,* which is a monumental work addressed to scholars. Review of *a.* J. Morgenstern, *Amer. Jour. of Theol.* 16:450, July 1912. DDL

C623a **Smith, Henry P.** *Religion of Israel, an historical study.* N. Y., 1914.

b **Barton, George A.** *Religion of Israel.* N. Y. and London, 1918. [Religious science and literature series.] (Brief bibliographies.)

c **Peters, John P.** *Religion of the Hebrews.* Boston and London, 1914. [Handbooks on the history of religions.] (Selected bibliography.)

d **Badè, William F.** *Old Testament in the light of today, a study in moral development.* Boston, 1915.

a. First class summary of the history of the Hebrew religion from the modern point of view. *b.* Less ambitious sketch in text-book form. Review, K. Fullerton, *Harvard Theological Rev.* 12:455, Oct. 1919. *c.* Much fuller presentation; adopts the critical, historical method but is conservative in tone. *d.* Non-technical, topical presentation of Hebrew religious thought addressed to the general reader.

JMPS

C624a **Darmesteter, James,** and **Mills, Lawrence H.,** tr. *Zend avesta.* 3 v. Oxford, 1880–87. [Sacred books of the east, v. 4, 23, and 31.]

b **Jackson, Abraham V. Williams.** *Zoroaster, the prophet of ancient Iran.* N. Y. and London, 1899. (Bibliography.)

c **Moulton, James H.** *Early Zoroastrianism.* London, 1913. [Hibbert lectures.]

a. Latest translation in English of the Persian sacred books. *b.* Attempt on the basis of later legends to reconstruct the life of the founder of Persia's early religion. Review, C. D. Buck, *Amer. Jour. of Theol.* 3:756, Apr. 1899. *c.* Argues for an earlier dating of the Avesta and of Zoroaster. Review, E. W. Hopkins, *Harvard Theological Rev.* 8:258, Apr. 1915.

AVWJ

CULTURAL HISTORY: ART

C681 **Perrot, Georges,** and **Chipiez, Charles.** *History of art.* 12 v. N. Y., 1883–94. Tr. by W. Armstrong and I. Gonino from v. 1–6 of *Histoire de l'art dans l'antiquité,* 10 v., Paris, 1881-1914. [1–2, *Ancient Egypt;* 3–4, *Chaldaea and Assyria;* 5–6, *Phoenicia and its dependencies;* 7–8, *Sardinia, Judaea, Syria, and Asia Minor;* 9, *Persia;* 10, *Phrygia, Lydia, Caria, and Lycia;* 11–12, *Primitive Greece, Mycenean art.* French original, v. 7, *La Grèce de l'épopée, la Grèce archaïque;* 8, *La Grèce archaïque, la sculpture;* 9, *La Grèce archaïque, la glyptique, la numismatique, la peinture, la céramique;* 10, *La Grèce archaïque, la céramique d'Athènes.*]

Best collection of material on ancient oriental art. While antiquated in part, there are still considerable portions for which more recent treatises do not exist.

ATO

C682a **Maspero, Sir Gaston C. C.** *Art in Egypt.* N. Y. and London, 1912. [Ars una series.] (Bibliographies.)

b **Petrie, Sir William M. Flinders.** *Arts and crafts of ancient Egypt.* Edinburgh, 1909; Chicago, 1910.

c **Fechheimer, Hedwig.** *Die Plastik der Ägypter.* 1914. New ed., as v. 1 of *Die Kunst des Ostens,* Berlin, 1920.

d —— *Kleinplastik der Ägypter.* Berlin, 1921. [Die Kunst des Ostens, v. 3.]

e **Jequier, G.** *Manuel d'archéologie égyptienne: les éléments de l'architecture.* Paris, 1924.

f **Capart, Jean.** *Lectures on Egyptian art.* Chapel Hill, N. C., 1928.

a. Excellent manual of art, with many, though small, illustrations. *b.* Deals especially with the minor arts. *c.* and *d.* Furnish in some 300 unusually beautiful plates the most important works of Egyptian art. An introduction to *c.* contains the most penetrating critical discussion of Egyptian sculpture to be found anywhere.   JHB
e. Valuable work by a competent scholar, illustrated. *f.* Brief general account, well illustrated, by the leading authority on Egyptian art.   ATO

PERIODICALS

For a subject so new and so rapidly increasing in information recourse must constantly be had to periodical literature. It is, therefore, particularly unfortunate that there is no American periodical which makes a practice of regularly reviewing the oriental publications. For original studies cf. (C941) *Journal of the American Oriental Society,* Boston, 1843 ff.; (C942) *Journal of the Royal Asiatic Society of Great Britain and Ireland,* London, 1833 ff.; (C943) *Journal Asiatique,* Paris, 1822 ff., published by the Société Asiatique; (C944) *Zeitschrift der deutschen Morgenländischen Gesellschaft,* Leipzig, 1847 ff.; (C945) *Rivista degli studi orientali* of the Scuola Orientale, Roma, 1907 ff. More specialized are (C951) *Mitteilungen der Vorderasiatischen Gesellschaft,* Leipzig, 1896 ff.; (C952) *Mitteilungen der Deutschen Orient-Gesellschaft,* Leipzig and Berlin, 1898 ff. The chief organ for such studies in America is (C953) *American journal of Semitic languages and literatures,* Chicago, 1895 ff., which is a continuation of (C953a) *Hebraica,* 11 v., Chicago, 1884–95. Valuable bibliographies, especially for Assyriology, are printed in (C954) *Journal of the Society of Oriental Research,* Chicago, 1917 ff.; and (C955) *Die orientalistische Literaturzeitung,* Leipzig, 1898 ff., is primarily devoted to reviews and bibliography.

Periodicals especially devoted to Egypt are (C961) *Journal of Egyptian archaeology,* London, 1914 ff.; (C962) *Ancient Egypt,* London, 1914 ff.; (C963) *Sphinx, revue critique embrassant le domaine entier de l'Égyptologie,* Upsala, 1896 ff.; (C964) *Recueil de travaux relatifs à la philologie et à l'archéologie égyptiennes et assyriennes, pour servir de bulletin à la Mission Française du Caire,* Paris, 1870 ff.; (C965) *Zeitschrift für ägyptische Sprache und Altertumskunde,* Leipzig, 1863 ff.; (C966) *Aegyptus rivista italiana di Egittologia e di papirologia,* Milano, 1920 ff.; (C967) *Annales du service des antiquités de l'Egypte,* Le Caire, 1900 ff.; (C968) *Bulletin de l'institut français d'archéologie orientale,* Le Caire, 1901 ff.

For Assyriology see (C971) *Revue d'Assyriologie et d'archéologie orientale,* Paris, 1884 ff.; (C972) *Babyloniaca,* Paris, 1906 ff.; (C973) *Zeitschrift für Assyriologie und verwandte Gebiete,* Leipzig and Berlin, 1886 ff.; (C974) *Beiträge zur Assyriologie und vergleichenden semitischen Sprachwissenschaft,* Leipzig, 1890 ff. For Syria there has recently been established (C976) *Syria, revue d'art oriental et d'archéologie publiée sous le patronage du Haut-Commissaire de la République Française en Syrie,* Paris, 1920 ff.

The number of periodicals more or less seriously devoted to the study of the Bible is legion, and the more popular often present excellent bibliographies and reviews and occasionally serious articles of merit. In the first rank are: (C981) *Journal of biblical literature,* N. Y., 1881 ff.; (C982) *Zeitschrift für die alttestamentliche Wissenschaft,* Giessen, 1881 ff., the standard German publication; (C983)

Revue biblique, Paris, 1892 ff., published by l'École Biblique at Jerusalem; (C984) *Journal of the Palestine Oriental Society,* Jerusalem, 1921 ff., a publication of international character. The following are specially devoted to research in the Holy Land: (C986) *Quarterly statement of the Palestine Exploration Fund,* London, 1869 ff.; and (C987) *Zeitschrift des Deutschen Palästina-Vereins,* Leipzig, 1878 ff.

Somewhat more popular articles, with reviews and bibliographies may be found in the following: (C991) *Expositor,* London, 1875 ff.; (C992) *Expository times,* Edinburgh, 1889 ff.; (C993a) *American journal of theology,* 24 v., Chicago, 1897–1920, continued as (C993b) *Journal of religion,* Chicago, 1920 ff.; (C994) *Harvard theological review,* Cambridge, Mass., 1908 ff.; (C995) *Princeton theological review,* Princeton, N. J., 1890 ff. Especially devoted to Jewish history are: (C996) *Jewish quarterly review,* v. 1–20, London, 1888–1908; v. 21 ff., Philadelphia, 1910 ff.; and (C997) *Revue des études juives,* Paris, 1880 ff. Cf. also periodicals listed in § G and § T.   ATO

SECTION D

ANCIENT GREECE AND THE HELLENISTIC WORLD

Editor

DONALD McFAYDEN

Professor of History, Washington University

CONTENTS

INTRODUCTION

This section lists the chief works upon the history of Greece and the Hellenistic states down to their conquest by Rome, and also the leading books and periodicals which treat of Greece and Rome conjointly. The outstanding histories of the ancient world as a whole have already been listed in § C. The history of Greece under Roman rule is treated in § E; its history under Byzantine rule in § H; its history in modern times in § T.

The important position occupied by the ancient Greeks in the history of civilization and of European culture requires that this section give unusual attention to literature, art, philosophy, and other phases of life besides the political. Not only for this reason, but also because of the wealth of materials resulting from the prolonged exploitation of this field of study, the number of titles of works cited in this section is exceptionally large. Even so, the specialist will note many omissions and will doubtless in many instances challenge the selection made.

In compiling the section two special classes of readers, in addition to the general reader, have been kept in mind: the teachers and students of history in schools and junior colleges; and those students in universities, a growing number, who enter the field of Greek history from the study of general history, economics, or sociology rather than, as formerly, from the study of the classical languages and literatures. For both classes there is an embarrassment of riches. On the one hand, there is at present issuing from the press a veritable flood of books designed to interest in things Hellenic the general reader and the student who has not received a classical training. On the other hand, the special student has before him a vast technical literature.

Since the limits of the section preclude an adequate account of either class of publications, an endeavor has been made to observe three principles. First, at the head of each group there has been named, where possible, one or more brief and interesting accounts of the topic with which the group deals, and at the end of the group there has been mentioned the most reliable and exhaustive treatise on the subject. Second, English translations of Greek authors, rather than editions of the text, have been cited. In some cases, however, either because no translation is available or because of important introductory essays or of commentary which the edition contains, editions of the Greek text have been cited. Contrary to practice elsewhere in this volume, it has not seemed essential to take the space necessary to give exact and complete titles of the numerous editions and transla- tions of the classic Greek authors. Third, in view of the large number of titles cited, the review notices have been reduced to the minimum, especially where the title affords adequate indication of the content of a work. In essential cases, how- ever, care has been taken to advise the reader of the bias or other peculiar qualities of a particular work.

BIBLIOGRAPHY, LIBRARY AND MUSEUM COLLECTIONS

D1 **Botsford, George W.,** and **Sihler, Ernest G.** *Hellenic civilization.* N. Y., 1915. [(B61) Records of civilization: sources and studies, ed. by J. T. Shotwell.] (Bibliographies.)

Primarily a source book, but even more useful for its bibliographies. This and the bibliographical notes in (D101a) G. W. Botsford, *Hellenic history* and similar works are intended for the non-technical student. DMCF

D2a **Engelmann, Wilhelm.** *Bibliotheca scriptorum classicorum, et graecorum et latinorum: alphabetisches Verzeichniss der Ausgaben, Uebersetzungen, und Erläuterungsschriften der griechischen und lateinischen Schriftsteller, welche vom Jahre 1700 bis zu Ende des Jahres 1846 besonders in Deutschland ge- druckt worden sind: sechste gänzlich umgearbeitete Auflage der Bibliotheca auctorum classicorum von Enslin.* 1847. 8th rev. ed. by E. Preuss, 2 v., Leipzig, 1880–82. Supplement by R. Klussman in (D3b) *Jahresbericht über die Fortschritte der klassischen Altertumswissenschaft,* v. 146, 151, 156, 165, 2 v. in 4, Leipzig, 1909–13.

b **Mayor, Joseph B.** *Guide to the choice of classical books.* 1874. 2nd rev. ed., London, 1879. New supplement, 1879–1896, London, 1896.

c **Masqueray, Paul.** *Bibliographie pratique de la littérature grecque des origines à la fin de la période romaine.* Paris, 1914.

140   A GUIDE TO HISTORICAL LITERATURE

d Marouzeau, Jules. *Dix années de bibliographique classique* (1914–1924).
2 v. Paris, 1927–28.

All these handbooks were designed for the student of classical literature rather than for the student of history. *a.* Extensive list of editions of classical authors and of works relating to them. Eighth edition covers the works published between 1700 and 1878. Klussmann's supplement carries the list down to 1896. *b.* Select list of works published before 1896. Under the heading 'Helps to the study of ancient authors' are cited the main books on Greek and Roman history, antiquities, etc. *c.* Select bibliography, critical and fairly full. Also cf. (B669) Sandys, *History of classical scholarship,* for a critical account of the chief historians of Greece who wrote prior to the end of the nineteenth century. *d.* Full bibliography of the texts of Greek and Roman writers, and of the discussions of them, whether in book or periodical form, which have appeared between 1914 and 1924. The second volume contains a bibliography of books and articles upon general classical topics.   DMCF

D3a *Year's work in classical' studies.* London, 1907 ff. [Classical Association of England.]

b *Jahresbericht über die Fortschritte der klassischen Altertumswissenschaft,
begründet von Conrad Bursian.* With its supplements, (*c*) *Bibliotheca
philologica classica* and (*d*) *Biographisches. Jahrbuch für Altertumskunde.*
Leipzig, 1874 ff.

Annuals. *a.* Each number consists of several readable essays by eminent English scholars describing the contributions in the various fields of classical scholarship published in the course of the previous year. The comments are usually illuminating, but the citation of new books and articles is rarely exhaustive. *b.* Most valuable bibliographical aid in the field. Each annual issue consists of three volumes, containing accounts of the progress made in the study respectively of (I) Greek authors, (II) Latin authors, and (III) *Altertumswissenschaft* (philology, history, etc.). Each volume contains two or more extended articles describing the work done in a specific field since that topic was last treated in the *Jahresbericht.* Thus v. 176 (1918) and v. 180 (1919) contain a description of the main books and articles on Greek history published between 1907 and 1916. The last treatment of this field had been in v. 135 (1907), in which the contributions published between 1903 and 1906 were discussed. A full index to v. 1–87 (1873–1895) was published as a separate volume. A list of the articles in v. 88–163 (1896–1913) is contained in v. 166 (1914).* A classified list of all

* V. 164-224 (1914-1929) contain bibliographies on the following topics:
176, 180, 218, Greek history; 201, Greek language; 184, 189, 193, 213, Greek inscriptions; 172, Greek religious institutions; 168, Sophists; 197, 216, Pre-Socratic philosophy, including the sophists; 187, 191, 195, Plato; 216, Aristotle; 174, 178, 191, 201, Greek lyric poetry; 174, 195, 207, Greek comedy; 166, 182, 207, Homer; 170, 191, Herodotus; 178, 195, 207, Thucydides; 178, 203, Xenophon; 166, Attic orators; 170, 211, 216, Greek rhetoricians; 170, 187, 219, Plutarch's *Moralia;* 219, Greek Patristics.
168, Roman history; 189, Roman Empire; 184, 213, Transition from ancient to medieval times; 176, Roman constitutional history; 201, 218, Roman military antiquities; 197, Roman private life; 176, 184, 205, 209. Old Latin inscriptions and the Italic dialects; 201, 205, Vulgar and late Latin; 188, Latin grammarians; 183, Latin rhetoricians; 175, 204, Latin satire; 171, 212, 217, Post-Augustan Latin poetry; 203, 208, Latin literature of the third and fourth centuries; 171, 175, Apuleius; 183, 212, Catullus; 167, 183, 204, Cicero's orations; 200, 204, 208, Cicero's philosophical works; 179, 204, Cicero's rhetorical works; 196 Horace; 188, Livy; 196, Lucretius; 167, 179, 200, Ovid; 183, Phaedrus and the Latin fable; 167, 192, Plautus; 196, 208, Propertius and Tibullus; 192, 212, Quintilian; 183, 192, 212, Sallust; 192, Seneca; 171, 200, Scriptores Historiae Augustae; 167, Tacitus; 192, Varro; 167, 196, Virgil; 220, Pliny the Younger; 220, Christian Latin poets.
186, Ancient mythology and religion; 172, 193, 209, Greek and Latin paleography; 193, Ancient music; 180, Ancient medicine; 222, Latin grammar and ancient rhetoric.

the articles in v. 1–198 (1873–1923), as well as a fuller bibliographical account of the set, will be found in D. McFayden, 'Fifty Years of Bursian's Jahresbericht' *Washington University studies, humanistic series,* 12:105–114, St. Louis, Mo., Oct. 1924. In addition to the three volumes just described, each annual issue of the *Jahresbericht* includes a fourth volume containing *c. Bibliotheca philologica classica,* a classified list of all books, articles, and important book reviews published anywhere throughout the world during the preceding year, and *d. Biographisches Jahrbuch für Altertumskunde,* biographies of classical scholars recently deceased, with lists of their works. The attention of the reader should be called also to (B15a) *Annual bulletin of historical literature,* and to the book reviews and 'Lists of books received' contained in the historical and classical periodicals.

DMCF

D4 Otto, Walter. *Kulturgeschichte des Altertums, ein Überblick über neue Erscheinungen.* München, 1925.

Excellent survey of recent publications in the various fields of the cultural history of the ancient nations, naturally with special attention to German works. Review, E. Hohl, *Philologische Wochenschrift,* 45:1291, Nov. 28, 1925.   GMD

D5 *Jahresberichte des Literarischen Zentralblattes über die wichtigsten wissenschaftlichen Neuerscheinungen des gesamten deutschen Sprachgebietes,* 1924 ff. Ed. by Hans Ruppert. Leipzig, 1925 ff.

Contains an annual record of German publications in classical philology.   DMCF

Library Collections.—The library of Harvard University contains the richest American collections not only for Greek archeology and history, including the Hellenistic period, but also for practically every other branch of Hellenic studies. There are also good collections in the libraries of the following universities: Yale (Curtius collection), Columbia, Princeton, Johns Hopkins, Cornell (Anthon collection), Chicago, Illinois (Dittenberger and Vahler collections), Michigan, Stanford, and California.

AHS

Museum Collections.—The most extensive collections of Greek and Roman art and antiquities on this continent are those in the Metropolitan Museum in New York, the Museum of Fine Arts in Boston, and the museum of the University of Pennsylvania. Other collections of importance may be found in the Fogg Art Museum at Harvard; in the Museum of Industrial Arts, Providence, R. I.; at Cornell University; at the University of Cincinnati; at the Randolph-Macon Woman's College, Lynchburg, Va.; at the University of Michigan; in Chicago at the Art Institute, the Field Museum, and the University of Chicago; in St. Louis at the Art Museum and at Washington University; at Stanford University; at the University of California; and at the Royal Museum of Art, Toronto, Canada.

DMCF

ENCYCLOPEDIAS AND WORKS OF REFERENCE

D21a Walters, Henry B. *Classical dictionary of Greek and Roman antiquities. biography, geography, and mythology.* Cambridge, Eng., and N. Y., 1916.

b Lübker, Friedrich. *Reallexikon des klassischen Altertums.* 1853. 8th rev. ed. by J. Geffcken, E. Ziebarth, and others, Leipzig, 1914.

c Smith, Sir William, ed. *Dictionary of Greek and Roman antiquities.* 1842 3rd rev. ed. by S. W. Wayte, and G. E. Marindin, 2 v., London, 1890–91.

d ——— *Dictionary of Greek and Roman biography and mythology.*
1844–49. 3rd rev. ed. by G. E. Marindin, 3 v., London, 1909.

e ——— *Dictionary of Greek and Roman geography.* 1854–57. 2nd rev.
ed., 2 v., London, 1878.

f **Daremberg, Charles,** and **Saglio, Edmond,** ed. *Dictionnaire des antiquités grecques et romaines d'après les textes et les monuments, contenant
l'explication des termes qui se rapportent. . . . à la vie publique et privée
des anciens.* 5 v. in 9, Paris, 1873–1919.

g **Pauly, August F. von.** *Realencyclopädie der classischen Altertumswissen-
schaft.* 1839–52. Rev. ed. begun by G. Wissowa and carried on by W.
Kroll and K. Witte. Pt. A v. 1–13 (to 'Lysimachides') ; pt. B v. 1–6 (R to
'Stluppi'), Stuttgart, 1895–1924. Supplements to pt. A, v. 1–4 (A to
'Ledon'), Stuttgart, 1903–24. (Bibliographies.)

a. Useful single volume dictionary of Greek and Roman biography, geography,
and antiquities. *b.* Best single volume dictionary of antiquities ; does not contain proper names. *c., d., e.* Still useful, though getting antiquated. *f., g.*
The most authoritative dictionaries. *f.* Contains no proper names save those of
deities. *g.* Still in progress. Contains biographical and geographical articles as
well as articles on antiquities. *c., d., e., f.,* and especially *g.* Valuable for their
references to the ancient sources.   DM F

D31 Whibley, Leonard, ed. *Companion to Greek studies.* 1905. 3rd rev. ed.,
Cambridge, Eng., 1916. [I. 1, H. F. Tozer, *Geography;* 2, A. J. B. Wace,
Ethnology; 3, D'Arcy W. Thompson, *Fauna;* 4, W. T. Thiselton-Dyer,
Flora. II. 1, R. D. Hicks, *Chronology;* 2, R. D. Hicks, *Chronological tables.*
III. 1, Sir R. C. Jebb, *Literature;* 2, H. Jackson and R. D. Hicks, *Philos-
ophy;* 3, J. Gow, *Science.* IV. 1, A. J. B. Wace, *Prehistoric art;* 2, F. C.
Penrose and E. A. Gardner, *Architecture;* 3, Sir C. Waldstein and R. C.
Bosanquet, *Sculpture;* 4, F. R. Earp, *Painting;* 5, A. H. Smith, *Vase paint-
ing;* 6, H. B. Walters, *Terracottas;* 7, H. B. Walters, *Bronze work;* 8, H. B.
Walters, *Gold and silver work;* 9, W. Ridgeway, *Gems;* 10, R. D. Archer-
Hind, *Music.* V. 1, E. A. Gardner, *Mythology and religion.* VI. 1, F. E.
Adcock and L. Whibley, *Constitutions;* 2, W. Wyse, *Law;* 3, M. O. B.
Caspari, *Finance;* 4, R. J. G. Mayor, *Population;* 5, R. J. G. Mayor, *Slaves
and slavery;* 6, H. J. Edwards, *Colonies;* 7, H. J. Edwards, *Commerce and
industry;* 8, W. Ridgeway, *Measures and weights;* 9, W. Ridgeway, *Money;*
10, Sir C. W. C. Oman, *War;* 11, A. B. Cook, *Ships;* 12, J. Gow, *Calendar.*
VII. 1, J. Gow, *Table of the relationships of a man;* 2, J. E. Harrison,
Ritual of birth, marriage, and death; 3, A. S. Wilkins, *Education;* 4, M. R.
James, *Books and writing;* 5, F. W. Cornish, *Position of women;* 6, Lady
Evans, *Dress;* 7, E. A. Gardner, *Daily life;* 8, A. J. B. Wace and E. A.
Gardner, *House and furniture;* 9, Sir T. C. Allbutt, *Medicine.* VIII. 1,
R. A. Neil and P. Giles, *Dialects;* 2, E. S. Roberts and E. A. Gardner,
Epigraphy; 3, E. H. Minns, *Palaeography;* 4, Sir R. C. Jebb, *Textual
criticism;* 5, A. W. Verrall, *Metre;* 6, J. E. Sandys, *History of scholarship.*]
(Bibliographies.)

Brief introductions to the several fields of Greek studies, written by leading
English scholars ; indispensable to the student of Greek history.   DMCF

D32 Gercke, Alfred, and **Norden, Eduard,** ed. *Einleitung in die Altertums-
wissenschaft.* 1910–12. 2nd ed., 3 v., Leipzig, 1912–14. 3rd rev. ed., Leipzig,
1921 ff. [1, A. Gercke, *Methodik;* E. Bethe, P. Wendland, E. Norden,
Griechische und römische Literatur; P. Kretschmer, *Sprache;* E. Bickel,
Antike Metrik. 2, E. Pernice, *Griechisches und römisches Privatleben;* F.
Winter, *Griechische Kunst;* S. Wide, *Griechische und römische Religion:*
A. Gercke, *Geschichte der Philosophie;* J. L. Heiberg, *Exakte Wissen-*

schaften und Medizin. 3, C. F. Lehmann-Haupt, K. J. Beloch, E. Korne-mann, *Griechische und römische Geschichte;* B. Keil, *Griechische Staatsalter-tümer;* K. J. Neumann, *Römische Staatsaltertümer.*]

Summarizes the state of scholarship in the various fields of classical learning. Each article is by an eminent specialist. In the third, enlarged edition the articles are entirely rewritten, often by new authors.   DMCF

D33 Hall, Frederick W. *Companion to classical texts.* Oxford, 1913. (Biblio-graphies.)

Will afford the historical student a clear idea of the nature of the problems involved in the establishment of the text of an ancient author.   DMCF

D34a Clinton, Henry F. *Fasti hellenici; the civil and literary chronology of Greece from the earliest accounts to the death of Augustus.* 3 v. Oxford, 1824–34.

b —————— *Epitome of the civil and literary chronology of Greece.* Oxford, 1851.

The fundamental works on the chronology of Greece in the historical period. In *a.* the source material is printed in full; in *b.* references only are given, though conclusions stated in *a.* are in some instances revised. For a more modern treat-ment cf. (D35) Kubitschek.   DMCF

D35 *Handbuch der Altertumswissenschaft, begründet von Iwan von Müller, fortgesetzt von Robert von Pöhlmann.* 9 v. in about 40. München, 1885 ff. Rev. ed., by Walter Otto, to be 10 v. in about 40, München, 1923 ff. [1. L. von Urlichs, *Grundlegung und Geschichte der klassischen Altertumswissen-schaft;* E. Hübner, *Römische Epigraphik;* W. Kubitschek, *Zeitrechnung des Altertums,* 1928; H. Nissen, *Griechische und römische Metrologie, in* the 2nd ed. of v. 1, 1892; Th. Birt, *Kritik und Hermeneutik, Abriss des antiken Buchwesens,* 3rd ed., 1913; W. Larfeld, *Griechische Epigraphik,* 3rd ed., 1913. 2. K. Brugmann and A. Thumb, *Griechische Grammatik,* 4th ed., 1913; 5th ed. in press; Fr. Stolz and J. H. Schmalz, *Lateinische Grammatik,* 5th ed., pt. 1, 1926; R. Volkmann and C. Hammer, *Rhetorik der Griechen und Römer;* H. Gleditsch, *Metrik der Griechen und Römer, mit einem Anhang über die Musik der Griechen,* 3rd ed., 1901. 3. F. Hommel, *Grundriss der Ethnologie und Geographie des alten Orients,* 1904–26; H. G. Lolling, *Hellenische Landeskunde und Topographie,* in the first ed. of v. 3, 1889; W. Judeich, *Topographie von Athen,* 2nd ed., 1905; (D103a) R. von Pöhlmann, *Griechische Geschichte,* 5th ed., 1914; (E43a) J. Jung, *Geographie von Italien und den römischen Provinzen,* 2nd ed., 1897; (E101) B. Niese, *Römische Geschichte,* 5th ed., 1923; (E683b) O. Richter, *Topo-graphie der Stadt Rom,* 2nd ed., 1901. 4. (D532d) G. Busolt and H. Swaboda, *Griechische Staatskunde,* 2 v., 1920–26; (D571i) I. von Müller and A. Bauer, *Griechische Privataltertü.ner und Kriegsaltertümer,* 2nd ed., 1893; H. Schiller, *Römische Staats-, Rechts-, und Kriegsaltertümer,* 2nd ed., 1893; M. Voigt and H. Blumner, *Römische Privataltertümer und Kulturgeschichte,* 3rd ed., 1911. 5. (D652b) W. Windelband and A. Goedeckemeyer, *Geschichte der abendländischen Philosophie im Altertum,* 4th ed., 1923; I. L. Heiberg, *Geschichte der Mathematik und der Naturwissenschaften im Alter-tum,* 1925; O. Gruppe, *Griechische Mythologie und Religionsgeschichte,* 1906; P. Stengel, *Griechische Kultusaltertümer,* 3rd ed., 1920; (E623) G. Wissowa, *Religion und Kultus der Römer,* 2nd ed., 1912. 6. K. Sittl, *Archäologie der Kunst, nebst einem Anhang über die antike Numismatik,* 2 v., 1895–97; H. Bulle, *Handbuch der Archäologie*:* (*A, Wesen und Methode der Archäologie,* 1913). 7. (D661g) W. von Christ, O. Stählin, and W. Schmid,

* This work when complete will replace the preceding.

Geschichte der griechischen Literatur bis auf die Zeit Justinians, 6th ed., 2 v. in 3, 1912–24. 8. (E661*b*) M. Schanz, *Geschichte der römischen Literatur bis zum Gesetzgebungswerk des Kaisers Justinian,* 1st to 3rd ed., 4 v. in 7, 1905–27. 9. (H662) K. Krumbacher, A. Erhardt, and H. Gelzer. *Geschichte der byzantinischen Literatur bis zum Ende des oströmischen Reiches,* 527–1453, 2nd ed., 1897**; (H661*a*) M. Manitius, *Geschichte der lateinischen Literatur im Mittelalter,* 3 v., v. 1, 1911, v. 2, 1923, v. 3, in preparation.]

This great series of authoritative treatises upon the various phases of classical scholarship, originally entitled *Handbuch der klassischen Altertumswissenschaft,* was founded by the late Professor von Müller of Munich. Hence it is usually referred to as 'Müller's Handbuch,' although in the most recent issues the name of its new general editor, Professor Otto, replaces that of Müller on the back of the volume. As originally contemplated by Müller, it was to consist of nine volumes, in the physical sense of the word volume. Volume II, the first to be issued, appeared in its first edition in 1885. The first edition of the second part of Manitius' contribution to the ninth volume appeared only in 1923, with a third part to follow. In the meantime the history of the series has been a most complicated one. Each individual treatise, indeed, has had its own history. Most of them have passed through two, three, or even six editions independently, and have been revised or rewritten at least once by hands other than those of the original authors. In some instances entirely new works have been substituted for the originals. Expansion has accompanied revision, until a treatise which in its first form occupied only a small part of a volume has often grown into a volume by itself, or a single volume has developed into several. In this respect, it should be said, the fate of the several treatises has been most uneven. Christ's book on Greek literature and Schanz's book on Roman literature are now the most exhaustive works in their several fields in any language, while the volumes on Greek history, Roman history, and ancient philosophy have remained in comparison mere outlines. To add to the bibliographer's confusion, the technical arrangement and numeration of the several parts of the series have been changed from time to time in some particulars, and an entire reorganization of the series is projected by its new editor. A proper bibliography of the series is for these reasons impossible in the space available. Only the most recent edition of each treatise has been cited above. For Otto's prospectus the reader may consult any volume issued since 1923. Those numbers of the series which are of most interest to the historical student are reviewed separately elsewhere in this book, as indicated by the cross reference numbers. DMCF

D36 Laurand, L. *Manuel des études grecques et latines.* 8 pt. in 1 v. Paris, 1914–19. Later ed. of several pt. [1, *Géographie, histoire, institutions grecques;* 2, *Littérature grecque;* 3, *Grammaire historique grecque;* 4, *Géographie, histoire, institutions romaines;* 5, *Littérature latine;* 6, *Grammaire historique latine;* 7, *Métrique, sciences complémentaires;* 8, *Tables méthodiques et alphabétiques.*] (Bibliographies.)

Arranged as a syllabus, with adequate directions to the literature; very useful. GMD

** To be replaced by a *Byzantinisches Handbuch,* which will constitute v. 10 in the Otto set. Its place in v. 9 will be taken by a new work, P. Lehman, *Das Fortleben der antiken Literatur im Mittelalter.*

GEOGRAPHY AND ATLASES

D41 Kiepert, Heinrich. *Manual of ancient geography.* London, 1881. Tr. by G. A. McMillan from *Lehrbuch der alten Geographie,* Berlin, 1878.

There is no good recent work on classical geography. For an excellent brief survey of Greek geography the reader may consult (D31) Whibley, *Companion to Greek studies* or the first chapter of (D101b) Oman, *History of Greece.* Grote's survey in the first chapter of pt. 2 of his (D121a) *History* is classic. The influence of geography upon the life of the ancient Greeks is discussed in the opening chapters of nearly every history; also very interesting in (D531d) Zimmern, *Greek commonwealth* and in (A47d) Newbigin, *Mediterranean lands.* For the history of geographical knowledge in antiquity, the works of Tozer, Bunbury, and Berger listed in (D657) furnish much information. For detailed questions in Greek topography, the reader may consult (D21e) Smith, *Dictionary of Greek and Roman geography* or (D21g) Pauly-Wissowa. A work on *Hellenische Landeskunde* is announced in the new Otto edition of (D35) *Handbuch der Altertumswissenschaft,* to replace that by H. G. Lolling.   DMCF

D42a Allinson, Francis G., and **Allinson, Anne C. E.** *Greek lands and letters.* Boston, 1909.

b Bosanquet, Ellen S. (Mrs. R. C.). *Days in Attica.* London, 1914. (Bibliography.)

Mentioned as examples of many charming books of travel and description which help the student to visualize the landscape and physical conditions in Greece.   DMCF

D43 Strabo. *Geography.* Ed. by A. Meinecke, 3 v., Leipzig, 1866. Ed. and tr. by Horace L. Jones, v. 1–6, London and N. Y., 1917–29, to be 8 v. [Loeb classical library.] (Bibliography.)

Principal ancient source for the geography of the ancient world. Chiefly a geographical account of the ancient world in the time of Augustus, accompanied by valuable historical information regarding the various regions and cities.

Of special value for topographical data of Greece is (D690d) Pausanias, *Description of Greece.*   DMCF

D46a Kiepert, Heinrich. *Atlas antiquus: zwölf Karten zur alten Geschichte.* 1854. 12th rev. ed., Berlin, 1902. 11th American rev. ed., Boston, 1892.

b Lord, John K., ed. *Atlas of the geography and history of the ancient world.* Boston, 1902. [Sanborn's classical atlas.]

c Sieglin, Wilhelm. *Schulatlas zur Geschichte des Altertums.* 1899. 5th ed., Gotha, 1906.

d Shepherd, William R. *Atlas of ancient history.* 1912. 2nd ed., N. Y., 1922

e Grundy, George B., ed. *Murray's classical atlas for schools.* 1904. Rev. ed., London, 1917.

f —— *Murray's handy classical maps.* London, 1899–1905. [*Gallia; Britannia; Hispania; Graecia; Asia Minor; Germania, Rhaetia, Illyria, Moesia, etc.; Italia; Palestine, Syria, and part of Mesopotamia; Eastern empires, including Egypt; Mare Aegaeum, Athens, Acropolis, etc.; Roman empire at various periods.*]

g Kampen, Albert. *Justus Perthes Atlas antiquus.* 1893. 8th ed., Gotha, 1906.

h *Atlas of ancient and classical geography.* N. Y., 1908. [Everyman's library.]

a. This famous atlas, made by one of the greatest of modern geographers, has been reproduced in numerous editions in almost every civilized country. All subsequent atlases for ancient history are based upon it in greater or less degree. Thus *b.* is in large part a revision of *a.* *c.* Inexpensive but good; lacks an index. *d.* Ancient history portion of the author's (A50a) *Historical atlas,* separately bound. *e.* Excellent atlas of newly constructed maps by various scholars, under the editorship of the foremost living English authority on ancient geography. *f.* Useful separate maps, 8 x 11 inches. *g.* and *h.* Convenient and inexpensive pocket atlases. All these atlases except *c.* are equipped with indexes. The maps in *e* and *f* are contour maps.   DMCF

SOURCE BOOKS AND COLLECTIONS OF SOURCES

D61a Thallon, Ida C., ed. *Readings in Greek history, from Homer to the battle of Chaeronea, a collection of extracts from the sources.* Boston, 1914. (Bibliographies.)

b Fling, Fred M., ed. *Source book of Greek history.* Boston, 1907. (Bibliography.)

These together with (D1) Botsford and Sihler, *Hellenic civilization,* are the best and fullest collections of extracts, in English translation, from the ancient sources for Greek history. Also cf. (C62).   DMCF

D62 Cary, Max. *Documentary sources of Greek history.* Oxford, 1927.

Brief but excellent account of the non-literary sources for Greek history. Fuller accounts will also be found in (C61) Wachsmuth, Schaefer, Strehl and Soltau, and (D121f) Busolt.   DMCF

D71a *Loeb classical library.* Ed. by Edward Capps, Thomas E. Page, and William H. D. Rouse, London and N. Y., 1912 ff.

b *Collection des universités de France, publiée sous le patronage de l'Association, Guillaume Budé, par la société d'édition Les Belles Lettres.* Paris, 1919 ff.

c *Fundació Bernat Metge: collecció catalana dels autors grecs i latins.* Barcelona, 1924 ff.

d *Bibliotheca scriptorum graecorum et romanorum Teubneriana.* About 570 v., Lipsiae, 1847 ff.

e *Oxford classical texts.* About 80 v. Oxford, 1894 ff.

f Pascal, Carlo, ed. *Corpus scriptorum latinorum Paravianum.* Augustae Taurinorum, 1916 ff.

g *Tusculum-Bücher.* München, 1923 ff.

Most complete modern collections of Greek and Roman literature in the original text. *a.* Gives the original text and a careful English translation on opposite pages. It is planned to include in this series practically every Greek and Latin author of importance. *b.* French counterpart to *a.;* gives the original text and French translation on opposite pages. The publishing house, Les Belles

Lettres, is also proceeding to issue a series of monographs on classical subjects entitled, *Collection d'études anciennes;* a series of texts, without translation, of less famous or hitherto unpublished Greek and Latin sources under the title *Nouvelle collection de textes et documents;* a series of commentaries on classical authors under the title *Collection de commentaires d'auteurs anciens;* also a *Collection de littérature générale,* to contain monographs upon general literature, including both ancient and subsequent literature; and a quarterly *Bulletin,* Paris, 1923 ff. *c.* Spanish counterpart to *b.* The text is accompanied by a translation into Catalan. *d., e.,* and *f.* Texts only, without translation or notes. *d.* Already includes nearly every Greek and Latin author of importance. *e.* Very excellent series in which special attention is paid to the results of textual criticism; contains only a part of Greek and Latin literature. *f.* New Italian series; characterized by extreme conservatism in matters of text; the manuscript reading is followed wherever it is at all possible and conjectural emendation is eschewed. *g.* Series of texts, with German translations.   DMCF

D72a *Oxford library of translations.* Oxford, 1902 ff.

   b *Bohn classical library.* London, 1848 ff.

   a. Contains translations of many classical authors; always scholarly and in every respect excellent. *b.* Old series in which a wide range of classical literature is represented. As a rule the translations are at best mediocre, both as to style and as to accuracy; but there are notable exceptions. Also cf. (B138*b*) *Everyman's library,* which includes only works of which the copyright has expired; the translations are always old ones, though in most cases they have received some revision by a recent scholar before being included in the series.
                                                                          DMCF

D73a Bury, John B. *Ancient Greek historians.* N. Y., 1909. [Lane lectures, Harvard University.]

   b Glover, Terrot R. *Herodotus.* Berkeley, 1924. [Sather classical lectures.]

   c Herodotus. *History.* Ed. with commentary by A. H. Sayce, books 1–3, London, 1883, and by R. W. Macan, books, 4–9, 4 v., London, 1895–1908. Commentary by W. W. How and J. Wells, 2 v., Oxford, 1912. Ed. and tr. by A. D. Godley, 4 v., London and N. Y., 1921–24. [Loeb classical library]. Tr. by G. C. Macaulay, 1890; reprint, 2 v., London, 1914. Tr. by G. Rawlinson, 1858–60; reprint, 2 v., London and N. Y., 1910 [Everyman's library]. Tr. by H. C. Cary, 1886; new ed., London, 1894 [Bohn classical library].

   d Thucydides. *History.* Ed. and tr. by C. F. Smith, 4 v., London and N. Y., 1919–23 [Loeb classical library]. Tr. by B. Jowett, 1881; 2nd rev. ed., 2 v., Oxford, 1900. Tr. by H. Dale, 1853–62 [Bohn classical library]; new ed., N. Y., 1888 [Harper's classical library]. Tr. by R. Crawley, 1874; new ed., London and N. Y., 1910 [Everyman's library]; rev. ed. by R. Feetham, London, 1903 [Temple classics].

   e Xenophon. *Works.* Ed. and tr. by various authors, London and N. Y., 1914–22 [Loeb classical library]. Ed. and tr. by H. G. Dakyns, v. 1–3, London, 1890–97. French tr. of *Anabasis,* with introduction, commentary, and maps, by A. Boucher, Paris, 1913.

   f Plutarch. *Lives.* Tr. by John Dryden, 1683–86; rev. ed. by A. H. Clough, 1859; new ed., 3 v., London and N. Y., 1910 [Everyman's library]. Ed. and tr. by B. Perrin, 11 v., 1914–24 [Loeb classical library].

g Aristotle. *Constitution of Athens.* Ed. with commentary by Sir J. E. Sandys, 1893; 2nd rev. ed., London, 1912. Tr. by Sir F. G. Kenyon, 1891; 3rd ed., London, 1920.

h *Hellenica Oxyrhynchia cum Theopompi et Cratippi fragmentis.* Ed. by B. P. Grenfell and A. S. Hunt, Oxonii, 1909. [Oxford classical texts.] Ed. by E. Kalinka, Leipzig, 1927 [Teubner series].

i Müller, Carl W. L. *Fragmenta historicorum graecorum.* 5 v. Parisiis, 1841-43.

j Jacoby, Felix. *Die Fragmente der griechischen Historiker.* V. 1, 2. Berlin, 1923-29.

a. Best account of Greek historiography in English. Review, Paul Shorey, *A.H.R.* 15:113, Oct. 1909. Cf. also (B61) Shotwell, *Introduction to the history of history;* R. C. Jebb, 'Speeches of Thucydides,' and H. G. Dakyns, 'Xenophon' in (D605a) Abbott, *Hellenica;* and (D301). *b.* Introduction to Herodotus for the general reader; discusses both his life and his book. Review, J. Wells, *Classical Rev.* 39:80, May 1925. *c., d., e., f.,* and *g.* Best editions and translations in English of the principal Greek historical works. *h.* Text of the important historical fragment recently discovered at Oxyrhynchus; not yet available in translation. For an account of this and other historical fragments recovered from Egyptian papyri, their contents, and the question as to their authorship, cf. (D91d) Powell and Barber, *New chapters in the history of Greek literature. i.* Contains the text of the existing fragments of lost Greek historical works. *j.* When completed will replace *i.*   DMCF

D81a Hicks, Edward L. *Manual of Greek historical inscriptions.* 1882. 2nd rev. ed. by G. F. Hill, Oxford, 1901.

b *Corpus inscriptionum graecarum.* Ed. by August Boeckh and others. 4 v. in 8, Berolini, 1828-77.

c *Inscriptiones graecae, consilio et auctoritate Academiae Litterarum Regiae Borussicae editae.* 14 v. Berolini, 1873 ff. [1-3, *Attica;* 4, *Argolis;* 5, *Laconia, Messenia, Arcadia;* * 6, *Elis and Arcadia;* 7, *Megara and Boeotia;* * 8, *Delphi;* 9, *Remainder of northern Greece;* * 10, *Epirus, Macedonia, Scythia;* ** 11, *Delos;* ** 12, *Islands of the Aegean, with the exception of Crete;* * 13, *Crete;* 14, *Sicily and Italy.*] V. 1-3 also appearing in an *editio minor,* Berolini, 1913-24. V. 11 is being completed in *Inscriptions de Délos,* published by the French Academy, 1926 ff.

d Michel, Charles. *Recueil d'inscriptions grecques.* Bruxelles, 1900. *Supplément,* 1912.

e *Recueil des inscriptions juridiques grecques.* Ed. by Rodolfe Dareste, Bernard Haussoullier, and Theodore Reinach. 2 v. in 5 pt. Paris, 1891-1904.

f Dittenberger, Wilhelm. *Sylloge inscriptionum graecarum.* 1883. 3rd rev. ed., 4 v., Lipsiae, 1915-22.

a. Gives the Greek text of the main inscriptions of historic interest, with full discussion of each. *b.* Usually cited as *C. I. G.* Published under the auspices of the Berlin Academy of Sciences. *c.* Published under the same auspices; intended to replace *b.* It is usually cited as *I. G.,* although v. 1-3 are often cited as *C. I. A.* (*Corpus inscriptionum Atticarum*). *d., e., f.* Other collections which are often referred to.   DMCF

---

* These volumes have not yet appeared.
** These volumes have appeared in part.

D91a **Mitteis, Ludwig,** and **Wilcken, Ulrich,** ed. *Grundzüge und Chrestomathie der Papyruskunde.* 2 v. in 4. Leipzig, 1912. (Bibliographies.)

b **Schubart, Wilhelm.** *Einführung in die Papyruskunde.* 1918. 2nd. ed., Berlin, 1920. (Bibliography.)

c **Wilcken, Ulrich.** *Griechische Ostraka aus Aegypten und Nubien, ein Beitrag zur antiken Wirtschaftsgeschichte.* 2 v. Leipzig, 1899.

d **Powell, John U.,** and **Barber, Eric A.,** ed. *New chapters in the history of Greek literature: recent discoveries in Greek poetry and prose of the fourth and following centuries, B. C.* Oxford, 1921.

e **Milligan, George,** ed. *Selections from the Greek papyri, ed. with tr. and notes.* Cambridge, Eng., 1910. (Bibliography.)

a. Standard treatise on the papyrus documents. V. 1, 1 and 2, 1. Describe the contributions made by the study of papyri to knowledge of the history and life of Ptolemaic and Roman Egypt. V. 1, 2 and 2, 2. Contain illustrative papyri with commentary. *b.* Another useful introduction to the study of papyri. *c.* Standard treatise on the *ostraca* or inscribed potsherds, found in Egypt and on the light they throw upon social conditions in Hellenistic Egypt. *d.* Describes the new fragments of Greek literature recovered among the Egyptian papyri. *e.* Contains a brief introduction on the nature of papyri, a list of the main published collections with the contractions by which they are customarily referred to, and illustrations of various types of non-literary papyri with English translation. For fuller lists of published papyrus collections, cf. *a.,* v. 1, 1, p. xxiii ff.; and *b.,* appendixes. Annual bibliographical records of papyrus publications appear in (C961) *Journal of Egyptian archaeology;* (C966) *Aegyptus, rivista italiana di egittologia e di papirologia;* and (D958) *Revue des études grecques.* DMCF

SHORTER GENERAL HISTORIES OF GREECE

D101a **Botsford, George W.** *Hellenic history.* N. Y., 1922. Later reprints. (Excellent bibliographies.)

b **Oman, Sir Charles W. C.** *History of Greece from the earliest times to the death of Alexander the Great.* 7th ed., London and N. Y., 1900. Later reprints.

c **Shuckburgh, Evelyn S.** *Greece from the coming of the Hellenes to A. D. 14.* London and N. Y., 1905. [Story of the nations.]

d **James, Henry R.** *Our Hellenic heritage.* 2 v. 1921–24. 1 v. London and N. Y., 1927.

e **Stobart, John C.** *The glory that was Greece, a survey of Hellenic culture and civilisation.* 1911. 2nd rev. ed., London, 1916. (Brief bibliography.)

f **Cotterill, Henry B.** *Ancient Greece, a sketch of its art, literature, and philosophy viewed in connexion with its external history from the earliest times to the age of Alexander the Great.* London and N. Y., 1913. [Great nations.]

g **Robinson, Cyril E.** *History of Greece.* London and N. Y., 1929.

Elementary histories. *a.* Most scholarly text-book on Greek history. Traces not only the political history but the evolution of all phases of Greek civilization down to the Roman conquest. Owing to its wide scope its literary style often suffers from condensation, with the result that it is a book to be studied rather than read and that most points are settled dogmatically without discussion; often their very existence being ignored. Review, W. S. Ferguson, *A.H.R.* 28:79, Oct. 1922. *b.* Readable narrative history of the older type, dealing almost exclusively with the political history. *c.* Excellent outline. *d.* Very interestingly written account, intended for those boys in the English public schools who do not read Greek. Ends at B. C. 338. Strongly to be recommended for the general reader. *e.* and *f.* In these books, which conclude at B. C. 323, political history is subordinated to the history of culture. *g.* Brilliantly written and up-to-date.

In addition, cf. (C101) for elementary works on ancient history, which contain sections devoted to Greece.   DMCF

D102a **Baumgarten, Fritz; Poland, Franz;** and **Wagner, Richard.** *Die hellenische Kultur.* 1905. 3rd rev. ed., Leipzig, 1913.

   b ——— *Die hellenistisch-römische Kultur.* Leipzig, 1913.

   c **Baumgarten, Fritz.** *Die antike Kultur.* Leipzig, 1922.

   d **Poland, Franz; Reisinger, Ernst;** and **Wagner, Richard.** *Culture of ancient Greece and Rome: a general sketch.* Boston, 1926. Tr. by J. H. Freeze from 2nd ed. of *Die antike Kultur.*

a. and *b.* Together constitute a history of the Greco-Roman world to the fall of Rome, as well as an admirable description of Greco-Roman civilization in all its aspects. Even those who do not read German will find these volumes extremely useful by reason of their illustrations, which are exceptionally numerous and well chosen and include a number of valuable restorations, e.g., the citadel of Tiryns, a Greek theater, the Acropolis, the Roman fora. *c.* An abridgment of *a.* and *b.* in a single volume.   DMCF

D103a **Pöhlmann, Robert von.** *Grundriss der griechischen Geschichte.* 1889. 6th rev. ed., München, 1926 [(D35) Handbuch der Altertumswissenschaft.]

   b **Wilcken, Ulrich.** *Griechische Geschichte im Rahmen der Altertumsgeschichte.* München, 1924. [Reimann, Weltgeschichte.]

   c **Hatzfeld, Jean.** *Histoire de la Grèce ancienne.* Paris, 1926.

a. Résumé in 370 pages; the account extends to B. C. 146; interesting for its unfavorable view of Greek democracy, which the author regards as essentially socialistic. Pöhlmann has developed this idea at length in his (D533f) *Geschichte der sozialen Frage und des Sozialismus in der antiken Welt.* *b.* Brilliant survey in 246 pages, by a distinguished papyrologist; especially valuable for its discussion of the relations of the Greeks to their oriental forerunners and contemporaries, and of the political and social institutions of the Greeks; includes the Hellenistic period. Review, J. Hammer, *A.H.R.* 31:302, Jan. 1926. *c.* Good survey with attention to economics and culture.   DMCF

LONGER GENERAL HISTORIES

D121a **Grote, George.** *History of Greece from the earliest period to the close of the generation contemporary with Alexander the Great.* 1846–56. 4th ed., 10 v., London, 1888. New ed., 12 v., London and N. Y., 1906 [Everyman's library].

   b **Curtius, Ernst.** *History of Greece.* 5 v. London, 1868–73. Rev. ed. by W. A. Packard, 5 v., N. Y., 1892. Reprint, 1907. Tr. by Sir A. W. Ward from *Griechische Geschichte,* 1857–67. 6th ed., 3 v., Berlin, 1887–89.

c Holm, Adolf. *History of Greece from its commencement to the close of the independence of the Greek nation.* 4 v. N. Y., 1894–98. Tr. by F. Clarke from *Griechische Geschichte von ihrem Ursprunge bis zum Untergang der Selbständigkeit des griechischen Volkes*, 4 v., Berlin, 1886–94.

d Abbott, Evelyn. *History of Greece.* 3 v. London and N. Y., 1895–1901.

e Bury, John B. *History of Greece to the death of Alexander the Great.* 1900. 2nd rev. ed., London, 1913.

f Busolt, Georg. *Griechische Geschichte.* 1885–88. 2nd rev. ed., v. 1–3, Gotha, 1893–1904. [Handbücher der alten Geschichte.]

g Beloch, Karl Julius. *Griechische Geschichte.* 1893–1904. 2nd rev. ed., 4 v. in 8, Strassburg, 1912–27.

Standard histories of Greece. The progress of archeology has naturally rendered the older ones greatly in need of revision, particularly in their earlier chapters. *a.* This great work still remains the best starting point for the serious study of Greek history in the classical period. Epigraphic evidence is of course neglected, for epigraphy was in its infancy in Grote's day. Indeed, many of the most interesting inscriptions had not yet been discovered. Furthermore, (D73*h*) *Hellenica Oxyrhynchia* and (D73*g*) Aristotle, *Constitution of Athens,* had not yet come to light. But after all ninety per cent of available information regarding fifth and fourth century Greece is derived from literary sources which were at Grote's disposal. These sources Grote analysed fully and with sound judgment, though naturally the methods of historical criticism have advanced somewhat since his day. The fact that Grote was himself a man of affairs is reflected in his keen criticism of Greek statesmen and their policies. His book is the classic defense of Greek democracy, 'a Liberal pamphlet in ten volumes.' *b.* German counterpart to Grote. Carries the story down to 338 B. C. Curtius was a distinguished archeologist. Grote never visited Greece but Curtius knew the country and its monuments intimately. His esthetic appreciation was superior to Grote's. On the other hand, writing in Berlin in the days of William I and Bismarck, he naturally lacked Grote's sympathy with Athenian democracy and Grote's interest in political and constitutional problems. From the point of view of the modern student, Curtius's *History* is inferior to Grote's in another respect. It is far less full in its citation and discussion of authorities, whereas Grote in his footnotes cites his sources in full and weighs their evidence. *c.* Dry, but valuable for its discussion of special points in the notes; carries the account to 146 B. C. *d.* Sound, well-written narrative covering the period to 403 B. C. *e.* Best political history of Greece in English. *f.* Sane and thorough handbook of the best German type, giving in the footnotes exhaustive justification for every statement in the text and taking full account of the archeological, as well as of the literary, evidence; for that reason indispensable for the serious student. The author intended to cover the history of Greece to 338 B. C. but died before he had finished his task. As it stands the work ends with the surrender of Athens in 404 B. C. *g.* Brilliant. Beloch applies the more penetrating methods of modern historiography to the criticism of the sources and of the conventional interpretations of them. Consequently, his book abounds in new suggestions; which, however, have not all won universal assent.

Also cf. (C121) *Cambridge ancient history;* (C124) Meyer, *Geschichte des*

Altertums; (C125) Cavaignac, *Histoire de l'antiquité;* and the volume by Ciccotti in (B168) Hartmann, *Weltgeschichte in gemeinverständlicher Darstellung.*

DMCF

MINOAN, MYCENEAN, AND HOMERIC AGES

D201a **Baikie, James.** *Sea-kings of Crete.* 1910. 3rd ed., London, 1920. (Brief bibliography.)

   b **Dussaud, René.** *Les civilisations préhelléniques dans le bassin de la mer Egée.* 1910. 2nd rev. ed., Paris, 1914.

   c **Tsountas, Chrestos,** and **Manatt, James Irving.** *Mycenaean age, a study of the monuments and culture of pre-Homeric Greece.* Boston, 1897.

   d **Burrows, Ronald Montagu.** *Discoveries in Crete and their bearing on the history of ancient civilisation.* 1907. 3rd ed., with addenda on the season's work of 1907. London, 1908. (Bibliography.)

   e **Hawes, Charles H.,** and **Hawes, Harriet Boyd.** *Crete, the forerunner of Greece.* 1909. 2nd ed., London and N. Y., 1911. [Harper's library of living thought.]

   f **Evans, Sir Arthur.** *Palace of Minos, a comparative account of the successive stages of the early Cretan civilization as illustrated by the discoveries at Knossos.* 2 v.; 2nd v. in 2 pts. London and N. Y., 1921–28.

   a. Interesting and accurate account of prehistoric Greece, for the general reader. *b.* More scholarly treatment of the same period. *c.* Most interesting account of the discoveries of Schliemann and his successors; written before Evans's excavations in Crete. *d.* Valuable for its discussion of moot points. These four works are bountifully illustrated. *e.* Excellent brief account of the work of Evans and his associates; not illustrated. *f.* This sumptuously illustrated volume is the first installment of what will be the definitive account of Evans's work. The volumes published carry the account to the end of the Middle Minoan Period.

   For a careful statement of the archeological evidence cf. (D683) Hall, *Aegean archaeology* and for Hall's reconstruction of the history on the basis of this evidence, his (C102c) *Ancient history of the Near East.* For recent summaries, cf. (C121) *Cambridge ancient history;* and Glotz, *Aegean civilization,* N. Y., 1925 [(B153a) *History of civilization*]; tr. by M. R. Dobie and E. M. Riley from *La civilisation égéenne* [(B153b) *L'évolution de l'humanité*]; review, D. M. Robinson, *A.H.R.* 29:588, Apr. 1924.   DMCF

D202a **Homer.** *Iliad.* Ed. by W. Leaf, 1886–88; 2nd ed., 2 v., London and N. Y., 1900–02. Tr. by A. Lang, W. Leaf and E. Myers, 1882; reprint, London, 1919. Ed. and tr. by A. T. Murray, v. 1, London and N. Y., 1925 [Loeb classical library].

   b ——— *Odyssey.* Ed. and tr. by A. T. Murray, 2 v., London and N. Y., 1919 [Loeb classical library]. Tr. by S. H. Butcher and A. Lang, 1879; reprint, London, 1920. Tr. by G. H. Palmer, 1890; rev. ed., Boston, 1921.

   c **Lang, Andrew.** *Homeric hymns, a new prose translation, with essays literary and mythological.* 1899. New ed., London and N. Y., 1915.

   d **Hesiod.** *Poems.* Tr. by A. W. Mair, Oxford, 1908 [Oxford library of translations].

e Evelyn-White, Hugh G., ed. and tr. *Hesiod, the Homeric hymns, and Homerica.* London and N. Y., 1914 [Loeb classical library]. (Bibliography.)

Best recent translations in English of the literature of the epic period.

DMCF

D203a Browne, Henry. *Handbook of Homeric study.* 1905. 2nd ed., London, 1908.

b Seymour, Thomas D. *Life in the Homeric age.* N. Y., 1907. (Brief bibliography.)

c Jebb, Sir Richard C. *Homer, an introduction to the Iliad and the Odyssey.* 1887. 7th ed., Glasgow, 1919.

d Leaf, Walter. *Troy, a study in Homeric geography.* London, 1912.

e ——— *Homer and history.* London, 1915. [Northwestern University, Harris lectures.]

f ——— *Strabo on the Troad, book xiii, cap. 1, edited with translation and commentary.* Cambridge, Eng., 1923.

g Chadwick, Hector Munro. *Heroic age.* Cambridge, Eng., 1912. [Cambridge archaeological and ethnological series.]

h Cauer, Paul. *Grundfragen der Homerkritik.* 1895. 3rd rev. ed., 2 v., Leipzig, 1921–23.

i Leaf, Walter. *Companion to the Iliad, for English readers.* London and N. Y., 1892.

j Murray, Gilbert. *Rise of the Greek epic.* 1907. 3rd rev. ed., Oxford, 1924.

k Lang, Andrew. *Homer and the epic.* London and N. Y., 1893.

l ——— *Homer and his age.* London and N. Y., 1906.

m ——— *World of Homer.* London and N. Y., 1910.

n Scott, John A. *Unity of Homer.* Berkeley, 1921. [Sather classical lectures, University of California.]

o Allen, Thomas W. *Homer, the origins and the transmission.* Oxford, 1924.

The reader can get an idea of the vastness of the literature upon the Homeric question and of the complexity of the issues involved by consulting (D3b) *Jahresbericht über die Fortschritte der klassischen Altertumswissenschaft,* v. 2, 3, 9, 13, 26, 34, 42, 46, 62, 92, 112, 117, 138, 157, 161, 182, 191, 207. To select from that literature books which will best serve to introduce non-technical students to the subject is difficult.   *a.* Still perhaps the best introduction to the Homeric question as a whole, although recent discussion has tended to a more conservative view as to the question of literary unity.

b. Best account in English of the civilization depicted in Homer. An excellent brief account of the same topic will be found in ch. 2 of *c.* So far the student is on relatively solid ground. *d.* and *e.* Attempt in an interesting way to relate the Trojan war and the details of the Homeric narrative to the known facts of geography. *f.* Should be studied in connection with *d.* Here the reader will feel less secure, though the geography at least is relatively certain. *g.* Derives more or less valuable surmises as to the historical bases of the Homeric narrative from a careful comparison of the Homeric with the Teutonic epic.

The questions, all-important to the historian, as to the date of the Homeric poems, the date of the civilization which they depict, and whether the poems and that civilization were contemporaneous, have produced extended controversy, which may be said to involve two questions: the relation of the civilization depicted in the poems to that of the Mycenean epoch, and the literary unity of the poems. The reader can lay a basis for the understanding of the first of these questions by consulting the books listed in (D201). The prime difficulty lies in the fact that, on any hypothesis, the Homeric poems must be dated somewhere between 1100 and 700 B. C., in the so-called 'Greek Middle Ages,' which is the darkest of all periods in Greek history. The second question has evoked a greater volume of discussion than any other in the whole range of literary criticism; yet an accepted solution seems about as far distant as ever. A brief review of the earlier phases of the discussion may be found in c. The more recent phases are well set forth from the unitarian point of view, by A. Shewan, 'Recent Homeric Literature,' Classical Philology, 7:190, Apr. 1912. There is an admirable survey of the subject in (D661g) Christ, Geschichte der griechischen Literatur. h. Best handbook for the serious student of the problem. Until recently the overwhelming tendency among scholars was to deny, not merely that the Iliad and the Odyssey had a common author, but that either poem is a literary unit. This tendency in the modern form is illustrated by i. and j. The latter is a provocative work of genius which has raised a storm of controversy of itself. Review of b. and j., H. Browne, Classical Rev. 22:185, Sept. 1908; of i., J. T. Sheppard, ibid., 26:260, Dec. 1912; P. Shorey, Classical Philology, 6:258, Apr. 1911. At present the tide seems to be turning the other way. The opposite or 'unitarian' view, so long championed almost single-handed by (k., l., and m.) Andrew Lang, is now vigorously maintained by (n.) Scott, (o.) Allen and others. Review of n., J. T. Sheppard, Classical Rev., 36:169, Nov. 1922; of o., J. A. Scott, Classical Philology, 20:83, Jan. 1925. The most recent summary of the Homeric question in all its phases, historical as well as literary, is that by J. B. Bury in (C121) Cambridge ancient history, v. 2, ch. 18, which also presents the unitarian view.   DMCF

GREECE BEFORE THE PERSIAN WARS

D251a Ure, Percy N. *Greek Renaissance.* London, 1921.

   b ——— *Origin of tyranny.* Cambridge, Eng., 1922. (Bibliographical footnotes.)

   c Hogarth, David G. *Ionia and the East.* Oxford, 1909.

   d Ramsay, Sir William M. *Asiatic elements in Greek civilization.* Edinburgh, 1927. [Gifford lectures.]

   a. Interesting study of the seventh and sixth centuries and the beginnings of Hellenic culture; naturally somewhat speculative in places. *b.* Defense of Ure's most startling thesis, that the early tyrants rose to power by reason of wealth acquired largely through manipulation of the new medium of exchange —coined money. Adverse review of *b.,* W. R. Halliday, Classical Rev. 36:172, Dec. 1922; Ure's reply, ibid. 37:27, Feb. 1923. *c* and *d.* Valuable discussions of the influence of the Orient on early Greece. For other aspects of the period, cf. (C121) Cambridge ancient history, v. 3; and Jardé, Formation of the Greek *people*, in (B153a) Ogden, History of civilization. Review of *c*, D. M. Robinson, *A.H.R.* 29:112, Oct. 1923; of *d*, W. M. Calder, *Classical Review*, 53:221, Dec. 1928.

DMCF

D252a Sanctis, Gaetano de. *Atthis, storia della repubblica ateniese dalle origini alla età di Pericle.* 1898. 2nd rev. ed., Torino and N. Y., 1912. [Biblioteca di scienze moderne.] (Bibliographical footnotes.)

b Linforth, Ivan M. *Solon the Athenian.* Berkeley, 1919. [University of California publications in classical philology.]

c Seltman, Charles T. *Athens, its history and coinage before the Persian invasion.* Cambridge, Eng., 1924. (Bibliography.)

a. Critical study of the early history of Attica. The first edition closed with the reforms of Clisthenes.   *b.* Study of the sources for Solon's life; contains a translation of the extant fragments of his writings.   *c.* Interesting but rather speculative attempt to utilize numismatic evidence for the elucidation of early Athenian history. Extended critical review, E. S. G. Robinson, *Numismatic Chronicle*, 5th series, 15–16: 329–341, 1924.   DMCF

D253 Stählin, Friedrich. *Das hellenische Thessalien, landeskundliche und geschichtliche Beschreibung Thessaliens in der hellenischen und römischen Zeit.* Stuttgart, 1924.

Authoritative book upon ancient Thessaly. Review, A. J. B. Wace, *Classical Rev.* 39:139, Aug. 1925.   DMCF

D254 Casson, Stanley. *Macedonia, Thrace and Illyria.* Oxford, 1926.

Review, A. J. B. Wace, *Classical Review*, 41:231, Dec. 1927.   DMCF

GREECE FROM THE PERSIAN WARS TO ALEXANDER

D301a Grundy, George B. *Great Persian war and its preliminaries, a study of the evidence, literary and topographical.* London, 1901.

b —— *Thucydides and the history of his age.* London, 1911.

c Cornford, Francis M. *Thucydides mythistoricus.* London, 1907.

d Hill, George F., ed. *Sources for Greek history between the Persian and Peloponnesian wars.* 1897. 2nd rev. ed., Oxford, 1907.

e Obst, Ernst. *Der Feldzug Xerxes.* Leipzig, 1913. [*Klio*, Beiheft, 12.]

f Lamb, Walter R. M. *Clio enthroned: a study of prose form in Thucydides.* Cambridge, 1914.

g Abbott, George F. *Thucydides: a study in historical reality.* London, 1925.

h Henderson, Gerard W. *Great War between Athens and Sparta.* London, 1926.

a. Critique of Herodotus's narrative in the light of the author's topographical studies.   *b.* Contains chapters on 'Economic background of Greek history,' 'Art of war amongst the Greeks of the fifth century,' and 'Causes and strategy of the Ten Years' War,' in addition to a life of Thucydides and a discussion of his book. Review, M. O. B. Caspari, *Year's work in classical studies*, 6:106, 1911. *c.* Brilliant attack upon the credibility of Thucydides, which has not proved entirely successful. Review, J. P. Postgate, *Classical Quar.* 1:308, Oct. 1907. *d.* Complete assemblage of the sources for the period in the original text.   *e.*

Study by a German scholar, which may profitably be read along with *a*. Also cf. (C121) *Cambridge ancient history*, v. 4. *f*. and *e*. Defend the credibility of Thucydides. Review of *e*, M. L. W. Laistner, *Classical Weekly*, 21:133; Mar. 5, 1928. *h*. Military history of the Peloponnesian War. Review, M. Cary, *Classical Review*, 41:179, Nov. 1927. Cf. also (B169a 2) G. Glotz, *La Grèce au Ve siècle*.   DMCF

D302a **Grant, Arthur J.** *Greece in the age of Pericles*. N. Y., 1897. [Chautauqua series.]

　　b **Abbott, Evelyn.** *Pericles and the golden age of Athens*. 1897. New ed., N. Y. and London, 1903. [Heroes of the nations.]

　a. Strongly to be recommended to the general reader.   *b*. Best single volume in English on the age of Pericles.   DMCF

D303a **Glover, Terrot R.** *From Pericles to Philip*. N. Y. and London, 1917.

　　b **Beloch, Karl Julius.** *Die attische Politik seit Perikles*. Leipzig, 1884.

　　c **Marshall, Frederick H.** *Second Athenian confederacy*. Cambridge, Eng., 1905. [Cambridge historical essays.]   (Bibliographical footnotes.)

　　d **Pickard-Cambridge, Arthur W.** *Demosthenes and the last days of Greek freedom, 384–322 B. C.* London and N. Y., 1914. [Heroes of the nations.]

　　e **Schaefer, Arnold D.** *Demosthenes und seine Zeit*. 1856–58. 2nd rev. ed., 3 v., Leipzig, 1885–87.

　　f **Kessler, Josef** *Isokrates und die panhellenische Idee*. Paderborn, 1911. [Studien zur Geschichte und Kultur des Altertums.]

　　g **Demosthenes.** *Public orations*. Tr. by A. W. Pickard-Cambridge, 2 v., Oxford, 1912 [Oxford translations]. Tr. by C. R. Kennedy, 5 v., London, 1852–63 [Bohn classical library]. *De corona* and *De falsa legatione*. Ed. and tr. by C. A. and J. H. Vince, 1926 [Loeb classical library].

　　h **Jebb, Sir Richard C.** *Attic orators from Antiphon to Isaeos*. 1876. 2nd ed., 2 v. London, 1893.

　　i **Aeschines.** *Speeches*. Ed. and tr. C. D. Adams, London, 1919 [Loeb classical library].

　　j **Isaeus.** *Orations*. Ed. and tr. E. S. Forster, London, 1927 [Loeb classical library].

　a. Suggestive sketch.   *b*. and *e*. Older works; still fundamental; valuable for their references to sources.   *c*. Study of the second Athenian empire, 378–354 B. C.   *d*. Best account in English of the period.   *f*. Study of the publicist who best represents the ideas which were to inspire Alexander the Great in the next generation. An edition and translation of the works of Isocrates by G. Norlin is announced for early publication in the Loeb classical library. *h*. Best account in English of the Attic orators, who are the main sources of information for the period.   DMCF

HELLENISTIC PERIOD

D351a **Mahaffy, Sir John P.** *Alexander's empire*. 1887. New ed., London and N. Y., 1898. [Story of the nations.]

　　b **Hogarth, David G.** *Philip and Alexander of Macedon*. London and N. Y., 1897.

c **Wheeler, Benjamin I.** *Alexander the Great: the merging of East and West in universal history.* London and N. Y., 1900. [Heroes of the nations.]

d **Kaerst, Julius.** *Geschichte des hellenistischen Zeitalters.* V. 1–2, 1, 1901–09. Rev. ed. of. v. 1,2, with title *Geschichte des Hellenismus,* Leipzig, 1917–26.

e **Niese, Benedictus.** *Geschichte der griechischen und makedonischen Staaten seit der Schlacht bei Chaeronea.* 3 v. Gotha, 1893–1903. [Handbücher der alten Geschichte.]

f **Bury, John B.; Barber, Edwin A.; Bevan, Edwyn; and Tarn, William W.** *Hellenistic age, aspects of Hellenistic civilization.* Cambridge, Eng., 1923. [J. B. Bury, *Hellenistic age and the history of civilization;* E. A. Barber, *Alexandrian literature;* E. Bevan, *Hellenistic popular philosophy;* W. W. Tarn, *Social question in the third century.*]

g **Tarn, William W.** *Hellenistic Civilization.* London, 1927.

h **Meyer, Eduard.** *Blüte und Untergang des Hellenismus in Asien.* Berlin, 1925.

The only major history of Greece, in English, which includes the whole Hellenistic age is (D121c) Holm. *a.* Interesting outline of the epoch. *b.* and *c.* Excellent biographies. Review of *b.*, B. Perrin, *A.H.R.* 3:128, Oct. 1897; of *c.*, *A.H.R.* 6:113, Oct. 1900. For an interesting discussion of the different points of view with which modern writers have approached the career of Philip, cf. J. R. Knipfing, 'German historians and Macedonian imperialism,' *A.H.R.* 26:657–671, July 1921. On Alexander's eastern campaigns, also cf. (U1122) *Cambridge history of India,* v. 1. *d.* and *e.* Most complete scholarly works on the period. *d.* The treatment is topical rather than narrative and, in general, does not extend beyond the period of the Diadochi. Review, B. Perrin, *A.H.R.* 8:100, Oct. 1902; 14:793, July 1909. *e.* Exhaustive compilation of the available data to B. C. 120. Review, W. S. Ferguson, *A.H.R.* 10:911, July 1905. *f.* The fourth of these excellent essays describes the growth of poverty and economic discontent in the third century as illustrated by a study of prices and wages and of the revolutions of Sparta. Review, W. S. Ferguson, *A.H.R.* 30:124, Oct. 1924. *g.* Best description of the Hellenistic age and its civilisation in English. *h.* Brilliant summary by a great authority. Review, J. Hammer, *Classical Weekly* 23:22, Oct. 21, 1929. DMCF

D352a Ferguson, William S. *Hellenistic Athens.* London, 1911. (Bibliography.)

b **Freeman, Edward A.** *History of federal government in Greece and Italy.* 1863. 2nd rev. ed., by J. B. Bury, London and N. Y., 1893.

c **Tarn, William W.** *Antigonos Gonatas.* Oxford, 1913.

d **Mahaffy, Sir John P.** *Empire of the Ptolemies.* London and N. Y., 1895.

e **Bouché-Leclercq, Auguste.** *Histoire des Lagides.* 4 v. Paris, 1903–07. (Bibliography.)

f ——— *Histoire des Séleucides,* 323–64 avant J.–C. 2 v. Paris, 1913–14. (Bibliography.)

g **Bevan, Edwyn R.** *House of Seleucus.* 2 v. London, 1902.

h ——— *History of Egypt under the Ptolemaic dynasty.* N. Y., 1928.

a. Pronounced by Professor Eduard Meyer the best book on its subject in any language; readable. Review, B. Perrin, *A.H.R.* 17:589, Apr. 1912. *b.* Describes the Achaean and other Greek leagues. *c.* Useful biography for the history of Macedonia and Greece in the third century B. C. *d, e,* and *h.* Scholarly accounts of Hellenistic Egypt. Review of *d,* B. Perrin, *A.H.R.* 1:704, July 1896. Also cf. Mahaffy, 'Egypt under the Ptolemaic dynasty,' v. 4 of (C203) Petrie, *History of Egypt;* review, G. S. Goodspeed, *A.H.R.* 5:549, Apr. 1900. *f.* and *g.* Authoritative monographs on Syria. Review of *g.,* J. I. Manatt, *A.H.R.* 9:126, Oct. 1903. Review of *h,* C. J. Kraemer, *Classical Weekly* 23:71, Dec. 16, 1929. DMCF

D353a **Holleaux, Maurice.** *Rome, la Grèce, et les monarchies hellénistiques au IIIᵉ siècle avant J.-C., 273–205.* Paris, 1921. [Bibliothèque des Écoles Françaises d'Athènes et de Rome.].

   b **Colin, Gaston.** *Rome et la Grèce de 200 à 146 avant Jésus-Christ.* Paris, 1905. [Bibliothèque des Écoles Françaises d'Athènes et de Rome.]

   c **Barbagallo, Corrado.** *Déclin d'une civilisation, ou la fin de la Grèce antique.*

Important studies of the relations of Rome with Greece, Macedon, and other Hellenistic states in the third and second centuries. The authors differ radically in their estimates of the extent and significance of Roman intervention in the East in earlier Hellenistic times. Review of *a.,* T. Walek, 'La politique romaine en Grèce et dans l'orient hellénistique au IIIᵉ siècle,' *Revue de philologie,* 49:28–54, 118–142, 1925; W. S. Ferguson, *A.H.R.* 28:81, Oct. 1922; S. Reinach, *Revue Archéologique,* 15:372, May 1922; of *b.,* G. Radet, *Revue des études anciennes,* 8:81, Jan. 1906. DMCF

D354a **Rostovtzeff, Michael I.** *A large estate in Egypt in the third century, B.C., a study in economic history.* Madison, Wis., 1922. [University of Wisconsin studies in the social sciences and history.]

   b **Schnebel, Michael.** *Die Landwirtschaft im hellenistischen Aegypten.* V. 1. München, 1925. [Münchener Beiträge zur Papyrusforschung und antiken Rechtsgeschichte.]

   c **Schubart, Wilhelm.** *Aegypten von Alexander dem Grossem bis auf Mohammed.* Berlin, 1922.

a. Based upon recently discovered papyri. Important contribution to agricultural history. An excellent illustration of Greek administrative activities in the Hellenistic states. Review, W. L. Westermann, *A.H.R.* 28:83, Oct. 1922. *b.* Authoritative handbook upon the economic system of Hellenistic Egypt. *c.* Excellent sketch by a distinguished papyrologist of Egyptian life in the Hellenistic and Roman periods. DMCF

GREEKS IN SICILY AND ITALY

D401a **Freeman, Edward A.** *Story of Sicily: Phoenician, Greek, and Roman.* 1892. 2nd ed., London and N. Y., 1894. [Story of the nations.]

   b ——— *History of Sicily from the earliest times.* 4 v. Oxford, 1891–94.

   c **Holm, Adolf.** *Geschichte Siciliens im Alterthum.* 3 v. Leipzig, 1870–98.

   d **Pais, Ettore.** *Storia della Sicilia e della Magna Grecia.* Torino, 1894. [Storia d'Italia dai tempi piu antichi alle guerre puniche, pt. 1.]

e Tillyard, Henry Julius W. *Agathocles.* Cambridge, Eng., 1908. [Cambridge historical essays.]

f Ciaceri, Emanuele. *Storia della Magna Grecia.* Roma, 1927.

a. Excellent single volume.   *b.* Ends with the death of Agathocles, 289 B.C. *c.* Valuable for its references to the original sources.   *d.* Comprehensive study of the Greek colonies in Italy and Sicily. Also cf. (E254*e*) Pais, *Ancient Italy.* *e.* Biography of the tyrant of Syracuse who from B. C. 317 to 289 was the dominant figure in Greek Sicily. *f.* Review, A. C. Johnson, *A.H.R.* 33:624, Apr. 1928.

DMCF

DIPLOMATIC, MILITARY, AND NAVAL HISTORY, INTERNATIONAL LAW

D501 Ferguson, William S. *Greek imperialism.* Boston, 1913. (Select bibliographies.)

Scholarly public lectures describing the successive Greek hegemonies. Review, W. L. Westermann, *A.H.R.* 19:848, July 1914.

DMCF

D502a Phillipson, Coleman. *International law and custom of ancient Greece and Rome.* 2 v. London, 1911. (Bibliography.)

b Tod, Marcus N. *International arbitration amongst the Greeks.* Oxford, 1913.

c Caldwell, Wallace E. *Hellenic conceptions of peace.* N. Y., 1919. [Columbia studies in history, economics, and public law.]

a. Standard work in English on the principles governing the interstate relations of Greece.   *b.* and *c.* Special studies. On the Panhellenic ideas of the fourth century, cf. (D303*f*) J. Kessler, *Isokrates und die panhellenische Idee.*

DMCF

D511a Kromayer, Johannes. *Antike Schlachtfelder: Bausteine zu einer antiken Kriegsgeschichte.* V. 1–4 in 5. Berlin, 1903–24.

b Kromayer, Johannes, and **Veith, Georg,** ed. *Schlachten-Atlas zur antiken Kriegsgeschichte: 120 Karten auf 34 Tafeln mit begleitendem Text.* Leipzig, 1922 ff.

A good account of the military history of Greece is given in the first half of v. 1 of (B511) Delbrück, *Geschichte der Kriegskunst.*   *a.* Studies of the battles of Mantinea, B.C. 362; Chaeronea, B.C. 338; Sellasia, B.C. 221; and Mantinea, B. C. 207 are contained in v. 1.   *b.* The Greek half of this work will contain plans of the main battles from B.C. 490 to B.C. 207, with full explanatory notes and bibliography on each battle. For studies of the battles in the Persian war, cf. (D301*a*) Grundy, *Great Persian war.*

DMCF

D521a Shepard, Arthur M. *Sea power in ancient history: the story of the navies of classic Greece and Rome.* Boston, 1924. (Bibliography.)

b Ormerod, Henry A. *Piracy in the ancient world, an essay in Mediterranean history.* London, 1924. [The ancient world.]

a. Convenient summary. Review, J. W. Pratt, *A.H.R.* 30:119, Oct. 1924.   *b.* Illuminating assemblage and presentation of hitherto scattered data already mainly familiar. Review, T. Frank, *A.H.R.* 31:342, Jan. 1926.

DMCF

CONSTITUTIONAL AND LEGAL HISTORY, POLITICAL THEORY

D531a Halliday, William R. *Growth of the city state, lectures on Greek and Roman history.* Liverpool, 1923.

b Fowler, William Warde. *City-state of the Greeks and Romans, a survey introductory to the study of ancient history.* 1893. Reprint, London, 1907. [Macmillan's manuals for students.]

c Fustel de Coulanges, Numa D. *Ancient city, a study on the religion, laws, and institutions of Greece and Rome.* 1874. 10th ed., Boston, 1901. Tr. by W. Small from *La cité antique, étude sur le culte, le droit, les institutions de la Grèce et de Rome,* 1864, 19th reprint, Paris, 1905.

d Zimmern, Alfred E. *Greek commonwealth: politics and economics in fifth century Athens.* 1911. 3rd rev. ed., Oxford, 1922.

e Wilamowitz-Moellendorf, Ulrich, and **Niese, Benedictus.** *Staat und Gesellschaft der Griechen und Römer.* 1910. [(B606) Hinneberg, Kultur der Gegenwart.] (Bibliography.) Enlarged and rev. ed., Berlin, 1923.

f Francotte, Henri. *La polis grecque, recherches sur la formation et l'organisation des cités, des ligues, et des confédérations dans la Grèce ancienne.* Paderborn, 1907. [Studien zur Geschichte und Kultur des Altertums.]

g Rose, Herbert J. *Primitive culture in Greece.* London, 1925.

Studies of the ancient city state, describing the evolution of its political and social structure. *a.* Good introduction. *b.* and *c.* Classics, emphasizing the parallels between the development of the Greek states and that of Rome. *c.* Exaggerates the importance of religious forces, though the importance of religion as consecrating and expressing the different stages in the evolution is easily underestimated by the modern student. *d.* Brilliant work; emphasizes the geographical and economic background. *e.* and *f.* Other excellent recent studies by eminent scholars. Review of *e.,* L. Whibley, *Classical Rev.* 26:86, May 1912. For a recent account of the rise of the Greek city state, cf. (C121) *Cambridge ancient history,* v. 3, especially ch. 26, by F. E. Adcock. *g.* Restatement of the importance of religious forces in the social and political development of Greece in the light of recent anthropology.   DMCF

Cf. also (B153*a*).

D532a Greenidge, Abel H. J. *Handbook of Greek constitutional history.* London and N. Y., 1896. [Handbooks of archaeology and antiquities.] (Brief bibliography.)

b Botsford, George W. *Development of the Athenian constitution.* Boston, 1893. [Cornell studies in classical philology.] (Bibliography.)

c Gilbert, Gustav. *Constitutional antiquities of Sparta and Athens.* London and N. Y., 1895. Tr. by E. J. Brooks and T. Nicklin from v. 1, *Handbuch der griechischen Staatsaltertümer,* 2 v., Leipzig, 1881–85; 2nd ed. of v. 1, 1893.

d Busolt, Georg. *Griechische Staats- und Rechtsaltertümer.* 1887. 2nd rev. ed., 1892; 3rd ed., under title *Griechische Staatskunde,* 2 v. München, 1920–27. [(D35) Handbuch der Altertumswissenschaft.]

e Kahrstedt, Ulrich. *Griechisches Staatsrecht.* V. 1, *Sparta und seine Symmachie,* Göttingen, 1922.

a. Good handbook for students.   *b.* Valuable as containing an account of the usually accepted theory concerning the origin of the clan system which forms the background of Greek political institutions.   *c.* Most detailed account in English of the Spartan and Athenian constitutions. V. 2 of original treats of the constitutions of the other Greek states.   *d.* and *e.* Recent authoritative treatises. For discussion of conclusions of *e.,* cf. V. Ehrenberg, 'Spartiaten und Lakedaimonier,' *Hermes* 59:23–72, 1924. For the latest sketches of the Spartan, Athenian, and other constitutions, cf. (C121) *Cambridge ancient history,* v. 3, ch. 22–24.

DMCF

D533a **Croiset, Alfred.** *Les démocraties antiques.* 1909. Rev. ed., Paris, 1916. [Bibliothèque de philosophie scientifique.]

  b **Croiset, Maurice.** *Aristophanes and the political parties at Athens.* London, 1909. Tr. by J. Loeb from *Aristophane et les partis à Athènes,* Paris, 1907.

  c **Whibley, Leonard.** *Political parties in Athens during the Peloponnesian war.* 1888. 2nd ed., Cambridge, Eng., 1889. [Cambridge historical essays.]

  d ———— *Greek oligarchies, their character and organization..* N. Y. and London, 1896.

  e **Calhoun, George M.** *Athenian clubs in politics and litigation.* Austin, Texas, 1913. [University of Chicago thesis.] (Bibliography.)

  f **Pöhlmann, Robert von.** *Geschichte der sozialen Frage und des Sozialismus in der antiken Welt.* 1893–1901. 3rd rev. ed. by F. Oertel, 2 v., München, 1924.

Studies of various aspects of the struggle between oligarchy and democracy in Greece.   *a.* Most readable sketch of the evolution of democracy in Greece.   *e.* Describes the large part played by the hetaerae in Athenian life.   *f.* Illuminating comparison between ancient democracy and modern socialism. Review, F. Granger, *Classical Rev.* 28:90, May 1914.

DMCF

D534a **Boeckh, August.** *Public economy of the Athenians.* Boston, 1857. Tr. by A. Lamb from 2nd ed. of *Die Staatshaushaltung der Athener,* 1817, 2nd ed., 1850, 3rd rev. ed. by M. Frankel, 2 v., Berlin, 1886.

  b **Francotte, Henri.** *Les finances des cités grecques.* Paris, 1909.

  c **Cavaignac, Eugène.** *Études sur l'histoire financière d'Athènes au V*ᵉ *siècle, le trésor sacré d'Eleusis jusqu'en 404.* Versailles, 1908.

  d ————.*Études sur l'histoire financière d'Athènes au V*ᵉ *siècle, le trésor d'Athènes de 480 à 404.* Paris, 1908. [Bibliothèque des Écoles Françaises d'Athènes et de Rome.]

a. Classic account of Athenian public finance; still valuable. V. 2. Provides a complete collection of the documentary sources available in 1886. *b.* More recent treatment.   *c.* and *d.* Special studies of Athenian finance.   DMCF

D551a **Adams, Charles D.,** ed. *Lysias, selected speeches.* N. Y., 1905. [Greek series for colleges and schools.]

  b **Lipsius, Justus H.** *Das attische Recht und Rechtsverfahren mit Benutzung des 'Attischen Processes' von M. H. E. Meier and G. F. Schömann,* 3 v. in 4. Leipzig, 1905–15.

  c **Beauchet, Ludovic.** *Histoire du droit privé de la république athénienne.* 4 v. Paris, 1896.

d **Vinogradoff, Sir Paul.** *Jurisprudence of the Greek city.* Oxford, 1922. [(B551a) Outlines of historical jurisprudence, v. 2.]

e **Bonner, Robert J.** *Lawyers and litigants in ancient Athens.* Chicago, 1927.

f **Calhoun, George C.** *Growth of criminal law in Greece.* Berkeley, 1927.

g **Weiss, Egon.** *Griechisches Privatrecht auf rechtsvergleichender Grundlage.* V. 1. *Allgemeine Lehre.* Leipzig, 1923.

a. Contains, on p. 534–543, an excellent brief account of Athenian legal procedure. Also cf. (D31) Whibley, *Companion to Greek studies.* *b.* and *c.* Standard works of reference on the subject. *d.* Most extensive work in English. Vinogradoff is more interested in law than in procedures. Review, G. Smith, *Classical Philology,* 19:284, July 1924; E. Barker, *E.H.R.* 39:424, July 1924. *e.* Excellent description by an eminent scholar who is also a barrister. *f.* Interesting, though some of its contentions in the early part are speculative. Review of *b* and *c,* A. R. Bellinger, *Classical Review,* 33:474, 1928. *g.* First volume of an extensive work on Greek private law.   DMCF

D561a **Barker, Ernest.** *Political thought of Plato and Aristotle.* London and N. Y., 1906.

b ——— *Greek political theory: Plato and his predecessors.* London, 1918.

c **Willoughby, Westel W.** *Political theories of the ancient world.* N. Y., 1903.

d **Myres, John L.** *Political ideas of the Greeks.* Cincinnati, 1927.

Standard works on Greek political theory. *b.* Revision and enlargement of the first half of *a.* Another good survey is in (H561) Dunning, *History of political theories ancient and mediaeval.* For the political writings of Plato, cf. (D654); for those of Aristotle cf. (D655). Also cf. Bradley, 'Aristotle's conception of the state' in (D605a) Abbott, *Hellenica.*   DMCF

ECONOMIC AND SOCIAL HISTORY

D571a **Mahaffy, Sir John P.** *Old Greek life.* N. Y., 1884. [History primers.]

b **Davis, William S.** *A day in old Athens, a picture of Athenian life.* Boston, 1914.

c **Tucker, Thomas G.** *Life in ancient Athens; the social and public life of a classical Athenian from day to day.* N. Y. and London, 1906. [Handbooks of archaeology and antiquities.]

d **Gulick, Charles B.** *Life of the ancient Greeks, with special reference to Athens.* N. Y., 1902. [Twentieth century text-books.] (Bibliography.)

e *British Museum Guide to the exhibition illustrating Greek and Roman life.* 1908. 2nd ed., London, 1920.

f **McClees, Helen.** *Daily life of the Greeks and Romans as illustrated in the classical collections of the Metropolitan Museum of Art, New York.* N. Y., 1924.

g **Gardiner, Edward Norman.** *Greek athletic sports and festivals.* London, 1910. [Handbooks of archaeology and antiquities.] (Bibliography.)

h **Becker, Wilhelm A.** *Charicles; or illustrations of the private life of the ancient Greeks.* 1845. 4th ed., London, 1874. Tr. by F. Metcalfe from *Charikles, Bilder altgriechischer Sitte zur genaueren Kenntniss des griechischen Privatlebens,* 1840. Rev. ed. by H. Göll, 3 v., Berlin, 1877–78.

i **Müller, Iwan von.** *Griechische Privataltertümer,* 1887. 2nd ed., with additional section on *Kriegsaltertümer,* by Adolf Bauer, München, 1893. [(D35) Handbuch der Altertumswissenschaft.]

a. Brief but interesting. *b.* Excellent for supplementary reading in high schools. *c.* Somewhat more scholarly but slightly less entertaining than *b.* *d.* For teachers and advanced students. *e.* and *f.* Contain illustrative material and pictures. *g.* Excellent. *h.* Classic; under the guise of a novel describes the daily life of an ancient Athenian. As a novel it is deadly, but its excursuses contain a vast assemblage of material. *i.* Best book of reference. DMCF

D572a Martin, Albert. *Les cavaliers athéniens.* Paris, 1886. [Bibliothèque des Écoles Françaises d'Athènes et de Rome.]

b **Clerc, Michel.** *Les métèques athéniens, étude sur la condition légale, la situation morale, et le rôle social et économique des étrangers domiciliés à Athènes.* Paris, 1893. [Bibliothèque des Écoles Françaises d'Athènes et de Rôme.] (Bibliography.)

c **Zaborowski-Moindron, Sigismond.** *Ancient Greece and its slave population.* Washington, D. C., 1913. [Report of the Smithsonian Institution, 1912, p. 597–608.] Tr. from *Revue anthropologique,* 21:245–258, 1911.

d **Donaldson, James.** *Woman, her position and influence in ancient Greece and Rome and among the early Christians.* London and N. Y., 1907.

Studies of social classes in Athens. For Greek slavery also cf. (C571a) Wallon, *Histoire de l'esclavage dans l'antiquité,* (C571b), Ward, *Ancient lowly,* and (C571c) Meyer, *Kleine Schriften.* DMCF

D573a Glotz, Gustave. *Ancient Greece at work: an economic history of Greece from the Homeric period to the Roman conquest.* London, 1927. [(B153a) History of civilization]. Tr. by M. R. Dobis from *Le travail dans la Grèce ancienne.* Paris, 1920.

b **Guiraud, Paul.** *La propriété foncière en Grèce jusqu'à la conquête romaine.* Paris, 1893.

c ———— *La main d'œuvre industrielle dans l'ancienne Grèce.* Paris, 1900. [Université de Paris, Bibliothèque de la Faculté des Lettres.]

d **Francotte, Henri.** *L'industrie dans la Grèce ancienne,* 2 v. Bruxelles, 1900–01. [Université de Liège, Bibliothèque de la Faculté de Philosophie et Lettres.]

e **Blümner, Hugo.** *Technologie und Terminologie der Gewerbe und Künste bei den Griechen und Römern.* 4 v. in 3, Leipzig, 1875–87. 2nd rev. ed. of v. 1, Leipzig, 1912.

f **Diels, Hermann.** *Antike Technik.* 1914. 2nd rev. ed., Leipzig, 1920. [*Wissenschaft und Technik bei den Hellenen; 2, Antike Türen und Schlösser; 3, Dampfmaschine, Automat, und Taxameter; 4, Antike Telegraphie; 5, Die antike Artillerie; 6, Die antike Chemie; 7, Die antike Uhr.*]

g **Neuburger, Albert.** *Die Technik des Altertums.* 1919. 2nd rev. ed., Leipzig, 1921.

h **Jardé, Auguste.** *Les céreales dans l'antiquité grecque.* Paris, 1925. [Bibliothèque des Écoles Françaises d'Athènes et de Rome.]

i **Calhoun, George M.** *The ancient Greeks and the evolution of standards in business.* Boston, 1926.

j ———— *Business life of ancient Athens.* Chicago, 1926.

a. This is the only good economic history of Greece in English. Review, W. L. Westermann, *A.H.R.* 26:493, Apr. 1921.   *b.* Discusses the methods and organization of Greek agriculture; very valuable to the student of Greek politics, for the economic background of Greek political organization.   *c., d.,* and *e.* Describe Greek industry; the last is an exhaustive book of reference.   *f.* Popular lectures, bountifully illustrated, on certain ancient inventions. Review, M. W. Humphreys, *Classical Weekly,* 15:20, Oct. 17, 1921.   *g.* More systematic account of ancient mechanical devices.   *h.* Careful study of the sources of food supply in ancient Greece.   *i* and *j.* Review, J. Hammer, *Classical Philology,* 22:114, Jan. 1927.   DMCF

D574a Haussoullier, Bernard.   *La vie municipale en Attique, essai sur l'organisation des dèmes au quatrième siècle.*   Paris, 1884.   [Bibliothèque des Écoles Françaises d'Athènes et de Rome.]

  b Poland, Franz.   *Geschichte des griechischen Vereinswesens.*   Leipzig, 1909.

Standard collections of data on two important aspects of social organization in Attica: the demes, and the religious, social, and industrial guilds.   Review of *b.*, W. H. D. Rouse, *Classical Rev.* 25:213, Nov. 1911.   DMCF

D575a Beloch, Karl Julius.   *Die Bevölkerung der griechisch-römischen Welt.*   Leipzig, 1886.   [Historische Beiträge zur Bevölkerungslehre.]

  b Cavaignac, Eugène.   *Population et capital dans le monde méditerranéen antique.*   Strasbourg, 1923.   [Publications de la Faculté des Lettres de l'Université de Strasbourg.]   (Bibliographical footnotes.)

a. Standard assemblage of materials upon the question regarding the size of the population in the ancient states.   *b.* Recent discussion of various aspects of the problem adducing certain evidence not hitherto considered.   Review, M. Besnier, *Revue des Quest. Hist.* 201:231, July 1924; G. H. Stevenson, *E.H.R.* 39:110, Jan. 1924.   DMCF

CULTURAL HISTORY: GENERAL

D601 Van Hook, Larue.   *Greek life and thought, a portrayal of Greek civilization.*   N. Y., 1923.   (Good bibliography.)

Best general survey.   Review, C. B. Gulick, *A.H.R.* 29:589, Apr. 1924.   Also cf. (D102).   DMCF

D602a Mahaffy, Sir John P.   *Social life in Greece from Homer to Menander.*   1874.   7th ed., 1890.   Reprint, London, 1907.

  b ——— *Greek life and thought from the age of Alexander to the Roman conquest.*   1887.   Rev. ed., London, 1896.

  c ——— *Silver age of the Greek world.*   Chicago, 1906.

  d ——— *Greek world under Roman sway from Polybius to Plutarch.*   London and N. Y., 1890.

  e ——— *Progress of Hellenism in Alexander's empire.*   Chicago, 1905.

a., b., and *c.* Together constitute a very suggestive history of Greek civilization.   *d.* Earlier edition of *c.*   *e.* Six lectures on as many aspects of Hellenistic culture.   DMCF

D603a Mahaffy, Sir John P. *What have the Greeks done for modern civilization?* N. Y. and London, 1909. [Lowell lectures.]

   b. Livingstone, Richard W., ed. *Legacy of Greece.* Oxford, 1921. [G. Murray, *Value of Greece to the future of the world;* W. R. Inge, *Religion;* J. Burnet, *Philosophy;* Sir T. L. Heath, *Mathematics and astronomy;* D'Arcy W. Thompson, *Natural science;* C. Singer, *Biology;* C. Singer, *Medicine;* R. W. Livingstone, *Literature;* A. Toynbee, *History;* A. E. Zimmern, *Political thought;* P. Gardner, *Lamps of Greek art;* Sir R. Blomfield, *Architecture.*].

   c *Our debt to Greece and Rome.* Ed. by George D. Hadzsits and David M. Robinson, Boston, 1922 ff. [*1, J. A. Scott, *Homer;* *2, D. M. Robinson, *Sappho;* *3A, F. L. Lucas, *Euripides;* *3B, J. T. Sheppard, *Aeschylus and Sophocles;* *4, L. E. Lord, *Aristophanes;* *5, C. D. Adams, *Demosthenes;* *6, L. Cooper, *Aristotle's Poetics;* 7, A. E. Zimmern, *Greek historians;* *8,F. G. Allinson, *Lucian;* 9, C. Knapp, *Plautus and Terence;* *10A, J. C. Rolfe, *Cicero;* 10B, N. G. McCrea, *Cicero as philosopher;* *11, K. P. Harrington, *Catullus;* 12, G. D. Hadzsits, *Lucretius;* *13, E. K. Rand, *Ovid;* *14, G. Showerman, *Horace;* *15, J. W. Mackail, *Virgil;* *16, R. M. Gummere, *Seneca;* 17, G. Ferrero, *Roman historians;* *18, P. Nixon, *Martial;* *19, A. E. Taylor, *Platonism;* *20, J. L. Stocks, *Aristotelianism;* *21, R. M. Wenley, *Stoicism;* *22, R. G. Kent, *Language and philology;* 23a, W. R. Roberts, *Greek rhetoric and literary criticism;* 23b, G. C. Fiske, *Roman rhetoric and literary criticism;* *24, W. W. Hyde, *Greek religion;* 25, G. J. Laing, *Roman religion;* *26, J. E. Harrison, *Mythology;* 27, C. H. Moore, *Theories regarding the immortality of the soul;* *28, J. T. Allen, *Stage antiquities;* 29, E. Barker, *Greek politics;* *30, F. F. Abbott, *Roman politics;* 31, R. Pound, *Roman law;* 32, M. I. Rostovtsev, *Economics and society;* *33, E. S. McCartney, *Warfare by land and sea;* 34, R. J. Deferrari, *Greek fathers;* *35, H. O. Taylor, *Greek biology and medicine;* *36, D. E. Smith, *Mathematics;* 37, H. R. Fairclough, *Love of nature;* 38, F. Cumont, *Astronomy and astrology;* 39, A. Fairbanks, *Fine arts;* *40, A. M. Brooks, *Architecture;* 41, A. P. Gest, *Engineering;* *42, C. B. Gulick, *Greek private life;* *43, W. B. McDaniel, *Roman private life and its survivals;* * 44, W. R. Halliday, *Folk lore;* 45, J. F. Dobson, *Greek and Roman education;* 46, A. F. West, *Christian Latin writers;* 47, P. Shorey, *Roman poetry and its influence upon European culture;* 48, G. S. Brett, *Psychology;* 49, T. Reinach, *Music;* *50, R. Lanciani, *Ancient and modern Rome;* 51, B. L. Ullman, *Ancient writing;* *52, E. H. Haight, *Apuleius;* *53, W. Rhys-Roberts, *Greek rhetoric and literary criticism.*]

   d *Das Erbe der Alten, Schriften über Wesen und Wirkung der Antike.* Ed. by Otto Immisch and others. Leipzig, 1910 ff. [First series: 1, G. Treu, *Hellenische Stimmungen in der Bildhauerei von einst und jetzt;* 2–3, W. Süss, *Aristophanes und die Nachwelt;* 4, R. Hirzel, *Plutarch;* 5, H. Steiger, *Euripides;* 6, L. Hahn, *Das Kaisertum;* 7, A. von Mess, *Caesar, sein Leben, seine Zeit, und seine Politik bis zur Begründung seiner Monarchie;* 8, J. Geffcken, *Kaiser Julianus;* 9–10, K. Borinski, *Das Antike in Poetik und Kunsttheorie vom Ausgang des klassischen Altertums bis auf Goethe und W. von Humboldt.* Second series: 1, O. Immisch, *Das Nachleben der Antike;* 2, L. Weniger, *Altgriechischer Baumkultus;* 3–4, K. Heinemann, *Die tragische Gestalten der Griechen in der Weltliteratur;* 5, E. Stemplinger, *Horaz im Urtheil der Jahrhunderte;* 6, K. Bapp, *Aus Goethes griechischer Gedankenwelt;* 7, E. Stemplinger, *Antiker Aberglaube in seinen modernen Ausstrahlungen;* 8, J. Jüthner, *Hellenen und Barbaren;* 9, F. Münzer, *Die politische Vernichtung des Griechentums;* 10, E. Stemplenger, *Antike und moderne Volksmedizin.*]

Discussions of the contributions of ancient Greece to modern civilization. *a.* Illuminating volume of lectures. *b.* Volume of essays, each by an eminent Eng-

* Volumes marked with an asterisk have already appeared.

lish specialist. Also cf. (C604) de Burgh, *Legacy of the ancient world.* *c.* Series of small books of high excellence; still in process of publication. Other volumes may be expected to appear rapidly. *d.* German counterpart to *c.*

DMCF

D604a Dickinson, Goldsworthy Lowes. *Greek view of life.* 1905. 7th ed., Garden City, N. Y., 1925.

b Livingstone, Richard W. *Greek genius and its meaning to us.* Oxford, 1912.

c Greene, William C. *Achievement of Greece, a chapter in human experience.* Cambridge, Mass., 1923. (Bibliography.)

d Burns, Cecil D. *Greek ideals, a study of social life.* London, 1917.

e Taylor, Henry O. *Ancient ideals, a study of intellectual and spiritual growth from early times to the establishment of Christianity.* 1896. 2nd ed., 2 v., N. Y., 1913.

f Cooper, Lane, ed. *Greek genius and its influence, select essays and extracts.* New Haven, 1917. (Bibliography.)

g Thomson, James A. K. *Greeks and barbarians.* London, 1921.

h Croiset, Maurice. *Hellenic civilization.* Tr. from the French by P. D. Thomas. London, 1925.

Group of brilliant books strongly to be recommended to readers who desire to gain a sympathetic understanding of the Greeks. *a., b.,* and *c.* Depict the ancient Greek view of life in general. *d.* Describes the conflict of ideals in ancient Greece. *e.* Illuminating history of ideals in the ancient period, including those of Greece. *f.* Volume of extracts from the above and similar works. *g.* Describes the aspects in which the Greeks were conscious of superiority to non-Greeks, a most important side of Greek national feeling. DMCF

D605a Abbott, Evelyn, ed. *Hellenica, a collection of essays on Greek poetry, philosophy, history, and religion.* London, 1880. [E. Myers, *Aeschylus;* E. Abbott, *Theology and ethics of Sophocles;* R. L. Nettleship, *Theory of education in Plato's Republic;* A. C. Bradley, *Aristotle's conception of the state;* W. L. Courtney, *Epicurus;* R. C. Jebb, *Speeches of Thucydides;* H. G. Dakyns, *Xenophon;* J. L. Strachan-Davidson, *Polybius;* F. W. H. Myers, *Greek oracles.*]

b Marett, Robert R., ed. *Anthropology and the classics.* Oxford, 1908. [A. J. Evans, *European diffusion of primitive pictography and its bearings on the origin of script;* A. Lang, *Homer and anthropology;* G. G. A. Murray, *Early Greek epic;* F. B. Jevons, *Graeco-Italian magic;* J. L. Myres, *Herodotus and anthropology;* W. W. Fowler, *Lustratio.*]

c Smyth, Herbert Weir, ed. *Harvard essays on classical subjects.* Boston, 1912. [G. H. Chase, *New criticism of Roman art;* C. B. Gulick, *Notions of humanity among the Greeks;* C. N. Jackson, *An ancient letter-writer—Alciphron;* C. H. Moore, *Greek and Roman ascetic tendencies;* M. H. Morgan, *Some aspects of an ancient Roman city;* C. P. Parker, *Plato and pragmatism;* E. K. Rand, *Ovid and the spirit of metamorphosis;* H. W. Smyth, *Greek conceptions of immortality from Homer to Plato.*]

d *Greek literature: a series of lectures delivered at Columbia University.* N. Y., 1912. [P. Shorey, *Study of Greek literature;* H. W. Smith, *Epic poetry;* E. D. Perry, *Lyric poetry;* J. R. Wheeler, *Tragedy;* E. Capps, *Comedy;* B. Perrin, *History;* C. F. Smith, *Oratory;* F. J. E. Woodbridge, *Philosophy;* H. W. Prescott, *Hellenistic literature;* G. Lodge, *Greek influence on Roman literature.*]

Four volumes of valuable miscellaneous essays. DMCF

D606 Lunn, Sir Henry, ed. *Aegean civilizations.* London, 1925. [Sir H. Lunn and others, *Debate on the imperialism of Athens and her downfall;* S. R. James, *Olympia;* S. R. James, *Tiryns and Mycenae;* J. Gow, *Pergamum;* W. Leaf, *Troy;* H. J. C. Knight, *Greek sculpture;* W. Sanday, *Exploration in the Levant;* Sir G. Greenhill, *Astronomy and navigation in the Odyssey;* S. R. James, *Syracuse;* W. Leaf, *Ithaca;* R. Caton, *Delphi, Delos, Cos;* W. A. Jamieson, *Rhodes and the Knights of St. John;* G. B. Grundy, *Marathon;* J. Gow, *Thessaly and Tempe;* G. B. Grundy, *Thermopylae;* L. R. Furneaux, *Mount Athos;* J. Gow, *Oracles;* S. R. James, *Knossos.*]

Volume of lectures, by leading British scholars, addressed to visitors to Greek lands. Each important site receives independent treatment.   DMCF

CULTURAL HISTORY: RELIGION

D621a Fairbanks, Arthur. *Handbook of Greek religion.* N. Y., 1910. [Greek series for colleges and schools.] (Bibliography.)

b —— *Mythology of Greece and Rome.* 1907. New ed., N. Y., 1912. [Twentieth century text-books.]

c Nilsson, Martin P. *History of Greek religion.* Oxford, 1925. Tr., with author's revisions, by F. J. Fielden, from the Swedish.

d Kern, Otto. *Die religion der Griechen.* V. 1. *Von den Anfängen bis Hesiod.* Berlin, 1926.

a. and *b.* Convenient introductory handbooks. Also cf. W. W. Hyde, 'Greek religion and its survival' in (D603c) *Our debt to Greece and Rome.* *c.* Brief survey of the whole period from Minoan times onward; careful, sane treatment of primitive religious elements in relation to Greek religion. Only the two concluding chapters on 'The civic religion' and 'The religion of the cultured classes and the religion of the peasants' relate to the strictly historic period. Well written; by a scholar who has contributed several important monographs to the subject. *d.* Full treatment of early Greek religion. Review, H. J. Rose, *Jour. of Hellenic Studies,* 47:136, 1927. Cf. also (D531g) Rose.   GMD

D622a Farnell, Lewis R. *Cults of the Greek states.* 5 v. Oxford, 1896–1909.

b Fox, William S. *Greek and Roman mythology.* Boston, 1916. [Mythology of all races, ed. by L. H. Gray, v. 1.] (Exhaustive bibiliography of Greek and Roman religion and mythology.) Rev. ed., Boston, 1928.

c Roscher, Wilhelm H., ed. *Ausführliches Lexikon der griechischen und römischen Mythologie.* V. 1–6, Leipzig, 1884–1925.

d Preller, Ludwig. *Griechische Mythologie.* 1854. 4th rev. ed., by Carl Robert, 2 v. in several pt., Berlin, 1920 ff.

e Cook, Arthur B. *Zeus, a study in ancient religion.* Cambridge, Eng., 1914.

a. Discussion of the public cults of Greece with full reference to the original sources. *b.* General survey of Greek and Roman mythology, with emphasis on hero tales. *c.* Contains extended articles by eminent scholars upon all aspects of Greek religion. It extends at present to the word 'Windgötter.' *d.* Exhaustive treatise. *e.* Encyclopedic study from all sources. Written from the comparative point of view.   HBA

D623a Harrison, Jane E. *Prolegomena to the study of the Greek religion.* 1903. 2nd ed., Cambridge, Eng., 1908.

  b —— *Themis, a study of the social origins of Greek religion; with an excursus on the ritual forms preserved in Greek tragedy by Professor Gilbert Murray, and a chapter on the origin of the Olympic games by Mr. F. M. Cornford.* 1912. 2nd rev. ed., Cambridge, Eng., 1927.

  c —— *Epilegomena to the study of Greek religion.* Cambridge, Eng., 1921.

Complementary books emphasizing the folklore and mystery elements in Greek religion and purporting to give an account of the genesis of some of the major deities as indicated in the popular art and beliefs of the Greeks. The political and cultural influences are subordinated; the general point of view is anthropological or folklorist rather than historical.   HBA

D624a Farnell, Lewis R. *Greek hero cults and ideas of immortality.* Oxford, 1921. [Gifford lectures.]

  b Foucart, Paul. *Recherches sur l'origine et la nature des mystères d'Eleusis.* Paris, 1895.

  c —— *Le culte de Dionysos en Attique.* Paris, 1904.

  d —— *Les mystères d'Eleusis.* Paris, 1914.

  e Rohde, Erwin. *Psyche: Seelencult und Unsterblichkeitsglaube der Griechen.* 1894. 7th and 8th rev. ed., Tübingen, 1921. English translation by H. B. Hillis, London, 1925.

a. Excellent introduction to the Greek views of the future life and to the native Greek mysteries. *b., c.,* and *d.* Describe in detail certain aspects of the most famous of the Greek mysteries. *e.* Standard work on the ancient mystery religions. For the mystery cults of the Roman empire cf. (E627).   HBA

D625a Farnell, Lewis R. *Higher aspects of Greek religion.* London and N. Y., 1912. [Hibbert lectures.]

  b Murray, Gilbert. *Five stages of Greek religion.* 1912. 2nd rev. ed., N. Y. and London, 1925. [Columbia University lectures.]

  c Campbell, Lewis. *Religion in Greek literature.* London and N. Y., 1898.

  d Caird, Edward. *Evolution of theology in the Greek philosophers.* 2 v. Glasgow, 1904. [Gifford lectures.]

  e Adam, James. *Religious teachers of Greece.* Edinburgh, 1908. [Gifford lectures.]

  f Moore, Clifford H. *Religious thought of the Greeks from Homer to the triumph of Christianity.* 1916. 2nd rev. ed., Cambridge, Mass., 1925. (Bibliography.)

Attempts to interpret the spiritual side of Greek religion. *a.* and *b.* Relatively brief. Also cf. the chapter on Greek religion in (D604a) Dickinson, *Greek view of life.*   HBA

CULTURAL HISTORY: EDUCATION, THOUGHT, PHILOSOPHY

D641a Mahaffy, Sir John P. *Old Greek education.* 1882. Reprint, London and N. Y., 1905. [Education library.]

  b Freeman, Kenneth J. *Schools of Hellas, an essay on the practice and theory of ancient Greek education from 600 to 300 B. C.* London, 1907.

c **Bosanquet, Bernard,** tr. *Education of the young in the Republic of Plato, translated into English with notes and introduction.* Cambridge, Eng., 1900.

d **Allinson, Anne C.** *Roads from Rome.* N. Y., 1913.

a. Best general survey.   *b.* Study of Hellenic education with detailed examination of the monumental and literary sources.   *c.* Plato's theory of higher education as elaborated in the *Republic;* also cf. (D605a) and (D654).   *d.* Contains an admirable sketch of Athens in the Roman imperial period as a university town.   HBA

D651 *Library of Greek thought.* Ed. by Ernest Barker. 9 v. to date. London and N. Y., 1923 ff. [F. M. Cornford, *Greek religious thought;* M. L. W. Laistner, *Greek economics;* A. J. Toynbee, *Greek historical thought;* A. J. Toynbee, *Greek civilization and character;* J. D. Denniston, *Greek literary criticism;* F. A. Wright, *Greek social life;* E. A. Bevan, *Greek religion;* H. D. Oakley, *Greek ethical thought;* A. J. Brock, *Greek medicine.*]

Useful series for the general reader. Each volume contains translations of the most significant passages in Greek literature which illustrate a given phase of thought, together with an introductory essay.   DMCF

D652a Mayor, Joseph B. *Sketch of ancient philosophy from Thales to Cicero.* 1881. Reprint, Cambridge, Eng., 1912.

b **Windelband, Wilhelm.** *History of ancient philosophy.* N. Y., 1899. Tr. by H. E. Cushman from 2nd ed. of *Geschichte der antiken Philosophie,* 1888; 4th rev. ed. by A. Goedeckemeyer, entitled *Geschichte der abendländischen Philosophie im Altertum,* München, 1923. [(D35) Handbuch der Altertumswissenschaft.]

c **Gomperz, Theodor.** *Greek thinkers, a history of ancient philosophy.* 4 v. London, 1901–12. Tr. by L. Magnus and G. G. Berry from *Griechische Denker, Geschichte der antiken Philosophie,* 1896–1902, 2nd rev. ed., 3 v., Leipzig, 1903–09.

d **Zeller, Eduard.** *History of Greek philosophy from the earliest period to the time of Socrates.* 2 v. London, 1881. Tr. by S. F. Alleyne from *Die Philosophie der Griechen in ihrer geschichtlichen Entwicklung,* 1844–52; 2nd ed., 1855–68; 3rd ed., 1869–81; 4th and 5th ed., 1889–1909; 5th, 6th, and 7th ed.. 3 v. in 6, Leipzig, 1920–23.

e —— *Socrates and the Socratic schools.* 1868. 3rd rev. ed., London, 1885. Tr. by O. J. Reichel from *idem.*

f —— *Plato and the older Academy.* 1876. 3rd rev. ed., London and N. Y., 1888. Tr. by S. F. Alleyne and A. Goodwin from *idem.*

g —— *Aristotle and the earlier Peripatetics.* 2 v. London, 1897. Tr. by B. F. C. Costelloe and J. H. Muirhead from *idem.*

h —— *Stoics, Epicureans, and Sceptics.* 1870. 3rd rev. ed , London, 1892. Tr. by O. J. Reichel from *idem.*

i —— *History of eclecticism in Greek philosophy.* London, 1883. Tr. by S. F. Alleyne from *idem.*

j **Ritter, August Heinrich,** and **Preller, Ludwig.** *Historia philosophiae Graecae et Romanae ex fontium locis contexta.* 1838. 9th rev. ed., Gotha, 1913.

k **Bakewell, Charles M.** *Source book in ancient philosophy.* N. Y., 1907.

a. Best brief sketch.   *b.* Perhaps the best single volume.   *c.* Most readable extended account of Hellenic philosophy.   *d., e., f., g., h.,* and *i.* Really a single work; best reference authority for the English speaking student. *j.* The great collection of source material. *k.* Selections from the sources in English translation.

For those who read German, the latest edition of (B642) Ueberweg, *Grundriss der Geschichte der Philosophie des Altertums* is the most valuable bibliographical guide and work of ready reference. The development of the central lines of Greek speculation throughout its course is well set forth in (D625*d*) E. Caird, *Evolution of theology in the Greek philosophers.*   HBA

D653a Burnet, John. *Greek philosophy, part I, Thales to Plato.* London, 1914.

b ——— *Early Greek philosophy.* 1892. 2nd ed., London, 1908.

c Cornford, Francis M. *From religion to philosophy.* London, 1912.

d Diels, Hermann. *Die Fragmente der Vorsokratiker.* 1903. 3rd rev. ed., 2 v., Berlin, 1912.

e Nestle, Wilhelm, ed. and tr. *Die Vorsokratiker, die Sokratiker, die Nachsokratiker.* 4 v. Jena, 1908–23.

a. Best brief book on pre-Aristotelian Greek philosophy. *b.* Best brief book on the pre-Socratics. *c.* Presents a competing view of the beginnings of Greek philosophy. *d.* Fullest collection of source material on the subject, with a German translation of all important fragments, in addition to the Greek text. *e.* Supplements *d.* with material for later periods.   HBA

D654a Plato. *Dialogues.* Tr. with analyses and introductions by B. Jowett, 1871. 3rd rev. ed., 5 v., N. Y. and London, 1892; reprint, 1925. American reprint, 4 v., N. Y., 1897.

b ——— *Republic.* Ed. with notes and essays by B. Jowett and L. Campbell, 3 v., Oxford, 1894. Ed. by J. Adam, 1902; reprint, 2 v., Cambridge, Eng., 1905–07. Tr. by J. L. Davies and D. J. Vaughan, 1852; 3rd ed., 1866; reprint, London and N. Y., 1895 [Golden treasury series]. Jowett's tr. in *a,* printed separately, 2 v. [Oxford library of translations.]

c ——— *Laws.* Ed. with notes by E. B. England, 2 v., London and N. Y., 1921. [University of Manchester publications.]

d ——— *Euthyphron, Apology, Crito, and Phaedo.* Tr. by F. J. Church, 1880; reprint, London and N. Y., 1906 [Golden treasury series]. Jowett's tr. in *a,* printed separately. [Oxford library of translations.]

e ——— *Phaedrus, Lysis, and Protagoras.* Tr. by J. Wright, 1848; reprint, London and N. Y., 1921. [Golden treasury series.]

f Nettleship, Richard L. *Lectures on the Republic of Plato.* Reprint, London, 1920. [1st ed. was v. 2 of *Philosophical lectures and remains,* ed. by G. R. Benson, 1897.]

g Taylor, Alfred E. *Plato.* N. Y., 1909. [Philosophies ancient and modern.]

h Grote, George. *Plato and the other companions of Socrates.* 1865. New ed., 4 v., London, 1885; reprint, 1888.

a. Standard English version. *b., d.,* and *e.* Translations in the Golden treasury series are excellent as well as inexpensive. Translations of many of Plato's dialogues are also in the Loeb and Everyman's libraries. The notes in the editions mentioned under *b.* and *c.* are of importance for the student of Plato's thought. *f.* Illuminating. *g.* Brief and reliable work for the general reader. *h.* T view of pre-Platonic Greek philosophy, followed by a detailed and erudite stud of the several dialogues. For Plato's political thought, cf. (D561); for his ideas on education cf. (D641c) and Nettleship's essay in (D605a) Abbott's *Hellenica.*

HBA

D655a Aristotle. *Works.* Tr. by various authors under the editorship of J. A. Smith and W. D. Ross. V. 1–3, in part; 4–6; 8–11. Oxford, 1900 ff. To be completed in 11 v.

b —— *Nicomachean ethics.* Ed. with essays and notes by Sir A. Grant, 1866; 4th rev. ed., London, 1885. Ed. by J. Burnet, London, 1905. Tr. by J. E. C. Welldon, London, 1892.

c —— *Politics.* Ed. with introductory essays and commentary by W. L. Newman, 4 v., Oxford, 1887–1902. Tr. by J. E. C. Welldon, 1883; 2nd ed., 1888; reprint, London, 1905. Tr. with introductory essays by B. Jowett, 2 v., Oxford, 1885; reprint, 1 v., Oxford, 1905 [Oxford library of translations].

d Butcher, Samuel H., ed. and tr. *Aristotle's theory of poetry and fine art, with a critical text and translation of the Poetics.* 1895. 4th ed,. London, 1911. (Bibliography.)

e Taylor, Alfred E. *Aristotle.* N. Y., 1912. [People's books.]

f Ross, William D. *Aristotle.* London, 1923. (Bibliography.)

a. Standard English version. Translations listed under *b.* and c. are excellent. Introductory essays in the editions listed under *b.* and *c.* contain valuable expositions of Aristotle's ethical and political thought. The essays in Newman's *Politics,* for example, constitute a scholarly review of the whole of Greek political science. For the political thought of Aristotle, also cf. (D561). *d.* Includes an expository introduction and commentary. *e.* and *f.* Short volumes; the first the more readable, the second the more comprehensive and technical.

HBA

D656a Hicks, Robert D. *Stoic and Epicurean.* London and N. Y., 1910. [Epochs of philosophy.] (Select bibliography.)

b Bevan, Edwyn. *Stoics and sceptics.* Oxford, 1913.

c Arnold, Edward V. *Roman Stoicism.* Cambridge, Eng., 1911. (Bibliography.)

d Bussell, Frederick W. *Marcus Aurelius and the later Stoics.* Edinburgh and N. Y., 1910.

e Inge, William R. *Philosophy of Plotinus.* 2 v. London and N. Y., 1918. [Gifford lectures.]

a. Admirable popular exposition. *b., c., d.,* and *e.* Works of more scholarly importance. Also cf. W. L. Courtney, 'Epicurus' in (D605a) Abbott, *Hellenica.*

HBA

D657a Heath, Sir Thomas L. *History of Greek mathematics.* 2 v. Oxford, 1921.

b Dreyer, John L. E. *History of the planetary systems from Thales to Kepler.* Cambridge, Eng., 1906.

c Heath, Sir Thomas L. *Aristarchus of Samos, the ancient Copernicus: a history of Greek astronomy to Aristarchus, together with Aristarchus's Treatise on the sizes and distances of the sun and moon, a new Greek text with translation and notes.* Oxford, 1913.

d Duhem, Pierre. *Le système du monde, histoire des doctrines cosmologiques de Platon à Copernic.* 5 v. Paris, 1913–17.

   e **Tozer, Henry F.** *History of ancient geography.* Cambridge, Eng., 1897. [Cambridge geographical series.]

   f **Bunbury, Sir Edward H.** *History of ancient geography among the Greeks and Romans, from the earliest ages till the fall of the Roman empire.* 1879. 2nd ed., 2 v., London, 1883.

   g **Berger, Hugo.** *Geschichte der wissenschaftlichen Erdkunde der Griechen.* 1887–93. 2nd rev. ed., Leipzig, 1903.

   h **Moon, Robert O.** *Hippocrates and his successors in relation to the philosophy of their time.* London and N. Y., 1923. [Fitzpatrick lectures.]

   i **Berthelot, Marcellin.** *Les origines de l'alchimie.* Paris, 1885.

   j **Lones, Thomas E.** *Aristotle's researches in natural science.* London, 1912.

Authoritative studies of Greek science. For summaries of various aspects of Greek science cf. (D603*b*) Livingstone, *Legacy of Greece;* (D603*c*) *Our debt to Greece and Rome;* and Heiberg's article in (D32) Gercke and Norden, *Einleitung in die Altertumswissenschaft.* The latter has been translated into English as *Mathematics and physical science in classical antiquity.* Oxford, 1922.

FB

CULTURAL HISTORY: LITERATURE

D661a Wright, Wilmer C. *Short history of Greek Literature from Homer to Julian.* N. Y., 1907. [Greek series for colleges and schools.] (Bibliographies.)

   b **Capps, Edward.** *From Homer to Theocritus, a manual of Greek literature.* N. Y., 1901. (Bibliography.)

   c **Livingstone, Richard W.,** ed. *Pageant of Greece.* Oxford, 1923.

   d **Murray, Gilbert.** *History of ancient Greek literature.* N. Y., 1897. [Short histories of the literatures of the world, ed. by E. Gosse.]

   e **Croiset, Alfred,** and **Croiset, Maurice.** *Abridged history of Greek literature.* N. Y. and London, 1904. Tr. by G. F. Heffelbower from *Manuel d'histoire de la littérature grecque à l'usage des lycées et collèges,* 1900, 5th ed., Paris, 1900.

   f —— *Histoire de la littérature grecque.* 1887–99. 3rd rev. ed., 5 v., Paris, 1910–21.

   g **Christ, Wilhelm von.** *Geschichte der griechischen Literatur bis auf die Zeit Justinians.* 1888. 6th ed. by O. Stählin and W. Schmid, 3 v., München, 1912–24. [(D35) Handbuch der Altertumswissenchaft.]

   h **Foster, Finley M. K.** *English translations from the Greek, a biblographical survey.* N. Y., 1918. [Columbia University studies in English and comparative literature.]

For an excellent brief sketch of Greek literature by Jebb cf. (D31) Whibley, *Companion to Greek studies.* Also cf. (D605*d*.) *a.* and *b.* Good elementary manuals. *b.* Contains illustrative extracts. *c.* Specimens in translation of the greatest Greek writers so woven together by comments of the editor as to form an excellent, concrete account of Greek literature; intended for the general reader. *d.* Brilliant as well as sound. *e.* Abridgement of *f. f.* and *g.* Standard works of reference. *h.* List of English translations of Greek authors. For select lists, cf. (D601) Van Hook, *Greek life and thought* and (D604*a*) G. L. Dickinson, *Greek view of life.*

DMCF

D662a Edmonds, John M., ed. and tr. *Lyra graeca, being the remains of all the Greek lyric poets from Eumelus to Timotheus, excepting Pindar.* V. 1–2, London and N. Y., 1922–24. To be 3 v. [Loeb classical library.] (Bibliography.)

b Pindar. *Odes and principal fragments.* Ed. and tr. by Sir J. E. Sandys. London and N. Y., 1915 [Loeb classical library]. (Bibliography.)

a. Text and translation of all extant fragments of the lyric poets, including those discovered among the Egyptian papyri, also of all references in ancient literature to their lives. Pindar is not included. *b.* Text and translation of the extant works of Pindar. The contribution of lyric poetry to knowledge of social conditions in the eighth and seventh centuries is well set forth in (D101a) Botsford, *Hellenic history,* ch. 8 and 9, and in (D1) Botsford, *Hellenic civilization,* ch. 5.   DMCF

D663a Goodell, Thomas D. *Athenian tragedy, a study in popular art.* New Haven, 1920. [Yale classical series.]

b Norwood, Gilbert. *Greek tragedy.* London, 1920.

c Moulton, Richard G. *Ancient classical drama, a study in literary evolution intended for readers in English and in the original.* 1890. 2nd ed., Oxford, 1898.

d Haigh, Arthur E. *Attic theatre; a description of the stage and theatre of the Athenians and of the dramatic performances at Athens.* 1889. 3rd rev. ed. by A. W. Pickard-Cambridge, Oxford, 1907.

e Flickinger, Roy C. *Greek theater and its drama.* 1918. 2nd ed., Chicago, 1922.

f Allen, James T. *Greek theater in the fifth century before Christ.* Berkeley, 1920. [University of California publications in classical philology.] (Bibliographical footnotes.)

a. Excellent introduction to Greek tragedy, for the general reader. *b.* Somewhat more technical manual. *c.* Earlier study of Greek and Roman tragedy and comedy which is still of value. *d.* Until recently the standard work in English upon the structure of the Athenian theater and the conduct of dramatic performances at Athens. Still of value, though in the main superseded by *e.,* which also discusses the origin of Athenian tragedy and comedy. *f.* Recent discussion of the vexed problems relating to the structure of the theater in which the plays of Aeschylus, Sophocles, Euripides, and Aristophanes were originally produced.   DMCF

D664a Aeschylus. *Tragedies.* Ed. and tr. by H. W. Smyth, v. 1, London and N. Y., 1922 [Loeb classical library]. Tr. by E. D. A. Morshead. 2 v., London and N. Y., 1908–11 [Golden treasury series].

b Sophocles. *Tragedies.* Ed. and tr. with commentary by Sir R. C. Jebb, 7 v., Cambridge, Eng., 1883–96; translation published separately, Cambridge, Eng., 1906. Ed. and tr. by F. Storr, 2 v., London and N. Y., 1912–19 [Loeb classical library].

c Euripides. *Tragedies.* Ed. and tr. by A. S. Way, 4 v., London and N. Y., 1912–13 [Loeb classical library]. *Alcestis, Bacchae, Electra, Hippolytus, Iphigenia in Tauris, Medea, Rhesus, Trojan Women,* tr. by G. Murray, London, 1902–14.

d Aristophanes. *Comedies.* Ed. and tr. by B. B. Rogers, 3 v., London and N. Y., 1924 [Loeb classical library]. *Acharnians, Knights, Peace, and Birds,* tr. by J. H. Frere, privately printed about 1840; reprint, London and N. Y., 1909 [Everyman's library].

   e **Menander.** *Comedies, principal fragments.* Ed. and tr. by F. G. Allinson, London and N. Y., 1921 [Loeb classical library].

   f **Murray, Gilbert.** *Euripides and his age.* London and N. Y., 1913
   [Home university library]. (Bibliography.)

   g **Decharme, Paul.** *Euripides and the spirit of his dramas.* London and
   N. Y., 1906. Tr. by J. Loeb from *Euripide et l'esprit de son théâtre,* Paris,
   1893.

   h **Legrand, Philippe E.** *New Greek comedy.* London and N. Y., 1917.
   Abridged tr. by J. Loeb from *Daos, tableau de la comédie grecque pendant
   la période dite nouvelle,* Paris, 1910 [Annales de l'Université de Lyon].

   i **Appleton, Reginald P.** *Euripides the idealist.* N. Y., 1927.

   The Greek dramatists have been translated into English times without number.
The above are especially to be recommended.   *b.* Jebb's edition and translation
of Sophocles are superb pieces of English scholarship.   *d.* Frere's translations
from Aristophanes are literary classics.   Inexpensive translations of Aeschylus,
Sophocles, and Euripides are also available in Everyman's library.   *f.* and *g.*
Interesting popular studies of the social background of Euripides and Menander
respectively. On Aeschylus and Sophocles cf. (D605a) Abbott, *Hellenica;*
on Aristophanes cf. (D533b) Croiset, *Aristophanes and the political parties at
Athens;* and on Euripides the volume by Lucas in (D603c) *Our debt to Greece
and Rome.* Browning's translations of Euripides's *Alcestis* and Euripides's
Herakles contained in his *Balaustion's adventure* and *Aristophanes' apology* respectively, Browning's translation of Aeschylus's *Agamemnon,* and Mrs. Browning's translation of Aeschylus's *Prometheus bound* are perhaps the most readily
accessible specimens of Greek tragedy in English.   DMCF

D665a Lang, Andrew. tr. *Theocritus, Bion, and Moschus, rendered into English prose with an introductory essay.* 1880. New ed., 1889; reprint,
   London and N. Y., 1901. [Golden treasury series.]

   b **Couat, Auguste.** *La poésie Alexandrine sous les trois premiers Ptolémées
   (324–222 av. J–C).* Paris, 1882.

   c **Körte, Alfred.** *Hellenistic poetry.* N. Y., 1928. Trans. from *Die hellen-
   istische Dichtung,* Leipzig, 1925.

   a. Besides an excellent translation of characteristic specimens of Alexandrian
poetry, this little volume contains an introduction characterizing Alexandrian
literature as a whole.   *b.* Fuller account of Alexandrian literature, interestingly written.   Also cf. Barber's chapter in (D351f).   TSD

CULTURAL HISTORY: ART

D681 Fowler, Harold N.; Wheeler, James R.; and **Stevens, Gorham P.**
   Handbook of Greek archaeology. N. Y., 1909. [Greek series for colleges and schools.] (Bibliography.)

   Best introduction to the study of Greek archeology and art.   A brief account
of the progress of Greek archeology in modern times and a chapter on pre-
Hellenic Greece are followed by brief, but scholarly and accurate accounts of
each of the major and the minor arts: architecture, sculpture, terra-cottas, coins,
etc.   More than 400 illustrations.   GHC

D682 Michaelis, Adolf. *Century of archaeological discoveries.* London and N. Y., 1908. Tr. by Bettina Kahnweiler from *Die archäologischen Entdeckungen des neunzehnten Jahrhunderts,* Leipzig, 1906.

Popular account by one of the most learned German classical archeologists; well translated. Traces clearly and interestingly the progress of the science of archeology during a most important period, with special emphasis on work in Greek and Roman lands. Somewhat colored by the writer's own views and interests.   GHC

D683 Hall, Harry R. H. *Aegean archaeology, an introduction to the archaeology of prehistoric Greece.* N. Y., 1915. [Handbooks to ancient civilizations.] (Excellent classified bibliography.)

Presents, in logical arrangement, the principal results of the exploration of the Bronze Age sites in the Aegean area, and attempts, with emphasis on the actual remains and avoidance of theorizing, to draw as complete a picture as possible of the Aegean age. Cf. (S201a) Minns, *Scythians and Greeks, a survey of ancient history and archaeology on the north coast of the Euxine.*   GHC

D684 Weller, Charles H. *Athens and its monuments.* N. Y., 1913. (Brief critical bibliography.)

Excellent illustrations, often from photographs by the author. Gives a clear idea of what is actually to be seen in Athens; provides an introduction to the difficult subject of topography of the ancient city. Disputed questions are frankly treated as such, and although the writer usually states his own opinion, the reader is provided with a clear exposition of the evidence and of the arguments advanced by others.   GHC

D685a Hill, George F. *Historical Greek coins.* London and N. Y., 1906.

b Head, Barclay V. *Historia numorum, a manual of Greek numismatics.* 1887. 2nd rev. ed., Oxford, 1911. (Excellent bibliography.)

c Gardner, Percy. *History of ancient coinage, 700–300 B. C.* Oxford, 1918.

a. Describes many Greek coins of historic interest. *b.* Exhaustive treatise; lists the extant coin types according to the cities by which they were issued. *c.* Describes in detail the rise and history of coinage in Greece as a whole.
                                                                          DMCF

D686 Gardner, Percy. *Principles of Greek art.* London and N. Y., 1914. (Rev. ed. of *Grammar of Greek art,* 1905.)

An attempt to formulate a 'grammar' or underlying principles of Greek art. These are discussed as they manifest themselves in architecture, sculpture, painting, and coins; many interesting and suggestive comparisons with other manifestations of the Greek spirit, especially with literary works. Chapters on 'Art in relation to history' and 'Coins in relation to history.'   GHC

D687 Anderson, William J., and Spiers, Richard Phené. *Architecture of Greece and Rome, a sketch of its historic development.* 1902. 2nd rev. ed., by R. P. Spiers, London, 1907. (Bibliography.)

Ch. 1–7. Trace the development of architecture in Greece from the Mycenean period to the post-Alexandrian age, and aim to give a consecutive historical account. Ch. 8. Discusses the secular architecture of the Greeks. Well-chosen illustrations, beautifully reproduced; useful glossary of technical terms.   GHC

D688 Chase, George H. *Greek and Roman sculpture in American collections.* Cambridge, Mass., 1924. [Lowell Institute lectures.]

Excellent and readable account of the outstanding characteristics of the several periods of classical sculpture as illustrated by specimens available in the United States. The most famous specimens in the European museums, together with the American specimens under discussion, are reproduced in photographs.

DMCF

D689a Gardner, Ernest A. *Handbook of Greek sculpture.* 1896–97. 2nd ed., London and N. Y., 1915. [Handbooks of archaeology and antiquities.] (Select bibliography.)

  b Collignon, Maxime. *Histoire de la sculpture grecque.* 2 v. Paris, 1892–97.

  c Furtwängler, Adolf. *Masterpieces of Greek sculpture, a series of essays on the history of art.* London, 1895. Ed. and tr. by Eugénie Sellers from *Meisterwerke der griechischen Plastik,* Leipzig, 1893.

a. The great value of this book lies in its orderly arrangement and its emphasis on the literary, as well as the monumental, sources for the study of Greek sculpture. Though somewhat dry in style, it contains good descriptions of most of the important works of the Greek sculptors and brief statements of the principal theories and controversies concerning them. The relation of the development of sculpture to the development of Greek civilization as a whole is well brought out.   *b.* Most readable history of Greek sculpture, written with characteristic French orderliness and clearness. Discoveries made since the book was written have added new material, but have not greatly altered the theories here propounded and discussed. Many excellent illustrations; references to original publications are freely given.   *c.* Controversial book, in which the attempt is made, on stylistic grounds, to increase the body of work attributed to the great Greek sculptors. Excellent as an example of critical method, but many of the theories here advanced have not met with general approval.   GHC

D690a Overbeck, Johannes. *Die antiken Schriftquellen zur Geschichte der bildenden Künste bei den Griechen.* Leipzig, 1868.

  b Jones, Henry Stuart, ed. and tr. *Select passages from ancient authors illustrative of the history of Greek sculpture.* London and N. Y., 1895.

  c Jex-Blake, Katharine, and **Sellers, Eugénie,** ed. and tr. *The elder Pliny's chapters on the history of art.* London and N. Y., 1896. (Bibliography.)

  d Pausanias. *Description of Greece.* Ed. and tr. by James G. Frazer. 1898. Reprint, 6 v., London and N. Y., 1913.

  e Loewy, Emanuel. *Inschriften griechischer Bildhauer.* Leipzig, 1885. (Bibliography.)

a. Indispensable for the study of Greek sculpture and painting.   *b.* Selection of important passages, accompanied by translations and references to modern discussions.   *c.* Contains the text of parts of books 34–36 of the *Naturalis historia,* with a translation and illuminating comments.   *d.* Mine of information for all questions connected with the 'Greek Baedeker.'   *e.* Though out of date, represents the only attempt to bring together the numerous signatures of Greek sculptors which have been preserved.   GHC

BIOGRAPHIES

D701a Hopkinson, Leslie W. *Greek leaders.* Boston, 1918.
b Bromby, Charles H. *Alkibiades.* London, 1905.

The story of Greece abounds in picturesque characters and the history of the classical period might easily be related in the form of a series of biographies. *a.* Successful attempt so to treat the subject in a small volume for the general reader. *b.* Readable biography intended also for the general reader.

Biographies of Greek statesmen, however, are apt to resolve themselves into histories of the periods in which their subjects lived, and hence in this section biographies are with these two exceptions listed under the histories of special periods. Cf. (252*b*) Solon, (301*b*) Thucydides, (302) Pericles, (303*d* and *e*) Demosthenes, (303*f*) Isocrates, (351*b* and *c*) Philip and Alexander, (352*c*) Antigonos Gonatas, (401*e*) Agathocles, (654*g* and *h*) Plato, (655*e* and *f*) Aristotle, (657*c*) Aristarchus of Samos. DMCF

ACADEMY AND UNIVERSITY PUBLICATIONS

The academy publications listed in other §§ frequently contain good articles in the field of classical studies. Doctoral dissertations and other monographs appear in (D921) *Harvard studies in classical philology,* Cambridge, Mass., 1890 ff.; (D922) *Cornell studies in classical philology,* N. Y., 1887 ff.; (D923) *University of California publications in classical philology,* Berkeley, 1904 ff.; and in the corresponding philological and historical series published by other American universities.

PERIODICALS

Aside from (D941a) *Klio, Beiträge zur alten Geschichte,* annual, with frequent *Beihefte,* Leipzig, 1901 ff., there is no periodical of importance devoted exclusively to ancient history. This is now supplemented by (D941*b*) *Die Antike, Zeitschrift für Kunst und Kultur des klassischen Altertums,* quarterly, Berlin, 1925 ff., and (D941*c*) *Gnomon, Kritische Zeitschrift für die gesamte klassische Altertumswissenschaft,* monthly, Berlin, 1925 ff. Research in these fields finds publication, for the most part, either in periodicals devoted to general literature or to history in general, which are listed in § B, or in those devoted to classical philology or archeology, of which the most important are here mentioned.

PHILOLOGY: *United States:* (D942a) *American journal of philology,* quarterly, Baltimore, 1880 ff., published under the auspices of the American Philological Association; (D942*b*) *Transactions and proceedings* of the same society, Hartford, Conn., and Cleveland, Ohio, 1869 ff.; (D943) *Classical philology,* quarterly, Chicago, 1906 ff., published by the University of Chicago; (D944) *Classical journal,* 9 no. a year, Chicago and Cedar Rapids, Iowa, 1905 ff., published by the Classical Association of the Middle West and South; (D945) *Classical weekly,* N. Y., 1907 ff., published by the Classical Association of the Atlantic States. The two journals last mentioned are designed primarily for teachers of classics in secondary schools, but they frequently contain valuable reviews and historical articles. The last named publishes frequent lists of current articles on classical subjects appearing in non-classical periodicals.

Great Britain and Ireland: (D946a) *Classical review,* 8 no. a year, London, 1887 ff., and (D946b) *Classical quarterly,* London, 1907 ff., both published under the auspices of the Classical Association. The *Quarterly* appears in Jan., Apr., July, and Oct., the *Review* in the remaining months of the year and, as its name suggests, is devoted mainly to book reviews. The *Quarterly* was instituted to relieve the *Review* of its longer articles. (D947)*Journal of Hellenic studies,* semi-annual, London, 1880 ff., published by the Society for the Promotion of Hellenic Studies; (D948) *Journal of philology,* annual, London, 1868–1920; (D949) *Hermathena,* annual, Dublin, 1874 ff., published by Trinity College, Dublin.

Germany and Austria: (D950a) *Berliner philologische Wochenschrift,* weekly, Berlin, 1881–1920; and (D950b) *Wochenschrift für klassische Philologie,* Berlin, 1884–1920, now combined as (D950c) *Philologische Wochenschrift,* weekly, Berlin, 1921 ff. These periodicals are devoted mainly to reviews of current books. Articles appear in (D951) *Berliner Studien für classische Philologie und Archaeologie,* 19 v., Berlin, 1884–98; (D952) *Hermes, Zeitschrift für klassische Philologie,* annual, Berlin, 1866 ff.; (D953) *Leipziger Studien zur classischen Philologie,* annual, Leipzig, 1878 ff.; (D954a) *Jahrbücher für Philologie und Pädagogik,* Leipzig, 1826–30; and its successors, (D954b) *Neue Jahrbücher für Philologie und Pädagogik,* Leipzig, 1831–97; (D954c) *Neue Jahrbücher für das klassische Altertum, Geschichte, und deutsche Litteratur und für Pädagogik,* Leipzig, 1898–1924; (D954d) *Neue Jahrbücher für Wissenschaft und Jugend-bildung,* Leipzig, 1925 ff.; (D955) *Philologus: Zeitschrift für das klassische Altertum und sein Nachleben,* annual, Göttingen and Leipzig, 1846 ff.; (D956) *Rheinisches Museum für Philologie,* quarterly, Frankfurt am Main, 1827 ff.; (D957) *Wiener Studien: Zeitschrift für klassische Philologie,* semi-annual, Wien, 1879–1919.

France: (D958) *Revue des études grecques,* quarterly, Paris, 1888 ff.; (D959) *Revue de philologie, de littérature, et d'histoire anciennes,* quarterly, Paris, 1845 ff.; (D960) *Revue des études anciennes,* annual, Bordeaux, 1899 ff.

Belgium: (D961a) *Le musée belge, revue de philologie classique,* quarterly, Louvain, 1897 ff. and its bibliographical supplement, (D961b) *Bulletin biblio-graphique et pédagogique du musée belge,* annual, Louvain, 1897 ff.

Netherlands: (D962) *Mnemosyne, bibliotheca philologica batava,* quarterly, Lugduni-Batavorum, 1852 ff.

Sweden: (D963) *Eranos, acta philologica suecana,* annual, Upsaliae and Goto-burgi, 1896 ff.

Italy: (D964) *Atene e Roma, bollettino della Società italiana per la diffusione e l'incoraggiamento degli studi classici,* Firenze, 1898 ff.; (D965a) *Rivista di filologia e d'istruzione classica,* quarterly, Torino, 1872 ff.; and its bibliographical sister (D965b) *Bollettino di filologia classica,* monthly, Torino, 1894 ff.; (D966) *Studi italiani di filologia classica,* quarterly, Firenze, 1893 ff.; (D967) *Rivista di storia antica e scienze affini,* quarterly, Messina, 1895–1910.

Greece: (D968)*Athēna,* annual, Athēnai, 1889 ff., published by Epistēmonikē Hetaireía; (D969) *Parnassós,* Athēnai, 1877 ff., published by Philologikòs Súllogos Parnassós, (D970) *Laographia,* quarterly, Athēnai, 1908 ff.

ARCHEOLOGY: The publications of the various schools at Athens are nat-urally of the utmost importance to the student of Greek history: (D971a) *Papers,* Boston, 1882–97, and (D971b) *Bulletin,* Boston, etc., 1883–1902, of the American

School of Classical Studies at Athens; (D972) *Annual of the British School at Athens*, London, 1894 ff.; (D973) *Mitteilungen des Kaiserlich Deutschen Archäologischen Instituts, Athenische Abteilung*, annual, Athens, 1876 ff.; (D974) *Jahreshefte des Oesterreichischen Archäologischen Institutes*, Wien, 1898 ff.; (D975) *Bulletin de correspondance hellénique*, annual, Athènes and Paris, 1877 ff., of the École Française d' Athènes; (D976) *Annuario della Scuola Archeologica di Atene e della Missioni Italiana in Oriente*, annual, Bergamo, 1914 ff.; (D977) *Ephēmerìs archaiologikē*, annual, Athēnai, 1837 ff., published by the Archaiologikē Hetaireía; and (D978) *Archaiologikon deltion*, annual, Athēnai, 1915 ff., published by the Greek government.

In addition the following archeological periodicals often contain articles upon Greek archeology:

United States: (D979) *American journal of archaeology*, quarterly, Concord, N. H., 1885 ff., published by the Archaeological Institute of America; the best journal in English for the student; reports promptly all new finds and new books; now the organ of the American School of Classical Studies at Athens; (D980) *Art and archaeology*, monthly, Washington, D. C., 1914 ff., published by the Washington Society of the Archaeological Institute, a popular, beautifully illustrated journal, especially to be recommended to the teacher and the general reader.

Great Britain: (D981a) *Archaeologia*, annual, London, 1770 ff., and (D981b) *Antiquaries' journal*, quarterly, London, 1921 ff., which is the successor of (D981c) *Proceedings of the Society of Antiquaries of London*, 36 v., London, 1843–1920, all published by the Society of Antiquaries of London, the first named is devoted to articles; (D982) *Journal of the British Archaeological Association*, annual, London, 1845 ff.; and (D983) *Archaeological journal*, London, 1844 ff., of the Royal Archaeological Institute of Great Britain and Ireland.

France: (D984) *Revue archéologique*, monthly, Paris, 1844 ff., important for its book reviews and reports of discoveries; (D985) *Comptes rendus des séances de l'Académie des Inscriptions et Belles-Lettres*, monthly, Paris, 1857 ff., which likewise reports recent discoveries; (D986) *Monuments et mémoires: publiée par l'Académie des Inscriptions et Belles-Lettres: Fondation Eugène Piot*, occasional, Paris, 1894 ff.; (D987) *Bibliothèque des Écoles françaises d'Athènes et de Rome*, occasional, Paris, 1876 ff., a series of monographs.

Germany and Austria: (D988) *Jahrbuch des Kaiserlich-Deutschen Archäologischen Instituts*, Berlin, 1886 ff.; (D989) *Archäologisch-epigraphische Mitteilungen aus Oesterreich-Ungarn*, 20 v. in 7, Wien, 1877–97, and its successor, (D974) *Jahreshefte des Oesterreichischen Archäologischen Institutes*, Wien, 1898 ff.

PAPYROLOGY: (D996) *Archiv für Papyrusforschung und verwandte Gebiete*, 6 v., Leipzig, 1900–20; (D997) *Studien zur Paläographie und Papyruskunde*, annual, Leipzig, 1901 ff.; (D998) *Studî della Scuola Papirologica*, Milano, 1915 ff.

EPIGRAPHY: Newly found inscriptions are recorded in (D958) *Revue des études grecques*.

NUMISMATICS: Most of the numismatic periodicals listed in §A contain articles of importance to the student of ancient Greece.   DMCF

SECTION E

ROME: THE REPUBLIC AND THE EMPIRE

Editor

ARTHUR EDWARD ROMILLY BOAK

Professor of Ancient History, University of Michigan.

CONTENTS

INTRODUCTION

The treatment in this section differs sharply from that in the preceding one on Ancient Greece, mainly because of the narrower range of literature available. Consequently fewer titles are listed and fuller attention is given to the characterization of the works cited. Another consideration is that a large part of the scholarly output in the field of Roman history is of the specialized monograph type, which it is impracticable to include in a work of so limited scope as the present. This is peculiarly unfortunate, as no adequate guide exists to the literature of Roman history. The section further differs from that on Greece in the marked emphasis on political, constitutional, and legal history and in the relatively small attention allotted to cultural topics. In this respect the section corresponds with substantial accuracy to the distribution of the available works in the two fields, and, indeed, to the relative importance of the topics in the two cases. To a considerable degree the differences between the two sections reflect the differences between the respective contributions of Greece and Rome in the history of the world.

Works on the general history of the ancient world are discussed in § C; those on the general history of classical antiquity in § D; those on the rise of Christianity in § F; those on the continuation of the empire in the East, that is, Byzantine history, in § H; those on the later history of the West and of Italy in §§ H and O.

BIBLIOGRAPHY

The current literature on Roman history is contained mainly in classical and historical periodicals, of which lists are appended to §§ B, C, and D, as well as to the present section. Brief annual bibliographies are given in (D3a) *Year's work in classical studies,* published by the English Classical Association, and in (B15a) *Annual bulletin of historical literature,* published by the English Historical Association. (B941f 10) *Revue des questions historiques* publishes an annual 'Chronique d'histoire ancienne grecque et romaine'; and (D959) *Revue de philologie* contains two very complete annual bulletins entitled 'Revue des comptes rendus d'ouvrages relatifs à l'antiquité classique,' and 'Revue des revues: bibliographie analytique des articles de périodiques relatifs à l'antiquité classique.' More complete, but somewhat more tardy in appearing, are the annual records of new publications in (D3b) *Jahresbericht über die Fortschritte der klassischen Altertumswissenschaft,* and, prior to 1918, in (B15b) *Jahresberichte der Geschichtswissenschaft.*

E1 Botsford, George W. *Syllabus of Roman history.* N. Y., 1915. (Select bibliographies.)

Designed to serve as a guide for the independent study of Roman history. Gives an outline of the field, divided into convenient epochs, with a topical analysis of each, and with brief lists of the sources and modern works bearing upon the several topics in each section. For a similar work on a somewhat more extended scale, cf. (D36) Laurand, *Manuel des études grecques et latines.*

AERB

E11a Rosenberg, Arthur. *Einleitung und Quellenkunde zur römischen Geschichte.* Berlin, 1921.

b Peter, Hermann W. G. *Die geschichtliche Litteratur über die römische Kaiserzeit bis Theodosius I und ihre Quellen.* 2 v. Leipzig, 1897.

Best introductions to the literature of Roman history; but reference may also be made to (C61) Wachsmuth, *Einleitung in das Studium der alten Geschichte;* to the surveys by Beloch and Kornemann in (D32) Gercke and Norden, *Einleitung in die Altertumswissenschaft;* and to the pertinent sections in (E101) Niese, *Grundriss der römischen Geschichte.*   AERB

Library collections.—The libraries best equipped for the study of Roman history are those of the larger universities. Of these, Harvard and Columbia have excellent, well-rounded collections. Chicago is particularly strong in editions of ancient authors and in dissertations; Princeton in texts, inscriptions, and papyri; Michigan in papyri, inscriptions, and archeological material; Illinois in texts, monographs, and archeological works. Cornell is especially well equipped on the early empire to the Flavians and on the third century, besides having good epigraphical and papyrological collections. Wisconsin and Johns Hopkins also have a good general equipment, and the former is, in addition, strong in the field of papyri. Yale has the Wheeler collection of about eight thousand volumes on Roman law.   AHS

Museum collections.—The principal collections of Roman art and antiquities in the United States and Canada are listed under this heading in § D.

ENCYCLOPEDIAS AND WORKS OF REFERENCE

E21a Jones, Henry Stuart. *Companion to Roman history.* Oxford, 1912. (Bibliographies.)

b Sandys, Sir John E., ed. *Companion to Latin studies.* 1910. 3rd rev. ed., Cambridge, Eng., 1921. [1, J. E. Sandys, *Geography of Italy;* 2, W. Ridgeway, *Ethnology of Italy;* 3, T. Ashby, *Topography of Rome;* 4, O. Keller, *Fauna;* 5, Sir W. T. Thiselton-Dyer, *Flora;* 6, J. S. Reid, *Chronology;* 7, W. W. Fowler, *Religion and mythology;* 8, F. H. Marshall, *Birth, marriage, and death; Position of women; Dress; Daily life; Agriculture; House and furniture;* 9, W. Murison, *Education;* 10, M. R. James, *Books and writings;* 11, J. S. Reid, *Roman constitution; Law;* 12, G. H. Stevenson, *Finance;* 13, F. H. Marshall, *Population; Orders of society; Slaves;* 14, B. W. Henderson, *Roman municipal system; Colonies; Roman provincial system; Alphabetic list of provinces;* 15, R. C. Bosanquet, *Industry and commerce; Roads and travel;* 16, W. Ridgeway, *Roman measures and weights; Roman money;* 17, E. H. Alton, *Roman army;* 18, W. W. Tarn, *Roman navy;* 19, J. H. Gray, *Roman public games; Roman theatre;* 20, C. Gutch, *Architecture;* 21, A. J. B. Wace, *Sculpture;* 22, A. H. Smith, *Terracottas;* 23, W. Ridgeway, *Engraved gems;* 24, F. R. Earp, *Painting and mosaic;* 25, A. W. Verrall, *Poetry to the end of the Augustan age;* 26, W. C. Summers, *Post-Augustan poetry;* 27, J. E. Sandys, *Prose from Cato to Cassiodorus;* 28, R. D. Hicks, *Roman philosophy;* 29, J. F. Payne, *Natural history and science; Medicine;* 30, J. E. Sandys, *Epigraphy;* 31, Sir E. M. Thompson, *Palaeography;* 32, J. P. Postgate, *Textual criticism;* 33, P. Giles, *Languages of Italy;* 34, A. W. Verrall, *Metre;* 35, J. E. Sandys, *History of Latin scholarship.*]

c Abbott, Frank F. *Handbook for the study of Roman history.* Chicago, 1906.

a. Written by one person; deals only with such aspects of Roman life as could be illustrated from material remains, and excludes those which could be studied satisfactorily in handbooks without illustrations. Introduction covers early Italian and Roman civilization; remaining chapters treat of architecture, war, religion, production and distribution, money, public amusements, and art. *b.* Very useful compilation of studies by various specialists. *c.* Brief manual to supplement his school text-book on Roman history.

Also cf. (E101) Niese, *Grundriss der römischen Geschichte.*. The general dictionaries and encyclopedias of classical studies listed in (D21) are all valuable for Roman history. The handbooks or introductions, (D32) Gercke and Norden, and (D33) Hall, and notably the volumes on Roman affairs in (D35) *Handbuch der Altertumswissenschaft,* are likewise useful for Roman studies.   AERB

E32a Sandys, Sir John E. *Latin epigraphy.* 1919. 2nd rev. ed. by S. G. Campbell. Cambridge, Eng., 1927.

b Cagnat, René. *Cours d'épigraphie latine.* 1885. 4th rev. ed., Paris, 1914. (Bibliography.)

c Egbert, James Chidester. *Introduction to the study of Latin inscriptions.* 1896. Rev. ed., N. Y., 1906.

a. Best guide in English to the study of Latin inscriptions; contains a good text of (E281*b*) *Res gestae Divi Augusti.* Review, C. Knapp, *Classical Weekly,* 13:212, May 1920. *b.* Standard work in French. *c.* Useful manual, similar in scope and arrangement to *b.* One may consult also with profit: H. Dessau, *Lateinische Epigraphik,* in (D32) Gercke and Norden, I, 10, 1927; and, for a special phase of the subject: H. B. Van Hoesen, *Roman cursive writing,* Princeton, 1915.

AERB

E33 Mommsen, Theodor. *Die römische Chronologie bis auf Caesar.* 1858. 2nd rev. ed., Berlin, 1859.

Pioneer modern work in this field; best introduction to the general problems of Roman chronology. For the advance in knowledge since Mommsen's work, and for the most careful use of the evidence bearing upon disputed points, one should consult Unger, *Zeitrechnung der Griechen und Römer* in (D35) *Handbuch der Altertumswissenschaft.*

AERB

E34a Clinton, Henry Fynes. *Fasti romani: the civil and literary chronology of Rome and Constantinople from the death of Augustus to the death of Justin II.* 2 v. Oxford, 1845–50.

b Peter, Karl L. *Zeittafeln der römischen Geschichte zum Handgebrauch und als Grundlage des Vortrags in höheren Gymnasialklassen mit fortlaufenden Belegen und Auszügen aus den Quellen.* 1841. 6th rev. ed., Halle, 1882.

c Fischer, Ernst W. *Römische Zeittafeln von Roms Gründung bis auf Augustus' Tod.* Altona, 1846.

d Goyau, Georges. *Chronologie de l'empire Romain.* Paris, 1891. [Nouvelle collection à l'usage des classes.]

a. Contains in v. 1 chronological tables from A.D. 15 to 578; and in v. 2 chronological and historical investigations. The same author's (D34*a*) *Fasti hellenici,* v. 3, which covers from B.C. 280 to A.D. 14, is also useful for Roman history. *b.* Similar work; briefer; intended for school use; covers from B.C. 753 to A.D. 476. *c.* and *d.* Useful tables for shorter periods. AERB

E35 *Prosopographia imperii romani saeculorum I, II, III, consilio et auctoritate Academiae Scientiarum Borussicae.* Ed. by E. Klebs, H. Dessau, and P. Rhoden, 3 v., Berolini, 1897–98.

Covers the period from the battle of Actium to the reign of Diocletian; list of Roman senators and of such equestrians as held imperial offices, together with members of their households. A few plebeians, Greeks, and other provincials of historical importance are included. Arranged alphabetically according to gentile names. Literary, inscriptional, and numismatic references to each are cited with great fullness. Very useful work of reference. AERB

GEOGRAPHY

E41 Plinius Secundus, Gaius, (The Elder). *Naturalis historia.* 1492. Ed. by Detlef Detlefsen, 6 v., Berlin, 1866–82. Tr. by John Bostock and H. T. Riley, 6 v., London, 1855–57; later reprints. [Bohn's classical library.]

Pliny the Elder, a Roman who had filled the highest civil and military offices, considered the most learned Roman of his time, published in 77 A. D. his *Natural history* in thirty-seven books. It is a compendium of natural science, derived from many sources. Books 2–6 deal with geography and ethnography, but consist chiefly of the divisions of various countries with a list of places in each.   AERB

E42a Ptolemaeus, Claudius. *Geographia.* 1533. Ed. by C. Müller, v. 1, pt. 1, Paris, 1883; ed. by C. Müller and C. T. Fischer, v. 1, pt. 2, Paris, 1901.

  b —— *Die Geographie des Ptolemaeus: Galliae, Germania, Raetia, Noricum, Pannoniae, Illyricum, Italia: Handschriften, Text, und Untersuchung.* Ed. by Otto Cuntz, Berlin, 1923.

Taken together, these three volumes constitute a complete scholarly edition of the text with full annotation and commentary. The numerous editions in Latin which appeared from 1475 onwards exercised notable influence in the age of discovery (cf. K41). Written by Ptolemy, an Alexandrine astronomer and mathematician, about A. D. 150 to accompany his maps. Together with these, the work sums up the geographical knowledge of the time, and marks the close of scientific geographical study in antiquity. Aimed to place accurately according to latitude and longitude all places from 10 degrees South to 60 degrees North between the western islands of Europe and Java and Sumatra. Books 2–7 consist of tables of latitude and longitude.

A richer store of ancient materials will be found in (D43) Strabo, *Geography.*
      AERB

E43a Jung, Julius. *Grundriss der Geographie von Italien und dem Orbis Romanus.* 1888. 2nd rev. ed., München, 1897. [(D35) Handbuch der Altertumswissenschaft.] (Good bibliography.)

  b —— *Die romanischen Landschaften des römischen Reiches, Studien über die inneren Entwicklungen in der Kaiserzeit.* Innsbruck, 1881.

  c Philippson, Alfred. *Das Mittelmeergebiet, seine geographische und kulturelle Eigenart.* 1904. 4th ed., Leipzig, 1922.

  a. The one comprehensive modern work on the geography of the Roman world. Deals with historical and physical geography, ethnography, the topography of cities, and the Roman administration. Incorporates much material from *b.*, but must be supplemented by *c.* for the physical geography, ethnography, and economic conditions of the Mediterranean lands. Review of *a.*, A. Riese, *Berliner philologische Wochenschrift,* 17:1481, Nov. 27, 1897.

For an account of geographical knowledge and literature in the Roman world, cf. (D41) Kiepert, (D657e) Tozer, (D657f) Bunbury, and (D657g) Berger, which may also be consulted for introductory accounts of the Roman roads and of the ancient works, such as Peutinger's table and the itineraries of the Roman empire, which furnish information concerning them. They likewise supply introductory information on the ancient routes of maritime trade and on the ancient accounts of voyages in strange seas, such as the *Periplus Maris Erythraei.*

Students of the geography and topography of Rome, Italy, and the provinces of the Roman empire may consult, with profit, modern guide books of the type of (B43a) Baedeker, narratives of travel, and such popular descriptive works as contain accounts of the climate, geography, and ancient monuments of these regions.

The best atlases of classical geography are listed in (D46). AERB

E44 Nissen, Heinrich. *Italische Landeskunde.* 2 v. in 3. Berlin, 1883–1902.

V. 1 Physical geography of Italy; takes up in turn its geographic regions and discusses the surface features, geological history, soil, climate, and vegetation of each. V. 2. Political geography, with introductory essays and historical and descriptive account of the towns of Italy, following the order of the old Roman regions. A careful work embodying a vast fund of general and detailed information. Review, v. 2, D. Detlefsen, *Berliner Philologische Wochenschrift,* 22:1619, Dec. 27, 1902.

For additional works on the geography of Italy, cf. (O41), especially Hofmann, *Das Land Italien und seine Geschichte.* AERB

E45a Sabin, Frances L. *Classical associations of places in Italy.* Madison, Wis., 1921.

  b Haight, Elizabeth H. *Italy old and new.* N. Y., 1922.

a. Collection of passages from Greek and Latin authors, with translations and explanations, illustrating the ancient life of 175 places in Italy. Maps and plans. Review, G. D. Hadzsits, *Classical Weekly,* 16:102, Jan. 1923. *b.* Account of travels in Italy with interpretations of Italian life, illustrating and illustrated by references to Latin literature. Review, W. B. McDaniel, *Classical Weekly,* 16:175, Apr. 1923. AERB

E46a Cervesato, Arnaldo. *Roman Campagna.* London and Boston, 1913. Tr. by L. Caico and M. Dove from *Latina tellus, la Campagna romana,* Roma, 1910.

  b Tomassetti, Giuseppe. *La Campagna romana, antica, medioevale, e moderna.* 4 v. Roma, 1910–26. V. 3 and 4, ed. by F. Tomassetti.

  c Ashby, Thomas. *Roman Campagna in classical times.* London, 1927.

a. Excellent illustrated account of the geography, climate, people, and daily life of the Roman campagna; extremely useful for the student of Roman history. *b.* V. 1. General presentation of the economic, administrative, and cultural conditions of the Campagna from the earliest times to the present. V. 2–3. Topographical data, following the Roman roads in alphabetical order to about twenty-five miles from the city. Not always dependable for the prehistoric period. Very valuable synthesis of modern literature on this region. Review, v. 1, G. Wissowa, *Berliner Philologische Wochenschrift,* 30:1097, Aug. 20, 1910; v. 4, T. Ashby, *Jour. Roman Studies,* 16:268, 1926. *c.* Embodies the results of thirty years' explorations; characterized by conscientious observations and accurate description. Review, R. Gardner, *Classical Rev.,* 42:36, Feb. 1928. AERB

E47 Beloch, Karl Julius. *Campanien, Geschichte und Topographie des antiken Neapel und seiner Umgebung.* 1879. 2nd rev. ed., Breslau, 1890.

Model work; perhaps the most valuable of several studies of special regions of Italy in ancient times. AERB

SOURCE BOOKS AND COLLECTIONS OF SOURCES

E61 Munro, Dana C., ed. *Source book of Roman history.* Boston, 1904.

Extracts from the ancient writers, in English translation, illustrating Roman history from the earliest times to Diocletian. The source books of Botsford, Davis, and Webster listed in (C62) are likewise useful for Roman history.

AERB

E62 Greenidge, Abel H. J., and **Clay, A. M.** *Sources for Roman history, B. C. 133–70.* Oxford, 1903.

Very complete collection of the literary and epigraphic material arranged under the heads of 'Internal history' and 'External history' for each year of the period covered.

AERB

Source materials.—It is to be regretted that there is, as yet, in English no good introduction to the sources of Roman history. Reference is made to the best foreign works in (E11). A brief description of the various types of sources, however, follows, together with indications where they may most conveniently be consulted.

a. The *literary sources* comprise both the historical works of Greek and Latin authors and their other writings which throw light upon the various aspects of life in the Roman world. For editions, translations, and critical estimates of the most important ancient writers on Roman history, cf. (E221–226, 281–285, 651–654, 688); for the works of other authors, cf. (E661–664) books listed on Roman literature. Texts and translations of the literary sources for Roman studies may be found in the collections listed in (D71–72). The existing fragments of the lost works of ancient historians are in the collections listed in (D73i and j) and in (E71). Carefully chosen selections from these sources, in translation, are in the works cited in (E61).

b. The *inscriptions* consist chiefly of laws, treaties, dedications, and honorary and funerary inscriptions. Their value lies in the contributions which they make to knowledge of the Roman administrative system as well as of social and economic conditions. The principal collections of Roman inscriptions are listed in (E81–83).

c. *Papyri* have been found in large numbers in Egypt. They comprise public records of all sorts, as well as private archives and correspondence. For the history of Roman Egypt they are invaluable. Of a similar character, but of minor importance are the *ostraka,* or records on potsherds, coming mostly from the same country. The principal publications of papyri and *ostraka* and bibliographies of the literature concerning them are referred to in (D91).

d. Roman *coins* are of importance for chronology, politics, economics, and the history of art. The chief works on Roman coins are listed in (E691–695). Current bibliographical notes and other recent data may be found in the numismatic periodicals listed in (A1041–1052) and, at intervals, in (D959) *Revue de Philologie.*

e. Under *archeological material* may be included whatever material remains of Roman civilization, outside of the preceding categories, have survived to the present. The catalogues of museums containing public and private collections are the best guides to material of this sort. For introductory handbooks reference may be made to (E21, 681–690). A bulletin of new discoveries appears yearly in (D979) *American Journal of Archaeology.*

E71 Peter, Hermann W. G., ed. *Historicorum romanorum reliquiae.* 2 v. Lipsiae, 1870–1905; rev. ed. of v. 1, Lipsiae, 1914.

Standard collection of the surviving fragments of the lost works of the ancient annalists and historians of Rome.   AERB

E81a Corpus inscriptionum latinarum. Ed. by Königliche Preussische Akademie der Wissenschaften. v. 1–15 in 36. Berolini, 1863–1920. 2nd ed., v. 1, 1–2, Berolini, 1893–1918. [1, *Inscriptiones antiquissimae;* 2, *Hispaniae;* 3, *Asiae, provinciarum Europae Graecarum, Illyrici;* 4, *Parietariae Pompeianae, Herculanenses, Stabianae;* 5, *Galliae Cisalpinae;* 6, *Urbis Romae;* 7, *Britanniae;* 8, *Africae;* 9, *Calabriae, Apuliae, Samnii, Sabinorum, Piceni;* 10, *Bruttiorum, Lucaniae, Campaniae, Siciliae, Sardiniae;* 11, *Aemiliae, Etruriae, Umbriae;* 12, *Galliae Narbonensis;* 13, *Trium Galliarum et Germaniarum Latinae;* 14, *Latii veteris;* 15, *instrumentum domesticum urbis Romae.*]

b *Ephemeris epigraphica, corpus inscriptionum latinarum supplementum.* Ed. by Kaiserlich Deutsches Archaeologisches Institut, Roemische Abteilung. V. 1–9. Berolini, 1872–1913.

c *Inscriptiones graecae ad res romanas pertinentes.* Ed. by Académie des inscriptions et belles lettres. V. 1, pt. 1–7; v. 3, pt. 1–6; v. 4, pt. 1–8, Paris, 1902–21.

d *Inscriptions latines de l'Algérie.* V. 1, *Inscriptions de la proconsulaire,* ed. by Stéphane Gsell, Paris, 1922.

e Ruggiero, Ettore de. *Dizionario epigrafico di antichità romane.* V. 1; v. 2, pt. 1–2; v. 3; v. 4, pt. 1–4, art. Italia, ed. by G. Cardinali. Roma, 1895–1928.

a. Chief collection of Latin inscriptions, which is supplemented by *b.*   *c.* Collection of Greek inscriptions important for Roman history.   *d.* More complete than the corresponding part of *a.*   *e.* Arrangement under appropriate titles of the historical information contained in the inscriptions.

Newly found inscriptions are published annually in (D984) *Revue Archéologique;* also separately printed as *Bulletin Épigraphique.* For references to publications of papyri and *ostraka,* cf. (D91). For collections of laws, edicts, and imperial constitutions, cf. (E551–552).   AERB.

E82a Dessau, Hermann, ed. *Inscriptiones latinae selectae.* 3 v. in 5. Berolini, 1892–1916.

b Orelli, Johann K., and **Henzen, Wilhelm.** *Inscriptionum latinarum selectarum amplissima collectio ad illustrandum romanae antiquitatis.* 3 v. Turici, 1828–56.

c Wilmanns, Gustav. *Exempla inscriptionum latinarum in usum praecipue academicum.* 2 v. Berolini, 1873.

a. Most valuable collection of Latin inscriptions in small compass; has notes and indexes; supersedes such older collections as *b* and *c.*   AERB

E83 Rushforth, Gordon McN. *Latin historical inscriptions, illustrating the history of the early empire.* Oxford, 1893. (Bibliography.)

Small but useful collection of inscriptions designed to serve as an introduction to Latin epigraphy and, at the same time, to illustrate the history of the principate. Notes and interpretations.   AERB

SHORTER GENERAL HISTORIES

E101a Niese, Benedictus. *Grundriss der römischen Geschichte nebst Quellenkunde.* 1888. 5th rev. ed. by E. Hohl, München, 1923. [(D35) Handbuch der Altertumswissenschaft.]   (Well selected bibliography.)

  b Cauer, Friedrich. *Römische Geschichte.* München, 1925. [Reimann, Weltgeschichte.]

a. Excellent reference book; concise, accurate, and sober narrative of the political history of Rome; gives very little space to economic, social, or cultural history; reliable estimates of sources; style is matter of fact; judgments seldom original and never profound.   *b.* Excellent brief summary from beginnings to Byzantine times.

For brief general histories of the ancient world, cf. (C101). The more extended and scholarly works of (C124) Meyer, and (C125) Cavaignac are also useful for the Roman period.   Especially deserving of mention is (C101i) Rostovtzeff, *History of the Ancient World,* v. 2.

E102a Pelham, Henry F. *Outlines of Roman history.* 1893. 4th rev. ed., London and N. Y., 1905. (Brief bibliography.)

  b Fowler, William Warde. *Rome.* N. Y. and London, 1912. [Home university library.]

a. Opens with the legendary history of Livy and Dionysius of Halicarnassus duly criticised; closes at A.D. 476. As constitutional questions are emphasized, it should be supplemented by studies in economic and social influences. Hellenistic civilization, as it met and influenced the Roman, receives but meager consideration. Treatment of the imperial period has been improved in the last edition, but is still inadequate. Good, readable account; written from the sources. Review, E. Harrison, *Classical Rev.* 20:279, June 1906.   *b.* Brief, brilliantly written, interpretation of Roman character and Roman history to the time of the Antonines.   CHO

E103 Boak, Arthur E. R. *History of Rome to 565 A. D.* 1921. 2nd rev. ed., N. Y., 1929. (Selected bibliography.)

Excellent text for college classes; based upon a thorough knowledge of the sources and a full examination of recent works. Concise and vigorous in style, clear, accurate, reasonable, well-organized, and sanely proportioned. The general reader will find the movement of the story somewhat retarded by the topical method, and the treatment of literary and social matters somewhat too terse and formal.   TF

E104 Frank, Tenney. *History of Rome.* N. Y. and London, 1923. [American historical series.] (Brief bibliography.)

Comprehensive, readable, and scholarly narrative to the death of Constantine, with short summary of the following century. Written particularly for general readers, but also adapted for use as a college text. Its special strength lies in its discussion of economic conditions. Review, A. E. R. Boak, *A.H.R.* 28:730, July 1923.   AERB

E105 Ferrero, Guglielmo, and **Barbagallo, Corrado.** *Short history of Rome.* 2 v. N. Y. and London, 1918–19. Tr. by G. Chrystal from Italian original.

Based to some extent upon (E255) Ferrero, *Greatness and decline of Rome.* The authors have measurably succeeded in their aim to present a unified history of Rome, but have given prominence to their favorite theories: for instance, concerning Rome's origin, a 'republican renascence' in Trajan's reign, and the 'barbaric' character of the late empire. The development of law, the imperial provinces, and the rise of Christianity are treated in a stimulating manner. Review of v. 1, F. F. Abbott, *A.H.R.* 24:504, Apr. 1919.   GAH

E106a Bloch, Gustave. *La république romaine, conflits politiques et sociaux.* Paris, 1913. [Bibliothèque de philosophie scientifique.]

 b ——— *L'empire romain, évolution et décadence.* Paris, 1922. [Bibliothèque de philosophie scientifique.]

 c Homo, Léon. *Primitive Italy and the beginnings of Roman imperialism.* N. Y., 1926. [(B153a) History of civilization.] Tr. by V. Gordon Childe from *L'Italie primitive et les débuts de l'impérialisme romain.* Paris, 1925. [(B153b) L'évolution de l'humanité.]

 d ——— *L'empire romain.* Paris, 1925.

 e Chapot, Victor. *Roman world.* N. Y., 1928. [(B153a) History of civilization.] Tr. by E. A. Parker from *Le monde romain.* Paris, 1927. [(B153b) L'évolution de l'humanité.]

a. Reliable manual of the development of the political and social institutions of Rome to the principate. Review, C. Jullian, *Revue des Études Anciennes,* 16:121, Jan. 1914. *b.* Work of erudition and ripe reflection; historical survey of the empire to the time of Theodosius, and a study of imperial institutions. Review, C. Jullian, *Revue des Études Anciennes,* 24:356, Oct. 1922. *c.* and *d.* Together form another good brief manual; one of the most recent available. *e.* In general a very successful survey, covering the phases of Roman expansion, the methods of Roman expansion, and descriptions of the various parts of the Roman empire. Review, D. Atkinson, *Classical Rev.,* 42:82, May 1928.   AERB

E107a Hartmann, Ludo M., and **Kromayer, Johannes.** *Römische Geschichte.* Gotha, 1919. [(B168b) Weltgeschichte in gemeinverständlicher Darstellung.]

 b Kromayer, Johannes. *Staat und Gesellschaft der Römer.* Leipzig. 1923. [(B606) Hinneberg, II, 4, Wilamowitz-Moellendorf and Niese.]

a. Covers the history of Rome and Italy from the earliest times to the fall of the Byzantine exarchate. Hartmann treats the early period and the decline of the ancient world; Kromayer the later republic and the principate. The special value of the work lies in the close association of home and foreign political history with the cultural, economic, constitutional, and legal developments. Review, C. Lecrivain, *Rev. Hist.* 137:244, July 1921. *b.* Supplants in this series the older survey with the same title by B. Niese. Treats the expansion of Rome in the three phases of city state, national state, and world state. Details of political history are omitted, but special stress is laid upon the general constitutional, economic, and social developments of each epoch. Independent and stimulating work. Review, R. Wagner, *Philologische Wochenschrift,* 44:856, Sept. 6, 1924.   AERB

LONGER GENERAL HISTORIES

E121 Duruy, Victor. *History of Rome and of the Roman people from its origin to the invasion of the barbarians.* 8 v. in 16. London and Boston, 1883–86. Ed. by J. P. Mahaffy and tr. by M. M. Ripley and W. J. Clarke from *Histoire des Romains depuis les temps les plus reculés.* 7 v. Paris, 1870–85.

An attempt to put in good narrative form the result of scholarly research a half century ago. Though obviously antiquated, it is the only extended work covering the whole history of both republican and imperial Rome that is worthy of citation, primarily because of its wealth of illustrations. A new and exhaustive treatment of Roman history will be found in (C121) *Cambridge ancient history,* especially v. vii ff.   GMD

PRE-ROMAN ITALY

E201a Modestov, Vasilii Ivanovich (Basile). *Introduction à l'histoire romaine; l'ethnologie préhistorique, les influences civilisatrices à l'époque préromaine et les commencements de Rome.* Paris, 1907. Tr., with revisions and additions by the author, by M. Delines from the Russian, 2 v., St. Petersburg, 1902–04.

b Montelius, Gustav Oscar. *La civilisation en Italie depuis l'introduction des métaux.* 2 v. Stockholm and Berlin, 1895–1910.

c ——— *Die vorklassische Chronologie Italiens.* Stockholm, 1912.

d Duhn, Friedrich K. von. *Italische Gräberkunde.* v. 1. Heidelberg, 1924.

a. Convenient collection and interpretation of the archeological evidence bearing upon the history of civilization in Italy in prehistoric times. Pt. 1. Deals with paleolithic, neolithic, bronze, and early iron ages in Italy as a whole. Pt. 2. Discusses, in great detail, the question of the origin and civilization of the Etruscans. In the main, the author has abstained from rash hypotheses, and most of his conclusions are supported by the evidence available to him and by subsequent discoveries. Review, A. Grenier, *Revue Archéologique,* 4th series, 9:305, March 1907. *b* and *c.* Of fundamental importance for the interpretation of the remains of prehistoric civilization in Italy. *d.* The great work on the interpretation of the archeological material found in early Italian cemeteries.   AERB

E202 Peet, Thomas Eric. *Stone and bronze ages in Italy and Sicily.* Oxford, 1909.

Careful, well illustrated description of the archeological material found in the paleolithic, neolithic, terramara, and Villanova sites of Italy. The discussions of cultural and ethnological questions are relatively full, clear, and sane; the conclusions agree in general with those of the best Italian archeologists. Since excavations are progressing rapidly and new interpretations of the material are constantly appearing, the results can naturally not be considered final, but at present the book affords the best introduction to the subject.   TF

E211a Randall-MacIver, David. *Villanovans and early Etruscans, a study of the early iron age in Italy as it is seen near Bologna, in Etruria, and in Latium.* Oxford, 1924.

b ——— *Iron age in Italy: a study of those aspects of the early civilization which are neither Villanovan nor Etruscan.* Oxford, 1927.

c **Grenier, Albert.** *Bologne villanovienne et étrusque, VIIIᵉ–IVᵉ siècles avant notre ère.* Paris, 1912. [Bibliothèque des Écoles Françaises d'Athènes et de Rome.]

d **Pinza, Giovanni.** *Storia delle civiltà antiche d'Italia dalle origine al V secolo avanti Cristo.* Milan, 1923.

a. Careful study and clear discussion of the evidence; well illustrated. Review, K. McK. Elderkin, *Amer. Jour. of Archaeology,* 29:325, July 1925. *b.* Resumes and completes *a;* a work of remarkable scholarship. Review, T. E. Peet, *Classical Rev.,* 42:80, May 1928. *c.* Thorough work, with special attention to the region of Bologna. *d.* Excellent handbook; sums up the results of archeological research in the early period of Italian culture. AERB

E212 Fell, Roland A. L. *Etruria and Rome.* Cambridge, Eng., 1924. [Thirlwall prize essay.] (Bibliography.)

Sound, scholarly work; excellent summary of the present state of knowledge in respect to the problems of Etruscan history and civilization. Review, L. R. Taylor, *Classical Philology,* 20:93, Jan. 1925. AERB

E213 Adams, Louise E. W. *Study in the commerce of Latium from the early iron age through the sixth century, B. C.* Northampton, Mass., 1921. [Smith College classical studies.] (Bibliography.)

Extremely careful collection, analysis, and interpretation of the archeological evidence. Review, A. E. R. Boak, *Classical Weekly,* 18:70, Dec. 1924. AERB

E214 Rosenberg, Arthur. *Der Staat der alten Italiker, Untersuchungen über die ursprüngliche Verfassung der Latiner, Osker, und Etrusker.* Berlin, 1913.

Very valuable study of the political institutions of the peoples of Italy prior to their absorption into the Roman state. Review, W. Soltau, *Berliner Philologische Wochenschrift,* 34:310, March 7, 1914. AERB

E215 Piganiol, André. *Essai sur les origines de Rome.* Paris, 1917. [Bibliothèque des écoles françaises d'Athènes et de Rome.]

Attempts to interpret early Roman civilization as the fusion of several clearly distinguishable cultures. Displays great ability but presents results which are questionable because of a too uncritical use of cultural comparisons and a tendency to interpret the evidence in the light of previously assumed hypotheses. Review, J. Toutain, *Rev. Hist.* 44:96; Jan.-April 1919. AERB

E216 Holland, Louise E. W. Adams. *Faliscans in prehistoric times.* Rome, 1925. [Papers and monographs of the American academy in Rome, v. 5.]

Useful study in regional culture based on archeological evidence. Review, E. S. McCartney, *Classical Weekly,* 21:156, March 26, 1928.

REGAL PERIOD AND THE REPUBLIC: ANCIENT WRITERS

E221 Livius, Titus. *Ab urbe condita libri.* 1469. Ed. by W. Weissenborn, 1850–51; rev. ed., pt. 1–4, by H. J. Müller, Lipsiae, 1881–1902; pt. 5, by W. Heraeus, Lipsiae, 1908–12. Ed. and tr. by B. O. Foster, v. 1–3 (books 1–7), London and N. Y., 1919–24. [Loeb classical library.] Tr. by W. M. Roberts, 6 v., London and N. Y., 1912–24. [Everyman's library.]

Livy, B. C. 59–A. D. 17, at first a rhetorician and philosopher, turned to historical writing after B. C. 31. He was a professed *laudator temporis acti,* sympathizing with the senatorial against the Caesarian party. His history, in 142 books, covered the period from the landing of Aeneas to the death of Drusus, B.C. 9. Books 1–10 (to B. C. 293), 21–45 (B. C. 218–167), and a fragment of 91 (on Sertorius) have been preserved; of the remainder there exist epitomes, *periochae*, and a few excerpts. Livy aimed to make his history a great work of art and in this he was preëminently successful, but his interest lay far more in the promotion of patriotism and the inculcation of sound moral doctrine than in the attainment of historical accuracy through a critical examination of his sources. These were chiefly the later annalists, although he frequently follows Polybius also. From his own time until the eighteenth century Livy's narrative was regarded as the canonical version of the history of the Roman republic.

WAO

E222 Appianus. *Historia romana.* 1551. Ed. by L. Mendelssohn, Lipsiae, 1879–81; rev. ed. of v. 2, by P. Viereck, Lipsiae, 1905. Ed. and tr. by Horace White, J. D. Denniston, and E. I. Robson, 4 v., London and N. Y., 1912–13. [Loeb classical library.]

Appian, flourished A. D. 116–160, an Alexandrian Greek, became a lawyer and an official at Rome in the latter part of his life. His almost exclusively military history is composed on a geographical basis partly modified by chronological considerations. Of the twenty-four books, covering the period from the founding of Rome to the time of Trajan: 6, Wars in Spain; 7, War with Hannibal; 11, Wars with the Seleucids; 12, Wars with Mithridates; 13–17, Civil Wars, B. C. 133–35, especially tainted and partisan; are preserved intact. Considerable portions exist of 8, including the Third Punic War, and 9, including the Illyrian Wars; of the remainder only excerpts and epitomes survive. Written without knowledge, judgment, or distinction of style, the work has value only as it faithfully reproduces sources, usually the later annalists, together with some few additions from documents of substantial importance. His unsupported authority is very unreliable. Review, E. Schwartz in (D21g) Pauly-Wissowa, *Realencyclopädie,* 2:216–237; (E11a) Rosenberg, *Einleitung ' und Quellenkunde zur römischen Geschichte,* 203–210.

WAO

E223 Dionysius of Halicarnassus. *De antiquitatibus romanorum quae supersunt.* 1546. Ed. by C. Jacoby, 4 v., Lipsiae, 1885–1905.

Dionysius of Halicarnassus, a resident of Rome after B. C. 30, published this work in B. C. 7. Covers in twenty books the history of Rome to B. C. 265, at which date the narrative of Polybius begins. Written in Greek to present to the Greek-speaking world the current version of the origins of Rome. Only books 1–10, part of 11, and a few scattered fragments of others have survived. Dionysius preserves a tradition which resembles closely that which appears in Livy. The historical value of his work is very slight, owing to his rhetorical treatment of his subject and his utter lack of historical sense. Review, E. Schwartz in (D21g) Pauly-Wissowa, *Realencyclopädie,* 1:934–961.

AERB

E224 Polybius. *Historiae.* 1609. Ed. by L. Dindorf, 1866–68; rev. ed. by T. Büttner-Wobst, 2 v., Lipsiae, 1882–89. Tr. by E. S. Shuckburgh, 2 v., London and N. Y., 1889; by W. R. Paton, 6 v., London and N. Y., 1924–27. [Loeb Classical Library.]

Polybius, about B. C. 210–138, an Achaean of Megalopolis, the son of a general of the Achaean Federation, was one of the greatest historians of ancient times.

Taken as a hostage to Rome in B. C. 167, he lived there, in close association with Scipio Aemilianus and other influential Romans, until B. C. 150. Without becoming disloyal to his own people, Polybius developed a great admiration for the Romans and set himself to the task of making clear to the world of his day the inevitability of the Roman conquest of the Mediterranean world. To this end he wrote the history of the Mediterranean states during the period of Roman expansion from B. C. 264 to 146. Of the forty books of this history only the first five, to B. C. 216, have survived intact; of the remainder there are considerable fragments, the most important of which is the account of the Roman constitution from book 6. Polybius wrote as an experienced statesman and soldier, with contempt for the bookworm historian, but with a passionate devotion to truth. The value of his work lies in its accuracy, its impartiality, and in the author's keen sense of political realities. Unfortunately, his hopeless style and other literary deficiencies have deprived his history in both ancient and modern times of the popularity which its solid qualities merit. Review, (D73a) Bury, *Ancient Greek historians,* 191–223.   AERB

E225a Caesar, Caius Julius. *Commentarii de bello gallico.* 1469. Ed. by T. Rice Holmes, London, 1914. Ed. and tr. by H. J. Edwards, London and N. Y., 1917. [Loeb classical library.]

    b ―――― *Commentarii de bello civili.* 1469. Ed. by F. Kraner, 1856; 3rd ed. by F. Hofmann, 1864; 11th ed. by H. Meusel, Berlin, 1906. Ed. and tr. by A. G. Peskett, London and N. Y., 1914. [Loeb classical library.]

Julius Caesar, B. C. 100–44, famous in his own time as an orator and man of letters, owes his reputation as an historian to his *Commentaries.* They are partisan works, but in general the accounts, except for certain exaggerations in the number of his barbarian enemies, are fair and accurate. Modestly termed *Commentarii,* as only the materials of history, not a finished literary product, these works rank among the greatest of memoirs, and are the finest specimens of the Stoic standards of style. *a.* The seven books, covering the conquest of Gaul and the invasions of Britain and Germany, B. C. 58–52, were probably written in B. C. 52–51 as a justification of his military and political policy against his critics in the senate, and as an appeal to public opinion over the head of the government to which his formal reports were made. *b.* This fragment in three, originally two, books, covers the events of the years B. C. 49–48, and was written towards the end of his life. The two works were connected by Hirtius, who added book 8 of the *Gallic war,* covering the years B. C. 51–50. The anonymous continuations are authoritative but on a lower literary level.   WAO

E226 Sallustius Crispus, Gaius. 1470. *C. Sallusti Crispi Catilina, Jugurtha, orationes et epistolae exceptae.* Ed. A. W. Ahlberg, Lipsiae, 1919. [Bibliotheca Teubneriana.] Tr. by J. C. Rolfe, London and N. Y., 1921. [Loeb classical library.]

Sallust, 86–35 B.C., was an ardent Caesarian and held high office through Caesar's favor. In 44 B.C. he retired from public life and devoted himself to historical writing. Taking Thucydides as his model, he wrote monographs on the Catilinarian Conspiracy and the Jugurthine War and five books of histories covering the years 78–67 B.C. Of the latter, only the speeches, letters and a quantity of small fragments survive. Although written from a partisan standpoint, his work is marked by a respect for accuracy unusual at the time and was based upon serious investigations. Under the empire Sallust ranked as the first among Roman historians.   AERB

REGAL PERIOD AND THE REPUBLIC: MODERN WRITERS

E241a Shuckburgh, Evelyn S. *History of Rome to the battle of Actium.* London and N. Y., 1894. Later reprints. (Bibliographies.)

   b How, Walter W., and **Leigh, Henry D.** *History of Rome to the death of Caesar.* London and N. Y., 1896. Later reprints.

   c Heitland, William E. *Short history of the Roman republic.* Cambridge, Eng., 1911.

a. and *b.* Thorough, detailed text-books by English scholars; written a generation ago; unfortunately not revised in later reprints. Review of *b.,* C. E. Bennett, *A.H.R.* 2:510, Apr. 1897. *c.* Not an abridgment of (E253), but a rewriting of the account on a smaller scale for students. Over half the volume is given to the period between B. C. 133 and B. C. 42, with which date the narrative terminates.
                                       GMD

E251a Niebuhr, Barthold G. *History of Rome.* 3 v. Cambridge, Eng., and London, 1828–42. Tr. by J. C. Hare and others from *Römische Geschichte,* 3 v., Berlin, 1812–32. Later editions and reprints of both original and translation.

   b Lewis, Sir George Cornewall. *Inquiry into the credibility of the early Roman history.* London, 1855.

   c Barbagallo, Corrado. *Il problema delle origini di Roma da Vico a noi.* Milano, 1926.

a. Today little inherent interest for the general reader and little intrinsic value for the student attaches to this famous work whose first appearance opened a new epoch in historical studies. The lasting significance of the work lay in the critical treatment of the literary sources for the early history of Rome, not in the constructive effort of the author to recreate that history. For Niebuhr and his work, cf. (E622d) Fowler, *Roman essays and interpretations,* 229–250. *b.* This remarkable study in historical criticism combats vigorously the principal conclusions of *a,* its own conclusions are negative. *c.* Vigorous assault upon current critical tendencies in the treatment of the literary tradition of antiquity regarding the early period of Roman history. Review, M. Besnier, *Rev. Crit.* 61:323, Sept. 1, 1927.   GMD

E252 Mommsen, Theodor. *History of Rome.* 1862. New ed., 4 v., London and N. Y., 1911. [Everyman's library.] Tr. by W. P. Dickson from *Römische Geschichte,* 1854–56. 12th–13th ed., 3 v., Berlin, 1920–23.

    Account of the growth of the Roman state from its origins to the death of Julius Caesar. Contains few discussions of problems or citation of authorities, but yet it reveals in the unhesitating confidence of the author's judgments a thorough mastery of all the available sources. Mommsen wrote under the smart of his disillusionment in the Revolution of 1848, and so he displays scant sympathy with the Gracchi, little respect for Cicero as a politician, a contempt for the decadent senate of the last century of the republic, but an overwhelming enthusiasm for Julius Caesar, who gave promise of founding a new era. Not limiting himself to political history, he gives, in special chapters, excellent surveys of the development of Roman social, economic, intellectual, and religious life.

Archeological discoveries and the progress of historical criticism have rendered antiquated the earlier part of this work, but the rest still demands consideration. The general method of treatment, the keen estimates of political situations and characters, and the crisp, vigorous style combine to ensure this work a place among the classics of historical literature. On Mommsen and his work, cf. (E622d) Fowler, *Roman essays and interpretations*, 250–268. AERB

E253 Heitland, William E. *Roman republic.* 3 v. Cambridge, Eng., 1909.

'Political study of the Roman republic,' in which 'literary, military, and economic history are only touched as bearing on public life,' and in which the author regards 'politics functionally rather than structurally.' In trying to show how political institutions worked, the author has frequently failed to show the reasons underlying them and why they developed as they did. Likewise, his disregard of economic history has led him to ignore the results of important work done in this field. The same criticism applies to phases, such as archeology, and to periods, such as that preceding the Punic Wars, in which he was not particularly interested. The Second Punic War takes up more than a third of v. 1, which is short and the least satisfactory of the three. The author's main interest is in the revolutionary era, to which he devotes about eight hundred pages. The work is free from sensationalism and startling novelties of interpretation. The style, while always readable, becomes more graphic towards the end. Review, F. F. Abbott, *A.H.R.* 15:833, July 1910. ABWt

E254a Pais, Ettore. *Storia critica di Roma durante i primi cinque secoli.* 4 v. Roma, 1898–1920.

b ———— *Ricerche sulla storia e sul diritto pubblico di Roma.* 4 v. Roma, 1915–21.

c ———— *Storia della colonizzazione di Roma antica.* V. 1. *Prolegomeni, le fonti, i libri imperiali regionum.* Roma, 1923.

d ———— *Ancient legends of Roman history.* N. Y., 1905. Tr. by M. E. Cosenza.

e ———— *Ancient Italy, historical and geographical investigations in central Italy, Magna Graecia, Sicily, and Sardinia.* Chicago, 1908. Tr. by C. D. Curtis from *Ricerche storiche e geographiche sull' Italia antica,* Torino, 1908. Republished, with additions and alterations, as *Italia antica, ricerche di storia e di geografia antica,* 2 v., Bologna, 1921.

f Pais, Ettore, and **Stella Maranca, F.,** ed. *Ricerche sulla storia e sul diritto romano.* Pt. 1–2, Roma, 1918. [1, E. Pais, *Dalle guerre puniche a Cesare Augusto, indagini storiche, epigrafiche, giuridiche;* 2, E. Ciaceri, *Processi politici e relazioni internazionali.*]

g Pais, Ettore, and **Stella Maranca, F.,** ed. *Collezione di testi e monumenti romani.* Pt. 1, E. Pais, *Fasti triumphales populi romani.* 1 v. in 2, Roma, 1920.

h ———— *Storia dell' Italia antica.* 2 v. Roma, 1925.

i ———— *Storia di Roma durante le guerre puniche.* 2 v. Roma, 1927.

a. Covers from the earliest times to the unification of Italy under Roman domination. Pais takes the view that the usually accepted literary sources for the early centuries of Roman history are utterly unreliable. Accordingly, after a destructive criticism of the traditions, he seeks to replace them by a thoroughly original reconstruction. Review, v. 1, A. S. Wilkins, *Classical Rev.* 12:419, Nov.

1898; 13:453, Dec. 1899. *b.* Supplement to *a*; deals with problems requiring more exhaustive discussion.   V. 3. Especially useful for chronological purposes; contains list of the tribunes.   Review, v. 3, *A.H.R.* 24:118, Oct. 1918.   *c.* Thorough study of source questions.   *d.* Volume of lectures delivered in the United States; relates chiefly to prehistoric and regal times.   Review, S. B. Platner, *A.H.R.* 11:872, July 1906.   *e.* Collection of essays and addresses on questions of the early history of Italy, chiefly the early republican period.   Review, C. H. Moore, *A.H.R.* 14:95, Oct. 1908.   *f.* Continuation of *b.* Pt. 1. Mainly relates to first century B. C. Pt. 2. Deals chiefly with history and geography of Alpine and sub-Alpine lands.   Review, pt. 1–2, H. S. Jones, *E.H.R.* 35:436, July 1920.   *g.* Eighteen pages of text and over five hundred pages of introductory and editorial material.   Review, R. V. D. Magoffin, *A.H.R.* 27:284, Jan. 1922.   *h.* Somewhat popular in character.   V. 1. Relates entirely to pre-Roman times.   V. 2. Deals mainly with Magna Graecia.   Other works by Pais are (D401*d*) *Storia della Sicilia e della Magna Grecia,* and (E436*b*) *Storia della Sardegna e della Corsica durante il dominio romano.*   Concerning Pais as an historian, cf. Giuseppe Piazza, 'L'opera storica di Ettore Pais,' *Nuova Antologia,* 279:160–168, May 16, 1918.   *i.* Continuation of *a* and *h.*   AERB

E255a **Ferrero, Guglielmo.**   *Greatness and decline of Rome.*   5 v.   London and N. Y., 1907–09.   Tr. by A. E. Zimmern and H. J. Chaytor from *La Grandezza e decadenza di Roma,* 5 v., Milano, 1902–07.

b ——— *Characters and events of Roman history from Caesar to Nero.* N. Y. and London, 1909.   Tr. by F. L. Ferrero.   [Lowell Institute lectures.]

c ——— *Ancient Rome and modern America, a comparative study of morals and manners.*   N. Y. and London, 1914.

d ——— *Ruin of the ancient civilization and the triumph of Christianity, with some consideration of conditions in the Europe of today.*   N. Y., 1921. Tr. by Lady Whitehead from *La ruine de la civilisation antique,* Paris, 1921.

a. Analyzes from the 'psychological and moral' point of view the causes of Rome's conquest of the Mediterranean world and the subsequent decay of the Roman political power and of Graeco-Latin civilization.   The narrative ends with the death of Augustus.   The early stages of Roman expansion are dismissed with a brief outline, but the period B.C. 80–A.D. 14 is treated in great detail.   The main thesis is that the Roman world-conquest was the result of 'the growth of a nationalist and mercantile democracy on the ruins of a federation of agricultural aristocracies.'   The work makes a popular appeal through its rhetorical style, its interpretation of social and economic conditions in terms understood by the public of today, its emphasis upon character analysis, and the positiveness of its judgments.   Yet its value is seriously impaired by the presence of unsound hypotheses and the lack of critical acumen in the judgment of sources.   Review, B. Perrin, *A.H.R.* 13:829, July 1908; 14:796, July 1909.   *b.* Series of lectures popularizing the views set forth in the latter part of *a.*   *c.* Collection of popular essays.   *d.* Interpretation of the movements of the third and fourth centuries, A.D.   Review, T. Frank, *A.H.R.* 28:84, Oct. 1922.   AERB

E256 **Sanctis, Gaetano de.**   *Storia dei Romani.*   V. 1–4.   Torino, 1907–22. [Biblioteca di scienze moderne.]

A work of surprising industry and accuracy, now reaching the end of the third Macedonian War.   The various parts differ somewhat in scope, purpose, and usefulness. V. 1–2. Written at the time when the question of the credibility of Rome's early annals was most vigorously discussed, it took the form of a critical analysis of early tradition. By the application of sound methods, it did great service in stemming the tide of over-reckless scepticism. In view of the rapid progress of Etruscan and early Roman archeology this part, despite its excellence, must be revised, but it is still perhaps the safest history of the early period. V. 3. Runs in a smooth narrative style, since the discussion of sources, which are fairly reliable for this period, is relegated to appendixes. Employs 1160 pages to cover the story of the years B. C. 260–200. As a narrative of political and military events it is incomparable for completeness and accuracy. The author, however, reveals insufficient interest in constitutional, social, and economic questions, and his judgments on the causes of Rome's political acts seem at times superficial and traditional. V. 4. Covers the first third of the second century, B. C. Review, v. 1–2, *A.H.R.* 13:316, Jan. 1908; v. 3, F. F. Abbott, *A.H.R.* 23:131, Oct. 1917; v. 4, A. E. R. Boak, 29:117, Oct. 1923. TF

E257 Piganiol, André. *La conquête romaine.* Paris, 1927. [(B169*b*) Peuples et civilisations.]

Clear and stimulating narrative of Roman history to the battle of Actium, particularly useful for its reconstruction of the early period. Review, T. Frank, *A.H.R.* 33:373, Jan. 1928. AERB

E271a Greenidge, Abel H. J. *History of Rome during the later republic and early principate.* V. 1, *From the tribunate of Tiberius Gracchus to the second consulship of Marius, B.C. 133–104.* London, 1904; N. Y., 1905. (Bibliography.)

b Carcopini, Jerome. *Autour des Gracques: études critiques.* Paris, 1928.

a. A knowledge of the earlier history and of the political situation at the beginning of the period treated is taken for granted, and the first 100 pages are devoted to a full survey of social and economic conditions in Rome and Italy during the late second century, B.C. Pages 101–276 cover the Gracchan movement, and include an excellent estimate of the motives and plans of the Gracchi. The rest of the volume is chiefly concerned with the early career of Marius. Scholarly, and, as a whole, very interesting. Review, F. F. Abbott, *Classical Philology,* 1:183, Apr. 1906. *b.* Series of related essays on Gracchan history, constituting one of the most important works on this period. Review, M. Cary, 43:82, May 1929. Cf. also Fritz Taeger, *Tiberius Gracchus: Untersuchungen zur römischen Geschichte und Quellenkunde,* Stuttgart, 1928. CWK, AERB

E272 Frank, Tenney. *Roman imperialism.* N. Y., 1914.

After a minute study of the sources and an analysis of the motives underlying Rome's territorial expansion under the republic, the author concludes that Rome deviated but seldom from the fetial rules of war and was non-aggressive, that in general until the second century an analogy to modern imperialism was lacking, and that commercialism as a motive hardly appeared before 123 B.C. Review, W. L. Westermann, *A.H.R.* 20:131, Oct. 1914. ABW

E273 Meyer, Eduard. *Caesars Monarchie und das Principat des Pompeius: innere Geschichte Roms von 66 bis 44 v. Chr.* 1918. 3rd rev. ed., Stuttgart, 1922.

A work of great distinction, marked by broad scholarship and keen character analysis. In contrast to (E252) Mommsen, the author holds no brief for Julius

Caesar as a savior of society, but stresses the importance of the career of Pompey as the true forerunner of the principate of Augustus. Suffers somewhat from a failure to understand democratic institutions. Review, E. Hohl, *Berliner Philologische Wochenschrift,* 39:865, Sept. 13, 1919.   AERB

E274 Marsh, Frank B. *Founding of the Roman empire.* Austin, Texas, 1922. 2nd rev. ed., Oxford, 1927. (Bibliography.)

Study of the transformation of the Roman republic into the principate of Augustus; covers in detail the period from the death of Sulla to A.D. 14; offers a careful and critical survey of constitutional problems and an interpretation of the aims of the leading statesmen of the time. Review, A. E. R. Boak, *Classical Journal,* 18:316, March 1923.   AERB

E275a Holmes, Thomas Rice. *Caesar's conquest of Gaul.* 1899. 2nd rev. ed., Oxford, 1911.

    b —— *Roman republic and the founder of the empire.* 3 v., Oxford and N. Y., 1923. (Bibliographical footnotes.)

    c —— *Architect of the Roman empire.* Oxford, 1928.

a. Indispensable companion to the study of Caesar's campaigns. Review, H. Meusel, *Berliner Philologische Wochenschrift,* 31:1467, Nov. 25, 1911. *b.* Essentially a study of the military history of the close of the republican period, B. C. 133–44, with particular reference to the career of Caesar. In this respect it is detailed and reliable, but the accompanying account of political movements is very superficial. Review, T. Frank, *Classical Philology,* 19:89, Jan. 1924. *c.* Thorough treatment of the history of the Second Triumvirate, yet presenting some questionable conclusions. Review, G. H. Stevenson, *Classical Review,* 42: 137, Sept. 1928.   AERB

THE PRINCIPATE AND THE AUTOCRACY: ANCIENT WRITERS

E281a Velleius Paterculus, Caius. *Ad M. Vinicium libri duo.* 1520. Ed. by R. Ellis, Oxford, 1898. Ed. and tr., together with *b.,* by F. W. Shipley, London and N. Y., 1924 [Loeb classical library].

    b Augustus. *Res gestae divi Augusti, ex monumentis Ancyrano et Apolloniensi.* Ed. by T. Mommsen, 1865; 2nd ed., Berlin, 1883.

a. Velleius Paterculus, a Caesarian, wrote, in A. D. 30, a short sketch of the civil wars and the principate to that date, with a strong bias in favor of Tiberius and Sejanus. *b.* Composed by Augustus shortly before his death and set up as a public inscription in Rome and the chief provincial cities, gave to the Roman world the interpretation he desired to have put upon his career. The fragments known as the *monumenta* of Ancyra and Apollonia must now be supplemented by those found recently at Antioch in Pisidia; cf. W. M. Ramsay and A. v. Premerstein, *Monumentum Antiochenum.* Leipzig, 1927. [*Klio,* Beiheft 19.]   AERB

E282 Cassius Dio Cocceianus. *Historia romana.* 1548. Ed. by U. P. Boissevain, 4 v., Berlin, 1895–1926. Tr. by H. B. Foster, 1905; revised by E. Cary, v. 1–9, London and N. Y., 1914–28 [Loeb classical library].

Dio Cassius, about A. D. 155–229, of Nicaea in Bithynia, twice consul, wrote this work in eighty books, extending from the founding of Rome to his own second consulship in A. D. 229. Of these, books 36–60 (B. C. 68 to A. D. 46) are preserved intact, together with portions of book 17 (end of Second Punic War), most of 79 and part of 80 (A. D. 217–219). The remainder can be fairly well reconstructed from the extensive epitome of Xiphilinus, for the period of the empire; the *Epitome of history* of Zonaras, for books 1–21 and 44–80; the Constantinian excerpts; and other late works. Dio's sources for the early republic were annalistic; for the late republic, the annalists combined with Polybius; for the years B. C. 68–30, mainly Livy; for the early empire, the annalists. The history of his own time is elaborately presented and for much of it he needed no literary authorities. He was a capable official and has preserved much information of high value on administrative matters. For the early periods he is practically useless, as the subject matter lay outside the range of his experience. For the empire, however, his authority is excellent. Review, E. Schwartz in (D21g) Pauly-Wissowa, *Realencyclopädie,* 3:1648–1722.   WAO

E283 Suetonius Tranquillus, Caius. *De vita duodecim Caesarum.* 1470. Ed. by M. Ihm, Leipzig, 1907. Ed. and tr. by J. C. Rolfe, 2 v., London and N. Y., 1914 [Loeb classical library]. (Bibliography.)

Suetonius, about A. D. 75–140, originally a lawyer, turned soon to scholarship. For a time secretary *ab epistulis* under Hadrian, he lost office with the fall of his patron, the praetorian prefect Sulpicius Clarus, to whom he had dedicated, about A. D. 120, his lives of the first twelve Caesars, Julius to Domitian. The form is that of the standard Alexandrian biography of men of letters, and it is unfair to demand of these 'lives' the qualities of history. They are designed rather to supplement the corresponding annals, and as such are of the highest value for the richness of their content. All kinds of available evidence are put under contribution: inscriptions, memoirs, official records, pamphlets, letters. The author often takes pains to consult the sources and to compare diverse data quite in the style of modern scholars. Unfortunately Suetonius drew heavily from the literature of the senatorial opposition, so that his portraits convey much of the partisan bias of his originals. Of psychological analysis there is hardly a trace; of a feeling for statesmanship, even less. The details given are objective, though often superficial if not trivial; the purpose is obviously honest; the method, thorough; accuracy is never sacrificed to fine writing. Review, A. Macé, *Essai sur Suétone,* Paris, 1900; F. Leo, *Die griechisch-römische Biographie,* Leipzig, 1901.   WAO

E284a Tacitus, Caius Cornelius. *Annales.* 1470. Ed. by C. D. Fisher, Oxford, 1906 [Scriptorum classicorum bibliotheca oxoniensis]. Tr. by G. G. Ramsay, 2 v., London, 1904–09.

b ―――― *Historiae.* 1470. Ed. by C. D. Fisher, Oxford, 1911 [Scriptorum classicorum bibliotheca oxoniensis]. Tr. by W. H. Fyfe, 2 v., Oxford, 1912 [Oxford translations]. Ed. and tr. by C. H. Moore, v. 1, London and N. Y., 1925 [Loeb classical library].

a and *b*. Together constituted a history of Rome from the accession of Tiberius in A. D. 14 to the death of Domitian in 96. Of this great historical work only fragments are preserved; of *a.,* a fairly complete narrative of Tiberius's reign, a portion of Claudius's, and most of Nero's; of *b.,* the story of the civil wars following the death of Nero, the insurrection of the Gallic chieftain Civilis, and the beginning of the siege of Jerusalem. As an historian, Tacitus leaves much to be desired; his method is that of the dramatist rather than the writer of history; he is more interested in the moral consequences of actions than in historical cause and effect. He concentrates attention on interesting individuals and illuminating scenes, but neglects political developments and economic factors. The personages of the court and the transactions of the senate interest him to the exclusion of the empire as a whole. In his accounts of campaigns he so subordinates strategic details to unimportant, but dramatic, incidents that Mommsen dubbed him 'the most unmilitary of historians.' Despite these defects as an historian, his brilliant style, his gloomy moral grandeur, and his power of description rank him among the foremost writers of Rome.

For his *Germania* and *Agricola,* cf. (P201).   DM

E285 Ammianus Marcellinus. *Rerum gestarum libri XXXI.* 1474. Ed. by C. U. Clark, 2 v., Berolini, 1910–15. Tr. by C. D. Yonge, 1862; reprint, London, 1894 [Bohn's classical library].

Ammianus Marcellinus, A. D. 330–400, a Greek from Antioch, held high rank in the imperial Roman army under the Emperor Constantius and his successors. Taking Tacitus as his model, he wrote, in Latin, a history which continued the work of that writer for the period A. D. 96–378. Unfortunately, only the part covering the years 353–378 has survived. Characterized by sound judgment and objectivity, it is the one reliable source for the history of this period, though the strained, rhetorical style has injuriously affected the popularity of the work. For the life of Ammianus and a detailed examination of the value of his history, cf. (E312) Gibbon, *Decline and fall,* ed. by Bury, 2:536–538, and W. Klein, *Studien zu Ammianus Marcellinus,* Leipzig, 1914. [*Klio,* Beiheft 13.]   AERB

THE PRINCIPATE AND THE AUTOCRACY: MODERN WRITERS

E301 Jones, Henry Stuart. *Roman empire, B. C. 29 to A. D. 476.* London and N. Y., 1908. [Story of the nations.]

Short, readable, well-proportioned account of the military and political history of imperial Rome. Does not over-stress the importance of the first century because of the wealth of source material available. The second century is adequately treated, and properly from the point of view that the government, while benevolent, was despotic and bureaucratic. Criticism may be directed at the lack of attention to social customs and to the situation of subject peoples. Review, W. A. Goligher, *E.H.R.* 23:541, July 1908. For a good brief account of the imperial period, cf. (E102) Pelham, *Outlines of Roman history.* For the best recent treatment of the period after Constantine, cf. (H121) *Cambridge medieval history,* v. 1, *The Christian Roman empire.*   GAH

E302 Bury, John B. *History of the Roman Empire from its foundation to the death of Marcus Aurelius.* London, 1893. Later reprints.

Excellent introductory text-book, with good maps, plans, and illustrations.
                                                                               AERB

E311 Merivale, Charles. *History of the Romans under the empire.* 1850–62. New ed., 8 v., London and N. Y., 1890.

Antiquated, diffuse, and ill-proportioned; only one volume is allowed for the century A. D. 70–180. Cited solely because there is no better extended narrative in English to cover the period from B. C. 60 to A. D. 180 and so link the work of (E252) Mommsen with that of (E312) Gibbon.   GMD

E312 Gibbon, Edward. *History of the decline and fall of the Roman empire.* 1776–81. Ed. with introduction, notes, appendixes, and index, by J. B. Bury, 7 v., London and N. Y., 1896. 1896–98; later reprints.

This classic work covers the twelve centuries intervening between the time of Marcus Aurelius and the capture of Constantinople by the Turks in 1453. For v. 4–7, cf. (H122). V. 1–3 relate to the period prior to the middle of the fifth century. The treatment is characterized by historical unity and a fine sense of proportion. The central theme is 'the triumph of barbarism and Christianity' which constitutes the outstanding development of these centuries. Although Gibbon preserves, for the most part, praiseworthy historical impartiality, his treatment of the rise of the Christian church has frequently been criticized as biased. Because of his success in combining so admirably an excellent literary style with strict attention to historical accuracy, Gibbon's work has not been superseded. The corrections and additions which modern scholarship has made are indicated in Bury's excellent notes and introduction, the latter of which also contains a good appreciation of the historical value of the author's work. For a fuller recital of the history of the empire in the East from the time of Arcadius, based upon later researches, cf. (H304a) Bury, *History of the later Roman empire.*   AERB

E313 Dessau, Hermann. *Geschichte der römischen Kaiserzeit.* V. 1–2, i. Berlin, 1924–26.

Covers at present the period from the death of Julius Cæsar to 69 A.D. Written for general readers, but in unattractive style; a work of great scholarship, though inadequately equipped with notes. On many topics, such as the treatment of the principate of Augustus as an unlimited monarchy, the author differs from the views generally held in the scholarly world. Review of v. 1, E. Hohl, *Philologische Wochenschrift,* 44:706, July 26, 1924; of v. 1, i, J. G. C. Anderson, *Class. Rev.* 41:142, Sept. 1927.   AERB

E314 Schiller, Hermann. *Geschichte der römischen Kaiserzeit.* 2 v. in 3. Gotha, 1883–87.

Sound, though not brilliantly written, political history of the ancient world from the assassination of Julius Cæsar to the division of the empire in A. D. 395. Practically the only extended narrative which makes complete use of the epigraphic evidence about imperial administration and institutions. The exhaustive treatment (2:23–119) of the régime set up by Diocletian and Constantine should be read by all students who wish to understand the institutional foundations of the early Middle Ages.   WSD

E315 Domaszewski, Alfred Von. *Geschichte der römischen Kaiser.* 1909. 3rd ed., 2 v., Leipzig, 1922.

Treats the history of the Roman empire from Augustus to Diocletian in a series of biographical sketches of the various emperors. Addressed to the German reading public and not to students of Roman history in particular. Lacks critical acumen; follows closely the literary authorities, without making use of other source materials. Ill-proportioned; the period from Augustus to Nerva occupies the whole of v. 1 and almost half of v. 2. The author's interest lies in the personalities of the emperors, and practically no attention is paid to social, economic, and religious conditions. Review, J. Beloch, *Hist. Zeit.* 107:115, 1911.

AERB

E321 Gardthausen, Viktor. *Augustus und seine Zeit.* 2 v. in 6. Leipzig, 1891–1904.

This monumental work aims to give a complete survey of the life of Augustus and of the social, political, intellectual, and religious world of his day. Characterized by thoroughness and sound judgment; its generous scale permits the author to give due prominence to the views of other writers which are at variance with his own. V. 1. Contains the text. V. 2. Reserved for the authorities and the author's notes on controversial points. Review, H. Schiller, *Wochenschrift für Klassische Philologie,* 8:1081, Oct. 1, 1891; 13:845, July 22, 1896; C. Benjamin, 22:1061, Sept. 27, 1905. Cf. also M. Gottschald, *Augustus und seine Zeit.* Leipzig, 1926.

AERB

E322a Henderson, Bernard. *Life and principate of the Emperor Nero.* London, 1903.

b ―――― *Life and principate of the Emperor Hadrian, A. D. 76–138.* London, 1923.

c ―――― *Five Roman emperors: Vespasian, Titus, Domitian, Nerva, Trajan.* Cambridge, 1927.

a. Scholarly study of the personality of Nero, and of the foreign and domestic policy of the Roman empire during his principate. Particularly successful in its treatment of the Armenian frontier problem, the Jewish War, and the revolt in Britain. However, in his attempt to rehabilitate the personal reputation of Nero, the author fails to be convincing. Review, E. Shuckburgh, *E.H.R.* 19:746, Oct. 1904. *b.* Another excellent study; on most points interprets Hadrian favorably. Review, by N. H. Baynes, *Nation* (London), 33:458, July 7, 1923. *c.* Together with the same author's *Civil war and the rebellion in the Roman empire,* 1908, covers the period between *a* and *b*; broad and scholarly treatment, subject to correction on minor points. Review, M. P. Charlesworth, *Classical Rev.,* 42:37, Feb. 1928.

AERB

E331 Seeck, Otto. *Geschichte des Untergangs der antiken Welt.* 6 v. in 2. Berlin, 1895–1920. 4th rev. ed. of v. 1, 1921–22; 2nd rev. ed. of v. 2–2, 1921.

The opening chapters deal with the reign of Diocletian and the accession of Constantine. V. 4–5. Treat of the dynasty of Constantine and the wars and disasters which culminated in the triumph of Alaric. V. 6. Covers the fifth century to 476 A. D. For most students, however, the invaluable parts are the long intervening essays, really special monographs, upon all the various causes, economic, biological, religious, as well as political, which undermined the Roman empire. In handling these topics the author often shows himself brilliant and highly illuminating, but sometimes eccentric and subjective to a dangerous degree. Very few readers, of whatever persuasion, will accept as final Seeck's analysis of early 'Christentum.' On the other hand the chapters on 'The emperor and his officials,' 'The public administration,' 'The new taxes,' 'Money and tribute,' and such a study as 'The extermination of the best' (showing how Roman society destroyed its own most valuable elements) are a stimulus and a delight to every serious student. The extensive notes are somewhat exasperatingly bound as supplements to the several volumes. A work of high and original significance, provided it is used by readers who can keep their sense of proportion when sometimes the author almost loses his own. For the barbarian invaders, cf. (H201) Dahn, *Die Könige der Germanen,* and (H202) Hodgkin, *Italy and her invaders.*

WSD

E332 Stein, Ernst. *Geschichte des spätrömischen Reiches.* V. 1. Vienna, 1928.

Solid work, based upon conscientious study of the sources and a mastery of modern investigations. Review, E. Hohl, *Hist. Zeit.,* 139:580, 1929. AERB

THE ROMAN PROVINCES: GENERAL WORKS

E341 Mommsen, Theodor. *Provinces of the Roman empire from Caesar to Diocletian.* 1886. 2nd ed., by F. Haverfield, 2 v., London, 1908. Tr. by W. P. Dickson from *Geschichte der Provinzen von Cäsar bis Diocletian,* 1885; 9th ed., Berlin, 1921.

Mommsen wrote this work as v. 5 of his (E252) *History of Rome.* Largely based on inscriptional evidence collected by the author himself and his colleagues in the compilation of (E81a) *Corpus inscriptionum latinarum.* Disregarding the details of provincial administration, he gives a masterly sketch of civilization in the various provinces under the principate. Thereby he seeks to show that the great achievement of the imperial government was the gift of three centuries of peace and prosperity to the provincials, and that the corrupt society of the court and capital did not constitute or even typify the Roman world of the time. As yet the work has no rival. Review, W. T. Arnold and T. F. Tout, *E.H.R.* 1:350, Apr. 1886.

For the details of provincial administration, cf. (E536a) Marquardt, *Römische Staatsverwaltung;* (E541a) Arnold, *Roman provincial administration;* and (E541c) Halgan, *Administration des provinces sénatoriales.* AERB

E346a Cromer, Evelyn Baring, Earl of. *Ancient and modern imperialism.* London and N. Y., 1910.

b Lucas, Sir Charles P. *Greater Rome and Greater Britain.* Oxford, 1912.

c Bryce, James, Viscount. *Ancient Roman empire and the British empire in India. The diffusion of Roman and English law throughout the world. Two historical studies.* London and N. Y., 1914. Reprinted from (B245a) *Studies in history and jurisprudence.*

Three studies, by English public officials of wide experience, which throw valuable light upon the problems of the Roman imperial government, by comparisons and contrasts with the administration of the British Empire. Review of *b.,* A. L. P. Dennis, *A.H.R.* 19:398, Jan. 1914. AERB

E351a Guiraud, Paul. *Les assemblées provinciales dans l'empire romain.* Paris, 1887.

b Carette, Ernest. *Droit romain, les assemblées provinciales de la Gaule romaine.* Paris, 1895.

a. Good, comprehensive treatment. May be supplemented by special articles in encyclopedias and dictionaries and, for Gaul, by *b.* AERB

E356 Josephus, Flavius. *Opera.* 1544. Ed. by B. Niese, 7 v., Berlin, 1887–95. Tr. by William Whiston, 1737, rev. ed. by A. R. Shilleto, 5 v., London, 1889–90 [Bohn's standard library.]

In this notable group of writings on the Jews and their history, the work entitled *Wars of the Jews* is the principal contemporary source for the struggle of the Jews with Rome, which ended in the destruction of Jerusalem in A. D. 70.

GMD

E357a Juster, Jean. *Les Juifs dans l'empire romain, leur condition juridique, économique, et sociale.* 2 v. Paris, 1914. (Bibliography.)

   b Bell, H. Idris. *Jews and Christians in Egypt, the Jewish troubles in Alexandria and the Athanasian controversy.* London, 1924.

   c Fuchs, L. *Die Juden Aegyptens.* Vienna, 1924.

a. Comprehensive and careful study, particularly valuable for the relations of the Jewish communities to the imperial authority. Review, G. F. Moore, *A.H.R.* 20:613, Apr. 1915. *b* and *c.* Interesting supplements to *a.*   AERB

AFRICA: CARTHAGINIAN AND ROMAN

E361a Tissot, Charles J. *Exploration scientifique de la Tunisie; géographie comparée de la province romaine d'Afrique.* 2 v. and atlas. Paris, 1884–88. V. 2., ed. by Salomon Reinach; 2nd ed., 1891.

   b Boissier, Gaston. *Roman Africa, archaeological walks in Algeria and Tunis.* London and N. Y., 1899. Tr. by Arabella Ward from *L'Afrique romaine*, 1895. 5th rev. ed., Paris, 1912.

   c Bouchier, Edmund S. *Life and letters in Roman Africa.* Oxford, 1913.

   d Graham, Alexander. *Roman Africa, an outline of the history of the Roman occupation of North Africa based chiefly upon inscriptions and monumental remains in that country.* London and N. Y., 1902.

   e Schulten, Adolf. *Das römische Afrika.* Leipzig, 1899.

a. Exhaustive study in historical geography. *b.* and *c.* Readable accounts, with special attention to cultural aspects. *b.* Written with notable charm and inspiration. *d.* Systematic historical narrative from the second century, B. C., to the fifth century, A. D. Review, F. W. Kelsey, *A.H.R.* 8:159, Oct. 1902. *e.* Brief sketch. Also cf. (E514) Cagnat, *L'armée romaine d'Afrique et l'occupation militaire de l'Afrique sous les empereurs.*   AERB

E371 Meltzer, Otto, and **Kahrstedt, Ulrich.** *Geschichte der Karthager.* 3 v. Berlin, 1879–1913.

In v. 1, Meltzer carries the history of the Carthaginians to B. C. 306, and in v. 2, to B. C. 218. V. 3. Completely new work by Kahrstedt; carries the narrative to the destruction of Carthage in B. C. 146. While Meltzer's writing is characterized by most careful discussion of both sources and modern works, Kahrstedt's is marked by an exceedingly radical and independent attitude towards his material. Both parts, however, are works of real scholarship. Review, v. 2, Adolf Bauer, *Hist. Zeit.* 79:72, 1897; v. 3, R. Oehler, *Berliner Philologische Wochenschrift*, 35:683, May 29, 1915.   AERB

E376 Gsell Stéphane. *Histoire ancienne de l'Afrique du Nord.* V. 1–8. Paris, 1913–29.

North Africa is used to denote that region of uniform geographic characteristics which stretches between the Sahara and the Mediterranean from the Gulf of Syrtis to the Atlantic Ocean. V. 1–4. Cover from prehistoric times to the fall of Carthage. Indispensable work. Review, F. F. Abbott, *A.H.R.* 23:839, July 1918; 25:701, July 1920. V. 5–6. Deal with native kingdoms; v. 7, with the Roman republic and native states. Review, J. J. Van Nostrand, *A.H.R.* 33:845, July 1928; 34:793, July 1929. AERB

EGYPT IN ROMAN TIMES

E391 Milne, Joseph Grafton. *History of Egypt under Roman rule.* London, 1898. 3rd rev. ed., 1924. [(C203) Petrie, History of Egypt, v. 5.] (Bibliography.)

Covers the period from Augustus to A. D. 668. Special chapters on administration, taxation, religious, social, and economic conditions. Valuable collection of references from inscriptions, papyri, and *ostraka* bearing on each emperor. Review, G. S. Goodspeed, *A.H.R.* 5:549, Apr. 1900. AERB

E392a Stein, Arthur. *Untersuchungen zur Geschichte und Verwaltung Aegyptens unter römisher Herrschaft.* Stuttgart, 1915.

b Oertel, Friedrich. *Die Liturgie, Studien zur ptolemäischen und kaiserlichen Verwaltung Aegyptens.* Leipzig, 1917.

Two of the more important recent studies of conditions in Egypt under Roman rule; based mainly on papyri. Also cf. (D91a) Mitteis and Wilcken, *Grundzüge und Chrestomathie der Papyruskunde;* (D91b) Schubart, *Einführung in die Papyruskunde;* (E694b) Vogt, *Römische Politik in Aegypten;* and (E515) Lesquier, *L'armée romaine d'Égypte.* AERB

ASIATIC PROVINCES OF ROME

E401 Hahn, Ludwig. *Rom und Romanismus im griechisch-römischen Osten, mit besonderer Berücksichtigung der Sprache, bis auf die Zeit Hadrians.* Leipzig, 1906.

Investigation of the influence of Rome upon the Greek and oriental population of her eastern provinces. AERB

E406a Ramsay, Sir William M. *Cities and bishoprics of Phrygia, being an essay of the local history of Phrygia from the earliest times to the Turkish conquest.* 1 v. in 2. Oxford, 1895–97.

b ——, ed. *Studies in the history and art of the eastern provinces of the Roman Empire.* Aberdeen, 1906. [Aberdeen University series.]

a. Together with the author's (C43b) *Historical geography of Asia Minor,* and other writings (cf. F241), furnishes a wealth of materials on conditions in Asia Minor in Roman times. Review, J. R. S. Sterret, *A.H.R.* 2:507, Apr. 1897. *b.* Papers by seven contributors dealing with Phrygia, Pisidia, Lycaonia and Isauria. Review, *Journal of Hellenic Studies,* 27:136, 1907. AERB

E407a Chapot, Victor. *La province romaine proconsulaire d'Asie depuis ses origines jusqu'à la fin du haut empire.* Paris, 1904. [Bibliothèque de l'École des Hautes Études.] (Bibliography.)

b —— *La frontière de l'Euphrate, de Pompée à la conquête arabe.* Paris, 1907. [Bibliothèque des Écoles Françaises d'Athènes et de Rome.]

a. Excellent study of municipal, provincial, and imperial institutions, political and religious. General political history of the province and the rise of Christianity in Asia receive more summary treatment. Review, W. Liebenam, *Berliner Philologische Wochenschrift,* 27:116, Jan. 26, 1907. *b.* Omits military operations; analyzes carefully Roman policy in its attempts to find a satisfactory eastern frontier. Particular attention is devoted to the system of frontier defence; based partly on the author's own researches. Review, E. Girland, *Byzantinische Zeit.* 18:567, 1909.   AERB

E411 Bouchier, Edmund S. *Syria as a Roman province.* Oxford, 1916. (Bibliography.)

Good, readable narrative. Review, R. V. D. Magoffin, *A.H.R.* 22:193, Oct. 1916.   AERB

E416a Brünnow, Rudolf E., and **Domaszewski, Alfred Von.** *Die provincia Arabia, auf Grund zweier in den Jahren 1897 und 1898 unternommener Reisen und der Berichte früherer Reisender beschrieben.* 2 v. Strassburg, 1904–05.

  b Musil, Alois. *Arabia Petraea.* 3 v. in 4. Wien, 1907–08. [Kaiserliche Akademie der Wissenschaften.]

a. Useful contribution to historical geography. *b.* Contains valuable reports of topographical and ethnographical studies in Moab and Edom.   AERB

EUROPEAN PROVINCES OF ROME

E431a Carcopino, Jérome. *La loi de Hiéron et les Romains.* Paris, 1919.

  b Jenison, Elsie S. *History of the province of Sicily.* Boston, 1919.

a. Concerned with the organization of the direct tax which the Roman republic levied on Sicily; fundamental for the study of direct taxation in all the provinces. Review, P. Roussel, *Revue des Études Anciennes,* 22:304, Oct. 1920. *b.* Useful summary.   AERB

E436a Bouchier, Edmund S. *Sardinia in ancient times.* Oxford, 1917. (Bibliography.)

  b Pais, Ettore. *Storia della Sardegna e della Corsica durante il dominio romano.* 1 v. in 2. Roma, 1923.

Accounts by competent scholars; *a,* the more readable, *b,* the more critical. Review of *a,* J. J. Van Nostrand, *A.H.R.* 33:208, Oct. 1917.   AERB

For the relations of Rome with Greece and the neighboring Balkan lands prior to B. C. 146, cf. (D353*a*) Holleaux, *Rome, la Grèce et les monarchies hellénistiques* and (D353*b*) Colin, *Rome et la Grèce.*

For the five centuries following B. C. 146 the history of Greece and of the other Balkan lands has been surprisingly neglected. The general reader will find little save (D602*d*) Mahaffy, *Greek world under Roman sway from Polybius to Plutarch,* ch. 1 in (H305) Finlay, *History of Greece,* and ch. 7 in (E341) Mommsen, *Provinces of the Roman Empire.* The student may begin with (E81*c*) *Inscriptiones graecae ad res romanas pertinentes* and the highly specialized monograph literature.   GMD

E451a Nischer, Ernst. *Die Römer im Gebiete des ehemaligen Österreich-Ungarn.* Wien, 1923. (Bibliography.)

b Wagner, Friedrich. *Die Römer in Bayern.* Munich, 1924.

c Reinhart, Ludwig. *Helvetien unter den Römern.* Berlin, 1924.

d Alföldi, Andreas. *Der Untergang der römischen Herrschaft in Pannonien.* 2 v. Leipzig, 1924–26.

e Pârvan, Vasile. *Dacie: recherches et découvertes archéologiques en Roumanie.* 2. v. Bucharest, 1924–25.

a. Popular account of the Roman conquest of the lands between the Adriatic and the Danube, and of their cultural conditions under Roman rule. Brief; based upon scientific studies; dependable. Review, G. Wolff, *Philologische Wochenschrift,* 44:986, Oct. 11, 1924. *b, c, d,* and *e.* Excellent studies on the Alpine and Danubian districts under Roman rule. AERB

E456 Koepp, Friedrich. *Die Römer in Deutschland.* 1905. 2nd ed., Bielefeld, 1912. [Monographien zur Weltgeschichte.] (Bibliography.)

Best and most complete general treatment of the subject; combines the literary, epigraphic, and archeological material; maps, plans, and illustrations. Review, E. Anthes, *Berliner Philologische Wochenschrift,* 33:1399, Nov. 1, 1913. AERB

E457 Knoke, Friedrich. *Die Kriegszüge des Germanicus in Deutschland.* 1887. 2nd rev. ed., Berlin, 1922.

Basic work on this subject; very detailed; overpositive upon disputed points. Review, G. Wolff,*Philologische Wochenschrift,* 42:849, Sept. 9, 1922. AEPB

E458 Staehelin, Felix. *Die Schweiz in römischer Zeit.* Basel, 1927.

Valuable study, based largely on archeological materials. AERB

E461 Desjardins, Ernest. *Géographie historique et administrative de la Gaule romaine.* 4 v. Paris, 1876–93. V. 4, ed. by A. Longnon.

Study of the historical geography, formation, and organization of the provinces, with their administrative systems, subdivisions, and municipal organization; supplemented by a detailed examination of the development of the Roman road system. Good maps. Also cf. (M124a) Bloch, *Les origines, la Gaule indépendante, et la Gaule romaine,* v. 1, pt. 2. AERB

E462 Jullian, Camille. *Histoire de la Gaule.* V. 1–8. Paris, 1907–26. (Bibliographical foot-notes.)

Exhaustive and authoritative treatment of the history of Gaul from B. C. 600 to the end of Roman rule. V. 7 and 8. Cover the history of Gaul under the Roman emperors who made their capital at Treves, (284–394 A.D.), giving a masterly sketch of the political, military, economic and social life of the period. Review, A. Grenier, *Jour. des Savantes,* 11:120, March 1927. Also cf. (B308) Déchellette, *Manuel d'archéologie préhistorique, celtique, et gallo-romaine.* For special works on Roman Britain, cf. (L202). AERB

E471a Bouchier, Edmund S. *Spain under the Roman empire.* Oxford, 1914. (Bibliographies.)

b Van Nostrand, John J. *Reorganization of Spain by Augustus.* Berkeley, 1916. [University of California publications in history.] (Bibliography.)

c Albertini, Eugène. *Les divisions administratives de l'Espagne romaine.* Paris, 1923.

a. Readable survey of the history, antiquities, and literature. *b.* Good brief study of the administration. *c.* Clear and complete, superseding earlier works.

AERB

DIPLOMATIC AND MILITARY HISTORY

E501 Taübler, Eugen. *Imperium romanum, Studien zur Entwicklungsgeschichte des römischen Reichs.* V. 1, *Die Staatsverträge und Vertragsverhältnisse.* Leipzig, 1913. (Bibliography.)

Remarkably acute study of Roman international relations; careful analysis of the various types of treaties which Rome contracted; redates some of the older treaties, the texts of which have been preserved in literary works. Review, W. Soltau, *Berliner Philologische Wochenschrift,* 34:778, June 20, 1914.

Of first rate importance is (D502a) Phillipson, *International law and custom of ancient Greece and Rome.*   AERB

E511 Grosse, Robert. *Römische Militärgeschichte von Gallienus bis zum Beginn der byzantinischen Themenverfassung.* Berlin, 1920. (Bibliography.)

Indispensable work, thorough and dependable. Review, O. Fiebiger, *Philologische Wochenschrift,* 41:659, July 9, 1921.

For useful materials for Roman military history, also cf. (B511b) Spaulding, Nickerson, and Wright, *Warfare;* (B511a) Delbrück, *Geschichte der Kriegskunst,* (D511a) Kromayer, *Antike Schlachtfelder,* and (D511b) Kromayer and Veith, *Schlachten-Atlas.*   AERB

E512 Domaszewski, Alfred von. *Die Rangordnung des römischen Heeres.* Bonn, 1908. [Sonderabdruck aus *Bonner Jahrbücher.*]

Fundamental study; based on inscriptional evidence; investigates the officers of the Roman army from Augustus to Diocletian as a means of interpreting imperial policy. Review, F. Frölich, *Berliner Philologische Wochenschrift,* 29:1279, Oct. 9, 1909.   AERB

E513a Cheesman, George L. *Auxilia of the Roman imperial army.* Oxford, 1914.

b Parker, H. M. D. *Roman legions.* Oxford, 1928.

c Reynolds, Paul K. Baillie. *Vigiles of imperial Rome.* Oxford, 1926.

a. Sound, comprehensive study; based largely on epigraphic evidence. Review, F. Haverfield, *Classical Rev.* 29:218, Nov. 1915. *b.* Scholarly, stimulating, and valuable. Review, A. M. Duff, *Classical Rev.* 43:33, Feb. 1929. *c.* Careful compilation. Review, *Jour. Roman Studies,* 15:295, pt. 2, 1925.   AERB

E514 Cagnat, René. *L'armée romaine d'Afrique et l'occupation militaire de l'Afrique sous les empereurs.* 1892. 2nd rev. ed., 1 v. in 2, Paris, 1912–13. [Ministère de l'instruction publique.] (Bibliography.)

Very important contribution to the study of Roman military history; based upon careful epigraphical and archeological studies. Pt. 1. Traces the military operations of the empire in Africa to Diocletian and treats the organization of the pre-Diocletian army. Pt. 2. Studies the frontier lines, fortifications, and military system of the fourth century. Review, G. L. Cheesman, *Classical Rev.* 28:105, May 1914.   AERB

E515 Lesquier, Maurice J. *L'armée romaine d'Égypte, d'Auguste à Diocletien.* Le Caire, 1918. [Mémoires publiées par les membres de l'Institut Français d'Archéologie Orientale du Caire.] (Bibliography.)

Work of great erudition and sound judgment; continues author's study of the military institutions of the Ptolemies. Review, H. I. Bell, *Journal of Egyptian Archaeology,* 6:222, July 1920. AERB

E516 Couissin, Paul. *Les armes romaines.* Paris, 1926.

Careful and competent investigation of the equipment of the Roman soldiers from the earliest times to the end of the empire. Makes good use of archeological evidence. Review, A. Blanchet, *Jour. des Savants,* p. 1, Jan. 1927. AERB

CONSTITUTIONAL AND LEGAL HISTORY

E531a Abbott, Frank F. *History and description of Roman political institutions.* 1901. 3rd ed., Boston, 1911. (Bibliographies.)

   b ———— *Roman politics.* Boston, 1923. [(D603c) Our debt to Greece and Rome.] (Bibliography.)

   c Homo, Léon. *Les institutions politiques romaines, de la cité à l'état.* Paris, 1927. [(B153b) L'évolution de l'humanité.]

a. This clearly and carefully written and well-arranged introduction is particularly helpful for its documentation. Appendixes contain pertinent Latin selections from epigraphical and literary sources. Review, T. Nicklin, *Classical Rev.* 17:324, July 1903. *b.* Well-written interpretation of the main currents of Roman political life; designed expressly for the general reader. Review, W. R. Halliday, *Classical Rev.* 38:36, Feb. 1924. *c.* Constitutional history of Rome from the founding to the age of Constantine I. The first part is excellent, the later, dealing with the later republic and empire, is much weaker and rather uncritical. Review, D. McFayden, *A.H.R.* 33:98, Oct. 1927. ABWt

E532 Greenidge, Abel H. J. *Roman public life.* London and N. Y., 1901. [Handbooks of archaeology and antiquities.] (Select bibliography.)

This standard and very useful handbook traces the development of the Roman constitution from the earliest period to that of the principate, and describes its workings in Rome, Italy, and the provinces under the developed republic and under the principate. Well arranged and convenient for reference. Review, T. Nicklin, *Classical Rev.* 16:360, Oct. 1902; F. Cauer, *Berliner Philologische Wochenschrift,* 22:977, Aug. 2, 1902. CWK

E533 Botsford, George W. *Roman assemblies from their origin to the end of the republic.* N. Y., 1909. (Extensive bibliography.)

The first few chapters are argumentative. In opposition to Mommsen, the author believes that both patricians and plebeians took part in the legislative assemblies, and that political class distinctions at Rome arose from economic causes. His argument is well-founded and very important. The rest of the book gives a very accurate and full description of the activities and functions of the assemblies, affording a complete history of comitial legislation. When this work appeared it was considered unusually conservative in its acceptance of annalistic sources on matters of legal records, but the trend of criticism has in general been favorable to Botsford's point of view. An indispensable reference book. Review, F. F. Abbott, *A.H.R.* 15:354, Jan. 1910. TF

E534a Gelzer, Matthias. *Die Nobilität der römischen Republik.* Leipzig, 1912.

b Münzer, Friedrich. *Römische Adelsparteien und Adelsfamilien.* Stuttgart, 1920.

a. Careful study of Roman political life; interesting and informative. Review, C. Bardt, *Berliner Philologische Wochenschrift,* 33:16, Jan. 4, 1913. *b.* Illuminating work bearing on the problem of traditional family politics in Rome; shows a deep understanding of the structure of Roman society and the influence of the aristocracy in Roman history. Review, E. Hohl, *Berliner Philologische Wochenschrift,* 40:1091, Nov. 13, 1920.   AERB

E535a Mommsen, Theodor. *Römisches Staatsrecht.* 1871–76. 3rd ed., 3 v. in 5, Leipzig, 1887–88. [Marquardt and Mommsen, Handbuch der römischen Altertümer.]

b ——— *Abriss des römischen Staatsrechts.* 1893. 2nd ed., Leipzig, 1907. [Binding, Systematisches Handbuch der deutschen Rechtswissenschaft.]

c ——— *Römisches Strafrecht.* Leipzig, 1899. [Binding, Systematisches Handbuch der deutschen Rechtswissenschaft.]

d ——— *Römische Forschungen.* 2 v. Berlin, 1864–78.

e ——— *Gesammelte Schriften.* 8 v. Berlin, 1905–13. [1–3, *Juristische Schriften;* 4–6, *Historische Schriften;* 7, *Philologische Schriften;* 8, *Epigraphische Schriften.*]

a. This exposition of the Roman constitution as a well-knit system of offices and institutions based upon certain clearly grasped, fundamental, legal conceptions was a wholly original idea at the time of the publication of this book. The subject is treated under four main divisions: the magistracy, the individual magistrates, the people, the senate. No sharp line is drawn between the early monarchy, the republic, and the empire, for these are regarded merely as stages of a continuous development, and the same legal conceptions underlie all alike. Mommsen's method is first to give a clear enunciation of basic legal ideas and then to proceed to a discussion of their practical application by the various organs of government. The chief weakness of such a treatment of constitutional history is that the desire to erect an all-embracing system and the consequent tendency to deduce a general law from the exceptional occurrence has done some violence to historical reality, and has led to a false emphasis of legal right above political fact. It is in the discussions of the senate and the principate that this weakness makes itself chiefly felt. The value of the work lies in its completeness, its logical thinking, its clarity, and its thoroughness in detail. Its appearance put the study of Roman constitutional history upon a scientific basis, and it is still an indispensable work, the starting point of all investigation in this field, partly because of its complete citation of the source materials on each topic. Deservedly it ranks as the greatest achievement of Mommsen's genius. *b.* Stimulating survey of the constitutional growth of the Roman state, with more emphasis on the process of development than in *a.* *c.* Classic work on Roman criminal law. *d.* Important contributions on problems of Roman history, chiefly in the republican period. *e.* General collection of Mommsen's contributions to periodical literature.   AERB

E536a Marquardt, Karl Joachim. *Römische Staatsverwaltung.* 3 v. Leipzig, 1873–78. [1, *Organisation des römischen Reichs,* 2nd ed., 1881; 2, *Finanz- und Militärwesen,* 2nd ed. by H. Dessau and A. von Domaszewski, 1884; 3, *Das Sacralwesen,* 2nd ed. by G. Wissowa. 1885.] [Marquardt and Mommsen, Handbuch der römischen Altertümer.]

b Madvig, Johann N. *Die Verfassung und Verwaltung des römischen Staates.* 2 v. Leipzig, 1881–82.

c Herzog, Ernst. *Geschichte und System der römischen Staatsverfassung.* 2 v. Leipzig, 1884–87.

a. Work of primary importance. *b.* and *c.* Other useful treatises. For much shorter but very suggestive discussion, cf. Neumann, *Römische Staatsaltertümer,* in (D32) Gercke and Norden, *Einleitung in die klassische Altertumswissenschaft.*   AERB

E537a Hardy, Ernest G. *Studies in Roman history.* 2 v. London, 1906–09. (Bibliographical foot-notes.)

b ———, ed. *Six Roman laws, translated with introduction and notes.* Oxford, 1911.

c ——— ed. *Roman laws and charters, translated with introduction and notes.* Oxford, 1912.

d ——— *Some problems in Roman history, ten essays bearing on the administrative and legislative work of Julius Caesar.* Oxford, 1924.

a. V. 1. Contains an essay on 'Christianity and the Roman government,' and six shorter studies on constitutional questions of the principate. Review, P. J. Healy, *A.H.R.* 11 :931, July 1906. V. 2. Essays on the armies and frontiers, and on the emperors of the year A. D. 68–69. *b.* Includes Lex Acilia and the Roman laws of the republic dealing with municipal administration; valuable commentary. *c.* Republication of *b.* with addition of three municipal charters from Spain. *d.* Collection of studies previously published in periodicals.   AERB

E538a Schulz, Otto T. *Das Wesen des römischen Kaisertums der ersten zwei Jahrhunderte.* Paderborn, 1916. [Studien zur Geschichte und Kultur des Altertums.]

b ——— *Vom Prinzipat zum Dominat, das Wesen des römischen Kaisertums des dritten Jahrhunderts.* Paderborn, 1919. [Studien zur Geschichte und Kultur des Altertums.]

c McFayden, Donald. *History of the title Imperator under the Roman Empire.* Chicago, 1920. (Bibliographical foot-notes.)

These two volumes really form a single study, the main thesis of which is that the right of appointment to the principate legally belonged to the Senate alone, and that the army had no constitutional authority therein. *b.* Contains a useful collection of materials bearing on this problem. Review of *a* and *b,* D. McFayden, *Classical Philology,* 17 :274, July 1922. *c.* Important re-study of this problem; corrects the conclusions of Mommsen.   AERB

E539a Mattingly, Harold. *Imperial civil service of Rome.* Cambridge, Eng., 1910. [Cambridge historical essays.] (Bibliography.)

b Stein, Arthur. *Der römische Ritterstand.* München, 1926. [Münchener Beiträge zur Papyrusforschung und antiken Rechtsgeschichte, 10.]

a. Outlines the general development of the service in the first and second centuries; takes up in greater detail the *procuratores provinciarum.* Convenient summary; contains little or nothing original. Review, O. Hirschfeld, *Wochenschrift für Klassische Philologie,* 28 :243, Feb. 27, 1911. *b.* Authoritative study of the equestrian order from the time of its formation as a social and political class in the time of the Gracchi until its disappearance in the fourth century. Review, J. G. C. Anderson, *Jour. Roman Studies,* 16 :251, pt. 2, 1926.   CWK

E540a Hirschfeld, Otto. *Untersuchungen auf dem Gebiete der römischen Verwaltungsgeschichte.* Berlin, 1876.

b ——— *Die kaiserlichen Verwaltungsbeamten bis auf Diocletian.* Berlin, 1905.

b. Second edition of *a.;* standard work on the officials employed in the administration of the Roman empire, their rank and duties, and the evolution of the offices. Deals with all the important departments of administration. Concludes with a valuable general survey which brings out the growth of despotism and centralization, and the great importance of Hadrian and Septimius Severus in administrative history. An important supplement to older works such as (E535a) Mommsen, *Staatsrecht.* Review, H. Peter, *Wochenschrift für Klassische Philologie,* 22:948, Aug. 30, 1905; V. Chapot, *Revue de Philologie,* 29:274, July 1905.

WDG

E541a Arnold, William T. *Roman system of provincial administration to the accession of Constantine the Great.* 1879. 3rd rev. ed. by E. S. Bouchier, Oxford, 1914. [Arnold prize essay.] (Brief bibliography.)

b ——— *Studies of Roman imperialism.* Ed. by E. Fiddes. Manchester, 1906. [Publications of the University of Manchester.]

c Halgan, Cyprien. *Essai sur l'administration des provinces sénatoriales sous l'empire romain.* Paris, 1898.

a. Good general survey of Roman imperial government. After a preliminary study of the growth of the empire and the treatment of subject territories and dependencies, the author discusses, under the three periods of the republic, the early empire, and the late empire, the general features of provincial government and the policy of particular emperors with respect to the provinces. Special chapters on the system of taxation, which is discussed separately for each of the above periods, and on the municipalities in the provinces. *b.* Posthumous publication of a series of essays which are fragments of a larger work that Arnold had intended to write on the government of the Roman empire. These sketches discuss part of the work of Augustus in his attempt to reorganize the government of Rome and the empire. The three chapters dealing with the powers of the principate, the relations of Augustus and the senate, and the domestic policy of Augustus are very keen treatments of these questions. The other four chapters discuss the provincial organization in Gaul; Spain; Arabia, Egypt, and Greece; and Asia Minor. Review of *a.* and *b.,* H. S. Jones, *E.H.R.* 22:325, Apr. 1907; of *a.,* 30:370, Apr. 1915. *c.* Useful monograph.

For the provincial administration, also cf. (E536a) Marquardt, *Römische Staatsverwaltung;* for other works on the provinces, cf. (E341–471). AERB

E542a Reid, James S. *Municipalities of the Roman empire.* Cambridge, Eng., 1913.

b Abbott, Frank Frost, and **Johnson, Allan.** *Municipal administration in the Roman empire.* Princeton, 1926.

a. Survey of the Roman empire as a vast federation of commonwealths, retaining many characteristics of the old city-state. Convenient synthesis of facts already familiar to scholars, but does not lack illuminating comments contributed by the author. Contains no maps, notes, or bibliography. Review, G. W. Botsford, *A.H.R.* 19:335, Jan. 1914; H. S. Jones, *E.H.R.* 28:758, Oct. 1913. *b.* Very useful reference work in two parts, the first giving a general topical treatment, and the second a valuable collection of documents with commentaries. Review, A. E. R. Boak, *A.H.R.* 33 :375, Jan. 1928. ABWt

E543 Liebenam, Wilhelm. *Städteverwaltung im römischen Kaiserreiche.* Leipzig, 1900.

Studies the municipal budget, the local administration, and the relation of the municipality to the state. Valuable collection of material; suffers somewhat from neglect of chronological development. Review, J. Toutain, *Rev. Hist.* 78 :336, March 1902. AERB

E544 Waltzing, Jean P. *Étude historique sur les corporations professionnelles chez les Romains depuis les origines jusqu'à la chute de l'Empire d'Occident.* 4 v. Louvain, 1895–1900. (Bibliographies.)

Shows how the *collegia,* at first purely private, were ignored by the state until their repression in the late republic. Under the early empire those which applied for and received official authorization were allowed to exist. The state imposed public duties to an increasing extent upon the *collegia* till, in the fourth century, they had become administrative institutions, membership in which was compulsory and hereditary. Very scholarly monograph; conclusions based largely on inscriptions and legal literature; indispensable basis for any further investigation of this subject. WDG

E551a Bruns, Carl Georg, ed. *Fontes iuris romani antiqui.* 1860. 7th rev. ed. by O. Gradenwitz, 2 v. in 1, Tubingae, 1909, with *Additamentum,* 2 v., Tubingae, 1912. [1, *Leges et negotia;* 2, *Scriptores;* 3, *Index;* 4, *Simulacra.*]

b Krueger, Paul; Mommsen, Theodor; and Studemund, Wilhelm F. A., ed. *Collectio librorum iuris antejustiniani.* 3 v. Berolini, 1877–90; 7th rev. ed. of v. 1, 1923. [1, *Gai Institutiones,* ed. by P. Krueger and W. Studemund; 2, *Ulpiani liber singularis regularum, Pauli libri quinque sententiarum, fragmenta minora saeculorum p. Chr. n. secundi et tertii,* ed. by P. Krueger; 3, *Fragmenta Vaticana, Mosaicarum et romanarum legum collatio,* ed. by T. Mommsen, *Consultatio veteris cujusdam jurisconsulti, Codices Gregorianus et Hermogenianus, Alia minora,* ed. by P. Krueger.]

c Huschke, Eduard, ed. *Jurisprudentiae antejustinianae quae supersunt.* 1861. 6th rev. ed. by E. Seckel and B. Kuebler, 2 v., Lipsiae, 1908–11. [Bibliotheca scriptorum graecorum et romanorum Teubneriana.]

d Girard, Paul F., ed. *Textes de droit romain.* 1890. 4th rev. ed., Paris, 1913.

e Muirhead, James, tr. *Institutes of Gaius and Rules of Ulpian, with translation, notes, etc.* 1880. Rev. ed., Edinburgh, 1904.

f Poste, Edward, tr. *Gai Institutiones: or, Institutes of Roman law by Gaius, with a translation and commentary.* 1871. 4th rev. ed. by E. A. Whittuck, with historical introduction by A. H. J. Greenidge, Oxford, 1904.

g Godefroy (Gothofredus), Jacques, ed. *Codex Theodosianus cum perpetuis commentariis.* 1665. Rev. ed. by J. D. Ritter, 6 v., Lipsiae, 1736–45.

h Mommsen, Theodor, and Meyer, Paul M., ed. *Theodosiani· libri XVI cum Constitutionibus Sirmondianis et leges novellae ad Theodosianum pertinentes; consilio et auctoritate Academiae Litterarum Regiae Borussicae* 2 v. Berolini, 1905. 2nd ed., pt. 1 (Books 1–6), by P. M. Meyer, 1923.

a. Particularly valuable for inscriptions bearing on Roman law. The edition of Gradenwitz is based on the fifth and sixth editions prepared by Mommsen. *b.* Best edition of such writings of Gaius and other Roman jurisconsults as have been preserved outside of the *Corpus iuris civilis* of Justinian. *c.* and *d.* Other editions; more convenient for most purposes. *e.* and *f.* Texts, with good English translations and valuable notes, of the Institutes of Gaius. This work was composed as a text-book for the study of Roman law, by an otherwise almost unknown jurist, about the close of the principate of Antoninus Pius, and published soon after his death. After a short introduction on the sources of law, it gives a survey of the whole private law, in four commentaries, treating the subject under the divisions of law of persons, law of things, and law of actions. *g.* Old edition, but still valuable for its commentaries. *h.* Standard edition of the Theodosian code which is a collection of imperial constitutions issued after the accession of Constantine the Great. It was published in A. D. 438 by Theodosius II in the Eastern Empire and by Valentinian III in the West. The constitutions are arranged in chronological order under appropriate titles. The Novels included in *h.* are those promulgated in the Eastern and Western Empire between A.D. 438 and 476.   AERB

E552a **Krueger, Paul,** and others, ed. *Corpus iuris civilis.* 3 v. Berolini, 1884–95. [1, *Institutiones,* ed. by P. Krueger, *Digesta,* ed. by T. Mommsen, 14th ed., 1922; 2, *Codex,* ed. by P. Krueger, 9th ed., 1914; 3, *Novellae,* ed. by R. Schoell and W. Kroll, 4th ed., 1912.]

b **Monro, Charles H.,** tr. *Digest of Justinian* (Books 1–16). 1896. 2nd rev. ed. by W. W. Buckland, 2 v., Cambridge, Eng., 1904–09.

c **Moyle, John B.,** tr. *Institutes of Justinian translated into English.* 1883. 4th ed., Oxford and N. Y., 1906.

An attempt to make a definitive codification of the Roman law was carried out, under the orders of the Emperor Justinian, by the quaestor Tribonian with the aid of a corps of eminent jurists. The aim was to bring into one harmonious, comprehensive system the statute law and the writings of the jurisconsults. The resulting compilation absorbed and deprived of legal validity all independent works. The *Code,* a compilation of imperial constitutions, was issued in 529, revised in 534. The *Digest,* or *Pandects,* issued in 533, in fifty books, contains extracts from the works of the jurisconsults systematically arranged. The *Institutes,* also published in 533, formed a text-book for the study of the Roman law and also enjoyed the force of law. The later constitutions of Justinian, 535–565, known as *Novellae,* each of which was an independent law, were never officially codified but have been preserved in private compilations.   AERB

E553a **Buckland, William W.** *Text-book of Roman law from Augustus to Justinian.* Cambridge, Eng., and N. Y., 1921.

b **Girard, Paul F.** *Manuel élémentaire de droit romain.* 1896. 6th rev. ed., Paris, 1918. (Bibliography.)

c **Czyhlarz, Karl, Ritter von.** *Lehrbuch der Institutionen des römischen Rechts.* 1888. 18th rev. ed. by M. San Nicolò, Wien, 1924. (Bibliography.)

d **Sohm, Rudolf.** *The institutes, a textbook of the history and system of Roman private law.* 1892. 3rd ed., Oxford and N. Y., 1907. Tr. by J. C. Ledlie from *Institutionen: Geschichte und System des römischen Privatrechts.* 1884. 17th rev. ed., by L. Mitteis and L. Wenger, München, 1923.

a. Exceptionally comprehensive and detailed account of pure Roman law, following the order of the *Institutes.* Review, F. de Zulueta, *Classical Rev.* 36:134, Aug. 1922. *b.* Brief preliminary survey of the constitutional and legal development of Rome; followed by an exposition of Roman civil law based on the arrangement of the *Institutes.* Companion to his edition of (E551*d*) *Textes de droit romain.* *c.* Particularly clear and well-organized introduction to Roman law as it appears in the Justinian codification. Concerned with the study of pure Roman law not for its own sake but only as a key to the law of the present day. *d.* Gives the student of law a thorough treatment of the Roman private law of the *Corpus iuris civilis.* After brief survey of the sources of Roman law, traces its historical growth under the republic and empire, and its influence in Europe, particularly in Germany, in medieval and modern times. Then follows a systematic presentation of Roman law at the culmination of its development in Justinian's codification.

For the later development and influence of Roman law, cf. the works of (H551*a*) Vinogradoff and (H551*c*) Savigny. AERB

E554a Krueger, Paul. *Geschichte der Quellen und Literatur des römischen Rechts.* 1888. 2nd ed., München, 1912. [Binding, Systematisches Handbuch der deutschen Rechtswissenschaft.]

b Clark, Edwin C. *History of Roman private law.* 3 pt. in 4 v. Cambridge, Eng., 1906–19. [1, *Sources;* 2, *Jurisprudence;* 3, *Private law in the regal period,* ed. by W. W. Buckland.]

c Roby, Henry J. *Roman private law in the times of Cicero and of the Antonines.* 2 v., Cambridge, Eng., 1902.

a. Most complete and servicable treatment of this subject. *b.* Pt. 1. Most detailed and reliable account in English of the same subject; useful chronological sketch. Pt. 2. Critical examination of the ideas of Roman jurists from point of view of English jurisprudence. Prepared to meet the needs of English students of law, but valuable as a general work of reference. Review, R. Pound, *Harvard Law Rev.* 28:535, March 1915. Pt. 3. Full presentation of available materials, with wise emphasis on the conjectural character of the conclusions offered. Review, F. de Zulueta, *Classical Rev.* 35:177, Nov. 1921. For the beginnings of Roman law the student should not fail to consult (I555*c*) Maine, *Ancient law.* *c.* Manual of Roman law which was in force under the late republic and under the principate to about A. D. 228. Exhaustive treatment; elaborate but clear. The text and notes form an invaluable commentary on legal passages in Roman authors of the period, dealing particularly with Cicero's private orations, to which four special studies are devoted. Review, S. G. Owen, *Classical Rev.* 18:174, Apr. 1904. For briefer account by Roby, cf. (H121) *Cambridge medieval history,* v. 2, ch. 3, which is accompanied by a useful bibliography. V. Siniaski, *Les XII tables au point de vue de la chronologie de Rome et de son calendrier,* Riga, 1926, for a new interpretation of the code of the XII Tables. AERB

E555a Cuq, Edouard. *Manuel des institutions juridiques des romains.* Paris, 1917. (Bibliography.)

b ―――― *Les institutions juridiques des Romains envisagées dans leurs rapports avec l'état social et avec les progrès de la jurisprudence.* 2 v. and index. Paris, 1891–1908. 2nd rev. ed., v. 1, 1904. (Bibliography.)

c Costa, Emilio. *Profilo storico del processo civile romano.* Roma, 1918.

d **Declareuil, J.** *Rome the law-giver.* London and N. Y., 1926. [(B153a) History of civilization.] Tr. from *Rome et l'organisation du droit.* Paris, 1924. [(B153b) L'évolution de l'humanité.]

a. Historical rather than doctrinal; differs from *b.* in giving separate treatment of historical development of individual institutions from the earliest times to the late empire, instead of dividing the discussion into studies of various periods. Review, P. Fournier, *Nouvelle Revue Historique du Droit Français et Étranger,* 42:69, 1918. *c.* Valuable, up-to-date, comprehensive historical survey of procedure in Roman private law. Review, L. Wenger, *Zeitschrift der Savigny-Stiftung für Rechtsgeschichte, Romanistische Abteilung,* 41:304, 1920. *d.* Brief survey of the Roman legal system in its various stages of development. In general dependable, but suffers from compression. Review, (London) *Times Lit. Suppl.* 26:298, Apr. 28, 1927.   AERB

E556a **Mitteis, Ludwig.** *Reichsrecht und Volksrecht in den östlichen Provinzen des römischen Kaiserreichs, mit Beiträgen sur Kenntniss des griechischen Rechts und der spätrömischen Rechtsentwicklung.* Leipzig, 1891. (Bibliography.)

b ────── *Römisches Privatrecht bis auf die Zeit Diokletians.* V. I. Leipzig, 1908. [Binding, Systematisches Handbuch der deutschen Rechtswissenschaft.]

c **Meyer, Paul M.** *Juristische Papyri: Erklärung der Urkunden zur Einführung in die juristische Papyruskunde.* Berlin, 1920. (Extensive bibliography.)

a. Treats the important problem of the conflict and coalescence of Roman and local legal principles and practices in the eastern Mediterranean world. Review, H. Lewy, *Berliner Philologische Wochenschrift,* 13:435, Apr. 1, 1893. *b.* Reveals the Roman law of the principate freed from the contamination resulting from Justinian's codification; describes the reception of Roman law in Germany, and the principles of the Pandects. Review, A. Manigh, *Berliner Philologische Wochenschrift* 29:1630, Dec. 25, 1909. *c.* Extremely useful chrestomathy; accompanied by excellent discussions and annotations. Review, L. Mitteis, *Zeitschrift der Savigny-Stiftung für Rechtsgeschichte, Romanistische Abteilung,* 41:309, 1920.   AERB

E557 **Strachan-Davidson, James L.** *Problems of the Roman criminal law.* 2 v. Oxford, 1912. (Bibliography.)

Written as a criticism and supplement to (E535c) Mommsen, *Römisches Strafrecht.* Marked by strikingly independent views; mainly concerned with the Ciceronian period. Primarily an examination of the steps whereby a criminal in Rome was brought to trial, the theories upon which the conduct of the trial was based, and the means whereby the sentence was executed. Review, J. S. Blake Reed, *Classical Rev.* 27:137, June 1913.   AERB

E558 **Buckland, William W.** *Roman law of slavery, the condition of the slave in private law from Augustus to Justinian.* Cambridge, Eng., 1908.

Standard work on the subject. Review, F. de Zulueta, *Classical Rev.* 23:116, June 1909.   AERB

E559 Sherman, Charles P. *Roman law in the modern world.* 1917. 2nd ed., 3 v., New Haven, 1922. (Exhaustive bibliography.)

V. 1. Treats the history of Roman law. V. 2. Manual of its legal principles. V. 3. Contains a subject guide and a very extensive bibliography. The work has been prepared for the general reader, the non-professional student, the student of law, and the teacher of law. Review, J. H. Drake, *Michigan Law Rev.* 16:281, 1918. AERB

ECONOMIC AND SOCIAL HISTORY

E571 Frank, Tenney. *Economic history of Rome.* 1920. 2nd rev. ed., Baltimore, 1927. (Bibliographical foot-notes.)

Based on a thorough study of sources; sane in its conclusions; no over-emphasis on the importance of the economic element. References to similar modern conditions are made, though the reader is warned of the impossibility of drawing exact parallels. Review, A. E. R. Boak, *Classical Weekly*, 14:61, Dec. 6, 1920. The second edition is carefully revised, and enlarged to cover the period to the fourth century A.D.; and includes good survey of the provinces. Review, D. McFayden, *Classical Jour.* 22:636, May 1927. GAH, AERB

E572 Louis, Paul. *Ancient Rome at work,* N. Y., 1927. [(B153a) History of civilization.] Tr. by E. B. F. Waring from *Le travail dans le monde romain.* Paris, 1912. [(B575) Histoire universelle du travail, ed. by G. Renard.] (Bibliography.)

Compact survey of the conditions of labor throughout twelve centuries of Roman history. Discusses the supply of free and slave labor, agricultural and industrial toil, the associations of workers, and allied questions. Review, J. Toutain, *Rev. Hist.* 112:108, Jan. 1913. AERB

E573 Heitland, William E. *Agricola, a study of agriculture and rustic life in the Greco-Roman world from the point of view of labour.* Cambridge, Eng., 1921. (Select bibliography.)

This comprehensive and thoughtful work presents the evidence upon the condition of the agricultural classes which is contained in the various authors of antiquity. These, from Homer to Apollinaris Sidonius, are examined in chronological order and interpreted in the light of the political and social conditions of the time in which each wrote. Less than half of the book is devoted to Greece prior to the Roman conquest and to the Roman republic; the rest deals with the empire to the close of the fifth century of the Christian era. On the basis of the literary evidence, supplemented by some inscriptions, the author concludes that, as far as agriculture is concerned, ancient civilization rested upon a foundation of slavery. While maintaining that slavery probably was essential to the development of Greco-Roman culture, he believes that the evils resulting from this system led, directly or indirectly, to its fall. Review, H. S. Jones, *E.H.R.* 37:569, Oct. 1922. AERB

E574a Rostovtzeff (Rostowzew), Michael. *Geschichte der Staatspacht in der römischen Kaiserzeit bis Diokletian.* Leipzig, 1904. [*Philologus,* Supplementband, 9:329–510.]

b ——— *Studien zur Geschichte des römischen Kolonates.* Leipzig, 1910. [Archiv für Papyrus Forschung und verwandte Gebiete, Beiheft 1.]

c ——— *Social and economic history of the Roman Empire.* Oxford, 1926.

a. German version, with considerable modifications, of the author's Russian work of similar title published in 1899. Treats the historical development of the public contract and the relation between its history in the Hellenic East and the Roman West; based on a thorough mastery of the material; handles important problems of ancient history from a broad historical standpoint. Review, W. Liebenam, *Berliner Philologische Wochenschrift,* 25:538, April 29, 1905. *b.* Discusses the Hellenistic and Roman systems of tenant-farming in Egypt, Sicily, Asia Minor, and Africa, the significance of the technical terms involved, and, to some extent, the general agrarian history. Demonstrates how greatly the Romans were influenced by Hellenistic practices. Thus the Roman emperors, adopting the Hellenistic theory that ownership of the soil pertained only to the ruler, took possession of the royal lands of the Ptolemies and the Seleucids, and attempted, like their Hellenistic predecessors, to deal with their *coloni* directly and not through the middlemen, the great landlords. The ancient oriental feudalism triumphed, however, in the third century, and the *coloni* became veritable serfs. Based on the papyri and inscriptions; thoroughly scientific in method; a contribution to social and economic history of the greatest value. Review, W. S. Ferguson, *Classical Philology,* 6:355, July 1911. *c.* Work of the highest importance; scholarly and stimulating treatment of the evolution of the social and economic life of the Roman empire; unique in its field. Advances some questionable hypotheses, but collects and coördinates a vast body of evidence bearing on the subject. Reviews, H. Last, *Jour. Roman Studies,* 16:120, 1926; M. Besnier, *Rev. Critique,* 61:19, Oct. 1, 1927.   WDG, AERB

E575 Persson, Axel W. *Staat und Manufaktur im römischen Reiche, eine wirtschaftsgeschichtliche Studie, nebst einem Exkurs über angezogene Götterstatuen.* Lund, 1923. [Skrifter utgiona av Vetenskafs-Societeten i Lund.]

Treats of industry in its relation to the state under the following headings: Ptolemaic Egypt, Egypt in the early empire, the empire apart from Egypt until the end of the principate, and conditions in the late empire. Despite some questionable interpretations, a valuable contribution to ancient economic history. Review, W. Ensslin, *Philologische Wochenschrift,* 45:1260, Nov. 14, 1925.   AERB

E576a Charlesworth, Martin P. *Trade-routes and commerce of the Roman empire.* 1924. 2nd rev. ed., Cambridge, Eng., 1925. (Select bibliography.)

b Pârvan, Vasile. *Die Nationalität der Kaufleute im römischen Kaiserreiche.* Breslau, 1909.

c Hatzfeld, Jean. *Les trafiquants italiens dans l'Orient hellénique.* Paris, 1919. [Bibliothèque des Écoles Françaises d'Athènes et de Rome.]

d Warmington, E. A. *The commerce between the Roman empire and India.* Cambridge, 1928.

a. Restricted to the first two centuries, A. D.; good collection of material; does not show satisfactory acquaintance with the results of modern research; contains some very questionable conclusions. Review, W. Ensslin, *Philologische Wochenschrift,* 45:1166, Oct. 24, 1925. *b.* Study of the inscriptional evidence relating to trade and commerce in the Roman Empire, showing the extent to which commerce was in the hands of the peoples of the eastern provinces. *c.* Treats the history of the diffusion of *negotiatores,* their activities, organization, and historical influence, as a phase of the expansion of Rome in the Near East.

Review, P. Roussel, *Revue des Études Anciennes,* 22:304, Oct. 1920. *d.* Deals chiefly with the period from Augustus to Marcus Aurelius. Good study of trade routes and of exports and imports, with elaborate but inconveniently arranged notes and references. Review, J. O. Thompson, *Classical Rev.* 43:84, May, 1928.

AERB

E577a Park, Marion E. *Plebs in Cicero's day, a study of their provenance and of their employment.* Cambridge, Mass., 1921.

b Brewster, Ethel H. *Roman craftsmen and tradesmen of the early Roman Empire.* Menasha, Wis., 1917. (Bibliography.)

Two useful studies of social life in Rome. *b.* Based on the writings of the Roman satirists of the first century, A. D. Review, F. W. Wright, *Classical Weekly,* 12:38, Nov. 11, 1918.

AERB

E581 Bloch, Leo. *Soziale Kämpfe im alten Rom.* 900. 4th ed., Leipzig, 1920. [Aus Natur und Geisteswelt.]

Brief work for general readers; based upon independent research; marked by well-considered opinions; fails to indicate the evidence upon which judgments are based. Review, F. Cauer, *Wochenschrift für Klassische Philologie,* 26:625, June 7, 1909.

AERB

CULTURAL HISTORY: GENERAL

E601a Bailey, Cyril, ed. *Legacy of Rome.* Oxford, 1923. [1, H. H. Asquith, *Introduction;* 2, C. Foligno, *Transmission of the legacy;* 3, E. Barker, *Conception of empire;* 4, H. S. Jones, *Administration;* 5, G. H. Stevenson, *Communciations and commerce;* 6, F. de Zulueta, *Science of law;* 7, H. Last, *Family and social life;* 8, C. Bailey, *Religion and philosophy;* 9, C. Singer, *Science;* 10, J. W. Mackail, *Literature;* 11, H. Bradley, *Language;* 12, G. McN. Rushforth, *Architecture and art;* 13, G. Giovannoni, *Building and engineering;* 14, W. E. Heitland, *Agriculture.*] (Bibliographies.)

b —— ed. *Mind of Rome.* Oxford, 1926. Contributions by C. Bailey, J. Bell, J. C. Harrington-Ward, T. F. Higham, A. N. Bryan-Brown, H. E. Butler, M. Platnauer, C. Singer.

a. Essays by several scholars on Roman civilization, with particular emphasis upon its contribution to later civilization. Designed for the general public but valuable to the special student. *b.* Attempts to interpret Roman thought by translations of characteristic passages of Roman literature with the commentaries necessary for their elucidation. Review, L. A. Constans, *Rev. Critique* 61:478, Dec. 15, 1927.

Cf. various volumes in (D603c) *Our debt to Greece and Rome,* and in (D603d) *Das Erbe der Alten;* and also (C604) de Burgh, *Legacy of the ancient world;* (D604e) Taylor, *Ancient ideals;* (D605c) Smyth, *Harvard essays on classical subjects;* and A. Grenier, *Roman spirit in religion, thought and art,* in (B153a) *History of civilization;* review, C. H. Moore, *A.H.R.* 31:159, Oct. 1925.   CERB

E602a Showerman, Grant. *Eternal Rome, the city and its people from the earliest times to the present day.* 2 v. New Haven, 1924. Also 1 v. ed., 1924. (Bibliography.)

b Davis, William S. *A day in old Rome, a picture of Roman life.* Boston, 1925.

c Giles, Alexander F. *Roman civilization.* London, 1926. [Through the eye.]

a. Illustration. and pen pictures furnishing a connected survey of the history and culture of the city of Rome. Review, C. U. Clark, *Amer. Jour. of Philology,* 46:287, July 1925; T. Ashby, *Classical Rev.* 39:130, Aug. 1925 *b.* Able and interesting account of the observations of a supposed visitor to Rome in A. D. 134; illustrated. *c.* Well illustrated and readable account of the main aspects of Roman civilization. GMD

E606a Fowler, William Warde. *Social life at Rome in the age of Cicero.* London, 1908; N. Y., 1909.

b Abbott, Frank F. *Common people of ancient Rome, studies of Roman life and literature.* N. Y., 1911.

c McDaniel, Walton B. *Roman private life and its survivals.* Boston, 1924. [(D603c) Our debt to Greece and Rome.] (Bibliography.)

a. The author's aim 'is only to give such a picture of society in general as may tempt a student to further and more exact inquiry.' He has been entirely successful. Based largely on the sources and especially on the correspondence of Cicero; recommended as an interesting general survey of the city and society which produced a Cicero and a Catiline. Review, H. N. Fowler, *Classical Philology,* 5:235, Apr. 1910; S. B. Platner, *A.H.R.* 14:795, July 1909. CHO

b. By interesting descriptions of the social, political, and economic position of the common people of Rome, in such things as their language, literary tastes, trade-guilds, and the high cost of living, and by emphasizing the many points of similarity between ancient and modern conditions, the author, in nine scholarly essays, has brought the past very close to the present. Review, F. B. R. Hellems, *Classical Philology,* 7:371, July 1912. ABWt

c. Readable, popular account of the life of the upper classes of Rome in the late republican and early imperial periods. Review, E. H. Haight, *Classical Jour.* 21:63, Oct. 1925. AERB

E611 Grupp, Georg. *Kulturgeschichte der römischen Kaiserzeit.* 2 v. München, 1903–04. 2nd rev. ed., v. 1, Regensburg, 1921. [1, *Untergang der heidnischen Kultur;* 2, *Anfänge der christlichen Kultur.*]

Readable, scholarly study of social conditions in all their aspects. Review, v. 1, J. P. Waltzing, *La Musée Belge,* 8:117, March 1904; 8:381, Oct. 1904. AERB

E612 Friedländer, Ludwig. *Roman life and manners under the early empire.* 4 v. London and N. Y., 1908–13. Tr. by L. A. Magnus, J. H. Freese, and A. B. Gough from 7th ed. of *Darstellungen aus der Sittengeschichte Roms in der Zeit von August bis zum Ausgang der Antoninen,* 1862–71; 9th and 10th rev. ed., by G. Wissowa, 4 v., Leipzig, 1921–23.

A work of genuine scholarship, sound and well-written without being over-ingenious or pedantic. Very few pertinent topics in the cultural history of Rome between B. C. 31 and A. D. 180 are omitted. Students of special topics will usually find a wealth of information. V. 4. Appendixes and notes containing much curious data. The general treatment is much more objective, although less philosophical, than in (E614) Dill, *Roman society,* and better adapted to reference purposes. WSD

E613 Tucker, Thomas G. *Life in the Roman world of Nero and St. Paul.* N. Y., 1910.

Popular work; written in pleasing style; shows thorough acquaintance with the literature of the period. Its scope is not as broad as the title indicates, as disproportionate emphasis is laid upon Rome and Italy. Weak in its treatment of the provinces, the lower classes, and the imperial administrative system. Review, *Classical Rev.* 25:88, March 1911.   AERB

E614a Dill, Sir Samuel. *Roman society from Nero to Marcus Aurelius.* 1904. 2nd rev. ed., London and N. Y., 1905. (Bibliographical foot-notes.)

b ——— *Roman society in the last century of the Western empire.* 1898. 2nd rev. ed., London and N. Y., 1899. (Bibliographical foot-notes.)

a. Penetrating and exceedingly well-written exposition of the Roman imperial age as reflected in the writings of the two Plinies, Juvenal, Martial, Tacitus, Suetonius, Marcus Aurelius, and, especially, Seneca, and in the great mass of inscriptional evidence. Stronger on the philosophical and religious side than on the political. Review, *A.H.R.* 11:125, Oct. 1905. *b.* Study of the social atmosphere of the dying empire. The examination of the causes which led paganism long to survive in the circles of the great senatorial families is acute and interesting. The world portrayed is essentially that of St. Jerome, Symmachus, and Ausonius, and therefore of conditions mainly in Italy and Romanized Gaul. Demonstrates that the men of the fifth century were by no means so effete and decadent as they are often represented, and that the invaded population often got on pretty well with the invaders. Review, F. A. Christie, *A.H.R.* 5:554, Apr. 1900.   WSD

E615 Glover, Terrot R. *Life and letters in the fourth century.* Cambridge, Eng., 1901.

Primarily a series of biographical sketches of prominent literary figures. While the literary interests of the time receive satisfactory treatment, economic conditions, law, language, and religion are neglected. Review, F. T. Richards, *Classical Rev.* 16:131, March 1902.   AERB

E616 Gorce, Denys. *Les voyages, l'hospitalité et la port des lettres dans le monde chrétien des IVᵉ et Vᵉ siècles.* 2 v. Paris, 1925.

Careful study, contributing to the general picture of the social life of the period. Review, P. de Labriolle, *Rev. Critique* 61:326, Sept. 1, 1927.   AERB

CULTURAL HISTORY: RELIGION

E621a Halliday, William R. *Lectures on the history of Roman religion from Numa to Augustus.* Liverpool, 1922; Boston, 1923. [Ancient world.]

b **Carter, Jesse Benedict.** *Religion of Numa, and other essays on the religion of ancient Rome.* London and N. Y., 1906.

c ——— *Religious life of ancient Rome, a study in the development of religious consciousness, from the foundation of the city until the death of Gregory the Great.* Boston, 1911. [Lowell Institute lectures.]

a. Excellent, popular manual. Review, C. Bailey, *Classical Rev.* 37:123, Aug. 1923. *b.* Brief, well-written survey of the religious development of the Romans from the earliest times to the age of Augustus. Review, S. B. Platner, *Classical Philology,* 2:224, Apr. 1907. *c.* Similar work, for longer period.   AERB

E622a Fowler, William Warde. *Roman festivals of the period of the republic, an introduction to the study of the religion of the Romans.* London and N. Y., 1899. [Handbooks of archaeology and antiquities.]

b ——— *Religious experience of the Roman people from the earliest times to the age of Augustus.* London, 1911. [Gifford lectures.]

c ——— *Roman ideas of deity in the last century before the Christian era.* London, 1914.

d ——— *Roman essays and interpretations.* Oxford, 1920.

a. Full and excellent description of Roman public religious rites. *b.* Describes the animism of the primitive Romans; traces the gradual inflow of Etruscan and Greek cults and religious ideas, the influence of this syncretized religion upon the individual and the state; ends with chapters on Vergil and the Augustan revival. Familiarity with historical sources, sound critical sense, profound knowledge of Rome's political history, keen insight into religious psychology, and wide reading in the recent literature of comparative religions combine to make the book a masterpiece in religious history. Illustrative and supporting references to sources often need to be supplied from (E623) Wissowa. Review, H. S. Jones, *E.H.R.* 27:340, Apr. 1912. *c.* Aims to discover intellectual conceptions of deity current among upper classes of society but especially in the minds of plebeians. Review, C. Bailey, *Classical Rev.* 28:241, Nov. 1914. *d.* Collection of studies, dealing chiefly with questions of religion and society.   TF

E623 Wissowa, Georg. *Religion und Kultus der Römer.* 1902. 2nd rev. ed., München, 1912. [(D35) Handbuch der Altertumswissenschaft.]

Most thorough discussion of the religious belief and worship of the Romans. A separate section for each of the gods makes the work most convenient for reference. Review, G. Showerman, *Amer. Jour. of Philology,* 24:75, 1903.   CHO

E624a Peterson, Roy M. *Cults of Campania.* Rome, 1919. [Papers and monographs of the American Academy in Rome.] (Bibliography.)

b **Taylor, Lily R.** *Local cults in Etruria.* Rome, 1925. [Papers and monographs of the American Academy in Rome.] (Bibliography.)

Detailed, thorough, scientific studies of the literary, epigraphical, numismatic, archeological, and topographical material bearing on the local cults. Treat pre-Roman, Roman, and oriental cults, and also the beginnings of Christianity. Review, G. Wissowa, *Philologische Wochenschrift,* 44:1104, Nov. 8, 1924.   AERB

E625 Beurlier, Emile. *Essai sur le culte rendu aux empereurs romains.* Paris, 1890.

Still the best comprehensive treatise on the subject, though corrected and supplemented by an extensive literature on special aspects of the imperial cult.   AERB

E626 Toutain, Jules François. *Les cults païens dans l'empire romain.* Pt. 1, *Les provinces latines.* V. 1–3. Paris, 1907–20. [1, *Les cultes officiels, les cultes romains et greco-romains;* 2, *Les cultes orientaux;* 3, *Les cultes indigènes, nationaux, et locaux, Afrique du Nord, péninsule iberique, et Gaule.*] (Bibliothèque de l'École des Hautes Études.)

Work of great detail and fundamental importance; based upon a painstaking study of the inscriptional evidence. Review, v. 1–2, E. Samter, *Berliner Philologische Wochenschrift,* 29:623, May 15, 1909; 33:1164, Sept. 13, 1913; v. 3, A. Grenier, *Rev. Hist.* 137:96, May, 1921.   AERB

E627a Cumont, Franz, ed. *Textes et monuments figurés relatifs aux mystères de Mithra.* 2 v. Bruxelles, 1896–99. (Bibliography.)

b —— *Mysteries of Mithra.* 1903. 2nd ed., Chicago, 1910. Tr. by T. J. McCormack from 2nd rev. ed. of *Les mystères de Mithra,* 1900. 3rd rev. ed., Bruxelles, 1913.

c —— *Oriental religions in Roman paganism.* Chicago, 1911. Tr. by G. Showerman from 2nd rev. ed. of *Les religions orientales dans le paganisme romain,* 1906, 2nd rev. ed., Paris, 1909.

d —— *Astrology and religion among the Greeks and Romans.* N. Y. and London, 1912. Tr. by J. B. Baker. [American lectures on the history of religions.]

e —— *After life in Roman paganism.* New Haven, 1922. [Silliman lectures.]

f Reitzenstein, Richard. *Die hellenistischen Mysterienreligionen, ihre Grundgedanken und Wirkungen.* 1910. 2nd ed., Leipzig, 1920.

a. Important work which began a long series of books and essays by the author, dealing with special cults or aspects of pagan religions. *b.* Embodies the conclusions reached in *a. c* and *d.* Best available general accounts on the subjects. *e.* Eight excellent lectures on as many aspects of the subject. Cumont, one of the foremost living scholars, is thoroughly familiar with all phases of the complex problem of the propagation of oriental religions in the western world. Most of his best work appears in brief articles in various French journals. While *a* is intended for the student, *b, c, d,* and *e* are readable as well as scholarly. For other cults, in addition to Mithraism, *c* should be supplemented by v. 2 of (E626) Toutain, and by *f,* a public address, richly elaborated with scholarly notes. WAH

E628a Glover, Terrot R. *Conflict of religions in the early Roman empire.* 1909. 3rd ed., London, 1909.

b Sihler, Ernest G. *From Augustus to Augustine, essays and studies dealing with the contact and conflict of classic paganism and Christianity.* Cambridge, Eng., and N. Y., 1923.

c Angus, Samuel. *Mystery-religions and Christianity, a study in the religious background of early Christianity.* London, 1925. (Extensive bibliography.)

d Halliday, William R. *Pagan background of early Christianity.* Liverpool, 1925. [Ancient world.]

Studies of the relations of Christianity with its rivals in the first four centuries and of the transition from paganism to Christianity. To a considerable degree the four works supplement one another in the topics discussed and in the distribution of emphasis. Review of *a, Athenaeum,* 2:234, Aug. 28, 1909; of *b,* F. A. Christie, *A.H.R.* 29:318, Jan. 1924. GMD

E629 Wendland, Paul. *Die hellenistisch-römische Kultur in ihren Beziehungen zu Judentum und Christentum.* 1907. 3rd. ed., Tübingen, 1912. [Handbuch zum Neuen Testament.] (Bibliographies.)

Brief study, but most important treatment of the subject. Also cf. (F646) Hatch, *Influence of Greek ideas and usages upon the Christian church;* and (F202) Clemen, *Primitive Christianity and its non-Jewish sources.* WAH

E630a Boissier, Gaston. *La religion romaine d'Auguste aux Antonins,* 1874. 5th ed., 2 v., Paris, 1900.

b ——— *La fin du paganisme, étude sur les dernières luttes religieuses en Occident au quatrième siècle.* 1891. 6th ed., 2 v., Paris, 1909.

Graced by an admirable style and permeated with an extensive knowledge of the literature, these masterly works still hold their place, though they should be supplemented by the more recent writings of (E614) Dill, and by later works listed in this subsection.   GMD

E631 Geffcken, Johannes. *Der Ausgang des griechisch-römischen Heidentums.* Heidelberg, 1920. [Religionswissenschaftliche Bibliothek.]

Very able treatment of the decline of paganism in the Roman empire from the end of the second century. Review, W. Capelle, *Literarisches Zentralblatt,* 71:849, 865, 881, Nov. 6, 13, 20, 1920.   AERB

CULTURAL HISTORY: EDUCATION, THOUGHT, PHILOSOPHY

For education and the advancement of learning and science, cf. (D21) encyclopedias and dictionaries of classical antiquity; (D32) Gercke and Norden, *Einleitung in die Altertumswissenschaft;* (D35) *Handbuch der Altertumswissenschaft;* (D641d) Allinson, *Roads from Rome;* and (E21b) Sandys, *Companion to Latin studies.*

For Roman philosophy, cf. the works on ancient philosophy listed in (D652) and (D656), especially those dealing with Epicureanism, Stoicism, and Neo-Platonism; and also (E661-664) the general works on Roman literature, and the works of (E614) Dill, and of (E630) Boissier.

E651 Lucretius, Carus Titus. *De rerum natura.* 1473. Ed. and tr. by H. A. J. Munro, 1864; 4th rev. ed., 3 v., London, 1886; later reprints.

In this didactic poem, Lucretius, a contemporary of Cicero, gives an interpretation of the universe from the point of view of Epicurean philosophy.   AERB

E652 Cicero, Marcus Tullius. *Scripta quae manserunt omnia,* ed. by C. F. W. Mueller, 4 v. in 10, Lipsiae, 1889-1902; later ed. of several parts [Bibliotheca scriptorum graecorum et romanorum Teubneriana]. *De finibus bonorum et malorum,* ed. and tr. by H. Rackham, London and N. Y., 1914 [Loeb classical library] *De officiis,* ed. and tr. by W. Miller, London and N. Y., 1913 [Loeb classical library]. *De senectute, de amicitia, de divinatione,* ed. and tr. by W. A. Falconer, London and N. Y., 1923 [Loeb classical library].

In his philosophic works, written in the years B. C. 46-44, Cicero aimed to give to the Roman world, in popular form, the substance of Greek philosophic thought from the point of view of the New Academy.   AERB

E653 Seneca, Lucius Annaeus. *Epistulae morales, Dialogi, Naturales quaestiones, de Ira, de Clementia, de Consolatione, de Tranquillitate animi, de Brevitati vitae, de Beneficiis.* 1515. Ed. by F. Haase, in *Opera quae supersunt,* 3 v., Lipsiae, 1852-53. *Dialogorum libros XII,* ed. by E. Hermes, Lipsiae, 1905. *De beneficiis libri VII, De clementia libri II,* ed. by C. Hosius, Lipsiae, 1900. *Naturalium quaestionum libros VIII,* ed. by A. Gercke, Lipsiae, 1907.

Seneca, died A. D. 65, philosopher, rhetorician, poet and statesman, gives in the above works a rhetorical, but sincere, discussion of moral questions from the Stoic point of view.   AERB

E654 Aurelius Antoninus, Marcus. *Tōn eis heauton (To himself).* 1558. Ed. by J. H. Leopold, Oxford, 1911. Ed. and tr. by C. R. Haines, London and N. Y., 1916 [Loeb classical library].

Twelve books, written in Greek between A. D. 166 and 176, in which the emperor expounds the ethical teachings of the Stoic system.   AERB

E655a Martha, Constant. *Les moralistes sous l'empire romain, philosophes et poètes.* Paris, 1864.

  b Degert, Antoine. *Les idées morales de Ciceron.* Paris, 1907. [Philosophes et penseurs.]

Among the more comprehensive works dealing exclusively with Roman philosophy.   AERB

E656 Gwynn, Aubrey. *Roman education from Cicero to Quintilian.* Oxford, 1926.

Good analysis of the main principles and ideals of Roman education. Review, J. W. Duff, *Jour. Roman Studies* 15:274, pt. 2, 1926.   HERB

CULTURAL HISTORY: LITERATURE

E661a Mackail, John W. *Latin literature.* London and N. Y., 1895. [University series.]

  b Schanz, Martin. *Geschichte der römischen Literatur bis zum Gesetzgebungswerk des Kaisers Justinian.* 4 v. in 7. München, 1890–1920. 3rd rev. ed., v. 1–3, 1907–22; 2nd rev. ed., v. 4, pt. 1, 1914. V. 4, pt. 2, completed by C. Hosius and G. Krueger. [(D35) Handbuch der Altertumswissenschaft.]

  a. Delightfully written historical and critical survey of Roman literature from its beginnings to the disappearance of classical Latin in the Middle Ages. Valuable for the broad treatment of various forces influencing Roman literature at different times, and for estimates of the literary values of works of individual authors. Lacks both biographical and bibliographical details, for which the student should consult *b.* Review of *a.,* J. P. Postgate, *Classical Rev.* 10:259, June 1896.   AERB

E662a Duff, John Wight. *Literary history of Rome from the origins to the close of the golden age.* 1909. 3rd ed., London, 1927. [Library of literary history.]

  b —— *Literary history of Rome in the silver age.* London, 1927. [Library of literary history.] (Bibliographies.)

  a. The thesis of this work is the distinctly Roman element in Latin literature. For this reason, p. 1–63 are devoted to the geographical environment and racial characteristics of the Romans. Each author is treated with special regard to his personality and experience. The treatment is original and the illustrative material well chosen. Review, K. F. Smith, *Amer. Jour. of Philology,* 31:222, Apr. 1910. *b.* Continues *a* to 138 A.D. Excellent work showing a highly satisfactory combination of knowledge, breadth of view, and appreciation. Review, J. W. Mackail, *Classical Rev.* 42:34, Feb. 1928.   AERB

E663a Leo, Friedrich. *Die römische Literatur des Altertums.* 1905. 2nd ed.,
Berlin, 1907. [(B606) Hinneberg, Die Kultur der Gegenwart.]

   b —— *Geschichte der römischen Literatur.* V. 1, *Archäische Literatur.*
Berlin, 1913.

   c **Norden, Eduard.** *Die römische Literatur.* Berlin, 1910. [(D32)
Gercke and Norden, Einleitung in die Altertumswissenschaft.]

   a. and *c.* Excellent introductions in very compact form. *b.* New work on
much more extensive scale.   AERB

E664 Teuffel, Wilhelm S. *History of Roman literature.* 2 v. London, 1873.
Tr. by W. Wagner from *Geschichte der römischen Litteratur,* 1870; 6th
rev. ed., by W. Kroll and others, 3 v., Leipzig, 1910–16; 7th ed., v. 2, 1920.
Another tr. by G. C. W. Warr, 2 v., London, 1891–92, reprint, 1900, from
5th German rev. ed. by L. Schwabe.

Unsurpassed for accuracy and comprehensiveness; a most dependable *vade-
mecum.*   AERB

CULTURAL HISTORY: ART

Some of the best studies of Roman art appear in general works on the history
of art listed in § B, and in works devoted to Greek and Roman art, such as (D682)
Michaelis, *Century of archaeological discoveries;* (D687) Anderson and Spiers,
Architecture of Greece and Rome; (D688) Chase, *Greek and Roman sculpture
in American collections;* (D690c) Jex-Blake and Sellers, *The elder Pliny's chapters on the history of art.*

E681a Amelung, Walther, and **Holtzinger, Heinrich.** *Museums and ruins of
Rome.* 1906. Reprint, 2 v., London, 1912. Ed. and tr. by Eugènie (Mrs.
S. Arthur) Strong from *Antike Kunst,* 1904; 2nd ed., 2 v., Stuttgart, 1912
[Moderne Cicerone, Rom.].

   b **Seta, Alessandro Della.** *Italia antica: dalla caverna preistorica al
palazzo imperiale.* 1922. 2nd ed. Bergamo, 1927.

   a. Small travelers' guide; amply illustrated; convenient, in the absence of
any systematic manual in English, as an introduction for the general reader and
the student. *b.* Admirably illustrated, popular, account of the material remains
of Roman civilization from the earliest times to the imperial period.   AERB

E682 Cagnat, René, and **Chapot, Victor.** *Manuel d'archéologie romaine.* 2 v.
Paris, 1916–20. (Bibliography.)

Not a compilation but an independent, erudite, and authoritative work by two
highly competent scholars whose mastery of the general field is unrivalled. V. 1.
Devoted to the various classes of monuments throughout the Roman world, and
to their decoration. V. 2. Continues the subject of decoration with its extensive ramifications; treats also of painting, mosaics, and the instruments of
public and private life. The material is thoroughly organized; descriptions are
clear and concise. Review, v. 1, D. M. Robinson, *Classical Weekly,* 12:44, Nov.
18, 1918.   JGW

E683a Platner, Samuel B. *Topography and monuments of ancient Rome.* 1904.
2nd rev. ed., Boston, 1911. [College Latin series.]

   b **Richter, Otto L.** *Topographie der Stadt Rom.* 1889. 2nd rev. ed.,
München, 1901. [(D35) Handbuch der Altertumswissenschaft.]

   c **Stannard, Harold.** *Rome and her monuments.* London and N. Y., 1923.

a. This excellent handbook still remains the most useful one on the subject in any language; indispensable to students of ancient history and archeology. Numerous references to ancient sources and to the voluminous controversial literature in books and periodicals; well illustrated. While based on *b,* it far surpasses that work. Review of *a.,* 1st ed., G. J. Laing, *Classical Rev.* 19:232, May 1905; 2nd ed., T. Ashby, *Journal of Roman Studies,* 2:278, 1912.   *c.* More recent manual.   JGW

E684 Frank, Tenney. *Roman buildings of the republic, an attempt to date them from their materials. Rome,* 1924. [Papers and monographs of the American Academy in Rome.]

Scientific study of the problem of dating early Roman buildings by examination of the building stone employed and the quarries from which this was obtained. Review, G. Hadzsits, *Amer. Jour. of Archaeology,* 29:449, Oct. 1925.   AERB

E685a Lanciani, Rodolfo. *Ancient Rome in the light of recent discoveries.* London and Boston, 1888.

b ——— *Pagan and Christian Rome.* London and Boston, 1893.

c ——— *Ruins and excavations of ancient Rome.* London and Boston, 1897.

d ——— *Wanderings in the Roman Campagna.* Boston, 1909.

e ——— *Wanderings through ancient Roman churches.* London and Boston, 1924.

f ——— *Forma urbis Romae.* 8 pt. Milano, 1893–1901.

g ——— *Storia degli scavi di Roma e notizie intorno le collezioni romane di antichità.* 4 v. Roma, 1902–12.

a, b, c, d, and *e.* Popular works adapted to serve as guides to the monuments of ancient Rome. *f.* The great archeological map of Rome; scale 1–1,000. *g.* Very important for students of Roman art and archeology. Detailed record of the researches and discoveries of monuments of antiquity made in Rome from the eleventh century to A. D. 1605, with location of such objects as found their way into museums, and list of authorizations to export issued in this period. Also cf. his *Ancient and modern Rome* in (D603c) *Our debt to Greece and Rome.*

AERB

E686 Walters, Henry B. *Art of the Romans.* London and N. Y., 1911. (Brief bibliography.)

Written by a competent scholar, for readers who are not specialists; primarily an introduction to the study of Roman art. The author's main thesis is that Roman art, like Roman literature, is Greek in form but essentially Roman in spirit and character. Best section is on sculpture. Excellent illustrations. Review, A. M. Daniel, *Journal of Roman Studies,* 1:241, 1911.   JGW

E687a Wickhoff, Franz. *Roman art, some of its principles and their application to early Christian painting.* London, 1900. Tr. by Mrs. A. Strong.

b Strong, Eugénie [Mrs. S. Arthur]. *Roman sculpture from Augustus to Constantine.* London, 1907.

c Bernoulli, Johann J. *Römische Ikonographie.* 2 v. in 4. Stuttgart, 1882–94.

a. Historical account of style in Roman art, both in painting and in sculpture, from about the period of Augustus to that of Constantine. Republication, with modifications, of the author's contribution, entitled 'Römische Kunst,' to the edition of *Die Wiener Genesis,* Wien, 1895. *b.* Good account of Roman portraiture and the more important monuments. Seeks to present the characteristically Roman element in Roman art. Review, A. M. Daniel, *Classical Rev.* 22:85, May 1908. *c.* Collection of Roman portraits. AERB

E688 Vitruvius Pollio. *De architectura libri decem.* 1486–92. Ed. by F. Krohn, Lipsiae, 1912 [Bibliotheca scriptorum graecorum et romanorum Teubneriana.] Tr. by M. H. Morgan, with illustrations and original designs prepared under the direction of H. L. Warren, Cambridge, Mass., 1914.

Written about B. C. 14; only surviving ancient work on architecture. Much of its value lies in the excerpts from Greek writers. AERB

E689a Martha, Jules. *L'art étrusque.* Paris, 1889.

b Poulsen, Frederick. *Etruscan tomb paintings, their subjects and significance.* Oxford, 1922.

c Dennis, George. *Cities and cemeteries of Etruria.* 1848. New ed., by W. M. Lindsay, 2 v., London, 1907.

d Ducati, Pericle, and **Giglioli, Giulio Q.** *Arte etrusca.* Roma, 1926.

a. Valuable compendium of Etruscan art in all its phases. May be supplemented by such works as *b* and *c.* *d.* Good introductory survey. AERB

E690a Frothingham, Arthur L. *Roman cities of North Italy and Dalmatia.* N. Y., 1910.

b Mau, August. *Pompeii, its life and art.* 1899. 3rd rev. ed., N. Y. and London, 1907. (Bibliography.) Tr. by F. W. Kelsey from MS. of *Pompeii in Leben und Kunst,* 1900, 2nd rev. ed., Leipzig, 1908.

a. Popular work; good account of the Roman remains in North Italy and Dalmatia; holds that the municipalities reproduced the buildings and architecture of Rome itself. Has some questionable theories regarding the dates and purposes of certain structures. Review, F. G. Moore, *Classical Weekly,* 4:36, Oct. 1910. *b.* Authoritative, well-written account of municipal life in Pompeii, based upon a careful study of the excavations. Indispensable for the student of Roman art, architecture, and private life. Review, F. von Duhn, *Berliner Philologische Wochenschrift,* 21:19; Jan. 5, 1901. AERB

E691a Hill, George F. *Historical Roman coins from the earliest times to the reign of Augustus.* London, 1909.

b Mattingly, Harold, and **Sydenham, Edward A.** *Roman imperial coinage.* V. 1, *Augustus to Vitellius.* V. 2, *Vespasian to Hadrian.* London, 1923–26.

c Mattingly, Harold. *Roman coins from the earliest times to the fall of the Western Empire.* London, 1928.

a. Useful study of Roman coin types illustrating special phases of Roman history. *b.* General historical sketch followed by sections on countermarks, denomination of coins, forgeries, and modern prices of coins; catalogue of coins arranged by reigns, mints, and dates. Review, D. Atkinson, *Classical Rev.* 39:84,

May 1925. Also cf. (E695*b*). *c*. Numismatic history of Rome, the first comprehensive study of Roman coinage since (E692) which it in large measure supersedes. Review, J. Toynbee, *Classical Rev.* 42:142, Sept. 1928.   AERB

E692 Mommsen, Theodor. *Geschichte des römischen Münzwesens.* Berlin, 1860. French tr. by Duc de Blacas, ed. by J. de Witte, *Histoire de la monnaie romaine*, 4 v., Paris, 1865–75. (Bibliography.)

Basic modern work on Roman numismatics. French translation contains many emendations and additions by Mommsen himself.   AERB

E693a Babelon, Ernest C. F. *Description historique et chronologique des monnaies de la république romaine vulgairement appelées monnaies consulaires.* 2 v. Paris, 1885–86.

 b Bahrfeldt, Martin. *Nachträge und Berichtigungen zur Münzkunde der römischen Republik, in Anschluss an Babelon's Verzeichniss der Consular-Münzen.* 2 v. in 1. Wien, 1897–1900.

 c Cohen, Henry. *Description historique des monnaies frappées sous l'empire romain communément appelées médailles impériales.* 1859–68. 2nd rev. ed., by H. Cohen and G. L. Feuardent, 8 v., Paris, 1880–92.

These three works cover the whole field of Roman numismatics, but should be supplemented by reference to catalogues of important collections and special studies.   AERB

E694a Vogt, Joseph. *Die alexandrinischen Münzen, Grundlegung einer alexandrinischen Kaisergeschichte.* 2 v. in 1. Stuttgart, 1924.

 **b ——— ** *Römische Politik in Aegypten.* Leipzig, 1924. [Der alte Orient, Beiheft.]

 c Schultz, Otto Th. *Rechtstitel und Regierungsprogramme auf römischen Kaisermünzen.* Paderborn, 1925. [Studien zur Geschichte des Altertums.]

 d Bernhardt, Max. *Münzkunde der römischen Kaiserzeit.* Halle, 1926.

a. V. 1. Discussion of the coinage of various emperors in its historical relations. V. 2. List of imperial coins of the Alexandrine mint. Best reference work on this subject. *b.* Study of the administrative system in Roman Egypt and of Roman policy there; the latter based largely on an interpretation of the Alexandrine coinage. Review, W. Kunkel, *Philologische Wochenschrift*, 45:996, Sept. 5, 1925. *c.* Deals with the period from Caesar to Septimius Severus. Attempts with considerable success to make use of the imperial coinage to interpret constitutional and political history. Review, W. Ensslin, *Philologische Wochenschrift* 46:1354, Dec. 4, 1926. *d.* Extremely valuable study of imperial numismatics.   AERB

E695a *Catalogue of the Roman coins in the British Museum: coins of the Roman republic,* ed. by Herbert A. Grueber, 3 v. London, 1910.

 b *Catalogue of the Roman coins in the British Museum: coins of the Roman empire. V. 1, Augustus to Vitellius,* ed. by Harold Mattingly, London, 1923.

 c *Catalogue of the Greek coins in the British Museum: coins of Alexandria and the nomes,* ed. by Reginald Stuart Poole, London, 1892.

 d Dattari, G. *Monete imperiali greche. Numi Augg. Alexandrini catalogo della collezione G. Dattari.* 2 v. in 1. Cairo, 1901.

a. and *b.* Illustrations and descriptions of coin types, together with studies of fundamental importance for the history of Roman numismatics. Review of *b.*, C. T. Seltman, *Journal of Roman Studies* 12:139, 1922. *c.* Valuable work of reference for the Greek coinage of Egypt from Augustus to Diocletian. *d.* In many respects more complete than *c.*   AERB

BIOGRAPHIES

In addition to the biographical works reviewed above, the following are among the most valuable and readable biographies of Roman personages.

Of ancient collective works, in addition to the lives of Roman statesmen in (D73f) Plutarch, there are (E701) Cornelius Nepos, *Vitae excellentium imperatorum,* ed. by E. O. Winstedt, Oxford, 1904 [Oxford classical texts]; (E702) *Scriptores historiae Augustae,* ed. by Hermann W. G. Peter, 1865, 2nd ed., 2 v., Leipzig, 1884; ed. and tr. by David Magie and others, v. 1-2, London and N. Y., 1922–24 [Loeb classical library], which contains lives of the emperors from Hadrian to Numerian; (E703) Sextus Aurelius Victor, *De Caesaribus,* ed., together with *De viris illustribus* and *Epitome de Caesaribus,* by Franz Piehlmayr, Leipzig, 1892, three works which include brief lives of prominent Romans from legendary times to the end of the republic and of the emperors from Augustus to Theodosius I.

Of modern collective studies there are (E711) Sir Charles W. C. Oman, *Seven Roman statesmen of the later republic: the Gracchi, Sulla, Crassus, Cato, Pompey, Caesar,* London, 1902; (E712) Theodor Birt, *Römische Charakterköpfe, ein Weltbild in Biographien,* Leipzig, 1913, a series of excellent sketches of prominent figures from the elder Scipio to Marcus Aurelius; (E713) Carl Bardt, *Römische Charakterköpfe in Briefen, vornehmlich aus caesarischer und traianischer Zeit,* Leipzig, 1913; and especially, (E714) Wilhelm K. A. Drumann, *Geschichte Roms in seinem Uebergange von der republikanischen zur monarchischen Verfassung, oder Pompeius, Caesar, Cicero, und ihre Zeitgenossen nach Geschlechtern und mit genealogischen Tabellen,* 1833–44, 2nd rev. ed. by P. Groebe, v. 1–5 in 6, Berlin, 1899–1919, which is an exhaustive study in the form of biographies arranged in alphabetical order according to *gentes,* and which is especially useful for its full references to the sources for each historical event.

(E720) B. H. Liddell Hart, *A greater than Napoleon: Scipio Africanus,* London and Boston, 1927.

For the republican period: (E721) Theodore A. Dodge, *Hannibal, a history of the art of war among the Carthaginians and Romans down to the battle of Pydna, 168 B. C., with a detailed account of the second Punic war,* 1891, 3rd ed., Boston, 1896 [Great captains]; (E722) Eugène Hennebert, *Histoire d'Annibal,* 3 v., Paris, 1870–91; (E723) Theodore Reinach, *Mithridate Eupator, roi de Pont,* Paris, 1890 [Bibliothèque d'archéologie, d'art, et d'histoire ancienne], German tr., by A. Goetz, with revisions by author, *Mithridates Eupator, König von Pontus,* Leipzig, 1895; (E731) Harold Bennett, *Cinna and his times, a critical and interpretative study of Roman history during the period 87–84 B. C.,* Menesha, Wis., 1923; (E732) Frank H. Cowles, *Gaius Verres, an historical study,* N. Y., 1917 [Cornell studies in classical philology]; (E741) Gaston Boissier, *Cicero and his friends, a study of Roman society in the time of Caesar,* London, 1897, tr. by A. D. Jones from *Ciceron et ses amis, étude sur la société romaine du temps de César,* 1865, 15th ed., Paris, 1910; (E742) James L. Strachan-Davidson, *Cicero and the fall of the Roman republic,* 1894, new ed., London and N. Y., 1903 [Heroes of the nations]; (E743) Ernest G. Sihler, *Cicero of Arpinum, a political and literary biography, being a contribution to the history of ancient civilization and a guide to the study of Cicero's writings,* New Haven, 1914; (E744) Torsten Petersson, *Cicero, a biography,* Berkeley, 1920 [Semicentennial publications of the University of California]; (E745) Alice H. Byrne, *Titus Pomponius Atticus,* Bryn Mawr, Penn., 1920; (E746) G. P. Baker, *Sulla the fortunate,* London, 1927; (E747) A. Schultess, *Sertorius,* Leipzig, 1926.

For the period of transition from the republic to the principate: (E751) William Warde Fowler, *Julius Caesar and the foundation of the Roman imperial system,* 1892, 2nd ed., London and N. Y., 1919 [Heroes of the nations]; (E752) James A. Froude, *Caesar, a sketch,* 1879, new ed., London and N. Y., 1890; (E753) Ernest G. Sihler, *Annals of Caesar, a critical biography with a survey of the sources, for more advanced students of ancient history and particularly for the use and service of instructors in Caesar,* N. Y., 1911; (E754) Theodore A. Dodge, *Caesar, a history of the art of war among the Romans down to the end of the Roman empire,* Boston, 1892 [Great captains]; (E755) Matthias Gelzer, *Caesar, der Politiker und der Staatsmann,* Stuttgart, 1921 [Meister der Politik]; (E761) Arthur E. P. B. Weigall, *Life and times of Cleopatra, queen of Egypt, a study in the origin of the Roman empire,* 1914, 2nd rev. ed., London and N. Y., 1924; (E771) John B. Firth, *Augustus Caesar and the organization of the empire of Rome,* London and N. Y., 1903 [Heroes of the nations]; (E772) Evelyn S. Shuckburgh, *Augustus, the life and times of the founder of the Roman empire, B. C. 63–A. D. 14,* London, 1903.

For the first century: (E781) John C. Tarver, *Tiberius the tyrant,* Westminster, 1902; (E782) Guglielmo Ferrero, *Women of the Caesars,* N. Y., 1911; (E783) Richard M. Gummere, *Seneca the philosopher and his modern message,* Boston, 1923 [(D603c) Our debt to Greece and Rome]. (E784) Roberto Paribeni, *Optimus Princeps: saggio sulla storia e sui tempi dell' imperatore Traiano,* Messina, 1927.

For the second century: (E791a) Wilhelm Weber, *Trajan und Hadrian,* Stuttgart, 1923 [Meister der Politik], and (E791b) *Untersuchungen zur Geschichte des Kaisers Hadrianus,* Leipzig, 1907; (E792) Ferdinand Gregorovius, *Emperor Hadrian, a picture of the Graeco-Roman world in his time,* London and N. Y., 1898, tr. by M. E. Robinson from *Der Kaiser Hadrian, Gemälde der römisch-hellenischen Welt zu seiner Zeit,* 1851, 3rd ed., Stuttgart, 1884; (E793) Otto T. Schulz, *Leben des Kaisers Hadrian,* Leipzig, 1904; (E794) Georges Lacour-Gayet, *Antonin le pieux et son temps,* Paris, 1888; (E795) Ernest E. Bryant, *Reign of Antoninus Pius,* Cambridge, Eng., 1895 [Thirlwall dissertation, Cambridge historical essays]; (E796) Ernest Renan, *Marc-Aurèle et la fin du monde antique,* 1881, 8th ed., Paris, 1899 [V. 7 of his Histoire des origines du christianisme]; (E797) Henry D. Sedgwick, *Marcus Aurelius, a biography told as much as may be by letters, together with some account of the Stoic religion and an exposition of the Roman government's attempt to suppress Christianity during Marcus's reign,* New Haven, 1921; (E798) Joseph M. Heer, *Der historische Wert der Vita Commodi,* Leipzig, 1904 [*Philologus,* Supplementband. 9:1–208].

For the third century: (E801) Maurice Platnauer, *Life and reign of the emperor Lucius Septimius Severus,* Oxford and N. Y., 1918; (E802) Henry J. Bassett, *Macrinus and Diadumenianus,* Menasha, Wis., 1920; (E803) John Stuart

Hay, *The amazing emperor Heliogabalus,* London, 1911; (E804) Richard V. Nind Hopkins, *Life of Alexander Severus,* Cambridge, Eng., 1907 [Prince Consort essay, Cambridge historical essays].

For the fourth century: (E811) Jakob C. Burckhardt, *Die Zeit Constantins des Grossen,* 1853, 3rd ed., Leipzig, 1898; (E812) John B. Firth, *Constantine the Great, the reorganisation of the empire and the triumph of the church,* London and N. Y., 1905 [Heroes of the nations]; (E813) Jules Maurice, *Constantin le Grand: l'origine de la civilisation chrétienne,* Paris, 1924; (E814) Alice Gardner, *Julian, philosopher and emperor, and the last struggle of paganism against Christianity,* 1895, new ed., London and N. Y., 1901 [Heroes of the nations]; (E815) Johannes Geffcken, *Kaiser Julianus,* Leipzig, 1914 [(D603d) Das Erbe der Alten]; (E816) Paul Allard, *Julien l'Apostat,* 3 v., Paris, 1900–03; (E817) Thomas Hodgkin, *Dynasty of Theodosius, or eighty years' struggle with the barbarians,* Oxford, 1889. AERB

ACADEMY, UNIVERSITY, AND SOCIETY PUBLICATIONS

The publications of the national academies of European countries listed in other §§ contain numerous articles relating to Roman history and allied subjects, as do also the series of publications issued by American universities listed as D921–923.

A special group of publications bearing on Roman history are the bulletins and reports of the various national schools established at Rome and those of the Italian government dealing with archeological discoveries in Italy. In addition to the publications of the French school edited in (D987) *Bibliothèque des Écoles Françaises d'Athènes et de Rome,* there are (E921) *Papers,* v. 1–10, London, 1902–27, of the British school in Rome; (E922) *Mitteilungen des Kaiserlichen Deutschen Archaeologischen Instituts, Römische Abteilung,* annual, Rom., 1886 ff., issued by the German school; the contributions of the American School of Classical Studies in Rome, which appear in (D979) *American Journal of Archaeology,* and in special volumes of (E923a) *Supplementary papers,* N. Y., 1905–08, and (E923b) *Papers and monographs,* N. Y., 1919 ff; (E924) *Notizie degli Scavi,* Roma, 1876 ff, published by the Accademia dei Lincei; and (E925) *Bolletino della Commissione Archeologica Communale di Roma,* Roma, 1872 ff.

PERIODICALS

Some periodicals enumerated in § C and nearly all those relating to philology and archeology listed in § D contain many articles in the field of Roman studies. In addition to (D941a) *Klio: Beiträge zur alten Geschichte,* special mention should be made of (E941) *Journal of Roman studies,* occasional, London, 1911 ff., published by the Society for the Promotion of Roman Studies; and (E942) *Revue des études latines,* quarterly, Paris, 1923 ff., which are devoted entirely to discussions of various aspects of Roman civilization.

Of particular importance for Roman history and archeology are (E951) *Limesblatt,* Trier, 44 nos., 1893–1926; (E952) *Der obergermanisch-rätische Limes des Römer-Reiches,* Heidelberg, 1893 ff., published by the German Reichslimes Commission; and (E953) *Der römische Limes in Oesterreich,* 16 v., Wien, 1900–26, issued by the Limescommission Oesterreichs and the Akademie der Wissenschaften in Vienna.

For Roman law, cf. (H956c) *Zeitschrift der Savigny-Stiftung für Rechtsgeschichte, Romanistische Abteilung.* AERB

SECTION F

HISTORY OF CHRISTIANITY

Editor

WILLIAM HENRY ALLISON

Professor Emeritus of Ecclesiastical History, Colgate-Rochester Divinity School

CONTENTS

INTRODUCTION

Since the study of the history of Christianity has, in recent years, broadened in scope so as to comprise almost everything which might be included in the term Christian civilization, it is difficult to delimit the books properly to be included in this field. In addition to general histories of Christianity, of the institutions of the Christian church, and of the wider ranges of its activities, there are listed in this section works on the history of the early church and on the history of the papacy. Many books which might be looked for in the present section are listed elsewhere: those which are devoted to religion in general rather than to Christianity in particular appear in § B; those whose contents relate to the history of the church in some specific period or region are appropriately assigned to the corresponding section of this *Guide*. In the main, the titles in

233

this section deal with the broader range of environmental relationships of Christianity rather than with the inner structure and procedure of its ecclesiastical institutions, thus reflecting the prevailing historical interest of the last fifty years. Yet the selection as a whole represents primarily the Christian religion as expressed in and through its institutions.

Though the advanced student and the expert will find directions for further study in many of the books here reviewed, the present section has been prepared with special attention to the interests of the general reading public. Two considerations have, chiefly, dictated this policy. The literature of church history is so extensive that much more space would have been required to meet all the needs of those engaged in intensive research. Moreover, the service to be rendered to pastors and to teachers engaged in religious education, which will increasingly direct attention to the history of the Church, has demanded consideration. For these same reasons, the selection of books has been restricted primarily to those which are available in English. Fortunately, in this field, an unusual proportion of the most important scholarly contributions published in other languages is accessible through translation. Abundant clues to a much wider literature, however, will be found in the works reviewed and especially in the bibliographies listed.

BIBLIOGRAPHY, LIBRARY COLLECTIONS

There is no comprehensive bibliography for the history of Christianity, but various parts of the subject are dealt with as separate topics in the bibliographies mentioned in many of the sections of this *Guide*. In the absence of special bibliographies for the history of the early church, the reader should consult bibliographies of literature on the New Testament and on the apostolic age which often extend into the post-apostolic period, and bibliographies of medieval history (cf. H1–4) which frequently include materials on the rise of Christianity. In the Middle Ages and in the period of the Reformation (cf. P4), the church was so closely related to the state that bibliographies for the political history of those eras will be found useful. The bibliographies in (H121) *Cambridge medieval history,* and (I121) *Cambridge modern history* provide good classified lists of titles, without critical comments.

F1 **Smith, Gerald B.,** ed. *Guide to the study of the Christian religion.* Chicago, 1916.

Prepared by Protestant scholars; represents very specifically the historical approach to the understanding of the Christian religion. Four successive chapters, 'The study of early Christianity,' by S. J. Case; 'The development and meaning of the Catholic church,' by F. A. Christie; 'The Protestant Reformation,' by G. Cross; and 'The development of modern Christianity,' by E. Gates, not only form a fairly adequate syllabus of the history of Christianity, but they suggest many problems confronting the present study of this subject, especially those relating to the development of thought and to the organization of society. Includes much bibliographical material, usefully arranged for introduction to studies in the field. For bibliographies of the Reformation in Germany, cf. (P4). Review, *Methodist Rev.,* 99:811, Sept. 1917. WHA

F2 Whitley, William T. *Baptist bibliography, being a register of the chief materials for Baptist history, whether in manuscript or in print, preserved in Great Britain, Ireland and the colonies.* 2 v. London, 1916–22.

Lists the material chronologically from 1526 to 1837. This and the noteworthy bibliography in (F383) Dexter, *Congregationalism of the last three hundred years as seen in its literature,* locate much material on Puritanism and related topics.

WHA

F3 Allison, William H., ed. *Inventory of unpublished material for American religious history in Protestant church archives and other repositories.* Washington, 1910. [Department of historical research, Carnegie Institution of Washington.]

Indispensable aid to research in American religious history. Review, F. A. Christie, *A.H.R.* 17:190, Oct. 1911.

Brief bibliographies for the various denominations will be found in the several volumes of (X622) *American church history* series, v. 12 of which contains a somewhat meager general bibliography of church history in the United States. This should be supplemented by (F64) Mode, *Source book and bibliographical guide for American church history.*

GMD

F4a Richardson, Ernest C. *Alphabetical subject index and index encyclopaedia to periodical articles on religion, 1890–1899.* N. Y., 1907. (Author index, 1911.)

b *Theologischer Jahresbericht, 1881–1913.* 33 v. Leipzig, 1882–1915.

Extremely valuable guides to current literature on the history of the Christian church and allied topics.

WHA

F5 Streit, Robert. *Bibliotheca missionum.* V. 1, *Grundlegender Teil,* Münster i. W. 1916. V. 2, 3, *Amerikanische Missionsliteratur, 1493–1919;* v. 4, 5, *Asiatische Missionsliteratur,* 1245–1699. Aachen, 1925–29.

Will form a complete bibliography of printed works relating to the history of Catholic missions and missionaries; v. 4–6 will deal respectively with Africa, Asia, and Oceanica. Includes voyages, relations, official documents, both governmental and ecclesiastical, compiled by the director of the missionary library at the Vatican. Arrangement is chronological; includes full bibliographical details, brief notice of the author, an analysis of the book with critical estimate, and an indication of leading European libraries in which copies may be found. V. 2 and 3, including 5600 titles, especially important for students of American history. Review, G. Allemang, *Rev. des Quest. Hist.* 107:485, Oct. 1927. WHA

F6 Gillett, Charles R., ed. *McAlpin collection of British history and theology.* 4 v. and index. N. Y., 1927–29.

Contains 2,500 pages of full titles of a valuable collection in the Union Theological Seminary Library of New York.

WHA

Library collections.—Probably the most important collections in the United States for the history of Christianity in general are to be found in the university and seminary libraries of Harvard (notably for the medieval church, the papacy, and the Greek Church), Yale, Columbia (Union Theological Seminary has special collections on French Protestantism, English church history, and Presbyterianism), Princeton, and Chicago, and at the Catholic University of America,

Washington, D. C., and the University of Illinois (including pamphlets and official publications of American denominations). The other larger university and theological seminary libraries almost without exception possess good collections for the field as a whole and sometimes highly valuable special collections, such as the President White collections on the Protestant Reformation, the Jesuits, the inquisition, the index, witchcraft, toleration, and relations of science and theology, in the Cornell University Library. The University of Missouri and Rutgers College have special collections on early church history; and Augustana College, Rock Island, Illinois, on the Reformation. As a rule, public libraries are inclined to neglect this field, but a few of the largest ones, such as the Library of Congress, New York Public Library, and Boston Public Library, contain many books on the subject.

Though the libraries of the theological seminaries often contain good collections of sources for the earlier history of the church, one naturally turns to them and to the various archives of the different religious groups for material bearing upon the more modern religious movements and the history of the several denominations.

Valuable Roman Catholic material will be found at the Catholic University of Notre Dame, Notre Dame, Indiana. Worthy of special mention are the Congregational Library at Boston, Mass.; the Presbyterian Historical Society at Philadelphia; collections on missions at Hartford Theological Seminary and at Yale Divinity School; a collection on Christian art, the Agnew Collection on the baptismal controversy, and one of the largest collections of Puritan literature at Princeton Theological Seminary; the Jenks Collection on Quakerism at Haverford College; Lutherana at Hartford Theological Seminary and at the Lutheran Theological Seminary, Mt. Airy, Penn.; the Samuel Colgate Baptist Historical Collection, also rich in Puritan pamphlets, at Hamilton, N. Y.; other collections on Baptist history at Princeton Theological Seminary and Crozer Theological Seminary, Upland, Penn. Most of the pamphlets gathered by William B. Sprague for his (F841) *Annals of the American pulpit* are also at Princeton, the rest being at Drew Theological Seminary, Madison, N. J., where are the Tyerman and the Osborn Collections on Wesley and Methodism. There are also collections on Methodism at Wesleyan University and Garrett Biblical Institute. Valuable collections on liturgics and hymnology will be found at the General Theological Seminary in New York City; the hymnological collection, including the library of F. M. Bird, at Union Theological Seminary, New York City; the Paine Hymnological Collection at Hartford Theological Seminary; the Lowell Mason Library of Church Music at the Yale Divinity School; a hymnological collection at Newberry Library, Chicago; collections of catechisms and varied liturgical material at the Lutheran Seminary at Mt. Airy.

An article on 'Theological libraries' in (F23b) *New Schaff-Herzog encyclopedia of religious knowledge,* 11:336–341, will locate many other special collections in the United States.

ENCYCLOPEDIAS AND WORKS OF REFERENCE

F21a Hastings, James, and others, ed. *Dictionary of the Bible, dealing with its language, literature, and contents, including the biblical theology.* 4 v. and extra v. with indexes. 1898–1904. Reprint, 5 v., Edinburgh and N. Y., 1911–12. (Valuable bibliographies.)

   b ——— *Dictionary of the Bible.* Edinburgh and N. Y., 1909 c ——— *Dictionary of Christ and the gospels.* 2 v. Edinburgh and N. Y., 1906–08. (Bibliographies.)

d ——— *Dictionary of the apostolic church.* 2 v. Edinburgh and N. Y., 1916–18. (Bibliographies.)

The positions adopted by most of the writers were somewhat conservative even at the beginning of the century and have now been still further left behind, but the work is marked by fulness, scholarship, and soundness of judgment and may still be regarded as, on the whole, the most useful of the Bible dictionaries. The historical articles are numerous and are always thorough and competent. Writers like Ramsay, Sayce, Hommel, Buhl, and others no less eminent deal at length with the most important subjects. Perhaps the most valuable feature of the book on the historical side is the great number of short articles on particular places, men, and events. The dictionary is stronger in its treatment of Old Testament than of New Testament history. Review, v. 1, *Amer. Jour. of Theol.* 3:84, Jan. 1899; v. 2. *Presbyterian and Reformed Rev.* 11:174, Jan. 1900; v. 3, *ibid.* 12:151, Jan. 1901; v. 4, *Amer. Jour. of Theol.* 7:111, Jan. 1903; v. 5, *ibid.* 9:522, July 1905. *b.* Independent work of similar character on a smaller scale. *c.* and *d.* Treat more fully many subjects relating to the early church. Review of *c., Amer. Jour. of Theol.* 12:144, Jan. 1908; 13:277, Apr. 1909. Review of *d., American Jour. of Theol.* 21:297, Apr. 1917; 24:148, Jan. 1920.

Also cf. (C21) Cheyne, *Encyclopaedia biblica.* EFS

F22 Hastings, James; Selbie, John A., and others, ed. *Encyclopaedia of religion and ethics.* 13 v. Edinburgh and N. Y., 1908–27. (Comprehensive bibliographies.)

This monument of erudition will be found serviceable not only because many articles belong distinctively to the history of the church, such as biographical sketches, surveys of religious movements and denominational history, but also because the articles on historical religion and ethics often treat specifically Christian forces and movements. The scholarship of the work is distinctly modern; keenly analytical and critical, it is generally constructive and represents the Protestant religious-historical school at its best. WHA

F23a Herzog, Johann J.; Plitt, Gustav L.; and **Hauck, Albert,** ed. *Realencyklopädie für protestantische Theologie und Kirche.* 1853; 3rd rev. ed., 24 v., including 2 v., *Ergänzungen und Nachträge,* Leipzig, 1896–1913. (Bibliographies.)

b Jackson, Samuel Macauley, and others, ed. *New Schaff-Herzog encyclopedia of religious knowledge, embracing biblical, historical, doctrinal, and practical theology, and biblical, theological and ecclesiastical biography from the earliest times to the present day.* 13 v., including index. N. Y. and London, 1908–14. (Bibliographies.)

While the first two editions of *a.* were important contributions to the encyclopedic literature of Christianity, the third edition with its supplementary volumes occupies a distinctive place in historiography. Represents Protestant point of view; its articles comprise almost the full scope of Christian history; particularly rich in biographical material and in surveys of movements and parties through the Christian centuries. WHA

b. Based on third edition of *a.* While many of the original articles in *a.* are condensed and translated for *b.,* supplementary material is frequently added by the editors so as to adapt the articles to the needs of English and American readers. New materials, the result of later investigation, are also incorporated. The articles on biblical subjects do not supersede those of the Bible dictionaries; those on church history are the most valuable feature of the work. Essentially Protestant in tone, though Roman Catholicism is represented by a number of articles by its own scholars.   GWRi

F24a Smith, Sir William and **Wace, Henry,** ed. *Dictionary of Christian biography, literature, sects, and doctrines, being a continuation of 'The dictionary of the Bible.'* 4 v. London, 1877–87.

b Wace, Henry, and **Piercy, William C.,** ed. *Dictionary of Christian biography and literature to the end of the sixth century A. D., with an account of the principal sects and heresies.* London, 1911.

a. Still the most complete and best patristic biographical work. Primarily a product of the learning of the Anglican church, but writers of other communions were also contributors. There is a broad range of subjects pretty thoroughly covering the fields indicated for the first eight centuries. Many of the articles need revision on account of later researches. Review, *Church Quar. Rev.* 27 :296, Jan. 1889.   *b.* Contains much of the material in *a* relative to the first six centuries, with condensations, revisions and additions. Review, *Independent,* 71 :1209, Nov. 30, 1911.   DSS

F25 —— *Catholic encyclopedia, an international work of reference on the constitution, doctrine, discipline, and history of the Catholic church.* Ed. by Charles G. Herbermann and others. 16 v. N. Y., 1907–14; supplement, 1922. (Bibliographies.)

Embodies the essence of the world's best Catholic scholarship; ranks among the best authorities on church history. While its main purpose is to set forth the leading aspects and achievements of Roman Catholicism, its scope includes much general religious history. For example, there is an article on each of the great Protestant denominations. Review, *Contemporary Rev.* 103 :593, Apr. 1913.   JWM

F26 Wetzer, Heinrich J., and **Welte, Benedict,** ed. *Kirchenlexikon oder Encyklopädie der katholischen Theologie und ihrer Hülfswissenschaften.* 13 v. 1847–60. 2nd ed., by Joseph, Cardinal Hergenröther and Franz Kaulen, 13 v., Freiburg im Breisgau and St. Louis, 1880–1903. French tr., with modifications, by J. Goschler, *Dictionnaire encyclopédique de la théologie catholique.* 1858–65. 3rd ed., 26 v., Paris, 1869.

Long recognized as the most important Roman Catholic encyclopedia in German; still valuable. Review, giving the history of previous works of a similar nature, (F974*a*) *Stimmen aus Maria Laach,* 24 :75, 1883.   WHA

F27a Baudrillart, Alfred, and others, ed. *Dictionnaire d'histoire et de géographie ecclésiastique.* Paris, 1909 ff. [Encyclopédie des sciences religieuses.] (Bibliographies.)

b Cabrol, Fernand, and others, ed. *Dictionnaire d'archéologie chrétienne et de liturgie.* Paris, 1903 ff. [Encyclopédie des sciences religieuses.] (Bibliographies.)

c Vacant, Alfred, and others, ed. *Dictionnaire de théologie catholique contenant l'exposé des doctrines de la théologie catholique, leurs preuves et leur histoire.* Paris, 1899 ff. [Encyclopédie des sciences religieuses.] (Bibliographies.)

Each of these works, which are appearing in fascicules, in its own field approximates the scale of the series as a whole, of which L. J. Paetow, cf. (H1a), *Guide to the study of medieval history*, p. 16, says, it 'will be the largest work of reference on religion in any language.' *a.* Colossal work, whether viewed in its *ensemble* or as a thesaurus of details in the history of the church; promises to be the most important treatise on ecclesiastical geography. Review, *Month*, 116:103, July 1910. *b.* Very important as dealing with aspects of the history of the church too largely ignored hitherto or touched upon only incidentally. Review, *Month*, 101:214, June 1903. *c.* Historical exposition of Roman Catholic theology in encyclopedic form, with special consideration of the interests of modern times; treats many subjects lying outside the direct domain of theology. Review, *Expository Times*, 15:361, May 1904. WHA

F28 ———— *Jewish encyclopedia, a descriptive record of the history, religion, literature, and customs of the Jewish people from the earliest times to the present day.* Ed. by Cyrus Adler, Isidore Singer, and others. 12 v. London and N. Y., 1901–06. Reprint, with slight changes, 1916. (Brief bibliographies.)

Indispensable repertorium for everything Jewish. The major articles are written by scholars of competence and frequently of eminence in their fields; the minor ones are generally adequate. There is much in it, also, that is of value to students of church history. The religious surroundings of nascent Christianity, the medieval philosophy and theology which influenced the schoolmen, the mysteries of the Cabala which attracted Christian scholars in the Renaissance, may serve as examples of a general character. Particular note may be made of the biographical articles, many of which give information not otherwise accessible. Review, H. P. Smith, *Amer. Jour. of Theol.* 11:653, Oct. 1907. GFM

F29 Dwight, Henry O.; Tupper, Henry Allen, Jr.; and Bliss, Edwin M., ed. *Encyclopedia of missions, descriptive, historical, biographical, statistical.* 1891. 2nd rev. ed., N. Y. and London, 1904.

Descriptive, historical, biographical, and statistical summary of Christian missions. Covers two general departments: first, the organized work of missions as represented by the principal missionary societies, their origin, history, emphasis, and achievements; second, the lands, races, and religious beliefs constituting the missionary challenge. Some five thousand cities, towns, and villages, important from the missionary viewpoint, are described. The second edition omits the maps. Appendixes contain lists of foreign missionary societies, Bible translations, and statistics covering Roman Catholic and Protestant activities. Needs further revision. Review, *Missionary Rev. of the World*, n.s., 18:61, Jan. 1905. HHW

ATLASES

F41a McClure, Edmund. *Historical church atlas.* London, 1897.

  b Heussi, Karl, and **Mulert, Hermann.** *Atlas zur Kirchengeschichte.* 1905. 2nd ed., Tübingen, 1919.

  c Dennis, James S.; Beach, Harlan P.; and **Fahs, Charles H.,** ed. *World atlas of Christian missions.* N. Y., 1911.

  d Beach, Harlan P., and **Fahs, Charles H.,** ed. *World missionary atlas, containing a directory of missionary societies, classified summaries of statistics, etc.* N. Y., 1925.

While the general historical atlases usually include considerable ecclesiastical data and many of the books reviewed in this section contain maps of varying serviceability, a comprehensive atlas for church history is a great desideratum. *The atlas of the historical geography of the United States* which is being prepared by the Department of Historical Research of the Carnegie Institution of Washington will include maps bearing upon American church history. *a.* and *b.* Convenient small atlases. *c.* Superseded by *d.;* still useful for historical purposes. *d.* Specialized work, locating Protestant (and in one instance, Roman Catholic and Eastern Orthodox) mission stations; rich in statistical and other information; brought up to 1923. WHA

SOURCE BOOKS, COLLECTIONS OF SOURCES, ARCHIVE PUBLICATIONS

F61 Ayer, Joseph C., Jr., ed. *Source book for ancient church history, from the apostolic age to the close of the conciliar period.* N. Y., 1913. (Bibliography.)

Excerpts, in English translation, from sources for church history for approximately the first eight centuries. The selections, though often much abbreviated, are wisely chosen and are classified according to the periods and rubrics employed in the standard text-books on church history. Review, W. W. Rockwell, *Harvard Theol. Rev.* 7:626, Oct. 1914. SJC

F62 Mirbt, Carl, ed. *Quellen zur Geschichte des Papsttums und des römischen Katholizismus.* 1895. 4th rev. ed., Tübingen, 1924. (Bibliographies.)

Convenient, well selected, scholarly collection; gives the Latin text of some of the most important sources for the history of the papacy and of Catholic doctrine. Indispensable to anyone who has not a large library at command. Review, P. J. Healy, *A.H.R.* 17:866, July 1912. SBF

F63 Kidd, Beresford J., ed. *Documents illustrative of the continental reformation.* Oxford, 1911.

Most serviceable, compact collection of important Reformation material. The choice of sources is made with great skill, and includes the most significant documents of the Scottish reformation. The sources, in whole or in extract, are given in the original Latin or French, while German material is translated. Brief introductions of value precede each selection. Review, *Church Quar. Rev.* 73:223, Oct. 1911. WHA

F64 Mode, Peter G., ed. *Source book and bibliographical guide for American church history.* Menasha, Wis., 1921.

Reasonably successful endeavor to bring together the most significant documents for the religious history of the thirteen colonies and of the United States, previously scantily represented in source books. Local areas, denominational and group activities, and general movements are treated. Quite important sources still unprinted or not easily accessible; but brings together material hitherto scattered, especially documents illustrating recent movements. Review, F. A. Christie, *A.H.R.* 27:582, Apr. 1922. WHA

F71a Roberts, Alexander, and **Donaldson, James,** tr. and ed. *Ante-Nicene Fathers: translations of the writings of the fathers down to A. D. 325.* 24 v. 1867–72. Supplement, ed. by A. Menzies, 1897. American ed. by A. C. Coxe, 8 v., Buffalo, 1885–86; v. 9, supplement, ed. by A. Menzies, N. Y., 1896; v. 10, supplement, ed. by E. C. Richardson, N. Y., 1899; new ed., 10 v., N. Y., 1911–19. [Original English ed. had title, *Ante-Nicene Christian library.*]

   b Schaff, Philip, tr. and ed. *Select library of the Nicene and post-Nicene fathers of the Christian church.* 14 v. N. Y., 1886–90.

   c Schaff, Philip, and **Wace, Henry,** tr. and ed. *Select library of the Nicene and post-Nicene fathers of the Christian church.* 2nd series. 14 v. N. Y., 1890–1900.

a. Translations from the Christian writings outside the New Testament down to the council of Nicaea. For the majority of these writings, still the source most accessible to the English reader; makes available to the classical scholar the contents of certain lengthy treatises; not up to date and some parts need revision. *b.* and *c.* Brought out in a more elaborate fashion with prolegomena, notes, and dissertations. The volumes are of very uneven quality; some, notably the edition of (F203) Eusebius by Dr. McGiffert and of Athanasius by Dr. Robertson, are of permanent value; others possess but little merit. One fault in both series is that words, especially Latin ones, are transliterated rather than translated, so that a false meaning frequently results.   FJFJ

F72a Migne, Jacques P. *Patrologiae cursus completus, series graeca.* 161 v. in 166. Lutetiae Parisiorum, 1857–66. Index, by F. Cavallera, Parisiis, 1912.

   b ———— *Patrologiae cursus completus, series latina.* 221 v. Parisiis, 1844–64.

   c ———— *Corpus scriptorum ecclesiasticorum latinorum.* V. 1–63. Vindobonae, 1866–1922. [Kaiserliche Akademie der Wissenschaften zu Wien.]

   d Geyer, Bernhardus, and **Zellinger, Johannes.** *Florilegium patristicum tam veteris quam medii aevii auctores complectens.* Bonn. 1906 ff.

a. and *b.* Indispensable for the student of church history. Not a work of scholarship, but a publishing enterprise; composed largely of reprints of older and inadequate editions; writings of each author are not always given completely; *a.* Extends to A. D. 863; includes Latin translations of the Greek text; these translations were also published separately. *b.* Includes writings down to about 1200. *c.* Attempts to provide definitive editions of all writings of Latin church fathers down to the seventh century. For English translations of the more important writings, cf. (F71). *d.* Incorporates results of careful textual study and offers valuable critical apparatus. First eighteen *fasciculi* thus far published are important selections ranging from the apostolic age to Thomas Aquinas.   WHA

F73 Mansi, Gian D., ed. *Sacrorum conciliorum nova et amplissima collectio.* 31 v. Florentiae and Venetiis, 1759–98. Rev. ed. by J. B. Martin and L. Petit, 56 v., Parisiis, 1901–24.

Begun as a supplement to N. Coleti, *Collectio conciliorum,* 23 v., Venetiis, 1728–33, this became an almost exhaustive collection of documents for the history of the councils, reaching into the council of Florence of 1438. The new edition brings the Latin texts to 1870 and the Greek texts to 1902. Criticized in F. Loofs,

'A new collection of *Acta conciliorum,* an appeal,' *Harvard Theol. Rev.* 16:187–195, Apr. 1922. Cf. (E541), (L94a), and (L94b).   WHA

F74 *Concilium Tridentinum: diariorum, actorum, epistularum, tractatum nova collectio.* [Societas Goerresiana (Görres-Gesellschaft.)] V. 1–10. Freiburg, 1901–24.

This, the supreme work of the Görres-Gesellschaft, will doubtless be considered the definitive source collection for the Council of Trent when finally completed. It represents sound scholarship and an almost amazing attention to details involving extensive investigation. Review, *Dublin Rev.* 152:198, Apr. 1903.   PG

F75a Jaffé, Philipp, ed. *Regesta pontificum romanorum . . . ad annum . . .* MCXCVIII. 1851. 2nd ed., 2 v., Lipsiae, 1885–88.

   b Potthast, August, ed. *Regesta pontificum romanorum, inde ab anno post Christum natum MCXCVIII ad annum MCCCIV.* 2 v. Berolini, 1874–75.

   c Kehr, Paul F., ed. *Regesta pontificum romanorum.* V. 1–7, pt. 2. Berolini, 1906–25. [Königliche Gesellschaft der Wissenschaften zu Göttingen.]

   d Pflugk-Harttung, Julius von, ed. *Acta pontificum romanorum inedita* [97–1198]. 3 v. Tübingen, 1881–88.

Most important collections of papal documents. Additional materials of importance are to be found in other collections of sources, especially (D987) *Bibliothèque des Écoles Françaises d'Athènes et de Rome;* and (P71a) *Monumenta Germaniae historica.*   GMD

F81a Denzinger, Heinrich J. D., ed. *Enchiridion symbolorum et definitionum et declarationum de rebus fidei et morum.* 1854. 10th rev. ed., by C. Barnwart, Freiburg, 1908.

   b Schaff, Philip. *Bibliotheca symbolica ecclesiae universalis: the creeds of Christendom, with a history and critical notes.* 1877. 4th rev. ed., 3 v., N. Y., 1884. (Full bibliographies.)

a. Convenient handbook with texts (all Latin except a few early Greek readings) of creeds, definitions, statements of theological propositions which have been condemned, and other official utterances chiefly of councils and popes. The latest edition extends to decrees of Leo XIII. Review, *Amer. Cath. Quar. Rev.* 33:756, Oct. 1908.   WHA

b. V. 1. 'History of creeds'; describes the circumstances of composition and the contents of over sixty creeds, confessions, and catechisms of all churches. The other volumes contain the texts of creeds and catechisms, with English translations; v. 2, Greek and Latin churches; v. 3, Evangelical Protestant churches. A very valuable work. Review, *Bibliotheca Sacra,* 35:203, Jan. 1878.

                                                                   RHN

F82 Holstenius, Lucas, ed. *Codex regularum monasticarum et canonicarum quas sancti patres monachis, canonicis, et virginibus sanctimonialibus servandas praescripserunt.* 1661. 2nd ed. by Marian Brockie, 6 v., Augustae Vindelicorum, 1759.

Most important collection of monastic rules.   GMD

F83 Gasparri, Petrus, Cardinal, ed. *Codex juris canonici Pii X Pontificis maximi jussu digestus Benedicti papae XV auctoritate promulgatus.* Romae, 1918.

Authoritatively revised body of canon law as officially recognized and promulgated by the Roman Curia.   WHA

SHORTER GENERAL HISTORIES

F101 Fisher, George P. *History of the Christian church.* N. Y., 1887. Later reprints.

Single volume on church history to about 1880; Protestant; terse and crowded with facts; well organized, clear in statement, accurate; evidences great learning and broad culture. Appreciation of social movements is deficient; consideration of the Eastern church is inadequate; contains good chapters on doctrine. The modern portion (from 1648) is inferior to the previous part. Antiquated in some particulars, but still useful. Review, *E.H.R.* 3:812, Oct. 1888.   RHN

F102 Newman, Albert H. *Manual of church history.* 2 v. Philadelphia, 1900–03. (Good bibliographies.)

The method of topical analysis, justified by its primary purpose as a text-book, doubtless interferes with facile reading of this book, but its wealth of material and the unusual amount of space devoted to the sects which have reacted against conventional catholicity and sought to express spiritual evangelicism through democratic media, make this one of the most distinctive of the general church histories. Review, J. W. Moncrief, *Amer. Jour. of Theol.*, 4:851, Oct. 1900; 7:394, Apr. 1903.   WHA

F103 Schubert, Hans von. *Outlines of church history.* London and N. Y., 1907. [Theological translation library.] Tr. by M. A. Canney from 3rd ed. of *Grundzüge der Kirchengeschichte,* 1904; 3rd ed., 1906; 7th rev. ed., Tübingen, 1921.

Based on a public course of lectures at the University of Kiel in 1896 and 1897. Not so much a narration as an interpretation; refers to facts rather than records them. The survey is on broad lines and the horizon is largely that seen from a German center; yet it is the church as the medium of general Western culture that predominates in the treatment. Translation contains a supplementary chapter by Alice Gardner, on 'Religious thought and life in England during the nineteenth century.' Review, *Rev. of Theol. and Phil.* 5:629, 1910.   WHA

F104 Walker, Williston. *History of the Christian church.* N. Y., 1918. (Good bibliography.)

One of the best single volume histories of the church in English; covers the whole field; includes the history of thought. Review, J. C. Ayer, Jr., *Amer. Jour. of Theol.* 23:240, Apr. 1919.   WWR

F105 Guignebert, Charles A. H. *Christianity, past and present.* N. Y., 1927. Tr. from *Le christianisme antique,* Paris, 1921; and *Le christianisme mediéval et moderne,* Paris, 1922.

More radical than (F103) Schubert, emphasizing especially the fact of transition and change. Differentiations in the successive periods are pointed out, while the process of development is analyzed with a recognition of accretions from without, so that the product as seen in western Christianity, both Roman Catholic and Protestant, is something other than the original Christianity. A thought-provoking book. Reviews, D. S. Muzzey, *Sat. Rev. of Lit.* 4:627, Feb. 25, 1928; J. H. Randall, *World Unity Magazine,* 3:67, Oct. 1928.   WHA

LONGER GENERAL HISTORIES

F121a Cheetham, Samuel. *History of the Christian church during the first six centuries.* London and N. Y., 1894. Later reprints. (Bibliographical foot-notes.)

b Hardwick, Charles. *History of the Christian church: the middle age.* 1853. 3rd ed. by W. Stubbs, London, 1872. Later reprints. (Bibliographical foot-notes.)

c —— *History of the Christian church during the reformation.* 1856. 3rd ed. by W. Stubbs, London, 1873. (Bibliographical foot-notes.)

d Cheetham, Samuel. *History of the Christian church since the reformation.* London, 1907. (Bibliographical foot-notes.)

These four volumes, forming a complete church history by Anglican scholars, rest on an independent study of the sources, to which constant references are made in extensive footnotes. The style is spirited and engaging, possessing high literary merit. The admirable topical arrangement, the many marginal headings, excellent indexes, and serviceable maps in *a.* and *b.* add to their value as manuals adapted to the use of students. Review of *a., Church Quar. Rev.* 40:212, Apr. 1895. *b.* and *c.* Should be used only in connection with works embodying the results of more recent researches. *d.* Particularly useful because it embraces a period often omitted or inadequately treated in similar works; marred somewhat, however, by the author's bias, which prevents his doing justice to some of the non-Anglican bodies. Review, *Church Quart. Rev.* 67:446, Jan. 1909. FWL

F122 *Epochs of church history.* Ed. by Mandell Creighton. London and N. Y., 1886–89. Later reprints. [1, A. Plummer, *Church of the early fathers;* 2, H. M. Gwatkin, *Arian controversy;* 3, A. Carr, *Church and the Roman empire;* 4, H. F. Tozer, *Church and the Eastern empire;* 5, (F705b) W. R. W. Stephens, *Hildebrand and his times;* 6, U. Balzani, *Popes and the Hohenstaufen;* 7, W. Hunt, *English church in the middle ages;* 8, R. L. Poole, *Wycliffe and early movements of reform;* 9, G. G. Perry, *History of the reformation in England;* 10, A. W. Ward, *Counter-reformation;* 11, H. O. Wakeman, *Church and the puritans;* 12, J. H. Overton, *Evangelical revival in the eighteenth century;* 13, H. W. Tucker, *English church in other lands;* 14, G. C. Brodrick, *History of the University of Oxford;* 15, J. B. Mullinger, *History of the University of Cambridge.*]

Convenient set of handbooks of uneven merit and disproportionate treatment. Many important phases are completely omitted, so that the series does not constitute a history of the Church as a whole, but space is thus given for fuller treatment of many subjects frequently touched upon but lightly in other general works. Over half the volumes are devoted to England. WHA

F123 *Ten epochs of church history.* Ed. by John Fulton. 10 v. N. Y., 1896–1900. [1, J. V. Bartlet, *Apostolic age;* 2, L. Waterman, *Post-apostolic age;* 3, W. P. Dubose, *Ecumenical councils;* 4, (H222c) C. L. Wells, *Age of Charlemagne;* 5, M. R. Vincent, *Age of Hildebrand;* 6, J. M. Ludlow, *Age of the crusades;* 7, (I201d) P. Van Dyke, *Age of the renascence;* 8, C. Locke, *Age of the great western schism;* 9, W. Walker, *Reformation;* 10, W. Clark, *Anglican reformation.*]

Fairly successful attempt to provide an authoritative and comprehensive account in readable style; usually conservative and moderately Protestant in tone. Review, v. 1, F. A. Christie, *A.H.R.* 6:537, Apr. 1901; v. 2, T. J. Shahan, *ibid.*

5:107, Oct. 1899; v. 3, *Church Quar. Rev.* 45:246, Oct. 1897; v. 4, J. W. Moncrief, *Amer. Jour. of Theol.* 2:912, Oct. 1898; v. 5, J. W. Moncrief, *ibid.* 1:218, Jan. 1897; v. 6, O. J. Thatcher, *ibid.* 1:1059, Oct. 1897; v. 7, F. Schevill, *ibid.* 2:428, Apr. 1898; v. 8, J. W. Moncrief, *ibid.* 1:499, Apr. 1897; v. 9, *Nation,* 73:18, July 4, 1901; v. 10, E. B. Hulbert, *Amer. Jour. of Theol.* 2:430, Apr. 1898.   HKR

F124a Alzog, Johann B. *Manual of universal church history.* 3 v. Cincinnati, 1874–78. Later reprints. Tr. by F. J. Pabisch and T. S. Byrne from 9th ed. of *Universalgeschichte der Kirche,* 1841; 10th ed. by F. X. Kraus, Mainz, 1882.

  b Hergenröther, Joseph, Cardinal. *Handbuch der allgemeinen Kirchengeschichte.* 1876. 6th ed. by J. P. Kirsch, 4 v., Freiburg im Breisgau, 1924–25. [Theologische Bibliothek.] (Bibliographies.) French tr. by P. Belet, *Histoire de l'église.* 7 v., Paris, 1880–92.

  c Funk, Franz X. von. *Manual of church history.* Ed. by W. H. Kent. 2 v. London, 1914. (Bibliography.) Tr. by P. Perciballi from *Lehrbuch der Kirchengeschichte,* 1886; 7th rev. ed. by K. Bihlmeyer, 2 v., Paderborn, 1921. [Wissenschaftliche Handbibliothek.]

  d Stebbing, George. *Story of the Catholic church.* 1915. 2nd ed., London and St. Louis, 1916.

a. Has been widely used as a standard Roman Catholic history of the church but has been largely supplanted by later works. Review of 1899 (Cincinnati) reprint of v. 1, F. A. Christie, *A.H.R.* 8:797, July 1903; *Catholic World* 28:283. *b.* Planned along lines which led inevitably to a complexity bordering upon confusion, somewhat cleared up by Dr. Kirsch's rearrangement of the material. Review, *Ecclesiastical Rev.* (Philadelphia), 27:682, Dec. 1902.   WHA

c. The interest, point of view, and emphasis are Roman Catholic; seven-tenths of the space devoted to early and medieval church history. The modern era is but scantily sketched, without even a thorough analysis of modern Roman Catholicism. Useful synoptical tables suffer from rigid adherence to six divisions fixed upon for the earlier time. Concise, objective, and descriptive rather than philosophical. The translation is very readable. Review, *Expository Times,* 26:222, Feb. 1915.

CHMO

d. Some Roman Catholic scholars prefer this to *c.,* as representing more fully British and American interests. Review, *Dublin Rev.* 158:397, Apr. 1916.

WHA

F125 Möller, Wilhelm E. *History of the Christian church.* 3 v. London and N. Y., 1892–1900. [1, A.D. 1–600, 4th ed., 1912; 2, *Middle ages,* 2nd ed., 1910; 3, *1517–1648, Reformation and counter-reformation.*] V. 1–2, tr. by A. Rutherfurd; v. 3, ed. by G. Kawerau, tr. by J. H. Freese from *Lehrbuch der Kirchengeschichte,* 3 v., Freiburg, 1889–94; 2nd ed. of v. 1 by H. von Schubert, 1897–1902; 2nd ed. of v. 2 by G. Kawerau, 1893; v. 2, rewritten by H. von Schubert, 1921; 3rd rev. ed. of v. 3 by G. Kawerau, 1907. (Good bibliographies.)

One of the best manuals of general church history down to the peace of Westphalia, by Protestant author. Marked by accurate scholarship, breadth and comprehensiveness of treatment, judicial temper, and by an unusual skill in grouping the materials in such a way as to emphasize the genetic relationship of events in a given period. Review of v. 1, *E.H.R.* 8:397, Apr. 1893; v. 2, 9:188, Jan. 1894; v. 3, (German ed.) F. Johnson, *Amer. Jour. of Theol.* 12:306, Apr. 1908.   FWL

F126 Schaff, Philip. *History of the Christian church.* 7 v. [V. 5, in two parts, by David S. Schaff.] N. Y., 1858–1910; 3rd ed. of v. 1, 1890; 8th ed. of v. 2, 1901; 5th ed. of v. 3, 1902; reprint of v. 4, 1899; 2nd ed. of v. 6, 1901; 3rd ed. of v. 7, 1898. (Full bibliographies.)

Most considerable attempt yet made in America to write a complete history of the church. Planned on a scale too large for completion by one man, it was carried by Dr. Philip Schaff to the close of the Reformation, omitting the later Middle Ages, 1073–1517. The omission has been supplied by his son. The point of view is evangelical Protestant; the method is the German scientific, with an abundance of critical notes. The work falls naturally into four parts: v. 1–3, early church to 600; v. 4, medieval period to 1073; v. 5, medieval church, 1049–1517; v. 6–7, Reformation in Germany and Switzerland. As a readable and generally accurate presentation of a vast subject and as a guide to wider reading it is unique among histories of the church in English. Review of v. 2, C. J. H. Ropes, *Andover Rev.* 1:218, Feb. 1884; v. 4, E. C. Smyth, *ibid.* 4:285, Sept. 1885; v. 5, pt. 1, J. W. Moncrief, *Amer. Jour. of Theol.* 12:305, Apr. 1908; pt. 2, A. H. Newman, *ibid.* 15:123, Jan. 1911; v. 6, C. C. Starbuck, *Andover Rev.* 11:108, Jan. 1889; v. 7, *ibid.* 19:259, Mar. 1893.   EE

F127 Sheldon, Henry C. *History of the Christian church.* 5 v. N. Y. 1894–95.

Planned to meet a need felt by both professional students and intelligent laymen for a church history midway between the small compendium and the ponderous works; the perspective is excellent; scant attention is given to doctrine. V. 3–5. Devoted to the modern church with special emphasis on its growth among English-speaking peoples. As a whole the tone is temperate, but at times the author shows decidedly his Protestant sympathies. While there is evidence of the use of the chief sources, too many conclusions are based on secondary writers. Review, *Methodist Rev.* 77:676, July 1895.   ACF

F128 Milman, Henry H. *History of Latin Christianity, including that of the popes to the pontificate of Nicolas V.* 6 v. 1854–55. Latest ed., 8 v., N. Y., 1903.

Based on a discriminating study of the sources. The author's claim to 'calm and rigid impartiality' was justified by praise from Catholics and Protestants alike. Like Gibbon's masterpiece, that of Milman has also become one of the classics of history. Both secular and ecclesiastical students acknowledge their indebtedness to his erudition. Later investigations have supplemented his learning, but have not materially changed his conclusions. Review, *Edinburgh Rev.* 107:26, Jan. 1858. There is a collection of reviews of this work in Moulton, *Library of literary criticism of English and American authors,* 6:536–539.   ACF

F129 Paget, R. Harold, ed. director. *Outline of Christianity: the story of our civilization.* 5 v. N. Y., 1926. V. 1, *Birth of Christianity,* ed. by E. F. Scott and B. S. Easton; v. 2, *Builders of the Church,* ed. by F. J. Foakes Jackson; v. 3, *Rise of the modern churches,* ed. by Shailer Mathews; v. 4, *Christianity and modern thought,* ed. by F. J. McConnell; v. 5, *Christianity today and tomorrow,* ed. by J. H. Finley. (Bibliographies.)

Work of collaboration, with many chapters by recognized specialists in the various fields, such as B. W. Bacon, C. H. Robinson, R. M. Jones, G. G. Coulton, W. H. Hutton, and G. A. Reisner, while the editors of the several volumes have contributed much of the text. Broadly conceived, it is prevailingly Protestant in outlook, although one chapter bears the official *imprimatur* of the Roman Catholic Church. Well-selected illustrations, some in color, increase the value of the work as a scholarly presentation to a popular audience of the influences of Christianity upon civilization. WHA

EARLY CHURCH

F201 Schürer, Emil. *History of the Jewish people in the time of Jesus Christ.* 5 v., Edinburgh, 1885–90. Reprint, 5 v., 1896. [Clark's foreign theological library.] Tr. by J. Macpherson, S. Taylor, and P. Christie from *Geschichte des jüdischen Volkes im Zeitalter Jesu Christi*, Leipzig, 1886–90, which was 2nd rev. ed. of his *Lehrbuch der neutestamentlichen Zeitgeschichte* (1874) ; 4th and 5th ed., 3 v. and index, Leipzig, 1907–20.

Most significant work dealing with the history of the Jews from B. C. 175 to A. D. 135,—a period of the utmost importance to the student of Christianity. Although the English edition has by no means been superseded, the special student should consult later German editions which are especially valuable in notes and the use of newly discovered inscriptions. Colorless exposition of facts; admirably organized and analyzed; rich in references to sources. Especially valuable for the discussion of the Messianic hope, the religious organization of Judaism, and the remarkable summary of Jewish religious literature to which all of v. 5 is devoted. Indispensable for thorough study of the field. Review of 3rd German ed., v. 1, *Amer. Jour. of Theol.* 7:344, Apr. 1903; v. 2–3, C. Clemen, *Amer. Jour. of Theol.* 3:595, July 1899. SM

F202 Clemen, Carl. *Primitive Christianity and its non-Jewish sources.* Edinburgh, 1912. Tr. by R. G. Nisbet from *Religionsgeschichtliche Erklärung des neuen Testaments.* 1909. 2nd ed., pt. 1, Giessen, 1924.

Summary and estimate of data assembled by comparative investigation. Employment of the case method prevents a philosophic presentation of the materials. The author insists upon discrimination between form and idea, granting dependence only in cases of similarity of idea. He thus undervalues the non-Jewish elements and does not adequately consider the influence of alien religions upon late Judaism. The translation is very faithful and readable. Review, S. J. Case, *Amer. Jour. of Theol.* 17:282, Apr. 1913. CHMO

F203 Eusebius of Caesarea. *Church history, translated with prolegomena and notes by A. C. McGiffert.* N. Y., 1890. (Full bibliography.) [(F71c) Select library of Nicene and post-Nicene fathers, second series.] Greek text, with Latin tr. by Rufinus, ed. by E. Schwartz and T. Mommsen, 3 v., Leipzig, 1903–09. [Pt. 2 of Eusebius' *Werke*, in *Die griechischen christlichen Schriftsteller der ersten drei Jahrhunderte*, herausgegeben von der Kirchenväter-Kommission der Preussischen Akademie der Wissenschaften.]

Fresh translation of one of the most important sources for the history of the early church by a master of the subject. The 72 pages of prolegomena furnish the best available account of the life and writings of Eusebius. The elaborate commentary omits nothing of importance. A first class work; indispensable for early church history; best introduction to a more careful study of the first three centuries. Review, M. B. Riddle, *Presbyterian and Reformed Rev.* 2:509, July 1891. JCA

F204 Wernle, Paul. *Beginnings of Christianity.* 2 v. London and N. Y., 1903–04. [Theological translation library.] Ed. by W. D. Morrison and tr. by G. A. Bienemann from *Die Anfänge unser Religion.* Tübingen, 1901.

Not an objective history of early Christianity, but a particular interpretation of that history. According to this thesis, the religion of Jesus and his immediate followers, including Paul, reveals the 'gospel' in its original purity, while the activities of the next generation in devising rites and institutions mark the beginning of a process of decline ultimately issuing in the establishment of Catholicism. A highly controversial work. Review, *Expository Times,* 12:542, Sept. 1901; 14:562, Sept. 1903; 15:460, July 1904.   SJC

F205 Weizsäcker, Carl von. *Apostolic age of the Christian church.* 1894–95. 2nd ed., 2 v., London and N. Y., 1899. [Theological translation library.] Tr. by J. Millar from 2nd rev. ed. of *Das apostolische Zeitalter der christlichen Kirche,* 1886; 2nd ed., 4 pt., Freiburg, 1891–92.

Still holds its place in virtue of its keen insight, grasp of historical and religious realities, and clear and vivid exposition. Represents, on the theological side, the views of a scholarship which had not yet caught the significance of the apocalyptic and Hellenistic factors in early Christianity. Needs to be largely supplemented by more recent books, but no student of Christian origins can afford to neglect it. Review, A. C. McGiffert, *Andover Rev.* 7:217, Feb. 1887.   EFS

F206 McGiffert, Arthur C. *History of Christianity in the apostolic age.* 1897. Rev. ed., N. Y., 1906. [International theological library.]

Standard work in its field. Not only a critical reconstruction of the history of the Christian movement from the death of Jesus to the end of the first century, but also essentially a critical introduction to the books of the New Testament. The point of view is that of the best historical scholarship of a generation ago as represented, for example, in the works of (F242, 532e, 641a, 661b) Harnack and (F205) Weizsäcker. Review, J. W. Platner, *Amer. Jour. of Theol.* 1:1025, Oct. 1897.   SJC

F207 Meyer, Eduard. *Ursprung und Anfänge des Christentums.* 3 v. Stuttgart, 1921–23. 5th ed. of v. 1, 1924; 5th ed. of v. 2, 1925; 3rd ed. of v. 3, 1923.

Eduard Meyer, the eminent historian of the ancient world, has latterly devoted himself to the investigation of primitive Christianity. His lack of specialized learning is sometimes apparent, but is not wholly a disadvantage. With his comprehensive knowledge of the life of antiquity he is able to view the Christian movement in its larger bearings, and has made many things clear and intelligible for the first time. In some respects the most notable of all recent contributions to New Testament study. Review of v. 1, F. A. Christie, *A.H.R.* 27:99, Oct. 1921.   EFS

F208a Case, Shirley Jackson. *Evolution of early Christianity, a genetic study of first-century Christianity in relation to its religious environment.* Chicago, 1914.

b ———— *Social origins of Christianity.* Chicago, 1923. (Bibliography.)

c **Jackson, Frederick J. Foakes.** *Studies in the life of the early church.* N. Y., 1924.

d **Scott, Ernest F.** *First age of Christianity.* N. Y., 1926.

a. and *b.* Discuss cogently the forces, individual and social, that affected the primitive faith, cultus, and ethic of the Christian group as it moved out into the wider circles of influence in the Mediterranean area. Review of *a.*, A. C. McGiffert, *Amer. Jour. of Theol.* 19:118, Jan. 1915; F. A. Christie, *A.H.R.* 20:616, Apr. 1915; of *b.*, E. F. Scott, *Jour. of Religion,* 4:320, May 1924. *c.* Appears to be meant for the lay, rather than the scholarly reader; treats somewhat sketchily the period from the death of Jesus to the times of Constantine.

TW

d. Presentation of the 'early Christian movement as a whole', this is both an introduction to the study of Christian origins and a harmonized epitome of the results of recent investigations using modern historical methods. Review, J. Johnson, *Bibliotheca Sacra* 85:243, Apr. 1925. WHA

F209 Dobschütz, Ernst von. *Christian life in the primitive church.* London and N. Y., 1904. [Theological translation library.] Ed. by W. D. Morrison and tr. by G. Bremner from *Die urchristlichen Gemeinden: sittengeschichtliche Bilder,* Leipzig, 1902.

From the New Testament and the writings of the apostolic fathers, the author collects data on early Christian worship, institutions, and social conditions, and so tries to construct pictures of life in the church generally and in the several communities. There is little in the book that is strikingly original, but the material is fully presented and skilfully arranged. Inadequate attention is given to the influence of pagan religion on Christian thought and custom. Review, A. W. Anthony, *Amer. Jour. of Theol.* 7:149, Jan. 1903; *Expository Times,* 16:97, Dec. 1904. EFS

F221a Duchesne, Louis M. O. *Early history of the Christian church from its foundation to the end of the fifth century.* 3 v. London and N. Y., 1909–24. Rev. ed. of v. 1–2, 1912–13. Tr. from 4th ed. of *Histoire ancienne de l'église,* 3 v., Paris, 1906–10; 4th ed. of v. 1, 1908; 3rd ed. of v. 2, 1906.

b ——— *L'église au VIe siècle.* Paris, 1925.

a. Most readable of the histories of the early church; English translation has much of the charm of the French original. Thoroughly scholarly work of the highest merit and singular impartiality. Exposition of controversies is lucid; objective statements of disputed matters should be constantly consulted. The author, probably the foremost French ecclesiastical historian of his generation, was a Roman Catholic. Review of v. 1–2, F. A. Christie, *A.H.R.* 18:351, Jan. 1913; of v. 3, P. Allard, *Revue des Quest. Hist.* 89:190, Jan. 1911. JCA

b. Continuation of *a,* but inferior to it; published posthumously. Review, F. Lot, *Rev. Critique* 61:179, May 1, 1927. WHA

F222 Gwatkin, Henry M. *Early church history to A. D. 313.* 2 v. London and N. Y., 1909.

Clear, pungent, and very readable. In spite of the monographic essay type of treatment, the reader is always kept aware of thought and action contemporary with the topics under discussion. The author's sound scholarship is limited only occasionally, but noticeably, by his ecclesiastical and theological prejudices. Checked with (F221) Duchesne's treatment of the period, the discussions are excellent. Review, P. V. M. Benecke, *E.H.R.* 25:559, July 1910. HBW

F223a Bright, William. *Age of the fathers, being chapters in the history of the church during the fourth and fifth centuries.* 2 v. London and N. Y., 1903.

b ———— *History of the church from the edict of Milan, A.D. 313 to the council of Chalcedon, A.D. 451.* 1860. 2nd ed., Oxford, 1869.

a. Appears without notes and accordingly might best be used in connection with *b.*, his earlier work, which covers the same period. Far more interesting in style, though the treatment is too detailed. Modern German investigations are ignored. Consequently the doctrinal controversies of the period are treated from what is at times an antiquated standpoint. Good description of the characters reveal an intimate knowledge of the sources. Review, A. E. Burn, *E.H.R.* 19:136, Jan. 1904.

JCA

F224 Kidd, Beresford J. *History of the church to A. D. 461.* 3 v. Oxford, 1922.

New and comprehensive survey of the history of the early church, by an Anglican. Special attention is given to the primary sources which are cited constantly and critically considered. Review, Alice Gardner, *E.H.R.* 38:95, Jan. 1923.

WHA

F225 Rainy, Robert. *Ancient catholic church from the accession of Trajan to the fourth general council, A.D. 98–451.* Edinburgh, 1902. [International theological library.] (Bibliography.)

Of extraordinary value for thorough analysis of the thought life of the church. Treats the whole period in three main divisions separated by the dates A.D. 180 and 313. Lucid presentation of Gnosticism, Montanism, and Manicheism; lacks extended discussion of organization, persecutions, and external expansion. Some chapters, e.g., ch. 4, 'Beliefs and sacraments,' require revision in the light of recent research. Indispensable to students. Reviews, E. B. Hulbert, *Amer. Jour. of Theol.* 6:585, July 1902.

JTMCN

F231a Rivington, Luke. *Primitive church and the see of St. Peter.* London, 1894.

b Bright, William. *Roman see in the early church, and other studies in church history.* London and N. Y., 1896.

c Shotwell, James T., and Loomis, Louise Ropes. *See of Peter.* N. Y., 1927. [Records of civilization, sources and studies.] (B61)

a and *b.* These works may be accepted as characteristic presentations of the opposing views of Catholics and Protestants on the relations of St. Peter to the foundation of the .Roman see. They marshal the available evidence and the various arguments on the questions whether St. Peter was bishop of Rome, whether he was the 'pope' of the apostolic church, and whether the bishops of Rome were acknowledged as popes in the primitive church. Both works, especially *b*, are polemic in character. The Roman Catholic side is presented in *a*, and the Protestant in the first six essays in *b*. Review of *b*, A. C. McGiffert, *A.H.R.* 2:106, Oct. 1896.

ARW, GMD

c. Probably the most complete presentation of the evidence bearing upon the rise of the papacy; with· critical questions regarding the relations of the papacy with the Petrine tradition on the one side, and the authority of the bishop of

Rome within the church on the other. Gives in English translation almost everything which can in any real sense be considered as historical source material for the subject. Reviews, F. A. Christie, *A.H.R.* 33:848, July 1928; J. M. Lenhart, *Cath. Hist. Rev.* 8:266, July 1928.   WHA

F232a Cadoux, Cecil John. *Early church and the world.* Edinburgh, 1925.

  b Haase, Felix. *Altchristliche Kirchengeschichte nach orientalischen Quellen.* Leipzig, 1925.

  a. Exposition of Christian teachings during the first four centuries in regard to the state, property, war, the family, and slavery. Review, F. Cabrol, *Rev. des Quest. Hist.* 106:197, Jan. 1927. *b.* Critical study of oriental sources for early church history. Review, A. Vincent, *Rev. des Quest. Hist.* 107:227, July, 1927.

                                                                    WHA

F241a Ramsay, Sir William M. *Church in the Roman empire before A. D. 170.* 1893. 6th ed., London, 1900. [Mansfield College lectures.]

  b ——— *St. Paul the traveller and the Roman citizen.* 1895. 5th ed., London, 1898.

  a. Pt. 1. Forms the basis of *b;* replete with fresh information on social and political history of the first century; written with fine historical imagination. Pt. 2. Investigates relations of the Church with the Roman government, between A. D. 64 and 170; gives a luminous discussion of the persecutions. The author holds that the Flavian policy of prosecution of Christians as political offenders, allowed to lapse by Hadrian and Antoninus, was rescinded by Marcus Aurelius. Discursive but scholarly. Review, *Expository Times,* 4:375, May 1893.   JTMCN

F242 Harnack, Adolf von. *Mission and expansion of Christianity in the first three centuries.* 1904. 2nd rev. ed., 2 v., London and N. Y., 1908. [Theological translation library.] Tr. by J. Moffatt from *Die Mission und Ausbreitung des Christentums in den ersten drei Jahrhunderten.* 1902. 4th rev. ed., 2 v., Leipzig, 1924.

  Far and away the most important work upon the spread of Christianity in the first three centuries. The second book sets out with great insight the various kinds of appeal made by the new religion and concludes with a brief sketch of Christianity in its complete form as a syncretistic religion. The fourth book, which fills v. 2, is an exhaustive presentation of all that is known about the actual spread of the Christian movement, the places where Christianity existed, and its relative strength. Eleven excellent maps illustrate the course of the development. Review, J. V. Bartlet, *Rev. of Theol. and Phil.,* 1:542, Feb. 1906.   ACMCG

F251a Workman, Herbert B. *Persecution in the early church, a chapter in the history of renunciation.* London, 1906. [Fernley lecture.]

  b Merrill, Elmer T. *Essays in early Christian history.* N. Y. and London, 1924. (Bibliographical foot-notes.)

  c Canfield, Leon H. *Early persecutions of the Christians.* N. Y., 1913. [Columbia University studies in history, economics, and public law.] (Bibliography.)

  d Gregg, John A. F. *Decian persecution.* Edinburgh, 1897. [Hulsean prize essay.] (Bibliography.)

e **Healy, Patrick J.** *Valerian persecution, a study of the relations between church and state in the third century, A.D.* Boston, 1905. (Bibliography.)

f **Mason, Arthur J.** *Persecution of Diocletian, a historical essay.* Cambridge, Eng., 1876.

a. Systematic survey; maintains a proper balance between the legal and historical aspects as against the ecclesiastical and experiential; based on a critical examination of traditions and occupies a middle position as to their value; furnished with copious references of the highest value and with critical appendixes. As to the legal question, it adopts Mommsen's judgment that Christianity itself was a crime, that persecution was a police matter rather than the result of special laws, and that the 'general persecutions' were seasons of special 'enforcement from high quarters.' Review, P. V. M. Benecke, *E.H.R.* 22:328, Apr. 1907. ARW

b. Especially valuable study of the persecutions by the Roman government; approached primarily from the Latin rather than from the Greek side. Review, K. Lake, *A.H.R.* 30:340, Jan. 1925. *c, d, e,* and *f.* Valuable intensive monographic studies of several persecutions. WHA

CHURCH IN THE MIDDLE AGES

F261 Lagarde, André. *Latin church in the middle ages.* N. Y., 1915. [International theological library.] (Excellent bibliographies.) Tr. by A. Alexander.

Useful handbook for medieval history. Some mystery attaches to the identity of the author who has no apparent academic position and, judging from internal evidence, may be a former priest who has become separated from Rome. History and institutions are handled, sometimes together, sometimes in separate chapters. As a whole the treatment is topical. The work is abreast of modern scholarship. The final chapter, on ecclesiastical writers, is a handy manual of medieval, ecclesiastical historiography. Review, H. H. Walker, *Amer. Jour. of Theol.* 20:609, Oct. 1916. For the history of the medieval church, especially in the early periods, cf. also (H121) *Cambridge medieval history;* (H122) Gibbon, *Decline and fall of the Roman empire;* (H304a) Bury, *History of the later Roman empire;* and (H202) Hodgkin, *Italy and her invaders.* JWT

F262 Flick, Alexander C. *Rise of the mediaeval church and its influence on the civilisation of western Europe from the first to the thirteenth century.* N. Y. and London, 1909. (Bibliographies.)

Popular but scholarly, relatively brief, non-theological survey of the development of the church. Review, C. H. Walker, *Amer. Jour. of Theol.* 15:640, Oct. 1911. HHW

F263a Jackson, Frederick J. Foakes. *Introduction to the history of Christianity, A.D. 590–1314.* N. Y., 1921. (Bibliographies.)

b **Workman, Herbert B.** *Church of the West in the middle ages.* 2 v. London, 1898–1900. [Books for Bible students.] (Bibliographies.)

c —— *Dawn of the reformation.* 2 v. London, 1901–02. [Books for Bible students.] (Bibliographies.)

d —— *Foundation of modern religion: a study in the task and contribution of the mediaeval church.* N. Y., 1916. [Cole lectures.]

a. Suggestive survey of the Middle Ages from the interpretative standpoint that 'a Christian ideal dominated society' and that a 'Church empire' was the dominant institution. A map shows the location of the principal sees and monasteries. Review, A. H. Sweet, *A.H.R.* 27:774, July 1922. *b.* Work of uneven merits; extends from Gregory the Great to the Avignon papacy. Its general attitude of appreciation is insufficiently restrained by critical judgment. Review, v. 1, J. W. Moncrief, *Amer. Jour. of Theol.* 3:800, Oct. 1899; v. 2, D. S. Schaff, *ibid.*, 5:159, Jan. 1901. *c.* The volumes cover the ages of Wiclif and Hus respectively. Review, J. W. Moncrief, *Amer. Jour. of Theol.*, 6:161, Jan. 1902; 8:203, Jan. 1904. *d.* Study of the outward environment and the inner life of the medieval church with more obvious correlation of medieval Christianity with modern life than in his previous works. Review, J. W. Moncrief, *Amer. Jour. of Theol.* 21:466, July 1917.

WHA

F271 Grisar, Hartmann. *History of Rome and the popes in the middle ages.* 3 v. London, 1911–12. Tr. by L. Cappadelta [pseud. of C. L. Dessoulavy] from *Geschichte Roms und der Päpste im Mittelalter.* V. 1. Freiburg im Breisgau, 1901.

Planned to comprise six volumes in the German edition, in which the period from the late fourth century to the middle of the fifteenth was to be covered. Only v. 1 has appeared. This brings the story down to the commencement of the pontificate of Gregory I, in 590. Scholarly; takes account of the more recent archeological discoveries which throw light on the history of the city of the popes. Depicts Rome as the head of Christendom; pays no attention to social or economic factors in the history of the city. Frankly Catholic in conception and presentation. Review of German ed., F. X. Kraus, *Historische Zeitschrift,* 88:288, March 1902; of tr., *Athenaeum* 2:247, Aug. 26, 1911; *Saturday Rev.,* 112:525, Oct. 21, 1911. Also cf. (O481a) Gregorovius, *Rome in the middle ages.* APE

F272 Rocquain, Felix. *La papauté au moyen âge: Nicolas Ier, Grégoire VII, Innocent III, Boniface VIII, étude sur le pouvoir pontifical.* Paris, 1881.

Essays on the influence of the great popes of the middle ages, a scholarly study in theocracy. Valuable appendixes on Innocent III's struggle with Otto of Brunswick, the papal registers, and (F75a) Jaffé, *Regesta pontificum.* HRS

F281a Salembier, Louis. *Great western schism.* London, 1907. Tr. from *Le grand schisme d'occident,* 1900; 5th rev. ed., Paris, 1921. [Bibliothèque de l'enseignement de l'histoire ecclésiastique.] (Full bibliography.)

b Valois, Noël. *La France et le grand schisme d'occident.* 4 v. Paris, 1896–1902. (Bibliography.)

c —— *La crise religieuse du XVe siècle, le pape et le concile, 1418–1450.* 2 v. Paris, 1909.

a. Brief survey of the schism of the papacy from its beginning in 1378 to the close of the Council of Constance; sympathetic with the Roman as opposed to the Avignon party. Review, A. Largent, *Rev. des Quest. Hist.* 69:671, Apr. 1901. *b.* Fuller account, favorable to the Avignon party. Review, A. Molinier, *Rev. Hist.* 80:101, Sept. 1902.. *c.* Continues *b.* from the close of the Council of Constance to the close of the Council of Basel; emphasizes diplomatic affairs. Review, J. W. Thompson, *A.H.R.* 15:839, July 1910. Cf. (F311a) Creighton, *History of the papacy,* and (F311b) Pastor, *History of the popes.* GMD

F291 Robinson, Charles H. *Conversion of Europe.* London and N. Y., 1917. (Bibliography.)

Carefully documented history of the conversion of the various countries of the British Isles and of the Continent; utilizes the sources and a portion of the French and German secondary literature. Best book in English on the subject. Review, J. P. Whitney, *E.H.R.* 33:557, Oct. 1918. WWR

REFORMATION AND COUNTER-REFORMATION

Excellent bibliographies of the Reformation will be found in (I121) *Cambridge modern history,* v. 1–3, in (I231a) Smith, *Age of the Reformation,* and in (I101) Hayes, *Political and social history of modern Europe,* 1:169–174. For special bibliographies of the Reformation in Germany, cf. (P4).

F301 Lindsay, Thomas M. *History of the reformation.* 2 v. London and N. Y., 1906–07. [International theological library.] (Bibliographical footnotes.)

Attractive in style, thoroughly studied, quiet in tone, generous in outlook; good treatment of the Reformation for those whose interests lie primarily in the fields of doctrine and of ecclesiastical politics. For the economic forces and social conditions of the age Lindsay has small care or understanding; nor does he treat, with any philosophical grasp, the intellectual revolution of the sixteenth century, as far as this lay outside the confessional battlefield. For further review of v. 1, cf. (P251). V. 2. Deals with the movement in countries other than Germany and with the Counter-Reformation. Review, W. W. Rockwell, *A.H.R.* 12:874, July 1907. PS

Works which deal with the Reformation as a political, economic, social, and intellectual movement, are listed in the subsection Reformation and Counter-Reformation in § I.

F311a Creighton, Mandell. *History of the papacy from the great schism to the sack of Rome.* 1st ed., 5 v., under title, *History of the papacy during the period of the reformation,* London, 1882–94; new ed., 6 v., 1897; new ed. cf. v. 1 and reprint cf v. 2–6, London, 1901.

  b Pastor, Ludwig von. *History of the popes from the close of the middle ages, drawn from the secret archives of the Vatican and other original sources.* V. 1–18, London and St. Louis, 1891–1930. Tr. by F. I. Antrobus and R. F. Kerr from *Geschichte der Päpste seit dem Ausgang des Mittelalters,* v. 1–14, Freiburg, 1886–1930. (Bibliographies.)

  c Ranke, Leopold von. *Ecclesiastical and political history of the popes of Rome during the sixteenth and seventeenth centuries.* 3 v. 1840. 2 v., Philadelphia, 1841. 4th ed., 3 v., London, 1866. Tr. by S. Austin from *Die römischen Päpste, ihre Kirche und ihr Staat im 16. und 17. Jahrhundert,* being v. 2–4 of *Fürsten und Völker von Süd-Europa,* 1834. 2nd ed., Berlin, 1838–39.

These works are of the highest excellence. *a.* Creighton, an Anglican, whose history appeared before *b.,* assembled a mass of material to study the causes of the Reformation. He sought to write the sober, unadorned truth, hence sacrificed interest and style to accuracy. His work is dry but never dull. *b.* Abounds in notes of vast erudition and in quotations direct from the documents. The style is masterful, vivid, and inspiring; the criticisms are cautious, scholarly, and self-reliant; the interpretations are characterized by a keen sense of fairness.

Creighton saw his problem in a larger unity, but Pastor has the warmer, subtler touch. In some instances Creighton is more conservative than Pastor. V. 14 of German edition covers the period to 1700; further volumes bringing the history down to 1800 are in preparation. The translation gives two volumes to each volume of the original. Also cf. Pastor's ed. of (P242a) Jannsen, *History of the German people at the close of the Middle Ages,* and his (P242b) *Erläuterungen und Ergänzungen zu Jannsens Geschichte.* c. Remains a standard work although lacking in the human interest of a and b. ACF

For the Renaissance and its relations with Christian life and thought, cf. works listed in subsection Renaissance in § I.

CHURCH IN MODERN TIMES

F351a MacCaffrey, James. *History of the catholic church in the nineteenth century, 1789–1908.* 1909. 2nd rev. ed., 2 v., Dublin and St. Louis, 1910.

b Nielsen, Fredrik. *History of the papacy in the XIXth century.* 2 v. N. Y., 1906. Tr. under the direction of A. J. Mason from *Pavedømmet i det nittende hundredaar,* 1878, 2nd rev. ed., 2 v., København, 1895–98.

c Nippold, Friedrich. *Papacy in the 19th century, a part of 'The history of Catholicism since the restoration of the papacy.'* N. Y. and London, 1900. Tr. by L. H. Schwab from *Katholizismus seit der Restauration des Papstthums,* Elberfeld, 1883. [V. 2 of 3rd ed. of *Handbuch der neuesten Kirchengeschichte,* 1st ed., 1 v., 1867; 3rd ed., 5 v. in 6, Elberfeld, Berlin, and Leipzig, 1880–1906.]

a. Probably the best account of the church's total activity in every country; admirable for scholarship, fair statement, and judgment. Especially valuable in relation to England, Ireland, and America, and for the relation of the church to social and educational problems. Review, *Amer. Cath. Quar. Rev.* 35:565, July 1910.   b. Richly detailed story; based on full documentary and literary sources; shows the fortunes of the papacy and of the French church in the Revolutionary and Napoleonic periods, and the development of ultramontanism since 1815. Review, R. M. Johnston, *A.H.R.* 12:377, Jan. 1907.   c. Without detail or delineations of the personalities involved; argumentative account of papal policy since 1814; expressed Prussian political feeling at the time of the 'Kulturkampf.' The purpose, as stated by the translator, is to rescue Catholicism from its papal caricature and to maintain its importance as a corrective to Protestant individualism. Review, *Nation* (N. Y.), 72:16, Jan. 3, 1901.   FAC

F361 Pullan, Leighton. *Religion since the reformation.* Oxford, 1923. [Bampton lectures.]

Scholarly analysis, always from the standpoint of Anglo-Catholicism, of the major forces and movements within Christendom, both eastern and western, since the beginning of the Reformation. Many strictures against Roman Catholicism and Protestantism; too much controlled by its point of view of the *via media.* Review, F. Cabrol, *Rev. des Quest. Hist.* 103:207, July 1, 1925.   WHA

F371 Newman, Albert H. *History of antipedobaptism from the rise of pedobaptism to A.D. 1609.* Philadelphia, 1896. (Bibliography.)

Standard account in English in respect to completeness. Deals with evangelical sects in the Middle Ages as well as with the Anabaptists of the Reformation and their evolution into Mennonite and Baptist denominations. Review, G. Anderson, *Amer. Jour. of Theol.* 2:184, Jan. 1898.   FAC

F381 Burrage, Champlin. *Early English dissenters in the light of recent re-search, 1550–1641.* 2 v. Cambridge, Eng., 1912.

Rich in material; invaluable in critical treatment of the sources for the formative period of English Separatism, not only in England but also in its temporary and permanent homes in the Netherlands and America. V. 2. Contains source material not readily accessible elsewhere. Review, W. H. Frere, *E.H.R.* 27:570, July 1912.   WHA

F382a Jones, Rufus M. *Studies in mystical religion.* London, 1909. [Rowntree series.]

b ——— *Spiritual reformers in the sixteenth and seventeenth centuries.* London, 1914. [Rowntree series.]

c **Braithwaite, William C.** *Beginnings of Quakerism.* London, 1912. [Rowntree series.]

d ——— *Second period of Quakerism.* London, 1919. [Rowntree series.]

e **Jones, Rufus M.,** and others. *Quakers in the American colonies.* London, 1911. [Rowntree series.]

f ——— *Later periods of Quakerism.* 2 v. London, 1921. [Rowntree series.]

g **Emmott, Elizabeth B.** *Short history of Quakerism (earlier periods).* London and N. Y., 1923.

h **Jones, Rufus M.** *New studies in mystical religion.* N. Y., 1927. [Ely lectures.]

i **Jones, Lester M.** *Quakers in action: recent humanitarian and reform activities of the American Quakers.* N. Y., 1929.

The first six of these items form the Rowntree series which furnishes an excellent complete history of the Quaker movement. They are of wider significance than the history of a mere denomination, for they deal with a movement of thought with far reaching influence in the fields of religion and politics. Of the several items the most significant is *b.* which, for original research and literary merit, outranks all other accounts of the Humanist mystics (Denck, Franck, Boehme, et al.) who sought in immediate experience of an inherent relationship of the divine and the human another basis of religious authority than the Lutheran or Calvinist systems offered. Indispensable for a knowledge of currents which found group organization through Fox in the Quaker movement. *g.* Shorter account of Quakerism to the end of the seventeenth century; based upon the preceding works. Review of *a*, W. R. Inge, *Hibbert Jour.* 8:208, Oct. 1909; of *b*, C. C. J. Webb, *E.H.R.* 30:140, Jan. 1915; G. L. Burr, *A.H.R.* 20:624, Apr. 1915; of *d*, W. T. Morgan, *Pol. Sci. Quar.* 35:671, Dec. 1925; of *e*, W. W. Fenn, *A.H.R.* 17:618, Apr. 1912; of *f*, W. W. Fenn, *A.H.R.* 28:309, Jan. 1923; V. D. Davis, *Hibbert Jour.* 21:202, Oct. 1922; of *g*, V. D. Davis, *ibid.* 21:825, July 1923.   FAC

h. More psychological than historical in interest, this yet belongs to the records of evolving mysticism, and may be considered a sequel to the Rowntree series, although not bibliographically connected with it. Review, A. C. Wyckoff, *Biblical Rev.* 13:303, Apr. 1928. *i.* Account of the adjustment of a Christian group, opposed in principle to war, to the realities of the World War, but continuing its activities and significance into the post-war period.   WHA

F383 Dexter, Henry M. *Congregationalism of the last three hundred years as seen in its literature, with special reference to certain recondite, neglected, or disputed passages.* N. Y., 1880. (Comprehensive bibliography.)

Series of discussions in early Congregational history; the result of the life-work of a competent scholar. Though needing correction at many points in view of subsequent investigations, it must always be valued by the student. Its largest permanent worth is in its appended 'Collections toward a bibliography of Con-gregationalism,' extending from 1546 to 1879 and including 7250 titles, which is not exhaustive but is indispensable to the student, especially as it indicates where most of the volumes listed could be found at the time of compilation. Review, C. A. Briggs, *Presbyterian Rev.* 1:762, Oct. 1880. wwa

EASTERN CHURCHES

F401a Adeney, Walter F. *Greek and eastern churches.* London and N. Y., 1908. [International theological library.]

b Burkitt, Francis C. *Early eastern Christianity, . . . the Syriac-speaking church.* London, 1904. [St. Margaret's lectures.]

c Duchesne, Louis M. O. *Churches separated from Rome.* London, 1907. [International Catholic library.] Tr. by A. H. Mathew from *Autonomies ecclésiastiques, églises séparées,* 1896. 2nd ed., Paris, 1905.

d Fortescue, Adrian. *Orthodox eastern church.* 1907. 3rd ed., London, 1911. Reissue, 1916. (Bibliography.)

e —— *Lesser eastern churches.* 3rd ed. N. Y., 1911.

f —— *Uniate eastern churches: the Byzantine rite in Italy, Sicily, Syria and Egypt.* Ed. by George D. Smith. London, 1923. (Bibliography.)

g Dampier, Margaret G. *Organization of the orthodox eastern churches.* London, 1910.

a. Introduction to the salient episodes of practically every aspect of Greek and Eastern church history; represents a mastery of much of the source material and the best of the secondary authorities. Noteworthy is the chronologically consecutive treatment of the Russian, the Syrian and Armenian, and the Coptic and Abyssinian churches. Review, E. W. Miller, *Amer. Jour. of Theol.* 13:478, July 1909. HBW

b. Relates not to the entire Christian movement in the East, but to Syriac Christianity, especially the church centering at Edessa and its literature. *c.* Primarily a study of conditions which led to separations from the see of Rome, with some consideration of variety of religious custom within the Roman communion. Review, G. Monod, *Rev. Hist.* 64:364, July 1897; *Amer. Cath. Quar. Rev.* 33:188, Jan. 1908. *d.* Roman Catholic exposition of the Orthodox Eastern Church, especially useful for its discrimination between the practices of the two systems. *e.* Carries the study over into the smaller eastern bodies, while *f,* a posthumous work, incomplete, treats those eastern churches which are now in communion with the See of Rome. *g.* Useful handbook of the constitutional systems of twelve autonomous national churches and metropolitanates of the Orthodox Eastern Church. Cf. also (H308a) Norden, *Das Papsttum und Byzanz;* (H308b) Bréhier, *Le schisme oriental;* (H352a) id. *L'église et l'orient au moyen âge.* WHA

MONASTICISM

F411a Workman, Herbert B. *Evolution of the monastic ideal from the earliest times down to the coming of the friars: a second chapter* (cf. F251a) *in the history of Christian renunciation.* London, 1913. (Bibliography.)

b Harnack, Adolf von. *Monasticism: its ideals and history.* 1901. New ed., N. Y., 1910. Tr. by E. E. Kellett and F. H. Marseille from *Das Mönchthum, seine Ideale und seine Geschichte,* 1881; 10th ed., Giessen, 1921.

c Eckenstein, Lina. *Woman under monasticism: chapters on saint-lore and convent life between A. D. 500 and A. D. 1500.* Cambridge, Eng., 1896.

a. Written in popular style. Not a general history of the monastic movement, but an effort to delineate the causes and motives which induced such large numbers of people to embrace the monastic state. Valuable as an introduction to the literature and the history of the subject. The section dealing with Eastern monasticism is unsatisfactory. Review, *E.H.R.,* 28:802, Oct. 1913.   *b.* Pamphlet containing a summary outline of the principal movements in monastic history down to the sixteenth century; its value is lessened by the author's subjectivism and his failure to connect monasticism with the ascetic movement in the early church. Review of 7th German ed., E. B. Krehbiel, *Amer. Jour. of Theol.* 12:294, Apr. 1908.   PJH

c. Notable and interesting study of the influence of monastic life upon the development of women. The central thesis is that the nunnery afforded to medieval woman the largest liberty attainable in that day. Based throughout on documentary material not easily accessible. Review, M. Wergeland, *Amer. Jour. of Theol.* 1:826, July 1897.   EE

F412a Butler, Edward Cuthbert. *Benedictine monachism, studies in Benedictine life and rule.* 1919. 2nd rev. ed., London and N. Y., 1924.

b Gasquet, Francis A., Cardinal. *English monastic life.* 1904. 6th ed., London, 1924. [Antiquary's books.] (Bibliography.)

c —— *Monastic life in the middle ages.* London, 1922.

a. Written by a Benedictine abbot in explanation and defense of the Benedictine system. Very clear exposition of the origins as planned by St. Benedict and of later developments as carrying out his spirit while departing in many ways from the formal detail of his establishments. Not a history of the order in its outward aspect, but a series of studies of various features of its organization, its discipline, and its influence. Written in a calm, judicial tone without controversial animus, but with due reference to controverted points. Especially interesting for its apologetic description of contemporary monasticism. Review, H. A. Wilson, *E.H.R.* 35:440, July 1920.   *b.* Convenient treatise, by an eminent Catholic scholar; gives clear idea of the material equipment, organization, and daily practice of English religious houses, with a list of them.   *c.* Collection of essays previously published in various periodicals; interesting studies on a wide variety of monastic topics; valuable when not of controversial character. Review, *E.H.R.* 37:611, Oct. 1922; S. M. Robinson, *Princeton Theol. Rev.* 21:135, Jan. 1923.   EE

F413 Coulton, George G. *Five centuries of religion,* v. 1, *St. Bernard, his predecessors and successors, 1000–1200 A. D.;* v. 2, *Friars and the dead weight of tradition.* Cambridge, Eng., 1923–27. [Cambridge studies in medieval life and thought.] (Valuable bibliography.)

Largely an interpretative description of medieval religion as it centered about the ascetic ideal and as it expressed itself in monasticism and related institutions. Based upon an extensive study of the sources; perhaps the most critical survey of monasticism which has yet appeared. Preface of v. 1 announced two other volumes as 'almost ready for the press,' while v. 2 indicates that a fourth volume is planned. Review of v. 1, E. W. Watson, *E.H.R.*. 39:259, Apr. 1924; of v. 2, S. M. Brown, *A.H.R.* 33:633, Apr. 1928; P. J. Healy, *Cath. Hist. Rev.* 8:262, July 1928.

WHA

F414 Montalembert, Charles F. R. comte de. *Monks of the west from St. Benedict to St. Bernard.* 7 v., Edinburgh, 1861–79. New ed. with introduction by F. A. Gasquet, 6 v., London, 1896. Tr. from *Les moines d'occident depuis Saint-Benôit jusqu'à Saint-Bernard,* 7 v., Paris, 1860–77.

Written at the time when the Romantic movement, which aimed not only at a fuller understanding of the Middle Ages but at their rehabilitation, was at its height. The purpose of the author was 'to vindicate the glories of one of the greatest institutions of Christianity.' He saw in monasticism, not something 'irrational and meaningless' but one of the great constructive and civilizing forces in the society of the Middle Ages. Death prevented the author from carrying out his full plan, and consequently the work contains an account merely of Benedictine and Irish monasticism. Though the work falls far short of being a scientific history, it deals with the institutional side of monasticism in such a broad and sympathetic spirit that it is still invaluable to the student. Best critical estimate is in Cardinal Gasquet's introduction to the new edition. Review, *E.H.R.* 11:400, Apr. 1896.

PJH

SOCIETY OF JESUS

F441a Campbell, Thomas J. *The Jesuits, 1534–1921: a history of the Society of Jesus from its foundation to the present time.* 2 v. N. Y., 1921. (Bibliography.)

b Boehmer, Heinrich. *Studien zur Geschichte der Gesellschaft Jesu.* V. 1, Bonn, 1914.

a. By a member of the Society; most comprehensive history of the Jesuits in English; deals with the rise of the Society of Jesus, the chief criticisms and attacks upon it, its suppression and restoration, its modern activities. Inadequately documented; throws little light upon the inner organization of the order. Review, P. Guilday, *A.H.R.* 28:304, Jan. 1923. *b.* This work by a Protestant has attracted favorable attention from the Jesuits themselves. Its chief contribution lies in its survey of formative influences in the religious environment of Loyola. Review, G. Krüger, *Harvard Theol. Rev.* 17:45, Jan. 1924.

WHA

F442a Astrain, Antonio. *Historia de la Compañia de Jesús en la asistencia de España.* V 1–5, to 1652, Madrid, 1902–16.

b Duhr, Bernhard. *Geschichte der Jesuiten in den Ländern deutscher Zunge.* V. 1–2 in 3, to 1648, Freiburg im Breisgau, 1907–13. (Bibliographical footnotes.)

c **Fouqueray, Henri.** *Histoire de la Compagnie de Jésus en France des origines à la suppression, 1528–1762.* V. 1–5, to 1645, Paris, 1910–24. (Bibliography.)

d **Venturi, Pietro Tacchi.** *Storia della Compagnia di Gesù in Italia.* V. 1, Roma, 1910.

e **Hughes, Thomas A.** *History of the Society of Jesus in North America, colonial and federal.* V. 1–2, to 1773, London and N. Y., 1907–17; *Documents,* v. 1 in 2, *ibid.,* 1908–10. (Bibliography.)

f **Pastells, Pablo.** *Historia de la Compañía de Jesús en la provincia del Paraguay.* V. 1, Madrid, 1912.

g —— *Misión de la Compañía de Jesús de Filipinas en el siglo XIX, relación histórica.* 3 v. Barcelona, 1916–17.

h **Taunton, Ethelred L.** *History of the Jesuits in England, 1580–1773.* London and Philadelphia, 1901.

All except *h.* are by Jesuit scholars and form part of a great enterprise to narrate the history of the Society in each country in the vernacular. Done largely from documentary and printed sources; differ widely in scholarship and tone; the best is *b.   a., b., c.,* and *d.* Chiefly important for the history of the Counter-Reformation.   *e., f.,* and *g.* Reveal some of the missionary activities of the Society. Review of *b.,* G. L. Burr, *A.H.R.* 13:850, July 1908; 19:143, Oct. 1913; of *c.,* G. L. Burr, *A.H.R.* 15:845, July 1910; 19:143, Oct. 1913; P. Smith, *A.H.R.* 28:736, July 1923; 31:512, Apr. 1926; of *e.,* B. C. Steiner, *A.H.R.* 13:597, Apr. 1908; 16:143, Oct. 1910; 23:662, Apr. 1918.   *h.* By a secular priest; emphasizes political activities, especially of Parsons; inadequate as general account of subject. Review, A. L. Cross, *A.H.R.* 8:130, Oct. 1902.   GMD

MISSIONS

Only a few distinctive works are included here for review. See above, Library collections, and (F29) *The Encyclopaedia of missions;* (F41d) *World atlas of Christian Missions;* (F242) Harnack, *Mission and expansion of Christianity;* (F291) Robinson, *Conversion of Europe.*

F451 Robinson, Charles H. *History of Christian missions.* Edinburgh and N. Y., 1915. [International theological library.]

Canon Robinson, editorial secretary of the Society for the Propagation of the Gospel in Foreign Parts and editor of *The East and the West* has produced one of the best single-volume histories of missions yet written. Restricted mainly to modern times and to Protestant missions; very uneven in value, but marked by the discriminating insight of a ripe scholar in mission statesmanship. Review. W. D. Mackenzie, *International Rev. of Missions,* 4:668, Oct. 1915.   DJF

F452 Dennis, James S. *Christian missions and social progress; a sociological study of foreign missions.* 3 v. N. Y., 1897–1906. Statistical supplement. *Centennial survey of foreign missions,* N. Y., 1902. (Bibliographies.)

Sociological survey; deals with modern conditions; forms a thesaurus of facts connected with the modern missionary movement and an index to a broad range of missionary history. Review, v. 1, W. E. Griffis, *Amer. Jour. of Theol.* 2:707, July 1898; v. 2, W. E. Griffis, *ibid.,* 4:231, Jan. 1900; v. 3, A. K. Parker, *ibid.* 11:362, Apr. 1907; supplement, A. K. Parker, *ibid.,* 7:193, Jan. 1903.   WHA

INSTITUTIONAL HISTORY

F531 Hatch, Edwin. *Organization of the early Christian churches.* 1882. 5th ed., 1895; reprint, London and N. Y., 1909. [Bampton lectures.]

The principal contribution lies in the suggestion that the position of the bishop, as it was in the year 200, was caused by the ordinary usage of societies at that time plus the effect of duties, charitable and religious, which the bishop was called upon to discharge. Review, *Bibliotheca Sacra,* 40:398, Apr. 1883.   HBW

F532a Lightfoot, Joseph B. *Christian ministry.* London, 1901. [Reprint of pp. 179–267 of his ed. of *Saint Paul's Epistle to the Philippians,* 1868; rev. ed., London, 1913.]

   b Sohm, Rudolph. *Kirchenrecht.* 2 v. München, 1892–1923. Reprint of v. 1, 1923; v. 2, ed. by E. Jacobi and O. Mayer. [Binding, Systematisches Handbuch der deutschen Rechtswissenschaft.] (Bibliography.)

   c Lowrie, Walter. *Church and its organization in primitive and catholic times: an interpretation of Rudolph Sohm's 'Kirchenrecht.'* V. 1, *Primitive age.* N. Y. and London, 1904.

   d Lindsay, Thomas M. *Church and the ministry in the early centuries.* London, 1902. [Cunningham lectures.]

   e Harnack, Adolf von. *Constitution and law of the church in the first two centuries.* London and N. Y., 1910. [Crown theological library.] Tr. by F. L. Pogson and ed. by H. D. A. Major from *Entstehung und Entwickelung der Kirchenverfassung und des Kirchenrechts in den zwei ersten Jahrhunderten,* Leipzig, 1910.

a. Investigation into the origin of the ministry, especially the episcopate. *b.* Exposition of the historical foundations of church polity. *c.* Primarily an exposition of *b.;* presses through some of its conclusions to an extreme almost revolutionary. *d.* Lays special emphasis upon the transitions in the ministry, especially in the direction of official functions. Review of *c.* and *d.,* with consideration of *b.,* A. V. G. Allen, *Amer. Jour. of Theol.* 8:799, Oct. 1904. *e.* In part an enlargement of the article on 'Verfassung, Kirchliche, . . .' in (F23a) *Realencyklopädie;* and in part a criticism of Sohm's views in *b.,* but more specifically as later elaborated in 'Wesen und Ursprung des Katholizismus,' Leipzig, 1909. [Abhandlungen der Philologisch-Historische Klasse der Königlichen Sächsischen Gesellschaft der Wissenschaften.] Review of *e.,* C. H. Walker, *Amer. Jour. of Theol.* 16:122, Jan. 1912.   JBA, WHA

F536 Allen, Alexander V. G. *Christian institutions.* N. Y., 1897. [International theological library.]

Convenient work; comprehensive in selection of topics; not limited to the period of the early church. The term 'Christian institutions' includes the organization or government, creeds, and worship of the Church. The author shows how these institutions, in their origin and in their development to modern times, 'are related to the spiritual life and to the growth of civilization.' The views are, in general, similar to those set forth in (F641, F242, F532e) more extended works of Harnack. Review, B. O. True, *Amer. Jour. of Theol.* 2:696, July 1898; E. K. Mitchell, *A.H.R.* 3:523, Apr. 1898.   GWRI

F541a Hefele, Carl J. von. *History of the Christian councils,* 5 v. (to 787). Edinburgh, 1871–96. 2nd rev. ed. of v. 1, 1894. Tr. and ed. by W. R. Clark, H. N. Oxenham, and E. H. Plumptre from *Conciliengeschichte,* 7 v., Freiburg, 1855–74; 2nd ed., 6 v., 1873–90. Continued (to 1534) by Joseph, Cardinal Hergenröther, v. 8–9, 1887–90. Also tr. from 2nd ed. and augmented by H. Leclercq, *Histoire des conciles,* v. 1–7 in 14 v., Paris, 1907–18. (Bibliographies.)

b Blatchford, Ambrose N. *Church councils and their decrees.* London and Boston, 1909.

a. Classic history of the councils of the church; an outstanding monument in ecclesiastical historiography. Presents in detail the circumstances under which the several councils met; gives the texts of their canons interwoven with the author's explanations; the interpretation is that dominant in the Vatican Council in which both author and continuator participated. Review, v. 8–9, E. Bacha, *Rev. des Quest. Hist.* 49:653, 1891.   *b.* Brief, indeed meagre, account of the more important councils, possibly with over-emphasis on the defects of the councils. For the councils of the fourth and fifth centuries, inferior to (F123, v. 3) Dubose, *Ecumenical councils.*   WHA

F546a Goyau, Georges, and others. *Le Vatican, les papes, et la civilisation, le gouvernement central de l'église.* Paris, 1895.

b Hilling, Nicholas. *Procedure at the Roman curia, a concise and practical handbook.* N. Y., 1907. Adapted tr. from *Die römische Kurie, ein kurzes Handbuch für die Kenntnis der gegenwärtigen Verfassung,* Paderborn, 1906.

c Mater, André. *L'église catholique, sa constitution, son administration.* Paris, 1906. (Bibliographies.)

a. Learned treatise on the church and the papacy; complete synthesis of what each has been and has done in the world from the beginning of Christianity up to our day. At the same time a work of history, of philosophy, of art and literature. Review, *Polybiblion,* 73:57, 1895.   PG

b. Concise, practical handbook of the organization and procedure of officials at the papal court; relates to the church as organized by the Council of Trent; intended to be helpful to a visitor at Rome; gives the Latin text of a number of important papal documents.   SBF

c. Analytical description of the organization of the Roman Catholic Church. The functions of the several officers and various features of organized activities are explained. The chapters on parochial organization, with their discussion of lay participation, are especially illuminating.   WHA

F551 Tardif, Adolph. *Histoire des sources du droit canonique.* Paris, 1887.

Hardly more than an introduction, but probably the most serviceable single volume as a guide to this important subject. Review, *Polybiblion,* 102:424, 1888.
                                                                        PG

F552 Zollmann, Carl. *American civil church law.* N. Y., 1917. [Columbia University studies in history, economics, and public law.]

Exhaustive study of the relations between church and state in America, especially in the field of law in which the interests of church and state come into contact and where they overlap. Religious liberty, incorporation of churches, schism, church decisions, tax exemption, and status of the clergy are among the subjects treated. Review, R. E. Cushman, *Amer. Pol. Sci. Rev.* 12:726, Nov. 1918.   WHA

F556 Watkins, Oscar D. *History of penance being a study of the authorities: (A) for the whole church to A. D. 450, (B) for the western church from A. D. 450 to A. D. 1215.* 2 v. London and N. Y., 1920.

Work of great learning and research with significant extracts from most documents bearing upon the subject. Each volume concludes with a summary review of the practice of penance for the period and region covered.   WHA

F557 Krehbiel, Edward B. *The interdict, its history and its operation, with especial attention to the time of Pope Innocent III, 1198–1216.* [American Historical Association, Adams prize essay.] (Bibliography.)

Good monograph; pays special attention to the scope of the interdict. Review, D. C. Munro, *A.H.R.* 15:644, Apr. 1910.   WHA

F561a Lea, Henry C. *History of the inquisition of the middle ages.* 3 v. N. Y., 1888. Tr. by S. Reinach as *Histoire de l'inquisition au moyen âge* from a copy revised and corrected by the author, 2 v., Paris, 1900–01.

b —— *Historical sketch of sacerdotal celibacy in the Christian church.* 1867. 3rd rev. ed., 2 v., N. Y. and London, 1907. (Bibliographical footnotes.)

c —— *History of auricular confession and indulgences in the Latin church.* 3 v. Philadelphia, 1896.

d —— *Studies in church history: the rise of the temporal power, benefit of clergy, excommunication, the early church and slavery.* 1869. 2nd ed., Philadelphia, 1883.

Lea's works constitute the most important contribution to European history made by any American scholar. They are based on original sources, and owe less than most histories to the investigations of other scholars. Lea's independence of judgment is fortified by great critical ability and a vast knowledge of medieval literature. *a.* Only important work on this subject; so thoroughly done that little has been left for later investigators beyond supplying additional details. Review, Lord Acton, *E.H.R.* 3:773, Oct. 1888. *b.* Good historical treatment of the subject. Review, *Quar. Rev.* 127:514, Oct. 1869. *c.* Vast mass of materials of the highest value; difficulties of organization and interpretation make it the least satisfactory of the author's works. Review, E. Emerton, *A.H.R.* 2:113, Oct. 1896. *d.* Especially valuable for the essay on excommunication.

For very adverse criticism, cf. P. M. Baumgarten, *Henry Charles Lea's historical writings: a critical inquiry into their method and merit,* N. Y., 1909. For other writings of H. C. Lea, cf. (N621a) *History of the inquisition of Spain;* (Y621) *Inquisition in the Spanish dependencies;* (N621b) *Chapters from the religious history of Spain connected with the inquisition;* (N263) *Moriscos of Spain, their conversion and expulsion;* and (H552) *Superstition and force.* Also, cf. (F562).   ACH

F562a Turberville, Arthur S. *Mediaeval heresy and the inquisition.* London, 1920. (Bibliography.)

b Vacandard, Elphège. *The inquisition, a critical and historical study of the coercive power of the church.* 1908. New ed., N. Y., 1915. Tr. by B. L. Conway from 2nd ed. of *L'inquisition, étude historique et critique sur le pouvoir coercitif de l'église,* 1907; 5th ed., Paris, 1909.

c **Fredericq, Paul,** ed. *Corpus documentorum inquisitionis haereticae pravitatis Neerlandicae: verzameling van stukken betreffende de pauselijke en bisschoppelijke inquisitie in de Nederlanden.* 5 v. Gent, 1889–1906.

a. Summarizes results of investigations since (F561) Lea's monumental works and deals more specifically with the doctrinal basis, especially the underlying doctrinal reasons for intolerance by medieval ecclesiastical authority. Averrhoism, Wyclifitism, and Hussitism are specifically treated. Review, *E.H R.* 36:144, Jan. 1921.   *b.* Careful study by a Roman Catholic scholar, very useful to supplement (F561) Lea's works, although not explicitly an answer to Lea. The abuses of and through the Inquisition are represented as individual or, if institutional, as non-ecclesiastical. Review, *Ecclesiastical Rev.* 39:103, July 1908. *c.* Important collection of documents of special interest in connection with (Q301) Motley, *Rise of the Dutch Republic.*   WHA

CULTURAL HISTORY: DOCTRINE, THOUGHT

F641a **Harnack, Adolf von.** *History of dogma.* 7 v. London and Boston, 1895–1900. [Theological translation library.] Tr. by N. Buchanan and others from 3rd ed. of *Lehrbuch der Dogmengeschichte,* 1886–90; 3rd rev. ed., 3 v., Freiburg, 1894–97; 6th ed., 3 v., Tübingen, 1922.

b ──── *Outlines of the history of dogma.* N. Y. 1893. Tr. by E. K. Mitchell from *Grundriss der Dogmengeschichte,* 1889–91; 6th ed., Tübingen, 1922. [Grundriss der theologischen Wissenschaften.]

c **Seeberg, Reinhold.** *Text-book of the history of doctrines.* 2 v. Philadelphia, 1905. Tr. by C. E. Hay from *Lehrbuch der Dogmengeschichte,* 2 v., 1895–98; 2nd-3rd rev. ed., 4 v. in 5, Leipzig, 1913–23.

d **Loofs, Friedrich.** *Leitfaden für seine Vorlesungen über Dogmengeschichte,* 1889. 4th rev. ed., *Leitfaden zum Studium der Dogmengeschichte,* Halle, 1906. (Bibliographical foot-notes.)

a. Monumental work; still the most valuable history of dogma. Its chief merits are its comprehensive survey of the whole field under discussion, its luminous analysis of the problems, its clear distinction between primary and secondary questions, and the wealth of learning and insight which are packed into its notes. Its limitations consist in the restricted nature of its subject-matter and the large amount of valuable material which is put into notes rather than in the text. Those who desire a history of theology which carries the subject down to the present will not find it in Harnack. In estimating the value of his work it must be remembered that he has not written the history of theology in general, but of dogma, that is, of those doctrines which have been made part of the authoritative teaching of the church. Hence much more space is given to the earlier period than to the later. V. 1 and 2 of the original carry the story only to the end of the trinitarian and christological controversies; v. 3, begins with Augustine and includes both the medieval and modern periods. The section on Protestantism is least satisfactory, but the whole work abounds in suggestion and stimulus and can be neglected by no one who desires to understand the history of thought in this most important field. *b.* Abridgment of *a.*   *c.* Covers about the same ground as *a.,* but from a more conservative point of view. Review, W. W. Rockwell, *Jour. of Religion,* 2:321, May 1922.   *d.* Excellent abstract, at some length, of the whole development; more serviceable than *b.*   WAB

F642 Fisher, George P. *History of Christian doctrine.* N. Y., 1896. [International theological library.]

A history of theology as well as of doctrine and dogma; extends into late nineteenth century; 'Modern theology' occupies over half the space. Expounds the principal thinkers with sound knowledge and insight, in compact, lucid style, with brief biographical notes and many short quotations. Fair-minded, not biased by theory or enthusiasms. Good treatment of the influence of philosophy, but not of other features of intellectual environment. A vast amount of information crowds the volume, which is for reference rather than continuous reading. Review, E. K. Mitchell, *A.H.R.* 2:332, Jan. 1897. RHN

F643a Gibbons, James, Cardinal. *Faith of our fathers, being a plain exposition and vindication of the church founded by Our Lord Jesus Christ.* 1876. 94th ed., Baltimore, 1925.

b Tixeront, Joseph. *History of dogmas.* 3 v. St. Louis, 1910–16. Tr. by H. L. Brianceau from 5th ed. of *Histoire des dogmes,* 3 v., Paris, 1905–12. [Bibliothèque de l'enseignement de l'histoire ecclésiastique.]

a. Clear and attractive presentation in popular, but authoritative, form of the principal tenets of the Roman Catholic Church by the late Cardinal Archbishop of Baltimore. *b.* Extends to the time of Charlemagne; by one of the earliest pupils of Duchesne, cf. (F221). Review, F. A. Christie, *A.H.R.* 19:390, Jan. 1914. SBF

F646 Hatch, Edwin. *Influence of Greek ideas and usages upon the Christian church.* Ed. by A. M. Fairbairn. 1890. 2nd ed., London, 1891. [Hibbert lectures.]

Principal attention is given to the relation of Greek religious, ethical, and philosophical thought to the theology and thought of the early church. Of special importance is the tenth lecture on the relation of the mystery cults to the development of Christian usages. Gave a stimulus to the study of Christian origins which was almost epoch-making. Review, *Expository Times,* 2:194, June 1891. GMD

F651a Workman, Herbert B. *Christian thought to the reformation.* London and N. Y., 1911. [Studies in theology.] (Select bibliography.)

b McGiffert, Arthur C. *Protestant thought before Kant.* London and N. Y., 1911. [Studies in theology.] (Bibliography.)

c Moore, Edward C. *Outline of the history of Christian thought since Kant.* N. Y., 1912. [Studies in theology.] (Bibliography.)

d McGiffert, Arthur C. *Rise of modern religious ideas.* N. Y., 1915.

a., b., and *c.* Series constituting a brief survey of the progress of Christian thought from the close of the apostolic age to the present. Brevity, competency in scholarship, and clarity of style attract the busy pastor and general reader for whom the series is primarily intended. Cf. (I232a) Beard, *Reformation of the sixteenth century.* Review of *a., Amer. Jour. of Theol.* 16:150, Jan. 1912; of *b., Westminster Rev.* 175:702, June 1911; of *c.,* E. Gates, *Amer. Jour. of Theol.* 17:296, Apr. 1913. *d.* Deals with the theological reconstruction of the second half of the nineteenth century, brought about by the collapse of older conceptions of God, nature, and the Bible. The disintegration of the older orthodoxy is traced while the movement toward reconstruction is followed through the idealistic philosophy, the rehabilitation of faith, and the principle of evolution to new ideas of God, a new social emphasis, and a new concept of authority in religion. Suggestive and helpful to those interested in the problems of readjustment. Review, A. C. Watson, *Amer. Jour. of Theol.* 20:305, Apr. 1916.

HHW

F652a Baudrillart, Alfred. *Catholic church, the renaissance, and protestantism.* London, 1908. [International Catholic library.] Tr. by Mrs. P. Gibbs from *L'église catholique, la renaissance, le protestantisme*, Paris, 1904.

b Balmes, Jaime Luciano. *Protestantism and catholicity compared in their effects on the civilization of Europe.* 1849. 10th ed., Baltimore, 1868. Tr. by C. J. Hanford and R. Kershaw from the French version (3 v., 1842–44) of *El protestantismo comparado con el catolicismo en sus relaciones con la civilizatión Europea,* 3 v., 1842–44; 6th ed., Barcelona, 1879.

c Troeltsch, Ernest. *Protestantism and progress, a historical study of the relation of protestantism to the modern world.* London and N. Y., 1912. [Crown theological library.] Tr. by W. Montgomery from *Die Bedeutung des Protestantismus für die Entstehung der modernen Welt,* München, 1911. [Historische Bibliothek.]

d Cadoux, Cecil John. *Catholicism and Christianity; a vindication of progressive Protestantism.* London, 1928.

a. Lectures intended as an interpretation of the influence of the Renaissance upon both Roman Catholicism and Protestantism. Turgidity of thought in the French may be responsible in part for a similar quality in the translation. Review, *Dublin Rev.* 144:428, Apr. 1909. WHA

b. Reply to (B602) Guizot, *History of civilization;* written in a broad spirit of philosophical and historical inquiry and interpretation. Review, (B23c) Larousse, *Grand Dictionnaire,* 13:309. GMD

c. Modern Protestantism, 'the religious metaphysic of freedom and of a faith based on personal conviction,' is here differentiated from early Protestantism, considered essentially medieval. Protestantism is studied in relation to politico-social institutions, economic organization, science, art, and religious feeling, and pronounced the form of religion most consonant with the modern spirit. Review, F. Palmer, *Harvard Theol. Rev.* 7:277, Apr. 1914. RHN

d. Most thorough survey of the historical, theological and ethical claims of Roman Catholicism using the presuppositions of liberal Protestanism as the baseline for measurements. Fully documented. A real contribution to the history of authority in religion. Review, (London) *Times Lit. Suppl.,* 27:976, Dec. 13, 1928.

WHA

F656a Harnack, Adolf von. *What is Christianity?* London and N. Y., 1901. [Theological translation library.] Tr. by T. B. Saunders from *Das Wesen des Christentums.* Leipzig, 1900. Later reprints.

b Loisy, Alfred. *The gospel and the church.* London, 1903. Tr. by C. Home from *L'évangile et l'église,* Paris, 1902.

c *Programme of modernism: a reply to the encyclical of Pius X, Pascendi dominici gregis, with the text of the encyclical in an English version, translated from the Italian by Rev. Father George Tyrrell, with an introduction by A. Leslie Lilley.* N. Y. and London, 1908. [Crown theological library.]

a. Interpretation, by an advanced German Protestant scholar, of the essential meaning and significance of Christ's teaching; stimulated considerable contemporary controversial literature, of which *b* is perhaps the most important. Review, G. B. Smith, *Amer. Jour. of Theol.* 7:182, Jan. 1903. *b.* Criticism of *a* by an eminent Roman Catholic modernist, a French Dominican, who attempted to bring Roman Catholic teaching into harmony with evolution and other modern doctrines, especially with the methods and results of historical criticism. *c.* Full translation of encyclical of Pius X against modernism, with a statement which is both an interpretation of modernism and a criticism of the papal interpretation in the encyclical. Review, H. C. Corrance, *Hibbert Jour.* 6:930, July 1908.

WHA

CULTURAL HISTORY: LITERATURE

F661a Krüger, Gustav. *History of early Christian literature in the first three centuries.* London and N. Y., 1897. Tr. by C. R. Gillett from *Geschichte der altchristlichen Litteratur in den ersten drei Jahrhunderten,* 1895; 2nd rev. ed., Freiburg, 1898.

b Harnack, Adolf von. *Geschichte der altchristlichen Litteratur bis Eusebius.* 2 pt. in 3 v., Leipzig, 1893–1904.

c Bardenhewer, Otto. *Geschichte der altkirchlichen Literatur.* 4 v. 1902–24. 2nd ed., Freiburg, 1913–24.

d Tixeront, Joseph. *Handbook of patrology.* 1920. 2nd ed., St. Louis, 1923. (Useful bibliographies.) Tr. from 4th French ed. of *Précis de patrologie,* Paris, 1918.

e Gebhardt, Oscar von; Harnack, Adolf von; and Schmidt, Carl, ed. *Texte und Untersuchungen zur Geschichte der altchristlichen Literatur.* 36 v. Leipzig, 1883–1913.

a. Accurate and complete; great wealth of scholarship compressed into brief notices of the various writings and their authors. Not to be used as an introduction or short-cut to a knowledge of the subject; but, to gather up and clarify the results of other reading, it is indispensable. English translation is excellent. Review, E. C. Richardson, *Presbyterian and Reformed Rev.* 9:171, Jan. 1898.

EFS

b. Outstanding Protestant work; especially valuable for location of manuscripts and discussion of chronology. *c.* Comprehensive survey; by an eminent Roman Catholic scholar. *d.* Unusually attractive presentation of what has usually been considered rather dreary material. The author's critical temper is admirable; full weight seems to be given to modern scholarship. *e.* Comprises a series of monographs, texts, critical discussions, and some extended treatises; invaluable for intensive study of the early literature. WHA

F671a Putnam, George Haven. *Censorship of the church of Rome and its influence upon the production and the distribution of literature; a study of the history of the prohibitory and expurgatory indexes, together with some consideration of the effects of protestant censorship and of censorship by the state.* 2 v. N. Y. and London, 1906–07. (Bibliography.)

b Reusch, Franz H. *Index der verbotenen Bücher, ein Beitrag zur Kirchen- und Literaturgeschichte.* 2 v. Bonn, 1883–85.

a. Best work in English on the subject; acknowledges its debt to *b,* which is a monumental work; lists books forbidden before 1500, and Italian, Dutch, Spanish, and papal indexes down to the second index of Leo XIII in 1900. Review, D. M. McIntyre, *Rev. of Theol. and Phil.* 3:225, Oct. 1907. DSS

CULTURAL HISTORY: ART AND LITURGY

F681 Strzyowski, Josef. *Origin of Christian church art: new facts and principles of research.* Oxford, 1923. (Bibliography.) Tr. by O. M. Dalton and H. J. Braunholtz from *Ursprung der christlichen Kirchenkunst.* Leipzig, 1920. [Olaus-Petri Foundation lectures, Upsala.]

Result of painstaking research into the genetics of Christian art; a book of which the author says it 'marks a pause, it is retrospective.' Attempts to free the history of art from 'false methods' whether philological, historical, philosophical, or esthetic. The discussion of the relations between representational and non-representational art is an especially valuable contribution to the history of the church. A chapter on 'Hiberno-Saxon Art in the time of Bede' has been added to the lectures. Review, C. H. Moore, *Architectural Record,* 56:375, Oct. 1924. WHA

F682a Duchesne, Louis Marie Olivier. *Christian worship: its origin and evolution: a study of the Latin liturgy up to the time of Charlemagne.* London and N. Y., 1903. Tr. from 3rd ed. of *Origines du culte chrétien: étude sur la liturgie latine avant Charlemagne.*

b Cabrol, T. R. Fernand. *Origines liturgiques.* Paris, 1906.

There seems to be no comprehensive work covering the history of all important phases of the Christian liturgy. Encyclopedias are the chief resource. Cf. F21 ff, especially F27b. While *a* is limited to the Latin church from the fourth to the ninth century, it covers a broad range of liturgical interest and is replete with specific historical information in this field. *b.* More philosophical and interpretative; its appendices are especially valuable historical contributions. WHA

BIOGRAPHIES

Probably no division of history is richer in biographical material than is church history, especially in its extension to cover the history of Christianity. The numerous biographical works on modern missions, in addition to their value for religious history, afford important contributions to the general history of many lands and peoples. As the primary importance of most biographies is clearly regional, these works are regularly to be sought in the appropriate section of this *Guide.* In those cases where the activities of the individual entered largely into the general history of his time the volumes concerning him are listed in the sections devoted to special periods.

In this section there are listed, in addition to lives of the more important popes, biographies of a few individuals whose activities were not confined to any particular country but belonged distinctly to the broader history of the church. There are also included the titles of some of the more important collective works of ecclesiastical biography and of biographies of eminent churchmen, chiefly of England and the United States which have not been included elsewhere. These latter have been selected primarily because of their value as methods of approach to important movements in the church rather than from consideration of the intrinsic value of the biography or of the importance of the individual who is its subject.

F701 Benson, Edward W. *Cyprian: his life, his times, his work.* London and N. Y., 1897. (Bibliography.)

Standard biography of Cyprian in English; the product of indefatigable industry in historical research as an avocation. The career of Cyprian is utilized as a revelation of the religious forces and movements of the third century, with well-balanced attention to sentiments as well as institutions. Invaluable for the study of persecution, the monarchic episcopate, and the element of unity in Catholicism. Review, F. Johnson, *Amer. Jour. of Theol.* 2:422, Apr. 1898.

WHA

F702a Bertrand, Louis. *Saint Augustine.* London and N. Y., 1914. Tr. by V. O'Sullivan from *Saint Augustin,* Paris, 1913.

b McCabe, Joseph. *Saint Augustine and his age.* London, 1902; N. Y., 1903. (Bibliography.)

a. Written from a sympathetic standpoint; based upon a study of the sources; highly eulogistic and tends at times to overstretch the scant historical facts by the power of a fervid imagination and gift of word painting. Attempts to reconstruct the historical framework for the figure of the hero. Suggestive and interesting, but not the product of profound scholarship. Review, *Nation (N. Y.),* 98:699, June 11, 1914. *b.* Sympathetic, balanced, and fascinating treatment of a great life. Consideration is given to the political, intellectual, and social background of the age and against this is projected the figure of the man himself. The volume is more than a biography; it pilots the reader through the currents and counter-currents of a period of challenging interest in the history of the church. Review, *Nation (N. Y.)* 76:318, Apr. 16, 1903. HHW

For a very complete bibliography on Augustine of Hippo, cf. article by E. Portalié in (F25) *Catholic encyclopedia,* 2:84 ff. For principal works of Augustine, translated into English, cf. (F71b) *Select library of the Nicene and post-Nicene fathers.* For Augustine as a theologian, cf. (F641) histories of dogma, especially (F641a) Harnack, *History of Dogma,* v. 5.

F703 Mann, Horace K. *Lives of the popes in the early middle ages.* 15 v. London, 1902–29.

By the leading English Roman Catholic authority in this field, who has usually worked from the sources, but without utilizing all the German secondary literature. Covers thus far Gregory I to Gregory X inclusive. The two volumes on Innocent III are as full a treatment as can be found in English. WWR

F704a Dudden, Frederick Homes. *Gregory the Great, his place in history and thought.* 2 v. London and N. Y., 1905. (Bibliographical preface.)

b Howorth, Sir Henry H. *Saint Gregory the Great.* London, 1912.

c Barmby, James. *Gregory the Great.* 1879. Reprint, London and N. Y., 1908. [The Fathers for English readers.]

a. Fullest life of Gregory the Great in English; by the chief Anglican authority on the subject. Review, *E.H.R.* 21:760, Oct. 1906. *b.* Pays special attention to archeological evidence. Review, *E.H.R.* 28:554, July 1913. *c.* Brief, popular life by an Anglican.

Also cf. (F703) Mann, *Lives of the popes of the early middle ages,* and for valuable bibliography, (F25) *Catholic encyclopedia,* 6:787. WWR

F705a Mathew, Arnold H. *Life and times of Hildebrand, Pope Gregory VII.* London, 1910. (Brief bibliography.)

b Stephens, William R. W. *Hildebrand and his times.* London and N. Y., 1898. Later reprints. [(F122) Epochs of church history.]

c Fliche, Augustin. *Saint Grégoire VII.* Paris, 1920. [Les saints.]

d —— *Les Prégrégoriens, études sur la polémique religieuse à l'époque de Grégoire VII.* Paris, 1916. (Bibliographies.)

Both *a* and *b*, though often made to serve 'as a brief account in English,' are very unsatisfactory. *a.* Though relatively recent, must be reckoned an incompetent compilation; how it seems to have been produced is shown in *Athenaeum* 1:755, June 25, 1910. *b.* Antedates much modern investigation. Review, C. C. Starbuck, *Andover Rev.* 12:673, Dec. 1889.   EWD
c. Lays emphasis upon the saintly character of Gregory; gives a highly partisan turn to the endless controversial questions in the narrative, which diminishes the usefulness of the book. *d.* Not strictly biographical but important for Gregory VII, as its thesis is that the work of Gregory was only the carrying out of ideas brought forward by his immediate predecessors. Marked by sound scholarly method.   EE

F706a Luchaire, Achille. *Innocent III.* 6 v. Paris, 1904–08. [1, *Rome et l'Italie,* 3rd ed., Paris, 1907; 2, *La croisade des Albigeois,* 2nd ed., Paris, 1906; 3, *La papauté et l'empire;* 4, *La question d'Orient;* 5, *Les royautés vassales du Saint-Siège;* 6, *Le concile de Latran et la réforme de l'église.*] (Bibliography.)

b Pirie-Gordon, Charles H. C. *Innocent the Great, an essay on his life and times.* London and N. Y., 1907. (Bibliography.)

a. Each volume deals with some large aspect of Innocent III's pontificate; all are small, have few notes, and display little sign otherwise of the erudition back of them. 'My aim,' the author said to critics, 'was not to be useful to a few dozen scholars, but to give people concerned about the past a clear understanding of the action of a great medieval pope.' That aim he achieved most worthily. Review, v. 1, E. Barker, *E.H.R.* 20:358, Apr. 1905; v. 2, T. F. Tout, *ibid.,* 21:615, July 1906; v. 4, E. Barker, *ibid.* 23:126, Jan. 1908; v. 5–6, E. Barker, *ibid.* 25:196, Jan. 1910. *b.* For its various shortcomings, cf. review, E. B. Krehbiel, *A.H.R.* 13:564, Apr. 1908.   EWD

F707a Jörgensen, Johannes. *Saint Francis of Assisi, a biography.* 1912. Rev. ed., N. Y., 1922. Tr. by T. O. Sloane from the Danish. (Valuable bibliography.)

b Sabatier, Paul. *Life of St. Francis of Assisi.* London and N. Y., 1894. Tr. by L. S. Houghton from *Vie de Saint-François d'Assise,* Paris, 1894. Many reprints of tr. and original.

c Cuthbert, Father (Hess, Lawrence Cuthbert). *Life of St. Francis of Assisi.* London and N. Y., 1912.

a. Perhaps the most scholarly life of St. Francis; utilizes results of recent intensive research pertaining to St. Francis and the Franciscans. Review, P. Robinson, *A.H.R.* 18:121, Oct. 1912. *b.* By the foremost Protestant authority on St. Francis; gave great stimulus to further studies. Sabatier is clear-sighted enough to see some things blended which other interpreters of St. Francis have seen only as good or bad. Review, A. G. Little, *E.H.R.* 9:747, Oct. 1894. *c.*

Sympathetic and suggestive; offers little new information. Review, *Nation*
(N. Y.), 97:312, Oct. 2, 1913.   WHA

F708a Jarrett, Bede. *Life of St. Dominic, 1170–1221.* London and N. Y., 1924.
b Guiraud, Jean. *Saint Dominic.* London, 1901. [The saints.] Tr. by
K. de Mattos from *Saint Dominique, 1170–1221,* 1898; 4th ed., Paris,
1901. [Les saints.]

c Drane, Augusta T. *History of St. Dominic, founder of the Friars
Preachers.* London and N. Y., 1891. 6th ed. (n.d.)

d Herkless, Sir John. *Francis and Dominic and the mendicant orders.*
London and N. Y., 1901. [World's epoch makers.] (Bibliography.)

It has been said that 'St. Dominic cannot be made a popular figure,' and no
fully satisfactory biography of him has yet appeared. *a.* Most recent fairly
creditable biography; by a writer who has published other studies in Dominican
history. *b.* Obviously the work of a Dominican protagonist; deficient in all
aspects outside the range of ultramontane interests, but admirable within that
range. *c.* In no sense a critical biography; as a character study its appeal is
limited. The historical sketch of the Dominican Order is more objective. *d.*
Not comparable with the larger biographies; better for St. Dominic than for
St. Francis; an interesting study. Review, *A.H.R.* 7:395, Jan. 1902.   WHA

F709a Loyola, Ignacio De. *Autobiography.* Tr. and ed. by John F. X. O'Conor.
N. Y., 1900. There are other English editions of this work, of which
the original was printed in (F801) *Acta sanctorum* and in the *Scripta*
of Saint Ignatius.

b —— *Spiritual exercises, Spanish and English, with a continuous commentary.* N. Y. 1916. Ed. and tr. by Joseph Rickaby from *Exercitia
spiritualia* [tr. from Spanish ms. by A. Frusius], Romae, 1548. Numerous other editions and translations.

c Joly, Henri. *Saint Ignatius of Loyola.* 1899. 2nd ed., London, 1906.
[The saints.] Tr. by M. Partridge from *Saint Ignace de Loyola,* Paris,
1898. [Les saints.]

d Thompson, Francis. *Saint Ignatius Loyola.* Ed. by John H. Pollen.
2nd ed., London and N. Y., 1910.

e Gothein, Eberhard. *Ignatius von Loyola und die Gegenreformation.*
Halle, 1895.

f McCabe, Joseph. *Candid history of the Jesuits.* London and N. Y.,
1913.

g Sedgwick, Henry D. *Ignatius Loyola, an attempt at an impartial biography.* N. Y., 1923.

h Van Dyke, Paul. *Ignatius Loyola, the founder of the Jesuits.* N. Y.,
1926.

a. and *b.* Important for the light they throw on the character of St. Ignatius.
c. Interpretative biography; subordinates the record of events to an analysis
of the character and motives of the saint. Style, clear and simple; rather
apologetic. Review, *Rev. des Quest. Hist.* 65:631, Apr. 1899. *d.* Most spiritedly
written and artistic life of Ignatius in English; a eulogy rather than a work
of critical scholarship, attractively illustrated.   APE
e. Sympathetic and scholarly effort by a German Protestant, to give a sound
account of the founder of the Jesuits and of their influence in the sixteenth
century. *f.* Sketch of the life of Loyola and of the later history of the Jesuits

by a former Catholic who now describes himself as neither a Catholic nor a Protestant. Review, *Nation* (N. Y.), 97:383, Oct. 23, 1913.   SBF

g. The author's effort as defined in the title seems successful. Based directly on the sources; presents the most important criticisms. Not a history of the Society of Jesus except in its earlier phases, but pays considerable attention to the most important of Loyola's immediate associates. Review, C. H. A. Wager, *Nation* (N. Y.), 118:652, June 4, 1924. *h.* Makes good use of the sources, but perhaps discounts too generously his own Protestantism, becoming almost over-sympathetic. Review, P. Smith, *A.H.R.* 32:587, Apr. 1927.   WHA

F710a Walker, Williston. *John Calvin, the organizer of reformed protestantism, 1509–1564.* N. Y. and London, 1906. [Heroes of the reformation.] (Critical bibliography.)

   b Reyburn, Hugh Y. *John Calvin, his life, letters, and work.* London and N. Y., 1914. (Bibliography.)

   c Doumergue, Émile. *Jean Calvin: les hommes et les choses de son temps.* 7 v. Lausanne, 1899–1927.

   d Calvin, John. *Opera.* Ed. by G. Baum, E. Cunitz and E. Reuss. 59 v. Brunsvigae, 1863–1900. [Corpus reformatorum.] (Extensive bibliographies in v. 59.)

a. Notwithstanding the mass of material published at Calvin's quatercentenary in 1909, this remains the best biography, well-balanced, candid, judicious; based on scholarly use of recent works and valuable source material. Review, *Nation* (N. Y.), 84:15, Jan. 3, 1907.   *b.* Next to *a.,* the most readable and useful. The author has used intelligently the Latin and French sources and shows keen analytical power and insight. Particularly good on Calvin after 1553, being fuller than *a.* for that period. Review, H. D. Foster, *Harvard Theol. Rev.* 8:574, Oct. 1915.   *c.* Mine of valuable material and opinion. Doumergue is a hero-worshiper, but painstaking, scholarly and frank. Review C. Borgeaud, *A.H.R.* 7:350, Jan. 1902; 9:797, July 1904; 12:127, Oct. 1906.   *d.* Standard complete edition; supersedes earlier collections; valuable for the history of the Reformation as well as for Calvin's life.

Works on Luther and Zwingli are listed in § P, and on English reformers in § L.   HDF

Collective biographical works.—(F801) *Acta sanctorum,* ed. by Jean Bollandus and others, 1. 1–67, Antwerp, Paris, etc., 1643 ff.; new ed., Paris, 1863 ff., v. 4. for November issued in 1926 carries the work to November 10 (cf. article 'Bollandists,' in (F25) *Catholic encyclopedia,* and (F801a) Hippolyte Delehaye, *Work of the Bollandists through three centuries, 1615–1915,* Princeton, N. J., 1922, tr. from *À travers trois siècles: l'oeuvre des Bollandistes, 1615–1915,* Bruxelles, 1920); (F802) Frederic W. Farrar, *Lives of the Fathers,* 2 v., Edinburgh, 1889; (F803) Sabine Baring-Gould, *Lives of the saints,* 1872–82, rev. ed., 16 v., Edinburgh, 1914; (F804) John H. Newman, *Lives of the English saints,* 1844–45; reprint, 6 v., London and N. Y., 1900–02; (F805) Agnes B. C. Dunbar, *Dictionary of saintly women,* 2 v., London, 1904–05; (F806) Ferdinand Piper, *Lives of the leaders of our church universal,* with additions and tr. by H. M. MacCracken, Philadelphia, 1879, reprint as *Lives of church leaders,* Cleveland, Ohio, 1900, abridged tr. from *Die Zeugen der Wahrheit,* 4 v., Leipzig, 1873–75; (F807) Annie E. McKilliam, *Chronicle of the popes from St. Peter to Pius X,* London 1912; (F808) William Cowan, *Pre-Reformation worthies,* London, 1897;

(F809) Anne Macdonnell, *Sons of Francis,* London and N. Y., 1902; (F810) Samuel E. Herrick, *Some heretics of yesterday,* Boston, 1885; (F811) Charles Platts, *Pioneers of our faith,* London, 1910.

(F821) Christopher Wordsworth, *Ecclesiastical biography, or lives of eminent men connected with the history of religion in England from the commencement of the Reformation to the Revolution,* 1810, 4th rev. ed., 4 v., London, 1853; (F822) Sir James Stephen, *Essays in ecclesiastical biography,* 1849, reprint, 2 v., London and N. Y., 1907; (F823) Samuel Parkes Cadman, *Three religious leaders of Oxford,* N. Y., 1916; (F824) Algernon Cecil, *Six Oxford thinkers,* London, 1909; (F825) Augustus B. Donaldson, *Five great Oxford leaders,* London, 1900; (F826) Charles S. Isaacson, *Story of the English cardinals,* London, 1907; (F827) Alfred Barry, ed., *Masters in English theology,* London, 1877; (F828) Albert H. Currier, *Nine great preachers,* Boston, 1912; (F829) Sir William Robertson Nicoll, *Princes of the church,* 1921, 3rd ed., London, 1921; (F830) Arthur C. Benson, *Leaves of the tree: studies in biography,* London and N. Y., 1911; (F831) Harold Begbie, *Painted Windows: studies in religious personality,* N. Y., 1922.

(F841) William B. Sprague, *Annals of the American pulpit,* 9 v., N. Y., 1857–69; (F842) Daniel D. Addison, *Clergy in American life and letters,* N. Y. and London, 1900; (F843) Williston Walker, *Ten New England leaders,* Boston, 1901; (F844) John W. Buckham, *Progressive religious thought in America, a survey of the enlarging Pilgrim faith,* Boston, 1919.

Biographies of individuals.—(F851) Gaetano Negri, *Julian the Apostate,* 2 v., N. Y., 1905, tr. by the Duchess Litta-Visconti-Arese from *L'imperatore Giuliano l'Apostata,* Milano, 1901; (F852) Robinson Thornton, *St. Ambrose, his life, times, and teaching,* 1879, reprint, London and N. Y., 1898; (F853) Peter Lechner, *Life and times of St. Benedict, patriarch of the monks of the west,* London and N. Y., 1900, tr. from *Leben des heiligen Benedict, Ordensstifters und ersten Abtes auf Monte Cassino,* Regensburg, 1857; (F854) Willibald, *Life of Saint Boniface,* tr. by G. W. Robinson, Cambridge, Mass., 1916 [Harvard translations]; (F855) Alfred H. Tarleton, *Nicholas Breakspear (Adrian IV), Englishman and pope,* London, 1896; (F856) Ernest Gilliat-Smith, *Saint Clare of Assisi, her life and legislation,* London and N. Y., 1914; (F857) Cecilia M. Ady, *Pius II (Aeneas Silvius Piccolomini), the humanist pope,* London, 1913; (F858) Henry C. Vedder, *Balthasar Hübmaier, the leader of the Anabaptists,* N. Y. and London, 1905 [Heroes of the Reformation].

(F881) Henry P. Liddon, *Life of Edward Bouverie Pusey,* 4 v., London and N. Y., 1893–97; (F882) Edmund S. Purcell, *Life of Cardinal Manning,* 1896, new ed., 2 v., London and N. Y., 1898; (F883) James Drummond and Charles B. Upton, *Life and letters of James Martineau,* 2 v., London and N. Y., 1902; (F884) Arthur C. Benson, *Life of Edward White Benson, sometime archbishop of Canterbury,* 2 v., London and N. Y., 1899; (F885) James S. Drummond, *Charles A. Berry, a memoir,* London, 1899; N. Y., 1900; (F886) Dorothea P. Hughes, *Life of Hugh Price Hughes,* London and N. Y., 1904; (F887) Harold Begbie, *Life of William Booth: founder of the Salvation Army,* 2 v., N. Y., 1920.

(F891) Alexander V. G. Allen, *Jonathan Edwards,* Boston, 1889; (F892) Walter Elliott, *Life of Father Hecker, founder of the Paulists,* N. Y., 1899; (F893) Peter Guilday, *Life and times of John Carroll, archbishop of Baltimore, 1735–1815,* 2 v., N. Y., 1922; (F894) Theodore T. Munger, *Horace Bushnell, preacher and theologian,* Boston, 1899; (F895) Alexander V. G. Allen, *Life and letters of Phillips Brooks,* 2 v., N. Y., 1900; (F896) A. Laveille, *Life of Cardinal Mercier,* N. Y., 1928.

WHA

SOCIETY PUBLICATIONS

(F921) *Papers,* v. 1–8, N. Y., 1888–97; 2nd series, v. 1 ff., N. Y., 1906 ff., published by the American Society of Church History, contain articles relating to the whole range of church history.

PERIODICALS

Theological journals usually devote some space to the history of ecclesiastical institutions as well as of religious thought, while Biblical journals (cf. § C) usually include the apostolic age and frequently extend their interest further into the history of the early church. (F4a) Richardson, *Alphabetical subject index . . . to periodical articles on religion,* is not only an index for the years covered, 1890–1899, but also a direct clue to periodicals in which such articles are to be found. The article on 'Periodical literature, Catholic,' in (F25) *Catholic encyclopedia,* 11 :669–696, gives a very comprehensive survey of Roman Catholic periodicals, arranged by countries. An even more inclusive article, 'Zeitschriften, theologische,' will be found in (F23a) *Realencyklopädie,* 24 :662–691.

Articles and review of books on church history will be found in the general historical journals and in other periodicals listed in other sections of this *Guide,* notably (C991) *Expositor;* (C992) *Expository times;* (C993a) *American journal of theology;* (C993b) *Journal of religion;* (C994) *Harvard theological review;* and (C995) *Princeton theological review,* with its predecessors extending from 1853.

Among the more important of the numerous special journals in this field, either for articles or book reviews or for both, are: (F941) *Methodist review,* bi-monthly, N. Y., 1818 ff., with different titles prior to 1884; (F942) *Bibliotheca sacra,* quarterly, Andover, Mass., and Oberlin, Ohio, 1884 ff.; (F943) *Lutheran quarterly,* Gettysburg, Penn., 1849 ff., with different titles prior to 1898; (F944) *Review and expositor, a Baptist theological quarterly,* Louisville, Ky., 1904 ff.; (F945) *Andover review, a religious and theological monthly* (Congregationalist), 19 v., Boston, 1884–93; (F946) *Constructive quarterly, a journal of the faith, work, and thought of Christendom,* 10 v., N. Y., 1913–22; (F947) *Christian union quarterly, interdenominational and international,* Baltimore, 1911 ff.; (F948) *Federal Council Bulletin,* N. Y., 1918 ff.

(F961) *Church quarterly review,* London, 1875, ff.: (F962) *Hibbert journal, a quarterly review of religion, theology, and philosophy,* London, 1902 ff.; (F963) *Review of theology and philosophy,* 10 v., Edinburgh, 1905–15 (F964) *International review of missions,* quarterly, Edinburgh, 1912 ff., valuable bibliographies.

(F971) *Historisches Jahrbuch,* quarterly, Münster and München, 1880 ff., extensive bibliographies; (F972) *Quellen und Forschungen aus dem Gebiete der Geschichte,* Paderborn, 1892 ff., chiefly devoted to history of the papacy, together with the preceding published by the Görres-Gesellschaft; (F973) *Zeitschrift für Kirchengeschichte,* quarterly, Gotha, 1876 ff. (F974a) *Stimmen aus Maria-Laach,* Freiburg im Breisgau, 1871–1914, continued as (F974b) *Stimmen der Zeit, katholische Monatschrift für das Geistesleben der Gegenwart, ibid.*, 1914 ff.

(F981) *Revue d'histoire ecclésiastique*, Louvain, 1900 ff., excellent bibliographies; (F982) *Études religieuses* (*Pères de la Compagnie de Jésus*), Paris, 1856 ff., with different titles prior to 1888; (F983) *La civiltà cattolica*, Roma, 1850 ff., Jesuit semi-monthly; (F984) *Analecta Bollandiana* (*Société des Bollandistes*), Bruxelles, 1882 ff., studies relating to (F801) *Acta sanctorum;* (F985) *Archivum franciscanum historicum,* quarterly, Quaracchi, 1908 ff.   WHA

SECTION G

HISTORY OF MOHAMMEDANISM AND OF MOSLEM PEOPLES

Editor

DANA CARLETON MUNRO *

Professor of Medieval History, Princeton University

CONTENTS

INTRODUCTION

It is difficult to segregate the books dealing with Moslem history, because of the wide extent of the conquests of Islam and its influence upon peoples in many parts of the world, from the seventh century onwards. Consequently, many books which are important for Moslem history are included in other sections of this *Guide,* notably §§ H, I, J, N, T, U, W.

There are relatively few excellent books in English on Moslem history, and not a large number in the other languages of Europe. As yet many of the sources have not been translated and few have been critically studied. Satisfactory histories by modern Moslem scholars are few. At the present time the number of western scholars working in this enormous field is comparatively small, and their publications are frequently too highly specialized to be in-

* Professor Munro wishes to make special acknowledgment of assistance received from Professor D. B. Macdonald.

cluded in this section. On the other hand, there are books of an elementary
character written by men not fitted for serious work, which do not deserve
mention.

BIBLIOGRAPHY

G1a Chauvin, Victor C. *Bibliographie des ouvrages arabes, ou relatifs aux
Arabes, publiés dans l'Europe chrétienne de 1810 à 1885.* 12 pt. Liége,
1892–1922.

b Gabrieli, Giuseppe. *Manuale di bibliografia musulmana.* Pt. 1. Roma,
1916. [Manuali coloniali pubblicati a cura del Ministero delle colonie.]

a. Includes Arabic works and works relative to Moslem history and literature. *b.* Touches upon all subjects connected with Moslems, their schools and
teachers. Deals also with Mohammedan chronology. Cf. also (G61) Caetani,
Annali dell' Islam.   RG

G2a Röhricht, Reinhold. *Bibliotheca geographica Palaestinae: chronologisches
Verzeichniss der auf die Geographie des Heiligen Landes bezüglichen
Literatur von 333 bis 1878, und Versuch einer Cartographie.* Berlin, 1890.

b Thomsen, Peter. *Systematische Bibliographie der Palästina-Literatur
[1895–1904].* V. 1, Leipzig, 1908. V. 2, *Die Palästina-Literatur; eine internationale Bibliographie* . . . [1905–09]. Leipzig, 1911.

Although covering thoroughly only Palestine, they contain many titles for
the geography of the Moslem world.   DCM

G3a *Orientalische Bibliographie* [1887–1911]. Ed. by A. Müller and others.
25 v. Berlin, 1888–1917.

b *Literatur-blatt für orientalische Philologie* [1883–86]. Ed. by E. Kuhn.
4 v. Leipzig, 1883–88.

c Friederici, Karl. *Bibliotheca orientalis* [1876–83]. 8 v. in 1. Leipzig,
1876–83.

d *Wissenschaftlicher Jahresbericht über die morgenländischen Studien
[1850–80].* 6 v. in 2. Leipzig, 1868–83. [Irregular supplement to (C944)
Zeitschrift der Deutschen Morgenländischen Gesellschaft.]

e Zenker, Julius T. *Bibliotheca orientalis.* 2 v. in 1. Leipzig, 1846–61.

f Massignon, L., ed. *Annuaire du monde musulman, statistique, historique,
social, et économique.* Paris, 1924 f.

a. Aims to give a complete inventory of books, articles, reviews, and monographs for Islam as well as for other branches of Oriental studies. Together
with *b, c, d,* and *e,* it forms a continuous bibliography of Oriental philology and
related subjects. *f.* Lists periodicals, schools, learned societies; summarizes events;
and includes bibliographical references to publications on Moslem countries. Cf.
also (T8001a) Masson, *Éléments d'une bibliographie française de la Syrie.* DCM

General reviews and summaries of new books and periodical literature for
Islam have been published in several periodicals, notably (B941f 9) *Revue historique,* 114:104, Sept. 1913; 138:94, Sept. 1921; (B941f 18) *Revue de l'histoire des
religions,* 71:47–127, Jan. 1915; 80:271–353, Nov. 1919; *Archiv für Religions-
wissenschaft;* 8:129–143, 1905; 11:339–368, 1908; 15:530–602, 1912; and (U942)
Asiatic review. Many articles in (G22a) *Encyclopedia of Islam* contain excellent

bibliographies. The following book lists in (B14a) *Bulletin* of the New York Public Library, are useful: 'List of books on Arabic poetry,' 12:7–31, Jan. 1908; 'Arabic drama,' 10:251–252, Apr. 1906; 'Muhammadanism,' 15:211–246, Apr. 1911; 'Arabia and the Arabs, Arabic philosophy, science, and literature,' 15:7–40 and 163–198, Jan. and March 1911; 'Muhammadan law,' 11:8–17, Jan. 1907; 'History of Egypt,' 32:11, Nov. 1928. Also cf. §§ C, H, T, W.

Library collections.—Probably the best place in the United States to use works on Moslem history is the New York Public Library, because of the bibliographies prepared by Professor Gottheil, and because of his readiness to assist students. The Harvard University Library also contains an excellent collection for the various important topics of Moslem history.   AHS

ENCYCLOPEDIAS AND WORKS OF REFERENCE

G21 Hughes, Thomas P. *Dictionary of Islam, being a cyclopaedia of the doc·trines, rites, ceremonies, and customs, together with the technical and theological terms, of the Muhammadan religion.* 1885. Reprint, London, 1896.

Within its field it still holds an important place and, since the original edition has become very rare, its anastatic reproduction is a service. Some articles have been rendered antiquated by recent discoveries. That by Steingass on 'Writing' should be compared with Moritz's article in (G22a) *Encyclopedia of Islam,* 1:381. Rubrics relating to the Koran are by far the most trustworthy and important; those on theology and language are often quite untrustworthy. Review, *Athenaeum,* 1:385, Mar. 20, 1886.   NS, DBM

G22a *Encyclopedia of Islam.* Ed. by Martijn T. Houtsma, A. Schaade, and others. Pt. 1–38 (A to Mahmud), pt. A–K (S to Tashkent). Leiden, 1908–24. (Extensive bibliographies.)

b Herbelot, Barthélemy d'. *Bibliothèque orientale, ou dictionnaire universel contenant généralement tout ce qui regarde la connoissance des peuples de l'Orient.* Paris, 1697.· 2nd ed., Maestricht, 1776, and *Supplément* by C. Visdelou and A. Galland, Maestricht, 1780.

c Beale, Thomas W. *Oriental biographical dictionary.* 1881. Rev. ed. by H. G. Keene, London, 1894.

d *Dictionnaire d'histoire et de géographie ecclesiastique.* V. 3, Art. *Arabie* by R. Aigran. Paris, 1924.

a. Unlike *b.* and *c.* and (G21), this encyclopedia is the result of collaboration by a large number of scholars, financially assisted by a union of academies of science. Intended to be a geographical, ethnographical, and biographical dictionary of the Muhammedan peoples. Appears in three languages: English, French, and German. Abounds in articles that are extremely well written, many of which are significant monographs. It was planned to have the encyclopedia complete in 45 parts in 1920, but the war has delayed its publication. Review, I. Goldziher, *Deutsche Literaturzeitung,* 29:2009, Aug. 8, 1909. In addition to the encyclopedias listed above, such information is to be found in all the larger encyclopedias, especially (F22) Hastings, *Encyclopaedia of religion and ethics,* (Cf. review of its articles on Mohammedanism by D. B. Macdonald, *Journal of religion,* 3:74, Jan. 1923), (B22b) *Encyclopaedia Britannica,* and (F28) *Jewish encyclopedia.*   NS

G23 Poole, Stanley Lane. *Mohammedan dynasties.* Westminster, 1894. Reprint, Paris, 1925.

Lists and genealogical tables of individual rulers; short introduction and valuable colored chart show interrelationships, succession, and geographical extension of the dynasties; accurate, indispensable.   WP

G24 Zambour, E. de. *Manuel de généalogie et de chronologie pour l'histoire de l'Islam.* 1927.

Contains genealogical tables and five maps, and supplements (G23) Poole.

DCM

GEOGRAPHY OF ARABIA AND OTHER MOSLEM LANDS

Books relating to the geography of Mohammedan lands other than Arabia will be found in § C, Ancient Near East, e.g. (C41) Hogarth, *Nearer East;* and (C42*b*) Smith, *Historical geography of the Holy Land;* § T, Southeastern Europe and Ottoman Empire, e.g. Cuinet, *Turquie d'Asie;* and § U, Central, Southern, and Eastern Asia; and § W, Africa. Reference should also be made to *Handbook of Arabia, Handbook of Mesopotamia,* and *Handbook of Syria and Palestine* in (J441*a*) *Peace handbooks.*

G41 Hogarth, David G. *Penetration of Arabia, a record of the development of western knowledge concerning the Arabian peninsula.* N. Y., 1904. (Bibliographies.)

Most comprehensive and authoritative study of Arabia as a whole, being a review of the explorations in the peninsula by Europeans since the Middle Ages, with descriptions of the country, its physical characteristics, climate, peoples, products, and government, derived from a great variety of sources. The various political divisions are discussed separately, with a brief account of the more recent history of each. Rough estimates of the population are given, the natives are characterized, and the presence of occasional foreign elements, Moslem and non-Moslem, is noted. Accuracy of the accounts of numerous travellers is frankly criticized. Very useful as a foundation for the more detailed study of the history of Arabia. Review, D. B. Macdonald, *Nation,* (N. Y.) 79:165, Aug. 25, 1904.   HCBr

G42a Doughty, Charles M. *Travels in Arabia Deserta.* 2 v. Cambridge, Eng., 1888. Verbatim reprint, London, 1920. New ed. with preface by T. E. Lawrence, 2 v., N. Y., 1923.

b Philby, Harry St. J. B. *Heart of Arabia, a record of travel and exploration.* 2 v. London, 1922.

c —— *Arabia of the Wahabis.* London, 1928.

d Rihani, Ameen F. *Ibn Sa'oud of Arabia.* London, 1928. Same with title, *Maker of Arabia,* Boston and N. Y., 1928.

e Musil, Alois. *Explorations in Arabia and Mesopotamia* [1908–1915]. 6 v. N. Y., 1926–28.

a. In some respects the best book on Arabian travel; deals primarily with the desert waste and the Bedouin. 'A tremendous picture of desert life and the desert mind.' 'No one has looked as narrowly at the land and life of Arabia as Doughty, and no one has painted them in literature with a touch so sensitive, so sincere, and so sure.' The author's style does not make easy reading. Very technical review, A. Sprenger, *Zeitschrift der Deutschen Morgenländischen Gesellschaft*, 42:321, 1888.   HCBr

b. Much information on geography and on habits of Bedouin, especially of the Wahabi and on their chief Ibn Sa'oud. Philby's observations enabled the Royal Geographical Society to chart extensive tracts hitherto unexplored. Review, C. Candler, *Nation* (London), 32:59, Oct. 4, 1922. *c.* Forms in effect a third volume of *b.*   DBM

d. Review, *Sat. Rev. of Lit.* 145:324, March 17, 1928. *e.* First-hand observations of Bedouin life and folk-lore. Excellent maps. Of highest importance for understanding a civilization which is rapidly passing away. Review, R. Geger, *Wiener Zeit. für die Kunde des Morgenlandes* 35:139, 1928.   DCM

G43 Le Strange, Guy. *Lands of the eastern caliphate, Mesopotamia, Persia, and Central Asia, from the Moslem conquest to the time of Timur.* Cambridge, Eng., 1905. [Cambridge geographical series.]

Historical and descriptive geography of Asia Minor, Mesopotamia, Persia, and Central Asia to the Indus and Jaxartes; synthesizes the numerous Arabic itineraries and systematic geographical works of the ninth to the twelfth centuries A.D., adding pertinent data from the historians and occasionally from modern books of travel. Contains sketch maps of all the provinces. Readable; frequent checking with the sources has proven it remarkably free from errors; indispensable for the non-Arabist, and almost so for the Arabist as well. Review, *Nation* (N. Y.), 81:360, Nov. 2, 1905.   WP

G44 Lammens, Henri. *Le berceau de l'Islam, l'Arabie occidentale à la veille de l'Hégire.* V. 1. Romae, 1914. [Scripta Pontificii Instituti Biblici.] (Bibliography.)

Lammens, a Jesuit, perceives the dependence of the earlier biographies of Mohammed on the interpretation of the Quran and tradition, but goes too far in deriving all tradition from exegesis. Like all his books it is a thesaurus of Arabic references. His best and least subjective book. In sketching the background of the Prophet's life, he rightly rejects the theory that the climate of Arabia has in historic times undergone a marked change through desiccation. His account of the Bedouins suffers somewhat from a tendency to exaggerate the defects of the Arab character. Review, T. Nöldeke, *Der Islam,* 5:205, 1914; A. H. Lybyer, *Bibliotheca sacra,* 73:156, 1916.   NS and DBM

G45 Dussaud, René. *Topographie historique de la Syrie, antique et médiévale.* Paris, 1927. (Bibliography.)

Review, L. Halphen, *Rev. de Synthèse Hist.* 45:92, June 1928.   DCM

ETHNOGRAPHY OF MOSLEM COUNTRIES

In the absence of commendable special works reference may be made to (G123) P. J. André, *L'Islam et les races* and to the books listed in this section under the sub-heading Geography (G41–44) and in the appropriate sub-sections in other sections of this *Guide* dealing with countries inhabited by Moslems.

COLLECTIONS OF SOURCES AND TRANSLATIONS OF SIGNIFICANT ARABIC AND PERSIAN TEXTS

G61 Caetani, Leone, Principe di Teano. *Annali dell' Islam.* 8 v. Milano, 1905–14.

Gives an analysis or translation of all the more important sources. The volumes published cover only the period to the year 35 of the Hegira.   DCM

G62 Lyall, Sir Charles J. *Translations of ancient Arabian poetry, chiefly pre-Islamic.* London, 1885.

Excellent collection of poems and fragments well translated and ably introduced. For the non-Arabist one of the best source books for this phase of early Arabic civilization.   MS

G63a Sale, George, tr. *The Koran, commonly called the Alcoran of Mohammed, translated into English immediately from the original Arabic.* London, 1734. Many later ed. Warne of London has good editions in print.

    b Marracci, Ludovico, ed. and tr. *Alcorani textus universus ex correctioribus Arabum exemplaribus summa fide, atque pulcherrimis characteribus descriptus, . . . in Latinum translatus, . . .* 2 v. Patavii, 1698.

    c Rodwell, John M., tr. *The Koran translated from the Arabic, the suras arranged in chronological order, with notes and index.* 1861. 2nd ed., London, 1876. Reprint, London and N. Y., 1909. [Everyman's library.]

    d Palmer, Edward H., tr. *The Qur'ân.* 2 v. Oxford, 1880. [Sacred books of the East.]

a. Not very readable but still useful. In the introduction there is a mass of material, useful too, but to be used with caution; the full commentary cannot be found elsewhere except in Arabic or in *b.* Sale is very largely based on *b.* and all later translations have been affected by Sale. *b.* Latin translation and commentary by Father Marracci, always to be mentioned with respect. *c.* Attempt at a chronological re-arrangement of the Koran, translated into more picturesque language than Sale's. Where it departs from *a.* and *b.* it is to be used with caution. *d.* More scholarly production than either *a.* or *c.,* but marred by strange slips, due apparently to mere carelessness. Palmer undoubtedly knew Arabic—the high, the middle, and the low,—better than any other translator of the Koran; but he seems to have translated at a gallop. His introduction is poor, but he gives a useful abstract of the contents of the Koran. There are no translations into other western languages which are any better than the above; the influence of Marracci and Sale is over them all.   DBM

G64a Lane, Edward W., tr. *Thousand and one nights.* 3 v. London, 1839–41. Ed. by E. S. Poole, with Harvey illustrations, 3 v., London, 1859. Rev. ed. by E. S. Poole, 3 v., London, 1883, and later reprints.

    b Payne, John, tr. *Book of the thousand nights and one night.* 9 v. London, 1882–84. [Villon Society.] *Together with Tales from the Arabic of the Breslau and Calcutta (1814–18) editions of the Book of the thousand nights and one night not occurring in the other printed texts of the work.* 4 v. London, 1884–89. [Villon Society.]

    c Burton, Sir Richard F., tr. *Plain and literal translation of the Arabian nights' entertainments . . . with introduction, explanatory notes, . . . and a terminal essay upon the history of the nights.* 10 v. Benares, 1885. *To-*

gether with Supplemental nights, with notes. 6 v. Benares, 1886–88. Later reprints of all or parts of both.

d **Torrens, Henry,** tr. *Book of the thousand and one nights, from the Arabic of the Egyptian manuscript as edited by W. H. Macnaghten, done into English.* V. I. Calcutta and London, 1838.

e **Henning, M.,** tr. *Tausend und eine Nacht.* 8 pt. Leipzig, 1900. [Reclam Universal-Bibliothek.]

The *Thousand and one nights* should be read by every student of Islam; there is no other such picture of Moslem life. Only three translations into English need to be specially considered. *a.* Incomplete but accurate; has a very valuable and full commentary. There are many editions of it in many different forms. The right and only complete editions are always in three large octavo volumes, with the Harvey illustrations and the full commentary, now published by Chatto and Windus; all others are incomplete in one way or another. *b.* Complete, but has no commentary. While it is exceedingly readable, its style hardly represents the tone of the original. There are several cheap, pirated reprints. *c.* Practically derived from *b.*, except as to the verse part, only touched up in Burton's manner. *d.* Translation only of the first fifty *Nights;* has many inaccuracies, yet it gives the style and tone of the original better than any other. *e.* There are no translations into western languages of especial importance other than those mentioned above, but Henning's is very complete and cheap. It is secondary, has no commentary, and is not very readable; a creditable German hack-production.   DBM

G65 Ibn Khallikān. *Biographical dictionary.* Tr. by Baron MacGuckin de Slane. 4 v. Paris, 1842–71. [Oriental Translation Fund.]

An admirable dictionary of national biography, written in the middle of the thirteenth century, containing 865 lives. The author gives biographies of those only whose death-dates he could ascertain, and omits also the caliphs, the companions of the Prophet, and the next generation to them; for the lives of such there were special means of information. Cf. (G663a) Nicholson, *Literary history of the Arabs,* p. 451.   DBM

G66 Ibn Khaldūn. *Les prolégomènes.* French tr. by Baron MacGuckin de Slane. 3 v. Paris, 1863–68. [Notices et extraits des manuscrits de la Bibliothèque Impériale.] New ed. announced, tr. by Baron de Slane, 3 v.. Paris, 1930 f.

Perhaps the most scientific book in all Arabic historical literature. It is the introduction to the author's *Universal history* and by far the most valuable part, covering all phases of Moslem civilization. Ibn Khaldūn was more scientific, less prejudiced, and more careful than Buckle. Cf. (G663a) Nicholson, *Literary history of the Arabs,* p. 437.   DBM

G67 Ibn At-Tiqtaqā. *Al-Fakhrī.* French tr. by Émile Amar. Paris, 1910.

Short history, written in A.D. 1302, and extending to the fall of Baghdad in A.D. 1258. It has a good political-constitutional introduction. Cf. (G663a) Nicholson, *Literary history of the Arabs,* p. 454.   DBM

G68 Bīrūnī. *Chronology of ancient nations; an English version of the Arabic text of the Athār-ul-Bākiya of Albīrūnī, or Vestiges of the past, collected . . . by the author in A.H. 390–1, A.D. 1000.* Tr. and ed. by C. E. Sachau. London, 1879. [Oriental Translation Fund.] Enlarged ed. with notes, etc., by E. C. Sachau, 2 v., London, 1888.

A book remarkable in Arabic literature for its strictly scientific attitude. Includes a mass of material on the calendar systems of Central Asia, not preserved in any other form. DBM

G69 Mas'ūdī ['Alī ibn Husain]. *Murūj adh-dhahab.* French tr. (with Arabic text) *Les prairies d'or,* by C. Barbier de Meynard and Pavet de Courteille. 9 v. Paris, 1861–78. [Collection d'ouvrages orientaux publiée par la Société Asiatique.]

Mas'ūdī, who died A.D. 956, was a traveller, a student of life, and an historian. His book professes to be a universal history from the creation to A.D. 947, but is really an encyclopedic hodgepodge of all that he had learned and observed in his wanderings; that is also its value. He was interested, in a critical way, in religious discussions, social and literary history, and what is now called folklore. Cf. (G663a) Nicholson, *Literary history of the Arabs,* p. 352. DBM

G70a Ibn Battūta [Muhammad Ibn 'Abd Allāh]. *Travels of Ibn Batūta; translated from the abridged Arabic manuscript copies preserved in the public library of Cambridge, with notes illustrative of the history, geography, botany, antiquity, etc. occurring throughout the work.* Ed. and tr. by S. Lee. London, 1829. [Oriental Translation Fund.]

b ——— *Voyages d'Ibn Batoutah.* French tr. (with Arabic text) by C. Defrémery and B. R. Sanguinetti. 1853–59. Reprint, 4 v., Paris, 1914. [Collection d'ouvrages orientaux publiée par la Société Asiatique.]

c ——— *Travels of Ibn Battūta.* Tr. by H. A. R. Gibbs. London, 1929.

Ibn Battūta died A. D. 1377. He left his native town, Tangier, when twenty-two years old and spent twenty-seven years in wanderings which extended from southern Russia to Timbuctoo, from Arabia to Buchara, and from India to China. His book shows him a combination of Marco Polo and Pepys. It gives an unsurpassed picture of certain phases of the Moslem civilization in its widest spread and illustrates vividly the cosmopolitanism of an educated, Arabic-speaking Moslem. *a.* Incomplete; useful only as an English version. Superseded by *b.* *c.* Part only; complete translation in progress. DBM

G71 Balādhūrī [Ahmad ibn Yahyā]. *Origins of the Islamic state.* Tr. by P. K. Hitti, N. Y., 1916. [Columbia University studies in history, economics, and public law.]

Translation, with annotations, of the first part of the *Futūh al-buldān* (Conquests of the countries), by Balādhūrī, who died A.D. 892. One of the oldest of the Arabic histories and a primary source for the first Moslem conquests. DBM

G72 Mawardī ['Ali ibn Muhammad]. *Les statuts gouvernementaux, ou règles de droit public et administratif.* French tr. by E. Fagnan. Alger, 1915.

The author died A.D. 1058. His book is a classical analysis of Moslem constitutional law and government. His statement of the nature of the caliphate is basic for all present day discussion. Cf. (G663a) Nicholson, *Literary history of the Arabs,* p. 337. DBM

G73 Damīrī [Muhammad ibn Musa]. *Hayāt al-Hayawān al-Kurba, a zoölogical lexicon.* Tr. by A. S. G. Jayakar. 2 v. London, 1906–08.

The author, a Cairene all his life, died A.D .1405. A book of beasts, philosophical, poetical, descriptive, traditional, legal, proverbial, medical, oneirocritical— everything but zoölogical. It is thus, beyond all praise, an enormous compilation of folk-lore, tradition, popular medicine, and racial psychology. This translation covers about three quarters of the original. Cf. also (G22a) *Encyclopedia of Islam,* 1:912; *Encyclopaedia Britannica,* 9th ed., 6:794. (B22b) DBM

G74 Hamd-Allāh Mustawfī. *Geographical part of the Nuzhat-al-qulūb composed by Hamd-Allāh mustawfi of Qazwīn in 740 (1340).* Ed. and tr. by G. Le Strange. 2 v. London, 1915–19. [1, Text; 2, Translation.] [E. J. W. Gibb Memorial.]

Good example of a Moslem cosmography though it gives most attention to Persia and Mesopotamia, with much sociology, tradition, folk-lore, and many popular marvels. Compiled in Persian in the middle of the fourteenth century, A. D. DBM

G75 Al-Hujwīrī ['Ali ibn Usman]. *Kashf al-Mahjūb: the oldest Persian treatise on Sūfiism.* Tr. by R. A. Nicholson from the text of the Lahore edition, compared with mss. in the India Office and British Museum. London, 1911. [E. J. W. Gibb Memorial.]

Classical treatise for all interested in mysticism. The author lived about the middle of the eleventh century A.D. Nicholson has made large use of this book in his (G626) *Mystics of Islam,* on p. 170 of which is a list of other similar translations from Persian and Arabic writers. DBM

G76a Tabarī [Muhammad ibn Jarir]. *Chronique, traduite sur la version persane d' Abou-'Ali-Mo'hammed Bela'mi, d'après les manuscrits de Paris, de Londres, et de Canterbury.* Tr. by H. Zotenberg. 4 v. Paris, 1867–74. [Oriental Translation Fund.]

b ——— *Geschichte der Perser und Araber zur Zeit der Sasaniden; aus der arabischen Chronik des Tabari übersetzt und mit ausführlichen Erläuterungen und Ergänzungen versehn.* Ed. and tr. by T. Nöldeke. Leyden, 1879.

The Arabic chronicle of Tabarī is the oldest and most celebrated of Moslem universal histories; extends from the creation to A. D. 915. *a.* Unfortunately through a Persian version only. *b.* Work of a great master who has supplied extensive notes and much supplementary material. Cf. classical article on Tabarī, *Encyclopaedia Britannica,* 9th ed., 23:1; (G663) Nicholson, *Literary history of the Arabs,* p. 350. DBM

G77a Abū-l-Fidā. *Géographie d'Aboulféda, traduite de l'Arabe en Français, et accompagnée de notes et d'éclaircissements by J. T. Reinaud and S. Guyard.* 2 v. Paris, 1848–83.

b ——— *Abulfedae annales Muslemici, Arabice et Latine, opera et studiis J. J. Reiskii.* Ed. by J. G. C. Adler. 5 v. Hafniae, 1789–94.

a. Minute but uninspired geographical conspectus of the Moslem world. *b.* Elaborate universal history; valuable for the times of the author, who died A.D. 1331. DBM

SHORTER GENERAL HISTORIES

G101a Gilman, Arthur. *The Saracens from the earliest times to the fall of Bagdad.* N. Y., 1887. [Story of the nations.] (Valuable annotated bibliography.)

b Ameer Ali, Syed. *Short history of the Saracens, being a concise account of the rise and decline of the Saracenic power and of the economic, social, and intellectual development of the Arab nation from the earliest times to the destruction of Bagdad and the expulsion of the Moors from Spain.* 1899. Rev. ed., London, 1921. (Bibliography.)

a. Popular account of Mohammed and Islam and the political history of the caliphate to 750, with brief sketch to 1258. *b.* Interesting because written from the standpoint of an enthusiastic Mohammedan. Review, *Athenaeum,* 1:493, Apr. 22, 1899; 1:595, May 13, 1899. For excellent brief surveys of early Moslem history, cf. (H122) Gibbon, *Decline and fall of the Roman empire,* ch. 50–52, 57; and (H121) *Cambridge medieval history,* v. 2, ch. 10–12, v. 4, ch. 10, with accompanying bibliographies.   JEW

LONGER GENERAL HISTORIES

G121 Müller, August. *Der Islam im Morgen—und Abendland.* 2 v. Berlin, 1885–87. [(B162) Oncken, Allgemeine Geschichte.]

Best political history of the Muslim world, but of the German *Handbuch* type and with no index. V. 1. Covers Mohammed, Islam, and the eastern and Fatimid caliphates to 1258. V. 2. Deals with the smaller eastern Muslim states, the Mongol invasions, and the Spanish Muslims, with brief surveys of the Ottoman, Mogul, and Persian empires. Written mainly from secondary material, with few footnotes. While the arrangement and the chapter headings are good, the discussion is primarily from the political viewpoint and sadly lacking in information on the social, economic, and intellectual sides. Many chapters are crowded with minor detail, largely military. Review, C. Snouck Hurgronje, *Deutsche Literaturzeitung,* 7:815, June 5, 1886.   JEW

G122a Muir, Sir William. *The caliphate: its rise, decline, and fall.* 1891. Rev. ed. by T. H. Weir, Edinburgh, 1915. (Bibliography.)

b Weil, Gustav. *Geschichte der Chalifen.* 5 v. Mannheim and Stuttgart, 1846–62.

c Huart, Clément I. *Histoire des Arabes.* 2 v. Paris, 1912–13. (Bibliographies.)

a. Still a useful book; not as full as *b.* Narrower in scope and less critical than (G121); also narrower than *c.,* and less concerned with cultural development; but the new edition, somewhat enlarged in text, is of value to English readers.   NS

G123 André, Pierre J. *L'Islam et les races.* 2 v. Paris, 1922. [1, *Les origines, le tronc, et la greffe;* 2, *Les rameaux; mouvements régionaux et sectes.*] (Bibliography.)

V. 1. General survey of the history of Islam; of little value. V. 2. Discusses the sects, schisms, and local movements which led to the formation of the separate states; valuable. Review, D. B. Macdonald, *Isis,* 6:563, 1924; C. Huart, *Rev. Hist.* 145:281, March 1924.   DCM

MOHAMMED

G201 Poole, Stanley Lane. *Speeches and table-talk of the prophet Mohammad, chosen and translated, with introduction and notes.* London, 1882. [Golden treasury series.]

Small book for the general reader. Excellent introduction on Mohammed and the Koran, followed by portions of the latter and materials from the traditions about the Prophet.   DCM

G202 Muir, Sir William. *Life of Mohammad from original sources.* 4 v. 1858–61. Rev. ed. by T. H. Weir, 1 v., Edinburgh, 1912.

Since this book was written many important sources have been published, and the judgment of the value of others has greatly changed. It is now recognized that many of the traditions which Muir used are late forgeries sprung from theological or legal controversies. In spite of this Muir's book is a valuable rendering of the orthodox traditional view of Mohammed. In addition it is well written. Review, *British Quart. Rev.* 36:255, Oct. 1862. Cf. Sir C. J. Lyall, 'Sir William Muir,' *Journal of Royal Asiatic Society*, N.S. 37:875–879, 1905.   MS

G203 Margoliouth, David S. *Mohammed and the rise of Islam.* N. Y., 1905. [Heroes of the nations.] (Bibliography.)

The essential facts of Mohammed's life and work and much source material are presented; the wide reading of Professor Margoliouth is evident on every page. Valuable preface. Pioneer effort to write the history of Mohammed and of the beginnings of Islam in social and economic terms. The non-Arabist will do well, if he weighs the advanced positions of this book with Bevan's conservative statements in (H121) *Cambridge medieval history*, v. 2, ch. 10. Review, J. R. Jewett, *A.H.R.* 11:880, July 1906. Cf. *Church Quart. Rev.* 62:357, July 1906.   MS

HISTORIES OF MOSLEM COUNTRIES

For Mohammedan Spain, cf. § N, especially (N203c) Dozy, *Spanish Islam;* for the Mohammedans in Sicily and southern Italy, cf. (O491b) Amari, *Storia dei Musulmani di Sicilia;* for Morocco, and the other North African states, and for Egypt since the eighteenth century, cf. § W; for Mohammedan rule in Palestine, Syria, and adjacent lands in the time of the Crusades, cf. § H, especially (H356) Poole, *Saladin;* for the Ottoman Turks and the lands they have occupied, cf. § T; for Persia, Central Asia, and India under Moslem rule, cf. § U.

G251 Hogarth, David G. *Arabia.* Oxford, 1922.

Very slight historical sketch from before Mohammed to the present; yet the only easily accessible source for medieval Arabia, its Turkish period, and its present situation (p. 82–131). Readable; without a single reference to an authority or a note. Review, D. B. Macdonald, *A.H.R.* 28:161, Oct. 1922.   DBM

G271 Poole, Stanley Lane. *History of Egypt in the middle ages.* London, 1901. [V. 6 of (C203) Petrie, *History of Egypt.*] (Bibliography.)

Presented for the first time the history of Egypt from 640 to 1517 in a continuous narrative apart from the general history of Islam. Too narrowly limited to Egypt; such isolation tends to obscure the historic movements. Sufficient attention is not given to the growth of ideas and the literary development, but the best sources are employed, and the extensive use of coins and illustrations gives a distinctive value to the work. Excellent illustrations, though the one map is very poor. Review, *Nation* (N. Y.), 73:326, Oct. 24, 1901.   NS

G272a Butler, Alfred J. *Arab conquest of Egypt and the last thirty years of the Roman dominion.* Oxford, 1902. (Bibliography.)

b Caudel, Maurice. *Les premières invasions arabes dans l'Afrique du Nord, 21–100 Heg., 641–718 J.-C. Journal asiatique,* 9th series, 13:102, 189, 385; 14:50, 187, 1899. Reprint, Paris, 1900.

c ——— *Les premières invasions arabes dans l'Afrique du Nord, 21–78 H., 641–697 J.-C.* Paris, 1900. [Bibliothèque d'archéologie africaine, v. 3.]

a. First full treatment; prefaced by an account of the history of Egypt under Romans and Persians from 609 A. D. Important for account of sources, chronology, and maps. Review, G. Le Strange, *E. H. R.* 18:546, July 1903. *b.* Part one only of the work planned; describes the Berbers and their country, and the early history of the Arabs, but does not take up their invasions into Africa. *c.* Reprint with some modifications.   DCM

G301a Le Strange, Guy. *Palestine under the Moslems, a description of Syria and the Holy Land from A.D. 650 to 1500, translated from the works of the mediaeval Arab geographers.* London and Boston, 1890. [Palestine Exploration Fund.]

b ——— *Baghdad during the Abbasid caliphate, from contemporary Arabic and Persian sources.* 1900. Reprint, Oxford and N. Y., 1924.

a. Very useful for the knowledge of conditions in Palestine under Muslim rule in the period before the crusades; especially full accounts of Jerusalem. *b.* Similar collection of contemporary descriptive accounts of Bagdad under the Abbasids.   DCM

G321 Lammens, Henri. *La Syrie, précis historique.* 2 v. Beyrouth, 1921. (Bibliography.)

History of Syria from the earliest times to the present day by a most competent scholar. French view of recent events. (Review, P. K. Hitti, *Amer. Jour. of Semitic Lang. and Lit.* 42:211, Apr. 1926.   DCM

G322 Gaudefroy-Demombynes, Maurice. *La Syrie à l'époque des Mameloukes d'après les auteurs Arabes, description géographique, économique, et administrative, précédée d'une introduction sur l'organisation gouvernementale.* Paris, 1923. [Bibliothèque archéologique et historique, v. 3.]

Supplements for Syria in the thirteenth and fourteenth centuries the treatment of the earlier period by Guy Le Strange in (G301) *Palestine under the Moslems* and (G43) *Lands of the eastern caliphate.* Largely a translation from Arabic sources. Excellent introduction on the organization of the Mameluk state. Review, D. C. Munro, *A.H.R.* 29:793, July 1924; D. B. Macdonald, *Isis,* 6:561, 1924.   DCM

G323 Gautier, Émile Félix. *L'islamisation de l'Afrique du Nord: les siècles obscurs du Maghreb.* Paris, 1927.

The use of the camel, introduced in the second or third century A.D., and the influence of the Arabs, transferred the power to the nomadic part of the population and destroyed the civilization. Review, J. Tramond, *Rev. de l'Hist. des Colonies françaises* 16:363, Mai-juin 1928. DCM

G324 Ribera, Julian, tr. *Historia de la conquista de España de Abenelcotía el Cordobás.* Madrid, 1926. [V. 2, *Collección de obras arabigas de historia y geografía,* publ. by the Royal Academy of Spain.]

The importance of this work was first pointed out by Dozy, cf. (G622, N203c), who made use of it. Review, D. B. Macdonald, *A.H.R.* 33:78, Oct. 1927. DCM

G325 Vonderheyden, M. *La Berbérie orientale sous la dynastie des Benoû'l-Arlab,* 800–909, Paris, 1927.

Study of the manner in which the people of North Africa became arabicized. Review, D. B. Macdonald, *A.H.R.* 34:799, July, 1929. DCM

G391a Hurgronje, Christiaan Snouck. *Nederland en de Islam.* 1911. 2nd ed., Leiden, 1915. French tr., *Politique musulmane de la Hollande,* Paris, 1912.

b —— *The Achehnese.* 2 v. Leiden and London, 1906. Tr. by A. W. S. O'Sullivan from *De Atjèhers,* 2 v., Leiden, 1893–94.

a. Authoritative, brief, and popular summary of Islamic doctrinal, legal, and political development, omitting accounts of sects, from Mohammed to the present time; followed by comparatively extended discussion of political and social problems presented by Mohammedanism in the Netherlands Indies. Contains definite political recommendations. Good sources for precise, even though general, information upon Khalifate and allied questions. Review, R. Basset, *Revue de l'histoire des religions,* 68:115, July 1913. VSC

b. Elaborate description, by a great master, of a modern Moslem community located in Sumatra. JHW

CONSTITUTIONAL AND LEGAL HISTORY

G531 Arnold, Sir Thomas W. *The caliphate.* Oxford, 1924.

Study of the caliphate as an institution tracing its vicissitudes through the ages. Review, D. S. Margoliouth, *E.H.R.* 40:143, Jan. 1925; D. B. Macdonald, *A.H.R.* 30:581, Apr. 1925. JEW

G551 Macdonald, Duncan B. *Development of Muslim theology, jurisprudence, and constitutional theory.* N. Y., 1903. [Semitic series.] (Bibliography.)

Best general introduction to the history and theory of the Mohammedan legal system. That system, like the Jewish, rested originally on religion and was administered by ecclesiastics. 'To be a statesman in the Muslim world meant also to be a jurist and theologian.' Hence the grouping of the three subjects in the title. The discussion of the 'obscure and difficult subject of Muslim theology, occupying nearly two thirds of the book' is excellent. Review, F. W. Williams, *A.H.R.* 9:137, Oct. 1903. JHW

G552 Juynboll, Theodor W. *Handleiding tot de kennis van Mohammedaansche wet volgens de leer der Sjâfi'itische school.* Leiden, 1903. German tr, *Handbuch des islāmischen Gesetzes,* Leiden, 1910. (Bibliography.)

The translation is a second edition, corrected, enlarged, but omitting some details peculiar to the Dutch East Indies. Best introduction to Muslim canon law. especially of the Shafi'ite school; accurate and detailed. As this ecclesiastical law lies behind all the jurisprudence of Islam and is the millennial ideal of the pious, deeply affecting political views, every one who has to do with Islam must take account of it. Excellent lists and definitions of technical terms. DBM

G553a Abdur Rahim. *Principles of Muhammedan jurisprudence according to the Hanafi, Maliki, Shafi'i, and Hanbali schools.* London, 1911.

b Ruston, F. H. *Maliki law.* London, 1916.

a. Best discussion of the Hanefite branch of law which predominates in Turkey, northern India, Central Asia, Egypt, and western Arabia. *b.* Important for the Malekite branch which predominates in North Africa. JHW

G554 Becker, Carl Hinrich. *Vom Werden und Wesen der islamischen Welt.* Leipzig, 1924.

Contains important studies of the development of the religion. DCM

CULTURAL HISTORY: GENERAL

G601 Lane, Edward W. *Account of the manners and customs of the modern Egyptians written in Egypt during the years 1833–1835.* 2 v. London, 1836. Many later editions; an excellent one. N. Y., 1908. [Everyman's library.]

Very careful, detailed, and admirably illustrated study of the life of the people of Cairo and, in a lesser degree, of lower Egypt. It stood alone as such a study of a people when it first appeared, and is still probably the best introduction to any Muslim community. The outlines hold for Islam everywhere. Somewhat weaker on the life of women and children and on mystical religion. Pre-folklore, and therefore uses the term 'superstitions' rather freely. Indispensable for any student of Islam. DBM

G602 Kremer, Alfred, Freiherr von. *Orient under the caliphs.* Calcutta, 1920. Tr. by S. Khuda Bukhsh from *Kulturgeschichte des Orients unter den Chalifen,* 2 v., Wien, 1875–77.

Kremer seems to have been primarily interested in Muslim jurisprudence. The humane principles of the Bagdad school impressed him. He examined with care the economic foundations of the Muslim state, its inner organizations, and its culture. Excellent translations make the section dealing with poetry very valuable. Kremer made us acquainted with the great poet and philosopher Abu-l Ala al Ma'arri. Ends with the fall of the Abbasid caliphate. The best review is the author's preface. NS

G603 Harrison, Paul W. *The Arab at Home.* N. Y., 1924.

Sympathetic account of life and customs; the outcome of fourteen years of medical service in Arabia and Mesopotamia. Review, G. E. Andrews, *Saturday Review of Literature,* 1:492, Jan. 31, 1925. DCM

CULTURAL HISTORY: RELIGION

G621 Hurgronje, Christiaan Snouck. *Mohammedanism, lectures on its origin, its religious and political growth, and its present state.* N. Y. and London, 1916. [American lectures on the history of religions.]

Excellent brief introduction. The sketch of the growth of the study of Mohammedanism and the statement on the present conditions and outlook for the future of the Mohammedan world are particularly worthy of notice. Review, *Nation* (N. Y.), 104:77, Jan. 18, 1917.   MS

G622 Dozy, Reinhart P. A. *Het Islamisme.* 1863. 3rd rev. ed. by H. W. van der Meij, Haarlem, 1900. French tr. by V. Chauvin, *Essai sur l'histoire de l'Islamisme,* Leyde and Paris, 1879.

Excellent, popular, yet not unscholarly sketch of Islam as a religious, not political, system and of its spread over the world. If in parts, notably in the life of the Prophet, it accepts too implicitly Mohammedan traditions at their face value, it is useful for an understanding of the faith as an actual living and expanding force today. To be used as an introduction, not as a final authority in scientific investigations. Review, T. Nöldeke, *Literarisches Zentralblatt,* 406, March 29, 1879.   WP

G623 Goldziher, Ignaz. *Vorlesungen über den Islam.* Heidelberg, 1910. [Religionwissenschaftliche Bibliothek.] French tr. by F. Arin, *Le dogme et la loi de l'Islam, histoire du développement dogmatique et juridique de la religion musulmane,* Paris, 1920.

Though brief, the best account of Mohammedanism as a religious and theological system, of the principles of its internal development, and of its absorption of foreign elements. Semi-popular, but every statement rests upon the author's previous penetrating, sympathetic, exhaustive special studies and upon a critical use of the recent researches of others. Noticeable are his keen yet cautious etymological deductions; his use of the traditions as evidence for the traditioner's own times when they cannot be accepted as statements of fact; and his wide acquaintance with the comparative fields while he abstains from unjustified and useless deductions. Review, E. Montet, *Revue de l'histoire des religions,* 63:367, May 1911; D. B. Macdonald, *Nation* (N. Y.), 93:168, August 24, 1911; D. B. Macdonald, *Isis,* 4:64, 1911.   WP

G624a Sell, Edward. *Faith of Islam.* 1880. 3rd rev. ed., London, 1908.

    b Bell, Richard. *Origin of Islam in its Christian environment.* London, 1926.

    a. Sketch of Mohammed and Mohammedanism from the point of view of a Christian missionary. In spite of this bias, of rather copious use of Indo-Persian terms and material, and of confusion in arrangement, considerable information may be culled from this volume.   MS

    b. Lectures on the Christian element in Islam; perhaps the most noteworthy, that on the part played by Christianity in the consolidation of Islam. Review, T. H. Weir, *History* 12:249, Oct. 1927.   HRS

G625a Macdonald, Duncan B. *Religious attitude and life in Islam.* Chicago, 1909. [Haskell lectures on comparative religion.]

    b ——— *Aspects of Islam.* N. Y., 1911. [Hartford-Lamson lectures.]

    c Ameer Ali, Syed. *Spirit of Islam, a history of the evolution and ideals of Islam, with a life of the prophet.* 1891. 2nd rev. ed., London, 1922. (Bibliography.)

    d Lammens, Henri. *L'Islam: croyances et institutions.* Beirut, 1926. Eng. tr. by E. D. Ross, London, 1929.

    a. Practically a source book, giving long extracts from (G66) Ibn Khaldun and from al Ghazzali, sometimes in actual translation, sometimes in condensed

English version. An excellent sketch of the moderate, generally accepted type of Moslem mysticism; complemented by (G626) Nicholson, *Mystics of Islam.* Review, *Nation* (N. Y.), 89:164, Aug. 19, 1909.   MS

b. Attempt to 'portray Islam in its broad outline, in its spirit and not in its details.' Excellent introduction to the subject; described as 'the most important general study.' Review, *Athenaeum,* 2:261, Sept. 2, 1911.   DCM

c. By a Mohammedan; one-sided but, just for that reason, necessary.   RG

d. Excellent popular account.   DCM

G626a **Nicholson, Reynold A.** *Mystics of Islam.* London, 1914. [Quest series.]

b **Carra de Vaux, Baron Bernard.** *Les penseurs de l'Islam.* 5 v. Paris, 1921–26.

a. Small book, but done with that conscientiousness for which the author is justly famous. Many quotations in excellent translation help to set forth in outline the essential features of more extreme Moslem mysticism, forming a complement to (G625a) Macdonald, *Religious attitude and life in Islam.* Review, *Athenaeum,* 1:403, Mar. 21, 1914.   MS

b. Covers a wide range of subjects and writers—theology, philosophy, geography, the natural sciences, law, sects, and modern liberalism. Not an exhaustive but a selective treatment of Islamic thought in various countries and periods. Review, L. Halphen, *Rev. Critique* 61:330, Sept. 1, 1927.   SBF

G627a **Burton, Sir Richard F.** *Personal narrative of a pilgrimage to El-Medinah and Meccah.* 3 v. 1855–56. Many later ed.; an excellent one, 2 v., London, 1913. [Bohn's popular library.]

b **Gaudefroy-Demombynes, Maurice.** *Le Pèlerinage à la Mekke.* Paris, 1923. [Annales du Musée Guimet, Bibliothèque d'études, v. 33.]

a. Racy, vivid, picturesque; often giving sides of life not in the more staid (G601) Lane, *Modern Egyptians,* but reliable even in details and producing the right impression as to the whole. Middle-class life in Cairo, Medina, and Mecca; sea-travel in a pilgrim ship; and desert travel in a pilgrim caravan described from the inside. The pilgrim ceremonial is recorded with careful detail and with a sympathetic study of its emotional effects. Burton's best book by far; indispensable. *b.* Study in religious history; very full collection of notes on the religious rites of the Muslim pilgrimage; considers especially how these rites have been adapted from ancient Arabia and adjusted to Islam. To this is prefixed a detailed description of the Ka 'ba and the surrounding sacred precinct, with an archeological history of the latter. Evidently intended for advanced students of Islam; but even they will feel the entire lack of plans and maps.

DBM

G628 **Depont, Octave,** and **Coppolani, Xavier.** *Les confrèries religieuses musulmanes.* Alger, 1897.

Fundamental work; indispensable as a source of knowledge on the origins and present constitutions of the Derwish fraternities. Frank in its exposition of French political and cultural aims. Antiquated in its introductory portions, ch. 1, and a part of ch. 2.   MS

G629 Doutté, Edmond. *Magie et religion dans l'Afrique du Nord.* Alger, 1908. [Publications de la Société Musulmane du Maghrib.]

Only book for Islam in its class, and a thesaurus at that. Elaborate study, both from Arabic texts and, at first hand, from the people, of folk-lore, beliefs, and usages in Muslim North Africa; almost equally valuable for the rest of the Muslim world. Illuminates magic and popular religion and the relation of the two, which is far more important for understanding Islam than Christendom.
                                                                                    DBM

G630 Weir, Thomas H. *Shaikhs of Morocco in the VIth century..* Edinburgh, 1904.

Good picture of the mystical, ecstatic, and miraculous religious life of the West, but true for all Islam, especially in its organization around saintly individuals and as affecting political action. Makes vivid a side of Muslim life very difficult and yet essential for us to realize. Review, *Asiatic Quar. Rev.* 3rd series, 18:420, Oct. 1904.   DBM

G631 Arnold, Sir Thomas W. *Preaching of Islam, a history of the propagation of the Muslim faith.* 1896. 2nd ed., N. Y. and London, 1913.

Fascinating development of the proposition that Islam has gained by far the larger number of its converts by missionary efforts. Authorities like Snouck Hurgronje do not consider the main thesis proven. In any case an astonishing amount of information on the spread of Islam in all parts of the globe is presented in most readable form. Review, R. Basset, *Revue de l'histoire des religions,* 77:302, Feb. 1918.   MS

CULTURAL HISTORY: THOUGHT AND PHILOSOPHY

G641 Browne, Edward G. *Arabian medicine.* Cambridge, Eng., 1921. [Fitz-patrick lectures.] (Bibliographical foot-notes.)

Admirable sketch by a thorough orientalist, linguist, and traveller, who has also had a complete medical training. Traces the beginnings and development of Muslim science as well as medicine and, while very accurate, gives a wealth of picturesque detail and anecdote. Explodes the misleading term 'Arabian' but unhappily retains it in the title. Best introduction in English.   DBM

G651 Boer, Tjitze J. de. *History of philosophy in Islam.* London, 1903. [Luzac's oriental religious series.] Tr. by E. R. Jones from *Geschichte der Philosophie im Islam,* Stuttgart, 1901.

Should preferably be read in the German original, as this translation is not quite adequate. Short, readable, thorough; reliable on both the Arabic and the philosophic sides; the only easily accessible introduction to the development of philosophy and of philosophical theology in Islam. Although many lines of investigation—in philosophy proper, in scholastic theology, in mystical philosophy—have been carried farther since it appeared, it is still the book with which to begin.   DBM

CULTURAL HISTORY: LITERATURE

G661 Huart, Clement I. *History of Arabic literature.* N. Y., 1903. [Short histories of the literature of the world.] (Bibliography.) Tr. by Lady Mary Loyd from *Littérature arabe,* Paris, 1902.

Handy reference work on books and writers for those who do not possess the larger histories of literature. Not a history of ideas or movements. Review, *Gunton's magazine,* 25:360, Oct. 1903.   WHW

G662a Brockelmann, Carl. *Geschichte der arabischen Litteratur.* 2 v. Weimar, 1898–1902.

b Pfannmüller, Gustav. *Handbuch der Islam-Literatur.* Berlin, 1923.

a. Not a real history of literature but a *catalogue raisonné* with biographical and historical details and outlines.   *b.* Comprehensive, systematic, critical history of Moslem religious literature; comparatively little on philosophy and science as western scholars have found it and judged it; consequently supplements *a.*   Review, J. Ruska, *Isis,* 6:425, 1924.   DBM

G663a Nicholson, Reynold A. *Literary history of the Arabs.* 1907. 2nd ed. N. Y., 1930. [Library of literary history.] (Bibliography.)

b —— *Translations of Eastern poetry and prose.* Cambridge, Eng., 1922.

a. History of the development of ideas in the literature of the Arabic language. Does not include Muslim writers of Persia; and for Persian writers of Arabic, who were numerous and important, it requires the supplementation of (G671) Browne. Written primarily as a general historical and literary introduction for students of Arabic, it is, especially when combined with Browne, the best existing history of Arabic literature for general purposes. The author, in contrast to Browne, sees things from the exterior and less intimate, though more critical, standpoint of the West. Review, Bouvat, *Journal Asiatique,* 10th series, 11:347, March 1908.   WHW
    b. On Islamic history and religion, morals and manners, culture and character. Something, too, on the heathen Arabs before Mohammed.   DBM

G671a Browne, Edward G. *Literary history of Persia.* 4 v. London and N. Y., 1902–29. [Library of literary history.]

b —— *History of Persian literature under Tartar dominion, A. D. 1265–1502.* Cambridge, Eng., 1920.

a. V. 1. General introduction to Persian literature. V. 2. History of that literature down to Sa'adi. V. 4. Discusses vernacular literature from 1500 to 1924. Includes Persian writers of Arabic; addresses itself chiefly to non-Orientalists; both volumes, especially v. 1, are useful to all students of Muslim literature, whether in Persian or in Arabic. The author sees the intellectual and literary achievements of Persian national genius from within. Review, F. Unwin, *Athenaeum,* 1:330, Mar. 14, 1903; 2:822, Dec. 29, 1906. *b.* Independent volume, but numbered in series as v. 3 of *a.* Volume 4 is also independent.
                                                                          WHW

CULTURAL HISTORY: ART

G681 Poole, Stanley Lane. *Story of Cairo.* London and N. Y., 1902. [Medieval towns.]

Illuminating archeological survey, chiefly architectural, with sufficient political and social setting, covering seventh to sixteenth centuries. Has chronological list of rulers and their buildings.   JEW

G682a Saladin, Henri, and **Migeon, Gaston.** *Manuel d'art musulman.* 2 v. Paris, 1907. [1, H. Saladin, *L'architecture;* 2, G. Migeon, *Les arts plastiques et industriels.*] 2nd rev. ed. of v. 2, Paris. 1926. (Bibliographies.)

  b Marcais, Georges. *Manuel d'art musulman: l'architecture, Tunisie, Algérie, Maroc, Espagne, Sicile.* 2 v. Paris, 1926.

a. V. 1. Contains, after a long prefatory chapter, five chapters on the individual schools of Mohammedan architecture, Syro-Egyptian, Moroccan, Persian, Ottoman, Indian. V. 2. Contains fourteen chapters on the other arts, from paintings and fabrics to ivory carvings and enameled glass; ends with a chapter on the influences of Mohammedan art on the arts of the West. The respective volumes are by authorities in their own fields. The 1594 illustrations are, for the most part, excellent.   HCB

b. Revision and amplification of first volume of *a;* abundantly illustrated and scholarly. Review, A. Vincent, *Rev. des Quest. Hist.,* 107:437, Oct. 1927. SBF

PERIODICALS

The following seven reviews are devoted especially to Moslem history and conditions: (G941) *Der Islam, Zeitschrift für Geschichte und Kultur des islamischen Orients,* Strassburg, 1910 ff.; (G942) *Mir Islama* (Russian), Petrograd, 1912–14; (G943) *Revue du monde musulman, publiée par la Mission Scientifique du Maroc,* Paris, 1906 ff., later changed in name to *Revue des études islamiques;* (G944) *Die Welt des Islams, Zeitschrift der Deutschen Gesellschaft für Islamkunde,* Berlin, 1913–19; (G945) *Revue de l'Islam,* Paris, 1896–1906; (G946) *Moslem world, a quarterly review of current events, literature, and thought among Mohammedans and the progress of Christian missions in Moslem lands,* London and N. Y., 1911 ff.; (G947) *Islamica, a journal devoted to the study of the language, arts, and civilization of the Islamic peoples,* Leipzig, 1924 ff.; issued as a supplement to (U948) *Asia Major.* In addition a great deal of material for the history and institutions of Islam is to be found in periodicals listed in §§ B, C, H, U, and W.   DCM

SECTION H

MEDIEVAL TIMES, 500–1500

Editor

Louis John Paetow *

Professor of Medieval History, University of California. Died, Dec. 22, 1928.

CONTENTS

INTRODUCTION

Although the history of the Middle Ages is a well-tilled field in which there are excellent manuals and standard histories, as well as many interesting books for the general reader, it is still obscured by the conception 'dark ages.' As the Renaissance was necessary to reveal the real nature of the ancient world so a new renaissance will be necessary to present the Middle Ages in their true light. It is possible that this revival may result from a scientific study of medieval Latin.

The Mediaeval Academy of America, founded in 1925, is promoting medieval studies in America by means of its quarterly journal, (H952) *Speculum.*

Since the books in this *Guide* are classified by countries or areas, and by subjects as well as by periods, the books included in this section for the period

* Professor Paetow wished to make special acknowledgment of assistance received from Professors Haskins, Munro, and Thorndike.

from about A. D. 500 to about A. D. 1500 are necessarily limited mainly to those which are general in scope or which deal with certain special topics not logically classified elsewhere. Many items of interest to students of medieval history, consequently must be sought in other sections, especially § F, History of the church, § G, Mohammedanism, and the sections on those countries which had their rise in the Middle Ages. Many books on the Renaissance will be found in § O, Italy, and some in § I, Modern history. Many books dealt with in § A, History and auxiliary sciences, are especially important for students of medieval history.

BIBLIOGRAPHY AND LIBRARY COLLECTIONS

H1a Paetow, Louis J. *Guide to the study of medieval history for students, teachers, and libraries.* Berkeley, Calif., 1917. Rev. ed. N. Y., 1930.

b Lees, Beatrice A. *Bibliography of medieval history, 400 to 1500 A. D.* London, 1917. [Leaflet no. 44 of the Historical Association.]

a. Best general bibliography of medieval history; comprehensive, scholarly, and critical. Designed primarily for use in university classes; contains topical outlines and references for beginners and general readers, as well as the more special bibliographies, sources, and works in foreign languages needed by advanced students. Particularly full on the side of medieval culture. *b.* Scholarly, convenient pamphlet of 47 pages; much briefer than *a.* but useful within its limits. CHH

H2a Chevalier, Ulysse. *Répertoire des sources historiques du moyen âge: bio-bibliographie.* 2 v. 1877–88. 2nd rev. ed., Paris, 1903–07.

b —— *Répertoire des sources historiques du moyen âge: topo-bibliographie.* 2 v. Paris, 1894–1903.

Indispensable guides to the special literature of medieval history, though far from complete and making no attempt to discriminate critically among the mass of references industriously collected. *a.* Deals with persons; the more serviceable. *b.* Covers topics as well as places. Both are somewhat out of date but nothing takes their place. CHH

H3 Potthast, August. *Bibliotheca historica medii aevi: Wegweiser durch die Geschichtswerke des europäischen Mittelalters bis 1500.* 1862. 2nd rev. ed., 2 v., Berlin, 1896.

Primarily a bibliography of medieval chronicles and biographies, including lives of saints, indicating in each instance the various editions and translations and the critical literature. Analyzes the great collections of such sources and lists the chronicles chronologically by countries. Long a standard work of reference; never accurate or complete; must be supplemented by more detailed and recent works for special countries. Review, D. C. Munro, *A.H.R.* 2:710, July 1897. Cf. also the bibliographies for special countries listed in other sections of this *Guide* and those in § B, General history. CHH

H4 Thompson, James Westfall. *Reference studies in medieval history.* 1907. 3rd rev. ed., 3 v., Chicago, 1923–24.

Limited to works in English; covers about A. D. 300 to 1500. Under about ninety general headings and several hundred sub-headings are listed a multitude of exact references. Excellent reader's guide, with helpful introduction.

GMD

Library collections.—In America, the best collection of books on medieval history is undoubtedly that of the Harvard University Library, which includes the unrivalled Riant collection on the crusades and the Latin East, and extensive collections on the history of the Byzantine Empire, of the Normans, and of medieval culture in its several phases. Probably next in order is the Princeton University Library which also has good collections on the crusades and the Byzantine Empire, followed by the university libraries of Cornell, Columbia, and Yale, in the East, of Chicago and Western Reserve in the Middle West, and of California in the Far West. Syracuse University possesses the Ranke collection, which is rich in works on medieval Germany and Italy. The Library of the Catholic University of America, Washington, D. C., should be mentioned especially for the history of medieval learning and philosophy.   AHS

WORKS OF REFERENCE

H21a Du Cange, Charles Du Fresne, Sieur. *Glossarium mediae et infimae latinitatis.* 3 v. 1678. Best ed., 7 v., Paris, 1840–50. Newest ed. by L. Favre, 10 v., Niort, 1883–87.

b Maigne D'Arnis, W. H. *Lexicon manuale ad scriptores mediae et infimae latinitatis.* 1858. Reprint, Paris, 1890.

c Schmidt, Charles. *Petit supplément au dictionnaire de Du Cange.* Strasbourg, 1906.

d Diefenbach, Lorenz. *Glossarium Latino-Germanicum mediae et infimae aetatis.* Frankfurt, 1857. *Novum Glossarium.* Ibid., 1867.

a. This glossary has long been the indispensable manual for every student of the period. Now a Committee of the Union Académique Internationale is preparing a glossary of medieval Latin to 1000 A.D. and other committees are preparing glossaries of later Latin for the separate countries. This work is participated in by the American Council of Learned Societies, which has a Committee on a Dictionary of Medieval Latin and a Committee on a Dictionary of Later Medieval British Latin; cf. (H951) *Archivum latinitatis,* and (H952) *Speculum.* *b.* Epitome of *a.* Very useful for those who do not have access to *a.* Definitions are given in Latin and French. *c.* Contains some additional words and many additional definitions of words in *a* drawn largely from sermons, poems, and university documents. *d.* Supplements to *a.*   DCM, LJP

H22a Gröber, Gustav, ed. *Grundriss der romanischen Philologie.* 2 v. in 4, Strassburg, 1888–1902. 2nd ed. of v. 1, Strassburg, 1904–06.

b Paul, Hermann, ed. *Grundriss der germanischen Philologie.* 2 v. in 3, 1891–93. 2nd rev. ed., 3 v. in 4, 1900–09; 3rd rev. ed., v. 1–6, Strassburg, 1911–16.

Fortunately the modern vernaculars, which took shape in the Middle Ages, have been studied much more scientifically than medieval Latin. The results have been epitomized in *a.* and *b.* For the study of medieval history from the sources, however, the vernaculars are of much less importance than Latin.   LJP

H23 Willard, James F. *Progress of medieval studies in the United States of America.* Bulletins 1–7. Boulder, Colorado, 1923–29.

These annual reports issued under the patronage of the University of Colorado and of the American Council of Learned Societies are very useful for all students of medieval history. They contain alphabetical lists of American medievalists and their writings. LJP

GEOGRAPHY

H41a [Deschamps, Pierre]. *Dictionnaire de géographie ancienne et moderne à l'usage du libraire et de l'amateur de livres, par un bibliophile.* Paris, 1870.

b Graesse, Johann G. *Orbis latinus, oder, Verzeichnis der wichtigsten lateinischen Orts- und Ländernamen.* 1861. Rev. ed. by F. Benedict, Berlin and N. Y., 1909.

For medieval geographical terms, especially their Latin forms, these manuals are essential. Cf. also (A48) Freeman, *Historical geography of Europe;* (K222) Beazley, *Dawn of modern geography;* and (A49, 50) historical atlases. LJP

H42 Wright, John K. *Geographical lore of the time of the crusades: a study in the history of medieval science and tradition in western Europe.* N. Y., 1925. (Excellent critical bibliography.)

Based on the sources; best introduction to geographical knowledge in the Middle Ages. LJP

H43 Newton, Arthur P., ed. *Travel and travelers in the middle ages.* N. Y., 1926. [(B153a) History of Civilization.]

A collection of public lectures by various speakers at the University of London on such topics as the geographical knowledge of the middle ages, Vikings, Arab travelers, and the opening of the trade routes to the Far East. LJP

SOURCE-BOOKS, COLLECTIONS OF SOURCES, ARCHIVE PUBLICATIONS

H61a Ogg, Frederic A. *Source book of mediaeval history: documents illustrative of European life and institutions from the German invasions to the renaissance.* N. Y., 1908.

b Robinson, James H. *Readings in European history.* V. 1. Boston, 1906. (Critical bibliographies.)

c Henderson, Ernest F. *Select historical documents of the middle ages.* London and N. Y., 1892. Later reprints. [Bohn's antiquarian library.]

d Thatcher, Oliver J., and **McNeal, Edgar H.** *Source book for mediaeval history.* N. Y., 1905. (Bibliography.)

e Coulton, George G. *From St. Francis to Dante: a translation of all that is of primary interest in the Chronicle of the Franciscan Salimbene, 1221–1288.* 1906. 2nd rev. ed., London, 1907. (Bibliography.)

f —— *Mediaeval garner, human documents from the four centuries preceding the reformation.* London, 1910.

g Duncalf, Frederic, and **Krey, August C.** *Parallel source problems in medieval history.* N. Y. and London, 1912. [Harper's parallel source problems.]

Each of these books contains translations of a number of representative extracts from historical sources. In choice of what is historically important and pedagogically possible there seems little to choose between them. Their merit is to get the reader away from the text-book and the secondary historian's type of statement, and to lend vividness and freshness to the study of the past.

a. Perhaps the most systematic arrangement, but does not adhere to a uniform method. Includes 83 narratives and documents of fair length, with introductions giving the historical setting. *b.* These 230 briefer selections are in part from later histories rather than from sources. Gives most attention to medieval culture. *c.* Practically limited to documents connected with English constitutional history and the empire and papacy, but has the merit of giving fully some of the latter, as the Rule of St. Benedict and the Golden Bull. *d.* Contains 325 brief selections dealing mainly with the empire and the papacy but also with feudalism, medieval law, monasticism, and the crusades. *e.* and *f.* Coulton shows the closest acquaintance with the sources and with the medieval mental attitude, but is a little too zealous in emphasizing unattractive features of the medieval church and of the Middle Ages. *g.* Represents a reaction against presenting the sources in detached fragments and is an experiment for more intensive study and critical training through grouping source material about a single problem or subject, such as the coronation of Charles the Great. Cf. (H353*a*) A. C. Krey, *First Crusade.*   LT

H62a Munro, Dana C., and **Sellery, George C.,** ed. and tr. *Medieval civilization: selected studies from European authors.* 1904. Enlarged ed., N. Y., 1907.

  b Langlois, Charles V., ed. *Lectures historiques: histoire du moyen âge, 395–1270.* 1890. 5th ed., Paris, 1912. (Bibliographies.)

  c Mariéjol, Jean H., ed. *Lectures historiques: histoire du moyen âge et des temps modernes, 1270–1610.* Paris, 1891.

a. Very clever skimming off of some of the cream of European scholarship and historical writing. The well-chosen selections from periodical literature as well as books, translated and adapted for the student and reader, are the stimulating and illuminating reflection of ripe scholarship upon the main features and problems of medieval history. *b.* and *c.* French prototypes of *a.* in which the selections are taken almost exclusively from French books.   LT

H63a Beeson, Charles H. *Primer of medieval Latin.* Chicago, 1925.

  b Harrington, Karl P. *Mediaeval Latin.* Boston, 1925.

Textbooks of well chosen selections of medieval Latin; include extracts from most of the leading chroniclers, contemporary accounts of important events, and a wide variety of illustrative material on the life of the times; illuminating introductory paragraphs, with bibliographical data, and necessary glossarial notes accompany the selections. Review of *a, b,* and similar works, C. U. Clark, *Speculum* 1:110, Jan. 1926.   LJP

Collections of sources.—Thus far practically all the important attempts to publish the sources of the history of the Middle Ages, such as (P71*a*) *Monumenta Germaniae historica,* have been national, and not international enterprises. As a consequence nearly all the important collections of medieval sources are listed in other sections of this *Guide,* cf. especially § F, Church history. Mention need here be made only of the most important sources for the crusades, the outstanding international enterprise of the Middle Ages, for the Byzantine Empire, and for the universities. (H71) *Recueil des historiens des croisades publié par les soins de l'Académie des Inscriptions et Belles-Lettres,* 16 v., Paris, 1841–1906; (H72) Société de l'Orient Latin, *Publications,* 10 v., Genève and Paris,

1877–89; (H76) *Byzantinae historiae scriptores,* or *Corpus byzantinae historiae,* 39 v. (or 47, or 23, or 27 according to arrangement), Parisiis, 1645–1711, reprint, Venetiis, 1729–33; revised as (H77) *Corpus scriptorum historiae Byzantinae,* 50 v., Bonnae, 1828–97; (H81) *Chartularium universitatis Parisiensis,* ed. by H. Denifle and E. Châtelain, 4 v., Parisiis, 1889–97, supplemented by the (H81a) *Auctarium chartularii universitatis Parisiensis,* by the same editors, 2 v., Parisiis, 1894–97; (H82) *Chartularium studii Bononiensis, documenti per la storia dell' università di Bologna dalle origini fino al secolo XV,* ed. by L. Nordi and E. Orioli, v. 1–8, Bologna, 1907–27; (H83) *Les statuts et privilèges des universités françaises depuis leur fondation jusqu'en 1789,* ed. by M. Fournier, 4 v., Paris, 1890–94.

SHORTER GENERAL HISTORIES

H101a Thorndike, Lynn. *History of medieval Europe.* Boston, 1917. Illustrated ed., with the title, *Medieval Europe,* London, 1920. Rev. ed., Boston, 1928. [Great nation series.] (Carefully selected bibliographies.)

b Thatcher, Oliver J., and **McNeal, Edgar H.** *Europe in the middle age.* N. Y., 1920. Rev. ed. of O. J. Thatcher and F. Schevill, *Europe in the middle age.* N. Y., 1896.

c Previté-Orton, Charles W. *Outlines of medieval history.* 1916. 2nd rev. ed., Cambridge, Eng., 1924.

These three books attempt to cover the period from about A. D. 400 to about A. D. 1500 in single volumes for use in the first years of college. *a.* Fresh and stimulating, written by a scholar who has devoted himself to the intellectual history of the Middle Ages. Much space is given to the history of culture. *b.* In its revised form this old text has been completely rewritten but the general plan has not been altered drastically. Marginal references to source-books constitute a valuable feature. *c.* Departs from the English custom of crowding historical text-books with political facts and touches upon many other phases of life in the Middle Ages.   LJP

H102a Munro, Dana C. *Middle ages, 395–1272.* N. Y., 1921. Rev. ed., D. C. Munro and R. J. Sontag, *Middle Ages, 395–1500.* N. Y., 1928. [Century historical series.] (Good bibliography.)

b Bémont, Charles, and **Monod, Gabriel.** *Medieval Europe from 395 to 1270.* N. Y., 1902. Tr. by M. Sloan, with notes and revisions by G. B. Adams, from *Histoire de l'Europe et en particulier de la France de 395 à 1270,* Paris, 1891. (Bibliographies.)

These text-books cut off the story of the Middle Ages somewhat arbitrarily at about 1270, a disadvantage which has disappeared in the revised edition of *a.* Both were written by well-known scholars, justly famed for their ability to teach. Both aim to present only the main features of medieval life. *a.* To be commended rather than *b,* not merely as a more recent work, but also as a better balanced treatment.   LJP

H103a Emerton, Ephraim. *Introduction to the study of the middle ages, 375–814.* Boston, 1888. (Bibliographies.)

b —— *Mediaeval Europe, 814–1300.* Boston, 1894. (Bibliographies.)

c —— *Beginnings of modern Europe, 1250–1450.* Boston, 1917.

For the reader who is not satisfied with a general survey in a single volume these books furnish the best outline of medieval history within a moderate compass. *a.* Written for comparatively young students. Very well done and forty-one years have not diminished its serviceability. *b.* and *c.* Written for more mature students. In *b.* the history of the empire and papacy is perhaps stressed unduly; in *c.* Spain and Eastern Europe are left out entirely. Review of *c.*, L. J. Paetow, *A.H.R.* 23:842, July 1918. Cf. also v. 1-3 of (B132) A. Hassall, *Periods of European history.*   LJP

H104a **Adams, George B.** *Civilization during the middle ages.* 1894. Rev. ed., N. Y., 1914.

  b **Hearnshaw, Fossey J. C.,** ed. *Mediaeval contributions to modern civilisation, a series of lectures delivered at King's College, University of London.* London, 1921; N. Y., 1922.

  c **Crump, C. G.,** and **Jacob, E. F.,** eds. *The legacy of the middle ages.* Oxford, 1926.

  d **Sellery, George C.,** and **Krey, August C.** *Medieval foundations of western civilization.* N. Y., 1929.

  e **Rand, Edward Kennard.** *Founders of the middle ages.* Cambridge, Mass., 1928. [Lowell Institute Lectures.]

  a. Much the best work upon the subject in the English language. In all qualities that make a good book—knowledge of the subject, coördination and interpretation of material, presentation—it is a superior work.   JWT
  b. Stimulating popular lectures, by ten London professors, on characteristic features of the Middle Ages and the debt which modern society owes to them in religion, philosophy, science, art, poetry, education, social institutions, economics, and politics. Review, G. C. Sellery, *A.H.R.* 28:86, Oct. 1922. *c.* Essays by various specialists on topics similar to those in *b.* Reviews, N. Neilson, *A.H.R.* 32:846, July 1927; Z. N. Brooke, *E.H.R.* 42:426, July 1927.   LJP
  d. Excellent text-book by teachers of long experience familiar with the needs of the class-room. Review, E. Emerton, *A.H.R.* 34:796, July 1929. *e.* Chapters on Ambrose the Mystic, Jerome the Humanist, Boëthius the Scholastic, The New Poetry, the New Education, and St. Augustine and Dante illustrate the appropriation of pagan classical culture by the church; thoughtful, witty, whimsical, and charming popularization by a ripe scholar. Review, A. P. Evans, *A.H.R.* 34:797, July 1929.   SBF

H105 **Loserth, Johann.** *Geschichte des späteren Mittelalters von 1197 bis 1492.* München, 1903. [Handbuch der mittelalterlichen und neueren Geschichte, ed. by Below and Meinecke.] (Excellent bibliographies.)

  Although a general political history of the period covered, it stresses the history of the church in its relations to the state. The author is a well-known Wyclif scholar. Italy, which is justly emphasized by E. Emerton in (H103*c*) *Beginnings of modern Europe,* is slighted by Loserth.   LJP

LONGER GENERAL HISTORIES

H121 *Cambridge medieval history.* Planned by J. B. Bury. Ed. by H. M. Gwatkin, J. P. Whitney, J. R. Tanner, C. W. Previté Orton, and Z. N. Brooke. N. Y., v. 1-6, 1911-29. (Extended bibliographies.)

  'Intended,' says the preface, 'as a comprehensive account of medieval times, drawn up on the same lines as the (I121) *Cambridge modern history* but with a few improvements of detail suggested by experience. It is intended partly for the general reader as a clear and, as far as possible, interesting narrative; partly for the student, as a summary of ascertained facts, with indications (not discussions) of disputed points; partly as a book of reference containing all that can reasonably be required in a comprehensive work of general history.' A portfolio of illustrative maps accompanies each volume.

Since each chapter is a separate monograph, complete coördination of material, proportion in distribution of space, and unity of the subject are difficult to achieve. In spite of these drawbacks, which seem to be unavoidable, the volumes constitute the most recent and most scholarly presentation of the history of the early Middle Ages in English. V. 1. 'The Christian Roman Empire' covers the fourth and fifth centuries. V. 2. 'The rise of the Saracens' extends from Justinian to Charlemagne. V. 3. 'Germany and the western empire' carries the narrative to 1079. V. 4. 'Eastern Roman Empire, 717–1453' includes eastern Europe and western Asia in the period. V. 5. 'Contest of Empire and Papacy' records events to the deaths of Louis VII of France, Henry II of England, and the Emperor Henry VI; treatment of the Third Crusade is only incidental. Not all the contributors are English. French, German, Russian, American, and other scholars have been enlisted. One hardly looks for great originality in a synthetic work but Peisker's chapter on the Huns, (v. 1, ch. 12) is a remarkable study in nomadism. Reviews, E. W. Dow, *A.H.R.* 17:592, Apr. 1912; 19:588, Apr. 1914; J. W. Thompson, 28:93, Oct. 1922; D. C. Munro, 29:749, July 1924; 32:574, Apr. 1927; G. M. Rushforth, *E.H.R.* 27:538, July 1912; E. W. Brooks, 29:336, Apr. 1914; 39:627, Oct. 1924; T. F. Tout, 42:110, Jan. 1927.   JWT

H122 Gibbon, Edward. *History of the decline and fall of the Roman empire.* 1776–81. Ed. with introduction, notes, appendices, and Index, by J. B. Bury. 7 v., London and N. Y., 1896–98; later reprints.

For v. 1–3 cf. (E312). V. 4–7. Deal with the medieval period. The continuation of the Roman Empire in the East is traced from the middle of the fifth century to the fall of Constantinople in 1453. The work is more than a history of the Byzantine empire, for it includes the history of Italy throughout the period from the point of view of the Roman tradition, and the history of the various peoples and states with which Byzantium was brought into relations. The history of the eastern branches of the Christian church and of their schism from Rome and also of the rise of Mohammedanism receives adequate attention. Though modern researches have added much to knowledge, Gibbon's account not only remains a classic but is still the best comprehensive survey for the whole medieval period of the history of the regions now called the Near East. Gibbon practically confined himself to political, religious, and institutional history, and failed to consider the important economic and cultural factors involved. For further consideration of Gibbon as an historian, cf. Bury's introduction in v. 1 of his edition of the work; cf. also two articles in F. Harrison, *Tennyson, Ruskin, Mill, and other literary estimates.*   GMD

BARBARIAN INVASIONS

H201 Dahn, Felix L. S. *Die Könige der Germanen: das Wesen des ältesten Königthums der germanischen Stämme und seine Geschichte bis zur Auflösung des karolingischen Reiches, nach den Quellen dargestellt.* 12 v. and index. V. 1-2, München, 1861, 2nd ed., Leipzig, 1911; v. 3-6, Würzburg, 1866-71, v. 6, 2nd ed., Leipzig, 1885; v. 7-12 and index, Leipzig, 1894-1911. (Bibliographies.)

Most complete history of the Germanic peoples from the beginning of the migrations to the dissolution of the Carolingian empire. Narrative history is confined within small compass and most of the emphasis is placed upon institutions. Well-written, monumental work, though encumbered with details and marred by decided and uncompromising opinions. Reviews, *Hist. Zeit.* 7:288, 1862; 16:177, 1866; 28:163, 1872; 56:79, 1886; 76:295, 1896; 78:193, 1897; 88:281, 1902. CWD

H202 Hodgkin, Thomas. *Italy and her invaders.* 8 v. in 9. 1880-99. 2nd thoroughly rev. ed. of v. 1 and 2, Oxford, 1892; 2nd slightly rev. ed. of v. 3 and 4, Oxford, 1896; 2nd slightly rev. ed. by R. H. Hodgkin, of v. 5 and 6, Oxford, 1916.

Most elaborate history of Italy and its barbaric invaders in the early Middle Ages which has been attempted in English since (H122) Gibbon, *Decline and fall.* The later volumes contain much matter which lay beyond the scope of Gibbon's work. Covers the period from the crossing of the Roman frontier by the Visigoths in 376 to the death of Charles the Great in 814. Digressive, 'the story of the invading nation' being 'treated as fully as that of the invaded land.' Primarily a narrative history; little space is given to institutions or to the life of the people. Its picturesque style, in spite of verbosity, has won it popularity among general readers, though it cannot be said to have greatly extended the scholar's knowledge or deepened his understanding of the obscure and difficult period with which it deals. Review, 2nd ed., v. 1 and 2, R. L. Poole, *E.H.R.* 9:187, Jan. 1894; 1. 3 and 4, H. M. Gwatkin, 1:154; Jan. 1886; 2nd ed., 1. 3 and 4, 12.183, Jan. 1897; v. 5 and 6, H. M. Gwatkin, 10:781, Oct. 1895, and *A.H.R.* 1:108, Oct. 1895; 2nd ed., v. 5 and 6, R. L. Poole, *E.H.R.* 32:306, Apr. 1917; v. 7 and 8, E. W. Brooks, 15:152, Jan. 1900, and *A.H.R.* 5:734, July, 1900.   CWD

H203a Jordanes. *Gothic history: English version with an introduction and a commentary by C. C. Mierow.* 1908. 2nd rev. ed., Princeton, 1915. Tr. from *Romana et Getica,* ed. by T. Mommsen, Berolini, 1882 [(P71a) Monumenta Germaniae historica]. (Bibliography.)

b Gregory, Bishop of Tours. *History of the Franks: selections with notes.* N. Y., 1916. [(B61) Shotwell, Records of civilization.] (Bibliography.) Tr. by E. Brehaut from *Historiae Francorum libri decem,* ed. by W. Arndt, M. Bonnet, and B. Krusch, Hannover, 1885 [(P71a) Monumenta Germaniae historica]. More popular ed. by H. Omont and G. Collon, 2 v., 1886-93, rev. ed. by R. Poupardin, Paris, 1913 [Collection de textes pour servir à l'étude et à l'enseignement de l'histoire]. *History of the Franks by Gregory of Tours.* Tr. with an intro. by O. M. Dalton, 2 v. Oxford, 1927.

c Paul the Deacon. *History of the Langobards.* Philadelphia, 1907. Tr. by W. D. Foulke from *Historia Langobardorum,* ed. by L. Bethmann and G. Waitz, Hannover, 1878 [(P71a) Monumenta Germaniae historica].

a. Jordanes, bishop of Ravenna in the sixth century, wrote when the ancient Latin culture had almost perished. His style is uncouth and barbarous. The method of exposition is singularly crude. The value of the work lies in the fact that it is the sole existing history of the East Goths, since the larger and far superior *History* of the Ostrogoths, by Cassiodorus, has unfortunately perished. Review, E. W. Brooks, *E.H.R.* 30:564, July 1915. JWT
b. Dalton has made the first complete English translation of the monumental history of Gregory of Tours. The work of Brehaut contains translations of most of the interesting passages usually quoted and a skeleton summary of the whole work. Review of Brehaut, A. C. Krey, *A.H.R.* 22:623, Apr. 1917.
c. This complete translation is accurate, but lacks distinction. An introduction, notes, and appendixes summarize the conclusions of the best modern authorities concerning the author's life, sources, etc. Review, E. H. McNeal, *A.H.R.* 13:378, Jan. 1908; E. W. Brooks, *E.H.R.* 22:826, Oct. 1907. CWD

H204a Bradley, Henry. *Story of the Goths from the earliest times to the end of the Gothic dominion in Spain.* London and N. Y., 1888. [Story of the nations.]

b Sergeant, Lewis. *The Franks, from their origin as a confederacy to the establishment of the kingdom of France and the German empire.* London and N. Y., 1898. [Story of the nations.]

a. Deals with both Visigoths and Ostrogoths. Brief sketch 'intended not for scholars, but for readers in whom little knowledge of general history is to be pre-supposed.' Based mainly upon (H122) Gibbon and (H202) Hodgkin. Fairly readable for so condensed a treatment. *b.* This convenient summary has been superseded by the chapters in (H121) *Cambridge medieval history* and the subject is more fully treated in v. 7 of (H202) T. Hodgkin, *Italy and her invaders.* Cf. also (P202) F. B. Gummere, *Germanic origins.* CWD

H205 Halphen, Louis. *Les barbares: des grandes invasions aux conquêtes turques du XIᵉ siècle.* Paris, 1926. [(B169b) Peuples et civilisations. Histoire générale.]

General survey of medieval history to the end of the eleventh century, with special reference to the movement of uncivilized peoples into the civilized Mediterranean area. Has many merits, of which the portrayal of the Asiatic background of early medieval history is the most prominent. Reviews, F. Duncalf, *A.H.R.* 32:573, Apr. 1927; F. M. Powicke, *History* 13:85, Apr. 1928. LJP

CHARLEMAGNE

H221a Einhard (or Eginhard). *Life of Charlemagne.* N. Y., 1880. [Harper's half-hour series.] Tr. by S. E. Turner from *Vita Karoli Magni,* ed. by G. Pertz, 1829; 6th rev. ed. by O. Holder-Egger, Hannover, 1911 [(P71a) Monumenta Germaniae Historica].

b Grant, Arthur J., ed. and tr. *Early lives of Charlemagne, by Eginhard and the Monk of St. Gall.* London and Boston, 1907. [King's classics.] Tr. from texts in P Jaffé, *Bibliotheca rerum germanicarum,* 6 v., Berolini, 1864–73.

c Éginhard. *Vie de Charlemagne.* Tr. by L. Halphen. Paris, 1923. [*Les classiques de l'histoire de France au moyen âge,* ed. by L. Halphen.]

This famous little biography, written by a contemporary of the great medieval emperor, is a mine of information for scholars, and a source of unending interest to the general reader because of its reflection of the civilization and the mental attitude of the times.   *a.* Probably most convenient of the English translations. *b.* Contains, in addition, materials from other chronicles.   *c.* Gives the Latin text and French translation on opposite pages, together with scholarly introduction and notes.   Review, F. M. Powicke, *E.H.R.* 39:307, Apr. 1924.   LJP

H222a Davis, Henry W. Carless. *Charlemagne (Charles the Great), the hero of two nations.* London and N. Y., 1899. [Heroes of the nations.]

b Hodgkin, Thomas. *Charles the Great.* London and N. Y., 1897. [Foreign statesmen.]

c Wells, Charles L. *Age of Charlemagne. (Charles the Great).* N. Y., 1898. [Ten epochs of church history.] (Bibliography.)

d Mombert, Jacob I. *History of Charles the Great (Charlemagne).* London and N. Y., 1888.

e Halphen, Louis. *Études critiques sur l'histoire de Charlemagne: les sources de l'histoire de Charlemagne, la conquête de la Saxe, le couronnement impérial, l'agriculture et la propriété rurale, l'industrie et le commerce.* Paris, 1921.

Of the biographies of Charlemagne by modern scholars *a., b., c.,* and *d.* are the best available in English.   *a.* Fairly complete; includes an excellent discussion of the civilization of the time; numerous illustrations.   *b.* Brief but well written and interesting.   *c.* Less valuable except for its fuller treatment of the activities of the church.   *d.* Still useful, though somewhat older than any of the preceding.   Very full and contains appendixes of value.   CWD

e. Eight studies which first appeared in *Revue historique,* 1917–20. Based upon a careful reëxamination of the sources, they upset many old theories and bring forth new facts which the author hopes to incorporate in a forthcoming large work on Charlemagne and Carolingian civilization. Review, C. W. David, *A.H.R.* 27:102, Oct. 1921.   LJP

NORMANS

H241a Haskins, Charles H. *Normans in European history.* Boston, 1915. (Bibliographies.)

b ——— *Norman institutions.* Cambridge, Mass., 1918. [Harvard historical studies.]

a. Popular presentation by a profound scholar. This work of absorbing interest combines with remarkable success exact scholarship, broad knowledge, and a high degree of literary art. While not neglecting the earlier and the later stages of Norman history, the author devotes himself in the main to the great achievements of the Normans in France and England and in southern Italy and Sicily between the close of the Viking age and the beginning of the thirteenth century. Reviews, *A.H.R.* 21:580, Apr. 1916; J. H. Round, *E.H.R.* 32:616, Oct. 1917.   *b.* This, on the other hand, is a work designed for scholars. Close-packed with fact, exhausting the sources, it is the definitive treatment of the institutions of Normandy in the eleventh and twelfth centuries. Throws light on English constitutional history. Reviews, G. B. Adams, *A.H.R.* 24:78, Oct. 1918; J. Tait, *E.H.R.* 33:388, July 1918; F. Liebermann, *Hist. Zeit.* 125:305, 1922. For the Normans in Italy, cf. (O492).   CWD

H242a Fowke, Frank R. *Bayeux tapestry reproduced in autotype plates, with historic notes.* London, 1875. [Arundel Society.]

b ——— *Bayeux tapestry, a history and description.* 1898. [Ex-libris series.] Reissued, London and N. Y., 1913. [Bohn's antiquarian library.]

c Belloc, Hilaire. *Book of the Bayeux tapestry, presenting the complete work in a series of colour facsimiles.* London and N. Y., 1914.

a. Elaborate publication. *b.* Good handy abridgement of *a.* The plates, though reduced in size, are well executed, and the usefulness of the volume is little impaired by the omission of much of the original printed matter. Reproduces the whole of the tapestry in 79 facsimiles with simple historical and descriptive notes. *c.* The reproduction in color is attractive, but the plates are on a somewhat smaller scale and not so clear in detail as the monochromes of *b.* The author's dating of the tapestry is not to be trusted. Review (severely critical but just) J. H. Round, *E.H.R.* 30:109, Jan. 1915.   CWD

BYZANTINE EMPIRE

H301a Harrison, Frederic. *Byzantine history in the early middle ages.* London and N. Y., 1900. [Rede lecture.] (Bibliographies.)

b Freeman, Edward A. *Byzantine empire.* 1879. 2nd ed., London and N. Y., 1892. [Historical essays, 3rd series, 1879, p. 231–277; 1892, p. 235–282.]

a. Brief analysis of the important characteristics of Byzantine history of the eighth, ninth, and tenth centuries, which summarizes the results of historical investigation, and suggests the possibilities of further study offered by this field. *b.* Brilliant general survey of Byzantine history, which emphasizes the continuity of Greek and Roman civilization. This essay, according to Frederic Harrison, 'is one of the most eloquent and impressive of all Professor Freeman's writings, and has exercised a deserved influence over English historical thought.'

FD

H302 Oman, Sir Charles W. C. *Story of the Byzantine empire.* London and N. Y., 1892. [Story of the nations.]

This popular, general history is a very interesting treatment of the Eastern Empire. The important phases of Byzantine history are clearly marked; the continuity of the story is never neglected; social, economic, intellectual, and artistic forces are discussed. Review, J. B. Bury, *E.H.R.* 8:327, Apr. 1893. Cf. p. 1–211 of (T102f) W. S. Davis, *Short history of the near east.*   FD

H303a Diehl, Charles. *History of the Byzantine empire.* Princeton, 1925. (Critical bibliography.) Tr. by G. B. Ives from *Histoire de l'empire byzantin.* Paris, 1920.

b ——— *Justinien et la civilisation byzantine au VIe siècle.* Paris, 1901. [Monuments de l'art byzantin.] (Bibliography.)

c ——— *Byzance, grandeur et décadence.* Paris, 1919. [Bibliothèque de philosophie scientifique.]

d ——— *Byzantine Portraits.* N. Y., 1927. Tr. by H. Bell from *Figures byzantines,* Paris, 1906.

e Hesseling, Dirk C. *Byzantium: Studiën over onze beschaving na de stichting van Konstantinopel.* Haarlem, 1902. Tr. into French, *Essai sur la civilisation byzantine,* with preface by G. Schlumberger, Paris, 1907.

Professor Diehl is the foremost French scholar in the field of Byzantine history, on which he has written many volumes. *a.* Of the works in one volume which survey the whole of Byzantine history this is undoubtedly the best. Review, D. C. Munro, *A.H.R.* 25 :741, July 1920; W. W. Hyde, *A.H.R.* 31 :818, July 1926. *b.* Sumptuous biography with very good illustrations. *c.* and *e.* Outstanding surveys, like *a.,* but of civilization rather than of narrative history. Each is brilliant and serves to supplement the other. *d.* Excellent essays. Review, D. C. Munro, *Speculum* 2 :350, July, 1927.   ACK

H304a Bury, John B. *History of the later Roman empire from Arcadius to Irene, 395 A.D. to 800 A.D.* 2 v. London and N. Y., 1889.

b ———— *History of the later Roman empire from the death of Theodosius I to the death of Justinian, A.D. 395 to A.D. 565.* 2 v. London, 1923. (Bibliography.)

c ———— *History of the eastern Roman empire from the fall of Irene to the accession of Basil I, A.D. 802–867.* London and N. Y., 1912. (Bibliography.)

Bury (died in 1927) was the leading English-speaking student of Byzantine history. *a.* Valuable exposition of the continuance and vigor of the Roman Empire and of the Greco-Roman culture in the East after the barbarian invasions. The author combats the use of the term 'Byzantine Empire.' Review, H. M. Gwatkin, *E.H.R.* 5 :578, July 1890. *b.* This welcome new work supersedes the first portion of *a,* which is out of print. It takes full account of the large amount of new material which has accumulated since 1889. Review, A. Gardner, *E.H.R.* 38 :428, July 1923.   LJP
c. Continues *a.* but is a much more comprehensive study of a shorter period. The author has investigated all known sources and utilizes the results of recent scholarship. In scope, the volume treats of the peoples that surrounded the empire, as well as of the events of the period and the institutions and civilization under the Amorian dynasty. Review, D. C. Munro, *A.H.R.* 18 :120, Oct. 1912. Cf. also v. 4–7 of (H122) Gibbon, *History of the decline and fall of the Roman empire,* edited by Professor Bury.   FD

H305 Finlay, George. *History of Greece from its conquest by the Romans to the present time, B. C. 146 to A.D. 1864.* 1844–61. Rev. ed. by H. F. Tozer, 7 v., Oxford, 1877. Reprint of v. 2 as *History of the Byzantine empire from DCCXVI to MLVII,* N. Y., 1906. [Everyman's library.]

V. 1–3. Devoted to the Eastern Empire. V. 4. Necessary to an understanding of the last phase of the empire, as it deals with the Latin and the other states formed after 1204. Notwithstanding the advance made by scholarship since its publication, this history remains the best comprehensive treatment in the English language of the Eastern Empire. Cf. (T7121) for later volumes.   FD

H306 Holmes, William G. *Age of Justinian and Theodora, a history of the sixth century A.D.* 2 v. London, 1905–07.

V. 1. Rather discursive treatment of the conditions of the empire before Justinian. V. 2. Deals with the events and circumstances of Justinian's reign. The work contains much information, but the author accepts too readily all evidence which indicates immorality and decadence. Review, E. W. Brooks, *E.H.R.* 21 :553, July 1906. Cf. (F704a) Dudden, *Gregory the Great.*   FD

H307a **Rambaud, Alfred N.** *L'empire grec au dixième siècle: Constantin Porphyrogénète.* Paris, 1870.

b **Neumann, Carl.** *Die Weltstellung des byzantinischen Reiches vor den Kreuzzügen.* Leipzig, 1894. French tr. by Renauld and Kozlowski, *Revue de l'Orient Latin,* v. 10, Paris, 1905.

These two books have marked epochs in the modern study of the Byzantine Empire by calling attention to the underlying forces within the empire to which its permanence was due. *a.* Systematic exposition of the events of the tenth century. *b.* Sweeping interpretative treatment of the following century. Both are brilliant contributions and while much of their material has been incorporated in more recent works, they still offer enough additional information to repay separate study.   ACK

H308a **Norden, Walter.** *Das Papsttum und Byzanz, die Trennung der beiden Mächte und das Problem ihrer Wiedervereinigung bis zum Untergange des byzantinischen Reichs, 1453.* Berlin, 1903. (Bibliographical footnotes.)

b **Bréhier, Louis.** *Le schisme oriental du XIe siècle.* Paris, 1899. (Bibliography.)

a. Large work; based upon the sources; studies the schism between the Latin and Greek churches and the attempts to reunite them as political rather than as religious problems. Special stress is placed on the thirteenth century, the Crusades, and the commercial expansion of Venice. *b.* Authoritative treatise, also based on contemporary sources, concerning the crisis of A. D. 1054 which definitely marked the separation of the Latin and Greek churches.   LJP

H309 **Vasiliev, Alexander A.** *History of the Byzantine empire.* V. 1, *From Constantine the Great to the epoch of the crusades.* Tr. from the Russian by Mrs. S. Ragozin. Madison, 1928. [University of Wisconsin studies in social sciences and history, no. 13.] (Critical bibliographies.) V. 2, 1929.

This bids fair to become the best general, strictly chronological, history of the Byzantine empire. Cf. also (H121) *Cambridge medieval history,* v. 4, *Eastern Roman empire.*   LJP

H310 **Baynes, Norman H.** *Byzantine empire.* London and N. Y., 1925. [Home university library.] (Bibliography.)

Brilliant little sketch. Extends only to capture of Constantinople by the crusaders in 1204. Review, H. I. Bell, *History* 11:151, July 1926.   LJP

CRUSADES

H351a **Archer, Thomas A.,** and **Kingsford, Charles L.** *The crusades, the story of the Latin kingdom of Jerusalem.* London and N. Y., 1895. [Story of the nations.]

b **Burr, George L.** *Year 1000 and the antecedents of the crusades. A.H.R.* 6:429–439. Apr. 1901.

c **Newhall, Richard A.** *The Crusades.* N. Y., 1927. [Berkshire studies in European history.]

d **Barker, Ernest.** *The Crusades.* London. 1923.

a. Still the best one-volume treatment of the subject in English. Style interesting and clear. Accounts of second and third crusades better than those of the first and later crusades. Description of institutions should be supplemented by reference to more recent investigations. *b.* Sparkling essay; summarizes the results of critical scholarship; brushes away a mass of legend.   ACK

c. Clear, scholarly sketch, designed to furnish a week's reading in a college course of general European history. *d.* Convenient reprint, with slight changes, of article in the Encyclopaedia Britannica.   LJP

H352a Bréhier, Louis. *L'église et l'orient au moyen âge: les croisades.* 1906. 4th enlarged ed., Paris, 1921. [Bibliothèque de l'enseignement de l'histoire ecclésiastique.] (Bibliography.)

b Kugler, Bernhard. *Geschichte der Kreuzzüge.* 1880. 2nd ed., Berlin, 1891. [(B162) Oncken, Allgemeine Geschichte.]

c Röhricht, Reinhold. *Geschichte der Kreuzzüge im Umriss.* Innsbruck, 1898.

d Michaud, Joseph F. *History of the crusades.* 3 v. London, 1852. Tr. by W. Robson from *Histoire des croisades,* 3 v., Paris, 1812–17. Many other ed.

e Wilken, Friedrich. *Geschichte der Kreuzzüge nach morgenländischen und abendländischen Berichten.* 7 v. Leipzig, 1807–32. (Bibliography.)

a. Devoted mainly to the crusades, but also treats of earlier relations between East and West, and relatively fully of the Christian missions in the East and the theoretical propagandists. Pays little attention to the influence of the crusades, either in the East or West. Review, E. Barker, *E.H.R.* 22:348, Apr. 1907. *b.* Excellent account of the political and military history, intended for the general public, but based upon careful study. Well illustrated. *c.* Excellent and convenient short sketch to A.D. 1291. *d.* and *e.* The most well known longer histories of the crusades. *d.* The basis for most of the writing on the crusades done in English during the nineteenth century. *c.* More scholarly, and in parts still valuable.   DCM

H353a Krey, August C. *First crusade: the accounts of eye-witnesses and participants.* Princeton, 1921.

b Sybel, Heinrich von. *Geschichte des ersten Kreuzzugs,* 1841; 2nd ed., Leipzig, 1881.

**c —— ** *History and literature of the Crusades.* London, 1861, ed. and tr. by Lady Duff Gordon.

d Röhricht, Reinhold. *Geschichte des ersten Kreuzzuges.* Innsbruck, 1901.

e Munro, Dana C. *Speech of Pope Urban II at Clermont,* 1095. *A.H.R.* 11:231–242, Jan. 1906.

f Duncalf, Frederic. *Peasants' crusade.* *A.H.R.* 26:440-453, Apr. 1921.

a. Most vivid account in English of the first crusade. Composed of translations of contemporary letters and chronicles, put together in such a way as to present a remarkably full narrative of the whole movement. An introduction, notes, and maps supply all the information necessary to the general reader in the use of these first-hand materials. *b.* Celebrated work, the publication of which marked an epoch in the historiography of the crusades. Applied critical methods, and for the first time based the narrative on strictly contemporary authorities. Still valuable. *c.* Pt. 1 a translation of four lectures on the Crusades delivered by von Sybel in Munich in 1855; pt. 2 a translation from the preface to von Sybel's 1841 edition; contains a criticism of the sources for the study of the First Crusade. *d.* Outline with copious notes; best guide to the subject. *e.* and *f.* Excellent critical articles which revise earlier judgments.

CWD

H354a Munro, Dana C.; Prutz, Hans; and **Diehl, Charles.** *Essays on the crusades.* Burlington, Vermont, 1903.

  b Munro, Dana C. *Children's crusade. A.H.R.* 19:516–524, Apr. 1914.

  a. In these three essays, Munro adduces proofs that the Syrian Franks were successful in adapting themselves to oriental conditions; Prutz traces the chief economic influences of the crusades upon the West; and Diehl studies Byzantine policy toward the crusaders and the Latin states to 1187. *b.* Scholarly account of this curious episode. Also cf. (H42) Wright, *Geographical lore of the time of the crusades.* FD

H355a Röhricht, Reinhold. *Geschichte des Königreichs Jerusalem, 1100–1291.* Innsbruck, 1898.

  b Stevenson, William B. *Crusaders in the east, a brief history of the wars of Islam with the Latins in Syria during the twelfth and thirteenth centuries.* Cambridge, Eng., 1907. (Bibliography.)

  a. Invaluable chronological account; especially commendable for thorough documentation of every item. A procession of facts little relieved by literary imagination. Part of this material is available in *b.,* but with the same faults of style. ACK

  b. Briefer and less satisfactory than *a.* which covers the same period. Treats the history of the Latin states as a phase of Mohammedan history; based largely on oriental sources; uninteresting and monotonous in style. The foot-notes show careful investigation of chronology and border warfare. Review, G. Le Strange, *E.H.R.* 23:346, Apr. 1908. FD

H356 Poole, Stanley Lane. *Saladin and the fall of the kingdom of Jerusalem.* London and N. Y., 1898. [Heroes of the nations.]

Interesting biography of Saladin; the story of the fall of Jerusalem is told chiefly from the oriental viewpoint. Rather eulogistic and may convey the impression that all Moslems were as chivalrous as his hero. The faithlessness of the Christians is too much emphasized. Good general description of the growth of the united Mohammedan power which crushed the Latin states. Review, C. L. Kingsford, *E.H.R.* 14:763, Oct. 1899. FD

H357 Pears, Sir Edwin. *Fall of Constantinople, being the story of the fourth crusade.* London, 1885; N. Y., 1886.

About one-half of this book describes the condition of the Byzantine Empire on the eve of the crusade; the other half, the crusade. The second part is based upon a careful study of the sources. Pears considers, probably wrongly, that this crusade made the later Turkish conquest 'both certain and easy' and that the conduct of the crusaders was due to a plot formed by Venice. Review, C. Oman, *E.H.R.* 2:155, Jan. 1887. Cf. (F706a) Luchaire, *Innocent III,* v. 4, *La question d'Orient.* DCM

H358a Miller, William. *Latins in the Levant, a history of Frankish Greece, 1204–1566.* London, 1908. (Bibliography.)

  b —— *Essays on the Latin Orient.* Cambridge, Eng., 1921. (Bibliographies.)

  c —— *Latin Orient.* London and N. Y., 1920. [(A295) Helps for students of history, no. 37.] (Useful bibliography.)

a. Excellent account of the dramatic attempts of the Latins to retain Greece and its islands (Crete excluded) against declining Byzantium and the advancing Turk. All available sources and nearly all the best secondary authorities have been used, while personal acquaintance with existing monuments gives spots of vivid color. The reader's perspective may be somewhat distorted by the writer's effort to include all the facts, and by the lack of correlation with the history of the rest of Europe. Review, J. B. Bury, *E.H.R.* 24:135, Jan. 1909. *b.* Reprint of 26 miscellaneous essays. Review, D. C. Munro, *A.H.R.* 27:570, Apr. 1922. *c.* In briefest outline of only 57 pages the whole history of Latin domination in the Near East is sketched from 1098 to 1797.   EHB

H359a Marzials, Sir Frank, tr. *Memoirs of the crusades by Villehardouin and De Joinville.* London and N. Y., 1908. [Everyman's library.] Tr. from Geoffroi de Ville-Hardouin, *La conquête de Constantinople,* 1584; ed. by Natalis de Wailly, 1872; 2nd ed., Paris, 1875; and J. de Joinville, *Mémoires,* 1546; ed. by Natalis de Wailly in *Oeuvres de Jean Sieur de Joinville comprenant l'Histoire de Saint-Louis,* Paris, 1867.

  b Joinville, Jean, Sire de. *Memoirs of the Lord of Joinville.* London, 1906. New English version, tr. by Ethel Wedgewood from *Mémoires,* 1546; ed. by Natalis de Wailly in *Oeuvres de Jean Sieur de Joinville comprenant l'histoire de Saint-Louis,* Paris, 1867.

  c *Chronicles of the crusades, being contemporary narratives of the crusade of Richard Coeur de Lion, by Richard of Devizes and Geoffrey de Vinsauf; and of the crusade of St. Louis, by Lord de Joinville . . .* tr. by J. A. Giles and T. Johnes. London, 1848.

These two masterpieces of early French literature are also the most important single sources for the events which they describe. Villehardouin's account is biased by the necessity of justifying the conduct of leaders on the fourth crusade, of whom he was one. Joinville accompanied Louis IX on his first crusade. *a.* Has translated only the portion of Joinville's account leading to the crusade. *b.* Based upon the standard editions by Natalis de Wailly, and is, therefore, better than *c.*   ACK

H360 Paetow, Louis J., ed. *The crusades and other historical essays presented to Dana C. Munro by his former students.* N. Y., 1928.

Eight of these twelve essays deal with the crusades and throw new light on the great German pilgrimage of 1064-65, the pope's plan for the first crusade, a neglected passage in the *Gesta,* Robert II of Flanders, Albert of Aachen, the Genoese colonies in Syria, Fulk of Neuilly, and John of Garland.   SBF

MILITARY HISTORY

H511 Oman, Sir Charles W. C. *History of the art of war in the middle ages.* 1898. 2nd rev. ed., 2 v., London and Boston, 1924.

Only authoritative English work, by a versatile scholar. Describes the continuity in the history of warfare, the development of tactics, the changes in equipment, and in methods of fortifications, and the growth of military tradition. Military affairs of central and eastern Europe are less extensively discussed than those of England and France. The 1st ed. stopped abruptly with 1375 without treating fully the beginnings of infantry or the introduction of gunpowder. The 2nd ed. supplies these omissions and extends to 1485. Well equipped with maps. Review, J. E. Morris, *E.H.R.* 14:129, Jan. 1899; T. F. Tout, *E.H.R.* 40:113, Jan. 1925. Also cf. (H602c) Paul Lacroix, *Military and religious life in the middle ages;* and especially the classic treatment of the subject in (B511) Delbrück, *Geschichte der Kriegskunst.*   RAN

LEGAL HISTORY AND POLITICAL THEORY

H551a Vinogradoff, Sir Paul. *Roman law in mediaeval Europe.* London and N. Y., 1909 [Harper's library of living thought.] (Bibliographies.)

   b Wigmore, John H., ed. *General survey of events, sources, persons, and movements in continental legal history.* Introduction by O. W. Holmes and E. Jenks. Boston, 1912. [V. 1 of Continental legal history series, published under the auspices of the Association of American Law Schools.] (Bibliographies.)

   c Savigny, Friedrich Karl von. *Geschichte des römischen Rechts im Mittelalter.* 6 v. 1815–31. 2nd ed., 7 v., Heidelberg, 1834–51. Tr. into French from 2nd ed. by C. Guenoux, *Traité de droit romain,* 4 v., 1839; 2nd ed., 8 v., Paris, 1855–60. V. 1 tr. into English by W. Holloway, *System of the modern Roman law,* v. 1., Madras, 1867.

   a. Remarkable short summary of modern research on this subject interspersed with many a new fact or interpretation from the researches of the author who was one of the foremost authorities on the history of law and of medieval institutions. Indispensable book because of its intrinsic value and because there is nothing else like it.   *b.* Aims to give a general survey of the legal history of western Europe in medieval and modern times. An ingenious and valuable patchwork chiefly composed of translations into English from leading European authorities such as Carlo Calisse, Jean Brissaud, Heinrich Brunner, and Richard Schroeder. There are extracts from the writings of Frederic W. Maitland, and a special contribution by Rafael Altamira.   *c.* Classic work which first placed the study of the history of Roman law upon a scientific basis.   LJP

H552 Lea, Henry C. *Superstition and force: essays on the wager of law, the wager of battle, the ordeal, torture.* 1886. 4th rev. ed., Philadelphia, 1892.

   These essays were by-products from the workshop of the famous American authority on the inquisition (cf. F561). Still valuable for a study of early Germanic law and for the history of forms of trial throughout the Middle Ages.   LJP

H553a Jenks, Edward. *Law and politics in the middle ages, with a synoptic table of sources.* 1898. 2nd ed., London, 1913.

   b Lindner, Theodor. *Die Veme.* 1888. New ed., Paderborn, 1896.

   a. Noteworthy essay based on the legal sources and a careful reading of modern writers on medieval institutions. Written in the heyday of speculation on early Germanic law by scholars who stuck too closely to the legal texts and did not read them in the light of all other sources of history. Jenks did not escape from the dangers of this unintentional narrowness. Review, J. Tait,

E.H.R. 13:750, Oct. 1898. *b.* Standard book on the secret, extra-legal forms of trial which were prevalent in distracted Germany in the fifteenth century.   LJP

H561 Dunning, William A. *History of political theories, ancient and mediaeval.* N. Y., 1902. (Bibliography.)

Standard book in English for a general survey of the subject. Review, J. Sullivan, *A.H.R.* 7:747, July 1902. For excellent short survey of medieval political theories, cf. Bk. 10 of (B561*b*) Janet, *Histoire de la science politique.*
   LJP

H562a Carlyle, Sir Robert W., and **Carlyle, Alexander J.** *History of medieval political theory in the west.* V. 1-5. Edinburgh, 1903-28. (Bibliography.)

   b Figgis, John N. *Political aspects of S. Augustine's City of God.* London, 1921. (Bibliography.)

   c Hearnshaw, Fossey J. C., ed. *Social and political ideas of some great mediaeval thinkers.* London and N. Y., 1923. (Bibliographies.)

   d Jarrett, Bede. *Social theories of the middle ages, 1200-1500.* London and N. Y., 1926.

a. For the history of political thought from Cicero to the end of the thirteenth century, this book supplies a want not fully met by any other book, for it provides a compendious historical account based on a careful examination of the extensive contemporary literature. Study of the general development of thought rather than of particular men; more systematic and detailed than the political part of (P561*a*) Gierke, *Genossenschaftsrecht* and more prosaic than (P561*b*) Maitland's brilliant translation thereof. Foot-notes contain extracts from contemporary writings, judiciously chosen and of great value. Review, J. Sullivan, *A.H.R.* 10:629, Apr. 1905; 15:836, July 1910; 21:784, July 1916; 28:92, Oct. 1922. Cf. also A. J. Carlyle, 'The sources of medieval political theory and its connection with medieval politics,' *A.H.R.* 19:1, Oct. 1913.   CHM
b. Posthumous collection of six essays which dissect Augustine's great contribution to political thought and trace its profound influence in medieval and even modern times.   *c.* Lecture by Ernest Barker, surveying medieval political thought, is followed by admirable lectures by different individuals on St. Augustine, John of Salisbury, St. Thomas Aquinas, Dante, Pierre du Bois, Marsilio of Padua, and John Wycliffe. Review, F. W. Coker, *Amer. Pol. Sci. Rev.* 18:184, Feb. 1924.   *d.* Interesting survey of medieval ideas concerning law, education, women, slavery, property, war, christendom, and art. Review, C. Johnson, *History,* 12:57, Apr. 1927.   LJP

H563 Dickinson, John, tr. *The statesman's book of John of Salisbury: being the fourth, fifth, and sixth books, and selections from the seventh and eighth books, of the Policraticus, translated into English with an introduction.* N. Y., 1927.

ECONOMIC AND SOCIAL HISTORY

H571a Heyd, Wilhelm von. *Geschichte des Levantehandels im Mittelalter.* 2 v. Stuttgart, 1879. (Bibliography.) Tr. into French, with additions by the author, by M. Furcy-Raynaud, *Histoire du commerce du Levant au moyen-âge,* 2 v., Leipzig, 1885-86; reprint, Leipzig, 1923.

   b Lybyer, Albert H. *Ottoman Turks and the routes of oriental trade. E.H.R.* 30:577-588, Oct. 1915.

a. The classic on the subject; upon it all subsequent work in the field must be based even though the published sources were not exhausted nor the unpublished documents utilized. Not only a history of medieval commerce but of medieval experiments in colonization as well; admirably conceived and brilliantly executed. The French edition, revised and enlarged by the author, is distinctly the better. Covers from the sixth century to the sixteenth. The historical background is sketched throughout in masterly fashion. *b.* Argues that the extension of Turkish power was not the cause of efforts to discover new trade routes in the fifteenth century. EHB

H572 Schaube, Adolf. *Handelsgeschichte der romanischen Völker des Mittelmeergebiets bis zum Ende der Kreuzzüge.* München, 1906. [(B170) Below and Meinecke, Handbuch der mittelalterlichen und neueren Geschichte.] (Bibliography.)

Extensive and laborious study devoted mainly to the commerce of the Italian peninsula. Inasmuch as Italy was the center of most of the commerce of the Middle Ages, this work really constitutes an invaluable guide to the whole subject of European trade to about 1250. Embodies the results of the writer's own wide researches and of those of a generation of historians and economists since (H571a) Heyd, to whom Schaube's debt is also considerable. Very useful tables of medieval weights and measures with modern equivalents are followed by a similar table of medieval media of exchange, which is open to serious criticism. Review, G. Yver, *Rev. Hist.* 99:394, Sept. 1908; H. Sieveking, *Hist. Zeit.* 99:364, 1907. Cf. pt. 2 of (B576a) C. Day, *History of commerce.* EHB, AHB

H573 Thompson, James W. *Economic and social history of the middle ages.* N. Y., 1928.

Fills a long-felt want in the teaching of medieval history. Covers the thousand years between 300 and 1300, and is intended primarily for the upper classes of colleges and universities. LJP

H574 Knight, Melvin M. *Economic history of Europe to the end of the middle ages.* Boston, 1926. (Bibliography.)

Slight but useful sketch. Two thirds of its 254 pages are devoted to the middle ages. Review, H. L. Gray, *A.H.R.* 32:568, Apr. 1927. LJP

H576 Pirenne, Henri. *Medieval cities, their origins and the revival of trade.* Princeton, 1925. (Bibliography.) Tr. by F. D. Halsey from author's MS. French ed., *Les villes du moyen âge: essai d'histoire économique et sociale,* Brussels, 1927.

Indispensable; only scholarly, comprehensive work in English on this important subject; contains the substance of lectures delivered by this eminent Belgian historian in several American universities in 1922. Review, H. W. C. Davis, *Econ. Hist. Rev.* 1:348, Jan. 1928. LJP

H577 *Medieval towns.* V. 1–36, N. Y., 1898–1923. [1, L. D. Gordon, *Assisi;* 2, T. Okey, *Avignon;* 3, A. Wiel, *Bologna;* 4, E. Gilliat-Smith, *Bruges;* 5, *id., Brussels;* 6, S. Lane Poole, *Cairo;* 7, C. W. Stubbs, *Cambridge;* 8, G. R. Sterling Taylor, *Canterbury;* 9, C. Headlam, *Chartres;* 10, W. H. Hutton, *Constantinople;* 11, M. D. Harris, *Coventry;* 12, D. A. Chart, *Dublin;* 13, O. Smeaton, *Edinburgh;* 14, E. Noyes, *Ferrara;* 15, E. G. Gardner, *Florence;* 16, C. M. Watson, *Jerusalem;* 17, H. B. Wheatley, *London;* 18, J. Ross, *Lucca;* 19, E. Noyes, *Milan;* 20, W. Gerrare, *Moscow;* 21, C.

Headlam, *Nuremberg;* 22, *id., Oxford;* 23, C. Foligna, *Padua;* 24, T. Okey, *Paris;* 25, M. Symonds and L. D. Gordon, *Perugia;* 26, J. Ross, *Pisa;* 27, Count Lützow, *Prague;* 28, N. Young, *Rome;* 29, T. A. Cook, *Rouen;* 30, Mrs. W. M. Gallichan, *Santiago de Compostela;* 31, W. M. Gallichan, *Seville;* 32, E. G. Gardner, *Siena and San Gimignano;* 33, H. Lynch, *Toledo;* 34, T. Okey, *Venice;* 35, A. Wiel, *Verona;* 36, C. Headlam, *Naples.*]

Convenient and, in some cases, excellent accounts of individual towns. The volumes are addressed primarily to the tourist and consequently abound in descriptive matter, but some attention is usually given to the history and institutions of the town.   GMD

H578 Clarke, Maude V. *The medieval city state: an essay on tyranny and federation in the later middle ages.* London, 1926.

Very significant book for the general reader. Confined to cities in Italy, Germany, the Netherlands, and Switzerland. Excellent complement of (H576) Pirenne, *Medieval cities,* which covers the early middle ages to the middle of the twelfth century. Reviews, E. H. Byrne, *A.H.R.* 33:101, Oct. 1927; C. W. Previté Orton, *E.H.R.* 42:641, Oct. 1927.   LJP

H581a Seignobos, Charles. *Feudal régime.* 1902. New ed., N. Y., 1926. Tr. by E. W. Dow, from *Le régime féodal.* [V. 2, ch. 1, of (B152) Lavisse et Rambaud, Histoire générale.]

b Giry, Arthur, and **Réville, André.** *Emancipation of the medieval towns.* N. Y., 1907. Tr. by F. G. Bates and P. E. Titsworth, from *Émancipation des villes, les communes, la bourgeoisie.* [v. 2, ch. 8, *ibid.*]

In the two chapters here rendered into English three European scholars of eminence have presented a clear summary view of medieval society in the feudal age. *a.* Explains the usages of feudalism; includes the life and status of the peasantry (manorial system) as well as that of the feudal nobility. *b.* Tells of the great struggle whereby the towns succeeded very largely in emancipating themselves from the restrictions of the feudal system during the eleventh, twelfth, and thirteenth centuries.   CWD

H582a Gautier, Léon. *Chivalry.* London, 1891. Tr. by H. Frith, from *La chevalerie,* 1884, 3rd ed., Paris, 1895.

b Warre Cornish, Francis. *Chivalry.* London and N. Y., 1901. [Social England series.]

c Davis, William Stearns. *Life on a mediaeval barony, a picture of a typical feudal community in the thirteenth century.* N. Y. and London, 1923.

d Meller, Walter C. *Knight's life in the days of chivalry.* N. Y., 1924.

e Schultz, Alwin. *Das höfische Leben zur Zeit der Minnesinger.* 1879–80. 2nd rev. ed., 2 v., Leipzig, 1889.

a. No work on the general topic of chivalry excels that of Gautier in fullness of treatment or wealth of illustration, though it is tinged with the literary and antiquarian bias of the author. The translation by Frith contains the illustrations as printed in the first French edition. *b.* Neither so full nor so well illustrated. *c.* The chief features of medieval society in northern France about A. D. 1220 are set forth in a story which describes the daily life of an imaginary fief. Young students especially will find this attempt to stimulate interest in medieval life very instructive. Review, F. Duncalf, *A.H.R.* 29:368, Jan. 1924.   *d.* Depicts the life of a medieval knight, from birth to death, by means of a great variety of examples drawn chiefly from medieval French literature.   Review, W. S. Davis, *A.H.R.* 30:583, Apr. 1925.   *e.* Interesting and valuable work in German.   ACK

H583 Abrahams, Israel. *Jewish life in the middle ages.* N. Y. and London, 1896.

Written largely from English sources; less valuable for the Continent. Fills excellently, with this limitation, a gap which (L1) Gross, *Sources and literature of English history,* p. 510 (1st ed.) deplored.   JWT

H584 Gasquet, Francis A., Cardinal. *Black death of 1348 and 1349.* London, 1908. 2nd ed. of *Great pestilence, A.D. 1348-9.* London, 1893.

Best general history in English of the black death from its entrance into southeastern Europe. The greater part of the work is devoted to the progress of the plague and the resulting desolation in England. Description of economic and social results is inadequate. Review, G. Kriehn, *A.H.R.* 14:569, Apr. 1909.
                                                                                        JFW

H585 Power, Eileen. *Medieval people.* London and N. Y., 1924.

Six short biographical studies which depict the life of a medieval peasant, a traveller, a prioress, a Paris housewife, a merchant, and a clothier. Review, W. S. Davis, *A.H.R.* 30:632, Apr. 1925.   LJP

H586 Tupper, Frederick. *Types of society in medieval literature.* N. Y., 1922. [Brown University, Colver lectures.]

Three delightful lectures on conditions of men, sins and sinners, and the eternal feminine.   LJP

CULTURAL HISTORY: GENERAL

H601 Maitland, Samuel R. *The dark ages: a series of essays intended to illustrate the state of religion and literature in the ninth, tenth, eleventh, and twelfth centuries.* 1844. 5th ed., with introduction by F. Stokes, London, 1890.

This series of essays, which first appeared in the *British Magazine* in 1835-38, deserved a new edition in our day because Maitland was among the first to create a reaction against the conception of 'dark ages.' The book has a decided ecclesiastical and controversial tone but is scholarly and contains many interesting side lights which attract all readers of medieval history.   LJP

H602a Lacroix, Paul. *Arts in the middle ages and at the period of the renaissance.* London, 1870. Translated by J. Dafforne from the 2nd rev. ed. of *Les arts au moyen âge et à l'époque de la renaissance,* 1869, 6th ed., Paris, 1877. [1st ed. of this and of three succeeding works appeared as single work under title, *Le moyen âge et la renaissance: histoire et description des moeurs et usages, du commerce et de l'industrie, des sciences, des arts, des littératures, et des beaux-arts en Europe,* 5 v., Paris, 1847-52.]

   b ―――― *Manners, customs, and dress during the middle ages and during the renaissance period.* London, 1874. Tr. from 3rd ed. of *Moeurs, usages, et costumes au moyen âge et à l'époque de la renaissance,* Paris, 1873.

c ———— *Military and religious life in the middle ages and at the period of the renaissance.* London 1874. Tr. from 2nd ed. of *Vie militaire et religieuse au moyen âge et à l'époque de la renaissance,* Paris, 1873.

d ———— *Science and literature in the middle ages and at the period of the renaissance.* London, 1878. Tr. from 2nd ed. of *Sciences et lettres au moyen âge et à l'époque de la renaissance,* Paris, 1877.

e **Parmentier, André E. E.** *Album historique, publié sous la direction de M. Ernest Lavisse.* 4 v. 1894–1907. Ed. de luxe, v. 1–3, Paris, 1901–02. 3rd ed. of v. 1, Paris, 1905.

Pictorial descriptions of medieval society; invaluable for historical pageantry. *a., b., c.,* and *d.* English translations contain the original illustrations. The material is chosen to illustrate manners, customs, and social interests of the period from a somewhat antiquarian point of view. Popular interest dominates both in the selection of illustrations and in the text. The later French editions are better than the earlier. *e.* More systematic presentation of social progress from ancient to modern times including all Europe. V. 1 and 2. Cover the Middle Ages.   ACK

CULTURAL HISTORY: EDUCATION, THOUGHT, PHILOSOPHY, SCIENCE

H641 **Mullinger, James B.** *Schools of Charles the Great and the restoration of education in the ninth century.* London, 1877. Anastatic reprints, N. Y., 1904, 1911. [Kaye prize essay.] (Bibliography.)

Based upon a conscientious reading of the sources; well written; deservedly maintains an honorable place among the modern books on early medieval Latin culture.   LJP

H642a **Rashdall, Hastings.** *Universities of Europe in the middle ages.* 2 v. in 3. Oxford, 1895. (Bibliographies.) (New ed. in preparation by H. H. E. Craster and F. M. Powicke.)

b **Denifle, Heinrich S.** *Die Universitäten des Mittelalters bis 1400.* V. 1, *Die Entstehung der Universitäten des Mittelalters bis 1400.* Berlin, 1885.

c **Packard, Francis R.,** ed. *School of Salernum, Regimen sanitatis salernitanum, the English version by Sir John Harington; with a history of the school of Salernum by Francis R. Packard, M.D., and a note on the prehistory of the Regimen sanitatis, by Fielding H. Garrison, M.D.* N. Y., 1920. (Bibliography.)

d **Norton, Arthur O.** *Readings in the history of education: mediaeval universities.* Cambridge, Mass., 1909. (Bibliography.)

e **Rait, Robert S.** *Life in the medieval university.* Cambridge, Eng., 1912. [Cambridge manuals of science and literature.] (Bibliography.)

f **Haskins, Charles H.** *Rise of universities.* N. Y., 1923. [Brown University, Colver lectures.] (Bibliography.)

g **Seybolt, Robert F.,** tr. *Manuale scholarium: an original account of life in the mediaeval university.* Cambridge, Mass., 1921. (Bibliography.)

h **Symonds, John A.** *Wine, women, and song: mediaeval Latin students' songs now translated into English verse with an essay.* 1884. 2nd ed., London, 1907. [King's classics.]

i **Paetow, Louis J.,** ed. and tr. *Two medieval satires on the university of Paris: La bataille des sept ars of Henri d'Andeli, and the Morale scolarium of John of Garland.* Berkeley, 1927. [Memoirs of the University of California, v. 4.]

The history of medieval universities was extremely obscure until the appearance of the books of Rashdall and Denifle, who began their researches independently. *a.* Standard work on medieval universities. Aims to cover the whole field but special stress is laid upon Oxford and Paris. Written chiefly from the constitutional side and with no attempt to treat fully the intellectual interests of masters and students nor to make the prominent figures stand out as life-like personalities. Review, G. B. Adams, *A.H.R.* 1:520, Apr. 1896. *b.* Denifle planned to complete his work in five volumes, the last three to be devoted to the university of Paris, but died in 1905 without realizing his plan. Though unfinished, his work is of great value because it is based upon an incredible amount of research in many European archives. Denifle is often controverted in a polemic tone in (P641*b*) Kaufmann, *Die Geschichte der deutschen Universitäten,* of which v. 1 is devoted to a general history of medieval universities to serve as a background for the study of German universities. *c.* Gives the Latin text and an old English translation of the short version of the famous *Regimen,* and states what is known of the school at Salerno, often referred to as the oldest university. *d.* Source-book containing English translations of illustrative original sources, bound together by the translator's explanations and comments. *e.* Readable and popular description of the life of medieval masters and students, based largely on the last chapter of *a.* *f.* Contains three lectures dealing respectively with the earliest universities, the medieval professor, and the medieval student. Cf. further the author's articles on 'Life of medieval students as seen in their letters,' *A.H.R.* 3:203–229, Jan. 1898, and 'The University of Paris in the sermons of the thirteenth century,' *A.H.R.* 10:1–27, Oct. 1904, which are both outstanding contributions based mainly on manuscript sources. *g.* English translation of the most important, although anonymous, source for German student life in the fifteenth century. *h.* Rather free, but delightful, translations of some Latin songs of medieval students, drawn largely from *Carmina Burana,* Stuttgart, 1847. *i.* Throws new light on studies and life in the University of Paris about the middle of the thirteenth century. LJP

H643 Haskins, Charles H. *The Renaissance of the twelfth century.* Cambridge, Mass., 1927. (Critical bibliography.)

First systematic treatment of the culture of the twelfth century. Art and the vernacular literature are not included. Devoted wholly to the Latin side of this renaissance which it presents in a masterly fashion. Combines literary excellence with profound scholarship. Should be read in connection with the author's (H657) *Studies in the history of mediaeval science,* and with his *Studies in mediaeval culture,* Oxford, 1929. Reviews, L. R. Loomis, *A.H.R.* 33:629, Apr. 1928; L. J. Paetow, *Speculum* 3:122, Jan. 1928; E. Faral, *Rev. Critique,* 61:304; and G. Sarton, *Isis* 10:62, March 1928. Cf. also (H645), Otto of Freising's *Two Cities,* next to Augustin's *De civitate Dei,* the most interesting philosophy of history produced in the middle ages; the translation is very careful, and the introduction and notes are invaluable to students who do not read Latin and German, and to the general reader. LJP

H646a Taylor, Henry O. *The mediaeval mind, a history of the development of thought and emotion in the middle ages.* 1911. 2nd rev. ed., 1914. 4th ed. (unaltered), 2 v., London and N. Y., 1925–27.

b ——. *Classical heritage of the middle ages.* 1901. 3rd ed., N. Y., 1911. (Bibliography.)

Best introductions to the history of medieval intellectual and emotional development from the patristic period through the time of Dante. Neither is a systematic nor an exhaustive treatment, and not written by a specialist in medieval
history. The author roves freely over the whole field of intellectual history; he
has written on ancient intellectual ideals (D604e) and has more recently entered
the field of modern thought (I232b). It is noteworthy that a man with such a
perspective has treated the Middle Ages with a sympathetic touch. Numerous
translations from medieval Latin writings, interspersed here and there, furnish
valuable illustrative material. Reviews, D. C. Munro, *A.H.R.* 17:117, Oct. 1911;
E. K. Rand, *Nation* (N. Y.) 93:7, July 6, 1911. Although there is some overlapping in the two books, *a.* does not supersede *b.* which has done much to demonstrate the continuity between ancient and medieval culture.   LJP

H647a Wulf, Maurice de. *History of medieval philosophy.* London and N. Y.,
    1909. Tr. by P. Coffey as 3rd ed. of *Histoire de la philosophie médiévale,
    précédée d'un aperçu sur la philosophie ancienne,* 1900; 4th rev. ed., Paris,
    1912; 5th rev. ed., 2 v., Paris, 1924–25, tr. by E. C. Messenger, History
    of mediaeval philosophy, 2 v., London and N. Y., 1926. (Bibliographies.)

  b Ueberweg, Friedrich. *Grundriss der Geschichte der Philosophie der
    mittleren oder der patristischen und scholastischen Zeit.* 1924. 11th ed.
    of pt. 2, *Die patristische und scholastische Philosophie,* ed. by B. Geyer,
    Berlin, 1928. [V. 2 of 11th rev. ed. of (B642e) Ueberweg, Grundriss der
    Geschichte der Philosophie.] (Bibliography.)

  c Baeumker, Clemens. *Die europäische Philosophie des Mittelalters.* 1909.
    2nd ed., Berlin, 1913. [Allgemeine Geschichte der Philosophie, p. 288–381,
    in (B606) Hinneberg, Die Kultur der Gegenwart, Teil 1, Abteilung 5.]
    (Bibliography.)

  d Picavet, François J. *Esquisse d'une histoire générale et comparée des
    philosophies médiévales.* 1905. 2nd rev. ed., Paris, 1907.

  e Hauréau, Barthélemy. *Histoire de la philosophie scolastique.* 2 v. in 3.
    Paris, 1872–80.

  f Gilson, Étienne. *La philosophie au moyen âge.* 2 v. Paris, 1922.

  a. Best manual for the historical student interested in medieval philosophy.
Simple, clear, and systematic treatment by a competent scholar. *b.* Presents the
best survey in general histories of philosophy. Unfortunately there is no English
translation of this latest and greatly improved edition of the work. *c.* Convenient short summary by one of the foremost medievalists in Europe. *d.*
Takes issue with *a.* on various points. Although important, its poor arrangement renders it almost useless for the ordinary student. *e.* This older and
fuller work is by no means superseded. *f.* Clear, readable sketch by an able
scholar. Review, J. H. Ryan, *Speculum* 1:6, Jan. 1926.   LJP

H648a Wulf, Maurice de. *Philosophy and civilization in the middle ages.*
    Princeton, 1922. [Princeton University, Vanuxem foundation lectures.]
    (Bibliography.)

  b —— *Mediaeval philosophy illustrated from the system of Thomas
    Aquinas.* Cambridge, Mass., 1922.

  a. Series of lectures designed by the author to supplement his (H647a) *History of medieval philosophy.* He has frequently contended that medieval
philosophy can be understood only when illuminated by a study of medieval
civilization as a whole. Emphasizes the relations of Thomistic philosophy with

politics and political thought. *b.* Supplements *a.* Clear and simple summary for the general reader of the cardinal philosophical, not theological, doctrines of Aquinas as typical of thirteenth century thought.   LJP

H649 Husik, Isaac. *History of mediaeval Jewish philosophy.* N. Y., 1916. (Bibliography.)

Valuable because it is the only book which presents the contributions of the Jews to medieval thought in a systematic form intelligible to the general reader. Begins with Isaac Israeli, who lived in Babylonia in the ninth and tenth centuries, culminates in the twelfth century with Maimonides, and traces the decline of Jewish philosophy in the fifteenth century in Spain, France, and Italy. Review, N. H. Adlerblum, *Journal of Philosophy,* 15:22, Jan. 3, 1918.   LJP

H650 Poole, Reginald Lane. *Illustrations of the history of medieval thought in the departments of theology and ecclesiastical politics.* 1884. Rev. ed., London and N. Y., 1920.

Reveals at every turn the author's direct contact with the sources. The revision involved few changes, a rare tribute to the quality of the original work. Though dealing with a difficult theme, it is singularly clear and interesting. Review, C. W. Previté-Orton, *E.H.R.* 36:587, Oct. 1921.   ACK

H651a Grabmann, Martin. *Die Geschichte der scholastischen Methode.* V. 1–2. Freiburg im Breisgau and St. Louis, Mo., 1909–11. (Bibliographical footnotes.)

b —— *Thomas von Aquin, eine Einführung in seine Persönlichkeit und Gedankenwelt.* Kempten, 1912. English tr. London, 1928.

c —— *Die Philosophie des Mittelalters.* Berlin, 1921. [V. 3 of Geschichte der Philosophie. Sammlung Göschen, 826.

d —— *Mittelalterliches Geistesleben: Abhandlungen zur Geschichte der Scholastik und Mystik.* München, 1926.

a. The author made a special study of the method of Thomas Aquinas, which led him to write a general history of scholastic method, beginning with patristic times. V. 1–2. Extend to the beginning of the thirteenth century; based on much learned research in printed and manuscript sources and throw considerable light on medieval intellectual life. The third and last volume is to deal with Thomas Aquinas and his contemporaries. In some measure its place may be supplied by *b.* *c.* Brief survey of whole period of scholastic philosophy with special attention to Thomas Aquinas. *d.* Collection of scattered essays dealing chiefly with Thomas Aquinas and his contemporaries.   LJP

H652 Baeumker, Clemens, ed. *Beiträge zur Geschichte der Philosophie des Mittelalters: Texte und Untersuchungen.* V. 1–27. Münster, 1891–1928.

This important collection deserves special mention because it has brought to light a host of hitherto unpublished, or badly or obscurely published, works by medieval authors, which illuminate various phases of the intellectual history of the Middle Ages. The editorial work is of high standard and the numerous monographs, explanatory treatises, and notes are scholarly.   LJP

H653 Eicken, Heinrich von. *Geschichte und System der mittelalterlichen Weltanschauung.* Stuttgart, 1887.

The central theme in this large book is the attempt to show that the ascetic ideal of the medieval church and its struggle for world dominion, apparently incompatible, are in reality harmonious. Hence it is, in large measure, a history of the ideas which determined the relations between church and state in the Middle Ages. The work reaches back into the Roman, Greek, and Jewish worlds of thought and extends to the Reformation. Its treatment is philosophical rather than historical, it takes for granted a thorough knowledge of the history of the Middle Ages, and does not furnish a systematic treatment of the intellectual history of that period. Review, W. Bernhardi, *Hist. Zeit.* 62:101, 1889.   LJP

H654 **Huizinga, Johan.** *Waning of the middle ages: a study of the forms of life, thought, and art in France and the Netherlands in the XIV*th *and XV*th *centuries.* London, 1924. (Bibliography.) Tr. from *Herfsttij der mid-deleeuwen, studie over levens- en gedachtenvormen der XIV*de *en XV*de *eeuw in Frankrijk en de Nederlanden,* 1919; 2nd ed., Haarlem, 1921.

Important study of the culture of this period, based on literature and art, with constant reference to earlier centuries of the middle ages. Not merely a translation from the Dutch edition, but an adaptation directed by the author. Review, C. L. Kingsford, *E.H.R.* 40:273, Apr. 1925; G. C. Sellery, *A.H.R.* 31:113, Oct. 1925.

H656 **Thorndike, Lynn.** *History of magic and experimental science during the first thirteen centuries of our era.* 2 v. N. Y., 1923. (Bibliographies.)

'This book aims to treat the history of magic and experimental science and their relations to Christian thought during the first thirteen centuries of our era, with especial emphasis upon the twelfth and thirteenth centuries.' A very notable contribution to the history of the natural sciences; demonstrates that this period was by no means such an age of retrogression or stagnation as is generally believed. Valuable to all students of medieval thought in all its phases. Although almost encyclopedic in scope, it is by no means merely a restatement of accumulated and previously digested matter, for it is based upon an independent reading of manuscript and printed sources. Its great size, and its biographical rather than topical arrangement, will make it more a book for reference than for continuous reading. Review, G. L. Burr, *A.H.R.* 29:118, Oct. 1923; F. M. Powicke, *E.H.R.* 40:111, Jan. 1925.   LJP

H657 **Haskins, Charles H.** *Studies in the history of mediaeval science.* Cambridge, Mass., 1924. 2nd ed., 1927. [Harvard historical studies.]

Professor Haskins has made strikingly original contributions to the history of medieval science in numerous articles published in various periodicals. This scattered material has been revised, and, together with several new studies, combined in a systematic manner under the following headings: 'The science of the Arabs,' 'Translations from the Greek,' 'The court of Frederick II,' 'Other studies.' That European scholars have long ago appreciated the high value of these studies may be seen in the article devoted to ten of them by C. V. Langlois, 'Travaux de Ch. H. Haskins sur la littérature scientifique en Latin du XIIe siècle,' *Journal des Savants,* n.s.17:57-73, March 1919. Review, L. Thorndike, *A.H.R.* 30:344, Jan. 1925. Also cf. (H602d) Lacroix, *Science and literature in the middle ages.*   LJP

H658a Little, Andrew G., ed. *Roger Bacon essays, contributed by various writers on the occasion of the commemoration of the seventh centenary of his birth.* Oxford, 1914. (Excellent bibliography.)

 b Steele, Robert. *Roger Bacon and the state of science in the thirteenth century.* Oxford, 1921. [Charles Singer, Studies in the history and method of science, 2:121–150.]

 c Charles, Émile. *Roger Bacon, sa vie, ses ouvrages, ses doctrines, d'après des textes inédits.* Bordeaux, 1861.

 d Burke, Robert B., tr. *Opus majus of Roger Bacon: a translation.* 2 v. Phila., 1928.

 e Newbold, William R. *Cipher of Roger Bacon,* edited by Roland Kent, Phila., 1928.

a. This collection of careful studies—some in French and German—by competent scholars, provides on the whole a sane estimate of Roger Bacon's importance in relation to physics, chemistry, mathematics, medicine, philosophy, philology, and English literature. Little's introduction gives a conservative statement of the known facts of Bacon's life. *b.* Discussion of Bacon's contributions to science by the editor of his unpublished works. *c.* Still the only biography in book form, now largely antiquated and should be supplemented and corrected by the literature suggested above. However, Charles was better informed concerning thirteenth century learning than some of his recent critics imagine. Cf. (H656) L. Thorndike, *History of magic and experimental science,* and his contributions to periodical literature listed in its bibliography, especially 'The true Roger Bacon,' *A.H.R.* 21:237–257, Jan. 1916; 21:468–480, Apr. 1916. *d.* First translation of Bacon's chief work, which has become a medieval Latin classic. Review, G. Sarton, *Isis,* 11:138, July 1928.   LJP

CULTURAL HISTORY: LITERATURE

H661a Manitius, Maximilianus. *Geschichte der lateinischen Literatur des Mittelalters.* V. 1–2, München, 1911–23. [(D35) Handbuch der Altertumswissenschaft.]

 b Ebert, Adolf. *Allgemeine Geschichte der Literatur des Mittelalters im Abendlande bis zum Beginne des XI Jahrhunderts.* 3 v. 1874–87. 2nd ed. of v. 1 and 2, Leipzig, 1889.

 c Norden, Eduard. *Die antike Kunstprosa vom VI Jahrhundert vor Christus bis in die Zeit der Renaissance.* 1898. 3rd reprint, 2 v. Leipzig, 1915–18.

 d Ker, William P. *Dark ages.* Edinburgh and N. Y., 1904. [(B662d) Saintsbury, Periods of European literature, v. 1.]

 e Saintsbury, George E. B. *Flourishing of romance and the rise of allegory: the twelfth and thirteenth centuries.* Edinburgh and N. Y., 1897. [*Id.,* v. 2.]

 f Snell, Frederick J. *Fourteenth century.* Edinburgh and N. Y., 1899. [*Id.,* v. 3.]

 g Smith, George Gregory. *Transition period.* Edinburgh and N. Y., 1900. [*Id.,* v. 4.]

 h Fiske, Christabel F., ed. *Vassar mediaeval studies, by members of the faculty of Vassar College.* New Haven, 1923.

 i Baldwin, Charles S. *Medieval rhetoric and poetic (to 1400) interpreted from representative works.* N. Y., 1928.

j Waddell, Helen. *Wandering scholars.* Glasgow and Boston, 1927. (Bibliography.)

a. First scientific attempt to deal on a comprehensive scale with medieval Latin literature. Gives a short sketch of the life of each author with proofs from the sources, followed by a treatment of each of his works with careful references to the extant manuscripts and editions as well as to modern appraisals of the works. *b.* Covers almost the same period comprised in v. 1 of *a.,* namely, from the sixth century to the tenth, but includes the vernacular literatures in the first portion of v. 3. Ebert gave his book a literary form instead of the mechanical arrangement adopted by *a.* In all technical details *a.* supersedes *b.* Cf. also (B671) Sandys, *History of classical scholarship,* which covers in part the same field as *c.,* but Norden is particularly interested in prose style and his book is not a manual for reference. He gives interesting interpretations but his treatment of the Middle Ages in v. 2 is determined too much by classical conceptions. *d., e., f., g.* Carry the subject to the beginning of the Renaissance. Devoted in large part to vernacular rather than to Latin literature, they constitute the most convenient general survey of medieval literature. Also cf. (H602d) Lacroix, *Science and literature in the middle ages. h.* Sixteen studies which deal principally with medieval literature and art. Review, *A.H.R.* 29:165, Oct. 1923. *i.* Indispensable for a study of medieval Latin literature. *j.* Brilliant, although somewhat subjective, study of the medieval Latin lyric. Most of the book is an introduction to a study of the Goliardi. Reviews, P. S. Allen, *Speculum* 3:109, Jan. 1928; E. F. J., *E.H.R.* 43:289, Apr. 1928.

LJP

H662 Krumbacher, Karl. *Geschichte der byzantinischen Litteratur von Justinian bis zum Ende des oströmischen Reiches, 527-1453 A.D.* 1890. 2nd rev. ed., München, 1897. [(D35) Handbuch der Altertumswissenschaft.] (Excellent bibliography.)

Krumbacher, with the assistance of A. Ehrhard and H. Gelzer, has endeavored in this pioneer work to give a fair picture of achievement in all branches of literature during the nine centuries between Justinian's accession and the fall of Constantinople, a period which, until comparatively recent times, was often underestimated or actually misrepresented. The broad field is explored with patience and thoroughness, every writer and type of literature is considered, and especial care is taken to point out the questions which still await the investigator. Review, W. Fischer, *Hist. Zeit.* 80:112, 1898. It is announced that this volume will be replaced in the *Handbuch der Altertumswissenschaft* by new works prepared by Professors A. Ehrhard and K. Dieterich, each assisted by other scholars.

HBD

H663a Bulfinch, Thomas. *Bulfinch's mythology: the age of fable, the age of chivalry, legends of Charlemagne.* Complete in 1 v., rev. and enlarged. N. Y., 1913. [Component parts appeared separately: *Age of fable,* Boston, 1855; *Age of chivalry,* Boston, 1859; *Legends of Charlemagne,* Boston, 1864; later eds. of each part.]

b Guerber, Hélène A. *Myths and legends of the middle ages, their origin and influence on literature and art.* London, 1909. Latest reprint, 1922.

a. Handy volume containing all the classic tales of Bulfinch which pertain to antiquity and the early Middle Ages—the northern myths, King Arthur and his knights, the Welsh popular tales called Mabinogion, the hero myths of the

British races, and the legends of Charlemagne.   *b.* Most convenient reference book on medieval legends for young readers.   LJP

H664 Comparetti, Domenico. *Vergil in the middle ages.* London and N. Y., 1895. Tr. by E. F. M. Benecke, from *Virgilio nel medio evo,* 1872; 2nd ed., 2 v., Firenze, 1896.

The use of Virgil's poetry during the Middle Ages, the attitude toward the poet, and incidentally the development of medieval literary appreciation are effectively treated. No similar work on any other writer of antiquity is available.
                                                                                  ACK

H665 Putnam, George H. *Books and their makers during the middle ages, a study of the conditions of the production and distribution of literature from the fall of the Roman empire to the close of the seventeenth century.* 2 v. N. Y., 1896–97. (Bibliography.)

Librarians, editors as well as writers in general, will find this work interesting and valuable. Though concerned primarily with the manufacture and publication of books, it also contributes important matter for the history of culture.   ACK

H666 Chambers, Edmund K. *Mediaeval stage.* 2 v. Oxford, 1903. (Bibliography.)

Brilliant book by an authority on the subject. Indispensable to the student of English literature and very valuable for the historian. Reviews, W. P. Ker, *E.H.R.* 19:145, Jan. 1904; W. L. Phelps, *Modern Language Notes,* 19:207, Nov. 1904.   JWT

CULTURAL HISTORY: ART

H681 Lethaby, William R. *Mediaeval art from the peace of the church to the eve of the renaissance, 312–1350.* 1904. Rev. ed., London and N. Y., 1912.

Handiest book on the subject in English. The illustrations are numerous, of good size, not trite, and remarkably lifelike. The text is not always sufficiently elementary for the novice, but to the reader with some slight general knowledge of art and architecture the volume will give interesting supplementary information on many topics. It perhaps exaggerates the oriental influence on medieval art. Also cf. (H602a) Lacroix, *Arts in the middle ages.*   LT

H682a Wulff, Oskar. *Altchristliche und byzantinische Kunst.* 2 v. Berlin, 1914–18. [F. Burger, Handbuch der Kunstwissenschaft.] (Bibliographies.)

   b Diehl, Charles. *Manuel d'art byzantin.* 1910. 2nd rev. ed., 2 v., Paris, 1925–26. (Bibliography.)

   c Dalton, Ormonde M. *Byzantine art and archaeology.* Oxford, 1911. (Bibliography.)

   d Millet, Gabriel. *L'art byzantin.* Paris, 1905. [(B682e) A. Michel, *Histoire de l'art,* 1:127–299.]

a. Best manual on Byzantine art; richly illustrated. V. 1. Early Christian art. Accepts Strzygowski's hypothesis of the oriental derivation of Christian art. V. 2. Byzantine art proper. Less subjective; includes recent material; provides a systematic survey. *b.* To achieve historical clearness, the author has unduly curtailed his treatment of monuments. *c.* A dictionary rather than a treatise; extensively lists the monuments but omits architecture. In his new book,

East Christian Art: a survey of the monuments, Oxford, 1925, Dalton treats architecture on pp. 70–159. d. Convenient sketch. Cf. (H684a) Jackson, *Byzantine and Romanesque architecture*.

CRM

H683a Porter, Arthur K. *Medieval architecture, its origin and development, with lists of monuments and bibliographies*. 1909. New ed., 2 v., New Haven, 1912.

   b ——— *Romanesque sculpture of the pilgrimage roads*. 10 v., Boston, 1923. (Bibliography.)

   a. 'Designed primarily' for 'the general reader' and 'to supply the tourist with a *vade mecum* of somewhat larger scope than has hitherto been attempted' but also 'not without value to the advanced student.' The volumes, however, are large and heavy to carry and do not completely cover medieval ecclesiastical architecture. After chapters on ancient, early Christian, Byzantine, Carolingian, and Lombard architecture, the work limits itself to Normandy and the Ile de France. The presentation is clear; the style readable and at times brilliant. The illustrations are numerous and accurate but a trifle cold. The work is a scholarly one, rejecting or questioning many previous views. It gives detailed classified descriptions of churches for the periods and areas treated, in order of importance. The development of architecture is closely associated with the general history of medieval civilization, the author's interpretation of which, while usually well informed, is not always to be accepted unquestioningly. Also cf. (O681e) Porter, *Lombard architecture*. *b*. Consists of 1 v. of text, and 9 v. containing hundreds of plates devoted respectively to 2, Burgundy; 3, Tuscany and Apulia; 4, Aquitaine; 5, Catalonia and Aragon; 6, Castile, the Asturias, and Galicia; 7, Western France; 8, Auvergne and Dauphiné; 9, Provence; 10, Ile-de-France. Valuable for the numerous plates and for urging an earlier chronology for the monuments; based on documents and inscriptions rather than archeological theory; the text will seem a confusing hodge-podge to most readers. LT

H684a Jackson, Sir Thomas G. *Byzantine and Romanesque architecture*. 1913. 2nd ed., 2 v., Cambridge, Eng., 1920.

   b ——— *Gothic architecture in France, England, and Italy*. 2 v., Cambridge, Eng., 1915.

   a. Well illustrated; one of the clearest expositions of the general development of architecture in the Byzantine and Romanesque periods; shows the effect of shrewd and careful personal observation. Has the fault, however, of neglecting recent architectural theories, and especially discussion of the oriental origin of the Byzantine and Romanesque styles. Review S. F. Kimball, *Dial*, 55:306, Oct. 16, 1913; G. M. Rushforth, *E.H.R.* 28:551, July 1913. *b*. Profusely illustrated; probably the best synthetic book of its kind in English today. Especially valuable on account of the writer's lack of a patriotic bias in discussing the moot questions of French and English Gothic. The table of dates is invaluable. Reviews, G. B. Brown, *E.H.R.* 31:478, July 1916; M. B. Medary, Jr., *Journal of the American Institute of Architects*, 4:301, July 1916; S. F. Kimball, *Dial*, 60:502, May 25, 1916.

GHE

H685a Viollet-Le-Duc, Eugène E. *Dictionnaire raisonné de l'architecture française du XIe au XVIe siècle.* 10 v. Paris 1858–68.

b Moore, Charles H. *Development and character of Gothic architecture.* 1890. 2nd rev. ed., N. Y. and London, 1899.

c Cram, Ralph A. *Substance of Gothic: six lectures on the development of architecture from Charlemagne to Henry VIII.* 1917. 2nd ed., Boston, 1925. [Lowell Institute lectures.]

a. Monumental work of special importance for the study of French Gothic architecture. *b.* One of the most important contributions to the study of organic French Gothic architecture, since the publication of *a.;* presents the material in the most synthetic way. The writer has, however, a strong bias in favor of French Gothic of the thirteenth century, and his treatment of the later styles in France, and above all, Gothic styles in other countries, is entirely unsympathetic. A knowledge of the work is essential to the student of Gothic, but should be supplemented by reading the works of others. Review, *Architectural Review* (American) 66:71, Dec. 1899. *c.* Represents an enthusiastic thesis in behalf, not merely of Gothic but of all medieval architecture and of the medieval point of view, emphasizing the spiritual, as well as physical aspects. It condemns in an unnecessary way, however, all periods since the Middle Ages. Reviews, C. Bragdon, *Review of Reviews,* 57:216, Feb. 1918; R. Burton, *Bookman,* 46:477, Dec. 1917.   GHE

H686 Adams, Henry. *Mont-Saint-Michel and Chartres, with an introduction by R. A. Cram.* Boston, 1913. 17th impression, 1927. [First privately printed in 1904.]

This book takes its title from two architectural monuments of the Middle Ages, but is rather a scholarly study of medieval civilization. It discusses literature, history and science, as well as architecture, and is especially valuable in reflecting the change of the medieval point of view between the Romanesque and Gothic periods. Equally invaluable for the student of art and of letters; interestingly written. Reviews, H. O. Taylor, *A.H.R.* 19:592, Apr. 1914; F. B. Luquiens, *Yale Review,* n.s. 3:826, July 1914; S. F. Kimball, *Dial,* 56:246, March 6, 1914.   GHE

H687 Reinach, Salomon. *Répertoire de peintures du moyen âge et de la renaissance, 1280–1580.* 5 v. Paris, 1905–22.

Not a work of historical literature but a classified art catalogue in the form of 3,590 line engravings of as many paintings dating between A.D. 1280 and 1580, each accompanied by a brief verbal identification and indication of bibliography. In each volume pictures dealing with the same subject, as the Annunciation or the Flagellation occur together. Such topics are repeated in the other volumes, but there are recapitulative indexes of artists, subjects, towns, and museums and galleries.   LT

H688a Labarte, Jules. *Histoire des arts industriels au moyen âge et à l'époque de la renaissance.* Text, 4 v., album, 2 v., 1864–66. 2nd ed., 3 v., Paris, 1872–75.

b Addison, Julia de Wolf. *Arts and crafts in the middle ages.* London and Boston, 1908. (Bibliography.)

a. Although this sumptuous old work is found in few American libraries it must be mentioned on account of its remarkable illustrations in color and its wealth of detail concerning such arts as sculpture in ivory, jewelry, miniature work in manuscripts, painting on glass, enameling, mosaic work and ceramic art. *b.* Convenient manual with good illustrations. Cf. (M681*a*) Enlart, *Manuel d'archéologie française.*   LJP

H689 Mâle, Émile. *Art et artistes du moyen âge.* Paris, 1928.

This important book, in describing medieval art, reveals interesting sidelights on the thought of the Middle Ages. Review, Henry Lemonnier, *Journal des Savants,* 97:103, Mar. 1928.   LJP

BIOGRAPHIES

The number of biographies of medieval personages listed here is very small since it is strictly limited to correspond with the topics treated in this section. The life of Theodoric the Ostrogoth is well portrayed in (H701) Thomas Hodgkin, *Theodoric the Goth,* N. Y., 1891 [Heroes of the nations], and in the beautifully illustrated book by (H702) Georg Pfeilschifter, *Die Germanen im römischen Reich: Theoderich der Grosse,* Mainz, 1910. 'The last of the Romans' is treated briefly by (H703) Hugh F. Stewart, *Boethius,* Edinburgh, 1891 [Hulsean essay], but no biography will ever displace the *Consolations of philosophy* by Boethius himself, of which the Latin text, with an English translation on opposite pages may be read in (H704) Boethius, *Theological tractates, with an English translation by H. F. Stewart and E. K. Rand; The consolation of philosophy, with the English translations of 'I. T.' (1609) rev. by H. F. Stewart,* London and N. Y., 1918 [Loeb classical library].

In the period before Charlemagne biographies of figures who had international influence are (H711) Helena Concannon, *Life of Saint Columban,* Dublin, 1915, St. Louis, 1916; (H712) Ernest Brehaut, *An encyclopedist of the dark ages: Isidore of Seville,* N. Y., 1912, [Columbia University studies in history]; (H721) George F. Browne, *Boniface of Crediton and his companions,* London, 1910; and the good book in French by (H722) Godefroid Kurth, *Saint-Boniface,* 1902, 4th ed., Paris, 1913, [Les saints]. The central figure of the Carolingian Renaissance has attracted many biographers: (H723) Andrew F. West, *Alcuin and the rise of Christian schools,* N. Y., 1892 [Great educators]; (H724) George F. Browne, *Alcuin of York,* London, 1908; and (H725) Charles J. B. Gaskoin, *Alcuin, his life and his work,* London, 1904.

One of the greatest men of the tenth century is presented by (H741) François J. Picavet, *Gerbert, un pape philosophe, d'après l'histoire et d'après la légende,* Paris, 1897; and of the eleventh by (H751) Richard W. Church, *Saint Anselm,* London, 1905. (H752) Charles W. David, *Robert Curthose. Duke of Normandy,* Cambridge, Mass., 1920, and (H753) Ralph B. Yewdale, *Bohemund I, prince of Antioch,* Princeton, 1924, are excellent studies of two leaders of the first crusade.

The most attractive figures of the twelfth century are Abelard and Bernard of Clairvaux. (H761) Joseph McCabe, *Peter Abélard,* N. Y. and London, 1901, is a stimulating but popular book which, however, should not be read as a substitute for Abelard's famous (H762) *Historia calamitatum, the story of my misfortunes, an autobiography,* tr. by H. A. Bellows, Saint Paul, 1922. The standard biography of Bernard is by (H763) Elphège Vacandard, *Vie de Saint-Bernard, abbé de Clairvaux,* 1895, 4th ed., 2 v., Paris, 1910, which can be used to check (H764) James A. C. Morison, *Life and times of Saint Bernard, abbot of Clairvaux, A. D. 1091-1153,* 1863, rev. ed., 1868, reprint, London, 1901; and (H765) Richard S. Storrs, *Bernard of Clairvaux,* 1892, reprint, N. Y., 1907.

Among the lives of the greatest scholastic philosophers the most notable in English are: (H781) Roger W. B. Vaughan, *Life and labours of Saint Thomas of Aquin,* 2 v., London, 1871-72, abridged ed. with same title, 1872, 2nd ed., London and N. Y., 1890, which still stands the test of time; and a newer sketch (H782) Placid Conway, *Saint Thomas Aquinas, of the Order of Preachers,* 1225-1274, London and N. Y., 1911. The following volumes of the French collection, *Les Grands Philosophes,* deserve mention: (H783) A. D. Sertillanges, *Saint-Thomas d'Aquin,* 1910, 3rd ed., 2 v., Paris, 1922; and (H784) Bernard Landry, *Duns Scot,* Paris, 1922. Also cf. (H648b) Wulf, *Mediaeval philosophy.*

The story of the man who tried and failed to make Burgundy a modern state is told by (H821) Ruth Putnam, *Charles the Bold, last duke of Burgundy, 1433-1477,* N. Y. and London, 1908 [Heroes of the nations]. (H841) Alice K. Welch, *Of six mediaeval women,* London, 1913, gives brief sketches of Roswitha, Marie de France, Mechthild of Magdeburg, Mahaut, countess of Artois, Christine de Pisan, and Agnes Sorel.   LJP

PERIODICALS

By far the most important periodical devoted to the Middle Ages is the venerable organ of the famous École des Chartes of Paris (H941) *Bibliothèque de l'École des Chartes: revue d'érudition consacrée spécialement à l'étude du moyen âge,* Paris, 1839 ff. Other more or less general reviews devoted to the study of the Middle Ages are (H942) *Le moyen âge: revue d'histoire et de philologie,* Paris, 1888 ff; (H943) *Münchener Archiv für Philologie des Mittelalters und der Renaissance,* München, 1913 ff. (H944a) *Studi medievali,* 4 v. Torino, 1904-13, ed. by F. Novati and R. Renier; continued as (H944b) *Nuovi studi medievali,* Bologna, 1923 ff. (H945) *Archiv für Literatur- und Kirchengeschichte des Mittelalters,* 7 v., Berlin, 1885-1900, ed. by H. Denifle and F. Ehrle.

To facilitate the production of a new dictionary of medieval Latin the Union Académique Internationale has begun the publication of (H951) *Archivum latinitatis medii aevi: bulletin Du Cange,* Paris, 1924 ff., ed. by H. Goelzer. The Committee on Medieval Latin Studies of the American Council of Learned Societies in 1925 evolved into the Mediaeval Academy of America. The Academy publishes a quarterly devoted to all phases of medieval culture, with special emphasis on medieval Latin, (H952) *Speculum, a journal of mediaeval studies,* Cambridge, Mass., 1926 ff., now edited by J. D. M. Ford.

For legal and church history, especially in the medieval period, invaluable articles and critical reviews appear in (H956a) *Zeitschrift für Rechtsgeschichte,* 13 v., Weimar, 1861-80, later published as (H956b) *Zeitschrift der Savigny-Stiftung für Rechtsgeschichte, Germanistische Abteilung,* Weimar, 1880 ff., (H956c) *Romanistische Abteilung,* Weimar, 1880 ff., (H956d) *Kanonistische Abteilung,* Weimar, 1911 ff.

In the special field of Byzantine history there are (H961) *Byzantinische Zeitschrift,* Leipzig, 1892 ff., founded by K. Krumbacher; (H962) *Byzantinisch-neugriechische Jahrbücher: internationales wissenschaftliches Organ,* ed. by Nikos A. Bees, Berlin, 1920 ff.; and (H963) *Byzantion: revue internationale des études byzantines,* Paris, 1924 ff. For the history of the crusades the Société de l'Orient Latin founded (H971a) *Archives de l'Orient Latin,* 2 v., Paris, 1881-84, revived as (H971b) *Revue de l'Orient Latin,* 12 v., Paris, 1893-1911.   LJP

SECTION I

MODERN EUROPE, 1450–1870

Editor

WILLIAM E. LINGELBACH

Professor of European History, University of Pennsylvania

CONTENTS

INTRODUCTION

The period dealt with in this section includes the four centuries from the Renaissance to the unification of Germany and Italy, approximately 1450–1870.

The growth of the spirit of nationality resulting in the rise of separate nations in modern times gradually destroyed even the semblance of unity which had characterized the history of western Europe in the Middle Ages. As a consequence European history during the modern period develops more distinctly along national lines. Important movements and events become associated more and more with particular peoples and countries. This tendency is in turn strongly reflected in the historical writing and research of the period. Students and scholars adapt themselves to the new conditions and direct their efforts along national lines. The vast mass of historical literature on the modern period is therefore not sufficiently general in its scope to appear in this section. Many works usually associated with the history of modern Europe and at first included in this section have upon a careful analysis of their contents been assigned by the editors to the sections on national history. Thus works on the Renaissance are for the most part included in §§ L (England), M (France), O (Italy) and P (Germany); those on the Reformation in §§ P (Germany) and F (History of Christianity); those on the French Revolution and Napoleon in § M (France), while those on the nineteenth century are still more widely distributed. On the other hand, the works on the history of international relations and on military history have been developed somewhat more fully in this section.

BIBLIOGRAPHY

There is no general bibliography for modern European history. For the purpose of the general reader, as well as of the college student, the bibliographies in the works listed in the subsection (I101 ff.), Shorter General Histories, will be found very serviceable because of discriminating selection and helpful critical comment. Fuller classified lists, without critical comments, appear in (I121) *Cambridge modern history,* and (B152) Lavisse et Rambaud, *Histoire générale.* Both are now somewhat out-of-date. More highly specialized lists will be found in the works discussed under special subjects in this section and in the sections on national history. Among the latter the following deserve notice here: (M2a) Molinier and others; (M3b) Caron; (M3c) Brière and Caron; (P1a) Dahlmann-Waitz; (Q1) Pirenne; (N5) Foulché-Delbosc, and (N3a) Sanchez-Alonso.

Library collections. The best collections on International Law are at the Carnegie Endowment for International Peace, at the Department of State, and at the Library of Congress, Washington, D. C.; the Olivart collection at Harvard University; Grotius collection, Columbia University; Wheaton collection, Brown University; Columbia library, Pan-American Union; Pitney collection, Princeton University; Georgetown University Foreign Science School; and at the Northwestern Law School. For military and naval sciences the best collections are at the United States War Department Library and the U. S. Army War College, Washington; the U. S. Military Academy, West Point; the U. S. Naval Academy, Annapolis; the U. S. Engineering School Library; Naval History Society, New York; U. S. Naval War College, Newport, R. I.; New York Public Library; Newberry Library, Chicago, Ill.; and the Library of Congress.   AHS

GEOGRAPHY AND ATLASES

I41a *Cambridge modern history atlas.* 1912. 2nd ed., Cambridge (Eng.) and N. Y., 1925.

b Hearnshaw, Fossey J. C., ed. *Macmillan's historical atlas of modern Europe.* London, 1920.

a. Accompaniment to (I121) *Cambridge modern history,* octavo in size. Maps are clear and well selected, but often faulty in detail. Review, A. F. Pollard, *E.H.R.,* 28: 598, July 1913; S. B. Harding, *A.H.R.,* 31: 562, Apr. 1926.   HRS

b. Convenient little atlas for the class room of historical maps accompanied by explanatory notes. Physical features are omitted and occasional inaccuracies have crept in. Review, W. A. Frayer, *A.H.R.,* 27: 143, Oct. 1921. Excellent historical atlases covering a wider field but useful for the period covered by this section will be found in A49 and A50. Of special interest here are (A50a) Shepherd, (A50d) *Putnam's,* and (A50f) Meyer.   WEL

SOURCE BOOKS AND COLLECTIONS OF SOURCES

161 Robinson, James H., and Beard, Charles A. *Readings in modern European history, a collection of extracts from the sources chosen with the purpose of illustrating some of the chief phases of the development of Europe during the last two hundred years.* 2 v. Boston, 1908–09. (Bibliography.)

Convenient, well-selected group of primary sources; covers a wide range of subjects, literary as well as political and economic. Review, S. B. Fay, *A.H.R.*, 14: 639, April 1909; 15: 196, Oct. 1909.

HLH

162 Postgate, Raymond W. *Revolution from 1789 to 1906. Documents selected and edited with notes and introduction.* Boston, 1921.

Volume of sources furnishing suggestive material for a comparative study of the successive revolutions from the French in 1789 to the Russian in 1905–06. Notes and introduction at times reveal a distinctly radical tendency which is also reflected strongly in the selection of the documents. Social changes are overemphasized at the expense of the political and national movements. Review, W. C. Abbott, *A.H.R., 27*: 554, Apr. 1922.

WEL

163 Hall, Walter P., and Beller, Elmer A., ed. *Historical readings in nineteenth century thought.* N. Y., 1928.

Well chosen selections from the writings of Huxley, Herbert Spencer and other influential nineteenth century thinkers, with brief introductions on the authors represented.

HRS

164a Dickinson, Edwin Dewitt. *Selections of cases and other readings on the law of nations chiefly as it is interpreted and applied by British and American courts.* London and N. Y., 1929.

b Scott, James Brown. *Cases on international law selected from decisions of English and American courts,* 1902. New ed. St. Paul, 1922. [American casebook series.] (Bibliography.)

Good examples of case books useful in the teaching of international law. Review of *a*, (London) *Times Lit. Suppl.*, 28: 869, Oct. 31, 1929. Larger collections of sources especially in the field of international relations will be found in (1507, 508, 509). Diplomatic instructions and correspondence; and treaty collections. HRS

SHORTER GENERAL HISTORIES

I101 Hayes, Carlton J. H. *Political and social history of modern Europe.* 1916. 2nd rev. ed., 2 v., N. Y., 1924. [V. 1, *1500–1815;* v. 2, *1815–1923.*] (Good critical bibliographies.)

Excellent synthesis; unique in quality; emphasizes the last century and economic factors. The unifying idea is the rise of the bourgeoisie; the dominating forces producing this development, the French Revolution and especially the Industrial Revolution, are constantly stressed. Important chapters are devoted to the Europeanizing of America, the penetration of Asia, and the partition of Africa. The second edition adds chapters on the World War, the peace settlement, the Russian revolution and the 'Latest Era.' Review, H. E. Bourne, *A.H.R., 22*: 638, Apr. 1917.

EEY

I102 Gooch, George P. *Annals of politics and culture, 1492–1899.* Cambridge (Eng.), 1901. Reprint, 1905.

Compact compilation of the facts of modern history; arranged chronologically; left-hand pages are devoted to politics, right-hand, to culture; many errors of facts, as well as numerous faults of judgment in selection. Review, *E.H.R.*, 17 : 20c Jan. 1902. CWD

I103 Robinson, James H., and **Beard, Charles A.** *Development of moder Europe, an introduction to the study of current history.* 2 v. 1907–08. Re. ed. Boston, 1929. (Bibliographies.)

Covers the period from Louis XIV to the opening of the twentieth century. Characterized by breadth of view and freedom of treatment. Its appearance marked a new departure in historical text-books and it had a wide influence upon history teaching; excellent example of the project method, and emphasis upon recent history. Review, S. B. Fay, *A.H.R.*, 14 : 188, Oct. 1908. HLH

I104a Turner, Edward Raymond. *Europe, 1450–1789.* N. Y., 1923.

b —— *Europe since 1789.* N. Y., 1924.

Texts forming with the author's (J104c) *Europe since 1870,* a series covering European history from the Renaissance to 1927. Straightforward narrative preserving a creditable balance between political, social and economic matters. Review of *a*, E. M. Hulme, *A.H.R.*, 29 : 757, July 1924; of *b*, E. E. Sperry, *A.H.R.*, 30 : 356, Jan. 1925. JES

I105a Higby, Chester P. *History of Europe, 1492–1815.* N. Y., 1927. (Bibliographies.)

b Hyma, Albert. *Short history of Europe, 1500–1816.* N. Y., 1928. (Bibliographies.)

c Gillespie, James E. *History of Europe, 1500–1815.* N. Y., 1928. (Bibliographies.)

Text-books covering the three centuries preceding the fall of Napoleon, each well organized, reliable and readable. *c.* Emphasizes the history of culture and institutions to a greater extent than do *a* and *b*. Review of *a*, T. Collier, *A.H.R.*, 33 : 110, Oct. 1927; of *b*, id., ibid., 34 : 638, Apr. 1929; of *c*, (London) *Times Lit. Suppl.*, 28 : 245, March 21, 1929; T. Collier, *A.H.R.*, 35 : 156, Oct. 1929. HRS

I106 Schevill, Ferdinand. *History of Europe from the reformation to the present day.* 1907. Rev. ed., N. Y., 1930.

Stands midway between the college texts listed in this subsection and the high school texts whose numbers preclude their consideration here. Mainly a narrative of political history. Three new chapters continue the story through the World War. Review, S. B. Fay, *A.H.R.*, 13 : 667, Apr. 1908. HLH

I107 Friedell, Egon. *Cultural history of the modern age.* V. 1. *The crisis of the European soul.* N. Y., 1930. Tr. by C. F. Atkinson from *Kulturgeschichte der Neuzeit,* 2 v., München, 1928.

Attempt to interpret the last four centuries of European history in the terms of Spengler's morphology of history, that is, in the rise, maturity and decay of cultural epochs. In place of the continuity of history, the author lays the emphasis upon the unity of well-defined periods characterized by a spirit and tone of their own. Characteristically, he begins the new age with the middle of the fourteenth century, the Black Death serving as a phenomenon of the illness and decay that marked the decline of the middle ages. The Renaissance is not a return to the classics but, according to the author, something new and modern; the Reformation 'not a creative religious movement,' but the glorification of 'work' which it sanctified, thus preparing the way for capitalism and Marxism. WEL

LONGER GENERAL HISTORIES

I121 *Cambridge modern history.* Planned by the late Lord Acton. Ed. by Sir Adolphus W. Ward, Sir G. W. Prothero and Stanley Leathes. 14 v. Cambridge, Eng., and N. Y., 1902–12. [1, *Renaissance; 2, Reformation; 3, Wars of religion; 4, Thirty years' war; 5, Age of Louis XIV; 6, Eighteenth century; 7, United States; 8, French revolution; 9, Napoleon; 10, Restoration; 11, Growth of nationalities; 12, Latest age; 13, Genealogical tables and lists and general index; 14, Atlas,* rev. ed., 1924.] (Extensive bibliographies.)

These fourteen bulky volumes represent the most ambitious project of co-operative writing on modern history yet attempted in English. A great many authors contributed, varying from 12 to 29 for the different volumes. Each volume was developed about what the editors regarded as the central idea or movement of one of twelve periods of modern history. Despite this, the work as a whole lacks unity. Even the individual volumes rarely show real unity of design or execution. The authors were for the most part specialists in the particular fields assigned to them but their contributions are of unequal merit. Individual chapters are often excellent; nearly all are accurate and scholarly; too many are dull and colorless. The bulk of the material relates to political and diplomatic rather than to social and economic history, though there are occasional chapters of great merit on these phases of history. The treatment of intellectual development, art and literature is inadequate and uneven.

There is a chronological table of events and a working index in each volume. The work is a vast storehouse of information; useful for reference and topical study rather than for general reading. Review of v. 1 and the plan of the work as a whole, M. Whitcomb, *A.H.R.,* 9: 142, Oct. 1903; E. W. Watson, *E.H.R.,* 18: 353, Apr. 1903. Other volumes were reviewed at the time of publication in these and other historical magazines. Cf. also the volumes devoted to modern history in the larger works on general history listed in § B.   WEL

I122 **Dyer, Thomas H.** *History of modern Europe from the fall of Constantinople.* 4 v. 1861–64. 3rd rev. ed., continued to 1900 by A. Hassall, 6 v., London, 1901. Reprint, 1907. (Bibliography.)

Compendious, compact with facts; useful for reference; not distinguished for merits of style; a chronicle unrelieved by vivid pictures or brilliant characterization; many of its judgments susceptible of modification in the light of more recent research. Review, J. P. Whitney, *E.H.R.,* 18: 559, July 1903.   TC

THE RENAISSANCE

Historical works dealing with the Renaissance are apt to stress its development in particular countries and are therefore noted in the sections devoted to national history, as for example the well-known works on the Italian Renaissance, (O251a) Burckhardt, and (O252a) Symonds; the former an original interpretation along philosophical and cultural lines, the latter a brilliant if none too reliable account of the various manifestations of the movement in Italy.

I201a **Hollings, Mary A.** *Europe in renaissance and reformation, 1453–1659.* London, 1909.

b **Hudson, William H.** *Story of the renaissance.* N. Y., 1912.

c **Hulme, Edward Maslin.** *Renaissance, the protestant revolution, and the catholic reformation in continental Europe.* 1914. Rev. ed., N. Y., 1917.

d **Van Dyke, Paul.** *Age of the renascence.* N. Y., 1897.

e **Tanner, Emmeline M.** *Renaissance and reformation, 1494–1610.* Oxford, 1908.

f **Allen, Percy S.** *Age of Erasmus.* Oxford, 1914.

g **Hyma, Albert.** *Christian renaissance: a history of the 'Devotio moderna.'* Grand Rapids, Mich., 1924. (Q621*b*)

a, b, and *d.* Small texts of uneven merit. *d.* Stresses the intellectual movement. *c.* Longer and not so much a narrative as it is a topical treatment somewhat crowded with detail. Despite frequent searching interpretations and excellent analyses there is no philosophical viewpoint or unity. The English reformation is not treated. Appendix contains useful lists of emperors, popes, genealogical tables, etc. Review, G. E. Sellery, *A.H.R.,* 20: 393, Jan. 1915. *e.* Clear but conventional presentation of the subject. *f.* Series of lectures in which the author sketches with considerable skill different phases of the world of Erasmus, its study, education, social conditions, north and south of the Alps. Review, H. D. Foster, *A.H.R.,* 20: 428, Jan. 1915; E. Bensly, *E.H.R.,* 30: 540, July 1915. *g.* Scholarly and original. Author claims the Renaissance is more than a humanistic movement, its roots were widespread throughout northern Europe where it was the precursor of the reformation. Review, E. W. Miller, *A.H.R.,* 30: 346, Jan. 1925.   WEL

I212a **La Croix, Paul.** *Middle ages and the renaissance.* 4 v. N. Y., 1875–78. Tr. from *Le moyen âge et la renaissance,* 5 v., 1848–51. Latest ed., Paris, 1884.

b **Monnier, Marc.** *Histoire générale de la littérature moderne: la renaissance de Dante à Luther.* Paris, 1884.

Works by foreign authors of the old-fashioned type on special phases of the renaissance.   WEL

I213a **Whitcomb, Merrick.** *Literary source-book of the renaissance.* 1900. 2nd ed., Philadelphia, 1903.

b **Woodward, William H.** *Studies in education during the age of the renaissance.* Cambridge (Eng.), 1914. (Bibliography.)

a. Convenient collection of sources in translation illustrating the literary and intellectual side of the Italian and German renaissance. Selections are apt and well chosen. Introduction to the German renaissance excellent. *b.* Very satisfactory exposition of the rise and development of humanistic educational theory and practice in Italy and of their spread to transalpine lands; based upon wide reading in the original sources and inspired by an intelligent conception of the general bearing of the subject upon the history of civilization.   WEL

Cf. (B671*a*) Sandys, (O253*a*) Robinson and Rolfe, (L667*a*) Einstein, (M661*f*) Tilley, and (O255) Cellini.

I214a **Drummond, Robert B.** *Erasmus; his life and character, as shown in his correspondence and works.* 2 v. London, 1873.

b **Emerton, Ephraim.** *Desiderius Erasmus of Rotterdam.* N. Y., 1899. [Heroes of the reformation.]

c **Froude, James Anthony.** *Life and letters of Erasmus.* 1894. 3rd ed., N. Y., 1912.

d **Lindeboom, J.** *Erasmus, Onderzoek naar zijne theologie en zijn gods-dienstig gemoedsbestaan.* Leiden, 1909.

e **Mestwerdt, P.** *Die Anfänge des Erasmus, Humanismus und 'Devotio moderna.'* Leipzig, 1917.

f **Smith, Preserved.** *Erasmus, a study of his life, ideals and place in history.* London and N. Y., 1923.

g **Huizinga, J.** *Erasmus.* N. Y. and London, 1924. [Great Hollanders.]

h **Allen, Percy S.** *Erasmus' services to learning.* London, 1926.

i **Major, Emil.** *Erasmus von Rotterdam.* Basel, 1926.

j **Mangan, John J.** *Life, character and influence of Erasmus of Rotterdam derived from a study of his works.* 2 v. N. Y., 1927.

a. Gives a translation of well-chosen letters and writings of Erasmus which serve as a basis for a fair and judicious estimate of the great scholar. Review, *Athenaeum,* p. 9, July 5, 1873. *b.* Restricted to a consideration of the attitude of Erasmus toward the revolt of Luther from Rome; not, therefore, a well-rounded biography; with also perhaps too easygoing an opinion of the theological revolution in Germany; but its special theme is finely illustrated by quotation from Erasmus' writings, especially from his letters. A charming volume always written with insight. Review, *A.H.R.,* 5:751, July 1900; P. S. Allen, *E.H.R.,* 15:578, July 1900. *c.* Vigorous and attractive lectures, marred by inaccuracies and prejudice; an attempt to interpret the age of the Renaissance through the opinions of Erasmus in conformity with the author's belief in the importance of the individual in history. Review, *Edinburgh Rev.,* 181:173, Jan. 1895. *d.* Work by a Dutch scholar stressing Erasmus' attitude toward the institutions, doctrines and sacraments of the church; interprets his character from the religious point of view. Lucid presentation, mainly theological. Review, *E.H.R.,* 25:613, July 1910. *e.* Penetrating analysis of the historical origins of Erasmus' religious outlook as moulded by Italian religions, humanism and the *devotio moderna* in Holland. Review, H. Baron, *Hist. Zeit.,* 132:413, 1925. *f.* Sympathetic appreciation with special reference to his relations with humanism and the reformation; a commendable and successful effort to present the personality of Erasmus not only as the product of the age but as typical of this critical and turbulent period. Review, E. Emerton, *A.H.R.,* 30:348, Jan. 1925. *g.* Brief but excellent popular biography by an eminent Dutch historian. His appraisement of Erasmus is less favorable than Allen's, but essentially fair. The outstanding cosmopolitan figure of his age, a 'citizen of the world' as he called himself, Erasmus does not readily fit into a national series. Review, E. Emerton, *A.H.R.,* 30:132, Oct. 1924. *h.* Brilliant and altogether favorable estimate of the contribution of Erasmus to learning and education. Review, J. P. Whitney, *E.H.R.,* 42:280, Apr. 1927. *i.* Charming account. Gives important information on the cultural and daily life of Erasmus. Review, W. Koehler, *Hist. Zeit.,* 134:441, 1926; E. W. Nelson, *Jour. Modern Hist.,* 1:88, Mar. 1929. *j.* New interpretation of Erasmus based on wide and careful study of his writings and the literature that has grown up around him; a psycho-analysis by a Catholic writer who seeks to explain the enigmatical conduct and writings of Erasmus by the claim that he was 'neurasthenic,' 'physically timid,' 'morbidly sensitive' and 'selfish to a degree.' Good illustrations and bibliography of Erasmus' writings, editions and translations. Review, E. Emerton, *A.H.R.,* 33:108, Oct. 1927.

WEL

I215a Nichols, Francis M. *Epistles of Erasmus from his earliest letters to his fifty-first year, arranged in order of time. English translation with a commentary.* 3 v. London and N. Y., 1901–18.

b Allen, Percy S. *Opus epistolarum Des. Erasmi Roterodami denuo recognitum et auctum.* V. 1–7, Oxford and N. Y., 1906–28.

a. Contains the epistles of Erasmus from his earliest letters to his fifty-first year in excellent translation and with full notes. Reviews, v. 1, *A.H.R.*, 7: 548, Apr. 1902; v. 1 and 2, P. S. Allen, *E.H.R.*, 17: 785, Oct. 1902; 20: 362, Apr. 1905; v. 2 and 3, E. Emerton, *A.H.R.*, 10: 686, Apr. 1905; 24: 669, July 1919; v. 3, J. P. Whitney, *E.H.R.*, 34: 103, Jan. 1919. *b.* Masterly edition of the epistles, accompanied by valuable notes, characterized by sound scholarship and fine literary sense. Reviews, v. 1–6, J. P. Whitney, *E.H.R.*, 23: 139, Jan. 1908; 25: 774, Oct. 1910; 31: 317, Apr. 1916; 42: 280, Apr. 1927; v. 1, 2 and 4, P. Smith, *A.H.R.*, 15: 841, July 1910; 28: 107, Oct. 1922; v. 5–7, E. Emerton, *ibid.*, 30: 351, Jan. 1925; 32: 311, Jan. 1927; 34: 870, July 1929. For a critical and appreciative survey of the recent literature on Erasmus, cf. E. W. Nelson, *Journal of Modern History,* 1: 88, March 1929.   WEL

THE REFORMATION AND COUNTER-REFORMATION

Other works in this field are listed in § F, History of Christianity, and in the sections on national history, especially §§ L, M, and P. Among them the following should be noted here as having a special interest to the student of modern history: (F23a) *Realencyclopädie,* (F124b) Hergenröther, (F301, P251) Lindsay, (F311a) Creighton, (F311b) Pastor, (F311c) Ranke, and (P242a) Janssen.

I231a Smith, Preserved. *Age of the reformation.* N. Y., 1920. (Excellent bibliography.)

b Mackinnon, James. *Luther and the reformation.* 4 v. London and N. Y., 1925–30.

a. Most readable and scholarly one-volume account in English based upon wide reading and critical research, especially on Luther, with new and valuable chapters on later interpretations of the Reformation. Places the movement in its proper relation to the economic and intellectual revolutions of the sixteenth century. Sometimes there is a lack of appreciation of the reformers' ideals and better side, perhaps true especially in the chapters on Calvin, which contain errors of fact and inference. Review, E. M. Hulme, *A.H.R.*, 26: 765, July 1921.   HDF

b. Fullest and most scholarly biography of Luther in English, presenting him in the rôle of a hero. Emphasizes the personal and theological aspects of the German reformation. Marked by certain inaccuracies of detail and a neglect of the significance of contemporary social, political and intellectual forces. Reviews, P. Smith, *E.H.R.*, 41: 597, Oct. 1926; 43: 628, Oct. 1928; E. W. Nelson, *A.H.R.*, 31: 507, Apr. 1926; 33: 861, July 1928; 34: 809, July 1929; 36: 115, Oct. 1930.   WEL

I232a Beard, Charles. *Reformation of the sixteenth century in relation to modern thought and knowledge.* 1883. 5th ed., London, 1907. Reprint, 1927. [Hibbert lectures.]

b Taylor, Henry O. *Thought and expression in the 16th century.* 2 v. London and N. Y., 1920.

c Allen, John W. *History of political thought in the sixteenth century.* London, 1928.

d Hearnshaw, Fossey J. C., ed. *Social and political ideas of some great thinkers of the renaissance and the reformation.* London, 1925.

e Stubbs, William. *Lectures on European history,* ed. by A. Hassall. London and N. Y., 1904.

f Murray, Robert H. *Political consequences of the reformation: studies in sixteenth century political thought.* London, 1926.

g O'Brien, George. *Essay on the economic effects of the reformation.* London, 1923.

a. Series of lectures from the Protestant viewpoint; not a history but an interpretation of the movement, a plea for the reconciliation of theology and the new knowledge. Cf. (F652*b*) Balmes.   EEY
b. Supplement to (H646*a*) Taylor, *Medieval mind,* with chapters on the development of letters, literature, art, science, and philosophy, and to the Lutheran, Zwinglian, Calvinist, and Anglican revolts from Rome; omits the Catholic Reaction. Brilliant and suggestive, particularly on poets, painters, and philosophers, but not always accurate. Review, E. M. Hulme, *A.H.R.,* 26: 501, Apr. 1921. *c.* Work of real scholarship and insight, though covering a large area. Review, H. J. Laski, *E.H.R.,* 44: 469, July 1929. *d.* Excellent studies by British scholars on Machiavelli, Luther, Nicholas of Cusa and others. Review, J. Dickinson, *Am. Pol. Sci. Rev.,* 21: 164, Feb. 1927. *e.* Lectures by the distinguished constitutional historian on the political and military history of the Reformation and on the Thirty Years' War. Review, H. D. Foster, *A.H.R.,* 10: 160, Oct. 1904. *f.* Erudite but lacking in care for detail or thorough research that makes for originality. There are many minor errors. Review, P. Smith, *E.H.R.,* 42: 308, Apr. 1927; J. Dickinson, *Am. Pol. Sci. Rev.,* 21: 164, Feb. 1927. *g.* Written to establish the thesis that the Reformation destroyed freedom and justice and 'enthroned the state as an absolute and unlimited sovereign.' Original in its recombination of old data rather than in the introduction of new material.   WEL, HRS
Cf. also, (P256*e*) Schapiro.

I235a Robertson, William. *History of the reign of the emperor Charles the fifth.* 3 v. 1769. Ed. by W. H. Prescott, 3 v., Boston, 1857. Prescott edition ed. by J. F. Kirk, 3 v., Philadelphia, 1872.

b Armstrong, Edward. *Emperor Charles V.* 2 v. London, 1902.

a. Appears in many editions, the best being that of Prescott, who added chapters on Charles' life at San Yuste. Long considered the 'classic' English biography of Charles, but now antiquated, inadequate and, in important particulars, unreliable, vitiated by a strong bias against Charles and strongly prejudiced religiously. Review, E. F. Henderson, *A.H.R.,* 9: 22, Oct. 1903. Cf. (A247) Fueter, p. 456, French edition. *b.* 'Does not profess to be a history of the reign, but of the man.' (Preface.) Portrays Charles as 'not quite a great man, nor yet quite a good man,' but essentially just and conscientious; a sympathetic study, but judicial, impassionate, free from exaggeration and partisanship, based on sound scholarship; the best recent life of Charles. Review, E. F. Henderson, *A.H.R.,* 9: 22, Oct. 1903; S. Leathes, *E.H.R.,* 18: 560, July 1903. Cf. (N251) Merriman, v. 3.   TC

I241a Ward, Adolphus W. *Counter reformation.* London, 1889. [Epochs of church history.]

b Maurenbrecher, Wilhelm. *Geschichte der katholischen Reformation.* V. 1, Nördlingen, 1880.

c Droysen, Gustav. *Geschichte der Gegenreformation.* Berlin, 1893. [Oncken: Allgemeine Geschichte.]

d **Philippson, Martin.** *La contre-révolution religieuse au 16ᵉ siècle.* Bruxelles, 1884. [Les origines de catholicisme moderne.]

e **Jourdan, George V.** *Movement towards catholic reform in the early sixteenth century.* London, 1914.

a. Convenient brief account of the outburst of reforming militant activity in the church in the latter part of the sixteenth century. General rather than profound, well-written and arranged with judicial intent despite its shortcomings in this respect. Review, *E.H.R.*, 4 : 600, July 1889. *b.* Scholarly account by a liberal Catholic historian. Review, H. Baumgarten, *Hist. Zeit.*, N. F., 10 : 154, 1881. *c.* Semipopular but scholarly, by a leading German historian. Like the other volumes in the series, it is well illustrated with contemporary engravings and woodcuts. *d.* General survey of subject rather than authoritative investigation. Review, P. Fredericq, *Rev. Hist.*, 34 : 316, July 1887. *e.* Attempt to evaluate the efforts to reform the church anterior to the reformation by such individuals as Savonarola, Colet, More, Erasmus, Lefèvre, and others.   EMH, WEL

SEVENTEENTH AND EIGHTEENTH CENTURIES

Historical works relating to general history in these two centuries are not numerous; even more than for other periods, historical writing, save in the field of political and economic theory and of international relations, is directly associated with national history.

I271a **Ogg, David.** *Europe in the seventeenth century.* London, 1925.

b **Guedalla, Philip.** *Partition of Europe, 1715–1815.* Oxford, 1914.

c **Hearnshaw, Fossey J. C.**, ed. *Social and political ideas of some great thinkers of the sixteenth and seventeenth centuries.* London, 1926.

a. Brief but fairly successful effort to treat the century as a whole, stressing the origins of the movements that came into prominence in the eighteenth century. Review, P. Geyl, *E.H.R.*, 40 : 611, Oct. 1925; H. R. Shipman, *A.H.R.*, 31 : 312, Jan. 1926. *b.* Entertainingly written, emphasizing the frequent changes in the political map. *c.* Series of eight excellent lectures by eminent scholars with an introductory lecture on the period by the editor. Review, C. H. McIlwain, *History,* 12 : 262, Oct. 1927. Cf. companion volume on Renaissance and Reformation (I232d).   WEL

I272a **Schlosser, Friederich C.** *History of the eighteenth century and of the nineteenth till the overthrow of the French empire.* 8 v. London, 1843–52. Tr. by D. Davidson from the 2nd and 3rd ed. of *Geschichte des achtzehnten Jahrhunderts und des neunzehnten bis zum Sturz des französischen Kaiserreichs. Mit besonderer Rücksicht auf die geistige Bildung.* 7 v., Heidelberg, 1835–48.

b **Immich, Max.** *Geschichte des europäischen Staatensystems von 1660–1789.* München, 1905. [(B170) Below and Meinecke.] (Good bibliography.)

a. Schlosser's work represents wide reading rather than research. Dominated by the ethics of Kant, history becomes with him applied morals. Hostile to aristocracy in every age, he is yet a stern judge of the enlightened despots and absolute monarchs. The first two volumes, devoted to thinkers and literary movements, show the author's understanding of the intimate relations between such writers and the political and social system of the century. In a sense the work is culture history.   GSF

b. Posthumous work in which author attempted to present the several states of Europe as a part of the whole European political system; in the words of the editors of the series, it is 'not so much a history of states as a history of the family of states.'

WHA

I273a Ward, Sir Adolphus W. *Collected papers, historical, literary, travel and miscellaneous.* 5 v. Cambridge (Eng.), 1921.

  b Acton, John Edward Emerich, Baron. *Lectures on modern history.* Ed. by J. N. Figgis and R. V. Lawrence. London, 1906.

a. First two volumes consist of interesting essays and reviews published from time to time on a great variety of historical subjects relating mainly to British and German history since the seventeenth century. Review, *E.H.R.*, 36 : 467, July 1921. *b.* Stimulating lectures to University audiences by a great scholar on a variety of subjects in modern history down to the French Revolution with a special lecture on the study of History. Review, *E.H.R.*, 22 : 164, Jan. 1907.   SBF

I274a Meiern, Johann G. von. *Acta pacis Westphalicae publica oder Friedenshandlungen und Geschichte.* 6 v. Hanover, 1734–36.

  b *Négotiations secrètes touchant la paix de Münster et d'Osnabrug, ou recueil général des préliminaires, instructions, lettres, mémoires, etc., concernant ces négotiations depuis 1642 jusqu'à leur conclusion en 1648 avec les dépêches de Mr. de Vautorte et autres pièces au sujet du même traité jusqu'en 1645 incl.* 4 v. La Haye, 1725–26.

Basic source materials for the negotiations and agreements of the peace of Westphalia. By way of supplement, cf. Johann L. Walther, *Universal-Register sowie über die Friedens-als Exekutionshandlungen,* Göttingen, 1740, a useful guide to names of persons associated with the peace negotiations.   HRS

I275a Archives Diplomatiques, Commission des. *Recueil des instructions données aux ambassadeurs et ministres de France depuis les traités de Westphalie jusqu'à la Révolution française.* V. 1–25, Paris, 1884–1929. [1. *Autriche,* ed. by A. Sorel; 2. *Suède,* ed. by A. Geffroy; 3. *Portugal,* ed. by Amedée de Caix de Saint Aymour; 4–5. *Pologne,* ed. by L. Farges; 6. *Rome,* pt. 1, ed. by G. Hanotaux; 7. *Bavière, Palatinat, Deux-Ponts,* ed. by A. Lebon; 8–9. *Russie,* pts. 1–2, ed. by A. Rambaud; 10. *Naples et Parme,* ed. by J. Reinach; 11–12. *Espagne,* pts. 1–3, ed. by A. P. V. Morel-Fatio with the collaboration of H. Leonardon; 13. *Dänemark,* ed. by A. Geffroy; 14. *Savoie-Sardaigne et Mantoue,* pts. 1–2, ed. by le comte Horric de Beaucaire; 16. *Prusse,* ed. by A. Waddington; 17. *Rome,* pt. 2, ed. by G. Hanotaux; 18. *Diète germanique,* ed. by B. Auerbach; 19. *Florence, Modène, Gênes,* ed. by É. Driault; 20. *Rome,* pt. 3, ed. by J. Hanoteau; 21–23. *Hollande,* ed. by L. André and É. Bourgeois; 24–25. *Angleterre,* pts. 1–2, ed. by G. J. Jusserand.] [Also as (M74*b*).]

  b *British diplomatic instructions, 1689–1789.* V. 1–5, London, 1922–28. [1. *Sweden, 1689–1723,* ed. by J. F. Chance; 2. *France, 1689–1721,* ed. by L. G. Wickham Legg; 3. *Denmark,* ed. by J. F. Chance; 4. *France, 1721–27,* ed. by L. G. Wickham Legg; 5. *Sweden, 1727–1789,* ed. by J. F. Chance.]

a. Classic introduction to the study of the diplomatic history of Europe from the treaty of Westphalia to the outbreak of the French Revolution in the form of instructions given to French ambassadors and ministers, arranged by countries, each volume with a masterly introduction giving the reader a luminous survey of French policy with regard to the state in question during a century and a half and fitting that policy into its place in the general history of Europe. A mine of invaluable source material. Reviews, *Rev. Hist.*, as follows: v. 1, by A. Sorel, 24: 368, March 1884; v. 2, by C. Bémont, 30: 386, March 1886; v. 3, by G. Monod and C. Bémont, 34: 283, July 1887; v. 4, 5, 6, by G. Monod, 38: 368, Nov. 1888; v. 6, by L. Farges and G. Monod, 39: 119, Jan. 1889; v. 7–9, by G. Monod, 44: 99, Sept. 1890; v. 10, by L. Farges, 52: 337, July 1893; v. 23, by G. Pagès, 146: 233, July 1924. *b.* Counterpart of *a.* Much less complete and informing, due in part to the fact that each French envoy was given most full instructions, 'in fact started for his destination with a regular plan of campaign in his pocket,' while the British envoy received his real instructions in a series of dispatches from a secretary of state, sent as detailed problems arose. Selections from these dispatches, with a short and not always satisfactory introduction, make up the volumes of *b.* Reviews of v. 1 and 2, H. Temperley, *E.H.R.*, 38: 281, Apr. 1923; 41: 603, Oct. 1926; of v. 3, W. F. Reddaway, *ibid.*, 43: 459, July 1928; of v. 4, R. Lodge, *ibid.*, 43: 433, July 1928; of v. 5, A. I. Andrews, *A.H.R.*, 34: 642, Apr. 1929.   HRS, WEL

I276a Stanhope, Philip H., 5th earl of. *History of the war of the Spanish succession in Spain.* London, 1832. Appendix comprising extracts from General Stanhope's letters.

   b Taylor, Frank. *Wars of Marlborough, 1702–1709.* Ed. by G. Winfried Taylor. 2 v. Oxford, 1921.

   c Murray, Sir George, ed. *Letters and dispatches of J. Churchill, first Duke of Marlborough, from 1702–1712.* 5 v. London, 1845.

   d Clark, George N. *Dutch alliance and the war against French trade, 1688–1697.* London, 1923.

   a. Holds a prominent place in history because it called forth Macaulay's brilliant but unreliable essay entitled, 'Lord Mahon's War of the Succession in Spain' in 1833.   TC
   b. Brilliantly written account of the principal war of Marlborough written from the military point of view and very favorable to him. Miss Taylor prepared the volumes for publication after the death of her father, adding references for the citations, while Sir John Fortescue wrote an appreciative introduction. Review, L. André, *Rev. Hist.*, 142: 96, Jan. 1923; G. N. Clark, *E.H.R.*, 32: 616, Oct. 1922.
   c. Valuable source material throwing light on other than military matters. *d.* Scholarly study of the important problem of trade warfare at sea as seen in the Anglo-French trade wars, based on extensive reading in Dutch archives and literature as well as upon a thorough knowledge of English sources. Review, C. Brinkmann, *E.H.R.*, 39: 287, Apr. 1924; F. G. Davenport, *A.H.R.*, 29: 548, Apr. 1924.   WEL
   Cf. also (I539a) Mahan, *Influence of sea power upon history, 1660–1783,* and (L524c and d) Corbett, *England in the Mediterranean,* and *England in the Seven Years' War.* For other works on the history of international relations in the seventeenth and eighteenth centuries, see (I501) ff.

I277a Noorden, Carl von. *Europäische Geschichte im 18. Jahrhundert. Erste Abtheilung: Der Spanische Erbfolge-Krieg.* 3 v. Düsseldorf, 1870–82.

   b Gerard, James W. *Peace of Utrecht: an historical review of the great treaty of 1713–14 and of the principal events of the war of the Spanish succession.* N. Y., 1885.

   c Weber, Ottocar. *Der Friede von Utrecht. Verhandlungen zwischen England, Frankreich, dem Kaiser und den Generalstaaten, 1710–1713.* Gotha, 1891.

a. Work of sound scholarship; extends only to 1710. Review of v. 1, A. Bier, *Hist. Zeit.*, 26: 427, 1871; of v. 2 and 3, F. Hirsch, *ibid.*, 33: 172, 1875; n. f., 13: 133, 1883. *b.* Semi-popular but useful book. Analyzes clearly the causes of the war and tells clearly the events of the war and negotiations for peace. No table of contents or text of treaty. Review, A. F. Allen, *Rev. Hist.*, 32: 386, Dec. 1886. *c.* Sound in scholarship, original and suggestive. Important letters and instructions in the appendixes. Review, A. Waddington, *Rev. Hist.*, 50: 422, Dec. 1892. APW

Cf. also (N301) Legrelle, *La diplomatie française et la succession d'Espagne.*

I278 Vaucher, Paul. *Robert Walpole et la politique de Fleury, 1731–1742.* Paris, 1924.

Valuable and scholarly monograph on international politics, dealing especially with the relations of England and France; perhaps the most informing book on the foreign policy of this period. Review, R. Lodge, *E.H.R.*, 40: 438, July 1925; W. T. Morgan, *A.H.R.*, 31: 515, Apr. 1926. HRS

I279a Waddington, Richard. *Louis XV et le renversement des alliances: préliminaires de la guerre de sept ans, 1754–56.* Paris, 1896.

b ———— *La guerre de sept ans; histoire diplomatique et militaire.* 5 v. Paris, 1899–1914.

c *Correspondance secrète du comte de Mercy-Argenteau avec l'Empereur Joseph II et le Prince de Kaunitz.* 2 v. Paris, 1889–90.

a. Best detailed survey of the diplomatic revolution of the eighteenth century by a scholar and diplomat with a good understanding of historical sources. An excellent introduction to *b.* Review, A. W. Ward, *E.H.R.*, 13: 792, Oct. 1898. *b.* The standard work on the history of the Seven Years' War in Europe. Review of v. 1, A. W. Ward, *E.H.R.*, 16: 395, Apr. 1901; v. 2, 20: 377, Apr. 1905; v. 4, 24: 161, Jan. 1909; v. 5, 30: 552, July 1915. *c.* Valuable first-hand materials on the development of the Austro-French alliance. Cf. also *Correspondance secrète entre Marie-Thérèse et le cte. de Mercy-Argenteau avec les lettres de Marie-Thérèse et de Marie Antoinette.* 3 v. Paris, 1874. WEL

I280a Sorel, Albert. *Eastern question in the eighteenth century, the partition of Poland and the treaty of Kainardji.* London, 1898. Tr. by F. C. Bramwell from 3rd ed. of *La question d'orient au XVIIIe siècle.* 1878. Paris, 1889.

b Lodge, Sir Richard. *Great Britain and Prussia in the eighteenth century.* Oxford, 1923.

a. Title too comprehensive. Very sketchy for period prior to 1756. Review, *E.H.R.*, 14: 191, Jan. 1899. *b.* Painstaking presentation of the bewildering changes in the relations between the two countries during the period without adequate reference to the larger national interests. Review, Basil Williams, *E.H.R.*, 39: 292, Apr. 1924. WEL

ERA OF THE FRENCH REVOLUTION AND NAPOLEON

There is no adequate bibliography in English of the historical writings of the revolutionary period. On the other hand, extensive lists are found in (I121) *Cambridge modern history*, v. 8, and more selected titles in (B152) Lavisse et Rambaud, *Histoire générale.* More critical and up-to-date are the bibliographical notes in the volumes covering the period from 1763 to 1815 in (M124*b*) v. 2,

Pariset, *La révolution, 1792–99,* and v. 3, *id., Le consulat et l'empire, 1799–1815.* See also the excellent bibliographical work of (M6*b*) Caron, (M3*c*) Brière, while for contemporary material in print on Paris and the Revolution consult the voluminous and scholarly volumes of Tourneux, *Bibliographie des sources bibliographiques de l'histoire de Paris pendant la Révolution.* Other works on the Revolution are discussed in § M.

Most of the brief surveys of the French Revolution and Napoleon devote considerable space to the history of Europe during the period and should be noted here although they are reviewed in the section on France, e.g., (M321*e*) Mathews, (M122) Madelin, (M324*a*) Taine, (M321*a*) Belloc. The same is true of the standard works on the political history of the Revolution by (M326*a*) Aulard, (M325*a*) Stephens, (M322*a*) Thiers, (M386*b*) Thibaudeau, and others.

I301a **Bourne, Henry E.** *Revolutionary period in Europe, 1763–1815.* N. Y., 1914. (Bibliography.)

  b **Gottschalk, Louis R.** *Era of the French Revolution (1715–1815).* Boston, 1929. (Bibliography.)

  c **Hazen, Charles D.** *French Revolution and Napoleon.* N. Y., 1917.

  d **Holt, Lucius H.,** and **Chilton, Alexander W.** *Brief history of Europe from 1789 to 1815.* N. Y., 1919.

  e **Rose, John H.** *Revolutionary and Napoleonic era.* Cambridge (Eng.), 1898.

  f **Stephens, Henry Morse.** *Europe, 1789–1815.* London and N. Y., 1893. [Periods of European history.]

a. Scholarly one volume text by a specialist in the history of the revolutionary period. It reflects not only the author's own researches and writing but an intimate acquaintance with the results of historical research in the field. Besides treating the progress of the revolutionary movement in France, the author stresses its broader character in its relation to European history. Entertainingly written but at times overburdened with details. Review, F. M. Fling, *A.H.R.,* 20: 848, July 1915. *b.* Good text intended as a general introduction to the study of European history of the late eighteenth century and of Napoleon. Presents the findings of the best European scholarship with here and there results of the author's own researches. Devotes relatively less attention to events outside France than does *a.* Review, E. Ellery, *A.H.R.,* 35: 105, Oct. 1929. *c.* Brief popular narrative written with the author's usual charm of style. *d.* Text in which military history is very satisfactorily summarized. *e.* Popular work by an English writer much interested in the international developments of the period, especially as they relate to the struggle between England and Napoleon. *f.* Mainly political in its interest and like *e* rather out-of-date.   WEL

I302a **Sybel, Heinrich von.** *History of the French Revolution.* 4 v. London, 1867–79. Tr. by W. C. Perry of v. 1–3, 3rd ed. of *Geschichte der Revolutionszeit von 1789–1800.* 1853–70. Rev. ed., 10 v., Stuttgart, 1897–1900.

  b **Sorel, Albert.** *L'Europe et la révolution française.* 8 v. Paris, 1895–1904.

  c **Masson, Frédéric.** *Le département des affaires étrangères pendant la révolution, 1787–1800.* Paris, 1877.

a and *b.* Indispensable for the international relations of the Revolution. Both are by eminent historical scholars but marred by strong nationalist prejudices. *b* is based on a wider study of the sources than was possible in Von Sybel's case. As a result it is both richer and more authoritative. It is also broader in scope, covering the field to the fall of Napoleon and devoting an entire volume (8) to the continental system. At the same time, it, too, is on many points superseded by later monographic studies. Review of French translation of *a*, *Rev. des Quest. Hist.*, 9: 516, Oct. 1870. Reviews of *b*, v. 1 and 2, C. Bémont, *Rev. Hist.*, 28: 352, July 1885, and of v. 2, C. Bémont and G. Monod, *ibid.*, 33: 359, March 1887; v. 3 and 4, G. Monod, *ibid.*, 49: 109, May 1892; v. 5 and 8, R. Reuss, *ibid.*, 86: 326, Nov. 1904; 89: 122, Sept. 1905. Cf. also important review of Sorel's work by P. Muret, *Rev. d'Hist. Mod. et Contemporaine*, 6: 724, Jan. 1905, and G. Monod, *Rev. Hist.*, 92: 91, Sept. 1906, who speaks of Sorel as 'le dernier des grands historiens généralisateurs, narrateurs, peintres et psychologues du XIXᵉ siècle.' *c*. Notable study of the organization and functioning of the Foreign Office during the years of the Revolution.   WEL

I311a Kircheisen, Friedrich M. *Bibliographie des napoleonischen Zeitalters.* Berlin, 1902.

b ——— *Bibliographie du temps de Napoléon comprenant l'histoire des États Unis.* V. 1–2, pt. 1, Paris, 1902–12.

a and *b*. Inadequate, but, taken together, an attempt at a scientific bibliography and at present the best available. Should be supplemented by the lists in (I315*b* and *c*) Fournier and (I121) *Cambridge modern history*, v. 9. Review of *b*, v. 1, O. Guerlac, *A.H.R.*, 14: 610, Apr. 1909; H. A. L. Fisher, *E.H.R.*, 28: 404, Apr. 1913. For a useful survey of the literature at the time of writing, and to some extent a supplement to Kircheisen, see G. M. Dutcher, 'Tendencies and opportunities in Napoleonic studies,' *A.H.A. Reports*, 1914, 1: 181, Washington.   WEL

I312a Rose, J. Holland. *Life of Napoleon the first.* 2 v. 1902. 8th rev. ed., 1 v., London, 1922.

b ——— *Napoleonic studies.* London, 1904–06.

a. Well written and scholarly, revising certain anti-Napoleonic traditions. In part based on archival materials resulting in new evidence on many disputed questions, but reflects the British point of view. Review, H. B. George, *E.H.R.*, 17: 597, July 1902; *A.H.R.*, 8: 565, Apr. 1903. *b*. Gleanings from the author's work on *a* in the form of essays on men and events of the Napoleonic period. Review, E. D. Adams, *A.H.R.*, 10: 658, Apr. 1905. Cf. (L357*c*) Rose, *William Pitt and the great war.*   FEM

I313a Fisher, Herbert A. L. *Studies in Napoleonic statesmanship.* Oxford and N. Y., 1903.

b ——— *Bonapartism.* Oxford and N. Y., 1908.

a. Consideration of Napoleonic administration in western Germany, suggestive, thoughtful and at times original. Review, A. W. Ward, *E.H.R.*, 18: 810, July 1903; J. H. Coney, *A.H.R.*, 9: 582, Apr. 1904. *b*. Lectures on Napoleon. Less judicious than *a*; the attempt to show an essential unity in the two Napoleonic régimes is not convincing. Review, V. Coffin, *A.H.R.*, 13: 870, July 1908.   WEL

I314a Ropes, John C. *The first Napoleon.* 1885. 3rd ed., Boston, 1886.

b Seeley, John R. *Short history of Napoleon the first.* London, 1886.

c Morris, William O. *Napoleon.* N. Y., 1893. [Heroes of the nations.]

d Johnston, Robert M. *Napoleon, a short biography.* N. Y., 1904.

e —— *Corsican.* N. Y., 1910.

f Lenz, Max. *Napoleon, a biographical study.* N. Y., 1907. Tr. by F. Whyte from *Napoleon,* Leipzig, 1905.

g Fisher, Herbert A. L. *Napoleon.* London and N. Y., 1912. [Home university library.]

a, b, c. Somewhat out-of-date but still stimulating short biographies. Review of *b,* Lord Acton, *E.H.R.,* 2 : 593, Oct. 1887. *d.* Successful attempt in small compass to show Napoleon in historical perspective. Review, T. A. Dodge, *A.H.R.,* 9 : 824, July 1904. *e.* Clever attempt to piece out a diary or autobiography from Napoleon's writings. *f.* Suggestive interpretation by a German scholar which suffers somewhat in translation. Review, G. S. Ford, *A.H.R.,* 13 : 868, July 1908. *g.* Remarkable for style, balance, fairness, and breadth of interpretation, a masterpiece among short biographies. Review, G. M. Dutcher, *A.H.R.,* 18 : 837, July 1913.   WEL

I315a Fournier, August. *Napoleon I, eine Biographie.* 3 v. 1886–89. 4th ed., Vienna, 1922.

b —— *Napoleon the first, a biography.* Ed. by E. G. Bourne. N. Y., 1903. Tr. by M. B. Corwin and A. D. Bissell from *Napoléon Ier,* tr. by E. Jaegli from *a.* Paris, 1892. (Bibliographies.)

c —— *Napoleon, a biography.* Intro. by H. A. L. Fisher. 2 v. London and N. Y., 1911. Tr. by A. E. Adams from 2nd ed. of *a.* 1904–06.

a. By a well-known Austrian authority, based on a thorough study of the sources, is fairly impartial and possesses distinct literary merit. Generally accepted as at present the best biography of Napoleon. Review, P. Bailleu, *Hist. Zeit.,* 94 : 372, 1905. *b* and *c.* Good English versions of *a.* *b.* Scholarly one volume translation, with discriminating bibliographies, in part compiled by E. G. Bourne. *c.* Based on Fournier's revision of 1904–06, which was virtually a rewriting of much of the original, in the light of his own investigations and those of Vandal, Chuquet and others. Includes valuable appendixes in which are printed many important letters of Napoleon and excellent critical bibliographies. Text of *a* somewhat reduced and added to by the translator. Review of *b,* F. L. Huidekoper, *A.H.R.,* 10 : 412, Jan. 1905; of *c,* H. E. Bourne, *ibid.,* 17 : 402, Jan. 1912; H. C. Gutteridge, *E.H.R.,* 28 : 173, Jan. 1913.   WEL, HRS

I316a Lanfrey, Pierre. *History of Napoleon the first.* 4 v. 1871–79. 2nd ed., 4 v., London and N. Y., 1894. Tr. from *Histoire de Napoléon Ier,* 5 v., Paris, 1867–75.

b Kircheisen, Friedrich M. *Napoleon I., sein Leben und seine Zeit.* v. 1–5, Munich, 1911–25.

a. Work by a French scholar hostile to Napoleon and his policies. Gives overmuch attention to moral and psychological aspects of the subject. Extends through the year 1811. Review, G. Fagniez, *Rev. Hist.,* 1 : 275, Jan. 1876 and a longer review by Henri Lot, *ibid.,* 1 : 311. *b.* Large work by a German historian projected in ten volumes and elaborately illustrated. Review of v. 4, R. Guyot, *Rev. Hist.,* 143 : 57, May 1923.   WEL

I317 Sloane, William M. *Life of Napoleon Bonaparte.* 4 v. 1894–96. 4th rev. ed., N. Y., 1910.

Large popular work by an American historian with profuse illustrations. These are omitted in the revision. Review, C. M. Andrews, *A.H.R.*, 3: 355, Jan. 1898; H. E. Bourne, *ibid.*, 16: 618, Apr. 1911.   WEL

I321a Driault, J. Édouard. *Napoléon et l'Europe.* 5 v. Paris, 1910–27. [1. *La politique extérieure du Premier Consul, 1800–1803; 2. Austerlitz la fin du Saint-Empire, 1804–1806; 3. Tilsit, France et Russie sous le premier empire. La question de Pologne, 1806–1809; 4. Le grand empire, 1809–1812; 5. La chute de l'empire: la légende de Napoléon, 1812–1815.*] [Bibliothèque d'histoire contemporaine.]

b —— *Napoléon en Italie, 1800–1812.* Paris, 1906. [Bibliothèque de l'histoire contemporaine.]

c —— *La politique orientale de Napoléon. Sebastiani et Gardane, 1806–1808.* Paris, 1904. [Bibliothèque de l'histoire contemporaine.]

a. Not a general study of the international relations of the period but a consideration of them in so far as they concern Napoleon. Brilliant and very suggestive but over-favorable to Bonaparte, crediting him with beneficent plans for Europe and liberty for the individual. An ambition to recreate the Roman empire with Rome as its capital explains much in Napoleon's policy in the belief of the author. The whole challenges comparison with (I302b) Sorel, by no means to the discredit of Driault. Review of v. 1 and 2, R. Reuss, *Rev. Hist.*, 105: 141, Sept. 1910; 112: 143, Jan. 1913; of v. 3 and 4, R. Guyot, *ibid.*, 133: 111, Jan. 1920; of v. 5, C. P. Higby, *A.H.R.*, 32: 862, July 1927. *b* and *c*. By-products of the larger work. Review of *b*, G. Monod, *Rev. Hist.*, 92: 111, Sept. 1906; H. A. L. Fisher, *E.H.R.*, 25: 205, Jan. 1910; of *c*, R. de Felice, *Rev. Hist.*, 93: 416, March 1907; G. Roloff, *Hist. Zeit.*, 96: 502, 1906.   HRS

I322a Vandal, Albert. *Napoléon et Alexandre Ier. L'alliance russe sous le premier empire.* 3 v. Paris, 1891–96.

b Tatischeff, Serge. *Alexandre Ier et Napoléon (1801–12) d'après leur correspondance inédite.* Paris, 1891.

Excellent and detailed studies of the relations of the two emperors. Unlike *b, a* concerns itself very little with contemporary diplomacy but seeks the explanation of Napoleon's conduct in the evolution of his ideas. Written with talent, simplicity and picturesqueness of style. Review of *a*, v. 1, L. Farges, *Rev. Hist.*, 46: 93, May 1913; v. 2 (which was awarded the Gobert prize), G. Monod, *ibid.*, 52: 356, Aug. 1893; v. 3, H. E. Bourne, *A.H.R.*, 2: 351, Jan. 1897. *b.* Concerns itself more with the policies and actions of the different governments, is frankly a partisan of the alliance, and for its break-up blames the English party rather than the ambitions of Napoleon and the Treaty of Tilsit itself. Review, L. Farges, *Rev. Hist.*, 46: 93, May 1891.   WEL

I323a Lefebvre, Armand. *Histoire des cabinets de l'Europe pendant le consulat et l'empire (1800–1815).* Précédée d'une notice par M. Sainte-Beuve et completée par M. Ed. Lefebvre de Béhaime. 3 v., 1845–47 (to 1808); 2nd ed., 5 v., Paris, 1866–69.

b Guyot, Raymond. *Le directoire et la paix de l'Europe (1795–9).* Paris, 1911.

a. Early and somewhat antiquated work with much interesting inside matter on the cabinets of Europe. Important in its influence on the historiography of the

First Empire and the origins of the Second. *b.* Work of sound scholarship, more objective and free from the bias manifest even in Sorel and Sybel. 'Learned' and 'critical' but marked by conspicuous fairness of tone. Review, J. H. Rose, *E.H.R., 27* : 788, Oct. 1912.   WEL

I 324a **Heckscher, Eli F.** *Continental system; an economic interpretation.* Oxford, 1922.

b **Melvin, Frank E.** *Napoleon's navigation system.* Philadelphia, 1919.

c. **Tarlé, Eugene.** *Le blocus continental et le royaume d'Italie: la situation économique de l'Italie sous Napoléon Iᵉʳ.* Paris, 1928.

a and *b.* Two notable contributions to the international history of Europe during the Napoleonic period. They bring out the far-reaching effects of the economic blockade as a belligerent weapon. *b.* Broader in its subject matter, it treats the Napoleonic navigation system, of which the continental system was a part, as a whole. Both studies are based on extensive research, *b* showing greater familiarity with French and English archives and a more conscientious use of the secondary authorities. On the other hand, the presentation of the material in *a* is more effective. The critical bibliography and study of the sources in *b* are of especial merit. Review of *a,* F. E. Melvin, *A.H.R., 29*: 328, Jan. 1923; of *b,* S. E. Morison, *A.H.R., 26*: 773, July 1921. *c.* Work by a Russian scholar and specialist in the field of commercial and economic history of the Napoleonic era. Presents new material on Italian industry under the influence of the continental system but fails to give due attention to the recent monographic studies in the field or to exploit adequately the archival material. Review, F. E. Melvin, *A.H.R., 34*: 587, Apr. 1929. For bibliographical comments on the writing and materials on the continental system, cf. M. Dunan, 'Le système continental'; *Revue des études napoléoniennes,* 2: 115, Jan. 1913; W. E. Lingelbach, 'Historical investigation and the commercial history of the Napoleonic era,' *A.H.R., 19*: 257, Jan. 1914. An able article on the working of the system is by P. Darmstädter, 'Studien zur napoleonischen Wirtschaftspolitik,' *Vierteljahrschrift für Social- und Wirtschaftsgeschichte,* 2: 559, 1904; 3: 112, 1905.   WEL

I 331a *Correspondance de Napoléon Iᵉʳ. Publiée par ordre de l'empereur Napoléon III.* 32 v. Paris, 1858–70. *Supplément.* Ed. by Baron du Casse. Paris, 1887.

b **Lecestre, Léon,** ed. *Lettres inédites de Napoléon (An VIII–1815). Lettres curieuses omises par la comité de publication.* 2 v. Paris, 1897.

c **Brotonne, Leonce,** ed. *Lettres inédites de Napoléon.* Paris, 1898.

d ———, ed. *Dernières lettres inédites de Napoléon.* 2 v. Paris, 1903.

e **Loyd, Lady Mary,** ed. *New letters of Napoleon I.* 1897. 2nd ed., N. Y., 1898.

f **Bingham, Denis A.,** ed. *Selection from the letters and dispatches of the first Napoleon.* 3 v. London, 1884.

g **Picard, Ernest,** and **Tuetey, Louis,** ed. *Unpublished correspondence of Napoleon I.* 3 v. N. Y., 1913. Tr. by L. S. Houghton from *Correspondance inédite de Napoléon I. conservée aux Archives de la Guerre.* 4 v. Paris, 1912–13.

h **Chuquet, Arthur,** ed. *Ordres et apostilles, 1799–1815.* 4 v. Paris, 1911–12.

a and *b*. Basic body of source material for the study of Napoleon; comprises the bulk of his letters, instructions, decisions, proclamations. Yet numerous papers, omitted purposely by the imperial commissioners from this publication, or discovered by later researches, have been published subsequently in *b, c, d, g,* and *h*. Critical introductions in *b* and *c,* dealing with the status of Napoleon's writings, are noteworthy. *g* and *h*. In both collections the documents are chiefly military in character, or grew out of military problems. Note the several series of soldiers' letters and related material separately published by Chuquet. *e* and *f*. Unsatisfactory selections in English translation, *e* from *b* and *f* from *a*. For critical comment on the value of some of these collections, and the destruction of letters and minutes, cf. J. B. Nye, 'The lost and new letters of Napoleon,' *E.H.R.,* 13 : 473, July 1898; A. du Casse, 'Étude sur la Correspondance de Napoléon Ier. Ses Lacunes,' *Rev. Hist.,* 31 : 326, July 1886; 32 : 350, Nov. 1886; 34 : 46, May 1887. For textual criticism, cf. A. Fournier, *Archiv für österreichische Geschichte,* 93 : 41, 1905.   FEM

For additional material on the Consulate and Empire, cf. (M831) ff.

NINETEENTH CENTURY, *1815–1870*

I401a **Fyffe, Charles A.** *History of modern Europe, 1792–1878.* 3 v., 1880–92. Popular ed., 1 v., London and N. Y., 1896, and 2 v., 1924.

b **Browning, Oscar.** *History of the modern world, 1815–1910.* 2 v., London, 1912.

c **Andrews, Charles M.** *Historical development of modern Europe.* 2 v. N. Y., 1896–98. Students' ed., 1 v., N. Y., 1900.

d **Hazen, Charles D.** *Europe since 1815.* 1909. Rev. and enl. ed., 2 v. and 1 v., N. Y., 1923. (Bibliography.)

e **Phillips, W. Alison.** *Modern Europe, 1815–1899.* London and N. Y., 1912. [(B132, v. 8.)]

f **Seignobos, Charles.** *Political history of Europe since 1814.* London and N. Y., 1899. Tr. by S. M. Macvane from *Histoire politique de l'Europe contemporaine,* Paris, 1897. 7th rev. and enl. ed., 2 v., Paris, 1924–26. (Bibliography.)

g **Schapiro, J. Salwyn.** *Modern and contemporary history.* 1919. Rev. and enl. ed., N. Y., 1929. (Bibliography.)

h **Fueter, Eduard.** *World history, 1815–1920.* London and N. Y., 1922. Tr. by S. B. Fay from *Weltgeschichte der letzten hundert Jahren,* 1815–1920. Zürich, 1921.

i **Davis, William S.** *Europe since Waterloo, 1815–1919.* London and N. Y., 1926.

j **Grant, Arthur J.,** and **Temperley, Harold W. V.** *Europe in the nineteenth century.* (*1789–1914.*) London and N. Y., 1927.

k **Flick, Alexander C.** *Modern world history. 1789–1920.*

a. Political, diplomatic and military survey of the countries of continental Europe from the outbreak of the Revolutionary wars in 1792 to the Congress of Berlin. Though interestingly written from a narrative and descriptive viewpoint, the author gives but little attention to social and economic factors; from the viewpoint of critical scholarship the work needs thorough revision. For continuation, cf. (J101) Gooch.   HCB

b. Based on the lectures and writings of the author who states that he has used the best authorities, but without footnotes, maps and bibliographies. Not well balanced but readable and interesting; comprehensive in scope, political rather than social and economic in interest. Review, *E.H.R., 27* : 826, Oct. 1912.   HW

c. Covers the period from 1815 to 1897. Narrative of political and diplomatic history, always well written and interesting, but superseded by more recent works in the field. Review, C. H. Levermore, *A.H.R., 2* : 354, Jan. 1897; 4 : 357, Jan. 1899.   JP

d. Excellent synthesis for college students and the general reader. The overemphasis of political history in the earlier edition is corrected to some extent in the revision by chapters on the Industrial Revolution and socialism. The revised edition carries the story through the World War and reconstruction to the summer of 1923. Review, F. Schevill, *A.H.R.,* 16 : 825, July 1911; F. M. Anderson, *A.H.R.,* 39 : 768, July 1924.   HCB

e. Emphasis is entirely upon political events; now out of date. *f.* Stresses the organization of the nations, governments and parties. Pt. 1 treats of domestic political history; pt. 2, of political phenomena common to various nations; pt. 3, of external relations between states. Still useful but the work as a whole now superseded by others. Review, T. Stanton, *A.H.R., 3* : 147, Oct. 1897; of 7th ed., E. N. Curtis, *A.H.R.,* 30 : 643, Apr. 1925; 32 : 315, Jan. 1927. *g.* College text especially adapted for courses in which events prior to 1870 are treated mainly as a basis for the study of subsequent developments. Suggestive paragraphs on literary movements are introduced here and there. Revised edition has many very worthwhile changes and a survey of the war and reconstruction based on recent research. Review, F. Schevill, *A.H.R.,* 24 : 276, Jan. 1919. *h.* Instead of giving brief descriptive chapters to individual countries, the author shows very effectively how modern industry, population increase, and the new colonial struggle for food and raw materials have influenced the political relations throughout the world. One of the most thoughtful, original and stimulating volumes on this period. Review, H. R. Shipman, *A.H.R.,* 28 : 358, Jan. 1923; of German original, G. N. Clark, *E.H.R.,* 37 : 617, Oct. 1922. *i.* Popular, nontechnical and journalistic in style and method, with undue emphasis upon particular individuals or topics, as for example, Napoleon III. Review, *Am. Pol. Sci. Rev., 21* : 207, Feb. 1927. *j.* Recent volume of real merit by specialists in diplomatic history, a field which is somewhat overemphasized; assumes considerable knowledge of the period on the part of the reader. Later chapters based on an unusual familiarity with the sources for the diplomatic history of the war and its antecedents. Review, J. A. Williamson, *History,* 14 : 84, Apr. 1929.   WEL

k. Broad-minded, accurate manual covering American affairs and those of European colonial empires as well as those of Europe. Stronger on facts than on generalization. Review, J. A. Williamson, *History,* 14 : 84, Apr. 1929.   HRS

Cf. also (1101) Hayes, v. 2, and (1104*b*) Turner.

1402a Stern, Alfred. *Geschichte Europas seit den Verträgen von 1815 bis zum Frankfurter Frieden von 1871.* 10 v. Stuttgart, 1894–1925.

   b Egelhaaf, Gottlob. *Geschichte des neunzehnten Jahrhunderts vom Wiener Kongress bis zum Frankfurter Frieden.* 2 v. Stuttgart, 1925.

a. Author has succeeded admirably in the gigantic task of writing the history of Europe from 1815 to 1870 from unused archival sources as well as from printed materials. It is impartial, well-balanced, lucidly written, correcting frequently the prejudices and errors of older writers. The most authoritative large general history of the period.   Review of v. 1–6, C. M. Andrews, *A.H.R.,* 4: 153, Oct. 1898; 7 : 357, Jan. 1902; 11 : 664, Apr. 1906; 17 : 374, Jan. 1912; 19 : 686, Apr. 1914; of v. 7–10, B. E. Schmitt, *ibid.,* 24 : 680, July 1919; 26 : 784, July 1921; 29 : 769, July 1924; 30 : 597, Apr. 1925.   SBF

b. Quite general in character after the manner of a popular text and not in the same class with *a.* Germany's rôle is over-emphasized. Companion work to the author's history of Europe during the contemporary period (J103). Review, O. Hintze, *Hist. Jahrbuch,* 46 : 663, 1926.   WEL

1403a Kirkpatrick, Frederick A., ed. *Lectures on the history of the nineteenth century.* Cambridge (Eng.), 1902.

 b Fisher, Herbert A. L. *Republican tradition in Europe.* London and N. Y., 1911. [Lowell institute lectures.]

 c Marriott, John A. R. *European commonwealth: problems historical and diplomatic.* Oxford and N. Y., 1918.

a. Seventeen university addresses by distinguished British scholars. Now somewhat out of date. Review, C. M. Andrews, *A.H.R.,* 10 : 448, Jan. 1905.   *b.* Outline history of democracy from the downfall of the Roman Empire to 1910 presented in attractive literary form. Period beginning with the French Revolution emphasized. Review, G. B. Hertz, *E.H.R.,* 26 : 803, Oct. 1911.   *c.* Essays dealing mainly with the nineteenth century European diplomacy. What unity the book has lies in the treatment of the principle of nationality. Review, A. I. Andrews, *A.H.R.,* 25 : 106, Oct. 1919; *E.H.R.,* 34 : 279, Apr. 1919.   WEL

1404a Marvin, Francis S. *Century of hope; a sketch of western progress from 1815 to the great war.* Oxford, 1919.

 b Wallace, William K. *Trend of history: origins of twentieth century problems.* N. Y., 1922.

 c Wallace, Alfred R. *Wonderful century; its successes and failures.* London and N. Y., 1898.

a. Attempt by a scientist to summarize the chief movements during the last century in politics, literature, social reforms, science and religion, regarded from the point of view of an optimist. Stimulating, but not without errors of detail. Review, *E.H.R.,* 34 : 453, July 1919.   HRS

b. Sketches the development of secular absolutism and the modern ideas of the state, the growth of industrialism, nationalism, socialism, the appearance of internationalism and imperialism, usually adequately indicating the interplay of theories and events. Review, H. E. Barnes, *A.H.R.,* 28 : 520, Apr. 1923.   WB

c. By a distinguished naturalist who writes in a field foreign to his own. The earlier portion of the book deals in a stimulating way with the material and intellectual progress of the nineteenth century, the later and larger part has little that is of historical interest, for the author gives free rein to his hobbies : phrenology, psychical research, anti-vaccination and kindred topics. Review, *A.H.R.,* 4 : 389, Jan. 1899.   GJ

1405a Webster, Charles K. *Congress of Vienna, 1814–15.* London, 1919. [Peace handbooks.] (Bibliography.)

 b Hazen, Charles D., Thayer, William R., and **Lord, Robert H.** *Three peace congresses of the nineteenth century;* and **Coolidge, Archibald C.,** *Claimants to Constantinople.* Cambridge (Mass.), 1917. (Bibliography.)

c **Phillips, W. Alison.** *Confederation of Europe, a study of the European alliances, 1813–1823; as an experiment in the international organization of peace.* 1914. 2nd enl. ed., London, 1919.

d **Cresson, William P.** *Diplomatic portraits.* N. Y., 1923.

a. Clear and satisfactory account of the preparation of the congress, its organization, its problems and work, by a specialist in the field. Review, E. Satow, *E.H.R.,* 34: 260, Apr. 1919. Cf. (L386d) Webster, and (L387e and h) Temperley. *b.* Suggestive and stimulating little volume on the three great congresses of the last century. The essays on the congress of Paris and the congress of Berlin articulate well with that on the claimants to Constantinople. Review, C. J H. Hayes, *A.H.R.,* 23: 155, Oct. 1917. *c.* Lectures on the European alliance after the overthrow of Napoleon. Author sees in the Holy Alliance a real attempt at international organization and paternal supervision over weaker states not unlike that of the United States in connection with the Monroe Doctrine. The parallels are often forced and the difference between the Holy Alliance and the Quadruple Alliance not clearly brought out. Review, H. W. V. Temperley, *E.H.R.,* 30: 359, Apr. 1915; W. S. Robertson, *A.H.R.,* 20: 153, Oct. 1914. *d.* Brief but stimulating pen-sketches of the leading diplomats of the restoration.   WEL

I406a Harrison, Frederic. *National and social problems.* N. Y., 1908.

b **Rose, J. Holland.** *Nationality in modern history.* London and N. Y., 1916.

c **Muir, Ramsay.** *Nationalism and internationalism: the culmination of modern history.* Boston, 1916. [J503a.]

a. Essays on history, war, imperialism and social and economic questions in which the author's leaning toward social regulation and control is often very evident. Review, *A.H.R.,* 14: 175, Oct. 1908. *b.* Traces the development of nationality in Europe from the days of Chaucer and Dante to recent times with a chapter each on 'Internationalism' and 'Nationality and Militarism.' Review, E. Krehbiel, *A.H.R.,* 22: 439, Jan. 1917. *c.* Thoughtful, well-balanced little volume of much popular interest. Cf. (K348) Hobson.   WEL

I407a Lord, Robert H. *Origins of the war of 1870. New documents from the German archives.* London and Cambridge (Mass.), 1924. [Harvard historical studies.]

b **Oncken, Hermann.** *Napoleon III and the Rhine. Origin of the war of 1870–71.* Introduction by F. Schevill. London and N. Y., 1928. Tr. by E. H. Zeydel from *Napoleon III und der Rhein, der Ursprung des Krieges von 1870 bis 1871.* Stuttgart, 1926, a separate issue of 120 pp. of v. 1 of *Die Rheinpolitik Kaiser Napoleons III von 1863 bis 1870 und der Ursprung des Krieges von 1870–71.* 3 v., Stuttgart, 1926.

c **Salomon, Henry.** *L'incident Hohenzollern; l'évènement, les hommes et les responsabilités.* Paris, 1922.

d **Sorel, Albert.** *Histoire diplomatique de la guerre franco-allemande.* 2 v. Paris, 1875.

a. Careful study of the immediate causes of the Franco-Prussian war with over two hundred documents not before published. Bismarck's diplomacy in connection with the candidacy for the Spanish throne and the Ems dispatch is sketched in a masterly fashion, but the policy and activity of the French war party and of the Paris press are handled less satisfactorily. Review, W. A. Frayer, *A.H.R.,*

30 : 817, July 1925. Cf. E. M. Carroll, French Opinion on War with Prussia in 1870, *A.H.R.*, 31 : 678–700, July 1926. *b*. Elaborate and scholarly introduction to an excellent collection of documents upon the subject. Review, R. H. Lord, *A.H.R.*, 32 : 109, Oct. 1926. *c*. Capable study assessing responsibility for the Franco-Prussian war ; a little new evidence from the Austrian archives is introduced. Review, J. V. Fuller, *A.H.R.*, 28 : 774, July 1923. *d*. Able work, but without the basis afforded by the archival materials used by *a, b* and *c*. Review, G. Monod, *Rev. Hist.*, 1 : 520, March 1876.   WEL

INTERNATIONAL RELATIONS AND DIPLOMACY

Among the publications on international history, the standard collections of treaties, and the diplomatic correspondence published by the respective governments are of especial importance. Most of these, like the great work begun by Georg de Martens (I507*a*) ff. and the invaluable series of state papers published by the different governments, are being kept up-to-date by the addition of one or two volumes a year. A recent guide to treaties is (B502*a*) Myers. Reference should be made to (X2*a*) Hasse, and (X907) for bibliographies of American state documents, to (X501–509, 902 and 905) for the diplomatic history of the United States ; to (L501–503) and (M501) for works on British and French foreign relations respectively, and to (B501) Hill, for general history of diplomacy.

I501a **Bourgeois, Emile.** *Manuel historique de politique étrangère.* 4 v. Paris, 1892–1926. [1, *Les origines, 1610–1789*, 7th ed., 1919; 2, *Les révolutions, 1789–1830*, 6th ed., 1920 ; 3, *Le temps présent, 1830–1877*, 5th ed., 1919 ; 4, *La politique mondiale, empire et nation, 1878–1919*, 2nd ed., 1927.]

 b **Debidour, Antonin.** *Histoire diplomatique de l'Europe depuis l'ouverture du congrès de Vienne jusqu'à la clôture du congrès de Berlin, 1814–1878.* 2 v. Paris, 1891.

a. Excellent work on international relations, despite its strong national bias, by a foremost French authority ; based on direct contact with the sources and a broad knowledge of the subject. Erudite and precise, bringing together a great mass of material in small compass, yet spirited and interesting both to the student and general reader. Review, v. 1, G. Monod, *Rev. Hist.*, 52 : 349, July 1893 ; of v. 2, *ibid.*, 70 : 97, May 1899 ; of v. 3, *ibid.*, 89 : 340, Nov. 1905. *b*. Widely used history of European diplomacy. Well organized, convenient, but inadequate, over-emphasizing the importance of the rôle played by France in diplomatic history. Continued in (J102). Review, G. Monod, *Rev. Hist.*, 45 : 103, Jan. 1891.   WEL

I502a **Mowat, Robert B.** *History of European diplomacy, 1451–1789.* London, 1928 ; N. Y., 1929.

 b ——— *Diplomacy of Napoleon.* London, 1924.

 c ——— *History of European diplomacy, 1815–1924.* London and N. Y., 1922.

 d ——— *History of European diplomacy, 1914–1925.* London and N. Y., 1927.

Brief popular manuals, readable and scholarly, but occasionally almost unintelligible in their attempt to do a difficult thing, to explain clearly the course of diplomacy during an era, at the same time omitting almost entirely material belonging to the domains of political and military history. Review of *a*, W. L. Dorn, *A.H.R.*, 35 : 334, Jan. 1930 ; of *b*, (London) *Times Lit. Suppl.*, 23 : 379, June 19,

1924; of *c*, B. E. Schmitt, *A.H.R.*, 28:740, July 1923; of *d*, C. Seymour, *ibid.*, 33:134, Oct. 1927.   HRS

I503a **Davis, George B.** *Elements of international law.* 1887. 3rd rev. ed., London and N. Y., 1908.

   b **Lawrence, Thomas J.** *Principles of international law.* 1895. 7th ed., by P. H. Winfield, London and N. Y., 1923. (Bibliography.)

   c **Fenwick, Charles G.** *International law.* London and N. Y., 1924. (Bibliographies.)

   d **Hall, William E.** *Treatise on international law.* 1880. 8th ed., by A. P. Higgins, Oxford, 1924.

   e **Hershey, Amos S.** *Essentials of international public law and organization.* 1912. Rev. ed., N. Y., 1927.

   f **Hyde, Charles C.** *International law, chiefly as interpreted and applied by the United States.* 2 v. Boston, 1922.

   g **Oppenheim, Lassa.** *International law.* 2 v., 1905–12. 4th ed. of v. 2, by A. D. McNair, London, 1926. (Bibliographies.)

   h **Phillimore, Sir Robert.** *Commentaries on international law.* 1854–61. 3rd ed., 4 v., London, 1875–89.

   i **Westlake, John.** *International law.* 2 v. Cambridge (Eng.), 1907–10.

   j **Fauchille, Paul.** *Traité de droit international public.* v. 1–2, Paris, 1921–26.

   k **Liszt, Franz E. von.** *Das Völkerrecht systematisch dargestellt.* 1898. 12th ed., Berlin, 1926.

a, b, c. Excellent short manuals. *d.* Well-known text, judicious and fair, but written from the British point of view. *e.* Emphasis on historic development, the first 156 pages being devoted to an historical survey on international relations to 1926. Packed with information and references to sources. Review, C. G. Fenwick, *Amer. Jour. Inter. Law, 22*:214, Jan. 1928. *f.* Excellent recent treatise, based on years of careful research. Scholarly in treatment and judicial in interpretation, seeking to present the official viewpoint on all questions of international law. Review, E. C. Stowell, *A.H.R., 27*:796, July 1922.   JWG

   g. Standard treatise by a high English authority, recently revised. The fourth part of v. 2 contains latest discussion on law of war, neutrality, and the legal settlement of disputes. Review of v. 2, 4th ed., *E.H.R., 42*:659, Oct. 1927. *h.* Early work of real distinction, devoting considerable attention to historical backgrounds.
                                        WEL

i. Standard work by an eminent English writer, valuable particularly for the student of history and of international law in its historical development and historical aspects. *j.* Originally an edition of H. Bonfils, *Manuel de droit international public,* Paris, 1894, but now practically a new work, one of the most valuable and up-to-date treatises on international law in the French language. *k.* Scholarly and solid German work.   HRS

I504a **Gentilis, Albericus.** *De legationibus libri tres.* 2 v. 1924. [1, Photographic reproduction of ed. of 1594; 2, Translation by G. F. Laing of Latin text.] 1st ed. Londini, 1585.

   b **Martens, Karl, Freiherr von.** *Manuel diplomatique ou précis des droits et des fonctions des agents diplomatiques; suivi d'un recueil d'actes et d'offices pour servir de guide aux personnes qui se destinent à la carrière politique.* 1822. 5th rev. ed., by F. H. Geffken, Leipzig, 2 v., 1866.

c **Heatley, David P.** *Internationalism and the study of international relations.* Oxford, 1919.

d **Satow, Sir Ernest.** *Guide to diplomatic practice.* 2 v. 1917. 2nd ed., London and N. Y., 1922. [Contributions to international law and diplomacy.]

e **Bryce, James, Viscount.** *International relations.* London and N. Y., 1922.

a. Celebrated treatise by the first systematic writer on diplomacy. Cf. Ernest Nys, 'Les commencements de la diplomatie et de la droit d'ambassade jusqu'à Grotius,' *Revue de droit internationale,* 16: 167, 1884. *b.* Important text-book of the rules and customs of the diplomatic service in the early nineteenth century. *c.* Somewhat disorderly but useful little book consisting of an essay on the machinery of diplomacy and the qualities of the good diplomatist with quotations to supplement the author's arguments and of a classified, but inadequate, list of books on various branches of diplomacy with extracts indicating their contents. Not without interest but almost a lecturer's notebook in print. Review, D. J. Hill, *A.H.R.,* 25: 698, July 1920; *E.H.R.,* 35: 629, Oct. 1920. *d.* Valuable and interesting survey of diplomatic practice by a distinguished British diplomatist; an historical and analytical discussion of many topics falling under the general heading, e.g., the attributes and immunities of diplomatic agents, use of Latin and French phrases and terms in diplomacy and treaties, the distinction between arbitration and mediation; the whole a veritable storehouse of knowledge. Review, J. B. Moore, *A.H.R.,* 23: 634, Apr. 1918; A. W. Ward, *E.H.R.,* 32: 418, July 1917. *e.* Brilliant lectures by the veteran British statesman on war and peace, particularly the causes of war and factors making for world peace. Review, G. G. Wilson, *A.H.R.,* 27: 766, July 1922. Cf. (J925) Publications of the World Peace Foundation, and those of (J921–924) The Carnegie Endowment for International Peace.

HRS

I505a **Grotius, Hugo (or Groot, Hugo de).** *Law of war and peace.* 2 v. in 4. Oxford and Washington, 1913–27. [1. Photographic reproduction of edition of 1646; 2. Text and translation.] [Classics of international law.] Tr. by F. R. Kelsey from *De jure belli ac pacis libri tres, in quibus jus naturae et gentium, item juris publici praecipua explicantur.* 1st ed., Parisiis, 1625. Earlier (abridged) translation with text, William Whewell, 4 v., Cambridge (Eng.), 1853. Many other editions.

b —— *Freedom of the seas; or the right which belongs to the Dutch to take part in the East Indian trade.* Oxford and N. Y., 1916. [Carnegie Endowment for International Peace.] Tr. with a revision of the Latin text of 1633, by R. V. Magoffin, from *De mare libero,* Lugduni, 1633. Many other editions.

c **Moore, John B.** *Digest of international law.* 8 v. Washington, 1906. [X502a]

d **Wharton, Francis,** ed. *Digest of the international law of the United States.* 3 v. 1886. 2nd ed., Washington, 1887.

e **Wheaton, Henry.** *Elements of international law.* 1836. Rev. and enl. ed. by A. B. Keith, London, 1929.

f —— *History of the law of nations in Europe and America from the earliest times to the treaty of Washington.* 1842. N. Y., 1845.

g **Butler, Sir Geoffrey,** and **Maccoby, Simon.** *Development of international law.* London, 1928.

a. Exhaustive and masterly treatise which entitles Grotius to be called the Father of International Law. Other important writers on the subject during the early period of its study were, in the seventeenth century, Zouche, Pufendorf, and Leibnitz; and in the eighteenth, Bynkershoek, Christian de Wolff, and the Swiss jurist Vattel, a most successful popularizer, whose writings were of great influence in the subsequent development of the science. Review, J. B. Scott, *Am. Jour. of Inter. Law,* 21 : 522, July 1927; of v. 1, pts. 2 and 3, C. van Hollenhoven, *ibid.,* 21 : 628, July 1927. *b.* Also a classic. Review, E. Wambaugh, *Am. Jour. of Inter. Law,* 10 : 942, Oct. 1916. *c.* Cf. (X502*a* and *b*) Moore, *International arbitrations.*

HRS

d. Earlier work of real merit. *e.* Worthy of mention as a treatise by a scholarly lawyer and a practical diplomat, the greatest of early American writers on the subject. *f.* Meritorious history of the science, written originally in French. Review of French original, N. Senior, *Edinburgh Rev.,* 77 : 303, Apr. 1843.

StGLS, HRS

g. Not strong on the development of legal theory or 'specifically legal doctrines and institutions, but has the merit of opening up a field of research hitherto greatly neglected by the historian and the lawyer.' Review, J. L. Brierly, *E.H.R.,* 44 : 667, Oct. 1929.

WEL

I 506a Oakes, Sir Augustus, and **Mowat, Robert B.** *Great European treaties of the nineteenth century.* Oxford, 1918.

b Hertslet, Sir Edward. *Map of Europe by treaty showing the various political and territorial changes which have taken place since the general peace of 1814.* 4 v. London, 1875–91.

c Albin, Pierre. *Les grandes traités politiques; recueil des principaux textes diplomatiques depuis 1815 jusqu'à nos jours avec des notes.* Paris, 1911.

a. Aims to present an historical summary of the events leading to the principal treaties 1815–1878 and gives the texts of the treaties. Review, C. Seymour, *A.H.R.,* 24 : 275, Jan. 1919. *b.* Useful collection comprising more than four hundred treaties and conventions showing the political and territorial changes from 1814–91. Each treaty is preceded by a table of contents and for each article there is a descriptive heading. Appendix contains copies of treaties or extracts from treaties, concluded before 1814, but alluded to in the body of the work as still valid. Numerous maps and charts and excellent index. Cf. (W311) Hertslet, *Map of Africa by treaty.* *c.* Convenient briefer collection. WEL, HRS

I 507a Martens, Georg F. von. *Recueil des principaux traités d'alliance, de paix, de trêve de neutralité, de commerce, de limites, d'échange, etc., conclus par les puissances de l'Europe tant entre elles, qu'avec les puissances et états dans d'autres parties du monde depuis 1761 jusqu'à présent.* 7 v. 1791–1801. 2nd enl. ed., by K. von Martens, 8 v., Gottingue, 1817–35.

b —— *Supplément au recueil etc. précédé de traités du XVIIIme siècle antérieurs à cette époque et qui ne se trouvent pas dans le corps universel diplomatique de Mrs. Dumont et Rousset et autres recueils généraux de traités.* 4 v. Gottingue, 1802–08.

c Martens, Georg F. von, and others. *Nouveau recueil de traités d'alliance etc. depuis 1808 jusqu'à présent.* 16 v. Gottingue, 1817–42.

d Murhard, Friedrich W. A. *Nouveau recueil général de traités, conventions et autres transactions remarquables, servant à la connaissance des relations étrangères des puissances et états dans leurs rapports mutuels.* 20 v. in 22. Gottingue, 1843–75.

e Samwer, Karl F. L., and others. *Nouveau recueil général de traités etc. Deuxième série.* 35 v. Gottingue, 1876–1908. General table and index volume for the entire series, Leipzig, 1910.

f Triepel, Heinrich von. *Nouveau recueil général de traités etc. Troisième série.* v. 1–19, Leipzig, 1908–29.

g Hopf, Julius. *Table générale du recueil des traités de G. F. Martens et de ses continuateurs.* (*1494–1874.*) 2 v. Gottingue, 1875–76.

h Martens, Karl von, and **Cusoy, Ferdinand de, Baron.** *Recueil manuel et pratique de traités etc. depuis l'année 1700 jusqu'à l'époque actuelle.* 7 v. Leipzig, 1846–57.

i Geffken, Friedrich H. *Recueil manuel et pratique de traités. Deuxième série.* 3 v. Leipzig, 1885–88.

j Dumont, Jean, Baron. *Corps universel diplomatique de droit des gens; contenant un recueil des traitez d'alliance, de paix de trêve, de neutralité, d'échange etc. qui ont été faits en Europe depuis le règne de l'empereur Charlemagne jusques à présent.* 8 v. Amsterdam, 1726–31.

k Rousset de Missy, Jean. *Supplément au corps universel diplomatique du droit des gens contenant un recueil des traitez d'alliance etc. qui ont échapé aux premières recherches de M. Du Mont. Continué jusqu'à présent.* 2 v. Amsterdam, 1739.

l Barbeyrac, Jean. *Histoire des anciens traitez ou recueil historique et chronologique des traitez répandus dans les auteurs Grec & Latin, & autres monuments de l'antiquité, depuis les tems les plus reculez jusques à l'empereur Charlemagne.* 2 v. in 1. Amsterdam, 1739.

m Wenck, Friedrich A. W. *Codex juris gentium recentissimi, e tabulariorum exemplorumque fide dignorum monumentis compositus.* 3 v. Lipsiae, 1781–95.

n Garden, Guillaume L., Comte de. *Histoire générale des traités de paix et autres transactions principales entre toutes les puissances de l'Europe depuis la paix de Westphalie. Ouvrage comprenant les travaux de Koch, Schoell etc. entièrement refondus et continués jusqu'à ce jour.* 15 v. Paris, 1848–87.

a, b, c, d, e, f, g. Taken together by far the most complete and extensive collection of international agreements and negotiations in existence (often referred to as Martens Collection of Treaties). *h, i.* Useful condensations of the above. *h,* Treaties 1760–1859; *i,* 1857–85. Cf. for years since the World War (J901) League of Nations, *Treaty series. j, k, l, m, n.* Helpful as supplementing the Martens series for the period before 1760. *j.* Cf. *b,* 1:lxiv for accounts of Dumont and discussions of this work. *n.* Covers period 1648–1814. V. 15 was added by author's son.

WEL

I 508a Hertslet, Lewis, and **Sir Edward,** and others. *Complete collection of the treaties, conventions and reciprocal regulations at present subsisting between Great Britain and foreign powers, and of the laws, decrees and orders in council, concerning the same, so far as they relate to commerce and navigation, to the repression and abolition of the slave trade, and to the privileges and interests of the high contracting parties, compiled from authentic documents.* 31 v. London, 1835–1927. Incorporated 1928 in (I509a) *British and foreign state papers.*

b Malloy, William W., and others. *Treaties, conventions, international acts, protocols and agreements between the United States of America and other powers, 1776–1923.* 3 v. Washington, 1910–23. (X902.)

c **Davenport, Frances G.** *European treaties bearing on the history of the United States and its dependencies (to 1648).* V. 1 and 2. Washington, 1910 and 1929. [Carnegie Institution of Washington, department of historical research.]

d **Clercq, Alexandre J. H. de,** and **Clercq, Etienne F. S. de.** *Recueil des traités de la France depuis 1713 jusqu'à nos jours.* V. 1–23, Paris, 1864–1917. [Bibliothèque diplomatique.] Publiés sous les auspices du ministre des affaires étrangères.

e **Roschinger, Heinrich V.,** ed. *Die Wirtschaftliche Verträge Deutschlands.* 3 v. Berlin, 1892–93.

f *Sammlung der Verträge und Verhandlungen über die Bildung und Ausführung des deutschen Handels- und Zollvereins.* 5 v. Berlin, 1845–71.

g Supplement: *Sammlung der Handels- und Schiffahrtsverträge Deutschlands mit dem Auslande von 1851–1872.* Berlin, 1872.

h *Handels- und Schiffahrtsverträge Deutschlands mit dem Auslande, 1872–1897.* 2 v. Berlin, 1897–98.

i *Die Handelsverträge des deutschen Reichs. Eine Zusammenstellung der geltenden Handels-, Zoll-, Schiffahrts-, und Konsularverträge des Reichs und einzelner Bundesstaaten mit dem Auslande.* Berlin, 1906.

j **Martens, Feodor F.** *Recueil des traités et conventions conclus par la Russie avec les puissances étrangères.* 15 v. St. Petersbourg, 1874–1909. [V. 1–4, avec l'Autriche, 1648–1877; 5–8, avec l'Allemagne, 1656–1888; 9–12, avec l'Angleterre, 1710–1895; 13–15, avec la France, 1717–1906.]

k **Neumann, Leopold von.** *Recueil des traités et conventions conclus par l'Autriche avec les puissances étrangères depuis 1763 à nos jours.* 6 v. Leipzig, 1855–59. *Nouvelle suite,* Neumann, L. von, and Plason, Adolphe la Woestyne, eds., v. 1–19 (7–24), Vienne, 1877 ff.

l *Österreichische Staatsverträge, England,* v. 1–2 (1526–1813) ed. by A. F. Pribram, Musbrüch, 1907; *Fürstentum Siebenbürgen* (1526–1690) ed. by R. Gooss. Wien, 1911; Niederlände, v. 1 (1636–1722) ed. by H. von Srbik, Wien, 1912. [Veröffentlichungen der Kommission für neuere Geschichte Österreichs.]

m **Calvo, Carlos.** *Recueil complet des traités, conventions, capitulations (etc.) de tous les états de l'Amérique latine compris entre le golfe du Mexique et le cap de Horn, depuis l'année 1493 jusqu'à nos jours, précédé d'un mémoire sur l'état actuel de l'Amérique, de tableaux statistiques, d'un dictionnaire diplomatique, avec une notice historique sur chaque traité important.* 11 v. Paris, 1862–68.

n **Reedtz, Holger de C.** *Répertoire historique et chronologique des traités conclus par la couronne de Danemark jusqu'à 1800, avec un extrait des principaux articles.* Gottingue, 1826.

o *Danske Tractater, 1751–1800; Danske Tractater efter 1800.* 3 v. Kjøbenhavn, 1882, 1874–85.

p **Rydberg, Olof S.,** and **Hallendorf, Carl J. H.** *Sveriges traktater med främmande Magter.* V. 1–15. Stockholm, 1877 ff.

q *Recueil des traités de la Norvège.* Kristiana, 1907.

r **Solar de la Marguerite, Clemente, Comte.** *Traités publics de la royale maison de Savoie avec les puissances étrangères depuis la paix de Chateau-Cambrésis jusqu'à nos jours.* 8 v. Turin, 1836–44.

s *Raccolta dei trattati e delle convenzioni commerciali in vigore tra l'Italia e gli stati stranieri.* Torino, 1862.

t *Raccolta dei trattati e delle convenzioni concliuse fra il regno d'Italia ed i governi esteri.* V. 1–17. Torino, 1865 ff.

u Lagemans, Evert G. *Recueil des traités et conventions conclus par la royaume des Pays-Bas avec les puissances étrangères depuis 1813 jusqu'à nos jours.* Continued by J. B. Breukelman. La Haye, 1858 ff. (V. 20, 1926.)

v Garcia de la Vega, Desire de, and **Busschere, Alphonse de.** *Recueil des traités et conventions concernant le royaume de Belgique.* V. 1-20, Bruxelles, 1850 ff.

w Testa, Ignaz von. *Recueil des traités de la Porte Ottomanne avec les puissances étrangères depuis le premier traité conclu, en 1536, entre Suleyman I et François I jusqu'à nos jours.* 11 v. Paris, 1864-1911.

Collections of treaties for particular nations. *b, d, j, l, o, q, r, s, t,* official collections. *a.* Standard English publication, well edited and kept up-to-date, includes post-war treaties. For the more recent of these, however, consult current volumes of (1509a) *British and foreign state papers.* There is an index for the first 22 volumes and a chronological and general index for v. 23-30. Continued in subseries of Parliamentary papers known as the *Treaty series,* London, 1892 ff. *b.* Standard collection of all American treaties since 1776. *c.* Thorough and scholarly work; a third volume will doubtless be published. Review, J. B. Moore, *A.H.R.,* 24:280, Jan. 1919; 35:376, Jan. 1930. Cf. also *Treaty series,* Washington, 1908 ff. *d.* Standard French collection giving treaties and diplomatic documents for the period from 1713 onward. *e, f, g, h, i.* Together these supply the main body of commercial treaties negotiated first under the auspices of the Customs Union and later by the Empire. The second part of *c* deals with international treaties from 1815 to 1905. For the legislative phases of German commercial treaties, etc., cf. Friedberg, Emil A., *Die Handelsgesetzgebung des deutschen Reiches,* 9th ed., Leipzig, 1908. *j.* Well edited with excellent historical introductions and notes. *m.* Scholarly and complete. Cf. (Y75a) Spanish translation. WEL, HRS

1509a *British and foreign state papers; compiled by the librarian and keeper of the papers, Foreign Office.* V. 1-120. London, 1832 ff.

b Ministère des affaires étrangères. *Documents diplomatiques.* Paris, 1861 ff.

c *Archives diplomatiques. Recueil mensuel international de diplomatie d'histoire.* Paris, 1861 ff. (Series 1. 1861-79; 2. 1880-1900; 3. 1901 ff.)

d *Das Staatsarchiv: Sammlung der officiellen Aktenstücke zur Geschichte der Gegenwart.* Hamburg and Leipzig, 1861 ff.

In addition to these regular publications under the auspices of the different foreign offices, the governments at frequent though irregular intervals publish parliamentary papers dealing with particular phases of the nation's foreign affairs. These are sometimes spoken of as the 'colored books.' Here should also be mentioned official collections such as (1275a) *Recueil des instructions,* and (1275b) *British diplomatic instructions.* For similar historical materials of an official character, cf. especially in the national sections, (901 ff.) Government publications.

WEL

MILITARY AND NAVAL HISTORY

The writing of military and naval history has been greatly stimulated by subventions and official researches under the direction of the historical section of the general staffs. Literally hundreds of volumes, based on sources difficult for the layman to interpret even if he obtains access to them, have been published in the last forty years as a result of the work of these sections. The volumes are always large, carefully done and liberally equipped with maps and plans. Moreover, stimulated by the encouragement and training given in the general staffs, not a few of the investigators have subsequently written valuable military histories on their own account. A suggestive summary of the historical work directed by the historical section of the general staffs in different countries is found in Ralph Magoffin's 'Historical work by army general staffs,' *A.H.R.*, 24: 630, July 1919. The article is, however, quite incomplete on the work of the French. It may be supplemented by Pierre Caron's 'L'histoire militaire de la Révolution et de l'Empire,' *Revue d'histoire moderne et contemporaine*, 2: 519, 1900–01, and by Jean Dany's 'La littérature militaire d'aujourd'hui,' *Revue de Paris*, Apr. 1, 1912, p. 611. For a select bibliography of the older books on military history since 1789, see Colonel Sir John F. Maurice, *War* (London, 1891), pp. 125–145.   WEL, DDI

I531 **Clausewitz, Karl von.** *On war.* 1873. Rev. ed., 3 v., London, 1908. Tr. by J. J. Graham, with introduction and notes by Colonel F. H. Maude, from *Vom Kriege* in Clausewitz' *Hinterlassene Werke über Krieg und Kriegsführung*, 10 v., Berlin, 1832–37.

Exhaustive treatise analogous in the history of military theory to Adam Smith's *Wealth of nations* in the history of economic thought. Clausewitz proceeds on the philosophy that states are always in a condition of struggle and that war is therefore only an intensive form of the continued conflict of opposing political and social ideals. On the purely military side he pronounces the destruction of the enemy's armed forces to be the immediate object of military operations and moral force rather than geometric manoeuvres to be the principal means of attaining that object. Clausewitz's doctrines have been subjected to much criticism since the World War by men like Captain B. H. Liddell Hart, Colonel J. F. C. Fuller, and General von Freytag-Loringhoven. Liddell Hart gives a summary of his criticism in his article 'Strategy' in the 14th ed. of (B22b) *Encyclopedia Britannica* and again in his *Remaking of modern armies* (Boston, 1928). Cf. also Fuller, *Foundations of the science of war* (London, 1926) and Freytag-Loringhoven, *Politik und Kriegsführung* (Berlin, 1918).   WEL, DDI

Cf. also works listed at (B511).

I532a **Colin, Jean.** *Transformations of war.* London, 1913. Tr. from *Les transformations de la guerre*, Paris, 1911. Another, partial translation as *France and the next war, a French view of modern war*, London, 1914.

b **Colin, Jean; Reboul, Frederic; Mangin, General; Franchet D'Esperey, Marshal; and Hanotaux, Gabriel.** 'Histoire militaire et navale,' *Histoire de la nation française* (Gabriel Hanotaux, ed., 15 v., Paris, 1925–27), v. 7–8.

c **Dodge, Theodore A.** *Great captains.* Boston, 1889.

d **Creasy, Sir Edward S.** *The fifteen decisive battles of the world, from Marathon to Waterloo.* 2 v. London, 1851. Many later editions; latest, N. Y., 1925.

e **Whitton, Frederick E.** *Decisive battles of modern times.* London and Boston, 1923.

a. By one of France's outstanding military historians. His work is distinguished by breadth of knowledge and a rare insight into the larger factors affecting the development of the art of war. *b.* Co-operative work, popular in character, by men of authority covering French military history to the end of the World War. *c.* History of the art of war as seen in the campaigns of Alexander, Hannibal, Caesar, Gustavus Adolphus, Frederick the Great, and Napoleon, stressing strategy rather than tactics. A model of condensation. *d.* Widely read popular account of what the author considers the decisive battles of the western world. *e.* An effort to do for recent history what *d* does for the longer period. The battles selected are Vicksburg, Sadowa, Mars la Tour, Tsushima, and the Marne.   WEL

I533a **Taylor, Frederick L.** *Art of war in Italy, 1494–1529.* Cambridge (Eng.), 1920. [Prince Consort prize essay.] (Bibliography.)

 b **Dodge, Theodore A.** *Gustavus Adolphus. A history of the art of war from its revival after the middle ages to the end of the Spanish Succession war, with a detailed account of the campaigns of the great Swede and the most famous campaigns of Turenne, Condé, Eugene, and Marlborough.* Boston, 1895.

 c *Die Kriege Friedrichs des Grossen.* Herausgegeben vom Grossen General-stabe, Abtheilung für Kriegsgeschichte. 3 pts. in 18 v., Berlin, 1890–1913. [Pt. 1, *Der erste schlesische Krieg, 1740–1742,* 3 v.; pt. 2, *Der zweite schlesische Krieg, 1744–1745,* 3 v.; pt. 3, *Der siebenjährige Krieg,* 12 v.]

 d **Horsetzsky, Adolf von, General.** *Short history of the chief campaigns of Europe since 1792.* London, 1909. Tr. by V. B. Ferguson from *Kriegs-geschichtliche Übersicht der wichtigsten Feldzüge der letzten 100 Jahre.* Wien, 1894.

 e **Goltz, Colmar, Freiherr von der.** *Kriegsgeschichte Deutschlands im neunzehnten Jahrhundert.* 2 v. Berlin, 1910–14.

a. Interesting book showing the rapid advance in the art of war during the operations conducted by Italians, French and Spanish in the period just before and after 1500. Review, *A.H.R., 27*: 144, Oct. 1921; J. E. Edmonds, *History, 7*: 132, July 1922. *b.* Conforms to the second rather than to the first part of the title. To the average reader it is a somewhat detailed survey of the military campaigns in western Europe in early modern times. Review, John Bigelow, Jr., *A.H.R., 1*: 331, Jan. 1896. *c.* Detailed, complete and thorough—a good example of the work of the historical section of the Great General Staff. *d.* Popular and inadequate survey of the military campaigns of the century beginning with the French Revolution by an Austrian officer. *e.* Good account of the military history of Germany from the beginning of the nineteenth century to the end of the War of 1870–71, with excessive emphasis on military operations.   HRS, WEL

I534a **Dumolin, Maurice.** *Précis d'histoire militaire.* 3 v., fascicules 1–15, and atlas, Paris, 1901–13.

 b **Dodge, Theodore A.** *Napoleon. A history of the art of war from the beginnings of the French Revolution to the battle of Waterloo, with a detailed account of the Revolutionary and Napoleonic wars.* 4 v. Boston, 1904–07.

 c **Yorck von Wartenburg, Count.** *Napoleon as a general.* 2 v. London, 1902. Tr. from *Napoleon als Feldherr,* 2 v., Berlin, 1885–86.

a. Good treatment in moderate space of the Revolution and Napoleon through the campaign of Wagram. *b.* The only extensive history written in English of Napoleon's whole military career. By an experienced soldier deeply read in the literature of military history and science. Not essentially a work based on research, but the judgments of the author are remarkably sound and perspicacious. Titles of separate volumes vary. Review, v. 1–2, F. L. Huidekoper, *A.H.R., 10*: 183, Oct. 1904; v. 3–4, *id., ibid., 13*: 578, Apr. 1908. *c.* Adhering strictly to his topic of Napoleon as a general, the author presents what was for his day an original and acceptable interpretation of Napoleon's generalship. Lacks maps and charts.   CDa

Other studies of this military history will be found in (M512) Phipps, and in (M513) Chuquet.

I535a Sargent, Herbert H. *Napoleon Bonaparte's first campaign*. Chicago, 1895.

  b ——— *Campaign of Marengo*. Chicago, 1897.

  c Clausewitz, Karl von. *Campaign of 1812 in Russia*. London, 1843. Tr. from *Der Feldzug von 1812 in Russland* in Clausewitz' *Hinterlassene Werke über Krieg und Kriegsführung*, 10 v., Berlin, 1832–37.

  d George, Hereford B. *Napoleon's invasion of Russia*. London, 1899.

  e Houssaye, Henri. *Jéna et la campagne de 1806*. 1912. 21st ed., Paris, 1918.

  f ——— *1814*. 1888. 65th ed., Paris, 1911.

  g ——— *1815, Waterloo, battle of*. London, 1900. Tr. by A. E. Mann from v. 3 of *1815*, 3 v., Paris, 1893–1905. Cf. also translation by S. R. Willis, N. Y., 1905.

  h Ropes, John C. *Campaign of Waterloo*. N. Y., 1892.

a, b, d. Popular accounts by writers in English of particular campaigns. *c*. Suggestive study of the Russian campaign by the famous military theorist, who was a participant on the Russian side. *e, f, g*. Works by the ablest and most popular of the French writers on the military history of Napoleon. *h*. Widely read popular work, well documented, with maps, critical notes and valuable appendixes of orders and dispatches. Review, F. C. Montague, *E.H.R.*, 8: 593, July 1893.   CDa

I536a Napier, Sir William F. P. *History of the war in the Peninsula and in the south of France from the year 1807 to the year 1814*. 6 v. 1824–40. Rev. ed., London, 1856; 6 v., London, 1905.

  b Oman, Charles. *History of the peninsular war*. 6 v. Oxford, 1902–22.

  c Grasset, Alphonse. *La guerre d'Espagne (1807–1813)*. Rédigée à la section historique de l'état-major de l'armée. V. 1–2, Paris, 1914–1925.

a. General Napier took part as an officer in the operations he describes. He also had access to the official papers, which he cites freely. Despite its strong English bias the work was for a long time the classic history of the Peninsular War. *b*. A distinctly modern history of the Napoleonic war in Spain differing widely in its point of view from that of *a*. The author used archival as well as published sources and made repeated journeys to Spain to study the country and the battlefields. The maps, careful reference to authorities, and reprints of important documents add greatly to the value of the work. Review, v. 1 and 2, E. M. Lloyd, *E.H.R.*, 17: 802, Oct. 1902; 19: 178, Jan. 1904; v. 3, T. A. Dodge, *A.H.R.*, 14: 131, Oct. 1908; v. 4 and 5, G. M. Dutcher, *A.H.R.*, 17: 830, July 1912; 20: 851, July 1915; v. 6, *E.H.R.*, 39: 472, July 1924.   OLS Jr

c. Comprehensive history in sixteen volumes from the French point of view was planned by A. Grasset under the direction of the French general staff, but only two volumes have as yet appeared. For the Spanish side of the war, cf. Arteche y Moro's *Guerra de la Independencia*, 13 v., Madrid, 1868–1902.   DDI

1537a Kinglake, Alexander W. *Invasion of the Crimea.* 8 v. Edinburgh, 1863–67.

b Hamley, Sir Edward B. *War in the Crimea.* London, 1890.

c Maurice, John F. *Russo-Turkish war of 1877, a strategical sketch.* London, 1905.

d *Der russisch-türkische Krieg 1877–1878 auf der balkan Halbinsel.* 7 v. Wien, 1902–11.

a. Vivacious work corresponding in importance to (1536a) Napier, but exhibiting exceedingly strong prejudices and an excessive use of invective and bombast. Its author, an amateur soldier who fought in the Crimean war, has taken far more pains to lay about at all and sundry, and especially Napoleon III and the French, than he has to weigh his evidence. Review, E. B. Hamley, *Edinburgh Rev.,* 117: 307, Apr. 1863; 128: 379, Oct. 1868; 141: 522, Apr. 1875; 153: 241, Jan. 1881; 167: 161, Jan. 1888. *b.* Masterly short survey by one of the outstanding British military theorists of the nineteenth century. Hamley, like Kinglake, a participant in the war, differs considerably from him in his interpretation. Review, *Blackwood's Edinburgh Magazine,* 148: 853, Dec. 1890. *c.* Excellent work by a competent authority on modern military history. *d.* German translation of the Russian staff account of the Russo-Turkish war.   CDa

1538a Sarcey, Francisque. *Le siége de Paris. Documents pour servir à l'histoire de la guerre de 1870–71.* 8 v. Paris, 1871.

b Moltke, Helmuth, Count von. *Franco-German war of 1870–71.* 2 v. London, 1893. Tr. from *Geschichte des deutsch-französischen Krieges 1870–71,* Berlin, 1891. New ed., 1 v., tr. and rev. by Archibald Forbes, London, 1907.

c Chuquet, Arthur. *La guerre, 1870–71.* Paris, 1895.

d *Franco-German war, 1870–71.* London, 1874–84. Tr. by F. C. H. Clarke from *Der deutsch-französische Krieg 1870–71.* Redigiert von der kriegsgeschichtlichen Abtheilung des grossen Generalstabes. 7 v., Berlin, 1872–80.

e *La guerre de 1870–71.* Redigée à la section historique de l'état-major de l'armée. V. 1–43, Paris, 1901–14.

f Pflugk-Harttung, Julius von. *Franco-German war, 1870–71.* London. Tr. and ed. by Sir John F. Maurice from *Krieg und Sieg 1870–71,* Berlin, 1895–96.

a. Valuable series of documents on the siege of Paris. *b.* Translation of the excellent work in German by a writer and thinker on military questions. *c.* Interesting work for the general reader by the able and popular French military historian. *d* and *e.* Outstanding examples of the work of the historical sections of the general staffs. The French claim that the German work is permeated with propaganda, while the Germans criticize the French work as overcrowded with detail and likewise nationalistic. *f.* Good translation with editorial comment of Pflugk-Harttung's somewhat hyper-nationalist work.   WEL

1539a Mahan, Alfred T. *Influence of sea power upon history, 1660–1783.* 1890. 32nd ed., Boston, 1928.

b —— *Influence of sea power upon the French Revolution and Empire, 1793–1812.* 2 v. 1893. 10th ed., Boston, 1898.

c —— *Sea power in its relation to the war of 1812.* 2 v. 1905. Good ed., Boston, 1919.

d ———— *Naval strategy compared and contrasted with the principles and practise of military operations on land.* Boston, 1911.

e Westcott, Allan. *Mahan on naval warfare.* Boston, 1918.

a, b, c. These remarkable studies by Admiral Mahan are more than mere accounts of naval tactics and strategy. They involve an interpretation of the events of international history from an entirely new viewpoint, namely that of sea power. The thesis that sea power proved itself to be the decisive factor in the wars of the French Revolution and of Napoleon is brilliantly sustained. The work is based on an intimate practical knowledge of naval matters, on much patient research, and upon sound scholarship. Admiral Mahan's conclusions have been widely accepted and his influence has been very great not only upon the writing on naval history but upon the actual policies of maritime powers. The volumes all have excellent maps and charts. *d.* Exposition of Mahan's theories of naval warfare with many historical examples. *e.* Volume of well-chosen selections from Mahan's writings.

Cf. also (L525) Mahan, *Life of Nelson;* (L524*a, b, c, d*) Corbett, works on the British navy; and (B521) Stevens and Westcott, *History of sea power.*

WEL, RHG

HISTORY OF GOVERNMENT, POLITICAL THEORY AND JURISPRUDENCE

I551a Bryce, James, Viscount. *Modern Democracies.* 2 v. N. Y., 1921. (K351).

b Burgess, John W. *Political science and comparative constitutional law.* Boston, 1890.

c Lowell, A. Lawrence. *Governments and parties in continental Europe.* 2 v. 1896. 5th ed., Boston, 1900. Later reprints.

d ———— *Greater European governments.* 1914. Rev. ed., Cambridge (Mass.), 1925.

e Ogg, Frederic A. *Governments of Europe.* 1913. 2nd rev. ed., London and N. Y., 1920. Later reprints.

a. The ripe fruit of years of observation, reading and thought by a scholar best situated and best equipped for the task of any man of his time; written primarily to give guidance to free peoples in establishing and improving their governments by showing the workings of democracy in its diverse forms. Its principal interest is an objective, unprejudiced and acute description of the existing institutions in the most advanced countries with the exception of Great Britain, which the author omits because of inability to be unprejudiced. Reviews, F. Ogg, *A.H.R.,* 27:91, Oct. 1921; E. Dawson, *Historical Outlook,* 13:102, Mar. 1922.   EPC

b. Classical treatment of the subject. Deals in its first volume with the theory and organization of the state and relationships of the then existing states of Europe to the geography of the continent; in its second, with the forms of government, the construction and rôle of the legislature, executive and judiciary under the constitutions of the United States, France, Germany and England. Review, *Annals Am. Acad.,* 1:681, 1890–91.   WEL

c. Thoughtful and scholarly treatment of the governments of France, Italy, Germany, Austria-Hungary and Switzerland with a brief account of the origin and development of each; now out of date but still valuable. Emphasis is upon political rather than historical problems. Review, J. Macy, *A.H.R.,* 2:729, July

1897. *d.* **Later form of c.** Clear concise statement of the organization and working of the governments of England, France, Italy, Germany and Switzerland, characterized by mature judgment and a sympathetic understanding of the many complex problems discussed. Review, *Amer. Pol. Sci. Rev.*, 20: 225, Feb. 1926.   JTY

c. Excellent one volume work stressing the comparative study of political institutions. Later edition radically different from the first; in it the governments of Great Britain and France receive much fuller treatment. Chapters on the governments of Austria-Hungary and some of the minor states are omitted. Instead the political institutions of republican Germany and Soviet Russia are briefly described. Brief historical introduction precedes the study of each government. Review, W. F. Dodd, *A.H.R.*, 19: 174, Oct. 1913.   WEL

I552 Dodd, Walter F. *Modern constitutions, a collection of the fundamental laws of twenty-two of the most important countries of the world, with historical and bibliographical notes.* 2 v. Chicago, 1909. (Bibliography.)

Standard collection of constitutional documents with admirable historical notes. Now slightly antiquated. Review, C. A. Beard, *Pol. Sci. Rev.*, 24: 524, Sept. 1909.   JTY

Cf. also (J531) McBain and Rogers, *Constitutions of Europe,* and (J532a) Graham and Binkley, *New governments of central Europe.*

I553a Dunning, William A. *History of political theories from Luther to Montesquieu.* N. Y., 1905.

b —— *History of political theories from Rousseau to Spencer.* N. Y., 1920.

a and *b* are volumes 2 and 3 of the author's *History of Political Theories.* (For v. 1, cf. (H561).) From thirty to fifty writers are discussed in each volume with special reference to their historical setting. The work is one of great merit, adhering strictly to its main purpose, which is the presentation of political theory as seen in its principal exponents. Review of *a*, A. H. Lloyd, *A.H.R.*, 11: 368, Jan. 1906; of *b*, E. Barker, *A.H.R.*, 26: 722, July 1921.   JTY

Cf. (J561) Merriam and Barnes, eds., *Political theories; recent times.*

I554a Merriam, Charles E. *New aspects of politics.* Chicago, 1925.

b Krabbe, Hugo. *Modern idea of the state.* N. Y., 1922. Tr. by G. F. Sabina and W. J. Shepard from *Die moderne Staatsidee,* 2nd ed., Haag, 1919.

c Coker, Francis W. *Readings in political philosophy.* N. Y., 1914.

Examples of shorter works on the history of political thought and theory of which there are many. Review of *b*, C. E. Merriam, *Amer. Pol. Sci. Rev.*, 16: 711, Nov. 1922.   WEL

For additional works in this field, cf. (B551) ff., and for works dealing with the different countries, the pertinent parts of the sections dealing with these national units.

I555a Austin, Sir John. *Province of jurisprudence determined, being the first part of a series of lectures on jurisprudence, or the philosophy of positive law.* 2 v. London, 1832. 2nd ed., 3 v., 1861–63. Many reprints and condensations.

b Holland, Thomas E. *Elements of jurisprudence.* 1880. 13th ed., Oxford, 1925.

  c **Maine, Sir Henry F.** *Ancient law—its connection with the early history of society and its relation to modern ideas.* London, 1861. New ed., with introduction and notes by Sir Frederick Pollock, 1906.

  d **Dillon, John F.** *Laws and jurisprudence of England and America.* Boston, 1895.

  e **Pound, Roscoe.** *Introduction to the philosophy of law.* New Haven, 1922.

  f **Berolzheimer, Fritz.** *World's legal philosophies.* Boston, 1912. Tr. by R. S. Jastrow from v. 2 of *System der Rechts-und-wirtschaftsphilosophie,* München, 1904–07. [Modern legal philosophy series.]

  g **Duguit, Léon.** *Law in the modern state.* London and N. Y., 1919. Tr. by F. and H. Laski, from *Les transformations du droit public,* Paris, 1913. [Modern legal philosophy series.]

  h **Stammler, Rudolph.** *Theory of justice.* London and N. Y., 1925. Tr. by I. Husik from *Die Lehre von dem rechtigen Rechte,* Berlin, 1902. Rev. ed., Halle, 1926.

  a. Founder of English analytical jurisprudence; the first to introduce the inductive treatment of the law. Although some of his conceptions, particularly those of law and sovereignty, have been discarded, nevertheless in defining the field of jurisprudence and abstracting law from morality and ethics, he made a unique contribution to the subject. Review, *Law Magazine and Review,* 22 : 234, Aug. 1861.   IH

  b. Develops the theories of Austin, superseding *a,* and supplies a logical scheme or framework for the arrangement of legal conceptions. Basis of his system is the classification rights. Review, A. V. Dicey, *Law Magazine and Review,* 237 : 352, Aug. 1880; A. Tulley, *ibid.,* 238 : 44, Nov. 1880.   *c.* Epoch-making treatise on the study of law by the founder of the historical school of jurisprudence. Review, Editor, *Law Magazine and Law Review,* 21 : 99, May 1861.   *d.* Lectures of a semi-popular character dealing with legal education, trial by jury, the origins, development and characteristics of common law; written constitutions, legislation, case law, codification and law reform. Protest against tendency to associate law too much with its moral surroundings making it dependent on moral and ethical speculation. Review, S. D. Thompson, *Amer. Law Review,* 29 : 276, Mar. 1895.   WEL

  e. Vigorous and logical presentation of the claims that the philosophy of law is a study not of abstractions but of humanity,—the product of economic and social progress. Cf. (B564), same author's enthusiastic treatment of juristic and philosophical interpretation of the history and principle of legal systems summarizing the work of the different schools of juridical thought from antiquity to our own times with comments upon their application to the social needs of to-day. Review, B. N. Cardozo, *Harvard Law Review,* 37 : 279, Dec. 1923.   WEL

  f. Faithful survey of the legal philosophers of modern times presenting the representative views of the leading modern writers of different continental countries on jurisprudence. The development of the law in relation to historic progress especially as it appears in the emancipation of different classes is emphasized with special stress upon the humanitarian character of the law. Review, H. Woodward, *Univ. of Penna. Law Review,* 61 : 349, March 1913.   IH

  g. Scholarly treatise by a leading French authority who holds 'that law is not a creation of the state but that it exists without the state' or is altogether independent of it and imposes itself on the state. Cf. author's article on 'Law and the State,' *Harvard Law Review,* 31 : 1–185, Nov. 1917.   JWG

  h. Work by foremost legal philosopher of Germany in which he takes issue with work by the historical and the law of nature school of jurisprudence and advocates a philosophical basis for law. See summary of Stammler's views by translator in the introduction and critiques by Geny and Dr. Wu in appendixes.   WEL

I556a Salmond, Sir John W. *Jurisprudence or the theory of the law.* 1902. 7th ed., London, 1924.

b Allen, Carlton K. *Law in the making.* Oxford, 1927.

c Holdsworth, Sir William S. *Some lessons from our legal history.* N. Y., 1928.

d Tourtoulon, Pierre de. *Philosophy in the development of law.* London and N. Y., 1922. Tr. by M. M. Read from *Les principes philosophiques de l'histoire du droit.* Paris, 1919. [Modern legal philosophy series.]

e Wigmore, John H. *Panorama of the world's legal systems.* 3 v. St. Paul, 1928. (Bibliography.)

f Cardozo, Benjamin N. *Growth of the law.* New Haven, 1924.

g —— *Paradoxes of legal science.* N. Y., 1928.

a. Philosophical treatise dealing with the nature, sources and elements of law by a trained jurist who emphasizes pure analytical or theoretical jurisprudence as opposed to the all inclusive treatises of the foreign school. Review, F. Pollock, *Law Quarterly Review,* 18: 431, Oct. 1902. *b.* Study of the processes in the making of law with special emphasis upon the influence of precedent. Review, *Law Quarterly Review,* 174: 736, Apr. 1928. *c.* Lectures by England's foremost legal historian. Review, F. Pollock, *Law Quarterly Review,* 179: 394, July 1929. *d.* Juristic history of modern Europe; shows evolutionary progress of law as a philosophy. Review, I. Husik, *Univ. of Penna. Law Review,* 71: 416, May 1923. *e.* Popular but scholarly treatment of the sixteen principal legal systems of the world with 500 illustrations of jurists, law courts and reproductions of important legal documents. Invaluable for the study of comparative law. Review, *Law Quarterly Review,* 179: 399, July 1929; J. P. Chamberlain, *A.H.R.,* 35: 86, Oct. 1919. *f.* Presents a thoroughly modern point of view, appealing not so much to the laymen as to the jurist and judge, for a philosophy of the law 'that will mediate between the conflicting claims of stability and progress.' Over against the claims of precedent and the letter of the statute, the author puts the necessity of adaptation to change and the principle of growth. Review, I. Husik, *Univ of Penna. Law Review,* 73: 327, March 1925. *g.* Interesting and illuminating discussions by a conscientious and progressive jurist and judge of such topics as stability and progress, meaning of justice, the individual and society, liberty and government.   IH

Other related works are (B245*a*) Bryce, (B551*a*) Vinogradoff, and (B564) Pound.

ECONOMIC AND SOCIAL HISTORY

Works in the field of economic history reviewed in other sections of this *Guide* but also of importance here are: (L572) Cunningham, (M582*b* and *c*) Levasseur, (M585) Pigeonneau, (P571) Roscher, and (S571) Mavor.

I571a Ogg, Frederic A. *Economic development of modern Europe.* 1917. New ed. by F. A. Ogg and W. R. Sharp, N. Y., 1926. (Bibliography.)

b Gibbins, Henry de B. *Economic and industrial progress of the century.* London and Philadelphia, 1901. [Nineteenth century series.]

c **MacGregor, David H.** *Evolution of industry.* N. Y., 1912. [Home university library.]

d **Byrn, Edward W.** *Progress of invention in the nineteenth century.* N. Y., 1900.

a. Clear, well-balanced survey of the economic history of modern Europe, especially of the last hundred years. The four parts of the book deal respectively with (1) antecedents of the nineteenth century development; (2) agriculture, industry, and trade since 1815; (3) population and labor; and (4) socialism and social insurance. In last edition six new chapters are added, dealing with the economic history of the war and reconstruction. Review, A. P. Usher, *Amer. Econ. Rev.,* 16:672, Dec. 1926; T. Veblen, *A.H.R.,* 24:273, Jan. 1919. *b.* Semi-popular account of industry and commerce in Europe and the United States from the Industrial Revolution to 1900, with over-much respect for the material side of progress. Review, *Athenaeum,* July 25:1903. *c.* Emphasis on interpretation rather than on the historical aspect of the subject. 'Full of facts and stuffed with ideas. . . .' Review, C. H. Hull, *Am. Econ. Rev.,* 3:95, March 1913. *d.* Good survey, covering a wide range and profusely illustrated. Review, *Quart. Jour. of Econ.,* 15:315, Feb. 1901. WEL

For other related works, cf. (B571*a*) Cunningham, (B571*c*) Weber, and (B106) Dietz.

I572 **Kovalevskii, Maksim Maksimovich.** *Die oekonomische Entwicklung Europas bis zum Beginn der kapitalistischen Wirtschaftsform.* 7 v. Berlin, 1901–14. Tr. from the Russian.

Work of considerable merit, often going into great detail, yet unique in the attempt to treat the subject for Europe as a whole. The last four volumes deal with the modern period. Review, v. 1, T. W. Page, *Pol. Sci. Quar.,* 17:336, June 1902; v. 2–7, G. Lapsley, *ibid.,* 18:346, June 1903; 23:162, March 1908; 24:703, Dec. 1909; 27:320, June 1912; 28:526, Sept. 1913; 30:134, March 1915. WEL

Cf. also (L583*b*) Mantoux, and (M581*a*) d'Avenel.

I573a **Clapham, John H.** *Economic development of France and Germany, 1815–1914.* Cambridge (Eng.), 1921.

b **Ashley, Percy W. L.** *Modern tariff history: Germany—United States—France.* 1904. 3rd rev. ed., London and N. Y., 1920. (Brief bibliographies.)

c **Hill, Charles E.** *Danish Sound dues and the command of the Baltic.* Durham, N. C., 1926.

d **Rand, Benjamin.** *Selections illustrating economic history since the Seven Years' War.* 1883. 5th ed., N. Y., 1911. (Bibliography.)

a. Thorough and well-organized account of agricultural and industrial progress stressing economic facts rather than economic opinions. Last chapter gives good survey of finance and financial institutions. Review, A. Law, *Scottish Hist. Rev.,* 18:297, July 1921; G. B. Diblee, *E.H.R.,* 36:605, Oct. 1921. *b.* Careful survey of modern tariff history. Story of the German tariff system is brought down from the formation of the Zollverein; that of the United States begins with the Tariff Act of 1789; that of France with the customs and navigation problems of the Revolution. Clear and scholarly with useful tables of statistics. Third edition brings the work done to 1914. Review, J. Viner, *Jour. of Pol. Econ.,* 29:259.

March 1921. *c.* Scholarly study based on extensive research in European and American archives; sets forth in a systematic manner the rôle of the Sound dues in the commerce and diplomatic relations of northern Europe. Review, W. Westergaard, *A.H.R.,* 32 : 585, Apr. 1927; W. F. Reddaway, *E.H.R.,* 43 : 116, Jan. 1927. *d.* Good selections of readings relating mainly to the Industrial Revolution.   WEL

I574a **Lindsay, William S.** *History of merchant shipping and ancient commerce.* 4 v. London, 1874.

b **MacPherson, Logan G.** *Transportation in Europe.* N. Y., 1910.

c **Patterson, James.** *History and development of road transport.* London, 1927.

d **Pratt, Edwin A.** *Rise of rail-power in war and conquest, 1833–1914.* London, 1915; Philadelphia, 1916. (Bibliography.)

a. Best general history of ocean commerce, particularly devoted to the development of shipping and commerce of England; scholarly and packed with information. Review, *Athenaeum,* p. 477, Oct. 10, 1874. *b.* Covers development of railway transportation in Europe in summary fashion; government control and inland waterways. Review, *Yale Rev.,* 19 : 332, Nov. 1910. *c.* Up-to-date study dealing mainly with England. *d.* Interesting study suggested by the World War; not a work of extensive research. Review, *Am. Econ. Rev.,* 6 : 364, June 1916.

WEL
Stimulating books on the theory and practice of international trade are: Bastable, C. F., *Theory of international trade,* London and N. Y., 1903; Taussig, F. W., *International trade,* N. Y., 1927; Griffin, C. E., *Principles of foreign trade,* N. Y., 1924; Culbertson, W. S., *International economic policies,* N. Y., 1925; Dennis, A. P., *Romance of world trade,* N. Y., 1926.

I575a **Hobson, John A.** *Evolution of modern capitalism; a study of machine production.* 1894. 2nd rev. ed., London and N. Y., 1917. [Contemporary science.]

b **Sombart, Werner.** *Der moderne Kapitalismus: historischsystematische Darstellung des gesamteuropäischen Wirtschaftslebens von seinen Anfängen bis zur Gegenwart.* 2 v. 1902. 4th ed., rev. and completed, 3 v. in 6 pts., München, 1921–27. (Bibliographies.)

c **Sée, Henri.** *Modern capitalism; its origin and evolution.* N. Y., 1928. Tr. by H. B. Vanderblue and G. F. Doriot from *Les origines du capitalisme moderne,* Paris, 1926. (Bibliography.)

d **Tawney, Richard H.** *Religion and the rise of capitalism: a historical study.* London and N. Y., 1926. [Holland memorial lectures.]

a. Study of the effects of the modern industrial and capitalistic régimes. Considers modern capitalism in a scientific spirit and stresses the benefits of the competitive principle. Cf. the author's (K348) *Imperialism,* a study in which modern imperialism is subjected to a searching criticism from the economic standpoint. Review, G. Gunton, *Pol. Sci. Quar.* 10 : 324, June 1895. *b.* Most important historical account in German of the development of modern capitalism in Europe from its origin to the present day; work of great scholarship; embraces studies in detail, and yet keeps a wide perspective; provoked much discussion upon its appearance. The later editions have been wholly rewritten and greatly enlarged; scarcely a tenth of the original work reappears. Review, G. von Below, *Hist.*

Zeit., 91 : 432, 1903; A. B. Johnson, *Pol. Sci. Quar.*, 18 : 354, June 1903. *c.* Good, popular account by a well-known French authority of the rise and development of capitalism from the sixteenth to the end of the nineteenth century. Review, R. H. Tawney, *Econ. Hist. Rev.*, 1 : 156, Jan. 1927. *d.* Stimulating volume; sees in the assertion of individualism and its tendency to stress economic virtues like integrity, hard work, temperance, efficiency and enterprise, the origins and growth of capitalism. Review, L. Febvre, *Rev. Critique*, 61 : 275, July 15, 1927; and T. R. Commaus, *Am. Econ. Rev.*, 17 : 63, March 1927, who says among other things, 'Tawney's memorable contribution in the book is his distinction between the early Puritanism and the later Puritanism; and in this he makes a much-needed correction of Max Weber, the pioneer in the field. . . .' SBF, WB

I576 **Gide, Charles,** and **Rist, Charles.** *History of economic doctrines from the time of the physiocrats to the present day.* London and N. Y., 1915. Tr. by R. Richards from 2nd rev. ed. of *Histoire des doctrines économiques depuis les physiocrates jusqu'à nos jours,* Paris, 1913.

'Distinctly the ablest and most interesting history of economics in existence. . . .' Good on French and German authors but rather less exhaustive on American contributors. Taussig not mentioned in the entire work. Review, 2nd French ed., *Jour. Pol. Econ.*, 22 : 104, Jan. 1914; review of Engl. tr., *Pol. Sci. Quar.*, 31 : 645, Dec. 1916. WEL

I58Ia **Marx, Karl.** *Capital: a critique of political economy.* 3 v. Chicago, 1906–09. V. 1, tr. by S. Moore and E. Aveling from 3rd German ed., ed. by F. Engels, rev. and amplified according to the 4th German ed. by E. Untermann; v. 2, tr. by E. Untermann from 2nd ed.; v. 3, tr. by E. Untermann from 1st ed., *Das Kapital: Kritik der politischen Oekonomie,* v. 1, 1867, 4th rev. ed. by F. Engels, Hamburg, 1890; v. 2, ed. by F. Engels, 1885, 2nd rev. ed., Hamburg, 1893; v. 3, ed. by F. Engels, Hamburg, 1894. (Bibliography.)

   b **Riazanov, D. (Goldendach),** ed. *Karl Marx and Friedrich Engels.* N. Y., 1927. Tr. by J. Kunitz from the Russian.

   c **Stammhammer, Josef,** ed. *Bibliographie der Socialpolitik.* 2 v. 1896–1912.

a. This important work is often called the Bible of socialism; in it are set forth the latter's basic ideas and doctrines. The volumes are difficult and often wearisome reading, despite the enthusiasm of the author. Frederick Engels revised the first volume and edited the other two from Marx's manuscripts and notes, but Untermann says that 'a large portion of the contents of *Capital* is as much a creation of Engels as though he had written it independently.' Review, *Jour. Pol. Econ.*, 17 : 546, Oct. 1909. *b.* Series of popular lectures incorporating new biographical material by the editor of the forthcoming new and complete edition of the works of Marx and Engels. Review, B. J. Stern, *Pol. Sci. Quar.*, 43 : 160, March 1928. *c.* Standard bibliography of the subject; should be supplemented by Hermann Beck, ed., *Bibliographie der Socialwissenschaften,* Dresden, 1905 ff. (I944f). WEL

I582a **Kirkup, Thomas.** *History of socialism.* 1892. 5th ed. rev. by E. R. Pease, 1913. New ed., London, 1920. (Bibliography.)

   b **MacDonald, J. Ramsay.** *Socialist movement.* London, 1911. (Bibliography.)

c **Sombart, Werner.** *Socialism and the social movement.* London and N. Y., 1909. Tr. by M. Epstein from 6th rev. ed. of *Sozialismus und soziale Bewegung,* Jena, 1908.

d **Spargo, John.** *Socialism: a summary and interpretation of socialist principles.* 1896. Rev. ed., N. Y., 1919.

e ——— *Karl Marx, his life and work.* 1910. Rev. ed., N. Y., 1912.

f **Kautsky, Karl.** *Economic doctrine of Karl Marx.* London, 1925.

g **Skelton, Oscar D.** *Socialism: a critical analysis.* Boston, 1911.

h **Bernstein, Eduard.** *Evolutionary socialism: a criticism and affirmation.* 1909. 2nd ed., London, 1912. Tr. by E. C. Harvey from *Voraussetzungen des Sozialismus und die Aufgaben der Sozialdemokratie,* Stuttgart, 1899. [Socialist library.]

i **Walling, William E.** *Socialism as it is: a survey of the world-wide revotionary movement.* N. Y., 1912.

j **Day, Henry C.** *Catholic democracy: individualism and socialism.* London, 1914.

k **Orth, Samuel P.** *Socialism and democracy in Europe.* N. Y., 1913. (Bibliography.)

l **Maurice, William.** *Social interpretation of history, a refutation of the Marxian interpretation of history.* N. Y., 1920.

m **Cole, George D. H.** *Social theory.* London and N. Y., 1920. [Library of social studies.] (Bibliography.)

n ——— *Guild socialism: a plan for economic democracy.* London and N. Y., 1921. (Bibliography.)

o **Ensor, Robert C. K.,** ed. *Modern socialism as set forth by socialists in their speeches, writings, and programmes.* 1904. 3rd ed., N. Y., 1910.

p **Longuet, Jean.** *La politique internationale du Marxisme.* Paris, 1918.

The above are typical of the many short works on one or other aspect of socialism. *a.* Treats the historic phases of the subject fairly well. Interpretative sections are moderately favorable to the socialist viewpoint. Review, *Nation,* 98: 299, March 19, 1914. *b.* Appreciative study by the first socialist Prime Minister of England; stresses the international aspects of economic matters which the author regards as fundamental in socialism. Cf. also the author's *Socialism and government,* 2 v., London, 1909; *Socialism and society,* London, 1905; and *Socialism: critical and constructive,* London, 1921. Review, *Jour. of Pol. Econ.,* 20: 202, Jan. 1912. *c.* Semi-popular work by a leading German authority. Review, C. V. Butler, *Econ. Jour.,* 18: 440, Sept. 1908. *d.* Elementary discussion of the principles of socialism sustaining the thesis that it is a result of economic conditions; moderate and judicious. Review, H. R. Seager, *Pol. Sci. Quar.,* 22: 166, March 1907. *e.* Good biography with much good material collected with the aid of Marx's daughter. The larger philosophic grasp is absent. Review, *Jour. of Pol. Econ.,* 19: 152, Feb. 1911. *f.* Sound, though sympathetic appreciation of Marxian doctrine by a leading socialist and historian. *g.* Forceful and well-sustained criticism of socialism, the best short reply. Review, J. E. Rossignol, *Jour. of Pol. Econ.,* 19: 798, Nov. 1911. *h.* Expresses the views of the 'revisionists' who wished to revise the old orthodox Marxian socialism with its 'catastrophic' aims, substituting what is sometimes called evolutionary socialism based on penetration and co-operation. Review, W. E. Lagerquist, *Econ. Bull.,* 3: 180, June 1910. *i.* Favorable to socialism but needs revision. Contains the author's presentation of the socialist views on war and peace. Review, *Annals Amer. Acad. of Pol. and Soc. Sci.,* 44: 198, Nov.

1912. *j.* Criticizes socialism as destructive of individualism; written from the standpoint of the Roman Catholic Church with suggestive chapters on the origin of society and the rights and duties of the state, land, labor, and capital. Review, *Nation,* 101 : 470, Oct. 14, 1915. *k.* Popular account with reprints of important socialist documents. Review, C. J. H. Hayes, *Pol. Sci. Quar.,* 28 : 679, Dec. 1913. *l.* By a socialist who opposes to Marx's 'class movement of producers' a 'social movement of consumers,' acting in a democratic state; written with reference to the World War and the Russian and German revolutions. *m* and *n.* By an advocate of guild socialism advocating in *n* a political system based upon functional representation. Review of *m,* H. E. Barnes, *Pol. Sci. Quar.,* 35 : 665, Jan. 1920; of *n,* R. G. Tugwell, *ibid.,* 36 : 702, Dec. 1921. *o.* Collection of twenty-nine articles by different writers. Review, M. S. Wildman, *Jour. of Pol. Econ.,* 13 : 298, Mar. 1905. *p.* Penetrating and sympathetic study of the French socialist group. Review, *Pol. Sci. Quar.,* 34 : 696, Dec. 1919.   WB

Considerable material closely related to this subsection will be found in § B, General history, especially in the corresponding subsection.

CULTURAL HISTORY

1601 Merz, John T. *History of European thought in the nineteenth century.* 4 v. Edinburgh, 1897–1914.

The work is divided into two parts comprising two volumes each. Part 1 deals primarily with scientific; part 2, with philosophical, literary, artistic and religious development. An outstanding example of the trend in the new history of emphasizing the importance of thought and intellectual movements. Well written in an objective vein and fully documented. Review of v. 1, 3, 4, J. E. Creighton, *Philosophical Rev.,* 6 : 415, July 1897; 22 : 661, Nov. 1913; 24 : 657, Nov. 1915; of v. 2, A. C. Armstrong, *ibid.,* 13 : 566, Sept. 1904.   EGS

1602 Höffding, Harald. *History of modern philosophy; a sketch of the history of philosophy from the close of the renaissance to our day.* 2 v. London and N. Y., 1900. Tr. by B. E. Meyer from German ed., *Geschichte der neueren Philosophie, eine Darstellung der Geschichte der Philosophie von dem Ende der Renaissance bis zum Schlusse des 19. Jahrhunderts,* 2 v., 1895–9; 2nd ed., Leipzig, 1921; tr. by F. Bendixen from *Den nyere filosofis historie en fremstilling af filosofiens historie fra renaissansens slutning til voredage,* 2 v., 1894–95; 3rd rev. ed., 10 v., Kjøbenhavn, 1921–22.

The English translation badly mars the author's interesting exposition of the chief movements in modern philosophy, with which he has skilfully combined an interpretation of the thinkers who have most definitely shaped modern thought both as to content and method. His own method, being both 'historical and comparative,' visualizes the 'personal equation,' which he considers 'of greater significance in philosophy than in any other department of science.' Notes at the end of each volume reveal especially cross connections between philosophy and its literature. Review, F. Thilly, *Philosophical Rev.,* 9 : 416, July 1900. WHA

1603 Marvin, Francis S., ed. *Unity series.* 8 v. Oxford, 1915 ff. [1, *Unity of western civilization; 2, Progress and history; 3, Recent developments in European thought; 4, Evolution of world peace; 5, Western races and the world; 6, Science and civilization; 7, England and the world; 8, Art and civilization.*]

Volumes giving the substance of series of public lectures on the above subjects delivered in Birmingham, England, by well-known scholars and authors. Reviews of v. 4, C. H. Levermore, *A.H.R.*, 27 : 282, Jan. 1922; of v. 7, (London) *Times Lit. Suppl.*, 25 : 275, Apr. 15, 1926; W. Bowden, *A.H.R.*, 32 : 153, Oct. 1926; v. 8, C. Moore, *A.H.R.*, 35 : 149, Oct. 1929.   HRS

I604a **Rogers, Arthur K.** *English and American philosophy since 1800.* N. Y., 1922.

b **Dewey, John.** *Reconstruction in philosophy.* N. Y., 1929.

c **Boutroux, Émile E. M.** *Historical studies in philosophy.* London, 1912. Tr. by F. Rothwell from *Études d'histoire de la philosophie*, 1897; Paris, 1925.

a. Surprisingly complete and very accurate account of the subject. Probably the best inclusive statement of English and American philosophy in the nineteenth century. Review, G. H. Sabine, *Philosophical Rev.*, 32 : 229, March 1923. *b.* Famous book, the aim of which is to exhibit the general contrasts between older and newer types of philosophic problems, rather than to make a partisan plea in behalf of any specific solution of these problems. Review, G. P. Adams, *Philosophical Rev.*, 30 : 519, Sept. 1921.   WEL

c. Brief studies of Socrates, Aristotle, Boehme, Descartes and Kant; especially interesting is the correlation of these five,—Hegel perhaps first discovered that Boehme belonged to such a galaxy,—with the dominant interests of modern thought. The articles on Aristotle and Kant will be found also in (B23*b*) *La grande encyclopédie*. Reviews, H. N. Gardiner, *Philosophical Rev.*, 7 : 191, March 1898; 22 : 224, March 1913.   WHA

BIOGRAPHY

So powerful was the force of nationalism throughout this period, almost all the names which might pertinently be entered in this section have rather been placed in the national sections. A few will be found in §§ B, F, and K; while Erasmus and Napoleon I are dealt with in the body of this section, (I214) and (I311) ff., respectively.

PERIODICALS

Many periodicals appropriate to this section appear in the periodical lists in other sections, particularly in §§ A, B, H, J, and K, and in the national sections. Here are listed a few of the more important journals in several special fields such as International Law and Diplomacy, Military and Naval History, Economic and Social History.

International Law and Diplomacy. (I941*a*) *American journal of international law*, Washington, 1907 ff. (monthly). [American Society of International Law] (B941*g*2) ; (I941*b*) *Annals of the American academy of political and social science*, Philadelphia, 1890 ff. (2 v. annually since 1895) ; (I941*c*) *International law association report*, London, 1873 ff.; (I941*d*) *Revue historique de droit français et étranger*, Paris, 1855 ff. Title varies; (I941*e*) *Revue du droit public et de la science politique en France et à l'étranger*, Paris, 1894 ff. (quarterly). Title varies; (I941*f*) *Revue de droit international et de législation comparée*, Bruxelles, 1869 ff.; (I941*g*) *La paix par le droit; revue de la paix*, Paris, 1890 ff. [Société des Nations] ; (I941*h*) *Annuaire de l'institut de droit international*, Paris, 1877 ff.; (I941*i*) *Niemeyer's Zeitschrift für internationales Recht*, Leipzig, 1890 ff. (monthly). Title varies.   WEL

Military and Naval History. (I942a) Military service institution of the United States, *Journal*, 61 v. N. Y., 1879–1917 (quarterly, 1879–1888; bi-monthly, 1889–1917); (I942b) United States naval institute, *Proceedings*, Annapolis, Md., 1874 ff.; (I942c) Royal united service institution, *Journal*, London, 1857 ff. (monthly); (I942d) *Naval chronicle*, 40 v., London, 1799–1818 (monthly); (I942e) *United service magazine*, 236 v., London, 1829–1920 (monthly). Title varies; incorporated with it are *Army and navy magazine* and the *Naval and military journal;* (I942f) *Spectateur militaire. Recueil de science, d'art et d'histoire militaires*, 296 v., Paris, 1826–1914 (monthly, 1826–82; semi-monthly, 1883–1914); (I942g) *Revue maritime: études historiques et scientifiques maritimes et militaires, questions économiques et sociales.* Paris, 1861–1914, 1920 ff. (monthly), (as *Revue maritime et coloniale*, 1861–96) [France. Ministère de la marine]; (I942h) *Revue militaire française*, Paris, 1825–1914, 1921 ff. (before 1899, irregular; 1899–1907, monthly; 1908–14, semi-monthly; formed in 1921 by union of *Journal des sciences militaires, Revue militaire des armées étrangères* and *Revue d'histoire*); (I942i) *Monatshefte für Politik und Wehrmacht*, 47 v. in 140, Berlin, 1871–1922 (with title *Jahrbücher für die deutsche Armee und Marine*, 1871–1918). [Gesellschaft für Heeres-Kunde]; (I942j) *Mittheilungen des k.k.Kriegs-Archivs, Abtheilung für Kriegsgeschichte*, Wien, 1881–1911. For a somewhat antiquated bibliography of military and naval periodicals, cf. *Publications of United States Adjutant General's office, Military information division*, List of principal military newspapers, magazines and periodicals, 1897. Appendix, 17 : 495.   RGA

Economic History. (I943a) *American journal of economics*, Cambridge, Mass., 1910 ff. (quarterly) [Bulletin of the American Economic Association]; (I943b) *Quarterly journal of economics*, Cambridge, Mass., 1886 ff., published by Harvard University; (I943c) *Journal of political economy*, Chicago, 1892 ff. (bi-monthly), published by the University of Chicago; (I943d) *Economic journal*, London, 1891 ff. (quarterly) [Royal Economic Society]; (I943e) *Economica*, London, 1921 ff. [London School of Economics and Political Science]; (I943f) *Revue économique internationale*, Paris and Brussels, 1904 ff. (quarterly); (I943g) *Jahrbücher für Nationalökonomie und Statistik*, Jena, 1863 ff. (monthly). Cf. also (B941f.6) *Economic history review*, (B941f.7) *Journal of economic and business history*, and (P956) *Jahrbuch für Gesetzgebung, Verwaltung, und Volkswirtschaft im deutschen Reich.*

Sociology. (I944a) *American journal of sociology*, Chicago, 1895 ff. (bi-monthly), published by the University of Chicago; (I944b) *Social forces*, Chapel Hill, N. C., 1922 ff., bi-monthly), published by the University of North Carolina; (I944c) *Revue de l'institut de sociologie*, Bruxelles, 1910 ff. (quarterly) [Institut de Sociologie, Institut Solvay]. Title varies; (I944d) *Zeitschrift für Socialwissenschaft*, 24 v., Berlin, 1898–1921 (monthly); (I944e) *Vierteljahrschrift für Sozial und Wirtschaftsgeschichte*, Leipzig, 1903 ff. (quarterly) with supplement *Bibliographie der Sozial- und- Wirtschaftgeschichte;* (I944f) *Bibliographie der Sozialwissenschaften*, Dresden, 1905 ff. (monthly) [International Institute of Social Bibliography].

Cf. (A13b) Grandin, A., *Bibliographie générale des sciences juridiques, politiques, économiques et sociales de 1800 à 1925–1926*, 3 v., Paris, 1926.

WEL, HRS

SECTION J

CONTEMPORARY TIMES, 1871-1930

Editor

FRANK MALOY ANDERSON

Professor of History, Dartmouth College

CONTENTS

INTRODUCTION

FOR no section of this *Guide* has the problem of selection been more difficult. There is scarcely a topic in the history of the period since 1871 which is not a live issue in class, partisan, national, or international interests and activities at the present moment. Consequently, though numerous works on the period have been produced by trained historians, often of the first rank, few of them are reasonably free from bias; many are written actually, if not avowedly, to support some cause or defend some person or thesis. Furthermore there has not been the lapse of time necessary to afford perspective and to permit accurate relative evaluation of forces and movements, which, as well as impartiality, are essential to true history.

Effort has been made to select those works which most nearly conform to the canons of correct historical writing, but some have been included because of their extensive circulation and of their effect in molding opinion or events. Occasionally a work is inserted, in spite of its defects, solely because it offers the most convenient statement on a particular topic. Unquestionably the numerous publications on the period, whether they emanate from a nation, a group, or an individual, include many that will have permanent value as historical sources. The selection of most of the works listed in this section, accordingly, has been determined by the test of their probable value to the future historian as source material.

The overwhelming importance of international affairs, diplomatic and military, in this period has rendered it impracticable to include more than a very few works on other topics. This deficiency is, in considerable measure, offset by books listed in § I and to a lesser degree in § B.

It is important to observe that works on certain topics which might be looked for in this section have been assigned to other sections. Books on the Balkan and Near Eastern questions will be found in § T; those on the Middle Eastern and Far Eastern questions in § U; those on the partition of Africa in § W; those on the expansion of Europe in § K; those on special fields of colonial activity in §§ U, V, W, and Z. The several sections devoted to the history of particular nations also include titles which relate to this period.

BIBLIOGRAPHY

For the period since 1871 there is no satisfactory bibliography covering the whole subject, but very useful and convenient bibliographical suggestions may be found in (J501a) Moon, *Syllabus on international relations;* (J501b) Krehbiel, *Nationalism, war, and society;* (B502a) Myers, *Manual of collections of treaties;* and in the works listed in (J101–106 and 441).

J1a *Subject index of the books relating to the European war, 1914–1918, acquired by the British Museum, 1914–1920.* London, 1922. [British Museum.]

b **Prothero, Sir George W.** *Select analytical list of books concerning the great war.* London, 1923.

c **Meyer, Herman H. B.** *Check list of the literature and other material in the Library of Congress on the European war.* Washington, 1918. [Library of Congress.]

d **Bulkley, Mildred E.** *Bibliographical survey of contemporary sources for the economic and social history of the war.* Oxford and N. Y., 1922. [(J571) Shotwell, Economic and social history of the world war.]

e **Lange, Frederick W. T.,** and **Berry, W. T.** *Books on the great war, an annotated bibliography of literature issued during the European conflict.* 4 v. in 2. London and White Plains, N. Y., 1915–16. Rev. ed. of v. 1–2, 1916.

f **Dutcher, George M.** *Selected critical bibliography of publications in English relating to the world war.* Philadelphia, 1918. [McKinley, Collected materials for the study of the war, 105–136.]

a. and *b.* Most useful general bibliographies for the World War. *b.* Contains eight thousand titles topically arranged   *c.* Titles merely arranged alphabetically. *d.* Valuable for its special field. *e.* Largely superseded by other works listed in this item. *f.* Brief list; arranged by topics; concise, critical comments; especially useful for the general reader; generally accessible. SBF

J2a Leblanc, Henri. *Collection Henri Leblanc, destinée à l'état: la grande guerre, iconographie, bibliographie, documents divers.* V. 1-11. Paris, 1916–25.

b Dubois, Jean, and **Appuhn, Charles.** *Catalogue méthodique du fonds allemand de la Bibliothèque [et Musée de la Guerre].* 4 v. Paris, 1921–24. [(J926) Société l'Histoire de la Guerre.]

c *Catalogue du fonds de la guerre: contribution à une bibliographie générale de la guerre de 1914.* 3 v. Paris, 1917–19. [Lyon, Bibliothèque Municipale.]

d Vic, Jean. *La littérature de guerre, manuel méthodique et critique des publications de langue française.* 5 v. Paris, 1918–23.

e Bloch, Camille. *Bibliographie méthodique de l'histoire économique et sociale de la France pendant la guerre.* Paris and New Haven, 1925. [(J571) Shotwell, Economic and social history of the world war.]

a. Classifies not only books and periodical literature, but also pictures, posters, etc. *b.* Admirable list, topically arranged, of works on the World War printed in Germany contained in the Bibliothèque et Musée de la Guerre at Vincennes, France, which with the Leblanc collection included, forms perhaps the most complete collection on the World War now in existence. *c.* Largely superseded by *a.* and *b.* *d.* Topical list of French books, with abundant annotations. *e.* Useful for French publications in its special field. SBF

J3a *Die Kriegsschuldfrage, ein Verzeichnis der Literatur des In- und Auslandes.* Leipzig, 1925. [Börsenverein der deutschen Buchhändler zu Leipzig.]

b *Literatur zur Kriegsschuldfrage.* 1923. 2nd rev. ed., Berlin, 1926. [Zentralstelle für Erforschung der Kriegsursachen.]

a. Best German bibliography, though very far from exhaustive, on the question of responsibility for the World War; contains about fifteen hundred titles arranged alphabetically by authors, with cross references but without annotations. *b.* Brief select list, arranged by countries; without comments. SBF

J4 Lumbroso, Alberto. *Bibliografia ragionata della guerra delle nazioni.* Roma, 1920.

Reviews a thousand books on the World War published prior to March 1916. SBF

J6 Hall, Hubert. *British archives and the sources for the history of the world war.* Oxford and New Haven, 1925. [(J571) Shotwell, Economic and social history of the world war.]

Describes the departments and bureaus of the British government in existence in the war period; gives general account of the British archives and of those of the various British dominions, of archival administration, and of archival research. Review, H. H. E. Craster, *E.H.R.* 41:160, Jan. 1926. GMD

J7 Sass, Johann. *Deutsche Weissbücher zur auswärtigen Politik, 1870–1914.* Berlin und Leipzig, 1928.

Full description of the German official collections of documents relating to international affairs from 1870 to 1914, and brief description of the similar collections of Austria, England, France, Italy and Russia. SBF

J8 Gooch, George P. *Revelations of European diplomacy.* London, 1927. *Supplements,* 1928–29.

A delightful *causerie* and not a formal bibliography. Selects the significant contributions of all the recent works on the World War and its causes. Notable for the author's breadth and fairness of mind. The *Supplements* bring the survey closely up to date. Review, B. E. Schmitt, *A.H.R.* 32:879, July 1927.   SBF

Library collections.—The larger university and public libraries usually have good collections on the World War, if not on this period as a whole; among the more important are those at Stanford University (Hoover collection), Harvard University, Clark University, Yale University, Union Theological Seminary (religious aspects of the period), Princeton University, University of Illinois, and in Library of Congress, and New York Public Library. There are some excellent private collections which are eventually destined to public libraries, and some libraries which have made considerable collections for the period have not yet completed their arrangement or published accounts of them.   AHS

ENCYCLOPEDIAS AND WORKS OF REFERENCE

Special attention should be called not only to the various year books listed in § B, but also to (B22b) *Encyclopaedia britannica,* of which the eleven supplementary volumes constituting the tenth edition and, even more, the three supplementary volumes of 1922 constituting the twelfth edition (Review, *Spectator,* 129:876, Dec. 9, 1922) and the three additional volumes of 1926 constituting the thirteenth edition (Review, C. K. Ogden, *Saturday Review of Literature,* 3:229, Oct. 23, 1926) are, in the main, excellently done and extremely useful for the portions of this period which they cover.

GEOGRAPHY

J41a Johnson, Douglas W. *Topography and strategy in the war.* N. Y., 1917.

b —— *Battlefields of the world war, western and southern fronts, a study in military geography.* Oxford and N. Y., 1921. [American Geographical Society, Research series.]

c Villate, Robert. *Les conditions géographiques de la guerre: étude de géographie militaire sur le front français de 1914 à 1918.* Paris, 1925. [Bibliothèque géographique.]   (Bibliography.)

Explain for the general reader better than anything else how the military operations of the World War in Europe were influenced by the character of the ground over which they were fought. *a.* Covers all European fields in very concise form. Review, R. H. Whitbeck, *A.H.R.* 23:702, Apr. 1918. *b.* Treats, in more detail, those of France, Belgium, Italy, and the Balkan peninsula except Rumania. On geography the author writes with authority; information on military matters is drawn chiefly from the better secondary accounts. Readable style; adequate maps and plans. Review, O. L. Spaulding, Jr., *A.H.R.* 27:563, Apr. 1922. *c.* Thorough analysis, illustrated by maps, sketches, and concrete examples, of the influence of geological, meteorological, and geographical factors, from Switzerland to the English Channel, upon the development of forms of warfare.   FMA

J42 Bowman, Isaiah. *New world: problems in political geography.* Yonkers-on-Hudson, N. Y., 1921. 4th ed., 1928. (Bibliography.)

Most valuable book in its field. The author is the director of the American Geographical Society and was the leading geographical expert with the American peace commission. Describes, with a wealth of information and scientific exactitude, but in simple and interesting style adapted to all readers, the important factors which constitute or seriously influence the political geography of the world as it has emerged from the war. Special attention is given to the British Empire, France, central and eastern Europe, and the Near East. Good printing, 65 well chosen illustrations, and 215 admirably designed maps add to its value. Review, R. H. Lord, *A.H.R.* 27:568, Apr. 1922.   FMA

The best modern atlases with large scale maps, embodying a wealth of detail, are listed in (B45), and those of more convenient type in (B46). By consulting successive editions of these works, recent changes in political boundaries may be traced. These changes are also usually shown with good small maps in the annual volumes of (B28*b*) *Statesman's year-book.*

ETHNOGRAPHY

For the relations of race to history and historical geography in recent times, reference may be made to (J42) Bowman, *New world;* (A47*a*) Dominian, *Frontiers of language and nationality in Europe;* (A47*b*) Newbigin, *Geographical aspects of Balkan problems,* and to the items listed as (J441).

SOURCE BOOKS, COLLECTIONS OF SOURCES, ARCHIVE PUBLICATIONS

J61 Clark, John Maurice; Hamilton, Walton H.; and Moulton, Harold G., ed. *Readings in the economics of war.* Chicago, 1918. [Materials for the study of economics.]

Excellent and illuminating compilation of about three hundred documents arranged in sixteen sections illustrating the economic and financial aspects of the causes and conduct of war and of the ensuing reconstruction. Review, E. L. Bogart, *A.H.R.* 24:477, Apr. 1919.   GMD

J62 Fauchille, Paul, ed. *La guerre de 1914: recueil de documents intéressant le droit international.* 2 v. Paris, 1916–17.

Useful collection illustrating the antecedents of the war and its first two years. Review, E. C. Stowell, *A H.R.* 23:397, Jan. 1918.   GMD

J71a Ministère des Affaires Étrangères. *L'alliance franco-russe: origines de l'alliance, 1890–1893; convention militaire, 1892–1899; et convention navale, 1912.* Paris, 1918.

 b ——— *Les accords franco-italiens de 1900–1902.* Paris, 1920.

 c ——— *Affaires du Maroc, 1901–1912.* 5 v. Paris, 1905–12.

 d ——— *Les affaires balkaniques, 1912–1914.* 3 v. Paris, 1922.

 e ——— *Documents diplomatiques français, 1871–1914.* Paris, 1929 ff.

Important Yellow books (Livres jaunes) containing diplomatic correspondence, officially published by the French ministry of foreign affairs. *a.* Gives, with satisfactory completeness, the genesis of the Dual Alliance and, very briefly, the military and naval conventions which followed it. *b.* Shows how France gave a free hand to Italy in return for a free hand in Morocco; its substance is well given in English in (J202) Coolidge's edition of Pribram. *c.* Five large volumes of detailed material concerning the extension of French control over Morocco and the diplomatic conflicts with Germany caused thereby. *d.* Incomplete collection of documents intended to show the pacific tendency of French policy during the Balkan Wars. *e.* Monumental publication of French diplomatic documents on the origins of the World War, similar to (J72a) German and (J75) British collections. Volumes are to appear simultaneously in each of the three series into which the collection is divided: first series, 1871–1900; second series, 1900–1911; third series, 1911–1914. Already (1930) the first volumes of each of the series have appeared; review of the first volume of the third series, B. E. Schmitt, *Jour. of Modern Hist.* 1:636, Dec. 1929.   SBF

J72a Lepsius, Johannes; Mendelssohn Bartholdy, Albrecht; and Thimme, Friedrich, ed. *Die grosse Politik der europäischen Kabinette, 1871–1914: Sammlung der diplomatischen Akten des Auswärtigen Amtes.* 40 v. Berlin, 1922–26.

b Schwertfeger, Bernhard. *Die diplomatischen Akten des Auswärtigen Amtes, 1871–1914: ein Wegweiser durch das grosse Aktenwerk der deutschen Regierung.* Berlin, 1923–24. New ed., 10 v., 1927.

a. Monumental publication of the most secret and important papers from the archives of the German foreign office. Contains the despatches received from German diplomatic representatives abroad, the marginal notes made thereon by Bismarck and his successors and by the German emperors, memoranda drawn up in the foreign office, and the instructions sent to German ambassadors and ministers. The documents appear to be selected with honesty and impartiality, with a view to giving an exact, detailed, and reliable record of German foreign policy. They reveal the inner springs of Germany's action, and in many cases place Germany in a more favorable light than has hitherto been generally believed. Indispensable for a knowledge of the underlying causes of the World War. Covers the documents down to July, 1914, where (J82a) Kautsky documents begin. Review, S B. Fay, *A.H.R.* 28:543, Apr. 1923; 30:136, Oct. 1924; 31:130, 520, Oct. 1925, April. 1926; 33:126, Oct. 1927; E. Bourgeois, *Rev. des Sciences Politiques,* Jan., Mar. 1924; F. Thimme and prominent Germans, *Archiv für Politik und Geschichte,* Jan. 1923; *Sonderheft,* 1–118, Jan. 1924; June, July 1924; Jan., Feb. 1925; M. Lhéritier, *Rev. Hist. de la Guerre Mondiale,* 4:97, Apr. 1926. *b.* Excellent summary, in narrative and explanatory condensed form, of the most important documents in *a.* Review, S. B. Fay, *A.H.R.* 30:136, Oct. 1924; 30:393, Jan. 1925.   SBF

J73 Schwertfeger, Bernhard, ed. *Zur europäischen Politik 1897–1914: unveröffentlichte Dokumente in amtlichem Auftrage.* 5 v. Berlin, 1919. 2nd ed., with title *Amtliche Aktenstücke zur Geschichte der europäischen Politik, 1885–1914 (Die Belgischen Dokumente zur Vorgeschichte des Weltkrieges): unveröffentlichte diplomatische Urkunden aus den belgischen Staatsarchiven, im Auftrage des Auswärtigen Amtes.* 5 v and 3 supplementary v. Berlin, 1924. [2nd ed.: 1, *Revanche-idee und Panslawismus, 1885–1893,* ed. by W. Köhler; 2, *Der Zweibund und der englisch-deutsche Gegensatz, 1897–1904,* ed. by W. Köhler; 3, *Die Politik König Eduards VII und die Marokkokrise, 1905–1907,* ed. by B. Schwertfeger; 4, *Die Balkanprobleme, die bosnische Krise, Albanien, der Panthersprung nach Agadir, 1908–1911,* ed. by A. Doren; 5, *Kriegstreibereien und Kriegsrüstungen, bis zur Schwelle des Weltkrieges, 1912–1914,* ed. by A. Doren; supplement: 1,

Belgische Aktenstücke, 1905–1914, Berichte der belgischen Vertreter in Berlin, London, und Paris an den Minister des Äusseren in Brüssel; 2, *Der Fehlspruch von Versailles Deutschlands Vorkriegspolitik, dargestellt auf Grund der belgischen Gesandschaftsberichte,* ed. by B. Schwertfeger; 3, *Der geistige Kampf um die Verletzung der belgischen Neutralität,* ed. by B. Schwertfeger]

Collection of documents published by the Germans from the Belgian archives after the German occupation of Belgium in 1914. They are of some historical value as showing the prevalent political gossip reported by the Belgian diplomatic representatives abroad to their home government, but must be used with caution, partly because they were selected by the Germans to prove the innocence of their own policies, and partly because the Belgian representatives were often not initiated into the inner secrets of the courts to which they were accredited and merely reported current but inaccurate diplomatic gossip. The supplementary volumes in the second edition reprint three small collateral collections originally published in 1915 (English tr., *Reports of the Belgian representatives in Berlin, London, and Paris to the minister of foreign affairs in Brussels, 1905–1914,* N. Y., 1915), 1919, and 1921.   SBF

J74a *Materialy po istorii Franko-Russikh otnoshenii za 1910–1914.* Moskva, 1922. [Materials for the history of Franco-Russian relations, 1910–1914.]

b **Marchand, René,** ed. *Un livre noir, diplomatie d'avant guerre d'après les documents des archives russes, novembre 1910–juillet 1914.* 2 v. Paris, 1922–23.

c **Stieve, Friedrich,** ed. and tr. *Der diplomatische Schriftwechsel Iswolskis, 1911–1914, aus den Geheimakten der russischen Staatsarchive.* 4 v. Berlin, 1924.

d —— *Iswolski im Weltkriege: der diplomatische Schriftwechsel Iswolskis aus den Jahren 1914–1917, neue Dokumente aus den Geheimakten der russischen Staatsarchive.* Berlin, 1925.

e —— *Isvolsky and the world war.* N. Y., 1926. Tr. by E. W. Dickes from *Iswolski und der Weltkrieg, auf Grund der neuen Dokumenten-Veröffentlichung des deutschen Auswärtigen Amtes,* 1924, 2d ed., Berlin, 1925.

f **Schreiner, George A.,** ed. *Entente diplomacy and the world: matrix of the history of Europe, 1909–14 . . . translated from the original texts in his possession by B. de Siebert . . . edited, arranged, and annotated.* N. Y. and London, 1921. Tr. from *Diplomatische Aktenstücke zur Geschichte der Ententepolitik der Vorkriegsjahre,* ed. by B. de Siebert, Berlin, 1921.

g **Adamov, E. A.** *Konstantinopol i Prolivy.* 2 v. Moskva, 1925–26. [Constantinople and the Straits.]

These collections of documents from the Russian archives, with the exception of *d* and *g,* mainly comprise the secret correspondence between the Russian minister of foreign affairs, Sazonov, and the Russian ambassadors in Paris and London, Izvolski and Benckendorff, during the years 1911 to 1914. As they consist of selected letters and telegrams, instead of forming a complete file, and as they were probably published partly with the aim of discrediting the old tsarist government and its capitalist allies, they must be used with caution. They are the mine from which many writers have quarried evidence to support the accusation that Izvolski and Poincaré must bear a large responsibility for the World War.   *a.* Original and most complete collection, mainly in Russian;

contains some documents not to be found in the other collections or anywhere else in print. *b.* French translation of a considerable part of the Izvolski correspondence in *a.* Review, S. A. Korff, *A.H R. 27* :796, July 1922; 28 :747, July 1923. *c.* Much more complete German translation of the Izvolski correspondence; contains some five hundred more documents than *b;* also includes a considerable number of despatches by or concerning Izvolski drawn directly from the Russian archives and not to be found in *a,* as well as German translation of the evidences of Russian corruption of the French press, published in *L'Humanité,* Paris, in January, 1924. *d.* Continuation of the Izvolski correspondence after the outbreak of the War; very valuable for the diplomatic history of the Allied Powers during the first two years of the War. *e.* Summarizes effectively the material in *c.* with the purpose of showing the responsibility of Izvolski and Poincaré. Review, *Times (London) Lit. Suppl.,* 87, Feb. 2, 1926. *f.* English translation, marred by partisan foot-notes and typographical emphasis, of selections from the correspondence of Sazonov and Benckendorff; skilfully arranged and of great value. These documents were filched from the Russian embassy in London by one of its secretaries, Siebert, and conveyed to the Germans. They throw very valuable light on the imperialist aims of the Entente Powers, especially of Russia and England, in China, Persia, Turkey, and the Balkans. Review, C. Seymour, *A.H.R. 28* :122, Oct. 1922. *g.* Admirable Russian account of Russia's historic mission to control the Bosphorus and the Dardanelles in the dozen years prior to the Bolshevist Revolution of 1917; two hundred and fifty pages of introduction are followed by six hundred and fifty pages of documents, mostly hitherto unpublished; valuable supplement to *d.*   SBF

J75 Gooch, George P., and **Temperley, Harold W. V.,** ed. *British official documents on the origins of the war, 1898–1914.* v. 1–6, 11. London, 1926 ff.

Planned as British counterpart of (J72a) *Die Grosse Politik,* but more restricted in scope; will be composed chiefly of unpublished correspondence. Every evidence points to the most complete frankness and to the excellence and reliability of the editorial work. V. 11. Issued first; edited by J. W. Headlam-Morley; covers June 28-August 4, 1914; practically a revised and greatly enlarged edition of the original British Blue Book later reprinted in (J81a) *Collected diplomatic documents;* includes every relevant document or annotation in the hands of the Foreign office in 1914 and also materials not then available. Enables the student to keep his finger on the pulse of the British government throughout the crisis. Volumes 1–5 cover British foreign relations from 1898 to 1909. Reviews, S. B. Fay, v. 11, *A.H.R. 32* :600, Apr. 1927; v. 1, 2, 33 :648, Apr. 1928; v. 4, 34 :340, Apr. 1929.   SBF

J76 Bittner, Ludwig; Pribram, Alfred F.; Srbik, Heinrich; and **Uebersberger, Hans,** ed. *Oesterreich-Ungarns Aussenpolitik von der Bosnischen Krise 1908 bis zum Kriegsausbruch 1914.* 9 v. Wien und Leipzig, 1930.

A very full collection of diplomatic documents on the origins of the World War from 1908 to 1914.   SBF

J77 Boghitschewitsch (Bogićević), M. *Auswärtige Politik Serbiens, 1903–1914.* 3 v. Berlin, 1928–31.

Unofficial collection of secret diplomatic documents from the Russian, Montenegrin, and other archives relating to Serbian foreign policy and throwing light on the origins of the World War.

SBF

J81a *Collected diplomatic documents relating to the outbreak of the European war.* London, 1915. [Parliament, Papers by command, cd. 7860.]

b Scott, James B., ed. *Diplomatic documents relating to the outbreak of the European war.* 2 v. N. Y. and Oxford, 1916. [Carnegie Endowment for International Peace.]

c Mach, Edmund von, ed. *Official diplomatic documents relating to the outbreak of the European war, with photographic reproductions of official editions of the documents, . . . introduction, daily summaries, cross-references, and foot-notes.* N. Y., 1916.

In these convenient collections are gathered the British Blue book and translations of the French Yellow book, the German White book, the Austrian Red book, the Russian Orange book, the Serbian Blue book, and the Belgian Gray book, in the very unsatisfactory and truncated form in which they were published in 1914 and 1915 for propagandist purposes soon after the outbreak of the war. They contain mainly documents relating to the period between the murder of the Austrian archduke and the beginning of hostilities and were thus intended to explain the immediate causes of the war. The German, Austrian, Russian, and English governments have subsequently issued the much more complete editions (J74a, c, and f, J75, and J76). a. Convenient and inexpensive. b. More complete and pretentious. Review, E. R. Turner, *A.H.R. 22*:657, Apr. 1917. c. Very useful because it contains facsimile reprints of the documents in the original language, as well as English translations which are classified chronologically instead of by countries. To be found in some libraries, but difficult to obtain at present because withdrawn from publication. Review, E. R. Turner, *A.H.R. 22*:658, Apr. 1917.

SBF

J82a Kautsky, Karl; Montgelas, Maximilian, Graf von; and **Schücking, Walther,** ed. *Outbreak of the world war: German documents.* N. Y. and Oxford, 1924. Tr. by Carnegie Endowment for International Peace, Division of International Law, from *Die deutschen Dokumente zum Kriegsausbruch, vollständige Sammlung der amtlichen Aktenstücke mit einigen Ergänzungen im Auftrage des Auswärtigen Amtes,* 4 v., Charlottenburg, 1919.

b Kautsky, Karl. *Guilt of William Hohenzollern.* London, 1920. Tr. from *Wie der Weltkrieg entstand,* Berlin, 1919.

c Staatsamt für Äusseres. *Austrian red book, official files pertaining to prewar history.* 3 v. London, 1920. Tr. from *Diplomatische Aktenstücke zur Vorgeschichte des Krieges 1914, Ergänzungen und Nachträge zum österreichisch-ungarischen Rotbuch,* 3 v., Wien, 1919.

d Gooss, Roderich. *Das Wiener Kabinett und die Entstehung des Weltkrieges, mit Ermächtigung des Leiters des deutschösterreichischen Staatsamtes für Äusseres auf Grund aktenmässiger Forschung.* 1919. 2nd ed, Wien, 1919.

e Romberg, Konrad Gisbert W., Freiherr von, ed. *Falsifications of the Russian orange book: actual exchange of telegrams between Paris and St. Petersburg at the outbreak of the war.* London and N. Y., 1923. Tr.

from *Die Fälschungen des russischen Orangebuches: der wahre Tele-grammwechsel, Paris-Petersburg, bei Kriegsausbruch,* Berlin, 1922.

f *Das russische Orangebuch von 1914 ergänzt durch inzwischen bekannt-gewordenen neuen Dokumente.* Berlin, 1925. [Zentralstelle für Erfor-schung der Kriegsursachen.]

g Schilling, Baron M. F. *How the war began in 1914, being the diary of the Russian foreign office from the 3rd to the 20th (old style) of July, 1914.* London, 1925. Tr. by W. C. Bridge from Russian original in *Krasnyi Arkhiv,* v. 4, 1923.

h Stieve, Friedrich, ed. *Das russische Orangebuch über den Kriegsaus-bruch mit der Türkei.* Berlin, 1926.

i Auswärtiges Amt. *German white book concerning the responsibility of the authors of the war.* N. Y. and Oxford, 1924. Tr. by Carnegie En-dowment for International Peace, Division of International Law, from *Deutschland schuldig? Deutsches Weissbuch über die Verantwortlichkeit der Urheber des Krieges,* Berlin, 1919.

j Wegerer, Alfred von, ed. *Das französische Gelbbuch von 1914.* Berlin, 1926.

a. Full and frank publication, edited with admirable precision, of all impor-tant documents which passed in and out of the German foreign office in July, 1914. Review, H. Delbrück, *Preussische Jahrbücher,* 179:71, Jan. 1920. *c.* Similar publication, edited by Dr. Gooss, from the Austrian foreign office; done with somewhat less completeness and precision. *b.* Summary and interpretation of *a,* with a strong socialist bias, seeking to place the responsibility for the war upon the German emperor and his advisers. *d.* Analogous summary and in-terpretation of *c.;* tends to place the responsibility upon Austria; also contains some valuable information not to be found in *c.* For review of *a, b, c, d,* and *i,* cf. (J261). *e.* and *f.* Contain a considerable number of secret telegrams, strik-ingly indicated in *e* by red type, which were omitted from the original Russian Orange book of 1914, and which show to what a large extent the Russian government of 1914 sought to conceal the truth as to its own share of respon-sibility for the war. Review of *e.,* H. W. C. Davis, *E.H.R.* 39:236, Apr. 1924. *g.* Vivid and very valuable diary of conversations, telegrams, and events in the Russian foreign office during the diplomatic crisis preceding the war, written by Sazonov's secretary. The English translation includes an unconvincing *apologia* by Sazonov himself, and an explanatory introduction by the author of the diary. *h.* Russian documents on the rupture with Turkey in 1914. *i.* Important new documents and arguments presented by the German government to the Paris peace conference in protest against the Treaty of Versailles. *j.* German translation of French Yellow book issued in December 1914 with twenty-six new documents and numerous corrections to others; useful until the French government shall publish a complete and adequate edition.   SBF

J83 Cumming, Caroline K., and **Pettit, Walter W.,** ed. *Russian-American relations, March, 1917–March, 1920: documents and papers.* N. Y., 1920. [League of Free Nations Association.]

Incomplete selection, chiefly of Russian documents; may be used with (S502*d*) Dennis, *Foreign policies of soviet Russia.* Review, *A.H.R.* 26:371, Jan. 1921.

J84a *Official German documents relating to the world war.* 2 v. N. Y. and Oxford, 1923. Tr. by Carnegie Endowment for International Peace, Division of International Law, from *Stenographische Berichte über die öffentlichen Verhandlungen des Untersuchungsausschusses der verfassung-gebenden deutschen Nationalversammlung, 15. Ausschuss,* 2 v., Berlin, 1920.

b *Preliminary history of the armistice: official documents published by the German national chancellery by order of the ministry of state.* N. Y. and Oxford, 1924. Tr. by Carnegie Endowment for International Peace, Division of International Law, from *Amtliche Urkunden zur Vorgeschichte der Waffenstillstandes, 1918, auf Grund der Akten der Reichskanzlei, des Auswärtigen Amtes, und des Reichsarchivs, herausgegeben vom Auswärtigen Amt und vom Reichsministerium des Innern,* 1922; 2nd rev. ed., with 41 new documents, Berlin, 1924.

a. Stenographic reports of the Reichstag investigating committee as to the responsibility of the men who involved Germany in the outbreak of the war and who directed its later conduct; especially valuable on the submarine warfare, with Bernstorff's despatches concerning the attitude of America. Review, C. Seymour, *A.H.R.* 29:374, Jan. 1924. *b.* Documents, from August to November, 1918, showing the confusion of mind among the German authorities just before the final military collapse; tends to show that the German army was not defeated by a 'stab in the back' from the socialists at home but by the military superiority of the Allies at the front.   SBF

J91 Martin, Lawrence, ed. *Treaties of peace, 1919–1923: maps compiled especially for this edition and a summary of the legal basis of the new boundaries.* 2 v. N. Y., 1924. [Carnegie Endowment for International Peace.]

Convenient collection of the peace treaties, from Versailles, 1919, to Lausanne, 1923, with very useful notes and maps.   GMD

SHORTER GENERAL HISTORIES

J101 Gooch, George P. *History of modern Europe,. 1878–1919.* London and N. Y., 1923.

Continues (I401a) Fyffe, *Modern Europe;* devoted exclusively to international affairs; best book on the period because of extensive research and judicial spirit. Only work listed in this subsection which makes thorough use of documentary material published in the first four years after the close of the World War. Interpretation is left chiefly to the reader, but the point of view of the author, that of a moderate opponent of British foreign policy from 1904 to 1914, does determine the emphasis. The literary style, while much above the average, is inferior to that of Fyffe and of the author's other books. Review, B. E. Schmitt, *A.H.R.* 29:136, Oct. 1923. Cf. also (J261) Fay, *Origins of the World War.*   FMA

J102 Debidour, Antonin. *Histoire diplomatique de l'Europe depuis le congrès de Berlin jusqu'à nos jours.* 2 v. Paris, 1916–17. [I, *La paix armée, 1878–1904;* 2, *Vers la grande guerre, 1904–1916.*] [Bibliothèque d'histoire contemporaine.] (Bibliographies containing chiefly French materials.)

Continuation of (I501b) standard manual; concise, well proportioned, clearly written. While rigidly confined to relations between European states, it is, within its field, remarkably comprehensive, though Anglo-German relations are somewhat neglected. Follows a strictly chronological method; pays little attention to personalities or economic conditions; assumes in the reader considerable knowledge of the general history of the period. The ardent French patriotism of the author is apparent, but he is always candid, usually restrained as to Germany, and frequently expresses strongly adverse judgments on England and Italy. V. 1. Better than v. 2. No references or maps; few footnotes. Review, C. Seymour, *A.H.R.* 22:655, Apr. 1917; 22:862, July 1917. FMA

J103 Egelhaaf, Gottlob. *Geschichte der neuesten Zeit, vom Frankfurter Frieden bis zur Gegenwart.* 1908. 9th rev. ed., continued to 1923, 2 v., Stuttgart, 1924.

Generally regarded as the best manual on the period in German; sane and reliable, though by no means inspiring; accords German history far more extensive treatment than that of other nations. Review, G. Roloff, *Hist. Zeit.* 102:147, 1908. WELr

J104a Holt, Lucius H., and Chilton, Alexander W. *History of Europe from 1862 to 1914, from the accession of Bismarck to the outbreak of the great war.* N. Y., 1917. (Bibliography.)

b Hazen, Charles D. *Fifty years of Europe, 1870–1919.* N. Y., 1919.

c Turner, Edward R. *Europe since 1870.* Garden City, N. Y., 1921. Rev. ed., 1927. (Bibliographies.)

d Mowat, R. B. *History of European diplomacy, 1914–1925.* N. Y., 1927.

e Slosson, Preston W. *Twentieth century Europe.* N. Y., 1927.

Text-books for college use. *a.* Written for war-time use; attention is concentrated chiefly on international relations; accounts of military operations by Chilton are especially good. Review, F. M. Anderson, *A.H.R.* 23:854, July 1918. *b.* About three-quarters is substantially identical with the corresponding portions of the author's *Modern European history,* which was a condensation from his (I401d) *Europe since 1815.* The other fourth is an admirable account of the World War in about twenty-five thousand words. Attention is concentrated on political and military affairs. Probably the best book of its size for the general reader. Review, F. M. Anderson, *A.H.R.* 25:319, Jan. 1920. *c.* Based on the author's (I104b) *Europe, 1789–1920,* but has numerous additions, and extends through the peace settlement. May also be commended to the general reader. Review, E. E. Sperry, *A.H.R.* 27:311, Jan. 1922; 32:921, July 1927. FMA

d. Accurate, skilfully proportioned, and objective outline. Review, C. Seymour, *A.H.R.* 33:134, Oct. 1927. *e.* Logical and attractively written survey. Review, W. E. Lingelbach, *A.H.R.* 33:117, Oct. 1927. SBF

J105a Seymour, Charles. *Diplomatic background of the war, 1870–1914.* New Haven, 1916. Reprint, 1923. (Useful bibliography.)

b Rose, John Holland. *Development of the European nations, 1870–1900* 1905. 6th rev. ed., *1870–1921,* 2 v. in 1, London and N. Y., 1922.

c Wallace, William K. *Thirty years of modern history.* London and N. Y., 1926.

a. Excellent brief narrative of diplomatic history; not overburdened with details; written in clear and interesting style. Review, E. R. Turner, *A.H.R.* 21:808, July 1916. *b.* Series of studies rather than a history of the period;

addressed to the general reader. Subsequent editions repeat the original unchanged, but with additional and usually inferior chapters on later events. Review, V. Coffin, *A.H.R.* 11:895, July 1906. *c.* Interpretation of events for the period approximately 1895–1925; includes discussions of such subjects as bolshevism, fascism, and the League of Nations. Review, *Times (London) Literary Supplement,* 518, Aug. 5, 1926. FMA

J106 Davis, William S., and others. *Roots of the war, a non-technical history of Europe, 1870–1914, A.D.* N. Y., 1918. (Bibliography.)

Surveys, in popular style and with little pretence to special originality, the history of the European states, 1870–1914, their diplomatic and colonial rivalries, and the causes of the World War. Information brought to light since the war shows that the views concerning responsibility for the war must be somewhat modified. The chapters by Professors Anderson and Tyler are, in general, more carefully done and more judicial in tone. Review, C.' Seymour, *A.H.R.* 24:94, Oct. 1918. CP, GMD

J107 Fullerton, William M. *Problems of power: a study of international politics from Sadowa to Kirk-Kilissé.* 1913. 2nd rev. ed., London and N. Y., 1914.

By an American who was formerly correspondent of the London *Times* at Paris. The author, writing on the eve of the war, was keenly aware of the international tension existing between France and Germany and devoted a great deal of his space to warning the English, French, and Americans of the danger of cherishing pacifist dreams of a world in which 'no international treaty, no diplomatic instrument or convention, is worth the paper on which it is written' (p. 167). The point of view is imperialistic and 'realistic,' rather contemptuous of parliamentary democracy and international idealism. The style is vivid and picturesque. Review, *Nation* (N. Y.), 97:337, Oct. 9, 1913. PWS

J108 Schmitt, Bernadotte E. *England and Germany, 1740–1914.* Princeton and London, 1916.

Devoted mainly to the development of antagonism between England and Germany from about 1897 to 1914, of which it is the best account for the general reader. Includes, as involved in the main theme, valuable accounts of the Morocco crises, the Bagdad railway, and German influence in Balkan affairs. Nearly all the evidence was gathered and the book partly written before the war began. Fair and candid; well written; based on extensive research. Review, S. B. Fay, *A.H.R.* 22:146, Oct. 1916. FMA

J109a Pinon, René. *France et Allemagne, 1870–1913.* 1913. Rev. ed., Paris, 1913.

  b Mévil, André. *De la paix de Francfort à la conférence d'Algésiras.* Paris, 1909.

a. Interesting and valuable short sketch, in support of the thesis that French policy until 1898 was on proper lines, involving neither close friendship nor a hostile attitude; but that afterwards France, to its own detriment, allowed itself to be drawn into the growing Anglo-German antagonism. The interpretation of events is rather favorable to Germany and M. Hanotaux, and somewhat hostile to England and M. Delcassé. *b.* Study of Franco-German relations, chiefly from about 1895 to 1906, by a well-informed journalist. Ably and energetically maintains the opposite thesis to that of *a*. The interpretation of the fall of Delcassé is noteworthy.   FMA

J110 Bullard, Arthur. *Diplomacy of the world war.* N. Y., 1916. (Bibliography.)

Widely circulated, especially in the United States, during the War; now antiquated. Includes a brief but interesting account of the events of European history since 1878· which explain the international friendships, enmities, and alignments behind the World War; a prophecy as to the outcome of the war; and a· rambling discussion of the relation of the United States to the conflict. Review, A. S. Hershey, *A.H.R.* 22:158, Oct. 1916.   OPC, GMD

LONGER GENERAL HISTORIES

J121 Zurlinden, Samuel. *Der Weltkrieg: vorläufige Orientierung von einem schweizerischen Standpunkt aus.* V. 1–2. Zürich, 1917–18. [1, *Die Wurzeln des Weltkrieges;* 2–3, *Die historische Grundlage des Weltkrieges;* 4, *Der Kriegsausbruch, Die Zentralmächte;* 5, *Die Staaten der Entente, Die Neutralen;* 6, *Die Schweiz im Weltkrieg, Der Krieg, Vorläufiges Endresultat.*]

An attempt on a large scale to reveal the setting of the World War rather than to recount the history of the war itself. Not a narrative to be read but a treasury of material to be consulted. V. 1. Primarily a discussion of ideas and principles, such as militarism and imperialism. V. 2. Surveys international relations from 1815 to 1908. Review, D. J. Hill, *A.H.R.* 23:646, Apr. 1918; 25:277, Jan. 1920.   GMD

ALLIANCES AND ENTENTES, 1871–1914

J201 Coolidge, Archibald C. *Origins of the triple alliance.* 1917. 2nd ed., N. Y., 1926. [University of Virginia, Barbour-Page lectures.]

Clear and closely studied survey of the conditions and events prior to 1882 that led to the formation of the Triple Alliance. Admirable on the basis of materials available in 1916; text of second edition is unchanged but notes at the end call attention to recent new material. Review, *A.H.R.* 23:430, Jan. 1918.
                                                                                       KRG

J202a Pribram, Alfred F. *Secret treaties of Austria-Hungary, 1879–1914.* 2 v. Cambridge, Mass., 1920–21. Ed. and tr. by A. C. Coolidge and others from *Die politischen Geheimverträge Oesterreich-Ungarns, 1879–1914, nach den Akten des Wiener Staatsarchivs,* v. 1, Wien, 1920.

   b Singer, Arthur. *Geschichte des Dreibundes.* Leipzig, 1914. French tr. by L. Suret, *Histoire de la triple alliance,* Paris, 1915.

   c Langer, William L. *Franco-Russian Alliance, 1890–1914.* Cambridge, 1929. [Harvard historical studies.] ·

   d Michon, Georges. *Franco-Russian Alliance, 1891–1917.* N. Y., 1929. Tr. from *L'alliance franco-russe, 1891–1917,* Paris, 1927.

a. One of the most important books on European diplomacy, 1870–1914. Most of the material came from the archives of Austria-Hungary and was previously unpublished. V. 1. Contains full and authentic texts of the secret treaties of Austria-Hungary and Bismarck's 'Reinsurance treaty' with Russia. V. 2.

Includes seven studies upon the negotiation of the Triple Alliance treaties, 1882–1912, and the most significant documents bearing on Austro-Russian relations, 1873–1877, the Franco-Russian alliance, and the Franco-Italian agreements of 1900–1902. The studies are thorough and dispassionate, but with an anti-Italian bias. They are for specialists. Review, L. Tryon, *Amer. Jour. Int. Law,* 16:741, Oct. 1922; v. 1, C. Seymour, *A.H.R.* 25:493, Apr. 1920.   *b.* Largely superseded by *a.*

FMA

c. Valuable analysis of the general diplomatic situation at the close of the nineteenth century which resulted in the Franco-Russian Alliance. Wisely draws attention to the influence of sea-power and Mediterranean questions upon diplomatic arrangements. *d.* Severely critical of the policy of the French government. Review, R. Turner, *A.H.R.* 33:874, July 1928.

SBF

J203 Friedjung, Heinrich. *Das Zeitalter des Imperialismus, 1884–1914.* **3 v.** Berlin, 1919–22.

At present this work by an Austrian historian is perhaps the most pretentious history of international relations in the period covered. Distinguished by breadth of view and by skilful interweaving of domestic and foreign policies; distinctly Anglophobe and somewhat anti-Magyar in tone. V. 1. Written before the recent deluge of source material; consequently out of date in many respects. V. 2–3. Revised by (cf. J202a) Professor A. F. Pribram; capital in importance; reflect the editor's wide knowledge of unpublished documents in the Vienna archives.

WLLr

J204a Lémonon, Ernest. *L'Europe et la politique britannique, 1882–1911.* 1910. 2nd rev. ed., Paris, 1912. [Bibliothèque d'histoire contemporaine.]

b Lanessan, Jean L. de. *Histoire de l'entente cordiale franco-anglaise: les relations de la France et de l'Angleterre depuis le XVIᵉ siècle jusqu'à nos jours.* Paris, 1916. [Bibliothèque d'histoire contemporaine.]

a. At the date of its publication, an interesting and important collection of material, but many of its conclusions have been rendered inadequate and obsolete by the large amount of new information recently divulged. Review, F. Salomon, *Hist. Zeit.* 106:150, 1911.   *b.* Emphasizes those influences and events which drew the two countries together; under the influence of the World War sympathies, contrary tendencies are rather freely and unhistorically discounted. Review, C. D. Hazen, *A.H.R.* 22:854, July 1917.

LBP

J205a Albin, Pierre. *La paix armée: l'Allemagne et la France en Europe, 1885–1894.* Paris, 1913. [Bibliothèque d'histoire contemporaine.]

b —— *La querelle franco-allemande: le 'coup' d'Agadir, origines et développement de la crise de 1911.* Paris, 1912. [Bibliothèque d'histoire contemporaine.]

c —— *La guerre allemande: d'Agadir à Sarajevo, 1911–1914.* Paris, 1915. [Bibliothèque d'histoire contemporaine.]

Written with careful attention to the distinction between evidence and opinion. *a.* and *b.* Originally designed to form, with a third volume which was in preparation, a series dealing in popular but sound and scholarly fashion with Franco-German relations from 1885 to 1911. Written before the war; favorable to France, but not marked by any pronounced hostility to Germany. *a.* Con-

tains valuable account of the Franco-Russian alliance. Review, *Revue Critique,*
n.s., 77:326, Apr. 25, 1914. *b.* One of the best brief books on the Morocco
crisis of 1911. Cf. (J206c) Tardieu, *Mystère d'Agadir.* *c.* Continuation of *b;*
describes the antecedents of the World War; written in the first year of the war.
Review, *Revue Critique,* n.s., 80:232, Oct. 9, 1915.   FMA

J206a Tardieu, André. *France and the alliances: the struggle for the balance
of power.* N. Y., 1908. French ed., *La France et les alliances, la lutte
pour l'équilibre,* 1909, 3rd rev. ed., Paris, 1910.

   b ———— *La conférence d'Algésiras: histoire diplomatique de la crise
marocaine, 15 janvier–7 avril 1906.* 1907. 3rd rev. ed., Paris, 1909. [Bib-
liothèque d'histoire contemporaine.]

   c ———— *Le mystère d'Agadir.* Paris, 1912.

   d Caillaux, Joseph. *Agadir, ma politique extérieure.* Paris, 1919.

   e Rüdiger, George von. *Die Bedeutung der Algeciras-konferenz unter
Berücksichtigung der europäischen Marokko-politik bis zur endgültigen
Lösung der Marokkofrage.* München, 1920.

a. Summary, not always chronological, of French foreign policy from 1871 to
1907. The tone is pitched rather high in praise of the policy of equilibrium, the
achievement of which restored to France her liberty of action; a somewhat
patronizing tone is adopted towards Germany. Within its limits, the book offers
the best account of international politics of this period as viewed by the French
governing classes at the time. Review, *A.H.R.* 14:825, July 1909. *b.* and *c.*
Most complete account of the Moroccan imbroglio; the author, at one time
foreign editor of *Le Temps,* was in close touch with the French foreign office
and very well informed. M. Tardieu can be an ardent controversialist, but in *b.*
he has written substantial and well-documented history, carrying the story down
to 1909. Review of *b.,* A. Lichtenberger, *Rev. Hist.* 94:349, July 1907. *d.* Decidedly more polemical, and sharply critical of French policy, though very illuminating. *e.* Serves as a German foil for *b.* Should be read with *c.* and
with (J205b).   BES

J207 Morel, Edmund D. *Morocco in diplomacy.* 1912. New ed., *Ten years of
secret diplomacy,* London, 1915. Later reprints.

This book attracted great attention because of its timely publication, an appearance of thorough documentation, the reputation of its author as a reformer,
and the vigor of its attack on Sir Edward Grey's support of France. Its interpretation can be safely accepted only where supported by other evidence. The
documents are omitted from the new edition. Review, *Athenaeum,* 1:332, March
23, 1912.   FMA

J208a Stuart, Graham H. *French foreign policy from Fashoda to Serajevo,
1898–1914.* N. Y., 1921. (Bibliography.)

   b Schefer, Christian. *D'une guerre à l'autre: essai sur la politique extérieure de la troisième république, 1871–1914.* Paris, 1920. (Bibliography.)

General surveys of French foreign policy in the pre-war period. *a.* Readable
account based mainly on French sources. Review, L. B. Packard, *A.H.R.*
27:317, Jan. 1922. *b.* By able French authority; excellent, discriminating, but
patriotic presentation. Review, F. M. Anderson, *A.H.R.* 26:329, Jan. 1921.
                                                                    GMD

J209 Barclay, Sir Thomas. *Turco-Italian war and its problems, with appendices containing the chief state papers bearing on the subject, with an additional chapter on Moslem feeling, by the Rt. Hon. Ameer Ali, P. C.* London, 1912.

Published during the war concerned; embodies useful documents; otherwise chiefly valuable for its contemporary point of view. Review, *Athenaeum,* 1:94, Jan. 27, 1912.   GMD

J210a Schiemann, Theodor. *Deutschland und die grosse Politik, 1901–1914.* 14 v. Berlin, 1902–15.

   b Gauvain, Auguste. *L'Europe au jour le jour.* 13 v. Paris, 1917–22.

   c —— *Les origines de la guerre européenne.* Paris, 1915.

   d —— *L'Europe avant la guerre.* Paris, 1917.

a. Reprint of weekly reviews of international affairs published in the *Kreuz-zeitung. b.* Similar reprint of articles from the *Journal des Débats* for the years 1908 to 1919. Review, G. B. Hurst, *E.H.R.* 33:427, July 1918; 34:126, Jan. 1919; 36:153, Jan. 1921. These two series are interesting for the presentation of the contemporary views of leading journalistic authorities in their respective countries. *c.* Study, written late in 1914, upon the course of events leading up to the war, and a reprint of his daily articles for the period between the assassination of the Austrian crown prince and the beginning of hostilities. *d.* Reprint of contemporary articles on leading international topics, 1908–1913. Review, F. Schevill, *A.H.R.* 23:167, Oct. 1917.   FMA, GMD

J211 *These eventful years, the twentieth century in the making, as told by many of its makers, being the dramatic story of all that has happened throughout the world during the most momentous period in all history.* Ed. by Franklin H. Hooper. 2 v. London and N. Y., 1924.

Attempt to relate the events and portray the changes which have taken place since 1900 in a series of eighty-four chapters by nearly as many contributors. As the authors were obviously chosen in many instances because what they wrote would be sure to attract attention, the contributions differ widely in value, but many are of decided merit. Review, A. Bullard, *A.H.R.* 30:821, July 1925.   FMA

J221 Steed, Henry Wickham. *Through thirty years, 1892–1922, a personal narrative.* 2 v. London and Garden City, N. Y., 1924.

Recollections and retrospective impressions of the talented journalist who represented the London *Times* at Berlin, Rome, and Vienna, and later, at the Paris peace conference. His extraordinary opportunities for gathering information and getting points of view make it probably the most valuable book of the kind, though its accuracy in points of detail is sometimes open to question. Review, L. S. Gannett, *Nation* (N. Y.), 120:46, Jan. 14, 1925.   FMA

J222a Grey, Sir Edward (Viscount Grey of Falloden). *Twenty-five years, 1892–1916.* 2 v. London and N. Y., 1925.

   b Asquith, Herbert H. (Earl of Oxford and Asquith). *Genesis of the war.* London and N. Y., 1923.

   c Haldane, Richard B., Viscount. *Before the war.* London and N. Y., 1920.

d Lutz, Hermann. *Lord Grey and the World War.* N. Y., 1928. Tr. by
E. W. Dickes from *Lord Grey und der Weltkrieg,* Berlin, 1927.

e Morley, John, Viscount. *Memorandum on resignation.* N. Y., 1928.

a. One of the most interesting of post-war recollections; remarkable alike for
charm of form, engaging frankness, and the revelation of the author's psychological qualities. That Sir Edward Grey aimed to be perfectly honest both in
his conduct of the foreign office and in the writing of these memoirs and that
he believed himself to have been honest, if not always wise, one can hardly doubt
who reads his work with an open and unbiased mind. But that he did things
in office which seem to lack candor and that he said many things in his book
which do not always appear to accord with the facts is likewise hardly open to
doubt. To attribute these, as many of his critics have done, to bad faith is to
misunderstand completely the man. Rather are they to be explained, partly by
the fact that no man's memory (not even Viscount Grey's, which was remarkably good) is absolutely trustworthy as to details ten years and more after
the events; partly by the fact that Sir Edward Grey did not always clearly grasp
situations with complete knowledge and understanding; and partly because he
had a tendency to rationalize disagreeable or repugnant facts which did not fit
in with the scheme of things as he liked to see them. Review, A. L. P. Dennis,
A.H.R. 31:323, Jan. 1926; M. Montgelas, *Die Kriegsschuldfrage,* 4:282, 377, 435,
May, June, July 1926; C. R. Beazley, *Foreign Affairs* (London), 7:172, Dec.
1925. *b.* Deals almost exclusively with Anglo-German relations and British
military preparations between 1905 and 1914; defends the policies of his ministry; supports his argument only by evidence already known. Review, S. B.
Fay, *New Republic,* 37:154, Jan. 2, 1924. *c.* In this brief, dignified, and restrained volume, the former British secretary of state for war reviews Anglo-
German diplomatic relations before the war, writes an extended commentary
on the memoirs of (J265a) Bethmann-Hollweg and (J396a) Tirpitz, and sketches
authoritatively the English military preparations, of which he was the chief
author between 1906 and 1914. Review, C. Becker, *Nation* (N. Y.), 110:692,
May 22, 1920.   SBF
d. Critical of *a;* seeks to give a key to Sir Edward Grey's policy prior to the
World War and during the crisis of July, 1914; based on an examination of the
most recent available documentary material, especially that in (J72a) and in
(J75). Review, S. B. Fay, *A.H.R.* 34:343, Jan. 1929. *e.* Dramatic personal narrative of the split in the British cabinet in July, 1914, of the reasons for Lord
Morley's resignation, and of the means by which the cabinet was persuaded to
approve war with Germany.   SBF

J223 Loreburn, Robert T. R., Earl. *How the war came.* London, 1919.

Devoted mainly to an analysis of British foreign policy from 1905 to 1914;
restrained and moderate statement of the point of view of the English liberals
who opposed the policy of Sir Edward Grey. Argues that while Germany must
be held morally responsible for starting the war there would have been no conflict if the English government, under the influence of Asquith, Grey, and Haldane and largely without the knowledge of the English people, had not departed
from its traditional policy by entering into intimate relations with France. Review, *Athenaeum,* p. 999, Oct. 10, 1919.   FMA

J224a Sarolea, Charles. *Anglo-German problem.* London, 1912. N. Y., 1915. (Bibliography.) French tr., by C. Grolleau, *Le problème anglo-allemand*, Paris, 1915.

b Cramb, John A. *Germany and England.* London and N. Y., 1914.

c Hovelaque, Émile. *Deeper causes of the war, with an introduction by Sir Walter Raleigh.* London and N. Y., 1916. Tr. by the author from *Les causes profondes de la guerre, Allemagne-Angleterre*, Paris, 1915.

a. Bitter attack on German militarism by a Belgian professor at Edinburgh; notable forecast of the war and its issues. Review, *Spectator,* 109:1064, Dec. 21, 1912.   HRS
b. Remarkable series of four lectures delivered in England in 1913 in aid of the campaign of Lord Roberts for conscription; published from the author's unfinished manuscript after his death. Acute and eloquent analysis of German thought, especially that of Treitschke, in regard to England during the generation before the World War. Published just as the war was beginning, Englishmen probably got from it their most vivid impressions of German feeling toward England as a factor in bringing on the war. Review, *Nation* (London), 15:594, July 18, 1914. *c.* Incisive, war-time analysis of German ideas and policies as exhibited in relations with England. Review, M. Smith, *A.H.R.* 24:677, July 1919.   FMA

J225 Dickinson, Goldsworthy Lowes. *International anarchy, 1904–1914.* London, 1926. (Bibliography.)

Admirable work; charmingly written; based on thorough and shrewd use of all the most recent material, including the new German documents. The author indicates effectively the selfish secret intrigues of all the Powers which caused the 'international anarchy' culminating in the World War and sees in an international organization like the League of Nations the only hope for the future. Review, *Times* (*London*) *Literary Supplement,* 127, Feb. 25, 1926; J. S. Schapiro, *Nation* (N. Y.), 123:39, July 14, 1926.   SBF

J231 Bourgeois, Émile, and Pagès, Georges. *Les origines et les responsabilités de la grande guerre, preuves et aveux.* 1921. 2nd ed., Paris, 1922. (Bibliographical foot-notes.)

One of the most important French studies upon the origin of the World War. Originally prepared for a senatorial commission of inquiry and amplified after the appearance of the German documents relating to the outbreak of the war; its authors had access to the archives of the ministry of foreign affairs. Pt. 2. By Pagès; valuable sketch of Franco-German relations, 1871–1904. Pt. 1, 3. By Bourgeois; cover 1904–1914. Pt. 4. Contains hitherto unpublished reports of French ambassadors at Berlin and a selection from the German documents with the Kaiser's annotations. Review, L. André, *Rev. Hist.* 140:241, July 1922.   FMA

J232a Poincaré, Raymond. *Les origines de la guerre.* Paris, 1921.

b Pevet, Alfred. *Les responsables de la guerre.* Paris, 1921.

c Morhardt, Mathias. *Les preuves, le crime de droit commun, le crime diplomatique.* Paris, 1924. [Société d'Études Documentaires et Critiques sur la Guerre.]

d Margueritte, Victor. *Les criminels.* Paris, 1925.

e Fabre-Luce, Alfred. *Limitations of victory.* N. Y., 1926. Tr. by C. Vesey from *La victoire,* Paris, 1924.

f Poincaré, Raymond. *Memoirs, 1912.* London, 1926. Tr. and adapted by Sir George Arthur from v. 1–2 of *Au service de la France, neuf annés de souvenirs.* 5 v. Paris, 1926–29.

a. Six lectures delivered in Paris in 1921. The first two sketch briefly Franco-German relations from 1870 and the origin of France's close relations with Russia and England. The other four give in more detail the author's interpretation of the critical years 1911–1914, with special attention to points which explain his own course and the policy of France as against the assertion of his critics that he allowed France to be dragged into the war by undue acquiescence in Russian intrigue over Balkan matters. Review, H. Buffenoir, *Revue Critique,* n.s., 88:438, Nov. 15, 1921. *b., c., d.,* and *e.* Representative of French criticisms, mostly by socialists, of Poincaré and of French foreign policy both preceding and following the World War. *f.* Practically Poincaré's reply to his critics; more complete statement than *a.* Review, *Times (London) Literary Supplement,* p. 381, June 10, 1926; v. 3 of French ed., *ibid.,* p. 530, Aug. 12, 1926. FMA

J233a Hazen, Charles D. *Alsace-Lorraine under German rule.* N. Y., 1917.

b Phillipson, Coleman. *Alsace-Lorraine, past, present, and future.* London and N. Y., 1918. (Bibliography.)

c Cerf, Barry. *Alsace-Lorraine since 1870.* N. Y., 1919. (Bibliography.)

d Wetterlé, Émile. *Behind the scenes in the Reichstag: sixteen years of parliamentary life in Germany.* N. Y., 1918. Tr. by G. F. Lees from *Les coulisses du Reichstag, seize années de vie parlementaire en Allemagne,* Paris, 1918.

a., b., and *c.* Provide some account of the history of Alsace-Lorraine, especially since 1870, and discuss the problem of its future. *a.* Strongly anti-German. Review, R. H. Fife, Jr., *A.H.R.* 23:894, July 1918. *b.* Aims at judicial impartiality. Review, C. D. Hazen, *A.H.R.* 24:667, July 1919. *c.* Pro-French. Review, *A.H.R.* 25:105, Oct. 1919. *d.* Recollections of an Alsatian clerical and deputy in the Reichstag. Review, R. H. Fife, Jr., *A.H.R.* 24:473, Apr. 1919. GMD

J241a Rachfahl, Felix. *Deutschland und die Weltpolitik, 1871–1914.* V. 1, *Die Bismarck'sche Aera.* Stuttgart, 1923.

b Becker, Otto. *Bismarck und die Einkreisung Deutschlands.* 2 v. Berlin, 1923–25. [1, *Bismarcks Bündnispolitik;* 2, *Das französisch-russische Bündnis.*]

c Valentin, Veit. *Deutschlands Aussenpolitik von Bismarcks Abgang bis zum Ende des Weltkrieges.* Berlin, 1921.

d Brandenburg, Erich. *From Bismarck to the world war.* N. Y., 1927. Tr. by A. E. Adams from the rev. ed. of *Von Bismarck zum Weltkriege; die deutsche Politik in den Jahrzehnten vor dem Kriege, dargestellt auf Grund der Akten des Auswärtigen Amtes.* Berlin, 1924. Rev. ed., 1927.

Of the numerous German works on the foreign policy of Bismarck and his successors these four are perhaps the best. *a.* Covers only the years 1871–1890, having been interrupted by the author's death. Contains no foot-notes or bibliographical references. Most thorough treatment of German policy, if not of European international relations, from 1870 to 1890. The author, though an admirer of Bismarck, endeavors, as a trained historian, to maintain strict impartiality, and does not conceal the chancellor's shortcomings and mistakes. *b.* Careful diplomatic narrative, based largely on (J72a) *Die grosse Politik;* strongly German in point of view; to be continued by a third volume on the Triple Entente. Review, J. V. Fuller, *A.H.R.* 32:115, Oct. 1926.   *c.* Originally undertaken at the request of the German foreign office; based to some extent on unpublished material as well as on source material published up to 1920; clear and fluent; critical and, in general, impartial. The four hundred pages are about equally apportioned to the pre-war period, the July crisis of 1914, and the diplomatic history of the war itself; the last two parts are the most valuable. Review, S. B. Fay, *A.H.R.* 31:141, Oct. 1924.   *d.* Best single volume on German foreign policy between 1890 and 1914. The author enjoyed free access to the German archives which have since been published in (J72a) *Die grosse Politik,* and clarifies scores of hitherto obscure or unknown episodes. Reveals the conflict of aims which often existed between Wilhelm II and his officials. Though written from the German point of view, admirably objective and not without severe criticisms of German diplomacy. Review, S. B. Fay, *A.H.R.* 30:362, Jan. 1925; (London) *Times Lit. Suppl.,* 26:239, Apr. 7, 1927.

WLLr, SBF

J242a Smith, Munroe. *Militarism and statecraft.* N. Y. and London, 1918.

   b Fuller, Joseph V. *Bismarck's diplomacy at its zenith.* Cambridge, Mass., 1922. [Harvard historical studies.] (Bibliography.)

   a. Series of penetrating and vigorously written essays by a biographer of Bismarck, to show how the German mind was militarized and Prussianized by Germany's military victories between 1864 and 1871 and by Bismarck's influence. Depicts the triumph of military strategy over diplomacy in Germany as a cause of the World War. Review, B. E. Schmitt, *A.H.R.* 24.278, Jan. 1919.   SBF

   b. Detailed study, marked by sound and extensive research, upon the diplomatic history of the years 1885–1888. The author argues that Bismarck then weakened the earlier favorable position of Germany and made almost certain an early formation of a Franco-Russian alliance. Review, B. E. Schmitt, *A.H.R.* 28:542, Apr. 1923.

FMA

J243a Hammann, Otto. *Der neue Kurs, Erinnerungen.* Berlin, 1918..

   b ——— *Zur Vorgeschichte des Weltkrieges, Erinnerungen.* Berlin, 1919.

   c ——— *Um den Kaiser, Erinnerungen.* Berlin, 1919.

   d ——— *Der missverstandene Bismarck, zwanzig Jahre deutscher Weltpolitik.* Berlin, 1921.

   e ——— *Bilder aus der letzten Kaiserzeit.* Berlin, 1922.

   f ——— *World policy of Bismarck, 1890–1912.* N. Y., 1927. Tr. from the German.

   This series comprises the memoirs of a man who was for many years director of the press bureau of the German foreign office. He writes well; shows unusually sound and fair judgment both as to men and events; and throws light on numerous disputed problems of pre-war diplomacy and domestic crises. An outstanding feature is the faithful portrayal of the characters of many leading Germans.   *a., b., c.,* and *e.* Cover respectively the years 1800–1896; 1897–1906;

1906–1909; 1909–1918. Review of *a* and *b*, A. C. Coolidge, *A.H.R.* 25:718, July 1920. *d*. Reprint of the chapters of *a*, *b*, and *c* which deal with foreign policy, revised in the light of the new evidence published between 1918 and 1921. Review, S. B. Fay, *A.H.R.* 27:152, Oct. 1921. *f*. Review, (London) *Times Lit. Suppl.* 26:239, Apr. 7, 1927. WLLr

J244a Eckardstein, Hermann, Freiherr von. *Lebenserinnerungen und politische Denkwürdigkeiten.* 3 v. Leipzig, 1919–21.

b —— *Ten years at the court of St. James', 1895–1905.* London, 1921. Tr. and ed. by G. Young from *a*.

a. Important contribution to knowledge of international affairs from 1895 to 1905, by a sagacious and well-informed member of the German embassy at London. Holds that German diplomacy was deflected into a wrong course by Wilhelm II, Bülow, and Holstein; throws much light on the projects for an Anglo-German alliance between 1898 and 1901. Review, A. C. Coolidge, *A.H.R.* 26:517, Apr. 1921. *b*. Abridged translation of *a*. FMA

J245a Reventlow, Ernest, Graf zu. *Deutschlands auswärtige Politik, 1888–1913.* 1914. 11th rev. ed., Berlin, 1918.

b —— *Politische Vorgeschichte des grossen Krieges.* 1919. 2nd ed., Berlin, 1919.

a. The first edition was, on the whole, a rather clear, fair, and restrained account of German foreign policy. It was probably the best one-volume book for the German general reader. Later editions, especially for the period after 1903, were much modified in the German war spirit. *b*. Continuation of *a;* deals chiefly with the policy of the Powers during the three years before the War; written from a strongly German point of view. Review, A. Walther, *Hist. Zeit.* 123:116, 1920. FMA

J251 Pribram, Alfred F. *Austrian foreign policy, 1908–1918.* London, 1923.

Brief and readable; written by a scholar thoroughly acquainted with unpublished Austrian archive material (cf., J202*a*). The account of the relations between Austria and Germany during the War and of the unavailing efforts of the peace party at Vienna to find some means of bringing the conflict to an end, though brief, is interesting and valuable. Review, H. W. C. Davis, *E.H.R.* 40:470, July 1925. SBF

J252 Andrássy, Julius, Graf. *Diplomacy and the war.* London, 1921. Tr. by J. H. Reece from *Diplomatie und Weltkrieg,* Wien, 1920.

Not an *apologia* but an exposition of the origins of the War and of the collapse of the Hapsburg monarchy. As one of the foremost Magyar statesmen the author was able to present valuable information, but naturally reveals the point of view of his people. Review, S. A. Korff, *A.H.R.* 27:795, July 1922. GMD

CRISIS OF 1914

J261 Fay, Sidney B. *Origins of the World War.* 2 v. N. Y., 1928. Rev. ed., 1930.

Unquestionably the most important and in general the most authoritative work upon the origin of the World War. It is based upon an unrivaled knowledge of the diplomatic correspondence and the personal narratives of leading diplomatists.

In method and in spirit it conforms closely to the highest standards of historical investigation and exposition. The style is direct, clear, and interesting. The first volume, covering 1871–1914, deals with the underlying causes of the war. Volume two, dealing with the immediate causes, is devoted wholly to the crisis of June 28 to August 4, 1914. Review, Renouvin, *For. Affairs*, 7:384, Apr. 1929; E. M. Earle, *New Republic*, 57:73, Dec. 5, 1928; P. W. Slosson, *A.H.R.* 34:336, Jan. 1929.

FMA

J263a Headlam, James W. *History of twelve days, July 24th to August 4th 1914, being an account of the negotiations preceding the outbreak of war based on the official publications.* London and N. Y., 1915.

b Stowell, Ellery C. *Diplomacy of the war of 1914: the beginnings of the war.* Boston, 1915.

c Oman, Sir Charles W. C. *Outbreak of the war of 1914–1918, a narrative based mainly on British official documents.* London, 1919.

d Renouvin, Pierre. *Immediate origins of the war, 28th June–4th August, 1914.* New Haven, 1928. Tr. by Theodore C. Hume from enlarged edition of *Les origines immédiates de la guerre, 28 juin–4 août 1914*, Paris, 1925. [Publications de la Société de l'Histoire de la Guerre.] (Bibliography.)

a. Digest of the then published diplomatic correspondence conducted by the belligerent powers during the twelve days preceding outbreak of the World War. Documents are quoted at length and the excerpts are, as a rule, wisely selected. The author, an English historical writer, argues the Allied case ably. Review, *Athenaeum*, 1:567, June 26, 1915; E. C. Stowell, *A.H.R.* 21:596, Apr. 1916.

OPC

b. Analytical study of the documents then available, by an American professor of international law; reaches conclusions unfavorable to Austria and Germany, favorable to Belgium and England. Review, T. S. Woolsey, *A.H.R.* 21:594, Apr. 1916.

GMD

c. Confined to the period, June 28 to August 4, 1914; first careful, well-documented, and dispassionate study of the subject which appeared after the war. Though it contains no significant revelations and now needs correction in the light of evidence subsequently disclosed, it still is a good book in English on the crisis. Review, *Spectator*, 122:262, March 1, 1919. *d.* One of the most objective and best documented accounts of the immediate causes of the World War. In remarkably few words it marshals the pertinent evidence and exhibits the recent state of knowledge as regards almost every significant aspect of the crisis which led to the war. Review, S. B. Fay, *A.H.R.* 31:354, Jan. 1926; J. W. Swain, *Hist. Outlook*, 20:247, May, 1929.

FMA

J264a Bausman, Frederick. *Let France explain.* 1922. 2nd ed., London and N. Y., 1923.

b Montgelas, Maximilian, M. K. D. Graf von. *Case for the central powers, an impeachment of the Versailles verdict.* London and N. Y., 1925. (Bibliography.) Tr. by C. Vesey from *Leitfaden zur Kriegsschuldfrage*, Berlin, 1923.

c Ewart, John S. *Roots and causes of the wars, 1914–1918.* 2 v. London and N. Y., 1925.

d Barnes, Harry Elmer. *Genesis of the world war, an introduction to the problem of war guilt.* N. Y., 1926. 2nd rev. ed., 1927. (Bibliography.)

e Wegerer, Alfred von. *Widerlegung der Versailler Kriegsschuldthese.* Berlin, 1928. Eng. trans., N. Y., 1930.

a. An American lawyer supports the thesis that while all the Great Powers contributed in some degree, the main responsibility for the World War lay with Russia and France, as their policy was controlled by Poincaré, Sazonov, and Isvolski, who deliberately worked for war. The documentation is elaborate but often deceptive. Review, B. E. Schmitt, *New Republic,* 33:255, Jan. 31, 1923. *b.* Appraised by highly competent authority as the most fair-minded German book on the origin of the World War. While this protest against article 231 of the Treaty of Versailles is marked in places by the usual characteristics of polemical writing, it is much above the general level of such books and is a real aid toward comprehension of the causes of the World War. Cf. (J82a).   *c.* By a Canadian jurist; deals with the remoter causes of the War and, less satisfactorily, with the crisis of 1914. Makes little use of materials not available in English and French; regards national self-interest as the dominant motive with each country; judgments with regard to Germany are sometimes too lenient. Review of *b* and *c,* S. B. Fay, *New Republic,* 44:49, Sept. 2, 925. *d.* Presents substantially the same conclusions as *a, b,* and *c;* most recent and most elaborate statement of the case for a minimum of German responsibility. Review, *Times (London) Literary Supplement,* 25:639, Sept. 30, 1926; B. E. Schmitt, *Foreign Affairs (N. Y.),* 5:12, Oct. 1926; G. L. Dickinson, *New Republic,* 47:284, July 28, 1926.   ᵀMA, GMD
e. Carefully documented examination or refutation of evidence on which the Versailles Peace Conference condemned Germany and her allies as responsible for the World War.   SBF

J265a Bethmann-Hollweg, Theobald von. *Reflections on the world war.* London and N. Y., 1920. Tr. by G. Young from *Betrachtungen zum Weltkriege,* 2 v., Berlin, 1919–20.

b—— *Kriegsreden.* Ed. by F. Thimme. Stuttgart, 1919.

c Jagow, Günther Gottlieb K. E. von. *Ursachen und Ausbruch des Weltkrieges.* Berlin, 1919.

d Schoen, Wilhelm E., Freiherr von. *Memoirs of an ambassador, a contribution to the political history of modern times.* London and N. Y., 1922. Tr. by C. Vesey from *Erlebtes: Beiträge zur politischen Geschichte der neuesten Zeit,* Stuttgart, 1921.

These apologetic volumes by former officials of the German foreign office deserve more serious consideration than they have commonly received. *a.* V. 1. Defends his policy before 1914. V. 2. More valuable; seeks to justify his policy during the World War; contains much information on the internal situation of Germany and on the impotence of the civilian chancellor in the face of the military authorities. Review, v. 2, S. B. Fay, *A.H.R.* 27:610, Apr. 1922. *b.* Review, M. W. Tyler, *A.H.R.* 25:549, Apr. 1920.   *c.* Jagow, secretary of state for foreign affairs in the months before the World War, seeks to justify Germany's policy as being defensive and a necessary consequence of the system of alliances. Review, W. Schotte, *Preussische Jahrbücher,* 179:155, Jan. 1920. *d.* Schoen, who was Germany's representative at Copenhagen and St. Petersburg, then secretary of state from 1907 to 1910, and ambassador at Paris from 1910 to 1914, writes with frankness, knowledge, and insight concerning Germany's foreign policy in the dozen years before the War. Review, G. Roloff, *Hist. Zeit.* 125:541, 1922. SBF

J266 Recouly, Raymond. *Les heures tragiques d'avant-guerre.* Paris, 1922.

Dramatic presentation of the personal elements in the crisis on the French side; based on interviews with ministers, other officials, and prominent individuals. SBF

J267a Barbagallo, Corrado. *Come si scatenò la guerra mondiale.* Milano, 1923. [Biblioteca della *Nuova rivista storica.*]

   b Bogitshevich (Bogićević), Milosh. *Causes of the war.* Amsterdam, 1919. Tr. from *Kriegsursachen, Beiträge zur Erforschung der Ursachen des europäischen Krieges mit spezieller Berücksichtigung Russlands und Serbiens,* Zürich, 1919. French tr., revised and enlarged, with bibliography, *Les causes de la guerre,* Paris, 1925.

a. Best critical account by an Italian of the immediate origins of the war. Review, G. Roloff, *Hist. Zeit.,* 130:637, 1924. *b.* Dr. Bogitshevich, Serbian *chargé d'affaires* at Berlin at the outbreak of the War, severely criticizes the policy of the Serbian prime minister, Pashitch, and prints many documents bearing upon the Serbian and Russian share of responsibility for the War. He has also written many articles in (J981) *Die Kriegsschuldfrage,* revealing the connection between Serbian officers in the secret 'Black Hand' and the assassination of Franz Ferdinand at Serajevo. SBF

J276a Dillon, Emile. *From the triple to the quadruple alliance: why Italy went to war.* London and N. Y., 1915.

   b *L'intervento dell'Italia nei documenti segreti dell'intessa.* Roma, 1923.

   c Solmi, Arrigo. *Le origini del patto di Londra. Politica* (Roma), 3:129–184, Nov. 30–Dec. 31, 1923.

a. Detailed story of the negotiations leading to Italy's entrance into the World War. The author represented the London *Telegraph* in Italy at that time and knew personally many of the leading men. Intensely anti-German. CP

b. Documents from the Russian archives, translated into Italian, revealing the negotiations leading to Italy's entry into the World War. *c.* Scholarly study; utilizes the documents in *b.* SBF

277a Visscher, Charles De. *Belgium's case: a juridical enquiry.* London and N. Y., 1916. (Bibliography.) Tr. by E. F. Jourdain from *La Belgique et les juristes allemands,* Paris, 1916.

   b Kurth, Godefroid. *Le Guet-apens prussien en Belgique.* Bruxelles, 1919.

a. By a professor of law in the University of Ghent; best discussion of Belgium's position in the war written during the conflict. Review, E. R. Turner, *A.H.R.* 22:660, Apr. 1917. *b.* Post-war statement of Belgium's case against Germany by a Belgian historian. Review, A. C. Krey, *A.H.R.* 26:363, Jan. 1921. Also cf. (Q353–354). GMD

WORLD WAR, 1914–1918: GENERAL

J281a Hayes, Carlton J. H. *Brief history of the great war.* N. Y., 1920. (Bibliography.)

   b Pollard, Albert F. *Short history of the great war.* London, 1920.

c Frothingham, Thomas G. *Guide to the military history of the world war, 1914–1918.* Boston, 1920.

d Howland, Charles R. *Military history of the world war.* 2 v. Fort Leavenworth, Kansas, 1923. [General Service Schools.] (Bibliography.)

a. Best history of the World War in one volume of medium size. The style, though without distinction, is clear, forceful, and interesting. Remarkably comprehensive; touches on almost every phase of world history during the war period. Good maps and plans. Review, W. S. Davis, *A.H.R. 26:91,* Oct. 1920. *b.* Valuable and interesting; somewhat smaller; not so wide in scope; designed especially for British readers; excellent maps. Review, G. B. Hurst, *E.H.R.* 35:477, July 1920; A. P. Scott, *A.H.R. 26:331,* Jan. 1921. *c.* Best short guide for the general reader to the military and naval operations of the war. A narrative synopsis devoted almost wholly to strategy and grand tactics. Official statements and reports, carefully checked, have served as the basis. Considerable, and sometimes too ready, use has been made of the post-war statements of the German military leaders. The style is simple, clear, interesting, and free from any excess as to details or technical terms. Many excellent sketch maps.

FMA

d. Gives clear idea of the strategy of the World War as a whole; includes all fronts and the relationship of each front to the general situation; pays special attention to army transportation and the placing of reserves; constantly indicates the bearing of the political situation upon military and naval operations; very valuable to students of the war. V. 2. Consists of one hundred and fifty maps, though not large ones.

TJW

J282 O'Neill, Herbert. *History of the war.* London, 1920.

Large volume; almost encyclopedic in scope and method of treatment; based upon wide reading and careful investigation; apparently to some extent the by-product of the author's activities as reviewer and journalist. Deals largely with military and naval operations, which are treated with clarity and with appreciation of tactical and strategical problems.

FMA

J283 Simonds, Frank H. *History of the world war.* 5 v. Garden City, N. Y., 1917–20.

Probably the best preponderantly military history of its size for the general reader. During the war the author was the leading American newspaper commentator on military affairs. He has a good eye for the really significant thing in military operations, does not overload his narrative with details, and has an exceptional gift for lucid and non-technical exposition. His opinions on disputed points have been considerably affected by French influences. Copiously illustrated; many of the numerous maps are highly and ingeniously graphic. Review, A. E. R. Boak, *A.H.R. 23:701,* Apr. 1918; 24:295, Jan. 1919.

FMA

J284a Buchan, John. *Nelson's History of the war.* 24 v. London and N. Y., 1915–19.

b ———— *History of the great war.* 4 v. London and N. Y., 1921–22.

c Repington, Charles à Court. *First world war, 1914–1918, personal experiences.* 2 v. London, 1920.

a. Each volume was issued within six months or less of the events described. The aim was to furnish the British public, at the earliest possible moment, in

small handy volumes, an approximately correct, interesting, and vivid narrative
of the war, more detailed where England participated directly, but including all
the military and naval operations. The author had unusual opportunities for
observation, especially at British headquarters. Better, perhaps, than any other
continuous narrative, it gives the contemporaneous atmosphere of the war. Each
volume has a valuable appendix of the more important documents, also numerous
maps and plans. *b*. Abridgement of *a;* recast in the light of additional information; lacks, however, the quality which gave *a* its greatest value. Review, C.
J. H. Hayes, *A.H.R.* 29:140, Oct. 1923; v. 1–2, G. B. Hurst, *E.H.R.* 37:472, July
1922. *c*. Chiefly a diary from September, 1915, to November, 1918, by the
foremost British newspaper military expert. Its remarkably vivid picture of
English high society includes opinions and special information on numerous
important topics imparted by many prominent persons, also the observations
and information gathered by the author on several visits to the western
front. Review, *Spectator*, 125:434, Oct. 2, 1920.   FMA

J285a *Times history of the war.* 22 v. London, 1914–21.

  b *Manchester Guardian history of the war.* 9 v. Manchester, Eng., 1915–
  20.

  c **Halsey, Francis W.**, ed. *Literary Digest history of the world war, compiled from original and contemporary sources: American, British, French,
  German, and others.* 10 v. N. Y. and London, 1919.

a. Most important work of its kind; issued in parts appearing within a few
weeks after the events described. The text has considerable worth, because
prepared by competent specialists, but the greatest value of the work lies in the
many pictures and maps, which have been prepared with great care, including
good portraits of nearly all the more prominent participants. While attention
is given chiefly to military and naval matters, other aspects of the war are not
neglected. *b*. Also good, but on less ambitious lines. Review, v. 1, *Athenaeum*,
2:7, July 3, 1915. *c*. Based chiefly on journalistic sources; usually well-
written; contains maps and illustrations; transitory in value. Review, G. F.
Zook, *A.H.R.* 25:720, July 1920.   FMA

J286a *History of the great war, based on official documents, by direction of the
Historical Section of the Committee of Imperial Defence.* London, 1922 ff.
1, J. E. Edmonds, *Military operations, France and Belgium, 1914,* v. 1–2
and 2 atlases; 2, *Campaign in Mesopotamia, 1914–1918,* v. 1–2, 1923–24;
3, *Medical services, diseases of the war,* v. 1, 1922; 4, *Medical services,
general history,* v. 2–4, 1923–25; 5, *Medical services, hygiene of the war,*
v. 1–2, 1923; 6, *Medical services, pathology,* 1923; 7, *Veterinary services,*
1925; for naval operations, cf. (J382); for aerial operations, cf. (J401a).

  b *Der Weltkrieg, 1914–1918, bearbeitet im Reichsarchiv.* V. 1–4, Berlin,
  1924 ff. [1, *Die Grenzschlachten im Westen; 2, Die Befreiung Ostpreus-
  sens; 3, Der Marne-Feldzug von der Sambre zur Marne; 4, Der Marne-
  Feldzug.*] (Bibliographies.)

  c *Der grosse Krieg in Einzeldarstellungen unter Benutzung amtlicher
  Quellen herausgegeben im Auftrage des grossen Generalstabes.* V. 1, 3, 5,
  10, 11, 19–21, 24, 26–28, 31, 33, 39, Oldenburg. 1918 ff.

  d *Les armées françaises dans la grande guerre: précis d'ensemble des opérations des armées françaises sur les différents fronts.* Paris, 1925 ff.
  [Service Historique de l'État-major.] [1, *La guerre de mouvement, les
  préliminaires, la bataille des frontières, opérations antérieures au 24 août
  1914.*]

Technical histories of the World War by members of the general staffs of the English, German, and French armies respectively, elaborate detailed studies based upon official records and also upon the printed materials available. Important orders or documents are often included and excellent maps are usually provided.

GMD

J291a Giraud, Victor. *Histoire de la grande guerre.* Paris, 1920.

    b Aulard, Francois V. Alphonse, and others. *Histoire politique de la grande guerre.* Paris, 1924.

a. Book of 760 medium-sized pages; one of the best of its size prepared for the French general reader; originally appeared in five parts, the first before the end of the war. The proportions are exceptionally good. While it is mainly military, other matters which influenced military events are included. Admirably executed maps and plans are inserted in the text. Review, pt. I, *Revue Critique,* n.s., 86:336, Sept. I, 1919. *b.* Written on lines similar to his (M326a) *Histoire politique de la révolution française,* emphasizing political and other topics rather than military ones.

FMA

J292 Hanotaux, Gabriel. *Histoire illustrée de la guerre de 1914.* 17 v. Paris, 1914–24.

Best work of its type; carefully studied attempt to write a substantial and reliable history; many maps and illustrations of the highest order. As a former minister of foreign affairs and a distinguished historian, the author obtained access to sources of information not yet open to other writers. In the earlier volumes he vigorously defends the French high command against adverse criticism.

FMA

J293 *La Belgique et la guerre.* 4 v. Bruxelles, 1924–25. [1, G. Rency, *La vie matérielle de la Belgique durant la guerre mondiale;* 2, J. Cuvellier, *L'invasion allemande;* 3, Lieut.-Col. Tasnier and Major van Overstraeten, *Les opérations militaires;* 4, A. de Ridder, *Histoire diplomatique, 1914–1918.*]

The positions of the contributors to this work give it a semi-official standing as a presentation of Belgium's participation and experiences in the World War. Written by competent scholars for the general reader rather than the student.

GMD

J301 Stegemann, Hermann. *Geschichte des Krieges.* 4 v. Stuttgart, 1918–21. (Bibliography.)

This widely-circulated book of some 2200 pages by a well known German literary man covers the entire history of the war in all parts of the globe. Soberly written and reflects the later disillusionment of the Germans, the first two volumes having appeared in the second half of the war and the last two only after the armistice. Though military operations occupy most of the space, a framework of the political events is also given. Blames the European system chiefly for the outbreak of the war; attempts no justification of the invasion of Belgium. Documentary appendixes and colored maps. Review, v. 1–3, *Preussische Jahrbücher,* 180:249, Apr. 1920.

WKS

J302a Baer, Casimir H. *Der Völkerkrieg, eine Chronik der Ereignisse seit dem 1 Juli, 1914.* 28 v. Stuttgart, 1914–23.

b Schwarte, Max, ed. *Der grosse Krieg, 1914–1918.* 10 v. Leipzig, 1921 ff. [1–3, *Der deutsche Landkrieg;* 4, *Der Seekrieg;* 5, *Der Osterreichisch-ungarische Krieg;* 8–9, *Die Organisationen der Kriegführung;* 10, *Die Organisationen für das geistliche Leben im Heere.*]

a. Perhaps the best example of the efforts of German publishers to furnish an illustrated running account of the World War during its progress. *b.* Most important unofficial coöperative history of the war yet issued in Germany. V. 6–7. Will contain an account of the diplomatic and political events and conditions written by Professor Hermann Oncken.   GMD

J303 Falkenhayn, Erich von. *German general staff and its decisions, 1914–1916.* N. Y., 1920. English ed., *General headquarters, 1914–1916, and its critical decisions,* London, 1920. Tr. from *Die oberste Heeresleitung, 1914–1916, in ihren wichtigsten Entschliessungen,* Berlin, 1920.

The chief of the German general staff from September 14, 1914 to August 29, 1916 describes the operations of Germany and her allies on the entire theater of war from Belgium to the Suez canal during these years. Clear and impressive account, with little detail, from the point of view of the general headquarters, of the problems that arose and the decisions that were taken. Review, J. Bigelow, *A.H.R.* 25:500, Apr. 1920; *Preussische Jahrbücher,* 180:249, Apr. 1920.
          FMF

J304 Hindenburg, Paul von. *Out of my life.* 2 v. N. Y. and London, 1921. Tr. by F. A. Holt from *Aus meinem Leben,* 1920, 13th ed., Leipzig, 1925.

Personal reminiscences covering the Austro-Prussian, Franco-Prussian, and World Wars. Tedious account; contains very little of value other than the decisions of a few large operations. Of civilian affairs, internal and external politics, and the handling of the many vital problems of supreme command which do not come under the head of tactics or strategy, Hindenburg shows utter lack of grasp. Written for home consumption, apparently without much reference to facts and figures. Review, J. Bigelow, *A.H.R.* 26:96, Oct. 1920.
          ST

J305a Ludendorff, Erich. *Ludendorff's own story, August 1914–November 1918: the great war from the siege of Liège to the signing of the armistice as viewed from the grand headquarters of the German army.* 2 v. N. Y., 1919. English ed., *My war memories, 1914–1918,* 2 v., London, 1919. Tr. from *Meine Kriegserinnerungen, 1914–1918,* 1919; 8th ed., Berlin, 1922.

b —— *General staff and its problems, the history of the relations between the high command and the German imperial government as revealed by official documents.* 1 v. in 2. London and N. Y., 1920. Tr. by F. A. Holt from *Urkunden der obersten Heeresleitung über ihre Tätigkeit, 1916–18,* 1920; 4th ed., Berlin, 1922.

c —— *Kriegführung und Politik.* 1922. 3rd ed., Berlin, 1923.

a. As chief of the operations section from 1904 to 1913, Ludendorff developed Schlieffen's plan of attack through Belgium; as deputy chief of staff of the second army he took part in the attack on Liège. Then, with Hindenburg, he was in command in Russia until 1916, when they were together given supreme command. Of secondary importance are his dealings with the civilian authorities of Germany and of her allies, on whom he places the blame for failure. The decline of the imperial and military authority, and the rise in power of the Reichstag are interwoven into a very interesting picture of the war as seen from the German headquarters. Review, W. Schotte, *Preussische Jahrbücher*, 179:159, Jan. 1920; J. Bigelow, *A.H.R.* 25:503, Apr. 1920; B. E. Schmitt, *Pol. Sci. Quar.* 35:440, Sept. 1920. *b.* Documents, chiefly political and mainly unpublished, in support of the narrative in *a.* Review, *Times (London) Literary Supplement*, Sept. 13, 1920. *c.* Third volume of *a,* with supplementary data and discussions. FMA, SBF

J306a **Stein, Hermann C. M. von.** *A war minister and his work, reminiscences of 1914–1918.* London, 1920. Tr. from *Erlebnisse und Betrachtungen aus der Zeit des Weltkrieges,* 1919; 2nd ed., Leipzig, 1919.

b **Freytag-Loringhoven, Hugo F. P. J., Freiherr von.** *Deductions from the world war.* London, 1918. Tr. from *Folgerungen aus dem Weltkriege,* 1917; 19th ed., Berlin, 1918.

c **Kuhl, Hermann von.** *Der deutsche Generalstab in Vorbereitung und Durchführung des Weltkrieges.* 1919. 2nd ed., Berlin, 1920.

d **Kann, Reginald.** *Le plan de campagne allemand de 1914 et son exécution.* Paris, 1923. [Collection de mémoires, études, et documents pour servir à l'histoire de la guerre mondiale.]

e **Hoffmann, Max von.** *War of lost opportunities.* London, 1924. N. Y., 1925. Tr. by A. E. Chamot from *Der Krieg der versäumten Gelegenheiten,* München, 1923.

a. These memoirs of the German minister of war throughout the conflict are brief in extent and slight in content. Review, *Hist. Zeit.* 123:149, 1920. *b.* Primarily a work of propaganda by the deputy chief of the German general staff. Review, *Spectator,* 120:90, Jan. 26, 1918. *c.* Excellent comparative study of the strategic plans and preparations of all the Great Powers by a member of the German general staff, written in its defense. Review, General Groener, *Preussische Jahrbücher,* 181:120, July 1920. *d.* Careful study and exposition of the plans of Schlieffen and Moltke, and of their attempted execution in 1914, for a war on two fronts—first the crushing of France through Belgium, then the reckoning with Russia. *e.* Severe criticism by Ludendorff's successor as chief of the general staff on the Eastern front, of the mistakes of the German general staff and of the high political authorities largely controlled by it. Review, O. G. Villard, *Nation* (N. Y.), 121:546, Nov. 11, 1925. SBF

J307 **Helfferich, Karl T.** *Der Weltkrieg.* 3 v. Berlin, 1919. [1, *Die Vorgeschichte des Weltkrieges;* 2, *Vom Kriegsausbruch bis zum uneingeschränkten U-Boot-Krieg;* 3, *Vom Eingreifen Amerikas bis zum Zusammenbruch.*]

Defense of the German imperial government by a distinguished financier who held high office during the war; omits inconvenient facts; must be classed as anti-democratic propaganda, not history. As a confirmed adherent of the monarchy he presents a version of events intended to show that the defeat and collapse of the Central Powers was not due to any mistakes made by the government or the military officials, but to internal dissensions and to the machinations of men like Erzberger. More impartial and useful is the account, written from inside knowledge, of the Bagdad railway and of Anglo-German projects for the Portuguese colonies. Review, C. Gauss, *A.H.R.* 25:496, Apr. 1920. WLLr, SBF

WORLD WAR, 1914–1918: WESTERN FRONT

J321a Doyle, Sir Arthur Conan. *British campaign in France and Flanders.* 6 v. London and N. Y., 1916–20.

b Maurice, Sir Frederick B. *Forty days in 1914.* London and N. Y., 1919.

c —— *Last four months, how the war was won.* London and Boston, 1919.

a. Based on official records, personal narratives, and eye-witness's accounts. Though admittedly incomplete, it will have some permanent value as a contemporary chronicle of operations from the eventful days at Mons and on the Marne in 1914 to the end at Mons in 1918. Detailed account; no attempt at tactical or strategic discussion; maps are inadequate. Review, *A.H.R.* 23:700, Apr. 1918; *Nation* (London), 25:146, May 3, 1919; 26:514, Jan. 10, 1920. *b.* and *c.* Clear and concise accounts of events based on inside information. The historical part of *b* and the discussions of policy and strategy in *c* are intensely interesting. *b.* Detailed; tells what happened to the British forces at Mons and at the Marne in 1914. Review, *Spectator,* 122:201, Feb. 15, 1919. *c.* Descriptions of battles reduced to the simplest terms; comprehensive account of Foch's great campaign in 1918. Review, *Nation* (London), 27:230, May 15, 1920.

TRH

J322a Sargent, Herbert H. *Strategy on the western front, 1914–1918.* Chicago, 1920. (Bibliography.)

b Lyon, Laurence. *Pomp of power.* London and N. Y., 1922.

a. Written by an American expert in military strategy; conclusions badly warped by author's thesis that the war should have been fought out on the Balkan front. Review, *A.H.R.* 26:792, July 1921. *b.* Account, written with a tone of authority, of the relations of British and French political personages to the conduct of the war, especially on the western front; published anonymously. Review, *A.H.R.* 29:143, Oct. 1923.

GMD

J323a Perris, George H. *Battle of the Marne.* London and Boston, 1920. (Bibliographical notes.)

b Kluck, Alexander H. R. von. *March on Paris and the battle of the Marne, 1914, with . . . maps and notes by the Historical Section (Military Branch) of the [British] Committee of Imperial Defence.* London and N. Y., 1920. (Bibliography.) Tr. from *Der Marsch auf Paris und die Marneschlacht, 1914,* Berlin, 1920.

a. The action of the eight allied armies is coupled with a much less complete description of the seven German armies in the first battle of the Marne. Lacks clearness, because each section of the battle is treated separately and in detail. The main German plan is not indicated, nor is Kluck's change of direction explained. The action of the west is overstressed at the expense of the east. Review, *Nation* (London), 27:648, Aug. 21, 1920.   ST

b. Technical account; written in 1918, by the German commander, mainly from his own papers and almost exclusively from German data. Review of *a.* and *b., Saturday Rev.,* 130:12, July 3, 1920.

GMD

J324a **Engerand, Fernand.** *Le secret de la frontière, 1815–1871–1914,* Charleroi, 1918. 6th ed., Paris, 1918.

   b **French, John D. P., Viscount.** *1914.* London and Boston, 1919.

   c **Whitton, Frederick E.** *Marne campaign.* London and Boston, 1917. [Campaigns and their lessons.] (Bibliography.)

   d **Dewar, George A. B.,** and **Boraston, John H.** *Sir Douglas Haig's command, December 19, 1915, to November 11, 1918.* 2 v. London, 1922. Boston, 1923.

a. One of the most important intensive studies on the early even*t*s of the World War. The head of the French parliamentary commission which investigated the loss of the Briey district deals with the French defeats of 1914 near the frontiers, ascribing them chiefly to excessive reliance on the theory of the offensive at any cost. Well documented; good maps. Review, W. D. Green, *E.H.R.* 35:265, Apr. 1919. *b.* Important personal narrative by the commander of the British army in France in 1914–1915; includes a continuous account of operations to Nov. 21, 1914, with some attention to matters of later date. In large part it is an amazingly frank expression of a man with a grievance; very severe on Kitchener, Asquith, Smith-Dorrien, and Lanrezac; adverse criticism is implied against Joffre; highly favorable to Foch, Haig, and Allenby. Especially valuable for the battles of Le Cateau and Ypres and the author's controversies with Kitchener; disappointing on the battle of the Marne. Review, T. R. Ybarra, *Yale Rev.* 9:90, Jan. 1920. *c.* Good critical study, by a British officer; subject to some amendment by information published later. Review, I. R. Pennypacker, *A.H.R.* 23:643, Apr. 1918. *d.* Strongly partisan and over-zealous argument that German defeat on the western front was due chiefly to Lord Haig. Dewar was close to Haig and thereby gained much valuable information, but it is probable that Haig had no knowledge of the claims put forth in his behalf. Review, *A.H.R.* 29:143, Oct. 1923; F. H. Simonds, *Pol. Sci. Quar.* 38:327, June 1923.   FMA

J325a **Gibbs, Sir Philip H.** *Soul of the war.* London and N. Y., 1915.

   b ——— *Battles of the Somme.* London and N. Y., 1917.

   c ——— *From Bapaume to Passchendaele, on the western front, 1917.* London and N. Y., 1918.

   d ——— *Open warfare, the way to victory.* London and N. Y., 1919.

   e ——— *Now it can be told.* N. Y., 1920. English ed., *Realities of war,* London, 1920.

   f **Palmer, Frederick.** *My year of the great war.* N. Y., 1915. English ed., *My year of the war, including an account of experiences with the troops in France, and the record of a visit to the grand fleet,* London, 1915.

   g ——— *My second year of the war.* N. Y. and London, 1917.

   h ——— *America in France.* N. Y., 1918. English ed., *America in France, the story of the making of an army,* London, 1919.

a., b., c., and *d.* Comprise the author's despatches as correspondent with the British army. Written subject to the censorship and partly to stimulate popular morale, they present a series of vivid, highly colored pictures of modern warfare into which the subjective element enters rather largely. Judged from the historical standpoint they are subject to limitations, though they possess value as revealing one phase of war psychology. Review of *a.,* F. F. Kelly, *Bookman,*

42:465, Dec. 1915; of *b.*, H. W. Nevinson, *Nation* (London), 21:18, Apr. 5, 1917; of *c.*, *Spectator*, 120:448, Apr. 27, 1918; of *d.*, *Dial*, 67:34, July 12, 1919. *e.* Constitutes an epilogue in which the author writes without restraint of the horrors of war as he witnessed them. Review, *New Republic*, 22:356, May 12, 1920. *f.*, *g.*, and *h.* Similar volumes by an American war correspondent. Review of *f.*, *Nation* (N. Y.), 101:694, Dec. 9, 1915; of *g.*, *A.H.R.* 23:898, July 1918; of *h.*, H. C. Bell, *A.H.R.* 24:712, July 1919.   WES

J326 Montgomery, Sir Archibald A. *Story of the fourth army in the battles of the hundred days, August 8th to November 11th, 1918.* London, 1920.

Thoroughly scientific account of a major military operation by a highly trained general staff officer, with every resource in the way of official data at his disposal. Interesting primarily to serious students of military history and to persons who participated in the operations described. Valuable reproductions of photographs and diagrams and a superb set of large scale maps. Review, *Spectator*, 125:213, Aug. 14, 1920.   WES

J327 Fuller, John F. C. *Tanks in the great war, 1914-1918.* London, 1920.

Authoritative account by the chief general staff officer of the tank corps in the British army for two years. Contains interesting descriptive material; debatable views on the military value of tanks. Review, *Spectator*, 124:391, March 20, 1920.   WES

J331a Malleterre, Pierre M. G. *Études et impressions de guerre.* 5 v. Paris, 1917-19.

b Palat, Barthélemy E. (Pierre Lehautcour). *La grande guerre sur le front occidental.* V. 1-12. Paris, 1917-27.

a. Consists of newspaper and review articles written in an historical spirit by a French officer forced into retirement by his wounds. The articles, while each is a separate study, make up a good account of the fighting on the western front to May 1918. Well adapted to the general reader because very clear and not overloaded with details. *b.* Very detailed military history by the author of many well-known books on the Franco-Prussian War. Its minute accounts of the positions and movements of many military units make it, in general, suitable only for specialists, but certain chapters, containing the author's general views, are of great interest and are adapted to the general reader. Very critical of the French high command and of French tactics; several passages have been deleted by the military censors. There are no plans in the text and the folding maps, while good for topography, do not show the positions of the troops. Review, v. 6, J. Isaac, *Rev. Hist.* 142:267, March 1923. V. 11. Completes narrative to close of 1916.   FMA

J332 Mangin, Joseph E. *Comment finit la guerre.* Paris, 1920.

One of the most valuable books on the military operations of the World War; by one of the ablest French generals; covers all the fighting on the western front, except 1915. Remarkable for its keen penetration, fullness of information, concentration on essentials, clear and interesting style, fairness, and inclusion of almost every matter of organization and policy which influenced military operations. Suitable for both the general reader and the specialist on military history. Review, G. B. Hurst, *E.H.R.* 36:475, July 1921.   FMA

J341 Feyler, Fernand. *La guerre européenne.* Paris, 1915.

Valuable study of the fighting on the western front to May 1915, by a Swiss officer, revised from current articles in *Journal de Genève.* The official, or virtually official, information given to the public is critically examined to bring out what really happened and the impression the public would get from the official statements. Too detailed for the general reader, but of great interest to the specialist in military history and those interested in the methods and the effect of propaganda.   FMA

J346 Essen, Léon van der. *Invasion and the war in Belgium from Liège to the Yser, with a sketch of the diplomatic negotiations preceding the conflict.* London, 1917. Tr. from *L'invasion allemande en Belgique de Liège à l'Yser,* Paris, 1917.

Written during the war by a professor of history in the University of Louvain, it exhibits as much impartiality as could be expected. It is so thoroughly documented that it will always be possible to correct statements based on sources which time proves to have been inadequate. Accounts of eye-witnesses have been used, but not followed blindly. Review, *Spectator,* 118:675, June 16, 1917.
                                                                                                           LFB

J347a Toynbee, Arnold J. *German terror in Belgium.* London and N. Y., 1917.
  b ——— *German terror in France: an historical record.* London and N. Y., 1917.

Attempts to show, from official sources available at the time, the nature and extent of the atrocities committed by the German armies in Belgium and France respectively during the opening months of the war. Better as propaganda than as history. Review of *b.,* A. C. Krey, *A.H.R.* 23:856, July 1918.   GMD

WORLD WAR, 1914–1918: EASTERN CAMPAIGNS

J351a Wilton, Robert. *Russia's agony.* London, 1918.
  b **Frantz, Gunther.** *Russlands Eintritt in den Weltkrieg: der Ausbau der russischen Wehrmacht und ihr Einsatz bei Kriegsausbruch, mit Genehmigung des Reichsarchivs und unter Benutzung amtlicher Quellen.* Berlin, 1924.
  c ——— *Russland auf dem Wege zur Katastrophe: Tagebücher des Grossfürsten Andrej und des Kriegsministers Poliwanow; Briefe des Grossfürsten an den Zaren.* Berlin, 1926.

a. Interesting popular account by the London *Times* correspondent in St. Petersburg, of political conditions and military preparations in Russia before and during the World War. Review, *Spectator,* 120:285, March 16, 1918.   *b.* Contains a large number of secret military telegrams captured by the Germans during the war and a valuable study, based on them, of Russia's strategic and political aims and preparations. Review, S. B. Fay, *A.H.R.* 30:646, Apr. 1925; H. Rothfels, *Hist. Zeit.* 132:122, 1925.   *c.* Presents evidence that the war aims of Russia were directed not merely toward the Balkans and the Straits but also to the crushing of Germany; also valuable for technical and strategic information furnished by the Russian minister of war.   SBF

J352a Knox, Sir Alfred W. F. *With the Russian army, 1914–1917, being chiefly extracts from the diary of a military attaché.* 1 v. in 2. London and N. Y., 1921.

b Gourko, Basil. *War and revolution in Russia, 1914–1917.* N. Y., 1919. English ed., *Memories and impressions of war and revolution in Russia, 1914–1917,* London, 1919.

These volumes are readable and supplement one another admirably. *a.* Extremely valuable commentary on Russian military operations and domestic conditions before and during the revolution; intimate personal glimpses of the Russian leaders are of special interest. Review, *Spectator*, 127:709, Nov. 26, 1921. *b.* Deals with the same events and conditions as *a*, but from the standpoint of a Russian military leader. Review, S. B. Fay, *A.H.R.* 24:695, July 1919.

WES

J353a Danilov, Iurii Nikiforovich. *Russland im Weltkrieg 1914–1915.* Jena, 1925. Tr. by Rudolf, Freiherr von Campenhausen.

b Denikin, Anton Ivanovich. *Russian turmoil: memoirs, military, social, and political.* London and N. Y., 1922. French ed., *La décomposition de l'armée et du pouvoir, février-septembre, 1917,* Paris, 1921.

c *Les alliés contre la Russie avant, pendant, et après la guerre mondiale.* Paris, 1926. Tr. from the Russian.

a. and *b.* Interestingly written accounts, with useful sketch-maps, by two leading officers in the tsar's army. Review of *b.*, *Nation* (London), 31:384, June 10, 1922. *c.* Contains studies of Russia's tragic part in the World War by sixteen officers and professors formerly in the military and naval academies. Though previously holding office under the tsar they were reconciled with the soviet authorities. Their thesis, supported by a considerable number of hitherto unpublished documents from the Russian war archives, is that Russia was exploited by her allies for their own selfish political and military interests.

SBF

J356a Stiénon, Charles. *Le mystère roumain et la défection russe,* Paris, 1918.

b Sturdza, Michel. *Avec l'armée roumaine, 1916–1918.* Paris, 1918. [Mémoires et récits de guerre.]

c Falkenhayn, Erich von. *Der Feldzug der neunten Armée gegen die Rumänen und Russen, 1916–1917.* 2 v. Berlin, 1920–21.

a. and *b.* Present Rumania's part in the war from the Rumanian point of view. *c.* Account of the campaign of the Central Powers against Rumania, by the officer in command.

GMD

J361a Kanner, Heinrich. *Kaiserliche Katastrophenpolitik, ein Stück zeitgenössischer Geschichte.* Leipzig, 1922.

b Nowak, Karl F. *Der Weg zur Katastrophe.* 1919. 25th ed., Berlin, 1922.

c —— *Collapse of central Europe.* London and N. Y., 1924. Tr. by P. Lochner and E. W. Dickes from *Der Sturz der Mittelmächte,* München, 1921.

d —— *Chaos.* München, 1923.

e Auerbach, Bertrand. *L'Autriche et la Hongrie pendant la guerre.* Paris, 1925.

a. and *b.* Brilliantly written journalistic accounts of the reckless Austrian political and military leadership which led to the war. Kanner, whose Vienna newspaper, *Die Zeit,* was suppressed, makes a very severe indictment. Nowak, an intimate friend of Conrad, the Austrian chief of staff, is apologetic. Review, of *a.,* S. B. Fay, *A.H.R.* 27:824, July 1922. *c.* and *d.* Graphic accounts of the political and military conditions which, respectively, led to the collapse of the Dual Monarchy and resulted from it. Review of *c., Spectator,* 133:197, Aug. 9, 1924; R. L. Duffus, *Book Review, N. Y. Times,* 10, Aug. 31, 1924. *e.* Scholarly analysis, based on documents, of the internal history of Austria-Hungary during the war, by a veteran student of the country. Review, P. Renouvin, *Revue d'Histoire de la Guerre Mondiale,* 4:66, Jan. 1926. For Italy's part in the World War, cf. (O411–412). SBF

J366a Feyler, Fernand. *Les campagnes en Serbie, 1914–1915.* Paris, 1925.

b ——— *La campagne de Macédoine, 1916–1918.* 2 v. Genève, 1920–21.

Studies by an able Swiss military expert (cf. J341) of the political as well as the military activities in the Balkan peninsula throughout the World War. Excellent maps and illustrations. SBF

J371 Dane, Edmund. *British campaigns in the Nearer East, 1914–1918, from the outbreak of the war with Turkey to the armistice.* 2 v. London and N. Y., 1919.

Succinct, readable account of political as well as military factors in the Nearer East. The narrative of military operations is preceded by a valuable and suggestive sketch of the origin, progress, and influence of German policy in Turkey. The volumes reveal an unusually keen appreciation of strategical values and of military motives and considerations of policy which led to the undertaking of the several campaigns. Review, *Spectator,* 123:777, Dec. 6, 1919. WES

J372a Nevinson, Henry W. *Dardanelles campaign.* London, 1918; N. Y., 1919. (Bibliography.)

b Callwell, Sir Charles E. *The Dardanelles.* London and Boston, 1919. [Campaigns and their lessons.] (Bibliography.)

c Masefield, John. *Gallipoli.* London and N. Y., 1916.

d Hamilton, Sir Ian S. M. *Gallipoli diary.* 2 v. London and N. Y., 1920.

a. and *b.* Both written from the English point of view, with little knowledge from enemy sources. *a.* By a newspaper correspondent who was on the spot during most of the campaign. Not a personal reminiscence, but a straightforward narrative utilizing accessible published materials. The author was an 'easterner', believing that the strategy of the Entente powers should have concentrated upon the Dardanelles. Review, *Nation* (London), 24:358, Dec. 21, 1918. *b.* More technical work; avoids the question of grand strategy; considers local strategical problems and those phases of the campaign which illustrate unusual forms of tactical work, and which afford lessons in 'amphibious warfare'. Review, H. W. Nevinson, *Nation* (London), 26:648, Feb. 7, 1920. RAN

c. Brilliant, non-technical defense of the British enterprise by a participant. Review, *Spectator,* 117:415, Oct. 7, 1916; F. Hackett, *New Republic,* 9:22, Nov. 4, 1916. *d.* Personal narrative of the British commander; prepared with elaborate care. Review, *Spectator,* 124:762, June 5, 1920; W. J. M. A. Maloney, *Nation* (N. Y.), 111:653, Dec. 8, 1920. GMD

J376a Massey, William T. *Desert campaigns.* London, 1918.

b —— *How Jerusalem was won, being the record of Allenby's campaign in Palestine.* London, 1919.

c —— *Allenby's final triumph.* London, 1920.

These three volumes, by the official correspondent of London newspapers with the Egyptian expeditionary force, comprise a practically continuous history of the British operations upon the Suez canal, in Palestine, and in Syria, down to the final Turkish *débâcle* in 1918. The description of desert warfare is valuable and interesting; comments upon the political aspects of the campaigns are most illuminating. The importance of these operations relative to those in other theaters is somewhat over-emphasized. Review of *a.*, *Spectator*, 120:544, May 25, 1918; of *b.*, *Nation* (London), 26:748, Feb. 28, 1920; of *c.*, *Athenaeum*, 889, Dec. 31, 1920.

WES

J377a Townshend, Sir Charles V. F. *My campaign in Mesopotamia.* 2 v. London and N. Y., 1920.

b Sandes, Edward W. C. *In Kut and captivity with the sixth Indian division.* London, 1919, N. Y., 1920.

c Candler, Edmund. *Long road to Baghdad.* 2 v. London and N. Y., 1919.

Taken together, these three well-written personal narratives provide a good account of all phases of the Mesopotamian campaigns. Review of *a.*, *Athenaeum*, 1:474, Apr. 9, 1920; of *b.*, *Athenaeum*, 2:912, Sept. 19, 1919; of *c.*, *Spectator*, 122:166, Feb. 8, 1919. Also cf. (J724) Callwell, *Life of Sir Stanley Maude*, and (J286) for the British official account.

GMD

J378a Dane, Edmund. *British campaigns in Africa and the Pacific, 1914–1918.* London and N. Y., 1919.

b Crowe, John H. V. *General Smuts' campaign in East Africa.* London, 1918.

c Buchanan, Angus. *Three years of war in East Africa.* London, 1919. Reprint, 1920.

d Fendall, Charles P. *East African Force, 1915–1919: an unofficial record of its creation and fighting career, together with some account of the civil and military administrative conditions in East Africa before and during that period.* London, 1921.

e Schnee, Heinrich. *Deutsch-Ost-Afrika im Weltkriege: wie wir lebten und kämpften.* Leipzig, 1919.

a. Convenient general account by a British writer. Review, *Times* (*London*) *Literary Supplement*, 728, Dec. 11, 1919.   *b.*, *c.*, and *d.* Good accounts of English participants in the East African campaigns.   *e.* Personal record of the German governor of East Africa. Also cf. (J762) Lettow-Vorbeck, *My reminiscences of East Africa.*

GMD

WORLD WAR, 1914–1918: NAVAL OPERATIONS

J381 Frothingham, Thomas G. *Naval history of the world war.* 3 v. Cambridge, Mass., 1924–26. [1, *Offensive operations, 1914–1915*; 2, *Stress of sea-power, 1915–1916*; 3, *United States in the war, 1917–1918.*]

Best account for the general reader; also important for the specialist. An unusually lucid attempt to point out how far the naval operations conformed to the requirements of naval strategy. Attention is everywhere focused on things which counted toward determining the length and outcome of the war. Though 'compiled from data provided by the Historical Section, United States Navy,' it is based largely on the personal narratives of Tirpitz, Churchill, Jellicoe, and Scheer and the British and German official naval histories. The literary style suffers from the extent to which the author quotes his sources. Admirably equipped with maps and plans. Review, E. Breck, *A.H.R.* 30:366, Jan. 1925; 31:138, Oct. 1925.   FMA

J382a Corbett, Sir Julian S., and **Newbolt, Sir Harry.** *Naval operations.* 4 v. London and N. Y., 1920–25.

    b Fayle, Charles Ernest. *Seaborne trade.* 3 v.   London and N. Y., 1920–24.

    c Hurd, Archibald S. *Merchant navy.* 2 v.   London and N. Y., 1921–24.

Three parts of the official *History of the Great War based on official documents, by direction of the Historical Section of the Committee of Imperial Defence.*   *a.* Elaborate work of the highest importance. Written with free access to British official documents; the opinions, however, which must often be read between the lines, are those of the writer. While very detailed, its clear and interesting style, free from any excess of technical terms, makes it suitable for the general reader as well as the specialist. Well equipped with maps and plans. Review, B. A. Fiske, *A.H.R.* 26:94, Oct. 1920; E. Breck, *A.H.R.* 27:562, Apr. 1922; 29:556, Apr. 1924.   *b.* and *c.* Similarly valuable works in their respective fields. Review of *b.*, E. Breck, *A.H.R.* 26:531, Apr. 1921; 28:750, July 1923; 30:145, Oct. 1924; of *c.*, E. Breck, *A.H.R.* 27:122, Oct. 1921; 30:861, July 1925; 32:603, Apr. 1927.   FMA

J383 Mantey, Eberhard von, ed. *Der Krieg zur See, 1914–1918, herausgegeben vom Marine-Archiv.* Berlin, 1920 ff. [1, O. Gross, *Der Krieg in der Nordsee,* v. 1–5, 1920–25; 2, R. Firle, *Der Krieg in der Ostsee,* v. 1, 1921; 3, E. Raeder, *Der Kreuzerkrieg in den ausländischen Gewässern,* 2 v., 1922–23.]

German general staff history of naval operations. The volumes thus far issued describe operations in the North Sea to June 1916, and in the Baltic to March 1915, and all the more distant operations in the first two years of the war. Technical and thorough.   GMD

J384 Thomazi, Auguste A. *La marine française dans la grande guerre, 1914–1918.* V. 1–4. Paris, 1924–29. [1, *La guerre navale dans la zone des armées du Nord;* 2, *La guerre navale dans L'Adriatique.*] [Collection de mémoires, études, et documents pour servir à l'histoire de la guerre mondiale.] (Bibliography.)

Written by a captain in the French navy who retired from active service to prepare this work. Careful, generally dispassionate study with less attention to technical details than would naturally have been expected from a naval expert. Review of v. 1, 2, E. Breck, *A.H.R.* 32:120, Oct. 1926.   GMD

J385 Amet, Jacques. *Le Jutland: bataille navale du 31 mai 1916.* Paris, 1923.

Supplants all earlier accounts of the campaign as it is based on published works, both British and German, not accessible to earlier writers. Written by a French naval officer; carefully critical; represents substantially the present consensus of judgment on the action and its results. Review, E. Breck, *A.H.R.* 29:335, Jan. 1924.

GMD

J391a Churchill, Winston L. S. *World crisis, 1911–1914.* London and N. Y., 1923.

b —— *World crisis, 1915.* London and N. Y., 1923.

c —— *World crisis, 1916–1918.* 2 v. London, 1927.

d —— *Aftermath.* London, 1929.

a, b, c and *d.* Practically a single work; brilliantly written; probably most important personal narrative dealing with the naval history of the World War. The most striking features are the description of British naval preparation in anticipation of war with Germany, the story of the control over naval operations during the early months of hostilities, and the spirited defence of the author's share in the Dardanelles expedition. Review, E. Breck, *A.H.R.* 29:137, Oct. 1923; 29:558, Apr. 1924; of *a.*, B. E. Schmitt, *Pol. Sci. Quar.* 38:690, Dec. 1923.

FMA

J392a Jellicoe, John R., Viscount. *Grand fleet, 1914–16: its creation, development, and work.* London and N. Y., 1919.

b —— *Crisis of the naval war.* London and N. Y., 1920.

These two books constitute a complete and remarkably candid narrative of the naval operations under Jellicoe's charge. *a.* Reveals, in ch. 4–10, which are addressed primarily to specialists, surprising defects in the British naval equipment during the earlier part of the World War. Gives, in ch. 12–15, matter-of-fact but vivid narrative of the battle of Jutland and Jellicoe's defense of his tactics. Review, B. A. Fiske, *A.H.R.* 25:280, Jan. 1920. *b.* Describes the methods employed against the German submarines in 1917–1918. Review, *Spectator*, 125:145, July 31, 1920.

FMA

J393 Sims, William S., and Hendrick, Burton J. *Victory at sea.* Garden City, N. Y., 1920.

Admiral Sims, who was in charge of American naval operations in European waters during the World War, gives a remarkably clear, concise, and illuminating account of the Anglo-American campaign against German submarines; describes the use of convoys, sub-chasers, mystery ships, and the mine barrage from Scotland to Norway. The first chapter is a perfectly frank statement of the naval situation when the United States entered the war, based on information furnished at the time to Sims by the British naval authorities. Review, *A.H.R.* 26:332, Jan. 1921.

FMA

J396a Tirpitz, Alfred P. F. von. *My memoirs.* 2 v. London and N. Y., 1919. Tr. from *Erinnerungen,* Berlin, 1919; 2nd rev. ed., Leipzig, 1920.

b —— *Politische Dokumente: der Aufbau der deutschen Weltmacht.* Stuttgart, 1924.

c —— *Politische Dokumente: Deutsche Ohnmachtspolitik im Weltkriege.* Hamburg, 1926.

a. Popular, vigorously written autobiography of Tirpitz, who was German naval minister from 1897 to 1916; throws much light on the building of the German navy; criticizes the political leadership of the German chancellors and the handling of the submarine campaign during the World War; contains numerous letters written from German headquarters in France in 1914–1915. The bitter tone of the book detracts from its value, and its comments on international politics must be treated with great caution, but it presents an interesting picture of the mentality of the high officials of the German government during the period concerned.   Review, H. Delbrück, *Preussische Jahrbücher,* 178:309, Oct. 1919; L. Roustam, *Revue Critique,* n.s. 87:161, May 1, 1920; C. Gauss, *A.H.R.* 25:499, Apr. 1920.   *b.* More technical but more valuable for the historian; consists mainly of documents relating to the upbuilding of the German navy and to the long negotiations with England, including the Haldane Mission of 1912, for an agreement for a mutual limitation of the rivalry in naval competition.   Review, A. Lajusan, *Revue d'histoire de la guerre mondiale,* 4:59, Jan. 1926.   *c.* Contains important documents concerning the management of the German navy during the World War; criticizes the policies of the civil authorities.

FMA, SBF

J397 Scheer, Reinhardt. *Germany's high sea fleet in the world war.* London and N. Y., 1920. Tr. from *Deutschlands Hochseeflotte im Weltkriege, persönliche Erinnerungen,* 1920. 3rd., ed., Berlin, 1922.

Account of the warfare in the North and Baltic seas and of the German submarine operations, combined with considerable personal narrative, by the German commander at the battle of Jutland.   The most valuable chapters are: 1–2, on the situation at the beginning; 10–11, on the battle of Jutland; 13–14, on the signficance of the submarine operations; 18, on the German naval command.   Review, *Spectator,* 124:458, Apr. 3, 1920.   FMA

WORLD WAR 1914–1918: AERIAL OPERATIONS

J401a Raleigh, Sir Walter A. *War in the air, being the story of the part played in the great war by the royal air force.* V. 1. Oxford, 1922. [History of the great war based on official documents, by direction of the Historical Section of the Committee Imperial Defence.]

   b Bingham, Hiram. *An explorer in the air service.* New Haven, 1920.

a. Official history of the British air service; interrupted by the author's death. Review, W. S. Holt, *A.H.R.* 28:318, Jan. 1923.   *b.* Personal narrative of an officer in the American air service.   Review, W. E. Stevens, *A.H.R.* 26:596, Apr. 1921.   GMD

WORLD WAR, 1914–1918: PARTICIPATION OF THE UNITED STATES

J411 McMaster, John B. *United States in the world war,* 2 v. N. Y. and London, 1918–20.

   Among the best of the contemporary accounts of the part played by the United States in the World War and in the making of the peace treaty.   Available official documents are drawn upon, but the most notable feature is the liberal use made of newspapers and editorial comments, both domestic and foreign.   These enable the reader to follow the trend of public opinion in the United States, as well as the unofficial attitude towards the United States abroad. Review, *A.H.R.* 24:496, Apr. 1919; 26:554, Apr. 1921.   WRW

J412 Bassett, John S. *Our war with Germany, a history.* N. Y., 1919.

Best short account of the share of the United States in the World War; gives concisely the most significant facts about nearly all the more important aspects of the subject. In the endeavor to avoid exaggeration and unwarranted national glorification, the style becomes sometimes a little dull. Review, *A.H.R.* 25:737, July 1920. FMA

J421a Scott, James B. *Survey of international relations between the United States and Germany, August 1, 1914–April 6, 1917, based on official documents.* N. Y. and Oxford, 1917.

b Robinson, Edgar E., and **West, Victor J.** *Foreign policy of Woodrow Wilson, 1913–1917.* N. Y., 1917.

c Barclay, Sir Thomas. *Le président Wilson et l'évolution de la politique étrangère des États-Units.* Paris, 1918.

d Viallate, Achille. *Les États-Unis d'Amérique et le conflit européen, 4 août 1914–6 avril 1917.* Paris, 1919.

e Hovelaque, Émile. *Les États-Unis et la guerre: de la neutralité à la croisade.* Paris, 1919.

f Grattan, C. Hartley. *Why we fought.* N. Y., 1929. (Bibliography.)

Aside from the documents quoted, none of these war-time books will possess permanent value, except as illustrations of war psychology and propaganda. *a.* Fully documented, scholarly presentation of the case of the United States against Germany. Review, C. N. Gregory, *A.H.R.* 24:494, Apr. 1919. *b.* and *c.* Less solid but more popular works of similar tendency though arranged as expositions of President Wilson's policy. Review, F. M. Anderson, *A.H.R.* 24:112, Oct. 1918. *d.* and *e.* Expositions of the circumstances and reasons leading to the entrance of the United States into the World War. *d.* Emphasizes the development of American foreign policy. *e.* Stresses the movement of public opinion. Review of *d.* and *e.*, G. F. Zook, *A.H.R.* 25:124, Oct. 1919.
GMD
f. Emphasizes the influence of Allied propaganda and minimizes idealistic motives as reasons for American participation in the World War. SBF

J422a Bernstorff, Johann H. A. H. A. Graf von. *My three years in America.* N. Y. and London, 1920. Tr. from *Deutschland und Amerika: Erinnerungen aus dem fünfjährigen Kriege,* Berlin, 1920.

b Lechartier, Georges. *Intrigues et diplomaties à Washington, 1914–1917.* Paris, 1919.

a. Comprehensive, well-informed, well-written review of the diplomatic relations between Germany and the United States between 1914 and 1917 by the German ambassador at Washington. Corrects much of the current misinformation about German propaganda and intrigues in the United States; gives a detailed account of President Wilson's attempts to mediate between the warring powers of Europe; contains many searching criticisms of Germany's policies. Review, E. E. Sperry, *A.H.R.* 26:98, Oct. 1920. *b.* Perhaps the best statement of the case against Bernstorff and the other agents of the Central Powers in the United States. Review, E. E. Sperry, *A.H.R.* 25:527, Apr. 1920. SBF

J423 House, Edward M. *Intimate papers of Colonel House arranged as a narrative by Charles Seymour.* 4 v. Boston and London, 1926–28.

Consists mainly of extensive extracts from the diary and correspondence of Colonel House skilfully arranged to tell the story of American and international events in which he had a part from about 1912 to June, 1919. Contains much important information not accessible elsewhere. Probably the most valuable book coming from a leading participant in international affairs during the World War period. Review, F. L. Paxson, *A.H.R.* 31:812, July 1926; S. P. Duggan, *Yale Rev.* 15:786, July 1926; B. E. Schmitt, *Pol. Sci. Quar.* 41:460, Sept. 1926. V. 3–4 are an invaluable record of the participation of the United States in the war and of the negotiations at the Peace Conference. Review, F. L. Paxson, *A.H.R.* 34:370, Jan. 1929.   FMA

J431a Thomas, Shipley. *History of the A. E. F.* N. Y., 1920.

    b Page, Arthur W. *Our 110 days' fighting.* Garden City, N. Y., 1920.

    c Wise, Jennings C. *Turn of the tide: American operations at Cantigny, Château Thierry, and the second battle of the Marne.* N. Y., 1920.

    d Chambrun, Jacques A. de Pineton, Comte de, and Marenches, Charles, Comte de. *American army in the European conflict.* N. Y., 1919. Tr. by the authors from *L'armée américaine dans le conflit européen,* Paris, 1919.

a. Best single volume of medium size upon the American army in the World War. Its author had an unusually extensive experience as a participant; gathered information from representatives of each combat division at the Army Intelligence School; had access to materials at Washington; and got much assistance from officers representing all branches of the service. Clear and interesting style; good maps. Review, *Review of Reviews* (N. Y.), 62:671, Dec. 1920. *b.* Valuable brief account, for the general reader, of the fighting done by American troops in the World War. Ch. 5. One of the best short descriptions of the Meuse-Argonne battle. Ch. 6. Gives short summaries of the history of each combat division. Good maps. *c.* One of the most valuable short studies upon American military operations in the World War. The American portion of the operations in the critical period between May 31 and August 6, 1918 is told in enough detail to be readily understood and is put into proper relation with the larger operations. The author was a participant, made special studies of the ground, and had access to the archives of the American general headquarters. *d.* Non-technical account by two French officers who were in a position to observe the American military operations. Review, *A.H.R.* 25:529, Apr. 1920.

The student of the military side of American participation in the World War will need to consult the growing accumulation of divisional and regimental histories.   FMA

J436a Crowell, Benedict, and Wilson, Robert F. *How America went to war, an account from official sources of the nation's war activities, 1917–1920.* 6 v. New Haven and London, 1921. [1, *Giant hand, our mobilization and control of industry and natural resources, 1917–1918;* 2–3, *Road to France, the transportation of troops and military supplies, 1917–1918;* 4–5, *Armies of industry, our nation's manufacture of munitions for a world in arms, 1917–1918;* 6, *Demobilization, our industrial and military demobilization after the armistice, 1918–1920.*

    b Clarkson, Grosvenor B. *Industrial America in the world war, the strategy behind the line, 1917–1918.* Boston, 1923.

a. Uncritical compilation of materials, chiefly from official sources and partly reprinted from public documents. Mr. Crowell was assistant secretary of war and director of munitions, 1917–1920. Review, v. 1–3, F. Schneider, Jr., *A.H.R.* 27:136, Oct. 1921; v. 4–6, F. Fritts, *A.H.R.* 28:339, Jan. 1923. *b.* Primarily an account of the work of the war industries board by the former director of the United States council of national defense. Review, *A.H.R.* 29:361, Jan. 1924.

GMD

PARIS PEACE CONFERENCE, 1919

J441a [*Peace*] *handbooks issued by the historical section of the foreign office,* ed. by Sir G. W. Prothero. 161 pt. in 25 v. London, 1920. (Bibliographies.)

b Anderson, Frank M. and **Hershey, Amos S.** *Handbook for the diplomatic history of Europe, Asia, and Africa, 1870–1914.* Washington, 1918. [National Board for Historical Service.] (Bibliographies.)

c Scott, Arthur P. *Introduction to the peace treaties.* Chicago, 1920. (Brief bibliography.)

a. Monographs prepared for the information and use of the British delegates to the Paris peace conference. Separate numbers deal with practically every state and colony or disputed area in the world. Each number presents a sufficient historical survey to indicate the present status of the areas, summarizes their international relations and problems, and contains a considerable amount of descriptive and statistical information. Convenient, sometimes excellent, introductions to the study of the regions concerned. Review, *A.H.R.* 26:135, Oct. 1920; 26:365, Jan. 1921; 26:582, Apr. 1921. *b.* Summary prepared for the information and use of the American delegates at the Paris conference; valuable manual of international relations since 1870. *c.* Outline history of the peace negotiations and analysis of the treaty provisions. Good handbook. Review, C. Seymour, *A.H.R.* 26:137, Oct. 1920.

GMD

J442a Harris, H. Wilson. *Peace in the making.* London and N. Y., 1920.

b Dillon, Emile J. *Inside story of the peace conference.* N. Y. and London, 1920.

a. Best journalistic account; has considerable historical value. The author, the special correspondent of the London *Daily News* at the Paris peace conference, was well informed, fair-minded, idealistic but practical. Review, *Nation* (London), 26:484, Jan. 3, 1920. *b.* As the most experienced international correspondent at the peace conference, the author might have written with knowledge and discrimination. Ignored by the leading statesmen, he took revenge in this bitter, partisan, and misleading book. It has no inside information, is badly arranged, and has importance only because it reflects the point of view of some of the small states, the Russian refugees, the Italians in part, and the bitterest enemies of Wilson, Clemenceau, and Lloyd George. Review, C. Seymour, *A.H.R.* 26:101, Oct. 1920.

FMA

J443 Temperley, Harold W. V., ed. *History of the peace conference of Paris.* 6 v. London, 1920–24. [British Institute of International Affairs.]

Coöperative work, written by a group of English and American historians, most of whom were present in some capacity at the peace conference. Not a definitive history of the conference, but the most helpful large work that has yet been published. V. 1–3. Deal with the settlement with Germany. V. 4–5. Consider the treaties relating to Austria, Hungary, and Bulgaria. V. 6. Treats the settlements affecting Turkey and the East. Review, C. Seymour, *A.H.R.* 26:535, Apr. 1921; 27:566, Apr. 1922; 30:369, Jan. 1925.   FMF

Cf. also R. C. Binkley, 'Ten years of Peace Conference history,' *Jour of Mod. Hist.*, 1:607–629, Dec. 1929.

J444a Baker, Ray S. *What Wilson did at Paris,* Garden City, N. Y., 1919.

b —— *Woodrow Wilson and world settlement, written from his unpublished and personal material.* 3 v. Garden City, N. Y., 1922.

c —— *Woodrow Wilson; life and letters. I, Youth; II, Princeton.* N. Y., 1927.

Sympathetic interpretations of Woodrow Wilson's efforts to realize American ideals in the peace negotiations after the World War. Review of *a.*, *Review of Reviews* (N. Y.), 61:106, Jan. 1920.   *b.* One of the leading representatives of the American press at Paris, possessing President Wilson's confidence and entrusted with his private collection of documents, the author writes with authority. His point of view, though friendly to President Wilson's aims, is not narrowly partisan or provocative. His presentation is fair, moderate, remarkably lucid, and admirably written. The treatment is comprehensive, popular but not journalistic, careful and accurate without the formalities of scholarship. The work is a valuable record by a discriminating and intelligent observer. Review, C. Seymour, *A.H.R.* 28:548, Apr. 1923.   LBP

c. First biography of President Wilson that can be regarded as of serious historical importance. Author has been given access to all of Mr. Wilson's papers. Review, C. Seymour, *A.H.R.* 33:898, July 1928.   SBF

J445a House, Edward M., and **Seymour, Charles,** ed. *What really happened at Paris, the story of the peace conference, 1918–1919, by American delegates.* N. Y., 1921.

b Haskins, Charles H., and **Lord, Robert H.** *Some problems of the peace conference.* Cambridge, Mass., 1920. [Lowell Institute lectures.] (Bibliographies.)

c Lansing, Robert. *Big four and others of the peace conference.* Boston, 1921.

d —— *Peace negotiations, a personal narrative.* Boston, 1921.

a. One of the most valuable books on the peace conference. Consists chiefly of sixteen lectures delivered at Philadelphia in 1920–1921 by former members of the staff of the American peace commission. Numerous questions and answers which followed the lectures are given in an appendix. Each speaker dealt with problems for which he had helped prepare the settlement at Paris. Nearly all the lectures are first-hand information presented in an historical rather than a controversial spirit. Review, C. Gauss, *A.H.R.* 28:123, Oct. 1922; *Nation* (London), 27:548, July 9, 1921.   *b.* Probably the most valuable book on the territorial aspects of the peace settlement of 1919. The authors, as American experts, helped to prepare several of the settlements they describe. Following an illuminating description of the working methods of the peace conference, consideration is given to each important territorial problem which had to be settled. Geography, population, national sentiments, economic condition, and strategic importance are described objectively and without excessive details. Arguments on controverted questions are summarized. The account of the Saar valley settlement has special value. Review, C. Day, *A.H.R.* 26:334, Jan. 1921. *c.* Impressions of the leading personalities of the peace conference. Review, C. Seymour, *A.H.R.* 27:612, Apr. 1922. *d.* Personal narrative and apologia of the American secretary of state as a delegate to the peace conference. Review, W. Lippmann, *New Republic,* 20:137, March 30, 1921; F. Frankfurter, *New Republic,* 26:198, Apr. 13, 1921. FMA

J451 Hanotaux, Gabriel. *Le traité de Versailles du 28 juin 1919: l'Allemagne et l'Europe.* Paris, 1919.

Not a history of the peace negotiations but a discussion and criticism of the peace terms from the point of view of the military security of France. Much emphasis is laid on the need for a strategic frontier between France and Germany, but the main thesis of the author is that France will never be secure while Prussia is allowed to remain the principal state in a unified Germany. The Allies should not have dealt with Germany but should have reorganized central Europe as a loose confederation of 'the Germanies'; and Prussia, at all events, should have been forbidden to hold lands west of the Rhine.

For German criticisms of the treaty, especially of article 231, cf. (J264*b*) Montgelas, *Case for the central powers,* and works listed in (J3*a*) *Die Kriegsschuldfrage.* PWS

J452 Tardieu, André P. G. A. *Truth about the treaty.* Indianapolis, 1921. Tr. from *La paix,* Paris, 1921.

Able and vigorous defense of the treaty of Versailles by Clemenceau's chief lieutenant and probably the best informed man, outside the 'big three', about the inside history of the Paris peace conference. Its chief concern is to explain and defend the French point of view; throws a great deal of light upon the processes of the conference, the desires and arguments of the French, British, and American delegates, and the reasons for the compromises which were made; more informing on territorial questions than on reparations or on the League of Nations. The French and English editions differ considerably, each omitting much that is in the other. Review, C. D. Hazen, *Pol. Sci. Quar.* 37:120, March 1922. FMA

J456a Keynes, John M. *Economic consequences of the peace.* London and N. Y., 1920.

b —— *Revision of the treaty, being a sequel to the Economic consequences of the peace.* London, 1922.

Publication at the most favorable moment, a remarkable literary quality, and the ill-founded belief that the author had exceptional opportunities for inside information, won for this book wide influence. Keynes was interested and informed only as to the economic aspects of the peace settlement. Assuming that Wilson, Clemenceau, and Lloyd George could do whatever they wished, he unsparingly condemned them, both intellectually and morally, because he believed the economic features of the treaty of Versailles unfair and unworkable. Historically the book has little value except as an acute criticism of the reparation articles of the treaty of Versailles and as an expression of what the enemies of the 'big three' believed about them in 1919. Review, A. A. Young,

New Republic, 21:388, Feb. 25, 1920. *b.* Rebuttal arguments in support of theses advanced in *a.* Review, *New Republic,* 30:24, March 1, 1922.   FMA

EVENTS SINCE THE TREATY OF VERSAILLES, 1919

J461a Toynbee, Arnold J. *World after the peace conference, being an epilogue to the 'History of the peace conference of Paris' and a prologue to the 'Survey of international affairs, 1920–1923.'* London and N. Y., 1925. [British Institute of International Affairs.]

   b —— *Survey of international affairs, 1920–1923.* London and N. Y., 1925. [British Institute of International Affairs.] (Bibliographies.)

   c —— *Survey of international affairs, 1924 ff* . London and N. Y., 1926 ff. [British Institute of International Affairs.]

Taken together, these works furnish the best historical account of international affairs since 1919; based as far as possible on official documents; objective in treatment. Review of *a.* and *b.,* B. E. Schmitt, *A.H.R.* 31:327, Jan. 1926; of *c.,* J. G. McDonald, *A.H.R.* 32:123, Oct. 1926.   GMD

J462a Gibbons, Herbert A. *Europe since 1918.* N. Y. and London, 1923.

   b Buell, Raymond L. *Europe: a history of ten years.* N. Y., 1928.

a. Readable outline of events including internal conditions of the countries as well as international relations; professedly dispassionate, but opens with a complete condemnation of the peace settlement, a theme which runs throughout the work. Review, W. MacDonald, *Nation* (N. Y.), 117:443, Oct. 17, 1923.
        GMD

b. Clear, candid, and very readable narrative; liberal and internationalist in point of view. Review, P. Slosson, *A.H.R.* 34:646, Apr. 1929.   SBF

J463a Kennedy, Aubrey L. *Old diplomacy and new, 1876–1922: from Salisbury to Lloyd-George.* London, 1922; N. Y., 1923. (Bibliography.)

   b Repington, Charles à Court. *After the war: London, Paris, Rome, Athens, Prague, Vienna, Budapest, Bucharest, Berlin, Sofia, Coblenz, New York, Washington: a diary.* London and Boston, 1922.

   c Fabre-Luce, Alfred. *La crise des alliances: essai sur les relations francobritanniques depuis la signature de la paix 1919–1922.* Paris, 1922. [Bibliothèque de la Société d'Études et d'Informations Économiques.]

a. Interesting volume by a correspondent of the London *Times;* chiefly important as a criticism of the 'new diplomacy' of Lloyd George during and after the World War; records personal observations of Russo-Polish War of 1920. Review, B. E. Schmitt, *A.H.R.* 28:744, July 1923. *b.* Valuable record of personal impressions and of numerous interviews with prominent and influential persons during 1921. Review, *Spectator,* 128:527, Apr. 29, 1922. *c.* Useful study of international affairs, with special reference to France and England, from the treaty of Versailles to the Genoa conference. Candid, penetrating analysis; somewhat critical of the policy of both the French and British governments. Review, *Rev. des. Quest. Hist.* 97:504, Oct. 1922.   FMA

J471a Sweetser, Arthur. *League of nations at work.* N. Y., 1920.

b Williams, Roth. *League of nations today, its growth, record, and relation to British foreign policy.* London and N. Y., 1923. (Brief bibliography.)

c Baker, Philip N. *League of Nations at work.* London, 1926.

d Bassett, John Spencer. *League of Nations: a chapter in world politics.* N. Y., 1928. (Bibliography.)

a. Descriptive study of the League and its organs; written before the first meeting of the assembly. Review, S. Wambaugh, *A.H.R.* 26:538, Apr. 1921. *b.* and *c.* Good accounts of the activities of the League; favorable in tone; intended for the general reader. Review of *b.*, *Times* (London) *Literary Supplement,* 394, June 14, 1923; of *c.*, *ibid.* 587, Sept. 9, 1926; of *d.*, S. B. Fay, (N. Y.) *Nation,* 127:184, Aug. 22, 1928.

GMD

J472 Visscher, Charles De. *Stabilization of Europe.* Chicago, 1924. [Harris Foundation lectures.] (Bibliographies.)

Discussion, by a Belgian professor of law, of the problem of avoidance of future wars, with special attention to the activities of the League of Nations; deals with the questions of nationalism, minorities, security, and international communications.

GMD

J473 Shotwell, James T. *War as an instrument of national policy and its renunciation in the Pact of Paris.* N. Y., 1929.

The historical portion of this book furnishes the clearest and most authoritative account of the origin of the Pact of Paris at present available. Review, Newton D. Baker, *A.H.R.* 34:842-3, July 1929.

FMA

DIPLOMATIC, MILITARY, AND NAVAL HISTORY, INTERNATIONAL LAW

J501a Moon, Parker T. *Syllabus on international relations.* N. Y., 1925. [Institute of International Education.] (Extensive bibliography.)

b Krehbiel, Edward B. *Nationalism, war, and society: a study of nationalism and its concomitant, war, in their relation to civilization and of the fundamentals and the progress of the opposition to war.* N. Y., 1916. (Bibliography.)

a. Convenient analytical outline of nationalism, imperialism, militarism, and diplomatic history, 1867–1920. Review, A. C. Flick, *Hist. Outlook,* 16:236, May 1925. *b.* Older, but still useful, syllabus of the topics indicated in the title. Review, G. E. Howard, *A.H.R.* 22:365, Jan. 1917.

A selection of the more important works on the diplomatic history of the period will be found in the sub-sections of this section, entitled 'Alliances and Ententes, 1871–1914,' 'Crisis of 1914,' and 'Paris Peace Conference.'

GMD

J502a Bloch, Ivan Stanislavovich. *Future of war in its technical, economic, and political relations: is war now impossible?* N. Y., 1899. Later reprints. Tr. by R. C. Long from v. 6 of Russian original. German tr., *Der Krieg,* 6 v., Berlin, 1899. French tr., *La guerre,* 6 v., Paris, 1898–1900.

b Liebknecht, Karl P. A. F. *Militarism.* N. Y., 1917. Tr. from *Militarismus und Antimilitarismus unter besonderer Berücksichtigung der internationalen Jugendbewegung.* Leipzig, 1907. 3rd ed., Zürich, 1911.

    c Nicolai, Georg F. *Biology of war.* N. Y., 1918. Tr. by C. A. Grande and J. Grande from *Die Biologie des Krieges: Betrachtungen eines deutschen Naturforschers.* Zürich, 1917.

    d Jordan, David Starr. *War and the breed: the relation of war to the downfall of nations.* Boston, 1915.

a. Marshals numerous facts, often technical, and arguments drawn chiefly from the history of the leading European powers in the nineteenth century. Alleged to have inspired Nicholas II to summon the first Hague peace conference. Review, *Nation* (N. Y.), 68:377, May 18, 1899. *b.* Forceful arraignment by prominent German socialist. Review, H. Neumann, *Survey,* 39:471, Jan. 26, 1918. *c.* Written in 1915 by a professor of physiology in the University of Berlin; argues that there is no longer biological justification for war; discusses how war may be abolished; remarkable book. Review, L. L. Bernard, *Amer. Jour. of Sociology,* 25:96, July 1919. The authors of *b* and *c* were imprisoned for writing these volumes which were prohibited in Germany. *d.* Perhaps the most significant of several works on pacifism and eugenics by this eminent American biologist.   GMD

J503a Muir, Ramsay. *Nationalism and internationalism, the culmination of modern history.* London and Boston, 1916. (I406c.)

    b Hayes, Carlton J. H. *Essays in nationalism.* N. Y. and London, 1926.

    c Moon, Parker T. *Imperialism and world politics.* .N. Y., 1926. (Bibliographies.)

a. In spite of obvious faults and the war-time atmosphere, a helpful survey of the development of nationalism and of internationalism chiefly since 1815. Review, H. J. Laski, *Dial,* 62:472, May 31, 1917. *b.* Keen analysis of the factors which have contributed to the growth of national ideas and of the effects of nationalism; hostile to nationalism as a creed. Review, *Times* (*London*) *Literary Supplement,* 530, Aug. 12, 1926. *c.* Outlines the history and effects of imperialistic world politics at the close of the nineteenth century and the beginning of the twentieth; clear, useful manual; good maps. Also cf. (K348) Hobson, *Imperialism.*   SBF

J504a Lane, Ralph Norman Angell (pseud. Norman Angell). *Great illusion: a study of the relation of military power in nations to their economic and social advantage.* 1910. 4th rev. ed., London and N. Y., 1913.

    b Mahan, Alfred T. *Armaments and arbitration, or, the place of force in the international relations of states.* N. Y. and London, 1912.

    c Coulton, George G. *Main illusions of pacificism: a criticism of Mr. Norman Angell and of the Union of Democratic Control.* Cambridge, Eng., 1916.

    d Brailsford, Henry N.. *War of steel and gold, a study of the armed peace.* 1914. 9th rev. ed., London and N. Y., 1917.

    e Key, Ellen K. S. *War, peace,. and the future: a consideration of nationalism and internationalism and of the relation of women to war.* N. Y. and London, 1916. Tr. by H. Norberg from *Kriget, freden, och framtiden,* Stockholm, 1914.

a. One of the most widely circulated pacificist publications prior to the World War; argues that war does not pay economically. Review, A. S. Hershey, *Amer. Pol. Sci. Rev.* 5:312, May 1911. *b.* and *c.* Replies to *a* and similar works.

Review of *b.*, *Nation* (N. Y.), 96:39, Jan. 9, 1913; of *c.*, Earl Cromer, *Spectator,* 116:413, March 25, 1916. *d.* Keen analysis of the balance of power between the rival alliances prior to 1914, which the author would replace by a new concert of Europe; written on the eve of the World War. Review, C. H. Levermore, *Amer. Econ. Rev.* 6:430, June 1916. *e.* Dispassionate survey of the problem of war and peace; English translation includes considerable supplementary material, especially on woman's relation to war. Review, T. D. A. Cockerell, *Dial,* 61:465, Nov. 30, 1916.

GMD

J505a Toynbee, Arnold J. *Nationality and the war.* London and N. Y., 1915.

b Fried, Alfred H. *Restoration of Europe.* London and N. Y., 1916. Tr. by L. S. Gannett from *Europäische Wiederherstellung,* Zürich, 1915.

c Dickinson, Goldsworthy Lowes. *Choices before us.* London and N. Y., 1917.

d Brailsford, Henry N. *League of nations.* London and N. Y., 1917.

Notable discussions, written during the progress of the World War, of the problems of post-war reorganization and reconstruction of the international order, especially in Europe. *a.* Devotes special attention to questions of geography and nationality. Review, *Athenaeum,* 1:419, May 8, 1915. *b.* Eminent German pacifist, who won the Nobel peace prize in 1911, argues for a coöperative union of Europe similar to the Pan-American Union. Review, F. A. Ogg, *Dial,* 61:350, Nov. 2, 1916. *c.* Incisive discussion of militarism and internationalism. Insists that international organization can succeed only if all great powers are included. Review, *Saturday Rev.* 124:129, Aug. 18, 1917. *d.* Excellent exposition of proposals for international organization to maintain peace; strong presentation of the case for a league of nations. Review, C. B. Burns, *International Jour. of Ethics,* 27:525, July 1917. Also cf. (K211) Lippmann, *Stakes of diplomacy.*

GMD

J506a Hull, William I. *Two Hague conferences and their contributions to international law.* Boston, 1908.

b Scott, James B. *Hague peace conferences of 1899 and 1907: a series of lectures delivered before the Johns Hopkins University in the year 1908.* 2 v. Baltimore, 1909.

c Higgins, Alexander P. *Hague peace conferences and other international conferences concerning the laws and usages of war.* Cambridge, Eng., and N. Y., 1909.

d Holls, Frederick W. *Peace conference at the Hague and its bearings on international law and policy.* 1900. Reprint, N. Y. and London, 1914.

e Choate, Joseph H. *Two Hague Conferences.* Princeton and London, 1913. [Princeton University, Stafford Little lectures.]

a. Concise record of the origin, procedure, and achievements of the two conferences; intended for the general reader. Review, A. S. Hershey, *A.H.R.* 14:384, Jan. 1909. *b.* Much fuller account; designed for the technical student. V. 2. Contains principal documents relating to the conferences and embodying their work. Review, *A.H.R.* 15:151, Oct. 1909. *c.* Edition of documents, extending from the Congress of Paris, 1856, to the Conference of London, 1909, with commentary by an English scholar. Review, *Saturday Rev.* 109:533, Apr. 23, 1910.

LL

d. Detailed narrative of the conference of 1899 by the secretary of the American delegation; based on official documents and personal observation. Valuable despite propensity to excessive laudation or reticence upon some important matters, owing to the author's official position. Review, G. L. Rives, *A.H.R.* 6:572, Apr. 1901. *e.* Two addresses by the chairman of the American delegation at the second conference.   FMA

J507a Schücking, Walther. *International union of the Hague conferences.* N. Y. and Oxford, 1918. [Work of the Hague.] [Carnegie Endowment for International Peace.] Tr. by C. G. Fenwick from *Der Staatenverband der Haager Konferenzen,* München, 1912.

b Wehberg, Hans. *Problem of an international court of justice.* N. Y. and Oxford, 1918. [Work of the Hague.] [Carnegie Endowment for International Peace.] (Bibliography.) Tr. by C. G. Fenwick from *Das Problem eines internationalen Staatengerichtshofes,* München, 1912.

Works, written by German scholars before the World War, dealing sympathetically with the work of the two Hague peace conferences and with their efforts to establish courts of an international character respectively. Review of *a.* and *b.,* G. G. Wilson, *A.H.R.* 24:687, July 1919.   GMD

J508 Hudson, Manley O. *Permanent court of international justice, and the question of American participation, with a collection of documents.* Cambridge, Mass., 1925. (Bibliography.)

Excellent historical and analytical account by a prominent advocate of American participation. Review, C. R. Fish, *A.H.R.* 30:863, July 1925.   GMD

J509a Garner, James W. *International law and the world war.* 2 v. N. Y. and London, 1920. [Contributions to international law and diplomacy.] (Bibliography.)

b —— *Recent developments in international law.* Calcutta, London, and N. Y., 1925. [Tagore law lectures.]

a. Exhaustive treatment of the problems of international law which arose in the course of the World War; intended for experts; best work on the subject. Review, E. C. Stowell, *A.H.R.* 26:526, Apr. 1921. *b.* Less technical in character; expounds the development of international law in the twentieth century, with reference both to war and to peace; admirable systematic exposition. Review, C. N. Gregory, *A.H.R.* 31:143, Oct. 1925.   GMD

The more important works on the military history of the period are listed in the sub-sections of this section, entitled 'World War: General,' 'World War: Western Front,' and 'World War: Western Campaigns.' Books on the naval history of the period appear in the sub-section 'World War: Naval Operations.'

CONSTITUTIONAL HISTORY AND POLITICAL THEORY

J531 McBain, Howard L., and Rogers, Lindsay, ed. *New constitutions of Europe.* Garden City, N. Y., 1922.

Brief introduction dealing with the principal political and social problems of the war and post-war periods, followed by English translations of the new constitutions of Germany, Austria, Prussia, Czechoslovakia, Jugoslavia, Russia, Poland, Free City of Danzig, Esthonia, and Finland. Constitutions of Belgium, France, and Italy are printed in an appendix which also contains the report of the (Bryce) Second Chamber Conference. Review, A. I. Andrews, *Amer. Pol. Sci. Rev.* 17:125, Feb. 1923.   LL

J532a Graham, Malbone W., and **Binkley, Robert C.** *New governments of Central Europe.* N. Y., 1924. [American political science series.]

b Ogg, Frederick A., and **Beard, Charles A.** *National governments and the world war.* N. Y., 1919. (Bibliographies.)

c Graham, Malbone W. *New governments of Eastern Europe.* N. Y., 1927.

a. Deals with the historical development and the post-war politics of Republican Germany, Austria, Hungary, Czechoslovakia, and Jugoslavia. About a third of the book consists of important constitutional documents which are not readily accessible elsewhere. Review, H. A. Yeomans, *Amer. Pol. Sci. Rev.* 19:183, Feb. 1925. *b.* Condensations of (I551e) Ogg, *Governments of Europe,* and (X532a) Beard, *American government and politics,* revised to show the structure and functioning of the governments of the principal belligerent powers with special reference to the changes produced by the War. Review, J. M. Callahan, *A.H.R.* 24:693, July 1919. Review of *c,* A. I. Andrews, *A.H.R.* 33:656, Apr. 1928.

LL

J561 Merriam, Charles E., and **Barnes, Harry Elmer**, ed. *History of political theories, recent times: essays on contemporary developments in political theory.* N. Y., 1924. (Bibliographies.)

Essays on recent political theory by students of the late Professor William A. Dunning; designed as a supplementary volume to Professor Dunning's (H561) *History of political theories.* Contains discussions of such topics as: 'Criticism of democracy,' 'The attack on state sovereignty,' 'Political theory and international law,' 'Proletarian political theory,' and 'Social psychology and political theory.' Most convenient summary of current thinking in the field. Review, R. G. Gettell, *A.H.R.* 30:574, Apr. 1925.

LL

ECONOMIC AND SOCIAL HISTORY

J571 Shotwell, James T., ed. *Economic and social history of the world war.* Oxford, etc., 1921 ff . [1, *British series,* v. 1-16, 1921 ff.; 2, *Austrian and Hungarian series,* v. 1-7, 1923 ff.; 3, *Belgian series,* v. 1-2, 1924 ff.; 4, *Bulgarian series;* 5, *Czechoslovak series,* v. 1, 1923; 6, *French series,* v. 1-15, 1924 ff.; 7, *German series;* 8, *Greek series;* 9, *Italian series,* v. 1-2, 1925; 10, *Netherlands series,* v. 1, 1923; 11, *Japanese series;* 12, *Rumanian series;* 13, *Russian series;* 14, *Scandinavian series;* 15, *Yugoslav series;* 16, *American series,* v. 1, 1926.[[Carnegie Endowment for International Peace.]

For the plan and present status of the series, cf. (J921a) Carnegie Endowment for International Peace, *Year book, 1925,* 150–165; and for a list of the volumes issued, *ibid.,* 216–218, supplemented by the *Annual report of the Director, Division of Economics and History, for 1925.* The project for this work dates from as early as 1915 and the development of its widespread international organization was undertaken promptly after the armistice. As general editor, Professor Shotwell has organized research and editorial committees in over a dozen countries, which include eminent scholars in history, economics, sociology, international law, and other fields. No effort on a similar scale has ever been made for coöperative research and publication with reference to any other movement in the world's history. The excellence of the volumes already published indicates that this series, which will extend to about two hundred volumes, will, when completed, be of the highest service, not only to scholars in the particular fields concerned, but also to the large number of officials, organizations, and individuals engaged in solving the various world problems discussed. Such volumes as are not published originally in English will be published in either abridged or complete translations in English. Several of the series, such as the Austrian, German, Belgian, and French, will be published in the languages of the respective countries.　　　　GMD

J572a **Bakeless, John.** *Economic causes of modern war: a study of the period 1878–1918.* N. Y., 1921. [Williams College, David A. Wells prize essays.] (Bibliography.)

b **Engerand, Fernand.** *L'Allemagne et le fer: les frontières lorraines et la force allemande.* 1915. 4th ed., Paris, 1916.

c —— *Le fer sur une frontière: la politique métallurgique de l'état allemand.* Paris, 1919.

a. Useful study, not only of the World War, but also of no less than twenty other conflicts within the period covered. Review, J. P. Goode, *A.H.R.* 28:116, Oct. 1922.　　*b.* and *c.* Studies of the conflict of economic interest on the Franco-German frontier during the past century with special reference to Lorraine. Review of *c.,* C. H. Haskins, *A.H.R.* 25:546, Apr. 1920.　　　　GMD

J573 **Noyes, Alexander D.** *Financial chapters of the war.* N. Y., 1916.

Contemporary study, by an American expert, of the interrelations of American and European finances during the first two years of the war. Review, E. W. Kemmerer, *A.H.R.* 22:871, July 1917.　　　　GMD

J574a **Parmelee, Maurice F.** *Blockade and sea power: the blockade, 1914–1919, and its significance for a world state.* N. Y., 1924.

b **Consett, Montagu W. W. P.,** and **Daniel, Octavius H.** *Triumph of unarmed forces, 1914–1918: an account of the transactions by which Germany during the great war was able to obtain supplies prior to her collapse under the pressure of economic forces.* London, 1923.

a. Study of the commercial restrictions enforced by the Allied Powers during the War, and of their removal after the War, followed by the author's personal views with reference to a world state. Review, E. C. Stowell, *A.H.R.* 30:576, Apr. 1925.　　*b.* Informing account, by the British naval attaché to the Scandinavian legations during the War. Review, J. A. Gade, *A.H.R.* 29:333, Jan. 1924.　　　　GMD

J575 **Gay, George I.** *Commission for relief in Belgium: statistical review of relief operations, five years, November, 1914, to August 31, 1919, and to final liquidation.* Stanford University, California, 1925.

Valuable statistical study; reveals the magnitude and nature of the relief operations. Review, *A.H.R.* 31:355, Jan. 1926.　　　　GMD

J576 **Gray, Howard L.** *War time control of industry: the experience of England.* N. Y., 1918.

Good study of the outstanding features of the case, based on careful researches. Considers the interests and acts of the government, of capital, and of labor. Review, A. Shortt, *A.H.R.* 24:96, Oct. 1918.　　　　GMD

J577 Gide, Charles, ed. *Effects of the war upon`French economic life: a collection of five monographs.* N. Y. and Oxford, 1923. [Carnegie Endowment for International Peace, Preliminary economic studies of the war.]

Essays on the merchant marine, textile industry, commercial policy, the effect of the war on the nation's finances, and the labor movement, by five French economists. Concise, dispassionate statements of the facts. Review, T. W. Page, *A.H.R.* 28:775, July 1923.
GMD

J578 Bogart, Ernest L. *Direct and indirect costs of the great world war.* N. Y. and Oxford, 1919. [Carnegie Endowment for International Peace, Preliminary economic studies of the war.] (Extensive bibliography.)

Probably represents the most careful and scientific study of the costs of the war which has yet been made. The author's methods as well as his conclusions will interest critical students. Indispensable introduction to further studies. Review, A. Comstock, *A.H.R.* 26:362, Jan. 1921.
WES

J579a Moulton, Harold G., and **McGuire, Constantine E.** *Germany's capacity to pay, a study of the reparation problem.* N. Y., 1923. [Institute of Economics, Investigations in international economic reconstruction.]

   b Pasvolsky, Leo, and **Moulton, Harold G.** *Russian debts and Russian reconstruction, a study of the relation of Russia's foreign debts to her economic recovery.* N. Y., 1924. [Institute of Economics, Investigations in international economic reconstruction.]

   c Moulton, Harold G. *Reparation plan: an interpretation of the Reports of the Expert Committees appointed by the Reparation Commission, November 30, 1923.* N. Y., 1924. [Institute of Economics, Investigations in international economic reconstruction.]

   d Moulton, Harold G., and **Lewis, Cleona.** *French debt problem.* N. Y., 1925. [Institute of Economics, Investigations in international economic reconstruction.]

   e Moulton, Harold G., and **Pasvolsky, Leo.** *World war debt settlements.* N. Y., 1926. [Institute of Economics, Investigations in international economic reconstruction.]

Very useful compilations of results of research by American experts in public finance and international trade. Review of *a.,* C. Snyder, *Amer. Econ. Rev.* 13:669, Dec. 1923; H. Hauser, *Rev. Hist.* 145:258, March 1924; of *b.,* E. A. Goldenweiser, *Amer. Econ. Rev.* 14:724, Dec. 1924; of *c.,* E. E. Agger, *Amer. Econ. Rev.* 14:730, Dec. 1924; of *d.,* *New Republic,* 44:137, Sept. 30, 1925; G. Soule, *ibid.,* 45:67, Dec. 2, 1925.
GMD

CULTURAL HISTORY

It has seemed impracticable to include in this section the customary subsections on cultural history. Many works listed in the preceding section (§ I) also include more or less of the period since 1871, as do also some works listed in § B, and in the several sections devoted to particular nations.

BIOGRAPHY

Among the more important or more interesting biographical or autobiographical works for the period not already listed in this or other sections are the following:

American.—(J701) Henry T. Allen, *My Rhineland journal,* Boston and London, 1923; (J702) Robert L. Bullard, *Personalities and reminiscences of the war,*

Garden City, N. Y., 1925; (J703) Charles G. Dawes, *Journal of the great war,* 2 v., Boston, 1921; (J704) Bradley A. Fiske, *From midshipman to rear admiral, a record of forty-nine years in the United States navy,* N. Y., 1919, London, 1920: (J705) James W. Gerard, *My four years in Germany,* N. Y. and London, 1917; (J706) Hugh Gibson, *Journal from our legation in Belgium,* Garden City, N. Y., 1917, English ed., *A diplomatic diary,* London, 1918; (J707) James G. Harbord, *Leaves from a war diary,* N. Y., 1925; (J708) Hunter Liggett, *Commanding an American army, recollections of the world war,* Boston, 1925; (J709) Henry Morgenthau, *Ambassador Morgenthau's story,* Garden City, N. Y. and London, 1918; (J710) Burton J. Hendrick, *Life and letters of Walter Hines Page,* 3 v., Garden City, N. Y., 1922–25.

British.—(J721) Francis L., viscount Bertie of Thame, *Diary, 1914–1918,* ed. by Lady Algernon Gordon Lennox, 2 v., London and N. Y., 1924, which records the experiences and activities of the British ambassador in Paris during the World War; (J722) Sir George W. Buchanan, *My mission to Russia and other diplomatic memories,* 2 v., London and Boston, 1923; (J723) John A., Baron Fisher, *Memories and records,* 2 v., London, 1919, N. Y., 1920; (J724) Sir Charles E. Callwell, *Life of Sir Stanley Maude,* London and Boston, 1920; (J725a) Sir William R. Robertson, *From private to field-marshal,* London and Boston, 1921; (J725b) *id., Soldiers and statesmen,* 2 v., London and N. Y., 1926; (J726) Sir James Rennell Rodd, *Social and diplomatic memories, 1884–1919,* 3 v., London and N. Y., 1922–25, which chronicles his career as British ambassador to Italy, 1908–1919.

French.—(J741) Alfred Dumaine, *La dernière ambassade de France en Autriche, notes et souvenirs,* Paris, 1921; (J742) Raymond Recouly, *Foch, the winner of the war,* N. Y., 1920, tr. by Mary C. Jones from *Foch, le vainqueur de la guerre,* Paris, 1919, English ed., *Foch, his character and leadership,* London, 1920; (J743) Joseph S. Galliéni, *Mémoires, défense de Paris, 25 août–11 septembre 1914,* Paris, 1920; (J744) Georges Louis, *Carnets, 1908–1917,* 2 v., Paris, 1926, the memoirs of the French ambassador to Russia.

German.—(J761) Karl, Graf von Hertling, *Ein Jahr in der Reichskanzlei: Erinnerungen an die Kanzlerschaft meines Vaters,* Freiburg-im-Breisgau, 1919; (J762) Paul E. von Lettow-Vorbeck, *My reminiscences of East Africa,* London, 1920, tr. from *Meine Erinnerungen aus Ostafrika,* Leipzig, 1920; (J763) Karl M., Fürst von Lichnowsky, *My mission to London, 1912–1914,* London and N. Y., 1918, tr. from *Meine Londoner Mission, 1912–1914,* Zürich, 1918; (J764) Jakob L. F. W. J., Graf von Pourtalès, *Am Scheidewege zwischen Krieg und Frieden, meine letzten Verhandlungen in Petersburg, Ende Juli 1914, veröffentlicht mit Genehmigung des auswärtigen Amtes,* Charlottenburg, 1919.

Russian.—(J781) Anatoliĭ Vasilevich Nekliudov, *Diplomatic reminiscences before and during the world war, 1911–1917,* London and N. Y., 1920, tr. by A. Paget from the French. (J782) Roman Romanovich, Baron Rosen, *Forty years of diplomacy,* 2 v., London and N. Y., 1922; (J783) Vladimïr Aleksandrovich Sukhomlinov [Suchomlinow], *Erinnerungen,* Berlin, 1924, tr. from *Vospominanija,* Berlin, 1924.

Other countries.—(J801) Henri G. S. A. O. de Blowitz, *Memoirs,* London and N. Y., 1903; (J802) Thomas G. Masaryk, *Die Weltrevolution, Erinnerungen und Betrachtungen, 1914–1918,* Berlin, 1925, tr. by C. Hoffmann from the Czechish.

SBF, FMA

GOVERNMENT PUBLICATIONS

The voluminous publications of (J901) League of Nations, Geneva, 1920 ff., are usually issued simultaneously in English and French. Catalogues of them are issued at frequent intervals, and may be obtained from the World Peace Foundation or from the Bureau of the League. Among the more important of them are: (J901a) *Records of the . . . assembly,* 1920 ff.; (J901b) *Minutes,* and other publications of the Permanent Mandates Commission, 1921 ff.; (J901c) *Treaty series,* 1920 ff.; and the following periodicals: (J901d) *Monthly summary of the League,* 1921 ff.; (J901e) *Quarterly bulletin of information on the work of international organizations,* 1922 ff.; (J901f) *Monthly bulletin of statistics,* 1919 ff.; and (J901g) *Official journal,* 1920 ff., which, with the exception of some months in 1921, includes the complete minutes of the sessions of the Council, and which also has numerous supplements. Annual reports on the several mandated territories are published by the governments holding the respective mandates.

(J902) *Publications* of the Permanent Court of International Justice, Leyde, 1922 ff., are issued concurrently in English and French, in five series. These, or information concerning them, may be obtained from the World Peace Foundation, as may also the various publications of (J903) International Labour Office, Geneva, 1919 ff., of which it will suffice to mention (J903a) *International labour review,* monthly, Geneva, 1921 ff.

ACADEMY AND SOCIETY PUBLICATIONS

The most important organization devoted to publication of works relating to the history of this period is the (J921) Carnegie Endowment for International Peace, with headquarters at 2 Jackson Place, Washington, D. C., which issues its publications with various imprints, including Washington, New York, New Haven, London, Oxford, and Paris. The more important groups of these publications are: (J921a) *Year book, 1911 ff.,* 1912 ff.; (J921b) books and pamphlets issued by its Division of Intercourse and Education, no. 1-19, 1914 ff.; (J921c) books and pamphlets issued by its European Bureau, no. 1-9, 1914 ff.; (J921d) books issued by its Division of International Law, v. 1-50, 1915 ff.; (J921e) pamphlets issued by its Division of International Law, no. 1-48, 1914 ff.; (J921f) *Classics of international law,* v. 1-19, 1911 ff.; (J921g) books issued by its Division of Economics and History, v. 1-22, 1915 ff.; (J921h) *Preliminary economic studies of the war,* no. 1-25, 1918 ff. issued by the same division, which also is publishing the monumental (J571) *Economic and social history of the war,* edited by Professor J. T. Shotwell. Since 1924 the Endowment has taken over and continued the publications of the American Association for International Conciliation, which are a pamphlet series entitled (J922a) *International conciliation,* no. 1-210, 1907 ff.; and another pamphlet series, (J922b) *Interamerican bulletin,* no. 1-28, 1914 ff. The Endowment also issues the publications, books and pamphlets, of (J923) American Institute of International Law, no. 1-8, 1916 ff.; and (J924) publications, pamphlet syllabi, no. 1-14, 1920 ff., of Institute of International Education. For a complete list of the preceding publications, a number of which are noted separately in this *Guide,* cf. the Endowment's (J921a) *Year book, 1925,* 203-232.

(J925) World Peace Foundation, 40 Mt. Vernon Street, Boston, Mass., besides publishing and assisting the circulation of various books, issues a valuable (J925a) bi-monthly pamphlet series, Boston, 1911 ff., which includes, since 1924, the unofficial (J925b) *Yearbook of the League of Nations, 1920 ff.*, Brooklyn, N. Y., and Boston, 1921 ff. The Foundation also handles, for the United States, the publications of the League of Nations, the International Labour Office, and the Permanent Court of International Justice.

(J926) Société de l'Histoire de la Guerre, Pavillon de la Reine, Château de Vincennes, Seine, publishes, in addition to (J975a) *Revue d'histoire de la guerre mondiale* and (J975b) *Bulletin mensuel de documentation internationale,* various volumes of bibliographical, documentary, and other materials relating to the World War.

(J927) Zentralstelle für Erforschung der Kriegsursachen, Luisenstrasse 31 a, Berlin NW 6, issues, in addition to (J981) *Die Kriegsschuldfrage,* occasional books and pamphlets.   GMD

PERIODICALS

Diplomatic documents for the period have been currently published in (I509c) *Archives diplomatiques* and in (I509d) *Das Staatsarchiv,* as well as in (I509a) *British and foreign state papers.* Since 1919 treaties and similar documents have been published by the League of Nations in its (J901c) *Treaty series.*

The monthly magazine (J941) *Current History,* N. Y., 1914 ff. furnishes a convenient record of current events in all parts of the world.

(J942) *Journal of modern history,* 1929 ff. quarterly, devoted to modern history, contains in addition to ordinary articles, excellent book reviews, lists of new books, and bibliographical articles.

(J951a) *Journal of race development,* 9 v., Worcester, Mass., 1910–19 and its successor, (J951b) *Journal of international relations,* 3 v. Worcester, Mass., 1919–22, have been superseded by (J951c) *Foreign affairs an American quarterly review,* N. Y., 1922 ff., which is of high value for articles and bibliographical notes on current international problems. The following British publications are useful to the student of contemporary history: (J961) *New Europe, a weekly review of foreign politics,* 17 v., 1916–20; (J962) *Foreign affairs, a journal of international understanding,* London, 1919 ff., published by the Union of Democratic Control.

Recently several periodicals, more or less propagandist, have been started in France to deal with the history of the World War and current problems, namely, (J971) *L'Europe nouvelle, revue hebdomadaire des questions extérieures, économiques, et littéraires,* Paris, 1918 ff.; (J972) *Les archives de la grande guerre,* Paris, 1919 ff., monthly; (J973) *Bulletin official de la Société d'Études Documentaires et Critiques sur la Guerre,* Paris, 1922–23, 1925 ff.; (J974) *Évolution, revue mensuelle des questions intéressant l'apaisement international et le rapprochement des peuples,* Paris, 1926 ff. (J926) Société de l'Histoire de la Guerre issues the quarterly (J975a) *Revue d'histoire de la guerre mondiale,* Paris, 1923 ff.; and (J975b) *Bulletin mensuel de documentation internationale,* Paris, 1922 ff., which records the accessions of (cf. J2a and b) Bibliothèque et Musée de la Guerre, and includes a select bibliography of new publications relating to the World War and its consequences. For Belgium there is (J976) *Revue belge des livres, documents, et archives de la guerre de 1914–1918, Bruxelles,* 1924 ff., monthly.

The following German periodicals, also more or less propagandist, contain valuable articles: (J981) *Die Kriegsschuldfrage*, Berlin, 1923 ff., issued by (J927) Zentralstelle für Erforschung der Kriegsursachen; (J982) *Europäische Gespräche, Hamburger Monatshefte für auswärtige Politik*, Hamburg and Stuttgart, 1923 ff.; and (J983) *Archiv für Politik und Geschichte*, Berlin, 1923 ff., monthly.

SBF, GMD

SECTION K

COLONIAL EXPANSION

Editors *

ARTHUR HERBERT BASYE

Professor of History, Dartmouth College

and

FRANK WESLEY PITMAN

Professor of History, Pomona College

CONTENTS

INTRODUCTION

Aside from exploration, the topics with which this section is concerned have received scant attention as fields of historical study until very recent times. Consequently, scarcely any works of magisterial character and few of enduring

---

* Professor Basye has been responsible for the materials prior to 1815 and Professor Pitman for the materials since that date.

value have been produced. Within the fields to which this section is principally devoted, the expansion of Europe and modern colonization in general and the general history and policy of the leading powers in their colonizing activities, there is, indeed, a paucity of works of moderately sound scholarship. Even the best informed and most accurate writers, whether of earlier or of recent times, do not escape from the tendency to champion the imperial interests of their own country or to expound the views of some particular group, party, or section. Propaganda and controversy rather than historical scholarship, consequently, give the prevailing tone to the literature of European expansion. The lists of works included under the several sub-headings in this section are, in general, limited to the more scholarly works in the respective fields and to the better representatives of the diverse views on the more important topics of controversial nature.

In the several sections of this *Guide* devoted to the history of the several principal colonizing nations will be found numerous works which devote more or less space to the activities overseas of the respective countries, namely: § L, England; § M, France; § N, Spain and Portgual; § O, Italy; § P, Germany; § Q, Netherlands and Belgium; and § S, Russia. Books relating to individual colonies will be found under the suitable sub-heading in the following sections: § R, Scandinavia; § U, Central, southern and eastern Asia; § V, Oceanica; § W, Africa; § X, United States; § Y, Hispanic America; § Z, British North America. Since they find no place in any of the sections just enumerated, works on the non-Spanish West Indies and on some scattered insular colonies are dealt with in a sub-section of this section. Among the special classes of books listed in this section are those on the European background of expansion, on the extension of geographical knowledge and exploration, on the development of commerce and of trading companies, and on the general subject of colonization. The history of land exploration is treated in the sections of this *Guide* devoted to the regions concerned. The history of maritime exploration, especially in the fifteenth and sixteenth centuries, and of Arctic and Antarctic exploration, especially in the past century, is allotted to this section. Space permits the citation of only the most outstanding works from the voluminous and usually excellent literature on these interesting topics.

GMD

BIBLIOGRAPHY

In addition to the bibliographies listed in this sub-section and § U, Central, southern, and eastern Asia; § V, Oceanica; § W, Africa; § Y, Latin America; and § Z, Canada, cf. (I121) *Cambridge modern history,* 1:693–699; 4:940–947; 5:895–902; 6:870–877; 7:753–784, 823–824; 9:883–891; 10:812–821, 871–878; 11:968–980; 12:927–948, 967–971, for good selected and classified lists. Lists of recent works, including government publications, appear in the section devoted to each colony in the annual issues of (B28b) *Statesman's year-book.* For the French colonies no special bibliography is available, but convenient lists will be found in (K407) E. Petit, *Organisation des colonies françaises.*

K1a Griffin, Appleton P. C. *Lists of books, with references to periodicals, relating to the theory of colonization, government of dependencies, protectorates, and related topics.* 1900. [Library of Congress.] 2nd rev. ed., Washington, 1901. [U. S. Bureau of Statistics.]

b Hill, Winifred C. *Select bibliography of publications on foreign colonisation, German, French, Italian, Dutch, Portuguese, Spanish, and Belgian, con-*

tained in the library of the Royal Colonial Institute. London, 1915. [Royal Colonial Institute.]

c **Lewin, Evans.** *Select list of recent publications . . . illustrating the constitutional relations between the various parts of the British empire.* London, 1926. [Royal Colonial Institute.]

d —— *Select bibliography of recent publications . . . illustrating the relations between European and coloured races.* London, 1926. [Royal Colonial Institute.]

e —— *Select list of publications . . . illustrating the communications of the overseas British empire, with special reference to Africa generally and the Bagdad railway.* London, 1927. [Royal Colonial Institute.]

a. Comprehensive list of about two thousand titles, including the leading works to 1900.   *b.* Contains an introduction by Evans Lewin, librarian of the Institute, emphasizing the need among Englishmen of a comparative study of colonization. Also cf. (K534) Keller, *Colonization,* 599–611, for selected lists on ancient, medieval, and modern colonization.   FWP

c, d, and *e.* Convenient recent bibliographies; they may be supplemented by reference to the quarterly bulletin, *Overseas Official Publications* (1927 ff.), issued as the official list of the Royal Colonial Institute, Northumberland Ave., London, W.C. 2, and obtainable from the librarian.   SBF

K2 Royal Colonial Institute, London, *Catalogue of the library,* ed. by James R. Boose. London, 1895.

Arranged in chronological order under the names of the various colonies; includes books, pamphlets, and magazines; separate lists of state papers, imperial and colonial, and of maps.   FWP

K3a Netherlands, Department Van Kolonien, Bibliotheek. *Catalogus van de boeken en kaarten uitmakende de bibliotheek,* ed. by Alexander Hartmann. 1885–92. New ed., 's Gravenhage, 1898.

b **Nijhoff, Martinus.** *List of the best books relating to Dutch East India.* The Hague, 1902.

a. Book lists only.   *b.* Brief selected list.   Also cf. (V2) Hooykaas, *Repertorium.*   GMD

K4a Decharme, Pierre. *Bibliographie critique de la colonisation allemande.* Paris, 1900. [Société des Études Historiques, Bibliothèque de bibliographies critiques.]

b **Brose, Maximilian.** *Die deutsche Koloniallitteratur von 1884–1895.* Berlin, 1897.

c —— *Die deutsche Koloniallitteratur im Jahre 1896–1913.* 18 v. Berlin, 1897–1914.

a. Critical list of books.   *b.* List mainly of periodical articles, supplemented by the annual publication *c.*   For other lists of books on German colonization, cf. (K421a) Townsend, *Origins of modern German colonialism,* and (K425) Hassert, *Deutschlands Kolonien.*   FWP

K5 Italy, Ministero degli Affari Esteri, Direzione Centrali degli Affari Coloniali. *Raccolta di pubblicazioni coloniali italiane, primo indice bibliografico.* Roma, 1911.

Bibliography of Italian works on Italian colonization down to 1911.   FWP

K6a Cundall, Frank. *Bibliographia jamaicensis, a list of Jamaica books and pamphlets, magazine articles, newspapers, and maps, most of which are in the library of the Institute of Jamaica.* 1895. 2nd rev. ed., Kingston and N. Y., 1902. Supplement, 1908.

b —— *Bibliography of the West Indies, excluding Jamaica.* Kingston, 1909.

Complementary publications which furnish the most complete lists for the history of the West Indies, especially the islands under British rule. GMD

K7a Chavanne, Josef and others. *Literatur über die Polar-Regionen der Erde.* Wien, 1878. [K. K. Geographischen Gesellschaft in Wien.]

b Pfaff, Christian G. F. *Bibliographica groenlandica.* Kjøbenhavn, 1890. [(K923) Meddelelser om Grønland.]

c Mill, Hugh R. *Antarctic bibliography.* London, 1901. [Antarctic manual, p. 517–586, published by the Royal Geographical Society.]

In addition to the above special bibliographies on polar exploration, use may be made of (K451) Greely, *Handbook of polar discoveries;* of (K481) Balch, *Antarctica;* and for more recent publications of the list appended to the article on 'Polar exploration' in (B22b) *Encyclopaedia Britannica.* GMD

Library collections.—For the history of exploration and of early trade and colonization, especially in the western hemisphere, there are highly valuable collections in the Harvard University Library, the John Carter Brown Library in Providence, and the New York Public Library; and less extensive collections in the Library of Congress, the Ayer collection of the Newberry Library, Chicago, the Clements Library at the University of Michigan, and, for the Spanish side, the H. E. Huntington Library in the Hispanic Society of America, New York City.

Extensive collections relating to exploration in more recent times exist in the library of the American Geographical Society, New York City, and in the library of the National Geographic Society, Washington. The latter library contains the Greely polar and sub-polar collection, which is undoubtedly the best in its field, of about 1500 separate works and 200 volumes of pamphlets. There are also good collections on polar exploration in the Boston Public Library and in the library of Bowdoin College.

In addition to good collections of general works on colonization and the history of colonies, the Library of Congress is especially useful for its collections of government publications issued both by the colonizing countries and by the colonies. AHS

ENCYCLOPEDIAS AND WORKS OF REFERENCE

K21 Schnee, Heinrich, ed. *Deutsches Kolonial-Lexikon.* 3 v. Leipzig, 1920. (Bibliographies.)

Ready for publication in 1914 and unchanged since the war, this encyclopedia stands as a monument to German colonization. Edited by a former governor of East Africa, it represented the work of eighty experts and was designed to furnish information of every description about the German colonies. With its photographs, maps, and diagrams, inserted after each topic, it forms an invaluable compendium. Review, P. Rohrback, *Preussische Jahrbücher,* 183:106, Jan. 1921.

MET

K22 Domville-Fife, Charles W. *Encyclopaedia of the British Empire.* 3 v. Bristol, Eng., 1924.

Convenient reference work. GMD

GEOGRAPHY AND ATLASES

K41a Nordenskiöld, Adolf Erik, Baron. *Facsimile atlas to the early history of cartography with reproductions of the most important maps of the fifteenth and sixteenth centuries.* Stockholm, 1889. Tr. from the Swedish by Capt. J. A. Ekelöf and C. R. Markham.

b ———— *Periplus, an essay on the early history of charts and sailing directions.* Stockholm, 1897. Tr. from the Swedish by F. A. Bather.

These two volumes by the famous discoverer of the north-east passage, although having separate titles, are virtually two parts of the same work. They were both published simultaneously in Swedish and English. They constitute the most useful single work in the field of cartography since they furnish a compendium of material otherwise practically unobtainable. *a.* Deals with maps and atlases. The introduction, illustrated by 85 inset maps, contains ten chapters: five devoted to (E42) Ptolemy and one each to the first maps of the new world, globes, map projections, the end of the early and the beginning of the modern period of cartography. A few changes in Nordenskiöld's conclusions result from later discoveries, notably the Waldseemüller map. The consensus of expert opinion assigns the Bologna Ptolemy, misdated 1462, to 1482 instead of 1472 as favored by Nordenskiöld. The atlas proper consists of 61 double folio pages which reproduce, by photolithography, the 27 maps of the first printed edition of Ptolemy with maps (Rome, 1490, reprint of edition of 1478) and 61 maps from later editions of Ptolemy and from other atlases, such as Mercator's and Ortelius's, down to the Wright-Hakluyt of 1599. *b.* Deals with portolans and sea charts. The introduction, including 100 inset maps, contains fifteen chapters, six on medieval portolans, and others on the forerunners of Ptolemy, the Periplus of Skylax, the charting of the Arctic and Pacific oceans and of the coast lines of Africa, Asia, and America. The atlas part reproduces a series of sea charts ranging from the Periplus of Skylax to Anson's map of the Pacific of 1748. FHH

K42a Marcel, Gabriel. *Cartes et globes relatifs à la découverte de l'Amérique du XVIᵉ au XVIIIᵉ siècle, 40 planches sur cuivre, texte.* 1 v. and atlas. Paris, 1893. [(K74) Schefer and Cordier, Recueil de voyages et de documents.]

b ———— *Choix de cartes et mappemondes des XIVᵉ et XVᵉ siècles, publiées avec introduction.* 16 planches. Paris, 1896. [(K74) Schefer and Cordier, Recueil de voyages et de documents.]

Excellent works of similar character to those of (K41) Nordenskiöld. GMD

K43 Robertson, Charles Grant, and **Bartholomew, John G.** *Historical and modern atlas of the British empire, specially prepared for students.* London, 1905. (Bibliography.)

Contains a series of historical maps illustrating the growth of the empire; orographical, economic, and political maps of the British isles and of the more important possessions; a gazetteer of British possessions; a chronological table of additions to and subtractions from the possessions of England; and index. EPce

K46 Herbertson, Andrew J., and Thompson, R. L. *Geography of the British empire.* 1912. 3rd rev. ed. by O. J. R. Howarth, Oxford, 1918. (Oxford geographies.)

Excellent manual; much information skilfully condensed in small compass.

GMD

K47 Meyer, Hans H. J., ed. *Das deutsche Kolonialreich; eine Länderkunde der deutschen Schutzgebiete.* 2 v. Leipzig, 1909–10. (Bibliographies.)

The editor, a geographer and a 'Kolonialpolitiker' of wide experience, has produced not a history but a geographical study of the German colonies. The work, written with the assistance of other specialists from a scientific and practical viewpoint, is painstakingly indexed and accompanied by many valuable plates and pictures. MET

K48 Fite, Emerson D., and Freeman, Archibald. *Books of old maps.* Cambridge, Mass., 1926.

Elaborate and handsome volume, reproducing 74 examples from the great libraries of America, the Vatican, British Museum, and Bibliothèque Nationale, delineating the geographical development of American history to the close of the Revolutionary War. Review, J. A. Robertson, *A.H.R.* 33:406, Jan. 1928.

FWP

ETHNOGRAPHY

K51 Thomas, Northcote W., ed. *Native races of the British empire.* V. 1–4, London, 1906–07. [1, N. W. Thomas, *Natives of Australia;* 2, A. Werner, *Natives of British Central Africa;* 3, C. Hill-Tout, *British North America;* pt. 1, *Far west, the home of the Salish and Déné;* 4, W. Crooke, *Natives of northern India.*] (Brief bibliographies.)

Series of convenient anthropological handbooks; accurate and popular. While the volumes are mainly compilations, the writers are, in each case, personally acquainted with the region and people considered. Review, v. 1, E. A. Parkyn, *Man,* 7:104, 1907; v. 2, F. Starr, *Amer. Anthropologist,* n.s., 9:593, July 1907; v. 3, A. F. Chamberlain, *ibid.,* n.s., 9:602, July 1907; v. 4, A. F. Chamberlain, *ibid.,* n.s., 9:604, July 1907. FWP

SOURCE BOOKS AND COLLECTIONS OF SOURCES

K61a Keith, Arthur Berriedale, ed. *Selected speeches and documents on British colonial policy, 1763–1917.* 2 v. Oxford and N. Y., 1918. [World's classics.]

b Egerton, Hugh E., ed. *Federations and unions within the British empire.* 1911. 2nd rev. ed., Oxford, 1924. (Bibliography.)

a. Well-chosen though inadequate selection from official documents and political addresses illustrating the constitutional evolution of the British Empire. Review, H. E. Egerton, *E.H.R.* 34:279, Apr. 1919. *b.* Edition of seven principal documents from the Articles of New England confederation of 1643 to the Union of South Africa act of 1909, with a good introduction, which is revised to date in second edition. Review, W. Macdonald, *A.H.R.* 17:189, Oct. 1911; *E.H.R.* 26:847, Oct. 1911. GMD

K62a Payne, Edward J., ed. *Voyages of the Elizabethan seamen to America, select narratives from the 'Principal Navigations' of Hakluyt.* 1880. Rev. ed., with additional notes, maps, etc. by C. R. Beazley, Oxford, 1907.

b Arber, Edward, ed. *Voyages and travels, mainly during the 16th and 17th centuries.* Ed. with introduction by C. R. Beazley, 2 v., Edinburgh and N. Y., 1903. [English garner, 2nd ed., v. 3–4 (1st ed., 1877–96).]

Narratives of voyages chiefly reprinted from (K71) Hakluyt. Convenient selections.   GMD

K71a Hakluyt, Richard, ed. *Divers voyages touching the discoverie of America and the islands adjacent unto the same, made first of all by our Englishmen and afterwards by the Frenchmen and Britons.* 1582. New ed. by J. W. Jones, London, 1850. [Hakluyt Society, 1st series, v. 7.]

b ———— *A discourse concerning western planting, written in the year 1584; now first printed from a contemporary manuscript, with a preface and an introduction by L. Woods.* Ed. by C. Deane. Cambridge, Mass., 1877. [Collections of the Maine Historical Society, 2nd series, v. 2.]

c ————, tr. *A notable historie containing foure voyages made by certayne French captaynes into Florida.* London, 1587. *Tr. from L'histoire notable de la Floride* (Paris, 1586) by René Goulaine de Laudonnière, ed. by M. Basanier.

d ————, ed. *De orbe novo Petri Martyris Anglerii . . . decades octo . . .* Parisiis, 1587. [New ed. of first complete ed. (Compluti, 1530) of Latin text.]

e ————, ed. *The principall navigations, voyages, [traffiques], and discoveries of the English nation, made by sea or over-land to the remote and farthest distant quarters of the earth at any time within the compasse of these 1600 yeares.* 1589. 2nd ed., 3 v., London, 1598–1600. Reprint of 2nd ed., 12 v., Glasgow, 1903–05. [Hakluyt Society, extra series, v. 1–12]; reprint, 8 v., London and N. Y., 1907. [Everyman's library.] Extracts reprinted in *Early English and French voyages, chiefly from Hakluyt, 1584–1608,* ed. by H. S. Burrage, N. Y., 1906. [Original narratives of early American history.]

f ———— *The discoveries of the world from their first originall unto the yeer . . . 1555; . . . written in the Portugal tongue by A. Galvano; . . . corrected, quoted, and . . . published in English.* Londini, 1601. Tr. from *Tratado . . . de todos os descobrimentos antigos & modernos* (Lisboa, 1563) by Antonio Galvano. New ed., including Galvano's text, by C. R. D. Bethune, London, 1862. [Hakluyt Society, 1st series, v. 30.]

g ———— *Virginia richly valued by the description of the maine land of Florida, her next neighbour.* London, 1609. Reissued as *Historie of the travailles, discovery, and conquest of Terra Florida,* 1611. Tr. from *Relacam vervadeira dos trabalhos q . . . Fernãdo de Souto . . . passarom no descobrimẽto . . . da Florida . . . per hũfidalgo Deluas* [the Gentleman of Elvas]. New ed. by W. B. Rye, London, 1851. [Hakluyt Society, 1st series, v. 9.]

These are the works of an Englishman who became interested in geographical studies while at Oxford, read all he could find on the subject, and after ten years began to publish in *a* the collections he had made. His collections, which are a mine of information for geography, discovery, and colonization, appear in their final form in the second edition of *e,* which Froude called 'the prose epic of the modern English nation.' *b.* Important document for the origins of the colonization movement in England. *d.* Edition of one of the most important works on early American exploration. *c., f.,* and *g.* Translations of three important accounts of explorations.   AHS

K72 Purchas, Samuel. *Hakluytus Posthumus, or Purchas his Pilgrimes: contayning a history of the world in sea voyages and lande travells by Englishmen and others.* 4 v. London, 1625. Reprint, 20 v., Glasgow, 1905–07 [Hakluyt Society, extra series, v. 14–33].

Frankly a continuation and supplement of (K71e) Hakluyt, based in part on manuscripts left by Hakluyt and including voyages of all nations. Despite the faults of the compiler, his collection is a rich storehouse of information, often unavailable from any other source. Contents listed in Boston Atheneum, *Catalogue.*   AHS

K73a Churchill, Awnsham, and **Churchill, John.** *Collection of voyages and travels . . . with general preface giving an account of the progress of navigation* [attributed to John Locke]. 4 v. 1704. 3rd ed., 6 v., London, 1744–46. Other editions. [V. 7–8, London, 1745–47, are known as the 'Harleian collection,' and two other v., ed. by John Harris, 1744–48, are usually added.]

  b Prévost D'Exiles, Antoine F., and others. *Histoire générale des voyages.* 1746–70. Rev. ed., by Dubois and others, 25 v., La Haye, 1747–80. Abridged ed. by J. F. de la Harpe, 32 v., 1780–86; later ed., 24 v., Paris, 1816.

  c Pinkerton, John. *General collection of the best and most interesting voyages and travels in all parts of the world, many of which are now first translated into English.* 17 v. London, 1808–14. (Bibliography.)

  a. Valuable set of voyages. John Locke participated in gathering the material. *b.* Most voluminous collection of voyages published with the exception of the (K921) Hakluyt Society. Two series, land and sea. Begins with Plato and Hippocrates, and includes the Middle Ages and the American discoveries. La Harpe's abridgement shows that each age depended on the work of a previous age. *c.* This useful collection of voyages, by a Scotchman, was the largest and best that had so far appeared in English. It includes many rare voyages not contained in earlier collections.   AHS

K74 Schefer, Charles H. A., and **Cordier, Henri,** ed. *Recueil de voyages et de documents pour servir à l'histoire de la géographie depuis le XIIIᵉ jusqu'à la fin du XVIᵉ siècle.* Paris, 1882 ff.

The twenty-third number, some numbers include more than one volume, was issued in 1917. This valuable series includes not only editions of narratives of voyages but also carefully documented original studies on the history of exploration. While several numbers relate to America, others deal with Africa and Asia, especially with the Levant.   GMD

K75 *Voyages de jadis et d'aujourd'hui.* Paris, 1924 ff. [1, P. Deslandres, ed., *Voyage de Bougainville autour du monde pendant les années, 1766, 1767, 1768, et 1769.*]

Initial issue of a new French collection of narratives of voyages of exploration.
                                                                                   GMD

K76a Navarrete, Martin Fernandez de. *Colección de los viages y descubrimientos que hicieron por mar los Españoles desde fines del siglo XV, con varios documentos inéditos concernientes á la historia de la marina castellana y de los establecimientos españoles en Indias,* 5 v. Madrid, 1825–37. 2nd ed. of v. 1–3, Madrid, 1858–80.

  b *Collecção de opusculos reimpresos relativos a historia das navegaçoes, viagens, e conquistas dos Portugueses.* 4 v. Lisboa, 1844–75. [Academia Real das Sciencias.]

a. Valuable work for the early voyages; constantly utilized since the days of Washington Irving.   *b.* Corresponding Portuguese collection; treats a wider field.   For collections on Spanish and Portuguese colonization, cf. (Y71–74).

IJC

K77a Commelin, Izaäk, ed. *Begin ende voortgangh van de Vereenighde Neder-lantsche Geoctroyeerde Oost-Indische Compagnie; vervatende de voor-naemste reysen, by de inwoonderen der selver provincien derwaerts gedaen.* 1645. New ed., 2 v., Amsterdam, 1646.

   b Renneville, René A. C. de, ed. *Collection of voyages undertaken by the Dutch East-India company, for the improvement of trade and navigation.* London, 1703. Tr. from v. 1 of *Recueil des voyages qui ont servi à l'établissement et aux progrès de la Compagnie des Indes Orientales, formée dans les Provinces Unies des Païs-Bas,* 5 v., Amsterdam, 1702–06. 2nd rev. ed., 7 v., Amsterdam, 1725; 10 v., Rouen, 1725. Reprint, 10 v., Amsterdam, 1730; 7 v., Amsterdam, 1754.

b. Practically a French translation of *a.,* with additions. Principal collection of narratives of voyages of Dutch explorers, but limited to expeditions undertaken by the Dutch East-India Company. For a vivid retelling of the experiences of some of the more important Dutch explorers, cf. (K252) Van Loon, *Golden book of the Dutch navigators.*

GMD

K81a *Calendar of state papers: colonial series, preserved in the Public Record Office.* V. 1–27. London, 1860 ff.

   b *Journal of the commissioners for trade and plantations, preserved in the Public Record Office.* V. 1–6. London, 1920 ff.

Extremely valuable for British trade and administration chiefly in America and the West Indies. *a.* Volumes published cover from 1574 to 1714. Review, v. 25, C. M. Andrews, *A.H.R.* 30:833, July 1925; v. 26, 31:778, July 1926. *b.* The years 1704 to 1734 have thus far been covered. Review, C. M. Andrews, *A.H.R.* 31:331, Jan. 1926; 31:778, July 1926.

GMD

SHORTER GENERAL HISTORIES

K101 Newton, Arthur P. *Introduction to the study of colonial history.* London and N. Y., 1919. [Helps for students of history.]

Very brief introductory survey, with bibliographical suggestions.   GMD

K102 Payne, Edward J. *History of European colonies.* 1877. Reprint, London and N. Y., 1889. [Historical course for schools, ed. by E. A. Freeman.]

Pioneer work; full of facts clearly presented in a rather unattractive guise. A most convenient and useful guide.   FJK

K103 Schäfer, Dietrich. *Kolonialgeschichte.* 1903. New ed., 2 v., Berlin, 1921. [Sammlung Göschen.]

Brief survey of the whole field of colonial history, almost solely from the political viewpoint. The work suffers from disproportion, the major part being devoted to German colonial enterprises. Review, J. E. Gillespie, *A.H.R.* 27:809, July 1922.   FWP

LONGER GENERAL HISTORIES

K121 Morris, Henry C. *History of colonization from the earliest times to the present day.* 2 v. N. Y. and London, 1900. (Bibliography.)

Readable narrative of the whole colonization movement; generally condemned by reviewers. No other work covers exactly this field and its usefulness lies largely in that fact. The quality of the work improves as the modern period is reached. Should be used with caution, owing to frequent mistakes. Review, C. Day, *A.H.R.* 6:533, Apr. 1901.   FJK

K122 Zimmermann, Alfred. *Die europäischen Kolonien, Schilderung ihrer Entstehung, Entwicklung, Erfolge, und Aussichten.* 5 v. Berlin, 1896–1903. (Bibliographies.)

Inferior compilation; apparently based on secondary sources; insufficiently provided with references. Cf. (K423) Zimmermann, *Geschichte der deutschen Kolonialpolitik.*   AGK

K123 Lannoy, Charles De, and **Linden, Herman Vander.** *Histoire de l'expansion coloniale des peuples européens.* 3 v. Bruxelles, 1907–21. [1, *Portugal et Espagne;* 2, *Néerlande et Danemark;* 3, *Suède.*] (Extensive bibliography.)

This projected study of European colonization from the Middle Ages to the present was unfortunately interrupted by the loss of Professor vander Linden's library and notes at Louvain in 1914. The history of the colonies themselves is narrated less fully than in (K122) Zimmermann. The valuable feature of the work is the treatment in the case of each nation of the European background, of the administration, economic life, and civilization of the colonies, and of the effect of expansion on the mother country. The authors used unpublished manuscripts only occasionally. Each volume contains maps. Review, v. 1, A. L. P. Dennis, *A.H.R.* 13:344, Jan. 1908; W. R. Shepherd, *Pol. Sci. Quar.* 23:526, Sept. 1908; v. 2, E. Hubert, *Rev. Hist.* 114:101, Sept. 1913; v. 3, H. E. Egerton, *E.H.R.* 37:614, Oct. 1922.   RGAn

EUROPEAN BACKGROUND AND EUROPEAN EXPANSION

K201 Cheyney, Edward P. *European background of American history, 1300–1600.* N. Y. and London, 1904 [(X122) American nation.] (Good bibliographies.)

This valuable volume includes illuminating chapters upon geographic conditions and influences, medieval trade, the background of oceanic discovery, and the political and religious organization of Europe, especially of England, at the beginning of the era of exploration and colonization. It unfortunately does not stress the social conditions. Review, V. Coffin, *A.H.R.* 10:858, July 1905. In connection with ch. 2 on the trade routes, students would do well to consult (H571b) Lybyer, 'Ottoman Turks and the routes of oriental trade.' For the European background in the seventeenth and eighteenth centuries cf. (I539a and b) Mahan, *Influence of sea power in history,* and *Influence of sea power upon the French Revolution and the empire.*   LHG

K202 Muir, Ramsay. *Expansion of modern Europe, the culmination of modern history.* 1917. 3rd rev. ed., Boston, 1923.

Inspired by the World War; strongly pro-British, pro-Ally, and anti-German. Aims, in the first place, to provide a broad survey of 'imperial expansion and the imperial rivalries of the greater states of western civilization' from the sixteenth century to the present; secondly, 'to bring out the political ideas which are implicit in, or which result from, the conquest of the world by western civilization . . . in particular . . . to direct attention to the significant new political form . . . the world state, embracing peoples of many different types, with a western nation-state as its nucleus'; and, thirdly, 'to display . . . the strife between two rival conceptions of empire; the old, sterile, and ugly conception . . . fully exemplified in Germany; and the nobler conception which regards empire as a trusteeship' exemplified chiefly by Great Britain. The conclusion is that the World War was unnecessary apart from the German conception of empire based upon the 'doctrine of power.' Review, G. M. Dutcher, *Historical Outlook*, 9:514, Dec. 1918; W. R. Shepherd, *A.H.R.* 23:387, Jan. 1918. CLB

K203 Abbott, Wilbur C. *Expansion of Europe, a history of the foundations of the modern world.* 2 v., 1918. Rev. ed., 1 v., N. Y., 1924. [American historical series.] (Good bibliographies.)

A world history, 1415 to 1789, in which the political and intellectual development of Europe is traced coincidently with the expansion or colonial movement. 'Within the dates given the work constitutes what is probably the best general history of European civilization available in English. . . . Many of the maps are novel and interesting.' This is one of the outstanding historical works of recent years, suitable for the use of both the student and the general reader. Review, W. R. Shepherd, *A.H.R.* 24:87, Oct. 1918. FJK

K204 Jeudwine, John W. *Studies in empire and expansion.* London and N. Y., 1923.

These studies of discovery and trade practically constitute a history of European expansion from the Northmen to the nineteenth century. Despite many statements of doubtful validity, the work contains considerable useful information. Review, H. E. Egerton, *E.H.R.* 39:160, Jan. 1924. AHS

K205 Poole, Reginald Lane. *History of the Huguenots of the dispersion at the recall of the Edict of Nantes.* London, 1880. [Lothian essay.]

Serves its avowed purpose of furnishing a 'compact index' to the literature of its subject available at the time of its publication. It further offers a useful and fairly complete summary of the fortunes of the Huguenots in the various countries in which they sought refuge, and gives in epitome the main consequences, chiefly economic and cultural, of Huguenot immigration. RHG

K211 Lippmann, Walter. *Stakes of diplomacy.* 1915. Popular ed., N. Y., 1917.

Perhaps the best example of an extensive literature upon the subject of colonial expansion as a factor in international relations. The proposed program of solution anticipated the scheme of mandates embodied in the treaty of Versailles. Review, *Nation* (N. Y.), 101:659, Dec. 2, 1915. For the application of the policy of mandates in Africa, cf. (W315) G. L. Beer, *African questions at the Paris Peace Conference.* GMD

K212 Beer, George L. *English-speaking peoples, their future relations and joint international obligations.* N. Y., 1917.

Important discussion of the past, present, and future relations of England with the United States and with the British self-governing dominions, with special reference to their joint relations to international affairs.   GMD

HISTORIES OF EXPLORATION

K221a Wetherill, Henry B. *World and its discovery.* Oxford, 1914. [Oxford geographies.]

b Spears, John R. *Master mariners.* N. Y. and London, 1912. [Home university library.] (Bibliography.)

a. Simple, comprehensive book, intended as a supplementary reader for school classes in geography. The chapters contain brief accounts of the exploration of Africa, Asia, America, and Australasia, with summaries of the narratives of the principal explorers. The sketch maps are strikingly clear.   *b.* Brief survey of achievements of the great navigators, especially in the age of discovery.

FHH

K222 Beazley, Charles Raymond. *Dawn of modern geography, a history of exploration and geographical science.* V. 1–2, London, 1897–1901; v. 3, Oxford, 1906; 2nd ed. of v. 1–2, London, 1905.

This excellent book is a history of medieval travel and geography, not of the age of discovery. The three volumes cover respectively A. D. 300 to 900; 900 to 1260; and 1260 to 1420. Accurate and entertaining; much the best work in the field. The treatment of the Norse voyages toward America antedates the recent revival of that controversy. Detailed criticism by Guy Le Strange, *E.H.R.* 12:538, July 1897; 17:338, Apr. 1902; 22:573, July 1907. Review, E. L. Stevenson, *A.H.R.* 12:867, July 1907. Cf. (U42a) Yule, *Book of Ser Marco Polo,* and (U2042a) Yule, *Cathay and the way thither.*   FHH

K226 Gathorne-Hardy, Geoffrey M. *Norse discoverers of America, the Wineland sagas translated and discussed.* Oxford and N. Y., 1921. (Bibliography.)

Dovetails together the relevant portions of the sagas; discusses the problems involved; latest treatment of the subject by a competent authority. Review, J. E. Olson, *A.H.R.* 27:325, Jan. 1922.   GMD

K231a Beazley, Charles Raymond. *Prince Henry the Navigator, the hero of Portugal and of modern discovery, 1394–1460.* N. Y., 1895. [Heroes of the nations.] (Bibliography.)

b Major, Richard H. *Life of Prince Henry of Portugal, surnamed the Navigator, and its results.* 1868. Abridged ed. as *Discoveries of Prince Henry the Navigator and their results.* London, 1877. (Bibliography.)

c Oliveira Martins, Joaquim P. *Golden age of Prince Henry the Navigator.* London, 1914. Tr. by James J. Abraham and William E. Reynolds from *Os filhos de Dom João I,* 1891; 2nd ed., 2 v., Lisboa, 1901.

a. One of the best biographies in a series which averages fairly high; a good picture of a remarkable man and his times; supersedes *b.;* far more dependable than *c.*   RBM

K232a Jayne, Kingsley G. *Vasco da Gama and his successors, 1460–1580.* London, 1910. (Bibliography.)

b Stephens, Henry Morse. *Albuquerque.* 1892. Reprint, Oxford, 1897. [Rulers of India series.] (Bibliography.)

Excellent biographies respectively of the discoverer of the sea-route to India, and of the great builder of Portuguese power in the East, with supplementary accounts of Portuguese possessions in the East to 1580. Review of *a. E.H.R.* 26:417, Apr. 1911. For fuller treatment of the Portuguese in India, cf. (U1221a) Whiteway, *Rise of the Portuguese Power in India.*   GMD

K233 Pigafetta, Antonio. *Magellan's voyage around the world: the original text, . . . with translation, notes, bibliography and index, by* J. A. Robertson. 2 v. and index. Cleveland, 1906. (Bibliography.)

Exact reprint of the earliest manuscript of the chronicle of the voyage, presented page by page with a translation. The extensive notes are scholarly and valuable. A very important book. Review, F. H. H. Guillemard, *E.H.R.* 23:146, Jan. 1908.   HRS

K234 Guillemard, Francis H. H. *Life of Ferdinand Magellan and the first circumnavigation of the globe, 1480–1521.* London, 1890. [World's great explorers and explorations.]

Standard biography, by the geographical editor of the Cambridge University Press. The appendixes contain genealogies, Magellan's wills, facts in regard to the personnel, the stores, and the equipment of his fleet, and the names of the men who returned to Seville on the *Victoria,* and other valuable information.
                                                                                    HRS

K241 Young, Filson. *Christopher Columbus and the new world of his discovery . . . with a note on the navigation of Columbus's first voyage by the Earl of Dunraven.* 2 v., 1906. 3rd ed., 1 v., N. Y., 1912.

Distinctly a popular book; based on a very superficial study of the sources; contains, however, rather full quotations from Columbus's own writings to illustrate his character and purposes. Of special value is the note of some thirty pages by the Earl of Dunraven interpreting obscure passages in the narratives of Columbus's first voyage. Review, E. G. Bourne, *A.H.R.* 12:656, Apr. 1906.   CHHg

K242a Winsor, Justin. *Christopher Columbus and how he received and imparted the spirit of discovery.* 1891. 5th rev. ed., Boston, 1892. (Bibliography.)

b —— — *Cartier to Frontenac . . . geographical discovery in the interior of North America in its historical relations, 1534–1700, with full cartographical illustrations from contemporary sources.* Boston, 1894. (Bibliography.)

Winsor's method was to gather all the available material, generally the printed material that passed through his hands as librarian, and then to mould it into shape in a continuous narrative. The result was a mine of information, especially biographical in *a.,* historical in *b.,* and in every case bibliographical and cartographical. On the other hand, such a method was fatal to style, so that these books are often hard reading. Winsor's attitude to Columbus was unfavorable. Cf. also his (X 431) *Mississippi basin* and *Westward movement.*
                                                                                    AHS

K243a Harrisse, Henry. *Bibliotheca americana vetustissima, a description of works relating to America published between 1492 and 1551.* N. Y., 1866.

b —— *Bibliotheca americana vetustissima, a description of works relating to America published between 1492 and 1551: additions.* Paris, 1872.

c —— *Fernand Colomb, sa vie, ses oeuvres: essai critique.* Paris, 1872.

d —— *Notes pour servir à l'histoire, à la bibliographie, et à la cartographie de la Nouvelle-France et des pays adjacents, 1545–1700.* Paris, 1872.

e —— *Jean et Sébastien Cabot, leur origine et leurs voyages, étude d'histoire critique suivie d'une cartographie, d'une bibliographie, et d'une chronologie des voyages au nord-ouest de 1497 à 1550, d'après des documents inédits.* Paris, 1882. [(K74) Schefer and Cordier, Recueil de voyages et de documents.]

f —— *Les Corte-Real et leurs voyages au Nouveau-monde d'après des documents nouveaux ou peu connus tirés des archives de Lisbonne et de Modène, suivi du texte inédit d'un récit de la troisième expédition de Gaspar Corte-Real.* Paris, 1883. [(K74) Schefer and Cordier, Recueil de voyages et de documents.]

g —— *Christophe Colomb: son origine, sa vie, ses voyages, sa famille, et ses descendants, d'après des documents inédits tirés des archives de Gênes, de Savonne, de Séville, et de Madrid; études d'histoire critique.* 2 v. Paris, 1884–85. [(K74) Schefer and Cordier, Recueil de voyages et de documents.]

h —— *Discovery of North America: a critical, documentary, and historic investigation, with an essay on the early cartography of the New world, including descriptions of two hundred and fifty maps or globes existing or lost, constructed before the year 1536; to which are added a chronology of one hundred voyages westward, projected, attempted, or accomplished between 1431 and 1504; biographical accounts of the three hundred pilots who first crossed the Atlantic; and a copious list of the original names of American regions, caciqueships, mountains, islands, capes, gulfs, rivers, towns, and harbours.* London and Paris, 1892.

i —— *Americus Vespuccius, a critical and documentary review of two recent English books concerning that navigator.* London, 1895.

j —— *John Cabot, the discoverer of North America, and Sebastian, his son; a chapter of the maritime history of England under the Tudors, 1496–1557.* London, 1896.

k —— *Diplomatic history of America: its first chapter 1452–1493–1494.* London, 1897.

l —— *Découverte et évolution cartographique de Terre Neuve et des pays circonvoisins, 1497–1501–1769, essais de géographie historique et documentaire.* Paris, 1900.

Henry Harrisse devoted a long lifetime to the study of the evidence bearing on the discovery and early exploration of America. Especially in the fields of bibliography and cartography he was acknowledged master among those of his generation. An indefatigable antiquary, his work was characterized by thorough scholarship and extraordinary perseverance in his search for materials. The character of the first six works listed is sufficiently indicated by their titles; most of the material is revised and reproduced in the later works cited. *g.* Series of critical essays on obscure questions relating to the early life of the admiral; must today be corrected by reference to (K244e) Vignaud, but it marked an epoch in the history of Columbian studies.　Review, L. Gallois, *Rev. Hist.* 35:381, Dec. 1887.　*h.* Quarto of 800 pages; luxuriously printed and illustrated; in a sense, a *résumé* of his previous works on the early navigators, with much new material added.　It includes a long and minute study on early American cartography, together with biographical and bibliographical information of all sorts which makes the volume indispensable to workers in this field. Review, E. J. Payne, *E.H.R.* 7:764, Oct. 1892; L. Gallois, *Rev. Hist.* 55:396, Aug. 1894.　*j.* Equally important for the events relating to the careers of the Cabots.　Review, N. E. Dionne, *A.H.R.* 1:717, July 1896.　*k.* Critical study of the papal bulls concerning Portuguese and Spanish explorations and of the treaty of Tordesillas.　Review, E. G. Bourne, *A.H.R.* 3:709, July 1898.　*l.* Cartographical study of Newfoundland from Cabot's landfall to Captain Cook's survey, with the author's final views on the Cabot controversy.　Review, G. P. Winship, *A.H.R.* 7:752, July 1902.　Cf. Vignaud, *Henry Harrisse, étude biographique et morale,* Paris, 1912. 　　　　　　　　　　　　　　　　CHHg

K244a Vignaud, Henry.　*La lettre et la carte de Toscanelli sur la route des Indes par l'ouest.*　Paris, 1901.　[(K74) Schefer and Cordier, Recueil de voyages et de documents.]　(Bibliography.)

　b ——— *Toscanelli and Columbus, the letter and chart of Toscanelli on the route to the Indies by way of the west, sent in 1474 to the Portuguese Fernam Martins, and later on to Christopher Columbus: a critical study on the authenticity and value of these documents and the sources of the cosmographical ideas of Columbus, followed by the various texts of the letter, with translations, annotations, several facsimiles, and also a map.* London, 1902.　(Bibliography.)

　c ——— *Critical study of the various dates assigned to the birth of Christopher Columbus: the real date, 1451.*　London, 1903.　(Bibliography.)

　d ——— *Études critiques sur la vie de Colomb avant ses découvertes: les origines de sa famille; les deux Colombo, ses prétendus parents; la vraie date de sa naissance; les études et les premières campagnes qu'il aurait faites, son arrivée en Portugal et le combat naval de 1476; son voyage au Nord; son établissement en Portugal; son mariage; sa famille portugaise.*　Paris, 1905.　(Bibliography.)

　e ——— *Histoire critique de la grande entreprise de Christophe Colomb, comment il aurait conçu et formé son projet, sa présentation à différents cours, son acceptation finale, sa mise à exécution, son véritable caractère.* 2 v.　Paris, 1911.　[Études sur la vie de Colomb, deuxième série.] (Bibliographies.)

　f ——— *Americ Vespuce, 1451–1512: sa biographie, sa vie, ses voyages, ses découvertes, l'attribution de son nom à l'Amerique, ses relations authentiques et contestées.*　Paris, 1917　[(K74) Schefer and Cordier, Recueil de voyages et de documents.]

　g ——— *Columbian tradition on the discovery of America and on the part played therein by the astronomer Toscanelli: a memoir addressed to the Professors Hermann Wagner of the University of Göttingen and Carlo Errera of Bologna.*　Oxford, 1920.

Henry Vignaud, by many years of critical investigation of the life and achievements of Christopher Columbus, attained a foremost place among students of the career of the great discoverer.　*a.* and *b.* His first important book, *b.* being a translation of *a.* with additional chapters and important alterations.　A rigorous and destructive criticism of the authenticity of the letter and map which Toscanelli supposedly addressed in 1474 to a Portuguese canon, Fernam Martins, a copy of which he later sent to Columbus. Review, E. G. Bourne, *A.H.R.* 8:341, Jan. 1903; G. Le Strange, *E.H.R.* 17:568, July 1902; 18:194, Jan. 1903. *c.* Critical study of the birth-date of Columbus. Review, E. G. Bourne, *A.H.R.* 10:148, Oct. 1904. *d.* Severe examination of various points in the Columbian tradition, generally to the disadvantage of Columbus. The main thesis is that the Genoese was an ignorant sailor who posed as a savant and an aristocrat, hoping to convince later generations that scientific considerations had led him to try to reach the Orient by sailing west. Vignaud pays a tribute to his energy, daring, and tenacity, but contends, that the real object of the voyage of 1492 was to seek an island in the Atlantic, and that only after all hope of finding it had gone did Columbus form the belief that he was in the Indies. Review, *A.H.R.* 11:140, Oct. 1905. *e.* Restatement of the conclusions reached in earlier studies, including the result of further research. Review, E. L. Stevenson, *A.H.R.* 17:610, Apr. 1912. *f.* Champions the Florentine navigator, and claims for him the merit of having first divined the true character of the lands which Columbus mistook for Asia. Review, H. P. Biggar, *E.H.R.* 34:553, Apr. 1919; G. T. Northup, *A.H.R.* 23:653, Apr. 1918. *g.* Reply to critics of *b.* and other works; reaffirms his conclusions on the object of Columbus's search. Review, E. L. Stevenson, *A.H.R.* 26:139, Oct. 1920. CHHg

K251 Heawood, Edward. *History of geographical discovery in the seventeenth and eighteenth centuries.* Cambridge, Eng., 1912. [Cambridge geographical series.]

Covers particularly the exploration of the Pacific and of the interior of the newly discovered continents. The material is well organized and as entertainingly presented as could reasonably be expected in a small book covering so large a field and involving such a mass of detail. The author is librarian of the Royal Geographical Society. Review, *E.H.R.* 28:611, July 1913; F. A. Golder, *A.H.R.* 19:145, Oct. 1913. The gap of two centuries between (K222) Beazley's work and this volume is conveniently bridged by (X205) Fiske, *Discovery of America,* though it is not an authoritative work. FHH

K252 Van Loon, Hendrik Willem. *Golden book of the Dutch navigators.* N. Y., 1916.

Lively accounts of Dutch voyages of exploration, made in the early part of the seventeenth century; based upon the original narratives. Review, G. F. Zook, *A.H.R.* 22:700, Apr. 1917. GMD

K256 Woollen, William Watson. *Inside passage to Alaska, 1792–1920, with an account of the North Pacific coast from Cape Mendocino to Cook Inlet, from the accounts left by Vancouver and other early explorers and from the author's journals of exploration and travel in that region, ed. from his original manuscripts by P. L. Haworth.* 2 v. Cleveland, 1924.

The records of early explorations of the northern Pacific coast of America are of distinct historical, as well as geographical, importance and are collected and annotated in this useful edition. Review, F. W. Howay, *Can. Hist. Rev.* 6:81, March 1925; E. S. Meany, *A.H.R* 31:181, Oct. 1925. FWP

K261 Buchan, John. *Last secrets, the final mysteries of exploration.* London and N. Y., 1923.

Brief popular account of some of the most sensational explorations in the twentieth century, including the North and South Polar expeditions, the attempts to ascend Mt. Everest, and the Younghusband expedition to Lhasa. Review, *Geographical Rev.* 15:167, Jan. 1925.   GMD

HISTORIES OF COMMERCE AND OF TRADING COMPANIES

K271 Macpherson, David. *Annals of commerce, manufactures, fisheries, and navigation, with brief notices of the arts and sciences connected with them: containing the commercial transactions of the British empire and other countries, from the earliest accounts to the meeting of the Union parliament in January, 1801; and comprehending the most valuable part of the late Mr. Anderson's History of commerce . . . with a large appendix.* 4 v. London, 1805.

Macpherson, as deputy keeper of the public records, was able to collect the authentic materials which make his annals a mine of reliable information for economic historians. The section, in v. 2–3, on the period, 1492–1760, is virtually a new edition of Adam Anderson, *Historical and chronological deduction of the origin of commerce,* 2 v., London, 1764. The material is collected under each year but a fairly good index, wherein matters are arranged chronologically under subjects, enables the student to trace development. For its statistical accounts the work remains useful for reference.   FWP

K272 Lindsay, William. *History of merchant shipping and ancient commerce.* 4 v. London, 1874–76.

V. 1–3. Divided chronologically, 1, to 1500; 2, to 1815; 3, to 1874. V. 4. Treats the history of steam navigation. A considerable part of the work as a whole relates to the development of trade and has been superseded. On the construction and operation of ships, the author has gleaned a great amount of interesting material. A useful source of information, though references to authorities are unfortunately infrequent. For highly valuable works on medieval commerce, cf. (H571a) W. von Heyd, *Histoire du commerce du Levant au moyen-âge* and (H572) A. Schaube, *Handelsgeschichte . . . bis zum Ende der Kreuzzüge.*
                                                                                 CD

K273 Schanz, Georg. *Englische Handelspolitik gegen Ende des Mittelalters.* 2 v. Leipzig, 1881.

Typical example of thorough German scholarship. V. 1. Deals with the trade relations of England with the various European countries during the reigns of Henry VII and Henry VIII, and with general conditions of trade, the staple, merchant adventurers, monetary conditions, etc. V. 2. Contains an introductory chapter devoted to statistical tables of tolls, exports and imports, etc.; and the documents upon which the various chapters of v. 1 are based, quoted in full in the original. Valuable especially for England; the conditions in the countries with which England had commercial relations are naturally treated with considerable fullness.   AHB

K291 Bonnassieux, Louis J. Pierre M. *Les grandes compagnies de commerce, étude pour servir à l'histoire de la colonisation.* Paris, 1892.

Survey of all the great commercial companies, classified by country and by date. The section devoted to the French companies is the largest and the best, including considerable original material from the French archives. Other sections are to be used with caution, since the author does not show acquaintance even with all the best secondary literature. Concluding sections discuss the general aspects of the earlier companies and of recent companies modelled after them.

CD

K292a Cawston, George, and **Keane, Augustus H.** *Early chartered companies. A. D. 1296–1858.* London and N. Y., 1896.

b Lucas, Sir Charles P. *Beginnings of English overseas enterprise: a prelude to the empire.* Oxford, 1917.

c Lingelbach, William E. *Merchant adventurers of England, their laws and ordinances, with other documents.* Philadelphia, 1902. [University of Pennsylvania, Translations and reprints from the original sources of European history, 2nd series, v. 2.]

d —— *Internal organization of the Merchant Adventurers of England.* Philadelphia, 1903. (Bibliography.)

e —— *Merchant Adventurers at Hamburg. A.H.R.* 9:265–287, Jan. 1904.

a. Short sketch of the Merchant Adventurers and later English commercial companies. Its value arises principally from the paucity of books on this subject. *b.* Chiefly an account of the Merchants of the Staple, the Eastland Merchants, and the Merchant Adventurers. Review, E. P. Cheyney, *A.H.R.* 23:381, Jan. 1918. *c.* Collection of previously unprinted documents concerning the Merchant Adventurers, with 'a brief history' which is almost the only continuous narrative of this influential but little understood organization from its origin to its dissolution. Review, A. L. Cross, *A.H.R.* 8:531, Apr. 1903. *d.* and *e.* Brief supplementary studies on the same subject.

EPC

K293 Scott, William Robert. *Constitution and finance of English, Scottish, and Irish joint-stock companies to 1720.* 3 v. Cambridge, Eng., 1910–12. (Bibliography.)

Only v. 1 and 2 are of interest to the student of colonial enterprise. The mechanics of finance in relation to trade and colonization, and the financial and economic background of the trading and planting companies, as well as the organization of the companies themselves, are ably treated in this well-documented work.

AHB

BRITISH COLONIZATION: HISTORY

K301 Robinson, Henry James. *Colonial chronology, a chronology of the principal events connected with the English colonies and India from the close of the fifteenth century to the present time, with maps.* London, 1892. (Brief bibliography.)

Convenient handbook. Contains general table, 1486–1891, in four parellel columns (Europe, America, Africa, and Asia with Australasia), and separate tables for each colony. Maps for 1592, 1692, 1792, 1892, and of principal colonies.

GMD

K302a **Barnard, Howard Clive,** ed. *Expansion of the Anglo-Saxon nations, a short history of the British empire and the United States.* London, 1920. (Bibliography.)

b **Robinson, Howard.** *Development of the British empire.* Boston, 1922. (Brief bibliographies.)

c **Williamson, James A.** *Short history of British expansion.* London, 1922. New ed., 2 v. 1930. (Excellent bibliographies.)

d **Woodward, William H.** *Short history of the expansion of the British empire, 1500–1902.* 1899. 2nd ed., Cambridge, Eng., 1902. N. Y., 1912. [Cambridge series for schools and training colleges.]

e **Higham, Charles S. S.** *History of the British empire.* London and N. Y., 1921.

a. Chapters by six different authors on the United States, India, the colonies in North America, Africa, and Australasia, and the lesser possessions. Good brief introductory text-book with maps and chronological table. *b.* Text-book for American colleges; contains excellent statements of main facts with little interpretation; good book for ready reference and for a straightforward account of the development of the empire. Review, W. P. Hall, *A.H.R.* 28:538, Apr. 1923; *Pol. Sci. Quar.* 38:183, March 1923. *c.* Relates 'the history of the British people in its external aspects. These include not merely colonization and the administration of tropical colonies but also movements which antedated, ran parallel to, and influenced both: foreign trade, the rise and decline of economic theories, religious and secular incentives to emigration, and broad changes in national character and outlook.' Rather detailed, but well written and reliable. Review, *Pol. Sci. Quar.* 38:183, March 1923. *d.* Formerly a standard text-book; superseded by *b.* and *c.* *e.* Good outline; very brief. Also cf. (L103) Muir, *Short history of the British commonwealth.* AHB

K303a **Lucas, Sir Charles P.,** ed. *Historical geography of the British colonies.* V. 1–7, Oxford, 1888–1923. [*Introduction,* H. E. Egerton, *Origin and growth of Greater Britain.* 1908, 2nd ed., 1920. (This introduction has taken the place of one written by Lucas in 1887.) 1, C. P. Lucas, *Mediterranean and eastern colonies,* 1888; 2nd ed. by R. E. Stubbs, 1906; 2, C. P. Lucas, *West Indies,* 1890; 2nd ed. by C. Atchley, 1905; 3, C. P. Lucas, *West Africa,* 1894; 3rd ed. by A. B. Keith, 1913; 4, C. P. Lucas, *South Africa,* pt. 1, *Historical—to the Boer War,* 1897, 2nd ed., 1913, pt. 2, *Historical—Boer War to the Union,* 1915; pt. 3, *Geographical,* 1897, 3rd ed. by A. B. Keith, 1913; (Z101a) 5, *Canada,* pt. 1, C. P. Lucas, *Historical—to 1763,* 1901, 2nd ed. 1916; (Z101b) pt. 2, H. E. Egerton, *Historical—since 1763,* 1908, 3rd ed., 1923; (Z41) pt. 3, J. D. Rogers, *Geographical,* 1911; pt. 4, J. D. Rogers, *Newfoundland,* 1911; 6, J. D. Rogers, *Australasia,* pt. 1, *Historical;* pt. 2, *Geographical,* 1907; 2nd rev. ed., by R. N. Kershaw, 1925; 7, (U1242a) P. E. Roberts, *India,* pt. 1, *Historical,* 1916; pt. 2, *Geographical,* 1920.] (Bibliographies.)

b **Rose, J. Holland; Newton, Arthur P.;** and **Benians, E. A.,** eds. *Cambridge history of the British empire.* To be in 8 v. V. 1, 4, 6, Cambridge, Eng., 1930.

a. This series, still in the process of expansion and revision, has from the first been a coöperative work, the product of a group of carefully trained writers, animated by a spirit of judicial impartiality. It aims to present the history of the British dominions with special emphasis upon geographical influences and features. The parts devoted exclusively to geography contain valuable descriptive material on a wide range of topics rather than investigations of the relations of geography to migration, settlement, and national development within the British empire. In the historical volumes, exploration and military history are emphasized. The introduction by Professor Egerton is well written as is also his volume on Canada. J. D. Rogers has presented the geography of Canada and the history and geography of Newfoundland and of Australasia with evidences of unusual mastery of source materials. One of the most stimulating volumes, that on South Africa, is contributed by the editor. The historical volume on India by P. E. Roberts is penetrating and commendable. LHG

b. Similar in conception to (I121) *Cambridge modern history.* Review, v. 1, G. M. Wrong, *A.H.R.* 35:103, Oct. 1929; v. 4, M. T. Titus, *A.H.R.* 35:851, July 1930. FWP

K304 Tilby, A. Wyatt. *English people overseas.* 6. v. London and Boston, 1908–14. 2nd ed. of v. 1–2, 1910. Later reprints. [1, *American colonies, 1583–1763; 2, British India, 1600–1828; 3, British North America, 1763–1867; 4, Britain in the tropics, 1527–1910; 5, Australasia, 1688–1911; 6, South Africa, 1486–1913.*] (Brief bibliographies.)

This interestingly written series covering the whole empire hardly reaches the standard of scholarship demanded by the critical historian. Mr. Tilby, however, approaches his task with breadth of view and with considerable appreciation of the larger historic forces involved. Review, v. 1–4, A. L. P. Dennis, *A.H.R.* 18:358, Jan. 1913. LHG

K305 Newton, Arthur P. *Colonising activities of the English Puritans: the last phase of the Elizabethan struggle with Spain.* New Haven, 1914. [Yale historical publications, miscellany.]

Survey of Puritan colonizing enterprises to 1660, with special reference to the activities of the Earl of Warwick and the Providence Company, and to anti-Spanish activities in the West Indies. Review, C. G. Calkins, *A.H.R.* 20:146, Oct. 1914. GMD

K306 Insh, George P. *Scottish colonial schemes, 1620–1686.* Glasgow, 1922.

Deals with enterprises in Newfoundland, Nova Scotia, New Galloway (Cape Breton), East New Jersey, and Stuart's Town, South Carolina. Appendixes of documents. First instalment of winning essay for Carnegie Essay Prize, 1920–1921. To be followed by a volume on the Darien scheme. Review, C. M. Andrews, *A.H.R.* 28:305, Jan. 1923. GMD

K307a Martin, Robert Montgomery. *History of the British colonies.* 5 v. London, 1834–35. New ed., entitled *British colonial library,* 10 v., London, 1844.

b McCulloch, John R. *Statistical account of the British Empire, exhibiting its extent, physical capacities, population, industry, and civil and religious institutions.* 2 v., 1837. 4th ed., 2 v. in 1, London, 1854.

Valuable for excellent descriptions of the colonies and compilations of data respecting them at the epoch of reform. GMD

K308a Dilke, Sir Charles W. *Greater Britain, a record of travel in English-speaking countries during 1866-7.* 1868. 2nd rev. ed., London, 1876.

b Froude, James A. *Oceana; or, England and her colonies.* London and N. Y., 1886.

c Freeman, Edward A. *Greater Greece and Greater Britain, and George Washington, the expander of England, two lectures, with an appendix on imperial federation.* London, 1886.

Notable works by eminent authors; now out of date; still valuable as records of conditions and opinions at the time of writing. *a.* Excellent record of travel with illuminating observations. Review, *Athenaeum,* 2:633, Nov. 14, 1868. *b.* Descriptive account of a visit to Australia and New Zealand, with a consequent discussion of imperial relations. Review, *Athenaeum,* 1:159, Jan. 30, 1886. *c.* Utilizes the analogy of Greek expansion without political connection to urge that a union of friendship, rather than imperial control, is the proper cohesive force for the British Empire. Review, *E.H.R.* 1:818, Oct. 1886.   GMD

K309 *All red series.* 6 v. London and Boston, 1907–13. [(V313a) B. R. Wise, *Commonwealth of Australia;* (V376) Sir A. P. Douglas, *Dominion of New Zealand;* W. L. Griffith, *Dominion of Canada;* (W436d) W. B. Worsfold, *Union of South Africa;* (K387c) A E. Aspinall, *British West Indies;* Sir J. B. Fuller, *Empire of India.*]

The growth of the British Empire historically and economically with special reference to recent progress is treated in separate volumes for the several principal units, each by a writer well acquainted with the region concerned. Not compendiums of information like (K303) Lucas or (K310) *Oxford survey,* but intended to popularize acquaintance with the essential facts of the history of the empire and its recent development.   GMD

K310 Herbertson, Andrew J., and **Howarth, Osbert, J. R.,** ed. *Oxford survey of the British empire, a description of the empire and its constituent territories in their geographical, economic, administrative, and social aspects.* 6 v. Oxford, 1914. [1, *British Isles and Mediterranean possessions;* 2, *Asia;* 3, *Africa;* 4, *America;* 5, *Australasia;* 6, *General survey.*]

Coöperative work intended for those whose special interest is the administration of the British Empire. Descriptive rather than historical; encyclopedic in scope, yet unified by a consistent plan. V. 1–5. Contain descriptive surveys, with emphasis on geographical and economic topics, prepared by experts familiar with the respective regions. V. 6. The most valuable to the historical student, though now somewhat out of date; contains, besides a convenient summary of imperial history by Professor H. E. Egerton, accounts of the British colonial office and its agencies and of the foreign office and its agencies. There is also discussion of general imperial problems, legal, educational, and commercial. Not least important are the chapters on imperial defence, and on 'The mapping of British territories.' Review, *Athenaeum,* 2:200, Aug. 15, 1914; *Nation* (N. Y.) 99:773, Dec. 31, 1914.   HET

K311 Lucas, Sir Charles P., ed. *Empire at war.* 5 v. Oxford and N. Y., 1921–26. [1, *Historical survey;* 2, *Canada and other American colonies;* 3, *Australasia;* 4, *African colonies;* 5, *Eastern and Mediterranean colonies.*] [Royal Colonial Institute.]

Designed to trace the growth of imperial coöperation in war time prior to the World War, to give a complete record of the effort made in the World War by each unit of the overseas empire, and to tell in what particular ways and to what extent each section of the empire was affected by the war. The participation of each colony is described by one of its own residents. Review, v. 1,

R. L. Schuyler, *A.H.R.* 28:112, Oct. 1922; v. 2, 29:771, July 1924; v. 3, 30:862, July 1925; v. 4, 31:171, Oct. 1925.

FWP

K312 Williamson, James A. *Builders of the empire.* Oxford, 1925.

Twenty good brief biographies of important figures in British imperial history from Cabot to Cecil Rhodes. Sound in scholarship, but commendable to younger readers.

GMD

BRITISH COLONIZATION: ADMINISTRATION

K321a Jenks, Edward. *Government of the British Empire, as at the end of the year 1917.* London and Boston, 1918.

b Hogan, Albert E. *Government of the United Kingdom, its colonies and dependencies.* 1908. 4th rev. ed., London, 1920.

Convenient recent manuals which include surveys of colonial administration. For an excellent older account, cf. (L548c) Lowell, *Government of England,* ch. 54–58.

GMD

K322 Todd, Alpheus. *Parliamentary government in the British colonies.* 1880. 2nd ed. by A. H. Todd, N. Y., 1894.

Authoritative study of parliamentary government in the British colonies prior to 1880, by the librarian of parliament, Ottawa, with additional data, relative to the years from 1880 to 1894, contributed by his son. The subject is viewed, in the main, from the angle of the chief executive in the colony. Appendixes supply statistical lists and pertinent legislative acts. Review, D. G. Ritchie, *E.H.R.* 10:815, Oct. 1895; *Nation* (N. Y.), 30:371, May 13, 1880; *ibid.* 58:389, May 24, 1894. Cf. (K349a) Keith, *Responsible government in the dominions,* and (K351) Bryce, *Modern democracies.*

HET

K323 Dilke, Sir Charles W. *Problems of Greater Britain.* 1890. 4th rev. ed., London and N. Y., 1890.

Systematic treatise on comparative government within the British Empire. Now valuable only as an excellent account of conditions at the time of writing. Review, *Athenaeum,* 1:237, Feb. 22, 1890.

GMD

K324 Bruce, Sir Charles. *Broad stone of empire, problems of crown colony administration, with records of personal experience.* 2 v. London and N. Y., 1910.

Exhaustive study of the health, laws, administrative systems, education, and religion of the British crown colonies. Overburdened with lengthy despatches and memoranda. The self-governing dominions are considered scarcely at all; but as a treatise on the government of tropical dependencies by one who was experienced as a colonial administrator it is of the highest value. Review, E. D. Adams, *Annals of the American Academy,* 38:649, Sept. 1911; *Athenaeum,* 2:664, Nov. 26, 1910.

FWP

K325 Porritt, Edward. *Fiscal and diplomatic freedom of the British oversea dominions.* Ed. by David Kinley. Oxford and N. Y., 1922. [Publications of the Carnegie Endowment for International Peace.] (Bibliography.)

Mainly the account of Canada's acquisition of sovereignty over her financial affairs and certain foreign relations. While the book shows wide research, the materials are poorly organized. Useful as a collection of source material and as a guide to the literature. Review, C. D. Allin, *Pol. Sci. Quar.* 38:152, March 1923; *A.H.R.* 28:314, Jan. 1923.   FWP

K326a Fuchs, Carl J. *Trade policy of Great Britain and her colonies since 1860.* London and N. Y., 1905. Tr. by C. H. M. Archibald from *Handelspolitik Englands und seiner Kolonien in den letzten Jahrzehnten,* Leipzig, 1893. [Schriften des Vereins für Socialpolitik.]

b Bérard, Victor. *British imperialism and commercial supremacy.* London and N. Y., 1906. Tr. by H. W. Foskett from *L'Angleterre et l'impérialisme,* 1900, 3rd ed., Paris, 1905.

c Schulze-Gaevernitz, Gerhart von. *Britischer Imperialismus und englischer Freihandel zu Beginn des zwanzigsten Jahrhunderts.* Leipzig, 1906. Reprint, München, 1915. (Bibliographical notes.)

d Ashley, William J., ed. *British dominions, their present commercial and industrial condition, a series of general reviews for business men and students.* London and N. Y., 1911. (Bibliography.)

e Drage, Geoffrey. *Imperial organisation of trade.* London, 1911.

Discussions of the problems of British colonial trade and of the commercial aspects of British imperialism between 1890 and 1914. *a.* and *c.* Marked by characteristic German thoroughness in the amassing of facts. *b.* Clever French journalistic observations. These three are important for the study of Chamberlain's policy of imperial preference, since *a.* and *b.* appeared in English translation and *c.* was published at the moment of culmination of that issue in British politics. *a.* Has suitable introduction to make it a political tract; statistics are not revised to date. Review, *Athenaeum* 1:748, June 17, 1905. *b.* Facts not always accurate. Review, *Athenaeum* 1:228, Feb. 24, 1906. *d.* and *e.* By British authorities. *d.* Collection of lectures on trade conditions and problems in the principal colonies, by eminent colonial officials. *e.* Published in anticipation of the imperial conference of 1911 and of the approaching revision of British commercial treaties. Valuable, impartial compilation of data. A survey of the history of British commercial policy is accompanied by discussions of both free trade and protection. Review, *Spectator,* 106:484, Apr. 1, 1911.   GMD

K327 Knowles, Lillian C. A. (Mrs. C. M. Knowles). *Economic development of the British overseas empire.* London and N. Y., 1924. [London School of Economics and Political Science, Studies in economics and political science.] (Bibliographical foot-notes.)

Three chapters on the empire as a whole are followed by more detailed study of the economic problems of India and of British tropical possessions. Very useful historical outline and systematic summary of a wealth of data. A companion volume to deal with the economic development of the self-governing dominions is announced. Review, H. E. Egerton, *Econ. Jour.* 35:133, March 1925; A. P. Usher, *Amer. Econ. Rev.* 15:306, June 1925.   FWP

K328 *British Empire, a survey.* Ed. by Hugh Gunn. 12 v. London, 1924. (Bibliographies.) [1, Sir C. P. Lucas, *Story of the empire;* 2, A. B. Keith, *Constitution, administration, and laws;* 3, E. Lewin, *Resources of the empire and their development;* 4, A. Balfour, and H. H. Scott, *Health problems;* 5, Thirteen contributors, *Dominions and dependencies;* 6, J. S. Mills, *Press and communications;* 7, Sir C. C. McLeod and A. W. Kirkaldy, *Trade, commerce, and shipping;* 8, H. Gunn, *Makers of the* *empire;* 9, Sir G. Lagden, *Native races;* 10, A. P. Newton, *Universities and educational systems;* 11, E. Salmon and A. A. Longden, *Literature and art;* 12, E. A. Belcher and J. A. Williamson, *Migration within the empire.*]

Best general descriptive survey of the administrative and cultural conditions and problems of the British Empire after the World War, by competent authorities in the several fields. The arrangement is topical, instead of regional as in (K310) *Oxford survey.* Each volume is an independent work; the first three are particularly important. Review, v. 1–4, O. D. Skelton, *Am. Pol. Sci. Rev.* 19:399, May 1925; R. L. Schuyler, *Pol. Sci. Quar.* 40:286, June 1925. GMD

K329 *Resources of the empire, a business man's survey of the empire's resources, prepared by the Federation of British Industries, with general introduction by Sir Eric Geddes.* 10 v. in 12, London, 1924. [1, J. R. Ainsworth-Davis, *Food supplies,* 2 v.; 2, S. J. Duly, *Timber and timber products;* 3, J. S. M. Ward, *Textile fibres and yarns;* 4, G. W. Andrew and others, *Fuel;* 5, W. A. MacLaren, *Rubber, tea, cacao, coffee, spices, and tobacco;* 6, E. C. Snow, *Leather;* 7, A. W. Ashe and H. G. T. Boorman, *Chemicals;* 8, pt. 1, M. S. Birkett, *Ferrous metals;* 8, pt. 2, N. M. Penzer, *Non-ferrous metals;* 9, E. R. Bolton and R. G. Pelly, *Oils, fats, waxes, and resins;* 10, W. T. Stephenson, *Communications.*] (Bibliographies.)

Like (K328) prepared in connection with the opening of the Wembley Exhibition. 'A compendious buyer's guide to our imperial resources.' Each volume complete in itself; data usually arranged by political divisions or units for each class of products. V. 8, pt. 1. Contains historical sketch of the iron and steel industry. The volumes on food supplies, chemicals, and communications are perhaps the more important. GMD

BRITISH COLONIZATION: HISTORY AND DISCUSSIONS OF POLICY

K341 Currey, Charles H. *British colonial policy, 1783–1915.* 1916. Reprint, Oxford and N. Y., 1924. (Bibliography.)

Very concise but excellent interpretative survey by an Australian. Review, *Spectator,* 117:533, Nov. 4, 1916. GMD

K342a Egerton, Hugh E. *Short history of British colonial policy.* 1897. 5th ed., London, 1918. (Bibliography.)

b Dickerson, Oliver M. *American colonial government, 1696–1765, a study of the British board of trade in its relation to the American colonies, political, industrial, administrative.* Cleveland, 1912. (Bibliography.)

c Basye, Arthur H. *Lords commissioners of trade and plantations, commonly known as the board of trade, 1748–1782.* New Haven, 1925. [Yale historical publications.] (Bibliography.)

a. Essential guide to the student of British colonization—probably the best comprehensive account of its subject.' Painstaking treatment of the evolution of British colonial policy from the period of beginnings down to 1895. Review, E. J. Payne, *E.H.R.* 13:778, Oct. 1898. Also cf. (K302c) Williamson, *Short history of British expansion.* LHG

b. and *c.* Excellent monographs on the home government side of colonial administration; based on extensive researches in the archival materials in London. Review of *b.*, C. M. Andrews, *A.H.R.* 17:841, July 1912. For extended studies of the development of British colonial policy both in the home country and in the colonies, prior to 1765, cf. the admirable works of (X202) Beer and (X201) Osgood. GMD

K343 Seeley, Sir John R. *Expansion of England: two courses of lectures.* 1883. 2nd ed., London, 1895. Later reprints.

The work of a man of vision, one of the first to point out the greatness and significance of the British empire. He protested against confining the study of English history to the British Isles and urged the consideration of imperial history. The first course surveys English expansion in the seventeenth and eighteenth centuries with special reference to the struggle with France; the second exhibits the growth of British power in India. Cf. the author's (L501a) *Growth of British policy.* FJK

K344a Grey, Henry George, Earl. *Colonial policy of Lord John Russell's administration.* 1853. 2nd ed., 2 v., London, 1853.

   b Adderley, Charles B., Baron Norton. *Review of 'The colonial policy of Lord John Russell's administration' by Earl Grey, 1853; and of subsequent colonial history.* London, 1869.

   c —— *Letter [to Disraeli] on the present relations of England with the colonies.* 1861. 2nd ed., London, 1862.

   d Childe-Pemberton, William S. *Life of Lord Norton (Right Hon. Sir Charles Adderley, K. C. M. G., M. P.), 1814–1905, statesman and philanthropist.* London, 1909.

   e Bodelsen, C. A. *Studies in mid Victorian imperialism.* Kjøbenhavn and London, 1924; N. Y., 1925. (Bibliography.)

   f Knaplund, Paul. *Gladstone and Britain's imperial policy.* N. Y., 1927.

For the history of the development of British thought and policy, these volumes should be read in succession to those of Buller and others listed in (K531) and in connection with those of (K308) Dilke, Froude, and Freeman, (K343) Seeley, (K322) Todd, and (K323) Dilke. They should in turn be followed by the works published since 1890 listed in this and the following sub-section. *a., b.,* and *c.* Most authoritative presentations of the two opposing policies of imperial relations with the colonies followed by the British government in the nineteenth century. *a.* Defence of the author's administration as colonial secretary; supports the policy of imperial interference and control. Review, *Edinburgh Rev.* 98:62, July 1853. *b.* Criticism of *a.*, by the Under-secretary for the colonies in the Derby-Disraeli ministry; advocates full local self-government in the colonies which possess representative institutions. Review, *Edinburgh Rev.* 131:51, Jan. 1870. *c.* Important political tract. *d.* Good biography; contains important contributions to the history of the changes of British thought and policy in colonial affairs. Review, *Athenaeum*, 1:195, Feb. 13, 1909. *e.* Well-documented and dispassionate account of British imperialism from its origin to about 1887. Especially important for its treatment of the sudden transition from separatism to imperialism during Gladstone's first administration. Review, H. H. Wrong, *Can. Hist. Rev.* 5:356, Dec. 1924; R. L. Schuyler, *Pol. Sci. Quar.* 40:640, Dec. 1925. GMD

f. Contrary to the view that Gladstone was indifferent to imperialism, this study, based on the Hawarden mss., sustains the view that Gladstone had a vital concern in the growth of an empire united by voluntary bonds. Review, H. C. Bell, *A.H.R.* 33:874, July, 1928. FWP

K345a Jenkyns, Sir Henry. *British rule and jurisdiction beyond the seas.* Ed. by Sir Courtenay Ilbert, Oxford, 1902.

b Goldman, Charles S., ed. *Empire and the century, a series of essays on imperial problems and possibilities, by various writers.* London and N. Y., 1905.

a. Gives the official colonial situation of 1899 as embodied in the records of parliament. Review, *Athenaeum,* 1:586, May 10, 1902.   EFH

b. Analysis of the British Empire as it was in 1905, having as its ultimate object the furtherance of closer union. The fifty contributors were all publicists of distinction, all 'believers in constructive imperialism' though differing as to specific proposals. Pt. 1. Discusses the various forces, constitutional, economic, military, etc., which act as bonds of union within the empire. Pt. 2. Considers the constituent parts of the empire as factors in the problems of imperial politics. Review, *Athenaeum,* 2:715, Nov. 25, 1905.   HET

K346 Holland, Bernard H. *Imperium et libertas, a study in history and politics.* London, 1901.

Divided into four parts, dealing respectively with the constitutional problems involved in the American Revolution, presented from the British point of view; with the history of Canada from 1763 to 1867; with the United Kingdom, advocating home rule as part of a general federalization of the United Kingdom and the British Empire; and with questions of imperial relations advocating the formation of an imperial council with certain executive powers. Appendixes give the Canadian Federation Act of 1867 and the Australian Federation Act of 1901. While frankly imperialist and, to a certain extent, propagandist, the book is written with learning and good temper, and in a sound literary style. Review, *Athenaeum,* 2:557, Oct. 26, 1901.   WLG

K347 Snow, Alpheus H. *Administration of dependencies: a study of the evolution of the federal empire, with special reference to American colonial problems.* N. Y. and London, 1902.

Traces the evolution of the conception of a federal empire in the English-speaking world, and shows how 'in both theory and practice, the men of the seventeenth and eighteenth centuries were half-consciously seeking an arrangement under which the sovereignty of the parent state could be brought into perfect harmony with the rights of self-government which had come to exist in the colonies.' Review, H. L. Osgood, *Pol. Sci. Quar.* 18:141, March 1903.   FWP

K348 Hobson, John A. *Imperialism, a study.* London, 1902, and N. Y., 1905.

Violent attack upon imperialism, under the guise of an economic treatise. Traces the economic origins of imperialism; investigates its theory and practice, regarded as 'a mission of civilization,' in its effect upon 'lower' or alien peoples; considers its political and moral reactions upon the Western nations engaging in it. Declares that 'the overflow of nationalism into imperial channels' has quenched the hope of a true internationalism. An appendix contains some valuable texts. Review, F. J. Goodnow, *Pol. Sci. Quar.* 17:523, Sept. 1902.
                      FWP

K349a Keith, Arthur Berriedale. *Responsible government in the dominions.* 1909. 2nd ed., Oxford, 1928.

b —— *Imperial unity and the dominions.* Oxford, 1916.

c —— *Dominion home rule in practice.* Oxford and N. Y., 1921. [World of to-day.]

d —— *War government of the British dominions.* Oxford and N. Y., 1921. [Carnegie Endowment for International Peace: Economic and social history of the World War.] (Bibliography.)

Valuable treatises on the respective topics by one of the most competent authorities. *a.* Discussion of the problems concerned. Review, *Athenaeum,* 1:224, Feb. 20, 1909. *b.* Review, *Spectator,* 116:778, Jan. 24, 1916. *c.* Summary of the subject. *d.* Shows how the British Empire was transformed in character and structure by the events of 1914–1919. Review, G. M. Wrong, *Amer. Pol. Sci. Rev.* 15:603, Nov. 1921; R. L. Schuyler, *Pol. Sci. Quar.* 37:147, March 1922; G. B. Hurst, *E.H.R.* 37:311, Apr. 1922. Also cf. his *Constitution, administration, and laws* in (K328) *British empire, a survey.*   FWP

K350a Lucas, Sir Charles P. *British empire, six lectures.* London, 1915.

   b Newton, Arthur P. *Old empire and the new.* London and Toronto, 1917. [Imperial studies series.]

   c Hearnshaw, Fossey J. C. *Democracy and the British empire.* London, 1920. N. Y., 1921.

   d Egerton, Hugh E. *British colonial policy in the XXth century.* London, 1922.

a. Brief historical survey, embodying an inventory of the situation at the time; excellent. Review, *Athenaeum* 1:350, Apr. 17, 1915. Also cf. his (E346) *Greater Rome and Greater Britain,* and his *Story of the Empire* in (K328) *British Empire, a survey. b.* Somewhat similar treatment, prepared as a study manual. *c.* Lectures showing how the British Empire is a democracy, how it differs from other empires and democracies, and why it may succeed where they failed. Review, *Spectator,* 126:109, Jan. 22, 1921. *d.* Not an adequate treatment, but presents useful materials on the relations of the dominions to the determination of imperial policy, on interrelation of foreign and colonial policy, and on the government of backward peoples. Review, A. L. P. Dennis, *A.H.R.* 28:745, July 1923.   GMD

K351 Bryce, James, Viscount. *Modern democracies.* 2 v. London and N. Y., 1921.

The author's last work; embodies his final judgments and ripe wisdom on democratic government. Special consideration is given to Canada, Australia, and New Zealand as well as to France, Switzerland, the United States, and the republics of ancient Greece and of South America. A comparative study of the highest value. Review, A. N. Holcombe, *Amer. Pol. Sci. Rev.* 15:433, Aug. 1921; G. B. Hurst, *E.H.R.* 37:135, Jan. 1922. Also cf. (K322) Todd, *Parliamentary government in the British colonies.*   GMD

BRITISH COLONIZATION: IMPERIAL FEDERATION

K361 Burt, Alfred L. *Imperial architects, being an account of proposals in the direction of a closer imperial union, made previous to the opening of the first colonial conference of 1887.* Oxford, 1913. (Bibliography.)

Convenient outline of the origins of the idea of imperial federation.   GMD

K362a Lorne, John G. E. H. D. S. Campbell, Marquis of (later ninth Duke of Argyll). *Imperial federation.* 1885. New ed., with an appendix, London, 1890. [Buxton, Imperial parliament.]

b Parkin, George R. *Imperial federation, the problem of national unity.* London and N. Y., 1892.

c Labillière, Francis P. de. *Federal Britain, or, unity and federation of the empire, with chapter on imperial defence by . . . Sir G. S. Clarke.* London, 1894.

a. Written shortly after his retirement from the governor-generalship of Canada; an early discussion of the subject.   *b.* The author, a Canadian, travelled widely in the interest of imperial federation; presents abundant material on the nature of the problem in its relation to England and the various colonies; criticizes the views of opponents; formulates the problem; offers no definite solution; suggests an extension of the privy council to include colonial representatives to advise and recommend measures toward imperial unity. Review, W. P. Trent, *Pol. Sci. Quar.* 8:174, March 1893.   *c.* Discussion of the problem by an Australian.

FWP

K363a Jebb, Richard. *Studies in colonial nationalism.* London, 1905.

b —— *Imperial conference, a history and a study.* 2 v. London and N. Y., 1911.

c —— *Britannic question, a survey of alternatives.* London and N. Y., 1913.

d —— *Empire in eclipse.* London, 1926.

e Pollard, Albert F., ed. *British Empire, its past, its present, and its future.* London, 1909. [League of the Empire.]

a. Presents the views held in the dominions on questions of trade and defense; published at the time of Mr. Chamberlain's proposals on these subjects. Review, *Athenaeum,* 1:494, Apr. 22, 1905.   *b.* Comprehensive and authoritative. Full accounts of the conferences of 1887, 1894, 1897, 1902, and 1907, laying special emphasis on the last, at which a constitution for the Imperial Conference was adopted. An appendix contains the resolutions adopted at the various sessions, arranged according to subject. Review, *Spectator,* 107:18, July 1, 1911. *Minutes of proceedings of the imperial conference,* and, *Papers laid before the conference* for each of the conferences mentioned above and for the later conferences of 1911, 1917, and 1921 will be found in *Parliamentary papers by command* for the year concerned.   *c.* Discusses, historically, philosophically, and practically, the two principal proposals made during the preceding fifty years for the reorganization of the British Empire. Strongly opposed to imperial federation. Mr. Jebb belongs to the school of imperialism which originated in the dominions and which looks forward to the transformation of the empire into a voluntary but permanent alliance of equal states, united by sentiment and common economic interests. Review, C. D. Allin, *Amer. Pol. Sci. Rev.* 8:120, Feb. 1914.   *d.* Eloquent plea for further coöperation within the empire in matters of foreign policy, defense, and trade.   *e.* Coöperative work, containing some good articles on the dominions.

RLS

K364a Curtis, Lionel. *Problem of the commonwealth.* London and N. Y., 1916.

b ——, ed. *Commonwealth of nations, an inquiry into the nature of citizenship in the British empire, and into the mutual relations of the several communities thereof.* 1916. Reprint, London, 1918.

   c **Worsfold, William Basil.** *Empire on the anvil, being suggestions and data for the future government of the British Empire.* London, 1916.

   a. Attempts to show what changes in the constitution of the British Empire would have to be made before British citizens domiciled in the dominions could enjoy the same control over the foreign policy of the empire as those domiciled in the United Kingdom. A clearly reasoned argument for the organic union of the empire by federation, advocating the establishment by written imperial constitution of an imperial cabinet responsible to an imperial parliament to be chosen by the electors of the United Kingdom and of the dominions. Proposes to vest in the federal government the control of foreign relations, imperial defence, and the administration of the dependencies. Review, C. Seymour, *A.H.R.* 22:644, Apr. 1917; R. L. Schuyler, *Pol. Sci. Quar.* 31:445, Sept. 1916. Cf. (K349*b*) Keith, *Imperial unity and the dominions.* *b.* Report incorporating criticisms of Curtis's views by the Round Table groups; includes historical studies of citizenship in the empire. Review, *Athenaeum,* 2:578, Dec. 1916. *c.* Similar discussion of imperial relations; by a student of South African conditions (cf. W436).   FWP

   K365a Hall, Hessel Duncan. *British commonwealth of nations, a study of its past and future development.* London, 1920.

   b **MacInnes, Charles M.** *British commonwealth and its unsolved problems.* London and N. Y., 1925. (Bibliography.)

   Discussions of the problem in the light of the changes wrought by the World War. *a.* Important work, by an Australian. *b.* Studies dominion status, crown colonial administration, and problems of India; offers suggestions toward imperial sympathy and understanding. Review, H. H. Wrong, *Can. Hist. Rev.* 6:245, Sept. 1925. Also cf. Keith, *Constitution, administration, and laws* in (K328) *British Empire, a survey.*   FWP

   K368a Hall, Walter P. *Empire to commonwealth: thirty years of British imperial history.*

   b **Zimmern, Alfred.** *The third British empire.* Oxford, 1926.

   c **Hurst, Sir Cecil; Smiddy, Timothy;** and others. *Great Britain and the dominions.* Chicago, 1928. [Harris Foundation lectures.]

   d **Morris, G. W.,** and **Wood, L. S.** *The English-speaking nations.* N. Y., 1924.

   a. Well written history of the development of the empire since 1897, effectively interpreting the significant personalities of its administration. Review, W. R. Livingston, *A.H.R.* 33:875, July, 1928. *b.* Clear, full, and reasoned exposition of the development and present status of the British commonwealth of nations. *d.* Able review of the growth of the empire and of the federative idea.   FWP

THE WEST INDIES AND OTHER INSULAR COLONIES

K381 Edwards, Bryan. *History, civil and commercial, of the British colonies in the West Indies.* V. 1-2 with atlas, London, 1793, 2nd ed., 1794; v. 3, *An historical survey of the French colony in the island of St. Domingo,* 1797; with reprints of v. 1-2, London, 1801; 5th ed., 3 v., London, 1819.

   Edwards resided in the West Indies for about twenty-five years and was familiar with both the French and English colonies. While the historical narrative of Edwards is being superseded by monographs based on official sources, the work remains of permanent value as an authoritative picture of economic and social life in the West Indies during the author's lifetime. His treatment of the slave trade, negroes, the cultivation and manufacture of West India staples, and of all the details of plantation economy is interesting and reliable. Excellent maps of each important island show the distribution of the great estates. The statistical tables of England's trade with the West Indies are authentic and do much to perpetuate the value of the work for reference. FWP

K382a **Watts, P. Arthur.** *Une histoire des colonies anglaises aux Antilles de 1649 à 1660.* Paris, 1925.

b ——— *Nevis and Saint Christopher, 1782–1784.* Paris, 1925.

a. Detailed study of British activities in the West Indies in the Cromwellian period which was a time of critical importance in the development of British policy and the extension of British power in the Caribbean region. *b.* Volume of documents chiefly from the Bancroft collection in the University of California relating mainly to the temporary rule of the French in these islands. Review, H. E. Egerton, *E.H.R.* 41:309 Apr. 1926. Also, cf. (K305) Newton, *Colonizing activities of the English Puritans;* and (Y421b) Williamson, *English colonies in Guiana and on the Amazon, 1604–1668.* GMD

K383 **Mims, Stewart L.** *Colbert's West India policy.* New Haven, 1912. [Yale historical publications: studies.] (Good bibliography.)

The prosperity of the French West Indies was so great in the eighteenth century that the English trade policy turned largely on the rivalry between the French and English islands in the Caribbean. The author set himself the task of tracing the sources of this prosperity and found them in the very definite policy of Colbert, which, 'established after a long and determined fight' was 'his most permanent contribution to the commerce of France.' Source material in the French archives has been used extensively. Review, C. H. Hull, *A.H.R.* 18:612, Apr. 1913. AHB

K384 **Higham, Charles S. S.** *Development of the Leeward Islands under the Restoration, 1660–1688, a study of the foundations of the old colonial system.* Cambridge, Eng., 1921. [Prince Consort prize essay.] (Select bibliography.)

Marks an important step in laying foundations for a really scientific history of the West Indies; based upon systematic investigation of manuscripts in the Public Record Office and private collections. About half the book relates the fortunes of the islanders resulting from European wars and alliances. The remainder is devoted to the topography and problems of navigation in the West Indies and to such topics as Caribs, slaves, sugar, colonial administration, attempts to enforce the navigation acts, colonial protests against them, and illicit trade. Particular attention is paid to Sir William Stapleton who governed the islands for fourteen years with eminent success. Review, V. Barbour, *A.H.R.* 27:162, Oct. 1921. FWP

K385a Pitman, Frank W. *Development of the British West Indies, 1700–1763*
New Haven, 1917. [Yale historical publications: studies.] (Bibliographical note.)

b —— *Slavery on British West India plantations in the eighteenth century.* Washington, 1926.

c Ragatz, Lowell J. *Fall of the planter class in the British Caribbean.*
N. Y., 1928. [Justin Winsor Prize Essay.]

a. Primarily a story of the economic development of the British islands, but the social and political sides of the story are also fully treated. The conflict between the British and foreign islands and that between various British interests have 'nowhere been treated in such fullness, with such continuity, and with so firm a grasp upon essentials' (Hull). The effect of these conflicts upon imperial policy, especially in its bearing upon the continental colonies, is clearly shown, and several interesting suggestions are advanced. Essential to a rounded knowledge of British policy. Review, C. H. Hull, *A.H.R.* 23:902, July 1918. The author is continuing his studies and plans to issue a second volume soon. AHB

b. "A highly valuable treatise", according to *A.H.R.* 32:388, Jan. 1927. *c.* Exceedingly valuable contribution to the commercial, agrarian, and social history of the West Indies based upon a thorough study of public and private sources, both printed and manuscript. Review, M. W. Williams, *A.H.R.* 35:131, Oct. 1929.

FWP

K386 Penson, Lillian M. *Colonial agents of the British West Indies, a study in colonial administration, mainly in the eighteenth century.* London, 1924.

Notable contribution to a subject which has long awaited competent treatment; valuable not only for its account of the development of the colonial agent, but also for its picture of the institutional and economic background out of which he came. Review, F. W. Pitman, *A.H.R.* 30:153, Oct. 1924; H. E. Egerton, *E.H.R.* 39:633, Oct. 1924. AHB

K387a Wrong, Hume. *Government of the West Indies.* Oxford, 1923. (Bibliography.)

b Walker, Henry de R. *West Indies and the empire, study and travel in the winter of 1900–1901.* London, 1901.

c Aspinall, Algernon· E. *British West Indies, their history, resources, and progress.* London, 1912. [(K309) All red series.]

d Harlow, Vincent T. *History of Barbados, 1625–1685.* Oxford, 1926.

a. Brief surveys of the government of each colony including British Guiana, British Honduras, and Bermuda, from the British occupation to date, but with special reference to the period since the abolition of slavery. Review, F. W. Pitman, *A.H.R.* 29:615, Apr. 1924. *b.* and *c.* Accounts of recent economic and political conditions and problems. GMD

d. Thorough, detailed, and careful history based on original sources. Review, F. W. Pitman, *A.H.R.* 33–165, Oct. 1927. FWP

K388 Gardner, William J. *History of Jamaica from its discovery by Christopher Columbus to the year 1872, including an account of its trade and agriculture; sketches of the manners, habits, and customs of all classes of its inhabitants; and a narrative of the progress of religion and education in the island.* 1873. New ed., by A. W. Gardner, London, 1909.

Good narrative history of the island with special attention to the period of English occupation, particularly the nineteenth century to 1872. Unlike the earlier historians of the West Indies, such as (K381) Edwards, who were supporters of slavery, the author, who was a Congregational clergyman in the island, writes in favor of emancipation and in sympathy with the negro. The governmental problem, culminating in the rebellion of 1865 and the abrogation of representative institutions, is recounted fully and fairly.   GMD

K389 Cundall, Frank. *Historic Jamaica.* Kingston and London, 1915.

Mr. Cundall, who has been secretary and librarian of the Institute of Jamaica since 1891, writes, in a cultured style and with scrupulous accuracy, accounts of hundreds of historic sites and landmarks in each of the parishes of the island. The narrative abounds in attractive personalities from pirates to preachers. The material is drawn mainly from local archives and monuments.   FWP

K390 Lefroy, Sir John H. *Memorials of the discovery and early settlement of the Bermudas or Somers Islands, 1515–1685, compiled from the colonial records and other original sources.* 2 v. London, 1877–79. (Bibliography.)

By a former Governor of the colony. Extended account of the early history of the islands, fully illustrated by the documents in full or in extracts. Unfortunately no adequate account of the later history of the colony exists. Review, *Athenaeum* 2:295, Sept. 8, 1877; 2:8, July 5, 1879.   GMD

K391 Westergaard, Waldemar. *Danish West Indies under company rule, 1671–1754; with a supplementary chapter, 1755–1917.* N. Y., 1917. (Bibliography.)

Scholarly and authoritative; based on source material; affords valuable comparisons with the history and development of the French and British islands. Review, C. L. Jones, *Amer. Pol. Sci. Rev.* 12:132, Feb. 1918; F. W. Pitman, *Jour. of Pol. Econ.* 26:669, June 1918.   AHB

K396 Boyson, V. F. *Falkland Islands: with notes on the natural history by Rupert Vallentin.* Oxford, 1924. (Bibliography.)

The chronicle of the slight annals, chiefly international, of these islands is based on thorough research in the sources and supplemented by a wealth of descriptive material. Includes important data on whaling and sealing in the South Atlantic. Review, R. L. Schuyler, *A.H.R.* 30:658, Apr. 1925.   FWP

K397 Hardman, William. *History of Malta during the period of the French and British occupations, 1789–1815.* Ed. with introduction and notes by J. H. Rose, London and N. Y., 1909.

Mainly a compilation of documents relating to the most critical period of the island's history. Valuable for international as well as local concerns.   GMD

K398 Orr, Charles W. J. *Cyprus under British rule.* London, 1918.

Interesting because of the unusual conditions under which Great Britain administers the island and because of the peculiar problems presented.   GMD

FRENCH COLONIZATION

K401a Deschamps, Léon. *Histoire de la question coloniale en France.* Paris, 1891.

  b ——— *Histoire sommaire de la colonisation française.* Paris, 1894.

a. Interesting study of French opinion on colonization from the great discoveries to the end of the Napoleonic era. Based on the official programs; on memoirs in the colonial archives, one of which is reproduced in the appendix; on general works from Rabelais to Rousseau; and on hundreds of special works by explorers, Jesuits, and others. Shows that over-centralization deadened the French colonial spirit. Elaborate subdivision of chapters detracts from clearness. Review, L. Farges, *Rev. Hist.* 50 :93, Sept. 1892; H. Hauser, *ibid.* 51 :156, Jan. 1893. *b.* Elementary survey of French colonization for use in commercial schools; convenient, concise summary of events, with statistics, ten maps, and several tables. Half the volume is devoted to the old colonial empire before 1815.   RGAn

K402 Lanessan, Jean L. de. *L'expansion coloniale de la France, étude économique, politique, et géographique sur les établissements français d'outre-mer.* Paris, 1886.

Detailed survey of French colonies and trading-posts; followed by general chapters on immigration, penal colonization, and administrative organization. Criticises excessive uniformity in the government of widely varied dependencies.
                                                                        CHCW

K403a Gaffarel, Paul. *Les colonies françaises.* 1879. 6th rev. ed., Paris, 1899. [Bibliothèque d'histoire contemporaine.]

  b Levasseur, Émile. *La France et ses colonies, géographie et statistique.* 3 v. Paris, 1890–93.

  a. Historical, physical, economic, and political survey of each of the French colonies. *b.* Similar collection of data by an eminent scholar.   CHCW

K404 Rambaud, Alfred, ed. *La France coloniale: histoire, géographie, commerce.* 1886. 7th ed., Paris, 1895.

Historical and geographical survey by collaborators. Special chapters deal with problems peculiar to different colonies; maps.   CHCW

K405 *Les colonies françaises. Publication de la commission chargée de préparer la participation du ministère des colonies à l'exposition universelle de 1900.* 6 v. Paris, 1900–02. [J. Charles-Roux, *Introduction générale;* 1, M. Dubois and A. Terrier, *Un siècle d'expansion coloniale;* 2, A. Arnaud and H. Méray, *Organisation administrative, judiciare, politique, et financière;* 3, C. Guy, *La mise en valeur de notre domaine colonial;* 4, H. Froidevaux, *L'oeuvre scolaire de la France dans nos colonies;* V. Tantet, *Survivance de l'esprit français aux colonies perdues;* 5, J. Imbart de la Tour, *Régime de la propriété;* Dorvault, *Régime de la main-d'oeuvre;* A. Lecomte, *L'agriculture aux colonies.*]

The introduction summarizes several topics connected with French colonial administration, such as protectorates, concessions, army colonization, railways, cables, and education. V. 1. ·Treats in detail colonial development from 1789 to 1900. Each chapter of history is accompanied by selected documents. Strongly nationalistic and anti-English. The other volumes are good topical treatments of the subjects indicated by their several titles.   CHCW

K406 Fallex, Eugène, and **Mairey, Alphonse.** *La France et ses colonies au début du XXe siècle.* 1908. Rev. ed., Paris, 1914. (Bibliographies.)

This excellent and widely used text-book was revised and corrected every two years up to the outbreak of the World War. Hence, in the portion (p. 307–420), devoted to the French colonies, it contains a compact and up-to-date survey of overseas France in 1914.   HAG

K407 Petit, Édouard. *Organisation des colonies françaises et des pays de protectorat.* 2 v. Paris, 1894–95. (Bibliographies.)

M Petit wrote from extended experience, both in the home service and in the colonies. In spite of the many changes that have taken place since its publication, this work remains of great value as a detailed analysis of the French system of colonial administration in its historical setting. Clear exposition of the circumstances under which the principles underlying the French system came to be adopted and how they have been constantly modified to suit local conditions. The development of every division of the legislative, administrative, and judicial machinery is traced for each colony. There are admirable chapters on the penal system, commerce, public utilities, religion, and education.   LFB

K408 Billiard, A. *Politique et organisation coloniales, principes généraux.* Paris, 1899.

Valuable treatise by a French colonial administrator in Algeria; deals with the question of governing native peoples, with various administrative problems, and with the principles by which colonial officials should be guided.   CHCW

K409 Girault, Arthur. *Principes de colonisation et de législation coloniale.* 1895. 3rd rev. ed., 3 v., Paris, 1907–08. (Bibliography.)

Professor Girault was charged, in 1891, by the French government, with the task of inaugurating the first course on colonial legislation in France. His book is largely the result of his first four years' experience in teaching it. This is, therefore, a pioneer book in elucidating principles from the unorganized mass of French colonial legislation. Review, L. Theureau, *Journal des Économistes,* 5th series, 23:452, Sept. 1895.   PLW

K410 Vignon, Louis. *Un programme de politique coloniale.* Paris, 1919.

Elaborate study of conditions, chiefly with regard to races such as negroes, Arabs, and Annamites. The author, professor at the École Coloniale, criticizes French lack of skill in dealing with native civilizations and efforts at governmental assimilation of races refractory to French methods.   CHCW

K411 Girault, Arthur. *Colonial tariff policy of France.* Ed. by C. Gide, Oxford and N. Y., 1916. [Carnegie Endowment for International Peace, Division of Economics and History.]

Critical account of the colonial trade policy of France. Pt. 1. Sketches the policy historically. Pt. 2. Describes and discusses the present relations of each French colony with the mother country. Chiefly valuable for its analysis of the causes and effects of the various colonial tariff policies of France. Review, F. W. Taussig, *Amer. Econ. Rev.* 7:155, March 1917; Simon Litman, *A.H.R.* 22:904, July 1917.   FWP

GERMAN COLONIZATION

K421a Townsend, Mary E. *Origins of modern German colonialism, 1871–1885.* N. Y., 1921. [Columbia University studies in history, economics, and public law.] (Bibliography.)

   b Hagen, Maximilian von. *Bismarcks Kolonialpolitik.* Gotha, 1923.

a. Valuable monograph; most recent study in English of the beginnings of German colonization. *b.* Exhaustive study based on all the published material   FWP

K422 Koschitzky, Max von. *Deutsche Kolonialgeschichte.* 2 v. Leipzig, 1887–88.

Stresses the colonial movement in its relations with internal politics of the Empire, as well as the acquisition of the several colonies and the resulting international complications. Primarily a detailed study of the colonial policy of the German Empire from 1871 to 1885, although one-half of v. 1 describes the early antecedents of colonial activity, such as the Hansa, and discusses emigration, missions, and trade as motives for colonization. Contains extracts from important documents, treaties, correspondence, and debates. Suffers from lack of documentation, of logical arrangement, and of index. MET

K423 Zimmermann, Alfred. *Die Geschichte der deutschen Kolonialpolitik.* Berlin, 1914.

Virtually v. 6 of (K122) Zimmermann, *Die europäischen Kolonien.* Written by an official prominent in the colonial service since 1893. Probably the best account of German colonial history, since it reflects the unusual opportunities of the author for observation of colonial affairs and for access to colonial records. Covers only the period from 1871 and presents primarily the external history of German colonialism. Presents the facts without bias or partisanship; discusses with authoritative detail the acquisition, administration, and economic significance of each of the colonies, with a thorough documentation, an index, appendixes, chronological tables, and valuable trade statistics. MET

K424 Chéradame, André. *La colonisaiton et les colonies allemandes.* Paris, 1905.

Sent to Germany in 1898 by the French Minister of Colonies to study German colonization, M. Chéradame produced this authoritative monograph. Based upon material drawn from the library of the Kolonial Gesellschaft; influenced very slightly, if at all, by French bias. Pt. 1. History of German colonial acquisition. Pt. 2. Description of the colonies and their economic importance, and a valuable discussion of the nature of colonial protectorates and of colonial administration in general. Well documented; contains valuable tables of statistics, eight large maps, but no index. MET

K425 Hassert, Kurt. *Deutschlands Kolonien: Erwerbungs- und Entwickelungsgeschichte, Landes- und Volkskunde, und wirtschaftliche Bedeutung unserer Schutzgebiete.* 1899. 2nd rev. ed., Leipzig, 1910. (Bibliography.)

Not so much a history as a geographic and economic study of the German colonies. Frankly attempts to advertise the German colonies to the German people; gives fifty pages of historical survey and a detailed, scientific description of the colonial lands and peoples. Excellent and thorough work illustrated with maps, diagrams, and pictures. For later data cf. (J441a) *Peace handbooks,* no. 42, which is the best compendium on the subject in English. MET

K426 Köbner, Otto. *Einführung in die Kolonialpolitik.* Jena, 1908. (Excellent bibliographies.)

A treatise rather than a history. Written by a professor of colonial law at the University of Berlin. Contains a discussion of the nature of colonialism, a survey of the colonial activity of other nations, a brief account of the external and internal history of the German colonial movement, and a detailed description of the administrative system of the German possessions overseas. Of great assistance to students; chiefly valuable in its suggestive rather than in its informative character. MET

K427a Zastrow, R. von, and **Dannert, Eduard,** eds. *Deutschland braucht Kolonien!* Berlin, 1925.

    b Schnee, Heinrich. *German colonization, past and future.* With an intro. by W. H. Dawson. London, 1926.

    a. Coöperative appeal for colonies by such men as Schnee, Seitz, and Solf. Valuable for German opinion relative to a revival of colonialism. FWP

    b. Popular and interesting sketch of the lost German colonies in Africa, with numerous illustrations, and with comparisons of conditions under former German rule and under present mandate rule; by the former governor of German East Africa. SBF

ITALIAN COLONIZATION

K441 Wallace, William K. *Greater Italy.* N. Y., 1917.

Excellent synthetic account of Italian achievement during the period of the Triple Alliance and the first years of the World War. While the volume is not free from error, the writer has succeeded in penetrating beneath the surface of events and in faithfully presenting the spirit and the ideals of the Italian people. An interpretation of Italy's colonial policy, useful for the general student, but unsatisfactory as a study of internal policy. In the treatment of home politics the statements of party writers have often been accepted with insufficient study of the sources. X

K442a Brunialti, Attilio. *Le colonie degli italiani, con appendice: I primi tentativi e le prime ricerche di una colonia in Italia, 1861–1882, di Giacomo Gorrini.* Torino, 1897.

    b Botarelli, Alberto. *Compendio di storia coloniale italiana.* Roma, 1914.

    c Italy, Ministero degli Affari Esteri, Direzione Centrale degli Affari Coloniali. *L'Africa italiana al parlamento nazionale, 1882–1905.* Roma, 1907.

    d Chiala, Luigi. *La spedizione di Massua, narrazione documentata, 1869–1887.* Torino, 1888.

    a. Still a valuable source for the student of Italy's colonial policy, being a clear, judicious view of the causes and vicissitudes of Italian expansion in Africa during the last quarter of the nineteenth century. Brunialti, in parliament, was one of the most earnest and consistent advocates of Italian colonial expansion, and in the present volume advocated colonization as a substitute for permanent emigration. Includes chapters on colonies under the Romans and in the Middle Ages, whose glories also influenced Italy to its recent colonial effort. The result of broad research, and enriched with copious bibliographical notes. Gorrini's appendix, reprinted from the *Biblioteca di scienze politiche e amministrative*, series 2, v. 9, is an excellent summary. *b.* Later manual; includes the acquisition of Libya. For other works on Libya cf. (W256). *c.* Full record of the development of Italian public opinion with regard to colonization, as reflected in parliament. Contains valuable maps and an index of parliamentary documents. *d.* Standard account of early Italian colonial effort in Africa and of the acquisition of Eritrea. X

K443 Colosimo, Gaspare. *Relazione al partamento sulla situazione politica, economica, ed amministrativa delle colonie italiane.* Roma, 1918.

Official report by Colosimo who was minister of the colonies. Best publication upon Italian colonial affairs during the earlier years of the World War. For colonial effort in Somalia, cf. (W386) G. Piazza, *Il Benadir.*   x

K444a Mondaini, Gennaro. *Manuel di storia e legislazione coloniale del regno d'Italia.* Roma, 1927.

   b Anon., *Il governo fascista nelle colonie.* Milano, 1925.

   c Guyot, Georges. *L'Italie devant le problème coloniale.* Paris, 1927.

a. Systematic and scholarly history of the Italian colonies written by an outstanding authority and devoting particular attention to the last decade. *b.* Severe criticism of the Fascist government in Somaliland, Eritrea, and Libya. *c.* Good survey of the history and status of Italian colonization.   FWP

ARCTIC EXPLORATION

K451 Greely, Adolphus W. *Handbook of polar discoveries.* 1896. 5th rev. ed., Boston, 1910. (Bibliographies.)

Very valuable digest and criticism, by the foremost authority on polar explorations, of all the important narratives of Arctic and Antarctic explorations by all nationalities since Elizabethan times. Particularly valuable for its succinct and precise indication of the contributions, geographic and scientific, made by each great explorer. Review, *Nation* (N. Y.), 83:493, Dec. 6, 1906; C. C. Adams, *N. Y. Times, Saturday Book Rev.* 11:845, Dec. 8, 1906.   FWP

K452 Scoresby, William, Jr. *Account of the Arctic regions, with a history and description of the northern whale-fishery.* 2 v. Edinburgh, 1820.

These volumes, the first in English on this subject, were the outcome of seventeen whaling voyages, in which Scoresby unceasingly made systematic scientific observations and explored eight hundred miles of East Greenland. His description of the known lands, Spitzbergen, Jan Mayen, and Greenland, remain practically unsurpassed in any single work, even today, while his comprehensive history of the northern whale-fishery is standard. Especially valuable were his hydrographical survey of the Greenland sea, description of polar ice, submarine temperature and meteorological observations. His terse but clear style has rarely been equalled by Arctic authors.   AWG

K453 Kotzebue, Otto von. *Voyage of discovery into the South Sea and Beering's Straits, for the purpose of exploring a north-east passage, undertaken in the years 1815–1818, at the expense of His Highness, . . . Count Romanzoff, in the ship Rurick.* 3 v. London, 1821. Tr. by H. E. Lloyd from *Entdeckungsreise in die Südsee und nach der Beringsstrasse zur Erforschung einer nordöstlichen Durchfahrt; unternommen in den Jahren 1815–1818 auf Kosten seiner Erlaucht des . . . Grafen Rumanzoff auf dem Schiffe Rurick,* 3 v., Weimar, 1821.

Cook's voyage, 1778, (cf. V104f) through Bering strait furnished no knowledge of the Alaskan coast. Kotzebue, whose explorations were chiefly directed to the coasts and islands of Bering sea, only reached Cape Krusenstern on the north shore of Kotzebue sound.   AWG

K454 Parry, Sir William E. *Journal of a voyage for the discovery of a north-west passage from the Atlantic to the Pacific, performed in the years 1819-20 in His Majesty's ships Hecla and Griper, with an appendix containing the scientific and other observations.* London, 1821.

This narrative has an important bearing on the evolution of knowledge of Arctic America. Parry's ships, which gained the bounty for sailing beyond 110° west, passed from Baffin bay to Melville sound and discovered many islands along the 75th parallel. Sabine's observations disclosed the notable fact that the ships passed north of the magnetic pole, which was approximately located for the first time. Parry's narrative is clearly written, but naturally suffers in style from its journalistic form. His second and third northwest voyages had unimportant results. AWG

K455a Franklin, Sir John. *Narrative of a journey to the shores of the polar sea, in the years 1819, 20, 21, and 22.* 1823. 3rd ed., 2 v., London, 1824. New ed., 1 v., N. Y., 1910 [Everyman's library].

b —— *Narrative of a second expedition to the shores of the polar sea, in the years 1825, 1826, and 1827, including an account of the progress of a detachment to the eastward by John Richardson.* London, 1828.

Franklin's journeys involved the outlining of the Arctic coast of North America, previously known only at the mouths of the Mackenzie and Coppermine rivers. *a.* The first expedition only traced Coronation Gulf through six degrees of longitude. *b.* The second expedition, however, charted the continent from 109° to 149° west longitude. The narratives of both officers are notable and excellently written. AWG

K456a McClure, Sir Robert J. L. *Discovery of the north-west passage by H.M.S. Investigator, Capt. R. M'Clure, 1850, 1851, 1852, 1853, 1854.* Ed. by Commander Sherard Osborn . . . from the logs and journals of Capt. Robert Le M. M'Clure. 1856. 4th ed., London, 1865.

b Armstrong, Sir Alexander. *Personal narrative of the discovery of the northwest passage, with numerous incidents of travel and adventure during nearly five years' continuous service in the arctic regions while in search of the expedition under Sir John Franklin.* London, 1857.

c Brown, John. *North-west passage, and the plans for the search for Sir John Franklin: a review.* 1858. 2nd ed., with sequel, London, 1860. (Bibliography.)

Franklin, 1846 and 1847, attaining Simpson's farthest, discovered the shortest route which skirts the continental coast. McClure was first to traverse the northerly passage, which involved loss of his ship. The crew escaped death through the timely visit of Pim, of Belcher's squadron engaged in the Franklin search. Disobedience of orders enabled McClure to make the passage, and extended controversy followed. *a.* McClure's own narrative. *b.* Account by the surgeon of his expedition. *c.* Most complete account. AWG

K457 Davis, Charles H., ed. *Narrative of the north polar expedition, U. S. ship Polaris.* Washington, 1876. [Navy department.]

Important as the only north-polar expedition sent forth by the United States government. The commander, Hall, followed Smith Sound, previously explored by Kane and Hayes, and charted the West Greenland waterways from Smith sound to the Arctic ocean. Later this route was selected by Nares, Peary, Cook,

Sverdrup, and MacMillan, and also for the northernmost international polar station, Lady Franklin bay, occupied by Greely for two years. Hall died after attaining a record north in the western hemisphere. Davis has well handled the material from various sources.   AWG

K458 Payer, Julius, Ritter von. *New lands within the arctic circle: narrative of the discoveries of the Austrian ship Tegetthoff, in the years 1872–1874.* 2 v. London, 1876. 1 v. N. Y., 1877. Tr. from *Die österreichisch-ungarische Nordpol-Expedition in den Jahren 1872–74, nebst einer Skizze der zweiten deutschen Nordpol-Expedition 1869–70 und der Polar-Expedition von 1871,* Wien, 1876.

This new (Franz Josef) land was proved, by later explorations, to be the most extensive eastern Arctic region discovered in three centuries, covering 20° of longitude and 2° of latitude. Its discovery was unique, being made without intent or effort, by a northeast passage expedition. Beset, never to be freed, the *Tegetthoff* drifted north a year, when Franz Josef Land was sighted. Audaciously Payer left the ship for five weeks and explored the central regions from Barents sea north to the Arctic ocean. The later expeditions of Leigh Smith, F. Jackson, Wellman, Baldwin, Duke of Abruzzi, Fiala, and Nansen have thoroughly explored the archipelago.   * AWG

K459a Nares, Sir George S. *Narrative of a voyage to the polar sea during 1875–6 in H.M. ships Alert and Discovery.* 2 v., London, 1878.

b Markham, Sir Albert H. *Great frozen sea, a personal narrative of the voyage of the Alert during the arctic expedition of 1875–6.* London, 1878.

a. Story of the final Arctic expedition of England. Among its extensive discoveries were Markham's record northing, described in *b.,* and surveys of Grinnell Land to the west and of Greenland to the east of Robeson channel.   AWG

K460 Nordenskiöld, Nils Adolf Erik, Friherre. *Voyage of the Vega round Asia and Europe, with a historical review of previous journeys along the north coast of the Old World.* 2 v. London, 1881; 1 v. N. Y., 1882. Tr. by A. Leslie from *Vegas färd kring Asien och Europa; jemte en historisk återblick på föregående resor längs Gamla Verldens Nordkust.* 2 v., Stockholm, 1880–81.

Account of the Swedish expedition which discovered and effected the northeast passage around Europe and Asia in 1878 and 1879.   GMD

K461 Nansen, Fridtjof. *Farthest north, being the record of a voyage of exploration of the ship Fram, 1893–96 and of a fifteen months' sleigh journey by Dr. Nansen and Lieut. Johansen.* 2 v., 1897. Popular ed., 1 v., N. Y., 1898. Tr. from *Fram over Polhavet, den norsk Polarfaerd, 1893–96,* 2 v., Kristiania, 1897.

This expedition was very successful; hydrographically it extended the Spitzbergen deep eastward to the Siberian islands.   AWG

K462 Sverdrup, Otto. *New land; four years in the arctic regions.* 2 v. London and N. Y., 1904. Tr. by E. H. Hearn from *Nyt land; fire aar i arktiske egne,* 2 v., Kristiania, 1903.

Failing to circumnavigate Greenland, Sverdrup turned to Jones sound, whence he explored the unknown west coast of Grinnell Land and islands to the west.

Filling in the blank between Greely fiord and Finlay island, he outlined the littoral western boundary of the main Northpolar basin. AWG

K463 Friis, Achton. *Danmark ekspeditionen til Grønlands nordostkyst.* København, 1909.

Popular account, by the artist, of the Mylius-Erichsen expedition in the *Danmark,* which closed the last gap in the coastline of Greenland. For official report, cf. (K923) *Meddelelser om Grønland,* v. 41–46, 52. AWG

K464a Peary, Robert E. *North pole, its discovery in 1909 under the auspices of the Peary Arctic Club.* N. Y., 1910.

b Cook, Frederick A. *My attainment of the pole, being the record of the expedition that first reached the boreal center, 1907–1909, with the final summary of the polar controversy.* N. Y., 1911.

c Helgesen, Henry T. *'North pole aftermath,' reply to some criticisms in the north pole controversy, Congressional record,* 63rd cong., 3rd sess., v. 52, pt. 6, appendix, 834–839. *Analyses of 'evidence' presented by Robert E. Peary to committee on naval affairs, 1910–11, ibid.,* 64th cong., 1st sess., v. 53, pt. 14, appendix, 268–327. *Peary and the north pole, ibid.,* 64th cong., 1st sess., v. 53, pt. 15, appendix, 1626–1646. *Dr. Cook and the north pole, ibid.,* 64th cong., 2nd sess., v. 54, pt. 6, appendix, 42–70.

d Hall, Thomas F. *Has the north pole been discovered? An analytical and synthetical review of the published narratives of the two Arctic explorers, Dr. Frederick A. Cook and Civil Engineer Robert E. Peary, U.S.N.; also a review of the action of the U. S. government.* Boston, 1917.

e MacMillan, Donald B. *Four years in the white north.* N. Y. and London, 1918.

a. and *b.* Gave rise to heated controversies. Thorough analyses of both accounts are contained in *c.* and *d.* While *b.* has been thoroughly discredited, doubts have also been thrown on *a.* because Peary's earlier reported discoveries of Crocker Land and Peary channel have both been eliminated by later explorers, the former land by MacMillan, whose account is in *e.,* and the waterway by Mylius-Erichsen (cf. K463) and also by Rasmussen. AWG

K465 Amundsen, Roald, and **Ellsworth, Lincoln.** *First flight across the Polar Sea.* London, 1927.

Somewhat bare recital of the voyage of the airship *Norge* in 1925 across the Arctic region around the North Pole, by two of the leaders of the expedition. Review, (London) *Times Lit. Suppl.* 26:135, Mar. 3, 1927. HRS

ANTARCTIC EXPLORATION

K481 Balch, Edwin Swift. *Antarctica.* Philadelphia, 1902.

History of Antarctic exploration up to 1901; although new data have been unearthed since its publication, it remains the most accurate compendium of early Antarctic explorations. The bibliographical notes may be relied on as accurate. To designate clearly the two big land masses of Antarctica, the writer christened them, in this book, respectively West Antarctica and East Antarctica. FWP

K482 Wilkes, Charles. *Narrative of the United States exploring expedition during the years 1838, 1839, 1840, 1841, 1842.* 5 v. Philadelphia, 1844. Many later ed.

Includes an account of the discovery in 1840 of the north coast of East Antarctica, whose dimensions were recognized by Wilkes to be continental and which he therefore christened 'Wilkes Land.' His cruise was one of the most remarkable on record and every statement he made about it has been recently corroborated. For the earlier voyage of Captain Cook who first crossed the Antarctic circle, cf. (V104*d*).   ESB

K483 Ross, Sir James Clark. *Voyage of discovery and research in the southern and antarctic regions during the years 1839–43.* 2 v. London, 1847.

Account of the discovery in 1841 of South Victoria Land, the Ross sea, and the Great Ice barrier. Important, but contains an unwarranted attack on Wilkes.
                                                                                ESB

K484a Gerlache de Gomery, Adrien V. J. de. *Voyage de la Belgica; quinze mois dans l'Antarctique.* 1902. 2nd ed., Paris, 1902.

b Nordenskjöld, Otto G., and **Anderson, Johann Gunnar.** *Antarctica or two years amongst the ice of the south pole.* London and N. Y., 1905. Tr. from *Antarktik, zwei Jahre in Schnee und Eis am Sudpol,* 2 v., Berlin, 1904.

c Drygalski, Erich von. *Zum Kontinent des eisigen Südens.* Berlin, 1904.

d Brown, Robert N. Rudmose; Mossman, Robert C.; Pirie, J. H. Harvey. *Voyage of the Scotia, being the record of a voyage of exploration in antarctic seas, by three of the staff.* Prefatory note by W. S. Bruce. London, 1906.

e Charcot, Jean Baptiste. *Journal de l'expédition antarctique français, 1903–1905; le Français au pôle sud.* Paris, 1906.

f —— *Voyage of the Why not? in the Antarctic, the journal of the second French south polar expedition, 1908–1910.* N. Y. and London, 1911. Tr. by P. Walsh from *Le Pourquoi pas? dans l'Antarctique,* Paris, 1910.

a. Account of the Belgian expedition to West Antarctica in 1898–1899 and of the exploration of the Gerlache strait. *b.* Describes the Swedish explorations in 1901–1903 along the east coast of West Antarctica. While in the ice, Nordenskjöld invented independently the names West Antarctica and East Antarctica for the two land masses of the south polar continent. *c.* Describes the German expedition of 1901–1903 which discovered Kaiser Wilhelm Land in East Antarctica. *d.* Tells the story of the Scotch expedition of 1902–1904 under William S. Bruce and the discovery of Coats Land on the eastern shore of Weddell sea. This part of the narrative sounds exactly like that of (K482) Wilkes. *e.* and *f.* Narrate the two French voyages, in 1903–1905 and 1908–1910 respectively, to the west coast of West Antarctica, which was surveyed and charted most thoroughly.   ESB

K485a Shackleton, Sir Ernest H. *Heart of the Antarctic, being the story of the British antarctic expedition, 1907–1909, with . . . an account of the first journey to the south magnetic pole by Professor T. W. Edgeworth David.* 2 v., 1909. Popular ed., 1 v., London, 1910.

b —— *South; the story of Shackleton's last expedition, 1914–1917.* London, 1919. N. Y., 1920.

Describe respectively Shackleton's voyage of 1907–1909, on which he reached latitude 88° 23' south, and his voyage of 1914–1917 in the Weddell sea, where his ship was crushed and whence he made a most marvelous retreat to boats. Review, Gen. A. W. Greely, *Science*, n.s., 31:828, May 27, 1910. ESB

K486 Amundsen, Roald E. G. *South pole: an account of the Norwegian antarctic expedition in the Fram, 1910–1912.* 2 v. London and N. Y., 1913. Tr. by A. G. Chater from *Sydpolen: den norske sydpolsfaerd med Fram, 1910–1912,* 2 v., Kristiania, 1912.

Narrates the author's voyage in 1910–1912 on which he discovered the South Pole. Reveals the admirable strategy and tactics of the discoverer. ESB

K487a Scott, Sir Robert F. *Voyage of the Discovery.* 2 v. London and N. Y., 1905.

  b —— *Scott's last expedition.* 2 v. London and N. Y., 1913. [1, *Journals of Captain Scott; 2, Reports of the journeys and scientific work;* both arranged by L. Huxley.]

  c Mawson, Sir Douglas. *Home of the blizzard, being the story of the Australasian antarctic expedition, 1911–1914.* 2 v. London and Philadelphia, 1915.

  d Davis, John King. *With the Aurora in the Antarctic, 1911–1914.* London, 1919.

  a. Story of the author's voyage of 1901–1904, on which he discovered King Richard Land. *b.* Narrates Scott's voyage of 1910–1912, on which he reached the South Pole just after Amundsen and perished on his return journey within a short distance of his base. Review, Gen. A. W. Greely, *Science,* n.s., 39:100, Jan. 16, 1914. *c.* Describes the Australian explorations in 1911–1914 of parts of Wilkes Land. Mawson verified the existence of Wilkes's antarctic continent. Review, Gen. A. W. Greely, *Science,* n.s., 41:360, March 5, 1915. *d.* Narrates the story of Mawson's ship in 1911–1914, and offers further proof of Wilkes's accuracy. Davis's excellent work at sea, coupled with Mawson's on land, verified completely Wilkes's Land. ESB

CONSTITUTIONAL AND ADMINISTRATIVE HISTORY AND METHODS

K531a Buller, Charles. *Responsible government for colonies.* London, 1840.

  b Lewis, Sir George Cornewall. *Essay on· the government of dependencies.* 1841. Ed. with introduction by Sir C. P. Lucas, Oxford, 1891.

  c Merivale, Herman. *Lectures on colonization and colonies delivered before the University of Oxford in 1839, 1840, and 1841.* 2 v., 1841–42. New ed., 1 v., London, 1861.

  d Wakefield, Edward Gibbon. *View of the art of colonization, with present reference to the British empire.* 1849. New ed. by J. Collier, Oxford, 1914.

  e Roebuck, John A. *Colonies of England: a plan for the government of some portion of our colonial possessions.* London, 1849.

Works written shortly after the publication, in 1839, of (Z532) Lord Durham's *Report.* The authors of *a.* and *d.* were associated with Lord Durham in Canada. *a.* Pamphlet discussing the governmental aspects of the colonial problem. *b.* Comparative study of colonization to ascertain the constitutional relations necessarily existing between a sovereign government and its dependencies and the advantages and disadvantages resulting to both parties from such relations. Discusses the character of a dependency, modes of acquiring dependencies, forms of their government, and reasons for governing territories in this manner. Full of suggestive thought; has scarcely been superseded by any later work. In this scholarly introduction Sir Charles Lucas has brought the treatment of the subject down to date. Review, *Pol. Sci. Quar.* 7:191, March 1892.   *c.* By a professor at Oxford who later became under-secretary of state for the colonies. Valuable as an early discussion of the problems, in their broader aspects, by a competent authority.   *d.* Combines, in matured form, views set forth in the preceding twenty years in scattered publications. Particularly valuable for suggestions on the treatment of land, labor, and social problems, especially with reference to the settlement of Australia.   *e.* Views on the question of colonial administration by an independent member of Parliament and active publicist familiar with Canadian affairs. Review of *d.* and *e., Edinburgh Rev.* 91:1, Jan. 1850.   FWP, GMD

K532 Roscher, Wilhelm G. F. *Kolonien, Kolonialpolitik und Auswanderung.* 1848. 3rd rev. ed., by R. Jannasch, Leipzig, 1885.

Roscher, a prominent political economist, combined an abstract treatment of the nature of colonization with an excellent historical survey of colonial systems. Jannasch, an influential promoter of the modern German colonial movement, added an account of the German colonies as they existed in 1885, thus rendering the book more concrete and of more practical value. Although somewhat out of date, Roscher's work is still recognized as one of the best general treatments of colonization in general.   MET

K533 Leroy-Beaulieu, Paul. *De la colonisation chez les peuples modernes.* 1874. 6th rev. ed., 2 v., Paris, 1908.

Voluminous and learned work by an economist whose chief interest was finance. Best thing of its kind; exhaustive so far as the aspects of colonization which it covers are concerned. The author has neither the breadth of outlook of (K532) Roscher nor his historic sense, and fails to afford as interesting or suggestive reading. General social aspects of colonization are ignored. Excellent trustworthy manual rather than a philosophic treatise.   AGK

K534 Keller, Albert G. *Colonization, a study of the founding of new societies.* Boston, 1908. (Bibliography.)

Omitting the more familiar story of British and French colonial activity, Professor Keller has treated the motives and results of colonization from Phoenician to modern times. Stress is laid upon the economic and social effect of colonization upon the mother countries, and upon the reciprocal effects of German, Portuguese, Spanish, Italian, and Russian colonization. Review, H. P. Judson, *A.H.R.* 14:861, July 1909.   FJK

K535 Reinsch, Paul S. *Colonial government, an introduction to the study of colonial institutions.* N. Y. and London, 1902. [Citizen's library of economics, politics, and sociology.] (Bibliographies.)

Pt. 1. Discusses motives and methods of colonization.   Pt. 2. Classifies, defines, and analyzes the forms of colonial government.   Pt. 3. Describes the institutions of colonial government both as to organs of colonial administration in the mother country and as to governmental machinery within the colonies themselves, from the legislatures through municipal and local governments to colonial law and the organization of colonial courts. Each topic is reduced to its simplest terms and expressed in clearest style as befits an introductory manual. Review, F. J. Goodnow, *Pol. Sci. Quar.* 17:523, Sept. 1902; *A.H.R.* 8:375, Jan. 1903.

EFH

K536 Reinsch, Paul S. *Colonial administration.* N. Y. and London, 1905. [Citizen's library of economics, politics, and sociology.]. (Bibliographies.)

This valuable comparative study of colonial systems aimed to give the American citizen a proper perspective in approaching colonial problems which were new to him in 1905. Gives briefly a broad survey of the most important activities of modern colonial governments such as finance, commerce, currency, banking and credit, agriculture, land policy, and labor. Concerned with the facts of administration rather than with principles. Review, *Athenaeum,* 2:684, Nov. 18, 1905.

FWP

K537a Ireland, Alleyne. *Tropical colonization, an introduction to the study of the subject.* N. Y. and London, 1899. (Full bibliography.)

b ———— *Far Eastern tropics: studies in the administration of tropical dependencies: Hong Kong, British North Borneo, Sarawak, Burma, the Federated Malay States, the Straits Settlements, French Indo-China, Java, the Philippine Islands.* Boston, 1905. (Bibliography.)

a. The author, an Englishman by birth, resided about twelve years in British tropical possessions, seven of them in the West Indies and South America. The sketch of English, French, and Dutch colonial methods is superficial. The secret of British success is shown to lie in the purity and efficiency of the civil service and in its independence from partisan politics. The culture system in Java and the coolie system in British Guiana are described; the necessity of some system of compulsory labor for exploiting the tropics is indicated. The popular notion that trade follows the flag is disproved from British trade statistics. While not profound or particularly useful in concrete suggestions, the book had a valuable influence in molding American opinion in the initial years of colonial administration. Review, *Nation* (N. Y.), 69:298, Oct. 19, 1899; E. R. A. Seligman, *Pol. Sci. Quar.* 15:141, March 1900. *b.* Collection of journalistic contributions. Contains early criticisms of American administration in the Philippines based on a very brief and inadequate sojourn in the islands. Review, J. A. Leroy, *Pol. Sci. Quar.* 21:288, June, 1906.

FWP

GOVERNMENT PUBLICATIONS

American.—(K901a) *United States Bureau of foreign commerce, Consular reports, commerce, manufactures, etc.,* v. 1–72, no. 1–275, Oct. 1880–Aug. 1903, Washington, 1880–1903. Continued, Sept. 1903–June 1905, by the Bureau of statistics, Department of commerce and labor; and July 1905–June 1910 by the Bureau of manufactures, Department of commerce and labor, with title (K901b) *Monthly consular and trade reports.* Continued in turn, from July 5, 1910, to Sept. 5, 1921, by (K901c) *Daily consular and trade reports;* and since then by (K901d) *Commerce reports,* weekly. (K902) *United States Department of commerce, Bureau of foreign and domestic commerce, Special consular reports,*

Washington, 1890 ff. was issued under different bureaus and titles until August, 1912, since which date the above title has been used. These include monographs compiled from the reports of consular officers, on selected commercial or industrial topics.

British.—(K904a) *Great Britain, Foreign office, Diplomatic and consular reports, annual series,* London, 1886 ff. [*Parliament, Papers by command*] ; and (K904b) *Great Britain, Foreign office, Diplomatic and consular reports, miscellaneous series,* London, 1886 ff. [*Parliament, Papers by command*] both contain information upon the history, administration, and commercial interests of British and foreign colonies. (K905) *Great Britain, Colonial office, Colonial reports,* London, annually, [*Parliament, Papers by command*] ; (K906) *Colonial office list,* London, 1862 ff., unofficial annual; and (K907) *Statistical abstract for the several British oversea dominions and protectorates,* London, 1865 ff. [*Parliament, Papers by command*], contain current statistics of the British colonies. The *Colonial office list* also contains lists of *Parliamentary papers* on colonization in general and on the individual colonies. Yearbooks, official or unofficial, with varying titles are issued in all the more important British colonies.

French.—The following annuals are useful for current information on the French colonies: (K909a) *France, Ministère de la marine et des colonies, Annuaire,* Paris, 1853–89, continued, in part, as (K909b) *France, Ministère des colonies, Annuaire,* Paris, 1887 ff.; (K910) *Annuaire colonial, annuaire agricole, commercial, et industriel des colonies françaises,* Paris, 1888 ff.; (K911) *Année coloniale,* ed. by C. Mourey and L. Brunel, v. 1–4 (all published), Paris, 1899–1905. There are also separate *Annuaires* for each of the more important colonies or groups of colonies.

Dutch.—Official annual reports on the Dutch colonies are published as (K914) *Jaarcijfers voor het Koninkrijk der Nederlanden: Kolonien,* 's Gravenhage, 1882 ff. (K915) *Regeerings-almanak voor Nederlandsche-Indië,* Batavia, 1834 ff. is an annual series of government almanacs for the Dutch East Indies. (K916) *Koloniaal verslag, 1847 ff.,* 's Gravenhage, 1850 ff. are annual reports, covering all the Dutch colonies, made by the colonial minister to the second chamber of the states-general, published in various forms and under various titles, the present title having been used since 1866. This same title has also formed part of the caption for numerous special reports on colonial questions, which, however, do not form part of this series. A good summary of recent data is (K917) *Handboek voor de kennis van Nederland en kolonien,* 's Gravenhage, 1922.   FWP

German.—(K918a) *Koloniales Jahrbuch, Beiträge und Mitteilungen aus dem Gebiete der Kolonialwissenschaft und Kolonialpraxis,* 11 v., Berlin, 1888–98, annual, continued as (K918b) *Beiträge zur Kolonialpolitik und Kolonialwirtschaft,* 5 v., Berlin, 1899–1903, then as (K918c) *Zeitschrift für Kolonialpolitik,* 9 v., Berlin, 1904–12, and finally as (K918d) *Koloniale Monatsblätter,* 2 v., Berlin, 1913–14; and (K919) *Deutscher Kolonial-Kalender und statistisches Handbuch,* 26 v., Berlin, 1889–1914, annual, furnished current information on the German colonies.

Polar exploration.—Considerable material on polar exploration is to be found in the British blue books and *Parliamentary papers.* The earlier of these are listed in (K456c) Brown, *Northwest passage,* 2nd ed., 1860. Each of the countries which participated in the maintenance of international circumpolar stations at dates between 1880 and 1895 has published careful reports of its own expedi-

tions at dates between 1885 and 1895. References to these will be found in
(K451) Greely, *Handbook of polar discoveries.* FWP

SOCIETY PUBLICATIONS

The Hakluyt Society, formed in 1846 to print 'rare and unpublished voyages
and travels,' has published (K921) *Works issued by the Hakluyt Society,* 1st
series, 100 v., London, 1847-98; 2nd series, v. 1-56, London, 1898 ff.; extra
series, 33 v., London, 1903-07. For list of issues to 1923 cf. extra pages at
end of v. 53, 2nd series. The works are not confined to Englishmen and frequently descriptions of some region by several travellers are included in one
volume. Among the voyagers represented are Columbus, da Gama, Hawkins,
Drake, Raleigh, Hudson. The extra series included (K71e) Hakluyt, *Voyages*
and (K72) Purchas, *Pilgrimes.* The works are well printed and well edited and
the texts are reliable.

The Linschoten-vereeniging, founded at the Hague to publish the works of
Dutch voyagers and travellers, has issued (K922) *Werken uitgegeven door de
Linschoten-vereeniging,* v. 1-23, 's Gravenhage, 1909 ff. Its restriction to Dutch
travellers makes it differ from the Hakluyt Society, but it provides otherwise
unavailable material. The set includes voyages of Linschoten, 3 v., Cornelis
May, Tasman, Henry Hudson, a volume on Cambodia and Laos, and Reizen in
Zuid-Afrika, 3 v. The work follows modern canons of editing. AHB

The Kommissionen for Ledelsen af de Geologiske og Geografiske Undersogelser
i Grønland has published (K923) *Meddelelser om Grønland,* v. 1-67, København,
1879 ff. It includes not only accounts of explorations in Greenland since the
foundation of the society, but also a wealth of other materials on the Arctic
regions. The collection is customarily published in Danish with a summary in
French, but occasional volumes are in English. GMD

PERIODICALS

British.—(K941) *Board of trade journal,* London, 1877 ff., monthly 1877-99,
weekly, 1900 ff., ed. by commercial department of the board of trade; (K941a)
Bulletin of the Imperial Institute, London, 1903 ff., issued as a quarterly supplement to the preceding; both are sources for current information upon the trade,
resources, and administration of the British colonies. (942a) *Proceedings of
the Royal Colonial Institute* 40 v., London, 1869-1909, is a repository of many
valuable papers on British colonial interests; continued as (K942b) *United empire, the Royal Colonial Institute journal,* London, 1910 ff., monthly. (K943)
Journal of the parliaments of the empire, London, 1920 ff., quarterly, issued under
the authority of Empire Parliamentary Association, United Kingdom Branch,
reviews current legislation of the United Kingdom and of the self-governing
dominions, and also includes parliamentary discussions of problems and policies,
and reports of the conference of the prime ministers of the empire in 1921.
(K944) *Round table, a quarterly review of the politics of the British commonwealth,* London, 1910 ff. is an admirable journal devoted to colonial interests.

French.—(K960) *Questions diplomatiques et coloniales, revue de politique
extérieure,* Paris, 1897 ff., quarterly, is valuable for questions of colonial concern.
(K961a) *La revue maritime, études historiques et scientifiques maritimes et militaires, questions économiques et sociales,* until 1896, *Revue maritime et coloniale,*
Paris, 1861 ff., is now published by the Service Historique de l'État-Major de la

Marine; it succeeded (K961b) *Revue coloniale,* 33 v. in 28, Paris, 1843–58, and (K961c) *Revue algérienne et coloniale,* 3 v., Paris, 1859–60; and it absorbed (K961d) *Nouvelles annales de la marine et des colonies,* 32 v., Paris, 1849–64. (K962a) *Bulletin de la Société des Études Coloniales et Maritimes,* 34 v., Paris, 1890–1909; continued as (K962b) *Revue des questions coloniales et maritimes,* Paris, 1910 ff., monthly; (K963) *La quinzaine coloniale, organe de l'Union Coloniale Française,* 24 v. in 29, Paris, 1897–1914; and (K964) *Revue de l'histoire des colonies françaises,* Paris, 1913 ff., quarterly, published by the Société de l'Histoire des Colonies Françaises, each deal mainly with French colonial affairs. In some of the more important French colonies there is published a *Journal officiel.*

German.—(K981) *Deutsches Kolonialblatt, Amtsblatt für die Schutzgebiete in Afrika und in der Südsee,* 30 v. in 28, Berlin, 1890–1919, semi-monthly, and (K982) *Deutsche Kolonialzeitung, Organ des Deutschen Kolonialvereins,* 31 v., Berlin, 1884–1914, weekly, were devoted to colonial questions. FWP

SECTION L

GREAT BRITAIN AND IRELAND

Editor

ARTHUR LYON CROSS

Hudson Professor of English History, University of Michigan

CONTENTS

INTRODUCTION

Not only have the sources for British history been more completely preserved than those for other European countries, but almost ever since the introduction of printing, there has been corresponding activity in their publication. Both from an earlier date and on a larger scale than other nations the government has taken an intelligent interest in the conservation and publication of official records. Societies, families, and individuals have liberally supplemented the work. British historical scholarship, in the last fifty years, has not only carried forward this work, but it has also been able to profit to a high degree from the accessibility of the original records, both in print and in the great manuscript collections.

Another peculiarity of British historiography, increasingly evident ever since the sixteenth century, is the wealth and high value of biographical works. Many of these are not works of entertainment or edification but scrupulous compilations of important primary materials, often presented in excellent literary form.

The great wealth of important works produced in the last half century has rendered most earlier publications in British history obsolete. Consequently the selection of titles in this section is almost entirely confined to works which have appeared within the last fifty years. For British relations with the nations of the European continent, reference should be made to the sections of this *Guide* devoted to the several countries and to § H, Medieval history, § I, Modern history, § J, Contemporary history. Works on British expansion overseas will be found in § K, Colonial expansion, § X, Central, Southern, and Eastern Asia, § V, Oceanica, § W, Africa, § X, United States, and § Z, Canada. For earlier publications of special interest, the reader should consult (B12) Adams, *Manual of historical literature*. More detailed reference to the literature of special topics will be found in the special bibliographies and in the bibliographies appended to the leading works in the several fields listed in this section.

BIBLIOGRAPHY AND LIBRARY COLLECTIONS

Fairly complete annotated bibliographies may be found at the end of each volume of (L121) Hunt and Poole, *Political history of England;* and of (L122) Oman, *History of England.* Fuller but less discriminating lists, unannotated, dealing with the period since 1485, will be found in (I121) *Cambridge modern history.* For general catalogues of all British publications, cf. (B3).

L1a Gross, Charles. *Sources and literature of English history, from the earliest times to about 1485.* 1900. 2nd rev. ed., N. Y., 1915.

    b *Bibliography of British History: Stuart Period, 1603–1714.* Ed. Godfrey Davies. Oxford, 1928.

Indispensable guides both to the sources and to later works on the earlier periods of English history. *a.* Over three thousand titles, carefully classified, with brief annotations and full index. A continuation is being prepared by a joint committee of the Royal Historical Society and of the American Historical Association.

ALC

b. Contains more than five thousand carefully selected titles, and, when supplemented by a similar volume on the Tudor Period, will form the continuation of *a.* Review, F. H. Relf, *Jour. of Mod. Hist.* 1:296, June 1929.   SBF

L2a Gardiner, Samuel R., and **Mullinger, James Bass,** ed. *English history for students, being the introduction to the study of English history, with a critical and biographical account of authorities.* 1881. 4th ed., London, 1903.

    b Cannon, Henry L. *Reading references for English history.* Boston, 1910.

a. The bibliographical section of 200 pp., contributed by Mullinger, excellent in its day, is still useful though antiquated. *b.* Convenient list of over two thousand works, including some important articles on English history, without critical comments, but with lists of topics and references for reading; includes poems and novels illustrative of English history, and also a good section on the empire. Review, R. C. H. Catterall, *A.H.R.* 16:399, Jan. 1911.

GMD

L3 Hall, Hubert, ed. *Select bibliography for the study, sources, and literature of English mediaeval economic history.* London, 1914. [Studies in economics and political science.]

As the phrase 'economic history' is liberally interpreted, the titles listed number more than three thousand. Accurate and skilful compilation including both sources and later works. While the bibliographical data are complete, critical information is, unfortunately, lacking. Review, E. P. Cheyney, *A.HR..* 20:134, Oct. 1914.

GMD

L4 Hall, Hubert, ed. *Repertory of British archives.* Pt. 1, London, 1920. [Royal Historical Society.]

This repertory, published under the auspices of the Royal Historical Society, will aim 'to assist historical students in locating such documents as may be useful for their studies,' including 'official documents not transferred to the Public Record Office' and local records as well. Review, C. M. Andrews, *A.H.R.* 27:813, July 1922.

ALC

L5a Bird, Samuel R. Scargill. *Guide to the principal classes of documents preserved in the Public Record Office.* 1891. 3rd ed., London, 1908. [Rolls series.]

b Giuseppi, M. S. *Guide to the manuscripts preserved in the Public Record Office.* 2 v. London, 1923–24.

Indispensable guides for the research student. *b.* Largely based on the last edition of *a*; v. I deals with the legal records, and v. II with State Papers and records of the public departments. Review of *b,* H. H. E. Craster, *E.H.R.* 39:454, July 1924; 40:474, July 1925.

GMD

L6a Hardy, Alfred L. *List of manorial court rolls in private hands.* 3 pt. London, 1907–10. 2nd ed. of pt. 1, London, 1913. [Manorial Society, Monographs, no. 1, 2, 4.]

b Hone, Nathaniel J. *Manor and manorial records.* London, 1906. [Antiquary's books.] (Bibliography.)

Both valuable for lists and descriptions of manorial records. Review of *b., Athenaeum,* 1:761, June 23, 1906. For further information cf. (L1) Gross, § 57.

ALC

L7a Buckley, John A., and **Williams, William T.** *Guide to British historical fiction.* London, 1912.

b Speare, Morris E. *Political novel, its development in England and in America.* Oxford and N. Y., 1924.

a. Designed primarily for teachers in elementary and secondary schools, but aims to be useful to 'students of history generally.' The list is 'representative and not exhaustive.' Covers the period from earliest times to 1900; each work is described in a brief note. The first section of (B10c) E. A. Baker, *Guide to historical fiction,* deals with the British Isles to the end of Victoria's reign. For a controversy as to the indebtedness of Buckley and Williams to an earlier

work of Baker, cf. *Athenaeum,* 1:164, 214, 254, 360, Feb. 8, 22, March 1, 29, 1913.
b. Study of political novels with special reference to Disraeli.   ALC

L8a His Majesty's Stationery Office. *Brief guide to government publications.*
London, 1925.

b Lees-Smith, Hastings B. *Guide to parliamentary and official papers.*
Oxford and N. Y., 1924. [London School of Economics and Political
Science Studies.] (Bibliographical footnotes.)

a. Brief description of the function, history, and publications of the Stationery
Office, the printer, publisher, and bookseller for the British government departments. Its publications, which began in 1786, consist of two classes, parliamentary papers and non-parliamentary papers. The latter include, in addition
to certain general works, such as (J441*a*) *Peace handbooks,* numerous scientific
and economic publications. *b.* Short account of the several series of official
documents issued by the British government, especially the various parliamentary
papers.   HRS

L9a *Catalogue of parliamentary papers, 1801–1900, with a few of earlier date.*
Ed. by Hilda V. Jones, London, 1904, supplement, 1901–20, 2 v., 1912–22.

b *General index to parliamentary papers, 1801–1852.* 3 v. London, 1833–52.

c *Alphabetical index to sessional papers, 1852–1899.* London, 1909.

d *Numerical list and alphabetical index to sessional printed papers.* London,
annual.

e *Consolidated list of parliamentary and Stationery Office publications.* London, annual.

a, b, and *c.* Useful guides for the student who has to seek information in
(L85) *Sessional papers.* For the period since 1899, he is either partially or
entirely dependent on the annual publications, *d* and *e.*   ALC

L10 Ponsonby, Arthur A. W. H. *English diaries, a review of English diaries
from the sixteenth to the twentieth centuries, with an introduction on diary
writings.* London and N. Y., 1923. (Bibliography.)

Accounts of diarists and diaries, with illustrative extracts. Some of those
noticed have never been printed.   ALC

L16a Livingstone, Matthew. *Guide to the public records of Scotland deposited
in H. M. General Register House, Edinburgh.* Edinburgh, 1905.

b Thomson, J. Maitland, ed. *Public records of Scotland.* Glasgow, 1922.

c Terry, Charles S. *Index to the papers relating to Scotland, described or
calendared in the Historical Mss. Commission's Reports.* Glasgow, 1908.

d ——— *Catalogue of the publications of Scottish historical and kindred
clubs and societies, and of the volumes relative to Scottish history issued
by His Majesty's Stationery Office, 1780–1908, with a subject-index.* Aberdeen, 1909. [Aberdeen University studies.]

e Nicolson, William. *English, Scotch, and Irish historical libraries, giving a
short view and character of most of our historians, either in print or
manuscript, with an account of our records, law-books, coins, and other
matters, serviceable to the undertakers of a general history of England.*
1696–1724. Rev. ed., 3 pt. in 1 v., London, 1776.

f Black, George F., ed. *List of works relating to Scotland.* N. Y., 1916.
[In part, reprint from *Bulletin of New York Public Library,* Jan.–Dec.
1914.]

a. Very useful classified list. *b.* Brief history and classified description. *c.* Takes up the *Reports,* volume by volume, and notes the materials relating to Scotland. *d.* Useful list, largely of documentary publications. *e.* Old introduction to British historiography, still useful, especially for Scotland. *f.* Lists the works in the New York Public Library relating to Scotland; classified by topic.

ALC

L17 *Reports from the committee appointed by His Majesty to execute the measures recommended in an address to the house of commons respecting the public records of Ireland.* 3 v. Dublin, 1813–25.

These fifteen reports, prepared between 1810 and 1825, are of basic importance to the student pursuing research in the public records of Ireland. ALC

Library collections.—The best rounded and largest collection in the United States for British history is in the Harvard University Library. Next in importance are probably the collections in the Library of Congress, New York Public Library, and the Library of the University of Michigan. There are good collections in the other larger university libraries, but they have not been built up so consistently. Boston Public Library and libraries of the Universities of Chicago, Cornell, and Minnesota have special collections for the seventeenth century. The Congregational Library of Boston possesses the library of Bishop Stubbs; Union Theological Seminary, the McAlpin collection on English church history; and Yale University, the Wagner collection which is valuable for English economic history.

AHS

ENCYCLOPEDIAS AND WORKS OF REFERENCE

L21 Low, Sidney J. M., and **Pulling, Frederick S.,** ed. *Dictionary of English history.* 1884. Rev. ed., enlarged, London and N. Y., 1928. (Bibliographies.)

Extremely convenient dictionary of brief articles on individuals, battles, treaties, institutions, and various other topics. While most of the items were evidently prepared by the editors, many bear the initials of the foremost English historians of the generation.

GMD

L22 Stephen, Leslie, and **Lee, Sir Sidney,** ed. *Dictionary of national biography.* 63 v. London, 1885–1900; *Supplement,* 3 v., 1901; *Index and epitome,* 1903; *Errata,* 1904. Slightly rev. ed., including 1901 supplement, 22 v., London, 1908–09; Supplement, 1901–1911, 3 v., 1912; Supplement, 1912–1921, H. W. C. Davis and J. R. H. Weaver, ed., London, 1927. (Valuable bibliographies.)

Invaluable work of the highest scholarship. As originally planned by the publisher, Mr. George Smith, the undertaking was to include biographies of all men and women who have made notable contributions to the life and the history of the British peoples. The term British was interpreted to comprise not only the United Kingdom but also the colonial field; it therefore became possible to include sketches of the more important leaders in American life before the revolt of the Thirteen Colonies. A further condition was that no person still living at the time of publication should have a place in the work. These conditions have been rigidly adhered to. The original plan was to close the work with the nineteenth century. In its present form it contains sketches of more than thirty thousand men and women. The task of preparation has been shared by about one thousand contributors. Indispensable as a book of reference, especially when information is sought concerning the less known characters, in which case it is frequently the only accessible source. Both the epitome and the reissue comprise the material in the first supplement as well as in the original. The epitome, an abridgement on the scale of one-fourteenth, is an extremely useful single volume manual for those who can not command access to the reissue, which is preferable to the original. Review, *E.H.R.* 5:783, Oct. 1890; of Suppl. 1912–1921, (London) *Times Lit. Suppl.* 26:827, Nov. 17, 1927.   LML

L23a *Who's who, an annual biographical dictionary.* V. 1–82, London, 1849 ff.

   b *Who was who: a companion to 'Who's who' containing the biographies of those who died during the period 1897–1916.* London, 1920.

   a. Standard work of its kind. Contains brief outlines of careers of eminent living Britons, especially titled persons, officials, and authors, usually compiled from data furnished by the individual concerned. Also includes some colonials and a few foreigners. With annual obituary list.   *b.* Convenient supplement to *a* and to (L22).   HLK

GEOGRAPHY AND ATLASES

L41 Ramsay, Sir Andrew C. *Physical geology and geography of Great Britain.* 1863. 6th ed., by H. B. Woodward, London, 1894.

Account of the geologic growth and change of the British Isles. Still authoritative in its large outlines of British geologic history, but antedates entirely the scientific studies in physical and human geography for Great Britain.   COS

L42 Mackinder, Halford J. *Britain and the British seas.* N. Y., 1902. 2nd ed., Oxford, 1907. [Regions of the world.] (Bibliographies.)

After twenty years still the standard geography of Britain. Readable; symmetrical; abundantly supplied with significant sketch maps, many of historical bearing; well organized for reference use. The chapters on 'Position of Britain,' on 'Historical Geography,' and on 'Metropolitan England' are especially significant. Review, *Spectator,* 88:593, April 19, 1902.   COS

L43 Gardiner, Samuel R., ed. *School atlas of English history.* London and N. Y., 1892.

Prepared as a companion to (L101a) his *Student's history of England.* In addition to maps of England, Scotland, and Ireland at various epochs, it contains maps of portions of Europe, and of other parts of the world illustrative of British interests and activities abroad. Plans of the more important battles are included. A very convenient manual.   GMD

L44a Mawer, Allen, and **Stenton, Frank M.,** ed. *Introduction to the survey of English place-names.* Cambridge, Eng. and N. Y., 1924. [English Place-Name Society, v. 1, pt. 1.]

   b Mawer, Allen, ed. *Chief elements used in English place-names.* Cambridge, Eng. and N. Y., 1924. V. 2, Buckinghamshire, 1925; v. 3, Bedfordshire and Huntingdonshire, 1926; v. 4, Worcestershire, 1927. [English Place-Name Society, v. 1, pt. 2.]

Prolegomena to a survey of place-names in all the English counties, which the society has been formed to undertake. Pt. 1. Sets forth the principles, methods, and present status of the study. Pt. 2. Catalogues some 650 elements, mostly

Old English, though about 100 are Old Norse. Both works reveal much interesting historical information. Reviews, L. M. Larson, *A.H.R.* 30:585, Apr. 1925; 33:680, Apr. 1928.

GMD

SOURCE BOOKS, COLLECTIONS OF SOURCES, ARCHIVE PUBLICATIONS

L61a Adams, George B., and **Stephens, Henry Morse**. *Select documents of English constitutional history.* 1901. New ed., N. Y., 1910. Later reprints.

b Medley, Dudley J. *Original illustrations of English constitutional history.* London, 1910.

Comprehensive collections of documents from the Saxon period to the end of the nineteenth century. *a.* The more comprehensive collection, wholly in English translations. Review, *Athenaeum,* 1:812, June 28, 1902. *b.* Gives translations of the French, but not of the Latin documents. Review, *ibid.* 1:759, June 25, 1910.

ALC

L62a Stubbs, William. *Select charters and other illustrations of English constitutional history, from the earliest times to the reign of Edward the First.* 1870. 9th rev. ed. by H. W. C. Davis, Oxford, 1913.

b Tanner, Joseph R. *Tudor constitutional documents, A.D. 1485–1603, with an historical commentary.* Cambridge, Eng., 1922.

c Prothero, Sir George W. *Select statutes and other constitutional documents illustrative of the reigns of Elizabeth and James I.* 1894. 4th ed., Oxford, 1913.

d Gardiner, Samuel R. *Constitutional documents of the Puritan revolution, 1625–1660.* 1889. 3rd rev. ed., Oxford, 1906.

e Robertson, Charles Grant. *Select statutes, cases, and documents to illustrate English constitutional history, 1660–1832, with a supplement, 1832–1894.* 1904. 2nd rev. ed., with additions to 1911, London, 1913.

These five volumes, taken together, cover the constitutional development of England from Saxon times to the twentieth century, with the exception of the reigns from Edward II to Edward IV inclusive, for which period the only available collections are those enumerated under (L61). The original texts of the documents are given (without translation of the Latin ones in *a.*) usually with a brief historical and bibliographical introduction in each case. Each volume also contains an excellent general introduction. Indispensable aids for the advanced student. Review of *b,* F. C. Dietz, *A.H.R.* 28:102, Oct. 1922; of *e,* A. L. Cross, *A.H.R.* 10:877, July 1905.

GMD

L63 Gee, Henry, and **Hardy, William J.** *Documents illustrative of English church history.* London and N. Y., 1896.

Useful collection of documents, in translation where necessary, illustrating the history of the English church prior to 1700, especially in its constitutional aspects.

GMD

L64 Bland, Alfred E.; Brown, Philip A.; and **Tawney, Richard H.** *English economic history, select documents.* London, 1914. (Bibliographies.)

Arranged in three chronological groups: 1000–1485, 1485–1660, 1660–1846, in each of which the documents are classified under topics. The selection is not limited to statutes or other official documents, but includes illuminating extracts from contemporary writings.   GMD

L65 Tawney, Richard H., and **Power, Eileen.** *Tudor economic documents, being select documents illustrating the economic and social history of Tudor England.* 3 v. London and N. Y., 1924. [University of London historical series, no. 4.]   [*1, Agriculture and industry; 2, Commerce, finance, and poor law; 3, Pamphlets, memoranda, and literary extracts.*]

Excellent selection from a wide range of sources on a well varied list of topics; well edited.   GMD

L66a Ballard, Adolphus. *British borough charters, 1042–1216.* Cambridge, Eng., 1913.

   b Ballard, Adolphus, and **Tait, James.** *British borough charters, 1216–1307.* Cambridge, Eng., 1923. (Bibliography.)

Contain Latin texts with translations and introductions. Excellent and useful collections of materials not easily accessible. Review cf. *a.*, J. Tait, *E.H.R.* 28:764, Oct. 1913; of *b.*, C. Johnson, *E.H.R.* 39:119, Jan. 1924.   GMD

L67a Cheyney, Edward P. *Readings in English history drawn from the original sources.* 1908. New ed., Boston, 1922.

   b White, Albert B., and **Notestein, Wallace.** *Source problems in English history.* N. Y. and London, 1915. [Harper's parallel source problems.]

   c Winbolt, Samuel E., and **Bell, Kenneth,** ed. *Bell's English history source books.* 21 v. London, 1913–27. Later ed. of several v.

   d Morgan, Robert B. *Readings in English social history from contemporary literature.* 5 v. 1921–22. New ed., 1 v., Cambridge, Eng., 1923.

a. Excellent selection, in translation where necessary, of over 450 brief extracts from contemporary sources illustrating the various phases of the national life. *b.* Groups of extracts from the sources, with translation when necessary, adequate for the study of eight typical questions ranging from the time of Alfred to the parliament act of 1911.   *c.* Handy volumes, each devoted to a separate epoch, covering the period from 449 to 1887; similar to *a.* but more comprehensive, especially for the later periods.   *d.* Useful collection covering the period from the beginning to 1837.   GMD

L68 Beard, Charles A. *Introduction to the English historians.* N. Y., 1906. (Bibliographies.)

In addition to collections of sources there have appeared several collections of extracts from later historians illustrating English history. Of these one of the most recent and best is this selection edited by Professor Beard. The extracts extend from the Saxon conquest to the nineteenth century and are chosen from the foremost works in English history. Review, C. T. Wyckoff, *A.H.R.* 12:416, Jan. 1907.   GMD

Collections of sources and archive publications.—The sources for the history of England are more varied and more continuously complete than those of any other European country. In (L1) Gross, *Sources and literature of English history* may be found a full list of printed sources, prior to 1485, with ample information as to their character, value, and location. As a matter of fact, in consequence of the public record act of 1837, most of the government records were, in 1856 to 1859, brought together in a building specially constructed for the purpose, the

Public Record Office, Fetter Lane, London. Until the publication of the proposed continuation, from 1485 to the present time, of Gross's monumental work, the student will have to seek elsewhere in various places for information concerning the sources of modern English history. There are extensive but rather undiscriminating lists, without comment, in the works mentioned in this section under the heading Bibliography.

The most complete collection of medieval chronicles is officially designated as (L71) *Rerum Britannicarum medii aevi scriptores, or chronicles and memorials of Great Britain and Ireland during the middle ages,* London, 1858–1911, but popularly known as the *Rolls series,* because published under the nominal direction of the master of the rolls. For an index of this series which extends from the earliest times to the reign of Henry VII, and which now includes 99 separate works in 243 v., cf. (L1) Gross, *Sources and literature,* appendix C. Besides chronicles, the *Rolls series,* has in more recent years included various other records; for example, calendars or chronological catalogues of divers sorts of state papers, in which cases the contents of the documents are sometimes presented in a very abbreviated form, sometimes at greater length, or even *in extenso.* The work now entrusted to the master of the rolls and his staff, of which the deputy keeper of the public records is the working head, was begun by the Record Commission appointed by parliament in 1800, which continued to operate till 1837. For list of its (L72) *Publications,* 92 v., London, 1802–69, cf. (L1) Gross, no. 538.

Among the documents in (L73) *Calendar of state papers, &c,* London, 1856 ff., which now includes all or parts of 30 separate works in 317 v., have been charter, patent, and close rolls and various state papers relating to domestic, foreign, and colonial affairs. The reign for which the materials have been most fully reproduced is that of Henry VIII for which there are (L73a) *Calendar of letters and papers, foreign and domestic, of the reign of Henry VIII,* 21 v., London, 1862–1910, ed. by J. S. Brewer, J. Gairdner, and R. H. Brodie, with many of the documents in a slightly abridged form; and also (L74) *State papers during the reign of Henry VIII,* 11 v., London, 1830–52, printed in full. For complete list of volumes in the five preceding items and of other documentary publications, cf. H. M. Stationery Office, List Q, *List of record publications,* of which the current issue may be obtained from British Library of Information, 44 Whitehall Street, New York.

The calendars of papers in the government archives are supplemented by more than 170 v. of Royal Commission on Historical Manuscripts, (L75) *Reports,* London, 1870 ff. [list in (L1) Gross, appendix B], dealing with materials to be found in private houses, cathedrals, colleges, municipalities, and other depositories. The commission has presented no *Report* since the seventeenth, but since 1899 has issued its publications under individual titles. One publication originally undertaken by the commission [14th *Report,* appendix, pt. 6] has been continued by the house of lords, namely, (L75a) *Manuscripts of the house of lords* [1693 ff.], v. 1–7, London, 1900–21. Many documents of a public character are still in private hands, owing to the fact that many officials were accustomed, in former times, to retain their papers at the end of their terms of service. Unfortunately, the reports in some of the early volumes are so brief as to be of little use; however, new and fuller calendars of these are promised for the future.

While legislation in the modern sense practically starts with Edward I, the official collections of statutes include a few earlier documents. Since it contains all the old laws, repealed and unrepealed, the student should use (L76) *Statutes of the realm* [1235–1713], 11 v., London, 1810–28 [Record Commission]. Statutes enacted since the accession of George I are printed in (L77a) *Statutes at large, from Magna Carta to . . . 1761, carefully collated and revised . . . by D. Pickering* [v. 1–24] *continued to . . . 1806* [v. 25–46], 46 v., Cambridge, Eng., 1762–1807; which is continued as (L77b) *Statutes of the United Kingdom . . .*, v. 47 ff., London, 1807 ff. Current legislation has also been printed under the title (L77c) *Public general statutes*, London, 1832–87, and (L77d) *Public general acts*, London, 1887 ff. Not to be confused with the above (L77a) are numerous other more or less complete collections entitled *Statutes at large*, printed at various dates since 1587. There are two recent editions of statutes in force: (L78a) *The statutes, revised edition*, v. 1–18, London, 1870–85, by A. J. Wood, G. K. Rickards, and others; and (L78b) *The statutes, second revised edition* [1235–1900], v. 1–20, London, 1888–1909.

Parliamentary records begin with (L79) *Rotuli parliamentorum*, 6 v., [London, 1777], and *Index*, 1832, or rolls of parliament, 1278–1503, which was issued by the house of lords. Although the text is faulty, 'having been printed from transcripts not collated with the originals,' it is an invaluable source, but can only be used by those familiar with old French. Beginning with 1509 and 1547 respectively, [cf. (L121, v. 6) Pollard, *Political history of England, 1547–1603*, p. 490] there are (L80) *Journals of the House of Lords*, London, 1767 ff., and (L81) *Journals of the House of Commons*, London, 1742 ff., (reprint, v. 1–34, 1803–20) containing, at the end of 1924, in 156 v. and 179 v. respectively, records of business transacted, petitions, etc., but no reports of debates after 1628. For debates it is necessary to turn to (L82) *Parliamentary or constitutional history of England* [1066–1660], 24 v., London, 1751–61, and the work which superseded it, (L83) *Parliamentary history of England* [1066–1803], 36 v., London, 1806–20, ed. by William Cobbett and J. Wright. This is based, at least in medieval and early modern times, on faulty and inadequate texts; the need for a new edition has been effectually demonstrated by Professor Notestein [cf. preface and introduction to (L83a) W. Notestein and F. H. Relf, *Commons debates for 1629*, Minneapolis, 1921; and also (L83b) W. Notestein, *Journal of Sir Simonds D' Ewes . . . of the Long Parliament*, v. 1, New Haven, 1923] and other students of the period. Under the title (L84) *Parliamentary debates*, London, 1812 ff., sometimes called *Hansard's Debates* from the government printer, it is continued in over 840 v. from 1803 to the present day. British government publications are divided into two classes, *Parliamentary papers* and *Non-parliamentary papers*. The former class, known as blue books, submitted at each session of parliament, are printed and published separately, but at approximately annual intervals the Stationery Office publishes (L9d) *Numerical list and alphabetical index to sessional printed papers*. The serially numbered and bound edition of (L85) *Sessional printed papers* is issued for official use only and is not placed on sale. Also cf. (L8).

The records of the privy council, so far as they have been printed, may be found in (L86) *Proceedings and ordinances of the privy council, 1386–1542, 7* v., London, 1834–37 [Record Commission], ed. by Sir N. Harris Nicolas; and in (L87) *Acts of the privy council of England, new series,* v. 1–35, London, 1890–

1927, ed. by Sir John R. Dasent and Sir H. C. Maxwell Lyte, which now covers the proceedings from 1542 to 1617.

Sources for the study of the legal side of English history are many and valuable. (L88a) *Complete collection of state trials* [1163-1820], 33 v. and index, London, 1809-28, ed. by W. Cobbett, T. B. Howell, and T. J. Howell, is extremely useful so far as it goes; however, the old custom of submitting the manuscript to the judge for revision often resulted in making him appear in a better light in the printed report than was the case in the actual conduct of the trial. A judicial commission, called the State Trials Committee, with the editorial assistance of J. Macdonell and J. E. P. Wallis, has undertaken the publication of (L88b) *State trials, new series*, London, 1883 ff., which continues the preceding work from 1820. Also to be recommended is (L88c) J. W. Willis-Bund, *Selection of cases from the state trials*, 2 v. in 3, Cambridge, Eng., 1879-82; of which v. 1 contains trials for treason, 1327-1660.

The 'official minutes,' or chief steps in trials in the common law courts, are to be found in the plea rolls, *e.g., coram rege, de banco,* and exchequer rolls, some of which have been printed by (L72) Record Commission, (L924) Pipe Rolls Society, and (L925) Selden Society. These have to be supplemented by the surviving accounts of the arguments of counsel and the discussion by judges of points of law, which must be sought in (L89) *Year books* [1292-1535], [for list of early printed ones, cf. *British Museum Catalogue*, v. *England*, p. 124-135], which are anonymous and written in old French. The most nearly complete edition is (L89a) *Les reports des cases*, 11 v., London, 1678-80, but the text is far from satisfactory. Various year books, previously unprinted, have of late, been published in (L71) *Rolls series* [with translations], by the (L925) Selden Society, and elsewhere; for a list see (L1) Gross, no. 2053. Also cf. William C. Bolland, (L89b) *Year books*, Cambridge, Eng., 1921, and (L89c) *Manual of year book studies*, Cambridge, Eng., 1925, for discussions of their origin, nature, and importance; and (L89d) H. G. Richardson, 'Year books and plea rolls as sources of historical information,' in (L922) *Transactions of the Royal Historical Society*, 4th series, 5:28-70, 1922, for an opposing point of view emphasizing the significance of the plea rolls. The year books were replaced, in the reign of Henry VIII, by (L90) *Reports* [described in (L553) *Select Essays in Anglo-American legal history*, v. 2, ch. 25], edited by various judges. Much information concerning existing law at successive periods may be obtained from the works of the leading law writers: (L91a) Glanvill, (L91b) Bracton, (L91c) Fortescue, (L91d) Littleton, (L91e) Coke, and (L91f) Blackstone [listed in A. L. Cross, 'A recent history of English law,' *Mich. Law Rev.* 9:6-12, Nov. 1910; and in (L1) Gross, cf. index under the several names].

For British international relations in the medieval and early modern period there was prepared at government expense (L92a) *Foedera, conventiones, litterae, et cujuscunque generis acta publica inter reges Angliae et alios quosvis imperatores, reges, pontifices, vel communitates* [1101-1654], v. 1-15, ed. by Thomas Rymer, v. 16-20, ed. by Robert Sanderson, Londini, 1704-35; 2nd ed. of v. 1-17 by George Holmes, 1727-29; 3rd ed., 10 v., Hagae Comitis, 1739-45; new ed. [1069-1383] by Adam Clark, Frederic Holbrooke, and John Caley, 4 v. in 7, Londini, 1816-69 [Record Commission]. For the several editions of this invaluable work, which vary considerably in content, the student will find (L92b) Sir T. D. Hardy, *Syllabus of documents in Rymer's Foedera*, 3 v., London, 1869-85 [*Calendar of*

state papers], an indispensable guide.   Unfortunately no suitable continuation of
Rymer's work exists, but for the period since the early nineteenth century, there
are available two excellent collections: (I509a) *British and foreign state papers,*
including documents since 1812; and (I508a) Hertslet, *Complete collection of the
treaties . . . between Great Britain and foreign powers,* useful for the period
since 1820.   Also, cf. (B28a) *Annual register,* which contains numerous documents on not only foreign but also internal and imperial affairs since 1758.

In addition to (L93a) *Collection of state tracts, published . . . in 1688 and
during the reign of William III . . .,* 3 v., London, 1705–07, there are two important printed collections of tracts primarily for the end of the seventeenth
century: (L93b) *Harleian miscellany,* ed. by W. Oldys, 8 v., 1744; new ed. by
T. Park, 10 v., London, 1808–13; and (L93c) *Somers tracts,* 16 v., 1748–52; rev.
ed. by Sir Walter Scott, 13 v., London, 1809–15, which contain useful reprints of
manuscripts and pamphlets from the libraries of two famous collectors, Edward
Harley, earl of Oxford, and John, Baron Somers.

For church history, (L94a) A. W. Haddan and William Stubbs, *Councils and
ecclesiastical documents relating to Great Britain and Ireland,* 3 v. in 4, Oxford,
1869–78, is very valuable so far as it goes, namely, to 870; for the later period
one has to resort to the less satisfactory (L94b) David Wilkins, *Concilia Magnae
Britanniae et Hiberniae, 446–1717,* 4 v., Londini, 1737.

For Scotland there are (L96a) *Acts of the parliaments of Scotland, 1124–1707,*
ed. by Thomas Thomson and Cosmo Innes, 11 v., Edinburgh, 1814–44, *General
index,* 1875; for v. 2–11 of which there is (L96b) a one-volume abridgement,
Edinburgh, 1908; (L96c) *Register of the privy council of Scotland,* ed. by J. H.
Burton, D. Masson, and P. H. Brown, v. 1–30, Edinburgh, 1877–1916, which now
covers the period, 1545–1684; (L96d) *Register of the great seal of Scotland,
registrum magni sigilli regum Scotorum,* ed. by J. M. Thomson and others, v.
1–11, Edinburgh, 1882–1914, which now covers the period, 1306–1668; (L96e)
Register of the privy seal of Scotland, registrum secreti sigilli regum Scotorum,
ed. by M. Livingstone and D. H. Fleming, v. 1–2, Edinburgh, 1908–1923, covering the years, 1488–1542; (L96f) *Exchequer rolls of Scotland, rotuli scaccarii
regum Scotorum,* ed. by J. Stuart, G. Burnett, and others, v. 1–23, Edinburgh,
1878–1908, covering the years, 1264–1600; (L96g) *Accounts of the lord high
treasurer of Scotland,* ed. by T. Dickson and Sir J. B. Paul, v. 1–11, Edinburgh,
1877–1916, covering the years, 1473–1566; (L96h) *Calendar of documents relating to Scotland preserved in Her Majesty's Public Record Office,* ed. by J. Bain,
v. 1–4, Edinburgh, 1881–1888, covering the years, 1108–1509; (L96i) *Calendar
of state papers relating to Scotland and Mary, queen of Scots, preserved in the
Public Record Office, the British Museum, and elsewhere in England,* ed. by J.
Bain and W. K. Boyd, v. 1–9, Edinburgh, 1898–1916, covering the years, 1547–
1588; and some other volumes in (L71) *Rolls series,* and (L73) *Calendar of
state papers.*

For Ireland there exist (L97a) *Statutes at large, passed in the parliaments
held in Ireland,* 8 v., Dublin, 1765; rev. ed. by J. G. Butler, 20 v., Dublin, 1786–
1801, covering the years, 1310–1800; (L97b) *Irish statutes, revised edition,*
London, 1885, which is an abridgement in a single volume; (L97c) *Calendar of
state papers, Ireland,* ed. by H. C. Hamilton, R. P. Mahaffy, and others, 24 v.,
London, 1860–1912, covering the years, 1509–1670; and various other volumes in
(L71) *Rolls series,* and (L73) *Calendar of state papers.*

For Wales extensive materials may be found in (L71) *Rolls series.* (L98) *Statutes of Wales,* ed. by Ivor Bowen, London, 1908, is a small volume containing all the statutes relating to Wales with a useful historical and legal introduction.

ALC, GMD

SHORTER GENERAL HISTORIES

L101a Gardiner, Samuel R. *Student's history of England.* 1890–91. Rev. ed., 3 v. in 1, London, 1923. (Brief bibliographies.)

b Tout, Thomas F. *Advanced history of Great Britain from the earliest times.* 1906. Rev. ed., London and N. Y., 1923. (Brief bibliographies.)

c Cheyney, Edward P. *Short history of England.* 1904. Rev. ed., Boston, 1918. (Brief bibliography.)

d Cross, Arthur L. *History of England and Greater Britain.* N. Y., 1914. Later reprints. (Bibliographies.)

e ——— *Shorter history of England and Greater Britain.* N. Y., 1920. Rev. ed., 1929. (Bibliographies.)

f Innes, Arthur D. *History of England and the British Empire.* 4 v. London and N. Y., 1913–15.

g Bright, James Franck. *History of England.* 5 v. London, 1899–1904.

h Green, John R. *Short history of the English people.* 1874. Illustrated rev. ed. by Mrs. J. R. Green and K. Norgate, 4 v., London and N. Y., 1892–94. Later reprints. New ed., with epilogue, 1815–1914, by Mrs. J. R. Green, London and N. Y., 1916.

i Larson, Laurence M. *History of England and the British commonwealth.* N. Y., 1924. [American historical series.] (Bibliographies.)

j Mowat, Robert B. *New history of Great Britain.* 3 v. in 1. Oxford and N. Y., 1921–22.

k Hulme, Edward M. *History of the British people.* N. Y. and London, 1924. (Bibliographies.)

l Trevelyan, George M. *History of England.* London and N. Y., 1926. (Bibliographies.)

m Dietz, Frederick M. *Political and social history of England.* N. Y. and London, 1927.

n Lunt, William E. *History of England.* N. Y., 1928. (Bibliographies.)

With the exception of Green, and possibly Bright, the authors' purpose was to write text-books. *a.* For many years the most substantial text-book for college use, and in spite of a multiplicity of details, it held the field until interest in more recent history made its slight treatment of the period since 1832 inadequate. Professor Gardiner remains, however, one of the great masters of English history, and his work must ever find a place in any reference collection. The illustrations, now published separately, are invaluable. *b.* Has few, if any, advantages over Gardiner, except its more equal proportions in the treatment of the several periods. The absence of illustrations is partly compensated by good sketch maps and plans. Review, R. C. H. Catterall, *A.H.R.* 13:193, Oct. 1907. Both these books, moreover, were written for students in the advanced forms of English schools, who were consequently already familiar with the main facts of English history. *c.* For the American who is beginning his study, this has proved to be the most successful of the many English histories for school use. Gives the broad sweep of events; emphasizes the effect of social and economic conditions on politics. So many details have been omitted, however, that the book lacks certain necessary vertebrae. Review, N. M. Trenholme, *A.H.R.* 10:851, July 1905. *d.* Replete with details, which make it particularly valuable as a book of reference, but which tend also to make it confusing to the student. The great contribution of Professor Cross is found in the admirable chapters on social, economic, and literary progress. Review, *A.H.R.* 20:620, Apr. 1915. *e.* Retains these chapters; adds a comprehensive survey of the empire and also an excellent chapter on the events leading to and including the World War. The political details have been brought down to an almost irreducible minimum for a college text. It therefore makes an excellent text, even though it lacks vividness and bears the mark of the pruning hook. Review, R. L. Schuyler, *Hist. Outlook*, 13:28, Jan. 1922. *f.* Attempts to treat the British Isles and the empire as a unit, but is not wholly successful; these volumes vary in merit, but all are heavy, and, in part, obscure. Review, B. S. Terry, *A.H.R.* 19:859, July 1914; 21:587, Apr. 1916. *g.* More readable and appeals to the general reader; with an acknowledged liberal bias, Bright has not been wholly detached in his treatment, particularly of the later period. Review, v. 1–4, Lord Acton, *E.H.R.* 3:798, Oct. 1888; v. 5, W. C. Abbott, *A.H.R.* 10:433, Jan. 1905. *h.* Stands in a class by itself; uneven in its merits as history, it is a great work of literature. As such it has no rival, and remains the envy and despair of all who wish to tell the story of England in graceful and dignified English. *i.* Well written and well arranged text of the conventional type, somewhat less detailed than *a.*, *b.*, and *e.*, particularly in its treatment of the medieval and early modern period. Review, W. E. Lunt, *A.H.R.* 30:126, Oct. 1924. *j.* and *k.* Distinct departures from the conventional text-book, but differ radically from one another. *j.* Well written and excellently illustrated; gives special attention to economic and social affairs; makes liberal use of source materials. *k.* Conscious imitation of *h.;* excels in the chapters devoted to social and economic conditions and especially in the many pages devoted to literary progress. The reduction of the political framework to such a degree as the plan and scope of the work demanded and the rather ornate style make it a difficult text for students who have not already acquired some knowledge of the political history. Review, C. E. Fryer, *A.H.R.* 30:339, Jan. 1925. *l.* Well proportioned except for the unusual space given to the pre-conquest period and the brevity of treatment of the period since 1815; ably written; each of the short, lucid paragraphs depicts vividly some significant event, condition, or movement; economic, social ,and cultural affairs are unusually well correlated with the political; a distinctive work. Review, E. P. Cheney, *A.H.R.* 33:570, Apr. 1927.   AHB

m. Emphasizes social and economic history. *n.* Lucid, interesting, instructive, and scholarly. Review of *l, m, n* and other recent English history text-books, G. Davies, *Jour. of Modern Hist.* 1:103, March 1929.   SBF

L102 Smith, Goldwin. *United Kingdom, a political history.* 2 v. N. Y. and London, 1899.

Based on the best secondary authorities; written near the close of his long life by an eminent scholar who was a keen observer and an active controversialist in political affairs. The narrative is vivid, vigorous, and illuminating, though the point of view is often unduly individualistic; closes with the reign of William IV.   GMD

L103 Muir, Ramsay. *Short history of the British commonwealth.* 2 v. (also in 6 pt.), London, 1920–22; 2 v., Yonkers, 1922–23.

Most recent attempt to trace in comparatively brief compass the development of the British nation into the present Commonwealth. Clearly written, with due subordination of details. Least effective in the treatment of medieval institutions, but very successful in linking together English and European relations. Review, *A.H.R.* 28:299, 738, Jan., July, 1923.   ALC

LONGER GENERAL HISTORIES

L121 Hunt, William, and **Poole, Reginald Lane,** ed. *Political history of England.* 12 v. London and N. Y., 1905–10. [1, T. Hodgkin, *To 1066;* 2, G. B. Adams, *1066–1216;* 3, T. F. Tout, *1216–1377;* 4, C. Oman, *1377–1485;* 5, H. A. L. Fisher, *1485–1547;* 6, A. F. Pollard, *1547–1603;* 7, F. C. Montague, *1603–1660;* 8, R. Lodge, *1660–1702;* 9, I. S. Leadam, *1702–1760;* 10, W. Hunt, *1760–1801;* 11, G. C. Brodrick and J. K. Fotheringham, *1801–1837;* 12, S. J. Low and L. C. Sanders, *1837–1901.*] (Excellent bibliographies.)

Coöperative work covering the history of England from the earliest times to the death of Queen Victoria. While the editors have exercised a general supervision in an effort to preserve uniformity, each volume forms a distinct unit and each may be procured separately. The undertaking was designed to embody the results of the most recent scholarship. Primarily a political narrative in chronological order, though religious, intellectual, social, and economic factors are not wholly left out of account. Perhaps too detailed and not entertaining enough for the general reader, while insufficiently documented for the special student. Still the most complete, authoritative, political narrative available covering the whole field to the close of the nineteenth century. Among the outstanding works are those of Adams, Tout, Fisher, Pollard, and Low and Sanders. Review, v. 1, L. M. Larson, *A.H.R.* 12:114, Oct. 1906; v. 2, G. T. Lapsley, *ibid.,* 11:639, Apr. 1906; v. 3, B. Terry, *ibid.* 12:613, Apr. 1907; v. 4, G. Kriehn, *ibid.* 14:570, Apr. 1910; v. 2, C. H. Haskins, *A.H.R.* 11:882, July, 1906; v. 3, C. L. Wells, *ibid.* 16:600, Apr. 1911; v. 7, W. C. Abbott, *ibid.* 13:349, Jan. 1908; v. 8, W. C. Abbott, *ibid.* 15:853, July 1910; v. 9, A. L. Cross, *ibid.* 15:141, Oct. 1909; v. 10, R. C. H. Catterall, *ibid.* 11:382, Jan. 1906; v. 11, R. C. H. Catterall, *ibid.* 12:139, Oct. 1906; v. 12, A. G. Porritt, *ibid.* 13:583, Apr. 1908.   ALC

L122 Oman, Charles, ed. *History of England.* 7 v. London and N. Y., 1904–13. [1, C. Oman, *England before the Norman Conquest;* 2, H. W. C. Davis, *England under the Normans and Angevins;* 3, K. Vickers, *England in the later Middle Ages;* 4, A. D. Innes, *England under the Tudors;* 5, G. M. Trevelyan, *England under the Stuarts;* 6, C. G. Robertson, *England under the Hanoverians;* 7, J. A. R. Marriott, *England since Waterloo.*] (Good bibliographies.)

This series also covers the period from the earliest times to the death of Queen Victoria. The majority of these volumes will probably prove more attractive to the mass of general readers than all but one or two of the works in (L121) Hunt and Poole, since they contain less detailed political narrative. This is also due to the obvious reason that the whole work is comprised in seven instead of twelve volumes; and to the fact that a far greater portion of the space is devoted to the non-political aspects of the subject, with condensation and generalization more in evidence. Trevelyan's *England under the Stuarts* is recognized as the most brilliant and suggestive single volume which has ever been written on the period. Another contribution of distinct literary charm is *England under the Normans and Angevins* by H. W. C. Davis. One who seeks a reasonably full narrative of political events will usually be better satisfied with the volumes edited by Hunt and Poole, while one who desires a more graphic and well-rounded picture of a given period will probably find the Oman series more to his liking. Both series are provided with maps. Review, v. 1, *Athenaeum*, 1:726, June 18, 1910; v. 2, C. H. Haskins, *A.H.R.* 11:882, July 1906; v. 3, C. L. Wells, *ibid.* 19:869, July 1914; v. 4, R. B. Merriman, *ibid.* 11:648, Apr. 1906; v. 5, W. C. Abbott, *ibid.* 11:378, Jan. 1906; v. 6, D. A. Winstanley, *E.H.R.* 26:801, Oct. 1911; v. 7, G. B. Hertz, *E.H.R.* 29:384, Apr. 1914.   ALC

L123 Lingard, John. *History of England from the first invasion by the Romans to the accession of William and Mary in 1688.* 8 v. 1819–30. 6th rev. ed., 10 v., London, 1854–55. Various reprints.

Although the author during his lifetime sought to keep his work abreast of modern learning by frequent revisions, the period relating to the middle ages is now largely superseded. He confined himself mainly to a sober political narrative, writing from the standpoint of a moderate Roman Catholic. His religious faith and his use of hitherto unpublished materials from the Vatican archives lend particular interest to his account of the Reformation. For a good estimate with references to attacks on him by ultramontane extremists, cf. (L22) *Dict. Nat. Biog.* 33:320.   ALC

L124a Ramsay, Sir James H. *Foundations of England or twelve centuries of British history, B. C. 55–A. D. 1154.* 2 v. London, 1898. (Bibliography.)

   b —— *Angevin Empire or the three reigns of Henry II, Richard I, and John, A. D. 1154–1216.* London and N. Y., 1903. (Bibliography.)

   c —— *Dawn of the constitution or the reigns of Henry III and Edward I, A. D. 1216–1307.* London and N. Y., 1908.

   d —— *Genesis of Lancaster or the three reigns of Edward II, Edward III, and Richard II, 1307–1399,* 2 v. Oxford, 1913. [Scholar's history of England, v. 5–6.] (Bibliography.)

   e —— *Lancaster and York, a century of English history, A. D. 1399–1485.* 2 v. Oxford, 1892. (Bibliography.)

Valuable series of laboratory handbooks; 'an English counterpart to the German (P215) *Jahrbücher.*' In a style which is simple, clear, and direct, the author presents a critical digest of the chronicles, adjusted, compared, and arranged in chronological order for a period of over fifteen hundred years. Unfortunately, however, he has made little use of the work of German scholars; he has also failed to check up the chronicles from other contemporary sources. Like (L241) Freeman, he is intolerant of the papacy but, unlike Freeman, he has no sympathy with the medieval church, and so fails to appreciate its influence for good. He attempts to reverse some popular notions and, in many respects, is refreshingly radical, delightfully modern, and for the most part convincing. Ramsay gives much attention to the fixing of battle sites; to medieval campaigning; and to medieval finance; but fails to treat commercial or economic development, intellectual or educational progress. The series is a worthy monument to forty years of unremitting labor. Review of *a.* and *b.,* W. H. Stevenson, *E.H.R.* 19:137,

Jan. 1904; of *c.*, G. T. Lapsley, *ibid.* 24:339, Apr. 1909; of *d.*, G. Baskerville, *ibid.* 30:130, Jan. 1915; of *e.*, T. F. Tout, *ibid.* 8:557, July 1893. BST

L125a Stubbs, William *Historical introductions to the Rolls Series.* Ed. by A. Hassall, London and N. Y., 1902.

b —— *Seventeen lectures on the study of mediaeval and modern history.* 1886. 3rd ed., Oxford, 1900.

a. The historical portions of Stubb's introductions to the chronicles which he edited for the (L71) Rolls Series are here available for the general reader. Vigor of style and unmatched grasp of the period bring the lives and times of Henry II and his sons as close as recent history. The accounts of the beginning of Angevin foreign policy, of Henry II's death, and of John's quarrel with the pope are classic. The editing is inadequate. Review, *E.H.R.* 18:191, Jan. 1903; G. B. Adams, *A.H.R.* 8:527, Apr. 1903. *b.* The first five of these selections from the lectures deal with (cf. A201) historiography and method; the remainder include studies of the court of Henry II, of canon law in England, and of the reigns of Henry VII and Henry VIII—a notable excursus of the great medievalist into the later period. Review, M. Creighton, *E.H.R.* 2:369, Apr. 1887. ABW

PREHISTORIC AND ROMAN TIMES

L201a Windle, Sir Bertram C. A. *Life in early Britain.* London, 1897. (Brief bibliography.)

b Ault, Norman. *Life in ancient Britain, a survey of the social and economic development of the people of England from earliest times to the Roman conquest.* London and N. Y., 1920.

c Mackenzie, Donald A. *Ancient man in Britain.* London, 1922.

a. Chiefly a description of material remains from prehistoric and early historic times, on the basis of which certain broad conclusions are drawn as to racial conditions in early Britain. Though the studies of later investigators have tended to discredit this account in some respects, the volume remains a convenient and fairly reliable manual of British archeology. In the absence of a recent scientific treatment of the subject, reference may be made to *b.* and *c.,* two popular works which must be used with caution. The best statements of current scientific conclusions will be found in the works on prehistory listed in § B. LML

L202a Holmes, Thomas Rice. *Ancient Britain and the invasions of Julius Caesar.* Oxford, 1907.

b Haverfield, Francis J. *Romanization of Roman Britain.* 1906. [Proceedings of the British Academy, v. 2.] 4th rev. ed. by G. Macdonald, Oxford, 1923.

c —— *Roman occupation of Britain.* Ed. by G. Macdonald. Oxford, 1924. [Ford lectures.] (Full bibliography.)

All things considered, the most scholarly studies on Celtic and Roman Britain respectively. Each work is a collection of special studies rather than a narrative. *a.* Covers the whole range from paleolithic times to the end of Caesar's second invasion. The latter half of the book is occupied with technical discussions. Review, F. N. Robinson, *A.H.R.* 13:833, July 1908; H. S. Jones, *E.H.R.* 24:114, Jan. 1909. *b.* First attempt by a competent scholar to summarize the results of recent researches concerning Roman rule in Britain. Review, J. B. Bury, *E.H.R.* 21:759, Oct. 1906. *c.* Though, in part, replacing some of the material in *b.*, does not entirely supersede it. After a survey of the history of the study of Roman Britain, the outstanding features of the conquest, the military occupation, the diffusion of culture, and the transition to Saxon England are set forth with accuracy and clarity. Review, M. Rostovtzeff, *A.H.R.* 30:337, Jan. 1925; S. N. Miller, *E.H.R.* 40:262, Apr. 1925.

The most complete information on Roman Britain is contained in the chapters contributed by Haverfield to the various volumes of (L441) *Victoria history of the counties of England.*   GMD

SAXON PERIOD

L221a Beda, Venerabilis. *Historiam ecclesiasticam gentis Anglorum, Historiam abbatum, Epistolam ad Ecgberctum, una cum Historia abbatum auctore anonymo . . . instruxit Charles Plummer.* 2 v. Oxonii, 1896.

  b Bede, Venerable. *Ecclesiastical history of the English nation.* London and N. Y., 1910. [Everyman's library.]

  c Plummer, Charles, ed. *Two of the Saxon chronicles parallel, with supplementary extracts from the others, . . . on the basis of an edition by John Earle (Oxford, 1865).* 2 v. Oxford, 1892–99.

  d *Anglo-Saxon chronicle.* Tr. by James Ingram. London and N. Y., 1913. [Everyman's library.] (Bibliography.)

Numerous editions of the original texts of these two most important sources for the history of the Saxon period have appeared, but *a* and *c* respectively are the best. Of the numerous translations of each, *b* and *d* respectively may be mentioned as handy and inexpensive.   GMD

L222a Thorpe, Benjamin. *Ancient laws and institutes of England, comprising laws enacted under the Anglo-Saxon kings from Æthelberht to Cnut, with an English translation of the Saxon; the laws called Edward the Confessor's; the laws of William the Conqueror; and those ascribed to Henry the First; also Monumenta ecclesiastica Anglicana, from the seventh to the tenth century; and the ancient Latin version of the Anglo-Saxon laws, with a compendious glossary.* 2 v. London, 1840. [Commissioners of the Public Records.]

  b Liebermann, Felix. *Die Gesetze der Angelsachsen.* 3 v., Halle, 1898–1916.

Much light on institutions may be gleaned from the Anglo-Saxon laws, although they are fragmentary in character, and—owing to the fact that oral tradition largely prevailed—consist mainly of confirmations of and departures from existing custom. *a.* Best edition containing English translation. *b.* Much better edition for the student who can read German. Review, v. 1, C. Gross, *A.H.R.* 3:525, Apr. 1898; G. B. Adams, *A.H.R.* 9:399, Jan. 1904; v. 2, *A.H.R.* 11:932, July 1906; W. E. Lunt, *A.H.R.* 18:387, Jan. 1913.   ALC

L223a Attenborough, Frederick L., ed. and tr. *Laws of the earliest English kings.* Cambridge, Eng., 1922.

  b Robertson, A. J. *Laws of the kings of England from Edmund to Henry I.* Cambridge, Eng., 1925.

a. Goes to the death of Aethelstan; embodies the results of the researches of (L222b.) Liebermann and others who have worked since (L222a) Thorpe's time. Makes the laws of the early period accessible in a new, scholarly English translation of the Anglo-Saxon. Review, L. M. Larson, *A.H.R.* 28:769, July 1923. *b.* Continuation of *a.*   ALC

L224 Plummer, Charles. *Life and times of Alfred the Great.* Oxford, 1902. [Ford lectures.] (Bibliography.)

Not a conventional biography but a series of lectures, constructed with great skill, dealing primarily with the sources for the history of English affairs in the ninth century. Includes the more prominent facts of Alfred's career, but makes no attempt to discuss his achievements in detail. Review, O. H. Richardson, *A.H.R.* 8:380, Jan. 1903.　　　　　　　　　　　　　　　　　　　　　　　　LML

NORMAN PERIOD

L241a Freeman, Edward A. *History of the Norman conquest of England, its causes and its results.* 6 v. Oxford, 1867–79.

b —— *Reign of William Rufus and the accession of Henry the First.* 2 v. Oxford, 1882.

Presents with elaborate detail Anglo-Norman history up to the Conquest, the Conquest itself, and its results to the accession of Henry I. Few historians have been subjected to such searching criticism, such pitiless analysis as Freeman. For much of this Freeman's imperious cock-sureness was quite as much to blame as his faulty methods and hasty judgments. Much of his work, however, is of real value and may not be dismissed with a sneer. His account of the succession of events and his background of antiquarian information abound with suggestion and can generally be relied on. What is also important, Freeman's text is good reading. Too often, however, he permits his dramatic imagination to make havoc of his data, as in his account of the battle of Hastings, or the death of Harold. More serious is Freeman's positive treatment of institutional history. He saw primitive institutions in the rigid outlines of the modern state, often distorted in the light of his own personal current sympathies or antipathies; and to him, the successive stages of development of free government in England seemed the result of a constant reversion to an original German type. The most searching as well as the most merciless critic of Freeman is J. Horace Round. Cf. his (L540a) *Feudal England.*　　　　　　　　　　　　　BST

L242 *Domesday-book, seu Liber censualis Wilhelmi Primi regis Angliae.* V. 1–2, ed. by Abraham Farley, London, 1783; v. 3–4, ed. by Sir Henry Ellis, London, 1816. [Record Commission.]

Best edition of the digested report of the great survey of 1086. Editions of select portions and special studies on Domesday book are listed in (L1) Gross, § 50a.　　　　　　　　　　　　　　　　　　　　　　　　　　　　ALC

EARLIER PLANTAGENET PERIOD

L251a Norgate, Kate. *England under the Angevin kings.* 2 v. London and N. Y., 1887.

b —— *Richard the Lion Heart.* London and N. Y., 1924.

c —— *John Lackland.* London and N. Y., 1902.

d —— *Minority of Henry the Third.* London, 1912.

The narrative is detailed and inaccurate; rarely gives a broad view of the significance of the material; neglects matters of religious or intellectual progress. *a.* Should have been called a History of the House of Anjou. As such it still has much value. Review, E. A. Freeman, *E.H.R.* 2:774, Oct. 1887. *b.* Favorable biographical picture of Richard, done from the chronicles. Lacks many of the essentials for a satisfactory history of England and Normandy during the reign. Review, C. H. Haskins, *A.H.R.* 30:384, Jan. 1925, C. Bémont, *Rev. Hist.* 147:47, Sept. 1924. *c.* Adds little to what is already known of this ungracious prince. The attempt to make a hero of John is not convincing. This may be said, also, of Miss Norgate's attempts to revise other conventional estimates of unpopular characters. Review, G. B. Adams, *A.H.R.* 9:352, Jan. 1904. *d.* Fullest account available for a most important era. Review, H. W. C. Davis, *E.H.R.* 29:145, Jan. 1914.   BST

L252 Green, Alice S. (Mrs. John R.). *Henry the Second.* London and N. Y. 1888. Later reprints. [Twelve English statesmen.]

Admirable monograph; combines picturesqueness with rare scholarship; reveals a thorough knowledge and evident use of the more important sources. In presenting the reign from the biographical point of view, the author has ably demonstrated her main thesis, the statesmanship of Henry—a statesmanship clearly meeting the unparalleled exigencies of the time and yet skilfully designed with a view to the future. Noteworthy are the stimulating and brilliantly conceived chapters devoted to the controversy with Becket and the revolt of the baronage. Review, *Athenaeum*, 12:149, Aug. 4, 1888.   WFG

L253 Salzmann, Louis F. *Henry II.* London and Boston, 1914. [Kings and queens of .England.] (Bibliography.)

Clear, direct account of the reign. Contains nothing new; lacks vividness and color; but is more than a mere catalogue of events. Every important phase of the reign is given attention, though with too little consideration for proportion and perspective, as in the treatment of the struggle with Becket. The use of the sources makes the book more interesting, and the many well-chosen illustrations add to its attractiveness. Review, C. H. Haskins, *A.H.R.* 20:190, Oct. 1914.

OWS

L254 Fitzneale, Richard. *De necessariis observantiis scaccarii dialogus, commonly called Dialogus de scaccario.* Ed. by A. Hughes, C. G. Crump, and C. Johnson. Oxford, 1902. (Bibliography.)

Best of the many printed editions of this famous description of the exchequer in the time of Henry II. The text may also be found in (L62a) Stubbs, *Select charters,* and a translation in (H61c) Henderson, *Select historical documents.*

ALC

L255 *Essays in medieval history presented to Thomas Frederick Tout.* Ed. by Andrew G. Little and Frederick M. Powicke. Manchester, 1925.

Twenty-eight special studies relating chiefly to English history from Henry II to Henry V.   GMD

LATER PLANTAGENET PERIOD

L271a Jenks, Edward. *Edward Plantagenet (Edward I) the English Justinian, or the making of the common law.* London and N. Y., 1902. [Heroes of the nations.] (Bibliography.)

   b Tout, Thomas F. *Edward the First.* London and N. Y., 1893. Several reprints. [Twelve English statesmen.]

a. First six chapters have practically nothing to do with Edward I, but, beginning with ch. 7, the events of the reign are discussed in some detail. Special emphasis is given to legal and constitutional matters. The outlook of the author is that of a lawyer. Review, G. E. Howard, *A.H.R.* 8:117, Oct. 1902.   *b.* Brief, well-balanced account; other aspects of the reign receive equal consideration with the constitutional. Review, G. W. Prothero, *E.H.R.* 9:565, July 1894.

OWS

L272 Mackinnon, James. *History of Edward the Third, 1327–1377.* London and N. Y., 1900.

Useful, because there are so few histories of the reign; readable; mainly political and military. Inadequate, because, though the author industriously read the sources, he lacked critical ability and sympathetic insight, and he failed to utilize modern studies on the reign. Review, O. H. Richardson, *A.H.R.* 6:125, Oct. 1900.

SKM

L273a Trevelyan, George M. *England in the age of Wycliffe.* 1899. New ed., London, 1904. Popular ed., 1909.

b Réville, André, and **Petit-Dutaillis, Charles.** *Le soulèvement des travailleurs d'Angleterre en 1381.* Paris 1898. [Mémoires et documents publié par la Société de l'École des Chartes, v. 2.]

c Oman, Sir Charles W. C. *Great revolt of 1381.* Oxford, 1906.

a. Interesting, popular study devoting its main attention to social and religious conditions during the early years of Richard II's reign, with a survey of the end of the reign of Edward III. The history of the Lollards is continued to 1520. In the main, the author presents an accurate picture of the times, but there are numerous errors in detail. His account of the Peasants' Revolt of 1381 was the first adequate history in English of that movement, but should be supplemented by *b., c.,* and other more recent works. Review of *a.,* J. Tait, *E.H.R.* 15:161, Jan. 1900.   *c.* Complete study of the peasant revolt written from the sources. Review, J. Tait, *E.H.R.* 22:161, Jan. 1907; *A.H.R.* 13:332, Jan. 1908.

SKM

LANCASTRIAN AND YORKIST PERIOD

L291a Wylie, James H. *History of England under Henry the Fourth.* 4 v. London and N. Y., 1884–98. (Bibliographies.)

b —— *Reign of Henry the Fifth.* 3 v. Cambridge, Eng., 1914–29. [1, 1413–1415; 2, 1415–1416; 3, 1416–1422, ed. W. T. Waugh.]

a. Most complete and authoritative history of this period, based on exhaustive study of practically all the available manuscript and printed material. On foreign affairs, the most recent continental studies were utilized so that the work was fully abreast of the results of modern scholarship. Written in annalistic fashion, with no effort at emphasis or proportion, in a style cumbered with archaic words and expressions, with innumerable digressions on persons and medieval customs, all fortified with elaborate footnotes. A mine of information and a great monument of scholarship. V. 4. Contains an appendix of extracts from documents in the Public Record Office and a complete index. Review, v. 1, C. Plummer, *E.H.R.* 1:786, Oct. 1886; v. 2, J. Tait, *E.H.R.* 9:761, Oct. 1894; v. 3, 12:351, Apr. 1897; v. 4, 14:551, July 1899.   *b.* Incomplete work of the same general character as that on Henry IV. There are fewer odd words and fewer digressions, a change which makes the narrative easier to follow. Review, C. L.

Kingsford, *E.H.R.* 30:138, Jan. 1915; 35:133, Jan. 1920; (London) *Times Lit. Suppl.* 28:835, Oct. 24, 1929.   SKM

L292a Scofield, Cora L. *Life and reign of Edward the Fourth, King of England and of France and Lord of Ireland.* 2 v. London and N. Y., 1923. (Bibliography.)

  b Gairdner, James. *History of the life and reign of Richard the Third, to which is added the story of Perkin Warbeck.* 1878. 3rd rev. ed., Cambridge, Eng., 1898.

  a. Exhaustive, scholarly study; chief emphasis on war and diplomacy; somewhat weighted with antiquarian detail. Review, R. A. Newhall, *A.H.R.* 29:541, Apr. 1924; C. L. Kingsford, *E.H.R.* 39:275, Apr. 1924.   ALC

  b. Excellent history of the times and a fair analysis of the character of Richard III, by the greatest authority on the period. The author admits Richard's abilities as a ruler, discounts many tales of his baseness, but in the main confirms the traditional, unfavorable verdict. Review, M. Bateson, *E.H.R.* 14:355, Apr. 1899.   SKM

L293a Fenn, Sir John, ed. *Original letters written during the reigns of Henry VI, Edward IV, and Richard III.* 5 v. London, 1787–1823.

  b Gairdner; James, ed. *Paston letters, 1422–1509 A. D.* 1872–75. Rev. ed., 6 v., London, 1904.

  c Archer-Hind, Mrs. ed. *Paston letters, 1424–1505–6, written by various persons of rank or consequence during the reigns of Henry VI, Edward IV, Richard III, and Henry VII, with précis of less important letters.* 2 v. London and N. Y., 1924. [Everyman's library.]

These editions of letters by or to members of the Paston family in Norfolk furnish no little information on public affairs, but are especially illuminating on domestic life and manners during the Wars of the Roses. *b.* Best edition. The editor's introduction admirably summarizes the information gleaned from the letters. *c.* Most recent edition; abridged; in cheap and convenient form.

GMD

L294 Kingsford, Charles L. *Prejudice and promise in fifteenth-century England.* Oxford, 1925. [Ford lectures.]

Presents and illustrates two theses: first, that the truth about the period has been distorted through the prejudice of the Tudor historical writers; second, that the truth can only be discovered from a study of the sources made with a view that this century was a 'seed-time of the future.' With these premises, the intellectual ferment, the social growth, the spirit of adventure, and the commercial enterprise of the time are well depicted.   GMD

TUDOR PERIOD

L301 Seebohm, Frederic. *Oxford reformers: John Colet, Erasmus, and Thomas More, being a history of their fellow-work.* 1867. 3rd rev. ed., 1877; new ed., by H. E. Seebohm, London and N. Y., 1914. [Everyman's library.] (Bibliography.)

The 'fellow-work' of the three friends in promoting the actual practice of Christianity among nations; their intimate conversation, correspondence, and daily life; and the analysis of the thought-currents, influences, and tendencies of this fascinating age, clearly and simply stated, make this book one of lasting value.   JEG

L302 Pollard, Albert F. *Henry VIII.* 1902. New ed., London and N. Y., 1905. (Bibliographical footnotes.)

Scholarly, well-written work, by one of the foremost students of English history. Professor Pollard has carefully worked in the vast stores of source material opened up since (L304) Froude's masterly writing, but he has been seriously criticized by competent students for his too favorable portraiture of the king. Review, J. Gairdner, *E.H.R.* 21:155, Jan. 1906; R. B. Merriman, *A.H.R.* 11:650, Apr. 1906.   PVBJ

L303 Brewer, John. *Reign of Henry VIII from his accession to the death of Wolsey.* Ed. by James Gairdner. 2 v. London, 1884.

Not designed as a complete history of the period, but a reprinting of the remarkable introductions to the (L73a) *Letters and papers* of the reign of Henry VIII which were written by their first editor, J. S. Brewer. Brilliant study, mainly of diplomatic history; the foundation of all later accounts. V. 2. Contains an elaborate discussion of Henry's divorce and of the fall of Wolsey for whom the author exhibits marked partiality. Review, *Spectator,* 57:949, 981, July 19, 26, 1884.   SKM

L304 Froude, James Anthony. *History of England from the fall of Wolsey to the defeat of the Spanish Armada.* 1856–93. New ed., 12 v. N. Y., 1899.

One of the really great historical works of the last century. Froude ransacked the collections at the British Museum, the Rolls House, and Simancas, thereby attaining unrivalled knowledge of the sources. He possessed rare political insight, a fascinating style, and a genius for vivid portrayal. Unfortunately his work is marred by numerous inaccuracies. He never comprehended the sanctity of inverted commas, and was curiously incapable of summarizing with precision. These defects—the word 'froudacity' was coined to describe them—make it extremely easy to criticize his work in detail; nevertheless, for a general picture of the period, the work remains unrivalled. His conception of Henry VIII, 'the majestic lord who broke the bonds of Rome,' was too flattering to win the approval of Froude's contemporaries; and even today, when the common verdict on his work is far more favorable, it is generally acknowledged that his judgments are saner on the period after the accession of Edward VI. The volume on Mary contains some of the finest passages in the whole work. Cf. Frederic Harrison, *Tennyson, Ruskin, Mill, and other literary estimates,* ch. 12, London, 1899.   RBM

L305 Merriman, Roger B. *Life and letters of Thomas Cromwell.* 2 v. Oxford, 1902. (Bibliography.)

Presents Cromwell as, in no sense, a hero of the Reformation, but as a patriotic statesman whose actions were invariably inspired by political motives. The letters, 'twenty-one of which have neither been printed nor calendared before,' constitute the second volume and more than one-fourth of the first. Review, *A.H.R.* 8:383, Jan. 1903.   PVBJ

L306 Pollard, Albert F. *England under Protector Somerset, an essay.* London, 1900. (Valuable bibliography.)

First important work to emanate from the pen of the foremost living authority on the Tudor period. Based on a thorough knowledge of the sources and secondary works; characterized by vigor, clarity, and great positiveness of expression. Highly favorable to Somerset; attributes to his successor, the Duke of Northumberland, a number of the mistakes previously credited to the Protector. The picture of Somerset as a defender of popular liberties is somewhat overdrawn and has been considerably toned down in his later volume in (L121) Hunt and Poole, *Political history of England.* Review, J. Gairdner, *E.H.R.* 16:151, Jan. 1901; E. P. Cheyney, *A.H.R.* 6:553, Apr. 1901.   RBM

L307 Creighton, Mandell. *Queen Elizabeth.* 1896. [Goupil illustrated series of historical volumes.] Popular ed., London and N. Y., 1899.

Forceful, lifelike character study of Elizabeth and her contemporaries, dealing with motives, policies, and accomplishments. Intended to portray, in a brilliantly interpretive essay, a character which the author believes shaped the course of events rather than to present a carefully annotated history of her time. The first edition was richly illustrated. Review, W. F. Tilton, *A.H.R.* 2:346, Jan. 1897.   JEG

L308 Cheyney, Edward P. *History of England from the defeat of the Spanish Armada to the death of Elizabeth, with an account of English institutions during the later sixteenth and early seventeenth centuries.* 2 v. N. Y. and London, 1914–26.

Standard authority on the last fifteen years of Queen Elizabeth. There is nothing startlingly new in the material collected or the point of view from which it is treated, but the sanity of the author's judgments, the soundness and thoroughness of his scholarship are evident on every page. Review, R. B. Merriman, *A.H.R.* 19:883, July 1914; 31:769, July 1926.   RBM

L309a *Tudor studies presented by the Board of Studies in History in the University of London to Albert Frederick Pollard.* Ed. by Robert W. Seton-Watson. London and N. Y., 1924.

b Liljegren, S. B. *Fall of the monasteries and the social changes in England leading up to the great revolution.* Lund, 1924. [Reprint from Universitets Arsskrift.]

a. Twelve essays, done from the sources, on administrative history and political thought chiefly in early Tudor times. Review, E. P. Cheyney, *A.H.R.* 30:805, July 1925. *b.* Good statement of the thesis that the economic changes resulting from the dissolution had far-reaching political significance; not a definitive work. Review, R. H. Tawney, *E.H.R.* 40:130, Jan. 1925.   GMD

STUART PERIOD

L321a Gardiner, Samuel. *History of England from the accession of James I to the outbreak of the Civil War, 1603–1642.* 1863–82 (under five different titles). New ed., 10 v., London and N. Y., 1901.

b —— *History of the great Civil War, 1642–1649.* 1886–91. New ed., 4 v., London and N. Y., 1901.

c —— *History of the Commonwealth and Protectorate, 1649–1656.* 1894–1903. New ed., 4 v., London and N. Y., 1903.

Gardiner spent forty years in writing his eighteen volumes and he left few lines that need to be erased. No historian has ever written with more minute accuracy, none has been at greater pains to search out all the evidence. He dealt with the most controversial period in English history, and though himself a descendant of Cromwell and historical heir to the Liberal traditions of Godwin, Carlyle, Forster, and Sanford, he contrived with effort to be just. He was not a constitutional historian, though when he turned aside to comment upon the constitution, he could be both searching and wise; he was not an historian of society, though occasional paragraphs make us wish that he had chosen to be; he was in no way a philosophic historian; he told the plain unvarnished tale of what came next. That history is a narrative of people and political events was to him not only a tradition but a creed; he believed that from a close sequence truth as to situations and persons would emerge. Nowhere was he more at home than in following through the turns of European diplomacy; he ransacked the archives of Europe that no clue to Jacobean policy might escape him. Chronological pursuit served his curiosity as to motives and conduct. Generations had vexed themselves as to whether Cromwell was honest and Gardiner settled that question. Into the motives and vacillations of Charles I he probed deeply, yet with all possible sympathy. Gardiner's work shows so much growth in insight that he is not always consistent. He had little knack of telling a story; he never stooped to be dramatic; he dealt with the most picturesque period in English history but his restrained pages give few portraits and those in quiet tones; hence he has been called dull. Yet his chapters seldom lack distinction and there are passages that come near to being a part of English literature. Cf. ·C. H. Firth, article in *Dict. Nat. Biog.*: 'Gardiner'; (L22) J. F. Rhodes, *Historical essays*, p. 143–150, N. Y., 1909; R. G. Usher, *Critical study of the historical method of S. R. Gardiner*, St. Louis, 1915; Wallace Notestein, 'Stuart period, unsolved problems,' *Am. Hist. Assn., Annual report, 1916*, p. 391–399.

WN

L322 Firth, Charles H. *Last years of the Protectorate, 1656–1658.* 2 v. London and N. Y., 1909.

Firth's continuation of (L321c) Gardiner is marked by the same elaborate research and painstaking accuracy. Firth has settled the question of Cromwell and the crown, has gathered together Cromwell's legislation, and has elucidated his Scottish policy. He edited numerous volumes of contemporary sources whose introductions constitute a considerable part of the best monographic literature on the Interregnum. Hence he was perhaps better qualified than Gardiner himself to deal with Cromwell's last years. He is more naturally impartial and writes with more lightness and ease. It is to be wished that he had not set himself to be so absolutely objective and had ventured to give more of his opinions. Review, *Athenæum*, 1:18, Jan. 29, 1910; W. C. Abbott, *A.H.R.* 15:851, July 1910.

WN

L323 Ranke, Leopold von. *History of England, principally in the seventeenth century.* 6 v. Oxford, 1875. Tr. by C. W. Boase and others from *Englische Geschichte vornehmlich im sechzehnten und siebzehnten Jahrhundert*, 6 v. and index, Berlin, 1859–69.

This work, although it contains a brief introductory survey from the earliest times to the death of Elizabeth and a supplementary outline of the reigns of Anne and the first two Georges, is devoted mainly to the seventeenth century, 1603–1702. Since the publication of (L321) Gardiner's monumental work it is less valuable than formerly for the period previous to the Restoration. Begun by a veteran worker in European history when he was over sixty years old, it is particularly notable for its ripe grasp of diplomatic history and foreign relations. From the standpoint of a general history its chief defect is its almost total neglect of the non-political aspects of the subject. Cf. (M252) Ranke, *Civil wars and monarchy in France.*   ALC

L324 Clarendon, Edward Hyde, Earl of. *History of the rebellion and civil wars in England.* 1702–04; 2nd ed. by B. Bandinel, 8 v., 1826; rev. ed. by W. D. Macray, 6 v., Oxford, 1888; many other editions.

Though Clarendon wrote of the time in which he himself lived, he should not be rated as a contemporary chronicler but rather as an historian. This work is based upon his *History,* written between 1646 and 1648, drawn from contemporary narratives as well as his own knowledge, and upon his *Life,* written between 1668 and 1670, based largely on memory. It was put together in less than a year, 'by the simple process of dovetailing the *History* into the *Life* and adding a certain amount of new material to supplement and complete the two' (Firth). As might be expected, it contains many inaccuracies and contradictions. It has become a classic because of the author's general knowledge of his time, because of his judgment on events and men and because of his style, which makes Clarendon's name great in literature as well as in history. Cf. C. H. Firth, 'Clarendon's History of the Rebellion,' *E. H. R.* 19:26, 246, 464, Jan., Apr., July 1904.   FHR

L325 Masson, David. *Life of John Milton narrated in connexion with the political, ecclesiastical, and literary history of his time.* 6 v. and index, Cambridge, Eng., 1859–94. New ed., v. 1–3, London, 1881–96.

Masson worked before (L321) Gardiner and (L322) Firth, and without the sources since made available. He used some materials in the Public Record Office, but mainly relied on the sources then in print. He touched only the surface of the pamphlet material of the Great Civil War. Consequently, much of his work now appears inaccurate and superficial. As a popularly written supplement to more recent works, Masson is still interesting and somewhat informing, especially on political and ecclesiastical theory. His sympathies usually correspond to those of Milton; he is insufficiently critical of the fallacies and contradictions in Milton's political works, and has a strong anti-royalist bias. Review, *Spectator,* 53:916, July 17, 1880.   TCP

L326 Hutchinson, Lucy. *Memoirs of the life of Colonel Hutchinson, governor of Nottingham, to which are added the letters of Colonel Hutchinson and other papers.* Ed. by J. Hutchinson. 1806. Rev. ed., with notes by C. H. Firth, 2 v., London, 1885. Reprint, N. Y., 1908. [Everyman's library.]

Mrs. Hutchinson, a woman of exceptional intellectual attainments, interestingly describes the landed gentry in Nottingham during the Puritan revolution and civil wars. Her bias against cavalier and Presbyterian in favor of her husband is largely corrected by Professor Firth's notes. Review, S. R. Gardiner, *E.H.R.* 1:173, Jan. 1886.   WTM

L327a Carlyle, Thomas. *Letters and speeches of Oliver Cromwell.* 1845. Ed. with notes by S. C. Lomas and introduction by C. H. Firth, 3 v., London, 1904. Many other editions.

b Firth, Charles H. *Oliver Cromwell and the rule of the Puritans in England.* London and N. Y., 1900. [Heroes of the nations.]

c Gardiner, Samuel R. *Oliver Cromwell.* 1899. [Goupil's illustrated series of historical volumes.] Popular ed., London and N. Y., 1901.

d —— *Cromwell's place in history.* London and N. Y., 1897.

e Morley, John, Viscount. *Oliver Cromwell.* N. Y., 1900.

f Roosevelt, Theodore. *Oliver Cromwell.* N. Y., 1900.

a. Epoch-making book, which practically revolutionized the prevailing conception of Cromwell and helped to destroy the Hume tradition. Carlyle utilized two-fifths of the space in explanations and interpretation, but for the most part permitted Cromwell to tell his own story. Especially valuable for Cromwell's Irish and foreign policies. The editor added many items to those printed by Carlyle, and re-edited others, as Carlyle was too favorable to Cromwell and exceedingly careless in copying manuscripts. The introduction is invaluable on this point. Review, R. C. H. Catterall, *A.H.R.* 10:646, Apr. 1905. *b.* Based upon a study of the sources; contains a satisfactory sketch of Puritanism; excellent for the military side and for Cromwell's domestic policy; Cromwell does not appear in so bold relief as in *c.* Review, S. R. Gardiner, *E.H.R.* 15:803, Oct. 1900. *c.* Clear, straightforward, scholarly biography written from source materials. Indicates that Cromwell was no hypocrite, although his opportunism frequently caused him to change his plans. Suggests that Puritan opposition to Anglicanism was probably directed more against its organization than its ceremonies. Review, C. H. Firth, *E.H.R.* 16:582, July 1901. WTM
d. Aims to show that Cromwell's work was premature and, so far as contemporary influence was concerned, rather destructive than constructive, though his efforts ultimately bore fruit. A penetrating study. Review, Goldwin Smith, *A.H.R.* 3:135, Oct. 1897. *e.* By a practiced biographer and man of letters, who, however, lacked the knowledge of the sources over which Gardiner and Firth gained such a recognized mastery. Aims to pass moral judgments on the men and events of the time. Review, G. Jones, *A.H.R.* 6:562, Apr. 1901. *f.* Based on very limited reading. Chiefly interesting as a reflection of the views of the author. Review, G. Jones, *A.H.R.* 6:562, Apr. 1901. ALC

L328 Pease, Theodore C. *Leveller movement, a study in the history and political theory of the English great civil war.* Washington, 1916. [H. B. Adams prize essay.] (Bibliography.)

Excellent contribution based on thorough research. Review, W. C. Abbott, *A.H.R.* 22:900, July 1917. ALC

L329a Burnet, Gilbert. *Bishop Burnet's History of his own time.* 1724–25. Ed. by M. J. Routh, *with the suppressed passages of the first volume, and notes by the earls of Dartmouth and Hardwicke, and Speaker Onslow, hitherto unpublished, to which are added the cursory remarks of Swift, and other observations,* 6 v., Oxford, 1823. V. 1–2, ed. by O. Airy, Oxford, 1897–1900. Many other ed.

b Foxcroft, Helen C., ed. *Supplement to Burnet's History of my own time, derived from his original memoirs, his autobiography, his letters to Admiral Herbert, and his private meditations, all hitherto unpublished.* Oxford, 1902.

a. For the period, 1660 to 1714, Bishop Burnet's account remains the 'cardinal authority,' despite (L323) Ranke's caustic criticisms. It is not a history, but the memoirs of a bustling churchman, usually more engrossed in politics than in religion. Strongly Whiggish and Low Church in tone, the work attempts to be fair to contemporaries as the variations in the printed work from the original draft sufficiently attest. Especially valuable for Anglo-Scottish relations, the Popish plot, and the preparations for William of Orange's expedition to England. Airy utilized the wide variety of sources made available since 1823, in his edition covering Charles II's reign. Reviews, H. O. Wakeman, *E.H.R.* 13:170, Jan. 1898; C. H. Firth, *ibid.*, 15:585, July 1900.   *b.* Indicates in what respects the printed work varies from the original manuscript. Review, R. S. Rait, *E.H.R.* 18:171, Jan. 1903. For the controversy over the earlier editions, see (L323) Ranke, *History of England,* 6:47–101, and O. Airy ed., *Bishop Burnet's History,* 1:vi–ix.

WTM

L330a Pepys, Samuel. *Diary.* Deciphered from the shorthand manuscript in the Bodleian library by John Smith, ed. by Richard G. Neville, Baron Braybrooke, 1825. Deciphered from his shorthand manuscript in the Pepysian library, Magdalene college, Cambridge, and ed. by Mynors Bright, 1875–79. Ed. by Henry B. Wheatley, 9 v., London and N. Y., 1893–99. Many other ed.

  b Evelyn, John. *Diary.* Ed. by William Bray, 1818–19. Ed. by William Upcott, 1827; rev. ed. by Henry B. Wheatley, 4 v., London, 1879. New ed. by Austin Dobson, 3 v., London and N. Y., 1906. (Bibliography.) Many other ed.

  a. The more complete edition by Wheatley entirely supersedes its predecessors. Originally kept in cipher, this diary, covering the years 1659–1669, is the most revealing and human document in the English language, and throws a flood of light on all aspects of the life of the Restoration period. Cf. (L22) *Dict. of Nat. Biog.,* 1st ed., 44:360–366; and (L10) Ponsonby, *English diaries,* 82–95.   *b.* The diary of a cultivated gentleman, one of the pioneers of the Royal Society, a royalist who was not in sympathy with the life at court. Not kept from day to day, but at irregular intervals. Next to *a.*, from which it differs so widely in character, the most notable diary of the century. Cf. (L22) *Dict. of Nat. Biog.,* 1st ed., 18:79–82; and (L10) Ponsonby, *English diaries,* 96–102.   ALC

L331 Airy, Osmund. *Charles II.* 1901. [Goupil's illustrated series of historical volumes.] Popular ed., London and N. Y., 1904.

  By-product of the authoritative edition of (L329a) Burnet, *History of my own time.* Scholarly, entertaining, and eminently judicial in portraying Charles II as selfish, deceitful, and depraved. Airy recognizes that Charles was able and insists that his own selfish interests always remained paramount. Fuller consideration of the political movements of the time would have afforded a truer estimate of the reign. Review, A. G. Porritt, *A.H.R.* 10:442, Jan. 1905.   WTM

L332a Lister, Thomas H. *Life and administration of Edward, first earl of Clarendon, with original correspondence and authentic papers never before published.* 3 v. London, 1837–38.

  b Craik, Sir Henry. *Life of Edward, earl of Clarendon, lord high chancellor of England.* 2 v. London, 1911.

  a. Despite its age this is still the standard biography of Clarendon. The work of a strong admirer; defends Clarendon's policy, even in ecclesiastical matters; probably unfair to both Charles II and Cromwell and perhaps to the other ministers of Charles II; needs correction, in the light of more recent knowledge, both in these matters and in the account of foreign policy after 1660. Its greatest value lies in the quotation of documents both in the text and in v. 3, in which are printed letters drawn from hitherto unpublished Clarendon papers. Review, *Athenaeum,* 1:353, 372, May 19, 26, 1838. *b.* Almost unqualified eulogy, which fails to supersede *a.* Review, *A.H.R.* 17:821, July, 1912. WTM

L333 Clarke, James S., ed. *Life of James the Second, king of England, &c., collected out of memoirs writ of his own hand, together with the king's advice to his son, and His Majesty's will, published from the original Stuart manuscripts in Carlton-House.* 2 v. London, 1816.

Often styled the autobiography of James II; really an eighteenth century compilation from notes left by James, probably by Lewis Innes though also ascribed to his brother Thomas. It is of uneven value, the best portion being that between 1678 and 1685, for in the account of these years the original manuscripts were most freely utilized. Some caution is necessary in using the other portions. Despite its one-sided view, it gives much information on Restoration history, especially on matters in which James was personally concerned. Review, *Edinburgh Rev.* 26:402, June 1816; (L323) Ranke, *History of England,* 6:31–45.

WTM

L334 Macaulay, Thomas Babington, Baron. *History of England from the accession of James II.* 5 v. 1849–61. Numerous reprints. Rev. ed. by E. P. Cheyney, 10 v., Philadelphia, 1898, reprint 1910 [Bibliophile ed.]; by C. H. Firth, 6 v., London and N. Y., 1913–15.

Macaulay's *chef d'oeuvre,* one of the most brilliant and popular pieces of serious historical writing in any language, covers twelve years, from 1685 to 1697. The style is animated, interesting, and often dramatic; for to Macaulay, the Anglo-French rivalry was a drama in which William III was the hero and Louis XIV, James II, and Marlborough in turn played the rôle of villain. The leading characters are too clearly drawn. Frequently the pictures are too favorable, often too dark, as of Princess Anne, Lady Marlborough, and William Penn. Despite its partisanship, the history is an enduring monument to the vast erudition, painstaking research, and literary genius of one who was never historically trained and whose Whiggish predilections were exceedingly strong.

Firth's edition is the best and is a triumph of the bookmaker's art, but unfortunately the text remains unedited and is not annotated. There are errors in identifying some of the illustrations, although the greatest disappointment arises from the failure to utilize original portraits, rather than engravings, for illustrations. The edition aids, however, in making even Macaulay's treatment more vivid. Reviews, W. C. Abbott, *A.H.R.* 19:612, Apr. 1914; 20:149, Oct. 1914; 20:662, Apr. 1915; 21:145, Oct. 1915. General criticisms of Macaulay's historical method may be found in John Paget, *New 'examen,' or, an inquiry into the evidence relating to certain passages in Lord Macaulay's History,* Edinburgh, 1861, reprinted in his *Paradoxes and puzzles,* Edinburgh, 1874; and in (A249a) Gooch, *History and historians in the nineteenth century,* 294–304. WTM

L335a Feiling, Keith. *History of the Tory party, 1640–1714.* Oxford and N. Y., 1924.

b Woods, Maurice. *History of the Tory party in the seventeenth and eighteenth centuries, with a sketch of its development in the nineteenth century.* London, 1924. (Bibliography.)

c Morgan, William T. *English political parties and leaders in the reign of Queen Anne, 1702–1710.* New Haven and London, 1920. [Yale historical publications. H. B. Adams, prize essay.] (Bibliography.)

Good recent studies of the early history of parties. *a.* Not merely a history of the Tory party written from sources, both printed and manuscript, but an interesting and detailed account of the political history of the post-restoration period. Emphasizes the political thought of the times as the basis of party history. Review, G. M. Trevelyan, *E.H.R.* 40:132, Jan. 1925; W. C. Abbott, *A.H.R.* 30:355, Jan. 1925. *b.* Covers a longer period; more philosophical; more Tory in bias; less well documented. Review of *a.* and *b.*, W. T. Morgan, *Hist. Outlook,* 16:129, March 1925. *c.* Detailed study of a brief but important period in the development of parties. Review, A. L. Cross, *A.H.R.* 26:132, Oct. 1920.

                                                                        EPCe

EIGHTEENTH CENTURY

L351a Stanhope, Philip Henry, Earl [earlier styled Lord Mahon]. *History of England, comprising. the reign of Queen Anne until the peace of Utrecht, 1701–1713.* 1870. 4th ed. 2 v., London, 1872.

b —— *History of England from the peace of Utrecht to the peace of Versailles, 1713–1783.* 1836–53. 5th ed., 7 v., London, 1858.

a. Written to fill the gap between (L334) Macaulay's history and *b.* Merely a chronological narrative; strongest on the diplomatic and military aspects. Although somewhat disappointing in style and in its treatment of domestic politics, it remains the most acceptable brief narrative for the period. *b.* Serious attempt to write the history of eighteenth century England. Purely political in scope; emphasizes the military, diplomatic, and colonial phases of English history. England's relations with India and America are treated at length, but Ireland, Scotland, and Wales are somewhat neglected. Although Tory in viewpoint, it is based upon the sources, printed and unprinted. Despite the failure to appreciate the influence of social and economic movements, it is the best narrative of the eighteenth century. Review, *Edinburgh Rev.* 64:232, Oct. 1836.   WTM

L352a Lecky, William E. H. *History of England in the eighteenth century.* 8 v. London, 1878–90.

b —— *History of England in the eighteenth century.* 1892. Reprint, 7 v., London and N. Y., 1913.

c —— *History of Ireland in the eighteenth century.* 1892. Reprint, 5 v., London and N. Y., 1913.

d —— *American revolution.* Ed. by J. A. Woodburn, N. Y., 1898. (Bibliography.)

e —— *French revolution.* Ed. by H. E. Bourne, N. Y., 1904.

a. This history differs from that of Stanhope mainly by its study of social and economic tendencies, by its emphasis upon Irish history and by its philosophic insight into political life. The first chapters are remarkable for their extensive grasp of English institutional life. The monarchy, the aristocracy, the trading classes, the press, all come under observation. Although Lecky neglects the first half of the century in his narrative, his fuller treatment of the American and French Revolutions is scholarly and luminous. His accounts of the American Revolution and the Wesleyan Revival are still, perhaps, the fairest summaries of these movements. Even better are the chapters dealing with Ireland, although in places intensely Irish in spirit; for here, even more than in the remainder of the book, his conclusions are based upon a laborious study of the unpublished materials in the British and Irish archives. Review, *Edinburgh Rev.* 148:81, July 1878; 156:203, July 1882; 166:346, Oct. 1887. *b.* and *c.* Later editions of *a.*, with the English and Irish sections arranged as separate works. *d.* and *e.* Editions of selected materials in *a.* relating to the two subjects concerned. Review of *d.*, E. C. Burnett, *A.H.R.* 4:762, July 1899.   WTM

L353a Coxe, William. *Memoirs of the life and administration of Sir Robert Walpole, earl of Orford, with original correspondence and authentic papers.* 1798. 3rd ed., 4 v., London ,1816.

b Morley, John, Viscount. *Walpole.* London and N. Y., 1889. Later reprints. [Twelve English statesmen.]

a. Written from the Whig standpoint; valuable for the original papers used; but commonplace and annalistic in treatment. *b.* This brief, interesting biography is a welcome relief from Coxe's dull pages. Based on the printed sources; skilfully interprets Walpole's career; unduly critical of Walpole's political rivals. The chapters on Tory supremacy from 1710 to 1714 and on the cabinet are particularly suggestive. Review, *E.H.R.* 6:193, Jan. 1891.   WTM

L354a Rosebery, Archibald, Earl of. *Lord Chatham, his early life and connections.* N. Y. and London, 1910.

b Ruville, Albert von. *William Pitt, earl of Chatham.* 3 v. London and N. Y., 1907. Tr. by H. J. Chaytor and M. Morison from *William Pitt, Graf von Chatham,* 3 v., Berlin, 1905.

c Williams, Basil. *Life of William Pitt, earl of Chatham.* 2 v. London and N. Y., 1913. (Bibliography.)

a. Least important of the three. Although the author occasionally borrows from the future in order to round out the sketches of some of his characters, the narrative stops at 1756, when Pitt finally attains to power. Colloquial style; particularly happy in portraitures of Chatham's early contemporaries; gives valuable information on his association with the Grenvilles. The picture drawn of Chatham himself is not particularly attractive or coherent and, perhaps because the story lacks an impressive climax, it fails to explain his greatness. Review, A. L. Cross, *A.H.R.* 16:609, Apr. 1911. *b.* Both its merits and defects stamp the author's nationality. Wide and careful reading, patient sifting of evidence, scrupulous attention to detail—in short, erudition above all else is apparent on every page. While his study of Chatham reveals an impartiality of which a British writer is scarcely capable, he fails to show that enthusiasm for the Great Commoner without which no picture can be drawn with complete truth. Though doing homage to his genius, particularly in the conduct of war, Ruville never quite understands why the Great Commoner cast a spell over his contemporaries. Chatham's character is dissected with a candor amounting at times almost to brutality. Ruville is singularly efficient in his understanding both of Chatham's political environment and of the pernicious effects which that environment had upon one who was instinctively superior to it. Review, *A.H.R.* 12:371, Jan. 1907. *c.* Williams is less concerned with fitting Chatham into the political setting, but is, rather, at pains to divorce him from it, presenting him wherever possible as a protagonist of popular government. Where Ruville sees him as a demagogue, Williams portrays him as the conscious mouthpiece of the articulate

forces outside parliament and gives convincing evidence that a sympathetic relationship with the people was one of the main channels, so to speak, of Chatham's
dramatic career. Incomparably the best work on Chatham; brings out more
clearly than any previous work the statesman's ever-increasing influence upon
public events during the period of his rise to power; relates the epic of his
triumphant ministry with precision and force. While not unaware of Chatham's
blemishes, the author steadily refuses to allow the grandeur of his hero to be
obscured by faults of character. The scholarship of the book is assured by the
use of an exceptionally wide range of historical material. Yet the success of
this biography is in large measure due to its charm of style. Chatham may be
truly said to live within its pages. Review, W. L. Grant, *E.H:R.* 29:379, Apr.
1914.   TWR

L355a Fortescue, Sir John, ed. *Correspondence of King George the Third from
    1760 to December, 1783.* 6 v. London, 1927–28.

b Fitzmaurice, Edmond G. Petty-Fitzmaurice, Baron. *Life of William,
    earl of Shelburne, afterwards first marquess of Lansdowne, with extracts
    from his papers and correspondence.* 3 v., 1875–76. 2nd rev. ed., 2 v.,
    London, 1912.

a. A definitive edition; the papers relate almost entirely to political and public
matters, but also throw much light upon the King's personality. Review of vols.
1 and 2, R. G. Adams, *A.H.R.* 33:641, Apr. 1928; of vols. 3–6, R. L. Schuyler,
(N. Y.) *Nation,* 127:91, July 25, 1928.   SBF

b. Neither an entertaining picture nor a scholarly study; yet of considerable
value, not only because of the large amount of manuscript material consulted, but
also by reason of the letters and other contemporary evidence interspersed throughout the narrative. Review, *Athenaeum,* 1:317, March 6, 1875; 1:257, Feb. 19, 1876.
                                                                          TWR

L356a Morley, John, Viscount. *Edmund Burke, a historical study.* London,
    1867.

b —— *Burke.* 1879. New ed., London, 1902. [English men of letters.]

c Samuels, Arthur P. I. *Early life, writings, and correspondence of the
    Rt. Hon. Edmund Burke.* Cambridge, Eng., 1923. (Bibliographical foot-
    notes.)

a. and *b.* These little books supplement each other admirably, as *a.* is a critical
study and *b.* biographical. Each is well written, although the author occasionally
seems somewhat too sympathetic with Burke and his philosophy. The chapters
in *a.* on the constitution and on the French Revolution are excellent. Review of *a.*,
Athenaeum, 2:723, Nov. 30, 1867; of *b.*, *ibid.* 2:335, Sept. 13, 1879. *c.* Not
easily readable, but presents valuable new materials.   WTM

L357a Rosebery, Archibald, Earl of. *Pitt.* London and N. Y., 1892. Later
    reprints. [Twelve English statesmen.]

b Rose, John Holland. *William Pitt and national revival.* London, 1911.

c —— *William Pitt and the great war.* London, 1911.

d —— *Life of William Pitt.* London, 1923; N. Y., 1924.

e Stanhope, Philip Henry, Earl. *Life of William Pitt.* 4 v. London,
    1861–62.

a. Brilliant little study, though not based on as extensive a range of sources
as *b.* and *c.* Pitt's greatness is not unduly magnified; nor are his weaknesses

concealed. The author's style is smooth and animated, his insight penetrating, and his portraitures, notably of Fox, are remarkable in their clearness and their deft and human touch. Review, S. Walpole, *E.H.R.* 7:177, Jan. 1892. *b.* and *c.* Constitute an exhaustive piece of work and contain a great deal of new information on his foreign policy, a feature of his life which Rosebery perhaps unduly slighted. Rose's authorship is a guarantee of diligence in searching out and examining materials. The diplomatic history of Europe from 1783 to Pitt's death in 1806 is consequently written with unparalleled fullness on the British side. The author's judgments are generally keen and convincing, but his chief defect is his strong partisanship, which makes these volumes something of an apology. Undoubtedly he substantiates Pitt's greatness; yet it is quite impossible to forget that his hero was assisted to power by an unscrupulous abuse of the royal influence, and that his early idealism was all but stifled by his unnatural alliance with the narrowest of monarchs. Review of *b.*, E. D. Adams, *A.H.R.* 17:134, Oct. 1911; H. E. Egerton, *E.H.R.* 26:589, July 1911; of *c.*, E. D. Adams, *A.H.R.* 18:137, Oct. 1912; C. T. Atkinson, *E.H.R.* 27:581, July 1912. *d.* Combines *b.* and *c.* in full in single volume reprint. TWR

e. Still an indispensable authority; chiefly valuable for extracts from unpublished correspondence and other manuscript material; by an admirer, but an admirer not without discrimination. Review, *Athenaeum* 1:457, Apr. 6, 1861; 1:358, March 15, 1862. ALC

NINETEENTH CENTURY

L381 Trevelyan, George M. *British history in the nineteenth century, 1782–1901.* London and N. Y., 1922. (Bibliography.)

Undoubtedly the best one-volume work available for the history of Great Britain during the last century. Excellently written. Although there are two fine chapters on conditions at the eve of the Industrial Revolution and although British lands overseas are not wholly neglected, the work is mainly a political history of England. Review, G. Hedger, *A.H.R.* 28:114, Oct. 1922. ALC

L382a Slater, Gilbert. *Making of modern England.* 1913. Rev. ed., Boston, 1915. (Bibliography.)

b Blease, Walter L. *Short history of English liberalism.* London and N. Y., 1913.

a. Straightforward narrative of the history of England from the beginning of the nineteenth century to the end of the first decade of the twentieth. Deals with social and economic rather than with political history, though the latter is not neglected when social and economic facts eventuated in political action. Review, *Nation* (N. Y.), 96:642, July 1913. WTL

b. Thoughtful, suggestive interpretation of social, religious, political, commercial, colonial, class, and diplomatic questions of the last century and a half in the light of a particular political philosophy. Liberalism is a term employed not to indicate a party or a policy, but an attitude of mind. The writer in his devotion to liberal ideas and their triumph perhaps does less than justice to other views. WTR

L383 Maxwell, Sir Herbert. *Century of empire, 1801–1900.* 3 v. London, 1909–11.

Narrative of the political history of the British empire from the Conservative and Unionist points of view, done in the style of the books of a generation ago.

Based on (B28a) *Annual register* and the familiar published correspondence, diaries, and similar papers. The author makes no attempt to discover the forces that shaped the direction of events; he is satisfied merely to tell the story of the events themselves. He is not a violent partisan and is able at times to see merits in men for whose political views he has little sympathy. Review, G. B. Hertz, *E.H.R.* 25:590, July 1910; 26:636, July 1911; E. D. Adams, *A.H.R.* 15:607, Apr. 1910; 16:388, Jan. 1911; 17:185, Oct. 1911. WTL

L384 **Fortescue, John W.** *British statesmen of the great war, 1793–1814.* Oxford, 1911. [Ford lectures.]

Seven vigorous papers by the historian of the (L511) British army. An opinionated book written by a man gifted as much with prejudice as with insight, but useful for its criticism of the military policies of British statesmen in the period of the Revolutionary and Napoleonic Wars. Review, E. D. Adams, *A.H.R.* 17:401, Jan. 1912; *E.H.R.* 27:608, July 1912. WTL

L385a **Maxwell, Sir Herbert.** *Life of Wellington, the restoration of the martial power of Great Britain.* 2 v. Boston, 1899.

b **Hooper, George.** *Wellington.* London and N. Y., 1889. [English men of action.]

a. Best biography of Wellington for the general reader. While the author is a civilian, he has made good use of the chief military authorities for the campaigns and, for the political and personal side of the subject, has made a considerable study of private papers. A readable and trustworthy work in spite of the fact that the treatment is colored by Tory sympathies. Review, *Spectator,* 83:957, Dec. 23, 1899. *b.* Best brief biographical sketch. ALC

L386a **Stewart** (afterwards **Vane**), **Charles William, Third Marquis of Londonderry,** ed. *Memoirs and correspondence of Viscount Castlereagh, second Marquis of Londonderry.* 12 v. London, 1848–53.

b **Alison, Sir Archibald.** *Lives of Lord Castlereagh and Sir Charles Stewart, the second and third marquesses of Londonderry, with annals of contemporary events in which they bore a part, from the original papers of the family.* 3 v. Edinburgh, 1861.

c **Brougham, Henry, Baron.** *Historical sketches of statesmen of the time of George III.* 3 v. London, 1839–43.

d **Webster, Charles K.** *Foreign policy of Castlereagh, 1815–1822, Britain and the European alliance.* London, 1925.

a. Chief source of information for Castlereagh. Grew out of the aim of the third marquis to defend the character and policies of his brother against the attacks in *c.,* cf. (L22) *Dict. Nat. Biog.,* 54:281, 358. *b.* Marked by intense Tory sympathies and excessively laudatory. Review, *Athenaeum,* 2:395, Dec. 14, 1861. *d.* Valuable contribution to diplomatic history; based on thorough research in all the principal European archives; judicial in tone; regards Castlereagh as founder of the system of congresses; good chapter on American relations. Review, R. B. Mowat, *E.H.R.* 40:445, July 1925; D. Perkins, *A.H.R.* 30:812, July 1925. ALC

L387a Stapleton, Augustus G. *Political life of the Right Honourable George Canning, 1822–1827.* 1831. 2nd rev. ed., 3 v., London, 1831.

   b —— *George Canning and his times.* London, 1859.

   c Stapleton, Edward J., ed. *Some official correspondence of George Canning, 1821–1827.* 2 v. London, 1887.

   d Phillips, Walter Alison. *George Canning.* London, 1903. [Little biographies.]

   e Temperley, Harold W. V. *Life of Canning.* London, 1905.

   f Marriott, Sir John A. R. *George Canning and his times, a political study.* London, 1903.

   g Bagot, Josceline. *George Canning and his friends, containing hitherto unpublished letters.* 2 v. London and N. Y., 1909.

   h Temperley, Harold W. V. *Foreign policy of Canning, 1822–1827.* London, 1925.

a. and *b.* Stapleton, who was Canning's private secretary, was naturally a supporter of his former chief. Neither is very well arranged. However, in connection with *c.*, edited by his son, they furnish much information not elsewhere available. *a.* Covers only the years from 1822 to 1827. Review, *Athenaeum,* 1 :67, Jan. 29, 1831. *b.* Exhibits the defect of a work written from memory some years after the event. *d., e.,* and *f.* Three good brief sketches. *f.* Devoted largely to Canning's foreign policy. Review of *d.,* E. D. Adams, *A.H.R.* 10:693, Apr. 1905; of *e.,* 11 :389, Jan. 1906; of *f.,* 9:410, Jan. 1904. *g.* A valuable contribution, but not a definitive work. *h.* Carries forward the narrative begun in (L386d) Webster, *Foreign policy of Castlereagh.* Review, D. Perkins, *A.H.R.* 31 :317, Jan. 1926.

ALC

L388 Halévy, Élie. *History of the English people.* v. 1–2. London and N. Y., 1924–27. (Bibliography.) Tr. by E. J. Watkin and D. A. Barker from v. 1–2 of *Histoire du peuple anglais au XIXe siècle,* v. 1–3, Paris, 1912–23.

The independent point of view of this scholarly work especially commends it. V. 1. Describes conditions in 1815 and analyzes the political stability of England in contrast with the revolutionary experiences of the continent. V. 2. Recounts events from 1815 to 1830. While the importance of Castlereagh in the first half of the period is emphasized, Canning's position in the latter half of the period is distinctly depreciated. V. 3. Carries the narrative to the election of 1841. Review, v. 1, J. H. Clapham, *E.H.R.* 28:176, Jan. 1913; v. 2, C. E. Fryer, *A.H.R.* 29:133, Oct. 1923; v. 3, 30:645, Apr. 1925; v. 2–3, J. H. Clapham, *E.H.R.* 40:138, Jan. 1925.

GMD

L389 Martineau, Harriet. *History of England during the thirty years' peace, 1816–1846.* 2 v. 1849–50. Later ed., 4 v., London, 1877–78.

This work, begun in 1846 by Charles Knight and later carried forward by George Lillie Craik, covered no more than the period 1815–1820, when in 1848 Harriet Martineau undertook the task and completed it before the end of the following year. In the later edition the whole book was revised by the last author and enlarged to cover the period 1790–1854. She attempts to write for a popular audience; emphasizes social and economic factors more than is done in most histories written in her time; and is plainly a Whig in sympathy. A source rather than a serious critical history.

WTL

L390a Walpole, Sir Spencer. *History of England from the conclusion of the great war in 1815.* 5 v. 1878–86. Rev. ed., 6 v., London, 1910–13.

   b ——— *History of twenty-five years, 1856–1880.* 4 v. London, 1904–08.

a. Detailed and complete narrative history of England from the close of the Napoleonic wars to the end of the Indian mutiny. Mainly a political history, but deals incidentally with economic changes and even religious controversies. The clear and vigorous treatment of such incidents as the Reform Bill controversy of 1832 have made it a standard work. Review, C. A. Fyffe, *E.H.R.* 2:809, Oct. 1887. *b.* Continuation of *a.,* carrying the narrative from the Indian mutiny to 1880. The change of title was made to emphasize the fact that in the former work the attention of the reader was directed mainly to the internal affairs of Great Britain, whereas in the later work at least equal attention is devoted to foreign affairs which affected British interests. V. 3–4. Cover the period since 1870; revised for the press by Sir Alfred Lyall after the author's death. Review, W. Hunt, *E.H.R.* 24:179, Jan. 1909.   **PWS**

L391a Trevelyan, George M. *Lord Grey and the reform bill, being the life of Charles, second Earl Grey.* London and N. Y., 1920.

   b ——— *Life of John Bright.* 1913. New ed., London and Boston, 1925.

These books must be read in full appreciation of the author's strong Liberal-Radical bias. *a.* Gives the only account of Grey's whole political career. Not so much a biography as a lively sketch of politics, policies, and personalities, with Grey as the central figure, and with the movement for parliamentary reform, from the time of the French Revolution to 1832, as the central theme. Review, W. Hunt, *E.H.R.* 35:457, July 1920. *b.* A political biography of distinction, as well from a literary as from an historical point of view. Surveys his attitude and activities in connection with the repeal of the corn laws, the Crimean War, the American Civil War, and the struggle for parliamentary reform. Illustrated by copious extracts from his speeches and letters. Review, A. G. Porritt, *A.H.R.* 19:351, Jan. 1914.   **HCB**

L392a Torrens, William M. *Memoirs of the Right Honourable William, second Viscount Melbourne.* 2 v. London, 1878.

   b Aspinwall, Arthur. *Lord Brougham and the whig party.* London and N. Y., 1927. [Publications of the University of Manchester, no. CLXXIX.]

a. Of recognized importance, both as a biography and as a work of reference, for the political history of England and Ireland; but seriously defective in several respects. Constructed from insufficient materials; marred by digressiveness, unwarranted conclusions, and carelessness with regard to precise fact and dates; must be used with caution. The later period of Melbourne's life is discussed on the basis of fuller evidence than is the earlier; the author has turned his personal knowledge of Irish affairs to account. Review, *Westminster Rev.,* July 1878.

b. Penetrating study of the party activities of Brougham; very searching as to his motives. Review, W. P. Hall, *A.H.R.* 33:646, Apr. 1928.   **ALC**

L393a Smith, George Barnett. *Sir Robert Peel.* London, 1881. [English political leaders.]

   b McCarthy, Justin. *Sir Robert Peel.* N. Y., 1891. [Prime ministers of Queen Victoria.]

c **Thursfield, James R.** *Peel.* London and N. Y., 1891. Later reprints. [Twelve English statesmen.]

d **Rosebery, Archibald, Earl of.** *Sir Robert Peel.* London and N. Y., 1899.

e **Parker, Charles Stuart,** ed. *Sir Robert Peel, from his private papers.* 3 v. London, 1891–99.

a., b., c., and *d.* Good brief popular accounts, of which *d.* is probably the best. *e.* Collection of extracts from the correspondence of Peel and his private and political associates so selected and arranged as to cover Peel's political career. Interspersed are brief notes offering sufficient narrative and comment to explain the incidents and political situations. An excellent piece of work; of the first importance both for domestic and foreign affairs. Review, S. Walpole, *E.H.R.* 6:793, Oct. 1891; E. Porritt, *A.H.R.* 4:721, July 1899. HCB

L394a Dalling, (Sir) Henry Lytton Bulwer, Baron, and **Ashley, Evelyn.** *Life of Henry John Temple, viscount Palmerston, with selections from his duties and correspondence.* 5 v. London, 1870–76; abridged ed. by E. Ashley, 2 v., London, 1879.

b **Martin, Basil Kingsley.** *Triumph of Lord Palmerston, a study of public opinion in England before the Crimean war.* London and N. Y., 1924. (Bibliography.)

a. Most important single work on Palmerston; cumbersome and ill-proportioned as a biography; extremely valuable for reference. V. 1 and 2. By Dalling. V. 3. By Ashley, from notes and materials by Dalling. V. 4 and 5. By Ashley. Dalling was not only a personal friend of Palmerston, but held diplomatic posts at several capitals at times when those capitals were focal points in his foreign policy. Ashley was Palmerston's private secretary from 1858 to 1865. The work, to a very large degree, possesses the peculiar value and exhibits the peculiar defects which might be anticipated from these circumstances, taken in conjunction with the dates of publication. Review, *Blackwood's Magazine,* 116:622, Nov. 1874; 119:482, Apr. 1876; *Quar. Rev.* 143:361, Apr. 1877. *b.* Deals mainly with England's entry into the Crimean war. Review, *E.H.R.* 39:639, Oct. 1924. HCB

L395a Reid, Stuart J. *Lord John Russell.* 1895. 4th ed., London, 1905. [Prime ministers of Queen Victoria.]

b **Walpole, Sir Spencer.** *Life of Lord John Russell.* 2 v. London and N. Y., 1891.

c **MacCarthy, Desmond,** and **Russell, Agatha,** ed. *Lady John Russell, a memoir with selections from her diaries and correspondence.* London, 1910; N. Y., 1911.

d **Russell, Rollo,** ed. *Early correspondence of Lord John Russell, 1805–1840.* 2 v. London, 1913.

e **Gooch, George P.** *Later Correspondence of Lord John Russell, 1840–1878.* 2 v. London, 1925.

a. Exceptionally good, brief, popular narrative, though perhaps too favorable to Russell. Least satisfactory in the treatment of Anglo-American relations, especially during the Civil War. Review, F. Bancroft, *A.H.R.* 1:349, Jan. 1896. ALC

b. Based upon Russell's political correspondence, speeches, and writings, from which lengthy quotations are printed. Avoids discursive history of the times;

exhibits only the part taken by Russell personally in Liberal reform and in Liberal foreign policy; confined to Russell's political opinions, conduct, and public character, on which it is authoritative. Review, J. R. Tanner, *E.H.R.* 6·175, Jan. 1891. *c.* Contains family letters, often bearing upon parliamentary and cabinet episodes, not printed elsewhere. Review, E. Porritt, *A.H.R.* 16:855, July 1911. CEF
d and *e.* On the death of Lord John Russell's son, Rollo, the editorship was taken over by Mr. Gooch. The letters contribute to the understanding of one of the leading English statesmen of the century, but reveal little new historical information. Mr. Gooch's historical introductions are excellent. Reviews, *A.H.R.* 20:632, Apr. 1915; E. D. Adams, *A.H.R.* 31:780, July, 1926. ALC

L396a Benson, Arthur C., and **Esher, Viscount,** ed. *Letters of Queen Victoria, a selection from Her Majesty's correspondence between the years 1837 and 1861.* 1907. New ed., 3 v., London, 1908.

b Buckle, George E., ed. *Letters of Queen Victoria, second series, a selection from Her Majesty's correspondence and journals, 1862–1885.* 3 v. London and N. Y., 1927.

a. Very valuable set of political letters selected from about eight hundred manuscript volumes of Victoria's official correspondence. They are chiefly to and from successive prime ministers and heads of cabinet departments. They touch upon every subject of political interest in England and abroad; illustrate the complex workings of ministerial responsibility in relation to the sovereign's personal authority, opinions, and desires. Review, *A.H.R.* 13:585, Apr. 1908. *b.* Similar in character; especially valuable for the international relations of the two decades. Review of v. 1, 2, H. C. Bell, *A.H.R.* 32:106, Oct. 1926; of v. 3, (London) *Times Lit. Suppl.* 27:35, Jan. 19, 1928. CEF

L397a Lee, Sir Sidney. *Queen Victoria.* 1902. 2nd ed., London, 1903.

b Strachey, Lytton. *Queen Victoria.* N. Y., 1921. (Bibliography.)

a. Somewhat perfunctory, condensed sketch enlarged from an article in (L22) *Dictionary of national biography.* Stresses the formation and the personnel of cabinets, the queen's official relations with her several prime ministers, her special interest in the foreign office and in the late-Victorian idea of empire. Chronicles, at the same time, the queen's family history, and that of her children and grand-children, describing all the visits made by the queen and her family to the con-tinent and her changing relations with other European rulers. Sir Sidney is frankness itself in his delineation of the queen's character, though he writes with a sober restraint appropriate to the subject. Review, C. W. Colby, *A.H.R.* 8:792, July 1903. *b.* Much more vivid portrait. Without overcrowding his sketch with inconsequential detail, the author achieves life-like pictures of the queen through a skilful setting of the trivial and familiar episodes of her family and public life. While not altogether kindly, his readable style makes this book, though of little use to the student, the best popular account of the queen. Only one third of the space is allotted to the forty years following the death of the Prince Consort. Review, C. E. Fryer, *A.H.R.* 27:351, Jan. 1922. CEF

L398 Paul, Herbert W. *History of modern England.* 5 v. London and N. Y., 1904–06.

Narrative of the political history of England from 1846 to 1895. Although it follows rather strictly the conventional chronicle of events, it is lifted far above mediocrity by the liveliness of the style and the very characteristic comments of the author. His judgments are shrewd and his wit is always keen, sometimes cruel. The accusation of undue cynicism and uncharitable verdicts is offset by generous enthusiasm for liberal and humane principles of government, as in his treatment of the case of Governor Eyre of Jamaica. While chief attention is devoted to the political events of later Victorian times, there are chapters on the literary and scientific life of the period. Review, G. T. Warner, *E.H.R.* 21:604, July 1906.

PWS

L399a McCarthy, Justin. *History of our own times from the accession of Queen Victoria to the general election of 1880.* 1879–80. Jubilee ed. with appendix to end of 1886, 2 v., London, 1887. Later reprints.

b ——— *History of our own times from 1880 to the diamond jubilee.* N. Y. and London, 1897.

c ——— *History of our own times from the diamond jubilee, 1897, to the accession of Edward VII.* 2 v. London and N. Y., 1905.

These successive volumes tell the story of the Victorian age, and form the chief literary monument of a gifted student of current events whose personal intimacy with leading politicians of the Liberal and Irish Nationalist parties afforded exceptional advantages for dealing with the political controversies of that period. It is a variegated chronicle rather than a history of the nation, still less of the empire. Though by no means free of minor inaccuracies, the volumes are eminently readable; the author's bias towards Liberalism has not led to any deliberate unfairness or distortion of fact. Review of *c.*, A. G. Porritt, *A.H.R.* 11:676, Apr. 1906.

PWS

L400a Gretton, Richard H. *Modern history of the English people, 1880–1910.* 2 v. London and Boston, 1913.

b Meech, Thomas C. *This generation: a history of Great Britain and Ireland, 1900–1925.* 2 v. London and N. Y., 1928.

a. Praiseworthy attempt to group into a single picture all aspects of English life at the turn of the century. Much attention is devoted to subtle changes in the general social atmosphere, such as the decreased influence of the ideal of respectability in the days of Edward VII as compared with the Victorian age. Events in literature and sport are set in close juxtaposition to political events. More emphasis is placed on the 'mafficking' in the streets of London than on the battle of Mafeking which caused it. The lack of arrangement and order has given some readers the impression that it is 'erratic and bizarre in its estimation of the relative importance of events' though others are impressed by its liveliness and originality. Review, G. B. Hertz, *E.H.R.* 28:618, July 1913; *Athenaeum,* 1:486, May 3, 1913.

PWS

b. Rather journalistic but of a superior type. While dealing with the war and foreign affairs, stresses chiefly domestic history in its varied phases. Review, (London) *Times Lit. Suppl.* 27:114, Feb. 16, 1928.

ALC

L401 Russell, George W. E. *Collections and recollections by one who has kept a diary.* N. Y. and London, 1898. Various reprints.

First appeared in 1897 in the form of articles in the *Manchester Guardian.* A golden treasury of rare and amusing anecdotes of prominent Englishmen, with many of whom Russell was intimately acquainted. Review, *Nation* (N. Y.), 67:36, July 1898.

GJ

L402 Morley, John, Viscount. *Life of William Ewart Gladstone.* 3 v. 1903. Reprint, 1 v., London and N. Y., 1921.

Two phases of Gladstone's life are brought together. One, dealing with his scholarly interests, depicts, almost day by day, his intellectual pursuits and studious recreation tinged deeply with the emotional and ecclesiastical spirit of his historical and speculative inquiries. The portrait as outlined sympathetically is of a lofty, subtle, yet quite baffling mind, struggling in the moral tempests of the Victorian era. The style bespeaks the elevated strain of the presentation. By contrast, Morley descends with Gladstone into the arena of statesmanship. Here his method is that of one practical politician writing as the disciple and adherent of another, explaining in matter-of-fact way election returns, party management and campaigning, the problems of cohesion within the Liberal ranks, and other outstanding features of the Liberal party's parliamentary and national history. Review, G. M. Wrong, *A.H.R.* 9:591, Apr. 1904.   CEF

L403 Monypenny, William F., and **Buckle, George E.** *Life of Benjamin Disraeli, Earl of Beaconsfield.* 6 v. London and N. Y., 1910–20.

Longest and, in many respects, the ablest of Victorian political biographies. Based upon the Disraeli-Beaconsfield papers, consisting of correspondence of Disraeli with his personal friends, his political colleagues, and Queen Victoria. Each chapter contains extracts from the papers, from public and parliamentary speeches, newspaper editorials, and Disraeli's own novels, the whole pieced together by editorial paragraphs in themselves admirably lucid and fair. Authoritative for Disraeli's career in English society as an author and statesman; invaluable for a knowledge of Conservative politics and for the inner management and direction of the Conservative party. Of particular interest is the opposition of Disraeli to Peel over the corn laws and the opposition to Gladstone over the Eastern Question and foreign and imperial policy. The absence of all reticence in the disclosure of motives, of dissensions, and disagreements within Conservative cabinets, and of the personal views and influence of Victoria, make the later volumes especially useful contributions to the study of recent cabinet government. Review, *A.H.R.* 16:627, Apr. 1911; A. G. Porritt, *A.H.R.* 18:585, Apr 1913; E. Porritt, *A.H.R.* 20:635, Apr. 1915; Lord Bryce, *A.H.R.* 26:672, July 1921.
                                                                                CEF

L404a Traill, Henry D. *Marquis of Salisbury.* N. Y., 1891. [Prime ministers of Queen Victoria.]

   b Cecil, Lady Gwendolen. *Life of Robert, Marquis of Salisbury.* 2 v., London, 1921.

a. Scholarly outline of Salisbury's parliamentary and official career up to 1892; with strong anti-Liberal bias.   CEF
   b. Written with a daughter's appreciation, but with studied restraint; perhaps too impersonal. Includes extracts from letters and other documents. Especially good on Salisbury's eastern policy. These volumes cover the period to 1880. Review, *Spectator,* 127:704, Nov. 26, 1921; J. L. Morison, *A.H.R.* 31:134, Oct. 1925.   ALC

L405a Oxford and Asquith, Herbert Henry, Earl of. *Fifty years of Parliament.* 2 v. London, 1926.

b Lowther, Rt. Hon. J. W., Viscount Ullswater. *A Speaker's Commentaries.* 2 v. London, 1925.

a. Valuable though not very revealing survey by a veteran statesman. Review, (London) *Times Lit. Suppl.* 25:683, Oct. 14, 1926. *b.* Entertaining reminiscences by one who was Speaker of the House of Commons from 1905 to 1921. Review, (London) *Times Lit. Suppl.* 24:685, Oct. 22, 1925. ALC

L406 Lee, Sir Sidney. *King Edward VII, a biography.* 2 v. London, 1925–27.

The official life, based on papers many of which have never hitherto been accessible. While it contains much that is indispensable to the student of the period, this is interspersed with arid stretches rather lacking in interest. Review of v. 1, A. L. P. Dennis, *A.H.R.* 30:818, July 1925; of v. 2, (London) *Times Lit. Suppl.* 26:711, Oct. 13, 1927. ALC

TWENTIETH CENTURY

L421 Hayes, Carlton J. H. *British social politics, materials illustrating contemporary state action for the solution of social problems.* Boston, 1913.

Convenient handbook of extracts from the parliamentary debates covering the whole field of social legislation in Great Britain from the workmen's compensation act of 1906 to national insurance in 1911. Brief sketch of the passage of the more important acts is given as well as quotations from their more salient clauses. WPH

L422 Metcalfe, Agnes E. *Woman's effort, a chronicle of British women's fifty years' struggle for citizenship, 1865–1914.* Oxford, 1917.

Confined to the history of the 'votes for women' campaign in Great Britain and practically to the years from 1906 to 1914. The author is an ardent supporter of the cause. Review, *Spectator,* 119:64, July 21, 1917. WPH

L431a Masterman, Charles F. G. *England after the war, a study.* London and N. Y., 1923.

b Siegfried, André. *Post-war Britain.* London and N. Y., 1924. Tr. by H. H. Hemming from *L'Angleterre d'aujourd'hui, son évolution économique et politique,* Paris, 1924.

a. Gloomy but sympathetic picture of the condition of the upper, middle, and lower classes. Perhaps the best of the British surveys of England in the years following the World War. Review, *Spectator,* 133:757, May 5, 1923. *b.* Discussion of the social, economic, and political problems of England from the close of the World War to the assumption of office by the Labor party, by an eminent French student of political affairs. ALC

ENGLISH LOCAL HISTORY

L441 *Victoria history of the counties of England.* Ed. by H. Arthur Doubleday and William Page. London, 1900 ff.

This vast undertaking was projected a quarter of a century ago, and its progress was for some years brought to a standstill by the World War. Although publication has since been resumed, the volumes issued—about 100—

constitute less than half the number contemplated in the original plan. The general editors of this coöperative work have been assisted by an advisory committee selected from eminent British scholars, by sectional editors, and by local investigators. Natural features and every aspect of history are treated for each of the English counties. Even in its unfinished state, it is a mine of information, not only for the counties, but also for various features of general English history. Review, A. L. Cross, *A.H.R.* 9:605, Apr. 1904.

Owing to the existence of this current enterprise, reference is omitted to the various older monumental county histories, for which cf. (L1) C. Gross, *Sources and literature of English history,* § 24.

ALC

WALES

L451 Edwards, Owen M. *Wales.* London and N. Y., 1902 [Story of the nations].

Very elementary account which undertakes to trace the history of Wales to the present; the first attempt at a continuous popular history of that country; not founded upon sources. The chapters devoted to the period since Henry VIII are often so brief as to become almost characterizations. Review, T. F. Tout, *E.H.R.* 17:401, Apr. 1902.

WAM

L452a Rhys, Sir John, and **Brynmor-Jones, Sir David.** *Welsh people, chapters on their origin, history, laws, language, literature, and characteristics.* 1900. 4th ed., London, 1906. (Useful bibliographical notes.)

b Stone, Gilbert. *Wales, her origins, struggles, and later history, institutions, and manners.* London and N. Y., 1915. [Great nations.] (Bibliography in preface.)

c Rees, William. *South Wales and the March, 1284–1415, a social and agrarian study.* Oxford and N. Y., 1924. (Bibliography.)

a. Survey of the development of the Welsh people and of their history, by eminent authorities. Full attention is given to the period prior to 1282; the treatment of certain topics is carried later. Review, R. Williams, *E.H.R.* 16:358, Apr. 1901. *b.* Practically a narrative history from the earliest times to Owen Glendower, with a concluding chapter outlining events to the present time. *c.* Valuable exposition of Welsh institutions and conditions in the period of the final establishment of English control. Review, J. G. Edwards, *E.H.R.* 40:601, Oct. 1925.

GMD

L453a Wheeler, R. E. M. *Prehistoric and Roman Wales.* Oxford, 1926.

b Ellis, T. P. *Welsh tribal law and custom in the middle ages.* 2 v. Oxford, 1926.

a. Substantial contribution by a competent scholar, with a chapter of conclusions. Review, (London) *Times Lit. Suppl.* 25:133, Feb. 25, 1926. *b.* A work of independent research which also embodies the results of previous investigations. The most complete study available of the Welsh legal system, though the volume is marred somewhat by careless or inaccurate citations. Review, F. N. Robinson, *A.H.R.* 33:104, Oct. 1927.

ALC

SCOTLAND

L461a Brown, Peter Hume. *History of Scotland.* 3 v. Cambridge, Eng., 1902–09. [1, *To the accession of Mary Stewart; 2, To the revolution of 1689; 3, To the disruption of 1843.*] [*Cambridge historical series.*] (Bibliographies.)

b Terry, Charles S. *History of Scotland from the Roman evacuation to the disruption, 1843.* Cambridge, Eng., 1920.

a. Comparatively brief account, not without defects, but the work of an able scholar; the most satisfactory general history of Scotland. Since critical treatment of the earlier period has led to the rejection of much that was previously accepted as authentic, the earlier chapters now need revision Concerned primarily with national movements; treats especially well religious and social history. V. 3. Contains the most attractive and the most masterly chapters. The account proper closes with the year 1843; a concluding chapter traces the events from that year to 1902. Review, v. 1, *E.H.R.* 15:403, Apr. 1900; v. 2, H. F. M. Simpson, *E.H.R.* 20:366, Apr. 1905; v. 3, R. S. Rait, *E.H.R.* 25:364, Apr. 1910. *b.* Scholarly but less readable, compendious work. Review, W. P. M. Kennedy, *A.H.R.* 26:756, July 1921.

Most histories of England give some attention to Scottish history. Special reference should be made to the works of (L124) Ramsay, (L304) Froude, (L321) Gardiner, (L329) Burnet, (L333) Macaulay, (L334) Stanhope.

WAM

L462 Lang, Andrew. *History of Scotland from the Roman occupation.* 4 v. Edinburgh and N. Y., 1900–07. (Bibliographies.)

Written from the sources by a versatile scholar and author. The narrative is livelier than that of (L461) Brown. The volumes end respectively with 1546, 1625, 1685, 1746. In the last three volumes the interest centers in turn on Mary Stuart, Montrose, and the Old Pretender. Review, v. 4, R. S. Rait, *E.H.R.* 25:364, Apr. 1910.

GMD

L463 Burton, John Hill. *History of Scotland from Agricola's invasion to the extinction of the last Jacobite insurrection.* 1867–70. New ed., 8 v., Edinburgh, 1905–06.

Making allowance for recent research in special fields, this is still the standard work for the period which it covers. The product of a well-equipped scholar; marked by careful investigation, a reasonably judicial tone, and attractiveness of presentation. Review, *Athenaeum*, 1:511, Apr. 20, 1867; 2:301, Sept. 3, 1870.

ALC

L464a Dunbar, Sir Archibald H. *Scottish kings, a revised chronology of Scottish history, 1005–1625, with notices of the principal events, tables of regnal years, pedigrees, calendars, etc.* Edinburgh, 1899. (Bibliography.)

b Maxwell, Sir Herbert E. *Early chronicles relating to Scotland.* Glasgow, 1912. [Rhind lectures.]

c Anderson, Alan O., ed. and tr. *Scottish annals from English chroniclers, A. D. 500 to 1286.* London, 1908. (Bibliography.)

d ———, ed. and tr. *Early sources of Scottish history, A. D. 500 to 1286.* 2 v. Edinburgh, 1922. (Bibliography.)

e Lawrie, Sir Archibald C., ed. *Early Scottish charters prior to A. D. 1153.* Glasgow, 1905.

f ———, ed. *Annals of the reigns of Malcolm and William, kings of Scotland, A. D. 1153–1214.* Glasgow, 1910.

g Bremner, Robert Locke. *Norsemen in Alban.* Glasgow, 1923.

Some of the most important recent scholarly contributions to the study of the earlier history of Scotland. *a.* Indispensable for the chronology. *b.* Critical survey of the chronicles and evaluations of their historical content. Review, R. S. Rait, *E.H.R.* 28:550, July 1913. *c.* Extracts from chronicles written in England or by Englishmen before 1291 relating to Scotland; translated and arranged by years; addressed to the reader rather than to the scholar; mainly valuable as an introduction to the sources. Review, T. F. Tout, *E.H.R.* 24:823, Oct. 1909. *d.* Similar compilation from the chroniclers of other nationalities, especially Celtic and Scandinavian, and from later chronicles in so far as they embody source materials originating before 1291. Review, F. N. Robinson, *A.H.R.* 29:120, Oct. 1923. *e.* and *f.* More scholarly compilations of sources materials, critically edited. Review of *f.* J. M. Thomson, *Scottish Hist Rev.* 8:189, Jan. 1911. *g.* Most recent account of the Norse invasions and occupation of Scottish territories down to the thirteenth century. Review, (London) *Times Literary Supplement,* 23:91, Feb. 14, 1924.   GMD

L465 Maxwell, Sir Herbert E. *Robert the Bruce and the struggle for Scottish independence.* 1897. Reprint, London and N. Y., 1909. [Heroes of the nations.]

Brief survey of earlier Scottish history is prefixed to this competent and readable account of the most heroic figure in early Scottish history.   GMD.

L466 Mackinnon, James, and **Mackinnon, James A. R.** *Constitutional history of Scotland from early times to the reformation.* London and N. Y., 1924. (Bibliographies.)

The treatment is divided into three periods: the early Celtic period to the eleventh century, the early feudal period to the war of independence, and the final period to the Reformation. The principal contribution will be found in the final section which includes accounts of the kingship, the administrative system, parliament, the burghs, and the church. Review, C. H. McIlwain, *A.H.R.* 30:128, Oct. 1924.   GMD

L467a Mackinnon, James. *Social and industrial history of Scotland from the earliest times to the union.* Edinburgh, 1920. (Bibliographies.)

b ——— *Social and industrial history of Scotland from the union to the present time.* London and N. Y., 1921. (Bibliographies.)

c Mackintosh, John. *History of civilisation in Scotland.* 1878–88. Rev. ed., 4 v., Paisley and London, 1892–96.

d Pagan, Theodora (Keith). *Convention of royal boroughs of Scotland.* Glasgow, 1927.

a. and *b.* Two informing surveys by one of the best-versed students of Scottish history; not definitive works. Review of *a.* and *b.,* C. Bémont, *Rev. Hist.* 147:63, Sept. 1924; of *b., E.H.R.* 37:301, Apr. 1922. *c.* Older work of somewhat larger scope which may still be read with some advantage. V. 1. Carries the narrative through the fifteenth century. V. 2–3. Deal respectively with the sixteenth and seventeenth centuries. V. 4. Relates to the eighteenth and nineteenth centuries. *d.* Chiefly valuable from the economic side. Hardly does justice to the constitutional importance of the royal boroughs. Review, C. H. McIlwain, *A.H.R.* 33:432, Jan. 1928.   ALC

L468a Graham, Henry G. *Social life of Scotland in the eighteenth century.* 2 v., 1899. Rev. ed., 1 v., London, 1909. *

   b Rogers, Charles. *Social life in Scotland from early to recent times.* 3 v. Edinburgh, 1884–86.

   a. Written by a well-equipped and judicious scholar in a pleasing style. Review, *Athenaeum*, 2:612, Nov. 4, 1899. Much superior to *b.*, which is a rather journalistic performance though useful as covering the whole period from early to modern times.   ALC

L469a Mathieson, William L. *Politics and religion, a study in Scottish history from the reformation to the revolution, [1550–1695].* 2 v. Glasgow and N. Y., 1902.

   b —— *Scotland and the union, a history of Scotland from 1695 to 1747.* Glasgow, 1905.

   c —— *Awakening of Scotland, a history from 1747 to 1797.* Glasgow, 1910.

   d —— *Church and reform in Scotland, a history from 1797 to 1843.* Glasgow, 1916.

Four brilliant interpretative studies of Scottish history with particular reference to religion and politics. Rather overburdened with detail in places but illuminated with generalizations which, though sometimes open to question, are, as a rule, worthy of serious consideration. Review of *a.*, G. T. Lapsley, *A.H.R.* 8:750, July 1903; of *b.*, A. L. Cross, *A.H.R.* 11:892, July 1906; of *c.*, J. Dall, *A.H.R.* 16:815, July 1911; of *d.*, *A.H.R.* 22:849, July 1917.   ALC

L470 Rait, Robert S. *Parliaments of Scotland.* Glasgow, 1924. (Bibliography.)

This valuable study by the historiographer royal for Scotland is the only work of importance on the subject. The historical narrative is supplemented by topical accounts of composition, powers, and procedure. Review, J. D. Mackie, *E.H.R.* 40:427, July 1925.   GMD

L471 Mackinnon, James. *Union of England and Scotland, a study of international history.* London and N. Y., 1896.

Survey of the relations of England and Scotland in the seventeenth and eighteenth centuries with detailed study of the period from 1695 to 1708. Best treatment of the parliamentary union, which was neglected not only by the older English historians but even by (L463) Burton. More recent works have, however, thrown additional light upon the subject. Review, *A.H.R.* 2:143, Oct. 1896.

                                                             GMD

L472a Innes, Cosmo. *Lectures on Scotch legal antiquities.* Edinburgh, 1872.

   b Robertson, Alexander. *Course of lectures on the government, constitution, and laws of Scotland, from the earliest to the present time.* London, 1878.

c **Cowan, Samuel.** *Lord chancellors of Scotland, from the institution of the office to the treaty of union.* 2 v. Edinburgh, 1911.

d **Omond, George W. T.** *Lord advocates of Scotland from the close of the fifteenth century to 1880.* 3 v. Edinburgh and London, 1883–1914.

a. Deals in somewhat brief and popular form with charters, parliament, the church, the old forms of law, rural occupations, and books. *b.* Addressed to a popular audience; by a barrister of Lincoln's Inn; chiefly on the period prior to 1688. *c* and *d.* Not so much works of collected biography as collections of biographical, antiquarian, and legal data.   ALC

IRELAND

L481a **Lawless, Emily.** *Story of Ireland.* 1887. 3rd rev. ed., London and N. Y., 1924. [Story of the nations.] (Brief bibliography.)

b **Dunlop, Robert.** *Ireland, from the earliest times to the present day.* Oxford, 1922.

c **Hayden, Mary,** and **Moonan, George A.** *Short history of the Irish people from the earliest times to 1920.* London and N. Y., 1921.

d **Gwynn, Stephen L.** *History of Ireland.* London, 1923.

e **Murray, Robert H.,** and **Law, Hugh.** *Ireland.* London, 1924. [Nations of to-day.] (Brief bibliography.)

f **D'Alton, Edward A.** *History of Ireland from the earliest times to the present day.* 3 v. in 6. Dublin and London, 1903–12.

g **Maxwell, Constantia.** *Short bibliography of Irish history.* London, 1923. [Hist. Association Leaflet No. 23.]

h **Kenney, James F.** *Sources for the early history of Ireland* [to 1172]. N. Y., 1929.

a. Long the best known brief survey; popular and superficial. *b.* Brief outline by a competent authority; not well proportioned; aims, with a fair degree of success, to hold an even balance between the British and Irish points of view. Review, L. M. Larson, *A.H.R.* 28:770, July 1923. *c.* Written from the Irish nationalist standpoint but fairly moderate in tone. Rather sketchy for the recent period. Review, A. L. Cross, *Yale Rev.* 11:428, Jan. 1922. *d.* Account from earliest times to entrance into League of Nations, by Irish author and politician, who is a moderate home ruler. Review, J. F. Kenney, *A.H.R.* 29:754, July 1924. *e.* Ch. 1–12 are by Rev. Dr. Murray and the remainder by Mr. Law, a former nationalist member of parliament. Review, (London) *Times Literary Supplement,* 23:168, March 20, 1924. *f.* Only recent attempt of importance at a more extended account of all Irish history since the earliest times; frequently open to criticism. Review, v. 1, G. H. Orpen, *E.H.R.* 19:565, July 1904.

Most histories of England give some attention to Irish history. Special reference should be made to the works of (L304) Froude, (L321) Gardiner, (L333) Macaulay, (L334) Lecky, (L399) McCarthy.   ALC

L482 **Joyce, Patrick W.** *Social history of ancient Ireland, treating of the government, military system, and law; religion, learning, and art; trades, industries, and commerce; manners, customs, and domestic life, of the ancient Irish people.* 2 v. London and N. Y., 1903. (Bibliography.)

Striking combination of learning and credulity; 'full of interesting facts and questionable inferences.' Review, *Athenaeum,* 2:712, Nov. 28, 1903.   ALC

L483a Green, Alice Stopford. *History of the Irish state to 1014.* London, 1925.

  b Orpen, Goddard H. *Ireland under the Normans, 1169–1216.* 2 v. Oxford, 1911.

  c —— *Ireland under the Normans, 1216–1333.* 2 v. Oxford, 1920.

  d Curtis, Edmund. *History of mediaeval Ireland from 1110 to 1513.* London, 1923; N. Y., 1924.

  e Gilbert, Sir John T. *History of the viceroys of Ireland, with notices of the castle of Dublin and its chief occupants in former times.* Dublin, 1865.

Scholarly narratives by specialists in the field. *a.* Based on extensive study, by an ardent champion of the Irish. *b* and *c.* Devoted primarily to the history of the Norman colonists. Review of *b,* J. Tait, *E.H.R.* 27:144, Jan. 1912; of *c,* F. M. Powicke, *E.H.R.* 36:451, July 1921. *d.* Emphasizes the history of the Celtic population in deliberate contrast to Orpen, upon whose scholarship he frequently relies. *e.* Useful for the period prior to 1509.   GMD

L484a Morris, William O'Connor. *Ireland, 1494–1868, with two introductory chapters.* 1896. Rev. ed. with additional chapter, 1868–1905, by R. Dunlop, Cambridge, Eng., 1909. [Cambridge historical series.] (Good bibliography.)

  b O'Connor, Sir James. *History of Ireland, 1798–1924.* 2 v. London and N. Y., 1925.

a. Better for the later than for the early period, which is treated in a rather confusing and illusive fashion. Generally impartial in tone, though written rather from the British standpoint. Review, W. A. Dunning, *A.H.R.* 2:515, Apr. 1897; G. H. Orpen, *E.H.R.* 12:162, Jan. 1897. *b.* By a former lord justice in appeal. Allowing for some Nationalist and religious sympathies, a well-balanced and valuable treatment.   ALC

L485a Bagwell, Richard. *Ireland under the Tudors, with a succinct account of the earlier history.* 3 v. London, 1885–90.

  b —— *Ireland under the Stuarts and during the interregnum.* 2 v. London and N. Y., 1909.

Exhaustive studies by a well equipped scholar; sound in judgment but heavy in treatment. Review of *a., Athenaeum,* 1:60, Jan. 9, 1886; of *b.,* R. Dunlop, *E.H.R.* 24:797, Oct. 1909.   ALC

L486 Hogan, James. *Ireland in the European system.* V. 1, London and N. Y., 1920.

This volume covering the years 1500–1557 is intended as the first instalment of an important study of Irish history in its international bearings. Review, H. Sée, *Rev. Hist.* 137:248, July 1921.   GMD

L487 MacNeill, John G. Swift. *Constitutional and parliamentary history of Ireland till the union.* Dublin and London, 1917.

Only convenient outline of the subject; starts with a long extract from the speech of Isaac Butt at the Home Rule Conference of 1873; makes considerable use of (L352) Lecky.   ALC

L491a Barker, Ernest. *Ireland in the last fifty years, 1866–1916.* 1916. 2nd rev. ed., Oxford, 1919.

b Hackett, Francis. *Ireland, a study in nationalism.* N. Y., 1918.

c Turner, Edward R. *England and Ireland in the past and at present.* N. Y., 1919. (Bibliography.)

d Henry, Robert M. *Evolution of Sinn Fein.* Dublin, London, and N. Y., 1920. [Modern Ireland in the making.]

a. Very concrete statistical account of such problems as the Irish church, Irish education, Irish agrarian and industrial development. Includes a brief chapter on the government of Ireland and also an inadequate chapter on Sinn Fein. *b.* Brilliant analysis of Anglo-Irish relationship. Presents in all frankness a keen, cynical indictment of English policy; deals with economic grievances and their political consequences in Ireland to-day; suggests as the only remedy the Sinn Fein program. Review, *Dublin Rev.* 164:129, Jan. 1919. *c.* Treats Anglo-Irish relationship with an air of studious and scholarly impartiality. Portrays English maladministration in all its various phases. England, however, in the twentieth century has made complete atonement. The treatment of Sinn Fein is quite inadequate and no longer up to date. Review, *Nation* (N. Y.), 109:661, Nov. 22, 1919. *d.* Study of the evolution during the early twentieth century of political thinking with which the Sinn Fein movement is very clearly and convincingly identified. Sinn Fein after 1916 is portrayed as the resultant of forces which expressed themselves earlier in such movements as the Gaelic League, the Labor League, and the Irish Volunteers. Review, E. R. Turner, *A.H.R.* 26:523, Apr. 1921. SML

L492a Phillips, Walter Alison. *Revolution in Ireland, 1906–1923.* London and N. Y., 1923.

b Desmond, Shaw. *Drama of Sinn Fein.* N. Y., 1923.

c O'Brien, William *Irish Revolution and how it came about.* London, 1923.

a. Aims to be impartial; may be read as a counterbalance to works of republican sympathizers such as *b.*, which is a glowing panegyric of the republican movement. Review of *a.*, *Spectator,* 131:800, No. 24, 1923. *c.* Written with strong feeling, by an Irish nationalist who favors a combination of Irishmen of all classes and creeds, and who broke with the majority of his party for consenting to a separate arrangement for Ulster. Throws much light on Anglo-Irish politics. Review, *Spectator,* 130:1009, June 16, 1923. ALC

L493 McNeill, Ronald. *Ulster's stand for union.* London, 1922.

Forceful presentation of the Ulster case by a prominent member of the British conservative party. ALC

DIPLOMATIC, MILITARY, AND NAVAL HISTORY

L501a Seeley, Sir John R. *Growth of British policy, an historical essay.* 1895. 2nd ed., 2 v., Cambridge, Eng., 1897.

b Burrows, Montagu. *History of the foreign policy of Great Britain.* 1895. New ed., Edinburgh, 1897.

a. Seeley was not a scientific historian addicted to research, but a thoughtful student who preferred to trace historical processes. Hence this posthumous work is an interpretation, not a narrative, of British diplomacy. Since it deals with facts generally known, there are few references; while the style is admirable, it suffers sometimes from repetition. No other book traces so clearly the evolution of national, as opposed to dynastic, foreign policy, the beginnings of which are ascribed to Elizabeth, the full realization to William III. Its tone is strongly imperialistic, in keeping with the author's (K343) *Expansion of England,* to which this book serves as a prelude. Review, H. M. Stephens, *A.H.R.* 1 :721, July 1896; S. R. Gardiner, *E.H.R.* 11 :159, Jan. 1896.   *b.* Slight for the period before the eighteenth century, this book complements *a.,* which it resembles in both the manner of treatment and the patriotic attitude of its author. The relation of naval policy to foreign affairs is well discussed. Review, H. M. Stephens, *A.H.R.* 1 :722, July 1896.   BES

L502 Ward, Sir Adolphus W., and **Gooch, George P.,** ed. *Cambridge history of British foreign policy, 1783–1919.* 3 v. Cambridge, Eng., 1922–23. (Bibliographies.)

Very useful presentation of British foreign policy. While devoted largely to European diplomacy, Anglo-American and other extra-European relations are treated with reasonable fullness. The coöperative nature of the undertaking insures competent contributions by specialists at some sacrifice of unity of treatment. The consideration of questions is frequently so rigidly from the point of view of British foreign policy as to leave an entirely inadequate or distorted conception of the case. A helpful feature is an introduction containing a sketch of England's foreign policy from 1066 to 1783. Review, H. W. C. Davis, *E.H.R.* 39:131, Jan. 1924; v. 1, E. D. Adams, *A.H.R.* 28:312, Jan. 1923; v. 2, 29:131, Oct. 1923; v. 3, 29:553, Apr. 1924; of work as a whole, B. E. Schmitt, *Pol. Sci. Quar.* 39:308, June 1924.   ALC

L503a Gooch, George P., and **Masterman, John H. B.** *Century of British foreign policy.* London, 1917. [Council for the Study of International Relations.] (Bibliography.)

   b Egerton, Hugh E. *British foreign policy in Europe to the end of the 19th century, a rough outline.* London, 1917.

a. Canon Masterman, in forty-one pages, has written a straightforward narrative of British relations with Europe from 1815 to 1901, with little mention of colonial controversies and almost no discussion of policy or its results. Gooch's sixty-six pages are a dispassionate survey of the period from 1902 to the outbreak of the World War. Though defending British policy, he understands the German case thoroughly, and if, in the end, he rejects it, he is sharply critical of the Triple Entente. A brilliant piece of condensation. Review, *Spectator,* 119:270, Sept. 15, 1917.   *b.* To refute the German charge that British policy has been conspicuous for 'perfidy and unscrupulousness,' the motives of British statesmen, chiefly in the nineteenth century, are exhibited in lengthy quotations from their speeches and correspondence. There is a connecting thread of narrative, but the volume will be most useful to those who have some knowledge of British diplomacy. Holds no brief for any political party; is often distinctly critical; argues that Great Britain has pursued a policy of peace, fulfilled her engagements, and sympathized with national aspirations. Review, W. A. Phillips, *E.H.R.* 33:118, Jan. 1918; *A.H.R.* 23:429, Jan. 1918. Cf. also (J108) Schmitt, *England and Germany, 1740–1914;* (I280b) Lodge, *Great*

Britain and Prussia; and (J101) Gooch, *History of modern Europe,* which furnishes much new information; and *Catalogue of printed books in the library of the foreign office* (London, 1926), a valuable special collection of about 30,000 printed volumes "on diplomacy, diplomatic history and relations, international law, and cognate subjects", chiefly since 1815.   BES

L511 Fortescue, John W. *History of the British army.* 13 v. in 20. London, 1899–1930.

This is, in the true sense, a history of the British army, beginning with the earliest times and reaching, in v. 13, the year 1870. While it gives in outline the history of the campaigns, this narrative is only for the purpose of furnishing the necessary background for a study of the development of the army. The writer, a civilian, apologizes for lack of military knowledge, but what he lacks in personal experience he has made up by sympathetic study. Well and interestingly written; on the whole, adequately documented for its purpose. The strong prejudices of the author lay his judgment, especially on persons, open to question. Valuable maps and plans. Review, v. 3, C. H. Van Tyne, *A.H.R.* 9:163, Oct. 1903; v. 5–6, E. A. Cruikshank, *A.H.R.* 16:816, July 1911; v. 8, 24:89, Oct. 1918; v. 9, 26:781, July 1921; v. 11, C. Bémont, *Rev. Hist.* 147:54 Sept. 1924; J. E. Morris, *E.H.R.* 39:299, Apr. 1924; v. 12, consisting of a book of maps, (London) *Times Lit. Suppl.* 26:705, Oct. 13, 1927.   OLS

L512 Newhall, Richard A. *English conquest of Normandy, 1416–1424, a study in fifteenth-century warfare.* New Haven and London, 1924. [Yale historical publications.]   (Bibliography.)

Valuable study of the organization, equipment, tactics, and strategy of the army of Henry V, and how it was financed; based on thorough use of sources. Review, C. L. Kingsford, *E.H.R.* 40:275, Apr. 1925; O. L. Spaulding, Jr., *A.H.R.* 30:804, July 1925.   GMD

L513 Firth, Charles H. *Cromwell's army, a history of the English soldier during the civil wars, the commonwealth, and the protectorate.* London, 1902. [Ford lectures.]

The writer is not a military man, but a civilian historian, who himself felt the need of information concerning the army in order to understand the general history of the period. Not a history, therefore, but a technical work prepared for the use of the student of history. Review, *A.H.R.* 8:167, Oct. 1902.   OLS

L514 Oman, Sir Charles W. C. *Wellington's army, 1809–1814.* London and N. Y., 1912.

Masterly work by the foremost historian of the (L536b) Peninsular War. Describes the organization of the British army in the Peninsula and of its German and Portuguese auxiliaries; some discussion of tactics; excellent characterizations of Wellington and his chief lieutenants. Ch. 1–2. Constitute a valuable critical essay on the literature of the Peninsular War. Review, F. L. Huidekoper, *A.H.R.* 18:804, July 1913.   GMD

L521a Hannay, David. *Short history of the royal navy, 1217–1815.* 2 v. London, 1898–1909.

   b Callender, Geoffrey. *The naval side of British history.* London, 1924.

a. Best popular history of the Royal navy. Clearly, though not brilliantly, written; contains not a few minor inaccuracies. Based upon a large, though not exhaustive, reading of the principal sources; suffers from omission of maps and plans. Review, C. T. Atkinson, E.H.R. 25:183, Jan. 1910.   COP
b. A fairly complete sketch. Aims to treat the whole development of English sea power rather than the naval side in the strictest sense. Review, (London) *Times Lit. Suppl.* 23:640, 16 Oct. 1924.   ALC

L522 Clowes, Sir William L., ed. *Royal navy, a history from the earliest times to the present.* 7 v. London and Boston, 1897–1903.

Best general history of the Royal navy. Most of the chapters were contributed by Clowes, although not a few were the work of his able assistants. Among the contributors on the naval wars with America were Admiral A. T. Mahan and Colonel Theodore Roosevelt. Treating naval history as a science, the writers have based their work on a wide reading of both printed and manuscript sources. They have emphasized three aspects of naval history: civil history, military history, and history of naval voyages and discoveries. For a less favorable view, cf. review, *Athenaeum*, 1:569, May 1, 1897; 2:180, Aug. 8, 1903. Review, F. Y. Powell, *E.H.R.* 13:342, Apr. 1898.   COP

L523 Oppenheim, Michael. *History of the administration of the royal navy and of merchant shipping in relation to the navy, 1509–1660, with an introduction treating of the preceding period.* London and N. Y., 1896.

Chiefly a collection of details, presented somewhat drily in a narrative form, relating to the civil history of the Royal navy prior to 1660. Based upon original sources. Review, A. T. Mahan, *A.H.R.* 2:719, July 1897.   COP

L524a Corbett, Sir Julian S. *Drake and the Tudor navy, with a history of the rise of England as a maritime power.* 2 v. London and N. Y., 1898.

   b ——— *Successors of Drake.* London and N. Y., 1900.

   c ——— *England in the Mediterranean, a study of the rise and influence of British power within the Straits, 1603–1713.* 2 v. London and N. Y., 1904.

   d ——— *England in the Seven Years' War, a study in combined strategy.* 2 v. London and N. Y., 1907.

The author's reputation will rest less upon his strictly historical work than on his mastery of naval strategy in a broad sense, the notable discussions of which in these volumes will influence the historical interpretation of the periods treated. 'The real importance of maritime power is its influence on military operations.' Wars are 'conducted by the ordered combination of naval, military, and diplomatic force' (Pitt's 'system'). Together the four works cover from the rise of England's naval power to the establishment of its full control of the sea. The two most illustrious seamen portrayed by the author are Drake, 'who has no rival . . . but Nelson,' and Blake, the great admiral of the Commonwealth. Review of *a.*, W. F. Tilton, *A.H.R.* 4:516, Apr. 1899; of *b.*, W. F. Tilton, 6:554, Apr. 1901; of *c.*, R. C. H. Catterall, 10:164, Oct. 1904; and of *d.*, T. W. Riker, 14:345, Jan. 1909.   GWA

L525 Mahan, Alfred T. *Life of Nelson, the embodiment of the sea power of Great Britain.* 1897. 2nd rev. ed., Boston, 1899.

One of the most scholarly of modern biographies; supersedes all the earlier books about Nelson. Of the writer's works, it best illustrates his unusual critical ability, literary power, and historical acumen. Review, *A.HR..* 4:719, July 1899.

COP

L526 Roscoe, Edward S. *History of the English prize court.* London, 1924.

Institutional study of the court, by its registrar, with special attention to its functioning during the World War. Review, C. M. Hough, *A.H.R.* 30:587, Apr. 1925.

GMD

L527 Albion, Robert G. *Forests and sea power: the timber problem of the royal navy, 1652–1862.* Cambridge, Mass., 1926.

An able and thorough study of a hitherto neglected problem. Review, E. L. Lord, *A.H.R.* 32:590, Apr. 1927.

ALC

CONSTITUTIONAL AND LEGAL HISTORY, POLITICAL THEORY

L531a Adams, George B. *Constitutional history of England.* N. Y., 1921. [American historical series.]

    b —— *Outline sketch of English constitutional history.* New Haven, 1918.

    c —— *Origin of the English constitution.* 1912 2nd rev. ed., New Haven, 1920.

    d —— *Council and courts of Anglo-Norman England.* New Haven, 1926.

a. This expansion of *b.,* intended for 'the general reader and college student,' will be of special value to the latter in advanced work. Knowledge of political history is assumed. A development of the author's feudal theory of constitutional origins, a brilliant account of seventeenth-century political theory and practice, and penetrating comparisons of things English and American are outstanding features. Half the book is on the twelfth, thirteenth, and seventeenth centuries, an apportionment strikingly appropriate to the subject. Review, E. R. Turner, *A.H.R.* 27:106, Oct. 1921. *c.* Not a description of institutions, but a chronological study of the forces which founded and developed the English constitution. The author approached English history after prolonged study of continental feudalism; his thesis is the significance of the feudal contract in the genesis of English limited monarchy. Review, B. Terry, *A.H.R.* 18:567, Apr. 1913. *d.* Posthumous volume; deals with the *Curia Regis,* lesser courts, origin of the common law and of common law courts; for some topics the treatment is carried into the thirteenth century.

ABW

L532 Maitland, Frederic W. *Constitutional history of England.* Cambridge, Eng., 1908.

Posthumous publication of lectures delivered in 1887–88 before Cambridge undergraduates 'reading for the law tripos.' The original investigation is largely in the history of law, and here was an 'advance program of Maitland's later work.' Public law is sketched at five periods, 1307, 1509, 1625, 1702, 1887, with connections established backwards and forwards precluding mere cross-sectioning, but hardly making a narrative of development. The foundation was laid for a newer synthesis than (L535) Stubbs's, one in which the English constitution will be brought into its true relation to the governmental evolution in continental states. A valuable book of reference. Review: G. B. Adams, *A.H.R.* 14:338, Jan. 1909; H. W. C. Davis, *E.H.R.* 24:341, April, 1909.   ABW

L533a Taswell-Langmead, Thomas P. *English constitutional history from the Teutonic conquest to the present time.* 1875. 8th rev. ed., by Coleman Phillipson, London, 1919.

b Medley, Dudley J. *Student's manual of English constitutional history.* 1894. 6th rev. ed., Oxford, 1925.

a. As a text-book this work has probably been more useful than any other on the subject because of its style and its successful arrangement—chronological, but with occasional and skilfully handled deviations where some particular topic seemed to require a continuous treatment. Its editors have added useful notes, but the text is substantially as the author left it in the second edition, 1879. The medieval portion has been superseded, but the chapters covering 1485 to 1689 are still of great value. The constitutional struggle is unfolded with striking power, and throughout illustrative material from contemporary sources is used with great skill. *b.* Aiming to present the results of recent investigation, this text has done much, since (L535) Stubb's work and in view of the inadequate editing of *a.*, to keep students abreast of recent scholarship. However, its topical arrangement, dealing with the several phases of government from earliest times to the present, does not give the reader a grasp of the developing constitution as a whole. The author is sometimes swamped with detail, and his presentation of divergent views, often with little discussion or conclusion, is confusing to the untrained reader. A book of reference. Review, A. G. Little, *E.H.R.* 10:555, July 1895; W. E. Lunt, *A.H.R.* 31:345, Jan. 1926.   ABW

L534 White, Albert B. *Making of the English constitution, 449–1485.* 1908. 2nd rev. ed., N. Y., 1925. (Bibliography.)

Brief text-book intended for college classes. Deals with the evolution of institutions, in three general periods, with special emphasis upon the judiciary. Scholarly work, but open to criticism in point of balance and apportionment of material. Much revised and rewritten in second edition. Review, *Nation* (N. Y.) 88:68, Jan. 1909; J. F. Baldwin, *A.H.R.* 31:563, Apr. 1926.   JFB

L535 Stubbs, William. *Constitutional history of England in its origin and development.* 3 v. Oxford, 1874–78. 6th ed. of v. 1, 1903; 4th ed. of v. 2, 1906; 5th ed. of v. 3, 1903.

With but slight work upon which to build, Stubbs produced 'one of the half-dozen most important historical works in the language.' From discovering sources to final synthesis, 'no other Englishman so completely displayed to the world the whole business of the historian.' His strong opinions, political and ecclesiastical, did not bias his scholarship, and his 'acute but wary reasoning' and genius for non-committal phrase, when needed, have kept his statements surprisingly impeccable. Yet he felt prevailing historical theories and German scholarship influenced him. For him England was a pure Teutonic state and its institutions developed with no important outside influence—thus Magna Carta was an Anglo-Saxon liberal movement and the House of Commons, a nationalized shire-court. Bishop Stubbs never adequately revised his history, and since his day a body of important work, bringing England more into its true relations with continental development, makes another great synthesis overdue. While Stubbs was strongest in the twelfth and thirteenth centuries, here the important recent work has been done; consequently he can today be read with least question in the section on the fourteenth and fifteenth centuries. Review, F. W. Maitland, *E.H.R.* 16:417, July 1901; (A249a) Gooch, *History and historians in the nineteenth century,* 340–346.   ABW

L536 Hallam, Henry. *Constitutional history of England from the accession of Henry VII to the death of George II.* 1827. 10th rev. ed., 3 v., London, 1861. Reprint, N. Y., 1897. [Hallam's work, v. 3–4.]

Extensively revised by the author. Various single volume editions, generally abridgments of the early editions, should be avoided. Long considered a standard authority, and even now not entirely superseded. Treating political controversies according to whig standards, it was praised by Macaulay for judicial impartiality, but was repudiated by tories and high churchmen. Review, *Quarterly Rev.* 37:194, Jan. 1828; *Edinburgh Rev.* 48:96, Sept. 1828.   JFB

L537 May, Thomas Erskine, Baron Farnborough. *Constitutional history of England since the accession of George the Third, 1760–1860.* 1861–63. 3rd ed., with supplementary chapter, 1861–1871, 1871; rev. ed., with continuation to 1911, by Francis Holland, 3 v., London and N. Y., 1912.

Intended as a sequel to Hallam, the work has merits of its own in point of trustworthiness, clearness of exposition, and excellence of style. The treatment deviates from chronology in favor of a topical arrangement of subjects, such as the crown, the houses of parliament, parties, the press, the church, political and civil liberty, and progress of legislation. There is a noticeable weakness in economic data, also a lack of interest in the colonies, and a failure to realize the drift of Ireland under the Union. The continuator is acknowledged to have made a valuable contribution to recent history. Review, C. E. Fryer, *A.H.R.* 17:832, July 1912; A. F. Pollard, *E.H.R.* 27:576, July 1912.   JFB

L538 Anson, Sir William R. *Law and custom of the constitution.* 1886–92. 4th rev. ed., 2 v. in 3, Oxford and N. Y., 1909; reissue, 1911; 5th rev. ed. of v. 1, by M. L. Gwyer, 1922.

Comprehensive work of high authority; follows a strictly analytical method. V. 1. On parliament: treats of constitutional law, the two houses of parliament, and the process of legislation.   V. 2.   On the Crown: deals with prerogative, councils, departments of government, armed forces, and the courts. Special attention has been given to the evolution of the cabinet. While the main object is to state the law regarding each institution as it now exists, this is done with a large amount of historical background. It must be admitted, however, that the author is not well versed in earlier history. Less literary than (L539) Dicey or (L548c) Lowell, the text is marked by abundant citations of statutes and law cases. Various documents appear in appendixes. Review, E. Porritt, *Am. Pol. Sci. Rev.* 4:196, May 1910.   JFB

L539 Dicey, Albert V. *Introduction to the study of the law of the constitution.* 1885. 8th ed., London, 1915.

This brilliant work inquires into the nature of constitutional law, how far it is really law and capable of being enforced, and refutes the saying of Tocqueville, 'the English constitution has no real existence.' Even conventions, which are not law, are shown to be not without binding force. There is further discussion, in their legal aspect, of such subjects as parliamentary sovereignty, martial law, and responsibility of ministers, with comment on recent changes. The author is an eminent advocate of the method of comparing the institutions of one country with those of another. His treatment of the *droit administratif* of France, as contrasted with the so-called 'rule of law' in England, betrays misunderstanding of French law; furthermore recent reforms in France have made the chapter out of date. Review, C. Elton, *Academy*, 29:229, Apr. 3, 1886; R. L. Schuyler, *Pol. Sci. Quar.* 30:325, June 1915.   JFB

L540a Round, John H. *Feudal England: historical studies of the XIth and XIIth centuries.* 1895. Reprint, London, 1909.

b Poole, Reginald Lane. *Exchequer in the twelfth century.* Oxford, 1912. [Ford lectures.]

c Hall, Hubert. *Antiquities and curiosities of the exchequer.* 1891. Reprint, London, 1898. [Camden library.]

d Ramsay, Sir James H. *History of the revenues of the kings of England, 1066–1399.* 2 v. Oxford and N. Y., 1926.

a. Reprint of papers; eight are 'territorial studies' on Domesday Book and subsequent surveys, by probably the greatest recent Domesday scholar; twenty-four are 'historical studies,' including a sharp attack on (L241a) Freeman's account of the battle of Hastings,—all noteworthy for acuteness, incisiveness, and accurate knowledge. Review, F. Pollock, *E.H.R.* 10:783, Oct. 1895. *b.* Best account of the early medieval English exchequer. Contains accurate descriptions of the early exchequer records, officials, and methods, with judicious discussions of disputed points such as the origin of the offices of treasurer, chancellor, and chamberlain. Review, F. Liebermann, *E.H.R.* 28:151, Jan. 1913. *c.* Older work; still valuable; includes account of early history of the public records. Review, G. T. Warner, *E.H.R.* 7:754, Oct. 1892. *d.* Posthumous publication; presents a wealth of statistical data with an exposition not always convincing. Review, M. H. Mills, *E.H.R.* 41:429, July 1926.   CHM

L541 McKechnie, William S. *Magna Carta, a commentary on the Great Charter of King John, with an historical introduction.* 1905. 2nd rev. ed., Glasgow, 1914. (Select bibliography.)

Only comprehensive commentary on the Great Charter in the light of modern research. Following a survey of events and conditions pertaining to the crisis, the main body of the work consists of an exposition of the text, chapter by chapter. The tendency of interpretation is away from the nationalist view toward an understanding of the document as a product of the feudal age. Criticisms made upon the first edition have been mainly overcome in the revision. Review, H. W. C. Davis, *E.H.R.* 21:150, Jan. 1906; H. L. Cannon, *A.H.R.* 11:137, Oct. 1905; 19:923, July, 1914.   JFB

L542a Baldwin, James F. *King's council in England during the middle ages.* Oxford, 1913. (Bibliography.)

b Dicey, Albert V. *Privy council.* 1860. Reprint, London and N. Y., 1887. [Arnold prize essay.]

c Palgrave, Sir Francis. *Essay upon the original authority of the king's council.* London, 1834. [Record commission.]

d Reid, Rachel R. *King's council in the North.* London and N. Y., 1921. (Bibliography.)

e Turner, E. Raymond. *The privy council of England in the seventeenth and eighteenth centuries.* 2 v. Baltimore, 1927–28.

f Fitzroy, Sir Almeric. *Memoirs.* 2 v. London, 1925.

a. Standard work. Contains the fullest and most trustworthy account of the council in the Middle Ages, its various forms, its organization and jurisdiction, the relation it bore to other organs of government, and the nature of its records; based on a fresh examination of the materials, printed and manuscript, from Henry III to Henry VIII; more exhaustive for the fourteenth and fifteenth centuries than for the periods before and after. Supersedes *b.* and *c.*, though these are both still valuable for certain points. Review of *a.*, T. F. Tout, *E.H.R.* 30:117, Jan. 1915; A. B. White, *A.H.R.* 19:867, July 1914.   CHM

d. Scholarly monograph, based on copious documentary material, both printed and manuscript. Describes the origin and development of the council of the North and its executive and judicial functions. Review, K. H. Vickers, *E.H.R.* 37:432, July 1922. *e.* After devoting three chapters to the development previous to 1603, the first volume deals with the years 1603–1679 and is preliminary to an extended study of the council and cabinet in the eighteenth century, to which the second volume is to some extent devoted. Reviews, A. L. Cross, *A.H.R.* 33:385, Jan. 1928; 34:117, Oct. 1928. *f.* Recollections of the clerk of the privy council, 1898 to 1923. Review, (London) *Times Lit. Suppl.* 24:565, Sept. 3, 1925.   ALC

L543 Evans, Florence M. G. (Mrs. C. S. S. Higham). *Principal Secretary of state, a survey of the office from 1558 to 1680.* Manchester, Eng., and N. Y., 1923. [Manchester historical series, v. 43.] (Bibliography.)

Excellent study so far as it goes, though much more research remains to be done on this large and important subject. Review, Conyers Read, *A.H.R.* 29:543, Apr. 1924; F. C. Montague, *E.H.R.* 39:280, Apr. 1924.   ALC

L544 McIlwain, Charles H. *High court of parliament and its supremacy, an historical essay on the boundaries between legislation and adjudication in England.* New Haven, 1910.

Illuminating essay and an important contribution both to political science and to constitutional history. Traces juristic ideas respecting the judicial and the legislative position of parliament, beginning with the medieval conceptions of a fundamental law and of the application of law by parliament as a court. The discussion of the transition of parliament from a body primarily judicial in character to a body primarily legislative, and the development of the seventeenth-century doctrine of parliamentary sovereignty constitute the kernel of the work. It also deals with the effects of these changes, incidentally presenting highly useful material from the political and judicial literature of the Tudor and Stuart periods. Review, G. B. Hertz, *E.H.R.* 26:408, Apr. 1911; J. F. Baldwin, *A.H.R.* 16:597, Apr. 1911.   WAM

L545a Pollard, Albert F. *Evolution of parliament.* London and N. Y., 1920.

b Pasquet, D. *Origin of the House of Commons.* Tr. by R. G. D. Laffan. Cambridge, Eng., 1925.

a. This work shows no trace of the persistent tradition of parliament's unbroken descent from some primitive democratic assembly of the Germanic peoples. It is a general history of parliament which follows evidence not theory; future additions or modifications will be mostly in detail. Parliament is shown as a post-conquest, king-made institution, most slowly attaining self-consciousness or democratic action of any sort. Other myths, some derivations from the parent tradition, are successfully attacked. The modern part—notably the sixteenth century, the author's special field—is more valuable than the medieval. There is much of interest to the student of American government. Review, J. Tait, *E.H.R.* 26:252, Apr. 1921; J. F. Baldwin, *A.H.R.* 27:108, Oct. 1921. ABW

b. A translation of a significant study, which is out of print in the original French edition. There are important additions by the author and a valuable introduction by G. Lapsley. Pasquet and Ludwig Riess, a German scholar, have contributed not a little to modify the traditional views as to the origin of the House of Commons, though their findings have not met with complete acceptance. Review, A. B. White, *A.H.R.* 32:353, Jan. 1927. ALC

L546a Pike, Luke O. *Constitutional history of the house of lords from original sources.* London and N. Y., 1894.

b Firth, Charles H. *The House of Lords during the civil war.* London and N. Y., 1910.

c Turberville, Arthur S. *House of Lords in the reign of William III.* Oxford, 1913.

d —— *House of Lords in the XVIIIth century.* London, 1927.

a. Valuable contribution on the development, composition, and functions of the Lords as a legislative house and court of law, from the modern point of view and based on extensive research. The chapters on the changes in the basis of the peerage from tenure to letters patent are particularly important. Review, T. F. Tout, *E.H.R.* 11:129, Jan. 1896. CHM

b. Really covers the period 1603 to 1661. An admirable survey. Discusses among other things government by a single house in comparison with the bicameral system. Review, W. C. Abbott, *A.H.R.* 16:608, Apr. 1911. *c.* Based largely on printed sources. Rather a narrative of the political activities of the House of Lords than a strictly constitutional study, though the latter is dealt with to some extent. Review, E. R. Turner, *A.H.R.* 19:887, July, 1914. *d.* Continuation of *b.* ALC

L547a Porritt, Edward, and Porritt, Annie G. *Unreformed house of commons: parliamentary representation before 1832.* 1903. 2nd ed., 2 v., Cambridge, Eng., 1909. [1, *England and Wales;* 2, *Scotland and Ireland.*] (Bibliography.)

b Seymour, Charles. *Electoral reform in England and Wales: the development and operation of the parliamentary franchise, 1832–1885.* New Haven, 1915. [Yale historical publications.] (Bibliography.)

a. Probably the most convenient comprehensive modern account of the representative system of the United Kingdom in and before 1832. For origins and development before the fourteenth century it is of little value; from the fifteenth to the nineteenth, excellent. V. 2. Particularly useful; contains much valuable information obtainable elsewhere only in widely scattered places. Review, C. G. Robertson, *E.H.R.* 19:167, Jan. 1904. CHM

b. Deals not only with franchise and redistribution acts, but also with the history and the political effects of all the other major factors of electoral reform in England from 1832 to 1885. Scholarly, discerning, and complete; recognized as the leading authority on the subject. Review, E. Porritt, *A.H.R.* 21:593, Apr. 1916.   JRH

L548a **Bagehot, Walter.** *English constitution.* 1867. Rev. ed., 1872. Reprint, London and N. Y., 1915. [Works and life of Walter Bagehot, ed. by Mrs. Russell Barrington, v. 5.]

   b **Low, Sidney J. M.** *Governance of England.* 1904. Rev. ed. with introductory essay, London and N. Y., 1915.

   c **Lowell, Abbott Lawrence.** *Government of England.* 1908. New ed. with additional ch., 2 v., N. Y., 1912.

   d **Trevelyan, George M.** *Two party system in English political history.* Oxford, 1926.

a. Classic exposition of the English parliamentary system just before the second reform act as it appeared to one of the acutest observers of the economic and political development of the nineteenth century. An essay rather than a detailed description; marked by some distrust of democratic institutions, but full of the keenest observations; in excellent literary form. Bagehot marks an epoch in the study of the English constitution in first emphasizing what since has become a commonplace—that the 'conventions of the constitution' are fully as important as the law for an understanding of the whole. *b.* This brilliant essay may be considered for the working constitution of twentieth-century England the nearest equivalent to that of the mid-Victorian period in *a*. It, too, deals more with actual government than with the paper constitution; chiefly important on the effects of the extensions of the franchise upon parliamentary government. Bagehot's England was still politically aristocratic; Low's had become democratic; this is probably the best account of the consequent political change, a shifting of power from the commons to the electorate resulting in a decline of the former in comparison with the cabinet. Review, *E.H.R.* 20:408, Apr. 1905. *c.* President Lowell's volumes have been received on both sides of the Atlantic as the standard work of the kind on the modern government of England. As in (X531) Lord Bryce's *American commonwealth,* 'government' is here taken in a broad sense to cover not merely the machinery of the state but the political and social conditions that lie behind. The book is really a political study of the present English people and their institutions, thus differing from narrower treatments like (L538) Sir William Anson's and also from unsystematic essays such as *a.* or *b*. Contains useful descriptions, more or less detailed, of the whole machinery of the state, constitutional and political; local, central, and imperial; judicial, educational, and ecclesiastical. Its unique value lies in the political and social chapters, which are filled with acute observations and comparisons with American conditions suggested by an intimate acquaintance with both English and American public life. Review, *A.H.R.* 14:140, Oct. 1908. *d.* An illuminating brief sketch.   CHM

L549a **Webb, Sidney,** and **Webb, Beatrice.** *English local government from the revolution to the municipal corporations act.* 4 v. London and N. Y., 1906–22. [1, *Parish and the county;* 2–3, *Manor and the borough;* 4, *Statutory authorities for special purposes.*]

   b ———— *History of liquor licensing in England principally from 1700 to 1830.* London and N. Y., 1903.

c ——— *English local government: the story of the King's highway.* London and N. Y., 1913. [English local government, v. 5.] (Bibliographical foot-notes.)

d ——— *English prisons under local government.* London and N. Y., 1922. [English local government, v. 6.] (Bibliographical foot-notes.)

e ——— *English poor law history:* Pt. 1, *The old poor law;* Pt. 2, *The last hundred years.* 3 v. London and N. Y., 1927–29. [English local government, v. 7.]

a. Copious and complete description and analysis of the subject from 1689 to 1835. V. 1. Deals with the two main forms of local government which existed everywhere in England. V. 2–3. Treat of the many and varied local bodies and authorities which stood out as exceptions to the control of the county. About one third deals with manorial courts and boroughs which lived on as tattered remnants of the manorial jurisdiction of past times. Two-thirds is given to a study of municipal corporations both in general and in ten selected cases. London, the greatest corporation of all, is given special treatment. V. 4. Study of over 1700 special organizations of municipal sort erected under eighteenth century statutes to meet new conditions of English life; also an illuminating general survey of local government in the period. Built solidly upon a prodigious mass of local sources, used with masterly thoroughness and presented systematically and judicially. Describes not only constitutional form and administrative procedure, but sets forth intimately and with local color the change going on from decade to decade and indicates the principles of growth. Well indexed. Review, v. 1–3, G. E. Howard, *A.H.R.* 12:631, Apr. 1907; 14:122, Oct. 1908; v. 4, W. Anderson, *Amer. Pol. Sci. Rev.* 17:487, Aug. 1923; J. H. Clapham, *E.H.R.* 39:288, Apr. 1924. *b., c., d.* Special studies supplementing *a.* Review of *b.,* E. Porritt, *A.H.R.* 9:861, July 1904; of *c.,* J. H. Clapham, *E.H.R.* 29:177, Jan. 1914. WTR

e. Completes the exhaustive work of the Webbs on English local government, nominally from 1688 to 1832, but really extending beyond these dates in both directions. Review of pt. 1, C. E. Fryer, *A.H.R.* 33:389, Jan. 1928; of pt. 2, (London) *Times Lit. Suppl.* 28:393, May 16, 1929. ALC

L551a Holdsworth, William S. *Sources and literature of English law.* Oxford, 1925.

b Winfield, Percy H. *Chief sources of English legal history.* Cambridge, Mass., 1925. (Bibliographies.)

c Jenks, Edward. *Short history of English law from the earliest times to the end of the year 1911.* Boston, 1912.

d Walsh, William F. *Outlines of the history of English and American law.* N. Y., 1923. (Bibliographies.)

e Potter, Harold. *Introduction to the history of English law.* 1923. 2nd rev. ed., London, 1926.

a. Covers period from Norman Conquest through the eighteenth century; intended as an introductory survey for students; emphasizes importance of legislation and of textbook writers. *b.* Valuable manual. Discusses training needed for studying the subject, bibliographical guides, sources of Anglo-Saxon law, influence of Roman law, statutes, public records, case law, text-books, etc. Review, B. H. Putnam, *A.H.R.* 31:763, July 1926. *c.* Good brief sketch of the development of English law. Deals with the subject chronologically in four periods. Its usefulness is somewhat impaired by the conscious omission of the origin and growth of the courts, and by occasional failure to define technical terms. Review, A. L. Cross, *Mich. Law Rev.* 11:262, Jan. 1913. *d.* and *e.* Both less technical than *c;* introductory works intended for students. *d.* Written for American law students; emphasizes substantive law. *e.* More stimulating, as well as briefer, treatment; greater emphasis on the history of institutions and procedure. Review of *d.* and *e.,* T. F. T. Plucknett, *Harvard Law Rev.* 37:643, March 1924. ALC, EPCE

L552 **Holdsworth, William S.** *History of English law.* V. 1–3, London, 1903–09. 3rd rev. ed., London, 1922–23; v. 4–9, London, 1924–26.

Most comprehensive history of English law. In addition to the history of procedure and of substantive rules of law, it treats very fully the courts, the literature of the law, and the education and careers of lawyers and judges. Devotes much space to both public law and political theory. V. 1. History of the courts and of their jurisdiction to the close of the nineteenth century. Best single work on the subject. Contains also a short, but satisfactory, summary of the development of the jury system. V. 2–3. Beginning with a long section on the Anglo-Saxon period, the development of English law is traced to 1485. Down to 1272 liberal use has been made of the works of (L532, 555) Maitland, although, even in this period, the author has made a considerable addition as the result of personal research. The chief contribution is in the period after 1272, for which it is unquestionably the best guide. V. 4–5. Deal mainly with the sources and development of law in the sixteenth century and the early seventeenth. V. 6. Devoted chiefly to the law of the seventeenth century. V. 7. Gives the history of the law of property. V. 8. Treats the law of obligations, mercantile law, and criminal law. V. 9. Deals with the law of status and with evidence, procedure, and pleading. While the work was announced to close with the seventeenth century, the history of several branches of the law is brought, more or less completely, down to the present. The combination of chronological and topical arrangement in the several volumes has rendered a considerable repetition inevitable; the student must, therefore, make frequent use of the cross references and the index. Copious citations of authorities in the foot-notes. The style is clear. Review, v. 1–3, H. D. Hazeltine, *E.H.R.* 27:341, Apr. 1912; A. L. Cross, *Mich. Law Rev.* 9:1, Nov. 1910, 24:1, Nov. 1925 (gives a list of errors in the work); v. 4–8, H. D. Hazeltine, *E.H.R.* 40:277, Apr. 1925, 41:449, July 1926. CCC, EPCE

L553 **Committee of the Association of American Law Schools,** ed. *Select essays in Anglo-American legal history.* 3 v. Boston, 1907–09. (Bibliographies.)

Consists of 76 essays, which have practically all been reprinted or translated from legal periodicals or treatises. In several instances the authors have revised their articles for this series. V. 1. 'General surveys' of the development of law in England and in the United States from the Anglo-Saxon period to the present. V. 2–3. 'A history of particular topics' under the divisions of sources, the courts, their organization and jurisdiction, procedure, equity, commercial law, contracts, torts, property (in general) and wills, descents, marriages. Thus the field covered is wide, but the method of treatment necessarily results in numerous gaps and in variations in style and points of view. Very convenient collection of trustworthy articles on the history of English law and procedure.

ccc

L554a Blackstone, Sir William. *Commentaries on the laws of England.* 1765–69. 9th ed., with author's latest revisions, 4 v., London, 1783. 23rd rev. ed. by J. Stewart, 4 v., London, 1854.

b Stephen, Henry J. *New commentaries on the laws of England, partly founded on Blackstone.* 1841–45. 16th rev. ed. by E. Jenks, 4 v., London, 1914.

a. Systematic exposition of the whole of English law, public and private, and a brief history of its development. As a presentation of the law of Blackstone's time, the work is in the main reliable. The portion dealing with origins, especially when an attempt was made to go back to the twelfth and thirteenth centuries, contains many errors and should be corrected by later works such as (L555a) Pollock and Maitland, and (L552) Holdsworth. Written for the general reader rather than the lawyer; the style is usually clear and forceful, unhampered by the endless technicalities which render so much of the earlier works unintelligible to the lay reader. The *Commentaries* were long regarded in the United States as a repository of English law and consequently served as a medium by which much of that law was transferred to America. The shallowness of much of his legal philosophy and his unbounded admiration for the spirit of English law called forth the bitter attacks of Bentham, Austin, and others. In recent years there has been a tendency to emphasize Blackstone's faults and overlook his merits. Heinrich Brunner, the eminent German student of English law, after mentioning this tendency, says 'Yet it can be boldly asserted that not one of the modern systems of law can boast of an exposition equal to that which the English law possesses in Blackstone.' *b.* Attempts to bring Blackstone down to date. ccc

L555a Pollock, Sir Frederick, and **Maitland, Frederic W.** *History of English law before the time of Edward I.* 1895. 2nd ed., 2 v., Cambridge, Eng., and Boston, 1899.

b Maitland, Frederic W. *Domesday book and beyond, three essays in the early history of England.* 1897. Reprint, Cambridge, Eng., 1907.

a. Scientific and philosophical exposition of English law in all its bearings upon the economic, political, social, and religious life of the people from the earliest times to 1272. Regarded as the highest attainment in English scholarship in this field from 1066 to 1272. The style is clear and vigorous, often highly dramatic, although an acquaintance with the language of jurisprudence is frequently essential to a full understanding of the theories. There are numerous comparisons with contemporary continental law and legal practices. Review, E. Fry, *E.H.R.* 10:760, Oct. 1895; H. Brunner, *Pol. Sci. Quar.* 11:534, Sept. 1896. *b.* Should be used to supplement the brief account of Anglo-Saxon law in *a.* Tends to exaggerate the prevalence of feudalism previous to the Conquest. Cf. G. B. Adams, 'Anglo-Saxon feudalism,' *A.H.R.* 7:11–35, Oct. 1901.

ccc

L556 Digby, Sir Kenelm E. *Introduction to the history of the law of real property, with original authorities.* 1875. 5th ed., Oxford, 1897.

Written for the general student of law. Pt. 1. 'The common and early statute law relating to land' gives a brief account of Anglo-Saxon land law, the transition to feudal tenure, and the incidents of feudalism in the twelfth and thirteenth centuries. Special attention is given to the legislation of Edward I. Pt. 2. 'Modern law of real property' is devoted primarily to a history of uses, the will, and modern conveyances. Contains copious extracts from Glanville, Bracton, the Year books, and the statutes in the original and in translations. Review, H. C. Lodge, *North Amer. Rev.* 121:429, Oct. 1875. ccc

L557a Stephen, Sir James Fitzjames. *History of the criminal law of England.* 3 v. London, 1883.

b —— *General view of the criminal law of England.* 1863. 2nd ed., London and N. Y., 1890.

a. Covers not only the history of each crime, but also the evolution of the courts which had criminal jurisdiction, and the origin and development of each important stage in criminal procedure. There are extended comparisons of English, Roman, French, and German law and practices. Stephen was an advocate of a strong central government, impatient with popular agitation, and freely expressed his opinions regarding modern legal practices in the light of his experience as a judge. In spite of numerous inaccuracies of statement and citation, due no doubt to haste imposed by other duties, his work remains the best general history of English criminal law. Review, *Blackwood's Magazine,* 133:731, June 1883. *b.* Earlier work of which *a* was an outgrowth and expansion. ccc

L558 Ault, Warren O. *Private jurisdiction in England.* New Haven, 1923. [Yale historical publications.]

Based on a study of the records. Review, James Tait, *E.H.R.* 39:427, July 1924. ALC

L559a *Laws of England, being a complete statement of the whole law of England.* Ed. by Earl of Halsbury and others. 31 v. London, 1907–17. Supplement, v. 1–14, London, 1910–24.

b *Encyclopaedia of the laws of England, being a new abridgement by the most eminent legal authorities.* Ed. by Alexander Wood Renton. 13 v. London, 1897–1903. 2nd rev. ed., by A. W. Renton and others, with general introduction by Sir Frederick Pollock, 15 v., 1906–09. Supplement, v. 16–17, 1913–19.

c *English and empire digest, with complete and exhaustive annotations, being a complete digest of every English case reported from early times to the present day, with additional cases from the courts of Scotland, Ireland, the empire of India, and the dominions beyond the seas, and including complete and exhaustive annotations giving all the subsequent cases in which judicial opinions have been given concerning the English cases digested.* Ed. by Earl of Halsbury, Sir Thomas W. Chitty, and others. V. 1–19, London, 1919–24.

a. States the law on each particular subject; arranged alphabetically; gives citations from the statutes. *b.* Useful short articles on various phases of the law, with helpful bibliographies. *c.* Alphabetically arranged; extends to rubric, "education." ALC

L561a Figgis, John N. *Theory of the divine right of kings.* 1896. 2nd ed., with three additional essays, Cambridge, Eng., 1914. [Cambridge historical essays.]

b McIlwain, Charles H., ed. *Political works of James I, reprinted from the edition of 1616.* Cambridge, Mass., 1918. [Harvard political classics.]

a. Standard treatise; aims to present the real historical explanation for a theory which has not always been dealt a full measure of justice. Review, W. A. Dunning, *A.H.R.* 2:371, Jan. 1897. *b.* Excellent edition of the writings of the most notorious British exponent of the theory. Review, R. G. Usher, *A.H.R.* 24:672, July 1919.

ALC

L562a Gooch, George P. *History of English democratic ideas in the seventeenth century.* Cambridge, Eng., 1898. [Cambridge historical essays.] New ed., with additions by H. J. Laski, London, 1927.

b ———— *Political thought in England from Bacon to Halifax.* London and N. Y., 1914. [Home university library.]

a. On the whole, a very satisfactory study of a most significant phase of English history. The author uses considerable original material, and brings together much information hitherto scattered or presented in connection with other subjects. He has been criticized mainly for minimizing or neglecting certain democratic tendencies at work previous to the Reformation, for not taking sufficiently into account economic factors and for over-emphasizing Pilgrim at the expense of other Puritan influences in New England. Review, F. Strong, *A.H.R.* 4:148, Oct. 1898; M. Lerner, *Pol. Sci. Quar.* 43:159, March 1928. *b.* Presents the subject in a broader, more compendious, and popular form.

ALC

L563a Laski, Harold J. *Political thought in England from Locke to Bentham.* London and N. Y., 1920. [Home university library.] (Good bibliography.)

b Davidson, William L. *Political thought in England, the utilitarians, from Bentham to J. S. Mill.* London and N. Y., 1915. [Home university library.] (Bibliography.)

c Barker, Ernest. *Political thought in England from Herbert Spencer to the present day.* London and N. Y., 1915. [Home university library.] (Bibliography.)

a. In parts, brilliant; as a whole, carefully written. This survey is admittedly indebted to (L651) L. Stephen, *History of English thought in the eighteenth century.* Laski's examination of Locke, limited to the two treatises on government, involves that of the principles of the revolution of 1688. More original is the chapter upon the early eighteenth century theories of church and state, written from the point of view of the author's own theory of sovereignty. The chapter upon Burke is dispassionate yet sympathetic and excellent. Review, T. C. Pease, *A.H.R.* 26:572, Apr. 1921. *b.* Sympathetic treatment throughout. Practically limited to a consideration of Bentham and the two Mills, to whom all but the last chapter are devoted. The topics most adequately treated are those on Bentham as a social reformer, James Mill as a politician, and J. S. Mill on *Liberty* and *Representative government.* J. S. Mill's *Political economy* and the works of Austin are inadequately treated. *c.* Extremely valuable survey of a field wherein such a work was greatly needed. The idealist school, represented by Green, Bradley, and Bosanquet, is shown to carry forward the conception that reason is the real dominating force in political development, an idea later re-examined in the brief consideration of the social psychologists, represented by (B587) Wallas, and MacDougal, *Social psychology.* The examination of Spencer is cogent, that of Maine less satisfactory, while Bryce, in many respects the greatest of all, is relegated to a footnote. Norman Angell, however, bulks large,—it would seem disproportionately so. The political philosophy of the author and his own original ideas stand out frequently as more illuminating than those of the writers discussed by him.   JSR

L564 Dicey, Albert V. *Lectures on the relation between law and public opinion in England during the nineteenth century.* 1905. 2nd ed., London, 1914.

Very suggestive discussion of the subject indicated by the title. Review, *E.H.R.* 20:829, Oct. 1905.   ALC

L565 Flournoy, Francis R. *Parliament and war: the relation of the British Parliament to the administration of foreign policy in connection with the initiation of war.* London, 1927.

A valuable contribution to an important but elusive subject. Review, R. B. Way, *A.H.R.* 33:688, Apr. 1928.   ALC

ECONOMIC AND SOCIAL HISTORY

L571a Usher, Abbott P. *Introduction to the industrial history of England.* Boston, 1920. (Bibliography.)

b Cheyney, Edward P. *Introduction to the industrial and social history of England.* 1901. Rev. ed., N. Y., 1920. (Bibliographies.)

c Tickner, Frederick W. *Social and industrial history of England.* London and N. Y., 1915.

d Waters, Charlotte M. *Economic History of England. 1066–1874.* Oxford, 1925.

a. In many respects a valuable survey of the subject; scholarly in treatment; marked by individual but sane and suggestive points of view; contains incisive criticisms of the socialistic interpretation of history. While extremely helpful for collateral reading, its apportionment of topics and its subtle discussions of disputed questions tend to make it over-difficult for the beginner. Review, A. L. Cross, *Hist. Outlook,* 11:244, June 1920.   ALC
b. Best brief handbook of English economic history, although, unfortunately, the new edition has not incorporated all that has been added to knowledge since 1901. The author's treatment is always judicious, his presentation lucid, his narrative entertaining. To many of the chapters is prefixed a brief indication of attendant political conditions. The last chapter in the new edition is an admirable account of developments from 1906 to 1920. Review, H. L. Gray, *A.H.R.* 26:568, Apr. 1921. *c.* Elementary and superficial sketch of social, artistic, literary, religious, and economic England, of little use save to the cursory reader. *d.* Well-illustrated text-book.   HLG

L572 Cunningham, William. *Growth of English industry and commerce.* 1882. 6th rev. ed., 2 v. in 3, Cambridge, Eng., 1915–21. (Bibliography.)

Cunningham was the first of modern scholars to formulate the history of English economic life, doing for it what (L535) Stubbs did for the early constitutional history of England. Always approaching his subject with a view to the larger aspects of social and national development, he imparted to his work something of a philosophic and monumental quality. Though not always lucid in arrangement or exhaustive in the statement of evidence, the volumes are indispensable to any student, incorporating in new editions, as they have, expanding research. In his description of the mercantile system of the Tudors and Stuarts, he has fewer rivals than in preceding or succeeding periods, and in temper of mind he was sympathetic with a strong central government. Review, *Athenaeum*, 2:111, July 22, 1882. HLG

L573a Ashley, Sir William J. *Introduction to English economic history and theory.* 1888–93. 5th ed., 2 v., London and N. Y., 1901.

b ——— *Economic organisation of England, an outline history.* London and N. Y., 1914.

a. Like (L572) Cunningham's work, a pioneer English economic history; highly valued for its clarity and for thorough treatment of certain subjects. The chapters on the canonist doctrine of usury and on the craft gilds are still valuable; but other parts of the book, such as the discussion of agricultural changes and the origin of the woolen industry, have been superseded. *b*. Series of lectures treating in a general way the successive stages of English economic organization and the social changes which have accompanied them. Newer points of view and maturer judgments appear; weighty in content; should be read along with (L571*b*) Cheyney's brief history. Review, *E.H.R.* 20:188, Jan. 1915. HLG

L574 Lipson, Ephraim. *Introduction to the economic history of England.* London, 1915. (Bibliography.)

Inasmuch as it embodies most of the information to be derived from recently printed sources, this is today the best manual of medieval English economic history to the reign of Elizabeth. Treats agriculture in a commonplace manner, finance and foreign trade inadequately. One-half of the book is devoted to industry; excellent on the early woolen industry. The new suggestions about the gild merchant and the origin of the crafts should be read in connection with (L575*a*) Gross and (L573*a*) Ashley respectively. Review, H. L. Gray, *A.H.R.* 21:571, Apr. 1916. HLG

L575a Gross, Charles. *Gild merchant, a contribution to British municipal history.* 2 v. Oxford, 1890.

b Salzman, Louis F. *English industries of the middle ages.* 1913. Rev. and illustrated ed., Oxford and N. Y., 1923. (Bibliographical foot-notes.)

c Kramer, Stella. *English craft gilds: studies in their progress and decline.* N. Y., 1927.

a. Scholarly, exhaustive work. Rejects the view that British municipal government was derived from the gild organization. Review, G. T. Warner, *E.H.R.* 6:757, Oct. 1891. ALC

b. Admirable little book on the beginnings and the early technique of various industries. Apart from utilizing the author's illuminating discoveries in manuscript sources, it summarizes the information contained in the economic chapters of (L441) *Victoria history of the counties of England* and in the considerable body of recently published records. Furnishes valuable statistical data. There is a good concluding chapter on the control of industry. Review, H. L. Gray, *A.H.R.* 20:136, Oct. 1914; 31:164, Oct. 1925. HLG

c. Scholarly supplement to previous investigations, particularly for the later period of gild history. Review, W. E. Lunt, *A.H.R.* 33:434, Jan. 1928. ALC

L576a Seebohm, Frederic. *English village community examined in its relations to the manorial and tribal systems and to the common or open field system of husbandry.* 1883. 4th ed., London and N. Y., 1890. Reprint, 1913.

b Gray, Howard L. *English field systems.* Cambridge, Mass. and London, 1915. [Harvard historical studies, v. 22.]

a. Viewing English history as a continuity from Roman Britain, Seebohm finds the origin of the English village in the Roman manorial system. Instead of being free the community was in serfdom under the lord of the manor. More recent investigations have shown this interpretation questionable, at least, in some respects. It has been, however, a valuable influence in modifying the older views which ascribed excessive importance to Germanic influences. Review, *Athenaeum,* 2:133, Aug. 4, 1883. *b.* More recent, exhaustive study, based upon fuller data; carefully analyzes the relative importance of Celtic and Germanic influences in the land systems in the different parts of England. Review, W. A. Morris, *A.H.R.* 21:783, July 1916. AHSW

L577a Vinogradoff, Sir Paul G. *Villainage in England, essays in English mediaeval history.* Oxford, 1892.

b ——— *Growth of the manor.* 1905. 2nd rev. ed., London and N. Y., 1911.

c ——— *English society in the eleventh century, essays in English mediaeval history.* Oxford, 1908.

The author of these three studies of first-rate importance, who had been professor of history in the University of Moscow, was professor of jurisprudence at Oxford from 1903 to 1925. *a.* Despite the Norman conquest and the attempts of lawyers to simplify the villain's status, the village community retained traces of its original freedom and these later expanded and developed. Review, *Athenaeum* 1:367, March 19, 1892. *b.* The division of the open field into strips was not manorial but essentially a communal institution. On the original township organization the manor was gradually superimposed, and society, at first democratic, became gradually divided into strata. The Domesday Book classification of persons is due to economic distinction. Review, F. G. Davenport, *A.H.R.* 11:361, Jan. 1906. *c.* Study of society in its political, economic, and juridical aspects; town life is omitted. Review, J. Tait, *E.H.R.* 24:333, Apr. 1909.

AHSW

L578a Bateson, Mary. *Mediaeval England, English feudal society from the Norman conquest to the middle of the fourteenth century.* London and N. Y., 1904. [Story of the nations.]

b Abram, Annie. *English life and manners in the later middle ages.* London and N. Y., 1913. (Bibliography.)

c ——— *Social England in the fifteenth century, a study of the effects of economic conditions.* London and N. Y., 1909. [Research library.] (Bibliography.)

d Denton, William. *England in the fifteenth century.* London, 1888.

e Green, Alice S. A. S. (Mrs. John R.). *Town life in the fifteenth century.* 2 v. N. Y. and London, 1894.

f Coulton, George Gordon. *The mediaeval village.* Cambridge, 1925.

g Salzman, Louis F. *English life in the middle ages.* Oxford Univ. Press, 1926.

a. Though small and devoted in the main to a description of social life, this excellent work includes enough narrative to furnish a distinct thread for the period. Review, E. Porritt, *A.H.R.* 9:782, July 1904. *b.* Best and fullest description of the more intimate sides of social life, with much information also upon business, education, and the church. Valuable illustrations. Review, *E.H.R.* 28:807, Oct. 1913. *c.* Similar work for the succeeding period. Review, *E.H.R.* 25:611, July 1910. *d.* Interesting and valuable but not well described by its title. Divided almost equally between an introductory essay on certain unfamiliar phases of earlier history and a sketch, from original sources, of rural conditions in the fifteenth and sixteenth centuries. Nothing on other sides of English history during the fifteenth century. Review, *Athenaeum,* 2:279, Sept. 1, 1888. *e.* Collection of spirited statements and interesting quotations from contemporary records, so arranged as to bring out various aspects of town life. Organization not very successful; statements frequently refer to centuries earlier or later than fifteenth; mainly useful as a book of reference and a series of detached descriptions. Review, J. Tait, *E.H.R.* 10:157, Jan. 1895.   EPC
f. A learned and readable work, aiming to show that the lot of the people of past times, in the humbler walks of life, was an unhappy one. Review, (London) *Times Lit. Suppl.* 24:37, Jan. 21, 1926. *g.* Sprightly rather general account, written primarily for school purposes. Review, N. Neilson, *A.H.R.* 32:912, July, 1927.
                                                                             ALC

L579 Tawney, Richard H. *Agrarian problem in the sixteenth century.* London and N. Y., 1912.

Enclosures and the introduction of capitalistic wool-raising checked the economic progress of the English peasantry and offset the abolition of labor services. The rise of competitive rents and the growth of the land market receive careful consideration. The statistics adduced furnish an inadequate basis for positive conclusions. Review, J. H. Clapham, *E.H.R.* 28:567, July 1913. AHSW

L580 Rogers, James E. Thorold. *History of agriculture and prices in England, 1259–1793.* 7 v. in 8. Oxford, 1866–1902.

Vast assemblage of materials. Critics have taken exception to many of the author's interpretations, for example, his belief in the prosperity of the medieval laborer, the over-emphasis of the depressing effect of seventeenth and eighteenth century legislation on the worker, and the antedating of the commutation of villein services. Review of v. 7, E. F. Gay, *A.H.R.* 8:769, July 1903. ALC

L581a Prothero, Rowland E., Baron Ernle. *English farming, past and present.* 1912. 3rd ed., with additional chapter, London and N. Y., 1922. 4th ed., London, 1927. (Bibliography.)

b —— *Pioneers and progress of English farming.* London and N. Y., 1888. (Bibliography.)

a. By far the most complete historical study of English farming; treated from the political, social, and legal points of view as well as from the economic.

The author skilfully demonstrates that the advent of scientific farming, labor saving machines, and the like exerted a powerful force in hastening the break-up of the medieval and the development of the modern agricultural life. His treatment of the enclosure movement, tithes, and the corn laws is suggestive, although the latter is weakened by a few inaccuracies. Valuable appendix of documents. Review, *A.H.R.* 19:860, July 1914.   *b.* Earlier work on which *a* is based.

WFG

L582a Botsford, Jay B. *English society in the eighteenth century as influenced from oversea.* N. Y., 1924. (Bibliography.)

  b Bowden, Witt. *Industrial society in England towards the end of the eighteenth century.* N. Y., 1925. (Bibliography.)

  c Jackson, Frederick J. Foakes. *Social life in England, 1750–1850.* N. Y., 1916. [Lowell lectures.]

  d Turberville, Arthur S. *English men and manners in the eighteenth century.* Oxford, 1926.

  e Williams, Judith Blow. *Guide to the printed materials for English social and economic history, 1750–1850.* 2 v. N. Y., 1926.

Recent studies of aspects of English social life in the eighteenth century.   *a.* Studies the reactions of trade upon domestic conditions. Review, A. L. Cross, *A.H.R.* 31:389, Jan. 1925.   *b.* Investigation of the consequences of the transition from handwork to the factory system. Review, W. T. Laprade, *A.H.R.* 31:808, July 1925.   *c.* Not a history, but a lively portraiture of different phases of social life based upon contemporary writings. Review, W. P. Hall, *A.H.R.* 22:438, Jan. 1917.   GMD
d. Suggestive survey, with excellent illustrations. Apologetic, but makes no effort to conceal faults of the period. Review, (London) *Times Lit. Suppl.* 25:711, Oct. 21, 1926.   *e.* Critical bibliography of, first, works written in England during the period 1750–1850, and, secondly, later works (to 1923) written in any language and dealing with the period in question. Very useful. Review, N. S. B. Gras, *Econ. Hist. Rev.* 1:165, Jan. 1927.   ALC

L583a Toynbee, Arnold. *Lectures on the industrial revolution of the 18th century in England.* 1884. New ed., London, 1908.

  b Mantoux, Paul. *La révolution industrielle au XVIIIe siècle: essai sur les commencements de la grande industrie moderne en Angleterre.* Paris, 1906. [Bibliothèque de la Fondation Thiers, v. 9.] (Bibliography.)

a. The work of a unique personality whose early death destroyed a career of great promise. Fragmentary, but marked by research and keen observation. Moderately socialistic in tone. Review, Sir Alfred (later Lord) Milner, (L22) *Dict. Nat. Biog.* 57:136.   *b.* Brilliant contribution, based on wide study and presented with unusual skill. Review, L. L. Price, *E.H.R.* 21:594, July 1906. English translation by Marjorie Vernon, London, 1929.   ALC

L584 Perris, George H. *Industrial history of modern England.* N. Y., 1914. (Bibliography.)

Best book on its subject for the period since 1760. Drawn from original sources to an unusual degree for an outline work. Emphasizes, perhaps over-emphasizes, the misery of the mass of the people in this particular period and the deleterious effect upon them of the Industrial Revolution. Review, *Athenaeum,* 2:142, Aug. 1, 1914.

EPC

L585 Porter, George R. *Progress of the nation in its various social and economical relations from the beginning of the nineteenth century to the present time.* 1836. Rev. ed. brought up to date, by F. W. Hirst, London, 1912.

Invaluable handbook of statistical information. Sociological data in regard to population, pauperism, emigration, crime, and education may be found here in abundance, as well as excellent summaries of progress during the period in trade, commerce, manufacturing, currency, banking, and taxation. Review, *Athenaeum,* 2:729, Oct. 1836; G. B. Hertz, *E.H.R.* 27:827, Oct. 1912.

WPH

L586a Hammond, John L., and **Hammond, Barbara.** *Village labourer, 1760–1832, a study in the government of England before the Reform Bill.* 1911. New ed., London and N. Y., 1920.

b —— *Town labourer, 1760–1832, the new civilisation.* London and N. Y., 1917. (Bibliography.)

c —— *Skilled labourer, 1760–1832.* London and N. Y., 1919.

These volumes describe in dark colors the condition of the English working classes during the Industrial Revolution. The authors have explored the hitherto unused records of the Home Office to such good effect that their vivid pages contain much that is new and important. They tell their story in terms of class struggle and they attribute the low wages and miseries of the period chiefly to the wickedness of the employers. Unsparing indictment of the English governing classes. Review, J. H. Clapham, *Econ. Jour.* 22:248, June 1912; 28:202, June 1918; 30:365, Sept. 1920.

GJ

L587 Nicholls, Sir George. *History of the English poor law.* 2 v., 1854. 2nd rev. ed., 1860; 3rd rev. ed., with supplementary v. by Thomas Mackay, 3 v., London and N. Y., 1898–99.

Standard work. Sir George Nicholls was the central figure in the reforms of 1834, and 'the father of the new system of poor law.' His knowledge of the practical workings of poor relief was unrivaled. His work covers the years 924 to 1853. Mackay's supplementary volume for the years 1834 to 1898 covers in part the same period, but follows a different method. Review, W. A. Spooner, *Econ. Rev.* 9:258 Apr. 1899; L. R. Phelps, *Econ. Jour.* 10:80, March 1900. GJ

L588 Hutchins, B. Leigh, and **Harrison, Amy (Mrs. F. H. Spencer).** *History of factory legislation.* 1903. 2nd rev. ed., London, 1911. [Studies in economics and political science.] (Select bibliography.)

Standard authority on this subject. The first edition contains extensive appendixes and bibliographies of factory legislation and other allied subjects, which have been greatly cut down in the second edition; this has a few added pages devoted to such minor advancements as were made between the dates in question. Review, A. P. Winston, *Jour. of Pol. Econ.* 11:650, Sept. 1903. WPH

L589a Holyoake, George J. *History of co-operation in England: its literature and its advocates.* 1875–79. 2nd rev. ed., 2 v., London, 1906.

b Wilkinson, John F. *Friendly society movement.* London, 1886.

c Webb, Sidney, and Webb, Beatrice. *History of trade unionism.* 1894. Rev. ed., with continuation to 1920. London and N. Y., 1920.

a. Detailed account of the coöperative movement from the early nineteenth century to 1906. Emphasis is laid on the earlier history of coöperation. Full description of American, as well as of British, endeavor in this direction is given, and the literature of coöperation is fully analyzed. Review, *Nation* (N. Y.), 21:315, Nov. 11, 1875. *b.* Social, moral, and educational influences of the friendly societies, or workingmen's benefit associations, are analyzed and their history traced from the middle of the eighteenth century to 1886. Emphasis is laid on the endeavor of these secret societies to gain legal recognition from the government. The relation of the American Odd Fellows to their British brethren is described. Review, *Athenaeum,* 2:8, July 3, 1886. *c.* Classic book in English economic history and the only one of importance on this subject. The first edition, widely advertised through the instrumentality of the Fabian Society, did much to popularize the trade union movement both in America and England. The second edition continued the story of British unionism to date, adding several hundred pages to the narrative. The well-known inclination of the authors toward a somewhat restricted view of the labor movement should render the reader cautious, not in respect to the reliability of the facts given, but against the non-inclusion of other facts germane to the subject but unfavorable to the trade union cause. Review, *Amer. Econ. Rev.* 10:834, Dec. 1920.   WPH

L590 Beer, Max. *History of British socialism.* 2 v., London, 1919–20.

Based upon his earlier work on the same subject in German. Most complete treatment of the subject; but the views of the author, an Austrian, are rather colored by his continental outlook. Perhaps inclined to over-stress the importance of British socialism in the period previous to the present century, and to include in his survey a movement so primarily political as Chartism. Review, *Nation* (London) 25:272, May 31, 1919; 27:562, July 31, 1920.   ALC

L591a Blanshard, Paul. *Outline of the British labor movement.* London and N. Y., 1923. (Brief bibliography.)

b Cole, George D. H. *Short history of the British working class movement.* 3 v. London, 1927.

a. Good sympathic sketch of the origin and aims of the Labor movement. *b.* Volumes 1. and 2 in the American edition are bound together. Volume 3 covers the period 1900–1927. A useful survey, somewhat influenced by the author's advocacy of guild socialism. Review of v. 1 and 2, C. F. Brand, *A.H.R.* 32:869, July 1927; of v. 3, (London) *Times Lit. Suppl.* 26:943, Dec. 15, 1927.   ALC

L592 Johnson, Stanley C. *History of emigration from the United Kingdom to North America.* London, 1913. [Studies in economics and political science.] (Bibliography.)

Deals with the period from 1763 to 1912; much more space is devoted to immigration to Canada than to the United States. An excellent resumé is given of both Canadian and American immigration laws and likewise of the public land policy of the two countries. A history of various colonization schemes during the nineteenth century is added. Review, E. A. Ross, *A.H.R.* 20:200, Oct. 1914.

WPH

L593 Jackman, William T. *Development of transportation in modern England.* 2 v. Cambridge, Eng., 1916. (Bibliography.)

Recounts the history of road, water, and railway transportation in England. The account of roads should be supplemented by the superior treatment in (L549c) Webb, *King's highway;* it fails to include the latter part of the nineteenth century. The development of canal and river navigation and the competition between canals and railways is well handled. The section devoted to railways is unfortunately less than one third of the book and is inadequate. Appendixes contain important statistical data. Review, J. H. Clapham, *E.H.R.* 32:611, Oct. 1917.

GMD

L594 Clapham, J. H. *An economic history of modern Britain: the early railway age, 1820–1850.* London, 1927.

The first of three volumes on British economic history since the Napoleonic Wars. Covers many topics and gives a complete picture of the period, social as well as economic in a narrow sense. Readable and corrective of many hitherto accepted views. Review, F. C. Dietz, *A.H.R.* 32:863, July 1927; also (London) *Times Lit. Suppl.* 26:169, March 17, 1927.

HRS

L596 Andréadès, A. *History of the bank of England.* London, 1909. 2nd ed. trans. by Christobel Meredith. Preface by H. S. Foxwell.

The standard work on the Bank of England; originally appeared in French in two volumes in 1904. Review, *Quart. Jour. of Econ.* 17:310, May 1909. ALC

CULTURAL HISTORY: GENERAL

L601 Traill, Henry D., ed. *Social England, a record of the progress of the people in religion, laws, learning, arts, industry, commerce, science, literature, and manners from the earliest times to the present day.* 1894–98. New illustrated ed., by H. D. Traill and J. S. Mann, 1901–04; also with title *Building of Britain and the empire, a record,* 6 v. in 12, London, 1909. (Bibliographies.)

Storehouse of information on the various subjects enumerated in its title. Extends to the year 1885. Its contents are treated mainly under four heads: political life, intellectual and religious interests, economic life, and social customs, with short sketches concerning Scotland and Ireland appended to each chapter. Much attention is paid to the art of war, naval history, agriculture, trade, and the fine arts. The writers who have coöperated in its production include, generally speaking, the ablest English scholars in their respective fields at the time of publication. The work is on the whole very good, though there is naturally much unevenness. Study and writing in these fields since its appearance have been largely critical rather than constructive and have, therefore, served rather to throw doubts on some of the statements than to supersede them by new knowledge. Valuable only as a wide collection of facts, critically examined and systematically arranged, not as a philosophy of history. Review, T. A. Archer, *E.H.R.* 9:721, Oct. 1894; J. Tait, *E.H.R.* 10:359, Apr. 1895; W. B. Weeden, *A.H.R.* 1:124, Oct. 1895.

EPC

L602a Barnard, Francis Pierrepont, ed. *Companion to English history, middle ages.* Oxford, 1902. (Bibliographies.)

  b Davis, Henry W. C., ed. *Mediaeval England, a new edition of Barnard's 'Companion to English history.'* Oxford and N. Y., 1924. (Bibliographies.)

  c *Shakespeare's England, an account of the life and manners of his age.* Ed. by Sir Walter Raleigh, Sir Sidney Lee, and Charles T. Onions. 2 v. Oxford, 1916.

Admirably illustrated coöperative works by eminent scholars. The various phases of court, town, and country life; of costume, architecture, and art; and of military, religious, and intellectual activities are concisely and clearly depicted. There are special chapters on handwriting, the book trade, heraldry, coinage, shipping, and commerce. *c.* Contains, in addition, excellent chapters on sports and pastimes and on the development of the theater. *b.* Partly rewritten revision of *a.*, published as a companion to *c.* Review of *b.*, N. Neilson, *A.H.R.* 29:756, July 1924; of *c.*, E. P. Cheyney, *A.H.R.* 22:372, Jan. 1917.   GMD

L603 Jusserand, Jean Jules. *English wayfaring life in the middle ages.* London, 1889. Various later ed. Tr. by L. T. Smith from *Les Anglais au moyen âge, la vie nomade et les routes d'Angleterre au XIVe siècle,* Paris, 1884.

Describes vividly and learnedly roads and bridges, lay and ecclesiastical wayfarers in the fourteenth century. Very valuable as a companion to Chaucerian studies. The author has added much material in the English translation. Review, *Athenaeum,* 1:277, March 2, 1889.   AHSW

L604 Notestein, Wallace. *History of witchcraft in England from 1558 to 1718.* Washington, 1911. [H. B. Adams prize essay.]

Scholarly monograph; based, to a large degree, on contemporary materials. Review, G. L. Burr, *A.H.R.* 18:129, Oct. 1912.   ALC

CULTURAL HISTORY: RELIGION

L621 Wakeman, Henry O. *Introduction to the history of the church of England.* 1896. 9th rev. ed., by S. L. Ollard, London, 1920.

Best brief account of the stages of church development to 1919. Scrupulous in statement and just in appreciations, while expounding a Catholic Anglicanism with an idealizing reverence which dims some realities of the lay world. Contains an excellent exposition of the system of life in the medieval church. Review, E. B. Hulbert, *Am. Jour. of Theol.* 1:1051, Oct. 1897.

Cf. § F for various works on general church history which contain materials pertinent to the religious history of the British islands.   FAC

L622 Stephens, William R. W., and **Hunt, William,** ed. *History of the English church.* 9 v. London, 1899–1910. [1, W. Hunt, *597–1066;* 2, W. R. W. Stephens, *1066–1272;* 3, W. W. Capes, *Fourteenth and fifteenth centuries;* 4, J. Gairdner, *From the accession of Henry VIII to the death of Mary;* 5, W. H. Frere, *1558–1625;* 6, W. H. Hutton, *1625–1714;* 7, J. H. Overton and F. Relton, *1714–1800;* 8–9, F. W. Cornish, *Nineteenth century.*] (Good bibliographies.)

This extensive coöperative history is distinguished by painstaking research, fullness of detail as to successions in prelacies and abbacies, diocesan statistics, and personalities; but is defective chiefly as to the development of institutions and religious thought and as to international relations. V. 1–2. Though lacking perspective and critical rigor, give the most complete existing account of the medieval period. V. 3. Skilfully and interestingly written; eminently judicial in the matter of Wiclif and the Lollards; admirably instructive as to diocesan and parochial administration, the organization of cathedral chapters, monastic and university life, and the social influence of the church. V. 4–5. The treatment of the sixteenth century is less satisfactory. Gairdner's minute knowledge of state papers and his acute interest make his narrative vital and valuable, but his presentation of affairs is as partisan as (L304) Froude's contrasted version. Frere, also, assuming modern Anglicanism as the norm, views the Puritans as interlopers and fails to understand their religious motives. V. 6. Less bias and more generosity belongs to Hutton's rather restricted account of the seventeenth century turmoil. V. 7. Rich in biographical matter and social history; valuable for the Methodist movement, the plans for an American episcopate, and the influence of the American and French Revolutions on the English Church. V. 8–9. Encyclopedic; enrich the chronicle of events by summaries of parliamentary debates and laws and by quotation of popular and journalistic comment; indispensable for the period subsequent to the Oxford movement. Review, v. 1–3, F. A. Christie, *A.H.R.* 7:342, Jan. 1902; v. 4, 8:348, Jan. 1903; v. 5, 10:636, Apr. 1905; v. 6, S. M. Jackson, 9:811, July 1904; v. 7, G. M. Rushforth, *E.H.R.* 22:177, Jan. 1907; v. 8–9, 26:605, July 1911.   FAC

L623 Makower, Felix. *Constitutional history and constitution of the church of England.* London and N. Y., 1895. Tr. from *Die Verfassung der Kirche von England,* Berlin, 1894. (Bibliography.)

Almost indispensable volume for English ecclesiastical and constitutional history and institutions; valuable for reference rather than reading, because of its elaborate descriptive 'conspectus of literature,' its numerous references, and its inclusion in foot-notes and appendixes of most of the important documents in whole or in part. Review, *Athenaeum,* 1:82, Jan. 19, 1905.   CHM

L624a Jessopp, Augustus. *Coming of the friars and other historic essays.* 1888. 7th ed., London, 1895.

   b Creighton, Mandell. *Historical lectures and addresses.* Ed. by Louise Creighton. London and N. Y., 1903.

   c Hutton, Edward. *The franciscans in England, 1224–1538.* London, 1927.

a. Accurate research illuminated by imagination and human sympathy. Deals with concrete local history in thirteenth-century England; the Mendicants' objects and methods; life in village, monastery, and university; and the extent of the Black Death. An account of the Muggletonians is added. Review, *Athenaeum,* 1:176, Feb. 9, 1889. *b.* Brief and informing lectures on various aspects of English church life, including the friars. Review, *E.H.R.* 19:826, Oct. 1904.

FAC

c. A good popular survey, not marked by extensive research. Review, *A.H.R.* 32:576, Apr. 1927.   ALC

L625a Gasquet, Francis A., Cardinal. *Old English Bible and other essays.* London, 1897.

b ———— *Eve of the reformation, studies in the religious life and thought of the English people in the period preceding the rejection of the Roman jurisdiction by Henry VIII.* 1899. 3rd ed., London, 1905.

c ———— *Henry VIII and the English monasteries, an attempt to illustrate the history of their suppression.* 1888. 6th ed., 2 v., 1895; popular rev. ed., 1 v., London, 1906. [Catholic standard library.]

d **Savine, A.** *English monasteries on the eve of the dissolution.* Oxford, 1909.

e **Snape, R. H.** *English monastic finances.* Cambridge (Eng.), 1926.

a. While the conclusions regarding the Wyclifite version do not meet with general acceptance, the point of view is interesting; other essays throw brilliant new lights on various aspects of medieval church life. Review, *Athenaeum,* 1 :833, June 26, 1897. *d* and *e* have made necessary some modification of Gasquet's conclusions.   ALC

b. Important contribution to the historical literature on the Reformation. Working largely from more recently available source material, the author very effectively upsets many of the preconceived ideas of religious life in England before the revolt from Rome. Scholarly and judicial. Review, *Athenaeum,* 1 :141, Feb. 3, 1900.   PVBJ

c. This judicious sifting, by an able historian, of the circumstances leading to the suppression of the monasteries has established a view with which other competent scholars largely agree. The discussion of the monasteries and their suppression in relation to social, economic, and political conditions is also of interest and value.   JEG

L626 Dixon, Richard W. *History of the church of England from the abolition of the Roman jurisdiction.* 6 v. Oxford, 1877–1902. 3rd ed. of v. 1–3, Oxford, 1895–1902. [1, *Henry VIII, 1529–1537;* 2, *Henry VIII, 1538–1547, Edward VI, 1547–1548;* 3, *Edward VI, 1549–1553;* 4, *Mary, 1553–1558;* 5, *Elizabeth, 1558–1563;* 6, *Elizabeth, 1564–1570.*]

Amplest and best history of the Church of England for the period 1529 to 1570. Marked by painstaking research, informing exposition, and a style clear and animated. Richly annotated with valuable quotations from sources. Its wealth of detail is skilfully constructed, with some lapses into the manner of a chronicle. Written with High Anglican prepossessions, its treatment of non-conformists under Elizabeth is fair-minded and makes adequate recognition of the influence of the continental reformation. Review, v. 3, G. G. Perry, *E.H.R.* 2 :165, Jan. 1887; v. 5–6, A. F. Pollard, *E.H.R.* 17 :577, July 1902.   FAC

L627 Perry, George G. *History of the church of England from the death of Elizabeth to the present time.* 1861–64. 6th rev. ed., 3 v., London, 1900.

At the time of its original publication a distinct contribution of high value. Still useful for information on many topics not reproduced in later works. The final volume is inferior to the other two.   EPCe

L628a Stoughton, John. *Church and state two hundred years ago, ecclesiastical affairs, 1660–3.* London, 1862.

b ———— *Ecclesiastical history of England from the opening of the long parliament to the death of Oliver Cromwell.* 2 v. London, 1867.

c —— *Ecclesiastical history of England: the church of the restoration.* 2 v. London, 1870.

d —— *Ecclesiastical history of England: the church of the revolution.* London, 1874.

e —— *Religion in England under Anne and the Georges, 1702–1800.* 2 v. London, 1878.

f —— *Religion in England from 1800 to 1850, a history with postscript on subsequent events.* 2 v. London, 1884.

Taken together, these volumes furnish the most complete survey of English religious history from 1640 to 1850. Specially useful for the treatment of non-conformists and dissenters, institutional questions, and the careers of important ecclesiastics.

EPce

L629a *Journal of John Wesley, A.M. sometime fellow of Lincoln College, Oxford, enlarged from original mss. with notes from unpublished diaries, annotations, maps, and illustrations.* Ed. by Nehemiah Curnock and others. 8 v. London and N. Y., 1909–16.

b Tyerman, Luke. *Life and times of the Rev. John Wesley, M.A., founder of the Methodists.* 1870. 6th ed., London, 1890.

c Winchester, Caleb T. *Life of John Wesley.* N. Y. and London, 1906.

a. Complete, authoritative edition with much supplementary manuscript materials. Numerous other more or less complete editions exist. Wesley himself compiled the *Journal* from his diaries. Important not merely for the rise of Methodism but also for many phases of English life and history in the eighteenth century. *b.* Long the standard biography; a storehouse of facts, derived from published and unpublished materials. 'Nothing, likely to be of general interest, has been withheld. Nothing, derogatory to the subject of these memoirs, has been kept back.' *c.* Excellent, brief work; based on original authorities; particularly admirable concerning the domestic society into which Wesley was born and the national society to which he preached.

WAG

L630a Ward, Monsignor Bernard N. *Dawn of the Catholic revival in England, 1781–1803.* 2 v. London and N. Y., 1909.

b —— *Eve of Catholic emancipation, being the history of the English Catholics during the first thirty years of the nineteenth century.* 3 v. London and N. Y., 1911–12.

a. Throws much light on the improved status of the Roman Catholics after the repeal of the penal laws, on the immigration of foreign priests, and on the resistance of the laity to clerical control and increased papal authority. Review, *E.H.R.* 25:204, Jan. 1910. *b.* Full and careful study. Review, S. B. Fay, *Nation* (N. Y.), 94:416, Apr. 25, 1912.

ALC

L631a Church, Richard W. *Oxford movement, twelve years, 1833–1845.* 1891. New ed., London and N. Y., 1904.

b Ward, Wilfrid P. *William George Ward and the Oxford movement.* London, 1889.

c Mathieson, William Law. *English church reform, 1815–1840.* London and N. Y., 1923.

a. Classic account, by a contemporary; aims not to criticize but to explain the movement by the religious and philosophical conditions of the time and to interpret the participants by reverent sympathy with their ideals. A masterpiece of Oxford culture. Review, *Athenaeum*, 1:367, March 21, 1891. *b.* Sympathetic account, by Ward's son, of the group who embraced Catholicism. Review, *Athenaeum*, 1:689, June 1, 1889. *c.* Collateral study of part of the same movement, devoted primarily to the ecclesiastical legislation of 1836–1840 and its antecedents; neither adequate nor sympathetic. Review, E. L. Woodward, *E.H.R.* 39:474, July 1924.   FAC

CULTURAL HISTORY: EDUCATION, THOUGHT, PHILOSOPHY

L641a Leach, Arthur F. *Schools of medieval England.* London, 1915. [The antiquary's books.] (Bibliography.)

   b ——— *English schools at the reformation, 1546–8.* Westminster, 1896.

   c Graham, Hugh. *Early Irish monastic schools: a study of Ireland's contribution to early medieval culture.* Dublin, 1923.

a. Very learned work; full of new information, particularly as to the number of schools in medieval England; marred by an unfortunate effort to score points against previous writers. Review, A. G. Little, *E.H.R.* 30:525, July 1915.   ALC

b. Chiefly a collection of sources, with long introduction summarizing the author's conclusions. Pioneer work of the highest value; but controversial in tone and not free from errors. Review, H. Rashdall, *E.H.R.* 12:566, July 1897.

                                                                                    GJ

c. A useful but not altogether authoritative work. Review, *A.H.R.* 29:791, July 1924.   ALC

L642 Mallet, Sir Charles E. *History of the University of Oxford.* 3 v. London, 1927.

Third volume, dealing with the eighteenth and nineteenth centuries, completes the work. Most comprehensi.e account of the subject; based chiefly on the printed materials. Review, H. H. E. Craster, *E.H.R.* 40:458, July 1925.

                                                                                    GMD

L651a Stephen, Sir Leslie. *History of English thought in the eighteenth century.* 1876. 3rd ed., 2 v., N. Y., 1902. (Bibliographies.)

   b ——— *English literature and society in the eighteenth century.* London and N. Y., 1904. [Ford lectures.]

a. Detailed, systematic, closely reasoned account of the chief currents and schools of English thought. It embraces a general consideration of the tendencies of the times, an analysis and critique of the ideas which shaped these tendencies, and some indication of the application of ideas to the questions of the day.   V. 1. Deals with the arguments of the English deists and the scepticism of Hume. V. 2. Analyzes the moral, political, economic, and literary currents of thought. The philosophies of Locke, Burke, Adam Smith, Priestley, and a host of other thinkers are scrutinized.   The work shows sincerity, insight, and evenness of judgment.   *b.* Slender, thoughtful book which treats literature as a mirror held up to reflect the movements of thought as affected by religious, social, political, and economic changes. Individual genius is not ignored. Pope, Addison, Swift, Chesterfield, Bolingbroke, Smollett, Defoe, Richardson, Goldsmith, and others are reviewed.   WTR

CULTURAL HISTORY: LITERATURE

L661a Moody, William Vaughn, and **Lovett, Robert Morss.** *History of English literature.* 1902. Rev. ed., N. Y., 1918. (Bibliography.)

 b Saintsbury, George E. B. *Short history of English literature.* N. Y. and London, 1898.

a. Shorter and less comprehensive than *b.*, but perhaps the best one-volume study for the general reader. *b.* Most inclusive of recent manuals of the history of English literature.

HEW

L662a *Cambridge history of English literature.* Ed. by Sir A. W. Ward and A. R. Waller. 14 v. Cambridge, Eng., 1907–16; N. Y., 1907–17. [1, *From the beginnings to the cycles of romance;* 2, *End of the middle ages;* 3, *Renascence and reformation;* 4, *Prose and poetry: Sir Thomas North to Michael Drayton;* 5–6, *Drama to 1642;* 7, *Cavalier and Puritan;* 8, *Age of Dryden;* 9, *From Steele and Addison to Pope and Swift;* 10, *Age of Johnson;* 11, *Period of the French revolution;* 12–14, *Nineteenth century.*] (Bibliographies.)

 b Garnett, Richard, and **Gosse, Edmund.** *English literature, an illustrated record.* 4 v. London and N. Y., 1903–04.

a. Uneven and not always well coördinated, but much the most complete and authoritative work on the subject. *b.* Valuable chiefly for its extraordinary wealth of illustrations.

HEW

L663 *Handbooks of English literature.* Ed. by John W. Hales. 11 v. London, 1894–1905. [1, F. J. Snell, *Age of Chaucer,* 2–3, *id., Age of transition;* 4–5, T. Seccombe and J. W. Allen, *Age of Shakespeare;* 6, J. H. B. Masterman, *Age of Milton;* 7, R. Garnett, *Age of Dryden;* 8, J. Dennis, *Age of Pope;* 9, T. Seccombe, *Age of Johnson;* 10, C. H. Herford, *Age of Wordsworth;* 11, H. Walker, *Age of Tennyson.*]

This series is uneven in merit. V. 1–3. Probably the least valuable studies. V. 4–5, 9, 10. Perhaps the best.

HEW

L664a Brooke, Stopford A. *English literature from the beginning to the Norman conquest.* London and N. Y., 1898. (Bibliography.)

 b Schofield, William H. *English literature from the Norman conquest to Chaucer.* N. Y. and London, 1906. (Bibliography.)

 c Saintsbury, George E. B. *History of Elizabethan literature.* London and N. Y., 1887. (Bibliography.)

 d Gosse, Edmund. *History of eighteenth century literature, 1660–1780.* London and N. Y., 1889. (Bibliography.)

 e Saintsbury, George E. B. *History of nineteenth century literature, 1780–1895.* London and N. Y., 1896.

Volumes of an incomplete series of histories of English literature. *a.* Best survey of this field. *b.* Standard history of this period. *c.* and *e.* Valuable in spite of a somewhat eccentric style and occasionally erratic judgments. *d.* Not always accurate in details, but probably the best one-volume study of the century.

HEW

L665 Jusserand, Jean J. *Literary history of the English people.* 2 v. in 3. N. Y. and London, 1895–1909; 2nd ed. of v. 1, 1907. [1, *From the origins to the renaissance; 2–3, From the renaissance to the civil war.*]

More than a history of English literature; a history of the cultural development of England in its literary aspects; includes, for the Middle Ages, writings in Latin and French as well as in English. Readable and illuminating though not always critical.   HEW

L666a Withington, Robert. *English pageantry, an historical outline.* 2 v. Cambridge, Mass., 1918–20.

  b Chambers, Edmund K. *Elizabethan stage.* 4 v. Oxford, 1923.

  c Ward, Sir Adolphus W. *History of English dramatic literature to the death of Queen Anne.* 1871. 2nd rev. ed., 3 v., London and N. Y., 1899.

a. Useful collection of interesting information. Review, C. L. Kingsford, *E.H.R.* 34:269, Apr. 1919; 36:612, Oct. 1921. *b.* Exhaustive, masterly study; continues (H666) E. K. Chambers, *Mediaeval stage.* Review, R. B. McKerron, *E.H.R.* 39:430, July 1924. *c.* This standard work has been supplemented but not superseded by later histories.   HEW

L667a Einstein, Lewis. *Italian renaissance in England, studies.* N. Y. and London, 1902. [Columbia University studies in comparative literature.] (Bibliography.)

  b Lee, Sir Sidney. *French renaissance in England, an account of the literary relations of England and France in the sixteenth century.* Oxford and N. Y., 1910. (Bibliography in preface.)

  c —— *Great Englishmen of the sixteenth century.* London and N. Y., 1904. [Lowell Institute lectures.] (Bibliographies.)

These three volumes combine high scholarship with readability; *b.* is the most scholarly work, and *a.* and *c.* are the more readable. *a.* Covers the various non-political phases of Italian influence in England in the sixteenth century with some emphasis on the literary tendencies. Review, S. B. Harding, *A.H.R.* 8:124, Oct. 1902. *b.* More strictly a literary study, though the broader aspects of the problem are not neglected. *c.* An illuminating lecture on the spirit of sixteenth century England is followed by able popular interpretations of More, Sydney, Raleigh, Spenser, Bacon, and Shakespeare.   HEW

L668a Elton, Oliver. *Survey of English literature, 1780–1830.* 2 v. London, 1912.

  b —— *Survey of English literature, 1830–1880.* 2 v. London and N. Y., 1920.

  c Cuncliffe, John W. *English literature during the last half century.* N. Y., 1919. (Bibliography.)

a. and *b.* Most important recent contribution to English literary history. *c.* Most convenient survey of recent literary developments in England.   HEW

CULTURAL HISTORY: ART AND MUSIC

L681a Prior, Edward S. *History of Gothic art in England.* London, 1900.

  b —— *Account of medieval figure-sculpture in England.* Cambridge, Eng., 1912. (Bibliography.)

c **Bond, Francis.** *Gothic architecture in England, an analysis of the origin and development of English church architecture from the Norman conquest to the dissolution of the monasteries.* London, 1905. (Bibliography.)

d **Thompson, Alexander H.** *Military architecture in England during the middle ages.* London and N. Y., 1912. (Bibliography.)

e **Gotch, John Alfred.** *Early renaissance architecture in England, a historical and descriptive account of the Tudor, Elizabethan, and Jacobean periods, 1500–1625, for the use of students and others.* 1901. 2nd rev. ed., London and N. Y., 1914. (Bibliography.)

These works will serve as an introduction to an extensive literature on English architecture to the beginning of the seventeenth century. The volumes are all amply illustrated with plans and photographic views. *b*. Included in this list, since sculpture was employed in the Middle Ages primarily for architectural ornamentation. GMD

L682a Chesneau, Ernest A. *English school of painting.* London and N. Y., 1895. [Fine art library.] Tr. by L. N. Etherington from *La peinture anglaise,* Paris, 1882.

b **White, Joseph W. Gleeson,** ed. *Master painters of Britain.* 4 v., 1898; 1 v., London, 1909.

c **Monkhouse, William Cosmo.** *British contemporary artists.* London and N. Y., 1899.

Satisfactory recent surveys of the history of painting in England are lacking, but the works mentioned will still be found of some service. For other than the most superficial treatment, the student should go directly to the biographical works relating to the leading artists, which are usually well illustrated and frequently ably written. References to these will be found in the proper articles in (L22) *Dict. Nat. Biog.* GMD

L691 Ford, Ernest. *Short history of English music.* London and N. Y., 1912.

This brief survey will afford an introduction to the subject which must, however, be pursued in biographies and other special studies, to the more important of which reference may be found in (B691*d*) Grove, *Dictionary of music and musicians.* GMD

BIOGRAPHY

In addition to the biographies which have already been listed and reviewed in this chapter, the following are among those of greater value and interest for the general reader.

Collections.—(L701) Agnes Strickland, *Lives of the queens of England,* 12 v., London, 1840–48, several later editions; (L702) Mary A. E. Green, *Lives of the princesses of England,* 6 v., London, 1849–55, reprint, 1857; (L703) Walter F. Hook, *Lives of the archbishops of Canterbury,* 12 v., London, 1860–76; (L704*a*) Charles Clive Bigham, *Chief ministers of England, 970–1720,* London, 1923, and (L704*b*) *Prime ministers of Britain, 1721–1921,* London, 1922.

Saxon period.—(L706) John B. Bury, *Life of St. Patrick and his place in history,* London and N. Y., 1905; (L707*a*) George F. Browne, *Augustine and his companions,* 1895, 2nd ed., London, 1897; (L707*b*) Edward L. Cutts, *Augustine of Canterbury,* London, 1895; (L707*c*) Arthur J. Mason, *Mission of St. Augustine to England according to the original documents,* Cambridge, Eng.,

1897; (L708) George F. Browne, *Theodore and Wilfrith*, London and N. Y., 1897; (L709) Charles Eyre, *History of St. Cuthbert*, 1849, 3rd ed., London, 1887; (L710) J. Armitage Robinson, *Times of Saint Dunstan*, Oxford, 1923 [Ford lectures]; also cf. (R701) L. M. Larson, *Canute the Great*, London and N. Y., 1912.

Norman and Anjevin period.—(L711) J. H. Round, *Geoffrey de Mandeville, a study of the anarchy*, London, 1892; (L712) A. J. Macdonald, *Lanfranc, a study of his life, work, and writing*, Oxford and N. Y., 1926; also cf. (H752) Charles W. David, *Robert Curthose, duke of Normandy*, Cambridge, Mass., 1920.

Early Plantagenet period.—(L716a) John Morris, *Life and martyrdom of Saint Thomas Becket*, 1859, 2nd rev. ed., 2 v., London and N. Y., 1885; (L716b) James C. Robertson, *Becket, archbishop of Canterbury, a biography*, London, 1859; (L716c) Robert A. Thompson, *Thomas Becket, martyr patriot*, London, 1889; (L716d) William H. Hutton, *S. Thomas of Canterbury, an account of his life and fame from the contemporary biographers and other chroniclers*, 1889, 3rd ed., London, 1910 [Makers of national history]; (L717) Sir George W. Prothero, *Life of Simon de Montfort*, London, 1877; (L718) Francis S. Stevenson, *Robert Grosseteste*, London and N. Y., 1899.

Later Plantagenet period.—(L726) Richard P. Dunn-Pattison, *Black Prince*, London, 1910; (L727) Sydney Armitage-Smith, *John of Gaunt*, Westminster, 1904; (L728a) Gotthard V. Lechler, *John Wiclif and his English precursors*, 1878, rev. ed., 2 v., London, 1884, tr. by P. Lorimer from *Johann von Wiclif und die Vorgeschichte der Reformation*, 2 v., Leipzig, 1873; (L728b) Reginald Lane Poole, *Wycliffe and movements for reform*, 1889, new ed., London and N. Y., 1896; (L729a) Charles L. Kingsford, *Henry V, the typical mediaeval hero*, London and N. Y., 1901 [Heroes of the nations]; (L729b) Robert B. Mowat, *Henry V*, London and Boston, 1915 [Kings and queens of England]; (L730) Mabel E. Christie, *Henry VI*, London and Boston, 1922 [Kings and queens of England]; (L731) Kenneth H. Vickers, *Humphrey, duke of Gloucester*, London, 1907.

Early Tudor period.—(L736a) Francis Bacon, Viscount St. Albans, *Historie of the raigne of King Henry the Seventh*, London, 1622, new ed. by J. Lawson Lumby, Cambridge, Eng., 1902 [Pitt Press series], also reprints in collected editions of Bacon's *Works;* (L736b) James Gairdner, *Henry the Seventh*, London and N. Y., 1889, later reprints [Twelve English statesmen]; (L736c) Gladys Temperley, *Henry VII*, London and Boston, 1914 [Kings and queens of England]; (L737) Martin A. S. Hume, *Wives of Henry the Eighth and the parts they played in history*, Edinburgh and N. Y., 1905; (L738) Paul Friedmann, *Anne Boleyn, a chapter of English history, 1527-1536*, 2 v., London, 1884; (L739) Arthur D. Innes, *Ten Tudor statesmen*, London, 1906; (L740a) George Cavendish, *Life of Cardinal Wolsey*, 1641, new ed., from original manuscript, by S. W. Singer, London, 1815, new ed., Boston, 1905; (L740b) Mandell Creighton, *Cardinal Wolsey*, London and N. Y., 1888, later reprints [Twelve English statesmen]; (L740c) Ethelred L. Taunton, *Thomas Wolsey, legate and reformer*, London and N. Y., 1902; (L741) William Roper, *Mirrour of vertue in worldly greatnes, or the life of Sir Thomas More*, 1626; new ed., London, 1903 [King's classics], London, 1924 [Blackie's English texts]; (L742) Albert F. Pollard, *Thomas Cranmer and the English reformation*, London and N. Y., 1904 [Heroes of the Reformation]; (L743) Joseph Gillow, *Literary and biographical history, or bibliographical dictionary, of the English Catholics from the breach with Rome in 1534 to the present time,* 5 v., London, 1885–1902; (L744) Dom Bede Camm, *Lives of the English martyrs declared blessed by Pope Leo XIII, 1886–1895,* 2 v., London, 1904–05; (L745) Edwin H. Burton and John Pollen, *Lives of the English martyrs, second series,* London, 1914; (L746) John Foxe, *Acts and monuments, popularly known as the Book of martyrs,* 1563, best ed., by S. R. Cattley and G. Townshend, 1837–41, 4th rev. ed., by J. Pratt and J. Stoughton, 8 v., London, 1877; (L747) Jean M. Stone, *History of Mary I, queen of England,* London, 1872; (L749) Francis Hackett, *Henry the VIIIth,* N. Y., 1929; (L750) A. F. Scott Pearson, *Thomas Cartwright and Elizabethan Puritanism,* Cambridge, 1925; (L751) Thomas McCrie, *John Knox,* Edinburgh, 1811.

Elizabeth and James I.—(L756a) Thomas F. Henderson, *Mary, queen of Scots, her environment and tragedy, a biography,* 2 v., London and N. Y., 1905; (L756b) Martin A. S. Hume, *Love affairs of Mary, queen of Scots, a political history,* London and N. Y., 1903; (L757) Martin A. S. Hume, *Great Lord Burghley, a study in Elizabethan statecraft,* London and N. Y., 1898; (L758) Algernon Cecil, *Life of Robert Cecil, first earl of Salisbury,* London, 1915; (L758a) Conyers Read, *Mr. Secretary Walsingham and the policy of Queen Elizabeth,* 3 v., Oxford and Cambridge, Mass., 1925; (L759) Sir Walter Runciman, *Drake, Nelson, and Napoleon, studies,* London and N. Y., 1919; (L760a) Sir Sidney Lee, *Life of William Shakespeare,* 1898, rev. ed., London and N. Y., 1916; (L760b) Sir Walter Raleigh, *Shakespeare,* London and N. Y., 1907 [English men of letters]; (L761a) James Spedding, *Letters and the life of Francis Bacon, including all his occasional works,* 7 v., London, 1861–74 [*Works,* v. 8–14]; (L761b) Richard W. Church, *Bacon,* London and N. Y., 1884 [English men of letters]; (L762) Philip H. Gibbs, *Romance of George Villiers, first duke of Buckingham, and some men and women of the Stuart court,* London, 1908.

Charles I, Commonwealth, and Protectorate.—(L771) Ida A. Taylor, *Life of Queen Henrietta Maria,* 2 v., London, 1905; (L772a) Elizabeth Cooper, *Life of Thomas Wentworth, earl of Strafford,* 2 v., London, 1874; (L772b) Henry D. Traill, *Lord Strafford,* London and N. Y., 1889 [English men of action]; (L773) William H. Hutton, *William Laud,* London and Boston, 1895 [English leaders of religion]; (L774) Goldwin Smith, *Three English statesmen* [Pym, Cromwell, Pitt], N. Y., 1867; (L775) George R. Stirling Taylor, *Modern English statesmen,* London, 1920; (L776) John Forster, *Statesmen of the Commonwealth of England,* 5 v., London, 1836–39; (L777) Charles E. Wade, *John Pym,* London, 1912; (L778) William W. Ireland, *Life of Sir Henry Vane the younger,* London, 1905; (L779a) Mark Pattison, *Milton,* London and N. Y., 1879, reprint, 1911 [English men of letters]; (L779b) Sir Walter Raleigh, *Milton,* London, 1900.

Restoration.—(L786) Frank R. Harris, *Life of Edward Montagu, first earl of Sandwich,* 2 v., London, 1912; (L787a) William D. Christie, *Life of Anthony Ashley Cooper, first earl of Shaftesbury,* 2 v., London and N. Y., 1871; (L787b) Henry D. Traill, *Shaftesbury,* London, 1888 [English worthies]; (L788) Violet Barbour, *Henry Bennet, earl of Arlington,* Washington, 1914 [H. B. Adams prize essay]; (L789) Winifred, Baroness Burghclere, *George Villiers, second duke of Buckingham,* London, 1903; (L790) Andrew Browning, *Thomas Osborne, earl of Danby and duke of Leeds,* Oxford, 1913 [Stanhope essay]; (L791) Lord Edmond Fitzmaurice, *Life of Sir William Petty,* London, 1895; (L792) Roger North, *Lives of Francis North, Baron Guilford; Sir Dudley North; and Dr.*

John North, together with the autobiography of the author, ed. by A. Jessopp, 3 v., London, 1890 [Bohn's standard library] ; (L793) Lord John Russell, *Life of William, Lord Russell,* 1819, 4th ed., London, 1853; (L794) Alexander C. Ewald, *Life and times of Algernon Sydney,* 2 v., London, 1873; (L795) Allan Fea, *King Monmouth,* London and N. Y., 1901; (L796) [Thomas Longueville], *Adventures of King James II of England,* with introduction by F. A. Gasquet, London and N. Y., 1904; (L797) Henry B. Irving, *Life of Judge Jeffreys,* N. Y., 1898; (L798) Helen C. Foxcroft, *Life and letters of George Savile, first marquis of Halifax,* 2 v., London and N. Y., 1898; (L799) Sir Almeric W. Fitzroy, *Henry, duke of Grafton, 1663–1690,* London, 1921; (L800) T. E. S. Clarke and Helen C. Foxcroft, *Life of Gilbert Burnet,* Cambridge, Eng., 1907; (L801) George E. B. Saintsbury, *Dryden,* 1881, reprint, London and N. Y., 1906 [English men of letters] ; (L802) Marion E. Grew, *William Bentinck and William III, the life of Bentinck, earl of Portland, from the Welbeck correspondence,* London, 1924.

Age of Anne.—(L811a) Garnet J., viscount Wolseley, *Life of John Churchill, duke of Marlborough, to accession of Queen Anne,* 2 v., London, 1894; (L811b) Stuart J. Reid, *John and Sarah, duke and duchess of Marlborough, 1660–1744, based on unpublished letters and documents at Blenheim palace,* London, 1914; (L811c) Christopher T. Atkinson, *Marlborough and the rise of the British army,* N. Y. and London, 1921; (L812) Hugh F. Elliot, *Life of Sidney, earl of Godolphin,* London and N. Y., 1888; (L813) Edward S. Roscoe, *Robert Harley, earl of Oxford,* London, 1902; (L814a) Thomas Macknight, *Life of Henry St. John, viscount Bolingbroke,* London, 1863; (L814b) Walter S. Sichel, *Bolingbroke and his times,* 2 v., London, 1901–02; (L814c) John C. Collins, *Bolingbroke, a historical study,* London, 1886; (L815) Leopold G. Wickham Legg, *Matthew Prior, a study of his public career and correspondence,* Cambridge, Eng., 1921.

Early Hanoverians.—(L821) Andrew Lang, *Prince Charles Edward Stuart, the Young Chevalier,* 1900, new ed., London and N. Y., 1903; (L822) Alice Shield, *Henry Stuart, cardinal of York, and his times,* London and N. Y., 1908; (L823) Evan E. Charteris, *William Augustus, duke of Cumberland,* London, 1913; (L824) Philip C. Yorke, *Life and correspondence of Philip Yorke, earl of Hardwicke,* 3 v., Cambridge, Eng., 1913; (L825a) Giles S. H. Fox-Strangways, earl of Ilchester, *Henry Fox, first Lord Holland; his family and relations,* 2 v., London, 1920; (L825b) Thad W. Riker, *Henry Fox, first Lord Holland, a study of the career of an eighteenth century politician,* 2 v., Oxford, 1911.

George III.—(L831) Horace Walpole, earl of Orford, *Letters,* 1820, new ed., by Mrs. Paget Toynbee, 16 v., Oxford, 1903–05, supplement, 2 v., Oxford, 1918; (L832a) Horace W. Bleackley, *Life of John Wilkes,* London and N. Y., 1917; (L832b) Sir William P. Treloar, *Wilkes and the City,* London, 1917; (L833) Walter S. Sichel, *Sheridan, from new and original material, including a manuscript diary by Georgiana, duchess of Devonshire,* 2 v., London, 1909; (L834) George Pellew, *Life and correspondence of Henry Addington, first Viscount Sidmouth,* 3 v., London, 1847; (L835) Samuel Smiles, *Lives of the engineers, comprising also a history of inland communication in Britain,* 3 v., London, 1861–62; (L836a) Robert I. Wilberforce and Samuel Wilberforce, *Life of William Wilberforce,* 5 v., London, 1838, abridged ed., 1 v., 1868; (L836b) Reginald Coupland, *Wilberforce, a narrative,* Oxford, 1923; (L837) Sir Samuel Romilly, *Memoirs, with a selection from his correspondence,* 1840, 3rd ed., 2 v., London,

1841; (L838a) Edward I. Carlyle, *William Cobbett, a study of his life as shown in his writings*, London, 1904; (L838b) F. E. Green and G. D. H. Cole, *Life of William Cobbett*, London, 1924; (L839) Charles M. Atkinson, *Jeremy Bentham, his life and work*, London, 1905; (L840) Alexander Bain, *James Mill, a biography*, London, 1882; (L841) Charles Buxton, *Memoirs of Sir Thomas Fowell Buxton*, 1848, new ed., London, 1872; (L842) Graham Wallas, *Life of Francis Place, 1771-1854*, N. Y. and London, 1898; (L843) Frank Podmore, *Robert Owen*, 2 v., London, 1906, N. Y., 1907, reprint, 1924; (L844) George Unwin, *Samuel Oldknow and the Arkwrights, the industrial revolution at Stockport and Marple*, Manchester, 1924 [University of Manchester publications].

Early Victorian period.—(L851) Walter Bagehot, *Biographical studies*, London, 1881; (L852) Lytton Strachey, *Eminent Victorians*, London and N. Y., 1918; (L853) James B. Atlay, *Victorian chancellors*, 2 v., London, 1906-08; (L854) Sir Theodore Martin, *Life of the Prince Consort*, 5 v., London, 1875-80; (L855) Benjamin Disraeli, earl of Beaconsfield, *Lord George Bentinck, a political biography*, London, 1852; (L856) Charles C. F. Greville, *Greville memoirs, a journal of the reigns of King George IV, King William IV, and Queen Victoria*, ed. by Henry Reeve, 1874-87, reprint, 8 v., London and N. Y., 1896-99; (L857) Sir Rowland Hill and George Birkbeck Hill, *Life of Sir Rowland Hill and the history of penny postage*, 2 v., London, 1880; (L858) Charles S. Parker, *Life and letters of Sir James Graham, second baronet of Netherby*, 2 v., London, 1907; (L859a) John, Viscount Morley, *Life of Richard Cobden*, 1881, 10th ed., London, 1903; (L859b) John A. Hobson, *Richard Cobden, the international man*, London and N. Y., 1919; (L860) George E. B. Saintsbury, *Earl of Derby*, London and N. Y., 1892 [Prime ministers of Queen Victoria]; (L861) Sir Herbert Maxwell, *Life and letters of George William Frederick, fourth earl of Clarendon*, 2 v., London, 1913; (L862) Thomas W. Legh, baron Newton, *Lord Lyons, a record of British diplomacy*, 2 v., London, 1913; (L863) Sir George O. Trevelyan, *Life and letters of Lord Macaulay*, 1876, rev. ed., London and N. Y., 1908; (L864a) Edwin Hodder, *Life and work of the seventh earl of Shaftesbury*, 3 v., London and N. Y., 1887; (L864b) John L. Hammond and Barbara Hammond, *Lord Shaftesbury*, London, 1923, N. Y., 1924 [Makers of the nineteenth century]; (L865) Sir Oliver Lodge, *Pioneers of Science*, 1893, new ed., London and N. Y., 1904; (L866) E. Francis Darwin, *Life and letters of Charles Darwin*, 3 v., London, 1887, 2 v., N. Y., 1888; (L867) E. T. Cook, *Life of Florence Nightingale*, 2 v., London, 1913.

Later Victorian period.—(L871) James, viscount Bryce, *Studies in contemporary biography*, London and N. Y., 1903; (L872) Lord Edmond Fitzmaurice, *Life of second earl Granville*, 2 v., London and N. Y., 1905; (L873a) Winston S. Churchill, *Lord Randolph Churchill*, 2 v., London and N. Y., 1906; (L873b) Archibald, earl of Rosebery, *Lord Randolph Churchill*, London and N. Y., 1906; (L874a) Richard B. O'Brien, *Life of Charles Stewart Parnell*, 2 v., London and N. Y., 1898; (L874b) John H. Parnell, *Charles Stewart Parnell, a memoir*, London and N. Y., 1914; (L875a) Warre B. Wells, *John Redmond, a biography*, London and N. Y., 1919; (L875b) Stephen Gwynn, *John Redmond's last years*, London and N. Y., 1919; (L876) Algar Labouchere Thorold, *Life of Henry Labouchere*, London, 1913; (L877) Bernard Holland, *Life of Spencer Compton, eighth duke of Devonshire*, 2 v., London and N. Y., 1911; (L878) Alfred G. Gardiner, *Life of Sir William Harcourt*, 2 v., London, 1923; (L879) Sir

Frederick Maurice and Sir George Arthur, *Life of Lord Wolseley,* London and N. Y., 1924; (L880) John H. Morgan, *John, viscount Morley, an appreciation and some reminiscences,* London and Boston, 1924; (L881) Sir Arthur Hardinge, *Life of Henry Howard Molyneux Herbert, fourth earl of Carnarvon, 1831–1890,* ed. by Elizabeth, countess of Carnarvon, 3 v., Oxford and N. Y., 1925; (L882) Osbert Burdett, *W. E. Gladstone: a psychological study,* London, 1927; (L883) H. A. L. Fisher, *James Bryce, 2* v., London, 1927.

Twentieth century.—(L886) Lord Newton, *Lord Lansdowne, a biography,* London and N. Y., 1929; (L887) John Alfred Spender, *Life of Sir Henry Campbell-Bannerman, 2* v., London, 1923; (L888) Sir George C. A. Arthur, *Life of Lord Kitchener, 3* v., London, 1920; (L889) Harold Spender, *Herbert Henry Asquith,* London, 1915; (L890a) Frank Dilnot, *Lloyd George, the man and his story,* London and N. Y., 1917; (L890b) Harold Spender, *The prime minister, life and times of David Lloyd George,* London and N. Y., 1920; (L890c) 'An independent liberal', *Lloyd George and the war, a personal history of his part in Armageddon,* London, 1917, N. Y., 1918; (L891a) Alfred G. Gardiner, *Prophets, priests, and kings,* London, 1914, and (L891b) *War lords,* London, 1915 [both, Wayfarer's library]; (L892a) 'A gentleman with a duster' [Harold Begbie], *Mirrors of Downing Street, some political reflections,* 1920, rev. ed., London, 1923; (L892b) *Glass of fashion, some social reflections,* London and N. Y., 1921; and (L892c) *Painted windows, a study in religious personality,* London, 1922; (L893) 'Iconoclast' [Mary A. Hamilton], *Man of tomorrow, J. Ramsay Mac-Donald,* London, 1923, N. Y., 1924; (L894) Earl of Ronaldshay, *Life of Lord Curzon, 3* v., London, 1928; (L895) J. A. Spender, *Life, Journalism, and Politics, 2* v., London, 1927; (L896) Lord Haldane, *Autobiography,* London and N. Y., 1929.

GOVERNMENT PUBLICATIONS

In Great Britain more than in any other country, the publication of the documentary sources for history has been carried on directly by the government. Furthermore, in Great Britain the existing institutions of government trace their development in unbroken continuity to dates far anterior to those in any other countries. In consequence of these two reasons, most publications which would normally appear under this rubric will be found in the subsection devoted to collections of sources. For the statutes, cf. (L76–78); for the various records of parliament cf. (L79–85); for court records cf. (L88–91); for diplomatic documents, cf. (L73, 74, 92), (I275b, 508a, 509a).

SOCIETY PUBLICATIONS

Various societies have been organized from time to time to print materials relating to British history. One of the earliest to be founded was the Camden Society (L921) *Publications,* London, 1838 ff., named in honor of the antiquary and historian, William Camden, 1551–1623. Beginning its activities in 1838, the society continued as an independent organization until 1897, when it was taken over by the Royal Historical Society (L922) *Transactions,* London, 1871 ff., which has continued the Camden series of publications, now over 200 v., of chronicles, letters, and other documents. The Early English Text Society (L923) *Publications,* London, 1864 ff., has made accessible many sources of importance. The Pipe Roll Society (L924) *Publications,* London, 1884 ff., was founded 'for the publication of the great rolls of the exchequer, commonly called the pipe rolls, and other documents prior to A. D. 1200.' The first pipe roll, or record of royal receipts, dates from 1130; then there is none extant until 2 Henry II, after which they continue in an annual series, unbroken with two exceptions, until 1832. The Selden Society (L925) *Publications,* London, 1888ff., named after the famous legal scholar, John Selden, 1584–1654, was founded 'to encourage the study and advance the knowledge of the history of English law.' It has published many valuable legal records, with excellent introductions. The Manorial Society (L926) *Publications,* London, 1907 ff., has printed manor rolls and similar documents. The Navy Records Society (L927) *Publications,* London, 1894ff., has already issued about 60 v. of important documents and studies relating to the history of the royal navy.

In addition there are numerous local societies such as the Surtees Society (L931) *Publications,* London, 1835 ff., named after a Durham antiquary, Robert Surtees, 1779–1834, which confines its activities to the northern counties of England; the Chetham Society (L932) *Remains, historical and literary, connected with the palatine counties of Lancaster and Chester,* Manchester, 1844ff., named after Humphrey Chetham, 1580–1653, a merchant and benefactor of Manchester; the William Salt Archaeological Society (L933) *Collections for a history of Staffordshire,* Birmingham, 1881ff., which takes its name from William Salt, 1805–1863, a Staffordshire antiquary; the Oxford Historical Society (L934) *Publications,* Oxford, 1885 ff.; and the Somerset Record Society (L935) *Publications,* London, 1887 ff., which have been the most important for their publishing activities.

For Scottish history over 80 v. of documentary and other source materials have been issued by the Scottish History Society (L936) *Publications,* Edinburgh, 1887 ff.

PERIODICALS

In addition to (B941f2) *English historical review,* and other general historical reviews listed in § B, and to the British archeological journals enumerated as (D981–983), there are the following periodicals which contain valuable material, documentary and monographic, relating to British history: (L941) *Gentleman's magazine,* 303 v., London, 1731–1907, with *General index,* 4 v., London, 1789–1821; (L942) *Notes and queries,* London, 1849 ff., with *General index* to each series of 12 v.; (L943) *History, a quarterly magazine and review for the teacher, the student, and the expert,* London, 1912 ff., (L944) *Archaeologia cambrensis, the journal of the Cambrian Archaeological Association,* London, 1846 ff.; (L945) *Scottish historical review,* Glasgow, 1903 ff.; (L946) *Journal of the Royal Society of Antiquaries of Ireland,* Dublin, 1890 ff., founded as (L946a) *Journal of the Kilkenny Archaeological Society,* Dublin, 1858–68, and continued as (L946b) *Journal of the Royal Historical and Archaeological Association of Ireland,* Dublin, 1869–1889; (L947) *Cambridge historical journal,* Cambridge, Eng., 1924 ff.; (L948) *Bulletin of the Institute of Historical Research,* London, 1923 ff.   ALC

SECTION M

FRANCE

Editor

HENRY ELDRIDGE BOURNE

Managing Editor, American Historical Review

CONTENTS

INTRODUCTION

France surpasses every other country on the continent of Europe in the unity and continuity of its history. Consequently, it is not surprising that the study of its history is second to none in thoroughness of organization and in the number and character of the works produced. No period of French national existence has been without its writers of history who have either equalled or surpassed their contemporaries in other lands. From Gregory of Tours through

Joinville, Froissart, Comines, Saint-Simon, Thiers, Michelet, and Lavisse to Hanotaux, the succession exhibits variety of genius and eminence of achievement. The versatility of interests and the standards of critical and literary attainment displayed by French historical scholars in the decade since the World War continue to exemplify the nation's best traditions.

So much, indeed, has been written in France upon almost every phase of French history that the task of keeping the list of titles within moderate proportions is peculiarly difficult. In some cases it is necessary to include books by English or American authors only, though an equally good or better book in French exists, in order that the list may be available for general library use. It is also necessary to omit many titles which would deserve a place in a fuller bibliography. Other books which might be looked for in this section will be found in those sections which treat periods of European history in which France played a leading part. For example, in § I, Modern Times, will be found works whose chief interest is their account of Napoleon and the policies of the First Empire. Works dealing with French colonization and colonial possessions will be found in §§ K, U, V, W, and Z.

BIBLIOGRAPHY

For general catalogues of publications in French cf. § B.

M1a Monod, Gabriel. *Bibliographie de l'histoire de France: catalogue méthodique et chronologique des sources et des ouvrages relatifs à l'histoire de France depuis les origines jusqu'en 1789.* Paris, 1888.

b Franklin, Alfred. *Les sources de l'histoire de France, notices bibliographiques et analytiques des inventaires et des recueils de documents relatifs à l'histoire de France.* Paris, 1877.

c *Catalogue de l'histoire de France.* 12 v. Paris, 1855–95. [Bibliothèque nationale.]

a. Monod intended to do for French history what Dahlmann [cf. (P1a) Dahlmann-Waitz] had done for German history. Pt. 1. Contains a list of bibliographies, works on the auxiliary sciences, names of collections, etc. Pt. 2. Contains lists of books by epochs. Review, C. Bémont, *Rev. Hist.* 28:158, Sept. 1888. *b.* Somewhat mechanical compilation; inadequate and antiquated; still a convenient guide within its limited field. Review, *Rev. des Quest. Hist.* 24:711, Oct. 1878. *c.* Most extensive list of works printed before 1875 on the history of France prior to 1875; though the main arrangement is chronological, separate sections are devoted to constitutional, diplomatic, military, religious, local, and colonial history, and to some minor topics. HEB

M2a Molinier, Auguste. *Les sources de l'histoire de France: des origines aux guerres de l'Italie, 1494.* 6 v. Paris, 1901–06. [Manuels de bibliographie historique.]

b Hauser, Henri. *Les sources de l'histoire de France: le XVIᵉ siècle, 1494–1610.* 4 v. Paris, 1906–15. [Manuels de bibliographie historique.]

c Bourgeois, Émile, and André, Louis. *Les sources de l'histoire de France: le XVIIᵉ siècle, 1610–1715.* 5 v. Paris, 1913–26. [Manuels de bibliographie historique.]

Planned as a critical catalogue of narrative sources, with accounts of authors and editions, and with brief critical discussions, to which were added references to noteworthy articles upon authors or editions. *b* and *c.* Scope enlarged to include other forms of historical material, notably memoirs. Review of *b*, J. W. Thompson, *A.H.R.* 21:792, July 1916; of *c*, *A.H.R.* 29:796, July 1924.   HEB

M3a Saulnier, Eugène, and **Martin, A.** *Bibliographie des travaux publiés de 1866 à 1897 sur l'histoire de la France de 1500 à 1789.* Pt. 1, Paris, 1927. [Confédération des Sociétés Scientifiques Françaises.]

b Caron, Pierre. *Bibliographie des travaux publiés de 1866 à 1897 sur l'histoire de la France depuis 1789.* 1 v. in 6 pt. Paris, 1907–12. [Société d'Histoire Moderne.]

c Brière, Gaston; Caron, Pierre; and others. *Répertoire méthodique de l'histoire moderne et contemporaine de la France, pour les années 1898–1906, 1910–1912.* 9 v. Paris, 1899–1924. [Société d'Histoire Moderne.]

d Caron, Pierre, and **Stein, Henri.** *Répertoire bibliographique de l'histoire de France.* V. 1, *1920–1921;* v. 2, *1922–1923.* Paris, 1923–27. [Confédération des Sociétés Scientifiques Françaises.]

a and *b*. Classified lists of books and articles, both in French and other languages, with references to reviews. *c*. Continuation of *a* and *b*; covers the period since 1500; planned to be completed through 1919. *d*. Continuation of *c*; to appear biennially; includes entire period of French history.   HEB

M4a Lasteyrie du Saillant, Robert C., Comte de, and others. *Bibliographie générale des travaux historiques et archéologiques publiés par les sociétés savantes de la France, dressée sous les auspices du ministère de l'instruction publique.* 6 v. Paris, 1888–1918. [Comité des Travaux Historiques et Scientifiques.]

b Lasteyrie du Saillant, Robert C., Comte de, and **Vidier, Alexandre.** *Bibliographie annuelle des travaux historiques et archéologiques publiés par les sociétés savantes de la France, dressée sous les auspices du ministère de l'instruction publique.* 3 v. in 9 pt. Paris, 1904–14. [Comité des Travaux Historiques et Scientifiques.]

a. V. 1–4. List publications previous to 1886. V. 5–6. List those from 1886 to 1900. *b.* Continuation of *a*; covers the years 1901–02 to 1909–10 inclusive.   HEB

M5a Lanson, Gustave. *Manuel bibliographique de la littérature française moderne, 1500–1900.* 1909–14. Rev. ed., 4 v. and index, Paris, 1921.

b Haskell, Daniel C. *Provençal literature and language, including the local history of southern France: a list of references in the New York Public Library.* N. Y., 1925. [Reprint, with additions, from *Bulletin of New York Public Library,* June 1921–Dec. 1922.]

a. Lists classified by periods, types of literature, and writers. *b.* An extensive booklist rather than a bibliography.   HEB

M6a Du Peloux, Charles, Vicomte. *Répertoire général des ouvrages modernes relatifs au dix-huitième siècle français, 1715–1789.* Paris, 1926.

b Caron, Pierre. *Manuel pratique pour l'étude de la révolution française.* Paris, 1912. [Manuels de bibliographie historique.]

a. Lists about a hundred thousand titles alphabetically by authors' names. Review, C. Becker, *A.H.R.* 32:357, Jan. 1927. *b.* Describes publications of official commissions, societies, etc., also national and local archives. Appendix contains an excellent concordance of the Republican and Gregorian calendars.   HEB

M7 Halphen, Louis. *L'histoire en France depuis cent ans.* Paris, 1914. (Bibliography.)

Short but clear characterization of the successive schools of the nineteenth century. Review, *Rev. Critique,* 79:58, Jan. 23, 1915. CHCW

M8 Hanoteau, Jean, and **Bonnot, Émile.** *Bibliographie des historiques des régiments français.* Paris, 1908.

Includes lists not only of printed sources but of manuscript material preserved at the French War Office. Indispensable for the study of military history. Review, *Rev. Hist.* 115:187, Jan. 1914. HEB

M9 Montandon, Raoul. *Bibliographie générale des travaux palethnologiques et archéologiques: époques préhistorique, protohistorique, et gallo-romaine.* 3 v. Paris, 1926.

Arranged by departments. Covers publications since the sixteenth century, and is well indexed. Review, A. Grenier, *Rev. Critique,* 61:407, Nov. 1, 1927. GMD

M11a Langlois, Charles V., and **Stein, Henri.** *Les archives de l'histoire de France.* 3 pt. in 1 v., Paris, 1891–93. [Manuels de bibliographie historique.]

b Schmidt, Charles. *Les sources de l'histoire de France depuis 1789 aux Archives Nationales.* Paris, 1907.

a. Indispensable guide to materials on French history in both French and foreign archives. Review, A. Molinier, *Rev. Hist.* 46:340, July 1891; 50:73, Sept. 1892; 54:98, Jan. 1894. *b.* More complete guide to the most important single collection of manuscripts for the period. GMD

Library collections.—In the United States, libraries especially rich in material on the history of France are those of Harvard University (good for all periods; extensive collections of revolutionary newspapers and of publications of local French historical societies), Cornell University (good for the period from the seventeenth century onward; President White collection on French Revolution, especially rich in pamphlets and newspapers), Princeton University (numerous revolutionary newspapers), University of California (Ledru Rollin collection of pamphlets on the Revolution, and library of the eminent Napoleonic scholar Fournier), Library of Congress, New York Public Library, Yale University, Columbia University (good for revolutionary and Napoleonic periods), University of Pennsylvania, Pennsylvania Historical Society (Maclure collection on French Revolution), University of Nebraska (good for the revolutionary period), and Leland Stanford Jr. University (Jarboe collection on French Revolution). The libraries of Union Theological Seminary, New York University (Baird collection on the Huguenots), and Bowdoin College, and the Newberry Library of Chicago each possess good collections on the Huguenots and the Wars of Religion. AHS

ENCYCLOPEDIAS AND WORKS OF REFERENCE
For leading French encyclopedias cf. (B23).

M21 Joanne, Paul B., ed. *Dictionnaire géographique et administratif de la France.* 7 v. Paris, 1890–1905.

Standard descriptive and statistical work; well-illustrated. Introduction by Élisée Reclus gives noteworthy survey of the structure of France, its population, and its products. WMD

M22 Lalanne, Ludovic. *Dictionnaire historique de la France.* 1872. 2nd rev. ed., Paris, 1877. (Bibliographies with some articles.)

Complete to close of 1876; contains brief articles on places, persons, and institutions connected with historical geography and civil, political, military, religious, and literary history. There are numerous lists of holders of offices and titles; the article 'France' includes a chronology of events by years. Extremely convenient handbook of ready reference; unfortunately antiquated; in view of its extended scope, it is not strange that omissions and errors occur.   GMD

M23a Chéruel, Pierre Adolphe. *Dictionnaire historique des institutions, moeurs, et coutumes de la France.* 1855. 8th rev. ed., 2 v., Paris, 1910.

b Marion, Marcel. *Dictionnaire des institutions de la France aux XVIIe et XVIIIe siècles.* Paris, 1923. (Bibliographies to more important articles.)

The scope of these dictionaries differs markedly as their titles imply. *a.* Covers all the centuries of French development, although references to conditions in the nineteenth are relatively few; repeatedly reprinted, but with little change, so that the work embodies on many subjects a state of knowledge long superseded; still useful if employed with discretion. *b.* More inclusive than its title suggests, since the term, institutions, is interpreted broadly; for example, articles on *agriculture* and *disette* are given on the ground that their phenomena often prompted governmental action; deals with the facts of periods prior to the seventeenth century only in so far as they are vital in explaining the institutions of the Bourbon monarchy; invaluable to students of the old régime. Review, F. M. Fling, *A.H.R.* 29:371, Jan. 1924; G. Pagès, *Rev. Hist.* 146:231, July 1924. HEB

M24a Robinet, Jean F. E.; Robert, Adolphe; and Le Chaplain, Julien. *Dictionnaire historique et biographique de la révolution et de l'empire, 1789–1815.* 2 v. Paris, 1899.

b Richardson, Hubert N. B. *Dictionary of Napoleon and his times.* London and N. Y., 1920.

a. Convenient handbook, but suffers badly from both omissions and errors. Review, R. Reuss, *Rev. Hist.* 72:350, March 1900; 73:325, July 1900. *b.* Similar in value.   GMD

M25 *Qui êtes-vous?* 3 v. Paris, 1908, 1909, 1924. (B702e)

Inadequate and sporadic efforts to establish a French *Who's who.* Review, C. Bémont, *Rev. Hist.* 145:321, March 1924.   GMD

GEOGRAPHY

M41a Blanchard, Raoul, and Todd, Millicent. *Geography of France.* Chicago, 1919.

b Davis, William M. *Handbook of northern France.* Cambridge, Mass., 1918.

a. Planned originally for use by American soldiers in France, but serviceable to the general reader as a compact statement. *b.* Pocket handbook prepared for use by American officers during the World War; description of geographical features of the western front with maps and diagrams.   WMD

M42a Vidal de la Blache, Paul. *Tableau de la géographie de la France.* Paris, 1903. [(M124a) Lavisse, *Histoire de France*, v. 1, pt. 1.]

b —— *La France de l'Est, Lorraine-Alsace.* 1917. 2nd ed., Paris, 1918.

c Brunhes, Jean. *Géographie humaine de la France: le cadre permanent et le facteur humain.* Paris, 1920. [(M123) Hanotaux, *Histoire de la nation française*, v. 1.]

d Brunhes, Jean, and Deffontaines, Pierre. *Géographie humaine de la France: géographie politique et géographie du travail.* Paris, 1926. [(M123) Hanotaux, *Histoire de la nation française*, v. 2.]

a. Valuable as a characteristic work of the master of the modern French school of geography. Readable and pleasing, but not sufficiently specific as to facts of topography and their meaning in relation to man. Review, G. Monod, *Rev. Hist.* 84:100, Jan. 1904. *b.* More intensive study dealing with the economic development of the two provinces as affected by their geographical characteristics and their political vicissitudes. Review, E. Welvert, *Rev. Critique,* 84:362, Dec. 1, 1917. *c.* More specific in treatment than *a,* but of similar character. Review, B. Auerbach, *Rev. Hist.* 136:268, March 1921. *d.* Continuation of *c*; notable treatment of the two topics considered. Review, P. Bigelow, *A.H.R.* 32:909, July 1927.

WMD

M43a Auerbach, Bertrand. *Le plateau lorrain, essai de géographie régionale.* Paris, 1893.

b Blanchard, Raoul. *La Flandre: étude géographique de la plaine flamande en France, Belgique, et Hollande.* Dunkerque, 1906. (Bibliographical footnotes.)

c Chantriot, Émile. *La Champagne: étude de géographie régionale.* Paris, 1906. (Bibliography.)

d Bleicher, Gustave. *Les Vosges, le sol et les habitants.* Paris, 1889. [Bibliothèque scientifique contemporaine.]

e Demangeon, Albert. *La Picardie et les régions voisines: Artois, Cambrésis, Beauvaisis.* Paris, 1905.

f Vacher, Antoine. *Le Berry: contribution à l'étude géographique d'une région française.* Paris, 1908. (Bibliography.)

Examples, of which *b, e,* and *f* are the best, of the work of the modern school of French geography, in which the historical element is strongly emphasized. This latter feature is largely due to the fact that the preparatory studies and qualifying examination for professors of geography and of history are the same.

WMD

M44a Longnon, Auguste H. *Formation de l'unité française, leçons professées au Collège de France en 1889–1890.* Ed. by H. F. Delaborde. Paris, 1922.

b Blanchard, Marcel. *Les routes des Alpes occidentales à l'époque napoléonienne, 1786–1815.* Grenoble, 1920.

a. These lectures, published posthumously, open with a discussion of the elements of Capetian geography and deal with the two main processes by which modern France was built up: the triumph of the monarchy over the feudatories and the extension of the frontiers towards what have been called the 'natural limits'. Valuable analytical index. Review, C. W. David, *A.H.R.* 28:533, Apr. 1923. *b.* Of special interest for the study of the trade relations with Italy under the Continental System. Review, H. Hauser, *Rev. Hist.* 137:110, May 1921.

HEB

M45a Longnon, Auguste H. *Les noms de lieux de la France: leur origine, leur signification, leurs transformations.* Pub. by Paul Marichal and Léon Mirot. Fasc. 1–5. Paris, 1920–1929.

b Dauzat, Albert. *Les noms de lieux, origine et évolution: villes et villages, pays, cours d'eau, montagnes, lieux-dits.* Paris, 1926. (Bibliography.)

c *Dictionnaire topographique de la France, comprenant les noms de lieux anciens et modernes.* V. 1–28. Paris, 1861–1913. [Ministère de l'instruction Publique: Comité des Travaux Historiques et des Sociétés Savantes.]

d *Guide officiel de la navigation intérieure.* 9th ed., Paris, 1925. [Ministère des Travaux Publics.]

a. Embodies an important part of the life work of the distinguished author. Editorial work well done. Review of Fasc. 1 and 2, E. G. Ledos, *Rev. des Quest. Hist.* 97:236, July, 1922; of 3, *ibid.*, 103:230, July 1, 1925. *b.* By a pupil of Gaston Paris, who often takes issue with Longnon. Includes explanation of 2700 names. Its method is a topical and synthetic study of the different factors entering into their determination. Review, E. G. Ledos, *Rev. des Quest. Hist.* 106:437, Apr. 1927.   GMD

c. Each volume deals with a single department. *d.* Description of canals and other waterways.   HEB

M46a Longnon, Auguste H. *Atlas historique de la France depuis César jusqu'à nos jours, avec un texte explicatif.* Pt. 1–3. Paris, 1885–89.

b Reclus, Onésime. *Atlas de la plus grande France, géographique, politique, économique, départemental, et colonial.* Paris, 1915.

a. The fifteen maps published cover only to the death of Charles V, 1380. Valuable work on monumental scale. Review, C. Bémont, *Rev. Hist.* 27:366, Jan. 1885; G. Monod, *ibid.* 40:107, May 1889.   HEB

b. One hundred and sixty maps of regional subdivisions with descriptive text; much statistical information.   WMD

M47a Brossard, Charles. *Géographie pittoresque et monumentale de la France.* 6 v. Paris, 1899–1906.

b Dubois, Marcel, and **Guy, Camille.** *La France.* Paris, 1906. [V. 5 of *Album géographique,* 5 v., Paris, 1896–1906.]

a. Numerous excellent half tones of landscapes and architecture, with descriptive text. *b.* Excellent smaller collection of pictures.   WMD

ETHNOGRAPHY

M51 Mathorez, Jules. *Les étrangers en France sous l'ancien régime.* V. 1, *Les causes de la pénétration des étrangers en France; les Orientaux et les Extra-Européens dans la population française.* Paris, 1919. [Histoire de la formation de la population française.]

Excellent historical study of the racial elements intermingled in the present population of France. The author has also published numerous periodical articles dealing with special phases of the same general subject. Review, T. Collier, *A.H.R.* 26:82, Oct. 1920. Also cf. (M582d) Levasseur, *La population française.*
                                                                                              GMD

SOURCE BOOKS, COLLECTIONS OF SOURCES, ARCHIVE PUBLICATIONS

M61a Zeller, Berthold, and **Luchaire, Achille.** *L'histoire de France racontée par les contemporains.* 65 v. Paris, 1880–90.

b Prou, Maurice; Molinier, Auguste E. L. M.; Langlois, Charles V.; and others, ed. *Collection de textes pour servir à l'étude et à l'enseignement de l'histoire.* V. 1–50. Paris, 1886–1925.

c Halphen, Louis, ed. *Les classiques de l'histoire de France au moyen âge.* V. 1–11. Paris, 1923–29.

a. These diminutive volumes form a useful collection of illustrative material excerpted from the writings of every age from the period of Roman Gaul to the death of Henry IV. The earlier selections are translated and the French of the later ones modernized. Review, G. Monod, *Rev. Hist.* 45:379, March 1891. *b* and *c.* Include chronicles, histories, treaties, and other documents in inexpensive *format. c.* Limited to Middle Ages; provides translations into modern French where necessary; over fifty other volumes announced. HEB

M62a Guénin, G., and **Nouaillac, J.** *Lectures historiques.* 3 v. Paris, 1921–25. [1, *L'ancien régime et la révolution, 1715–1800;* 2, *Le consulat, l'empire, et la restauration, 1800–1830;* 3, *La France et les grandes puissances du monde, 1830–1880.*]

b Cahen, Léon, and **Guyot, Raymond.** *L'œuvre législative de la révolution.* Paris, 1913. [Bibliothèque d'histoire contemporaine.]

c Cahen, Léon, and **Mathiez, Albert.** *Les lois françaises de 1815 à nos jours, accompagnées des documents politiques les plus importants.* 1906. 2nd rev. ed., Paris, 1919.

d Mautouchet, Paul. *Le gouvernement révolutionnaire, 10 août 1792–4 brumaire an IV.* Paris, 1912. [Collection de textes sur l'histoire des institutions et des services publics de la France moderne et contemporaine.] (Bibliography.)

e Cochin, Augustin, and **Charpentier, Charles.** *Les actes du gouvernement révolutionnaire, 22 août 1793–27 juillet 1794.* Paris, 1920. [Société d'Histoire Contemporaine.]

a. Well-chosen readings selected from contemporary memoirs, journals, letters, etc. V. 3. Contains also, as its title suggests, similar readings upon the principal countries of the world, including the United States. Review, C. Bémont, *Rev. Hist.* 139:280, March 1922; C. Richard, *ibid.* 145:275, March 1924; *Rev. des Quest. Hist.* 105:462, Oct. 1926. *b* and *c.* Useful collections of the principal legislative acts of their respective periods. Review of *b*, *A.H.R.* 19:397, Jan. 1914; of *c*, F. M. Anderson, *A.H.R.* 26:133, Oct. 1920. *d.* Contains the laws on the organization and operation of the revolutionary government from August 10, 1792, to the period of the Directory, with a substantial descriptive introduction. Review, H. E. Bourne, *A.H.R.* 18:166, Oct. 1912. *e.* Chiefly administrative circulars. Review, P. Caron, *La Révolution Française,* 75:56, Oct. 1922.

For a list of other similar collections of documents illustrative of French history, cf. *Rev. d'Hist. Moderne,* 2:144, 145 footnote, March 1927. HEB

M63a Hélie, Faustin A. *Les constitutions de la France: ouvrage contenant, outre les constitutions, les principales lois relatives au culte, à la magistrature, aux élections, à la liberté de la presse, de réunion, et d'association, à l'organisation des départements et des communes, avec un commentaire.* 4 pt. in 1 v., Paris, 1875–79.

b Anderson, Frank M. *Constitutions and other select documents illustrative of the history of France, 1789–1907.* 1904. 2nd rev. ed., Minneapolis, 1908. (Bibliography.)

c Legg, Leopold G. Wickham. *Select documents illustrative of the history of the French revolution: the constituent assembly.* 2 v. Oxford, 1905. (Bibliography.)

a. Standard collection of the French texts of the French constitutions and constitutional laws; partly superseded by the works listed under (M62), and by the official publication (M903).   GMD
b. Begins with the decree creating the national assembly on June 17, 1789, and ends with the papal encyclical of January 6, 1907; contains nearly 300 documents; translations are from the best French texts and are well done. Review, H. E. Bourne, *A.H.R.* 10:407, Jan. 1905. *c.* Made up of extracts, in French, from the *procès-verbaux* and newspapers of the period from 1789 to 1791, with the texts of the constitutional laws. Review, F. M. Anderson, *A.H.R.* 11:196, Oct. 1905.
                                                                            FMF

M64 Fling, Fred M., and **Fling, Helene D.** *Source problems on the French revolution.* N. Y. and London, 1913. [Harper's parallel source problems.] (Bibliography.)

Presents four problems: the oath of the tennis court, the royal session of June 23, the insurrection of October 5 and 6, and the flight to Varennes. Offers enough source material upon each problem to enable the student to assemble a sufficient body of sifted evidence upon which to base sound critical conclusions. Review, W. E. Lingelbach, *A.H.R.* 19:619, Apr. 1914.   HEB

M71a Laurière, Eusèbe J. de, and others, ed. *Ordonnances des roys de France de la troisième race, recueillies par ordre chronologique, avec des renvoys des unes aux autres, des sommaires, des observations sur le texte, et cinque tables.* 21 v. and index. Paris, 1723–1847.

b —— *Ordonnances des rois de France: règne de François Ier.* V. 1–10. Paris, 1887–1908.

c Jourdan, Athanase J. L.; Crusy, —— **de;** and **Isambert, François A.,** eds. *Recueil général des anciennes lois françaises, depuis l'an 420 jusqu'à la révolution de 1789.* 28 v. and index. Paris, 1822–33.

d Duvergier, Jean B. and others, ed. *Collection complète des lois, décrets, ordonnances, règlements et avis du conseil d'état, publiée sur les éditions officielles du Louvre; de l'Imprimerie nationale, par Baudouin; et du Bulletin des lois; (de 1788 à 1824 inclusivement, par ordre chronologique) continuée depuis 1824, avec un choix d'actes inédites, d'instructions ministérielles, et des notes sur chaque loi.* 24 v. and annual v. Paris, 1824 ff. 2nd ed., with the following alterations of title: '*De 1788 à 1830 . . . continuée depuis 1830*', 30 v. and annual v., Paris, 1834 ff.; *Table* 1788–1830, 2 v., 1834; 1831–1889, 4 v., 1890; 1890–1899, 1 v., 1900.

a. Covers the reigns of Hugh Capet to Louis XII inclusive. The work of Laurière's successors was stopped by the Revolution after the publication of v. 14; it was resumed and completed under the auspices of the Academy of Inscriptions.

For the early reigns, the collection was at first meagre, but was made more complete by supplements in subsequent volumes. *b.* Continuation of *a* under auspices of Academy of Moral and Political Sciences. *c.* Contains a wider variety of documents and extends over the whole period prior to the Revolution; besides laws, there are decisions of parliament, protests, and diplomatic acts. *d.* Not as complete as its title implies, but the most convenient single collection for the period since the outbreak of the Revolution. HEB

M72a Bouquet, Martin, and others, ed. *Recueil des historiens des Gaules et de la France: Rerum gallicarum et francicarum scriptores.* 24 v. in 25. Paris, 1738–1904. New ed. of v. 1–19 by Leopold Delisle, Paris, 1869–80.

b *Recueil des historiens de la France.* V. 1–13 in 14. Paris 1899–1923.

a. One of the historical collections begun by Dom Bouquet of the Benedictine abbey of Saint-Germain-des-Près. The work was interrupted by the Revolution and resumed under the auspices of the Academy of Inscriptions. More comprehensive than the title implies; even the earlier volumes, besides annals, chronicles, and histories, contained letters, *diplomata,* and ecclesiastical documents; with v. 21 its inclusiveness became more striking; the series was definitely concluded with v. 24 in 2 pt. *b.* New series, under the same auspices; divided into four sections: 1, *diplomes,* 2, *pouillés,* 3, *obituaires,* 4, *documents financiers.* In the second series, 8 v. of ecclesiastical tax records, etc., have been published, the earlier edited by Auguste Longnon; the other volumes belong to the third and fourth series. Review of *b,* section 2, v. 8, B. A. Pocquet du Haut-Jussé, *Rev. des Quest. Hist.* 101:465, Apr. 1, 1924. HEB

M73 *Collection de documents inédits sur l'histoire de France.* More than 280 v. Paris, 1836 ff.

Projected by Guizot when minister of public instruction in 1834; since 1881 carried forward by the Comité des Travaux Historiques et Scientifiques. Six series of publications have been undertaken: 1, chronicles, memoirs, journals, etc.; 2, charters; 3, correspondence, political and administrative documents; 4, documents of the revolutionary period; 5, documents relating to philology, philosophy, etc.; 6, archeological publications. Series 2, 3, and 4 have proved to be the most important. In series 3 notable publications are: *Lettres, instructions, et mémoires de Colbert,* ed. by Pierre Clément, 8 v. in 10, Paris, 1861–82, and *Correspondance des controleurs généraux des finances avec les intendants des provinces, 1683–1715,* ed. by Arthur M. de Boislisle and P. de Brotonne, 3 v., Paris, 1874–97. To series 4 belong *Recueil des actes du comité de salut public, avec la correspondance officielle des représentants en mission et le registre du conseil exécutif provisoire,* ed. by François Alphonse Aulard, v. 1–26, Paris, 1889–1925, indispensable for the study of the government of the mid-period of the Revolution; *Recueil des actes du directoire exécutif,* ed. by Antonin Debidour, v. 1–4, Paris, 1910–17, equally valuable for the period of the Directory but unfortunately broken off by the death of the editor, the last document bearing date of February 3, 1797; and *Procès-verbaux du comité d'instruction publique de la convention nationale,* ed. by James Guillaume, 6 v., Paris, 1891–1907, important for the study of the efforts at educational reconstruction which preceded the organization of the new system of public schools and the Napoleonic university. For descriptive list of the contents of v. 1–177 of the *Collection,* cf. (M1*b*) Franklin, *Les sources de l'histoire de France.* HEB

M74a Clercq, Alexandre J. H. de, and **Clercq, Jules de,** ed. *Recueil des traités de la France, publié sous les auspices du ministère des affaires étrangères.* V. 1–23 (v. 23 in 2 pt.). Paris, 1864–1917.

b Sorel, Albert; Hanotaux, Gabriel; and others, ed. *Recueil des instructions données aux ambassadeurs et ministres de France depuis les traités de Westphalie jusqu'à la révolution française, publié sous les auspices de la commission des archives diplomatiques au ministère des affaires étrangères.* V. 1–25 in 26. Paris, 1884–1929.

c *Les origines diplomatiques de la guerre de 1870–1871: recueil de documents publié par le ministère des affaires étrangères.* V. 1–19. Paris, 1910–27.

d Basdevant, Jules. *Recueil des traités et conventions en vigueur entre la France et les puissances étrangères.* 3 v. Paris, 1918–20.

a. Includes treaties from 1713 to the close of 1906. *b.* Arranged by states; now includes the principal states of Europe except Turkey and Great Britain. *c.* These documents are of special interest because, for this period, the archives of the ministry are not yet fully open; v. 1. Begins with December 25, 1863. V. 19. Ends with December 9, 1867. *d.* Carefully edited under the direction of the ministry of foreign affairs.   HEB

M81 Mavidal, Jérôme; Laurent, Émile; and others, ed. *Archives parlementaires, 1787–1860: recueil complet des débats des chambres françaises.* Series 1, 1787–1799, v. 1–82, Paris, 1879–1913; series 2, 1800–1860, v. 1–137, Paris, 1862–1913.

As in November, 1860, Emperor Napoleon III authorized the publication of a stenographic report of current debates in the legislative chambers in the official journal, then (M901) *Moniteur universel,* it was appropriate that an effort should be made to publish the debates from the beginning of parliamentary institutions at the time of the Revolution. Series 2, undertaken first, now extends to July 17, 1839. The method followed in v. 1–71 of series 1 was severely criticized by historical scholars (cf. *Rev. Hist.* 81:433–436, March 1903), because the editors in endeavoring to reproduce a speech, not printed by the author at the time, constructed a species of mosaic on the basis of a comparison of reports in various newspapers without indicating the sources. The annexes, containing the reproductions of speeches that were printed, were useful. Beginning with v. 72, sources have been carefully indicated. Series 1 has now reached January 4, 1794; series 2, July 17, 1839.   HEB

M82 *Collection de documents inédits sur l'histoire économique de la révolution française.* Approximately 100 v. Paris, Orléans, Rennes, etc., 1906 ff.

This collection is also (cf. M73) under the auspices of the Comité des Travaux Historiques et Scientifiques, but is directly administered by the Commission de Recherche et Publication des Documents Relatifs à la Vie Économique de la Révolution, appointed in 1903, when the French parliament, upon the recommendation of Jean Jaurès, voted the creation of such a collection. The field was divided into general topics, for each of which a series of documentary publications was projected: for example, 1, economic situation according to the *cahiers;* 2, feudal rights; 3, national property, including records of the sales of ecclesiastical and emigrants' estates; 4, industry; 5, money and paper money; 6, problems of subsistence, including supply of grain and flour and other necessaries; 7, public assistance; 8, commerce; 9, taxation. Thus far the collection is richest in volumes in series 1, 3, and 6.

To facilitate the work of editing, the Commission has prepared collections of laws and administrative acts relating to each of several series with the subtitle: *Instruction, recueil de textes, et notes*, Paris, 1907 ff., which are valuable instruments of work irrespective of the documents to which they serve as an introduction. The Commission also published a periodical *Bulletin d'histoire économique de la révolution*, Paris, 1906 ff., which contains many documents in the general field. Review, Pierre Caron, *A.H.R.* 13:501, Apr. 1908; H. E. Bourne, *ibid.* 32:315, Jan. 1928; of particular vs. C. Day, *ibid.* 15:377, Jan. 1910. HEB

M83a Lacroix, Sigismond, ed. *Actes de la commune de Paris pendant la révolution.* Series 1, 7 v. and index, Paris, 1894–99; series 2, v. 1–8, Paris, 1900–14.

b Aulard, François Alphonse, ed. *La Société des Jacobins: recueil de documents pour l'histoire du club des Jacobins de Paris.* 6 v. Paris, 1889–97.

c ———, ed. *Paris pendant la réaction thermidorienne et sous le directoire: recueil de documents pour l'histoire de l'esprit public à Paris.* 5 v. Paris, 1898–1902.

d ———, ed. *Paris sous le consulat: recueil de documents pour l'histoire de l'esprit public à Paris.* 4 v. Paris, 1903–09.

e ———, ed. *Paris sous le premier empire: recueil de documents pour l'histoire de l'esprit public à Paris.* V. 1, Paris, 1912.

Most notable publications in the *Collection de documents relatifs à l'histoire de Paris pendant la révolution· française, publiée sous le patronage du conseil municipal. a.* Planned to include the records as far as August 10, 1792, but the death of the editor stopped the work at November 10, 1791. V. 8. Includes some material, collected by Lacroix and edited by R. Farge, to February 24, 1792. *c, d,* and *e.* Contain excerpts from the journals of the day, selections from reports of police agents, and similar material for the study of public opinion; now completed as far as June 12, 1805. HEB

M84a Schmidt, Wilhelm Adolf. *Tableaux de la révolution française, publiés sur les papiers inédits du département et de la police secrète de Paris.* 3 v. Leipzig, 1867–71.

b ——— *Pariser Zustände während der Revolutionszeit von 1789–1800.* 3 v. Jena, 1874–76. French tr. by P. Viollet as *Paris pendant la révolution d'après les rapports de la police secrète, 1789–1800,* 4 v., Paris, 1880–94.

c Caron, Pierre. *Paris pendant la terreur: rapports des agents secrets du ministère de l'intérieur.* V. 1–2. Paris, 1910–14. [Société d'Histoire Contemporaine.]

a. Covers the whole period of the Revolution; even includes documents for the Consulate and the Empire; not a complete collection, however, for it contains only 201 documents out of 1463 belonging to the period covered by *c. b.* Abridged revision of *a.* Review, A. Stern, *Rev. Hist.* 3:196, Jan. 1877. *c.* Plans to bring together only the reports of the secret agents or observers of the ministry of the interior from September 2, 1793, to the end of Germinal, year II; provided with a comprehensive introduction and helpful notes. V. 2. Extends to January 16, 1794. Cf. (I331). HEB

M85a *Correspondance de Napoléon Ier, publiée par ordre de l'empereur Napoléon III.* 32 v. Paris, 1858–70.

b Lecestre, Léon, ed. *Lettres inédites de Napoléon Ier, an VIII–1815.* 1897. 2nd ed., 2 v., Paris, 1897.

c Brotonne, Léonce de, ed. *Lettres inédites de Napoléon Ier.* Paris, 1898.

d ――――, ed. *Dernières lettres inédites de Napoléon Ier.* 2 v. Paris, 1903.

e Picard, Ernest, and **Tuetey, Louis,** ed. *Correspondance inédite de Napoléon Ier, conservée aux archives de la guerre.* V. 1–4, Paris, 1912–13.

a. Official collection selected by two commissions appointed by Napoleon III. The second commission, over which Prince Napoleon presided, was appointed on February 3, 1864, because the emperor held that the first commission had not been sufficiently rigorous in excluding letters which might tarnish his uncle's fame. *b.* Intended to include as many as possible of the suppressed letters, but the editor was not permitted to make full use of the letters preserved in the archives of the ministry of war and had to rely upon the minutes preserved in the Archives Nationales. *c* and *d.* Add many more letters. *e.* Includes the letters in the archives of the ministry of war, previously withheld. V. 4. Closes with 1811. HEB

SHORTER GENERAL HISTORIES

M101a Adams, George B. *Growth of the French nation.* N. Y., 1896. Later reprints.

b Bainville, Jacques. *History of France.* N. Y., 1926. Tr. by Alice and Christian Gauss from *Histoire de France,* Paris, 1924.

c Davis, William S. *History of France from the earliest times to the treaty of Versailles.* Boston, 1919. (Bibliography.)

d Duclaux, Mary. (Agnes Mary F. Robinson, formerly Mrs. James Darmesteter.) *Short history of France from Cæsar's invasion to the battle of Waterloo.* N. Y. and London, 1918. (Bibliographies.)

e Duruy, Victor. *History of France.* 1889. Tr. and abridged from 17th ed. of *Histoire de France,* 2 v., Paris, 1856; 22nd ed., 1908, by M. Carey and continued by J. Franklin Jameson; rev. ed., continued to 1919, by Mabell S. C. Smith, N. Y., 1920. Another tr., with continuation to 1914, by L. Cecil Jane and Lucy Menzies, 2 v., London and N. Y., 1917 [Everyman's library].

f Hassall, Arthur. *France, mediaeval and modern, a history.* Oxford, 1918.

g Headlam, Cecil. *France.* London, 1913. [Making of the nations.]

h Malet, Albert. *Nouvelle histoire de France.* Paris, 1922. Abridged ed. by P. R. Doolin, N. Y., 1927.

i Reinach, Joseph. *Francia, histoire illustrée de la France.* Paris, 1921. (Brief bibliography.)

a. Best brief history of France in English; well-balanced, presenting social as well as political elements in the growth of the nation. Review, C. H. Haskins, *A.H.R.* 2:335, Jan. 1897. *b.* Great popular success in France; written from the nationalist point of view, the first half an apologia of the old monarchy; as a whole characterized by passages of brilliant interpretation; interest centers in the higher politics of government and foreign affairs; slight attention to the economic and social development. Review, F. M. Anderson, *A.H.R.* 31:819, July

1926. *c.* Originally planned for instruction of American soldiers in the World War; devotes about half the space to period since 1789. Review, C. H. C. Wright, *A.H.R.* 26:313, Jan. 1921. *d.* Sparkling with brilliant comment and interpretation; not so crowded with details as to obscure the main currents of national development; reveals long and intimate knowledge of French life and literature. Review, C. D. Hazen, *A.H.R.* 24:660, July 1919. *e.* Has long served as a text; still useful as a compendium of moderate dimensions. *f.* Brief chronicle; recounts chiefly political and military events. Review, K. Francke, *A.H.R.* 24:721, July 1919. *g.* Similar to *f*; well-illustrated; treatment of modern period superficial and disproportionately brief, giving only fifteen pages to the years from 1815 to 1871. *h.* Well-balanced narrative by competent scholar; numerous wisely chosen illustrations. *i.* Written to explain the development of the French people to the soldiers of the French, British, and American armies in the World War; able and suggestive, although not wholly free from discarded views upon points of detail.   HEB

LONGER GENERAL HISTORIES

M121a Kitchin, George W. *History of France.* 1873–77. 4th rev. ed., 3 v., Oxford, 1899–1903. (Bibliography.)

b MacDonald, John R. Moreton. *History of France.* 3 v. London and N. Y., 1915. (Bibliographies.)

a. Sober, uninspired narrative of the details of French political history from B.C. 58 to the Revolution; convenient and reliable compendium; displays a rather narrowly English point of view. Economic, social, and intellectual developments are unduly neglected. *b.* Comprehensive and fairly well-proportioned survey of the growth of the French people and their civilizations from the origins to 1871. Seriously defective in accuracy and some of its generalizations are loose and careless, but it conveys the sense of life, movement, and human interest. Review, C. D. Hazen, *A.H.R.* 21:573, Apr. 1916.   LBP

M122 Funck-Brentano, Frantz, ed. *National history of France.* 6 v. London and N. Y., 1913 ff. Tr. from *Histoire de France racontée à tous,* 8 v., Paris, 1911 ff. [*1, F. Funck-Brentano, *Earliest times;* *2, F. Funck-Brentano, *Middle ages;* *3, L. Batiffol, *Century of the renaissance;* *4, J. Boulenger, *Seventeenth century;* *5, C. Stryienski, *Eighteenth century;* *6, L. Madelin, *Revolution;* 7, L. Madelin, *Consulate and the empire;* *8, J. Lucas-Dubreton, *Restoration and the July monarchy;* 9, R. Arnaud, *Revolution of 1848 and the second empire;* *10, R. Recouly, *Third republic.*] (Bibliographies.)

Coöperative work by competent scholars; written in lively and interesting style; provides an appreciation of the national life in the successive periods rather than a mere narrative of political history. Consideration is given to literature, art, and social and economic affairs. Frequently use is made of illustrative extracts from the sources, especially in the earlier volumes. V. 1. Explains the racial elements blended to form the French people; the narrative extends from prehistoric times to the advent of the Capetians. Review, M. Besnier, *Rev. des Quest. Hist.* 105:474, Oct. 1926; C. W. David, *A.H.R.* 32:910, July 1927. V. 2. Distinctly superior to v. 1, as the author is a master of this field; vivid and intensely interesting appreciation of the civilization of feudal France from the tenth century to the end of the fifteenth; resembles (M224*d*) Luchaire, *Social*

* Indicates volumes already published.

France at the time of Philip Augustus, but covers more ground; particularly suggestive chapters on numerous cultural topics. Review, L. Halphen, *Rev. Hist.* 143:219, July 1923. V. 3. Clear, well-proportioned presentation. Review, E. M. Hulme, *A.H.R.* 22:640, Apr. 1917. V. 4. The selection of topics for treatment is, on the whole, satisfactory, although the royal mistresses receive more attention than the condition of the common people and a page is given to a noted duellist while a line suffices for La Salle. V. 5. Similar to v. 4 in character. Review, H. E. Bourne, *A.H.R.* 22:706, Apr. 1917. V. 6. Now usually considered the best single volume on the Revolution; brilliantly written; conclusions should be accepted with caution; inadequate on work of the Constituent Assembly and on the wars. Review, *E.H.R.* 32:155, Jan. 1917. V. 8. Emphasizes personalities and episodes. Review, R. Durand, *Rev. Critique,* 94:259, July 1, 1927. V. 10. Written by a brilliant journalist, whose contacts with public men, not only in France but in other countries, have been unusually numerous and intimate, its narrative often possesses the interest of recollections. Party controversies in France are skilfully and justly portrayed, but in foreign politics the attitude is distinctly nationalist. Review, *Rev. des Quest. Hist.* 108:247, Jan. 1928.

JWT, FMF, HEB

M123 Hanotaux, Gabriel, ed. *Histoire de la nation française.* 15 v. Paris, 1920 ff. [*1, G. Hanotaux, *Introduction générale;* J. Brunhes, *Géographie humaine de la France;* *2, J. Brunhes and P. Deffontaines, *Géographie politique et géographie du travail;* *3, P. Imbart de la Tour, *Histoire politique des origines à 1515;* *4, L. Madelin, *Histoire politique de 1515 à 1804;* *5, G. Hanotaux, *Histoire politique de 1804 à 1920;* *6, G. Goyau, *Histoire religieuse;* *7, J. Colin, *Histoire militaire et navale des origines aux croisades;* F. Reboul, *Des croisades à la Révolution;* *8, C. Mangin, *Histoire militaire et navale de la constituante au directoire;* L. F. M. F. Franchet d'Espérey, *Du directoire à la guerre de 1914;* G. Hanotaux, *La guerre de 1914–1918;* *9, R. Pinon, *Histoire diplomatique 1515–1928;* *10, G. Martin, *Histoire économique et financière;* *11, L. Gillet, *Histoire des arts;* *12, F. Picavet, *La littérature en langue latine;* J. Bédier, *Les chansons de geste;* A. Jeanroy, *La littérature de langue française des origines à Ronsard;* *13, F. Strowski, *Histoire des lettres de Ronsard à nos jours;* *14, E. Picard, *Histoire des sciences, introduction générale;* H. Andoyer and P. Humbert, *Histoire des mathématiques, de la mécanique, et de· l'astronomie;* C. Fabry,· *Histoire de la physique;* A. Colson, *Histoire de la chimie;* *15, M. Caullery, *Histoire des sciences biologiques;* R. Lote, *Histoire de la philosophie.*]

Instead of the chronological treatment customary in coöperative histories, an encyclopedic or topical arrangement and distribution of assignments is adopted. Since the volumes present syntheses and conclusions rather than learned discussions, notes and references are omitted and the scholarly standing of the authors is relied upon as adequate assurance that the conclusions have been reached by scientific processes. Handsomely printed and abundantly illustrated with portraits, scenes, and reproductions of great works of art. V. 1. Hanotaux's exposition of the historical rôle of France reveals somewhat too strongly the effects of the World War upon thought. The anthropogeography of France is admirably set forth (cf. M42c). V. 2. Cf. (M42d). V. 3. Much more than a political history; includes the social, economic, and intellectual development of medieval France. Review, C. Petit-Dutaillis, *Rev. Hist.* 139:260, March 1922. V. 4. Review, T. Collier, *A.H.R.* 30:133, Oct. 1924. V. 6. Restricted space prevents

* This series is now completed.

adequate consideration of the counter influences of religion and other elements of national growth. Review, T. Collier, *A.H.R.* 28:88, Oct. 1922. V. 7. Gives slight attention to the navy; illuminating sections on army organization, weapons, and tactics; summary descriptions of military operations. Review, O. L. Spaulding, Jr., *A.H.R.* 31:769, July 1926. V. 8. Similar to v. 7; gives liberal space to the period from 1815 to 1914. V. 9. Review, (London) *Times Lit. Suppl.* 28:463, June 13, 1929. V. 10. Gives special attention to the rise of capitalism and to economic conditions during the World War. Review, H. Sée, *Rev. Hist.* 155:341, July 1927. V. 11. Review, F. Kimball, *A.H.R.* 28:733, July 1923. V. 12. Contributions by Picavet and Bédier deserve special attention. Review, F. M. Warren, *A.H.R.* 27:547, Apr. 1922. V. 13. Review, A. Schinz, *A.H.R.* 29:320, Jan. 1924. V. 14. Review, C. Barus, *A.H.R.* 30:589, Apr. 1925. V. 15. Review, W. Riley, *A.H.R.* 31:761, July 1926. JWT, AS, HEB

M124a Lavisse, Ernest, ed. *Histoire de France depuis les origines jusqu'à la révolution.* 9 v. in 18. Paris, 1900–11. [V. 1, pt. 1, P. Vidal de la Blache, *Tableau de la géographie de la France;* pt. 2, G. Bloch, *Les origines, la Gaule indépendante, et la Gaule romaine;* v. 2, pt. 1, C. Bayet, C. Pfister, A. Kleinclausz, *Le Christianisme, les barbares, Mérovingiens, et Carolingiens;* pt. 2, A. Luchaire, *Les premiers Capétiens, 987–1137;* v. 3, pt. 1, A. Luchaire, *1137–1226;* pt. 2, C. V. Langlois, *1226–1328;* v. 4, pt. 1, A. Coville, *1328–1422;* pt. 2, C. Petit-Dutaillis, *1422–1492;* v. 5, H. Lemonnier, *1492–1559;* v. 6, J. H. Mariéjol, *1559–1643;* v. 7, E. Lavisse, *Louis XIV, 1643–1685;* v. 8, pt. 1, E. Lavisse and others, *Louis XIV, 1685–1715;* pt. 2, H. Carré, *Louis XV, 1715–1775;* v. 9, pt. 1, H. Carré and others, *Louis XVI, 1774–1789;* pt. 2, *Tables alphabétiques.*] (Bibliographies.)

b —— *Histoire de France contemporaine depuis la révolution jusqu'à la paix de 1919.* 10 v. Paris, 1920–22. [V. 1, P. Sagnac, *1789–1792;* v. 2, G. Pariset, *1792–1799;* v. 3, G. Pariset, *1799–1815;* v. 4, S. Charléty, *1815–1830;* v. 5, S. Charléty, *1830–1848;* v. 6, C. Seignobos, *1848–1859;* v. 7, C. Seignobos, *1859–1875;* v. 8, C. Seignobos, *1875–1914;* v. 9, H. Bidou and others, *La grande guerre;* v. 10, *Index.*]

a. Most successful example of coöperative historical writing yet attempted. The plan departs from that of either (B152) *Histoire générale* or (I121) *Cambridge modern history.* With the exception of v. 2, pt. 1, and v. 8, pt. 1, each volume (technically enumerated as a half-volume) is entrusted to a single author. This assures greater harmony of treatment. The plan also exhibits the extended scope of recent historical studies, including, as it does, besides narrative history of politics and war, the growth of institutions, manners, economic conditions, religion, literature, and the arts. These are not treated incidentally, but receive distinct sections of volumes. For example, v. 8, pt. 1, on the later years of Louis XIV, has seven parts or books. Of its 480 pages only 147 are given to politics and war. The authors offer positive contributions to historical knowledge rather than a rewriting for the general public of the work of other scholars. Critical apparatus has, however, not obtruded. In one or two instances the distribution of space has been questioned, notably the excessive condensation in v. 2, pt. 1. It was not to be expected that equality of attainment should have been reached throughout the series, but the level is remarkably high. The contributions of Vidal de la Blache, Luchaire, Langlois, Petit-Dutaillis. Lemonnier, Sagnac, and, of course, Lavisse himself are noteworthy. Review, v. 1, pt. 2, v. 2, pt. 2, v. 3, pt. 1, 2, *A.H.R.* 7:177, Oct. 1901; v. 4, pt. 2, F. M. Fling, *A.H.R.* 8:747, July 1903; v. 1, pt. 1; v. 2, pt. 1; v. 4, pt. 1; v. 5, pt. 1; v. 5, pt. 2; v. 6, pt. 1; v. 6, pt. 2; v. 7, pt. 1; v. 7, pt. 2; v. 8, pt. 1, J. W. Thompson, *A.H.R.* 9:342, Jan. 1904; 9:345, Jan. 1904; 8:119, Oct. 1902; 9:147, Oct. 1903; 10:387, Jan. 1905; 10:387, Jan. 1905; 11:376, Jan. 1906; 12:130, Oct. 1906; 13:859, July 1908; 14:579, Apr. 1909; v. 8, pt. 2; v. 9, pt. 1, H. E. Bourne, *A.H.R.* 15:857, July 1910; 16:615, Apr. 1911.

b. Worthy continuation of *a*, on the same plan, but by a smaller number of historians. Its publication, with the exception of the index volume, was fortunately completed before the death of its distinguished editor. The final chapter appended to v. 9 by M. Lavisse furnishes not only a fitting conclusion to the combined series, but also to the writer's career as an historian. His skilful synthesis of the basic factors in French history leads, in spite of the devastation of the World War, to optimistic predictions for his nation's future. V. 1. Model of balanced and scholarly treatment. The other volumes deserve similar praise. V. 9. M. Gauvain recounts the diplomacy of the World War; M. Bidou, military operations. V. 10. Index for both *a* and *b*. Review, v. 1–2, H. E. Bourne, *A.H.R.* 27:301, Jan. 1922; v. 3, W. E. Lingelbach, 27:304, Jan. 1922; v. 4–7, F. M. Fling, 27:306, Jan. 1922; v. 8–9, F. M. Anderson, 27:560, Apr. 1922; 28:315, Jan. 1923.   HEB

M125a Michelet, Jules. *History of France.* 2 v. in 1. London, 1844–46. [Foreign library.] Partial tr. (to 1454) by W. K. Kelly from *Histoire de France,* 19 v., Paris, 1833–46, 1855–67. Many later ed. Later partial tr. (to 1483) by G. H. Smith, 2 v., N. Y., 1887.

b ———— *Historical view of the French revolution.* 1848. Later ed., London, 1902. Partial tr. by C. Cocks from *Histoire de la révolution française,* 7 v., 1847–53; rev. ed. 9 v., Paris, 1883–87.

a. Although belonging to the mid-nineteenth century, Michelet's work is still regarded as the greatest masterpiece of French historical literature. He was at his best in v. 1–6, which bring the narrative to the close of the reign of Louis XI. From 1846 for a decade, he turned to *b*, a work second only to *a*. When he resumed the original task, his mind had become embittered by the triumph of reaction under the Second Empire and his volumes progressively lost in value. The place which *a* holds is due not alone to his genius as a writer, but to the fact that he was the first to work in the national archives in the modern sense of the phrase. He gave more attention to local and provincial history than any of his predecessors. He was also the first to show in his famous 'Tableau de France' the relation between the physical make-up of France and its history.

HEB

EARLY AND MEDIEVAL TIMES TO 1483

For prehistoric, Celtic, and Roman times cf. (B308) Déchellette, *Manuel d'archéologie préhistorique, celtique, et gallo-romaine;* (E461) Desjardins, *Géographie historique et administrative de la Gaule romaine;* and (E462) Jullian, *Histoire de la Gaule.*

M221 Fustel de Coulanges, Numa D. *Histoire des institutions politiques de l'ancienne France.* 6 v. 1882–92. Rev. ed. by C. Jullian, 6 v., Paris, 1905–14.

Remarkable for comprehensiveness of research, suggestiveness of interpretation, and quality of style. The reputation of Fustel de Coulanges had been made by his (D531c) *Ancient city* when the loss of his professorship at Strasbourg, owing to the Franco-Prussian War, diverted him to the field of medieval history. His thesis was that the real foundations of European society were Roman and that German influence in history has been much exaggerated. This conviction was sometimes pushed to such lengths that even French scholars disagreed with him. The sections of special value deal with land tenure and social texture. Review, (A249a) Gooch, *History and historians in the nineteenth century,* pp. 209–213; (A247) Fueter, *Geschichte der neueren Historiographie,* pp. 560–565; E. Jenks, *E.H.R.* 12:209, Apr. 1897.

JWT

M222 Guilhiermoz, Paul. *Essai sur l'origine de la noblesse en France au moyen âge.* Paris, 1902.

Brilliant exposition of many of the institutional, economic, and social conditions prevailing at the height of the middle ages. Finds the origin of the feudal nobility in chivalry; combats its derivation either from the Roman aristocrats or German conquerors. Review, *Rev. Hist.* 78:338, March 1902.

JWT

M223 Flach, Jacques. *Les origines de l'ancienne France: X^e et XIe siècles.* 4 v. Paris, 1886–1917. (Bibliographies.)

With the possible exception of (M222) Guilhiermoz, the most original contribution to knowledge of the sources and development of the feudal régime made within the last generation. Although his emphasis upon the influence of the Celtic clan has been opposed with success by other historians, his volumes form an immense storehouse of information, so thorough were his researches in every species of material printed and unprinted. He was a professor of law and his treatment is often legalistic, but his work is eminently historical. Review, G. B. Adams, *A.H.R.* 9:777, July 1904; 23:841, July 1918; F. M. Powicke, *History* 3:129, 193, Oct. 1918, Jan. 1919.

JWT

M224a Luchaire, Achille. *Histoire des institutions monarchiques de la France sous les premiers Capétiens, 897–1180.* 1884. 2nd rev. ed., 2 v., Paris, 1891.

   b —— *Manuel des institutions françaises: période des Capétiens directs.* Paris, 1892. (Bibliographies.)

   c —— *Les communes françaises à l'époque des Capétiens directs.* 1890. Rev. ed. by L. Halphen, Paris, 1911.

   d —— *Social France at the time of Philip Augustus.* London and N. Y., 1912. Tr. by E. B. Krehbiel from *La société française au temps de Philippe-Auguste,* Paris, 1909.

a. Traces the history of the Capetian monarchy from its rise in 987 to its position of power under Philip Augustus, 1180, delineating the mechanism of administration. Review, C. Bémont, *Rev. Hist.* 24:372, Jan. 1884. *b.* One of the most essential books; presents the main features of French medieval institutions; a model of lucidity. Review, A. Molinier, *Rev. Hist.* 51:107, Jan. 1893. *c.* Of equal authority for its subject. Review, E. W. Dow, *A.H.R.* 17:652, Apr. 1912. *d.* Omits meticulous references to documents; synthesizes the results of a lifetime of study in a series of brilliant lectures. Review, *Nation* (N. Y.), 95:83, July 25, 1912.

JWT

M231a Cartellieri, Alexander. *Philipp II, August, König von Frankreich.* 4 v. in 5. Leipzig, 1899–1922. (Bibliographies.)

   b Hutton, William H. *Philip Augustus.* London and N. Y., 1896. [Foreign statesmen.]

a. Authoritative history by a German scholar, although its solid qualities are outshone by the French counterpart, written by Luchaire as v. 3, pt. 1 of (M124*a*) Lavisse, *Histoire de France.* Review, C. Bémont, *Rev. Hist.* 141:71, Sept. 1922; L. Halphen, *ibid.* 143:227, July 1923. *b.* Small book; chiefly valuable as the only modern account in English. Review, W. Walker, *A.H.R.* 2:370, Jan. 1897. JWT

M232a Petit-Dutaillis, Charles. *Étude sur la vie et le règne de Louis VIII, 1187–1226.* Paris, 1894. [Bibliothèque de l'École des Hautes Études.]

   b Perry, Frederick. *Saint Louis (Louis IX of France) the most Christian king.* London and N. Y., 1901. [Heroes of the nations.]

   c Langlois, Charles V. *Le règne de Philippe III le Hardi.* Paris, 1887.

   d Boutaric, Edgard. *La France sous Philippe le Bel, étude sur les institutions politiques et administratives de moyen âge.* Paris, 1861.

a. Long book on a short reign; chapters dealing with French intervention in England in the reign of John are the most valuable. Review, A. Molinier, *Rev. Hist.* 59:115, Sept. 1895. *b.* Only convenient and modern account in English of St. Louis, but the treatment is inferior. Review, J. W. Thompson, *A.H.R.* 7:129, Oct. 1901. For better account, cf. (M124*a*) Lavisse, *Histoire de France,* v. 3, pt. 2; also cf. (H359*b*) Joinville, *Memoirs. c.* One of the best histories of a single reign yet written. Both the political and institutional conditions of France under Philip III were critical. The French monarchy was the most powerful in Europe, and yet the weakness of the king imperilled the crown and the Sicilian Vespers compromised France as never before. This double condition is clearly analyzed. Review, C. Bémont and G. Monod, *Rev. Hist.* 34:285, May 1887; A. Molinier, *ibid.* 40:373, May 1889. *d.* In a measure superseded by Langlois's treatment in (M124*a*) Lavisse, *Histoire de France,* v. 3, pt. 2; nevertheless it has substantial merits, particularly in the sections dealing with administration.

                                                      JWT

M233 Delachenal, Roland. *Histoire de Charles V.* V. 1–4. Paris, 1909–28.

The disastrous reign of Philip VI of Valois still awaits an historian, but that of his brilliant grandson, Charles V, has been to M. Delachenal an object of study for many years. V. 3. Closes with 1368. V. 5. Announced as completed at his death in 1923; has unfortunately not yet been published. The work is a model both in matter and in manner. Review, T. F. Tout, *E.H.R.* 25:156, Jan. 1910; J. F. Baldwin, *A.H.R.* 15:588, Apr. 1910.   JWT

M234a Froissart, Jean. *Chronicles of England, France, . . .* 2 v., London, 1523–25; many later ed., notably by W. P. Ker, 6 v., London and N. Y., 1901–03. [Tudor translations]; Oxford, 1927 ff., and abridged ed. by G. C. Macaulay, 1895, 2nd ed., London and N. Y., 1913 [Globe edition]. Tr. by John Bourchier, Baron Berners, from *Chroniques,* 4 v., Paris, 1495 (?); several later ed., notably by S. Luce and G. Raynaud, v. 1–11, Paris, 1869–99 [Société de l'Histoire de France], and by Baron Kervyn de Lettenhove, 25 v. in 26, Bruxelles, 1867–77 [*Oeuvres de Froissart publiées avec les variantes des divers manuscrits,* v. 1–25: Académie royale de Belgique]. Another tr. by T. Johnes, 4 v., Hafod, 1803–05; later reprints, notably abridged ed. by H. P. Dunster, London and N. Y., 1906 [Everyman's library].

b Monstrelet, Enguerrand de. *Chronicles . . . containing an account of . . . memorable events that happened in the kingdom of France, as well as in other countries . . . beginning at the year MCCCC . . . and continued by others to the year MDXVI.* 5 v. Hafod, 1809; 13 v., London, 1810; several later ed. in 2 v., including London and N. Y., 1867. Tr. by T. Johnes from *Chroniques,* Paris, 1500 (?); best ed. by L. Douet-d'Arcq, 6 v., Paris, 1857-62 [Société de l'Histoire de France].

a. Froissart, whose narrative covers the years 1327–1400, remains the most widely read of medieval chroniclers. He portrays with incomparable art the manners, incidents, and personages of his time. His were the impressions of an observer of genius, who travelled extensively and who questioned the principal actors in the drama of the Hundred· Years' War. His outlook, however, was limited. He had slight knowledge of the condition of the peasants, and felt little sympathy with their sufferings. Nor does he treat political events with much greater understanding. Book I of his *Chronicle* exists in three redactions: the first written from the English, the others from the French, point of view. The edition by Luce and Raynaud is the most authoritative, but is complete only to 1385. The Berners translation is from the first printed edition by A. Vérard, 1495 (?). Review, (M2a) Molinier, *Sources de l'histoire de France,* 1:4–18.

b. Monstrelet owes his fame primarily to the fact that he was a continuator of Froissart. His own narrative covers the years from 1400 to 1444. He wrote from the Burgundian point of view, although he affects an attitude of impartiality. He has nothing of the magic of his predecessor's style and overloads his account with wearisome details, but he had knowledge at first hand of the great crisis in French· affairs, and·so his pages cannot be neglected.

HEB

M235a Beaucourt, Gaston L. E. du Fresne, Marquis de. *Histoire de Charles VII.* 6 v. Paris, 1881–91.

b Lowell, Francis C. *Joan of Arc.* Boston, 1896.

a. The arrangement of the volumes is awkward and the narrative diffuse. The treatment is strongly tinged by monarchist and confessional prejudice: the first leads to palliation of the weaknesses and follies of Charles VII; the second, to distortion of the career of Joan and to misrepresentation of contemporaneous ecclesiastical conditions, especially the relations of the crown to the reforming councils. Review, A. Molinier, *Rev. Hist.* 45:358, Jan. 1891. A better, though much briefer, treatment of the reign is found in (M124a) Lavisse, *Histoire de France,* v. 4, pt. 2. *b.* An honor to American scholarship and probably the best biography in English of the Maid. Review, B. S. Terry, *A.H.R.* 2:131, Oct. 1896. For other biographies, cf. (M718); for the sources, cf. (M926a). JWT

M236a Willert, Paul F. *Reign of Lewis XI.* London and N. Y., 1876. (Historical handbooks.)

b Kirk, John F. *History of Charles the Bold, Duke of Burgundy.* 3 v. Philadelphia, 1864–68.

c Champion, Pierre. *Louis XI.* 2 v. Paris, 1927.

a. Characterized by a certain sketchiness, but redeemed by evidence of solid scholarship. In the light of work recently done by French historians, and of literature cited in (M124a) Lavisse, *Histoire de France,* v. 4, pt. 2, the treatment is antiquated. *b.* Written at a time when romanticism dominated· historical writing. Readable, but now superseded by (H821) Putnam, *Charles the Bold.* . JWT

c. By a scholar well known for his studies of fifteenth century France; emphasis laid upon the rôle of Louis XI in promoting territorial unity and upon his interest in efficient administration. Not an apology, and yet it presents as mere idiosyncrasies those qualities commonly pointed out by hostile writers as the king's characteristics. Does not describe Louis as a political genius, but, rather, as an able royalist lawyer, with ideas of order, combined with a land-greedy, hard-bargaining peasant. Contains an illuminating discussion of printed and manuscript sources. Review, Petit-Dutaillis, *Rev. Hist.* 157:89, Jan. 1928; R. A. Newhall, *A.H.R.* 33:635, Apr. 1928. RAN

M237 Comines, Philippe de. *Memoirs . . . containing the histories of Louis XI and Charles VIII, Kings of France, and of Charles the Bold, duke of Burgundy.* . . . 1855. New ed., 2 v., London, 1901–04 [Bohn's standard library]. Tr. by A. R. Scoble from *Mémoires* . . . , Paris, 1523; ed. by L. M. E. Dupont, 3 v., Paris, 1841–48 (Société de l'Histoire de France); best critical ed. by B. de Mandrot, 2 v., Paris, 1901–03 [Collection de textes pour servir à l'enseignement de l'histoire.] Another excellent ed. by Joseph Calmette and G. Durville, 3 v., Paris, 1924–27. Another tr., *History of Comines, Englished by Thomas Danett, anno 1596,* ed. by C. Whibley, 2 v., London and N. Y., 1897 [Tudor translations].

Comines was a Belgian by birth and long in the service of both Charles the Bold and Louis XI. He wrote these reminiscences of the year 1464 to 1498 late in life. His work is primary for the history of the times. He is the first French writer who manifests a marked influence of the Italian Renaissance. He is sometimes called the French Machiavelli, and in many ways he is a counterpart of the Florentine. The raciness of style, the intimacy of his revelations, the candor not unmixed with cynicism,—all these qualities make Comines highly interesting. Review, (M2a) Molinier, *Sources de l'histoire de France,* 5:5. Review of Calmette and Durville ed., v. 1, B. A. Pocquet du Haut-Jussé, *Rev. des Quest. Hist.* 102:488, Apr. 1925. JWT

SIXTEENTH CENTURY, 1483–1610

M251a Grant, Arthur J. *French monarchy, 1483–1789.* 1900. 4th ed., 2 v., Cambridge, Eng., 1925. [Cambridge historical series.] (Bibliography.)

b Bridge, John S. C. *History of France from the death of Louis XI.* V. 1–4. Oxford, 1921–29. [1, *Regency of Anne of Beaujeu, 1483–1493;* 2, *Reign of Charles VIII, 1493–1498.*] (Bibliographies.)

a. Satisfactory manual of political, diplomatic, and military history; very little is said of social or economic conditions. Review, *A.H.R.* 6:836, July 1901. b. Promises to be one of the most pleasing narrative histories of France in English; very readable; based upon the latest scholarly monographs; enlivened by frequent quotations from the best sources. Primarily concerned with personalities, politics, diplomacy, and war. Review, R. A. Newhall, *A.H.R.* 27:816, July 1922; 30:130, Oct. 1924; of v. 1, C. Petit-Dutaillis, *Rev. Hist.* 145:223, March 1924; of v. 3, 4, R. A. Newhall, *A.H.R.* 35:837, July 1930. RAN

M252 Ranke, Leopold von. *Civil wars and monarchy in France in the sixteenth and seventeenth centuries, a history of France principally during that period.* 2 v. London, 1852. Partial tr. by M. A. Garvey from *Französische Geschichte vornehmlich im sechzehnten und siebzehnten Jahrhundert,* 1852–59, 5 v., Leipzig, 1868–74 [v. 8–12 of Ranke, *Sämmtliche Werke*].

This monumental work covers the history of France from the accession of Francis I to the end of the reign of Louis XV in 1774, but its substance is comprehended between the inception of the French civil wars in 1562 and the termination of the reign of Louis XIV in 1715. Unfortunately the English version stops at 1593. Though an immense amount of new research has been done since its appearance, this work is still far from obsolete. Ranke was so profound a master of the sources of his subject, and his reasoning faculties were so potent and acute, that his historical judgments still stand. Characterized, like all his works, by brilliant analysis, unusual interpretative faculty, and cogent synthesis. The style is sinewy and vigorous. Cf. (L323) Ranke, *History of England principally in the seventeenth century.* JWT

M253a Viénot, Jean. *Histoire de la réforme française des origines à l'édit de Nantes.* Paris, 1926.

b Imbart de la Tour, Pierre. *Les origines de la réforme.* 3 v. Paris, 1905–14.

a. Popular history of the French Reformation from the Protestant standpoint; particularly valuable for the period after 1538, which Imbart de la Tour did not live to study. Thoroughly reliable; emphasizes the purely religious and political sides of the movement; much less on social and intellectual history than in *b* or in (M124a, v. 6), Mariéjol. *b.* Largely social and cultural; breadth of treatment, depth of insight, richness of knowledge, and charm of presentation give it high authority. V. 1. Economic and statistical survey of France about 1500. V. 2. Deals with the crisis in the church caused by the Renaissance. V. 3. Begins the history of the Reformation, carrying it up to 1538, when the influence of Calvin became decisive. Review, H. Hauser, *Rev. Hist.* 90:354, March 1906; 103:317, March 1910. PS

M254a Baird, Henry M. *History of the rise of the Huguenots of France.* 1879. Reprint, 2 v., N. Y., 1907.

b ———— *Huguenots and Henry of Navarre.* 2 v. N. Y., 1886.

c ———— *Huguenots and the revocation of the edict of Nantes.* 2 v. N. Y., 1895.

Written by a warm admirer of the Huguenots; well-informed; clear and readable; still useful, though in part superseded. Review of *b*, J. G. Black, *Rev. Hist.* 35:136, Sept. 1887. PS

M255 Romier, Lucien. *Les origines politiques des guerres de religion.* 2 v. Paris, 1913–14.

These volumes, based on an extended exploration of a score of Italian, Swiss, Belgian, as well as French archival collections, supply an entirely new foundation for the history of France under Henry II, 1547–1559. They describe the transition from the pacific expansion of the Reformed party to the militant Protestantism of the 'sixties. A minute and careful analysis of the Guise and Montmorency factions reveals the rivalries, purely political in character, which aggravated the religious revolt, after it had been provoked by the decision of the monarch to commit himself to one of the two confessions. Review, P. Bondois, *Rev. Hist.* 114:159, Sept. 1913; 116:364, July 1914. WLD

M256a Armstrong, Edward. *French wars of religion.* 1892. 2nd ed., London, 1904.

b Thompson, James Westfall. *Wars of religion in France, 1559–1576: the Huguenots, Catherine de Medici, and Philip II.* 1909. 2nd ed., Chicago, 1914.

c Rocquain, Félix. *La France et Rome pendant les guerres de religion.* Paris, 1924.

d Palm, Franklin C. *Politics and religion in sixteenth-century France, a study of the career of Henry of Montmorency-Damville, uncrowned king of the south.* Boston, 1927. (Bibliography.)

a. Brief, philosophical discussion of the political aspect of these wars. *b.* Thorough and detailed study of the subject; impartial and generally reliable. Review, H. Hauser, *Rev. Hist.* 102:332, Nov. 1909.   PS

c. Exposition of the attitude of the papacy to French affairs from 1559 to 1598 by a veteran historian of the papacy. Review, P. Van Dyke, *A.H.R.* 31:124, Oct. 1925. *d.* First adequate study of one of the most influential of the *Politiques,* who did so much to save the French monarchy from the consequences of the Religious Wars. Montmorency's career has a double interest, for his personal ambitions illustrate the desire, so late to disappear, of the greater feudal nobles· to recover a relative independence of the crown. Review, T. Collier, *A.H.R.* 33:638, Apr. 1928.   HEB

M257a Sichel, Edith. *Women and men of the French renaissance.* 1901. 2nd ed., London and N. Y., 1911. (Brief bibliography.)

b —— *Catherine de' Medici and the French reformation.* 1905. 2nd ed., London and N. Y., 1911. (Brief bibliography.)

c —— *Later years of Catherine d' Medici.* 1908. 2nd ed., London and N. Y., 1911. (Brief bibliography.)

Deal chiefly with the personal side of the period; written with much charm; richly illustrated with contemporary portraits. Review of *b,* E. Armstrong, *E.H.R.* 21:375, Apr. 1906; of *c, Nation* (N. Y.), 87:262, Sept. 17, 1908.   HEB

M258a Van Dyke, Paul. *Catherine de Médicis.* 2 v. N. Y., 1922. (Bibliography.)

b Mariéjol, Jean H. *Catherine de Médicis, 1519–1589.* Paris, 1920. (Brief bibliography.)

a. Studiously impartial biography; written with literary skill; based upon a considerable amount of new materials. Decidedly the author belongs to the older, objective, external school of biographers, rather than to those whose intensely penetrating methods have earned them, from Dr. Crothers, the name of 'the Satanic school'. Review, T. Collier, *A.H.R.* 28:536, Apr. 1923; H. Hauser, *Rev. Hist.* 142:239, March 1923. *b.* One of the foremost students of the period presents the queen as a weak character, guided and forced into a policy of violence by those about her. A new view ably argued, but contested by reviewers. Review, H. Hauser, *Rev. Hist.* 137:85, May 1921.   PS

M259a Willert, Paul F. *Henry of Navarre and the Huguenots in France.* London and N. Y., 1893. Later reprints. [Heroes of the nations.]

b Poirson, Auguste. *Histoire du règne de Henri IV.* 1856. 3rd rev. ed., 4 v., Paris, 1865–66.

a. Best brief life in English; painstaking, fair-minded, frank; reveals the two sides of Henry's character and career; emphasizes facts rather than interpretations; fails to show why he 'still retains the first place in the memory and affection of his people'. Review, M. A. S. Hume, *E.H.R.* 9:578, July 1894. *b.* Still the only comprehensive work in French.   HDF

M260 Sully, Maximilien de Béthune, Duc de. *Memoirs.* 1756; rev. ed., 4 v., London, 1856 [Bohn library]. Tr. by Charlotte Lennox from rev. ed., by Abbé P. M. de l'Écluse des Loges, 3 v., Londres, 1747, of *Mémoires des sages et royales oeconomies d'estat, domestiques, politiques, et militaires de Henry le Grand . . . et des servitudes utiles, obéissances convenables et administrations loyales de Maximillan de Béthune . . .*, v. 1–2, Amstelredam, 1638; v. 3–4, Paris, 1662. Several later ed.

Sully had already prepared two versions of his memoirs before 1638, when he caused v. 1–2 to be printed in his own château. The version of 1638 contains large elements of invention designed to enhance his reputation and to reply to works which had appeared since the first version was written, sometime before 1617. The most colossal is the 'grand dessein' which still imposes upon unwary writers on international affairs and leagues of nations. The English translation of 1856 is considerably revised from the one of 1756, which was based upon the version in narrative form by the Abbé de l'Écluse, who completely rearranged the materials in order to secure chronological sequence. The *Memoirs* have been reprinted several times in French collections; they are considered of high historical value if used with caution. Review, (M2*b*) Hauser, *Sources de l'histoire de France,* 4:24–30.   HEB

SEVENTEENTH CENTURY, 1610–1715

M271 Hanotaux, Gabriel. *Histoire du cardinal de Richelieu. 2 v.* Paris, 1893–96.

These two volumes, representing the completed portion of a projected four volume work, follow the Cardinal's career to the fall of Marie de Médicis, May 6, 1617. His dominant traits, ambition and force, are stressed in the picture of the youthful Richelieu, sketched by a hand trained in the schools of politics and research. A masterly summary of the development of French institutions and of conditions prevailing in 1614 occupies half of v. 1. Review, G. Monod, *Rev. Hist.* 53:98, Sept. 1893; 63:131, Jan. 1897.   RHG

M272 Avenel, Georges d', Vicomte. *Richelieu et la monarchie absolue.* 1884–90. 2nd ed., 4 v., Paris, 1895.

The work of one who regards Richelieu as the 'creator of a pure despotism', a statesman who destroyed provincial and other liberties of great value and long standing in order to create the absolute monarchy. The Cardinal's religious, naval, military, and foreign policies are viewed with high favor. A scholarly work in every respect; its thesis is summarized in 4:419 ff. Review, C. Bémont, *Rev. Hist.* 24:375, March 1884; C. Bémont and G. Monod, *ibid.* 34:98, May 1887; L. Farges and G. Monod, *ibid,* 43:109, May 1890.   RHG

M273a Perkins, James B. *France under Mazarin, with a review of the administration of Richelieu.* 2 v. N. Y. and London, 1886.

b ———— *France under the regency, with a review of the administration of Louis XIV.* Boston, 1892.

c ———— *France under Louis XV.* 2 v. Boston, 1897.

d ———— *France in the American Revolution.* Boston, 1911.

This series covers the history of France from the death of Henry IV to the reign of Louis XVI. Written in a fashion which arouses and sustains interest and based on documentary material, the narrative portions are particularly valuable, the descriptions of economic and social conditions hardly less so. Best and most useful survey of the Bourbon period in English. Review of *a*, *Nation* (N. Y.), 43:215, Sept. 9, 1886; of *b*, *ibid.*, 55:307, Oct. 20, 1892; of *c*, H. E. Bourne, *A.H.R.* 3:535, Apr. 1898; of *d*, D. J. Hill, *A.H.R.* 17:160, Oct. 1911.

RHG

M274 Hassall, Arthur. *Louis XIV and the zenith of the French monarchy.* London and N. Y., 1895. Later reprints. [Heroes of the nations.] (Brief bibliography.)

Careful and convenient narrative of the career of Louis XIV; not an adequate picture of the France of 1660 to 1715; too closely confined to military and political affairs; unduly neglects the social, economic, and intellectual developments. Review, J. B. Perkins, *A.H.R.* 1:335, Jan. 1896.   LBP

M275 Clément, Pierre. *Histoire de Colbert et de son administration.* 1874. 3rd ed., 2 v., Paris, 1892.

Represents the profound and accurate investigations of a scholar who, as editor of Colbert's *Lettres, instructions, et mémoires* (8v. in 10, Paris, 1861–82, in (M73) *Collection de documents inédits*), was a master of the documents of the period from 1660 to 1683. Specialized studies have replaced or elaborated portions of this book, but as a whole it is still unsurpassed.   LBP

M276 Saint-Simon, Louis de Rouvroy, Duc de. *Memoirs . . . on the times of Louis XIV and the regency.* 4 v., Boston, 1899 [Versailles ed.]. Abridged tr. by K. P. Wormley from *Mémoires*, 21 v., Paris, 1829–30; several later ed., notably by P. A. Chéruel and A. Regnier, 20 v., Paris, 1856–58; and new ed. by A. and J. Boislisle and L. Lecestre, 41 v. Paris, 1879–1928. [(M706) Les grands écrivains de la France.]

At once a classic among literary memoirs and perhaps the most important single work on the latter part of the reign of Louis XIV and the Regency, 1692–1723. In the remarkable new edition the material from St. Simon's pen is supplemented by a vast and erudite commentary consisting of a series of special investigations into important topics of court life and governmental institutions which incorporate the best results of recent scholarship.   LBP

M277 Farmer, James. *Versailles and the court under Louis XIV.* N. Y., 1905.

Entertaining, instructively written, and generally reliable picture of the activities and surroundings of 'le grande monarque'. Based upon a considerable acquaintance with the source material which is so selected and presented as to restore faithfully the life, color, and even more serious aspects of the grandiose scenes of this period. Review, J. W. Thompson, *A.H.R.* 11:658, Apr. 1906.   LBP

M278a Dedieu, Abbé Joseph. *Le rôle politique des protestants français* (1685–1715). Paris, 1920.

b —— *Histoire politique des protestants français* (*1715–1749*). 2 v., Paris, 1925.

In *a* the emphasis is upon the part played by Huguenot refugees, especially in England and Holland, during the long struggle against Louis XIV. Through the fortunate discovery of papers in the British Record Office the author is able to describe with precision the rôle of leaders like Pierre Jurieu, who organized an elaborate system of espionage in France. He attributes to refugee promptings the worst phase of the Camisard outbreaks. *b* is not so much a history of what the Protestants did as it is of the official policy towards them, whether of the ministry or of provincial governors or of intendants. It is based upon documents in the archives at Paris, and upon the abundant printed material in the *Bulletin de l'histoire du protestantisme français*. Review of *b* by Henri Hauser, *Revue Critique*, 92:188, May 15, 1925.   HEB

EIGHTEENTH CENTURY: OLD REGIME, *1715–1789*

M291 Sorel, Albert. *Montesquieu.* Chicago, 1888 [Great French writers.] Tr. by M. B. and E. P. Anderson from *Montesquieu,* 1887, 2nd ed., Paris, 1889 [(M707a) Les grands écrivains français].

If it were only in view of Montesquieu's influence on Alexander Hamilton, this sober analysis by one of the foremost historians of France, who never loses the point of view of the historian, could not be too highly recommended.   AS

M292a Morley, John, Viscount. *Voltaire.* London and N. Y., 1871. Later reprints.

b —— *Rousseau.* 2 v. London and N. Y., 1873. Later reprints.

c —— *Diderot and the encyclopaedists.* 2 v. London and N. Y., 1878. Later reprints.

These three 'studies in the literary preparation of the French Revolution' are justly considered classics in English-speaking countries. Morley's wise emphasis on the constructive elements, especially in *a*, is likely to be misinterpreted by Anglo-Saxon readers. *b*. His judgment of Rousseau's personality, based upon the *Mémoires* of Madame d'Épinay, then considered authentic, has been profoundly modified by the study of facts brought to light within recent years. Cf. *Philosophical Rev.* 26:214–227, Jan. 1917.   AS

M293a Higgs, Henry. *Physiocrats, six lectures on the French économistes of the 18th century.* London and N. Y., 1897. (Brief bibliography.)

b Say, Léon. *Turgot.* Chicago, 1888. [Great French writers.] Tr. by M. B. Anderson from *Turgot,* 1887, 2nd ed., Paris, 1891. [Les grands écrivains français.] Another tr. by G. Masson, London, 1888.

c Schelle, Gustave, ed. *Oeuvres de Turgot et documents le concernant, 1778–1781.* 5 v. Paris, 1913–23.

d Weulersse, Georges. *Le mouvement physiocratique en France de 1756 à 1770.* 2 v. Paris, 1910. (Bibliography.)

Of these works on the Physiocrats, *c* is the most important. *a*. Affords the most convenient account from the English point of view. Review, W. J. Ashley, *A.H.R.* 2:725, July 1897. *b*. Contains, of course, much history of general administrative matters, but Turgot was so closely identified with the larger aspects of the Physiocratic movement that his administrative work was in great measure an application of its principles. Review, G. Monod and C. Bémont, *Rev. Hist.* 37:146, May 1888. *c.* Authoritative edition of Turgot's works. Review of v. 5, A. Lesort, *Rev. des Quest. Hist.* 104:485, Apr. 1, 1926. *d.* Brings much new material to bear on the subject; traces the history of the movement in sumptuous detail during its critical years. Review, J. H. Hollander, *A.H.R.* 17:657, Apr. 1911.

APU

M294 Lowell, Edward Jackson. *Eve of the French revolution.* Boston, 1892. Later reprints. (Bibliography.)

Clear, readable account of some of the complex factors which produced the Revolution. Especially valuable for its comprehensive point of view, its moderation, and its simple and lucid exposition of the intellectual influence exerted by Montesquieu, Voltaire, Rousseau, and the encyclopedists. Perhaps weak on the economic side in view of the emphasis which recent scholarship has given to this part of the background of the Revolution. Review, *Nation* (N. Y.), 57:311, Oct. 26, 1893.

LBP

M295 Tocqueville, Alexis C. H. M. Clérel de. *Old régime and the revolution.* N. Y., 1856. Tr. by J. Bonner from *L'ancien régime et la révolution,* 1856; 7th ed., Paris, 1866; new ed. with introduction and notes by G. W. Headlam, Oxford, 1904. Another tr. by H. Reeve, 1856, 3rd ed., London, 1888.

Still one of the most valuable works on the eighteenth century; deals almost exclusively with the old régime; based upon a wide study of documents, though unfortunately few references are given. Tocqueville was one of the first to see that the Revolution was a logical development of the centralization of the eighteenth century. He also affirmed, what recent scholarship has proved (cf. M301), that peasant landed properties were widespread in France before the Revolution.

PLW

M296 Wahl, Adalbert. *Vorgeschichte der französischen Revolution: ein Versuch.* 2 v. Tübingen, 1905–07.

One of several important contributions that German scholarship has made to the history of the Revolution within a generation; suffers from the author's hostility to that movement. V. 1. Deals with the history of France under Louis XV and Louis XVI; emphasizes the conditions which characterized the old régime. V. 2. Begins with the assembly of the notables and ends with the elections to the states general. Review, v. 1, T. Ludwig, *Hist. Zeit.* 96:82, 1906.

FMF

M297a MacLehose, Sophia H. *Last days of the French monarchy.* Glasgow, 1901. (Bibliography.)

    b ——— *From the monarchy to the republic in France, 1788–1792.* Glasgow, 1904. (Bibliography.)

Well-developed, documented, interesting narratives; give little attention to economic factors or to the deeper social movements of the period; concentrate attention upon events in Versailles and Paris. No better accounts in English within the same compass. Review of *a, Athenaeum,* 1:39, Jan. 11, 1902; of *b,* H. E. Bourne, *A.H.R.* 10:885, July 1905; L. G. W. Legg, *E.H.R.* 20:406, Apr. 1905.

HEB

M298 Chérest, Aimé. *La chute de l'ancien régime, 1787–1789.* 3 v. Paris, 1884–86.

Most detailed treatment that has yet been written of the period between the calling of the notables and the July revolution of 1789. Does not, however, rest upon sufficient research; the sources used are not always the best, and they are not treated critically; nevertheless, an important and suggestive work. Review, G. Monod, *Rev. Hist.* 27:121, Jan. 1885; 31:129, May 1886. FMF

M299a Babeau, Albert A. *Le village sous l'ancien régime.* 1878. 3rd rev. ed., Paris, 1882.

b ——— *La ville sous l'ancien régime.* 1880. 2nd rev. ed., 2 v., Paris, 1884.

c ——— *La province sous l'ancien régime.* 2 v. Paris, 1894.

d ——— *Les voyageurs en France depuis la renaissance jusqu'à la révolution.* Paris, 1885.

Best of numerous volumes on the old régime by the same writer. *a.* Based mainly upon documents drawn from the archives of Champagne, consequently the author's conclusions upon conditions in France as a whole should be received with caution; contains, however, much valuable detailed information. Review, *Rev. Hist.* 10:197, May 1879. *b* and *c.* The author's later work has a broader basis and is more authoritative. Review of *b,* G. Fagniez, *Rev. Hist.* 14:111, Sept. 1880; of *c,* G. Monod, *ibid.* 55:371, July 1894. d. Records the principal impressions of foreign travelers in France. HEB

M300a Carré, Henri. *La fin des parlements, 1788–1790.* Paris, 1912. (Bibliography.)

b ——— *La noblesse de France et l'opinion publique au XVIIIe siècle.* Paris, 1920. (Bibliography.)

a. After an introductory chapter describing the parlements on the eve of the Revolution, this work of ripe scholarship deals with the period between September, 1788, and October, 1790, when the parlements were finally abolished. A concluding chapter describes the fortunes of the individual members during the later Revolution. Review, *A.H.R.* 28:165, Oct. 1912. *b.* Most complete account available of the nobility, both court and provincial, and especially of the tide of public opinion which set in against them and overwhelmed them during the Revolution. Successfully controverts the numerical estimates of the nobility popularized by (M324a) Taine. Review, H. E. Bourne, *A.H.R.* 26:573, Apr. 1921; G. Pagès, *Rev. Hist.* 142:77, Jan. 1923. FMF

M301 Luchitskii [Loutchisky], Ivan Vasilévich. *L'état des classes agricoles en France à la veille de la révolution.* Paris, 1911.

The author here presents briefly the results of long researches in French local archives and gives for the first time a basis sufficiently broad and scientific to (M295) Tocqueville's much discussed statement that peasant properties were a characteristic feature of prerevolutionary France. Indispensable for the study of the peasant question and, incidentally, of the distribution of the lands of the clergy and the nobles. Review, M. Marion, *Rev. d'Hist. Moderne,* 17:481, Nov. 1912. HEB

M302a Picard, Roger. *Les cahiers de 1789 et les classes ouvrières.* Paris, 1910.

b Denys-Buirette, A. *Les questions religieuses dans les cahiers de 1789.* Paris, 1919.

The increase in the number of published *cahiers* through the efforts of the (cf. M82) Commission on the Economic History of the Revolution is making possible such studies as these in the state of public opinion upon important questions at the outbreak of the Revolution. *a.* Includes every phase of the industrial question and also commerce both domestic and foreign. *b.* Deals with such aspects of the religious problem as property, taxation, debts of the clergy, relations of church and state. HEB

M303a Rocquain, Félix. *Revolutionary spirit preceding the French revolution.* London, 1891; N. Y., 1892 (Social Science series). Abridged tr. by J. D. Hunting from *L'esprit révolutionnaire avant la révolution, 1715-1789.* Paris, 1878.

b Roustan, Marius. *Pioneers of the French revolution.* London and Boston, 1926. Abridged tr. by F. Whyte from *Les philosophes et la société française au XVIIIe siècle,* Lyon, 1906. [Annales de l'Université de Lyon.]

c Sée, Henri. *L'évolution de la pensée politique en France au XVIIIe siècle.* Paris, 1925.

d Martin, Gaston. *La franc-maçonnerie française et la préparation de la révolution.* 1926. 2nd ed., Paris, 1926.

e Cochin, Augustin. *Les sociétés de pensée et la démocratie: études d'histoire révolutionnaire.* Paris, 1921. [Collection Armand Colin.]

f ——— *Les sociétés de pensée et la révolution en Bretagne, 1788–1789.* 2 v. Paris, 1925.

g Mornet, Daniel. *La pensée française au XVIIIe siècle.* Paris, 1928.

Each deals from a different point of view with the antecedents of the Revolution. *a.* Recounts the struggles which, since the Regency, shook the government; seeks, incidentally, to show that the fabric of the old régime was tottering before the philosophers put the match to the inflammable material. Review, P. Foncin, *Rev. Hist.* 9:238, Jan. 1879. *b.* Contends, on the other hand, that the philosophers created the Revolution, but fails to make clear the process by which their ideas reached the masses. Review, H. Hauser, *Rev. Hist.* 94:82, May 1907; H. E. Bourne, *Pol. Sci. Quar.* 41:635, Dec. 1926. *c.* Deals, in ch. 6, with this interesting problem from the experience of a scholar whose knowledge of the documents, including the *cahiers,* is unrivalled. Review, G. Pagès, *Rev. Hist.* 152:81, 1926. *d.* Notable contribution to the subject for it succeeds in tracing for the first time, from local archives and records of masonic lodges, the exact influence of that society upon the reform movement prior to 1789 and upon the early course of the Revolution. Its conclusions are that although the masons had much to do with the formulation of a common programme and its embodiment in the *cahiers,* and though their hand may be seen in the choice of deputies, they were not fomentors of disorder. Review, H. Sée, *Rev. Hist.* 152:94, May 1926; R. Durand, *Rev. Critique,* 43:69, Feb. 1928. *e* and *f.* These and other works by the same author throw additional light on the problem. Review of *e,* E. Welvert, *Rev. Critique,* 88:193, May 15, 1921; of *f,* J. de la Monneraye, *Rev. des Quest. Hist.* 107:123, July 1927; Gaston Martin, *Augustin Cochin et la Révolution,* Toulouse, 1926, p. 61. *g.* Brief but valuable. HEB

THE REVOLUTION, 1789–1799

M321a Belloc, Hilaire. *French revolution.* London and N. Y., 1911. [Home university library.]

b Gardiner, Bertha M. *French revolution, 1789–1795.* London and N. Y., 1882. Later reprints. [Epochs of modern history.]

c Johnston, Robert M. *French revolution, a short history.* N. Y., 1909.

d Mallet, Charles E. *French revolution.* London and N. Y., 1893. Later reprints. [University extension manuals.]

e Mathews, Shailer. *French revolution, 1789–1815.* 1900. Rev. ed., N. Y. and London, 1923.

f Bradby, E. D. *Short history of the French revolution, 1789–1795.* Oxford, 1926.

Short, popular works; the best are *b, d, e,* and *f;* none is adequate; each author fails either in breadth of view or in knowledge of the subject. A satisfactory single-volume history of the French Revolution, composed in a critical, scholarly spirit, is yet to be written. Review of *c,* W. E. Lingelbach, *A.H.R.* 15:411, Jan. 1910; of *e,* C. D. Hazen, *ibid.* 7:141, Oct. 1901; *History,* 10:186, July 1925; of *f, A.H.R.* 32:650, Apr. 1927.

Also cf. (M122, v. 6) Madelin, *French revolution.*　　　　　　FMF

M322a Thiers, Louis Adolphe. *History of the French revolution.* 1838. New ed., 5 v., London, 1895. Tr. by F. Shoberl from *Histoire de la révolution française,* 10 v., Paris, 1823–27. New illustrated ed., 2 v., Paris, 1882. Numerous other ed. and tr.

b Carlyle, Thomas. *French revolution, a history.* 3 v. London, 1837. Ed. by J. H. Rose, 3 v., London and N. Y., 1902; ed. by C. R. L. Fletcher, 3 v., London and N. Y., 1902; tr. with introduction by F. A. Aulard, as *Histoire de la révolution française,* 3 v., Paris, 1912.

a. Long the most popular history of the French Revolution. Those pages which treat questions of finance and commerce may even now be read to advantage. As originally published, it played a part in the political history of France, for it revived the revolutionary tradition and united the liberals for the overthrow of Charles X. *b.* As these volumes were completed in 1837, the question of their value for the present generation of readers is pertinent. No one would consult them for information upon matters in which Carlyle was not interested, such as the financial collapse which occasioned the Revolution or the social and civil institutions which grew out of it. Nevertheless, so eminent an authority as Professor Aulard regards Carlyle's work as good history. He believes that Carlyle was a true interpreter who discerned in the common people the real hero of the epic struggle. He adds that he was as well documented as the best informed of French writers in that time when the archives were still closed. The opinion of the two most recent English editors is substantially the same. Rose remarks that Carlyle 'shows us the workings of the human heart as no other historian of institutions and no microscopic analyst, like Taine, has ever done or ever will do'. Such annotated editions as those of Rose and Fletcher are useful because Carlyle's individual statements often require the correction of later knowledge.　　HEB

M323 Blanc, Louis. *History of the French revolution of 1789.* 11 v. Philadelphia, 1848. Tr. by W. K. Kelly from v. 1–2 of *Histoire de la révolution française,* 12 v., Paris, 1847–62.

Although many years have passed since this work was written, it is still the most satisfactory detailed history of the whole Revolution. Its narrative is continued to the end of the Convention; based on the sources, which the author cites throughout. Rendered antiquated, in parts, by monographic studies of recent years, but even when these studies give a fuller and more satisfactory account the general outline of the author's work as a rule remains sound.

Also cf. (M124*b*) Lavisse, *Histoire de la France contemporaine,* v. 1–2; and (M125*b*) Michelet, *Historical view of the French revolution.*   FMF

M324a Taine, Hippolyte A. *Origins of contemporary France.* 2 v. N. Y., 1876–94. [1, *Ancient régime;* 2–4, *French revolution;* 5–6, *Modern régime.*] Tr. by J. Durand from *Les origines de la France contemporaine,* 6 v., 1875–94 [1, *L'ancien régime;* 2–4, *La révolution;* 5–6, *La régime moderne*]; rev. ed., 11 v. and index, Paris, 1899–1914.

   b Aulard, François V. Alphonse. *Taine, historien de la révolution française.* Paris, 1907.

   c Cochin, Augustin. *La crise de l'histoire révolutionnaire: Taine et M. Aulard.* Paris, 1909.

a. Work of immense influence upon opinions held in the English-speaking world concerning the destruction of the old régime and the beginnings of the new. Its influence in France has been scarcely less marked, although from the first competent scholars protested at the defects of Taine's method. The work had its origin in 1870 and 1871, years of disaster and humiliation, when the author was moved by a sense of duty to point out to his fellow citizens the faults of attitude and organization that led to the catastrophe. He was engaged twenty years on the task and died leaving it incomplete. He believed that his methods of investigation were rigidly scientific, but Professor Aulard has shown in *b* that his researches were controlled by fixed ideas and that the bases of his conclusions were inadequate. As his work proceeded it was more and more affected by violent prejudices against the revolutionaries and their types of thought. It nevertheless remains of suggestive value for its acute observations and striking analyses. *c.* Attempt to refute *b.* Review of *a,* v. 1, A. Sorel, *Rev. Hist.* 2:281, July 1876; v. 2, A. Gazier, *ibid.* 8:453, Nov. 1878; v. 3, G. Monod, *ibid.* 16:414, July 1881; (B244) Morley, *Critical miscellanies,* 3:261; of *b, Rev. Hist.* 97:141, Jan. 1908; A. Mathiez, *Rev. d'Hist. Moderne,* 8:257, Jan. 1907.   HEB

M325a Stephens, Henry Morse. *History of the French revolution.* 2 v. London and N. Y., 1886–91; reprint, 1902.

   b ——— *Principal speeches of the statesmen and orators of the French revolution, 1787–1795, edited with introduction, notes, and indices.* 2 v. Oxford, 1892.

a. Incomplete; carries the narrative only to the opening phases of the reign of terror; fullest treatment in English for internal affairs in the period covered; sympathetic and fair toward the revolutionary movement; based on wide reading, but shows evidences of hasty and uncritical conclusions. Review, A. H. Johnson, *E.H.R.* 2:387, Apr. 1887; Lord Acton, *ibid.* 7:382, Apr. 1892. *b.* Contains important speeches of Mirabeau, Vergniaud, Barère, Danton, Robespierre, and others dealing with many important events and ideas of the Revolution.   FMF

M326a Aulard, François V. Alphonse. *French revolution, a political history, 1789–1804.* 4 v. London and N. Y., 1910. Tr. by B. Miall from *Histoire politique de la révolution française, origines et développement de la démocratie et de la république, 1789–1804,* 1901.

b ——— *L'éloquence parlementaire pendant la révolution française.* 1882–86. Rev. ed., 3 v., Paris, 1905–07. [1, *Les orateurs de l'assemblée constituante; 2–3, Les orateurs de la législative et de la convention.*]

c ——— *Les grands orateurs de la révolution: Mirabeau, Vergniaud, Danton, Robespierre.* Paris, 1914.

d ——— *La révolution française et le régime féodal.* Paris, 1919.

These are but a few of the contributions made to the study of the Revolution by the most distinguished investigator and writer in that field. From 1886 to 1922 Professor Aulard occupied the chair of the history of the Revolution established at the Sorbonne by the city of Paris. He has edited many important collections of documents (cf. M73, 83) and the magazine, (M931a) *La Révolution Française. a.* After he leaves the period of the Constituent the scope of his work broadens, and it becomes especially valuable for its analyses of the currents of public opinion, its description of party organization, and its explanation of the mechanism of government. Does not deal with other phases of the movement. Review, H. E. Bourne, *A.H.R.* 7:567, Apr. 1902. *b.* Sketches the life of each orator; explains his methods, politics, and policies; quotes choice extracts from famous speeches. *c.* Compilation from *b* with revisions of detail. *d.* This little book on the abolition of feudalism is suggestive for its indication of the present position of studies upon the situation immediately before the Revolution and upon the consequences of the legislation of March and May, 1790. Review, H. E. Bourne, *A.H.R.* 25:545, Apr. 1920.   FMF

M327 Jaurès, Jean, ed. *Histoire socialiste, 1789–1900.* 12 v. Paris, 1901–09. [1, J. Jaurès, *La constituante, 1789–1791;* 2, *ibid., La législative, 1791–1792;* 3–4, *ibid., La convention, 1792–1794;* 5, G. Deville, *Thermidor et directoire, 1794–1799;* 6, P. Brousse and H. Turot, *Consulat et empire, 1799–1815;* 7, R. Viviani, *La restauration, 1814–1830;* 8, E. Fournière, *Le règne de Louis-Philippe, 1830–1848;* 9, G. Renard, *La république de 1848, 1848–1852;* 10, A. Thomas, *Le second empire, 1852–1870;* 11, J. Jaurès, *La guerre franco-allemande, 1870–1871;* L. Dubreuilh, *La commune, 1871;* 12, J. Labusquière, *1871–1900.*] Rev. ed. of v. 1–4, by A. Mathiez, 8 v., Paris, 1922–24.

Attempts to explain the origins of contemporary France from the socialist standpoint; addressed to the working class. The necessity of cheap publication is reflected unfavorably in flimsy paper, poor cuts (the work is profusely illustrated), and typographical errors. There is an almost entire absence of critical apparatus. Nevertheless, it is a serious historical undertaking and has real importance, though the volumes are of very unequal value. Of the original edition, the five volumes by Jaurès, of which four are on the Revolution, and v. 9 are the best; v. 8 and v. 10 have suggestive features; the rest are of little consequence, descending in some cases to mere partisan polemic. Among the more striking contributions by Jaurès are his studies on subsistence and wages, his discussion of intellectual and social conditions in Germany and England as well as in France, and his analysis of Marat. V. 9. Perhaps the best in the series; accompanied by a supplementary volume of *Notes et références,* Paris, 1906. The author is the leading authority on 1848, and nothing better has been written on that period. Review, v. 1, G. Monod, *Rev. Hist.* 78:354, March 1902; v. 2, G. Monod, *ibid.* 80:353, Nov. 1902; v. 3–4, R. Reuss, *ibid.* 89:101, Sept. 1905; v. 5–6, R. Reuss, *ibid.* 95:109, Sept. 1907; v. 7–8, A. Lichtenberger, *ibid.* 94:331, July 1907; v. 9, E. Driault, *ibid.* 98:326, July 1908; v. 12, E. Driault, *ibid.* 103:113, Jan. 1910; v. 1–5, P. Sagnac, *Rev. d'Hist. Moderne*, 4:279, Jan. 1903; 6:404, March 1905; 7:158, Nov. 1905; v. 7–9, J. Ceby, *ibid.* 8:378, 617, Feb., May 1907; 10:54, March 1908. The revised edition of the portion on the Revolution is fully annotated in the light of later researches. The original arrangement of volumes has been altered. Review, v. 1–4, R. Reuss, *Rev. Hist.* 145:68, Jan. 1924. ENC

M328 Mathiez, Albert. *French revolution.* N. Y., 1928. Tr. by C. A. Phillips from *La révolution française*, 3 v. Paris, 1922–27.

Brief but comprehensive treatment; composed in a fresh and vigorous style; especially valuable because it embodies conclusions reached in many research studies of the author, one of the ablest and most productive scholars now devoted to the subject; an ardent admirer of Robespierre, his essays have thrown new light upon the career of that statesman, as well as damaged the reputation of his rival Danton. This history, originally projected for three small volumes, the last to close with the founding of the Empire, will extend to four. V. 1. Admirable example of lucid brevity of statement; ends at August 10, 1792. V. 2–3. Since the ground is more controversial, the author has found it impossible to maintain the same proportions, so that v. 3 closes with the fall of Robespierre, rather than with the coming of the Empire. Review, C. Cristol, *A.H.R.* 28:356, Jan. 1923; 30:641, Apr. 1925; 33:185, Oct. 1927. *E.H.R.* 43:299, Apr. 1928; V. 3, R. Durand, *Rev. Critique* 62:117, Mar. 1928.	HEB

M329 Kerr, Wilfred B. *Reign of terror, 1793–1794.* Toronto, 1927.

The theme is the class struggle between the urban proletariat and the bourgeoisie, from the overthrow of the monarchy to the death of Robespierre and the 'fall of the sansculotte régime'. Since the author regards the economic factor as primary, it is surprising that he treats with such brevity the history of the supply of the necessaries of life, the application of the maximum, and the administration of the system of requisitions. He regards as inevitable, if not always justified, the sanguinary repressions carried out by the revolutionary tribunal and by the 'proconsuls of the Terror'. Among the leaders of the period the author's admiration is reserved for Marat, by whose death 'revolutionary France lost her ablest intelligence'. Review, (London) *Times Literary Supplement*, 27:52, Jan. 26, 1928.	HEB

M330 Henderson, Ernest F. *Symbol and satire in the French revolution.* N. Y. and London, 1912.

Reproduces numerous contemporary caricatures and prints; elucidates them, not with individual explanations, but by a continuous narrative. Review, *A.H.R.* 18:802, July 1913.	GMD

M340 Baldensperger, Fernand. *Le mouvement des idées dans l'emigration française* (1789–1815). 2 v. Paris, 1924.

A study of French emigration during the Revolution from a new point of view, the intellectual and moral reaction of the émigrés to the calamity which had overwhelmed them, and, at the same time, to their new environment, whether this was

London, or Scotland, or far away America. It is a literary history of the emigration, based upon records in almost as many libraries and local archives as there were cities where émigrés resided. The author believes that the evolution of ideas which he describes was one of the forces, if not the chief force, in the development of the Romantic movement. Review, by E. Estève, *Revue Critique,* 94:223, June 15, 1927.   HEB

M341a Sagnac, Philippe. *La législation civile de la révolution française, 1789–1804, essai d'histoire sociale.* Paris, 1898. (Bibliography.)

   b ——— *La révolution du 10 août 1792; la chute de la royauté.* Paris, 1909.

   c Seligman, Edmond. *La justice en France pendant la révolution.* 2 v. Paris, 1901–13. 2nd ed. of v. 1, 1913. (Bibliography.)

   a. Important contribution to the study of the constructive work of the Revolution, never before adequately treated. It established the position of the author, who later succeeded Professor Aulard (cf. M326) at the Sorbonne, as one of the most productive students of the period. Review, H. Sée, *Rev. Hist.* 74:393, Nov. 1900. *b.* Of smaller compass; most complete and satisfactory study of August 10, 1792; traces the growth of opposition to the king from the time of the invasion of the Tuileries on June 20; includes critical discussion of the sources of information for the subject. *c.* Excellent work; based on a careful study of the best monographs and sources. V. 1. Describes the courts in 1789; explains the rôle of the parlements and their abolition, the organization of the new judicial system, and its methods of administration. V. 2. Deals with the creation of the new extraordinary courts for political offenders; describes the trial and execution of Louis XVI; closes with the organization of the revolutionary tribunal in March 1793. Review, R. Reuss, *Rev. Hist.* 79:121, May 1902; 114:311, Nov. 1913.   FMF

M342 Vingtrinier, Emmanuel. *La contre-révolution, première période, 1789–1791.* 2 v. Paris, 1924–25.

   These volumes deal with the earliest of four periods which the author proposes to study. They furnish the first coherent picture of what the enemies of the Revolution actually attempted and of their successes and failures. These conspiracies are commonly treated only as incidents in the general development of the struggle. The principal subject of these two volumes is the work of the Count of Artois and his partisans with Turin as a base of operations. Review, G. Pariset, *Rev. Hist.* 152:213, March 1926.   HEB

M343a La Rocheterie, Maxime de. *Life of Marie Antoinette.* 2 v. London and N. Y., 1893; reprint, 1906. Tr. by C. H. Bell from *Histoire de Marie Antoinette,* 1890; 2nd ed., 2 v., Paris, 1892.

   b La Rocheterie, Maxime de, and **Du Fresne, Gaston, L. E., Marquis de Beaucourt,** ed. *Lettres de Marie Antoinette: recueil des lettres authentiques de la reine.* 2 v. Paris, 1895–96. [Société d'Histoire Contemporaine.]

   a. Based largely on contemporary correspondence and presented in popular form. The writer is anti-revolutionary in sympathy. His attitude is thus stated in the preface: 'Marie Antoinette was not a sinner, neither was she a saint. She was a pure and charming woman, somewhat heedless and frivolous, but always chaste . . . a true queen by reason of the dignity of her bearing and the splendor of her majesty, a true woman in virtue of the seductiveness of her manners and the tenderness of her heart, till she became a martyr, through the extremity of her trials and her triumphant death'. Review, G. Monod, *Rev. Hist.* 43:374, July 1890. b. Important collection, carefully edited. Also cf. (M366c, 785). EEY

M344a Gosselin, Louis L. T. (pseud. G. Lenôtre). *Flight of Marie Antoinette.* London and Philadelphia. 1906. Tr. by Mrs. R. Stawell from *Le drame de Varennes, juin 1791, d'après des documents inédits et les relations des témoins oculaires,* 1906; 22nd ed., Paris, 1908.

b ——— *Romances of the French revolution.* 2 v. London and N. Y., 1908. Partial tr. by F. Lees from *Paris révolutionnaire vieilles maisons, vieux papiers.* 5 v., Paris, 1900–23; numerous reprints.

c ——— *Robespierre's rise and fall.* London, 1927. Tr. by Mrs. R. Stawell from *Robespierre et la Mère de Dieu,* Paris, 1926.

The author, utilizing with dramatic skill the results of genuine research, deals with that which is personal and incidental in the Revolution. The tales are fascinating, and add to the reader's appreciation of the human elements which entered into the great struggle, even if they may not always be dignified as history. Review of *a, Saturday Rev.* 103:241, Feb. 23, 1907; of *b, ibid.* 107:404, March 27, 1909; J. Guirand, *Rev. des Quest. Hist.* 106:481, Apr. 1927. *c.* Interesting for the *petits faits* which bear upon the careers of the minor characters in the Robespierre drama, but embodying a partisan view of the principal figure. Review, (London) *Times Literary Supp.* 26:826, Nov. 17, 1927. HEB

M345a Young, Arthur. *Travels during the years 1787, 1788, and 1789, undertaken more particularly with a view of ascertaining the cultivation, wealth, resources, and national prosperity of the kingdom of France.* 2 v. Bury St. Edmund's, 1792. 2nd ed. 2 v. London, 1794. Abridged ed. by M. Betham-Edwards, 1889; 4th ed., London, 1892 [Bohn's standard library].

b **Rigby, Edward.** *Letters from France in 1789.* Ed. by his daughter, Lady Eastlake. London, 1880.

c **Morris, Gouverneur.** *Diary and letters.* Ed. by A. C. Morris. 2 v. N. Y., 1888.

d **Moore, John.** *Journal during a residence in France from . . . August to . . . December 1792, to which is added an account of the most remarkable events that happened at Paris from that time to the death of the late King of France.* 1793. New ed., 2 v., London, 1793; 2 v., Boston, 1794; 2 v., Philadelphia, 1794.

a. Young was a famous English agriculturalist whose *Travels* consist of a journal kept during three journeys through France in 1787, 1788, and 1789. The original edition contains also a second part giving in successive chapters a mass of information upon soil, climate, courses of crops, size of farms, rents, and prices. For the student of economic history this is even more valuable than the journal republished in the Betham-Edwards edition. The journal for 1789 gives many curious pictures of the revolutionary movement in the provinces. *b.* Rigby, another English traveller, reached Paris on July 7, 1789, on the eve of the uprising which led to the fall of the Bastille and the collapse of royal authority. He left the city on July 19 and as soon as he reached Geneva he wrote a letter to his family giving an account of the critical days in Paris. He gives in other letters glimpses of the regions through which he passed, leaving the impression that the country was highly cultivated and prosperous. *c.* Morris was minister to France after the retirement of Jefferson. His official position, as well as influential friends, offered him opportunities of obtaining valuable information, which he recorded in his diary and letters. *d.* By an eminent Scotch physician and author; possesses unusual interest for the period of the second revolution in the summer and fall of 1792. FMF

M361a Charavay, Étienne. *Le général La Fayette, 1757–1834, notice biographique.* Paris, 1898. [Société de l'Histoire de la Révolution Française.] (Bibliography.)

    b Tuckerman, Bayard. *Life of General Lafayette, with a critical estimate of his character and public acts.* 2 v. N. Y., 1889.

    c Bardoux, Agénor. *Études sociales et politiques: la jeunesse de La Fayette, 1757–1792.* Paris, 1892.

    d ——— *Études sociales et politiques: les dernières années de La Fayette, 1792–1834.* Paris, 1893.

    e Sedgwick, Henry Dwight. *La Fayette.* Indianapolis, 1928. (Bibliography.)

a. Scholarly work based on a study of the sources, with elaborate footnotes, and appendix containing letters of La Fayette. The author does not claim to have exhausted the material or to have said the last word on every disputed point. His work is favorable to La Fayette, but by no means a eulogy. Review, A. Lichtenberger, *Rev. Hist.* 67:339, July 1898. *b.* Gives a popular presentation of La Fayette's career. The author recognizes that La Fayette has suffered 'as much from the exaggerated praises of his admirers as from the bitter attacks of his enemies', and tries to be impartial. His estimate of La Fayette's character is high. *c* and *d.* Emphasize La Fayette's personal character, for which the author's admiration is without bounds. He regards him as a 'sort of paladin of the Round Table'. Review, L. Farges, *Rev. Hist* 50:363, Nov. 1892; 52:351, July 1893.

EEY

e. A sketch rather than a full length portrait, done in a pleasing style. Deals chiefly with La Fayette's rôle in the two revolutions, American and French. The story is often told in the words of his letters. In such a biography, with its requirements of brevity, the most difficult task is the setting, which for an important part of La Fayette's career is the history of the first three years of the French Revolution. Here the author occasionally fails to give sharpness of outline to his picture. HEB

Also cf. (X734) Tower, *Marquis de La Fayette in the American revolution,* and (M807).

M362a Loménie, Louis L. de, and **Loménie, Charles de.** *Les Mirabeau: nouvelles études sur la société française au XVIIIe siècle.* 5 v. Paris, 1879–91.

    b Stern, Alfred. *Das Leben Mirabeaus.* 2 v. Berlin, 1889. French tr. by M. Lespes and others, as *La vie de Mirabeau,* 2 v., Paris, 1895–96.

    c Barthou, Louis. *Mirabeau.* London and N. Y., 1913. Tr. from *Mirabeau,* Paris, 1913 [Figures du passé]. (Bibliography.)

a. Fascinating study of French society in the eighteenth century as reflected in the life of one of the most extraordinary families of the period. V. 1–2. Devoted to the Marquis de Mirabeau and his brothers. V. 3–5. Relate to the Mirabeau of Revolutionary fame; based on a mass of manuscript material; most complete life of the great Frenchman that has yet been written. *b.* Professor Stern's work supplements *a,* because of his researches in the archives of Berlin, Vienna, and Neufchatel, as well as of Paris, although he did not have at his disposal the great mass af manuscript material which Charles de Loménie used. His work is more scientific and a better guide for the investigator. The French translation is really a second edition, for the author took advantage of its publication to revise his work. Review of *a* and *b,* H. M. Stephens, *E.H.R.* 7:587, July 1892. *c.* Best single-volume biography of Mirabeau in English; contains several hitherto unpublished letters of Mirabeau. Review, *E.H.R.* 29:407, Apr. 1914. Also, cf. (M811). FMF

M363 Fling, Fred M. *Mirabeau and the French revolution.* V. 1, *Youth of Mirabeau.* N. Y. and London, 1908. (Bibliography.)

This unusually instructive piece of biographical study covers Mirabeau's life up to his imprisonment at the Chateau d'If on September 20, 1774. By a complete and careful discussion of the evidence contained in family letters and papers it seeks to explain the development of Mirabeau's character and qualities. Review, R. C. H. Catterall, *A.H.R.* 15:371, Jan. 1910. HEB

M364 Bradby, E. D. *Life of Barnave.* 2 v. Oxford, 1915. (Bibliography.)

Excellent biography of one of the most interesting and important characters of the early Revolution; based upon a thorough study of all the material, both printed and manuscript. Because of Miss Bradby's full treatment of Barnave's activities in the national assembly, it becomes one of the best accounts of that period in English. Review, E. Ellery, *A.H.R.* 21:348, Jan. 1916; J. H. Clapham, *E.H.R.* 30:733, Oct. 1915. FMF

M365 Ellery, Eloise. *Brissot de Warville: a study in the history of the French revolution.* Boston, 1915. [Vassar semi-centennial series.] (Bibliography.)

The author has brought together all the data on Brissot to be found in printed and manuscript sources and has produced a definitive life. The work throws light upon several phases of the Revolution, because before Brissot, as a member of the legislative assembly and of the convention, became a national figure, he had played a notable part in the early municipal assembly of Paris, had edited an influential newspaper, *Le patriote français,* and had founded La Société des Amis des Noirs, the French anti-slavery society. Review, *A.H.R.* 22:848, July 1917. Also cf. (M796). FMF

M366a Belloc, Hilaire. *Danton, a study.* London and N. Y., 1899.

b —— *Robespierre, a study.* 1901. New ed., London and N. Y., 1927.

c —— *Marie Antoinette.* 1909. 5th ed., London, 1923. 2nd American ed., N. Y., 1924.

Works of interpretation rather than of original research. The author's purpose is to paint as vivid a picture as may be on the basis of facts already gathered by others, in the case of Danton, by Bougeart, Robinet, and Aulard; in the case of Robespierre by Hamel. *a.* Danton is pictured as a reformer, a man of practical sense, and above all a tribune. Review, *Nation* (N. Y.), 69:281, Oct.

12, 1899. Also cf. (M800). *b*. Robespierre is presented as 'a man of insufficient capacity bent into the narrowest gauge' whose success was due to the possession 'to an inhuman degree of the potentiality of intense conviction'. Review, F. M. Fling, *A.H.R.* 7:780, July 1902. Also cf. (M814). *c*. Marie Antoinette stands out as an object of pity, a victim of an inexorable fate, of accidents which 'drove her with a precision that was more than human, right to her predestined end'. Review, P. F. Willert, *E.H.R.* 25:620, July 1910. Also cf. (M343, 785).

For additional biographical works and memoirs for the revolutionary period, cf. (M791–817). EEY

NAPOLEONIC PERIOD, 1799–1815

For the biographies of Napoleon and for the diplomatic and military history of the period, cf. § I, Modern times.

M381a Browning, Oscar. *Napoleon, the first phase: some chapters on the boy-hood and youth of Bonaparte, 1769–1793.* 1905. Rev. ed., as *Boyhood and youth of Napoleon,* London and N. Y., 1906.

b —— *Fall of Napoleon.* London and N. Y., 1907. (Brief bibliography.)

c Chuquet, Arthur. *La jeunesse de Napoléon.* 3 v. Paris, 1897–99. Rev. ed. of v. 1, 1898.

d Vandal, Albert, Comte. *L'avènement de Bonaparte.* 2 v. Paris, 1902–07. Many reprints.

a and *b*. Contain much of the latest results of French scholarship. The story is told by an admirer of Napoleon with sufficient completeness to enable the reader to form his own conclusions. Review of *a, A.H.R.* 11:385, Jan. 1906; of *b,* T. A. Dodge, *A.H.R.* 13:138, Oct. 1907. *c*. Recounts, in a masterly way, and after most thorough research, the incidents of Bonaparte's life until the capture of Toulon. Appendixes contain abundant notes and documents. Review, R. Reuss, *Rev. Hist.* 67:125, May 1898; 69:114, Jan. 1899; 70:374, July 1899. *d*. Tells with equal authority the story of Brumaire and of the constructive work of the consulate. Chuquet is more impartial in attitude, but Vandal's admiration of the First Consul may be in part due to his contempt for the Directory. Review, H. A. L. Fisher, *E.H.R.* 23:379, Apr. 1908. HEB

M382a Masson, Frédéric. *Napoléon et sa famille.* 13 v. Paris, 1897–1919.

b —— *Napoléon à Sainte-Hélène, 1815–1821.* Paris, 1912.

c Masson, Frédéric, and **Biagi, Guido.** *Napoléon inconnu: papiers inédits, 1786–1793, accompagnés de notes sur la jeunesse de Napoléon, 1769–1793 par Frédéric Masson.* 2 v. Paris, 1893. New ed. as *Manuscrits inédits de Napoléon, 1786–1791,* Paris, 1907, and F. Masson, *Napoléon dans sa jeunesse,* Paris, 1907.

By one of the ablest, as well as the most devoted, of Napoleonic scholars; most important of his many works, which also include four on Josephine, one on Marie Louise, and one on the king of Rome, dealing with the personal aspects of the emperor's career. *a*. Napoleon's relatives escape with little credit from the full statement of facts and the searching analysis of situations. Review, B. Monod, *Rev. Hist.* 74:339, Nov. 1900; G. Monod, *ibid,* 94:106, May 1907. *c*. These manuscripts of the youthful Corsican offer an opportunity to discover any possible indications of budding genius before his achievements at Toulon. HEB

M383a Rose, John Holland. *Personality of Napoleon.* N. Y. and London, 1912. [Lowell lectures.]

b Rosebery, Archibald P. P., Earl of. *Napoleon, the last phase.* N. Y. and London, 1900.

a. Series of compact, critical analyses of Napoleon the man, Jacobin, warrior, emperor, lawgiver, thinker, world-ruler, and exile, by a highly competent English scholar. Based on an extensive acquaintance with the literature of the Napoleonic period; presents in attractive form and in sympathetic spirit the most important aspects of this subject. Review, R. L. Poole, *E.H.R.* 18:404, Apr. 1903. *b.* Brilliant discussion of Napoleon's sojourn at St. Helena, his character, and his place in history. Important as a penetrating and valuable analysis of the literature of the much-discussed treatment of Napoleon by his captors, and also of Napoleon's own efforts in this 'last phase' to justify his course and create a legend for the influencing of historical judgment. Unlike many English opinions of Napoleon this estimate is eminently balanced and fair. Review, T. A. Dodge, *A.H.R.* 6:565, Apr. 1901.   LBP

M384a Ludwig, Emil. *Napoleon.* London and N. Y., 1926. Tr. by Eden and Cedar Paul from *Napoleon,* Berlin, 1925.

b Geer, Walter. *Napoleon and his family: the study of a Corsican clan.* 3 v. N. Y., 1927–29. [1, *Corsica-Madrid, 1769–1809;* 2, *Madrid-Moscow, 1809–1813;* 3, *Moscow-Saint Helena, 1813–1821.*]

c Driault, Edouard. *La vraie figure de Napoléon.* Paris, 1928.

a. Not a complete account of Napoleon's public career or of the Napoleonic period, but a psychological study, an interpretation of character. Brilliant, almost glittering in style; a vivid portrayal, often keenly analytical. Though the exact historian may object to the use of the methods of fiction, as, for example, a number of imaginary soliloquies, still the work must be regarded as one of the noteworthy books about Bonaparte. Review, E. Achorn, *A.H.R.* 32:860, July 1927; (London) *Times Literary Supplement,* 26:325, May 12, 1927.   HRS
b. The first two of three volumes which deal with Napoleon's family 'as it influenced his plans, his acts, and his fate.' Illuminating with many more facts than appear in *a,* and those worked skilfully into a coördinated record. Review of v. 1, (London) *Times Literary Supplement,* 27:38, Jan. 19, 1928; of v. 2, E. Achorn, *Journ. of Mod. Hist.* 1:129, March 1929.   HEB
c. By the leading Napoleonic scholar in France today, the author of the well-known volumes on *Napoleon et l'Europe.* His aim is to present a rounded picture of Napoleon, following his tempestuous career step by step. At times the rush of events, described in a swift style, leaves the reader breathless, but the final impression is true to the life of the period.   CLL

M385a Broadley, Alexander M. *Napoleon in caricature, 1795–1821,* . . . *with an introductory essay on pictorial satire as a factor in Napoleonic history* by J. Holland Rose. 2 v. London, 1910; N. Y., 1911.

b Wheeler, Harold F. B., and **Broadley, Alexander M.** *Napoleon and the invasion of England, the story of the great terror, with numerous illustrations from contemporary prints, caricatures, etc.* 2 v. London, 1907; N. Y., 1908.

a. Richest in the caricatures published in England, the works notably of Rowlandson, Gillray, and the two Cruikshanks; include also chapters on the work of French, German, and other continental artists; many illustrations in color. Review, *Athenæum*, 2:672, Nov. 26, 1910. *b*. Also chiefly interesting for illustrative materials. Review, *Athenæum*, 2:396, Oct. 5, 1907. HEB

M386a Thiers, Louis Adolphe. *History of the consulate and the empire of France under Napoleon.* 1845–62. New ed., 12 v., London and Philadelphia, 1893–94. Tr. by D. F. Campbell and J. Stebbing from *Histoire du consulat et de l'empire,* 20 v., Paris, 1845–62, with two supplementary v. containing atlas and index; new illustrated ed., 5 v. and atlas, Paris, 1878–83. Many other ed.

b Thibaudeau, Antoine C., Comte. *Le consulat et l'empire, ou Histoire de la France et de Napoléon Bonaparte de 1799 à 1815.* 10 v. Paris, 1834–35. 2nd ed., 18 v., Paris, 1837–38.

a. As a history, superior to the author's (M322*a*) *History of the French revolution.* Like that work it exercised an important political influence, for its cult of 'glory' enhanced the Napoleonic legend, much to the advantage of the Third Napoleon. Thiers's experience as minister under Louis Philippe gave him a firmer grasp of administrative questions, so that his comments on finance and commerce are valuable. He is also noted for his skill in describing battles and campaigns. *b.* Still important because the author was one of Napoleon's ablest officials and had ample opportunities to know the inner history of the period. While he was in exile he began a work entitled *Histoire générale de Napoléon* (v. 1–6, Paris, 1827–28), and its sixth volume is the first volume of this later and completed work. Also cf. his (M854) *Bonaparte and the consulate.* HEB

M391 Lanzac de Laborie, Léon de. *Paris sous Napoléon.* 8 v. Paris, 1905–13. [1, *Consulat provisoire et consulat à temps;* 2, *Administration: les grands travaux;* 3, *La cour et la ville: la vie et la mort;* 4, *La religion;* 5, *Assistance et bienfaisance: approvisionnement;* 6, *Le monde des affaires et du travail;* 7, *Le Théâtre-Français;* 8, *Spectacles et musées.*]

Product of careful research; touches every phase of the life of the city from the advent of Napoleon to the fall of the empire. Because of the peculiar relationship of Paris to France, these studies have more than a local value and illustrate the tendencies of French society during the period, especially in v. 4 and 6. V. 6 Throws some light on the great economic struggle with England and its consequences for French industry. Review, v. 1–5, *A.H.R.* 14:127, Oct. 1908; 14:581, Apr. 1909; v. 6–8, G. M. Dutcher, *A.H.R.* 15:860, July 1910; 16:854, July 1911; 18:837, July 1913. HEB

M392 Anchel, Robert. *Napoléon et les juifs.* Paris, 1928. (Bibliography.)

This volume possesses the double interest of showing how a community so unique as that of the Jews was affected by the grant of liberty in 1790 after centuries of restriction, and how Napoleon sought to remedy the anarchy in the Jewish religious organization which had been the consequence. The author believes that in this effort Napoleon was moved by his genius for order and that Jewish worship suffered no more from his will to control than did the Catholic church from the Organic Articles. Part of his legislation, however, was prompted by the apparent necessity of checking usury and of protecting the peasants, especially of Alsace, against Jewish money-lenders. The laws of 1808 introduced a "régime of oppression." HEB

M401a Talleyrand-Perigord, Charles Maurice de, Prince de Benevent. *Memoirs.* 5 v. N. Y. and London, 1891–2. Tr. by R. Ledos de Beaufort and Mrs. Angus Hall from *Mémoires,* ed. by J. V. A. duc de Broglie, 5 v., Paris, 1891–2.

    b Lacour-Gayet, Georges. *Talleyrand, 1754–1838.* V. I., 1754–1799. Paris, 1928.

    a. The authenticity of these memoirs was at first the subject of animated controversy: cf. J. Flammermont, *Rev. Hist.* 48:72–80, Jan. 1892; P. Bertrand, *ibid.* 48:301–316, March 1892; J. Flammermont, *La Révolution Française,* 23:385–409, Nov. 1892. The possibility of controversy was increased by the fact that only copies of the original manuscript, authenticated by Talleyrand's literary executors, remained. No one was supposed to know more of what passed behind the scenes during the Napoleonic régime than Talleyrand, yet his memoirs added practically nothing to existing information. The memoirs are detailed for only two phases of Talleyrand's activity, his work at the Congress of Vienna and his embassy in London after the establishment of the July Monarchy. Here they are made up largely of his correspondence.

    b. By the author of a well-known life of Napoleon. A critical examination of Talleyrand's 'Memoirs' as well as a biography of their writer, disposing of many of the legends skilfully embodied in this *apologia.* Its conclusions are based upon much new material drawn partly from private collections. A work of deep interest, but the most abiding impression is not so much of Talleyrand's intellectual power as of his almost uncanny wickedness.   HEB

M402 Pasquier, Étienne Denis, Duc de. *History of my time: memoirs of Chancellor Pasquier.* 3 v. London and N. Y., 1893–94. Tr. by C. E. Roche from v. 1–3 of *Histoire de mon temps: mémoires du Chancelier Pasquier,* ed. by E. A. G., duc d'Audiffret-Pasquier, 6 v., 1893–95.

    These memoirs are regarded as an historical work of the first order. Pasquier's career was of extraordinary length, beginning in the parlement of Paris before the Revolution and closing in 1862 under the Second Empire. His narrative becomes detailed only after the time when he rallied to the new régime in 1806. The volumes which have been translated end with the second Restoration. The others carry the story through the Revolution of 1830, and it is understood that further volumes are in manuscript. Review, J. H. Robinson, *A.H.R.* 1:140, Oct. 1895.   HEB

    For other memoirs of the Napoleonic period, cf. (M831–855).

1815–1870

M411 Bourgeois, Émile. *History of modern France, 1815–1913.* 2 v. Cambridge, Eng., 1919. [Cambridge historical series.] (Good bibliography.)

    Careful study, by one of the most prominent authorities on modern France; centers about the growth of French democracy during the nineteenth century; indicates in detail the various obstacles that this development encountered; remarkably fair in judgments and conclusions. The chapters on the Second Republic and the Second Empire are especially valuable. Review, *E.H.R.* 34:618, Oct. 1919.   JMSA

M412a Weill, Georges. *La France sous la monarchie constitutionelle, 1814–1848.* 1902. Rev. ed., Paris, 1912. (Bibliography.)

b —— *Histoire du parti republicain en France de 1814 à 1870.* Paris, 1900. (Bibliography.)

c —— *Histoire du mouvement social en France, 1852–1914.* 1904. 3rd ed., Paris, 1924.

a. Excellent survey of political, economic, social, religious and cultural life during the reigns of Charles X and Louis Philippe; clear and exact in treatment. Review, F. N. Anderson, *A.H.R.* 18:168, Oct. 1912. *b.* Gives a single chapter to the Restoration and lays the greatest emphasis on the years 1830 to 1852; well documented with references to letters, memoirs, and contemporary literature. Review, G. Monod, *Rev. Hist.* 73:342, July 1900. *c.* Useful complement to the two preceding works. Review, A. Lichtenberger, *Rev. Hist.* 97:131, Jan. 1908.

JMSA

M413 Duvergier de Hauranne, Prosper L. *Histoire du gouvernement parlementaire en France, 1814–1848.* 10 v. Paris, 1857–72.

The author was active in the public life of France from 1825 to about 1870. His work is a very detailed, although not a scholarly, account of French political history from 1814 to August 1830; particularly valuable for the period of the Martignac ministry; based partly on the author's experiences and partly on newspapers, pamphlets, and private papers of the period. JMSA

M414 La Gorce, Pierre de. *La restauration: Louis XVIII.* Paris, 1926.

Not a definitive work but an excellent survey of the reign. Review, *Rev. des Quest. Hist.* 106:241, Jan. 1927; C. H. Pouthas, *Rev. d'Hist. Moderne,* 1:310, Aug. 1926.

GMD

M421 Hillebrand, Karl. *Geschichte Frankreichs von der Thronbesteigung Louis Philipps bis zum Falle Napoleon's III.* V. 1–2, Gotha, 1877–79; index, 1898. [(B161) Geschichte der europäischen Staaten.]

Originally planned to consist of five volumes. V. 2. Carries the narrative only to the fall of the July monarchy in 1848. Still one of the standard histories of the period, particularly valuable for the later chapters. The writer made use of German and Italian sources. Review, v. 1, A. Böhtlingk, *Hist. Zeit.* 42:173, 1879; v. 2, ibid. 45:153, 1881. PLW

M422 Thureau-Dangin, Paul. *Histoire de la monarchie de juillet.* 7 v. Paris, 1884–92. Various reprints.

Complete narrative of the reign of Louis Philippe; strongly monarchical; covers in considerable detail the external and internal policy; particularly valuable are the chapters on the foreign policy and on the years 1847 and 1848. The author had access to private papers belonging to prominent men of the time, and makes numerous references to contemporary pamphlets and newspapers. Review, v. 6–7, G. Monod, *Rev. Hist.* 49:371, July 1892. JMSA

M423 Blanc, Louis. *History of ten years, 1830–1840.* 2 v. London, 1844–45. Tr. by W. K. Kelly from *Révolution française: histoire de dix ans, 1830–1840,* 5 v., Paris, 1841–44; numerous later ed.

The author was one of the famous radicals and socialists of the mid-nineteenth century. The introduction contains a clear and correct estimate of the political importance of the Charter of 1814. The ensuing chapters embody a wealth of information concerning the radical movements of the time, but statements in regard to the author's political opponents and the more moderate republicans are biased.   JMSA

M424 Allison, John M. S.   *Thiers and the French monarchy, 1797–1848.* Boston and London, 1926.

This volume, to be followed by another for the period of the empire, closes with the Revolution of 1848. By the use of the collections of Thiers's papers, at Aix-en-Provence as well as at Paris, the author has been able to throw new light upon the earlier career of Thiers, especially of his life before residence at Paris began. The extraordinary mental energy and intense individuality of the man engage the interest of the reader. Enough is told of the constitutional monarchy to furnish the setting for the experiences of one of its foremost political leaders. Review, (London) *Times Literary Supplement,* 25:707, Oct. 21, 1926.   HEB

M431a La Gorce, Pierre de.   *Histoire de la seconde république française.* 2 v. Paris, 1886.

> **b** —— *Histoire du second empire.* 7 v. Paris, 1894–1905. Various reprints.

a. Compact but satisfactory account; more concerned with internal affairs than with foreign policy. Although the author is strongly conservative, he is remarkably fair to the republicans. Review, G. Monod and C. Bémont, *Rev. Hist.* 34:111, May 1887. *b.* Excellent and impartial; takes a high place among the historical writings of the last fifty years; especially valuable for its authoritative account of the foreign policy of the Second Empire. V. 6–7. Commendable treatment of the origin of the War of 1870. Review, C. M. Andrews, *A.H.R.* 1:731, July 1896; 2:356, Jan. 1897; 5:131, Oct. 1899; 7:148, Oct. 1901; 11:671, Apr. 1906.
                                                                              JMSA

M432 Tocqueville, Alexis C. H. M. Clérel de.   *Recollections.* London and N. Y., 1896. Tr. by A. T. de Mattos from *Souvenirs,* Paris, 1893.

These memoirs, which cover only from February 1848 to October 1849, are literally recollections jotted down from time to time during the years 1850 and 1851 after the author's retirement from public life. Their chief value lies in the pen pictures, drawn with Thucydidean sharpness of outline, which they give of the men of 1848 with whom Tocqueville had been intimately associated. About one-quarter of the book deals with the author's ministry of foreign affairs, June–October, 1849. Review, T. de Puymaigre, *Rev. des Quest. Hist.* 54:232, July, 1893.   PLW

M433a Simpson, Frederick A.   *Rise of Louis Napoleon.* 1909. New ed., London and N. Y., 1925. (Extensive bibliography.)

> **b** —— *Louis Napoleon and the recovery of France, 1848–1856.* London and N. Y., 1923. (Excellent critical bibliography.)

> **c Guedalla, Philip.** *Second empire: Bonapartism, the prince, the president, the emperor.* London and N. Y., 1922. (Bibliography.)

a. Perhaps the most convenient account of Louis Napoleon as a pretender; the author holds that this period affords the clue to his success in 1848 and to his subsequent career. Review, W. Miller, *E.H.R.* 26:404, Apr. 1911. *b.* Carries the story to 1856; additional volumes are promised. Both are scholarly, well-written works; based in part on diplomatic correspondence and other unpublished material; there is nothing better in English; the standpoint is, in general, sympathetic. Review, W. Miller, *E.H.R.* 38:290, Apr. 1923. *c.* Less satisfactory; brilliantly written but unanalytical résumé grounded chiefly on memoirs and secondary sources. As a picture of externals, it is full of color, even to excess; the story has no hero. Review, R. Guyot, *Rev. Hist.* 143:74, May 1923. ENC

M434a Ollivier, Émile. *L'empire libéral: études; récits, souvenirs.* 17 v. Paris, 1895–1915.

b —— *Franco-Prussian war and its hidden causes.* Boston, 1912. Tr. of extracts from *a* by G. B. Ives.

a. Elaborate account of the Second Empire by the leader of the 'tiers parti' and the head of the responsible ministry of Napoleon III in 1870; a defence of his acts and policies; decidedly biased and should be used with caution. In his discussion of the aggressive foreign policy of Napoleon III the author does not stress enough the existence and influence of a war party in France. V. I. Contains an interesting study of the development of the principle of nationalities. Review, *Rev. Hist.* 58:369, Aug. 1895; 103:110, Jan. 1910. *b.* Made up of selections translated from the later volumes of *a.* Review, M. Smith, *A.H.R.* 19:153, Oct. 1913. JMSA

M435 Beyens, Napoleon, Baron. *Le second empire vu par un diplomate belge.* 2 v. Paris, 1925–26.

Based upon the papers of the author's father, for forty years in the Belgian legation at Paris, and for thirty-one years its head. Interesting chiefly for the light that it throws upon the schemes of Napoleon III to recover the "Natural Limits" and to annex Belgium. Review, *Rev. des Quest. Hist.* 103:502, Oct. 1, 1925; 106:242, Jan. 1927; Raymond Guyot, *Rev. Hist.* 151:241, March 1926. HEB

M436 Laronze, Georges. *Histoire de la commune de 1871, d'après des documents et les souvenirs inédits. La justice.* Paris, 1928.

A work of deep interest, which, as the sub-title indicates, deals chiefly with the administration of justice during the period of the Commune. Other chapters describe the opening and closing scenes of the insurrection and portray the character of the government. The author has had access to archival collections closed to his predecessors. He has also utilized many private papers and has obtained important evidence from living witnesses. Review, (London) *Times Literary Supplement,* 27:543, July 26, 1928. HEB

THE THIRD REPUBLIC

M441a Wright, Charles H. C. *History of the third French republic.* Boston, 1916. (Bibliography.)

b Bodley, John E. C. *France.* 2 v. 1898. New ed., 1 v., London and N. Y., 1907. French tr. as *La France: essai sur l'histoire et le fonctionnement des institutions politiques françaises,* Paris, 1901.

c Buell, Raymond L. *Contemporary French politics.* N. Y. and London, 1920.

d Wendell, Barrett. *France of today.* 1907. 2nd ed., N. Y., 1912. [Lowell lectures.]

a. Brief, modest, dispassionate statement of purely political events to 1914. The author has no desire to be philosophical or entertaining but he succeeds in being lucid and reliable. Review, C. D. Hazen, *A.H.R.* 22:156, Oct. 1916. *b.* Result of fifteen years' painstaking preparation, with the best opportunities; considered in England as the best authority on France at the close of the nineteenth century. A book of political discussion rather than of information, severe for republican politicians, decidedly conservative in tone, with a personal bias in favor of the Napoleonic system. Review, W. J. Ashley, *A.H.R.* 4:353, Jan. 1899. *c.* Model of fairness, sympathy, and completeness; passes in review the numerous groups and the outstanding questions in French politics, with a brief sketch of their antecedents in the recent past. Review, F. A. Ogg, *Amer. Pol. Sci. Rev.* 15:116, Feb. 1921. *d.* Contains 'impressions' in the form of popular lectures, but their author was a keen observer; demolishes the legend of French 'frivolity'. Although not systematic or exhaustive, the eight chapters cover all the main aspects of French life. Combined with *a,* it provides an excellent introduction to the subject. Review, J. Sullivan, *Amer. Pol. Sci. Rev.* 2:659, Nov. 1908.

ALG

M442a Zévort, Edgar. *L'histoire de la troisième république.* 4 v. Paris, 1896–1901.

b Simond, Émile. *Histoire de la troisième république.* 4 v. Paris, 1913–22.

c Lhéritier, Michel. *La France depuis 1870.* Paris, 1922.

a. Study of political history through the presidency of Carnot; accurate in treatment but with more attention to administrative and parliamentary details than to broad policies. Review, *A.H.R.* 2:372, Jan. 1897; 2:754, July 1897; 5:133, Oct. 1899. CHCW

b. Mediocre narrative from 1887 to 1906; favors the church, the army, the navy, and colonial development; useful only as a detailed account in continuation of *a.* Review, F. M. Anderson, *A.H.R.* 27:353, Jan. 1922; 28:361, Jan. 1923. *c.* Brief history of the period; intended as a guide; comprehensive in scope; includes accounts of the economic, social, and intellectual phenomena of the Third Republic as well as a description of the origin and growth of its institutions and political parties. Review, *Rev. Critique,* 91:65, Feb. 1, 1924; F. M. Anderson, *A.H.R.* 29:373, Jan. 1924. HEB

M443a Hanotaux, Gabriel. *Contemporary France.* 4 v. London and N. Y., 1903–09. Tr. by J. C. Tarver and E. Sparvel-Bayly from *Histoire de la France contemporaine,* 4 v., Paris, 1903–08.

b —— *Histoire de la fondation de la troisième république.* V. 1–4, Paris, 1925–26. [1–2, *Le gouvernement de M. Thiers, 1871–73; 3–4, L'échec de la monarchie et la fondation de la république, mai 1873–mai 1876.*]

a. Notable book on the establishment and early years of the Third Republic to 1882; written by a man who lived through this period, knew its principal figures, and later held distinguished positions in the French government. Some of the book is, consequently, based on personal observation, some of it on unusual access to private papers; portions represent a considerable amount of scholarly research, but there is, perhaps, too much dependence placed upon memoirs and reminiscences. Rich in descriptions of personalities, particularly of Thiers and Gambetta. Its style reveals the French characteristics of flexibility, subtlety, and accuracy of touch, with flashes of philosophic insight and brilliant generalization. In general its qualities of judgment are sound and shrewd, although sometimes, especially with reference to foreign affairs, there is a tendency to over-refinement. Unfortunately the English translation is not only somewhat abridged but is also very faulty in rendering. Review, v. 1, C. F. A. Currier, *A.H.R.* 9:206, Oct. 1903; v. 3–4, F. M. Anderson, *A.H.R.* 13:589, Apr. 1908; 15:864, July 1910.   LBP

b. New edition of *a;* narrative slightly revised in v. 1–2; important additional source materials utilized in v. 3–4. Review, *Rev. des Quest. Hist.* 103:506, Oct. 1925; 106:493, Apr. 1927.   GMD

M444 Thiers, Louis Adolphe. *Memoirs, 1870–1873.* London, 1915; N. Y., 1916. Tr. by F. M. Atkinson from *Notes et souvenirs, 1870–1873,* Paris, 1903.

Highly important personal narrative of his diplomatic activities in 1870–1871 and of his administration of the French government from 1871 to 1873; succinct, clear, and dispassionate. Review, C. D. Hazen, *A.H.R.* 22:652, Apr. 1917.

JMSA

M445 Washburne, Elihu B. *Recollections of a minister to France, 1869–1877.* 2 v. N. Y., 1887.

Contains interesting and important anecdotes and descriptions of Paris and the leading citizens of France. Written by the minister of the United States to France who remained in Paris during the siege of 1870–1871.   JMSA

LOCAL HISTORY

M481 Albert-Petit, Armand, ed. *Les vieilles provinces de France.* V. 1–9. Paris, 1911–26. [1, A. Albert-Petit, *Normandie;* 2, R. Reuss, *Alsace;* 3, L. Febvre, *Franche-Comté;* 4, C. Dufayard, *Savoie;* 5, P. Boissonnade, *Poitou;* 6, Colonna di Cesari Rocca and L. Villat, *Corse;* 7, P. Gachon, *Languedoc;* 8, J. Calmette and P. Vidal, *Rousillon;* 9, G. Morizet, *Lorraine.*]

These little volumes afford a convenient introduction to regional history upon which reliance must be placed to such a considerable extent for either a comprehensive or a detailed picture of pre-revolutionary France. The volumes are of uneven excellence, those on Normandy and Alsace, especially the latter, being by far the best. Each province, by its very nature, presents special difficulties and each has received a distinctive treatment. Considerable emphasis has been placed upon social and economic history, geographic factors, and the perplexing problems of origins. In most instances the period before the Revolution, in some cases even the period prior to Louis XIV, occupies the major portion of the volume. Review, v. 1, G. de Beaurepaire, *Rev. des Quest. Hist.* 91:195, Jan. 1912; v. 2, *ibid.* 95:667, Apr. 1914; v. 4, L. Alloing, *ibid.* 96:669, Oct. 1914; v. 7, L. Halphen, *Rev. Hist.* 140:264, July 1922; v. 9, L. André, *Rev. Critique,* 94:129, Apr. 1, 1927.

Since these volumes (except Corsica) are devoid of bibliographical information, one must turn elsewhere for the sources and literature of French provincial

608   A GUIDE TO HISTORICAL LITERATURE

history, notably to the bibliographical essays upon the French provinces printed from time to time in (B941*f*12) *Revue de synthèse historique,* of which that for Normandy by H. Prentout is perhaps the most valuable (19:52, 203, Aug., Oct. 1909; 20:37, 188, 306, Feb., Apr., June 1910). SRP

M482a Devic, Claude, and **Vaissète, Joseph.** *Histoire générale du Languedoc.* 5 v. Paris, 1730–45. Rev. ed. by E. Dulaurier and others, with continuation from 1643 to 1790, by E. Roschach, 16 v. in 18, Toulouse, 1872–1905.

   b La Borderie, Arthur le Moyne de, and **Pocquet, Barthélemy.** *Histoire de Bretagne.* 6 v. Rennes, 1896–1914.

   c Kleinclausz, Arthur. *Histoire de Bourgogne.* 1909. 2nd ed., Paris, 1924.

   d Parisot, Robert. *Histoire de Lorraine (Duché de Lorraine, Duché de Bar, Trois-Evêchés) des origines à 1919.* 3 v. and index. Paris, 1919–25.

It is impossible to construct any brief list from the numerous monographs and special studies in French provincial history which will fairly represent the erudition lavished thereon by both French and foreign writers. These four titles are samples of French scholarship. *a.* Monumental work; one of the best of the Benedictine historical enterprises; greatly amplified in the new edition; leaves little to be desired in either scope or accuracy. Review, G. Monod, *Rev. Hist.* 32:114, Sept. 1886. *b, c,* and *d.* Not such examples of exhaustive scholarship as *a,* although all three are successful compilations and helpful guides. Review of *b,* L. Duchesne, *Rev. Hist.* 66:182, Jan. 1898; of *c,* J. Guiraud, *Rev. des Ques. Hist.* 87:358, Jan. 1910; of *d,* E. W. Dow, *A.H.R.* 25:259, Jan. 1920; 28:352, Jan. 1923; E. Welvert, *Rev. Critique,* 92:163, May 1, 1925. SRP

M483a Lodge, Eleanor C. *Gascony under English rule, 1154–1453.* London, 1926. (Bibliography.)

   b Marsh, Frank B. *English rule in Gascony, 1199–1259, with special reference to the towns.* Ann Arbor, Mich., 1928.

a. Sample contribution of foreign scholarship to French local history; popular account based upon researches into the political, social, and economic conditions; particularly valuable on town life in the fourteenth century. Review, H. Johnstone, *E.H.R.* 42:606, Oct. 1927. *b.* Another treatment of the same problem, emphasizing the dependence of English rule upon the wine trade.

Corresponding contributions on English relations with Normandy may be found in (H241*a* and *b*) Haskins, *Normans in European history,* and *Norman institutions.* HRS

M491a Poëte, Marcel. *Une vie de cité: Paris de sa naissance à nos jours.* V. 1–2 and *Album,* Paris, 1924–27. [1, *La jeunesse, des origines aux temps modernes;* 2, *La cité de la Renaissance, du milieu du XVᵉ à la fin du XVIᵉ siècle.*]

   b Bournon, Fernand. *Paris: histoire, monuments, administration, environs de Paris.* Paris, 1887.

   c Hoffbauer, Fedor, and others. *Paris à travers les âges; aspects successifs des principales vues et perspectives des monuments et quartiers de Paris le XIIIᵉ siècle jusqu'à nos jours fidèlement restituées d'après les documents authentiques.* 2 v. Paris, 1875–82.

a. Noteworthy addition to the literature on Paris. V. 1. Of special value to students of medieval history, whether political, social, or economic, covering as it does in authoritative detail the annals and life of the most important city in continental Europe from its first settlements down to the middle of the fifteenth century. The chapters on 'Roman Paris in the early Christian centuries', on the 'Hansa of the Water Merchants' in the twelfth century, and on the expansion of commerce and industry in the thirteenth, and the excellent account of the career of Étienne Marcel are of great interest. The author, in his introduction, gives a critical account of the sources utilized, but adds no footnotes or references in the text itself. Review, L. Halphen, *Rev. Hist.* 147:229, Nov. 1924. V. 2. Similar, but more detailed, in treatment. Review, W. S. Davis, *A.H.R.* 33:178, Oct. 1927. The *Album,* which is a companion to v. 1 and 2, contains six hundred illustrations, based on the documents, and an historical account of the city. *b.* Hitherto the most convenient account of the city and its history. Review, G. Monod and C. Bémont, *Rev. Hist.* 36:162, Jan. 1888. *c.* More comprehensive; very valuable for its authoritative reconstruction of the city in plans and illustrations.

WSD

M492 Reuss, Rodolphe. *Histoire de Strasbourg depuis ses origines jusqu'à nos jours.* Paris, 1922.

Admirable example of a history of a city; shows at how many points the experience of Strasbourg touched and illustrated the history of Europe, especially in the struggles of the Reformation and of the Counter-Reformation, in the advance of the French toward the Rhine, and in the French Revolution; stops at the treaty of Frankfort. Review, C. Pfister, *Rev. Hist.* 140:247, July 1922.

HEB

DIPLOMATIC, MILITARY, AND NAVAL HISTORY

Since the principal contributions to the history of French foreign relations have been written from the point of view of Europe in general rather than of France they are listed in §§ I and J. Especially cf. (I302b) Sorel, *L'Europe et la révolution;* (I323b) Guyot, *Le directoire et la paix;* (I321a) Driault, *Napoléon et l'Europe;* (I501a) Bourgeois, *Manuel historique de politique étrangère;* (J208a) Stuart, *French foreign policy from Fashoda to Serajevo.*

M501 Masson, Frédéric. *Le département des affaires étrangères pendant la révolution, 1787–1804.* Paris, 1877.

Valuable for its description of the organization of the department and of the changes brought about by the vicissitudes of the Revolution, and for biographical details of the personnel, ministers, chiefs of division, and other employees. No account is given of the agents of the department abroad. Criticized for an unsympathetic attitude toward the Revolution.

HEB

M511 Wilkinson, Spenser. *French army before Napoleon.* Oxford, 1915. (Brief bibliography.)

The purpose of these seven lectures is to show that General Bonaparte, upon taking command in Italy in 1796, found a fully developed instrument and a new art of using it, both being the product of the study and discussion of generals of the old régime after the conclusion of the Seven Years' War. The author gives a full analysis of Guibert's *Essai général de tactique* (2 v., Londres, 1772), and explains its formative influence, especially upon the drill-book of 1791, which remained the standard text until 1830. He also describes the modifications of the army made during the Revolution. Review, W. B. Wood, *E.H.R.* 31:328, Apr. 1916; *A.H.R.* 21:852, July 1916.   HEB

M512 Phipps, Ramsay W. *Armies of the first French republic and the rise of the marshals of Napoleon I.* V. 1–2. Oxford and N. Y., 1926. [1, *Armée du Nord; 2, Armées de la Moselle, du Rhin, de Sambre-et-Meuse, de Rhin-et-Moselle.*]

Interesting book by a British army officer, not only a biographical dictionary of Napoleon's leading generals, but a military history of Northern France and Belgium during the period, with much information as to the organization of the armies and their control by the government. Review of v. 1, (London) *Times Lit. Suppl.* 25:733, Oct. 28, 1926; R. Loky, *Rev. des Quest. Hist.* 106:235, Jan. 1927; F. L. Huidekoper, *A.H.R.* 34:120, Oct. 1928; v. 2, (London) *Times Lit. Suppl.* 28:525, July 4, 1929.   HRS

M513 Chuquet, Arthur. *Les guerres de la révolution.* 11 v. Paris, 1886–96. [1, *La première invasion prussienne; 2, Valmy; 3, La retraite de Brunswick; 4, Jemappes et la conquête de la Belgique, 1792–1793; 5, La trahison de Dumouriez; 6, L'expédition de Custine; 7, Mayence; 8, Wissembourg; 9, Hoche et la lutte pour l'Alsace, 1793–1794; 10, Valenciennes; 11, Hondschoote.*] Later ed. of several v.

In a sense v. 3 of the author's (M381c) *La jeunesse de Napoléon,* on the siege of Toulon, may be grouped with this series. Most authoritative treatment of the wars of the earlier Revolution. As soon as v. 1 appeared it was recognized that a contribution of high order was being made to historical literature, for the author displayed a mastery of his materials and ability to weave into a lucid and interesting narrative their thousand scattered details. V. 1. Contains a careful survey of the condition of the French and Prussian armies in the summer of 1792. V. 2, 9, 10. Regarded as of special interest for their accounts of critical military operations. Review, v. 1, G. Monod and C. Bémont, *Rev. Hist.* 31:128, May 1886; v. 2, 34:104, May 1887; v. 3, 34:289, July 1887; v. 4, 45:99, Jan. 1891; v. 5, 46:92, May 1891; v. 6, 49:113, May 1892; v. 7, 50:357, Nov. 1892; v. 8, 53:103, Sept. 1893; v. 9, 54:116, Jan. 1894; v. 10, 56:351, Nov. 1894; v. 11, 60:381, March 1896.   HEB

M514 Desbrière, Édouard. *Projets et tentatives de débarquement aux îles britanniques, 1793–1805.* 4 v. in 5. Paris, 1900–02.

Noteworthy example of the publications of the Historical Section of the French General Staff, which has undertaken to publish the documents which bear upon all the campaigns of France since the eighteenth century. This collection is essential to the study of the development of Napoleon's plans for the invasion of England, and the documents which it embodies, as well as Captain Desbrière's interpretations, enable the historian to appraise the legends which have grown up about Napoleon's famous gesture. Review, R. Reuss, *Rev. Hist.* 76:123, May 1901; 79:132, May 1902; 81:115, Jan. 1903.   HEB

M521a Tramond, Johannès. *Manuel d'histoire maritime de la France des origines à 1815.* 1916. 2nd rev. ed., Paris, 1925. (Bibliographies.)

   b **La Roncière, Charles de.** *Histoire de la marine française.* V. 1–5. Paris, 1898–1920.

   a. Of broader interest than the title suggests; general history of the French navy and merchant marine; written by a teacher in the naval school at Brest;

does not deal in detail with the medieval period; stops at 1815. Review, C
Pfister, *Rev. Hist.* 124:348, March 1917; C. Bémont, *ibid.* 155:188, May 1927.
b. Work not only of genuine erudition but of great human interest; richly illus-
strated from contemporary material of all kinds. Does not begin with the
thirteenth century, when France first had a war fleet, but goes back to the Gallo-
Roman period and even beyond; emphasizes the exploits of the navy rather than
its organization. V. 5. Includes the period of the Thirty Years' War and of
Colbert. Review, J. S. Corbett, *A.H.R.* 5:744, July 1900; 6:546, Apr. 1901;
16:115, Oct. 1910; 28:110, Oct. 1922.   HEB

CONSTITUTIONAL AND LEGAL HISTORY

M531a Sait, Edward M. *Government and politics of France.* Yonkers-on-
Hudson, 1920. [Government handbooks.] (Bibliography.)

b Barthélemy, Joseph. *Government of France.* N. Y., 1924. Tr. by J.
B. Morris from *Le gouvernement de France,* 1919, 2nd rev ed., Paris,
1924.

a. Excellent handbook; describes the present governmental organization and
methods of political action. Review, F. A. Ogg, *Amer. Pol. Sci. Rev.* 15:116,
Feb. 1921. *b*. By a distinguished French scholar; second edition is preferable,
because of additions. The translation was made from the first edition, but the
translator was able to incorporate certain revisions suggested by the author.
Review, *Pol. Sci. Quar.* 40:326, June 1925.

Also cf. (M441*b*) Bodley, *France,* and (M441*c*) Buell, *Contemporary French
politics.*
HEB

M532 Holtzmann, Robert. *Französiche Verfassungsgeschichte von der Mitte
des neunten Jahrhunderts bis zur Revolution.* München, 1910. [Handbuch
der mittelalterlichen und neueren Geschichte.] (Bibliographies.)

Excellent handbook; divided into three parts: 'The age of the feudal system',
843–1180; 'The age of the growing royal power', 1180–1437; and 'The age of
the absolute monarchy', 1437–1789. The origin and nature of the various social
groups and political institutions are described. Dr. Holtzmann was a professor
at the University of Strassburg before the World War. Review, F. M. Powicke,
E.H.R. 25:761, Oct. 1910.
FMF

M533a Chénon, Émile. *Histoire générale du droit français public et privé des
origines à 1815.* V. I, *Période gallo-romaine, période franque, période
féodale et coutumière.* Paris, 1926. [Sources du droit, Droit public.]
(Bibliographies.)

b Viollet, Paul. *Droit public: histoire des institutions politiques et administratives de la France.* 3 v. Paris, 1889–1903. (Bibliographies.)

c —— *Droit public: histoire des institutions politiques et administratives
de la France: le roi et ses ministres pendant les trois derniers siècles de
la monarchie.* Paris, 1912. (Bibliographies.)

d Cheruel, Pierre Adolphe. *Histoire de l'administration monarchique en
France, depuis l'avènement de Philippe-Auguste jusqu'à la mort de Louis
XIV.* 2 v. Paris, 1855.

a. Scholarly work of great value, dealing chiefly with *droit privé;* unfortunately left unfinished at the death of the author in 1927. Review, J. de la Monneraye, *Rev. des Quest. Hist.* 108:206, Jan. 1928.
HEB

b. Manual for the serious student; treats of the public law of France down to the Revolution; by a man both of great learning and of originality and largeness of view. The author succeeded to a remarkable degree in seeing institutions as they were in actual life, and produced a work that is very human, as well as highly competent. Review, A. Molinier, *Rev. Hist.* 83:89, Sept. 1903. *c.* Displays the same qualities in dealing with the functions of the king and his ministers down to the Revolution. Review, H. Hauser, *Rev. Hist.* 111:83, Sept. 1912. *d.* General survey by an able student of the seventeenth century; deals chiefly with period since 1500.   EWD

M534a Aubert, Félix. *Histoire du parlement de Paris de l'origine à François Ier, 1250–1515.* 2 v. Paris, 1894.

    b Ducoudray, Gustave. *Les origines du parlement de Paris et la justice aux XIIIe et XIVe siècles.* Paris, 1902.

    c Maugis, Édouard. *Histoire du parlement de Paris, de l'avènement des rois Valois à la mort d'Henri IV.* V. 1–3. Paris, 1913–16.

    d Glasson, Ernest. *Le parlement de Paris: son rôle politique depuis le règne de Charles VI jusqu'à la révolution.* 2 v. Paris, 1901.

The history of the parlement of Paris, long very obscure, has at last become clearer; and Aubert's share in the clarification is considerable, especially as to procedure. In most respects, however, his work needs control and supplement from other studies, notably *b* on the origins, *c* on the fifteenth and sixteenth centuries, *d* on the later political rôle of the parlement, and (M300a) Carré, *La fin des parlements.* *a.* In part a republication of the author's previous work, *Le parlement de Paris de Philippe le Bel à Charles VII, 1314–1422,* 2 v., Paris, 1887–89. Review of *a,* R. Delachenal, *Rev. des Quest. Hist.* 59:324, Jan. 1896; of *b,* A. Molinier, *Rev. Hist.* 80:106, Sept. 1902; of *c,* C. Pfister, *ibid.* 115:153, Jan. 1914; 119:385, July 1915; 123:141, Sept. 1916; of *d,* G. Monod, *ibid.* 78:131, Jan. 1902.   EWD

M535 Monnet, Émile. *Histoire de l'administration provinciale, départementale, et communale en France.* Paris, 1885.

Convenient introduction to the history of French local administration; needs careful correction by the results of researches both in the broader field of administration and in local history. Review, C. Bémont, *Rev. Hist.* 27:375, March 1885.
                                                                                                     GMD

M551a Esmein, Adhémar. *Cours élémentaire d'histoire du droit français.* 1892. 15th rev. ed., Paris, 1925.

    b Glasson, Ernest. *Histoire du droit et des institutions de la France.* 8 v. Paris, 1887–1903. (Bibliographies.)

a. Handbook, addressed primarily to first-year law students in France, by a scholar who could give not only much systematized information but also a constructive general view. Useful for many besides those to whom it was addressed. Review, R. Saleilles, *Rev. Hist.* 56:389, Nov. 1894. *b.* Exhaustive general account, packed with information and discussion about both the law and institutions of France and about the documents and works thereon. Even more encyclopedic and detailed than would appear from the title and accompanying data, since the author only reached in v. 7 the end of feudalism and had but begun on the monarchical period in v. 8, when death interrupted the task. The learning and good sense put into the work assure it a permanent place; but its usefulness would be greatly enhanced by an appropriate index. Review, v. 1-3, L. Huberti, *Hist. Zeit.* 68:526, 1892; v. 4-7, G. Monod, *Rev. Hist.* 48:376, March 1892; 53:330, Nov. 1893; 58:128, May 1895; 63:131, Jan. 1897.

EWD

ECONOMIC AND SOCIAL HISTORY

M571 Vuitry, Adolphe. *Études sur le régime financier de la France avant la révolution de 1789.* 3 v. Paris, 1877-83. [1, *Les impôts romains dans la Gaule du V* ͤ *siècle, le régime financier de la monarchie féodale au XI* ͤ*, XII* ͤ*, et XIII* ͤ *siècles; 2, Philippe le Bel et ses trois fils, 1285-1328; 3, Les trois premiers Valois, 1328-1380.*]

The term 'régime financier' is, of course, interpreted in its feudal meaning so that much space is accorded coinage problems of the fourteenth century. One of the most careful detailed studies of feudal fiscal institutions. The feudal revenues and administrative machinery are traced in more detail than is possible in the general histories of institutions like (M533*b*) Viollet, but the development of the parlement of Paris and of the local officials is treated at greater length in various special works of recent date. Review, *Rev. Hist.* 8:181, Sept. 1878; C. Bémont, *ibid.* 22:386, July 1883.

APU

M572a Stourm, René. *Les finances de l'ancien régime et de la révolution: origines du système financier actuel.* 2 v. Paris, 1885.

b —— *Les finances du consulat.* Paris, 1902.

c **Gomel, Charles,** *Les causes financières de la révolution française.* 2 v. Paris, 1892-93.

d —— *Histoire financière de l'assemblée constituante.* 2 v. Paris, 1896-97.

e —— *Histoire financière de la législative et la convention.* 2 v. Paris, 1902-05.

a and *b.* Constitute a continuous analysis and narrative of the history of government finance during the critical period. The main purpose is to give in full the historical setting for the origins of the existing system. The period of the Revolution is marked by the determination of principles: the consulate established the institutions that are the basis of the present system. Review of *a, Rev. Hist.* 27:374, March 1885; of *b, ibid.* 81:112, Jan. 1903.

APU

c. Opens with the ministry of Turgot. *c, d,* and *e.* All three works of value because of the author's experience as an administrator. At times wander too far into the political field; attitude often hostile to the Revolution; the problems are studied chiefly from printed sources. Review of *c,* L. Farges, *Rev. Hist.* 50:361, Nov. 1892; 53:339, Nov. 1893; of *e,* R. Reuss, *Rev. Hist.* 83:106, Jan. 1903; 89:103, Sept. 1905.

HEB

M573a Marion, Marcel. *Histoire financière de la France depuis 1715.* 4 v. Paris, 1914-25. [1, *1715-1789; 2, 1789-1792; 3, 1792-1797; 4, 1797-1818.*]

b —— *La vente des biens nationaux pendant la révolution, avec étude spéciale des ventes dans les départements de la Gironde et du Cher.* Paris, 1908.

c —— *Les impôts directs sous l'ancien régime, principalement au XVIII* ͤ *siècle.* Paris, 1910. [Collection de textes sur l'histoire des institutions et des services publics de la France moderne et contemporaine.] (Bibliography.)

d **Vialay, Amédée.** *La vente des biens nationaux pendant la révolution. française.* Paris, 1908.

a. Designed originally as a comprehensive study of the financial history of modern France; brought to a conclusion with the reëstablishment of the national credit in 1818 and the payment of the war indemnity. In v. 1-3, which reach the collapse of the revolutionary paper money, the treatment is more detailed than that in (M572) Stourm's volumes, but v. 4, covering twenty years, is more summary. Does not turn aside from the theme to describe the general history of the Revolution. The author's attitude towards the financial policies of the Revolution is that of a severe critic. He shows once more, as earlier in *b,* that the over-issue of assignats dissipated the immense resources which the state sought to find in the lands of the church and of the emigrant nobles. His exposition of the financial history of the old régime is equally illuminating, especially his re-examination of the case against Calonne. Review of *a,* R. Reuss, *Rev. Hist.* 135-81, Sept. 1920; 140:76, May 1922; of *b, ibid.* 100:337, March 1909. *c.* Includes brief account of each of the direct taxes and a collection of texts which bring into relief their defects and the evils incident to their administration, together with the efforts of the government to remedy the situation. A most convenient instrument for the study of the system. Review, F. M. Fling, *A.H.R.* 16:614, Apr. 1911. *d.* Especially valuable for sales in the department of the Côte d'Or and in the municipality of Paris. The statistics in regard to the comparative value of real estate before, during, and after the Revolution are illuminating. The author is convinced that the larger part of the rural properties of the second, or emigrant, origin was sold in small parcels and passed into the hands of the peasants. Review, G. Monod, *Rev. Hist.* 99:98, Sept. 1908.

HEB

M581a Avenel, Georges d', Vicomte. *Histoire économique de la propriété, des salaires, des denrées, et de tous les prix en général, depuis l'an 1200 jusqu'en l'an 1800.* 6 v. Paris, 1894-1913.

b —— *Paysans et ouvriers depuis sept cents ans.* Paris, 1899.

a. Attempt to describe the changes in cost of living throughout the period 1200 to 1800; painstaking and, in many features, scholarly. The data are insufficient and too widely dispersed over the total area to afford a basis for significant general averages. The materials offer many interesting illustrations of particular prices and wages, and these are of genuine utility if one is cautious in respect to generalization. Although the work is imposing, there are many price materials in manuscript that are not utilized. Review, v. 1-2, E. Castelot, *Rev. Hist.* 61:128, May 1896; v. 3-4, R. Reuss, *Rev. Hist.* 70:348, July 1899. Much of the general descriptive matter in v. 3 and 4 of *a* is embodied in the convenient small volume *b.* Review, *A.H.R.* 5:387, Jan. 1900.

APU

M582a Levasseur, Émile. *Histoire des classes ouvrières et de l'industrie en France avant 1789.* 1859. 2nd rev. ed., 2 v., Paris, 1900-01.

b —— *Histoire des classes ouvrières et de l'industrie en France depuis 1789 à 1870.* 1867. 2nd rev. ed., 2 v., Paris, 1903-04.

c —— *Histoire du commerce de la France.* 2 v. Paris, 1911-12. (Bibliography.)

d ——— *La population française: histoire de la population avant 1789 et démographie de la France comparée à celle des autres nations au XIXe siècle, précédée d'une introduction sur la statistique.* 3 v. Paris, 1889–92.

a and *b.* Constitute the most substantial achievement in the presentation of the economic history of France. The more important manuscript sources have been effectively utilized and the new edition is greatly enlarged. Levasseur possessed critical capacity of the highest order and notable power of concise description. Review of *a*, G. Fagniez, *Rev. Hist.* 80:387, Dec. 1902. *c.* Combined with *a* and *b*, forms a substantially comprehensive survey of the economic history of France. V. 2. Deals with the period since 1789. *d.* Contains, in addition to a full analysis of nineteenth century vital statistics, chapters on the history of population in France and many chapters dealing with conditions in other countries, so that it is a work of great value both to the historian and to the statistician. Review, C. Juglas, *Journal des Économistes,* 12:292, Nov. 1892.   APU

M583a Lachapelle, Georges. *Les finances publiques après la guerre, 1919–1924.* Paris, 1924.

b Peel, George. *Financial crisis of France.* London and N. Y., 1925.

c Macdonald, William. *Reconstruction in France.* N. Y. and London, 1922.

a and *b.* Two of the most instructive books provoked by the financial crisis of 1924 and 1925. The theme of both is the financial policy pursued after the World War closed, which led the country to the verge of bankruptcy. *b.* Devotes three preliminary chapters to the system of taxation which prevailed in France from 1789 to the World War; also discusses the budget of expenditure for the same period. *c.* Describes the process by which the government, after the close of the World War, succeeded in restoring the means of transportation, the industrial equipment, and the housing, in the regions devastated by the struggle; includes an explanation of the methods of financing the whole undertaking. Review, (London) *Times Literary Supplement,* 21:606, Sept. 28, 1922.   HEB

M584 Hayem, Julien, ed. *Mémoires et documents pour servir à l'histoire du commerce et de l'industrie en France.* V. 1–9. Paris, 1911–25.

These volumes, which form a continuing series, include essays and monographs, by the editor and the scholars he has associated with him, upon many phases of French economic life, chiefly of the eighteenth century. They deal with particular industries and centers of trade, utilizing local records and archives, and offer pertinent illustrations of phases of the general economic development of the country. More detailed indication of the topics will be found in the following notices: *Rev. Hist.* 113:84, May 1913; 116:122, 170, May 1914; 126:370, Nov. 1917; 133:283, March 1920; 149:115, May 1925; 151:122, Jan. 1926. Review, v. 9, F. W. Pitman, *A.H.R.* 31:764, July 1926; v. 8–9, J. Letaconnoux, *Rev. d'Hist. Moderne,* 1:232, June 1926.   HEB

M585 Pigeonneau, Henri. *Histoire du commerce de la France.* 2 v. Paris, 1885–88.

Written before the importance and complexity of economic factors were as generally emphasized as at present, this book nevertheless retains its usefulness. Closely confined to maritime trade; clear account of the origin and development of French seaborne commerce, with special reference to the great companies. Review, C. Bémont, *Rev. Hist.* 27:367, March 1885; G. Monod, *ibid.* 40:108, May 1889.   LBP

Cf. (M582c) Levasseur and (K291) Bonnassieux, *Les grandes compagnies de commerce.*

M591a Vaissière, Pierre de. *Gentilshommes campagnards de l'ancienne France: étude sur la condition, l'état social, et les moeurs de la noblesse de province du XVIe au XVIIIe siècle.* 1903. 3rd ed. Paris, 1904.

   b Ducros, Louis. *French society in the eighteenth century.* London, 1926. Tr. by W. deGeijer from *La société française au XVIIIe siècle d'après les mémoires et correspondances du temps,* Paris, 1922.

a. The Revolution often did not content itself with destroying its victims, it sought to rob them of the respect of posterity. So it was with the old nobility which, since that time, has been represented as essentially parasitic, if not lazy and disorderly. In this book the author presents, in pages full of life and color, the results of his studies upon the manners, the social status, and the economic condition of the provincial nobility from the sixteenth century to the Revolution. It is not surprising that his conclusions are favorable to the French country gentleman, for it was chiefly the court nobility whose conduct gave point to the strictures of the Revolutionary orators. Review, H. Hauser, *Rev. Hist.* 84:88, Jan. 1904. Cf. (M300b) Carré, *La noblesse de France.*   HEB

b. Divided into three parts, the first dealing with society at Versailles, the second with life in Paris, and the third with the provinces, including the country gentlemen described in *a.* Chapters on the provinces are of particular interest. Its material is drawn from a wide variety of material by a scholar known from his familiarity with the eighteenth century. Review, A. J. Grant, *History,* 11:256, Oct. 1926.   HRS

M592 Fagniez, Gustave. *L'économie sociale de la France sous Henri IV, 1589–1610.* Paris, 1897.

Brilliant and scholarly work on a difficult subject; presents a vivid picture of the chaos and misery of France at the end of the Wars of Religion; recounts, in orderly detail, the efforts of Henry IV and his associates to better conditions. Careful appraisal reveals the first Bourbon, in spite of his many failures, as an active participant in a general economic, and more especially commercial, renaissance. Review, G. Monod, *Rev. Hist.* 65:345, Nov. 1897.   RHG

M593a Sargent, Arthur J. *Economic policy of Colbert.* London and N. Y., 1899. [Studies in economics and political science.] (Bibliography.)

   b Usher, Abbott P. *History of the grain trade in France, 1400–1710.* Cambridge, Mass., 1913. [Harvard economic studies.] (Bibliography.)

a. Brief but brilliant essay; pioneer work, in English; analyzes closely and lucidly the real significance of Colbert's position in French economic development; emphasizes his influence as more than that of a pettifogging bureaucrat dominated by mercantilist doctrine; considers him a great financier working to lay a broad foundation for French economic growth. Review, W. G. P. Smith, *E.H.R.* 15:197, Jan. 1900. *b.* Very detailed and thorough investigation into the complex internal economy of early modern France; important as a contribution to the study of the economic background of the Revolution; closely documented, but somewhat involved in style. The first part is devoted to a topical study of various phases of the subject; the second traces, by periods, the national and local regulations of the movement of grain. Review, *A.H.R.* 19:874, July 1914.   LBP

M594a Martin, Germain. *La grande industrie sous le règne de Louis XIV, plus particulièrement de 1660 à 1715.* Paris, 1899.

  b —— *La grande industrie en France sous le règne de Louis XV.* Paris, 1900. [Bibliothèque de la Société des Études Historiques.]

  a. Useful manual, comprehensive in scope, conveniently arranged in topical form; important because it is almost the only available treatise covering this subject as a whole. Yet it is in many respects inaccurate and careless, as the use of documents and the citations from other books are not always reliable. Review, Rouxel, *Journal des Économistes,* 5th series, 38:295, Apr. 1899; R. Reuss, *Rev. Hist.* 70:365, July 1899.   LBP

  b. Continuation of *a;* much better done; shows manufacturing well developed. Review, H. Hauser, *Rev. Hist.* 74:334, Nov. 1900.   GMD

M595a Sée, Henri. *L'évolution commerciale et industrielle de la France sous l'ancien régime.* Paris, 1925. (Bibliographies.)

  b —— *Economic and social conditions in France during the eighteenth century.* N. Y., 1927. Tr. by E. H. Zeydel from *La France économique et sociale au XVIIIᵉ siècle,* Paris, 1925. (Bibliographies.)

  c Ballot, Charles. *L'introduction du machinisme dans l'industrie française.* Paris, 1923. [Comité des travaux historiques et scientifiques, *Notices, inventaires, documents.*]

  a. Scholarly history of commerce and industry in France in the seventeenth and eighteenth centuries. The large monographic literature of recent years has been fully utilized, and there is, thus, a notable wealth of carefully selected material and a substantial revision of many judgments. The history of commerce is more carefully handled than in many earlier French works, and as industry and commerce are here drawn together within the compass of a single volume the narrative achieves a balance and comprehensiveness that is quite fresh. Review, E. Laurain, *Rev. des Quest. Hist.* 106:218, Jan. 1927.   APU

  b. Primarily designed as a guide to younger scholars, or a convenient summary for the general reader; also valuable to more advanced students for its presentation of the progress of investigation upon many controversial questions touching eighteenth-century France; best brief treatment of the economic and social condition of the century at that time. Review of *a* and *b,* H. Hauser, *Rev. Hist.* 150:242, Nov. 1925; of *b,* H. E. Bourne, *A.H.R.* 31:351, Jan. 1926.   HEB

  c. By tracing exactly the beginnings of the more important machines, especially in the silk industry, the author shows that the general introduction of machinery was well advanced at the outbreak of the Revolution. He also makes clear that the French movement was more than a reflection of English tendencies. His technical competence adds to the clearness of his presentation, and his work must be regarded as a notable contribution to the history of the industrial revolution. A victim of the World War, his manuscript was completed by a fellow student, Claude Gével. Review, E. Welvert, *Rev. Critique* 91:372, Sept. 15, 1924.   APU

M596a **Nussbaum, Frederick L.** *Commercial policy in the French revolution: a study of the career of G. J. A. Ducher.* Washington, D. C., 1923. [American Historical Association: Herbert Baxter Adams prize.] (Bibliography.)

   b **Mathiez, Albert.** *La vie chère et le mouvement social sous la terreur.* Paris, 1927.

   c **Lefebvre, Georges.** *Les paysans du Nord pendant la révolution française.* 2 v. Paris, 1924.

a. Illustrates, by means of an examination of the career of Ducher, the constructive work along economic lines accomplished during the Revolution; also brings out a difference, hitherto little noticed, between the economic policy of the Gironde and the Mountain, the former being anti-mercantilist and the latter mercantilist. Incidentally it exhibits a phase of American influence, for Ducher had made a special study of the American customs system. Review, E. Ellery, *A.H.R.* 29:765, July 1924.   EEY

b. Invaluable treatment of the shortage of food and other necessaries of life, and of the repercussions of this problem in the factional struggles of 1792 and 1793; especially interesting is the rôle of Jacques Roux and the *Enragés.* Review, H. Sée, *Rev. Hist.* 155:374, July 1927. *c.* Most complete monograph that has yet appeared upon the history of the peasants of a particular department during the Revolution; opens with a detailed description of conditions under the old régime. The problem of land ownership, both before the Revolution and as affected by the sales of ecclesiastical and emigrant property, is dealt with descriptively and by statistical tables which fill v. 2; also includes the experience of the department with the legislation fixing maximum prices. Review, H. Sée, *Rev. Hist.* 147:90, Sept. 1924.   HEB

M597a **Louis, Paul.** *Histoire du parti socialiste en France, 1871–1914.* Paris, 1922.

   b —— *Histoire du mouvement syndical en France, 1789–1910.* 1907. 3rd rev. ed., Paris, 1921. [Bibliothèque d'histoire contemporaine.]

   c —— *Le syndicalisme français d'Amiens à Saint-Étienne, 1906–1922.* Paris, 1924. [Bibliothèque d'histoire contemporaine.]

a. Excellent sketch of the vicissitudes of the socialist groups up to the time when the 'unified' party was constituted. Review, *Rev. Hist.* 141:112, Sept. 1922. *b.* Deals with the trade union movement historically from the point of view of a scholar in deep sympathy with the extreme aims of syndicalism. *c.* Continuation of *b.* Review, G. Bourgin, *Rev. Hist.* 148:280, March 1925.   HEB

M598a **Sée, Henri.** *La vie économique de la France sous la monarchie censitaire, 1815–1848.* Paris, 1927. (Bibliography.)

   b **Pirou, G.** *Les doctrines économiques en France depuis 1870.* Paris, 1925. [Collection Armand Colin.]

a. Excellent survey of the development of agriculture, industry and the use of machinery, organization of the working classes, and commerce. Review, J. M. S. Allison, *A.H.R.* 33:186, Oct. 1927; H. Hauser, *Rev. Critique,* 94:443, Dec. 1. 1927. *b.* Brief exposition.   GMD

CULTURAL HISTORY: GENERAL

M601 Guizot, François P. G. *History of civilization in France from the fall of the Roman empire.* 3 v. London and N. Y., 1846. [V. 2–4 of *History of civilization from the fall of the Roman empire to the French revolution.*] Tr. by W. Hazlitt from *Histoire de la civilisation en France depuis la chute de l'empire romain,* 5 v., 1829–32 [V. 2–6 of *Cours d'histoire moderne professé à la Faculté de Lettres*] ; 15th ed., 4 v., Paris, 1884.

The author's original plan was never carried out, because he was drawn into public administration by the Revolution of 1830. The treatment stops with the fourteenth century. The insight and grasp which Guizot displayed in organizing and interpreting masses of social facts opened a new era in historical investigation and writing. May still be read with advantage.

Cf. (B602) Guizot, *History of civilization in Europe.*   HEB

M602a Rambaud, Alfred. *Histoire de la civilisation française.* 2 v. 1885–87. 11th ed. of v. 1, Paris, 1909; 10th ed. of v. 2, Paris, 1907.

b —— *Histoire de la civilisation contemporaine en France.* 1888. 6th rev. ed., Paris, 1901.

a and *b.* Packed with information upon every phase of the subject; originally intended as a manual for the use of students in the French lycées, but more likely to be useful to teachers. Review, C. Bémont and G. Monod, *Rev. Hist.* 29 :386, Nov. 1885; 33 :364, March 1887; 37 :151, May 1888.   HEB

M603a Tilley, Arthur, ed. *Medieval France, a companion to French studies.* Cambridge, Eng., and N. Y., 1922. (Bibliographies.)

b —— *Modern France, a companion to French studies.* Cambridge, Eng., and N. Y., 1922. (Bibliographies.)

These volumes represent the coöperative method applied within brief compass. They include accounts of the general history of France during the medieval and the modern periods, the first written by C. V. Langlois, and the second divided between MM. Hauser, Bourgeois, Aulard, and Weill. There are also chapters upon the church, the army, architecture, literature, and economic life. In *a* there is a sketch of the geography of France by Professor Gallois. The majority of the writers are French, representing some of the best known names in French scholarship. Their work, as well as that of their English collaborators, offers a ready means of learning authoritative conclusions upon many phases of French historical development. Review of *a,* A. C. Howland, *A.H.R.* 28 :532, Apr. 1923; of *b, E.H.R.* 39 :639, Oct. 1924.   HEB

M604a Evans, Joan. *Life in mediaeval France.* London and N. Y., 1925. (Bibliography.)

b Langlois, Charles V. *La vie en France au moyen âge de la fin du XIIᵉ siècle au milieu du XIVᵉ siècle.* V. 1–3, Paris, 1924–27. [1, *D'après des romans mondains du temps* (1st ed., 1903) ; 2, *D'après des moralistes du temps* (1st ed., 1908) ; 3, *La connaissance de la nature et du monde d'après des écrits en français à l'usage des laïcs.* 1928.] (Excellent bibliographies.)

a. Selections from contemporary chansons and the more lively chronicles illustrate the more picturesque aspects and incidents of medieval life in France; grouped under such headings as: feudal society, monasticism, and the crusades;

useful notwithstanding many questionable generalizations; excellent illustrations. Review, E. W. Dow, *A.H.R.* 31:306, Jan. 1926; T. S. R. Boase, *History,* 11:241, Oct. 1926.   HRS

b. Life in medieval France is illustrated by admirably edited selections from contemporary texts; useful to students who can read the French of the period. Review, C. W. David, *A.H.R.* 30:633, Apr. 1925; 31:560, Apr. 1926; E. Faral, *Rev. Critique,* 94:303, Aug. 15, 1927.   GMD

M611 Guérard, Albert L. *French civilization from its origins to the close of middle ages.* London and Boston, 1920. (Bibliography.)

Well-arranged and useful work of popularization; convenient, comprehensive survey of the background of early French history; reviews, in about three hundred pages, the various forces which have molded France and its inhabitants, even from prehistoric times; touches upon ethnology, literature, art, philosophy, the church, feudalism, the communes, etc. Review, C. H. C. Wright, *A.H.R.* 26:755, July 1921.   CHCW

M612 Dill, Sir Samuel. *Roman society in Gaul in the Merovingian age.* London, 1926. Ed. by C. B. Armstrong and others.

Posthumous publication; like his earlier works (E614) on Roman society under the empire, readable, informing, and suggestive; fills a gap in the treatment of French history in English; unfortunately does not give consideration to the results of various recent critical studies on the period; more favorable to the church than many histories of Merovingian times. Review, N. H. Baynes, *E.H.R.* 42:269, Apr. 1927; L. Halphen, *Rev. Hist.* 155:382, July 1927.

Also cf. (H203*b*) Gregory of Tours, *History of the Franks.*   HRS

M613 Tilley, Arthur. *Dawn of the French renaissance.* Cambridge, Eng. and N. Y., 1918.

Elaborate study, reaching back into Italy; includes history scholarship, literature, and art; scholarly and accurate but with much unimportant and confusing detail. Review, E. M. Hulme, *A.H.R.* 24:466, Apr. 1919.   CHCW

M614 Guérard, Albert L. *French civilization in the nineteenth century, a historical introduction.* London and N. Y., 1914. (Bibliographies.)

Interesting, but not entirely adequate, study of the development of French civilization during the past century and its relation to the political developments of the time; useful for the student both of French literature and of French history. Review, *Athenaeum,* 1:191, Feb. 7, 1914.   .   JMSA

M615a Bracq, Jean C. *France under the republic.* 1910. 2nd rev. ed., N. Y., 1916.

b Baillaud, Benjamin, and others. *Un demi-siècle de civilisation française, 1870–1915.* Paris, 1916.

c Huddleston, Sisley. *France and the French.* London and N. Y., 1925. [(B137*b*) Modern world.]

a. Readable survey of the general progress of French civilization since 1870; written in vindication of the Third Republic; useful and well-referenced synthesis of varied material, especially that dealing with intellectual, social, and religious developments. A fair sense of proportion is maintained, but the writer, a Protestant, although moderate in the treatment of religious questions, is inclined to glorify the achievements and policies of the Republic without discrimination. Review, J. T. Shotwell, *A.H.R.* 16:624, Apr. 1911.   ALG

b. Composed of chapters by twenty specialists each of whom treats his chosen portion of the field of French culture under the Third Republic. Review, J. T. Shotwell, *A.H.R.* 22:379, Jan. 1917.   *c.* Recent, popular survey by English publicist. Review, R. M. Lovett, *New Republic* 45:193, Jan. 6, 1926.   GMD

CULTURAL HISTORY: RELIGION

M631a Galton, Arthur. *Church and state in France, 1300–1907.* London, 1907. (Bibliography.)

b Sloane, William M. *French revolution and religious reform: an account of ecclesiastical legislation and its influence on affairs in France from 1789 to 1804.* N. Y., 1901. [Morse lectures.]

c La Gorce, Pierre de. *Histoire religieuse de la révolution française.* 5 v. Paris, 1909–23. Various reprints.

a. Lucid survey of a vast and difficult field. The first three chapters give a clear account of Gallicanism under the old régime. The other chapters are a convenient abridgement of (M632) Debidour, thus made available to English readers. The author, a liberal English clergyman, makes a much better case for the civil constitution of the clergy than is usual with English historians. Review, *Athenaeum*, 1:472, Apr. 20, 1907. *b.* Brief survey; favorable to the church. Review, S. Mathews, *A.H.R.* 7:778, July 1902. *c.* Comprehensive work by one of the ablest living French historians; sympathetic in its attitude toward the church. Review, v. 1–4, *A.H.R.* 15:384, Jan. 1910; 18:583, Apr. 1913; 27:791, July 1922; v. 5, E. L. Woodward, *E.H.R.* 39:298, Apr. 1924; v. 1, P. Pisani, *Rev. des Quest. Hist.* 86:613, July 1909; v. 3–5, R. Reuss, Rev. Hist. 140:77, May 1922; 145:91, Jan. 1924.   ALG

M632a Debidour, Antonin. *Histoire des rapports de l'église et de l'état en France de 1789 à 1870.* Paris, 1898. [Bibliothèque d'histoire contemporaine.] (Bibliographies.)

b —— *L'église catholique et l'état sous la troisième république, 1870–1906.* 2 v. Paris, 1906–09. [Bibliothèque d'histoire contemporaine.] (Bibliographies.)

Although frequently marred by a polemical tone (the author is an outspoken anti-clerical), these volumes are scholarly as well as exhaustive. The conservative Académie des Sciences Morales et Politiques gave a prize to *a,* which is sufficient guarantee of impartiality. Contain all that is essential to the understanding of the problems involved in the relation between church and state in France. Review of *a,* A. Lichtenberger, *Rev. Hist.* 67:350, July 1898; C. Pfister, *ibid.* 74:178, Sept. 1900; C. L. Wells, *A.H.R.* 6:362, Jan. 1901; of *b,* A. Lichtenberger, *Rev. Hist.* 94:336, July 1907; E. Driault, *ibid.* 103:119, Jan. 1910.   ALG

M633a Mathiez, Albert. *Rome et le clergé français sous la constituante: la constitution civile du clergé, l'affaire d'Avignon.* Paris, 1911.

b —— *Les origines des cultes révolutionnaires, 1789–1792.* Paris, 1904. [Bibliothèque d'histoire moderne.]

c —— *La théophilanthropie et le culte décadaire, 1796–1801: essai sur l'histoire religieuse de la révolution.* Paris, 1903. [Bibliothèque de la Fondation Thiers.]

a. In research, criticism, and synthesis, the most scholarly volume that has yet been written on the religious history of the Revolution. Seeks to show that the majority of the French clergy were ready to put the civil constitution of the clergy into effect if it could be done canonically, that is, under papal authority. The difficulty was to persuade the pope to consent to the termination of his own jurisdiction in France. Review, P. Pisani, *Rev. des Quest. Hist.* 90:521, July 1911; H. E. Bourne, *A.H.R.* 16:852, July 1911. *b* and *c.* Illuminating accounts of the revolutionary cults. Review, G. M. Dutcher, *A.H.R.* 10:409, Jan. 1905; 10:189, Oct. 1904.   FMF

M634a Boulay de la Meurthe, Alfred, Comte. *Histoire de la négociation du concordat de 1801.* Tours, 1920.

   b —— *Histoire du rétablissement du culte en France, 1802–1805.* Tours, 1925.

   c ——, ed. *Documents sur la négociation du concordat et sur les autres rapports de la France avec le Saint-Siège en 1800 et 1801.* 5 v. Paris, 1891–97. [Société d'Histoire Diplomatique.]

   d Lévy-Schneider, L. *L'application du concordat par un prélat d'ancien régime, Mgr. Champion de Cicé, archevêque d'Aix et d'Arles, 1802–1810.* Paris, 1921.

By the preparation of *c* (Review, L. Farges and G. Monod, *Rev. Hist.* 48:102, Jan. 1892; 50:95, Sept. 1892; 52:352, July 1893; 65:341, Nov. 1897), the author was eminently qualified to deal authoritatively in *a* with the intricate manoeuvres out of which came the settlement of the schism in the French church. The narrative closes with the signature of the agreement on September 8 and the exchange of ratifications two days later. Review, R. Reuss, *Rev. Hist.* 140:97, May 1922. *b.* Deals with the difficulties which deferred the full application of the concordat for several months, the problem of dissident and emigrant bishops, and the negotiations which brought Pope Pius VII to Paris for the coronation of Napoleon. Review, R. Guyot, *Rev. Hist.* 151:228, March 1926. *d.* Illustrates the difference between a law and its application, for Champion de Cicé, a liberal ecclesiastic under the old régime, displayed in the reëstablished church great skill and patience in reconstituting in practice much of the position lost through the Revolution and not legally restored by the concordat. Review, C. Guignebert, *Rev. Hist.* 140:236, July 1922.   HEB

CULTURAL HISTORY: EDUCATION, THOUGHT, PHILOSOPHY

M641a Compayré, Gabriel. *Histoire critique des doctrines de l'éducation en France depuis le seizième siècle.* 1879. 7th ed., 2 v., Paris, 1904.

   b Liard, Louis. *L'enseignement supérieur en France de 1789 à 1893.* 2 v. Paris, 1888–94.

a. Has long been the standard history of the development in France of educational theory and of educational institutions as well; prefaced by a substantial sketch of education prior to the sixteenth century. Rabelais is the first writer whose doctrines are described in detail. The treatment does not cover the latter part of the nineteenth century. *b.* Equally authoritative description of higher education; opens with a detailed statement of the condition of the universities before the changes incident to the Revolution began. Its value is enhanced by the large number of illustrative documents in the appendixes. Review, G. Monod, *Rev. Hist.* 38:380, Nov. 1888; 55:382, July 1894.   HEB

M646 Lévy-Bruhl, Lucien. *History of modern philosophy in France.* Tr. from French manuscript by G. Coblence. Chicago, 1899. (Bibliography.)

Surveys French philosophy from Descartes to the close of the nineteenth century; gives special attention to the eighteenth century; series of essays rather than well-proportioned systematic history. Review, D. Irons, *Philosophical Rev.* 9:429, July 1900.   GMD

M651a Bergson, Henri, and others. *La science française.* 2 v. Paris, 1915. [Ministère de l'Instruction Publique.] (Bibliography.)

b Wigmore, John H., ed. *Science and learning in France, with a survey of opportunities for American students in French universities: an appreciation by American scholars.* [N. Y.] 1917. [Society for American Fellowships in French Universities.]

a. Records of French contributions to science and learning in twenty fields by as many experts. Review, *A.H.R.* 21:853, July 1916. *b.* Appreciative survey of higher education and research in France at the beginning of the World War. Review, C. H. Van Tyne, *A.H.R.* 23:391, Jan. 1918.   GMD

CULTURAL HISTORY: LITERATURE

M661a Saintsbury, George. *Short history of French literature from the earliest texts to the close of the nineteenth century.* 1882. 7th rev. ed., Oxford, 1917.

b Nitze, William A., and **Dargan, Edwin Preston.** *History of French literature from the earliest times to the great war.* N. Y., 1922; London, 1923. (Bibliography.)

c Strachey, Giles Lytton. *Landmarks in French literature.* 1912. Reprint, London and N. Y., 1923. [Home university library.] (Brief bibliography.)

d Wright, Charles H. C. *History of French literature.* 1912. New ed., N. Y., 1925. (Extensive bibliography.)

e —— *Background of modern French literature.* Boston, 1926. (Bibliography.)

f Tilley, Arthur. *Literature of the French renaissance.* 2 v. Cambridge, Eng. and N. Y., 1904.

g —— *From Montaigne to Molière, or, the preparation for the classical age of French literature.* 1908. 2nd rev. ed., Cambridge, Eng. and N. Y., 1923.

h Wright, Charles H. C. *French classicism.* Cambridge, Mass., 1920. [Harvard studies in Romance languages.]

a, b, c, d, and *e.* Popular short histories of French literature intended for English readers. Review of *a, Athenaeum* 2:522, Oct. 21, 1882; of *b,* J. J. Smertenko, *Nation* (N. Y.) 117:93, July 25, 1923; of *c,* H. Salpeter, *ibid.* 117:198, Aug. 22, 1923; of *d, ibid.* 94:640, June 27, 1912; of *e, A.H.R.* 31:825, July 1926. *f* and *g.* Tilley (cf. M603, 613), long recognized as an authority on the literary history of the French renaissance, has done more than any other writer to keep the English public informed on this period of French literature. Review of *f, Athenaeum,* 1:647, May 27, 1905; of *g, Spectator,* 102:182, Jan. 20, 1909. *h.* Useful treatise addressed to students rather than to the general reader. Review, F. Baldensperger, *Rev. Critique* 88:178, May 1, 1921.   AS

M662a Brunot, Ferdinand. *Histoire de la langue française des origines à 1900.*
V. 1–5, 7, and 9, pt. 1, in 9. Paris, 1905–27. [*1, *De l'époque latine à*
la renaissance; *2, *Le seizième siècle;* *3, *La formation de la langue*
classique, 1600–1660, 2 pt.; *4, *La langue classique, 1660–1715,* 2 pt.; *5,
Le français en France et hors de France au XVIIe siècle; 6, *Le XVIIIe*
siècle, pt. 1, *La philosophie et la langue;* pt. 2, *L'époque post-classique:*
tradition et nouveautés; *7, *La propagation du français en France jusqu'à*
la fin de l'ancien régime; 8, *La propagation du français en Europe: le*
français langue universelle; 9, *La révolution et l'empire,* *pt. 1, *Le français, langue nationale;* pt. 2, *Mouvement interne de la langue: perte de*
l'hégémonie en Europe.] (Bibliographies.)

b Brunetière, Ferdinand, and others. *Histoire de la littérature française*
classique, 1515–1830. 4 v. in 6. Paris, 1904–17.

c Faguet, Émile. *Histoire de la littérature française.* 2 v. Paris, 1900.
19th ed. of v. 1, 1916; 20th ed. of v. 2, 1913.

d Lanson, Gustave. *Histoire de la littérature française.* 1894. 18th rev.
ed., Paris, 1924. Illustrated ed., 2 v., Paris, 1923.

a. Masterly work, on a very broad basis; constantly connects the history of the
French language with social and political history. Review, v. 1–2, H. Chatelain,
Rev. d'Hist. Littéraire de la France, 13:742, Oct. 1906; v. 5–7, E. Bourciez, *Rev.
Critique* 85:166, May 1, 1918; 93:311, Aug. 15, 1926; v. 9, pt. 1, L. Brandin, *Rev.
d'Hist Moderne* 2:388, Sept. 1927. *b.* Keen and erudite work; strongly colored
by the religious, often reactionary, views of the author, that is, he exalts the
literature of the time of Louis XIV at the expense of that of post-revolutionary
France and especially of realism. *c.* Very genial presentation; wholly free from
any such bias as *b. d.* Admirable, succinct survey; embodies the critical and
philosophical results of the author's remarkable knowledge of both the literature
itself and the sources for its history; text is somewhat modified in the excellently
illustrated edition. Review, *Rev. Hist.* 144:263, Nov. 1923.   AS .

M663a Petit de Julleville, Louis, ed. *Histoire de la langue et de la littérature*
française des origines à 1900. 8 v. Paris, 1896–99. [1–2, *Moyen âge;*
3, *Seizième siècle;* 4, *Dix-septième siècle, 1601–1660;* 5, *Dix-septième*
siècle, 1661–1700; 6, *Dix-huitième siècle;* 7, *Dix-neuvième siècle, période*
romantique, 1800–1850; 8, *Dix-neuvième siècle, période contemporaine,*
1850–1900.]

b Bédier, Joseph, and **Hazard, Paul,** ed. *Histoire de la littérature française illustrée.* 2 v. Paris, 1923–24. (Bibliographies.)

a. Scholarly and very readable coöperative work; topics were allotted to specialists by chapters, not by volumes. As a rule, the chapters are excellent, though
some—for instance, the one on Victor Hugo—are less good. *b.* Coöperative
work similar to *a;* Bédier was especially in charge of medieval, and Hazard of
modern, French literature. After the period of romanticism, the chapters are
less satisfactory, owing chiefly to the formidable amount of material. For the
most recent period and for recent bibliography, it supplements *a,* which stops in
1900. Both *a* and *b* are very intelligently illustrated. Review of *b, Rev. Hist.*
144:262, Nov. 1923.

For a much briefer and less complete treatment, cf. v. 12–13 of (M123) Hanotaux, *Histoire de la nation française,* in which Picavet's contribution on the Latin
writings of French authors is very important as it supplements and corrects the
older accounts in (M664) *Histoire littéraire de la France,* and Strowski's treatment of the recent period should also be noted.   AS

M664 Rivet de la Grange, Antoine, and others. *Histoire littéraire de la France: ouvrage commencé par des religieux Bénédictins de la Congrégation de Saint Maur, et continué par des membres de l'Institut (Académie des Inscriptions et Belles Lettres).* V. 1–36. Paris, 1733–1927. [1, *I*er *au IV*e *siècles;* 2, *V*e *siècle;* 3, *VI*e *et VII*e *siècles;* 4–5, *VIII*e *et IX*e *siècles;* 6, *X*e *siècle;* 7–8, *XI*e *siècle;* 9–15, *XII*e *siècle;* 16–23, *XIII*e *siècle;* 24–36, *XIV*e *siècle.*] (Indexes in v. 15, 23, 32.)

Contains very careful and elaborate studies by different scholars; among the most valuable is v. 30, Gaston Paris, *Romans de la table ronde* (1888). Review, v. 35–36, *Rev. Hist.* 139:280, March 1922; 149:107, May 1925; 155:433, July 1927.

AS

M665 Smith, Justin H. *Troubadours at home, their lives and personalities, their songs and their world.* 2 v. N. Y. and London, 1899. (Bibliography.)

Mentions about one hundred and ten troubadours; treats fifty in some detail; offers abundant information on the period, on the historical circumstances, and especially on the present appearance of the land of the troubadours. Not the least valuable are the specimens of the early poetry of France. Review, F. M. Warren, *A.H.R.* 5:559, Apr. 1900.

AS

M666 Lalou, René. *Contemporary French literature.* N. Y., 1924; London, 1925. Tr. by W. A. Bradley from *Histoire de la littérature française contemporaine, 1870 à nos jours, 1922;* 65th rev. ed., Paris, 1925. (Bibliography.)

Best known manual dealing with recent French literature. Review, P. Arbelet, *Rev. d'Hist. Moderne* 2:145, March 1927.

GMD

CULTURAL HISTORY: ART

M681a Enlart, Camille. *Manuel d'archéologie française depuis les temps Mérovingiens jusqu'à la renaissance.* 3 v. Paris, 1902–16. 2nd rev. ed. of v. 1, in 2 pt. and index, Paris, 1919–21; 3rd rev. ed. of v. 1, pt. 1, Paris, 1927. (Bibliographies.)

b Mâle, Émile. *L'art religieux du XII*e *siècle en France: étude sur les origines de l'iconographie du moyen âge.* Paris, 1922. (Bibliography.)

c —— *Religious art in France, XIII century, a study in mediaeval iconography and its sources of inspiration.* London and N. Y., 1913. Tr. by D. Mussey from *L'art religieux du XIII*e *siècle en France: étude sur l'iconographie du moyen âge et sur ses sources d'inspiration,* 1898; 3rd rev. ed., Paris, 1909. (Bibliography.)

d —— *L'art religieux de la fin du moyen âge en France: étude sur l'iconographie du moyen âge et sur ses sources d'inspiration.* Paris, 1908.

e Gonse, Louis. *L'art gothique: l'architecture, la peinture, la sculpture, le décor.* Paris, 1890.

f —— *La sculpture française depuis le XIV*e *siècle.* Paris, 1895.

g Hourticq, Louis. *Art in France.* N. Y., 1911. [Ars una, species mille: general history of art.] Tr. from *Histoire générale de l'art, France,* Paris, 1911 [Ars una, species mille]. (Bibliographies.)

h Ward, William H. *Architecture of the renaissance in France: a history of the evolution of the arts of building, decoration, and garden design under classical influence from 1495 to 1830.* 2 v. London and N. Y., 1911.

a. Excellent book, in which the methods of French builders in the Middle Ages are described and the historical development of medieval art in France is portrayed. The point of view is technical and historical, rather than esthetic. Review, A. Molinier, *Rev. Hist.* 80:91, Sept. 1902; L. Halphen, *ibid.* 125:108, May 1917; 133:102, Jan. 1920; 138:240, Nov. 1921. *b, c,* and *d.* Discuss the content of medieval art, not its technical methods or its esthetic value. Especial stress is laid upon the literary sources of inspiration of medieval art. The plan is well worked out and the numerous illustrations excellent. Review of *c,* B. Monod, *Rev. Hist.* 72:359, March 1900; of *d,* L. Hourticq, *ibid.* 103:358, March 1910. *e* and *f.* Richly illustrated; treat the development of architecture, and of glass-painting, sculpture, and other arts which attended it. *e.* Not limited to the Gothic period. Review, G. Monod, *Rev. Hist.* 45:371, March 1891. *g.* Illustrated handbook; covers a very large field in an astonishingly successful and thorough manner. Review, *Athenaeum* 1:695, June 17, 1911. *h.* Of high character and well illustrated. Review, W. R. Lethaby, *E.H.R.* 27:353, Apr. 1912.

Also cf. (H686) Adams, *Mont-Saint-Michel and Chartres.*   HNF

M682 Dimier, Louis, and **Réau, Louis.** *Histoire de la peinture française.* 5 v. Paris, 1926–27.

Fully illustrated; covers from 1300 to 1790; by well-known French authorities.
GMD

BIOGRAPHIES

The French have, doubtless, excelled all other peoples in the art and practice of writing memoirs. Works of this type are not infrequent in the medieval period and abound for the modern period. They differ considerably in interest for the general reader but still more widely in their value to the critical historian who must, in each instance, determine carefully the questions of authenticity and credibility. A large proportion of the more important memoirs for the period prior to 1815 will be found in one or more of the following collections: (M701) François P. G. Guizot, ed., *Collection des mémoires relatifs à l'histoire de France depuis la fondation de la monarchie française jusqu'au XIIIᵉ siècle, avec une introduction, des suppléments, des notices, et des notes,* 31 v., Paris, 1823–35, in which the earlier works are presented in translations into modern French; (M702) Claude B. Petitot, Alexandre Petitot, Bernard L. J. Monmerqué, and others, ed., *Collection complète des mémoires relatifs à l'histoire de France depuis le règne de Philippe-Auguste jusqu'à la Paix de Paris, 1763, avec des notices sur chaque auteur et des observations sur chaque ouvrage,* 131 v. (series 1, 52 v.; series 2, 79 v.), Paris, 1819–29; (M703) Joseph F. Michaud and Jean J. F. Poujoulat, ed., *Nouvelle collection des mémoires pour servir à l'Histoire de France depuis le XIIIᵉ siècle jusqu'à la fin de XVIIIᵉ, précédés des notices . . . , suivis de l'analyse de documents qui s'y rapportent,* 32 v. (series 1, 12 v.; series 2, 10 v.; series 3, 10 v.), Paris, 1836–39 (the publisher's remainder of the series was sold with new title pages dated 1850); (M704) Jean F. Barrière and Mathurin F. Adolphe de Lescure, ed., *Bibliothèque des mémoires relatifs à l'histoire de France pendant le XVIIIᵉ siècle, avec avant-propos et notices,* 37 v. (series 1, 28 v.; series 2, 9 v.), Paris, 1846–81 (*Table alphabétique des noms propres,* by Alfred Marquiset, Paris, 1913 [Revue des bibliothèques supplément 9]); (M705) Saint-Albin Berville and Jean F. Barrière, ed., *Collection des mémoires relatifs à la révolution française, avec des notices et des éclaircissements historiques,* 60 v., Paris, 1820–27. Both (M702) Petitot and Monmerqué, and (M703) Michaud and Poujoulat, are marred by defects in editing, although in this respect the latter is an improvement upon the former of which it is in part a reproduction. (M704) Barrière and Lescure, embodies, in addition to others, a number of the memoirs printed in (M705) Berville and Barrière.

Later and better critical editions of many memoirs in the preceding series (M701–705), together with standard editions of other memoirs are included in (M926) *Publications* of the Société de l'Histoire de France. Numerous other memoirs and materials of a biographical nature have been issued by (M929b) Société d'Histoire Contemporaine, by other historical societies, national, provincial, and local, and by societies devoted to the study of special periods or subjects. The best critical editions of a few of the most important memoirs are to be found in (M706) *Les grands écrivains de la France,* Paris, 1862 ff., which also includes excellent editions of works important to the student of history as well as to the student of literature. These editions are usually supplemented with valuable introductions, notes, and commentaries. Excellent brief lives of the leading French authors, written by eminent scholars and littérateurs, appear in a supplementary series (M707a) *Les grands écrivains français,* Paris, 1887 ff., of which some volumes have been translated in the series (M707b) *Great French writers,* Chicago, 1887 ff. More recently there has been launched (M708) *Figures du passé,* Paris, 1913 ff., a series of biographies, also by distinguished writers and scholars, of the principal personages in French political history, most of which have appeared in English translation though not as a series. A few outstanding works from the eight series mentioned above are listed elsewhere in this section.

The following list is an attempt to select from the wealth of resources some of the works of biographical and autobiographical character, in addition to those already listed in this section, which are of special importance either because of their interest for the general reader or because of their value to the student of history.

Medieval period. In addition to (H221a) Einhard, *Life of Charlemagne,* and (H359b) Joinville, *Memoirs,* there are: (M711) Ferdinand Lot, *Études sur le règne de Hugues Capet et la fin du Xe siècle,* Paris, 1903 [Bibliothèque de l'École des Hautes Études]; (M712) Christian Pfister, *Études sur le règne de Robert le Pieux, 996–1031,* Paris, 1885 [Bibliothèque de l'École des Hautes Études]; (M713) Henri Malo, *Un grand feudataire, Renaud de Dammartin et la coalition de Bouvines: contribution à l'étude du règne de Philippe-Auguste,* Paris, 1898; (M714) Élie Berger, *Histoire de Blanche de Castille, reine de France,* Paris, 1895 [Bibliothèque des Écoles Françaises d'Athènes et de Rome]; (M715a) Marius Sepet, *Saint Louis,* Paris, 1898 [Les Saints]; (M715b) Louis S. Le Nain de Tillemont, *Vie de Saint Louis, roi de France,* ed. by J. de Gaulle, 6 v., Paris, 1846–51 [Société de l'Histoire de France]; (M716) François T. Perrens, *Étienne Marcel, prévôt des marchands, 1354–1358,* Paris, 1875 [Histoire générale de Paris]; (M717) Siméon Luce, *Histoire de Bertrand du Guesclin et de son époque: la jeunesse de Bertrand, 1320–1364,* 1876, 2nd ed., Paris, 1882; (M718a)[1] Jules Quicherat, *Aperçus nouveaux sur l'histoire de Jeanne d'Arc,* Paris, 1850; (M718b) Marius Sepet, *Jeanne d'Arc,* Paris, 1869; later ed.; (M718c) Siméon Luce, *Jeanne d'Arc à Domremy: recherches critiques sur les origines de la mission de la Pucelle, accompagnées de pièces justificatives,* 1886, 2nd ed., Paris, 1887; (M718d) Henri A. Wallon, *Jeanne d'Arc,* 1860, 6th ed., 2 v., Paris, 1893; (M718e) Andrew Lang, *Maid of France, being the story of the life and death of*

[1] Also cf. (M 235b, 926a).

Jeanne d'Arc, London and N. Y., 1908, later ed.; (M718f) Anatole France, *Vie de Jeanne d'Arc*, 2 v., Paris, 1908, illustrated ed., 4 v., Paris, 1909–10; (M719) Pierre Clément, *Jacques Coeur et Charles VII, l'administration, les finances, l'industrie, le commerce, les lettres, et les arts au XVe siècle: étude historique, précédée d'une notice sur la valeur des anciennes monnaies françaises,* 1853, 3rd rev. ed., 2 v., Paris, 1865; (M720a) Louis XI, roi de France, *Lettres*, ed. by Joseph Vaesen, Étienne Charavay, and B. de Mandrot, 11 v., Paris, 1883–1909 [Société de l'Histoire de France]; (M720b) Pierre Champion, *Louis XI,* 2 v., Paris, 1927 [Bibliothèque du XVe siècle]; (M721) Olivier de la Marche, *Mémoires du maître d'hôtel et capitaine des gardes de Charles le Téméraire,* ed. by H. Beaune and J. d'Arbaumont, 4 v., Paris, 1883–89 [Société de l'Histoire de France]; (M722) Albert Lecoy de la Marche, *Le roi René, sa vie, son administration, ses travaux artistiques et littéraires,* 2 v., Paris, 1875; (M723) Henri L. J. Forgeot, *Jean Balue, cardinal d'Angers, 1421?–1491,* Paris, 1895 [Bibliothèque de l'École des Hautes Études]; (M724) Charles VIII, roi de France, *Lettres,* ed. by P. Pelicier, 5 v., Paris, 1898–1905 [Société de l'Histoire de France]; (M725) Adrien J. V. Le Roux de Lincy, *Vie de la reine Anne de Bretagne, femme des rois de France Charles VIII et Louis XII, suivie de lettres inédites et de documents originaux,* 4 v., Lyon and Paris, 1860–61; (M726) Marie A. René de Maulde La Clavière, *Histoire de Louis XII,* 6 v., Paris, 1889–93.

Sixteenth century. (M731) Jacques Joffrey (pseud. Le Loyal Serviteur), *La très joyeuse, plaisante, et récréative histoire du gentil seigneur de Bayart,* 1527; new ed. by J. Roman, Paris, 1878 [Société de l'Histoire de France]; (M732) *Journal d'un bourgeois de Paris sous le règne de François Premier, 1515–1536,* ed. by Ludovic Lalanne, Paris, 1854 [Société de l'Histoire de France]; later ed. by V. L. Bourrilly, Paris, 1910 [Collection de textes pour servir à l'étude et à l'enseignement de l'histoire]; (M733) Antoine de Bourbon and Jehanne d'Albret, *Lettres, 1538–1572,* ed. by Achille L. de Vimeux, Marquis de Rochambeau, Paris, 1877 [Société de l'Histoire de France]; (M734a) Martin du Bellay and Guillaume du Bellay, *Mémoires,* ed. by V. L. Bourrilly and F. Vindry, 4 v., Paris, 1908–19 [Société de l'Histoire de France]; (M734b) V. L. Bourrilly, *Guillaume du Bellay, seigneur de Langey, 1491–1543,* Paris, 1905; (M735a) Pierre de Bourdeille, seigneur de Brantôme, *Oeuvres complètes,* ed. by Ludovic Lalanne, 11 v., Paris, 1864–82 [Société de l'Histoire de France]; (M735b) Ludovic Lalanne, *Brantôme, sa vie et ses écrits,* Paris, 1896 [Société de l'Histoire de France]; (M736a) Comte Jules Delaborde, *Gaspard de Coligny, amiral de France,* 3 v., Paris, 1879–82; (M736b) Erich Marcks, *Gaspard von Coligny: sein Leben und das Frankreich seiner Zeit,* v. 1, pt. 1, Stuttgart, 1892; (M736c) Arthur W. Whitehead, *Gaspard de Coligny, admiral of France,* London, 1904; (M737) Blaise de Montluc, maréchal de France, *Commentaires et lettres,* ed. by Alphonse de Ruble, 5 v., Paris, 1865–72 [Société de l'Histoire de France]; also ed. by P. Courteault, 3 v., Paris, 1911–25 [Collection de textes pour servir à l'étude et à l'enseignement de l'histoire]; (M738) Pierre de l'Estoile, *Mémoires-journaux, 1574–1610,* ed. by G. Brunet and others, 12 v., Paris, 1875–96; (M739a) Guillaume de Saulx, seigneur de Tavannes, *Mémoires.* 1625; Paris, 1823 [(M702) Petitot, *Collection*]; Paris, 1838 [M703) Michaud, *Collection*]; (M739b) Jean de Saulx, Vicomte de Tavannes, *Mémoires de Gaspard de Saulx, seigneur de Tavannes,* 1657; 3 v., Paris, 1822 [(M702) Petitot, *Collection*]; Paris, 1838 [(M703) Michaud, *Collection*]; (M739c) Léonce Pingaud, *Les Saulx-Tavannes,* Paris, 1876; (M740) Marguerite de Valois, *Mémoires et lettres,* ed. by F. Guessard, Paris, 1842 [Société de l'Histoire de France]; (M741) Pierre de Vaissière, *Récits du temps des troubles (XVIᵉ siècle):* v. 1, *De quelques assassins: Jean Poltrot, seigneur de Méré; Charles de Louviers, seigneur de Maurevert; Jean Yanowitz, dit Besme; Henri III et les 'Quarante-Cinq'; Jacques Clément;* v. 2, *Une famille: les d'Algère,* Paris, 1912–14; (M742) Jacques A. de Thou, *Mémoires,* 1620; Paris, 1823 [(M702) Petitot, *Collection*]; Paris, 1839 [(M703) Michaud, *Collection*]; (M743a) Philippe de Mornay, seigneur du Plessis-Marly, *Mémoires et correspondance,* 12 v., Paris, 1824–25; (M743b) Charlotte du Plessis-Marly, *Mémoires: édition revue sur les manuscrits, publiée avec les variantes et accompagnée de lettres inédites de M. et Mme. du Plessis-Mornay et de leurs enfants,* 2 v., Paris, 1870–73 [Société de l'Histoire de France], abridged tr. by Lucy Crump, with the title, *A Huguenot family in the XVI. century,* London and N. Y., 1925 [Broadway translations]; (M744) Théodore Agrippa d'Aubigné, *Mémoires,* 1729; new ed. by Ludovic Lalanne, Paris, 1854; (M745) Henri IV, roi de France, *Recueil des Lettres missives,* ed. by Jules Berger de Xivrey and Joseph Guadet, 9 v., Paris, 1843–76 [Collection de documents inédits].

Seventeenth century. (M751a) François A., duc d'Estrées, maréchal de France, *Mémoires sur la régence de Marie de Médicis, 1610–1616, et sur celle d'Anne d'Autriche, 1643–1650,* 1666; ed. by Paul Bonnefon, Paris, 1910 [Société de l'Histoire de France]; (M751b) Louis Batiffol, *Marie de Médicis and the French court in the XVIIth century,* London and N. Y., 1908, tr. by Mary King and ed. by H. W. Carless Davis from *La vie intime d'une reine de France au XVIIᵉ siècle,* Paris, 1906; (M752) Henri, duc de Rohan, prince de Léon, *Mémoires,* 1644; 2 v., Paris, 1822 [(M702) Petitot, *Collection*]; Paris, 1837 [(M703) Michaud, *Collection*]; (M753a) Armand J. du Plessis, cardinal, duc de Richelieu, *Mémoires,* 1823; ed. by Charles P. M., comte Horric de Beaucaire, François Bruel, and Robert Lavollée, v. 1–7 (to 1627), Paris, 1907–26 [Société de l'Histoire de France]; (M753b) *id., Lettres, instructions diplomatiques et papiers d'état,* ed. by Denis M. L. Avenel, 8 v., Paris, 1853–77 [Collection de documents inédits]; (M753c) Gustave C. Fagniez, *Le père Joseph et Richelieu, 1577–1638,* 2 v., Paris, 1894; (M754) François de Bassompierre, maréchal de France, *Journal de ma vie: mémoires,* 1665; ed. by Marie J. A. de La Cropte, marquis de Chantérac, 4 v., Paris, 1870–77 [Société de l'Histoire de France]; (M755a) Jules, Cardinal Mazarin, *Lettres à la reine, à la Princesse Palatine, . . . pendant sa retraite hors de France, 1651–2,* ed. by J. Ravenel, Paris, 1836 [Société de l'Histoire de France]; (M755b) *id., Lettres pendant son ministère,* ed. by Pierre Adolphe Chéruel and Comte Georges d'Avenel, 9 v., Paris, 1872–1906 [Collection de documents inédits]; (M756) Mathieu Molé, premier président au parlement de Paris, *Mémoires,* ed. by Aimé L. Champollion-Figeac, 4 v., Paris, 1855–57 [Société de l'Histoire de France]; (M757a) Jean F. Paul de Gondi, Cardinal de Retz, *Oeuvres* (*Mémoires,* 1st ed., 1717, in v. 1–5), ed. by Alphone Feillet, Jules Gourdault, and François R. Chantelauze, 10 v., Paris, 1870–96 [Les grands écrivains de la France]; (M757b) Louis Batiffol, *Le cardinal de Retz: ambitions et aventures d'un homme d'esprit au XVIIᵉ siècle,* Paris, 1927 [Figures du passé]; (M758) Nicolas Joseph Foucault, *Mémoires,* ed. by F. Baudry, Paris, 1862 [Collection de documents inédits]; (M759) Esprit Fléchier, *Mémoires sur les Grands-jours d'Auvergne en 1665,* 1844; ed. by Pierre Adolphe Chéruel, 1856, 2nd ed., Paris, 1862; (M760a) Louis XIV, roi de France, *Mémoires pour l'instruc-*

tion du dauphin, ed. by Charles Dreyss, 2 v., Paris, 1860; (M760b) Louis XIV, *Mémoires pour les années 1661 et 1666, suivis des reflexions sur le métier de roi, des instructions au duc d'Anjou et d'un projet de harangue,* ed. by Jean Longnon, Paris, 1923. (Collection des chefs-d'oeuvre méconnus); (M761) Auguste Geffroy, ed., *Madame de Maintenon d'après sa correspondance authentique; choix de ses lettres et entretiens,* 2 v., Paris, 1887; (M762) Charlotte Élisabeth, duchesse d'Orléans, 'Princesse Palatine', *Correspondance extraite de ses lettres publiées par M. de Ranke et M. Holland,* tr. and ed. by Ernest Jaeglé, 1880, 2nd rev. ed., 3 v., Paris, 1890; (M763) Philippe de Courcillon, marquis de Dangeau, *Journal, avec les additions inédites du duc de Saint-Simon, 1684–1720,* ed. by Eudoxe Soulié, L. E. Dussieux, and others, 19 v., Paris, 1854–60; (M764) Henri de La Tour d'Auvergne, Vicomte de Turenne, maréchal de France, *Mémoires,* ed. by Paul Marichal, 2 v. (to 1659), Paris, 1909–14 (Société de l'Histoire de France); (M765a) Marie de Rabutin-Chantal marquise de Sévigné, *Lettres de Mme. de Sévigné, de sa famille, et de ses amis,* ed. by Louis J. N. Monmerqué, 14 v. and album, Paris, 1862–68 (Les grands écrivains de la France); (M765b) *id., Letters from the marchioness de Sévigné to her daughter, the Countess de Grignan,* 10 v., London, 1927, reprint of Marie de Rabutin-Chantal, marquise de Sévigné. *Letters to her daughter, the Countess de Grignan,* tr. from the French, 7 v., London, 1801. (M765c) *id., Lettres inédites à Mme. de Grignan, sa fille,* ed. by Charles Capmas, 2 v., Paris, 1876 (Les grands écrivains de la France); (M766) François VI, duc de la Rochefoucauld, prince de Marsillac, *Oeuvres complètes (Mémoires,* 1st ed., 1662, in v. 2), ed. by D. L. Gilbert and Jules Gourdault, 3 v., Paris, 1868–84.

Eighteenth century. (M771) Claude L. H., duc de Villars, maréchal de France, *Mémoires, accompagnés de correspondance inédites,* 1734; ed. by Charles P. M. marquis de Vogüé, 6 v. in 8, Paris, 1884–1904 (Société de l'Histoire de France); (M772a) Renè L. de Voyer de Paulmy, marquis d'Argenson, *Journal and memoirs,* Boston, 1901; London, 1902; (Versailles ed.), abridged tr. by Katharine P. Wormeley from *Journal et mémoires,* 1785; ed. by Edme. J. B. Rathéry, 9 v., Paris, 1859–67 (Société de l'Histoire de France]; (M772b) *id., La France au milieu du XVIIIᵉ siècle, 1747–1757, d'après son Journal: extraits publiés avec notice bibliographique,* ed. by Armand Brette, Paris, 1898; (M773) Edmond J. F. Barbier, *Chronique de la régence et du règne de Louis XV, 1718–1763, ou, Journal de Barbier,* 8 v., Paris, 1857, reprint, 1885; (M774) Louis F. A. du Plessis, duc, de Richelieu, maréchal de France, *Mémoires authentiques, 1725–1757,* ed. by A. de Boislisle, Paris, 1918 [Société de l'Histoire de France]; (M775a) François J. de Pierre, Cardinal de Bernis, *Memoirs and letters,* 2 v., London and Boston, 1902 [Versailles ed.], tr. by Katharine P. Wormeley from *Mémoires et lettres, 1715–1758,* ed. by Frédéric Masson, 2 v., Paris, 1878; (M775b) Frédéric Masson, *Le cardinal de Bernis depuis son ministère, 1758–1794: la suppression des jésuites, le schisme constitutionnel,* Paris, 1884; (M776) Étienne F., duc de Choiseul-Stainville, *Mémoires,* ed. by Fernand Calmettes, Paris, 1904; (M777) Stephen G. Tallentyre (pseud. of Evelyn B. Hall), *Life of Voltaire,* 2 v., London, 1903; (M778) Jean Jacques Rousseau, *Correspondance générale,* ed. by Théophile Dufour, v. 1–9 (to 1763), Paris, 1924–28; (M779) Gustave Schelle, *Du Pont de Nemours et l'école physiocratique,* Paris, 1888; (M780) *id., Turgot,* Paris, 1909; (M781) Comte Dominique J. Garat, *Mémoires historiques sur la vie de M. Suard, sur ses écrits, et sur le XVIIIᵉ siècle,* 1820, 2nd ed., 2 v., Paris, 1821;

(M782) Stéphanie Félicité Ducrest de Saint-Aubin, comtesse de Genlis, *Memoirs illustrative of the history of the eighteenth and nineteenth centuries,* 8 v., London, 1825–26, tr. from *Mémoires inédites sur le dix-huitième siècle et la révolution française, depuis 1756 jusqu'à nos jours,* 10 v., Paris, 1825; abridged ed., Paris, 1878 [(M704) Barrière, *Bibliothèque,* v. 15]; (M783) Siméon P. Hardy, '*Mes loisirs': journal d'événements tels qu'ils parviennent à ma connaisance,* ed. by Maurice Tourneux and Maurice Vitrac, v. 1, *1764–1773,* Paris, 1912 [Mémoires et documents relatifs aux XVIIIe et XIXe siècles]; (M784a) Marie L. E. Vigée Lebrun, *Memoirs,* N. Y., 1903, London, 1904, tr. and ed. by Lionel Strachey; (M784b) *id., Souvenirs jusqu'à 1789,* ed. by Pierre de Nolhac, Paris, 1910; (M785)[1] Pierre de Nolhac, *La dauphine Marie Antoinette,* Paris, 1896; cheaper reprints; (M786) Abbé André Morellet, *Mémoires sur le dix-huitième siècle et sur la révolution,* 1821; 2nd rev. ed., 2 v., Paris, 1822.

Revolution. (M791) Jean S. Bailly, *Mémoires d'un témoin oculaire de la révolution,* 1804; new ed., 3 v., Paris, 1821–22 [(M705) Berville and Barrière, *Collection*]; (M792) Paul F. J. N., vicomte de Barras, *Memoirs,* 4 v., London and N. Y., 1895–96, tr. by Charles E. Roche from *Mémoires,* ed. by Georges Duruy, 4 v., Paris, 1895–96; (M793) Bertrand Barère, *Mémoires,* ed. by Hippolyte Carnot and Pierre J. David, 4 v., Paris, 1842–43; (M794) Antoine F., marquis de Bertrand de Molleville, *Mémoires particuliers pour servir à l'histoire de la fin du règne de Louis XVI,* 1797; 2nd ed., 2 v., Paris, 1816; (M795) Marquis Louis J. A. de Bouillé, *Souvenirs et fragments pour servir aux mémoires de ma vie et de mon temps, 1769–1812,* ed. by P. L. de Kermaingant, 3 v., Paris, 1906–11 [Société d'Histoire Contemporaine]; (M796)[2] Jean P. Brissot, *Mémoires, 1754–1793,* 1830–32; ed. by Claude Perroud, 2 v., Paris, 1910 [Mémoires et documents relatifs aux XVIIIe et XIXe siècles]; (M797a) Hippolyte Carnot, *Mémoires sur Carnot par son fils,* 1861–63; 2 v., Paris, 1893; (M797b) Comte Lazare N. M. Carnot, *Correspondance générale,* ed. by Étienne Charavay and Paul Mautouchet, v. 1–4, Paris, 1892–1907 [Collection de documents inédits]; (M798) Mme. Jean B. Cavaignac, *Les mémoires d'une inconnue, 1780–1816,* Paris, 1894; (M799) Léon Cahen, *Condorcet et la révolution française,* Paris, 1904 [Bibliothèque d'Histoire Contemporaine]; (M800a)[3] Louis Madelin, *Danton,* London and N. Y., 1921, tr. by Lady Mary Loyd from *Danton,* Paris, 1914 [Figures du passé]; (M800b) Albert Mathiez, *Danton et la paix,* Paris, 1919; (M801) Gabriel G. Ramon, *Frédéric de Dietrich, premier maire de Strasbourg sous la révolution française,* Paris, 1919; (M802) Comte Mathieu Dumas, *Memoirs of his own time including the revolution, the empire, and the restoration,* 2 v., London and Philadelphia, 1839, tr. from *Souvenirs de 1770 à 1836,* ed. by Comte Christian L. Dumas, 3 v., Paris, 1839; (M803) Adrien Duquesnoy, député du tiers état de Bar-le-Duc, *Journal sur l'assemblée constituante, 3 mai 1789–3 avril 1790,* ed. by Robert de Crèvecoeur, 2 v., Paris, 1894 [Société d'Histoire Contemporaine]; (M804) Louis Madelin, *Fouché, 1759–1820,* 2 v., Paris, 1901; (M805) Alphonse Dunoyer, *Public prosecutor of the Terror, Antoine Quentin Fouquier-Tinville,* London and N. Y., 1913, tr. by A. W. Evans from *Fouquier-Tinville, accusateur public du tribunal révolutionnaire, 1746–1795,* Paris, 1912; (M806) Comte Dominique J. Garat, *Mémoires sur la révolution, ou exposé de ma conduite dans les*

[1] Also cf. (M343, 366c).
[2] Also cf. (M365).
[3] Also cf. (M366a).

affaires et dans les fonctions publiques, An III [1795]; ed. by E. Maron, Paris, 1862; (M807)[1] Marie J. P. R. Y. G. de Motier, marquis de La Fayette, *Memoirs, correspondence, and manuscripts,* 3 v., London and N. Y., 1837, tr. from *Mémoires, correspondance, et manuscrits,* ed. by George W., marquis de La Fayette, 6 v., Paris, 1837–38; (M808) Comte de Lort de Sérignan, ed., *Un duc et pair au service de la révolution, correspondance intime du duc de Lauzun, général Biron, 1791–1792,* Paris, 1906; (M809a) Ernest Belfort Bax, *Jean-Paul Marat, the people's friend,* London and Boston, 1901; (M809b) Louis R. Gottschalk, *Jean Paul Marat, a study in radicalism,* N. Y. and London, 1927; (M810) Baron Pierre V. Malouet, *Mémoires,* ed. by Baron Victor P. Malouet, 1868, 2nd rev. ed., 2 v., Paris, 1874; (M811)[2] Étienne Dumont, *Great Frenchman and the little Genevese,* London and N. Y., 1904, tr. by Elizabeth, Lady Seymour, from *Souvenirs sur Mirabeau et sur les deux premières assemblées législatives,* ed. by J. L. Duval, Paris, 1832; (M812) Roger Merlin, *Merlin de Thionville d'après des documents inédits,* 2 v., Paris, 1927; (M813) Louis M. de Larevellière-Lépeaux, *Mémoires publiés par son fils,* 3 v., Paris ,1895; (M814a)[3] Ernest Hamel, *Histoire de Robespierre,* 3 v., Paris, 1865–67; (M814b) J. A. Paris, *La jeunesse de Robespierre et la convocation des états généraux en Artois,* Arras, 1870; (M814c) Albert Mathiez, *Fall of Robespierre and other essays,* N. Y., 1927, tr. by C. A. Philipps from *Autour de Robespierre,* Paris, 1925; (M814d) Georges Michon, *Correspondance de Maximilien et Augustin Robespierre,* Paris, 1926; (M815) Marie L. V. de Donissan, marquise de la Rochejacquelein, *Mémoires,* 1815, 9th ed., 2 v., Paris, 1860; (M816) Jeanne M. P. Roland, *Appeal to impartial posterity,* London, 1795; N. Y., 1798; tr. from *Appel à l'impartiale postérité, ou recueil des écrites qu'elle a rédigés pendant sa detention aux prisons de l'Abbaye et de Sainte-Pélagie,* Paris, 1795; ed. by Claude Perroud with the title *Mémoires,* 2 v., Paris, 1905; (M817) Henriette L. marquise de La Tour du Pin de Gouvernet, *Recollections of the revolution and the empire,* N. Y., 1920; London, 1921, tr. by Walter Geer from *Journal d'une femme de cinquante ans, 1778–1815,* ed. by Comte Aymar de Liedekerke-Beaufort, 2 v., Paris, 1913. (M818) Anna Bowman Dodd, *Talleyrand, the training of a statesman, 1754–1838,* N. Y. and London, 1927.

Consulate and empire. (M831) Jérôme Bonaparte, roi de Westphalie, *Mémoires, avec la correspondance de la reine Cathérine et la correspondance du roi avec Napoléon,* ed. by Baron P. E. Albert DuCasse, 7 v., Paris, 1861–66; (M832) Joseph Bonaparte, roi d'Espagne, *Mémoires et correspondance politique et militaire,* ed. by Baron P. E. Albert DuCasse, 1853–54; 3rd ed., 10 v. and album, Paris, 1856–58; (M833) Théodore Iung, *Lucien Bonaparte et ses mémoires, 1775–1840,* 3 v., Paris, 1882–83; (M834) Louis A. Fauvelet de Bourrienne, *Private memoirs of Napoleon Bonaparte during the periods of the directory, the consulate, and the empire,* 1830; new ed. by R. W. Phipps, 4 v., London and N. Y., 1885; many reprints, tr. from *Mémoires sur Napoléon, le directoire, le consulat, l'empire, et la restauration* 10 v., Paris, 1829; many reprints; (M835) Comte Jean A. C. Chaptal de Chanteloup, *Mes souvenirs sur Napoléon,* ed. by Comte Emmanuel A. Chaptal de Chanteloup, Paris, 1893; (M836) Louis A. H. de Bourbon-Condé, duc d'Enghien, *Correspondance, 1801–1804, et documents sur son enlèvement et sa mort,* ed. by Comte Alfred Boulay de la Meurthe, 4 v., Paris, 1904–13; (M837a) Baron Agathon J. F. Fain, *id., Manuscrit de l'an III, 1794–*

---

[1] Also cf. (M361).   [2] Also cf. (M362, 363).
[3] Also cf. (M366b).

1795 . . . , 1828, 2nd ed., Paris, 1829; (M837*b*) *id., Manuscrit de 1812* . . . , 2 v., Paris, 1827; (M837*c*) *id., Manuscrit de 1813* . . . , 1824, 3rd ed., 2 v., Paris, 1829; (M837*d*) *id., Manuscript of 1814* . . . , London, 1823; another ed., London, 1834, tr. from *Manuscrit de 1814* . . . , 1823, 4th ed., Paris, 1830; (M837*e*) *id., Mémoires,* ed. by P. Fain, Paris, 1908; (M838) Martin M. C. Gaudin, duc de Gaëte, *Mémoires, souvenirs, opinions, et écrits,* 1826–34; reprint, 3 v., Paris, 1926; (M839) Baron Gaspard Gourgaud, *Sainte-Hélène: journal inédit de 1815 à 1818,* ed. by Vicomte Emmanuel H. de Grouchy and Antoine Guillois, 2 v., Paris, 1899; (M840) Hortense, reine de Hollande, *Mémoires,* ed. by Jean Hanoteau, 3 v., Paris, 1927; (M841) Antoine R. C. M., comte de La Forest, ambassadeur de France en Espagne, *Correspondance, 1808–1813* [*1814*], ed. by Charles A. Geoffroy de Grandmaison, 7 v., Paris, 1905–13 [Société d'Histoire Contemporaine] ; (M842) Emmanuel, comte de Las Cases, *Mémorial de Sainte Hélène: journal of the private life and conversations of the emperor Napoleon at Saint Helena,* 8 v. in 4, London and N. Y., 1823, tr. from *Mémorial de Sainte-Hélène: journal de la vie privée et des conversations de l'empereur Napoléon à Sainte Hélène,* 8 v. in 4, Londres, 1823; new ed., 4 v., Paris, 1894–95; (M843) Antoine M. Chamans de Lavalette, *Memoirs,* 2 v., London, 1831; 1 v., London and Philadelphia, 1894, tr. from *Mémoires et souvenirs,* 2 v., Paris, 1831; (M844) Jean B. A. M., baron de Marbot, *Memoirs,* 2 v., London and N. Y., 1892, new ed., 2 v., N. Y., 1908, abridged tr. by A. J. Butler from *Mémoires,* 3 v., Paris, 1891; (M845) Baron Alfred A. Ernouf, *Maret, duc de Bassano,* 1878; 2nd ed., Paris, 1884; (M846) Comte André F. Miot de Melito, *Memoirs between the years 1788 and 1815,* 2 v., London, 1881; 1 v., N. Y., 1881; tr. by Mrs. Cashel Hoey and John Lillie from *Mémoires,* ed. by Wilhelm A. Fleischmann, 1858; 3rd ed., 3 v., Paris, 1873; (M847) Baron Claude F. de Méneval, *Memoirs illustrating the history of Napoleon I from 1802 to 1815,* 3 v., London and N. Y., 1894, tr. by Robert H. Sherard, from *Mémoires pour servir à l'histoire de Napoléon I*er *depuis 1802 jusqu'à 1815,* ed. by Baron Napoléon J. E. de Méneval, 3 v., Paris, 1894; (M848) Comte François N. Mollien, *Mémoires d'un ministre de trésor public, 1780–1815,* 1845; new ed. by Charles Gomel, 3 v., Paris, 1898; (M849) Jacques M. de Norvins, *Souvenirs d'un historien de Napoléon: mémorial,* ed. by Léon de Lanzac de Laborie, 3 v., Paris, 1896–97; (M850) Claire E. J. G. de Vergennes, comtesse de Rémusat, *Memoirs, 1802–1808,* 3 v. (also 1 v.), London and N. Y., 1880, tr. by Mrs. Cashel Hoey and John Lillie from *Mémoires, 1802–1808,* ed. by Paul L. E. de Rémusat, 3 v., Paris, 1879–80, many reprints; (M851) Comte Pierre L. Roederer, *Autour de Bonaparte: journal: notes intimes et politiques d'un familier des Tuileries,* ed. by Maurice Vitrac, Paris, 1909 [Bibliothèque du vieux Paris] ; (M852) Anne J. M. Savary, duc de Rovigo, *Memoirs illustrative of the history of the emperor Napoleon,* 4 v., London, 1828, tr. from *Mémoires pour servir à l'histoire de l'empereur Napoléon,* 8 v., Paris, 1828; rev. ed. by Désiré Lacroix, 5 v., Paris, 1900–01; (M853) Philippe P., comte de Ségur, *Histoire et Mémoires,* 8 v., Paris, 1873, abridged ed., with title *Un aide de camp de Napoléon: mémoires,* by Comte Louis de Ségur, 3 v., Paris, 1894–95; (M854) Comte Antoine C. Thibaudeau, *Bonaparte and the consulate,* London and N. Y., 1908, tr. and ed. by George K. Fortescue from *Mémoires sur le consulat, 1799 à 1804, par un ancien conseiller d'état,* Paris, 1827; (M855) Graf Aleksandr Antonovich Balmain, *Napoleon in captivity: the reports of Count Balmain, Russian commissioner on the island of St. Helena, 1816–1820,* tr. and ed. by Julian Park, N. Y., 1927.

1815–1870. (M861) Edmond de Lignères, comte d'Alton-Shée, *Mes mémoires, 1826–1848,* 2 v., Paris, 1868–69; (M862) François A. R., vicomte de Chateaubriand, *Memoirs,* 6 v., London and N. Y., 1902, tr. by Alexander L. Teixeira de Mattos from *Mémoires d'outre-tombe,* 1849–50; new ed. by Edmond Biré, 6 v., Paris, 1910; (M863) Amable G. P. Brugière, baron de Barante, *Souvenirs, 1782–1866,* ed. by Claude de Barante, 8 v., Paris, 1890–1901; (M864) Jean B. S. J., comte de Villèle, *Mémoires et correspondance,* 5 v., Paris, 1887–90; (M865) Comte Adolphe M. P. de Circourt, *Souvenirs d'une mission à Berlin en 1848,* ed. by Georges Bourgin, 2 v., Paris, 1908–09 [Société d'Histoire Contemporaine]; (M866) Charles M., marquis de Salaberry, *Souvenirs politiques sur la restauration, 1821–1830,* ed. by Comte de Salaberry, 2 v., Paris, 1900 [Société d'Histoire Contemporaine]; (M867a) François P. G. Guizot, *Mémoires pour servir à l'histoire de mon temps,* 8 v., Paris, 1858–67; (M867b) Agénor Bardoux, *Guizot,* Paris, 1894 [Les grands écrivains français]; (M868) Charlotte L. E. A. d'Osmond, comtesse de Boigne, *Memoirs,* 3 v., London and N. Y., 1907-08, tr. from *Récits d'une tante: mémoires,* ed. by Charles Nicoullaud, 4 v., Paris, 1907-08; (M869) Esprit V. E. B., comte de Castellane, maréchal de France, *Journal, 1804–1862,* 5 v., Paris, 1895–97; (M870) Comte Louis M. Molé, *Life and memoirs, 1781–1855,* v. 1–2, London and N. Y., 1925, tr. by Arthur Chambers, from *Le comte Molé, 1781–1855: sa vie, ses mémoires,* ed. by Marquis de Noailles, 4 v., Paris, 1922–25; (M871) Dorothée de Courlande, duchesse de Dino, duchesse de Talleyrand-Périgord, *Memoirs,* 3 v., London and N. Y., 1909–10, tr. from *Chronique de 1831 à 1862,* ed. by Princesse Radziwill, née Castellane, 4 v., Paris, 1909–10; (M872) Vicomte Jacques M. Cavaignac and Louis E. Cavaignac, *Souvenirs et correspondance, 1808–1848,* Paris, 1898; (M873) Achille C. L. V., duc de Broglie, *Personal recollections, 1785–1820* [actually 1832], 2 v., London, 1887; tr. and ed. by Raphael Ledos de Beaufort from *Souvenirs, 1785–1870* [actually 1832], ed. by Jacques V. A., duc de Broglie, 4 v., Paris, 1886; (M874) Comte Émile F. Fleury, *Souvenirs, 1837–1867,* 2 v., Paris, 1897–98; (M875) Alfred P. F., comte de Falloux, *Memoirs,* 2 v., London, 1888; tr. by C. B. Pitman from *Mémoires d'un royaliste,* 2 v., Paris, 1888; new ed., 1925; (M876) Comte Horace de Viel-Castel, *Memoirs,* 2 v., London, 1888, tr. by C. Bousfield from *Mémoires sur le règne de Napoléon III, 1851–1864,* ed. by L. Léouzon Le Duc, 6 v., Berne and Paris, 1881–84; (M877) Victor Duruy, *Notes et souvenirs, 1811–1894,* 2 v., Paris, 1901, new ed., 1923; (M878) Gabriel Monod, *La vie et la pensée de Jules Michelet, 1798–1852,* 2 v., Paris, 1923; (M879) Baron Georges E. Haussmann, *Mémoires,* 3 v., Paris, 1890–93; (M880) Vicomte Ferdinand de Lesseps, *Recollections of forty years,* 2 v., London, 1888; 1 v., N. Y., 1888, tr. by C. B. Pitman from *Souvenirs de quarante ans dédiés à mes enfants,* 2 v., Paris, 1887; (M881) Charlemagne E. de Maupas, *Mémoires sur le second empire,* 2 v., Paris, 1884–85; (M882) Napoléon III and Napoléon J. Bonaparte, prince Napoléon, *Correspondance inédite,* ed. by Ernest d'Hauterive, Paris, 1925; (M883) Gustave Rothan, *Souvenirs diplomatiques,* 1882–90, 2nd ed., 7 v., Paris, 1883–93.

Third Republic. (M891) Maurice Réclus, *Jules Favre, 1809–1880,* Paris, 1912; (M892) Marie C. A., vicomte de Meaux, *Souvenirs politiques, 1871–1877,* Paris, 1905; (M893a) Léon M. Gambetta, *Gambetta: life and letters,* London and N. Y., 1910, tr. by V. Montagu from *Gambetta par Gambetta: lettres intimes et souvenirs de famille,* ed. by Pierre B. Gheusi, Paris, 1909; (M893b) Paul E. L. Deschanel, *Gambetta,* London, 1920, tr. from *Gambetta,* Paris, 1919; (M894) Alfred N.

Rambaud, *Jules Ferry*, Paris, 1903; (M895) Charles L. de Saulses de Freycinet, *Souvenirs, 1848–1893*, 2 v., Paris, 1912–13; (M896) Hippolyte A. Taine, *Life and letters*, 3 v., Westminster and N. Y., 1902–08; abridged tr. by Mrs. R. L. Devonshire and E. Sparvel-Bayly from *H. Taine, sa vie et sa correspondance*, 4 v., Paris, 1902–07; (M897) Henry M. Hyndman, *Clemenceau, the man and his time*, London and N. Y., 1919; (M898) Sisley Huddleston, *Poincaré: a biographical portrait*, London and N. Y., 1924. HEB

GOVERNMENT PUBLICATIONS

(M901) *Moniteur universel*, Paris, 1789–1868, daily, throughout its existence published a record of debates in the French legislative chambers, and during most of its career was the national official journal. It was superseded by (M902) *Journal officiel de la république française*, Paris, 1869 ff., daily, which includes, in addition to records of legislative debates, texts of laws and decrees, occasional bills or reports upon bills, and administrative documents.

(M903) *Recueil des lois constitutionnelles et organiques de la république française*, latest ed., Paris, 1924, is a collection of French constitutions and organic laws, published at intervals by the government.

(M904) *Les livres jaunes*, v. 1–213, Paris, 1856–1928, contain diplomatic documents selected from official correspondence, reports, and instructions bearing upon international problems, published from time to time by the ministry of foreign affairs. (M905) *Exposé de la situation de l'empire presenté au sénat et au corps législatif*, 10 v., Paris, 1861–69, which dealt, among other things, with the international situation during the later years of the Second Empire, is sometimes classified with the Yellow Books.

(M906) *Bulletin des lois*, Paris, 1793 ff., biweekly, now published under the auspices of the ministry of justice, prints the complete text of all laws, whether of general or local interest; indexes have been published from time to time.

Among publications of the ministry of finance is (M907) *Bulletin de statistique et de législation comparée*, Paris, 1877, monthly, which contains decrees and laws bearing upon finances, with tables of imports and exports for France and for the countries which have been its principal customers. HEB

ACADEMY, UNIVERSITY, AND SOCIETY PUBLICATIONS

The publications of two of the academies belonging to the Institut de France contain materials useful to the historian. In addition to miscellaneous publications, the Académie des Sciences Morales et Politiques maintains two serials; (M921a) *Mémoires*, Paris, 1796 ff., and (M921b) *Comptes rendus des séances et travaux*, Paris, 1840 ff. In like manner, the Académie des Inscriptions et Belles Lettres issues two serials: (M922a) *Mémoires*, Paris, 1803 ff., and (M922b) *Comptes rendus des séances*, Paris, 1857 ff.

Many valuable historical monographs, including some relating to France, have been issued in (M923) *Bibliothèque de l'Ecole Pratique des Hautes Études: sciences philologiques et historiques*, Paris, 1869 ff. Not a few historical works have also appeared among the various publications issued by the several French universities.

France possesses about three hundred historical societies, general and local, over two hundred of which undertake publications of some sort; several issue periodicals and other important works. Of preëminent importance is the Société de l'Histoire de France, founded in 1833, whose constitution requires the publication each year of three volumes of chronicles, memoirs, correspondence, and other materials relating to the history of France prior to 1789. These (M926) *Publications,* Paris, 1834 ff., have included excellent editions of many notable works such as (H359b) Joinville, (M234a) Froissart, (M234b) Monstrelet, and (M926a) *Procès de condamnation et de réhabilitation de Jeanne d'Arc,* 5 v., Paris, 1841–49, ed. by Jules Quicherat; and several other works listed in this section in the subsection 'Biographies'. Some works included in the *Publications* are now out of print; some have been superseded by later critical editions, especially in the series (M61b) *Collection de textes pour servir à l'étude et à l'enseignement de l'histoire.* The society has also published (M927a) *Bulletin,* 18 v., Paris, 1834–62, and (M927b) *Annuaire historique,* 27 v., Paris, 1836–63, which were merged in (M927c) *Annuaire-bulletin,* Paris, 1863 ff.

Among the other more important general historical societies are: Société de l'Histoire du Protestantisme Français, founded in 1852, which issues (M928) *Bulletin,* Paris, 1852 ff., monthly; Société d'Histoire Contemporaine, founded in 1890 and merged in 1922 with the Société de l'Histoire de France, which issued (M929a) *Assemblée générale,* 24 v., Paris, 1891–1914, and (M929b) *Publications,* 63 v., Paris, 1892–1921, of which the more important numbers are listed separately in this section under the subsection 'Biographies'; Société d'Histoire Moderne, founded in 1901, which issues (M930a) *Revue d'histoire moderne,* Paris, 1926 ff., bimonthly, a continuation of (M942), and (M930b) *Publications,* v. 1–20, Paris, 1903–25; Société de l'Histoire de la Révolution Française, founded in 1888. which issues (M931a) *La révolution française, revue d'histoire moderne et contemporaine,* Paris, 1881 ff., quarterly; and (M931b) *Publications,* v. 1–44, Paris, 1888–1927; Société des Études Robespierristes, founded in 1908, which issues (M932a) *Annales révolutionnaires,* 15 v., Paris and Besançon, 1908–23, changed to (M932b) *Annales historiques de la révolution française,* v. 16 ff., Reims, 1924 ff., bimonthly, and (M932c) *Bibliothèque d'histoire révolutionnaire,* v. 1–22. Paris and Besançon, 1911–26; Société des Études Napoléoniennes, founded in 1923, which publishes (M933) *Napoléon, revue des études Napoléoniennes* (founded as *Revue des études Napoléoniennes*), Paris, 1912–1926, bi-monthly, from 1929 as monthly; Société d'Histoire de la Révolution de 1848, founded in 1904, which publishes the review (M934a) *La révolution de 1848,* Paris, 1904 ff., and (M934b) *Bibliothèque de "La Révolution de 1848",* v. 1–7, Paris, 1908–12.

Among the local historical societies which issue publications of importance, the following may perhaps be selected for special mention: Société de l'Histoire de Paris et de l'Île-de-France, founded in 1874, which publishes (M936a) *Bulletin,* Paris, 1874 ff., (M936b) *Mémoires,* v. 1–48, Paris, 1875–1925, and (M936c) *Documents,* v. 1–27, Paris, 1877–1913; Société des Archives Historiques de la Gironde, founded in 1858, which issues (M937) *Archives historiques du département de la Gironde,* v. 1–66, Paris, 1859–1927; Société Historique de Gascogne, founded in 1859, which publishes (M938a) *Revue de Gascogne,* Auch, 1860 ff., and (M938b) *Archives historiques de la Gascogne,* Paris, 1883 ff.; Société de l'Histoire de Normandie, founded in 1869, which issues (M939) *Publications,* Paris, 1870 ff.

HEB

PERIODICALS

In addition to the general historical periodicals published in France, listed in § B and § I, and to those more specially devoted to French history listed as publications of academies and societies (cf. M921–939), there are the following which relate primarily to modern French history: (M941) *Revue de la révolution: revue mensuelle historique, philosophique, économique, littéraire, et artistique*, 16 v., Paris, 1883–89; (M942) *Revue d'histoire moderne et contemporaine*, 19 v., Paris, 1899–1914; and (M943) *Revue historique de la révolution française*, 15 v., Paris, 1910–18, 1922–23, which was merged in (M932b) *Annales historiques de la révolution française*.

The following are important for special fields: (M951) *Nouvelle revue historique de droit français et étranger*, Paris, 1855 ff.; (M952) *Revue d'histoire littéraire de la France*, Paris, 1894 ff., published by the Société d'Histoire Littéraire de la France; and (M953) *Revue des cours et conférences*, Paris, 1892 ff., which is especially important for linguistics and literature.

In addition to the reviews published by local historical societies, the following are among the more important journals devoted to local history: (M961) *Revue de Bretagne, de Vendée, et d'Anjou*, Nantes, 1857 ff., published by the Société des Bibliophiles Bretons et de l'Histoire de Bretagne; (M962) *Annales de Bretagne*, Rennes, 1885 ff., published by the Faculté des Lettres de l'Université de Rennes; (M963) *Anjou historique*, Angers, 1900 ff.; (M964) *Annales de l'Est*, Nancy, 1887 ff., published by the Faculté des Lettres de l'Université de Nancy; (M965) *Annales du midi, revue archéologique, historique, et philologique*, Toulouse, 1889 ff.; and (M966) *Revue historique de Bordeaux*, Bordeaux, 1908 ff., bimonthly.

HEB

SECTION N

SPAIN AND PORTUGAL

Editor

ROGER BIGELOW MERRIMAN

Professor of History, Harvard University

CONTENTS

SPAIN AND PORTUGAL: INTRODUCTION

The chief interest in Spanish and Portuguese history centers in the fifteenth and sixteenth centuries, when Spain attained to the foremost rank among European nations, controlled important European territories outside the peninsula, and when both Spain and Portugal built up vast colonial empires. Consequently, in the present section, that period receives special attention, but effort has been

638

made to indicate also some of the more important works for the other parts of the history of these two countries, with some emphasis upon institutional development and recent conditions.

For the general history of Spain and Portugal and their relations to other nations in the successive periods, cf. § E, Rome; § H, Medieval history; § I, Modern history; and § J, Contemporary history. For matters associated with the religious history of the peninsula, cf. §.F, Church history and § G, Moslem history. For Spanish rule over other parts of Europe, cf. § O, Italy; § P, Germany; and § Q, Netherlands and Belgium. Spanish and Portuguese activities in the age of discovery are dealt with in § K, Colonial expansion; the history of their colonizing activities in § U, Central and Southern Asia; § V, Oceanica; § W, Africa; and § Y, Hispanic America.

SPAIN: BIBLIOGRAPHY

N1a Antonio, Nicolás. *Bibliotheca Hispana vetus, sive, Hispani scriptores qui ab Octaviani Augusti aevo ad annum Christi M.D. floruerunt.* 2 v. Roma, 1696. 2nd ed. by F. P. Bayer, 2 v., Matriti, 1788.

b —— *Bibliotheca Hispana nova, sive, Hispanorum scriptorum qui ab anno M. D. ad MDCLXXXIV. floruere notitia.* 2 v. Roma, 1672. 2nd ed. by T. A. Sánchez, J. A. Pellicer, and R. Casalbón, 2 v., Matriti, 1788. (V. 1, 1783, by misprint.)

Two and a half centuries ago, Spain led the world in the field of historical bibliography. Antonio's works have rightly been described as 'incomparably superior to any previous bibliography,' 'still unsuperseded and indispensable.' (Cf. M. Menendez y Pelayo, *La ciencia española,* Madrid, 1887–88, 1:50 ff.). But in the succeeding period this early promise was not fulfilled; and while the other western European nations made rapid strides in the science of historical bibliography, Spain lagged painfully behind. Consequently, down to 1919, there was nothing for Spain comparable to (M1) Monod for France or (P1a) Dahlmann-Waitz for Germany. *a.* Includes both Spanish and Portuguese writings to 1500. *b.* Includes publications from 1500 to 1672 (2nd ed., to 1684). RBM

N2a Almirante, José. *Bibliografía militar de España.* Madrid, 1876.

b Boissonnade, Prosper. *Les études relatives à l'histoire économique de l'Espagne.* Paris, 1913. (First published in *Revue de synthèse historique,* 25:83–93, Aug. 1912.)

c Ballester y Castell, Rafael. *Las fuentes narrativas de la historia de España durante la edad media, 417–1474.* Palma de Mallorca, 1908.

d Massó y Torrents, José. *Historiografia de Catalunya en Català durant l'epoca nacional. Revue Hispanique,* 15:486–613, Dec. 1906.

e Morel-Fatio, Alfred. *Historiographie de Charles-Quint.* V. 1. Paris, 1913. [Bibliothèque de l'École des Hautes Études, v. 202.]

f Palmer, Thomas W., Jr. *Guide to the law and legal literature of Spain.* Washington, 1915. [Library of Congress.]

Bibliographies of special topics have been constantly produced, of which these six are of special value. *b.* Covers down to 1453. *c.* and *d.* Contain brief critical accounts of the medieval chroniclers. *e.* Very notable critical work, on a much larger scale, for the materials on the first half of the sixteenth century.

RBM

N3a Sánchez Alonso, B. *Fuentes de la historia española, ensayo de bibliografía sistemática de las monografías impresas que ilustran la historia política nacional de España, excluídas sus relaciones con América.* Madrid, 1919. [Junta para ampliación de estudios e investigaciones científicas. Centro de estudios históricos.]

    b Ballester y Castell, Rafael. *Bibliografía de la historia de España, catálogo metódico y cronológico de las fuentes y obras principales relativas a la historia de España desde los orígenes hasta nuestros días.* Gerona, 1921.

    a. Makes good most of the previous deficiencies in Spanish historical bibliography. Comprises 6,783 titles, arranged in sections and subsections corresponding to the great chronological subdivisions of Spanish history; includes articles in historical journals and reviews as well as independent volumes; this latter feature of the work will prove a priceless boon to all students of Spanish history. Though no critical estimate of the works cited is given in the text, reference is often made to reviews by specialists in the periodicals; there are two useful indexes of authors and of subjects. By far the most valuable general bibliography that Spain has produced since the days of (N1) Nicolás Antonio, and it should inaugurate a new era in the study of Spanish history. *b.* Students who are not familiar with the principal standard Spanish histories and collections of sources will find this convenient to use in conjunction with *a.* Its arrangement of titles is different from that of *a.,* to which it constantly refers. It pays little attention to foreign books, and is pitiably weak on recent Spanish history; but its summaries and critical estimates of important authorities are often very valuable.

    Mention should also be made of the bibliography and notes in (N123*b*) Ballesteros, *Historia de España.* It lists many titles, particularly monographs of a highly special nature, which are not found in *a.,* and the references to the text give valuable indications of their contents. Professor Ballesteros's heroic determination to keep abreast of the times obliges him to be constantly putting forth additional lists of titles, as the successive volumes of his work appear, with the consequence that it is not always perfectly easy to find what one wants; there are, moreover, occasional misprints. These defects, however, can be easily remedied when his work is complete, and in the meantime he has earned the lasting gratitude of every serious student of Spanish history.   RBM

N4 Foulché-Delbosc, Raymond, and **Barrau-Dihigo, Louis.** *Manuel de l'hispanisant.* V. 1, 2. N. Y., 1920–26.

    First two volumes of a more special work which scholars have long needed. V. 1 gives 'repertoires,' general and special—that is, bibliographies, biographical collections, catalogues, indexes, and descriptions of public or private archives, etc.; v. 2, the 'collections' of various kinds. Includes Portugal as well as Spain; in fact, much of the material is grouped according to the three chief linguistic divisions of the peninsula—Castilian, Catalan, and Portuguese. A model of thoroughness and precision, which will prove indispensable to the specialist; it will probably be useful to the general reader as a bibliography of bibliographies, and still more as a table of contents of the more important collections.   RBM

N5 Foulché-Delbosc, Raymond. *Bibliographie hispanique.* V. 1–13, 1905–1917. N. Y., 1909–1917. [Hispanic Society of America.]

    Annual list of titles of all books, pamphlets, and articles on Spanish, Portuguese, and Latin American history and literature that have appeared during the year under review. Lists of current publications relating to Spanish history appear in (N942) *Revista de archivos, bibliotecas, y museos* and (N943) *Revista de filología española.*

RBM

N6a Hidalgo, Dionisio. *Diccionario general de bibliografía española.* 7 v. Madrid, 1862–81.

  b *Boletín de la librería.* Madrid, 1873 ff., monthly.

  c *Bibliografía española, revista general de la imprenta, de la librería, y de las industrias que concurren á la fabricación del libro.* Madrid, 1901–22 ff., semi-monthly. [Asociación de la librería.]

  d *Bibliografía general española e hispano-americana.* Madrid, 1923 ff.

  a. Attempt at a general list of all works published in Spain. *b.* and *c.* Supplementary periodical lists of all current publications issued in Spain. *d.* Continuation of *c.*

GMD

Library collections.—The most important collections in the United States on Spanish and Portuguese history are to be found in the library of the Hispanic Society of America, New York City. The library of W. H. Prescott forms the nucleus of the collection in the Harvard College Library; of George Ticknor, of that in the Boston Public Library; and of H. C. Lea, of that in the University of Pennsylvania Library. There are also good collections in the libraries of the University of California, Stanford University, and the University of Texas.

AHS

SPAIN: ENCYCLOPEDIAS

N21a *Diccionario enciclopédico hispano-americano de literatura, ciencias, y artes.* 23 v. in 24, Barcelona, 1887–98. Apéndice, 5 v., Barcelona, 1898–1910.

  b *Enciclopedia universal ilustrada europeo-americana.* 65 v. in 67. Barcelona, 1912–1929.

Leading recent Spanish encyclopedias. *b.* In most respects distinctly the better. Contains in v. 21 a good series of maps illustrating Spanish history.

RBM

SPAIN: GEOGRAPHY

N41 Blázquez y Delgado-Aguilera, Antonio. *España y Portugal.* 1914. 2nd ed., with title *Península Ibérica,* Barcelona, 1921. [Vidal de la Blache and Camena d'Almeida, Curso de geografía, v. 3.]

Best and most recent general account of the geography and physiography of the Iberian peninsula; thorough and scientific; contains 181 admirable illustrations.

RBM

SPAIN: COLLECTIONS OF SOURCES

The most important manuscript collections in the Iberian peninsula are those in the castle of Simancas (mostly on the sixteenth and seventeenth centuries); at Madrid, in the Biblioteca Nacional, the Archivo Histórico Nacional, and the Real Academia de la Historia; at the Escorial; at Seville, in the Archivo de Indias (chiefly valuable for the American colonies); at Barcelona, in the Archivo de la Corona de Aragón (largely unexplored and especially rich on the medieval period). The names of the different published guides and catalogues of these archives will be found in (N4) Foulché-Delbosc and Barrau-Dihigo, *Manuel de l'hispanisant.* There are also numerous private collections.

N61a Morel-Fatio, Alfred. *Bibliothèque Nationale, Département des Manuscrits, Catalogue des manuscrits espagnols et des manuscrits portugais.* 2 v. Paris, 1881–92.

    b Gayangos, Pascual de. *Catalogue of the manuscripts in the Spanish language in the British Museum,* ed. by E. A. Bond. V. 1–4, London, 1875–93.

Catalogues of the two most important collections of manuscripts for Spanish history located outside of Spain. The collection in the Bibliothèque Nationale is very valuable, and that in the British Museum even more so. The latter contains duplicates of many of the manuscripts in Simancas and Madrid.　　RBM

N62 *Colección de documentos inéditos para la historia de España.* Ed. by M. F. Navarrete and others. 112 v. Madrid, 1842–95. [Real Academia de la Historia.]

By far the most important collection of miscellaneous historical material for Spanish history; carefully and accurately transcribed. The bulk of it concerns the reigns of Charles V and Philip II; there is practically nothing on the ancient or medieval periods and but little on Bourbon Spain; the realms of the crown of Aragon, moreover, receive but scant attention. For students of the sixteenth century, however, the collection is invaluable; it contains the full text of many important letters of the period of Philip II, which are sometimes rather inaccurately summarized in translation, in the English (L73) *Calendar of State Papers, Spanish.* A rather meager index of v. 1–102 was published in 1891; an excellent table of contents appears on pp. 113–179 of v. 2 of (N4) Foulché-Delbosc and Barrau-Dihigo.　　RBM

N63 Finke, Heinrich, ed. *Acta Aragonensia, Quellen zur deutschen, italienischen, französischen, spanischen, zur Kirchen- und Kulturgeschichte aus der diplomatischen Korrespondenz Jaymes II, 1291–1327.* 3 v. Berlin, 1908–24.

Contains an account of the Aragonese archives, in addition to being one of the most important publications of manuscript materials extracted from them. The documents and accompanying editorial materials contribute much information on the ecclesiastical history of Aragon and on the nation's diplomatic relations in the important period when it was extending its power and enterprises in the islands of the Mediterranean and in Italy. Review, T. F. Tout, *E.H.R.* 24:141, Jan. 1909; 39:598, Oct. 1924.　　GMD

SPAIN: SHORTER GENERAL HISTORIES

N101a Díaz Carmona, Francisco. *Elementos de la historia de España.* 2nd ed., 2 v., Granada, 1904–05.

    b Ballesteros y Beretta, Antonio. *Síntesis de historia de España.* 1920, 2nd ed., Madrid, 1924.

a. Probably the best-proportioned and most accurate history of Spain in Spanish suitable for advanced high school or freshman college work. It carries the narrative to the reign of Alfonso XII. *b.* Outline by one of the most eminent living Spanish historians, author of (N123b).　　CEMCG

N102a Hume, Martin A. S. *Spanish people, their origin, growth, and influence.* N. Y., 1901. [Great peoples series.] (Brief bibliography.)

    b Chapman, Charles E. *History of Spain, founded on the Historia de España . . . of Rafael Altamira.* N. Y., 1918. (Brief bibliography.)

c **Sedgwick, Henry D.** *Spain: a short history of its politics, literature, and art from earliest times to the present.* Boston, 1925.

a. 'An analysis or the Spanish people, built up about a condensed outline of the history of Spain from the earliest times to the present day.' The best portions are the chapters devoted to the times between the end of the Moorish régime and the accession of the Bourbons, 1250–1700. The treatment of the eighteenth and nineteenth centuries is hasty and unsatisfactory. Cf. (N260a) Hume, *Spain, 1479–1788.* Review, B. P. Bourland, *A.H.R.* 7:337, Jan. 1902. *b.* Serviceable condensation of (N123a) in English. Two brief concluding chapters, thirty-seven pages, based upon other secondary works and upon personal observation, are devoted to the period since 1808. Review, *A.H.R.* 24:720, July 1919. *c.* Popular account, interestingly written.

CEMCG

SPAIN: LONGER GENERAL HISTORIES

N121a **Rosseeuw Saint-Hilaire, Eugène.** *Histoire d'Espagne depuis les premiers temps historiques jusqu'à la mort de Ferdinand VII.* V. 1–5 (corresponding to v. 1–4 of the 2nd ed.), 1837–40. 2nd rev. ed., 14 v., Paris, 1844–79.

b **Lafuente, Modesto.** *Historia general de España desde los tiempos más remotos hasta nuestros días.* 30 v. 1850–67. Cheaper ed., 15 v., 1861–69. Illustrated ed., 6 v., 1877–82. Rev. ed., with continuation, by J. Valera and others, 25 v., Barcelona, 1887–91.

Both these works are good typical products of the period in which they were written. They make reasonably good use of chronicles and memoirs (Lafuente also cites an occasional document) ; they give a mass of interesting detail, and are in general fairly accurate as far as they go; the constitutional, social, and economic sides of the story, however, are largely neglected, and the subsequent discovery of manuscript material has necessarily modified a number of their verdicts. Lafuente ('Fray Gerundio') was apparently incited to undertake his task by the appearance of the first volume of Rosseeuw Saint-Hilaire ; indeed, he sometimes followed the latter's work more closely than the canons of modern historical scholarship would approve. Both authors carry the story from the earliest times to 1833.

RBM

N122 **Cánovas del Castillo, Antonio,** ed. *Historia general de España escrita por individuos de número de la Real Academia de la Historia.* 18 v. Madrid, 1891–99.

It does not seem likely that this ambitious work will ever be completed. Of the eighteen volumes which compose it one is devoted to geological and prehistoric times, two to the period from the barbarian invasions to the coming of the Moors, three to the periods from 1065 to 1312 and from 1350 to 1390, two to the Catholic Kings, nine to the reigns of Charles III and Charles IV, and one to the early development of the Castilian navy; all the rest of the story is as yet untouched. Like all collaborated enterprises, the work is very uneven; constitutional, social, and economic developments are inadequately described; and a disproportional amount of space is devoted to the history of Castile.

RBM

N123a Altamira y Crevea, Rafael. *Historia de España y de la civilización española.* 1900–11. 3rd rev. ed., 4 v., Barcelona, 1913–14. (Extensive bibliography.)

b Ballesteros y Beretta, Antonio. *Historia de España y de su influencia en la historia universal.* V. 1–5, Barcelona, 1918–29. (Valuable bibliographies.)

c —— *Sevilla en el siglo XIII.* Madrid, 1913.

a. Marks an epoch in Spanish historiography. The narrative portions, on which the older historians concentrated their efforts, are reduced to the narrowest limits; the author devotes the bulk of his space to social, institutional, and cultural developments, and shows that he has kept in close touch with the recent tendencies of historical scholarship beyond the Pyrenees. Begins with prehistoric origins and carries the story to the Napoleonic invasion. Review, *Rev. Hist.* 87:156, Jan. 1905; 109:158, Jan. 1912. *b.* Altamira's work is being largely superseded by that of Professor Ballesteros, whose fourth volume extends to 1700; the two which are still to be published will carry the story to the present day. This very able and comprehensive work is a remarkably successful attempt to include every phase of Spanish history; profusely illustrated; references for every important fact. Review, *Rev. Hist.* 142:89, Jan. 1923. The author, who is professor at Madrid, and a recognized leader of the younger school of Spanish historians, has also written *c.*, a delightful volume. He is also preparing a monumental work in four volumes on the reign of Alfonso X. RBM

N124 Diercks, Gustav. *Geschichte Spaniens von den frühesten Zeiten bis auf die Gegenwart.* 2 v. Berlin, 1895–96.

Compact account, in some 1100 pages, of the historical evolution of Spain from the settlements by the Phoenicians to the birth of Alfonso XIII. Much space is devoted to the internal development of the country; each of the five books into which the volumes are divided ends with a chapter on the institutions and civilization of the period in question. V. 1. Better than v. 2. There is no bibliography or other indication of the sources used; the work is marred by occasional errors of detail. Review, K. Haebler, *Hist. Zeit.* 76:524, 1896; 79:509 1897. CHHg

SPAIN: ANCIENT AND MEDIEVAL

N201 Lembke, Friedrich W.; Schäfer, Heinrich; and Schirrmacher, Friedrich W. *Geschichte von Spanien.* 7 v. Hamburg and Gotha, 1831–1902 (V. 1 by Lembke, v. 2–3 by Schäfer, and v. 4–7 by Schirrmacher). [Geschichte der europäischen Staaten.]

Probably the principal large scale and scientific history of Spain in a language other than Spanish, but it carries the story only to 1516. The volumes of Lembke and Schäfer merit consultation on nearly every serious point which arises in the study of ancient and medieval Spain. They knew the classical, Arabic, Byzantine, and medieval sources; and although Lembke's portion of the work was composed nearly a century ago, its judgments are sound and are frequently corroborated by epigraphic and manuscript material since discovered and analyzed. CEMCG

N202 Burke, Ulick R. *History of Spain from the earliest times to the death of Ferdinand the Catholic.* 1895. 2nd rev. ed. by Martin A. S. Hume, 2 v., London and N. Y., 1900.

Hardly comparable with other general histories, even of the period covered. The style is brilliant in places but strikingly uneven. The author's prejudices are defiantly displayed, his statements are often inaccurate, and his moralizing is frequently neither tranquil nor substantial. Review, C. H. Haskins, *A.H.R.* 6:167, Oct. 1900.   CEMCG.

N203a Conde, José Antonio. *History of the dominion of the Arabs in Spain.* 3 v. London, 1854–55. Tr. by Mrs. Jonathan Foster from French translation by J. Lacroix de Marleé, 3 v., Paris, 1825, of *Historia de la dominación de los Arabes en España,* 3 v., Madrid, 1820–21.

b Makkarî. *History of the Mohammedan dynasties in Spain, extracted from the Nafhu-t-tíb min ghosni-l-Andalusi-r-rattíb . . . translated . . . and illustrated with critical notes . . . by Pascual de Gayangos.* 2 v. London, 1840–43. [Oriental translation fund.]

c Dozy, Reinhart P. A. *Spanish Islam, a history of the Moslems in Spain.* London, 1913. Tr. and ed. by F. G. Stokes from *Histoire des musulmans d'Espagne,* 4 v., Leyde, 1861. (Bibliography.)

d Coppée, Henry. *History of the conquest of Spain by the Arab-Moors, with a sketch of the civilization which they achieved and imparted to Europe.* 1881. 2nd ed., 2 v., Boston, 1892.

e Lane-Poole, Stanley, and **Gilman, Arthur.** *Moors in Spain.* 1886. New ed., N. Y., 1911. [Story of the nations.]

f Whishaw, Bernard and **Whishaw, Ellen M.** *Arabic Spain, sidelights on her history and art.* London, 1912. (Bibliography.)

These six titles have been selected as the most notable, in various ways, of the numerous books on Moorish Spain. The first four are all large works. *c.* Unquestionably the greatest; it corrects many of the errors of *a* and *b.* (the introduction to Stokes's translation contains a temperate estimate of both these books), and marks an epoch in the study of Spanish Islam. Much material, however, may still be derived from *a.* and *b.,* but it should be used with the utmost caution. *b.* The author, a Moroccan, died A. D. 1632. He had much interest in literature; but this rendering is, unfortunately, abridged in that respect. Cf. (G663a) R. A. Nicholson, *Literary history of the Arabs,* p. 413. *d.* Frankly based on *b.;* a readable work on a lower intellectual plane. *e.* and *f.* The best of the shorter histories of Spanish Islam. The appropriate chapters of (G122c) C. Huart, *Histoire des Arabes,* and of (G101b) Ameer Ali, *Short history of the Saracens,* are also useful; the latter is written from the standpoint of an enlightened Moslem of today.

The name of Francisco Codera stands first among the list of Spanish-Arabic scholars of recent years; most of his works, however, are of too special a nature to be mentioned here.

The reader should be warned against the three pretentious volumes of (N203g) S. P. Scott, *History of the Moorish empire in Europe,* 3 v., Philadelphia, 1904; to all intents and purposes they are valueless.   RBM

N204a Swift, Francis Darwin. *Life and times of James the First, the Conqueror, king of Aragon, Valencia, and Majorca, count of Barcelona and Urgel, lord of Montpellier.* Oxford, 1894. (Bibliography.)

b Tourtoulon, Charles, Baron de. *Études sur la maison de Barcelone: Jacme Ier le conquérant.* 2 v. Montpellier, 1863–67.

a. One of the few thoroughly reliable and scholarly monographs in English on a medieval Spanish subject. Every important statement is backed up by a wealth of references to manuscript and printed sources; there are five valuable appendixes, and fourteen printed documents. For the purposes of the serious student, it supersedes *b.*, which is longer and more brilliant. Review of *a.*, M. A. S. Hume, *E.H.R.* 10:147, Jan. 1895.   RBM

N205 Mérimée, Prosper. *History of Peter the Cruel.* 2 v. London, 1849. Tr. from *Histoire de Don Pèdre Ier, roi de Castille,* 1843; 2nd ed., Paris, 1865.

Opens with a review of the reign of Alfonso XI of Castile, 1312–1350, and a brief survey of the state of Spain at its close. The tragic story of King Peter is wonderfully well told. The hand of the skilled novelist is recognized in the record of a series of dramatic episodes. The translation is poor. The second French edition should be used.   RBM

N206 Calmette, Joseph. *Louis XI, Jean II, et la révolution catalane, 1461–1473.* Toulouse, 1902. (Excellent bibliography.)

Masterly diplomatic study, by the foremost living authority, on the relations of France and Spain on the eve of the Italian wars. The scholarship and thoroughness of the author leave nothing to be desired: his political judgments are of the shrewdest: and his story is brilliantly told. Contains three appendixes and thirty-five well selected *pièces justificatives.* Review, G. Monod, *Rev. Hist.* 81:325, Mar. 1903.   RBM

SPAIN: GREATNESS AND DECAY, 1469–1700

N251 Merriman, Roger B. *Rise of the Spanish empire in the old world and in the new.* V. 1–3. N. Y., 1918–26. [1, *Middle Ages;* 2, *Catholic Kings;* 3, *Emperor.*] (Bibliographies.)

A history of Spain 'from the standpoint of the great empire which sprang from her,' which seeks to demonstrate the continuity of the development of Spanish territorial expansion from the early Middle Ages to its climax in the sixteenth century. V. 1. Provides the necessary background for the great drama of the sixteenth century. It falls naturally into three nearly equal divisions: the rise of the medieval kingdoms of Castile and Aragon; the development of the Mediterranean empire of the Catalans and Valencians; and an analysis and description of the social, religious, and constitutional life of the peninsula in the Middle Ages. V. 2. Here the writer arrives at the main part of his story. He recounts the peninsular aspects of the astonishing reign of the Catholic Kings, and the movement of expansion to the Canaries and the New World, to North Africa and Italy. V. 3. The climax of the story; describes the reign of Charles V; reveals Spain as the foremost power in Europe and the conqueror of the New World. V. 4. Will carry the account to the death of Philip II. Reviews, B. Moses, *A.H.R.* 24:83, Oct. 1918; P. Smith, *A.H.R.* 31:508, Apr. 1926.   CHHg

N252 Prescott, William H. *History of the reign of Ferdinand and Isabella the Catholic.* 3 v. Boston, 1838. Rev. ed. by J. F. Kirk, 1873; further rev. [Montezuma] ed. by W. H. Munro, 4 v., Philadelphia, 1904.

Unquestionably the masterpiece of one of America's greatest historians; published before the author had completed his forty-second year, and while his eyesight, though seriously impaired, still enabled him to read and write during a portion of the day. Characterized by profound learning, deep insight, and the finest kind of historical honesty; the style is dignified and sonorous—it might perhaps be regarded today as somewhat pompous—but the book makes delightful reading. Though produced more than eighty years ago, it is still of high value to scholars. Much new material has been uncovered, but Prescott made such good use of everything—both in print and in manuscript—that was accessible in his day, that his work will long remain the indispensable foundation for all special research on the reign of the Catholic Kings.   RBM

N253 Irving, Washington. *Chronicle of the conquest of Granada.* 1829. New ed., London and N. Y., 1910. [Everyman's library.]

This charming and very famous work is rather of literary than of historical value; the Fray Antonio Agapida, on whose manuscript the author states that it is based, is a totally fictitious personage. Together with *The Alhambra* (1832) it was the product of a three years' stay in Spain, during which the author absorbed the atmosphere and romantic traditions of the region he describes. Though the facts, as he gives them, should be controlled by the use of more recent and scientific works, one can still catch the spirit of the last great struggle of Cross and Crescent in the peninsula better, perhaps, in Irving's pages than anywhere else.
                    RBM

N254 Plunket, Irene L. *Isabel of Castile and the making of the Spanish nation, 1451–1504.* 1915. Reissue, N. Y., 1919. [Heroes of the nations.] (Bibliography.)

Pleasant and truthful character sketch, supplemented by well-chosen selections from the narrative, literary, and artistic history of the period. Review, *A.H.R.* 25:88, Oct. 1919.   RBM

N255 Boissonnade, Prosper. *Histoire de la réunion de la Navarre à la Castille, essai sur les relations des princes de Foix-Albret avec la France et l'Espagne, 1479–1521.* Paris, 1893.

A scholar's book, written for the use of scholars. The author has spared no pains in exploring all the available sources of information; his paragraphs are both long and extraordinarily compact; the average reader soon becomes bewildered by the wealth of detail. Review, A. Molinier, *Rev. Hist.* 53:96, Sept. 1893.   RBM

N256 Haebler, Konrad. *Geschichte Spaniens unter den Habsburgern.* V. 1, *Geschichte Spaniens unter der Regierung Karls I (V).* Gotha, 1907. [Geschichte der europäischen Staaten.]

The outstanding merit of this volume, which continues (N201) Lembke, Schäfer, and Schirrmacher, *Geschichte von Spanien,* is that the emphasis is thrown on the internal development of Spain under the emperor—a much neglected subject; the treatment of foreign affairs is cut down to the smallest possible proportions.

The author has also written half a dozen other monographs on Spanish economic history and bibliography, and knows his field well. There is much solid stuff in the book, but the verdicts on Charles and his policy are too favorable. Haebler entirely ignores the strictures of the critics of his earlier works, who have pointed out his tendencies in this direction and given adequate reasons for disagreeing with him. Review, R. B. Merriman, *A.H.R.* 13:342, Jan. 1908. Also cf. the lives of Charles V by (I235*a*) Robertson and (I235*b*) Armstrong.   RBM

N257 Prescott, William H. *History of the reign of Philip the Second, king of Spain.* 3 v. Boston, 1855–58. Rev. ed. by J. F. Kirk, 1874; further rev. [Montezuma] ed. by W. H. Munro, 4 v., Philadelphia, 1904.

This history, which, save for a few details about Philip's private life and family, only carries the story to the year 1573, was the last important work which Prescott undertook. His eyesight troubled him far more when he was engaged on it than in the period when he wrote his (N252) *Ferdinand and Isabella,* and the material was so vast that he was unable to go through it with the same thoroughness. The fact that the book was unfinished has militated somewhat against its success; and it has been superseded by later works to a degree that does not hold true of Prescott's first work. The estimate of Philip is, on the whole, sane and just, and the work abounds in splendid passages, but it can never attain the same rank with *Ferdinand and Isabella.*   RBM

N258 Forneron, Henri. *Histoire de Philippe II.* 1880–82. 3rd ed., 4 v., Paris, 1887. (Bibliography.)

By all odds the best general account of the reign of Philip II. The author corrects the excessive severity of the judgments of the ultra-protestant historians of the period; on the other hand he makes no attempt to whitewash the king, and pitilessly exposes his many mistakes. M. Forneron is not a plodder; he aims at brilliant characterization; if his work is a little weak on the administrative and constitutional sides, it is only because he obviously preferred to leave these parts of the story to be treated by someone else. Review, L. Pingaud, *Rev. Hist.* 17:423, Nov. 1881; 24:409, Mar. 1884.   RBM

N259 Bratli, Carl G. V. *Filip II af Spanien, hans liv og personlighed.* København, 1909. French tr. and 2nd ed., *Philippe II, roi d'Espagne étude sur sa vie et son caractère,* Paris, 1912. (Bibliography.)

Not a biography, but a series of essays on the historical literature concerning Philip and on some of the more disputed phases of his life and reign. Marred by numerous minor slips and errors of detail; the point of view is frankly apologetic. Review, R. B. Merriman, *A.H.R.* 18:128, Oct. 1912.   RBM

N260a Hume, Martin A. S. *Spain, its greatness and decay, 1479–1788.* 1898. 2nd ed., Cambridge, Eng., 1899. [Cambridge historical series.] (Bibliography.)

   b ——— *Philip II of Spain.* 1897. New ed., London, 1911. [Foreign statesmen.] (Bibliography.)

   c ——— *Court of Philip IV: Spain in decadence.* N. Y., 1907.

   d Morel-Fatio, Alfred. *Études sur l'Espagne.* 4 v. Paris, 1888–1925.

Major Hume, editor of the Spanish series of the (L73) *Calendars of state papers,* utilized his knowledge of things Spanish, acquired in the Record Office and by long residence in Spain, to publish various volumes on the history of the Iberian peninsula. All are very readable; addressed to the general public rather than to specialists and scholars. Superficiality, frequent inaccuracies of statement, and lack of method and of thoroughness in the study of the sources are found, more or less, in all his works. *a.* Sketch of Spanish history from the beginning of the reign of Philip II to the end of that of Charles III, preceded by an introduction of 98 p. by Edward Armstrong which traces briefly the antecedent work of the Catholic Kings and Charles V. A useful supplement on special topics, especially of literary or social interest, may be found in *d.* *b.* Unquestionably Hume's *chef d'oeuvre* and one of the best of the series to which it belongs. He wrote, on this occasion at least, with clearness and impartiality, and the limitations of space to which he was subjected saved him from making the numerous errors of detail which disfigure some of his more special works. *c.* One of the last, most loosely written, and most readable of Hume's works. The reader is given a succession of 'close-up' views of seventeenth-century Spain, its foreign and domestic policy, its economic and social crises, its court intrigues, public scandals, and private amusements, over a period of some forty-five years.

CHHg

N261 Stirling-Maxwell, Sir William. *Don John of Austria, or passages from the history of the sixteenth century, 1547–1578.* 2 v. London, 1883.

These two sumptuous volumes, brought out after the author's death, by Sir George William Cox, read more like a novel than like serious history. Sir William's aim was to depict vividly the most notable personalities and dramatic scenes of the second half of the sixteenth century, and he succeeded admirably. He spared neither pains nor expense to make his work accurate and complete; he went through large masses of manuscript material with the utmost care, and resided for long periods in Spain. Save for narrative history and the study of personalities, the book is of little value; within those limits, however, it is all that could be desired. Review, J. G. Black, *Rev. Hist.* 25:146, May 1884.

RBM

N262a Pidal, Pedro José, Marqués de. *Historia de las alteraciones de Aragon en el reinado de Felipe II.* 3 v. Madrid, 1862–63. Tr. by J. G. Magnabal as *Philippe II, Antonio Perez, et le royaume d'Aragon,* 2 v., Paris, 1867.

b Mignet, François Auguste. *Antonio Perez and Philip II.* London, 1846. Tr. by W. F. Ainsworth from *Antonio Perez et Philippe II,* 1845; rev. ed., Paris, 1881.

a. The scholarship is sound, the judgments sane, and there is an admirable appendix of documents at the end of each volume. Completely supersedes *b.,* which is a brilliant book.

RBM

N263 Lea, Henry C. *Moriscos of Spain, their conversion and expulsion.* Philadelphia, 1901.

By-product of the author's (N621a) *History of the inquisition of Spain;* characterized by the same profound research. Lea traces, in some 340 pages, the fortunes of the converted Moors from the conquest of Granada to their expulsion in 1609, and closes with a chapter on the heavy economic penalties to which this episode condemned the Spanish state. Review, C. H. Toy, *A.H.R.* 7:346, Jan. 1902.

CHHg

N264a Cánovas del Castillo, Antonio. *Historia de la decadencia de España desde el advenimiento de Felipe III al trono hasta la muerte de Carlos II.* 1854. 2nd ed., with preface by J. Pérez de Guzmán, Madrid, 1910.

b —— *Bosquejo histórico de la casa de Austria en España.* 1868. 2nd ed., with preface by J. Pérez de Guzmán, Madrid, 1911.

a. Notable book, written in 1854, when he was twenty-six years of age, by one of the greatest scholars and statesmen that Spain produced in the nineteenth century. Cánovas was the first Spaniard to undertake any serious work on the period of his country's decline, which he characterizes as 'no less worthy of study than that of Rome'; and it was but natural that his book should be disfigured by numerous errors and inaccuracies, which he acknowledged, with characteristic frankness, in *b.* The *Decadencia,* however, reveals profound political insight and touches of real genius. RBM

N265 Taillandier, Saint-René, Madame. *La princesse des Ursins: une grande dame française à la cour d'Espagne sous Louis XIV.* Paris, 1926. [Figures du passé.]

Based on archival and other unpublished material. RBM

SPAIN: EIGHTEENTH CENTURY

N301 Legrelle, Arsène. *La diplomatie française et la succession d'Espagne.* 4 v. Paris, 1888–92; 2nd ed., 6 v., 1895–99.

Work of profound research and abundant citation; most complete history of the question of the Spanish succession. Written from a French point of view; displays the deepest admiration and sympathy for Louis XIV; and presents a correspondingly unfavorable view of William III and the coalition. In the introduction to v. 1 is a comprehensive review of previous works, old and modern, on the subject. Review, A. Morel-Fatio, *Rev. Hist.* 41:421, Nov. 1889; L. Farges, *ibid.* 48:88, Jan. 1892; 50:90, Sept. 1892; 51:335, Mar. 1893. CHHg

N302 Parnell, Arthur. *War of the succession in Spain during the reign of Queen Anne, 1702–1711.* 1888. Cheaper reissue, London, 1905. (Bibliographies.)

Thorough study, based on a careful exploration of manuscript sources, but generally ignoring the background of contemporary European politics. Its special contribution is the elucidation of events in the years of 1705–1707 centering about the pretended exploits of the Earl of Peterborough. CHHg

N303 Baudrillart, Alfred. *Philippe V et la cour de France.* 5 v. Paris, 1890–1901.

Making use of extensive correspondence in Spanish archives, the existence of which was for the most part previously unknown, Baudrillart presents a picture of the relations between France and Spain in the first half of the eighteenth century truer in all essential details than that of any of his predecessors. He is perhaps inclined, at times, to judge the activities of the French government in too favorable a light, and to exaggerate the immediate advantages which French influence brought to Spain and the Spaniards. The volumes offer a series of incisive portraits of the leading personalities of the time. Review, A. Pribram, *Hist. Zeit.* 70:304, 1893. CHHg

N304 Armstrong, Edward. *Elisabeth Farnese, "the termagant of Spain."* London, 1892.

Study of European diplomacy in the first half of the eighteenth century. Based largely on the letters of Alberoni and the despatches of English ambassadors at Madrid; covers a period of complicated diplomatic cross-currents and intrigues, when the personal influence and dynastic ambitions of the Spanish queen were dominant factors in international politics. Interesting and well-written; important for the Bourbon family compacts, the relations between England and Spain before 1739, and the beginnings of the Austrian hegemony in Italy. Review, A. W. Ward, *E.H.R.* 8:162, Jan. 1893.   CHHg

N305a Rousseau, François. *Règne de Charles III d'Espagne, 1759–1788.* 2 v. Paris, 1907. (Bibliography.)

   b Ferrer del Río, Antonio. *Historia del reinado de Carlos III en España.* 4 v. Madrid, 1856.

   c Danvila y Collado, Manuel. *Reinado de Carlos III.* 6 v. Madrid, 1893–96. V. 3–6 are v. 9–13 of (N122) Cánovas del Castillo, *Historia general de España.*

a. Latest and best history of the reign, more impartial in spirit and critical in method than the more extensive lives, *b.* and *c.* Although in many ways a commentary and criticism of these earlier works, Rousseau's volumes represent much independent study and research. The author regards Spain as dominated throughout by the political and intellectual influence of France. Review, W. H. Hutton, *E.H.R.* 22:809, Oct. 1907.   CHHg

SPAIN: NINETEENTH CENTURY

N351 Clarke, Henry Butler. *Modern Spain, 1815–1898.* Cambridge, Eng., 1906. [Cambridge historical series.] (Bibliography.)

Thorough and accurate, somewhat meticulous, and overcrowded with detail. The author's standpoint is genuinely objective, and he knows the facts. Unquestionably the safest book in English on which to lay the foundations for a study of nineteenth-century Spain. Review, *E.H.R.* 22:410, Apr. 1907.   RBM

N352 Hume, Martin A. S. *Modern Spain, 1788–1898.* 1900. 2nd ed., N. Y., 1906. [Story of the nations.]

One of the most entertaining, but likewise superficial, volumes that Hume produced (cf. N260). Based rather on hearsay than research; places far too much emphasis on palace intrigues; serves, however, to give the 'atmosphere' of one phase of the period under review. Review, E. G. Bourne, *A.H.R.* 7:151, Oct. 1901.   RBM

N353 White, George Frederick. *A century of Spain and Portugal, 1788–1898.* London, 1909. (Bibliography.)

Readable, though not particularly accurate, narrative. The author, who is a military man, obviously delights in battles and revolutions and tends to group his story around them.   RBM

N354 Baumgarten, Hermann. *Geschichte Spaniens vom Ausbruch der französischen Revolution bis auf unsere Tage.* 3 v. Leipzig, 1865–71. [Staatengeschichte der neuesten Zeit.] (Bibliographical footnotes.)

This careful, painstaking, and, on the whole, accurate work carries the story from the accession of Charles IV to the end of the first Carlist war, 1839. Primarily a narrative history, written in a manner at present out of date; no other works covers the same field with equal thoroughness. For the period of the Peninsular War it should be supplemented by the works of (1536a) Napier and (1536b) Oman.   RBM

N355a Duncan, Francis. *English in Spain, or the story of the war of succession between 1834 and 1840. Compiled from the letters, journals, and reports of Generals W. Wylde, Sir Collingwood Dickson, W. H. Askwith; Colonels Lacy, Colquhoun, Michell, and Major Turner, R. A.; and Colonels Alderson, Du Plat, and Lynn, R. E., commissioners with Queen Isabella's armies.* London, 1877.

b Bollaert, William. *Wars of succession of Portugal and Spain from 1826 to 1840 with résumé of the political history of Portugal and Spain to the present time.* 2 v. London, 1870.

a. Readable, though occasionally prolix collection of papers relating to the Carlist war of 1834–40. Major Duncan seems skilfully to have welded the disparate material he had available into an accurate and impartial record of an interesting episode in modern Spanish history. Useful as a commentary on all the military activities of the war; it contains illustrations and a military map. V. 2 of *b.* Another work of similar character.   RBM

N356 Strobel, Edward Henry. *Spanish revolution, 1868–1875.* Boston, 1898.

Terse and direct in style; precise in statement. Reviews in simple fashion the developments from September 19, 1868, the outbreak of the revolution, down to the restoration of the Bourbons in January, 1875. Attributes to Castelar a larger part than the famous orator really played in shaping the course of the constitutional debates and republican fortunes.   CHHg

N357 Becker, Jerónimo. *Historia de las relaciones exteriores de España durante el siglo XIX.: Apuntes para una historia diplomática.* V. 1, 2. 1800–1868. Madrid, 1924.

Valuable for the study of general European history as well as for Spanish history. Review, *A.H.R.* 30:595, Apr. 1925.   RBM

N358 Ramírez, Wenceslao, Marqués de Villa-Urrutia. *La reina gobernadora: Doña María Cristina de Borbón.* Madrid, 1925.

Primarily diplomatic and military affairs; emphasizes personal rather than economic factors.   RBM

SPAIN: TWENTIETH CENTURY

N401 Meynadier, Robert. *Les étapes de la royauté d'Alphonse XIII.* Paris, 1914.

Accurate and well-informed summary of the political history of Spain, 1904–1914. There is not much head or tail to it; it is thrown together rather than composed, but it contains much valuable material. The portrait of the young king is highly favorable.   RBM

N402a Lavondès, Raymond. *La question Catalane.* Montpellier, 1908. [University of Montpellier dissertation.] (Bibliography.)

b Archer, William. *Life, trial, and death of Francisco Ferrer.* N. Y., 1911.

c Hernández Villaescusa, Modesto. *La revolución de Julio en Barcelona, hechos, causas, y remedios.* 1909. 2nd ed., Barcelona, 1910.

a. Clear, sane, and scholarly treatment of the Catalan question, in which the historical background is particularly well done. The sole defect of the book, from the point of view of the student of modern conditions, is that it came out before the Ferrer case reached its conclusion, and consequently furnishes no information in regard to that dramatic episode. There is, however, already a considerable literature concerning the Ferrer case, of which *b.* gives a good account, highly favorable to Ferrer, and *c.* presents the opposite point of view.

RBM

SPAIN: NAVAL HISTORY

N521 Fernández Duro, Cesáreo. *Armada Española desde la unión de los reinos de Castilla y de Aragón.* 9 v. Madrid, 1895–1903.

Captain Fernández Duro, retired, had already achieved distinction as an historian of the Spanish navy (his *Marina de Castilla* in (N122) *Historia general de España* summarizes the naval history of Castile down to 1476), when he entered upon this monumental record of Spanish naval activities from the last quarter of the fifteenth century to the end of the first third of the nineteenth. The work is an accurate and scholarly compendium of political history, biography, geography, colonial history, and many other aspects of national life which were affected by the growth and decline of the Spanish navy, and of the many wars, on both shores of the Atlantic and in the Mediterranean, in which Spain from time to time was engaged. Much fresh documentary material; excellent illustrations; numerous maps.

RBM

SPAIN: CONSTITUTIONAL AND LEGAL HISTORY

N531 Marichalar, Amalio, Marqués de Montesa, and **Manrique, Cayetano.** *Historia de la legislación y recitaciones del derecho civil de España.* 9 v. Madrid, 1861–72.

Minute chronological study of all the legislation recorded in Spanish history, with copious citation of texts, down to the nineteenth century. A detailed chapter of narrative history precedes each of the social and legal surveys of the successive chronological periods. Not a profound piece of juristic analysis, but rather a generally dependable compilation. Analytical tables of contents serve in lieu of indexes.

RBM

N532 Pérez Pujol, Eduardo. *Historia de las instituciones sociales de la España Goda.* 4 v. Valencia, 1896.

The fruit of thirty years of laborious research; intended to serve as the first portion of an intensive survey of the history of legal and political institutions; published after the author's death. Written in a fine, attractive style; embraces the political, social, and institutional history of Roman and Gothic Spain; supersedes, in large measure, the Visigothic portions of (H201) Felix Dahn, *Könige der Germanen.* Review, R. Altamira, *Rev. Hist.* 66:383, March 1898.

RBM

N533a Colmeiro, Manuel. *Historia de la economía política en España.* 2 v. Madrid, 1863.

b ——— *Curso de derecho político, según la historia de León y Castilla.* Madrid, 1873.

c ——— *Cortes de los antiguos reinos de León y de Castilla. Introducción.* 2 v. Madrid, 1883–84.

d *Cortes de los antiguos reinos de León y de Castilla.* 5 v. Madrid, 1861–1903. [Real Academia de la Historia.]

e *Actas de las cortes de Castilla.* Madrid, 1877 ff. [Comisión de Gobierno Interior.]

f **Danvila y Collado, Manuel.** *El poder civil en España.* 6 v. Madrid, 1885–86.

Manuel Colmeiro, 1818–1894, was professor of constitutional history at the University of Madrid, a prominent figure in the Spanish literary world, and also a participant in public life. *a.* First serious effort of a Spanish scholar to bring together and classify the vast amount of material available on this subject. Still well worth consulting at the outset of an investigation. *b.* Methodical *résumé* of the medieval institutional history of Castile and Leon; an admirable foundation for more special work in this field. *c.* Indispensable guide to *d.*, which contains the records of proceedings of the Castilian cortes from the beginning to 1559. Far fuller and more reliable than the corresponding portion of *f.*, which may still be profitably consulted for the proceedings of the cortes of the eastern kingdoms (which with the exception of Catalonia to 1479 have not yet been published) and for the development of the other institutions of Castile; it should be used, however, with the utmost caution. *e.* Continuation of *d.*, now covering to 1620. RBM

N534a Hinojosa, Eduardo de. *El régimen señorial y la cuestión agraria en Cataluña durante la edad media...* Madrid, 1905.

b ——— *Estudios sobre la historia del derecho Español.* Madrid, 1903.

a. 'One of the most remarkable books produced by the Spanish historical school in many years,' and unquestionably Hinojosa's masterpiece. It gives the most profound and penetrating analysis of the position of the Catalonian serf, supported by illuminating comparisons with conditions in other lands. The sources, in manuscript and in print, and the works of other authorities, both Spanish and foreign, are carefully scrutinized and compared. Hinojosa's other works, especially *b.*, are all indispensable for the student of Spanish jurisprudence. Review of *a., Rev. Hist.* 85:447, July 1904; of *b.,* R. Altamira, *ibid.* 97:385, March 1908. RBM

N535 Gounon-Loubens, Jules. *Essais sur l'administration de la Castille au XVIᵉ siècle.* Paris, 1860.

Though written over sixty years ago, the best general sketch of the social, constitutional, and economic condition of Spain under Charles V and Philip II. Based almost entirely on contemporary writers and printed sources; a model of accurate, painstaking scholarship. Some of its conclusions, especially on the economic side, have been modified as a result of the subsequent discovery of new material; but the book as a whole remains indispensable. RBM

N536 **Mayer, Ernst.** *Historia de las instituciones sociales y políticas de España y Portugal durante los siglos V á XIV.* V. 1. Madrid, 1925.

To be completed by a second volume. This is the first of a series of volumes intended by the jurists of the Centro de Estudios Históricos to supplement the (N946) *Anuario de historia del derecho español.* RBM

SPAIN: ECONOMIC AND SOCIAL HISTORY

N571 **Klein, Julius.** *The mesta, a study in Spanish economic history, 1273–1836.* Cambridge, Mass., 1920. [Harvard economic studies, v. 21.] (Valuable bibliography.)

Scholarly analysis of the significance of the great sheep-owning organization which, from the later Middle Ages through the Napoleonic invasions, served as the backbone of the foremost industry of the country. Has a technical glossary, illustrations, and a map of the migration routes and pasturage areas. Review, A. Morel-Fatio, *Rev. Hist.* 137:98, May 1921. RBM

SPAIN: CULTURAL HISTORY: GENERAL

N601 **Mariéjol, Jean H.** *L'Espagne sous Ferdinand et Isabelle: le gouvernement, les institutions, et les moeurs.* Paris, 1892. [Bibliothèque d'histoire illustrée.] (Bibliographies.)

By all odds the best general picture of the political, social, and administrative system of the Spanish kingdoms in the period of the Catholic Kings. The book is so entertainingly written that the casual reader might be deceived into thinking it superficial: careful perusal, however, will speedily reveal the sound and thorough scholarship which forms the basis for the entire work. Characterized by an admirable objectivity; helpful and precise footnotes; well selected illustrations. Review, *Rev. Hist.* 51:436, March 1893. RBM

N602 **Desdevises du Dezert, Georges.** *L'Espagne de l'ancien régime.* 3 v. Paris, 1897–1904. [1, *La société;* 2, *Les institutions;* 3, *La richesse et la civilisation.*] (Bibliography.)

By far the best general picture available of the social, constitutional, and economic conditions of Spain in the eighteenth century. The fullest possible citation of authorities and a wealth of picturesque detail reveal the unusual extent of the author's reading. Review, R. Reuss, *Rev. Hist.* 64:344, July 1897; H. Léonardon, *ibid.* 86:156, Sept. 1904. RBM

N603 **Calvert, Albert F.** *Spanish series.* 22 v. London and N. Y., 1907–21. [1, *Granada and the Alhambra;* 2, *Seville;* 3, *Toledo;* 4, *Murillo;* 5, *Spanish arms and armour;* 6, *Escorial;* 7, (with W. M. Gallichan) *Cordova;* 8, (with C. G. Hartley) *Prado;* 9, *Goya;* 10, (with C. G. Hartley) *Velasquez;* 11, *Leon, Burgos, and Salamanca;* 12, *Valladolid, Oviedo, Segovia, Zamora, Avila, and Zaragoza;* 13, (with C. G. Hartley) *El Greco;* 14, *Madrid;* 15, *Royal palaces of Spain;* 16, *Valencia and Murcia;* 17, *Galicia;* 18, *Royal tapestries at Madrid;* 19, *Vizcaya and Santander;* 20, *Catalonia and the Balearic Islands;* 21, *Sculpture in Spain;* 22, *Spanish royal tapestries.*]

This series on the different cities and regions of Spain and on the fine arts in Spain, is chiefly valuable for its admirable illustrations, which occupy over five times as much space as the text. The printed pages are pleasantly written descriptions, with occasional mention of significant historical facts, and serve as an adequate introduction to the pictorial portion which follows. The reader can get an excellent idea of the characteristic Spanish landscape, and of Spain's principal architectural monuments by glancing through the different volumes which compose this series. That on Granada and the Alhambra is a particularly satisfactory one.   RBM

SPAIN: CULTURAL HISTORY: RELIGION

N621a Lea, Henry C. *History of the inquisition of Spain.* 4 v. N. Y. and London, 1906–07.

b —— *Chapters from the religious history of Spain connected with the inquisition.* Philadelphia, 1890.

c **Schäfer, Ernst.** *Beiträge zur Geschichte des spanischen Protestantismus und der Inquisition im sechzehnten Jahrhundert, nach den Originalakten in Madrid und Simancas bearbeitet.* 3 v. Gütersloh, 1902. (Bibliography.)

d **Régne, Jean.** *Catalogue des actes de Jaime I, Pedro III, Alfonso· III, et Jaime II, rois d'Aragon, concernant les juifs, 1213–1327.* 4 pt. Privas, 1924.

a. These massive volumes are unquestionably one of the greatest monuments of American historical scholarship. Their outstanding characteristics are direct dependence on the sources, great wealth of illustrative detail, and complete freedom from polemic or bias; Lea sought merely to describe the actual workings of the inquisition; he seldom stopped to moralize. The partisan attitude of previous writers rendered this task exceedingly difficult to perform; Lea achieved it in such fashion that it will never have to be done again. The book will never, in all probability, be thoroughly studied except by scholars; certain chapters, however, will prove permanently interesting and important for the intelligent general reader. Perusal of the one on 'Protestantism' in v. 3 will dispense everyone but the specialist from the necessity of using *c*. *b.* Earlier studies by Lea in the same field. Review of *a.,* G. L. Burr, *A.H.R.* 11:887, July 1906; 12:359, Jan. 1907; 12:625, Apr. 1907; 13:337, Jan. 1908; of *c.,* H. C. Lea, *A.H.R.* 8:529, Apr. 1903. For other works by Lea and for criticisms of his methods and views, cf. (F561, 562). *d.* Opens an important field of investigation. Review, *Rev. Hist.* 148:117, Jan. 1925.   RBM

SPAIN: CULTURAL HISTORY: LITERATURE

N661a Fitzmaurice-Kelly, James. *History of Spanish literature.* London and N. Y., 1898. [Short histories of the literatures of the world.] French tr. by Henry D. Davray, *Histoire de la littérature espagnole,* Paris, 1904. [Histoire des littératures.] *New history of Spanish literature.* London and N. Y., 1926. (Bibliography.)

b —— *Bibliographie de l'histoire de la littérature espagnole.* Paris, 1913. [Histoires des littératures.]

c **Clarke, Henry Butler.** *Spanish literature: an elementary handbook.* 1893. New ed., London, 1909. (Bibliography.)

d **Mérimée, Ernest.** *Précis d'histoire de la littérature espagnole.* Paris, 1908.

e **Wolf, Ferdinand J.** *Studien zur Geschichte der spanischen und portugiesischen National-litteratur.* Berlin, 1859. Spanish tr. by Miguel de Unamuno and Marcelino Menéndez y Pelayo, *Historia de las literaturas castellana y portuguesa,* 2 v., Madrid, 1895–96.

f Amador de los Ríos, José. *Historia crítica de la literatura española.*
7 v. Madrid, 1861–65.

g Blanco García, Francisco. *La literatura española en el siglo XIX.* 3 v.
Madrid, 1891–94. 3rd ed. of v. 1–2, Madrid, 1909–10.

h Cejador y Frauca, Julio. *Historia de la lengua y literatura castellana.*
14 v. Madrid, 1915–22.

a. Sober, critical, and accurate review of the Spanish literary field: enlarged
and improved in American, Spanish, and French editions, and in the 'new history'
of 1926.   *b.* Indispensable guide to the literature of Spanish literary history.   *c.*
A suitable handbook.   *d.* Very good manual, written by a keen French critic.   *e.*
Masterly study of the early period only. The Spanish edition contains additions
and corrections.   *f.* Critical, but not entirely reliable, study of Spanish literature
prior to the sixteenth century.   *g.* Extended and useful treatise, written with
an ecclesiastical bias.   TWB
   h. Especially valuable for recent and contemporary literature; devotes seven
volumes to the period 1849–1920.   RBM

SPAIN: CULTURAL HISTORY: ART

N681a Dieulafoy, Marcel A. *Art in Spain and Portugal.* N. Y., 1913. [Ars
Una series.]   (Good bibliographies.)   Tr. of *Histoire générale de l'art,*
v. 5, *Espagne et Portugal,* Paris, 1913.

b Mayer, August L. *Geschichte der spanischen Malerei.*   1913.   2nd ed.,
2 v., Leipzig, 1923. (Bibliography.)

c Gade, John A. *Cathedrals of Spain.* Boston, 1911.

d Byne, Arthur, and **Stapley, Mildred.** *Spanish architecture of the sixteenth century.* N. Y. and London, 1917. [Publications of the Hispanic
Society of America.]

a. Useful introductory handbook with a great variety of small but well-chosen
illustrations.   *b.* Solid history of Spanish painting from the earliest times to
the present day; half-tone illustrations.   *c.* An artist's account, with numerous
illustrations of typical Romanesque, Gothic, and Renaissance ecclesiastical architecture.   *d.* Admirable description of the plateresque and Herrera styles. Also
cf. (N603) Calvert, *Spanish series,* of which various volumes contain abundant
illustrations of Spanish architecture, and others are devoted to the leading
Spanish artists and art collections.   SBF

SPAIN: GOVERNMENT PUBLICATIONS

   The Spanish government has published verbatim records of the proceedings of
the Cortes since 1810. The original title, (N901) *Diario de las discusiones y
actas de las Cortes,* Cadiz and Madrid, 1811 ff. has been slightly modified several
times.

SPAIN: PERIODICALS

   Of periodical publications, (N941) *Boletín de la Real Academia de la Historia,*
Madrid, 1877 ff., deserves first mention; it is a vast mine of historical information, and contains articles, documents, and bibliographical notes. The most
valuable of the Spanish reviews for historical students is (N942) *Revista de
archivos, bibliotecas, y museos,* Madrid, 1871 ff., index, 1871–1910, Madrid, 1911–13,
edited by a committee of the most eminent scholars in Spain. Its recent numbers

are far more valuable than the earlier ones. Each number contains lists of current publications relating to Spanish history, as does also (N943) *Revista de filología española,* Madrid, 1914 ff. Two notable periodicals, devoted exclusively to Spanish topics, but published in France, are (N944) *Revue hispanique,* Paris, 1894 ff., edited by R. Foulché-Delbosc, which since 1905 has been the official organ of the Hispanic Society of America; and (N945) *Bulletin hispanique,* Paris, 1899 ff., which is published by a group of well known French scholars, mostly from the South. The history of law is treated in (N946) *Anuario de historia del derecho español,* Madrid, 1924 ff., issued by the Centro de Estudios Históricos.

PORTUGAL: BIBLIOGRAPHY

N1001a Figanière, Jorge Cesar de. *Bibliographia historica portugueza.* Lisboa, 1850.

  b Bernardes Branco, Manoel. *Portugal e os estrangeiros.* 4 pts. in 2 v. Lisboa, 1879. Rev. ed. of pt. 1, 3 v., Lisboa, 1893–95.

  c Brito Aranha, Pedro W. de. *Bibliographie des ouvrages Portugais pour servir à l'étude des villes . . . des institutions . . . du Portugal . . .* Lisbonne, 1900.

  d Faria, Antonio de Portugal de. *Portugal e Italia.* 2 v., Leorne, 1898.

  e Albrecht, Johannes. *Beiträge zur Geschichte der portugiesischen Historiographie des sechszehnten Jahrhunderts.* Halle, 1915.

The historical bibliography of Portugal is still in a most unsatisfactory condition. There are a number of old-fashioned works on the subject, such as *a.,* but they are naturally quite out of date, both as regards matter and arrangement. *b.* and *c.* Most valuable for general bibliographical information. *d.* and *e.* Useful to the specialist; *d.* being a catalogue of Italian books and of manuscripts in Italian libraries which deal with Portuguese affairs. The reader is reminded that (N4) Foulché-Delbosc and Barrau-Dihigo, *Manuel de l'hispanisant,* treats of Portugal as well as Spain. RBM

N1002 Silva, Innocencio F. da. *Diccionario bibliographico portuguez . . . applicaveis a Portugal e ao Brasil.* V. 1–22, Lisboa, 1858–1922.

Lists Portuguese publications in general. The original work occupies v. 1–7, while the supplement forms v. 8–22. GMD

Portugal: Library Collections.—Fair collections of material on Portuguese history will be found in the libraries listed earlier in this section as containing good collections on Spanish history. AHS

PORTUGAL: ENCYCLOPEDIAS

N1021 Pinheiro Chagas, Manuel. *Diccionario popular, historico, geographico, mythologico, biographico, artistico, bibliographico, e litterario.* 16 v. Lisboa, 1876–90.

Most important encyclopedic work for Portugal. GMD

PORTUGAL: COLLECTIONS OF SOURCES

The chief collection of Portuguese archives is at Lisbon in the Torre do Tombo. For further information, cf. (N4) Foulché-Delbosc and Barrau-Dihigo, *Manuel de l'hispanisant.*

Among the more important printed collections of documentary sources are (N1061) M. F. de Barros, Visconde de Santarem, *Quadro elementar das relações politicas e diplomaticas de Portugal com as diversas potencias do mundo, desde o principio da monarchia portugueza até aos nossos dias,* 18 v., Paris and Lisboa, 1842–76, of which the later volumes were edited by L. A. Rebello da Silva and J. da Silva Mendes Leal; (N1062) L. A. Rebello da Silva and others, *Corpo diplomatico portuguez, contendo os actos e relações politicas e diplomaticas de Portugal com as diversas potencias do mundo desde o seculo XVI. até os nossos dias,* 14 v., Lisboa, 1862–1910; (N1063a) J. Ferreira, Visconde de Borges de Castro, *Collecção dos tratados, convenções, contratos, e actos publicos celebrados entre a coroa de Portugal e as mais potencias desde 1640 até ao presente,* 8 v., Lisboa, 1856–58, continued by a (N1063b) *Supplemento,* 22 v. in 24, Lisboa, 1872–80, edited by Borges de Castro and J. F. J. Biker, and (N1063c) *Nova collecção de tratados . . .,* Lisboa, 1890 ff.

PORTUGAL: SHORTER GENERAL HISTORIES

N1101 Stephens, Henry Morse. *Portugal.* 1891. 4th ed., with continuation to 1908 by M. A. S. Hume, London and N. Y., 1908. [Story of the nations.] (Bibliography in preface.)

By all odds the best short account in English of the history of Portugal; one of the best volumes of the series to which it belongs; written entirely from printed material. The importance of Portugal's relations to England is somewhat over-emphasized. The author had real love and enthusiasm for his subject and tells his story simply and effectively. RBM

N1102 Young, George. *Portugal old and young, an historical study.* Oxford, 1917. [History of belligerents.]

Essay on the racial antecedents and political development of the Portuguese people; epigrammatic, antithetical, not always trustworthy, and often contradictory. Most of the brilliant generalizations of the writer are stimulating but untrue. The tone throughout is anti-clerical, anti-Spanish, and strongly British. The best part of the book is the account, at the end, of recent Portuguese history, including the revolution and the World War. CHHg

N1103 Diercks, Gustav. *Das moderne Portugal.* Berlin, 1913. [Veröffentlichungen des allgemeinen Vereins für deutsche Literatur.]

Descriptive rather than historical work; mentioned here because its author is well versed in Iberian affairs, because of the admirable chapter on 'Geschichtliche Erinnerungen,' and because it is one of the sanest books that has been written about Portugal since the installation of the republican regime. CEMCG

N1104 Oliveira Martins, Joaquim Pedro. *Historia de Portugal.* 1879. 10th ed., 2 v., Lisboa, 1920. (Bibliography.)

Complete narrative history of Portugal down to 1816. While there are no references through the work, there is at the end a long bibliographical note, in which the author reveals his bitter prejudices against the colonial policies of his country. CEMCG

PORTUGAL: LONGER GENERAL HISTORIES

N1121a Herculano, Alexandre. *Historia de Portugal desde o começo da monarchia até o fim do reinado de Affonso III.* 1846–53. 4th ed., 4 v., Lisboa, 1875–88.

b McMurdo, Edward. *History of Portugal.* 3 v. London, 1888–89.

a. Embraces the history of Portugal in all its phases from the earliest times until 1279; worthy to be ranked among the great national histories produced in the nineteenth century. Exceptionally good for its treatment of feudal institutions and the social conditions of Portugal and western Spain. *b.* V. 1. Covers the same field as *a.;* owes far more to *a.* than the introduction would give reason to think. V. 2 and 3. Carry the story to 1740; considerably less satisfactory. There is, however, no other history of Portugal in English which covers the ground with the same detail.   RBM

N1122 Schäfer, Heinrich. *Geschichte von Portugal.* V. 1–4, Hamburg; v. 5, Gotha, 1836–54. [Geschichte der europäischen Staaten.] Tr. of v. 1–2, with brief supplementary summary for later times, by H. Soulange-Bodin as *Histoire de Portugal,* 1846; new ed., Paris, 1858.

Without doubt the best general history of Portugal in a language other than Portuguese; still of great value; carries the story from 1095 to 1820.   RBM

N1123 Almeida, Fortunato de. *História de Portugal.* V. 1–4. Coimbra, 1922–26.

Published volumes come down to 1816.   RBM

PORTUGAL: HISTORY OF SPECIAL PERIODS

N1201a Suárez Inclán, Julián. *Guerra de anexión en Portugal durante el reinado de Don Felipe II.* 2 v. Madrid, 1897–98.

b Prestage, Edgar. *Diplomatic relations of Portugal with France, England, and Holland from 1640 to 1668.* Watford, Eng., 1925. (Bibliographical foot-notes.)

a. Standard, indeed the only important, authority on the subject with which it deals. Practically the entire book is devoted to the years 1578–82; the military events of 1580–81 are related· with great fulness. The author utilized a number of documents previously unknown, and published the most important of them in an appendix; they are chiefly concerned with naval and military details. *b.* Valuable monograph on the international aspects of the restoration of Portuguese independence. Review, G. Jones, *A.H.R.* 31:824, July 1926.   RBM

N1202a Carnota, John Athelstane Smith, Conde da. *Memoirs of the Marquis of Pombal, with extracts from his writings.* 2 v. London, 1843. 2nd ed., with title, *Marquis of Pombal,* London, 1871.

b Gomes, Francisco Luiz. *Le marquis de Pombal, esquisse de sa vie publique.* Lisbonne, 1869.

c Duhr, Bernhard, S. J. *Pombal, sein Charakter und seine Politik.* Freiburg, 1891.

d Menezes, Carlos J. de. *Os Jesuitas e o Marques de Pombal.* 2 v Porto, 1893.

e Du Hamel de Breuil, Comte Jean. *Un ministre philosophe, Carvalho, Marquis de Pombal.* Rev. Hist. 59:1–35, Sept. 1895; 60:1–27, 272–306, Jan., March 1896.

a. and *b.* On the whole the most satisfactory general accounts of the great eighteenth-century minister. *b.* The more impartial; justly appraises Pombal's virtues and his immense services to the state; but is by no means blind to his faults. Among the numerous monographs on the period, *c., d., e.* are specially valuable.   RBM

N1203 Carnota, John Athelstane Smith, Conde da. *Memoirs of Field-Marshal the Duke of Saldanha.* 2 v. London, 1880.

Interesting biography of one of the foremost figures in the stormy history of nineteenth-century Portugal, with a number of the most important of his letters. May be profitably read in conjunction with v. 1 of (N355*b*) Bollaert, *Wars of succession.*   RBM

PORTUGAL: CONSTITUTIONAL HISTORY

N1531 Gama Barros, Henrique da. *Historia da administração publica em Portugal nos seculos XII a XV.* 3 v. Lisboa, 1885–1914. (Copious bibliographical references.)

Standard constitutional and social analysis of medieval Portugal. Unfortunately there is no parallel work for medieval Castile or the eastern Spanish kingdoms. Book 1. Analyzes the written and customary law. Book 2. Contains a study of the administrative system and a methodical review of the royal powers and those of the royal assistants. The succession problem is acutely surveyed. Book 3. Admirable summary of the economic history of medieval Portugal.   CEMCG

N1532 Nerêa, M. P. *O poder real e as cortes.* Coimbra, 1923.

Careful discussion of an important and complicated subject.   RBM

N1533 Prestage, Edgar. *The royal power and the cortes in Portugal.* Watford, 1927.

Brief but penetrating analysis.   RBM

PORTUGAL: CULTURAL HISTORY: LITERATURE

N1661a Braga, Theophilo. *Manual da historia da litteratura portugueza.* Porto, 1875.

  b ——— *Curso de historia da litteratura portugueza.* Lisboa, 1885.

  c ——— *Historia da litteratura portugueza.* V. 1–4, 6–8, 8A, 9–14, 17–22, 24–30. Porto, 1870–1909. Later ed. of some v.

  d Mendes dos Remedios, Joaquim. *História da literatura portuguêsa desde as origens até á atualiaade.* 1898. 5th ed., Lisba, 1921. (Bibliography.)

  e Michaëlis de Vasconcellos, Carolina. *Geschichte der portugiesischen Litteratur.* Strassburg, 1894. [Groeber, Grundriss der romanischen Philologie.]

  f Bell, Aubrey, F. G. *Portuguese literature.* Oxford, 1922.

a. and *b.* Brief summaries by one of the foremost masters of the subject. *b.* Contains interesting selections from the texts. *c.* Monumental work; planned to extend to thirty-two volumes; really several separate but complementary works under a common title.   *d.* Convenient and popular manual.   *e.* Typical product of the best German literary scholarship.   *f.* Convenient and interesting manual. Review, C. K. Jones, *Hisp. Amer. Hist. Rev.* 7:94, Feb. 1927.   TWB

PORTUGAL: PERIODICALS

The most valuable of the Portuguese historical periodical publications similar in scope to (N941) is (N1941) *Archivo (Arquivo) historico portuguez,* v. 1-9, Lisboa, 1903-14, ed. by J. da Silva Pessanha and A. Braamcamp Freire.   RBM

SECTION O

ITALY

Editor

THEODORE FRANCIS JONES

Professor of European History, New York University

CONTENTS

INTRODUCTION

The selection of books presented in this section has been subjected to certain important restrictions. Works for the ancient period to the fall of the Roman Empire in the West have been assigned to § E, and those dealing with the history of the Catholic church in general and with the papacy to § F. Furthermore, books which present Italy in its relations to the general History of Europe in

663

the medieval, modern, and contemporary periods have been assigned to §§ H, I, and J respectively.

The field covered by this section is, therefore, that of the internal affairs of Italy since the close of the fifth century, excluding the history of the papacy. Through this period down until as late as 1860 Italy was 'a geographical expression' rather than a unit in historical development. Consequently, there are extraordinarily few works dealing with the history of Italy as a whole, in comparison with the wealth of materials for countries like England and France.

Throughout a large part of the period concerned, Italy was more or less under the domination of other countries, or its affairs were closely bound up with the activities of other nations such as Germany, Austria, Spain, and France. Accordingly, the histories of those countries (cf. §§ M, N, P) contain much material important for the history of Italy.

The division of Italy into petty states, until after the middle of the nineteenth century, has had an important effect upon the production of historical works concerning Italy. There is a vast wealth of sectional and local histories and of biographies of individuals of provincial or minor importance. Nearly all the best work in the field of Italian history has, consequently, been of a local rather than of a national character.

Although one of the most important movements of general character in the history of Europe, the Renaissance, with its revival of learning and its development of art, was primarily Italian in origin and development, its historical treatment has been provincial rather than national. Even in the case of the Risorgimento, the movement which produced the unification of Italy, while the output of literature of local or biographical character has been extraordinary, there have appeared remarkably few competent studies of the movement as a whole or in its national aspects.

BIBLIOGRAPHY

O1a **Pagliaini, Attilio.** *Catalogo generale della libreria italiana dall' anno 1847 a tutto il 1899.* 3 v. Milano, 1901–10. *Indice,* 3 v., Milano, 1910–22. *Supplemento,* 1900–1910, 2 v., Milano, 1912–14. *Secondo supplemento,* 1911–1920, 2 v., Milano, 1925–1928.

b **Biblioteca Nazionale Centrale di Firenze.** *Bolletino delle pubblicazioni italiane ricevute per diritto di stampa.* Firenze, 1886 ff.

There exists no single work nor any combination of works furnishing a complete record of the books issued from the Italian press. Several older works furnish some contribution to the bibliography of the earlier period. *a.* General catalogue of books published in Italy or in Italian from 1847 to 1920. *b.* Though practically a library accession list, the most satisfactory monthly record of newly published books in Italian. GMD

O2a **Croce, Benedetto.** *Storia della storiografia italiana nel secolo decimo nono.* 2 v. Bari, 1921.

b **Bresslau, Harry.** *Quellen und Hilfsmittel zur Geschichte der romanischen Völker im Mittelalter.* Strassburg, 1901. [(H22a) Gröber, Grundriss der romanischen Philologie, v. 2, pt. 3, especially p. 447–450 and 479–503.]

c **Balzani, Ugo, Conte.** *Early chroniclers of Europe: Italy.* London and N. Y., 1883. Tr. by author's wife from MS of *Le cronache italiane nel medio evo,* 1884; 3rd ed., Milano, 1909.

d Manno, Antonio, Barone, and **Promis, Vincenzo.** *Bibliografia storica degli stati della monarchia di Savoia.* V. 1–9. Torino, 1884–1913.

e Cicogna, Emmanuele Antonio. *Saggio di bibliografia veneziana.* Venezia, 1847.

f Soranzo, Girolamo. *Bibliografia veneziana, compilata in aggiunta e continuazione del Saggio di E. A. Cicogna.* Venezia, 1885.

The lack of a complete bibliography for Italian history, like (P1a) Dahlmann-Waitz for Germany, is painfully obvious. For purposes of general reference, the sales catalogues of works on Italian history issued by Ulrico Hoepli of Milan are sometimes helpful. *a.* Very suggestive history and criticism of Italian historical writing in the past hundred years by a distinguished philosopher. *b.* Valuable for the medieval period. Cf. also (H1a) Paetow, *Guide to the study of medieval history. c.* Useful introduction to medieval Italian chroniclers. *d., e.,* and *f.* Comprehensive bibliographies for two of the former Italian states. For the modern period, there are available the bibliographies in the various volumes of (I121) *Cambridge modern history.* For the Risorgimento, the short bibliography in (O351c) Rinaudo, *Il risorgimento italiano* is serviceable. TFJ

O3a Calvi, Emilio. *Biblioteca di bibliografia storica italiana, catalogo tripartito delle bibliografie finora pubblicate sulla storia generale e particolare d'Italia.* Roma, 1903. *Supplemento, 1903–06, Rivista delle Biblioteche,* 17:129–143, 1906.

b *Annuario bibliografico della storia d'Italia dal sec. IV dell' e. v. ai giorni nostri.* 8 v. Pisa and Pavia, 1903–10. [Supplement to *Studi storici,* v. 11–18.]

c Cipolla, Carlo, Conte. *Pubblicazioni sulla storia medioevale italiana, 1890–1910.* Venezia, 1891–1911. [Appendix to (O965) *Nuovo archivio veneto,* n.s., v. 1–20.] *Indici,* 1890–1898, ed. by G. Giomo, Venezia, 1903; *Indici,* 1899–1910, ed. by E. Pastorello, Venezia, 1916.

a. The three sections in which this bibliography is arranged deal respectively with printed works, manuscripts and documents, and statutes. *b.* Abortive attempt at an annual bibliography of publications on Italian history since the fourth century. *c.* More successful work of similar sort but limited to the Middle Ages. GMD

O4a Calvi, Emilio. *Bibliografia generale di Roma.* V. 1; 1, supplements; 2, pt. 1; 5, pt 1. Roma, 1906–13.

b *Bibliografia periodica romana, bollettino bibliografico delle pubblicazioni italiane e straniere edite su Roma.* V. 1–5, Roma, 1910–14.

a. Of this incomplete bibliography for Roman history since the fall of the Empire, two parts relate to the Middle Ages, one to the sixteenth century, and one to the Risorgimento. *b.* Semi-annual index of articles on Roman history in periodicals. GMD

O5a *Pubblicazioni edite dallo stato o col suo concorso (1861–1923): Indice generale.* Roma, 1924.

b *Pubblicazioni edite dallo stato o col suo concorso: Spoglio dei periodici e delle opere collective (1901–25); Parte prima: Scritti biografici e critici o comunque riferentisi a singole persone o alle loro opere.* Roma, 1926.

Both issued by a committee of the Ministry of Finance. *a.* Check list of the publications issued by the Italian state or with state subvention since the foundation of the state to 1923. b. Subject index to periodicals and collective works issued by the state in the twentieth century.   TFJ

O6a **Tonelli, Luigi.** *La critica.* Roma, 1920. [Fondazione Leonardo per la Cultura Italiana : Guide bibliographiche, v. 4.]

b **Egidi, Pietro.** *La storia medioevale.* Roma, 1922. [*Id.*, v. 8–9.]

c **Solmi, Arrigo.** *La storia del diritto italiano.* Roma, 1922. [*Id.*, v. 10.]

d **Fumagalli, Giuseppe.** *La bibliografia.* Roma, 1923. [*Id.*, v. 11–12.]

Most important volumes for the historian in this series of guides which furnish critical and bibliographical surveys of the work of Italian scholars since 1861. *a.* Relates to the history of literature. *b.* Deals with the history of Italy from the invasions to 1500; especially good for its account of the activities of historical societies. *c.* Much of the material included relates to constitutional and economic history. *d.* Surveys bibliographical publications. Review, H. Baron, *Hist. Zeit.* 133 :325, 1925.   TFJ

Library collections.—Several American libraries are fairly rich in material for the study of Italian history. Among these are the following : Cornell University Library, which has the largest collection in the United States of literature upon the age of Dante and of Petrarch; University of Illinois Library, which has the Cavagna-Sanguiliani library of about 40,000 volumes in Italian history, literature, and art, providing a notable opportunity for research; and Harvard College Library, which also has a large Dante collection and is well provided with published source material. It is strong in the history of Venice and of Florence, and its collection of municipal *Statuti* numbers over 350 volumes. Perhaps next in importance are Brown University Library, which has the Chambers Dante collection, New York Public Library, Princeton University Library, and the Library of Congress.   AHS

ENCYCLOPEDIAS AND WORKS OF REFERENCE

O21 *Nuova enciclopedia italiana.* 1841–51. 6th rev. ed., by Gerolamo Boccardo, 25 v. in 26, Torino, 1875–88. *Supplemento,* ed. by S. Pagliani, 5 v. in 6, Torino, 1889–99.

Leading general encyclopedia in Italian; not as comprehensive and not always as critical as the best of the type in English, German or French; often gives the historical student information not found elsewhere.

In 1925 a wealthy Italian senator established the Istituto Giovanni Treccani to undertake the publication in the course of the ensuing ten years of a new Italian encyclopedia in thirty-two volumes under the editorship of Giovanni Gentile and others. Two volumes have appeared to date : *Enciclopedia italiana di scienze, lettere ed arti,* Milano e Roma, 1929 ff.   TFJ

O22a **Garollo, Gottardo.** *Dizionario biografico universale.* 2 v. Milano, 1907.

b *Chi è? Annuario biografico italiano.* Ed. by G. Biagi. V. 1 only, Roma, 1908. New ed., by A. F. Formiggini, *Dizionario degli Italiani d'oggi,* Roma, 1928.

A good national biography for Italy is wholly lacking, and information must be sought in the general biographical dictionaries. *a.* Very superficial; valuable only because it contains a larger relative proportion of Italian names than other general biographical dictionaries. *b.* Useful as the only source of its kind for contemporary biography.   TFJ

GEOGRAPHY

O41a Deecke, Wilhelm. *Italy, a popular account of the country, its people, and its institutions.* London and N. Y., 1904. Tr. by H. A. Nesbitt from *Italien,* Berlin, 1899. [Kirchhoff and Fitzner, Bibliothek der Länderkunde.]

b Strafforello, Gustavo. *La patria: geografia dell' Italia.* 5 v. in 31. Torino, 1890–1905.

c Hofmann, Albert von. *Das Land Italien und seine Geschichte, eine historisch-topographische Darstellung.* Stuttgart, 1921.

a. Comprehensive and trustworthy account of Italy as a geographical unit and as a nation; less popular than the title might indicate. As a general introduction to the study of Italy, it is of real value. The illustrations are excellent and well-chosen. *b.* Similar, but, although much larger, of somewhat more popular, gazetteer-like character. *c.* Provided with maps; combines a description of the physical characteristics of each section of Italy with a general historical survey. Review, H. Philipp, *Philologische Wochenschrift,* 42:441, May 1922. TFJ

O42 Nitti, Francesco S. *La ricchezza dell'Italia.* 1904. 2nd rev. ed., Roma, 1905. [R. Istituto d'Incoraggiamento di Napoli: Atti.]

This exposition of the economic resources and weaknesses of Italy, made by a distinguished economist after long study, contains much of interest to the historical student. The second edition merely summarizes the results of the much longer first edition. TFJ

ETHNOGRAPHY

O51a King, Bolton, and Okey, Thomas. *Italy today.* 1901. Rev. ed., London, 1909. (Bibliography.) Italian tr. and 3rd ed., *L'Italia d'oggi,* Bari, 1910.

b Villari, Luigi. *Italian life in town and country.* N. Y. and London, 1902. [Our European neighbors.]

a. Critical survey of the Italian people in the twentieth century; often severe, but sympathetic. The chapters on economic conditions are of particular value. As a study by foreigners, it deserves comparison with *b.,* an attempt by an Italian to perform a similar task. Villari's account of Italian education is authoritative, for the author is the son of Pasquale Villari (cf. O121), one of the makers of modern Italian education. TFJ

COLLECTIONS OF SOURCES AND ARCHIVE PUBLICATIONS

To the Italian archives no single guide exists. (O71) Giuseppe Mazzatinti, *Gli archivi della storia d'Italia,* v. 1–9, Rocca San Casciano, 1897–1915, is a useful guide to the archives of secondary importance only. For the larger archives, consult (B32a) *Minerva,* especially v. 28–29, 1926–28, under the name of the city concerned. Also cf. (O72) Charles H. Haskins, 'Vatican archives,' *A.H.R.* 2:40–58, Oct. 1896.

A large amount of valuable historical material has been published in Italy by various organizations under direct governmental control. The Istituto Storico Italiano, founded in 1883, has published 58 v. of (O76) *Fonti per la storia d'*

Italia, Roma, 1887 ff., a collection largely of unedited material for the history of medieval Italy as a whole. A collection of (O77) *Corpus statutorum italicorum*, v. 1–9, Roma, 1912–16, has been begun under the editorship of Pietro Sella.

In 1833 Charles Albert, King of Sardinia, following the example of the German and French commissions for the publication of materials for the national history, created the Regia Deputazione sopra gli Studi di Storia Patria (changed in 1861 to Regia Deputazione sopra gli Studi di Storia Patria per le Antiche Province e la Lombardia), which has issued (O81) *Monumenta historiae patriae*, 22 v., Augustae Taurinorum and Cremonae, 1836–1901. In 1862, older organizations were amalgamated by royal decree as the Reale Deputazione sugli Studi di Storia Patria per le Provincie di Toscana, dell'Umbria, e delle Marche, which has published 12 v. of (O82) *Documenti di storia italiana*, Firenze, 1867 ff., and (O967) *Archivio storico italiano*. The Reale Deputazione Veneta di Storia Patria, formed in 1873, has published 39 v. of (O83) *Monumenti storici*, Venezia, 1876 ff.; (O84) *I diarii di Marino Sanuto*, 58 v. in 59, Venezia, 1879–1903, edited by R. Fulin, F. Stefani, and others, which cover, with extraordinary fulness, the years 1496 to 1533; and (O85) *Miscellanea di storia veneta*, v. 1–31, Venezia, 1881 ff. Organizations of less official standing have issued collections of documents for the history of Genoa, Parma, Romagna, Rome, Naples, and Sicily; and local historical societies, which are numerous in Italy, have occasionally published volumes of documents. Some further details concerning these collections will be found in (A3a) Langlois, *Manuel de bibliographie historique*, § 452.

The works of Italian chroniclers from 500 to 1500 were collected by Lodovico A. Muratori in (O91) *Rerum italicarum scriptores*, 25 v. in 28, Mediolani, 1723–51. A much needed revision of this invaluable collection has been undertaken under the editorial supervision of G. Carducci, 1835–1907, and V. Fiorini, and more than 228 parts have thus far appeared (Città di Castello and Bologna, 1900 ff.); in 1923 its publication was taken over by the Istituto Storico Italiano. The precious (O92) *Relazioni degli ambasciatori veneti al senato*, 15 v. Firenze, 1839–63, were issued under the editorship of Eugenio Albèri, by a private society.

Several foreign governments have long maintained schools in Rome, some of which have done good work in publishing historical material, but largely for the history of the popes. The Preussisches Historisches Institut, founded in 1888, is largely devoted to the publication of material in Italian archives for German and papal history, cf. (O953); and in coöperation with the Istituto Storico Italiano, has published (O93) *Regesta chartarum Italiae*, 18 v., Roma, 1907–23, a series of analyses of early diplomatic material in various archives. Notice also (O94) *Calendar of state papers and manuscripts relating to English affairs, existing in the archives and collections of Venice and in other libraries of North Italy*, London, 1864 ff., of which 28 v. have appeared, under the editorship of Rawdon L. Brown, Horatio R. F. Brown, and Allen B. Hinds, covering the years 1202 to 1643 and (O95) *Calendar of state papers and manuscripts relating to English affairs, existing in the archives and collections of Milan*, v. 1, London, 1912, edited by Allen B. Hinds, which are both published by the British government. (cf. L73).

TFJ

SHORTER GENERAL HISTORIES

O101a Jamison, Evelyn M., and others. *Italy, mediaeval and modern, a history.* Oxford, 1917. (Selected bibliography.)

b Sedgwick, Henry D. *Short history of Italy, 476–1900.* Boston, 1905.

c Trevelyan, Janet P. *Short history of the Italian people from the barbarian invasions to the attainment of unity.* N. Y. and London, 1920. (Selected bibliography.)

Best summaries in English of the history of the Italian peninsula; popular in tone and easily read. None of them pretends to be based on original research, to present new facts, or to give new interpretation. *a.* Coöperative work by various English scholars; very brief on recent history, but good for the period 1528 to 1789. *b.* Written with an amusing touch, occasionally too light for accuracy; brief but more satisfactory on the intellectual and artistic developments at the close of the Middle Ages than *c.* *c.* Handles the nineteenth century with greater assurance and with a greater regard for comprehensiveness; narrative extends to 1915; some excellent illustrations and several good maps.   EHB

LONGER GENERAL HISTORIES

O121 Villari, Pasquale, ed. *Storia politica d'Italia scritta da una società di amici.* 8 v. Milano, 1874–82. [1, F. Bertolini, *Storia antica;* 2, F. Bertolini, *I barbari;* 3, F. Lanzani, *I comuni fino al 1313;* 4, C. Cipolla, *Le signorie italiane dal 1313 al 1530;* 5, A. Cosci, *Preponderanze straniere, 1530–1789;* 6, A. Franchetti, *Italia dal 1789 al 1799;* 7, G. de Castro, *Italia dal 1799 al 1814;* 8, F. Bertolini, *Italia dal 1814 al 1878.*]

Still probably the best popular history of Italy in Italian.   TFJ

MEDIEVAL PERIOD

O201a Cotterill, Henry B. *Medieval Italy during a thousand years, 305–1313, a brief historical narrative with chapters on great episodes and personalities and on subjects connected with religion, art, and literature.* London, 1915. [Great nations.]

b —— *Italy from Dante to Tasso, 1300–1600, its political history as viewed from the standpoints of the chief cities, with descriptions of important episodes and personalities and of the art and literature of the three centuries.* London and N. Y., 1919.

c Villari, Pasquale. *Barbarian invasions of Italy.* 2 v. London and N. Y., 1902. Tr. by L. Villari from *Le invasioni barbariche in Italia,* 1901; 2nd ed., Milano, 1905.

d —— *Mediaeval Italy from Charlemagne to Henry VII.* London, 1910. Tr. by C. Hulton from *L'Italia da Carlomagno alla morte di Arrigo VII,* Milano, 1910.

Good histories of medieval Italy for the general reader. *a.* and *b.* Well illustrated; quote few authorities, but are, on the whole, of a high grade. The treatment of the Italian communes is unsatisfactory. *c.* and *d.* Though these summaries of the results of modern research make no pretense to great erudition, the general reader will find them of high excellence. For Villari's other works, cf. (O121) and (O472). For the period of the invasions the reader is especially referred to (H202) Hodgkin, *Italy and her invaders.*   TFJ

O202a Hegel, Carl. *Geschichte der Städteverfassung von Italien seit der Zeit der römischen Herrschaft bis zum Ausgang des zwölften Jahrhunderts.* 2 v. Leipzig, 1847. Italian tr., *Storia della costituzione dei municipi italiani,* Milano, 1861.

 b Hartmann, Ludo M. *Geschichte Italiens im Mittelalter.* 4 v. in 6. Leipzig, 1897–1915. 2nd rev. ed. of v. 1, Gotha, 1923 [Allgemeine Staatengeschichte]. (Critical bibliography.)

a. Admirably written work; very significant in its day; still one of the most suggestive accounts of the retrogression and reconstruction of municipal institutions in Italy from the Roman Empire to the thirteenth century under the influence of Goth, Lombard, Frank, the Church, and the German Roman Empire. *b.* Skilful, scholarly survey of Italian history from 475 to 1002, left incomplete by the recent death of its distinguished author. V. 1. Notable chiefly for the study of the administrative and legal phases of the period ending with the death of Justinian, especially of Theodoric's reign. V. 2. Discusses critically the process by which Italy was freed from Byzantine control only to be enslaved by the Frank. V. 3. Extended treatment of the Frankish period. V. 4. Incomplete; pt. 1, devoted to the Ottos, with emphasis on the social and economic life. The author discusses interestingly the question of the profit to Germany of domination in Italy; unlike Sybel, Below, and others, he thinks the Italian connection was of great value. Review, C. Cipolla, *Rivista Storica Italiana,* 15:269, 1898; 17:426, 1900; 21:163, 1904. EHB

O203 Butler, William F. *Lombard communes, a history of the republics of North Italy.* London and N. Y., 1906.

Covers in detail the history of the communes to the middle of the fourteenth century. Interestingly written; well illustrated; founded almost entirely on earlier works, some of which have long since been superseded. Contains a full and good account of relations of the different towns with the Empire and the Papacy. Fails to give a clear picture of the origin and growth of communal governments, and deals only in a cursory fashion with economic developments which were of such great importance in the history of the Lombard towns.

EHB

O204 Sismondi, Jean C. L. Simonde de. *History of the Italian republics in the middle ages: entirely recast and supplemented in the light of subsequent historical research.* London and N. Y., 1906. Tr. by W. Boulting from *Histoire des républiques italiennes du moyen âge.* 16 v. 1809–18. Rev. ed., 10 v., Paris, 1840.

For many years the standard work on the subject. This abridged English edition is useful for securing a general view of the medieval Italian republics from the invasions to the sixteenth century. It must always be used with caution and, if possible, in connection with good histories of the individual states; no mere revision of the work could embody nearly all the results of the century of research that has altered the historical point of view since Sismondi wrote. Boulting has succeeded in giving new life to a memorable work. EHB

O205a Huillard-Bréholles, Jean L. Alfonse. *Historia diplomatica Friderici Secundi.* 7 v. in 12. Parisiis, 1852–61.

 b Kington, Thomas L. (later **Oliphant, T. L. Kington**). *History of Frederick II, emperor of the Romans.* 2 v. London, 1862.

c **Winkelmann, Eduard.** *Kaiser Friedrich II.* 2 v. Leipzig, 1889–97. [(P215*b*) Jahrbücher der deutschen Geschichte.]

d **Allshorn, Lionel.** *Stupor Mundi: life and times of Frederick II, emperor of the Romans, king of Sicily and Jerusalem, 1194–1250.* London, 1912.

a. For the career in Italy of the Emperor Frederick II, King of the Two Sicilies, the series of essays that form the preface and introduction to this great collection of source material is still the best authority.   *b.* Based on *a.;* still the most complete work in English, but now somewhat antiquated, although not replaced by *d.*, which largely follows it.   *c.* Contains much of Italian interest; careful and detailed, but goes only to 1233.   JCH

O206 Jordan, Édouard. *Les origines de la domination angevine en Italie.* Paris, 1909.

For the dramatic period in Italian history between 1250 and 1285 there is no better authority than this admirable book, which is in theory a history of Charles of Anjou's career in Italy, but is also a history of all Italy for the period. Review, R. Poupardin, *Rev. Hist.* 109:360, March 1912.   TFJ

O207a Grandgent, Charles H. *Dante.* N. Y., 1916. [Master spirits of literature.] (Bibliography.)

b **Toynbee, Paget.** *Dante Alighieri, his life and works.* 1900. 4th ed., London and N. Y., 1910. (Bibliography.)

c **Zingarelli, Nicola.** *Dante.* Milano, 1899–1904. [Storia letteraria d'Italia scritta da una società di professori.]

d **Hauvette, Henri.** *Dante: introduction à l'étude de la Divine comédie.* 1911. 2nd rev. ed., Paris, 1912.

e **Koch, Theodore W.** *Cornell University Library catalogue of the Dante collection.* 3 v. (V. 3 ed. by M. Fowler.) Ithaca, 1898–1921.

a. Illuminating study of Dante and his times by one who excels in his understanding of what is essential and of permanent importance.   *b.* Gives in a sympathetic manner the information useful for the student.   *c.* Most comprehensive account of Dante viewed in relation to his times.   *d.* Hauvette's attempt to fix the setting of the *Divine comedy* and to explain clearly and simply its significance is the best work in French. These works are, perhaps, the best for the general reader; students seeking fuller information should consult *e.* for further guidance.   EBB

RENAISSANCE PERIOD

O251a Burckhardt, Jakob C. *Civilisation of the period of the renaissance in Italy.* 2 v. 1878. New ed. from 15th German ed., London, 1929. Tr. by S. G. C. Middlemore from *Die Kultur der Renaissance in Italien,* 1860; 16th ed. by W. Goetz, Leipzig, 1927.

b **Voigt, Georg.** *Die Wiederbelebung des classischen Altertums, oder, das erste Jahrhundert des Humanismus.* 1859. 3rd ed., by M. Lehnert, 2 v., Berlin, 1893.

c **Geiger, Ludwig.** *Renaissance und Humanismus in Italien und Deutschland.* Berlin, 1882. [(B162) Oncken, Allgemeine Geschichte.]

These three classic works in German on the Italian Renaissance are still of fundamental importance, although not entirely in agreement with more recent historical research. Burckhardt and Voigt were the two German scholars who, in the middle of the nineteenth century, practically formulated the conception of the Renaissance as a period in European history. *a.* Probably still the best single work of its scope. A philosophic history; presupposes, on the art of the reader, a considerable knowledge of facts and events; frankly omits treatment of the artistic development of Italy; largely indifferent to economic changes. *b.* Emphasizes the importance of the revival of the classic tradition. *c.* Continues the Burckhardt tradition; contains an excellent account of Italian humanism, largely from the viewpoint of literary influence.   HLG

O252a **Symonds, John A.** *Renaissance in Italy.* 4 pt. in 5 v. 1875–81. 2nd rev. ed., 5 pt. in 7 v., N. Y., 1887–88. [1, *Age of the despots;* 2, *Revival of learning;* 3, *Fine arts;* 4–5, *Italian literature;* 6–7, *Catholic reaction.*]

   b —— *Short history of the renaissance in Italy,* adapted by Lieut. Col. A. Pearson. N. Y., 1894.

   c Taylor, Rachel A. *Aspects of the Italian renaissance.* London and N. Y., 1923.

   d Emerton, Ephraim. *Humanism and tyranny, studies in the Italian trecento.* Cambridge, Mass., 1925.

   a. These volumes are the most ambitious undertaking of a talented literary historian, not greatly given to original investigation. All are admirably written. Many parts, however, are antiquated, notably the volume on the fine arts. Better is the account of Italian literature, with its happy appreciations and translations, and best is the treatment of the revival of learning, borrowing largely, as it does, from (O251b) Voigt. The part on the Catholic reaction, first issued in 1887, deals with the middle of the sixteenth century. *b.* A dull condensation; lacks the vivifying qualities of the larger work. *c.* Attractive presentation of the intellectual and spiritual sides of the Renaissance, suggestive of Symonds in both merits and defects. Review, F. Schevill, *A.H.R.* 29:122, Oct. 1923. *d.* Presents well-chosen examples of political thought and practice in fourteenth-century Italy. Review, G. C. Sellery, *A.H.R.* 32:92, Oct. 1926.   HLG

O253a **Robinson, James H.,** and **Rolfe, Henry W.** *Petrarch, the first modern scholar and man of letters; a selection from his correspondence with Boccaccio and other friends, designed to illustrate the beginnings of the renaissance.* 1898. 2nd rev. ed., N. Y. and London, 1914.

   b Nolhac, Pierre de. *Petrarch and the ancient world.* Boston, 1907. [Humanists' library.] Abridged tr. from *Pétrarque et l'humanisme,* 1892; 2nd rev. ed., 2 v., Paris, 1907. [Bibliothèque littéraire de la renaissance.] (Bibliography.)

   c Körting, Gustav. *Petrarca's Leben und Werke.* Leipzig, 1878. [Geschichte der Litteratur Italiens im Zeitalter der Renaissance.]

   d Hollway-Calthrop, Henry C. *Petrarch, his life and times.* N. Y., 1907.

   e Tatham, Edward H. R. *Francesco Petrarca, the first modern man of letters, his life and correspondence.* 2 v. London and N. Y., 1925–1928.

   a. Charming volume; limited in scope principally to a study of Petrarch's letters. Extracts, in good translation, portray him in relation to his age. The authors discuss his attitude toward the Italian language, his devotion to the classics, his interest in travel, and the influence of medieval ideals on his political and religious beliefs. There is an excellent introductory chapter on the Renais-

sance.   *b.* Valuable though inferior to *c.*, which is still the best detailed account of the life and influence of the first great humanist.   *d.* Good, popular
biography.   *e.* Attempt, by an English clergyman, to present a biography of
Petrarch that will appeal to both scholars and the public.   V. *2.* Closes at 1346.

JHP

O254a **Hutton, Edward.** *Giovanni Boccaccio, a biographical study.* London
and N. Y., 1910.   (Bibliography.)

   b Hauvette, Henri. *Boccace, étude biographique et littéraire.* Paris, 1914.
(Bibliography.)

   a. Only general English work on Boccaccio since (O252*a*, v. 4) Symonds'
sketch.   Not first-rate in scholarship or literary criticism, it is yet sympathetic
and useful.   An appendix contains descriptive notes on each of the stories of
the *Decameron*.   HLG
   b. Excellent, scholarly literary biography.   Ample attention to the sources and
contents of the *Decameron* and to his other literary works does not prevent
adequate consideration of the strictly biographical elements.   GMD

O255a **Cellini, Benvenuto.** *Autobiography of Benvenuto Cellini.* 1888.   New
ed., N. Y., 1910 [Harvard classics].   Tr. by J. A. Symonds from *La vita
di Benvenuto Cellini da lui medesimo scritta,* Colonia (Naples), 1728.

   b ———— *Life of Benvenuto Cellini.* 2 v. London and N. Y., 1910.
(Bibliography.)   Tr. by R. H. H. Cust from ed. by Orazio Bacci, Firenze,
1901.

   c ———— *Memoirs of Benvenuto Cellini, a Florentine artist, writen by himself.* Tr. by Anne Macdonell. London and N. Y., 1906. [Everyman's
library.]

   d ———— *Memoirs of Benvenuto Cellini.* Tr. by T. Roscoe, rev. ed., London and N. Y., 1927. [World's classics.]

   As a contemporary record of the Italian Renaissance, Cellini's autobiography
is invaluable.   It is not in the accuracy with which he records the events of his
life—far from it—but in the unconscious exposition of the development of a
genius unhampered by social conventions, that the great interest of his book lies.
a. Symonds's translation is a classic, but expurgated.   *b.* Cust's two volumes
are translated from the best text in print and are supplied with excellent notes
and illustrations.   *c* and *d.* Convenient, cheap editions.   TFJ

O256a **Castiglione, Baldassare, Conte.** *Book of the courtier.* 1561.   Latest
ed, with introduction by Walter Raleigh, London, 1900 [Tudor transla-
tions].   Tr. by Sir Thomas Hoby from *Il cortegiano,* 1528; best ed. by
V. Cian, Firenze, 1894 [Biblioteca scolastica di classici italiani].

   b Cartwright, Julia (Mrs. Henry Ady). *Baldassare Castiglione, the perfect courtier, his life and times, 1478–1529.* 2 v. London and N. Y.,
1908.   (Bibliography.)

   a. Castiglione was a leading figure in the brilliant court of Guidobaldo da
Montefeltro at Urbino, in the first decade of the sixteenth century.   In the
Cortegiano he outlined the requirements of culture, courtesy, and ideals for the
true gentleman of the age.   It thus gives a remarkably attractive picture of
the finest sides of that Italian civilization of the Renaissance, which was soon
to become the model for Europe.   *b.* Best biography in English of Castiglione.

TFJ

O257 **Leva, Giuseppe De.** *Storia documentata di Carlo V in correlazione all'Italia.* 5 v. Venezia, Padova, and Bologna, 1863–94.

For the Italian side of Charles the Fifth's reign this is the authoritative book; the result of thorough research; contains a large amount of unedited source material; unfortunately left incomplete by the author's death. For a modern work in English on the same period, cf. (I235b) Armstrong, *Emperor Charles the Fifth.*

TFJ

FROM THE RENAISSANCE TO THE RISORGIMENTO

O301 **Vernon, Katherine Dorothea.** *Italy from 1494 to 1790.* Cambridge, Eng., 1909. [Cambridge historical series.]

Mrs. Vernon, joint author with E. M. Jamison in (O101a) *Italy, medieval and modern,* in this volume fills a distinct need for English readers. Passes briefly over the period of wars from 1494 to 1559; devotes over 400 pages to the period 1559 to 1790, for which in English there is little else available. Handles well a difficult and unattractive period; usually good in perspective and in detail. Review, W. R. Thayer, *A.H.R.* 15:125, Oct. 1909.

TFJ

O302 **Orsi, Pietro.** *Modern Italy, 1748–1898.* 1900. 3rd rev. ed., 1748–1922, London and N. Y., 1923. [Story of the nations.] Tr. by M. A. Vialls from *L'Italia moderna; storia degli ultimi 150 anni fino alla assunzione al trono di Vittorio Emanuele III,* 1901; 3rd ed., Milano, 1910. (Bibliography.)

For the study of Italy in the eighteenth century, there are few books of general scope and outstanding value. A popular account is given in the earlier portion of this manual by Orsi. (O301) Vernon, *Italy from 1494 to 1790* devotes the third part to this period. Cosci, 'Preponderanze straniere' in (O121) Villari, *Storia politica d'Italia* covers the century in some detail, but is already out of date. Probably the best recent treatment is (O351d) Tivaroni, *Storia critica del risorgimento italiano,* v. I, entitled 'L'Italia prima della rivoluzione francese.'

TFJ

O303a **Gaffarel, Paul.** *Bonaparte et les républiques italiennes, 1796–1799.* Paris, 1895. [Bibliothèque d'histoire contemporaine.]

b **Driault, Édouard.** *Etudes napoléoniennes: Napoléon en Italie, 1800–1812.* Paris, 1906. (Bibliography.) (I321b)

c **Pingaud, Albert.** *La domination française dans l'Italie du nord, 1796–1805: Bonaparte, président de la république italienne.* 2 v. Paris, 1914.

d —— *Les hommes d'état de la république italienne, 1802–1805, notices et documents biographiques.* Paris, 1919. [Bibliothèque de l'Institut Français de Florence.] (Bibliography.)

e **Madelin, Louis.** *La Rome de Napoléon: la domination française à Rome de 1809 à 1814.* Paris, 1906.

f **Weil, Maurice H.** *Le Prince Eugène et Murat, 1813–1814, opérations militaires, négociations diplomatiques.* 5 v. Paris, 1901–02. (Bibliography.)

There is a scarcity of good works of general character on the history of Italy during the revolutionary and Napoleonic age. The best recent works on the period are by French scholars; the volumes noted above, although limited in scope, are of great value. It will be useful for a general view to consult the separate volumes of (O121) Villari's coöperative history and of (O351d) Tivaroni, *Storia critica,* and the appropriate chapters in (I121) *Cambridge modern history.*

RISORGIMENTO

O351a King, Bolton. *History of Italian unity, being a political history of Italy from 1814 to 1871.* 2 v. London, 1899. (Bibliography.) Italian tr. by A. Comandini, *Storia dell' unità italiana,* 2 v., Milano, 1909–10.

b Thayer, William R. *Dawn of Italian independence: Italy from the Congress of Vienna, 1814, to the fall of Venice, 1849.* 2 v. Boston, 1892.

c Rinaudo, Costanzo. *Il risorgimento italiano, conferenze con appendice bibliografico.* 1910. 2nd ed., 2 v., Città de Castello, 1911. (Excellent bibliography in 2nd ed.)

d Tivaroni, Carlo. *Storia critica del risorgimento italiano, 1735–1870.* 9 v. Torino, 1888–1897.

a. Best work in English covering the entire Risorgimento period, although dull and somewhat inaccurate as a chronicle of events; shows a strong Mazzinian bias. *b.* Faithful interpretation of the awakening of the national spirit, but as a narrative it is already out of date. *c.* Much more trustworthy and readable. *d.* Still the fullest and best general history; comparatively impartial; quotes from contemporary documents freely. The author himself participated as a Garibaldian in the revolutionary movements of 1860 and 1867. Cf. also v. 7 and 8 of (O121) *Storia politica d'Italia.*

x

O352 Comandini, Alfredo. *Italia nei cento anni del secolo XIX, 1801–1900, giorno per giorno illustrata.* 4 v. Milano, 1900–20.

One of the most important and useful works published on the Risorgimento; an accurate chronicle of the principal events in all parts of Italy from 1801 to 1900; a work of vast erudition. Profusely illustrated with instructive facsimiles of documents and medals, and with views and portraits principally from Comandini's own collection of prints, the richest in existence for the period; indexes of the illustrations are given at the end of each volume. V. 4. 1861 to 1900, issued in parts, has not yet been completed.

x

O353 Bianchi, Nicomede. *Storia documentata della diplomazia europea in Italia dall'anno 1814 all'anno 1861.* 8 v. Torino, 1865–72.

Contains a vast number of important unpublished official documents, and has long constituted one of the principal sources for historians of the Risorgimento. The documents are from state archives; unfortunately some have been proved to contain serious errors of transcription. A work to be consulted rather than read.

x

O354a Cavour, Camillo Benso di. *Lettere edite ed inedite, raccolte ed illustrate da Luigi Chiala.* 6 v. Torino, 1883–87. Index by C. Isaia, Torino, 1887. Many later ed.

b —— *La politique du Comte Camille de Cavour de 1852 à 1861, lettres inédites avec notes par Nicomède Bianchi.* Turin, 1885.

c —— *Nouvelles lettres inédites, recueillies et publiées avec notes historiques par Amédée Bert.* Rome, 1889. Many later ed.

d ——— *Count Cavour and Madame de Circourt, some unpublished corre-spondence.* London, 1894. Tr. by A. J. Butler from *Cavour et la comtesse de Circourt; lettres inédites, publiées par Comte C. Nigra,* Turin, 1891.

e ——— *Nuove lettere inedite del Conte Camillo di Cavour, con prefazione e note di E. Mayor.* Torino, 1895.

f ——— *Discorsi parlamentari.* Ed. by Giuseppe Massari. 11 v. V. 1–4, Torino; v. 5–10, Firenze; v. 11, Roma, 1863–72. Index by Raffaelo Biffoli, Roma, 1885.

g ——— *Gli scritti del conte di Cavour, nuovamente raccolti e pubblicati da Domenico Zanichelli.* 2 v. Bologna, 1892. [Biblioteca di scrittori politici italiani.]

h ——— *Il carteggio Cavour-Nigra dal 1858 al 1861.* 2 v. Bologna, 1927.

Cavour's letters, speeches, and writings form a primary source of the first importance for the history of the Risorgimento, especially during the years 1860 and 1861. *a.* Chiala's long prefaces are of the highest order of scholarship and are still among the best writings upon the Risorgimento. The other collections of letters are interesting. A great number of Cavour's most important letters are still unpublished. *g.* The collected parliamentary speeches and writings are indispensable. *h.* First two volumes of Cavour's correspondence with Count Nigra, his most intimate political associate. x

O355a Thayer, William R. *Life and times of Cavour.* 2 v. Boston, 1911.

b Ruffini, Francesco. *La giovinezza del conte di Cavour.* 2 v. Torino, 1912.

c Whyte, Arthur J. *Early life and letters of Cavour, 1810–1848.* Oxford and N. Y., 1925.

d Matter, Paul. *Cavour et l'unité italienne.* 3 v. Paris, 1922–27. [Bibliothèque d'histoire contemporaine.] (Bibliographical footnotes.)

a. Best work in English on modern Italy; most complete life of Cavour in any language. Cf. also (O351*b*). As an exposition of Cavour's character and statesmanship, it is a model of sound judgment and scholarship. Review, H. N. Gay, *A.H.R.* 18:143, Oct. 1912. *b.* For the first thirty-five years of Cavour's life, Ruffini's work is indispensable, being of excellent scholarship, and giving many letters unknown to Thayer. Review, H. N. Gay, *A.H.R.* 18:809 July, 1913. *c.* In the absence of an English translation of *b.,* the general reader will find this a readable and scholarly substitute. Review, K. R. Greenfield, *A.H.R.* 31:170, Oct. 1925. *d.* Sympathetic account, the best in French, of Cavour's early career; based partly upon original French archival material, but uncritical. Review, H. N. Gay, *A.H.R.* 29:134, Oct. 1923; G. Bourgin, *Rev. Hist.* 145:104, Jan. 1924; 155:425, July 1927. Cf. also (O363*c*) Martinengo-Cesaresco, *Cavour.* For a French view of Cavour's diplomacy, cf. (M431*b*) La Gorce, *Histoire du second empire,* 2:211–449; 3:1–212. x

O356a Garibaldi, Giuseppe. *Scritti politici e militari, ricordi e pensieri inediti raccolti su autografi, stampe, e manoscritti, da Domenico Ciampoli.* Roma, 1907.

b ——— *Epistolario, con documenti e lettere inedite, 1836–1882, raccolto ed annotato da E. E. Ximenes.* 2 v. Milano, 1885.

c —— *Autobiography.* 3 v. London, 1889. Tr. by A. Werner, with supplement by J. W. Mario from *Memorie autobiografiche,* 1888; 2nd rev. ed., Torino, 1907.

d **Guerzoni, Giuseppe.** *Garibaldi, con documenti editi ed inediti.* 2 v. Firenze, 1882.

e **Mario, Jessie W.** *Garibaldi e i suoi tempi.* Milano, 1884. French tr., *Garibaldi et son temps,* Paris, 1884.

Indispensable primary sources for the history of the Risorgimento are Garibaldi's letters and autobiographical writings. *a.* The best of his letters, although full of errors in transcription and printing, and very far from complete. The appended 'ricordi e pensieri' are of considerable value. *b.* Contains several important letters not published in *a.* Both should be used in connection with *c.* Garibaldi's judgments of men and events written in his later years, though always sincere, must be accepted with caution. *d.* Guerzoni's biography is one of the best. *e.* Was carefully corrected by Carducci.

x

O357a **Trevelyan, George M.** *Garibaldi's defence of the Roman republic.* London and N. Y., 1907. (Bibliography.) Italian tr. by E. B. Dobelli, *Garibaldi e la difesa della repubblica romana,* Bologna, 1909.

b —— *Garibaldi and the thousand.* London and N. Y., 1909. (Bibliography.) Italian tr. by E. B. Dobelli, *Garibaldi e i mille,* Bologna, 1910.

c —— *Garibaldi and the making of Italy.* London and N. Y., 1911. (Bibliography.) Italian tr. by N. Zanichelli, Bologna, 1911.

d —— *Manin and the Venetian revolution of 1848.* London and N. Y., 1923.

a., b., and *c.* Brilliantly written volumes, giving a vivid and generally correct account of Garibaldi's aspirations and achievements from 1848 to 1861. They contain, however, many inaccuracies of fact. Trevelyan's judgments were based on too hasty an examination of evidence to possess positive value for the historian. Review of *a.,* H. N. Gay, *A.H.R.* 14:134, Oct. 1908; of *b.,* W. R. Thayer, 15:613, Apr. 1910; of *c.,* 17:376, Jan. 1912. *d.* Valuable account, for English readers, of the heroic defense of Venice against the Austrian attack; lacks some of the dramatic element of the author's trilogy on Garibaldi. Not a final authority. Review, H. N. Gay, *A.H.R.* 29:552, Apr. 1924; W. Miller, *E.H.R.* 39:135, Jan. 1924.

x

O358a **Mazzini, Giuseppe.** *Scritti editi ed inediti.* V. 1–52. Imola, 1906–29. (*Epistolaria,* v. 1–29; *Scritti politici,* v. 1–18; *Scritti letterari,* v. 1–5.) [Edizione nationale.]

b —— *Life and writings of Joseph Mazzini.* 1864–70. New ed., 6 v., London, 1890–91. A partial tr. from *Scritti editi ed inediti di Giuseppe Mazzini,* ed. by G. Mazzini and A. Saffi, 18 v., Milano and Roma, 1861–91.

c *Protocollo della Giovine Italia, Congrega centrale di Francia.* V. 1–6, Imola, 1916–23. [*Appendice agli Scritti editi ed inediti di Giuseppe Mazzini.*]

a. Monumental work, edited by a royal commission and published at the expense of the Italian government. Ranks with (O354) Cavour's letters and speeches before all other primary sources for the making of modern Italy. Presents a continuous record of over forty years of lofty, national propaganda and untiring political agitation. When completed it will comprise one hundred volumes, of which these forty come down to 1848. The editing represents vast research and the highest critical scholarship; the notes, particularly those to the letters, are abundant. The only indexes are those of names of persons in the volumes of letters; nevertheless, for the period covered, it supersedes the Italian edition of *b.* which contains a fair subject index in each volume.   *c.* Valuable collection of material for the period 1840 to 1848 published under the same auspices as *a.*   x

O359a **King, Bolton.** *Mazzini.* London and N. Y., 1902. [Temple biographies.]   (Bibliography.)   Italian tr. by Maria P. Pascolato, *Mazzini,* Firenze, 1903.

   b **Mario, Jessie W.** *Della vita di Giuseppe Mazzini.* Milano, 1886.

   c **Luzio, Alessandro.** *La madre di Giuseppe Mazzini.* Torino, 1919.

   d ——— *Giuseppe Mazzini, carbonaro.* Torino, 1920.

   e ——— *Carlo Alberto e Giuseppe Mazzini: studi e ricerche di storia del risorgimento.* Torino, 1923.

   f ——— *Garibaldi, Cavour, Verdi: nuova serie di studi e ricerche sulla storia del risorgimento.* Torino, 1924.   (Bibliography.)

   a. and *b.* Best biographies of Mazzini.   *c.* and *d.* Of a distinctly higher grade of scholarship and rich in unpublished documents and letters; both, however, relate only to Mazzini's earliest years of political agitation.   *e.* and *f.* Valuable essays on various topics in Risorgimento history, largely concerned with Mazzini; based on original investigation and of high scholarship. Review of *f.,* H. N. Gay, *A.H.R.* 29:331, Jan. 1924.   x

O360a **Ricasoli, Barone Bettino.** *Lettere e documenti.* Ed. by M. Tabbarini and A. Gotti.   11 v.   Firenze, 1887–96.

   b **Gotti, Aurelio.** *Vita del Barone Bettino Ricasoli.* Firenze, 1894.

   c **Hancock, E. K.** *Bettino Ricasoli and the risorgimento in Italy.* London, 1926.

   a. As a primary source for the Risorgimento, Ricasoli's letters come next in importance after (O354) Cavour's letters and (O358) Mazzini's writings; they cover chiefly his correspondence between 1829 and 1880. Indispensable for the history of Tuscany and for the first years of the Kingdom of Italy. V. 11. Contains a good index and an anthology of Ricasoli's views on many topics. Review, Zanichelli, *Archivio Storico Italiano,* series 5, 19:1, 1897.   *b.* Best biography.   *c.* Valuable biography in English. Review, H. N. Gay, 32:870, July 1927.   x

O361a **Luzio, Alessandro.** *I martiri di Belfiore e il loro processo.* 2 v.   1905. 2nd ed., 1 v., Milano, 1908.

   b ——— *Antonio Salviotti e i processi del ventuno.* Roma, 1901.

   c ——— *Il processo Pellico-Maroncelli secondo gli atti officiali segreti.* Milano, 1903.

   d ——— *Nuovi documenti sul processo Confalonieri.* Roma, 1908.

   e ——— *Le cinque giornate di Milano nelle narrazioni di fonte austriaca.* Roma, 1899.

   f ——— *Felice Orsini, saggio biografico.* Milano, 1914.

The author has spent many years in a study of Austrian rule in Italy, and has published these important works on the subject. The most valuable is *a.*

which is based upon wide research in Austrian and Italian archives. Although relating solely to anti-Austrian conspiracies centering in Mantua, and to the imprisonment, torture, and execution of the conspirators, it throws a flood of light upon the whole Austrian system of oppression in Italy. Written with a severe historical method, it is nevertheless one of the most moving works upon the Risorgimento. The two editions differ considerably both in the text and in the documentation. Review, H. N. Gay, *A.H.R.* 12:644, Apr. 1907. x

O362a Cesare, Raffaele de. *La fine di un regno dal 1855 al 6 settembre, 1860; per Memor; con prefazione di R. de Cesare.* 1895. 2nd ed., *La fine di un regno, 1848–1860, Napoli e Sicilia,* 2 v., 1900; 3rd rev. ed., with new documents and index, 3 v., Città di Castello, 1909.

b —— *Last days of papal Rome, 1850–1870.* London and N. Y., 1909. Abridged tr. by H. Zimmern from *Roma e lo Stato del Papa dal ritorno di Pio IX al 20 settembre, 1850–1870,* 2 v., Roma, 1907.

c Johnston, Robert M. *Roman theocracy and the republic, 1846–1849.* London and N. Y., 1901. (Bibliography.)

d Bourgeois, Émile, and **Clermont, Émile.** *Rome et Napoleon III, 1849–1870, étude sur les origines et la chute du second empire.* Paris, 1907. (Bibliography.)

a. Best work on the last years of the Two Sicilies; based upon many unpublished documents in private archives, but also upon gossip; a series of detached studies rather than a complete history; favorable to the revolution, but moderate in tone. The scientific method which generally characterizes recent Italian work upon the Risorgimento is lacking and the volumes are not free from personal prejudice. Many errors have been corrected and much new material added in the later editions. In the first edition the author used the pen-name of Memor. *b.* Of similar character; best upon this period for the Papal States. Review, W. R. Thayer, *A.H.R.* 15:388, Jan. 1910. x

c. One of the few books in English on the condition of the Papal States in the early days of Pius IX's rule, but marred by lack of sympathy and careless haste. Review, W. R. Thayer, *A.H.R.* 7:576, Apr. 1902. *d.* Good account of Oudinot's expedition in 1849 and of Lesseps's mission, primarily with reference to their influence on international politics. TFJ

O363a Martinengo-Cesaresco, Countess Evelyn. *Italian characters in the epoch of unification.* 1890. Rev. ed., London and N. Y., 1901.

b —— *Liberation of Italy, 1815–1870.* London, 1895.

c —— *Cavour.* London and N. Y., 1898. [Foreign statesmen.]

d —— *Lombard studies.* London, 1902.

The author of these highly interesting books is an Englishwoman, married to a Lombard noble of ancient lineage. She has a remarkable talent for combining distinction of style with general accuracy of fact. *a.* Especially in its latest edition, probably her most lasting work, and, as a secondary source on the Risorgimento, of great value to the English reader. In writing short biographies of heroes of the period, such as Sigismondo Castromediano, the Poerios, and Nino Bixio, she has re-created the heroic spirit of the age with surprising success. Review, W. R. Thayer, *A.H.R.* 7:605, Apr. 1902. *b.* An enthusiastic story, well-told, but now out-of-date. *c.* Her biography of Cavour was the first written in English. Although wholly outclassed in thoroughness of research and completeness by (O355a) Thayer, *Life and times of Cavour,* is still, in its brief way, an excellent book. *d.* Interesting but rather desultory sketches of the history and civilization of her adopted province.   x

UNITED ITALY SINCE 1870

O401a Underwood, F. M. *United Italy.* London, 1912. (Brief bibliography.)

b Croce, Benedetto. *History of Italy, 1871–1915.* Oxford, 1929. Tr. by Cecilia M. Ady from *Storia d'Italia dal 1871 al 1915,* Bari, 1928.

a. Perhaps the best popular book in English on the history of Italy between 1870 and the World War; it makes no pretense to erudition. Particularly useful to English readers are the biographical sketches of many distinguished Italians of the period. Review, *Nation* (N. Y.), 96:367, Apr. 10, 1913. Cf. (K441) Wallace, *Greater Italy,* a work of similar character, with particular reference to recent Italian colonization. *b.* Latest work of Italy's best-known living scholar; of exceptional value and interest.   TFJ

O402 *Cinquanta anni di storia italiana: pubblicazione fatta sotto gli auspicii del governo per cura dallo R. Accademia dei Lincei.* 3 v. Milano, 1911. (Bibliographies.)

Mine of scholarly information upon the progress of Italy from 1861 to 1911; a collection of monographs, each by a specialist, upon population, railway, army, navy, education, industry, commerce, finance, emigration, etc.   x

O403a Billot, Albert. *La France et l'Italie, histoire des années troublées, 1881–1899.* 2 v. Paris, 1905.

b Pingaud, Albert. *Italie depuis 1870.* Preface by É. Denis. Paris, 1915. [Bibliothèque d'histoire et de politique.] (Bibliography.)

c Zimmern, Helen, and **Agresti, Antonio.** *New Italy.* London, 1918; N. Y., 1920.

a. Study of the relations between Italy and France during a period of strained friendship, by the French ambassador at Rome at the time; prudent in character, and in the nature of memoirs. *b.* Survey of Italian history and diplomacy from 1870 to the World War, written for the French public at the moment when Italy entered the war on the side of the Entente allies. Review, A. Chuquet. *Revue Critique,* n.s., 81:114, Feb. 19, 1916. *c.* Later survey of the same period.   TFJ

O404 Crispi, Francesco. *Memoirs of Francesco Crispi.* 3 v. London and N. Y., 1912–14. Tr. by M. Prichard-Agnetti from v. 1–3 of *Memorie e documenti,* ed. by T. Palamenghi-Crispi, 5 v., Milano, 1911–24.

Recounting the career of Italy's most prominent political figure from Cavour's death to 1896, these memoirs are of great interest to the student of modern Italian history. They must be used with the greatest care; they were perhaps prepared for publication by Crispi himself, in order to present his own career in the most favorable light, and his nephew, the editor, has clearly the tendency to exalt his uncle's memory by suppressing his weaker points and vilifying his contemporaries. Unfavorable review, *Nation* (N .Y.), 96:55, Jan. 16, 1913.

x

O405 Tittoni, Tommaso. *Italy's foreign and colonial policy; a selection from the speeches delivered in the Italian parliament, by the Italian foreign affairs minister, Senator Tommaso Tittoni, during his six years of office, 1903–1909.* London, 1914; N. Y., 1915. Tr. by Baron Bernardo Quaranta di San Severino from *Sei anni di politica estera, 1903–1919,* Roma, 1912.

Exposes, in a way designed to please all sides, his management of the relations of Italy with its partners in the Triple Alliance and with the Entente. Important, not for the facts, but for the way in which those facts were presented to the Italian public. TFJ

O406 Giolitti, Giovanni. *Memoirs of my life.* London, 1923. Tr. by Edward Storer from *Memorie della mia vita, con uno studio di Olindo Malagodi,* 2 v., Milano, 1922.

Autobiography of an Italian statesman who was five times prime minister between 1892 and 1913, and for twenty years the chief political power in the peninsula. Especially interesting for his account of Italy's entrance into the World War, which he opposed. TFJ

O411a Gay, Harry Nelson, ed. *Italy's great war and her national aspirations, by Mario Alberti, General Carlo Corsi, Armando Hodnig, Tomaso Sillani, Attilio Tamaro, and Ettore Tolomei; with an introductory chapter by H. Nelson Gay.* Milan, 1917.

b Trevelyan, George M. *Scenes from Italy's war.* London and Boston, 1919.

a. In small compass gives excellent survey of the motives and ideals of Italy in the early years of the World War. Review, *A.H.R.* 24:127, Oct. 1918. *b.* Striking account of Italy's part in the World War, written from the personal experiences of its distinguished author (cf. O357) who served as chief of the British Red Cross in Italy. TFJ

O412a Cadorna, Luigi, Conte. *La guerra alla fronte italiana fino al . . . 9 novembre 1917.* 2 v. Milano, 1921.

b Capello, Luigi. *Note di guerra.* 2 v. Milano, 1920.

c Regio Esercito Italiano: Comando Supremo. *Battle of the Piave, June 15–23, 1918.* London, 1920. Tr. by M. P. Agnetti from *La battaglia del Piave,* Roma, 1920.

d Page, Thomas Nelson. *Italy and the world war.* N. Y., 1920.

Histories of the Italian part in the World War are as yet incomplete and colored by personalities. *a.* Account of the Italian campaign until his retirement, by the foremost Italian military commander. Since he lost the chief command after the disaster of Caporetto, the author has naturally made of his volumes something of a personal apology. *b.* Capello was in command during the greater part of the war on the eastern front, and in that capacity captured Gorizia; after the collapse of his front at Caporetto, he was also retired; his memoirs are valuable, but even more of a personal defense than *a.* *c.* Official history of the battle of the Piave, with good maps. *d.* Interesting history of the Italian campaign by the American ambassador to Italy; well-written, but panegyrical and uncritical. TFJ

For other aspects of Italy's diplomacy and part in the World War, see § J.

O413 Lémonon, Ernest. *L'Italie d'après-guerre, 1914–1921.* Paris, 1922. [Bibliothèque d'histoire contemporaine.]

Well-informed account, from the French point of view, of Italian history from the beginning of the World War to the days preceding the fascist movement. Valuable on the economic side; the author's thesis is that Italy's future lies in agricultural, rather than industrial, development. TFJ

O421 Tittoni, Tommaso. *Modern Italy, its intellectual, cultural, and financial aspects.* N. Y., 1922. [Institute of Politics publications.]

Noteworthy description of Italy at the conclusion of the World War by one of the foremost Italian statesmen, at the time president of the senate, given as a series of lectures before the Institute of Politics at Williamstown. The views represent not merely the interest of an Italian but an Italian of a particular party. TFJ

O422a Villari, Luigi. *Awakening of Italy, the fascista regeneration.* London and N. Y., 1924.

b Prezzolini, Giuseppe. *Fascism.* Tr. by K. MacMillan. N. Y., 1927.

c Gay, Harry Nelson. *Strenuous Italy.* N. Y., 1927.

d Mussolini, Benito. *My autobiography.* N. Y., 1928.

e Sturzo, Luigi. *Italy and Fascismo.* Tr. by B. B. Carter.

f Salvemini, Gaetano. *Fascist dictatorship in Italy.* 2 v. N. Y., 1927–28.

g Nitti, Francesco Saverio. *Bolshevism, fascism, and democracy.* Tr. by M. M. Green. N. Y., 1927.

In the inevitable absence of objective treatments of the period of Italian history since the World War, it is only possible to cite a few of the leading books describing for English readers the Fascist régime in generally sympathetic tone, namely, *a, b, c,* and *d*; and the leading criticisms of the régime, namely, *e, f,* and *g*. TFJ

SAVOY

O431a Ricotti, Ercole. *Storia della monarchia piemontese.* 6 v. Firenze, 1861–69.

b Carutti, Domenico. *Storia della diplomazia della corte di Savoia.* 4 v. Roma, 1875–80.

Two most complete histories of the House of Savoy; both are almost wholly political, and rather old-fashioned; both are based on research among primary sources. *a.* Written immediately after the unification, by a professor of history at the University of Turin; sound in scholarship, although distinctly patriotic in tone. *b.* History of Piedmontese diplomacy from 1494 to 1773 by a distinguished member of the Piedmontese diplomatic service who had free entry to the archives of the foreign office at Turin. TFJ

NORTH ITALIAN CITY STATES

O441a Allen, A. M. *History of Verona.* London, 1910. [States of Italy.] (Bibliography.)

b Muir, Dorothy. *History of Milan under the Visconti.* London, 1924. (Bibliography.)

c Ady, Cecilia M. *History of Milan under the Sforza.* London, 1907. [States of Italy.] (Bibliography.)

d Heywood, William. *History of Perugia.* London and N. Y., 1910. [States of Italy.]

a., c., and *d.* Scholarly and attractive accounts, in the same series under the able editorship of Edward Armstrong, of the history of three Italian cities, all of great interest. *c.* Of special value. *b.* Somewhat similar work covering a period of the history of Milan antecedent to that narrated in *c.*   TFJ

O442 Gardner, Edmund G. *Dukes and poets in Ferrara, a study in the poetry, religion, and politics of the fifteenth and early sixteenth centuries.* London and N. Y., 1904. (Bibliography.)

Perhaps the best volume in English on the development of a small Italian Renaissance state, one of the half-dozen which contributed most to the progress of the arts.   HLG

O443a Gardner, Edmund G. *Story of Siena and San Gimignano.* London and N. Y., 1904. [(H577) Mediaeval towns.] (Bibliography.)

b Douglas, Robert Langton. *History of Siena.* London, 1902; N. Y., 1903. (Bibliography.)

c Schevill, Ferdinand. *Siena, the history of a mediaeval commune.* N. Y., 1909. (Bibliography.)

Three histories of Siena well worth attention. *a.* Careful and useful, with little or no consideration of the economic side. *c.* Generally very excellent, especially with regard to economic development.   TFJ

GENOA

O451a Canale, Michele G. *Nuova istoria della repubblica di Genova, del suo commercio e della sua letteratura dalle origini all' anno 1797.* 4 v. Firenze, 1858–64.

b ——— *Storia del commercio, dei viaggi, delle scoperte e carte nautiche degli Italiani.* Genova, 1866.

c Caro, Georg. *Genua und die Mächte am Mittelmeer, 1257–1311.* 2 v. Halle, 1895–99. (Bibliography.)

a. Standard history of Genoa; incomplete, closes at 1528; old-fashioned, uncritical, and free from all references to authorities; well written, often dramatic; compiled partly from unpublished records in the Genoese archives. *b.* Old, standard book on Italian commerce, both just before and after the Commercial Revolution. *c.* Praiseworthy and successful attempt to depict the rôle of Genoa in the Middle Ages in its broadest aspects, without narrow specialization. Best critical study of Genoa as a Mediterranean power.   EHB

VENICE

O461a Hazlitt, William C. *History of the Venetian republic, her rise, her greatness, and her civilisation.* 1860. 4th rev. ed. by F. J. Payne, 2 v., London, 1915.

b Romanin, Samuele. *Storia documentata di Venezia.* 10 v. Venezia, 1853–61. 2nd ed. of v. 1–4, Venezia, 1912–13.

c **Kretschmayr, Heinrich.** *Geschichte von Venedig.* V. 1–2, Gotha, 1905–20. [Allgemeine Staatengeschichte.]

d **Diehl, Charles.** *Une république patricienne: Venise.* Paris, 1915. [Bibliographie de philosophie scientifique.]

a. Best extended history in English of Venice. The first edition was very modest in its worth, but through successive revisions it has, in its latest form, assumed great value. *b.* Long the authoritative history in Italian; based largely on research in Venetian archives. *c.* More recent work; exhaustive study, based on the sources which are fully described in an appendix to v. 1, and which are submitted to careful critical analysis. V. 1. Treats the origins and closes with the capture of Constantinople in 1204. V. 2. Deals with the period of Venetian greatness. V. 3. Announced to complete the narrative. Constitutional and economic developments receive full consideration and are frequently presented in a new light, as is also the case with the fine arts. Written with feeling for the dramatic interest of the subject. Review, v. 1, F. Schevill, *A.H.R.* 12:864, July 1907. *d.* Attractive in style; particularly good for the relations between Venice and the East. Review, C. Pfister, *Rev. Hist.* 121:159, Jan. 1916. Also cf. Rawdon Brown's excellent account of Venetian commerce at its period of greatness, in the preface to v. 1 of (O94) *Calendar of state papers, Venetian.*

TFJ

O462a Brown, Horatio F. *Life on the lagoons.* 1884. 5th ed., London, 1909.

b ——— *Venetian studies.* 1887. Rev. ed., *Studies in the history of Venice,* 2 v., London and N. Y., 1907.

c ——— *Venice, an historical sketch of the republic.* 1893. 2nd rev. ed., London, 1895. (Bibliography.)

d ——— *Venetian republic.* London, 1902. [Temple primers.] (Bibliography.)

e **Molmenti, Pompeo G.** *Venice, its individual growth from the earliest beginnings to the fall of the republic.* 6 v. Chicago, 1906–08. Tr. by H. F. Brown from *La storia di Venezia nella vita privata,* 1880; 5th ed., 3 pt., 1903–08. 7th ed., Bergamo, 1927–.

No modern writer in English had a deeper knowledge of Venetian history than Horatio Brown, who combined attractiveness of style with sound learning. For five years, 1900 to 1905, he edited v. 8–12 of (O94) *Calendar of state papers, Venetian,* for the British government, and gained an unrivalled knowledge of the Venetian archives. *b.* Twenty essays on various topics in Venetian history, all of interest, although possibly those which deal with Venetian policy in the Levant are most suggestive. *d.* Best brief handbook on the subject. *e.* More recently he has translated Molmenti's classic volumes on Venetian private life. Review, F. Schevill, *A.H.R.* 12:866, July 1907.

TFJ

FLORENCE

O471a Hyett, Francis A. *Florence, her history and art to the fall of the republic.* London and N. Y., 1903. (Bibliography.)

b **Perrens, François T.** *History of Florence under the domination of Cosimo, Piero, Lorenzo de' Medicis, 1434–1492.* London, 1892. Abridged tr. by H. Lynch from *Histoire de Florence depuis ses origines jusqu'à la chute de la république,* 9 v., Paris, 1877–90; 2nd ed. of v. 1–6, Paris, 1902.

c **Davidsohn, Robert.** *Geschichte von Florenz.* V. 1–4 in 9. Berlin, 1896–1927. (Bibliographies.) Italian tr. of v. 1–2 *Storia di Firenze,* 2 v., Firenze, 1907–09.

d —— *Forschungen zur Geschichte von Florenz.* V. 1–4, Berlin, 1896–1908.

e **Young, George F.** *The Medici.* 2 v. London, 1909. (Bibliography.)

f **Roth, Cecil.** *The last Florentine republic.* London, 1925.

a. Sympathetic account of the history of Florence to the siege of 1529–1530. The chapters on Florentine art and literature are especially full, and the one on trade gilds is also useful. *b.* Most recent complete history of Florence prior to 1531; already antiquated; the reader would better turn at once to more modern specialized works, such as *c.* and *d.* and that of (O472) Villari. *c.* Splendid and perhaps definitive history, which has reached the middle of the fourteenth century; the latest parts issued are devoted to a critical discussion of Florentine industry, commerce, banking, and social life, about 1350. Reviews, G. Salvemini, *Rev. Hist.* 68:354, Dec. 1898; G. Baskerville, *E.H.R.* 26:371, Apr. 1911; (London) *Times Literary Supplement,* 23:796, Nov. 27, 1924. *d.* Invaluable, especially on the economic side. *e.* Fair, recent account of the Medici period. *f.* Scholarly history of Florence as the center of Italian politics from 1527–1530.

FJFJ

O472a **Villari, Pasquale.** *Two first centuries of Florentine history, the republic and parties at the time of Dante.* London, 1894–95. Tr. by L. Villari from *I primi due secoli della storia di Firenze,* 2 v., Firenze, 1894.

b —— *Life and times of Girolamo Savonarola.* 1888. 3rd popular ed., London, 1899. Tr. by L. Villari from *La storia di Girolami Savonarola e de' suoi tempi,* 1859–61; 3rd ed., 2 v., Firenze, 1898.

c —— *Life and times of Niccolò Machiavelli.* 1878–83. Rev. ed., 1892; popular ed., 2 v., London, 1898. Tr. by L. Villari from *Niccolò Machiavelli e i suoi tempi,* 1877–82; 3rd rev. ed., 3 v., Milano, 1912–14.

d **Schnitzer, Joseph.** *Savonarola, ein Kulturbild aus der Zeit der Renaissance.* 2 v. München, 1924.

Pasquale Villari, 1827–1917, is undoubtedly the most widely known of recent historians of Italian nationality. A fugitive from Naples after the 1848 revolution, he settled in Florence as professor of history at the Istituto di Studii Superiori. His long life was divided between service to the Italian state and scientific investigation of its history. *a.* His last important production; its value, though great, is today lessened by the deeper research of (O471c and d) Davidsohn. *b.* Youthful work; while of great merit and full of vivid description, is perhaps too enthusiastic in tone. *c.* His best work; perhaps the best book on that period of Italian history available in English. Cf. (O121) and (O201c and d) for Villari's other works. *d.* Most authoritative of the recent biographies of Savonarola; the result of many years of careful study.

TFJ

O473a Machiavelli, Niccolò. *Historical, political, and diplomatic writings.* 1882. 2nd ed., 4 v., Boston, 1891. Tr. by C. E. Detmold from *Tutte le opere di Nicolo Machiavelli cittadino ed secretario fiorentino,* 1550; most complete ed., *Opera di Niccolò Machiavelli,* 8 v., 1813; most recent and best ed., though incomplete, by L. Passerini, G. Milanesi, and P. Fanfani, *Opere di Niccolò Machiavelli,* 6 v., Firenze, 1873-77.

   b ⸺ *Il principe, edited by L. Arthur Burd, with an introduction by Lord Acton.* Oxford, 1891. (Bibliography.)

The principal writings of Machiavelli are: *Il principe di Niccholo Machiavello al Magnifico Lorenzo di Piero de' Medici,* 1532; *Discorsi sopra la prima deca di Tito Livio,* 1531; *Historie fiorentine,* 1532; *Libro della arte della guerra,* 1521. There have been various editions of each of these, as well as of the author's collected works, both in Italian and in translations in many languages. An acquaintance with the writings of this famous statesman and political philosopher is indispensable to an understanding of the spirit of Florence—or, indeed, of Italy—in the early sixteenth century. In spite of his bad reputation, Machiavelli was a zealous Italian patriot, trying to find the surest way to expel the foreigner and unify Italy. *b.* Best annotated edition of the 'Prince' which deserves special attention. Cf. (O472c) Villari, *Life and times of Niccolò Machiavelli.*

                                                                          TFJ

O474a Guicciardini, Francesco. *Historie of Guicciardin, conteining the warres of Italie and other partes.* 1579. 3rd ed., London, 1618. Tr. by G. Fenton from *L'historia d'Italia,* 1561; best ed. by A. Gherardi, v. 1-4, Firenze, 1919.

   b ⸺ *Counsels and reflections.* London, 1890. Tr. by N. H. Thomson from *Ricordi politici e civili.* First published in *c.* Later ed., *Ricordi politici e civili, introduzione e note di Adolfo Faggi,* Torino, 1921. [Collezione di classici italiani.]

   c ⸺ *Opere inedite.* Ed. by G. Canestrini. 10 v. Firenze, 1857-67.

   d **Ranke, Leopold von.** *Zur Kritik neuerer Geschichtschreiber.* Leipzig, 1824.

To understand the spirit of Florence in the sixteenth century one should also read Guicciardini as well as (O473) Machiavelli, the two men being Florence's most famous political philosophers. Guicciardini was a cynical searcher of human motives, telling an interminable story with keen and analytic power, but strikingly destitute of national and ethical ideals. *b.* Deserves special comparison with Machiavelli's *Prince.* *d.* Furnishes a severe criticism of Guicciardini as historian; written in Ranke's youth. For a more recent appraisal of Guicciardini as historian, cf. E. Fueter, 'Guicciardini als Historiker,' *Hist. Zeit.* 100:486-540, 1908.

                                                                          TFJ

ROME AND PAPAL STATES

O481a Gregorovius, Ferdinand. *History of the city of Rome in the middle ages.* 8 v. in 13. London, 1894-1902. Tr. by A. Hamilton from 4th ed. of *Geschichte der Stadt Rom im Mittelalter vom fünften bis zum sechzehnten Jahrhundert,* 1859-72; 6th ed., 8 v., Stuttgart, 1922.

   b **Duchesne, Louis.** *Beginnings of the temporal sovereignty of the popes, A. D. 754-1073.* London, 1908. [International Catholic library.] Tr. by A. H. Mathew from *Les premiers temps de l'état pontifical,* 1898; 2nd ed., Paris, 1904.

c **Halphen, Louis.** *Études sur l'administration de Rome au moyen âge, 751–1252.* Paris, 1907. [Bibliothèque de l'École des Hautes Études.]

d **Boüard, Alain de.** *Le régime politique et les institutions de Rome au moyen âge, 1252–1347.* Paris, 1920. [Bibliothèque des Écoles françaises d'Athènes et de Rome.] (Bibliography.)

a. Standard history of the city of Rome from about 400 to 1534. *b.* Critical history of the early growth of the temporal possessions of the pope, by an eminent Catholic scholar. *c.* Short study of highest value. Review, R. Poupardin, *Rev. Hist.* 95:104, Sept. 1907. *d.* Best work on Roman medieval commune.

For books that deal primarily with the history of the papacy, the reader is referred to § F. For the Roman republic of 1848–49, cf. (O357a) Trevelyan, *Garibaldi's defense of the Roman republic.* TFJ

NAPLES AND SICILY

O491a **Gay, Jules.** *L'Italie méridionale et l'empire byzantin depuis l'avènement de Basile Ier jusqu'à la prise de Bari par les Normands, 867–1071.* Paris, 1904. [Bibliothèque des Écoles Françaises d'Athènes et de Rome.] (Bibliography.)

b **Amari, Michele.** *Storia dei Musulmani di Sicilia.* 3 v. in 4. Firenze, 1854–72.

Standard authorities for the earlier medieval history of Naples and Sicily. *a.* Authoritative work on two centuries of the general history of southern Italy, with special reference to the decline of Byzantine power. Clear, scholarly account, based upon a sound knowledge of printed sources and of modern researches. *b.* Still the most important contribution to the subject; scholarly and critical; based on the Arabic sources, of which Amari was a recognized master. Where, however, Latin sources were used, its value has been somewhat superseded by more recent investigations. JCH

O492a **Chalandon, Ferdinand.** *Histoire de la domination normande en Italie et en Sicile.* 2 v. Paris, 1907.

b **Caspar, Erich.** *Roger II, 1101–1154, und die Gründung der normannisch-sicilischen Monarchie.* Innsbruck, 1904.

c **Curtis, Edmund.** *Roger of Sicily and the Normans in lower Italy, 1016–1154.* London and N. Y., 1912. [Heroes of the nations.] (Bibliography.)

For the Norman period in the history of southern Italy much good work has been done in recent years; cf. § H and the bibliography in (H241a) Haskins, *Normans in European history,* p. 247. *a.* This elaborate and scholarly work covers from the arrival of the Normans to the close of the period in 1197. The author shows ample evidence of his mastery of the printed, and investigation of the unprinted, sources. The first part of the book, devoted to political history, remains the best complete work on the period; the second part, on institutions and civilization, is less satisfactory. *b.* Standard work on the reign. *c.* Useful, popular account. JCH

O493a **Johnston, Robert M.** *Napoleonic empire in southern Italy and the rise of the secret societies.* 2 v. London and N. Y., 1904. (Bibliography.)

b **Colletta, Pietro.** *History of the kingdom of Naples, 1734–1825.* 2 v. Edinburgh, 1858. Tr. by S. H. Horner from *Storia del reame di Napoli, dal 1734 sino al 1825,* 2 v. (also 4 v.), Capolago, 1834. Many later ed.

c **Croce, Benedetto.** *Storia del regno di Napoli.* Bari, 1925. [Scritti di storia letteraria e politica.] (Bibliography.)

a. Interesting and suggestive treatment, although marred by haste, of the reconstruction of the Two Sicilies under the rule of Joseph Bonaparte and Joachim Murat, and of the early years of the Bourbon restoration. It largely supersedes *b.* which was long a notable work, but is now to be avoided as extremely prejudiced. Review of *a.*, H. N. Gay, *A.H.R.* 10:661, Apr. 1905. *c.* Latest exposition of Neapolitan history; by one of the most distinguished of living Italian historians. For the last years of the Kingdom of the Two Sicilies, cf. (O362a) R. de Cesare, *La fine di un regno.*   TFJ

NAVAL HISTORY

O521a **Manfroni, Camillo.** *Storia della marina italiana dalle invasioni barbariche al trattato di Ninfeo.* Livorno, 1899.

b ———— *Storia della marina italiana dal trattato di Ninfeo alla caduta di Costantinopoli.* 2 v. Livorno, 1902.

c ———— *Storia della marina italiana dalla caduta di Costantinopoli fin alla battaglia di Lepanto.* Roma, 1897.

Four excellent volumes upon the history of Italian sea-power from the invasions to 1571; written largely from primary sources, although not always with the best critical judgment; from the nature of the subject, the history is chiefly that of separate cities.   TFJ

CONSTITUTIONAL AND LEGAL HISTORY

O531 **Mayer, Ernst.** *Italienische Verfassungsgeschichte von der Gothenzeit bis zur Zunftherrschaft.* 2 v. Leipzig, 1909. (Bibliography.)

Admirable account, by a jurist, of constitutional development in Italy from the latest imperial period to about 1500; written wholly from the sources, with little reference to secondary authorities. V. 1. Treats of land tenure and persons. V. 2. Deals with administration and justice. The chapter devoted to the early history of municipalities should be supplemented by (O202) Hegel, *Geschichte der Städteverfassung von Italien.*   TFJ

O551 **Pertile, Antonio.** *Storia del diritto italiano dalla caduta dell' impero romano alla codificazione.* 1873–87. 2nd rev. ed., 6 v. in 8 and index, Torino, 1892–1903. (Bibliography.)

Standard history of legal development in Italy. Cf. (O6c) Solmi, *La storia del diritto italiano.*   TFJ

ECONOMIC AND SOCIAL HISTORY

O571a **Schulte, Aloys.** *Geschichte des mittelalterlichen Handels und Verkehrs zwischen Westdeutschland und Italien mit Ausschluss von Venedig.* 2 v. Leipzig, 1900. [Badische Historische Kommission.]

b ———— *Die Fugger in Rom, 1495–1523, mit Studien zur Geschichte des kirchlichen Finanzwesens jener Zeit.* 2 v. in 1. Leipzig, 1904.

c **Simonsfeld, Henry.** *Der Fondaco dei Tedeschi in Venedig und die deutsch-venetianischen Handelsbeziehungen.* 2 v. Stuttgart, 1897.

a. and *c.* Two outstanding books on Italian commerce before the Commercial Revolution. *a.* With one volume of text and one of published source material, covers the history of medieval commerce over the northwestern Alpine passes. *c.* Classic account of the trade relations between Venice and the southern German towns. *b.* Detailed, critical account of the Italian side of the Fugger Bank at its moment of greatest activity and influence; perhaps the best monograph on Italian banking in the late Renaissance.

Also cf. (H571a) Heyd, *Histoire du commerce du Levant au moyen-âge;* (H572) Schaube, *Handelsgeschichte der romanischen Völker des Mittelmeergebiets bis zum Ende der Kreuzzüge;* and the histories of (O451) Genoa, (O461–462) Venice, (O471) Florence. Works listed under the following numbers: (O402, 413, 421, 521, 531) contain more or less material on economic and social history.   TFJ

CULTURAL HISTORY: RELIGION

For works on the history of the papacy and on the religious history of Italy, cf. § F. For lives of Savonarola, cf. (O472).

CULTURAL HISTORY: THOUGHT AND PHILOSOPHY

In the absence of good general works surveying these topics, reference may be made to the lives and works of the following persons listed under the numbers affixed: (O255) Cellini, (O256) Castiglione, (O472–473) Machiavelli, (O474) Guicciardini, (O822) Galileo, (O823) Giordano Bruno. For the intellectual history of the Renaissance period in Italy, much valuable material is embodied in the works listed under (O251–252). Also cf. (A243) Croce, *History, its theory and practice.*

CULTURAL HISTORY: LITERATURE

O661a Gaspary, Adolf. *Geschichte der italienischen Literatur.* 2 v. Strassburg, 1885–88. Italian tr. by N. Zingarelli and Vittorio Rossi, *Storia della letteratura italiana,* 2 v., Torino, 1887–91; rev. ed. of v. 2 by V. Rossi, 1901. English tr. of small part by H. Oelsner, *History of early Italian literature to the death of Dante,* London, 1901. [Bohn's standard library.] (Bibliography.)

b **Bartoli, Adolfo.** *Storia della letteratura italiana.* 7 v. in 8. Firenze, 1878–89.

c *Storia letteraria d'Italia, scritta da una società di professori.* 9 v. in 11. Milano, 1897–1913. [1, C. Giussani, *Letteratura romana;* 2a, F. Novati, *Le origini;* 2b, G. Bertoni, *Il duecento;* 3, N. Zingarelli, *Dante;* 4, G. Volpi, *Il trecento;* 5, V. Rossi, *Il quattrocento;* 6, F. Flamini, *Il cinquecento;* 7, A. Belloni, *Il seicento;* 8, T. Concari, *Il settecento;* 9a and b, G. Mazzoni, *L'ottocento.*]

d **Hauvette, Henri.** *Littérature italienne.* 1906. 2nd ed., Paris, 1914. [Histoire des littératures.]

e **Rossi, Vittorio.** *Storia della letteratura italiana per uso dei licei.* 1900. 4th ed., 3 v. Milano, 1910. (Excellent bibliographies.)

f **D'Ancona, Alessandro,** and **Bacci, Orazio.** *Manuale della letteratura italiana.* 1909. Rev. ed., 6 v., Firenze, 1919–21. [Collezione scolastica.] (Bibliography.)

g **Sanctis, Francesco de.** *Storia della letteratura italiana.* 1870. New ed. by B. Croce, 2 v., Bari, 1912; Eng. tr. by J. Refern in preparation.

a. For the history of Italian literature, this is still unequalled for original material, and for clearness and taste of presentation, but extends only to the end of the sixteenth century. The Italian translation is better than the German original. *b.* Also useful, especially for the earlier period, although of uneven merit. *c.* This coöperative history has great fulness of detail; each volume was prepared by a specialist; the work as a whole lacks symmetry. *d.* Best study in French; makes no pretense to completeness; interest is centered in the greatest writers, especially in the Renaissance. *e.* Excellent manual; presents the results of the most recent investigation. *f.* Also excellent; contains many extracts.   EBB

g. By many critics, including Croce, considered the best general study.   TFJ

English readers will find a good survey of Italian literature of the Renaissance in (O252a) Symonds, *Renaissance in Italy,* v. 4–5. For works on Dante, cf. (O207), on Petrarch, cf. (O253), on Boccaccio, cf. (O254).

CULTURAL HISTORY: ART

O681a Cummings, Charles A. *History of architecture in Italy from the time of Constantine to the dawn of the renaissance.* 2 v. Boston, 1901. (Bibliography.)

b Anderson, William J. *Architecture of the renaissance in Italy.* 1896. 4th rev. ed., London and N. Y., 1909. (Bibliography.)

c Ricci, Corrado. *Baroque architecture and sculpture in Italy.* London and N. Y., 1912.

d —— *Architecture and decorative sculpture of the high and late renaissance in Italy.* N. Y., 1923.

e Porter, Arthur K. *Lombard architecture.* 3 v. and atlas. New Haven, 1915–17. (Bibliography.)

For the history of Italian architecture as a whole, cf. general histories of architecture in § B. *a.* Facile summary of Italian architecture in the Middle Ages; written prior to the valuable researches of Porter and others; richly illustrated. *b.* Popular study; written from the point of view of the practising architect; the estimates, especially for the later period, need revision in the light of more recent studies; the datings have been revised by later researches, partly embodied in *c.* and *d.* *c.* and *d.* Primarily volumes of illustrations, with informative legends and a brief introductory text; measurably abreast of current research. *e.* Monumental work which incorporates the author's extensive studies in the documents and monuments of the Lombard style and in the iconographic materials. A volume of general summary is followed by two large volumes of detailed studies of each individual building and by a large atlas of illustrations. Porter's more general works (cf. H683) are also useful for the architecture of Italy.   FK

O686 Vasari, Giorgio. *Lives of the most eminent painters, sculptors, and architects.* 10 v. London, 1912–15; N. Y., 1912–16. Tr. by G. du C. de Vere from *Le vite dei più eccellenti pittori, scultori, ed architetti.* 1550. 12th ed., Firenze, 1893.

In his day, 1511–1574, Vasari was considered an excellent artist himself; but today his great reputation depends wholly upon his work as biographer of the famous artists of Italy from Cimabue to Sansovino. Although often based on gossip and full of plagiarisms, this work still remains a mine of information and interest. As, in a sense, the father of the history of art, Vasari well deserves attention.   HLG

O687a Crowe, Sir Joseph A., and **Cavalcaselle, Giovanni Battista.** *New history of painting in Italy, from the second to the sixteenth century.* 3 v., 1864–66. 2nd ed. by Langton Douglas, S. A. Strong, G. de Nicola, and T. Borenius, *History of painting in Italy, Umbria, Florence, and Siena, from the second to the sixteenth century.* 6 v., London, 1903–14. Another ed. by Edward Hutton, 3 v., London and N. Y., 1908–09.

b ———— *History of painting in north Italy, Venice, Padua, Vicenza, Verona, Ferrara, Milan, Friuli, Brescia, from the fourteenth to the sixteenth century.* 2 v., 1871. New ed. by Tancred Borenius, 3 v., London and N. Y., 1912. (Bibliography.)

c Morelli, Giovanni (Lermolieff, Ivan). *Italian painters, critical studies of their works.* 2 v. London, 1892–93. Tr. by C. J. Ffoulkes from *Kunstkritische Studien über italienische Malerei,* 3 v., Leipzig, 1890–93.

d Berenson, Bernhard. *Venetian painters of the renaissance.* 1894. 3rd ed., N. Y., 1903.

e ———— *Florentine painters of the renaissance.* 1896. 3rd rev. ed., N. Y., 1909.

f ———— *Central Italian painters of the renaissance.* 1897. 2nd rev. ed., N. Y., 1909.

g ———— *North Italian painters of the renaissance.* N. Y., 1907.

h Venturi, Adolfo. *Storia dell' arte italiana.* 7 v. in 10. Milano, 1901–15.

i Toesca, Pietro. *Storia dell'arte italiana.* V. 1, *Il Medioevo.* Torino, 1927.

a. In its first edition, the earliest complete survey of Italian painting; written in the midst of hardship, by an English enthusiast, advised by an Italian friend. It showed sound judgment and became the accepted English history of Italian painting. The vast amount of investigation in the ensuing forty years was embodied in the notes of the new edition. The four volumes which Douglas revised embody the results of his scholarship and research, but the other two volumes are less well done. Hutton's edition is less expensive. *b.* Supplementary work of similar character. *c.* Morelli, whose work was originally published in German under the pseudonym of Ivan Lermolieff, was the founder of the modern scientific method of attribution of paintings based on internal evidence. The English translation covers only his studies on the Borghese and Doria galleries in Rome and the Munich and Dresden galleries. *d., e., f.,* and *g.* Berenson's volumes represent the continuation of the Morellian method. Each of these small books, without illustrations, contains, first, general characterizations of the work of the school and of the individual masters, which afford the most penetrating and suggestive brief analyses of their style, and, secondly, lists of the works of each master which are accepted as authentic by Berenson, in the exercise of his critical method of attribution by internal evidence. As a whole, they remain the most discriminating and reliable body of judgments. *h.* Monumental work; lavishly illustrated; an encyclopedic storehouse of material. For each master there is a brief summary of all the documentary knowledge, and then an attempt to reconstruct the work of the master by the aid of internal evidence. While full of suggestion, the attributions are generally regarded as less reliable than Berenson's. Venturi is, however, especially valuable on the art of Ferrara, Modena, and the Marches. FK

i. Outstanding volume covering the history of Italian art from its beginnings to the thirteenth century, by the professor of medieval art at the University of Rome; complete and philosophical. TFJ

BIOGRAPHIES

Among many excellent biographies of personages of note in Italian history, beyond those already listed, may be mentioned the following of special interest: For the eleventh century: (O721) Nora Duff, *Matilda of Tuscany*, London, 1909. For the twelfth, (O731) Adolf Hausrath, *Arnold von Brescia*, Leipzig, 1891; reprint, Leipzig, 1895 [Weltverbesserer im Mittelalter.] For the thirteenth, (O741) Friedrich Stieve, *Ezzelino von Romano*, Leipzig, 1909.

For the fourteenth century: (O761) Edmund G. Gardner, *Saint Catherine of Siena*, London and N. Y., 1907; (O762) John Temple-Leader and Giuseppe Marcotti, *Sir John Hawkwood (L'Acuto), Story of a condottiere*, Florence and London, 1889, tr. by Leader Scott (Mrs. L. E. Baxter) from *Giovanni Acuto (Sir John Hawkwood), la storia d'un condottiere*, Firenze, 1889; (O763) Hans Spangenberg, *Can Grande della Scala*, 2 v., Berlin, 1892-95; (O764) Emmanuel Rodocanachi, *Cola di Rienzi, histoire de Rome de 1342 à 1354*, Paris, 1888.

For the fifteenth century: (O781) Edward Hutton, *Sigismondo Pandolfo Malatesta, Lord of Rimini*, London and N. Y., 1906; (O782) Katharine D. Ewart (Mrs. H. M. Vernon), *Cosimo de' Medici*, London and N. Y., 1899 [Foreign statesmen]; (O783) Edward Armstrong, *Lorenzo de' Medici*, London and N. Y., 1896 [Heroes of the nations]; (O784) Conte Pietro D. Pasolini dall'Onda, *Caterina Sforza*, 3 v., Roma, 1893, abridged French tr. by M. Hélys (M. Léra), Paris, 1912; (O785) Ferdinand Gregorovius, *Lucrezia Borgia*, 1874, 3rd rev. ed., 2 v. in 1, Stuttgart, 1875, French tr. by P. Regnaud, 2 v., Paris, 1876; (O786) William H. Woodward, *Cesare Borgia*, London, 1913.

For the sixteenth century: (O801) Eugène Müntz, *Leonardo da Vinci*, 2 v., London and N. Y., 1878, tr. from ms. of *Léonard de Vinci*, Paris, 1899; (O802) Sir Joseph A. Crowe and Giovanni B. Cavalcaselle, *Raphael, his life and works*, 2 v., London, 1882-85; (O803) Crowe and Cavalcaselle, *Titian, his life and times*, 2 v., London, 1877; (O804) Georg Gronau, *Titian*, London and N. Y., 1904, tr. by A. M. Todd from *Tizian*, Berlin, 1900; (O805) Herman F. Grimm, *Life of Michael Angelo*, 1865, new ed., 2 v., Boston, 1896, tr. by (O806) Julia Cartwright (Mrs. Henry Ady), *Beatrice d'Este, Duchess of Milan*, 1899, later ed., London and N. Y., 1912; (O807) *id., Isabella d'Este, Marchioness of Mantua*, 1903, reprint, London and N. Y., 1923; (O808) Edward Hutton, *Pietro Aretino, the scourge of princes*, London and Boston, 1922; (O809) Pierre Gauthiez, *Jean des Bandes Noires*, Paris, 1901; (O810) Cecily Booth, *Cosimo I, duke of Florence*, Cambridge, Eng., 1921.

For the seventeenth century: (O821) Alexander Robertson, *Fra Paolo Sarpi*, 1893, 2nd ed., London, 1894; (O822) John H. Fahie, *Galileo, his life and work*, London, 1903; (O823) Domenico Berti, *Giordano Bruno*, 1861, rev. ed., Torino, 1889.

For the eighteenth century: (O841) Costanzo Rinaudo, *Carlo Emanuele I*, Torino, 1891; (O842) Pietro Calà Ulloa, *Di Bernardo Tanucci e de' suoi tempi*, 2nd ed., Napoli, 1875; (O843) Eugène Bouvy, *Le comte Pietro Verri, 1728-1797, ses idées et son temps*, Paris, 1889.

For the nineteenth century: (O861) Alfred von Reumont, *Gino Capponi*, Gotha, 1880; (O862) Alessandro di Ancona, *Federigo Confalonieri*, 1896, 2nd ed., Milano, 1898; (O863) Giuseppe Ricciardi, *Storia dei fratelli Bandiera*, Firenze, 1862; (O864) Giovanni Baldasseroni, *Leopoldo II, granduca di Toscana, e i suoi tempi*, Firenze, 1871; (O865) Domenico Berti, *Di Vincenzo Gioberti, riformatore politico e ministro,* Firenze, 1881; (O866) A. Anzilotti, *Gioberti,* Firenze, 1922; (O867) Massimo, Marchese d'Azeglio, *Recollections,* tr. by A. Maffei from *I miei ricordi,* 1866, best ed., 3 v., Firenze, 1899; (O868) Dominique Battesti, *Un patriote italien: Massimo d'Azeglio,* Paris, 1913; (O869) Giovanni Visconti-Venosta, *Memoirs of youth, things seen and known, 1847–1860,* Boston, 1914, tr. by W. Prall, from *Ricordi di gioventù, cose vedute o sapute, 1847–1860,* 1904, 3rd ed., Milano, 1906; (O870) Marco Minghetti, *I miei ricordi,* 3 v., Roma, 1888–90.

TFJ

GOVERNMENT PUBLICATIONS

Among the official publications of the Italian government the following are of interest to the historian: (O901) *Gazzetta ufficiale del regno d'Italia,* Torino, Firenze, Roma, 1860 ff., which gives the text of royal decrees, and a statement of various administrative acts; (O902) *Atti parlamentari,* in two divisions, for the senate and chamber of deputies, and, under each division, in various series, of which the following are noteworthy: (O902a) *Discussioni* (debates), (O902b) *Disegni di legge* (legislation), and (O902c) *Documenti* (material from various ministries submitted to parliament). Among the *Documenti* are to be found the (O902d) *Documenti diplomatici,* presented by the Ministry of Foreign Affairs, and commonly called 'green books.' (O903) *Annuario statistico italiano,* Roma, 1878 ff., published about once in two years by the Ufficio centrale di statistica, gives convenient information on the statistics of population, government, bureaus, finance, industry, commerce, etc.

The historical section of the general staff, Corpo di Stato Maggiore, Ufficio Storico, has published (O904) *Relazione e rapporti finali sulla campagna di 1848,* 3 v., Roma, 1910; (O905) *Sulla campagna di 1849,* Roma, 1911; (O906) *Sulla campagna di 1859,* 6 v., Roma, 1910–12; and (O907) *Sulla campagna di 1866,* 2 v., Roma, 1875–95. TFJ

ACADEMY AND SOCIETY PUBLICATIONS

For academy and society publications relating to Italian history, cf. (O76–93).

PERIODICALS

Among the periodicals of general character in Italian, several frequently contain articles of an historical nature. Among these the most important are (O941) *Nuova antologia di lettere, scienze, ed arti,* semi-monthly, Firenze and Roma, 1866 ff. (*Indici, 1866–1895,* Roma, 1901); and (O942) *Rivista d'Italia,* monthly, Roma and Milano, 1898 ff.

(O951) *Rivista storica italiana,* quarterly, Torino, 1884 ff. (*Indice, 1884–1901,* 2 v., Torino, 1904), which formerly limited its scope to book reviews and bibliographical data on Italian history and has consequently been the indispensable means of keeping abreast with the subject, began in 1923 a new series as a general historical review. (O952) *Bollettino dell' Istituto Storico Italiano,* Roma, 1886 ff., is the organ of the Institute auxiliary to its publication of (O76) *Fonti per la storia d'Italia,* and, since 1923, of the new edition of (O91) Muratori. A similar journal devoted primarily to materials concerning the relations of the Teutonic nations with Italy, especially in the Middle Ages, is (O953) *Quellen und Forschungen aus italienischen Archiven und Bibliotheken herausgegeben vom Königlichen Preussischen Historischen Institut in Rom,* 20 v., Rom, 1898 ff. (index of v. 1–17 in v. 17). Another general historical review was (O954)

Studi storici, Pisa, Torino, and Pavia, 22 v., 1891–1914; and a new one is (O955) *Nuova rivista storica,* quarterly, Milano, 1917 ff.

There are also a large number of periodicals of provincial, local, and specialized character, of which the more important are: (O961) *Miscellanea di storia italiana,* Torino, 1862 ff. (indexes in v. 15 and 31), originally published by the Regia Deputazione di Storia Patria, but since 1895 by the Regia Deputazione sopra gli Studi di Storia Patria per le Antiche Provincie e la Lombardia, which has also issued (O961a) *Biblioteca di storia italiana recente,* Torino, 1907 ff.; (O962) *Biblioteca della Società Storica Subalpina,* Pinerolo, 1899 ff., for the history of Piedmont; (O963) *Archivio storico lombardo,* quarterly, Milano, 1874 ff. (*Indici, 1874–1903,* 2 v., Milano, 1894–1905); (O964) *Archivio veneto,* quarterly, 40 v., Venezia, 1871–90 (*Indice generale* forms v. 39–40), continued as (O965) *Nuovo archivio veneto,* quarterly, Venezia, 42 v., 1891–1921 (*Indice, 1891–1910,* 2 v., Venezia, 1901–1911); then as (O966a) *Archivio veneto-tridentino,* quarterly, Venezia, 1922–26; and again as (O966b) *Archivio veneto,* 1927 ff.; (O967) *Archivio storico italiano,* Firenze, 1842 ff. (*Indice, 1842–1907,* 6 v., Firenze, 1857–1909), now published by Regia Deputazione Toscana di Storia Patria; (O968) *Archivio della Reale Società Romana di Storia Patria,* Roma, 1877 ff. (*Indice, 1877–1902,* 2 v., Roma, 1888–1903); (O969) *Archivio storico per le province napoletane pubblicato a cura della Società di Storia Patria,* quarterly, Napoli, 1876 ff. (*Indice generale, 1876–1900,* 2 v., Napoli, 1897–1902); (O970) *Archivio storico siciliano,* quarterly, Palermo, 1873 ff.

For the Risorgimento, several specialized periodicals have published an enormous quantity of important documents and inaugurated the critical study of that epoch. Among the more important are: (O981) *Rivista storica del risorgimento italiano,* ed. by B. Manzone, 3 v., Torino, 1895–1900, continued, by the same editor, as (O982) *Il risorgimento italiano, rivista storica,* Torino, 1908 ff., until 1914 the organ of the Società Nazionale per la Storia del Risorgimento Italiano, since which date its organ has been (O983) *Rassegna storica del risorgimento,* Roma and Aquila degli Abruzzi, 1914 ff.

(O991) *Memorie storiche militari, comando del Corpo di Stato Maggiore, Ufficio Storico,* 10 v. in 11, Roma and Città di Castello, 1909–14, contains a series of military studies of the first importance. TFJ

SECTION P

GERMANY, AUSTRIA, AND SWITZERLAND

Editor
SIDNEY BRADSHAW FAY
Professor of History, Harvard University

CONTENTS

INTRODUCTION

The history of Germany has been subjected to a great amount of detailed scrutiny, owing partly to the fact that the modern school of historical writing largely developed from Ranke and the students whom he trained, and partly to the local patriotism which has led investigators to deal at length with the history of the hundreds of little states comprised within the old Holy Roman Empire, as well as with the history of the nation as a whole. A large part of this vast historical literature is noted in (P1a) Dahlmann-Waitz, *Quellenkunde,* an invaluable bibliographical guide to which all students of German history should have recourse. There are also helpful but uncritical lists of books in the chapters dealing with Germany in (H121) *Cambridge medieval history* and (I121) *Cambridge modern history.*

As the history of the Holy Roman Empire in the Middle Ages is, to a large extent, the history of Europe and of the relations of church and state, for many of the works which one might expect to find mentioned in this section, the reader should consult §§ F, H, I, J, M, and O. Similarly for the German colonies, reference should be made to §§ K and V. The more important works on the history of Austria before 1918 are given below, but for the bibliography of the parts of the Austro-Hungarian Monarchy which became independent as the result of the World War, cf. §§ S and T.

BIBLIOGRAPHY

P1a **Dahlmann, Friedrich C.,** and **Waitz, Georg.** *Quellenkunde der deutschen Geschichte.* 1830. 8th rev. ed. by Paul Herre, Leipzig, 1912.

b **Loewe, Victor.** *Bücherkunde der deutschen Geschichte: kritischer Wegweiser durch die neuere deutsche historische Literatur.* 1900. 5th ed., Berlin, 1919.

c **Ulrich, Hermann.** *Die besten deutschen Geschichtswerke.* Leipzig, 1923. [Kleine Literaturführer.]

d *Jahresberichte der deutschen Geschichte, 1918 ff.* Ed. by V. Loewe and others. Breslau, 1920 ff.

a. The slender guide to German historical literature which Dahlmann prepared for the convenience of his students in 1830, and which was given by Waitz in 1869 an improved arrangement and enlarged size, has swelled in its eighth edition in 1912, through the coöperation of forty-two historical experts, into a gigantic but invaluable compendium. Classifies virtually all works of any importance on German history in the German language which appeared prior to 1912; less complete in listing non-German works. Less important titles are printed in smaller type, but otherwise there is no indication as to relative importance and value of the works cited. Indispensable for the bibliography of any phase of German history. *b.* Small, critical guide, complementary to *a.* Instead of aiming at comprehensiveness, it selects a few of the most important works on German history and indicates very satisfactorily their character and value by brief descriptive notes; it will, therefore, be often more convenient for the beginner and is more up to date. *c.* Contains a good introductory sketch of German historiography, and useful critical or descriptive notes on each work. In size and comprehensiveness stands midway between *a.* and *b.,* but includes some mention of other countries besides Germany. Designed to guide the general student rather than the specialist. *d.* Continues (B15b) *Jahresberichte der Geschichtswissenschaft,* but for Germany only. Annual volume with full record of the books and periodical articles published in the year. For critical reviews and for more recent publications, the student should consult the current periodicals noted at the close of this section. For general catalogues of all German publications, cf. (B5).   SBF

P2a Wattenbach, Wilhelm. *Deutschlands Geschichtsquellen im Mittelalter bis zur Mitte des dreizehnten Jahrhunderts.* 1858. 6th rev. ed., 2 v., Berlin, 1893–94. 7th ed., v. 1, Stuttgart and Berlin, 1904.

b Lorenz, Ottokar. *Deutschlands Geschichtsquellen im Mittelalter seit der Mitte des dreizehnten Jahrhunderts.* 1870. 3rd rev. ed., 2 v., Berlin, 1886–87.

c Jansen, Max, and **Schmitz-Kallenberg, Ludwig.** *Historiographie und Quellen der deutschen Geschichte bis 1500.* 2nd ed., Leipzig, 1914. [(A294) Meister, Grundriss der Geschichtswissenschaft.]

a. and *b.* These two works together form a comprehensive, critical survey of medieval German historiography, including literary and cultural history. The sources for each period are systematically coördinated and critically appraised; the best modern editions are indicated. Indispensable to every great library and invaluable as guides to the thorough student. *c.* More recent, briefer survey of the same literature. JWT

P3a Wegele, Franz X. von. *Geschichte der deutschen Historiographie seit dem Auftreten des Humanismus.* München, 1885. [Geschichte der Wissenschaften in Deutschland.]

b Guilland, Antoine. *Modern Germany and her historians.* London and N. Y., 1915. Tr. from *L'Allemagne nouvelle et ses historiens,* Paris, 1899.

c —— *German historical publications, 1914–1920.* A.H.R. 25:640–659, July 1920.

d Below, Georg A. H. von. *Die deutsche Geschichtsschreibung von den Befreiungskriegen bis zu unseren Tagen.* 1916. 2nd rev. ed., München, 1924. [(B170) Below and Meinecke, Handbuch der mittelalterlichen und neueren Geschichte.] (Bibliographical footnotes.)

e Wolf, Gustav; Schäfer, Dietrich; Delbrück, Hans. *Nationale Ziele der deutschen Geschichtsschreibung seit der französischen Revolution.* Gotha, 1918.

f Acton, John E. E. D., Baron. *German schools of history.* E.H.R. 1:7–42, Jan. 1886. Reprint in his (B243b) *Historical essays and studies.*

g Westphal, M. *Die besten deutschen Memoiren: Lebenserinnerungen und Selbstbiographien aus sieben Jahrhunderten.* Leipzig, 1923. [Kleine Literaturführer.]

a. Attempt to give a bibliographical and yet philosophical account of the development of historical writing in Germany since the Middle Ages. Still useful, though somewhat out of date. *b.* By a Swiss professor; gives an admirable and severely critical, though not unsympathetic, account of the writings and influence of Niehbuhr, Ranke, Mommsen, Sybel, and Treitschke; supplemented by *c.* *d.* and *e.* Contain penetrating studies of the growth of historical writing in Germany and the influence upon it of nationalistic conceptions since the French Revolution. Review of greatly enlarged 2nd ed. of *d.,* G. P. Gooch, E.H.R. 40:159, Jan. 1925. *f.* Scholarly critique of the character and value of German historical work. *g.* Useful annotated bibliography of the best memoirs, reminiscences, and autobiographies written by Germans or translated from foreign languages into German.

Also cf. the biographies of German historians in (P21) *Allgemeine deutsche Biographie;* (A249a) Gooch, *History and historians in the nineteenth century;* and the brilliant work of (A247) Fueter, *Geschichte der neueren Historiographie.* Excellent bibliographical material will also be found in the volumes of (A294) Meister, *Grundriss der Geschichtswissenschaft.* SBF

P4a Wolf, Gustav. *Quellenkunde der deutschen Reformationsgeschichte.* 2 v. Gotha, 1915–22.

   b Robinson, James Harvey. *Study of the Lutheran revolt.* A.H.R. 8:205–216, Jan. 1903.

   c Harvey, Andrew Edward. *Martin Luther in the estimate of modern historians.* Amer. Jour. of Theology, 22:321–348, July 1918.

   d Stern, Alfred. *Histoire d'Allemagne, publications relatives à la Réforme.* Rev. hist. 115:128–140, Jan. 1914; 132:305–320, Nov. 1919.

   e Kieffer, George L.; Rockwell, William W.; Pannkoke, Otto H. *List of references on the history of the reformation in Germany.* N. Y., 1917.

   a. Indispensable for the study of the German Reformation; contains a critical estimate of the more important works in German, but neglects some valuable English works. V. 1. History of the historiography of the Reformation, with a bibliography of the background of the Reformation from the Council of Constance to Luther. V. 2. Accounts of the sources for the study of religious life during the Reformation, and of the biographies of the leading reformers. Review, G. Krüger, *Harvard Theol. Rev.* 17:3, Jan. 1924. Too severe review, P. Kalkoff, *Hist. Vierteljahrschrift,* 19:261, 1919. A more philosophical view of many of the authors discussed may be found in (A247) Fueter, *Historiographie.* Good summaries of Reformation literature will be found in *b., c., d.,* and *e.*

                                                                                        SBF

P5 Borchard, Edwin M. *Guide to the law and legal literature of Germany.* Washington, 1912. [Library of Congress.]

   Useful, critical bibliography by an American legal expert; gives an account of the more important works on German legal history and philosophy, the civil codes, commercial law, social insurance and labor legislation, and civil and criminal procedure.   SBF

P6 Loewe, Victor. *Das deutsche Archivwesen: seine Geschichte und Organisation.* Breslau, 1921.

   Recent manual of information useful to those undertaking research in German archives. Review, *E.H.R.* 40:159, Jan. 27, 1925.   SBF

P7 *Katalog der Bibliothek des Reichstages,* ed. by E. Blömeke and J. Müller. 5 v. Berlin, 1890–99.

   Best guide to German government publications.   HRS

P11a Charmatz, Richard. *Wegweiser durch die Literatur der österreichischen Geschichte.* Stuttgart, 1912.

   b Krones, Franz X. von. *Grundriss der österreichischen Geschichte mit besonderer Rücksicht auf Quellen- und Literaturkunde.* Wien, 1882.

   a. Best recent general bibliography of Austrian history. *b.* Though somewhat out of date, still useful for its bibliographical references and critical account of the older sources.

   Cf. (S1) Kerner, *Slavic Europe,* for works on Slavic nationalities which at any time have been under Hapsburg rule; recent; comprehensive; especially convenient for those who do not read Slavic languages.   SBF

P12 *Katalog des Verlages der K. K. Hof- und Staatsdruckerei.* Wien, 1911.
Complete to end of 1910; best guide to Austrian government publications.

HRS

P16a Barth, Hans. *Bibliographie der schweizer Geschichte enthaltend die selb-
ständig erschienen Druckwerke zur Geschichte der Schweiz.* 3 v. Basel,
1914–15. [Allgemeine Geschichtforschende Gesellschaft der Schweiz.]

  b Brandstetter, Josef L. *Repertorium über die in Zeit- und Sammelschriften
der Jahre 1812–1890 enthaltenen Aufsätze und Mitteilungen schweizer-
geschichtlichen Inhaltes.* Basel, 1892. Continuation, 1891–1900, by H.
Barth, Basel, 1906. [Allgemeine Geschichtforschende Gesellschaft der
Schweiz.]

  c Wyss, Georg von. *Geschichte der Historiographie in der Schweiz.*
Zürich, 1895.

a. Comprehensive and altogether admirable bibliography of Swiss history;
mentions some 30,000 works published to the close of 1913. Review, G. Meyer
von Knonau, *Hist. Zeit.* 116:516, 1916. *b.* Classifies historical articles published in Swiss periodicals from 1812 to 1900. *c.* Gives reliable characterizations of Swiss chroniclers; an excellent guide to the works and lives of Swiss
historians up to about 1850. SBF

Library collections.—For German history the collection in the Library of
Harvard University is the best in New England, or in fact in the United States.
It contains works selected from the libraries of many German scholars and is
especially rich in complete sets of documentary sources, of local historical society
magazines, and of the more general academy and learned society publications of
Germany as well as of other countries. It has been even said to be a better
collection than any in Europe with the exception of the Royal Library in Berlin
and of the City Library in Frankfort-on-the-Main. Of interest to the literary
historian is the Carlyle collection of books annotated by Carlyle and used by him
in writing his (P303) *Frederick the Great.* The Library of the Harvard Law
School is rich in German legal literature of all sorts. The Boston Public Library
may sometimes be used to supplement the Harvard collections. The Boston
Athenaeum contains some (incomplete) sets of recent German newspapers.

In New York, Columbia University Library has fairly complete sets of German
government documents, such as the stenographic reports of the debates in the
Reichstag and in the state legislatures of Prussia, Saxony, and Bavaria. It is
rich in books and pamphlets on recent German political parties and politics and
on the Pan-German movement. For literary history it contains the Calvin
Thomas collection—which is very extensive on Goethe—and an unusually valuable
collection on modern German literature. The New York Public Library, aside
from its excellent general collection, is distinguished by the large number of
foreign language works on German history, especially works in the Slavic languages to be found nowhere else in the United States. The library of Princeton
University is rich in sets of historical periodicals and publications of learned
societies; that of the University of Pennsylvania is especially useful on German
commerce; and that of Cornell University on medieval German culture and on
the German Reformation.

The Library of Congress, very weak in German history a quarter of a century
ago, has been rapidly making up for its former deficiency by purchasing very

extensively both individual books and valuable sets, especially those relating to legal and political history.

The library of the University of Chicago, supplemented by the valuable collections in the Newberry Library, is especially rich in German medieval history. Other libraries which have good general collections on German history, including many of the most important periodicals, are those of the Universities of Illinois, Michigan, Wisconsin, and Minnesota.

Good collections for the history of Switzerland will be found in the libraries of Harvard and Johns Hopkins Universities.   AHS

ENCYCLOPEDIAS AND WORKS OF REFERENCE

For the leading general encyclopedias published in German, cf. (B24).

P21 *Allgemeine deutsche Biographie, herausgegeben durch die Historische Commission bei der königlichen Akademie der Wissenschaften* (zu München). Ed. by Rochus, Freiherr von Liliencron, Franz X. von Wegele, and others, 56 v., Leipzig, 1875–1912. (Bibliographies.)

Invaluable dictionary of national German biography. Articles often written by scholars of first rank. Includes prominent Germans from earliest times to end of nineteenth century.   SBF

P22a *Biographisches Jahrbuch und deutscher Nekrolog, 1896–1913.* Ed. by Anton Bettelheim, 18 v. Berlin, 1897–1917. Continuation, Stuttgart, 1925 ff.

b *Deutsches biographisches Jahrbuch, herausgegeben vom Verbande der Deutschen Akademien, Ueberleitungsbände.* v. 1, 1914–1916. Stuttgart, 1925.

c *Wer ist's? Unsere Zeitgenossen* . . . Ed. by Hermann A. L. Degener. Leipzig, 1905 ff.

Volumes of current biographical information. *a.* Annual necrology, with convenient biographical sketches. *b.* Continuation of *a.* Two other transition volumes will give biographies of Germans who died between 1916 and 1920; the regular series of this necrology will then begin with the record of notable Germans who died after 1920. *c.* The German *Who's Who;* its annual appearance has been interrupted, so that only eight volumes have appeared.   SBF

P31a Wurzbach, Constantin von. *Biographisches Lexikon des Kaisertums Oesterreich, enthaltend die Lebensskizzen der denkwürdigen Personen, welche seit 1750 in den österreichischen Kronländern geboren wurden oder darin gelebt und gewirkt haben.* 60 v. Wien, 1856–91.

b *Neue österreichische Biographie, 1815–1918.* Ed. by Anton Bettelheim, pt. 1, v. 1–2; pt. 2, v. 1, Wien, 1923–25.

Best, though inadequate, dictionaries of biography for Austria, that is, for the German lands formerly under Hapsburg rule. Review of *b,* G. G. Picavet, *Rev. Hist.* 151:112, Jan. 1926.   SBF

P36a Galerie Suisse. Ed. by E. Secrétan, 3 v., Lausanne, 1873–80.

b *Dictionnaire historique et biographique de la Suisse* . . . *publié sous la direction de Marcel Godet, Henri Türler, Victor Attinger.* V. 1–5, Neuchâtel, 1921–30.

a. Somewhat antiquated biographical dictionary for Switzerland. *b.* More comprehensive, with excellent illustrations and brief bibliographies; v. 5 extends through "Scheveney."   SBF

GEOGRAPHY

P41a Partsch, Josef F. M. *Central Europe.* N. Y., 1903. Tr. by C. Black, abridged by E. A. Reeves, from ms. of *Mitteleuropa,* Gotha, 1904.

b Kretschmer, Konrad. *Historische Geographie von Mitteleuropa.* München, 1904. [(B170) Below and Meinecke, Handbuch der mittelalterlichen und neueren Geschichte.]

c Hofmann, Albert Von. *Das deutsche Land und die deutsche Geschichte.* Stuttgart, 1921.

a. Thoroughly satisfactory brief outline of the main features of the economic geography of central Europe; includes the Netherlands, Belgium, Switzerland, Serbia, Rumania, and Bulgaria, as well as the central empires; written from the point of view of a geologist; contains sketches, maps, and diagrams. *b.* Most valuable book on German historical geography; covers the physical, political, and cultural geography of Germany from the period of the migrations to the middle of the eighteenth century, with clarity, fulness, and precision. *c.* Detailed study of the influence of geographical factors in the history of central Germany.   SBF

P42a Penck, Albrecht. *Das Deutsche Reich.* Wien, 1887. [V. 1, pt. 1 of Länderkunde des Erdteils Europa, ed. by A. Kirchhoff.]

b Supan, Alexander G. *Oesterreich-Ungarn.* Wien, 1889. [V. 1, pt. 2 of Länderkunde des Erdteils Europa, ed. by A. Kirchhoff.]

c Egli, Johann J., and others. *Die Schweiz.* Wien, 1887. [V. 1, pt. 2 of Länderkunde des Erdteils Europa, ed. by A. Kirchhoff.]

Three excellent selections, relating to German lands, from a standard work on the geography of Europe. For other works on the Austrian lands, cf. § T.
SBF

SOURCE BOOKS, COLLECTIONS OF SOURCES, ARCHIVE PUBLICATIONS

P66 Oechsli, Wilhelm, ed. *Quellenbuch zur schweizer Geschichte.* 2 v. Zurich, 1893–1900. 2nd ed. of v. 1, Zürich, 1901. Small ed., Zürich, 1909.

Compendious and important source book for documents illustrating Swiss political and constitutional history from the origins to recent times.   RCB

P71a *Monumenta Germaniae historica inde ab anno Christi quinquentesimo usque ad annum millesimum et quinqentesimum, auspiciis Societatis Aperiendis Fontibus Rerum Germanicarum Medii Aevi.* Ed by Georg. H. Pertz and others. 120 v. Hannoverae and Berolini, 1826–1925. [Folio series: *Scriptores.* 30 v.; *Leges,* 5 v.; *Diplomata,* 1 v. Quarto series: *Auctores antiquissimi,* 15 v.; *Scriptores rerum Merovingicarum,* 7 v.; *Scriptores rerum Langobardicarum et Italicarum,* 1 v.; *Deutsche Chroniken,* 6 v.; *Libelli de lite imperatorum et pontificum,* 3 v.; *Gesta pontificum Romanorum,* 1 v.; *Leges,* 18 v.; *Diplomata Karolinorum,* 1 v.; *Diplomata regum et imperatorum Germaniae,* 4 v.; *Epistolae,* 7 v.; *Epistolae saec. XIII e regestis pontificum Romanorum selectae,* 3 v.; *Poetae Latini Medii Aevi,* 4 v.; *Necrologia Germaniae,* 6 v.; Indices, 1 v. Octavo series: *Scriptores rerum Germanicarum, nova series,* 4 v.; *Epistolae selectae,* 3 v.]

b *Die Geschichtschreiber der deutschen Vorzeit in deutscher Bearbeitung.* Ed. by Georg H. Pertz, Jakob Grimm, and others. Berlin, 1849 ff. New ed., by W. Wattenbach, O. Holder-Egger, and M. Tangl. Leipzig, 1884 ff.

a. Embodies all the principal sources for the history of medieval Germany from the time of the Germanic invasions until the fourteenth century when the vernacular language began to supplant Latin. In a very essential way the *Monumenta* is an expression of the spirit of that new Germany which was born of the Napoleonic wars, and its conception was coeval with the founding of the University of Berlin. The original projector was Freiherr vom Stein. When peace came in 1815 the idea materialized in the establishment of a commission of the ablest historians of Germany to edit all the known sources and to discover unknown ones. At first a private enterprise, the design was soon subsidized by the German governments. For many years the chief direction of the *Monumenta* was under Georg Heinrich Pertz, who edited the earlier volumes and established the lines of editorial policy. He was succeeded by Georg Waitz, after whose death in 1886 the direction was vested in a commission, which has undertaken a smaller quarto reprint of the original volumes and has re-edited many of the sources in the light of more recent research. Almost every notable medievalist of Germany is represented among the editors of the *Monumenta.* For literature bearing on the origin of the work, cf. (P313a) Seeley, *Life and times of Stein,* pt. 9, ch. 3; (A249a) Gooch, *History and historians in the nineteenth century,* ch. 5, with bibliography there cited; (P313d) Ford, *Stein and the era of reform in Prussia,* 322–326. *b.* Series of over ninety volumes of German translations of the most important medieval chronicles and histories. Begun in 1849, the project languished until Wattenbach undertook the direction of the series in 1873, when German national sentiment was at high pitch owing to the Franco-German War. While a translation is deficient when compared with an original source, nevertheless these volumes are valuable for use by those who have difficulty in reading medieval Latin and convenient for rapid survey. Each volume has been done by an accomplished scholar so that the version may be relied upon.

JWT

P76 *Nuntiaturberichte aus Deutschland nebst ergänzenden Aktenstücken. Abteilung I, 1533–1559, herausgegeben durch das Königliche Preussische Historische Institut im Rom und die Königliche Preussische Archivverwaltung,* Gotha, 1892 ff. *Abteilung 2, 1560–1572, herausgegeben von der Historischen Kommission der Kaiserlichen Akademie der Wissenschaften,* Wien, 1897 ff. *Abteilung 3, 1572–1585, herausgegeben vom Königlichen Preussischen Historischen Institut zu Rom,* Berlin, 1892 ff.; *1558–1590, herausgegeben von der Görres-Gesellschaft,* Paderborn, 1895 ff. [*Quellen und Forschungen aus dem Gebiete der Geschichte, in Verbindung mit ihrem historischen Institut in Rom herausgegeben von der Görres-Gesellschaft.*] *Abteilung 4, 17. Jahrhundert, herausgegeben vom Königlichen Preussischen Historischen Institut zu Rom.* Berlin, 1895 ff.

More than twenty volumes issued. When complete the four series will include the reports of the papal nuncios in Germany during the Reformation and Counter-Reformation, from 1533 to 1648.   SBF

P81 *Publikationen aus den Königlichen Preussischen Staatsarchiven, veranlasst und unterstützt durch die königliche Archivverwaltung.* Leipzig, 1878 ff.

About ninety volumes of valuable archival materials from territories which have come under Prussian rule.   SBF

P91 *Fontes rerum Austriacarum, österreichische Geschichtsquellen, herausgegeben von der Historischen Kommission der Kaiserlichen Akademie der Wissenschaften in Wien.* Wien, 1855 ff. [Abteilung 1, Scriptores; Abteilung 2, Diplomataria et acta.]

Austrian equivalent of (P71*a*), though the materials relate more largely to the modern than to the medieval period. Over seventy volumes have been issued.

SBF

P96a *Quellen zur schweizer Geschichte, herausgegeben von der Allgemeinen Geschichtsforschenden Gesellschaft der Schweiz.* Basel, 1877 ff.

  b Kopp, J. E., and others, ed. *Amtliche Sammlung der älteren eidgenössischen Abschiede.* 32 v. Luzern, Basel, Zürich, Bern, 1839–1905.

a. Extensive collection of sources in about forty volumes. *b.* Official collection of all the recesses of the diet from 1245 to 1848. The successive volumes appeared with various modifications of title, were the work of many different editors, were published at several different places, and have appeared without regard to chronological sequence.

RCB

SHORTER GENERAL HISTORIES

P101 Bryce, James, Viscount. *Holy Roman empire.* 1864. Rev. ed., N. Y., 1904; London, 1919.

History of the imperial idea from the founding to the fall of the Holy Roman Empire and a description of the Empire as an institution, woven into an outline of the political history of Germany; thoughtful, sane, and stimulating. Though written when he was still a very young man, the author never surpassed the art of clear, succinct presentation of political theory and history manifested in this masterpiece. Review, J. W. Thompson, *Historical Outlook,* 13:125, Apr. 1922.

EWD

P102a Henderson, Ernest F. *Short history of Germany.* 1902. Rev. ed. 2 v. in 1, N. Y., 1916. (Bibliographies.)

  b —— *History of Germany in the middle ages.* London and N. Y., 1894. (Bibliography.)

a. Best history of Germany in English; by a capable writer who knows the Germans sympathetically and writes with life and spirit. Deals mostly with events, and only very inadequately with thought and institutions; not based on original investigation, but on the best secondary German works. Review, F. Schevill, *A.H.R.* 8:110, Oct. 1902.   *b.* More detailed political narrative to A. D. 1272.

EWD

P103 Gebhardt, Bruno, ed. *Handbuch der deutschen Geschichte.* 1891–92. 6th rev. ed. by A. Meister, 3 v., Berlin, 1922–23. (Valuable bibliographies.)

This very useful storehouse of systematized information, which goes under the name of Gebhardt, is really the work of a number of capable German scholars. Most compact, accurate, well-balanced, and useful compendium of facts concerning German history.

EWD

P104a Schäfer, Dietrich. *Deutsche Geschichte.* 1910. 9th ed., 2 v., Jena, 1922.

  b Kaemmel, Otto. *Deutsche Geschichte.* 1889. 3rd rev. ed., 2 v., Leipzig, 1911.

    c **Jäger, Oskar.** *Deutsche Geschichte.* 1909. 5th ed., 2 v., München, 1919.

    d **Heyck, Eduard.** *Deutsche Geschichte.* 3 v. Bielefeld, 1905–06.

Semi-popular, but written by scholars of sound ability. *a.* Perhaps the most successful and readable of the group; treats military events but briefly; economic matters are subordinated; 'History is no struggle for a feeding place' said Schäfer. Review, E. F. Henderson, *A.H.R.* 16:594, Apr. 1911. *b.* and *c.* Have many illustrations and are more educational and patriotic in purpose. *d.* Readable; illustrated with more than a thousand pictures well selected to depict the life and culture of the German people in all its aspects.   EWD

LONGER GENERAL HISTORIES

P121a **Lamprecht, Karl G.** *Deutsche Geschichte.* 12 v. in 16 pt. Berlin, 1891–1901. Later ed. of various volumes. (Bibliography.)

    b —— *Deutsche Geschichte zur jüngsten deutschen Vergangenheit.* 1901–04. Later ed., 2 v. in 3, Berlin and Freiburg, 1905–11.

    c —— *Deutsche Geschichte der jüngsten Vergangenheit und Gegenwart.* V. 1–2, Berlin, 1912–13.

    d —— *Deutsches Wirtschaftsleben im Mittelalter: Untersuchungen über die Entwicklung der materiellen Kultur des platten Landes auf Grund der Quellen zunächst des Mosellandes.* 3 v. in 4. Leipzig, 1885–86.

Lamprecht, after cultivating history for some years, developed a conviction that the workers in that field were on the wrong track and ought to be turned from the old way, *alte Richtung,* into a new way, *neue Richtung.* What the new way should be he tried to show chiefly by *a,* and by various articles and pamphlets written in reply to critics, or in explanation or justification of his views. Failing to gain acceptance for his views—indeed finding them, by the end of the century, all but universally rejected—he devoted the remainder of his life mostly to training at Leipzig a body of students for the exemplification and furtherance of the new sort of history. The Lamprecht way involves, among other things, less concern with the individual human, and more emphasis upon humans in the mass; the use of psychology not exactly as a 'helping science,' but for a science of history; and, on this foundation, a search for the typical, for the general, and for law in history. For an estimate of Lamprecht's work at the height of the controversy, cf. E. W. Dow, 'Features of the new history,' *A.H.R.* 3:431–448, Apr. 1898; for a helpful appraisal, written a dozen years later, cf. A. B. Show, *History Teacher's Magazine,* 4:215, Oct. 1913. *b.* and *c.* Continuations of *a.* *d.* Earlier special study.   EWD

P122 **Zwiedineck-Südenhorst, Hans von,** ed. *Bibliothek deutscher Geschichte.* 24 v. Stuttgart and Berlin, 1876–1912. [O. Gutsche and W. Schultze, *Von der Urzeit bis zu den Karolingern,* 2 v., 1894–96; E. Mühlbacher, *Unter den Karolingern,* 1896; M. Manitius, *Unter den sächsischen und salischen Kaisern,* 1889; J. Jastrow and G. Winter, *Im Zeitalter der Hohenstaufen,* 2 v., 1893–1901; T. Lindner, *Unter den Habsburgern und Luxemburgern,* 2 v., 1888–93; V. Kraus and K. Kaser, *Im Ausgange des Mittelalters, 1438–1519,* 2 v., 1888–1912; G. Egelhaaf, *Im 16. Jahrhundert bis zum Augsburger Religionsfrieden,* 2 v., 1887–92; (P271c) M. Ritter, *Im Zeitalter der Gegenreformation und des dreissigjährigen Krieges,* 3 v., 1889–1908; H. von Zwiedineck-Südenhorst, *Im Zeitraum der Gründung des preussischen Königtums,* 2 v., 1890–94; (P304) R. Koser, *König Friedrich der Grosse,* 2 v., 1893–1903; (P311b) K. T. von Heigel, *Vom Tode Fried-*

richs des Grossen bis zur Auflösung des alten Reichs, 2 v., 1899–1911;
(P331h) H. von Zwiedineck-Südenhorst, *Von der Auflösung des alten bis
zur Errichtung des neuen Kaiserreiches,* 3 v., 1897–1905.] Later ed. of some
volumes.

Series of large volumes. Each of the component parts is devoted to a separate period in the history of Germany and written by an acknowledged master
of the field, but addressed to the general reader rather than to the scholar.
Neither sources nor authorities are cited, although it is evident that each author
was conversant with both; consequently the volumes will prove unsatisfactory
to the scholar who wishes to ascertain and to verify sources and authorities.

JWT

GERMANIC ORIGINS

P201a Tacitus, Caius Cornelius. *De Germania, edited with introduction, notes,
and a map,* by H. Furneaux. Oxford, 1894.

   b Church, Alfred J., and **Brodribb, William J.,** tr. *Agricola and Germany
of Tacitus.* 1868. Rev. ed., 1877; reprint, London, 1885.

a. Tacitus was the first historian who attempted to give a large and sustained
account of the institutions of the primitive Germans, as Caesar, a century and
a half earlier, in his (E225a) *Gallic wars,* endeavored briefly to describe them.
Herein lies his great value. But an understanding of Tacitus's account is fraught
with grave difficulties, partly owing to the natural inability of a cultured Roman
wholly to understand the manners and institutions of barbarians who were yet
far from being an object of fear to Rome; partly owing to Tacitus's terse and
sometimes almost cryptic style, and his difficulty in using the Latin tongue to
describe things so totally foreign to Roman experience. A signal example of
this is the chapter which attempts to describe ancient German agriculture and
the primitive German village community. To this day historians do not agree
in their understanding of what Tacitus meant. Besides this commentary of Furneaux, which is the best for English students, there are other excellent commentaries in German by Müllenhoff, Schweizer-Sidler, and Holtzmann. Good
English translations of *a.* may be found in *b.,* and in University of Pennsylvania,
Translations and reprints, v. 6, no. 3.   JWT

P202 Gummere, Francis B. *Germanic origins, a study in primitive culture.*
N. Y., 1892.

Clear and interesting study of the nature of primitive Germanic institutions;
now somewhat out of date, but still valuable for its description of the more
important characteristics of early German life. The author was primarily a
student of English literature and leans much upon Anglo-Saxon literary sources
and the sagas for his exposition. His use of the historical sources is sometimes
deficient.   JWT

MIDDLE AGES TO 1493

For works on the Germanic invasions, Charlemagne, the Crusades, and the
Holy Roman Empire in its wider aspects, cf. §§ F, H. O.

P211a Stubbs, William. *Germany in the early middle ages, 476–1250.* Ed. by
A. Hassall, London and N. Y., 1908.

   b —— *Germany in the later middle ages, 1200–1500.* Ed. by A. Hassall,
London and N. Y., 1908.

These two volumes are a double series of lectures on the history of medieval
Germany by the late William Stubbs, Regius professor of history in Oxford and

bishop of Oxford, published after his death. The lectures were originally delivered at Oxford forty years before the author's death, and long before he had reached the high point of his powers as a scholar. Except in a few paragraphs, as for instance those upon feudalism, the treatment is in narrative form and jejunely factual. Stubbs was not, at this writing, the consummate master of sources that he later became, nor was he yet acquainted with works of German scholarship. He wisely suppressed the publication of these amateurish lectures during his lifetime. Cf. adverse review, O. J. Thatcher, *A.H.R.* 14:167, Oct. 1908; 14:847, July 1909.   JWT

P212a Gerdes, Heinrich. *Geschichte des deutschen Volkes und seiner Kultur im Mittelalter, 919–1250.* 3 v. Leipzig, 1891–1908.

    b Hampe, Karl. *Deutsche Kaisergeschichte in der Zeit der Salier und Staufer.* 1909. 8th ed., Leipzig, 1922. [Bibliothek der Geschichtswissenschaft.]

    a. V. 1. Devoted to the history of Germany under the Saxon dynasty; v. 2, to the Salian epoch; v. 3, to that of the Hohenstaufen. Each volume is divided into two parts: pt. 1, dealing with the political history of the period; pt. 2, with the social, economic, and cultural history. Every chapter is supplemented by full citations from the sources. All in all, probably the best general survey of the history of Germany in the feudal age. *b.* Admirable book, with almost French sense of proportion and clarity of expression; predominantly a political history. The characterization of individuals is noteworthy.   JWT

P213a Raumer, Friedrich von. *Geschichte der Hohenstaufen und ihrer Zeit.* 1823–25. 5th ed., 6 v., Leipzig, 1878.

    b Giesebrecht, Wilhelm von. *Geschichte der deutschen Kaiserzeit.* 5 v. 1855–88. New ed., with continuation by B. von Simson, 6 v., Leipzig, 1877–95.

    a. Product of the romantic school in the early part of the nineteenth century, written with enthusiasm, even passionate admiration, for the epoch; but even after discounting this *leit-motiv* of romanticism, the work remains one of the most valuable surveys of German history in the highest feudal age. *b.* At once a monument of erudition and a work of art. Lord Acton has described it as 'the only critical history of the Middle Ages which is a popular classic.' The author was one of Ranke's first and most brilliant pupils, the second member of that trinity of scholars with Waitz and Sybel. He looked back to the Saxon, Salian, and Hohenstaufen times as Germany's golden age. His prose epic attained enormous popularity among thousands of readers, owing to its exalted tone and glowing style, while its solid scholarship has always commanded respect. Giesebrecht labored for thirty-four years upon this *magnum opus* and left it unfinished. It terminates with the reign of Frederick Barbarossa. Unfortunately Giesebrecht omitted to cite his sources in footnotes, but partial compensation is made for this omission by penetratingly critical appendixes. On the author's personality, cf. (P3*f*) Lord Acton, *German schools of history,* and obituary article, *E.H.R.* 5:306–310, Apr. 1890; (A249*a*) Gooch, *History and historians in the nineteenth century,* 122–127; (A247) Fueter, *Geschichte der Historiographie,* 489–490 (German ed.), 610–612 (French ed.)   JWT

P214 Nitzsch, Karl W. *Geschichte des deutschen Volkes bis zum Augsburger Religionsfrieden.* Ed. by G. Matthäi. 1883–85. 2nd ed. 3 v., Leipzig, 1892.

Nitzsch possessed a gift of interpretation which at times amounted almost to divination. His capacity for making the dry bones of historical institutions live, his insight into the real significance of movements, his analysis of motives and perception of the drift of currents in history is very remarkable. A pioneer work in the economic, social, and even psycho-social interpretation of medieval German history. (P121) Lamprecht owed much to Nitzsch's suggestions, which he did not always acknowledge.

JWT

P215a Ranke, Leopold von, ed. *Jahrbücher des deutschen Reiches unter dem sächsischen Hause.* 6 v. Berlin, 1837–40.

b *Jahrbücher der deutschen Geschichte herausgegeben durch die Historische Kommission bei der Königlichen Akademie der Wissenschaften* [zu München]. 36 v. Berlin, 1862–1909.

These volumes depict the history of medieval Germany by the reigns of the sovereigns. The arrangement of matter is by years. Each volume was intended to be and is a well-nigh exhaustive summary of each and all of the events of importance, critically examined and tersely narrated. The treatment is almost wholly factual. Footnotes abound and there are often valuable appendixes. The volumes are not so much designed to be read as to be studied; they constitute an immense and indispensable repository of information. This great series, whose plan is now being imitated for the kings of medieval France, was originally projected by Ranke and later revised under the patronage of the Bavarian Academy. Waitz's *Jahrbücher des deutschen Reichs unter König Heinrich I.* was the first volume to appear. The series begins with the Carolingian mayors in 687 and extends through the reign of Frederick II in 1250, though there are gaps in the reigns of Frederick Barbarossa and Frederick II. Though the task was begun in Ranke's seminar, the method has been pursued by his pupils in their own seminars, and many a prominent German historical scholar won his spurs by this kind of solid and substantial research.

JWT

P216 Fisher, Herbert A. L. *Medieval empire.* 2 v. London and N. Y., 1898.

Less a study of the empire as a set of ideas and institutions than a series of studies on political development and practice, to 1250, in the regions where the emperors were ascendant. The best portions concern Germany—imperial legislation and finance, partibility of fiefs, expansion eastward, and the church. The rôle ascribed to the empire is principally that of generator of ills, deep and abiding ills. For some corrective of the arraignment, cf. review, G. Blondel, *Rev. hist.*, 86:142, Sept. 1904; and *A.H.R.* 4:704, July 1899. For a valuable study contrasting the feudalism of Germany with that of France, cf. J. W. Thompson, 'German feudalism,' *A.H.R.* 28:440–474, Apr. 1923.

EWD

P217. Thompson, James Westfall. *Feudal Germany.* Chicago, 1928.

Very scholarly but clear and attractively written solid volume comparing the development of feudalism on both sides of the Rhine. Review, E. Emerton, *A.H.R.* 34:104, Oct. 1928.

SBF

P231a Schulze, Eduard Otto. *Die Kolonisierung und Germanisierung der Gebiete zwischen Saale und Elbe.* Leipzig, 1896.

    b Sommerfeld, Wilhelm von. *Geschichte der Germanisierung des Herzogtums Pommern oder Slavien bis zum Ablauf des dreizehnten Jahrhunderts.* Leipzig, 1896.

    c Wendt, Georg. *Die Germanisierung der Länder östlich der Elbe.* Liegnitz, 1884.

    d Thompson, James Westfall. *East German colonization in the middle ages.* Washington, 1917. [American Historical Association, Annual report, 1915, 123–150.]

a., b., and *c.* Regional monographs giving the best account in German of East German colonization—the conquest and settlement of the territory east of the Saale and Elbe rivers, once peopled by Slavonic tribes. They may be supplemented by *d.* and also by the following detailed studies by the same author: 'The German church and the conversion of the Baltic Slavs,' *Amer. Jour. of Theology,* 20:205–230, Apr. 1916; 20:372–389, July 1916; 'The Cistercian order and colonization in mediaeval Germany, *ibid.,* 24:67–93, Jan. 1920; 'Dutch and Flemish colonization in mediaeval Germany,' *Amer. Jour. of Sociology,* 24:159–186, Sept. 1918; 'Early trade relations between the Germans and the Slavs,' *Jour. of Pol. Econ.* 30:543–558, Aug. 1922.   SBF

RENAISSANCE, REFORMATION, AND COUNTER-REFORMATION, 1493–1648

P241 Mentz, Georg. *Deutsche Geschichte im Zeitalter der Reformation, der Gegenreformation, und des Dreissigjährigen Krieges, 1493–1648.* Tübingen, 1913.

Best summary of political events in Germany during the Reformation and Counter-Reformation; fully abreast with the results of the latest research. Review, W. Mechler, *Zeitschrift für Kirchengeschichte,* 35:590, 1914.   PS

P242a Janssen, Johannes. *History of the German people at the close of the middle ages.* 17 v. London, 1896–1925. Tr. by A. M. Christie and M. A. Mitchell from *Geschichte des deutschen Volkes seit dem Ausgang des Mittelalters,* 8 v. 1876–94. Rev. ed. by L. von Pastor, 18th ed., v.1–4; 16th ed., v. 5–6; 14th ed., v. 7–8; Freiburg, 1897–1904. 20th ed., Freiburg, 1913 ff.

    b Pastor, Ludwig von, ed. *Erläuterungen und Ergänzungen zu Janssens Geschichte des deutschen Volkes.* V. 1–10. Freiburg, 1898–1920.

a. The later editions revised by Pastor improve markedly on the older edition from which the English version was made. Janssen combined a wonderful fullness of material and apparent objectivity with a strong Catholic bias. He let the sources speak, but only those sources he had carefully selected. But, withal, the work is an indispensable aid to the student, especially for the sixteenth century and the first half of the seventeenth century. It made a great sensation when first published, and gave Nietzsche the idea, since widely adopted, that the Reformation was a blight on culture and prosperity. Reviews by Protestant critics, M. Lenz, *Hist. Zeit.,* 50:231, 1883; A. Kluckhohn, *ibid.* 63:1, 1889; H. Delbrück, *Preussische Jahrbücher,* 53:529–550, 1884. Also cf. (A247) Fueter, *Historiographie,* 571–575, (German ed.), 715–719 (French ed.). Janssen replied to his earlier critics in two volumes: *An meine Kritiker*, 1882, rev. ed., Freiburg, 1891; and *Ein zweites Wort an meine Kritiker*, Freiburg, 1883. For a friendly estimate of him, cf. Ludwig von Pastor, *Johannes Janssen, 1829–1891, ein Lebensbild*, 1893, 2nd ed., Freiburg, 1894. *b*. Important series of supplementary monographs by Catholic scholars.

PS

P243a Seton-Watson, Robert W. *Maximilian I, Holy Roman emperor.* Westminster, 1902. [Stanhope historical essay.]

 b Ulmann, Heinrich. *Kaiser Maximilian I.* 2 v. Stuttgart, 1884–91.

a. Popular, yet reasonably reliable biography; well illustrated; relies largely on *b.*, but shows knowledge of subsequent research. *b.* Well-written work of great research; marred only by one fault, its excessively romantic idealization of the emperor and of his contemporaries, Sickingen and Hutten. PS

P244a Brant, Sebastian. *Ship of fools.* 1509. Ed. by T. H. Jamieson, 2 v. Edinburgh and N. Y., 1874. Tr. by Alexander Barclay from J. Locher's Latin version (1497) of *Das Narrenschiff*, 1494; ed. by F. Zarncke. Leipzig, 1854 and by K. Goedeke, Leipzig, 1872.

 b Stokes, Francis G., ed. *Epistolae obscurorum virorum: the Latin text with an English rendering, notes, and an historical introduction.* London, 1909.

 c Hutten, Ulrich von. *Opera.* Ed. by E. Böcking. 5 v., Lipsiae, 1859–62.

 d Sastrow, Bartholomew. *Social Germany in Luther's time, being the memoirs of Bartholomew Sastrow.* Westminster, 1902. Abridged tr. by A. D. Vandam of *Bartholomew Sastrow, Herkommen, Geburt, und Lauf seines ganzen Lebens*, ed. by G. C. F. Mohnicke, 3 v., Greifswald, 1823–24.

 e Barack, Karl A., ed. *Zimmerische Chronik.* 1869. 2nd rev. ed., 4 v., Freiburg, 1881–82.

These five sources each give an excellent picture of a different side of German social life at the opening of the sixteenth century. *a.* Written by a native of Strasbourg; one of the most popular satires of the day. *b.* Stokes's edition of the famous *Letters of obscure men* contains an excellent introduction and translation. *c.* Satirical dialogues and other writings which obtained a very wide reading because of their cleverness and because the author wrote in German as well as Latin. Cf. (P4*a*) Wolf, *Quellenkunde*, 376–388, and (P741*a* and *b*) for lives of Hutten. *d.* Reveals the life of a Mecklenburg bourgeois. *e.* The Zimmern chronicle is not merely a family history; it contains a great variety of information about other South German families and events, and many interesting anecdotes and observations; an excellent index facilitates its use. SBF

P251 Lindsay, Thomas M. *History of the reformation.* 2 v. N. Y., 1906–07. [V. 1. *Reformation in Germany.*] [International theological library.] (Bibliographical foot-notes.)

Excellent compendium of the ecclesiastical history of the period; well written, genial, attractive. The author's warmly Protestant sympathies do not make him unfair, and he is particularly notable as giving one of the first generous and trustworthy accounts of the sects, Anabaptists and Unitarians. Save for an excellent introduction on the political and cultural conditions of the time, his interests are closely confined to religion. Though he has read widely, he has not always mastered the whole literature of the subject and he is capable of making mistakes. Review, P. Smith, *Amer. Jour. of Theology*, 13:267, Apr. 1909. For v. 2, cf. (F301). PS

P252 Ranke, Leopold von. *History of the reformation in Germany.* 3 v. London, 1845–47. Later ed. by R. A. Johnson, 1 v., London and N. Y., 1905. (Bibliography.) Tr. by S. Austin from *Deutsche Geschichte im Zeitalter der Reformation*, 1839–47. 4th–6th ed., 6 v., Leipzig, 1867–82.

In some respects the best work of the greatest of historians. The completely objective method, the exhaustive use of sources, the philosophical (Hegelian) treatment of man's past as an intelligible whole, the keen criticism of documents, the fine psychological discrimination, make Ranke's work stand long after all its contemporaries have fallen. Save where he has been corrected by later discoveries and in part superseded by the more social, economic interests of this generation, his work still stands supreme. Review, (P3f) Lord Acton, *German schools of history;* (A247) Fueter, *Geschichte der Historiographie,* 472–485 (German ed.), 589–605 (French ed.) ; Hans F. Helmolt, *Leopold von Rankes Leben und Wirken*, Leipzig, 1921. PS

P253 Bezold, Friedrich von. *Geschichte der deutschen Reformation.* Berlin, 1890. [(B162) Oncken, Allgemeine Geschichte in Einzeldarstellungen.]

Useful, popular treatment, slightly past its prime; distinguished by the author's breadth of interest, fairness of attitude, and good selection of illustrations; lacks references to authorities. Review, G. Egelhaaf, *Hist. Zeit.* 70:125, 1892. SBF

P256a Bax, Ernest Belfort. *German society at the close of the middle ages.* London and N. Y., 1894. [Social side of the reformation in Germany].

b —— *Peasants war in Germany, 1525–1526.* London and N. Y., 1899. [Social side of the reformation in Germany.]

c —— *Rise and fall of the Anabaptists.* London and N. Y., 1903. [Social side of the reformation in Germany.]

d **Kautsky, Karl.** *Communism in central Europe in the time of the reformation.* London, 1897. Tr. by J. L. and E. G. Mulliken from *Der Kommunismus im Mittelalter und im Zeitalter der Reformation,* Stuttgart, 1894.

e **Schapiro, Jacob Salwyn.** *Social reform and the reformation.* N. Y., 1909. [Columbia University, Studies in history, economics, and public law.] (Bibliography.)

f **Klingner, Erich.** *Luther und der deutsche Volksaberglaube.* Berlin, 1912. [Palaestra, v. 56.]

g **Fay, Sidney B.** *Roman law and the German peasant. A.H.R.* 16:234–254, Jan. 1911.

h **Below, Georg A. H. von.** *Die Ursachen der Rezeption des römischen Rechts in Deutschland.* München, 1905. [Historische Bibliothek.]

i —— *Die Ursachen der Reformation, mit einer Beilage: Die Reformation und der Beginn der Neuzeit.* München, 1917. [Historische Bibliothek.] (Bibliographical foot-notes.)

a., b., c., and *d.* Bax and Kautsky write from the socialist standpoint; the works of both are popular, warped by bias, and lacking in scholarship; Kautsky is more reliable but less readable than Bax. *e.* Discusses the causes of the Peasants' Revolt and gives in translation the Utopian programs current in Luther's day. Review, S. B. Fay, *A.H.R.* 15:127, Oct. 1909. *f.* Excellent presentation of the superstitions so characteristic of the sixteenth century. Review, W. Köhler, *Zeitschrift für Kirchengeschichte,* 33:39, 1917. *g.* Corrects exaggerated notion of the evil effects of the Roman law on the German peasant. *h.* and *i.* Penetrating studies by one of Germany's most distinguished economic historians.

For the extensive literature in German on the Peasants' War of 1525 and its causes, cf. (PI*a*) Dahlmann-Waitz, *Quellenkunde,* 8th ed., no. 2173 ff., 6776 ff., 7704 ff., 7877 ff.; and Wilhelm Stolze, 'Neuere Literatur zum Bauernkriege,' *Hist. Zeit.* 105:296–315, 1910.

SBF

P261a McGiffert, Arthur C. *Martin Luther, the man and his work.* N. Y., 1911.

b Köstlin, Julius. *Martin Luther, sein Leben und seine Schriften.* 1875. 5th rev. ed. by G. Kawerau, 2 v., Berlin, 1903.

c —— *Life of Luther.* 1883. Reprint, N. Y., 1913. Tr. of *Luthers Leben,* 1882, 10th ed., Leipzig, 1892.

d Smith, Preserved. *Life and letters of Martin Luther.* 1911. 2nd ed., Boston, 1914. (Bibliography.)

e Hausrath, Adolf. *Luthers Leben.* 1903–04. New ed. by H. von Schubert, 2 v., Berlin, 1924.

f Grisar, Hartmann. *Luther.* 6 v. London, 1913–17. (Bibliography.) Tr. by E. M. Lamond from *Luther,* 3 v., Freiburg, 1911–12; 3rd rev. ed., 3 v., Freiburg, 1924–26.

g Schreckenbach, Paul, and **Neubert, Franz.** *Martin Luther, ein Bild seines Lebens und Wirkens.* 1917. 2nd rev. ed., Leipzig, 1918.

a. Popular, charmingly written biography, based on the more obvious sources, particularly *e.,* from which several errors are copied. Many inaccuracies in the work as it appeared in the *Century Magazine* were corrected in the book, and some rash judgments have been rectified by the author himself in later writings. Review, P. van Dyke, *A.H.R.* 17:598, Apr. 1912. *b.* Standard work in point of research and minute detail. It owes its excellence in part to numerous revisions, for it was harshly criticised at first by Knaake and Seidemann. *c.* Translated from earlier edition of the German original and in no wise represents the scholarship of Köstlin's later work. *d.* Reviewed by A. C. McGiffert, *A.H.R.* 17:396, Jan. 1912, as 'an admirable biography to be commended for both its fairness and its accuracy.' *e.* Most beautiful of all the lives of Luther, and, except that it is marred by too much love for him to be fair to his enemies and by some inaccuracies (mostly corrected by Schubert), the best. Review, W. Köhler, *Hist. Zeit.* 96:469, 1906. *f.* Gives a Catholic view of Luther; moderate and scholarly. *g.* Notable chiefly for the wealth of illustrations; 384 pictures, all authentic and many rare. Review, *Archiv für Reformationsgeschichte,* 14:16, 1917.

PS

P262a Luther, Martin. *Werke: kritische Gesammtausgabe.* Ed. by J. K. F. Knaake, G. Kawerau, and others. V. 1–71, Weimar, 1883–1927.

b Denifle, Heinrich S. *Luther and Lutherdom, from original sources.* Somerset, Ohio, 1917. Tr. by R. Volz from 2nd rev. ed. of *Luther und Luthertum in der ersten Entwickelung, quellenmässig dargestellt,* 2 v. and 2 supplementary v. Mainz, 1904–09.

c *Lutherstudien zur vierten Jahrhundertfeier der Reformation; veröffentlicht von den Mitarbeitern der Weimarer Lutherausgabe.* Weimar, 1917.

d Luther, Martin. *Luther's primary works.* Tr. by H. Wace and C. A. Buchheim. London, 1896.

e —— *Luther's correspondence and other contemporary letters.* Tr. and ed. by Preserved Smith and C. M. Jacobs. v. 1–2, Philadelphia, 1913–18.

a. Standard edition; not all the volumes numbered 1 to 53 have appeared, while some numbers represent more than one volume. Review, P. Smith, *Amer. Jour. of Theology,* 13:259, Apr. 1909. *b.* Severe criticism of *a.* by a Catholic. *c.* Contains valuable information regarding *a.* *d.* Excellent version of a few of Luther's more important treatises. *e.* Translation, with valuable notes, of Luther's more important letters. V. 2. Covers the years 1521 to 1530. Review, W. W. Rockwell, *A.H.R.* 19:680, Apr. 1914; M. Reu, *ibid.* 25:90, Oct. 1919. PS

P263 Berger, Arnold E. *Martin Luther in kulturgeschichtlicher Darstellung.* 3 v. in 4. Berlin, 1895–1921. [Geisteshelden, ed. by A. Bettelheim.]

This biography is, in some respects, the most philosophic of all works on Luther. It essays to put him into the frame of the civilization of his time and to trace his influence on the subsequent history of thought. Review, F. Gess, *Hist. Zeit.* 80:306, 1898; G. von Below, *ibid.* 126:483, 1922. PS

P271a Gardiner, Samuel R. *Thirty years' war, 1618–1648.* 1874. Reprint, London and N. Y., 1903. [Epochs of modern history.]

b Gindely, Anton. *History of the thirty years' war.* 2 v. N. Y., 1884. Tr. by A. Ten Brook from *Geschichte des dreissigjährigen Krieges,* 4 v., Prag, 1869–80.

c Ritter, Moritz. *Deutsche Geschichte im Zeitalter der Gegenreformation und des dreissigjährigen Krieges.* 3 v. Stuttgart, 1889–1908. [(P122) Zwiedineck-Südenhorst, Bibliothek deutscher Geschichte.]

a. Good, brief sketch by a great English historian, based on a knowledge of English as well as German sources. *b.* Somewhat antiquated; best on the earlier, Bohemian, period of the war; the English translation is unsatisfactory. *c.* Scholarly and fair-minded work; based on an enormous collection of sources made by the author and only partly accessible to Gindely; the standard history of Germany from 1555 to 1648; supersedes the more popular illustrated volume by G. Winter in (B162) Oncken series. Review, F. Rachfahl, *Hist. Zeit.* 103:349, 1909. For the Thirty Years' War, also cf. §§ I, M, Q, R. SBF

PRUSSIA AND AUSTRIA, 1648–1815

For Germany's part in the general European wars and international relations of this period, cf. § I.

P281 Atkinson, Christopher T. *History of Germany, 1715–1815.* London, 1908. (Brief bibliography.)

Clear and accurate outline of the political and military history of Germany from the Peace of Utrecht to the fall of Napoleon, by a military historian; makes some use of English sources, but does not pretend to be a work of original research nor to give any account of institutional and social development. Review, A. W. Ward, *E.H.R.* 24:809, Oct. 1909. SBF

P282 Erdmannsdörffer, Bernhard. *Deutsche Geschichte vom Westphälischen Frieden bis zum Regierungsantritt Friedrichs des Grossen, 1648–1740.* 2 v. Berlin, 1892–93. [(B162) Oncken, Allgemeine Geschichte in Einzeldarstellungen.]

V. 1. By far the best general history of Germany in the second half of the seventeenth century, a field which the author mastered by his publication of documents on the Great Elector. V. 2. The period from 1688 to 1740 is sketched more rapidly and less satisfactorily. Erdmannsdörffer gives an excellent, clear, impartial account not only of the Holy Roman Empire as a whole, but of the principal states within it. In the chapters on Prussia, which hold a prominent place, he corrects the excessively patriotic tendency of his teacher Droysen. He refrains from trying to make past history serve a present political purpose as Droysen, Sybel, and Treitschke had done. Review, A. Pribram, *Hist. Zeit.* 73:329, 1894; and valuable obituary notice, *ibid.* 87:56, 1901.

SBF

P286a Marriott, Sir John A. R., and Robertson, Charles Grant. *Evolution of Prussia, the making of an empire.* Oxford, 1915. (Bibliography.)
b Tuttle, Herbert. *History of Prussia.* 4 v. Boston, 1884–96.

a. Best book in English covering the whole period of the rise and development of Brandenburg-Prussia and the Prussianization of Germany under the Hohenzollern dynasty; objective, but slight in the treatment of institutions. Review, M. Smith, *A.H.R.* 24:677, July 1919. *b.* V. 1, which is the best, although somewhat out of date, gives much attention to the development of Prussian institutions. In the later volumes the author expanded so fully the diplomatic history that he had only reached the second year of the Seven Years' War at the time of his death. Two supplementary chapters on the Prussian campaign of 1758 were published posthumously in *A.H.R.* 3:1, Oct. 1897; 3:230, Jan. 1898. As a newspaper correspondent in Berlin, Tuttle had excellent opportunities for collecting material for his history and for observing Prussian politics and institutions at close range. He draws some comparisons between English and Prussian development, and shows a healthy reaction against the excessively patriotic propagandist work of Droysen, which covers precisely the same period, but with much more detail and with far greater research. V. 4. Contains a biographical sketch and appreciation of Tuttle by Herbert B. Adams. Review, U. G. Weatherly, *A.H.R.* 2:145, Oct. 1896.

SBF

P287a Ranke, Leopold von. *Memoirs of the house of Brandenburg and history of Prussia during the seventeenth and eighteenth centuries.* 3 v. London, 1849. Tr. by Sir A. and Lady Duff-Gordon from *Neun Bücher preussischer Geschichte,* 3 v., Berlin, 1847–48.
b —— *Genesis des preussischen Staates.* Berlin, 1874.
c —— *Zwölf Bücher preussischer Geschichte.* 5 v. Berlin, 1874.

a. Written in masterly fashion. Ranke's attitude is that of a conservative, divine-right monarchist, with a just admiration for the work of the Hohenzollern rulers. *b.* Ranke, much later in life, after the establishment of the German Empire, expanded the first book of *a.* into four books dealing with the earlier history of Brandenburg-Prussia. *c.* Consists of *b.* together with the other eight books of the original Prussian history, i.e., *a.*

SBF

P288 Droysen, Johann G. *Geschichte der preussischen Politik.* 5 pt. in 14 v. Leipzig, 1855–86; 2nd ed. of v. 1–7, Leipzig, 1868–72.

Both a *magnum opus* of prodigious research and a propagandist pamphlet of gigantic dimensions. In the course of his political life and as a result of his historical studies Droysen had become convinced that the German people could only achieve liberty and unity through accepting Prussian leadership. 'Prussia's mission' was to replace Austria as the controlling state in Germany; 'Hohenzollern or Hapsburg' is the significant title of the last chapter of his first volume. Throughout the work, especially in the earlier volumes, he contrasts Prussia, working for reforms, progress, interior efficiency, and patriotism, on the one hand, with Austria on the other, unprogressive, empty, and impotent. Convinced of Prussia's mission to regenerate and unite Germany, he wished by his history to convince his countrymen likewise. He therefore imputes patriotic national German motives to Hohenzollern rulers who in reality were actuated only by narrow Prussian self-interest. Even admitting the bias of his subjective and idealized conception of Prussia's conscious effort to accomplish her 'manifest destiny,' it nevertheless remains true that Droysen was the first, on the basis of solid historical documents, clearly and sharply to show the fundamental facts of Prussia's growth and greatness. At the author's death in 1884, his history was broken off with the year 1757. For estimates of Droysen and his work, cf. (A247) Fueter, *Geschichte der neueren Historiographie,* 492–496 (German ed.), 615–619•(French ed.); (A249a) Gooch, *History and historians in the nineteenth century,* 134–140.   SBF

P289 Prutz, Hans. *Preussische Geschichte.* 4 v. Stuttgart, 1900–02.

Prutz shows a healthy reaction against the Droysen method and school of history. His opening pages are devoted to a severely critical and illuminating criticism of his predecessors and to an annihilation of current patriotic legends. He gives relatively more attention to the East Prussian lands and less than the other historians to the central and western Hohenzollern territories. His history, which extends from the origin of Brandenburg-Prussia to the death of William I in 1888, is the best general account. Well-balanced, scholarly, readable, stimulating, scientifically impartial, and severely critical.   SBF

P290a Koser, Reinhold. *Geschichte der brandenburgischen Politik bis zum Westphälischen Frieden von 1648.* Stuttgart, 1913.

    b Hintze, Otto. *Die Hohenzollerns und ihr Werk: fünfhundert Jahre vaterländischer Geschichte.* Berlin, 1915.

a. Koser, like Prutz, corrects Droysen's tendency. His outline of Prussian policy moves clearly and rapidly forward and embodies brilliantly the results of the latest scholarship. Unfortunately it was cut short by the author's death in 1914 and reaches only to 1648. *b.* This centenary volume is no mere panegyric. Emphasizes the monarchy and the military system as the bases on which the Hohenzollern power has rested. Compact with reliable information, especially in regard to the economic and institutional development of Prussia. Review, J. Ziekursch, *Hist Zeit.* 116:288, 1916.   SBF

P296a Waddington, Albert. *Histoire de Prusse.* 2 v.   Paris, 1911–22.

b —— *Le Grand Électeur, Frédéric Guillaume de Brandenbourg, 1640–88.*
2 v.   Paris, 1905–08.

a. Admirable example of the best French historical scholarship.   V. 1. Deals
with the development of Brandenburg-Prussia to 1688; based partly on the
author's own researches in the archives of France and Prussia, and partly on the
best recent German scholarship.   V. 2. Covers from 1688 to 1740.   Judicious
and sympathetic attempt to explain to French readers the reasons for Prussia's
growth and the remarkable character of her rulers.   Review of v. 1, A. W. Ward,
E.H.R. 27 :558, July 1912; of v. 2, R. Lodge, *ibid.* 37 :590, Oct. 1922.   *b.* Both
a biography of the man and a history of the measures by which he contributed
so much to the formation of an organic Brandenburg-Prussian state.   Distinguished by the same thorough scholarship, judicious impartiality. and charm of
style as *a.,* for which it formed the preliminary study.   SBF

P297a Philippson, Martin. *Der Grosse Kurfürst Friedrich Wilhelm von
Brandenburg.* 3 v.   Berlin, 1897–1903.

b Erdmannsdörffer, Bernhard, and others, ed.   *Urkunden und Aktenstücke
zur Geschichte des Kurfürsten Friedrich Wilhelm von Brandenburg.*
Berlin, 1864 ff.

c Meinardus, Otto, ed.   *Protokolle und Relationen des brandenburgischen
Geheimen Rates aus der Zeit des Kurfürsten Friedrich Wilhelm.*   Leipzig,
1889 ff.   [Publikationen aus den königlichen preussischen Staatsarchiven.]

a. Though the best biography in German of the Great Elector, it does not make
the real man stand forth; pedestrian and uncritical; but gives a good account of
the Great Elector's remarkable administration and the measures by which he
built up the army, the finances, the prosperity, and the administrative machinery
which raised his country from weakness to strength.   *b.* Contains, in more than
twenty volumes, the text of the Great Elector's diplomatic negotiations with
foreign powers and also the documents for the history of the struggle with the
estates through the defeat of which absolutism was established in Prussia;
provided with admirable introductions and indexes by the editors.   *c.* Contains
an abstract of the privy council records; the seven volumes already published
cover the years 1640 to 1665.   They deal with all possible questions of foreign
and domestic policy, are provided with excellent introductions and indexes, and
form an exceedingly interesting and valuable source for the study of the period.
                                                                              SBF

P301a Lavisse, Ernest. *Études sur l'histoire de Prusse.* 1879.   7th ed., Paris,
1916.

b —— *Youth of Frederick the Great.*   London, 1891; tr. by S. L. Simeon;
Chicago, 1892; tr. by M. B. Coleman from *La jeunesse du grand Frédéric,*
1891, 3rd ed., Paris, 1899.

c —— *Le grand Frédéric avant l'avènement.*   Paris, 1893.   (Bibliography.)

Lavisse was one of the first French historians to deal in a scientific, scholarly
fashion with Prussian history; he presents his results with characteristic charm
of style.   *a.* Deals with the early history of Brandenburg, but may be regarded
as superseded by the more recent work of (P296a) Waddington.   *b.* and *c.*
Analyze with skill and sympathy the Crown Prince's psychological development
at the harsh court of his father.   SBF

P302a Reddaway, William F. *Frederick the Great and the rise of Prussia.* N. Y. and London, 1904. [Heroes of the nations.]

    b Young, Norwood. *Life of Frederick the Great.* London and N. Y., 1919.

a. Good, sympathetic, traditional view of Frederick, with the merit of using and quoting the recently published volumes of Frederick's correspondence. Review, E. F. Henderson, *A.H.R.* 10:652, Apr. 1905. *b.* Written during the World War when the fruits of Prussianism appeared all too patent; portrays Frederick as a physical coward, an incompetent commander, an inveterate hypocrite, a treacherous friend, and an oppressive despot. In spite of the belittling spirit ·in which Frederick is treated, the work rests on a careful reading of the sources; and in spite of minor inaccuracies and many exaggerations, has a certain historical value in correcting the hero worship of Carlyle and Prussian hagiographers.   SBF

P303 Carlyle, Thomas. *History of Friedrich II of Prussia, called Frederick the Great.* 6 v. London, 1858–65. Many later ed. including centenary ed. of *Works* (v. 12–19) by H. D. Traill. N. Y., 1900.

Carlyle's biography, written in his characteristic jerky style, will always stand as an interesting monument of English literature and a fascinating example of the author's theory of heroes in history. Since Carlyle worked in Chelsea with such books as he could collect in his own study, and made no effort to examine any archives, his account of diplomatic negotiations is well-nigh worthless. Since, on the other hand, he had tramped over many of Frederick's battlefields and made a careful analysis of the military narratives left by Frederick himself and by other military leaders, his accounts of the battles are still valuable and show satisfactorily the elements of Frederick's genius in war. V. 1. Contains a sketch of Frederick's ancestors who helped to build up the Prussian state of 1740.   SBF

P304 Koser, Reinhold. *König Friedrich der Grosse.* 2 v. 1893–1903. [(P122) Zwiedineck-Südenhorst, Bibliothek deutscher Geschichte.] 4th and 5th ed., including *Friedrich der Grosse als Kronprinz,* 1886, 4 v., Stuttgart, 1912.

Koser, for many years director of the Prussian archives, combined an aptitude for detailed scholarly research and interesting popular presentation. Of his numerous contributions to Prussian history from the eleventh to the nineteenth century, most notable is this work, which is both a biography of the king and a history of his times. Warmly sympathetic with the subject, yet not unduly inclined to magnify Frederick at the expense of the others; corrects Droysen; embodies the best scholarship. Likely long to stand as the definitive biography of Prussia's most remarkable ruler.   SBF

P305a Preuss, Johann D. E., ed. *Oeuvres de Frédéric le Grand.* 31 v. in 33 and atlas. Berlin, 1846–57. There are earlier collections by other editors.

    b Droysen, Johann G.; Volz, G. B.; and others, ed. *Politische Korrespondenz Friedrichs des Grossen.* Berlin, 1879 ff.

    c Schmoller, Gustav F. von and others, ed. *Acta borussica: Denkmäler der Preussischen Staatsverwaltung im 18. Jahrhundert, herausgegeben von der Königlichen Akademie der Wissenschaften.* Berlin, 1892 ff.

The three most important collections of sources for Prussian history in the eighteenth century. *a.* Written wholly in French; contains chiefly Frederick's literary correspondence with Voltaire, d'Argens, and others, as well as with his own relatives; his poetic and philosophic works; his essay on the art of war illustrated by his own drawings; and his history of Brandenburg and of his own times.   *b.* Written partly in French and partly in German; valuable for diplomatic and military history as well as for the king's own personality. About forty volumes have appeared, covering the years 1740–1777.   *c.* Consists of about twenty-five volumes.   Owes its inspiration to the well known German economic historian, Gustav Schmoller, and consists of a series of monographs each in several volumes, by different authors.   Each series contains a selection of the more important documents, accompanied by invaluable introductions.   The more important series so far published deal with the organization of Prussia's administrative boards, now complete to 1758, by Schmoller and Hintze; grain trade, by Naudé; trade, tariff, and excise policy, by Rachel; the silk industry,. by Schmoller and Hintze; and coinage, by Schrötter.   SBF

P306a Arneth, Alfred, Ritter von. *Geschichte Maria Theresia's.* 10 v. Wien, 1863–79.

   b Bright, James Franck. *Maria Theresa.* London and N. Y., 1897. [Foreign statesmen.]

   c ——— *Joseph II.* London and N. Y., 1897. [Foreign statesmen.]

   d Guglia, Eugen. *Maria Theresia, ihr Leben und ihre Regierung.* 2 v. München, 1917.

   e Mitrofanov, Paul von. *Joseph II, seine politische und kulturelle Tätigkeit.* 2 v. Wien, 1910. Tr. from the Russian by V. von Demelič.

   a. Formless collection of original material for the history of Austria, very valuable for the student; not a biography, strictly speaking, of the Empress.   *b.* and *c.* Based mainly on *a.;* taken together, give a thoroughly readable and satisfactory brief account of Austria from 1740 to the French Revolution.   *d.* Recent and successful attempt to picture, for the two-hundredth anniversary of Maria Theresa's birth, her personality and place in history, and the social and intellectual conditions of her time; scholarly but popular.   *e.* Good portrayal of the personality and complex problems of Joseph II.   Review, H. von Voltelini, *Hist. Zeit.* 106:375, 1911.   SBF

P307a Temperley, Harold W. V. *Frederic the Great and Kaiser Joseph: an episode of war and diplomacy in the eighteenth century.* London, 1915. (Bibliography.)

   b Ranke, Leopold von. *Die deutschen Mächte und der Fürstenbund.* Leipzig, 1875.

   a. Excellent sketch of the diplomatic rivalry between Prussia and Austria, from 1763 to 1779.   *b.* One of Ranke's most masterly studies in diplomatic history; covers the second half of the eighteenth century.   Contrary to the Prussian school of historians who regard Frederick the Great's league of princes, Fürstenbund, as a patriotic national German effort to unite Germany, Ranke shows it was merely a narrowly selfish Prussian effort on Frederick's part to strengthen his own kingdom.   SBF

P311a Häusser, Ludwig. *Deutsche Geschichte vom Tode Friedrichs des Grossen bis zur Gründung des deutschen Bundes.* 1854–57. 4th ed., 4 v., Berlin, 1869.

b Heigel, Karl T. von. *Deutsche Geschichte vom Tode Friedrichs des Grossen bis zur Auflösung des alten Reichs.* 2 v. Stuttgart, 1899–1911. [(P122) Zwiedineck-Südenhorst, Bibliothek deutscher Geschichte.]

c Meinecke, Friedrich. *Das Zeitalter der deutschen Erhebung, 1795–1815.* 1906. 2nd ed., Bielefeld, 1913. [Monographien zur Weltgeschichte.]

d Ford, Guy S. *Hanover and Prussia, 1795–1803: a study in neutrality.* N. Y., 1903. [Columbia University, Studies in history, economics, and public law.]

a. By a German liberal of 1848; well written and, though not up to the demands of modern scholarship, still valuable. *b.* Cool, dispassionate, and fully abreast of modern scholarship. *c.* Brief sketch; brilliant and suggestive. *d.* Detailed study of the years when Prussia was under weak leaders and drifting toward the maelstrom of 1805–1806.   GSF

P312a Gooch, George P. *Germany and the French revolution.* London and N. Y., 1920.

b Fisher, Herbert A. L. *Studies in Napoleonic statesmanship: Germany.* Oxford, 1903. (Bibliographies.)

a. Study of the impact of the French Revolution on the German thinkers and writers, great and small, revealing much that is valuable and suggestive to those who have not the author's wide range of reading. *b.* Series of excellent essays on the political effects of the revolutionary and Napoleonic period on Germany, and of the rise and fall of the states created in Germany by Napoleon. Review, J. H. Coney, *A.H.R.* 9:582, Apr. 1904.   GSF

P313a Seeley, Sir John R. *Life and times of Stein,* or *Germany and Prussia in the Napoleonic age.* 2 v. London and Boston, 1879.

b Pertz, Georg H. *Das Leben des Ministers Freiherrn vom Stein.* 6 v. Berlin, 1849–55.

c Lehmann, Max. *Freiherr vom Stein.* 3 v. 1902–05. New ed., 1 v., Leipzig, 1921.

d Ford, Guy S. *Stein and the era of reform in Prussia, 1807–1815.* Princeton, 1922.

a. Clear, judicious, readable synthesis of the best German works then available. The biographic element and final results are somewhat lost when the narrative expands into a history of the times. *b.* More a documentary compilation than a biography; still valuable for source material. *c.* A great biography. The controversy it has aroused by its criticism of the military nobles and by its emphasis on French influence on Stein's reforms prevent its being called definitive. Scholars can form a judgment by weighting the criticisms of Ernst von Meier, which are discussed by Hintze, *Forschungen zur brandenburgischen Geschichte,* 21:313–326, 1908. *d.* Brief, popular treatment in English; utilizes the latest scholarship on the man and his period. Review, S. B. Fay, *A.H.R.* 27:794, July 1922.   GSF

P314a **Cavaignac, Jacques M. E. Godefroy.** *La formation de la Prusse contemporaine.* 2 v. Paris, 1891–98. [1, *Les origines, le ministère de Stein, 1806–1808; 2, Le ministère de Hardenberg, le soulèvement, 1808–1813.*]

  b **Hardenberg, Karl August, Fürst von.** *Denkwürdigkeiten.* Ed. by Leopold von Ranke. 5 v. Leipzig, 1877.

  c **Ranke, Leopold von.** *Hardenberg und die Geschichte des preussischen Staates,* 1793–1813. 3 v. Leipzig, 1879–81.

a. Digests a great mass of literature; trustworthy and informing but strongly French in its interpretation of the period. Stein makes no appeal to the author because he did not have a logical program, but Hardenberg is much more sympathetically treated. Review, v. 2, U. G. Weatherly, *A.H.R.* 4:149, Oct. 1898.   *b.* Of Hardenberg there is unfortunately no adequate biography. Ranke's volumes remain a great source, and in the biographical comment are distinguished by Ranke's grasp of international politics and his preëminent ability in illuminating them.   *c.* Second edition of the biographical and political history included in *b.*

GSF

P315a **Henderson, Ernest F.** *Blücher and the uprising of Prussia against Napoleon, 1806–1815.* N. Y. and London, 1911. [Heroes of the nations.]

  b **Lehmann, Max.** *Scharnhorst.* 2 v. Leipzig, 1886–87.

  c **Meinecke, Friedrich.** *Das Leben des Generalfeldmarschalls Hermann von Boyen.* 2 v. Stuttgart, 1895–99.

  d **Delbrück, Hans.** *Das Leben des Feldmarschalls Grafen Neidhardt von Gneisenau.* 1882. 3rd ed., 2 v., Berlin, 1908.

  e **Ulmann, Heinrich.** *Geschichte der Befreiungskriege, 1813 und 1814.* 2 v. München, 1914–15.

a. Popular account; useful because it is available in English; does not rise to any high standard as a military or historical study.   *b.* Model biography; will stand as the definitive life of the greatest Prussian military thinker.   *c.* Outstanding for its keen analysis of character and fine synthesis of contemporary thought. Boyen's name is attached to the decree of September 3, 1814, instituting universal military service, for an account of which cf. G. S. Ford, 'Boyen's military law,' *A.H.R.* 20:528–538, Apr. 1915.   *d.* Gneisenau was Blücher's brains. Delbrück's biography is good, but is touched with the author's tendency to over-refined argumentation and his attempts to force and justify brilliant generalizations. Both Delbrück and Lehmann are especially competent in presenting military problems.   *e.* Centennial publication, strongly nationalistic, and though an outstanding work, supplements the older work of Wilhelm Oncken, *Das Zeitalter der Revolution, des Kaiserreiches, und der Befreiungskriege,* 2 v., 1884–86, in (B162) Oncken, *Allgemeine Geschichte in Einzeldarstellungen.*   GSF

BISMARCK AND GERMAN UNITY, 1815–1890

P321a **Priest, George M.** *Germany since 1740.* Boston, 1915. (Brief bibliography.)

  b **Ward, Sir Adolphus W.,** and for v. 2, **Wilkinson, Spenser.** *Germany 1815–1890.* 3 v. Cambridge, Eng., 1916–18. [Cambridge historical series.] (Bibliography.)

  c **Meinecke, Friedrich.** *Weltbürgertum und Nationalstaat, Studien zur Genesis des deutschen Nationalstaates.* 1907. 7th ed., München, 1928.

a. Clear and readable brief sketch of German national development. *b.* Much longer and very useful narrative; crammed with facts and information; impartial and serene in its scholarly detachment; lacks distinctness and vividness in narration. In the fullness of his own knowledge of German affairs, Ward has too often forgotten the need of emphasizing the significant facts in the mass of detail. V. 3. Contains a convenient chapter on intellectual and social life. Review, v. 1, G. S. Ford, *A.H.R.* 22:706, Apr. 1917; v. 3, G. M. Dutcher, *Historical Outlook,* 11:155, Apr. 1920. *c.* Profound and brilliant study of the development of the German national idea. The last edition contains studies of German problems resulting from the World War. SBF

P322 Treitschke, Heinrich von. *History of Germany in the nineteenth century.* V. 1–7, London and N. Y., 1915–19. Tr. by E. and C. Paul from *Deutsche Geschichte im neunzehnten Jahrhundert.* 1879–94. Later ed., 5 v., Leipzig, 1919–23.

By common consent Treitschke's work is still the best general acoount of Germany from 1815 to 1848 and one of the most brilliant pieces of historical writing in the German language. Its intense Prussian nationaiistic tone and the author's scholarship and eloquence gave the work wide reading and great influence. Cultural factors are given due weight, and such an organization as the Zollverein is nowhere better treated. The reader must keep a critical attitude, but may lay aside prejudices aroused by the association of Treitschke's name with Bernhardi during the World War. It was in his treatises on politics and his dithyrambic lectures at Berlin that Treitschke played the rôle of high priest of Prussian militarism. The chapter on Treitschke in (P3*b*) Guilland, *Modern Germany and her historians* tempers any enthusiasm aroused by his historical writing. Review, M. Smith, *A.H.R.* 29:127, Oct. 1923. GSF

P331a Sybel, Heinrich von. *Founding of the German empire by William I, based chiefly upon Prussian state documents.* 7 v. N. Y., 1890–98. Tr. by M. L. Perrin, G. Bradford, and H. S. White from *Die Begründung des deutschen Reiches durch Wilhelm I,* 1889–94, 6th rev. ed., 7 v., München, 1904.

b Lorenz, Ottokar. *Kaiser Wilhelm und die Begründung des Reiches, 1866–1871.* Jena, 1902.

c Maurenbrecher, Wilhelm. *Gründung des deutschen Reiches, 1859–1871.* 1892. 4th rev. ed., Leipzig, 1910.

d Stolze, Wilhelm. *Die Gründung· des deutschen Reiches im Jahre 1870.* München, 1912.

e Brandenburg, Erich. *Die Reichsgründung.* 2 v. Leipzig, 1916. (Critical bibliography.)

f Friedjung, Heinrich. *Der Kampf um die Vorherrschaft in Deutschland, 1859 bis 1866.* 1897. 10th ed., 2 v., Stuttgart, 1916–17.

g Oncken, Wilhelm. *Das Zeitalter des Kaisers Wilhelm.* 2 v. Berlin, 1890–92. [(B162) Oncken, Allgemeine Geschichte.]

h Zwiedineck-Südenhorst, Hans von. *Deutsche Geschichte von der Auflösung des alten bis zur Errichtung des neuen Kaiserreiches, 1806–1871.* 3 v. Stuttgart, 1897–1905. [(P122) Bibliothek deutscher Geschichte.]

i Denis, Ernest. *La fondation de l'empire allemand, 1852–1871.* Paris, 1906.

j Ziekursch, Johannes. *Politische Geschichte des neuen deutschen Kaiserreiches.* 3 v. Frankfurt a. M., 1925–30.

a. Quasi-official Prussian account; covers from 1848 to July 1870. Sybel used archival material not available to others but by no means everything, for Bismarck made reservations and nothing in the archives between 1868 and 1870 was open to Sybel. Still fundamental, but no longer the last word in content and interpretation. Certain limitations are revealed by such parallel works as *b., c., d.,* and *e.,* and above all by the brilliant work of an Austrian in *f.* Popular accounts of the same period are given by a North German in *g.* and from the Austrian point of view in *h.*   *i.* Brief, clear account by a French scholar. For estimates of Sybel's work, cf. (P3*b*) Guilland, *Modern Germany and her historians,* ch. 3; (A247) Fueter, *Historiographie,* 535 (German ed.), 668 (French ed.); F. Meinecke, *Hist. Zeit.* 75:390, 1895.   GSF

j. To be in three volumes; first volume covers the founding of the German empire, 1859 to 1870; the second, the Bismarck period to 1890; and the third, the age of William II, 1890 to 1918; one of the best recent histories of the period.

SBF

P336a Goyau, Georges. *Bismarck et l'Église, le Culturkampf, 1870–1887.* 4 v. Paris, 1911–13.

b Friedrich, J. *Ignaz von Döllinger.* 3 v. München, 1899–1901.

a. Most thorough and complete study of the highly controversial subject of Bismarck's struggle with the Catholic church.   *b.* Exhaustive biography of the leader of the old Catholic movement in Germany; valuable for the attitude of the German Catholics during the *Kulturkampf.*   GMD

P341a Bismarck, Otto, Fürst von. *Bismarck the man and the statesman, being the reflections and reminiscences of Otto, Prince von Bismarck written and dictated by himself after his retirement from office.* 2 v. N. Y. and London, 1899. Tr. by A. J. Butler from *Gedanken und Erinnerungen,* ed. by Horst Kohl, 2 v., Stuttgart, 1898.

b —— *Anhang zu Gedanken und Erinnerungen.* 2 v. Stuttgart, 1901.

c —— *The Kaiser vs. Bismarck: suppressed letters by the Kaiser and new chapters from the autobiography of the Iron Chancellor, with a historical introduction by C. D. Hazen.* N. Y., 1920. *New chapters of Bismarck's autobiography,* London, 1921. Tr. by B. Miall from *Gedanken und Erinnerungen,* v. 3, Stuttgart, 1922.

d Busch, Moritz. *Bismarck, some secret pages of his history, being a diary kept during twenty-five years' official and private intercourse with the great chancellor.* 2 v. N. Y., 1898. German ed., *Tagebuchblätter,* 3 v. Leipzig, 1899.

e Kohl, Horst, ed. *Die politischen Reden des Fürsten von Bismarck; historisch-kritische Gesammtausgabe.* 14 v. Stuttgart, 1892–1904.

f Poschinger, Heinrich von. *Fürst Bismarck und die Parlamentarier.* 3 v. Breslau, 1894–95.

g —— *Fürst Bismarck und der Bundesrat, 1876–1890.* 5 v. Stuttgart, 1896–1901.

h —— *Fürst Bismarck und die Diplomaten, 1852–1890.* Hamburg, 1900.

i Hofmann, Hermann. *Fürst Bismarck, 1890–1898.* 1913–14. 11th ed., 3 v., Stuttgart, 1922.

a. Not a consecutive narrative nor a real autobiography but an exposition of a series of topics in the terms which Bismarck wished to impress on posterity, 'Bismarck on parade.' Review, Munroe Smith, *A.H.R.* 4:536, Apr. 1899; G. S.

Ford, 'Bismarck as historiographer,' *American Historical Association, Annual report,* 1909, 127–139. *b.* Contains selections from Bismarck's correspondence with Emperor William I and others. *c.* Continuation of *a.,* but withheld from publication until 1921 on account of its severe strictures upon William II; deals largely with Bismarck's dismissal in 1890; gives his side of the quarrel. *d.* Undress view of Bismarck by his Boswell, based on Busch's earlier works published in 1878 and 1884, which were chiefly valuable as the first important effort in Bismarck's behalf to take the public into confidence. Review, C. H. Levermore, *A.H.R.* 4:531, Apr. 1899. *e., f., g.,* and *h.* The more important collections of source material on Bismarck. *i.* Collection of articles written or inspired by Bismarck and printed in the *Hamburger Nachrichten* after his dismissal, defending his policies and criticising his successors. For other Bismarck literature, cf. (P1a) Dahlmann-Waitz, no. 11970–11985, and 12131–12137, especially 11980 for criticisms of *a.*   GMD, SBF

P342a Robertson, Charles Grant. *Bismarck.* London, 1918. [Makers of the nineteenth century.] (Bibliography.)

b Marcks, Erich. *Bismarck, eine Biographie.* V. 1, *Bismarcks Jugend, 1815–1848.* Stuttgart, 1909.

c Matter, Paul. *Bismarck et son temps.* 3 v. Paris, 1905–08. 2nd rev. ed. of v. 1 and 2, Paris, 1912–14. [Bibliothèque d'histoire contemporaine.]

d Lenz, Max. *Geschichte Bismarcks.* 1902. 4th ed., Leipzig, 1914.

e Egelhaaf, Gottlob. *Bismarck, sein Leben und sein Werk.* 1911. 3rd rev. ed., Stuttgart, 1922.

f Headlam, James W. *Bismarck and the foundation of the German empire.* 1899. 3rd rev. ed., N. Y. and London, 1922. [Heroes of the nations.]

g Singer, Arthur. *Bismarck in der Literatur, ein bibliographischer Versuch.* Würzburg, 1909.

a., b., and *c.* Respectively the best biographies of Bismarck in English, German, and French. *a.* Takes high rank for objectivity, scholarship, and clarity. *b.* Marcks, favorably known for his biography of *Kaiser Wilhelm I.,* Leipzig, 1905, was a happy choice to write the official biography, and his work when completed promises to be standard. *c.* Sound, inclusive, and well documented; lacks something of the crispness expected of the best French historical writing. *d.* Reprint from (P21) *Allgemeine deutsche Biographie;* very stimulating because it sees and solves problems in Bismarck's career from the broad standpoint of European history. *e.* Better for the period after 1871. *f.* Clear and generally acceptable, except as modified by fuller information since its publication. *g.* Excellent Bismarck bibliography.   GSF

P346a Morris, William O'Connor. *Moltke, a biographical and critical study.* 1893. 2nd ed., London, 1894.

b Jähns, Max. *Feldmarschall Moltke.* 1894–1900. 2nd ed., 2 v., Berlin, 1906. [Geisteshelden.]

c Bigge, Wilhelm. *Feldmarschall Graf Moltke ein militärisches Lebensbild.* 2 v. München, 1900.

d Moltke, Helmuth, Graf von. *Gesammelte Schriften und Denkwürdigkeiten.* Ed. by Stanislaus von Leszczynski. 8 v. in 7. Berlin, 1891–93.

e ——— *Militärische Korrespondenz.* 4 v. Berlin, 1892–1902. [Moltkes militärische Werke, herausgegeben vom Grossen Generalstabe.]

f Roon, Albrecht, Graf von. *Denkwürdigkeiten aus dem Leben des Generalfeldmarschalls Kriegsministers Grafen von Roon.* 1892. 5th rev. ed., 3 v., Breslau, 1905.

These volumes afford insight into Prussian military policy during the period of unification and into the conduct of the campaigns from 1864 to 1871, as well as giving personal accounts of Bismarck's two principal co-workers. GMD

P347 Hohenlohe-Schillingsfürst, Chlodwig, Fürst zu. *Memoirs.* 2 v. London and N. Y., 1906. Tr. by G. W. Chrystal from *Denkwürdigkeiten,* ed. by Friedrich Curtius, 2 v. Stuttgart, 1906.

Prepared from the diaries and papers of the chancellor, with copious extracts. Chiefly valuable for his Bavarian premiership, 1866–1870; his membership in the Reichstag, 1870–1874; his ambassadorship at Paris, 1874–1885; and his governorship of Alsace-Lorraine, 1885–1894; less informing on his chancellorship, 1894–1900. Accurate in facts; broad in its range of acquaintance and information; calm and sincere in tone; one of the most enlightening contributions to the history of the German Empire. The English translation is wretched; students must consult the original. Review, Munroe Smith, *A.H.R.* 13:356, Jan. 1908. GMD

P348a Ponsonby, Sir Frederick, ed. *Letters of the Empress Frederick.* N. Y., 1928.

b Meisner, H. O., ed. *Kaiser Friedrich III, das Kriegstagebuch von 1870–71.* Berlin, 1926.

a. Interesting record of the life of Queen Victoria's daughter at the Prussian court, giving a pathetic account of the sickness and death of her husband, Emperor Frederick III, of her "persecution" by Bismarck, and of her distress at the unfilial conduct of her son, later Emperor William II. *b.* Complete edition, replacing the extracts published by Geffcken in 1888, of the Emperor Frederick's War Diary, which caused a bitter conflict with Bismarck. SBF

GERMANY SINCE 1890

For this period also cf. § J.

P351a Hammer, Simon C. *William the Second as seen in contemporary documents and judged on evidence of his own speeches.* London and Boston, 1917. Tr. from *Wilhelm II et blad av Tysklands nyeste historie,* Kristiania, 1915.

b Hill, David J. *Impressions of the Kaiser.* N. Y. and London, 1918.

c Bernstein, Herman, ed. *Willy-Nicky correspondence, being the secret and intimate telegrams exchanged between the Kaiser and the Tsar.* N. Y., 1918.

d Levine, Isaac D., and **Grant, Neil F.,** ed. *The Kaiser's letters to the Tsar, copied from government archives in Petrograd.* London and N. Y., 1920.

e Gauss, Christian, ed. *The German emperor as shown in his public utterances.* N. Y., 1915.

f Wilhelm II. *My memoirs, 1878–1918.* London and N. Y., 1922. Tr. by T. R. Ybarra from *Ereignisse und Gestalten aus den Jahren 1878–1918.* Leipzig, 1922.

g Ludwig, Emil. *Kaiser Wilhelm II.* N. Y., 1926. Tr. by E. C. Mayne from *Wilhelm der Zweite.* Berlin, 1925.

Of the innumerable biographies of Emperor William II most of those written before 1914, especially in Germany, are excessively laudatory. Those written since that date are excessively condemnatory. *a.* Perhaps the best brief sketch in English is that translated from the Norwegian of Hammer. It is lively in style, quotes largely from the Kaiser's own speeches, and shows considerable insight into his character and personality. The bias against him is much less than in most books written since 1914. An artistic portrait by a publicist rather than an historian. Review, C. J. H. Hayes, *A.H.R.* 23:892, July 1918. *b.* Shows a more pronounced bias due to the World War; but has considerable value. The conclusions of a lawyer and historian who, as American ambassador to Germany, had excellent opportunities for coming into close contact with the Kaiser and observing him at close range. The second half of the book dealing with the Kaiser's responsibility for the war is of less value than the earlier chapters. Review, R. H. Fife, *A.H.R.* 25:274, Jan. 1920. *c.* Remarkable collection of letters in the original English in which they were written by William II and Nicholas II, who signed themselves respectively 'Willy' and 'Nicky.' They were found in Russia after the Bolshevist revolution and throw a flood of light on the German emperor's character and efforts at personal secret diplomacy. Review, S. B. Fay, 'The Kaiser's secret negotiations with the Tsar, 1904–05,' *A.H.R.* 24:48–72, Oct. 1918. *d.* Further instalment of the Willy-Nicky correspondence, covering the years 1894 to 1914, but unfortunately lacking the Tsar's replies. For an understanding of the significance of the Kaiser's letters and of the political circumstances under which each was written, cf. (J72a) *Die Grosse Politik.* *e.* One of the best keys to the Kaiser's character is to be found in his numerous speeches; of these Gauss has made an excellent and judicious representative selection. *f.* Of little value except for the light which it sheds on the writer's personality. *g.* Written with literary skill; somewhat hostile. SBF

P352a Waldersee, Alfred, Graf von. *A field-marshal's memoirs, from the diary, correspondence and reminiscences,* London, 1924. Tr. by F. Whyte from *Denkwürdigkeiten,* 3 v. Stuttgart, 1923.

b Moltke, Helmuth von. *Erinnerungen, Briefe, Dokumente, 1877–1916.* Ed. by Eliza von Moltke. Stuttgart, 1922.

These two memoirs, by men who were chiefs of the German general staff, throw much new valuable light on William II and his interference in military matters. *a.* Waldersee, at first one of William's intimate friends and influential advisers, contributed to the overthrow of Bismarck in 1890; but, failing to be appointed Chancellor in his place, he reveals in later pages much bitter criticism of the Kaiser. *b.* Moltke, of a more noble and generous character, betrays in these letters to his wife and other papers his incapacity for the task of chief of staff and the difficulty and thanklessness of serving such a ruler as William II. Review of *a., Living Age,* 317:204, Apr. 28, 1923; of *b., ibid,* 317:38, Apr. 7, 1923. SBF

P361a Bülow, Bernhard, Fürst von. *Imperial Germany.* 1914. 2nd rev. ed., London and N. Y., 1917. Tr. by M. A. Lewenz, from *Deutsche Politik,* 1913; 2nd ed., Berlin, 1916.

b Haller, Johannes. *Die Aera Bülow, eine historisch-politische Studie.* Stuttgart, 1922.

a. Foreign and domestic policies under William II are reviewed by a practised diplomatist and a vigorous champion of Germany's international position. The treatment of home policies is, in part, a defense of the author's chancellorship. Bülow presents throughout the aristocratic and nationalistic attitude of 1913, but is statesmanlike in tone and unsparingly critical of German political weaknesses. Review, F. Meinecke, *Hist. Zeit,* 117:98, 1917.   *b.* Severe but penetrating review of *a* and of Bülow's policy. Also cf. G. P. Gooch, 'Baron von Holstein, 'the mystery man,' of the German foreign office, 1890–1906,' *Cambridge Hist. Jour.* 1:61–84, 1923, a valuable study on Bülow's influential advisor.   RHF

P362a Fife, Robert H. *German empire between two wars, a study of the political and social development of the nation between 1871 and 1914.* N. Y., 1916.

  b Collier, Price. *Germany and the Germans from an American point of view.* N. Y., 1913.

  a. Excellent survey; includes penetrating and well-balanced discussions of the clash between liberal and reactionary elements in Germany's foreign affairs, domestic politics, and municipal and educational systems. Review, F. A. Ogg, *A.H.R.* 22:157, Oct. 1916.   *b.* Presents entertainingly trenchant, though often superficial, criticisms of political and social conditions.   SBF

P363a Dawson, William H. *German empire, 1867–1914, and the unity movement.* 2 v. London, 1919.

  b —— *Evolution of modern Germany.* 1908. Rev. ed., London and N. Y., 1919.

  c —— *German socialism and Ferdinand Lassalle: a biographical history of German socialistic movements during this century.* 1888. 3rd rev. ed., London and N. Y., 1899. [Social science series.]

  d —— *Bismarck and state socialism, an exposition of the social and economic legislation of Germany since 1870.* 1890. 2nd ed., London, 1891. [Social science series.]

  e —— *Social insurance in Germany, 1883–1911, its history, operation, results, and a comparison with the national insurance act, 1911.* London and N. Y., 1912.

  f —— *Germany and the Germans.* 2 v. London, 1894.

  g —— *Industrial Germany.* London, 1912. [Nation's library.]

  h —— *Municipal life and government in Germany.* 1914. 2nd ed., London and N. Y., 1916.

  All Dawson's works present the balanced views of a British economist, with first-hand knowledge of German sources and conditions. They are matter-of-fact in tone, but rich in material and accurate in detail.   *a.* Painstaking *résumé* of his earlier studies, with the addition of more political narrative. Review, B. E. Schmitt, *A.H.R.* 24:268, Jan. 1920.   *b.* Very valuable analysis of German industrial and commercial growth to 1905; later edition needed little alteration except in statistics.   *d.* Sequel to *c.*   RHF

P364a Veblen, Thorstein. *Imperial Germany and the industrial revolution.* N. Y. and London, 1915.

  b Barker, J. Ellis. *Modern Germany.* 1907. 6th rev. ed., London and N. Y., 1919.

  c —— *Foundations of Germany, a documentary account revealing the causes of her strength, wealth, and efficiency.* 1916. Rev. ed., London, 1918.

a. Veblen investigates the industrial differences between England and Germany from a standpoint hostile to capitalism. He develops historically novel and interesting views on the influence of Germany's borrowing industrial technique from English experience. His work is somewhat impaired by an obscure style, digressions, and an inability to appreciate German idealism; but it is a valuable contribution to the explanation of Germany's industrial development. Review, S. B. Fay, *Amer. Econ. Rev.* 6:353, June 1916; G. S. Ford, *A.H.R.* 21:801, July 1916. *b.* Presents a full account of Germany's growth viewed as a danger to Great Britain. *c.* Topical outline of German policies with extensive quotations from German rulers and statesmen.   RHF

P371 Hurd, Archibald S., and **Castle, Henry.** *German sea power, its rise, progress, and economic basis.* London and N. Y., 1913.

Shrewd, careful analysis of German naval history, equipment, and resources to 1913. Dispassionately written, abundantly illustrated by statistics, and prophetic of the danger threatening England. Review, *Nation* (N. Y.), 98:434, Apr. 16, 1914.   RHF

P372a Bernhardi, Friedrich von. *Germany and the next war.* N. Y., 1914. Tr. by A. H. Powles from *Deutschland und der nächste Krieg*, Stuttgart, 1911.

b Usher, Roland G. *Pan-Germanism.* Boston, 1913. (Bibliography.)

c Bourdon, Georges. *German enigma, being an inquiry among Germans as to what they think, what they want, what they can do.* London, 1914. Tr. by B. Marshall from *L'Enigme allemande*, Paris, 1914.

d Andler, Charles, ed. *Les origines du Pangermanisme, 1800 à 1888; Le Pangermanisme continental sous Guillaume II de 1888 à 1914; Le Pangermanisme colonial sous Guillaume II; Le Pangermanisme philosophique, 1800 à 1914.* 4 v. Paris, 1915–17. [Collection de documents sur le Pangermanisme.]

e Wertheimer, Mildred S. *Pan-German League, 1890–1914.* N. Y., 1924. [Columbia University, Studies in history, economics, and public law.] (Bibliography.)

a. Defends war as a biological and historical necessity; an urgent, though reasoned, plea by an ardent militarist, for strengthening national forces. *b.* Interprets views and intentions of Pan-German nationalism, with many undocumented statements and hypotheses. *c.* Republishes from *Figaro*, 1913, with candid but conciliatory discussion, interviews containing the ideas of many leaders in all branches of German life. *d.* Collection of texts; includes many insignificant authorities; a strong, cumulative documentation of the aggressive and progressive spirit of Pan-Germanism. Review, R. G. Usher, *A.H.R.* 23:165, Oct. 1917. *e.* Shows that the Pan-German League had fewer members and less influence in Germany than has usually been supposed. Review, B. E. Schmitt, *A.H.R.* 30:394, Jan. 1925.   RHF, SBF

P373a Rohrbach, Paul. *German world policies.* N. Y., 1915. Tr. by E. von Mach from *Der deutsche Gedanke in der Welt*, Berlin, 1912.

b —— *Germany's isolation, an exposition of the economic causes of the war.* Chicago, 1915. Tr. by P. H. Phillipson from *Der Krieg und die deutsche Politik*, Berlin, 1914.

c Naumann, Friedrich. *Central Europe.* N. Y., 1917. (Bibliography.) Tr. by C. M. Meredith from *Mittel-Europa*, Berlin, 1916.

a. Reviews Germany's errors, triumphs, and ambitions from the standpoint of a professedly peaceful Pan-German. *b.* Written in part during the World War; is increasingly militant. *c.* Plea for closer political and economic union of Teutonic allies; presents interesting historical and economic material; based on the military situation of the first years of the war. Review, G. Pollak, *Nation* (N. Y.), 103:557. Dec. 14, 1916. RHF

P380a **Max von Baden, Prince.** *Memoirs.* 2 v. N. Y., 1928. Tr. by W. M. Calder and C. W. H. Sutton from *Erinnerungen und Dokumente*, Stuttgart, 1927.

b **Scheidemann, Philip.** *Memoirs: the making of new Germany.* 2 v. N. Y., 1929. Tr. from the German.

a. Personal reminiscences of one of Germany's most liberal pre-war rulers, who, as Chancellor in 1918, tried to preserve his country from collapse but failed to prevent the downfall of the Kaiser. Review, (London) *Times Lit. Suppl.* 27:693, Oct. 4, 1928. *b.* Lively account of the rise of one of the most influential leaders of the Social Democratic Party; gives a detailed account of various German peace-moves during the war, and of the overthrow of the monarchy and the establishment of the republic, in which the author took a prominent part. Criticises severely *a*, and is complementary to it. SBF

P381a **Noske, Gustav.** *Von Kiel bis Kapp: zur Geschichte der deutschen Revolution.* Berlin, 1920.

b **Bouton, Stephen Miles.** *And the Kaiser abdicates, the German revolution, November, 1918–August, 1919.* 1920. Rev. ed. New Haven, 1921.

c **Lutz, Ralph H.** *German Revolution, 1918–1919.* Stanford University, California, 1922. [Stanford University Publications.] (Bibliography.)

a. Noske recites his part in the revolution, interweaving a strong apologia for his acts as minister of defense; events are told in great detail, in a strongly personal style. Review, R. H. Lutz, *A.H.R.* 26:794, July 1921. *b.* By an American newspaper correspondent who witnessed many of the events of the German revolution; the narrative is serious, well documented, and sympathetic with efforts for democratic rule. Review, C. Becker, *Nation* (N. Y.), 115:632, Dec. 6, 1922. *c.* Careful monograph, based on wide study of documents, by a member of the American military commission in Berlin in March and April, 1919. Review, R. H. Fife, *A.H.R.*, 29:337, Jan. 1924. RHF

P382a **Coar, John F.** *The old and the new Germany.* N. Y., 1924.

b **Kraus, Herbert.** *Germany in transition.* Chicago, 1924. [Harris lectures.]

c **Gooch, George P.** *Germany.* London and N. Y., 1925. [Modern world.]

a. and *b.* Careful, thoughtful, and sympathetic studies respectively by an American professor and an East Prussian jurist of the working of the new German constitution, and of the political and social problems which have beset Germany since its adoption. *c.* Concise and very informing account of German political and intellectual development from the founding of the German Empire to the beginning of 1925 by a sympathetic student of German affairs. Gives special attention to the shifting preoccupations of the German mind before, during and after the World War, and an excellent analysis of present-day conditions in Germany. SBF

P383a **Luehr, Elmer.** *New German republic.* N. Y., 1929.

b **Quigley, Hugh,** and **Clark, R. T.** *Republican Germany.* N. Y., 1928.

c **Angell, James W.** *Recovery of Germany.* New Haven, 1929. [Publications of the Council on Foreign Relations.]

a and *b.* Two of the best and most readable accounts of the establishment and the development of the new German republic during the first ten years of its existence. *a* gives more attention to the financial problems and to the reorganization of German industry. *c.* Very careful and scholarly but readable analysis of Germany's financial and economic recovery and of the working of the Dawes Plan; contains a summary of the Young Plan and gives reasons for believing that Germany can meet the payments stipulated in it; based on a very thorough and meticulous use of statistics and on personal investigations in Germany.   SBF

LOCAL HISTORY

The literature on the smaller German states is so vast that no account can be given of it here, except to list some of the best works, in addition to those given above (P286–305) on Brandenburg-Prussia: (P401) Hermann Waeschke, *Anhaltische Geschichte,* 3 v., Köthen, 1912–13; (P402a) Friedrich von Weech, *Badische Geschichte,* 1890, 2nd ed., Karlsruhe, 1896; (P402b) Edmond Rebmann, Eberhard Gothein, and Eugen von Jagemann, *Das Grossherzogtum Baden in allgemeiner, wirtschaftlicher und staatlicher Hinsicht dargestellt.* 1885. 2nd ed., 2 v., Karlsruhe, 1912; (P403) Johann Looshorn, *Geschichte des Bistums Bamberg,* 7 v., München, 1886–1910; (P404a) Sigmund von Riezler, *Geschichte Bayerns,* 8 v., Gotha, 1878–1914; (P404b) Michael Doeberl, *Entwicklungsgeschichte Bayerns,* 3 v., München, 1906–18, 3rd ed. of v. 1, 1916; (P405) Otto von Heinemann, *Geschichte von Braunschweig und Hannover,* 3 v. in 2, Gotha, 1882–92; (P406) Anton Horne, *Geschichte von Frankfurt am Main,* 1882, 4th ed., Frankfurt, 1903; (P407) Christoph von Rommel, *Geschichte von Hessen,* 10 v., Marburg and Cassel, 1820–58; (P408) Otto Vitense, *Geschichte von Mecklenburg,* Gotha, 1920 [(B 161) Allgemeine Staatengeschichte]; (P409) Martin Wehrmann, *Geschichte von Pommern,* 1903–06, 2nd ed., 2 v., Gotha, 1919–21; (P410) Ludwig Häusser, *Geschichte der Rheinischen Pfalz,* 2 v., Heidelberg, 1845; (P411) Colmar Grünhagen, *Geschichte Schlesiens,* 2 v., Gotha, 1884–86; (P412) Georg Waitz, *Schleswig-Holsteins Geschichte,* 2 v., Göttingen, 1851–52 (P413a) Christoph von Stälin, *Würtembergische Geschichte,* 4 v., Stuttgart and Tübingen, 1841–73; (P413b) Paul F. Stälin, *Geschichte Württembergs,* 2 v., Gotha, 1882–87. For details on these and other local histories, cf. (P1a) Dahlmann-Waitz, especially no. 1079–1273, 1469–1692, and (P1b) Loewe.   SBF

AUSTRIA

For bibliography of Austria cf. (P1a) Dahlmann-Waitz and (P11a) Charmatz, and for geography cf. (P41a) Partsch. Much of the history of Austria, as the leading state in the Holy Roman Empire, is to be found in most of the works on German history noted in this section. Materials relating to territories which were portions of the former Austro-Hungarian Empire will be found in §§ S and T. Also cf. §§ F, H, I, J, and O.

P421 Léger, Louis P. M. *History of Austria-Hungary.* London, 1889. Tr. by Mrs. B. Hill from 1st ed. Also ed. by W. E. Lingelbach, Philadelphia, 1907 [History of the nations]. (Bibliography.) Tr. from *Histoire de l'Autriche-Hongrie depuis ses origines jusqu'à l'année 1878*, 1879; 6th rev. ed. to 1918, Paris, 1920. (Bibliography.)

Account, by a veteran in eastern European matters and a strong sympathizer with the Slavs, less of Austria as a unity than of Austria as a diversity. What the author more or less looked forward to in the earlier editions—the ruin of Austria by Germans and Magyars and the rise from the ruin of the component peoples—he has been able in the latest edition to portray as a reality. EWD

P422a Kralik, Richard. *Oesterreichische Geschichte.* 1913. 3rd ed., Wien, 1914.

b Krones, Franz X. von. *Handbuch der Geschichte Oesterreichs von der ältesten bis zur neuesten Zeit, mit besonderer Rücksicht auf Länder-Völkerkunde, und Culturgeschichte.* 1876–79. New ed., 5 v., Berlin, 1880–81. (Extensive bibliographies.)

c Huber, Alfons. *Geschichte Österreichs.* V. 1–5, to 1648, Gotha, 1885–96; v. 6, to 1705, by O. Redlich, Gotha, 1921. [(B 161) Heeren and Uckert series.]

a. Readable, popular survey on the monarchy from a clerical, conservative point of view, by an Austrian for fellow Austrians, with many quotations from the original sources. *b.* Comprehensive examination of Austrian political development in the light of ethnic and geographic factors. The curious conclusion is reached that these factors are such as to render unity of government necessary for the peoples concerned. *c.* Competent, sober account, with reference rather to events than to institutions. EWD

P431 Coxe, William. *History of the house of Austria, . . . 1218 to 1792.* 1807. With continuation to 1849 by W. K. Kelly, and tr. in appendix of Count F. von Hartig's account of revolution of 1848, 1853. New impression. 4 v., London, 1893–95.

Until the translation of the work by (P421) Léger, this was the only general history of Austria-Hungary accessible in English. Now mostly out of date, but still useful at least for Hartig's account of the revolution of 1848. EWD

P432 Srbik, Heinrich, Ritter von. *Metternich, der Staatsmann und der Mensch.* 2 v. München, 1925.

Monumental and erudite work on the dominant figure in the Hapsburg monarchy in the first half of the nineteenth century, but too encyclopedic to be readable as a biography. SBF

P436a Friedjung, Heinrich. *Oesterreich von 1848 bis 1860.* 2 v. 1908-12. 4th ed. of v. 1, Stuttgart, 1918.

b Andrássy, Julius, Graf. *Ungarns Ausgleich mit Oesterreich vom Jahr. 1867.* Leipzig, 1897.

c Eisenmann, Louis. *Le compromis austro-hongrois de 1867, étude sur le dualisme.* Paris, 1904. (Bibliography.)

d Burián, Stephan, Graf. *Austria in dissolution.* London, 1924. Tr. by Brian Lunn from *Drei Jahre aus der Zeit meiner Amtsführung im Kriege.* Wien, 1923.

  e **Redlich, Joseph.** *Austrian War Government.* New Haven, 1929. Tr. from *Oesterreichische Regierung und Verwaltung im Weltkriege,* Wien, 1927. [(J571) Shotwell, Economic and Social history of the world war.]

These five works give an account of the internal conflicts between the nationalists under Hapsburg rule, especially during three of the most violent crises, the revolutions of 1848, the compromise of 1867 which established the Dual Monarchy, and its final collapse in the World War.   *a.* Gives the point of view of a patriotic but scholarly German Austrian; *b.,* that of a Magyar statesman and leading minister; *c.,* that of a scientific historian; and *d.,* that of the Austro-Hungarian minister of foreign affairs in the time of the World War who furnishes a vivid account of his experiences, of the abortive peace proposals, and of the conflict of nationalities. *e.* Careful study of the government of Austria during the World War, with an introduction on the constitution and administration of Austria-Hungary from 1867 to 1914.   Review, (London) *Times Lit. Suppl.* 26:722, Oct. 20, 1927.   SBF

P437a Redlich, Joseph. *Emperor Francis Joseph of Austria.* N. Y., 1929.

  b **Bagger, Eugene.** *Francis Joseph, emperor of Austria, king of Hungary.* N. Y., 1927.

  c **Ernest, Otto.** *Franz Joseph as revealed by his letters.* London, 1927. Tr. from the German by Agnes Blake.

  a. Very readable and sympathetic biography, showing, however, the emperor's deficiencies, by a scholar thoroughly familiar with the subject. *b.* More popular and journalistic account than *a.* *c.* Well-chosen selection of the emperor's letters. Review, (London) *Times Lit. Suppl.* 26:631, Sept. 22, 1927.   SBF

P441a Steed, Henry Wickham. *Hapsburg monarchy.* 1913. 4th ed., London, 1919.

  b **Schierbrand, Wolf von.** *Austria-Hungary, the polyglot empire.* N. Y., 1917.

  c **Drage, Geoffrey.** *Austria-Hungary.* London and N. Y., 1909.

  a. Steed wrote his book in 1912–1913, after ten years of observation and study on the ground as correspondent of the London *Times.* His treatment is highly interpretative, living, and suggestive. *b.* Aims at both description and interpretation; most useful possibly on the Jewish question. *c.* Primarily descriptive, with useful tables and maps.   EWD

P442a Auerbach, Bertrand. *Les races et les nationalités en Autriche-Hongrie.* 1898. 2nd rev. ed., Paris, 1917. [Bibliothèque d'histoire contemporaine.]

  b **Gayda, Virginio.** *Modern Austria, her racial and social problems with a study of Italia Irredenta.* London and N. Y., 1915. Abridged tr. by Z. M. Gibson and C. A. Miles from the 2nd ed. of *L'Austria di Francesco Giuseppe, la crisi di un impero,* 1913, 2nd ed., Torino, 1915, together with a study of the Italian irredentist question specially written by the author for this English edition.

  c **Goričar, Josef,** and **Stowe, Lyman B.** *Inside story of the Austro-German intrigue, or, How the world war was brought about.* Garden City, N. Y., 1920.

  a. Auerbach, long professor of geography in the University of Nancy, and competent also in history, treated the racial and national elements of Austria-Hungary in ways that leave little to be desired; comprehensively, with abundant and precise detail, without bias, and very clearly. Review, G. Pollak, *A.H.R.* 23:639, Apr. 1918. *b.* Very readable analysis by an Italian of good education and considerable experience in political life. *c.* Goricar was fourteen years in the Austro-Hungarian diplomatic service. With the advantage derived from that position, and with the sympathies natural to a high-spirited Slav, he weaves a living story. EWD

SWITZERLAND

For other works containing material on Swiss history, cf. §§ H, I, and J; for Zwingli and Calvin, cf. § F; for bibliography, cf. (P16) Barth and others; and for geography, cf. (P42c) Egli.

P461a McCrackan, William D. *Rise of the Swiss republic.* 1892. 2nd ed., N. Y., 1901. (Bibliography.)

   b Dändliker, Karl. *Short history of Switzerland.* London and N. Y., 1899. Tr. and rev. by E. Salisbury from 2nd ed. of *Lehrbuch der Geschichte des Schweizervolkes*, 1874; 2nd ed., Zürich, 1889.

   c Hug, Lina, and **Stead, Richard.** *Switzerland.* N. Y. and London, 1890. [Story of the nations.]

   d Oechsli, Wilhelm. *History of Switzerland, 1499–1914.* Cambridge, Eng., 1922. Tr. by E. and C. Paul from author's ms. [Cambridge historical series.] (Bibliography.)

   e Martin, William. *Histoire de la Suisse: Essai sur la formation d'une confédération des états.* Paris, 1927.

a. and *b.* Best brief general narratives in English for the use of students. *c.* More popular in style and contains many well-chosen illustrations. *d.* Embodies the ripe scholarship of one of the greatest Swiss historians; by far the best concise account of Switzerland since the time the cantons became virtually independent of the Holy Roman Empire. Review, J. M. Vincent, *A.H.R.* 28:534, Apr. 1923. RCB
e. Short well-written volume on the growth of Swiss national independence and internal unity, emphasizing economic causes of this growth. SBF

P466 Dierauer, Johannes. *Geschichte der schweizerischen Eidgenossenschaft.* 5 v. Gotha, 1887–1919. 3rd ed. of v. 1 and 2, Gotha, 1919–20; 2nd ed. of v. 3, Gotha, 1920. [(B 161) Heeren and Uckert series.] French tr. by A. Reymond, *Histoire de la confédération suisse,* v. 1–4, Lausanne and Paris, 1910–13.

Takes very high rank among more recent authorities as the best detailed history of Switzerland; covers the whole range of Swiss history from Roman times to 1848. Well written, judicious, objective, painstakingly accurate, and thorough in research. Movements and events, more than individuals, fascinate the author. Both the German and French editions contain exhaustive critical notes upon the sources. Review, A. B. Faust, *A.H.R.* 18:362, Jan. 1913; 24:683, July 1919.

RCB

P467a Dändliker, Karl. *Geschichte der Schweiz, mit besonderer Rücksicht auf die Entwicklung des Verfassungs- und Kulturlebens.* 3 v. 1884–87. 4th rev. ed. of v. 1, Zürich, 1901; 3rd rev. ed. of v. 2 and 3, Zürich, 1902–03. (Bibliographies.)

   b Muyden, Berthold van. *Histoire de la nation suisse.* 3 v. Lausanne and Paris, 1899–1901.

c Gagliardi, Ernst. *Geschichte der Schweiz von den Anfängen bis auf die Gegenwart.* 2 v. Zürich, 1920.

a. Conceived on the same large scale as (P466) Dierauer; ably executed; covers Swiss history from the time of the lake dwellers to 1885. *b.* Widely read, popular history of Switzerland from the earliest times; originally published in serial form. *c.* New general history which embodies scholarly researches in readable form; emphasizes the firm foundation of freedom and the community of aspect of peasant and town life in Switzerland in contrast to the territorial and imperial development in Germany. Review, R. Reuss, *Rev. Hist.* 139:100, Jan. 1922. RCB

P471a Oechsli, Wilhelm. *Geschichte der Schweiz im neunzehnten Jahrhundert.* 2 v. Leipzig, 1903–13.

b Curti, Theodor. *Geschichte der Schweiz im XIX. Jahrhundert.* 1902. 2nd ed., Neuenburg, 1904.

Both are valuable for the nineteenth century as a whole, and may be used for this later period to supplement (P466) Dierauer, (P467a) Dändliker and (P467b) Muyden. Review of *a.,* C. Borgeaud, *A.H.R.* 10:419, Jan. 1905. RCB

P481a Vincent, John M. *Government in Switzerland.* N. Y. and London, 1900. [Citizen's library of economics, politics, and sociology.] (Critical bibliography.)

b Brooks, Robert C. *Government and politics of Switzerland.* Yonkers, 1918. [Government handbooks.] (Critical bibliography.)

c Bonjour, Félix. *Real democracy in operation, the example of Switzerland.* N. Y., 1920.

a. Description of the cantonal and federal governments. Appendixes include the federal constitution of 1874 in English. *b.* Designed as text-book; convenient for the general reader. Contains initiative and referendum tables from 1874 to 1918; frequent comparisons with government and politics of the United States; and discussions of Swiss army system, social legislation, nationalization of railroads, international relations, political parties, and *Landesgemeinden.* *c.* Describes the mechanism of democratic institutions peculiar to Switzerland and explains their effects. Also cf. (K351) Bryce, *Modern democracies,* especially v. 1, ch. 27–32. RCB, SBF

P482 His, Eduard. *Geschichte des neueren schweizerischen Staatsrechts.* V. 1, *Die Zeit der Helvetik und der Vermittlungsakte, 1793–1813.* Basel, 1920.

Of the highest rank; gives systematic and connected account of the history of Swiss public law during the period of the Helvetic Republic and the Act of Mediation. RCB

DIPLOMATIC, MILITARY, AND NAVAL HISTORY

Most works dealing with these phases of German history will be found in §§ H, I, J, and K. For diplomatic history reference should also be made to the following items in the present section: (P307) for the relations between Frederick the Great and Joseph II; (P314b) for the Napoleonic period; (P341, 342, 347) for the establishment of the German empire; (P373, 436d, 442e) for the World War and its antecedents. For military history: (P231) the medieval struggle with the Slavs; (P271) Thirty Years' War; (P315) War of Liberation; (P346)

Seven Weeks' War and Franco-German War; (P352, 372a) the army under William II. For naval history, primarily under William II: (P371).

CONSTITUTIONAL AND LEGAL HISTORY, POLITICAL THEORY

P531 Conrad, Johannes and others, ed. *Handwörterbuch der Staatswissenschaften.* 1890–94. 3rd rev. ed., 8 v., 1909–11; 4th rev. ed. by L. Elster and others, V. 1–8, Jena, 1921–29. (Bibliographies.)

Invaluable encyclopedia of legal, economic, and historical information and reliable statistics. The articles, which relate chiefly to Germany, are contributed by some of Germany's foremost scholars and experts. The 3rd ed. is still very useful and contains some good articles not reproduced in the 4th ed.   SBF

P536 Waitz, Georg. *Deutsche Verfassungsgeschichte.* 8 v. Kiel, 1844–78. Later ed., Berlin; 3rd ed. of v. 1 and 2, 1880–82; 2nd ed. of v. 3 and 4, 1883–85; 2nd rev. ed. of v. 5 by K. Zeumer, 1893; 2nd rev. ed. of v. 6 by G. Seeliger, 1896.

Marks an epoch in modern German historiography. Waitz was one of Ranke's earliest and ablest pupils. His preliminary studies as a medievalist were made upon Henry I, the (P215a) *Jahrbücher* of whose reign he published in 1837. He succeeded Pertz in 1876 in the direction of (P71a) *Monumenta,* and died in 1886. His seminar both at Kiel and Göttingen was year after year devoted to the study of medieval German institutions, and his 'D V G,' as it is often cited, was thirty-four years in preparation. Waitz sifted and weighed every source for his subject. Almost nothing, however small, has escaped his scrutiny. As a history of German institutions from the earliest times to the middle of the twelfth century, his work is without a peer. Many pages contain only a few lines of text, the residue of the page being covered with notes. Waitz's chief defect was a lack of historical imagination, so that not without justice Mr. Herbert Fisher has characterized the work as a 'vast and orderly museum of desiccated antiquities.' He possessed immense industry, vast erudition, great capacity for coördination of his data, but it was (P214) Nitzsch who first clearly interpreted these materials and showed the genetic development of medieval German history which Waitz had failed to perceive. For literature upon Waitz, cf. (A249a) Gooch, *History and historians in the nineteenth century,* 117–122; (A247) Fueter, *Historiographie,* 487 (German ed.), 608 (French ed.) ; Sybel, *Hist. Zeit.* 56:482, 1886; G. Monod, *Rev. Hist.* 31:382, July 1886; his life by his son Eberhard Waitz, *Ein Lebens- und Charakterbild,* Berlin, 1913.   JWT

P537a Meister, Aloys. *Deutsche Verfassungsgeschichte von den Anfängen bis ins 15. Jahrhundert.* 1907. 3rd rev. ed. Leipzig, 1922. [(A294) Meister, Grundriss der Geschichtswissenschaft.] (Bibliographies.)

b Hartung, Fritz. *Deutsche Verfassungsgeschichte vom 15. Jahrhundert bis zur Gegenwart.* 1914. 2nd rev. ed. Leipzig, 1922. [(A294) Meister, Grundriss der Geschichtswissenschaft.] (Bibliographies.)

Excellent outlines of German constitutional history and useful introduction to the materials and the study of the subject.   GMD

P541a Howard, Burt E. *German empire.* N. Y., 1906.

b Krüger, Fritz K. *Government and politics of the German empire.* Yonkers, 1915. [Government handbooks.] (Critical bibliography.)

   c Hue de Grais, Robert Graf. *Handbuch der Verfassung und Verwaltung in Preussen und dem deutschen Reiche.* 1881. 22nd ed., Berlin, 1914.

   d Laband, Paul. *Das Staatsrecht des deutschen Reiches.* 1876–82. 5th rev. ed., 4 v., Tübingen, 1911–14. (Bibliographies.)

   e Salomon, Felix, ed. *Die deutschen Parteiprogramme.* 1907. 3rd rev. ed., 3 v., Leipzig, 1920. (Bibliography.)

   f Emerson, Rupert. *State and sovereignty in modern Germany.* New Haven, 1928.

a. Admirable analysis, well documented from German constitutional authorities, of the German imperial constitution of 1871; strictly juridical, without historical setting or theoretical development. *b.* Brief and objective presentation of the organization of the empire. *c.* and *d.* Authoritative German works on the constitutional law and administration of the German empire. *c.* Convenient manual. *d.* Extended treatise. *e.* Presents well selected documentary material for party history from 1845 to 1920. Also cf. the works of (P362a) Fife, (P363) Dawson, (P364a) Veblen, and (P364b and c) Barker. The most readable brief account in English of the German government is in (I551c) Lowell, *Governments and parties in continental Europe.*   RHF

f. Careful analysis of the philosophic conceptions and constitutional theories which have been at work during the past century and a half in shaping the development of constitutional forms in Germany. Review, (London) *Times Lit. Suppl.* 28:267, Apr. 4, 1929.   SBF

P542 Brunet, René. *New German constitution.* N. Y., 1922; London, 1923. Tr. by J. Gollomb from *La constitution allemande du 11 août 1919,* Paris, 1921. [Bibliothèque politique et économique.] (Bibliographical foot-notes.)

Text of the Weimar republican constitution, with a clear, readable, and acute exposition; prefaced by an able analysis of the economic and social forces which overthrew the old imperial government. Review, A. N. Holcombe, *Amer. Pol. Sci. Rev.* 16:700, Nov. 1922.   SBF

P546a Huber, Alfons. *Oesterreichische Reichsgeschichte: Geschichte der Staatsbildung und des öffentlichen Rechts.* 1895. 2nd rev. ed. by A. Dopsch, Wien, 1901.

   b Luschin von Ebengreuth, Arnold. *Oesterreichische Reichsgeschichte.* 2 v. Bamberg, 1895–96.

Excellent scholarly text-books published in response to a law of 1893 which placed Austrian constitutional history and public law among the required studies for prospective jurists in Austria.   EWD

P551 Schröder, Richard K. H. *Lehrbuch der deutschen Rechtsgeschichte.* 1889. 6th rev. ed. by E. von Künssberg, Leipzig, 1922. (Excellent bibliography.)

Learned, methodical, accurate; embodies the latest researches; presents the whole of German legal history in compact form; most useful of the many German text-books on the subject.   SBF

P552a Brunner, Heinrich. *Deutsche Rechtsgeschichte.* 2 v. Leipzig, 1887–92. 2nd ed. of v. I, Leipzig, 1906.

   b —— *Grundzüge der deutschen Rechtsgeschichte.* 1901. 8th rev. ed. by E. Heymann, Leipzig, 1921.

a. Magisterial work of great erudition and acumen, but of highly technical treatment and difficult style. Must often be read with caution, partly owing to ı predilection for minimizing the influence of Roman institutions and partly because of a disposition to advance theories which have little basis in reality. b. Outline of German legal history. Much smaller and more readable text-book than that of (P551) Schröder. JWT

P553a Huebner, Rudolf. *History of Germanic private law.* Boston, 1918. [Continental legal series.] (Bibliography.) Tr. by F. S. Philbrick from 2nd ed. of *Grundzüge des deutschen Privatrechts,* 1908; 4th ed., Leipzig, 1922.

    b Grimm, Jakob. *Deutsche Rechtsalterthümer.* 1828. 4th rev. ed. by A. Heusler and R. Huebner, 2 v., Leipzig, 1899.

    c —— *Weisthümer.* Ed. by R. Schröder and others. 7 v. Göttingen. 1840–78.

a. Traces the development of the several parts of German private law from their origin to the present time as part of the actual law of Germany. The author belongs to the moderate section of the so-called Germanistic school, and follows (P561) Gierke in a general way, though he pays careful heed to opposing views and attempts to state his conclusions with impartiality. *b.* Grimm, one of the editors of the great German dictionary, has collected in this volume of legal antiquities a wealth of interesting law and folk-lore drawn largely from his philological researches and his *c.,* an invaluable edition of the German peasant legal maxims, customs, and 'dooms,' the first three volumes of which were published during his lifetime. SBF

P561a Gierke, Otto F. von. *Das deutsche Genossenschaftsrecht.* 4 v. Berlin, 1868–1913. (Bibliographies.)

    b —— *Political theories of the middle ages.* Cambridge, Eng., 1900. Tr. by F. W. Maitland from part of v. 3 of *a.,* entitled *Die publicistischen Lehren des Mittelalters.*

    c —— *Johannes Althusius und die Entwicklung der naturrechtlichen Staatstheorien, zugleich ein Beitrag zur Geschichte der Rechtssystematik.* 1880. 3rd rev. ed., Breslau, 1913.

a. and *b.* These masterpieces of industry, erudition, and acute analysis trace, in marvelous fashion, the difficult course of the evolution of the legal capacity of the community through German history. Remarkable examples of a combination of astounding capacity for minute research in the history of political ideas with the faculty of broad generalization in the field of systematic theory. Broadly speaking, the significance of Gierke's theory is his development of the doctrine that the state and the group are real and actual personalities, as distinguished from the *persona ficta.* *c.* Discusses the political ideas of this remarkable but forgotten writer, and then traces in minute detail the development of these ideas down to the time of Rousseau. CEM

ECONOMIC AND SOCIAL HISTORY

P571 Roscher, Wilhelm. *System der Volkswirtschaft, ein Hand- und Lesebuch für Geschäftsmänner und Studierende.* 5 v. in 6. Stuttgart, 1883–94. Many later ed. of the different volumes by W. Stieda and others, Stuttgart, 1901–22. (Valuable bibliography.)

In his own time Roscher was reckoned as an economist. Were he living to-day he would be called an economic historian, for he was one of the pioneers in this form of historical interpretation. He was profoundly influenced by Ritter, the geographer, and by the new currents of economic and social interpretation in the middle of the nineteenth century. The volumes are interesting and suggestive reading, but sometimes difficult because of the wide geographical and chronological areas over which he ranges in a single paragraph. Written before the theory of evolution had penetrated into the representation of history, and before the biological or organic nature of human society was appreciated, the early editions are antiquated to-day. The revised edition, however, incorporates the large results of modern historical research. The notes are mines of classified information. Review, *Hist. Zeit.* 33:417, 1895. JWT

P572a Inama-Sternegg, Karl T. von. *Deutsche Wirtschaftsgeschichte.* 3 v. in 4. Leipzig, 1879–1901. 2nd ed. of v. 1, Leipzig, 1909.

   b —— *Die Ausbildung der grossen Grundherrschaften in Deutschland während der Karolingerzeit.* Leipzig, 1878.

a. First sustained history of any European country expressive of the new historical interpretation which arose in the later decades of the nineteenth century. Its freshness and suggestiveness have not been staled by lapse of time nor by the appearance of many similar works. Indispensable for an understanding of the economic foundations of the feudal régime. *b.* Smaller monograph a by-product of his *magnum opus;* deals with the origins of the landed feudal aristocracy during the Carolingian epoch. JWT

P573a Kötzschke, Karl Rudolph. *Grundzüge der deutschen Wirtschaftsgeschichte bis zum 17. Jahrhundert.* 1908. 2nd rev. ed., Leipzig, 1923 [(A294) Meister, Grundriss der Geschichtswissenschaft.] (Valuable bibliography.)

   b Sieveking, Heinrich. *Grundzüge der neueren Wirtschaftsgeschichte vom 17. Jahrhundert bis zur Gegenwart.* 1907. 4th rev. ed., Leipzig, 1923 [(A294). Meister, Grundriss der Geschichtwissenschaft.] Bibliographies.)

   c Dopsch, Alfons. *Die Wirtschaftsentwicklung der Karolingerzeit vornehmlich in Deutschland.* 1912–13. 2nd ed., 2 v., Weimar, 1921–22.

a. Guide to the study of medieval German economic history rather than an actual history itself. Important movements or conditions are characterized in broad generalizations. Whether for rapid survey or for intense special research, the work is of great value to the student. Perhaps no other single book is more satisfactory for the subject. *b.* Of similar character and value for the modern period. *c.* Dopsch belongs to the younger school of Austrian economic historians. He almost possesses the faculty of divination in his perception of economic and social values in history, and has reread much of the history of the Carolingian period in new terms. While extremely suggestive, the work abounds in radical ideas, as for instance the remarkable interpretation of Charlemagne's capitulary *De Villis.* The sensation made by the appearance of this work has not yet subsided. The cautious student will do well to read attentively the reviews of this work by C. Brinkmann, *Vierteljahrschrift für Sozial- und Wirtschaftsgeschichte,* 10:546, 1912; S. Hertzberg-Frankel, *Hist. Zeit* 112:159, 1914; A. Hofmeister, *ibid.,* 120:109, 1919. JWT

576a **Below, Georg von.** *Das ältere deutsche Städtewesen und Bürgertum.* 1898. 2nd ed., Bielefeld, 1906. [Monographien zur Weltgeschichte.]

b **Hegel, Karl.** *Städte und Gilden der germanischen Völker im Mittelalter.* 2 v. Leipzig, 1891.

c —— *Die Entstehung des deutschen Städtewesens.* Leipzig, 1898.

d **Preuss, Hugo.** *Die Entwicklung des deutschen Städtewesens.* V. 1. Leipzig, 1906.

a. This illustrated little volume gives in interesting popular form the ripe scholarship of one of Germany's ablest students of medieval institutions. For Below's numerous more specialized monographs and his critiques of the views of others on medieval towns, cf. his works listed in (P1a) Dahlmann-Waitz. *b.* represents the conclusions of a scholar who has written on the cities of Italy and on the constitutional history of Frankfort and Cologne and has edited the series of German town chronicles; it includes chapters on the English towns and seeks to prove that municipal constitutions were not derived from the gilds. *c.* and *d.* Excellent general accounts of the development of town organization and life. SBF

577a **Schäfer, Dietrich.** *Die deutsche Hanse.* 1902. 2nd ed., Bielefeld, 1914. [Monographien zur Weltgeschichte.]

b **Lindner, Theodor.** *Die deutsche Hanse, ihre Geschichte und Bedeutung.* 1898. 4th ed., Leipzig, 1911.

c **King, Wilson.** *Chronicles of three free cities, Hamburg, Bremen, Lübeck.* London and N. Y., 1914.

d **Daenell, Ernst R.** *Die Blütezeit der deutschen Hanse, hansische Geschichte von der zweiten Hälfte des XIV. bis zum letzten Viertel des XV. Jahrhunderts.* 2 v., Berlin, 1905–06.

a., b., and *c.* Scholarly but very readable general accounts of the Hanseatic League. *a.* Illustrated; by a man who has inspired and edited many monographs by others on German commercial and maritime history. *c.* The author was American consul at Bremen. *d.* More detailed account of the most flourishing period of the Hanseatic League; based on the rich source material which has been published by the Verein für Hansische Geschichte, cf. (P926a and b, 972). SBF

578a **Schmoller, Gustav F. von.** *Mercantile system and its historical significance illustrated chiefly from Prussian history.* N. Y. and London, 1896. [Economic classics.] Tr. by W. J. Ashley from part of *Studien über die wirtschaftliche Politik Friedrichs des Grossen,* Leipzig, 1884.

b **Below, Georg von.** *Territorium und Stadt: Aufsätze zur deutschen Verfassungs-, Verwaltungs-, und Wirtschaftsgeschichte.* 1900. 2nd ed., München, 1923. [Historische Bibliothek.] (Rich bibliography.)

c —— *Der deutsche Staat des Mittelalters, ein Grundriss der deutschen Verfassungsgeschichte.* V. 1. 1914. 2nd ed., Leipzig, 1925.

d **Keutgen, Friedrich.** *Der deutsche Staat des Mittelalters.* Jena, 1918.

a. In this small monograph Professor Schmoller shows the connection and interdependence between economic and political arrangements which go hand in hand, supporting one another, through various stages in Prussia: village, town, territory, and national state. Mercantilism is not merely an economic policy; it is also essentially political, and, as such, a powerful factor in state-building.

This essay is merely a chip from Schmoller's workshop; for his numerous works
on economic theory and history cf. (P1a) Dahlmann-Waitz. Schmoller belonge
to the younger historical school of German economists and his writings illustrate
how powerful a factor the state may be in the field of economics. As professor
as editor of Prussian archival material, and as editor and frequent contributor
to (P956) *Jahrbuch für Gesetzgebung, Verwaltung, und Volkswirtschaft im
deutschen Reich,* he has exercised a great influence over the minds of economists
politicians, officials, and the educated public in Germany. *b.* Below, many of
whose views differ sharply from those of Schmoller, explains clearly the rise
of the large patrimonial estates in eastern Germany, their great contrasts to
those west of the Elbe, and the formation of the new territorial states with their
new organs of government at the close of the Middle Ages. He illustrates in
detail one of those states in coincident economic and political development—
from town to territory—of which Schmoller speaks. It is rich in its contribution to German agrarian history of the later Middle Ages. Both editions are
useful, as the second omits two chapters of the first and adds three new ones
c. and *d.* Discuss the question of the 'dualism' between town and territorial state
and the rise of the latter upon the ruins of the former; both reviewed by E
Rosenthal, *Hist. Zeit.* 119:372, 1918; 121:296, 1920.   SBF

P579a Strieder, Jacob. *Studien zur Geschichte kapitalistischer Organizations-
formen: Monopole, Kartelle, und Aktiengesellschaften im Mittelalter und
zu Beginn der Neuzeit.* München, 1914. (Bibliography.)

b Ehrenberg, Richard. *Das Zeitalter der Fugger: Geldkapital und Credit-
verkehr im 16. Jahrhundert.* 1896. 3rd ed., 2 v., Jena, 1922.

c ——— *Grosse Vermögen, ihre Entstehung und ihre Bedeutung.* 1902
Rev. ed., Jena, 1905.

d Wiebe, Georg. *Zur Geschichte der Preisrevolution des 16. und 17 Jahrhunderts.* Leipzig, 1895.

e *Fugger News-Letters, being a selection of unpublished letters from the
correspondents of the house of Fugger during the years 1568–1605.* 2
series; N. Y., 1924–26. Tr. by P. de Chary from *Fugger-Zeitungen,* ed
by Victor Klarwill, Wien, 1923. (Bibliography.)

a. Brilliant and important; discusses a hitherto neglected field, the beginnings
of German capitalism in the fifteenth and sixteenth centuries. Review, F. Rörig
Hist. Vierteljahrschrift, 19:110, 1919. *b.* Very valuable history of banking
mining, and commercial enterprise of the first great family of German capitalists
in Luther's day. Review, K. Rathgen, *Hist. Zeit.* 82:120, 1898. *c.* Traces, in
interesting and popular fashion, the fascinating story of the rise and power of
such great fortunes as those of the Fugger, Rothschild, Krupp, Siemens, and
Parish families. Also cf. (I575b) Sombart, *Der moderne Kapitalismus. d*
Based on wide statistical studies; best account of the perplexing rise of prices
in the sixteenth and seventeenth centuries. *e.* Contains interesting reports or
all sorts of subjects sent to Augsburg by agents of the Fugger banking house
from the various parts of the world where their trading was done, and also
copies of news sheets circulated by a sixteenth century news-collecting agency.
        SBF

P581a Knapp, Theodor. *Gesammelte Beiträge zur Rechts-und Wirtschaftsgeschichte vornehmlich des deutschen Bauernstandes.* Tübingen, 1902. (Bibliography.)

b ———— *Neue Beiträge zur Rechts-und Wirtschaftsgeschichte des Würtembergischen Bauernstandes.* 2 v. Tübingen, 1919.

In these volumes a modest schoolmaster has made a remarkable contribution to the understanding of the complex economic, legal, and political condition of the peasantry in southwestern Germany at the close of the Middle Ages. By taking a few villages as concrete examples, he analyzes with a wealth of material the tangle of burdens to which the peasant was subject, and performs for this part of Germany somewhat the same service as Seebohm performed for England in (L576a) *English village community.* Review of *b.*, V. Ernst, *Hist. Zeit.* 126:303, 1922.

SBF

P582a Knapp, Georg F. *Die Bauernbefreiung und der Ursprung der Landarbeiter in den älteren Teilen Preussens.* Leipzig, 1887.

b ———— *Die Landarbeiter in Knechtschaft und Freiheit.* Leipzig, 1891.

These two volumes, though somewhat out of date and too optimistic in their conclusions, still give the best general account of the emancipation of the Prussian peasantry during the great reform period of the Napoleonic era. For an excellent review of the subject in English and the more recent literature, cf. (P313d) Ford, *Stein and the era of reform in Prussia*, ch. 6–7.   SBF

P591a Mehring, Franz. *Geschichte der deutschen Sozialdemokratie.* 2 v. 1897–98. 12th ed., 4 v., Stuttgart, 1922.

b Milhaud, Edgard. *La démocratie socialiste allemande.* Paris, 1903. [Bibliothèque d'histoire contemporaine.]

c Bernstein, Eduard. *Ferdinand Lassalle as a social reformer.* London and N. Y., 1893. [Social science series. Tr. by E. M. Aveling from *Biographische Einleitung* in v. 1 of F. Lassalle, *Reden und Schriften*, ed. by E. Bernstein, Berlin, 1892.

d Oncken, Hermann. *Lassalle, eine politische Biographie.* 1904. 4th ed., Stuttgart, 1923. (Bibliography.)

e Bebel, August. *Reminiscences.* V. 1–2, N. Y., 1911–12. Tr. by Ernest Untermann from *Aus meinem Leben*, 3 v. (v. 3 by K. Kautsky), Stuttgart, 1910–14.

f Bevan, Edwyn R. *German social democracy during the war.* London, 1918.

g Hayes, Carlton J. H. *History of German socialism reconsidered. A.H.R.* 23:62–101, Oct. 1917.

a. Standard authority on the German social democratic party by one of its more moderate members.   *b.* Gives the point of view of a keen Swiss observer. *c.* One of the best of the older accounts of Lassalle and his influence, by a newspaper correspondent for many years a resident in London. Also cf. the author's (I582h) *Evolutionary socialism. d.* Not only an excellent portrait of Lassalle, based to some extent on new material, but also an illuminating account of his political significance.   *e.* Autobiography of the veteran leader of the party from its early days to the eve of the World War; full of personal interest and valuable political information.   *f.* Good account of the vicissitudes and internal conflicts of the German social democratic party during the war to the final split of the party. *g.* Thoughtful revaluation of the German socialist movement. Also cf. (P363*c, d,* and *e*) Dawson's works on Lassalle and on state socialism.   SBF

CULTURAL HISTORY: GENERAL

P601a Richard, Ernst. *History of German civilization.* N. Y., 1911.

   b Francke, Kuno. *Glimpses of modern German culture.* N. Y., 1898.

   c —— *German ideals of today and other essays on German culture.* Boston, 1907.

a. Best treatment of its subject now available in English; uneven in style and treatment; well condensed; throws many interesting sidelights on German life and history. Review, C. von Klenze, *A.H.R.* 17:649, Apr. 1912. *b.* and *c.* Somewhat antiquated, as they consist chiefly of impressionistic sketches of books, plays, and men talked of between 1894 and 1907, but they contain flashes of keen insight into German character.   GMP

P606a Henne Am Rhyn, Otto. *Kulturgeschichte des deutschen Volkes.* 1886. 3rd ed., 2 v., Berlin, 1898.

   b Scherr, Johannes. *Deutsche Kultur- und Sittengeschichte.* 1852–53. 12th rev. ed., 3 v., Leipzig, 1909.

a. Purely descriptive, without any guiding thought or ultimate philosophizing; extremely comprehensive in the presentation of many phases of German culture and civilization; profusely illustrated. *b.* Comprehensive, more animated account; lays emphasis on individual figures; attempts for the first time to portray the development of the national elements in German culture.   GMP

P607a Steinhausen, Georg. *Geschichte der deutschen Kultur.* 1904. 3rd rev. ed., 2 v., Leipzig, 1929.

   b ——, ed. *Monographien zur deutschen Kulturgeschichte.* 12 v. Leipzig, 1899–1905.

   c ——, ed. *Deutsches Leben der Vergangenheit in Bildern.* 2 v. Leipzig, 1907–08; index to *b.* and *c.,* Jena, 1909.

All these works contain reproductions of many interesting woodcuts and copperplates. *a.* The author utilizes the monographs of *b.* and adds much new material. His work as a whole is heavy reading, but is admirably balanced in the relative weight given to the social, economic, literary, and other factors in German civilization. Review, A. Rapp, *Hist. Zeit.* 115:365, 1916. *b.* Vary greatly in merit; the best are v. 2, by Steinhausen himself on the merchant; and v. 6, by Bartels on the peasant. *c.* Supplements to *b.*   GMP

P608 Freytag, Gustav. *Bilder aus der deutschen Vergangenheit.* 1859–62. 37th ed., 4 v. in 5, Leipzig, 1923.

Few errors of fact have ever been discovered in Freytag's pictures, which retain all their original color and vividness. Very valuable and unique presentation of a long series of historical events and figures by a man of great literary skill.   GMP

P609a Biedermann, Karl. *Deutschland im achtzehnten Jahrhundert.* 1854–80. 2nd rev. ed., 4 v., Leipzig, 1880; index, 1881.

b —— *Deutsche Volks- und Kulturgeschichte.* 1885–86. 4th ed., 3 v., Wiesbaden, 1891.

a. Biedermann's greatest work on German thought and culture. *b.* Has a far greater range, as it covers the whole field, but it sacrifices the cultural for the political. Presents, especially, the rise of constitutional government and the unification of modern Germany with clarity and with the authority of a man who took an active part in the political affairs of his time. GMP

P611 Lichtenberger, Henri. *Germany and its evolution in modern times.* N. Y., 1913. Tr. by A. M. Ludovici from *L'Allemagne moderne,* 1907; 12th ed., Paris, 1915.

Appreciative interpretation, based on Lamprecht and other German sources. Valuable especially for discussion of religion, philosophy, and art, by a French scholar with esthetic discrimination. RHF

P616 Mayer, Franz M. *Geschichte Oesterreichs mit besonderer Rücksicht auf das Kulturleben.* 1874. 3rd rev. ed., 2 v., Wien, 1909. (Bibliography.)

Attempts to give, in the narrowest possible compass, a comprehensive view of Austrian civilization in all aspects; deals mostly, however, with the German factors therein; very useful, though far from faultless. EWD

CULTURAL HISTORY: RELIGION

P621 Hauck, Albert. *Kirchengeschichte Deutschlands.* V. 1–5. 1887–1920. 4th ed., v. 1–4, Leipzig, 1904–13.

This monumental church history views the church from all angles and as the greatest organism of human society in the Middle Ages. It is at once a history of religious theory or dogma, of ecclesiastical organization, of intellectual development, and of medieval Germany's economic and social condition in the light of the church's activity and influence; fully documented; a mine of information and an admirable guide to further study. The second part of v. 5, which deals with the Council of Constance was edited by H. Boehmer who will continue the work. Review, E. Vogt, *Hist. Zeit.,* 118:104, 1917.

For the Reformation and Counter-Reformation in Germany, cf. (P241–263); for the *Kulturkampf,* cf. (P336). JWT

CULTURAL HISTORY: EDUCATION

P641a Paulsen, Friedrich. *German universities and university study.* N. Y., 1906. Tr. by Frank Thilly and William W. Elwang from *Die deutschen Universitäten und das Universitätsstudium,* Berlin, 1902. (Bibliography.)

b **Kaufmann, Georg H.** *Die Geschichte der deutschen Universitäten.* 2 v. in 1. Stuttgart, 1888–96. (Bibliography.)

c **Paulsen, Friedrich.** *Geschichte des gelehrten Unterrichts auf den deutschen Schulen und Universitäten vom Ausgang des Mittelalters bis zur Gegenwart.* 1885. 3rd rev. ed., by Rudolf Lehmann, 2 v., Berlin, 1919–21.

a. Contains a brief sketch of the development of German universities, followed by a full account of their organization and methods at the beginning of the twentieth century. *b.* Authoritative and well-documented history of the origins of the German universities and their development to the close of the Middle Ages. *c.* Describes the development of German universities since the Middle Ages, and thus serves as a continuation of *b.;* at the same time it gives a philosophic outline of the growth of ideas and intellectual life in Germany in modern times. For a bibliography of the individual universities, cf. (P1a) Dahlmann-Waitz, no. 2998–3103. SBF

CULTURAL HISTORY: LITERATURE

P661a Scherer, Wilhelm. *History of German literature.* 2 v. Oxford, 1886. Tr. by Mrs. F. C. Conybeare from 3rd ed. of *Geschichte der deutschen Literatur,* 1883, 15th ed. by E. Schroeder, Berlin, 1922. (Bibliography.)

    b Francke, Kuno. *History of German literature as determined by social forces.* 1896. (Original title, *Social forces in German literature, . . .*) 4th rev. ed., N. Y., 1901.

    c Robertson, John G. *History of German literature.* N. Y., 1902.

    a. Ends with the death of Goethe; has never been excelled in brilliance and suggestiveness; but Scherer treats theories of his own as if they were facts. *b.* Offers an excellent bridge from the study of German history to that of German literature; broad in outline and in execution; based on sound knowledge and comprehension. Review, R. M. Meyer, *Euphorion,* 4:560, 1897; *Nation* (N. Y.), 63:331, Oct. 29, 1896. *c.* More conventional in its array of a host of authors and their works, but gives a very useful and reliable account of German literature from the earliest times down to 1900. Review, J. S. Nollen, *Modern Language Notes,* 19:17, Jan. 1904. GMP

CULTURAL HISTORY: ART

P681a Knackfuss, Hermann. *Deutsche Kunstgeschichte.* 2 v. Berlin, 1888.

    b Lübke, Wilhelm. *Geschichte der deutschen Kunst von den frühesten Zeiten bis zur Gegenwart.* Stuttgart, 1890.

    c Dehio, Georg G. *Geschichte der deutschen Kunst.* 1919–21. 2nd ed., 3 v. Berlin, 1921–24.

    d —— *Handbuch der deutschen Kunstdenkmäler.* 5 v. Berlin, 1905–12; 2nd ed., v. 1, *Mitteldeutschland,* 1914; v. 2, *Nordostdeutschland,* 1922; 3rd ed., v. 3, *Süddeutschland,* 1925.

    a. and *b.* Though somewhat out of date, still useful as works covering the whole history of German art. More modern accounts, including some in English or English translation, are indicated among the general histories of art in § B. Volumes on all the leading German artists will be found in (B686a) Knackfuss, *Künstler-Monographien.* *c.* Ripe work of a former Strasbourg professor, sound in scholarship, masterly in presentation, and accompanied by excellent illustrations. Review, Carl Neumann, *Hist. Zeit.* 123:81, 1921; 126:279, 1922. *d.* Each volume deals with one of the five regions into which the author divides Germany; within each are noted, alphabetically according to places, all the existing artistic monuments with brief notes on each; a kind of topographical dictionary of German art. SBF

BIOGRAPHY

The best biographies of the most important medieval emperors are: (P701) Hans Prutz, *Kaiser Friedrich I,* 3 v., Danzig, 1871–74; (P702) Friedrich W.

Schirrmacher, *Kaiser Friedrich der Zweite,* 4 v., Göttingen, 1859–65; for Frederick II also cf. (O205); (P703) Oswald Redlich, *Rudolf von Hapsburg,* Innsbrück, 1903; (P704) Emil Werunsky, *Geschichte Kaiser Karls IV und seiner Zeit,* 3 v., Innsbrück, 1880–92; (P705) Christopher Hare [pseudonym of Mrs. Marian Andrews], *A great emperor, Charles V, 1519–1558,* London and N. Y., 1917.

Other important biographies for the medieval period are: (P721) Otto von Heinemann, *Albrecht der Bär,* Darmstadt, 1864, an account of the beginnings of Brandenburg as an important territory; (P722) Karl Hampe, *Geschichte Konradins von Hohenstaufen,* Innsbrück, 1894, dealing with the end of Hohenstaufen rule in Italy.

Notable biographies of the Reformation period, in addition to those mentioned above (P243 and 261), are (P741a) David F. Strauss, *Ulrich von Hutten,* 1858, 4th ed., Leipzig, 1878; (P741b) Paul Kalkoff, *Ulrich von Hutten und die Reformation,* Leipzig, 1920 [Quellen und Forschungen zur Reformationsgeschichte]; valuable for German humanism; (P742) Georg Ellinger, *Philipp Melanchthon,* Berlin, 1902; (P743a) Samuel M. Jackson, *Huldreich Zwingli,* N. Y. and London, 1900 [Heroes of the Reformation series]; (P743b) Rudolf Stähelin, *Huldreich Zwingli,* 2 v., Basel, 1895–97; (P744) Erich Brandenburg, *Moritz von Sachsen,* Leipzig, 1898; (P745) Karl Lohmeyer, *Herzog Albrecht von Preussen,* Danzig, 1890.

Three very different treatments of the Wallenstein problem may be found in: (P761a) Leopold von Ranke, *Geschichte Wallensteins,* 1869, 6th ed., Leipzig, 1910, an old but still valuable general account; (P761b) Heinrich, Ritter von Srbik, *Wallensteins Ende,* Wien, 1920, a recent critical study; (P761c) Johann C. F. von Schiller, *Wallensteins Lager, Die Piccolomini, Wallensteins Tod,* Tübingen, 1799–1800, a great trilogy, of which, and of the translation into English by S. T. Coleridge (London, 1800), there are numerous later editions.

Good biographies of two men who helped the Great Elector create the Brandenburg-Prussian state are: (P781) Karl Spannagel, *Konrad von Burgsdorff,* Berlin, 1903; (P782) Bernhard Erdmannsdörffer, *Graf Georg Friedrich von Waldeck,* Berlin, 1859.

Notable biographical studies of men of the eighteenth century are: (P801) Edmond Pfleiderer, *G. W. Leibniz als Patriot, Staatsmann und Bildungsträger,* Leipzig, 1870; (P802) Alfred, Ritter von Arneth, *Prinz Eugen,* 1858, 2nd ed., 3 v., Wien, 1864; (P803) Paul Haake, *König August der Starke,* München, 1902; (P804) H. de Catt, *Frederick the Great, the memoirs of his reader, Henri de Catt, 1758–1760,* 2 v., London, 1916; Boston, 1917; abridged tr. by F. S. Flint from *Unterhaltungen mit Friedrich dem Grossen, Memoiren und Tagebücher von Heinrich de Catt,* ed. by R. Koser, Leipzig, 1884; (P805) Christian W. von Dohm, *Denkwürdigkeiten meiner Zeit, oder Beiträge zur Geschichte des letzten Viertels des 18. und des Anfangs des 19. Jahrhunderts,* 5 v., Hannovei, 1814–19.

In addition to the biographies mentioned above (P313–315) there are also for the regeneration period: (P821) Eugen Guglia, *Friedrich von Gentz,* Wien, 1901; (P822) Paul Bailleu, *Königin Luise,* 1908, new ed., Berlin, 1922; (P823) Bruno Gebhardt, *Wilhelm von Humboldt als Staatsmann,* 2 v., Stuttgart, 1896–99; (P824) Johann G. Droysen, *Das Leben des Feldmarschalls Grafen Yorck von Wartenburg,* 3 v., 1851–52, 11th ed., 2 v., Leipzig, 1913; (P825) W. von Unger, *Blücher,* 2 v., Berlin, 1907–08; (P826) Ernst Müsebeck, *Ernst Moritz Arndt,*

Gotha, 1914; (P827) Wilhelm Scherer, *Jakob Grimm,* first published in *Preussische Jahrbücher,* 14–16, reprint, 1865, 2nd ed., Berlin, 1885.

Besides the works listed above (P336–352) there are the following lives of important leaders of the last hundred years: (P841) Paul Hassel and Friedrich Meinecke, *Joseph Maria von Radowitz,* 2 v., Berlin, 1905–13, valuable for the revolution of 1848 and the reign of Frederick William IV; (P842) *Denkwürdigkeiten aus dem Leben Leopolds von Gerlach,* 2 v., Berlin, 1891–92, throws valuable light on Bismarck's early public life; (P843) Hermann Oncken, *Rudolf von Bennigsen,* 2 v., Stuttgart, 1910; (P844) E. Hüsgen, *Ludwig Windthorst,* Köln, 1907; and (P845) Ludwig von Pastor, *August Reichensperger,* 2 v., Freiburg, 1899, the best biographies of three of the most important parliamentary leaders in the new German Empire; (P846) Adolf Hausrath, *Treitschke,* N. Y. and London, 1914; (P847) Erich Dombrowski, *German leaders of yesterday and today,* N. Y. and London, 1920, tr. from v. 1 of *Das alte und das neue System,* new ed., Berlin, 1919; (P848) Bernhard Huldermann, *Albert Ballin,* Oldenburg, 1922, an interesting story of the rise of the Hamburg-Amerika Line and a biography of one of the Kaiser's ablest advisers.

Intimate pictures of William II and his court circle are given by (P849) Johannes Haller, *Aus dem Leben des Fürsten Philipp zu Eulenburg-Hertefeld,* Berlin, 1924; and by (P850) Count Robert Zedlitz-Trützschler, *Twelve years at the imperial German court,* London and N. Y., 1924, tr. by A. Kalisch from *Zwölf Jahre am deutschen Kaiserhof,* Berlin, 1923. Of little historical value except as an apologetic revelation of his own personality is (P851) Crown Prince Wilhelm, *Memoirs of the Crown Prince of Germany,* N. Y., 1922, tr. from *Erinnerungen,* ed. by K. Rosner, Stuttgart, 1922. The Kaiser's relations to the foreign office, to the diplomatic corps, and to international policy are revealed in (P852) Alfred von Kiderlen-Wächter, *Der Staatsmann und Mensch, Briefwechsel und Nachlass,* 2 v., Stuttgart, 1924, ed. by E. Jäckh.

For the post-war political and economic reconstruction, see (P871) Rochus von Rheinbaben, *Stresemann,* the man and the statesman, N. Y., 1929, tr. from the German; (P872a) Harry Graf Kessler, *Walther Rathenau, sein Leben und sein Werk,* Berlin, 1928; and (P872b) Walther Rathenau, *Briefe,* 2 v. Dresden, 1926.

Among biographies of men prominent in Austrian history, are: (P881) George B. Malleson, *Life of Prince Metternich,* London, 1888, 2nd ed., London, 1895; (P882) *Memoirs of Count Beust,* 2 v., London, 1887, tr. by H. de Worms from *Aus drei Viertel-Jahrhunderten: Erinnerungen und Aufzeichnungen, von Friedrich Ferdinand, Graf von Beust,* 2 v., Stuttgart, 1887; (P883) Eduard von Wertheimer, *Graf Julius Andrássy, sein Leben und seine Zeit,* 3 v., Stuttgart, 1910–13, invaluable for the foreign and domestic policy of Austria-Hungary in the second half of the nineteenth century; (P884) Albert, Freiherr von Margutti, *Emperor Francis Joseph and his times,* London, 1921, tr. from *Vom alten Kaiser, persönliche Erinnerungen an Franz Joseph I,* 1921, 5th ed., Wien, 1922, the best picture of the old emperor in his latter days, 1900–1917, by an intimate official; (P885) Freiherr von Musulin, *Das Haus am Ballplatz,* München, 1924, the recollections of an Austro-Hungarian diplomat of Croatian birth; (P886) Conrad von Hoetzendorf, *Aus meiner Dienstzeit, 1906–1918,* v. 1–5, Wien, 1921–25, a mass of valuable documents of all sorts, political and military, for the years 1906–14 during which Conrad was chief of the Austrian .general staff; (P887) Graf Ottokar Czernin, *In the World War,* London and N. Y., 1919, tr. from *Im Welt-*

kriege, Berlin, 1919; (P888) Prince Ludwig Windischgraetz, *My memoirs,* London and N. Y., 1921, tr. by Constance Vesey from *Vom roten zum schwarzen Prinzen,* Berlin, 1920.   SBF

GOVERNMENT PUBLICATIONS

The laws of the North German Confederation were published in (P901) *Bundes-gesetzblatt des norddeutschen Bundes,* Berlin, 1867-71; and of the German empire in (P902) *Reichs-gesetzblatt,* Berlin, 1871 ff. The proceedings of the Reichstag appear in (P903) *Stenographische Berichte des deutschen Reichstages,* Berlin, 1871 ff.

Official statistics on a great variety of subjects are published in the voluminous (P911) *Statistik des deutschen Reiches, herausgegeben vom kaiserlichen statistischen Amte (vom statistischen Reichsamte),* Berlin, 1873 ff., of which there is a convenient annual summary, (P912) *Statistisches Jahrbuch für das deutsche Reich, herausgegeben vom kaiserlichen statistischen Amte (vom statistischen Reichsamte),* Berlin, 1880 ff. which includes comparative statistics of other countries. Cf. also (J7) Sass, *Deutsche Weissbücher.*   SBF

ACADEMY AND SOCIETY PUBLICATIONS

Die Königliche Akademie der Wissenschaften in Berlin has issued (P921a) *Abhandlungen,* Berlin, 1815 ff.; (P921b, *Abhandlungen, Philosophische-historische Klasse,* Berlin, 1908 ff.; (P921c) *Sitzungsberichte,* Berlin, 1882 ff. Die Königliche Bayerische Akademie der Wissenschaften [zu München] has published (P922a) *Abhandlungen, Historische Klasse,* München, 1833 ff., and (P922b) *Sitzungsberichte, Philosophische-philologische-historische Klasse,* München, 1871 ff. Die Kaiserliche Akademie der Wissenschaften [zu Wien] has printed (P923) *Sitzungsberichte, Philosophisch-historische Klasse,* Wien, 1848 ff. Of less importance are the publications of the academies in Heidelberg and Erfurt, and of the royal societies of Göttingen, Leipzig, and Prague.

Der Verein für Hansische Geschichte has published (P926a) *Hansische Geschichtsquellen.* Halle, 1875 ff., and (P926b) *Hansisches Urkundenbuch,* Halle, 1876 ff.

La Société d'Histoire et d'Archéologie de Genève has issued (P936) *Mémoires et Documents,* Genève, 1841 ff.   SBF

PERIODICALS

The most important periodicals published in Germany which contain materials of historical value, because of their general scope, are listed in § B. To them may be added (P941a) *Archiv der Gesellschaft für Ältere Deutsche Geschichtskunde,* 12 v. Frankfurt and Hannover, 1824-74, continued as (P941b) *Neues Archiv der Gesellschaft für Ältere Deutsche Geschichtskunde,* 1876 ff., issued by the editors of (P71a) *Monumenta* for the publication of studies collateral to their editorial work. (P942) *Mitteilungen aus der historischen Litteratur, herausgegeben von der Historischen Gesellschaft in Berlin,* Berlin, 1873 ff., quarterly, ed. by F. Hirsch and others, which contains critical reviews; (P943) *Historisch-politische Blätter für das katholische Deutschland,* München, 1838 ff., semi-monthly, ed. by Guido Görres and others; (P946) *Deutsche Rundschau,* Berlin, 1874 ff., monthly, ed. by Julius Rodenberg and others, though dealing with literary and other subjects, contains many popular but valuable historical articles;

(P947) *Preussische Jahrbücher*, Berlin, 1858 ff., monthly, ed. by Rudolf Haym. Heinrich von Treitschke, Hans Delbrück, and others, contains numerous historical, political, and literary articles.

Periodicals devoted to legal and economic history include: (P956) *Jahrbuch für Gesetzgebung, Verwaltung, und Volkswirtschaft im deutschen Reich*, Leipzig, 1871 ff., ed. by G. Schmoller and others, which is indispensable for economic history and for its critical reviews; (P957) *Zeitschrift für die gesamte Staatswissenschaft*, Tübingen, 1844 ff. Also cf. (H956) *Zeitschrift der Savigny-Stiftung für Rechtsgeschichte*.

Germany maintains numerous local historical reviews, of which many are issued by local historical societies. Among the more important of these are (P961) *Zeitschrift für die Geschichte des Oberrheins*, Karlsruhe, 1850 ff.; (P962) *Westdeutsche Zeitschrift für Geschichte und Kunst*, Trier, 1882 ff., quarterly; (P963) *Annalen des Historischen Vereins für den Niederrhein*, Köln, 1855 ff.; (P964) *Zeitschrift für vaterländische Geschichte und Altertumskunde, herausgegeben von dem Verein für Geschichte und Altertumskunde Westfalens*, Münster, 1838 ff.; (P965) *Zeitschrift des Historischen Vereins für Niedersachsen*, Hannover, 1851 ff.; (P966a) *Archiv für die sächsische Geschichte*, 18 v., Leipzig, 1863–79 ff., continued as (P966b) *Neues Archiv für sächsische Geschichte*, Dresden, 1880 ff.; (P967a) *Märkische Forschungen, herausgegeben von dem Vereine für Geschichte der Mark Brandenburg*, 20 v., Berlin, 1841–87, continued as (P967b) *Forschungen zur brandenburgischen und preussischen Geschichte*, Leipzig, 1888 ff.; (P968) *Hohenzollern-Jahrbuch*, 20 v., Leipzig, 1897–1916, sumptuously illustrated; (P969) *Baltische Studien, herausgegeben von der Gesellschaft für pommersche Geschichte und Alterumskunde*, Stettin, 1832 ff.; (P970) *Altpreussische Monatsschrift*, Königsberg, 1864 ff.; (P971) *Zeitschrift des Vereins für Geschichte und Altertum Schlesiens*, Breslau, 1856 ff.; (P972) *Hansische Geschichtsblätter, herausgegeben vom Verein für Hansische Geschichte*, Leipzig, 1871 ff.

Among the more important Austrian historical periodicals are (P981) *Archiv für österreichische Geschichte, herausgegeben von der Historischen Kommission der Kaiserlichen Akademie der Wissenschaften*, Wien, 1848 ff.; (P982) *Mitteilungen des Instituts für österreichische Geschichtsforschung*, Innsbrück, 1880 ff., ed. by E. Mühlbacher.

For Swiss history there are the following: (P991a) *Anzeiger für schweizerische Geschichte, herausgegeben von der Allgemeinen Geschichtsforschenden Gesellschaft der Schweiz*, Bern, 1870 ff., bi-monthly, ed. by Gustaf Tobler; (P991b) *Jahrbuch für schweizerische Geschichte, herausgegeben auf Veranstaltung der Allgemeinen Geschichtsforschenden Gesellschaft der Schweiz*, Zürich, 1876 ff., annual, ed. by Gerold Meyer von Knonau; (P991c) *Zeitschrift für schweizerische Geschichte, herausgegeben von der Allgemeinen Geschichtsforschenden Gesellschaft der Schweiz*, Zürich, 1921 ff.; (P992) *Basler Zeitschrift für Geschichte und Altertumskunde*, Basel, 1902 ff.   SBF

SECTION Q

THE NETHERLANDS AND BELGIUM

Editor
JOHN FRANKLIN JAMESON

CONTENTS

INTRODUCTION

Little attention has been paid by Americans and Englishmen to Dutch and Belgian history except to the period illuminated by the genius of Motley, and there is a distinct lack of good books in English on the subject. Most good books on Dutch history have been written in Dutch and have not been translated into English, yet, since few Americans read Dutch, this section contains but a small representation of these volumes. It also contains mention of fewer books on the history of the Netherlands, Holland and Belgium, in the Middle Ages than might be expected, because in that period their history merges with that of Germany, of France, and of all western Europe in general. In this, as in so many other parts of medieval history, the reader must be on his guard against reading into the past the geography of the present day. Modern 'Holland' and Belgium are, in their present form and bounds, the creation of modern times in which their history is closely interwoven with that of other nations of western Europe. Consequently materials relating to the history of the Low Countries will also be found in §§ H, I, J, L, M, N, P.

The reader may be reminded that a narrative midway in length between the short manuals for Belgian history and the longer series by (Q121) Blok and (Q161) Pirenne may be obtained from the following chapters of (I121) *Cambridge Modern History*, 1:13; 3:6,7,19; 4:24,25; 5:7,8; 6:18; 10:16; 11:23; 12:9, chapters mostly by the Reverend George Edmundson; but these give little account of the important period, 1795-1815, when Dutch and Belgian history were merged in that of the French Republic and of the Napoleonic Empire. For Dutch and Belgian colonial expansion, cf. §§ K, V, W.

BIBLIOGRAPHY

Q1 Pirenne, Henri. *Bibliographie de l'histoire de Belgique, catalogue méthodique et chronologique des sources et des ouvrages principaux relatifs à l'histoire de tous les Pays-Bas jusqu'en 1598 et à l'histoire de Belgique jusqu'en 1830.* 1895. 2nd ed., Bruxelles, 1902.

A model volume; lists both sources and later authorities; indicates the books of most importance by asterisks, though without further comment. There is no similar manual for Dutch history. For the modern period of both Dutch and Belgian history, there are good bibliographies, lists without comment in, (I121) *Cambridge modern history*, 1:761-769; 3:798-809; 4:931-947; 5:809-818, 9:804, 850; 10:848-851; 11:956-958; 12: 888-890.   JFJ

Q2a *Bibliographie nationale, dictionnaire des écrivains belges et catalogue de leurs publications, 1830–1880.* Ed. by A. de Koninck and others. 4 v. Bruxelles, 1886–1910.

b *Bibliotheca belgica, bibliographie générale des Pays-Bas.* Ed. by F. Vander Haeghen and others. Gand, 1880 ff. [Pt. 195 issued 1921.]

c *Bibliographie de Belgique, bulletin mensuel des publications belges ou relatives à la Belgique, 1875 ff.* Bruxelles, 1875 ff.

In the absence of any comprehensive work or series of works listing all publications issued within the present Belgium, mention may be made of *a.* as a convenient reference work for publications during the first half century of the Belgian kingdom. *b.* and *c.* Current lists of all publications issued in Belgium.

GMD

Q3a Abkoude, Johannes van. *Naamregister van de bekendste en meest in gebruik zynde Nederduitsche boeken, welke sedert het jaar 1600 tot het jaar 1761 zyn uitgekomen.* 1762. Rev. ed. by R. Arrenberg, with continuation to 1787, 2 v., Rotterdam, 1788.

b —— *Alphabetische naamlijst van boeken, welke sedert het jaar 1790 tot en met het jaar 1832 in Noord-Nederland zijn uitgekomen.* Ed. by J. de Jong. 's Gravenhage, 1835.

c Brinkman, Carel L. *Alphabetische naamlijst van boeken, plaat- en kaartwerken die gedurende de jaren 1833 tot en met 1849 in Nederland uitgegeven of herdrukt zijn.* Amsterdam, 1858.

d *Brinkman's catalogus der boeken, plaat- en kaartwerken, die gedurende de jaren 1850-1920 in Nederland zijn uitgegeven of herdrukt.* Ed. by R. van der Meulen. V. 1-6, Amsterdam and Leiden, 1883-1920.

e *Brinkman's alphabetische lijst van boeken, landkaarten, en verder in den boekhandel voorkomende artikelen.* Amsterdam and Leiden, 1846 ff.

f *Nederlandsche bibliographie, lijst van nieuw verschenen boeken, 1856 ff.* Utrecht, 1856 ff.

a., b., c., and *d.* Taken together, these four works furnish a substantially complete list of all publications in the Dutch language issued since 1600. *e.* and *f.* Respectively, annual and monthly current lists of all publications issued in the Netherlands.

GMD

Library collections.—A large special collection of books in the Dutch language is in the Tank library, in the possession of the State Historical Society of Wisconsin at Madison. It contains some five thousand volumes, comprising many volumes of history of the Netherlands and European countries, together with the greater part of the legislative and executive enactments of the Republic and of the provinces of Holland, Zeeland, and Utrecht up to the year 1800. The collection has many eighteenth-century periodicals, and much material for the history of Dutch Protestantism. The Boston Athenaeum has a special collection of about fifteen hundred volumes on Dutch history; the Library of Congress, for Belgium and the Netherlands, about the same number. Princeton has five thousand manuscripts of the seventeenth and eighteenth centuries; the University of Michigan, much source material; the New York Public Library, eighteenth and nineteenth-century pamphlets; the New York State Library about a thousand volumes. Harvard University has good collections on both Dutch and Belgian history.

AHS

ENCYCLOPEDIAS AND WORKS OF REFERENCE

Q21 Prins, Anthonij Winkler, ed. *Geïllustreerde encyclopaedie.* 1870-82. 4th rev. ed., by H. Zondervan, 16 v., Amsterdam, 1914-22.

Standard Dutch encyclopedia.

JFJ

Q22a Molhuysen, Philip C.; Blok, Petrus J.; and others, ed. *Nieuw Nederlandsch biografisch woordenboek.* V. 1-6, Leiden, 1911-24.

b *Biographie nationale.* V. 1–24, Bruxelles, 1866–1928.

Excellent national biographical dictionaries compiled by competent scholars. *a.* Supersedes older works for the northern Netherlands; each volume alphabetized separately; about half completed. *b.* Prepared and published by (cf. Q81) Académie Royale des Sciences, des Lettres, et des Beaux-Arts de Belgique. Now complete to end of S.

JFJ

GEOGRAPHY AND ATLASES

Q41 Beekman, A. A., and others. *Geschiedkundige atlas van Nederland.* 's Gravenhage, 1914 ff.

Of all atlases of the historical geography of a single nation, this is the most elaborate and one of the most scholarly. Prepared under official auspices. Nearly eighty sheets thus far issued, making about half the atlas. Each section, when completed, is accompanied by a volume of learned letter-press.

JFJ

Q42 Jourdain, Alfred, and **Stalle, Léopold C. F. van.** *Dictionnaire encyclopédique de géographie historique du royaume de Belgique.* 1896. 2nd ed., 2 v., Bruxelles, 1896.

Mainly a gazetteer, yet containing a good deal of historical geography.

JFJ

Q43 Essen, Léon van der, and others. *Atlas de géographie historique de la Belgique.* Bruxelles and Paris, 1927 ff.

An atlas of high quality, with full historical letter press. In progress, but the fascicles are not proceeding in regular numerical order.

COLLECTIONS OF SOURCES: ARCHIVE PUBLICATIONS

Documentary historical publications of the Dutch government are prepared under the auspices of the Advisory Commission on National Historical Publications (Commissie van Advies voor 's Rijks Geschiedkundige Publicatiën), which was established in 1902 and proceeds upon an excellent systematic plan. It has published collections of sources for various periods and aspects of Dutch history, but the most important series is (Q71) *Gedenkstukken der algemeene geschiedenis van Nederland van 1795 tot 1840, 22* v., 's Gravenhage, 1905-22, ed. by H. T. Colenbrander, drawn from various foreign as well as Dutch archives. The royal family has published a very important series, (Q76) *Archives ou correspondance inédite de la maison d'Orange-Nassau,* ed. by G. Groen van Prinsterer and others 27 v., Utrecht and Leiden, 1835–1919.

Documentary historical publications for Belgium are issued by the Commission Royale d'Histoire, established in 1834, and connected with the Académie Royale des Sciences, des Lettres et des Beaux-Arts de Belgique. It has issued, in quarto and octavo series, (Q81) *Publications,* 179 v., Bruxelles, 1836 ff., containing materials for the various portions of Belgian history.

SHORTER GENERAL HISTORIES

Q101 Edmundson, George. *History of Holland.* Cambridge, Eng., 1922. [Cambridge historical series.]   (Bibliography.)

By the Englishman best versed in modern Dutch history; covers from 1361 to 1913; fills in excellent fashion, though somewhat drily, the need for a narrative in English of all Dutch history since the Middle Ages. Review, *A.H.R.* 27:815, July 1922; A. Waddington, *Rev. Hist.* 143: 259, July 1923.   JFJ

Q102 Gosses, Izaak H., and Japikse, Nicolaas. *Handboek tot de staatkundige geschiedenis van Nederland.* 's-Gravenhage, 1916–20.   (Bibliographies.)

These very competent scholars have divided their task—Gosses, professor at Groningen, covering the earlier period; Japikse, secretary of the Historical Commission, that from 1568 onward. They give a condensed political history of the northern Netherlands, the present kingdom, from Roman times to 1914, with quite full data on sources. Review, R. Putnam, *A.H.R.* 24:663, July 1919.   RP

Q111 Linden, Herman Vander. *Belgium, the making of a nation.* Oxford, 1920. Tr. by S. Jane from *Vue générale de l'histoire de Belgique,* Paris, 1918. [Ch. 13, 14, 15, written specially for the English ed.]

Good account for the reader who simply desires to place modern Belgium in the history of Europe, and has not time for (Q161) Pirenne. Beginning with the Belgae as seen by the Romans, the author traces the foundation of the principalities, the growth of the cities with the type of democracy developed, the consolidation with Burgundy, the effort to force the stoutly individual provinces into one form, the revolt against Spain, its reaction, the revolution, the unfortunate connection with Holland, and finally the establishment of the modern kingdom. Review, *A.H.R.* 26:355, Jan. 1921.   RP

Q112 Essen, Léon van der. *Short history of Belgium.* 1916. 2nd rev. ed., with chapter 'Belgium during the great war,' Chicago, 1920. (Bibliography.)

Useful in essential opinions. The author follows (Q161) Pirenne, but the outline is convenient for an English reader who wishes much in brief compass. It differs from (Q111) Vander Linden, in being half as long and in containing, in this second edition, eleven pages written after the armistice, thus bringing the narrative down to the evacuation of Belgium by the Germans. The writer, a refugee from a Belgian university, was made a lecturer in the University of Chicago during the war and thus knows the Americans to whose use the volume is dedicated. Review, *A.H.R.* 21:847, July 1916. RP

Q113 Cammaerts, Émile. *Belgium from the Roman invasion to the present day.* N. Y. and London, 1921. [Story of the nations.]

Popular account of the history of Belgian civilization and of national development. JFJ

Q120 Putnam, Ruth. *Luxemburg and her neighbors, a record of the political fortunes of the present grand duchy from the eve of the French revolution to the great war, with a preliminary sketch of events from 963 to 1780.* 1918. 2nd ed., N. Y. and London, 1919. (Bibliography.)

After a competent survey of the earlier history, the events of the revolutionary and Napoleonic period, the effects of the Congress of Vienna and of the later liberation of Belgium are well described. The latest edition has additions on the developments since 1914. Review, *A.H.R.* 24:665, July 1919.

JFJ

LONGER GENERAL HISTORIES

Q121 Blok, Petrus J. *History of the people of the Netherlands.* 5 v. N. Y. and London, 1898–1912. Tr. by O. A. Bierstadt and R. Putnam from *Geschiedenis van het Nederlandsche volk,* 8 v., Groningen, 1892–1908; 2nd ed., 4 v., Leiden, 1912–15. German tr. by O. G. Houtrouw, *Geschichte der Niederlande,* 6 v., Gotha, 1902–18. [(B161) Allgemeine Staatenge-schichte.] (Excellent critical bibliography of sources.)

The author long held the chair of Dutch history at Leiden. Among books covering the whole of Dutch history, it ranks as the standard account. The long story is told correctly, but somewhat drily and without illumination. In the English version the original eight volumes are reduced to five, in consultation with the author, by omission of local matter, while preserving general, and especially social and literary history. RP

Q161 Pirenne, Henri. *Histoire de Belgique.* 6 v. Bruxelles, 1900–26. German tr. by F. Arnheim, *Geschichte Belgiens,* v. 1–4, Gotha, 1899–1913. [(B161) Allgemeine Staatengeschichte.]

Absolutely indispensable to the student of Belgian history. The writer, the leading professor of history in Belgium (Ghent), traces with affectionate appreciation, but discriminatingly, the development of the region and nation now called Belgium and makes manifest the elements of unity it has possessed through the ages. The work is an adequately documented, reliable, eminently agreeable narrative, written with great skill and sound historical judgment. V. 1–4. Extend to 1648; appeared in French, 1900-11, and also in German, before the World War. V. 5. Covers period, 1648-1790; completed in November, 1915, but owing to the author's imprisonment by the Germans not published until 1921; v. 6, 1792-1830. Review, v. 2, R. Putnam, *A.H.R.* 8: 340, Jan. 1903; v. 3, 13: 340, Jan. 1908; v. 4, 17: 367. Jan. 1912; v. 5, T. Collier, 27: 294, Jan. 1922; v. 6, J. M. S. Allison, 33: 854, July 1927.   RP

MIDDLE AGES

Q251 Pirenne, Henri. *Belgian democracy, its early history.* Manchester, Eng., 1915. [University of Manchester publications.]   Tr. by J. V. Saunders from *Les anciennes démocraties des Pays-Bas,* Paris, 1910.

The translation makes a pleasant and valuable little volume which can be used advantageously in connection with (Q111) Vander Linden's political narrative. Belgian democracy was, from the inception of the towns and the acquisition of precious chartered privileges, very jealous of its own rights and nowise inclined to universal brotherhood.   Review, *A.H.R.* 21: 345, Jan. 1916.   RP

Q252 Ashley, Sir William J. *James and Philip van Artevelde.* London, 1883. [Lothian prize essay.]

Written in youth by one afterwards prominent as an economic historian. Sketches the history of Flanders before Jacques van Artevelde; describes his work from 1337 to 1345 in liberating the workmen of Ghent from the domination of capitalistic oligarchy, and the ensuing constitutional changes; shows how his son, Philip, made his victory permanent. Written with great economic insight and placed in proper setting of contemporary European history.   JFJ

Q253 Putnam, Ruth. *A mediaeval princess, being a true record of the changing fortunes which brought divers titles to Jacqueline, countess of Holland.* N. Y., 1904. (Bibliography.)

Jacoba of Bavaria, 1401-1436, countess of Holland, Zeeland, and Hainaut, whose four husbands were a French prince, a duke of Brabant, an English prince, and a Dutch lord, was an international figure and an interesting person. Her unsuccessful struggle with Philip V., duke of Burgundy, brought about the fateful entrance of the Burgundian house into Dutch-Belgian history. The author weaves around her a picturesque and entertaining narrative of the complications of the time. Review, B. Terry, *A.H.R.* 10: 917, July 1905.   JFJ

SIXTEENTH AND SEVENTEENTH CENTURIES

Q301 Motley, John Lothrop. *Rise of the Dutch republic, a history.* 1856. Latest ed., 3 v., N. Y., 1913.

The author, a brilliant literary Bostonian, spent several years of study in Dutch and other European archives before publishing. His enthusiasm and warmth of feeling and his admirable style combine with the intrinsic charm of the subject to make one of the most interesting books of history. The author's ardor for the Dutch and for his hero, William the Silent, often caused him to be less than just to Spain and to Philip II. The present-day reader would like a fuller treatment of constitutional and economic development. The work opens with the abdication of Charles V in 1555 and ends with the assassination of William in 1584.   JFJ

Q302 Motley, John Lothrop. *History of the United Netherlands, from the death of William the Silent to the twelve years' truce, 1609.* 1861-68. Latest ed., 4 v., N. Y., 1909.

Published while the author was American minister in Vienna; covers that portion of the Eighty Years' War with Spain during which the Dutch Republic was winning actual independence and an assured position in Europe. The scope is wider than that of (Q301); contains much diplomatic as well as military and naval history. The narrative is not less epic, for the hero is now the Dutch nation. JFJ

Q303 Fruin, Robert Jacobus. *Tien jaren uit den tachtigjarigen oorlog, 1588-1598.* 1861. 6th ed., 's Gravenhage, 1904.

Regarded as a masterpiece of one who was the foremost Dutch historian of his time. 'Ten years out of the Eighty Years' War' for Dutch independence.

JFJ

Q304 Motley, John Lothrop. *Life and death of John of Barneveld, advocate of Holland, with a view of the primary causes and movements of the thirty years' war.* 1874. Latest ed., 2 v., N. Y. and London, 1904.

Motley intended to broaden his field still more and write a history of the Thirty Years' War. He achieved only this connecting link toward that work. It recounts the history of the Netherlands republic during the Twelve Years' Truce with Spain and is mainly occupied with the struggle between two political and religious parties, the Orange party, headed by Count Maurice of Nassáu, and the party of the burgher aristocracy, headed by Johan van Oldenbarnevelt. The narrative is brilliant, but Motley is plainly a partisan of the latter. For a criticism of the work, cf. Groen van Prinsterer, *Maurice et Barnevelt, étude historique,* Utrecht, 1875. JFJ

Q305a Putnam, Ruth. *William the Silent, prince of Orange, the moderate man of the sixteenth century: the story of his life as told from his own letters, from those of his friends and enemies, and from official documents.* 2 v. N. Y., 1895. (Bibliography.)

b ——— *William the Silent, prince of Orange, 1533-1584, and the revolt of the Netherlands.* N. Y. and London, 1911. [Heroes of the nations.] (Bibliography.)

a. A lighter product than (Q306) Blok or (Q307) Rachfahl, but the fruit of industrious research in original sources and entertaining reading. Many picturesque details sometimes hinder the narrative, and the insight into political situations is not profound. Review L. M. Salmon, *A.H.R.* 1:329, Jan. 1896. *b.* Preferable for most readers. Compressed from *a* and rewritten with the use of additional material printed between 1895 and 1910. JFJ

Q306 Blok, Petrus J. *Willem de Eerste, prins van Oranje.* 2 v. Amsterdam, 1919-20. [Nederlandsche historische bibliothek, ed. by H. Brugmans.]

Compact biography of William the First; Blok discards the adjective 'Silent.' One of a series of finely illustrated monographs covering most periods of the modern history of the Netherlands. Corrects many errors, is very readable as well as authoritative, and should appear in English. Contains a careful, critical, yet sympathetic, commentary on all earlier biographies. RP

Q307 Rachfahl, Felix. *Wilhelm von Oranien und der niederländische Aufstand.*
3 v. Halle. 1906-08, Haag, 1924.

By a noted German scholar, professor successively in Königsberg and in Freiburg
(d. 1925). By reason of his death the work, which had reached the year 1568,
will not be carried further. It is very elaborate, especially on the side of William's
relations with Germany. It blends history and biography successfully, and is highly
authoritative. Review, H. Brugmans, *Hist. Zeit.* 100:153, 1908; R. Häpke, 136:
149, 1927.

Q308 Edmundson, George. *Anglo-Dutch rivalry during the first half of the
seventeenth century.* Oxford, 1911. [Ford lectures.] (Bibliography.)

Careful and interesting study of the conflicting economic interest of the English
and Dutch in the period indicated; makes clear that the Anglo-Dutch wars of the
latter half of the century were inevitable. The appendix contains a number of
short, useful monographs, e.g., 'The merchant adventurers,' 'The British troops
in Dutch service.' Review, R. C. H. Catterall, *A.H.R.* 17:398, Jan. 1912.
                                                                                                EWP

Q309 Muller, Pieter Lodewijk. *Onze gouden eeuw: de republiek der Vereenigde
Nederlanden in haar bloeitijd geschetst.* 3 v. Leiden, 1896–98.

'Our golden age'; excellent account, finely illustrated, of the political and cultural history of the Dutch republic in the seventeenth century.   JFJ

Q310 Lefèvre-Pontalis, Germain Antonin. *John de Witt, grand pensionary of
Holland, or, twenty years of a parliamentary republic.* 2 v. London, 1885.
Tr. by S. E. and A. Stephenson from *Vingt années de république parlementaire au dix-septième siècle, Jean de Witt, grand pensionnaire de Hollande.* 2 v. Paris, 1884.

Not a biography so much as a history of the foreign and domestic affairs of
the United Provinces during de Witt's administration. The result of long, profound, and conscientious study on the part of an able scholar, who has approached
his subject sympathetically; holds high position among studies dealing with the
seventeenth century. Review, J. A. Wijnne, *Rev. Hist.* 28:417, June 1885.
                                                                                                EWP

Q311 Geddes, James. *History of the administration of John de Witt, grand
pensionary of Holland.* V. 1. London, 1879.

Covers de Witt's life to 1654. Dutch historians regard it as unworthy of
the subject. Geddes's search through the manuscript and printed sources in the
Hague, London, and Paris was far from exhaustive; his appraisal of the material utilized was not always critical. Though he shed new light on the nature
of the early Dutch republic, he did not approach the problems confronting the
Dutch leaders with the sympathetic understanding they deserve. Review, P.
Bondois, *Rev. Hist.* 17:418, Oct. 1881.   EWP

EIGHTEENTH CENTURY AND AFTER

Q351a Van Loon, Hendrik W. *Fall of the Dutch republic.* 1913. 2nd ed.,
Boston, 1924. (Bibliography.)

b —— *Rise of the Dutch kingdom, 1795–1813.* Garden City, N. Y.,
1915. (Bibliography.)

a. The author, a scholar of Dutch birth, long resident in America, invests
with much interest a period commonly thought dull. The first quarter gives an

excellent sketch, much needed by English readers, of the political, economic, and social development of the Netherlands from the times celebrated by Motley down into the eighteenth century. Then follows the political history of the later period to the extinction of the old Dutch Republic by the revolutionary French in 1795. Written with much insight; bright and unconventional style. Review, H. T. Colenbrander, *A.H.R.* 19:616, Apr. 1914. *b.* With heightened faults of style, gives a brisk sketch of the events from 1795 to 1815—Batavian Republic, King Louis, incorporation in Napoleon's empire, liberation, and the founding of the modern constitutional kingdom.   JFJ

Q352a Colenbrander, Herman T. *De patriottentijd, hoofdzakelijk naar buitenlandsche bescheiden.* 3 v. 's Gravenhage, 1897–99.

b —— *De Bataafsche republiek.* Amsterdam, 1908. [Brugmans, Nederlandsche historische bibliotheek.]

c —— *Schimmelpenninck en Koning Lodewijk.* Amsterdam, 1911. [Brugmans, Nederlandsche historische bibliotheek.]

d.—— *Inlijving en opstand..* Amsterdam, 1913. [Brugmans, Nederlandsche historische bibliotheek.]

e Edler, Friedrich W. *Dutch republic and the American revolution.* Baltimore, 1911. [Johns Hopkins University studies in historical and political science, v. 39, pt. 2.]

f Wijk, F. W. van. *De republiek en Amerika, 1776–1782.* Leiden, 1921.

g Renaut, Francis P. *Les Provinces-Unies et la guerre d'Amérique, 1775–1787.* V. 1, 2, 3, and 5; to be 6 v. Paris, 1924–25.

a. The time of the patriots' is the period in Dutch history, 1776 to 1787, marked chiefly by the struggle between the partisans of the stadholder, favorable to England, and the patriot party, favorable to France. The author, now professor at Leiden, gives an excellent account, characterized by learning, intelligence, and insight. Appendixes contain nearly 300 documents from various European archives. *b, c,* and *d.* Give excellent treatment of the ensuing periods, 1787 to 1815; handsomely illustrated. *e.* Contains some account of the earlier years covered in *a;* for readers who have no knowledge of Dutch. *f.* Supplements *e. g.* More exhaustive than *e* and *f* but does not entirely replace them; important for extensive use of archive materials. Review, A. Hyma, *A.H.R.* 32:135, Oct. 1926.   JFJ

Q353 Sanger, Charles P., and Norton, Henry T. J. *England's guarantee to Belgium and Luxemburg, with full text of the treaties.* N. Y. and London, 1915.

The authors, a London barrister and a fellow of Trinity College, Cambridge, intended this little book 'to give all the information which will enable the reader to form an opinion as to the treaty obligations of England toward Belgium and Luxemburg.' It examines not only the words of the treaties but the historical circumstances under which they were made, and thus surveys the international position of Belgium and Luxemburg from 1815 to 1887. The texts of the five treaties of 1837, 1867, and 1870 are given.   JFJ

Q354 Corti, Egon Caesar, Count. *Leopold I. von Belgien.* Wien, Leipzig, München, 1922. Tr., *Leopold I. of Belgium.* London, 1923.

Leopold's wide family connections (e.g., uncle of Queen Victoria), his sagacity, and his experience, gave him great influence in Europe, and his biography is of value to European history in general as well as to Belgian history. Much use made of his correspondence with Archduke John and other Austrian public men.   JFJ

Q355 Whitlock, Brand. *Belgium, a personal narrative.* 2 v. N. Y., 1919.

Two moving volumes by a consummate literary artist, who was American minister to Belgium when the World War broke out, and who, in that position, performed invaluable services. Occupying this favorable post of observation until the United States also entered the war, he gives with great skill an authentic and unforgettable picture of the events and conditions. The detailed narrative of an acute and sympathetic eyewitness, fortified by numerous contemporary documents, it can never lose its value. Review, D. C. Munro, *A.H.R.* 25:107, Oct. 1919. For other works relating especially to Belgium during the World War, cf. (J277, 293, 346, 347a, 705).   JFJ

DIPLOMATIC AND NAVAL HISTORY

Q501 Vreede, George Willem. *Inleiding tot · eene geschiedenis der nederlandsche diplomatie.* 6 v. Utrecht, 1856-65.

Covers only parts of the field, but very carefully. V. 1–3. Relate to the period 1572–1650. V. 4–6. Deal with the diplomacy of the Batavian Republic and of the reign of Louis Bonaparte, 1795–1810.   JFJ

Q521 Jonge, Johannes Cornelius de. *Geschiedenis van het nederlandsche zeewezen.* 1833–48. 3rd ed., 5 v., Zwolle, 1869.

Standard work on Dutch naval history, to 1810.   JFJ

CONSTITUTIONAL HISTORY

Q531 Fruin, Robert Jacobus. *Geschiedenis der staatsinstellingen in Nederland tot den val der republiek.* 1901. 2nd rev. ed., by H. T. Colenbrander, 's Gravenhage, 1922. (Bibliographies.)

Of great value for political institutions of the Netherlands to 1795. Much of (Q102) Gosses and Japikse also is constitutional history.   JFJ

Q532 Poullet, Edmond. *Histoire politique nationale: origines, développements, et transformations des institutions dans les anciens Pays-Bas.* 2nd rev. ed., 2 v., Louvain, 1882-92.

Constitutional history of the whole area, with special interest in the portion now Belgium. Still highly regarded.   JFJ

ECONOMIC HISTORY

Q571 Diferee, Hendrik C. *De geschiedenis van den nederlandschen handel tot den val der republiek.* 3 pt. Amsterdam, 1905–08.

On Dutch commerce and commercial policy to 1795.   JFJ

CULTURAL HISTORY: RELIGION

Q621a Moll, Willem. *Kerkgeschiedenis van Nederland voor de hervorming.* 6 v. Utrecht, 1864–71. German tr., by P. Zuppke, *Die vorreformatorische Kirchengeschichte der Niederlande.* 2 v. Leipzig, 1895.

   b Hyma, Albert. *Christian renaissance: a history of the 'Devotio moderna.'* Grand Rapids, Mich., 1924. (Bibliography.) (I201g)

a. Standard work for the fifteenth century. *b.* Chiefly a study of the Brethren of the Common Life from 1380 to 1520. Review, E. W. Miller, *A.H.R.* 30:346, Jan. 1925.   JFJ

Q622 Knappert, Laurentius. *Geschiedenis der hervormde kerk onder de republiek en het koninkrijk der Nederlanden.* 2 v. Amsterdam, 1911–12.

Standard work for the period since the Reformation. JFJ

CULTURAL HISTORY: LITERATURE

Q661 Prinsen, Jacob. *Handboek tot de nederlandsche letterkundige geschiedenis.* 1916. 2nd ed., 's Gravenhage, 1920. (Bibliography.)

Latest of several excellent treatises in Dutch on the history of Dutch literature; a good work in moderate compass. JFJ

CULTURAL HISTORY: ART

Q681 Valentiner, Wilhelm R. *Art of the Low Countries: studies..* N. Y., 1914. Tr. by Mrs. Schuyler Van Rensselaer from *Aus der niederländischen Kunst,* Berlin, 1914.

Useful work which may be mentioned in the absence of a complete history of Dutch and Belgian art. The English edition contains some additional matter. JFJ

SOCIETY PUBLICATIONS

The chief Dutch historical society is the Historisch Genootschap te Utrecht, founded in 1845. Its earlier publications comprised three series: (Q921) *Berigten* (proceedings), 7 v., Utrecht, 1846-62; (Q922) *Codex diplomaticus neerlandicus,* 6 v. in 9, Utrecht, 1852-62; (Q923) *Kronijk* (documents mostly), 30 v., Utrecht, 1846–76. A general (Q923a) *Register* to all these was published in 1877. The Society's later series (Q924) *Werken* (documents), v. 1-109, Utrecht, 1863 ff., contains a wealth of materials from public and private sources. The publications of this society take high rank in respect to scholarship.

PERIODICALS

The leading Dutch historical journal is (Q941) *Bijdragen en mededeelingen voor vaderlandsche geschiedenis en oudheidkunde,* v. 1-48, Utrecht, 1877 ff., the organ of (cf. Q921) Historisch Genootschap te Utrecht.

The record of proceedings of (cf. Q81) Commission Royale d'Histoire was styled (Q971) *Compte rendu,* v. 1-70, Bruxelles, 1837-1901, and subsequently has been called (Q971a) *Bulletin,* v. 71-91, Bruxelles, 1902-27, for which 4 v. of general indexes, (Q971b) *Table générale,* covering v. 1-59 have been published. A general historical periodical for Belgium has recently been started, (Q972) *Revue belge de philologie et d'histoire,* Bruxelles, 1922 ff. JFJ

SECTION R

SCANDINAVIAN COUNTRIES

Editor

LAURENCE MARCELLUS LARSON

Professor of History, University of Illinois

CONTENTS

INTRODUCTION

The historical literature of the northern countries is relatively large and includes a number of individual works that embody the highest traditions of scientific scholarship. Nearly all these, however, have been written by native Scandinavian scholars and only a few are accessible in translated form. Among non-Scandinavian writers the Germans have shown the greatest interest in northern fields; such translations of Scandinavian historical writings as have been made are therefore likely to be found in the German language.

BIBLIOGRAPHY

No general work listing all Scandinavian publications and no bibliography of all Scandinavian writings on history or of all writings on Scandinavian history exist. The more important books dealing with the modern history of the northern countries are listed in the bibliographies appended to the various volumes of (I121) *Cambridge modern history.* Lists of current publications dealing

758

with Scandinavian affairs and subjects are published annually in (R946) *Arkiv för nordisk filologi.*

R1a Erichsen, Balder V. A., and **Krarup, Alfred.** *Dansk historisk bibliografi.* V. 1; 2, pt. 1; and 3, København, 1917 ff.

b Bay, Jens Christian, ed. *Denmark in English and American literature, a bibliography.* Chicago, 1915. [Danish American Association.]

c Bruun, Christian W. *Bibliotheca danica, systematisk fortegnelse over den danske literatur fra 1482 til 1830.* V. 1–4, Kjøbenhavn, 1877–1902.

d *Dansk bogfortegnelse for aarene 1841 ff.* Ed. by F. Fabricius, J. Vahl, and H. Ehrencron-Müller. V. 1–8, Kjøbenhavn, 1861–1921.

e *Dansk bogfortegnelse,* 1861 ff. København, 1861 ff.

a. The trustees of the Carlsberg Fund have undertaken to publish this bibliography of Danish historical literature to be issued in three volumes. *b.* Valuable list of some fourteen hundred titles of books and articles in the English language dealing with Danish literature, history, and public affairs. *c.* and *d.* Lists of all Danish publications. *e.* Periodical publication, cumulated annually, of all current Danish publications, with a supplement for Icelandic publications.

The Danish Historical Society publishes annually a list of historical publications in (R941) *Historisk Tidsskrift.* The literature of Iceland is dealt with extensively by Halldór Hermannsson in (R949) *Islandica.* LML

R2a Pettersen, Hjalmar. *Bibliotheca norvegica.* 3 v. in 4. Christiania, 1899–1918.

b *Norsk bogfortegnelse.* Ed. by M. Nissen and others. V. 1–9, with indexes. Kristiania, 1848–1923.

c *Aarskatalog over norsk litteratur, 1902 ff.* Kristiania, 1903 ff.

d *Norsk bogfortegnelse, 1883 ff.* Christiania, 1884 ff.

a. Descriptive catalogue of all books printed in Norway from 1643 to 1813 and of books in other languages relating to Norway. *b.* Norwegian literature, historical and otherwise, published since 1814, has been listed in this series of volumes prepared by various editors under this common title. V. 9. Continues the work to 1920. *c.* and *d.* Annual catalogues of works printed in Norway, published by the Norske Boghandlerforening (Associated Book Dealers of Norway) and the library of the University of Christiania respectively.

There seems to be no bibliography covering the entire field of Norwegian history, but an annual historical bibliography is now published in the Norwegian (R942) *Historisk Tidsskrift.* For the literature of the Middle Ages, Hermannsson's bibliographies in (R949) *Islandica* will be found of great value. For the modern period prior to 1814 bibliographical materials for Norway will be found most conveniently in Danish sources. LML

R3a Linnström, Hjalmar. *Svenskt boklexikon, åren 1830–1865.* 2 v. Stockholm, 1883–84.

b *Svensk bok-katalog för åren 1866 ff.* Ed. by C. J. Broberg and others, Stockholm, 1878 ff.

c *Arskatalog för svenska bokhandeln, 1861 ff.* Stockholm, 1862 ff.

d *Svensk bokförteckning, 1913 ff.* Stockholm, 1913 ff.

e Warmholtz, Carl Gustaf, and others. *Bibliotheca historica sueo-gothica, eller förtekning uppå så väl trykte, som handskrifne böcker, tractater och skrifter, hvilka handla om svenska historien, eller därutinnan kunna gifva ljus, med critiska och historiska anmärkningar.* 15 v. in 6. Upsala and Stockholm, 1782–1817. Index volume, Leipzig and Upsala, 1889.

a. List of all Swedish publications for the period indicated in the title. No single work or series of volumes lists earlier publications in Swedish. *b.* Continuation of *a.* *c.* Supplements *b.;* annual catalogue of works printed in Sweden, published by the Svenska Bokförläggareföreningen (Associated Publishing Houses of Sweden). *d.* Similar monthly book list published by the Svenska Bokhandlareföreningen (Associated Book Dealers of Sweden). *e.* Extensive bibliography of Swedish historical literature, including manuscript sources.

Annual lists of writings on Swedish history are published by the Swedish Historical Society in (R943) *Historisk Tidskrift.* For a review of publications relating to Swedish history published between 1903 and 1915, cf. article by A. Ganem, *Rev. Hist.* 133:287–318, March 1920.   LML

Library collections.—The most noteworthy collection of Scandinavian historical materials in the United States is the Icelandic collection [(R11) *Catalogue,* Cornell University Library, 1914] bequeathed by Willard Fiske to the Cornell University Library. Important collections are also to be found in the libraries of Harvard University (Maurer collection), Yale University (Count Riant collection), of the Universities of Wisconsin, Illinois, Chicago (Stensland collection), Minnesota (Bang collection), Texas (Palm collection), and of Augsburg Seminary, Minneapolis, (Heggtveit collection).   AHS

ENCYCLOPEDIAS AND WORKS OF REFERENCE

R21a *Nordisk familjebok, konversationslexikon och realencyklopedi.* Ed. by N. Linder and others. 20 v. Stockholm, 1876–99. 2nd rev. ed. by B. Meijer and T. Westrin, 34 v., Stockholm, 1904–22; supplement, v. 34–38, Stockholm, 1922–26.

b *Salmonsens store illustrerede konversationsleksikon.* Ed. by J. C. Blangstrup. 19 v. Kjøbenhavn, 1893–1911. 2nd ed., Kjøbenhavn, 1915 ff. (V. 23, issued 1927..)

c *Illustreret norsk konversationsleksikon.* Ed. by H. Nyhus and others. 6 v. 1907–13. 2nd rev. ed. by A. Krogvig, with title changed to *Aschehougs konversationsleksikon, Kristiania,* 1920 ff. (V. 9 issued 1925.)

Respectively the leading Swedish, Danish, and Norwegian encyclopedias; thoroughly revised editions of all are in course of publication.   HH

R22a *Dansk biografisk lexikon, tillige omfattende Norge for tidsrummet, 1537–1814.* Ed. by C. F. Bricka and others. 19 v. Kjøbenhavn, 1887–1905.

b *Dansk biografisk haandleksikon.* Ed. by S. Dahl and P. Engelstoft. V. 1–2; 3, pt. 1, Kjøbenhavn, 1920–26.

c Ehrencron-Müller, H. *Forfatterlexikon omfattende Danmark, Norge, og Island indtil 1814.* Kjøbenhavn, 1924 ff.

a. Biographical dictionary of great excellence covering Danish history from the year 1,000 to the close of the nineteenth century. It also serves the same purpose for Schleswig-Holstein prior to 1864, and for Iceland since the sixteenth century. *b.* Contains more names (about 6,000) than *a.*, but the biographies are usually shorter; illustrated. *c.* To contain sketches, with bibliographical details, of all Danish, Norwegian, and Icelandic authors, without regard to their literary importance, who lived before 1814 and whose writings have to any extent appeared in print. Vol. V (1927) carries the subject matter to Muusmann. LML

R23a *Biographistk lexikon öfver namnkunnige svenska män.* Ed. by V. F. Palmblad, P. Wieselgren and others. 23 v. in 12. Stockholm and Upsala, 1835–57; rev. ed. of v. 1–8 by K. F. Werner, 1874–76.

b *Svenskt biografiskt lexikon, ny följd.* Ed. by H. O. Wieselgren and others. 10 v. Orebro and Stockholm, 1857–1907.

c *Svenskt biografiskt lexikon.* Ed. by B. Boëthius. Stockholm, 1917 ff.

a. Begun under the direction of V. F. Palmblad, but the principal contributor was Peter Wieselgren, who wrote nearly half the biographies and contributed largely to *b.*, of which he was one of the editors. *b.* Supplement to a. *c.* Planned on a large scale. V. 9. (1930) Carries the subject matter down only to Cronstedt. HH

R24a *Norsk biografisk leksikon.* Ed. by E. Bull, A. Krogvig, and G. Gran. Kristiania, 1922 ff. (V. 4, to Guld, issued 1929.)

b *Illustreret biografisk leksikon over kjendte norske mænd og kvinder.* Ed. by Nanna With. Kristiania, 1920.

a. Deals with Norwegian persons from the earliest times down to the present day; treats of prominent men at considerable length. *b.* Norwegian 'Who's Who.' HH

R25 Carpelan, Tor, ed. *Finsk biografisk handbok.* 2·v. Helsingfors, 1903.

Biographical dictionary for Finland; in the Swedish language. LML

GEOGRAPHY AND ATLASES

R41a *Økonomisk-geografisk atlas over Norge med en oversigt over de kulturelle og økonomiske forhold sælig næringsveiene.* Ed. by P. Nissen. Kristiania, 1921.

b *Norges land og folk topografisk-statistisk beskrevet.* Ed. by A. N. Kiær and others. 19 v. Kristiania, 1884–1921.

a. Contains sectional maps of Norway with abundant detail and considerable supplementary data. *b.* Government publication describing in detail the various Norwegian counties; of particular value for its excellent series of maps. LML

R42a *Nordisk familieboks karta över Sverige.* Stockholm, 1919.

b Anrich, Carl J., and others, ed. *Svenska turistenföreningens atlas över Sverige, 48 kartor och 7 profiler samt fullständigt alfabetisktnamnregister.* Stockholm, 1923.

c Zetterstrand, S. and **Lagrelius, A.,** ed. *Sverige i 32 kartblad, skala 1:500,000, med fullständigt namnregister utarbetad vid Generalstabens Litografiska Anstalt.* Stockholm, 1916.

d *Generalstabens kartor över Sverige.*

e Hildebrand, E. and **Selander, N.** *Atlas till allmänna och svenska historien.* 4 pts. in 1 v. Stockholm, 1883.

f Ahlenius, K. and **Sjögren, O.** *Sverige: geografisk, topografisk, statistisk beskrifving.* 6 pts. Stockholm, 1908–22.

a. Contains twelve excellent maps of sections of Sweden which include detail for adjacent regions in Denmark, Norway, and Finland; index. *b.* Shows physical features; includes considerable general information. c. Admirable atlas of Sweden in sections based on d., which includes about 300 separate sheets embodying the most detailed information. e. Atlas of general and of Swedish history. f. Most complete and up-to-date descriptive account of Sweden and its resources.   GMD

R43 Braun, Gustav. Die nordischen Staaten: Norwegen, Schweden, Finnland: eine soziologische Länderkunde. Breslau, 1924. (Bibliography.)

Excellent brief survey of the geographical factors characteristic of these countries. A companion volume dealing with the economic factors is announced. Review, M. Jefferson, Geographical Rev. 15:333, Apr. 1925.   GMD

R44 Atlas de Finlande. 3 v. Helsinki, 1911.

Comprehensive atlas for Finland.   LML

R45 Nansen, Fridtjof. In northern mists: Arctic exploration in early times. 2 v. N. Y. and London, 1911. Tr. by A. G. Chater from Nord i taakeheimen, Kristiania, 1911. (Bibliography.)

This work, by an eminent Norwegian explorer and scientist, is a history of the age-long effort to penetrate the mysteries of the Arctic world. Begins with the journey of Pytheas into the northern waters in the fourth century B.C. and closes with the voyages of Cabot and Cortereal. Discusses a number of important problems in early Scandinavian history.   LML

COLLECTIONS OF SOURCES

R61a Danske samlinger for historie, topografi, personal- og literaturhistorie. Ed. by C. Bruun and others. 12 v. in 6. Kjøbenhavn, 1865–79.

b Langebek, Jacob and others, ed. Scriptores rerum danicarum medii aevi. 9 v. Hafniae, 1772–1878.

c Jorgensen, Ellen, ed. Annales danici medii aevi, editio nova. Kjøbenhavn, 1920.

d Gertz, M. C. Scriptores minores historiae danicae medii aevi. V. 1–2. Kjøbenhavn, 1917–22.

a. Collection containing miscellaneous source materials, mostly from the modern period. b. Three volumes of the Scriptores were published before Langebek's death; but the later editors made extensive use of the materials that Langebek had collected and had in large part prepared for publication. c. New critical edition of the Danish annals; well indexed. Review, E.H.R. 39:145, Jan. 1924. d. Includes the Latin historical literature of medieval Denmark, except Saxo and the Annals.   LML

R62 Diplomatarium norvegicum: oldbreve til kundskab om Norges indre og ydre forholde, sprog, slaegter, saeder, lovgivning og rettergang i middel- alderen. Ed. by C. C. A. Lange. 17 v. Christiania, 1847–1913.

Collection of charters and related documents from the Middle Ages and the sixteenth century.   LML

R63a Handlinger rörande Sveriges historia, ur utrikes arkiver. Ed. by A. Fryxell. 4 v. Stockholm, 1836–43.

b Svenskt diplomatarium: diplomatarium suecanum. Ed. by J. G. Liljegren, and B. E. Hildebrand. V. 1–5. Stockholm, 1828–65. Index to v. 1–2, by K. H. Karlsson, Stockholm, 1910.

c *Svenskt diplomatarium från och med år 1401.* Ed. by C. Silfverstolpe, Karl H. Karlsson, and Sven Tunberg. V. 1–6. Stockholm, 1875–1921.

a. Includes chiefly diplomatic reports and letters from the sixteenth and seventeenth centuries. b. Carries the publication of Swedish charters from 817 down to 1350. c. Published by the national archives; supplements b.; at present covers from 1401 to 1420. **LML**

SHORTER GENERAL HISTORIES

R101 Stefánsson, Jón. *Denmark and Sweden, with Iceland and Finland.* N. Y. and London, 1917. [Story of the nations.]

This attempt to gather the salient facts of Scandinavian history into a single volume has not been wholly successful; the treatment is very brief and is limited almost entirely to political events. The most satisfactory chapter is that devoted to Iceland, in which the author has brought together much important information on the early history of the Icelandic people. **LML**

R102 Ottosen, Johan. *Vor historie, den nordiske folkestamme gennem tiderne.* 3 v. København, 1901–04.

Though mainly a history of Denmark, takes extensive account of the entire Scandinavian field; also gives due attention to the proper relation of the northern countries to the larger events and movements of European history. Beginning with an introductory section tracing the ethnic and linguistic background of the Scandinavian peoples, the narrative is continued to the close of the war of 1864. In the matter of scholarship it takes high rank. **NHD**

R103 Bain, Robert Nisbet. *Scandinavia, a political history of Denmark, Norway, and Sweden from 1513 to 1900..* Cambridge, Eng., 1905. [Cambridge historical series.]

The author's chief interest lies in the struggle of the Swedes, first with the Danes and later with the Russians, for the control of the Baltic Sea. Beginning with the accession of Christian II, he traces the decline of Danish power, the swift rise of Sweden under the leadership of the Vasas, and the collapse of the Swedish empire in the reign of Charles XII. The greater part of the work is consequently devoted to the larger political events of the sixteenth and seventeenth centuries; for this period Bain's history is perhaps the best account in the English language. Though the author presents the subject from a Swedish point of view, he is usually fair in his conclusions and is never guilty of offensive partisanship. Review, L. M. Larson, *A.H.R.* 11:190, Oct. 1905; *Nation* (N. Y., 81:150, Aug. 17, 1905. **LML**

DENMARK

R201 Dahlmann, Friedrich C., and **Schäfer, Dietrich.** *Geschichte von Dänemark.* 5 v. Hamburg, 1840–1902. [(B161) Allgemeine Staatengeschichte.]

Written by two eminent German scholars; presents the German point of view on Dano-German relations. V. 1–3. Written by Dahlmann; cover the period from the legendary age to the partial dissolution of the Kalmar union in 1523. V. 4–5. By Professor Schäfer; carry the narrative down to the close of the Reformation period, 1648. Though less attractive in style than the earlier three, Schäfer's volumes show a more careful use of materials made available by Danish scholars and are of greater historical value. Review, G. von der Ropp, *Hist. Zeit.* 76:142, 1896. **NHD**

R202 Steenstrup, Johannes C. H. R., and others. *Danmarks riges historie.* 8 v. in 6. København, 1896–1907.

Most important general history of Denmark that has ever been written. Eight scholars, each the leading specialist in his particular period, have coöperated in producing it. It would be hard to find anywhere a work of equal volume covering more than a thousand years in which historical authority and literary presentation have been more successfully combined. The authors of the closing volume, A. D. Jörgensen and N. Neergaard, both Slesvigers, have won unstinted praise from German scholars for the manner in which they have handled the details of the Slesvig-Holstein question. Altogether, this history of the Danish realm is a worthy monument to Danish historiography. Review, D. Schäfer, *Hist. Zeit.* 83:329, 1899; 86:517, 1901; 95:519, 1905. NHD

R203 Friis, Aage, and others. *Det danske folks historie.* 8 v. København, 1926–1929.

A notable coöperative undertaking having as its purpose to write the history of the Danish people in the terms of our own time and in the light of the most recent historical research. The emphasis is placed on social rather than on political development. Eighteen scholars are engaged in the enterprise. Review of vol. 7, W. Westergaard, *A.H.R.* 33: 294–96, Jan. 1928; of vols. 4, 5, 6, 8, W. Westergaard, *A.H.R.* 36: 104, Jan. 1930. LML

ICELAND

R251 Gjerset, Knut. *History of Iceland.* N. Y. and London, 1924.

Only adequate history of Iceland in the English language; traces the social, economic, and political development of Iceland from the years of settlement in the ninth century to the present day. The story of the recent struggle for political independence is told in some detail and the institutions of the new state are clearly and adequately described. Review. M. W. Williams, *A.H.R.* 29:753. July 1924. LML

R252a Maurer, Konrad. *Island von seiner ersten Entdeckung bis zum Untergang des Freistaats.* München, 1874.

    b Poestion, Joseph C. *Island, das Land und seine Bewohner nach den neuesten Quellen.* Wien, 1885.

    c Herrmann, Paul. *Island: das Land und das Volk.* Leipzig, 1914. [Aus Natur und Geisteswelt.]

    d Thoroddsen, Thorvaldur. *Geschichte der islandischen Geographie.* V. 1–2. Leipzig, 1897–98. Tr. by A. Gebhardt from *Landfraedissaga Islands,* 4 v., Reykjavik, 1892–1904.

There is no important work in French or German covering the entire history of the Icelandic people. *a.* Classic among its kind, but deals with only the first four centuries of Icelandic history (to 1262). *b.* Largely descriptive; in its day a very creditable publication. *c.* Covers the same ground as *b.,* though somewhat more briefly; brings the discussion more nearly down to date and is a thoroughly reliable and useful summary. *d.* Gives more historical information than the title indicates; it is, in a certain sense, a history of Icelandic civilization down to the middle of the eighteenth century. The last two volumes of this work have not been translated. HH

NORWAY

R301 Gjerset, Knut. *History of the Norwegian people.* 2 v. N. Y., 1915. (Bibliographical foot-notes.)

Without question the most satisfactory account of Norwegian history that has thus far appeared in the English language. Believing that the proper theme of an historian is the life and collective activities of a people, the author has written with commendable fulness on such topics as political institutions, colonizing activities, intellectual culture, and religious movements. Includes an account of the Norwegian emigration to the American Northwest in the second half of the nineteenth century. The conflict with Sweden, which culminated in the revolution of 1905, is frankly presented from the Norwegian viewpoint, though without any trace of hostility to the Swedish people. Review, L. M. Larson, *A.H.R.* 21:578, Apr. 1916.

LML

R302a Sars, Johan E. W. *Udsigt over den norske historie.* 4 v. in 2. Christiania, 1873–91.

b —— *Norges politiske historie, 1815–1885.* Kristiania, 1904.

a. Marked an epoch in the study of Norwegian history. In opposition to the prevailing views of a common Scandinavian cultural life, Sars made a vigorous and scholarly presentation of nationalism. *b.* In a sense a continuation of *a.* The most important fact of this period was the dispute between Norway and Sweden as to their rights as partners in the Union, a contest in which Sars himself took an active part. The Norwegian side of the dispute is stated with a clarity and a precision that is not to be found in any other historical work of the time.

KG

R303 Bugge, Alexander, and others. *Norges historie fremstillet for det norske folk.* 6 v. in 12. Kristiania, 1909–17.

Compendious work; written by some of Norway's ablest historians; covers the whole field of Norwegian history from 800 to 1905. Based on the latest research, it gives a trustworthy account of the people's political history and cultural development. The first part, covering the period 800 to 1030, is the work of Dr. Alexander Bugge, who devotes particular attention to the activities of the Norsemen in the British Isles, a field in which he brings to light much that is new and valuable also to students of English history. The volume by J. E. Sars on the new development of Norway, and the struggle for national independence, 1814 to 1905, ranks with the best works of this eminent historian. The various phases of the union with Denmark are treated with the same scholarly ability.

KG

SWEDEN

R351a Hildebrand, Emil, and others. *Sveriges historia intill tjugonde seklet.* 11 v. in 6. Stockholm, 1903–10.

b Hildebrand, Emil, and **Stavenow, Ludvig,** ed. *Sveriges historia till våra dagar.* Stockholm, 1919 ff.

a. One of the more recent standard surveys of the entire field of Swedish history. It is for Sweden approximately what (L121) Hunt and Poole, *Political history of England* is for that country. While its scientific and literary value is, like that of every coöperative publication, somewhat uneven, none the less, this work represents much of the best in Swedish synthetic historiography. The authoritative and lucid account of the prehistoric civilization of Sweden, the new and unified treatment of the personality and the work of Gustavus Vasa, the excellent survey of the reign of Charles XII, the suggestive interpretation of eighteenth-century Swedish parliamentarism, and the very thorough study of nineteenth-century Swedish history are perhaps the most valuable portions of the work. The series is copiously illustrated and has numerous maps and reproductions of original documents. *b.* Revised edition of *a.* with chapters covering the period since 1900. To be completed in 15 volumes. Review, v. 2, D. J. Bjork, *A. H. R.* 32:844, July 1927.   EJ

R352 Watson, Paul B. *Swedish revolution under Gustavus Vasa.* Boston, 1889. (Bibliography.)

Most detailed treatment in English of this important movement. Though the author adheres to the traditional Swedish view of Christian II and the larger policies of that Danish king, he has, nevertheless, succeeded in bringing out the real (political and economic) motives that impelled Gustavus to break with Rome. The narrative is written in a somewhat rhetorical style and reveals distinctly the author's Protestant bias. Review, A. W. Ward, *E.H.R.* 6:383, Apr. 1891.   EJ

R353 Fletcher, Charles R. L. *Gustavus Adolphus and the struggle of Protestantism for existence.* N. Y. and London, 1890. [Heroes of the nations.]

'A political monograph rather than a genuine biography,' this work is devoted almost entirely to the participation of Sweden in the Thirty Years' War. Though based chiefly on non-Swedish authorities, it was, at the time of its publication, a useful addition to the rather scant literature in English on this subject. The viewpoint is that of a somewhat militant Protestant.   EJ

R354a Bain, Robert Nisbet. *Charles XII and the collapse of the Swedish empire, 1682–1719.* N. Y., 1895. [Heroes of the nations.]

b —— *Gustavus III and his contemporaries, 1746–1792.* 2 v. London, 1894.

In both works the statecraft of the eighteenth century with its endless intrigues is well depicted and the conditions in Sweden during the periods covered are adequately set forth. *a.* Only satisfactory monograph thus far written in English on the career of Charles XII. While emphasizing the heroic element in the great Charles, the author does not overlook the king's intellectual and moral qualities. Review, A. Hassall, *E.H.R.* 12:370, Apr. 1897. *b.* Though lacking somewhat in color, a comprehensive treatment covering not only the internal political conflicts of the age but also the very involved foreign relations of the Swedish monarchy. As a rule the author has been able to find plausible reasons for justifying the revolutionary measures of the king. Review, *Athenaeum,* 1:43, Jan. 12, 1895.   EJ

FINLAND

R401 Schybergson, Magnus G. *Geschichte Finlands.* Gotha, 1896. [(B161) Allgemeine Staatengeschichte.] Tr. by F. Arnheim, in somewhat condensed form, from *Finland's historia, 1887–89,* 2nd rev. ed., 2 v., Helsingfors, 1903.

The main theme is the material and intellectual development of Finland during the long conflict between Sweden and Russia. The political history of the nineeenth century, with its many problems due to continued pressure from the mperial government at Leningrad, is treated with evident caution, though from a distinctly nationalist point of view. Review of Swedish original, F. Arnheim, *Hist. Zeit.* 64:565, 1890. In its revised form Schybergson's history deals chiefly with the modern period and is less concerned with the general history of the Swedish monarchy. A supplementary chapter continues the narrative through the reign of Alexander III, 1881–1894. The author's recent volume in the same series, *Politische Geschichte Finlands, 1809–1919,* (Gotha-Stuttgart, 1925), emphasizes the recent period of liberation and national independence.   LML

R402 Fisher, Joseph R. *Finland and the tsars, 1809–1899.* 1899. 2nd rev. ed., with supplementary chapter relating to the events of 1900, London, 1901.

Devoted to the antecedents of the constitutional conflict between the tsar and the Finnish people which began in 1899. Though the problem is presented from a Finnish point of view, the author's discussion is objective and shows no undue hostility toward the Russian government.   LML

CONSTITUTIONAL AND LEGAL HISTORY

R531 Larson, Laurence M., tr. *King's mirror.* N. Y., 1917. [Scandinavian monographs.] (Bibliography.) Tr. from *Speculum regale, Konungs skuggsjá,* ed. by R. Keyser, P. A. Munch, and C. R. Unger, Christiania, 1848.

Norwegian didactic treatise dating from the thirteenth century; of general value for the light that it sheds on intellectual conditions in the North in the later Middle Ages. Of particular value is the discussion of kingship and the relation of church to state. Review, C. Peterson, *A.H.R.* 23:886, July 1918.   NHD

R532a Aall, Anathon and **Gjelsvik, Nikolaus.** *Die norwegisch-schwedische Union: ihr Bestehen und ihre Lösung.* Breslau, 1912. (Bibliography.)

b Jordan, Louis. *La séparation de la Suède et de la Norvège.* Paris, 1906. (Bibliography.)

c Mohn, Jacques Alfred. *La Suède et la révolution norvégienne.* Paris, 1906.

a. Elaborate study by two Norwegian scholars of the Scandinavian union, its essential character, and the problems to which it gave birth; the viewpoint is Norwegian. *b.* Objective and fairly definite statement of the same subject by a French student of Scandinavian affairs. *c.* Composed almost entirely of letters, somewhat revised, written from Stockholm to the *Journal de Genève* during the years 1903–1905. The viewpoint is Swedish.   LML

R533 Brækstad, Hans L. *Constitution of the kingdom of Norway.* London, 1905.

Translation of the Norwegian constitution, with brief historical introduction.
LML

R534 Fahlbeck, Pontus. *La constitution suédoise et le parlementarisme moderne.* Paris, 1905.

Study of the Swedish system of government in its historical development with particular attention to the growth of popular control since the adoption of the constitution of 1809.   LML

ECONOMIC AND SOCIAL HISTORY

R571 Drachmann, Povl, and **Westergaard, Harald.** *Industrial development and commercial policies of the three Scandinavian countries.* Oxford and N. Y., 1915. [Carnegie Endowment for International Peace.]

Important contribution to the economic history of the Northern countries by two eminent Danish economists. Covers the nineteenth century and the first decade of the twentieth. Review, G. Cassel, *Economic Jour.* 25:587, Dec. 1915.

LML

R572 Hill, C. E. *The Danish Sound dues and the command of the Baltic.* Durham, N. C., 1926.

The author states his purpose to be "to show the origin, the growth, the fixation, and misfit, and the abolition of the Sound dues." His volume is a very satisfactory presentation of an important subject, one that interested the capitals of Europe for four hundred years and even figured in the diplomacy of our own country. Review, W. Westergaard, *A. H. R.,* 32: 585–86, Apr., 1927; J. H. Wuorinen, *Hist. Outl.,* 19:80. Apr. 1928.

LML

CULTURAL HISTORY: GENERAL

R601 Leach, Henry G. *Scandinavia of the Scandinavians.* N. Y., 1915.

This handbook describes modern conditions and recent progress in the northern countries. Though not a large volume, it contains a mass of pertinent information and takes high rank as a work of reference. Review, *Nation* (N. Y.), 101:603, Nov. 18, 1915.

LML

R602a Montelius, Oscar. *Civilization of Sweden in heathen times.* London and N. Y., 1888. Tr. by F. H. Woods from 2nd rev. ed. of *Om lifvet i Sverige under hednatiden,* 1873, 2nd ed., Stockholm, 1878.

b ——— *Kulturgeschichte Schwedens von den ältesten Zeiten bis zum 11. Jahrhundert nach Christus.* Leipzig, 1906.

c ——— *Meisterstücke im ·Museum Vaterländischer Altertümer zu Stockholm.* 2 pts.. Stockholm, 1913.

a. By an eminent Swedish archeologist; covers the period from earliest appearance of man in Sweden to the close of the viking age. Though the author's conclusions have been modified on many important points by later research, his book remains the most recent scientific work in English on this subject. *b.* Revised and enlarged edition of *a.* Review, *Hist. Zeit.* 99:176, 1907. *c.* Twenty large plates with commentary.

EJ

R603a Bugge, Alexander. *Die Wikinger: Bilder aus der nordischen Vergangenheit.* Halle, 1906. Tr. by H. Hungerland from *Vikingerne,* 2 v., Kobenhavn, 1904–06.

b Williams, Mary W. *Social Scandinavia in the viking age.* N. Y., 1920. (Bibliography.)

The common theme of these two works is the state of civilization in the North at the close of the heathen age. They differ in this, however, that while *b.* describes the social relations in the northern homelands, *a.* is chiefly concerned with the newer civilization in the Scandinavian colonies. In its own field and subject, *b.* has no important rival in English historical literature. Review of *b.,* L. M. Larson, *A.H.R.* 26:496, Apr. 1921.

LML

R604a Weitemeyer, Harold S. L., ed. *Denmark; its history and topography, language, literature, fine arts, social life, and finance.* London, 1891. (Bibliographies.)

    b Carlsen, Johan; Olrik, Hans; and **Starcke, Carl N.,** ed. *Le Danemark, état actuelle de sa civilisation et de son organisation sociale.* Copenhague, 1900. Tr. from *Danmark's Kultur ved Aar 1900,* København, 1900.

These volumes are each a series of essays prepared by Danish authors, scientists, and artists describing in popular fashion the main currents and events in the national, cultural, and economic life of the Danish people during the nineteenth century. *b.* The more valuable; to it nearly a hundred specialists contributed; gives reliable information on every important phase of Danish life and progress in recent years. Review of *b.,* A. Friis, *Hist. Zeit.* 93:324, 1904.

NHD

R605 Rygh, Oluf. *Norske oldsager.* Christiania, 1885.

Description of the antiquarian treasures of Norway dating from the stone age to the viking period. Profusely illustrated; French and Norwegian text.   LML

R606 Konow, Sten and **Fischer, Karl,** ed. *Norway: official publication for the Paris exhibition, 1900.* Kristiania, 1900. (Bibliographies.)

Survey of the political, economic, and intellectual conditions in Norway at the end of the nineteenth century together with a brief review of Norwegian history. As an authoritative *résumé* of important data the work will commend itself to all readers who desire concise but reliable information.   KG

R607 *Sweden, historical and statistical handbook.* Ed. by G. Sundbärg in Swedish, 1898, in French, 1900, in English, 1904. 2nd ed. by A. J. J. Guinchard, in English, Swedish, and German, 2 v., Stockholm, 1914. (Bibliographies.)

This work is described in the preface as 'a handbook giving a cross-sectional view of the economic and cultural life of Sweden.' A brief outline reflecting the important achievements of recent Swedish historical scholarship is contributed by a popular writer, while the larger specialized fields of history, such as the constitution, law, literature, and industry, have been treated by recognized authorities in those fields.   EJ

R608a Mechelin, Leopold H. S., ed. *Notices sur la Finlande, publiées à l'occasion de l'Exposition Universelle à Paris en 1900.* Helsingfors, 1900.

    b Reade, Arthur. *Finland and the Finns.* N. Y., 1917.

These volumes deal with the larger features of social life in Finland, giving information on such subjects as agriculture, transportation, industries, finance, administration, and intellectual culture. The authors have drawn freely from historical sources, but the chapters devoted specifically to historical narrative are brief and of only slight value. *b.* Has a further value as a discussion of certain great movements which have reshaped Finnish society during the past century. Review, *Nation* (N. Y.), 106:351, March 28, 1918.   LML

CULTURAL HISTORY: RELIGION

R621a Mortensen, Karl A. *Handbook of Norse mythology.* N. Y., 1913. Tr. by A. C. Crowell from *Nordisk mythologie.*

    b Craigie, William A. *Religion of ancient Scandinavia.* London, 1914. [Religions ancient and modern.]

c ——— *Icelandic sagas.* Cambridge, Eng., and N. Y., 1913. [Cambridge manuals of science and literature.]

Brief but exceedingly useful manuals of a popular character, prepared by prominent students of Scandinavian culture in the Middle Ages.   LML

CULTURAL HISTORY: LITERATURE

R661 Mogk, Eugen. *Geschichte der norwegisch-isländischen Literatur.* 1893. 2nd ed., Strassburg, 1904. [(H22b) Paul, Grundriss der germanischen Philologie.]

One of the most satisfactory studies of early northern literature and literary history.   LML

BIOGRAPHIES

The number of important biographies in the English language dealing with Scandinavian subjects is not great. In addition to those listed above the following may be noted: (R701) Laurence M. Larson, *Canute the Great,* N. Y. and London, 1912 [Heroes of the nations]; (R702) Mary Hill, *Margaret of Denmark,* London, 1898; (R703) John L. Stevens, *History of Gustavus Adolphus,* N. Y. and London, 1884; (R704) Francis W. Bain, *Christina, Queen of Sweden,* London, 1890; (R705) John A. Gade, *Charles the Twelfth,* Boston, 1916; (R706) Sofie Elkan, *An exiled king, Gustaf Adolf [IV] of Sweden,* 2 v., London, 1913, tr. by M. E. Koch from the Swedish. For Charles XIV, Bernadotte, there are (R707) Christian Schefer, *Bernadotte roi, 1810–1818–1844,* Paris, 1899; and (R708) Hans Klaeber, *Marschall Bernadotte, Kronprinz von Schweden,* Gotha, 1910. A notable work of Norwegian biography is (R709) Gerhard Gran, *Nordmaend i det nittende aarhundrede,* 3 v., Kristiania, 1914; biographical sketches of the great leaders in Norwegian progress during the nineteenth century.   LML

ACADEMY AND SOCIETY PUBLICATIONS

For the study of prehistoric times, especially in Scandinavia, the Kungliga Vitterhets Historie och Antikvitets Akademien, besides occasional publications, has issued (R921a) *Månadsblad,* 10 v., Stockholm, 1872–1905, continued by the annual (R921b) *Fornvännen,* Stockholm, 1906 ff.

For nearly a century the Kongelige Nordiske Oldskrift-selskab (Royal Society of Northern Antiquarians) has published a valuable yearbook, devoted to early Scandinavian history (R926a) *Annaler for nordisk oldkyndighed og historie,* 23 v., Kjøbenhavn, 1836–63, and a continuation of it (R926b) *Aarbøger for nordisk oldkyndighed og historie,* Kjøbenhavn, 1866 ff. Extensive collections of materials for the history of the Northern countries have been published by (R927) Selskabet for Udgivelse af Kilder til Dansk Historie, [*Publications*], København, 1884 ff.; (R928) Samfund til Udgivelse af Gammel Nordisk Litteratur, *Aarsberetning,* København, 1879 ff.; (R931) Norske Historiske Kildeskriftfond, *Skrifter,* Kristiania, 1852 ff.; (R936) Svenska Fornskriftsällskapet, *Samlingar,* Stockholm, 1844 ff.; Kongligt Samfundet för Utgifvande af Handskrifter rörande Skandinaviens Historia; (R937a) *Samling af instructioner rörande den civila förvaltningen i Sverige och Finnland,* Stockholm, 1856 ff.; (R937b) *Handlingar rörande Skandinaviens historia,* 40 v., Stockholm, 1816–60, *Register,* 1865; continued as (R937c) *Historiska Handlingar,* Stockholm, 1861 ff.; (R938) Svenska Litteratursällskapet i Finland, *Skrifter,* Helsingfors, 1886 ff.   LML

PERIODICALS

The Scandinavian kingdoms have their respective historical societies, each of which publishes an historical review: (R941) *Historisk Tidsskrift*, published by Dansk Historisk Forening, Kjøbenhavn, 1840 ff.; (R942) *Historisk Tidsskrift*, published by Norsk Historisk Forening, Kristiania, 1871 ff.; (R943) *Historisk Tidskrift*, published by Svenska Historiska Föreningen, Stockholm, 1881 ff. Among the local historical societies which publish reviews or yearbooks the most important are Bergens Historiske Forening, (R944) *Skrifter*, Bergen, 1895 ff.; and Upplands Fornminnesförening, (R945) *Tidskrift*, Stockholm, and Upsala, 1871 ff. Useful materials especially bibliographical, appear in (R946) *Arkiv för nordisk filologi*, Christiania and Lund, 1883 ff. Important historical materials are also published in (R947) *Nordisk Tidsskrift*, Stockholm, 1881 ff. The American-Scandinavian Foundation in its review, (R948a) *American-Scandinavian review*, N. Y., 1913 ff., and in its series of (R948b) *Monographs*, N. Y., 1914 ff., publishes historical materials in English. Cf. also the bibliographies by Halldór Hermannsson in the annual publication (R949) *Islandica*, Cornell University Library, Ithaca, N. Y., 1908 ff.

LML

SECTION S

RUSSIA, POLAND, CZECHOSLOVAKIA, AND THE BORDERLANDS

Editors

ROBERT HOWARD LORD

Formerly Professor of History, Harvard University

and

ROBERT JOSEPH KERNER

Professor of History, University of California

CONTENTS

772

RUSSIA AND POLAND: INTRODUCTION

In the selection of titles of works to be listed in this section, emphasis has been placed upon the period since the beginning of the eighteenth century when the affairs of Russia and Poland began to be a matter of lively concern to the nations of western Europe. The extraordinary developments in both Polish and Russian affairs since the opening of the twentieth century explain, if they do not justify, the disproportionate number of titles on the most recent period in the history of the two peoples.

Though the great mass of works dealing with the history of Russia and of Poland are in languages unfortunately little known to western readers, it has seemed desirable to mention a few of them which are of outstanding importance. Most of the works listed, however, are those written in English, French, or German, or which have been translated into one of these languages. The unusually small number of titles in English appearing in this section is due to the scarcity of works of first-rate importance or of reasonable soundness of scholarship. Both French and German scholars have quite surpassed English and American writers in their contributions to the history of these two countries.

For the international relations of Russia and Poland, the reader should also consult § I, Modern history and § J, Contemporary history. Various works mentioned in § P, Germany; § R, Scandinavia; and § T, Southeastern Europe and Ottoman empire, are essential for an understanding of certain phases of Russian and Polish history. Works on Russian expansion and relations in Asia are also listed in § U, Asia.

RUSSIA: BIBLIOGRAPHY

S1 Kerner, Robert J. *Slavic Europe, a selected bibliography in the western European languages, comprising history, languages, and literatures.* Cambridge, Mass., 1918. [Harvard bibliographies.]

Excellent guide to the works in western languages not only on Russia but also on Poland and the other Slavic countries. RHL

S2a Mezhov, Vladimir Izmaïlovich. *Russkaia istoricheskaia bibliografiia, 1800–1854.* [Russian historical bibliography, 1800–1854.] 3 v. S. Peterburg, 1892–93.

  b Lambin, Petr Petrovich, and **Lambin, Boris Petrovich.** *Russkaia istoricheskaia bibliografiia, 1855–1864.* 10 v. in 6. S. Peterburg, 1861–84.

  c Mezhov, Vladimir Izmaïlovich. *Russkaia istoricheskaia bibliografiia, 1865–1876.* 8 v. S. Peterburg, 1882–90.

  d Bestuzhev-Riumin, Konstantin Nikolaevich. *Quellen und Literatur zur russischen Geschichte von der ältesten Zeit bis 1825.* Mitau, 1876. Also published in v. 1 of his *Russische Geschichte,* Mitau, Pt. 1–3, 1873–76, and (complete) *ibid.,* 1877. Both tr. by T. Schiemann from *Russkaia istoriia,* v. 1, S. Peterburg, 1872.

  e Artsimolovich, E. V., ed. *Ukazatel' knig po istorii i obshchestvennym voprosam.* [Guide to books on history and public questions.] S. Peterburg, 1910.

  f Voznecenskiĭ, S. *Programma chteniia po russkoi istorii. Ukazatel literatury.* [Program of reading in Russian history. A guide to the literature.] Petrograd, 1923.

The instruments of Russian bibliography are cumbersome, heterogeneous, and seldom of highest quality; but with the combined aid of the above, which are historical bibliographies and of the general bibliographies listed in (S3), one can make a nearly exhaustive survey of the historical literature published in Russia in books and periodicals down to 1887. While not faultlessly exact, these works are well-indexed and comparatively easy to use. *a.* and *c.* Equipped with copious and precious references to critical reviews of the works listed. *d.* Old but still very useful; describes the various kinds and collections of sources and the chief secondary works. For publications since 1887, one must fall back on brief, select bibliographies like *e.,* a usable volume compiled by a group of Russian scholars; on the historical journals (S941–947); and on the current general bibliographies (S3*d* and *f*). RHL

f. This handbook of 296 pages owes its special usefulness to the fact that it includes references to many books issued since the publication of the bibliographies listed above. GTR

S3a Sopikov, Vasiliĭ Stepanovich. *Opyt rossiĭskoi bibliografii.* [Attempt at a Russian bibliography.] 5 v. 1813–21. Rev. ed., 5 pts. in 2 v., S. Peterburg, 1904–06. Index, 1908.

  b Neustroev, Aleksandr Nikolaevich. *Ukazatel' k russkim povremennym izdaniiam i sbornikam, 1703–1802.* [Guide to Russian periodical publications and collections, 1703–1802.] S. Peterburg, 1898.

  c *Sistematicheskaia rospis' knigam prodaiushchimsia v knizhnom magazinie A. I. Glazunova, 1855–1866.* [Systematic catalogue of books for sale at the bookstore of A. I. Glazunov, 1855–1866.] Ed. by P. A. Efremov. S. Peterburg, 1867. Pribavleniia, 1867–1887. [Supplements, 1867–87.] Ed. by P. A. Efremov and V. I. Mezhov, 5 v., S. Peterburg, 1869–89.

d *Knizhnyĭ Viestnik.* [Book news.]   S. Peterburg, 1884–1915.

e *Knizhnaia lietopis'.* [Book chronicles.]   S. Peterburg and Moskva, 1907 ff.

f *Osteuropäische Bibliographie,* Breslau, 1928 ff.

Bibliographies of Russian publications in general. Unfortunately they do not combine to form a complete series. Of special value to the historian are *Supplements* 2–5 of *c*. which were edited by V. I. Mezhov and which also serve to supplement his historical bibliography (S2*c*). *d* and *e*. Weekly lists of all current publications. *d.* Incomplete, hard to use, with annual index sometimes, but not always. *e.* Since 1926 weekly; attempts to chronicle all new books and periodicals as registered at the state bureaus of the press. *f.* Valuable bibliographical annual; volume for 1923, covering years 1920–1923, appeared in 1928. RHL

Library collections.—Among American libraries Harvard has the most complete collection on Russian history; but there are also extensive and valuable collections in the Library of Congress (Yudin collection, especially for Asiatic Russia), the New York Public Library, and the libraries of Cornell (Schuyler collection), Yale (Sumner Smith collection), and the University of Pennsylvania (Charlemagne Tower collection). Columbia and Stanford University libraries have specialized in the collection of materials on the Russian Revolution.   AHS

RUSSIA: ENCYCLOPEDIAS

S21 *Entsiklopedicheskĭĭ slovar.* [Encyclopedic dictionary.]   Ed. by I. E. Andreevskĭĭ.   41 v. in 82, S. Peterburg, 1890–1904. 2 suppl. v. in 4, *ibid.*, 1905–07.   New ed., *Novy entsiklopedicheskĭĭ slovar, ibid.*, 1911 ff.

Published jointly by the firms of F. A. Brockhaus (Leipzig) and I. A. Efron (St. Petersburg), and usually cited as Brockhaus-Efron. The standard work. The new edition had reached v. 29 (to Otto) in 1917, but has not, apparently, been completed.   RHL

S22 *Bol'shaia sovetskaia entsiklopediia.* [Great Soviet Encyclopedia.]   9 v., Moscow, 1926 ff.

A general encyclopedia, embodying a re-valuation of knowledge on the grand scale from the Soviet-Russian point of view.   GTR

RUSSIA: GEOGRAPHY

S41a **Semenov, Petr Petrovich,** ed.   *Geografichesko-statisticheskĭĭ slovar rossĭĭskoĭ imperĭĭ.*   [Geographical and statistical lexicon of the Russian empire.]   5 v.   S. Peterburg, 1863–85.   (Bibliographies.)

b **Semenov-Tian-Shanskĭĭ,** V.P., ed.   *Rossĭia, polnoe geograficheskoe opisanĭe.*   [Russia, a complete geographical description.]   v. 1–3, 5–7, 9, 14, 16, 18, 19, S. Peterburgh, 1899–1914.   (Bibliographies.)

Large collaborative works.   *a.* Contains articles, partly of an historical nature, on every province, district, city, and larger village of the empire.   *b.* Planned to extend to 20 v., but has never been completed; consists of a series of excellent monographs on the great regions into which Russia may be divided, dealing with their geography, history, demography, economic development, etc. Copious maps; illustrations.   RHL

RUSSIA: ETHNOGRAPHY

S51a Niederle, Lubor. *La race slave, statistique, démographie, anthropologie.*
1911. 2nd rev. ed., Paris, 1916. Tr. by L. Leger from *Slovansky svet.*
V Praze, 1909. (Bibliography.)

b Šafařík, Pavel Josef. *Slavische Altertümer.* 2 v. Leipzig, 1843–44. Tr.
by Mosig von Aehrenfeld from *Slovanské starožitnosti,* V. Praze, 1837.

c Niederle, Lubor. *Manuel de l'antiquité slave.* V. I, *L'histoire.* Paris, 1923.
V. 2, *La civilisation,* 1926. [Collection de manuels publiée par l'Institut
d'Études Slaves.] (Bibliography.)

d —— *Slovanské starozitnosti.* [Slavonic antiquities.] V. 1–6, V. Praze,
1902 ff. (Bibiography.)

e Pypin, Aleksandr Nikolaevich and **Spasovich, Vladimir Danilovich.**
Geschichte der slavischen Literaturen. 2 v. in 1. Leipzig, 1880–84. Tr.
by T. Pech from *Istoriïa slavianskikh literatur,* S. Peterburg, 1879–81. V. 1
also tr. by E. Denis, *Histoire des littératures slaves,* Paris, 1881.

These works deal with the whole group of Slavic peoples. *a.* Offers an
excellent brief survey of each of these nations from the standpoint of anthropology, language, and general demography. *b.* Pioneer and epoch-making work;
remains even today of capital importance for the study of Slavic origins and
antiquities; though for the present state of the innumerable controversies be-
setting those fields, one will do well to consult *c.*, a good recent manual, or *d.*,
a monumental work which is still incomplete. *e.* Very notable work; reviews
the literary and cultural history of all the Slavs except the Great Russians.

RHL

RUSSIA: COLLECTIONS OF SOURCES

Of the multifarious and voluminous publications carried on by official bodies
(especially the Archeographical Commission, created in 1835, and the local
archeographical commissions), the numerous historical societies, and private
persons, a few outstanding examples follow. The Archeographical Commission
has published (S71) *Polnoe sobranie russkikh lietopiseĭ,* 23 v. Moskva, 1841–
1918, containing the old Russian chronicles; (S72) *Russkaia istoricheskaia
biblioteka,* 37 v., S. Peterburg, 1872–1924, comprising many narratives and documents of the Muscovite period; and a dozen other collections relating to legal
and economic history, and to the history of western and southern Russia.
Under the auspices of the ministry of foreign affairs, F. Martens published his
(S81) *Recueil des traités et conventions conclus par la Russie avec les puissances
étrangères,* 15 v., St. Pétersbourg, 1874–1909 (in French, or German, and Russian
in parallel columns), which is copiously supplemented by valuable documents
published in (S921) *Sbornik.*

Several of the great noble families have published important collections of
papers, such as (S91) *Arkhiv Kniazia Vorontsova* [Archives of Prince
Vorontsov], 40 v., Moskva, 1870–95.

Since the Revolution of 1917, there has been published a considerable amount of
source-material dealing with two subjects: revolutionary movements in Russia,
and the foreign relations of the Imperial Government. Some account of the
materials last named will be found in § J, Contemporary History. Of the materials
dealing with the history of revolutionary activities, the most important are: (S92)

Materialy po istorii vozstaniia Dekabristov (Materials on the history of the uprising of the Decembrists), v. 1–3, 5, 8, Moscow and Leningrad, 1926–27; (S93) *1905 god. Materialy i dokumenty* (The year 1905. Materials and Documents), 7 v., Moscow and Leningrad, 1925–27; (S94) *Padenie tsarskovo rezhima* (Downfall of the tsarist régime. Stenographic reports of the examinations and the testimony rendered in the year 1917 before the Extraordinary Investigating Commission of the Provisional government), 7 v., Leningrad, 1924–26; (S95) *1917 g. v Materialakh u dokumentakh* (The year 1917 in materials and documents), 7 v., Moscow and Leningrad, 1925–28. Some of the most valuable sources for Russian social history thus far published in any Western European language have appeared in (S96) *Quellen und Aufsätze zur russischen Geschichte,* 7 v., Leipzig, 1920–27; partial list of titles in *A.H.R.* 32:407, Jan. 1927. GTR

RUSSIA: SHORTER GENERAL HISTORIES

S101a Morfill, William R. *Russia.* 1890. 6th rev. ed., N. Y., 1904. [Story of the nations.] (Bibliography.)

b Beazley, Charles Raymond; Forbes, Nevill; and Birkett, George A. *Russia from the Varangians to the bolsheviks.* Oxford, 1918. (Brief bibliography.)

Both works cover the same field, giving a sketch of the whole history of the country. *a.* Full of material, sometimes irrelevant; incoherent and unsystematic. *b.* Has the faults of all composite works. The first section is thin and does not emphasize the points vital for the later development. The latter portions are more satisfactory, especially the treatment of modern times, but lack coherence. RPB

S102 Platonov, Sergieĭ Fedorovich. *History of Russia.* N. Y., 1925. (Bibliography.) Tr. by E. Aronsberg and ed. by F. A. Golder, from *Uchebnik russkoĭ istorii,* 2 pt., Sanktpeterburg, 1909–10, many later ed.

Model text-book; clear, concise, well-proportioned, scholarly; admirably adapted to a first study of the subject. Written before 1917, however, it had to be reticent on certain subjects; the last forty years are treated very briefly; English edition closes with 1923. Excellent maps; genealogical tables. RHL

S103 Pares, Sir Bernard. *History of Russia.* New York, 1926.

This is a fuller account than the English translation of (S102) Platonov, but in its later chapters runs rather too heavily to political matters, and gives too little consideration to such basic subjects as the land problem and the growth of machine industry. Review, A. S. Kaun, *New Republic,* 48:198, 6 Oct. 1926; and B.H.S., in *E.H.R.,* 42:654, Oct. 1927. Cf. also (B137b3) Makeev and O'Hara. GTR

RUSSIA: LONGER GENERAL HISTORIES

S121a Rambaud, Alfred N. *Popular history of Russia from the earliest times to 1877.* 3 v. Boston, 1879–82. Tr. by L. B. Lang from *Histoire de la Russie,* 1877; 7th rev. ed., continued to 1917, by Émile Haumant, Paris, 1917. (Bibliography.) New ed. of translation with continuation by G. Mercer Adam to 1904, 2 v., N. Y., 1904.

b Stählin, Karl. *Geschichte Russlands von den Anfängen bis zur Gegenwart.* V. 1. Stuttgart, 1923.

a. Has long passed for the best general sketch of the subject extant in any western language; by a great historian; brilliantly written; well-organized. Deals primarily with political and diplomatic affairs, though other topics are touched upon. Anti-German bias evident, also distinct propaganda in favor of French alliance. Treatment of the nineteenth century sketchy and unsatisfactory.

b. Based on a thorough and critical utilization of the results of Russian scholarship; more up-to-date than *a.* and, through the larger attention paid to internal development and social conditions, more in line with present historical tendencies. V. 1. Extends to Peter the Great. Review, F. Andreae, *Hist. Zeit.* 131:147, 1925. RHL

S122 Schiemann, Theodor. *Russland, Polen, und Livland bis ins 17. Jahrhundert.* 2 v., Berlin, 1886–87. [(B162) Oncken, Allgemeine Geschichte.]

Solid and readable book, based everywhere on original sources. Emphasizes particularly the international and diplomatic relations of the three countries. Livonia gets rather too much space. Fairly dispassionate, but author's Germanic sympathies crop out here and there. Well illustrated. RPB

S123 Kliuchevskiĭ, Vasiliĭ Osipovich. *History of Russia.* 4 v. London and N. Y., 1911–26. Tr. by C. J. Hogarth from *Kurs russkoĭ istoriĭ,* 4 pts., Moskva, 1904–10. Pt. 5 (1762 to 1907), Peterburg, 1921.

Fundamental work by a great specialist. Deals with internal dynastic, institutional, and social history of Russia, touching on the cultural side to some extent as well. Especially valuable for the growth of the appanage system, the rise of Muscovite autocracy, and the development of serfdom. Political and peripheral history neglected. The author is inclined to minimize the historical importance of the individual. The translation is most unsatisfactory. Review, G. R. Noyes, *Nation* (N. Y.), 97:310, Oct. 2, 1913. RPB

S124a Solov'ev, Sergieĭ Mikhaĭlovich. *Istoriia Rossii s drevnieĭshikh vremen.* [History of Russia from the most ancient times.] 29 v. Moskva, 1851–79. Last and most convenient ed., 7 v., S. Peterburg, 1893–97.

b Kostomarov, Nikolaĭ Ivanovich. *Istoricheskiia monografii i izsliedovaniia.* [Historical monographs and researches.] 1872–89. New ed., 21 v. in 8. S. Peterburg, 1903–06.

c Platonov, Sergieĭ Federovich. *Lektsii po russkoĭ istorii.* [Lectures on Russian history.] 1900. 7th ed., S. Peterburg, 1910.

d Pokrovskiĭ, M. N. *Russkaia istoriia s dreveneĭshikh vremen.* [Russian history from the earliest times.] 6th ed., 4 v., Leningrad, 1924.

These are, perhaps, the three most important general histories in Russian that have never been translated into western languages. *a.* Solov'ev's monumental work, which stops at 1780, is probably the greatest achievement of Russian historiography. Although based on certain theories no longer accepted by Russian scholars (e.g. the clan system as the key to the interpretation of medieval Russian history) it still retains eminent value as the most exhaustive and scholarly history of the country and a vast mine of source material, largely reproduced verbatim. *b.* In the form of detached monographs, Kostomarov's voluminous studies also cover nearly the whole of Russian history down to the nineteenth century. His cardinal theory—the federal nature of the early Russian state—has proved untenable; but his essay upon the origins of the autocracy, his emphasis upon the democratic factor in early Russian history and upon the distinction between Great and Little Russians, and his pioneer work in Little Russian history, were contributions of lasting value.   *c.* Standard text-book of Russian history, especially full and authoritative upon the sixteenth century and the revolutionary period, 1604–13.   SAK

d. Closes with the beginning of the twentieth century; frankly materialistic in its point of view, and very highly regarded by Russians of this school of thought.

GTR

RUSSIA: HISTORY THROUGH THE SIXTEENTH CENTURY

S201a Minns, Ellis H. *Scythians and Greeks, a survey of ancient history and archaeology on the north coast of the Euxine.* Cambridge, Eng., 1913. (Bibliographies.)

b Rostovtsev, Mikhail Ivanovich. *Iranians and the Greeks in south Russia.* Oxford and N. Y., 1922. (Bibliography.)

a. Work of monumental industry and erudition; aims to give a complete survey of all the material illustrating the history and civilization of southern Russia in ancient times.   Review, J. L. Myres, *A.H.R.* 19:843, July 1914.   *b.* Advances very interesting views as to the importance of the ancient Greco-Iranian civilization of the south, both from the standpoint of general European history and as helping to explain the precocious development of the early Russian (Kievan) state.   Review, D. M. Robinson, *A.H.R.* 29:114, Oct. 1923.   RHL

S202 Thomsen, Vilhelm. *Relations between ancient Russia and Scandinavia and the origin of the Russian state.* Oxford, 1877.

In the famous historical controversy between Normannists and Anti-Normannists, that is, between those who affirmed and those who denied that the original Russians, the Russian state, and the first Russian dynasty were of Scandinavian origin, these lectures have remained the classic statement on the Normannist side.   For Anti-Normannist arguments, see especially (S421a) Hrushevskyï.

RHL

S203a Leger, Louis, tr. and ed. *Chronique dite de Nestor, traduite sur le texte slavon-russe, avec introduction et commentaire.* Paris, 1884. [Publications de l'École des Langues Orientales Vivantes.] Best ed. of original by Shakhmatov, *Poviest' vremennykh liet,* Petrograd, 1916.

b Michell, Robert, and **Forbes, Nevill,** tr. and ed. *Chronicle of Novgorod, 1016–1471.* London, 1914. [(L921) Camden society, 3rd series, v. 25.] Best ed. of original, *Novgorodskaia lietopis' po sinoda nomu kharateĭnomu spisku,* Sanktpeterburg, 1888. [Imperial Archeographical Commission.]

These are the only Russian chronicles that have been translated into western languages, and two of the best.   *a.* The so-called Nestor, really a highly composite work, which forms the chief source for Russian history down to 1113, is one of the finest monuments of medieval historiography.   *b.* The Novgorodian chronicle gives a vivid picture of the great trading republic of the north. Review, R. H. Lord, *A.H.R.* 21:140, Oct. 1915.   RHL

S204a Curtin, Jeremiah. *Mongols in Russia.* Boston, 1908.

b Hammer-Purgstall, Joseph, Freiherr von. *Geschichte der Goldenen Horde in Kiptschak.* Pesth, 1840. (Bibliography.)

a. Really a narrative history of Russia throughout the Middle Ages, containing full details about princes, politics, and wars—and nothing else.   *b.* Should be consulted by those interested in the organization and internal history of the Mongol state in Russia.   RHL

RUSSIA: HISTORY OF SEVENTEENTH AND EIGHTEENTH CENTURIES

S251a Bain, Robert Nisbet. *Slavonic Europe, a political history of Poland and Russia from 1447 to 1796.* Cambridge, Eng., 1908. [Cambridge historical series.]   (Bibliography.)

b ———— *First Romanovs, 1613–1725.* London, 1905.

c ———— *Pupils of Peter the Great, a history of the Russian court and empire from 1697 to 1740.* Westminster, 1897.   (Bibliography.)

d ———— *Daughter of Peter the Great, a history of Russian diplomacy and of the Russian court under the empress Elizabeth Petrovna, 1741–1762.* Westminster, 1899.   (Bibliography.)

e ———— *Peter III, emperor of Russia, the story of a crisis and a crime.* Westminster, 1902.   (Bibliography.)

The author, for many years assistant librarian of the British Museum, was a learned man and an accomplished linguist, but a mediocre historian. His books, written in haste, carelessly, and without plan or system, are crowded with useless details and devote too much space to military and diplomatic history, court affairs, and biographical trivialities. They contain a great deal of information not readily accessible in English, and many well-drawn portraits. Bain was generally inclined to take a very favorable view of his leading characters.   *a.* Most important of his works; useful text-book, relating very fully the age-long and momentous struggle between Russia and Poland. Review, R. C. H. Catterall, *A.H.R.* 14:110, Oct. 1908.   *d.* Review, A. W. Ward, *E.H.R.,* 15:383, Apr. 1900.   RHL

S252a Waliszewski, Kazimierz. *Ivan the Terrible.* Philadelphia, 1904. Tr. by Lady Mary Loyd from *Ivan le Terrible,* Paris, 1904.   (Bibliography.)

b ———— *Les origines de la Russie moderne; la crise révolutionnaire, 1584–1614.* Paris, 1906.   (Bibliography.)

c ———— *Le berceau d'une dynastie; les premiers Romanov, 1613–1682.* Paris, 1909.   (Bibliography.)

d ———— *Peter the Great.* 2 v. London, 1 v. N. Y., 1897. Tr. by Lady Mary Loyd from *Pierre le Grand,* Paris, 1897.

e ———— *L'héritage de Pierre le Grand, règnes des femmes, gouvernement des favoris, 1725–1741.* Paris, 1900.

f ———— *La dernière des Romanov, Élisabeth Ire, impératrice de Russie, 1741–1762.* Paris, 1902.

g ———— *Romance of an empress, Catherine II of Russia.* N. Y., 1894. Tr. from *Le roman d'une impératrice, Catherine II de Russie,* Paris, 1893. (Bibliography in French ed.)

h ———— *Story of a throne, Catherine II of Russia.* 2 v. London, 1895. Tr. from *Autour d'un trône, Catherine II de Russie,* Paris, 1894.

i ———— *Paul the First of Russia.* London, 1913. Tr. from *Le fils de la grande Catherine, Paul Ier empereur de Russie,* Paris, 1912. (Bibliography in French ed.)

j ———— *Le règne d'Alexandre Ier.* 3 v., Paris, 1923–25.   (Bibliography.)

Waliszewski, a Pole long resident in France, has produced a series of monographs covering nearly three centuries of Russian history. Based on extensive researches, admirably fair, and full of originality and insight, his books are also written in brilliant style and make excellent reading. Avoiding the usual tedious details of wars and diplomacy, he excels in portraying such characters as Catherine II or Peter and in analyzing political and social conditions. Unfortunately, however, he sometimes seems to sacrifice truth to romanticism, sober fact to epigram. Reviews, of *c*, O. Wardrop. *E.H.R.* 25:173, Jan. 1910; of *f*, H. Hauser, *Rev. Hist.* 80:345, Nov. 1902; of *g*, L. Farges, *ibid.* 51:338, Mar. 1893.

RHL

S253 Schuyler, Eugene. *Peter the Great.* 2 v. N. Y., 1884.

Perhaps the best work on Russian history yet produced by an American. Schuyler was not a Motley or a Prescott; but he thoroughly mastered the vast literature of his subject, he did some archival research, and his biography of Peter, though rather overloaded with anecdotes, is accurate, judicious, substantial, and entertaining.

RHL

S254a Brückner, Alexander. *Katharina die Zweite.* Berlin, 1883. [(B162) Oncken, Allgemeine Geschichte.]

    b Bil'Basov, Vasiliĭ Aleksieevich. *Geschichte Katharina II.* 4 pt. in 3 v. Berlin, 1891–93. Tr. by M. von Pezold and 'P. v. R.' from v. 1 and 2 of *Istorïia Ekateriny Vtoroi,* S. Peterburg, 1890–91; rev. ed., 2 v., Berlin, 1900.

    c —— *Katharina II, Kaiserin von Russland, im Urtheile der Weltliteratur.* 2 v. Berlin, 1897. Tr. from v. 12 of *Istorïia Ekateriny Vtoroĭ,* Berlin, 1900, which was the first publication of the original Russian text.

a. Learned, dry, and ill-proportioned; useful chiefly in respect to Catherine's personal history, character, and foreign policy. *b.* Planned on a grand scale; promised to be the standard life of the empress; has remained a torso, owing to difficulties with the censorship; carries the narrative only to 1764. *c.* Immense critical bibliography of the literature on Catherine II.

RHL

RUSSIA: HISTORY OF NINETEENTH CENTURY

S301a Skrine, Francis H. *Expansion of Russia, 1815–1900.* 1903. 3rd ed., Cambridge, Eng., 1915. [Cambridge historical series.] (Bibliography.)

    b Kornilov, Aleksandr Aleksandrovich. *Modern Russian history . . . from the age of Catherine the Great to the present.* 1917. Rev. ed., 2 v. in 1, N. Y., 1924. Tr. by A. S. Kaun, with continuation to 1917, from *Kurs russkoĭ istorïi XIX vieka,* Moskva. 1912. (Bibliography.)

Both these histories of Russia in the nineteenth century are clear, objective, and scholarly. Both deal mainly with politics. *a.* Much the better on foreign policy, wars, and territorial expansion, which Kornilov treats only in the most perfunctory fashion. Review, A. C. Coolidge, *A.H.R.* 9:617, Apr. 1904. *b.* Though wretchedly translated, an excellent basis for a detailed intensive study of the internal development during this period, on which subject Skrine is inadequate. Review, A. C. Coolidge, *A.H.R.* 23:148, Oct. 1917.

RHL

S302 Schiemann, Theodor. *Geschichte Russlands unter Kaiser Nikolaus I.* 4 v. Berlin, 1904-19.

Professor Schiemann's *magnum opus*—based largely on archive materials, soberly and judiciously written, and scrupulously fair—is likely to remain the classic work on the age of Nicholas.   V. 1.   Devoted to Alexander I.   Review, J. B. Bury, *E.H.R.* 24:385, Apr. 1909; 28:792, Oct. 1913.   RHL

RUSSIA: HISTORY IN THE TWENTIETH CENTURY

S351a Miliukov, Pavel Nikolaevich. *Russia and its crisis.* Chicago, 1905. [Crane lectures.]

b ——— *Essais sur l'histoire de la civilisation russe.* Paris, 1901. Tr. by P. Dramas and D. Soskice of 1st pt. of *Ocherki po istorïi russkoï kul'tury,* 3 pts. in 4 v., S. Peterburg, 1896–1903.   (Bibliographies.)

c ——— *Russia to-day and to-morrow.* N. Y., 1922.

Excellent retrospects of Russia's historical development viewed in the large. *a.* Describes the growth of the empire, its political and religious traditions, and the nationalist, liberal, socialist, and revolutionary movements.   Review, C. E. Fryer, *A.H.R.* 11:678, Apr. 1906.   *b.* Surveys successively the growth of the population, and the economic, political, and social evolution.   Review, O. Wardrop, *A.H.R.* 17:808, Oct. 1902.   SAK

c. Chiefly a review of the second Russian revolution, 1917, and the Bolshevik experiment by a veteran leader of Russian Liberalism.   Review, S. A. Korff, *A.H.R.* 28:126, Oct. 1922.   RHL

S352a Kulczycki, Ludwik. *Geschichte der russischen Revolution.* 3 v. Gotha, 1910–14.   Tr. by A. Schapire-Neurath from *Rewolucya rosyjska,* Lwów, 1908.

b Olgin, Moissaye J. *Soul of the Russian revolution.* N. Y., 1917.

Both these works review the history of the revolutionary movement in Russia from a standpoint decidedly sympathetic to the revolutionaries.   *a.* Kulczycki, an erudite and dispassionate scholar, marshals the long array of revolutionary thinkers, schools, and parties of the nineteenth century, with elaborate analyses of their theories, tactics, and mutual relations.   Review, A. C. Coolidge, *A.H.R.* 16:819, July 1911; 17:378, Jan. 1912.   *b.* More popular; devoted mainly to a vivid narrative of the first revolution, 1905, and the period down to the outbreak of the second, 1917.   SNH

S353a Baring, Maurice. *A year in Russia.* London, 1907.

b ——— *Russian people.* 1911. 2d ed., London, 1914.

c Pares, Sir Bernard. *Russia and reform.* London, 1907.

a. Vivid psychological picture of the sentiments of a capable foreign observer in Russia in 1905.   *b.* and *c.* Attempts to interpret to English readers the causes of the first Russian revolution and the reasons for its failure.   For both observers they are social (lack of cohesion) and psychological (extreme individualism combined with lack of the pressure of public opinion).   The discussion is preceded in each case by an historical sketch, but Baring discusses the subject throughout in its historical continuity, while Pares deals primarily with the reactions of the various classes of society.   *b.* The more readable.   *c.* The more solid.   RPB

S354 Martov, L., and others.   *Obshchestvennoe dvizhenïe v nachalïe XX⁹⁰ stolietïia.*   [Social movement at the beginning of the 20th century.]   4 v., Moskva, 1909–14.

This collaborative socialist work forms the most comprehensive and detailed history yet published of the revolution of 1905. Though strongly colored by partisanship, it offers an unrivalled mine of information, especially on conditions and movements among the workingmen, the peasants, the radical *intelligentsia* and the non-Russian nationalities.   RHL

S355a Dillon, Emile J. *Eclipse of Russia.* N. Y., 1918.

b Hötzsch, Otto. *Russland, eine Einführung auf Grund seiner Geschichte vom japanischen Kriege bis zum Weltkrieg.* 1913. 2nd rev. ed., Berlin, 1917. (Bibliography.)

Both books review the reign of Nicholas II: *a.,* in a rambling, journalistic way; *b.,* in systematic and scholarly fashion. *a.* Dillon, long the dean of foreign correspondents in Russia and the close friend of Count Witte, has very interesting information on international politics, particularly on the tsar's relations with the kaiser. Review, S. B. Fay, *A.H.R.* 24:475, Apr. 1919. *b.* Hötzsch passes as the leading German expert on Russia. Review, K. Stählin, *Hist. Zeit.* 119:283, 1919.   SAK

S356a Paléologue, Georges Maurice. *An ambassador's memoirs.* 3 v. London and N. Y., 1923–25. Tr. by F. A. Holt from *La Russie des tsars pendant la grande guerre.* 3 v, Paris, 1922.

b Wilcox, E. H. *Russia's ruin.* London and N. Y., 1919.

c Williams, Mrs. Ariadna (Tyrkóva). *From liberty to Brest-Litovsk, the first year of the Russian revolution.* London, 1919.

a. Day-to-day observations of the French ambassador from July 20, 1914 to May 17, 1917. Extremely interesting, but neither unbiased nor altogether candid. Review, S. B. Fay, *A.H.R.* 28:319, Jan. 1923. *b.* Wilcox, an Englishman long resident in Russia, gives his personal reaction upon events during the war and the revolution down to the beginning of 1918. Makes extensive use of Russian newspapers and published documents. *c.* Mrs. Williams, a prominent Russian social worker and an active member of the liberal Cadet party, writes from a standpoint inevitably influenced by the bitter conflict between liberals and socialists. Nevertheless, this detailed, well-documented narrative is of much interest, especially for the early period of the revolution of 1917.   SNH

S357a Antonelli, Étienne. *Bolshevik Russia.* N. Y., 1920. Tr. by C. A. Carroll, from *La Russie bolchéviste,* Paris, 1919.

b Ransome, Arthur. *Russia in 1919.* N. Y., 1919. Also issued as *Six weeks in Russia in 1919.* London, 1919.

**c ——— ** *Crisis in Russia.* London, 1921.

d Russell, Bertrand. *Bolshevism; practice and theory.* N. Y., 1920.

e Zagorskiĭ, Simon. *La république des Soviets, bilan économique.* Paris, 1921.

f Mackenzie, Frederick A. *Russia before dawn.* London, 1923.

g International Labour Office. *Labour conditions in soviet Russia, systematic questionnaire and bibliography prepared for the mission of enquiry in Russia.* London, 1920. (Bibliography.)

a. Exceptionally impartial and well-balanced analysis of the principles and methods of the bolsheviks, based chiefly on their own statements. Covers only the first year of the communist régime. *b.* and *c.* Ransome, a British journalist favorably disposed to the bolsheviks from the outset, spent a long time in soviet Russia and enjoyed unusually close contact with its leaders. Hence his surveys of the situation during two successive years have a peculiar interest and value. *c.* The more objective in statement. *d.* Bertrand Russell went to Russia frankly in sympathy with the bolshevik experiment. He found much to oppose in the dictatorship of the proletariat, as it had developed by 1920. Among the many visitors to soviet Russia, this writer was especially well-equipped to interpret the political philosophy of bolshevism to western readers. Review, *a., b., c., d.,* G. T. Robinson, *Pol. Sci. Quart.* 36:454, Sept. 1921. *e.* Most complete and well-documented study that has yet appeared of the economic aspects of the communist régime; with unfavorable conclusions. *f.* Probably the best picture of conditions since the adoption of the 'new economic policy,' 1921–23. *g.* The great merit of this volume is that it contains a nearly exhaustive bibliography of soviet Russia through 1919.   SNH

S358a. Kerensky, Alexander. *The catastrophe.* N. Y. and London, 1927.

b Trotzkiï, Lev D. [Pseud. of Bronstein, Lev D.] *History of the russian revolution to Brest-Litovsk.* London, 1919.

c Denikin, A. I. *Russian turmoil: memoirs, military, social and political.* London, 1922.

For the Revolution of 1917, no general work of sound scholarship is yet available; reference is here made to certain writings of three conspicuous partisans whose testimony will have some permanent value as source material.   GTR

S359 Golder, Frank Alfred, ed. *Documents of Russian history, 1914–1917.* N. Y., 1927.

A useful collection of materials, drawn in considerable part from Russian newspapers, for the period from the outbreak of the war to the accession of the Bolsheviki. See also: "Russian: Collections of Sources," above. Review, S. N. Harper in *A.H.R.,* 33:915, July, 1928.   GTR

RUSSIA: THE JEWS

S401 Dubnov, Semen Markovich. *History of the Jews in Russia and Poland from the earliest times until the present day.* 3 v. Philadelphia, 1916–20. Tr. by I. Friedlaender from original MS. (Bibliography.)

While attempting to trace the intellectual and religious life of his people, the author devotes himself mainly to the story of their persecutions and sufferings, which have seldom been set forth more powerfully. Review, *A.H.R.* 22:626, Apr. 1917; 24:726, July, 1919; 26:833, July, 1921.   RHL

RUSSIAN BORDERLANDS: UKRAINE

S421a Hrushevśkyï (Hruševśkyj or Grushevskiï), Mikhail. *Geschichte des ukrainischen Volkes.* V. 1, Leipzig, 1906. Tr. by F. Nossig and I. Franko from v. 1 of *Istoriia Ukraïny-Rusy,* 8 v., Lviv, 1898–1917. (Critical bibliographies.)

b ——— *Abrégé de l'histoire de l'Ukraine.* Paris, 1920.

c Rudnytśkyï (Rudnyćkyj or Rudnitskiï), Stefan. *Ukraine, the land and its people.* N. Y., 1918. Tr. from *Ukraina, Land und Volk,* Wien, 1916. (Bibliography.)

a. The history of the little known people called Ukrainians or Ruthenians or Little Russians received its first detailed treatment in Professor Hrushevśkyï's eight volumes, which go down to 1650. His German volume, which deals with the Kievan empire, should be familiar to students of early Russian history because of its critical discussion of many controverted questions. Hrushevśkyï combines great erudition with an ardent and sometimes too audacious Ukrainian nationalism. *b.* Almost the only general survey of the subject in a western language. *c.* The elementary facts in the Ukrainian problem today are well set forth.   RHL

RUSSIAN BORDERLANDS: BALTIC STATES

S441a Seraphim, Ernst, and Seraphim, August. *Geschichte Liv-, Est-, und Kurlands . . . bis zur Einverleibung in das russische Reich.* 1895. 2nd rev. ed., as *Livländische Geschichte,* 3 v., Reval, 1897–1904.

b Seraphim, Ernst. *Baltische Geschichte im Grundriss.* Reval, 1908. (Bibliography.)

c Walters, M. *Lettland, seine Entwicklung zum Staat und die baltischen Fragen.* Rom, 1923.

d Ruhl, Arthur. *New masters of the Baltic.* N. Y., 1921.

e Harrison, E. J. *Lithuania, past and present..* London, 1922.

a. and *b.* Written from a German Junker standpoint. *a.* Fully detailed history of the Baltic provinces. Review, *Hist. Zeit.* 77 :523, 1896. *b.* Clear, well-planned outline abridged from *a.* Review, O. Hötzsch, *Hist. Vierteljahrsschrift,* 11 :131, Apr. 1908. *c.* Lettish view of Baltic history. *d.* Informal but illuminating account of conditions since the World War and the rise of the new Baltic republics. *e.* The most considerable work yet published in English on Lithuania; marked by extreme and quite uncritical sympathy for the country and by grave historical inaccuracy. For the earlier history of Lithuania, cf. the works on Poland listed in this §. For Finland, cf. § R.   RHL

RUSSIAN BORDERLANDS: TRANSCAUCASIA

S461 Brosset, Marie Félicité. *Histoire de la Géorgie depuis l'antiquité jusqu'au XIXᵉ siècle, avec introduction, additions, et éclaircissements.* 2 pt. in 4 v. S. Pétersbourg, 1849–57.

Only connected account of the history of the country in any language except Georgian. Comprises an edition and translation of the Georgian chronicle, with notes and appendices which contain abundant citations from other sources. Conscientiously done; the translation is fairly reliable; but the basic and only manuscript used is of inferior quality, and much documentary material has since been published which Brosset did not have at his disposal. No criticism of the chronicle, from the point of view of either its genesis or its tendency. Much supplementary material of historical importance is to be found in Brosset's other works, of which an excellent analysis is contained in L. Brosset, *Bibliographie analytique des ouvrages . . . de M. F. Brosset.* S. Pétersbourg, 1887.   RPB

S462 Djavakhishvili (Djavakhov), I. A. *Kartuli eris istoria.* [History of the Georgian people.] Vol. 1, 2, 4. Tiflis, 1908, 1913, 1924.

Sole critical history of Georgia to be found in any language. V. 1–2. Carry the account down to the death of Queen Tamara, 1212. V. 4. Deals with the fifteenth and part of the sixteenth century. It is the author's intention to carry the account up to the year 1801. Based upon a critical examination of all available sources, native, occidental, and oriental, since the author holds to a sharply nationalistic viewpoint, the connections and position of Georgia with the surrounding countries are not very well brought out. Additional materials on the economic development of the realm and on the criticism of local sources are to be found in the author's other works, which are all in Georgian.   RPB

S463a Baddeley, John F. *Russian conquest of the Caucasus.* London and N. Y., 1908.

b Freshfield, Douglas W. *Exploration of the Caucasus.* 2 v. London and N. Y., 1896.

c ———— *Travels to the Central Caucasus and Bashan including visits to Ararat and Tabreez and ascents of Kazbek and Elbruz.* London, 1869.

d Déchy, Móricz von. *Kaukasus: Reisen und Forschungen im kaukasischen Hochgebirge.* 3 v. Berlin, 1905–07.

e Merzbacher, Gottfried. *Aus den Hochregionen des Kaukasus: Wanderungen, Erlebnisse, Beobachtungen.* 2 v. Leipzig, 1901.

a. Very excellent book, much the best in any language on the subject. Contains a good sketch of the annexation of Georgia by Russia and of the subsequent developments, though most of the narrative is devoted to the mountain folk. The account runs to 1871. *b., c., d.,* and *e.* Contain observations on recent conditions and much about topography and ethnography. *b.* Magnificent illustrations.   RPB

RUSSIAN BORDERLANDS: ASIATIC RUSSIA

S481a Rambaud, Alfred. *Expansion of Russia, problems of the East and problems of the Far East.* 1900. 2nd rev. ed., N. Y., 1904. [Contemporary thought series.]

b Krausse, Alexis. *Russia in Asia, 1558–1899.* 1899. 2nd rev. ed., London and N. Y., 1901. (Bibliography.)

a. Concise and fair outline sketch of Russia's empire-building in Asia before the great setback of 1904–1905. *b.* Far more detailed account; written in rather slipshod style and marred by virulent Russophobia. Review, A. C. Coolidge, *A.H.R.* 5:345, Jan. 1900. Cf. § U for works on the Middle Eastern question, on Far Eastern relations, and on the war with Japan.   RHL

S482a Azïatskaia Rossïia, izdanïe pereselencheskago upravlenïia glavnago upravlenïia zemleustroĭstva i zemledielïia. [Asiatic Russia, published by the colonization department of the department of agriculture.] 3 v. and atlas, S. Peterburg, 1914. (Bibliography.)

b Wright, George F. *Asiatic Russia.* 2 v. N. Y., 1902. (Bibliography.)

c Price, Morgan P. *Siberia.* London and N. Y., 1912.

a. For a thorough study of Siberian questions no other source of information equals this sumptuous work, with its chapters written by experts. *b.* Good account of Siberian geography, ethnography, and history. *c.* Price describes, with the authority of a widely-travelled and keen observer, the social and economic conditions and vast potentialities of the country.   RHL

S483 Kennan, George. *Siberia and the exile system.* 2 v. N. Y., 1891.

This famous work of an American traveller and journalist supplies the most vivid picture and the most crushing indictment of a system whose rigors it did much to mitigate. Though somewhat overcolored in parts, it may in the main be taken as a true description.   RHL

RUSSIA: DIPLOMATIC HISTORY

S501a Aleksinskiĭ, Grigoriĭ. *Russia and the great war.* London and N. Y., 1915. Tr. by M. Miall from original MS.

b —— *Russia and Europe.* N. Y., 1917. Tr. by B. Miall from original MS.

More or less repeat each other; seem largely colored by political aims.   *a.* Discusses and justifies Russia's participation in the World War. Review, F. A. Golder, *A.H.R.* 21:369, Jan. 1916.   *b.* Surveys Russia's position among the nations and the attitude of the Russian people towards western civilization.

SAK

S502a Korff, Sergiĕ Aleksandrovich, Baron. *Russia's foreign relations during the last half century.* N. Y., 1922. [Institute of Politics, Williams College.]

b Dennis, Alfred L. P. *Foreign policies of Soviet Russia.* N. Y., 1924.

a. Reviews Russia's relations with each of the powers from 1878 to 1917 clearly and critically. Scarcely abreast of the post-war literature on the subject. Review, R. H. Lord, *A.H.R.* 28:120, Oct. 1922.   *b.* Comprehensive and illuminating survey of six years of Bolshevik foreign policy, based on wide researches and on material much of which is ordinarily inaccessible; scholarly and impartial. Review, A. Bullard, *A.H.R.* 29:772, July 1924.   RHL

RUSSIA: CONSTITUTIONAL HISTORY

S531a Kovalevskiĭ, Maksim Maksimovich. *Modern customs and ancient laws of Russia.* London, 1891. [Ilchester lectures.]

b —— *Russian political institutions, the growth and development of these institutions from the beginnings of Russian history to the present time.* Chicago, 1902...

c Sergieevich, Vasiliĭ Ivanovich. *Lektsiĭ i izsliedovaniia po istorĭ russkago prava.* [Lectures and researches on the history of Russian law.] S. Peterburg, 1883.

d —— *Russkiia iuridicheskiia drevnosti.* [Russian legal antiquities.] 2 v. S. Peterburg, 1890–93.

e Gradovskiĭ, Aleksandr Dmitriĕvich. *Nachala russkago gosudarstvennago prava.* [Principles of Russian public law.]   3 v.   S. Peterburg, 1875–83.

The three authors here grouped together represent respectively the standpoint of the sociologist, the historical jurist, and the constitutional lawyer.   *a.* Devoted mainly to the history of the family, the peasant commune, and the folkmoots of early Russia.   *b.* General sketch of the constitutional evolution of Russia, which, defective as it is, is probably the best thing of the sort in English. Review, A. C. Coolidge, *A.H.R.* 8:131, Oct. 1902.   *c.* and *d.* Best survey in Russian is furnished by the two works of Sergieevich, who was much influenced by the German historical school and who largely employed the comparative method. His researches, notable particularly as first bringing out fully the importance of the early popular assemblies, were epoch-making in Russian constitutional history. *e.* Describes and analyzes, in masterly fashion, the institutions of the empire in the second half of the nineteenth century. Long the classic text-book of Russian public law; through its objectivity, it helped powerfully to further the struggle for constitutional freedom.   SAK

RUSSIA: ECONOMIC AND SOCIAL HISTORY

S571 Mavor, James. *Economic history of Russia.* 1914. 2nd rev. ed., 2 v., London and N. Y., 1926.

Best general survey of the economic history of Russia; valuable particularly on the questions of serfdom, the emancipation, and modern industrialism.   V. 2. Contains an excellent and detailed account of the revolutionary movements of the last century; new edition covers the earlier movements in the present century. Review, R. J. Kerner, *A.H.R.* 21:575, Apr. 1916.   RHL

S572a Wittschewsky, Valentin. *Russlands Handels-, Zoll-, und Industriepolitik von Peter dem Grossen bis auf die Gegenwart.* Berlin, 1905.

b Tugan-Baranovskiĭ, Mikhail Ivanovich. *Geschichte der russischen Fabrik.* Berlin, 1900. [Sozialgeschichtliche Forschungen.] Tr. and rev. ed. by B. Minzès from *Russkaia fabrika v proshlom i nastoiashchem,* S. Peterburg, 1898.

Excellent and authoritative monographs. *a.* Supplies the only coherent account of the commercial and industrial policy of the Russian government in the past two centuries. If the eighteenth century is treated too briefly, the work of Cancrin, Bunge, Vyshnegradskiĭ, and Witte is dealt with fully and admirably. *b.* Written from the social rather than the strictly economic standpoint; describes the penetration of the western factory system into Russia, its struggle with the native forms of industry, its effects upon social life, and the changing attitude of Russian society towards industrial problems.   RHL

S573a Bieliaev, Ivan Dmitrïevich. *Krest'iane na Rusi.* [Peasants in old Russia.] 1879. 4th ed., Moskva, 1903.

b Simkhovitch, Vladimir G. *Die Feldgemeinschaft in Russland.* Jena, 1898.

c Maslov, Petr Pavlovich. *Die Agrarfrage in Russland.* Stuttgart, 1907. Tr. by M. Nachimson of part of V. 1 of *Agrarnyĭ vopros v Rossii,* 2 v., S. Peterburg, 1905–08.

d Hindus, Maurice G. *Russian peasant and the revolution.* N. Y., 1920. (Bibliography.)

a. One of the first results of scientific historical research on the subject of the Russian peasantry; has remained an outstanding authority, particularly on the earlier periods and the development of serfdom. *b.* Traces the history of Russian village communism; makes accessible to western students the fruits of Russian investigations on that complicated question; attacks the system as an evidence of backwardness and a source of material distress. *c.* Analyzes the land question from the socialist standpoint; describes the peasant movements down to and through the revolution of 1905. This book enjoyed great popularity in Russia, and sent its author to prison. *d.* Up-to-date and popular presentation for western readers of the 'sphinx' of Russia, the peasantry in its every-day life and as a political factor. Review, M. Rostovtsev, *A.H.R.* 26:364, Jan. 1921.   SNH

S574a Kovalevskiĭ, Vladimir Ivanovich, ed. *La Russie à la fin du 19ᵉ siècle.* Paris, 1900. Tr. by S. Rocher from *Rossïia v kontsie XIX vieka,* S. Peterburg, 1900. [Commission impériale de Russie à l'Exposition universelle de Paris.]

   b Raffalovich, Arthur, ed. *Russia, its trade and commerce.* London, 1918.

   a. One of the most useful books of reference on Russia's recent economic development and resources is this extensive, semi-official work prepared for the Paris exposition by a large group of specialists headed by Kovalevskiĭ, Witte's assistant in the ministry of finance. A comprehensive survey of every branch of economic life, with copious statistics, maps, and diagrams. *b.* Also a collaborative work; covers the same ground much more briefly, but with statistics coming down to 1914.   RHL

RUSSIA : CULTURAL HISTORY: GENERAL

S601a Wallace, Sir Donald Mackenzie. *Russia.* 1877. Last rev. ed., London, 1912.

   b Leroy-Beaulieu, Anatole. *Empire of the tsars and the Russians.* 3 v. London and N. Y., 1893–96. Tr. by Zenaïde A. Ragozin from 3rd ed. of *L'empire des tsars et les Russes, 1881–89;* 4th rev. ed., 3 v., Paris, 1897–98.

   These two works long passed as the classic descriptions of Russian life by foreign observers. Valuable especially for their analyses of peasant conditions and the famous *mir* system. [Cf. review of Wallace in (B12a) Adams, *Manual of historical literature,* 1882, p. 397; 1888, p. 427.] Today both works are somewhat out of date, although Wallace has appended to his later editions chapters on contemporary events.   SAK

S602a Drage, Geoffrey. *Russian affairs.* 1904. 2nd ed., London, 1904.

   b Williams, Harold W. *Russia of the Russians.* London and N. Y., 1914. [Countries and peoples series.]

   c Wiener, Leo. *Interpretation of the Russian people.* N. Y., 1915. (Bibliography.)

   d Aleksinskiĭ, Grigoriĭ. *Modern Russia.* 1913. Cheaper ed., London, 1914, N. Y., 1915. Tr. by B. Miall from *La Russie moderne, traduit du manuscrit russe, par Mme. Aimée Lavaasky,* Paris, 1912.

   a. Good on economic side, gives a detailed account, with copious statistics, of the development of agriculture, commerce, industry, and finance down to 1904. Much of this has, however, lost its value with the lapse of time. The chapters on political conditions are marred by numerous mistakes, misstatements, and misprints, and there are grave errors even in the documentary appendix. *b.* Most satisfactory of these general descriptions of Russia early in the twentieth century. Its value lies particularly in its account of political conditions just before the World War, and in its illuminating survey of contemporary Russian art, music, literature, press, and theater. *c.* Vivid interpretation of the character, ideals, and spirit of the Russian people. *d.* Describes pre-war internal conditions from the socialist standpoint. Review, R. H. Lord, *A.H.R.* 19:632, Apr. 1914.

                                                                                   SAK

RUSSIA: CULTURAL HISTORY: RELIGION

S621a Makarii (Macarius), Metropolitan of Moscow. *Istoriia russkoi tserkvi.* [History of the Russian church.]   12 v.   S. Peterburg, 1858–83.

 b Palmieri, Aurelio. *La chiesa russa: le sue odierne condizioni e il suo riformismo dottrinale.* Firenze, 1908.   (Bibliographical foot-notes.)

 c Conybeare, Frederick C. *Russian dissenters.* Cambridge, Mass., 1921. [Harvard theological studies, v. 10.]

a. The Metropolitan Makarii's monumental work has much the same importance for Russian church history as (S124a) Solov'ev's for political history. The longest and fullest account though stopping with 1667; based on careful investigation; a vast storehouse of source materials. *b.* Most searching analysis of modern conditions in the state church; marked by great learning, complete objectivity, and rather pessimistic conclusions. *c.* The dissenting, rationalist, and mystic sects, which have swarmed in Russia since the seventeenth century, are very competently treated.   RHL

RUSSIA: CULTURAL HISTORY: THOUGHT AND PHILOSOPHY

S641 Masaryk, Thomas G. *Spirit of Russia: studies in history, literature, and philosophy.* 2 v.   London and N. Y., 1919.   Tr. by E. Paul and C. Paul from *Zur russischen Geschichts- und Religionsphilosophie,* 2 v., Jena, 1913.   (Bibliography.)

Best history of Russian thought published in English.   Traces with equal interest and skill the currents of religious, philosophical, social, and political thought, and the interplay of foreign influences.   The author is at his best in dealing with the revolutionary movement and the various socialistic schools, but he also succeeds in being fair to the ideology of autocracy and reaction.
                                                                                          SAK

RUSSIA: CULTURAL HISTORY: LITERATURE

S661a Kropotkin, Petr Aleksieevich. *Russian literature.* 1905.   Reprinted as *Ideals and realities in Russian literature,* N. Y., 1915.   (Bibliographies.)

 b Olgin, Moissaye J. *Guide to Russian literature, 1820–1917.* N. Y., 1920.

 c Wiener, Leo. *Anthology of Russian literature from the earliest period to the present time.* 2 v.   N. Y. and London, 1902–03.

a. Reviews, in picturesque and illuminating fashion, and with thorough command of the subject, the whole history of Russian literature, with attention concentrated upon the great masters.   *b.* Not so much a history as a guide-book, introducing one to a large gallery of writers, describing their chief works, emphasizing their social tendencies and influence, and giving comments of authoritative Russian critics on each.   The great merit of the book is its full treatment of contemporary literature.   *c.* Extremely happy selection and translation of characteristic passages from the leading Russian writers.   RHL

RUSSIA: CULTURAL HISTORY: ART

S681a Réau, Louis. *L'art russe des origines à Pierre le Grand.* Paris, 1921.   (Bibliography.)

 b —— *L'art russe de Pierre le Grand à nos jours.* Paris, 1922.   (Bibliography.)

c **Kondakov, N. P.** *The Russian icon.* Tr. and abridged from the Russian manuscript, by E. H. Minns. Oxford, 1927.

Scholarly, well-proportioned, and beautifully illustrated; splendid contributions to the cultural history of Russia, providing as nearly adequate a synthesis as the present state of investigation permits. Review of *a*. E. Duchesne, *Rev. Hist.* 142:259, March 1923.   RHL

c. Westerners have long had some acquaintance with Russian literature and Russian music. This authoritative and excellently illustrated work will help to open to them the third great field of Russian cultural achievement.   GTR

S691a Montagu-Nathan, M. *History of Russian music.* London, 1914.

b **Pougin, Arthur.** *Short history of Russian music.* London, 1915. Tr. by Lawrence Haward from *Essai historique sur la musique en Russie.* Paris, 1904.

a. The more systematic of the two works, and better on the latest period.
b. Better written and more illuminating.   RHL

RUSSIA: BIOGRAPHIES

In addition to the titles listed above, mention should be made of the following biographical works: (S701) N. I. Kostomarov, *Russische Geschichte in Biographien,* Leipzig, 1886, deals with the chief personages in Russian history down to 1613. A famous enigma is treated by (S741) E. Shchepkin, 'Wer war Pseudodemetrius I?', *Archiv für slavische Philologie,* 20:224-325, 21:99-169, 558-606; 22:321-432; Berlin, 1898-1900; and (S742) T. H. Pantenius, *Der falsche Demetrius,* Leipzig, 1904. (S743) William Palmer, *The patriarch and the tsar,* 3 v., London, 1871-73, traces the stormy career of Nikon. The *Memoirs of Catherine II* have at last been authoritatively published by the Academy of Sciences, in v. 12 of her complete works (S744), *Sochineniia imperatritsy Ekateriny II,* 12 v., S. Peterburg, 1901-07.

On the monarchs and ministers of more recent times, the following works are important: (S761) Grand Duke Nikolaĭ Mikhaĭlovich, *L'empereur Alexandre Ier,* 2 v., St. Pétersbourg, 1913; (S762) N. K. Shil'der, *Aleksandr I,* 4 v., S. Peterburg, 1897-98, and (S763) *Nikolaĭ I,* 2 v., ibid., 1903; (S764) S. S. Tatishchev, *Aleksandr II,* 2 v., ibid., 1903; (S765) *Lettres et papiers du chancelier comte de Nesselrode,* 11 v., Saint-Pétersbourg, 1904-12; (S766) K. P. Pobiedonostsev, *Reflections of a Russian statesman,* London, 1898; the *Memoirs* of (S767) Count Witte, Garden City, 1921, and of (S768) Aleksandr Izvolskiĭ, London, 1921. For persons connected with the liberal or revolutionary movements: (S781) Aleksandr Herzen, *Memoirs,* 4 v., N. Y., 1924-25; (S782) Prince Kropotkin, *Memoirs of a revolutionist,* Boston, 1899; (S783) Aylmer Maude, *Life of Tolstoy,* 2 v., London, 1908-10, N. Y., 1910; and (S784) Alice S. Blackwell, *Little grandmother of the Russian Revolution, reminiscences and letters of Catherine Breshkovsky,* Boston, 1917.

RUSSIA: SOCIETY PUBLICATIONS

(S921) *Sbornik* [Magazine] of the Imperial Russian Historical Society, 148 v., S. Peterburg, 1867-1916, is devoted exclusively to the publication of documentary materials and is extraordinarily valuable for the history of Russia's foreign relations. Much of the material in it is in French or other western languages. (S922) *Chteniia* [Readings] 264 v., Moskva, 1846–1918, of the Moscow Historical Society are a rich mine of material.

RUSSIA: PERIODICALS

The more important periodicals of general interest for Russian history are: (S941) *Russkii arkhiv* [Russian archives), Moskva, 1863–1917; (S942) *Russkaia starina* [Russian antiquities], S. Peterburg, 1870–1917; (S943) *Istoricheskii viestnik* [Historical messenger], S. Peterburg, 1880–1917; (S944) *Zhurnal ministerstva narodnago prosvieshcheniia* [Journal of the ministry of public instruction], S. Peterburg, 1834–1917; (S945) *Russkii istoricheskii zhurnal* [Russian historical journal], Petrograd, 1917 ff.; (S946) *Krasnyi Arkhiv* [Red archives], Moskva, 1922 ff; (S947) *Slavonic review,* London, 1922 ff; (S948) *Revue des études slaves,* Paris, 1921 ff; (S949) *Ost-Europa,* Berlin, 1925 ff.

POLAND: BIBLIOGRAPHY

S1001a Finkel, Ludwik. *Bibliografia historyi polskiej.* [Bibliography of Polish history.]   1 v. in 3.   Kraków, 1891–1906.   Dodatek I [Supplement I], Kraków, 1906.   Dodatek II, zeszyt I [Supplement II, section I] Kraków, 1914.

b Recke, Walter, and **Wagner, Albert M.** *Bücherkunde zur Geschichte und Literatur des Königreichs Polen.* Warschau and Leipzig, 1918.

a. Covers Polish history to 1815; a model of its kind. The original work and the first supplement exhaustively cover the literature published down to 1900; the second supplement, the publications (original sources only) of 1901–1910. For later works consult the current bibliographies of Polish history printed semiannually in (S1941) *Kwartalnik historyczny.   b.* Useful for those unable to read Polish.   Also cf. (S1) Kerner, *Slavic Europe.*   RHL

S1002a Estreicher, Karol J. T. *Bibliografia polska.* 27 v. Kraków, 1870–1929.

b *Bibliografia polska, 19 stulecia, lata 1881–1900.* V. 1–4, Kraków, 1906–16.

a. V. 1–7. Alphabetical list of all publications in Polish, 1800–1870.   V. 8–11. Similar chronological lists, 1455–1889.   V. 12–24. Similar alphabetical list for the period prior to 1800, but complete only through Sh.   *b.* Supplement completed in 1916.   GMD

Library Collections.—The best collections on Polish history in the United States are at Harvard University and in the New York Public Library.   AHS

POLAND: ENCYCLOPEDIAS

S1021a Orgelbrand, Samuel. *Encyklopedja powszechna.* [Universal encyclopedia.] Warszawa, 1859–68. New ed., with maps and illustrations, 16 v. and supplements, 2 v., 1898–1912.

b Gloger, Zygmunt. *Encyklopedia staropolska.* [Encyclopedia of Old Poland.] 3 v., Warsawa, 1900–03.

a. Standard Polish encyclopedia.   *b.* Especially valuable for historical articles.   RHL

POLAND: GEOGRAPHY

S1041a Romer, Eugeniusz. *Geograficzno-statystyczny atlas Polski.* 1916. [Geographical and statistical atlas of Poland.] 2d ed., Lwow and Warszawa, 1921. (Bibliographies.)

b Sulimierski, Filip; Chlebowski, Bronisław, and Walewski, Władysław, ed. *Słownik geograficzny królestwa polskiego i innych krajów słowiańskich.* [Geographical lexicon of the kingdom of Poland and other Slavic countries.] 15 v. and 2 supplements. Warszawa, 1880–1914.

Both works deal with the whole area of historic Poland. *a.* Best introduction to Polish problems today. Contains about seventy well-constructed maps, with explanatory texts (in Polish, French, and English in the 2nd ed.), illustrating every side of Polish life: physiography, history, administration, religious and linguistic distribution, economic development, education, etc. *b.* Contains an (often very extended) historical account of every province, district, city, and village of old Poland.   RHL

POLAND: SHORTER GENERAL HISTORIES

S1101a Morfill, William R. *Poland.* 1893. Reprint, N. Y., 1924. [Story of the nations.]

b Slocombe, G. E. *Poland.* London, 1916. [Nations' histories.] (Bibliography.)

c Orvis, Julia S. *Brief history of Poland.* Boston, 1916. (Bibliography.)

d Lewinski-Corwin, Edward H. *Political history of Poland.* N. Y., 1917.

a. Extraordinary medley of sound observations, picturesque quotations from the sources, pedantic digressions, and sheer trivialities. *b.* Apparently written with no knowledge of Slavic languages. Careful, well-planned, matter-of-fact little book; good particularly on constitutional and social development. *c.* Probably the clearest, best-balanced, most satisfactory work on the subject in English. Review, R. H. Lord, *A.H.R.* 22:701, Apr. 1917. *d.* Much longer and more detailed than the others; based on wider acquaintance with Polish sources and with Polish life; suffers from an excess of patriotic and partisan prejudice. Review, R. J. Kerner, *A.H.R.* 23:846, July 1918.   RHL

S1102a Mickiewicz, Adam, Count. *Histoire populaire de Pologne publiée avec préface, notes, et chapitre complémentaire,* by Ladislas Mickiewicz, Paris, 1867.

b Brandenburger, Clemens. *Polnische Geschichte.* Leipzig, 1907. [Sammlung Göschen.]

c Missalek, Erich. *Geschichte Polens.* Breslau, 1911.

Three general histories of Poland in western languages other than English. *a.* Presents an early nineteenth century Polish point of view regarding the old Polish state. An interpretation of Poland's history by a patriot steeped in its past, who was also its greatest poet. Interesting and valuable. *b.* and *c.* Good brief outlines, well-informed, well-proportioned, German in viewpoint but fair. *b.* Slightly longer, more interesting, more biased.   JSO

S1103a Waliszewski, Kazimierz. *Poland the unknown.* London, 1919. Tr. from *La Pologne inconnue,* Paris, 1919.

b Winter, Nevin O. *Poland of today and yesterday; a review of its history, past and present, and of the causes which resulted in its partition, together with a survey of its social, political, and economic conditions to-day.* Boston, 1913. (Bibliography.)

Two recent informal reviews of Polish history. *a.* Aims to expose the falsity of Russian and German interpretations of that history, especially of Poland's fall. As one of the few works in any western language presenting the Polish viewpoint, this book is important—but brilliant and provocative rather than convincing. Review, R. H. Lord, *A.H.R.* 26:316, Jan. 1921. *b.* Agreeable combination of history and travel, without great value. JSO

POLAND: LONGER GENERAL HISTORIES

S1121a Szujski, Józef. *Dzieje Polski.* [History of Poland.] 4 v. Lwów, 1862–66. Rev. ed. in his *Dziela* [Collected works] series II, v. 1–4, Kraków 1894–95.

b Bobrzyński, Michał. *Dzieje Polski w zarysie.* [History of Poland in outline.] 1879. 3rd rev. ed., 2 v., Warszawa, 1887–90. (Bibliography.)

c Sokołowski, August, and Inlender, Adolf. *Dzieje Polski illustrowane.* [Illustrated history of Poland.] 4 v. Wiedeń, 1896–1901.

d Lewicki, Anatol. *Zarys historji polskiej.* [Outlines of the history of Poland.] 1884. 8th ed., Kraków, 1919.

e Polish Academy of Sciences (of Cracow). *Encyclopedya polska,* tom V, część I.-dział VI: *Historya polityczna Polski,* część I, *Wieki średnie;* część II, *Od r. 1506 do r. 1775.* [Polish encyclopedia, v. 5, pt. 1, section 6: *Political history of Poland;* pt. 1, *Middle ages;* pt. 2, *1506–1775.*] Kraków, 1920–23. (Valuable bibliographies.)

a. Among the standard histories of Poland in Polish, Szujski's ranks as both an historical and a literary masterpiece. In the main it represents the views of the democratic school, which idealized the old Polish republic, emphasized the (at that time) unparalleled liberties it accorded, and traced Poland's downfall not so much to internal as to external causes (the wickedness of her neighbors). *b.* Bobrzyński, on the other hand, a leader of the 'Cracow school,' preached the bitterest 'truths' to his compatriots, assuring them that their history was mainly a tissue of mistakes, negligences, and failures, and that they had only themselves to blame for their misfortunes. Among more recent and less philosophic works, *c.* offers perhaps the most satisfactory longer history of the country in Polish, while *d.,* an ever popular handbook, furnishes the best short account. *e.* Very valuable collaborative work, presenting the latest fruits of Polish scholarship. Not yet completed. RHL

POLAND: HISTORY TO SIXTEENTH CENTURY

S1201a Roepell, Richard, and Caro, Jacob. *Geschichte Polens.* V. 1 (Roepell), Hamburg, 1840; V. 2–5 (Caro), Gotha, 1863–88. [Geschichte der europäischen Staaten.]

b Zivier, Ezechiel. *Neuere Geschichte Polens.* V. 1, 1506–1572, Gotha, 1915. [Geschichte der europäischen Staaten.]

a. Roepell and Caro were pioneers in applying modern critical methods to Polish medieval sources. Their work, which is a model of scholarly investigation and synthesis, of clearness, fairness, and objectivity, still passes as the most complete history of Poland in the Middle Ages (down to 1506). *b.* Continuation of *a.*, though scarcely equal to it. Very detailed study of the age of the last two Jagellonian kings, based largely on new materials from foreign archives.

RHL

POLAND: HISTORY IN SEVENTEENTH AND EIGHTEENTH CENTURIES

S1251a Bain, Robert Nisbet. *The last king of Poland and his contemporaries.* N. Y., 1909.

b Kalinka, Waleryan. *Der vierjährige polnische Reichstag, 1788–1791.* 2 v. Berlin, 1896–98. Tr. by Marie Dohrn from *Sejm czteroletni, 1880–81*, 4th ed., Kraków, 1895.

c Lord, Robert H. *Second partition of Poland.* Cambridge, Mass. 1915 [Harvard historical studies.] (Bibliography.)

d Gardner, Monica M. *Kościuszko, a biography.* London and N. Y., 1920.

Four books on the last period of the old republic. *a.* Scholarly, independent, and discriminating study of King Stanislas and his period. Rather indulgent to the king. *b.* Careful, detailed account, from the sources, of the last independent diet of old Poland; severely critical towards the leaders of that time, but highly important for an understanding of that crucial period. *c.* Only adequate account in any language of the second partition and the movement for national regeneration which preceded it. The introduction contains a brilliant background sketch of conditions before the first partition. Review, S. B. Fay, *A.H.R.* 21:590, Apr. 1916. *d.* Only biography in English of Poland's greatest hero. Not profound, but careful and pleasing. JSO

POLAND: HISTORY IN NINETEENTH AND TWENTIETH CENTURIES

S1301a Privat, Edmond. *L'Europe et l'odyssée de la Pologne au XIXe siècle.* Lausanne, 1918.

b Feldman, Wilhelm. *Geschichte der politischen Ideen in Polen seit dessen Teilungen, 1795–1914.* München, 1917. In part, tr. from *Dzieje polskiej myśli politycznej w okresie porozbiorowym*, 3 v., Kraków, 1914, 1916; Warszawa, 1920. (Bibliographies.)

Both books review the history of the Polish question during the past century, but from rather different angles. *a.* Privat, a Swiss scholar and an ardent friend of Poland, dwells chiefly upon the shifting policies of the great powers. *b.* Well-documented; traces the evolution of ideas and movements among the Poles themselves, and the rise of the present political parties. An excellent introduction to current Polish politics.

RHL

S1302a Cleinow, Georg. *Die Zukunft Polens.* 2 v., Leipzig, 1908–14.

b Dmowski, Roman. *La question polonaise.* Paris, 1909. Tr. by V. Gasztowtt from *Niemcy, Rosya, i kwestya polska*, Lwów, 1908.

c Bernhard, Ludwig. *Die Polenfrage.* 1907. 3d rev. ed., Leipzig, 1920.

a. Although marred by anti-Polish bias, furnishes a detailed and useful account of the economic and political development of Russian Poland from 1863 to 1914. *b.* Analyzes the Polish problem as it appeared to one of the foremost of Polish politicians—the leader of the national democrats—on the eve of the World War. He advocated a *rapprochement* with Russia and a united front against Germany. *c.* Professor Bernhard—a German, but relatively fair—describes the course and results of the protracted struggle between the Poznanian Poles and the Prussian government.   RHL

POLAND: CONSTITUTIONAL HISTORY

S1531a Kutrzeba, Stanislaw. *Grundriss der polnischen Verfassungsgeschichte,* Berlin, 1912. Tr. by W. Christiani from v. 1 of 3rd ed. of *Historya ustroju Polski w zarysie,* 4 v., Lwów, 1911–17 (1st ed. 1905).

b Hüppe, Siegfried. *Verfassung der Republik Polen.* Berlin, 1867.

c Konopczyński, Władysław. *Liberum veto.* Kraków, 1918. [In Polish.]

a. An outline rather than a detailed account. Fills a great gap in historical literature. It led to prolonged polemics and has undergone considerable revision, but it ranks as one of the most important achievements of recent Polish historiography. V. 2–4. Not translated; deal with the institutions of Lithuania, and of Poland since 1795. *b.* Although old and marred by Prussian prejudice, retains a certain value as the fullest description of the constitution of the republic just before the partitions. *c.* Brilliant monograph on that most discussed and most interesting institution of old Poland, the *liberum veto.*
RHL

POLAND: CULTURAL HISTORY: GENERAL

S1601 Brandes, George. *Poland, a study of the land, people, and literature.* London and N. Y., 1903.

One of the best pictures of Polish nationalism struggling against Russian oppression. Views Poland as 'the symbol of human freedom.'   JSO

S1602a Piltz, Erasmus, ed. *Poland; her people, history, industries, finance, science, literature, art, and social development.* London, 1919. Tr. from *Petite encyclopédie polonaise,* Lausanne, 1916. (Bibliography.)

b ——— *Polen, Entwickelung und gegenwärtiger Zustand.* Bern, 1918.

c Comité des Publications Encyclopédiques sur la Pologne. *Encyclopédie polonaise.* Lausanne, 1916–20. [1, *Géographie et ethnographie;* 2, *Territoire et population;* 3, *Vie économique;* 4, pt. 1, *Régime politique et administratif dans la Pologne prussienne.*] V. 1, and 2 pt. of v. 3 have been reprinted in English by the Polish National Committee of America, Geneva, 1921.

All these works are collaborative enterprises undertaken by groups of Polish scholars during the World War; intended to supply the outside world with the fullest information about 'unknown Poland.' *a.* Brief, compendious manual. Nowhere else can one find so much information about Poland packed into one volume in English. *b.* At greater length (1036 p.) covers the same ground, with particularly valuable chapters on social and cultural conditions. *c.* Unfinished; as far as it goes, the most exhaustive and authoritative publication; includes an interesting atlas.   RHL

S1603a Boswell, A. Bruce. *Poland and the Poles.* London and N. Y., 1919.

b Pember, Mrs. Devereux [pseudonym, Roy Devereux]. *Poland reborn,* N. Y., 1922.

c **Phillips, Charles.** *New Poland.* London and N. Y., 1923.

d **Winter, Nevin O.** *New Poland.* Boston, 1923. (Bibliography.)

In very similar manner describe the new Polish republic: its political, economic, boundary, and nationality problems, and its social, intellectual, and artistic life—all from a decidedly sympathetic standpoint.   RHL

POLAND: CULTURAL HISTORY: RELIGION

S1621a **Kantak, Ks. Kamil.** *Dzieje kościoła polskiego.* [History of the Polish church.] V. 1–2, Gdańsk-Poznań, 1912–14.

b **Krasiński, Walerjan.** *Historical sketch of the rise, progress, and decline of the reformation in Poland.* 2 v. London, 1838–40.

c **Wotschke, Theodor.** *Geschichte der Reformation in Polen.* V. 1, Leipzig, 1911.

d **Fox, Paul.** *Reformation in Poland, some social and economic aspects.* Baltimore, 1924. [Johns Hopkins University studies in history and political science, series.] (Bibliography.)

a. By a Catholic scholar; a great work, which is planned to extend to 9 v., but now reaches only to 1400.   *b.* Most complete account of the Protestant movement in Poland; written from a Protestant standpoint.   *c.* Throws light on many questions, but is sadly prejudiced in favor of the Protestant cause and weak on the political and social issues involved.   *d.* Excellent study of the political, social, and economic causes of the growth of Protestantism down to 1573. Review, R. H. Lord, *Slavonic Rev.* 4:238, June 1925.   RHL

POLAND: CULTURAL HISTORY: LITERATURE

S1661a **Brückner, Alexander.** *Geschichte der polnischen Litteratur.* 1901. 2nd ed., Leipzig, 1909. [Die Litteraturen des Ostens.]

b **Gardner, Monica M.** *Adam Mickiewicz, the national poet of Poland.* London and N. Y., 1911.

c —— *Poland, a study in national idealism.* London, 1915.

d **Dyboski, Roman.** *Periods of Polish literary history.* London and N. Y., 1923. [Ilchester lectures.]

e —— *Modern Polish literature.* London and N. Y., 1924. [Lectures delivered at King's College, University of London.]

a. Delightful book, full of knowledge, ideas, and geniality; reviews the history of Polish literature with thorough consideration of the political, social, and intellectual influences at work.   *b.* and *c.* Excellent introductions to that brilliant galaxy of nineteenth century poets, so little known to the outside world, whose genius and patriotism kept the national spirit of Poland alive even in the darkest period of its captivity.   *d.* and *e.* Clear and concise surveys of literary history; *d.*, going to the latter half of the nineteenth century, and *e.* dealing with the last fifty years.   RHL

POLAND: BIOGRAPHIES

Polish history is poorly supplied with good biographies. Among the best in Polish are: (S1701) A. Prochaska, *Król Władysław Jagiełło,* 2 v., Kraków, 1908, and (S1702) *Dzieje Witołda W. Księcia Litwy* [History of Vitovt, Grand

Prince of Lithuania], Wilno, 1914; (S1703) T. Korzon, *Dola i niedola Jana Sobieskiego* [Good and ill fortunes of John Sobieski], 3 v., Kraków, 1898, and (S1704) *Kościuszko,* 1894, 2nd ed., Kraków, 1906. Among the few that have been translated are (S1751) S. Askenazy, *Le prince Joseph Poniatowski, 1763–1813,* Paris, 1921; and (S1752) H. Lisicki, *Le marquis Wielopolski, 1803–1877,* 2 v., Vienne, 1880.

POLAND: ACADEMY AND SOCIETY PUBLICATIONS

While Poland until recently has had no government to organize and assist such enterprises, the Academy of Sciences at Cracow, with its numerous commissions, has carried on an immense and invaluable work in publishing materials for Polish history. Among its most notable enterprises are: (S1921) *Scriptores rerum polonicarum,* 22 v., Cracoviae, 1872–1917; (S1922) *Monumenta medii aevi historica res gestas Poloniae illustrantia,* 18 v., *ibid.,* 1874–1908; and (S1923) *Acta historica res gestas Poloniae illustrantia ab anno 1507 usque ad annum 1795,* 12 v., *ibid.,* 1878–1910. Much has also been done by historical and scientific societies at Lemberg, Posen, Warsaw, and elsewhere.

POLAND: PERIODICALS

The leading ones are (S1941) *Kwartalnik historyczny* [Historical quarterly], Lwów, 1887 ff., and (S1942) *Przeglad historyczny* [Historical survey], Warszawa, 1905 ff.

CZECHOSLOVAKIA: BIBLIOGRAPHY AND ENCYCLOPEDIAS

S2001a Zíbrt, Čeněk, and Volf, Josef. *Bibliografie české historie.* [Bibliography of Czech history.] V. 1–5. v Praze, 1900–12. [Česká Akademia.]

b Tobolka, Zdeněk V., ed. *Česká bibliografie.* [*Czech bibliography.*] 1902 ff. v Praze, 1903 ff. [Česká Akademia.]

c *Übersicht über die Leistungen der Deutschen Böhmens auf dem Gebiete der Wissenschaft, Kunst, und Literatur im Jahre 1891–1897.* 7 v. Prag, 1893–99. [Gesellschaft zur Förderung Deutscher Wissenschaft, Kunst, und Literatur in Böhmen.]

d Čapek, Thomas, and Čapek, Anna V. *Bohemian (Čech) bibliography, a finding list of writings in English relating to Bohemia and the Čechs,* N. Y., 1918.

e Bestaux, Eugène. *Bibliographie tchèque, contenant . . . ouvrages sur la Tchéco-slovaquie, en langues diverses (à l'exclusion des langues slaves).* v. 1. Prague, 1920.

a. Monumental and authoritative for the period prior to 1679. *b.* Current bibliography. *c.* Select lists, in a limited field, of current publications. *d.* Convenient for those who use only English. *e.* Useful for titles in western European languages.

Also cf. (S1) Kerner, *Slavic Europe;* J. Šusta, 'Bulletin historique: histoire de Tchécoslovaquie,' *Rev. Hist.,* 149: 212–238, July 1925; 150: 67–89, Sept. 1925, which covers publications from 1904 to 1925; and (S2923) *Český časopis historický,* which not only publishes reviews of all important current works for Czech history but also contains an annual bibliography of historical publications relating to Czechoslovakia (interrupted from 1916 to 1922, but the gap is covered by a summary in 1922).   RJK

S2021a Rieger, František L., and Malý, Jakub, ed. *Slovník naučný.* [Encyclopedia.] 12 v. v Praze, 1860–90.

b *Ottův slovník naučný.* [Otto's Encyclopedia.] 27 v., and supplement, 1 v. v Praze, 1888–1909.

a. Indispensable and authoritative; contains articles on many historical and literary topics treated in no other work. *b.* More recent publication of similar character.   RJK

For works on the geography and ethnography of Czechoslovakia, cf. the publications listed under (T41) and (T51).

CZECHOSLOVAKIA: COLLECTIONS OF SOURCES AND ARCHIVE PUBLICATIONS

Fortunately a large proportion of the documents printed in the several collections of materials for Czech history is in Latin, German, or other western European language. Among the more important collections are (S2071) *Archiv český, čili staré písemné památky české i moravské* [Czech archives, or old Czech and Moravian written records], v. 1–32, v Praze, 1840–1918, ed. by František Palacký, J. Kalousek, and others, a somewhat miscellaneous collection of documents chiefly from the fifteenth and sixteenth centuries; (S2072) *Prameny dějin českých: Fontes rerum bohemicarum,* v. 1–6, Pragae, 1873–1907, ed. by František Palacký and J. Emler; (S2073) *Staré paměti dějin českých: Monumenta historiae bohemica,* 5 v. in 11, Pragae, 1864–69, ed. by Anton Gindely; (S2074) *Codex diplomaticus et epistolaris regni Bohemiae,* v. 1–2, Pragae, 1904–12, ed. by Gustav Friedrich, which contains documents down to 1230; (S2075) *Codex diplomaticus et epistolaris Moraviae,* v. 1–13, Olomucii and Brunae, 1836–97, ed. by A. Boczek and others, which includes materials to 1407; (S2076) *Regesta diplomatica necnon epistolaria Bohemiae et Moraviae,* 4 pt. in 6 v., Pragae, 1855–92, ed. by J. C. Erben and J. Emler, with documents down to 1346; (S2077) *Monumenta vaticana res gestas bohemicas illustrantia,* v. 1, 2, and 5, Pragae, 1903–07, ed. by Ladislaus Klicman, Jan B. Novák, and Kamill Krofta, of which the volumes published relate to the fourteenth century; (S2078) *Sněmy české od léta 1526 až po naši dobu: Die böhmischen Landtagsverhandlungen und Landtagsbeschlüsse vom Jahre 1526 an bis die Neuzeit,* v. 1–11, v Praze, 1877–1910, ed. by Anton Gindely and others, covering proceedings to 1611; (S2079) *Zemské sněmy a sjezdy moravské, . . . 1526–1628* [Records of Moravian diets and provincial congresses], v. 1–3, v Brne, 1900–05, ed. by F. Kameníček; (S2080) *Deutsche Chroniken aus Böhmen,* 3 v., Prag, 1879–84, ed. by L. Schlesinger and H. Gradl; (S2081) *Kronika česko-slovenská* [Czechoslovak chronicles], v. 1 in 2 pt., v Praze, 1921–23, ed. by J. V. Šimak; (S2082) *Sbirka pramenu českého hnuti náboženského ve XIV. a XV. stoleti* [Collection of sources for the Czech religious movement in the fourteenth and fifteenth centuries], v. 1–9, v Praze, 1909–20 [Česká Akademie], of which v. 9 contains Huss's correspondence, ed. by V. Novotný; (S2091) *Diplomatiché dokumenty o československém státu* [Diplomatic documents of the Czechoslovak state], Paris, 1918, ed. by W. Tobolka.   RJK, GMD

CZECHOSLOVAKIA: GENERAL HISTORIES

S2101a Maurice, Charles Edmund. *Bohemia from the earliest times to the foundation of the Czecho-Slovak republic in 1918.* 1896. 2nd rev. ed., London and N. Y., 1922. [Story of the nations.]

b **Pekař, Josef.** *Dějiny naší říše* [History of our state]. 1914. Rev. ed entitled *Dějiny československé* [Czechoslovak history], Praha, 1921.

a. Best general popular account in English; dwells particularly on the period down to 1620 but includes, in the revised edition, a short outline to 1918. *b.* Secondary school text-book, by the leading Czech national historian, who brings the story down to date. The only connected general account of the history of the Czechoslovaks thus far written. Review, J. Šusta, *Rev. Hist.*, 149: 216, July 1925.

RJK

S2102a Lützow, Franz H. V., Graf von. *Bohemia, an historical sketch.* 1896 Reprint, London and N. Y., 1909. [Everyman's library.]

b **Monroe, Will S.** *Bohemia and the Čechs: the history, people, institutions and the geography of the kingdom, together with accounts of Moravia and Silesia.* Boston, 1910. (Bibliography.)

a. Brief general history based chiefly on the more detailed works of Czech and German historians; its main portion concludes with the battle of White Mountain in 1620. *b.* A fervid admirer of the Czechs devotes a third of his book to a summary sketch of Czech history, and the remainder to description, based largely on his impressions as a traveler. Popular, useful, generally authoritative; scanty material on the political situation.   CS

S2121a Novotný, Václav, ed. *České dějiny* [Czech history]. V. 1–3 in 5 v v Praze, 1910–16. [1, V. Novotný, *To 1192;* 2, V. Novotný, *1192–1437,* 3, R. Urbánek, *1438–1457*].

b **Bretholz, Bertold.** *Geschichte Böhmens und Mährens.* V. 1–4. Reichenberg, 1921–24. [Deutsche Gesellschaft für Wissenschaft und Kunst in Brünn.]

Best general longer histories of Bohemia in Czech and German respectively *a.* More than a modernization of (S2201a) Palacký's monumental national history, erudite presentation of recent researches and views. Review, J. Šusta, *Rev. Hist.* 149: 216, July 1925. *b.* Broader in scope, but written on a distinctly smaller scale emphasizes German influences; at present ends with 1917. Reviews v. 1–2, J Loserth, *Hist. Zeit.*, 130: 329, 1924; v. 3–4, H. Ritter von Srbik, *Hist. Zeit.* 133: 289, 294, 1925; J. Šusta, *Rev. Hist.*, 149: 218, July 1925.   RJK

S2122a Denis, Ernest. *Études d'histoire bohême: Huss et la guerre des Hussites* 1878. New ed., Paris, 1918.

b ——— *Fin de l'indépendance bohême.* 2 v. Paris, 1890. [1, *Georges de Podiebrad;* 2, *Les premiers Habsbourgs.*] Tr. into Czech, with author's added notes and corrections, by J. Vančura, as *Konec samostatnosti české* v Praze, 1892.

c ——— *La Bohême depuis la Montagne-Blanche.* 2 v. Paris, 1903.

Together, these three works form an authoritative general history of the Czechs largely political in nature, from the beginning of the fifteenth century to the end of the nineteenth; by one of the foremost scholars in the field of Czech history Based on critical study of published Czech and German sources; the scientific value of the conclusions is not vitiated by the author's Czech and Protestant sympathies. Reviews of *a,* *Hist. Zeit.*, 41: 305, 1879; G. Fagniez, *Rev. Hist.*, 8: 122 Sept. 1878; of *b,* *Rev. Hist.*, 47: 399, Nov. 1891; I. Goll, *Rev. Hist.*, 51: 354, March 1893; of *c,* R. Reuss, *Rev. Hist.*, 86: 371, Nov. 1904; B. Bretholz, *Hist. Zeit.* 95: 110, 1905.   CS, GMD

CZECHOSLOVAKIA: PERIOD OF THE NATIONAL KINGS

S2201a Palacký, František. *Geschichte von Böhmen.* 5 v. Prag, 1836–67. Tr. into Czech as *Dějiny národu českého w čechách a w morawě,* 1848–67; 5th ed., 5 v., v Praze, 1900.

b Bachmann, Adolf. *Geschichte Böhmens.* 2 v. Gotha, 1899–1905. [(B161) Geschichte der europäischen Staaten.]

a. Classic national history of Bohemia to 1526; both a cause and a result of the national revival in the middle of the nineteenth century; completely superseded in scholarship by (S2121a) Novotný. Review, v. 4, G. Voigt, *Hist. Zeit.,* 5: 398, 1861; v. 5, *ibid.,* 20: 203, 1868. *b.* Best presentation of the German point of view in opposition to *a;* account ends at 1526; continued by (S2261a) Bretholz, *Neuere Geschichte Böhmens.* Review, v. 2, J. Loserth, *Hist. Zeit.,* 99: 621, 1907.   RJK

S2221a Dudík, Beda F. *Mährens allgemeine Geschichte.* 12 v. and indexes. Brünn, 1860–88. Published simultaneously in Czech.

b Bretholz, Bertold. *Geschichte Mährens.* V. 1 in 2 pt. Brünn, 1893–95. Published simultaneously in Czech.

Both works published under patronage of the provincial authorities. *a.* By Benedictine scholar; gives liberal attention to cultural developments; packed with facts; though not a first-class work, it is the best history of the country to 1350. Review, v. 7, I. Goll, *Rev. Hist.,* 6: 438, March 1878. *b.* More recent and scholarly but German in tone; extends only to 1197. Review, I. Goll, *Rev. Hist.,* 71: 349, Nov. 1899; W. Erben, *Hist. Zeit.,* 77: 140, 1896.   GMD

S2241a Lützow, Franz H. V., Graf von. *Life and times of Master John Hus.* 1909. 2nd ed., London and N. Y., 1921. (Bibliography.)

b —— *Hussite wars.* London and N. Y., 1914.

Give in connected sequence and with a wealth of detail, the story of the great Czech national and religious movement. Carefully documented by this learned patriot, they present, without political prejudice, Hus as the champion of Czech nationalism. Review of *b,* R. J. Kerner, *A.H.R.,* 20: 842, July 1915.   CS

CZECHOSLOVAKIA: PERIOD OF HAPSBURG RULE

S2261a Bretholz, Bertold. *Neuere Geschichte Böhmens.* V. 1, Gotha, 1920. [(B161) Geschichte der europäischen Staaten.]

b Rezek, Antal, and Svatek, Josef. *Dějiny čech a moravy nové doby.* [History of Bohemia and Moravia in modern times.] V. 1–4, v Praze, 1892–97.

a. Continues (S2201b) Bachmann, *Geschichte Böhmens* from 1526 to 1576; better in style but not so sound in scholarship. Reviews, R. F. Kaindl, *Hist Zeit.,* 130: 560, 1924; J. Šusta, *Rev. Hist.,* 149: 218, July 1925. *b.* Best history of the country in the seventeenth and eighteenth centuries from the nationalist point of view. Review, I. Goll, *Rev. Hist.,* 51: 352, March 1893; 61: 117, May 1896; 71: 349, Nov. 1899.   GMD

S2321a Beneš, Edvard. *Le problème autrichien et la question tchèque: étude sur les luttes politiques des nationalités slaves en Autriche.* Paris, 1908. (Bibliography.)

b Tobolka, Zdeněk V., ed. *Česká politika.* [Czech politics.] V. 1–5, v Praze, 1908–13.

a. Keen presentation of the Czech question in the setting of Austrian history from 1848 to 1907; ablest work of its sort. *b.* Best detailed account of Czech and Austrian politics from 1848 to 1906. V. 3. Mainly from the pen of Karel Kramář, a leading Czech statesman. RJK

CZECHOSLOVAKIA: THE REPUBLIC

S2361a **Nosek, Vladimír.** *Independent Bohemia, an account of the Czecho-Slovak struggle for liberty.* London and N. Y., 1918. (Bibliography.)

b **Čapek, Thomas.** *Origins of the Czechoslovak state with particular reference to the 1918 upheaval.* N. Y., 1926.

Deal with the antecedents and beginnings of the republic. *a.* Serviceable because of extensive quotations from published documents. *b.* Most recent convenient summary of the subject. RJK

S2371a **Eisenmann, Louis.** *La Tchèco-Slovaquie.* Paris, 1921. [États contemporains.] (Bibliography.)

b **Císař, Jaroslav,** and **Pokorný, František,** ed. *Czechoslovak republic, a survey of its history and geography, its political and cultural organization, and its economic resources.* London, 1922.

a. Ablest general survey of the Czechoslovak Republic; written in a non-Slavic language by a distinguished French historian who is a specialist on the recent history of Central Europe. Review, R. Guyot, *Rev. Hist.,* 143: 89, May 1923. *b.* Handy general survey of the republic by Czechs who had access to official documents. RJK

CZECHOSLOVAKIA: THE SLOVAKS

S2381 **Botto, Julius.** *Slováci, vývin ich národného povedomia.* [Slovaks, the evolution of their national consciousness.] 2 v. Turčiansky Svätý Martin, 1906–10.

Despite its journalistic character, the best general account of Slovak politics in the nineteenth century. RJK

S2382 **Seton-Watson, Robert W.** *New Slovakia.* Prague, 1924.

Best statement of the situation and problems of the Slovaks in the present republic. Review, C. E. Maurice, *Contemporary Rev.,* 126: 257, Aug. 1924. GMD

CZECHOSLOVAKIA: DIPLOMATIC HISTORY

S2501a **Masaryk, Tomáš G.** *New Europe: the Slav standpoint.* London, 1918. Published simultaneously in Czech and French, and later in German.

b ―― *Making of a state: memories and observations, 1914–1918.* London and N. Y., 1927. Tr. by H. W. Steed from the Czech. German tr. by C. Hoffmann, *Die Weltrevolution: Erinnerungen und Betrachtungen, 1914–1918,* Berlin, 1925.

c **Beneš, Edvard.** *Five years of Czechoslovak foreign policy.* Prague, 1924. Tr. from *Problémy nové Evropy a žahranicni politika česko-slovenská,* v Praze, 1924.

a. Survey of the European situation at the close of the World War with special reference to the position and interests of the Czechoslovaks, by the president of their republic. *b.* Recollections and political observations on the World War, with special reference to Czech affairs. Review, A. I. Andrews, *A.H.R.,* 33: 657, Apr.

1928. *c.* Outline and discussion of the international relations of the Czechoslovak republic in its earliest years by its minister of foreign affairs. GMD

CZECHOSLOVAKIA: ECONOMIC AND SOCIAL HISTORY

S2571a Gruber, Josef, ed. *Czechoslovakia, a survey of economic and social conditions, translated from Czech manuscripts by A. Brož, S. V. Klíma, and J. J. Král.* N. Y., 1924.

b Textor, Lucy E. *Land reform in Czechoslovakia.* London, 1923.

a. Collection of articles by national scholars edited by a professor in the University of Prague; rich in statistical data. *b.* Incorporates the results of personal investigations in the country by an American scholar. GMD

CZECHOSLOVAKIA: CULTURAL HISTORY

S2601 Nosek, Vladimír. *Spirit of Bohemia: a survey of Czecho-slovak history, music, and literature.* London, 1926. (Bibliographies.)

Useful and informing synopses of topics indicated in the title, especially of music; includes notable account of Czechoslovak effort during the World War. Review, (London) *Times Lit. Suppl.,* 25 : 904, Dec. 9, 1926. HRS

S2661a Lützow, Franz H. V., Graf von. *History of Bohemian literature.* 1899. 2nd ed., London, 1907. [Short histories of the literatures of the world.] (Bibliography.)

b Flajšhans, Václav. *Písemnictví české slovem i obrazem.* [Czech literature in word and picture.] v Praze, 1901.

c Vlček, Jaroslav. *Literatura na Slovensku.* [*Literature in Slovakia.*] v Praze, 1881. [Knihovna československá.]

d Frýdecký, František. *Slovensko literarni od doby Bernolákovy.* [Literary history of Slovakia since the time of Bernolák.] Moravska Ostrava, 1920.

a. First attempt in English at a history of Czech literature. Though somewhat out of date and now out of print, parts (ch. 3, 5, 7) are still valuable. *b.* Standard literary history in Czech; accurate, original, scientific; recognized as the authority in the field. *c.* Brief; excellent account of the beginnings of Slovak literature prior to 1880. *d.* Sheds much light on modern Slovak literature and culture in general. LZL

CZECHOSLOVAKIA: BIOGRAPHIES

Among the best biographies of eminent Czechoslovaks are: (S2701) Václav Novotný, *Mistr Jan Hus, život a učení* [Master John Hus, his life and teaching], 2 v., v Praze, 1919–21; (S2721) Jan Kvačala [Johann Kvacsala] *Johann Amos Comenius, sein Leben und seine Schriften,* Leipzig, 1892, abridged ed., Berlin, 1914 [Die grossen Erzieher]; (S2722) A. Patera and Jan Kvačala, ed., *Jana Amosa Komeského korrespondence,* 2 v., v Praze, 1892–98 [Česká Akademie]; (S2741) Jaroslav Vlček, *Pavel Josef Šafařík,* v Praze, 1896; (S2761) Hélène Tourtzer [Turcer], *Louis Stúr et l'idée de l'indépendance slovaque, 1815–1856,* Cahors, 1913; (S2762) Josef Pekař, *František Palacký,* v Praze, 1912; (S2763) Tomáš G. Masaryk, *Karel Havlíček,* 1896, 2nd ed., v Praze, 1904; (S2801*a*) Edvard Beneš, ed., *T. G. Masarykovi, k šedesatym narozeninam* [To T. G. Masaryk in honor of his sixtieth birthday], v Praze, 1910; (S2801*b*) J. Doležal, *Masarykova cesta životní* [Masaryk's cycle of life], 2 v., v Brne, 1920–21. RJK, GMD

CZECHOSLOVAKIA: ACADEMY AND SOCIETY PUBLICATIONS

Česká Akademie Císaře Františka Josefa pro Vědy, Slovesnost, a Umění v Praze, now Česká Akademie Věd a Umění [Czech Academy of Sciences and Arts], issues (S2921) *Historický archiv,* v Praze, 1893 ff., and numerous other publications. Among the many societies which publish works relating to history and allied subjects are: Královská Česká Společnost Nauk [Die Königliche Böhemischen Gesellschaft der Wissenschaften], which issues (S2922a) *Abhandlungen* [*Rozpravy*], 50 v., Prag, 1775–1884; (S2922b) *Abhandlungen* [*Rozpravy*]: *Klasse für Philosophie, Geschichte, und Philologie,* 4 v., Prag, 1885–91; (S2922c) *Sitzungsberichte* [*Věstnik*], 26 v., Prag, 1859–84; (S2922d) *Sitzungsberichte* [*Věstnik*]: *Klasse für Philosophie, Geschichte, und Philologie,* Prag [v Praze], 1885 ff.; (S2922e) *Jahresberichte* [Výroční zprávy], Prag [v Praze], 1875 ff.; Klub Historický [Historical Club, originally History Seminar of Karlova Universita], which issues (S2923) *Český časopis historický* [Czech historical magazine], v Praze, 1894 ff.; Museum Království Českého, which publishes (S2924) *Časopis* [Magazine], v Praze, 1827 ff.; Gesellschaft zur Förderung Deutscher Wissenschaft, Kunst, und Literatur in Böhmen, since 1924 Deutsche Gesellschaft der Wissenschaften und Künste für die Tschechoslowakische Republik, which issues (S2925) *Deutsche Arbeit, Zeitschrift für das geistige Leben der Deutschen in Böhmen,* Prag, 1901 ff., and other publications; Verein für Geschichte der Deutschen in Böhmen, which publishes (S2926) *Mitteilungen,* Prag, 1862 ff., and has issued other works from time to time; and Deutscher Verein für die Geschichte Mährens und Schlesiens, whose organ was (S2927a) *Notizenblatt,* Brünn, 1855–96, continued by (S2927b) *Zeitschrift,* Brünn, 1897 ff.   RJK, GMD

SECTION T

SOUTHEASTERN EUROPE AND SOUTHWESTERN ASIA: THE BALKANS AND THE NEAR EAST SINCE THE RISE OF THE OTTOMAN TURKS

Editors

ALBERT HOWE LYBYER

Professor of History, University of Illinois

AND

ROBERT JOSEPH KERNER

Professor of Modern History, University of California

CONTENTS

INTRODUCTION

The earliest history of Southwestern Asia is dealt with in § C, and that of Southeastern Europe and the establishment of its sway over Southwestern Asia in the Hellenistic period in § D. In the next age both Southeastern Europe and Southwestern Asia passed under the rule of the Roman empire, so that the books relating to them in this period are listed in § E. Works on the continuation of the Roman empire in the East, that is, on Byzantine history, and on the great western enterprises in the East known as the Crusades, are noted in § H. With the rise of Mohammedanism a steadily increasing portion of Southwestern Asia passed from Byzantine to Moslem rule, and consequently the treatment of its history passes to § G.

The transition from the conditions prevailing in Southeastern Europe and Southwestern Asia in the Middle Ages to those in modern times is marked by the rise of the Ottoman Turks at the close of the thirteenth century just after the great era of crusading enterprise had ended. The history of the Near East, that is, of Southeastern Europe and of Southwestern Asia, in modern times has been characterized by the steady spread of Ottoman sway over these regions through nearly four centuries, followed by its decline and the emergence of the local populations into independent nationalities in the last two centuries and a half. These two movements furnish the subject matter for this section. The central theme is Ottoman history: the dominant issues are the Eastern Question and the revival of the submerged nationalities.

The Eastern Question, or more recently the Near Eastern Question, is, in its broadest sense, the continuous complex of problems arising from the decline of Ottoman power. In a narrower and equally familiar usage it signifies the whole group of diplomatic and military relations of the leading European nations with the Ottoman empire and its successors. In either case the phrase is most commonly applied to the kaleidoscopic changes in the period since the outbreak of the Serbian revolt in 1804. Since the major part of these problems have concerned the peoples of Southeastern Europe, the narrower phrase, Balkan Question, is also frequently employed. The successive acute phases of the Eastern Question have led to the production of many hasty historical sketches, usually of propaganda nature; of valuable analyses of current situations by competent observers; of an enormous mass of historical materials, still widely scattered and often difficult of access; and of a few seasoned works by sound and impartial scholars. In addition to the typical books selected for mention in this section, the student should consult various works listed in §§ I and J and in the sections devoted to the several nations whose international policies have involved them in the Eastern Question.

The scientific study of Ottoman Turkish history is in a very imperfect state. The main streams of European historiography have long flowed elsewhere. The Turks are Mohammedans and their tongue is a mixture of three Asiatic vernaculars. The materials for their story lie scattered through a score of literatures. Their own histories have been translated inadequately into European languages and are only beginning to be submitted to severe scrutiny, chiefly by German and Austrian scholars. It is true, furthermore, that all parts of the vast areas at any time dominated by Turkey have been of perennial interest, and have steadily attracted travelers of every description, hundreds of whom have been moved to write intelligently and a few with critical scholarship concerning the lands, the peoples, their cultures, and their histories. Many compilers and narrators have labored long at fuller and sounder accounts, and a few great scholars have produced extended histories.

A scholar's bibliography for the study of the nations of the Near East would contain very few works in English. A bibliography comprised of English works alone, in spite of some excellent contributions, would give the student an inadequate introduction to the very complicated history of this corner of the world. In view of the objects of this volume, it has seemed wise to compromise by taking the middle course. The controversial character of many of the subjects involved, the limitations in space, and the quality of the material have made it advisable to give preference to general accounts rather than to special studies, to present selections of typical works rather than exhaustive lists, and to cite mainly works in English and the more familiar languages rather than in the vernaculars of the several nationalities, though a few characteristic works in the native languages, written from the national points of view, have been included. As the reawakening of these nationalities has taken place largely within the past hundred years, the major portion of the books included deals with comparatively recent events. Citations have been included of the more important collections of sources because a large proportion of the materials included is of international rather than national import and because many of the documents printed are in western European languages.

It should be borne in mind throughout this section that some knowledge of antecedent conditions and events is particularly necessary to an accurate understanding of recent changes and current problems in the Near East.

AHL, RJK

NEAR EAST: BIBLIOGRAPHY

T1a Bengescu (Bengesco), George. *Essai d'une notice bibliographique sur la question d'orient: orient-européen, 1821–1897.* Paris, 1897.

b New York Public Library. *List of works in the New York Public Library relating to the Near Eastern question and the Balkan states, including European Turkey and modern Greece.* N. Y., 1910. [Reprint from *Bulletin*, Jan.-May, 1910.]

c Yovanovitch (Jovanović), Vojislav M. *Engleska bibliografija o istočnom pitanju u Evropi.* [English bibliography of the Eastern question in Europe, 1481–1906.] Beograd, 1908. [Srbska Kraljevska Akademija, Spomenik, v. 48.]

d Mikhov [Michoff], Nikola V. *Bibliographie de la Turquie, de la Bulgarie, et de la Macédoine.* 2 v. Sofia, 1908–13.

e —— *Sources bibliographiques sur l'histoire de la Turquie et de la Bulgarie.* 2 v. Sofia, 1914–24.

Useful works in the absence of a complete bibliography of the Near East and the Eastern Question; should be supplemented by bibliographies mentioned elsewhere in this section. *a.* Most thorough for the period covered. Review, *Rev. Hist.*, 66: 241, Jan. 1898. *b, c,* and *e.* Lists of limited compass and moderate size. *d.* Only an introductory pamphlet. Review of *e,* E. Gerland, *Hist. Zeit.*, 131: 158, 1925. Cf. also W. L. Langer, 'Recent books on the History of the Near East,' in *Journal of Modern History,* I, 420–441, Sept. 1929. AHL, RJK

Library Collections.—The collections of materials to be found in American libraries on the history of the Near East and of its several nationalities probably rank in the following order of importance: Harvard University, Library of Congress, New York Public Library, Columbia University, University of Chicago, Stanford University, and University of Michigan. AHS

NEAR EAST: ENCYCLOPEDIAS AND WORKS OF REFERENCE

Among the general encyclopedias special attention should be directed to (B22b) *Encyclopaedia Britannica;* the supplementary volumes forming the twelfth edition record fully the eastern campaigns during the World War. The most recent internal history of the several countries is, however, not always as adequately treated either in these volumes or in the fourteenth edition. (G22a) *Encyclopedia of Islam* is providing, in an unprecedentedly thorough and scholarly way, articles on cities which have been under Moslem sway, on important Mussulman individuals, and on the institutions of Mohammedan religion and rule. AHL

T21 Bell, H. T. Montagu, ed. *Near East year book and who's who.* London, 1927.

'A survey of the affairs, political, economic, and social of Yugoslavia, Roumania, Bulgaria, Greece, and Turkey.' Valuable for reference; annexes include recent Near Eastern treaties and agreements; who's who section lacks Turkish names.

AHL

NEAR EAST: GEOGRAPHY

T41a *Die österreichische Monarchie in Wort und Bild.* 24 v. Wien, 1886–1902.

b Umlauft, Friedrich. *Die österreichisch-ungarische Monarchie: geographisch-statistisches Handbuch für Leser aller Stände.* 1876. 3rd rev. ed., Wien, 1897.

Useful descriptions of those portions of the former Austro-Hungarian monarchy which have been especially involved in the Balkan and Near Eastern questions. *a.* Monumental coöperative publication in German and Magyar; contains, in addition to geographical material, much political, economic, and cultural history for all parts of the former Austro-Hungarian monarchy. Though the various sections differ in quality and impartiality, all are convenient summaries and some are important contributions. *b.* Useful for statistical data.

For a concise geographical treatise by an able scholar, cf. (P42b) Supan, *Österreich-Ungarn.*

RJK

T42 Cvijić, Jovan. *La péninsule balkanique, géographie humaine.* Paris, 1918.

Indispensable for the advanced student. The author, a famous Serb geographer, studies the peninsula as the connecting link between Europe and Asia; determines the lines of approach and areas of isolation; and examines with meticulous detail the climate, vegetation, and ethnography, as well as the prevailing social and mental types. Review, F. Schevill, *A.H.R.,* 24:690, July 1919. Also cf. (J441a) *Peace handbooks,* and (A47b) Newbigin, *Geographical aspects of Balkan problems.*

FS

NEAR EAST: ETHNOGRAPHY

T51a Auerbach, Bertrand. *Les races et les nationalités en Autriche-Hongrie.* 1898. 2nd rev. ed., Paris, 1917. [Bibliothèque d'histoire contemporaine.]

b *Die Völker Oesterreich-Ungarns: ethnographische und culturhistorische Schilderungen.* 12 v. in 15. Wien, 1881–85. [1, K. Schober, *Die Deutschen in Nieder- und Ober-Oesterreich, Salzburg, Steiermark, Kärnthen, und*

Krain; 2, J. Bendel, *Die Deutschen in Böhmen, Mähren, und Schlesien;* 3, J. H. Schwicker, *Die Deutschen in Ungarn und Siebenbürgen;* 4, J. Egger, *Die Tiroler und Vorarlberger;* 5, P. Hunfalvy, *Die Ungarn oder Magyaren;* 6, I. Slavici, *Die Rumänen in Ungarn, Siebenbürgen, und der Bukowina;* 7, J. Wolf and W. Goldbaum, *Die Juden;* 8, J. Vlach and J. A. Helfert, *Die Čecho-Slaven;* 9, J. Szujski, *Die Polen und Ruthenen in Galizien;* 10, J. Šuman, *Die Slovenen;* J. Starè, *Die Kroaten im Königreiche Kroatien und Slovonien;* 11, T. Stefanović Vilovsky, *Die Serben im südlichen Ungarn, in Dalmatia, Bosnien, und in der Herzegovina;* J. Czirbusz, *Die südungarischen Bulgaren;* 12, J. H. Schwicker, *Die Zigeuner in Ungarn und Siebenbürgen.*]

c Niederle, Lubor. *La race slave: statistique, démographie, anthropologie.* 1911. 2nd rev. ed., Paris, 1916 [Nouvelle collection scientifique]. (Bibliography.) Tr. by L. Leger from *Slovansky svet,* v Praze, 1909.

Representatives of the best works on the complicated, controversial subject of nationalities in the former Austro-Hungarian monarchy. Generally fair, comprehensive, and sound. *a* and *c.* Though professedly impartial, reveal sympathies for the Slavs and other racial minorities. *a.* Best of the group. Review, E. Bourgeois, *Rev. Hist.,* 71 : 396, Nov. 1899. *b.* More popular; uneven in quality; attempts an impartial presentation of the question by means of monographic studies of the several national groups by competent scholars.

Also cf. works listed under (T1051) and (T2051).   RJK

T52 Laveleye, Émile, Baron de. *Balkan peninsula.* London, 1887. Tr. by Mrs. Thorpe from *La péninsule des Balkans: Vienne, Croatie, Bosnie, Serbie, Bulgarie, Roumélie, Turquie, Roumanie . . . ,* 1886; new ed., 2 v., Bruxelles, 1888.

Excellent survey of the peoples and conditions in the Balkans at a critical period in their history, by a professor in the University of Liége. Review, C. Bémont, *Rev. Hist.,* 31 : 364, July 1886. For recent changes in the population of the Balkans, cf. A. A. Pallis, 'Racial migrations in the Balkans during 1912–24,' *Geographical Journal,* 66 : 315–331, Oct. 1925.   GMD

NEAR EAST: COLLECTIONS OF SOURCES

Many of the collections of sources for diplomatic history listed in §§ I and J contain extensive materials relating to the Eastern Question, notably (J72a) *Die grosse Politik der europäischen Kabinette, 1871–1914,* v. 2, for the Near Eastern crisis, 1876–1878, and the Congress of Berlin; v. 5–6, for Bulgarian complications, 1885–1888; v. 12, for Crete and the Turkish question, 1895–1899; v. 22, for the Macedonian reforms, 1904–1907; v. 25–27, for the Turkish revolution, the Bosnian crisis, and the Austro-Russian rivalry in the Balkans, 1907–1911; v. 33–36, for the Balkan Wars, 1912–1914; and also (J75) *British Documents,* v. 4, 5, for the Near East, 1903–1909, and for the Anglo-Russian negotiations, 1903–1907, relating to Persia, Afghanistan, and Tibet.   SBF

NEAR EAST: SHORTER GENERAL HISTORIES

T101 Schevill, Ferdinand. *History of the Balkan peninsula from the earliest times to the present day.* N. Y., 1922. (Bibliography.)

General history of the Balkan peninsula; founded on an extensive literature in the Western European languages; written in excellent style. Review, A. H. Lybyer, *A.H.R.,* 28 : 528, Apr. 1923.   RJK

T102a Seton-Watson, Robert W. *Rise of nationality in the Balkans.* London, 1917. (Bibliography.)

b Forbes, Nevill; Toynbee, Arnold J.; Mitrany, David; and Hogarth, David G. *The Balkans: a history of Bulgaria, Serbia, Greece, Rumania, Turkey.* Oxford, 1915.

c Miller, William. *The Balkans, Roumania, Bulgaria, Servia, and Montenegro.* 1896. 3rd rev. ed., London and N. Y., 1923. [Story of the nations.]

d —— *Ottoman empire, 1801–1913.* 1913. 3rd rev., entitled *Ottoman empire and its successors, 1801–1927,* Cambridge, Eng., 1927. [Cambridge historical series.] (Bibliography.)

e Iorga [Jorga], Nicolae. *Histoire des états balcaniques jusqu'à 1924.* Paris, 1925.

a. Standard work in English on the general historical evolution of the Balkan nations prior to 1913. Comprehensive and brilliant. Review, *Saturday Rev.,* 124:288, Oct. 13, 1917. *b.* Commendable, lucid, historical treatment, with emphasis on recent events. Review, F. Schevill, *A.H.R.,* 21:807, July 1916. *c* and *d.* Substantially identical works, furnishing good general historical accounts of each of the Balkan states from their beginnings to 1922. Review of *c,* E. A. Grosvenor, *A.H.R.,* 3:387, Jan. 1898; of *d,* F. J. Bliss, *A.H.R.,* 19:355, Jan. 1914. *e.* By an eminent Rumanian historian; similar to *b* and *c.* RJK

NEAR EAST: GENERAL HISTORIES OF THE EASTERN QUESTION

T201a Driault, Édouard. *La question d'orient depuis ses origines jusqu'à nos jours.* 1898. 8th rev. ed., Paris, 1921. [Bibliothèque d'histoire contemporaine.] (Bibliographies.)

b Ancel, Jacques. *Manuel historique de la question d'orient, 1792–1923.* Paris, 1923. [Bibliothèque d'histoire et de politique.] (Bibliographies.)

a. Has been, since its first publication, the standard exposition in French of the Eastern Question, which concept the author enlarges to include the whole field of the political decline of Islam. Much used by later writers. The successive editions show little change beyond the addition of a few pages to bring the story up to date. Reviews, S. Lane-Poole, *E.H.R.,* 14:805, Oct. 1899; A. H. Lybyer, *A.H.R.,* 23:388, Jan. 1918; R. Guyot, *Rev. Hist.* 143:85, May 1923. *b.* Good recent historical survey and introduction. Review, *Rev. Hist.,* 150:114, Sept. 1925. AHL

T202a Marriott, Sir John A., Jr. *Eastern question: an historical study in European diplomacy.* 1917. 3rd rev. ed., Oxford and N. Y., 1924. (Bibliographies.)

b Holland, Sir Thomas E. *European concert in the eastern question: a collection of treaties and other public acts, edited with introduction and notes.* Oxford, 1885.

a. Concise history of the relations of Turkey with the nations of western Europe; noteworthy for its comprehensiveness and breadth of vision; two thirds of the book deal with events since 1800. Review, A. H. Lybyer, *A.H.R.,* 23:388, Jan. 1918. *b.* Mainly a collection of important nineteenth-century documents relating to Turkey, including the principal treaties between 1826 and 1885. AHL

T221a Goriainov, Sergïi M. *Le Bosphore et les Dardanelles: étude historique sur la question des détroits, d'après la correspondance diplomatique déposée aux archives centrales de Saint-Pétersbourg et à celles de l'empire.* Paris 1910. Tr. from Russian original of 1908.

b Puaux, René. *Constantinople et la question d'orient.* Paris, 1920.

a. Important contribution to the diplomatic history of one of the most critical problems in the Eastern Question. Review, K. Stählin, *Hist. Zeit.*, 108: 406, 1912. *b.* Discussion of more recent aspects of the same question by a French journalist who has published several works on the Greek phases of the Eastern Question.

GMD

T301a Cahuet, Albéric. *La question d'orient dans l'histoire contemporaine, 1821–1905.* Paris, 1905.

b Bamberg, Felix. *Geschichte der orientalischen Angelegenheit im Zeitraume des Pariser und des Berliner Friedens.* Berlin, 1892. [(B162) Oncken, Allgemeine Geschichte in Einzeldarstellungen.]

c Choublier, Max. *La question d'orient depuis le traité de Berlin: étude d'histoire diplomatique.* 1897. 2nd rev. ed., Paris, 1899.

Careful studies of the question during limited periods in the nineteenth century. Review of *c*, A. D. Xénopol, *Rev. Hist.*, 74: 374, Nov. 1900.   AHL

NEAR EAST: EASTERN QUESTION AT THE BEGINNING OF THE TWENTIETH CENTURY

T331 Tyler, Mason W. *European powers and the Near East, 1875–1908.* Minneapolis, 1925. [University of Minnesota, Studies in the social sciences.]

Posthumous monograph, with supplementary chapter on the Baghdad Railway, edited by G. S. Ford from the author's draft and submitted to reading by E. M. Earle (cf. T381); and a chapter on the Balkans, 1904–1908, by W. S. Davis, based on Professor Tyler's notes. Shows excellent judgment and understanding; unbiased and clear. Review, R. J. Kerner, *Slavonic Rev.*, 5: 461, Dec. 1926.

HRS

T332 Pears, Sir Edwin. *Forty years in Constantinople: recollections, 1873–1915.* London and N. Y., 1916.

Personal impressions of Near Eastern events; emphasizes the influence of Great Britain and her ambassadors.   AHL

T351a Pinon, René. *L'Europe et l'empire ottoman: les aspects actuels de la question d'orient.* Paris, 1909.

b ———— *L'Europe et la Jeune Turquie: les aspects nouveaux de la question d'orient.* Paris, 1911.

c Fehmi, Youssouf. *La révolution ottomane, 1908–1910.* Paris, 1911.

a and *b.* French publicist describes and interprets fairly the stirring period from 1907 to 1911. *c.* Turkish view of the revolutionary period.   AHL

T352a Abbott, George F. *Turkey in transition.* London, 1909.

b ———— *Turkey, Greece, and the great powers, a study in friendship and hate.* London, 1916; N. Y., 1917. (Bibliography.)

The author, a member of a British family long resident in the region, narrates clearly and vigorously, with full expression of personal opinion, the events of eight or nine momentous years about 1908 to 1916; often takes exception to the policies of European diplomats and statesmen.   AHL

T361a Brailsford, Henry N. *Macedonia, its races and their future.* London, 1906.

b Bérard, Victor. *La Macédoine.* 1897. 3rd ed., Paris, 1903.

c Amadori-Virgilj, Giovanni. *La questione rumeliota (Macedonia, Vecchia Serbia, Albania, Epiro) e la politica italiana.* Bitonto, 1908. [Biblioteca italiana di politica estera.]

d Weigand, Gustav. *Ethnographie von Makedonien: geschichtlich-nationaler, sprachlich-statistischer Teil.* Leipzig, 1924.

a. Fairest and most impartial statement of the much vexed Macedonian question; written by an Englishman. *b, c,* and *d.* Similar attempts at impartial study of the question by a Frenchman, an Italian, and a German respectively. Review of *d,* F. Geyer, *Hist. Zeit.,* 134:430, 1926. RJK, GMD

T371a International Commission to Inquire into the Causes and Conduct of the Balkan Wars. *Report.* Washington, 1914. [Carnegie Endowment for International Peace.]

b Young, George [pseud. **Diplomatist**]. *Nationalism and war in the Near East.* Oxford and N. Y., 1915. [Carnegie Endowment for International Peace.]

a. Made by a commission chosen by the trustees of the Carnegie Endowment. Considers, among other things, the ethnography and national aspirations of the various Balkan peoples, the wars themselves, and the policy adopted by each of the combatants. The final chapters are devoted to a consideration of the economic, moral, and social consequences of the wars. Though the trustees of the Endowment hoped to secure a fair, non-partisan statement, it has been adversely criticized by Greeks and Serbs. Review, F. Schevill, *A.H.R.,* 20:638, Apr. 1915. *b.* Undoubtedly the best account of the Balkan Wars, their causes and their political, economic, and moral results. The work aims to be impartial, and, on the whole, succeeds very well. It is philosophical rather than narrative in character and thus presupposes a knowledge of the essential facts of the historical evolution of the Near East.

Also cf. (J71d) *Documents diplomatiques: les affaires balkaniques, 1912–1914,* the French yellow book on the diplomatic history of the Balkan Wars. SPD

T372a Gueshoff [Geshov, Guéchoff], Ivan E. *Balkan League.* London, 1915. Tr. by C. C. Mincoff from *L'alliance balkanique,* Paris, 1915.

b Panaretoff, Stephen [pseud. **Historicus**]. *Bulgaria and her neighbors, an historic presentation of the background of the Balkan problem, one of the basic issues of the World War.* N. Y., 1917.

c Protić, Stojan [pseud. **Balkanicus**]. *Aspirations of Bulgaria.* London, 1915. Tr. from the Serbian.

d Cassavetti, Demetrius J. *Hellas and the Balkan wars.* London, 1914.

a. For the English reader, the Bulgarian side has the advantage of being defended, in the matter of the diplomacy of the Balkan wars, by one of the important participants, I. E. Geshov. His little work is written with skill and moderation, as well as with knowledge. As he had resigned before the second war, he was in a position to condemn the later mistakes of his countrymen. Review of *a* and *d, Athenaeum,* 25, Jan. 1916. *b.* Another good statement of the Bulgarian point of view, though the emphasis is upon the Macedonian question. *c.* Best presentation of the case for Serbia. *d.* Stout volume; mainly devoted to the exploits of the Greeks; gives only a summary statement of the causes of the wars and of the diplomatic complications. Review, N. D. Harris, *Amer. Pol. Sci. Rev.,* 8:685, Nov. 1914. ACC

T381 **Earle, Edward M.** *Turkey, the great powers, and the Bagdad railway, a study in imperialism.* N. Y., 1923. (Bibliographies.)

Based on conferences with many individuals associated with the enterprise as well as upon thorough research; interestingly written; calm and dispassionate. The interpretation is rather critical of British and French opposition to the enterprise, somewhat apologetic as regards German policy, and decidedly pro-Turkish. Review, A. I. Andrews, *Amer. Pol. Sci. Rev.,* 18:410, May 1924.   FMA, AHL

T382 **Buxton, Noël,** and **Leese, C. Leonard.** *Balkan problems and European peace.* N. Y., 1919.

Chiefly important for British diplomatic documents relating to Bulgaria's entrance into the World War, presented by Mr. Buxton, who was British special envoy in the Balkans.   GMD

T391a **Toynbee, Arnold J.** *Western question in Greece and Turkey, a study in the contact of civilisations.* 1922. 2nd ed., London and Boston, 1923.

b **Panaretoff, Stephen.** *Near Eastern affairs and conditions.* N. Y., 1922. [Williams College, Institute of Politics publications.]

c **Armstrong, Hamilton Fish.** *New Balkans.* N. Y., 1926.

d —— *Where the east begins.* N. Y., 1929.

e **Stoddard, Theodore Lothrop.** *New world of Islam.* N. Y., 1921. (Bibliographical foot-notes.)

a. Intensive study of a single current problem in the Eastern Question. Recent relations of Greeks and Turks, especially from 1919 to 1922, are investigated from the point of view of the contact of civilizations rather than of political rivalries. Based on careful study and extensive observations; accurate and impartial; sympathetic with Near Eastern peoples, especially with the Turks; considers western intervention a serious obstacle to the pacification of the Near East. Review, A. H. Lybyer, *A.H.R.,* 28:753, July 1923. *b.* Situation of the Balkan peoples in 1922 treated as the product of fifteen centuries of history; excellent exposition; fair and dispassionate, though inevitably colored by the desire of the author, a Bulgarian, to present as good a case as possible for his country. Review, A. H. Lybyer, *Amer. Pol. Sci. Rev.,* 16:695, Nov. 1922. *c.* Optimistic survey of the post-war period, with special reference to new nationalistic developments in the Balkan peninsula. Review, R. J. Kerner, *Slavonic Rev.,* 6:230, June 1927. *d.* Discusses sympathetically and clearly the new dictatorship in Jugoslavia, the return of Venizelos in Greece, the peasant régime in Rumania, Albanian problems, and the broad trend of events in the Balkans since the World War. *e.* Comprehensive survey of present factors on the Moslem side in the Eastern Question. Recent political and other movements in Turkey and other parts of the Moslem world are described with substantial accuracy. Review, A. H. Lybyer, *A.H.R.,* 27:322, Jan. 1922.   AHL

T396 **Bagger, Eugene S.** *Eminent Europeans: studies in continental reality.* N. Y. and London, 1922. (Bibliographies.)

Collection of interesting biographies of contemporary celebrities in eastern and southeastern Europe, by a liberal Magyar journalist.   RJK

NEAR EAST: ECONOMIC HISTORY

T571 **Dudescu [Dudesco], Jean N.** *L'évolution économique contemporaine des pays balkaniques, Roumanie, Bulgarie, et Serbie.* Paris, 1915. (Bibliography.)

Best general treatise on the economic evolution of the Balkan countries. The development and contemporary conditions of agriculture, commerce, and finances are treated accurately and impartially, and with abundant statistical data.   RJK

NEAR EAST: CULTURAL HISTORY: RELIGION

T621 Greene, Joseph K. *Leavening the Levant.* Boston, 1916.

Excellent survey of American Protestant missionary work in Turkey and of the conditions with which it attempts to deal.   AHL

NEAR EAST: PERIODICALS

Besides various important periodicals listed in §§ C and G, the following also deserve mention as devoting considerable space to authoritative articles on the Near East, especially in recent times: (T941) *The Orient,* Constantinople, 1910–22, weekly, published by American missionaries, especially valuable for its news from inside Constantinople during the World War and for its selected translations from local newspapers; (T942) *Near East, a weekly journal of oriental politics, literature, finance, and commerce,* London, 1908 ff., extremely useful for political and economic news, opinions, letters, and book reviews; (T951) *Echos d'Orient, revue bimestrielle de théologie, de droit canonique, de liturgie, d'archéologie, d'histoire, et de géographie orientales,* Paris, 1897 ff., until 1904 entitled *Echos de Nôtre-Dame de France;* (T952) *Correspondance d'Orient, politique, économique, et financière,* Paris, 1908 ff.; (T961) *Österreichische Monatsschrift für den Orient,* 44 v., Wien, 1883–1918; (T971) *Oriente moderno,* Roma, 1921 ff.; which contains extensive monthly accounts and discussions of political, economic, and cultural events in the Near East. Numerous articles on current affairs appear in general reviews listed in §§ B and J.

Among the publications devoted to the discussion of Balkan affairs are (T981a) *Balkan review,* 4 v., London, 1919–21, continued as (T981b) *Eastern Europe,* London, 1921 ff.; (T982a) *Balkan-Revue: Monatsschrift für die wirtschaftlichen Interessen der südost-europäischen Länder,* Berlin, 1914–18, title changed to (T982b) *Südost: Balkan-Revue,* Berlin, 1918 ff.; (T983a) *Bulletin de l'Institut pour l'Étude de l'Europe sud-orientale,* 10 v., Bucarest, 1914–23, continued as (T983b) *Revue historique du sud-est européen,* Bucarest, 1924 ff., ed. by Professor N. Iorga.   AHL, RJK

TURKEY: BIBLIOGRAPHY

No adequate or reasonably complete bibliography on the Ottoman Turks exists. Reference, however, may be made to the lists in (I121) *Cambridge modern history,* and (B152) Lavisse and Rambaud, *Histoire générale,* and also to the works cited in (T1043) Banse, *Die Türkei,* (T1121) Hammer, *Geschichte des osmanischen Reiches,* (T1123) La Jonquière, *Histoire de l'empire ottoman,* and (T1371b) Mears, *Modern Turkey.* Various bibliographies listed in §§ G and W should also be consulted. An annotated bibliography, based upon the extensive Ottoman collection in the library of Harvard University, is in preparation.   AHL

T1001 Auboyneau, Gaston, and **Fevret, A.** *Essai de bibliographie pour servir à l'histoire de l'empire ottoman: livres turcs, livres imprimés à Constantinople, livres étrangers à la Turquie mais pouvant servir à son histoire.* V. 1, *Religion, moeurs, et coutumes.* Paris, 1911.

This fragment represents the only considerable attempt to provide a bibliography on the Ottoman Turks.   AHL

TURKEY: GEOGRAPHY

T1041 Hubbard, Gilbert E. *Day of the crescent: glimpses of old Turkey.* Cambridge, Eng., and N. Y., 1920.

Fairly readable condensations of accounts by western European visitors to the Ottoman Empire prior to the nineteenth century, including several not listed in (T1042). Reviews, *Spectator*, 124:768, June 5, 1920; A. H. Lybyer, *A.H.R.*, 26:129, Oct. 1920. AHL

T1042a Schiltberger, Johannes. *Bondage and travels of Johann Schiltberger, a native of Bavaria, in Europe, Asia, and Africa, 1396–1427.* London, 1879. [Hakluyt Society.] (Bibliography.) Tr. by J. B. Telfer from *Reisen des Johannes Schiltberger aus München in Europa, Asia, und Afrika von 1394 bis 1427, zum ersten Mal nach der gleichzeitigen Heidelberger Handschrift herausgegeben und erläutert von Karl Friedrich Neumann,* München, 1859; critical ed., by V. Langmantel, *Reisebuch,* Stuttgart, 1885. [Bibliothek des litterarischen Vereins in Stuttgart.]

b La Brocquière, Bertrandon de. *Travels of Bertrandon de la Brocquière . . . to Palestine, and his return from Jerusalem overland to France, during the years 1432 and 1433.* London, 1807. Later ed., London, 1847. [Bohn's Antiquarian library.] Tr. by T. Johnes from *Voyage d'outremer et retour de Jérusalem en France par la voie de terre pendant le cours des années 1432 et 1433 . . . ouvrage extrait d'un manuscrit de la Bibliothèque Nationale, remis en Français moderne,* ed. by P. J. B. LeGrand d'Aussy, Paris, 1804. [Mémoires de l'Institut.] New ed., by C. Schefer, Paris, 1892. [(K74) Schefer and Cordier, Recueil de voyages.]

c Busbecq, Ogier Ghislain de. *Legationis turcicae epistolae quattuor.* Paris, 1589. Several later ed. English tr. in Charles T. Forster and Francis H. Blackburne Daniell, *Life and letters of Ogier Ghiselin de Busbecq,* 2 v., London, 1881.

d Montagu, Lady Mary Wortley. *Letters written during her travels in Europe, Asia, and Africa, to persons of distinction.* Ed. by Mary Astell. London, 1763. Several later ed. Also in her *Letters and works* ed. by Lord Wharncliffe, 1837; rev. ed., 2 v., London, 1887; and in her *Letters, 1709 to 1762,* London and N. Y., 1906 [Everyman's library].

e Kinglake, Alexander W. *Eöthen: or, traces of travel brought home from the East.* London, 1844. Numerous later ed., including London and N. Y., 1908 [Everyman's Library].

Probably the best known of the many accounts left by travelers in Turkish lands prior to the twentieth century. *a.* Account by a captive at the Battle of Nicopolis, 1396; first printed about 1475 and often reissued. *b.* Record by a native of Guyenne, later in the service of Philip the Good of Burgundy. *c.* A native of Flanders, who spent his life in the service of the Emperor Charles V. and his successors, vividly records his intelligent observations while representing the Hapsburgs at Constantinople from 1554 to 1562. Review, *Athenaeum,* 1:456, Apr. 2, 1881. *d.* Written in sprightly fashion by the wife of the British ambassador at Constantinople from 1716 to 1718. *e.* This classic record of travel recounts a tour by the historian of the Crimean War made in 1835, soon after his leaving Cambridge. GMD

T1043 Banse, Ewald. *Die Türkei, eine moderne Geographie.* 1916. 3rd ed., Braunschweig, 1919. (Bibliography.)

Treats, by topics, of the area included in Turkey in 1913; best existing general survey; well-selected illustrations. AHL

T1044a Grosvenor, Edwin A. *Constantinople.* 1895. 2nd ed., 2 v., Boston, 1900.

b Hutton, William H. *Constantinople: the story of the old capital of the empire.* 1900. 3rd ed., London and N. Y., 1909. [Mediaeval towns.]

c Young, George. *Constantinople.* London and N. Y., 1926.

d Dwight, Harry G. *Constantinople, settings and traits.* N. Y. and London, 1926. Rev. ed. of *Constantinople, old and new.* N. Y., 1915. (Bibliography.)

e Johnson, Clarence R., ed. *Constantinople today, or, the pathfinder survey of Constantinople: a study in oriental social life.* N. Y. and London, 1922.

f Lybyer, Albert H. *Constantinople as capital of the Ottoman empire.* American Historical Association, *Annual report, 1916,* 1 : 371–388.

a. Abundantly illustrated historical and descriptive account. Review, *Spectator,* 76: 19, Jan. 4, 1896. *b.* Briefer historical and descriptive work. Review, *Spectator,* 85: 935, Dec. 22, 1900. *c.* Spirited historical narrative. Review, *Saturday Rev.,* 141: 578, May 1, 1926. *d.* Sympathetic, well-stated, and well-illustrated description. *e.* Scientific survey of conditions, with statistics. Review, M. M. Patrick, *Nation,* 116: 497, Apr. 25, 1923. *f.* Brief historical survey. AHL

TURKEY: ETHNOGRAPHY

T1051a Rycaut, Sir Paul. *Present state of the Ottoman empire.* London, 1668. Many later ed. with title, *History of the present state of the Ottoman empire.* Also reprinted in (T1201*d*) Knolles, *Generall historie of the Turkes,* 6th ed.

b Eliot, Sir Charles N. E. [pseud. **Odysseus**]. *Turkey in Europe.* 1900. Rev. ed., London, 1908.

c Pears, Sir Edwin. *Turkey and its people.* 1911. 2nd ed., London and N. Y., 1912.

a. Quaint earliest extended description in English. *b.* Eliot, after many years' residence in Turkey and much travel, discussed with thoughtful discernment the traits, ideas, religions, etc., of the different peoples. *c.* The author discussed the same topics as are found in *b* after a still longer residence and different opportunities for observation. AHL

TURKEY: COLLECTIONS OF SOURCES

T1071a Testa, Ignaz, Freiherr von, and others, ed. *Recueil des traités de la Porte ottomane avec les puissances étrangères, depuis le premier traité conclu, en 1536, . . . jusqu'à nos jours.* 11 v. Paris, 1864–1911.

b Noradounghian, Gabriel, Effendi, ed. *Recueil d'actes internationaux de l'empire ottoman.* 4 v. Paris, 1897–1903. (Bibliography.)

a. Ignaz von Testa worked a life-time collecting and editing the treaties of Turkey with the different powers and himself published those with France and Austria. *b.* Collection of many of the treaties found in *a,* together with other treaties and documents from 1300 to 1902, published in chronological order. Review, v. 1, G. F. Hertzberg, *Hist. Zeit.,* 85: 148, 1900. AHL

T1072 Schopoff, A., ed. *Les réformes et la protection des chrétiens en Turquie, 1673–1904: firmans, bérats, protocoles, traités, capitulations, conventions, arrangements, notes, circulaires, règlements, lois, mémorandums, etc.* Paris, 1904. (Bibliography.)

Convenient collection of materials on this important question. GMD

No other important collection of documents relating primarily to Turkish history has yet appeared, but the historical publications and collections of documents issued by the (T2921) Hungarian, (T4922) Croatian, and (T3921) Rumanian national academies contain much material which relates to Turkey.

On the international relations of Turkey in the past century a wealth of material may be found in the English (L85) *Blue books,* the French ('M904) *Livres jaunes,* and the corresponding publications of other governments; especially cf. (T1081*a*) *Lausanne conference on Near Eastern affairs, 1922–1923: records of proceedings and draft terms of peace,* London, 1923 [Parliament, Papers by command, Cmd. 1814]; and (T1081*b*) *Treaty of peace with Turkey and other instruments signed at Lausanne on July 24, 1923 . . . and subsidiary documents forming part of the Turkish peace settlement,* London, 1923 [Parliament, Papers by command, Cmd. 1929].   AHL

TURKEY: GENERAL HISTORIES

T1101a **Poole, Stanley Lane,** and others. *Story of Turkey.* 1888. New ed. London and N. Y., 1922. [(B136) Story of the nations.]

   b **Creasy, Sir Edward S.** *History of the Ottoman Turks from the beginning of their empire to the present time.* 2 v. London, 1854–56. Later ed. Rev. ed. by A. C. Coolidge with continuation to 1905 by W. H. Claflin, Philadelphia, 1906. [(B135) Lodge, History of nations.]

   c **Eversley, George J. S. L., Baron.** *Turkish empire, its growth and decay.* 1917. 2nd ed., entitled *Turkish empire from 1288 to 1914,* with four additional chapters, 1914–1922, by Sir Valentine Chirol, London and N. Y., 1923.

a. Most accessible history of Turkey in English; generally reliable but very inadequate, especially for the nineteenth century; includes condensed accounts of Turkish government and literature. Review, *Spectator,* 61 : 1562, Nov. 10, 1888. *b.* Fuller and better balanced, except that relatively the military side is overemphasized, while religious and cultural topics are neglected; the first edition, called out by the Crimean War, carried the story to about 1840; succinct continuations bring it to 1905. *c.* Well-proportioned narrative from the Turkish origins until the close of the World War. Due to the author's long personal acquaintance with the Balkan countries, his treatment of the European affairs of the Ottoman Empire is superior to that of Asiatic questions. Review, *Saturday Rev.,* 124 : 309, Oct. 20, 1917; (London) *Times Lit. Suppl.,* 22 : 50, Jan. 25, 1923.

AHL

T1121 **Hammer-Purgstall, Joseph, Freiherr von.** *Geschichte des osmanischen Reiches.* 10 v. 1827–35. 2nd rev. ed., 4 v., Pesth, 1834–36. French tr. by J. J. Hellert, *Histoire de l'empire ottoman depuis son origine jusqu'à nos jours,* 18 v. and atlas, Paris, 1835–43; and by L. Dochez, *Histoire de l'empire ottoman . . . traduit de l'allemand sur le deuxième édition,* 3 v., Paris, 1840–42. (Bibliographies.)

Hammer was the first western historian who could use readily the Arabic, Persian, and Turkish writings. An indefatigable collector of books, manuscripts, and classified information, he prepared a great work, with abundant notes and lists, which has since been used to replace all older writings as a general reservoir of Turkish history prior to 1774. While he attacked some critical problems and compared his sources, he was not a successful critic; nor did he use sufficiently the writings of westerners preserved in books and archives.   AHL

T1122 Zinkeisen, Johann W. *Geschichte des osmanischen Reiches in Europa.* 7 v. Hamburg and Gotha, 1840–63. [(B161) Geschichte der europäischen Staaten.]

The author, unable and not caring to read oriental material in the original, made full use of western writings. He excluded for the most part the Asiatic and African areas of Turkey, and introduced extensive descriptions of government, manners, and customs. More critical and comprehensive than (T1121) Hammer, his work has been undeservedly less used. Death prevented the author from continuing his narrative from 1812 to 1861 in an eighth volume. No auxiliary material aside from footnotes, and an index by another hand.   AHL

T1123 La Jonquière, A., Vicomte de. *Histoire de l'empire ottoman depuis les origines jusqu'au traité de Berlin.* 1 v. 1881. Rev. ed., entitled *Histoire de l'empire ottoman depuis les origines jusqu'à nos jours,* 2 v., Paris, 1914 [Duruy, Histoire universelle]. (Bibliography.)

The first edition consists of a brief, clear, well-proportioned, and dispassionate sketch of Turkish history, concluding with a survey of existing conditions. The latest edition is twice as long; almost the entire increase is devoted to the period from 1881 to 1913 and to an extensive expansion of the survey. Some maps are included. Review, A. H. Lybyer, *A.H.R.,* 20: 195, Oct. 1914.   AHL

T1124 Iorga [Jorga], Nicolae. *Geschichte des osmanischen Reiches.* 5 v. Gotha, 1908–13. [(B161) Geschichte der europäischen Staaten.]

An attempt, by a Rumanian professor of history, to write Turkish history on a large scale with a view to bringing out, as (T1121) Hammer and (T1122) Zinkeisen did not do, the part played by the Christian subjects of the sultan. Review, J. Loserth, *Hist. Zeit.,* 103: 639, 1909.   AHL

TURKEY: HISTORY PRIOR TO 1900

T1201a Chalcocondylas, Laonicus. *De origine et rebus gestis Turcorum.* Tr. by C. Clauser from the Greek. Basileae, 1556. French tr. by B. de Vigenère, *L'histoire de la décadence de l'empire grec et establissement de celuy des Turcs,* Paris, 1584; with continuations to 1612 by Thomas Artus and to 1661 by F. E. de Mézeray, 2 v., Paris, 1662. First ed. of Greek text, with Latin translation by C. Clauser, in v. 2 of *Historiae byzantinae scriptores tres,* Coloniae Allobrogum, 1615; also in (H76) *Corpus byzantinae historiae,* 1650, 2nd ed., 1729; in (H77) *Corpus scriptorum historiae byzantinae,* pt. 31, Bonnae, 1843; and in (F72a) Migne, *Patrologia graeca,* v. 159, Paris, 1866.

b Leunclavius [Löwenklau], Johannes, tr. *Annales sultanorum Othmanidarum a Turcis sua lingua scripti,* with continuations to 1588 and *Pandectes historiae Turcicae.* Francofurdi, 1588. Also appended to editions of 1650, 1729, and 1866 of (T1201a) Chalcocondylas. German ed., *Neuwe Chronica türckischer Nation,* Franckfurt am Mayn, 1590.

c —— *Neuwer musulmanischer Histori türckischer Nation von ihrem Herkommen, Geschichten und Thaten, drey Bücher.* Franckfurt am Meyn, 1590. Latin ed., *Historiae musulmanae Turcorum de monumentis ipsorum exscriptae libri XVIII,* Francofurti, 1591.

d Knolles, Richard. *Generall historie of the Turkes.* 1603. 6th ed., with title, *Turkish history from the original of that nation . . . ,* with continuations to 1699 by Sir Paul Rycaut and others, 3 v., London, 1687–1700.

The chief sources of knowledge of early Ottoman history in western Europe in the second half of the sixteenth century and in the seventeenth century. These great works, unrivalled for more than two centuries, furnished reservoirs from which many lesser writers drew. *a.* The author was the first historian of the Near East who wrote primarily not of the decline of the Byzantine empire, but of the rise upon its ruins of the Ottoman state. Artus made use of *b*. *b.* Leunclavius was editor and translator of the first Ottoman histories by Turkish writers known in western Europe. The *Annals* were condensed by Gaudier-Spiegel from a Turkish manuscript probably of Muhiyeddin Ali, extending to 1549 A.D., which had been brought to Vienna in 1550 by the interpreter Beck of Leopoldsdorf. Leunclavius supplemented the *Annals* with an outline to 1588 A.D. and added in the *Pandects* extensive notes which have not yet lost all value. Review, Horawitz, article Leunclavius, *Allgemeine deutsche Biographie*, 18: 488; also cf. F. Giese, 'Einleitung zu meiner Textausgabe der altosmanischen anonymen Chroniken te' wārīh-i āl-i 'osmān,' *Mitteilungen zur osmanischen Geschichte*, 1: 65 ff., 1922. *c.* Woven of two strands, one probably the same account as in *b*, and the other similar to the work of the Ottoman historian Neshri. Cf. P. Wittek, 'Zum Quellenproblem der ältesten osmanischen Chroniken, mit Auszügen aus Nešrī,' *Mitteilungen zur osmanischen Geschichte*, 1: 78 ff., 1922. *d.* The author made use of the Latin versions of *a* and *b*, with other works, in preparing what is still the longest history of Turkey in English. He did not possess the materials nor the training for scientific criticism, but faithfully summed up western knowledge of Turkey in spirited and sonorous English. AHL

T1211a Gibbons, Herbert A. *Foundation of the Ottoman empire: history of the Osmanlis up to the death of Bayezid I, 1300–1403.* Oxford, 1916. (Comprehensive bibliography.)

b Pears, Sir Edwin. *Destruction of the Greek empire and the story of the capture of Constantinople by the Turks.* London, 1903. (Bibliography in preface.)

c Schlumberger, Gustave. *Le siège, la prise, et le sac de Constantinople par les Turcs en 1453.* Paris, 1914.

a. Written with cleverness and shrewdness, but with a little too much eagerness to discover new points of view. It would possess a greater degree of finality if it had been based upon a critical study of the early•Ottoman historians in the original language. Review, A. H. Lybyer, *A.H.R.*, 22: 140, Oct. 1916. *b.* The story of 1453 told from contemporary narratives and personal investigations on the ground; continues his (H357) *Fall of Constantinople*. Review, D. C. Munro, *A.H.R.*, 9: 354, Jan. 1904. *c.* Careful monograph on the same subject by a French specialist in the field. AHL, GMD

TURKEY: HISTORY SINCE 1900

T1371a Price, Clair. *Rebirth of Turkey.* N. Y., 1923.

b Mears, Eliot G. *Modern Turkey: a politico-economic interpretation, 1908–1923 inclusive, with selected chapters by representative authorities.* N. Y., 1924. (Extensive bibliography.)

c Toynbee, Arnold J., and **Kirkwood, Kenneth P.** *Turkey.* London, 1926. N. Y., 1927. [(B137*b*) Modern world.]

a. Sketch of Turkish history, 1907-1922, by a friendly newspaper correspondent. *b.* Substantial and comprehensive survey, including historical chapters, by Mr. Mears and eighteen others, with chronology, documents, maps, and illustrations. Review, E. Turlington, *A.H.R.*, 31: 353, Jan. 1926. *c.* Excellent summary of recent events. Review, (London) *Times Lit. Suppl.*, 25: 455, July 8, 1926. AEL

TURKEY: DIPLOMATIC HISTORY

T1501a Pélissié du Rausas, G. *Le régime des capitulations dans l'empire otto-man*. 2 v. Paris, 1902–05.

  b Brown, Philip M. *Foreigners in Turkey: their juridical status*. Princeton, 1914. (Bibliography.)

  a. Lengthy discussion of the special international agreements under which foreigners might trade and reside in Turkey; includes Egypt. *b*. Brief, practical statement of the same regulations.   AHL

T1502 Verney, Noël, and Dambmann, George. *Les puissances étrangères dans le Levant, en Syrie, et en Palestine*. Paris, 1900.

  Comprehensive analysis of the political and economic activities of the various national groups of foreigners who have dealt with Turkey, including the service of the public debt, the construction and operation of railways and other public works, and participation in trade and navigation.   AHL

TURKEY: CONSTITUTIONAL AND LEGAL HISTORY

T1531a Hammer-Purgstall, Joseph, Freiherr von. *Des osmanischen Reichs Staatsverfassung und Staatsverwaltung*. 2 v. Wien, 1815.

  b Ohsson, Ignatius M. d'. *Tableau général de l'empire ottoman*. 7 v. Paris, 1788–1824.

  The history of Turkey is illuminated greatly by an understanding of secular and religious law and organization. *a*. Hammer translated freely certain fundamental documents of the old unsystematic Turkish constitution, and explained the scheme of official organization. *b*. The author, an Armenian native of Turkey, translated, with ample illustrative comments, the fundamental religious law which influenced all phases of Turkish living; and, parallel with *a*, described the official hierarchy of the empire.   AHL

T1536 Lybyer, Albert H. *Government of the Ottoman empire in the time of Suleiman the Magnificent*. Cambridge, Mass., 1913. [Harvard historical studies.] (Bibliography.)

  Using chiefly materials written by westerners, the author describes the main elements of the twofold Turkish organization, secular and religious, which gave aggressive strength in the great days and patient endurance in the period of decline. Review, H. D. Jenkins, *A.H.R.*, 19: 141, Oct. 1913.   GMD

T1551a Heidborn, A. *Manuel de droit public et administratif de l'empire ottoman*. 2 v. in 4 pt. Vienne, 1908–12.

  b Young, George. *Corps de droit ottoman: recueil des codes, lois, règlements, ordonnances, et actes les plus importants du droit intérieur, et d'études sur le droit coutumier de l'empire ottoman*. 7 v. Oxford, 1905–06.

  a. Admirable systematic study of Turkish organization and law. V. 2. Discussion of Ottoman finances; closes at 1912. *b*. Competent translation of Ottoman legislation after the 'reforms'; enables Westerners to grasp the legal basis of the new régime.   AHL

TURKEY: BIOGRAPHIES

Eighteenth century: (T1721) Albert Vandal, *Le Pacha Bonneval*, Paris, 1885; (T1722) *id.*, *Une ambassade française en orient sous Louis XV: la mission du Marquis de Villeneuve, 1728–1741*, Paris, 1887; (T1723) Louis Bonneville de

Marsangy, *Le chevalier de Vergennes, son ambassade à Constantinople,* 2 v., Paris, 1894; (T1724) Léonce Pingaud, *Choiseul-Gouffier: la France en orient sous Louis XVI,* Paris, 1887.

Nineteenth century: (T1741a) Stanley Lane Poole, *Life of the Right Honourable Stratford Canning, Viscount Stratford de Redcliffe . . . from his memoirs and private and official papers,* 2 v., London and N. Y., 1888; (T1741b) *id., Life of Lord Stratford de Redcliffe,* London and N. Y., 1890; (T1742) Sir Henry G. Elliot, *Some revolutions and other diplomatic experiences,* ed. by his daughter, London and N. Y., 1922; (T1743) Sidney Whitman, *Turkish memories,* London and N. Y., 1914. The course of domestic affairs, as well as of international relations, in the nineteenth century appears in (T1761) Ali Haydar Midhat Bey, *Life of Midhat Pasha, a record of his services, political reforms, banishment, and judicial murder,* London, 1903; (T1762) Sir Edwin Pears, *Life of Abdul Hamid,* London, 1917 [Makers of the nineteenth century].

Twentieth century: (T1781) Hālidah Adib Khānum [Halidé Edib], *Memoirs,* London and N. Y., 1926; (T1791) Ahmad Djemal Pasha, *Memories of a Turkish statesman, 1913–1919,* London and N. Y., 1922; (T1792) Otto Liman von Sanders, *Five years in Turkey,* Annapolis, Md., 1927, tr. from *Fünf Jahre Türkei,* 1920, 2nd ed., Berlin, 1922; (T1793) Harry Stuermer, *Two war years in Constantinople: sketches of German and Young Turkish ethics and politics,* London and N. Y., 1917, tr. by E. Allen and the author from *Zwei Kriegsjahre in Konstantinopel: Skizzen deutsch-jungtürkischer Moral und Politik,* Lausanne, 1917; as well as for (J709) Morgenthau, *Ambassador Morgenthau's story.*   GMD

TURKEY: PERIODICALS

(T1941) *Mitteilungen zur osmanischen Geschichte,* Wien, 1921 ff., gives promise of clearing up many of the critical problems relating to Turkish history and historians.   AHL

HUNGARY: BIBLIOGRAPHY AND ENCYCLOPEDIAS

T2001a Szabó, Károly, and Hellebrant, Arpad. *Régi magyar könyvtár [1473–1711].* [Old Magyar library.] 3 series in 4 v. Budapest, 1879–98. [Magyar Tudományos Akadémia.]

b Petrik, Géza. *Bibliographia Hungariae, 1713–1860, seu, catalogus librorum in Hungaria, et de rebus patriam nostram attingentibus extra Hungariam editorum . . . : Magyarország bibliographiája. . . .* 4 v. Budapest, 1888–97.

c Petrik, Géza, and Kiszlingstein, Sándor. *Bibliographia hungarica: Magyar könyvészet, 1860–1875, 1876–1885, 1886–1900.* 3 v. Budapest, 1885, 1890, 1903.

d Rényi, Károly, and Steinhofer, Károly, ed. *Magyar könyvkereskedök évkönyve, magyar könyvészet.* [Magyar bookseller's annual, Magyar bibliography.] Budapest, 1902 ff.

e Kertbeny, Károly M. [Benkert, Károly M.], and Petrik, Géza. *Ungarns deutsche Bibliographie, 1801–1860: Verzeichniss der in Ungarn und Ungarn betreffend im Auslande erschienenen deutschen Drucke.* 2 v. in 1. Budapest, 1886.

f Kont, Ignace. *Bibliographie française de la Hongrie, 1521–1910, avec un inventaire sommaire des documents manuscrits.* Paris, 1913. *Supplément,* by A. Leval, Budapest, 1914. [*Revue de Hongrie,* Jan., Feb., March, 1914].

g *Magyar könyv-szemle.* [Magyar book review.] Budapest, 1903 ff.

Few nations have so efficiently organized their bibliographical apparatus as the Magyars. These compilations, which are all general bibliographies, are typical. *a, b,* and *c.* Form a series covering publications prior to 1900; continued by *d* and *g. e* and *f.* Each covers efficiently the special field indicated by its title.   RJK

T2002 Gragger, Robert, ed. *Bibliographia Hungariae.* V. 1, *Historica.* Leipzig, 1923. [Ungarische Bibliothek.]

Includes publications in non-Magyar languages from 1861 to 1921, relating to Hungary, the Austro-Hungarian monarchy, and its participation in the World War. Useful as the only important contribution specifically to the historical bibliography of Hungary. Additional volumes are planned to include geographical and literary publications. Review, *E.H.R.,* 40: 319, Apr. 1925.   GMD

HUNGARY: ENCYCLOPEDIAS

T2021 *A Pallas nagy lexikona az összizes ismeretek enciklopédiája.* [Pallas's grand . . . encyclopedia.] 16 v. and supplement, 2 v. Budapest, 1893–1904.

Standard Magyar encyclopedia; supplement completes data to 1904.   GMD

T2022 Jáznigi, Sándor [Alexander]. *Das geistige Ungarn, biographisches Lexikon.* Ed. by O. von Krücken [pseud.] and I. Parlagi. 2 v. Wien, 1918.

Convenient biographical dictionary for Hungary.   RJK

HUNGARY: GEOGRAPHY, ETHNOGRAPHY

T2041 Lóczy, Lajos [Louis], ed. *Geographical, economic, and social survey of Hungary.* Budapest, 1919. [Publications of the Hungarian Geographical Society.]

Brief but thorough summary of a much larger Magyar work written by numerous distinguished scholars. Gives in dry outline the essential facts of the geography, history, finances, industries, agriculture, and commerce of Hungary before 1918, gathered for the most part from official sources and intended for government propaganda.   RJK

T2051a Seton-Watson, Robert W. [pseud. Scotus Viator]. *Racial problems in Hungary.* London, 1908. (Bibliography.)

b —— *German, Slav, and Magyar, a study in the origins of the great war.* London, 1916. (Bibliography.)

a. Indictment of the Magyar anti-Slav and anti-Rumanian policy before the World War; based for the most part on official statistics and publications and on local investigations. Review, K. Uhlirz, *Hist. Zeit.* 103: 609, 1909. *b.* Later treatment, on similar lines, of Austro-Hungarian relations with the Southern Slavs. Review, Lord Cromer, *Spectator,* 117: 158, Aug. 5, 1916.

For the classic statement of the Magyar point of view, cf. P. Hunfalvy, *Die Ungern oder Magyaren,* v. 5 of (T51*b*) *Die Völker Oesterreich-Ungarns;* Review, E. Sayous, *Rev. Hist.,* 24: 420, March 1884.   RJK, GMD

HUNGARY: COLLECTIONS OF SOURCES

T2061 Marczali, Henrik, ed. *Enchiridion fontium historiae hungarorum: A magyar történet kútföinek kézikönyve.* Budapest, 1901. (Bibliographies.)

Useful manual of the sources, both national and foreign, for Hungarian history, with illustrative extracts, from the beginning to 1867. Review, I. Kont, *Rev. Hist.*, 82 : 441, July 1903.   GMD

Collections of sources and archive publications.—Much material in the following publications is in Latin or one of the modern languages of western Europe or in a translation into one of these languages. The principal publication of the national sources for Hungarian history is (T2071) *Monumenta Hungariae historica: Magyar történelmi emlékek,* Budapest, 1857 ff., a collection now numbering over one hundred volumes, issued under the auspices of · (T2921) *Magyar National Academy.* This publication has been issued in four principal series: (T2071a) *Diplomataria: Okmánytárak,* which includes documents drawn from the archives in Brussels, London, and Naples; (T2071b) *Scriptores: Irók;* (T2071c) *Acta extera: Diplomácziai emlékek,* which includes materials for the fourteenth and fifteenth centuries; (T2071d) *Monumenta comitialia regni Hungariae: Magyar órszággyülési emlékek,* the proceedings of the Hungarian diet since 1526, which are now complete to the earlier part of the seventeenth century, and its supplement (T2071e) *Monumenta comitialia regni Transylvaniae: Erdélyi órszággyülési emlékek,* which has been completed from 1540 to the end of the seventeenth century. Outside these principal series the collection contains several other publications, including (T2071f) *Codex diplomaticus hungaricus andegavensis: Anjoukori okmánytár,* 6 v., Budapest, 1879–91, which relates chiefly to the earlier part of the fourteenth century, and (T2071g) *Archivum Rakoczianum: Rákóczy Ferencz levéltára;* 10 v., Budapest, 1873–89, and (T2071h) *Monumenta turco-hungarica: Török-Magyarkori történelmi emlékek,* pt. 1, 9 v., Budapest, 1863–73; pt. 2, v. 1–4, Budapest, 1893–1908.

For the earlier chroniclers it is necessary, however, to consult (T2072) *Historiae hungaricae fontes domestici,* 4 v., Lipsiae and Quinque-Ecclesiis, 1881–85, ed. by Matthias Florianus [Mátyás Florián]. An exhaustive collection of the sources both in Magyar and all other languages for the Magyar conquest and settlement of Hungary, is contained in (T2073) *A magyar honfoglalás kútföi* [Sources for the conquest of Hungary], Budapest, 1900, ed. by Julius Pauler and Alexander Szilágyi, and published by the Hungarian Academy. The Hungarian Institute in Rome, established by Bishop Vilmos [William] Fraknói, has published (T2074) *Monumenta Vaticana historiam regni Hungariæ illustrantia: Vatikáni magyar okirattár,* first series, v. 1–6 in 8 v., second series, 2 v., Budapestini, 1885–91, in which the distribution of materials between the two series is determined by the year 1526. (T2075) *Recueil des traités de la Hongrie avec les puissances étrangères,* v. 1, Budapest, 1921, contains a catalogue of Hungarian treaties from 973 to 1526.   GMD

HUNGARY: GENERAL HISTORIES

T2101a Yolland, Arthur B. *Hungary.* London and N. Y., 1917. [Nations' histories.] (Brief bibliography.)

b Vámbéry, Ármin, and **Heilprin, Louis.** *Story of Hungary.* London and N. Y., 1886. [(B136) Story of the nations.]

c **Alden, Percy,** ed. *Hungary of today, by members of the Hungarian government.* London, 1907.

d **Bovill, W. B. Forster.** *Hungary and the Hungarians.* Edinburgh and N. Y., 1908.

Most easily accessible accounts in English of the history of Hungary before the World War. Sympathy with the Magyars colors all four works. *a.* Handiest and most recent account; devotes comparatively more space to the modern period. *b.* Skilfully written; older; treats the earlier period more fully. *c.* Coöperative publication, with propagandist tendencies. *d.* Popular survey of Magyar history and culture. RJK

T2102a Sayous, Édouard. *Histoire générale des Hongrois.* 1877. 2nd rev. ed. by A. E. Sayous and J. Dolenecz, Paris, 1900. (Bibliography.)

b **Marczali, Henry.** *Magyarország története.* [Hungarian history.] Budapest, 1911.

a. Fully documented history of the Magyars from the earliest times, with decreasing emphasis on the modern period. Based upon careful studies and monographs of the author; tinged by Magyar sympathies, but scholarly in method. The second edition is considerably abridged but includes a brief continuation to 1900. Review, L. Leger, *Rev. Hist.,* 79: 175, May 1902. *b.* Brilliantly written brief national history; strongly patriotic in tone. RJK

T2103 Teleki, Pál [Paul], Gróf. *Evolution of Hungary and its place in European history.* N. Y., 1923. [Williams College, Institute of Politics publications.] (Bibliography.)

Survey of the history of Hungary by a Magyar scholar and statesman; dwells particularly on circumstances following the World War; includes discussions of the racial and economic problems of Hungary before and since the war. Review, R. J. Kerner, *A.H.R.,* 29: 160, Oct. 1923. RJK

T2121 Knatchbull-Hugesson, Cecil Marcus, Baron Brabourne. *Political evolution of the Hungarian nation.* 2 v. London, 1908.

Written in popular style; rests mainly on the best Magyar works accessible; strongly nationalistic. RJK

T2122 Acsády, Ignácz. *A magyar birodalom története: a kútfok alapján a müvelt közönség számára.* [History of the Magyar empire.] 2 v. Budapest, 1904. (Excellent bibliography of Magyar sources.)

Publication subsidized by the Hungarian ministry of education. The development of the Magyar state idea is the main thesis. In v. 1, covering the period of national kings, to 1490, the author champions royal authority against oligarchy; in v. 2, the national side against the Hapsburgs. Social problems, like serfdom, are treated in a liberal spirit; the greatest defect of the work is insufficient interest in the non-Magyar races, and occasional unfairness to them. Eminently readable. ESBr

T2123 Szilágyi, Sándor [Alexander], ed. *A magyar nemzet története.* [History of the Hungarian nation.] 10 v. Budapest, 1895–98.

The monumental national history; a coöperative work; strongly nationalist in tone; published on the occasion of the national millenary. RJK

HUNGARY: HISTORY UNDER HAPSBURG RULE

T2261 Marczali, Henrik [Henry]. *Hungary in the eighteenth century, with an introductory essay on the earlier history of Hungary by Harold W. V. Temperley.* Cambridge, Eng., 1910. Rev. and tr. by the author and A. B. Yolland from v. 1 of *Magyarország története II József korában,* 3 v., Budapest, 1882–88 [Magyar Tudományos Akadémia].

Written as introduction to an extended history of the reign of Joseph II. Scholarly analysis of the society of Hungary, covering economic conditions, the social system, nationality, the church, the royal power, and government. Based upon the archives of the royal chancellery, royal council, and the treasury, which for the period are illuminating and authoritative. Reviews, R. H. Lord, *A.H.R.,* 16: 123, Oct. 1910; I. Kont, *Rev. Hist.,* 106: 391, March 1911. Reviews of original work, *Rev. Hist.,* 39: 411, March 1889; L. Mangold, *Hist. Zeit.,* 67: 331, 1891.

CS

T2321a Bertha, Sándor [Alexander] de. *La Hongrie moderne de 1849 à 1901: étude historique.* Paris, 1901.

b Eisenmann, Louis. *La Hongrie contemporaine,. 1867–1918.* Paris, 1921.

a. Strongly nationalistic account. Review, A. Lichtenberger, *Rev. Hist.,* 78: 124, Jan. 1902. *b.* Excellent account, by a well-known French historian, of the political development of Hungary during its membership in the Dual Monarchy.

RJK, GMD

HUNGARY: HISTORY IN THE TWENTIETH CENTURY

T2371a Jászi, Oszkár [Oscar]. *Der Zusammenbruch des Dualismus und die Zukunft der Donaustaaten.* Wien, 1918. Tr. by S. von Hartenstein from 2nd ed. of Magyar original.

b Szilassy, Gyula [Julius], Báró. *Der Untergang der Donau-Monarchie: diplomatische Erinnerungen.* Berlin, 1921.

c Károlyi, Michael, Gróf. *Fighting the world, the struggle for peace.* London and N. Y., 1925. Tr., by E. W. Dickes, from *Gegen eine ganze Welt, mein Kampf um den Frieden,* München, 1924.

a. Political pamphlet by one of the foremost liberals of Hungary, written before the defeat of the Central Powers in the World War had become apparent. Emphasizes the political bankruptcy of the dualistic system; advocates a close political confederation of the five major nationalities of Austria-Hungary. CS

b. Revelations by Magyar magnate and diplomatist with intimate knowledge of the Austro-Hungarian foreign office; important for years 1908–1919; explains Magyar relations to the World War and the collapse of the Dual Monarchy. Review, R. J. Kerner, *A.H.R.,* 28: 159, Oct. 1922. *c.* Significant memoirs, chiefly of the period of the World War, by a consistent opponent of the prevailing nationalist policy; closes with his assumption of power in October, 1918. Review, C. J. H. Hayes, *New Republic,* 42: 269, Apr. 29, 1925. RJK

T2381 Jászi, Oszkár [Oscar]. *Revolution and counter-revolution in Hungary.* London, 1924. Tr., by E. W. Dickes, from *Magyariens Schüld, Ungarns Sühne, Revolution und Gegenrevolution in Ungarn,* München, 1923, tr. by A. Gas from Magyar original.

Most convenient account in English of events in Hungary following the close of the World War; allowance must be made for the liberal bias of the author who was a member of the Károlyi cabinet. GMD

HUNGARY: CONSTITUTIONAL HISTORY

T2531a Andrássy, Gyula [Julius], Gróf. *Development of Hungarian constitutional liberty.* London, 1908. Tr. by C. A. Ginever and I. Ginever from *A magyar állam fennaradásának és alkotmányos szabadságának okai,* 2 v., Budapest, 1901.

b Marczali, Henrik [Henry]. *Ungarische Verfassungsgeschichte.* Tübingen, 1910. (Bibliography.)

a. Extends only to 1619; aims to explain the development and preservation of constitutional liberty in Hungary, with continual comparisons with England; presupposes considerable knowledge of political history. Review, A. C. Coolidge, *A.H.R.,* 15:359, Jan. 1910. *b.* Brief standard work. Review, K. Uhlirz, *Hist. Zeit.,* 106:642, 1911.   RHL

HUNGARY: CULTURAL HISTORY, LITERATURE

T2661 Riedl, Frigyes [Frederick]. *History of Hungarian literature.* London and N. Y., 1906. Tr. by C. A. Ginever and I. Ginever from MS. in Magyar. [Short histories of the literatures of the world.] (Brief bibliography.)

Text-book intended for the English-reading public. Traces Magyar literature from the earliest monuments to the beginning of the twentieth century, thus leaving out contemporary Magyar literature altogether. Its judgments and conclusions can be generally accepted as conforming to the best standards of Magyar academic criticism.   ESBr

T2662a Kont, Ignace. *La Hongrie littéraire et scientifique.* Paris, 1896.

b —— *Histoire de la littérature hongroise.* Budapest and Paris, 1900. (Bibliography.)

c —— *Geschichte der ungarischen Litteratur.* Leipzig, 1906. [Die Litteraturen des Ostens in Einzeldarstellungen.] (Bibliography.)

Good manuals. *a.* Includes survey of Magyar historical writing in both Latin and Magyar; also deals with scientific activities and higher education. Review, E. Sayous, *Rev. Hist.,* 62:143, Sept. 1896. *b.* Adapted from three recent works by the Magyar scholars, C. Horváth, A. Kardos, and A. Endrödi. Review, L. Leger, *Rev. Hist.,* 79:175, May 1902.   GMD

HUNGARY: BIOGRAPHIES

(T2701) Sándor [Alexander] Szilágyi and others, *Magyar történeti életrajzok, a Magyar Tudományos Akadémia és Magyar Történelmi Társulat megbízásából* [Magyar historical biographies, published under the auspices of the Magyar Academy of Sciences and the 'Magyar Historical Society], Budapest, 1885 ff., a series of volumes usually appearing annually which contains numerous biographical articles varying greatly in length and value. Among the biographies of Magyar personages important in history are: (T2751) Vilmos [William] Fraknói, *Mathias Corvinus, König von Ungarn, 1458–1490,* Freiburg im Breisgau, 1891, tr. from *Mátyás király élete,* Budapest, 1890; (T2752) Sándor [Alexander] Márki, ed., *Mátyás király emlékkönyv* . . . [King Mathias Corvinus memorial], Budapest, 1902, a collection of brief monographs on the reign of about forty Magyar authors; (T2781) Sándor [Alexander] Márki, *II Rákóczi Ferencz,* Budapest, 1910; (T2782) Ladislaus, Freiherr Hengelmüller von Hengervár, *Hungary's fight for national existence, or the history of the great uprising led by Francis Rakoczi II, 1703–1711,* London and N. Y., 1913, tr. from *Franz Rákóczi und sein Kampf für Ungarns Freiheit, 1703–1711,* v. 1, Stuttgart, 1913; (T2801) Ede Somogyi, *Ludwig Kossuth, sein Leben und Wirken,* Leipzig, 1894; (T2802) Sándor [Alexander] Márki, *I Ferencz József Magyarország királya* [Francis Joseph I, Hungarian king], Budapest, 1907; (T2803) Menyhért, Gróf Lonyay, *Graf Stephan Széchenyi und seine hinterlassenen Schriften,* Budapest, 1875, tr. by A. Dux from the Hungarian; (T2804) G. Steinbach, *Franz Deák,* Wien, 1888. Special reference should be made to (P883) Wertheimer, *Graf Julius Andrássy.*   RJK

HUNGARY: ACADEMY PUBLICATIONS AND PERIODICALS

In addition to (T2071) *Monumenta Hungariae historica,* most historical publications in Hungary are issued by (T2921) Magyar Tudományos Akadémia [Magyar National Academy], Budapest, 1831 ff., and many of its other publications contain materials useful to the historian. Among the works issued under its auspices few are of greater usefulness than (T2922) Ede Margalits, ed., *Horvát történelmi repertorium* [Repertory of Croatian history], 2 v., Budapest, 1900–02, which is a list of the historical publications, especially those relating to Hungary, of (T4922) Croatian National Academy with brief summaries of contents.

The standard Hungarian historical review is (T2941) *Századok, a Magyar Történelmi Társulat közlönye* [The centuries: organ of the Magyar Historical Society], Budapest, 1867 ff. (T2942) *Magyar történelmi tár* [Collection of Magyar historical documents], 25 v., Budapest, 1855–78, organ of the commission for editing (T2071) *Monumenta Hungariae historica,* devoted to the publication of briefer miscellaneous documents. Other periodicals especially devoted to Hungary which contain articles and current bibliographical information relating to its history are: (T2951a) *Literarische Berichte aus Ungarn,* 4 v., Budapest, 1877–80, continued as (T2951b) *Ungarische Revue,* 15 v., Budapest, 1881–95, published by (T2921) Magyar National Academy; (T2952) *Ungarische Rundschau für historische und soziale Wissenschaften,* 5 v., München, 1912–17, quarterly; (T2953) *Ungarische Jahrbücher,* Berlin, 1921 ff., quarterly; (T2961) *Revue de Hongrie,* Budapest, 1908 ff., monthly, organ of the Société Littéraire Française de.Budapest; (T2962) *Revue des études hongroises et finno-ongriennes,* Paris, 1923 ff., quarterly, published under the auspices of (T2921) Magyar National Academy; and (T2971) *Hungarian nation,* Budapest, 1920 ff., published in English.   RJK, GMD

RUMANIA: BIBLIOGRAPHY AND ENCYCLOPEDIAS

T3001a Bianu, Ioan, and **Hodos, Nerva.** *Bibliografia românéscă veche, 1508–1830.* [Old Rumanian bibliography.] V. 1–3 in 8 pt., Bucuresci, 1898–1912. [Academia Româna.]

  b Bengescu [Bengesco], George. *Bibliographie franco-roumaine du XIXe siècle.* 1895. 2nd rev. ed., with supplement, 1895–1906, Paris, 1907.

  a. Fundamental bibliography for Rumania; excellent; arranged chronologically. Review, pt. 1, A. D. Xénopol, *Rev. Hist.,* 73: 353, July 1900. *b.* Useful for French publications about Rumania.

Also cf. (T3072) Hurmuzaki, *Documente privitóre la istoria Rominilor,* v. 10, for a comprehensive bibliography of Rumanian history contributed by Professor N. Iorga in 1897. From time to time excellent surveys of current publications relating to Rumanian history have appeared in (B941f) *Revue historique* and (T3921a) *Analele.*   RJK

T3021 Diaconovich, Corneliu. *Enciclopedia română, publicată din însărcinarea si sub auspiciile Asociatiunii pentru Literatura Română si Cultura Poporuli Român* [Rumanian encyclopedia, published under the direction and under the auspices of the Association for Rumanian Literature and for the Culture of the Rumanian People]. 3 v. Sibiiu, 1898–1904.

Only important Rumanian work of encyclopedic character. GMD

RUMANIA: GEOGRAPHY AND ATLASES

T3041 Sturdza [Stourdza], Alexandru A. C. *La terre et la race roumaines depuis leurs origines jusqu'à nos jours.* Paris, 1904. (Brief bibliography.)

Somewhat voluminous compilation. Reliable geographical and statistical information; the historical chapters are not critical, but are animated by a nationalistic bias. Well-illustrated; good maps. MSH

T3046 Comnène, Nicolae P. *Rumania through the ages, an historical, political, and ethnological atlas.* Lausanne and Paris, 1919.

Handy historical atlas of twenty-three maps with text in English and French; drawn up for Rumanian propaganda purposes; illustrates the stages in the growth of Rumania; the historical background for the boundary changes is brief and inadequate. RJK

RUMANIA: COLLECTIONS OF SOURCES

A portion of the material in the following collections is in western European languages. (T3071) Theodorŭ Codrescu, ed., *Uricariul sau colectiune de diferite acte care pot servi la istoria Rominilor* [Historical miscellany, or collection of various acts relating to Rumanian history], 25 v., Iasi, 1852–96, is an unarranged collection of miscellaneous materials, poorly edited and without index, but still useful; title frequently varies from volume to volume. (T3072) Eudoxiu, Baron de Hurmuzaki, *Documente privitore la istoria Rominilor* [Documents relating to Rumanian history], v. 1–19 in 30 pt. and supplement, v. 1–2 in 9 pt., Bucuresci, 1876–1922 [Academia Română], contains an invaluable, though incomplete, collection of materials gathered from various national archives and other sources, Rumanian and foreign, covering from 1199 to 1849, but relating mainly to the sixteenth, seventeenth, and eighteenth centuries. The various volumes were edited, after Baron Hurmuzaki's death in 1874, by the foremost Rumanian historical scholars, including Densusianu, D. A. Sturdza, Bogdan, and Iorga. Professor Nicolae Iorga has also edited (T3073) *Acte si fragmente cu privire la istoria Rominilor adunate din depositele de manuscrise ale apusuluĭ* [Acts and fragments relating to Rumanian history collected from depositories of manuscripts in western countries], 3 v., Bucuresti, 1895–97, which is drawn largely from the archives in Paris and Berlin for the period from 1367 to 1772. (T3074) Ghenadie Petrescu, the primate of Rumania, Dimitrie A. Sturdza, Dimitrie C. Sturdza, and G. Colescu-Vartic, *Actes et documents relatifs à l'histoire de la régénération de la Roumanie: Acte si documente relative la istoria renascerei României*, 10 v. in 12 pt., Bucuresci, 1888–1909, includes an extensive collection of treaties relating to Rumania since the fourteenth century and supplements (T3072) with documents for the period from 1844 to 1866. For later Rumanian treaties Trandafir G. Djuvara has edited (T3075) *Traités, conventions, et arrangements internationaux de la Roumanie actuellement en vigueur*, Paris, 1888 [Ministère des Affaires Étrangères].

The chronicles for earlier Rumanian history have been collected and edited by Ioanŭ Bogdan in (T3081a) *Cronicele moldovenesti înainte de Ureche* [Moldavian chronicles before Ureche], Bucuresti, 1891, and (T3081b) *Cronice inedite atingetóre de istoria Românilor* [Unpublished chronicles relating to Rumanian history], Bucuresti, 1895. The chronicle of Gregory Ureche, written about 1640, has been edited with a French translation by Émile Picot under the title (T3082) *Chronique de Moldavie depuis le milieu du XIVe siècle jusqu'à l'an 1594*, Paris, 1878. (T3083) Michail Kogălniceanu, *Cronicele Românŭ, seŭ letopisetele Moldaviei si Valahieĭ* [Chronicles of Rumania, or annals of Moldavia and Wallachia], 1846–52, 2nd rev. ed., 3 v., Bucuresci, 1872–74.

The editing of parliamentary proceedings prior to the daily publication of legislative debates has been undertaken in (T3086) *Analele parlamentare ale Românieĭ* [Parliamentary annals of Rumania], v. 1–9, 1832–1840, Bucuresti, 1890–99.

For the reign of Carol I, Dimitrie A. Sturdza has edited (T3091) *Trei-deci de ani de domnie ai Regelui Carol I, cuvîntări si acte* [Thirty years of the reign of King Carol I, addresses and acts], 2 v., Bucuresti, 1897 [Academia Română], and Nicolae Iorga, (T3092) *Correspondance diplomatique roumaine sous le roi Charles Ier, 1866–1880*, Paris, 1923 [Ministère des Affaires Étrangères]. GMD

RUMANIA: GENERAL HISTORIES

T3101 Iorga [Jorga], Nicolae. *History of Roumania: land, people, civilization.* London and N. Y., 1926. Tr. by Joseph McCabe from *Histoire des Roumains et de leur civilisation*, 1920; 2nd rev. ed., Bucarest, 1922. (Brief bibliography.)

Able, brilliant summary; sketches in broad outlines the history and culture of the Rumanians and synthesizes admirably their geography, ethnography, and cultural evolution. Review, (London) *Times Lit. Suppl.*, 25 : 890, Dec. 2, 1926.

RJK

T3121a Xénopol, Alexandru D. *Istoria Rominilor din Dacia Traiană.* [History of the Rumanians of Trajan's Dacia.] 6 v. Iassi, 1888–93.

b ——— *Domnia luĭ Cuza-Vodă.* [Reign of Cuza.] 2 v. Iasi, 1896.

c ——— *Histoire des Roumains de la Dacie Trajane depuis les origines jusqu'à l'union des principautés en 1859.* 2 v. Paris, 1896.

a. Generally considered the standard national history for Rumania prior to 1859. Written when much of the documentary evidence for a complete and scholarly history was not yet available. It also reveals the influence of the old Roman continuity theory, and does not admit that Slavic influences were of serious importance. Social, economic, and cultural conditions receive special consideration. Review, N. Iorga, *Rev. Hist.*, 53 : 153, Sept. 1893. *b.* Continues *a* to 1866. *c.* Abridgement of *a.* Review, J. Loserth, *Hist. Zeit.*, 81 : 341, 1898. MSH

T3122a Iorga [Jorga], Nicolae. *Geschichte des rumänischen Volkes im Rahmen seiner Staatsbildungen.* 2 v. Gotha, 1905. [(B161) Geschichte der europäischen Staaten.] (Critical bibliography.)

b ——— *Histoire des Roumains de Transylvanie et de Hongrie.* 2 v. Bucarest, 1915–16.

a. Iorga, the most distinguished living Rumanian historian, has written the best general history of his people covering the period from the earliest times to the end of the nineteenth century. Scholarly and authentic; based on primary sources;

thoroughly historical and complete for the period prior to 1878. Review, A. D. Xénopol, *Rev. Hist.*, 96: 120, 1908; *Hist. Zeit.*, 99: 178, 1907. *b.* Only good history of the subject.   RJK

RUMANIA: HISTORY BEFORE 1822

T3201a Hurmuzaki, Eudoxiu, Baron de. *Fragmente zur Geschichte der Rumänen.* Ed. by D. A. Sturdza. 5 v. Bucuresci, 1878–86. [Rumänischen Cultus- und Unterrichts-Ministerium.]

  b Urechiă, Vasilie A. *Istoria Românilor.* [History of the Rumanians.] 13 v. Bucuresci, 1891–1902.

  a. Collection of articles ranging over the whole field of Rumanian history; published posthumously. Review, v. 3, J. Loserth, *Hist. Zeit.*, 57: 176, 1887; A. D. Xénopol, *Rev. Hist.*, 28: 395, July 1885. *b.* Based on his lectures in the University of Bucharest; not primarily a narrative account, but an assemblage of materials of widely varying value; relates to the period from 1774 to 1822. Review, A. D. Xénopol, *Rev. Hist.*, 50: 388, Nov. 1892; 73: 375, July 1900.   GMD

RUMANIA: HISTORY SINCE 1822

T3301 Damé, Frédéric. *Histoire de la Roumanie contemporaine depuis l'avènement des princes indigènes jusqu'à nos jours, 1822–1900.* Paris, 1900. [Bibliothèque d'histoire contemporaine.] (Brief bibliography.)

  Though a generation old and indulgent toward Russia, still remains best detailed account of the period in any western language. Review, A. Lichtenberger, *Rev. Hist.*, 75: 381, March 1901.   RJK

T3351a Clark, Charles U. *Greater Roumania.* N. Y., 1922. (Bibliography.)

  b —— *Bessarabia, Russia, and Roumania on the Black Sea.* N. Y., 1927.

  c Babel, Antony. *La Bessarabie: étude historique, ethnographique, et économique.* Paris, 1927.

  d Szász, Zsombor de. *Minorities in Roumanian Transylvania.* London, 1927.

  a. Best recent work in English. General survey of politics and culture; gives the Rumanian version of events from the World War to 1922. Review, F. Schevill, *A.H.R.*, 27: 823, July 1922. *b.* Favorable to the Rumanian side of the controversy with Russia over Bessarabia. Review, S. Panaretoff, *A.H.R.*, 33: 119, Oct. 1927. *c.* Descriptive study of Bessarabia by a Swiss scholar; also favorable to the Rumanian cause. Reviews, (London) *Times Lit. Suppl.*, 26: 168, March 17, 1927; A. I. Andrews, *A.H.R.*, 32: 919, July 1927. *d.* Hostile account of the Rumanization of Transylvania. Review, (London) *Times Lit. Suppl.*, 26: 431, June 23, 1927. Also cf. *Rumania* in (J441a) *Peace handbooks.*   RJK, HRS

RUMANIA: ECONOMIC HISTORY

T3571a Ionescu, Dimitrie B. *Die Agrarverfassung Rumäniens, ihre Geschichte und ihre Reform.* Leipzig, 1909. [Staats- und Sozialwissenschaftliche Forschungen.]

  b Evans, Ifor L. *Agrarian revolution in Roumania.* Cambridge, Eng., and N. Y., 1924.

  Brief studies of the land-holding and peasant problems before and after the World War.   GMD

T3572 Rommenhoeller, C. G. *La grande Roumanie: sa structure économique, sociale, financière, politique, et particulièrement ses richesses.* La Haye, 1926.

Storehouse of information, by the Rumanian consul-general in Berlin, about the commercial, agricultural, and mineral wealth and industry of Rumania. Useful chapters also on politics and the new constitution. Review, (London) *Times Lit. Suppl.*, 25: 961, Dec. 30, 1926.   HRS

RUMANIA: CULTURAL HISTORY: LITERATURE

T3661a Densusianu, Ovid. *Histoire de la langue roumaine.* V. 1–2. Paris, 1901–14.

   b Adamescu, George. *Istoria literaturii române.* Bucuresci, 1913.

   c Alexics, György. *Geschichte der rumänischen Litteratur.* Leipzig, 1906. [Die Litteraturen des Ostens in Einzeldarstellungen.]

a. Incomplete but generally considered the most thorough study of the history of the Rumanian language. *b.* Handbook of all literary manifestations in the Rumanian language; especially satisfactory for the more recent period. *c.* Convenient brief manual.   MSH, GMD

RUMANIA: BIOGRAPHIES

The following are among the most important biographies in the field of Rumanian history: (T3711) Ioanŭ Bogdan, *Vlad Tepec* [Vlad the Impaler], Bucuresci, 1896, for the fifteenth century; (T3721) Nicolae Iorga, *Scurtă istorie a luĭ Mihaĭ Viteazul* [Life of Michael the Brave], Bucuresci, 1900, for the sixteenth century.

For the nineteenth century: (T3801) Nicolas Ypsilanti, *Mémoires,* ed. by D. G. Kambouroglous, Athènes and Paris, 1901; (T3802) George, Principe Bibescu, *Roumanie d'Andrinople à Balta-Liman, 1829–1849, règne de Bibesco,* 2 v., Paris, 1893–94, published also in Rumanian; (T3803) Alexandrŭ A. C. Sturdza, *De l'histoire diplomatique des Roumains, 1821–1859: règne de Michel Sturdza, prince régnant de Moldavie, 1834–1849,* Paris, 1907; (T3804a) Sidney Whitman, ed., *Reminiscences of the King of Roumania,* London and N. Y., 1899, which is an abridged translation of (T3804b) *Aus dem Leben König Karls von Rumänien: Aufzeichnungen eines Augenzeugen* [ed. by Georg Schaefer], 4 v., Stuttgart, 1894–1900, which carries the narrative only to 1881; (T3805) Paul Lindenberg, *König Karl von Rumänien, ein Lebensbild dargestellt, unter Mitarbeit des Königs,* 1906, new ed., 2 v., Berlin, 1923; (T3806) Titu Maiorescŭ, *Discursuri parlamentare* [Parliamentary speeches], 3 v., Bucuresti, 1897–99, speeches from 1866 to 1888 of the parliamentary spokesman of King Carol I; (T3807) D. Iancovici, *Take Jonesco,* Paris, 1919; (T3808) Take Ionescŭ [Jonesco], *Souvenirs,* Paris, 1919.

RJK, GMD

RUMANIA: ACADEMY PUBLICATIONS

The extensive publications of (T3921) Academia Română, Bucuresci, 1866 ff., contains valuable historical materials. In addition, this institution has published numerous historical works not prepared under its immediate direction. Full reference to these publications will be found in the academy's annual, (T3921a) *Analele,* Bucuresci, 1867 ff., and more conveniently in (T3921b) Dimitrie A. Sturdza, *L'activité de l'Académie Roumaine de 1884 à 1905,* Bucarest, 1905, and (T3921c) *Publicatiunile Academiei Române, 1866–1906,* Bucuresci, 1906.

RJK, GMD

RUMANIA: PERIODICALS

In spite of some short-lived attempts Rumania has no periodical devoted exclusively to history, but the following have included history as one of their fields: (T3941) *Columna lui Traian* [Column of Trajan], 7 v., Bucuresci, 1870-83, which, with variations of title, was published at three different intervals within the years indicated; (T3942) *Revista pentru istorie, archeologie, si filologie,* quarterly, 7 v., Bucuresci, 1883-93; (T3943) *Arhiva,* Iasi, 1890 ff.; (T3944) *Anuarul Institului de Istorie Naţională,* Cluj, 1922 ff., published by the University of Cluj [Klausenburg]; (T3945) *Buletinul,* Bucuresti, 1907 ff., issued by the national Comisiunea Monumentelor Istorice.

Among the more important Rumanian reviews which contain materials useful to the historian are: (T3951) *Convorbiri literare* [Literary colloquies], Iassi and Bucuresti, 1867 ff., organ of the literary society Jounimea [Youth]; (T3952) *Viată romînească„ revistă literară si stiintifică* [Rumanian life: literary and scientific review], Iasi, 1905 ff.

The only periodical of importance relating chiefly to Rumania that has been published outside the country is (T3961a) *Rumänische Revue,* 8 v., Budapest, 1885-92, continued as (T3961b) *Rumänische Jahrbücher,* 2 v., Hermannstadt, 1893-94.

RJK, GMD

JUGOSLAVIA: BIBLIOGRAPHY

T4001a Novaković, Stojan. *Srbska bibliografija za noviju književnost.* [Serbian bibliography of modern literature.] Beograd, 1869.

b *Glasnik srbskoj geografskog društva.* [Bulletin of the Serbian Geographical Society.] Beograd, 1910 ff.

c Ivanić, Ivan. *Essai de bibliographie française, anglaise, et allemande sur la Serbie et les Serbes.* London, 1907.

d Petrović, Nikola S. *Essai de bibliographie française sur les Serbes et les Croates, 1544-1900.* Belgrade, 1900.

e Odavić, Rista J. *Essai de bibliographie française sur les Serbes, Croates, et Slovènes depuis le commencement de la guerre actuelle.* Paris, 1918.

f Kukuljević-Sakcinski, Ivan. *Bibliografia hrvatska.* [Croatian bibliography.] U Zagrebu, 1860. *Dodatak* (supplement), U Zagrebu, 1863. [Bibliografia jugoslavenska.]

g Simonić, Franc. *Slovenska bibliografija.* [Slovenian bibliography.] V. 1. V Ljubljani, 1903-05.

h Zbornik Slovenske Matice. [Magazine of Slovenian Foundation.] V Ljubljani, 1899 ff.

i *Bibliograf popis novih knjiga i periodičnih publikacija u kraljevini Srba, Hrvata, i Slovenaca.* [Bibliography of new books and periodicals published in the kingdom of the Serbs, Croats, and Slovenes.] Beograd, 1926 ff.

a. Covers from 1741 to 1867; continued in *b* and in (T4921a) *Spomenik* of Serbian Royal Academy. Neither *a* nor *f* are satisfactory for their respective fields; but *g,* which covers from 1550 to 1900 and is continued in *h,* is more adequate. *c, d,* and *e.* Useful within their limited fields. An adequate current bibliography, long needed, will apparently be provided by *i.* Also cf. (S1) Kerner, *Slavic Europe.*

RJK

JUGOSLAVIA: GEOGRAPHY

T4041a Kanitz, Felix P. *Serbien: historisch-ethnographische Reisestudien aus den Jahren 1859–1868.* Leipzig, 1868.

b —— *Das Königreich Serbien und das Serbenvolk von der Römerzeit bis zur Gegenwart.* 3 v. Leipzig, 1904–14. V. 2–3, ed. by B. Jovanović.

c Mallat, Joseph. *La Serbie contemporaine: études, enquêtes statistiques.* 2 v. Paris, 1902.

d Krebs, Norbert. *Beiträge zur Geographie Serbiens und Rasciens: Ergebnisse zweier . . . im Jahre 1916 durchgeführten Studienreisen.* Stuttgart, 1922.

Good contributions to the geography and ethnography of Serbia. **GMD**

JUGOSLAVIA: GENERAL HISTORIES

T4101 Vukičević, Milenko M. *Istorija Srba, Hrvata, i Slovenaca.* [History of the Serbs, Croats, and Slovenes.] 1902. 7th rev. ed., 2 v., Beograd, 1920.

Text-book in Serbian for secondary schools; contains brief outline of Jugoslav history from the earliest times to 1918. **RJK**

T4102 Wendel, Hermann. *Der Kampf der Südslawen um Freiheit und Einheit.* Frankfurt am Main, 1925. (Bibliography.)

Enthusiastic account of the origins of the Jugoslav kingdom written in sentimental style. Review, A. Vaillant, *Rev. Critique,* 61 : 25, Jan. 15, 1927. **SBF**

T4111a Seton-Watson, Robert W. *Southern Slav question and the Habsburg monarchy.* London, 1911. (Bibliography.)

b Südland, L. von [pseud. of Pilar]. *Die südslawische Frage und der Weltkrieg: übersichtliche Darstellung des Gesamt-Problems.* Wien, 1918. (Bibliography.)

a. Still the best work in English on the southern Slavs in the former Austro-Hungarian monarchy; written from the point of view of the Croats and in favor of Serbo-Croat unity. Review, J. Loserth, *Hist. Zeit.,* 111 : 451, 1913. *b.* By an anti-Serbian Croatian; shows strong religious and pro-Austrian bias; though well-documented, does not estimate properly the movement which led to the formation of Jugoslavia. Review, J. Loserth, *Hist. Zeit.,* 127 : 326, 1923. **RJK**

T4112a Picot, Émile. *Les Serbes de Hongrie, leur histoire, leurs privilèges, leur église, leur état politique et social.* Prague, 1873–74.

b Samassa, Paul. *Der Völkerstreit im Habsburgerstaat.* Leipzig, 1910.

c Radonić [Radonitch], Jovan. *Histoire des Serbes de Hongrie: études historiques et économiques.* Paris, 1919.

a and *b.* Valuable discussions of the condition of the Jugoslavs in Hungary at the respective dates of publication. *c.* Well-documented study of the Serbian element in the Banat. **GMD**

JUGOSLAVIA: HISTORY OF SERBIA

T4201 Stanojević, Stanoje. *Istorija srbskoga naroda.* [History of the Serb nation.] 1908. 2nd rev. ed., Beograd, 1910. (Bibliographies.)

Best general political history of the Serbs, by a distinguished native scholar; thoroughly documented; extends to 1910; includes two chapters on the cultural evolution. **RJK**

T4202a **Temperly, Harold W. V.** *History of Serbia.* London and N. Y., 1917. (Bibliography.)

b **Jelenić, Djordje** [pseud. George Y. Devas]. *La nouvelle Serbie: origines et bases sociales et politiques, renaissance de l'état et son développement historique, dynastie nationale et revendications libératrices.* Paris, 1918. (Bibliography.)

c **Denis, Ernst.** *La grande Serbie.* 1915. New ed., Paris, 1919. [Bibliothèque d'histoire et de politique.]

All four were written during the World War and in a sympathetic tone. *a.* Without question the best history of Serbia in English. Fair and impartial; begins with the entrance of the Southern Slavs into the Balkan peninsula; closes with the opening of the Balkan wars in 1912. Review, R. J. Kerner, *A.H.R.,* 23: 135, Oct. 1917. *b.* Most comprehensive work in French. *c.* By one of the foremost French students of Slavic history.

SPD

T4203a **Ranke, Leopold von.** *History of Servia and the Servian revolution.* London, 1847. Later reprints. Tr. by Mrs. A. Kerr from *Geschichte Serbiens bis 1842,* Leipzig, 1844, being 2nd rev. ed. of *Die serbische Revolution,* Hamburg, 1829.

b —— *Serbien und die Türkei im 19. Jahrhundert.* Leipzig, 1879.

c **Kállay, Benjamin von.** *Geschichte der Serben von den ältesten Zeiten.* Budapest, 1878. Tr. by J. K. Schwicker from *A szerbek története,* Budapest, 1877.

d —— *Die Geschichte des serbischen Aufstandes, 1807–1810.* Ed. by L. von Thallóczy; tr. by S. Beigel. Wien, 1910.

Earlier works which subordinate the general history of Serbia to the treatment of the revolt at the beginning of the nineteenth century. *a.* Utilizes manuscript materials. *b.* Abridgement, revision, and continuation of *a* to 1867; almost unrivalled by later works for disinterestedness and impartiality. Reviews, *Hist. Zeit.,* 44: 555, 1880; L. Leger, *Rev. Hist.,* 17: 195, Sept. 1881. *c.* Extends to the beginning of the nineteenth century. Reviews, Zieglauer, *Hist. Zeit.,* 42: 375, 1879; L. Leger, *Rev. Hist.,* 10: 475, July 1879. *d.* Continuation of *c.* Based on first-hand acquaintance with the land and people, and upon Serbian materials not accessible to Ranke. Includes life, by the editor, of Kállay who was for some time in charge of the administration of Bosnia. Review, J. Loserth, *Hist. Zeit.,* 108: 401, 1912.

GMD

T4206a **Mijatović [Miyatovich], Chedomil.** *Servia and the Servians.* 1908. New ed., London and Boston, 1911.

b **Lazarović-Hrebelianović, Stephan, Prince,** and **Lazarović-Hrebelianović, Eleanor, Princess.** *Servian people, their past glory and their destiny.* 2 v. N. Y., 1910.

c **Waring, Miss L. F.** *Serbia.* London and N. Y., 1917. [Home university library.] (Bibliography.)

a. Popular account of all phases of Serbian life; excellent, readable introduction. *b.* Long, rather diffuse, descriptive work; comprehensive in scope. *c.* Brief survey of Serbian history, conditions, and problems.

MWT

T4211a **Jireček, Constantin.** *Geschichte der Serben.* V. 1–2. Gotha, 1911–18. [(B161) Allgemeine Staatengeschichte.]

b —— *Staat und Gesellschaft im mittelalterlichen Serbien, Studien zur Kulturgeschichte des XIII.–XV. Jahrhunderts.* Wien, 1912. [Denkschriften der Kaiserlich Akademie der Wissenschaften, phil.-hist. Cl., v. 56, 58.]

Fundamental studies by the leading scholar in the field. *a*. Detailed record of the political vicissitudes of the Serb peoples; includes the 'Montenegrins; narrative terminated at 1537 by author's death. Review, J. Loserth, *Hist. Zeit.*, 110: 161, 1913; 123: 142, 1921. *b*. Presents the completest picture to be found of the internal situation of a medieval Balkan state. Political and legal institutions and social classes are treated in detail and the strength and weakness of medieval Serbia assessed for the first time on a plan other than guesswork. FS

JUGOSLAVIA: HISTORY OF THE CROATS

T4261a Šišić, Ferdo [Ferdinand]. *Geschichte der Kroaten*. V. 1. Zagreb, 1917. (Bibliography.)

b ——— *Hrvatska provijest*. [Croatian history.] V. 1–3. Zagreb, 1906–13. [Matica Hrvatska.]

c Klaić, Vjekoslav. *Povjest Hrvata od najstarijih vremena do svršetka XIX. stoljeca*. [History of Croatia from the earliest times to the nineteenth century.] V. 1–5. Zagreb, 1899–1911.

a and *b*. Written by a distinguished native historian; planned to extend to the end of the nineteenth century; scholarly and impartial. *a*. Extends to 1102. *b*. The successive volumes end at 1526, 1790, 1847. *c*. Also by a competent native scholar; more extended in scope than *b*, but the narrative has not been completed beyond 1608. RJK, GMD

JUGOSLAVIA: HISTORY OF THE SLOVENES

T4281a Gruden, Josip. *Zgodovina slovenskoga naroda*. [Annals of the Slovene nation.] 6 v. Celovec, 1910–16.

b Vošnjak, Bogumil. *Bulwark against Germany: the fight of the Slovenes, the western branch of the Jugoslavs, for national existence*. London, 1917. Tr. by F. S. Copeland.

By distinguished native scholars. *a*. Conventional work, but the standard Slovene history; does not extend beyond the seventeenth century. *b*. Though written for propaganda purposes, virtually the only good account in English of Slovene history. RJK

JUGOSLAVIA: HISTORY OF MONTENEGRO

T4291a Gopčević, Spiridion. *Geschichte von Montenegro und Albanien*. Gotha, 1914. (Brief bibliography.)

b Devine, Alexander. *Montenegro in history, politics, and war*. London and N. Y., 1918. (Bibliography.)

c Stevenson, Francis S. *History of Montenegro*. London, 1912.

There is no authoritative history of Montenegro in any language. *a*. Best in German. Review, J. Loserth, *Hist. Zeit.*, 116: 318, 1916. *b*. Most recent in English; a plea for the existence of Montenegro as an independent state; forty-five pages on 'Montenegrin history previous to 1905; remainder on Montenegro's part in the Balkan Wars and the World War. *c*. Fuller account of Montenegro's history. SPD

JUGOSLAVIA: HISTORY IN NINETEENTH AND TWENTIETH CENTURIES

T4301a Novaković, Stojan. *Die Wiedergeburt des serbischen Staates, 1804–1813.* Sarajevo, 1912. Tr. by G. Grassl. [Zur Kunde des Balkanhalbinsel.]

b Jakšić [Yakschitch], Gregory. *L'Europe et la résurrection de la Serbie, 1804–1834.* 1907. 2nd ed., Paris, 1917.

Older histories of the Serb revolt (cf. T4203) are entirely superseded by these recent works constructed with the aid of an immense body of new material. *a.* Authentic version of Black George's heroic enterprise. *b.* Carries the story of the rebellion through the period of Miloš; sketches the actual foundations of the Serb state.

FS

T4371a Marković [Marcovitch], Lazar, ed. *Serbia and Europe, 1914–1920.* London, 1920, N. Y., 1921.

b Price, W. H. Crawfurd. *Serbia's part in the war.* V. 1. London, 1918.

c Rivet, Charles. *En Yougoslavie.* Paris, 1919.

d Vesnić [Vesnitch], Milenko R. *La Serbie à travers la grande guerre.* Paris, 1921.

e Vouksanovitch, R. *Le Monténégro dans les guerres balkanique et mondiale.* Pau, 1918.

a. 'A collection of articles published in *La Serbie,* in Geneva, between 1916 and 1919' on Serbian politics, the Jugoslav movement, the war with Austria-Hungary, and Serbian relations with the other Balkan states and the Great Powers. Review, R. J. Kerner, *A.H.R., 27*:154, Oct. 1921. *b.* Includes introductory chapter on Austro-Serbian relations before 1914. *c.* Record of a journey made shortly after the armistice of 1918; an antidote to the Pan-Serb view. *d.* Collection of addresses and articles written from 1914 to 1919 by the Serbian minister in Paris; deals with Serbian history and aspirations. *e.* Depicts the expiring glories of the little state.

BES, GMD

T4381a Mousset, Albert. *Le royaume des Serbes, Croates, et Slovènes.* Paris, 1921.

b —— *Le royaume serbe croate slovène: son organisation, sa vie politique, et ses institutions.* Paris, 1926.

c Beard, Charles A., and **Radin, George.** *Balkan pivot: Yugoslavia.* N. Y., 1929.

a. Good general survey of Jugoslavia. *b.* Together with a second volume to follow, an enlarged rewriting of *a.* Study not only of Jugoslav foreign policy and party politics, particularly since the establishment of the triune monarchy, but also of the organization and institutions of the state; includes such topics as the church and art. Review, (London) *Times Lit. Suppl.,* 25 : 894, Dec. 9, 1926. *c.* Admirably clear and discriminating description of the government and administration of Jugoslavia.

RJK, HRS

JUGOSLAVIA: DIPLOMATIC AND MILITARY HISTORY

T4501a Račić [Rachitch], Vojislav V. *Le royaume de Serbie, étude d'histoire diplomatique et de droit international.* Paris, 1901.

b Fournier, August. *Wie wir zu Bosnien kamen.* Wien, 1908.

c Cvijić, Jovan. *L'annexion de la Bosnie et la question serbe.* Paris, 1909.

a. Diplomatic history of the establishment of the Serbian kingdom. *b.* Approved Austrian views presented by an eminent Austrian historian. *c.* Corresponding exposition of Serbian views.

GMD

JUGOSLAVIA: CULTURAL HISTORY; LITERATURE

T4661a Popović, Pavle. *Jugoslovenska književnost.* [Jugoslav literature.] Cambridge, Eng., 1918.

b Stanoyevich [Stanojević], Beatrice Stevenson, ed. *Anthology of Jugoslav poetry: Serbian lyrics.* Boston, 1920.

a. Small book; treats the regional literatures of the Jugoslavs for the first time as one organic whole. Discusses works written or printed in Cyrillic, Glagolitic, Latin, and Gothic scripts, or orally perpetuated. Illuminating description of the nine cycles of national epic poetry, twelfth to nineteenth centuries, of which the most important are those of Nemanjić, of Kosovo, and of Prince Marko. *b.* Collection of translations from the much-admired South-Slavonic popular poetry.

LZL

T4662a Jagić, Vatroslav. *Die slawischen Sprachen.* Leipzig, 1908. [Die Kultur der Gegenwart.]

b Murko, Matthias. *Geschichte der älteren südslawischen Litteraturen.* Leipzig, 1908. [Die Litteraturen des Ostens.] (Bibliography.)

c Stanoyevich [Stanojević], Milivoy S. *Early Jugoslav literature, 1000–1800.* N. Y., 1922. [Columbia University Slavonic studies.] (Bibliography.)

a and *b.* Good summaries of the respective subjects by competent scholars. Review of *b,* W. Christiani, *Hist. Zeit.,* 103:637, 1909. *c.* Small volume with ample references to the best sources.

GMD

JUGOSLAVIA: BIOGRAPHY

Among the biographical works in the field of Jugoslav history for the eleventh century are: (T4701) M. Mesić, *Dimitar Zvonimir, kralj hrvatski* [Demetrius Zvonimir, king of Croatia], Zagreb, 1876; (T4702) P. Grebenarović and T. Koliška, *Kral Uroš I veliki* [King Urosh I the Strong], Beograd, 1897; for the thirteenth century, (T4721) A. Gavrilović, *Sveti Sava, pregled života i rada* [Saint Sava, review of his life and speeches], Beograd, 1900; for the fourteenth century, (T4741) Émile de Borchgrave, *L'empereur Étienne Douchan et la péninsule balcanique au XIVᵉ siècle,* Bruxelles, 1884; for the nineteenth century, (T4801) M. Vukičević, *Karadjordje* [Kara George], v. 1, *1752–1804,* Beograd, 1907; (T4802) M. Gavrilović, *Miloš Obrenović,* 2 v., Beograd, 1908–09; (T4821) M. Hartley, *Man who saved Austria, the life and times of Baron Jellačić,* London, 1912; (T4841) S. Jovanović, *Svetozar Marković,* Beograd, 1903; (T4842) Vladimir Zagorsky, *François Racki et la renaissance scientifique et politique de la Croatie, 1828–1894,* Paris, 1909; for religious history (T4861) Voyeslav Yanich and C. Patrick Hankey, *Lives of the Serbian saints,* London, 1921.   RJK

JUGOSLAVIA: ACADEMY PUBLICATIONS

Three national academies—Serb, Croat, Slovene—have been instrumental in publishing much important material on the history of the Jugoslavs. A considerable portion of these materials has a wider usefulness for European history, especially for Austrian and Venetian affairs; and many of the documents or contributions are in western European languages. Srbska Kraljevska Akademija [Serbian Royal Academy], issues (T4921a) *Spomenik* [Memoirs], Beograd, 1888 ff., and (T4921b) *Sbornik za istoriju, jezik, i književnost srbskoga naroda* [Magazine of Serbian national history, language, and literature.] Beograd, 1902 ff.

Academia Scientiarum et Artium Slavorum Meridionalium, or Jugoslavenska Akademija Znanosti i Umjetnosti [Croatian National Academy of Sciences and Arts], includes among its publications (T4922a) *Gradja za povjest književnosti hrvatska* [Materials for the history of Croatian literature], v. 1–9, u Zagrebu, 1897–1920; (T4922b) *Stari pisci hrvatski* [Ancient Croatian writers], v. 1–12, u Zagrebu, 1869 ff.; (T4922c) *Ljetopis* [Yearbook], v. 1–38, u Zagrebu, 1867–1924; (T4922d) *Rad* [Publications], v. 1–232, u Zagrebu, 1867–1926; (T4922e) *Starine* [Antiquities], v. 1–36, u Zagrebu, 1869–1918; (T4922f) *Zbornik za narodni život i običaje južnih slavena* [Magazine of the national life and customs of the southern Slavs], v. 1–25, u Zagrebu, 1896–1924; (T4922g) *Monumenta historico-juridica Slavorum meridionalium,* v. 1–8, Zagrabiae, 1877 ff.; (T4922h) *Monumenta spectantia historiam Slavorum meridionalium,* 33 v., Zagrabiae, 1868–1913; (T4922i) T. Smičiklas, ed., *Codex diplomaticus regni Croatiae, Dalmatiae, et Slavoniae,* v. 1–14, Zagrabiae, 1904–14. A catalogue and epitome of the historical portions of these publications is provided by (T2922) Margalits, *Horvát történelmi repertorium.*

Slovenska Matica [Slovene Foundation] publishes (T4923) *Letopis* [Yearbook], v Ljubljani, 1866 ff.
RJK, GMD

BULGARIA: BIBLIOGRAPHY AND ENCYCLOPEDIAS

T5001a Teodorov-Balan, A. *B" lgarski knigopis za sto godini, 1806–1905.* [Century of Bulgarian bibliography.] Sofia, 1909. [B" lgarskoto Knizhovno Druzhestvo.]

b Ivanov, Iordan. *B" lgarski periodicheski pechat, 1844–1890.* [Bulgarian periodical press.] V. 1. Sofia, 1893.

c Narodna Biblioteka [National Library]. *Bibliograficheski biuletin.* [Bibliographical bulletin.] Sofia, 1897 ff.

d Kersopulov, Jean G. *Essai de bibliographie franco-bulgare, 1613–1910.* Paris, 1912. [Extrait de la *Revue des Bibliothèques,* 21: 269–335, July–Sept. 1911.]

With *a* and *b* general Bulgarian bibliography is splendidly organized. *c.* Record of current publications. *d.* Useful special bibliography. Also cf. (S1) Kerner, and (T1d) Mikhov.
RJK

T5021 Kasurov, L., ed. *Enciklopedicheski rěčnik.* [Encyclopedic dictionary.] Plovdiv, 1899 ff.

BULGARIA: GEOGRAPHY AND ATLASES

T5041a Ishirkov [Ischirkoff], Anastas. *Bulgarien: Land und Leute.* 2 v. Leipzig, 1916–17. [Bulgarische Bibliothek.]

b Grothe, Hugo. *Bulgarien: Natur, Volkstum, Staat, Geistesleben, Wirtschaft: ein Beitrag zur Landeskunde.* Wien, 1921. [Angewandte Geographie.]

Brief compendiums of geographical, ethnographical, and other data. GMD

T5046 Rizov, Dimitŭr, ed. *Bulgarians in their historical, ethnographical, and political frontiers.* Berlin, 1917. (Brief bibliography.)

Atlas of forty maps with text in English, German, French, and Bulgarian; issued by the Bulgarian minister in Berlin for propaganda purposes; contains facsimiles of many important maps. RJK

BULGARIA: SHORTER GENERAL HISTORIES

T5101a Jireček, Constantin. *Geschichte der Bulgaren.* Prag, 1876. Tr. from *Dějiny naroda bulharského,* v Praze, 1876.

b —— *Das Fürstenthum Bulgarien: seine Bodengestaltung, Natur, Bevölkerung, wirtschaftliche Zustände, geistige Cultur, Staatsverfassung, Staatsverwaltung, und neueste Geschichte.* Wien, 1891.

a. Not yet superseded; utilizes an amazing wealth of sources in treating the whole history of the Bulgars to the date of publication. Review, F. Hirsch, *Hist. Zeit.,* 38: 549, 1877. *b.* Voluminous continuation to the election of Prince Ferdinand in 1887, but chiefly valuable for thorough account of economic, social, and cultural conditions. Also cf. *Bulgaria* in (J441a) *Peace handbooks.* FS

T5102a Gleichen, Lord Edward. *Bulgaria and Romania.* London and Boston, 1924. [(B137a) *Nations of today.*] (Brief bibliography.)

b **Bousquet, Georges.** *Histoire du peuple bulgare depuis les origines jusqu'à nos jours.* Paris, 1909.

c **Antonov, Beltscha.** *Bulgarien . . . 679–1917, eine knappe Darstellung . . .* Berlin, 1917.

d **Zlatarski [Slatarski], Vasili N.,** and **Stanev [Staneff], Nikola.** *Geschichte der Bulgaren.* 2 v. Leipzig, 1917–18. [Bulgarische Bibliothek.] Tr. by H. K. Swischtoff from the Bulgarian.

a. Best account in English. *b* and *c.* Convenient manuals in French and German respectively. *c.* Contains useful maps. *d.* Brief work by Bulgarian scholars. Despite its faults, most competent account since (T5101a) Jireček. Review, E. Gerland, *Hist. Zeit.,* 123: 326, 1921. GMD

BULGARIA: HISTORY SINCE 1870

T5331a Landemont, Ambroise, Comte de. *L'élan d'un peuple: la Bulgarie jusqu'au traité de Londres, 1861–1913.* Paris, 1914.

b **Ancel, Jacques.** *L'unité de la politique bulgare, 1870–1919.* Paris, 1919.

c **Stanev [Staneff], Nikola.** *Histoire de Bulgarie, 1878–1912.* Paris, 1924.

a. Survey of the development of independent Bulgaria to the close of the first Balkan war. *b.* Strong indictment of Bulgarian imperialism. Review, F. Bertrand, *Rev. Critique,* 86: 473, Dec. 15, 1919. *c.* Good account by a native scholar. GMD

T5351 Monroe, Will S. *Bulgaria and her people, with an account of the Balkan wars, Macedonia, and the Macedonian Bulgars.* Boston, 1914. (Bibliography.)

After devoting a quarter of the volume to a hasty geographical and historical survey, the author provides interesting chapters on economic and cultural conditions and on his own experience in the Balkan wars. He believes that Bulgaria 'was betrayed, attacked, and traduced by her treacherous allies' in the Second Balkan War. Useful contribution to the literature of the subject in English. RJK

T5371 **Ivanov, Iordan.** *Les Bulgares devant le Congrès de la Paix, recueil de documents historiques, ethnographiques, et diplomatiques.* Berne, 1919. 2nd rev. ed. of *Les Bulgares et leurs manifestations nationales,* Berne, 1919.

The Bulgarian case before the Paris Peace Conference ably presented by a professor in the University of Sofia. Includes the question of the Dobrudja. Contains maps.

RJK

T5381a **Gentizon, Paul.** *Le drame bulgare de Ferdinand à Stamboulisky.* Paris, 1924.

b **Radoslavov [Radoslawoff], Vasili.** *Bulgarien und die Weltkrise.* Berlin, 1923.

c **Lamouche, Léon.** *La Bulgarie.* Paris, 1923. [Les états contemporains.] (Bibliography.)

a. By a French journalist who spent two years in the Balkans; surveys the reign of Ferdinand and treats in fuller detail events from 1918 to 1923. General tone is anti-Bulgar. Review, G. Cahen, *Rev. Hist.,* 151: 275, March 1926. *b.* Treatment of the same period by a member of the Bulgarian National Academy. *c.* Brief, convenient statement of recent political changes and economic conditions; by the Bulgarian consul general in Paris. Review, G. Cahen, *Rev. Hist.,* 146: 260, July 1924.

GMD

BULGARIA: DIPLOMATIC HISTORY

T5501 **Chaunier, Auguste.** *La Bulgarie, étude d'histoire diplomatique et de droit international.* Paris, 1909. (Bibliography.)

Useful survey of international aspects of Bulgarian history from 1878 to 1908. Good collection and interpretation of printed sources. Problems of international law are fully treated, especially the relation of Bulgaria to Turkey. Pro-Bulgarian in tone.

MWT

BULGARIA: BIOGRAPHIES

Among biographical works for Bulgarian history are (T5751) A. F. Golovin, *Fürst Alexander I von Bulgarien, 1879–1886,* Wien, 1896; (T5752) Egon C. Corti, *Alexander von Battenberg, sein Kampf mit den Zaren und Bismarck, nach des ersten Fürsten von Bulgarien nachgelassenen Papieren und sonstigen ungedruckten Quellen,* Wien, 1920; (T5753) Eumène Queillé, *Les commencements de l'indépendance bulgare et le prince Alexandre: souvenirs d'un Français de Sofia,* Paris, 1910; (T576i) Ardern G. Hulme Beaman, *M. Stambuloff,* London, 1895; (T5771) John MacDonald, *Czar Ferdinand and his people,* London, 1913; and (T5772) Alexandre Hepp, *Ferdinand de Bulgarie intime,* Paris, 1909.

RJK

BULGARIA: ACADEMY PUBLICATIONS

B″ lgarsko Knizhovno Druzhestvo [Bulgarian Literary Society], which published (T5921) *Periodichesko spisanie* [Periodical publications], 22 v., Braila and Sofia, 1870–1910, has since 1911 been superseded by B″ lgarska Akademiia na Naukitie [Bulgarian National Academy of Sciences], which issues (T5922a) *Lietopis* [Yearbook], Sofia, 1899 ff., and (T5922b) *Spisanie: klon historiko-filologichen* [Publications: historical-philological series], Sofia, 1911 ff.

RJK, GMD

BULGARIA: PERIODICALS

Among the more important Bulgarian periodicals are: (T5941) *Izviestiia na B" lgarskiia Arkheologicheski Institut* [Bulletin of the Bulgarian Archeological Institute], Sofia, 1921 ff., which includes materials on both ancient times and the Middle Ages, with each article summarized in either French or German; (T5942) *B" lgarski pregled* [Bulgarian review], Sofia, 1893 ff.; and (T5943) *Makedonski pregled* [Macedonian review], Sofia, 1924 ff., which is the organ of the Make-donski Naučen Institut [Macedonian Institute of Sciences], and contains French abridgements of the articles.   RJK, GMD

ALBANIA: BIBLIOGRAPHY

T6001a **Manek, Franz; Pekmezi, Georg;** and **Stolz, Alfred.** *Albanesische Bibliographie.* Wien, 1909.

   b **Legrand, Émile L. J.** *Bibliographie albanaise, description raisonée des ouvrages publiés en albanais ou relatifs à l'Albanie du quinzième siècle à l'année 1900.* Paris, 1912.

General bibliographies covering practically the whole period; useful and valuable as far as they go, but leave the task of preparing a comprehensive bibliography far from completed. *b.* Posthumous work, completed by Henri Gûys.   RJK

ALBANIA: COLLECTIONS OF SOURCES

T6071 **Thallóczy, Ludwig von; Jireček, Constantin;** and **Sufflay, Emil von.** ed. *Acta et diplomata res Albaniae mediae aetatis illustrantia.* V. 1, *Annos 344–1343, tabulamque geographicam continens.* Vindobonae, 1913.

Several leading Balkan scholars collaborated on this digest of almost one thou-sand documents relating to the medieval history of Albania. A model of accurate and enlightened scholarship; should serve as the starting-point for an era of Albanian studies; includes materials from printed and unprinted sources; contains careful index of persons and places. Three more volumes are planned to carry the work through the fifteenth century.   FS

ALBANIA: HISTORY IN THE TWENTIETH CENTURY

T6351a **Durham, Mary Edith.** *Burden of the Balkans.* London, 1905.

   b ———— *High Albania.* London, 1909.

   c ———— *Struggle for Scutari: Turk, Slav, and Albanian.* London, 1914.

   d ———— *Twenty years of Balkan tangle.* London, 1920.

   e **Peacock, Wadham.** *Albania, the foundling state of Europe.* London and N. Y., 1914.

a, b, c, and *d.* Treat, from different angles, substantially the same subject, Albanian customs and religion, together with the pressing national and political problems of the day. Attempt to probe the Albanian soul, and, though casual and unsystematic, have the quality of fresh notes taken on the spot by an intelligent and sympathetic traveler. *c* and *d.* Belong more particularly to the field of politics. *c.* Treats of the Albanian interest in the Balkan wars of 1912–1913. *d.* Reviews a twenty years' experience in the Balkans, with the object of showing that the World War was a deliberate Russian plot. *e.* Full of sympathy for the backward Albanian; presents sparkling descriptions of people and country.   FS

T6352a Gopčević, Spiridion. *Das Fürstenthum Albanien.* Berlin, 1914.

b Godart, Justin. *L'Albanie en 1921.* Paris, 1922.

c Stickney, Edith P. *Southern Albania or Northern Epirus in European international affairs, 1912–1923.* Stanford University, 1926.

a. Work of a Serb publicist and ethnologist; anti-Albanian, but basic study of the peoples and resources of Albania. *b.* Description of recent conditions by French observer. *c.* Careful documentary study; best treatment of international relations of Albania since its independence. Review, A. H. Lybyer, *A.H.R., 33* : 188, Oct. 1927. Also cf. (J441a) *Peace handbooks.* GMD

ALBANIA: BIOGRAPHIES

The life of the Albanian national hero is told in (T6721) Julius Pisko, *Skanderbeg,* Wien, 1894. GMD

MODERN GREECE: BIBLIOGRAPHY

T7001a Sathas, Kōnstantinos N. *Neoellēnikē filologia: biografiai tōn en tois grammasi dialampsantōn Hellēnōn, 1455–1821.* [Modern Greek philology: Biographies of Greeks distinguished in literature.] En Athēnais, 1868.

b Vretos, Andreas P. *Neoellēnikē filologia: ētoi katalogos tōn . . . typōthentōn bibliōn par' Hellēnōn eis tēn homiloumenēn, ē eis tēn archaian hellēnikēn glōssan [1453–1821].* [Modern Greek philology: catalogue of books printed by Greeks in the vernacular or in the ancient Greek tongue.] 1845. 2nd rev. ed., 2 v., En Athēnais, 1854–57.

c Koromēlas [Coromilas], Dēmētrios A. *Catalogue raisonné des livres publiés en Grèce, 1868–1872; 1873–1877.* 2 v. Athènes, 1873–78.

d *Timologion bibliōn [apo 1895].* [Noteworthy books.] En Athēnais, 1895 ff.

a. Preferable to *b. c.* Useful for its limited period. *d.* Current bibliography. Unfortunately no comprehensive work is available for the important years, 1821–1868, or for the years 1878–1894. RJK, GMD

T7002a Legrand, Émile L. J. *Bibliographie hellénique, ou description raisonnée des ouvrages publiés par des Grecs aux XVᵉ et XVIᵉ siècles.* 4 v. Paris, 1885–1906. V. 4 ed. by H. O. Pernot.

b —— *Bibliographie hellénique, ou description raisonnée des ouvrages publiés par des Grecs au dix-septième siècle.* 5 v. Paris, 1894–1903.

c —— *Bibliographie hellénique, ou description raisonnée des ouvrages publiés par des Grecs au dix-huitième siècle: œuvre posthume completée et publiée par Louis Petit et Hubert Pernot.* V. 1. Paris, 1918.

d —— *Bibliographie ionienne: œuvre posthume publiée par Hubert Pernot.* 2 v. Paris, 1910.

Monumental work; planned to cover all publications by Greeks since the introduction of printing; includes numerous biographical sketches of Greek authors. Review of *b,* A. D. Xénopol, *Rev. Hist., 73* : 359, July 1900. GMD

MODERN GREECE: COLLECTION OF SOURCES

In addition to (H76) *Byzantinae historiae scriptores* and (H77) *Corpus scriptorum historiae byzantinae,* (T7071) Kōnstantinos N. Sathas, ed., *Mesaiōnikē bibliothēkē* [Medieval library], 7 v., En Venetia, 1872–94, and (T7072) Kōnstantinos N. Sathas, ed., *Mnēmeia hellēnikēs historias: Documents inédits relatifs à l'histoire de la Grèce au moyen âge,* 9 v., Paris, 1880–90, contain some materials for early modern times as well as for the Middle Ages.

For the period of the World War, reference should be made to the Greek white books, notably (T7081) *Diplōmatika engrapha* [Diplomatic documents], 2 v., En Athēnais, 1917. GMD

MODERN GREECE: GENERAL HISTORIES

T7101 Bikēlas, Dēmētrios. *La Grèce byzantine et moderne.* Paris, 1893.

Best account in French of Greek history since 1453, and best balanced survey in any language of the whole of Greek history from the Middle Ages to the present day. RJK

T7102 Lhéritier, Michel. *La Grèce.* Paris, 1921. [Collection des états contemporains.]

Good, extremely concise historical and descriptive account; chiefly valuable as the most recent work of the sort. Review, *Rev. Hist.,* 141: 114, Sept. 1922.

  GMD

T7121 Finlay, George. *History of Greece from its conquest by the Romans to the present time, B. C. 146 to A.D. 1864.* 1844–61. Rev. ed. by H. F. Tozer, 7 v., Oxford, 1877.

Cf. (H305) for review of v. 1–4. V. 4. Deals with the Turkish conquest. V. 5–7. Relate to modern Greece. Finlay was an actor in the drama he describes, and naturally reveals certain prejudices. He exaggerates the defects of the revolutionary leaders in whom he sees only the darker side as contrasted with the glorious aspirations of the people, but this is wholesome exaggeration. For the constitutional development of modern Greece prior to 1864, no better authority is available. AEP

T7122a Mendelssohn-Bartholdy, Karl W. P. *Geschichte Griechenlands von der Eroberung Konstantinopels durch die Türken im Jahre 1453 bis auf unsere Tage.* 2 v. Leipzig, 1870–74. [Staatengeschichte der neuesten Zeit.]

b Hertzberg, Gustav F. *Geschichte Griechenlands seit dem Absterben des antiken Lebens bis zur Gegenwart.* 4 v. Gotha, 1876–79. [(B161) Geschichte der europäischen Staaten.] [1, *395–1204;* 2, *1204–1470;* 3, *1470–1821;* 4, *1821–1878.*]

a. Best extended account in German of Greek history since 1453; not carried beyond 1835 because of author's death, but cf. his valuable article, 'Die Verwaltung König Otto's in Griechenland und sein Sturz,' *Preussische Jahrbücher,* 14: 365–392, 1864. Review, G. F. Hertzberg, *Hist. Zeit.,* 25: 227, 1871; 35: 204, 1876. *b.* Also good; briefer than *a* for the period covered therein; likewise briefer than (T7121) Finlay, to which it corresponds approximately in scope; useful both as having been written later and as extending to a later date than either *a* or Finlay. Review, F. Hirsch, *Hist. Zeit.,* 36: 677, 1876; 39: 376, 1878; 41: 562, 1879; 44: 542, 1880.

  GMD

T7123a Paparrhēgopoulos, Kōnstantinos. *Historia tou hellēnikou ethnous apo tōn archaiotatōn chronōn mechri tōn kath' hēmas.* [History of the Greek people from the earliest times to the present.] 1860–74. 2nd rev. ed., by A. P. Kōnstantinidēs, 5 v. and atlas, En Athēnais, 1885–87.

b Lampros, Spyridōn P. *Historia tēs Hellados, met' eikonōn, apo tōn archaiotatōn chronōn mechri tēs basileias tou Othōnos.* [Illustrated history of Greece from the earliest times to the reign of Otho.] 6 v. En Athēnais, 1886–1903.

a. Still read as a classic by Greeks everywhere. Modeled on Grote and Gibbon, but not without judicious discrimination and sufficient originality and independence of judgment. Especially valuable as an authority on the period following the fall of Constantinople in 1453. The account of the forces that led to the revival of Hellenism after the Turkish invasion is masterly and the discussion of klephts and klephtic lore is of much value. *b.* Only rival of *a.* Review of *a* and *b,* P. Karolidēs, *Rev. Hist.,* 39: 139, Jan. 1889.   AEP

MODERN GREECE: HISTORY SINCE 1821

T7301 Phillips, Walter Alison. *War of Greek independence, 1821 to 1833.* London and N. Y., 1897.

Classic account in English; makes full use of material in English archives; pro-English in tone; somewhat critical of the Greek leaders. Review, J. I. Manatt, *A.H.R.,* 3: 537, Apr. 1898.   MWT

T7321a Miller, William. *History of the Greek people, 1821–1921.* London, 1922. [History of the people's series.]

   b ——— *Modern Greece.* London, 1928.

a. Convenient survey of Greek history from the War for Independence through the World War by a well-known English historian of the Near East. *b.* After a sketch of Greek history to the death of George I in 1913, deals in detail with subsequent events. Though packed with facts, often fails to interpret material. Excellent chapters on Greek politics. Review (London) *Times Lit. Suppl.,* 27: 303, April 26, 1928.   RJK, HRS

MODERN GREECE: DIPLOMATIC HISTORY

T7501 Driault, Édouard, and Lhéritier, Michel. *Histoire diplomatique de la Grèce de 1821 à nos jours.* 5 v. Paris, 1925–26.

Well-proportioned work by French historians well acquainted with the field; most useful recent addition to the literature of the diplomatic history of the Near East. Review, W. Miller, *History,* 12: 81, Apr. 1927.   GMD

MODERN GREECE: ECONOMIC HISTORY

T7571a Andreadēs, Andreas M. *Les progrès économiques de la Grèce.* Paris, 1919.

   b **Tsouderos, E. J.** *Le relèvement économique de la Grèce.* Paris, 1920.

Recent presentations of conditions and problems by competent Greek authorities.
        GMD

GREECE: CULTURAL HISTORY: LITERATURE

T7661a Dietrich, Karl. *Geschichte der byzantinischen und neugriechischen Literatur.* Leipzig, 1902. [Die Literaturen des Ostens.]

   b **Pernot, Hubert O.** *Études de littérature grecque moderne.* 2 v. Paris, 1916–18. (Bibliographical foot-notes.)

   c **Rodd, Sir James Rennell.** *Customs and lore of modern Greece.* London, 1892.

a. Based on careful and exhaustive study; shows broad and comprehensive understanding of the forces which have molded Modern Greece from the classical age to the present day. Probably exaggerates the importance of Byzantinism; makes no allowance for a renaissance in Constantinople, signs of which clearly appeared just before the Turkish avalanche. The author would have reversed his judgment of many of the literary men of his day, had he been able to foresee the later development of these men. Should be supplemented by *b* and *c*. *c*. Excellent account of village festivals, popular superstitions, and folk songs; contains faithful translations of some of the songs. AEP

MODERN GREECE: BIOGRAPHIES

The following biographies in the field of modern Greek history may be noted: (T7701) Phōtios Chrysanthopoulos, *Bioi Peloponnēsiōn andrōn kai tōn exōthen eis tēn Peloponnēson elthontōn sungraphentes* [Coöperative biographies of Peloponnesian men and immigrants into the Peloponnesus], ed. by S. Andropoulos, En Athēnais, 1888, which relates especially to the period of the struggle for independence; (T7721) D. Thērianos, *Adamantios Koraēs,* 3 v., Tergestē [Trieste], 1889–90, which treats the cultural history of Greece from the Turkish conquest but with special emphasis on the age of Koraēs [Coray], 1748–1833; (T7722) Kōnstantinos Paparrhēgopoulos, *Geōrgios Karaiskakēs* (in his *Historikai pragmateiai*), En Athēnais, 1889; (T7741) Tryphōn Evangelidēs, *Historia tou Othōnos, basileōs tēs Hellados, 1832–1862, kata tas neōtatas pēgas* [History of Otto, king of Greece, from the latest sources], En Athēnais, 1893; (T7761) Walter Christmas, *King George of Greece,* London and N. Y., 1914, tr. from the Danish by A. G. Chater; (T7781) Léon Maccas, *Constantin Ier, roi des Hellènes,* Paris, 1917; (T7782) George M. Mélas, *Ex-King Constantine and the war,* London, 1920; (T7783) Paxton Hibben, *Constantine I and the Greek people,* N. Y., 1920; (T7784) Prince Nicholas [brother of Constantine I], *My fifty years,* London, 1926; (T7791) Herbert A. Gibbons, *Venizelos,* 1920, 2nd rev. ed., Boston, 1923 [Modern statesmen series]; (T7792) C. Kerofilas, *Eleftherios Venizelos, his life and work,* London, 1915, tr. by B. Barstow. RJK, GMD

MODERN GREECE: PERIODICALS

Greek periodicals, though not numerous, are often of high grade. Of these special mention may be made of (T7941) *Neos hellēnomnēmōn* [Modern Greek recorder], Athēnēsin, 1904 ff., quarterly, founded by S. P. Lampros (cf. T7123b); (T7942) *Deltion* [Tablet], En Athēnais, v. 1–3, 1882–89, published by Historikē kai Ethnologikē Hetairia tēs Hellados, for medieval and modern Greece; and (T7943) *Epetēris Hetaireias Byzantinōn Spoudōn* [Annual of the Society of Byzantine Studies], En Athēnais, 1924 ff. Also cf. periodicals listed in § D, which occasionally include materials relating to medieval and modern Greece, notably (D977) *Ephēmeris archaiologikē.*

(T7951) *Byzantinisch-neugriechische Jahrbücher, internationales wissenschaftliches Organ,* Berlin-Wilmersdorf, 1920 ff., and similar periodicals listed in § H, afford some materials for the history of the Greeks in modern times.

RJK, GMD

SOUTHWESTERN ASIA: BIBLIOGRAPHY

T8001a **Masson, Paul.** *Éléments d'une bibliographie française de la Syrie (géographie, ethnographie, histoire, archéologie, langues, littératures, religions).* Paris, 1919. [Chambre de Commerce de Marseille: Congrès français de la Syrie.]

b Pratt, Ida A. *Armenia and the Armenians: a list of references in the New York Public Library. Bulletin of the New York Public Library,* 23: 123–143, 251–277, 303–335, March-May 1919.

In the absence of any comprehensive bibliography for southwestern Asia reference may be made to these two special bibliographies and also to the bibliographies listed elsewhere in this *Guide* under the following numbers: (T1*a, b,* and *c*), (T1001), and (G1–3).

For current bibliographical data it is necessary to consult various periodicals listed in §§ C and G. AHL

SOUTHWESTERN ASIA: GEOGRAPHY

T8041a Cuinet, Vital. *La Turquie d'Asie: géographie administrative, statistique, descriptive, et raisonnée de chaque province de l'Asie-Mineure.* 4 v. and index. Paris, 1891–1900.

b —— *Syrie, Liban, et Palestine: géographie administrative, statistique, descriptive, et raisonnée.* 1 v. in 4 pt. Paris, 1896–1900.

c Lynch, Harry F. B. *Armenia, travels and studies.* 2 v. London and N. Y., 1901. (Extended bibliography.)

d Dana, Lanice P. *Arab-Asia: a geography of Syria, Palestine, Irak, and Arabia.* Beirut, 1923.

All have appropriate maps. *a* and *b.* Survey Asiatic Turkey of the later years of the nineteenth century, province by province, considering each as occupied and used by man. *c.* Handles thoroughly the Armenian plateau country, both Turkish and Russian, with full consideration of the inhabitants; well-chosen illustrations. Review, *Spectator,* 87: 355, Sept. 14, 1901. *d.* Convenient manual.

Also cf. (C41) Hogarth, *Nearer East,* (T1043) Banse, *Die Türkei,* and (J441*a*) *Peace handbooks,* for the whole region, and (C42*b*) Smith, *Historical geography of the Holy Land.* AHL

T8042a Sykes, Sir Mark. *Through five Turkish provinces.* London and N. Y., 1900.

b —— *Dar-ul-Islam: a record of a journey through ten of the Asiatic provinces of Turkey.* London and N. Y., 1904.

c —— *Caliph's last heritage, a short history of the Turkish empire.* London and N. Y., 1915.

d Burton, Isabel. *Inner life of Syria, Palestine, and the Holy Land, from my private journal.* 2 v. London, 1875.

a, b, and *c.* Vivid descriptions of a series of journeys into most parts of Asiatic Turkey in the opening years of the twentieth century; of special interest because of the part played by the author in the Anglo-French partition agreement of 1915. *c.* Subtitle is misleading as work is chiefly descriptive. Review of *a, Athenaeum,* 2: 644, Nov. 17, 1900; of *b, Spectator,* 93: 396, Sept. 17, 1904; of *c,* A. H. Lybyer, *A.H.R.,* 21: 844, July 1916; of *a, b,* and *c,* Shane Leslie, *Mark Sykes, his life and letters* (London and N. Y., 1923). *d.* Excellent earlier work; lively record of keen observations of conditions about 1870, by the wife of Sir Richard Burton (cf. G627*a*), the famous traveler and orientalist. Review, *Athenaeum,* 2: 18, July 3, 1875. AHL, HRS

T8043 Vivien de Saint Martin, Louis. *Histoire des découvertes géographiques des nations européennes dans les diverses partis du monde . . . , première série: Asie-Mineure.* 2 v. Paris, 1845. Reprinted as *Description historique et géographique de l'Asie Mineure . . . , 2 v.,* Paris, 1852. (Chronological annotated bibliography.)

Only volumes published in a projected series of forty-three, of which nine were allotted to Asia Minor. Contains chronological history of travels in Asia Minor, 1536–1844; describes the land, its resources, and population. AHL

T8044 Meistermann, Barnabas. *Guide to the Holy Land.* London, 1923. Tr. from *Guide de terre sainte,* 2nd ed., Paris, 1923.

Excellent recent guide book with good maps and plans of buildings; especially useful for historical topography; by a Franciscan long familiar with the country. Review, *Rev. Critique,* 91 : 9, Jan. 1, 1924. HRS

T8045 *Handbook of Arabia, compiled by the Geographical Section of the Naval Intelligence Division, Naval Staff, Admiralty.* V. 1, *General.* London, 1920.

Best general summary of geographical data relating to Arabia and guide to further study. GMD

SOUTHWESTERN ASIA: COLLECTIONS OF SOURCES, ARCHIVE PUBLICATIONS

Considerable material relating to Southwestern Asia may be found in the collections of sources listed in §§ I and J. Especial attention, however, should be directed to (J72a) *Die grosse Politik der europäischen Kabinette, 1871–1914,* v. 10, for the Armenian massacres; and v. 14, pt. 2, 25, 27, 31, and 37, for the Baghdad railway; and to (J75) *British Documents,* v. 5. SBF

SOUTHWESTERN ASIA: GENERAL WORKS

T8101a Mathews, Basil J., ed. *Riddle of nearer Asia.* London and N. Y., 1919. (Bibliographies.)

b Loder, John de Vere. *Truth about Mesopotamia, Palestine, and Syria.* London, 1923.

a. Written as introduction for missionaries to the region; both anti-Moslem and anti-Turk; careful work based on personal acquaintance with the area; useful manual. *b.* Intelligent summary of events during and since the World War; includes important official documents. Review, A. J. Toynbee, (London) *Nation,* 34 : 19, Oct. 6, 1923. GMD

ARMENIA

T8251a Aslan, Kevork. *Armenia and the Armenians from the earliest times until the great war, 1914.* London and N. Y., 1920. Tr. by P. Crabitès from the French.

b Morgan, Jacques de. *Histoire du peuple arménien depuis les temps les plus reculés de ses annales jusqu'à nos jours.* Paris, 1919.

a. Recent, concise, scholarly manual of the whole period of Armenian history. Review, D. Magie, *A.H.R.,* 25 : 748, July 1920. *b.* Fuller and better account by able French scholar; emphasizes ancient and medieval periods; gives scant attention to modern times. GMD

T8252a Tournebize, Henri François. *Histoire politique et religieuse de l'Arménie.* V. 1, *Depuis les origines jusqu'à la mort de leur dernier roi, l'an 1393.* Paris, 1910.

b Basmadjian, K. J. *Histoire moderne des Arméniens depuis la chute du royaume jusqu'à nos jours, 1375–1916: les guerres russo-turques, les guerres russo-persanes, les guerres perso-turques, les soulèvements des Arméniens, la question d'orient, et principalement la question arménienne.* Paris, 1917.

a. Only volume published; extended scholarly account of Armenia in ancient and medieval times by a Jesuit professor in a college at Beirut. *b.* Detailed history of the Armenians in modern times by an Armenian scholar; serves as a continuation to *a.*   GMD

MESOPOTAMIA: IRAQ

T8301 Coke, Richard. *Heart of the Middle East.* London, 1925; N. Y., 1926.

Brief outline of principal historical facts since ancient times affecting Mesopotamia and adjacent regions. About half the volume, however, relates to the period since the World War; favors British control, though critical of some aspects of British administration. Review, *Saturday Rev.,* 140: 166, Aug. 8, 1925.

GMD

T8302 Longrigg, Stephen H. *Four centuries of modern Iraq.* Oxford and N. Y., 1925.

Excellent account of period from 1500 to 1900, based largely on Arab and Turk sources, written by a British administrator in the area; valuable information on Turkish provincial administration. Reviews, E. M. Earle, *A.H.R.,* 31: 829, July 1926; R. Loky, *Rev. des Quest. Hist.,* 105: 458, Oct. 1926.   GMD

SYRIA AND LEBANON

T8341 Stein, Leonard J. *Syria.* London and N. Y., 1925.

Good, dispassionate, brief survey of conditions and events following the World War. Review, (London) *Times Lit. Suppl.,* 25: 222, March 18, 1926.

For a consecutive history of Syria from the close of the Crusades to the establishment of the French administration under the mandate, cf. (G321) Lammens, *La Syrie, précis historique,* v. 2.   GMD

T8342a Gontaut-Biron, R., Comte de. *Comment la France s'est installée en Syrie, 1918–1919.* Paris, 1923.

b Burckhard, Charles. *Le mandat français en Syrie et au Liban.* Paris, 1925.

c Aboussouan, Benoît. *Le problème politique syrien.* Paris, 1925.

a. Chronicle of events; strongly anti-British. Review, S. Reinach, *Rev. Critique,* 90: 182, May 15, 1923. *b.* General survey of the French administration. *c.* Discussion of the situation by an Arab doctor of laws.   GMD

PALESTINE: ZIONISM

T8381 Worsfold, William Basil. *Palestine of the mandate.* London, 1925.

Favorable description of British administration by an observer fully conversant with the problems of governing dependencies. Review, *Spectator,* 135: 1195, Dec. 26, 1925.   GMD

T8401a Sokolow, Nahum. *History of Zionism, 1600–1918. 2 v.* London and N. Y., 1919.

b Stein, Leonard J. *Zionism.* London and N. Y., 1925.

a. Good, comprehensive account; supplemented with numerous documents in v. 2. Review, *Spectator,* 121 : 365, March 22, 1919; 123 : 445, Oct. 4, 1919. *b.* Excellent, concise history of both the Zionist movement and Jewish settlement in Palestine, by an English Jew associated with the Zionist movement; contains documents on British relations to Palestine. Review, A. J. Toynbee, *Nation* (London), 37 : 178, May 9, 1925.   GMD

ARABIA

T8421 Jacob, Harold F. *Kings of Arabia, the rise and set of the Turkish sovranty in the Arabian peninsula.* London, 1923.

General account of recent events in Arabia with special attention to the kingdom of the Hedjaz.   GMD

T8422a Jung, Eugène. *Les puissances devant la révolte arabe, la crise mondiale de demain.* Paris, 1906.

b —— *La révolte arabe.* 2 v. Paris, 1924–25. [1, *De 1906 à la révolte de 1916; 2, De juin 1916 à nos jours, la lutte pour l'indépendance.*]

Chronicle and discuss events in Arabia since the beginning of the twentieth century; by a French colonial civil servant.   GMD

T8431a Philby, Harry St. J. B. *Heart of Arabia, a record of travel and exploration.* 2 v. London and N. Y., 1922.

b Lawrence, Thomas E. *Seven pillars of wisdom.* London, 1926.

c —— *Revolt in the desert.* London and N. Y., 1927.

d Graves, Robert. *Lawrence and the Arabs.* London, 1927.

a. Highly important account of extensive explorations in connection with a British political mission among the Wahabis in 1917; presents a wealth of information, much new, especially on the history of the Wahabis. Review, E. Candler, (London) *Nation,* 32 : 59, Oct. 14, 1922. *b.* Published only in costly limited edition; complete personal narrative; rich in observations on Arab character, conditions, and problems; work of the first importance. *c.* Abridgement of *b,* retaining its best qualities. Review, P. Bigelow, *A.H.R.,* 32 : 873, July 1927; (London) *Times Lit. Suppl.,* 26 : 151, March 10, 1927. *d.* Vivid account of the life of Lawrence, who gave some assistance to its preparation; emphasizes his part in the Arab revolt; in many ways supplements *c;* excellent illustrations and maps. Review, (London) *Times Lit. Suppl.,* 26 : 903, Dec. 1, 1927.   GMD, HRS

SOUTHWESTERN ASIA: GOVERNMENT PUBLICATIONS, PERIODICALS

The governments at present existing in Southwestern Asia and the governments of the several outside countries with administrative, diplomatic, or economic interests in the region have issued numerous official publications rich in information on its conditions, problems, and recent history. For current conditions in the several mandated territories, the reports of the administering powers to the Mandates Commission of the League of Nations are of the first importance.

Many of the journals listed in §§ C and G contain materials relating to recent conditions in the various regions of Southwestern Asia. Besides these, attention may be called to (T8941) *Revue des études arméniennes,* Paris, 1920 ff.   GMD

SOUTHEASTERN EUROPE AND SOUTHWESTERN ASIA 851

Several handbooks relating to the regions of the administrative powers in the Middle East. Compilation of the Volume of 1941 are of the first importance. Many of the journals listed in §3 C. and to contain materials relating to recent conditions in the various regions of Southwestern Asia. Besides these attention may be called to (785 a-c) *Levant* for discussion purposes, Vera (1028 ff.) *Orbis*

SECTION U

ASIA, INCLUDING INDIA, CHINA, AND JAPAN

Editor

WILLIAM HENRY ALLISON

Professor Emeritus of Ecclesiastical History, Colgate-Rochester Divinity School

CONTENTS

INTRODUCTION

Although Central Asia was long considered the cradle of the human race, and although historically a genetic unity might be sought about which to gather the materials for this section, actually this portion of the world is to-day one of those most separate from the forces and interests which are dominant in the world as a whole. Approach to this region is largely made not only geographically but historically through India or through China, while even these great areas of the largest continent appeal to western peoples primarily not through their indigenous culture but because of their potentialities in the international world of to-day and to-morrow. We are not much interested in the history of Southern Asia before European imperialism laid its hand upon India, nor does the history of the peoples of eastern Asia appeal to us prior to the development of western intercourse in the nineteenth century. The earlier history of these regions has not yet received adequate consideration from the western world, yet their ancient and medieval elements have possibly persisted full more than have classical and medieval civilization survived in the life of Europe and America. We may expect an enlarging knowledge of this .past as native scholars acquire the sounder historical methods of the West, and through their coöperation our scholars gain more direct access to the sources of information. Thus far the handicap of language limitation has been most serious, while the few who have acquired in special fields an adequate linguistic facility, have usually lacked both breadth of knowledge and a proper historical method for authoritative results.

As already suggested, it has been primarily through interest in international relations that historical works have been produced. Consequently the books written have been too largely propaganda and even trained historians almost invariably show bias. Prior to 1900 scarcely a work in this field by a native was available for readers of western languages, but of late, the number of such works has increased rapidly. Some of them are remarkably well done, but most of them are frankly inspired by national interests and the remainder are obviously if not obtrusively tendential.

Books in western languages on India and the Far East have usually been the product of some momentary interest, a recent journey or contemporary events.

Consequently the works have been ephemeral. A few only of the older histories are worth citation at the present day and these primarily because the author was a specially favored or skilled observer, whose narrative becomes valuable as contemporary evidence for events and conditions at the date of writing, as for instance, Marco Polo in the thirteenth century, Kaempfer in the seventeenth, Wells Williams in the nineteenth, or even Reinsch in the twentieth.

Most of the works listed in this section, therefore, are materials for history rather than histories. The selection of titles for inclusion has been necessarily determined more by the topics on which references might be expected than by the quality of the books. The best works are undoubtedly the more recent monographs bearing upon international relations. The vastness and the complexities of the range of history in this section have led to the devotion of relatively more space to titles and less to evaluations than elsewhere in this GUIDE. Some inferior and antiquated books are cited merely because they are widely circulated.

Other works related to this section will be found in §§ B, General history; C, Near East in ancient times; D, Ancient Greece and the Hellenistic world; E, Rome: the republic and the empire; G, History of Mohammedanism and of Moslem peoples; J, Contemporary times; K, Colonial expansion; S, Russia and its borderlands.

ASIA: BIBLIOGRAPHY

U1 United States—Library of Congress. *Select list of books (with references to periodicals) relating to the Far East.* Compiled under direction of Appleton Prentiss Clark Griffin, chief bibliographer. Washington, 1904.

A list so useful that now twenty-five years later it should be brought up to date.

WHA

U2a Mezhov, Vladimïr Izmaïlovich. *Bibliographie asiatica.* 2 v. St. Petersbourg, 1891–94.

b Luzac's *Oriental list and book review.* London, 1891 ff.

c Deutsche Morgenländische Gesellschaft. *Orientalische Bibliographie.* Berlin, 1888 ff.

d Egerton, C., ed. *Asiatica. A record of literature dealing with the East and with Africa.* London, 1928 ff.

a. Comprehensive survey in French of the literature bearing upon all Asia with the exception of Siberia; includes references to articles in Russian periodicals. *b.* A trade list, but valuable for bibliographical purposes. *c.* Largely philological in interest, but rich in historical references. *d.* Classified list of current works, with some brief reviews and bibliographical data.

WHA

U3a Cordier, Henri. *Bibliotheca sinica. Dictionnaire bibliographique des ouvrages relatifs à l'empire chinois.* 2 v. Paris (1878), 1881–85. (For later eds., cf. (U2001a).

b —— *Bibliotheca japonica; dictionnaire bibliographique,* etc. Paris, 1912.

c —— *Bibliotheca indosinica: dictionnaire bibliographique des ouvrages relatifs à la peninsule Indo-chinoise.* 4 v. Paris, 1912–15.

These are brought together as forming the most comprehensive bibliography of the Far East. *a* and *b* are reviewed at U2001a and U3001b respectively.

WHA

Library Collections.—The libraries of Harvard, Yale, 'Columbia (including Union Theological Seminary), Cornell and the University of California contain good collections on the Far East; Harvard has much on India and Yale much on Central Asia. Yale has probably the best collection on Japan and Cornell the best on China, though its Wason Collection is limited primarily to works in English. There are good collections at the Library of Congress and in the Newberry Library, Chicago, while the White Collection of Orientalia in the public library of Cleveland, Ohio, deserves special mention. The Day Missions Library at Yale and the Missionary Research Library, New York City, are the most complete on Christian missions and extend into the environmental area.

AHS

ASIA: ENCYCLOPEDIAS

U21 Herbelot, Barthélémy d'. *Bibliothèque orientale, ou dictionnaire universel, contenant généralement tout ce qui regarde la connaissance. des peuples de l'Orient.* Paris, 1697. Enl. ed. by C. Visdelou and A. Galand. 4 v. La Haye, 1777–79.

Typical product of an age of erudition. Relatively more material for §G, *Mohammedanism and Moslem peoples,* but even in its inaccuracies preserving many milestones of accumulative learning as to Persia, Central Asia and lands beyond.

WHA

U22 Balfour, Edward Green. *Cyclopædia of India and of eastern and southern Asia, commercial, industrial and scientific: products of the mineral, vegetable and animal kingdoms, useful arts and manufactures.* 3 v. 1858. 3rd ed., 5 v., Madras, 1885.

Replete with data as to geography and the natural products of these regions and interpretative of vernacular names in many dialects; its biographical and historical contribution is less than its ethnographical; the aggregate of information is substantial.

WHA

ASIA: GEOGRAPHY

U41a Keane, Augustus Henry. *Asia.* v. 1, *Northern and eastern Asia;* v. 2, *Southern and western Asia.* 1882. 2nd ed. rev. to 1905 and 1908, London, 1906–09. [Stanford's Compendium of geography and travel.]

b Reclus, Élisée. *The earth and its inhabitants. Asia.* 4 v. N. Y., 1882–95. Ed. and tr. by E. G. Ravenstein and A. H. Keane from v. 6–9 of *Nouvelle géographie universelle; la terre et les hommes.* 19 v. Paris, 1876–94.

a. Standard authority prior to the World War; marked by the author's minute care and wide learning. Treatment includes physical, biological, political, ethnological and statistical geography, the last much out of date. Review, *Chinese Recorder,* 13: 397, Nov.-Dec., 1882. *b.* Detailed physical and human geography of the continent by one of the greatest geographers of modern times, with many illustrations and also statistical tables. Appreciative summary of the life and work of Reclus by P. Kropotkin will be found in *The Geographical Journal* (London), 26: 337–343 (1905).

APB

U42a Polo, Marco. *The book of Ser Marco Polo, the Venetian, concerning the kingdoms and marvels of the East.* Tr. and ed. by Colonel Sir Henry Yule from *Livre de Marco Polo.* 2 v. 1871. 3rd ed., rev. by H. Cordier, London, 1903. (Bibliography.)

b Cordier, Henri. *Ser Marco Polo: notes and addenda to Sir Henry Yule's edition, containing the results of recent research and discovery.* N. Y., 1920.

c **Komroff, Manuel,** ed.　*Contemporaries of Marco Polo.*　N. Y., 1928. (Bibliography.)

d **Bernier, Francis.**　*Travels in the Mogul empire.*　London, 1826. 2nd ed., rev. by V. A. Smith, London and N. Y., 1914. Tr. on basis of I. Brock's version (1826) and annotated by A. Constable (1891), from *Voyages de François Bernier . . . contenant la description des états du Grand Mogul, de l'Hindoustan, du royaume de Kachemire,* &c. 2 v. Amsterdam, 1699.

a. Third edition, under Cordier's revision, is still an authoritative work on Marco Polo and his travels, with which European knowledge of central and eastern Asia may be said to have begun. Written *c.* 1298 and first printed in 1477, it is especially important for the conditions prevailing in China during the Yuan dynasty when Kublai Khan ruled as emperor. The critical comment, including identification of places visited by Marco Polo, continued in *.b,* which is partly 'addenda' and 'corrigenda' of *a,* is of great service to the student. Review of *a, Edinburgh Rev.,* 135 : 1, Jan. 1872; G. P. Marsh, *Nation* (N. Y.), 21 : 135, 152, Aug. 26, Sept. 2, 1875. Review of *b,* B. Laufer, *A.H.R.,* 26 : 499, Apr. 1921. *c.* English translation of some of the journals of travelers who penetrated Asia in the middle ages: The Journey of Friar John of Pian de Carpini to the Court of Kuyuk Khan, 1245–47; the Journal of Friar William of Rubruck, 1253–55; the Journal of Friar Odoric, 1318–30; the Travels of Rabbi Benjamin of Tudela, 1160–73. Review of several recent editions of Marco Polo and of *c, Geog. Rev.,* 18 : 521, July 1928. *d.* One of the classics of travel brought under critical examination by a modern scholar. Review by ·D. H. Buel, *Geog. Rev.,* 1 : 72, Jan. 1916.　　　　　　　　　　　　　　　　　　　　　　　　　NTJ, WHA

U43a Rockhill, William Woodville.　*Diary of a journey through Mongolia and Thibet in 1891 and 1892.*　Washington, 1894.

b **Vámbéry, Arminius.**　*Travels in central Asia.*　London, 1864; N. Y., 1865.

c **Pumpelly, Raphael.**　*Explorations in Turkestan, with an account of the basin of eastern Persia and Sistan.*　(Expedition of 1903.)　Washington, 1905.

d ――――　*Explorations in Turkestan; expedition of 1904.*　Washington, 1908.

While these works are primarily accounts of travels and explorations, they abound in the geographical and archeological information useful for the student of history and particularly reveal conditions in the regions visited. For Vámbéry, see (U708) *Story of my Struggles,* and for Pumpelly (U709), *My Reminiscences.* Review of *d,* C. R. Gillett, *N. Y. Times Sat. Rev.,* 14 : 194, Apr. 3, 1909.

　　　　　　　　　　　　　　　　　　　　　　　　　　　　　　　　WHA

U44a Stein, Sir Marc Aurel.　*Serindia.*　5 v.　Oxford, 1921.

b ――――　*Ancient Khotan.*　2 v.　Oxford, 1907.

c ――――　*Ruins of desert Cathay.*　2 v.　London, 1912.

d **Hedin, Sven.**　*Through Asia.*　2 v.　London, 1898; N. Y., 1899. Tr. by J. T. Bealby from the Swedish.

e ――――　*Trans-Himalaya. Discoveries and adventures.*　3 v.　London and N. Y., 1909–13.

a. Detailed scientific account of recent explorations in central Asia and western China where once flourished a great Buddhist civilization which has now disappeared under the sands of the desert. Description of a vast collection of manuscripts in many languages, of frescoes and paintings on silk, and of many articles which throw light on the life, customs and history of the people. Review by C. W. Bishop, *Geog. Rev.*, 12: 660, Oct. 1922. *b.* Rich in both archeological and ethnographic material, while giving much information on early history of Central Asia. *c.* Enters more definitely into the realm of historical knowledge, especially archeology, than do *d* and *e,* which are more specifically narrative and description of travel, of entrancing interest, by the eminent Swedish explorer. Review of *c,* M. Bloomfield, *A.H.R.,* 18: 113, Oct. 1912; of *e, N. Y. Times Sat. Rev.,* 14: 817, Dec. 25, 1909; 18: 386, July 6, 1913; 18: 679, Nov. 30, 1913.

WHA

U45a Clifford, Hugh. *Further India.* London, 1904. [Story of exploration.] (Bibliography.)

b Gerini, Colonel G. E. *Researches on Ptolemy's geography of eastern Asia (Further India and Indo-Malay archipelago).* London, 1909. [Asiatic Society Monographs.]

c Bretschneider, Emil. *Medieval researches from eastern Asiatic sources.* 2 v. London, 1910.

a. Narrative of the exploration of Burma, Malaya, Siam and Indo-China, including some of the activities of the Portuguese and French as well as those of the Dutch and English East India Companies. Review, *Asiatic Quar. Rev.,* 3rd ser., 19: 196, Jan. 1905. *b.* Invaluable for a critical study of place-names. *c.* Reprints, with some additions, of three articles: 'Notes on Chinese medieval travelers to the West'; 'Notes on the medieval geography and history of central and western Asia, drawn from Chinese and Mongol writings and compared with observations of western authors in the middle ages'; 'Chinese intercourse with the countries of central and western Asia during the fifteenth century'; important for their presentation of the materials for the history of the Yuan or Mongol dynasty. Review, W. T. Swingle, *AHR.* 26: 724, July 1921.

GMD

U46 Wright, Arnold. *Early English adventurers in the east.* London, 1917.

Limited to the period from Drake's circumnavigation of the globe to the founding of Calcutta, that is. primarily to the seventeenth century. Shows the beginnings of the eastern trade, the rivalries with the Dutch and the steady penetration of British influence; the narrative is constructed largely about such personalities as Henry Middleton, William Hawkins, Sir Thomas Roe, and Mathune Courthope, who, if not great in statesmanship or in character, remain of dramatic interest.

WHA

ASIA: ETHNOGRAPHY

U51a Bastian, Adolf. *Die Voelker des oestlichen Asien. Studien und Reisen.* v. 3, *Reisen in Siam im Jahre 1863;* v. 5, *Reisen im indischen Archipel; Singapore, Batavia, Manila und Japan;* v. 6, *Reisen in China von Peking zur mongolischen Grenze und Rückkehr nach Europa.* Jena, 1867–71.

b Buxton, L. H. Dudley. *Peoples of Asia.* London, 1925. [(B153a, v. 14) History of civilization.] (Bibliography.)

a. This writer of numerous monographs is interested primarily in ethnology as he relates his travels. *b.* Cautious work which may be described as a blend of somewhat traditional views and more recent hypotheses, but recognizing the many racial and cultural elements infiltrating into Asia. Chapter on India particularly satisfying and of interest to the non-professional reader. Reviews of *b,* *A.H.R.* 31: 498, Apr. 1926; C. W. Bishop, *Geog. Rev.* 18: 169, Jan. 1928.

WHA

ASIA: GENERAL HISTORIES

U1o1a Webster, Hutton. *History of the Far East.* Boston, 1923. (Bibliography.)

b Steiger, George Nye; Beyer, H. Otley; and Benitez, Conrado. *History of the Orient.* Boston, 1926. (Bibliography.)

c Hannah, Ian Campbell. *Eastern Asia, a history, being a second edition of A brief history of eastern Asia, entirely rewritten.* London, 1911.

d Gowen, Herbert H. *Asia: a short history from the earliest times to the present day.* Boston, 1926. (Bibliography.)

e Prothero, George W., ed. *Peace handbooks.* (Volume) 12. no. 67, *China;* no. 68, *Mongolia;* no. 69, *Manchuria;* no. 70, *Tibet;* no. 71, *Kiaochow and Weihaiwei;* no. 73, *Japan;* no. 74, *Siam.* London, 1920.

f Vinacke, Harold Monk. *History of the Far East in modern times.* N. Y., 1928. [Borzoi historical series.] (Bibliographies.)

g Treat, Payson J. *The Far East. A political and diplomatic history.* N. Y. and London, 1928. [Harper's historical series.] (Bibliographies.)

a. and *b.* Text-books convenient for acquiring an acquaintance with the ordinary essentials of the subject. Review of *b, Chinese Recorder,* 58: 790, Dec. 1927. *c.* Summary history of most of the regions, except Persia, included in this section. The earlier work (1900) gives more details. Review, E. H. Parker, *Asiatic Quar. Rev.,* 3rd ser. 32: 426, Oct. 1911. *d.* In a fair-sized volume the reader is carried quickly over the broader areas of Asiatic history. Developments effected by the contacts with the occidental world and conditions since the World War are emphasized. Review, G. H. Blakeslee, *Atlantic's Bookshelf,* Sept. 1926. *e.* Present in brief and accurate outline the events of recent years which form the background of conditions in the Far East as they appeared at the time the Peace Conference was called in 1918. Review, C. Constant, *Rev. Hist.,* 142: 271, March-Apr. 1923. *f.* Representative work of the so-called "new history" with special attention paid to economic and social, including cultural, elements, but also well-proportioned treatment of internal politics and foreign affairs. The term "Far East" is here restricted to China, Japan and Korea, with a chapter on "The Far Eastern Republic of Siberia." cf. (U351) H. K. Norton, *Far eastern republic of Siberia.* Story begins virtually with the opening of China and Japan, devoting most space to the last forty years. Review, K. S. Latourette, *A.H.R.,* 34: 649, Apr. 1929. *g.* Sub-title rather disclaims any conscious attempt to adjust this treatise to the 'new history,' though the Preface acknowledges the advisability of including 'as much of the historical and cultural background as would be essential for the understanding of recent events.' The first parts of about equal length deal successively with China and Japan to 1895, i.e., through the Sino-Japanese war. The remaining part, comprising about two-fifths of the space, presents "The Far East, 1895–1927." Review, K. S. Latourette, *A.H.R.,* 34: 347, Jan. 1929. Review of *f* and *g* (London) *Times Lit. Suppl.,* 28: 128, Feb. 21, 1929.   NTJ, WHA

U121 Grousset, René. *Histoire de l'Asie.* 3 v. Paris, 1921–22. (Bibliographies.)

Admirable example of the selection of details to suggest the widening horizons of history, based on recent special works. The first volume sketches the history of the Orient largely as Europe entered into relation with it up through the period of the Crusaders. The second volume deals with ancient India, China to the Mongol conquest and the civilization of Indo-China. The concluding volume treats the Mongol Empires and then Persia, India and China since the Mongol conquest; a final chapter gives an epitome of Japanese history to the restoration of the Mikado. Review, P. M. Oursel, *Rev. Hist.*, 144: 274, Nov.-Dec., 1923.

WHA

U122 Krause, Friedrich E. A. *Geschichte Ostasiens.* 3 v. Göttingen, 1925. (Bibliography at end of v. 2.)

Most successful attempt thus far to treat the history of Eastern Asia comprehensively and with a reasonable degree of unity and balance. This is accomplished in part by making the history of Chinese civilization (*Kultur*) central, but recognizing that throughout, the history of China extends to other lands and peoples. Begins the modern history (v. 2) with the closer relations of East Asia with Europe. Review, F. W. Williams, *A.H.R.*, 32: 81, Oct. 1926; O. Franke, *Hist. Zeit.*, 134: 411, 1926.

WHA

ASIA: PERSIA

Almost all the great world movements have been related to Persia; cf. therefore §§ B, General history; C, Near East in ancient times; D, Ancient Greece and the Hellenistic world; E, Rome; G, Mohammedanism and Moslem peoples; and J, Contemporary times. The New York Public Library has published a list of its books relating to Persia (1915).

U301a Gutschmid, Alfred von. *Geschichte Irans und seiner Nachbarländer von Alexander dem Grossen bis zum Untergang der Arsaciden.* Tübingen, 1888.

b Nöldeke, Theodor. *Aufsätze zur persischen Geschichte.* Leipzig, 1887.

c Huart, Clement. *Ancient Persia and Iranian civilization.* N. Y., 1927. [(B153a, v. 31) History of civilization.] (Bibliography.) Tr. by M. R. Dobie from *La Perse antique et la civilisation iranienne.* Paris, 1925. [(B153b, v. 24, L'évolution de l'humanité.] (Bibliography.)

a and *b*. German originals, later revised by T. Nöldeke, from which reduced translations were made as Section II and Sections I and III respectively of Part I, 'Ancient Iran,' of the article on 'Persia' in the ninth edition of the (B22b) *Encyclopædia Britannica. c.* Introduction gives concise but interesting account of the oldest languages of Persia, including the deciphering of the Avesta. The history is sketched through the Sassanids, A.D. 651, with some particular attention to the religions and the arts in the successive periods. Reviews of French ed., R. W. Rogers, *A.H.R.*, 31: 301, Jan. 1926. On the ancient Persians cf. also (C451–453).

WHA

U302a Malcolm, Sir John L. C. *History of Persia from the most early period to the present time.* 2 v. 1815. Rev. ed., London, 1829.

b Markham, Sir Clements. *General sketch of the history of Persia.* London, 1871.

c Sykes, Percy Molesworth. *History of Persia.* 2 v. 1915. 2nd ed., London, 1921.

d Jackson, A. V. Williams. *Persia past and present.* N. Y., 1906.

e Wilson, Sir Arnold T. *Persian gulf.* Oxford, 1928. (Bibliography.)

a. Long the authoritative history in English until it was partly supplanted by *b*, which brought the history down to the treaty with England in 1857. *c.* Most comprehensive history of modern Persia, combining the advantages derived from over twenty years of residence and travel in the country, a knowledge and appreciation of the source material, and the methods of scientific historical scholarship. Distinctly sensitive to historical forces, ancient and modern; brings the story to 1906, the attainment of constitutional government. Review, C. R. Beazley, *A.H.R.*, 21 : 339, Jan. 1916. *d.* More a description of the people than a history. Review, G. M. Bolling, *A.H.R.*, 12 : 602, Apr. 1907. *e.* First history of this arm of the sea and its shores from early times until the twentieth century. Interests of rival powers are traced, the place of piracy and the slave trade, and the growth of British influence which the author favors. Summary of scientific research in the Persian Gulf adds to the comprehensive scope of the book. Review, C. V. H. Engert, *A.H.R.*, 34 : 560, Apr. 1929. WHA

U303a Browne, Edward Granville. *Year among the Persians.* . . . (1887–8). London, 1893. New ed., with memoir by Sir E. Denison Ross, Cambridge (Eng.), 1926.

b —— *Persian revolution of 1905–9.* Cambridge (Eng.), 1910.

c Bérard, Victor. *Révolutions de la Perse. Les provinces, les peuples et le gouvernement du roi des rois.* Paris, 1910.

d Balfour, James M. *Recent happenings in Persia.* London, 1922.

e Mirza, Youel Benjamin. *Iran and the Iranians.* Baltimore, 1913.

b. Rather intimate account by a learned British sympathizer with Persian national aspirations, who in *a* had shown that a prepared mind can see much in a single year. Review of *a*, (London) *Times Lit. Suppl.*, 25 : 925, Dec. 16, 1926; review of *b*, A. V. W. Jackson, *A.H.R.*, 16 : 634, Apr. 1911. *c.* Graphic description of the political life of Persia especially in the nineteenth century under the domination of the Kadjiar Turks, with a brief account of the revolution which the author treats as effective in 1907. Review, *Rev. Hist.*, 106 : 206, Jan.-Feb. 1911. *d.* Account chiefly of conditions after the World War as seen through the eyes of the British chief assistant to the financial adviser to the Persian government. *e.* Tells the story of the political crisis which brought constitutional government, but treats primarily the cultural features of Persian life as interpreted by a Persian. WHA

U304a Curzon, George N. *Persia and the Persian question.* 2 v. London, 1892.

b Shuster, William M. *Strangling of Persia.* N. Y., 1912.

c Desmorgny, Gustave. *La question persane et la guerre.* Paris, 1916.

a. Most definite work on political and economic conditions of forty years ago. Written by a young man who became a distinguished British publicist and statesman. Review, *Asiatic Quar. Rev.*, n.s. 4 : 562, Oct. 1892. *b.* Somewhat biased account by an American adviser of the Persian government of how Persia was caught between the policies, economic and political, of British and Russian imperialism. Review, *N. Y. Times Sat. Rev.*, 17 : 401, July 7, 1912. *c.* Brief study of the conflict of English, Russian, German and Persian interests and the sphere of French influence in the midst of them. WHA

U305a Clemen, Carolus, ed. *Fontes historiae religionis persicae.* Bonnae, 1920. [Fontes historiae religionum.]

 b —— *Die griechische und lateinische Nachrichten über die persische Religion.* Giessen, 1920.

a. Collection from Greek and Latin writers of all passages relating to the Persian religion. *b.* Largely a critical commentary on these texts and an interpretation of their significance.   WHA

U306a Dhalla, Maneckji Nusservanji. *Zoroastrian civilization from earliest times to downfall of the last Zoroastrian empire, 651 A.D.* N. Y., 1922.

 b —— *Zoroastrian theology from earliest times to the present day.* N. Y., 1914. (Bibliography.)

a. The most comprehensive presentation in English of over three millennia of Iranian civilization; a comparative study, in the successive main periods of Persian history, of the various phases of the intellectual, social, political, economic, æsthetic and religious interests. Review, R. Levy, *E.H.R.,* 38:582, Oct. 1923. *b.* One of the best expositions of Zoroastrian theology and ethics; a study by a high priest of the Parsis, along the lines of scientific scholarship, of the historic development of Zoroastrianism, including its communal solidarity, its syncretism and modern reform movements.   WHA.

U307a Edwards, Edward, compiler. *Catalogue of the Persian printed books in the British museum.* London, 1922.

 b Browne, Edward Granville. *Catalogue of the Persian manuscripts in the library of the university of Cambridge.* Cambridge, Eng., 1896.

 c —— *Literary history of Persia from the earliest time until Firdawsi.* London, 1902. (G671a)

 d —— *Literary history of Persia from Firdawsi to Sa'di.* London, 1906.

 e —— *History of Persian literature under Tartar dominion (A.D. 1265–1502).* Cambridge, Eng., 1920. (G671b)

 f —— *Press and poetry of modern Persia.* Cambridge, Eng., 1914.

a, and *b.* Distinctively bibliographical. *c, d,* and *e.* Treat successive phases of the literary history of Persia and form the most exhaustive survey of ancient and medieval Persian literature to be found in English. Review of *c, Asiatic Quar. Rev.,* 3rd ser., 15:429, Apr. 1903; of *d, ibid.,* 23:205, Jan. 1907; of *e,* A. V. W. Jackson, *Nation* (N. Y.), 111:508, Nov. 3, 1920. *f.* Takes up certain very recent phases of that literary development. Review, D. N. Singh, *Asiatic Rev.,* n.s. 6:338, Apr. 1915.   WHA

ASIA: AFGHANISTAN.

U321a Malleson, George Bruce. *History of Afghanistan.* 1878, 2nd ed., London, 1879.

 b Tate, George P. *Kingdom of Afghanistan.* London, 1911. (Bibliography.)

 c Hamilton, Angus. *Afghanistan.* N. Y. and London, 1906. (Reprint, Boston, 1910. [Oriental series.])

a. Covers the whole course of Afghan history from the tenth century to the beginning of England's second Afghan war. *b.* Treats the history largely in relation to the external powers, especially from the eighteenth century onward.

c. Excellent account of author's travels as a correspondent through Afghanistan and neighboring regions with a wealth of descriptive and statistical matter. The historical materials are contained in two chapters on Anglo-Afghan relations since the second Afghan war and in appendixes of documents. Admirably illustrated; excellent maps. Review, *Asiatic Quar. Rev.,* 3rd ser., 24: 193, July 1907.

WHA, GMD

U322 Ikbal, Faqir Syed. (Sirdar **Ikbal Ali Shah.**) *Afghanistan of the Afghans.* London, 1928.

Especially well-informed description of the life of the Afghan people, with brief account of the geography and history of the land and an interpretation of the governmental policy of King Amanullah Khan as favorable to adjustment to modern world conditions, though restrained by some naturally conservative elements in the population. Review, (London) *Times Lit. Suppl., 27*: 179, March 15, 1928.　　　WHA

U323a Bellew, Henry W. *Races of Afghanistan, being a brief account of the principal nations inhabiting that country.* Calcutta, 1880.

b —— *Inquiry into the ethnography of Afghanistan.* Woking, 1891.

Two studies of the ethnology of Afghanistan by a British officer who became Surgeon-General of the Bengal army; invaluable contribution to the subject. *b.* Prepared for and presented to the Ninth International Congress of Orientalists (London, 1891).　　　WHA

ASIA: TIBET AND CENTRAL ASIA KHANATES

U331a Chavannes, Edouard. *Documents sur les Tou-kine (Turcs) occidentaux.* St. Petersburg, 1903. Additional notes from T'oung Pao, 1904.

b Cahun, Léon. *Introduction à l'histoire de l'Asie: Turcs et Mongols, des origines à 1405.* Paris, 1896.

a. Account of the empire established by the western Turks in Bokhara and adjacent countries between the sixth and eighteenth centuries, A.D. Full translation of all the Chinese sources relating to the Turks during that period. *b.* Remarkably clear, lively and forceful sketch of the 'Tartar' peoples in ancient and medieval times, based on all sources available at the date of composition. Noteworthy for boldness, shrewdness, felicity and originality of expression. Review, *Asiatic Quar. Rev.,* 3rd ser. 1: 203, Jan. 1896.　　　WEC, AHL

U332a Wessels, C. *Early Jesuit travellers in central Asia, 1603–1721.* The Hague, 1924.

b Huc, Evariste Régis. *Travels in Tartary, Thibet, and China, during the years 1844–5–6.* 2 v. London (1852). Tr. by W. Hazlitt from *Souvenirs d'un voyage dans la Tartarie, le Thibet et la Chine.* New ed., 2 v., Paris, 1925–26. Reprint of accounts of Huc and Gabet, newly edited and introduction by Paul Pelliot, London, 1928.

c O'Donovan, E. *The Merv oasis; travels and adventures east of the Caspian during the years 1879–80–81.* 2 v. London, 1882; N. Y., 1883. (Epitomized in *Merv. A story of adventures and captivity,* N. Y., 1893.)

d Czaplica, Mary A. C. *Turks of central Asia in history and at the present day.* Oxford. 1918. (Bibliography.)

a. Erudite work with valuable chronological summaries, making available in English indispensable information from primarily Portuguese sources. Review,

P. Pelliot, *T'Oung Pao,* 241 : 386 (1925–26) ; *Cath. Hist. Rev.,* n.s. 6 : 162, Apr.
1926. *b.* In 1844, two Lazarist fathers, MM. Gabet and Huc, were sent, in connection with the establishment by the Pope of an Apostolic Vicariate of Mongolia, to
obtain information as to the country. Penetrating Thibet, they were deported
through China to Hong Kong. Some time later, Abbé Huc wrote this account of
his journey and experiences, 'M. Gabet having written his account a little earlier.
See (U335*a*) T. H. Holdich, *Tibet the mysterious.* Review of latest French ed.,
Asiatica, 1 : 28, Jan. 1928. *c.* Journalist's account, with large map, from observations made during residences in the land. *d.* Primarily an ethnological inquiry
into the Pan-Turanian question ; bibliography extends into a wider field. Review,
Saturday Rev., 127 : 331, Apr. 5, 1919.   WHA

U333a Skrine, Francis Henry Bennett and **Ross, Edward Denison.** *Heart of
Asia. A history of Russian Turkestan and the central Asian khanates
from the earliest times.* London, 1899.

  b Lansdell, Henry. *Russian central Asia.* 2 v. London and N. Y., 1885.
  (Bibliography.)

  c Marvin, Charles. *Reconnoitring central Asia.* 1884. 3rd ed., London,
  1886.

  d Skrine, Clarmont P. *Chinese central Asia.* Boston, 1926.

a. First half of this book contains a valuable consecutive history of central
Asian events from the earliest times to 1865 by Professor Ross. In the latter
half Mr. Skrine describes Russian expansion in central Asia, traces events from
1865 to 1899, and describes the existing situation from first-hand observation.
Not unfriendly to Russia. Review, *Asiatic Quar. Rev.,* 3rd ser., 8 : 429, Oct. 1899.

GMD

b. Somewhat dependent upon Russian literary sources, but primarily upon the
author's personal observations, when partly as an agent of the British and Foreign
Bible Society and the Religious Tract Society, he traveled extensively in the
region east of the Caspian. *c.* Account of the penetration of the region between
the Caspian and India by European explorers and governmental agents and so a
propædeutic to the early contacts of European governments, specifically British
and Russian, with the khanates. Begins with Vámbéry's journey in disguise to
Khiva and Bokhara in 1863. See (U708) Vámbéry, *Story of my struggles.*
d. Account of a two and a half years' sojourn in Chinese Turkestan, well illustrated, interestingly written, with much information as to the geography, archeology and customs of the region.   WHA

U334a Schuyler, Eugene. *Turkistan: notes of a journey in Russian Turkistan,
Khokand, Bukhara, and Kuldja.* 2 v. 6th ed., London, 1877 ; 3rd Amer.
ed., N. Y., 1882.

  b Barthold, W. *Turkestan down to the Mongol invasion.* 2nd ed., London,
  1928. Tr. from the Russian by author and H. A. R. Gibb. [E. J. W.
  Gibb memorial.]

  c Vámbéry, Arminius. *History of Bokhara.* London, 1873. Tr. of
  *Geschichte Buchara's oder Transoxaniens von den frühesten Zeiten bis
  auf die Gegenwart.* 2 v. Stuttgart, 1872.

  d Olufsen, Ole. *Emir of Bokhara and his country.* London, 1911.

a. Narration of a journey into central Asia, including territory recently an-
nexed, its avowed purpose being a comparison of 'the state of the inhabitants
under Persian rule with that of those still living under the despotism of the

Khans.' Review, *Rev. Hist.*, 10: 148, May-June, 1879. *b.* Although called a second edition, there seems to have been previously only the original Russian edition (1900). Gives more in detail than is elsewhere available in English the history of Turkestan from the first Moslem invasion till the early phases of the Mongol conquests under Ghingis-Khan. Review, *Asiatica*, 1: 287, Aug.-Oct. 1928. *c.* Comprehensive and scholarly work, based on original sources, comprising the first history in English of this region. Schuyler, in *a* (v. i, App. 2), gives a translation of a long adverse review of *b* by Professor W. Gregorief, cited as from 'Journal of the Ministry of Public Instruction,' Nov. 1873. For allusion to this, see Appendixes 1 and 2 of (U708) Vámbéry, *Story of my struggles,* especially 2: 467, 483. Review of *c, Saturday Rev.,* 35: 20, Jan. 4, 1873.

WHA

d. Describes thoroughly but not exhaustively 'present day' conditions; largely ethnographical and geographical.   AIA

U335a Holdich, Sir Thomas H. *Tibet the mysterious.* London and N. Y., 1906. [Story of exploration.]

b Younghusband, Sir Francis. *India and Tibet; a history of the relations which have subsisted between the two countries from the time of Warren Hastings to 1910, with a particular account of the mission to Lhassa of 1904.* 1905. 3rd ed., London, 1906.

c Waddell, L. Austine. *Lhassa and its mysteries with a record of the expedition of 1903-1904.* N. Y., 1905.

d Bell, Sir Charles. *Tibet past and present.* Oxford, 1924.

a. Popular account, with maps and illustrations, of exploration of Tibet, with special attention to the work of (U332b) Huc and Gabet. Review, *N. Y. Times Sat. Rev.,* 11: 801, Dec. 1, 1906. *b.* Chiefly account of the 1904 expedition which the author commanded, with six chapters on earlier relations and two chapters on more recent events. Believes English aim has been 'to accomplish a single purpose—the establishment of ordinary neighborly intercourse with Tibet.' Review, *Asiatic Quar. Rev.,* 3rd ser., 32: 429, Oct. 1911.   GMD
c. Result of long study of Tibet from its borders as well as a product of experiences and observations in the British expedition under Younghusband. Review, *Saturday Review,* 100: 56, July 8, 1905. *d.* This work, with maps and good illustrations, records the results of wide observation by a diplomat in the British service who does not ignore the Tibetan point of view. Contains valuable historical information as to the distant past, but is especially valuable for its contribution from the author's extended personal knowledge of conditions, made more reliable by his thorough acquaintance with the native language. Review, S. K. Hornbeck, *A.H.R.,* 30: 827, July 1925.   WHA

ASIA: MONGOLIA

There are a number of books not listed here which give accounts of individual travelers in Mongolia. Some of the works included in other sub-sections, such as U101 and U121 ff., and U331 ff., include material pertinent to Mongolia.

U341a Andrews, Roy Chapman. *On the trail of ancient man. With an introduction and a chapter by Henry Fairfield Osborn.* N. Y. and London, 1926.

b Bouillane de Lacoste, Commandant de. *Au pays sacré des anciens Turcs et des Mongols.* Paris, 1911.

a. Although this work retains much of the atmosphere of the popular periodicals in which much of the material first appeared and its scientific contribution belongs more to paleontology and to anthropology than to historiography, this is a valuable propædeutic for the historical study of Mongolia. It is an account by its leader of the Central Asiatic Expedition of the American Museum of Natural History (New York, 1921 ff.). Review, S. Beach, *Independent,* 117: 302, Sept. 11, 1926. *b.* Journal of the leader of an expedition sent under the auspices of the Minister of Public Instruction (France), aided by several French learned societies.

WHA

U342a Howorth, Sir Henry H. *History of the Mongols from the 9th to the 19th century.* 4 parts in 5 v. London, 1876–1927.

b Curtin, Jeremiah. *The Mongols. A history.* Boston, 1908.

c Korostovetz, Iwan J., and Hauer, Erich. *Von Cinggis Khan zur Sowjet Republik. Eine kurze Geschichte der Mongelei unter besonderer Berücksichtigung der neuesten Zeit.* Berlin, 1926.

d Bouvat, Lucien. *L'empire Mongol (deuxième phase).* Paris, 1927. [Histoire du monde, E. Cavaignac, ed.] (Bibliographical footnotes.)

a. Main part appeared in four volumes, 1876–88, a posthumous supplement and index appearing almost forty years later. Interest is ethnological and historical; only to a limited extent does it extend beyond the sixteenth century. The successive 'parts' take up the Mongols proper, the so-called Tartars, and the Mongols of Persia, so the geographical range is extensive. Doubtless will long remain, for all but specialists, the chief source of most of our knowledge of most of the peoples of central Asia and their history. Review of pt. 1, *Chinese Recorder,* 8: 179, March 1877; of pt. 2, *Rev. Hist.,* 10: 148, May 1879; of pt. 3, *Chinese Recorder,* 18: 381, May 1890; of pt. 4, *A.H.R.,* 34: 199, Oct. 1928; *E.H.R.,* 44: 331, Apr. 1929. *b.* Dedicated to President Roosevelt who wrote its 'Foreword,' this is a popular presentation of the Mongols from their earliest appearance, veiled in myth, up through their expulsion from China; account of activities in western Asia ends with 1266. Review, W. W. Rockhill, *A.H.R.,* 13: 562, Apr. 1908. *c.* By a Russian diplomat and fortified by an appreciative Introduction by Otto Franke, this is one of the best and most comprehensive studies of Mongolia. Review, J. Hashagen, *Hist. Zeit.,* 136: 403 (1927). *d.* Sketches the history from the close of the Crusades, emphasizing Timour and the dynasty he founded and also Baber and the Mongol dynasty of India. Especially valuable for the fifteenth century. Review, A. H. Lybyer, *A.H.R.,* 33: 681, Apr. 1928.

WHA

U343a Carruthers, Douglas. *Unknown Mongolia. A record of travel and exploration in north-west Mongolia and Dzungaria.* 2 v. London, 1913. (Bibliography.)

b Perry-Ayscough, Henry G. C., and Otter-Barry, Robert B. *With the Russians in Mongolia.* London and N. Y., 1914.

a. Account by one who is a geographer—a gold-medallist of the Royal Geographical Society—rather than an historian; yet the work throws much light upon the life of man. Three chapters on 'sport' contributed by J. H. Miller, deal with game, not games. Review, *Dial,* 57: 142, Sept. 1, 1914. *b.* Primarily a contribution to the Far Eastern Question, with a suspicious eye directed toward Russia, yet descriptive of the land and the people. Review, *Athenaeum,* 1: 335, March 7, 1914.

WHA

U344 Consten, Hermann. *Weideplätze der Mongolen im Reiche der Chalcha.* 2 v. Berlin, 1920.

Valuable account of conditions in Mongolia with special reference to recent relations of Mongolia with China and Russia. The first volume was written before and the second volume after the World War.   WHA

U345 *Outer Mongolia treaties and agreements.* Washington (D. C.), 1921. [Pamphlet series of the Carnegie Endowment for International Peace. Division of international law. No. 41.]

Texts of various treaties and agreements relating to Mongolia or with Mongolia as one party from February 1881 (extracts only) to June 1915. For additional texts listed in this but not printed, consult (U2062b) MacMurray.   WHA

ASIA: FAR EASTERN REPUBLIC

U351 Norton, Henry K. *Far eastern republic of Siberia.* London, 1923.

Author is inclined to sympathy with the revolution and is hostile to the intervention; but he presents facts and his interpretation of them rather judicially and moderately. Review, *Amer. Pol. Sci. Rev.,* 18: 202, Feb. 1924.   HMV

ASIA: MANCHURIA

U361a Hosie, Sir Alexander. *Manchuria; its people, resources, and recent history.* N. Y., 1904. [Also Oriental series, Boston, 1910.]

   b Hoshino, T. *Economic history of Manchuria.* Seoul, 1920.

   c Clyde, Paul Hibbert. *International rivalries in Manchuria, 1689–1922.* Columbus, O., 1926. [Ohio State University studies.]

a. Resident British consul at Newchwang for almost five years just before the close of the last century gives an account of his travels into central Manchuria and along its eastern frontiers, with the results, also, of a somewhat intensive study of the physical factors and the products of Manchuria. *b.* Very readable survey of the natural resources, industries and commerce of Manchuria, with a little material relating to the political history. A companion volume to (U3379). *c.* Although this story begins with the treaty of Nerchinsk, there is little to tell of international matters for two hundred years; most of this monograph is concerned with the period from the Chino-Japanese war through the Washington Conference of 1921. Review, C. W. Young, *A.H.R.,* 33: 137, Oct. 1927.
                                                                         WHA

ASIA: MALAY PENINSULA AND STRAITS SETTLEMENTS

U381a Skeat, Walter William, and **Blagden, Charles Otto.** *Pagan races of the Malay peninsula.* 2 v. London and N. Y., 1906. (Bibliography.)

   b Annandale, Nelson, and **Robinson, Herbert.** *Fasciculi malayenses.* London and N. Y., 1903.

   c Evans, Ivor H. N. *Studies in religion, folk-lore, & custom in British North Borneo and the Malay peninsula.* Cambridge (Eng.), 1923.

   d —— *Papers on the ethnology and archæology of the Malay peninsula.* Cambridge (Eng.), 1927.

a. Work in descriptive ethnography; a definite contribution to a scientific survey of the races of south-eastern Asia. Its main divisions are devoted respectively to race, manners and customs, religion, and language. Review, *Asiatic Quar. Rev.*, 3rd ser., 23 : 190, Jan. 1907. *b.* These 'contributions to the ethnography of the Malay peninsula' are the results of an expedition following that of Skeat (cf. *a*). Review, W. L. H. Duckworth in *a*, 1 : 96 ff. *c.* More than half this work in ethnology deals with the inhabitants of the Malay peninsula. Based on investigation made by the author; much of the material has appeared in periodicals not readily accessible. *d.* Supplementary to the latter part of *c.* Review, *Asiatica*, 1 : 32, Jan. 1928.

WHA

U382a Dennys, Nicholas B. *Descriptive dictionary of British Malaya.* London, 1894.

b Harrison, Cuthbert Woodville. *Illustrated guide to the Federated Malay States.* 1910. 3rd impression, London, 1920. (Bibliography.)

c *Handbook to British Malaya.* (London, 1926 ff.)

d Winstedt, Richard O., Ed. *Malaya. The Straits Settlements and the federated and unfederated Malay states.* London, 1923.

a. While primarily limited to the portion of Malaya under British control or direct influence, some material from the independent native states is included. A number of articles, some of them considerably revised, are transferred from Crawfurd, *Descriptive Dictionary of the Indian Archipelago,* (1856). Review, E. J. Eitel, *China Review,* 21 : 282, Jan.-Feb. 1895. *b.* While planned for the tourist, this brings together much descriptive material. Review, (Millard's) *Weekly Review,* 18 : 146, Sept. 17, 1921. *c.* Convenient manual issued by authority of the government, well illustrated and with map, with a brief history and description of the physical character, the governmental administration and the general economics of the Straits Settlements and the federated and unfederated Malay states.

WHA

d. Includes brief historical accounts of the several units, and a series of carefully topical chapters descriptive of the characteristics and resources of these lands, by competent authorities.

GMD

U383a Newbold, Thomas J. *Political and statistical account of the British settlements in the Straits of Malacca, viz., Pinang, Malacca, and Singapore; with a history of the Malayan states on the peninsula of Malacca.* 2 v. London, 1839.

b Cameron, John. *Our tropical possessions in Malayan India.* London, 1865.

c Swettenham, Sir Frank A. *British Malaya, an account of the origin and progress of British influence in Malaya.* London, 1907.

d Wright, Arnold, and **Reid, Thomas H.** *Malay peninsula, a record of British progress in the middle east.* London, 1912.

a. Long the standard work on the Malayan peninsula, this contains much material of permanent worth. *b.* Considerable historical information, but more distinctively a descriptive account of the region. Contains what may be considered a contemporary account of the Confederate privateer *Alabama* at Singapore and its operations in the Straits. *c.* Largely an account of the operations of British administration in the Malay states, with considerable personal information from the author who rose to be the governor of the Straits Colony and high commissioner for the Federated Malay States. Review, *Asiatic Quar. Rev.,* 3rd ser., 23 : 185, Jan. 1907. *d.* Probably the best study of the whole history of the British

administration from its beginning to 1909. Has made large use of records of
East India Company and other official sources.   WHA

U384a Sidney, Richard J. H. *Malay land.* London, 1926.

  b —— *In British Malaya to-day.* London (1927).

Journalistic and often conversational presentations of life in modern Malaya.
Review of *a, Asiatic Rev.,* n.s. 23 : 529, July 1927.   WHA

U385a Buckley, Charles Burton. *Anecdotal history of old times in Singapore.*
    2 v. Singapore, 1902.

  b Makepeace, Walter; Brooke, Gilbert E.; and Braddel, Roland St. J.,
    eds. *One hundred years of Singapore.* 2 v. London, 1921.

  a. Largely comprised of articles published in the *Singapore Free Press,* but revised with considerable additional information. The historical material extends
from 1819 to the transfer to the Colonial Office, April 1, 1867. *b.* Comprehensive
history of the capital of the Straits Settlements for the century following its
foundation in 1819. Both these works have much material bearing upon Sir
Stamford Raffles. Cf. U705–U707.   WHA

ASIA: SIAM AND FRENCH INDO-CHINA

U391a Crawfurd, John. *Journal of an embassy from the governor-general of*
    India to the courts of Siam and Cochin China; exhibiting a view of the
    actual state of those kingdoms. London, 1828.

  b The Crawfurd Papers. *Collection of official records relating to the mis-*
    sion of Dr. John Crawfurd sent to Siam by the government of India in
    the year 1821. Bangkok, 1915.

  c Bowring, Sir John. *Kingdom and people of Siam; with a narrative of*
    the mission to that country in 1855. 2 v. London, 1857.

  a. The author was commissioned by the Marquis of Hastings, Governor-
general of India, to undertake a mission to the courts of Siam and Cochin China
in the interest of the revival of commercial intercourse with those regions. The
Journal is not only a record of the mission but also an account and description of
many things Siamese. *b.* Brings together the official papers connected with the
mission underlying *a.* *c.* Extensive account of Siam and its people, drawn to some
extent from (U392*b*) Pallegoix, with the personal journal of Bowring's visit to
Siam.   WHA

U392a Turpin, François Henri. *Histoire civile et naturelle du royaume de Siam,*
    et des revolutions qui ont bouleversé cet empire jusqu'en 1770. 2 v. Paris,
    1771.

  b Pallegoix, Jean Baptiste. *Description du royaume Thai ou Siam.* 2 v.
    Paris, 1854.

  c Launay, Adrien. *Siam et les missionnaires français.* Tours, 1896.

There is a considerable literature in French on Siam and French relations
with that country. *a.* Was for some time a chief authority upon Siam. English
translation of its second volume was recently brought out (Bangkok, 1908), which
indicates that it still has some value. *b.* Largely supplanted the much older work
of Turpin, and remains as one of the standard histories; much used by later
writers. *c.* Devoted primarily to the history of the Roman Catholic missions in

Siam, it has an admirable introductory survey of the land and its people, while the history of the missions is necessarily involved in that of the country itself.

WHA

U393 Wood, William Alfred Rae. *History of Siam from the earliest time to the year A.D. 1781, with a supplement dealing with more recent years.* London, 1926. (Bibliography in Introduction.)

The most comprehensive treatise in English on the early history of Siam, its interest lying primarily in political affairs. There is no adequate work covering the last century and a half of Siamese history; the works whose titles promise such material are largely descriptive rather than historical contributions.

WHA

U394a Graham, A. W. (Walter Armstrong). *Siam: a handbook of practical, commercial, and political information.* 1912. Rev. ed., 2 v., London, 1924. (Bibliography.)

b Smyth, H. Warrington. *Five years in Siam.* 2 v. London, 1898.

c Campbell, John G. D. *Siam in the twentieth century, being the experiences of a British official.* London, 1902.

d Carter, A. Cecil, ed. *Kingdom of Siam.* N. Y. and London, 1904.

e Thompson, Peter A. *Lotus land, being an account of the country and the people of southern Siam.* Philadelphia and London (1906). Republished as *Siam, an account of the country and the people.* Boston, 1910. [Oriental series.]

f Le May, Reginald. *An Asian arcady, the land and peoples of northern Siam.* Cambridge (Eng.), 1926; Boston, 1927.

These books are grouped as being works of a descriptive character, fairly obvious in the titles. They contain relatively little narrative history. Review of *a, Nature,* 89: 138, Apr. 11, 1912. *b.* Falls within the years 1891–96, and *c,* within 1899–1901, so its title may be a little misleading. Review of *c, Asiatic Quar. Rev.,* 3rd ser., 14: 206, July 1902. *d.* Prepared as a part of the exhibit of Siam at the Louisiana Purchase Exposition (St. Louis, 1904). Review, W. Rice, *Dial,* 38: 91, Feb. 1, 1905. *e* and *f.* Deal respectively with the southern and northern parts of Siam. Review of *e, Athenaeum,* 2: 506, Oct. 27, 1906. WHA

U395a Lemire, Charles. *La France et le Siam. Nos relations de 1662 à 1903.* Paris, 1903.

b Seauve, Le Capitaine. *Les relations de la France et du Siam (1680–1907).* Paris, 1907.

c Berjdan, A. *Le Siam et les accords Franco-Siamois.* Paris, 1927.

d Nathabanja, Luang. *Extra-territoriality in Siam.* Bangkok, 1924.

a, b, and *c.* Monographs treating the international relations between France and Siam. *d.* Belongs more definitely to the sphere of international law, but brings together much useful historical material. WHA

U396a Lanessan, Jean Marie Antoine de. *L'Indo-Chine française.* Paris, 1889.

b —— *Colonisation française en Indo-Chine.* Paris, 1895.

c Lemire, M. Charles D. *Les cinque pays de l'Indo-Chine française.* Paris, 1900.

d Faque, L. *L'Indo-Chine française.* Paris, 1910.

e Russier, Henri E. E., and Brenier, Henri. *L'Indochine française.* Paris, 1911. Rev. ed., Saigon, 1915.

f Baudesson, Henry. *Indo-China and its primitive people.* London (1919). Tr. from French by E. A. Holt.

a and *b.* Professor Lanessan's books on Indo-China, where he served four years as Governor General, have never been replaced. He laid the foundations of the system under which the five provinces have been governed since 1891. The value of his two volumes lies in his authoritative presentation of administrative and economic problems. Review of *a,* J. B. Perkins, *Pol. Sci. Quar.,* 4: 332, June 1889. *c* and *d.* Brief compendiums of general information prepared for French readers and decidedly partial. *e.* Handbook on the French possessions in eastern Asia, mainly a census of the productive elements in the five regions. FWW
f. Intimate study of the primitive people dwelling in the uplands and more secluded regions of Indo-China. Review, *Asiatic Rev.,* n.s. 15: 656, Oct. 1919; C. C. Adams, *Geog. Rev.,* 11: 154, Jan. 1921. WHA

U397a Aymonier, Étienne. *Le Cambodge.* 3 v. Paris, 1900–04.

b Leclère, Adhémard. *Histoire du Cambodge.* Paris, 1914.

c Groslier, George. *Recherches sur les Cambodgiens.* Paris, 1921.

a. Third volume of this work contains the historical portion of the fullest general account of Cambodia yet in print; it gives also a comprehensive description of the Group at Angkor, the most stupendous ruins in Asia. *b.* Scholarly, thoroughly documented, but very dull. *c.* Study of Khmer civilization based on archeological researches; assembles a mass of data and illustrations not to be found elsewhere. FWW

U398 Maybon, Charles B. *Histoire moderne du pays d'Annam; 1592–1820.* Paris, 1919.

Covers .the period of the dual government and the inroads of Spanish missionaries and Portuguese pirates before the French occupation. Based on native authorities, accurate, fairly impartial as to European prejudices, but not alluring to the uninstructed reader. Review, *New China Rev.,* 2: 315, June 1920. FWW

U399 Reinach, Lucien de. *Le Laos.* 2 v. 1901. Posthumous ed., rev. by P. C. Dupontes, Paris, 1911.

Brief summary of political history and causes of the French seizure of the Mekong valley from Siam. .Ethnological material quite ample but not at first hand. V. 2 consists wholly of documents of political importance and brief reports on products. FWW

ASIA: MIDDLE EASTERN QUESTION

U401a Chirol, Valentine. *Middle eastern question or some political problems of Indian defence.* N. Y., 1903.

b Hamilton, Angus. *Problems of the Middle East.* London, 1909.

c Popowski, Josef. *Rival powers in central Asia.* Westminster, 1893. Tr. by A. B. Brabant and ed. by C. E. D. Black from *Antagonismus der englischen und russischen Interessen in Asien,* Wien, 1890.

d Rouire, Fernand. *La rivalité anglo-russe au XIXe siècle en Asie.* Paris, 1908.

a. Chirol, an able correspondent of the London *Times,* describes conditions in Persia, around the Persian Gulf, and along the frontiers of India in 1902–03.

Rich in facts, emphasizes the Persian question, dispassionate, but keenly insistent on conservation of British power and influence in Asia. Review, *Asiatic Quar. Rev.*, 3rd ser., 18: 207, July 1904. *b.* Collection of occasional articles, of which the more important relate to the Persian situation in 1907. Review, *Spectator*, 103: 166, July 31, 1909. *c.* The Austrian author attempts to prove that England cannot single-handed withstand Russia in Asia and argues that Russia is vulnerable only through the Caucasus, and that England and the central European monarchies should unite against Russia. Valuable only as an outsider's view of Anglo-Russian rivalry. Review, *Asiatic Quar. Rev.*, n.s. 7: 234, Jan. 1894. *d.* Clear, impartial historical account of developments affecting Arabia, Persia, Afghanistan, and Tibet, culminating in the Anglo-Russian agreement in 1907 which is carefully analyzed. Review, E. Driault, *Rev. Hist.*, 100: 122, Jan.-Feb. 1909.

GMD

U402a Holdich, Sir Thomas H. *Gates of India, being an historical narrative.* 1910. 2nd ed., London, 1914.

   b ——— *Indian borderland, 1880–1900.* 1901. 2nd ed., London, 1909.

   a. Historical survey of the northwestern approaches to India from ancient times to the first Afghan war, with special reference to explorations of the region in the early nineteenth century, notably by the American Masson. Holdich believes England must be strong enough to close the gates or guard them. Review, A. C. Yate, *Asiatic Quar. Rev.*, 3rd series, 31: 194, Jan. 1911. *b.* Account of events affecting the northwestern borderland with special reference to frontier delimitations for Afghanistan and Baluchistan in which author had important part.

GMD.

U403a Valikhanof, Captain; Venivkof, M.; and others. *Russians in central Asia.* London, 1865. Tr. from the Russian by John and Robert Michell.

   b Curzon, George Nathaniel. *Russia in central Asia in 1889 and the Anglo-Russian question.* London and N. Y., 1889.

   c ——— *Frontiers.* Oxford, 1907.

   a. Valikhanof was in the Russian service, but himself was 'the son of a Kirghiz Sultan and a native of the Steppe.' He and other travelers describe the Russian occupation of the Kirghiz Steppe and the relations of the Russian government with the khanates in the middle of the nineteenth century.   WHA
   b. Excellent record of observations during journey along the Trans-Caspian railway soon after its opening, to determine its effects. Basic to all later British writings and activities relating to the Middle East. England may concede Russian position north of Hindu Kush, but must follow definite policy of safeguarding its own interests. Review, *Asiatic Quar. Rev.*, 9: 231, Jan. 1890. *c.* Romanes· lecture illustrating the problems of frontiers from his expert knowledge of the Indian frontier.

GMD

ASIA: FAR EASTERN QUESTION

Bibliographical Note: In addition to the general works relating to the Far East there are numerous books containing sections or references to Eastern Asia which supply information not available elsewhere. In many cases the books mentioned here contain bibliographical data not only of supplementary source material but also of contemporary pamphlets and periodical literature of the utmost value to students, collectors and librarians. The collections of the various historical societies, especially those of Massachusetts, Rhode Island and Connecticut, contain much information relating to the early American contacts with the Far East as well as to the domestic conditions in the various ports there. In the generation prior to the American Civil War there were published many volumes by American naval and merchant marine officers and some notable contributions by missionaries. Only a few works are specifically mentioned: S. E. Morison, *Maritime history of Massachusetts,* Boston, 1921; C. O. Paullin, *Diplomatic negotiations of American naval officers, 1778–1883,* Baltimore, 1912; and the series of articles by the same author in the U. S. Naval Institute Proceedings, 1910–11, under the general title 'American Naval Vessels in the Orient'; Jared Sparks, *Life of John Ledyard,* Cambridge (Mass.), 1828; E. Fanning, *Voyages around the world,* N. Y., 1833; E. Roberts, *Embassy to the eastern courts of Cochin-China, Siam and Muscat,* N. Y., 1837; F. W. Taylor, *The flag ship; or a voyage around the world in the U. S. ship "Columbia,"* N. Y., 1840; 9th ed., 1847; J. Quincy, *Journals of Major Samuel Shaw,* Boston, 1847 (very important); P. Parker, *Journal of an expedition from Singapore to Japan,* London, 1838; J. W. Spalding, *The Japan expedition. Japan and around the world,* N. Y., 1855; W. W. Wood, *Fankwei; or the San Jacinto in the seas of India, China and Japan,* N. Y., 1859; W. Barrett, *Old merchants of New York,* N. Y., 1863; R. Pumpelly, *Across America and Asia,* N. Y., 1870; J. R. Young (ed. by May D. R. Young), *Men and memories,* 2 v., N. Y., 1901. TD

U421a Curzon, George N. *Problems of the Far East.* 1894. Rev. ed., Westminster, 1896.

b Chirol, Valentine. *Far eastern question.* London and N. Y., 1896.

c Leroy-Beaulieu, Pierre. *Awakening of the east. Siberia-Japan-China.* London, 1900. Tr. by Richard Davey from *La renovation de l'Asie.* Paris, 1900.

d Little, Archibald. *Far East.* Oxford, 1905.

a. Examination of the political, social and economic conditions in Japan, Korea and China by the keen observer who thoroughly believed in the beneficence of British imperialism and who later became Viceroy of India. Review, E. J. Eitel, *China Rev.,* 21: 352, March-Apr. 1895. *b.* Journalistic surveys of the situation in the Far East at the end of the Chinese-Japanese war, with special reference to its demands upon British policy. Review, *Asiatic Quar. Rev.,* 3rd ser., 1: 447, Apr. 1896. *c.* Description of conditions in Siberia, China and Japan, with some attention to past history, but special interest in transformation *in esse* and *in posse.* Much of the book appeared earlier in *Revue des Deux Mondes.* *d.* Result of long and intimate acquaintance with China, including the language, and of many journeys from 1860 onward. Devoted primarily to China, yet nearly half the chapters treat of the 'dependencies' (Manchuria, Mongolia, Turkestan, Tibet), the 'whilom dependencies' (Indo-China, Corea), and the 'buffer kingdom' (Siam), with a final chapter on Japan. Valuable maps. Review, *Asiatic Quar. Rev.,* 3rd ser., 20: 402, Oct. 1905. WHA

U422a Hatch, Ernest F. G. *Far eastern impressions.* London, 1904.

b Millard, Thomas F. *New Far East.* N. Y., 1906.

c Cotes, Everard. *Signs and portents in the Far East.* London, 1907.

d Coleman, Frederick. *Far East unveiled; an inner history of events in Japan and China in the year 1916.* London and N. Y., 1918.

e Reinsch, Paul S. *Intellectual and political currents in the Far East.* Boston, 1911.

a, b, c, d. Successive journalistic interpretations of first-hand impressions during approximately the first decade and a half of the present century. Japan, Korea and China are to the forefront of attention, with British, American and Russian influences and interests ever present more or less conspicuously. Review of *a*, H. E. Coblentz, *Dial*, 39: 378, Dec. 1, 1905; of *b* and *c*, P. S. Reinsch, *Amer. Pol. Sci. Rev.*, 1: 650, Aug. 1907; 2: 301, Feb. 1908; of *d*, *Spectator*, 121: 181, Aug. 17, 1918.

WHA

e. Series of brilliant essays describing and interpreting contemporary thought and political development in the Far East and India. Based on research and on observations and interpretations of friends native of or residing in countries dealt with. Accurate estimate of conditions, forces, and tendencies. At the time when it was written, the retarding and opposing internal forces had not fully manifested themselves and the external developments which were destined shortly to impede some movements and accelerate others could not be foreseen. Review, A. B. Hart, *Amer. Pol. Sci. Rev.*, 6: 268, May 1912.

SKH

U423a Hornbeck, Stanley K. *Contemporary politics in the Far East.* N. Y., 1916.

b Brown, Arthur Judson. *Mastery of the Far East. Korea's transformation and Japan's rise.* 1919. Rev. ed., N. Y., 1921.

a. Author wrote this book after a period of residence in China as a teacher in government colleges. It has the merit of the author's personal familiarity with the events which led up to and included the presentation of the Twenty-one Demands; shows an exceptional critical faculty in the use of political sources. Style excellent and dramatic. At time of publication, the best and most impartial study of its subject. While some new material has since become available, it remains of great permanent value and may be reckoned among the books essential for an understanding of the course of events in the Far East since 1898. Publicist's treatment rather than a historian's. Review, B. E. Schmitt, *Amer. Pol. Sci. Rev.*, 11: 150, Feb. 1917.

TD

b. Careful and unusually impartial account, though not entirely free from some pro-Korean bias, of Korean affairs since the Chino-Japanese war; the best comprehensive treatment of the case. Last third of volume is discussion of influence of Christian missions with special reference to Korea. The author, who has long been the secretary of the Board of Foreign Missions of the Presbyterian Church of the United States, has twice visited the Far East and has written several other books based upon his close study of Far Eastern affairs. Review, H. L. Joly, *Asiatic Rev.*, n.s. 16: 144, Jan. 1920.

GMD

U424a Gibbons, Herbert A. *New map of Asia, 1900–1919.* N. Y., 1919.

b Bland, John O. P. *China, Japan and Korea.* N. Y., 1921.

c Wood, Ge-Zay. *China, the United States, and the Anglo-Japanese alliance.* N. Y. (1921).

d King-Hall, Stephen. *Western civilization and the Far East.* 1924. 2nd ed., London, 1925.

e Harris, Norman D. *Europe and the east.* Boston, 1926. (Bibliography.)

a. Readable, rabidly anti-British, but in general, reliable account of recent events; so saturated with the author's zeal for self-determination and self-government of the Asiatic peoples as to be a demonstration of a hypothesis rather than a history. Review, E. Huntington, *Geographical Rev.*, 9: 145, Feb. 1920.

GMD.

b. Narrative of developments in the second decade of this century. First part, a political survey, contains much recent history; second part consists of impressions from personal investigations. Pessimistic as regards democracy and self-government in China. Review, C. D. Bruce, *Asiatic Rev.*, n.s. 27: 553, July 1921. *c.* Centers about the Anglo-Japanese alliances, 1902 ff., presenting fairly China's objections to this method of meeting the Far Eastern question. Appendixes comprise documents including the texts of the Anglo-Japanese agreements of 1902, 1905 and 1911. Review, G. N. Steiger, *Amer. Pol. Sci. Rev.*, 16: 331, May 1922. *d.* Excellent survey of the history, external and internal, and the social and economic developments of China and Japan, with more attention to Japanese domestic and foreign policies. More optimistic regarding the future of democracy in China than is *b.* Review, S. K. Hornbeck, *A.H.R.*, 30: 825, July 1925.

WHA

e. Compact, comprehensive and impartial summary of European activities in the Far East from the early part of the nineteenth century to 1922. Review, (London) *Times Lit. Suppl.*, 26: 383, June 2, 1927.

HRS

U425 Morse, Hosea B., and **Macnair, Harley F.** *Far eastern international relations.* Shanghai, 1928.

Considerable portion of this many-paged volume consists of an abridgment, largely through omission of the less important material, of the author's three-volume work (U2503*a*) with the addition of later material for China and considerable material for Japan, Russian Asia, Siam and the Philippines. Students of the book should balance some of the treatment of controversial factors and episodes of recent days by other works representing other points of view. Review, G. H. Blakeslee, *A.H.R.*, 34: 844, July 1929.

WHA

U426a Franke, Otto. *Die Grossmächte in Ostasien von 1894 bis 1914.* Braunschweig, 1923.

    b Driault, Edouard. *La question d'Extrême-Orient.* Paris, 1908. [Bibliothèque d'histoire contemporaine.]

    c Cateliani, Enrico L. *La penetrazione straniera nell'estremo Oriente, sue forme giuridiche ed economiche.* 1915. Firenze, 1925. [Biblioteca coloniale.]

    d Pasvolsky, Leo. *Russia in the Far East.* N. Y., 1922.

Grouped as offering typical approaches to the subject from several national points of view. Review of *a*, S. K. Hornbeck, *A.H.R.*, 30: 143, Oct. 1924; of *b*, H. Hauser, *Rev. Hist.*, 101: 113, May-June 1909; of *c*, A. A. Bernardy, *Archivio Storico Italiano*, Anno 74, 2: 201, 1916; of *d*, T. B. Partington, *Asiatic Rev.*, n.s. 18: 691, Oct. 1922; *Amer. Pol. Sci. Rev.*, 16: 523, Aug. 1922.

WHA

U427a Chirol, Sir Valentine. *The occident and the orient.* Chicago (1924). [Lectures on Harris foundation.]

    b Soyeshima, Michimasa, and **Kuo, Ping Wen.** *Oriental interpretations of the far eastern problem.* Chicago, 1925. [Lectures on Harris foundation.]

a. Illuminating presentation in six lectures of the relations between East and West with special attention to the perils from racial prejudice and the superiority complex. Recent conditions in the Ottoman empire, Egypt and India (Gandhi and non-participation) are passed in rapid review; the principles of protectorate and mandate are analyzed; the significance of Bolshevism in the problem is indicated. Review, A. H. Lybyer, *A.H.R.*, 30 : 631, Apr. 1925. *b.* Deals with Japan in its relations with the Far East and with the United States, while Dr. Kuo similarly presented China's positions. Review, *Am. Pol. Sci. Rev.*, 20 : 447, May 1926. WHA

U428a Buell, Raymond Leslie. *The Washington conference,* 1922. N. Y. and London, 1922.

b Ichihashi, Yamato. *The Washington conference and after.* Stanford University, California, and London. 1928. (Appendixes of documents and bibliography.)

a. Contemporary account, somewhat journalistic in character but based on careful reading; the only available well-rounded account of the Conference until the appearance of *b.* Review, G. H. Blakeslee, *Am. Pol. Sci. Rev.*, 16 : 669, Nov. 1922. KSL

b. Account of the Conference in its two aspects—Conference on limitation of armament and Conference on the Pacific and the Far East. Written some years after the Conference and so with some advantage over *a* in the perspective of the years. Review, E. T. Williams, *A.H.R.*, 34 : 840, July 1929. WHA

U431a Callahan, James Morton. *American relations in the Pacific and in the Far East, 1784–1900.* Baltimore, 1901. [Johns Hopkins University studies in historical and political science.]

b Foster, John W. *American diplomacy in the Orient.* Boston, 1903.

c Millard, Thomas F. *America and the far eastern question.* N. Y., 1909.

d —— *Our eastern question—America's contact with the Orient and the trend of relations with China and Japan.* N. Y., 1916.

e —— *Democracy and the eastern question. The problem of the Far East as demonstrated by the great war, and its relations with the United States of America.* N. Y., 1919.

f Dennett, Tyler. *Americans in eastern Asia.* N. Y., 1922.

g —— *Roosevelt and the Russo-Japanese war.* N. Y., 1925.

a. Monograph, tracing the development of American commercial interests in the nineteenth century, with some attention to exploration and colonization and the influence of the United States in opening the closed Far East. WHA

b. Includes relations with China, Japan, Korea, Hawaii, Samoa, and the Philippines. Appendixes contain the texts of a number of treaties and conventions, all of which are easily accessible elsewhere. A popular resumé of the subject with numerous citations to books and documents. Useful to the beginner as supplying background for more specialized study. Review, T. S. Woolsey, *A.H.R.*, 9 : 180, Oct. 1903. WWMCL

c, d, e. By the former editor of *Millard's Review;* mainly significant for their presentation of a mass of evidence in support of the author's animadversions to Japanese policy. *e.* Discusses present-day politics in the Far East on a less restricted scale than *d.* Author states the case for democracy as illustrated by the Republic of China and advocates a strong oriental policy by the United States to offset the growing influence of Japan, which he frankly regards as a menace to any healthy democratic political development in the Far East. Review of *c,* E. C. Elliott, *Amer. Pol. Sci. Rev.*, 4 : 124, Feb. 1910; of *d,* H. R. Mussey, *Pol. Sci.*

Quar., 32:603, Dec. 1917; of *e*, S. K. Hornbeck, *Amer. Pol. Sci. Rev.*, 14:515, Aug. 1920.   NTJ

f. Investigation of the development of American policy in China, Japan and Korea to 1900; at the time of publication, was the most complete work in the field. Both supplements and is supplemented by (U2503*a*) Morse. Attention may be directed to the author's paper, as supplemental, on 'Seward's Far Eastern Policy,' *A.H.R.*, 28:45–62, Oct. 1922. Review, F. W. Williams, *A.H.R.*, 28:563, Apr. 1923. *g.* Continuation of *f.* Review, A. C. Coolidge, *A.H.R.*, 31:156, Oct. 1925.   WHA

ASIA: CONSTITUTIONAL, LEGAL, POLITICAL, AND ECONOMIC HISTORY

U531a Ireland, Alleyne. *Far eastern tropics.* Boston, 1905. (Bibliography.)

   b Dutcher, George M. *Political awakening of the east. Studies of political progress of Egypt, China, Japan and the Philippines.* N. Y., 1925. [Bennett lectures, Wesleyan University.]

a. Studies in the administration of tropical dependencies, including Hong Kong, British Borneo, Burma, the Federated Malay States, French Indo-China and the Philippines, representing part of the results of an examination in the Far East, of colonial administration, especially in southeastern Asia. Hostile to the American experiment in the Philippines. Review, *Pol. Sci. Quar.*, 22:315, June 1907. *b.* Portrays 'the penetration of modern ideas and methods among the peoples of the East.' Limited primarily to the political forces, it yet pays considerable attention to social influences. Review, K. S. Latourette, *A.H.R.*, 31:174, Oct. 1925.

                                                                  WHA

U571a Milburn, William. *Oriental commerce.* 2 v. London, 1813.

   b Eldridge, Frank R., Jr. *Trading with Asia.* N. Y., 1921. (Bibliography.)

a. Contents of these large quartos are adequately expressed in the descriptive language of the title page: 'A geographical description of the principal places in the East Indies, China and Japan, with their produce, manufactures, and trade, including the coasting or country trade from port to port; also the rise and progress of the trade of the various European nations with the eastern world, particularly .that of the English East India Company, from the discovery of the passage round the Cape of Good Hope to the present period; with an account of the Company's establishments, revenues, debts, assets, &c. at home and abroad. Deduced from authentic documents, and founded upon practical experience obtained in the course of seven voyages to India and China.' *b.* While primarily a text-book for students of commerce, this is a convenient manual for a rapid survey of the general economics, the products, industries and markets of central, southern and eastern Asia. Review, *Boston Transcript*, p. 6, Dec. 31, 1921.

                                                                  WHA

U572 King, Franklin H. *Farmers of forty centuries, or permanent agriculture in China, Korea and Japan.* Madison, Wis., 1911.

Careful, if incomplete, survey of irrigation and farming methods in the Far East by a specialist in scientific agriculture. Remains the most useful statement of the sources of China's economic wealth and husbandry. Review, *Nation* (N. Y.), 96:213, Feb. 27, 1913.   FWW

ASIA: CULTURAL HISTORY

U601a Dickinson, Goldsworthy Lowes. *Essay on the civilization of India, China and Japan.* London, 1914.

b Rihbany, Abraham Mitrie. *Wise men from the east and from the west.* Boston, 1922.

c Moore, Edward Caldwell. *West and east; the expansion of Christendom and the naturalization of Christianity in the orient in the nineteenth century.* N. Y., 1920. [Dale lectures, Oxford, 1913.]

d Sarkar, Benoy Kumar. *Futurism of young Asia and other essays on the relations between the east and the west.* Berlin, 1922.

a. Brief but well-balanced study. Review, F. W. S. Browne, *International Jour. Ethics,* 25 : 424, Apr. 1915. *b* and *c.* Representing respectively the eastern and the western points of view, these dwell upon the religious phases; placed here because of their broader interest and for the comparison which they set forth, both similarities and contrasts. Both authors believe that East and West have much to learn, each from the other. Review of *b, N. Y. Times Book Rev.,* p. 13, Jan. 7, 1923; of *c,* (London) *Times Literary Supplement,* p. 566, Sept. 2, 1920. *d.* Here are brought together many papers by one of the outstanding representatives of modern Asia, whose *Leitmotif* in this volume is 'war against colonialism in politics and against *orientalisme* in science.' Most of the articles have appeared in American or Indian periodicals; much of the material has been presented in lectures at educational centers in the United States, Paris and Berlin. WHA

U602 Laufer, Berthold. *Sino-Iranica.* Chicago, 1919. [Anthropological series.]

This publication of the Field Museum of Natural History, Chicago, is a distinct contribution to the history of early civilization. Its primary purpose is 'to trace the history of all objects of material culture in their migration from Persia to China (Sino-Iranica) and others transmitted from China to Persia (Irano-Sinica).' Bibliographical references are a convenient supplement to (U3*a*) Cordier. Review, W. T. Swingle, *A.H.R.,* 26 : 725, July 1921. WHA

U621a Davids, Thomas William Rhys. *Buddhism, being a sketch of the life and teachings of Gautama the Buddha.* 1877). Rev. ed., London, 1903. [Non-Christian religious systems.]

b —— *Buddhism, its history and literature.* 1896. 3rd ed., rev., N. Y. and London, 1909. [American lectures on history of religions.]

c Eliot, Sir Charles Norton Edgecombe. *Hinduism and Buddhism; an historical sketch.* 3 v. London, 1921.

a and *b.* Standard works, intended for a general public, setting forth the general principles of Buddhism as interpreted by one of the most eminent of scholars in the history and philosophy of religion. Review, *Asiatic Quar. Rev.,* 3rd ser., 2 : 209, July 1896. WHA

c. Very useful contribution to the study of Buddhism in the Far East, although Japanese Buddhism is omitted; but religious activity in Ceylon, Burma, Siam, Tibet and China is expounded by a capable eye-witness. Review, E. W. Hopkins, *A.H.R.,* 27 : 572, Apr. 1922. EWH

U622 Anesaki, Masaharu. *Religious and social problems of the Orient.* N. Y., 1923. [Earl lectures.]

Four lectures dealing with the cultural contacts between the Far East and the West with the resulting mutual reactions in ethics, religion and in social structures. WHA

U641 Grousset, René. *Histoire de la philosophie orientale—Inde—Chine—Japon.* Paris, 1923.

Hindu, Buddhist and Chinese thought are successively and successfully treated in their logical development. Moslem thought Grousset excludes from his discussion as a branch of Greek philosophy, and theosophy as a modernism directly opposed to Hindu doctrine. Review, P. M. Oursel, *Rev. Hist.,* 144: 274, Nov. 1923. WHA

U681a Fenollosa, Ernest Francisco (and **Mary Fenollosa,** ed.) *Epochs of Chinese and Japanese art. An outline history of east Asiatic design.* 2 v. N. Y., 1911.

  b Binyon, Laurence. *Painting in the Far East.* 1908. 3rd rev. ed., N. Y., 1923.

a. Richly illustrated analysis and interpretation of Chinese and Japanese art, centering its interest in the influence of Buddhism upon the art of these peoples. Review, *Athenaeum,* 2: 484, Oct. 26, 1912. *b.* Devoted primarily to pictorial art in China and Japan, but covering somewhat Asian painting in general. Throws much light upon cultural conditions at various stages of development. Review, *Nation* (N. Y.), 87: 637, Dec. 24, 1908. WHA

ASIA: BIOGRAPHY

Most of the biographical works included in this Section are distributed among the subsections devoted respectively to India, China and Japan, while the biographical subsections of §§ B, General history; C, Near East in ancient times; G, Mohammedanism and Moslem peoples; and K, Colonial expansion, as well as of those treating European lands which have had interests in Asia, will contain pertinent references. The autobiographical and biographical literature of the diplomats and missionaries who have shared in the opening of the Far East and India is extensive and important, but such material for the leading native personages in any Western language is scanty. For these latter, though primarily for India and exclusive of China and Japan, (U701) H. G. Keene's revised edition (London, 1894) of T. W. Beale's *Oriental Biographical Dictionary,* Calcutta, 1881, will be found convenient. (U702) *Who's Who in the Far East,* Hong Kong, 1906 ff., is a current biography of important people in that region. Among many biographies the following may be mentioned: (U703) H. Lamb, *Genghis Khan, the emperor of all men,* London, 1928; (U704) V. A. Smith, *Akbar, the great Mogul, 1542–1605,* Oxford, 1917; (U705) D. C. Boulger, *Life of Sir Stamford Raffles,* London, 1897; (U706) H. E. Egerton, *Sir Stamford Raffles,* London, 1900; (U707) R. Coupland, *Raffles, 1781–1826,* Oxford, 1926; (U708) A. Vámbéry, *The Story of my struggles,* 2 v., N. Y., 1904; (U709) R. Pumpelly, *My reminiscences,* 2 v., N. Y., 1918; (U710) S. Hedin, *My life as explorer,* N. Y., 1925; (U711) J. W. Foster, *Diplomatic memoirs,* 2 v., Boston, 1909; (U712) D. Christie, *Thirty years in Moukden, 1883–1913,* London, 1914.

ASIA: PERIODICALS

The following extend in their interest into more than one of the larger regions of Asia: (U941) (*Asia,* originally *Journal of the American Asiatic Association*), N. Y., 1898 ff.; (U942) *Asiatic review* (earlier *Asiatic quarterly review*), London, 1886 ff.; (U943) *Journal of the Royal Asiatic Society,* London, 1834 ff.; (U944) *Journal asiatique,* Paris, 1822 ff.; (U945) *L'Asie française,* Paris, 1901 ff.; (U946) *Asien* (organ of the Deutschasiatische Gesellschaft), Berlin, 1901 ff.; continued as *Ostasiatische Rundschau,* Berlin, 1920 ff.; (U947) *Wiener Zeitschrift für die Kunde des Morgenlandes,* Vienna, 1887 ff.; (U948) *Asia major* (Journal devoted to the study of the languages, arts and civilization of the Far East and Central Asia), Leipzig, 1924 ff.; (U949) *Asiatic researches,* 20 v., Calcutta, 1788–1839; (U950) *Journal of the Central Asian Society,* London, 1914 ff.; (U951) *Der neue Orient,* Berlin, 1917 ff.; (U952) *The new East,* Tokio, 1917 ff.; (U953) *Millard's Review of the East,* now *Chinese weekly review,* Shanghai, 1917 ff.; (U954) *T'oung pao . . . ou Archives concernant l'histoire, les langues, la géographie et l'ethnographie de l'Asie orientale,* Leyden, 1890 ff.; (U955) *Revue indo-chinoise,* Hanoi, 1900 ff.; (U956) *Bulletin de l'École Française d'Extrême-Orient,* Paris, 1901 ff.

INDIA: BIBLIOGRAPHY AND ENCYCLOPEDIAS

While many of the works listed in this sub-section contain bibliographies, special attention is called to those in (U1122) *Cambridge history of India.* The various catalogues of the Library of the India Office and guides of various sorts to the government documents (cf. U1901 ff.) are of service primarily to those who can visit London, but others will derive information and clues to knowledge from them.

The only encyclopedia devoted primarily to India also covers other parts of Asia and so appears as (U22), Balfour, *Cyclopædia of India and of eastern and southern Asia.* The leading general encyclopedias, such as (B22b) *Encyclopædia Britannica,* and universal geographies, like (B42a) Reclus, and encyclopedias of religion and of missions, such as (F22) Hastings, *Encyclopædia of religion and ethics,* and (F29) Dwight and others, *Encyclopedia of missions,* all contain much material on India.

U1001 Campbell, Francis B. F. *Index-catalogue of bibliograph-works (chiefly in the English language) relating to India.* London, 1897.

Compiled largely from references which the editor met in secondary sources; useful key to lists of official documents, reports, catalogues and periodicals.

WHA

INDIA: GEOGRAPHY AND ETHNOLOGY

U1041a Hunter, Sir William W. (director). *Statistical survey of British India.* 128 v. Various places, 1875–86.

b ———, ed. *Imperial gazetteer of India.* 9 v., 1881; 2nd ed., 14 v., London, 1885–87; 3rd ed., J. S. Cotton et al., eds., 26 v., Oxford, 1907–09.

c ——— *Indian empire, its peoples, history and products.* 1882. 3rd ed., London, 1893. (Bibliographies.)

d ——— *Brief history of the Indian peoples.* 1882. 23rd ed., W. H. Hutton, ed., Oxford, 1903. Rev. reprint of 23rd ed., G. M. Dutcher, ed., in (B135, v. 5) Lodge, *History of the nations.*

e ——— *Atlas of India.* London, 1894.

a. Under appointment in 1869 from Lord Mayo, Hunter began the collection of information on the topographical, ethnical, agricultural, industrial, administrative and medical aspects of each of the 240 districts in British India. Hunter himself compiled and edited the materials for Bengal and Assam, but others did the work for the remaining thirteen provinces. Only a few volumes deal with a portion of the native states. No such complete survey had previously been undertaken in any country, though it was modeled in part on Bonaparte's survey of Egypt. Hunter digested these materials with additions to cover the native states, in *b,* in the first two editions of which the article 'India' filled a complete volume. This was enlarged and published separately in *c;* later it was largely rewritten and expanded to fill vs. 1–4 of the third edition of *b.* The historical chapters were also detached and published as *d.* Hunter's work was fundamental and invaluable, although it of course needs to be corrected and supplemented by later information. *e.* This atlas is still useful; that constituting v. 26 of *b* is fifteen years later. Review of *b,* v. 2, *A.H.R.,* 14: 333, Jan. 1909; of *c, Asiatic Quar. Rev.,* n.s. 5: 537, Apr. 1893.   GMD

U1042a Hamilton, Walter. *East-India gazetteer; containing particular descriptions of . . . Hindostan, and the adjacent countries, India beyond the Ganges, and the eastern archipelago.* 2nd ed., 2 v., London, 1828.

  b Thornton, Edward. *Gazetteer of the territories under the government of the East India company, and of the native states on the continent of India.* 4 v. London, 1854.

  c Pharaoh and Co. *Gazetteer of southern India, with the Tenasserim provinces and Singapore.* Madras, 1855.

  d Baness, J. Frederick. *Index geographicus Indicus.* London and Calcutta, 1881.

a, b, c. Of an encyclopedic nature, alphabetically arranged though limited primarily to geographical interests. *d.* Practically an indexed atlas of India, but containing considerable geographical, economic and statistical information.   WHA

U1043a Patterson, George. *Geography of India.* 2 v. London, 1909.

  b Holdich, Sir Thomas H. *India.* London, 1904. [Regions of the world.]

  c Cunningham, Alexander. *Ancient geography of India.* v. 1. *The Buddhist period.* London, 1871.

a. Perhaps the best manual for purely geographical information. *b.* Good summary of other books with many useful maps. Disproportionate attention to the frontiers of which alone the author had expert knowledge. Good chapters on railways, minerals and climate. Review, *Asiatic Quar. Rev.,* 3rd ser., 19: 423, Apr. 1905.   GMD
c. Blend of geographical and historical inquiry concerning the times especially of Alexander's campaigns and of the travels, a millennium later, of Hwen Thsang, a Chinese pilgrim.   WHA

U1044a *Statistical abstract relating to British India.* London, 1840 ff.

  b Reed, Sir Stanley, ed. *Indian year book.* Bombay and London, 1914 ff.

  c Williams, L. F. Rushbrook. *India in 1917–1918* (ff.). Calcutta, 1919 ff.

a. Contains current and recent statistics, the successive numbers usually covering about a decade. *b* and *c.* Useful annuals, replete with information, including statistics, *c,* prepared and published under 26th section of Government of India

Act of 1919, a report on moral and material progress of India, invaluable for current economic, social, and political events and conditions, including the "unrest." The successive volumes are most convenient in which to trace the recent history.

GMD

U1045a (**Murray's**) *Handbook for travellers in India, Burma and Ceylon including all British India, the Portuguese and French possessions, and the protected native states.* 2 v., 1859. 11th ed., London, 1924.

b **Baedeker, Karl.** *Indien. Handbuch für Reisende.* Leipzig, 1914.

Convenient information primarily for the traveler, but much of it historical. Review of *a*, C. MacLeod, *Asiatic Rev.*, n.s. 21 : 160, Jan. 1925. There are also special Murray's Handbooks for Bombay (2nd ed., 1881), Bengal (2nd ed., 1882), Madras (2nd ed., 1879), and the Punjab (1883).

WHA

U1051a *Census of India, 1901.* v. 1, *India* (ethnographic appendices by H. H. Risley). Calcutta, 1903.

b *Census of India, 1911.* v. 1, *India,* Pt. 1, report by E. A. Gait, Calcutta, 1913.

c **Grierson, George A.,** ed. *Linguistic survey of India.* 10 v. Calcutta, 1903–1922. v. 1, Pt. 1, *Introductory, 1927.* (Bibliography).

d **Risley, Sir Herbert H.** *People of India.* 1908. 2nd rev. ed., by W. Crooke, London, 1915.

The first synchronous enumeration of India was made for February 17th, 1881, and a decennial census has been taken thereafter. That for 1921 is being published. Of the voluminous publication for each decennial census, the introductory general report volumes, *a* and *b,* are of special value, notably in the case of Risley's materials on ethnography, which he rewrote in more popular form as *d*. The book is fully illustrated and in the second edition has the 1911 census figures. The subject of castes receives full and authoritative treatment, but it should be supplemented for this topic by (U1204*a*) Ketkar. Review of *b*, M. Jefferson, *Geog. Rev., 7* : 196, March 1919; of *d, Calcutta Rev.,* 126 : 305, Apr. 1908.   GMD

c. Devoted specifically to linguistics; a vast undertaking, rich in its ethnographic contribution, contains much folk-lore derived from the primitive peoples of India.

WHA

U1052a **Elliot, Sir Henry M.** *Memoirs on the history, folklore, and distribution of the races of the northwestern provinces of India.* 2 v. London, 1869.

b **Risley, Sir Herbert H.** *Tribes and castes of Bengal.* 2 v. Calcutta, 1892.

c **Crooke, William.** *Tribes and castes of the northwestern provinces and Oudh.* 4 v. Calcutta, 1896.

d ———— *Natives of northern India.* Calcutta, 1907.

e **Thurston, Edgar,** and **Rangachari, K.** *Castes and tribes of southern India.* 7 v. Madras, 1909.

f **Russell, Robert V.,** and **Lai, R. B. H.** *Tribes and castes of the central provinces of India.* London, 1916.

In recent years there has been a noticeable revival of interest in the ethnography of India and historical clues have been followed, in part redressing the balance after probable over-emphasis upon philological considerations. Monographic works upon limited fields are abundant. The works listed here survey the fairly broad areas indicated in their titles. Review of *d, Asiatic Quar. Rev.*, 3rd ser., 24 : 402, Oct. 1907; of *e, Calcutta Rev.*, 130 : 132, Jan. 1910.   WHA

INDIA: COLLECTIONS OF SOURCES

Most of the collections of sources for the study of Indian history have been brought out by the government, some of the more important being listed in (U1901 ff.).

U1061a Khan, Shafaat Ahmad. *Sources for the history of British India in the seventeenth century.* London, 1926.

   b *Indian records, with a commercial view of the relations between the British government and the Nawabs Nazim of Bengal, Behar and Orissa.* London, 1870.

   c Mukherji, Panchanandas, ed. *Indian constitutional documents (1600– 1918).* 2 v. 2nd enl. ed., Calcutta, 1918. [Indian citizen series.]

a. Bibliography of manuscript material, transcripts and calendars of documents. Preface states twofold aim: 'supplying a critical analysis of essential data for the study of seventeenth century British India,' and 'bringing within one purview all the materials lying scattered in various record offices in England.' Review, *E.H.R.,* 42 : 316, Apr. 1927. *b.* Documents are presented in anti-British or pro-Indian settings; useful glossary of Hindu terms included. *c.* Contains not only documents relating to India, such as acts of Parliament, but also important speeches, especially such as set forth governmental policies. Introduction points out many of the main features of constitutional development.   WHA

U1062 M'Crindle, J. W., ed. and tr. *Ancient India as described in classical literature.* Westminster, 1901.

Fullest excerpts are from Strabo, Pliny and Aelian; two sections present material treating of the Brahmans; more or less incidental notices are also collected. The book is the last in a series of six (listed in the introduction to this volume), which offer translations from the Greek and Latin classics of passages 'which throw any light upon the distant past of India.' Review, *Asiatic Quar. Rev.,* 3rd ser., 12 : 417, Oct. 1901.   WHA

U1063a Forrest, George W., ed. *Selections from the letters, despatches, and other state papers preserved in the foreign department of the government of India, 1772–1785.* 3 v. Calcutta, 1890.

   b Payne, Charles H., ed. *Scenes and characters from Indian history as described in the works of some old masters.* London, 1925.

   c Muir, Ramsay. *Making of British India, 1756–1858.* Manchester (Eng.), London and N. Y., 1915.

   d Anderson, G., and **Subedar, M. B.** *Expansion of British India, 1818– 1858.* London and N. Y., 1918.

a. Valuable collections of original sources for the history of the administration of Warren Hastings in India, chiefly drawn from the secret proceedings of the select committee of the governor's council, edited with excellent introductions.

GMD

b. Brief selections from early writers (Plutarch to Tavernier), giving intimate touches of events and men (Alexander to Aurangzeb). *c.* Basic material consists of documents—despatches, treaties, statutes, letters, etc.—with introductory statements distributed chiefly at the beginning of the several chapers. Review, A. L. P. Dennis, *A.H.R.*, 21 : 798, July 1916. *d.* Collection of excerpts from memoranda, correspondence, despatches and other documents and from important secondary sources. Review, W. H. Hutton, *Asiatic Rev.*, n.s. 14: 376, July 1918; *E.H.R.*, 33 : 424, July 1918.

WHA

INDIA: GENERAL HISTORIES

U1101a Duff, C. Mabel. (Mrs. W. R. Rickmers.) *Chronology of India, from the earliest times to the beginning of the sixteenth century.* Westminster, 1899.

b Burgess, James. *Chronology of modern India for four hundred years from the close of the fifteenth century, A.D. 1494–1894.* Edinburgh, 1913.

a. Effort to list year by year the most important events from the earliest time to A.D. 1530. Needs many additions and corrections in the light of recent research. Many dates are still doubtful. Review, *Asiatic Quar. Rev.*, 3rd ser., 8: 213, July 1899. *b.* Accurate and reliable account year by year of the most important events from 1494 to 1894. Review, *Asiatic Rev.*, n.s. 1: 415, Apr. 1913.

GMD

U1102a Trotter, Lionel J. *History of India from the earliest times to the present day.* 1874. 3rd rev. ed. brought up to 1911 by W. H. Hutton. London, 1917.

b Smith, Vincent A. *Oxford history of India, from the earliest times to the end of 1911.* 1919. 2nd ed. rev. and continued to 1921 by S. M. Edwardes, Oxford, 1923. (Bibliographies.)

c —— *Oxford student's history of India.* 1908. 10th ed. rev. by H. G. Rawlinson, Oxford, 1926.

d Dutt, Romesh Chunder. *Brief history of ancient and modern India.* 3rd rev. ed., Calcutta, 1908.

e Ali, A. Yusuf. *Making of India.* London, 1925. (Bibliography.)

First two are English writers who are convinced supporters of British rule in India; the last two represent native points of view; all rise far above the propagandist level. *a.* Gives major attention to the period since 1760. Review, *Asiatic Rev.*, n.s. 12: 426, Nov. 15, 1917. Both *b* and *c* are well-proportioned, but the latter is the only one of the first three of these works which more than sketches the early and Mohammedan periods. Account of British rule in *a* is briefer than in *b*, perhaps more readable, but not always so discriminating. Review of *b*, *Asiatic Rev.*, n.s. 15: 654, Oct. 1919; of *c*, W. H. Hutton, *Asiatic Rev.*, n.s. 16: 713, Oct. 1920.

GMD

d. Useful for the novice as it is a brief manual following the syllabus prescribed for those preparing for the matriculation for Calcutta University. *e.* Successful attempt to set forth in relatively brief compass the constructive factors which have been evident in the long history of India. The story is brought up to the middle of 1925.

WHA

U1121a Mill, James. *History of British India.* 9 v. 1848. 5th ed., 10 v., London, 1858. (v. 6–9 have title, *History of British India. From 1805 to 1835.* By Horace H. Wilson.)

b Marshman, John C. *History of India from the earliest period to the close of Lord Dalhousie's administration.* 3 v. 1863–67. 2nd ed., London, 1867. Abridgment, 1876; 3rd ed., continued, London, 1893.

A GUIDE TO HISTORICAL LITERATURE

c **Wheeler, J. Talboys.** *History of India from the earliest ages.* 4 v. in 5. London, 1867–81.

a. Mill attempted to produce a classic, but he had no first-hand knowledge of Indian languages or literatures. The first two volumes of introductory material, therefore, give a deceptive appearance of erudition. The main narrative begins with 1740; disproportionate space and animus are devoted to Warren Hastings; the work ends with the death of Cornwallis, 1805. Wilson corrected the worst errors and prejudices by his notes and added volumes 7–9. continuing the account to Bentinck's retirement. Volume 10 is the Index. *b.* Although superseded for the earlier periods, this account of the British period is still one of the best. The abridgment has been extended to 1891. Review of abridgment, *Academy,* 9: 260, March 18, 1876.

GMD

c. While the author's primary interest is the political history of India, the earlier volumes treat comprehensively the literature and the life of the people; it might be called the history of the civilization of India. It extends through the middle of the eighteenth century.

WHA

U1122 *Cambridge history of India.* Cambridge, Eng., and N. Y., 1922 ff. v. 1, 1922; v. 3, 1928. (Extensive bibliographies, chronological and genealogical tables.)

Planned for six volumes, a collaborated work by acknowledged experts in the several fields. Authoritative, embodying the results of many recent researches not elsewhere readily available. Well provided with maps and illustrations. The work now reaches the middle of the sixteenth century, with one earlier period yet to be covered. Review of v. 1, M. Bloomfield, *A.H.R.,* 28: 727, July 1923; of v. 3, M. T. Titus, *A.H.R.,* 35: 117, Oct. 1929.

WHA

U1123 **Jackson, Abraham V. W.,** ed. *History of India.* 9 v. London, 1906–07. [1, R. C. Dutt, *From the earliest times to the sixth century B.C.* Cf. U1102d. 2, V. A. Smith, *From the sixth century B.C. to the Mohammedan conquest, including the invasion of Alexander the Great.* Cf. U1201b. 3, S. Lane-Poole, *Mediæval India from the Mohammedan conquest to the reign of Akbar the Great.* Cf. U1213a. 4, id., *From the reign of Akbar the Great to the fall of the Moghul empire.* Cf. U1213a. 5, Sir H. M. Elliot, *The Mohammedan period as described by its own historians.* Cf. U1211b. 6, Sir W. W. Hunter, *From the first European settlements to the founding of the English East India Company.* Cf. U1243b. 7, id., *The European struggle for Indian supremacy in the seventeenth century.* Cf. U1243b. 8, Sir Alfred C. Lyall, *From the close of the seventeenth century to the present time.* Cf. U1242d. 9, A. V. W. Jackson, *Historic accounts of India by foreign travellers, classic, oriental and occidental.*]

An edition *de luxe,* limited to one thousand copies, related to other and previous works in various ways, partly indicated above. In general they are abridged reprints of standard works, with some new matter, usually as appendixes. The last volume had not appeared independently before. The editor of the series and the writers of the several volumes form a group of unusual authoritative strength for the fields covered.

WHA

INDIA: ANCIENT AND MOHAMMEDAN PERIODS

U1201a **Rapson, Edward J.** *Ancient India, from the earliest times to the first century, A.D.* Cambridge (Eng.), 1914.

b **Smith, Vincent A.** *Early history of India from 600 B.C. to the Muhammedan conquest including the invasion of Alexander the Great.* 1904. 4th ed., rev. by S. M. Edwardes, Oxford, 1924. (Bibliography.)

c Havell, Ernest B. *History of Aryan rule in India from the earliest times to the death of Akbar.* N. Y. (1918).

a. Best brief popular account. Review, *Calcutta Rev.*, n.s. 3: 129, Jan. 1925. *b.* Standard history of the whole pre-Mohammedan period—careful, accurate, and scholarly. (U1122) *Cambridge history of India* will cover the ground in greater detail, but will not supersede this work, which is also included in (U1123). Review, G. M. Bolling, *A.H.R.*, 11: 121, Oct. 1905.   GMD
c. Especially valuable as mediating between the political and cultural history of India and so preparing the mind for a more adequate appreciation of the profound problems inherent in the varied 'situations' in that land and population. Review, *Asiatic Rev.*, n.s. 15: 459, July 1919.   WHA

U1202a Dutt, Romesh Chunder. *History of civilization in ancient India, based on Sanscrit literature.* 3 v. Calcutta, 1889–90; 2 v., London, 1893.

b Davids, T. W. Rhys. *Buddhist India.* N. Y., 1903. [Story of the nations.]

c Aiyangar, S. Krishna. *Ancient India.* 1911. London, 1913.

d Banerjee, Gauranga Nath. *Hellenism in ancient India.* 1919. 2nd rev. and enl. ed., Calcutta, 1920. (Bibliographies.)

a. Popular account of Indian civilization; needing corrections, but valuable chiefly for its effort to depict the social background. Review, *Asiatic Quar. Rev.*, n.s. 8: 221, July 1894. *b.* Description of social, political, and religious conditions in early India (sixth and fifth centuries, B.C.), as portrayed in the Buddhist books. Picture very different from that given in the contemporary Brahman books and therefore of the greatest importance. It probably errs in dating some of the Buddhist material too early. Review, G. M. Bolling, *A.H.R.*, 10: 136, Oct. 1904.   GMD
c. Collection of papers, including lectures dealing with the early history of India. Most of the contents have been rightly called 'rather materials for history than history itself.' These enter the realm of history, chronology and literature. Chapter on the history and government of the Cholas, a medieval dynasty, is considered by the writer of the Introduction as an especially valuable contribution. Review, *Asiatic Rev.*, n.s. 1: 416, Apr. 1913. *d.* Primarily a study of the Hellenistic influence upon the art of ancient India. Review, P. M. Oursel, *Rev. Hist.*, 139: 124, Jan.-Feb. 1922.   WHA

U1203a Vaidya, Chintāmana V. *Epic India.* Bombay, 1907.

b Rawlinson, Hugh G. *Indian historical studies.* London and N. Y., 1913.

c —— *Intercourse between India and the western world from the earliest times to the fall of Rome.* 1916. 2nd ed., Cambridge (Eng.), 1926. (Bibliography.)

d Waley, Adolf. *Pageant of India.* London, 1927.

a. Description of the social, political, intellectual and religious conditions of India as described in the two great epics, the Mahabharata and the Ramayana (B.C. 400 to A.D. 400). Not sufficiently critical, but gives much which is not available elsewhere.   GMD
b. Most of the papers collected here present phases of ancient conditions, but a few treat medieval and later periods of Indian life. Review, *Asiatic Rev.*, n.s. 3: 129, Jan. 1914; F. Edgerton, *A.H.R.*, 19: 579, Apr. 1914.   WHA

c. Written from original sources most of which are available in M'Crindle's six volumes of translations, (U1062), from the Greek and Roman writers relating to India. Review, *A.H.R., 22*: 620, Apr. 1917.   GMD

d. Graphic and vivid narrative of India from nomadic days to the death of Aurangzeb. Concerned primarily with the conflicts among the rulers of India and their rivals. Review, *E.H.R., 43*: 465, July 1928.   WHA

U1204a Ketkar, Shridhar V. *History of caste in India; evidence of the laws of Manu on the social conditions in India during the third century A.D., interpreted and examined, with an appendix on radical defects of ethnology.* Ithaca, N. Y., 1909.

b —— *Essay on Hinduism, its formation and future, illustrating the laws of social evolution as reflected in the history of the formation of Hindu community.* London, 1911.

c Upendranatha Ghosal. *History of Hindu political theories. From the earliest times to the end of the first quarter of the seventeenth century A.D.* London and Calcutta, 1923.

a. Scholarly monograph by a Hindu on the laws of Manu which 'enjoy a greater prestige in India and are regarded as authoritative on the matter of caste.' He dates this work in the third century A.D. and incidentally furnishes much information on the general questions of caste and its history. *b.* Sociological study of the relation between caste and Hinduism, with constant reference to the differing character of Christianity and Mohammedanism. Concludes that caste is not an indispensable factor in Hinduism, and that Hinduism really expresses better than Christianity or Mohammedanism the cosmopolitanism toward which the world is advancing. Review, *Asiatic Quar. Rev.*, 3rd series, 34: 204, July 1912.   GMD

c. Study of the ancient and medieval literature of India to ascertain the fundamental theories of government therein expressed. Review, F. Edgerton, *A.H.R., 29*: 267, Jan. 1924.   WHA

U1205a Law, Narendra Nath. *Aspects of ancient Indian polity.* Oxford, 1921.

b Majumdar, Ramesh Chandra. *Corporate life in ancient India.* Calcutta, 1918. 2nd rev. and enl. ed., Poona, 1922.

c Banerjea, Pramathanath. *Public administration in ancient India.* London and N. Y., 1916.

d Mookerji, Radhakumud. *Local government in ancient India.* 1919. 2nd rev. and enl. ed., Oxford, 1921.

e Dutt, Binode Behari. *Town planning in ancient India.* Calcutta, 1925.

f Viswanatha, S. V. *International law in ancient India.* Bombay, London and N. Y., 1925.

Group of monographic studies in political science, the product of the interest of natives of India, trained in western scientific methods, in historical genetics. *a.* Although recognizing various forms and types of states, this study generally keeps close to the regal organization and the close relation in ancient India between religion and the state. *b.* First edition was doctoral dissertation which has been considerably revised and expanded. The corporate activities are traced in economic, political, religious and social life. Review, V. A. Smith, *E.H.R., 35*: 150, Jan. 1920. *c.* Doctoral dissertation setting forth the main facts as to the administrative system of ancient India, primarily from B.C. 500 to A.D. 500. *d.* While apparently dealing with a more restricted interest than *c,* this work deals with institutions that are closer to the life of the people and thus more reflective of the democratic principle. Review, E. J. Rapson, *E.H.R.*, 35: 260, Apr. 1920. *e*. As India is preëminently a land of villages, a study of the historical bases for village reconstruction possesses practical as well as scholarly value. Review, P. Geddes, *Asiatic Rev.*, n.s. 22: 505, July 1926. *f*. Study of the body of custom operative in the relations between states in ancient India.   WHA

U1211a **Elliot, Sir Henry M.** *Bibliographical index of the historians of Muhammedan India.* v. 1, *General histories.* Calcutta, 1849.

   b ———— *History of India, as told by its own historians. The Muhammadan period.* Ed. by John Dowson. 8 v., London, 1867–77.

   c **Bayley, Sir Edward C.** *History of India as told by its own historians. The local Muhammadan dynasties. Gujarat.* London, 1886.

a and *b*. For these works we may best quote from (U1102c) V. A. Smith, *Oxford student's history of India*, p. 109; 'The best view of Muhammadan sources of Indian history. . . . The editors were pioneers in the subject and naturally could not attain perfection, especially in the earlier volumes, but the errors in detail are as nothing compared with the benefits conferred on students by such a library of translations.' *c*. History, supplementary to b, of one of the independent Mohammedan monarchies of the medieval period.   WHA

U1212a **Manucci, Niccolo.** *General history of the Mogul empire, from its foundation by Tamerlane to the late emperor Orangzeb.* London, 1709. Tr. from the French of F. Catrou's version of *Storia do Mogor en tres partes.*

   b ———— *Storia do Mogor; or, Mogul India, 1653–1708.* Tr. with introduction and notes, by William Irvine. 4 v. London, 1907–08. [Indian text series.] (Bibliography.)

   c ———— *A Pepys of Mogul India, 1653–1708.* London, 1913.

   d **Irvine, William.** *Later Mughals.* Ed. and v. 2 augmented by J. Sarkar. 2 v., Calcutta, 1921–22.

   e **Kennedy, Pringle.** *History of the great Moghuls; or, A history of the badshahate of Delhi from 1398 A.D. to 1739, with an introduction concerning the Mongols and Moghuls of central Asia.* 2 v. Calcutta, 1905–11.

   f **Erskine, William.** *History of India under the two first sovereigns of the house of Taimur, Báber and Humáyun.* 2 v. London, 1854.

a and *b*. Form one of the most important sources for our knowledge of this period of Indian history and throw much light upon the Mogul empire. Review of *b*, v. 1 and 2, *Asiatic Quar. Rev.*, 3rd ser., 25: 188, Jan. 1908. *c*. Abridgment of *b*, limited chiefly to such portions as represent Manucci's own observations. Introduction to *b* gives the relations between Catrou's work and Manucci's manuscript. Review, *Asiatic Rev.*, n.s. 3: 266, Feb. 1914. *d*. Death of author cut this history of the Mogul empire off at about 1738, so it covers only about three decades instead of approximately the entire eighteenth century as planned. Will be more serviceable to critical writers in the future than to the average reader. Review, *E.H.R.*, 37: 448, July 1922; 38: 305, Apr. 1923. *e*. Sub-title more accurately presents the scope of this work, which the writer planned for those not particularly informed in Indian history. It includes the period of Baber, Akbar, Jahangir and Aurangzeb. Part 1 is an especially useful survey in about one hundred pages of Mongol history in central Asia. *f*. Covers in much detail the period from 1494 to 1596. Few if any of the previous workers in this period of Indian history were as well equipped as Erskine in language and in acquaintance with the source material.   WHA

U1213a Lane-Poole, Stanley. *Mediæval India under Mohammedan rule, 712–1764.* N. Y., 1903. [Story of the nations.]

  b Vaidya, Chintāmana V. *History of mediæval Hindu India.* 3 v. Poona, 1921–26.

  c Prasad, Ishwari. *History of medieval India from 647 A.D. to the Mughal conquest.* Allahabad, 1925.

  d Sarkar, Jadumath. *History of Aurangzib, based on original sources.* Calcutta, 1912. Reissue, 4 v., London and N. Y., 1920.

  a. Good account of Muslim India treated through the lives of its great rulers; emphasizes military affairs and building; many illustrations of coins and architecture. Review, F. W. Williams, *A.H.R.,* 9: 139, Oct. 1903.   JEW
  b. Comprehensive survey of the history of India from the seventh to the twelfth century inclusive, with detailed account of the very confusing period between A.D. 600 and 800. Constant criticism of its inferences is necessary, as it has an anti-Buddhist bias.   GMD
  c. Carries the history three centuries further than does *b,* and also is better adapted for use by those not already somewhat well informed, although it is in no sense an elementary work. Review, F. Edgerton, *A.H.R.,* 31: 566, Apr. 1926.
  d. Much more a history of this ruler's career and of India in his time than a biography.   WHA

U1214a Aiyangar, S. Krishna. *South India and her Muhammadan invaders.* Oxford, 1921.

  b Oaten, Edward F. *European travellers in India during the fifteenth, sixteenth and seventeenth centuries.* London, 1909. (Bibliography.)

  a. Six lectures at the University of Madras on the condition of southern India on the eve of the Mohammedan invasion. Review, G. C. O. Haas, *A.H.R.,* 27: 825, July 1922. *b.* Includes some material relating to travelers who themselves left no account of their travels as such and considerable material from men whose writings are almost basic for an understanding of medieval India. Review, E. H. Parker, *Asiatic Quar. Rev.,* 3rd series, 34: 196, July 1912.   WHA

INDIA: PORTUGUESE AND FRENCH PERIODS

U1221a Whiteway, Richard S. *Rise of the Portuguese power in India, 1497–1550.* Westminster, 1899.

  b Campos, J. J. A. *History of the Portuguese in Bengal.* Calcutta and London, 1919.

  Relatively brief, somewhat critical sketches of the Portuguese power in India, largely political in their interest.   WHA

U1222a Alboquerque, Afonso. *Commentaries of the great Afonso Dalboquerque, second viceroy of India.* 4 v. London, 1875–84. Tr. with notes and introduction, by Walter de Gray Birch, from the Portuguese edition of 1774 of *Commentarios do grande Afonso Dalbuquerque.* Lisboa, 1774. [Hakluyt Society.]

  b Barros, Joao de. *Geschichte der Entdeckungen und Eroberungen der Portugiesen im Orient, vom Jahr 1415 bis 1534.* 5 v. Braunschweig, 1821. Tr. by D. W. Soltau from the Portuguese. Lisbon, 1552–1615.

c Biker, Julio F. J. *Collecçao de tradados e concertos de pazes que o Estado da India Portuguesa fez com os Reis e Senhores com quem teve relaçoes nas partes da Asia e Africa Oriental desde o principio da conquista a te seculo XVIII.* 14 v. Lisboa, 1881–87.

a. Forms not only the main source for the biography of Dalbuquerque but also for our knowledge of the beginnings of the development of Portuguese power in India until it was well established in Goa. *b.* German translation of the classic Portuguese history of their activities in the Orient in the fifteenth and sixteenth centuries. *c.* Extensive collections of treaties and agreements on the part of the Portuguese government in India from the fifteenth to the eighteenth century.

WHA

U1231 *Catalogue des manuscrits des anciennes archives de l'Inde française.* 2 v. (1922) 2nd ed., Paris, 1926.

Important source of information concerning French colonial interests centering at Pondichéry, as it is a calendar of the documents as well as a catalogue. It extends from 1690 through the Napoleonic period.   WHA

U1232a Castonnet des Fosses, Henri. *L'Inde française avant Dupleix.* Paris, 1887. [La France dans l'Extrême Orient.]

  b Weber, Henry. *La compagnie française des Indes (1604–1875).* Paris, 1904. (Bibliography.)

  c Kaeppelin, Paul. *La compagnie des Indes Orientales et François Martin.* Paris, 1908. [Les origines de l'Inde française.]

Scholarly works based largely on archival material, dealing primarily with the history of the company and its commercial activities rather than with the political aspects of the enterprise. Relative scope is indicated in the titles, but *c* is by far the most extended work. Review of *c*, *Rev. Hist.*, 101: 107, May-June 1909.

GMD

U1233a Malleson, George B. *History of the French in India, from the founding of Pondichery.* 1868. 2nd rev. ed., London, 1893; reissue, Edinburgh, 1909.

  b —— *Final French struggle in India.* 1878. 2nd ed., London, 1884.

  c —— *Decisive battles of India, from 1746 to 1849 inclusive.* 1883. 4th ed., London, 1888.

  d Rapson, Edward J. *Struggle between England and France for supremacy in India.* London, 1887.

  e Dodwell, Henry. *Dupleix and Clive; the beginning of empire.* London, 1920. (Bibliography.)

  f Martineau, Alfred A. *Dupleix et l'Inde française.* Paris, 1920.

a, b, and *c.* Malleson is the standard English authority on Dupleix and the French side of the struggle for India. His books are based on a fair amount of contemporary material, mostly printed. He is rather detailed on military operations and political developments in India, not so full on the commercial activities of the Companies or on the European background. Review of *b*, *Rev. Hist.*, 10: 150, May-June 1879.   GMD

d. Admirable brief sketch of the rivalry of these powers for the control of India with analyses of their policies and of the causes underlying the final outcome of the struggle. Review, *Rev. Hist.*, 36: 463, Mar.-Apr. 1888.   WHA

e. Based on Madras, Bengal and India Office manuscripts; covers 1740–67, traces

English indebtedness to French for imperialistic ideas and methods; corrects Malleson and other earlier writers. Best account of Anglo-French rivalry in India at present available, but written from customary Anglo-Indian point of view.

GMD

f. Martineau, a former governor in French India, uses much documentary material previously unexploited. This volume covers the life of Dupleix to 1741 and two future volumes will complete the study. Review, G. Pagès, *Rev. Hist.,* 142:73, Jan.-Feb. 1923. WHA

INDIA: BRITISH PERIOD

U1241 **Thornton, Edward.** *History of the British empire in India.* 6 v. London, 1841–45; 2nd ed. of v. I, London, 1858.

Thornton wrote with personal knowledge gained as an official in India; made no attempt to display his learning, literary skill or prejudices; commenced his account almost abruptly at 1740 and closed it with Ellenborough's recall, 1844.

GMD

U1242a **Roberts, Paul E.** *History of British India under the company and the crown.* Oxford, 1923. (Earlier, *India,* 2 v., Oxford, 1916–20; originally v. 7, pts. 1 and 2 of (K303) C. Lucas, *Historical geography of the British dependencies.*)

   b. **Frazer, Robert W.** *British India.* 1897. 2nd ed., N. Y., 1898. [Story of the nations.]

   c **Innes, Arthur D.** *Short history of the British in India.* London, 1902. (Bibliography.)

   d **Lyall, Sir Alfred C.** *Rise and expansion of the British dominion in India.* 1893. 5th rev. ed., London, 1910.

a. Never really a contribution to historical geography, as its original association suggests, this work, based largely upon documentary materials, is one of the most reliable accounts for the whole period of British rule up to its publication. Review of pt. 1, *Asiatic Rev.,* n.s. 11:234, Feb. 1917; of pt. 2, *ibid.,* 17:549, July 1921. *b.* Intended as a popular account in a much-read series, but does not reach the scholarly standard of *c,* which is thoroughly sound though unpretentious. Review of *b, A.H.R.,* 3:388, Jan. 1898. *d.* Lyall's masterly essay extended to 1849 in the first edition, but was continued to 1907 in the fifth. His pride in the British achievement is unconcealed. He was himself one of the most eminent British civilians in India in his generation. Review, *Asiatic Quar. Rev.,* n.s. 5:528, Apr. 1893. GMD

1243a **Elphinstone, Mountstuart.** *Rise of the British power in the east.* London, 1887.

   b **Hunter, Sir William W.** *History of British India.* (v. 2 completed and ed. by P. E. Roberts.) 2 v. London and N. Y., 1899–1900.

   c **Rawlinson, Hugh G.** *British beginnings in western India, 1579–1657.* Oxford, 1920.

   d **Basu, B. D.** *Rise of the Christian power in India.* 5 v. and Index. Calcutta, 1923.

   e **Tilby, A. Wyatt.** *British India, 1600–1828.* 1908. 2nd rev. ed., Boston, 1911. [English people overseas.] (K304, v. 2.)

a. This posthumous fragment covers some points well, but does not extend beyond the close of the struggle with France in 1763. *b.* Incomplete work, extending only to 1708, but a master-piece by a competent hand, done from the sources, and without a rival for the period covered. Review, *Asiatic Quar. Rev.*, 3rd ser., 8: 220, July 1899; 11: 200, Jan. 1901.   GMD

c. Study from the sources of one episode in the early history, the establishment of the British factory at Surat. Review, W. C. Abbott, *A.H.R.*, 27: 144, Oct. 1921. *d.* The 'Christian Power' is the British governmental system as imposed upon India. Rather characteristic exposition, from the anti-British point of view, of the history of India in the period of British domination through the end of the East India Company's rule. *e.* Readable summary of the development of British interest and control of India through the Napoleonic period. Review, A. L. P. Dennis, *A.H.R.*, 18: 358, Jan. 1913.   WHA

U1251a Foster, William, ed. *Early travels in India, 1583-1619.* London, 1921. (Bibliography.)

b Wheeler, James Talboys. *Early records of British India; a history of the English settlements in India.* London, 1878.

c Foster, Sir William, ed. *Embassy of Sir Thomas Roe to India, 1615-19, as narrated in his journal and correspondence.* 1899. Rev. ed., London, 1926. [Hakluyt Society.] (Bibliography.)

a. Original narratives of seven English travelers into India during the reigns of Akbar and Jahangir—Fitch, Muldenhall, Hawkins, Finch, Withington, Coryat and Terry—with valuable introductions and notes. Review, W. C. Abbott, *A.H.R.*, 27: 296, Jan. 1922. *b.* Narrative history from 1600 to 1700 built upon records, accounts of early travelers, and various documents which are represented by copious extracts. *c.* The student of Indian history may well tarry in this vestibule at the British entrance with so competent a guide as Sir William. The new edition omits a bit of relatively unimportant material and adds some of significance, chiefly letters. Review, *E.H.R.*, 43: 152, Jan. 1928.   WHA

U1252 Dutt, Romesh C. *Economic history of British India.* 2 v. 1902. 4th ed., London, 1916.

By former native member of civil service and of Bengal legislative council. While approving in general British rule in India, he criticizes its economic policy for narrowing the sources of national wealth, for destroying or restricting native manufactures, and for excessive and erratic land taxes; for draining instead of developing the wealth of the country.   GMD

U1253a Stevens, Henry. *Dawn of British trade to the East Indies as recorded in the court minutes of the East India company, 1599-1603; with introduction by Sir G. Birdwood.* London, 1886.

b Birdwood, Sir George and **Foster, William**, etc. *(First letter book.) Register of letters &c. of the Governor and company of merchants trading into the East Indies, 1600-1619.* London, 1893.

c Sainsbury, W. Noel, ed. *Calendars of state papers, colonial series, East Indies, China, Japan, and Persia,* 1513-1634. 5 v. London, 1862-92.

d Danvers, F. C., and **Foster, William**, eds. *Letters received by the East India company from its servants in the East, 1602-1617.* London, 1896-1902.

e Sainsbury, Ethel Bruce, ed. *Calendar of the court minutes, etc., of the East India company, 1635-67.* 7 v. Oxford, 1907-25.

f Foster, William, ed. *English factories in India; a calendar of documents in the India office, British museum and public record office (1618-69).* 13 v. Oxford, 1906-27.

g East India Company. *Collection of treaties and engagements with the native princes and states of Asia concluded, on behalf of the East India company, by the British governments in India; . . . also copies of sunnuds, or grants, of certain privileges and immunities to the East India company, by the Mogul, and other native princes of Hindustan, with index.* London, 1812.

Excellently prepared collections of fundamentally important original documents or abstracts of them. Much of the material in *c* is better presented in the other collections, especially in *d* and *e*. The full introductions to the several volumes taken together furnish the most complete contribution yet made to the narrative history of the East India Company for the period prior to 1670. Reviews of *e* and *f* by A. L. P. Dennis in *A.H.R.*, with a few exceptions indicated by [ ], as follows: *e.* (1635–39) 13: 856, July 1908; (1640–43) 16: 607, Apr. 1911; (1644–49) 17: 819, July 1912; (1650–54) 20: 844, July 1915; (1655–59) 23: 891, July 1918; (1664–67) 31: 313, Jan. 1926. *f.* (1618–21) 12: 881, July 1907; (1622–23) 14: 380, Jan. 1909; (1624–29) 15: 135, Oct. 1909; (1630–33) 16: 605, Apr. 1911; (1634–36) [*Asiatic Quar. Rev.*, 3rd ser., 32: 405, Oct. 1911; (1637–41) *ibid.* 34: 426, Oct. 1912]; (1642–45) 19: 395, Jan. 1914; (1646–50) 20: 878, July 1915; (1651–54) 21: 793, July 1916; (1655–60) [W. C. Abbott] 27: 296, Jan. 1922; (1661–64) 29: 546, Apr. 1924; (1665–67) 31: 572, Apr. 1926; (1668–69) [P. E. Roberts, *E.H.R.*, 43: 114, Jan. 1928].   GMD

U1254a Willson, Beckles. *Ledger and sword or the honourable company of merchants of England trading to the East Indies.* (*1599–1874*). 2 v. London and N. Y., 1903.

b Foster, William. *The East India house. Its history and associations.* London, 1924.

c —— *John company.* London, 1926.

a. Popular account of the history of the East India Company; the human interest predominates. The material presented after the accession of Victoria is very scant. *b* and *c*. Interesting accounts of the London headquarters of the Company, the personnel employed there—e.g., Charles Lamb, James and John Stuart Mill—with miscellaneous data vitalizing the routine of this great business enterprise. Review of *b*, H. Das, *Asiatic Rev.*, n.s. 20: 359, Apr. 1924.   WHA

U1261 Busteed, Henry E. *Echoes from old Calcutta, being chiefly reminiscences of the days of Warren. Hastings, Francis, and Impey.* 1882. 4th ed., Calcutta and London, 1908.

Author has tried to give historically accurate pictures of Anglo-Indian life in Calcutta in the latter half of the eighteenth century. One essay deals with the Black Hole. Each succeeding edition of this interesting book is marked with numerous additions and improvements. Review, W. K. Firminger, *Calcutta Rev.*, 127: 615, Oct. 1908.   GMD

U1271a Kaye, Sir John W. *History of. the Sepoy war in India, 1857–1858.* 3 v. London, 1864–76.

b Malleson, George B. *Indian mutiny of. 1857.* 3 v. 1878–90. 9th ed., London, 1896.

c Holmes, Thomas R. E. *History of the Indian mutiny.* 1883. 5th rev. and enl. ed., London, 1898.

d Forrest, George W. *History of the Indian mutiny.* 3 v. Edinburgh, 1904–12.

a. Based on a careful use of private sources. Full account of the Sepoy army, the mutiny and its spread, the campaign and the character of individual Englishmen. Indispensable to the military student. Review, *Rev. Hist.,* 3 : 154, Jan.-Feb. 1877. *b.* Continuation of *a,* which was left unfinished by Kaye. The completed work, which served as the standard history, was issued as Kaye and Malleson, *History of the Indian Mutiny,* 6 v., 1896. This is a blending of Malleson's three volumes of continuation with Kaye's first two volumes. *c.* Good brief account, partly narrative, of chief campaigns and events, largely interpretative of problems and personalities. Based partly on Kaye and Malleson, partly on intimate private and public sources. Good maps. Review, *Asiatic Quar. Rev.,* 3rd ser., 5 : 440, Apr. 1898. *d.* Narration, fully and simply told, of military campaigns, heroic deeds and persons, gathered from official despatches, fortified by private letters and diaries of the actors in the drama. Good maps.   WTR

U1272a Hunter, Sir William W. *India of the queen and other essays.* London, 1903.

b Fraser, Lovat. *India under Curzon & after.* London, 1911.

a. Five essays on the India of the queen and four on England's work in India. Thoughtful and valuable contribution, combining strong convictions of the necessity and justice of England's rule in India with warm sympathy for the native interests and aspirations. Review, *Asiatic Quar. Rev.,* 3rd ser., 16 : 200, July 1903.   GMD
b. Eulogistic but useful review of the chief events and results of Lord Curzon's Viceroyalty by the editor, at the time, of *The Times of India.* Review, *Pol. Sci. Quar.,* 31 : 188, March 1916.   HRS

U1301 Cunningham, Joseph D. *History of the Sikhs, from the origin of the nation to the battles of the Sutlej.* 1849. Rev. ed., London and N. Y., 1918. (Bibliography.)

Work of a British official long resident and in contact with the people whose history he studied and wrote. Devotes half the space to the period from the rise of Ranjit Singh to the close of the first Sikh war, 1809–46. Appendixes and, in the second edition, introduction and notes by Crooke give added value. Review, W. H. Hutton, *Asiatic Rev.,* n.s. 15 : 652, Oct. 1919.   WHA

U1302a Duff, James C. Grant. *History of the Mahrattas.* 3 v., 1826. 2nd rev. ed., with introduction by S. M. .Edwardes, 2 v., London, 1921. (Bibliography.)

b Kincaid, Charles A., and **Parasnis, Rao B. D. B.** *History of the Maratha people.* 3 v. London and N. Y., 1918–25.

a. By a British official of long residence in India. Practically begins with Sivaji, while the second volume deals exclusively with the period of the three Maratha wars with the British, 1772–1819. Review, *Calcutta Rev.,* 135 : 442, Oct. 1912. *b.* Although written by Kincaid, the assistance of his collaborator, through his learning and his collection of materials for the history, contributes greatly to the value of this work. More favorable to Sivaji than was *a.* Edwardes, in his introduction to the revised edition of *a,* thinks Duff's position has been vindicated by later research. Review of *b,* P. E. Roberts, *E.H.R.,* 34 : 597, Oct. 1919; 39 : 285, Apr. 1924; 41 : 604, Oct. 1926.   GMD, WHA

U1303a Gribble, James D. B.   *History of the Deccan.*   2 v.   London, 1896–1924. (v. 2 ed. and finished by Mrs. M. Pendlebury.)

b Aiyer, K. V. Subrahmanya.   *Historical sketches of ancient Dekhan.* Madras, 1917.

c Tod, James.   *Annals and antiquities of Rajasthan, or the central and western Rajput states of India.*   1829–32.   2nd ed., with introduction and notes, by W. Crooke.   3 v.   London and N. Y., 1920.   (Bibliography.)

d Landon, Perceval.   *Nepal.*   2 v.   London, 1928.

a. Long interval between the two volumes.   Based primarily upon Elliot and Dowson, (U1211*b*), but makes no adequate use of the material offered by epigraphy, numismatics, and manuscript histories of the dynasties now available for the critical student.   The author's daughter completed the work which is brought down to 1883.   *b.* Treats the early and medieval periods, the last of its five books being an exposition of the political, social and economic organization.

WHA

c. Gives the author's personal observations of the land, people, customs, etc., recording the annals of Mewar, Marwar, Bikaner, Jaisalmer, Amber, and Haravati, which are chiefly valuable for the two centuries preceding 1820.   Review, *Rev. Hist.*, 118: 162, Jan.-Feb. 1915.

GMD

d. Fascinating account in almost sumptuous form of this north Indian region extending from Mount Everest along the southern slopes of the Himalayas.   Review, *Asiatica*, 1: 283, Aug.-Oct. 1928.

WHA

INDIA: CEYLON

U1341a *Ceylon handbook & directory and compendium of useful information.* Colombo, 1868 ff.

b Tennent, Sir James Emerson.   *Ceylon.   An account of the island physical, historical, and topographical with notices of its natural history, antiquities and productions.*   2 v.   London, 1859.

a. Useful reference work, under varying titles, abounding with statistics and current facts; considerable history presented in tabular form.   *b.* More satisfactory as a description of physical factors than in its historical data, as these latter are not subjected to adequate critical testings.

WHA

U1342a Pieris, Paulus E.   *Ceylon: the Portuguese era, being a history of the island for the period 1505–1658.*   2 v.   Colombo, 1913.   (Bibliography.) [Rewritten, much condensed, and published as *Ceylon and the Portuguese, 1505–1658*.   Tellippalai, Ceylon, 1920.]

b ——— *Ceylon and the Hollanders, 1658–1796.*   Tellippalai, Ceylon, 1918. (Bibliography.)

c ———, and **Fitzler, M. A. H.**   *Ceylon and Portugal.*   [Pt. 1, *Kings and Christians, 1539–1552*.]   From the original documents at Lisbon.   Leipzig, 1927.

Probably no one has devoted himself more assiduously to the study of the Portuguese in Ceylon than has Pieris, who has given the results of his researches in these books.   *a* and *b.* Form a consecutive history of Ceylon for approximately three centuries, *a,* being based upon an unpublished history by Queiroz (1617–88) who was Provincial of the Jesuits at Goa.   Review of *a,* E. W. Hopkins, *A.H.R.*, 27: 287, Jan. 1922; of *b,* C. Day, *A.H.R.*, 25: 318, Jan. 1920.   *c.* Source book, giving in English translation many illuminating documents.

WHA

INDIA: BURMA

U1351a Hall, Daniel G. E. *Early English intercourse with Burma (1587–1743).* London and N. Y., 1928. (Bibliography.)

b Cocks, Samuel W. *Short history of Burma.* London, 1910.

c Phayre, Sir Arthur Purves. *History of Burma, including Burma proper, Pegu, Taungu, Tenesserim, and Arakan, from the earliest times to the end of the first war with British India.* London, 1883.

d Harvey, Godfrey Eric. *History of Burma, from the earliest times to 10th March, 1824, the beginning of the English conquest.* London, 1925. (Bibliography.)

e Nisbet, John. *Burma under British rule—and before.* 2 v. Westminster, 1901.

a. Scholarly and interesting account of this early period, based on the best sources, which are used critically.   WHA

b. Cocks, who was in educational service in Burma, gives brief readable survey down to 1886, with half the book on the period after 1752. *c.* Phayre was British commissioner for many years. He has written a more scholarly but less readable book, of which the latter half deals with the years 1752–1826.   GMD

d. Far more scholarly work than the preceding, being based largely upon the inscriptions and Burmese chronicles. Review, *E.H.R.,* 41 : 476, July 1926.

WHA

e. Compilation of much descriptive material with brief historical introduction, but written with first-hand knowledge of an official. Review, *Asiatic Quar. Rev.,* 3rd ser., 14 : 421, Oct. 1902.   GMD

U1352a Ireland, Alleyne. *Province of Burma. Colonial administration in the Far East.* 2 v. N. Y., 1907. (Bibliography.)

b Marshall, Harry I. *The Karen people of Burma; a study in anthropology and ethnology.* Columbus, O., 1922. (Bibliography.)

a. Critical yet readable account giving full attention to economic matters and the native states as well as to the administrative system which is the central theme of his study; contains useful appendixes of documents and statistics. Probably the most thorough and scientific account of a European colony in Asia yet produced; apparently chose Burma as ideal subject for such a masterly investigation.   GMD

b. Systematic and authoritative study by a missionary who gathered his materials and observations during seventeen years' residence among this people. The distribution, origin, characteristics, language, dress, the domestic, social and religious life, and the recent progress of the Karen are fully discussed. Footnotes, numerous pictures and a glossary add to the value of the work.   WHS

INDIA: POLITICAL AND ADMINISTRATIVE HISTORY

U1531a Forrest, George W. *Administration of Warren Hastings, 1772–1785.* Calcutta, 1892.

b Martin, Montgomery, ed. *Despatches, minutes, and correspondence of the Marquess Wellesley during his administration in India.* 5 v. London, 1836–37.

c Owen, Sidney J. *Selection from the despatches, treaties, and other papers of the Marquess Wellesley during his government of India.* Oxford, 1877.

d Roberts, Paul E. *India under Wellesley.* London, 1929.

e Colchester, Reginald C. E. A. *History of the Indian administration of Lord Ellenborough.* London, 1874.

f Law, Sir Algernon, ed. *India under Lord Ellenborough.* London, 1926.

g Arnold, Sir Edwin. *Marquis of Dalhousie's administration of British India.* 2 v. London, 1862–65.

a. Reprint of the scholarly introduction to (U1063*a*). *b.* Contains little editorial addition. *c.* Bulk of volume is copious selections from the state papers, but preceded by surveys of Wellesley's administration by the editor and in the form of a 'memorandum' by the (later) Duke of Wellington. *d.* Both a narrative history and a consideration of imperial policy in a crucial period of England's relations with India. Review, R. G. Burton, *Saturday Review,* 148: 546, Nov. 9, 1929. *e.* Ellenborough's letters to the Queen and the correspondence of Ellenborough and the Duke of Wellington during the former's governor-generalship of India. *f.* Very recent study, much later than *e,* having the advantage over the earlier work not only in the greater wealth of available materials and in the advance of historical criticism, but also from the fact of fifty more years in the development of the British governmental policy itself. Review, *E.H.R.,* 43: 153, Jan. 1928. *g.* Review of the administration which closed the 'Hundred Years' of the East India Company's domination; deals particularly with the annexation of the Punjab and some other regions, and the relation of annexations and administration to the great Mutiny so soon to follow.   WHA

U1532a Campbell, Sir George. *Modern India: a sketch of the system of civil government.* London, 1852.

b Chesney, George. *Indian polity; a view of the system of administration in India.* 1868. 2nd rev. ed., London, 1870.

c Strachey, Sir John. *India. Its administration & progress.* 1888. 4th ed. rev. by Sir Thomas W. Holderness, London, 1911.

d Tupper, Charles Lewis. *Our Indian protectorate. An introduction to the study of the relations between the British government and its Indian feudatories.* London and N. Y., 1893.

a. Excellent work for the period just before the mutiny. *b.* After a resumé of the British in India, this describes in successive 'books' the constitution of the Indian government, the civil administration, the army, the public works and the financial system as they were two generations ago. Review, L. L. Price, *Econ. Jour.,* 5: 387, Sept. 1895. *c.* Originally a course of lectures delivered at the University of Cambridge, setting forth the governmental system in India, the successive editions have introduced the necessary changes in the exposition of the British administration at the times of issue. Review, *Asiatic Quar. Rev.,* 3rd ser., 16: 202, July 1903. *d.* By tracing the history of the Indian governmental institutions, as well as the history of the British administration, the writer sets forth what he considers the justification for the continuation of the dual control through the use of natives as well as the British system. Review, *Asiatic Quar. Rev.,* n.s. 6: 493, Oct. 1893.   WHA

U1533a Ilbert, Sir Courtenay P. *Government of India, being a digest of the statute law relating thereto.* 1898. 3rd ed., Oxford, 1915.

b Cross, Cecil M. P. *Development of self-government in India. 1858–1914.* Chicago, 1922. (Bibliography.)

   c Thakore, Balvantrai K. *Indian administration to the dawn of responsible government, 1765–1920.* Bombay, 1922.

   d Cotton, Sir Henry J. S. *New India; or, India in transition.* 1885. Rev. ed., London, 1907.

a. Comprises an historical introduction (which was revised and separately published as *The Government of India; a brief historical survey of parliamentary legislation relating to India,* Oxford, 1922), a summary of existing law, and a digest of statutory enactments relating to the government of India. Especially valuable for its judicial and legal material. Review, *Calcutta Rev.,* 3rd ser., 5: 197, Oct. 1922. *b.* Objective presentation of the experimentation in self-government in India from the transfer of the government to the Crown until the World War. The successive reform measures are presented and the result of their operation critically examined. Review, V. Lovett, *Asiatic Rev.,* n.s. 19: 345, Apr. 1923. *c.* Fair-minded in the presentation of the governmental history, its pro-Indian point of view predominates; yet its recognition of the existence of conflicting groups is something of a corrective. Review, *Asiatic Rev.,* n.s. 24: 165, Jan. 1928.

WHA

d. Thoughtful volume by a liberal Anglo-Indian treating sympathetically Indian problems and aspirations and suggesting the spirit which should guide England in relation to them.

GMD

U1534a Chirol, Sir Valentine. *Indian unrest.* London, 1910.

   b —— *India old and new.* London, 1921.

   c Macdonald, J. Ramsay. *Government of India.* London, 1919; N. Y., 1920.

   d Curtis, Lionel. *Papers relating to the application of the principle of dyarchy to the government of India.* Oxford, 1920.

a. Searching masterly analysis of the causes and consequences of Indian discontent by one who knows India thoroughly. *b.* The background of unrest and the influence of the World War on Indian reform are described impartially from a wealth of intimate knowledge. Review, C. H. VanTyne, *A.H.R.,* 28: 129, Oct. 1922.

WTR

c. Written by a leader of the British labor party who was soon to become prime minister, and put into final form after the Montagu-Chelmsford Report; chiefly important for its interpretation of Indian conditions from a point of view different from that of the Government. Review, *Asia,* 20: 822, Sept. 1920; B. K. Sarkar, *Pol. Sci. Quar.,* 35: 296, June 1920. *d.* Exposition of the Government of India Act of 1919, intended in part to assist the civil servants in the operation of the system set up by that Act. Its forms are quite varied, including letters, comments and memoranda, making a very comprehensive discussion of the principles of dyarchy and their application to India.

WHA

U1535a Lajpat, Raya. *Young India; an interpretation and a history of the nationalist movement from within.* N. Y., 1916.

   b —— *Political future of India.* N. Y., 1919.

   c Sultan Muhammad Shah, Aga Khan. *India in transition.* London and N. Y., 1918.

   d Banerjee, Debendra Nath. *Indian constitution and its actual working.* Bombay, London, N. Y., 1926.

a and *b.* Author is a prominent Indian long identified with the Indian national movement. As a fiery patriot he wrote these little books to justify the Indian cause before the court of world opinion. His consuming nationalism led him to do less than justice to British rule in India. The books are not sound history; they are valuable historical material. They reveal effectively the intense spirit and the ideals which actuate the extreme nationalist leaders. Review of *a*, *Dial*, 61: 318, Oct. 19, 1916.   WTR

c. The Aga Khan, a prominent Indian nobleman, is head of the Ismaili Mohammedans. His book, written just before the Montagu-Chelmsford Report and the new Government of India Act, is an acute, intelligent and valuable analysis of Indian conditions. A federalized India, with much more self-government but within the British Empire, is advocated. Review, W. Johnson, *Asiatic Rev.*, n.s. 14: 524, Oct. 1918.   GMD

d. Primarily an analysis of the governmental system as provided for under the several Government of India Acts, but with special attention to the system as set up by the Act of 1919. Review, *Calcutta Rev.*, 3rd ser., 20: 353, Aug. 1926.

WHA

U1536a Lovett, Sir Verney. *History of the Indian nationalist movement.* London, 1920.

    b Ilbert, Sir Courtenay P., and **Lord Meston.** *New constitution of India.* London, 1923. [Rhodes lectures, University of London, 1921–22.]

    c Craddock, Sir Reginald. *The dilemma in India.* London, 1929.

a. Written from observations during over thirty years in the Indian civil service, with strong convictions as to the beneficence of the British administration, but with copious quotations from Indian nationalists. *b.* Three lectures each by two especially able men, presenting the main features of the government of India as set up under the Act of 1919. *c.* Account, by a well-informed officer long in the Indian service, of the administration in the last few years and too much limited by that experience. Review, (London) *Times Lit. Suppl.*, p. 755, Oct. 3, 1929.

WHA

INDIA: ECONOMIC HISTORY

Considerable material relating to the economics of India, where this intertwines with politics, will be found in many previous items in this section, as U1041*a* and U1252.

U1571a Moreland, William H. *India at the death of Akbar, an economic study.* London and N. Y., 1920. (Bibliography.)

    b ——— *From Akbar to Aurangzeb; a study in Indian economic history.* London and N. Y., 1923.

a Very important historical inquiry into the basic conditions affecting human life in India at the beginning of the seventeenth century. *b.* Continuation of the study through the next half century. Review of *a* and *b*, P. E. Roberts, *E.H.R.*, 35: 455, July 1920; 39: 434, July 1924.   WHA

U1572a Morison, Sir Theodore. *Economic transition in India.* London, 1911.

    b Radhakamal Mukerjee. *Foundations of Indian economics.* London and N. Y., 1916.

    c Pillai, Padmanabha. *Economic conditions in India.* London, 1925.

a. Attractively written volume based upon the theses that India stands economically where Europe stood before the industrial changes of the nineteenth century, that in some centers the industrial revolution has already been accomplished, that further industrialism is to be desired and that India must seek capital abroad to reorganize her industry—a book comparatively free from partisanship in a highly controversial field. Review, J. M. Keynes, *Economic Journal*, 21 : 426, Sept. 1911. *b*. Valuable study of village industries, undertaken to prove that for the welfare of the masses the cottage and workshop industries should not be super-seded by the factory. Over-enthusiastic about the virtues of the village com-munity. Review, Sir James Douie, *Economic Journal*, 27 : 255, June 1917.   HRS

c. The *motif* of this book is stated as the study of 'the economic life of India with special reference to her industrial organization, and to take stock of the possibilities of developing Indian industries on modern lines.' It attempts to discover the precise nature of the organized industrial life of the past and the proper proportion of agriculture and manufactures. Review, *Asiatic Rev.*, n.s. 21 : 352, Apr. 1925.   WHA

U1573a Wadia, Pestonji A., and **Joshi, Gulabbhai N.** *Wealth of India.* London, 1925.

    b Trevaskis, Hugh Hennedy. *Land of the five rivers. An economic history of the Punjab from the earliest time to the year of grace 1890.* Oxford, 1928. (Bibliography.)

a. Account of the physical enviroment, population, social institutions, agricul-tural conditions, industries, etc., of India. *b*. Well-organized presentation of the main facts, subordinating the political to the economic history. Review, *Asiatic Rev.*, n.s. 24 : 506, July 1928; *E.H.R.*, 44 : 344, Apr. 1929.   WHA

U1574a Baden-Powell, Baden H. *Land-systems of British India, being a manual of the land-tenures and of the systems of land-revenue administration prevalent in the several provinces.* 3 v. Oxford, 1892.

    b —— *Short account of the land revenue and its administration in British India; with a sketch of the land tenure.* 1894. 2nd rev. ed. by T. W. Holderness, Oxford, 1907.

    c —— *Indian village community.* London and N. Y., 1896.

a. Standard work on this complex subject, which is presented with full measure of recognition of the historical conditions and forces which have been indissolubly merged with the economic problems. The author's fund of knowledge is put into more compact form in *b*, a very serviceable handbook. Review of *a*, *Asiatic Quar. Rev.*, n.s. 4 : 250, July 1892; of *b*, *ibid*. 3rd ser., 24 : 400, Oct. 1907. *c*. Study of the village community in its relation to the tribal and provincial organization; in many particulars it is also a study of land tenure.   WHA

U1575a Webb, Montague de P. *India and the empire. A consideration of the tariff problem.* London and N. Y., 1908.

    b Smith, H. B. Lees. *India and the tariff problem.* London, 1909.

    c Shah, N. J. *History of Indian tariffs.* Bombay and London, 1924.

a. Exposition of India as an economic factor in the British imperial system. Review, T. Morison, *Economic Journal*, 18 : 424, Sept. 1908. *b*. Consideration of the demand in India for preferential tariffs. *c*. Doctoral dissertation, setting forth at length the evolution of the governmental fiscal policy with special reference to tariffs.   WHA

U1581 Lyall, Sir Alfred C. *Asiatic studies.* 1882. New ed., 2 v., London, 1899.

Eleven essays, ten relating to India and dealing with social and economic as well as religious conditions, intended mostly for English readers; somewhat speculative as to the analogy between English dominion in Asia and the vanished empire of Rome.	SEB

U1582a Mitter, Dwarka Nath. *Position of woman in Hindu law.* Calcutta, 1913. (Bibliography.)

    b Mayo, Katherine. *Mother India.* N. Y., 1927.

    c Iyer, C. S. Ranga. *Father India. A reply to Mother India.* London, 1927.

    d Mukerji, Dhan Gopal. *Son of Mother India answers.* N. Y., 1928.

  a. Comprehensive work dealing with the status of woman in India; as it traces the various stages in the development of woman's place in society, its contribution is distinctly historical. *b.* Probably no other book on the life of India has been more provocative of controversy. On the one hand it has taken things out of their historical and sociological settings for observation and analysis, which has led to inferences, explicit or inevitable, and these have led to prejudiced conclusions. On the other hand it has exposed real evils, and when a spade has been used for individual or social brutality, it has not been alluded to merely as a certain implement used in agriculture. *c* and *d.* Replies to *b* from the Hindu point of view. Review of the controversy as well as of *b,* E. F. Rathbone, *Hibbert Journal,* 27 : 193, Jan. 1929. Review of *b,* L. F. R. Williams, *Asiatic Review,* n.s. 23 : 637, Oct. 1927; of *c,* P. P. Pillai, *ibid.,* 24 : 164, Jan. 1928; of *d,* H. K. Norton, *Saturday Review of Literature,* 5 : 430, Dec. 1, 1928.	WHA

INDIA: CULTURAL HISTORY

U1601a Barnett, Lionel. *Antiquities of India.* London, 1913.

    b Mitra, Panchanan. *Prehistoric India. Its place in the world's culture.* 1923. 2nd rev. and enl. ed., Calcutta, 1927.

    c Macdonell, Arthur Anthony. *India's past. A survey of her literatures, religions, languages and antiquities.* Oxford, 1927. (Bibliographies.)

  a. Following a brief history of India, with a convenient tabulated chronology to A.D. 1200, there is a study of the early social groups in their organization, the Vedic and the non-Vedic rituals and other elements in the primitive culture. Review, *Nation* (N. Y.), 99 : 440, Oct. 8, 1914. *b.* Contributions from Indian data to our knowledge of primitive Indian civilization. *c.* Useful introduction to Indian ancient civilization through its literature. Review, R. J. Deferrari, *Cath. Hist. Rev.,* 8 : 280, July 1928; H. Das, *Asiatic Rev.,* n.s. 23 : 692, Oct. 1927.	WHA

U1602a Law, Narendra N. *Promotion of learning in India during Muhammadan rule (by Muhammadans).* London and N. Y., 1916.

    **b —— ** *Promotion of learning in India by European settlers (up to about 1800 A.D.).* London and N. Y., 1915.

    c Mayhew, Arthur. *Education in India. A study of British educational policy in India, 1835–1920, and of its bearing on national life and problems in India to-day.* (London), 1926.

  a. Scholarly survey of the evidence for the development of education in India under Mohammedan influence. Review, E. W. Hopkins, *A.H.R.,* 23 : 136, Oct.

1917. *b.* Deals primarily with the introduction of European methods and institutions for education during the long period when there was little interest anywhere in general education. *c.* Survey and analysis of the educational problems and the attempts to solve them during the period, brought to an end in 1920, when the educational organization was a corporate part of the British administration.

WHA

U1621a Crooke, William. *Introduction to the religion and folklore of northern India.* Allahabad, 1894. 2nd ed., 2 v., 1896. New ed., 1 v., *Religion and folklore of northern India.* (Oxford), 1926. (Bibliography.)

  b Hopkins, Edward W. *Religions of India.* Boston, 1898. Reprint, 1902. (Bibliography.)

  c Pratt, James B. *India and its faiths.* Boston, 1915.

  a. Especially valuable as it points out the differences between the religion, customs and folklore of the peasantry and those of the Brahman priesthood. Review, N. M. Panzer, *Asiatic Rev.,* n.s. 22 : 510, July 1926.   WHA

  b. Comprehensive manual for students, conservatively interpreting the religious beliefs and literature of the peoples of India; an estimate of these religions; the origin and development of various theological and moral conceptions within them; and their relation to one another.   SEB

  c. Sympathetic study of the religions of India by an American professor of philosophy and competent student of the psychology of religion.   WHA

U1622a Bloomfield, Maurice. *Religion of the Veda.* N. Y., 1896.

  b Monier-Williams, Sir Monier. *Brahmanism and Hinduism; or religious thought and life in India, as based on the Veda and other sacred books of the Hindus.* 1887. 4th enl. and improved ed., London, 1891.

  **c ——— ** *Indian wisdom.* 1875. Rev. ed., London, 1893.

  d Davids, Thomas W. Rhys. *Lectures on the origin and growth of religion as illustrated by some points in the history of Indian Buddhism.* 3rd ed., London, 1897.

  e Macauliffe, Max A. *Sikh religion. Its gurus, sacred writings and authors.* 6 v. Oxford, 1909.

  a. Six lectures giving an introduction to the study of the Veda. Author opposes the view that the monotheistic tendency in Vedic religion is of Semitic origin and credits the priestly caste alone with the philosophy of the Upanishads. Review, *Nation* (N. Y.), 86 : 469, May 21, 1908.   EWH

  b and *c.* These approach the religious views through the literature, with one of the most competent of scholars as guide. Interest in *c* is philosophical and ethical as well as religious. Review of *c, Asiatic Quar. Rev.,* n.s. 6 : 248, July 1893.

  d. One of the standard works by a leading authority on the history of religion.

  e. Especially valuable for its translations from the sacred writings and for the biographical sketches of the Sikh gurus, saints and authors. Review, *Asiatic Quar. Rev.,* 3rd series, 28 : 201, July 1909.   WHA

U1623a Farquhar, John N. *Modern religious movements in India.* London, 1913.

  b Noble, Margaret E. (The Sister Nivedita.) *Footfalls of Indian history.* London and N. Y., 1915.

  c Lajpat Raya. *Arya Samaj; an account of its origin, doctrines and activities, with a biographical sketch of its founder.* London and N. Y., 1915.

a. Book of great value. Gives the only complete account of modern religious tendencies in India, tracing their growth and evaluating their results. *b.* Although not explicitly a work on religion, its religious interest is paramount; especially valuable as an interpreter of the relations between Indian religion in its expressional aspects and Indian culture. Review, *E.H.R.*, 30: 759, Oct. 1915. *c.* Account of one of the most widely known of the modern religious movements of India and of its founder. Review, *Asiatic Rev.*, n.s. 7: 346, Oct. 1915; E. P. Buffet, *E.H.R.*, 30: 574, July 1915.   WHA

U1641a **Launay, Adrien.** *Histoire des missions de l'Inde.* Paris, 1898. [Société des Missions étrangères.]

b **Capuchin Mission Unit.** *India and its mission.* London, 1923.

c **Richter, Julius.** *History of missions in India.* Edinburgh and London, (1908). Tr. by S. H. Moore from *Indische Missionsgeschichte,* Gütersloh, 1906.

d **Chatterton, Eyre.** *History of the church of England in India since the early days of the East India company.* London, 1924. (Bibliographies.)

a. Launay has been the historian *par excellence* of Roman Catholic missions in Asia. This great work presents that history for India from the negotiations in 1775, which led to the entrance of the *Missions étrangères* into India, to the proclamation of the hierarchy in 1887. The last volume consists of illustrations and valuable maps. *b.* Primarily a brief history of Roman Catholic missions in India. Admirable chapters on the country, its political history, the non-Christian religions, native manners and customs, education, literature and the arts, besides one on Protestant missions. *c.* Most comprehensive survey of the missionary history of India, Roman Catholic and Protestant. *d.* Account of the development of the Anglican missionary movement in India, from the time of chaplains in the factory of the East India Company to the time when an autonomous 'Church of India in communion with the Church of England' appeared about to arrive.   WHA

U1661a **Manning, Mrs.** [C. Speir.] *Ancient and medieval India.* 2 v. London, 1869.

b **Farquhar, John N.** *Outline of the religious literature of India.* London, 1920. (Bibliography.)

c **Frazer, Robert Watson.** *Literary history of India.* N. Y., 1898. New ed., London, 1920.

d **Winternitz, Moritz.** *Geschichte der indischen Litteratur.* 3 v. Leipzig, 1908–22.

a. Relatively early attempt to present in as simple form as the material permits considerable of the literature of ancient and modern India.   WHA
b. Brief history of Hindu religious literature, especially valuable for enumeration of modern works. Indispensable guide to the development of Hindu religious thought. Review, T. W. Arnold, *Asiatic Rev.*, n.s. 16: 717, Oct. 1920.   EWH
c. Most readable popular account, the best general introduction for the layman. Review, *Asiatic Quar. Rev.*, 3rd ser., 6: 202, July 1908. *d.* Only critical, detailed, scholarly account of Indian literature.   GMD

U1681a **Havell, Ernest B.** *Indian sculpture and painting.* 1908. Rev. ed., London, 1928.

b ———— *Ideals of Indian art.* London, 1911.

c ———— *Handbook of Indian art.* London, 1920.

a. Well illustrated presentation of both the ideals and the products, the technique and the cultural background of the art of India, showing that these are different from their western parallels. Review, *Asiatica,* 1 : 279, Aug.-Oct. 1928. *b* and *c.* Excellent introductions to the elements of Indian art, especially in their historical and religious relations. Review of *b,* F. W. Gookin, *Dial,* 52 : 277, Apr. 1, 1912; of *c, N. Y. Times Book Rev.,* 70 : 13, Feb. 13, 1921.   WHA

U1682a **Rao, T. A. Gopinatha.** *Elements of Hindu iconography.* 2 v. of 2 pts. each. Madras, 1914.

 b Foucher, Alfred. *Beginnings of Buddhist art and other essays in Indian and Central-Asian archæology.* Tr. from the French by L. A. and F. W. Thomas. Paris and London, 1917.

 c Blacker, J. F. *ABC of Indian art.* London, 1922.

a and *b.* Scholarly, scientific and comprehensive treatises of the subjects indicated in their titles. *c.* Popular guide for the leading centers where the products of Indian art are especially to be found.   WHA

INDIA: BIOGRAPHY

U1701 **Buckland, Charles E.** *Dictionary of Indian biography.* London, 1906. (Bibliography.)

Convenient reference work of over 2500 biographical sketches of individuals connected with the history and literature of India since about 1750 A.D. Review, *Asiatic Quar. Rev.,* 3rd ser., 22 : 205, July 1906.   WHA

U1702 **Hunter, Sir William W.,** ed. *Rulers of India.* 28 v. Oxford, 1890 ff. (a) V. A. Smith, *Asoka, the Buddhist emperor of India;* (b) Radhakumuda Mukhopadhyaya, *Harsha;* (c) S. Lane-Poole, *Babar;* (d) G. B. Malleson, *Akbar and the rise of the Mughal empire;* (e) W. W. Hunter, *Aurangzeb and the decay of the Mughal empire;* (f) H. M. Stephens, *Albuquerque;* (g) G. B. Malleson, *Dupleix and the struggle for India by the European nations;* (h) id., *Lord Clive and the establishment of the English in India;* (i) L. J. Trotter, *Warren Hastings and the founding of the British administration;* (j) H. G. Keene, *Madhu Rao Sindhia and the Hindu reconquest of India;* (k) L. B. Bowring, *Haidar Ali and Tipu Sultan and the struggle with the Musalman powers of the south;* (l) W. S. Setin-Karr, *The Marquess of Cornwallis and the consolidation of British rule;* (m) W. H. Hutton, *Marquess Wellesley;* (n) Sir J. F. G. Ross-of-Bladensburg, *Marquess of Hastings;* (o) J. Bradshaw, *Sir Thomas Munro and the British settlement of the Madras presidency;* (p) J. S. Cotton, *Mountstuart Elphinstone;* (q) Lady A. I. Ritchie, *Lord Amherst and the British advance eastwards to Burma;* (r) Sir L. Griffin, *Ranjit Singh and the Sikh barrier between our growing empire and central Asia;* (s) D. C. Boulger, *Lord William Bentinck and the company as a governing and non-trading power;* (t) L. J. Trotter, *Earl of Auckland;* (u) Sir R. Temple, *James Thomason;* (v) C. S. Hardinge, Viscount, *Viscount Hardinge and the advance of the British dominions into the Punjab;* (w) Sir A. Colvin, *John Russell Colvin, the last lieutenant-governor of the northwest under the company;* (x) Sir W. W. Hunter, *The Marquess of Dalhousie and the final development of the company rule;* (y) Sir O. T. Burne, *Clyde and Strathnairn and the suppression of the great revolt;* (z) Sir H. S. Cunningham, *Earl Canning and the transfer of India from the company to the crown;* (aa) Sir C. U. Aitchison, *Lord Lawrence and the reconstruction of India under the crown;* (bb) Sir W. W. Hunter, *The Earl of Mayo and the consolidation of the queen's rule in India.*

Series as a whole is more a history of India, especially of the British administration, than a series of biographies, yet in most of the volumes the man's whole career is to some extent covered. Many of the sketches are by men unusually well qualified to interpret their subjects.   WHA

(U1711) E. S. Holden, *The Mogul emperors of Hindustan, 1398–1707,* N. Y., 1895; (U1712) J. J. Higginbotham, *Men whom India has known,* Madras, 1874; (U1713) W. F. B. Laurie, *Sketches of some distinguished Anglo-Indians,* London, 1888; (U1714) M. Griffith, *India's princes,* London, 1894; (U1715) G. P. Pillai, *Representative Indians,* London, 1897; (U1716) S. Jehangir, *Representative men of India,* London (1890); (U1717) D. N. Bannerjee, *India's nation builders,* London (1919); (U1718) Sir John Kaye, *Lives of Indian officers,* London, 1867; (U1719) G. B. Malleson, *Founders of the Indian empire, Clive, Warren Hastings, and Wellesley,* London, 1882; (U1720) F. B. Bradley-Birt, *Twelve men of Bengal in the nineteenth century,* London, 1910.

(U1731) W. W. Rockhill, *Life of the Buddha,* London, 1884; (U1732) D. R. Bhandarkar, *Asoka,* Calcutta, 1925; (U1733) *Memoirs of Zehired-Dīn Muhammed Bābur, emperor of Hindustan written by himself in the Chaghatāi Tūrki and translated by John Leyden and William Erskine; annotated and revised by Sir Lucas King,* 2 v., London, 1921; (U1734) F. G. Talbot, *Memoirs of Baber emperor of India,* London, 1909; (U1735) S. M. Edwardes, *Babur, diarist and despot,* London, 1926; (U1736) L. F. R. Williams, *Empire builder of the sixteenth century,* London, 1918; (U1737) Gul-Badan Begam (Princess Rose-body), *History of Humāyūn,* London, 1902; (U1738) F. A. Noer, *Emperor Akbar,* 2 v., Calcutta, 1890; (U1739) V. A. Smith, *Akbar the great Mogul, 1542–1605,* Oxford, 1917; (U1740) B. Prasid, *History of Jahangir,* London, 1922; (U1741) J. Sarkar, *Shivaji and his times,* London and N. Y., 1919.

(U1751) Sir J. Malcolm, *Life of Robert, Lord Clive,* 3 v., London, 1836; (U1752) Sir A. J. Arbuthnot, *Lord Clive: the foundation of British rule in India,* London, 1899; (U1753) Sir George Forrest, *Life of Lord Clive,* 2 v., London and N. Y., 1918; (U1754) G. R. Gleig, *Memoirs of the life of Warren Hastings,* 3 v., London, 1836; (U1755) E. A. Bond, ed., *Speeches of the managers and counsel in the trial of Warren Hastings,* London and N. Y., 4 v., London, 1859; (U1756) Sir C. Lawson, *Private life of Warren Hastings,* London and N. Y., 1895; (U1757) G. W. Hastings, *Vindication of Warren Hastings,* London and N. Y., 1909; (U1758) G. B. Malleson, *Life of the Marquess Wellesley,* London, 1889; (U1759) R. R. Pearce, *Memoirs and correspondence of . . . Richard Marquess Wellesley,* 3 v., London, 1846; (U1760) Editor of 'The Windham Papers,' *The Wellesley papers. The life and correspondence of Richard Colley Wellesley Marquess Wellesley,* 2 v., London, 1914; (U1761) *Journal and correspondence of William, Lord Auckland,* 4 v., London, 1861–62; (U1762) Sir W. Lee-Warner, *Life of the marquis of Dalhousie,* 2 v., London, 1904; (U1763) L. J. Trotter, *Life of the marquis of Dalhousie,* London, 1889; (U1764) Sir T. E. Colebrooke, *Life of Mountstuart Elphinstone,* 2 v., London, 1884; (U1765) Sir H. B. Edwards, *Life of Sir Henry Lawrence,* 3rd ed., London, 1873; (U1766) J. J. M. Innes, *Sir Henry Lawrence, the pacificator,* Oxford, 1898; (U1767) Sir W. W. Hunter, *Life of the earl of Mayo, fourth viceroy of India,* London, 1876; (U1768) A. C. Lyall, *Life of the Marquis of Dufferin and Ava,* 2 v., London, 1905; (U1769) Earl of Ronaldshay, *Life of Lord Curzon,* 3 v., London, 1928.

(U1781) H. Pearse, *Memoir of the life and military services of Viscount Lake,*

Edinburgh, 1905; (U1782) G. R. Gleig, *Life of Major General Sir Thomas Munro,* 3 v., London, 1830; (U1783) Sir A. J. Arbuthnot, *Major General Sir Thomas Munro,* 2 v., London, 1881; (U1784) Sir W. F. P. Napier, *Life and opinions of General Sir Charles James Napier,* 4 v., London, 1857; (U1785) W. B. Bruce, *Life of General Sir Charles Napier,* London, 1885; (U1786) W. Brock, *Biographical sketch of Sir Henry Havelock,* N. Y., 1858; (U1787) J. C. Marshman, *Memoirs of Major-General Sir Henry Havelock,* 1860, new ed., London, 1881; (U1788) A. Forbes, *Havelock,* London and N. Y., 1891; (U1789) R. S. Rait, *Life and campaigns of Hugh first Viscount Gough Field-Marshal,* 2 v., Westminster, 1903; (U1790) H. Morris, *Life of Charles Grant,* London, 1904; (U1791) H. Fraser, *Memoir and correspondence of General James Stuart Fraser,* London, 1885; (U1792) G. W. Forrest, *Life of Field-Marshal Sir Neville Chamberlain,* Edinburgh, 1909; (U1793) Sir F. J. Goldsmid, *James Outram,* 2 v., London, 1881; (U1794) E. Gambier-Parry, *Reynell Taylor,* London, 1880; (U1795) Sir W. Lee-Warner, *Memoirs of Field Marshal Sir Henry Wylie Norman,* London, 1908; (U1796) T. H. Thornton, *Colonel Sir Robert Sandeman,* London, 1895; (U1797) Sir Donald Stuart, *Account of his life,* London, 1903; (U1798) Lord Roberts, *Forty-one years in India,* 2 v., N. Y. and London, 1897.

(U1801) J. H. Rylie, *Ralph Fitch, England's pioneer to India and Burma,* London, 1899; (U1802) N. L. Hallward, *William Bolts, a Dutch adventurer under John Company,* Cambridge, Eng., 1920; (U1803) G. Smith, *Alexander Duff,* 2 v., N. Y., 1879; (U1804) E. Judson, *Life of Adoniram Judson,* N. Y., 1883; (U1805) Sir M. E. Grant Duff, *Sir Henry Maine: his life,* London, 1892; (U1806) Sir G. Campbell, *Memoirs of my Indian career,* London, 1893; (U1807) W. W. Hunter, *Life of Brian Houghton Hodgson, British resident at the court of Nepal,* London, 1906; (U1808) A. Forbes, *Colin Campbell, Lord Clyde,* London, 1895; (U1809) P. Sykes, *The Right Hon. Sir Mortimer Durand,* London, 1926; (U1810) F. H. Skrine, *Life of Sir William Wilson Hunter,* London and N. Y., 1901; (U1811) H. G. Keene, *Servant of "John Company,"* London, 1897; (U1812) Sir M. Durand, *Life of Sir Alfred Comyn Lyall,* Edinburgh, 1913; (U1813) Sir O'Moore Creagh, *Autobiography,* London (1925); (U1814) Sir Joseph Fahrer, M.D., *Recollections of my life,* Edinburgh, 1900; (U1815) Sir O. T. Burne, *Memories,* London, 1907; (U1816) J. N. Gupta, *Life and work of Romesh Chunder Dutt,* London and N. Y., 1911; (U1817) Sir Surendranath Banerjea (Surendranātha Vandyopādhyaya), *A nation in the making, being the reminiscences of fifty years of public life in Bengal,* Oxford, 1925; (U1818) R. Rolland, *Mahatma Gandhi: the man who became one with the universal being,* N. Y. and London, 1924. WHA

INDIA: GOVERNMENT PUBLICATIONS

It is of course impossible to list here the innumerable British governmental publications relating to India, whether products of the home administration (Crown, Parliament, India Office) or of the authorities in India. The bibliographies in this sub-section (U1001) and especially in works dealing with governmental matters will be found serviceable. Special mention may be made of (U1901) *Acts passed by the Governor General of India in council* (annual), Calcutta; (U1902) *Hand-book to the records of the government of India in the imperial record department, 1748 to 1859,* Calcutta, 1925; (U1903) *General catalogue of all publications of the government of India and local administration,* Calcutta, 1892 ff.; (U1904) S. C. Hill, ed., *Catalogue of the home miscel-*

laneous series of the India office records, London, 1927; (U1905) India-Foreign department, *Collection of treaties, engagements, and sanads relating to India and neighbouring countries,* 7 v., 1876; 11 v., Calcutta, 1892. WHA

INDIA: PERIODICALS AND SOCIETY PUBLICATIONS

Many of the periodicals listed above under Asia in U941 ff. and in B941, I941, K941, contain material relating to India.

(U1941) *Asiatic annual register,* 12 v., London, 1799–1811; (1942) *Asiatic journal and monthly register,* 3 series, London, 1816–45; (U1943) *Calcutta review,* Calcutta, 1844 ff.; (U1944) *Indian antiquary,* Bombay, 1872 ff.; (U1945) *Indian review,* Madras, 1900 ff.; (U1946) *Journal of Indian history* (University of Allahabad), London, 1921 ff.; (U1961) *Transactions,* 1788–1839; *Journal,* 1832–64; *id,* pt. 1, *History,* 1865–1904; *Journal and proceedings,* 1905 ff., Calcutta [Asiatic Society of Bengal]; (U1962) *Journal,* London, 1867–1915 [East India Association]; (U1963) *Transactions,* London, 1918–23, *Journal,* London, 1841 ff. [Royal Asiatic Society of Great Britain and Ireland, Bombay Branch]. WHA

CHINA: BIBLIOGRAPHY AND ENCYCLOPEDIAS

Valuable bibliographies relating in part to China will be found in B2 ff., U1 ff., and U3001 ff. Cordier's article on the works on China, *Revue Historique,* 18: 143–170, Jan.-Feb., 1882, is still valuable for the older literature. Useful information on recent activities, including bibliographical data, will be found in articles in the *American Historical Review* as follows: K. S. Latourette, 'Chinese Historical Studies during the past seven years,' 26: 703 ff., July 1921; W. T. Swingle, 'Chinese Historical Sources,' *ibid.,* pp. 717 ff.; A. W. Hummel, 'What the Chinese are doing in their own History,' 34: 715 ff., July 1929.

U2001a Cordier, Henri. *Bibliotheca sinica. Dictionnaire bibliographique des ouvrages relatifs à l'empire chinois.* 2 v. 1881–85. 2nd rev. and enl. ed., 4 v., Paris, 1904–08. *Supplément,* 1895. 2nd rev. and enl. ed., 1922–24.

b Wieger, Léon. *La Chine à travers les âges, hommes et choses. Index biographique. Index bibliographique.* Sienhsien, 1920.

a. Only reasonably complete bibliography for China in any European language. Contains titles of periodical articles as well as books; without critical comment, but enumerates the various editions. Arranged topically, with some chronological tables. Indispensable to the careful student of things Chinese. Later editions and supplement supply some lacunæ in original work. Review, A. Wylie, *China Review,* 7: 339, March-April 1879, from *Trübner's Oriental Record.* KSL

b. Epitome of Chinese history by a Jesuit doctor of medicine, with translations from Chinese authors of the several dynasties. Biographical index gives brief notices of about 4,500 persons and bibliographical index refers to about a thousand Chinese works. Review, W. T. Swingle, *A.H.R.,* 26: 725, July 1921. GMD

U2002a Wylie, Alexander. *Notes on Chinese literature.* 1867. 2nd ed., Shanghai, 1901. Reprint from original ed., 1922.

b Möllendorff, P. G., and O. F. von. *Manual of Chinese bibliography.* Shanghai, 1876.

c Williams, Frederick Wells. *Best hundred books on China.* New Haven, 1924.

d China Institute in America. *One hundred selected books on China.* Revised list. Bulletin 6. N. Y., 1928.

a. Brief notes on about two thousand Chinese books, with list of translations of Chinese works into European languages prior to first edition. Review, W. T. Swingle, *A.H.R.*, 26: 723, July 1921.   GMD

b, c, and *d.* Convenient lists of limited range.   WHA

U2021a Couling, Samuel. *Encyclopædia sinica.* Shanghai, 1917.

   b Ball, J. Dyer. *Things Chinese, or, notes connected with China.* 1892. 5th rev. ed., London, 1926.

a. Gives in alphabetical order short account of the chief places, objects, events and persons connected with China and Chinese history. Suffers somewhat from having been produced, not by a group of specialists, but almost entirely by the compiler and his wife. Review, *Journal* (North China Branch, Royal Asiatic Society), 49: 193, 1918; H. L. Joly, *Asiatic Rev.*, n.s. 14: 536, Oct. 1918.

                                                   KSL

b. Topical presentation, in alphabetical order, of much information, largely sociological, concerning the Chinese. Review of 4th ed., *Chinese Recorder,* 35: 201, Apr. 1904.   WHA

CHINA: GEOGRAPHY

U2041a Stanford, Edward. *Atlas of the Chinese empire.* 1908. 2nd rev. ed., Philadelphia, 1917.

   b Dingle, Edwin J., ed. *New atlas and commercial gazetteer of China.* Shanghai, 1917.

   c Hosie, Sir Alexander. *New commercial map of China. With handbook.* (Scale 1 : 3,000,000.) London, 1922.

Serviceable atlases and map for ordinary use, though first edition of *a* is out of date. The maps which in *b* are bilingual, are based upon the best surveys; the technique is unusually satisfactory. Review of *a,* J. C. Gibson, *Chinese Recorder,* 40: 105, Feb. 1909; of *b, ibid.,* 49: 117, Feb. 1918.   WHA

c. The most accurate map of China in the English language to date, being based upon many years of travel and observation on the spot. Review, *Asiatica,* 1 : 39, Jan. 1928.   AWH

U2042a Yule, Sir Henry. *Cathay and the way thither, being a collection of mediæval notices of China.* 1866. 2nd rev. ed. by H. Cordier. 4 v. London, 1913–16. [Hakluyt society, *Works,* ser. 2, v. 33, 37, 38, 41.] (Bibliography.)

   b Anville, Bourguignon d'. *Nouvel atlas de la Chine, de la Tartarie chinoise et du Thibet.* La Haye, 1736.

a. Important supplement to Yule's edition of (U42*a*) *Book of Ser Marco Polo;* contains an essay on medieval intercourse with China and extracts from the narratives of Ibn Batuta, John de Marignolli, Odoric de Pordenone, and Goës. Review, D. S. Margoliouth, *E.H.R.*, 33 : 268, April 1918.   GMD

b. D'Anville engraved this collection of maps of China by provinces, under the direction of Emperor Kang-hi; based on materials collected by Mailla (cf. U2121*c*) and others. The atlas was prepared to accompany (U2121*b*) J. B. DuHalde, *Description géographique.*   GMD, AWH

U2043a Reclus, Elisée, and **Onésime.** *L'empire du milieu; le climat, le sol, les races, la richesse de la Chine.* Paris, 1902. (Bibliography.)

   b Huc, Evariste R. (Abbé). *Chinese empire.* 2 v. 1855. 2nd ed., London, 1857. Tr. from *L'empire chinois,* 2 v., 1854. 2nd ed., Paris, 1857.

c Carnegie Institution of Washington. *Research in China.* 3 v. in 4. Washington, 1907–13. [Publication No. 54.]

d Richard, Louis. *Comprehensive geography of the Chinese empire and dependencies.* 1908. 2nd ed., Shanghai, 1927. Tr., rev. and enl. by M. Kennelly, from *Géographie de l'empire de Chine.* Chang-hai, 1905. (Bibliographies.)

a. Well organized account of China with special attention to the human geography. Good maps. *b.* Sequel to the author's (U332b) *Travels in Tartary, Thibet, and China.* Account of journey from Thibet to Canton by author, who had earlier resided fourteen years in various parts of China. *c.* Scientific results of the Carnegie expedition to China in 1903–04. WHA

d. Best readily available book on the geography of China. Full geographical description of each of the provinces, some account of the older government of China, and a brief survey of the history of the country. Its information is in compact form, with Chinese characters for the names used as well as their romanization. The maps leave much to be desired. Review of French ed., E. H. Parker, *Asiatic Quar. Rev.,* 3rd ser., 21 : 403, Apr. 1906. KSL

U2044a Imperial Japanese Government Railways. *Official guide to eastern Asia.* [v. 1, *Manchuria and Chosen,* 1913; v. 4, *China.*] Tokyo, 1915.

b Cook, Thomas & Son, publishers. *Cook's handbook for tourists to Peking, Tientsin, Shan-Hai-Kwan, Dalny, Port Arthur, and Seoul.* London, 1910.

c Crow, Carl. *Travelers' handbook for China including Hongkong.* 4th rev. ed., N. Y., 1926.

Authoritative guide-books containing some geographical, sociological and historical information, with excellent maps and plans. Review of *a, Asiatic Rev.,* n.s. 14 : 400, July 1918. WHA

CHINA: ETHNOLOGY

U2051a Clarke, Samuel R. *Among the tribes in south-west China.* London, 1911.

b Shirokogoruff, S. M. *Anthropology of northern China.* Shanghai, 1923.

c Chi Li. *Formation of the Chinese people. An anthropological inquiry.* Cambridge (Mass.), 1928.

a. Written with primary interest in Christian missions and for a popular audience, this is especially valuable in its presentation of the non-Chinese races. Review, E. H. Parker, *Asiatic Quar. Rev.,* 3rd ser., 32 : 414, Oct. 1911. *b* and *c.* Highly technical anthropological studies of Chinese groups. Review of *c, Chinese Recorder,* 59 : 793, Dec. 1928; B. Laufer, *A.H.R.,* 34 : 650, Apr. 1929. WHA

CHINA: COLLECTIONS OF SOURCES

U2061a McNair, Harley F. *Modern Chinese history; selected readings; a collection of extracts from various sources chosen to illustrate some of the chief phases of China's international relations during the past hundred years.* Shanghai, 1923. (Bibliographies.)

b Wieger, Léon, ed. *Rudiments de parler et de style chinois.* Paris, 1903. [Textes historiques, v. 10 and 11, in 3 v.]

a. Prepared primarily for Chinese students acquainted with the English language; includes material representative of various points of view and covers period of modern Western intercourse through the Washington Conference. Review, E. T. Williams, *A.H.R.*, 29 : 605, Apr. 1924. *b.* Selected texts, Chinese and French translation in parallel column, containing such extracts from Chinese sources as the editor, a Jesuit missionary, considered interesting and instructive for a missionary in China. His great care, he assures us, has been 'not to alter the naïve realism' of the texts.   WHA

U2062a **Hertslet, Sir Edward,** ed. *China treaties: treaties. etc., between Great Britain and China; and between China and foreign powers, and orders in council, rules, regulations, acts of parliament, decrees, etc., affecting British interests in China.* 2 v. 1896. 3rd rev. ed., by Godfrey E. P. Hertslet, London, 1908. [v. 1, *Treaties, 1689–1907;* v. 2, *Orders in council, regulations, etc., 1855–1907.*]

   b **MacMurray, John Van A.,** ed. *Treaties and agreements with and concerning China, 1894–1919.* 2 v. Oxford, 1921. [Publication of the Carnegie Endowment for International Peace.]

   c **Inspectorate General of Customs.** *Treaties, conventions, etc., between China and foreign states.* 2 v. 1908. 2nd ed., Shanghai, 1917.

a. Somewhat limited in usefulness by omission, partly deliberate, of certain classes of texts, it remains the standard reference book for treaties and agreements to which China was a party from 1689 to 1894, and for British orders in council and similar documents concerning China from 1855 to 1907. Review, *Asiatic Quar. Rev.*, 3rd series, 27 : 193, Jan. 1909. *b.* Beginning where the first edition of *a* closed, it supplements and replaces earlier compilations. Its accuracy, convenience in form, and above all, its inclusion of many quasi-public commitments, such as loan contracts, the texts of which are not elsewhere readily accessible, make it a source indispensable for the analysis and handling of present Far Eastern problems. *c.* In some particulars more useful than *a.* It includes some treaties and conventions never ratified, but having historical significance, although none such as may be considered pending. Some additions, appropriately distributed in the second edition, are also separately printed as a quasi-supplement to the first edition.   WHA

CHINA: GENERAL HISTORIES

U2101a **Douglas, Robert K.** *China.* 1885. 4th ed., N. Y., 1912. [Story of the nations. Reprinted in (B135) Lodge.]

   b **Parker, Edward Harper.** *China. Her history, diplomacy, and commerce from the earliest times to the present day.* 1901. 2nd ed., London, 1917.

   c **Pott, Francis Lister Hawks.** *Sketch of Chinese history.* 1903. 4th ed., London, 1923.

a. Arranged somewhat as a sociological and economic survey, but with the successive topics treated historically. Brief review, *Chinese Recorder,* 52 : 355, May 1921.   WHA

b. Not a complete history, but a collection of interesting essays and notes; shows marked prejudice against Americans. Review, *Chinese Recorder,* 49 : 477, July 1918; *Asiatic Review,* n.s. 12 : 439, Nov. 15, 1917. *c.* Excellent brief outline rather than narrative, brought well down by successive editions. Review, *Chinese Recorder,* 35 : 203, Apr. 1904.   KSL

U2102a Boulger, Demetrius C. *Short history of China.* London, 1893.

b MacGowan, John. *History of China from the earliest days down to the present.* London, 1897. 2nd ed., *Imperial history of China, being a history of the empire as compiled by Chinese historians.* Shanghai, 1906.

a. Author disclaims this as an abridgment of his larger work, *History of China,* but alterations in the treatment consist primarily in changes of phraseology, not of interpretation. Review, *Asiatic Quar. Rev.,* n.s. 6: 502, Oct. 1893. WHA

b. Full summary of the traditional Chinese accounts, dealing almost exclusively with political history. Particularly good for events before the nineteenth century, although quite inadequate in treatment of Chinese origins—a field in which the Chinese have done much in the past ten years. Review, F. H. James, *Chinese Recorder,* 29: 299, June 1898. KSL

U2103a Li Ung Bing, and Whiteside, Joseph, eds. *Outline of Chinese history.* Shanghai, 1914.

b Gowen, Herbert H. *Outline history of China.* 2 v. London, 1914. Rev. ed., Boston, 1917. (Bibliography.)

c ——, and Hall, Josef W. *Outline history of China.* N. Y., 1926.

a. First attempt by a Chinese scholar educated abroad to construct a resumé of Chinese history. Good maps and illustrations, but the native authorities consulted are all secondary and the estimates commonplace. Too much like European histories of China in arrangement and in disproportionate space given the Manchu dynasty. Review, *Chinese Recorder,* 45: 777, Dec. 1914. FWW

b. Compact story of .China, abounding in names and facts, at times seeming to lose in these the main thread of events. Carefully compiled and useful as a brief work of reference. Review, *Dial,* 56: 150, Feb. 16, 1914. KSL

c. Based in part on *b,* but rewritten and with much additional material, that on the more recent history being by Hall. It inadequately reflects the work recently done by the Chinese on their ancient history and it is not based on the original sources. Review, *Chinese Recorder,* 58: 278, Apr. 1927. WHA

U2104a Giles, Herbert A. *China and the Manchus.* Cambridge (Eng.) and N. Y., 1912.

b Hsieh, Pao Chao. *Government of China, 1644–1911.* Baltimore, 1925. (Bibliography.)

a. Brief history concerning the last three centuries. Review, E. H. Parker, *Asiatic Rev.,* n.s. 1: 196, Jan. 1913. *b.* Primarily a description of the governmental system under the Manchu (Tsing) dynasty rather than an account of its operation, but traces developing customs and institutions back into the areas of historical interest. Review, F. W. Williams, *A.H.R.,* 31: 527, Apr. 1926. WHA

U2105a Latourette, Kenneth S. *Development of China.* 1917. 4th ed., Boston, 1929. (Bibliography.)

b Williams, Edward T. *China yesterday and to-day.* (1923) Rev. ed., N. Y., 1927. (Bibliography.)

c —— *Short history of China.* N. Y., 1928. [Harper's historical series.] (Bibliographies.)

a. Following a succinct resumé of the ancient history of China, a chapter on the culture of the old empire at the beginning of its contact with the West is as good as anything ever written on it within the same space. Last half of book gives essential facts of China's history since the Opium War and their relation to her political reconstruction. Excellent introduction to the study of Chinese history. Review, S. K. Hornbeck, *A.H.R.*, 22:857, July 1917; 30:177, Oct. 1924. FWW

b and *c*. Works of a careful modern student of Chinese life and history. *b* is more a social survey, carried out along historical lines, and has been rated as the best general survey of Chinese civilization now to be had in English. *c*. Traces the successive historical stages, but does not incorporate the results of Chinese critical studies of the past ten years. Both works successfully carry out the author's desire 'to interpret Chinese history to Western students.' Review of *b*, *Chinese Recorder*, 55:47, Jan. 1924. WHA

U2121a Se-ma Ts'ien. *Mémoires historiques de Se-ma Ts'ien.* 5 v. Paris, 1895–1905. Tr. from the Chinese into French by E. Chavannes.

b Du Halde, Jean B. *General history of China.* 4 v. London, 1736. Tr. by R. Brookes from *Description géographique, historique, logique, politique, et physique de l'empire de la Chine et de la Tartarie chinoise.* 4 v. Paris, 1735; 2nd ed., La Haye, 1736.

c Mailla, Joseph A. M. M. de. *Histoire générale de la Chine, ou annales de cet empire; traduites du Tong-Kien-Kang-mou.* Ed. by J. B. G. A. Grosier and M. A. A. le R. Deshautesrayes. 13 v. Paris, 1777–85.

d Batteux, Charles, and others, ed. *Mémoires concernant l'histoire, les sciences, les arts, les moeurs, et les usages des Chinois, par les missionaires de Pekin.* 17 v. Paris, 1776–1814.

a. First of the formal twenty-four dynastic histories by one who has been called the Herodotus of China, and for whom the claim has been made that he is the earliest genuine historian. This work formed the model for all subsequent official dynastic histories. Review, *Asiatic Quar. Rev.*, 3rd ser., 3:435, Apr. 1897; 9:415, Apr. 1900; 13:191, Jan. 1902; 21:181, Jan. 1906. WHA

b, c, and *d*. Monumental works, composed from materials furnished by Jesuit missionaries to China in the eighteenth century, from which many later sinologues have drawn liberally. *b*. Compiled from missionary letters, reports and documents, affording the most complete information concerning China which had yet reached the western world. *c*. While working on the materials referred to above, Mailla found access to materials of prime importance. He translated or rather abstracted the *Tong-Kien-Kang-mou*, or annals of the earlier dynasties, so his completed manuscript covered the history of China from B.C. 2935 to the eighteenth century and was finally extended to A.D. 1780, when it was printed. Mailla arrived in China in 1703, sent his manuscript to France in 1737, and died in Peking in 1749. The history, condensed from that manuscript, fills v. 1–11, the index v. 12, and a *Description topographique,* prepared by Grosier, v. 13. *d*. Bertin, the controller-general of finances, even after the suppression of the Jesuits in France, maintained correspondence with Jesuit missionaries in China, especially Père Amiot, obtaining from them, and from two young Chinese who came to France to study, the body of materials which he engaged Batteux to edit. Several savants, including Joseph de Guignes, collaborated and continued the publication. GMD

U2122 Cordier, Henri. *Histoire générale de la Chine et de ses relations avec les pays étrangers depuis les temps les plus anciens jusqu'à la chute de la dynastie mandchoue.* 4 v. Paris, 1920–21.

Based mainly upon (U2121c) Mailla's great history, this summary of four thousand years of China's annals preserves a better proportion than most European efforts of the same kind. Cordier's own studies on medieval central Asia and the early travelers from the west make the second and third portions authoritative and important. Last volume recounts the European and Japanese wars from a French standpoint. A work of considerable importance. Review K. S. Latourette, *A.H.R.*, 27 : 575, Apr. 1922.   FWW

U2123a Williams, Samuel Wells. *Middle kingdom; a survey of the geography, government, literature, social life, arts, and history of the Chinese empire and its inhabitants.* 1848. Rev. ed., 2 v., N. Y., 1904.

    b Brinkley, Frank. *China; its history, arts and literature.* 4 v., Boston, and Tokyo (1902). [Oriental series, v. 9–12.]

a. The standard general work on every phase of China, rewritten in 1883. Derives main value from author's encyclopedic information, his long experience in China as editor, missionary, and diplomatist, and the penetration of his judgment. Two chapters, bringing the record down to 1896, were added by his son in 1900. Its descriptions of the institutions of China apply only to the last century. Review, *Westminster Rev.*, 49 : 131, Apr. 1848; of rev. ed., *China Rev.*, 12 : 195, Nov.-Dec. 1883.   FWW

    b. Not so authoritative as author's similar work (U3121) on Japan ; the more important sections are those dealing with art. Review, W. E. Griffis, *A.H.R.*, 8 : 795, July 1903.   KSL

CHINA: SPECIAL PERIODS

U2201a Hirth, Friedrich. *Ancient history of China to the end of the Chou dynasty.* N. Y., 1908.

    b Parker, Edward H. *Ancient China simplified.* London, 1908.

    c Maspero, Henri. *La Chine antique.* Paris, 1927. [Histoire du monde, v. 4.] (Bibliographies.)

a. Eight chapters on the obscure beginnings of Chinese history and the turmoil of the Chou period condensed with due regard to relative importance of the problems involved. Controversial topics are discussed with temperance in a series of brief essays introduced in proper chronological sequence into the narrative. Review, E. H. Parker, *Asiatic Quar. Rev.*, 3rd ser., 26 : 197, July 1908. *b.* Attempt by a brilliant and unconventional English scholar to give English readers 'an intelligible notion of what Chinese antiquity really was.' As *Kulturgeschichte* it is excellent, being based on Chinese sources unbiased by the researches or opinions of other Europeans. Value of the author's scholarship is somewhat impaired by prejudices. Review, *Academy,* 75 : 344, Oct. 10, 1908.   FWW

    c. Recent work with excellent perspectives ; differentiates between the periods in which our knowledge is ample and those in which it is relatively restricted. Proportionately more space is given to sociological description than to historical narrative, but considerable attention is given to processes which belong to both these spheres of interest. Considered the best work on ancient China in any western language, although a comparable work in Chinese is the *Ku Shih Pien* (Discussions in ancient history) by Ku Chieh-kang, Peking, 1926. Review, B. Laufer, *A.H.R.*, 33 : 903, July 1928.   WHA

U2231 Hail, William James. *Tseng Kuo-fan and the Taiping rebellion with a short sketch of his later career.* New Haven, 1927. (Valuable bibliography.)

Especially important, showing the overlapping of two personalities, Tseng Kuo-fan and Li Hung Chang, who together span sixty years of active history before the Boxer uprising. Review, *Chinese Recorder,* 58 : 724, Nov. 1927. WHA

U2241a Volpicèlli, Zenone (pseudonym, **Vladimir**). *China-Japan war compiled from Japanese, Chinese, and foreign sources.* N. Y., 1896.

b Gérard, Auguste. *Ma mission en Chine (1893–1897).* Paris, 1918.

a. Contemporary compilation, making major use of Japanese materials; only considerable work in English on the subject. GMD

b. Illuminating exposition by the French minister to China of Chinese international relations during four of the most important years of the Manchu period. WHA

U2242a Pott, Francis Lister Hawks. *Outbreak in China; its causes.* N. Y., 1900.

b Smith, Arthur Henderson. *China in convulsion.* 2 v. N. Y., 1901.

c Clements, Paul Henry. *Boxer rebellion; a political and diplomatic review.* N. Y., 1915. (Bibliography.)

a. Contemporary statement of the situation by the president of St. John's College, Shanghai. *b.* Author went to China in 1872 as an American missionary and was present in Peking during the Boxer siege. His treatment of the Boxer movement is still unsurpassed. Review, A. Schade van Westrum, *Book Buyer,* 23 : 560, Jan. 1902. *c.* Careful historical study of all phases of the movement. Review, S. K. Hornbeck, *A.H.R.,* 21 : 601, Apr. 1916. GMD

U2243a Bland, John O. P., and **Backhouse, E.** *China under the empress dowager; being the history of the life and times of Tzu Hsi.* Philadelphia, 1910. Abridged ed., Boston, 1914.

b Kent, Percy Horace. *Passing of the Manchus.* London, 1912.

c Dingle, Edwin J. *China's revolution: 1911–1912. A historical and political record of the civil war.* Shanghai, 1912.

a. Authentic account, based on well translated documents, of the acts and opinions of the palace group in Peking during the last fifty years of the Manchu dynasty. Of romantic as well as historical interest, this biographical work of Chinese writers throws much light upon the Boxer uprising. Review, (N. Y.) *Nation,* 92 : 214, March 2, 1911; C. Bone, *London Quarterly Rev.,* 116 : 65, July 1911. FWW

b. Valuable account, by a careful writer, of the beginnings of the Chinese awakening, the immediate causes which brought about the revolution of 1911, the course which the revolution took, the abdication of the dynasty, and the introduction of Yuan-shih-kai into office as first president of the republic of China. NTJ

c. Comprehensive story of the revolution of 1911 by one who had intimate personal knowledge of much of China's life both inside and outside the areas best known to Europeans. Review, *Saturday Review,* 114 : 555, Nov. 2, 1912. WHA

U2251a Bland, John O. P. *Recent events and present policies in China.* Philadelphia, 1912.

b Blakeslee, George Hubbard, ed. *China and the far east.* N. Y., 1910. [Clark university lectures.]

c ———, ed. *Recent developments in China.* N. Y., 1913. [Clark university addresses.]

d Reinsch, Paul S. *American diplomat in China.* Garden City, N. Y., 1922.

e Woodhead, Henry G. W. *Truth about the Chinese republic.* London (1925).

a. Rather over-confident survey, with many interesting illustrations, of political conditions in China in the revolutionary period which produced the Republic. Review, E. H. Parker, *Asiatic Review,* n.s. 2: 201, July 1913.   WHA

b and *c.* Addresses by natives of eastern Asia and by persons who through residence or travel in China were competent to speak with authority on the various Far Eastern questions. Range of information and opinion is wide; the views expressed mainly interesting as illustrating state of opinion at the time. Review of *b, Nation* (N. Y.), 90: 510, May 19, 1910; cf. *c, American Pol. Sci. Rev.,* 8: 291, May 1914.   GMD

d. Chinese affairs, especially international relations, as seen by the American minister to China during six years of official residence, 1913–19. Review, W. W. McLaren, *Amer. Pol. Sci. Rev.,* 16: 505, Aug. 1922.   *e.* Editor of (U2941) *China year book* and of the *Peking and Tientsin Times* gives his description and interpretation of events in connection with the formation of the Republic and more recently, but with inadequate appreciation of the Chinese points of view.   WHA

U2252a Ariga, Nagao. *La Chine et la grande guerre européenne.* Paris, 1920.

b Wheeler, William Reginald. *China and the world-war.* N. Y., 1919. (Bibliography.)

c Wood, Ge-Zay. *Shantung question, a study in diplomacy and world politics.* N. Y., 1922.

a. By a Japanese professor of international law who had by 1920 served for more than seven years as a legal adviser to the Chinese Republic. Consists largely of state papers from Chinese archives, many previously unpublished; well arranged with explanatory texts.   LRM

b. Brief survey of Chinese affairs, internal and external, during the World War. Contains considerable documentary material in the text and appendixes. Review, *Asia,* 19: 696, July 1919.   WHA

c. Careful study of the situation from 1897 through the Washington Conference by a Chinese. Apologetic and litigious animus evident, but does not seriously impair historical reliability of this book. Review, A. P. L. Dennis, *A.H.R.,* 28: 342, Jan. 1923.   GMD

CHINA: INTERNATIONAL RELATIONS

U2501a Hunter, William C. *The "fan kwae" at Canton before treaty days, 1825–1844.* 1882. 2nd ed., Shanghai, 1911.

b Koo, Vi Kyuin Wellington. *Status of aliens in China.* N. Y., 1912. [Columbia University studies in history, economics and public law.]

c Baudez, Marcel. *Essai sur la condition juridique des étrangers en Chine.* Paris, 1913. (Bibliography.)

d Tyau, Minchien Tuk Zung. *Legal obligations arising out of treaty relations between China and other states.* Shanghai, 1917. (Bibliography.)

a. Important account of conditions when Canton was the only port open to foreigners. Review, *China Rev.,* 11 : 190, Nov.-Dec. 1882. *b.* Rather extensive monograph by a Chinese, an important part of whose education was obtained in America; later he became English secretary to the President of China and Chinese minister to the United States. It treats the status of aliens in China as a class and from the Chinese point of view. Review, P. J. Treat, *Amer. Pol. Sci. Rev.,* 7 : 298, May 1913. *c.* Doctoral thesis, presented to the faculty of law of the University of Paris, treating the privileges accorded foreigners, the consular courts and the concessions. *d.* Doctoral thesis presented to the University of London, deals with the provisions in the various treaties and conventions, 1689–1915, respecting political and economic matters and general arrangements including the right of protection, religious toleration, reciprocity, most-favored nation principle and treaty interpretation. Review, *Chinese Recorder,* 49 : 538, Aug. 1918.

WHA

U2502a Tchen Ki Chan. *Le politique de la porte ouverte en Chine.* Paris, 1912. (Bibliography.)

b Tai, En Sai. *Treaty ports in China.* N. Y., 1918.

c Bau, Mingchien Joshua. *Open door doctrine in relation to China.* N. Y., 1923. [Knights of Columbus historical series.] (Bibliography.)

d —— *Foreign relations of China; a history and a survey.* N. Y. (1921).

a, b, and *c.* Group of monographs setting forth the principles and the working of the open-door policy, and to some extent, its admission into international law. Review of *b, Chinese Recorder,* 49 : 808, Dec. 1918; of *c,* G. N. Steiger, *Amer. Pol. Sci. Rev.,* 17 : 662, Nov. 1923; E. T. Williams, *A.H.R.,* 20 : 376, Jan. 1924.

WHA

d. Survey of diplomatic history of China and of the policies of western powers, followed by studies of Japan's policy and the impairment of China's sovereignty. New problems arising since the World War are considered and a program proposed for China's foreign policy. Review, T. Dennett, *Pol. Sci. Quar.,* 38 : 520, Sept. 1923.

GMD

U2503a Morse, Hosea Ballou. *International relations of the Chinese empire.* 3 v. London and N. Y., 1910–18. (Bibliography.)

b Keeton, George William. *Development of extraterritoriality in China.* 2 v. London and N. Y., 1928.

a. Political history of modern China by an American commissioner in the maritime customs service; with good maps, and documented with materials previously unpublished. Extends from some three hundred fifty years before the opening of Peking to foreigners through the Russo-Japanese war. Estimates differ as to its impartiality; inadequate use of American sources. Review of v. 1, E. H. Parker, *Asiatic Quar. Rev.,* 3rd ser., 31 : 404, Apr. 1911; of v. 2 and 3, *Chinese Recorder,* 50 : 626, Sept. 1919.

FWW, WHA

b. Comprehensive historical account with considerable documentary material. Review, H. B. Morse, *E.H.R.,* 44 : 479, July 1929. Cf. (U2532*b*) Chu.

WHA

U2504a Willoughby, Westel W. *Foreign rights and interests in China.* 1920. Rev. and enl. ed., 2 v., Baltimore, 1927. (Bibliographical foot-notes.)

   b —— *China at the conference; a report.* Baltimore, 1922.

   c Whyte, Sir Frederick. *China and foreign powers; an historical review of their relations.* London, 1927.

a. Scholarly analysis of the international commitments of China and foreign claims therein, by an acknowledged authority in political science who had been recently constitutional adviser to the Chinese government. Practically indispensable to students of the Far Eastern question; considers extra-territoriality, commercial rights, leases, concessions, loans, railways and spheres of influence. Review, E. B. Drew, *Amer. Pol. Sci. Rev.,* 14: 727, Nov. 1920; review of 2nd ed., R. B. Buell, *ibid.,* 21: 669, Aug. 1927. *b.* Not so much a narrative as a handbook of classified information and documents on Chinese problems and the action of the Washington Conference of 1921–22 with regard to them. Author was adviser to the Chinese delegation at the Conference. Review, T. Dennett, *A.H.R.,* 27: 798, July 1922.   GMD

c. Excellent survey of the more recent Chinese and British relations. Review, *Hist. Outlook,* 18: 395, Dec. 1927.   WHA

U2505a Williams, Frederick Wells. *Anson Burlingame and the first Chinese mission to foreign powers.* N. Y., 1912.

   b Latourette, Kenneth S. *History of early relations between the United States and China, 1784–1844.* New Haven. [Transactions of the Connecticut Academy of Arts and Sciences, v. 22.] (Bibliography.)

   c Hoo Chi-tsai. *Les bases conventionnelles des relations modernes entre la Chine et la Russie.* Paris, 1918. (Bibliography.)

   d Douglas, Sir Robert K. *Europe and the Far East.* 1904. Rev. ed., with additional chapters (1904–12) by J. H. Longford. N. Y. (1924).

a. Interesting account of an important event in the early diplomatic history of China. Review, C. E. Hesselgrave, *Independent,* 73: 1173, Nov. 21, 1912. *b.* Analytical, critical, detailed and thoroughly documented account of trade and other relations for six decades. Review, *Journal,* North China Branch, Royal Asiatic Society, 49: 174 (1918). *c.* Doctoral thesis (University of Paris); scholarly presentation of the diplomatic relations between China and Russia from the middle of the nineteenth century to the treaty of St. Petersburg, 1881, although also extending back in some particulars to the treaty of Nerchinsk of 1689 and forward to the secret alliance of 1896.   WHA

d. Scholarly production, though with noticeable British bias and little attention to American interests or influence; narrative of the political and diplomatic phases of China's intercourse with the Occident, chiefly since the beginning of the nineteenth century. Review, K. Asakawa, *A.H.R.,* 10: 918, July 1905.   KSL

U2506a Cordier, Henri. *L'expédition de Chine de 1857–58.* Paris, 1905. [Bibliothèque d'histoire contemporaine.]

   b —— *L'expédition de Chine de 1860.* Paris, 1906. [Bibliothèque d'histoire contemporaine.]

   c —— *Histoire des relations de la Chine avec les puissances occidentales, 1860–1902.* 3 v., Paris, 1901–02.

These works by one of the greatest sinologues survey with characteristic comprehensiveness and accuracy the diplomatic history of China during almost half a century. Well documented not only with texts of treaties, but with much from the official negotiations and correspondence. Review of *c, Rev. Hist.,* 77:119, Sept. 1901; 78:225, Mar. 1902; 80:126, Sept. 1902. WHA

CHINA: CONSTITUTIONAL AND POLITICAL HISTORY

U2531a **Martin, Robert Montgomery.** *China; political, commercial, and social.* 2 v. London, 1847.

b **Brunnert, Ippolit Semenovich,** and **Hagelstrom, V. V.** *Present day political organization of China.* Shanghai, 1912. Tr. by A. Beltchenke and E. Moran, from *Sovremennaia polititches kaia organizatsiia kitaia.* Peking, 1910.

These books are both photographs of conditions just before considerable changes took place but are of value for the times depicted. *a.* Official report to the British government on the geography, early history and commercial organization of China.
WHA
b. Exhaustive summary of the political framework of China as reorganized at the end of the last dynasty. Its four sections cover the imperial, administrative, provincial and honorary categories of the former governmental system, with Chinese characters attached to all proper names. Review of Russian edition, *T'oung Pao,* 11:693, 1910. FWW

U2532a **Yen, Hawkling L.** *Survey of constitutional development in China.* N. Y., 1911. [Columbia University studies in history, economics and public law, v. 40.]

b **Chu Ao-hsiang.** *Le régime des capitulations et la réforme constitution- nelle en Chine.* Cambridge (Eng.), 1915. [Université Catholique de Louvain. École des Sciences Politiques et Sociales.] (Bibliography.)

c **Tyau, Minchien T. Z.** *China's new constitution and international prob- lems.* Shanghai, 1918.

d —— *China awakened.* N. Y., 1922.

e **Cheng, Sih-gung.** *Modern China, a political study.* Oxford, 1919.

f **Vinacke, Harold Monk.** *Modern constitutional development in China.* Princeton, 1920. (Bibliographical foot-notes.)

g **Hsü, Shu-hsi.** *China and her political entity; a study of China's foreign relations with reference to Korea, Manchuria and Mongolia.* N. Y., 1926.

a. Exposition of the leading schools of Chinese political philosophy, of the ancient feudalism, of the principles of public law as set forth by Confucius in 'The Spring and Autumn'; a brief characterization of the two millennia of the absolutism of the old régime; a brief statement of essential facts in the recent movement for a written constitution. *b.* Doctoral dissertation tracing the history of many treaties of China with western nations, which placed the subjects of these nations residing in China under the jurisdiction of the diplomatic agents of those nations—one form of extraterritoriality. Cf. (U2503*b*) Keeton. WHA

c and *d.* By one of the ablest of the younger generation in understanding and advocacy of Chinese interests. Review of *c,* L. B. Evans, *Amer. Pol. Sci. Rev.,* 13:512, Aug. 1919; of *d, Chinese Recorder,* 53:275, Apr. 1922. *e.* Partly written while author was a student in England during the World War and partly after his service as member of the Chinese delegation at the Paris Conference. Material valuable but somewhat inarticulated, Chinese viewpoint predominant. Has useful appendixes of documents. Review, R. M. McElroy, *A.H.R.,* 27:125, Oct. 1921.
GMD

f. Beginning with the reform edicts of the emperor Kwang Hau in 1898, the various constitutional documents and their evolution are analyzed. Review, *Amer. Pol. Sci. Rev.,* 15 : 313, May 1921. *g.* Doctoral dissertation, dealing primarily with modern developments in China's relations with other nations, especially Japan, but not neglectful of the long distant past where this enters into the more recent historical situation. Review, W. Hung, *Chinese Recorder,* 58 : 723, Nov. 1927; L. P. L. Woo, *Cath. Hist. Rev.,* n.s. 7 : 534, Oct. 1927.   WHA

CHINA: SOCIAL AND ECONOMIC HISTORY

U2551a Doolittle, Justus. *Social life of the Chinese. A daguerreotype of daily life in China.* London, 1868.

   b Simon, G. Eugène. *China: its social, political, and religious life.* London, 1887. Tr. from *La cité chinoise.* 1885. 7th ed., Paris, 1891.

   c Headland, Isaac Taylor. *Court life in China; the capital, its officials and people.* N. Y., 1909.

a and *c.* Deal with the aspects of the social life as indicated in their titles. Review of *c,* E. H. Parker, *Asiatic Quar. Rev.,* 3rd ser., 29 : 428, Apr. 1910. *b.* Title of French work may be misleading as the book is a description of the Chinese social state under the captions 'The Family,' 'Work,' 'The State,' 'Government,' and an analytical account of a relatively small family group or community in the province of Fo-Kien.   WHA

U2552a Smith, Arthur Henderson. *Village life in China; a study in sociology.* N. Y. (1899).

   b Leong, Y. K., and **Tao, L. K.** *Village and town life in China.* N. Y. and London, 1915. [University of London. Studies in economics and political science.]

a. Product of personal observation by an American missionary who went to China in 1872. Deals chiefly with North China. Review, *Chinese Recorder,* 31 : 202, Apr. 1900. *b.* First author describes the internal workings of a Chinese village and the second the administration of towns. This is carefully done, with proper attention to the Chinese family system. Review, Shosanken, *Asiatic Rev.* n.s. 7 : 98, July 1915.   WHA

U2553a Gamble, Sidney David. *Peking, a social survey.* N. Y. (1921).

   b Anderson, Adelaide Mary. *Humanity and labour in China.* London, 1928.

a. Thorough social survey conducted with the assistance of John Stewart Burgess and under the auspices of the Princeton University Center in China and the Peking Young Men's Christian Association; reliable Chinese investigators gathered much of the information, which was supplemented by government reports. Review, *Chinese Recorder,* 53 : 127, Feb. 1922. *b.* Account of modern conditions of labor in the most important industrial centers of China, with special interest in movements for constructive reform.   WHA

U2571 Chen Huan-Chang. *Economic principles of Confucius and his school.* 2 v. N. Y., 1911. [Columbia University studies in history, economics and public law.] (Bibliographical appendixes.)

Extensive treatise, the product of a Confucianist mandarin, well versed in Chinese lore and literature and with western scientific training. Review, *Chinese Recorder,* 43 : 365, 430, June, July, 1912.   WHA

U2572a Lee, Mabel Ping-Hua. *Economic history of China, with special reference to agriculture.* N. Y., 1921. [Columbia University studies in history, economics and public law.] (Chinese bibliography.)

b Morse, Hosea Ballou. *Chronicle of East India company trading to China, 1635–1834.* 4 v. Oxford, 1926. v. 5, *Supplementary, 1742–1774.* 1929.

a. Scientific survey of agrarian economics with voluminous and well-arranged translations of the source material. *b.* Written very largely from the official sources and containing much information, commercial, financial and political, the narrative is entertainingly told. Many documents, including correspondence, distributed through the work; good maps and illustrations. The supplementary volume fills gaps where the treatment was inadequate in the original work. Review, J. H. Clapham, *E.H.R.*, 42:289, Apr. 1927; of v. 5, K. S. Latourette, *A.H.R.*, 35:169, Oct. 1929. WHA

U2573a Chen, Shao-Kwan. *System of taxation in China in the Tsing dynasty, 1644–1911.* N. Y., 1914. [Columbia University studies in history, economics and public law.] (Chinese bibliography.)

b Huang, Hanliang. *Land tax in China.* N. Y., 1918. [Columbia University studies in history, economics and public law.] (Bibliography.)

Two doctoral dissertations, the results of scientific study of taxation in China. Review of *a*, A. P. Winston, *Amer. Econ. Rev.*, 5:119, March 1915; of *b*, *Chinese Recorder*, 50:561, Aug. 1919. WHA

U2574a United States—Department of Commerce. Julean Arnold, ed. *China. A commercial and industrial handbook.* Washington, 1926. [Trade promotion series, No. 38.]

b Jernigan, Thomas R. *China's business methods and policy.* London, 1904. (Bibliography.)

c —— *China in law and commerce.* N. Y. and London, 1905.

d Morse, Hosea Ballou. *Trade and administration of the Chinese empire.* 1908. 3rd rev. ed., London and N. Y., 1921.

a. Authoritative manual, with brief geographical and historical sketches and detailed reports, largely by United States consular and other officials, regarding the trade and industries of China. *b* and *c*. Author, a former American consul at Shanghai, describes the broader aspects of the conditions,—political, legal, social, commercial,—under which business is transacted in China, the later work being somewhat more detailed. Review of *b*, *Spectator*, 94:121, Jan. 28, 1905; of *c*, E. H. Parker, *Asiatic Quar. Rev.*, 3rd ser., 20:414, Oct. 1905. *d.* Partly descriptive of the administrative system of China, but primarily of trade and economics. Later editions have reflected some of the political changes in and since the Revolution of 1911. Review, E. H. Parker, *Asiatic Rev.*, n.s. 17:735, Oct. 1921. WHA

U2575a Sargent, Arthur John. *Anglo-Chinese commerce and diplomacy (mainly in the nineteenth century).* Oxford, 1907. (Bibliography.)

b Chu, Chin. *Tariff problem in China.* N. Y., 1916. [Columbia University studies in history, economics and public law.]

c See, Chong Su. *Foreign trade of China.* N. Y., 1919. [Columbia University studies in history, economics and public law.]

d Smith, Cades Alfred Middleton. *British in China and far eastern trade.* London, 1920.

a. Confining itself primarily to the history of commerce, especially British trade with China, this work shows clearly the basic part which commerce has played in China's foreign relations. It carries the story through the Boxer period. Review, *Asiatic Quar. Rev.,* 3rd ser., 25: 392, Apr. 1908. *b.* Exposition of the tariff system in China and its administration with special attention to the complications which have come from tariff agreements in treaties with foreign powers. Review, A. P. Winston, *Amer. Econ. Rev.,* 6: 928, Dec. 1916. *c.* Author modestly describes this valuable and rather extensive treatise as 'a humble attempt to trace briefly the development of China's commercial relations with the outside world from the earliest period to the present time, and to explain certain forces at work in that development.' Fair presentation of the case from the Chinese point of view, although not adequately recognizing difficulties emanating from China itself in the international situations which arose. Review, *Chinese Recorder,* 51: 434, June 1920. *d.* Much information regarding China's financial and commercial methods, presented with much human interest. Many specific details illustrate the larger movements which are treated; chapter on 'Britons who have served China' deserves special mention. Review, *Chinese Recorder,* 52: 433, June 1921.   WHA

U2576a Overlach, Theodore William. *Foreign financial control in China.* N. Y., 1919. (Bibliography.)

    b Wagel, Srinivas R. *Finance in China.* Shanghai, 1914.

    c —— *Chinese currency and banking.* Shanghai, 1915.

a. Historical examination of foreign encroachment, setting forth in successive chapters the interest and policy of Great Britain, Russia, France, Germany, Japan and the United States. An apologetic for international control. Review, *Chinese Recorder,* 50: 484, July 1919. *b* and *c.* Substantial treatises presenting the economic conditions of China in the early days of the Republic. *b* is the more general survey, including currency and banking, which are treated more exhaustively in *c.*   WHA

U2577a Kent, Percy Horace Braund. *Railway enterprise in China.* London, 1907.

    b Laboulaye, Édouard de. *Les chemins de fer de Chine.* Paris, 1911.

    c Hsu, Mongton Chih. *Railway problems in China.* N. Y., 1915. [Columbia University studies in history, economics and public law.] (Bibliographies.)

    d Stringer, Harold. *China: a new aspect.* London, 1929.

a. History of the beginnings of railways in China, with the opposition to the enterprise, the extension of the railways and the development of the State system. Valuable appendixes of documents. Review, *Nation* (N. Y.), 87: 82, July 23, 1908. *b.* Material gathered chiefly about the contracts or agreements under which the railroads have been constructed and administered. *c.* Critical study of railway development in China, with special reference to the political and economic problems involved, especially through the methods of foreign loans. Review, A. P. Winston, *Amer. Econ. Rev.,* 6: 121, March 1916. *d.* Especially valuable as stressing the significance of the avenues of communication, in particular the railways, in their bearing upon the foreign relations of China. Review, (London) *Times Lit. Suppl.,* 28: 803, Oct. 17, 1929.   WHA

CHINA: CULTURAL HISTORY

U2601a Hunter, William C. *Bits of old China.* 1885. 2nd ed., Shanghai, 1911.

b Smith, Arthur Henderson. *Chinese characteristics.* 1890. N. Y., 1918.

c Denby, Charles. *China and her people; being the observations, reminiscences, and conclusions of an American diplomat.* 2 v. Boston, 1906. [Travel lovers' library.]

d Giles, Herbert A. *Civilization of China.* N. Y., 1911. [Home university library.] (Bibliography.)

e Ross, Edward Alsworth. *Changing Chinese; the conflict of oriental and western cultures in China.* N. Y., 1911.

f Bashford, James Whitford. *China; an interpretation.* 1916. Rev. and enl. ed., N. Y., 1919. (Bibliography.)

g Werner, Edward T. C. *China of the Chinese.* London and N. Y., 1919. [Countries and peoples.]

h Hovelaque, Émile Lucien. *China.* London and N. Y., 1923. Tr. by Mrs. Laurence Binyon from *Les peuples d'Extrême-Orient. La Chine.* Paris, 1920. [Bibliothèque de philosophie scientifique.]

i High, Stanley. *China's place in the sun.* N. Y., 1922.

j Monroe, Paul. *China: a nation in evolution.* N. Y., 1928. (Bibliography.)

k Wilhelm, Richard. *Soul of China.* Tr. of text by J. H. Reece; of poems by A. Waley. N. Y., 1928.

This group of books is but a part of a much larger number written by Europeans or Americans who have visited or resided in China. Inevitably they are influenced by the limitations of opportunity for observation, by the special interests of the several authors, and to some extent by restrictions, usually self-imposed, upon freedom of utterance. Review of *a, Chinese Recorder,* 16: 230, June 1885; of *b, Asiatic Quar. Rev.,* n.s. 10:481, Oct. 1895; of *c,* J. W. Foster, *Atlantic,* 97: 543, Apr. 1906; of *d, Oriental Rev.,* 2:435, May 1912; of *e, ibid.,* 2: 169, Jan. 1912; of *f, Journal* (North China Branch, Royal Asiatic Society), 48:229, 1917; of *g,* L. Giles, *Asiatic Rev.,* n.s. 16:723, Oct. 1920; of *h, Oriental Rev.,* 56:606, Sept. 1925; of *i,* N. Peffer, *Nation* (N. Y.), 114:537, May 3, 1922; of *j, Chinese Recorder,* 59:450, July 1928; of *k, A.H.R.,* 34:651, Apr. 1929.

WHA

U2621a Parker, Edward Harper. *Studies in Chinese religion.* London, 1910.

b Clennell, Walter James. *Historical development of religion in China.* 1917. Rev. ed., London, 1926.

c Groot, Jan Jakob Maria de. *Religious system of China. Its ancient forms, evolution, history, and present aspect. Manners, customs, and social institutions connected therewith.* 4 v. Leyden, 1892–1901.

d Granet, Marcel. *La religion des Chinois.* Paris, 1922. [Science et civilisation.]

a. Professor of Chinese at the Victoria University of Manchester presents the early spiritual ideas of China; Taoism, Confucianism, Buddhism, Mohammedanism and the early contacts with Christianity are considered. Review, *Asiatic Quar. Rev.,* 3rd ser., 31: 179, Jan. 1911. *b.* Somewhat subjective exposition, with perhaps over-emphasis upon the elements in eastern religions similar to those with which the occidental world is familiar. Review, E. H. Parker, *Asiatic Rev.*, n.s. 12: 80, July 1917.

WHA

c. This standard work on the religious practices of China quotes extensively from Chinese sources, giving both Chinese text and translation, and also includes observations of the author on practices current when the book was written.

KSL

d. Relatively brief exposition of Chinese religion in its rural setting, in its forms expressive of the feudal relationships of Chinese life, in its official forms, and in its relations with Taoism and Buddhism. Review, *Chinese Recorder*, 41: 428, June 1910.

WHA

U2622a Legge, James. *Religions of China; Confucianism and Taoism described and compared with Christianity.* London, 1880; N. Y., 1881.

b Douglas, Sir Robert Kennaway. *Confucianism and Taoism.* London, 1879. [Non-Christian religious systems.]

c Soothill, William Edward. *Three religions of China.* London and N. Y., 1913. [Expositor's library.]

d Giles, Herbert Allen. *Confucianism and its rivals.* N. Y., 1915. [Hibbert lectures, second series.]

This group represents comparative studies of the religious systems of China, with Christianity generally included explicitly in the comparison. All the authors were professors in English universities and the works, except *b*, were first given as lectures. Review of *d*, H. H. Scullard, *Hibbert Jour.*, 14: 217, Oct. 1915.

WHA

U2623a Legge, James. *Life and teachings of Confucius, with explanatory notes.* London, 1867. [Chinese classics. cf. (U2661a).]

b —— *Life and works of Mencius, with essays and notes.* London, 1875. [Chinese classics. cf. (U2661a).]

c Dawson, Miles Menander, ed. *Ethics of Confucius.* N. Y. and London, 1915.

a and *b.* Not merely biographies of Confucius and Mencius, but introductions to their writings and to the study of them, by the professor of Chinese literature at Oxford. *c.* Arrangement of the sayings of Confucius and some of his disciples to set forth his and their teachings upon 'the superior man.' It interprets Confucianism as not a religion but an ethical system. Review, T. C. Chao, *Chinese Recorder*, 49: 606, Sept. 1918.

WHA

U2624a Edkins, Joseph. *Chinese Buddhism; a volume of sketches, historical, descriptive, and critical.* 1880. 2nd rev. ed., London, 1893. [Trübner's oriental series.]

b Beal, Samuel. *Buddhism in China.* London, 1884. [Non-Christian religious systems.]

c Johnston, Reginald Fleming. *Buddhist China.* London, 1913.

d McGovern, William Montgomery. *Introduction to Mahāyāna Buddhism, with especial reference to Chinese and Japanese phases.* London and N. Y., 1922.

e Pratt, James Bissett. *Pilgrimage of Buddhism.* N. Y., 1928.

a. Following a life of Buddha and a sketch of the history of Buddhism in China, the author expounds the religion and philosophy of Buddhism with some special attention to its development in China. Review, *China Rev.*, 9: 112, Sept.-

Oct. 1880. *b.* While primarily an exposition of Buddhist doctrines and customs in China, this brief work sets forth many of the mutual influences of India and China. *c.* Historical, descriptive, and illustrated account of Buddhism in China, with special interest in the schools, monasticism and pilgrimages. Review, *Dial,* 56: 305, Apr. 1, 1914. *d.* Exposition of the so-called 'northern' school of Buddhism which became predominant in China and Japan. Review, (London) *Times Lit. Suppl.,* 21 : 42, Jan. 19, 1922.   WHA
  e. Very readable general introduction to Buddhism.   AWH

U2625a Stauffer, Milton T., ed. *Christian occupation of China.* Shanghai, 1922.

  b Latourette, Kenneth Scott. *History of Christian missions in China.* N. Y., 1929.

  a. Commonly called the 'China Survey,' a mine of accurate information, primarily concerning the Christian (Protestant) missionary movement, but with other valuable historical data. Annual survey. *b.* Most comprehensive history of the subject. The 'religious background of the Chinese,' the 'outstanding characteristics of Christianity,' Roman Catholic, Russian Orthodox, and Protestant missions are treated in well-proportioned manner and the changes of recent years up to 1926 described and analyzed.   WHA

U2641a Reichwein, Adolf. *China and European intellectual and artistic contacts in the eighteenth century.* London and N. Y., 1925. [(B153a) History of civilization.] Tr. by J. C. Powell from *China und Europa,* Berlin, 1923.

  b Tsuchida, Kyoson. *Contemporary thought in Japan and China.* London, 1927. [Library of contemporary thought.]

  a. Probably throws as much light upon eighteenth century Europe as upon Chinese thought and art, but these latter are brought out in somewhat unusual perspective and relief by the European reactions to them. Review, K. S. Latourette, *A.H.R.,* 31 : 129, Oct. 1925. *b.* Gives brief summaries of the philosophical ideas of contemporary thinkers and emphasizes the lack of connection in thought between the Chinese and the Japanese; represents the contemporary thought of both these people as largely the effort 'to reconstruct their systems on the basis of Western philosophies, keeping scarcely any of their own traditional ideals.'

        WHA

U2642 Kuo, Ping Wen. *Chinese system of public education.* N. Y., 1915. [Teachers College, Columbia University, Contributions to education.] (Bibliography.)

  Monograph describing ancient education system and its decadence; the development of education for over two thousand years (to A.D. 1842) under the successive dynasties; the influence of the West upon Chinese education until its reorganization under the Republic. Review, *Chinese Recorder,* 49: 122, Feb. 1918.

        WHA

U2661a Legge, James. *Chinese classics: with a translation, critical and exegetical notes, prolegomena and copious indexes.* 5 v. in 8. Hong Kong and London, 1861–72. 2nd rev. ed., Oxford, 1893–95.

  b Soothill, William Edward. *Analects of Confucius.* N. Y., 1910.

  c Giles, Lionel. *Sayings of Confucius.* London, 1907.

  d ——— *Sayings of Lao-tzu.* 1904. London, 1926.

 e **Fung, Yu-Lan.** *Comparative study of life's ideals.* Shanghai, 1925.

 f **Li Po.** *Works of Li Po, the Chinese poet.* Tr. into English verse by Shigeyoshi Oblata. N. Y., 1922. (Bibliography.)

 g **Ayscough, Mrs. Florence,** tr. *Fir-flower tablets; poems translated from the Chinese.* Boston, 1921.

 a. Carefully edited translations of the most important classics of Chinese literature. In the second edition, only v. 1 and 2 are revised, v. 3–5 being reprints. Review of v. 1, J. Edkins, *Asiatic Quar. Rev.,* n.s. 6: 256, July 1893.   GMD

 b, c, d, e, f, and *g.* Group of somewhat representative writings in English translation; *b* and *c,* the most readable versions of the Analects; *d,* the best English translation of the *Tao Te Ching; e,* the best comparative study of the Eastern and Western world view in English. Review of *b, Chinese Recorder,* 42: 174, March 1911; *Asiatic Quar. Rev.,* 3rd series, 32: 416, Oct. 1911. Review of *c,* E. H. Parker, *Asiatic Quar. Rev.,* 3rd ser., 25: 410, Apr. 1908; of *d, id., ibid.,* 19: 207, Jan. 1905; of *g, Bookman,* 54: 378, Dec. 1921.   AWH

U2662a Giles, Herbert Allen. *History of Chinese literature.* N. Y., 1901. [Short histories of the world.] (Bibliographical note.)

 b **Buss, Kate.** *Studies in the Chinese drama.* Boston, 1922.

 a. Thoroughly competent scholar gives account of a few hundred leading Chinese works, with translated extracts. Review, W. T. Swingle, *A.H.R.,* 26: 724, July 1921.   GMD

 b. Brief introduction to an understanding of the Chinese drama through attention to its historical evolution, its relation to Chinese life and religion,—its actors, its music, its costumes and symbolic designs. Review, *Chinese Recorder,* 53: 543, Aug. 1922.   WHA

U2681a Bushell, Stephen Wootton. *Chinese art.* 2 v. 1905–06. 2nd rev. ed., London, 1909.

 b **Giles, Herbert Allen.** *Introduction to the history of Chinese pictorial art.* 1905. 2nd enl. ed., Shanghai, 1918.

 c **Ferguson, John Calvin.** *Outlines of Chinese Art.* Chicago, 1919. [Scammon lectures.]

 d **Hetherington, A. L.** *Early ceramic wares of China.* N. Y., 1922.

These works will serve as an introduction to the more important forms of Chinese art and to the essential facts of their historical development. See also (U681) and (U3681). Review of *a, Chinese Recorder,* 40: 590, Oct. 1909; of *b,* H. L. Joly, *Asiatic Rev.,* n.s. 15: 137, Jan. 1919; of *c,* F. Ayscough, *Chinese Recorder,* 51: 202, March 1920.   GMD

CHINA: BIOGRAPHY

(U2701) H: A. Giles, *Chinese biographical dictionary,* London and Shanghai, 1898; (U2702) M. E. Burton, *Notable women of modern China,* N. Y., 1912; (U2703) J. Quincy, *Journals of Major Samuel Shaw, the first American consul at Canton. With a life of the author,* Boston, 1847; (U2704) D. Abeel, *Journal of a residence in China, and the neighboring countries, from 1829 to 1833,* N. Y., 1834; (U2705) G. B. Stevens, *Life, letters and journals of the Rev. and Hon. Peter Parker,* Boston, 1896; (U2706) F. W. Williams, *Life and letters of Samuel Wells Williams, missionary, diplomatist, sinologue,* N. Y. and London, 1889;

(U2707) S. Lane-Poole, *Life of Sir Harry Parkes . . . sometime Her Majesty's minister to China and Japan,* 2 v., London and N. Y., 1894; (U2708) L. Oliphant, *Narrative of the earl of Elgin's mission to China and Japan in the years 1857, '58, '59,* 2 v., Edinburgh, 1859; (U2709) H. B. Loch (Lord Loch), *Personal narrative of occurrences during Lord Elgin's second embassy to China in 1860,* London, 1900; (U2710) A. E. Hake, *Story of Chinese Gordon,* N. Y., 1884; (U2711) D. C. Boulger, *Life of Gordon,* 2 v., London, 1896; (U2712) R. B. Forbes, *Personal reminiscences,* 3rd ed., Boston, 1892; (U2713) A. Michie, *The Englishman in China during the Victorian era, as illustrated in the career of Sir Rutherford Alcock,* 2 v., Edinburgh, 1900; (U2714) P. W. Sergeant, *The great empress dowager of China,* London, 1910; (U2715) J. O. P. Bland, *Li Hung-Chang,* London, 1917; (U2716) H. Croly, *Willard Straight,* N. Y., 1924.

CHINA: PERIODICALS

(U2941) *China year book,* London and N. Y., 1912–19; Peking, 1921 ff.; (U2942) *China mission year book,* Shanghai, 1910 ff.; (U2943) *North China herald,* Shanghai, 1850 ff.; (U2944) *Chinese recorder,* Foochow and Shanghai, 1868 ff.; (U2945) *China review,* Hongkong, 1872–1901; (U2946) *Chinese repository,* Canton, 1832–51; (U2947) *China,* London, 1902–15; (U2948) *China weekly review* (Millard's), Shanghai, 1917 ff.; (U2949) *Chinese social and political science review,* Peking, 1916 ff.; (U2950) *Chinese students' monthly,* Baltimore, etc., 1905 ff. (U2961) *Journal,* Shanghai, 1858 ff. [North China Branch, Royal Asiatic Society.] Cf. also U941 ff.

WHA

JAPAN: BIBLIOGRAPHY AND ENCYCLOPEDIAS

Some of the bibliographies of (U1 ff.) Asia and (U2001 ff.) China contain material for the history of Japan, as do many of the works listed in § B, General history, and § V, Oceanica. For the current bibliography of Japan, which (U3001c) Nachod has brought up to date, cf. bibliographies in such periodicals as (U2d) *Asiatica,* (U954) *T'oung pao,* (U956) *Bulletin de l'École Française d'Extrême-Orient,* and (U3963) *Bulletin de la Société Franco-Japonaise de Paris.*

U3001a Wenckstern, Friedrich von. *Bibliography of the Japanese empire.* 2 v. London, 1895 and Tokyo, 1907. [v. 1] *being a classified list of all books, essays, and maps in European languages relating to Dai Nihon (Great Japan) published in Europe, America, and in the East from 1859–93 A.D. (VIth year of Ansei—XXVIth of Meiji) to which is added a facsimile-reprint of Léon Pagès: Bibliographie japonaise, depuis le XVe siècle jusqu'à 1859.* London, 1905. [v. 2] *comprising the literature from 1894 to the middle of 1906 (XXVII–IXLth year of Meiji), with additions and corrections to the first volume and a supplement to Léon Pagès' Bibliographie japonaise. Added is a list of the Swedish literature on Japan by Miss Valfrid Palmgren.* Tokyo, 1907.

b Cordier, Henri. *Bibliotheca japonica. Dictionnaire bibliographique des ouvrages relatifs à l'empire japonaise rangés par ordre chronologique jusqu'à 1870, suivi d'un appendice renfermant la liste alphabétique des principaux ouvrages paru de 1870 à 1912.* Paris, 1912. [Publications de l'École des Langues Orientales Vivantes, series 5, v. 8.]

c Nachod, Oskar, compiler. *Bibliography of the Japanese empire, 1906–1926.* 2 v. London, 1928.

a. Books are listed under subject headings. No works in the Russian language are included. In both these respects it differs from *b,* in which the arrangement of titles is chronological up to 1870, and alphabetical from 1870 to 1912. *b.* Includes a careful revision and continuation of Pagès and was the more up-to-date; but both *a* and *b* are supplemented by *c,* which is an exhaustive classified list of the literature issued up to 1926 since the publication of *a,* of which it is a continuation. Special attention is directed to its section (8) on bibliography and to its inclusion of Russian works, concerning which see its Preface, p. 7. It represents one form of bibliographical presentation at its best, classified, with continuous enumeration, but the binder's designation of the volumes as 3 and 4 (continuing Wenckstern's two volumes), complicates citation needlessly.

WHA

U3002a Gay, Helen K. *Reading list on Japan.* Albany, N. Y., 1898. [State library bulletin, Bibliography, No. 6.]

b New York—Public Library Reference Department. *List of works in the New York public library relating to Japan.* N. Y., 1906.

Both need to be brought up to date, yet useful especially for the general reader.

WHA

U3021a Chamberlain, Basil Hall. *Things Japanese, being notes on various subjects connected with Japan.* 1890. Reprint of 5th ed. 1905, rev., with 2 appendixes, London and Kobe, 1927. (Bibliographies.)

b Papinot, E. *Historical and geographical dictionary of Japan.* Tokyo, 1910. Tr. of *Dictionnaire d'histoire et de géographie du Japon,* Tokyo, 1906.

a. Readable compilation of useful and interesting information about Japan, based on personal knowledge and on the best authorities at the time of writing. Much of the information could not be elsewhere obtained so readily. Review, E. H. Parker, *China Rev.,* 18: 381, May-June 1890; of 5th ed. rev., *Japan Weekly Chronicle,* n.s. no. 1343, p. 326, Sept. 29, 1927. HMV

b. Based on a smaller French work (Hongkong, 1899); items defined or explained are chiefly biographical or geographical, but also comprise historical, cultural and bibliographical data, accompanied by maps and illustrations. Inadequate definitions are given in some cases, as of the *jito, shugo, sho,* and other important but difficult terms, yet the work is indispensable to all foreign students of Japanese history. KA

U3022a Greene, Daniel Crosby; and others, eds. *Christian movement· in Japan including Korea and Formosa.* Yokohama, 1903–04; Tokyo, 1905 ff.

b Takenobu, Y.; and others, eds. *Japan year book.* Tokyo, 1905 ff.

a. Annual survey of events, followed by more detailed accounts of the activities of the various missions, churches and other religious organizations; social and literary activities are recorded, with statistical and other information, including personnel. *b.* Of somewhat more general scope; a repertory of general information and current statistics, covering in all numbers since 1914 the Japanese territories as well as the Japanese islands. WHA

JAPAN: GEOGRAPHY AND ETHNOLOGY

U3041a Imperial Japanese Government Railways. *Official guide to eastern Asia, transcontinental connections between Europe and Asia.* 5 v. Tokyo, 1913–17. [1, *Manchuria and Chosen;* 2, *South-western Japan;* 3, *North-eastern Japan.*]

b Chamberlain, Basil Hall; and others. *Handbook for travellers in Japan.* 1881. 9th rev. ed., London, 1913. [(B43*b*) Murray's hand-books.]

c **Terry, T. Philip.** *Terry's Japanese empire including Korea and Formosa, with chapters on Manchuria, the Trans-Siberian railway and the chief ocean routes to Japan.* 1914. 3rd ed., rev., Boston, London and Tokyo, 1928.

Excellent travellers' guides, well provided with maps and plans. Introductory sections as well as occasional paragraphs furnish good digests of information on history, art, literature, and other topics. Review of *a, Asiatic Rev.,* n.s. 14 : 400, July 1918; of *b,* E. J. Eitel, *China Rev.,* 19 : 329, March-Apr. 1891; of *c, Japan Weekly Chronicle,* n.s. no. 1403 : 646, Nov. 22, 1928. GMD

U3051 **Rein, Johannes Justus.** *Japan: travels and researches undertaken at the cost of the Prussian government.* London, 1884. Tr. from *Japan nach Reisen und Studien im Auftrage der königlich preussischen Regierung dargestellt.* 1880. 2nd rev. ed., Leipzig, 1905.

Translation made after some revision of the original German work. Rather comprehensive survey of the physical geography of Japan is followed by a fuller treatment of the Japanese people, including the history in general and the ethnography, with some details of local topography. WHA

U3052 **Batchelor, John.** *Ainu life and lore. Echoes of a departing race.* Tokyo (n.d.) (1927?).

Representing intimate and long acquaintance, during approximately fifty years as a missionary among the Ainu, this practically supplants two earlier works by the same author. WHA

JAPAN: COLLECTIONS OF SOURCES

U3061a **Japan—Ministère des Affaires Étrangères.** *Traités et conventions entre l'empire du Japon et les puissances étrangères.* 2 v. Tokyo, 1908. (Earlier eds. in various European languages, 1854 ff.)

b **Rundall, Thomas,** ed. *Memorials of Japan in the XVI and XVII centuries.* London, 1850. [Hakluyt Society.]

c **McLaren, Walter Wallace,** ed. *Japanese government documents. 1867–1889.* Tokyo, 1914. [Asiatic Society of Japan. Transactions, v. 42, pt. 1.]

a. Texts of treaties and other agreements directly between the government of Japan and other countries; second volume contains the texts of international conventions to which Japan adheres. The language is generally that of the other contracting power, but in some instances is also given in English (or) and French. *b.* Part 1 consists of a sixteenth century description of the Japanese empire from 'The Firste Books of Relations of Moderne States' (Harleian Mss. 6259); pt. 2 of six letters of William Adams, 1611–17, correspondence which 'in the sequel . . . led to the opening of commercial intercourse between England and Japan.' Editor has appended explanatory notes. *c.* English text of official documents covering over two decades of modern Japan, dealing largely with the internal organization, including that of local government; contains also a number of memorials expressive of some unofficial opinion. Review, W. R. Shepherd, *Pol. Sci. Quar.,* 33 : 131, March 1918. WHA

JAPAN: GENERAL HISTORIES

U3101a **Brinkley, Frank,** and **Kikuchi, Dairoku, Baron.** *History of the Japanese people from the earliest times to the end of the Meiji era.* 1912. N. Y., 1915.

b **Asakawa, Kanichi,** ed. *Japan. From the Japanese government history.* Philadelphia, 1906. [History of nations.] (Bibliography.)

a. Most complete, and in some respects the best single volume work covering the whole range of Japanese history, but has the faults of exaggerated nationalistic point of view held by officials. Review, K. Asakawa, *A.H.R.*, 21 : 600, Apr. 1916.

GMD

b. Consists of the 'History of the Empire of Japan' compiled for the Imperial Japanese Commission of the Chicago exposition of 1893, but slightly revised and enlarged, bringing the history down to 1906.

WHA

U3102a Murray, David. *Story of Japan.* 1894. Rev. ed., A. W. Vorse, continuing the history to close of 1905, and supplementary chapters by Baron K. Kaneko, *Japan.* 6th ed., with supplementary chapter by J. H. Longford. London and N. Y., 1920. [Story of the nations.]

    b Longford, Joseph H. *Story of old Japan.* London, 1910. (Bibliography.)

    c —— *Japan of the Japanese.* N. Y., 1912.

    d —— *Evolution of new Japan.* Cambridge (Eng.) and N. Y., 1913. [Cambridge manuals of science and literature.] (Brief bibliography.)

    e Saito, Hisho. *History of Japan.* London, 1912. Tr. by Elizabeth Lee from *Geschichte Japans.* Berlin, 1912.

    f Davis, Frederick Hadland. *Japan, from the age of the gods to the fall of Tsing-tau.* London and N. Y., 1916.

    g Gubbins, John Harington. *Japan.* London, 1920. [Peace handbooks.]

    h Gowen, Herbert Henry. *Outline history of Japan.* N. Y., 1927. (Bibliography.)

    i Scherer, James A. B. *Romance of Japan through the ages.* N. Y., 1927.

a. Popular account of Japan and its history by one who from 1873 to 1879 was special adviser to the Imperial minister of education. Review, *Oriental Rev.*, 2 : 308, March 1912.

WHA

b. Narrative history of Japan from earliest time to the Restoration, 1868. Introductory chapter on the country and people, with appendixes containing chronological and other useful data. Uncritical, but most readable and lucid. Review, *Oriental Rev.*, 1 : 212, Apr. 10, 1911.

WWM

c and *d.* Descriptive accounts rather than analytical studies. Review of *c, Oriental Rev.*, 2 : 561, July 1912; *d,* K. Kato, *Japanese Student,* 1 : 208, June 1917.

RLB

e. Concise, elementary; three-quarters of space given to period prior to 1868. Review, L. Reiss, *Hist. Zeit.*, 109 : 631, 1912.

GMD

f, g and *h.* Good, brief, popular, narrative histories. Review of *h, A.H.R.*, 33 : 738, July 1928.

WHA

i. Popular, written to make clear 'the historical evolution of Japan.' Not original but a suggestive outline emphasizing the spiritual and æsthetic as well as the social and political forces in Japan's history. Review, (London) *Times Lit. Suppl.*, 26 : 465, July 7, 1927.

HRS

U3103 Hara, Katsuro. *Introduction to the history of Japan.* N. Y., 1920. [Yamato society publication.]

Not a conventional text-book compiled from known works, but a highly individual though quite catholic interpretation of history written by a master who is professor in the University of Kyoto,—the first general history of Japan that has been written with any real knowledge of a large part of its contents, although the reader should beware of the author's views of the important institutions of the *sho-yen* and the *jito*. Treatment of the cultural development is fresh and vigorous. Review, P. J. Treat, *A.H.R.*, 26: 539, Apr. 1921. KA

U3104 Koch, W. *Japan: Geschichte nach japanischen Quellen und ethnographische Skizzen.* Dresden, 1904.

Compact critical sketch of the history of Japan (with considerable correction of earlier writers in European languages), to the Anglo-Japanese alliance of 1902, followed by 'ethnographic sketches,' alphabetically and topically arranged.

WHA

U3121a Brinkley, Frank. *Japan, its history, arts, and literature.* 8 v. 1901–02. Reprint, Boston, 1910. [Oriental series.]

b Murdoch, James. *History of Japan.* 3 v. 1903–26. Rev. and ed. by J. H. Longford, London, 1926. [1, *From the origin to the arrival of the Portuguese in 1542 A.D.*, Yokohama, 1910; 2, *During the century of early foreign intercourse, 1542–1651*, Kobe, 1903; 3, *The Tokugawa epoch, 1652–1868*.]

a. Reliable and perhaps the fullest good account in English of the subjects with which it deals, by an editor of the *Japan Advertiser;* particularly important for the art, customs and cultural history of the older Japan. Review, W. E. Griffis, *A.H.R.*, 8: 154, Oct. 1902. *b*. Standard and authoritative work, well written and based upon careful research in both Japanese and Chinese sources, chiefly, although not entirely, concerned with political history. Review of v. 1, K. Asakawa, *A.H.R.*, 16: 630, Apr. 1911; of v. 2, E. H. Parker, *Asiatic Quar. Rev.*, 3rd ser., 17: 423, Apr. 1904; of v. 3, *Transactions* (Japan Society London), 23: 214, 1925–26. KSL

U3122 Kaempfer, Engelbert. *History of Japan, together with a description of the kingdom of Siam, 1690–92.* 1727. 2nd ed., 3 v., Glasgow, 1906. Tr. by J. G. Scheuchzer from Ms. of De beschryving van Japan . . . benevens eene beschryving van het koningryk Siam.

By a physician of the Dutch East India Company who spent two years on the island of Deshima in the harbor of Nagasaki; an eager observer and student, he went on two of the annual embassies to Yedo. His book, therefore, is of great interest and contains a summary of the history of Japan up to the time of writing, and a description of the country, its plants and animals, its religions and its language. Review, *Saturday Review*, 102: 17, July 7, 1906. KSL

U3123a Charlevoix, Pierre François Xavier de. *Histoire et description générale du Japon.* Paris, 1736.

b La Mazelière, Antoine Rous, Marquis de. *Le Japon, histoire et civilisation.* 8 v. Paris, 1907–23.

a. By a Jesuit father, based only upon material in European languages. Contains description of the country and its people and customs, and gives brief account of the history of the land, especially during the sixteenth and seventeenth centuries; is particularly valuable for its narrative of early Christian missions in Japan and of the persecution that put an end to them. The work is by no means infallible and must be used with discrimination. KSL

b. Comprehensive survey of the entire range of Japanese history, with exposition of the most important features of Japanese civilization. Review of various volumes, K. Asakawa, *A.H.R.*, 13: 837, July 1908; 16: 134, Oct. 1910; of v. 7 and 8, W. E. Soothill, *E.H.R.*, 40: 298, Apr. 1925. Also cf. (U3121a) Brinkley, *Japan.*   LRM

JAPAN: HISTORIES OF PERIODS, REGIONS, OR TOPICS

U3201a Munro, Neil Gordon. *Prehistoric Japan.* 1908. 2nd ed., Yokohama, 1911.

    b Nachod, Oskar. *Geschichte von Japan.* v. 1, bk. 1. *Die Urzeit (bis 645 n. Chr.)* Gotha, 1906. [(B161) Allgemeine Staatengeschichte.] (Bibliography.)

a. Beginning with a brief and very cautious statement concerning the paleolithic phase, the writer brings the reader the evidence, supported by many illustrations, of the developing culture of man in Japan, the ceramic material being especially rich in contribution to our knowledge. Concluding chapters deal with prehistoric religion and ethnology. *b.* One of the earlier works using modern scientific historical method, although relying largely upon sources in translation. Review, C. E. Maitre, *Rev. Hist.*, 96: 316, sup. vol. 1908.   WHA

U3202a Asakawa, Kanichi. *Early institutional life of Japan.* Tokyo, 1903.

    b Bertin, Louis Émile. *Les grandes guerres civiles du Japon. Les minamoto & les taira—les mikados & les siogouns (1156–1392) précédé d'une introduction sur l'histoire ancienne & les légendes.* Paris, 1894.

    c Yamada, Nakaba. *Ghenkō—The Mongol invasion of Japan.* London, 1916. (Bibliography.)

    d Nagaoka, H. *Histoire des relations du Japon avec l'Europe aux XVIe et XVIIe siècles.* Paris, 1905.

a. Study of the reform of A.D. 645 to explain the origins of feudalism in Japan. The reform is described as 'a supreme effort of the theory of divine succession, which had been almost obliterated, to once more assert itself by striking down the tribal organism and substituting for it a new state modelled after a foreign [Chinese] example, and by converting the powers claimed and lost by the emperor into public powers of the new state.' Review, G. W. Knox, *A.H.R.*, 11: 128, Oct. 1905.   LRM
b. Deals with the successive civil wars among contending clans to the abdication of the dynasty of the South. An 'epilogue' summarizes briefly the history to the restoration of the Mikado. Interesting illustrations. *c.* Covers the Mongol invasion in the thirteenth century, with an introduction on the antecedent relations with Korea and the aggressiveness of Kublai Khan. Review, *Asiatic Rev.*, n.s. 12: 72, July 1917; J. H. Gubbins, *E.H.R.*, 31: 640, Oct. 1916. *d.* Good account of the rise and fall of Christianity in Japan and the commercial relations of Japan with Europe to 1800. Review, H. Hauser, *Rev. Hist.*, 94: 392, July-Aug. 1907.   WHA

U3203a Nachod, Oskar. *Die Beziehungen der Niederländischen Ostindischen Kompagnie zu Japan im 17. Jahrhundert.* Leipzig, 1897.   ·

    b Feenstra Kuiper, J. *Japan en de buitenwereld in de achttiende eeuw.* 's-Gravenhage, 1921. [v. 3 of *Werken uitgegeven door de Vereeniging het Nederlandsch Economisch-Historisch Archief.*] (Bibliography.)

    c Chijs, Jacobus A. Vander. *Neerlands streven tot Openstelling van Japan voor den wereldhandel. Uit officieele, grootendeels onuitgegeven beschieden toegelicht.* 's-Gravenhage, 1921.

These three volumes taken in order give the history of the Dutch intercourse with Japan in the seventeenth, eighteenth, and nineteenth centuries, and are of special value since during most of the period the Dutch were the only outside people in contact with Japan. Review of *b*, V. S. Clark, *A.H.R.*, *27*: 156, Oct. 1921.

GMD

U3204 Aston, William G., tr. *Nihongi, chronicles of Japan from the earliest times to A.D. 697.* 2 v. London, 1896. [Transactions and proceedings of the Japan Society, London.]

One of the most important sources for the earliest history of Japan, reaching back into the mythology and ancient folklore. Excellent notes. Review of v. 1, *Asiatic Quar. Rev.*, 3rd ser., 2: 204, July 1896.

WHA

U3241 Hawks, Francis L. *Narrative of the expedition of an American squadron to the China seas and Japan, performed in the years 1852, 1853, and 1854, under the command of Commodore M. C. Perry, United States navy, by order of the government of the United States. Compiled from the original notes and journals of Commodore Perry and his officers, at his request and under his supervision.* 3 v. Washington, 1856. [Published by order of the Congress of the United States.]

Official account of the Commodore Perry expedition. Well illustrated with lithographs and woodcuts. The correspondence, etc., relative to this expedition was also printed in Executive document no. 34, 33rd Congress, 2nd session, (Senate).

WHA

U3251a Yamaguchi, Ken. *Kinsé Shiriaku. A history of Japan, from the first visit of Commodore Perry in 1853 to the capture of Hakodate by the Mikado's forces in 1859.* Tr. from the Japanese by E. M. Satow. 3 v. in 1, 1873. Rev. ed. with supplementary notes by Shuziro Watanabe. Tokyo, 1906.

   b Gubbins, John H. *Progress of Japan, 1853–1871.* Oxford, 1911.

a. Of special interest as giving an account from the Japanese point of view of the early phases of the modern contact of Japan with western civilization. WHA

b. Concise account of Japan in her transitional years. Although undue stress is laid on the attitude of the great nobles toward public questions, with a consequent under-emphasis on the work of the leading samurai, and although the extent to which the emperor was controlled by the western clans might have been brought out more clearly, the account is substantially accurate. Twenty-three appendices include the texts of several treaties. Review, *Oriental Rev.*, 2: 245, Feb. 1912.

HMV

U3252a Mossman, Samuel. *New Japan, the land of the rising sun; its annals during the past twenty years, recording the remarkable progress of the Japanese in western civilization.* London, 1873.

   b McLaren, Walter Wallace. *Political history of Japan during the meiji era, 1867–1912.* London and N. Y., 1916.

   c Latourette, Kenneth Scott. *Development of Japan.* N. Y., 1918. (Bibliography.)

   d Gubbins, John H. *Making of modern Japan, an account of the progress of Japan from pre-feudal days to constitutional government & the position of a great power.* . . . London, 1922.

a. Narrative history, year by year, from 1853 through the Japanese embassy to Europe for the investigation of western civilization. WHA *b.* Survey of the evolution of existing political institutions of Japan, a critical examination of these institutions, and a history of Japanese politics, domestic and foreign, from 1890 to 1913. Scholarly indictment of the spirit and methods of the Japanese constitutional monarchy. Author is especially qualified by training as an economist and by a long residence and study in Japan. Illuminating accounts of political personalities. Author considers the mainspring of Japanese policy to be 'the strength of the military oligarchy,' which in turn is 'explained by the inherent chauvinism of the Japanese.' 'Japanese predominance in Eastern Asia has become the foundation of the national policy.' Review, P. J. Treat, *A.H.R.*, 22 : 859, July 1917; W. R. Shepherd, *Pol. Sci. Quar.*, 33 : 131, March 1918.   SKH

c. Valuable essay on the development of Japan as a cultural state. Rather inadequate treatment of the history before 1853, but more satisfactory account of events since, related without prejudice and with due emphasis upon essential factors in the process of national reconstruction. Review, P. J. Treat, *A.H.R.*, 24 : 128, Oct. 1918.   FWW

d. The first chapters include the same material as in author's (U3251*b*) *Progress of Japan.* Then the progress of Japan to 1920 is discussed, but internal developments since 1895 are not treated. The new constitutional system is seen in more favorable light than by many authors. Foreign affairs are emphasized throughout and attention paid to economic development. Review, *Saturday Review*, 134 : 680, Nov. 4, 1922.   HMV

U3253a Dyer, Henry. *Dai Nippon. A study in national evolution.* 1904. 2nd ed., London and N. Y., 1905. (Bibliography.)

   b McGovern, William M. *Modern Japan; its political, military, and industrial organization.* London, 1920.

   c Okakura, Kakuzo. *Awakening of Japan.* 1904. N. Y., 1921. (Original English ed., *Ideals of the East,* London, 1903.)

   d Tsurumi, Yusuke. *Present day Japan.* N. Y. and London, 1926.

   e Bellesort, André. *Le nouveau Japon.* Paris, 1916.

a. Written at the time of Russo-Japanese war by the chief agent in organizing what became the Imperial College of Engineering; thoughtful interpretation of the political, economic and social evolution of modern Japan.   WHA

b. Entire volume is built around the conception of the bureaucratic or oligarchic control in Japan, the types of organization mentioned in the sub-title being discussed to show how a narrow oligarchy gained, maintains and uses its power. The successes rather than the failures of the Japanese bureaucracy are emphasized. With minor exceptions the book is accurate and gives a true picture of modern Japan. Review, R. H. Akagi, *Japan Rev.*, 4 : 275, July 1920.   HMV

c. A leader in the reactionary movement against the subordination of indigenous Japanese culture points out the intellectual and moral qualities of Japan in its modern transition, with keen analysis of the situation within and without. Review, *Asiatic Quar. Rev.*, 3rd ser., 16 : 426, Oct. 1903. *d.* Six lectures, interpreting to American audience the changing Japanese life; the old and the new—intellectual currents—the modern literature—the impact upon the Japanese mind of the American immigration law. Review, *N. Y. Times Book Review*, p. 20, Dec. 26, 1926. *e.* Somewhat journalistic, but contains rather unusual expositions of modern Japanese life.   WHA

U3254a Okuma, Shigenobu, Count, and others. *Fifty years of new Japan.*
1909. 2nd ed., 2 v. London, 1910. Tr. by M. B. Huish from *Kaikoku gojunen shi,* Tokyo, 1907–08.

b Satow, Sir Ernest M. *Diplomat in Japan; the inner history of the critical years in the evolution of Japan.* . . . London, 1921.

a. Covers practically all the important phases of modern Japanese life, including also an outline of the history of the period. Mine of information, but as a whole the work must be described as a high-class piece of special pleading obviously written for foreign consumption. Appendix contains the text of the constitution. Review, K. Asakawa, *A.H.R.,* 15 : 868, July 1910.   WWM

b. This work, by an official of the British Legation at Tokio and later British minister at Peking, covers the earlier part, 1862–69, of his career in Japan and reveals much of the inner history of what the author terms 'the critical years in the evolution of Japan when the ports were opened and the monarchy restored.' Review, *Transactions* (Japan Society, London), 18 : 111, 1921.

U3261a Hershey, Amos S. *International law and diplomacy of the Russo-Japanese war.* N. Y. and London, 1906.

b Asakawa, Kanichi. *Russo-Japanese conflict, its causes and issues.* Boston, 1904.

c Historical Section of Committee of Imperial (British) Defense. *Russo-Japanese war, official history, naval and military.* London, 1910–1912 (?)

d United States Cavalry Association, ed. *German official account of the Russo-Japanese war.* 5 v. Fort Leavenworth, Kan., 1912.

e Ariga, Nagao. *La guerre Russo-Japonaise au point de vue continental et le droit international.* Paris, 1908.

a. Fair and authoritative treatment of questions in international law raised during the war, particularly with respect to neutral rights and obligations; covers also the diplomatic phases of the struggle, its causes and conclusion, and the attempt to safeguard Chinese neutrality. Review, T. S. Woolsey, *A.H.R.,* 12 : 652, Apr. 1907.   HMV

b. Exposition of the antecedents of the war by a Japanese scholar resident in the United States. Review, *Nation* (N. Y.), 80 : 98, Feb. 2, 1905. *c* and *d.* British and German staff histories of the war, the latter the more thorough. The Russian and Japanese staff histories are available in French. There is no good book in English on this war for the general reader, who must consult general works on the period. Cf. (U431*g*) T. Dennett, *Roosevelt and the Russo-Japanese war.*

                    GMD
e. Comprehensive account of the war, constructed largely from the Japanese official documents, giving much information on the conduct of the war and the Japanese administration of affairs to the establishment of peace. Review. *Pol. Sci. Quar.,* 14 : 353, June 1899.   WHA

U3271 Young, A. Morgan. *Japan under Taisho Tenno, 1912–1926.* N. Y. and London, 1928.

Account of fourteen momentous years, too near for proper evaluation; with major interest in Japanese policies in continental Asia and the World War and minor in the great earthquake and other events at least temporarily significant. Review, *Journal,* Royal Institute of International Affairs, 8 : 78, Jan. 1929.

                    WHA

U3272 **Kawabe, Kisaburo.** *The press and politics in Japan: a study of the relation between the newspaper and the political development of modern Japan.* Chicago, 1921. (Bibliography.)

Able volume in a little worked field. The average work on the history and politics of Japan has tended to ignore the powerful influence of the press in developing and guiding public opinion. Dr. Kawabe endeavors to show how the press has steadily gained in influence, that its present dominating position gives assurance that the democratic movement cannot be successfully obstructed. Interesting translations and incidents of early journalism are given. Review, *Japan Rev.*, 5 : 148, June 1921. GMF

U3273a **Blakeslee, George H.**, ed. *Japan and Japanese-American relations.* N. Y., 1910. [Clark university addresses.]

　b **Treat, Payson J.** *Early diplomatic relations between the United States and Japan, 1853–1865.* Baltimore, 1917. [Albert Shaw lectures.]

　a. Addresses by Americans and Japanese, all competent observers, with wide range both of information and opinion. Review, *N. Y. Japan Rev.*, 1 : 113, Aug. 1913. GMD
　b. Most intensive and scholarly study yet made of a limited period of American political relations with Japan. Draws on practically all available published sources, especially Japanese, which are used critically. Use of the unpublished diplomatic archives of the American government would not materially alter the conclusions. Author stresses the pacific and altruistic aspects of American polity at least as far as the facts warrant, and minimizes somewhat the sterner aspects of American economic and nationalistic expansion. Review, F. W. Williams, *A.H.R.*, 23 : 687, Apr. 1918. TD

U3301a **Imbault-Huart, Camille.** *L'ile Formose. Histoire et description.* Paris, 1893. (Bibliographical introduction by H. Cordier.)

　b **Campbell, William.** *Formosa under the Dutch described from contemporary records.* London, 1903. (Bibliography.)

　c **Davidson, James W.** *Island of Formosa, past and present.* London, N. Y. and Yokohama, 1903.

　d **Takekoshi, Yosaburo.** *Japanese rule in Formosa.* Tr. by G. Braithwaite. London and N. Y., 1907. (Bibliography.)

　a. Outlines clearly the history of the land through the Dutch, Tartar and Chinese periods to the time when Japanese occupation was impending; with chapters on the political organization and the life of the people. *b.* Consists of selections from the ecclesiastical records and correspondence, extending from 1624 to 1675, with some later data. WHA
　c. Useful history of the island, under the Dutch, Chinese, and Japanese, including a description of the abortive French expedition of 1884–85 and the ephemeral Formosan republic of 1895, by an American consul to Formosa. Review, E. H. Parker, *Asiatic Quar. Rev.*, 3rd ser., 16 : 204, July 1903. *d.* Defense of Japanese policy, with emphasis upon the resources of Formosa, and the land, financial, and police policy of the Japanese government. The writer does not believe Formosa ready for a constitution. Review, *Asiatic Quar. Rev.*, 3rd ser., 24 : 198, July 1907. RLB

U3302a Leavenworth, Charles S. *Loo Choo islands.* Shanghai, 1905.

 b Simon, Edmund M. H. *Beiträge zur Kenntnis der Riukiu-Inseln.* Leipzig, 1913. (Excellent bibliography.)

Brief descriptions of these islands, the customs of the people, their history, especially in relation to Japan. Review of *a, Chinese Recorder, 36:* 469, Sept. 1905.   WHA

JAPAN: KOREA (CHOSEN)

U3371 Courant, Maurice. *Bibliographie coréenne: tableau littéraire de la Corée, contenant la nomenclature des ouvrages publiés dans ce pays jusqu'en 1890 ainsi que la description et l'analyse detaillés des principaux d'entre ces ouvrages.* 3 v. Paris, 1894–96.

After extended introduction on books, writing and printing in Korea, this arranges the literature of Korea in nine books, of which the sixth book deals with history and biography and the ninth with international relations. Other books deal with language, literature, religion, manners and customs, etc. Over three thousand titles, with explanatory notes. Cf. also (U421 ff.) *Far Eastern Question.*

                           GMD

U3372a Hulbert, Homer B. *History of Korea.* 2 v. Seoul, 1905.

 b Hamilton, Angus. *Korea.* 1904. 2nd rev. ed., Boston, 1910. (Oriental series, v. 13.]

 c Longford, Joseph H. *Story of Korea.* N. Y., 1911. (Bibliography.)

a. Probably the best history of Korea in English as the author had access to the historical documents of the former Korean government and was well acquainted with the Korean language.   BWB

b. Account of the history, commerce, and people of Korea by a British journalist, published just before the outbreak of the Russo-Japanese war; revised edition contains an introduction by Percival Lowell, supplementary chapters by Major Herbert E. Austin and Viscount Masatake Terauchi (who are pro-Japan), and a concluding chapter by F. A. McKenzie (who is pro-Korean). An excellent presentation of contemporary opinions and in that way, a source of value. *c.* Historical account of Korea from earliest times by a professor of Japanese in King's College, London. Accurate, balanced, critical treatment, based on the best sources. Review, E. H. Parker, *Asiatic Quar. Rev.,* 3rd ser., 33: 202, Jan. 1912.   TD

U3373a Bishop, Mrs. Isabella L. Bird. *Korea & her neighbors. A narrative of travel, with an account of the recent vicissitudes and present condition of the country.* 2 v. London, 1898. 1 v. N. Y., 1898.

 b Bourdaret, Émile. *En Corée.* Paris, 1904.

 c Ladd, George Trumbull. *In Korea with Marquis Ito.* London and N. Y., 1908.

Results of visits to Korea from 1898 to 1907, popular but graphic.   HRS

U3374a Wilkinson, W. H. *The Corean government: constitutional changes, July 1894 to October 1895. With an appendix on subsequent enactments to 30th June, 1896.* Shanghai, 1897.

 b *Treaties, regulations, etc., between Corea and other powers, 1876 to 1889.* Shanghai, 1891.

 c Chung, Henry, ed. *Korean treaties.* N. Y., 1919.

d *Korea. Treaties and agreements.* Washington (D. C.), 1921. [Pamphlet series of the Carnegie Endowment for International Peace. Division of international law. No. 43.]

e *Annual report for* (1907) *on reforms and progress in Korea.* Seoul, 1908 ff.

f *Annual report on administration of Chosen.* Keijo, 1924 ff.

a. This volume is divided into two parts, of which the first is descriptive of 'The Old System' and the second of 'The Reorganized Administration.' *b.* Gives the official texts of the treaties in the languages in which they were drawn up and an English translation where there was no official text in English. WHA

c. Collection of treaties and conventions between Korea and other powers from 1876 to 1910, arranged by countries. GMD

d. Texts of upwards of twenty treaties and agreements between Korea and China, Japan, Russia, and Great Britain (separately or in several combinations), from September 1882 to August 1910. *e* and *f.* Cover officially from the Japanese administrative point of view the whole range of governmental activity from 1907 to 1923 in very readable form. Illustrations and usually a large map are included. WHA

U3375a Allen, Horace Newton. *Chronological index.* Seoul, 1901.

b Rockhill, William Woodville. *China's intercourse with Korea from the XV th century to 1895.* London, 1905.

a. Summary, for popular use, of the chief events in Korea's contacts with the outside world. A 'Supplement' (1903), brings the data through 1902. *b.* Brief monograph, portions of which had been published in periodicals, setting forth the nature of Korea's relationship to China up to the Chino-Japanese war, especially as revealed in the 'official Chinese ˙publications and writings of Chinese holding official positions.' WHA

U3376a Hulbert, Homer B. *Passing of Korea.* N. Y., 1906.

b McKenzie, Frederick A. *Tragedy of Korea.* London, 1908.

a. One of the most dramatic books on Korea in English. Gives much information about the life, arts, and customs of the Korean people and traces the events almost up to the time of the annexation of Korea by Japan. Strongly pro-Korean and anti-Japanese. Review, K. K. Kawakami, *N. Y. Times Sat. Rev.,* 11 : 749, 1906. *b.* Observations by an English journalist who was in Korea while guerilla fighting was being carried on between scattered bands of Koreans and the Japanese military. Review, F. A. Ogg, *Dial,* 45 : 289, Nov. 1, 1908. BWB

U3377a Cynn, Hugh Heung-Wo. *Rebirth of Korea, the reawakening of the people, its causes, and the outlook.* N. Y., 1920.

b McKenzie, Frederick A. *Korea's fight for freedom.* N. Y., 1920.

c Chung, Henry. *Case of Korea, a collection of evidence on the Japanese dominion in Korea and on the development of the Korean independence movement.* N. Y., 1921 ; London, 1922.

d Ireland, Alleyne. *The new Korea.* N. Y., 1926.

a. Clear and yet restrained statement of the issues in the Korean independence movement of 1919, by an outstanding Christian leader among the younger generation, who now serves as general secretary of the Y. M. C. A. for Korea. Review. *Chinese Recorder,* 51 : 503, July 1920. BWB *b.* Another account of the independence movement; while partisan in interest, it is marked by effort at exactness and accuracy; critical of the Japanese military control. Review, W. W. McLaren, *Am. Pol. Sci. Rev.*, 14: 518, Aug. 1920.

WHA

c. Presentation of the case for Korea by an ardent exponent of Korea's cause. Review, P. J. Treat, *Am. Pol. Sci. Rev.*, 15: 612, Nov. 1921.

BWB

d. Based in part upon the (U3374*e*) *Annual reports on reforms and progress,* but also upon a careful study in the country itself and many contacts with many well-informed people there, this is a favorable account of the Japanese adminis-tration of Korea, especially under the Governor-Generalship of Viscount Saito. Review, M. Willis, *Pol. Sci. Quar.*, 42: 489, Sept. 1927.

WHA

U3378 Dallet, Charles. *Histoire de l'église de Corée précédé d'une introduction sur l'histoire, les institutions, la langue, les moeurs et coutumes coréennes.* 2 v. Paris, 1874.

The introduction of almost two hundred pages covering the subjects indicated on the title page, while needing critical revision, has been much relied upon, directly or indirectly, by almost all later writers upon the earlier history of Korea. The tragic story of the French Roman Catholic missionaries is carried from their arrival in 1784 through the French expedition to Korea in 1866, with some later data.

WHA

U3379 [Hoshino, T.] *Economic history of Chosen.* Seoul, 1920.

Illustrated; covers the general physical features, the administrative changes introduced by the Japanese government, and the economic development in agri-culture, the industries, commerce and finance.

WHA

JAPAN: CONSTITUTIONAL AND POLITICAL HISTORY

U3531a Japan (Government). *Constitution of the empire of Japan.* N. Y. (1889).

b Ito, Hirobumi, Count. *Commentaries on the constitution of Japan.* Tr. by Baron M. Ito, 1889. 2nd ed., Tokio, 1906.

c Nakano, Tomio. *Ordinance power of the Japanese emperor.* Baltimore, 1923. (Bibliography.)

d Oda, Yorodzu. *Principes de droit administratif du Japon.* Paris, 1928.

e Kitazawa, Naokichi. *Government of Japan.* London and Princeton, 1928.

a. Convenient text in English of the constitution, the imperial speech at its promulgation, the Law of the Houses, the Law of Election and the Law of Finance, all of 1889. *b.* Explanatory comment on the constitution, with text of various laws. Second edition records some amendments. Review, G. Hunt, *Pol. Sci. Quar.*, 6: 367, June 1891. *c.* Critical study of the constitutional authority of the emperor, with emphasis upon its character as the embodiment of the demo-cratic spirit rather than as autocracy. *d.* Masterly analysis of the theoretical and practical aspects of the administrative system of the modern Japanese empire.

WHA

e. Clear exposition of Japanese governmental practices and conceptions. Re-view, (London) *Times Lit. Suppl.*, 28: 246, March 21, 1929.

HRS

U3532a Kawakami, Kiyoshi Karl. *Political ideas of modern Japan.* Iowa City, Iowa, 1903. [State Univ. of Iowa, Studies in sociology, economics, politics and history.] (Bibliography.)

    b Uyehara, George E. *Political development of Japan, 1867–1909.* London, 1910. [London School of Economics and Political Science: studies in economics and political science.]

    c Iwasaki, Uichi. *Working forces in Japanese politics, a brief account of political conflicts.* N. Y., 1921. [Columbia Univ., studies in history, economics and public law.]

    a. Critique upon the governmental system rather than a description of it, but valuable for its analysis of political principles as operative in Japan.   WHA

    b. This treatise should be called 'Constitutional government in Japan.' After laying his foundations in a discussion of the Japanese nation, and of the Restoration and constitutional movements, author analyzes carefully and authoritatively the theoretical and actual system established under the constitution of 1889. The book contains a chronology of Japanese history, a chart of the ministries (1890–1910), and the text of the constitution. Review, *Pol. Sci. Quar.,* 27: 561, Sept. 1912. *c.* The forces 'whose interplay is Japanese politics' are found to be: the emperor, the genro (elder statesmen), the peers, the bureaucrats, the militarists, the political parties, the capitalists, and the workers. Suggestive rather than conclusive and should be considered as a preliminary study. The chapters on the capitalists, the workers, and the relations between the parties and the capitalists contain the only material that cannot be obtained better elsewhere. Review, *A.H.R.,* 26: 867, July 1921.   HMV

U3533 Stead, Alfred, ed. *Japan by the Japanese.* London and N. Y., 1904.

    Many documents are quoted, and most of the information, covering all phases of the constitutional organization and functioning of the Japanese state, is presented by highly qualified Japanese.   WHA

JAPAN: ECONOMIC HISTORY

U3571 Yoshitomi, Macaomi. *Étude sur l'histoire économique de l'ancien Japon des origines à la fin du XIIᵉ siècle.* Paris, 1927. (Bibliography.)

    Important study of the economic bases of ancient Japan, including the economic institutions,—land tenure, taxes, currency, agriculture, industry and commerce,—with much information as well on early migrations, development of villages, and social organization in general.   WHA

U3572a Viallate, Achille. *L'avenir économique du Japon.* Paris, 1907. (Brief bibliography.)

    b Dautremer, Joseph. *Japanese empire and its economic conditions.* 1910. 2nd ed., N. Y., 1915. Tr. from *L'empire Japonaise et sa vie économique.* 1910. 3rd ed., Paris, 1919.

    c Uyehara, Shigeru. *Industry and trade of Japan.* London, 1926.

    a. Very concise essay on economic, especially industrial, development and problems. Convenient manual of facts, now considerably out of date.   GMD

    b. More detailed and comprehensive compilation, describing the geography of the empire, the racial origins of its people, government and administration, and economic situation. Third French edition contains supplement showing effect of the World War on Japan's economic condition.   RLB

c. Japanese ambassador to the court of St. James in a brief introduction calls this an 'exhaustive account of the development of Japanese industry and trade since the Restoration of 1868.' Valuable as showing trends as well as conditions.   WHA

U3573a Yamawaki, Haruki, compiler. *Japan in the beginning of the 20th century.* Tokyo, 1903–04.

b Igarashi, Eikichi, and **Takahashi, Hide-Omi.** *National wealth of Japan.* Tokio, 1906.

a. Readable account, liberally interspersed with statistics, of the economic affairs of Japan, prepared originally for the Fifth Domestic Exhibition at Osaka and used also the following year in connection with the Japanese participation in the St. Louis Exposition of 1904. *b.* Well-organized presentation of the national wealth of Japan soon after the Russo-Japanese war, first, of the land as a whole secondly, as distributed among the provinces.   WHA

JAPAN: CULTURAL HISTORY

U3601a Morse, Edward S. *Japan, day by day, 1877, 1878–79, 1882–83.* 2 v. Boston, 1917.

b Robertson-Scott, John W. *Foundations of Japan, notes made during journeys of 6,000 miles in the rural districts as a basis for a sounder knowledge of the Japanese people.* N. Y., 1922.

a. Illuminating records of a Japan that is past, from personal observations and contacts which incidentally yield a wealth of varied information. Review, P. Bigelow, *A.H.R.,* 23 : 688, April 1918.   GMD

b. Valuable source-book regarding the life and character of rural Japanese of all classes, abounding in anecdote and verbatim conversations. Author's intimate knowledge of rural conditions in Europe enables him to make interesting comparisons; a keen observer, although without a knowledge of the Japanese language. Review, *Saturday Review,* 133 : 467, May 6, 1922.   GMF

U3602a Hearn, Lafcadio. *Japan, an attempt at interpretation.* London and N. Y., 1904.

b Couperus, Louis. *Nippon.* N. Y. (1926). Tr. by John de La Valette from the Dutch, *Nippon,* 's Gravenhage, 1925.

a. Classical interpretation of the Japanese by a distinguished man of letters who lived for many years in Japan, although it has been criticised as idealistic. No other book gives a better introduction to the subject. Makes clear how Shintoism (ancestor-worship) has been the basis of the organization of the family, of laws regarding property and succession, and of every other important feature of the social order. Review, *Pol. Sci. Quar.,* 20 : 573, Sept. 1905.   LRM

b. Contrast to *a,* far less enthusiastic about things Japanese, but a thoughtful interpretation. Lacks the more intimate penetration of Hearn, but does not ignore 'Bushido'; cf. (U3603*b*) and (U3622*a*). Review, L. Bryson, *New Republic,* 51 : 288, Aug. 3, 1927.   WHA

U3603a Okakura-Yoshisaburo. *Life and thought of Japan.* London, 1913.

b Nitobe, Inazo Ota. *Bushido, the soul of Japan; an exposition of Japanese thought.* 1899. 10th rev. ed., N. Y., 1905.

c —— *Japanese nation, its land, its people, and its life, with special consideration to its relations with the United States.* N. Y., 1912.

a. Popular interpretation of some of the moral and religious aspects of Japanese life, obviously intended for a western audience, with some attention to the effect of Chinese Buddhism on Japanese life and the influence of Shintoism and emperor worship upon Japanese character. Review, *Saturday Review,* 117 : 52, Jan. 10, 1914. RLB

b. Classical effort by a Japanese scholar to expound the ideals of his people to western readers. Fails to indicate what period he is discussing, shows no interest in Buddhist influence and gives no idea of the real life of the *samurai.* Review, *Asiatic Quar. Rev.,* 3rd ser., 21 : 414, Apr. 1906. *c.* Series of lectures explaining important elements of Japanese life to Americans in an interesting manner. Review, *N. Y. Times Sat. Rev.,* 17 : 609, Oct. 20, 1912. GMD

U3604a Lamairesse, E. *Le Japon. Histoire, religion, civilisation.* Paris, 1892.

b Itchikawa, Daiji. *Die Kultur Japans.* 3 eds., Berlin, 1907.

a. Somewhat general survey of Japanese civilization with relatively more space devoted to religious aspects, especially valuable are the analyses of the various sects of Buddhism in Japan. *b.* Readable, popular, illustrated description of Japanese civilization. WHA

U3621a Knox, George William. *Development of religion in Japan.* N. Y. and London, 1907. [American lectures on the history of religions.] (Bibliography.)

b Harada, Tasuku. *Faith of Japan.* N. Y., 1914. [Hartford-Lamson lectures on the religions of the world.]

a. Scholarly lectures by a former missionary who became an authority on the history of religion. Review, *Nation* (N. Y.), 85 : 37, July 11, 1907. WHA

b. Exposition of Japanese ethical and religious concepts without particular reference to their place in the several religious systems. Review, *Biblical World,* 44 : 294, Oct. 1914. GMD

U3622 Okakura-Yoshisaburo. *The Japanese spirit.* London and N. Y., 1905.

Able essay in exposition of present-day thought in Japan, with special reference to the contribution of religious ideals toward the common stock of Japanese intellectual and æsthetic interests. Review, *Asiatic Quar. Rev.,* 3rd ser., 20 : 406, Oct. 1905. WHA

U3623a Lloyd, Arthur. *Wheat among the tares. Studies of Buddhism in Japan.* London and N. Y., 1908.

b —— *Creed of half Japan; historical sketches of Japanese Buddhism.* N. Y., 1912.

c Reischauer, Augustus K. *Studies in Japanese Buddhism.* N. Y., 1917.

a. Brief exposition of Buddhism, with perhaps over-confident attempts at historical derivations of ideas in Japanese Buddhism. Review, *Chinese Recorder,* 40 : 224, Apr. 1909. WHA

b. Introduction to the complicated and interesting subject of Buddhism in Japan. Review, *Oriental Rev.,* 2 : 628, Aug. 1912. *c.* Scholarly study by an American mission teacher in Tokyo. Review, *Chinese Recorder,* 49 : 53, Jan. 1918. GMD

U3624a Aston, William G. *Shinto (the way of the gods).* N. Y., 1905.

b Kato, Genchi. *Study of Shinto, the religion of the Japanese nation.* Tokyo, 1926. [Meiji society.] (Bibliography.)

a. Treatise on the Shinto religion, minute and careful study of its ritual and ceremonies, past and present. Review, *Asiatic Quar. Rev.,* 3rd ser., 21 : 407, Apr. 1906. LRM

b. Fair-minded interpretation by a Shintoist, of Shintoism as religious patriotism, culminating in mikadoism, loyalty to the emperor as head of a 'constitutional, yet theocratico-patriarchal' government. Review, *Chinese Recorder,* 59 : 51, Jan. 1928. WHA

U3625a Florenz, Karl. *Die historischen Quellen der Shinto-religion aus dem altjapanischen und chinesischen übersetzt und erklärt.* Göttingen, 1919.

b Schurhammer, George. *Shin-to der Weg der Götter in Japan. Der Shintoismus nach den gedruckten und ungedruckten Berichten der japanischen jesuiten Missionäre des 16. und 17. Jahrhunderts.* Bonn, 1923.

a. Source book, with translations into German of Kojiki, Nihongi, and Kogushūi, with useful foot-notes, explanatory and critical. *b.* German and English text in parallel columns; many illustrations, including full-page colored plates and explanations of them. WHA

U3626a Crasset, Jean. *Histoire de l'église du Japon.* 2 v. 1689. 2nd ed., Paris, 1715. (Tr. into English, German, Portuguese and Italian.)

b Pagès, Léon. *Histoire de la religion chrétienne au Japon depuis 1598 jusqu'à 1651, comprenant les faits relatifs aux deux cent cinq martyrs béatifiés le 7 juillet 1867.* 2 v. Paris, 1869–70.

c Haas, Hans. *Geschichte des Christentums in Japan.* 2 v. Tokyo, 1902–04.

d Delplace, L. *Le catholicisme au Japon.* 2 v. Bruxelles, 1909–10. [1, *S. François-Xavier et ses premiers successeurs, 1540–1593; 2, L'ère des martyrs 1593–1660.*] (Bibliographical foot-notes.)

Accounts of early (Jesuit) missions in Japan, each later work in part relying upon and supplementing its predecessors. WHA

U3627 Cary, Otis. *History of Christianity in Japan.* 2 v. N. Y., 1909. [1, *Roman Catholic and Greek Orthodox missions; 2, Protestant missions.*]

There is a large amount of rather ephemeral literature related to Christian missions in Japan; reference to much of this will be found in the annual (U3022a) *Christian movement in Japan,* while general works on missions (cf. F451 ff.) will include material on Japan. The present title is selected as the most adequate and comprehensive work in English for missions in Japan. Review, *Chinese Recorder,* 41 : 303, Apr. 1910. WHA

U3641a Kikuchi, Dairoku. *Japanese education.* London, 1909.

b Lombard, Frank Alanson. *Pre-meiji education in Japan, a study of Japanese education previous to the restoration of 1868.*

a. Deals exhaustively with all phases of education in Japan up to 1908, revealing its highly organized and nationalistic character. Chapters on elementary education and the observations on the position of women, and on text books, are of special interest. Review, *Spectator,* 103 : 815, Nov. 20, 1909. LRM

b. Study, more intensive than *a,* of the educational influences and processes of ancient and feudal Japan. Review, P. Monroe, *Educational Rev.,* 53 : 192, Feb. 1917. WHA

U3661a Aston, William G. *History of Japanese literature.* N. Y., 1899. [Short histories of the literatures of the world.] (Brief bibliography.)

b Florenz, Karl A. *Geschichte der japanischen Litteratur.* Leipzig, 1906.

a. Survey by periods, from earliest times, with brief notices of the more important works and their authors, and with illustrative abstracts in admirable translation. Short chapter on literature of the Meiji era with reference to western influence. Pioneer work in its field, done intelligently and sympathetically.

GMD

b. Substantial single-volume survey of Japanese literature by chronological periods, with copious extracts in German translation.   WHA

U3662a Chamberlain, Basil H. *Japanese poetry.* London, 1911. Enlargement of *Classical poetry of the Japanese,* London, 1880.

b Davis, F. Hadland. *Myths and legends of Japan.* London, 1912.

a. Translations of poems of various types, including ballads of the eighth century A.D., classic shorter poems of a later period, medieval dramas, and specimens of the modern epigrammatic form. Review of the shorter work, *China Rev.,* 9: 236, Jan.-Feb. 1881.   LRM

b. Interesting collection of tales of Japan selected to serve as the basis for a long comprehensive study. There are numerous other collections of Japanese stories told in English, among the transmitters being W. E. Griffis, A. B. Mitford, Lafcadio Hearn, Grace James and Yei Theodora Ozaki. Review, *Asiatic Rev.,* n.s. 1: 193, Jan. 1913.   WHA

U3681a Japan—Bureau of Religions. *Handbook of the old shrines and temples and their treasures in Japan.* Tokyo, 1920.

b Japan—Commission Impériale à l'Exposition Universelle de Paris, 1900. *Histoire de l'art du Japon.* Paris, 1900.

c Otto, Alexander F., and **Holbrook, Theodore S.** *Mythological Japan; or, The symbolisms of mythology in relation to Japanese art.* Philadelphia, 1902.

a. Illustrated manual containing valuable historical descriptive and interpretative information on many phases of Japanese art, arranged regionally. *b.* Prepared as part of the Japanese exhibit at the exposition at Paris in 1900. Folio, containing numerous illustrations, some full page and in colors, with descriptive text, presenting the information generally in historical order. *c.* *Édition de luxe,* with exquisite illustrations.   WHA

U3682a Morrison, Arthur. *Painters of Japan.* 2 v. London, 1911.

b Taki, Sei-Ichi. *Three essays on oriental painting.* London, 1910.

c Anderson, William. *Descriptive and historical catalogue of a collection of Japanese and Chinese paintings in the British museum.* London, 1886. (Bibliography.)

a. Folio volumes with copious illustrations, some .in colors, and text interpretative of Japanese painting in its historical and æsthetic aspects. Review, L. Binyon, *Saturday Review,* 112: 427, Sept. 30, 1911. *b.* Description by a Japanese art critic of characteristics of Japanese painting and of Chinese landscape painting. Excellent illustrations. *c.* While primarily a guide to the collection which was gathered by the author, this still holds the position stated in the prefatory note by Sidney Colvin, 'the most complete account which at present exists of the general history of the subject.'   WHA

U3683a Audsley, George Ashdown. *Ornamental arts of Japan.* 2 v. N. Y., 1883–84.

b ——, and **Bowes, James Lord.** *Keramic art of Japan.* 2 v., Liverpool, 1875. 1 v. ed., London, 1881.

a. Édition de luxe, with many illustrations, some in colors, with text by one of the greatest authorities on oriental art. Includes drawing, painting, engraving and printing; embroidery and textile fabrics; lacquer, incrusted work, metal work, cloisonné; modelling and carving; the emblems of heraldry. *b.* Introductory essay describing the characteristics of Japanese art in general, followed by the consideration of the keramic art of Japan. Well-executed plates. WHA

U3684 Cram, Ralph Adams. *Impressions of Japanese architecture and the allied arts.* N. Y., 1905; London, 1906.

Discerning analysis and evaluation of art in Japan, emphasizing its architecture. Review, *Public Opinion,* 39: 666, Nov. 18, 1905. WHA

U3685a Anesaki, Masaharu. *Buddhist art in its relation to Buddhist ideals with special reference to Buddhism in Japan.* Boston, 1915. (Bibliography.)

b With, Karl. *Buddhistische Plastik in Japan bis in den Beginn des 8. Jahrhunderts n. Chr.* 1919. 3rd ed., Wien, 1922.

a. Masterly lectures. Review, *Journal* (North China Branch, Royal Asiatic Society), 48: 203, 1917. *b.* Collection of 224 half-tone reproductions of examples of early Buddhist plastic art. WHA

JAPAN: BIOGRAPHY

(U3701) K. R. Isaki, ed., *Who's who hakushi in great Japan,* Tokyo, 1921 ff.; (U3702) C. Lanman, *Japan: its leading men,* Boston, 1886; (U3703) J. Morris, *Makers of Japan,* London, 1906; (U3711) R. C. Armstrong, *Just before the dawn; the life and work of Ninomiya Sontoku,* N. Y., 1912; (U3712) Sir R. Alcock, *Capital of the tycoon: a narrative of a three years' residence in Japan,* 2 v., London, 1863; (U3713) W. E. Griffis, *Townsend Harris, first American envoy in Japan,* Boston, 1895; (U3714) S. Shimada, *Life of Ii Naosuke,* Tokyo, 1888; (U3715) Prince Hirobumi Ito, *A maker of new Japan. Marquis Ito's experience,* Nagasaki, 1904; (U3716) K. Nakamura, *Prince Ito, the man and statesman, a brief history of his life,* 1841–1909, N. Y., 1910; (U3717) A. M. Pooley, ed., *The secret memoirs of Count Tadasu Hayashi,* N. Y. and London, 1915; (U3718) A. Gérard, *Ma mission au Japon,* Paris, 1919.

JAPAN: PERIODICALS AND SOCIETY PUBLICATIONS

Some of the most important periodicals for Japan are listed in this section at U941 ff.

(U3941) Y. Takenobu, ed., *Japan year book,* Tokyo, 1905 ff.; (U3942) *Japan weekly chronicle,* Kobe, 1897 ff.; (U3943) *Japan magazine,* Tokyo, 1910 ff.; (U3944) *Deutsche-Japan post,* Yokohama, 1902–14; (U3945) *Japan weekly mail,* Yokohama, 1882–1913; Tokio, 1913–1917; (U3946) *Japan Evangelist,* Tokyo, 1893–1925; superseded by *Japan Christian quarterly;* (U3947) *Economic review,* Kyoto, 1926 ff.

Among the societies which print important material relating to Japan are the Japan Society, London, (U3961) *Transactions and proceedings,* London, 1892 ff.; Korea Branch, Royal Asiatic Society, (U3962) *Transactions,* Seoul, 1900 ff.; Société Franco-Japonaise de Paris, (U3963) *Bulletin,* Paris, 1902 ff. WHA

SECTION V

OCEANICA

Editor

GEORGE HUBBARD BLAKESLEE

Professor of History and International Relations
Clark University

CONTENTS

INTRODUCTION

Few books treat of the Pacific islands as a whole. Each important archipelago, however, has its distinct literature, which in a few cases, notably that of the Philippines, is full and scholarly; but in others, especially that of the French islands, is very meager. The German works descriptive of the physical features and native life of the former German islands have rarely been excelled for accuracy and thoroughness. On Australasia there is a considerable collection of scholarly works; on the Netherlands Indies there are many standard works in Dutch, although few in English. With the exception of accounts of exploring voyages, but little information on the Pacific islands, except the Dutch East Indies and the Philippines, is available for the period prior to the nineteenth century. During the past century, however, the literature of the subject has increased steadily in volume and in value. These later works fall, for the most part, into three classes: studies of the native races, accounts of European colonization, and discussion of international relations.

BIBLIOGRAPHY

There is no good general bibliography for the Pacific islands. Several of the histories in this field contain limited bibliographies; among the best selected short lists are those in (V22a) *Peace handbooks.*

V1a Griffin, Appleton P. C., ed. *List of books relating to Hawaii, including references to collected works and periodicals.* Washington, 1898. [Library of Congress.]

b ——— *List of books, with references to periodicals, on Samoa and Guam.* Washington, 1901. [Library of Congress.]

c ——— *List of books, with references to periodicals, on the Philippine Islands in the Library of Congress; with chronological list of maps in the Library of Congress by P. Lee Phillips.* Washington, 1903. [Library of Congress; also 57th congress, 2nd session, senate document no. 74.]

d Leroy, James A. *The Philippines, 1860–1898, some comment and bibliographical notes.* Cleveland, 1907. [(V211) Blair and Robertson, Philippine Islands, 52:112–207.]

e Robertson, James A. *Bibliography [of the Philippine Islands].* Cleveland, 1908. [(V211) Blair and Robertson, Philippine Islands, v. 53.]

f Pardo de Tavera, Trinidad H. *Biblioteca filipina: ó sea, catálogo razonado de todos los impresos, tanto insulares como extranjeros, relativos á la historia, la etnografía, la lingüística, la botánica, la fauna, la flora, la geología, la hidrografía, la geografía, la legislación, etc., de las islas Filipinas, de Joló y Marianas.* Washington, 1903. [Library of Congress; also 57th congress, 2nd session, senate document no. 74.]

g Retana, Wenceslao Emilio. *Epítome de la bibliografía general de Filipinas.* [In v. 1–4 of Retana, Archivo del bibliófilo filipino, recopilación de documentos históricos, científicos, literarios, y políticos y estudios bibliográficos, 5 v., Madrid, 1895–1905.]

h Torres y Lanzas, Pedro. *Catálogo de los documentos relativos a las Islas Filipinas existentes en el archivo de Indias de Sevilla.* V. 1, 1493–1572, preceded by *Historia general de Filipinas por el Pablo Pastells.* Barcelona, 1925.

Comprehensive bibliographies for the several American possessions in the Pacific. *d, e, f,* and *g.* Contain valuable critical notes; these, combined with *h,* form one of the most complete critical bibliographies available for any country. *h.* Series to cover period to 1898 in 19 v. Review, L. Araujo-Costa, *Rev. des Questions Hist.* 104:463, Apr. 1, 1926.   GHB

V2a Hooykaas, J. C. *Repertorium op de koloniale litteratuur, of, systematische inhoudsopgaaf van hetgeen voorkomt over de koloniën in mengelwerken en tijdschriften van 1595 tot 1865 uitgegeven in Nederland en zijne overzeesche bezittingen* . . . Ed. by W. N. Du Rien. 2 v. Amsterdam, 1877–80.

b *Repertorium op de literatuur betreffende de Nederlandsche koloniën, voor zoover zij verspreid is in tijdschriften en mengelwerken: 1, Oost-Indië, 1866–1893; 2, West-Indië, 1840–1893.* Ed. by Alexander Hartmann. 's Gravenhage, 1895. Supplements, 1894–1915, 1916–1920, 1921–1925, ed. by A. Hartmann, W. J. P. J. Schalker, and W. C. Muller, 6 v., 's-Gravenhage, 1901–26.

a. Most important bibliography for the Netherlands Indies, both East and West, though chiefly limited to periodical articles. *b.* Continuation of *a.* GHB

V3 Hocken, Thomas M. *Bibliography of literature relating to New Zealand.* Wellington, N. Z., 1909.

Only work at all adequate for Australasia; includes a Maori bibliography.
                                                                    GHB

Library collections.—The best general collections on Oceanica, in the continental United States, are in the library of the American Board of Commissioners for Foreign Missions, Boston, and in the Newberry Library, Chicago. Good collections exist in the Library of Congress, Harvard University Library, New York Public Library, and Stanford University Library.

The Honolulu collections of books, manuscripts, newspapers, periodicals, and miscellaneous historical material relating to Oceanica, especially to Polynesia, are unusually complete. These are contained in the libraries of the Bishop Museum, the Hawaiian Historical Society, and the Board of Archives, and in the Carter Library, the Missionary Memorial Library, which contains one of the best collections relating to missionary enterprises in the Pacific, and the Wilcox Library at Lihue, island of Kauai.

For Philippine material, the best collection of printed Filipiniana is that of the Philippine Library and Museum, Manila, which, besides possessing almost all the books published on the Philippines and an excellent assortment of old and modern newspapers, owns one hundred thousand pages of manuscript copied from the originals in the Archivo General de Indias, Seville. For the student of the present-day Philippines, the library of the Bureau of Insular Affairs, War Department, Washington, is probably the best in the continental United States; it is especially rich in official documents issued by the United States and Philippine governments since 1898; it also contains many other modern works, including some Philippine newspapers. It possesses, however, very little of the old and rare material. The Library of Congress also has a good Philippine collection. Aside from government libraries, the Ayer collection of the Newberry Library, Chicago, is the best in printed books and manuscripts. Harvard University (Forbes collection), University of Michigan (Worcester library), and the New York Public Library also possess excellent material for the study of the Philippines. AHS

ENCYCLOPEDIAS AND WORKS OF REFERENCE

V21a *Encyclopaedie van Nederlandsch-Indië.* Ed. by P. A. van der Lith and others. 1894–1905. 2nd rev. ed., by J. Paulus and others, 4 v., 's-Gravenhage, 1917–21.

b *Deutsches Kolonial-Lexikon.* Ed. by Heinrich Schnee. 3 v. Leipzig, 1920.

c *Illustrated Australian encyclopaedia.* Ed. by Arthur W. Jose and Herbert J. Carter. 2 v. Sydney, 1925–26.

a. Standard work of reference on the Dutch East Indies, by thoroughly competent collaborators; covers all subjects of interest and importance relating to the islands; emphasizes contemporary conditions. Addressed to the general reader rather than to the specialist, the articles are comprehensive and compact, avoiding disputed issues. Includes historical surveys for each of the larger territorial divisions, biographies covering all persons prominent in the history of the islands, and special articles on particular periods or institutions. Supplementary articles to the second edition appear every few months. Review, *De Indische Gids*, 1906, pt. 1, p. 624–629. *b.* Includes the former German Pacific islands, as well as the German African colonies; scholarly; printed as written in 1914. GHB

V22a *Pacific Islands.* London, 1920. [V. 22 of (J441a) Peace handbooks issued by the historical section of the British Foreign Office, no. 139–147. Cf. also no. 80, 82–88.] (Good selected bibliographies.)

b *Stewart's [annual] handbook of the Pacific islands, a reliable guide to all the inhabited islands of the Pacific Ocean, for traders, tourists, and settlers, with a bibliography of island works.* Sydney, 1907–1923.

c Brigham, William T. *Index of the islands of the Pacific Ocean.* Honolulu, 1900. [Memoirs, B. P. Bishop Museum.]

a. Authoritative summaries of the history, geography, and economic and political conditions of the Pacific islands to 1917. For material 1917–1923, consult *b.*, which contains description, statistics, and extracts from government reports and from important magazine and newspaper articles. *c.* Alphabetical list of the charted islands, with brief descriptions where possible.   GHB

GEOGRAPHY

In lieu of treatises on the geography of the Pacific, and of its various islands, reference may be made to (V214b) for the Philippines; (V104) for Australasia; (V421a and b) for the Dutch possessions; and (V451a) for the former German possessions, now the mandated islands.

ETHNOGRAPHY

V51a Skinner, Henry D. *Morioris of Chatham Islands.* Honolulu, 1923. [Memoirs, B. P. Bishop Museum.] (Bibliography.)

b Best, Elsden. *The Maori.* 2 v. Wellington, 1924.

c Cowan, James. *Maoris of New Zealand.* Christchurch, N. Z., and London, 1910. [Makers of Australasia.]

d Seligmann, Charles G. *Melanesians of British Guinea.* Cambridge, Eng., 1910.

e Rivers, William H. R., ed. *Essays on the depopulation of Melanesia.* Cambridge, Eng., 1922.

f Skeat, Walter W., and Blagden, Charles O. *Pagan races of the Malay Peninsula.* 2 v. London, 1906. (Bibliography.)

g Spencer, Sir Baldwin, and Gillen, Francis J. *Northern tribes of central Australia.* London and N. Y., 1904.

h —— *Across Australia.* 2 v. London, 1912.

i —— *Native tribes of the northern territory of Australia.* London, 1914.

Accounts of the native races of the Pacific, their history, culture, characteristics, geographic relations, and future possibilities. *a., b.,* and *c.* Deal with Polynesia. *d.* and *e.* Deal with Melanesia, *e.* discussing especially the results of contact of Melanesians with Europeans. *f.* Describes the tribes of the Malay Peninsula, giving a good general picture of the Malay world. *g., h.,* and *i.* Accounts of the native races of Australia. Cf. (V52; V53a and b; V292b and c.)   HEG

V52a Pritchard, William T. *Polynesian reminiscences, or life in the South Pacific islands.* London, 1866.

b Romilly, Hugh H. *Western Pacific and New Guinea: notes on the natives, Christian and cannibal, with some account of the old labour trade.* 1886. 2nd ed., London, 1887.

Contemporary accounts of life in the southern and western islands of the Pacific, some decades past, by resident British officials. *a.* By son of one of earliest British missionaries, himself consul at Samoa and Fiji; period covered, 1843 to 1863; deals with Samoa, Fiji, and early history of Tahiti; description, personal experiences, valuable history. *b.* By the deputy commissioner of the Western Pacific; much information on native customs; written in entertaining style. Cf. (V51*a, b, c, d,* and *e;* V53*a* and *b;* and V292*b* and *c*).   GHB

V53a Ellis, William. *Polynesian researches during a residence of nearly eight years in the Society and Sandwich Islands.* 1829. 2nd rev. ed., 4 v., London, 1832–34; N. Y., 1833.

b Williams, John. *Narrative of missionary enterprises in the South Sea islands, with remarks upon the natural history of the islands, origin, languages, traditions, and usages of the inhabitants.* London and N. Y., 1837. Later reprints.

c Brown, George. *George Brown, D.D., pioneer-missionary and explorer, an autobiography, a narrative of forty-eight years' residence and travel in Samoa, New Britain, New Ireland, New Guinea, and the Solomon Islands.* London, 1908.

a. Description of the natives of the Polynesian islands and their customs, especially those of the Society and Hawaiian groups, with a history of early missionary activities. Authoritative and interesting. *b.* By a member of the London Missionary Society; an account of work and personal experiences in the South Seas when Christianity was being introduced, especially in Rarotonga and Samoa. *c.* Dr. Brown, known as "the grand old man" of the Melanesian region, presents an unusually valuable description of these islands from about 1860 to 1908.   GHB

V54 Brown, J. MacMillan. *Peoples and Problems of the Pacific.* 2 v., London, 1927.

A general survey of Pacific races, particularly of the Polynesians. Discusses geography, history, ethnology. Conclusions regarding origin and relations of native races out of accord with those of other writers.   HEG

V55 Henry, Teuira. *Ancient Tahiti.* Honolulu, 1928. [B. P. Bishop Museum.]

Comprehensive treatise on the history and culture of the Society Islanders.   HEG

V56 Roberts, Stephen H. *Population problems of the Pacific.* London, 1927. (Bibliography.)

Scholarly study of conditions among native races of the Pacific, stressing problems arising from migrations and causes and remedies for depopulation.   GHB

GENERAL·WORKS ON THE PACIFIC

V101a Scholefield, Guy H. *The Pacific, its past and future, and the policy of the great powers from the eighteenth century.* London, 1919.

b Colquhoun, Archibald R. *Mastery of the Pacific.* N. Y. and London, 1902.

Two volumes dealing with the Pacific islands as a whole. *a.* Strictly historical; the best work in this field; scholarly and reliable; British viewpoint; thorough use of British, Australian. and New Zealand sources; not adequate for

American relations and policy.   *b.*   Largely descriptive; illustrated; may serve
as a popular introduction to further study; becoming antiquated.   GHB

V102a Fletcher, Charles Brunsdon.   *Problem of the Pacific.*   London, 1919.

  b Bancroft, Hubert H.   *The new Pacific.*   1899.   3rd rev. ed., N. Y., 1915.

  c Roosevelt, Nicholas.   *The restless Pacific.*   N. Y., 1928.

  d Blakeslee, George H.   *The Pacific area: an international survey.*   Boston,
  1929.

Deal with the Pacific in its wider meaning, including the nations on its borders
as well as its islands.   *a.*   The policies and rivalries of the great powers of the
Pacific: the British Empire, Germany, the United States, and Japan.   Useful for
information and points of view, but impressionistic in style, strongly anti-German
in attitude, and lacking in systematic presentation.   *b.*   Lengthy survey of the
countries and islands of the Pacific as of 1899.   Much of the material, especially
of a statistical nature, now antiquated; popular and superficial; written under the
influence of the emotions of the Spanish war; poorly organized.   *c.*   Emphasizes
the geographic and economic fundamentals of the Pacific area, and its strategic
factors.   GHB

d.   The history and the present status of the international issues which are pressing for settlement in the Pacific area, and the factors which are most important
in the relations of the leading countries.   Valuable for its information and its
measured statements of opinion.   SBF

V103 Callahan, James M.   *American relations in the Pacific and the Far East,
1784–1900.*   Baltimore, 1901.   [Johns Hopkins University studies in historical and political science.]

Only historical survey of American relations, diplomatic and commercial,
throughout the entire Pacific.   Extensive footnotes referring to government documents and other source material.   Needs to be revised and brought up to date.
Review, H. Bingham, *A.H.R.*   6:827, July, 1901.   GHB

V104a Wood, George Arnold.   *Discovery of Australia.*   London, 1922.   (Critical bibliographies.)

  b Kitson, Arthur.   *Captain James Cook, R. N., F. R. S., the circumnavigator.*   London, 1907.   Condensed, popular ed. with title, *Life of Captain
  James Cook, the circumnavigator,* London, 1911.

  c Hawkesworth, John, ed.   *Account of the voyages undertaken for making
  discoveries in the southern hemisphere and performed by Commodore
  Byron, Captain Wallis, Captain Carteret, and Captain Cook (from 1764–
  1771) drawn up from the journals which were kept by the several com-
  manders and from the papers of . . . J. Banks.*   3 v.   London, 1773.

  d Cook, James.   *Captain Cook's journal during his first voyage round the
  world made in H. M. bark Endeavor, 1768–71, a literal transcription of
  the original mss., with notes and introduction.*   Ed. by Sir W. J. L. Wharton, London, 1893.

  e ———   *Voyage towards the South Pole and round the world, performed
  in His Majesty's ships, the Resolution and Adventure, in the years 1772,
  1773, 1774, and 1775.*   1777.   4th ed., 2 v., London, 1784.

  f Cook, James, and King, James.   *Voyage to the Pacific Ocean, undertaken, by the command of His Majesty, for making discoveries in the
  northern hemisphere; performed under the direction of Captains Cook,
  Clerke, and Gore, in His Majesty's ships the Resolution and Discovery, in*

the years 1776, 1777, 1778, 1779, and *1780 . . . 1784.* 2nd ed., 3 v. and atlas, London, 1785.

g Favenc, Ernest. *History of Australian exploration from 1788 to 1888, compiled from state documents, private papers, and the most authentic sources of information, issued under the auspices of the governments of the Australian colonies.* London and Sydney, 1888.

h Scott, Ernest. *Life of Captain Matthew Flinders, R. N.* Sydney, 1914. (Bibliography.)

i Lee, Ida. *Early explorers in Australia, from the log-books and journals, including the diary of Allan Cunningham, botanist, from March 1, 1817, to November 19, 1818.* London, 1925.

Histories of exploration in the Pacific. *a.* Scholarly, many maps, carries the history to about 1800. Review, A. H. Abel-Henderson, *A.H.R.* 31 :172, Oct., 1925. *b.* Best life of Cook, recent, based on manuscripts, well written. *c.* Personal narratives of the pioneer British explorers in the Pacific. *d.* Authoritative edition. The authorship of the work with similar title originally published in 1771 is an unsettled question. For Cook's log, cf. (V914a) *Historical Records of New South Wales,* v. 1, pt. 1. *e.* and *f.* Cook's narratives of his second and third voyages, considerably altered by uncritical and unreliable editing. There are numerous popular reprints of a collection of Cook's three voyages in a single volume. The original manuscripts, in London, have never been published, but were used by Kitson in writing his life of Cook. *g.* Detailed narrative; written from the sources. *h.* Exhaustive, scholarly, largely based on manuscript sources; covers from about 1795 to 1803. Author is professor of history in the University of Melbourne. Review, A. L. P. Dennis, *A.H.R.* 20 :881, July 1915. *i.* Valuable source material.   GHB

V105a Bywater, Hector C. *Sea-Power in the Pacific, a study of the American-Japanese naval problem.* London and Boston, 1921.

b Golovin, Nikolaî Nikolaevich and **Bubnov, Aleksandr Dimitrïevich.** *Problem of the Pacific in the twentieth century.* Tr. by C. Nabokoff from the Russian. London, 1922. (Bibliography.)

Discussions of naval problems of the Pacific. Although the greater part of each work deals with temporary conditions, the study of the strategic factors of the Ocean and of the military importance of various islands is of permanent value. Review of *a.,* Admiral W. S. Sims, *Atlantic Monthly,* 128 :704, Nov. 1921; of *b, Saturday Rev.* 134 :16, July 1, 1922.   GHB

V106a Young, William Allen. *Christianity and civilization in the South Pacific, the influence of missionaries upon European expansion in the Pacific during the 19th century.* London and N. Y., 1922. [Robert Herbert memorial prize essay.]

b Martin, K. L. P. *Missionaries and annexation in the Pacific.* London, 1924.

Scholarly surveys. *a.* Concentrates on the history of New Guinea. *b.* Deals mainly with Tahiti, New Zealand, and Fiji.   GHB

THE PHILIPPINES

V201a Barrows, David P. *History of the Philippines.* 1905. 4th rev. ed., Yonkers, 1924.

b Fernández, Leandro H. *Brief history of the Philippines.* Boston, 1919.

Short histories of the Philippines. *a.* Excellent for rapid survey. The 4th ed. covers events to 1924. Recommended for its sane viewpoint and its recognition of important historical events. The American position is clearly stated. *b.* Elementary history by a Filipino author; intended for school use in the Philippine Islands; generally dependable.

JAR

V211 Blair, Emma H. and Robertson, James A., ed. *.Philippine Islands, 1493–1898: explorations by early navigators, descriptions of the islands and their peoples, their history and records of the Catholic missions, as related in contemporaneous books and manuscripts, showing the political, economic, commercial, and religious conditions of those islands from their earliest relations with European nations to the beginning of the nineteenth century, translated from the originals, edited and annotated.* 55 v. Cleveland, 1903-09. (Bibliography.)

Invaluable and monumental collection of source material for the history of the Philippines before and during the Spanish régime. Excellent historical introduction by E. G. Bourne, 1:19-87. The introductions to the individual volumes, taken together, furnish a good detailed account of the Spanish occupation. Review, v. 1-5, J. A. LeRoy, *A.H.R.* 9:149, Oct. 1903.

GHB

V212a Morga, Antonio de. *Philippine Islands, Moluccas, Siam, Cambodia, Japan, and China, at the close of the sixteenth century.* London, 1868. [Hakluyt Society.] Tr. by H. E. J. Stanley from *Sucesos de las Islas Philipinas, Mexici ad Indos,* 1609; rev. ed. by José Rizal, Paris, 1890. Better English tr. in (V211) Blair and Robertson, *Philippine Islands,* v. 15-16.

b Rios Coronel, Hernando de los. *Memorial, y relacion para su Magestad, del procurador general de las Filipinas, de lo que conuiene remediar, y de la riqueza que ay en ellas, y en las Islas del Maluco.* Madrid, 1621. French tr. in M. Thevenot, *Relations de divers voyages curieux,* Paris, 1696. English tr. of essential parts in (V211) Blair and Robertson, *Philippine Islands,* v. 19.

c Alvarez de Abreu, Antonio. *Extracto historial del expediente que pende en el Consejo Real y Supremo de las Indias, á instancia de la ciudad de Manila y demás de las Islas Philipinas, sobre la forma en que se ha de hacer y continuar el comercio y contratacion de los texidos de China en Nueva España.* . . . Madrid, 1736. English tr. of extracts in (V211) Blair and Robertson, *Philippine Islands.*

d Comyn, Tomás de. *State of the Philippine Islands, being an historical, statistical, and descriptive account of that interesting portion of the Indian archipelago.* London, 1821. Tr. by W. Walton from *Estado de las Islas Filipinas en 1810 brevemente descrito,* Madrid, 1820. Reprint of tr. forms p. 357-458 of A. Craig, *Former Philippines through foreign eyes,* N. Y., 1917.

e Mas, Sinibaldo De. *Informe sobre el estado de las Islas Filipinas en 1842.* 3 v. Madrid, 1843. English tr. of excerpts of v. 1-2 and of practically the whole of v. 3 in (V211) Blair and Robertson, *Philippine Islands.*

f Sancianco y Goson, Gregorio. *El progreso de Filipinas, estudios económicos, administrativos, y politicos. Parte económica.* Madrid, 1881.

g Montero y Vidal, José. *Historia general de Filipinas desde el descubrimiento de dichas islas hasta nuestros días.* 3 v. Madrid, 1887-95.

Best and most representative works in Spanish written by secular persons. From them much of the Spanish régime in the Philippines may be followed. Translation of *a* and translated excerpts of all the others, except *f*, appear in (V211) Blair and Robertson, *Philippine Islands. a.* By one of the highest officials; best of all the early works; gives an excellent survey of the Spanish conquest, the early government, and the natives, both before and at the time of the conquest. This volume has a distinctly modern tone. *b.* By the procurator for the Philippines, who had access to all documents bearing on the islands. Important historically and economically. *c.* Most important single work for the commerce of the Philippines up to 1736; written for the private use of certain Spanish officials. *d.* By an authority on financial, economic, and commercial matters. *e.* Survey made, by order of the Spanish government, to aid government officials; embraces many different subjects, some of which are treated in a mediocre manner. By far the most valuable part is the rare third volume which was issued secretly for the sole use of the government; it is very important to the student of Spanish-Filipino relations. *f.* Useful both for administrative matters of its period and for its economic data. *g.* Best modern Spanish general history of the Philippines; includes considerable bibliographical and documentary material. The author was more of an annalist than an historian.

JAR

V213a **Chirino, Pedro.** *Relacion de las Islas Filipinas i de lo que en ellas an trabaiado los padres de la Compañia de Iesus.* Roma, 1604. English tr. in (V211) Blair and Robertson, *Philippine Islands,* v. 12–13.

b **Aduarte, Diego.** *Historia de la provincia del Sancto Rosario de la Orden de Predicadores en Philippinas, Iapon, y China.* Manila, 1640. 2nd ed., Zaragoça, 1693. English tr. and synopsis in (V211) Blair and Robertson, *Philippine Islands,* v. 30–32.

c **Colin, Francisco.** *Labor evangelica, ministerios apostolicos de los obreros de la Compañia de Jesus, fundacion y progressos de su provincia en las islas Filipinas.* Madrid, 1663. 2nd ed. by Pablo Pastells, 3 v., Barcelona, 1904.

d **Combes, Francisco.** *Historia de las islas de Mindanao, Iolo, y sus adyacentes, progresos de la religion y armas católicas.* . . . Madrid, 1667. 2nd ed. by P. Pastells and W. E. Retana, Madrid, 1897.

e **Santa Cruz, Baltasar de.** *Tomo segundo de la historia de la provincia del Santo Rosario de Filipinas, Iapon, y China del Sagrado orden de Predicadores.* Zaragoça, 1693.

f **San Agustin, Gaspar de.** *Conquistas de las Islas Philipinas: la temporal, por las armas del Señor Don Phelipe segundo el prudente; y la espiritual, por los religiosos del Orden de nuestro padre San Augustin: fundacion y progressos de su provincia del santíssimo nombre de Jesus. Parte primera.* Madrid, 1698.

g **San Antonio, Juan Francisco de.** *Chronicas de la apostolica provincia de San Gregorio de religiosos Descalzos de N. S. P. San Francisco en las Islas Philipinas, China, Japon, etc.* 3 v. Sampaloc, 1738–44.

h **Murillo Velarde, Pedro.** *Historia de la provincia de Philipinas de la Compañia de Jesus; segunda parte, que comprehende los progresos de esta provincia desde el año de 1616 hasta el de 1716.* Manila, 1749.

i **Concepción, Juan de la.** *Historia general de Philipinas, conquistas espirituales y temporales de estos españoles dominios, establecimientos progressos, y decadencias.* 14 v. Manila and Sampaloc, 1788–92.

j **Diaz, Casimiro.** *Conquistas de las islas Filipinas: la temporal por las armas de nuestros Católicos reyes de España y la espiritual por los religiosos de la Orden de San Agustin, y fundación y progresos de la provincia del santísimo nombre de Jesus de la misma órden. Parte segunda.* Ed. by Tirso López. Valladolid, 1890.

k Delgado, Juan J. *Historia general sacro-profana, política y natural de las islas del poniente llamadas Filipinas.* Manila, 1892.

l Martinez de Zúñiga, Joaquin. *Estadismo de las islas Filipinas, ó mis viajes por este pais.* Ed. by W. E. Retana. 2 v. Madrid, 1893.

While most of these works are primarily concerned with Christian missions in the Philippines, they narrate much of the secular history and are very important to the student. The authors of *a., c., d., h.,* and *k.* were Jesuits; of *b.* and *e.,* Dominicans; of *f., i., j.,* and *l.,* Augustinians; and of *g.,* Franciscan. (V211.) Blair and Robertson, *Philippine Islands* contains translations of *a.* and *b.,* and translated excerpts of all the others. All are important for the culture of the natives, especially *a., c.,* and *g.* The map accompanying *h.* was the best that had yet appeared. *e.* Supplements *b.;* covers the years 1637–1669; the third part, for the period, 1669–1700, by Vicente Salazar, Manila, 1742, and the fourth part, for the years 1700–1765, by Domingo Collantes, Manila, 1783, are less important. *i.* Remarkably free from bias; a work by an ecclesiastic. *j.* Supplements *f.;* comprises the years 1616–1694. *k.* Written between 1751 and 1754; has a wide sweep; remarkable for its description of the animal and vegetable life of the Philippines. *l.* Significant for its racy description of the Philippines in 1800. JAR

V214a Jagor, Feodor. *Travels in the Philippines.* London, 1875. Tr. from *Reisen in den Philippinen, Berlin,* 1873. Better tr. by Austin Craig, entitled *Jagor's travels in the Philippines,* published in *The former Philippines through foreign eyes,* p. 1–356, Manila, 1916; N. Y., 1917. Spanish tr. by S. Vidal y Soler, Madrid, 1875.

b Foreman, John. *Philippine Islands: a political, geographic, ethnographical, social, and commercial history of the Philippine archipelago.* 1890 3rd rev. ed., London and N. Y., 1906.

Old, standard works. *a.* Correct appraisement of the Philippines toward the end of Spanish rule, by a trained observer and keen student. *b.* Written by a British subject of many years' residence in the Philippines; has been much overrated, although it contains much useful material.

The best monograph on Spanish governmental institutions in the Philippines is (Y532c) Cunningham, *Audiencia of the Spanish colonies as illustrated by the audiencia of Manila, 1583–1800.* Berkeley, 1919. JAR

V231a Le Roy, James A. *Americans in the Philippines, a history of the conquest and first years of occupation, with an introductory account of the Spanish rule.* 2 v. Boston, 1914. (Bibliography.)

b Worcester, Dean C. *The Philippines, past and present.* 1914. 2nd rev. ed., 2 v., N. Y., 1914. 2 v. in one, 1921.

c Elliott, Charles B. *The Philippines to the end of the military régime, America overseas.* Indianapolis, 1916.

d —— *The Philippines to the end of the Commission government, a study in tropical democracy.* Indianapolis, 1917. (Bibliography.)

e Williams, Daniel R. *The United States and the Philippines.* Garden City, N. Y., 1924.

f Forbes, W. Cameron. *The Philippine Islands.* 2 v. Boston and N. Y., 1928.

Standard works for the study of the American régime. *a.* Published posthumously; unfinished; brings the history to the opening years of the twentieth century; a sober, analytical treatment from the sources; indispensable for the closing years of Spanish control and the opening years of American occupation. Review, D. P. Barrows, *A.H.R.* 20:181, Oct. 1914. *b*. Closes with the first year of Harrison's governorship; vigorous, lacks unity, sometimes prolix and biased, but gives much first-hand information of value. Review, F. W. Williams, *Amer. Pol. Sci. Rev.* 8:705, Nov. 1914. *c*. and *d*. Pleasantly written; excellent complements to *a*, *b*, and *e;* generally reliable; end with the passage of the Jones bill in 1916. Review, C. H. Cunningham, *Amer. Pol. Sci. Rev.* 12:129, Feb. 1918. *e*. Measured, earnest account of relations between the United States and the Philippines; especially valuable for the period since the beginning of the Harrison régime; conservative in tone. Williams lived for many years in the Philippines, first as an official, later as a practising lawyer. *f*. Study and vindication of the occupation of the islands by the United States; government and administration; people, both Christian and non-Christian; underlying forces in the progress of the modern Philippines; independence movement; basic documents in the appendix.

For the formulation of American policy toward the Philippines, cf. Olcott, *William McKinley* [(X701) American statesmen series]. For a hostile estimate of the earlier years of American administration, by a competent British observer, cf. (K537*b*) Ireland, *Far Eastern tropics.*   JAR

V232a *Wood-Forbes commission: condition in Philippine Islands, report of the special mission to the Philippine Islands to the secretary of war.* Washington, 1921. [67th congress, 2nd session, house document no. 325.] Reprint, *N. Y. Times Current History*, 15:678–694, Jan. 1922.

   b *Filipino appeal for freedom: the Philippine parliamentary mission's statement of actual conditions in the Philippine Islands and a summary of Philippine problems. Washington*, 1923 [67th congress, 4th session, house document no. 511.]

   c Harrison, Francis Burton. *Corner-stone of Philippine independence: a narrative of seven years.* N. Y., 1922.

   d Russell, Charles Edward. *Outlook for the Philippines.* N. Y., 1922.

   e Kalaw, Maximo M. *Case for the Filipinos.* N. Y., 1916.

   f —— *Self-government in the Philippines.* N. Y., 1919.

   g Mayo, Katherine. *Isles of fear: the truth about the Philippines.* N. Y., 1925.

   h Gabaldon, Isauro. *My reply to Miss Mayo's articles, speech in the house of representatives. Congressional Record*, 66:1167–1173, Jan. 3, 1925.

   i Storey, Moorfield, and Lichauco, Marcial P. *Conquest of the Philippines by the United States, 1898–1925.* N. Y. and London, 1926.

   j Roosevelt, Nicholas. *The Philippines: a treasure and a problem.* N. Y., 1926.

Discussions of the Harrison administration and of recent political conditions. *a*. Embodies the results of painstaking, thorough investigation. Its conclusions are definite; its recommendations, clear-cut and authoritative; its brevity, commendable. *b*. In part an answer, by the Filipino majority, to *a*, with which it should be read. Both reports touch matters discussed by *c* and *d*, but neither of the latter can be recommended for fairness of treatment or historical accuracy. Review of *a*, *b*, *c*, and *d*, C. C. Batchelder, *Foreign Affairs*, 2:488, March 1924; of *c* and *d*, H. P. Willis, *New Republic*, 32:103, Sept. 20, 1922. *e* and *f*. Kalaw's two volumes, covering in general the period from 1896 to 1919, present the radical Filipino viewpoint in a brilliant manner. *g*. Vigorous account by a publicist, of general conditions in the Philippines; first syndicated through various newspapers; expresses a distinctively American viewpoint; should be read with *e* and *f*, and with *i*. The title is ill-chosen. Review, W. F. Johnson, *North Amer. Rev.*, 221:560, March 1925. *h.* Only a partial answer to *g*, which is called an insult to the Filipino people. Gabaldon, a former commissioner for the Philippines to the United States, is a Spanish-Filipino mestizo, one of the classes denounced by Miss Mayo. *i.* Latest survey of American relations with the Philippines, by an American anti-imperialist and a Filipino advocate of independence. *j.* Summary and partial survey of conditions by a publicist for the *New York Times;* somewhat popular in tone; advises caution and mature judgment before changing status of the Philippines; compares problems with those in Dutch East Indies and with Dutch procedure. Review, *Amer. Pol. Sci. Rev.* 21:464, May 1927; *Hisp. Amer. Hist. Rev.* 7:482, Nov. 1927; *Pol. Sci. Quar.* 42:624, Dec. 1927. JAR

V241a Malcolm, George A., and Kalaw, Maximo M. *Philippine government, development, organization, and functions.* Manila and N. Y., 1923.

b Fernández, Leandro H. *Philippine Republic.* N. Y., 1926. [Columbia University Studies in history, economics and public law.] (Bibliography.)

c Laurel, José P. *Local government in the Philippine Islands.* With an introduction by Máximo M. Kalaw. Manila, 1926.

d Kalaw, Máximo M. *Development of Philippine politics* (1872–1920). Manila, 1927. (Bibliography.)

a. Admirable and informing work; Malcolm is an associate justice of the Philippine Supreme Court; and Kalaw is a professor of Political Science in the Philippine University. *b.* A study of armed resistance against Spain and the United States and attempts at self-government; revolutionary government; restrained in tone; recommended. *c.* Based on a series of lectures on municipal government in the University of the Philippines; the appendices present several prime sources recommended for study, as the municipality is the governmental unit of the islands. *d.* The best work of this author, who here attempts with considerable success to portray the political development of the Philippines from the inside and from the strictly Filipino viewpoint; background sketched lightly; utilizes manuscript material hitherto not used; should be read especially with *b*.

JAR

V242a Miller, Hugo H. and Storms, Charles H. *Economic conditions in the Philippines.* 1913. Rev. ed., Boston, 1920.

b Reyes, José S. *Legislative history of America's economic policy toward the Philippines.* N. Y., 1923. [Columbia University, Studies in history, economics, and public law.] (Bibliography.)

Valuable for the history of the Philippines in interpreting present-day conditions. Review of *b.*, J. A. Robertson, *A.H.R.* 29:385, Jan. 1924. JAR

V243a Le Roy, James A. *Philippine life in town and country.* N. Y. and London, 1905.

b Carpenter, Frank G. *Through the Philippines and Hawaii.* Garden City, N. Y., 1925.

c Laubach, Frank C. *People of the Philippines, their religious progress and preparation for spiritual leadership in the Far East.* N. Y., 1925. (Excellent bibliography.)

d *Survey of the educational system of the Philippines.* [Philippine Islands: Board of educational survey.] Manila, 1925.

Descriptions of social and religious conditions. *a.* Best single introduction to general social conditions in the Philippines, and still essentially accurate. *b.* Descriptions made on the spot, somewhat hurriedly, by a well-known publicist; treats mainly of the Philippines. Serviceable, but should be checked with other accounts. *c.* Best volume yet published on Protestant missionary and educational work in the Philippines. Discusses various social factors that have a bearing on the work of Protestant missions. Sympathetic viewpoint. Laubach has been a missionary of the American Board of Commissioners for Foreign Missions since 1916. *d.* Mainly the work of Paul Monroe, chairman of the board; in part historical; authoritative; important for study of social conditions.   JAR

HAWAII, GUAM, AND SAMOA

V251 Alexander, William D. *Brief history of the Hawaiian people.* 1892. 2nd ed., N. Y., 1899. [Brief historical series.]

Brief, detailed history, from 1778 to 1890; describes customs and civil policy of ancient Hawaiians; authoritative, standard work.   HEG

V252 Castle, William R., Jr. *Hawaii past and present.* 1913. 2nd rev. ed., N. Y., 1927.

Survey of the history of Hawaii; account of economic, political, and social conditions; and description of the various islands, by a member of one of the influential families of Hawaii.   GHB

V253 Kuykendall, Ralph S. *History of Hawaii.* With introductory chapters by Herbert E. Gregory. N. Y., 1926.

Brief detailed history of Hawaii to 1926; historical development, and economic, political, and social growth and present conditions. Most recent and carefully written history of Hawaii, based upon documents many of which were available for the first time. Review, N. D. Harris, *Pol. Sci. Quar.* 42:645, Dec. 1927.   KCL

V261 Ellis, William. *Narrative of a tour through Hawaii, or Owhyhee, with remarks on the history, traditions, manners, customs, and language of the Sandwich Islands.* 1826. 2nd rev. ed., London, 1827.

Clearest picture of early conditions; interesting first-hand experience. Cf. (V53*a* and *b*) Ellis, *Polynesian researches,* and Williams, *Narrative of missionary enterprises.*   HEG

V262 Blackman, William F. *Making of Hawaii, a study in social evolution.* 1899. New ed., N. Y., 1906. (Bibliography.)

Story of the development of a primitive race through contact with civilized peoples; reliable and informative. Review, *A.H.R.* 5:786, July 1900.   HEG

V271a Carpenter, Edmund J. *America in Hawaii, a history of United States influence in the Hawaiian Islands.* Boston, 1899.

b Liliuokalani. *Hawaii's story by Hawaii's queen.* Boston, 1898.

Accounts of American relations with the islands. *a.* Outlines events preceding 1889; treats more fully the reign of Liliuokalani, the revolution of 1893, and steps leading to annexation; takes the American point of view. Review, *A.H.R.* 5:786, July 1900. *b.* Written from the standpoint of the royal family; a complement to *a.*   HEG

V272 Palmer, Albert W. *Human side of Hawaii.* Boston, 1924.

Valuable for presentation of the problems of Hawaii, especially those arising from the peculiar racial and industrial situation in the islands.

GHB

V281 Cox, Leonard M. *Island of Guam.* 1904. 4th rev. ed., by M. G. Cook, Washington, 1917. [Navy department.] (Bibliography.)

Only reliable recent work upon Guam. Written by naval officers. Brief history, 1521 to 1916; description of island, social and economic conditions, and operation of government.

GHB

V291 Watson, Robert M. *History of Samoa.* Wellington, N. Z., 1918.

Introductory survey of Samoan history to 1917. Cf. (V451a) W. Sievers, *Die Schutzgebiete in der Südsee.*

GHB

V292a Churchward, .William B. *My consulate in Samoa: a record of four years' sojourn in the Navigators Islands, with personal experiences of King Malietoa Laupepa, his country, and his men.* London, 1887.

b Stair, John B. *Old Samoa, or flotsam and jetsam from the Pacific Ocean.* London, 1897.

c Turner, George. *Samoa a hundred years ago and long before, together with notes on the cults and customs of twenty-three other islands in the Pacific.* London, 1884.

Older histories. *a.* By a British consul; valuable for local history and the rivalry of the great powers, 1881–1885, and for description of native life and customs; well written. *b.* Record of the habits and customs of the native Samoans, 1838–1845, by one of the earliest missionaries. *c.* Description of Samoan life before serious modifications were introduced by the whites. Cf. (V53c) Brown, *Autobiography;* (V52a) Pritchard, *Polynesian reminiscences;* and (V53b) Williams, *Narrative of missionary enterprises.*

GHB

V293a Stevenson, Robert Louis. *Footnote to history: eight years of trouble in Samoa.* N. Y., 1892. Later reprints.

b Henderson, John B., Jr. *American diplomatic questions.* N. Y. and London, 1901.

Accounts of Samoa in world politics. *a.* Describes accurately, yet fascinatingly, the most critical years, 1884–1892. *b.* Survey of the entire period of American-German-British rivalry, 1872–1900, from the viewpoint of American diplomacy, forms pt. 3.

GHB

V294 Crose, William M. *American Samoa, a general report by the governor.* 1913. Rev. ed. by H. F. Bryan, Washington, 1927. [Navy department.] (Short bibliography.)

Survey of conditions, including historical summary, issued by the Navy Department 'for information of the general public.' This pamphlet, originally written in 1912, is the only recent publication on American Samoa. GHB

AUSTRALASIA

V301a Jenks, Edward. *History of the Australasian colonies.* 1896. 3rd rev. ed., Cambridge, Eng., 1912. [Cambridge historical series.]

b Jose, Arthur W. *History of Australasia, from the earliest times to the present day, with a chapter on Australian literature.* 1899. Latest rev. ed., Sydney, 1926.

c Scott, Ernest. *Short history of Australia.* 1916. 5th ed., London and N. Y., 1927. (Bibliography.)

Best short histories of Australasia. *a.* Especially useful on legal and constitutional questions. Cf. (V104) works on the discovery of Australia; and (V702) Sir Henry Parkes, *Fifty years in the making of Australian history.*

Also cf. volumes on Australasia in (K303) Lucas, *Historical geography of the British colonies;* (K304) Tilby, *English people overseas;* (K307a) Martin, *History of the British colonies;* (K310) Herbertson and Howarth, *Oxford survey of the British Empire;* (K309) *All red series;* (K311) *British empire series;* and (K329) *Resources of the Empire series.* ALPD

V302a Coghlan, Timothy A., and Ewing, Thomas T. *Progress of Australasia in the nineteenth century.* London and Philadelphia, 1902. [Nineteenth century series.]

b Dunbabin, Thomas. *Making of Australasia, a brief history of the origin and development of the British dominions in the South`Pacific.* London, 1922. [Making of the British Empire.]

Additional one-volume histories dealing mainly with the period before the Commonwealth. *a.* In largest part a history of the individual states with emphasis upon economic development. *b.* Good for the early history; meager and unsatisfactory treatment of the period since about 1850. GHB

V306a Bean, Charles E. W. *Official history of Australia in the War of 1914–18.* V. 1, 2, 3, 7, 8, and 12. Sydney, 1921–29.

b *Official history of New Zealand's effort in the Great War.* v. 1–3. Auckland, 1921–22.

Detailed narrative histories based upon official records and other sources.
GHB

V312 Rusden, George W. *History of Australia.* 1883. 3rd ed., 3 v., Melbourne, 1908.

Standard political history, from prehistoric times to 1897, narrative and detailed, based on sources. ALPD

V313a Wise, Bernard R. *Making of the Australian Commonwealth, 1889–1900, a stage in the growth of the Empire.* London and N. Y., 1913.

b Turner, Henry G. *First decade of the Australian Commonwealth, a chronicle of contemporary politics, 1901–1910.* Melbourne, 1911.

a. Well-documented, yet lively, account of the decade during which federation was the dominant issue in Australian politics, by an eye-witness whose political sympathies color somewhat his interpretation of events. *b.* Valuable contemporary record; the author allows his anti-labor point of view to affect his treatment of controversial subjects. Cf. the historical introduction to (V342b) Quick and Gerran, *Annotated constitution of the Australian Commonwealth.* ALPD

V321a Barton, George B. *History of New South Wales from the records.* v. 1, *Governor Phillip, 1783–1789.* Sydney, 1889.

b Britton, Alexander. *History of New South Wales from the records,* v. 2, *Phillip and Grose, 1789–1794.* Ed. by F. M. Bladen. Sydney, 1894.

c Collins, David. *Account of the English colony in New South Wales.* 2 v. 1798–1802. 2nd ed., abridged, 1 v., 1804. Ed., with an introduction and notes by J. Collier, London, 1910.

a. and *b.* Authoritative and detailed accounts of the early years of Australia, published by the government of New South Wales; they follow closely the official records. Cf. (V914a) *Historical records of New South Wales,* ed. by Bladen and Britton. *c.* Valuable as a contemporary chronicle of the first years of colonization, 1788 to 1801; by a former judge advocate and secretary of the colony.

GHB

V323a Turner, Henry G. *History of the colony of Victoria from its discovery to its absorption into the Commonwealth of Australia.* 2 v. London and N. Y., 1904.

b Jenks, Edward. *Government of Victoria, Australia.* London and N. Y., 1891.

a. Standard history; the author's personal views unduly influence his presentation of controversial topics. *b.* Scholarly, though somewhat technical, history of constitutional and legal development in Victoria, and a detailed description of the organs of government in 1890.

GHB

V325a Mills, Richard C. *Colonization of Australia, 1829–1842: the Wakefield experiment in empire building, with an introduction by Graham Wallas.* London, 1915. [University of London, Studies in economics and political science.] (Bibliography.)

b Price, A. Grenfell. *Foundation and settlement of South Australia, 1829–1845: a study of the colonization movement based on the records of the South Australian government and on other authoritative documents.* Adelaide, 1924.

a. Indispensable study of the Wakefield system with emphasis on its political aspect, based on careful study of best sources. *b.* Presents the geographical aspect of historical development; colonial rather than imperial in viewpoint. Review, A. H. Abel-Henderson, *A.H.R.* 30:395, Apr. 1925; W. K. Hancock, *E.H.R.* 40:449, July 1925. Cf. (V701) Garnett, *Life of Edward Gibbon Wakefield.*

ALPD

V327 Battye, James S. *Western Australia, a history from its discovery to the inauguration of the Commonwealth.* Oxford, 1924.

Outstanding historical work, clear, impartial, and based upon documentary material in both Australia and England. Review, C. D. Allin, *A.H.R.* 30:599, Apr. 1925; W. K. Hancock, *E.H.R.* 40:449, July 1925.

GHB

V329a West, John. *History of Tasmania.* 2 v. Launceston, 1852.

b Fenton, James. *History of Tasmania from its discovery in 1642 to the present time.* Hobart, 1884. (Bibliography.)

c Walker, James B. *Early Tasmania, papers read before the Royal Society of Tasmania between the years 1888 to 1899.* 1902. 2nd ed., Hobart, 1914.

d Giblin, R. W. *Early History of Tasmania: the geographical era, 1642–1804.* London, 1928.

a. and *b.* Old works, but the only available histories of the island. *c.* Studies, by a local scholar, on the aborigines, exploration, and settlement to 1804. *d.* A Tasmanian writer traces the development of European knowledge concerning the island from its discovery by Tasman to 1804.

GMD

V336a Murray, Sir John Herbert P. *Papua, or British New Guinea.* London and N. Y., 1912.

b ——— *Papua of today: an Australian colony in the making.* London, 1926.

By the lieutenant governor of Papua. *a.* Describes the country and native life and contains a history of the Australian administration. *b.* Reviews the progress made with the dual problem of developing natural resources and of preserving the Papuan and raising him to the highest civilization of which he is capable—'how the civilization of the 20th century can be introduced among people of the Stone Age.' ECP

V341 Sweetman, Edward. *Australian constitutional development.* Melbourne, 1925.

Most recent scholarly study of the subject for the earlier period. Review, C. D. Allin, *A.H.R.* 31:173, Oct. 1925; A. B. Keith, *E.H.R.* 40:624, Oct. 1925.
GHB

V342a Moore, William Harrison. *Constitution of the Commonwealth of Australia.* 1902. 2nd ed., Melbourne and London, 1910.

b Quick, Sir John and **Garran, Robert R.** *Annotated constitution of the Australian Commonwealth.* Sydney and Melbourne, 1901.

Best works on general constitutional law in the Australian Commonwealth. Each contains a long historical introduction. *a.* Describes topically the various features and agencies of the government. *b.* Exhaustive commentary on the constitution, clause by clause. GHB

V346a Atkinson, Meredith, ed. *Australia, economic and political studies by various writers.* Melbourne and London, 1920.

b Wise, Bernard R. *Commonwealth of Australia.* 1909. 2nd ed., London, 1913. [All red series.]

c Ferrin, Augustin W. *Australia, a commercial and industrial handbook.* Washington, 1922. [Bureau of foreign and domestic commerce.] (Bibliography.)

Studies of present conditions in the commonwealth. *a.* Good survey; thirteen essays by different authorities upon significant aspects of Australian life and culture. *b.* Useful and well organized economic and legislative summary from point of view of the Labour party. *c.* Survey of economic, social, and political conditions by the recent American trade commissioner to Australia. GHB

V347a Northcott, Clarence H. *Australian social development.* N. Y., 1918. [Columbia University, Studies in history, economics, and public law.] (Bibliography.)

b Reeves, William P. *State experiments in Australia and New Zealand.* 1902. Reprint, 2 v., London, 1923; N. Y., 1925.

c St. Ledger, Anthony J. J. *Australian socialism, an historical sketch of its origin and developments.* London, 1909.

d Clark, Victor S. *Labor movement in Australasia, a study in social democracy.* N. Y., 1906.

a. Sociological interpretation of recent democratic tendencies based on source material. Tends to dogmatize and concludes with vague program of economic progress. *b.* Careful topical account, for 1881 to 1902, of social legislation, by former agent general of New Zealand in London. Generally favorable to the progressive movement. Review, P. H. Douglas, *Amer. Pol. Sci. Rev.* 20:208, Feb. 1926. *c.* By a Commonwealth senator; opposed to state socialism and the Labour party. *d.* Earlier study of the causes and results of the labor movement by an American investigator. Review, W. F. Willoughby, *Amer. Pol. Sci. Rev.* 2:144, Nov. 1907.   ALPD

V348a Thwing, Charles F. *Human Australasia: studies of society and of education in Australia and New Zealand.* N. Y., 1923.

  b Willard, Myra. *History of the white Australia policy.* Melbourne, 1923. [University of Melbourne publications, no. 1.]

  a. Evaluation of Australasian culture, education, literature, and contributions to civilization, by an eminent American educator.   *b.* Detailed and scholarly study of the leading policy of Australia. Review, *A.H.R.* 29:631, Apr. 1924.   GHB

V349 Roberts, Stephen H. *History of Australian land settlement, 1788–1920.* Melbourne, 1924.

Interesting and scholarly presentation of a technical subject. The development of Australia is traced with thoroughness, following the steps of the progress of land settlement. Review, A. H. Abel-Henderson, *A.H.R.* 30:395, Apr. 1925.

                                                         GHB

V351a Condliffe, John B. *Short history of New Zealand.* Christchurch, N. Z., 1925.

  b Reeves, William P. *Long white cloud, Ao tea roa.* 1898. Rev. ed. by C. J. Wray, with title *New Zealand, Ao tea roa,* Boston, 1925.

  c Rusden, George W. *History of New Zealand.* 1883. 2nd ed., 3 v., Melbourne and London, 1895.

  a. Survey of the main features of the economic, constitutional, and political history of New Zealand.   *b.* Standard one-volume history of New Zealand; continued up to date in new edition. *c.* Detailed political narrative, based on sources. Prejudiced favorably to the Maori; contains some inaccuracies. Review, *Athenaeum,* 2:171, Aug. 11, 1883.   ALPD

V352 Marais, J. S. *Colonization of New Zealand.* London, 1927.

Scholarly work, based on sources, describing early settlements of New Zealand in their relation to the theory of colonization. Favorable to the New Zealand Company. Reviews, Sir Henry Lambert, *E.H.R.* 43:146, Jan. 1928; P. Knaplund, *A.H.R.* 33:445, Jan. 1928; *Pol. Sci. Quar.* 43:151, March 1928.   GHB

V353 Harrop, A. J. *England and New Zealand.* London, 1926.

Study of British policy toward New Zealand to 1855; well documented and based on sources. .Review, E. N. W., *E.H.R.* 43:146, Jan. 1928.   GHB

V361a McNab, Robert. *Murihiku: a history of the South Island of New Zealand and the islands adjacent and lying to the South, from 1642 to 1835.* Christchurch, N. Z., 1909.

  b ——— *Old whaling days, a history of southern New Zealand from 1830 to 1840.* Christchurch, N. Z., and London, 1913.

Early history of the South Island of New Zealand, based upon extensive research in various collections, including the whaling records in New England. America's part in the early history of the southern Pacific is nowhere better presented than in these volumes.   HEG

V371 Hight, James and **Bamford, Harry D.** *Constitutional history and law of New Zealand.* Christchurch, N. Z., 1914. (Bibliography.)

Standard work in this field; furnishes a full description of the organization and operation of the government.   GHB

V376 Douglas, Sir Arthur P. *Dominion of New Zealand.* London, 1909. [All red series.]

Comprehensive survey, with summary of statistical and general information as of January 1, 1908. ALPD

V377a Scholefield, Guy H. *New Zealand in evolution, industrial, economic, and political.* London, 1909.

b Lusk, Hugh H. *Social welfare in New Zealand: the result of twenty years of progressive social legislation and its significance for the United States and other countries.* N. Y., 1913.

c Le Rossignol, James E. and **Stewart, William D.** *State socialism in New Zealand.* N. Y., 1910. [Library of economics and politics.]

d Siegfried, André. *Democracy in New Zealand, with an introduction by W. D. Stewart.* London, 1914. Translated from *La démocratie en Nouvelle Zélande,* Paris, 1904.

a. Description of the country and people, followed by a history of economic and industrial development and a discussion of state activities and of unsettled economic problems. *b., c.,* and *d.* Discuss the results of state socialism. *b.* Maintains that it "has proved a great success," while *c.* and *d.* are more skeptical. *d.* Has a valuable introduction by a member of the New Zealand ministry, who is also a co-author of *c.;* an impartial study. Review of *b.* and *d., Spectator,* 113:528, Oct. 17, 1914. Cf. (V347*b*) Reeves, *State experiments in Australia and New Zealand;* and (V347*d*) Clark, *Labor movement in Australasia.* GHB

V381 Burton, John W. *Fiji of to-day.* London, 1910.

Manners and customs; brief generalized history; mainly discussion of missions and possibility of relapse from Christian teaching. Cf. (V22*a*) *Peace handbooks,* no. 144; (V52*a*) Pritchard, *Polynesian reminiscences;* and (V101*a*) Scholefield, *The Pacific.* HEG

BRITISH BORNEO

V391 Baring-Gould, Sabine and **Bampfylde, Charles A.** *History of Sarawak under its two white rajahs, 1839–1908.* London, 1909.

Detailed history, based upon the correspondence of the two British rajahs and upon the official records. Cf. (V741*a*) St. John, *Life of Sir James Brooke.*

GHB

FRENCH POSSESSIONS

V401a Caillot, A. C. Eugène. *Les Polynésiens orientaux au contact de la civilisation.* Paris, 1909.

b —— *Histoire de la Polynésie orientale.* Paris, 1910.

These works are complementary. They treat of French Polynesia, including the islands of Tahiti, Tuamotus, Gambier, Tubuai, Rapa, and Rurutu. *a.* Mainly geographical and ethnological; outlines history of important events. *b.* Historical, based on documents. Cf. (V22*a*) *Peace handbooks,* no. 145; (V52*a*) Pritchard, *Polynesian reminiscences;* and (V53*a*) Ellis, *Polynesian researches.* HEG

V406a Deschanel, Paul. *La politique française en Océanie à propos du canal de Panama.* Paris, 1884.

b —— *Les intérêts français dans l'Océan Pacifique.* Paris, 1888.

Valuable for history of the policies of the great powers, especially in the 'eighties,' and of the international relations in the Pacific, from the French point of view. Extensive descriptions of the French archipelagoes and their administration.

GHB

V411 Christian, Frederick W. *Eastern Pacific lands: Tahiti and the Marquesas Islands.* London, 1910.

Description of islands, people, and customs, with incidents of travel. Includes account of the annexation of the Cook group and other islands to New Zealand. Disappointing, but the best work in English; the appendix contains information of value.

GHB

V416a Bourge, Georges. *Les Nouvelles-Hébrides de 1606 à 1906.* Paris, 1906. (Bibliography.)

b Jacomb, Edward. *France and England in the New Hebrides.* Melbourne, 1914.

Works on the New Hebrides and the Anglo-French condominium. *a.* Brief history to 1906; general description of archipelago; laudatory of the French New Hebrides Company. *b.* Exposure of the failure of the condominium. Cf. (V22a) *Peace handbooks,* no. 147; and (V22b) *Stewart's handbook of the Pacific, 1923.*

GHB

DUTCH POSSESSIONS

V421a Cabaton, Antoine. *Java, Sumatra, and the other islands of the Dutch East Indies.* London and N. Y., 1911. Tr. by B. Miall from *Les Indes néerlandaises,* Paris, 1910.

b *Manual of Netherlands India, Dutch East Indies; compiled by the geographical section of the naval intelligence division, naval staff,* [British] admiralty. London, 1920. (Bibliography.)

c Fowler, John A. *Netherlands East Indies and British Malaya: a commercial and industrial handbook.* Washington, 1923. [Bureau of foreign and domestic commerce, special agents series, no. 218.]

Descriptions, with brief historical sketches, of all of the Dutch East Indies. Cf. (V22a) *Peace handbooks,* no. 82–88.

CD

V431a Crawfurd, John. *History of the Indian archipelago, containing an account of the manners, arts, languages, religions, institutions, and commerce of its inhabitants.* 3 v. Edinburgh, 1820.

b Raffles, Sir Thomas Stamford. *History of Java.* 1817. 2nd ed., 2 v., London, 1830.

Long the standard works in English; though antiquated, still useful to those who do not read Dutch. *a.* By a British official in Malaysia. *b.* By the British lieutenant governor of Java, 1811 to 1815; a history of the island until the arrival of the British forces, and a description of country, people, and languages.

CD

V432a Meinsma, Johannes J. *Geschiedenis van de Nederlandsche Oost-Indische bezittingen.* 3 v. in 1. Delft and 's Hage, 1872–75.

b Deventer, Marinus L. van. *Geschiedenis der Nederlanders op Java.* 1886–87. 2nd ed., 2 v., Haarlem, 1895.

There is no general history even in Dutch covering all periods and all possessions of the Netherlands East Indies. *a.* The best one, although somewhat antiquated; convenient because of the extent of the ground it covers. *b.* Best history on Java alone; deals, however, only with the period of the East India Company.

CD

V433a Jonge, Johan K. J. de, and others, ed. *De opkomst van het Nederlandsch gezag in Oost-Indië, verzameling van onuitgegeven stukken uit het Oud-koloniaal Archief.* 13 v. with index. 's-Gravenhage, 1862–88; supplement, ed. by L. W. G. de Roo, 2 v., 's-Gravenhage, 1909.

b Tiele, Pieter A. and **Heeres, Jan E.,** ed. *De opkomst van het Nederlandsch gezag in Oost-Indië: 2e reeks, buitenbezittingen.* 3 v. 's-Gravenhage, 1886–95.

c Deventer, Marinus L. van. *Het Nederlandsch gezag over Java en onder-hoorigheden sedert 1811.* V. 1. 's-Gravenhage, 1891.

d Chijs, Jacobus A. van der. *Nederlandsch-Indisch plakaatboek, 1602–1811.* 17 v. Batavia and s'Hage, 1885–1900. [Bataviaasch Genootschap van Kunsten en Wetenschappen.]

The essential Dutch sources for the history of Java and some of the older Dutch possessions.

CD

V434a Kemp, Pieter H. van der. *De teruggave der Oost-Indische koloniën, 1814–1816.* s'-Gravenhage, 1910.

b —— *Oost-Indië's herstel in 1816.* 's-Gravenhage, 1911.

c —— *Het Nederlandsch-Indisch bestuur in 1817, tot het vertrek der Engelschen.* 's-Gravenhage, 1913.

d —— *Het Nederlandsch-Indisch bestuur in het midden van 1817.* 's-Gravenhage, 1915.

e —— *Het Nederlandsch-Indisch bestuur van 1817 op 1818.* 's-Gravenhage, 1917.

f —— *Oost-Indië's inwendig bestuur van 1817 op 1818, Falck als minister, weduwenfondsen, onderwijs, wetenschap, kunst, kerk en zending, slavernij, verblijfrecht, handel, scheepvaart.* 's-Gravenhage, 1918.

There is an embarrassing variety of special studies on different islands and for various periods. The most important are these six volumes covering the history of the Dutch East Indies in the period of the restoration of Dutch control from 1814 to 1818. They are based on original sources and are thoroughly reliable.

CD

V441 Gonnaud, Pierre. *La colonisation hollandaise à Java, ses antécédents, ses caractères distinctifs.* Paris, 1905. (Bibliography.)

Limited to Java, but covers a broad stretch of time, tracing the development of Dutch colonization in the island down to the present century.

CD

V442a Day, Clive. *Policy and administration of the Dutch in Java.* N. Y. and London, 1904.

b Chailley-Bert, Joseph. *Java et ses habitants: la société indigène; la société européenne; la concurrence économique, Européens et Orientaux, la question chinoise; la concurrence politique, Hollandais et Javanais; l'éducation des indigènes; l'Institut Botanique de Buitenzorg.* Paris, 1900.

a. Excellent work; based on thorough and critical study of the literature and sources of the subject; displaces earlier works in English. The culture system, its abolition, and the modern economic policy in Java are carefully treated. Devoted primarily to land, labor, and fiscal problems rather than to legal and political institutions. Preëminent as the most instructive treatise in English

upon Dutch colonial policy. Review, P. S. Reinsch, *A.H.R.* 10:391, Jan. 1905;
C. C. Plehn, *Jour. of Pol. Econ.* 13:122, Dec. 1904. *b.* Another useful work;
by a competent French authority on colonial administration in the East. FWP

MANDATED ISLANDS

V451a Sievers, Wilhelm. *Die Schutzgebiete in der Südsee.* (Extensive bibliography.) [V. 2, p. 301–496, (K47) Meyer, Das deutsche Kolonialreich, 2 v., Leipzig, 1910.]

b Parkinson, Richard H. R. *Dreissig Jahre in der Südsee, Land und Leute, Sitten und Gebräuche im Bismarckarchipel und auf den deutschen Salomoninseln.* Ed. by B. Ankermann. Stuttgart, 1907.

c Neuhauss, Richard. *Deutsch Neu-Guinea.* 3 v. Berlin, 1911.

Histories and descriptions of the former German islands, now administered under mandates. *a.* Accurate description of the islands and their native peoples. *b.* Scholarly, detailed account. *c.* V. 1. Best, fairest, most intimate account of the administration, natives, and culture of former German New Guinea. V. 2. Ethnographical atlas. V. 3. Collection of missionary narratives.

For the best short history of German policy and of diplomatic issues, cf. (K423) Zimmermann, *Geschichte der deutschen Kolonialpolitik.* Also cf. (V22a) *Peace handbooks,* no. 146; (V291–294) works on Samoa; and annual reports printed by the several mandatories and submitted to the council of the League of Nations. GHB

DIPLOMATIC AND MILITARY HISTORY

For works on general diplomatic history of the Pacific, cf. (V101), (V102), (V103), (V105), and (U421); for diplomatic relations affecting Samoa, (V293), the French possessions, (V406), the condominium in the New Hebrides, (V416). The military activities of Australia and New Zealand in the World War are recounted in (V306).

CONSTITUTIONAL AND LEGAL HISTORY

Some account of the constitutional and legal history of the Philippines will be found in (V241); of Australia, in (V323b), (V341), (V342); of New Zealand, in (V371); of the Dutch East Indies, in (V441), (V442).

ECONOMIC AND SOCIAL HISTORY

There will be found some contributions to the economic and social history of the Philippines in (V212b, c, d, f), (V242), and (V243a); of Australia, in (V346), (V347), (V348), (V349); of New Zealand, in (V361b), (V376), (V377); of the Dutch East Indies, in (V421c), (V441), (V442).

CULTURAL HISTORY: RELIGION

Mention may be made of the following works which deal in a general way with religious affairs in the Pacific islands: (V53) and (V106); while the following relate specifically to the Philippines: (V213) and (V243c).

CULTURAL HISTORY: EDUCATION

Educational developments in Australia and New Zealand are studied in (V248a)

CULTURAL HISTORY: LITERATURE

There is a brief survey of Australian literature in (V301b).

BIOGRAPHIES

The following biographies are of historical value: (V701) Richard Garnett, *Life of Edward Gibbon Wakefield*, London and N. Y., 1898; (V702) Sir Henry Parkes, *Fifty years in the making of Australian history*, 2 v., London and N. Y., 1892; (V703) Charles E. Lyne, *Life of Sir Henry Parkes*, London, 1897; (V721) George C. Henderson, *Sir George Grey, pioneer of empire in southern lands*, London and N. Y., 1907; (V722) James Milne, *Romance of a pro-consul* [Sir George Grey], London, 1911; (V723) James Drummond, *Life of R. J. Seddon*, London, 1907; (V741a) Sir Spenser R. St. John, *Life of Sir James Brooke, Rajah of Sarawak*, London, 1879; and an abridgement, (V741b) *Rajah Brooke, the Englishman as ruler of an eastern state*, London and N. Y., 1899 [Builders of Greater Britain]; (V761) Sophia Raffles, *Memoir of the life and public services of Sir Thomas Stamford Raffles, by his widow*, London, 1830; (V762) Hugh E. Egerton, *Life of Sir Stamford Raffles*, London, 1900; (V771) Charles E. Russell and E. B. Rodriguez, *Hero of the Filipinos, the story of José Rizal, poet, patriot, and martyr*, N. Y. and London, 1923; (V772) Walter Murdock, *Alfred Deakin, a sketch*, London, Bombay, Sydney, 1923. Cf. (V53c) George Brown, *Autobiography*.

GHB

GOVERNMENT PUBLICATIONS

Due to the limited number of reliable books and magazines on the Pacific islands, government publications are of especial value. For the Pacific as a whole, much detailed information, especially as to physical conditions, may be found in (V901) *Pacific islands pilot*, 1916, 2nd ed., 2 v., Washington, 1920. A careful examination of trade and economic resources is given in (V902) *British and Australian trade in the South Pacific*, by the inter-state commission of Australia, Melbourne, 1918. For the bearing of the Washington Conference, 1921–22, on the Pacific islands, cf. (U428) *Conference on limitation of armament*. Valuable material (relating to the Pacific islands about 1840 is found in (K482) Wilkes, *Narrative of the United States exploring expedition*.

For the American possessions, important government publications are listed and described in (V1) the bibliographies issued by the Library of Congress. Current information may be obtained from the following annual reports: (V906a) *Report of the governor general of the Philippine Islands*, Washington, 1918 ff. [War department]; (V906b) *Report of the governor of Hawaii*, Washington, 1900 ff. [Department of the interior]; (V906c) *Report of the governor of Guam*, Washington, 1900 ff. [Navy department]; (V906d) *Report of the governor of American Samoa* [Navy department]. The first three are published annually at Washington; the fourth may be examined in typewritten form at the navy department. Valuable bulletins and reports are published by the government of the Philippines, Manila, which usually may be obtained from the bureau of insular affairs, Washington. (V907) *Official Gazette*, weekly, Manila, 1902 ff., contains recent laws, executive orders, proclamations, and decisions of the supreme court of the islands. Economic conditions and racial problems in Hawaii are discussed at length in (V908) *Labor problems in Hawaii: hearings before the committee on immigration and naturalization,* 2 v., Washington, 1923 [67th congress, 4th session, house report no. 1717]. For Samoa, a valuable sketch is (V909) *American Samoa; joint hearings before the committee on territories and insular possessions, U. S. Senate, and the committee on insular affairs,* H.R., Washington, 1928.

For the British possessions and dominions, there is considerable governmental material. Of greatest value are (V911a) *Official year book of the Commonwealth of Australia,* annual, Melbourne, 1908 ff., ed. by G. H. Knibbs; and (V911b) *New Zealand official year-book,* annual, Wellington, N. Z., 1892 ff. The states of New South Wales and Victoria issue separate yearbooks. An excellent survey of the debates of the Commonwealth and state parliaments of Australia and of the New Zealand parliament is given in (K943) *Journal of the parliaments of the Empire.* The full debates of the Australian Commonwealth and New Zealand parliaments are published under the titles (V912a) *Commonwealth parliamentary debates,* Melbourne, and (V912b) *New Zealand parliamentary debates,* Wellington, N. Z.; these are popularly called Australian and New Zealand Hansards. British (L85) *Sessional papers* should be consulted; they contain annual reports on the colonies, statistical abstracts of their trade, and occasional reports on non-British possessions. The titles of these papers may be found in (L9e) *Consolidated list of parliamentary and stationery office publications.* The Commonwealth of Australia issues (V913) *Annual report on Papua,* Melbourne, 1889 ff. (V914a) *Historical records of New South Wales,* v. 1–7 in 8, Sydney, 1892–1901, covers the years 1762 to 1811, edited by F. M. Bladen, with the exception of v. 1, part 2, which was prepared by Alexander Britton. (V914b) *Historical records of Australia,* Sydney, 1914 ff., edited by J. Frederick Watson, is being published by the library committee of the Commonwealth parliament; the following volumes have already appeared: series 1, v. 1–26; series 3, v. 1–6; series 4, v. 1. Robert McNab is editing (V914c) *Historical records of New Zealand,* v. 1–2, Wellington, N. Z., 1908–14.

For the eastern French islands there is the official (V916) *Annuaire des établissements français de l'Océanie,* Papeete, 1863 ff.; and for the French colonies as a whole, the official (K910) *Annuaire colonial.* Recent changes in the Anglo-French condominium are given in (V917a) *Protocol respecting the New Hebrides, signed at London on August 6, 1914, by representatives of the British and French governments,* London, 1922 [Treaty series, 1922, no. 7]; or, better, in (V917b) *Protocol . . . and papers relating to it,* Melbourne, 1923 [Parliament of the Commonwealth of Australia, 1923, 2nd session].

For the Dutch East Indies the following government publications should be mentioned: (V918a) *Yearbook of the Netherlands East Indies,* Batavia, 1916 ff., compiled by the sub-department of industry and commerce at Buitenzorg; (V918b) *Staatsblad van Nederlandsch-Indië,* Batavia, 1847 ff.; (K917) *Handboek voor de Kennis van Nederland en Koloniën;* and (K915) *Regeeringsalmanak voor Nederlandsch-Indië.*

There is a rapidly accumulating list of official papers on the mandated islands. Conditions under the German régime are described officially, with statistics, in the last German reports on their colonies: (V919a) *Die deutschen Schutzgebiete in Afrika und der Südsee,* annual, Berlin, 1910–14. The parliament of the Commonwealth of Australia published (V919b) *Interim and final reports of the Royal commission on late German New Guinea,* Melbourne, 1920, of which a full summary is given in (V22b) *Stewart's handbook of the Pacific islands, 1921,* 271–317. The terms of the mandates are given in (J901g) *Official Journal, League of Nations*, Jan.-Feb., 1921. This monthly journal frequently contains material on the mandates. Each mandatory publishes an annual report for each of its mandates; these should be read in connection with (J901b) *Permanent mandates commission, minutes,* and other official papers on the mandates, published by the League of Nations at Geneva. For recent conditions in the New Zealand mandate, see the full (V919c) *Report of Royal Commission concerning the administration of Western Samoa,* Wellington, 1928.　　　　GHB

SECTION W

AFRICA

Editors

MASON WHITING TYLER *

Associate Professor of History, University of Minnesota

and

ARTHUR IRVING ANDREWS

CONTENTS

INTRODUCTION

Africa is hardly more conceivable as an historical than as a geographical unit. Geographically the Sahara divides the continent even more emphatically than the Mediterranean separates it from Europe. Almost equally is Egypt cut off from the Barbary States. The Suez isthmus, on the contrary, has seen the crossing of extraneous cultures to influence, as did the Greek and the Moham-

---

* Died March 15, 1923. Professor Tyler completed the original preparation of the section; the work of revision, which he would normally have performed, has been done by Professor Andrews.

medan, part of the African lands, but only part. From the North, likewise came the Roman domination and, much later, the real wave of European expansion, overflowing much of the African continent, but creating no distinctive civilization in Africa, however much or little its inhabitants were civilized.

No indigenous civilization has dominated, even temporarily, the whole continent; indeed, none has asserted itself with assurance of permanence as paramount in any portion. Wherever, as in Egypt, such a culmination has, at times, seemed possible, Asiatic and European influences have overwhelmed it. None of these could fuse the continent into a whole, an entity. Three forces, in turn, have, however, brought about something of union between the eastern and western parts of Africa above the Sudan and Sahara: the Roman Empire, the Mohammedan conquests, and the more recent expansion of European states. Of these the Mohammedan tide swirled into many eddies even south of the desert, but European penetration has threatened to split up all Africa and to draw all fragments under European rule and civilization. Consequently Africa remains partitioned among various races and civilizations in different stages of development.

Few are the books that deal with Africa north of the Sahara that contain also any attempt to describe the South. Specialists on Egypt are seldom more than strangers to the Barbary states. Few books on Africa were produced before 1830; the great mass belong to the nineteenth and twentieth centuries, scattered unevenly over sections and periods. Few are in English, and they hardly the best. Few, too, are the students who have attempted specialization upon the African fields—really great writers are conspicuously lacking. Exceedingly few are those who have mastered thoroughly the essential basic facts underlying the African continent and revealing its special characteristics considered as a whole.

On the other hand, certain portions of Africa, more than others, have received attention from writers: Egypt and South Africa obviously from English writers; Northern Africa, especially Algeria and Morocco, from the French. But these lean heavily toward the descriptive, toward the journalistic and the picturesque, the tourist's standpoint and not that of the thoroughly equipped student. The more interested a great state may be in the lands and ports of Africa, the more its citizens write about European, not native, interests. Missionaries, explorers, scientists, and traders are apt to relegate their historical matter to an introductory chapter or two; publicists of world reputation are even more apt to describe Africa merely as a field for the imperialism and expansion of European states.

Much space is usually devoted to descriptions of manners and customs. Probably, it is true, these manners and customs furnish the only possible clues to the historical development of the natives concerned. Few men in the English-writing world, few, indeed, outside of it, have shown a major interest in the historical development of Africa or have tended toward an African, instead of a European, orientation.

For works on ancient Egypt cf. § C; on Carthaginian and Roman North Africa, § E; on Mohammedan rule in Africa, § G; and for such general works on colonization as include material on Africa, § K.   AIA

BIBLIOGRAPHY

There is no good critical bibliography of modern Africa as a whole. The bibliographies in (1121) *Cambridge modern history*, 11:973–977, 12:927–948,

969–971, are mere book-lists without comment. A brief list, indicating the most important books by asterisks, is given in the appendix to (W103*b*) Harris, *Intervention and colonization in Africa* and a briefer list, with comments on books mentioned, in the appendix to (W101*a*) Johnston, *Colonization of Africa by alien races.* There are excellent lists in (J441*a*) *Peace handbooks,* and in G. L. Swiggett, ed., *Training for foreign service, Bulletin, 1921, no. 27, Bureau of Education, Department of Interior,* p. 90–95, 114–118, Washington, 1922, prepared by A. I. Andrews and G. F. Andrews, but these leave much of Africa without treatment. For the most recent books the lists in (B28*b*) *Statesman's year book* are valuable.

W1a Schunke-Hollway, Henry C. *Bibliography of books pamphlets, maps, magazine articles, etc., relating to South Africa with special reference to geography, from the time of Vasco da Gama to the formation of the British South Africa Company in 1888.* Capetown, 1898. [Transactions of the South African Philosophical Society, 10:131–294.]

b Mendelssohn, Sidney. *Mendelssohn's South African bibliography, being the catalogue raisonné of the Mendelssohn library of works relating to South Africa . . . together with notices of a large number of important works not as yet included in the collection . . . a bibliography of South African periodical literature, and of articles on South African subjects in periodical literature . . . also a complete list of the British parliamentary blue-books on South Africa, a cartography of South Africa, etc.* 2 v. London, 1910.

Together these give a useful, well-selected collection of books available on South Africa. AIA

W2a Playfair, Sir Robert Lambert. *Bibliography of Algeria from the expedition of Charles V in 1541 to 1887.* London, 1889. [Royal Geographical Society, Supplementary papers, II, pt. 2.]

b ——— *Supplement to the bibliography of Algeria, from the earliest times to 1895.* London, 1898. [Royal Geographical Society.]

c Playfair, Sir Robert Lambert, and **Brown, Robert.** *Bibliography of Morocco from the earliest times to the end of 1891.* London, 1892. [Royal Geographical Society, Supplementary papers, III, pt. 3.]

d Ashbee, Henry S. *Bibliography of Tunisia from the earliest times to the end of 1888 including Utica and Carthage, the Punic wars, the Roman occupation, the Arab conquest, the expeditions of Louis IX and Charles V, and the French protectorate.* London, 1889. [Partly reprinted from Alexander Graham and Henry S. Ashbee, *Travels in Tunisia,* London, 1887.]

e Playfair, Sir Robert Lambert. *Bibliography of the Barbary states: Tripoli and the Cyrenaica.* London, 1889. [Royal Geographical Society, Supplementary papers, II, no. 4.]

f Meakin, Budgett. *Bibliography of books on Morocco before 1889.* [In (W236*a*) Meakin, *Moorish Empire.*]

g Rouard de Card, Edgard. *Livres français des XVIIe et XVIIIe siècles concernant les États Barbaresques.* Paris, 1911. *Supplément,* Paris, 1917.

h Jacqueton, Gilbert. *Les archives espagnoles du Gouvernement Général de l'Algérie, histoire du fonds et inventaire.* Alger, 1894.

a., b., c., d., and *e.* This collection covers the ground up to the dates of publication with very great thoroughness and forms the starting point for any student of North African history. *f.* Annotated list based upon one man's judgment.

g. Small but well-chosen collection; useful for the student of the centuries concerned. *h.* Guide to a section of the archives in Algiers.   AIA

W3 Bruel, Georges. *Bibliographie de l'Afrique Équatoriale Française.* Paris, 1914. [Gouvernement général de l'Afrique Équatoriale Française.]

Reasonably full and well-selected; therefore indispensable.   AIA

W4 Grandidier, Guillaume. *Bibliographie de Madagascar.* 2 v. Paris, 1905–06.
Standard and indispensable.   AIA

W5a Minutilli, Federico. *Bibliografia della Libia, catalogo alfabetico e metodico di tutte le pubblicazioni . . . esistenti sino a tutto il 1902 sulla Tripolitania, la Cirenaica, il Fezzan, e le confinanti regioni del deserto.* Torino, 1903.

b Ceccherini, Ugo. *Bibliografia della Libia, in continuazione alla "Bibliografia della Libia" di F. Minutilli.* Roma, 1915. [Ministero delle Colonie.]

a. Upon Libia a multitude of monographs and articles exist, of which the titles may be found in *a.* and in *b.,* its continuation.   HNG

W6 Luke, Harry C. *Bibliography of Sierra Leone, prefaced by an essay on the origin, character, and peoples of the colony and protectorate.* 1910. 2nd rev. ed., Oxford and N. Y., 1925.

Includes many works which also relate to West African regions adjacent to Sierra Leone.   GMD

Library Collections.—No library in the United States seems to have made a special effort to collect works either on Africa as a whole or on any particular section of it during modern times. There are fairly good collections, however, to be found in the library of Harvard College and in the New York Public Library. The collections of government documents in the Library of Congress should be especially noted because of the importance of this class of materials for the study of Africa and its recent history. The American Geographical Society in New York City has an extensive collection of works on African exploration. The student of Africa will also find in the collections on the history of missions, such as that in the library of Union Theological Seminary, New York City, useful materials relating to the native races, to explorations, and to contemporary problems and conditions.   AHS

GEOGRAPHY

W41 Keane, Augustus H. *Africa.* 1895. 2nd ed., 2 v., London, 1907–09. [Stanford's Compendium of geography and travel.]

Excellent geography of Africa, probably furnishing the best introduction to the subject. Treats of the history, resources, and administration of Africa to 1907. Good maps of the various regions. For the British colonies, cf. Africa in (K310) *Oxford survey of the British empire,* a collaborative survey of high merit with excellent brief bibliographies, and (K303) Lucas, *Historical geography of the British colonies,* v. 3 and 4.   MWT

ETHNOGRAPHY

W51 Molema, S. M. *Bantu, past and present, an ethnographical and historical study of the native races of South Africa.* Edinburgh, 1920. (Bibliography.)

Good general survey; half historical, including ethnographical studies; half on contemporary conditions and problems. Though written by a Bantu, it relies on secondary sources, particularly upon the accounts of white men.   AIA

W52a Dennett, Richard E. *At the back of the black man's mind, or, notes on the kingly office in West Africa.* London and N. Y., 1906.

b Ellis, Alfred B. *Tshi-speaking peoples of the Gold Coast of West Africa, their religion, manners, customs, laws, language, etc.* London, 1887.

c —— *Ewe-speaking peoples of the Slave Coast of West Africa, their religion, manners, customs, laws, languages, etc.* London, 1890.

d —— *Yoruba-speaking peoples of the Slave Coast of West Africa, their religion, manners, customs, laws, language, etc.* London, 1894.

e Crawford, Daniel. *Thinking black, 22 years without a break in the long grass of Central Africa.* 1912. 2nd ed., London and N. Y., 1913.

a. Really a series of notes on the religion and politics of the negro tribes in the valley of the Congo and the Niger. The author has considerable respect for the negro mind and presents the best case for these peoples. *b., c.,* and *d.* Other standard works on the West African negro, somewhat old, but still of great value for the ethnography and social conditions of the west coast negro. *e.* Lively missionary account, nobly presenting the humanitarian view of the negro and his future.
MWT, GMD

COLLECTIONS OF SOURCES

No systematic attempt has been made to publish in collected form the sources for the history of Africa as a whole. Perhaps the most important single work of general scope is (W311) Hertslet, *Map of Africa by treaty.* Even for the various political units· there has been little systematic work, though in nearly every case some publications have been issued. The most extensive of these works are: (W61) G. M. Theal, *Records of the Cape Colony, from February 1793, copied for the Cape government from manuscript documents in the Public Record Office, London,* v. 1–36, London, 1897–1905; (W62) G. M. Theal, *Records of South-Eastern Africa, collected in libraries and archive departments in Europe,* v. 1–9, London, 1898–1903; (W63) Alfred Grandidier and others, *Collection des ouvrages anciens concernant Madagascar,* v. 1–9, Paris, 1903–10, which includes records of exploration and descriptive works from Portuguese, Dutch, English, French, and other sources from 1500 to 1800; (W64) G. Esquer, *Collection de documents inédits sur l'histoire de l'Algérie,* v. 1–3, Paris, 1923–25, thus far devoted to the earlier years of French occupation.

SHORTER GENERAL HISTORIES

W101a Johnston, Sir Harry H. *History of the colonization of Africa by alien races.* 1899. 2nd rev. ed., Cambridge, Eng., 1913. [Cambridge historical series.] (Bibliography.)

b —— *Opening up of Africa.* London and N. Y., 1911. [Home university library.]

c Lucas, Sir Charles P. *Partition and colonization of Africa.* Oxford, 1922. (Brief bibliography.)

a. General account of the division and colonization of Africa by the European powers, writen by a great authority on Africa. Packed with facts and somewhat dry; an excellent introduction to the subject. The treatment of the colonial enterprises of the various powers is uniform and fair. The edition of 1913 should be used. Review, E. K. Alden, *A.H.R.* 5:134, Oct. 1899. *b.* Briefer, readable account of the subject by the same author.   *c.* Best and most recent brief survey from the earliest times to about 1920 by a competent authority. Review, Basil Williams, *A.H.R.* 29:146, Oct. 1923.   Cf. (B121) *New Larned history for ready reference,* articles on Africa and on its several political sub-divisions.   GMD

W102a Keltie, Sir John Scott. *Partition of Africa.* 1893. 2nd rev. ed., London, 1895.   (Bibliography.)

   b White, Arthur S. *Development of Africa, a study in applied geography.* 1890. 2nd rev. ed., London, 1892.

   a. Very valuable and authoritative account of African development up to about 1895; especially important for early explorations and colonization.   *b.* Less important but useful.   AIA

W103a Gibbons, Herbert A. *New map of Africa, 1900–1916, a history of European colonial expansion and colonial diplomacy.* N. Y., 1916.   Later reprints.

   b Harris, Norman D. *Intervention and colonization in Africa.* Boston, 1914.   (Bibliography.)

   c Woolf, Leonard S. *Empire and commerce in Africa, a study in economic imperialism.* London, 1919.

   Three comparatively recent books of the popular order all emphasizing European imperialism, *a.* lightly, the others heavily. Of the latter, *b.* is not so severe, *c.* is more sober and scholarly even though didactic and somewhat prejudiced. *c.* Decidedly the best.   *a.* and *b.* Compromised by many errors in facts and by shallowness in interpretations. Review of *a.,* N. D. Harris, *A.H.R.* 22:873, July 1917; of *b,* C. S. Allen, *Amer. Pol. Sci. Rev.,* 9:389, May 1915.   *b,* completely revised, has been published as *Europe and Africa,* N. Y., 1927.   AIA

W104 Powell, E. Alexander. *Last frontier, the white man's war for civilisation in Africa.* N. Y., 1912.

   Travel-sketches, by an American correspondent, of journeys in Africa in the years just preceding the war. Somewhat impressionistic; valuable because of its readable qualities and its graphic pictures of conditions in the various European colonies; it contributes little in the way of history.   AIA

NORTH AFRICA BEFORE 1830

W201a Poole, Stanley Lane. *Barbary Corsairs.* London and N. Y., 1890. [Story of the nations.]   (Bibliography.)

   b Playfair, Sir Robert Lambert. *Scourge of Christendom: annals of British relations with Algiers prior to the French conquest.* London, 1884.

   a. Although betraying some bias and evincing a slight tendency to rely on secondary and untrustworthy sources, this book is the best account, all things considered, of the Barbary pirates from the beginnings to the French conquest. Its illustrations are unusually valuable and its treatment of material well proportioned.   *b.* Especially valuable for Anglo-Algerian relations. Contains many extracts from contemporary documents.   AIA

W202 Piquet, Victor. *Les civilisations de l'Afrique du Nord: Berbères, Arabes, Turcs.* 1909. 2nd ed., Paris, 1917.   (Bibliography.)

   Best general history of the people of North Africa from earliest times to the nineteenth century.   GFA

W203 Mercier, Ernest. *Histoire de l'Afrique septentrionale, depuis les temps les plus reculés jusqu'à la conquête française, 1830.* 3 v. Paris, 1888–90.

Standard history of North Africa; based in large part upon African native sources; a carefully written summary of events from the earliest times to the French conquest. Though the earliest sections are most valuable the whole work should be consulted.

AIA

W204a Al Bakrī (Abu Obeid Abdulla el Be!:ri). *Description de l'Afrĭque septentrionale, texte arabe,* ed. by W. MacGuckin, Baron de Slane, Alger, 1857; French tr. by W. MacGuckin, Baron de Slane, Paris, 1859 [Extrait du *Journal Asiatique*], rev. ed., Alger, 1913.

b Edrīsī (Abu Abdulla Mohammed el Edrisi). *Nuzhat al-Mushtāk.* De *geographia universali* [abridged Arab text), Romae, 1592; *Géographie d'Edrisi traduite de l'arabe en français et accompagnée de notes,* by Amédée Jaubert, 2 v., Paris, 1836–40; *Description de l'Afrique et de l'Espagne, par Edrîsî, texte arabe, avec une traduction, de notes et un glossaire,* by R. Dozy and M. J. de Goeje, Leyde, 1866.

c Ibn Khaldūn (Abu-Zeid Abd-er-Rahman-ibn-Mohammed ibn Khaldoun). *Histoire des Berbères et des dynasties musulmanes de l'Afrique septentrionale, texte arabe,* ed. by W. MacGuckin, Baron de Slane, 2 v., Alger, 1847–51; French tr. by W. MacGuckin, Baron de Slane, 4 v., Alger, 1852–56. New ed. of French tr., with notice of Ibn Khaldūn, bibliography, and index, by Paul Casanova, v. 1–2, Paris, 1925–27.

a. Description of Africa especially of the northwestern section written by a Spanish Arab of the eleventh century. *b.* General geographical description of the world written about 1150 by a native of Ceuta who, after extensive travels, settled and wrote in Sicily. The portion on Africa which has been published separately is especially full and valuable. *c.* Third section of a general history of Mohammedan peoples of which (G66) *Les prolégomènes* is the first part. The author was a native of Tunis who had travelled widely in Mohammedan lands and who wrote at Cairo near the end of the fourteenth century. A very important source of information on North African history in the Middle Ages, with special emphasis on Morocco. Accounts of distinguished Mohammedan leaders prior to the thirteenth century will be found in (G65) Ibn Khallikān, *Biographical dictionary.*

AIA, GMD

W205a Leo Africanus, Joannes. *Geographical historie of Africa, written in Arabicke and Italian by Iohn Leo a More . . . before which . . . is prefixed a generall description of Africa, and also a particular treatise of all the maine lands and isles vnderscribed by Iohn Leo.* 1600. Rev. ed. by R. Brown, 3 v., London, 1896. [Hakluyt Society.] Tr. by John Pory from *Della descrittione dell' Africa et delle cose notabili che ivi sono,* Venetia, 1550. [G. B. Ramusio, Delle navigationi et viaggi, v. 1.]

b Mármol Carvajal, Luis del. *Descripción general de Affrica, con todos los sucessos de guerras que a avido entre los infieles y el pueblo christiano y entre ellos mesmos desde que Mahoma inveto su secta, hasta el año del Señor 1571.* 3 v. Granada and Malaga, 1573–99. French tr. by N. Perrot, sieur d'Ablancourt and others, *L'Afrique de Marmol,* 1653, rev. ed., 3 v., Paris, 1667.

Both written in the sixteenth century by natives of Granada. Basic works on north African history; quite comprehensive; used directly or indirectly by most later writers on North Africa. *a.* Contains much first hand information. The original edition in Italian, published by Ramusio, is still much the best. *b.*

Copied freely from *a.*, but contains a great deal of original material collected at first hand. The original Spanish edition is preferable to the French translation.

AIA

W206a Haedo, Diego de. *Topographia e historia general de Argel, etc.* Valladolid, 1612. French tr. by Dr. Monneneau and A. Berbrugger, of description of Algiers, *Revue Africaine,* 14:364, 15:473, 1870–71, by M. de Grammont, of epitome of the kings of Algiers, *Revue Africaine,* 24:37, 25:120, 1881–82.

b Dan, Pierre. *Histoire de Barbarie et de ses corsaires, des royaumes, et des villes d'Alger, de Tunis, de Salé, et de Tripoly; ou il est traitté de leur gouvernement, de leurs moeurs, de leurs cruautez, de leurs brigandages, de leurs sortileges, et de plusieurs autres particularitez remarquables.* 1637. 2nd rev. ed., Paris, 1649.

c Busnot, Dominique. *History of the reign of Muley Ismael, the present king of Morocco, Fez, Tafilet, Sous, etc.* London, 1715. Tr. from *Histoire du règne de Mulay Ismael, roy de Maroc, Fez, Tafilet, Souz, etc.,* Rouen, 1714.

a. Contains, in addition to a full description of North African places, an epitome of the kings of Algiers which is of first importance for North African events in the sixteenth century. Frequently cited. *b.* and *c.* Useful sources; utilized frequently by later writers without acknowledgment. Each invaluable for its particular century. AIA

W207a Laugier de Tassy, N. *Histoire du royaume d'Alger, avec l'état présent de son gouvernement, de ses forces de terre et de mer, de ses revenus, police, justice, politique, et commerce.* Amsterdam, 1725. Later editions.

b Morgan, Joseph. *Complete history of Algiers, to which is prefixed an epitome of the general history of Barbary,* etc. 1728–29. Reprint, London, 1731. Also reprinted as *Compleat history of the piratical states of Barbary.* London, 1750.

c Shaw, Thomas. *Travels or observations relating to several parts of Barbary and the Levant.* 1738. 2nd ed., 'with great improvements,' London, 1757; 3rd rev. ed., 2 v., Edinburgh, 1808.

d Chenier, Louis Sauveur de. *Present state of the empire of Morocco; its animals, products, climate, soil, cities, ports, provinces, coins, weights, and measures; with the language, religion, laws, manners, customs and character of the Moors; the history of the dynasties since Edris; the naval force and commerce of Morocco; and the character, conduct, and views, political and commercial, of the reigning emperor.* 2 v. London, 1788. Abridged tr. from *Recherches historiques sur les Maures, et histoire de l'empire de Maroc,* 3 v., Paris, 1787.

e Rotalier, Charles de. *Histoire d'Alger et de la piraterie des Turcs dans la Méditerranée, à dater du XVIᵉ siècle.* 2 v. Paris, 1841.

a. Somewhat plagiarized from (W205a) Leo Africanus and (W205b) Mármol; gives abundant historical data; readable. *b.* Valuable paraphrases (especially in the 1750 ed.) of *a.* without credit; useful, nevertheless, for North African history. *c.* Described by (W2) Playfair as 'One of the most valuable works ever written on North Africa'; well reflects conditions in the eighteenth century; valuable documentary appendix. *d.* Uses Arab sources freely; despite some errors, valuable for seventeenth-century conditions in western North Africa. *e.* Rather thorough account of North Africa during the Turkish period; based upon Turkish and European sources; faulty but usable. AIA

W208 Martin, Alfred G. P. *Quatre siècles d'histoire marocaine, au Sahara de 1504 à 1902, au Maroc de 1894 à 1912, d'après archives et documentations indigènes.* Paris, 1923.

One of the few really historical works available which contain material on the native side; important for African development. Review, D. S. Margoliouth, *E.H.R.* 39:122, Jan. 1924. GFA

W209 Ismael, Hamet. *Histoire du Maghreb.* Paris, 1923. (Bibliography.)

Good general history of Morocco throughout the whole Mohammedan period down to 1907. GMD

NORTH AFRICA SINCE 1830

W231a Piquet, Victor. *La colonisation française dans l'Afrique du Nord, Algérie, Tunisie, Maroc.* 1912. 2nd rev. ed., Paris, 1914. (Bibliography.)

b Pinon, René. *L'empire Méditerranée; l'entente franco-italienne, la question marocaine, Figuig, le Touât, la Tripolitaine, Bizerte, Malte, Gibraltar.* 1904. 5th ed., Paris, 1912.

a. Although somewhat out of date, by far the most useful single work covering all French North Africa. A work limited to 530 pages covering so broad a field can be scarcely more than an outline, but it is remarkably complete. Historical, political, economic, and social developments are well treated. *b.* Careful study of the international questions connected with French Africa, Tripoli, Malta, and Gibraltar. GFA, AIA

W232 Bernard, Augustin, and others. *L'Afrique du Nord, conférences organisées par la Société des Anciens Élèves et Élèves de l'École Libre des Sciences Politiques.* Paris, 1913. [Bibliothèque d'histoire contemporaine.]

Collection of ten lectures on Algeria, Tunisia, Morocco, French West Africa, Egypt, and Tripolitania, prepared by some of the ablest French authorities. Excellent, though brief, surveys of the history and conditions in each of these countries on the eve of the World War. MWT

W233a Sloane, William M. *Greater France in Africa.* N. Y. and London, 1924.

b Wickersham, George W. *Spring in Morocco and Algiers.* N. Y. and London, 1923.

Two accounts of the same mission by two of the members. *a.* Result of a five weeks semi-official visit to French North Africa, interestingly told. The historical and political portions appear to have been hastily written and without sufficient knowledge of the subject. Review, G. F. Andrews, *A.H.R.* 30:648, Apr. 1925. *b.* Short, interesting survey of country and people. Less pretentious than *a.*, but free from noticeable errors. GFA

W236a Meakin, Budgett. *Moorish empire, a historical epitome.* London and N. Y., 1899. (Bibliography, listed separately as W2f.)

b —— *Land of the Moors, a comprehensive description.* London and N. Y., 1901.

c —— *The Moors, a comprehensive description.* London and N. Y., 1902.

d —— *Life in Morocco and glimpses beyond.* London, 1905.

a. Best history of Morocco, but to be used with caution as the author's training and equipment were inadequate. He knew the country and people well at first hand, but not the historical sources. Good, elaborate chronological chart and illustrations, but a perversely original system of transliteration. Review, *Nation* (N. Y.) 70:346, May 3, 1900. *b., c.,* and *d.* Of less value but not to be disregarded.   DBM

W237a Mackenzie, Donald. *Khalifate of the West, being a general description of Morocco.* London, 1911.

   b Ashmead-Bartlett, Ellis. *Passing of the Shereefian empire.* Edinburgh and N. Y., 1910.

Of no great authority but two of the few works picturing the transitional era from native rule to foreign protectorate. *a.* The more descriptive. *b.* The better narrative. Review, D. S. Margoliouth, *E.H.R.* 39:123, Jan. 1924. Cf. also (J207) Morel, *Morocco in diplomacy.*   AIA

W238a Bernard, Augustin. *Le Maroc.* 1912. 6th rev. ed., Paris, 1921. [Bibliothèque d'histoire contemporaine.] (Bibliography.)

   b Goulven, Joseph. *Le Maroc; les ressources de ses régions, sa mise en valeur.* 1919. 2nd ed., Paris, 1920.

a. General history of Morocco from early times to the establishment of the protectorate. Particular attention is given to political, religious, and social questions; to the character and distribution of the population; and to the history of the Moroccan question. *b.* Very valuable account of the natural resources, economic development, and possibilities of Morocco with numerous and useful illustrations and an excellent map.   GFA

W239 Piquet, Victor. *Le Maroc, géographie, histoire, mise en valeur.* 1918. New ed., Paris, 1920.

Most comprehensive handbook treating of all matters of interest with regard to Morocco. Excellent maps.   GFA

W240a Aubin, Eugène. *Morocco of today.* London, 1906. Tr. from *Le Maroc d'aujourd'hui,* Paris, 1904.

   b Harris, Walter B. *Morocco that was.* London, 1921.

   c —— *Tafilet, the narrative of a journey of exploration in the Atlas mountains and the oases of the north-west Sahara.* Edinburgh, 1895.

a. Illuminating short account of travel in southern Morocco; also some very interesting side-lights on life in northern Morocco. The exceptional value of the book, however, lies in the detailed description of the machinery of government under the Makhzen before the establishment of the protectorate. *b.* Not as carefully written as *a.;* the reminiscences of a man who was very close to the government of the Makhzen before the establishment of the protectorate. The book is filled with anecdotes which throw considerable light on conditions and personalities in Morocco before 1911. *c.* Only detailed description of Tafilet, a portion of the Moroccan hinterland; gives an interesting account of political conditions at the close of the reign of Moulay Hassan.   GFA

W241a Touton, Max. *Notre protectorat marocain.* Poitiers, 1923.

   b Britsch, Amédée. *Le maréchal Lyautey, le soldat, l'écrivain, le politique.* Paris, 1921. [Les cahiers de la victoire.[(Bibliography.)

a. Historical, economic, social, and military study of Morocco, descriptive rather than narrative, from the French point of view. Good reference book for recent events. *b.* Brief account, too chronological in some places, too eulogistic in others, of the remarkable work of the great French colonial administrator. Review, A. I. Andrews, *A.H.R.* 27:356, Jan. 1922. AIA

W246a Wahl, Maurice. *L'Algérie.* 1882. 5th rev. ed. by A. Bernard, Paris, 1908.

   b Gaffarel, Paul. *L'Algérie, histoire, conquête, et colonisation.* Paris, 1883. (Bibliography.)

   c Pember, Mrs. Devereux, [pseudonym, Roy Devereux]. *Aspects of Algeria, historical, political, colonial.* London and N. Y., 1912. (Brief bibliography.)

   a. For many years the standard work on modern Algeria. Some useful material in the early editions was discarded in the later ones. It contains particularly valuable chapters on the various native peoples as well as on the European populations. *b.* Not so scholarly; requires more revision in view of passing years, but assists materially toward giving readers a truly African orientation; historical section inferior. *c.* Slightly better than the average book in English; devotes some chapters to a rather sketchy, ill-connected, and faulty historical account; interspersed with some descriptive matter of value. GFA, AIA

W251a Loth, Gaston. *La Tunisie et l'œuvre du protectorat français.* Paris, 1907.

   b Lanessan, Jean L. de. *La Tunisie.* 1887. 3rd ed., Paris, 1917.

   c Broadley, Alexander M. *Last Punic war: Tunis past and present, with a narrative of the French conquest of the Regency.* 2 v. London, 1882.

   d Sladen, Douglas. *Carthage and Tunis, the old and new gates of the Orient.* 2 v. London and N. Y., 1906.

   a. Published under the auspices of the government; the best general book on Tunisia in one volume. Twenty-six pages are devoted to the history from early times; the organization of the government under the protectorate is fully set forth; adequate chapters deal with political, social, and economic conditions. *b.* Devoted almost exclusively to economic matters which are set forth in great detail by the author, perhaps the best qualified French authority on this subject. *c.* Though anti-French, it gives valuable information on the situation in Tunis just before and during the French occupation. *d.* Similar to *c.* but later; inferior even in scholarly arrangement; prolix. GFA, AIA

W256a McClure, W. K. *Italy in North Africa, an account of the Tripoli enterprise.* London, 1913; Philadelphia, 1914.

   b Braun, Ethel. *New Tripoli and what I saw in the hinterland.* London, 1914.

   a. The author was in Tripoli during a few months in 1911 and 1912, and made good use of his opportunities. The reader will find an excellent account of local conditions at that time. Considerable space is given to political history and political questions. Well illustrated; excellent maps. *b.* Interesting description of the making of the new Italian colony, its progress and problems. Based mainly on conversations with Italians and others in Libya; possibly a little over-hopeful of good results from the new rule. GFA

EGYPT AND THE SUDAN

W261a Weigall, Arthur E. P. B. *History of events in Egypt from 1798 to 1914.* London, 1915.

b Dicey, Edward. *Story of the khedivate.* N. Y., 1902.

c Charles-Roux, François. *L'Angleterre et l'expédition française en Égypte.* 2 v. Paris, 1925. [Société Royale de Géographie d'Égypte.]

Two general accounts of Egypt during the nineteenth century. *a.* Popular treatment; for the latter part of the period based on the writings of Cromer and other English partisans of the occupation. *b.* More independent piece of work, based on the personal views and experiences of the author who, as a journalist closely in touch with most of the leading persons of Egypt from 1875 to 1900, was in a good position to learn much regarding the course of events. *c.* Exhaustive study by an author of other works on English and French relations with Egypt. MWT

W262 Freycinet, Charles de. *La question d'Égypte.* Paris, 1905.

Account of the relations of England and France toward Egypt during the decade before the establishment of British control. Written distinctly from the French point of view and to some extent as a defence of the author's policy as premier, January to July 1882. Its value lies in the numerous documents and bits of inside information. MWT

W263a Blunt, Wilfrid S. *Secret history of the English occupation of Egypt, being a personal narrative of events.* London, 1907.

**b —— ** *Gordon at Khartoum.* London, 1911.

a. Somewhat opinionated account of the revolt of Arabi Pasha and of the Egyptian nationalist movement in the seventies and early eighties, by one who knew well the nationalist leaders in these events. An apology, but overdrawn, vehement, and exaggerated in some respects. *b.* Continuation of *a.* but less valuable. MWT, AIA

W264 Milner, Alfred, Viscount. *England in Egypt.* 1892. 13th ed., London, 1920.

Thorough discussion and defence of the British position in Egypt much along the lines of (W266) Cromer, *Modern Egypt,* but written some fifteen years previously. Based on observations while under-secretary of finance in Egypt from 1889 to 1892. For many years the standard descriptive account of political, administrative, and economic conditions in Egypt. Though badly out of date in many respects and but slightly revised in later editions, it is still one of the most valuable works for the understanding of the establishment of British control in Egypt of which it heartily approves. GMD

W265a White, Arthur S. *Expansion of Egypt under Anglo-Egyptian condominium.* London, 1899.

b Colvin, Sir Auckland. *Making of modern Egypt.* 1906. 4th ed., London, 1909.

Both, particularly *b.,* are in sympathy with the work and ideas of the Cromer administration. *a.* Account of the international relations of Egypt and of Egyptian problems about 1899, with valuable statistics. *b.* Survey of the whole British occupation down to about 1906; readable but superficial. AIA

W266 Cromer, Evelyn Baring, Earl. *Modern Egypt.* 2 v. London and N. Y., 1908. Later reprints.

Standard account of British rule in Egypt, from its beginning to 1907, by its organizer; an appraisal and study of its results as well as an autobiography of the author. Accepted generally as authentic and trustworthy for the earlier years of British control. The later chapters, three, in particular, dealing with Egyptian nationalism and presenting the personal viewpoint of the writer, should be compared with other discussions of the subject. Review, J. S. Reeves, *Amer. Pol. Sci. Rev.* 2:638, Nov. 1908. GFA

W267a Alexander, John R. *Truth about Egypt.* London and N. Y., 1911.

  b Low, Sidney. *Egypt in transition.* London, 1914.

These books help to dispel the clouds of controversy over Egypt at a critical time by supplying information, documentary and otherwise, on the native parties and Turkish officials. AIA

W268a Chirol, Sir Valentine. *Egyptian problem.* London, 1920. Later reprints.

  b Worsfold, William Basil. *Future of Egypt.* London, 1914. [Nations library.] (Bibliography.)

a. Probably the most authoritative treatment of recent Egyptian problems. Frankly critical of certain phases of Egyptian rule and exceedingly fair towards the aspiration of the Egyptian nationalists. The first half of the book is devoted to an account of British control in Egypt since 1900; the second half, to an analysis of the problems since 1914. The views of Chirol should be studied with those of (W266) Cromer and his followers, which have been briefly and conveniently summarized in *b.* For the most recent developments, cf. (W315) G. L. Beer, *African questions at the Paris Peace Conference;* (U427a) Chirol, *Occident and the Orient;* and (U531b) Dutcher, *Political Awakening of the East.* MWT, AIA

W269a Elgood, Percival G. *Egypt and the army.* London and N. Y., 1924.

  b Harris, Murray. *Egypt under the Egyptians.* London, 1925.

  c Hayter, Sir William. *Recent constitutional developments in Egypt.* Cambridge, Eng., 1924.

a. By a British army officer who has held important administrative posts in Egypt. Somewhat over-critical study of British policy in Egypt during the World War and immediately after, together with a useful survey of events during the same period. Review, *A.H.R.* 30:148, Oct. 1924. *b.* Critical analysis of present-day conditions in Egypt, but neither prompted by venom nor wholly pessimistic in its outlook. *c.* Valuable information given by a former legal adviser to the Egyptian government. GMD, AIA

W281 MacMichael, Harold A. *History of the Arabs in the Sudan, and some account of the people who preceded them and of the tribes inhabiting Dárfūr.* 2 v. Cambridge, Eng., 1922. (Bibliography.)

Keeps well the promise of its title; based upon original sources throughout; gives much valuable detail on ethnology, anthropology, and folklore. V. 2. Consists of translations, analyses, and commentaries on the original historical-genealogical documents of the Arabs in the Sudan, and forms a very suggestive study of historical method bearing on the value of such materials. Most readable and interesting to any historical student, although loaded with references and notes. Review, *Near East,* 21:866, June 29, 1922.   DBM

W282 Budge, Sir Ernest A. T. Wallis. *Egyptian Sûdân, its history and monuments.* 2 v. London and Philadelphia, 1907. (Bibliography.)

General study of the Egyptian Sudan from the earliest times to the present with an account of the geography and present problems of the region. The author, a well-known Egyptologist, is inclined to stress the earlier period, but the account of the later years is clear and adequate for general purposes.

MWT

W283a Wingate, Sir Francis R. *Mahdiism and the Egyptian Sudan, being an account of the rise and progress of Mahdiism and of subsequent events in the Sudan to the present time.* London and N. Y., 1891.

  b Churchill, Winston L. Spencer. *River war, an historical account of the reconquest of the Soudan.* Ed. by F. W. Rhodes. 2 v., 1899. Rev. ed., 1 v., London and N. Y., 1902. (Bibliography.)

  c Steevens, George W. *With Kitchener to Khartum.* London and N. Y., 1898.

a. Detailed account of the rise of the Mahdi and of his conquest of the Sudan in 1884–1885. Careful study with emphasis on the military side.   *b.* Readable story of the recovery of the Sudan by Anglo-Egyptian troops. The author, who was then a newspaper correspondent, gives a good detailed account of the progress of the expedition.   *c.* Brilliantly written and deserving of notice, though less important.

MWT, AIA

W284 Martin, Percy Falcke. *Sudan in evolution, a study of the economic, financial, and administrative conditions of the Anglo-Egyptian Sudan.* London, 1921.

Good study of developments in the Sudan since the hectic days of the Mahdi and Gordon.   AIA

AFRICAN EXPLORATION

W291a La Roncière, Charles Bourel de. *La découverte de l'Afrique au moyen âge, cartographes et explorateurs.* 2 v. Le Caire, 1925. [Société Royale de Géographie d'Égypte.]

  b Wiener, Leo. *Africa and the discovery of America.* 3 v. Philadelphia, 1920.

a. Prepared and published under the patronage of King Fuad. Exhaustive collection and study of the data with regard to European knowledge of Africa from Roman times to the fifteenth century, with various early maps.   GMD

b. Ethnological-linguistic study of great suggestiveness. Review, v. 1. E. L. Stevenson, *A.H.R.* 26:102, Oct. 1920.   V. 2 and 3. D. B. Macdonald, *A.H.R.* 28:734, July 1923.   AIA

W292a *Africa and its exploration as told by its explorers: Mungo Park, Clapperton, the Landers, Livingstone. . . .* London, 1891.

  b Brown, Robert. *Story of Africa and its explorers.* 4 v. London and N. Y., 1911.

a. Excellent selection from the works of the African explorers of the early nineteenth century, knit together to give a history of the opening up of Africa.

b. Popular but well written, with much matter of historical value. Contains many references and illustrations. AIA

W293a Park, Mungo. *Travels in the interior districts of Africa, performed in the years 1795, 1796, and 1797.* London 1799. New ed., with an account of a subsequent mission to that country in 1805, 2 v., London, 1816.

b Thomson, Joseph. *Mungo Park and the Niger.* London, 1890. [World's great explorers and explorations.]

a. Detailed account of Park's exploration. *b.* Both a biography of Park and a history of the exploration and European control of the Niger, about half the book is devoted to the latter topic. It therefore provides an excellent introduction to the subject of West Africa to about 1885. MWT

W294a Barth, Heinrich. *Travels and discoveries in North and Central Africa.* 5 v. London, 1857–58. 3 v. N. Y., 1857–59. Abridged ed., 1 v. Philadelphia, 1859. Tr. from *Reisen und Entdeckungen in Nord- und Central-Afrika in den jahren 1849 bis 1855,* 5 v. 1857–59; condensed ed., 2 v., Gotha, 1859–61.

b Nachtigal, Gustav. *Sahărâ und Sûdân, Ergebnisse sechsjähriger Reisen in Afrika.* 3 v. Berlin, 1879–89.

a. Somewhat abridged translation of the German account of one of the most valuable expeditions undertaken in Africa, which was carried out under English auspices in the years 1849 to 1855. It is still one of the most valuable sources for the regions around Timbuctoo and Lake Chad and in northern Nigeria, especially during the period preceding the arrival of Europeans. Knowledge of these regions during the Middle Ages is largely based on information acquired by Barth. *b.* Account of an important later expedition from Tripoli to Lake Chad and thence eastward to the Nile. MWT

W295a Livingstone, David. *Missionary travels and researches in South Africa: including a sketch of sixteen years' residence in the interior of Africa, and a journey from the Cape of Good Hope to Loanda on the west coast; thence across the continent, down the river Zambesi, to the eastern ocean.* 1857. New ed., London, 1899.

b —— *Last journals of David Livingstone in Central Africa from 1865 to his death, continued by a narrative of his last moments and sufferings . . . by H. Waller.* 2 v. London, 1874.

Valuable as a personal record of heroic labors in the opening-up of Africa and as a source of information on South and Central Africa before the coming of the white man and on the early relations of Boers, English, and natives.
MWT

W296a Johnston, Sir Harry H. *Livingstone and the exploration of Central Africa.* London, 1891. [World's great explorers and explorations.]

b Hughes, Thomas. *David Livingstone.* London, 1889. [English men of action.] N. Y., 1902. [Heroes of history.]

a. Not merely a biography of Livingstone but a presentation of a wealth of information on the peoples and conditions in Central and Southern Africa. Some of this information is now out of date, but the residue will prove sufficient for practical purposes if checked by a good modern historical geography. The treatment of Livingstone is full, enthusiastic but judicious. *b.* Briefer and strictly biographical. MWT

W297a Stanley, Sir Henry M. *How I found Livingstone: travels, adventures, and discoveries in Central Africa, including an account of four months' residence with Dr. Livingstone.* 1872. Centenary ed., N. Y., 1913.

b —— *Through the dark continent, or, the sources of the Nile, around the great lakes of equatorial Africa, and down the Livingstone River to the Atlantic Ocean.* 1878. Reprint, 2 v., N. Y., 1906.

c —— *In darkest Africa, or, the quest, rescue, and retreat of Emin, governor of Equatoria.* 2 v. N. Y., 1890. 2 v. in 1, N. Y., 1913.

d Stanley, Dorothy, ed. *Autobiography of Sir Henry Morton Stanley.* Boston, 1909.

a., b., and *c.* Personal records of explorations in Central Africa in 1871–72, 1874–77, and 1887–89, respectively. *d.* Fascinating volume edited by his wife, containing interesting biographical material and well-selected passages from the explorer's own works. Its value lies in its hints as to Stanley's maturer views regarding British policy in Central Africa. For Stanley's work in establishing the Congo Free State, cf. (W402). SBF

W298a Speke, John H. *Journal of the discovery of the source of the Nile.* Edinburgh, 1863.

b Baker, Sir Samuel W. *Albert Nyanza, great basin of the Nile, and explorations of the Nile sources.* 2 v. London, 1866. New ed., 1 v., Philadelphia, 1870.

c Burton, Sir Richard F. *Lake regions of Central Africa, a picture of exploration.* 2 v. London, 1860.

These three eminent explorers describe their searches for the Nile sources, and present valuable information on the natives, their legends, tribal customs, etc. AIA

W299 Schweinfurth, Georg A. *Heart of Africa, three years' travels and adventures in the unexplored regions of Central Africa from 1868 to 1871.* 2 v. N. Y., 1874. Tr. by E. E. Frewer from *Im Herzen von Afrika, Reisen und Entdeckungen im centralen Aequitorial-Afrika während der Jahren 1868 bis 1871,* 2 v. Leipzig, 1874.

Much of the knowledge regarding the peoples of this region is based on Schweinfurth. His data are undoubtedly substantially correct, though he lost his field notes and appears to have written mainly from memory. MWT

W300a Frobenius, Leo. *Voice of Africa, being an account of the travels of the German Inner African Exploration Expedition in the years 1910–1912.* 2 v. London, 1913. Tr. by R. Blind from *Und Afrika sprach, Bericht über den Verlauf der dritten Reise-Periode der deutschen inner-afrikanischen Forschungs-Expedition in den Jahren 1910–1912.* Berlin, 1912. [v. 3 of Deutsche inner-afrikanische Forschungs-Expedition.]

b Mecklenburg-Schwerin, Duke Adolphus Frederick of. *In the heart of Africa.* London and N. Y., 1910. Tr. by G. E. Maberly-Oppler from *Ins innerste Afrika,* 1909; new ed. by J. Hennings, Berlin, 1910.

Some of the best work in African exploration during the years immediately preceding 1914 was done by German explorers. These volumes describe two of these German expeditions. *a.* Account of exploration in West and Central Africa; especially valuable in its treatment of the native races of these regions. *b.* Record of an expedition which crossed Central Africa in 1907 to 1908 following approximately the route of the second Stanley expedition. It should be read in connection with (W297b) H. M. Stanley, *Through the dark continent.* Review, *Athenaeum,* 2:695, Dec. 3, 1910. MWT

EUROPEAN RELATIONS IN AFRICA

W311 Hertslet, Sir Edward. *Map of Africa by treaty.* 1894–95. 3rd rev. ed., continued to the end of 1908, by R. W. Brant and H. L. Sherwood, 3 v., London, 1909.

The great storehouse of documents regarding the division of Africa among the European powers. Copies of all the important treaties and diplomatic correspondence are given; illustrated by numerous maps. MWT

W312a Darcy, Jean. *France et Angleterre, cent années de rivalité coloniale, l'Afrique.* Paris, 1904.

b Lebon, André. *La politique de la France en Afrique, 1896–98: mission Marchand, Niger, Madagascar.* Paris, 1901.

a. Most usable French account of the colonial struggle between England and France in Africa. The earlier portions of the book are based on unpublished sources. The tone is strongly French, certain of the righteousness of France's cause. Its scope extends from the conquest of Algiers to Fashoda, 1830 to 1898. *b.* Account of the last years of this struggle, presented from the French point of view. The author was minister for the colonies at the time. MWT

W313 Beyens, Napoléon Eugène, Baron. *La question africaine.* Bruxelles, 1918.

Recent work on international problems in Africa. The main value of the book lies in the author's ability to lift the curtain somewhat from before the mysteries of international diplomacy in Africa. The point of view is decidedly Belgian and the emphasis is on the Congo problem. MWT

W314 Carton De Wiart, Edmond. *Les grandes compagnies coloniales anglaises du 19ᵉ siècle.* Paris, 1899. (Excellent bibliography.)

Account of the four British chartered companies of the late nineteenth century, three of which, the British East Africa, the British South Africa, and the Niger companies, operated in Africa. An account of each of the companies is given; and a discussion of development by chartered companies is added. The tone is distinctly favorable to the companies; the best introduction to this method of administration. MWT

W315 Beer, George L. *African questions at the Paris Peace Conference, with papers on Egypt, Mesopotamia, and the colonial settlement.* Ed. by Louis H. Gray. N. Y. and London, 1923. (Bibliography.)

The author was the expert on African affairs attached to the American Commission at the Peace Conference. The volume is not a complete discussion of African questions but of those relating to the German colonies, middle Africa, and Egypt. In each case the conditions are described and the questions elucidated with thorough knowledge and acumen. The chief documents relating to Africa in the actions of the Peace Conference are included. Review, H. A. Gibbons, *A.H.R.* 29:603, Apr. 1924.

For the conditions in the several African portions of the British empire during the World War and for their participation in the struggle, cf. (K311) Lucas, *Empire at War.* A wealth of data on African conditions and questions will be found in various numbers of (J441a) *Peace handbooks.* Also cf. (J42) Bowman, *New world* for exceedingly valuable chapter on present conditions in Africa and their historical antecedents. GMD

W316 **Weinthal, Leo**, ed. *Story of the Cape to Cairo railway and river route from 1887 to 1922.* 4 v. London, 1923.

Includes contributions by General Jan Smuts, Sir F. L. Lugard, Sir Percy Gironard, Sir Percy Fitzpatrick, Sir Lionel Phillips, Sir Alfred Sharpe, Professor Flinders Petrie, and others. Valuable discussions of conditions in each country along the route. AIA

PORTUGUESE AFRICA

W331 **Marvaud, Angel**. *Le Portugal et ses colonies, étude politique et économique.* Paris, 1912. [Bibliothèque d'histoire contemporaine, Collection du Musée social.]

Partly historical, but mainly devoted to the recent history of the Portuguese colonies, the international questions involved, and contemporary problems. Perhaps the best general account, though naturally over-favorable to Portuguese policies and somewhat suspicious of Great Britain. MWT, AIA

W332 **Vasconcellos, Ernesto J. De.** *As colonias portuguezas, geografica, fisica, politica, e economica.* 1903, rev. ed., Lisboa, 1921.

A political manual rather than an historical study; somewhat useful in view of the scarcity of works in the field. AIA

GERMAN AFRICA

W341a **Lewin, Percy Evans.** *Germans and Africa, their aims on the Dark Continent and how they acquired their African colonies.* London, 1915.

b **Zimmermann, Emil.** *German empire of Central Africa as the basis of a new German world-policy.* London and N. Y., 1918. Tr., with an introduction by Edwyn Bevan, from *Das deutsche Kaiserreich Mittelafrika als Grundlage einer neuen deutschen Weltpolitik,* Berlin, 1917.

c **Calvert, Albert F.** *German African empire.* London, 1916.

d —— *Southwest Africa during the German occupation, 1884–1914.* 1915, 2nd ed. London, 1916.

e —— *Cameroons.* London, 1917.

f —— *German East Africa.* London, 1917.

g —— *Togoland.* London, 1918.

a. Primarily an historical account. Despite the war atmosphere, the book is reasonably fair and contains many facts germane to the development of Africa. Much is said of native contact with Europeans, this latter European side being uppermost. *b.* Extreme statement of the significance and possibilities of German colonial possessions in Africa, written during the World War. For the fate of these possessions at the close of the war, cf. (W315) G. L. Beer, *African questions at the Paris Peace Conference. c.* Good brief survey of the German African Empire with much statistical information. The historical side receives scant treatment. *d., e., f.,* and *g.* Little manuals with fragments of historical content. Reflect war psychology, but give some valuable data on conditions. MWT, AIA

W351a Eveleigh, William. *South-West Africa.* London, 1915.

   b Rohrbach, Paul. *Südwest-Afrika.* Berlin, 1907. [Deutsche Kolonial-wirtschaft, v. 1.]

a. Brief and readable general account of the colony, its history, resources, and development. Written during the World War but, in general, fair to the Germans. Takes moderate view as to the future possibilities of the colony. *b.* Storehouse of general information, presenting the German point of view. MWT

W356a Peters, Karl. *Die Gründung von Deutsch-Ostafrika, Kolonialpolitische Erinnerungen und Betrachtungen.* Berlin, 1906.

   b Fonck, H. *Deutsch-Ostafrika.* Berlin, 1909.

a. Brief account of his work by the founder of German East Africa. Virtually an autobiography of Peters's life in the middle eighties. The only good account from the German side of the founding and early years of the colony. *b.* Treats of later years and problems of the colony. MWT

WEST AFRICA

W361a Kingsley, Mary H. *Travels in West Africa, Congo Français, Corisco, and Cameroons.* London and N. Y., 1897.

   b ——— *West African studies.* London and N. Y., 1899.

Few people knew West Africa as well as Miss Kingsley, few books of travel are as interesting as hers. *a.* Primarily descriptive and ethnographical. *b.* For general purposes, the more valuable; it treats of the people and problems of West Africa, the international rivalries for the region, its economic development, and the defects of crown colony government. For accounts of British possessions in West Africa, cf. (K303) Lucas, *Historical geography of the British colonies,* v. 3. MWT

W366a Johnston, Sir Harry H. *Liberia.* 2 v. N. Y., 1906. (Bibliography.)

   b Reeve, Henry F. *Black republic, its political and social conditions to-day.* Ed. by Sir Alfred Thorpe. London, 1923.

a. General study of the history, resources, and geography of Liberia, with many illustrations. The result of careful study and exploration by a British traveler and consular official with extensive African experience. Long considered the standard account in English of the republic. MWT
b. An even less kindly judgment is passed on the negro republic by a British official who served many years in neighboring colonies. GMD

W371a Claridge, William W. *History of the Gold Coast and Ashanti, from the earliest times to the commencement of the twentieth century.* 2 v. London, 1915. (Bibliography.)

   b Reeve, Henry F. *Gambia, its history, ancient, mediaeval, and modern, together with its geographical, geological, and ethnographical conditions.* London, 1912.

a. Complete history, with much supplementary information, of the regions to 1900; continued with an introduction by Sir Hugh Clifford, governor of Gold Coast, carrying the account to 1915. Review, *Spectator,* 115:750, Nov. 27, 1915. *b.* Exhaustive compilation of materials by a colonial official long familiar with the region. Review, *Spectator,* 108:656, Apr. 27, 1912. GMD

W372a Mockler-Ferryman, Augustus F. *Imperial Africa, the rise, progress, and future of the British possessions in Africa,* v. 1, *British West Africa.* London, 1898. [Imperial library.]

b Morel, Edmund D. *Nigeria, its peoples and its problems.* London, 1911.

a. Excellent *résumé* of the history of British possessions in West Africa to 1898. Other materials in the book are largely obsolete. *b.* Graphic account of the Niger territories, particularly Northern Nigeria, to about 1910; rather favorable to British rule and less polemic than other works by the same author.

MWT, AIA

W373a Orr, Charles W. J. *Making of Northern Nigeria.* London, 1911. (Bibliography.)

b Schultze, Arnold. *Sultanate of Bornu.* London and N. Y., 1913. Tr. by P. A. Benton from *Das Sultanat Bornu mit besonderer Berücksichtigung von Deutsch-Bornu,* Essen, 1910. (Bibliography.)

a. Not merely a careful and detailed account of the development and present problems of Northern Nigeria but also a valuable treatment of the administration of one of the most successful crown colonies. *b.* Gives useful information on the history of the region prior to the entry of Europeans. MWT

W376a François, Georges. *L'Afrique Occidentale Française.* Paris, 1907. [Gouvernement général de l'Afrique Occidentale Française, Notices publiées par le Gouvernement général à l'occasion de l'Exposition coloniale de Marseille.]

b Olivier, Marcel. *Le Sénégal.* Paris, 1907. [Gouvernement Général de l'Afrique Occidentale Française, Notices publiées par le Gouvernement général à l'occasion de l'Exposition coloniale de Marseille.]

Brief historical introductions are given, but the main body of each book is devoted to problems of administration and economic development, with full discussion in each case. Valuable statistics and tables. MWT

W377 Schweitzer, Albert. *On the edge of the primeval forest, experiences and observations of a doctor in equatorial Africa.* London, 1922. Tr. by C. T. Campion from *Zwischen Wasser und Urwald: Erlebnisse und Beobachtungen eines Arztes im Urwalde Äquatorialafrikas,* 1922, 4th ed., Berlin, 1923.

The author abandoned a successful career as professor of theology at the University of Strassburg and as an eminent organist to become a doctor in French Equatorial Africa. This fascinating little volume embodies his experiences from 1913 to 1916 and many valuable observations on native and colonial problems.

GMD

W378a Gatelet, Auguste L. C. *Histoire de la conquête du Sudan français, 1878–1899.* Paris, 1901.

b Gautier, Émile F. *La conquête du Sahara, essai de psychologie politique.* Paris, 1910.

c Germain, José, and **Faye, Stéphane.** *Un fils de France, le général Laperrine, grand Saharien.* Paris, 1922.

d Gautier, Emile F. *Le Sahara.* Paris, 1923. (Bibliographies.)

e Haardt, Georges M., and **Audouin-Debreuil, Louis.** *Le raid citroën, la première traversée du Sahara en automobile, de Touggourt à Tombouctou par l'Atlantide.* Paris, 1923.

a., b., and *c.* Accounts of the extension of French control from Algeria across the Sahara into the Sudan and the Niger valley. General Laperrine was the most active officer in conduct of these enterprises. *d.* Combines a presentation of the most recent French activities in the Sahara with a valuable scientific geographical treatise on the desert. Review, G. M. Wrigley, *Geographical Rev.* 15:92, Jan. 1925. *e.* Remarkable as a record of achievement rather than as a story. **GMD, AIA**

EAST AFRICA

W381a Wylde, Augustus B. *Modern Abyssinia.* London, 1901.

> **b Skinner, Robert P.** *Abyssinia of to-day, an account of the first mission sent by the American government to the court of the King of Kings, 1903–1904.* London and N. Y., 1906.

a. General account of the peoples and problems of Abyssinia by the British consul for the Red Sea. Gives a brief account of Abyssinian history and modern policies, mixed with accounts of travel, hunting, and the customs of the people. Opposed to French influence in Abyssinia, friendly to Italy. *b.* Rather light in tone; borrows freely from earlier works; supplements *a.* in historical as well as in descriptive matter. **MWT, AIA**

W386 Piazza, Giuseppe. *Il Benadir.* Roma, 1913. (Bibliography.)

Good account of the Italian colonizing enterprise in Somaliland. **HNG**

W391a Pearce, Francis B. *Zanzibar, the island metropolis of eastern Africa.* London, 1920. (Bibliography.)

> **b Lyne, Robert N.** *Zanzibar in contemporary times, a short history of the southern East in the nineteenth century.* London, 1905. (Bibliography.)

a. By the British resident at Zanzibar; one of the latest works on the subject, with some historical content; of considerable importance. *b.* Not so recent but valuable owing to its intensive study of conditions in Zanzibar. **AIA**

W392a Lugard, Sir Frederick J. D. *Rise of our East African empire, early efforts in Nyasaland and Uganda.* 2 v. Edinburgh, 1893.

> **b** ——— *Dual mandate in British tropical Africa.* Edinburgh, 1922.

> **c McDermott, P. L.,** ed. *British East Africa, or Ibea, a history of the formation and work of the Imperial British East Africa Company.* 1893. Rev. ed., London, 1895.

a. Exceedingly valuable in presenting the problems ·in the early development of Central Africa and Uganda. The author, who was one of the earliest administrators under the British company in Uganda, describes his experiences during the period 1888 to 1893. *b.* Of less value; useful on international complications, as well as upon British rule, in tropical Africa. *c.* The editor was secretary of the British East Africa Company; his book gives valuable documents. **MWT, AIA**

W393 Eliot, Sir Charles. *East Africa protectorate.* London, 1905.

Practically a state paper, giving a general description of the protectorate, written by the high commissioner for East Africa (Kenya), 1901 to 1904. The author is enthusiastic over the possibilities of the region which he considers a 'true white man's land.' Presents many suggestions for further development, some of which met with decided opposition in England. **MWT**

W394a Johnston, Sir Harry H. *Uganda protectorate, an attempt to give some description of the physical geography, botany, zoology, anthropology, languages, and history of the territories under British protection in East Central Africa, between the Congo Free State and the Rift Valley and between the first degree of south latitude and the fifth degree of north latitude.* 2 v. London, 1902.

b Harrison, Mrs. J. W. (Alexina Mackay). *A. M. Mackay, pioneer missionary of the Church Missionary Society to Uganda.* London and N. Y., 1890. Later reprints.

c Tucker, Alfred R. *Eighteen years in Uganda and East Africa.* 1908. Rev. ed., 2 v., London, 1911.

a. Deals with the history, material resources, and peoples of Uganda. V. 2. Entirely devoted to a detailed account of the native races. Supplies a wealth of detail on all phases of the region. *b.* Well written account by Mackay's sister, who later published a briefer and more popular account, utilizing different materials, under a slightly different title. *c.* Account by the Anglican bishop of Uganda. MWT, AIA

BELGIAN CONGO

W401 Keith, Arthur Berriedale. *Belgian Congo and the Berlin act.* Oxford, 1919.

Excellent example of moderate and careful discussion of the Congo problem. The development of the Congo Free State and its transformation into the Belgian Congo, the international status of the region, and the economic and social problems are historically treated with great fairness and scholarship. MWT

W402 Stanley, Sir Henry M. *Congo and the founding of its Free State, a story of work and exploration.* London and N. Y., 1885.

Deals almost entirely with his own work done in the early development of the Free State. The international phases of the task are but slightly treated. There is a good deal of information, however, on conditions in the Congo region in the early eighties. For Stanley's other works, cf. (W297). MWT

W403a Morel, Edmund D. *King Leopold's rule in Africa.* London, 1904.

b Wack, Henry W. *Story of the Congo Free State, social, political, and economic aspects of the Belgian system of government in Central Africa.* N. Y. and London, 1905.

Two examples of the polemic literature aroused by King Leopold's management of the Congo Free State. The value of both books lies mainly in the documents cited. *a.* Passionately critical of this rule, basing criticism on British reports and an analysis of the defence by the Free State. *b.* Defends the Congo administration and cites a number of documents to prove the contention. MWT, AIA

W404 Johnston, Sir Harry H. *George Grenfell and the Congo, a history and description of the Congo Independent State and adjoining districts of Congoland, together with some account of the native peoples and their languages, the fauna and flora; and similar notes on the Cameroons and the island of Fernando Pô, the whole founded on the diaries and researches of the late Rev. George Grenfell.* 2 v. London, 1908.

This book is primarily the biography of an English missionary who, for a quarter-century after 1878, was a great power in the Congo region. A great storehouse of information on the Congo, its races, and problems, and on conditions under the Congo Free State. The attitude is moderately critical. GFA

W405 Alexander, Boyd. *Boyd Alexander's last journey, with a memoir by Herbert Alexander.* London and N. Y., 1912.

Exceedingly interesting first-hand information of real value on the Belgian Congo.

GFA

W406 Daye, Pierre. *L'empire colonial belge.* Paris, 1923.

Based on recent journey in the Congo region. Deals discriminatingly with the various problems.

GMD

SOUTH AFRICA

W431a Theal, George M. *History and ethnography of Africa south of the Zambesi.* 11 v. 1888–1919. 4th rev. ed., London, 1915–19.

b —— *South Africa.* 1894. 8th rev. ed., N. Y., 1916. [Story of the nations.]

c Cory, George E. *Rise of South Africa, a history of the origin of South African colonisation and of its development towards the east from the earliest times to 1857.* V. 1–5, London and N. Y., 1910–30.

a. Monumental work, written with deep scholarship and wealth of detail, covering the history of South Africa from the earliest days to the modern period. The published volumes carry the history into the eighties, the fourth edition containing additional volumes as well as revision of the earlier volumes. *b.* One volume account, the narrative of events preceding 1873 being condensed from *a.* with a continuation to June 1916. *c.* Scholarly account of early South Africa up to 1853. Another volume may be expected. Review, H. E. Egerton, *E.H.R.* 26:621, July, 1910; 29:410, Apr. 1914; 35:289, Apr. 1920. Also cf. (K303) Lucas, *Historical Geography of the British colonies,* v. 4, of which pt. 2 contains one of the best accounts of the War of 1899–1902.

MWT, GMD

W432 Bryce, James, Viscount; Brooks, Sidney; and others. *Briton and Boer, both sides of the South African question.* N. Y. and London, 1900.

Series of articles originally published in the *North American review;* v. 169, 1899, dealing with the causes of the war in South Africa and with the reaction of the war on European politics.

MWT

W433a Williams, Basil. *Cecil Rhodes.* London and N. Y., 1921. [Makers of the 19th century.] (Bibliography.)

b Michell, Sir Lewis. *Life and times of the Right Honorable Cecil John Rhodes, 1853–1902.* 2 v. N. Y. and London, 1910.

a. Excellent brief account by a sympathetic writer; based on sources; carefully written; practically a history of South Africa in the years preceding the Boer War. *b.* The authorized biography, much longer and less readable, but with many citations from Rhodes's correspondence and with other contemporary detail.

MWT

W434 Kruger, Paul. *Memoirs of Paul Kruger, four times president of the South African Republic, told by himself.* Tr. by A. Teixeira de Mattos, ed. by A. Schowalter. London and N. Y., 1902.

These memoirs naturally take a one-sided view of the relations between the Transvaal and England. At times Kruger's feelings drive him into extreme statements which, however, are generally given as opinion and not as fact. The best part of the book is that devoted to the negotiations preceding the Boer War.

The tone is more repressed, many documents are quoted, and the presentation has distinct historical value. The book also supplies a valuable picture of Kruger, the man.   MWT

W435a Doyle, Sir Arthur Conan. *War in South Africa, its cause and conduct.* London and N. Y., 1902.

   b ——— *Great Boer War.* 1900. Rev. ed., N. Y., 1902.

   c Hobson, John A. *War in South Africa, its causes and effects.* London, 1900.

   d Amery, Leopold C. M. S., ed. *Times history of the war in South Africa, 1899–1902.* 7 v. London, 1900–09. (Excellent bibliography.)

   e Maurice, Sir John Frederick, and **Grant, Maurice H.,** ed. *History of the war in South Africa, 1899–1902, compiled by direction of His Majesty's Government.* 4 v. and 4 v. of maps. London, 1906–10.

   f De Wet, Christiaan Rudolf. *Three years' war.* N. Y., 1902.

a. Good concise account written just at the close of the war. *b.* and *c.* Fuller contemporary accounts. The final edition of *b.* covers the whole period of the war. *a.* and *b.* Frank presentations of the English point of view. *c.* Though by an Englishman, is inclined to present favorably the case for the Boers. *d.* Thorough, detailed, longer account. *e.* Official British narrative prepared by the army general staff, with full use of documentary materials. Especially important for military operations. *f.* Best known and probably the most satisfactory account of the struggle from the Boer side, by one of the leading Boer generals.   MWT, GMD

W436a Worsfold, William Basil. *South Africa, a study in colonial administration and development.* 1895. 2nd rev. ed., London, 1897.

   b ——— *Lord Milner's work in South Africa from its commencement in 1897 to the peace of Vereeniging in 1902, containing hitherto unpublished information.* London, 1906.

   c ——— *Reconstruction of the new colonies under Lord Milner.* 2 v. London, 1913.

   d ——— *Union of South Africa, with chapters on Rhodesia and the native territories of the High Commission.* London, 1912. [All red series.]

a. Good treatment of the conditions and administrative developments immediately before the Boer war. Review, *Spectator,* 75:695, Nov. 16, 1895. *b.* and *c.* These works, with a wealth of documentary material, give the best account and defence of Lord Milner's and of England's policy in South Africa just before and after the Boer war. The author is avowedly a partisan of the Milner policy, but is reasonably fair to its opponents. Their value lies in the quotations from documents, letters, reports, and newspaper articles, that make them almost source books of South African history. *d.* Useful account of the establishment of the Union and of certain related topics.   MWT, GMD

W437a Brand, Robert H. *Union of South Africa.* Oxford, 1909.

   b Walton, Sir Edgar H. *Inner history of the national convention of South Africa.* Capetown, London, and N. Y., 1912.

   c Newton, Arthur Percival, ed. *Select documents relating to the unification of South Africa.* London and N. Y., 1924. [University of London, Historical series.]

   d Williams, Basil, ed. *Selborne Memorandum, a review of the mutual relations of the British South African colonies in 1907, with an introduction.* Oxford and N. Y., 1925.

a. Brief, clear, and useful. While more a descriptive than an historical work, there is a good account of the negotiations for union and of the problems arising at that time. *b.* Useful on the formation of the Union. *c.* Compilation of indispensable sources for the subject. *d.* Survey of the South African situation on the eve of Union by the British high commissioner. MWT, GMD

W438a Spender, Harold. *General Botha, the career and the man.* 1916. 2nd ed., London, 1919.

b Buxton, Sidney Charles, Earl. *General Botha.* London, 1924.

a. Brief biography, by an English liberal, decidedly eulogistic. It is also a history of South Africa from 1902 to 1914, from the standpoint of the conforming Boers. Despite the absence of documents, the work is carefully done, distinctly fair to all parties, and forms as good a brief account of recent phases of South African history as may be found. *b.* The author, as governor-general of South Africa during the World War, was thoroughly acquainted with the later phases of General Botha's career so that his work supplements *a.*
MWT, GMD

W439a Nathan, Manfred. *South African commonwealth.* Capetown, 1919; London, 1920.

b Dawson, William H. *South Africa: people, places, and problems.* London and N. Y., 1925.

a. Recent discussion of the working of the Union, including the various political and social problems involved. Review, *Spectator,* 124:429, March 27, 1920. *b.* Still more recent work; favorable presentation of South Africa and its prospects; frank discussion of current issues, especially the native problem. GMD

W440 Eybers, G. W., ed. *Select constitutional documents illustrating South African history, 1795–1910.* London and N. Y., 1918. (Bibliography.)

Thoroughly well-arranged collection; practically indispensable to the serious student.
AIA

W451 Ingram, J. Forsyth. *Natalia, a condensed history of the exploration and colonisation of Natal and Zululand from the earliest times to the present day.* London, 1897.

Convenient outline of events in these two countries down to the incorporation of the latter with the former.
GMD

W456 Ellenberger, D. Fred., and **Macgregor, James C.** *History of the Basuto, ancient and modern, compiled by D. Fred Ellenberger and written in English by James C. Macgregor . . . under the auspices of the Basutoland government.* London, 1912.

Serious attempt, however imperfect, to give Basuto history; based largely upon tradition and Basutoland records.
AIA

W461 Hensman, Howard. *History of Rhodesia compiled from official sources.* Edinburgh, 1900.

Useful account of the beginnings of British occupation and rule in this territory.
GMD

W462a Johnston, Sir Harry H. *British Central Africa, an attempt to give some account of a portion of the territories under British influence north of the Zambesi.* 1897. 2nd ed., London, 1898.

b Duff, Hector L. *Nyasaland under the foreign office.* London, 1903.

a. Probably the standard work on the regions under British rule lying just north of the Zambesi. Contains a wealth of material on the history, natural resources, and peoples of the region. Some of the details need correction and the book is somewhat out of date. b. Later book covering a portion of the region.   MWT

ISLANDS

W481 Keller, Konrad. *Madagascar, Mauritius, and the other East-African islands.* London, 1901. Tr. by H. A. Nesbitt from *Die. ostafriken Inseln,* Berlin, 1898.

English translation of a careful German work dealing with the East African islands. Full on the geography and contemporary problems; the historical section is brief.   MWT

W482a Grandidier, Alfred, ed. *Histoire physique, naturelle, et politique de Madagascar.* V. 1–39 (in part), Paris, 1875–1915.

    b Oliver, Samuel P. *True story of the French dispute in Madagascar.* London, 1885.

    c You, André. *Madagascar, histoire, organisation, colonisation,* Paris, 1905.

    d Grandidier, Guillaume. *Le Myre de Vilers, Duchesne, Galliéni: quarante années de l'histoire de Madagascar, 1880–1920.* Paris, 1923.

    a. Monumental enterprise published by the French government. Many of the volumes comprise two or more parts; part or all of twenty-five of the first thirty-nine volumes have been issued. Thus far the volumes are devoted to scientific and descriptive material, and the promise of the title that the political history shall be treated has not yet been fulfilled. *b.* Presents the English view of French exploitation of Madagascar in the latter half of the nineteenth century. *c.* Recounts the history and describes the governmental organization from the French point of view. *d.* Supplies in brief space the historical account of the French occupation which is still lacking in *a.*   MWT, GMD

CONSTITUTIONAL AND LEGAL HISTORY

W531 Stigand, Chauncey H. *Administration in tropical Africa.* London, 1914.

Best introduction to the problems confronting a European administrative officer in tropical Africa. In the discussion of these problems there is a wealth of information regarding methods of administration past and present, the culture, ideals, and government of the natives.   MWT

CULTURAL HISTORY: RELIGION

W621 Le Chatelier, A. *L'Islam dans l'Afrique occidentale.* Paris, 1899. (Brief bibliography.)

Study of the conquest and penetration of Islam into West Africa during the last two centuries. As this development in West Africa is apparently quite similar to that elsewhere, the book will supply some light on East Africa for which no such studies have been made. The author is inclined to see in Islam the spreading religion in Africa and to welcome its advent.   MWT

BIOGRAPHIES

Relatively few biographies deal with persons important in the history of Africa at large. These include lives of explorers such as (W701) Henry W: Little,

H. M. Stanley, London and Philadelphia, 1890, also cf. (L888) Sir George Arthur, *Life of Lord Kitchener.*

In addition to the biographical works already reviewed in this section which are useful for a particular area, mention may be made of the following for South African history in the last quarter of the nineteenth century: (W751) Percy A. Molteno, *Life and times of Sir J. C. Molteno, first premier of Cape Colony,* 2 v., London, 1900; (W752) John Martineau, *Life and correspondence of Sir Bartle Frere,* 2 v., London, 1895; (W753) Sir William F. Butler, *Life of Sir. George Pomeroy-Colley,* London, 1899; (W754) Howard Hensman, *Cecil Rhodes,* Edinburgh, 1901; (W755) Sir Thomas E. Fuller, *Cecil John Rhodes,* London and N. Y., 1910; (W756) Francis Reginald Statham, *Paul Kruger and his times,* London and Boston, 1898.

The lives of the following missionaries throw considerable light on South African history: (W761) Sir George W. Cox, *Life of John William Colenso, Bishop of Natal,* 2 v., London, 1888; (W762) William D. Mackenzie, *John Mackenzie,* London, 1902.

For the French occupation in North Africa reference should be made to (W801) Count Henry d'Ideville, *Memoirs of Marshal Bugeaud, from his private correspondence and original documents, 1784–1849,* 2 v., London, 1884, tr. by C. M. Yonge from *Le maréchal Bugeaud d'après sa correspondance intime et des documents inédits,* 3 v., Paris, 1882.

GOVERNMENT PUBLICATIONS

For African questions of international character the British blue books, the French yellow books, and the German white books are of prime importance, as are publications of the League of Nations for the period since 1919. The British, French, German, and other governments and the governments of their several colonies have issued numerous other publications which cover the entire gamut of African affairs from diplomatic correspondence to reports on sleeping-sickness in various districts. These are the raw materials from which many books on Africa are wrought. Lists of the more important of these publications are given in the bibliographies in (B28b) *Statesman's year-book,* (I121) *Cambridge modern history,* and (J441a) *Peace handbooks.* Year-books were published by almost all the English, French, and other colonies down to 1914, since then intermittently, though in most cases regular publication has now been resumed. These year-books are mines of information on the regions covered.

The laws and ordinances of the various colonies, especially since the close of the nineteenth century, have usually been regularly published by the government concerned, as have also full reports of the debates in the several South African parliaments.

MWT, GMD

SOCIETY PUBLICATIONS

Special mention may be made of (W921a) *Renseignements coloniaux et documents,* Paris, 1895 ff. and of (W921b) *L'Afrique française, bulletin mensuel,* Paris, 1891 ff., both issued by the Comité de l'Afrique Française et le Comité du Maroc.

PERIODICALS

There are few periodicals devoted to material on Africa and these are only in part historical in character. Perhaps the most important, because of its valuable articles and useful collections of documents, is (W941) *Revue africaine, journel des travaux de la Société Historique Algérienne,* Constantine and Alger, 1856 ff.; besides which mention may be made of (W942) *Revue algérienne et tunisienne de législation et de jurisprudence, fondée par l'Ecole de Droit d'Alger,* Alger, 1885 ff., and (W943) *Revue tunisienne,* Tunis, 1894 ff., originally published by Association Tunisienne des Lettres, Sciences, et Arts, now Institut de Carthage. These all relate primarily to North Africa, with especial reference to the French occupation.

The leading journal in English devoted to African questions in general is (W951) *Journal of the African Society,* London and N. Y., 1901 ff.   AIA

X

UNITED STATES

Editor

MARCUS WILSON JERNEGAN

Professor of American History, University of Chicago

CONTENTS

INTRODUCTION

The wealth of literature devoted to the history of the United States and of the earlier development of its several component regions is very extensive in view of the comparatively short period of time involved. Scarcely any section, period, or topic has escaped attention, and for a considerable proportion of them there are works of sound scholarship and literary finish. Though the current output of writings of an historical character was notable in each successive period of

American history, there has been, since the organization of the American Historical Association in 1884, an extraordinary development of productive historical scholarship with reference to every period from the pre-Columbian times to the present decade. On the other hand, since the early period of settlement on the continent, comparatively few writers, other than Americans, have devoted their attention to American history.

The embarrassment of riches has presented a difficult problem of selection to the editor of this section. In planning this *Guide* it was recognized at the outset that the existence of the special bibliographies for American history listed under (X1) would make it unnecessary and undesirable to give in this section treatment proportional to that accorded other fields in this volume. Consequently it was determined to limit the choice of titles in this section chiefly to important standard works and to the more valuable special studies. It has seemed desirable, however, to include certain items of less permanent value, because they discuss important topics which have not as yet received authoritative or definitive treatment.

In accordance with this plan no attempt is made to give, in this section, anything like a complete list of even the important histories and special studies in this field which have been published in the past fifty years. These often appear in large series, as for example in (X122) *American nation* and (X123) *Chronicles of America* series; in those issued by the large universities (cf. X931–934); in (X921*b*) *Annual reports* of the American Historical Association; in (B941*f*) *American historical review* and other periodicals; and in the proceedings of historical societies (cf. X1*c*). Many of these are of marked interest to the scholar and have influenced the more general histories in the making. Doubtless in the building up of American historical writing, some of the works omitted here are as important as those that are mentioned. There are listed only such works of general interest or of general character and such more important and useful special studies as are likely to be of service to public libraries, secondary schools, and colleges. Specialists have various bibliographical aids and guides (cf. X1) for their particular use.

Notice should be taken of certain other principles of inclusion and exclusion. More space has been given to political and constitutional history than to other fields. In some fields the title of a single general work has been considered sufficient. For other special fields it has seemed necessary to refrain from citing any titles, on the ground of limitation of space. There are thus omitted most state and local histories, and all detailed military and naval histories; and with few exceptions, monographs on narrow fields of study, text-books, other than college texts, most biographies, and works of a partially historical character in allied fields. These omissions, while regrettable, are not so serious as might seem, because sufficient other bibliographical aids are readily available, by means of which the reader or student may solve most of his problems.

The reviews are purposely, and for recent publications, necessarily, brief. For nearly all important works references are given which will enable the reader to obtain longer and more critical evaluations, if needed.

BIBLIOGRAPHY

X1a Channing, Edward; Hart, Albert B.; and **Turner, Frederick J.** *Guide to the study and reading of American history.* 1896. Rev. ed., Boston and London, 1912.

b Larned, Josephus N., ed. *Literature of American history: a bibliographical guide in which the scope, character, and comparative worth of books in selected lists are set forth in brief notes by critics of authority.* Boston, 1902. [American Library Association annotated lists.]

c Griffin, Appleton P. C. *Bibliography of American historical societies, the United States and the Dominion of Canada.* Washington, 1907. [American Historical Association, Annual Report, 1905, v. 2.]

d Richardson, Ernest C., and **Morse, Anson E.** *Writings on American history, 1902.* Princeton, 1904.

e McLaughlin, Andrew C.; Slade, William A.; and **Lewis, Ernest D.** *Writings on American history, 1903.* Washington, 1905. [Carnegie Institution of Washington, Publications.]

f Griffin, Grace G. *Writings on American history, 1906 ff., a bibliography of books and articles on United States and Canadian history published during the year, with some memoranda on other portions of America. 1906-08, N. Y.,* 1908-10; *1909-11,* in American Historical Association, *Annual reports,* for respective years. Washington, 1911-13; *1912-17,* New Haven, 1914-19; *1918 ff.,* in American Historical Association. *Annual reports,* for respective years, Washington, 1921 ff.

g Bradford, Thomas L., and **Henkels, Stanislaus V.** *Bibliographer's manual of American history, containing an account of all state, territory, town, and county histories relating to the United States of North America, with verbatim copies of their titles, and useful bibliographical notes.* 5 v. Philadelphia, 1907-10.

Invaluable for supplementing the list of books given in this section. *a.* Provides classified lists of books devoted to bibliographies, indexes, catalogues, reference books, general and special histories, geography, special topics, including constitutional, diplomatic, political, economic, social, and religious history, and also books on travel, biography, state and local history, literature, education, music, fine arts, etc. Review, M. W. Jernegan, *A.H.R.* 18:589, Apr. 1913. *b.* Contains signed evaluations or reviews of over four thousand books. Review, *A.H.R.* 8:171, Oct. 1902. *c.* Includes tables of contents of the published proceedings of all important historical societies in the United States from their foundation; elaborate subject index. Review, *A.H.R.* 13:647, Apr. 1908. *d, e,* and *f.* Annual lists of books published relating to American history, with short reviews or indications where reviews may be found, of some of the more important works. Also include titles of articles in leading magazines, historical, general, and local. Items are arranged partly chronologically by periods, sections, or states; partly topically for such subjects as constitutional, diplomatic, economic, social, and cultural history. Very useful supplements to *a, b,* and *c. g.* Useful, though incomplete. Review, *A.H.R.* 13:384, 908, Jan., July 1908; 14:617, Apr. 1909.

In (X121) Winsor, *Narrative and critical history of America* there are exhaustive bibliographical essays on the sources of information for the history of America to about 1850. To each volume of (X122) Hart, *American nation* series is appended a well-selected, classified list of authorities with critical comments. For competent reviews of current publications, cf. (B941f) *American historical review* and other journals listed in the sub-section on periodicals in this section. For general catalogues of American publications, cf. (B2). MWJ

X2a Hasse, Adelaide R. *Materials for a bibliography of the public archives of the thirteen original states, covering the colonial period and the state period to 1789.* Washington, 1908. [American Historical Association, *Annual report, 1906, 2*:239–572.]

   b —— *Index of economic material in documents of the states of the United States.* 13 v. in 16. Washington, 1907–22. [1, *California;* 2, *Delaware;* 3, *Illinois;* 4, *Kentucky;* 5, *Maine;* 6, *Massachusetts;* 7, *New Hampshire;* 8, *New Jersey;* 9, *New York;* 10, *Ohio,* 2 pt.; 11, *Pennsylvania,* 3 pt.; 12, *Rhode Island;* 13, *Vermont.*] [Carnegie Institution of Washington.]

   c Bowker, Richard R. *State publications, a provisional list of the official publications of the several states of the United States from their organization.* N. Y., 1908. Originally issued in 4 pt., 1899–1908.

   a. Gives titles of the printed sources, such as charters, laws, records, and other official publications, arranged by states. *b.* Subject classifications of the materials under a wide range of topics, such as land, education, state institutions, etc. *c.* Indispensable guide to the student who needs to consult this group of sources. Review, *A.H.R.* 15:417, Jan. 1910. MWJ

X3a Swanton, Walter I. *Guide to United States government publications.* Washington, 1918. [Bureau of Education, Bulletin, 1918, no. 2.]

   b Clarke, Edith E. *Guide to the use of United States government publications.* Boston, 1918. (Bibliography.)

   c Everhart, Elfrida. *Handbook of United States public documents.* Minneapolis, 1910. (Bibliography.)

   a. Latest and most complete guide in compact and summary form. *b.* Textbook for use in library training schools; helpful also as an introduction to the use of government documents. *c.* Supplements *b* with a clear and readable treatment of the various series of publications. Changes in the organization of governmental departments and bureaus, made since 1909, render it less valuable for publications issued since that date. For lists of United States public documents, cf. (X907–908). HRS

X4a Van Tyne, Claude H., and **Leland, Waldo G.** *Guide to the archives of the government of the United States in Washington.* 1904. 2nd rev. ed. by W. G. Leland, Washington, 1907. [Carnegie Institution of Washington, Publications.]

   b *Handbook of manuscripts in the Library of Congress,* ed. by Gaillard Hunt and others. Washington, 1918.

   c *Check list of collections of personal papers in historical societies, university and public libraries, and other learned institutions in the United States.* Washington, 1918. [Library of Congress.]

   d *Manuscripts in public and private collections in the United States.* Washington, 1924. New and enl. ed. of *c.* [Library of Congress.]

The student who wishes to make use of the manuscript sources for American history should begin by consulting these guides. *a.* Indispensable for research workers in the large collections of the various departments of the national government. *b.* The Library of Congress is the repository for the papers of most of the presidents and important statesmen, and contains a very large general collection of national, state, and local manuscripts. *c* and *d.* Give the names of important public men, showing where their letters and other papers are deposited.

In addition to *a,* (X926) *Publications* of the Carnegie Institution of Washington include similar guides to the materials relating to American history preserved in domestic and foreign archives and libraries. The reports of the Public Archives Commission, 1900 ff., and of the Historical Manuscripts Commission, 1896 ff., of the American Historical Association are published in its (X921*b*) *Annual reports* for the years indicated. The former series includes surveys of important official archives in the several states; the latter series contains descriptions of the printed guides to manuscripts in the possession of public and semi-public institutions, and also in private hands. A bibliography of these two series appeared in (X921*b*) American Historical Association, *Annual report, 1912,* 315–319. Sections are given in each volume of (X1*d, e,* and *f*) *Writings on American history* listing the printed descriptions of archives and manuscript collections published in the year concerned.   MWJ

X11 Jameson, John Franklin. *History of historical writing in America.* Boston, 1891.

Four lectures, given at different times and later revised, with the titles: 'The historians of the seventeenth century'; 'The historians of the eighteenth century'; 'From the Revolution to the Civil War'; and, 'Since the Civil War.' Brilliant study of the work and characteristics of the principal American historians prior to 1891, with observations on the general problem of writing history, particularly as applied to America.   MWJ

X12 Bassett, John S. *Middle group of American historians.* N. Y., 1917.

After an introductory chapter on the early progress of the writing of history in the United States, author considers the work of certain mid-nineteenth century historians: Sparks, Bancroft, Prescott, Motley, and Peter Force, the compiler. Descriptive and biographical details; brief critical estimates of the work of the various authors; excellent within its limited scope. Review, M. A. DeW. Howe, *A.H.R.* 22:879, July 1917.   MWJ

Library Collections.—Because of its resources in both manuscript and printed materials the most important single collection for the history of the United States is in the Library of Congress. All the larger university libraries have extensive collections, and in nearly every case excel in one or more special fields; but undoubted preëminence, both for size of the general collection and for importance of the special collections, belongs to Harvard; second place should probably be assigned to Yale; and special mention should be made of Cornell University (Sparks collection) and Marietta College (Stimson collection) ; but for the South, the Middle West, and the Pacific Coast, respectively, the libraries of Johns Hopkins University, of the University of Wisconsin, including that of the State Historical Society, of the University of California, including the great H. H. Bancroft collection, and the Henry E. Huntington Library, San Marino, Cal., are of the highest importance. Many public libraries are well supplied with works both in general American history and in local history, but special mention is merited by the New York Public Library, Boston Public Library, and the groups of public and semi-public libraries in Philadelphia and Chicago.

For local history the state libraries and the libraries of the state historical societies are rich in resources, for example, Massachusetts, Connecticut, New York, Pennsylvania, Virginia, South Carolina, Illinois, Minnesota, and Washington. Some local historical societies, such as the Essex Institute, Salem, Mass., possess notable collections in special fields. In selected fields of earlier American history, the library of the American Antiquarian Society, Worcester, Mass.; the John Carter Brown Library, Providence, R. I.; the Hispanic Society of America, New York; the William L. Clements Library at the University of Michigan; and the Newberry Library of Chicago are of priceless importance.

For fuller lists of special collections in American history, cf. W. D. Johnston and I. G. Mudge, *Special collections in libraries in the United States,* 34–36, 38–52, Washington, 1912. [Bureau of Education, Bulletin 495.]   AHS

ENCYCLOPEDIAS AND WORKS OF REFERENCE

X21 McLaughlin, Andrew C., and **Hart, Albert B.,** ed. *Cyclopedia of American government.* 3 v. N. Y. and London, 1914. (Bibliographies.)

Work of very great value; contains articles prepared by competent specialists. Includes the following broad topics: land and people, theories and principles, history, organization of government, functions of government. Much of the material is of permanent value, but in some instances revision is essential to cover developments since the time of publication. The articles are supplemented by useful maps, charts, and tables. There are numerous cross references and a detailed index. Review, H. B. Learned, *A.H.R.* 20:411, Jan. 1915; J. A. Fairlie, *Amer. Pol. Sci. Rev.* 9:793, Nov. 1915; E. M. Sait, *Pol. Sci. Quar.* 30:177, March, 1915.   CEM

X25 *Appleton's cyclopedia of American biography,* ed. by James Grant Wilson and John Fiske. 6 v. N. Y., 1886–89. Later reprints. Supplements: v. 7, ed. by J. G. Wilson, 1900; v. 8, ed. by J. E. Homans, 1918; v. 9, ed. by J. E. Homans and H. M. Linen, 1922.

Includes some names from American countries other than the United States. Despite obvious faults, still the best work of its kind. Review, *Nation (N. Y.),* 48:349, Apr. 25, 1889.   GMD

X26 Johnson, Allen, ed. *Dictionary of American biography.* v. 1–5. N. Y., 1928 ff.

Produced under the auspices of the American Council of Learned Societies, with the British (L22) *Dictionary of national biography* the model for both scope and scholarship, the volumes thus far published must gratify all who have coöperated financially and in varied service toward the attainment of the high ideal. Most of the useful data sought after in such works will be not only found, but found accurate, in the sketches and longer articles; while the careers are usually traced in ways so that the distinctive personality and the social and historical setting contribute to a biographical understanding and evaluation. Planned for twenty volumes and to appear at the rate of three volumes annually, the first volume appeared promptly and was received with universal and significant acclaim; if the desired rate of publication is not fully attained, any delay will be for the interest of the high scholarly character of the work. Review of v. 1 and 2, A. M. Schlesinger, *A.H.R.* 35:119, Oct. 1929; of v. 3, 35:624, Apr. 1930.   WHA

X28 *Who's who in America, a biographical dictionary of notable living men and women of the United States.* Chicago, 1899 ff. (B702b.)

Current biographical dictionary, revised and reissued biennially, of notable men and women of the United States, especially those engaged in political, literary, and academic pursuits.   GMD

X29 Jameson, John Franklin. *Dictionary of United States history.* Boston, 1894.

Excellent single volume work, covering topics and biography.   MWJ

GEOGRAPHY AND ATLASES

X41a Semple, Ellen C. *American history and its geographic conditions.* Boston, 1903. (Bibliography.)

  b Brigham, Albert P. *Geographic influences in American history.* Boston 1903.

  c —— *United States of America: studies in physical, regional, industrial and human geography.* N. Y., 1927.

a. Pioneer work; still preëminent in its field; defines the relationship between historical facts and the natural environment in which history unfolds. The discussion is confined to a few of the major events of American development, which are freshly illuminated by details. Personalities figure little, and political and social institutions appear either as results of the environment, or as make-weights which may influence or modify, but can rarely determine events. Also cf. the author's (A42e) *Influences of geographic environment.*   DSW

b. While Miss Semple approaches the problem primarily from the human or historical side, Professor Brigham, as a physiographer, follows a geographic plan. With skill, accuracy, and conciseness, he presents an array of geographic data with which he couples the events and facts of the nation's history. Review of *a* and *b,* A. B. Hart, *A.H.R.* 9:571, Apr. 1904. *c.* Series of essays on climate, population, racial composition, agriculture, forests, commerce, etc. Review, E. L. Wood, *Miss. Val. Hist. Rev.,* 15:150, June 1928.   MWJ

X46 Fox, Dixon R., ed. *Harper's atlas of American history, selected from 'The American nation series,' with map studies.* N. Y. and London, 1920.

Contains 128 maps selected from (X122) Hart, *American nation* series; a good introduction and twenty-seven map studies; best available atlas of American history. Review, A. B. Hulbert, *A.H.R.* 26:584, Apr. 1921.

Numerous other volumes listed in this section contain good maps. Special reference should be made to (X121) Winsor, *Narrative and critical history of America* for reproductions of maps of the period of discovery and colonization, and to (X134) Avery, *History of the United States,* both for excellent reproductions of early maps and for carefully drawn maps and plans for the period down to 1806.

To meet the need for an accurate, scholarly work, the Department of Historical Research of the Carnegie Institution of Washington has for some years been engaged in the preparation of materials for an (X47) *Atlas of the historical geography of the United States,* though publication has not yet begun. It will include maps and charts illustrating the nation's economic and social progress.
                                                                     GMD

X48 *Statistical atlas of the United States: ninth census,* ed. by Francis A. Walker, 1874; *eleventh census,* ed. by Henry Gannett, 1898; *twelfth census,* ed. by Henry Gannett, 1902; *thirteenth census,* ed. by Charles S. Sloane, 1914; *fourteenth census,* ed. by Charles S. Sloane, Washington, 1925.

Contain numerous maps and charts with explanatory text relating to the distribution and movement of population, occupations, and economic resources and their development.   GMD

ETHNOGRAPHY

X51 Faust, Albert B. *German element in the United States with special reference to its political, moral, social, and educational influence.* 2 v. 1909. New enl. ed., 2 v. in 1, N. Y., 1927. (Elaborate bibliography.)

Most complete account yet made of any one racial element in the American population. V. 1. Mainly an outline of the settlement of Germans within the United States; includes a discussion of the reasons for migration; attention is given to the work of the Germans in defense of the frontier during the American Revolution, and in later wars of the United States. V. 2. Largely a discussion of the influence of the Germans on American development. The result of extensive study; much more than a popular presentation of the subject. The evidence, however, is not always convincing that the alleged good influence was due wholly to the racial factor rather than to other factors, such as mixed blood, environment, and Americanization. Review, O. Kuhns, *A.H.R.* 15:615. Apr. 1910; 33:697, Apr. 1928.   MWJ

X52 Ford, Henry J. *Scotch-Irish in America.* Princeton, 1915. (Bibliography.)

Covers the history of the Scot in Ulster and the causes of the migration to America; describes the various settlements made in the New England, Middle, and Southern colonies and in the West. Estimates the influence of this racial group in the occupation and defense of the frontier, in the development of the Presbyterian Church, and the influence of their racial and religious ideas on the American Revolution, on education, and other social and political institutions. Excellent presentation of the subject, but, like most studies of this type, tends to overemphasize the influence of the racial stock in question. Review, *A.H.R.* 20:886, July, 1915.

There are numerous studies of racial elements of the population appearing as books or as articles in reviews and in proceedings of societies devoted to racial history. For French, Irish, Italian, Scotch, Scandinavian and other racial studies, consult the bibliographies mentioned, especially (X1a) Channing, Hart, and Turner, *Guide,* 318, 392, 528; and (X101f) Schlesinger, *New viewpoints in American history,* 21–22.   MWJ

X53a Woodson, Carter G. *The negro in our history.* 1922. 4th rev. ed., Washington, 1927. (Bibliographical foot-notes.)

   b Brawley, Benjamin. *Social history of the American negro, being a history of the negro problem in the United States, including a history and study of the republic of Liberia.* N. Y., 1921. (Bibliography.)

Two recent works which cover various aspects of the history of negro slavery in America; convenient introductions; the bibliographies furnish guidance to the extensive literature of the subject. Also cf. (X585). For current publications, cf. (X952) *Journal of negro history.*   GMD

X54a Miner, William H. *American Indians north of Mexico.* Cambridge, Eng., 1917. (Bibliography.)

b Smithsonian Institution, Bureau of American Ethnology. *Annual report, 1879–80 ff.* Washington, 1881 ff.

c Field [Columbian] Museum, Chicago. *Publications, anthropological series.* Chicago, 1895 ff.

a. Good, brief, popular manual. Review, J. R. Swanton, *A.H.R.* 23:436, Jan. 1918. Perhaps the best recent scholarly summaries of information on the American Indian are: Farrand, *Basis of American history* in (X122) Hart, *American nation;* (Y51) Brinton, *American race;* (Y53a) Wissler, *American Indian;* and (Z51b) Hodge, *Handbook of American Indians.* These works will furnish references to the extended literature on the subject. *b.* and *c.* Both series of publications include a wealth of materials on the American Indian. See also (X123, 1).

GMD

X56a Fairchild, Henry P. *Immigration, a world movement and its American significance.* 1913. Rev. ed., N. Y., 1925. (Bibliography.)

b Hourwich, Isaac A. *Immigration and labor, the economic aspects of European immigration to the United States.* N. Y. and London, 1912; 2nd ed., N. Y., 1922.

c Commons, John R. *Races and immigrants in America.* 1907. New ed., N. Y., 1920. (Bibliography.)

d Mayo-Smith, Richmond. *Emigration and immigration; a study in social science.* 1890. Reprint, N. Y., 1912. (Bibliography.)

e Jenks, Jeremiah W., and **Lauck, William Jett.** *Immigration problem, a study of American immigration conditions and needs.* 1911. 6th rev. ed., by R. D. Smith, N. Y. and London, 1926.

a. Brief, convenient survey of immigration to the United States from the historical, sociological, and economic points of view. A review of the colonial period is followed by four chapters dealing with the history of immigration and, in particular, immigration legislation, from 1873 to the modern period. Separate chapters are also given to the volume, racial character, causes, effects, and the social and industrial aspects of immigration, such as problems of exploitation, pauperism, crime, wages, and standards of living. *b.* Gives another point of view on many questions; anti-restrictionist; contains a mass of historical and statistical material. *c., d.,* and *e.* Treat the problem from other angles; the more recent data being supplied in *e.*

EA

X57a Abbott, Edith. *Immigration: select documents and case records.* Chicago, 1924. [University of Chicago social service series.]

b —— *Historical aspects of the immigration problem.* Chicago, 1926.

a. Includes documents of both public and private origin arranged in three groups, dealing with the immigrant's journey from Europe to America; with admission, exclusion, and expulsion; and with domestic immigration problems. Material in the first two groups is chiefly historical, in the third, chiefly sociological. Useful source book and compendium of data. Review, H. P. Fairchild, *A.H.R.* 30:372, Jan. 1925.

GMD

b. Supplements *a.* Period of 'old immigration' is covered, ending with 1882. Valuable illustrative material. Review, H. P. Fairchild, *A.H.R.* 32:661, Apr. 1927.

MWJ

X58a Stephenson, George M. *History of American immigration, 1820–1924.* N. Y., 1926.

b Garis, Roy L. *Immigration restriction. A study of the opposition to and regulation of immigration into the United States.* N. Y., 1927. (Extensive bibliography.)

a. Useful as presenting the subject historically rather than sociologically. Review, *Amer. Pol. Sci. Rev.,* 20:465, May 1926.   GMD

b. Chief emphasis is after 1880. Chinese and Japanese immigration are treated in a chapter each. Review, H. P. Fairchild, *A.H.R.* 33:422, Jan. 1928.   MWJ

Cf. also (L592) Johnson.

SOURCE BOOKS, COLLECTIONS OF SOURCES, ARCHIVE PUBLICATIONS

The following source books are well-chosen and excellently edited selections of materials for the topics indicated by their titles: (X61) Edna Kenton, *Jesuit relations and allied documents,* N. Y., 1925, extracted from (X72a) Thwaites's edition; (X62a) William MacDonald, *Select charters and other documents illustrative of American history, 1606–1775,* N. Y., 1899; (X62b) *Select documents illustrative of the history of the United States, 1776–1861,* N. Y. and London, 1897; (X62c) *Select statutes and other documents illustrative of the history of the United States, 1861–1898,* N. Y. and London, 1903; abridged in (X62d) *Documentary source book of American history, 1606–1926,* 1908, 3rd rev. ed., N. Y., 1928; (X63) Paul S. Reinsch, *Readings on American federal government,* Boston, 1909, illustrating the processes of government; (X64) Charles A. Beard, *Readings in American government and politics,* 1909, Rev. ed., N. Y., 1925; (X65) Allen Johnson, *Readings in American constitutional history, 1776–1876,* Boston, 1912; (X66) Guy S. Callender, *Selections from the economic history of the United States, 1765–1860, with introductory essays,* Boston, 1909; (X67) Ernest L. Bogart and Charles M. Thompson, *Readings in the economic history of the United States,* N. Y. and London, 1916; (X68) Albert B. Hart, *American history told by contemporaries,* [1492–1929], 5 v., N. Y. and London, 1897-1929; (X69) Jesse L. Bennett, *Essential American tradition,* N. Y., 1925, illustrating the development of American ideals; (X70) Samuel E. Morison, *Sources and documents illustrating the American revolution, 1764-1788, and the formation of the federal constitution,* Oxford, 1923; (X70a) A. C. McLaughlin and others, eds., *Source problems in United States history,* N. Y. and London, 1918; (X70b) Kirk H. Porter, *National party platforms,* N. Y., 1924. Several of the preceding source books have been reprinted one or more times.

Extended lists of printed collections of documentary sources will be found in (X1a) Channing, Hart, and Turner, *Guide to the study and reading of American history.* The following may be cited as among the most useful: (X71a) J. Franklin Jameson, ed., *Original narratives of early American history, reproduced under the auspices of the American Historical Association,* 19 v., N. Y., 1906–17; (X71b) *Privateering and piracy in the colonial period: illustrative documents, edited under the auspices of the National Society of the Colonial Dames of America,* N. Y., 1923; (X72a) Reuben G. Thwaites, *Jesuit relations and allied documents: travels and explorations of the Jesuit missionaries in New France, 1610–1791: the original French, Latin, and Italian texts, with English translations and notes,* 73 v., Cleveland, 1896–1901; (X72b) *Early western travels, 1748–1846: a series of annotated reprints of some of the best and rarest contemporary volumes of travel, descriptive of the aborigines and social and economic conditions in the middle and far west, during the period of early American settlement,* 32 v., Cleveland 1904–07; (X72c) John B. McMaster, *Trail makers, library of history and exploration,* 17 v., N. Y., 1903–06; (X73) Leo F. Stock, *Proceedings and debates of the British parliaments respecting North America,* v. 1, *1542–1688,* v. 2, *1689–1702,* Washington, 1924–26, [Department of Historical Research, Carnegie Institution of Washington]; (X74) Worthington C. Ford and Gaillard Hunt, *Journals of the continental congress, 1774–1789, edited from the original records in the Library of Congress,* v. 1–25, *1774–1783,* Washington, 1904–22; (X75) Edmund C. Burnett, *Letters of members of the continental congress,* v. 1–4, *1774–1779,* Washington, 1921–28 [Department of Historical Research, Carnegie Institution of Washington]; (X76) Peter Force, *American archives: a collection of authentic state papers . . . forming a documentary history of the North American colonies,* 9 v., Washington, 1837–53, valuable for the years 1774–1776; (X77) Max Farrand, *Records of the federal convention of 1787,* 3 v., New Haven, reprint, 1923; (X78a) Paul Leicester Ford, *The federalist, a commentary on the constitution of the United States, by Alexander Hamilton, James Madison, and John Jay, edited with notes, illustrative documents, and a copious index,* N. Y., 1898; (X78b) *Pamphlets on the constitution of the United States, published during its discussion by the people, 1787–1788, edited with notes and a bibliography,* Brooklyn, N. Y., 1888; (X78c) *Essays on the constitution of the United States, published during its discussion by the people, 1787–1788,* Brooklyn, N. Y., 1892, supplementing the preceding; (X79) Francis N. Thorpe, *Federal and state constitutions, colonial charters and other organic laws of the states, territories, and colonies now or heretofore forming the United States of America, compiled and edited under the act of congress of June 30, 1906,* 7 v., Washington, 1909; (X80) Walter L. Fleming, *Documentary history of reconstruction, political, military, social, religious, educational, and industrial, 1865 to the present time,* 2 v., Cleveland, 1906–07; (X80a) John R. Commons, ed., *Documentary history of American industrial society,* 11 v., Cleveland, 1910–11.

Among the more important collections of the writings of American statesmen are: (X81) Sir William Johnson, *Papers,* ed. by James Sullivan and Alexander C. Flick, v. 1–6, Albany, N. Y., 1921–29 [University of the State of New York, Division of Archives and History]; (X82) Benjamin Franklin, *Writings,* ed. by Albert H. Smyth, 10 v., N. Y. and London, 1905–07; (X83) Samuel Adams, *Writings,* ed. by Harry A. Cushing, 4 v., N. Y. and London, 1904–08; (X84) Richard Henry Lee, *Letters,* ed. by James C. Ballagh, 2 v., N. Y., 1911–14 [National Society of the Colonial Dames of America]; (X85a) George Washington, *Writings,* ed. by Worthington C. Ford, 14 v., N. Y. and London, 1889–93; (X85b) *Diaries,* ed. by John C. Fitzpatrick, 4 v., Boston, 1925 [Mount Vernon Ladies' Association of the Union]; (X86) Alexander Hamilton, *Works,* ed. by Henry Cabot Lodge, 9 v., N. Y. and London, 1885–86; (X87) John Adams, *Works,* ed. by Charles Francis Adams, 10 v., Boston, 1850–56; (X88) Thomas Jefferson, *Works,* ed. by Paul Leicester Ford, 12 v., N. Y. and London, 1904–05; (X89) James Madison, *Writings,* ed. by Gaillard Hunt, 9 v., N. Y. and London, 1900–10; (X90) James Monroe, *Writings,* ed. by Stanislaus M. Hamilton, 7 v., N. Y. and London, 1898–1903; (X91a) John Quincy Adams, *Writings,* ed. by Worthington C. Ford, v. 1–7, N. Y., 1913–17; (X91b) Andrew Jackson,

Correspondence, ed. by John S. Bassett, v. 1–4, Washington, 1926 ff [Carnegie Institution of Washington, Publications]; (X92) Henry Clay, *Works,* ed. by Calvin Colton, 6 v., N. Y., 1857, new ed., 7 v., N. Y., 1897; (X93a) John C. Calhoun, *Works,* ed. by Richard K. Crallé, 6 v., N. Y., 1851–56; (X93b) *Correspondence,* ed. by John Franklin Jameson, Washington, 1900 [American Historical Association, Annual report, 1899]; (X94a) Daniel Webster, *Works,* ed. by Edward Everett, 6 v., Boston, 1851; (X94b) *Writings and speeches,* 18 v., Boston, 1903 [National edition]; (X95) Millard Fillmore, *Papers,* ed. by Frank H. Severance, 2 v., Buffalo, N. Y., 1907 [Publications of the Buffalo Historical Society]; (X96) James Buchanan, *Works,* ed. by John Bassett Moore, 12 v., Philadelphia and London, 1908–11; (X97) Abraham Lincoln, *Complete works,* ed. by John G. Nicolay and John Hay, 2 v., N. Y., 1894, rev. ed., 12 v., N. Y., 1905; (X98) Charles Sumner, *Works,* 15 v., Boston, 1870–83; (X99) Jefferson Davis, *Letters, papers, and speeches,* ed. by Dunbar Rowland, 10 v., Jackson, Miss., 1923 [Mississippi Department of Archives and History]; (X100a) Woodrow Wilson, *College and state: educational, literary, and political papers, 1875–1913,* ed. by Ray Stannard Baker and William E. Dodd, 2 v., N. Y. and London, 1924; (X100b) *New democracy: presidential messages and addresses and other papers, 1913–1917,* ed. by R. S. Baker and W. E. Dodd, 2 v., N. Y. and London, 1926; (X100c) *Messages and papers,* ed. by Albert Shaw, 2 v., N. Y., 1924.

SHORTER GENERAL HISTORIES

X101a Smith, Goldwin. *The United States, an outline of political history, 1492–1871.* N. Y. and London, 1893. Later reprints.

b Wilson, Woodrow. *History of the American people.* 5 v. N. Y., 1902. Later reprints.

c Sparks, Edwin E. *United States of America.* 2 v. N. Y. and London, 1904. [Story of the nations.]

d Elson, Henry W. *History of the United States of America.* 1904. New ed., N. Y. and London, 1923. (Bibliography.)

e Farrand Max. *Development of the United States from colonies to a world power.* Boston, 1918. (Bibliographies.)

f Schlesinger, Arthur M. *New viewpoints in American history.* N. Y., 1922. (Bibliographies.)

g MacDonald, William. *Three centuries of American democracy.* N. Y., 1923. (Bibliography.)

h Wertenbaker, Thomas J. *American people: a history.* N. Y., 1926.

i Becker, Carl. *United States: an experiment in democracy.* N. Y., 1920.

j Faÿ, Bernard, and Claflin, Avery. *American experiment.* N. Y., 1929.

k Adams, Ephraim D. *Power of ideals in American history.* New Haven, 1913.

a. Incisive presentation, brief, largely interpretive. Review, *Nation* (N. Y.), 57:292, Oct. 19, 1893. *b.* Brilliantly written; the text, sufficient for one substantial volume, has been embellished and enlarged, by the publisher, with elaborate illustrations to fill five volumes. Review, F. J. Turner, *A.H.R.* 8:762, July 1903. *c.* Ably written and helpful narrative covering the period from 1781 to about the end of the nineteenth century; suggestive and entertaining. Review, J. A. Woodburn, *A.H.R.* 10:883, July 1905. *d.* Somewhat extended, substantial narrative, addressed to the general reader. Review, E. E. Sparks, *A.H.R.* 10:377, Jan. 1905. *e.* Brief narrative; skilfully written; tends to emphasize recent interests and novel interpretations at the expense of the conventional. Review, T. C. Smith, *A.H.R.* 24:478, Apr. 1919. *f.* Topical presentation of interpretations elaborated during the preceding thirty years. Review, R. W. Kelsey, *A.H.R.* 28:131, Oct. 1922. *g.* Clear, brief chronological account of the major facts of political history. Review, M. W. Jernegan, *A.H.R.* 29:378, Jan. 1924. Also cf. (1121) *Cambridge modern history,* v. 7, devoted to the United States, with chapters contributed by recognized British and American authorities. Review, J. F. Jameson, *A.H.R.* 9:365, Jan 1904.   ACMCL

h. Fair, interesting and interpretative outline of American history. Review, W. K. Boyd, *A.H.R.* 32:881, July 1927. *i.* Stimulating and penetrating reflections on traits and tendencies in American history. Review, A. C. McLaughlin, *A.H.R.* 26:337, Jan. 1921. *j.* Discusses the historical factors which have produced the United States of the twentieth century. Review, *N. Y. Times,* Feb. 3, 1929. *k.* Lectures on such topics as nationality, anti-slavery, manifest destiny, religion and democracy. Review, E. B. Greene, *A.H.R.* 19:928, July 1914.   MWJ

X102a Bassett, John S. *Short history of the United States, 1492–1920.* 1913. Rev. ed., N. Y., 1921. (Bibliographies.)

b Forman, Samuel E. *Our republic, a brief history of the American people.* N. Y., 1922. (Bibliographies.)

c Harlow, Ralph V. *Growth of the United States,* N. Y., 1925. (Bibliography.)

d Pease, Theodore C. *United States.* N. Y., 1927.

Single-volume text-books for college classes; each somewhat exceeds eight hundred pages in length; each contains maps. *a.* Lucid narrative; gives major attention to period from 1829 to 1898. Review, W. MacDonald, *A.H.R.* 19:642, Apr. 1914. *b.* Reduces to a minimum the space allotted to period prior to 1783. Subordinates military and political affairs to economic and social development; gives special attention to the South and West. Review, J. A. Woodburn, *A.H.R.* 28:550, Apr. 1923. *c.* Readable account; devotes half the space to the period since 1850; political and economic affairs are stressed. Review, W. R. Waterman, *Hist. Outlook* 16:336, Nov. 1925.   GMD

d. Impartial, with unusual emphasis on the World War.   AOC

X103a Muzzey, David S. *United States of America.* 2 v. Boston, 1922–24. (Bibliography.)

b Caldwell, Robert G. *Short history of the American people.* 2 v. N. Y. and London, 1925–27. (Bibliography.)

c Martin, Asa Earl. *History of the United States.* v. 1, 1783–1865. Boston, 1928.

Works planned to narrate American history in two substantial volumes; readable and scholarly. *a.* Almost exclusively a history of the national period, as only single chapters are allotted to the colonial background and to the Revolution. V. 2. Begins in 1865. Review, N. W. Stephenson, *Historical Outlook,* 14:72, Feb. 1923; 16:177, Apr. 1925. *b.* Mere narrative is subordinated to interpretation. Extends to 1921. Review of v. 1, F. F. Stephens, *A.H.R.* 31:528, Apr. 1926.   GMD

c. Well-written text covering political, economic and social history. Review, J. A. Krout, *A.H.R.* 34:609, Apr. 1929.   MWJ

X104 Beard, Charles A. and **Mary E.** *Rise of American civilization. 2 v.* N. Y., 1927.

Emphasis is on tendencies, movements and major aspects of life, mainly accounted for by the action of social and economic forces. Brilliantly written. The material is often selected and interpreted to illustrate the authors' main thesis. Review, J. P. Bretz, *A.H.R.* 33:140, Oct. 1927.   MWJ

X111a Greene, Evarts B., and **Fish, Carl R.** *Short history of the American people.* 2 v. N. Y., 1913–22. [1, E. B. Greene, *Foundations of American nationality;* 2, C. R. Fish, *Development of American nationality,* rev. ed., 1924.] (Bibliographies.)

b Farrand, Max. *The United States.* 3 v. [1, W. T. Root, *Colonial beginnings* (announced) ; 2, M. Farrand, *Growth of the nation* (announced) ; 3, C. R. Lingley, *Since the civil war,* N. Y., 1920. Rev. ed., 1926.] (Bibliographies.)

c Hockett, Homer C., and **Schlesinger, Arthur M.** *Political and Social history of the United States.* 2 v. N. Y., 1925. [1, H. C. Hockett, *1492–1828;* 2, A. M. Schlesinger, *1829–1925.*] (Bibliographies.)

Excellent coöperative efforts to provide text-books suitable for college classes ; well-written ; scholarly ; embody the results of recent research ; social and economic topics are emphasized ; may be heartily commended to the general reader. *a.* Professor Greene has supplied the best single-volume account of the colonial and revolutionary periods. Review, C. M. Andrews, *Pol. Sci. Quat.* 38:141, March 1923; v. 2, C. W. Spencer, *A.H.R.* 19:651, Apr. 1914. *b.* V. 3. Review, U. B. Phillips, *A.H.R.* 27:620, Apr. 1922. *c.* Review, R. F. Nichols, *Hist. Outlook,* 17:36, Jan. 1926; T. C. Pease, *Miss. Val. Hist. Rev.* 13:110, June 1926.

Also cf. (B138*a*) *Home university library:* No. 47, Charles M. Andrews, *Colonial period,* review, H. V. Ames, *A.H.R.* 18:814, July 1913; No. 67, William MacDonald, *From Jefferson to Lincoln,* review, F. M. Anderson, *A.H.R.* 19:176, Oct. 1913.   MWJ

X112 Hart, Albert B., ed. *Epochs of American history.* 3 v. N. Y., 1891–93. [1, R. G. Thwaites, *The colonies, 1492–1750,* 5th rev. ed., 1910; 2, A. B. Hart, *Formation of the union, 1750–1829,* 7th rev. ed., 1925; 3, Woodrow Wilson, *Division and reunion, 1829–1889,* 5th rev. ed., with continuation to 1918, by E. S. Corwin, 1920.] New ed., 4 v., N. Y., 1918–29. [1, M. W. Jernegan, *American colonies, 1492–1750;* 2, A. B. Hart, *Formation of the union, 1750–1829;* 3, Woodrow Wilson, *Division and reunion, 1829–1889;* 4, J. S. Bassett, *Expansion and reform, 1889–1926.*] (Extensive bibliographies.)

These volumes were among the earlier attempts to combine the work of distinguished scholars in a broad outline of American history. Notwithstanding all that has been done in the field in the past forty years, the older volumes retain their high place, while the series has been greatly strengthened by the addition of the volumes by Professors Bassett and Jernegan. It now presents an excellent view, by epochs, of the development of the nation, from a political, economic and social standpoint. The treatment is evenly sound and lucid throughout. Review of v. 1, (new ed.), W. T. Root, *A.H.R.* 35:378, Jan. 1930.   JPB

X113 *American history series.* 7 v. N. Y., 1892–1902. [1, G. P. Fisher, *Colonial era;* 2, W. M. Sloane, *French war and the revolution;* 3, F. A. Walker, *Making of the nation, 1783–1817;* 4, J. W. Burgess, *Middle period, 1817–1858;* 5–6, J. W. Burgess, *Civil war and the constitution, 1859–1865;* 7, J. W. Burgess, *Reconstruction and the constitution, 1866–1876.*]

Covers briefly the whole history of the United States to 1877; emphasis is almost entirely on political and constitutional history. The four volumes by Professor Burgess give a connected account of constitutional developments from about the end of the war of 1812 to the end of reconstruction. Review, v. 4, C. H. Levermore, *A.H.R.* 2:746, July 1897; v. 5–6, W. G. Brown, *A.H.R.* 8:368, Jan. 1903; v. 7, W. G. Brown, *A.H.R.* 8:150, Oct. 1902.   ACMCL

X114 Dodd, William E., ed. *Riverside history of the United States.* 4 v. Boston, 1915. [1, C. L. Becker, *Beginnings of the American people;* 2, A. Johnson, *Union and democracy;* 3, W. E. Dodd, *Expansion and conflict;* 4, F. L. Paxson, *New nation.* New ed., 1924.] (Bibliographies.)

Excellent coöperative history, very readable; interprets rather than chronicles American history, with emphases on the West and South as factors rather than on New England and the Seaboard. Review, W. MacDonald, *A.H.R.* 21:351, Jan. 1916.   MWJ

LONGER GENERAL HISTORIES

X121 Winsor, Justin, ed. *Narrative and critical history of America.* 8 v. Boston, 1884–89. [1, *Aboriginal America;* 2, *Spanish explorations and settlements in America from the fifteenth to the seventeenth century;* 3, *English explorations and settlements in North America, 1497–1689;* 4, French explorations and settlements in North America, and those of the Portuguese, Dutch, and Swedes, 1500–1700;* 5, *English and French in North America, 1689–1763;* 6–7, *United States of North America, 1763–1850;* 8, *Later history of British, Spanish, and Portuguese America.*]

Justin Winsor, librarian of Harvard University, was learned in American history, especially its bibliography, and experienced in editing coöperative histories. Such works are most often useful in summing up the knowledge already attained rather than in setting forth new facts or adding new thoughts. Winsor's great work admirably summarizes American knowledge of American history as it stood about 1880. Each of the chapters of narrative, most of which are still good, is accompanied with a mass of valuable bibliographical information respecting sources and authorities, as then known. These give the work most of its great present value. The narratives, however, stop at 1850; and, besides the lapse of years since that date, the interest of historians and the public has shifted greatly since 1880. Review (X11), Jameson, *Historical writing in America,* 156–158; v. 1, *Nation* (N. Y.), 49:134, Aug. 15, 1889; v. 6, 47:12, July 5, 1888; v. 7, 47:316, Oct. 18, 1888.   JFJ

X122 Hart, Albert Bushnell, ed. *The American nation: a history from original sources by associated scholars.* 28 v. N. Y. and London, 1904–18. (Valuable bibliographies.) [1, E. P. Cheyney, *European background of American history, 1300–1600;* 2, L. Farrand, *Basis of American history, 1500–1900;* 3, E. G. Bourne, *Spain in America, 1450–1580:* 4, L. G. Tyler, *England in America, 1580–1652;* 5, C. M. Andrews, *Colonial self-government, 1652–1689;* 6, E. B. Greene, *Provincial America, 1690–1740;* 7, R. G. Thwaites, *France in America, 1497–1763;* 8, G. E. Howard, *Preliminaries of the revolution, 1763–1775;* 9, C. H. Van Tyne, *American revo-*

lution, 1776–1783; 10, A. C. McLaughlin, *Confederation and the constitution, 1783–1789;* 11, J. S. Bassett, *Federalist system, 1789–1801;* 12, E. Channing, *Jeffersonian system, 1801–1811;* 13, K. C. Babcock, *Rise of American nationality, 1811–1819;* 14, F. J. Turner, *Rise of the new West, 1819–1829;* 15, W. MacDonald, *Jacksonian democracy, 1829–1837;* 16, A. B. Hart, *Slavery and abolition, 1831–1841;* 17, G. P. Garrison, *Westward extension, 1841–1850;* 18, T. C. Smith, *Parties and slavery, 1850–1859;* 19, F. E. Chadwick, *Causes of the civil war, 1859–1861;* 20, J. K. Hosmer, *Appeal to arms, 1861–1863;* 21, J. K. Hosmer, *Outcome of the civil war, 1863–1865;* 22, W. A. Dunning, *Reconstruction, political and economic, 1865–1877;* 23, E. E. Sparks, *National development, 1877–1885;* 24, D. R. Dewey, *National problems, 1885–1897;* 25, J. H. Latané, *America as a world power, 1897–1907;* 26, A. B. Hart, *National ideals historically traced, 1607–1907;* 27, F. A. Ogg, *National progress, 1907–1917;* 27 (i.e. 28), D. M. Matteson, *Analytic index.*]

This is the first, as it is the best, of the coöperative histories of the United States written on a large scale. Presents a comprehensive, fairly consecutive, reasonably well-proportioned survey of the history of the country from the discovery down to 1917. A notable group of twenty-four scholars was associated with the editor in the work, so that each volume was written by a specialist in the particular period which it treats. The first twenty-six volumes were published within a three-year period. In 1918 a supplementary volume followed, covering the history for the most recent years. A general index completed the series. Naturally the volumes vary in value, but the average of excellence is high. The series immediately took its place as a standard work, which position it still holds. It has proved very acceptable to the general reader, but its chief service probably has been as collateral reading for college classes. The scope of the work is primarily political and constitutional, but economic, religious, social, diplomatic, and military phases are also treated. The notes and maps are especially valuable. Review, each volume, *A.H.R.*, v. 10–13, July 1905–Apr. 1908; series, M. Farrand, *A.H.R.* 13:591, Apr. 1908.   HVA

X123 Johnson, Allen, ed. *Chronicles of America.* New Haven, 1918–21. (Brief bibliographies.) [1, E. Huntington, *Red man's continent;* 2, I. B. Richman, *Spanish conquerors;* 3, W. Wood, *Elizabethan sea-dogs;* 4, W. B. Munro, *Crusaders of New France;* 5, M. Johnston, *Pioneers of the Old South;* 6, C. M. Andrews, *Fathers of New England;* 7, W. W. Goodwin, *Dutch and English on the Hudson;* 8, S. G. Fisher, *Quaker colonies;* 9, C. M. Andrews, *Colonial folkways;* 10, G. M. Wrong, *Conquest of New France;* 11, C. L. Becker, *Eve of the revolution;* 12, G. M. Wrong, *Washington and his comrades in arms;* 13, M. Farrand, *Fathers of the constitution;* 14, H. J. Ford, *Washington and his colleagues;* 15, A. Johnson, *Jefferson and his colleagues;* 16, E. S. Corwin, *John Marshall and the constitution;* 17, R. D. Paine, *Fight for a free sea;* 18, C. L. Skinner, *Pioneers of the old Southwest;* 19, F. A. Ogg, *Old Northwest;* 20, F. A. Ogg, *Reign of Andrew Jackson;* 21, A. B. Hulbert, *Paths of inland commerce;* 22, C. L. Skinner, *Adventurers of Oregon;* 23, H. E. Bolton, *Spanish borderlands;* 24, N. W. Stephenson, *Texas and the Mexican war;* 25, S. E. White, *The forty-niners;* 26, E. Hough, *Passing of the frontier;* 27, W. E. Dodd, *Cotton kingdom;* 28, J. Macy, *Anti-slavery crusade;* 29, N. W. Stephenson, *Abraham Lincoln and the Union;* 30, N. W. Stephenson, *Day of the Confederacy;* 31, W. Wood, *Captains of the civil war;* 32, W. L. Fleming, *Sequel of Appomattox;* 33, E. E. Slosson, *American spirit in education;* 34, B. Perry, *American spirit in literature;* 35, S. P. Orth, *Our foreigners;* 36, R. D. Paine, *Old merchant marine;* 37, H. Thompson, *Age of invention;* 38, J. Moody, *Railroad builders;* 39, B. J. Hendrick, *Age of big business;* 40, S. P. Orth, *Armies of labor;* 41, J. Moody, *Masters of capital;* 42, H. Thompson, *New South;* 43, S. P. Orth, *The* *boss and the machine;* 44, H. J. Ford, *Cleveland era;* 45, S. J. Buck, *Agrarian crusade;* 46, C. R. Fish, *Path of empire;* 47, H. Howland, *Theodore Roosevelt and his times;* 48, C. Seymour, *Woodrow Wilson and the world war;* 49, O. D. Skelton, *Canadian dominion;* 50, W. R. Shepherd, *Hispanic nations of the New World.*]

Attempts to tell the complete story of America in its broadest way, in such a manner as will meet the approval of scholars and at the same time attract and entertain the general reader, for whom the series is primarily intended; seems to fulfill both requirements admirably. There are fifty volumes by thirty-five writers of different points of view and of varying degrees of ability in historical writing. Though the editors have not hesitated to call in the popular writer, the best volumes come from the pens of well-known historical students, who speak with the authority of assured mastery of both the field in question and the methods of historical work. All phases of history are covered—political, constitutional, military, religious (though inadequately), economic, literary, educational. The account is brought down through the administration of Woodrow Wilson. Review, various volumes, *A.H.R.* v. 24-28, July 1919—Oct. 1922.   DRA

X134 Avery, Elroy M. *History of the United States and its people from their earliest records to the present time.* V. 1-7. Cleveland, 1904-10. *Index,* Tarrytown, N. Y., 1915. (Bibliographies.)

Intended 'to meet the wants of men and women of general culture rather than those of professional historical students.' Originally announced to be completed in twelve, later sixteen, volumes, but stopped with the seventh volume at 1806. Rich in admirably selected illustrations, important facsimiles, and numerous excellent maps and plans, which alone make the work invaluable to historical students. Review, v. 1, 2, 3, W. R. Shepherd, *A.H.R.* 10:852, July 1905; 12:657, Apr. 1907; 13:612, Apr. 1908; v. 6, *A.H.R.* 15:620, Apr. 1910.   GMD

X135 Channing, Edward. *History of the United States.* V. 1-6. N. Y. and London, 1905-25. To be completed in 8 v. (Bibliographies.)

This admirable work is already the most complete and satisfactory history of the United States on an extended scale which has come from the hand of a single competent scholar and writer. V. 1. Deals with the period of expansion and settlement prior to 1660. V. 6. Brings the narrative down to 1865. Throughout, the author is sure of his facts and constantly shows intimate familiarity with the sources. He is singularly free from inaccuracies and exaggerations, and is skillful in the clear and orderly presentation of complicated happenings. Yet the author by no means conceals his likes and dislikes. At times there is a disproportionate selection of material,—certain men and events being treated too fully or too scantily. Review, v. 1, E. G. Bourne, *A.H.R.* 11:390, Jan. 1906; v. 2, *A.H.R.* 14:364, Jan. 1909; v. 3, C. H. Van Tyne, *A.H.R.* 18:603, Apr. 1913; v. 4, J. S. Bassett, *A.H.R.* 23:189, Oct 1917; v. 5, D. R. Fox, *A.H.R.* 27:589, Apr. 1922; v. 6, D. R. Fox, *A.H.R.* 31:151, Oct. 1925.   WJW

COLONIAL PERIOD

X201a Osgood, Herbert L. *American colonies in the seventeenth century.* 3 v. N. Y., 1904-07.

b —— *American colonies in the eighteenth century* 4 v. N. Y., 1924-25.

Most important single contribution to the history of the continental American colonies. *a.* V. 1-2. Deal with the colonies settled under corporate and proprietary authority, without regard to the connection with the executive powers in England. V. 3. Discusses the relations of all the colonies with the home government and the beginnings of the system of royal control. The mode of approach is impersonal and objective; the treatment of facts is strictly scientific; and the interest is confined to those features that are legal, institutional, and administrative. Contains nothing on social, intellectual, and economic conditions; omits all mention of the West India colonies; frankly disclaims all intention of discussing the larger problem of British colonial administration. Though the work is thus limited in scope, it is very thorough and detailed in all that concerns the matter of which it treats. Review, C. M. Andrews, *A.H.R.* 11:397, Jan. 1906; 13:605, Apr. 1908. *b.* Continuation of *a,* published posthumously under the competent editorship of Professor D. R. Fox. Covers the years 1689–1763; varies slightly in general features from *a,* though the range of interests is somewhat broader and the treatment usually fuller. The point of view is that of the thirteen continental colonies, not that of England or of its other imperial interests. Review, C. M. Andrews, *A.H.R.* 31:533, Apr. 1926.

For relations between the British and French colonies in North America, cf. (Z201) Parkman, *Works.*   CMA

X202a Beer, George L. *Commercial policy of England toward the American colonies.* N. Y., 1893. [Columbia University, Studies in history, economics, and public law.] (Bibliography.)

    b —— *Origins of the British colonial system, 1578–1660.* N. Y., 1908.

    c —— *Old colonial system, 1660–1754.* Pt. 1, *Establishment of the system, 1660–1688.* 2 v. N. Y., 1912.

    d —— *British colonial policy, 1754–1765.* N. Y., 1907. Reprint, 1922.

The author began the study of British colonial policy when a student at Columbia University. *a.* His doctoral dissertation; still the only complete outline of the commercial aspects of British colonization in America. *b., c.,* and *d.* In 1904 he undertook an examination of the manuscript material in the Public Record Office and elsewhere in England, with the intention of rewriting his early essay on a much larger scale. He died before completing his task, leaving unfinished the portion treating of the important years from 1688 to 1754. The four volumes issued treat the subject largely from the standpoint of the British archives and take into less account the condition prevailing in the colonies themselves. The view is, therefore, somewhat one-sided. Written in a very compact, closely reasoned, almost legal style, and give up the full meaning only after careful study. In thoroughness of treatment and in the skill with which the old British colonial policy is interpreted as a fundamental feature of early American history, these volumes, for the periods under consideration, are epoch-making contributions. Review of *b.,* C. M. Andrews, *A.H.R.* 14:808, July 1909; H. L. Osgood, *Pol. Sci. Quar.* 24:127, March 1909; of *c.,* W. T. Root, *A.H.R.* 18:798, July 1913; O. M. Dickerson, *Pol. Sci. Quar.* 28:515, Sept. 1913; of *d.,* C. H. Hull, *A.H.R.* 14:817, July 1909; E. B. Greene, *Pol. Sci. Quar.* 23:326, June 1908.   CMA

X203 Bolton, Herbert E., and **Marshall, Thomas M.** *Colonization of North America, 1492–1783.* N. Y., 1920.

Successful attempt to portray the whole process of the colonization of North America, including Mexico, Canada and the West Indies. Review, V. W. Crane, *A.H.R.* 26:540, Apr. 1921.   MWJ

X204 Bancroft, George. *History of the United States of America from the discovery of the continent* [*to 1789*]. 1834–82. Author's last revision, 6 v. N. Y., 1883–85.

V. 1 of the first edition appeared in 1834; v. 10, in 1874. In 1882, at the age of eighty-two, Bancroft added two volumes on the formation of the constitution. The last revision carries the story from colonial origins to the adoption of the constitution. This work, by one of the great American historians, is built upon a mass of original sources; facts are set forth honestly and, in general, with accuracy; the style, however, is heavy. As a continuous history it is too detailed and lacks proportion; scant space is given to the important period from 1690 to 1750. The author's attitude is provincial and partisan; he saw in America the unfolding of the principles of democracy under divine guidance; he viewed England as a tyrant. In spite of this, his work is important because it grasps the buoyant spirit of American democracy. Review (X11), Jameson, *Historical writing in America*, 100–110; (X12) Bassett, *Middle group of American historians*, 138–210. WTR

X205 Fiske, John. *Historical writings.* Standard library ed., 12 v., Boston, 1902. [1–3, *Discovery of America*, 1892; 4–5, *Old Virginia and her neighbors*, 1897; 6, *Beginnings of New England*, 1889; 7–8, *Dutch and Quaker colonies in America*, 1899; 9, *New France and New England*, 1902; 10–11, *American revolution*, 1891; 12, *Critical period of American history, 1783–1789*, 1888.]

These volumes, covering the period from the discovery to 1789, constitute the most popular work on early American history. All are distinguished by a charm of style and an emphasis on the picturesque in the choice of subjects; parts fail to measure up to the standards of accuracy and fairness of judgment required of critical historians. Fiske is at his best in the *Discovery of America*. Review, E. G. Bourne, *Pol. Sci. Quar.* 8:163, March 1893. *The Dutch and Quaker Colonies* gave him another subject in which he achieved a high degree of success; that of contrasting the rise of a colony founded on trade (New York) and one founded on religious enthusiasm (Pennsylvania). Review, J. A. Doyle, *A.H.R.* 5:572, April 1900. The history of the colonies from Maryland southward is brought together in *Old Virginia and her neighbors* (review, L. G. Tyler, *A.H.R.* 3:734, July 1898), and of the New England colonies to 1689, in the *Beginnings of New England*. *New England and New France* was written to introduce the history of French colonization of America, to bring the French and English movements together in an account of the French and Indian War (review, R. G. Thwaites, *A.H.R.* 8:359, June 1903), and, finally, to link up with the volumes upon the *Revolution* and the *Critical period*. Also, cf. (Z201) Parkman, *Works*. EJB

X206 Doyle, John Andrew. *English colonies in America.* 5 v. N. Y., 1882–1907.

These volumes, written by an Englishman, are still of value. The work is sound and penetrating, especially for political history. Review of v. 4, 5, C. M. Andrews, *A.H.R.* 13:360, Jan. 1908. See also, *ibid.*, 198. MWJ

REVOLUTIONARY PERIOD

X231a Trevelyan, Sir George O. *Early history of Charles James Fox.* 1880. New ed., London and N. Y., 1908.

b ―――― *American revolution.* 1899–1907. New ed., 4 v., N. Y., 1905–12.

c ―――― *George the Third and Charles Fox, the concluding part of the American revolution.* 2 v. London and N. Y., 1912–14. Published together with *b.* in uniform ed., 6 v., N. Y., 1920–22.

This series of volumes is an English Whig's history of the American Revolution. The author is over sympathetic, if anything, with the Americans, but he knows his Englishmen best. Pictures the Revolution as a family quarrel, which it was only in part; shows little interest in some aspects which make an especial appeal to the American. The growth of constitutional theories, of political ideals; contests between the seaboard and back-countries, and even industrial and social movements of importance get but slight, if any, notice. The English side of such matters is often very well done, and the author's rich store of knowledge of the English individuals who enacted the events related is one of the fascinating things in this work. He is a master of the imponderables. There is evident lack of knowledge of some important monographs and little use of manuscript sources, but there is a mastery of the printed sources; a comprehensive synthesis of easily accessible facts. Written in a quaint style, now too rapidly disappearing, but whose charm will never die; allusion and epigram are the chief ornaments, but they are never tawdry. The work is not one in which to learn history but to enjoy it. Review of *b,* F. J. Turner, *A.H.R.* 5:141, Oct. 1899; 9:818, July 1904; J. Bigelow, Jr., 13:874, July 1908; of *c,* C. H. Van Tyne, *A.H.R.* 17:827, July 1912; 20:629, Apr. 1915.   CHVT

X232a Fisher, Sydney G. *Struggle for American independence.* 2 v. Philadelphia and London, 1908.

b Van Tyne, Claude H. *History of the founding of the American republic.* V. 1, *Causes of the war of independence;* v. 2, *War of independence, American phase.* Boston, 1922–29.

a. Continuation and enlargement of *True history of the American revolution* in (X703) *True biographies and histories.* Emphasizes phases which the author contends have been neglected by other writers, particularly the treatment of the loyalists by the patriots; lacks judicial poise; contains important material not easily found elsewhere. Review, J. A. Woodburn, *A.H.R.* 14:143, Oct. 1908. *b.* Plans to include one more volume continuing the history to 1789. First volume begins with suitable introductory description of American colonial governments, of political conditions, and of imperial problems, and then deals with the period of controversies between the colonies and Great Britain down to the battle of Lexington. The product of scholarly investigation and literary skill; appeals to the general reader as well as to the specialist. V. 2 extends to 1779. Review, A. M. Schlesinger, *A.H.R.* 28:327, Jan. 1923.   ACMCL

X233a Van Tyne, Claude H. *England and America: rivals in the American revolution.* N. Y., 1927.

b Baldwin, Alice M. *New England clergy in the American revolution.* Durham, N. C., 1928.

c Faÿ, Bernard. *Revolutionary spirit in France.* N. Y., 1927. Tr. by R. Guthrie from *L'esprit révolutionnaire et aux États-Unis à la fin du XVIIIᵉ siècle.* Paris, 1925.

a. This volume discusses such topics as 'Struggle for the Truth,' merchants, lawyers, church and dissenters, soldiers and diplomats; interesting and frank presentation of the topics mentioned. Review, F. J. Hinkhouse, *A.H.R.* 33:885, July 1928. *b.* Important study of the political and religious ideas of the clergy and their influence on revolutionary thought. Review, E. B. Greene, *A.H.R.* 34:136, Oct. 1928. *c.* Examination of the revolutionary state of mind which produced a bond of sympathy between France and America, 1774–1799, ideas, opinions and beliefs, aspirations, as expressed in books, eighteenth century revolutionary psychology. Review of French ed., C. Becker, *A.H.R.* 30:810, July 1925.   MWJ

X241 Andrews, Charles M. *Colonial background of the American revolution: four essays in American colonial history.* New Haven and London, 1924.

Traces the nature of British colonies in America and their relation to the Mother Country in the early years, the general colonial policy of Great Britain in the period when mercantilism held full sway; the changed policy with the assumption of imperialist plans after the defeat of the French, and the general implications of the American Revolution. The author, who speaks from years spent in mastery of the details, interprets the Revolution along broad, general lines from the standpoint both of England and of the colonies. Pleads for a reassessment of the Revolution by Americans who are urged to look on the question not only as one involving independence for the thirteen colonies but as a world problem in British colonial policy. Review,. W. T. Root, *A.H.R.* 30:832, July 1925.   ACMCL

X242 Alvord, Clarence W. *Mississippi Valley in British politics, a study of the trade, land speculation, and experiments in imperialism culminating in the American revolution.* 2 v. Cleveland, 1917. (Bibliography.)

The Treaty of Paris, 1763, which closed the Seven Years' War, gave to Great Britain the West and Canada. 'What was to be. done with them? . . . How could there be a reconciliation between the various interests clamoring for consideration? The Indian rights must be protected; the claims of various colonies to the West must be considered; the influence of the great land companies of different colonies must not be neglected; there were the fur traders who opposed western colonization; and these latter were supported by British and American land speculators in eastern lands who feared the effect of opening the West; and last of all there were the imperial interests to be conserved. . . . Successive administrations worked on this problem; three distinct plans [for a western policy] were developed and partially adopted. . . . These pages contain a history of the development of these plans.' (Preface.) Very careful study based on the sources; well written. Admirable and important work, emphasizing, perhaps over emphasizing, the influence of the West in the series of events that led up to the Revolution. Review, C. L. Becker, *A.H.R.* 22:671, Apr. 1917. Cf. (Z201) Parkman, *Conspiracy of Pontiac.*   CLB

X243a Egerton, Hugh E. *Causes and character of the American revolution.* Oxford and N. Y., 1923. [Histories of the nations.]

b Schlesinger, Arthur M. *Colonial merchants and the American revolution, 1763–1776.* N. Y., 1918. [Columbia University, Studies in history, economics, and public law.] (Bibliography.)

c McIlwain, Charles H. *American revolution, a constitutional interpretation.* N. Y., 1923.

d Adams, Randolph G. *Political ideas of the American revolution: Britannic-American contributions to the problem of imperial organization, 1765–1775.* Durham, N. C., 1922.

a. Summary of the causes of the Revolution; by an eminent English authority on British colonial history; considers the administrative system of the American colonies, the economic background, and the political blundering of the home government during two reigns; has a valuable chapter on American loyalists. Clear-cut presentation makes it a book readable on both sides of the Atlantic. Review, C. L. Becker, *A.H.R.* 29:344, Jan. 1924. *b.* Admirable study of American reactions to British commercial policy; based on extensive research; thoroughly impartial; important contribution to the study of the causes of the Revolution. Review, C. M. Andrews, *A.H.R.* 24:104, Oct. 1918. *c.* Potent argument in support of the thesis that the central problem in the genesis of the American Revolution was the determination of the exact nature of the constitution of the British Empire. After searching examination of a wealth of judicial precedents drawn largely from Ireland's relations with the English king and parliament, the author reaches the conclusion that 'there was a *bona fide* constitutional issue which preceded the American Revolution, and from which it in part resulted.' He contends that, strictly from the legal standpoint, the colonists had a number of good constitutional precedents to support their position. Review, E. S. Corwin, *A.H.R.* 29:775, July 1924. *d.* Describes various plans set forth by Revolutionary leaders to reconcile colonial autonomy with imperial unity. Review, S. E. Morison, *E.H.R.* 38:114, Jan. 1923; C. H. Van Tyne, *A.H.R.* 28:367, Jan. 1923.

For the history of the Revolution, also cf. (X671*b*) M. C. Tyler, *Literary history of the American Revolution,* and the appropriate sections of the works of (X121) Winsor, (X122) Hart, (X123) Johnson, (X204) Bancroft, (X205) Fiske, (X134) Avery, and (X135) Channing. MWJ

X244a Frothingham, Richard. *Rise of the republic of the United States.* 1872. 10th ed., Boston, 1910.

b Friedenwald, Herbert. *Declaration of Independence, an interpretation and analysis.* N. Y. and London, 1904.

c Hazelton, John H. *Declaration of Independence, its history.* N. Y., 1906. (Bibliography.)

d Becker, Carl L. *Declaration of Independence, a study in the history of political ideas.* N. Y., 1922.

a. Interesting and scholarly study in constitutional history; based largely on the sources; traces certain phases of development, particularly the movement toward union, from early times to the establishment of the government under the constitution. *b.* Interpretation of events and analysis of the document. Review, *A.H.R.* 11:422, Jan. 1906. *c.* Elaborate monograph, richly documented and illustrated with facsimiles, on the development of conscious sentiment for independence, and on the drafting, signing, and later history of the document. Review, G. E. Howard, *A.H.R.* 11:913, July 1906. *d.* Most recent study of the origins and meaning of the Declaration; emphasizes the political and philosophical setting of the document. Review, M. S. Brown, *A.H.R.* 28:761, July 1923. ACMCC

X245 Van Tyne, Claude H. *Loyalists of the American revolution.* N. Y., 1902.
Brief objective account in a series of essays, the only general work on the subject. Review, V. Coffin, *A.H.R.* 8:776, July 1903.   MWJ

X251a Jameson, John Franklin. *American revolution considered as a social movement.* Princeton, N. J., 1926.

b Humphrey, Edward F. *Nationalism and religion in America, 1774–1789.* Boston, 1924. (Bibliography.)

a. Deals with the social implications and consequences of the revolution, such as the effect on landholding, industry, slavery, religion and education. Review, A. Nevins, *A.H.R.* 32:167, Oct. 1926.   MWJ
b. Valuable study of religious elements in the Revolution, of nationalization of American churches, and relations of church and state; despite the title, relates to institutions rather than to ideas. Review, J. T. Adams, *A.H.R.* 30:155, Oct. 1924.
                                                                    GMD

X252 Nevins, Allan. *American states during and after the revolution, 1775–1789.* N. Y., 1924. [Knights of Columbus historical series.] (Bibliography.)

Convenient compilation of data on the transition from colonies to states, the framing and working of the state constitutions, and of political and economic developments in the several states and sections. Review, S. E. Morison, *A.H.R.* 30:611, Apr. 1925.   GMD

NATIONAL PERIOD, TO CLOSE OF THE CIVIL WAR

X261a McMaster, John Bach. *History of the people of the United States, from the revolution to the civil war.* 8 v. N. Y., 1883–1913.

b —— *History of the people of the United States during Lincoln's administration.* N. Y., 1927.

a. This work broke new ground in American history by undertaking to present the development of the people. The idea was not original, as J. R. Green had just done the same thing for the English people, but McMaster made a definite contribution to historical method by seeking much of his material from the newspapers. He allowed his new material to determine the order and proportion of his narrative, before a searching critique had been built up to test its possibilities. The result is a work brimming with new facts and fresh slants on American history, but oblivious of deeper tendencies of intellectual, spiritual, and industrial growth. Particularly commendable are the attention given to western affairs, in which the author was a pathfinder, and the treatment of popular sentiment at crises when the people were actively interested in public affairs, as at the time of the Genêt episode. Interesting in style and picturesque in detail, it holds the general reader. Can be neglected by no student of the field it covers. Review, C. R. Fish, *Miss. Val. Hist. Rev.* 1:31, June 1914; v. 8, C. H. Levermore, *A.H.R.* 19:363, Jan. 1914.   CRF
b. Constitutes a ninth volume of *a.* Written from the standpoint of war and public opinion, as reflected in the newspapers. Review, C. W. Ramsdell, *A.H.R.* 33:156, Oct. 1927.   MWJ

X262 Adams, Henry. *History of the United States of America* [*during the administrations of Jefferson and Madison*]. 9 v. N. Y., 1889–91. Reprint, 3 v., 1929.

Covers a limited, but very important period—one especially suited to the talent of the author. V. 1. Contains exceptionally valuable account of the state of society in 1800. The strength of the work as a whole is in the elaborate and scholarly treatment of the diplomatic discussions and controversies in the decade before the War of 1812. Foreign archives were searched and no pains were spared to get the materials so that the story might be fully and rightly told. The style is always good, often brilliant. One of the very best pieces of work American historians have produced. Review, *Nation* (N. Y.), 49:480, 504, Dec. 12, 19, 1889; 50:376, 395, May 8, 15, 1890; 51:405, 424, Nov. 20, 27, 1890; 52:322, 344, Apr. 16, 23, 1891.　　　　　ACMCL

X263 Morison, Samuel E. *Oxford history of the United States, 1783–1917.* 2 v. Oxford and N. Y., 1927.

Emphasis on diplomatic, political, commercial and cultural relations of Great Britain and the United States. Characterized by its accuracy, breadth of vision and charm of style. Designed for English readers, its choice of and emphasis on topics are largely controlled by this purpose. Review, F. L. Paxson, *A.H.R.* 33:889, July 1928.　　　　　MWJ

X264 Schouler, James. *History of the United States of America, under the Constitution.* v. 1–5, 1880–91, rev. ed., N. Y., 1894; v. 6, 1899; v. 7, 1913.

Though the early portions of the work are somewhat antiquated, probably no set of volumes by a single author gives more well-selected information on the strictly political and constitutional history of the country. Social history is not altogether slighted. The style is often peculiar, but is rarely heavy or discouraging to the general reader. The period covered is from 1783 to 1877. Review, v. 6, W. A. Dunning, *A.H.R.* 5:771, July 1900; v. 7, H. B. Learned, *A.H.R.* 19:665, Apr. 1914.　　　　　ACMCL

X266a Beard, Charles A. *Economic interpretation of the constitution of the United States.* N. Y. 1913.

b —— *Economic origins of Jeffersonian democracy.* N. Y., 1915.

Elaborate efforts to present the economic interpretation of history in application to these two subjects; emphasizes class, industrial, and financial interests. Review of *a.*, W. E. Dodd, *A.H.R.* 19:162, Oct. 1913; J. H. Latané, *Amer. Pol. Sci. Rev.* 7:697, Nov. 1913; of *b.*, C. H. Hull, *A.H.R.* 22:401, Jan. 1917; F. I. Schechter, *Amer. Pol. Sci. Rev.* 10:175, Feb. 1916.　　　　　ACMCL

X267a Davis, Jefferson. *Rise and fall of the confederate government.* 2 v. N. Y., 1881.

b —— *Short history of the Confederate States of America.* N. Y., 1890.

These two works, by the leader of the southern confederacy, give adequately the southern point of view of the struggle between the North and South.　　ACMCL

NATIONAL PERIOD, SINCE THE CIVIL WAR

X291a Beard, Charles A. *Contemporary American history, 1877–1913.* N. Y., 1914. (Bibliography.)

b Haworth, Paul L. *United States in our own times, 1865–1924.* 1920. Rev. ed., N. Y., 1930. (Bibliography.)

c Paxson, Frederic L. *Recent history of the United States, [1877–1924].* 1921. Rev. ed., Boston, 1926. (Bibliographies.)

d Shippee, Lester B. *Recent American history, [1865–1923].* N. Y., 1924. (Bibliographies.)

Brief, readable accounts, by competent scholars; written as text-books for college classes. Review of *a, A.H.R.* 20:179, Oct. 1914; of *b,* B. B. Kendrick, *A.H.R.* 26:349, Jan. 1921; of *c,* B. B. Kendrick, *A.H.R.* 27:594, Apr. 1922; of *d,* T. C. Pease, *A.H.R.* 30:619, Apr. 1925.

For similar brief works on the period, cf. (X114, v. 4) Paxson, *New nation,* and (X111b., v. 3) Lingley, *Since the Civil war.* GMD

X296a Rhodes, James Ford. *History of the United States, from the compromise of 1850 [to 1897.]* 1893–1919. New ed., 8 v., N. Y., 1920. (Bibliographical foot-notes.)

b ——— *McKinley and Roosevelt administrations, 1897–1909.* N. Y., 1922. (Bibliographical foot-notes.)

a. Best history of its period; one of the really great works in American historiography. V. 1–5. Contain a detailed, accurate, and dispassionate account of the causes and events of the Civil War, the more remarkable because the author lived through the period. V. 6–7. Cover the years of political reconstruction at the South, but give less than enough space to other events occurring between 1865 and 1877. The book seems, indeed, to have been conceived as a history of the Civil War and its immediate consequences, and was originally completed as *A History of the United States from the compromise of 1850 to the final restoration of home rule at the South in 1877.* V. 8 and *b.* Contain brief sketches of topics in American history after 1877; not only change the scale of treatment elsewhere followed, but are less comprehensive. Review, v. 1–3, A. C. McLaughlin, *A.H.R.* 1:366, Jan. 1896; v. 4, 5, W. A. Dunning, *ibid.,* 5:371, Dec. 1899; v. 5, W. G. Brown, *ibid.,* 11:181, Oct. 1905; v. 6–7, W. G. Brown, *A.H.R.* 12:680, Apr. 1907; v. 8, F. L. Paxson, *A.H.R.* 25:525, Apr. 1920; of *b,* F. L. Paxson, *A.H.R.* 28:565, Apr. 1923. FLP

X297 Oberholtzer, Ellis P. *History of the United States since the Civil war.* V. 1–3. N. Y., 1917–26.

Dr. Oberholtzer takes up the story at the close of the civil war. Of the five volumes announced, the three issued cover only twelve years, corresponding roughly to v. 6–7 of (X296) Rhodes's work. Readable, detailed, but not always judicial. Review, v. 1, W. A. Dunning, *A.H.R.* 23:676, Apr. 1918; v. 2, E. Stanwood, *A.H.R.* 28:337, Jan. 1923; v. 3, *ibid.,* 33:162, Oct. 1927. GMD

X298 Bowers, Claude G. *The tragic era; the revolution after Lincoln.* Boston, 1929.

Sharp criticism of Northern policy of reconstruction. Review, C. R. Lingley, *A.H.R.* 25:382, Jan. 1930. MWJ

X299 Sullivan, Mark. *Our times: the United States, 1900–1925.* v. 1–3, N. Y., 1927–30.

Panorama of American life and ideas in best journalistic style, planned for four volumes. Review of v. 1 and 2, C. R. Lingley, *A.H.R. 32*:626, Apr. 1927; *33*:704, Apr. 1928. MWJ

X301a Buck, Solon J. *Granger movement, a study of agricultural organization and its political, economic, and social manifestations, 1870–1880.* Cambridge, Mass., 1913. [Harvard historical studies.] Bibliography.)

b Haynes, Frederick E. *Third party movements since the civil war, with special reference to Iowa: a study in social politics.* Iowa City, 1916. [State Historical Society of Iowa.] (Bibliography.)

a. Best discussion of the subject. Review, K. L. Butterfield, *A.H.R. 19*:667, Apr. 1914. *b.* Deals with the Liberal Republican, Farmers', Greenback, Populist, and Progressive movements. The unity of the work, as a study of unrest in the Middle West, is indicated by omission of the Prohibition and Socialist parties. Review, S. J. Buck, *A.H.R. 22*:415, Jan. 1917. GMD

HISTORIES OF SECTIONS

X351 Palfrey, John G. *History of New England.* 5 v. Boston, 1858–1890.

The author was a Boston Unitarian minister and Harvard professor of Biblical literature turned historian. Gives the essential facts of the history of the Puritan colonies in America; interprets Puritanism under the spell of its ideals; the frontiers of Puritanism in Rhode Island, New Hampshire, and Maine receive scant consideration. Review (XII) Jameson, *Historical writing in America,* 113, 123–124. EJB

X352a Adams, James T. *Founding of New England.* Boston, 1921.

b —— *Revolutionary New England, 1691–1776.* Boston, 1923.

c —— *New England in the republic, 1776–1850.* Boston, 1926.

a. Searching examination of the early history of New England; exhibits the political, social, and religious activities of the founders. Review, S. E. Morison, *A.H.R. 27*:129, Oct. 1921. *b.* Continuation of *a;* allots two-thirds of the space to the years before the Stamp Act. Able, interesting presentation of the social, economic, and political forces which brought about independence; based on extensive examination of the sources. Review, E. B. Greene, *A.H.R. 29*:343, Jan. 1924. *c.* Continuation of *b.;* displays similar gifts for research, narration, and analysis; especially important as dealing with a period hitherto less fully studied than the two earlier ones. MWJ

X353 Weeden, William B. *Economic and social history of New England, 1620–1789.* 2 v. 1890. 2nd ed., Boston, 1891.

Pictures the local life of the people, their manners, morals, habits of thought, conduct; describes wages, prices, finances, roads, inns, travel; considers many-sided economic activities: agriculture, ship-building, fur-trading, fishing, distilling, home-spun industries. The business and methods of Hull, Pepperell, Faneuil, and Amory as merchant chiefs are depicted. The African slave trade, the West Indian commerce, illegal trade, and privateering are all described.

There is a wealth of detail and much color. The facts are dealt with by periods; the material is not systematically organized; weak on the relation of the economic life of the section to the English commercial system and the West Indian trade. Review, *Nation* (N. Y.), 51:365, Nov. 6, 1890.   WTR

X371 Mathews, Lois K. (Mrs. M. B. Rosenberry.) *Expansion of New England, the spread of New England settlement and institutions to the Mississippi River, 1620–1865.* Boston, 1909.

Most successful of those studies of racial stocks upon which an understanding of American history must be built up. The aim is not to evaluate the contribution of the people of New England, but to show tangibly just where that element penetrated. Based on the examination of many classes of material. The valuable results, made graphic by maps, will serve as a basis on which other studies may safely rest. Review, *A.H.R.* 15:618, Apr. 1910.   CRF

X381a Bruce, Philip A. *Economic history of Virginia in the seventeenth century; an inquiry into the material condition of the people, based upon original and contemporaneous records.* 2 v. N. Y. and London, 1895. (Bibliography.)

b —— *Social life of Virginia in the seventeenth century, an inquiry into the origin of the higher planting class, together with an account of the habits, customs, and diversions of the people.* Richmond, Va., 1907. Rev. ed., Lynchburg, Va., 1927. (Bibliography.)

c —— *Institutional history of Virginia in the seventeenth century, an inquiry into the religious, moral, educational, legal, military, and political condition of the people, based on original and contemporaneous records.* 2 v. N. Y. and London, 1910. (Bibliography.)

These volumes, pertaining to a single colony in the seventeenth century, are indispensable to the student of the history of the South as a section, since they illustrate fundamental characteristics of all the southern colonies, with respect to local government, land, labor, crops, religion, education, and other problems. Review of *a*, A. Brown, *A.H.R.* 1:538, Apr. 1896; of *b*, F. J. Turner, *A.H.R.* 13:609, Apr. 1908; of *c*, *A.H.R.* 16:139, Oct. 1910.   MWJ

X391 *The South in the building of the nation: a history of the southern states designed to record the South's part in the making of the American nation, to portray the character and genius, to chronicle the achievements and progress, and to illustrate the life and traditions of the southern people.* 13 v. Richmond, Va., 1909–13. (Bibliographies.) [1–3, J. A. C. Chandler, ed., *History of the states;* 4, F. L. Riley, ed., *Political history;* 5, J. C. Ballagh, ed., *Economic history, 1607–1865;* 6, J. C. Ballagh, ed., *Economic history, 1865–1910;* 7, J. B. Henneman, ed., *History of the intellectual life;* 8, E. Mims, ed., *History of southern fiction;* 9, T. E. Watson, ed., *History of southern oratory;* 10, S. C. Mitchell, ed., *History of the social life;* 11–12, W. L. Fleming, ed., *Southern biography;* 13, J. W. McSpadden, ed., *Index and study courses.*]

Handy reference work, but, like most coöperative works, uneven in style and value. The contributing authors number about one hundred. V. 4–8. Contain many critical and scholarly essays of considerable value. V. 11–12. Give numerous biographical sketches, averaging about a page in length. Some of the contributors are scholars of first rank.   CSB

X392 Brown, William G. *Lower South in American history.* N. Y., 1902.

Three of the eight articles in this volume relate directly to the subject and furnish suggestive explanations of the political influence of this section in the four decades preceding the Civil War. Review, J. W. Perrin, *A.H.R.* 10:192, Oct. 1904.   GMD

X393 Phillips, Ulrich B. *Life and labor in the old south.* Boston, 1929.

Valuable study of social and economic conditions in the ante-bellum South. Brief treatment of the colonial period with detailed study of individual plantations in different sections of the South after 1815. Social groups are described and negro slavery analyzed. Larger view of developments, tendencies, and variations in different periods is subordinated to an analysis of particular and local conditions. Review, W. K. Boyd, *A.H.R.* 35:133, Oct. 1929.   AOC

X401 Schwab, John C. *Confederate States of America, 1861–1865, a financial and industrial history of the South during the civil war.* N. Y., 1901. [Yale bicentennial publications.]   (Bibliography.)

Deals with both the Confederate government and the governments of the constituent states in their financial operations. Excellent, impartial study; based on extensive researches. Review, E. A. Smith, *A.H.R.* 7:579, Apr. 1902.
                                                                          GMD

X421 Turner, Frederick J. *Frontier in American history.* N. Y., 1920. (Bibliographical foot-notes.)

Most of the thirteen essays conveniently collected and reprinted in this volume are interpretations of particular geographical regions which at one time or another have been parts of the American frontier, or expositions of the ideals which the frontier has produced. Especially noteworthy are 'The significance of the frontier in American history,' 1893, one of the most suggestive essays in American historical writing, 'The old West,' 1908, and 'Social forces in American history,' the presidential address delivered before the American Historical Association in 1910. Practically indispensable for the student of American history. Review, A. Johnson, *A.H.R.* 26:542, Apr. 1921.   StGLS

X422 Paxson, Frederic L. *History of the American frontier, 1763–1893.* Boston, 1924. Reprint, 1925.

Declares 'the frontier with its continuous influence is the most American thing in all America'; shows, in some sixty chapters, the place of the frontier and of the West in the development of the United States. Begins with the narrow hem of settlement along the Atlantic littoral in the latter part of the eighteenth century; traces the details of discovery, diplomacy, war, exploration, penetration, and legislation until the year 1893. Essentially a narrative history rather than a discussion of movements and tendencies; the epic of western development from the up-country of the original colonies to the Cow Country. Awarded the Pulitzer Prize for the best book of the year on the history of the United States. Review, H. C. Dale, *A.H.R.* 30:603. Apr. 1925.   MWJ

X431a Winsor, Justin. *Mississippi basin: the struggle in America between England and France, 1697–1763.* Boston, 1895.

   b —— *Westward movement: the colonies and the republic west of the Alleghanies, 1763–1798.* Boston, 1897.

These two volumes, together with his (K242b) *Cartier to Frontenac,* cover adequately a period and phase of American history that has not been treated so fully by any other historian. Winsor's style is heavy and dry, but his narrative is weighty with facts and is, therefore, indispensable to one desiring knowledge of the period covered. Later monographs on various phases of western history have revised many of Winsor's interpretations. The cartographical illustrations from contemporary sources are extremely valuable and, though not always entirely trustworthy, are still the most accessible collection of maps for the history of the region. Review of *a., Nation* (N. Y.), 61:67, July 25, 1895; of *b.,* F. J. Turner, *A.H.R.* 3:556, Apr. 1898.   CWA

X432a Roosevelt, Theodore. *Winning of the West.* 1889–1900. Sagamore ed., 6 v., N. Y., 1900. [1, *Spread of English-speaking peoples; 2, In the current of the revolution; 3, War in the Northwest; 4, Indian wars, 1784–1787; Franklin, Kentucky, Ohio, and Tennessee; 5, St. Clair and Wayne; 6, Louisiana and Aaron Burr.*] Other eds. and reprints.

   b Henderson, Archibald. *Conquest of the old Southwest, the romantic story of the early pioneers into Virginia, the Carolinas, Tennessee, and Kentucky, 1740–1790.* N. Y., 1920.

   c Hinsdale, Burke A. *Old Northwest, the beginnings of our colonial system.* 1888. New ed., N. Y., 1899.

   a. Most important of Roosevelt's historical writings; vividly describes the westward movement across the Alleghanies and into the Mississippi valley and beyond, from the years following the peace of 1763 through the explorations of Lewis and Clark and of Pike. Highly expressive of Roosevelt's vigor and of his strong likes and dislikes; based upon much research, especially in the great collections of western materials; weaker on the diplomatic side; neglects the materials in the British Public Record Office. The later chapters are the least original. Review, F. J. Turner, *A.H.R.* 2:171, Oct. 1896. *b.* and *c.* Brief works on the regions south and north of the Ohio, respectively. Review of *b.,* C. W. Alvord, *A.H.R.* 26:116, Oct. 1920; of *c, Nation* (N. Y.), 46:513, June 21, 1888.   StGLS

X433a Hulbert, Archer B. *Frontiers: the genius of American nationality.* Boston, 1929.

   b Crane, Verner W. *Southern frontier, 1670–1732.* Philadelphia, 1929.

   c Whitaker, Arthur P. *Spanish-American frontier, 1783–1795: the westward movement and the Spanish retreat in the Mississippi valley.* Boston, 1927.

   d Rister, Carl C. *Southwestern frontier, 1865–1881.* Cleveland, 1928.

   a. Describes factors, causes and influences that have unified the American people. *b.* Scholarly and exhaustive study of the expansion of, and rivalry for, the Carolina frontier, and the genesis of Georgia. *c.* Survey of the struggle for the Natchez district with an account of frontier intrigue. Review, *A.H.R.* 33:671, Apr. 1928. *d.* Unified account of the section comprising parts of Kansas, Indian territory, Texas, and New Mexico. Review, J. B. Hedges, *A.H.R.* 34:625, Apr. 1929.
          MWJ

X441a Paxson, Frederic L. *Last American frontier.* N. Y., 1910. (Bibliography.)

   b Goodwin, Cardinal. *Trans-Mississippi West, 1803–1853, a history of its acquisition and settlement.* N. Y. and London, 1922. (Bibliographies.)

c **Coman, Katharine.** *Economic beginnings of the Far West: how we won the land beyond the Mississippi.* N. Y., 1912. (Bibliography.)

d **Schafer, Joseph.** *History of the Pacific Northwest.* N. Y. and London, 1905.

a. Traces the development of the region stretching from the Mississippi to the Pacific coast; brings out in strong relief the influence of the growing West upon the evolution of the nation; gives the story of the forces that divided the Trans-Mississippi region into territories and states and filled it with a farming, mining, and commercial people. Review, M. Farrand, *A.H.R.* 15:892, July 1910. *b, c,* and *d.* Useful monographs; supplement *a,* with fuller details on their respective subjects. Review of *b,* P. C. Phillips, *A.H.R.* 28:330, Jan. 1923; of *c,* F. L. Paxson, *A.H.R.* 18:821, July 1913; of *d,* F. H. Hodder, *A.H.R.* 11:949, July 1906. Also cf. (Y486*b* and *c*) Smith, *Annexation of Texas* and *War with Mexico.*   CWA

X451 Bancroft, Hubert H. *Works.* 39 v. San Francisco, 1882–90. (Bibliographies.) [1–5, *Native races,* 1st ed., 1874–76; 6–8, *History of Central America;* 9–14, *History of Mexico;* 15–16, *History of the north Mexican states and Texas;* 17, *History of Arizona and New Mexico;* 18–24, *History of California;* 25, *History of Nevada, Colorado, and Wyoming;* 26, *History of Utah;* 27–28, *History of the northwest coast;* 29–30, *History of Oregon;* 31, *History of Washington, Idaho, and Montana;* 32, *History of British Columbia;* 33, *History of Alaska;* 34, *California pastoral;* 35, *California inter pocula;* 36–37, *Popular tribunals;* 38, *Essays and miscellany;* 39, *Literary industries.*]

This large work, covering the history and to some extent the anthropology of Central America, Mexico, and the Far West of the United States and Canada, represents the life work of a great historical collector and pioneer, aided by numerous assistants. Although the history, as is shown by the copious footnotes, has been drawn from a great variety of sources and, in general, is fairly satisfactory, some of the volumes have been composed by authors without special equipment. One may therefore expect to find an unequal style and occasional inaccuracies. The work, as a whole, is of chief value for reference purposes, and to historical students undertaking further investigation in one of the many fields covered. For fuller discussion of the merits and defects of this great series, cf. (XII) Jameson, *Historical writing in America,* 152–156, and the following reviews: *Nation* (N. Y.), 36:85, Jan. 25, 1883; 41:283, Oct. 1, 1885; 46:492, June 14, 1888; 50:179, Feb. 27, 1890; 50:204, March 6, 1890.

                                                                                         JFR

X461 *American commonwealths.* Ed. by Horace E. Scudder. 18 v. Boston, 1885–1908. [1, J. Royce, *California;* 2, A. Johnston, *Connecticut,* rev. ed., 1903; 3, J. P. Dunn, Jr., *Indiana,* rev. ed., 1905; 4, L. W. Spring, *Kansas,* rev. ed., 1907; 5, N. S. Shaler, *Kentucky;* 6, A. Phelps, *Louisiana;* 7, W. H. Browne, *Maryland,* rev. ed., 1904; 8, T. M. Cooley, *Michigan.* rev. ed., 1905; 9, W. W. Folwell, *Minnesota;* 10, L. Carr, *Missouri;* 11, F. B. Sanborn, *New Hampshire;* 12, E. H. Roberts, *New York,* rev. ed., 1904; 13, R. King, *Ohio.* rev. ed., 1903; 14, I. B. Richman, *Rhode Island;* 15, G. P. Garrison, *Texas;* 16, R. E. Robinson, *Vermont;* 17, J. E. Cooke, *Virginia,* rev. ed., 1903; 18, R. G. Thwaites, *Wisconsin.*]

Of the eighteen volumes in this series, twelve appeared in the original editions between the years 1883 and 1892. By the standards of historical productions of those years they are, in most cases, excellent and scholarly works. As a rule, there have been few changes made in the revised editions; in some cases a chapter of continuation has been added. The greatest emphasis is usually on the formative period of the state's history. Some of the volumes are written in such a manner as to give them a special interest; for instance, Josiah Royce, *California*, is almost a psychological interpretation of California history from 1846 to 1856, and N. S. Shaler, *Kentucky* is largely a study of geographic influences. As brief, popular, and readable accounts of the formation of the various states, most of them are unmatched even today. Additional volumes have recently been announced as in preparation.

TCP

X471a Nichols, Jeannette P. *Alaska: a history of its administration, exploitation, and industrial development during its first half century under the rule of the United States.* Cleveland, 1924. (Bibliography.)

  b Greely, Adolphus W. *Handbook of Alaska, its resources, products, and attractions in 1924.* 3rd rev. ed., N. Y., 1925.

a. History of American rule in Alaska, 1867–1912. Review, F. L. Paxson, *A.H.R.* 29:579, Apr. 1924. *b.* Authoritative work of reference. Review, *Saturday Review of Literature*, 1:782, May 25, 1925.

For works on Hawaii, Samoa, Guam, and the Philippines, cf. § V; on Porto Rico, the Virgin Islands, and the Canal Zone, cf. § Y.

GMD

DIPLOMATIC, MILITARY, AND NAVAL HISTORY

X501a Fish, Carl R. *American diplomacy.* 1915. 4th rev. ed., N. Y., 1923. [American historical series.] (Bibliographical foot-notes.)

  b Adams, Randolph G. *History of the foreign policy of the United States.* N. Y., 1924. (Bibliography.)

  c Johnson, Willis F. *America's foreign relations.* 2 v. N. Y., 1916.

  d Hill, Charles E. *Leading American treaties.* N. Y., 1922.

  e Wright, Quincy. *Control of American foreign relations.* N. Y., 1922.

a. Designed for use as a text in college classes; best brief general survey of the subject; based largely upon recent monographs; somewhat weak as to international law. The method is strictly narrative and chronological, although topical leads are in places indicated. Eminently readable; generally judicious; well-balanced; maps illustrate territorial and boundary problems. Review, J. S. Reeves, *A.H.R.* 21:609, Apr. 1916.

JSR

b. Treated by topics, arranged substantially in chronological order; one third of the space allotted to the period since 1897; attempts to give a popular epitome of the results of research. Review, H. B. Learned, *A.H.R.* 30:835, July 1925. *c.* More detailed chronicles of occurrences and transactions; generally accurate; popular and readable. Review, J. S. Reeves, *A.H.R.* 22:397, Jan. 1917. *d.* Gives the historical setting and chief provisions of fifteen important treaties from 1778 to 1898, with special reference to territorial expansion. Review, G. G. Wilson, *A.H.R.* 27:827, July 1922. *e.* Deals with laws and precedents to illustrate the relations of constitutional and international law in American practice. Review. J. Dickinson, *Amer. Pol. Sci. Rev.* 17:123, Feb. 1923.

For books on relations with Hispanic America, the Monroe Doctrine, Pan-Americanism, the Far East, and the United States and the World War, cf. respectively (Y501–505), (Y521), (Y526), (U421 ff.), (U2501 ff.), (U3273), and (J411 ff.).

GMD

X502a Moore, John Bassett. *Digest of international law, as embodied in diplomatic discussions, treaties, and other international agreements, international awards, the decisions of municipal courts, and the writings of jurists, and especially in documents, published and unpublished, issued by the presidents and secretaries of state of the United States, the opinions of the attorneys-general, and the decisions of courts, federal and state.* 8 v. Washington, 1906. (1505c)

b ——— *History and digest of the international arbitrations to which the United States has been a party, together with appendices containing the treaties relating to such arbitrations, and historical and legal notes on other international arbitrations ancient and modern, and on the domestic commissions of the United States for the adjustment of international claims.* 6 v. Washington, 1898.

c ——— *Principles of American diplomacy.* N. Y. and London, 1918.

a. Reference work; embodies a vast mass of documentary material; indispensable to the study of American foreign policy and diplomatic relations; Review, J. B. Scott, *Amer. Jour. of International Law,* 1:254, Jan. 1907. *b.* Another compilation of first-rate importance. Review, E. I. Renick, *A.H.R.* 4:563, Apr. 1899. GMD

c. Discusses principles rather than events. Review, A. S. Hershey, *A.H.R.* 24:131, Oct. 1918. MWJ

X503a Coolidge, Archibald C. *United States as a world power.* N. Y., 1908. Later reprints.

b.**Blakeslee, George H.** *Recent foreign policy of the United States, problems in American coöperation with other powers.* N. Y., 1925. [Wesleyan University, Bennett lectures.]

a. Excellent survey of the international relations of the United States in the years immediately following 1898; shows the emergence of the United States as a world power. Review, A. S. Hershey, *A.H.R.* 14:372, Jan. 1909. *b.* Admirable account and discussion of the problems of American diplomacy with special reference to the incumbency of Mr. Hughes as secretary of state, 1921–1925. Review, C. E. Martin, *Amer. Pol. Sci. Rev.* 19:833, Nov. 1925. GMD

X504a Dealey, James Q. *Foreign policies of the United States. Bases and developments.* N. Y., 1927.

b **Sears, Louis M.** *History of American foreign relations.* N. Y., 1927.

c **Latané, John H.** *History of American foreign policy.* N. Y., 1927.

d **Garner, James W.** *American foreign policies.* N. Y., 1928.

e **Howland, Charles P.** *Survey of American foreign relations, 1928.* New Haven, 1928.

f **Dennis, Alfred L. P.** *Adventures in American diplomacy, 1896–1906.* N. Y., 1928.

Group of recent works. *a.* Discusses especially factors affecting developments, geographic, political and social ideals. Review, H. B. Learned, *A.H.R.* 32:889, July 1927. *b.* Useful general account, mainly chronological. Review, J. M. Callahan, *A.H.R.* 33:448, Jan. 1928. *c.* Interpretative survey of foreign policies. Review, J. B. Moore, *A.H.R.* 32:887, July 1927. *d.* Discusses policies in relation to isolation and international peace. Review, L. M. Sears, *A.H.R.* 33:923, July 1928. *e.* Coöperative work giving a survey of disputed points of policy. Review, E. S. Brown, *A.H.R.* 34:628, Apr. 1929. JFR *f.* Treats of the evolution of the United States as a world power. Impartial and authoritative. Review, R. B. Way, *A.H.R.* 34:368, Jan. 1929. MWJ

X506a Dunning, William A. *British empire and the United States, a review of their relations during the century of peace following the treaty of Ghent.* N. Y., 1914.

b Mowat, Robert B. *Diplomatic relations of Great Britain and the United States.* London and N. Y., 1925.

c. Bigelow, John. *Breaches of Anglo-American treaties, a study in history and diplomacy.* N. Y., 1917.

d Wrong, George M. *United States and Canada, a political study.* N. Y., 1921. [Wesleyan University, Bennett lectures.]

e Bemis, Samuel F. *Jay's treaty, a study in commerce and diplomacy.* N. Y., 1923. [Knights of Columbus historical series.] (Bibliography.)

f Adams, Ephraim D. *Great Britain and the American Civil War.* 2 v. London and N. Y., 1925. (Bibliographical foot-notes.)

a. Makes no pretence of offering results of personal research, but is based on careful study of general works and presents a composite, illuminated by the author's broad scholarship, keen and sane judgments of events and men in both countries, and by his customary pleasing style. Exact in the statement of accepted facts of diplomatic history; offers an excellent general survey of British-American relations, 1814–1914. Review, F. L. Paxson, *A.H.R.* 20:648, Apr. 1915. EDA

b. Corresponding volume by an English scholar. Review, E. D. Adams, *A.H.R.* 31:796, July 1926. *c.* Investigates whether the United States has been guilty of bad faith; in general the verdict is for acquittal. Review, J. B. Moore, *A.H.R.* 23:194, Oct. 1917. *d.* Primarily a comparative study of the political and constitutional development of the two neighbor nations. Review, R. L. Borden, *Can. Hist. Rev.* 2:272, Sept. 1921. *e.* Important monograph; reviews antecedent relations. Review, *A.H.R.* 29:345, Jan. 1924. f. Scholarly and impartial; based upon thorough examination of British policy and opinion during the Civil War, upon researches in diplomatic correspondence, much of the material hitherto unavailable for publication, and on the public press of the period, from which the author freely quotes. Demonstrates that the government of Great Britain maintained a 'generally correct neutrality' while the more liberal element and leaders gave their support to the Northern cause. Adds much to knowledge regarding the relation between the two nations at a very critical time. Review, G. M. Trevelyan, *A.H.R.* 31:154, Oct. 1925. GMD

X507a Chadwick, French E. *Relations of the United States and Spain, diplomacy.* N. Y., 1909.

b Yela Utrilla, Juan F. *España ante la independencia de los Estados Unidos.* 1922. 2nd ed., 2 v., Lérida, Spain, 1925.

a. Valuable study of relations between Spain and the United States since 1763, with special reference to the causes of the war of 1898, at which date the narrative closes. Review, *A.H.R.* 16:148, Oct. 1910. Continued by (X522*b*). *b.* Important contribution to the diplomatic history of the War for Independence and to the relations between the United States and Spain. V. 2. Made up of documents, notably the correspondence of Aranda, the Spanish ambassador at Paris. Review, S. F. Bemis, *A.H.R.* 31:794, July 1926. For additional works on relations between the United States and Spain, cf. (Y496–498); on relations between the United States and Mexico, cf. (Y486). GMD

X508 *Albert Shaw lectures on diplomatic history, Johns Hopkins University.* V. 1–14. Baltimore, 1900–29. [1, J. H. Latané, *Diplomatic relations of the United States and Spanish America;* 2, J. M. Callahan, *Diplomatic history of the southern Confederacy;* 3, (Y486e) J. S. Reeves, *American diplomacy under Tyler and Polk;* 4, E. J. Benton, *International law and diplomacy of the Spanish-American War;* 5, (Y486d) E. D. Adams, *British interests and activities in Texas, 1838–1846;* 6, C. O. Paullin, *Diplomatic negotiations of American naval officers, 1778–1883;* 7, F. A. Updyke, *Diplomacy of the War of 1812;* 8, W. R. Manning, *Early diplomatic relations between the United States and Mexico;* 9, (U3273b) P. J. Treat, *Early diplomatic relations between the United States and Japan, 1853–1865;* 10, (Y498a) I. J. Cox, *West Florida controversy, 1798–1813;* 11, (Y506) P. A. Martin, *Latin America and the war;* 12, S. F. Bemis, *Pinckney's treaty: a study of America's advantage from Europe's distress, 1783–1800;* 13, B. S. Williams, *State security and the league of nations;* 14, J. F. Rippy, *Rivalry of the United States and Great Britain over Latin America.*]

Important contributions to the history of the foreign relations of the United States; each volume presents the results of documentary researches. Review, v. 1, *A.H.R.* 6:146, Oct. 1900; v. 2, J. W. Foster, *A.H.R.* 7:379, Jan. 1902; v. 6, G. G. Wilson, *A.H.R.* 18:153, Oct. 1912; v. 7, K. C. Babcock, *A.H.R.* 21:157, Oct. 1915; v. 8, G. L. Rives, *A.H.R.* 21:825, July 1916; v. 12, I. J. Cox, *A.H.R.* 32:616, Apr. 1927.

For monographs on the relations of the Netherlands to the American Revolution, cf. (Q352e, f, and g); of Spain, (X507b); of France, (X734). GMD

X509a. Rippy, J. Fred. *United States and Mexico.* N. Y., 1926.

　b Rives, George L. *United States and Mexico, 1821–1848.* 2 v. N. Y., 1913.

　c Smith, Justin H. *War with Mexico.* 2 v. N. Y., 1919.

a. Gives the first comprehensive and scholarly survey of the diplomatic relations of the United States and Mexico. Review, J. M. Callahan, *A.H.R.* 32:899, July 1927. *b.* Detailed and thorough study mainly concerning diplomatic history. Review, J. S. Reeves, *A.H.R.* 19:659, Apr. 1914. *c.* Most comprehensive and scholarly history of the Mexican war. Review, E. C. Barker, *A.H.R.* 25:729, July 1920.
MWJ

X510a Hill, Howard C. *Roosevelt and the Caribbean.* Chicago, 1927.

　b Jones, Chester Lloyd. *Caribbean interests of the United States.* N. Y., 1916.

a. Well-written story of Roosevelt's part in American expansion and 'benevolent imperialism.' Review, P. M. Brown, *A.H.R.* 33:421, Jan. 1928. *b.* General account of political and economic conditions and American activities in the Caribbean region. Review, A. G. Robinson, *A.H.R.* 22:418, Jan. 1917. MWJ

X511a Huidekoper, Frederic L. *Military unpreparedness of the United States, a history of American land forces from colonial times until June 1, 1915.* N. Y., 1915. (Bibliographical notes.)

　b Ganoe, William A. *History of the United States army.* N. Y. and London, 1924.

a. Though written for propaganda purposes, this well-documented volume provides a fairly satisfactory brief history of the army of the United States.

Review, *A.H.R.* 21:604, Apr. 1916. *b.* Only direct effort to write a complete history of the military organization of the United States and its operations; not altogether successful. Review, O. L. Spaulding, Jr., *A.H.R.* 30:399, Jan. 1925.

Abundant citations of special works on the history of military and naval operations in the wars of the United States prior to the World War will be found in the bibliographies listed in (X1). For American participation in the World War, cf. (J411 ff.).

GMD

X512a Ropes, John C. *Story of the civil war.* 4 v. N. Y. and London, 1894–1913.

b Shannon, Fred Albert. *Organization and administration of the union army, 1861–1865.* 2 v. Cleveland, 1929.

a. Standard history of the Civil War. Review, J. H. Wilson, *A.H.R.* 5:592, Apr. 1900. *b.* Important and scholarly work. Review, *A.H.R.* 34:621, Apr. 1900.

MWJ

X521a Maclay, Edgar S. *History of the United States navy, 1775–1901.* 1894. Rev. ed., 3 v., N. Y., 1898–1901.

b Spears, John R. *History of our navy from its origin to the present day, 1775–1897.* 4 v. N. Y., 1897.

c —— *Our navy in the war with Spain.* N. Y., 1899.

d Paullin, Charles O. *Navy of the American revolution, its administration, its policy, and its achievements.* Cleveland, 1906. (Bibliography.)

a., b., and *c.* Principal histories of the United States navy and its operations. Review of *a, Nation* (N. Y.), 58:455, June 14, 1894; 60:35, Jan. 10, 1895; 66:499, June 30, 1898; of *b.,* A. T. Mahan, *A.H.R.* 3:747, July 1898; of *c.,* T. A. Dodge, *A.H.R.* 4:750, July 1899. *d.* Best account of the navy during the Revolutionary War; stresses the administration rather than the operations. Review, C. H. Van Tyne, *A.H.R.* 12:666, Apr. 1907.

GMD

X522a Mahan, Alfred T. *Sea power in its relations to the war of 1812.* 2 v. Boston, 1905. Reprint, 1919.

b Chadwick, French E. *Relations of the United States and Spain: the Spanish-American war.* 2 v. N. Y., 1911. (Bibliography.)

Special studies of capital importance, by recognized authorities. *a.* Review, G. Hunt, *A.H.R.* 11:924, July 1906. *b.* Continuation of (X507a). Review, A. W. Greely, *A.H.R.* 17:857, July 1912.

For other special works on the United States navy and its operations, cf. bibliographies listed in (X1).

GMD

CONSTITUTIONAL, POLITICAL, AND LEGAL HISTORY AND POLITICAL THEORY

X531 Bryce, James, Viscount. *American commonwealth.* 1888. Rev. ed., 2 v., N. Y., 1910. Later reprints.

Written by an observer with extraordinary range and keenness of vision, with sympathetic interest, and with great powers of lucid and interesting exposition; marked an epoch in the description of American institutions; still remains the most brilliant and authoritative study of the American government. The exposition of the workings and spirit of the governmental organization is remarkable for its insight and clearness. Of special significance is the discussion of the less formal characteristics of government, such as the party system, public opinion, and the social forces conditioning the operation of the governmental system. Review, *Nation* (N. Y.), 48:12, 34, Jan. 3, 10, 1889; H. J. Ford, *Amer. Pol. Sci. Rev.* 5:476, Aug. 1911. CEM

X532a Beard, Charles A. *American government and politics.* 1913. 4th rev. ed., N. Y., 1924. (Bibliography.)

   b Ogg, Frederic A., and Ray, Perley Orman. *Introduction to American government.* 1922. 3rd rev. ed., N. Y., 1928. [Century political science series.] (Bibliographies.)

   c Munro, William B. *Government of the United States, national, state, and local.* 1919. 2nd rev. ed., N. Y., 1925. (Bibliographical foot-notes.)

   Principal standard text-books on American government, national, state, and local. *a.* Devotes relatively more space to governmental functions and to proposals for reform. Review, C. Meriwether, *A.H.R.* 16:400, Jan. 1911; C. G. Haines, *Amer. Pol. Sci. Rev.* 5:141, Feb. 1911. *b.* Best on the descriptive side; has introductory discussion of political theory. Review, A. C. Hanford, *Amer. Pol. Sci. Rev.* 16:509, Aug. 1922. *c.* Well-balanced, judicious discussion; more concerned with principles than with problems. Review, *Amer. Pol. Sci. Rev.* 19:650, Aug. 1925. LL

X533a Long, Breckinridge. *Genesis of the constitution of the United States of America.* N. Y., 1926.

   b Schuyler, Robert L. *Constitution of the United States; an historical survey of its formation.* N. Y., 1923.

   c Farrand, Max. *Framing of the constitution of the United States.* New Haven, 1913.

   d Corwin, Edward S. *The Constitution and what it means today.* 1920. 3rd rev. ed., Princeton, N. J., 1924.

   e Horwill, Herbert W. *Usages of the American constitution.* Oxford and N. Y., 1925.

   f Stevens, Charles E. *Sources of the constitution of the United States, considered in relation to colonial and English history.* 1894. 2nd rev. ed., N. Y. and London, 1894.

   g Warren, Charles. *Making of the constitution.* Boston, 1928.

   a. Through an examination of the principal experiments in government in North America and of the more important constitutional documents between 1620 and 1787, traces the antecedents of the various provisions of the constitution. Review, *Amer. Pol. Sci. Rev.* 20:452, May 1926. *b.* Brief survey of the chief precedents for the constitution and of its framing and adoption. Review, B. F. Shambaugh, *A.H.R.* 29:609, Apr. 1924. *c.* Brief, authoritative account of the constitutional convention of 1787; suitable for the general reader, valuable to the more special student. Review, W. F. Dodd, *A.H.R.* 19:401, Jan. 1914. *d.* Useful exposition of the various clauses of the constitution; shows the difference between the original and present meanings. *e.* Well-written treatise by an English journalist; deals systematically with extra-constitutional practices according to which the government is actually conducted.

Useful presentation of neglected points of view and of materials not conveniently accessible elsewhere. Review, E. S. Corwin, *Amer. Pol. Sci. Rev.* 20:436, May 1926. *f.* Covers much the same field as *a,* which by no means displaces it. Review, H. A. Cushing, *Pol. Sci. Quar.* 9:545, Sept. 1894.   LL

g. Authoritative. Largely a day-to-day account of proceedings in the Federal Convention. Review, A. C. McLaughlin, *Yale Law Journal,* 38:559, Feb. 1929.

MWJ

X536a Landon, Judson S. *Constitutional history and government of the United States.* Boston, 1889.

b Curtis, George T. *Constitutional history of the United States from their declaration of independence to the close of their civil war.* 2 v. N. Y., 1889–96. V. 2, ed. by J. C. Clayton. (Bibliography.)

c Thorpe, Francis N. *Constitutional history of the United States, 1765–1895.* 3 v. Chicago, 1901.

d ———— *Constitutional history of the American people.* 2 v. N. Y. and London, 1898.

Though the best available works on the subject, all are incomplete and inadequate. *a.* Best single volume on the subject. Review, *Nation* (N. Y.), 48:453, May 30, 1889. *b.* V. 1. Treats the period of the Revolution and Confederation; the better of the two. Review, D. H. Chamberlain, *A.H.R.* 2:549, Apr. 1897. *c.* V. 1–2. Chiefly a description of the framing and adoption of the federal constitution and the first ten amendments. V. 3. Recounts the history of the Civil War amendments. Review, T. C. Smith, *A.H.R.* 7:152, Oct. 1901. *d.* Chiefly a study of the evolution of the state constitutions. Review, A. D. Morse, *A.H.R.* 4:734, July 1899.   GMD

X537 Holst, Hermann E. von. *Constitutional and political history of the United States.* 1876–92. New ed., 8 v., Chicago, 1899. (Bibliography.) Tr. by J. J. Lalor and others from *Verfassung und Demokratie der Vereinigten Staaten von Amerika,* 4 v., Düsseldorf and Berlin, 1873–91.

V. 1. Covers the period from 1750 to 1832; the treatment is semi-philosophic, hardly narrative. V. 2–7. Chiefly taken up with the anti-slavery struggle which is ably treated. V. 8. Index. The writer was an unflinching defender of free-labor and of the northern cause, not sparing denunciation of what he disliked. The latter half of the work covers the period from 1850 to 1861. There is not a very large degree of calm discussion of constitutional problems in these later volumes, but the elaborate and able treatment is of great service. Review, v. 4–5, *Nation* (N. Y.), 41:198, Sept 3, 1885; v. 6, 50:33, Jan. 9, 1890; v. 7, 55:32, July 14, 1892.   ACMCL

X538 Randall, James G. *Constitutional problems under Lincoln.* N. Y., 1926.

Scholarly and important study of such topics as treason, habeas corpus, martial law, conscription, confiscation, emancipation, state and federal relations. Review, C. R. Fish, *A.H.R.* 33:419, Jan. 1928.   MWJ

X541a Stanwood, Edward. *History of presidential elections.* Boston, 1884.

b —— *History of the presidency.* 1898. Rev. ed., 2 v., Boston, 1928.

c McKee, Thomas H. *National conventions and platforms of all political parties, 1789 to 1905; convention, popular, and electoral vote, also the political complexion of both houses of congress at each biennial period.* 1892. 6th rev. ed., Baltimore, 1906.

b. Based on *a;* broader in scope. Comprehensive account of party platforms, presidential campaigns, and national elections, supplemented by statistics; careful reflections upon policies and candidates; leading work of reference on presidential elections; usually sound in conclusions. Two chapters interesting from the standpoint of generalization are: 'The convention system,' and 'The evolution of the presidency,' the latter slightly elaborated in the latest condition. Review, *Nation* (N. Y.), 39:402, Nov. 6, 1884; E. C. Burnett, *A.H.R.* 4:391, Jan. 1899; H. B. Learned, *A.H.R.* 22:677, Apr. 1917. *c.* Gives platforms of political parties and some other useful material. HBL

X542a Learned, Henry B. *President's cabinet; studies in the origin, formation; and structure of an American institution.* New Haven, 1912. (Valuable bibliography.)

b Hinsdale, Mary L. *History of the President's cabinet.* Ann Arbor, Mich., 1911. [University of Michigan historical studies.] (Bibliography.)

a. Traces the origin of the cabinet in England; regards the origin of the American cabinet as an historical development rather than an accident. The origin and structure of each department is dealt with in successive chapters. Best authority for the structure of the cabinet. Review, *A.H.R.* 17:846, July 1912. *b.* Systematic discussion of the origin of the cabinet, its development under successive presidents, the principles on which the cabinet has been constructed, and the relations of the cabinet to the president and congress. Review, *A.H.R.* 17:844, July 1912. HMW

X543a Wilson, Woodrow. *Congressional government, a study in American politics.* 1885. New ed., with introduction by Ray Stannard Baker, Boston, 1925.

b Alexander, De Alva S. *History and procedure of the house of representatives.* Boston, 1916.

c Follett, Mary P. *Speaker of the house of representatives.* N. Y., 1896. (Bibliography.)

a. Belongs chiefly in the field of political science; discusses brilliantly the methods of congressional procedure; dwells on the character of congressional as distinguished from cabinet form of government. Review, *Nation* (N. Y.), 40:142, Feb. 12, 1885. *b.* Based on fourteen years' experience as a member of the house, and upon the familiar printed sources. Well-organized; impartial; very useful. Review, W. MacDonald, *A.H.R.* 22:177, Oct. 1916; G. W. Rutherford, *Amer. Pol. Sci. Rev.* 10:775, Nov. 1916. *c.* Study of the history of an office which is often called the second office in influence and power in the United States. Begins with the colonial speaker and treats of the development of the office and the character and influence of the great speakers. Can be profitably read with *a.*

ACMCL

X544a Holcombe, Arthur N. *State government in the United States.* N. Y., 1916. Rev. ed., 1926. (Bibliography.)

b Dodd, Walter F. *State government.* 1922. Rev. ed., N. Y., 1928. [Century political science series.] (Bibliographies.)

c Mathews, John M. *American state government.* N. Y. and London, 1924. (Bibliographies.)

Standard works; written as text-books for college use. *a.* Gives substantially equal space to historical development of state governments, to extent and methods of popular control, and to descriptions of structure and functions of state governments; somewhat out of date. Review, J. A. Fairlie, *Amer. Pol. Sci. Rev.* 11:344, May 1917. *b.* Chiefly descriptive, with some consideration of problems. Review, H. Lindley, *A.H.R.* 28:589, Apr. 1923. *c.* Also primarily descriptive; most recent and perhaps the best in both style and treatment. Review, R. H. Wells, *Amer. Pol. Sci. Rev.* 9:196, Feb. 1925.

LL

X546 Woodburn, James A. *American politics: political parties and party problems in the United States, a sketch of American party history and of the development and operations of party machinery, together with a consideration of certain party problems in their relations to political morality.* 1903. 3rd rev. ed., N. Y. and London, 1924. (Brief bibliographies.)

About one-half is a well-proportioned survey of the history of political parties leading up to the conclusion that party divisions in the United States have corresponded roughly 'to certain broad distinctions of mind and character'—namely, conservatism and radicalism. A separate treatment of minor parties in a concluding chapter isolates even the liberal republicans and other promising independent movements from the regular narrative. There follows an analysis of American party machinery and of its operations and, in a third part, a presentation of ethical problems in party politics intended to inspire a more adequate sense of American political duties as well as political rights. Review, M. S. Brown, *A.H.R.* 9:168, Oct. 1903.

ACCO

X547a Merriam, Charles E. *American party system, an introduction to the study of political parties in the United States.* N. Y., 1922. (Bibliographical foot-notes.)

b Brooks, Robert C. *Political parties and electoral problems.* N. Y., 1923. (Bibliographies.)

c Holcombe, Arthur N. *Political parties of to-day.* N. Y., 1924. (Bibliography.)

d Robinson, Edgar E. *Evolution of American political parties, a sketch of party development.* N. Y., 1924. (Bibliographies.)

a. Most recent attempt to deal scientifically with the American party system; written by the leading academic authority on the subject in the United States; analytical rather than descriptive. Disproportionate space given to discussion of the spoils system. Review, *A.H.R.* 28:370, Jan. 1923. *b.* Chiefly a discussion of the organization and activities of parties. Review, P. O. Ray, *Amer. Pol. Sci. Rev.* 18:400, May 1924. *c.* Studies composition of the Republican and Democratic parties and factors determining party alignment. Review, R. S. Boots, *Amer. Pol. Sci. Rev.* 19:199, Feb. 1925. *d.* Probably best recent short history of the political party as a social phenomenon. Treats the development of parties from the point of view of the sociologist, hence interpretive rather than merely descriptive. Review, *A.H.R.* 30:607, Apr. 1925.

LL

X551a Haines, Charles G. *American doctrine of judicial supremacy.* N. Y., 1914.

b Beard, Charles A. *Supreme court and the constitution.* N. Y., 1912.

c Carson, Hampton L. *History of the supreme court of the United States, with biographies of all the chief and associate justices, 1790–1902.* 2 v. Philadelphia, 1902.

d Warren, Charles. *Supreme court in United States history.* 3 v. Boston, 1922. Rev. ed., 2 v., 1926.

a. Discussion of the origin and development of the American practice of judicial review of legislative acts; gives a brief statement of historical background; traces the main movements and the outstanding discussions or controversies concerning the exercise of this power. Important as a brief but useful study in constitutional history. Review, W. F. Dodd, *Amer. Pol. Sci. Rev.* 9:168, Feb. 1915. In this connection attention may be called to *b.* and *c.* and to (X758) Beveridge, *Life of Marshall.* Review of *b.,* W. F. Dodd, *A.H.R.* 18:380, Jan. 1913. *d.* Most exhaustive and authoritative treatment of the subject; by competent legal authority. Review, E. S. Corwin, *A.H.R.* 28:134, Oct. 1922.   ACMCL

X552a McLaughlin, Andrew C. *Courts, the constitution, and parties: studies in constitutional history and politics.* Chicago, 1912. [Power of a court to declare a law unconstitutional; Significance of political parties; Political parties and popular government; Social compact and constitutional construction; Written constitution in some of its historical aspects.]

b Warren, Charles. *Congress, the constitution, and the supreme court.* Boston, 1925.

a. Scholarly and interesting articles of solid value; by an eminent authority. Review, C. A. Beard, *A.H.R.* 18:378, Jan. 1913. *b.* Discusses whether congress or the supreme court should determine questions of constitutionality; conclusions support the supreme court. Review, A. T. Mason, *Amer. Pol. Sci. Rev.* 20:440, May 1926.   CEM

X553a Willoughby, Westel W. *Constitutional law of the United States.* 2 v. N. Y., 1910. Abridgement in 1 v., 1912.

b Evans, Lawrence B. *Leading cases on American constitutional law.* 1915. 2nd rev. ed., Chicago, 1925.

c Hall, James P. *Cases on constitutional law, selected from decisions of state and federal courts.* 1913. New ed., St. Paul, 1926. [American casebook series.]

a. Still the best systematic statement and commentary on the ruling law of the constitution. Review, T. R. Powell, *Pol. Sci. Quar.* 26:545, Sept. 1911. *b.* and *c.* Best recent casebooks.   LL

X554 Warren, Charles. *History of the American bar.* Boston, 1911. (Bibliographies.)

Nearly one-half of this informing volume is devoted to the colonial bar, the remainder to the federal bar and the state bars of New York and New England prior to the Civil War. The treatment is not merely biographical, but deals also with the environment of the bar and the development of the law. Review, R. Foster, *A.H.R.* 17:616, Apr. 1912.   LDW

X561a Merriam, Charles E. *History of American political theories.* N. Y. and London, 1903. Reprint, 1926. [Citizen's library of economics, politics, and sociology.] (Bibliography.)

    b ——— *American political ideas, studies in the development of American political thought, 1865–1917.* N. Y., 1920. (Bibliographical foot-notes.)

These two rather small volumes provide the only scholarly and well planned treatment of the main phases of American political theory. There is no attempt to build up a philosophy to the writer's own liking, no depreciation of theorists whose thinking is not the writer's own. Gives detached and scholarly analyses of the influential writers whose work, whether consciously so intended or not, expressed a particular school of thought or was influential in American history. Certain periods as well as specific writers are thus analyzed. Review of *a.*, W. W. Willoughby, *A.H.R.* 8:767, July 1903; of *b.*, *A.H.R.* 26:551, Apr. 1921.

ACMCL

X562a Ostrogorskiĭ, Moiseĭ Iakovlevich. *Democracy and the organization of political parties.* 2 v. N. Y. and London, 1902. Reprint, 1908. Tr. by F. Clarke from *La démocratie et l'organisation des partis politiques,* 2 v., Paris, 1903.

    b ——— *Democracy and the party system in the United States, a study in extra-constitutional government.* N. Y., 1919. (Bibliography.)

    c Macy, Jesse. *Party organization and machinery.* 1904. Later ed., N. Y., 1912. [American state series.] (Bibliographies.)

    d Lowell, Abbott Lawrence. *Public opinion and popular government.* 1913. New ed., N. Y. and London, 1926. [American citizen series.]

    e Ford, Henry J. *Rise and growth of American politics, a sketch of constitutional development.* N. Y. and London, 1898.

a. Scholarly analysis by a keen Russian scholar, a firm believer in democracy and in the great American experiment. V. 1. Study of democratic origins and organization in England. V. 2. Shows a remarkable understanding of the forces that have influenced American political development. Deftly sketches in clear bold strokes the rise of parties and the growth of party machinery. Then analyzes the results of the extra-constitutional system which makes for control by the professional politician and his plutocratic ally without giving the advantage of 'party government' in the European sense. Concludes that stereotyped parties have long outlived their principles and their usefulness; advocates single issue alignment and organization in their stead. Review, A. L. Lowell, *A.H.R.* 8:519, Apr. 1903. *b.* Very valuable condensation of *a* to suit the needs of the average intelligent reader; incorporates new data for the first decade of the twentieth century. Review, J. Macy, *Amer. Pol. Sci. Rev.* 5:472, Aug. 1911. *c.. d.,* and *e.* Good studies of their respective special subjects. Review of *c.*, C. E. Merriam, *Pol. Sci. Quar.* 20:545, Sept. 1905; of *d.*, J. M. Mathews, *Amer. Pol. Sci. Rev.* 8:307, May 1914; of *e.*, J. W. Perrin, *A.H.R.* 4:592, Apr. 1899.

ACCO

ECONOMIC AND SOCIAL HISTORY

X571a Bogart, Ernest L. *Economic history of the United States.* 1907. Rev. ed., N. Y. and London, 1922. [Longmans' commercial text-books.] (Bibliography.)

    b Van Metre, Thurman W. *Economic history of the United States.* N. Y., 1921. (Bibliography.)

c **Lippincott, Isaac.** *Economic development of the United States.* 1921. New ed., N. Y. and London, 1927. (Bibliographies.)

d **Faulkner, Harold U.** *American economic history.* N. Y. and London, 1924. [Harper's historical series.] (Bibliographies.)

e **Jennings, Walter W.** *History of economic progress in the United States.* N. Y., 1926. (Bibliography.)

Text-books for college use; will also interest the general reader. *a.* Description of the colonial period is brief; nearly half of the space is devoted to the period since 1860; generally well-balanced; for the most part, factual and objective; simple style. Little attempt at an analysis of the underlying factors or at a broad interpretation in terms of the organic development of the economic organization of the country; the economic life is seldom related to the broader political and social movements. Review, G. S. Callender, *A.H.R.* 19:156, Oct. 1913.   cww

b. Uses the chronological method in studying the economic forces that have shaped the history of the United States; reveals keenness of analytical power in relating historical development to economic forces. Review, A. C. Ford, *Amer. Econ. Rev.* 12:122, March 1922.   *c.* Comprehensive record of the economic development of the United States from 1492 to 1920; contains a wealth of factual material which is shot through with causal explanation. While the outline is chronological, the method used is topical. Review, V. S. Clark, *A.H.R.* 27:583, Apr. 1922.   *d.* Though the author approaches the subject as an historian, his interpretation is based upon a thorough mastery of economic principles. Well-proportioned, topical treatment in three periods, divided at 1789 and 1861, with emphasis on the last period. Review, A. P. James, *A.H.R.* 30:371, Jan. 1925.   *e.* 'An explanation of the economic life of the people' in thirty-five well-chosen topical chapters, arranged in five periods, separated by the years 1776, 1815, 1861, and 1900; emphasis on the last two. Review, W. MacDonald, *N. Y. Times Book Review,* 3, March 14, 1926.   COF

X576 Dewey, Davis R. *Financial history of the United States.* 1903. 10th rev. ed., N. Y. and London, 1928. [American citizen series.] (Bibliographies.)

Traces the evolution, from the colonial period to 1922, of such topics as money, loans, taxation, tariff, debts, banks and banking, panics, etc. The arrangement is mainly chronological, and is skilfully carried out to avoid repetition and to present in proper proportion the main facts. Sufficient political background is given as a setting for the subject, and there are careful analyses of congressional votes on important bills by geographical sections. The effect of wars on financial development is especially well elucidated. Review, J. C. Schwab, *A.H.R.* 9:166, Oct. 1903.   MWJ

X577a Stanwood, Edward. *American tariff controversies in the nineteenth century.* 2 v. Boston, 1903.

b **Taussig, Frank W.** *Tariff history of the United States.* 1888. 7th rev. ed., N. Y. and London, 1923.

c ——— *Some aspects of the tariff question.* Cambridge, Mass., 1915. [Harvard economic studies.]

a. Fairly detailed and careful study of the legislative history of the various tariff acts and the congressional debates thereon from 1789 down to and including the tariff of 1922; by an avowed, though not extreme believer in protection. There is no serious analysis of the economic effects of the tariff on particular industries; tends to exaggerate the influence of the tariff in periods of prosperity or depression. Review, C. H. Hull, *A.H.R.* 9:832, July 1904. For a scholarly analysis of the economic effects of the tariff, cf. *b* and *c*. Review of *c*, J. H. Gray, *A.H.R.* 21:371, Jan. 1916. CWW

X578a Noyes, Alexander D. *Forty years of American finance.* N. Y., 1909.

b Hibbard, Benjamin H. *History of the public land policies.* N. Y., 1924.

a. Best available account of the subject. Review, *Pol. Sci. Quar.* 24:566, Sept. 1909. *b.* General sketch of the historical development of the federal land policies. Of chief value for the period after 1860. Review, R. G. Wellington, *A.H.R.* 30:837, July 1925. MWJ

X581a Treat, Payson J. *National land system, 1785–1820.* N. Y., 1910. (Bibliography.)

b Ford, Amelia C. *Colonial precedents of our national land system as it existed in 1800.* Maaison, 1910. [Bulletin of the University of Wisconsin.] (Bibliography.)

c Ise, John. *United States forest policy.* New Haven, 1920. (Bibliography.)

d ———— *United States oil policy.* New Haven, 1926.

e Wellington, Raynor G. *Political and sectional influence of the public lands, 1828–1842.* Cambridge, Mass., 1914. (Bibliography.)

f Stephenson, George M. *Political history of the public lands, from 1840 to 1862, from pre-emption to homestead.* Boston, 1917. (Bibliography.)

a. Covers satisfactorily the early history of the land system; deals mainly with the laws and their workings. The important topics treated are the origin of the public domain and federal land system, the history of land sales, the credit system, the surveys, land grants for public and private purposes, and the influence of the land system on the westward movement. Review, B. H. Hibbard, *A.H.R.* 16:643, Apr. 1911. May be supplemented by *b., c,. d., e.,* and *f.,* which are necessary for a more extended view of the national land system and its influence. Review of *b.,* P. J. Treat, *A.H.R.* 16:394, Jan. 1911; of *c.,* C. A. Beard, *Nation* (N. Y.), 112:187, Feb. 2, 1921; of *e., A.H.R.* 20:434, Jan. 1915; of *f.,* R. G. Wellington, *A.H.R.* 24:301, Jan. 1919. MWJ

X582 Bidwell, Percy W., and **Falconer, John I.** *History of agriculture in the northern United States, 1620–1860.* Washington, 1925. [Carnegie Institution of Washington, Publications.] (Bibliography.)

Treats of evolution of labor-saving machinery and change from self-sufficiency and economy to era of specialized industry. Review, N. S. B. Gras, *A.H.R.* 31:329, Jan. 1926. MWJ

X583a Clark, Victor S. *History of manufactures in the United States, 1607–1860.* Washington, 1916. [Carnegie Institution of Washington, Publications.] (Extensive bibliography.)

b Tryon, Rolla M. *Household manufacturers in the United States, 1640–1860, a study in industrial history.* Chicago, 1917. (Excellent bibliography.)

c Cole, Arthur H. *American wool manufacture.* 2 v. Cambridge, Mass., 1926. (Bibliography.)

a. Thorough, comprehensive, interpretative history of American manufactures down to 1860. Of the twenty chapters, nine cover the colonial period and eleven the period between 1790 and 1860; each of these periods is treated separately under topical headings. The conclusions, in the main, supported, as they are, by scholarly method and a broader basis of fact than has heretofore been available, are well-balanced and the interpretations are keen and illuminating. Review, C. W. Wright, *A.H.R.* 22:384, Jan. 1917.   RMT
b. Best treatment of the subject; emphasis is historical rather than economic. Review, P. W. Bidwell, *A.H.R.* 23:177, Oct. 1917.   *c.* Excellent example for much-needed studies of other industries. Review, C. Day, *A.H.R.* 32:133, Oct. 1926.
                                                                GMD

X584a Commons, John R. and others, ed. *Documentary history of American industrial society.* 11 v. Cleveland, 1910–11. (Bibliography.)

   b ———, and others. *History of labour in the United States.* 2 v. N. Y., 1918. Reprint, 1921. (Extensive bibliography.)

   c Carlton, Frank T. *History and problems of organized labor.* Boston, 1911. (Bibliographies.)

   d Ely, Richard T. *Labor movement in America.* 1886. Rev. ed., N. Y., 1905.

a. Valuable sources published with appropriate introductions. V. 1–2. Especially important compilation of documents, edited by U. B. Phillips, on the plantation and the frontier, with particular attention to negro labor. V. 3–4. Labor conspiracy cases, 1806–1842. V. 5–10. Labor movement, 1820–1880. Review, J. W. Bryan, *A.H.R.* 15:876, July 1910; A. H. Stone, *A.H.R.* 16:137, Oct. 1910; G. E. Barnett, *A.H.R.* 16:359, Jan. 1911; 17:167, Oct. 1911; G. S. Callender, *A.H.R.* 19:93, Oct. 1913.   *b.* Not a detailed record of the many labor organizations and institutions, but rather an account of the movements, philosophies, and conditions. After an introduction by Professor Commons, the work is chronologically divided into six parts written by as many authors. Excellent coöperative work. Facts have been carefully checked. Review M. B. Hammond, *A.H.R.* 24:698, July 1919.   *c.* and *d.* Earlier brief treatises; still useful. Review of *c.*, *Nation* (N. Y.), 93:421, Nov. 2, 1911; of *d.*, *Nation* (N. Y.) 43:293, Oct. 7, 1886.
                                                                HAM

X585a Phillips, Ulrich B. *American negro slavery, a survey of the supply, employment, and control of negro labor as determined by the plantation régime.* N. Y. and London, 1918. (Bibliographical foot-notes.)

   b Locke, Mary S. *Anti-slavery in America, 1619–1808.* Boston, 1901. [Radcliffe College monographs.] (Bibliography.)

   c Adams, Alice D. *Neglected period of anti-slavery in America, 1808–1831.* Boston, 1908. [Radcliffe College monographs.] (Bibliography.)

   d Siebert, Wilbur H. *Underground railroad from slavery to freedom.* N. Y., 1898. (Bibliography.)

a. Best single volume on slavery; written by a southern scholar of considerable northern training and experience; based on the best material available; generally fair, accurate. Includes a brief history of the slave trade and the introduction of slavery into the colonies; development and spread of tobacco, cotton, and sugar culture; the domestic slave trade; plantation management, labor, life, and tendencies; economic aspects of slavery; town slaves, free negroes, slave crime, slave codes and their enforcement. Review, T. D. Jervey, *A.H.R.* 25:117, Oct. 1919. For the early history of the anti-slavery movement, cf. *b.* and *c.* For a later phase of the subject, cf. *d.* Review, S. T. Pickard, *A.H.R.* 4:557, Apr. 1899.   CSB

X591a Johnson, Emory R., and others. *History of domestic and foreign commerce of the United States.* 2 v. Washington, 1915. [Carnegie Institution of Washington, Publications.] (Extensive bibliography.)

   b Morison, Samuel E. *Maritime history of Massachusetts, 1783-1860.* Boston, 1921.

   a. In 1902 a coöperative economic history of the United States was undertaken by some of the leading economists of the country under the auspices of the Department of Economics and Sociology of the Carnegie Institution of Washington. This was the first of the twelve proposed divisional summaries to be published. Professor Johnson describes the development of American commerce to 1789; T. W. Van Metre, the internal commerce, the coastwise trade, and the fisheries; G. G. Huebner, the foreign trade since 1789; and D. S. Hanchett, government aid and commercial policy. Trustworthy and careful studies; based upon first-hand study of documentary material; present no new conclusions, but rather a convenient and satisfactory collection of materials. Review, J. F. Crowell, *A.H.R.* 22:382, Jan. 1917. *b.* Admirable monograph; adds new materials; illuminates the history of American shipping. Review, T. W. Van Metre, *A.H.R.* 27:600, Apr. 1922.   ELB

X592 Meyer, Balthasar H., ed. *History of transportation in the United States before 1860.* Washington, 1917. [Carnegie Institution of Washington, Publications.] (Extensive bibliography.)

   Essentially an elaborate summary of monographs by various writers within its field; this fact determines its character and scope. On the one hand, it is silent, for example, upon Mississippi River traffic after 1820; on the other, it is rich in details upon the construction and operation of many roads, river improvements, canals, and railroads throughout the eastern half of the United States from colonial times to the middle of the nineteenth century. Data concerning tolls and transportation rates, capitalization, costs, and financial results are particularly copious; generalizations are few but well considered. Review, St. G. L. Sioussat, *A.H.R.* 23:409, Jan. 1918.   UBP

X593 Dunbar, Seymour. *History of travel in America, showing the development of travel and transportation, . . . together with a narrative of the human experiences and changing social conditions that accompanied this economic conquest of the continent.* 4 v. Indianapolis, 1915. (Extensive bibliography.)

   More than four hundred reproductions of 'early engravings, original contemporaneous drawings, and broadsides' comprise the most valuable part of this work; but, unfortunately, the locations of the originals are not indicated. The text consists of a popular description of methods and conditions of travel and transportation from the beginnings of settlement to the construction of the first transcontinental railroad. The value of the work for reference use is impaired by the utter inadequacy of the index. Review, M. Farrand, *A.H.R.* 21:150, Oct. 1915.   SJB

CULTURAL HISTORY: GENERAL

X601a Eggleston, Edward. *Beginnings of a nation, a history of the source and rise of the earliest English settlements in America, with special reference to the life and character of the people.* N. Y., 1896.

b ———— *Transit of civilization from England to America in the seventeenth century.* N. Y., 1901.

Written as parts of what the author called 'A history of life in the United States,' a work which he did not live to finish. Based on a good deal of research; brilliant and interesting in style. *a.* Tells the story of early Virginia, Maryland, and New England. Review, H. L. Osgood, *A.H.R.* 2:528, Apr. 1897. *b.* Deals with the knowledge, beliefs, and habits of the early colonists; with folk-lore, tradition, education, and similar topics. Review, B. Wendell, *A.H.R.* 6:802, July 1901. Also cf. (X353) Weeden, *Economic and social history of New England, 1620-1789;* and (X381) Bruce, works on Virginia in the seventeenth century. Also cf. (X123, v. 9) C. M. Andrews, *Colonial folkways.*
ACMCL

X602 Schlesinger, Arthur M., and Fox, Dixon R., eds. *History of American life.* To be in 12 v. N. Y., 1927-30. [v. 1, H. I. Priestley, *Coming of the white man, 1492-1819;* v. 2, T. J. Wertenbaker, *First Americans, 1607-1690;* v. 3, J. T. Adams, *Provincial society, 1690-1763;* v. 6, C. R. Fish, *Rise of the common man, 1830-1850;* v. 8, A. Nevins, *Emergence of modern America.*] (Bibliographies.)

This series stresses the economic, social, and cultural phases of American history, largely to the exclusion of political, constitutional, diplomatic and military history. The volumes so far published are excellent within the limits set. Reviews, v. 1, I. J. Cox, *A.H.R.* 35:374, Jan. 1930; v. 2, R. H. Gabriel, *ibid.,* 33:661, Apr. 1928; v. 3, C. A. Herrick, *ibid.,* 33:665; v. 6, C. S. Boucher, *ibid.,* 33:893, July 1928; v. 8, R. E. Turner, *ibid.,* 33:675, Apr. 1928. MWJ

X603 Gabriel, Ralph H., ed. *Pageant of America, a pictorial history of the United States.* 15 v. New Haven, 1926 ff. [1, C. Wissler, C. L. Skinner, and W. Wood. *Adventurers in the wilderness;* 2, R. H. Gabriel, *Lure of the frontier;* 3, R. H. Gabriel, *Toilers of land and sea;* 4, M. Keir, *March of commerce;* 5, M. Keir, *Epic of industry;* 6, W. Wood, *Winning of freedom;* 7, W. Wood, *In defense of liberty;* 8, F. A. Ogg, *Builders of the republic;* 9, J. S. Bassett, *Makers of a new nation;* 10, L. A. Weigle, *American idealism;* 11, S. T. Williams, *American spirit in letters;* 12, F. J. Mather, Jr., C. R. Morey, and W. J. Henderson, *American spirit in art;* 13, T. F. Hamlin, *American spirit in architecture;* 14, O. S. Coad and E. Mims, Jr., *American stage;* 15, J. H. Krout, *Annals of American sports.*]

Each volume contains approximately six hundred and fifty illustrations and sixty thousand words of text. The selection of illustrations, maps, and facsimiles has been made by experts with every care for historical accuracy. Attention has also been given to providing readable as well as accurate narratives. The aim of the work as a whole is to present a comprehensive picture of the development of American life. Review, M. W. Jernegan, *A.H.R.* 32:326, Jan. 1927; 33:663, 918, Apr., July, 1928; 35:137, 879, Oct. 1929, July 1930. GMD

X606 Pollard, Albert F. *Factors in American history.* London and N. Y., 1925. [Watson lectures.]

Lectures, by an English historian, addressed to an English audience; synthetic survey of American life and history since Independence, chiefly political; sympathetic in tone; stresses English influences and parallels. Review, T. J. Wertenbaker, *A.H.R.* 31:578, Apr. 1926. GMD

X611 Nevins, Allan. *American social history as recorded by British travellers.* N. Y., 1923.

Well-chosen extracts from 1789 to 1922, arranged in four period groups, with good introductory chapters. Review, M. L. Bonham, Jr., *A.H.R.* 29:778, July 1924. GMD

CULTURAL HISTORY: RELIGION

X621 Rowe, Henry K. *History of religion in the United States.* N. Y., 1924.

Attempt, in brief compass, to interpret the significance of the religious element in American history. Review, C. B. Coleman, *A.H.R.* 30:829, July 1925.

For other works dealing with the religious history of the United States, cf. § F. GMD

X622 Schaff, Philip; Potter, Henry C.; Jackson, Samuel M., ed. *American church history series, consisting of a series of denominational histories published under the auspices of the American Society of Church History.* 13 v. N. Y., 1893–97. [1, H. K. Carroll, *Religious forces of the United States;* 2, A. H. Newman, *Baptist churches;* 3, W. Walker, *Congregational churches;* 4, H. E. Jacobs, *Evangelical Lutheran church;* 5, J. M. Buckley, *Methodists;* 6, R. E. Thompson, *Presbyterian churches;* 7, C. C. Tiffany, *Protestant Episcopal church;* 8, E. T. Corwin, *Reformed church, Dutch;* J. H. Dubbs, *Reformed church, German;* J. T. Hamilton, *Unitas fratrum, or Moravian church;* 9, T. O'Gorman, *Roman Catholic church;* 10, J. H. Allen, *Unitarian movement since the reformation;* R. Eddy, *Universalism;* 11, G. Alexander, *Methodist Episcopal church, South;* J. B. Scouller, *United Presbyterian church;* R. V. Foster, *Cumberland Presbyterian church;* T. C. Johnson, *Southern Presbyterian church;* 12, B. B. Tyler, *Disciples of Christ;* A. C. Thomas and R. H. Thomas, *Society of Friends in America;* D. Berger, *United Brethren in Christ;* S. P. Spreng, *Evangelical association;* S. M. Jackson, *Bibliography of American church history, 1820–1893;* 13, L. W. Bacon, *History of American Christianity.*] (Bibliographies.)

The plan of this series emphasizes the protracted denominational phase of American Christianity. The initial volume differentiates among some forty groups; recognizes over one hundred and forty denominations; presents statistical information largely drawn from the eleventh federal census, 1890. The seven volumes dealing with the larger denominations, while lacking all reference to recent events, remain the best histories of these bodies in America which have yet appeared. V. 6. Contains an especially valuable appendix of documents. Review, S. M. Jackson, *A.H.R.* 1:357, Jan. 1896. V. 13. Well-balanced account of the general religious history of America. WHA

CULTURAL HISTORY: EDUCATION, THOUGHT, PHILOSOPHY

X641 Cubberley, Elwood P. *Public education in the United States, a study and interpretation of American educational history.* Boston, 1919. (Bibliography.)

Text-book; best volume on the subject; emphasizes period since 1890. Also cf. (B641*b*) Monroe, *Cyclopedia of education.*   MWJ

X651 Riley, Isaac Woodbridge. *American thought from Puritanism to pragmatism and beyond.* 1915. 2nd rev. ed., N. Y., 1923. (Bibliography.)

Useful survey of American philosophical thought from colonial times to the present. Review, W. T. Bush, *Jour. of Philosophy, Psychology, and Scientific Methods,* 12:715, Dec. 23, 1915.   GMD

CULTURAL HISTORY: LITERATURE

X661a Bronson, Walter C. *Short history of American literature.* 1900. Rev. ed., Boston, 1919. (Bibliography.)

   b Cairns, William B. *History of American literature.* N. Y., 1912.

   c Boynton, Percy H. *History of American literature.* Boston, 1919. (Bibliographies.)

   d Pattee, Fred L. *History of American literature with a view to fundamental principles underlying its development.* Boston, 1896.

   e —— *American literature since 1870.* N. Y. 1915.

a., b., and *c.* Excellent brief accounts; written as text-books. Review of *b.,* *Nation* (N. Y.), 95:313, Oct. 3, 1912. *d.* and *e.* Somewhat more extended accounts, written on broader lines. Review of *e., Nation* (N. Y.), 102:77, Jan. 20, 1916; W. C. Bronson, *A.H.R.* 21:830, July 1916.   FEF

X662a Wendell, Barrett. *Literary history of America.* N. Y., 1900.

   b Parrington, Vernon L. *Main currents of American thought.* 2 v. N. Y., 1927.

a. Original and interesting brief account. Review, W. C. Bronson, *A.H.R.* 6:807, July 1901. *b.* This important work surveys biographically the rise of American thought, interprets the economic forces, political theories, and general cultural ideas. Review, *N. Y. Times,* May 1, 1927.   MWJ

X666 *Cambridge history of American literature.* Ed. by William P. Trent, John Erskine, Stuart P. Sherman, and Carl Van Doren. 4 v. N. Y. and London, 1917–21. (Extensive and valuable bibliographies.)

V. 1–2. Composed as a single chronological survey; as nearly unified in general scheme and treatment as a joint work of many specialists can be expected to become. The contributions are uneven in scale, method of treatment, and effectiveness, but taken as a whole they amount to a more comprehensive and substantial treatment than any other. V. 3–4. Mainly series of special essays, each being a complete survey of one phase of the cultural history of the United States. In them is to be found the chief contribution and the chief distinction of the work. Review, W. C. Bronson, *A.H.R.* 24:100, Oct. 1918; 24:702, July 1919; 26:812 July 1921.   PHB

X671a Tyler, Moses Coit. *History of American literature during the colonial time.* 1878. Rev. ed., 2 v., N. Y. and London, 1897. (Bibliographical foot-notes.)

    b —— *Literary history of the American revolution, 1763–1783.* 2 v. N. Y. and London, 1897. (Bibliographical foot-notes.)

Studies of marked value and interest, thorough in scholarship, felicitous in style, classic for their period. Review of *a., Nation* (N. Y.), 28:16, Jan. 2, 1879; of *b.,* P. L. Ford, *A.H.R.* 2:738, July 1897.   GMD

X676a Quinn, Arthur H. *History of the American drama from the beginning to the civil war.* N. Y. and London, 1923.

    b —— *History of the American drama, from the civil war to the present day.* 2 v. N. Y., 1928. (Bibliography.)

    c Hornblow, Arthur. *History of the theatre in America from its beginnings to the present time.* 2 v. Philadelphia and London, 1919.

a. Based on extensive research; treats with great thoroughness the evolution of the American drama. Review, F. L. Pattee, *A.H.R.* 29:773, July 1924. *b.* Continuation of *a.* Scholarly study. *c.* Chronicle rather than history of American playhouses, actors, and theatrical productions. Review, *A.H.R.* 25:554, Apr. 1920.
                    MWJ

CULTURAL HISTORY: ART

X681 Dunlap, William. *History of the rise and progress of the arts of design in the United States.* 1834. Rev. ed. by F. W. Bayley and C. E. Goodspeed, 3 v., Boston, 1918. (Bibliography.)

Standard work, to 1834; greatly enlarged in revised edition. Review, (London) *Times Literary Supplement,* 636, Dec. 19, 1918.   MWJ

X682 Isham, Samuel. *History of American painting.* N. Y. and London, 1905. [History of American art.] (Bibliography.)

Readable account, by an American artist; well-illustrated. Review, *Nation* (N. Y.), 81:508, Dec. 21, 1905.   GMD

X683 Taft, Lorado. *History of American sculpture.* 1903. Rev. ed., N. Y. and London, 1924. [History of American art.] (Bibliography.)

Standard account; by an American sculptor; fully illustrated. Review, *Nation* (N. Y.), 77:486, Dec. 17, 1903.   GMD

X684 Kimball, Fiske. *Domestic architecture of the American colonies and of the early republic.* N. Y., 1922.

Valuable treatment; based on extensive documentary researches. Review, N. M. Isham, *A.H.R.* 29:147, Oct. 1923.   GMD

X691 Elson, Louis C. *History of American music.* 1904. Rev. ed., N. Y. and London, 1915. [History of American art.] (Bibliography.)

Good introduction to the subject by a competent authority. Review, *Nation* (N. Y.), 78:276, Apr. 7, 1904.   GMD

BIOGRAPHIES

Extended lists of biographical and autobiographical works in American history will be found in (X1a) Channing, Hart, and Turner, *Guide to the study and reading of American history*. References to lives of the leading personalities in American history will be found by consulting the index under the person's name in (X1b) Larned, *Literature of American history*. For later publications, cf. section on 'Biography' in each annual volume of (X1d, e, and f) *Writings on American history*. See also (X25), (X26), (X28).

(X701) *American statesmen,* ed. by John T. Morse, Jr., 1882–1900, Standard library ed., 32 v., Boston, 1898–1900; second series, 8 v., Boston, 1905–17, contains lives of thirty-four statesmen from Franklin to McKinley, written by scholars and men of affairs. A series of twenty lives of similar excellence for the period of the slavery controversy and of the Civil War is (X702) *American crisis biographies,* ed. by Ellis P. Oberholtzer, 20 v., Philadelphia, 1904–15. Of more uneven character is the series of (X703) *True biographies and histories,* 13 v., Philadelphia, 1899–1919, which contains lives of eleven individuals from Penn to Grant. With a few exceptions made to round out the lists given earlier in this section, the following titles represent a selection from the more important works of individual biography or autobiography which have appeared since the beginning of the present century.

Colonial period: (X721) Kenneth B. Murdock, *Increase Mather, the foremost American Puritan,* Cambridge, 'Mass., 1925; (X722) Everett Kimball, *Public life of Joseph Dudley, a study of the colonial policy of the Stuarts in New England, 1660–1715,* N. Y. and London, 1911 [Harvard historical studies]; (X723) Bernard Faÿ, *Franklin: the apostle of modern times,* Boston, 1929.

Revolutionary period: (X731) Ralph V. Harlow, *Samuel Adams, promoter of the American Revolution: a study in psychology and politics,* N. Y., 1923; (X732) William Wirt Henry, *Patrick Henry: life, correspondence, and speeches,* 3 v., N. Y., 1891; (X733) Varnum L. Collins, *President Witherspoon,* 2 v., Princeton, 1925; (X734) Charlemagne Tower, *Marquis de la Fayette in the American Revolution,* 2 v., Philadelphia, 1894, reprint, 1926; (X735) Rupert Hughes, *George Washington,* 3 v., N. Y., 1925–1930; (X736) Gilbert Chinard, *Thomas Jefferson, the apostle of Americanism,* Boston, 1929; (X737) Moncure D. Conway, *Life of Thomas Paine,* 2 v., 1893, new ed., 1909; (X738) James A. James, *Life of George Rogers Clark,* Chicago, 1928.

National period, 1789–1829: (X751) William Maclay, *Journal, 1789–1791,* ed. by Edgar S. Maclay, N. Y., 1890, important for the proceedings of the first senate; (X752) William Plumer, *Memorandum of proceedings in the United States senate, 1803–1807,* ed. by Everett S. Brown, N. Y. 1923 [University of Michigan publications]; (X753) Claude G. Bowers, *Jefferson and Hamilton, the struggle for democracy in America,* Boston, 1925; (X754) Henry Adams, *Life of Albert Gallatin,* Philadelphia, 1879; (X755) William C. Bruce, *John Randolph of Roanoke, 1773–1833,* 2 v., N. Y., and London, 1922; (X756) Samuel E. Morison, *Life and letters of Harrison Gray Otis, federalist, 1765–1848,* 2 v., Boston, 1913; (X757) S. H. Wandell and M. Minnigerode, *Aaron Burr, a biography compiled from rare and in many cases unpublished sources,* 2 v., N. Y. and London, 1925; (X758) Gaillard Hunt, *Life of James Madison,* N. Y., 1902; (X759) Albert J. Beveridge, *Life of John Marshall,* 4 v., Boston,

1916–19; (X760) John Quincy Adams, *Memoirs, comprising portions of his diary from 1795 to 1848*, ed. by Charles Francis Adams, 12 v., Philadelphia, 1874–77; (X761) Samuel F. Bemis, ed., *American secretaries of state and their diplomacy*, 10 v., N. Y., 1927–29.

National period, 1829–1861: (X781) Thomas H. Benton, *Thirty years' view, or, a history of the working of the American government for thirty years, from 1820 to 1850*, 2 v., N. Y. and London, 1854–56, later reprints; (X782) John S. Bassett, *Life of Andrew Jackson*, 2 v., Garden City, N. Y., 1911; reprint, 1 v., 1925; (X783) Martin Van Buren, *Autobiography*, ed. by John C. Fitzpatrick, Washington, 1920 [American Historical Association, *Annual report*, 1918]; (X784) Lyon G. Tyler, *Letters and times of the Tylers*, Richmond and Williamsburg, Va., 1884–96; (X785) James K. Polk, *Diary*, ed. by Milo M. Quaife, 4 v., Chicago, 1910 [Chicago Historical Society, Collections]; (X786) Eugene I. McCormack, *James K. Polk, a political biography*, Berkeley, Cal., 1922; (X787) Paul R. Frothingham, *Edward Everett, orator and statesman*, Boston, 1925; (X788) Bernard C. Steiner, *Life of Roger Brooke Taney, chief justice of the United States supreme court*, Baltimore Md., 1922; (X789) Allen Johnson, *Stephen A. Douglas, a study in American politics*, N. Y., 1908; (X790) Ulrich B. Phillips, *Life of Robert Toombs*, N. Y., 1913; (X791) Allan Nevins, *Fremont: the West's greatest adventurer*, 2 v., N. Y., 1928; (X792) H. J. Eckenrode, *Jefferson Davis, president of the South*, N. Y., 1923.

Civil War and reconstruction, 1861–1877: (X811) John G. Nicolay and John Hay, *Abraham Lincoln, a history*, 10 v., N. Y., 1890, reprint, 1917; (X812) Godfrey R. B., Baron Charnwood, *Abraham Lincoln*, 1916, 3rd ed., London and N. Y., 1917 [Makers of the nineteenth century]; (X813) Nathaniel W. Stephenson, *Lincoln; an account of his personal life, especially of its springs of action as revealed and deepened by the ordeal of war*, Indianapolis, 1922; (X814) Carl Sandburg, *Abraham Lincoln, the prairie years*, 2 v., N. Y., 1926; (X814a) William E. Barton, *Life of Abraham Lincoln*, 2 v., N. Y., 1925; (X814b) Albert J. Beveridge, *Abraham Lincoln, 1809–1858*, 2 v., Boston, 1928; (X815) Frederic Bancroft, *Life of William H. Seward*, 2 v., N. Y. and London, 1900; (X816) Gideon Welles, *Diary*, ed. by Edgar T. Welles, 3 v., Boston, 1911, reprint, 1925; (X817) Sir Frederick Maurice, *Robert E. Lee, the soldier*, Boston, 1925; (X818) George F. R. Henderson, *Stonewall Jackson and the American civil war*, 2 v., London and N. Y., 1898; (X819) Ulysses S. Grant, *Personal memoirs*, 2 v., N. Y., 1885–86, 2nd ed., 1895; (X820) Ellis P. Oberholtzer, *Jay Cooke, financier of the civil war*, 2 v., Philadelphia, 1907; (X821) James G. Blaine, *Twenty years of Congress, from Lincoln to Garfield*, 2 v., Norwich, Conn., 1884–86.

National period, 1877–1901: (X841) Charles R. Williams, *Life of Rutherford Birchard Hayes*, 2 v., Boston, 1914; (X842) John Bigelow, *Life of Samuel J. Tilden*, 2 v., N. Y. and London, 1895; (X843) Theodore C. Smith, *Life and letters of James Abram Garfield*, 2 v., New Haven, 1925; (X844) Grover Cleveland, *Presidential problems*, N. Y., 1904; (X845) Robert M. McElroy, *Grover Cleveland, the man and the statesman*, 2 v., N. Y. and London, 1923; (X846) John Sherman, *Recollections of forty years in the house, senate, and cabinet, an autobiography*, 2 v., Chicago and London, 1895; (X847) George F. Hoar, *Autobiography of seventy years*, 2 v., N. Y., 1903; (X848) Louis A. Coolidge, *An old fashioned senator, Orville H. Platt*, N. Y. and London, 1910; (X849) Carl Schurz, *Reminiscences*, 3 v., N. Y., 1907–08; (X850) DeAlva S. Alexander, *Four famous New Yorkers: the political careers of Cleveland, Platt,*

Hill, and Roosevelt, N. Y., 1923 [Political History of the State of New York, v. 4]; (X851) Thomas C. Platt, *Autobiography,* ed. by Louis J. Lang, N. Y., 1910; (X852) Herbert D. Croly, *Marcus Alonzo Hanna, his life and work,* N. Y., 1912; (X853) Andrew D. White, *Autobiography,* 2 v., N. Y., 1905; (X854) Royal Cortissoz, *Life of Whitelaw Reid,* 2 v., N. Y., 1921; (X855) Allen S. Will, *Life of Cardinal Gibbons, archbishop of Baltimore,* 2 v., N. Y., 1922; (X856) Wm. Jennings Bryan, *Memoirs,* Philadelphia, 1925; (X857) M. R. Werner, *Bryan,* N. Y., 1929; (X858) W. R. Thayer, *John Hay,* 2 v. Boston, 1915.

National period, 1901–1925: (X871) Theodore Roosevelt *Autobiography,* N. Y., 1913; (X872) Joseph B. Bishop, *Theodore Roosevelt and his time shown in his own letters,* 2 v., N. Y., 1920; (X873) *Selections from the correspondence of Theodore Roosevelt and Henry Cabot Lodge, 1884–1918,* 2 v., N. Y. and London, 1925; (X874) William Lawrence, *Henry Cabot Lodge, a biographical sketch,* Boston, 1925; (X875) William E. Dodd, *Woodrow Wilson and his work,* Garden City, N. Y., 1920; (X876) David Lawrence, *True story of Woodrow Wilson,* N. Y., 1924; (X877) William Allen White, *Woodrow Wilson,* Boston, 1924; (X878) James Kerney, *Political education of Woodrow Wilson,* N. Y., 1926; (X879) Burton J. Hendrick, *Life and letters of Walter Hines Page,* 3 v., Garden City, N. Y., 1922–25. Cf. (J444) Baker, *Woodrow Wilson.*   MWJ

GOVERNMENT PUBLICATIONS

The acts and resolutions of Congress, treaties, and executive proclamations are published in (X901) *Statutes at large,* v. 1–43, Washington, 1845–1925, of which v. 1–8, issued 1845–46, contain the acts from 1789 to 1845, and v. 9–43, containing the acts since 1845, have been issued currently since 1851. The treaties are collected in convenient form in (X902) *Treaties, conventions, international acts, protocols, and agreements between the United States of America and other powers, 1776–1909,* ed. by William M. Malloy, 2 v., Washington, 1910; v. 3, *1910–1923,* Washington, 1923. (I508*b*)

The messages of the presidents and some other executive documents, are collected in (X903) *Compilation of the messages and papers of the presidents, 1789–1897,* ed. by James D. Richardson, 10 v., Washington, 1896–99. Though originally issued by authority of congress, this work has passed into private hands and is frequently reissued with continuations to date. An edition complete to 1924 was issued in 20 v., N. Y., 1924.

Congressional debates may be consulted in the following series: (X904*a*) *Debates and proceedings in the congress of the United States,* usually cited by its half-title, *Annals of Congress* [*1789–1824*], 42 v., Washington, 1834–56; (X904*b*) *Register of debates in congress* [*1824–1837*], 14 v. in 29, Washington, 1825–37; (X904*c*) *Congressional globe* [*1833–1873*], 46 v. in 111, Washington, 1834–73; (X904*d*) *Congressional record* [*1873 ff.*], Washington, 1874 ff., of which most volumes are issued in several parts, v. 69 concludes in 1925; (X905) *American state papers: documents, legislative and executive, of the congress of the United States,* 38 v., Washington, 1832–61, contains public documents, arranged in ten classes, extending in the several classes to dates between 1823 and 1838. The regular congressional series of (X906) *Public documents,* Washington, 1817 ff., begins with the fifteenth congress in 1817, and at the close of the sixty-eighth congress in 1925, had reached serial number 8521.

In consulting this vast mass of materials and additional public documents issued by the several executive departments, or under other auspices, the student will be aided by (X907) *Checklist of United States public documents, 1789–1909,* v. 1, *Lists of congressional and departmental publications,* 3rd ed., by Superintendent of Documents, Washington, 1911; (X908a) *Descriptive catalogue of the government publications of the United States, September 5, 1774–March 4, 1881,* ed. by Benjamin Perley Poore, Washington, 1885; (X908b) *Comprehensive index to the publications of the United States government, 1881–1893,* ed. by John G. Ames, 2 v., Washington, 1905; (X908c) *Catalogue of the public documents,* ed. by Superintendent of Documents, v. 1–13, 1893–1917, Washington, 1896–1922, which is continued by (X908d) *Document index* for each session, and by (X908e) *Monthly catalogue.*

The decisions and opinions of the supreme court of the United States are published under the authority of the court itself in (X909) *United States reports,* v. 1–268, 1790–1925, Philadelphia and Washington, 1790–1926, of which v. 1–90, to 1874, are usually cited by the names of their reporters, Dallas, v. 1–4; Cranch, v. 5–13; Wheaton, v. 14–25; Peters, v. 26–41; Howard, v. 42–65; Black, v. 66–67; Wallace, v. 68–90.

For the history of the Civil War, the government has issued an enormous compilation (X916) *Official records of the Union and Confederate armies,* 130 v., Washington, 1880–1901, and (X917) *Official records of the Union and Confederate navies,* 30 v., Washington, 1894–1922.

UNIVERSITY AND SOCIETY PUBLICATIONS

The American Historical Association, founded in 1884, includes in its membership most American teachers and writers of history. A large amount of valuable monographs, catalogues of documentary collections, publications of sources, and other materials is to be found in its (X921a) *Papers,* 5 v., N. Y. and London, 1885–91, and in its (X921b) *Annual reports, 1889 ff.,* Washington, 1890 ff. The *Annual report, 1912,* 305–339, contains (X921c) *Classified list of publications of the American Historical Association, 1884–1912,* Washington, 1914; and the *Annual report, 1914,* v. 2, contains (X921d) *General index to papers and annual reports of the American Historical Association, 1884–1914,* Washington, 1918, compiled by David M. Matteson, which are indispensable aids to the utilization of these valuable materials. The organ of the association is (B941f) *American historical review.*

For a list of numerous local and special historical societies in the United States and of their publications, cf. (X1c) Griffin, *Bibliography of American historical societies.*

(X926) *Publications* of the Carnegie Institution of Washington contain a valuable series of guides to archival materials in Washington (cf. X4a), London, Paris, and other places relating to the history of the United States, prepared by its Department of Historical Research. The *Publications* also include the contributions to the economic history of the United States (cf. X2b, 582, 583a, 591a, 592), prepared by the Institution's Department of Economics and Sociology, and some other works useful to the student of American history, notably (X926a) Adelaide R. Hasse, *Index to United States documents relating to foreign affairs, 1828–1861,* 3 v., Washington, 1914–21.

Several of the leading universities in the United States publish series of monographs devoted, in whole or in part, to history, of which the following deserve special mention: (X931) *Johns Hopkins University studies in historical and political science,* Baltimore, 1883 ff., relating especially to the history of the United States, colonial and southern; (X932) *Columbia University studies in history, economics, and public law,* N. Y., 1891 ff., relating only in a minor degree to the United States, for which it deals mainly with economic and sectional matters; (X933) *Harvard historical studies,* N. Y. and London, 1896–1911, Cambridge, Mass. 1912 ff., in which the volumes relating to the United States are in many cases concerned with administrative subjects; (X934) *University of California publications in history,* Berkeley, Cal., 1911 ff., devoted primarily to the history of the Pacific coast and of the former Spanish possessions in America.

PERIODICALS

In addition to (B941f1) *American historical review,* (B941f4) *Historical outlook,* (B941h1) *Political science quarterly,* (B941h3) *American political science review,* and other periodicals listed in § B, which, though general in character, give liberal attention to the history of the United States, there are older periodicals devoted to the general field of American history, notably (X941) *Historical magazine and notes and queries concerning the antiquities, history, and biography of America,* ed. by H. B. Dawson and others, 23 v., Boston, 1857–75, and (X942) *Magazine of American history,* v. 1–30, N. Y., 1877–93, v. 30–46, Mount Vernon, N. Y., 1901–17. Of great value to the historian is also (X943) *Niles weekly register* (after 1837, *Niles' national register*), 76 v., Baltimore, 1811–49.

Among periodicals devoted primarily to special localities or subjects, as indicated by their respective titles, are: (X951) *Mississippi Valley historical review,* quarterly, Cedar Rapids, Iowa, 1914 ff.; (X952) *Journal of negro history,* quarterly, Washington, 1916 ff.; (X953) *American Catholic historical researches,* 29 v. in 36, Pittsburg and Philadelphia, 1884–1912; (X954) *Catholic historical review, for the study of the church history of the United States,* quarterly, Washington, 1915 ff.; (X955) *New England quarterly: an historical review of New England life and letters,* Portland, Me., 1928 ff.

There are also numerous historical magazines published under various state, association, and local auspices. For a list of these and of other American historical periodicals, cf. Augustus H. Shearer, 'American historical periodicals.' American Historical Association, *Annual report, 1916,* 1:469–484.   MWJ

SECTION Y

HISPANIC AMERICA

Editor

ISAAC JOSLIN COX

Professor of History, Northwestern University

CONTENTS

INTRODUCTION

While works dealing with colonization in general and with exploring activities carried on by the Spaniards and the Portuguese appear in § K, general works on the colonizing enterprises of Spain and Portugal are allocated to this section, as well as publications dealing with the history of the several nations which have come into existence in Central and South America. The selection of titles has been, in general, confined to the best books in English, to the most important collections of documents, and to the leading secondary works in Spanish and Portuguese.

Though all the Hispanic American countries have extensive published collections of sources and voluminous histories dealing with the colonial period and the Wars of Independence, not many of their annalists have ventured to sift the mass of polemical and partisan writings, of government reports, and of press discussion that have burdened the years of national existence. Consequently the number of citations of national histories is limited. Even those mentioned seldom bring the account down to the present generation.

Books of travel and descriptive accounts of parts of Hispanic America are legion. Of the older ones those of outstanding character have been listed because of their observations on political conditions, ethnography, and pre-Columbian culture. Of the later ones there have been selected only a very few of unusual value for the insight which they afford into political and social affairs.

Special notice should be taken of the inclusion in this section of works on the Spanish occupancy of territories now within the United States, and on the Monroe Doctrine, Pan-Americanism, and the relations between the United States and its southern neighbors. Various books listed in § X contain some materials relevant to the subject of this section. Special reference should be made to works mentioned in § N for the European background for Hispanic American history.

BIBLIOGRAPHY

Y1a Goldsmith, Peter H. *Brief bibliography of books in English, Spanish, and Portuguese, relating to the republics commonly called Latin America.* N. Y., 1915.

b Keniston, Hayward. *List of works for the study of Hispanic-American history.* N. Y., 1920. [Hispanic Society of America, Hispanic American series.]

c Hoskins, Halford L. *Guide to Latin-American history.* Boston, 1922.

d Jones, Cecil Knight. *Hispanic American bibliographies, including collective biographies, histories of literature, and selected general works.* Hispanic American Historical Review, 3:414–442, 603–634; 4:126–156, 297–324, 522–552, 783–813, Aug. 1920–Nov. 1921; also issued separately, Baltimore, 1922.

Brief but useful general works. *a.* Lists about 200 books of miscellaneous character, with critical estimate of each. *b.* Very useful for the period prior to 1830. *c.* Classified lists of titles and a useful syllabus outline with topical references. *d.* Includes for some countries references to government documents.

To supplement these brief guides and the special bibliographies enumerated in the following items, the student must refer to the library catalogues and to the lists issued by publishers and book dealers, notably by Casa Editorial América of Rufino Blanco-Fombona, Madrid. For specific regions and periods and for topics that touch upon the relations of the United States with Hispanic America, the student should consult book lists prepared by Philip Lee Phillips and others for the Library of Congress, the Pan-American Union, and the New York Public Library. The publications of the United States Government contain important documentary material relating to Mexico, Central America, the West Indies, and occasionally to the South American countries, which may be traced through references in the books treated in this section. Reference should be made to the bibliographies for their respective fields contained in the various comprehensive histories and monographs listed in this section. (Y996) *Hispanic American historical review* contains lists and reviews of books in the field which appeared since its publication.   IJC

Y2a Medina, José T. *Biblioteca hispano-americana, 1493–1810.* 7 v. Santiago de Chile, 1898–1907.

b Weber, Friedrich. *Beiträge zur Charakteristik der älteren Geschichtsschreiber über Spanisch-Amerika, eine biographisch-bibliographische Skizze.* Leipzig, 1911. [Beiträge zur Kultur- und Universalgeschichte.]

c *El libro y el pueblo, revista mensual bibliografica, órgano del Departmento de Bibliotecas de la Secretaria de Educación de Mexico.* Mexico, 1922 ff.

a. Most important general bibliography for Hispanic American history in the colonial period. *b.* Gives useful information concerning the personalities of early writers in the field of Spanish American history and archeology. *c.* A periodical valuable for current bibliography not only of Mexico, but of Hispanic America in general. IJC

Y3a Sánchez, Manuel Segundo. *Bibliografía venezolanista, contribucion al conocimiento de los libros extranjeros relativos a Venezuela y sus grandes hombres.* Caracas, 1914.

b René-Moreno, Gabriel. *Biblioteca boliviana.* Santiago de Chile, 1879; supplement for 1879–99, 1900; supplement for 1900–08, 1908; supplement for 1602–1879, 1900.

c ——— *Biblioteca peruana.* 2 v. Santiago de Chile, 1896.

d Posada, Eduardo. *Bibliografía bogotana.* V. 1. Bogotá, 1917. [Biblioteca de historia nacional, v. 16.]

The more important national bibliographies for Spanish American states. *a., b.,* and *c.* Fairly complete to the dates of publication for Venezuela, Chile, and Peru. *d.* Chiefly valuable for Colombian history from 1808 to 1820. IJC

Y4a Ramiz Galvão, Benjamin F. *Catalogo da exposição de historia do Brazil realizada pela Bibliotheca Nacional do Rio Janeiro a 2 de Dezembro de 1881.* 2 v. Rio de Janeiro, 1881. *Supplemento,* 1883.

b Sacramento Blake, Augusto V. A. do. *Diccionario bibliographico brazileiro.* 7 v. Rio de Janeiro, 1883–1902.

Best general bibliographies for Brazil. *a.* Now largely superseded by *b.* IJC

Y5a Salas, Carlos I. *Bibliografía del General Don José de San Martin y de la emancipación sudamericana.* 5 v. in 3. Buenos Aires, 1910. *Errores y omisiones,* Buenos Aires, 1912.

b Torres Lanzas, Pedro. *Independencia de América, fuentes para su estudio, catalogo de documentos conservados en el Archivo General de Indias de Sevilla.* Primera serie, 6 v., Madrid, 1912; segunda serie, v. 1, Sevilla, 1924.

a. Perhaps the most complete bibliography of printed works on the Wars of Independence in Hispanic America. Items arranged in alphabetical order; name and place index for each volume. *b.* A calendar rather than a catalogue; some items are complete enough to serve in lieu of the originals. V. 6 contains complete biographical and geographical index of the series. IJC

Y6a Bolton, Herbert E. *Guide to materials for the history of the United States in the principal archives of Mexico.* Washington, 1913. [Carnegie Institution of Washington, Publication no. 163.]

b Shepherd, William R. *Guide to materials for the history of the United States in Spanish archives, Simancas, the Archivo Historico Nacional, and Seville,* Washington, 1907. [Carnegie Institution of Washington, Publication no. 91.] (General bibliography.)

c Robertson, James A. *List of documents in Spanish archives relating to the history of the United States which have been printed or of which transcripts are preserved in American libraries.* Washington, 1910. [Carnegie Institution of Washington, Publication no. 124.] (Bibliography.)

d Hill, Roscoe R. *Descriptive catalogue of the documents relating to the history of the United States in the Papeles procedentes de Cuba deposited in the Archivo General de Indias at Seville.* Washington, 1916. [Carnegie Institution of Washington, Publication no. 234.] (Bibliography.)

e Pérez, Luis Marino. *Guide to the materials for American history in Cuban archives.* Washington, 1907. [Carnegie Institution of Washington, Publication no. 83.]

f Chapman, Charles E. *Catalogue of materials in the Archivo General de Indias for the history of the Pacific Coast and the American Southwest.* Berkeley, 1919. [University of California, Publications in history.]

These guides to certain archives and archival materials also furnish considerable general bibliographical data. *f.* Calendars over six thousand documents relating to explorations and colonization in the areas indicated. Review, R. R. Hill, *A.H.R.* 25:139, Oct. 1919.　　　　　　　　　　　IJC

Library collections.—The libraries of the leading universities of California and Texas have notable collections of local interest. The Bancroft Library of the University of California has long been known and appreciated. The Braziliana in Leland Stanford, Jr., University Library number some ten thousand volumes. The University of Texas has recently acquired the library of the famous Mexican scholar and bibliophile, Genaro Garcia—an unrivalled collection for Mexico, with much rare material for Hispanic America in general and for Spain. The published works in these libraries and the wealth of manuscript material available in Austin and in Berkeley make visits to these places necessary for the serious student of the history of the regions once included in the viceroyalty of New Spain.

For the Middle West, Chicago is the best working center. The Ayer collection of the Newberry Library of Chicago is especially good for manuscript materials and for rare and costly books relating to the colonial history of Mexico and to the aborigines. The John Crerar Library, the University of Chicago, and Northwestern University have important general collections on Hispanic America. The University of Illinois and the University of Michigan also have good collections.

The Library of Congress is naturally the repository for official publications of the several countries and for recent works relating to the field, but its general collections are also very complete. The Catholic University of Washington has recently come into possession of the library of the noted Brazilian scholar, Oliveira Lima, a collection of some thirty thousand volumes, easily the best in the country on Brazil. A third extensive collection in Washington is the Columbus Memorial Library.

The several larger libraries in Baltimore and Philadelphia contain fair collections on Hispanic America, but far better are those of Harvard University (legal works and Montt collection for Chile); Yale University (Bingham and Wagner collections); the American Antiquarian Society at Worcester (especially for

Mexico) ; the John Carter Brown Library at Providence (publications before 1800) ; Brown University Library (Church collection of 3500 v.) ; and Cornell University (H. H. Smith collection).

New York City is richly favored with the collections of Columbia University, of the New York Public Library (especially for Mexico), and above all, of the munificently endowed Hispanic Society of America, with its numerous maps manuscripts, and early books.

AHS

ENCYCLOPEDIAS AND WORKS OF REFERENCE

The standard works of reference for Hispanic America are (N21a) *Diccionario enciclopédico Hispano-Americano* and (N21b) *Enciclopedia universal ilustrada Europeo-Americana*.

Y21a Koebel, William H., ed. *Anglo-South American handbook, incorporating Mexico and Central America, 1921.* London, 1921.

b —— *Anglo-South American handbook, 1922: including Central America, Mexico, and Cuba.* London, 1922.

Compilations of current data, geographical, historical, political, financial, and commercial.

GMD

GEOGRAPHY AND ATLASES

Y41a Keane, Augustus H. *Central and South America.* Ed. by Sir Clements R. Markham, 1901. 2nd rev. ed., London, 1909–11. [1, *South America;* 2, *Central America and West Indies.*] [Stanford's compendium of geography and travel.]

b Bowman, Isaiah. *South America, a geography reader.* Chicago, 1915. [Lands and peoples series.]

c Shanahan, E. W. *South America: an economical and regional geography* London, 1927. (Bibliography.)

a. Gives information on the physical features, natural resources, and people, in an encyclopedic style with many maps and illustrations. *b.* Intended as a school text but serviceable to the general reader; much information attractively presented.

LFU

c. A survey based largely on economic interpretation. Review, (London) *Times Lit. Suppl.* 26:134, Mch. 3, 1927.

SBF

Y42 General Drafting Co., Inc. *Atlas América latina.* N. Y., 1919.

Contains numerous maps on a sufficiently large scale, together with statistical and other material of commercial nature printed in English, Spanish, and Portuguese in parallel columns.

GMD

ETHNOGRAPHY

Y51 Brinton, Daniel G. *American race, a linguistic classification and ethnographic description of the native tribes of North and South America.* N. Y., 1891. (Bibliographical foot-notes.)

About two thirds of the volume are devoted to a comprehensive treatment of aboriginal culture in Hispanic-America. The author attempts also to show the relationships between the native groups and their extent upon the arrival of the Europeans. A scholarly work, carefully documented; the best on the subject.

MWW

Y52a Joyce, Thomas A. *South American archaeology, an introduction to the archaeology of the South American continent with special reference to the early history of Peru.* London and N. Y., 1912.

   b ——— *Mexican archaeology, an introduction to the archaeology of the Mexican and Mayan civilizations of pre-Spanish America.* London and N. Y., 1914. [Handbooks to ancient civilizations.]

   c ——— *Central American and West Indian archaeology, being an introduction to the archaeology of the states of Nicaragua, Costa Rica, Panama, and the West Indies.* London and N. Y., 1916. (Critical bibliography.)

Contain little that is new, but furnish readable and scholarly summaries of the results of the labors of earlier scholars whose writings are not easily accessible. The influence of geography and the location of the aboriginal groups with relation to one another receive considerable attention. Many excellent illustrations. About half of *b.* is devoted to Mayan culture. Review of *a.*, W. C. Farabee, *A.H.R.* 18:116, Oct. 1912; of *b.*, *Dial*, 57:303, Oct. 16, 1914; of *c.*, *Literary Digest*, 55:39, Nov. 17, 1917.

For other works containing material on ethnography and related topics, cf. (Y201, 202, 203, 204, 241).

MWW

Y53a Wissler, Clark. *American Indian, an introduction to the anthropology of the New World.* 1917. 2nd ed., N. Y., 1922. (Bibliography.)

   b Church, George E. *Aborigines of South America.* Ed. by Sir Clements R. Markham. London, 1912.

a. Best general account of the aborigines of North and South America, with classifications based on cultural and physical characteristics as well as linguistic connections. *b.* Devoted to the less advanced tribes; based mainly on personal experience and study during a long residence in South America; many of the author's conclusions are now untenable.

IJC

COLLECTIONS OF SOURCES: ARCHIVE PUBLICATIONS

Y71a *Colección de documentos inéditos, relativos al descubrimiento, conquista, y organización de las antiguas posesiones españolas de América y Oceanía, sacados de los Archivos del Reino, y muy especialmente de las Indias.* Ed. by Joaquin F. Pacheco, Francisco de Cárdenas, and Luis Torres de Mendoza. 42 v. Madrid, 1864–84. [Colección de documentos inéditos de Indias.]

   b *Colección de documentos inéditos relativos al descubrimiento, conquista, y organización de las antiguas posesiones españolas de ultramar.* Segunda series. 19 v. Madrid, 1885–1926. [Colección de documentos inéditos de ultramar.]

   c *Colección de documentos inéditos pera la historia de Ibero-América.* 3 v. Madrid, 1927 ff.

a. Continued by *b.* These two series are composed of documents drawn from that portion of the Archivo General known as the Patronato Real. The documents were originally selected by the historian, Juan Bautista Muñóz, as the most valuable of the archive for the period of the early conquest, but the portion printed does not always constitute the most valuable part of the collection and comprises only a small fraction of the material available for the period. Cf. (Y491a) Chapman, *Founding of Spanish California*, 438. *c.* Supplements *a* and *b.*

IJC

Y72 *Collecçao de monumentos ineditos para a historia das conquistas dos Portuguezes em Africa, Asia, e America.* Ed. by Rodrigo J. de Lima Felner. 16 v. Lisboa, 1858–98. [Academia Real das Sciencias.]

The series that for the Portuguese corresponds most nearly in character to **Y71.** IJC

Y73 *Recopilación de leyes de los reinos de las Indias.* 1st ed., 4 v., Madrid, 1681; 2nd ed., 4 v., Madrid, 1754; 3rd ed., 4 v., Madrid, 1774; 4th ed., 3 v., Madrid, 1791; 5th ed., 2 v., Madrid, 1841.

Standard collection, indispensable for the legal study of Spanish colonization.

IJC

Y74 *Memorias de los vireyes que han gobernado el Perú durante el tiempo del coloniaje español.* Ed. by M. A. Fuentes. 6 v. Lima, 1859.

General accounts of their respective administrations prepared by ten viceroys of Peru between 1609 and 1796; an excellent source for administrative details.

IJC

Y75a Calvo, Carlos, ed. *Colección completa de los tratados . . . de todos los estados de la América Latina.* 11 v. Paris, 1862–69. V. 1–11 have title,. *América Latina, colección historica completa . . .* Cf. (I508m).

b Aranda, Ricardo, ed. *República del Perú, colección de los tratados, convenciones, capitulaciones, armisticios, y otros actos diplomaticos y politicos celebrados desde la independencia hasta el dia, precedida de una introducción que comprende la época colonial.* 14 v. in 13, Lima, 1890–1911.

a. V. 1–6. Give treaties of the colonial period. V. 7–10. Contain the geographical memoir of Don Andres de Oyarvide, who directed the reconnaissance made in 1784–1791 to determine the demarcation line between the Spanish and Portuguese possessions in South America, under the treaty of 1777. *b.* These documents cover Peru's relations with other countries during the nineteenth century, with a brief introduction for the colonial period, and form a useful contribution to diplomatic relations among American nations. Similar publications have been issued in several other countries of Hispanic America. IJC

Y76a *Colección de documentos relativos a la vida publica del Libertador de Colombia y de Peru, Simón Bolívar.* 22 v. Caracas, 1826–33.

b Blanco, José F. and **Azpurúa, Ramón,** ed. *Documentos para la historia de la vida pública del Libertador de Colombia, Perú, y Bolivia.* 14 v. Caracas, 1875–78.

c O'Leary, Daniel F. *Memorias del General O'Leary.* Ed. by Simon B. O'Leary. 32 v. Caracas, 1879–88.

d Lecuna, Vicente, ed. *Papeles de Bolívar.* Caracas, 1917.

e Blanco-Fombona, Rufino, ed. *Cartas de Bolívar, 1823, 1824, 1825, con un apéndice que contiene cartas de 1801 a 1822.* Madrid, 1921.

a. Published under the direction of three editors, whose work was then taken over by General José Felix Blanco, an active participant in the struggle for independence, with the intention of republishing it in an enlarged edition. Official duties and the lack of funds kept him from his purpose and in 1864 he turned the task over to Ramón Azpurúa, 'the original inspiration of the project,' with injunction to publish as soon as possible. Difficulties accumulated, however, and it was not till 1875 that the completed project, *b.*, was turned over to the nation and publication accomplished under the patronage of President Antonio Guzmán Blanco. This 'Illustrious American and Regenerator' devised for himself many notable monuments but none more useful than this collection, which, as is fitting, commonly bears the name of Azpurúa. It is supplemented by *c.*, or rather over-shadowed by that notable collection of Bolivar's personal correspondence. O'Leary, after his arrival in Venezuela in 1818, was the Liberator's chief of staff and, despite injunctions to the contrary, carefully preserved the mass of corre-spondence that came into his possession, and his son published it, also under the patronage of Guzmán Blanco. V. *28, Apendice* (sometimes numbered v. *29*). Exceedingly scarce, since the greater part of the edition was destroyed at the order of the distinguished patron. Some of the volumes are being reprinted in the *Biblioteca Ayacucho,* Madrid, 1915 ff., under the editorship of R. Blanco-Fombona. Also cf. (Y3*a*) Segundo Sanchez, *Bibliografía venezolanista,* 255–267. *d.* and *e.* Contain some new material, supplemented by selections from *a., b.,* and *c.* For additional documentary publications on the Wars of Independence, cf. (Y77, 78, 83*c*, 87, 97).   IJC

Y77a *Documentos del Archivo de San Martín.* 12 v. Buenos Aires, 1910–11.

  b *Documentos del archivo de Belgrano.* 6 v. Buenos Aires, 1913–16.

  c *Documentos del archivo de Pueyrredón.* 4 v. Buenos Aires, 1912.

  d Carranza, Adolfo P., ed. *San Martín, su correspondencia, 1823–1850.* 3rd ed., Buenos Aires, 1911. [Museo Histórico Nacional.]

  a., b., and *c.* Documents selected from the Museo Mitre in Buenos Aires and published under its auspices. *d.* Letters exchanged by San Martín with his intimate friends in the period following his retirement.   IJC

Y78 *Archivo Santander.* Ed. by Ernesto Restrepo Tirado. 14 v. Bogotá, 1913–18. [Academia de la Historia.]

Definitive edition of Santander's correspondence to June, 1826. Made up chiefly of letters to and from Santander, forming part of the Santander archive, a collection until lately in possession of his descendants but now under the control of the Colombian government. While the correspondence proper extends only from 1813 to 1826, there are biographical fragments and other data concerning Santander from 1792 to 1837. The material from the archive is supplemented from (Y76*c*) O'Leary and other sources.   IJC

Y79 Manning, William R., ed. *Diplomatic correspondence of the United States concerning the independence of the Latin-American nations.* 3 v., N. Y. and London, 1925. [Carnegie Endowment for International Peace.]

Important collection. Materials are classified by the countries from which the correspondence originated, and then arranged chronologically.   GMD

Y81a *Documentos para la historia argentina.* 14 v. Buenos Aires, 1913–21. [Buenos Aires, Universidad Nacional, Facultad de Filosofía y Letras, Sección de Historia.]

  b *Documentos relativos á los antecedentes de la independencia de la Repúb-lica Argentina.* 3 v. in 2. Buenos Aires, 1912–13. [Buenos Aires, Universidad Nacional, Facultad de Filosofía y Letras, Sección de Historia.]

  c *Documentos relativos á la organización constitucional de la República Argentina.* 4 v. Buenos Aires, 1911–14. [Buenos Aires, Universidad Nacional, Facultad de Filosofía y Letras, Sección de Historia.]

a. One of a notable series of publications undertaken by the National University of Argentina, under the leadership and with the active participation of Norberto Piñero, José Nicolás Matienzo, and Ridolfo Rivarola, who have held in succession the post of dean of the Faculty of Philosophy and Letters in that institution. The work of gathering material and preparing it for publication has been under the immediate direction of Luis María Torres, who brought out v. 1–9, and of Emilio Ravignani, who succeeded him. Most of the volumes relate to the last century of the colonial period, with emphasis on the years following 1778. V. 8, 13, and 14. Relate to the events of the revolution, for the years 1815–1824. Among the topics treated are trading conditions, census returns of Buenos Aires and of Montevideo, food supply and prices, early elections during the Wars of Independence, local politics in the province of Buenos Aires, and the early diplomatic relations of the province. While most of the material centers about Buenos Aires, there is a valuable contemporary report on the region east of the Paraguay. The archives of Buenos Aires and vicinity have been drawn upon for documents, and these have been supplemented from the General Archives of the Indies at Seville. Not the least valuable feature of the series is the scholarly introductions to the volumes by the directors, and by Ricardo Levene, Diego Luis Molinari, Carlos Correa Luna, and others. *b.* Should be used with v. 8, 13, and 14 of *a.* *c.* Relates to the period of constitution-making that followed the overthrow of Rosas. These works, together with others centering around other provinces of the republic, published under the same auspices, should receive the attention of the careful student. IJC

Y82 *Revista del archivo general administrativo, ó colección de documentos para servir al estudio de la historia de la República Oriental del Uruguay.* Ed. by Pedro Mascaró and Isidoro De María. 10 v. Montevideo, 1885–1921.

Collection relating chiefly to the colonial period. IJC

Y83a *Colección de documentos inéditos para la historia de Chile, desde el viage de Magallanes hasta la batalla de Maipó, 1518–1818.* Ed. by José T. Medina. 30 v. Santiago de Chile, 1888–1902.

b *Colección de historiadores de Chile y documentos relativos a la historia nacional.* Ed. by Luis Montt and José T. Medina. 45 v. Santiago de Chile, 1861–1923.

c *Colección de historiadores i de documentos relativos a la independencia de Chile.* 26 v. Santiago de Chile, 1900–14,

a. Edited by the well known Chilean bibliographer; extends only to 1567; very complete for that period. *b.* Devoted largely to the *actas* of the *cabildo* of Santiago; carries the record to 1684. *c.* Most important collection for the period of the Chilean revolt from Spain. IJC

Y86 *Biblioteca de historia nacional.* Ed. by Eduardo Posada and Pedro M. Ibáñez. V. 1–40. Bogotá, 1902–27.

Coöperative collection, embracing a wide variety of material for the history of Colombia; carefully annotated; presented in attractive form, under the auspices of the Academia Nacional de Historia. IJC

Y87 *Documentos para los anales de Venezuela desde el movimiento separatista de la Unión Colombiana hasta nuestros días.* 12 v. Caracas, 1889–1909. [Academia Nacional de la Historia, Caracas.]

V. 1–7. Give the story of the separation of Venezuela from its neighbor, Colombia, up to 1830. V. 8–11. Continue the story to 1840. V. 12. Largely extracts from newspapers, 1813–1842; ends with an account of the transfer of Bolivar's remains to Caracas.   IJC

Y96a *Documentos para la historia de Méjico.* 21 v. in 19. Méjico, 1853–57.

  b García Icazbalceta, Joaquin, ed. *Colección de documentos para la historia de México.* 2 v. México, 1858–66.

  c ——, ed. *Nueva colección de documentos para la historia de México.* 5 v. in 3. México, 1886–92.

  d García Pimentel, Luis. *Documentos históricos de Méjico.* 5 v. Méjico, 1903–07.

  e Cuevas, Mariano. *Documentos inéditos del siglo XVI para la historia de México.* México, 1914. [Publicación hecha bajo la dirección de Genaro García por el Museo nacional de arqueología, historia, y etnología.]

  f García, Genaro and Pereyra, Carlos, ed. *Documentos inéditos ó muy raros para la historia de México.* 35 v. México, 1905–11.

a. Compiled by Manuel Orozco y Berra; first published in pamphlet form in *Diario oficial* of Mexico. Relates to all periods of Mexican history, but principally to the colonial. For an alphabetical list of these documents, cf. (Y1*d*) Jones, *Hispanic American bibliographies,* 831. *b.* Relates to the conquest; includes the famous *Historia* of Padre Motolinía. *c.* Supplements *b.,* with which it forms a worthy monument to the editor's historical and bibliographical activities. Cf. (Y1*d*) Jones, *Hispanic American bibliographies,* 835. *d.* V. 1–2. Published by the son of the preceding editor from his father's manuscripts; relate to the sixteenth century; contain another text of Motolinía. V. 3–5. Relate to the nineteenth century; Luis González Obregón, long the efficient director of the Archivo General y Público de la Nación, México, assisted in editing them. *e.* Supplements *b., c.,* and *d.* Should be used in connection with (Y622) Cuevas, *Historia de la iglesia en México. f.* Valuable collection devoted mainly to the national period, especially to intervention and foreign wars. A few ecclesiastical items of the colonial period are included. The materials were drawn from the editor's private collection, now owned by the University of Texas.   IJC

Y97a Hernández y Dávalos, Juan E., ed. *Colección de documentos para la historia de la guerra de independencia de México de 1808 a 1821.* 6 v. México, 1877–82.

  b García, Genaro, ed. *Documentos historicos mexicanos, obra conmemorativa del primer centenario de la independencia de México.* 7 v. Mexico, 1910–12. [Museo nacional de arqueologia, historia, y etnologia.]

a. Especially good for the struggle for independence up to 1814; fragmentary for the rest of the war. Includes only a small part of the seventy-five volumes of manuscripts collected by the editor. For an alphabetical index of all these manuscripts, cf. (Y1*d*) Jones, *Hispanic American bibliographies,* 830. *b.* Supplements *a.* for the outbreak of the revolt. After García left the Museo, v. 7 was added to the collection, but he expressly disclaimed responsibility for it.   IJC

SHORTER GENERAL HISTORIES

Y101a **Webster, Hutton.** *History of Latin America.* Boston, 1924. (Brief bibliography.)

b **Sweet, William W.** *History of Latin America.* N. Y., 1919. Later reprints. (Brief bibliographies.)

c **James, Herman G.,** and **Martin, Percy A.** *Republics of Latin America, their history, governments, and economic conditions.* 1923. Rev. ed., N. Y. and London, 1924. (Good bibliographies.)

d **Robertson, William S.** *History of the Latin-American nations.* 1922. Rev. ed., N. Y. and London, 1925. (Good bibliographies.)

e **Shepherd, William R.** *Hispanic nations of the New World, a chronicle of our southern neighbors.* New Haven, 1919. [Chronicles of America.] (Bibliography.)

a. Brief well-written sketch; intended for use in secondary schools. *b.* Concise text based on secondary works in English; well written. Unfortunate errors in the original edition have largely been corrected in later impressions. Review, W. R. Shepherd, *A.H.R.* 24:741, July 1919. *c.* Brief historical treatment of each country, followed by a full and somewhat technical discussion of governmental topics. Introductory chapters give a *résumé* of the Iberian background and of the colonial period and the Wars of Independence. Somewhat briefer and better arranged than *d.* Review, W. R. Manning, *A.H.R.* 29:386, Jan. 1924. *d.* Longer, wider in range of materials, superior in scholarship, but less readable. Distinctly a book for advanced college classes. Gives more adequately proportionate treatment to Brazil. The correlation with developments and events outside Latin America is inadequate. Review, W. R. Shepherd, *A.H.R.* 28:343, Jan. 1923. *e.* Excellent suggestive introduction; begins about 1783. In lieu of details of narrative and political history, the book presents valuable points of view and interpretations of significant movements. Review, W. S. Robertson, *A.H.R.* 25:560, Apr. 1920.

IJC

Y102 **Akers, Charles E.** *History of South America, 1854–1904.* 1904. Rev. ed., with additional chapter bringing the history to the present day [1911]. London, 1912.

Readable narrative of the political events, especially in the southern countries, from 1854 to 1904, prefaced by a short account of the preceding period, with slight attention to economic development. Review, H. Bingham, *A.H.R.* 10:671, Apr. 1905. For a brief summary of political events in South America, cf. contributions of F. A. Kirkpatrick in (1121) *Cambridge modern history,* v. 11, 12.

EEB

Y103 **Dawson, Thomas C.** *South American republics.* 2 v. N. Y. and London, 1903–04. [Story of the nations.] (Bibliography.)

Written in a simple, graphic style. After a brief introductory chapter on the discoveries and conquests, the author relates the history of each country separately, with about equal attention to the colonial period and the period of independence. The authorities utilized for the earlier period, while secondary and few in number, are generally reliable. For post-revolution times, however, the material and information was gathered during several years' diplomatic service in South America. Well-chosen illustrations. Review, H. Bingham, *A.H.R.* 9:584, Apr. 1904; 10:671, Apr. 1905.

JBL

A GUIDE TO HISTORICAL LITERATURE

Y104 García Calderón, Francisco. *Latin America, its rise and progress.* N. Y., 1913. Later reprints. [South American series.] Tr. by B. Miall from *Les démocraties latines de l'Amérique,* Paris, 1912.

Brilliant interpretation of the life, thought, history, and problems of the Latin American democracies by a Peruvian diplomat and scholar. At times abstruse; its broad generalizations probably deserve further testing; by far the most stimulating book of its kind. Review, R. R. Hill, *Pol. Sci. Quar.* 28:700, Dec. 1913.   JFR

Y105a Barros Arana, Diego. *Compendio de historia de América.* 2 v. Santiago, 1865. Later abridged editions.

   b Navarro y Lamarca, Carlos. *Compendio de la historia general de América.* 2 v. Buenos Aires, 1910–13. (Extensive bibliographies.)

   a. Work of merit but biased. Though emphasis is placed upon Spanish America, the portions of the continent settled by the Portuguese, French, and English receive attention. Unfortunately, the history ends with the close of the Hispanic-American wars of independence.   JBL

   b. Intended for a text in the schools of Argentina; well illustrated and provided with maps. Beginning with prehistoric man in America, the story of the South American states is brought down to 1828; of Mexico and the West Indies, to the twentieth century. Review, W. R. Shepherd, *A.H.R.* 18:594, Apr. 1913; 21:377, Jan. 1916.   LFU

LONGER GENERAL HISTORIES

Y121 Hume, Martin A. S., ed. *South American series.* 14 v. London and N. Y., 1907–17. [1, G. F. Scott-Elliott, *Chile;* 2, C. R. Enock, *Peru;* 3, *id., Mexico;* 4, W. A. Hirst, *Argentina;* 5, Pierre Denis, *Brazil,* tr. by B. Miall; 6, W. H. Koebel, *Uruguay;* 7, James Rodway, *Guiana, British, Dutch, and French;* 8, L. V. Dalton, *Venezuela;* 9, (Y104) F. García Calderón, *Latin-America;* 10, P. J. Eder, *Colombia;* 11, C. R. Enock, *Ecuador;* 12, P. Wallé, *Bolivia,* tr. by B. Miall; 13, W. H. Koebel, *Paraguay;* 14, *id., Central America.*]

Noteworthy series, designed to give a correct account of each country with special regard to commercial conditions. Brief history of each, followed by a detailed description of physical features, social conditions, industries, facilities for travel and transportation, and natural resources. 1. Review, *Nation* (N.Y.), 88:63, Jan. 21, 1909. 2–3. By a civil and mining engineer; good for the general reader. Review of 2, *Nation* (N.Y.), 88:63, Jan. 21, 1909; *A.H.R.* 13:664, Apr. 1908. Review of 3, *Nation* (N.Y.), 90:401,Apr. 21, 1910. 4. Good, but shows a decided British bias. Review, *Nation* (N.Y.), 94:287, March 21, 1912. 5. One of the best of series. Review, *Nation* (N.Y.), 94:287, Mar. 21, 1912. 6. Review, *Nation* (N.Y.), 93:417, Nov. 2, 1911. 8. Review, *Nation* (N.Y.), 96:59, Jan. 16, 1913. 10. The author has a longer and more intimate acquaintance with his subject than some other contributors to the series; valuable data in appendix. Review, *Nation* (N.Y.), 97:458, Nov. 13, 1913. 11. Good for the general reader. Superior to 2 and 3. Review, *Nation* (N.Y.), 98:641, May 28, 1914. 12. Review, *Athenaeum,* 2:139, Aug. 1, 1914. 13. Review, *Spectator,* 118:392, March 31, 1917. 14. Review, *Pol. Sci. Quar.* 33:310, June 1918.   LFU

DESCRIPTIVE WORKS CONTAINING HISTORICAL MATERIALS ESPECIALLY FOR THE ABORIGINAL AND COLONIAL PERIODS

Y201a **Humboldt, Alexander von.** *Personal narrative of travels to the equinoctial regions of the new continent, during the years 1799–1804* . . . 7 v. in 8, London, 1814–29. Tr. by Helen M. Williams from *Voyage aux régions équinoxiales du nouveau continent fait en 1799–1804,* 3 v., Paris, 1809–25. [Voyage de Humboldt et Bonpland, pt. 1.] Numerous later editions, of which the translation from the same original by T. Ross, 3 v., London, 1847 [Bohn's scientific library], is most common and usable.

b —— *Political essay on the kingdom of New Spain . . . with physical sections and maps.* 4 v. London, 1811–22. Tr. by J. Black from *Essai politique sur le royaume de la Nouvelle Espagne,* 2 v. and atlas, Paris, 1811–12. [Voyage de Humboldt et Bonpland, pt. 3.]

c —— *Island of Cuba.* N. Y., 1856. Tr. by J. S. Thrasher from a Spanish tr. of *Essai politique sur l'ile de Cuba,* 2 v., Paris, 1826. [Extracted from original of *a.*]

d **Pons, François R. J. de.** *Voyage to the eastern part of Terra Firma, or the Spanish Main, in South-America, during the years 1801, 1802, 1803, and 1804.* 3 v. N. Y., 1806. Tr. by an American gentleman from *Voyage à la partie orientale de la Terre-Ferme, dans l'Amérique Méridionale, fait pendant les années 1801, 1802, 1803, et 1804, contenant la description de la capitainerie générale de Caracas,* 3 v., Paris, 1806.

a., b., and *c.* The most accurate accounts of the state of Hispanic America for the period of transition from subjection to independence; the observations on colonial institutions are eminently sane; the style heightens the charm of the matter. Review of *b., Edinburgh Rev.* 19:164, Nov. 1811. *d.* Also by a painstaking observer and accurate chronicler. The account is limited to Venezuela.

JFO'H

Y202a **Darwin, Charles R.** *Journal of researches into the natural history and geology of the countries visited during the voyage of H. M. S. Beagle round the world, under the command of Capt. Fitz Roy, R.N.* London, 1839. Many later ed. and reprints. Reprint, London and N. Y., 1908. [Everyman's library.]

b **Bates, Henry W.** *Naturalist on the river Amazons: a record of adventures, habits of animals, sketches of Brazilian and Indian life, and aspects of nature under the equator, during eleven years of travel.* 2 v. London, 1863. Many later ed. Reprint, London and N. Y., 1910. [Everyman's library.]

c **Belt, Thomas.** *Naturalist in Nicaragua: a narrative of a residence at the gold mines of Chontales, journeys in the savannahs and forests, with observations on animals and plants in reference to the theory of evolution of living forms.* London, 1874. Later ed. Reprint, London and N. Y., 1911. [Everyman's library.]

d **Herndon, William Lewis** and **Gibbon, Lardner.** *Exploration of the valley of the Amazon, made under direction of the Navy Department.* 2 v. and 2 atlases. Washington, 1853–54. [Senate executive document, no. 36, 32nd congress, 2nd session; and House executive document, no. 53, 33rd congress, 1st session, 1854.]

a., b., and *c.* Notable descriptions of sections of Central and South America by eminent scientific observers; valuable for geographical, social, and economic, as well as other scientific data. *d.* V. 1. By Herndon. V. 2. By Gibbon. Besides contributions to scientific knowledge and to the determination of the international status of the Amazon—a subject then of diplomatic interest—this work forms an important link in Inter-American cultural relations. Cf. (Y502c) Robertson, *Hispanic American relations with the United States*, 330–336. Also cf. (K482) Wilkes, *Narrative of the United States exploring expedition.*   IJC

Y203 Stephens, John L.   *Incidents of travel in Central America, Chiapas, and Yucatan.* 2 v. N. Y., 1841. Numerous later ed. and reprints.

Important for the conditions observed at the time of writing, but more especially for the first modern contribution to the study of Mayan civilization. GMD

Y204a Squier, Ephraim George.   *Nicaragua, its people, scenery, monuments, and the proposed inter-oceanic canal.* 2 v., N. Y. 1852.

b ——— *Notes on Central America, particularly the states of Honduras.* N. Y., 1855.

c ——— *States of Central America, their geography, topography, climate, population, resources, productions, commerce, political organization, aborigines, etc., etc., comprising chapters on Honduras, San Salvador, Nicaragua, Costa Rica, Guatemala, Belize, the Bay Islands, the Mosquito Shore, and the Honduras inter-oceanic railway.* N. Y., 1858.

No more scholarly works on Central America have appeared than those by Squier, whose best contribution is archeological and sociological; but the historical sketches which he occasionally includes are not without value, for, though most of them are based upon other authorities, at times he writes from firsthand information. Useful maps and illustrations.   *c.* Squier's most comprehensive work in this field; an amplification of *b.;* adds historical sketches of Belize, the Bay Islands, and the Mosquito Shore, with especial attention to British encroachments.   MWW

Y205a Squier, Ephraim George.   *Peru, incidents of travel and exploration in the land of the Incas.* London, 1877.

b Bandelier, Adolph F. A.   *Islands of Titicaca and Koati, illustrated.* N. Y., 1910 [Hispanic Society of America.]

c Bingham, Hiram.   *Inca land, explorations in the highlands of Peru.* Boston, 1922.

d Bowman, Isaiah.   *Andes of southern Peru, geographical reconnaissance along the seventy-third meridian.* N. Y., 1916. [American Geographical Society.]

e ——— *Desert trails of Atacama.* Ed. by G. M. Wrigley, N. Y., 1924. [American Geographical Society, Special publication, no. 5.]

a. and *b.* Valuable observations on the Incas and their culture by able students of the American aborigines.   *b.* Excellently illustrated.   *c.* Latest of several works by the author on exploring expeditions in South America in which he participated. Valuable for the account of the ancient Inca capital and of other Inca remains. Review, M. H. Saville, *Literary Rev.* 3:365, Jan. 6, 1923.   *d.* and *e.*   Also based upon exploring expeditions in South America in which the author participated; contain important geographical, social, and economic data. Also, cf. (Y381b) Markham, *Incas of Peru.*   IJC

SPANISH COLONIZATION

Y231 Bolton, Herbert E. and **Marshall, Thomas M.** *Colonization of North America, 1492–1783.* N. Y., 1920. (Bibliographies.)

New interpretation of the field, with adequate presentation of the Hispanic American colonial factors; sometimes overloaded with local names and minor events. Review, V. W. Crane, *A.H.R.* 26:540, Apr. 1921.   IJC

Y232 Bourne, Edward G. *Spain in America, 1450–1580.* N. Y. and London, 1904. [American nation.] (Valuable classified bibliography.)

Decidedly best concise work on the establishment and early development of the Spanish colonies. Accurate in the facts given, logical in the development of the subject, and reliable in its deductions. The political, economic, and cultural phases of the conquest and colonization are given proportional attention; comparisons are made with the colonial policies of other nations, to show the strength and weakness of the Spanish system. Review, M. Oppenheim, *A.H.R.* 11:394, Jan. 1906.

Also cf. (K123) Lannoy and Vander Linden, *Histoire de l'expansion coloniale des peuples européens,* v. 1; (K533) Leroy-Beaulieu, *De la colonisation chez les peuples modernes;* (K534) Keller, *Colonization,* ch. 4–9.   EEB

Y233 Robertson, William. *History of the discovery and settlement of America.* 1777. Ed. by John Frost, N. Y., 1837. (Bibliography.)

Robertson gave practically the first impetus to any sympathetic treatment in English of the Spanish conquest in America; he also gave to historical science a respect for the background of history. Portions of his work relating to colonial institutions are still readable. His chief faults are those of his time and environment: narrow religious views and dependence upon printed sources, since few manuscript sources were available to him.   JFO'H

Y234a Helps, Sir Arthur. *Spanish conquest in America and its relation to the history of slavery and to the government of colonies.* 1855–61. Rev. ed. by M. Oppenheim, 4 v., London and N. Y., 1900–04.

b —— *Life of Las Casas, 'the apostle of the Indies.'* 1867. 2nd ed., London, 1868.

c MacNutt, Francis A. *Bartholomew de Las Casas, his life, his apostolate, and his writings.* N. Y. and London, 1909.

d Simpson, Lesley Byrd. *The encomienda in New Spain. Forced native labor in the Spanish colonies, 1492–1550.* Berkeley, 1929. (Good bibliography.) [University of California Publications in History. Vol. 19.]

a. Pioneer work; makes admirable use of sources; presents clearly and correctly many fundamentals of the Spanish conquest in America. The discursive character of the work and its moral purpose, manifested in the author's bitter condemnation of slavery and of the encomienda system, constitute notable defects. The author is partial in his treatment of certain Spaniards, such as Balboa and Las Casas. Review, G. P. Winship, *A.H.R.* 10:641, Apr. 1905. *c.* Preferable to *b.* *d.* A thoroughly documented treatise with valuable appendices. A valuable corrective for *a, b,* and *c.*   CWH

Y235 Watson, Robert Grant. *Spanish and Portuguese South America during the colonial period.* 2 v. London, 1884.

Useful, readable, but not altogether scientific narrative of the chief episodes in the conquest and settlement of South America. Based on secondary authorities, and on some printed sources.   CWH

Y236 Herrera y Tordesillas, Antonio de. *Historia general de los hechos de los Castellanos en las islas i tierra firme del mar oceano.* 5 v., Madrid, 1601–15. Later ed.

The work covers from 1492 to 1554 and is divided into eight decades. The English version, 6 v. London, 1725–26, by Stevens is worthless and only includes the first five decades. Cf. (X121) Winsor, *Narrative and critical history of America,* 2:67–68, 563; (B2b) Sabin, *Dictionary of books relating to America,* 8–243 lists twenty editions; (B6c) *Catalogue of the John Carter Brown Library,* v. 2, pt. 1, p. 9, ed. 1922; (B2h) Stevens, *Bibliotheca historica,* p. xiii, and no. 892, where an incomplete title is given.   LFU

Y237a Prescott, William H. *History of the conquest of Mexico.* 3 v. N. Y., 1843. Rev. ed. by J. F. Kirk, 1873; further rev. [Montezuma] ed. by W. H. Munro, 4 v., Philadelphia, 1904. Illustrated by Keith Henderson, with introduction by T. A. Joyce (cf. Y52), 2 v., N. Y., 1922.

   b ——— *History of the conquest of Peru.* 2 v. N. Y., 1847. Rev. ed. by J. F. Kirk, 1874; further rev. [Montezuma] ed. by W. H. Munro, 3 v., Philadelphia, 1904.

   c Richman, Irving B. *Spanish conquerors, a chronicle of the dawn of empire overseas.* New Haven, 1919. [Chronicles of America.]

a. and *b.* Prescott's classics have often been reprinted and are still the broadest general treatment in their respective fields. Prescott used a wealth of manuscript sources, but did not sufficiently discriminate between the violently partisan accounts which he found; and he exaggerated the cultural development of the Aztecs. Monograph corrections of Prescott will continue to appear as new material is found and old material more impartially sifted. To this end the publications of the (Y921) Cortés Society and the introduction and illustrations in the Henderson-Joyce edition are worthy of careful consideration. *c.* Vivid recent sketch of the same subjects. Review, E. B. Greene, *A.H.R.* 25:294, Jan. 1920.   JFO'H

Y238a MacNutt, Francis A., tr. and ed. *Letters of Cortes, the five letters of relation from Fernando Cortes to the Emperor Charles V.* 2 v. N. Y. and London, 1908. (Bibliography.)

   b ——— *Fernando Cortes and the conquest of Mexico, 1485–1547.* N. Y. and London, 1909. [Heroes of the nations.]

   c Sedgwick, Henry Dwight. *Cortes the conqueror; the exploits of the earliest and greatest of the gentlemen adventurers in the New World.* London, 1927. (Brief bibliography.)

b. Virtually an expansion of a biographical introduction which the author prefixed to *a.;* fairly good popular account. Review, G. P. Winship, *A.H.R.* 15:670, Apr. 1910; *Nation* (N. Y.), 90:16, Jan. 6, 1910.   LFU

   c. Study favorable to Cortes, devoted primarily to the conquest. Review, (London) *Times Lit. Suppl.* 26:707, Oct. 13, 1927.   HRS

Y239a Graham, Robert G. B. Cunninghame. *Hernando de Soto, together with an account of one of his captains, Gonçalo Silvestre.* London, 1903.

b —— *Bernal Diaz del Castillo, being some account of him taken from his True history of the conquest of New Spain.* London, 1915.

c —— *Conquest of New Granada, being the life of Gonzalo Jimenez de Quesada.* London, 1922. (Brief bibliography.)

d —— *Conquest of the River Plate.* London, 1924. (Brief bibliography.)

e —— *A vanished arcadia, being some account of the Jesuits in Paraguay, 1607 to 1767.* 1901. 2nd rev. ed. London, 1924.

a., b., and *c.* Popular biographies of Conquistadores, by an Englishman familiar with Hispanic America; based, in considerable part, on a few original sources. Review of *c.,* I. J. Cox, *A.H.R.* 28:364, Jan. 1923. *d.* and *e.* Other works of similar type dealing with colonial origins in the regions indicated. IJC

Y240a Moses, Bernard. *Establishment of Spanish rule in America, an introduction to the history and politics of Spanish America.* N. Y. and London, 1898.

b —— *South America on the eve of emancipation, the southern Spanish colonies in the last half-century of their dependence.* N. Y. and London, 1908.

c —— *Spanish dependencies in South America, an introduction to the history of their civilisation.* 2 v. N. Y. and London, 1914.

d —— *Spain's declining power in South America, 1730–1806.* Berkeley, 1919. [Semicentennial publications of the University of California.]

c. and *d.* Intended to supplant *a.* and *b.* respectively. They are an interesting introduction to the colonial history of South America, based mainly on printed sources. The author's failure to note editions of books occasionally makes it difficult to trace the sources for some statements, but the volumes, as a whole, are exceedingly useful for the average reader. Review of *a.,* E. G. Bourne, *A.H.R.* 5:166, Oct. 1899; of *b., A.H.R.* 14:164, Oct. 1908; of *c.,* W. R. Shepherd, *A.H.R.* 21:169, Oct. 1915; of *d.,* W. S. Robertson, *A.H.R.* 25:309, Jan. 1920.

JFO'H

Y241a Bandelier, Adolph F. A. *Gilded man (El Dorado) and other pictures of the Spanish occupancy of America.* N. Y., 1893.

b —— *Papers of the Archaeological Institute of America, American series.* 5 v., Boston and Cambridge, Mass., 1881–92.

c Hackett, Charles W., ed. *Historical documents relating to New Mexico, Nueva Vizcaya, and approaches thereto, to 1773,* collected by Adolph F. A. Bandelier and Fanny R. Bandelier; Spanish texts and English translations; edited with introductions and annotations. V. 1, 2. Washington, 1923–26. [Carnegie Institution of Washington.]

a. Five essays, not thoroughly scientific in character, but based upon historical sources and supplemented by noteworthy archeological investigations of the author. The first two essays relate to the legends of El Dorado and of the Seven Cities of Cíbola. The last three essays are of more local interest. Review, *Nation* (N. Y.), 57:489, Dec. 28, 1893. *b.* Entirely composed of reports and monographs by Bandelier on his archeological researches and ethnographic investigations in southwestern United States and Mexico. *c.* Publication, intended to extend to four volumes, of transcripts of manuscripts in Mexican and Spanish archives made by Bandelier and his wife, to which are added some documentary materials from other sources. Review of v. 1, F. W. Hodge, *A.H.R.* 29:563, Apr. 1924; v. 2, A. S. Aiton, *Hisp. Amer. Hist. Rev.* 8:229, May 1928.   CWH

WARS OF INDEPENDENCE

Y261a Robertson, William S. *Rise of the Spanish-American republics as told in the lives of their liberators.* N. Y. and London, 1918. (Good bibliography.)

   b ———— *Francisco de Miranda and the revolutionizing of Spanish America.* Washington, 1908. [American Historical Association, Report, 1907, 1:189–539.] (Good bibliography.)

   c ———— *Life of Miranda,* Chapel Hill (N. C.), 1929. [University of North Carolina Publications.] (Bibliography.)

   a. Though subject to the limitations of the biographical method of historical writing, this is perhaps at once the fullest and most trustworthy account in English of the rise of the Spanish American republics. Based mainly on original sources; deals in a spirit of fairness and detachment with the numerous controversial questions involved.   *b.* More extended study of an early phase of the revolution. In various historical and political science journals Professor Robertson has also published articles on the early international relations of the American states.   JBL

   c. Based on sources recently discovered in England and now in the possession of the Venezuelan government, it largely supersedes *b.*   IJC

Y262a Ducoudray-Holstein, H. L. V. *Memoirs of Simon Bolivar, president liberator of the republic of Colombia, and of his principal generals, comprising a secret history of the revolution, and of the events which preceded it, from 1807 to the present time.* French ed., *Histoire de Bolivar . . . continuée jusqu'à sa mort par A. Viollet.* 2 v., Paris, 1831. 2 v. London, 1830. Boston, 1829.

   b Petre, Francis L. *Simon Bolivar, 'el libertador,' a life of the chief leader in the revolt against Spain in Venezuela, New Granada, and Peru.* London and N. Y., 1910. (Brief bibliography.)

   c Mancini, Jules. *Bolivar et l'émancipation des colonies espagnoles des origines à 1815.* Paris, 1912. Spanish tr. by Carlos Docteur, Paris, 1914.

   d Lemly, Henry Rowan. *Bolívar, liberator of Venezuela, Colombia, Ecuador, Peru, and Bolivia. . . .* Boston, 1923.

   e Sherwell, Guillermo A. *Simón Bolívar, el libertador, patriot, warrior, statesman, father of five nations: a sketch of his life and his work.* Washington, 1921. (Bibliography.)

   f ———— *Antonio José de Sucre, gran mariscal de Ayacucho, hero and martyr of American independence: a sketch of his life.* Washington, 1924.

   a. Bitterly biased account of the great Liberator, written by a disappointed soldier of fortune. Contains a mass of anecdotes, for the years 1814–1816, during which the author was in the service of Bolivar; may be used with caution by one who is familiar with the events of the period.   IJC

   b. Not a thorough study; based on a few sources and the better secondary works; the best biography in English of this leader. Review, *Nation* (N. Y.) 91:367, Oct. 20, 1910.   LFU *c.* The author was well fitted for his task by sympathy, training, and long diplomatic experience in South America, but unfortunately he did not live to complete the work. One of the best interpretations of the early years of the struggle for independence. More than a third of the volume is devoted to the preliminaries of the conflict. *d.* More popular account, with many quotations from the sources. *e.* and *f.* Popular biographies; sympathetic rather than discriminating.   IJC

Y263a Mitre, Bartolomé. *Historia de San Martín y de la emancipación sud-americana.* 1887–88. 2nd rev. ed. by Félix Lajouane, 4 v., Buenos Aires, 1890.

    b ——— *Emancipation of South America, being a condensed translation by William Pilling of the History of San Martin.* London, 1893.

b. Epitome of *a.,* furnishing a survey of the separation of the Spanish colonies in South America from the motherland. Although it devotes some attention to the conditions that provoked the revolution and mentions other Spanish American patriots, notably Bolivar, yet the story centers about San Martin.   WSR

HISPANIC AMERICA SINCE INDEPENDENCE

Y281a Markham, Sir Clements R. *War between Peru and Chile, 1879–1882.* London, 1882.

    b Maurtua, Victor M. *Question of the Pacific.* Philadelphia, 1901. Tr. and enlarged by F. A. Pezet from *La cuestión del Pacífico,* Lima, 1901.

    c Bulnes, Gonzalo. *Guerra del Pacífico.* 3 v. Valparaiso, 1912–19.

    d ———. *Chile and Peru, the causes of the war of 1879.* Santiago de Chile, 1920.

a. and *b.* Written from the Peruvian viewpoint. *c.* Most recent and de-tailed account, by a Chilean, describing the causes of the war, the occupation of Peruvian territory by Chilean soldiers, and the negotiations for peace. *d.* Eng-lish translation of the first four chapters of *c.*   WSR

Y282 *Report and accompanying papers of the Commission appointed by the Presi-dent of the United States 'to investigate and report upon the true divisional line between the Republic of Venezuela and British Guiana.'* 9 v. Wash-ington, 1896–97.

Contains historical summaries of early settlement in the disputed region, to-gether with documentary and cartographical information of historical value. V. 4. Atlas. Review of v. 1–4, S. M. Macvane, *A.H.R.* 3:580, Apr. 1898. V. 5–6. British papers. V. 7–9. Venezuelan papers.   GMD

Y283 Bryce, James, Viscount. *South America, observations and impressions.* 1912. Rev. ed., N. Y., 1914.

Based upon a brief journey through South America, yet its last five chapters contain material of interest to students of American history and politics, presented with the author's habitual broad sympathy and sound scholarship. Review, W. R. Shepherd, *A.H.R.* 18:406, Jan. 1913.   JBL

Y284a Blakeslee, George H., ed. *Latin America.* N. Y., 1914. [Clark University addresses.]

b ———, ed. *Mexico and the Caribbean.* N. Y., 1920. [Clark University addresses.]

c Warshaw, Jacob. *New Latin America.* N. Y., 1922. (Brief bibliography.) 2nd ed. 1926.

a. Contains twenty-nine articles dealing with Latin America and its relations with the United States. Review, *A.H.R.* 20:679, Apr. 1915. *b.* Contains twenty-three articles, more closely related in subject matter than are those in *a.* Review, W. F. McCaleb, *A.H.R.* 26:817, July 1921. In both volumes the articles are popular and suggestive rather than scholarly and scientific. CWH

c. Comprehensive summary of recent developments; presents conclusions that are generally well founded and expressed with sympathetic insight. Review, C. H. Haring, *Pol. Sci. Quar.* 37:164, March, 1923. IJC

BRAZIL

Y301 Kidder, Daniel P., and **Fletcher, James C.** *Brazil and the Brazilians portrayed in historical and descriptive sketches.* 1857. 9th rev. ed., Boston, 1879.

Written by two scholarly missionaries who spent nearly a quarter of a century in Brazil; based on keen and accurate observation and careful examination of the most important printed works then existing. By far the most complete and satisfactory account in English of social, political, religious, and economic conditions in Brazil during the reign of Dom Pedro II. PAM

Y302a Varnhagen, Francisco A. de. (Visconde de Porto Seguro.) *Historia geral do Brazil, isto é do descobrimento, colonisação, legislação, e desenvolvimento deste estado, hoje imperio independente.* 2 v. 1854–57. 2nd ed., Rio de Janeiro, 1877; 3rd rev. ed. of v. 1, by Capistrano de Abreu, Rio de Janeiro, 1906.

b Southey, Robert. *History of Brazil.* 3 v. London, 1817–22.

a. Still regarded as the standard history of Brazil for the colonial period, and one fully revealing Varnhagen's gifts as an historian. The author, a Brazilian diplomatist, ransacked the libraries and archives of Europe, especially the great collection in the Torre do Tombo at Lisbon, for material for this work and for numerous monographs on early Brazilian history. The work is not always judicial, notably towards the Jesuits; over-emphasizes details, and is faulty in perspective, but will long remain a quarry for later writers. The thoroughly annotated revision of Capistrano de Abreu, himself a scholar and historian of distinction, unfortunately extends through less than a third of the original work. *b.* Readers who can use only English texts will derive much profit from Southey's work. Continued by (Y303c). PAM

Y303a Oliveira Lima Manoel de. *Evolution of Brazil compared with that of Spanish and Anglo-Saxon America.* Ed. by P. A. Martin. Palo Alto, 1914. [Stanford University publications.] (Detailed bibliographical notes.)

b ——— *Dom João VI no Brazil, 1808–1821.* 2 v. Rio de Janeiro, 1908.

c Armitage, John. *History of Brazil from the period of the arrival of the Braganza family in 1808 to the abdication of Dom Pedro the First in 1831; compiled from state documents and other original sources; forming a continuation to Southey's history of that country.* 2 v. London, 1836.

a. Six lectures by the most eminent living historian of Brazil, dealing with various topics of the social, political, and intellectual development of his country during the colonial and revolutionary periods.   WSR

b. Covers a decisive period and conforms to the most exacting standards of historical criticism. Embodies the results of exhaustive researches in London, Vienna, Paris, and Rio de Janeiro which have led to a revised judgment on many persons and events of the period and to a rehabilitation of John VI.   *c.* Readable, and in the main, accurate account covering the same eventful period and extending the narrative over the turbulent years of Pedro I. The author terms his work an 'archive of experiments, tending to show how the advantages of government can best be secured to the governed.' One of the very few books of enduring value in English on Brazil.   PAM

Y304 Nabuco, Joaquim. *Um estadista do imperio, Nabuco de Araujo, sua vida, suas opinioes, sua época.* 3 v. Paris and Rio de Janeiro, 1898–1900.

Admirable biography of a distinguished statesman and juriconsult and a scholarly contribution to the constitutional history of the Brazilian empire. During his long political life, ending in 1878, Nabuco de Araujo conscientiously assembled an immense mass of material dealing with every phase of contemporary political life. From this his son, a famous publicist, man of letters, and diplomat, prepared the present work. It deals with the Paraguayan war, the abolition of negro slavery, and the development of the parliamentary system. Scholarly and analytic, with abundant documentation; colorful and dramatic in style.   PAM

Y305 Malheiro Dias, Carlos, and others, ed. *Historia da colonizaçao portuguesa de Brazil, ediçao monumental comemorativa do primeiro centenario da independencia do Brazil.* V. 1–3. Porto and Rio de Janeiro, 1921–25.

So far, only v. 1 of the proposed 6 v. of this monumental coöperative work has appeared; it is devoted to the precursors of Cabral. Carlos Malheiro Dias writes an introduction and then follow four chapters, each contributed by a separate author. Sumptuous work, elegantly printed, with numerous illustrations and facsimile maps of high artistic merit, but with a distressingly long list of errata. Promises to be serviceable in a field where comparatively little material is available.   IJC

SPANISH NATIONS OF SOUTH AMERICA

Y331a Levene, Ricardo. *Lecciones de historia Argentina.* 1913. 4th rev. ed., 2 v., Buenos Aires, 1919.

b Pelliza, Mariano A. *Historia Argentina.* 5 v. Buenos Aires, 1888–97.

c Estrada, José M. *Lecciones sobre la historia de la república Argentina.* 1896. 2nd ed., 2 v., Buenos Aires, 1898.

d López, Vicente F. *Historia de la república argentina, Su origen, su revolución, y su desarollo politico hasta nuestros dias.* 10 v. 1883–1893; 2nd ed., 13 v. Madrid, 1926 ff.

a. Good epitome of the history of Argentina; equipped with foot-notes; emphasizes diplomatic, political, and military history. Economic conditions and literary tendencies receive some attention. For certain matters Levene may be supplemented by *b* and *c.* *d.* The first ten volumes, covering the period to 1829 were completed by the author before his death.   WSR

Y332 Quesada, Ernesto. *La época de Rosas, su verdadero carácter historico.* Buenos Aires, 1898.

According to the author this is only a fragment of the story of civil strife in Argentina, but it forms a fairly complete and useful study of the Argentine dictator.   IJC

Y341 Acevedo, Eduardo. *Manual de historia Uruguaya.* V. 1–3, Montevideo,. 1916–19 [V. 2, 3, title: Historia del Uruguay].

Voluminous narrative based on extensive documentary sources, to which, however, there are few definite references. Economic affairs and administrative problems receive considerable attention. The annals of Uruguay frequently serve to explain much that is true of all Hispanic America. V. 1. Gives the story to the movement for independence. V. 2–3. Continue the narrative to 1851.

IJC

Y351 Thompson, George. *War in Paraguay, with a historical sketch of the country and its people and notes upon the military engineering of the war.* London, 1869.

By a lieutenant-colonel of engineers in the struggle; gives valuable source material for the Lopez régime in Paraguay.   LFU

Y361a Galdámes, Luís. *Estudio de la historia de Chile.* 1906–07. 2nd ed., 2 v., Santiago de Chile, 1911. 7th ed., illustrated, 1929.

    b Hancock, Anson U. *History of Chile.* Chicago, 1893. [Latin-American republics.] (Bibliography.)

a. Well-balanced compendium of Chilean history; begins with a brief account of the Araucanians. The conquest, the colonial, the revolutionary, and post-revolutionary periods each receive proportionate attention. Political and constitutional development to 1906 is treated fairly although the author is chauvinistic. Much space is given to the social, economic, cultural, and religious affairs and but little to military operations.   *b.* Well-proportioned account.   EEB

Y362a Barros Arana, Diego. *Historia general de Chile.* 16 v. Santiago de Chile, 1884–1902.

    b ——— *Un decenio de la historia de Chile, 1841–1851.* 2 v. Santiago de Chile, 1905–06.

a. Standard history of Chile and one of the best of the great national histories of South America. Covers the period to 1833. *b.* Devoted to the administration of General Bulnes.   IJC

Y371 Argüedas, Alcides. *Historia general de Bolivia, el proceso de la nacionalidad, 1809–1921.* La Paz, 1922.

Detailed description of Bolivia's development during the nineteenth century. The work of a keen-minded social philosopher. Inadequately documented. Events since 1900 are only briefly sketched.   IJC

Y381a Markham, Sir Clements R. *History of Peru.* Chicago, 1892. [Latin-American republics.] (Bibliography.)

    b ——— *Incas of Peru.* London, 1910.

Not only did Markham possess wide information and broad scholarship, but through residence and travel he gained an intimate acquaintance with the geography and archeology of the country. *a.* Excellent; well illustrated; contains chapters on the people, literature, resources, and trade of Peru together with an appendix giving statistical information and a translation of the constitution of 1860. *b.* Best brief description in English of the Incas. For other works on the Incas, cf. (Y205).

JBL

Y382a Lorente, Sebastián. *Historia del Peru bajo la dinastia austriaca, 1598–1700.* Paris, 1870.

b ——— *Historia del Perú bajo los Borbones, 1700–1821.* Lima, 1871.

c ——— *Historia del Perú desde la proclamacion de la independencia.* V. 1, 1821–1827, Lima, 1876.

Together with these volumes, written by a Peruvian, form the most comprehensive history of the country.

JBL

Y391 González Suárez, Federico. *Historia general de la República del Ecuador.* 9 v. and atlas, Quito, 1890–1904.

Compendious account, based on archival sources, with special emphasis on the colonial period and the Wars of Independence; marked ecclesiastical bias.

IJC

Y401 Groot, José M. *Historia eclesiástica y civil de Nueva Granada.* 1869–70. 2nd rev. ed., 5 v., Bogotá, 1889–93.

Extended annals with marked attention to ecclesiastical matters; based on archival sources; account ends at 1831.

IJC

Y411a Baralt, Rafael Maria, and Diaz, Ramón. *Resúmen de la historia de Venezuela desde el descubrimiento . . . hasta el año de 1797.* Paris, 1841.

b ——— *Resúmen de la historia de Venezuela desde el año de 1797 hasta el de 1830; tiene al fin un breve bosquejo histórico que comprende los años de 1831 hasta 1837.* 2 v. Paris, 1841. 2nd ed. of *a.* and *b.* combined, 3 v., Curazao, 1887.

Annalistic histories; prevailingly ecclesiastical in point of view. Also, cf. (Y201d) Pons, *Voyage to the eastern part of Terra Firma.*

IJC

Y412a Humbert, Jules. *Les origines vénézuéliennes, essai sur la colonisation espagnole au Vénézuéla.* Paris, 1905. [Bibliothèque des universités du Midi.]

b ——— *Histoire de la Colombie et du Vénézuéla des origines jusqu'à nos jours.* Paris, 1921.

a. Historical survey of the colonial period, with some attention to social and economic details. *b.* Well-ordered sketch, presenting alternately the development of each republic.

IJC

Y421a Rodway, James. *History of British Guiana from the year 1668 to the present time.* 3 v. Georgetown, 1891–94. [1, 1668–1781; 2, 1782–1833; 3, 1833–1893.]

b **Williamson, James A.** *English colonies in Guiana and on the Amazon, 1604–1668.* Oxford, 1923.

c *Encyclopaedie van Nederlandsch West-Indië.* Ed. by H. D. Benjamins. J. F. Snelleman, 's Gravenhage, 1914–17.

a. Most complete work on the subject. *b.* Important monograph; supplements (K305) Newton, *Colonizing activities of the English Puritans.* *c.* Compendious reference work for Dutch Guiana as well as the island colonies.

GMD

SPANISH WEST INDIES

Y431a Rodway, James. *West Indies and the Spanish Main.* London and N. Y., 1896.

b Fiske, Amos K. *West Indies, a history of the islands of the West Indian archipelago, together with an account of their physical characteristics, natural resources, and present condition.* London and N. Y., 1899. [Story of the nations.]

c Hill, Robert T. *Cuba and Porto Rico, with the other islands of the West Indies; their topography, climate, flora, products, industries, cities, people, political conditions, etc.* London and N. Y., 1898. Reprint, 1899.

a. Perhaps the best general treatment of the subject, but far from satisfactory. Long study and residence in the region gave the author a rich command of detail, but his viewpoint is strictly British and he is careless and uncritical. Review, *A.H.R.* 2:187, Oct. 1896. *b.* Very unsatisfactory; based on few sources and those entirely English. Review, E. G. Bourne, *A.H.R.* 4:763, July 1899. *c.* Has still less historical value, but the descriptions contained in it are perhaps above the average.

JFR

Y432a Wright, Irene A. *Early history of Cuba, 1492–1586.* N. Y., 1916.

b Johnson, Willis Fletcher. *History of Cuba.* 5 v. N. Y., 1920.

c Guerra y Sánchez, Ramiro. *Historia de Cuba . . . V.* 1, 1492–1607, v. 2, Habana, 1921–25.

d Chapman, Charles E. *A history of the Cuban Republic.* N. Y., 1927.

a. Based on manuscript sources, which are not generally available. Promising pioneer study. *b.* Popular account. Useful in the absence of other detailed works in English attempting to cover the entire field of Cuban history, domestic and foreign. V. 5. Devoted to a physical description of the island. *c.* This first volume of what promises to be the standard history of Cuba covers, in spite of the title, the period of discovery and early conquest only as far as 1555; gives some attention to geographical and ethnographical conditions and to the administrative and economic policy of Spain. Manuel Abril y Ochoa writes the prologue. *d.* Straightforward attempt, based on abundant evidence, to describe actual conditions in Cuba, and therefore bound to provoke bitter controversy. Review, William E. Shea, *A.H.R.* 33:167, Oct. 1927.

IJC

Y433a Callahan, James M. *Cuba and international relations, a historical study in American diplomacy.* Baltimore, 1899. [Johns Hopkins University studies in historical and political science.]

b Robinson, Albert G. *Cuba and the intervention.* N. Y., 1905.

a. Historical sketch, covering the field to the date of publication, but containing many gaps that sources now available will supply. The value of the work is much impaired by its lack of documentation. Review, *Nation* (N. Y.), 70:325, Apr. 26, 1900. *b.* Definite account of the events of the first American intervention in Cuba, by an experienced newspaper correspondent. Sane and well-grounded comments, based largely on personal experience.

IJC

Y434a Brau, Salvador. *Puerto Rico y su historia, investigaciones críticas.*
1888. Rev. ed., Valencia, 1894.

b Van Middeldyk, Rudolph A. *History of Puerto Rico from the Spanish
discovery to the American occupation.* Ed. by M. G. Brumbaugh. N. Y.,
1903. [Expansion of the republic series.] (Bibliography.)

c Rowe, Leo S. *United States and Porto Rico, with special reference to
the problems arising out of our contact with the Spanish-American civilization.* N. Y., 1904.

a. Admirable work by one of the greatest Porto Rican historians. His name
is strangely omitted from *b.* which is a brief, popular sketch based upon Spanish
and other secondary authorities. Review, G. P. Winship, *A.H.R.* 9 :208, Oct.
1903. *c.* Valuable treatment of the formative years following 1898. Review,
J. B. Moore, *Pol. Sci. Quar.* 20 :720, Dec. 1905. JFR

Y435 Schoenrich, Otto. *Santo Domingo, a country with a future.* N. Y., 1918.
(Bibliography.)

Combination of historical sketch and guide-book; not wholly satisfactory as
either. Review, *A.H.R.* 24 :502, Apr. 1919. IJC

Y436 Davis, H. P. *Black democracy; the story of Haiti.* N. Y. and Toronto,
1928. (Bibliography.)

Historical account with accompanying notes, documents and illustrations. Review, Arthur Ruhl, *Sat. Rev. of Lit.* 5 :3, July 28, 1928. IJC

CENTRAL AMERICA

Y441 Anderson, Charles L. G. *Old Panama and Castilla del Oro.* 1911;
Boston, 1914. (Bibliography.)

Largely concerned with the careers of Columbus, Pedrárias, Drake, Morgan,
and others connected with the Isthmus. Readable and, on the whole, reliable.
Contains reproductions of rare maps and pictures. Review, *A.H.R.* 17 :863, July
1912. MWW

Y442 Bancroft, Hubert H. *History of Central America.* 3 v. San Francisco,
1882–87. [*Works,* v. 6–8.] (Extensive bibliography.)

The author at times failed to make the most of the wealth of material which
he had gathered, but the careful documentation enables the reader to check up
and supplement statements. On the whole, the book is impartial, accurate, and
readable, and is decidedly the best general history of Central America that has
yet appeared. Its scope is from the discovery by Europeans to 1887. V. 1–2.
Devoted to the colonial period. MWW

Y443a Fernández Guardia, Ricardo. *History of the discovery and conquest of
Costa Rica.* N. Y., 1913. Tr. by H. W. VanDyke from *Historia de Costa
Rica, el descubrimiento y conquista.* San Jose, 1905.

b Gómez Carillo, Agustín. *Compendio de historia de la América Central.*
Madrid, 1892.

c —— *Elementos de la historia de Centro-América.* 1887. 5th rev. ed.
Guatemala, 1895.

d Montúfar y Rivera Maestre, Lorenzo. *Reseña histórica de Centro-
América.* 7 v. Guatemala, 1878–87.

a. Stories of the conquistadores, drawn from the archives of the Indies at Seville, with illustrations, some footnotes, and references. Review, *Outlook,* 105:330, Oct. 11, 1913. LFU

b. Fairly impartial survey of Central American history, including its social and economic phases. Authorities are occasionally cited. *c.* Much briefer survey, but of the same general character. *d.* Diffuse account showing strong liberal bias. Deals almost exclusively with political and military events; covers the period from independence to 1858. For other works on Central America, cf. those of (Y202*c*) Belt, (Y52*c*) Joyce, (Y203) Stephens, and (Y204) Squier.

MWW

MEXICO

Y461 Fortier, Alcée, and **Ficklen, John R.** *Central America and Mexico.* Philadelphia, 1907. [History of North America.] (Bibliography.)

Narrates the history of Central America, Mexico, Texas, New Mexico, and Arizona in the order named. To some extent, based on original sources, with a few documents in the appendixes. In addition to the works listed in this subsection, cf. those by (Y52*b*) Joyce, (Y201*b*) Humboldt, (Y241*b*) Bandelier, (Y241*c*) Hackett, and (Y284*b*) Blakeslee. LFU

Y462 Priestley, Herbert I. *Mexican nation, a history.* N. Y., 1923. (Bibliography.)

Scholarly treatment of the subject, the best in a single volume. Primarily political, but with some attention to economic and social affairs. Review, W. F. McCaleb, *A.H.R.* 29:583, Apr. 1924. IJC

Y463 Bancroft, Hubert H. *History of Mexico.* 6 v. San Francisco, 1883–88. [*Works,* v. 9–14.] (Extensive bibliography.)

This has, in general, the faults and the excellencies of the same author's (Y442) *Central America.* Covers from the Spanish discovery to 1887; more than half the work is devoted to the colonial era. MWW

Y464a Alamán, Lucas. *Disertaciones sobre la historia de la República Mejicana, desde la época de la conquista . . . hasta la independencia.* 3 v. Méjico, 1844–49.

b —— *Historia de Méjico desde los primeros movimientos que prepararon su independencia en el año de 1808, hasta la época presente.* 5 v. Méjico, 1849–52.

a. Summarizes the history of Spain and of the Mexican conquest and occupation, with valuable appendixes. Review, (Y463) Bancroft, *History of Mexico,* 4:821. *b.* Most important work on the separatist movement in Mexico; includes discussion of the outcome of the revolution and of the problems confronting the new Mexican nation. Accurate and usually impartial, the author is occasionally pro-Spanish. HIP

Y465a Hannay, David. *Diaz.* N. Y., 1917. [Makers of the nineteenth century.] (Bibliography.)

b Corti, E. Caesar, Count. *Maximilian and Charlotte of Mexico.* V. 2. New York, 1928. Trans. by C. A. Phillips from the German edition (Vienna, 1924).

Best book yet printed in English on this great dictator; moderate in tone; free from heroics; not well balanced; contains many errors in statement; lacks appreciation of the serious problem before Diaz and of his real accomplishment. Like most English writers on Hispanic America the author fails to discern the American attitude toward the southern republics, and underrates the importance of American infiltration into Mexico. Review, J. H. Smith, *A.H.R.* 22:890, July 1917.   HIP

b. Based on materials, including 'Maximilian's private library, now available in the Austrian archives; poor historical introduction but excellent character sketches. Review, N. Andrew Cleven, *Miss. Vcl. Hist. Rev.* 15:286, Sept. 1928.   IJC

Y466a Jones, Chester Lloyd. *Mexico and its reconstruction.* N. Y. and London, 1921. (Bibliography.)

b McCaleb, Walter F. *Present and past banking in Mexico.* N. Y. and London, 1920. (Bibliography.)

c —— *Public finances of Mexico.* N. Y. and London, 1921.

d Thompson, Wallace. *People of Mexico, who they are and how they live.* N. Y. and London, 1921.

Four works, relating mainly to recent events, compiled and published under the auspices of Mr. E. L. Doheny. *a.* Based on extensive research in libraries and on personal interviews, supplemented by observations in Mexico itself. Conclusions are conservative and well grounded, essentially practical in character. The writer has made extensive use of *b., c.,* and *d.* Review, W. F. McCaleb, *Amer. Pol. Sci. Rev.* 16:333, May 1922.   IJC

Y467 Trowbridge, Edward D. *Mexico today and tomorrow,* N. Y., 1919.

Issued when caustic comment on Mexico was rife. Popular account, friendly in tone, of the primitive civilization and of historical events, but in no sense a history. The most valuable part concerns Madero's revolution and Carranza's program; the latter the author does not sufficiently characterize. The 'tomorrow' part has not yet come reasonably near realization. Review, *Hispanic American Hist. Rev.* 3:189, May 1920.   HIP

SPANISH BORDERLANDS

Y481a Bolton, Herbert E. *Texas in the middle eighteenth century, studies in Spanish colonial history and administration.* Berkeley, 1915. [University of California publications in history.] (Excellent bibliography.)

b —— *Spanish borderlands, a chronicle of old Florida and the Southwest.* New Haven, 1921. [Chronicles of America.] (Bibliography.)

a. Collection of essays based on extensive documentary research in local records; thoroughly scholarly. Review, *A.H.R.* 21:816, July 1916. The author has also edited numerous volumes of documents and has inspired a number of excellent monographs on the part of his students, most of which have appeared from the University of California press, or in the *Southwestern Historical Quarterly.* *b.* Summarizes in popular form the results of these labors. Review, J. A. Robertson, *A.H.R.* 27:580, Apr. 1922. Also cf. (Y241c) Hackett, *Historical documents relating to New Mexico.*   IJC

Y482a Garrison, George P. *Texas, a contest of civilizations.* Boston, 1903.
[American commonwealths.]

   b ——— *Westward extension, 1841–1850.* N. Y. and London, 1906.
[American Nation.]   (Bibliography.)

   c Stephenson, Nathaniel W. *Texas and the Mexican war, a chronicle of
the winning of the Southwest.* New Haven, 1921. [Chronicles of America.]   (Bibliography.)

   a. Scholarly *résumé,* based on source material and monographs. Some of this
material with additions was utilized in *b.* Review of *a.,* F. L. Riley, *A.H.R.*
9:586, Apr. 1904; of *b.,* J. S. Reeves, *A.H.R.* 12:673, Apr. 1907.   *c.* Treats of
the same period in a popular vein. Review, J. H. Smith, *A.H.R.* 27:618, Apr.
1922.   IJC

Y486a Rives, George L. *United States and Mexico, 1821–1848, a history of
the relations between the two countries from the independence of Mexico
to the close of the war with the United States.* 2 v. N. Y., 1913.
(Bibliography.)

   b Smith, Justin H. *Annexation of Texas.* 1911. Reprint, N. Y., 1919.
(Bibliography.)

   c ——— *War with Mexico.* 2 v. N. Y., 1919.   (Bibliography.)

   d Adams, Ephraim D. *British interests and activities in Texas, 1838–
1846.* Baltimore, 1910. [Shaw lectures on diplomatic history.]

   e Reeves, Jesse S. *American diplomacy under Tyler and Polk.* Baltimore,
1907. [Shaw lectures on diplomatic history.]

   f Garber, Paul N. *Gadsden treaty.* Philadelphia, 1923.   (Bibliography.)

   g Rippy, James Fred. *United States and Mexico.* N. Y., 1926. [Borzoi
historical series.]   (Bibliography.)

   a. Careful, impartial study based upon recent monograph literature and other
printed materials and the papers of the United States department of state. Not
definitive, but excellent, comprehensive account. Review, J. S. Reeves, *A.H.R.*
19:659, Apr. 1914.   GMD
   b. Written from a minute study of a wide range of sources. Reasonably
adequate treatment of the local history of Texas; detailed treatment of the
foreign relations of the Republic of Texas and of the diplomacy of the United
States, England, France, and Mexico concerning Texas; close analysis of the
political history of annexation in the United States—presidential, congressional,
and popular. The book maintains a high standard of accuracy, is notably non-
partisan, and is a healthy antidote to (X759) John Quincy Adams and (X537)
Von Holst. Review, E. C. Barker, *A.H.R.* 17:626, Apr. 1912.   ECB
   c. Most exhaustive treatise, and most substantially documented account of the
Mexican war published in any language; the fruit of a dozen years' research.
The treatment involves Mexican history for the first half of the nineteenth
century, preceded·by a sketch of colonial conditions. The most valuable parts of
the work are those which treat of the actual antecedents of hostilities, their development, conclusion, and consequences. Generous space is given to the popular
attitude in Mexico and in the United States. Review, E. C. Barker, *A.H.R.*
25:729, July 1920.   HIP
   d. Series of lectures based on thorough documentary researches. Contains
supplementary chapter on 'English interest in the annexation of California.'
Review, J. H. Smith, *A.H.R.* 16:151, Oct. 1910; *A.H.R.* 16:402, Jan. 1911. *e.*

Good, brief, comprehensive series of lectures, which must now be checked and supplemented by the books mentioned herewith and by other later researches. Review, St. G. L. Sioussat, *Amer. Pol. Sci. Rev.* 2:655, Nov. 1908. For authoritative, if not definitive, treatment of Polk's policies, cf. (X786) McCormac, *James K. Polk.*

GMD

f. Carefully documented study of negotiations between the United States and Mexico for the period immediately following the Mexican War. Review, J. F. Rippy, *A.H.R.* 30:651, Apr. 1925. Supplemented by *g.*, which continues the account to 1878, with a brief sketch of subsequent relations. IJC

Y491a Chapman, Charles E. *Founding of Spanish California, the northwestward expansion of New Spain, 1687–1783.* N. Y., 1916. (Extensive bibliography.)

b ——— *History of California: the Spanish period.* N. Y., 1921. (Bibliography.)

c Cleland, Robert G. *History of California: the American period.* N. Y., 1922.

d Richman, Irving B. *California under Spain and Mexico, 1535–1847: a contribution toward the history of the Pacific coast of the United States, based on original sources (chiefly manuscript) in the Spanish and Mexican archives and other repositories.* Boston, 1911. (Valuable bibliography.)

a. Based upon sources largely new. Review, I. B. Richman, *A.H.R.* 22:389, Jan. 1917; *Catholic World,* 104:390, Dec. 1916. *b.* and *c.* Form a popular and comprehensive history of the state. Reviews, J. Schafer, *A.H.R.* 27:804, July 1922; 28:334, Jan. 1923. IJC

d. Narrative, with exceptionally full notes; based upon the sources found in the archives of Seville and Mexico City; ten reproductions of early maps and charts. Review, F. J. Teggart, *A.H.R.* 17:156, Oct. 1911. LFU

Y492 Bolton, Herbert E., ed. *Historical Memoirs of New California by Fray Francisco Palóu.* 4 v. Berkeley, 1927.

Carefully edited translation, preceded by a comprehensive introduction, of the most complete narrative of early missionary activity in California. Review by Fr. Zephyrin Englehardt, in *A.H.R.* 33:668, Apr. 1928. IJC

Y496 Robertson, James A., ed. *Louisiana under the rule of Spain, France, and the United States, 1785–1807: social, economic, and political conditions of the territory represented in the Louisiana purchase, as portrayed in hitherto unpublished contemporary accounts by Dr. Paul Alliot and various Spanish, French, English, and American officials, translated or transcribed from the original manuscripts . . .* 2 v. Cleveland, 1911. (Bibliography.)

Collection of illuminating contemporary accounts. Review, P. Butler, *A.H.R.* 17:166, Oct. 1911. Also cf. (X507) Chadwick, *Relations of the United States and Spain.* GMD

Y497a Bolton, Herbert E., ed. *Arredondo's historical proof of Spain's title to Georgia, a contribution to the history of one of. the Spanish borderlands.* Berkeley, Calif., 1925.

b Bolton, Herbert E., and **Ross, Mary.** *Debatable land, a sketch of the Anglo-Spanish contest for the Georgia country.* Berkeley, Calif., 1925. (Bibliography.)

a. Edition and translation of an eighteenth century manuscript from the Archives of the Indies. *b.* Excellent historical introduction to *a.* Review of *a.* and *b.*, V. W. Crane, *A.H.R.* 31:176, Oct. 1925. IJC

Y498a Cox, Isaac J. *West Florida controversy, 1798–1813, a study of American diplomacy.* Baltimore, 1918. [Shaw lectures on diplomatic history.] (Bibliographical foot-notes.)

b Fuller, Hubert B. *Purchase of Florida, its history and diplomacy.* Cleveland, 1906. (Bibliography.)

c Pratt, Julius W. *Expansionists of 1812.* N. Y., 1925.

a. Based on sources; frequent and full footnotes, maps, and an index; a thorough and exhaustive study for the period indicated, with an adequate review of supplemental events from 1763 to 1819. Review, P. J. Hamilton, *A.H.R.* 24:105, Oct. 1918; *Nation* (N.Y.), 107:593, Nov. 16, 1918.   LFU
b. Based largely on American sources, adds little new information, fails to grasp matters not immediately related to Florida but highly pertinent to the negotiations. Review, *A.H.R.* 12:404, Jan. 1907.   *c.* Includes all phases of the expansionist movement in the United States at the beginning of the nineteenth century, but chiefly valuable for the controversies over the Floridas. Review, K. C. Babcock, *A.H.R.* 31:364, Jan. 1926.   GMD

DIPLOMATIC HISTORY: MONROE DOCTRINE, PAN-AMERICANISM

Y501 Paxson, Frederic L. *Independence of the South ·American republics, a study in recognition and foreign policy.* 1903. 2nd rev. ed., Philadelphia, 1916. (Good bibliography in 1st ed.)

Scholarly monograph on the policy of recognition during the Wars of Independence. Review, W. C. Ford, *A.H.R.* 9:383, Jan. 1904.   LFU

Y502a Latané, John H. *United·States and Latin America.* Garden City, N. Y., 1920.

b Stuart, Graham H. *Latin America and the United States.* N. Y., 1922. [Century political science series.] (Bibliographies.)

c Robertson, William S. *Hispanic-American relations with the United States.* Ed. by D. Kinley. N. Y. and London, 1923. [Carnegie Endowment for International Peace.] (Bibliography.)

d Ugarte, Manuel. *Destiny of a continent.* Ed. by J. F. Rippy. N. Y., 1925. (Bibliography.) Tr. by Mrs. Allison Phillips from *El destino de un continente,* Madrid, 1923.

a. Authoritative diplomatic treatise. After a short *résumé* of the Hispanic American movement for independence—a part of the work that needs to be substantially revised—the author continues with the history of the recognition of the Latin American states. He then reviews, largely also from a diplomatic standpoint and from the standard printed sources, the most important questions that have arisen in the past century between the United States and Cuba, Mexico, Panama, and the Caribbean countries. Review, W. R. Shepherd, *A.H.R.* 26:351, Jan. 1921.   *b.* Covers much the same ground as *a.,* but with less attention to earlier events and with fuller treatment of issues affecting relations between the United States and the more progressive countries of South America, of the Monroe Doctrine, and of Pan-Americanism.   *c.* Valuable and exhaustive treatment of some, but not all, relations between the United States and its southern neighbors. Review, L. S. Gannett, *Nation* (N.Y.), 18:400, Apr. 9, 1924; W. R. Manning, *A.H.R.* 29:363, Jan. 1924.   EEB *d.* Comprehensive, but biased summary of what may be termed the workings of 'Yankee imperialism' in each of the Hispanic American countries. Valuable for the point of view, which well offsets that given in *c.*   IJC

Y503a Johnson, Willis F. *Four centuries of the Panama canal.* N. Y., 1906.

b Keasbey, Lindley M. *Nicaragua canal and the Monroe doctrine: a political history of isthmus transit, with special reference to the Nicaragua canal project and the attitude of the United States government thereto.* N. Y., 1896.

c Williams, Mary W. *Anglo-American Isthmian diplomacy, 1815–1915.* Washington, 1916. [American Historical Association, Winsor prize essay.] (Bibliography.)

a. Though partisan and containing many inaccuracies, useful because of its comprehensiveness. Review, J. R. Smith, *A.H.R.* 12:684, Apr. 1907.   MWW

b. History of the isthmus and of canal projects from the discovery to 1896. For period prior to 1865 there is full documentation from United States government publications and other sources, but for the more recent period has few references and has apparently relied on newspapers, etc. 'Written avowedly from the Monroe doctrine standpoint,' with full attention to diplomatic questions. Favors Nicaragua rather than Panama project. Review, G. L. Rives, *A.H.R.* 2:750, July 1897.   GMD

c. Thorough treatise. Gives the history of British acquisitions in Central America and the consequent long diplomatic controversy over the Clayton-Bulwer treaty and its interpretation. Satisfactory documentation is necessarily lacking for the two Hay-Pauncefote treaties and the canal tolls controversy. Review, *A.H.R.* 22:185, Oct. 1916.   EEB

Y504 Jones, Chester Lloyd. *Caribbean interests of the United States.* N. Y., 1916. (Bibliography.)

Broad general treatment, brilliant at times, and always suggestive, but somewhat imperialistic and shows too little consideration for Hispanic American susceptibilities. Written from the economic angle; lacking in proportion and accuracy. Reviews, A. G. Robinson, *A.H.R.* 22:418, Jan. 1917; J. M. Callahan, *Amer. Pol. Sci. Rev.* 11:159, Feb. 1917.   JFR

Y505 Munro, Dana G. *Five republics of Central America: their political and economic development and their relations with the United States.* N. Y., 1918. [Carnegie Endowment for International Peace.] (Bibliography.)

Sympathetic and scholarly study of contemporary Central America. Best work on the subject. Review, C. L. Jones, *Amer. Pol. Sci. Rev.* 13:507, Aug. 1919.   MWW

Y506 Martin, Percy A. *Latin America and the war.* Baltimore, 1925. [Shaw lectures on diplomatic history.]

The diplomatic history of eight of the more important Latin American countries during the World War is competently treated in as many chapters. Two additional chapters deal with the other countries. The resulting problems are discussed in a concluding chapter. Some attention is also given to the economic and political affairs of the several countries during the period. Review, C. B. Dana, *A.H.R.* 31:816, July 1926.   GMD

Y521a Hart, Albert B. *Monroe doctrine, an interpretation.* Boston, 1916. (Bibliography.)

b Root, Elihu. *Real Monroe doctrine.* Amer. Jour. of International Law, 8:427–442, July, 1914.

c Tucker, George F. *Monroe doctrine, a concise history of its origin and growth.* Boston, 1885.

d Reddaway, William F. *Monroe doctrine.* Cambridge, Eng., 1898.

e Edgington, Thomas B. *Monroe doctrine.* Boston, 1904.

f Kraus, Herbert. *Die Monroedoktrin in ihren Beziehungen zur amerikanischen Diplomatie und zum Völkerrecht.* Berlin, 1913. (Bibliography.)

g Thomas, David Y. *One hundred years of the Monroe doctrine, 1823–1923.* N. Y., 1923.

h Alvarez, Alejandro. *Monroe doctrine, its importance in the international life of the states of the New World.* N. Y. and London, 1924. [Carnegie Endowment for International Peace.] (Bibliography.)

i Perkins, Dexter. *The Monroe Doctrine, 1823–1826.* Cambridge, 1927. [Harvard historical studies.]

a. Comprehensive study. Pt. 1–3. Devoted to a condensed history of the doctrine. Pt. 4–6. Its interpretation. Pt. 7. Survey of the books on the subject. The author maintains that neither the Monroe doctrine nor its bases are now what they were at the beginning. In this he does not meet with universal assent. Review, *A.H.R.* 21:827, July 1916. *b.* Best statement of the contrary view. JBL

c. Long the best treatise and still useful. *d.* By an Englishman; deals fully with origins; presents new views. Review, G. F. Tucker, *A.H.R.* 4:180, Oct. 1898. *e.* Not so good, but useful for history of application and amplification of the doctrine; includes the Calvo doctrine. *f.* By a German who carried on researches in the United States; most exhaustive treatment of the subject. Review, T. S. Woolsey, *A.H.R.* 19:657, Apr. 1914. GMD

g. Critical review of the policy of the United States, replete with facts otherwise not easily accessible. Readable and well organized. Review, J. M. Callahan, *Amer. Jour. of International Law,* 18:655, July 1924; C. N. Gregory, *A.H.R.* 30:161, Oct. 1924. *h.* Pt. 1. Gives an historical sketch of the development of the doctrine since its announcement, followed by thirty-one documentary annexes. Pt. 2. Compilation of declarations of statesmen and publicists regarding ·the doctrine, about equally divided between those from the United States and from Hispanic America. Review, W. P. Cresson, *Amer. Jour. of International Law,* 19:221, Jan. 1925. *i.* 'A model in historical research and interpretation,' presenting clearly and definitely the origin and reception of the doctrine. Review, W. C. Ford, *A.H.R.* 33:416, Jan. 1928. IJC

Y526a Fried, Alfred H. *Pan-Amerika: Entwickelung, Umfang, und Bedeutung der pan-amerikanischen Bewegung, 1810–1910.* Berlin, 1910. (Bibliography.)

b Lockey, Joseph B. *Pan-Americanism, its beginnings.* N. Y., 1920. (Extensive bibliography.)

c Inman, Samuel G. *Problems in Pan-Americanism.* 1921. 2nd rev. ed., N. Y., 1926. (Bibliography.)

d Myers, Denys P. *New Pan Americanism.* 3 pt. Boston, 1916–17. [World Peace Foundation, pamphlet series: pt. 1, v. 6, no. 1, Feb. 1916; pt. 2, v. 6, no. 2, Apr. 1916; pt. 3, *Central American League of Nations,* v. 7, no. 1, Feb. 1917.] (Bibliography.)

e Manning, William R., ed. *Arbitration treaties among the American nations, to the close of the year 1910.* N. Y. and London, 1924. [Carnegie Endowment for International Peace.]

A satisfactory account of the Pan-American movement has yet to be written. *a.* This brief sketch by a militant pacifist fails to appreciate the difficulties encountered by the movement. Review, *Amer. Jour. of International Law,* 5:553, Apr. 1911. *b.* Detailed, suggestive, and generally reliable study of Pan-Americanism from 1809 to 1830; based upon a thorough use of the printed sources. Review, W. S. Robertson, *A.H.R.* 26:559, Apr. 1921. *c.* Some chapters of this book treat of Pan-Americanism in its political aspects, but the emphasis is primarily upon its social influences. A useful contribution to a better understanding of the Hispanic American countries and their problems. Review, C. E. Chapman, *Pol. Sci. Quar.* 38:144, March 1923. *d.* Collections of speeches and documents expounding the policy of the Wilson administration, dealing with relations between the United States and Mexico since 1913, and with movements for Central American union since 1902. *e.* Useful collection. Review, *Amer. Jour. of International Law,* 18:870, Oct. 1924. IJC

Y527a Rippy, J. Fred. *Latin America in world politics, an outline survey.* N. Y., 1928.

b Haring, Clarence H. *South America looks at the United States.* N. Y., 1928.

a. A study based on familiar materials, supplemented by the author's extensive use of sources. Emphasizes external reaction to Hispanic America rather than the reverse. Sane and detached views. Review, J. B. Lockey, *A.H.R.* 34:148, Oct. 1928. *b.* A well-balanced series of essays, depicting contemporary sentiment. Based on careful study and personal contacts. Review, J. H. Latané, *Yale Rev.* 17:827, July 1928. IJC

CONSTITUTIONAL HISTORY

Y531a Desdevises du Dezert, Georges N. *Vicerois et capitaines généraux des Indes espagnoles à la fin du XVIIIᵉ siècle. Rev. hist.* 125:225–264, July 1917; 126:14–60, 225–270, Sept., Nov. 1917.

b —— *L'église espagnole des Indes à la fin du dix-huitième siècle. Revue hispanique,* 39:112–293, Feb. 1917.

a. Valuable materials culled from official reports and papers in the archives at Seville. Gives general description of different provinces, with data on population, towns, resources, etc. Furnishes for each viceroyalty and captaincy-general a list of governors for the period and an account of commercial, agricultural, social, and cultural developments. A lively picture of the details of viceregal government; shows how the system broke down of its own weight. *b.* Discussion of the ecclesiastical institutions. EEB

Y532a Smith, Donald E. *Viceroy of New Spain.* Berkeley, 1913. [University of California publications in history.] (Bibliography.)

b Priestley, Herbert I. *José de Gálvez, visitor-general of New Spain, 1765–1771.* Berkeley, 1916. [University of California publications in history.] (Bibliography.)

c **Cunningham, Charles H.** *Audiencia in the Spanish colonies as illustrated by the audiencia of Manila, 1583–1800.* Berkeley, 1919. [University of California publications in history.] (Bibliography.)

d **Fisher, Lillian E.** *Viceregal administration in the Spanish-American colonies.* Berkeley, 1926. [University of California publications in history.] (Bibliography.)

Four valuable studies of Spanish colonial institutions. *a.* Review, R. R. Hill, *A.H.R.* 19:384, Jan. 1914. *b.* Study of the custom of visitations; based on sources; thorough and scholarly. Review, R. R. Hill, *A.H.R.* 23:199, Oct. 1917. *c.* Monograph on one of the audiencias in the viceroyalty of New Spain. Review, *Miss. Val. Hist. Rev.* 8:406, Mar. 1922. *d.* Systematic topical study; done largely from the sources; very useful.   LFU

Y533 **Blackmar, Frank W.** *Spanish colonization in the Southwest.* Baltimore, 1890. [Johns Hopkins University studies in historical and political science.]

Useful, suggestive, and in some respects valuable work. Not based on exhaustive examination and use of the sources; various later monographs have improved upon or supplemented much that appears in the book. The treatment of the several fields is not well-proportioned. Review, W. P. Trent, *Pol. Sci. Quar.* 7:547, Sept. 1892.   CWH

Y541a **Rodriguez, José I.**, ed. *American constitutions, a compilation of the political constitutions of the independent nations of the New World, with short historical notes and various appendixes.* 2 v. Washington, 1906–07. [International Bureau of the American Republics.]

b **Arosemena, Justo**, ed. *Constituciones politicas de la America Meridional reunidas i comentadas.* 2 v. Havre, 1870.

c **Dodd, Walter F.**, ed. *Modern constitutions, a collection of the fundamental laws of twenty-two of the most important countries of the world, with historical and bibliographical notes.* 2 v. Chicago, 1909. Reprint, 1912. (Bibliography. (1552)

d **Carranza, Arturo B.**, ed. *Digesto constitucional americano, constituciones nacionales, 1900–01.* Rev. ed., 2 v., Buenos Aires, 1910.

a. Contains the texts of the American constitutions that were in force at the date of publication. Has the text in the original language and English translation in parallel columns. This collection may be supplemented by *b., c.,* and *d.,* the last of which is a convenient Spanish text.   WSR

Y551 **Rowe, Leo S.** *Federal system of the Argentine republic.* Washington, 1921. [Carnegie Institution of Washington.] (Bibliography.)

Brief, comprehensive study of constitutional government in Argentina, with some attention to historical fundamentals, by a scholar who has gained his information from personal visits and who is familiar with the limitations of practical administration.   IJC

Y552 **Stuart, Graham H.** *Governmental system of Peru.* Washington, 1925. [Carnegie Institution of Washington.] (Brief bibliography.)

Well-proportioned study of governmental conditions in actual practice.   IJC

Y561 **James, Herman G.** *Constitutional system of Brazil.* Washington, 1923. [Carnegie Institution of Washington.] (Bibliography.)

Brief historical summary of constitutional development, followed by a detailed description of present day government, federal and state. Review, *Amer. Pol. Sci. Rev.* 18:649, Aug. 1924.   IJC

ECONOMIC HISTORY

Y571a Haring, Clarence H. *Buccaneers in the West Indies in the XVII century.* N. Y., 1910. (Bibliography.)

b —— *Trade and navigation between Spain and the Indies in the time of the Hapsburgs.* Cambridge, Mass., 1918. [Harvard economic studies.] (Bibliography.)

a. Critical treatment based largely upon British sources. Review, V. Barbour, *A.H.R.* 16:637, Apr. 1911. *b.* Much more significant and equally careful and accurate. Based upon published collections of documents and manuscripts examined by the author in the archives of Seville and in various libraries of Madrid. Best treatment of the subject in any language. Review, C. H. Cunningham, *A.H.R.* 25:299, Jan. 1920; F. A. Kirkpatrick, *E.H.R.* 33:539, Oct. 1918.

JFR

CULTURAL HISTORY: GENERAL

Y601 Shepherd, William R. *Latin America.* N. Y., 1914. [Home university library.] (Brief bibliography.)

Brief, but one of the most valuable critical surveys of Hispanic American conditions both before and since independence. It is best appreciated by the scholar and investigator, but it is equally valuable and essential to the general reader and student. Review, *A.H.R.* 21:376, Jan. 1916.

IJC

Y602 Ross, Edward A. *South of Panama.* N. Y., 1915.

Study of considerable merit describing the west coast countries of South America with glimpses at Argentina. It is perhaps unduly frank and severe in interpreting sociological conditions as the author views them. Review, *Nation* (N. Y.), 101:210, Aug. 12, 1915.

JFO'H

CULTURAL HISTORY: RELIGION

Y621 Lea, Henry C. *Inquisition in the Spanish dependencies: Sicily, Naples, Sardinia, Milan, the Canaries, Mexico, Peru, and New Granada.* N. Y. and London, 1908.

By-product of the author's great (N621a) *History of the inquisition of Spain.* Unsurpassed for the student who does not read Spanish. The author acknowledges his great indebtedness to Medina for Peruvian materials, and to David Fergusson and Riva Palacio for Mexican materials. Review, G. L. Burr, *A.H.R.* 13:847, July 1908.

HIP

Y622 Cuevas, Mariano. *Historia de la Iglesia en Mexico.* 4 v. Tlalpam, México, 1921–26. (Bibliography.)

The fruit of long research in the archives of Mexico and of Europe, especially in Seville; a valuable survey of ecclesiastical activity in Mexico up to 1800. Review, H. I. Priestley, *A.H.R.* 29:585, Apr. 1924. Also cf. (Y531b) Desdevises du Dezert, *L'église espagnole des Indes.* For lives of Las Casas, cf. (Y234b and c).

IJC

CULTURAL HISTORY: LITERATURE

Y66ia Coester, Alfred L. *Literary history of Spanish America.* N. Y., 1916.
(Bibliography.)

   b ———— *Bibliography of Spanish-American literature.* Romanic Review,
3:68–101, Jan. 1912.

   c Goldberg, Isaac. *Studies in Spanish-American literature.* N. Y., 1920.

   d ———— *Brazilian literature.* N. Y., 1922.

   e Walsh, Thomas, ed. *Hispanic anthology, poems translated from the
Spanish by English and North American poets.* N. Y. and London, 1920.
[Hispanic Society of America.]

  a. Survey of the literature of the Spanish American nations during the colonial,
revolutionary, and national periods, with a chapter on the 'Modernist movement.'
The text is illustrated by quotations, especially from the poetry of Spanish
Americans. Its brief bibliography is supplemented by *b. c.* and *d.* Contain
sketches and appreciations of prominent Hispanic American writers. *e.* Includes
some characteristic selections from their works.   WSR

Y662a Moses, Bernard. *Spanish colonial literature in South America.* London
and N. Y., 1922. [Hispanic Society of America.] (Bibliography.)

   b Quesada, Vicente Gaspar. *La vida intelectual en la América española
durante los siglos XVI, XVII, y XVIII.* Buenos Aires, 1910.

  a. Agreeable and entertaining appraisal. Review, *A.H.R.* 29:616, Apr. 1924.
b. Six scholarly monographs about intellectual life in the Spanish-American
colonies, with a prefatory description of legislation regarding the press and traffic
in books. The monographs describe activities of the regular and the secular
clergy, colonial printing presses and journalism, and literary productivity in the
separate administrative regions. Some attention is paid to censorship and to
higher education. Useful footnotes.   WSR

SOCIETY PUBLICATIONS

The Cortes Society has undertaken the publication of a series of (Y921)
*Documents and narratives concerning the discovery and conquest of Latin
America,* v. 1–5, N. Y., 1917–22. The volumes are well edited and serviceable but
are unfortunately issued in limited editions. The published volumes deal with
the early occupation of Mexico, Peru, and Brazil.

PERIODICALS

Valuable historical material may be found in all sorts of Hispanic American
publications, including newspapers and professional journals. Some of the briefer
and more interesting articles are translated in (Y941) *Inter America, English,*
N. Y., 1917 ff. For recent events, the files of (Y942) *La Reforma social:
revista mensual de cuestiones sociales, economicas, politicas, parlamentarias, esta-
disticas, y de higiene publica,* Habana and N. Y., 1914 ff. will be found useful.

Each country has at least one organization devoted to history, frequently more,
all printing material of popular as well as of professional interest. Among current journals there may be mentioned for Brazil (Y946a) *Revista trimensal do*

Instituto Historico e Geographico Brazileiro, Rio de Janeiro, 1906 ff., previously published as (Y946*b*) *Revista trimensal de historia e geographia,* Rio de Janeiro, 140 v., 1839 ff. A number of state capitals have similar publications. For Argentina, the chief publications of this class are (Y951*a*) *Anales de la Facultad de Derecho y Ciencias Sociales, Universidad de Buenos Aires,* Buenos Aires, 1902–21; continued as (Y951*b*) *Revista de la Facultad de Derecho y Ciencias Sociales, Universidad de Buenos Aires,* Buenos Aires, 1922 ff.; and (Y952) *Revista de derecho, historia, y letras,* Buenos Aires, 1898 ff. El Archivo y Museo Histórico Nacional of Uruguay publishes (Y956) *Revista histórica,* Montevideo, 1907 ff. In Chile there are (Y961) *Revista de derecho, jurisprudencia, y ciencias sociales,* Santiago de Chile, 1903 ff.; (Y962) *Revista chilena de historia y geografía,* Santiago de Chile, 1911 ff.; and (Y963) *Anales de la Universidad de Chile,* Santiago de Chile and Valparaiso, 1846 ff. Peru has made a number of attempts to maintain an historical publication, (Y966) *Mercurio peruano,* Lima, 1918 ff., a general journal being the most recent. (Y971) *Boletín de historia y antigüedades,* Bogotá, 1902 ff., and (Y976) *Boletín de la Academia Nacional de la Historia,* Caracas, 1912 ff., represent the northern republics.

(Y981) *Cuba contemporánea,* Habana, 1913 ff., and (Y982) *Revista bimestre cubana,* Habana, 1910 ff., published by Sociedad Económica de Amigos del País, combine historical and literary articles, while (Y983) *Anales de la Academia de la Historia,* Habana, 1919 ff. deals entirely with historical topics; (Y986) *Centro América, organo de publicidad de la Oficina Internacional Centro-Americana,* Ciudad de Guatemala, 1909 ff., and (Y987) *Repertorio americano,* San José de Costa Rica, 1920 ff., are two modern organs of Central America. (Y991) *Anales del Museo Nacional de México,* México, 1877 ff., and (Y992) *Boletín de la Sociedad Mexicana de Geografia y Estadistica,* Mexico, 1839 ff., publish historical articles of importance, as does (Y993) *Revista mexicana de derecho internacional,* Mexico, 1919, v. 1–5, 1919–1923, and (Y994) *El México antiguo, international review of Mexican archaeology, ethnology, folklore, prehistory, ancient history, and linguistics,* Mexico, 1923 ff.

Articles dealing with Hispanic America frequently appear in the principal general reviews published in Spain and France (cf. § N and § M). The unfortunately interrupted (Y996) *Hispanic American Historical Review,* Baltimore, 1918–22, 1926 ff., is helpful for all fields of Hispanic American history. A similarly wide range is covered in (Y997) *Boletin del Centro de Estudios Americanistas,* Sevilla, 1913 ff. (Y998) *Journal de la Société des Américanistes de Paris,* Paris, 1895 ff. is useful for the whole field of American studies, especially archeology and linguistics of the native races, and also contains an annual 'Bibliographie américaniste,' prepared by P. Rivet. IJC

SECTION Z

BRITISH NORTH AMERICA

Editor
GEORGE MACKINNON WRONG
Professor of History, Emeritus, University of Toronto

CONTENTS

INTRODUCTION

There is a fairly abundant literature of Canadian history. Canada has been the meeting-place of French, British, and American influences. Consequently, Canadian history has attracted the attention, not only of native Canadian, but also of French, British, and American writers. Some of these contributions to Canadian history, such as (Z201) Parkman's great series of narratives, reach a very high level; others, while containing the results of conscientious research, are on a lower plane. The reader is reminded, therefore, that not all the books listed below are recommended with the same degree of emphasis; of some of them all that can be said is that they are the best available in a particular field. Many works on the general history of English colonization listed in § K and also various works on the history of the United States listed in § X should be consulted for information on Canada and its relations to the British Empire and the United States.

BIBLIOGRAPHY

Z1 Wrong, George M.; Langton, Hugh H.; and **Wallace, William Stewart,** ed. *Review of historical publications relating to Canada.* 22 v. Toronto, 1896–1919. [University of Toronto studies in history.]

Annual volumes of book reviews for the years 1896–1918; continued as the quarterly (Z941) *Canadian historical review.* Each number is indexed, and there are index volumes for v. 1–10 and 11–20. The scope includes not only history, but government, geography, statistics, economics, ethnology, archeology, etc. Contributors are usually Canadian specialists, whose judgment, especially on works originating outside of Canada, is most valuable. The most complete available bibliography of Canadian history is in (Z125) *Canada and its provinces,* v. 23, and useful bibliographical aids are also to be found in individual volumes of (Z123) *Chronicles of Canada.*   CEF

Library collections.—There is no national library in Canada, but, so far as Canadian history is concerned, the Library of Parliament and the Library of the Public Archives at Ottawa take the place of a national library. The latter is particularly rich in pamphlet material. The Library of the City of Montreal contains the excellent Gagnon collection of Canadiana, and an equally fine collection is to be found in the Bibliothèque de St. Sulpice in Montreal. The Toronto Public Reference Library contains perhaps the most complete collection of books relating to Canada. In the United States, the libraries most complete in Canadiana are the Harvard University Library, to which Francis Parkman bequeathed his books, and the Library of Congress.   AHS

WORKS OF REFERENCE

Z21a *Canadian almanac and miscellaneous directory..* Toronto, 1850 ff.
  b *Canada year book.* Ottawa, 1885 ff.

a. Devoted to Canadian information of a general character. *b.* Annual publication of the Dominion Bureau of Statistics. Very full and reliable.   wsw

Z22 Hopkins, John Castell, ed. *Canadian annual review of public affairs, 1901 ff.* Toronto, 1902 ff.

The Canadian 'Annual register.' Exhaustive annual digest of the current history of Canada. Sometimes diffuse in style and lacking in perspective; nevertheless accurate and impartial. Each volume contains a fair index.   wsw

GEOGRAPHY

Z41 Rogers, John D. *Canada, part III, geographical.* Oxford, 1911. [(K303) Lucas, Historical geography of the British colonies.] (Bibliographies.)

Concise sketch. Besides giving an accurate and reasonably complete statement of the geography, as progressively revealed by exploration, it suggests geographical explanation of the course of settlement in the past and of its probable future direction. The maps are inadequate. Review, W. L. Grant, *Rev. Hist. Pubs. Canada,* 16:108, 1912.   HHL

Z42 **Wallace, William Stewart.** *By star and compass: tales of the explorers of Canada.* Toronto, 1922.

Introduction to the history of Canadian exploration. Beginning with the Scandinavians and ending with Sir John Franklin, the author links together some seventeen episodes in a way calculated to attract and hold the interest of readers.

JBB

Z43a **Dawson, Samuel E.** *The Saint Lawrence, its basin and border-lands; the story of their discovery, exploration, and occupation.* London and N. Y., 1905. (Bibliography.)

 b **Burpee, Lawrence J.** *Search for the western sea, the story of the exploration of north-western America.* Toronto, 1908. (Bibliography.)

a. Story of the discovery, exploration and occupation not only of the St. Lawrence river, but of the Great Lakes and the Mississippi, by the early explorers, especially Cartier, Champlain, Radisson, La Salle, Hennepin, and Du Lhut. Well illustrated, and, though not a work of original research, is trustworthy and written in a clear and vigorous style. Review, *Rev. Hist. Pub. Canada,* 10:27, 1906. Cf. (K242b) Winsor, *Cartier to Frontenac.*   WLG

b. Excellent account of the history of geographical exploration in Canada from the discovery of Hudson Bay to the beginning of the nineteenth century. Though not infallible, the book is by far the most authoritative on its subject. Supplements *a.;* the two books cover fairly well the history of discovery in Canada. Review, J. H. Coyne, *Rev. Hist. Pubs. Canada,* 13:117, 1909.   WSW

ETHNOGRAPHY

Z51a **White, James,** ed. *Handbook of the Indians of Canada.* Ottawa, 1913. [Geographic Board of Canada, tenth report, appendix; also Canada, Parliament, 1911–12, Sessional papers 21 a.]

 b **Hodge, Frederick W.,** ed. *Handbook of American Indians, north of Mexico.* 2 v. Washington, 1912. [Smithsonian Institution, Bureau of American Ethnology, Bulletin 30.] (Bibliography.)

a. Reprint of those parts of *b.* which relate to Indians resident in Canada, with the addition of special articles on topics peculiarly Canadian. Authoritative.

HHL

Z52 **Siegfried, André.** *Race question in Canada.* London, 1907. Tr. from *Le Canada, les deux races, problèmes politiques contemporains,* Paris, 1906.

Most discriminating and original study, by an outsider, of the complex French-Canadian problem. Written with fairness and, on the whole, with accuracy. Except for some overstatements it is a notable piece of work. Review, W. L. Grant, *Rev. Hist. Pub. Canada,* 11:144, 1907.   HG

ARCHIVE PUBLICATIONS

A great deal of the most important original material in Canadian history is to be found in the publications of the national and provincial archives departments. First in importance are the Public Archives of the Dominion of Canada which has issued (Z61) *Reports,* Ottawa, 1872 ff., for which a partial list of content will be found in (X1b) J. N. Larned, *Literature of American history,* no. 3462 ff.; and (Z62) *Publications,* Ottawa, 1909 ff., of which v. 1 is an index of the *Reports* from 1872 to 1908. The archives departments of the following provinces have also issued valuable publications and *Reports:* (Z63) Nova Scotia, Halifax, 1869 ff.; (Z64) Quebec, Québec, 1921 ff.; (Z65) Ontario, Toronto, 1903 ff.; and (Z66) British Columbia, Victoria, 1914 ff.

SHORTER GENERAL HISTORIES

Z101a Lucas, Sir Charles P. *Canada, part I, New France.* 1901. 2nd ed., Oxford, 1916. [(K303) Lucas, Historical geography of the British colonies.] (Bibliographies.)

b Egerton, Hugh E. *Canada, part II, the history from 1763.* 1908. 3rd ed., Oxford, 1923. [(K303) Lucas, Historical geography of the British colonies.] (Bibliographies.)

a. Covers the period of French rule. Review, *Rev. Hist. Pubs. Canada,* 6:21, 1902. *b.* Covers the period of British rule, Review, W. B. Munro, *ibid.* 13:34, 1909. The volumes are on the scale of books for secondary schools; but they are clearly and carefully written, and the references to authorities are useful for the mature student.

GMW

Z102a Bourinot, Sir John G. *Canada under British rule, 1760–1900.* 1901. Rev. ed. continued to 1905 by G. M. Wrong, Cambridge, Eng., 1909. [Cambridge historical series.] (Bibliography.)

b Grant, William Lawson. *History of Canada.* 1914. Rev. ed., Toronto, 1922.

c Roberts, Charles G. D. *History of Canada.* Boston, London, and Toronto, 1897.

a. Written in brief compass for the general reader. Review, *Rev. Hist. Pubs. Canada,* 6:44, 1902. *b.* Intended for secondary schools. *c.* Well-written, but not always accurate. Review, *ibid.* 2:27, 1898.

WSW

LONGER GENERAL HISTORIES

Z121 Garneau, François X. *History of Canada, from the time of its discovery till the union year, 1840–41.* 3 v. 1860. 3rd rev. ed., 2 v., Montreal, 1866. Tr. by A. Bell from *Histoire du Canada depuis sa découverte jusqu'à nos jours,* 3 v., Québec, 1845–48; 6th rev. ed. by H. Garneau, 2 v., Paris, 1920.

In the latest edition, Mr. Hector Garneau has brought up to date the work of his grandfather. The plan and ideas of the original have been retained, but new paragraphs have been inserted with much skill, and many notes and appendixes added. The result is a very scholarly and broad-minded treatment of Canadian history from 1534 to 1841. Review, v. 1, W. L. Grant, *Rev. Hist. Pubs. Canada,* 18:23, 1914; v. 2, W. L. Grant, *Can. Hist. Rev.* 2:78, March 1921.

WLG

Z122 Kingsford, William. *History of Canada.* 10 v. Toronto, 1887–98.

Written late in life by an author whose career had been that of an engineer. Embodies the result of many years of labor in the Canadian archives at Ottawa but its execution is defective; inaccurate, and sometimes incoherent. Any writer on the history of Canada should consult it, if only on account of the author's industry; but the book should be regarded as suggesting topics for inquiry rather than presenting trustworthy history. The narrative includes the French period and ends with the year 1841. Review, v. 8, G. M. Wrong, *A.H.R.* 1:550, Apr. 1896; v. 8–10, *Rev. Hist. Pubs. Canada,* 1:10, 1897; 2:18, 1898; 3:18, 1899.

GMW

Z123 Wrong, George M., and Langton, Hugh H., ed. *Chronicles of Canada.* 32 v. Toronto, 1914–16. [1, S. Leacock, *Dawn of Canadian history;* 2, *id., Mariner of St. Malo-Cartier;* 3, C. W. Colby, *Founder of New France—Champlain;* 4, T. G. Marquis, *Jesuit missions;* 5, W. B. Munro, *Seigneurs of old Canada;* 6, T. Chapais, *Great intendant—Talon;* 7, C. W. Colby, *Fighting governor;* 8, W. Wood, *Great fortress;* 9, A. G. Doughty, *Acadian exiles;* 10, W. Wood, *Passing of New France—Montcalm;* 11, *id., Winning of Canada—Wolfe;* 12, *id., Fathers of British Canada;* 13, W. S. Wallace, *United Empire Loyalists;* 14, W. Wood, *War with the United States;* 15, T. G. Marquis, *War chief of the Ottawas;* 16, L. A. Wood, *War chief of the Six Nations—Brant;* 17, E. Raymond, *Tecumseh, the last great leader of his people;* 18, A. C. Laut, *Adventurers of England on Hudson Bay;* 19, L. J. Burpee, *Pathfinders of the Great Plains—La Vérendrye and his sons;* 20, S. Leacock, *Adventurers of the Far North;* 21, L. A. Wood, *Red River colony;* 22, A. C. Laut, *Pioneers of the Pacific Coast;* 23, *id., Cariboo trail;* 24, W. S. Wallace, *Family compact;* 25, A. D. De Celles, *'Patriotes' of '37;* 26, W. L. Grant, *Tribune of Nova Scotia— Joseph Howe;* 27, A. MacMechan, *Winning of popular government;* 28, A. H. U. Colquhoun, *Fathers of confederation;* 29, J. Pope, *Day of Sir John Macdonald;* 30, O. D. Skelton, *Day of Sir Wilfrid Laurier;* 31, W. Wood, *All afloat;* 32, O. D. Skelton, *Railway builders.* (Good bibliographies.)

Best general introduction to Canadian history from the beginning of the French period to modern times. Popular and picturesque in style, scientific in method. The series is necessarily uneven, but many of the volumes are of high merit. V. 3, 5, 6, and 11. An excellent survey of the period up to 1763. V. 13 and 24. The most judicial short accounts of the early history of Ontario. V. 12, 26, 27, 28, 29, and 30. A group of books, written by experts, which give an excellent view of Canadian political development. V. 9 and 25. Candid, discriminating, and reasonable surveys of controversial subjects. Detailed criticism of all these volumes may be found in (Z1) *Review of historical publications relating to Canada,* v. 19–21, 1915–17.

WPMK

Z124 Scott, Duncan C., and Edgar, Pelham, ed. *Makers of Canada.* 1904–11. University ed., 21 v. in 11, Toronto, 1912. New series, v. 1–2, Toronto, 1916–23. [1 N. E. Dionne, *Champlain;* 2, A. Leblond de Brumath, *Bishop Laval;* 3, W. D. Le Sueur, *Count Frontenac;* 4, H. R. Casgrain, *Wolfe and Montcalm;* 5, A. G. Bradley, *Lord Dorchester;* 6, J. N. McIlwraith, *Sir Frederick Haldimand;* 7, D. C. Scott, *John Graves Simcoe;* 8, Lady Edgar, *General Brock;* 9, S. Leacock, *Baldwin, Lafontaine, Hincks;* 10, G. Bryce, *Mackenzie, Selkirk, Simpson;* 11, J. W. Longley, *Joseph Howe;* 12, N. Burwash, *Egerton Ryerson;* 13, Sir J. G. Bourinot, *Lord Elgin;* 14, J. Hannay, *Wilmot and Tilley;* 15, G. R. Parkin, *Sir John A. Macdonald;* 16, R. E. Gosnell and R. H. Coats, *Sir James Douglas;* 17, C. Lindsey, *William Lyon Mackenzie;* 18, A. D. DeCelles, *Papineau, Cartier;* 19, J. Lewis, *George Brown;* 20, A. Shortt, *Lord Sydenham;* 21, L. J. Burpee and A. G. Doughty, *Index and Dictionary.* New series: 1, J. W. Longley, *Sir Charles Tupper;* 2, W. L. Smith, *Pioneers of old Ontario.*]

This series consists of biographies of twenty-eight leading figures in Canadian history, beginning with Champlain, who died in 1635, and ending with Sir Charles Tupper, who died in 1915. Originally published in separate volumes in an *édition de luxe,* the lives are now collected in eleven volumes, the last of which consists of a valuable index and dictionary—a convenient guide to Canadian history. The volumes vary in quality. Probably the best are v. 7, 8, 15, and 20. In large measure, the series has been superseded by (Z123) *Chronicles of Canada,* but the volumes still have value in giving details not found in the briefer *Chronicles.* The index volume makes easy the use of the whole series as a unit. This helps to correct the breaks in the record, inevitable in a series of biographies. Review, v. 4, *A.H.R.* 11:416, Jan. 1906; all v., *Rev. Hist Pubs. Canada,* various dates, cf. *Indexes.*

GMW

Z125 Shortt, Adam, and **Doughty, Arthur G.,** ed. *Canada and its provinces, a history of the Canadian people and their institutions, by one hundred associates.* 23 v. Toronto, 1914–17. [1–2, *New France, 1534–1760;* 3–4, *British dominion, 1760–1840;* 5, *United Canada, 1840–1867;* 6–8, *The Dominion: political evolution;* 9–10, *The Dominion: industrial arts;* 11–12, *The Dominion:missions, arts and letters;* 13–14, *Atlantic provinces;* 15–16, *Province of Quebec;* 17–18, *Province of Ontario;* 19–20, *Prairie provinces;* 21–22, *Pacific province;* 23, *General index, manuscript sources, bibliography, chronological outlines, historical tables.*] (Excellent bibliography.)

Most important and comprehensive history of Canada. Written on a coöperative plan by a large number of experts, it covers the field from the days of the early explorers to the twentieth century. Not only does it deal with history in its usual aspects—political, constitutional, economic, and ecclesiastical—but it embraces also authoritative sections on such subjects as banking, the post-office, public finance, constitutional law, national defence, physical geography, shipping, highways, arts, and letters. Naturally the execution is uneven, and there is some padding. In the last volume is to be found a general index, together with chronological outlines and historical tables, of a most complete sort, and a bibliography of the primary and secondary sources, including manuscript material, which is fuller and more accurate than anything else in print. Review, *A.H.R.* 21:190, Oct. 1915; *Rev. Hist. Pubs. Canada,* 19, *passim,* 1915.

WPMK

FRENCH PERIOD

Z201 Parkman, Francis. *Works.* 12 v. Boston, 1893. Centenary ed. 13 v., Boston, 1922. [1, *Pioneers of France in the New World, 1865;* 2, *Jesuits in North America in the seventeenth century, 1867;* 3, *LaSalle and the discovery of the great west, 1869;* 4, *Old régime in Canada, 1874;* 5, *Count Frontenac and New France under Louis XIV, 1877;* 6–7, *Half century of conflict, 1892;* 8–9, *Montcalm and Wolfe, 1884;* 10–11, *Conspiracy of Pontiac and the Indian war after the conquest of Canada, 1851;* 12, *Oregon trail, 1849.*]

The writings of Parkman deal with French activities in North America during the colonial period, especially with the great struggle between France and England for the upper hand in the New World. They do not give a well-rounded survey of this subject, but make up a series of brilliant monographs on various phases of French colonial enterprise during the seventeenth and eighteenth centuries. Without exception, all the volumes combine sound historical scholarship with remarkable literary attractiveness. The narration is based, for the most part, upon first-hand materials and it is written with rare descriptive power. Parkman's strong New England sympathies occasionally blurred his perspective, hence he did not always render full justice to the ideals and achievements of the Gallic race; his highly imaginative temperament carried him at times into paroxysms of rhetoric; yet after a generation has passed his books still remain unsurpassed in general interest and value by anything else of their kind. WBM

Z202 **Wrong, George M.** *Fall of Canada, a chapter in the history of the seven years' war.* Oxford, 1914. (Bibliography.)

Study of the last phase of the conquest of Canada in 1760. Based on the best French and British sources. Impartial, readable, and thorough. Review, W. B. Munro, *A.H.R.* 20:898, July 1915. WW

BRITISH PERIOD PRIOR TO CONFEDERATION

Z241a **Bradley, Arthur G.** *Making of Canada.* N. Y., 1908.

b **Coupland, Reginald.** *Quebec act, a study in statesmanship.* Oxford and N. Y., 1925. (Bibliographical footnotes.)

a. Brilliant and interesting account of the history of Canada from the British conquest to the War of 1812. Accuracy in historical details, however, is unfortunately not always observed. Review, *Rev. Hist. Pubs. Canada,* 13:30, 1909. *b.* Detailed study not only of the act but also of the administration of French Canada in the earlier years of British rule. Review, D. McArthur, *A.H.R.* 31:338, Jan. 1926. WSW

Z242a **Lucas, Sir Charles P.** *History of Canada, 1763–1812.* Oxford, 1909.

b ——— *Canadian war of 1812.* Oxford, 1906.

These two volumes provide a scholarly survey of the first half-century of British rule in Canada. *a.* Review, *Rev. Hist. Pubs. Canada,* 14:41, 1910. *b.* Contains a series of admirable maps. Review, E. Cruikshank, *ibid.* 11:74, 1907. WSW

Z243 **Morison, John L.** *British supremacy and Canadian self-government, 1839–1854.* Glasgow and Toronto, 1919.

Penetrating study of Canadian politics during the fifteen years following the publication of Lord Durham's report. Review, A. Shortt, *Can. Hist. Rev.* 1:77, March 1920. WSW

BRITISH PERIOD SINCE CONFEDERATION

Z271 **Pope, Sir Joseph.** *Memoirs of Sir John Alexander Macdonald, first prime minister of the Dominion of Canada.* 2 v. London, 1894, Ottawa, 1895.

Interesting, accurate, and authoritative. The author was Macdonald's private secretary for ten years and possessed his immense collection of private papers. The book throws new light on Canadian politics from 1844 to 1891. Especially important is the correspondence on the Washington treaty, 1871. Naturally, the point of view is pro-Macdonald. Review, *Canadian Magazine,* 4:253, 1895. AHUC

Z272 **Willison, John S.** *Sir Wilfrid Laurier and the liberal party, a political history.* 2 v. Toronto and London, 1903.

Impartial and well-written narrative of Laurier and liberalism down to 1902. The anti-clerical movement in Quebec, including the famous Guibord case, is fully described. The chapters dealing with tariff policy, imperial relations, and commercial union with the United States show insight and intimate knowledge. Indispensable for the history of the Dominion since 1867. Review, *Rev. Hist. Pubs. Canada,* 8:36, 1904.

AHUC

Z273 Skelton, Oscar D. *Life and letters of Sir Wilfrid Laurier.* 2 v. Toronto, 1921. London and N. Y., 1922.

Authorized life of Laurier, based upon his papers. Written by a pronounced admirer, but otherwise scholarly and trustworthy. Review, A. Shortt, *Can. Hist. Rev.* 3:77, March 1922; G. M. Wrong *A.H.R.* 28:570, Apr. 1923.

WSW

Z274 Steele, Harwood E. R. *Canadians in France, 1915–1918.* London, 1920

Only account in one volume which gives a detailed description of the part which the Canadians took in the World War. Lacks maps; is too full of superlatives; deals only with the actual fighting; has little about organization behind the line. Review, F. H. Underhill, *Can. Hist. Rev.* 1:328, Sept. 1920.

FHU

Z275 Miller, John O., ed. *New era in Canada, essays dealing with the up-building of the Canadian commonwealth.* London, N. Y., and Toronto, 1917.

Series of essays on present-day Canadian problems. Stephen Leacock writes on 'Democracy and social progress'; Sir John Willison on 'Immigration and settlement'; Sir Edmund Walker on 'East and West,' etc. On the whole, the essays are remarkable for their insight and suggestiveness. Review, *Rev. Hist. Pubs Canada,* 22:68, 1919.

WSW

Z276 *'The Times' book of Canada: development since confederation; political, agriculture, mining, fisheries, forestry, railways, industries, finance, education, literature.* London, 1920.

Series of chapters on various phases of recent and current Canadian history, written by several anonymous but competent authorities. Shows signs of haste in preparation, but is unusually interesting and informing. Review, *Can. Hist Rev.* 1:421, Dec. 1920.

WSW

FRENCH CANADA

Z301 Bracq, Jean Charlemagne. *Evolution of French Canada.* N. Y., 1924. (Bibliography.)

Somewhat one-sided historical survey written with the purpose of proving the excellent quality of the French Canadian stock and its remarkable advance to meet modern demands. Based on extensive reading, with a rather uncritical use of authorities; contains a wide range of material to prove the cultural progress of French Canada. The author, a Protestant, is mildly anticlerical. Review, W. B. Munro, *A.H.R.* 30:378, Jan. 1925; G. M. Wrong, *Can Hist. Rev.* 5:365, Dec. 1924.

GMW

HUDSON'S BAY COMPANY AND OTHER CHARTERED COMPANIES

Z321a Bryce, George. *Remarkable history of the Hudson's Bay Company, including that of the French traders of north-western Canada and of the North-west, X Y, and Astor fur companies.* 1900. 3rd ed., N. Y., 1910. (Bibliography.)

b Laut, Agnes C. *Conquest of the great Northwest, being the story of the adventurers of England known as the Hudson's Bay Company; new pages in the history of the Canadian Northwest and western states.* 1908. 6th ed., 2 v. in 1, N. Y. and Toronto, 1918.

a. Story of western Canada from the foundation of the Hudson's Bay Company to the transfer of Rupert's Land to the Dominion. Chiefly valuable for the light it throws on the methods and life of the fur traders. Some errors of fact or interpretation have been corrected by later and more completely informed writers. Review, *Rev. Hist. Pubs. Canada,* 5:124, 1901.   *b.* Based on documentary material in Hudson's Bay House and the Public Record Office, London. Supplements *a.;* more complete in exploration, particularly to the west of the Rocky mountains, as well as in the history of the North West Company. Occasionally sacrifices dull facts to the dramatic story. Review, *ibid.* 13:101, 1909.

LJB

Z322 **Davidson, Gordon C.** *North West Company.* Berkeley, Calif., 1918. [University of California publications in history.] (Bibliography.)

Written partly from manuscript and printed sources. Describes early explorations of the Northwest, including those of Mackenzie, Thompson and others, but its chief value consists in the account of the fur trade and of the competition with the Hudson's Bay Company and the X. Y. Company. Not a finally adequate history but a useful contribution to the subject.   GMW

NEWFOUNDLAND

Z341a **Prowse, Daniel W.** *History of Newfoundland from the English, colonial, and foreign records.* 1895. 2nd ed., London, 1896.

   b **Smith, Frederick E., Earl of Birkenhead.** *Story of Newfoundland.* 1901. Rev. ed., London, 1920.

a. Fullest account of the history of Newfoundland hitherto published, but now somewhat antiquated. Its statements should be used with caution. Review, G. Stewart, *Rev. Hist. Pubs. Canada,* 1:21, 1897.   *b.* Sketch of the history of Newfoundland brought up to 1920. Another good outline of Newfoundland history, written by J. D. Rogers, is in (K303) Lucas, *Historical geography of the British colonies.*   WSW

LABRADOR

Z361a **Gosling, William G.** *Labrador, its discovery, exploration, and development.* London, 1910.

   b **Grenfell, Wilfred T.,** and others. *Labrador, its country and its people.* 1909. New ed., N. Y., 1913. (Bibliography.)

a. Affords some outline of leading facts of Labrador history.   *b.* Authoritative account, largely descriptive, based on long acquaintance with the region, with special sections by other competent hands. Review, *Nation* (N. Y.) 90:243, March 10, 1910.   GMD

CONSTITUTIONAL HISTORY

Z531 **Kennedy, William P. M.,** ed. *Documents of the Canadian constitution, 1759–1915.* London, N. Y., and Toronto, 1918.

The selection is not always judicious, some important documents having been omitted, and others of little importance included, but the volume is the most comprehensive and useful of its kind. Review, W. L. Grant, *A.H.R.* 26:597, Apr. 1921.   WSW

Z532 Lucas, Sir Charles P., ed. *Lord Durham's report on the affairs of British North America.* 3 v. Oxford, 1912.

Most famous state paper ever issued with regard to Canadian affairs, edited by an experienced official of the Colonial Office. V. 1. Introduction; penetrating analysis, by a master hand, of the problems confronted by Lord Durham in 1838. V. 2. Text of the report, with valuable notes. V. 3. Selection from the many appendixes to the original report. Review, *Rev. Hist. Pubs. Canada,* 17:59, 1913.

GMW

Z533 Kennedy, William P. M. *Constitution of Canada, an introduction to its development and law.* London, N. Y., and Toronto, 1922. (Bibliographies.)

Best outline of Canadian constitutional development. Review, C. Martin, *Can. Hist. Rev.* 4:162, June 1923.

WSW

Z534 Porritt, Edward. *Evolution of the Dominion of Canada, its government and its politics.* Yonkers, 1918. [Government handbooks.] (Bibliography.)

This book falls roughly into three sections: geography, vital statistics, economics; historical growth of the constitution; actual working of federal and provincial government. There are errors in perspective, proportion, insight, and fact, but the last part of the work is one of the best general accounts of the actual government of Canada. Review, W. S. Wallace, *A.H.R.* 24:286, Jan. 1919.

WPMK

BIOGRAPHIES

There are many excellent biographies, apart from those listed above, which have an importance for Canadian history. For the French period, the most noteworthy are perhaps (Z701) N. E. Dionne, *Samuel Champlain,* 2 v., Quebec, 1891–1906; (Z702) Henri Lorin, *Le Comte de Frontenac,* Paris, 1895; (Z703) Thomas Chapais, *Jean Talon,* Québec, 1904; and (Z704) Thomas Chapais, *Le marquis de Montcalm,* Québec, 1911, all in French. There are several lives of Wolfe: that by (Z741) Beckles Willson, London, 1909, is the most recent. For the early days of British rule, (Z742) W. S. Wallace, ed., *Maseres Letters, 1766–1768,* Toronto, 1919, may be referred to. The political struggle culminating in self-government is illustrated by (Z743) Charles Lindsey, *William Lyon Mackenzie,* 2 v., Toronto, 1862; (Z744) A. D. DeCelles, *Papineau,* Montréal, 1905; (Z745) J. A. Chisholm, *Speeches and public letters of Joseph Howe,* 2 v., Halifax, 1909; (Z746) Stuart J. Reid, *Earl of Durham,* 2 v., London and N. Y., 1906; and (Z747) George M. Wrong, *Earl of Elgin,* London, 1905. For the confederation period, reference should be made to (Z771) Alexander Mackenzie, *Life and speeches of George Brown,* Toronto, 1882; (Z772) Sir Charles Tupper *Recollections of sixty years,* London and N. Y., 1914; (Z773) John Boyd, *Sir George Etienne Cartier,* Toronto, 1914; and (Z774) O. D. Skelton, *Life and times of Sir A. T. Galt,* Toronto, 1920; and (Z775) W. L. Grant and F. Hamilton, *George Monro Grant,* Edinburgh and Toronto, 1905. For constitutional history since confederation, (Z776) C. R. W. Biggar, *Sir Oliver Mowat,* 2 v., Toronto, 1905, is important. (Z777) W. T. R. Preston, *Life and times of Lord Strathcona,* London, 1914; and (Z778) Walter Vaughan, *Life and work of Sir William Van Horne,* N. Y., 1920, illustrate material development. The annual publication,

(Z801) *Who's who in Canada, including the British possessions in the western hemisphere*, Toronto, 1906 ff., contains brief sketches of living celebrities, frequently with portraits. It must be consulted through the index, as the arrangement is not alphabetical.

SOCIETY PUBLICATIONS

Valuable historical materials are published by the Royal Society of Canada, (Z921) *Proceedings and transactions*, Montreal and Ottawa, 1882 ff. The oldest historical society in Canada is the Literary and Historical Society of Quebec, whose (Z922a) *Transactions*, Quebec, 1829 ff. and volumes of (Z922b) *Historical documents*, Quebec, 1838 ff. include valuable original documents; but the society now shows less activity. The same is true of the Société Historique de Montréal, which has also issued some important (Z923) *Mémoires*, Montréal, 1859 ff. The Historical Societies of the following provinces annually issue publications: (Z924) Ontario, *Annual report*, Toronto, 1898 ff.; (Z925) New Brunswick, *Collections*, Saint John, 1894 ff.; and (Z926) Nova Scotia, *Collections*, Halifax, 1879 ff., which are, however, largely of local interest, as are also the publications issued by the numerous local historical societies found in various parts of the Dominion, particularly in Ontario. Of peculiar importance is the Champlain Society, whose (Z927) *Publications*, Toronto, 1907 ff. include manuscript and rare printed materials relating chiefly to the period of exploration.

PERIODICALS

There are two journals in Canada devoted exclusively to Canadian history; (Z941) *Canadian historical review*, Toronto, 1920 ff., quarterly, and (Z942) *Bulletin des recherches historiques*, Lévis, Québec, 1895 ff., monthly.

INDEX I

In each section throughout the manual, as far as varying conditions have permitted, the following plan has been observed in the arrangement and numeration of titles:

1–20	Bibliography, Library and museum collections.
21–40	Encyclopedias, and Works of Reference.
41–50	Geography and atlases.
51–60	Ethnography.
61–100	Source books, collections of sources, archive publications.
101–120	Shorter general histories.
121–200	Longer general histories.
201–500	Histories of special periods, regions, or topics.
501–530	Diplomatic, military, and naval history, international law.
531–570	Constitutional and (551) legal history, (561) political theory.
571–600	Economic and (581) social history.
601–620	Cultural history, general.
621–640	" " religious.
641–660	" " education, thought, philosophy.
661–680	" " literature.
681–700	" " art, (691) music.
701–900	Biography.
901–920	Government publications.
921–940	Academy, university, and society publications.
941–1000	Periodicals.

Under the several headings briefer works are usually placed first and the larger works last. Aside from a few exceptional cases limitation of space has prevented the inclusion of articles in periodicals and of local and provincial histories; the same restriction has been observed, though to a somewhat less degree, in the case of biographies. The great majority of the biographical works included in the regular lists are those dealing with rulers or important ministers, which are in the nature of things historical in character. At the end of the main list in most sections will be found a short paragraph giving in the briefest form the authors and titles of a few additional biographies.

The problem of allocation of titles to sections has presented difficulties. It has seemed best to reserve the general chapters, *e.g.,* those on medieval history, modern history, contemporary times, for works of more general scope or for those relating, to a large degree, to the history of two or more countries. In the sections devoted to particular countries or regions, will be found works which deal more specifically with these areas.

INDEX II

Authors, Periodicals, and Academy Publications Cited

Aall, A. A. F., Norweg.-schwed. union R532a

Aarboger for nordisk hist. R926b

Aarskatalog over norsk litt. R2c

Abailard, P., Historia calamitatum H762

Abbott, Edith, Immigration X57a, b

Abbott, Evelyn, Greece D121d; Hellenica D605a; Heroes of the nations B711a; Pericles B711a1, D302b

Abbott, F. F., Common people of Rome E606b; Handbook E21c; Municipal admin. E542c; Rom. pol. institutions E531a; Rom. politics D603c30, E531b

Abbott, G. F., Thucydides D301g; Turkey, Greece and gt. powers T352b; Turkey in transition T352a

Abbott, W. C., Expansion K203; Writing of history A283a

Abdur Rahim, Principles of Muham. jurisprudence G533a

Abeel, D., Journal U2704

Abelard. See Abailard

Abhandlungen d. Akademie d. Wiss., Berlin, P921a, b, c; Bayer. Akademie P922a, b; (Rozpravy) S2922a, b

Abkoude, J. v., Naamregister Q23a, b

Aboussouan, B., Problème pol. syrien T8342c

Abrahams, I., Jewish lit. B360b; Jew. life H583

Abram, A., English life L578b; Social England L578c

Abū al Fidā, Annales G77b; Géographie G77a

Academia das Sciencias de Lisboa, Corpo dipl. N1062; Monumentos ineditos Y72

Academia de Hist. Nac., Boletin Y971

Academia Nac. Hist., Boletin Y976

Academia Română, Publications T3072, T3921a, b, c

Academia Scient. Art. Slavorum Merid., Publications T4922a-i

Académie d. Inscriptions, Comptes rendus D985, M922b; Mémoires M922a; Monuments D986

Académie d. Sciences Morales et Pol., Comptes rendus M921b; Mémoires M921a

Académie d. Sciences, Belgique, Biog. nationale Q22b; Bulletins Q971a; Compte rendu Q971; Publications Q81; Table générale Q971b

Accounts, Lord high treasurer, Scotland L96g

Acevedo, E., Manual hist. Uruguaya Y341

Acsády, I., A Magyar birodalom története T2122

Acta, Albaniae T6071

Acta extera (Mon. Hungariae hist.) T2071c

Acta hist. Poloniae S1923

Acta Sanctorum F801

Actas d. las Cortes de Castilla N533e

Acte, Istoria Rominilor T3073

Actes et documents, Roumanie T3074

Acton, Lord, Essays B243a, b; German schools of hist. P3f; Lectures on mod. hist. I273b

Acts of Parliaments of Scotland L96a, b

Acts, Gov. Gen'l. India U1901

Adair, E. R., Sources, hist. of council A295.51

Adam, G. M., Spain and Portugal B135.8

Adam, J., Relig. teachers D625e

Adamescu, G., Istoria liter. romăne T3661b

Adamov, E. A., Konstantinopol J74g

Adams, Alice D., Neglected period X585c

Adams, C. D., Demosthenes D603c5; Lysias D551a

Adams, C. K., Manual B12a

Adams, E. D., Brit. interests, Texas X508.5, Y486d; Gt. Brit. and Amer. civil war X506f; Power of ideals X101k

Adams, G. B., Civilization H104a; Constitutional hist. L531a, b, c; Council and courts L531d; England 1066-1216, L121.2; Eur. hist. B102a; Growth Fr. nation M101a; Select docs. L61a